A LITERARY HISTORY of ENGLAND

Edited by

ALBERT C. BAUGH

Second Edition

PRENTICE-HALL, INC., Englewood Cliffs, New Jersey 07632

PRENTICE-HALL INTERNATIONAL, INC., *London*
PRENTICE-HALL OF AUSTRALIA, PTY. LTD., *Sydney*
PRENTICE-HALL OF CANADA, LTD., *Toronto*
PRENTICE-HALL OF INDIA PRIVATE LIMITED, *New Delhi*
PRENTICE-HALL OF JAPAN, INC., *Tokyo*
PRENTICE-HALL OF SOUTHEAST ASIA PTE. LTD., *Singapore*
WHITEHALL BOOKS LIMITED, WELLINGTON, *New Zealand*

Preface to the First Edition

The purpose of the present book will be sufficiently apparent—to provide a comprehensive history of the literature of England, an account that is at once scholarly and readable, capable of meeting the needs of mature students and of appealing to cultivated readers generally. While the literature of England is commonly thought of as literature in English, it is not likely that any one will quarrel with the fact that some mention is made of writings in Latin and French during the medieval period, at a time when these languages served as vernaculars for certain classes. The Latin writings of the Renaissance and later periods, however, have been omitted for lack of space. Nor will any one object to the inclusion of Scottish and Irish writers who do not belong geographically to England. Custom sufficiently sanctions including them. The original plan brought the history to an end with the year 1939 (the outbreak of the Second World War); but delay in publication caused by the war has permitted reference to a few events of a date subsequent to 1939.

The extent of English literature is so great that no one can hope to read more than a fraction of it, and the accumulated scholarship—biographical, critical, and historial—by which writers and their works, and the forms and movements and periods of English literature have been interpreted, is so vast that no single scholar can control it. A literary history of England by one author, a history that is comprehensive and authoritative over the whole field, is next to impossible. Hence, the plan of the present book. A general harmony of treatment among the five contributors, rather than rigid uniformity of plan, has seemed desirable, and there is quite properly some difference of emphasis in different sections. Thus, there is more of strictly philological matter in the section on Old English literature, and more of political, economic, and social history in the treatment of the Nineteenth Century and After. It is hoped that the approach to the different sections will seem to be that best suited to the literature concerned.

Since it is expected that those who read this history or consult it will wish for further acquaintance with the writings and authors discussed, it has been a part of the plan to draw attention, by the generous use of footnotes, to standard editions, to significant biographical and critical works, and to the most important books and articles in which the reader may pursue further the matters that interest him. A few references to very recent publications have been added in proof in an effort to record the present state of scholarly and critical opinion.

Each of the five authors has had a free hand in dealing with his own period, but each has profited by the criticism and suggestions made by one or more of his collaborators. It is a pleasure also to record other obligations. Professor Arthur G. Brodeur has read most of the Old English section. Professors Clarence G. Child and MacEdward Leach have read the Middle English portion, Dr. Hope Emily Allen the chapters on the *Ancrene Riwle* and Richard Rolle, Professor William Roach the chapters on Arthurian romance. Professors Rodney M. Baine and Walter J. Bate made corrections in the manuscript of Book III, and Professors Donald F. Bond and Arthur Friedman helped with the proofs as well as the copy of this section. Professor Frederick L. Jones read the chapter on Shelley, Professor Mary S. Gardiner the chapter on evolution, and Professor Arthur C. Sprague the chapters on the drama in Book IV. To all these friends and colleagues the authors gratefully acknowledge their indebtedness for helpful criticism and suggestions.

It is with deep sorrow that we record the untimely death of Professor Tucker Brooke just as the galley proof of his chapters had begun to arrive. By his passing the world has lost a distinguished scholar, and his collaborators have lost a loyal friend. If there are any whom he would have thanked, they will know that their help would have been generously acknowledged, had he lived. Professor Sherburn and Professor Chew have given valuable assistance on the proofs of this part of the book, and the general editor is most grateful to them for sharing with him the responsibility for the final correction of these chapters.

Finally, Mrs. Chew has read all the proof with a keen eye for misprints; Mrs. Baugh has likewise read the proof and has devoted many hours to verifying the references in the Middle English section. To them the editor cannot leave unexpressed his personal indebtedness, though formal acknowledgment of their help is something which they least desire.

A.C.B.

NOTE TO SECOND EDITION

The reception of the *Literary History of England* has been so gratifying as to call for a number of successive printings, and these have permitted minor corrections to be made. The present edition has a further aim—to bring the book in line with the most recent scholarship. Small changes have been made in the plates wherever possible, but most of the additions, factual and bibliographical, are recorded in a Supplement. The text, Supplement, and Index are correlated by means of several typographical devices. Explanations of these devices appear on each part-title page as well as at the beginning of the Supplement and the Index.

The editor regrets that the authors of Books II, III, and IV did not live to carry out the revisions of those books, but their places have been ably taken by the scholars whose names appear with theirs in the list of collaborators. It has been the desire of the editor, as well as of those who have joined him, that each of these books should remain essentially as the original author wrote it, and we believe that other scholars would concur. Any new points of view, it is hoped, are adequately represented in the Supplement.

A. C. B.

Contents

BOOK II. THE RENAISSANCE

Part I. The Early Tudors (1485-1558)

Part II. The Reign of Elizabeth (1558-1603)

Part III. The Early Stuarts and The Commonwealth (1603-1660)

BOOK III. THE RESTORATION AND EIGHTEENTH CENTURY
(1660-1789)

PART I. THE RISE OF CLASSICISM

PART II. CLASSICISM AND JOURNALISM

PART III. THE DISINTEGRATION OF CLASSICISM

BOOK IV. THE NINETEENTH CENTURY
AND AFTER
(1789-1939)

List of Abbreviations

AJP	American Journal of Philology
Archiv	Archiv für das Studium der neueren Sprachen und Literaturen
ARS	Augustan Reprint Society
CBEL	Cambridge Bibliography of English Literature (4v, Cambridge, 1941; Supplement, 1957)
CFMA	Les Classiques français du moyen âge
CHEL	Cambridge History of English Literature (14v, 1907–17)
CL	Comparative Literature
E&S	Essays and Studies by Members of the English Association
EETS	Early English Text Society, Original Series
EETSES	Early English Text Society, Extra Series
EHR	English Historical Review
EIC	Essays in Criticism
ELH	ELH, A Journal of English Literary History
ELN	English Language Notes
EML Series	English Men of Letters Series
ES	English Studies
ESt	Englische Studien
GR	Germanic Review
HLQ	Huntington Library Quarterly
Hist. Litt.	Histoire littéraire de la France (38v, 1733–1941, in progress)
JAAC	Journal of Aesthetics and Art Criticism
JEGP	Journal of English and Germanic Philology
JHI	Journal of the History of Ideas
KSJ	Keats-Shelley Journal
LTLS	(London) Times Literary Supplement
MA	Medium Ævum
MLN	Modern Language Notes
MLQ	Modern Language Quarterly
MLR	Modern Language Review
MP	Modern Philology
MS	Medieval Studies
N&Q	Notes and Queries
NCF	Nineteenth-Century Fiction
PMLA	Publications of the Modern Language Association of America
PQ	Philological Quarterly

REL	Review of English Literature
RES	Review of English Studies
RLC	Revue de littérature comparée
RR	Romanic Review
SAB	Shakespeare Association Bulletin
SATF	Societé des anciens textes français
SEL	Studies in English Literature, 1500–1900 (Rice Univ.)
SF&R	Scholars' Facsimiles and Reprints
ShS	Shakespeare Survey
SP	Studies in Philology
SQ	Shakespeare Quarterly
SRen	Studies in the Renaissance
STS	Scottish Text Society
UTQ	University of Toronto Quarterly
VP	Victorian Poetry
VS	Victorian Studies

BOOK I
The Middle Ages

~⊙~

PART I
The Old English Period
(to 1100)

I[1]

Folk, State, and Speech

England and the English, state and folk,[2] are not old as historians reckon time. Tacitus set down the English name, it is true, as early as A.D. 98, but the Anglii of the *Germania*[3] were only a Germanic tribe of the Jutland peninsula, politically independent but culturally *part* of a nationality, not yet a nationality in their own right. They won cultural independence and national status by migration. In the fifth and sixth centuries of our era the Angles, like many another Germanic tribe of that day, gave up their old seats and sought land and loot within the bounds of the Roman Empire. If Bede is right, the whole tribe left home in this migration, and parts of at least two neighboring tribes, the Saxons and the Jutes, took ship in the same move.[4] All three tribes settled anew in the Roman province of Britannia, the eastern half of which they overran, from the Channel to the Firth of Forth. The western half held out longer against them, though without help from Rome, who had withdrawn her legions from Britannia one after another until, early in the fifth century, the land was left stripped of troops. Not until the ninth century did Cornwall yield to English arms, and further north the Welsh kept their freedom, more or less, until 1282, over 200 years after the English lost theirs at Hastings. But by the end of the sixth century most of the geographical area now known as England had fallen into the hands of

Migration to Britain

1 Bibliography: A. H. Heusinkveld and E. J. Bashe, *A Bibliographical Guide to Old English,* Univ. of Iowa Humanistic Studies, iv, 5 (Iowa City, 1931); see also the Old English section (1. 51-110) of the *CBEL*, and W. L. Renwick and H. Orton, *The Beginnings of English Literature to Skelton* (1940), pp. 133-252. Literary history: recent works are E. E. Wardale's *Chapters on Old English Literature* (1935) and C. W. Kennedy's *The Earliest English Poetry* (1943); an older work, S. A. Brooke's *English Literature from the Beginning to the Norman Conquest* (1898). The best treatment remains A. Brandl's *Englische Literatur*, in H. Paul's *Grundriss der germ. Philologie*, 2ed., 11. Band, 1. Abteilung, vi. Abschnitt (Strassburg, 1908), a work which, in spite of its title, deals almost wholly with Old English; also issued separately under the title *Geschichte der altenglischen Literatur*. Poetic texts: the corpus of Old English poetry was first edited by C. W. M. Grein, under the title *Bibliothek der ags. Poesie;* R. P. Wülcker's rev. ed. of this (1883-1898) is still standard; it is cited sometimes as Grein-Wülcker, sometimes as Wülcker or Wülker; a new collection in six volumes, *The Anglo-Saxon Poetic Records,* edited by G. P. Krapp and E. V. K. Dobbie, begun in 1932, was completed in 1953; we cite it as Krapp-Dobbie. Prose texts: the corpus of Old English prose still wants collecting, though a number of texts have been published in the *Bibl. der ags. Prosa*, the *Early English Text Society* series, and elsewhere.

2 Political history: F. M. Stenton, *Anglo-Saxon England* (Oxford, 1943); see also R. G. Collingwood and J. N. L. Myres, *Roman Britain and the English Settlements* (Oxford, 1936); R. H. Hodgkin, *A History of the Anglo-Saxons* [to A.D. 900] (2v, Oxford, 1935); Charles Oman, *England before the Norman Conquest* (1910).

3 Cap. 40; cf. K. Malone, *Namn och Bygd.* xxii (1934). 26-51.

4 *Hist. Eccl.* 1. 15. The *j* of *Jutes* (from Bede's *Iutae*) is in origin a blunder, by confusion of *I* and *j*. A better form would be *Iuts* or *Euts*, but these forms are current among the learned only.

the Germanic tribesmen, and these, whatever their tribe, had begun to think of themselves as members of a larger unit, a new nationality which went by the English name. The old tribal name *Angl(i)i* in its extended or generic sense, denoting the Germanic inhabitants of Britain irrespective of tribe, first appears in the writings of Pope Gregory the Great (d. 604).[5] The rise of this national name marks the beginnings of English national (as distinct from tribal) feeling.

By this time, indeed, the tribes no longer existed as such. When the Roman mission which Gregory had sent out reached England in the year 597, the missionaries did not find any tribal organizations of Angles, Saxons, and Jutes; they found a number of kingdoms, each autonomous but those south of the Humber drawn together, loosely enough, through their recognition of the *imperium* or overlordship of the reigning king of Kent. Earlier holders of such a personal imperium had been a king of Sussex and a king of Wessex, and later holders would be kings of various realms north and south of the Humber, until in the ninth century King Egbert would win it permanently for the royal house of Wessex.[6] We know nothing of the political connections of the various Germanic settlements in Britain before the rise of the first imperium, but we have little reason to think that any tribal organization, as such, outlived the migration from Germany. It seems altogether likely that the settlements started their respective careers as mutually independent political units, and that the tribal affiliations of given migrants or groups of migrants had little practical importance even at the time of migration, and soon became a matter of antiquarian and sentimental interest only.[7] No tribal loyalties, therefore, stood in the way of the English nationalism which, by virtue of geographical and cultural community, early came into being. On the religious side, moreover, this nationalism was fostered, not hindered, by the conversion to Christianity in the seventh century: the Roman missionaries organized a Church of England, not separate churches of Kent, Wessex, and the like, and in the year 664, at the synod of Whitby, the Romanizers, led by Wilfrid of York, won the field over their Irish rivals, ensuring thereby the religious unification of all England in a single Church.[8]

On the political side, it is true, English nationalism could hardly win much ground so long as the various kingdoms kept their autonomy, subject only to the shifting imperium of one or another of the many royal houses. But this particularistic system of government broke down for good and all in the ninth and tenth centuries. In the ninth Egbert set up and Alfred

[5] The Pope presumably had the term, directly or indirectly, from the English themselves. Certainly *Saxones* was the generic term current among the insular Celts, and on the Continent, in and before Gregory's day, and in setting this old and familiar term aside in favor of *Angli*, Gregory must have been trying to conform to English usage (which with good reason might be held authoritative here). The Pope's example was followed by Gregory of Tours and other writers of the seventh and eighth centuries.

[6] Bede, *op. cit.*, II. 5; see also *OE Annals* under A.D. 827. With the *imperium* went the title *Bretwalda* "ruler of Britain."

[7] Cf. J. N. L. Myres, in *Roman Britain and the English Settlements*, pp. 347-348.

[8] See S. J. Crawford, *Anglo-Saxon Influence on Western Christendom* (Oxford, 1933), pp. 48-49; cf. J. L. G. Meissner, *Celtic Church in England after the Synod of Whitby* (1929).

clinched the overlordship of the kings of Wessex, while in the tenth these kings took for title *Rex Anglorum* "King of the English." The other royal houses died out or lost their kingly rank and function; Alfred's followers on the throne won back the Danelaw; the former English and Danish kingdoms in Britain became mere provinces of a kingdom of England; in sum, an English nation replaced the old imperium. The political nationalism which grew up hand in hand with the new nation found focus, naturally enough, in the person of the king, and to this day English patriotism has not lost its association with the crown. But this is not the place to tell the tale of English nationalism in the tenth and eleventh centuries.[9] It will be enough to mention one of its many fruits, the "King's English" or standard written speech which had grown current all over England by the end of the tenth century. In this form of Old English nearly all the vernacular writings of the period were set down, and the scribes, in copying older writings, usually made them conform to the new standard of speech, though they might let an old spelling, here and there, go unchanged.

England, with its national king (descendant of Alfred, the national hero), its national Church (founded by a papal mission and in communion with Rome), its national speech (the King's English), and its old and rich ·national literature, stood unique in the Europe of the year 1000. No other modern European state reached full nationhood so early. And yet this English nationhood did not come too soon. Indeed, if it had not been reached early it might not have been reached at all, for the eleventh was a century of political disaster. The state succumbed to foreign foes, and for more than 200 years of French rule the only weapon left to the English was the strong nationalism handed down to them from the golden days of the past. But for this nationalism, the English language in particular would hardly have survived as such, though it might have lingered on for centuries in the form of mutually unintelligible peasant dialects, and with the triumph of French speech England would have become a cultural if not political province of France, doomed to a fate not unlike that which in later times actually befell Ireland at English hands. The nationalism which saved England from such a fate owed much of its strength, of course, to the rich literary culture of the centuries before Hastings, a culture marked from the beginning by free use of the mother tongue (alongside Latin) as a medium of expression. To this mother tongue, and to the literature of which it was the vehicle, let us now turn.[10]

English history (as distinguished from prehistory) begins in the year 597. *The* The Roman and Irish missionaries taught the English to make those written *Mother* records from which the historians glean their knowledge of early England. *Tongue*

[9] The tale is told by R. W. Chambers, *EETS*, 186 (1932). lxi-lxxx. See also Chambers, *Man's Unconquerable Mind* (1939), pp. 70-87. Chambers fails to point out that Old English nationalism was summed up and given official expression in the legal formula *an Christendom and an cynedom æfre on ðeode* "one Church and one state always in the land." See F. Liebermann, *Gesetze der Angelsachsen*, 1 (1903). 385.

[10] A standard guide to the language of the period is the *Old English Grammar* of J. and E. M. Wright (3ed., Oxford, 1925).

and the particular records written in the vernacular give us our earliest documentation of the mother tongue. Then as now this tongue went by the English name.[11] Its nearest kinsman was the speech of the Frisians. Closely kindred tongues, too, were Saxon and Franconian (or Frankish), the two main dialects of Low German.[12] The dialects of High German, and those of Scandinavian, had features which made their kinship to English less close. English was akin to all these neighboring tongues, and to Gothic, in virtue of common descent from Germanic, a language which we know chiefly through its offspring, as it had split up into dialects at a date so early that the records of it in its original or primitive state are few. Germanic in turn was an offshoot of Indo-European, a hypothetical tongue which we know only through the many languages which are descended from it. To the Indo-European family of languages belonged, not only English and the other children of Germanic, but also Latin (with its offspring, the Romance languages), Greek, the various Celtic and Slavic languages, Persian, Sanskrit (with other languages of India), Armenian, Albanian, Lithuanian, Latvian, etc.[13] Here, however, the kinship is so remote that it is overshadowed by a connection of another kind: a fellowship, so to speak. Latin, for instance, is only remotely linked to English by common descent from Indo-European, but it is closely linked to English by common participation in European life. The fellowship between English and Latin, it must be added, has always been one-sided; Latin has done the giving, English the taking, and this because Latin, the language of the Church and the vehicle of classical culture, had much to give and found little if anything that it needed to take.[14]

That English has many words taken from Latin is a fact familiar to everyone. Such words began coming in even before the migration to Britain (e.g., *street* and *cook*), and they have kept coming in ever since. Less familiar, perhaps, are the so-called semantic borrowings: native words with meanings taken from Latin. Two examples will have to serve: *gōd-spell*

[11] Throughout historical times the adj. *English* (used in the absolute construction) has been the regular name for the language spoken by the Germanic inhabitants of Britain. From the seventeenth century onward, the adj. *Anglo-Saxon* (a learned coinage of modern times) has had more or less currency as a synonym of *English*; among scholars it was commonly used to denote the earliest forms of English, but this meaning has never become familiar to the general public, and most scholars now call the language in all stages by the name which it has always had among those who spoke it: namely, *English*. See K. Malone, *RES*, v (1929). 173-185. When qualification by period is thought needful, a suitable qualifying term may be prefixed. See K. Malone, *English Journal*, College Edition, XIX (1930). 639-651. The usual division by periods gives *Old English* (beginnings to 1100), *Middle English* (1100 to 1500), and *Modern English* (1500 to present day). Linguistically speaking, this division is not accurate, but all divisions in the nature of the case are more or less arbitrary.

[12] The chief modern representatives of the Franconian dialect of Low German are Dutch and Flemish.

[13] The traditional classification here followed is figurative (for a language is no plant or animal and neither begets nor brings forth offspring). Classification in biological terms, moreover, like any other way of ordering phenomena, stresses some features at the cost of others. If, however, we bear all this in mind, we may accept the linguistic family tree as a legitimate device, serving a useful purpose.

[14] Here we must distinguish between classical and medieval Latin. The former took nothing from English; the latter (more precisely, that variety of medieval Latin current in England) became more or less colored, in time, by its English setting.

(modern *gospel*), literally "good news," is a translation of Latin *evangelium* (itself taken from Greek), and its meaning is restricted accordingly; *þing* (modern *thing*) originally had in common with Latin *res* the meaning "(legal) dispute, lawsuit," whereupon, in virtue of the equation thus set up, other meanings of *res* came to be given to the Old English word, including the meaning most common today.[15] But the fellowship with Latin affected English idiom and style as well as vocabulary; thus, the Latin *mundo uti* "live" reappears in the *worolde brucan* of *Beowulf*.

The fellowship of English with French began much later (toward the *French* end of the Old English period), but has proved just as lasting, and French comes next to Latin in the list of foreign tongues that have set their mark on English speech. The only other important medieval fellowship was that with Danish (as it was then called) or Scandinavian (as we call it now). *Danish* Here matters were complicated by the kinship of the two tongues. Both Danish and English went back to Germanic, and often one could not tell whether a given word was native English or of Viking importation, so much alike were the two languages. The Scandinavian origin of many of our most familiar words, however, can be proved by earmarks of one kind or another (e.g., *sky* and *take*). The fellowship with Danish, beginning in the ninth century, was at its height in the tenth and eleventh; after that it lessened, and though it never died out it has played only a small part in modern times.

Fellowship with foreign tongues is no peculiarity of English; all languages have connections of this kind, though some are more friendly than others. Such fellowships markedly affect the stock of words (including formative prefixes and suffixes), but as a rule leave almost or altogether unchanged the sounds and inflexions. Their effect on syntax, idiom, and style is hard to assess with precision. In the Old World of medieval times, four great linguistic cultural empires flourished side by side: Latin, Arabic, Sanskrit, and Chinese.[16] The languages of western Europe (whether Celtic, Germanic or Romanic) gave their allegiance to Latin, and English yielded with the rest,[17] but the Latinizing forces did not reach the height of their power in English until the Middle Ages were dead and gone. The medieval Englishman, meekly though he bowed before imperial speech, clung stubbornly to his linguistic heritage.

So much for externals. What of the mother tongue in its own right? Texts written partly or wholly in English (including glosses) have come down to us from the seventh century onward, and by the eleventh their number has greatly grown. From them we learn that the language was not uniform throughout the country but fell into dialects. Our records show *Dialects* four main dialects: one northern, commonly called Northumbrian; one midland, known as Mercian; and two southern, Kentish and West Saxon. The

---

[15] These and other examples may be found in S. Kroesch's paper, "Semantic Borrowing in Old English," *Studies . . . in honor of Frederick Klaeber* (Minneapolis, 1929), pp. 50-72.
[16] Greek had a medieval empire too, but it was a mere shadow of its Hellenistic self.
[17] Of all the western tongues, Icelandic alone held out against Latinization.

last of these is abundantly represented in the texts; it served as a basis for standard Old English speech. The other dialects are recorded rather meagerly, but the texts we have are enough to give us some idea of the dialectal distinctions. Other dialects than these presumably existed, but for want of texts we know little or nothing about them. The Old English dialects, unlike their descendants, the dialects of modern times, had undergone no great differentiation, and their respective speakers understood each other with ease. The Old English standardization of speech came about, not from any linguistic need but as a by-product and symbol of national unity: the King's English won for itself a prestige that proved overwhelming.

The Place of Old English

We shall not undertake to give in this history a detailed or even a systematic description of Old English speech. We shall do no more than mark, as best we can, where Old English stands on the road from Germanic times to the twentieth century. Here the classical or standard speech of A.D. 1000 will serve as our basis of comparison, and we shall compare this stage of Old English with primitive Germanic on the one hand and current English on the other. With our terms so defined, the temporal place of Old English is midway between Germanic and the speech of today. But mere lapse of time means little, since the tempo of change varies markedly down the years. Let us look at a few particulars each for itself. And first the matter of differentiation.

Independence

In the year 100, Germanic was already split up into dialects, but these dialects had not yet grown far apart, and the unity of the language was still unbroken. More precisely, the Anglo-Frisian or proto-English dialect had no independent existence, but was merely a regional form of Germanic. By the year 1000 a revolutionary change had taken place. English had become a language in its own right, fully developed and self-sufficient; in the process it had grown so unlike its Continental kinsmen that their respective speakers could not understand each other. No comparable change took place after the year 1000; since that date the language has simply kept the independence which it earlier won. In other words, the differentiation of English from the other Germanic tongues, a process which has been going on without a break for some 1500 years, was of the utmost importance in its early stages, but became relatively unimportant after English won its independence and established itself as a going concern. In the matter of differentiation, then, the fundamental changes took place in the first, not in the second of our two periods—before, not after A.D. 1000.

Simplified Forms

Next we take up the simplification of the inflexional system. Germanic was a highly inflected speech; Germanic and Latin were at about the same stage or level of inflexional complexity. Modern English, on the other hand, has a rather simple inflexional system and relies largely on word order and particles, devices not unknown to Germanic but less important than they are today in expressing syntactical relationships. How far had simplification gone by the year 1000? Among the nouns it had gone pretty far, though grammatical gender did not break down until Middle English times.[18] Among the adjectives, simplification went more slowly: the elaborate double system of adjectival inflexion characteristic of Germanic and kept to this day in German was kept in Old English too, and was not wholly given up until the fifteenth century. Much the same may be said of the demonstratives: *that* in Old English still had twelve forms as against the three current today (*the, that, those*),[19] and *this* still had ten forms as against the two of today (*this, these*). In the inflexion of the personal pronouns, however, the beginnings of the modern three-case system appear as early as the text of *Beowulf*, where we find the datives *me, þe, him* used now and then as accusatives; thus, *him* thrice occurs in accusative constructions (lines 963, 2377, 2828). This use led later to the loss of the personal (and interrogative) accusative forms, the old dative forms doing duty for both cases.[20] The Germanic system of verb inflexion also underwent marked simplification in Old English.[21]

This loss or reduction of many inflexional endings did not occur as a *Stress* strictly inflexional change, but made part of a change much wider in scope, and phonetic rather than inflexional in kind. English shared with the other Germanic tongues a system of pronunciation by which the first syllable of a word was stressed at the expense of the other syllables;[22] these, by progressive weakening, underwent reduction or were lost. Most of the many monosyllabic words in Old English go back to Germanic words of two or more syllables, and most of the dissyllabic words go back to Germanic polysyllables. The tendency to reduce or get rid of the unstressed syllables set in more than once in Old English times; thus, the so-called Middle English leveling of the inflexional endings actually took place in the tenth century, though traditional spelling kept the old distinctions in the texts (more or

---

[18] Nearly all Old English nouns belonged to one of three declensions: *a*-stems, *ō*-stems and *n*-stems. In the plural all these had a three-case system of inflexion: one form for the nom. and acc., one for the gen. and one for the dat. (Modern English has a two-case system: one form for nom. dat. acc., another for gen.). In the singular, the *ā*-stems had a three-case inflexion parallel to that of the plural. (Modern English likewise has a two-case system parallel to that of the plural). The other two declensions, however, had a two-case inflexion of the singular: one form marked the nom., the other the oblique case. (The neuter *n*-stem nouns had a different two-case system: one form for the nom. acc., the other for gen. dat.). Moreover, by the year 1000 the distinction between nom. and oblique had been lost in the singular of *ō*-stems, and tended to be lost in the singular of *n*-stems. The consequent inability of speakers to make case distinctions in these declensions may have had something to do with the Middle English tendency to give *a*-stem inflexion to the *ō*-stem and *n*-stem nouns. At any rate, this tendency existed and was carried through (to the incidental destruction of grammatical gender), and the modern inflexion of nouns is only a somewhat simplified form of the old *a*-stem inflexion. Other Germanic declensions, of which only remnants or traces appear in Old English, were *i*-stems, *u*-stems, *s*-stems, *r*-stems, *þ*-stems, *nd*-stems, and monosyllabic consonant stems.

[19] But the indeclinable definite article *the* occurs in Old English times (notably in annal 963 of the Laud text of the *Annals*).

[20] But the neut. acc. forms *hit* and *hwæt* were kept, and did duty for the dat. as well.

[21] Thus, the passive was lost, except for the form *hatte*; the dual was lost; the three persons were no longer distinguished except in the indicative singular, and even here only in the present tense (in the preterit the second person had a distinctive form, but the first and third persons were identical).

[22] But the inseparable preverbs did not take the stress (e.g., *be* in *becuman* "become"), and the prefixes *be-, for-,* and *ge-,* whether used as preverbs or not, usually lost whatever accent they may once have had (e.g., *forbod* "prohibition").

less) for 200 years thereafter. Nor did the year 1000 mark the end of such changes; the tendency has kept up to this day. It goes with our emphatic or dynamic style of utterance, a style which strengthens the strong and weakens the weak to gain its characteristic effects. The rhythm of English speech has always been apt for emphasis, but has lent itself less readily to indifference. In the quietest of conversations the points still come too strong for a really smooth flow; the dynamic style natural to the language makes itself felt in spite of everything. Perhaps the likewise hoary English taste for litotes has had the function of neutralizing the emphasis with which even an understatement must be uttered. And the quiet low voice which the English take such pains to cultivate may have a like function. In Old English verse the dynamic quality of ordinary speech rhythm was sharpened by alliteration and reinforced by an ictus which (unlike that of Latin verse) never did violence to the natural stress pattern. In effect the verse rhythm was a heightened prose rhythm; by virtue of this heightening, the words of the poet gained in strength and worth.

Stock of Words Finally we come to the development of the English vocabulary. Germanic was a speech well suited to those who spoke it, but its stock of words fell woefully short of meeting the needs of a civilized people. Many new scientific, technical, and learned terms had to be coined by the English after their conversion to Christianity and their adoption of that civilization which the missionaries brought up from the south. Indeed, the change from barbarism to civilization had marked effects on every aspect of English life, and names had to be found for all the new things that kept pouring in. The English rose magnificently to the occasion. They gave new meanings to old words, and made new words by the thousand. A good many Latin words were taken over bodily, but most of the new words were coinages, minted from the native wordstock whether inspired by Latin models or of native inspiration.[23] This creative linguistic activity made English an instrument of culture equal to the needs of the time. By the year 1000, this newcomer could measure swords with Latin in every department of expression, and was incomparably superior to the French speech that came in with William of Normandy.[24] But the shift from English to French in cloister

[23] On the Old English wordstock, see A. C. Baugh, *History of the English Language* (1935), pp. 75-80 and 101-110. Note also Professor O. Vocadlo's characterization of Old English: "The language of Wessex as it was developed by Alfred and his followers was certainly the most refined and cultured speech among all early Teutonic dialects. ... with its rich vocabulary, which conformed to a Latin pattern in the formation of native abstract words and was a fit tool even for the subtleties of philosophical and theological thought, [it] was no doubt the only fully developed vernacular language in Europe: the only medieval language which at an early period developed a remarkable nomenclature of science, religion and philosophy out of its own resources" (*Studies in English by Members of the English Seminar of the Charles University*, Prague, 1933, p. 62).

[24] Sir James Murray, in *The Evolution of English Lexicography* (1900), p. 14, puts the matter thus: "In literary culture the Normans were as far behind the people whom they conquered as the Romans were when they made themselves masters of Greece." Not until the twelfth century did the development of French into a literary language get well under way. In other important aspects of culture, too, the English were ahead of the Normans. As R. W. Chambers points out, in his *Continuity of English Prose* (1932), "the Norman conquerors were amazed at the wealth of precious things they found in England—a land which in that respect,

and hall brought about a great cultural decline among the hapless English, and when their speech at last rose again in the world it had been stripped of much of its cultural freight and now turned to Latin or French for words that it would never have needed if only it could have kept its own. By turning to foreign stores the language built up anew its lessened word stock, but at heavy cost. From that day to this it has gone the easy way, borrowing from others instead of doing its own creative work, until its muscles have become flabby for want of exercise, while the enormous and ever increasing mass of foreign matter taken into its system has given it a chronic case of linguistic indigestion.

In sum, the English language became a vehicle of civilization in Old *Summary* English times, but during the twelfth and thirteenth centuries, the great medieval centuries, it lost rather than gained cultural ground, and its remarkable recovery in the fourteenth and succeeding centuries took place in such a way that permanent damage was done. Thanks to this recovery, English has kept its function as a vehicle of civilization, but in so doing it was merely holding fast to an Old English inheritance. Today we carry on, but we owe our cultural tradition to the pathfinding work of the men of oldest England.

---

they said, surpassed Gaul many times over. England reminded them of what they had heard of the riches of Byzantium or the East. A Greek or a Saracen would have been astonished, said William of Poitiers, at the artistic treasures of England" (p. lxx). Again, "English jewellery, metal-work, tapestry and carving were famed throughout Western Europe. English illumination was unrivalled, . . . Even in stone-carving, those who are competent to judge speak of the superiority of the native English carver over his Norman supplanter" (*ibid.,* p. lxxvii). The verdict of one of "those who are competent to judge" reads thus: "in the minor arts the Norman conquest was little short of a catastrophe, blotting out alike a good tradition and an accomplished execution, and setting in its place a semi-barbaric art which attempted little and did that little ill" (A. W. Clapham, *English Romanesque Architecture before the Conquest* [1930], p. 77). See also M. Schapiro, *Gazette des Beaux-Arts,* VI Series, XXIII (1943). 146.

II
Anglo-Latin Writings

Composition in a foreign tongue has always been something of a *tour de force*. Few people ever master a language not their own, and writings done in an alien speech rarely rise above the level of school exercises. Now and then some genius transcends these limitations, but, even so, his work usually remains an aesthetic curiosity, of little consequence in the literary scheme of things. The Anglo-Latin writings [1] which we shall now take up make no exception to the general rule. They have their importance in the history of English culture, but they cannot be reckoned triumphs of literary art.

The custom of composing in Latin came to England with the missionaries of the Church, and the English converts (more precisely, those of them in training for holy orders) learned to read and write Latin as part of their professional education. Christianity, though Jewish in origin, had grown up in the Hellenistic world, and Greek accordingly became the language of the early Church. In the course of the third century, however, this linguistic unity was lost: Greek, kept in the east, yielded to Latin in the west as the masses there gradually gave up their native tongues and took the idiom of their Roman rulers. Into this *lingua franca* of the west St. Jerome translated the Bible; in this common speech his contemporary St. Augustine of Hippo [2] and other Church fathers wrote. By A.D. 597, when the conversion of the English began, a rich Christian literature in the Latin tongue had come into being. The Church made this literature accessible to the converts, along with secular and pagan literature in the same tongue. [3]

We know very little about the state of Latin learning among the English before the synod of Whitby. [4] After that synod (one of the great turning-

---

[1] The most convenient bibliography of Anglo-Latin writings for students of English literature is the section called "Writings in Latin" of the *CBEL* (1. 98-110). But the Anglo-Latin part of this section (it includes Celto-Latin writings as well) is incomplete and badly organized. By inadvertence F. J. E. Raby's *History of Secular Latin Poetry in the Middle Ages* (Oxford, 1934) is not listed in this section, though it is duly listed later (1. 281). It will here be cited as "Raby 1934," and the same author's *History of Christian-Latin Poetry . . .* (Oxford, 1927) will be cited as "Raby 1927."

[2] Jerome died in A.D. 420; Augustine, in A.D. 430.

[3] Some indication of the particular works current in early England may be had from the study of J. D. A. Ogilvy, *Books Known to Anglo-Latin Writers from Aldhelm to Alcuin* (Cambridge, Mass., 1936). We have no like study of vernacular writers, though learned sources for many Old English writings have been suggested, as will appear below, *passim*.

[4] See above, p. 4. From the witness of Bede (*Hist. Eccl.*, III. 3, 27) and from investigations into the sources of Anglo-Latin and vernacular writings, it looks as if the instruction which the Irish gave to their English pupils went beyond the elementary stage. We have no reason to credit the Roman mission, however, with anything more than elementary instruction in reading, writing, and singing.

points in English history) the reigning pope sent Theodore of Tarsus to *First*
England to serve as Archbishop of Canterbury and to make as fruitful as *Period*
possible the victory of the Romanizers at Whitby. With Theodore went
his fellow-monk, Abbot Hadrian, as chief helper in the work. Both were
men of learning, at home in Latin and Greek. They set up at Canterbury
a monastic school which worked wonders. Within a generation England
became the chief seat of scholarship in western Europe, and that golden
age of the English Church began through which the English people made
the greatest of all their contributions to civilization. During this momentous
period England led the world and set the course of history as she was not
to do again until modern times.[5]

The great service which the scholarship of the golden age rendered to us
and to all men was the preservation and transmission of classical culture.
This culture, long in decline, seemed doomed in its ancient western seats,
where barbarization proceeded apace. Luckily it found, first in Ireland and
then in England, a haven of refuge. Here Christianity soon won the hearts
of the heathen, and with the new faith came Mediterranean civilization, of
which the Church had made herself the bearer. In particular, monasticism
flourished, and the monks learned to read and copy the books that kept the
past alive. Further than this most of the monks did not go, but some took
the next step and composed works of their own in the Latin tongue. The
first Englishman of note to do this was Aldhelm; with him we begin our
brief survey of Anglo-Latin writings.

Aldhelm or Ealdhelm (d. 709)[6] was a man of Wessex, a kinsman of the *Aldhelm*
West Saxon king. He began his studies under the Irish scholar Maeldub,
but got most of his training at Canterbury under Theodore and Hadrian.
He gained a remarkable command of Latin, and learned some Greek besides, and even a little Hebrew. His duties as monk, as abbot of Malmesbury,
and finally as bishop of Sherborne did not keep him from doing a substantial amount of writing. He is said to have composed in English as well
as Latin, but his vernacular compositions have not come down to us; presumably they were thought of as trifles, unworthy of written record. For the
same reason only scraps have survived of Aldhelm's rhythmical Latin verse;
i.e., verse done in isosyllabic lines.[7] Nearly all we have of his poetry is in
hexameters, and belongs to the classical quantitative tradition.

---

[5] See S. J. Crawford, *Anglo-Saxon Influence on Western Civilization 600-800* (Oxford,
1933). See also W. Wattenbach, *Deutschlands Geschichtsquellen im Mittelalter* (3ed., Berlin,
1873), I. 102; L. von Ranke, *Sämmtliche Werke* 3ed., xxxvII (Leipzig, 1907). 11-13; K. Malone,
JHI, 1 (1940). 292-293; J. W. H. Atkins, *English Literary Criticism, the Medieval· Phase*
(Cambridge, 1943), p. 38. The student would do well to read, besides, the chapter on the
golden age in R. H. Hodgkin's *History of the Anglo-Saxons* (Oxford, 1935). The latest study
of these matters is that of W. Levinson, *England and the Continent in the Eighth Century*
(Oxford, 1946).

[6] R. Ehwald, *Aldhelmi Opera* (Berolini, 1919; *Mon. Germ. Hist., Auct. Antiq.*, xv).

[7] See Ehwald, *ed. cit.*, pp. 520-521, where the items are brought together. Ehwald also
includes in his edition (pp. 523-537) five *Carmina Rhythmica* by pupils of Aldhelm: four by
Æthilwald, one by a pupil whose name is not known. For a discussion of these poems see
Raby 1927, pp. 144-145 and Raby 1934, 1. 172-174. Rhythmical verse must be kept apart
from accentual verse, of which it was a forerunner. A truly accentual Latin versification
developed too late in the Middle Ages to come within the scope of this chapter.

Aldhelm's major poem is *De Virginitate* (2904 lines), a versification of a prose treatise of his which bears the same name. He also wrote a number of short *Carmina Ecclesiastica* (428 lines in all), and 100 versified riddles, done on the model of the 100 *Enigmata* of Symphosius,[8] but departing from these in various ways.[9] Aldhelm incorporated his riddles into the learned prose treatise which he wrote on versification, a treatise which took the form of a letter to King Ealdfrith of Northumbria, whence its title *Epistola ad Acircium*.[10] In it Aldhelm set forth in some detail the principles of metrics as he understood them, with many examples drawn indiscriminately from classical and postclassical writings, sacred and profane. A few other letters of Aldhelm's also survive.

Aldhelm wrote Latin well, by the standards of his own time. His taste for rare words, involved expression, and stylistic display reflects that of the age, and should not be held against him personally.[11] He had great gifts, but his education proved too much for them. Overawed by the postclassical literary culture which his teachers hammered into him, he took it as he found it and made it his own, without thought of criticism. What else could be expected of a man who was but one remove from barbarism? His writings won the admiration of many (e.g., Bede), and later writers were more or less influenced by him, especially in the composition of Latin and vernacular riddles.[12] The cultural developments in northern England, however, proved more important for Anglo-Latin letters; to these developments let us now proceed.

Benedict Biscop

Benedict Biscop (628-690), a Northumbrian monk of noble birth, happened to be in Rome, on the second of his five journeys to the Continent, when the Pope made Theodore Archbishop of Canterbury. At the Pope's request, Biscop accompanied Theodore to England, and helped him start his work there, serving two years as abbot of the monastery at Canterbury. After his return to his native Northumbria, Biscop founded at Wearmouth a Benedictine monastery on the Roman model; a few years later he estab-

---

[8] For the text of Symphosius see R. T. Ohl, *The Enigmas of Symphosius* (Philadelphia, 1928). The editor prints the Latin text and an English translation on opposite pages. In his Introduction (pp. 20-23) he sketches briefly the influence of Symphosius on Anglo-Latin writers.

[9] Thus, the riddles of Symphosius are all the same length (three lines), whereas those of Aldhelm vary greatly in length. Aldhelm's riddles were edited by J. H. Pitman, *Yale Studies in English*, LXVII (1925). The editor gives an English translation in blank verse, and in his introduction discusses Aldhelm's style and influence.

[10] Ehwald, *ed. cit.*, pp. 33-204. For an explanation of the curious name *Acircius*, see Ehwald, p. 61.

[11] That this taste was no peculiarity of Celto-Latin writers seems clear. Certainly Aldhelm's training at Canterbury did not teach him the error of his ways. Cf. J. W. H. Atkins, *op. cit.*, pp. 41-42.

[12] This influence went with that of Symphosius; see the discussions of Ohl and Pitman mentioned above. Besides the riddles of Aldhelm, we have 40 Latin riddles by Tætwine (d. 734), to which his contemporary Hwætberht or Eusebius added 60 in order to bring the total to the conventional century. Wynfrith or Boniface (d. 755) and Alcuin (d. 804) also wrote riddles; the former must be reckoned a disciple of Aldhelm. On the riddles associated with Bede, see F. Tupper, "Riddles of the Bede Tradition," *MP*, II (1905). 561-572. For a study of wider scope see E. von Erhardt-Siebold, *Die lateinischen Rätsel der Angelsachsen* (Heidelberg, 1925); the author notes that "the Latin riddles give ... a picture of an amazingly developed culture in Old England. They ... bear witness, further, to the amazing amount of reading done by their clerical authors" (pp. 3-4).

lished a sister monastery at Jarrow. These foundations soon became centers of learning unequaled in western Europe. For them, in repeated journeys to Rome, Biscop brought together a library adequate to the needs of scholarship. In his own teaching he applied the lessons he had learned at Canterbury and elsewhere, and his successor, Abbot Ceolfrid, kept up the good work. Under these two masters Bede, "the teacher of all the Middle Ages," [18] and many other Englishmen got a training comparable to that given by Theodore and Hadrian at Canterbury. The English golden age reached its height in the double monastery of Wearmouth-Jarrow.

The Venerable Bede (673-735), the greatest of Biscop's pupils and the chief Anglo-Latin writer of the golden age, entered the monastic school at Jarrow when he was seven years old, and spent the rest of his life in this monastery, becoming a deacon at 19, a priest at 30; he.performed the regular duties of a Benedictine monk up to his last illness. His writings are too many to be listed here; [14] they include grammatical and critical handbooks like *De Metrica Arte*, scientific treatises like *De Ratione Temporum*, commentaries on various books of the Bible (canonical and apocryphal), homilies, saints' lives, and verse. Many of his books had a wide circulation in medieval Europe and held their own for centuries as the authoritative treatments of their respective subjects. At present, however, Bede's fame rests chiefly on a work of his latter years, the *Historia Ecclesiastica Gentis Anglorum* ("Church History of the English People").[15] This work is our primary source of information about the most momentous period in English history: the period of change from barbarism to civilization. In other words, Bede is not only first among English historians in point of time; he is also first in importance.

The story of the great change found in Bede a worthy teller. The merits of Bede as a historian have often been pointed out and need not be dwelt upon here. In assessing his merits as a writer we must bear in mind that he was first of all the scholar, not the literary artist. He undertook the labor of composition to set forth historical truth, not to provide aesthetic delight. But it remains a pleasure to read the *History*. Bede wrote Latin with the

Bede (margin)

[18] W. Wattenbach, *loc. cit.*
[14] Bede lists nearly all of them himself at the end of the *Hist. Eccl.* Editions: J. A. Giles, *Works of Venerable Bede* (12v, 1843-1845); J. P. Migne, *Ven. Bedae Opera Omnia* (Paris, 1850-1851), in *Patrologiae Cursus Completus* (Sec. Ser.), xc-xcv (but Vol. xcv is only partly devoted to Bede); *Expositio Actuum Apostolorum et Retractatio*, ed. M. L. W. Laistner (Cambridge, Mass., 1940). See also M. L. W. Laistner, *A Hand-List of Bede Manuscripts* (Ithaca, N. Y., 1943), reviewed by N. Ker, *MA*, xiii (1944). 36-40; and C. W. Jones, *Bedae Pseudepigrapha* (Ithaca, N. Y., 1939). See also R. W. Chambers, "Bede," in *Proc. Brit. Acad.*, xxii (1936). 129-156. For a discussion of Bede's grammatical and critical writings, see J. W. H. Atkins, *op. cit.*, pp. 43-51. For a discussion of his Latin poetry, see Raby 1927, pp. 146-149 and Raby 1934, I. 174-175. The only vernacular poem of Bede's that has come down to us, the *Death Song*, is taken up below, p. 44.
[15] Ed. C. Plummer, *Bedae Opera Historica* (Oxford, 1896), and J. E. King, *Baedae Opera Historica* (Loeb Classical Library, 1930). Both these editions also give the *Vita Beatorum Abbatum* (the lives of the abbots of the double monastery at Wearmouth-Jarrow), the letter to Archbishop Egbert, and Cuthbert's letter on the death of Bede. The Loeb edition gives Latin text and English translation on opposite pages. Another translation: Everyman's Library No. 479, with an admirable introductory essay by Vida D. Scudder. Concordance: P. F. Jones, *A Concordance to the Hist. Eccl. of Bede* (Cambridge, Mass., 1929).

competence to be expected of a gifted man whose life had been spent in speaking, reading, writing, and teaching that tongue. His Latin style was no miracle, *pace* Hodgkin.[16] It lacks the showiness of Aldhelm's style because Bede, unlike Aldhelm, did not care for show. The style, in its strength and simplicity, reflects the man.

Bede included in his *History,* alongside the events commonly reckoned historical, many miracles, visions, and other matters which strike the modern reader as unhistorical enough. Here we must allow for the credulity of the age and, in particular, for the influence of Pope Gregory's *Dialogues.* Yet even here Bede makes every effort to be accurate. He admits wonders only after he has investigated them and found them well authenticated. His standards of verification are not ours, of course. If today a victim of snakebite were to drink down some scrapings of Irish books and get well, we should not conclude that the scrapings had worked the cure. But Bede in accepting this conclusion not only echoed the medical science of his day; he also paid tribute to the sanctity and miracle-working power of the sister island. Certainly no Irishman could outdo Bede in reverence for Ireland. He realized to the full, Romanizer though he was, how much the English owed to their Irish teachers, and he showed himself deeply grateful and appreciative.

Most of the unhistorical matter in Bede's *History* belongs to legend in the technical sense; that is, to hagiography. Besides the incipient or abbreviated saints' lives scattered through the work, Bede wrote saints' lives as such, notably two lives of St. Cuthbert, the shorter in hexameters, the longer in prose.[17] Bede's contemporaries Felix and Eddi also wrote saints' lives,[18] and thenceforth this kind of biography flourished in England as elsewhere in Christendom.[19] Secular biography is exemplified in Bishop Asser's *Life of King Alfred,*[20] but many centuries were to pass before this genre really began to flourish.[21]

One of Bede's pupils, Egbert, became Archbishop of York and there set up a cathedral school which in time eclipsed Wearmouth-Jarrow as a center

---

[16] *Op. cit.* I. 354.

[17] Here Bede was presumably imitating the fifth-century poet Sedulius, who balanced his *Carmen Paschale* with a prose *Opus Paschale.* Compare Aldhelm's two versions of *De Virginitate,* likewise inspired by the example of Sedulius.

[18] For Felix, see below, p. 75. Edition of Eddi: B. Colgrave, *The Life of Bishop Wilfrid, by Eddius Stephanus:* text, translation, and notes (Cambridge, 1927). As early as 713 some monk of Whitby (name unknown) had written a life of Gregory the Great; it was edited in 1904 by (Cardinal) F. A. Gasquet.

[19] Other hagiographies of the golden age: Æthelwulf, *Carmen de Abbatibus Cellae Suae,* in T. Arnold's edition (*Rolls Ser.,* 75) of Simeon of Durham's *Hist. Eccl.* Dunhelmensis (1882), Appendix I. 265-294; Alcuin, *De Pontificibus et Sanctis Ecclesiae Eboracensis Carmen,* in Wattenbach and Duemmler, *Monumenta Alcuiniana* (Berlin, 1873), pp. 80-131, and in J. Raine, *The Historians of the Church of York and its Archbishops* (*Rolls Ser.,* 71), I. 349-398; Alcuin, *Vita Sancti Willibrordi* (prose and verse), in Wattenbach and Duemmler, *ed. cit,* pp. 35-79, and in Migne, *Patr. Lat.,* CI. 694-724; Willibald, *Vita Bonifatii,* in *Mon. Germ. Hist., Scriptorum,* II. 331-353 (translation by G. W. Robinson, Cambridge, Mass., 1916); the anonymous *Vita Alchuini Abbatis* in Wattenbach and Duemmler, *ed. cit.,* pp. 1-34.

[20] Ed. W. H. Stevenson, *Asser's Life of King Alfred* (Oxford, 1904). Translations: by A. S. Cook (Boston, 1906); by L. C. Jane (1924).

[21] The first autobiography by an Englishman is the *Vita ... Willibaldi ...* in T. Tobler, *Descriptiones Terrae Sanctae ...* (Leipzig, 1874), pp. 1-55. Willibald died in A.D. 786.

of learning. Of the Englishmen trained at York the greatest was Alcuin *Alcuin* (735-804).[22] The writings of Alcuin have no great literary worth, it is true, but the man himself remains one of the most important figures in the cultural history of the West. He owes his importance to the part he played in the revival of learning which took place under Charles the Great: the so-called Carolingian Renaissance. Thanks to this revival, the culture of classical antiquity did not die out in western Europe but was transmitted to later generations and became the foundation upon which modern civilization was built. But Charles could not set the revival going out of the resources of his own empire, where only remnants of classical culture survived. He had to turn to Italy, to Ireland, and above all to England for teachers and cultural leadership generally. And for captain of his little troop of scholars he chose Alcuin, who reformed and built up the court school of Charles on the model of the cathedral school at York, and had a hand in founding other centers of learning, notably the one at Tours, where he served as abbot. The success of the Carolingian Renaissance was largely due to Alcuin's able leadership. But no revival of learning would have been possible, even so, had not the great reform of the Gallican and German churches, earlier in the eighth century, prepared the way. This reform was the work of Boniface, another Englishman. To Alcuin and Boniface, then, we of the West owe so much that they will always remain major figures in the history of our culture.[23]

While English missionaries and scholars were busy bringing civilization *Second* back to the Continent, Viking raids were laying low the cultural centers of *Period* England. During the ninth century the destruction went so far that, in King Alfred's words,[24] whereas

men from abroad used to seek wisdom and learning here in this country, ... now, if we were to have such wisdom and learning, we could get them only from outside. So utterly had book-learning fallen away in England that there were very few, this side the Humber, who knew how to interpret their [Latin] service-books in English, or even how to translate from Latin into English a written message; and I think there were not many beyond the Humber.

The good King made great efforts to revive the learning of the golden age, but not until the latter part of the tenth century did Latin scholarship again begin to flourish in England. At that time, under the leadership of the three bishops Dunstan, Æthelwold, and Oswald, backed by King Edgar,

[22] Ed. J. P. Migne, *Alcuini Opera Omnia* (Paris, 1863), in *Patrologia Cursus Completus* (Ser. Lat. Prior), Vols. c and ci; [W.] Wattenbach and [E.] Duemmler, *Monumenta Alcuiniana* (Berlin, 1873), sixth volume of P. Iaffe's *Bibl. Rerum Germ.* See also *Mon. Germ. Hist.*, for poems and letters: poems in *Poetae Latini Aevi Carolini*, I and IV; letters in *Epistolarum*, IV. See A. F. West, *Alcuin and the Rise of the Christian Schools* (1892); C. J. B. Gaskoin, *Alcuin: His Life and his Work* (1904); R. B. Page, *The Letters of Alcuin* (1909). W. S. Howell, *The Rhetoric of Alcuin and Charlemagne*: introduction, text, translation, and notes (Princeton, 1941). On the verse see Raby 1927, pp. 159-162 and Raby 1934, I. 178-187, and for criticism J. W. H. Atkins, *op. cit.*, pp. 51-58.
[23] For a brief discussion see Raby 1927, pp. 154-158; see also Atkins, *op. cit.*, p. 61. For fuller treatment see S. J. Crawford, *op. cit.*, and W. Levinson, *op. cit.*
[24] From the Preface of his translation of Gregory's *Cura Pastoralis.*

a monastic reform took place which brought about, among other things, a marked renewal of scholarly activity.[25] The learning of late Old English times, however, was chiefly concentrated in the south and west: at Glastonbury, Winchester, Canterbury, Worcester, and other centers. Monasticism in the north had been so thoroughly uprooted by the Danes that in spite of the efforts of Archbishop Oswald of York it did not come back into its own until the twelfth century.

In this second period of learned activity the Anglo-Latin writings seem to have been chiefly in prose. Frithegoda of Canterbury and Wulfstan of Winchester wrote verse, it is true,[26] but, apart from their compositions, little except prose has come down to us. The prose writings of the period follow the pattern laid down in the golden age, though not without variation. Hagiography continues to flourish.[27] Historical writing proper is represented by the *Chronica* of the ealdorman Ethelwerd [28] and the *Historia Novorum in Anglia* of Eadmer.[29] We also find translations from English into Latin, foreshadowings of the decline in vernacular letters which lay ahead.[30] The most active field, however, came to be that of monastic education and discipline. Here Æthelwold led the way with his *De Consuetudine Monachorum*, but his pupil Ælfric, best known for vernacular writings, composed the fundamental schoolbooks needed for teaching Latin to the oblates. These books, the *Grammar*, the *Glossary*, and the *Colloquy*,[31] gave to the masters in the monastic schoolrooms admirable tools. The *Colloquy* in particular is so good that even today we have nothing better to offer to would-be learners of a foreign tongue. Nothing of comparable merit can be found among the schoolbooks current at this time on the Continent.

---

[25] Consult D. Knowles, *The Monastic Order in England: A History of its Development* . . . *943-1216* (Cambridge, 1940); J. A. Robinson, *The Times of St. Dunstan* (Oxford, 1923). See also F. Tupper, *MLN*, VIII (1893). 344-367.

[26] See Raby 1927, pp. 152-153. Bibliography in *CBEL*, I. 107.

[27] Hagiographies of the second period: B.'s life of Dunstan, in W. Stubbs, *Memorials of St. Dunstan; Rolls Ser.*, 63 (1874), pp. 3-52 (but Stubbs thinks that B. was a Continental Saxon, not an Englishman); Osbern's life of Dunstan, in Stubbs, *ed. cit.*, pp. 69-161; Eadmer's life of Dunstan, in Stubbs, *ed. cit.*, pp. 162-249; Ælfric's life of Æthelwold, in J. Stevenson's edition (*Rolls Ser.*, 2) of the *Chronicon Monasterii de Abingdon*, II (1858). 253-266; Wulfstan of Winchester's life of Æthelwold (prose with appended verses), in Migne, *Patr. Lat.*, CXXXVII. 79-114; Frithegoda of Canterbury's life of Wilfrid (verse), in Raine, *ed. cit.*, I. 105-159; Eadmer's life of Wilfrid, in Raine, *ed. cit.*, I. 161-226; the anonymous life of Oswald, in Raine, *ed. cit.*, I. 399-475; Eadmer's life of Oswald, in Raine, *ed. cit.*, II. 1-59; Eadmer's life of Anselm, in M. Rule's edition (*Rolls Ser.*, 81) of Eadmer's *Historia Novorum* (1884), pp. 303-440; the anonymous life of Edward the Confessor, ed. H. R. Luard (1858; *Rolls Ser.*, 3), pp. 387-435.

[28] *Monumenta Historica Britannica* (1848), pp. 499-521. As Ethelwerd was a layman, one would not expect him to write good Latin; the thing to wonder at is his ability to write Latin at all. So far as we know, western Europe possessed no other Latin-writing layman of royal blood *c.* 1000.

[29] Ed. M. Rule, *ed. cit.*, pp. 1-302. Eadmer's work is well done, but does not live up to its title; it amounts to a life of Anselm, told by a devoted follower of his.

[30] Thus, we have a translation into Latin of the *Old English Annals*. Colman's life of Bishop Wulfstan of Worcester was written in English but survives only in a Latin translation (by William of Malmesbury). See R. W. Chambers, *EETS*, 186 (1932), pp. lxxxiii-iv.

[31] Ed. J. Zupitza, *Ælfrics Grammatik und Glossar* (Berlin, 1880); W. H. Stevenson, *Early Scholastic Colloquies* (Oxford, 1929), pp. 74-102 (Stevenson's book includes other Anglo-Latin colloquies as well); G. N. Garmonsway, *Ælfric's Colloquy* (1931).

Ælfric's other Latin works, though written with characteristic competence, have less cultural importance.[32]

If the golden age is marked by a fusion of cultures, the period with which we are now dealing shows an ever growing predominance of the Mediterranean over the native component in the fusion-product. By the eleventh century English monastic life had come to differ little from that of western Europe in general. The medieval world was fast becoming a cultural unit, dominated by a Church international in outlook and centralized in administration. To this trend of things the Church of England, by her devotion to the Papacy and her missionary efforts in behalf of papal supremacy, had made the decisive contribution, through Wilfrid, Boniface, and a host of other workers in the field. In the cataclysm which was about to sweep the English nation into foreign bondage, one element of the national life stood firm: Anglo-Latin letters. The literature of learning held its own, and even made forward strides, because its linguistic medium and scholarly pattern were already international.

[32] Bibliography in *CBEL*, I. 91-92.

III

The Old Tradition:[1] Poetic Form

Speakings
and
Writings

Few things of man's begetting outlast for long the times that give them birth, and works of literary art share the fate of the rest. The loss is the heavier when (as in Old English) much of the artistic activity takes the shape of *speakings;* that is, literary compositions designed for oral rendition (sung or said) and as a rule not circulated in written form.[2] No speakings, of course, could come down to us unless they happened to get recorded, and even then the chances would be all against their survival, for most of the old manuscripts perished long ago, victims of the years.[3] One might therefore reasonably expect to find the Old English literary records (or what is left of them) made up chiefly of *writings;* that is, compositions designed for circulation in written form. And when the records are studied, this expectation is more than fulfilled; indeed, the student may seek long before he finds any speakings at all. The few that survive are our oldest literary heirlooms, for the literary art of the English (as of the other Germanic peoples) before their conversion to Christianity found expression in speakings only.

Runes

The English of heathen times knew how to write, it is true. They brought with them from the Continent a *futhark* or runic alphabet of twenty-four letters, and to this in the course of time they added several new signs of their own. But the runes were epigraphic characters, and their use was therefore limited to inscriptions, cut or hammered out on hard surfaces (e.g., the pommel of a sword, the sides of a monumental stone, the top or sides of a box). This kind of writing is obviously not well suited to the recording of literary compositions, which (unless very short) need more space than a runemaster would be likely to find available. Moreover, even if a suitable

---

[1] The chief work on the Germanic literary tradition is A. Heusler's *Die Altgermanische Dichtung* (Berlin, n.d. but copyright 1926). For the Germanic background in general, J. Hoops's *Reallexikon der germanischen Altertumskunde* (4v, Strassburg, 1911-1919) is useful.

[2] Speakings are also known as "oral literature," a subject treated at length by H. M. and N. K. Chadwick, *The Growth of Literature.* The actual and hypothetical speakings of Old English are discussed in Vol. 1 of this work (Cambridge, 1932). The authors, however, take for speakings many compositions which others interpret as writings.

[3] Only eight Old English MSS with much vernacular poetry in them have survived. These are the Corpus MS, more precisely MS CCCC 201, at Corpus Christi College, Cambridge (whence the abbreviation CCCC); the so-called Paris Psalter, or MS Fonds Latin 8824 of the Bibliothèque National in Paris; the Vercelli Book, or Codex cxvii of the cathedral chapter library at Vercelli in northern Italy; the Exeter Book, preserved in the library of Exeter Cathedral; MS Junius 11 (often called the Cædmon MS) at the Bodleian Library, Oxford; and three MSS in the Cotton collection at the British Museum: Vitellius A xv (2nd MS, the Nowell or *Beowulf* codex), Otho A vi (the Boethius MS), and Tiberius B 1. Nearly all these MSS, moreover, have come down in a more or less damaged or mutilated state.

hard surface could be found, it would hardly be used to put a poem on
unless there were some very special reason for making such a record. Be it
added that runemasters were few and far between, and presumably drew
good pay for cutting an inscription; in other words, epigraphic writing
was expensive. The poets, for their part, would naturally be interested in
making their compositions known to the public (i.e., in uttering them, or
having them uttered, before audiences), not in making records of them
which few would see and fewer could read. Certainly no English poems of
heathen times have come down to us in the form of runic inscriptions, and
we have no reason to think that such poems were ever so recorded in English (though Scandinavian cases of the kind are known).

With the introduction of Christianity a great change took place. The
missionaries brought parchment, pen and ink, and the custom of writing
literary compositions down. They also brought the Roman alphabet.[4] The *The*
English futhark, epigraphic though it was in origin and history, might *Roman*
perfectly well have been used for writing with pen and ink on parchment, *Alphabet*
but the foreign missionaries and their English pupils associated the Roman
alphabet with this kind of writing and used it, not only in copying Latin
texts, but also in making English texts. Yet the old runes were not given
up for centuries. They were kept alongside the new letters, and the co-
existence of two kinds of writing naturally led to overlapping. On the one
hand, letters might be used in inscriptions; on the other, runes might be
used in manuscripts. The two runes *thorn* and *wynn,* indeed, were added
to the alphabet, as symbols for sounds wanting in postclassical Latin but
common in English. And the new practice of recording literary compositions
had its effect on native epigraphy: thus, the *Dream of the Rood* won epigraphic as well as manuscript record.[5]

In Old English times the Church monopolized the production of manu- *MSS*
scripts. A layman might know how to read; he might even be an author
(like King Alfred). But it would hardly occur to him to undertake the
work of a scribe, any more than it would occur to the ordinary reader or
author of today to undertake the work of a printer. The making of manuscripts was in the hands of the Church because the art or craft of writing
on parchment with pen and ink was part of the professional equipment of
the well-trained cleric, and of him alone. And the monopoly was strengthened by the workings of supply and demand. The Church made manuscripts
chiefly though not wholly for her own use; the readers of the day were
mostly clerics. Old English literature as we have it (not as it was) therefore
reflects the tastes and professional interests of the clergy; from the MSS
we get a one-sided picture of the literary art of those days. Poems that the

---

[4] Most of the Old English MSS were written in the so-called insular hand, a minuscule
script developed by the Irish out of half-uncial and brought to England by Irish missionaries
in the seventh century. Toward the end of the Old English period the insular hand lost favor,
and the so-called Caroline minuscule script, already dominant on the Continent, became
fashionable in England as well.

[5] Runes were used for some alliterative verses inscribed on the Franks Casket (eighth
century?). Text in Krapp-Dobbie, VI. 116.

clerics for any reason disliked or disapproved of did not get recorded, unless they happened to strike the fancy of some nonconformist scribe or anthologist who had the courage of his heterodoxy. Moreover, since little space was available, items thought of as trivial or as less important stood little chance of inclusion in a MS miscellany. Few things in lighter vein could be expected to come down to us under such conditions, and in fact the tone of the extant literary monuments is prevailingly serious and edifying.

Authors   Departures from the normal pattern we owe, no doubt, to the likes and dislikes of individual makers or takers of MSS. In many cases pride of authorship may have played a part; certainly a clerical author had ways of getting his compositions written down, even if he did not write them down himself, and the bulk of what we have was presumably composed as well as written down by clerics. A few compositions seem wholly secular, and two of them (*Wife's Lament* and *Eadwacer*) purport to be by women. But even here we cannot be certain of lay authorship; in every period of English literature clergymen have composed works secular enough in tone and spirit, and a male author might perfectly well make a woman his mouthpiece. The case is otherwise when the composition is definitely heathen (rather than secular); here clerical authorship must be ruled out. Unluckily no compositions of this kind, on the literary level, have come down to us, except a few spells (or charms), and most of these, in their recorded form, show more or less of a Christian coloring. On the other hand, we cannot safely presume clerical authorship of every work religious in tone or subject. Cædmon was a farmhand (Hild made him a monk *after* God had made him a poet), and other religious pieces besides his may well have been composed by men who had never taken holy orders or monastic vows. Our uncertainties are the greater since in most cases we do not know so much as the name of the author of a given work, and even if we happen to know the author's name we may be little the wiser; thus, our knowledge of the poet Cynewulf is limited to what we can glean from his poems. This want of biographical information, however, need not disturb us overmuch. Literary art in Old English times was highly traditional, and the personal history of the author did not come out in his compositions so markedly as it does in times when originality rather than mastery of a conventional mode wins the prizes.

Old English writings might be in prose or verse; speakings were restricted to verse, in early times at least.[6] We set the prose aside for the time being. The verse, writings and speakings alike, was regularly composed in the alliterative measure that had come down to the English from their Germanic forefathers. Before taking up the poetic kinds (or genres) cul-

---

[6] It seems unlikely that the English of heathen times cultivated the prose speaking or anecdote as a literary art-form; certainly we have no evidence of the existence of such an art-form then, though it may have developed in later times. See C. E. Wright, *The Cultivation of Saga in Anglo-Saxon England* (Cambridge, 1939), and K. Malone, *English Studies*, xxiii (1931). 110-112.

tivated in this measure, it will be needful to consider the measure itself, and the style that went with it.

Old Germanic verse makes many problems for the prosodist, and none *Short* of the methods of scansion proposed need be taken as definitive.[7] Here we *Verse* shall deal briefly with the main points. The rhythm of the verse grew *and Line* naturally out of the prose rhythm (as we saw above), by a process of metrical heightening and lowering. A metrically heightened syllable is called a *lift* (German *hebung*); a metrically lowered syllable, a *drop* (German *senkung*). Only a syllable that took or might take a main stress in the prose rhythm was subject to metrical heightening; in the same way, only a syllable that lacked or might lack stress in the prose rhythm was subject to metrical lowering. We do not know just how the metrical heightening and lowering were brought about, but time as well as stress played a part, and such verse as was sung or chanted necessarily made use of pitch patterns different from those of ordinary speech. The metrical heightening might be reinforced by alliteration [8] or rime, giving a *major* lift. A lift not so reinforced is a *minor* lift. The basic metrical unit was the short verse, made up of a varying number of syllables, at least one of which was a lift. Usually the short verse had two lifts. Such a verse might stand alone or in series. We illustrate with a passage from a legal text, *Hit Becwæð:* [9]

ne plot ne ploh,	nor plot nor plowland,
ne turf ne toft,	nor sod nor site,
ne furh ne fotmæl,	nor furrow nor foot-length,
ne land ne læse,	nor tillage nor pasturage,
ne fersc ne mersc,	nor fresh [water] nor marsh,
ne ruh ne rum,	nor rough [land] nor open [land],
wudes ne feldes,	of wood nor of field,
landes ne strandes,	of land nor of strand,
wealtes ne wæteres.	of wold nor of water.

Here we have nine short verses in series. The first six verses make a group, and the last three verses make another group; grouping by twos (giving long verses or *lines*) does not occur in this passage. The verses are not linked one to another by alliteration; each verse is a closed system so far as alliteration goes. Six verses have alliteration, two have rime, and one dispenses with both these aids.

Passages like that from *Hit Becwæð* were exceptional in Old English.

[7] A recent study: J. C. Pope, *The Rhythm of Beowulf* (1942). Earlier studies: E. Sievers, *Altgermanische Metrik* (1893); A. Heusler, *Deutsche Versgeschichte* I (1925). See also K. Malone, *ELH*, VIII (1941). 74-80.

[8] Two syllables are said to alliterate if each begins with the same sound. But in Old English verse only lifts were included in an alliterative pattern. Morover, the consonant combination *sk* (*sc*) for alliterative purposes was reckoned a single sound, and alliterated with itself only; similarly with the combinations *st* and *sp*. On the other hand, all vowels and dipthongs, for alliterative purposes, were reckoned the same sound.

[9] F. Liebermann, *Die Gesetze der Angelsachsen*, I (1903). 400. The text was also printed by F. Grendon, *Jour. of Amer. Folk-Lore*, XXII (1909). 179-180. The title *Hit Becwæð* "[he] bequeathed it" comes from the first two words of the text; compare *Habeas Corpus* and the like.

Ordinarily the short verses were grouped by twos, and a given verse occurred as the *on-verse* (first half) or the *off-verse* (second half) of a line. Here alliteration could not be dispensed with, for the line was an alliterative unit. A short verse included in a line is commonly called a *half-line*. A good example of an Old English line of poetry is *Beowulf*, 1725,

> hu mihtig God   manna cynne
> how mighty God to mankind.

Here *hu mihtig God* is the on-verse, *manna cynne* the off-verse. The two halves of the line are bound together by alliteration: the stave (i.e., the alliterating sound) is *m*. The line has four lifts, two in each half; two of the lifts are major, two are minor. The second and third lifts have no drop between them, but they have a pause between them which separates them more sharply than a drop could do. A more unusual (though not rare) type is *Beowulf*, 2987,

> heard swyrd hilted, ond his helm somod
> hard sword hilted, and his helm besides.

Here the two halves are doubly bound by alliteration: *heard, hilted* and *helm* are linked by the *h*-stave, *swyrd* and *somod* by the *s*-stave. There are five lifts: three in the on-verse, two in the off-verse. The first three lifts are juxtaposed, and so are the last two. All the lifts are major. Yet a third type is *Beowulf*, 2995,

> landes ond locenra beaga;   ne ðorfte him ða lean oðwitan
> of land and linked rings;   he needed not to blame him for those rewards.

Here we have six lifts, three in each half-line. Three lifts are major, three minor. Each lift is accompanied by one or more drops. Many other varieties occur, but the fundamental features of the line remain the same.

It is easier to determine the lift-pattern of a line than to divide its half-lines into feet (or measures). Here it is customary to distinguish between the half-lines of normal length (as in *Beowulf*, 1725) and so-called swollen or abnormally long half-lines (as in *Beowulf*, 2995). According to Sievers, a normal half-line had two feet; a swollen half-line, three feet. According to Heusler and Pope, however, each half-line, whether normal or swollen, had two feet. Heusler recognized only one kind of foot: this began with a main stress and included also a subordinate stress. Sievers, however, recognized four kinds of feet. To these he gave no names, but we shall call them classes 1, 2, 3, and 4. In class 1 (e.g., *drýhten* "lord") the stress came at the beginning; in class 2 (e.g., *begóng* "circuit") the stress came at the end; in class 3 (e.g., *féa* "few") the foot was monosyllabic; in class 4 (e.g., *wélþùngen* "excellent") the foot was polysyllabic, with initial main stress and medial or final subordinate stress.[10] Both Heusler and Sievers began

Lifts

*Sievers,
Heusler,
Pope*

---

[10] Here the acute accent marks main stress; the grave, subordinate stress. Sievers did not include in his system a polysyllabic foot with initial or medial subordinate stress and final main stress: e.g., *fùl arǽd* "quite inexorable" (*Wanderer* 5).

the half-line, on occasion, with an *onset* of one or more syllables reckoned as anacrusis: a kind of running start that belonged indeed to the half-line but made no part of the podic pattern. For Heusler this pattern was the same in every foot: two beats to the measure, whatever the number of syllables in the foot. The first or stronger beat coincided with the main stress of the prose rhythm. The second or weaker beat coincided with the subordinate stress of the prose rhythm, if such a stress occurred; otherwise, the weaker beat fell on an unstressed syllable, or on a pause (metrically a rest) in the prose rhythm, and served to heighten the syllable or the rest as the case might be. We illustrate Heusler's system of scansion with the on-verse of *Beowulf*, 1173:

beo wið Geatas glæd   be kind to the Geatas.

Here *beo wið* made the onset, *Geatas* the first foot, and *glæd* the second foot. The stronger beats fell on the alliterating syllables. The weaker beat of the first foot fell on the ending of *Geatas;* that of the second foot, on the rest after *glæd*. For Sievers the half-lines fell into five types. In type *A*, both feet were of class 1; in type *B*, both were of class 2; in type *C*, the first was of class 2, the second was of class 1; in type *D*, the first was of class 3, the second was of class 4; in type *E*, the first was of class 4, the second was of class 3. Examples of these types follow, all taken from on-verses of *Beowulf*. The onset is set off by double diagonals; the feet are divided by single diagonals.

A 1987 hu // lómp eow on / láde   how went it with you on the road?
B 1939 þæt hit scéa / denmǽl   that it the damascened sword
C 1192 him was fúl / bóren   the cup was borne to him
D 2705 for // wrát / Wédra hèlm   The Weders' lord cut through
E 1160 gléomànnes / gýd   the gleeman's song.

Pope's system of scansion may be described as a modification of Heusler's. According to Pope, each half-line had two feet, sung or chanted in 4/8 time (normal verse) or 4/4 time (swollen verse). The first foot of a half-line might be heavy or light. The second foot was regularly heavy. The light foot of Pope answers to the onset of Heusler; its lifts (one main and one subordinate) were both weak, and were excluded from the alliterative pattern of the line. We illustrate with *Beowulf*, 264a:

gebàd wíntra wòrn   he lived many years.

Here *gebad* makes the first foot, *wintra worn* the second. The first foot is light; it begins with a rest beat which takes the main stress. The second foot is heavy; it has *two* major lifts.

The systems of Sievers, Heusler, and Pope are outlined here for the information of the reader, but the student will do well enough in reading if he follows the natural rhythm of the lines, with due heed given to the lift-patterns and in particular to those syllables which the poets by alliteration and rime marked for heightening.

We have already seen that the short verse, the basic metrical unit, usually occurred by twos—that is, in *lines,* the two parts of which were linked by alliteration. Old English verse in all periods was almost exclusively *linear* (that is, made up of lines). In the oldest linear verse the end-stopped style prevailed: every line ended with a syntactical pause and every sentence made either a line or a couplet (i.e., a two-line unit). This pre-classical style of composition was kept, almost intact, in the mnemonic parts or thulas (i.e., metrical name-lists) of *Widsith,* where one sentence runs to six lines but all the others make either a single line or a couplet each. The *Leiden Riddle* likewise was done (though with less strictness) in the old style, and many one-line and two-line units occur in the spells. Otherwise, only relics of the pre-classical style may be found in the monuments.[11] Formulas like *Beowulf,* 456,

> Hroðgar maþelode, helm Scyldinga
> Hrothgar spoke, the helm of the Scyldings,

seem to reflect such a style, and other one- or two-line formulas occur in the laws and elsewhere. One might have expected to find end-stopping used a good deal in the gnomic verses, but here the clerical writers have given us the traditional material in remodeled form.[12] A few pieces of gnomic wisdom, however, have come down to us in lines or couplets. *Exeter Gnomics,* 158,

> licgende beam læsest groweð
> a fallen tree grows least

may serve to illustrate the one-line gnomic, while *Age mec,* 117-118,

> biþ þæt selast þonne mon him sylf ne mæg
> wyrd onwendan þæt he þon wel þolige
>
> that is best, when one himself cannot
> amend his fate, that he then put up with it

exemplifies the two-line gnomic. Somewhat similar in style is the linear formula of consolation used six times in *Deor.* Such formulas, nevertheless, regularly appear in a setting dominated by the run-on style of linear composition. In general, a plurilinear unit of classical Old English poetry was held together, not by uniformities of rhythmical or alliterative pattern, nor yet by uniformities of grouping (i.e., strophic structure), but by the use of run-on lines.

Yet the classical style grew out of the older, end-stopped style of composition, and kept what could be kept of the earlier technic. In the matter of plurilinear units the poverty of the old style was marked: only the two-line unit or couplet existed. The richness of the classical style in plurilinear units is no less marked: we find many such units of three, four, five, six, or

---

[11] The *Riming Poem* relies on rime rather than syntax to mark its three quatrains, 21 couplets and 33 single lines as separate and distinct units, and can hardly be taken as a survival or revival of the old end-stopped style of composition.

[12] See A. Heusler, *Zeitschrift des Vereins für Volkskunde,* xxvi (1916). 52.

seven lines; indeed, there was no limit to the number of lines permissible in making such a unit. This great change was brought about with the least possible disturbance to the old order. We illustrate with *Beowulf*, 639–641:

> Ðam wife þa word wel licodon,
> gilpcwide Geates. Eode goldhroden
> freolicu folccwen to hire frean sittan.

> To that woman those words were pleasing,
> the proud speech of the Geat. She went, gold-adorned,
> the noble folk-queen, to sit by her lord.

Here we have a three-line unit, made up of two sentences, each a line and a half long. Sentences of this length were forbidden to the oldest poets, but it would have been easy for them to say the same thing in two one-line sentences, as follows:

> Ðam wife þa word wel licodon.
> Folccwen eode to hire frean sittan.

These lines bring out, besides, the starkness of the old style. It may well have been a wish to make this style less bare which led to the expansion of the sentences beyond the linear limits; if so, the new plurilinear units were a mere by-product of a process set going for reasons unconnected with plurilinear structure.

In this connection we distinguish two kinds of run-on line. In the first, *Run-On* the sentence goes on to the next line without a syntactical pause; in the *Style* second, it goes on with a syntactical pause. The second kind of run-on line has obviously kept something of the old end-stopped style, and presumably grew out of the linear sentence. We further distinguish three stages in the development of the run-on style. The early stage is exemplified in the amnemonic parts of *Widsith* (the mnemonic parts, as we have seen, exemplify the end-stopped style). Here the plurilinear units vary in number of lines, but this variation is held within comparatively narrow limits: no unit longer than nine lines occurs. All the natural divisions of the poem end with a line; not one ends with an on-verse (i.e., in the middle of a line). Single lines and couplets make a respectable proportion of the whole. Most of the run-on lines are of the second kind mentioned above; that is, they end with a syntactical pause, though not with a full stop. *Beowulf* may serve to illustrate the middle stage of the run-on style. Here some of the plurilinear units are of great length; their length may be so great, indeed, that they no longer can be felt as units and include diverse matters. Single lines and couplets are infrequent. The fits (or cantos, as some prefer to call them) all end with a line, but some of the natural divisions end with an on-verse: thus, the Finn and Ingeld episodes, and one of the speeches.[13] Six of the speeches begin with an off-verse. *Judith* exemplifies the late stage of the run-on style. Here one can hardly speak of plurilinear units at

---

[13] Line 389. But here the text seems to be defective.

all, or indeed of clean-cut units of any kind, apart from the fits. If we follow the punctuation of Wülcker, only 11 of the 350 lines end with a full stop, and three of these mark the end of a fit. Since the sentences usually begin and end in the middle of a line, the syntactical and alliterative patterns rarely coincide at any point, and the matter is presented *en masse,* so to speak. The verses give the effect of a never-ending flow, but this continuous effect is gained at a heavy structural cost.[14]

ariation   So far as one can tell, the technic of adornment or elaboration was essentially the same in pre-classical and classical poetry. The starkness of the pre-classical style went naturally with its end-stopped lines, which left little room for ornamentation, but any room left did not fail to be used. Sheer adornment, it is true, may have been wanting in the oldest poetry: equivalents and attributives may have been put in, first of all, for the sake of the additional information which they gave. But if this was their origin, their original function soon became secondary. The use of equivalents for poetical purposes is technically known as *variation.* We illustrate, first, with a few linear formulas. In *Beowulf,* 3076,

Wiglaf maðelode, Wihstanes sunu,

the on-verse gives us needful information: namely, that the next passage is to be a speech by Wiglaf. The off-verse may be said to give us further information about the speaker, but since this same information had been given to us earlier (in line 2602) the chief function of the off-verse is hardly informative but rather poetic or (if you will) stylistic. More precisely, since we know already that Wiglaf is Wihstan's son, the off-verse serves primarily to repeat the subject in variant form, and, technically speaking, *Wihstanes sunu* is a variation of *Wiglaf.* The repetition includes the predicate as well (for *maðelode* is to be understood after *Wihstanes sunu*), but not in variant form; not formally, indeed, at all. We may therefore put the line into modern English as follows:

Wiglaf spoke, the son of Wihstan [spoke].

It will be seen that the variation, though appositive on the face of it, is felt rather as a repetition that involves the sentence as a whole. The term *apposition* therefore does not adequately describe the device, and the use of a special term *variation* seems quite in order. In *Widsith,* 1,

Widsið maðolade, wordhord onleac,

the off-verse repeats the predicate (not the subject) in variant form, and we may put the line into current speech as follows:

Widsith spoke, [he] unlocked the word-hoard.

Here the variation can hardly be said to give us any further information, and its function is strictly poetic or stylistic.

[14] In this history a poem in the run-on style the stage of which is not specified may be presumed to belong to the middle stage. See, further, K. Malone, *RES,* xix (1943). 201-204.

In both the examples which we have considered, the variation may be called *inner*, since it varies something already expressed in the same sentence. In *Beowulf*, 360,

> Wulfgar maðelode to his winedrihtne,

we have a case of *outer* variation: *his winedrihtne* "his lord" varies something already expressed, indeed, but not in the same sentence; we know only from the context who Wulfgar's lord is. In outer variation no parallelism of grammatical construction is to be expected as between the variation and the thing varied. Even in inner variation, indeed, such parallelism need not be thoroughgoing. In *Beowulf*, 1458,

> þæt wæs an, foran, ealdgestreona,

the adverb *foran* varies the adjective *an*, and the line means "that was unique, [that was] to the fore, among old treasures." In *Beowulf*, 2377-2378,

> hwæðre he him on folce freondlarum heold,
> estum, mid are, oð ðæt he yldra wearð,

"but he backed him up, in the tribe, with friendly teachings, [he backed him up] with kindnesses, [he backed him up] with help, until he grew older," the prepositional phrase *mid are* varies the simple case-forms *freondlarum* and *estum*. Here the variants, though loosely synonymous, are not identical in meaning (a state of things often found in the technic of variation). But more nearly synonymous variants may differ in grammatical construction. Thus, in *Andreas*, 1074b-1076,

> him seo wen gelah,
> syððan mid corðre carcernes duru
> eorre æscberend opene fundon,

"that expectation played them false when the company, the angry spearmen, found the doors of the prison open," the prepositional phrase *mid corðre* varies the nominative plural *æscberend* (here we have also a case in which the variation precedes the thing varied). Such variations in *mid* (or in the simple dative) presumably arose out of ordinary accompaniment: *A with B* was another way of saying *A and B*. When a variation happened to be almost or altogether identical in meaning with the thing varied the machinery of accompaniment might still be used, even though in such cases this machinery perforce lost its proper meaning and became a mere form of words.

Stereotypes of another kind were the *kennings*, a characteristic feature of **Kennings** Old Germanic poetical diction. These arose as variations, but in many cases became so familiar that they could be used without previous mention of the thing varied. A kenning may be described as a two-member (or two-term) circumlocution for an ordinary noun: such a circumlocution might take the form of a compound, like *hronrad* "sea" (literally "riding-place of the whale"), or of a phrase, like *fugles wynn* "feather" (literally

"bird's joy").[15] Alongside the kenning we find the *heiti,* a one-term substitute for an ordinary noun: e.g., *ash* or *wood* in the sense "spear" (the
weapon-name being varied in terms of material, like *iron* for "sword").
The heiti differed from the kenning in that it was simplex, not composital
or phrasal, but it resembled the kenning in that it arose as a variation. In
their use of kenning and heiti the English poets showed a characteristic
classical restraint. These stylistic features did not have in England the
luxuriant growth that they had in Iceland (whence come their names).
One may note in passing that the circumlocutions for verbs, like *grundwong
ofgyfan* "die" (literally "give up the earth"), were markedly fewer in number
than those for nouns, and did not give rise to a technical term parallel to
kenning.[16]

Poetic adornment might also take attributive form. The adjective in such
a phrase as *fealu flod* "fallow flood" is not without descriptive value and
presumably came into use, as part of the phrase, because it had descriptive
value, but it early became a standing or conventional poetic epithet by
virtue of frequent use in such phrases. Many standing expressions like
fealu flod may be found in Old English poetry. Thus, a *þeoden* "prince"
is commonly and conventionally illustrious: he is a *mære þeoden.* The
device is not limited to poetry, of course, but the poets made much use of
it and not a few expressions of the kind belong definitely to poetic diction.

oetical | In general it may be noted that the vocabulary and phraseology of poetry
)iction | differed greatly from that of prose. Words and phrases may be marked as
poetical by occurrence, dialectal form, or both. Thus, the word *mece* "sword"
is doubly marked: it does not occur in prose (apart from glosses) and its
dialectal form is Anglian (i.e., Northumbrian or Mercian).[17] Poetic diction,
though out of fashion at the moment, is still with us, and the phenomenon,
as such, hardly needs explanation here. The Anglian dialectal forms are
another matter. Nearly all the Old English poetry extant has come down to
us in West Saxon versions. In these versions, however, Anglian forms often
occur, and some words, like *mece,* never take the West Saxon form which
one would expect in a West Saxon setting. This feature, characteristic of
so many Old English poetical texts, is commonly explained on the theory
that the poems were first composed and recorded in an Anglian dialect,
and that the scribes who made the West Saxon versions sometimes copied
an Anglian dialectal form mechanically instead of substituting the equivalent
West Saxon forms. Fixed forms like *mece* are explicable on the theory that
the Anglian dialects held a certain prestige in metrical composition, and
that the fixed forms served to give poetic flavor, for a West Saxon audience
at least.

As in any traditional period, so in Old English times poetic effects could

---

[15] A modern parallel: *Monty's moonshine* "artificial daylight."

[16] Sometimes *kenning* is applied to verbal as well as to nominal circumlocutions. The most
detailed study of Old English kennings is that of Hertha Marquardt, *Die altenglischen Kenningar* (Halle, 1938); see also K. Malone, *MLN,* LV (1940). 73-74.

[17] The corresponding West Saxon dialectal form *mæce* occurs, be it noted, in the prose
compound *mæcefisc* "mullet."

be had, more or less mechanically, by using words and turns of phrase not customary in prose but familiar to the poet's audience as part of the stylistic tradition of poetry. Such words and turns of phrase need not be labeled archaic; certainly they were very much alive in the mouths of the poets and in the ears of their hearers.[18] A given poet was reckoned worthy if he handled with skill the stuff of which, by convention, poems must be made. This stuff was not merely stylistic, however; matter as well as manner was prescribed. And that brings us to another part of our subject.[19]

[18] For want of evidence we cannot tell (in most cases) whether a given word or turn of phrase had earlier been used in prose, though now restricted to poetry.

[19] Many stylistic features must here be left out, for want of space. Thus, we include no discussion of familiar rhetorical devices like litotes or understatement. For further discussion, see especially A. C. Bartlett, *The Larger Rhetorical Patterns in Anglo-Saxon Poetry* (1935) and the pioneer paper by J. Kail, "Ueber die parallelstellen in der angelsächsischen Poesie," published in *Anglia*, XII (1889). 21-40. The most important recent article on the subject is that of L. D. Benson, *PMLA*, LXXXI (1966). 334-341. On the oral-formulaic theory in general, see H. L. Rogers, *English Studies*, XLVII (1966). 89-102.

IV

The Old Tradition: Popular Poetry

hulas

The oldest Germanic verses extant are two metrical lists of names, re-corded in works of the first and second centuries of our era. Such a metrical list is technically known as a *thula*.[1] Tacitus in his *Germania* (A.D. 98) gives us a two-line thula the names of which appear, of course, in Latinized form.[2] This thula has for us a special interest for another reason: it is our first record of the English name. The thula reads thus:

> Reuding*i*, Auiones, Anglii, Varini,
> Eudoses, Suardones, U*n*ithones.

A like thula, giving our earliest record of the Saxon name, is set down in the *Geography* of Claudius Ptolemy (*c.* A.D. 150):[3]

> Saxones, Sigulones, Sabalingii, Cobandi,
> Chali, Phunusii, Charudes.

In both cases the alliteration shows that we have to do with verse, and verse of this kind is well evidenced, later on, in vernacular sources. Thus, the pedigree of King Cynric of the West Saxons is given metrical form in the following thula:[4]

> Cynric [wæs] Cerdicing, Cerdic Elesing,
> Elesa Esling, Esla Gewising,
> Gewis Wiging, Wig Freawining,
> Freawine Friðugaring, Friðugar Bronding,
> Brond Bældæging, Bældæg Wodening.

The King's descent from Woden could be told in correct verses all the better for being fictitious—the names were chosen to fit the alliterative rules. More elaborate are the three thulas of the sixth century incorporated in *Widsith*. The first of these (lines 18-33 of the poem) falls into two parts: a five-couplet unit and a six-line unit. The first couplet may serve to show the structure and subject-matter of this thula:[5]

---

[1] The term comes from Iceland, where the genre flourished. The metrical name-lists of *Widsith* were first called thulas by Heusler and Ranisch, *Eddica Minora* (1903), p. lxxxix.
[2] Cap. 40. For a full discussion of the passage, see K. Malone, *Namn och Bygd*, xxii (1934). 26-51. For the Latin text, see p. 317 of the standard edition of the *Germania*, that of R. P. Robinson (1935).
[3] II, 11, 7. See K. Malone, *Namn och Bygd*, xxii (1934). 30-31.
[4] *OE Annals*, ed. Earle-Plummer (1892), pp. 16 (A.D. 552), 20 (A.D. 597). See also R. W. Chambers, *Beowulf, An Introduction* (2ed., 1932), pp. 316-317. The suffix *ing*, used 10 times here, means "son of."
[5] *Widsith*, ed. K. Malone (1936), pp. 67-68; see also pp. 12-20.

Ætla weold Hunum, Eormanric Gotum,
Becca Baningum, Burgendum Gifica

Attila ruled the Huns, Ermanric the Goths,
Becca the Banings, Gifica the Burgundians.

The first thula is a list of kings; each king (30 are listed) is identified in terms of the tribe he rules. The second thula, as we have it, consists of twenty lines (57-64, 68-69, 75, 79-87): ten single lines and five couplets. Its first two lines (a couplet) sufficiently indicate its pattern:

Ic wæs mid Hunum ond mid Hreðgotum,
mid Sweom ond mid Geatum ond mid Suþdenum

I was with the Huns and with the Hreth-Goths,
with the Swedes and with the Geats and with the South-Danes.

This thula is a list of tribes (54 are listed), given in terms of the personal experiences of the speaker. The third thula as it stands is made up of nine lines (112-118, 123-124), of which the first reads

Hehcan sohte ic ond Beadecan ond Herelingas
I sought out Hehca and Beadeca and the Herelings.

This thula gives us a list of 28 men (presumably heroes); as in the second thula, they are listed in terms of the personal experiences of the speaker.

Such terms are to be taken as no more than a part of the mnemonic machinery. In general, thula composition seems to have had a highly practical purpose: that of making it easier to remember the names listed. It follows that the names in the lists were thought worth remembering, and in fact the mnemonic material given in the thulas is weighty matter. It meant much to a West Saxon king that he trace his descent from Gewis, the eponym of the tribe, and from Woden, the chief god of the tribe. We have reason to think that his political hold would have been strengthened likewise by belief that he had Wig and Freawine for ancestors, and we may presume that some of the other names in his genealogy were meaningful to our forefathers even though they are only names to us. In sum, the thula which gave Cynric's genealogy was a political poem of the first importance. The upstart West Saxon dynasty gained thereby in rank and worth: thenceforth its kings could face as equals the kings of the ancient Mercian house.[6] The importance of the thulas of *Widsith* lay elsewhere. The first thula embodied historical, the second ethnological lore; the third seems devoted to figures of story rather than (or more than) history. And many names in all three presumably brought to mind in the hearer things that we miss, or know little of. The artistic worth of a list has always lain in the associations which its names evoke. Every name is an allusion for those who know it, and a series of names makes a series of allusions. The names gathered in the thulas of *Widsith* stand for a world now long for-

[6] Compare the Chadwicks, *op. cit.*, p. 271, note 2.

gotten, the Germanic world of the migration period. Much of that world
still lived in the England of the *Widsith* poet, and the old thulas had then
a rich allusiveness which we see but darkly and know but in part.

Runic
Poem

Beside the thulas we set the *Runic Poem,* another example of mnemonic
verse.[7] Its practical value for would-be runemasters is comparable to that
of ABC poems for learners of the alphabet. The runes were learned by
name, and in a fixed order. The name of the rune gave one the clue to its
phonetic value, and its place in the sequence gave one the clue to other
values which need not be gone into here. It seems altogether likely that the
runes from the first were learned by means of a poem in which each rune-
name began a section, though in the original poem the sections may have
been quite brief—possibly no more than a short verse each. From this
original poem the three runic poems extant were presumably descended.
For the Norwegian and Icelandic runic poems we refer the reader to the
edition of Dickins. The English poem is much more elaborate than the
other two. We illustrate with the first section, devoted to the first rune:

> Feoh byþ frofur fira gehwylcum;
> sceal ðeah manna gehwylc miclun hyt dælan
> gif he wile for drihtne domes hleotan.

> Valuables are a joy to every man;
> yet every man must needs be openhanded with them
> if he is minded to win favor with the Lord.

Feoh is the name of the *f*-rune, and accordingly begins the section and sets
the stave for the first line of the section. Moreover, the section has *feoh* for
its theme. This theme is treated in a manner reminiscent of the riddles.
We can turn the section into a riddle, indeed, by putting *ic eom* for *feoh byþ*:

> I am a joy to every man;
> yet every man must needs be openhanded with me
> if he is minded to win favor with the Lord.

The poem is 94 lines long. It consists of 29 sections, devoted to as many
runes: 19 three-liners, seven four-liners, two two-liners, one five-liner (the
last section). The section quoted above is representative of the whole, though
the run-on style is much more pronounced in some of the other sections.
The two-liners make up in length of line for shortness in number of lines.
The *Runic Poem,* like the thulas, started as a speaking, but in its present
form it is better classified as a writing. Its literary elaboration may well
have taken place under the influence of the riddles, of which more anon.
If so, the poem as it stands hardly antedates the eighth century and may
be much later. The eleventh-century MS Cotton Otho B x in which the
poem came down was lost by fire in 1731, and for our text we must rely
on Hickes.[8]

---

[7] The best ed. is that of B. Dickins, *Runic and Heroic Poems* (Cambridge, 1915).
[8] G. Hickes, *Linguarum Veterum Septentrionalium Thesaurus* (Oxford, 1705), I. 135.

Another notable piece of mnemonic verse, the Old English *Menologium* Meno-
or calendar poem,[9] is recorded in the eleventh-century MS Cotton Tiberius logium
B I. This MS is commonly localized at Abingdon, but there are indications
that the menologist himself lived in Kent; note, for instance, the poet's special knowledge of the Canterbury minster (line 105). The poem is 231
lines long. It is written in standard Old English (i.e., West Saxon) of the
later period, and the poet seems to have flourished *c.* A.D. 1000. At the end
of the poem we are told what practical purpose it is meant to serve: "now
ye can find the feast days of the saints that one is duty bound to keep in this
kingdom (i.e., England) nowadays." For sources the menologist presumably
used church calendars and the like. The want of English saints in the
poem[10] indicates that one was not then duty bound to keep their days; the
older saints were more important. But the poet gives much that he need
not have included: the four seasons and the English names of ten of the
twelve months, with striking poetical descriptions of nature attached.[11]
We think it possible that in making his poetical calendar he drew not only
on Latin sources but also on a now lost native mnemonic poem of popular
character, a poem in which the months and seasons (but not the saints'
days) were named and characterized by descriptions not unlike those of
the *Menologium*.[12] This possibility must serve as our excuse for considering
the Old English calendar poem in the present chapter. In any case the
menologist was no mere clerk, learned in Church Latin only. He was
steeped in classical Old English poetry, as his style and choice of words
reveal. Yet another example of mnemonic verse, Cynewulf's *Fates of the
Apostles,* will be taken up with the other works of that poet.

The English of old, unlike their Continental contemporaries, made legal *Legal*
records in the mother tongue as well as in Latin. The laws of King Æðel- *Verse*
birht of Kent were set down in English as early as A.D. 602 or 603, and this
king's example was widely followed by English rulers of later times.
Many charters, wills, and other legal documents in the vernacular have Hit
come down to us as well.[13] One of these, *Hit Becwæð,* is metrical through- Becwæð

---

[9] Ed. R. Imelmann (Berlin, 1902); Krapp-Dobbie, VI. 49-55. See also H. Henel, "Ein
altenglisches Prosa-Menologium," in (Förster's) *Beiträge zur englischen Philologie,* XXVI (1934).
71-91. The work which Henel here edits is obviously a prose companion-piece to our poem,
though it cannot be reckoned literary and therefore will not be taken up in our chapter on
Old English literary prose.

[10] One English saint (Cuthbert) appears in the prose Menologium; see Henel, p. 71.

[11] The months are not named (whether in English or Latin) in the prose Menologium,
though the seasons are duly named (in English).

[12] The seasons in Old English: *winter, lencten, sumor, hærfest.* The months: earlier and
later *iula* (Dec. and Jan.), *sol* (Feb.), *hlyda* (Mar.), *easter* month (Apr.), *þrymilce*
(May), earlier and later *liþa* (June and July), *weod* month (Aug.), *halig* month (Sept.),
winterfylleð (Oct.), *blot* month (Nov.). The menologist gave only the Latin names of January
and July, but the English names can readily be inferred from those of December and June.

[13] The best English editions of the laws are those of F. L. Attenborough, *The Laws of
the Earliest English Kings, edited and translated* (Cambridge, 1922), and A. J. Robertson,
The Laws of the Kings of England from Edmund to Henry I, edited and translated (Cambridge, 1925). A more complete edition is that of F. Liebermann, *Die Gesetze der Angelsachsen*
(3v, Halle, 1903-1916). Most of the charters and wills may be found in the volumes of A. J.
Robertson (*Anglo-Saxon Charters,* Cambridge, 1939) and D. Whitelock (*Anglo-Saxon Wills,*
Cambridge, 1930); these may be supplemented by A. C. Napier and W. H. Stevenson, *Craw-*

out.[14] It falls into 46 short verses, nine of which were quoted above (p. 23). The text gives us the answer of a nameless landowner to some plaintiff who had laid claim to the defendant's land. It is addressed, not to any court but to the plaintiff, who is told his claim has no merit and is urged to drop the suit. More precisely, the defendant says: (Sec. 1) that the previous owner, now dead, had a clear title; (Sec. 2) that he, the defendant, got it from the previous owner; (Sec. 3) that he, the defendant, would never give it up to the plaintiff; (Sec. 4) that he would keep it all his life, just as the previous owner had done without challenge to his ownership. The fifth and last section reads:

> Do swa ic lære:
> beo ðe be þinum and læt me be minum;
> ne gyrne ic þines,
> ne læðes ne landes,
> ne sace ne socne,
> ne ðu mines ne ðærft, ne mynte ic ðe nan ðing.

Do as I say: keep to thine and leave me to mine; I crave nothing of thine, neither ground nor land, neither sake nor soke; neither hast thou need of mine, nor have I aught in mind for thee.

The text is one of A.D. 1000 or thereabouts. For the historian of literature its chief interest is metrical; note in particular the author's use of rime instead of alliteration to bind together the two halves of the line *beo ðe ... minum*, a use familiar in Middle English but rare in Old English alliterative poetry. As a piece of self-expression, too, the poem is worthy of note. The author speaks vigorously and to the point and makes his case come alive.

Many other legal texts are metrical in spots. Short verses, alone or in series, are scattered here and there through the prose, and sometimes one comes upon a line or even a series of lines. Thus, the author of *Gerefa* brings his treatise to a metrical end: [15]

> Fela sceal to holdan hames gerefan
> and to gemetfæstan manna hyrde.
> Ic gecende be ðam ðe ic cuðe;
> se ðe bet cunne, gecyðe his mare.

> Many things are required of a loyal overseer
> and dependable director of men.
> I have set forth [the subject] as best I could;
> Let him who knows [it] better make more of it known.

Jord Collection of Early Charters and Documents (Oxford, 1895), and F. E. Harmer, *Select English Historical Documents of the Ninth and Tenth Centuries* (Cambridge, 1914). The earlier collections of Thorpe, Kemble, and Birch are also still useful, though they must be used with caution.

[14] See also Heusler, *Altgerm. Dichtung,* p. 66. For a contrary view, see Liebermann, III. 236.
[15] Liebermann, I. 455.

The following passage from *Rectitudines* may also be quoted: [16]

> Laga sceal on leode luflice leornian,
> lof se ðe on lande sylf nele leosan.

> The laws of the realm he must lovingly learn
> who is unwilling to lose his good name in the land.

In the *Gerefa* passage the third line has only three lifts and the fourth follows an alliterative pattern quite unusual though probably old,[17] while in the *Rectitudines* passage the alliteration foreshadows Middle English and ignores classical Old English practice. Such irregularities are common in the linear verse of legal texts. By its end-stopping too this verse is marked as non-classical; here it harks back to earlier times. The short verses usually have a two-beat pattern. Examples: *ægðer ge dæde ge dihtes* "both in act *Tags* and in aim" (with alliteration); *æt ræde ne æt dæde* "by rede nor by deed" (with rime). As the examples indicate, we have to do with traditional formulas of one kind or another. Such tags are still common in legal phraseology, though the modern tags more often than not are without alliteration or rime, and consequently are not thought of as verse. Want of rime and alliteration in an Old English tag does not mean, of course, that the tag is unmetrical; it means that we cannot be sure of the tag's metrical character unless the context points to metrical treatment. The stock of verse formulas varied more or less down the centuries; some old formulas went out, and others came in. Thus the tag *ne sace ne socne* in *Hit Becwæð* is late. Metrically speaking, nevertheless, it is of a piece with prehistoric English formulas, and its introduction cannot be looked upon as a metrical innovation. Setting their age aside, we classify the formulas in terms of the relationship between the members. This relationship may be of sound or sense. In terms of sound, the two members of a typical formula may be free (e.g., *ne gyrne ic þines*) or bound by rime (e.g., *landes ne strandes*) or alliteration (e.g., *ne plot ne ploh*). Again, they may be symmetrical (e.g., *ne turf ne toft*) or asymmetrical (e.g., *ne furh ne fotmæl*). A symmetrical formula may be simple (e.g., *ne ruh ne rum*) or compound (e.g., *on ceapstowe oððe cyricware* "at marketplace or churchmeeting"). The members of a compound formula may be linked by a common first element (e.g., *oferseah and oferhyrde* "oversaw and overheard") or second element (e.g., *on scipfyrde, on landfyrde* "in ship-army, in land-army"); here the relationship is one of both sound and sense. The same holds of complete identity (e.g., *hand on hand* "hand in hand") and partial identity in asymmetrical formulas (e.g., *ne cyse ne cyslyb* "nor cheese nor cheese-rennet"). So also in cognate constructions (e.g., *to ræde gerædan* "advisably advise, wisely decide"). Meaningful relationships may be of contrast (e.g., *ær oððe æfter* "before or after") or of likeness (e.g., *healdan and wealdan* "hold and

---

[16] Liebermann, I. 452. Other single or double lines will be found in *I Cnut*, 2 and 25 (Lieb., I. 280 and 304); *II Cnut*, 38 (Lieb., I. 338); *X Æðelred*, Prol. I (Lieb., I. 269); *Excom.*, 2 (Lieb. I. 438); *Geþyncðo*, 3 (Lieb. I. 456); etc.

[17] See K. Malone, *Beiblatt zur Anglia*, XLVIII (1937). 351-352.

rule") or of mere association (e.g., *manige menn* "many men"). Other classifications might be made (have been made, indeed),[18] but these will serve well enough to bring out the characteristic features of the short verses. The metrical formulas here taken up belonged, for the most part, to everyday Old English speech, which made more use of short verses, and had a greater awareness of the metrical side of speech, than is the case in current English. If these short verses may be counted by the hundred in legal writings, the reason is not far to seek: everybody uses stereotyped expressions but the legal mind has a particular fondness for them. It was above all in legal texts, then, that these fragments of popular metrical speech found place and held out against the literary verse and prose which imposed itself nearly everywhere else.[19] Yet in a few spells and sayings likewise the popular verse-form managed to keep a precarious foothold.

Spells and Sayings

Versified wisdom, like versified tags and name-lists, is old in English; older than the language, indeed. But it had to pay for the privilege of written record. The clerics who wrote down what we have of it made fewer changes, interestingly enough, in the spells than in the sayings. They presumably feared that a spell would not work unless they kept the old wording, while they knew a saying would hold good whatever the wording.

We begin with the supernatural or magical wisdom of the spells (or charms). In Grendon's collection,[20] thirteen are wholly or partly in English verse. Of these, two (A 21 and 22) are obviously variants of the same spell. We thus have twelve spells to consider. Two survive in MSS of the tenth century;[21] nine are recorded in MSS of the eleventh century;[22] one, written in a hand of *c.* 1100, occurs in a MS of the tenth century.[23] We have no way of knowing who made these spells, when or where they took shape,

---

[18] Liebermann, II. 77-78. See also D. Bethurum, *MLR*, xxvii (1932). 263-279.

[19] See below, p. 101, for the rhythmical prose of Ælfric.

[20] F. Grendon, "The Anglo-Saxon Charms," *Jour. of Amer. Folk-Lore*, xxii (1909). 105-237. Item A 15 II of the collection is not a spell but the legal poem *Hit Becwæð*, which we took up above.

[21] From BM MS Regius 12 D xvii we have *Wið Wæterælfadle* "against waterelf sickness" (Grendon, B 5, p. 194; Krapp-Dobbie, vi. 124-125). From BM MS Harley 584 we have *Wið Cynnel* "against scrofula" (Grendon, A 9, p. 170; see also F. P. Magoun, Jr., *Arkiv för nordisk Filologi*, lx [1945]. 98-106).

[22] From BM MS Cotton Caligula A vii we have *Æcerbot* "acre-boot, field-remedy" (Grendon, A 13, pp. 172-176; Krapp-Dobbie, vi. 116-118). From BM MS Harley 585 we have: (1) *Wið Færstice* "against a sudden stitch in the side" (Grendon, A 1, pp. 164-166; Krapp-Dobbie, vi. 122-123), here called *Stice*; (2) *Wið Dweorh* "against a dwarf" (Grendon, A 2, p. 166; Krapp-Dobbie, vi. 121-122); (3) *Wið Ceapes Lyre* "against loss of cattle" (Grendon, A 22, p. 184; Krapp-Dobbie, vi. 123), here called *Lyre* when distinguished from its variant *Þeofend* but otherwise called *Bethlem;* (4) *Nigon Wyrta Galdor* "nine wort spell" (Grendon, B 4, pp. 190-194; Krapp-Dobbie, vi. 119-121), here called *Wyrta;* (5) *Wið Lætbyrde* "against slow birth" (Grendon, E 1, pp. 206-208; Krapp-Dobbie, vi. 123-124), here called *Lætbyrd*. From the Corpus Christi College Cambridge MS 41 we have: (1) *Wið Ymbe* "against a swarm of bees" (Grendon, A 4, p. 168; Krapp-Dobbie, vi. 125); (2) *Siðgaldor* "hap spell" (Grendon, A 14, pp. 176-178; Krapp-Dobbie, vi. 126-128); (3) *Wið Feos Nimunge* "against cattle theft" (Grendon, A 16, pp. 180-182; Krapp-Dobbie, vi. 125-126), here called *Garmund;* (4) *Wið Ceapes Þeofende* "against cattle theft" (Grendon, A 21, p. 184; Krapp-Dobbie, vi. 126), here called *Þeofend* when distinguished from its variant *Lyre* but otherwise called *Bethlem*.

[23] *Wið Wennum* "against wens" (Grendon, A 3, p. 166; Krapp-Dobbie, vi. 128), BM MS Regius 4 A xiv. This spell will here be called *Wenne*.

and how (if at all) the originals differed from the texts we have, apart from the ordinary linguistic changes down the years. We do not even know whether our texts were drawn from oral or written sources, though their ultimate source was presumably oral tradition. Strictly Christian spells like *Bethlem* may go back to a heathen original, but we need not make this presumption, since such spells might perfectly well have come into being in Christian times. Heathen elements in the spells are presumably old. Christian elements may reflect substitutions or additions. Much of the matter cannot be tied to religious belief, and is better classified as pseudo-science. In this history we take up the spells as examples of literary art, and leave to others the manifold non-literary problems which a student of spells must face.[24]

Our spells make a literary group of their own, not only in subject-matter but also in versification and style. They reflect a tradition independent of classical Old English poetry, but allied to legal verse and to pre-classical end-stopped linear verse.[25] Nearly all our twelve spells include prose as well as verse. In the verse parts a line may be followed by a short verse, a short verse by a line. Alliteration may be heaped up, or may be wanting. A line may be made up wholly, or almost wholly, of lifts. The three-lift verse, too, is in use here: a verse-pattern longer than the short verse but shorter than the line. A poem may show much greater variety in line pattern than would be possible in classical poetry. Run-on lines are rare. The familiar classical device of variation is avoided. We find, instead, repetition, and serial effects not unlike those achieved in the thulas of *Widsith* or in certain passages of *Beowulf* (e.g., lines 1392 ff., 1763 ff.). The *epitheton ornans* and other commonplaces of the classical style are likewise rare in the spells. These vary much in literary merit, but they all have freshness and go. We will look at a few of them.

The 13-line spell *Wenne* is marked by humor and lightness of touch. We quote in modernized form the first four and the last three lines: *Wenne*

> Wen, wen, wen-chicken,
> here thou shalt not build nor have any homestead,
> but thou shalt [go] north from here, to the near-by hill.
> There thou hast a wretch of a brother. . . .
>
> Do thou become as small as a linseed grain,
> and much smaller, like a handworm's hipbone,
> and become so small that thou become nothing at all.

Note the humorous shift of stress in *chicken*, a shift which makes the word rime with *wen*. The thrice repeated *become* is also of stylistic interest. But the reader can make his own commentary.

---

[24] There is a useful study by F. P. Magoun, Jr., *Archiv*, CLXXI (1937). 17-35, with bibliography; see also L. K. Shook, *MLN*, LV (1940). 139-140.

[25] Traces of strophic arrangement have been found by I. Lindquist (*Galdrar*, Göteborgs Högskolas Årsskrift, XXIX [1923]), and F. P. Magoun, Jr. (*ESt*, LXXII [1937]. 1-6).

Bethlem   The two variants of *Bethlem* have some importance for the textual critic, and are therefore given here (the same translation will serve for both):

Lyre

Bæðleem hatte seo buruh,
Þe Crist on acænned wæs.
Seo is gemærsod geond ealne middangeard.
Swa þyos dæd for monnum mære gewurþe.

Þeofend

Bethlem hattæ seo burh ðe Crist on geboren wes.
Seo is gemærsod ofer ealne middangeard.
Swa ðeos dæd wyrþe for monnum mære.

Bethlehem is called the town that Christ was born in.
It has become famous the world over.
So may this deed become famous in men's sight.

Lyre gives us the better text, but the two non-classical verses with which it began displeased somebody, and he made them into one line by putting *geboren* for *acænned*. Evidently a Christian spell could not always hold its own against the classical tradition.

Garmund   The following passage from *Garmund* is quoted for its metrical and stylistic features:

Garmund, godes ðegen,
find þæt feoh and fere þæt feoh
and hafa þæt feoh and heald þæt feoh
and fere ham þæt feoh

Garmund, God's thane,
find the cattle and bring the cattle
and have the cattle and hold the cattle
and bring home the cattle.

Here the alliteration, the two three-lift verses, and the repetitions are worthy of special note. The appeal to Garmund was addressed, one may suspect, to Godmund in heathen times.

Lætbyrd   The verses of *Lætbyrd* have power and poetry beyond expectation. We find space for a couplet only. A woman unable to feed her newborn child takes "part of her own child's caul," wraps it in black wool, and sells it to chapmen, saying:

I sell it, may ye sell it,
this black wool and seed of this sorrow.

Siðgaldor   The four long spells are *Siðgaldor* (40 lines), *Æcerbot* (38 lines of verse and much prose), *Wyrta* (63 lines of verse, followed by a short prose passage), and *Stice* (27 lines of verse, preceded and followed by a few words of prose). Of these, the first seems wholly Christian; in style as well as matter it stands closer to classical religious poetry than do the other spells. Among other things it gives us lists of biblical worthies, a feature reminiscent of the thulas. Except for a few lines it has little artistic merit. *Æcerbot* **Æcerbot** is Christian for the most part, but has passages (often quoted) that almost certainly go back to heathen times. Thus, the line *eorðan ic bidde and upheofon* "I pray to earth and to high heaven" has a strongly Christian context but nevertheless is unmistakably heathen. The famous line,

> Erce, Erce, Erce, eorþan modor,

whatever it means, surely appeals to mother earth, and the noble, hymn-like passage,

> Hal wes þu, folde, fira modor,
> beo þu growende on godes fæþme,
> fodre gefylled firum to nytte,

> Hale be thou, earth, mother of men,
> be thou with growing things in God's embrace,
> filled with food for the good of men,

takes us back to agricultural fertility rites, solemn ceremonies of immemorial antiquity.

Wyrta names nine worts or plants that have virtue against poisons (par- **Wyrta** ticularly snake-bite), aches and pains, infections, and demons.[26] We are told that these nine worts counteract as many devils, poisons and infections, but no list of nine devils is given. We do get a list of nine kinds of poison, followed by another list of six kinds of swelling or blister:

> Now these nine worts are potent . . .

> against the red poison, against the runl [27] poison,
> against the white poison, against the blue poison,
> against the yellow poison, against the green poison,
> against the dark poison, against the blue poison,
> against the brown poison, against the purple poison;

> against worm-swelling, against water-swelling,
> against thorn-swelling, against thistle-swelling,
> against ice-swelling, against poison-swelling.

Next comes a passage devoted to the cardinal points:

> if any poison come flying from the east
> or any come from the north
> or any from the west over the people.

Nothing harmful was expected from the south, it would seem. The passages quoted show the serial effects characteristic of the literary art of the spells, an art marked by repetition and parallelism. The versification, too,

[26] On the names of the worts, see H. Meroney, *MLN*, LIX (1944). 157-160.
[27] The meaning of *runl* is unknown, but it seems to be a color word.

with its mixture of line and short verse, is interesting. Running water also
has virtue, against snake-bite at least, and a couplet is added accordingly:

> Ic ana wat ea rinnende
> and þa nygon nædran behealdað.

> I alone know running water
> and that [i.e., running water] nine adders look to.[28]

The boast befits our learned spellman, but boasting is a conventional feature
of spells as of epics. The best known passage in this spell, however, has yet
to be quoted:

> A snake came creeping, tried to slit a man open.
> Then Woden took nine glory-rods;
> then he struck the adder, so that it burst into nine.

This narrative or "epic" passage, done in the pre-classical end-stopped style,
is a precious relic of English heathendom; unluckily we do not know the
Woden myth which it summarizes.

Stice

Wyrta has come down to us markedly imperfect; perhaps the disorder
was there from the start. *Stice,* however, is well built as it stands. First come
some directions, in prose. Then we get a pseudo-scientific explanation of the
stitch: spear-casts made by evil spirits (female, it would seem) cause these
sudden pains, and the magic weapon must be drawn out of you before
you can get relief. This explanation is given in highly poetical dress: the
women, loud and bold, have ridden over the hill, overland; you must protect yourself to stave off this attack. Here the spellman inserts, for the first
time, the oft-repeated curative formula,

> ut, lytel spere, gif her inne sie !
> out, little spear, if thou be in here,

which also serves as a kind of refrain, marking the end of the passage. But
your shield fails you: the magic dart pierced you

> when the mighty women drew up their forces
> and [when] they hurled yelling spears.

The spellman now comes to help you. He promises to fight the evil spirits
with weapons of his own:

> Six smiths sat,
> murderous spears they made;
> out, spear, not in, spear!

> If there be in here a bit of iron,
> the work of a witch, away it shall melt!

The incantation then proceeds in serial form (compare that quoted above
from *Wyrta*). The whole makes a little masterpiece of its kind.

[28] The second line of this couplet agrees in alliterative pattern with the last line of *Gerefa*
(see above, p. 36).

So much for the spells. We go on to the sayings. The term *sayings* is **Gnomic**
here taken to mean versified words of stock everyday wisdom: short, pithy, **Verse**
homespun generalizations about the common concerns of life, whether proverbial, descriptive, or moralizing. The sayings that won record in Old English times are found (1) imbedded here and there in a number of texts, and
(2) brought together in gnomic poems. Four such poems are extant. Three
of them are recorded in the Exeter Book, a MS of *c.* 980; [29] they go by the
collective name *Exeter Gnomics* (206 lines in all, as usually reckoned), and
are distinguished by the letters *A, B, C*. The fourth, set down in the eleventh-
century MS Cotton Tiberius B 1, is called *Cotton Gnomics* (66 lines).[30] The
imbedded sayings must first, of course, be winnowed out. Here the author
or compiler of the text may help us. Thus, the compiler of the (Latin) laws
attributed to Edward the Confessor quotes

> Bugge spere of side oððe bere
> buy spear from side or bear

as a proverbial expression current among the English.[31] In the same way,
a nameless correspondent of St. Boniface (the great English missionary of
the eighth century) calls the following couplet *saxonicum verbum:*

> Oft daedlata dome foreldit,
> sigisitha gahuem; suuyltit thi ana.[32]

> Oft a sluggard puts off decision,
> Lets all his chances slip; so he dies alone.

More commonly, however, no such help is forthcoming, and we must go by
internal evidence alone. A gnomic passage once found, we need to know
besides (if possible) whether the generalization was original with the author
or common literary property. The latter is normally to be presumed, in
virtue of the traditional and conventionalized character of Old English
literary art. And sometimes we have special reasons for coming to this conclusion. Thus, *Beowulf*, 1384b-1385,

> selre bið æghwæm
> þæt he his freond wrece þonne he fela murne

> it is better for every man
> to avenge his friend than to mourn [over him] much,

---

[29] Facsimile edition: *The Exeter Book of Old English Poetry* (London, 1933). Printed edition
with Old English text and modern English rendering: Part I, by I. Gollancz (*EETS*, 104);
Part II, by W. S. Mackie (*EETS*, 194).

[30] The four gnomic poems are best studied in the edition of Blanche C. Williams, *Gnomic
Poetry in Anglo-Saxon* (New York, 1914). Here, too, Miss Williams gives a thorough treatment
of the imbedded sayings.

[31] Liebermann, *ed. cit.*, I. 638-639. The popular character of this saying is reflected in its
metrical form; note the rime *spere—bere* and the irregular alliteration. The saying seems to
mean "pay wergeld or take the consequences," though the reference may equally well be to
Danegeld or to tribute generally.

[32] H. Sweet, *Oldest English Texts*, p. 152. The couplet (which we may name *Verbum*) is
obviously early, and keeps something of the old end-stopped style, but has a classical and
even bookish ring; note in particular the use of variation. We reckon it a writing, not a speaking.

fits Old Germanic morality but clashes with Christian morality. It seems unlikely, then, that the pious poet himself gave birth to this generalization; the chances are that he was quoting a stock piece of popular wisdom, handed down from heathen times.[33]

In studying the four gnomic poems we have to consider not only the individual sayings which these poems embody but also the poems as such. These are primarily compilations of traditional sententious wisdom, but the clerical compilers have more or less remodeled their material to make it fit the classical run-on linear style (though now and then they fail to do this and the older versification stands out). Sometimes, too, we find a single saying expanded or developed at some length, and not a few passages are homiletic or reflective rather than gnomic in character. Christian piety has made its way into the gnomic matter besides, and the poems as a whole give us a remarkable mixture of old and new. While the nature of the material makes a clean-cut structural pattern impossible, most of the sayings fall, more or less loosely, into groups, and certain passages are built up systematically enough. The sayings are so little organized in the Cotton Gnomics that the old term "gnomic verses" seems appropriate; the gnomic monuments of the Exeter Book, however, are properly poems rather than mere collections of verses.[34]

Bede's Death Song   Markedly different from all these is that famous piece of pious wisdom, the so-called *Death Song* of the Venerable Bede (d. 735), preserved to us by having been quoted in the *Epistola Cuthberti de Obitu Bedae.*[35] The modern rendering which follows is based on the text of the *Epistola* found in MS St. Gall 254 (ninth century):[36]

> Before the needful journey [i.e., death] no one becomes
> wiser in thought than he needs to be
> to think over, ere his going hence,
> what of good or evil about his spirit,
> after his day of death, may be decided.

This five-line poem of a single sentence evidently belongs to the classical, not the pre-classical style of composition. The thought as it stands is Christian, and Bede had Doomsday in mind. Yet the point of view needs but a slight shift to give us words that would befit Bede's heathen forefathers, who prized above all else that good name after death which may be had by living worthily, and not otherwise. An old ideal of conduct here held its own by taking new shape.

[33] For the sake of completeness we mention here two metrical proverbs, recorded in the BM MSS Cotton Faustina A. x and Regius 2 B. v. One proverb comes to two lines, the other to one line of verse. They are based on Latin originals. Texts in Krapp-Dobbie, VI. 109.

[34] For a study of the structure of one of these poems, see K. Malone, *MA*, XII (1943). 65-67.

[35] The standard study of Cuthbert's letter is that of E. V. K. Dobbie, *Columbia Univ. Stud. in English and Compar. Lit.*, CXXVIII. (1937). 49-129.

[36] The *Death Song* has been edited by A. H. Smith, *Three Northumbrian Poems* (1933), but this edition needs a few corrections in the light of Dobbie's study.

V
The Old Tradition: Courtly Poetry

So far, we have dealt with verse that reflects the traditional lore of oldest *Scop or* England. Such verse was popular in that it belonged to the people as a *Gleeman* whole. We come now to verse more personal in character and more limited in aim. At an early date Germanic kings began to keep professional poets, with functions not wholly unlike those of the poet laureate or official poet of later times. Among the English a court poet was called a *scop* or *gleeman*.[1] We are lucky enough to have in *Widsith* an early English poem on the Widsith scop.[2] From this poem (named after its hero) we learn something of the career and the repertory of an ideal gleeman, creature of a seventh-century poet's fancy.[3] The poem consists of a prologue (9 lines), a speech by Widsith (125 lines), and an epilogue (9 lines). The speech is built up round three old thulas and a thula-fragment (47 lines in all; see above, p. 32), which the author puts in his hero's mouth; to these are added 78 lines of the author's own composition.[4] Structurally the speech falls into five parts: an introduction, three fits or main divisions, and a conclusion. Each fit comprises (1) a thula and (2) passages added by the author.[5] The thulas were put in Widsith's mouth to bring out his knowledge of history, ethnology, and heroic story. Several of the added passages serve the same purpose. Other passages bring out the hero's professional experience and first-hand information (as do the second and third thulas); more particularly, they emphasize his success in his chosen calling. Thus, we are told of his professional performances:

> When Scilling and I, with sure voice, as one,
> made music, sang before our mighty lord,
> the sound of harp and song rang out;
> then many a man, mindful of splendor,
> those who well could know, with words spoke and said
> that they never heard a nobler song. (lines 103-8)

[1] See L. F. Anderson, *The Anglo-Saxon Scop* (Toronto, 1903).
[2] Recent edition: K. Malone, *Widsith* (1936). See also Lascelles Abercrombie, "*Widsith* as Art," *Sewanee Rev.*, XLVI (1938). 124-128. The edition of R. W. Chambers (*Widsith*, Cambridge, 1912) will always remain the best presentation of nineteenth-century Continental Widsithian scholarship. This scholarship is now largely out of date, because of the great advances made during the present century in our understanding of the poem; for crucial particulars, see K. Malone, *JEGP*, XXXVIII (1939). 226-228, XLIII (1944). 451, and XLV (1946). 147-152. But Chambers' book still has more than historical interest.
[3] For recent speculations about the author of *Widsith*, see especially W. H. French, *PMLA*, LX (1945). 623-630.
[4] Or 74, if lines 14-17 be rejected, as they commonly are.
[5] For a fuller analysis, see K. Malone, *ELH*, v (1938). 49-66.

Even the critics thought highly of Widsith's art! From this passage we learn, incidentally, that the scop sang his poems to the accompaniment of the harp. Whether Scilling was Widsith's harpist or a fellow scop (in which case the performance was a duet) we cannot tell; it has even been conjectured, indeed, that Scilling was the name of Widsith's harp.[6] The author makes it clear that his hero was composer as well as performer (though he would hardly have understood the distinction we make between these offices). Widsith sings in mead-hall about his own experiences (lines 54-56), and he composes and sings a poem in praise of his patroness, Queen Ealhhild (lines 99-102). We may safely presume that an actual scop would do as much for the kings who made him welcome at their courts and gave him gifts. The relationship between a scop and his royal patron comes out in the epilogue of our poem:[7]

> As gleemen go, guided by fortune,
> as they pass from place to place among men,
> their wants they tell, speak the word of thanks,
> south or north find someone always
> full of song-lore, free in giving,
> who is fain to heighten his favor with the worthy,
> do noble deeds, till his day is ended,
> life and light together; below he wins praise,
> he leaves under heaven a lasting fame. (lines 135-43)

The word of thanks is to be taken as a poem in honor of the prince, whose fame could hardly have been expected to last unless celebrated in song; poetry was then the only historical record. We conclude that the scop had the important function of immortalizing his patron by singing his praises. These poems of praise, handed down by word of mouth, and making part of the repertory of many a gleeman, were meant to keep the prince's name and deeds alive in the minds of men forever.

But the scop had another function, older and even more important: that of entertainer. In *Beowulf* we get descriptions of the entertainment. From these we gather that a gleeman's performance was short, and made part of a celebration which included amusements of other kinds. Thus, the royal scop sang one morning out of doors, in an interval between horse-races (864-918); the day before, he had sung at a feast in the hall (489-498). A given song might deal with contemporaries (witness the gleeman who celebrated, the morning after the deed, Beowulf's triumph over Grendel), or it might deal with figures of the past. But always, so far as we know, its theme was high and its tone earnest. The entertainment which the scop had to offer made demands on the audience; it could not be enjoyed without keen participation in thought and feeling; there was little about it restful

---

[6] W. J. Sedgefield, *MLR*, xxvi (1931). 75. In humbler circles the performer played his own accompaniment, as we learn from Bede's story of Cædmon.

[7] The metrical translations of *Widsith* 103-108 and 135-143 are taken, by permission, from K. Malone, *Ten Old English Poems* (Baltimore: Johns Hopkins Press, 1941).

or relaxing. The scop held his hearers because he and they were at one: schooled and bound in the traditions of a poetry that gave voice to their deepest loyalties and highest resolves. The theme that moved them most was the theme of sacrifice, dominant in the old poems and strong in the life which these poems reflected and glorified. King and dright [8] made a com- *King and* pany of warriors held together by the bond of sacrificial friendship. The *Dright* king shared his goods with the dright and took them into his very household; the dright shielded him with their bodies on the field of battle, and if he fell they fought on, to victory or death, deeming it base to give ground or flee when their lord lay slain. The famous speech of Byrhtwold in *Maldon* tells us more than pages of exposition could: [9]

> Thought shall be the harder, heart the keener,
> mood shall be the more, as our might lessens.
> Here lies our earl, all hewn to earth,
> the good one, on the ground. He will regret it always,
> the one who thinks to turn from this war-play now.
> My life has been long. Leave I will not,
> but beside my lord I will sink to earth,
> I am minded to die by the man so dear. (lines 312-19)

But the theme of sacrifice need not take the form which it takes in *Maldon*. And other themes might be used, as we have seen. Whatever the theme, the old poems had strength in them to stir the heart and steel the mood. The scop sang of heroes and called his hearers to the heroic life. He held out no false hopes: heroism leads to hardship, wounds, and death. But though all must go down in defeat at last, the fight is worth making: the hero may hope for a good name among men. The value set upon the esteem of others, and in particular upon fame, marks this philosophy social and secular (heathen is hardly the word). The gleemen who taught it in song were upholding the traditional morality of the English people, a way of life known to us from the pages of Tacitus. The entertainment that the scops gave was *ei blot for lyst*.[10] The old poems, and the new ones composed in the same spirit, kept alive for hundreds of years after the conversion to Christianity the old customs, conventions, and ideals of conduct. In so doing they did not stand alone, of course; many other things in English life made for conservatism. But they had a great and worthy part to play in the preservation of the nobler features of our Germanic heritage. It must not be thought, however, that the scops were conservators and nothing more. It was they who made the important stylistic shift from pre-classical to classical; the clerics who produced most of the classical poetry extant simply carried on and elaborated a style the basic features of which had already been set by the scops. Moreover, the personal themes which the scops favored,

---

[8] Comitatus, body of retainers.
[9] From K. Malone, *Ten Old English Poems* (Baltimore: Johns Hopkins Press, 1941), by permission.
[10] "Not merely for pleasure," the old motto of the Royal Theatre in Copenhagen.

courtly though their setting and heroic though their appeal, opened the way
to the lyricism of *Wife's Lament* and *Eadwacer.*

Deor

Only one poem definitely attributed to a specific scop has come down to
us. This poem, commonly called *Deor* after its reputed author, is recorded
in the Exeter Book.[11] The *terminus ad quem* of its composition is therefore
A.D. 980 or thereabouts; a *terminus a quo* will be set below. The poem belongs to the first stage of the run-on style. It is 42 lines long, and falls into
seven sections of varying length. The sections are all mutually independent;
each is complete in itself and could perfectly well stand as a separate poem,
without change. Nevertheless the seven sections make a well-knit whole, as
we shall see. We quote the last section, where the reputed author speaks in
the first person:

> That I will say, of myself to speak,
> That the Heodenings had me a while for scop,
> the king held me dear; Deor they called me.
> For many winters my master was kind,
> my hap was high, till Heorrenda now,
> a good man in song, was given the land
> that my lord before had lent to me.
> That now is gone; this too will go. (lines 35-42)

The last line is the so-called formula of consolation. It tells us (1) that the
misfortune set forth in the other lines of the section has now been overcome or outlived, no matter how; and (2) that the misfortune, whatever
it may be, of the present moment will pass likewise. The moral is: bear
your troubles in patience; they cannot last forever. In the section quoted,
the author mentions a misfortune of his own; in the first five sections, he
mentions as many pieces of adversity that befell others; each section gives
us a new victim (or victims), but ends with the same formula of consolation. The various misfortunes taken up were drawn from Germanic story.
This parallelism in theme, source, and treatment links the sections and gives
unity to the poem.

The sixth section, however, goes its own way. It reads,[12]

> The man that is wretched sits bereft of gladness,
> his soul darkens, it seems to him
> the number of his hardships is never-ending;
> he can bethink him, then, that through this world
> God in his wisdom gives and withholds;
> to many a man he metes out honor,
> fame and fortune; their fill, to some, of woes. (lines 28-34)

---

[11] The only separate edition is that of K. Malone (1933). See also K. Malone, *Acta Phil.
Scand.,* IX (1934). 76-84, *English Studies,* XIX (1937). 193-199, and *MP,* XL (1942). 1-18; L.
Whitbread, *MLN,* LV (1940). 204-207, LVII (1943). 367-369, LXII (1947). 15-20.
[12] The metrical translations of *Deor* 28-34 and 35-42 are taken, by permission, from K.
Malone, *Ten Old English Poems* (Baltimore: Johns Hopkins Press, 1941).

This poetry is timeless and nameless. The victim of misfortune stands for mankind in general, and his troubles are left unspecified. The consolation offered has a correspondingly generalized character. We are told (1) that woe, like weal, comes from God, who knows what is best for us, and (2) that our troubles are of this world (and therefore sure to come to an end). The marked differences between this section and the others have led many to reject it as interpolated. But it sums up admirably the theme of the poem and seems appropriate enough as a concluding passage. We incline to the opinion that it was composed for that purpose. If so, the section with which the poem now ends is best taken as an afterthought on the part of the poet. Certainly it differs from the first five sections in that it is no allusion but a plain summary account of the particular misfortune with which it deals.

Deor bears no likeness to the poems of praise that we hear about in *Beowulf* and *Widsith,* and cannot be reckoned typical of the gleeman's art. The last section comes under the head of personal experience, however, and verses dealing with such experiences are credited to Widsith, as we have seen. The theme of *Deor,* then, does not lie outside a scop's traditional range, though the treatment shows marked originality and the poem therefore makes difficulties for historians of literature, who can find no pigeonhole into which it will fit. If the reputed author actually composed the poem, the date of composition could hardly be set later than the sixth century, and only one section of his poem (the last) has survived: a sixth-century poet could not have composed the general section with its Christian coloring, nor yet the first five sections, which belong to a later stage of English poetic tradition, a stage marked by the use of German sources (compare *Waldere* and *Genesis B*). Most recent commentators have been unwilling to take the consequences of a sixth-century dating, and therefore make the scop Deor into a literary fiction, or, if historical, into a mere mouthpiece of the poet, not the poet himself.[13] The problems involved are too formidable for discussion here. It will be enough to say that *Deor* as it stands cannot plausibly be dated earlier than the ninth century and may have been composed as late as the tenth.

Another poem composed by a scop is that to which scholars have given the name *The Fight at Finn's Borough,*[14] or *Finn* for short. Only a fragment of this poem has survived: 46 lines and 2 half-lines. If the whole came to about 300 lines,[15] then we have somewhat less than a sixth of the text; if the poem was longer, the part we have is proportionately smaller. Our fragmentary text of uncertain date is known to us only from the faulty

Finn

---

[13] R. Imelmann, *Forschungen zur ae. Poesie* (1920), pp. 254-257, contends that the *Deor* poet was familiar with the ninth eclogue of Virgil and gave himself a pen-name in imitation of Virgil.

[14] The text of Hickes reads *Finnsburuh* (one word), but this can hardly be right; see F. P. Magoun, Jr., *Zeitschrift für deutsches Altertum,* LXXVII (1940). 65-66. The poem is included in most editions of *Beowulf* by way of appendix. B. Dickins also includes it in his *Runic and Heroic Poems* (Cambridge, 1915).

[15] For this bold and doubtful conjecture, see F. Klaeber, *Beowulf* (3ed., 1936), p. 236.

transcription of Hickes; [16] the manuscript leaf from which he took it has vanished. A poem which dealt with the same events (possibly the very poem of which we have a fragment) was known to the *Beowulf* poet, who calls it a "gleeman's song" (1160a). The author of *Beowulf* does not give us the text of this song, in whole or in part, but from his own treatment of the theme (1063-1159a) we learn something of the events on which the song was based. In style the Finn episode of *Beowulf* is consonant (for obvious artistic reasons) with the poem of which it makes a part, and differs correspondingly from the Finn fragment, which belongs to the early stage of the run-on style (see above, p. 27). Episode and fragment are not directly comparable in plot, since they deal with different stages of the action. It is customary to reconstruct the plot of the old tale by putting fragment and episode together. Unluckily the beginning of the action nowhere survives, and can be reconstructed only by conjecture. In the following summary of the plot, the conjectural items are bracketed:

King Hnæf of the Danes, with 60 followers, is in Frisia, [on a visit to] his sister Hildeburh, wife of King Finn of the Frisians. [Trouble arises between hosts and guests. The Danes take possession of a hall at Finn's seat, possibly Finn's own hall, and make ready to defend themselves. A Danish sentry (or wakeful warrior) rouses King Hnæf before dawn to report that he sees a light outside and to ask what it means.] Hnæf replies that an attack upon the hall is about to begin. He rouses his men and they take their appointed places to await the onslaught. The Danes hold the doors of the hall without loss to themselves for five days. *Here the fragment ends and the episode begins.* The Danes go over to the offensive [presumably in a sortie] but lose heavily, being reduced to a *wealaf* "remnant of disaster"; King Hnæf himself falls in the struggle. The Frisians too have had severe losses, including Finn's own son. The fight is a stalemate and Hengest, the spokesman for the *wealaf* and its informal leader, comes to terms with Finn. The Danes swear allegiance to Finn and are guaranteed the same rights and privileges that Finn's other followers have. In particular, anyone who taunts them for following their lord's slayer is to be put to the sword. The bodies of the fallen on both sides are then burned with appropriate rites. Life at Finn's court on the new basis continues the winter through. With spring, travel by sea again becomes possible, and Hengest is eager to go but his thoughts are not so much on the voyage itself as on the vengeance he would like to wreak on the "children of the Eotens" [i.e., the Frisians]. Eventually Guthlaf and Oslaf [presumably with the rest of the *wealaf*] get away by sea [to Denmark] and whet their compatriots at home against Finn. A Danish fleet-army attacks and slays Finn at his stronghold and bears off much booty to the ships. Queen Hildeburh goes back to her native land with the Danish victors. We are not told what became of Hengest.

This is not the place to discuss the many problems of fragment and episode.[17] We limit ourselves to the literary treatment of the theme. Both

---

[16] G. Hickes, *Ling. Vett. Sept. Thesaurus*...(1705). I: 192-193.
[17] For recent discussions, see K. Malone, *ELH*, x (1943). 257-284; *MA*, xiii (1944). 88-91; *RES*, xxi (1945). 126-127; and *MP*, xliii (1945). 83-85, together with the references to other studies there given.

fights are mentioned in the episode, but obviously the interest of the *Beowulf* poet centered, not in the fighting but in the tragic situation of Hildeburh and Hengest during the period between the two battles. The hapless queen makes a pathetic figure; husband and brother wage war against each other, and son and brother fall, fighting on opposite sides. Hers is a woman's tragedy; she can do nothing to keep her nearest and dearest from killing each other. The poet lays stress on her sorrow and her innocence. She did not deserve the fate that befell her.

The tragedy of Hengest (and of the *wealaf* [18] as a whole, for whom he stands) strikes deeper. The Danes not only made terms with their lord's slayer; they actually entered that slayer's service, became his men. This debarred them from carrying out their last and most solemn obligation to Hnæf: that of avenging his death. Indeed, they were now honor-bound to defend Finn against attack. The poet pictures Hengest in a kind of mental rebellion against his unhappy fate. He is eager to see the last of Frisia, but above all he yearns to wreak that vengeance on the Frisians which he cannot honorably wreak. We are told nothing more about him, and we need not speculate on his further activities. The tragedy of the *wealaf* as a whole, however, seems to have been resolved by the voyage of Guthlaf and Oslaf to Denmark. Though the Danes in Finn's service could not honorably turn upon him themselves, they could incite their fellow Danes to do so; such was the legalistic ethics prevalent in those days among the Germanic tribesmen. Whether Finn let the *wealaf* go that summer or whether they took advantage of an opportunity to desert, we have no means of knowing. In any case Guthlaf and Oslaf could hardly have made the voyage to Denmark without a crew, and the *wealaf* was the only crew available.

What of the gleeman's song on which the episode is based? Did its author see eye to eye with the *Beowulf* poet? Here we must go by the fragment. From this it would seem that the scop did not dwell on the early events and was hurrying on to something else. Hnæf's answer when he saw the light outside,[19]

> Here day dawns not, here a dragon flies not,
> and here the horns of this hall burn not,
> but here they bear forward, birds of prey croak,
> the greycoat yells, the gory spear shouts,
> shield answers shaft. Now shines this moon,
> wandering, on the earth; now woe-deeds arise,
> that will bring to a head this hatred between peoples.
> But waken now, warriors mine,
> take up your shields, think only of fighting,
> join battle in front, be bold-hearted (lines 3-12),

---

[18] Danish survivors.
[19] The metrical rendering of lines 3-12 of the *Finn* fragment is taken, by permission, from K. Malone, *Ten Old English Poems* (Baltimore: Johns Hopkins Press, 1941).

the manning of the doors (13-17), the challenge and reply with which the fight begins (18-27), are done with breadth and leisure, but then the tempo changes. The fight between challenger and defender, though elaborately introduced, is not reported in detail; the scop finds it enough to tell us that Garulf, the challenger (Finn's man), lost his life, and even this information is not given separately, but is incorporated in a brief description of the sounds and sights that go with battle (28-36). The course of the fight for five days is then disposed of in six lines (37-42) taken up chiefly with praise of Hnæf's following. The tempo slows again with the last lines of the fragment (43-48), which report, in indirect discourse, a dialogue between Hnæf and a wounded Dane. We surmise that the crisis of the battle is at hand, but here the fragment breaks off. The *Beowulf* episode makes clear the further course of the struggle. The Danes took the offensive after their long and successful defensive stand. The object of their sortie may have been to win through to the shore and take ship for home, or perhaps they had run short of water and needed a fresh supply. Whatever their reason for sallying forth, the sortie cost them dear: their king and many others fell and the company of sixty was reduced to a mere *wealaf* of, say, twenty or thirty men. As total destruction loomed before them, one of the retainers, Hengest by name, took command, not by inherited right but as a born leader who rose to the emergency. Under his leadership the Danes rallied, fought Finn to a standstill, and regained the shelter of the hall, where they held out against all the forces Finn could bring to the attack. In all likelihood the major part of the old lay was devoted to this stirring, heroic struggle, with Hengest as hero. The expression "Hengest himself" in line 17 of the fragment points to the centrality of this character in the poem, and his actual centrality in the *Beowulf* episode completes the demonstration. But we have no reason to think that the fighting proper was played down in the lay as it is in *Beowulf*. On the contrary, the lay first of all told the story of the battle, though of course the scop's interest was not in military tactics but in heroic deeds.

Hengest's heroism, however real, was far from ideal, as the *Beowulf* episode shows. The greatness of the man was marred by a tragic flaw. He and his fellows of the *wealaf*, rather than throw away their lives round the dead body of Hnæf, as the code prescribed, chose to live on, and even to enter the service of their lord's slayer. Why should a scop celebrate such a man in song? One may surmise that the lay of Hengest was first composed and sung by a scop in service at the Kentish court. If the Hengest of story was the man who began the English settlement of Britain (and many scholars have been of this opinion),[20] the scops of the kings of Kent might be expected to sing his virtues and to overlook or minimize his faults. And it is not without weight that the hero Hengest appears in English but not in Continental story.

[20] See especially E. Björkman, *Studien über die Eigennamen im Beowulf* (Halle, 1920), pp. 60-61.

The famous English scholar Alcuin in a letter of the year 797 (No. 124 *Lost* in Duemmler's edition) [21] bears incidental witness to the existence of a song *Songs* about Ingeld, the unfortunate king of the Heathobards mentioned in *Beowulf* and *Widsith*. This king sacrificed honor, love, and life itself in a fruitless attempt to avenge a defeat which the Danes had inflicted upon his tribe.[22] From allusions in extant literature and elsewhere we may infer with certainty that many other songs composed by scops were once current in England, though their texts have not come down to us. Sometimes the allusions give us a good idea of the events celebrated in an old poem, but often we must go to Iceland or Denmark or Germany for the story, and often we search in vain for further information. It would be interesting and worth while to make a list of songs once sung by English gleemen, but now lost. We find it safer, however, to list some of the heroes that were celebrated in these lost songs. In so doing, we begin with the Goths. The Gothic heroes fall into three groups: early, middle, and late. The early heroes are those mentioned as such by Jordanes, the sixth-century historian of the Goths, who tells us [23] that their deeds were celebrated in song. Three of these heroes, Emerca, Fridla, and Wudga (Widia), find place in *Widsith;* presumably they became known to the English through the scops. We add King Eastgota and his son Unwen to the early group; they are later in date than the ancient heroes in Jordanes' list, but lived too early (third century) to be put with the middle group, and the *Widsith* poet associates them with Emerca and Fridla. The chief hero of the middle group, and of the Goths in general, is King Ermanric, who figures largely in *Widsith,* and is mentioned in *Beowulf* and *Deor.* He flourished in the fourth century. To the middle group also belong Wulfhere and Wyrmhere, mentioned in *Widsith* as leaders of the Vistula Goths in their warfare against the Huns; these heroes presumably flourished c. A.D. 400. The case of Hama makes difficulties; in *Widsith* he goes with the early hero Wudga, while in *Beowulf* he goes with Ermanric. In all likelihood *Widsith* gives us the older tradition here, while the *Beowulf* allusion reflects the beginning of a process carried through in later times, a process whereby the gigantic figure of Ermanric drew various Gothic heroes into his circle, irrespective of chronology.[24]

---

[21] *Monumenta Germaniae Historica . . . Epistolarum,* IV (Berolini, 1895). 183. The passage may be translated thus: "The words of God are to be read at a corporate priestly meal. There it is proper to hear a reader, not a harper; sermons of the fathers, not songs of the heathen. What [has] Ingeld [to do] with Christ? Narrow is the house: and it cannot hold both. The heavenly king will not have to do with so-called kings, heathen and damned, because that king reigns in heaven, world without end, while the heathen one, damned, laments in hell. . . ." See also No. 21, *ed. cit.,* p. 59: audiantur in domibus vestris legentes, non ludentes in platea "readers in your houses, not players in the street are to be heard."

[22] The tale of Ingeld is the subject of a *Beowulf* episode (lines 2014-2069a) and a *Widsith* passage (lines 47-49). See K. Malone, *MP,* XXVII (1930). 257-276; *Anglia,* LXIII (1939). 105-112; *GR,* XIV (1939). 235-257; *ELH,* VII (1940). 39-44; *JEGP,* XXXIX (1940). 76-92; and *Essays and Studies in Honor of Carleton Brown* (1940), pp. 1-22.

[23] *Getica,* cap. V.

[24] Monograph: C. Brady, *The Legends of Ermanaric* (Berkeley, 1943); reviewed by K. Malone, *MLN,* LIX (1944). 183-188 and *JEGP,* XLIII (1944). 449-453; by P. W. Souers, *Speculum,* XX (1945). 502-507.

The only Gothic hero of the late period is Theodric, the conqueror of Italy; he is mentioned in *Waldere*.[25]

Three Burgundian heroes are mentioned in *Widsith:* Gifica, Guðhere and Gislhere. The fall of Guðhere in battle against the Huns may well have been the subject of an English song. The Frankish hero Sigemund, son of Wæls, together with Sigemund's nephew Fitela, was celebrated in song by a scop, according to the *Beowulf* poet, who gives us (lines 874-897) some idea of the deeds celebrated. But Sigemund's famous son Sigfrid or Sigurd seems to have been unknown to the English, and the tale of the Wælsings was not combined with that of the Burgundians as it was in the Icelandic *Völsungasaga* and the German *Nibelungenlied*. The Frankish king Theodric, eldest son of Clovis, appears twice in *Widsith* and his rule over the Mærings (the Visigoths of Auvergne?) is mentioned in *Deor*. He answers to the Hugdietrich of German story.[26] The Langobards held a high place in English song, if we may judge by *Widsith*, where no less than six Langobardish heroes appear: the ancient kings Ægelmund and Hun(d)gar, of whom a tale is told by Paulus Diaconus, the historian of the Langobards;[27] another ancient king Sceafa; two later kings, Eadwine and Ælfwine, the Audoin and Alboin of the historians; and a king or kemp Elsa otherwise unknown. Hagena, King of the Rugians, appears in *Widsith* 21, where he is coupled with a certain Henden, King of the Glomman. The line may well be an allusion to the Hild story, in which father and lover fight about the lady.[28] Wada, King of the Hælsings, was still sung in Chaucer's day, and his inclusion in *Widsith* indicates that the scops sang him too. Many Scandinavian heroes, besides, figured in English song. We learn of them chiefly in *Beowulf*, the major Old English poetic monument. Only one English hero found much favor with the scops, it would seem, but they made amends by composing two songs in his honor. King Offa, who ruled the English in Sleswick, before their migration to Britain, won fame both as a fighter and as a wife-tamer. His fight is told of in *Widsith* (38-44); his marriage, in *Beowulf* (1933-1962). At the opposite extreme from Offa stands King Attila of the Huns, the only non-Germanic hero whom the scops celebrated in song. We end our list with Weland the smith, the only mythological character included (unless Wada and Sceafa are mythical, as some scholars think).[29]

The heroes listed have much in common. First of all, their nationality is Germanic; even Attila may be looked upon as Germanic by adoption. For

---

[25] If the Beadeca of *Widsith* is rightly identified with King Totila, we have another Gothic hero of the latest or Italian period.

[26] See K. Malone, in *Acta Phil. Scand.,* IX (1934). 76-84, and *ESt,* LXXIII (1939). 180-184.

[27] The tale answers, in part, to the "Helgakviður" of the *Elder Edda;* see K. Malone, *Amer. Jour. Philology,* XLVII (1926). 319-346, and *MLQ,* I (1940). 39-42.

[28] For the various versions of this and other tales referred to here, see M. G. Clarke, *Sidelights on Teutonic History in the Migration Period* (Cambridge, 1911).

[29] Many other names might be added (e.g., those of eponyms and others from the royal genealogies), but we have given enough to serve the purposes of this history.

many centuries the English had enjoyed political independence, but cul-turally they still belonged to a commonwealth of nations, the Germania of their Continental forefathers. Within that commonwealth they were at home, and felt the Goth, the Swede, the Langobard alike to be cultural fellow-countrymen. Secondly, the heroes all flourished in a period thought of as heroic in some special or exclusive sense, though without definition. This period ended with Ælfwine, the Langobardish conqueror of Italy. When it began we cannot say with precision. The heroic period answers roughly to the great migration of the Germanic tribes in the third, fourth, fifth, and sixth centuries, a migration which overthrew the Roman Empire in the west and ushered in the Middle Ages. For the Romans and the Romanized peoples of western Europe this period was one of disaster; for the Germanic tribes it was a period of glorious achievement, a heroic age indeed. Thirdly, the heroes all fought their way to glory: their repu-tation was based on prowess in battle. A king might win martial fame, it is true, by good leadership or good luck in warfare, but personal courage remained the chief virtue of every hero, be he king or kemp. Along with courage a king must have generosity; his dright, loyalty to him. The two virtues went together: a niggardly king could not win or keep loyal fol-lowers, and faithless followers could not expect generous gifts from their lord. The king gained riches through inheritance and war; he gave land, weapons, and other valuables away in order to build up a large and loyal body of followers, by whose help he could win new victories and fill or swell his hoard. A dright was recruited from the whole Germanic world; the fame of a generous and victorious king would draw to his court many a *wrecca* "adventurer" from many a tribe. The king's fellow-tribesmen nevertheless made the backbone of his following. Fourthly, the heroes nearly always belonged to the upper classes of society; they could and did boast of distinguished fathers and forefathers. The society in which they lived, however, aristocratic though it was, had hardly begun that differentiation of classes so marked in the modern world: high and low thought and acted much alike; they had much the same cultural background, viz., that of the peasant. One may compare the peasant culture reflected in the *Iliad* and the *Odyssey,* a way of life simple and dignified, with much form and cere-mony upon occasion, but with many freedoms (e.g., boasting) that good manners now forbid.

Much more might be said about these heroes and the songs in which their heroic deeds found record, but we must go on to the tenth century, when nameless followers of the tradition of the scops composed two poems of praise which posterity has found worthy of admiration. These poems deal with contemporary events, not with events of the heroic age, and so far as we can tell they give us accurate historical information. They illustrate, therefore, a feature not always found in works of literary art, but character-istic of the tradition which the scops set going: the poet as historian.

Brunanburg　　Under the year 937 in the *Old English Annals* is recorded a poem of 73 lines in praise of King Athelstan of England and his brother Edmund.[30] The occasion for the poem was a battle which the brothers fought and won "at Bruna's borough (stronghold)," against an invading force of Scots and Vikings, led by Kings Constantine and Anlaf. The poet, after praising the brothers and telling of their foes' losses on the field of battle, goes on to praise the English army: [31]

> 　　　　　　　　　　　The West-Saxons
> pressed on in force all the day long,
> pushed ahead after the hostile army,
> hewed the fleeing down from behind fiercely,
> with mill-sharp swords. The Mercians withheld
> the hard handplay no whit from a man
> of those that with Anlaf came over the waves,
> by ship invaded our shores from abroad,
> warriors doomed to die in warplay. . . . (lines 20-28)　.

He continues with the flight of Constantine and Anlaf, told with relish and elaborated with passages of exultation. The last section (lines 57-73) falls into three parts: (1) the triumphant homecoming of the brothers; (2) the fate of the bodies of the slain; and (3) the following historical comment:

> 　　　　　　　　　　　So vast a slaughter
> of men never yet was made before this
> on this island of ours with the edge of the sword
> (if we take for true what is told us in books
> or by the old and wise), since from the east hither
> the Angles and Saxons came up, to these shores,
> over broad waters sought Britain out,
> the keen warsmiths, overcame the Welshmen,
> the worshipful kemps, and won the land. (lines 65-73)

The poem is done with high technical skill. The transitions in particular show the poet's mastery of his medium. Noteworthy, too, is a nationalism which goes beyond loyalty to the king's person or to the reigning dynasty. The reference to books, alongside oral tradition, marks the poet a clerk rather than a scop and his poem a writing rather than a speaking.[32] The verses belong, however, to the tradition of the scops in matter and manner. Like the scops, the author is not concerned to describe the course of the battle in any detail; he has made a poem of praise which happens to be a battlepiece as well because victory served as an occasion for praise. If this poem falls short of greatness, brilliant though the poet's performance, its

[30] The best edition of *Brunanburg* is that of A. Campbell (1938).

[31] The metrical translations from *Brunanburg* here quoted are taken, by permission, from K. Malone, *Ten Old English Poems* (Baltimore: Johns Hopkins Press, 1941).

[32] Reference to sources is of course a conventional feature, in writings and speakings alike.

occasion must take the blame, in part at least. Defeat, not victory, found the old poets at their best.[33]

Such a defeat was the battle of Maldon, and the poem so named rises   Maldon magnificently to the tragic occasion. The battle was fought in the year 991 at the estuary of the Blackwater (or Panta) in Essex near Maldon. The hero of the poem is Byrhtnoth, Earl of Essex, leader of the English fyrd (militia); the poet does not name the leaders of the Viking invaders. The text of the poem, preserved in the Oxford MS Rawlinson B 203 (eighteenth century),[34] has come down to us incomplete: it wants both beginning and end. The beginning presumably told of the arrival of the Viking fleet and the measures for defense taken by the Earl. We have no way of knowing what form the end took; possibly the author left his work unfinished. It seems unlikely that any great proportion of the poem has been lost: the 324½ lines that survive give us the meat of the matter. *Maldon* (like *Brunanburg*) was presumably composed shortly after the event which it commemorates: the fall of Byrhtnoth and his dright in battle against the Danes at Maldon. The later differs from the earlier poem markedly—much more than the difference in theme would lead one to expect. We illustrate with the transitions. The *Maldon* poet leans heavily on the connective *þa* "then." In *Brunanburg* this connective does not occur (unless line 53 gives us an instance); the earlier poet does his structural dovetailing so deftly that he must shun a crude device like *þa*—it would spoil the finished effect he aims at. But such deftness would defeat the purpose of the later poet, who is telling a tragic tale with high simplicity; he gains his effects the better for his loose composition.[35] The action of *Maldon* divides naturally into two parts: the course of the battle before (1-184) and after (185-325) the fall of Byrhtnoth. Another two-fold division, equally natural, is that made in terms of the hero's generalship; here the turning-point comes at line 96, when the Earl has made the mistake of withdrawing the holders of the

[33] No less than 13 other poems, occasional in theme, were included in the *Old English Annals*. Seven of these deal with events of the tenth century; six, with events of the eleventh. Some of them resemble *Brunanburg* in that they are panegyrics, done in correct classical verse. They lack the brilliance and fervor of *Brunanburg*, however, and their shortness gives them something of an annalistic character. The other poems incorporated in the *Annals* have a certain interest because of their departure from the classical tradition in style and technic; one notes in particular the growing use of rime and the growing freedom in alliteration (e.g., *st* need not be an alliterative unit). Their artistic worth is negligible. Some of the 13 poems were presumably composed or quoted by the annalists themselves (more precisely, by the original compilers of the annalistic material sent round to the monasteries); others seem to be interpolations, or insertions made by readers. Note K. Jost's demonstration (*Anglia*, XLVII [1923]. 105-123) that two of the poems were composed by Archbishop Wulfstan of York. Such compositions led to the metrical chronicles of Middle English times.

[34] Cotton Otho A XII, the old MS in which *Maldon* found record, was badly burned in the fire of 1731; only fragments remain. Luckily J. Elphinston had copied the poem several years earlier. His copy, now in the Rawlinson collection at Oxford, has served directly or indirectly, as the basis for all editions of the poem. The latest and best separate edition of *Maldon*, that of E. V. Gordon (London, 1937), is based directly on Elphinston's transcript.

[35] The same striving for naturalness comes out in the *Maldon* poet's preference for the early stage of the run-on style, and in his departures from the rigorously classical versification and technic favored by the *Brunanburg* poet. The freedoms found in *Maldon*, be it added, mark no breakdown of the classical tradition; they exemplify, rather, normal and proper variation within that tradition.

ford and letting the Vikings cross the river. The two schemes of division may be combined into a threefold scheme: first the English have the upper hand (1-95); after Byrhtnoth's mistake in generalship but before his fall, the issue of the battle hangs in the balance (96-184); after his fall the English lose the day (185-325). The hero's fatal error grew out of his martial spirit, to which the foe cunningly and successfully appealed. Here lies the tragic flaw which made possible the catastrophe. But it was the flight of the cowardly Godric, mounted on the hero's horse, that precipitated and ensured defeat for the English. Others followed his example (many misled by his mount into thinking it was the Earl himself that fled) and the faithful retainers who stood their ground were left in hopeless case. To their stand lines 202-325 are devoted, over a third of the poem. But this proportion should not mislead us. The thane who dies fighting to the last by his lord's body makes a noble figure, a figure that the scops loved to draw, but he is not a hero in his own right. His devotion typifies that of the dright as a whole, and serves to exalt the lord who won such loyalty. Earl Byrhtnoth is the hero of *Maldon*. But the poet does more than glorify a hero. He glorifies the institution: the relationship of lord and dright that gives rise to the heroism which he celebrates. The poem belongs to the tradition of the scops, and most of it might be put back into heathen times with little or no change in word or thought. Only one truly Christian passage occurs, the prayer of the dying hero:

> I thank thee, O God, Governor of peoples,
> for all the blessings that on earth were mine.
> Now, mild Master, I most have need
> that thou grant to my ghost the grace of heaven,
> that my soul have leave to seek thee out,
> depart in peace, pass into thy keeping,
> Prince of angels. I pray it of thee
> that the fiends of hell afflict her not.[36] (lines 173-80)

These moving words befit the hero, who, as we know from history, was a man of deep Christian piety. He and the cleric who composed the poem in his praise held warfare righteous if in a good cause, and what better cause could be found than defense of church and state, hearth and home against heathen invaders? Our poet upheld and glorified the heroic traditions of his forefathers with a clear conscience; he felt no conflict (in Byrhtnoth's case, at least) between these traditions and Christianity.

The heroic point of view, and the stylistic conventions that go with it, are manifest in the poet's account of the fighting. The battle in *Maldon*, like the battles in the *Iliad*, takes the form of single combats between champions; the common soldiers are ignored. Over a fourth of the poem is made up of speeches. Contrast *Brunanburg*, where neither single combats nor

---

[36] Taken, by permission, from K. Malone, *Ten Old English Poems* (Baltimore: Johns Hopkins Press, 1941).

speeches occur. Both poems are properly described as poems of praise, but they evidently represent different species of this genus. *Maldon* bears some likeness to the epic, *Brunanburg* to the panegyric of the ancients. The differences, however, are too great to admit of southern inspiration in either case. We must presume, rather, a differentiation within the tradition of the scops.

VI

Religious Poetry: Cædmon and His School

English religious poetry begins with a sharpness unusual in the history of literature. An elderly illiterate farmhand of Yorkshire, Cædmon by name, who had never learned how to make verses and would flee for shame when, at entertainments, his turn came to sing, suddenly began to compose poems of a kind hitherto not known in English: religious narrative verse on themes drawn from Holy Writ. The story of Cædmon is told in Bede; [1] it is so familiar that we need not tell it again here. Cædmon served as lay brother and, later, as monk in a monastery at Strenæshalc (Whitby?) under the abbess Hild; his literary activity thus falls between the years 657 and 680 (Hild's term as abbess). Bede gives a Latin paraphrase of Cædmon's first poem, the so-called *Hymn*, and texts of the poem in a dialect of the Northumbrian English native to the poet have come down to us in MSS of Bede's work. The following translation into modern speech is based on the Moore MS text, printed in A. H. Smith's edition: [2]

Hymn

Now [we] shall praise the heaven-realm's Keeper,
God's might and his mood-thought,
the work of the glory-Father, as he of each wonder,
the eternal Lord, the beginning ordained.
He first made to the children of men
heaven for roof, the holy Creator.
Then the middle-yard mankind's Keeper,
the eternal Lord, afterwards created
for men, the earth, the Ruler almighty.

This poem obviously belongs to the early stage of the classical run-on style (see above, p. 27); every line but the eighth ends with a pause, and every sentence ends with a line. The poet made use of a fully developed system of variation. He adapted the technic of the scops to his own purposes neatly enough: royal epithets like *ruler, lord, keeper* became epithets for God by qualification with *almighty, eternal, mankind's* and *heaven-realm's*. To speak more generally, Cædmon took God for his theme and sounded his praises much as a scop would sound the praises of his royal patron. And just as the scop celebrated the heroic deeds of the prince he served (or of that

---

[1] *Hist. Eccl.* IV. xxiv.
[2] *Three Northumbrian Poems* (1933), pp. 38, 40. But the editor's punctuation might be improved. For the history of the text, see E. V. K. Dobbie, *Columbia Univ. Stud. in English and Comp. Lit.*, No 128 (1937), pp. 10-48.

prince's forefathers), so Cædmon celebrated the glorious works of the prince *he* served: namely, God. As Bede informs us,

he sang about the creation of the world, and the origin of mankind, and the whole tale of Genesis; about the exodus of Israel from Egypt and entry into the Promised Land; about many other tales of Holy Writ; about the incarnation, passion, resurrection and ascension into heaven of the Lord; about the coming of the Holy Ghost and the work (doctrina) of the apostles. He made many songs, too, about the terror of doomsday to come and the horror of hell-fire but the sweetness of the kingdom of heaven; but also many others about divine benefits and judgments.

Thereby the pious poet provided the body of monks with entertainment suitable for the monastic refectory, though modeled after the worldly entertainment with which the scops had long regaled the body of retainers in the royal beer-hall.[3] Like the scops again, Cædmon could not read or write, and learned by word of mouth the stories he put into verse. But his poems, in virtue of their matter, were deemed highly edifying, and scribes took them down from the first. The poems of Cædmon make a bridge between speakings and writings: they were composed as speakings, but at once became writings too.

We cannot point to any particular source of Cædmon's *Hymn,* other than divine inspiration and Christian tradition.[4] There exists, however, in the Bodleian library at Oxford, a famous MS called Junius 11 and made up of verse obviously based, for the most part, on Holy Writ.[5] This verse was long attributed to Cædmon, although nowadays it is customary to put the poems of the Junius MS under the head "school of Cædmon"—a label which denies their Cædmonian authorship. We take up these and related poems here. The MS as it stands is divided into two books: the first given over to verse dealing with Old Testament story; the second, to verse about Christ and Satan. According to Gollancz (p. xviii),

Junius MS

The writing of Book I belongs to the last quarter of the tenth or the early years of the eleventh century. No long interval divided the writing of Book II from that of the earlier portion.

Book I was done by one scribe, who had no hand in the copying of Book II, carried out by three scribes "less than a generation"[6] later. Many leaves have been lost from Book I, which therefore has come down to us markedly incomplete; in Book II no such losses took place. Book I is profusely il-

---

[3] But worldly poems composed by scops were still being sung in refectories long after Cædmon's day, as we learn from Alcuin's letter (see above, p. 53). The performer of such a song might be a scop turned monk, or a scop who was spending the night at a monastery. We do not know to what extent (if at all) court poets, or others who followed the courtly tradition, gave performances for the general public (at markets and like places).

[4] But see Sir Israel Gollancz, facsimile ed. *Cædmon MS* (Oxford, 1927), pp. lxi-lxii.

[5] Edition of MS: see Krapp-Dobbie I. Editions of individual poems: F. Holthausen, *Die ältere Genesis* (Heidelberg, 1914); B. J. Timmer, *The Later Genesis* (Oxford, 1948); F. A. Blackburn, *Exodus and Daniel* (Boston, 1907); M. D. Clubb, *Christ and Satan* (New Haven, 1925). See also Clubb, *MLN,* XLIII (1928). 304-306.

[6] Clubb, *ed. cit.,* p. xii.

lustrated, though the artists did not finish their work, leaving many pages blank; Book II is written solid except for the lower half of two pages. We set the second book aside for the moment. The MS text of the first book is divided into 55 fits. With fit·42 the tale shifts from Genesis to Exodus; with fit 50, from Exodus to Daniel. Modern philologists accordingly divide the book into three independent poems. *Genesis,* the first of these, is by far the longest; it comes to 2936 lines.

Genesis

The poem opens with a few lines in praise of God, lines which lead naturally to a short passage in which is depicted the happy lot of the angels in heaven. Next we are told of the discontent and rebellion of Satan and his crew, God's wrath, the creation of hell to house the rebels, their overthrow and expulsion from heaven, and God's design to make the world as a means of filling with "better people" (95) the space left empty in heaven by the transfer of the wicked angels to their new abode.

The better people were presumably the souls of the blessed, the elect of the seed of Adam (as yet uncreated). The world was to be made as a breeding-place for these. Pope Gregory the Great gave a like interpretation to the story of the fall of the angels, and our poet doubtless got his ideas on the subject, directly or indirectly, from Gregory's writings. With line 103 the story of the world and man begins, a story based on the biblical narrative; more specifically, the poet's source was St. Jerome's Latin translation of the Scriptures, commonly called the Vulgate. This the poet follows faithfully from its beginning to Gen. 22:13; here the poem breaks off. We do not know whether it was left unfinished or once had a continuation now lost.

Genesis
A *and* B

Through loss of MS leaves our text has gaps in several places. Lines 235-851 do not belong to the poem at all, but make a great interpolation taken from a later poem on the same subject; this poem was an English version of a Low German (more precisely, an Old Saxon) original. We therefore distinguish between the *Earlier Genesis* or *Genesis A* (lines 1-234 and 852-2936) and the *Later Genesis* or *Genesis B* (lines 235-851). Of the later poem only that part survives which was interpolated into *Genesis A;* of its original, three fragments survive, one of which answers to lines 790-817a of the interpolation. The beginning of *Genesis B* is lost, but the interpolated verses from it dealt with the temptation and fall of Adam and Eve: Gen. 2:16-17 and 3:1-7. Into this story the German author had inserted an account of the fall of the angels, and our text therefore gives us two versions of this event: the rather short and simple version at the beginning of *Genesis A,* and the long, striking version in *Genesis B.* Of the two Genesis poems, the later has great poetic power; indeed, the speech of Satan to the fallen angels bears comparison with *Paradise Lost* in vigor if not in finish. The poet of *Genesis A* outdid his German fellow in craftsmanship but lacked his genius, and the poem is hardly what one would expect of Cædmon. It is worthy of particular note that Bede's list of Cædmon's poems begins, not with the fall of the Angels, but with the creation of the world. From Bede's list and discussion one gathers, further, that Cædmon's poems, like those of the scops, were many and short, not few and long. By its shortness the *Hymn,* Cædmon's authorship of which is certain, lends support to this interpretation of Bede's words. Moreover, the *Hymn* belongs to the early, *Genesis A* to the middle stage of the run-on style. We conclude that Cædmon hardly composed the latter poem, though its author may well have been inspired by Cædmon's songs to undertake a metrical paraphrase of Genesis which would differ from Cædmon's work by reproducing the sacred text in detail. Such a reproduction would of necessity make a long poem, and long poems of this kind would win favor among the clerics, at the expense of short poems, because of their completeness—little or nothing said in Holy Writ, however trivial or by the way, was left out. Again, though both short and long poems were composed for didactic entertainment in refectory, the long poems presumably followed the pattern traditional for monastic meals: they were meant to be read aloud, not sung to the accompaniment of the harp. Certainly the middle and late stages of the run-on style do not go well with musical performance. Ecclesiastical authority might be expected to favor poems for reading, as against poems that were performed after the secular courtly fashion; the latter, though not worldly in theme, had at least a touch of worldliness in performance. It was the practice of reading aloud, we may add, which made possible the rapid development of the run-on style in Old English poetry, freeing the poet as it did from the limitations imposed by musical performance. And the taste for long poems, aroused by the metrical paraphrasts and nourished by study of the *Æneid,* led to extended treatment of secular themes like those of *Beowulf* and *Waldere.*

With Bradley [7] we think that the author of *Genesis A* was a clerk who, as he wrote, had before him a copy of the Vulgate. But he had other sources besides. Gollancz has noted (p. lvii) that

in the poet's treatment of *Genesis* generally, one can trace the use of commentaries and legendary additions, as for example, the story that the raven sent out from the ark perched upon the floating bodies of the dead and so did not return,

and we saw above that the poet began with the fall of the angels, a story which he did not find in Genesis. Moreover, he drew freely from the tradition of the scops, not indeed for matter but for stylistic motifs and devices, and phraseology in general. Thus, the battles of Genesis are described after the manner of the scops. We quote the following passage by way of illustration:

---

[7] *Collected Papers of Henry Bradley* (Oxford, 1928), p. 248. In *DNB,* VIII. 200, Bradley put the matter thus: "a servile paraphrase of the biblical text can only have proceeded from a writer who was able to read his Latin Bible; to a poet who, like Cædmon, had to depend on his recollection of extemporised oral translation, such a performance would have been absolutely impossible."

> There was hard play there,
> exchange of deadly spears, great roar of battle,
> loud war clamor. With hands they drew,
> the heroes, from sheaths the ringed swords,
> the strong-edged [swords]. There it was easy to find
> booty for the fighter who had not had
> enough of combat. (lines 1989-95)

Typical here is the description of the victor: the one who wins booty (i.e., the battle) is the one who is not willing to stop fighting. Dogged does it— such was the spirit of the English then, even as now. The earlier *Genesis,* whether by Cædmon or not, is commonly reckoned a product of the Northumbrian school of poets which Cædmon brought into being, and is commonly dated *c.* 700. The later *Genesis* cannot be earlier than its German original, a poem of the ninth century, and cannot be later than the Junius MS. We know nothing of the translator.

Exodus   The second poem of Book 1 is known as *Exodus;* it has no name in the MS. It is 591 lines long by the reckoning of Blackburn, who in his edition rightly followed the pointing of the MS; earlier editors printed the poem in 589 lines.

We divide the text into the following parts: an introductory period on the Mosaic law (1-7); an epitome of the career of Moses (8-29); a sketch of events in Egypt that led up to the departure of the Hebrews (30-55); the march of the Hebrews to the Red Sea (56-134); the Egyptian pursuit and the rearguard set by the terrified Hebrews (135-246); the passage of the Red Sea and the destruction of the Egyptian army (247-515); conclusion (516-591).[8]

A digressive or episodic passage of more than 80 lines (362-446) on Noah and Abraham follows the description (310-353a) of the order of march of the Hebrew tribes; a short passage (353b-361) on the common ancestry of the tribes serves to tie the digression, loosely enough, to the main story. Through loss of MS leaves the text has two serious gaps: one between lines 141 and 142 and one (fit 48) between lines 446 and 447. The poet's theme is not Exodus as a whole but the passage of the Red Sea by the Israelites, or, better, the heroic leadership of Moses in this passage. Noteworthy are lines 208 ff., in which the despair of the fugitives at the approach of the Egyptian host changes to courage when Moses bids them "make up their minds to perform deeds of valor" (218b). Unluckily the battle-scene (fit 48) is lost. The poet gives much space to speech-making by his hero; the speeches are reported now in direct, now in indirect discourse. In general, the poet follows English heroic tradition: Moses answers to a Germanic king and the picked fighters of the Hebrews answer to a Germanic dright. For his story the poet relies chiefly on chapter 14 of Exodus. A few verses elsewhere in Exodus are used too, and some use is made of other books of Moses, notably Genesis. But the author goes much further afield. Modern

---

[8] The conclusion makes problems too involved for discussion here; see Gollancz, pp. lxxv-lxxix, whose conjectural rearrangement of the lines cannot surmount the obstacle of *swa* 549.

investigators have emphasized his learning and his originality, as reflected in style and in sundry details of the text.[9] The freedom with which he treated his main source finds extreme illustration in lines 447-515, based on a single Bible verse: Exod. 14:28. The half-line *flod blod gewod* "blood filled the flood" (463b) reveals a fondness for striking metrical effects. Now and again the poet's wording seems fanciful or even strained, as when he calls the Hebrews seamen (333) because they were crossing the Red Sea (on foot). But it would be a mistake to reckon the poem precious; [10] it departs somewhat from the classical mean characteristic of most Old English poetry, but remains traditional on the whole. The difficulties which the text makes come chiefly from its faulty transmission, and for this the poet cannot rightly be blamed. Date and authorship are unsolved problems. Gollancz was so impressed by the poet's learned preciosity (as he took it) that he suggested authorship "if not by Aldhelm, then by one of his school, and certainly by a kindred spirit" (p. lxix), but he admitted that the text bore marks of Anglian origin. The scanty evidence points to a Northumbrian clerk of the Age of Bede, when learning was at its height in Old England. Since the poem belongs to the middle stage of the run-on style, it can hardly have been composed earlier than *c.* 700.

The third and last poem of Book 1 is that called *Daniel*. It has no title in the MS. By Blackburn's count it comes to 764 lines; earlier editors wrongly made two lines of line 224. **Daniel**

Author or scribe divided the text into six fits. The first of these falls into two parts: an introduction, on Hebrew history down to the war with Nebuchadnezzar (1-41a); and the story of that war, with its consequence, the Babylonian captivity of the Jews, to which is added an account of the three Hebrew children, Hananiah, Mishael, and Azariah, with their training for Nebuchadnezzar's service (41b-103). The second part of the fit is based on the first chapter of Daniel, much of which, however, the poet leaves out; in particular, he fails to mention Daniel. The next fit likewise falls into two parts: it begins with a condensed paraphrase (104-167) of Daniel 2, in which we learn of Nebuchadnezzar's first dream (about the image) and Daniel's success with it after the Chaldean wise men had failed; then comes a versification of Dan. 3:1-18, the story of the golden image which the king sets up and which the three Hebrew children refuse to worship, though the king threatens to cast them into a fiery furnace (168-223). Through loss of a MS leaf the poet's paraphrase of Dan. 3:2-6 is wanting here. The third fit falls into three parts: first, a paraphrase of Dan. 3:19-27, telling how the king carried out his threat and how an angel came down into the furnace and saved the children (224-278); next, the apocryphal prayer of Azariah (279-332); last, a repetition of the rescue story, the angel's coming being represented

---

[9] Obviously he knew his way about in a monastic library, with its Latin classics, Church fathers, martyrologies, commentaries and miscellanies. In particular, he has been credited with knowledge of Avitus, Sedulius, Jerome, Josephus, Augustine, Bede, and Ealdhelm. The following studies are worth listing: L. L. Schücking, *Untersuchungen*, etc. (Heidelberg, 1915); S. Moore, *MP*, IX (1911). 83-108; J. W. Bright, *MLN*, XXVII (1912). 13-19 and 97-103; R. Imelmann, *Forschungen* etc. (Berlin, 1920).

[10] Imelmann, *op. cit.*, pp. 390-408, gives a needful corrective for the extravagances of Schücking and his followers.

as in answer to Azariah's prayer (333-361). The fourth fit too falls into three parts: it begins with the apocryphal Song of the Three Youths in praise of God (362-408), continues with a paraphrase of Dan. 3:24-29, in which the story of the angel is told a third time (409-485), and ends with a passage of transition to the next fit (486-494). The fifth fit versifies Daniel 4, telling of Nebuchadnezzar's second dream (about the tree) and Daniel's interpretation (495-674). The last fit versifies Daniel 5, on Belshazzar's feast (675-764); through loss of a MS leaf the end of this fit is missing. The poet seems not to have versified the story of Daniel in the Lions' Den (Daniel, 6).

Daniel
A *and* B

The second and third parts of the third fit make an interpolation into our poem. We therefore distinguish *Daniel A* (1-278 and 362-764) and *Daniel B* (279-361). The former poem belongs to the early stage of the run-on style. This may mean that it was composed early, but its author may have lived later and used the older style simply because he preferred it. The poem is no masterpiece, but shows good workmanship; the transitions especially are well done. The old link between fits three and four is lost, replaced by the interpolation. The repetitious treatment of the angel in *Daniel A* makes problems too knotty for this history. The poet does not follow his source slavishly; he leaves much out, and sometimes puts things in, as when he has Nebuchadnezzar wake up from a drunken sleep (116). He expands freely when he likes, and even includes a lyric piece: the Song of the Three Youths. His source here was not the Vulgate, but a canticle the Latin text of which is preserved in the so-called *Vespasian Psalter*.[11] We have no evidence, however, that the poet's English version of the Song once existed free of its setting in *Daniel A*. The Song does not fall into five-line stanzas, as some have maintained. *Daniel A* presumably goes back to early Northumbria (*c.* 700?).

Azariah

The interpolator took *Daniel B* from a poem which the philologists call *Azariah*.[12] A copy of this poem has come down to us in the Exeter Book. More precisely, the compiler of that MS miscellany included part of a poem on the third chapter of *Daniel,* presumably the part he liked best; certainly he left out the beginning, for his text begins, abruptly enough, with the introduction to the prayer of Azariah. The part preserved in the Exeter Book comes to 191 lines. Of these, lines 28-29 make what is left of a defective passage that answers to *Daniel,* 307-312; the missing words were recorded on the lost part of folio 53.

The poem as we have it consists of the introduction to the prayer of Azariah (1-4), the prayer (5-48), the rescue by the angel (49-67a), the introduction to the Song of the Three Youths (67b-72), the Song (73-161a), the outcry of the heathen at the miracle (161b-165), the report of the miracle, made to Nebuchadnezzar by his *eorl* (166-179a), and the king's reaction: he went to see the miracle

---

[11] H. Sweet, *Oldest English Texts* (EETS, 83). pp. 414-415. The canticle was drawn from the Roman Breviary.

[12] Ed. W. Schmidt, *Bonner Beiträge,* XXIII (1907). 40-48. See also editions of the Exeter Book. The latest of these is Krapp-Dobbie, III.

with his own eyes and then told the youths to come to him, whereupon they left the furnace in triumph (179b-191).

Daniel B is so like *Azariah,* 1-72 that we cannot speak of two poems but must reckon the two texts mere variants of the same original. The likenesses of *Daniel A* to the corresponding parts of *Azariah* need another explanation. The evidence indicates that the *Azariah* poet had before him, not only the Vulgate text but also a copy of *Daniel A.* This copy he drew upon freely at the beginning of the Song of the Three Youths, but less and less as he proceeded; in making his version of the Song he followed the Canticle text but took the Vulgate text into account as well. He expanded his sources with reflective and devotional matter much more freely than did the *Daniel* poet. We reckon the report of the *eorl* to Nebuchadnezzar a piece of conventional English heroic machinery; it may have been suggested by ⁺he speech of the counselor in *Daniel A* (416 ff.), but bears little likeness ⁻o that speech. Azariah belongs to the middle stage of the run-on style. It ⱽas composed later than *Daniel A,* and earlier than the time of compilation of the Exeter Book. Its author followed in the tradition set going by Cædmon, and may well have been a Northumbrian clerk, but of this we cannot be sure. If he was Northumbrian, his poem can hardly have been composed later than *c.* 875.

Another poem based on Old Testament story is *Judith;* it has come down to us in the Nowell codex, BM Cotton Vitellius A xv, 2d MS (late tenth century).[13] The poet had for source the Vulgate text of the apocryphal book of Judith. Unluckily only the last part of the poem survives: 348 lines and 2 half-lines, making a little more than three fits. If we go (as we must) by the MS numbering, the complete poem made at least 12 fits; the fragment we have begins toward the end of the ninth fit, and versifies Judith 12:10 to 16:1. We cannot tell whether the poet stopped here or composed a thirteenth fit, answering to the canticle of thanksgiving in Judith, 16. If such a fit 13 ever existed, it has been lost. **Judith**

The tenth fit (15-121) deals with the feast at which Holofernes became drunk and with his death at the hands of Judith. The eleventh fit (122-235) deals with the return of Judith and her maid to Bethulia, bringing the head of Holofernes; the joyous welcome Judith got from the Hebrews; her speech exhorting them to go forth to battle; and their attack upon the Assyrian host. The twelfth fit (236-350) deals with the hesitation of the Assyrians, though under attack, to wake Holofernes; their terror and flight when at last one of them ventured into the general's tent and found his headless body; the slaughter the Hebrews made and the booty they took; finally the spoils awarded to Judith and the praise she gave to God.

The poem belongs to the last stage of the run-on style (see above, p. 27). Its author shows himself a master of his medium. Indeed, he has produced a *tour de force.* In spite of the many swollen lines (nearly a fifth of the

---

[13] This codex, better known as the *Beowulf* MS, is now available in facsimile: *Early English MSS in Facsimile* xii (Copenhagen, 1963), ed. K. Malone.

whole), the long periods, the frequent variations and descriptive details, we find the tempo swift, the action sharp and straightforward. An elaborate and sophisticated style, made for epic breadth and leisure, is here seized upon and forced to yield effects akin to those of the scops, though without that singing quality which the gleeman's older and simpler art had kept. The heroic tone of *Judith* goes without saying. The battle scenes have rightly been praised, but owe less to the poet than to tradition. The scene of drunken revelry (15 ff.), however, stands unmatched in Old English. The poet has not hesitated to depart from his source when his art is served thereby. His fondness for rime is worthy of note. We take him to have been an Angle (Mercian) of the tenth century, though Saxon authorship is possible.

Christ and Satan

The second book of the Junius MS is given over to some 733 lines of verse, a poem which Grein aptly called *Christ and Satan;* it has no name in the MS.

The text is divided into 12 fits. The first of these begins with a brief account of Creation (attributed to the Son) and the fall of the angels (1-33); then come a lament by Satan (34-50), a reproachful reply by his crew (51-64), and a homiletic passage (65-74). Satan's second lament makes the second fit (75-125). The third fit gives us two more laments of Satan: the third (126-159) and the fourth (160-189). The fourth fit is a short homily inspired by the fate of the fallen angels (190-224). With the next fit (225-255) Satan begins a fifth lament, which he finishes in the first part (256-279) of the sixth fit. The rest of this fit (280-315) and the whole of the seventh (316-365) make a kind of homily on the sorrows of hell and the joys of heaven. The eighth fit repeats in résumé the story of the fall of the angels (366-379a) and begins the story of Christ's harrowing of hell (379b-442). This story is finished in the ninth fit (443-469), which ends with Christ's speech to the souls he has rescued from hell and taken up to heaven (470-513); in this speech Christ tells of the creation and fall of man, of his resolve to save man, and of his incarnation and earthly life. The tenth fit is devoted to the Resurrection (514-557). The eleventh fit tells of the Ascension, Pentecost, the fate of Judas, and Christ's kingdom in heaven, to which men too may come (558-597). The twelfth fit goes on to Doomsday (598-643), gives yet another reminder of the joys of the saved (644-664), and adds an account of Christ's temptation in the wilderness (665-710); the fit ends with Satan's return to hell and to the curses of his followers after his failure to tempt Christ (711-733).

This poem makes many problems which cannot be taken up here.[14] Apart from the faulty transmission of the text, we must reckon with a scheme of presentation anything but straightforward. The sequence, chronological in the main, does great violence to chronology on occasions. Thus, the temptation of Christ comes at the end of the poem, and the fall of man is not spoken of until long after the event (410-421 and 481-488). In telling the story of Christ from Creation to Doomsday, the poet plays action down and situation up. His interest lies, not in the narrative but in the punishments and rewards of the life to come, and he pictures these over and over, using

---

14 See the discussions in the editions of Clubb and Gollancz cited above (p. 61).

all the devices at his command, and constantly hammering home the moral: we should follow Christ, not Satan. The laments put in Satan's own mouth make clear in dramatic fashion the folly of choosing such leadership as his. The Satan of this poem is not the defiant and indomitable leader of *Genesis B*, but a leader broken by defeat, who must swallow the curses of his own dright. The fate of Satan and his crew serves as the supreme object-lesson by which mankind may take warning. On the positive side, Christ's rejection of Satan's lordship in the temptation scene serves as the supreme example which all men should follow when faced with the temptations of earthly life. This scene therefore makes a fitting end for the poem, and we cannot accept the view of Gollancz that the poet after finishing his poem tacked the temptation on by way of afterthought. No immediate sources have been found for this remarkable work. The author drew on Christian tradition, as known to him from the Bible and elsewhere. He handled his material with a freedom which suggests that he wrote without having any books before him; he seems to have relied on his memory of the events and to have given rein to his fancy. His verses have power and vividness, but too much should not be made of their originality: the poet combines lyric, dramatic, and epic in typical Old English fashion. We reckon the poem Anglian in origin, and of the ninth century, but we do not set even so loose a date as this with confidence. We agree with all recent authorities that Cædmon did not compose *Christ and Satan*. The clerk who made the poem belonged to Cædmon's school, but learned from another school as well: that of Cynewulf. The work of this school will be considered in the next chapter.

VII

Religious Poetry: Cvnewulf and His School

Nearly all Old English poetry is anonymous. One poet, however, had a habit of signing his verses, and from these signatures we know his name: Cynewulf.[1] His motive was not vainglory but (as he himself explains) hope that those who liked his poems would name him in their prayers. The signatures took the form of runes, woven in the verses towards the end but not at the very end of a given poem. From them we learn that the poet spelt his name indifferently *Cynewulf* and *Cynwulf*. Since he did not use the spelling *Cyniwulf* we infer that he lived after weak medial *i* had become *e*. The date of this sound-shift varies with the dialect. Other linguistic evidence, however, marks Cynewulf an Angle, and only the Northumbrian and Mercian dialects need be considered. Northumbrian weak *i* was kept until the middle of the ninth century, while Mercian variants with *e* appear early in that century, and this *e* may go back to the last years of the eighth. The earliest possible time for Cynewulf, then, is the last quarter of the eighth century, and the ninth makes a safer date. Of the man we know nothing except what we glean from his work. We have four poems of his: a list, a sermon, and two legends (i.e., saints' lives). We take them in the order given.

The Fates of the Apostles   *The Fates of the Apostles* is a poem of 122 lines, recorded in the Vercelli Book [2] (late tenth century). It falls into two parts: the list proper, in which are named the places or countries where the twelve apostles taught and died (1-87); and the poet's signature with accompanying verses (88-122). Unlike the *Menologium,* our poem does not include the feast-days of the twelve, but we need not infer with Krapp (p. xxxii) that "the motive which inspired its composition was, therefore, purely literary and devotional." A certain learned, antiquarian spirit also enters in, and such a list, though without dates, obviously had practical (didactic) worth besides. No single source answers precisely to lines 1-87, and such a source will hardly be found: Cynewulf starts by telling us he "gleaned far and wide" how the apostles "made their virtue known," and one naturally infers that the poet made a compilation drawn from various sources. Name-forms like *Petrus*

---

[1] See S. K. Das, *Cynewulf and the Cynewulf Canon* (Calcutta, 1942); K. Jansen, *Die Cynewulf-Forschung* (Bonn, 1908); K. Sisam, "Cynewulf and his Poetry," *Proc. Brit. Acad.*, XVIII (1932). 303-331. The texts are edited by A. S. Cook, *The Christ of Cynewulf* (Boston, 1900), and *The OE Elene* ... (New Haven, 1919); W. Strunk, *The Juliana of Cynewulf* (Boston, 1904); G. P. Krapp, *Andreas and the Fates of the Apostles* (Boston, 1906). On the so-called *Christ* see especially Brother Aug. Philip, *PMLA,* LV (1940). 903-909.

[2] Facsimile edition by Max Förster (Rome, 1913); printed verse texts in Krapp-Dobbie, II.

and *Paulus* point to Latin sources, and like lists in Latin have been pointed out by Krapp and by Sisam. The poem has a so-called epic opening consonant with the worth of the theme. The following passage is representative:

> Certain ones in Rome,
> bold ones and brave, gave up their lives
> through Nero's cruel cunning,
> Peter and Paul; that apostleship
> is widely honored among the nations. (lines 11-15)

The personal part of the poem (88-122) makes more than a fourth of the whole. The disproportion springs from the author's eagerness to win the prayers of others, an eagerness which drives him to repeat, after the runic passage, the request for prayers which he had already made before that passage. Art here yields to soul's need! Otherwise the poem is marked by good craftsmanship. The riming half-line *nearwe searwe* (13b) is worthy of note.

The Ascension (otherwise known as *Christ B*) is a poem of 427 lines recorded in the Exeter Book. The poem is divided into five fits. These we analyze as follows:

Ascension

I. Exhortation to an "illustrious man" (the poet's patron?) to make every effort to understand why the angels at the nativity did not appear in white robes (1-10a); the contrast here between nativity and ascension (10b-19a); the throng [before the ascension] in Bethany (19b-34); Christ's farewell to his followers (35-51); the ascension and the song of the angels (52-66); the two angels appear to the disciples and explain the event (67-77).

II. The parting words of the angels to the disciples (78-87); Christ assumes his seat in heaven amid rejoicing on high (88-93); the disciples return to Jerusalem and await Pentecost as Christ had bidden before he ascended (94-107); white-robed angels (i.e. splendor) befit Christ's return to his throne above (108-118); song of angels, celebrating Christ's harrowing of hell and return to heaven with the redeemed souls (119-146); lyric passage (with rime) on the plan of salvation and man's need to choose between good and evil (147-160).

III. Man should thank God for his gifts, the greatest of which is the hope of salvation, held out at the ascension (161-187); Christ's earthly life, from nativity to ascension, made our salvation possible (188-193); of this Job sang, using the figure of a bird [Job 28:7], but the Jews could not understand (194-219); Christ divides gifts among men; no one gets all spiritual wisdom, for fear of pride harming him (220-246).

IV. God by gifts honors his creatures, whose worth reflects God himself, our sun (247-258); the Church is likened to the moon; after the ascension she shone forth over the earth (259-264a); through the gift of the Holy Ghost [at Pentecost] the Church was enabled to withstand the persecutions which began after the ascension (264b-272); the six leaps of Christ (conception, nativity, crucifixion, burial, descent into hell, ascent into heaven), referred to by Solomon [Song 2:8] (273-304); so ought we to leap from strength to strength until we reach heaven through holy works; to that end we must choose the good and reject the evil; God will help us against devils; we must keep watch all our lives and pray to God, our benefactor, to whom be praise and glory for ever (305-339).

V. If God helps us, we need not fear devils (340-343a); Doomsday is near, when we shall be judged by our deeds (343b-346a); Christ's first coming was in humility [the angels did not appear in white robes]; his second coming will be in judicial sternness, and many will be punished (346b-357); runic passage (the poet's signature) on Doomsday (358-368a); the destruction of the world by fire (368b-375); be mindful of the soul's need now, before it is too late (376-384); the terrors of Doomsday (385-410); life is like a voyage, and heaven is like a port made ready for us by Christ when he ascended (411-427).

In this poem Cynewulf versified the conclusion of Gregory the Great's sermon on the ascension (the 29th of his gospel homilies).[3] Lines 220-246 owe much to another source, presumably an English poem not unlike the extant *Gifts of Men* (see below, p. 83). The Bible and other works seem to have been used more or less besides. The poet treated his matter with freedom and artistic skill, though of course his thought is derivative and traditional enough. This versified sermon must be reckoned successful. In structure it is governed by its chief source.

Juliana

Juliana is a poem of the Exeter Book. It comes to 731 lines as we have it, but through loss of MS leaves two passages are wanting: one before folio 70 (between lines 288 and 289), the other before folio 74 (between lines 558 and 559). The poem is made up of seven fits. These may be outlined as follows:

I. Under the Roman emperor Maximian (A.D. 305-311), persecutor of the Christians, there lived in Nicomedia a pagan official named Heliseus [Eleusius], who fell in love with the young and beautiful Christian virgin Juliana; she wished to keep her virginity, but her pagan father Africanus betrothed her to Heliseus; she refused to marry him unless he turned Christian; he protested to her father, who expostulated with her (1-104).

II. Juliana replied, holding her ground; Africanus argued further with her but could not move her; he turned her over to Heliseus for judgment; her betrothed, after pleading with her in vain, had her stripped and scourged; he then urged apostasy upon her with threats; she defied him and his false gods (105-224).

III. Heliseus had Juliana hanged on a tree by the hair and beaten for six hours; he then threw her into prison; a devil visited her there in angel form, to persuade her to yield; at her prayer a voice from heaven revealed the tempter's identity and gave orders that she seize the fiend and not let him go until he had confessed all; she obeyed and thereby forced the wretch to reveal the secrets of deviltry (225-344).

IV. The fiend continues his confessions (345-453).

V. He concludes; at his entreaty Juliana lets him go back to hell (454-558).

VI. An angel saved Juliana from the fire into which her persecutor had thrown

---

[3] For the Latin text see Migne, *Patrologia Latina*, LXXVI. 1218.

her; she was then put into a vat of boiling lead but took no hurt; 75 pagans were killed by the lead as it splashed; the judge then ordered that her head be cut off (559-606).

VII. Juliana's martyrdom; her persecutor's death by drowning; Juliana's burial and the honors paid to her then and now; personal ending, with runic signature and plea for prayers in the poet's usual style (607-731).

It is worthy of note that beheading (i.e., a normal form of execution) killed the saint, whereas the various (unhistorical) tortures left her unharmed. The poet had for source a Latin prose life of St. Juliana not substantially different from that printed in the Bollandist *Acta Sanctorum* under the martyr's feast-day, February 16. He followed his source in the main, but left out certain objectionable features of the lady's conduct, and used phraseology drawn from English heroic tradition. His departures from his source show ·a critical eye; his own verses, a practised hand. *Juliana* is not prentice work, as some scholars seem inclined to think. In particular, we do not blame the poet for keeping the miraculous instruction by which his heroine holds the devil fast in her clutches, grotesque though the scene to the modern reader. The poem's weakness lies elsewhere: it is hack work, verse done to order (or so we make bold to conjecture).

    The author did better with the legend of St. Helen (mother of Con- Elene stantine) and the true Cross. *Elene* is a poem of the Vercelli Book. It comes to 1321 lines. The MS text is marked for division into 15 fits. We summarize these as follows:

I-II. Constantine wins a battle by the sign of the cross, revealed to him in a dream, and becomes a Christian (1-193).

III. He learns Christian lore, especially the story of Calvary, and sends his mother Elene to seek the burial-place of the cross on which Christ died. Elene makes her way to Jerusalem by sea and land (194-275).

IV-VIII. Elene and the Jews; by keeping one of them, Judas, in a pit, without food, she finally makes him agree to help find the burial-place (276-708).

IX. Judas is led to Calvary but, not knowing just where the Cross is buried, prays to God for a sign (709-802).

X. God makes the sign; Judas digs in the spot indicated and finds three crosses 20 feet down; they are brought to Elene, and the true Cross is identified by another miracle: it brings a dead man back to life (803-894).

XI. War of words between Satan and Judas (895-967).

XII. Constantine rejoices when messengers from Elene bring the news; he orders a church built on the spot where the Cross was found; Elene sees to this; Judas is baptized (968-1043).

XIII. Judas is made bishop of Jerusalem; his name is changed to Cyriacus; Elene longs for the nails by which Christ was fastened to the Cross; Judas prays to God for a sign, God answers the prayer, and the nails are found; the people rejoice and Elene thanks God (1044-1147).

XIV. Elene seeks advice about the nails; a wise man suggests that they be made into a bit for Constantine's horse. Elene gives treasure to Cyriacus before leaving for Rome; she urges regular observance of the day (May 3) when the Holy Rood was found; the poet calls down blessings upon those mindful of this festival (1148-1236).

XV. In a rimed passage the poet tells of his art; in a runic passage he signs his name; he ends with a passage on Doomsday (1237-1321).

This legend differs from the usual saint's life in that the interest attaches to a deed not linked with the saint's death. The Latin text which lay before Cynewulf as he wrote has not come down to us. If Carleton Brown is right,[4] it was of Irish origin; certainly it differed in some details from any extant version of the legend. The name-form *Cyriacus* (instead of *Quiriacus*) indicates that Cynewulf's immediate source stood close to the Greek original: no unexpected feature of an early Irish Latin text. In regular Old English fashion, Cynewulf took much from native heroic set pieces: e.g., the admirable but conventional descriptions of voyage and battle, heroic names and all.[5] His own contribution looms larger in the less poetical parts; he told his tale clearly and simply, as Old English poets go. Here he doubtless owed something to his Latin source (the suggestion is Sisam's), though he was far from modeling his style on that of Latin prose. The *inventio sanctae crucis* ends with line 1236, and the riming and runic passages of the last fit are commonly taken to be autobiographical, along with the runic signatures in the other poems. Sisam is probably right in taking 1259 f. to mean that the poet had a patron, and it seems plausible to infer from 1237 f. that Cynewulf was old when he composed *Elene,* though this age, coupled with divine inspiration (1251), reminds one of Cædmon and may have been put in by way of imitation of Bede's familiar story. Otherwise, we learn that the poet felt himself a sinner, in need of prayers, when his thoughts turned to doomsday: information accurate enough, no doubt, but too vague to help us much. The various runic passages make formidable problems which we cannot deal with here.[6]

The work of Cynewulf marks a new stage in the history of English religious poetry. This had begun with paraphrases of biblical story. It now went on to themes more pointedly didactic. Cynewulf himself versified exemplary deeds of saints and a sermon on the ascension. We do not know whether he took the lead in departing from Cædmon's themes, or whether he was following someone else.[7] In any case, the school which goes by his

---

[4] *ESt,* XL (1909), 1-29. See also F. Holthausen, *Zeitschrift für deutsche Philologie,* XXXVII (1905). 1-19, with the references there given.

[5] The poet's Francan, Hugas, Hreðgotan, and Hunas did not actually fight in the ranks of Maxentius at the Milvian bridge, where Constantine by tradition had his vision of the cross.

[6] See Sisam's discussion and R. W. V. Elliott, *English Studies,* XXXIV (1953). 49-57.

[7] The author of *The Dream of the Rood* probably lived before Cynewulf, but this poem is a thing apart.

name greatly widened the scope of vernacular verse. We have looked at Cynewulf's own poems. We now take up the poems of others on kindred themes.

The English hermit St. Guthlac early became the subject of a Latin life by Felix, a monk of Croyland.[8] This life served as source for an English prose life of the saint. Two English verse lives have likewise come down to us; they are known as *Guthlac A* and *B*,[9] and are recorded together in the Exeter Book. One passage in *A* (between lines 368 and 369) and the last few lines of *B* have been lost by mutilation of the MS. *A* comes to 818 lines, divided into eight fits; *B*, to 561 lines, divided into seven fits. In each poem the first fit makes a kind of prologue. In *B* this prologue is devoted to the story of Adam and Eve; Guthlac is introduced toward the end of the fit. In *A* the prologue begins with the bliss of heaven, and goes on to the problem of how to attain this bliss: some of the ways of leading one's life on earth are considered, and finally the poem comes to the hermit's way. Guthlac is not introduced until the second fit. In both poems Guthlac is plagued by devils, but is sustained by forces of good and dies in the odor of sanctity. Grein wrongly attached the first 29 lines of *A* to the preceding poem about doomsday, which ends with a passage on the life eternal. *B* seems to be based chiefly on the Latin life. It has been attributed to Cynewulf on stylistic grounds, but since his signature is wanting we find it safer to attribute the poem to some Anglian who belonged to the same school. *A* is commonly reckoned earlier; its author owed little if anything to Felix, but relied on oral tradition, though making use of literary sources in giving literary form to this tradition.

Yet another legend, known to scholars as *Andreas*, has come down to us in the Vercelli Book.[10] Its 1722 lines of verse are divided into 15 fits. The poem tells how St. Andrew at God's bidding rescued St. Matthew from the cannibal Mermedonians, and, after suffering much at their hands through the machinations of Satan, called forth upon them a miraculous flood which made them see the error of their ways. When they had taken for theirs the true faith, Andrew left them, but God bade him turn back and stay with the converts a week longer. He then went away for good, to their great grief. The poem ends with a choral song in praise of God, put in the mouths of the erstwhile cannibals. The poet had for source a Latin version (of which two fragments survive) of the Greek apocryphal *Acts of Andrew and Matthew*. He treats his source with a freedom for which he apologizes in a well-known passage (1478-1489a): his paraphrase is selective rather than inclusive. The verses make lively reading. They may lack polish, but they have vigor to spare. Like most Old English religious poets, the author leans

Guthlac

Andreas

---

[8] Text printed by P. Gonser, *Anglistische Forschungen*, xxvii (1909).
[9] Good texts will be found in editions of the Exeter Book. For a discussion, see G. H. Gerould, *MLN*, xxxii (1917). 77-89.
[10] Ed. G. P. Krapp, *Andreas and the Fates of the Apostles* (Boston, 1906). A prose life of St. Andrew also existed, ed. J. W. Bright, in his *Anglo-Saxon Reader* (4ed., 1917), pp. 113-128. For the Latin source-material, see F. Blatt, *Die lateinischen Bearbeitungen der Acta Andreae et Matthiae* (Giessen, 1930).

hard on heroic tradition for the phraseology of poetic elaboration, and for purple passages in general. The epic opening,

> What! we have learned of the twelve under the stars
> in days of yore, heroes rich in glory,
> thanes of the Lord. Their might did not fail
> in warfaring, when banners clashed,
> after they scattered as the Lord himself,
> high king of the heavens, had set their portion.
> Those were famous men the earth over,
> brave folk-leaders and bold in fight,
> doughty warriors, when shield and hand
> on the field of battle defended helmet, . . .

is not unlike that of *Beowulf,* though it would be wrong to presume borrowing: both poets drew from a common stock of heroic formulas. The military metaphor need not disturb us more here than in "Onward Christian Soldiers," or Eph. 6:10-17.

Phoenix   From legend we go to fable. Mediterranean (originally Eastern) lore about beasts and birds early made its way to England, where the poets, like their sources, put it to allegorical and didactic use. *Phoenix* is the most notable composition of this kind in Old English. The poem is recorded in the Exeter Book. It has 677 lines, divided into eight fits.[11]

The first fit pictures an earthly paradise in the east. The second describes the life of a fabulous bird, the phoenix, in this paradise, and tells of its flight to Syria, every 1000 years, to renew its youth. The process of renewal (by fire) is explained in the third fit. In the fourth we get a description of the new bird, risen from the old bird's ashes; then comes an account of the departure of the phoenix for its old home. With the fifth fit the bird returns to its paradise, and the author begins (381) an allegorical treatment of the fable: the phoenix is likened (1) to the elect of Adam's seed, and (2) to Christ. This comparison, together with pertinent digressions (such as the story of Adam and Eve), takes up the rest of the poem to lines 661b-666, which make a conventional ending in praise of God (compare *Andreas* 1718-1722) but are followed by a second ending, in macaronic verse, on the rewards of the good in the life to come.

Lines 1-380 are based on the *De Ave Phoenice* of Lactantius (*fl. c.* 300).[12] The allegorical comparisons, etc., were drawn from various learned sources; in part, from the author's fancy. The verse, though rising to no heights, is competently done and makes pleasant reading. The poet was evidently a clerk and presumably an Angle; he lived in Cynewulf's day or thereabouts. Earlier scholars had more precise views, but the old datings go beyond our scanty evidence. As Sisam remarks in another connection,[13]

---

[11] Ed. A. S. Cook, *Elene, Phoenix and Physiologus* (New Haven, 1919). For the eleventh-century *Phoenix,* see F. Kluge, *ESt,* VIII (1885). 474-479, and Cook, *ed. cit.,* pp. 128-131.

[12] O. F. Emerson compares the Latin and English poems in *RES,* II (1926). 18-31.

[13] *Proc. Brit. Acad.,* XVIII (1932). 307. See also R. Imelmann, *Forschungen zur ae. Poesie* (1920), p. 239.

Elaborate linguistic and metrical tests have been applied to establish the chronological order of Old English poems. Because these tests leave out of account differences of authorship, of locality, of subject, and of textual tradition, the detailed results, whether of relative order or of absolute date, are little better than guess-work hampered by statistics.

Unnatural natural history is further represented by a poem called *Bestiary* or *Physiologus*,[14] recorded in the Exeter Book. The name, which does not appear in the MS, is that of the poet's source. The poem, 179 lines long, falls into three fits, but most of the third fit is wanting, through loss of a MS leaf at some stage in the transmission of the text. The three fits are devoted respectively to panther, whale, and partridge; these have been thought to stand for the creatures of land, sea, and air. In the first fit (1-74), after an introductory passage on the lower animals in general, the panther's looks and ways are described and given allegorical interpretation: the beast itself is likened to Christ; its foe the dragon, to Satan. The whale (75-163) does not get so good a character; it is credited with passing for an island to entice unwary sailors, who "land" only to drown when the creature dives. Another trick of the whale's when hungry is to send forth a sweet scent from its open mouth, thereby luring its prey into its very jaws, which it then shuts upon them. In the allegory the whale stands for the devil and his crew of tempters; the whale's mouth for hell. The poet's treatment of the partridge (164-179) cannot be made out from the text as it stands, because of the loss of so many lines. The verses end with a passage (175-179) which seems to be of general application, like the introductory passage (1-8a) already mentioned. We thus have reason to think the poem complete, except for the lacuna in the third fit. The author presumably did not try to paraphrase the whole of his source, but restricted himself to three of the creatures considered in the pseudo-scientific book from which he drew. His poem might well have been written by the author of *Phoenix*. Whether it was or not, it belongs to the same period and reflects a like taste. In later times we find fuller and more elaborate treatment of unnatural natural history; see below, p. 161.

The Bestiary

[14] Ed. A. S. Cook, *ed. cit.*

VIII
Religious Poetry: Poems on Various Themes

Dream
of the
Rood

Old English religious poetry was not confined to biblical paraphrase, homily, legend, and allegory. Many other types are found. We take up first the dream or vision, exemplified in the *Dream of the Rood* (i.e., dream about the Cross), a 156-line poem of the Vercelli Book. Fragments of an older version have come down to us as a runic inscription on the great stone cross at Ruthwell in Dumfriesshire, Scotland. In the following, the two versions will be called *R* (Ruthwell) and *V* (Vercelli). The most recent editors of the *Rood* [1] date *R* early in the eighth, *V* late in the ninth century. [2] In any case, *R* belongs to the classical period of Old English poetry. Unluckily, little of it is left, and all editions of the *Rood* have been based on *V*. The poem is in the first person throughout.

It falls into three parts: the opening words of the dreamer (1-27), the words spoken by the Rood (28-121), and the words of the dreamer after the dream is over (122-156). The speaker begins with his dream, in which he saw the True Cross and it spoke to him, telling him its history from the time when it was a tree growing in the woods to the time when, centuries after it bore Christ on Calvary, it was found [by St. Helen, who is not named] and made an object of worship (28-94). The Rood goes on to urge the dreamer to promote its cult (95-121); here the practical point and purpose of the dream comes out. With the Rood's speech the dream presumably ends, though the dreamer's waking is passed over. The dreamer now explains how his dream about the Rood has changed his life; ever since, he has devoted himself to the cult of the True Cross, and hopes to win a heavenly home thereby. The poem ends with a short passage about Christ (144b-156): "may the Lord be a friend to me, he who. . . ." In this passage Christ's passion, death, harrowing of hell, and ascension are touched upon. This ending takes the place of the lines in praise of God with which so many devotional poems end.

The *Rood* is one of the glories of Old English literature; indeed, of English literature as a whole. The introductory words of the dreamer could hardly be bettered, and the story of the Cross on Calvary has overwhelming poetic power and beauty. We quote a few lines: [3]

[1] B. Dickins and A. S. C. Ross (1934). For further references, see the bibliography in their edition. See also the monograph of H. Bütow, *Das ae. "Traumgesicht vom Kreuz"* (Heidelberg, 1935).

[2] If the southern coast of Strathclyde continued to be held by the English after the Battle of Nechtansmere (685), an English inscription might well have been cut at Ruthwell as late as the eighth century. C. L. Wrenn, in *Trans. Philological Soc.* for 1943, pp. 19-22, dates *R* at the end of the eighth century.

[3] Taken, by permission, from K. Malone, *Ten Old English Poems* (Baltimore: Johns Hopkins Press, 1941).

It was many years ago—I remember it still—
that I was felled, afar, at the forest edge,
borne off from my roots. Evil men took me; ...
When I saw the ends of the earth shaking
I dared not bow or break, against
the word of God. All at once I might
have struck his foes down, but I stood fast there. ...
I quaked when he clasped me, but I could not bow to earth,
nor fall to the ground; it was my fate to stand.
As a rood I was raised; I bore my Ruler up,
the King of the skies; I could not bow down.
They pierced me with dark nails; the places are on me still,
the wicked wounds are open. Not one of them dared I harm.
They railed at us both. I was all running with blood,
as he gave up the ghost, with gore from his side.
A heavy burden I bore on that hill,
My lot was hard.... (lines 28-30, 35-38, 42-51)

Modern readers like the first 77 lines best, but the poem makes an organic whole, and the later passages on the cult of the Rood were essential to the poet's purpose. The final passage begins in the middle of a line, but otherwise the poem belongs to the early stage of the run-on style. Its author was a Northumbrian, as the dialect of R reveals. The story of Cædmon may have inspired him to choose the vision form. If, as Dickins and Ross suggest (p. 19), "the occasion for the revision of the poem was the gift of a piece of the True Cross to Alfred in 885," we may owe version V to a West Saxon reviser. We cannot be sure of this, however; we cannot be sure, indeed, that V represents any substantial revision or expansion of R. No definite source of the poem has been found, though various influences have been pointed out,[4] and it seems likely that the Rood, in both conception and execution, belongs to the short list of original Old English religious poems.

The poems which we shall next consider are not readily classified except   Advent by subject. First we take The Advent (or Nativity; also known as Christ A); a poem recorded in the Exeter Book.[5] Its beginning is lost; what we have left comes to 439 lines, divided into five fits. The last of these fits is devoted, in part, to praise of the Trinity, but the rest of the poem is given over to the theme of Advent: that season of the Christian year so named, not the nativity proper. The season is marked by joyful expectancy, and the poet has caught this expectant mood. The note of wonder, too, is sounded again and again. Much of the text is best described as hymn-like. Hortatory and expository passages also occur, as well as two dialogues: one between Mary and dwellers in Jerusalem, the other between Mary and Joseph. The latter opens in a way reminiscent of secular heroic poetry, but this poem owes

[4] See especially M. Schlauch, Essays and Studies in Honor of Carleton Brown (1940), pp. 23-34.
[5] Ed. A. S. Cook, The Christ of Cynewulf (Boston, 1900). A more accurate text is that of Krapp-Dobbie, III.

less than most to the tradition of the scops; in style it marks a stage at which religious verse had reached maturity and independence. The poem is based, in large part, on antiphons of the Breviary. The dialogue between Joseph and Mary on the Conception goes back, ultimately, to Matt. 2:18-25; its immediate source has not been found. The poet is sometimes too medieval for the modern stomach, as when he likens Mary to a door, the key to which God alone holds and uses, but most of the poem makes good reading still. The anonymous author in all likelihood was an Angle of the ninth century. The ascription of this poem to Cynewulf rests on no evidence worthy of the name.

Harrowing of Hell   *The Harrowing of Hell* is a poem of the Exeter Book.[6] It comes to 137 lines, though a hole in the MS has done some damage to the text. The poem opens with the visit of the Marys to Christ's tomb on Easter morning, but soon (23b) shifts to hell, where John the Baptist serves as spokesman for the souls held there until the harrowing. John makes a short speech (26-32) before the harrowing; he predicts the coming of Christ. After the harrowing has begun, we are told who await release:

> Adam and Abraham, Isaac and Jacob,
> many a bold leader, Moses and David,
> Isaiah and Zachariah,
> many patriarchs and a throng of heroes too,
> the company of prophets, a host of women,
> many virgins, a countless multitude of folk. (lines 44-49)

When John sees Christ enter he makes a second speech. This falls into two parts: first, words of thanks to Christ, followed by apostrophes to Gabriel, Mary, Jerusalem, and Jordan (59-106); secondly, a prayer to Christ, asking that he have mercy upon the captives in hell and that he baptize them (107-134). At this point a scribe seems to have skipped an uncertain number of lines; the extant text continues with three lines (135-137) obviously spoken, not by John but by somebody else who is supporting John's plea that the captives be baptized. Here the poem breaks off. The lost conclusion presumably told of the baptism of the captives and their triumphant translation to heaven. Lines 1-23a are based on the biblical account of the resurrection. The rest of the poem goes back to the second part of the apocryphal gospel of Nicodemus, but this can hardly be called a source in any strict sense, as our text differs markedly from it in detail. The poem is anonymous and the date of its composition is uncertain.

Doomsday Poems   Three poems on Doomsday have come down to us from Old English times. We distinguish them as *A, B, C.*[7] The first, *Doomsday A,* is recorded in the eleventh-century MS 201, Corpus Christi College, Cambridge. The

---

[6] Dissertations: J. H. Kirkland (1885), J. Cramer (1896); the latter's also published as an article in *Anglia,* XIX (1897). 137-174. Text in Cramer; also in editions of Exeter Book.

[7] See G. Grau, [Morsbach's] *Studien zur englischen Philologie,* XXXI (1908). Editions: *A,* Hans Löhe, *Be Domes Dæge (Bonner Beiträge,* XXII, 1907); *B,* not separately edited, but included in editions of the Exeter Book; *C,* not separately edited, but included in A. S. Cook, *The Christ of Cynewulf* (Boston, 1900).

poet for the most part follows closely his Latin original, a poem *De Die Judicii* attributed to Bede. The greater length of the English version (308 lines for the 157 of the Latin) reflects in a few passages some expansion of the source but more commonly a mere effort to reproduce in full the thoughts there expressed. The English version seems to have been done in the tenth century. Its author used standard West Saxon speech, though a few Anglian forms occur. We cannot name or plausibly localize the poet, but can say that he made an effective English version of the Latin poem. *Doomsday B* is a poem of 119 lines, recorded in the Exeter Book. The scribe marked two fits, lines 1-80 making the first, lines 81-119 the second. The anonymous author drew on Christian tradition, as handed down in Latin poems, prose treatises, etc.[8] His verses show good workmanship, for the most part, but no great poetic gift. They were hardly composed earlier than the ninth century, and later composition is possible enough. *Doomsday C* (also known as *Christ C*) is likewise a poem of the Exeter Book. It makes a text 798 lines long, and divided into seven fits. Various connections and parallels have been pointed out;[9] as a whole, *C*, like *B*, rests on Christian tradition, not on a single source. The poet takes up the resurrection of the dead, their assembly for judgment, the destruction of the world, the second coming of Christ, the separation of the souls into two groups (sheep and goats), the words of Christ to each group, the punishments of hell and the rewards of heaven, together with much homiletic matter and many details which need not be listed here. In developing his theme the poet does not follow a rigorous order, and the poem gives us a combination, familiar in Old English, of narrative, description, reflection, exhortation and rhapsody. The verses show a practised and skilful hand; they include eloquent and beautiful passages, but nothing that deserves the name great. Swollen verses appear not infrequently. We know nothing of the poem's authorship; the old attribution to Cynewulf lacks evidential basis. The time of composition cannot be set with precision, but the poem is neither early nor late.

Closely linked in theme to the Doomsday poems is *Soul and Body,* a poem in which wicked and righteous souls speak to their respective (dead) bodies.[10] The poem falls naturally into two fits: in the first (lines 1-129) the wicked soul speaks; in the second (130-169), the righteous. The first fit has come down to us in two MSS: Vercelli and Exeter. The two texts differ more or less in wording and even in number of lines. *V* comes to 126 lines, *E* to 121; putting them together, we reach our total of 129. The second fit appears in Vercelli only, where through loss of one or more MS leaves it breaks off in the middle of a sentence. The poem begins with a prologue

Soul and Body

---

[8] For an attempt to specify the sources more narrowly see Grau, pp. 176-180. The homiletic tone of the poem is worthy of note.

[9] See Cook, ed., pp. 170-225 and Grau, pp. 48-83. See also R. Willard, *PMLA*, XLII (1927). 314-330.

[10] Ed. Wülker, II. 92-107. A recent discussion of the body and soul theme is that of E. K. Heningham, *An Early Latin Debate of the Body and Soul* (1939). The same author discusses the relationship between the Old English poem and the Middle English material in *PMLA*, LV (1940). 291-307.

of eight lines about soul and body in general. Then we are told (9-14) of the approach of the wicked soul: the poet thus sets the scene for the action of the first fit, though he confuses matters somewhat by explaining here (instead of in the prologue) that a soul must visit its dead body weekly for 300 years. Lines 15-16 announce the wicked soul as speaker, and the speech itself takes up lines 17-103. In the speech the soul reproaches its body for the damnation which will be its lot on Doomsday. In lines 104-109 we are told of the soul's return to hell uncomforted: the body cannot speak, or help the soul in any way, now that it is dead; the soul's reproaches have come too late. Next we learn in detail (110-127a) what happens to a dead body, and the fit ends with two generalizations: the body is destined to be food for worms, and every wise man is mindful of that. The second fit of course has no prologue. It begins with the approach of the righteous soul (130-134). The souls of the righteous are then announced as speakers (135-137) and the beginning of their speech follows (138-169): they give the body as much praise as the wicked soul gave it blame. Unluckily the rest of the speech (and poem) is lost. In spite of inconsistencies and rough spots (some of which may safely be attributed to faulty transmission) the poet does what he set out to do: he brings home with power the lesson that life on earth, vain in itself, has the grim function of determining our lot in the life to come. We do not know where, when, or by whom the poem was made. Its theme is one old and familiar in medieval literature, though the righteous soul rarely figures in such compositions.[11]

In Middle English the soul and body theme also occurs in dialogue form: the soul blames the body and the body replies in kind (see below, p. 162). The dialogue, a literary genre handed down from antiquity, was much used in Old and Middle English alike for didactic purposes. We take up here Solomon the two Old English metrical dialogues between Solomon and Saturn.[12] Both and are recorded in the tenth-century MS 422, CCCC, pp. 1-6 (first poem) and Saturn 13-26 (second poem). The first 93 lines of the first poem are also recorded, in a hand of c. 1100, on the margins of pp. 196-198 of MS 41, CCCC. Through loss of leaves and other damage the text of MS 422 is markedly defective; that of MS 41 is late, fragmentary, and poor. The poems come to 169 and 336 lines respectively, as we have them, but the first poem may be incomplete, while four serious lacunae mar the second poem. The poems seem to have different authors. The first poem may well have been composed somewhat later than the second; both probably belong to the ninth century, though the tenth remains a possibility. The scanty evidence indicates that the authors were Angles. The first poem, though a dialogue in form, comes close to being a monologue in fact; Solomon does nearly all

---

11 Two late and fragmentary versions (at Worcester and Oxford respectively) of an address of soul to body have been edited by R. Buchholz, in *Erlanger Beiträge*, vi (1890). The Oxford fragment of 25 lines is better known under the title *The Grave*. For a different interpretation of the Oxford fragment, see L. Dudley, *MP*, xi (1914). 429-442.

12 Ed. R. J. Menner, *The Poetical Dialogues of Solomon and Saturn* (MLA Monograph, xiii, 1941). By way of appendix Menner also prints a fragment of a prose dialogue. See also K. Sisam, *MÆ*, xiii (1944). 28-36.

the talking. His subject is the Lord's Prayer, the virtues of which, as a whole and letter by letter (or rune by rune), he explains in detail, with much use of highly figurative speech. These virtues are magical: the author evidently conceived of the Latin text of this prayer as a kind of spell. His poem has little artistic worth. The author of the second poem moved on a higher level. He made a true dialogue, in which Saturn and Solomon discuss matters of weight. Saturn personifies heathen wisdom (eastern and northern alike); Solomon, Christian (and Jewish) wisdom. Their dialogue is a contest, won, of course, by the representative of Christianity. The whole makes a worthy example of reflective religious poetry. Witness the following passage:

> A little while the leaves are green;
> then, afterwards, they fade, they fall to earth,
> and rot away; they turn to dust. (lines 136-8)

The immediate Latin sources on which the authors drew have not come down to us. These sources belonged to Oriental rather than to Roman Christian tradition, it would seem, and Irish transmission has been suggested.[13]

We go on to eleven somewhat shorter didactic or reflective poems, more *Eleven* or less religious in tone or inspiration. The compiler of the Exeter Book *Shorter* included in his poetic miscellany a number of such poems. Five of them *Poems* make a sequence in the MS: *Wanderer* (115 lines), *Gifts of Men* (113), *A Father's Teachings* (94), *Seafarer* (124), and *Overmood* (84). Another sequence consists of three gnomic poems (already considered; see above, p. 43), and *Fates of Men* (98 lines), *Wonders of Creation* (102) and *Riming Poem* (87). We include here the fragmentary *Admonition* as well, on the strength of lines 3-7, which agree strikingly with *Wanderer*, 11-18.[14] We add from the Vercelli Book the fragment *Falseness of Men* (47 lines) and from MS 201, CCCC, the exhortation to godly life commonly called *Lar* (80 lines).[15]

Of these poems, *Wanderer* and *Riming Poem* are least marked by *Wanderer* specific reference to God and the Faith. It would be wrong, however, to *and* infer that their Christianity served only for garnish. Both poets made their *Riming* central theme the vanity of worldly achievement; more particularly, the *Poem* inevitable end which awaits lord and dright. For both poets the grace of God was the only gleam of hope in the life of men on earth. They differed, it is true, in method of presentation. The wanderer begins in the depths; only by retrospect does he give us glimpses of his earlier success and happiness. The riming poet, on the contrary, starts with birth and ends with

---

[13] Like most contests of wisdom, the dialogue includes diverse matters, such as riddles, out-of-the-way lore, etc. See Menner's admirable discussion, *ed. cit.*, and his papers in *JEGP*, XXXVII (1938). 332-354 and *Studies . . . in Honor of F. Klaeber* (Minneapolis, 1929), pp. 240-253.

[14] The rest of this 20-line fragment seems to be based on the Nicene Creed. We call attention, besides, to the nine-line poem on almsgiving and the eight-line poem on the size of Pharaoh's army. All these poems may be found in editions of the Exeter Book.

[15] Renamed *An Exhortation to Christian Living* in Krapp-Dobbie, VI. 67.

death and the grave; he traces point by point the curve, first rising, then falling, of a distinguished earthly career,[16] and he follows this scheme so strictly that his poem has a certain stiffness, while *Wanderer* flows free by virtue of its looser structure.

Riming Poem got its name from the fact that its half-lines are systematically bound together into lines by rime as well as by alliteration. Now and then its author, like many other Old English poets, uses rime for ornamental rather than structural purposes. Neither the structural nor the ornamental riming helps much in dating or localizing the poem. The events set forth are given autobiographical form, but the poet's career, though it has a courtly setting, is highly generalized: so much so, indeed, that the speaker loses his individuality and becomes a mere representative of mankind. Much less abstract is the art of the *Wanderer* poet, who puts most of his verses in the mouth of a kemp (the wanderer) made homeless by the death of his lord.[17] Here, too, the characters are nameless and the events happen in no particular spot and at no particular time. The wanderer may be described as an old soldier turned sage. His dearly bought wisdom takes two main forms: (1) gnomic sayings, and (2) reflections on the transitory nature of all earthly things. The reflections at times amount to lamentations, but the poem is no elegy. The following passage is characteristic:[18]

> The tried kemp must grasp how ghastly it will be
> when the weal of this world stands waste wholly,
> as now in many a spot through this middle earth
> the wind-blown walls stand waste, befrosted,
> the abodes of men lie buried in snow,
> the wine-halls are dust in the wind, the rulers
> dead, stripped of glee; the dright all fell,
> by the wall the proud sought shield. . . . (lines 73-80)

Seafarer

Seafarer purports to give the poet's own experiences but is representative if not indeed symbolic in meaning. The author describes vividly his hardships at sea; he explains but vaguely why he would set out anew:

> Deep goes the mood that drives my soul
> to fare from home, that, far away,
> I may find the stead where strangers dwell. . . .
> So, now, my soul soars from my bosom,
> the mood of my mind moves with the sea-flood,
> over the home of the whale, high flies and wide
> to the ends of the earth; after, back to me
> comes the lonely flier, lustful and greedy,
> whets me to the whale-way, whelms me with his bidding
> over deep waters. Dearer, then, to me

[16] Compare the so-called sermon of Hrothgar in *Beowulf*, 1724-1768.
[17] For a recent study of *Wanderer* see B. F. Huppé, *JEGP*, XLII (1943). 516-538.
[18] The quotations from *Wanderer* and *Seafarer* are taken, by permission, from K. Malone, *Ten Old English Poems* (Baltimore, 1941).

the boons of the Lord than this life that is dead
in a land that passes; I believe no whit
that earthly weal is everlasting. (lines 36-38, 58-67)

Lines 64-67, however, give us a hint that the speaker thought the soft life
of a landsman incompatible with heavenly bliss; in ascetic mood he chose,
instead, the hard life of a seaman.[19] The call of the sea in this poem has
nothing in common with the romantic glamor of modern feeling; it is a
call to suffering, toil, privation. Only by denying oneself here can one win
salvation hereafter. Seafaring thus represents and symbolizes the sterner
side of the Christian way of life. After this autobiographical section, the
poet gives us conventional reflections about death, fame and God. Of particular interest is the chronological primitivism implicit in lines 80 ff. *Riming
Poem, Wanderer,* and *Seafarer* are compositions of unusual poetic power and
beauty. We cannot name their authors, and we do not know just when
or where these authors lived. The other eight poems named above have less
interest for the modern reader, and we shall leave them without discussion
here.

The Psalter held so important a place in Christian devotions that one , **The Paris**
might expect to find an Old English metrical version of the whole body of **Psalter**
psalms. Such a version in fact once existed, but it has not come down to us
intact. Fragments of it were included in a Benedictine service-book of the
eleventh century,[20] and Psalms 51 to 150 were recorded in the so-called
Paris Psalter, an eleventh-century MS which survives in a mutilated state.[21]
The author of the metrical psalms [22] departed widely from classical versification; so much so, indeed, that we must take him to have been indifferent
to classical poetic tradition (or perhaps even ignorant of that tradition).
His verses may reflect a development of the popular pre-classical style as
independent of the classical movement as is the versification of the spells.
In any case, we have no right to measure these verses by classical standards
and stigmatize them as irregular. Their metrical peculiarities give us no
evidence of value in setting time or place of composition. The translation
is not without literary merit.

An independent metrical version of *Psalm 50* (*51*) in the Kentish dialect *The*
is recorded in the tenth-century MS Cotton Vespasian D 6. The paraphrast *Kentish*
begins with a prologue about David, Nathan, Uriah, and Bathsheba (1-25). *Psalm*
The psalm proper (31-145) is preceded by an introduction (26-30) and followed by a conclusion (146-153) announcing David as speaker of the psalm
and emphasizing his penitence. Then comes an epilogue (154-157) in the
form of a prayer. The whole makes a neatly rounded work of art, some-

[19] For a somewhat different interpretation see O. S. Anderson, *The Seafarer* (Lund, 1937).
See also S. B. Liljegren, *Studia Neophilologica,* xiv (1942). 145-159.
[20] See E. Feiler, *Das Benediktiner-Offizium* (Heidelberg, 1901). The text of the fragments
is in Krapp-Dobbie, vi. 80-86.
[21] Text in Krapp-Dobbie, v. 3-150.
[22] Aldhelm, according to the late Eduard Sievers; see *Exeter Book of Old English Poetry*
(1933), p. 2, n. 3. The attribution will have weight with those who accept Sievers' *Schall-
analyse.*

thing more than a translation. Another poem in the Kentish dialect, a 43-line hymn in praise of God, is set down in the same MS.[23] Both these Kentish texts are sprinkled with West Saxon forms. Both poems are best given a tenth-century dating.

Pater-nosters   Metrical versions of the Lord's Prayer, the Gloria Patri, and the Apostles' Creed were composed in Old English. Three such versions of the Lord's Prayer have survived; we call them the Exeter, Junius, and Corpus Pater-nosters, from the MSS in which they are recorded. The *Exeter Paternoster* (Exeter Book) comes to 11 lines; the *Junius* (Bodleian, Junius 121), to 36 lines; the *Corpus* (CCCC 201), to 123 lines.[24] In the longer versions, each clause of the prayer obviously inspired a passage of verse. A like expansion of the Latin text marks the *Junius Gloria Patri* of 57 lines (Bodleian, Junius 121, and CCCC 201) and the *Junius Apostles' Creed* of 58 lines (Junius 121).[25] The three-line *Cotton Gloria Patri* (Cotton Titus D xxvii) shows no expansion.[26]

We end our survey of Old English religious poetry with five items of some interest for one reason or another. The *Macaronic Poem* (CCCC 201),[27] also known as *Call* (or *Summons*) *to Prayer*, is 31 lines long. Its interest for us lies in its macaronic form: each on-verse is in English, each off-verse in Latin (but two off-verses are wanting). The *Cotton Prayer* of 79 lines[28] is commonly divided into three, on grounds which we think insufficient. The *Exeter Prayer* of 118 lines,[29] also called *Age Mec* from its first two words, goes beyond the precative form as it proceeds and becomes a kind of complaint; it ends, however, on a note of resignation, expressed in words of aphoristic wisdom (quoted above, p. 26). The mixture of genres does not keep the poem from having power and artistic distinction.

Thureth   A poem hard to classify is *Thureth*,[30] in which a *halgungboc* "dedication book" makes an 11-line speech, informing the reader that a certain Thureth had had it made in gratitude to God and in God's honor. One may compare King Alfred's metrical prologue to the *Pastoral Care*, and inscriptions like those on the Brussels cross (*rod is min nama* "rood is my name") and the Alfred Jewel (*Ælfred mec heht gewyrcan* "Alfred had me made"). The

Stanzaic Poem   *Stanzaic Poem*[31] on fasting is of interest because it is the only Old English poem divided into regular stanzas. It is made up of 26 eight-line stanzas, one six-line stanza (the fourth), one nine-line stanza (the fifteenth), and

---

[23] The two Kentish poems are in Krapp-Dobbie, vi. 87-94.
[24] Texts in Krapp-Dobbie, iii. 223-224 (Exeter), vi. 77-78 (Junius), vi. 70-74 (Corpus).
[25] Texts in Krapp-Dobbie, vi. 74-77 (Gloria), 78-80 (Creed).
[26] Text in Krapp-Dobbie, vi. 94.
[27] Text in Krapp-Dobbie, vi. 69-70.
[28] Cotton Julius A 2; the first 15 lines are also in Lambeth Palace Library MS 427. Text in Krapp-Dobbie, vi. 94-96.
[29] Exeter Book. Text in Krapp-Dobbie, iii. 215-218.
[30] MS Cotton Claud. A iii (eleventh century). Text in Krapp-Dobbie. vi. 97; see also A. S. Napier, *Trans. Philol. Soc.* for 1903-1906, p. 299.
[31] British Museum Add. MS 43703 (Nowell's sixteenth-century copy of the now fragmentary MS Cotton Otho B xi). Text in Krapp-Dobbie, vi. 98-104.

one incomplete stanza at the end, where the poem breaks off in the middle of line 230. Each stanza makes a unit of thought and ends with a full stop. The poem is an exhortation to the faithful to keep the fasts prescribed by the Church, especially Ember days and Lent. It was presumably composed in the tenth century.

IX

Secular Poetry

The triumph of Christianity in England had literary effects which went beyond the composition of vernacular religious poems. The new faith, and the southern culture which came to the English with that faith, brought about great changes in the treatment of secular themes as well, and led to the use of themes not characteristic of the old native tradition. Such a theme **Durham** is the *encomium urbis* exemplified in the *Durham Poem,*[1] a 20-line fragment **Poem** in praise of the city of Durham. The fragment as we have it belongs to the early twelfth century, in all likelihood, but it may represent a revision of the earlier composition referred to in line 19 of the text.[2] The verses have little merit, but are worthy of mention as the only surviving Old English example of a type of poem familiar in classical antiquity.

Ruin A contrasting theme, which we may call *de excidio urbis* (or *arcis*), is exemplified in *Ruin,*[3] a poem of the Exeter Book. The poem is commonly printed in 48 or 49 lines; we cannot be sure of the number because of the defective state of folio 124. The loss of many words of the text makes interpretation harder, too, of course. The poet describes the decay and destruction of a city (or stronghold), and contrasts its present desolation with its presumable splendor in the past. This theme has obvious kinship to that of *Wanderer,* 73-105, and a Latin poem of the sixth century, the *De Excidio Thoringiae* of Venantius Fortunatus, begins in much the same vein.[4] The *Ruin* poet's mention of hot baths has led many to identify with Bath the ruin described,[5] but since the poem is of the nameless timeless kind we doubt that its author had in mind one site only: the ruin which he made his subject was (we think) a creation of his own, though in describing it he drew on his knowledge of actual ruins. His poem departs from the usual Old English pattern in that the reader or hearer must himself supply the obvious moral: all earthly things perish. But possibly the lost passage at the end was a moralizing one. We reckon the poem secular: Wyrd, not God,

---

[1] MS: Camb. Univ. Lib. H. 1. 27. Printed text and study: M. Schlauch, *JEGP*, XL (1941). 14-28.

[2] Line 20 in the text as printed in Krapp-Dobbie, VI. 27, where line 10 is divided into two lines.

[3] See C. A. Hotchner, *Wessex and Old English Poetry* ... (1939); for criticism of this unconvincing dissertation see Joan Blomfield, *MA*, IX (1940). 114-116 and S. J. Herben, *MLN*, LIX (1944). 72-74. The text is in N. Kershaw, *Anglo-Saxon and Norse Poems* (Cambridge, 1922).

[4] So first A. Brandl, *Archiv*, CXXXIX (1919). 84.

[5] Identification with Hadrian's Wall has been proposed by S. J. Herben; see *MLN*, LIV (1939). 37-39.

brought the ruin about (contrast *Wanderer*, 85). It does not follow, however, that the poet was a heathen. We believe that his Wyrd answers to
the Fate of classical antiquity and that in attributing the destruction to
Fate he was conforming to some classical literary model. We do not know
when or where the poet flourished, but we do know from his poem that he
had poetic power.

Of much interest are the 95 metrical riddles of the Exeter Book.[6] Through *Riddles*
loss of leaves and other damage to the MS the text of many of these riddles
is defective. Most of the editors combine the 68th and 69th riddles, but in
the MS they are clearly distinguished. On the other hand, the 2nd and 3rd
riddles make one in the MS. The Exeter scribe recorded two versions of
the 30th riddle, while the 35th riddle survives also in a Northumbrian
version elsewhere recorded.[7] The riddles vary in length from one line (No.
69) to over 100 lines (No. 40). In general they must be reckoned literary
(not popular) compositions; they are done in the classical Old English
poetic style. Two are translations of extant Latin originals: No. 35 translates
Aldhelm's 33rd riddle, *Lorica;* No. 40, his 100th, *Creatura.* Several more go
back, with varying degrees of probability, to Latin riddles in the collection
that goes by the name of Symphosius.[8] Many others may well have been
based on specific Latin sources; certainly the composition of Latin riddles
in verse had a vogue among English clerics in the seventh and eighth centuries, though most of these riddles have not come down to us.[9] Not a few
of the Old English riddles have poetic worth. We call attention to Lascelles
Abercrombie's happy modernization of the eighth riddle.[10] Other riddles
give us examples of the *double entente* (No. 44), and one even incorporates
a joke (No. 42). A certain dry humor marks the lines on the bookworm
(No. 47):

> A moth ate words. To me that seemed
> an odd happening, when I found it out,
> that the crawling thing swallowed up the speech of a man,
> a thief in darkness [ate] noble discourse
> and its strong support [i.e., parchment]. The thieving guest
> was none the wiser for swallowing those words.

Here (as in other cases) the riddle form was stretched to include something merely paradoxical, and even this only by identification of the ink-
marks with the words they symbolize. Many of the riddles are in the first
person, the speaker being the solution personified. The collection was formerly begun (as still in Tupper's edition) with the poem of 19 lines now

---

[6] One of these, the 90th, is in Latin. Ed. F. Tupper, *The Riddles of the Exeter Book* (Boston,
1910); A. J. Wyatt, *Old English Riddles* (Boston, 1912).
[7] In Leiden Univ. MS Voss 106; ed. A. H. Smith, *Three Northumbrian Poems* (1933).
[8] See above, p. 14.
[9] See above, p. 14. For discussion of other riddles see especially *MLR*, xxxi (1936). 545-547;
Neophilologus, IV (1919). 258-262, XIII (1928). 293-296, xxvi (1941). 228-231, xxvii (1942).
220, xxix (1945), 126-127; xxxi (1947). 65-68; *Studia Neophilologica*, XIV (1942), 67-70;
MLN, LIV (1939). 259-262; *MA*, xv (1946). 48-54.
[10] *Poems* (1930), p. 16.

known as *Eadwacer*. The so-called 60th riddle in all likelihood does not belong to the collection either, but makes the first section of the poem known as *Lover's* or *Husband's Message*. We know nothing of the authorship of the riddles, though they were presumably composed by clerics. We give the collection an eighth century dating, but not with certainty.

Love Poems

Three love poems have come down to us in the Exeter Book: the poems *Eadwacer* and *Lover's Message* mentioned above, and a poem of 53 lines called *Wife's Lament* or *Complaint*.[11] Two of these, *Eadwacer* and *Wife's Lament*, purport to be by women. *Eadwacer* is one of the most obscure poems in the English language. We make no attempt to interpret it, but quote two passages remarkable for their power and beauty:[12]

> I waited for my wanderer, my Wulf, hoping and fearing:
> when it was rainy weather and I sat wretched, weeping;
> when the doughty man drew me into his arms—
> it was heaven, yes, but hateful too.
>
> Wulf, my Wulf, waiting for thee
> hath left me sick, so seldom hast thou come;
> a starving mood, no stint of meat. (lines 9-15)

The Wife's Lament

The *Wife's Lament* likewise makes trouble for the interpreter, though here the difficulties are far less serious.[13] The poem is in the first person throughout. The speaker is a woman who has lost her husband's favor and has been forced, by him, to live alone, in a cheerless wooded spot. She applies several uncomplimentary epithets to the house she lives in: *herh-eard* "heathenish abode," *eorð-scræf* "hole in the ground, tomb, hovel," *eorð-sele* "hut." Such terms of denunciation need not be taken too literally. Her unhappiness finds expression in the following passage (among others):

> Fallen is this house: I am filled with yearning.
> The dales are dim, the downs [i.e., hills] are high,
> the bitter yards with briars are grown,
> the seats are sorrowful. I am sick at heart,
> he is so far from me. There are friends on earth,
> lovers living that lie together,
> while I, early and all alone,
> walk under the oak tree, wander through these halls. (lines 29-36)

She tries to console herself by reflecting that

> it is the way of a young man to be woeful in mood,
> hard in his heart's thought, . . . (lines 42-3)

---

[11] See R. Imelmann, *Forschungen zur ae. Poesie* (Berlin, 1920), pp. 1-314. The author includes also *Wanderer* and *Seafarer* in this investigation.

[12] The quotations from *Eadwacer* and *Wife's Lament* are taken, by permission, from K. Malone, *Ten Old English Poems* (Baltimore: Johns Hopkins Press, 1941).

[13] Ed. N. Kershaw, in *Anglo-Saxon and Norse Poems* (Cambridge, 1922).

and by drawing a picture of such a man (her husband) himself alone and
in misery, but she finds this picture not so consoling after all, and ends
with the dismal saying,

> hard is the lot
> of one that longs for [one's] love in vain. (lines 52-3)

The lyricism of *Eadwacer* and the *Wife's Lament,* wholly secular though
it be, has little in common with the personal poetry of native tradition,
the poetry of the scops, and one is tempted to look to classical antiquity
for models. Here Virgil's story of Dido comes at once to mind, while the
pages of Ovid give us other analogues.[14] We cannot take these classical tales
for sources, but they may well have suggested a like literary treatment of
native tales otherwise unknown to us. Imelmann sets the years 781-830 as
the period within which these poems were composed.

The *Lover's Message* makes other difficulties.[15] The MS text falls into *The*
four clearly marked sections: of these the first (17 lines) and the third (13 *Lover's*
lines) are intact; the second (11 to 13 lines) and the fourth (28 or 29 lines) *Message*
are defective, because of a great hole in folio 123. The first section is usually
but (we think) wrongly taken to be a separate poem, the so-called 60th
riddle. In form, the *Lover's Message* is a speech, made by a 'stick of wood
upon which a lover had cut (presumably in runes) a message to his lady.
The stick explains how the man with his knife made it into a messenger,
and then addresses the lady directly in that capacity (line 14), with mention
of its journey to her from overseas, and with many pleas in the lover's behalf. The lady's answer is not given, but from the tone of the speaker we
may infer that she said yes. The speech ends with a runic passage not altogether clear. The riddle (No. 30, second version) which immediately precedes *Lover's Message* in the MS likewise has a wooden object for speaker
and speeches by inanimate objects are characteristic of the riddles, as we
have seen. We remember, too, that a piece of wood (the Cross) made a
speech in *Dream of the Rood.* Our poet seems to have taken this device
and used it in his own way, with striking effect. His suitor gives us a foretaste, not so much of medieval as of modern love-poetry. The go-between,
the emphasis on privacy, and the deferential tone remind one, it is true, of
the later *service des dames,* while the setting is courtly enough, but the man
proposes, and intends, marriage, not seduction, and he is the lady's equal,
not her servant. The plain implication that the lady can do as she likes, even
to the point of making a journey overseas to join her lover, gives to the
poem a curiously modern touch. This touch would be removed, of course,
if we took the lovers for man and wife, but the lover's pleas would then
lose all point. The poem shows much literary merit, in spite of its mutila-

---

[14] See Imelmann, pp. 188-307, and H. Reuschel, Paul u. Braune's *Beiträge zur Geschichte
der deutschen Sprache u. Lit.,* LXII (1938). 132-142.
[15] Also known as the *Husband's Message.* Ed. N. Kershaw, in *Anglo-Saxon and Norse
Poems* (Cambridge, 1922).

tion. It was composed not later than c. 950. We know nothing of its author or of his sources.

A different kind of plea is that made by the scribe who copied the last part of the text of the Old English translation of Bede's *History* recorded in CCCC 41, a MS commonly dated c. 1030. At the end of this text the copyist added a 10-line poem of his own, a plea to readers of rank, urging his claims to patronage.[16] This versified advertisement for patrons he made as conspicuous as possible by writing every other line in red ink. Incidentally his verses show that he expected noble readers. We know of no other nation of western Europe which, in the first half of the eleventh century, could boast of a reading public that included laymen of noble rank.

A 17-line fragment of a poem in honor of Aldhelm (the famous English prelate and scholar) has come down in the tenth-century MS 326, CCCC. This poem is written in a curious mixture of English, Latin, and Greek not unsuited to its subject: Aldhelm had a weakness for showing off his learning. The anonymous poet probably wrote in Canterbury at a date not much earlier than that of the MS. The mixture of tongues in his poem reminds one of the charters, and differs from macaronic verse.[17]

The metrical writings of King Alfred will be taken up along with the prose in which they are imbedded.

Beowulf

The influence of southern culture on English secular poetry has shown itself chiefly, so far, in the choice and treatment of subject-matter, but two of the heroic poems that survive show marked influence in other ways as well. One of these poems, *Waldere*,[18] has come down in a state so fragmentary that we must set it aside for the moment. The other, however, *Beowulf*,[19] with its 3182 lines, gives us a broader basis for judgment. This famous poem, the chief literary monument of the Old English period, is the fourth article in the Nowell codex (see above, p. 67). The MS text is divided into a prologue and 43 fits. We look first at the theme of the poem. For this the poet turned to the heroic age of the Germanic peoples; more precisely, to heroes of the fifth and sixth centuries. And he chose for his setting Scandinavia, that motherland (or *vagina nationum,* as Jordanes puts it) from which so many Germanic tribes, the English among them, had gone forth down the years.[20] The poem thus celebrated, not contemporary deeds of heroism, but events of a past already remote, already glorified by a tradition centuries old. This tradition in its beginnings made part of the cultural baggage which the Germanic settlers in Britain brought with

---

[16] Text in Krapp-Dobbie, VI. 113.
[17] Text in Krapp-Dobbie, VI. 97-98.
[18] Ed. F. Norman (1933). See also *MA,* x (1941). 155-158.
[19] Facsimile ed.: J. Zupitza, *EETS,* 77 (London, 1882). Best printed editions: in English, F. Klaeber (Boston, 1922; 3ed. 1936); in German, E. von Schaubert (Paderborn, 1940), also referred to as 15th ed. of Heyne-Schücking's *Beowulf.* Most comprehensive study: R. W. Chambers, *Beowulf, An Introduction* . . . (Cambridge, 1921; 2ed. 1932). See also W. W. Lawrence, *Beowulf and Epic Tradition* (Cambridge, Mass., 1928) and H. Schneider, *Das germanische Epos* (Tübingen, 1936). A good recent verse translation is that of C. W. Kennedy (Princeton, 1940).
[20] See K. Malone, in *Namn och Bygd,* XXII (1934). 41, 51.

them from Sleswick. It had taken a shape specifically English by the eighth century, when in all likelihood *Beowulf* was composed.[21] In drawing from it, the poet followed his own needs, not modern taste; too many critics have scolded him for this.[22] The action of the poem falls into two main parts. In part one, the hero Beowulf, then young, goes from his homeland to Heorot, the hall of King Hrothgar of the Danes, in order to cleanse it of Grendel, a troll who for years had haunted it at night; he overcomes Grendel singlehanded and afterwards slays Grendel's mother, who sought to avenge her son. In part two, the hero, now grown old, goes out to defend his own kingdom of Geatland against the ravages of a dragon; with the help of a faithful young kinsman he kills the dragon but himself falls in the fight. These idealized folk-tales are not told in isolation, or for their own sakes; they make part of an elaborate complex of fact and fable, matters of pith and moment, involving the fortunes of three Scandinavian kingdoms, those of the Geats, the Danes, and the Swedes, over a period of several generations. The poet has painted a vast canvas. And in glorifying his hero he has not forgotten to glorify as well the heathen Germanic courtly culture of which that hero was the flower. He gives us a spiritualized picture of the Germanic heroic age, an age the memory of which the English of the poet's day cherished as their very own. We believe that *Beowulf* was meant to serve a purpose not unlike that which the *Æneid* of Virgil served: each poem exalted a past which by tradition or fiction belonged to the cultural heritage of the poet's nation. In each poem, moreover, this exaltation of the past took place under the influence of a foreign culture: pagan Greece in the *Æneid,* Christian Rome in *Beowulf.* The English poet accordingly pictures a society heathen and heroic, but strongly colored by Christian ideals of thought and deed. In particular, the hero is made as Christ-like as the setting would permit: highminded and gentle, he fights chiefly against monstrous embodiments of the forces of evil, and in the end lays down his life for his people. But the Christianity known to the poet had itself been strongly colored by the culture of classical antiquity. Latin was the language of the Church in Old England, and Roman poets were read and studied by learned clerics like the author of *Beowulf.* We believe that the English poet knew the *Æneid* and was influenced by it in designing and composing his own poem.[23] Alongside this influence, which made for epic breadth and leisure, we put the influence of English religious poems like *Genesis,* likewise marked by length and fullness in their narrative art. The *Beowulf* poet certainly showed originality when, in celebrating a secular hero of the Germanic past, he did not compose a song after the manner traditional to the scops (who before him had monopolized

---

21 A recent discussion of the date of *Beowulf* is that of D. Whitelock, *The Audience of Beowulf* (Oxford, 1951). pp. 22-29. See also H. M. Flasdieck, *Anglia,* LXIX (1950). 169-171.
22 See J. R. R. Tolkien, *Proc. Brit. Acad.* XXII (1936). 245-285 and K. Malone, *RES,* XVII (1941). 129-138. See also J. R. Hulbert, *MP,* XLIV (1946). 65-75.
23 See T. B. Haber, *A Comparative Study of the* Beowulf *and the* Æneid (Princeton, 1931). See also A. Brandl, *Archiv,* CLXXI (1937). 165-173.

such themes), but used, instead, an elaborate, sophisticated narrative form reminiscent of the *Æneid*. In doing so, however, he was only carrying into the secular field a process of amplification and complication which, as we have seen, had already set in among the composers of English religious verse.

More striking is the originality of *Beowulf* in structure. The two main parts balance each other admirably, exemplifying and contrasting as they do the heroic life in youth and age. By treating in full two chapters only of Beowulf's career, the poet makes his tale marvelously simple, at bottom. The elaboration, which Grundtvig has aptly likened to the multitudinous embellishments of a Gothic cathedral, not only lends richness and variety to the action, but also makes the hero and his deeds part of the age in which he and they are set. Since the scene is laid in Scandinavia, most of the allusions and episodes deal with Scandinavian history and story, but other quarters of Germania are brought into the picture as well. Eormenric and Hama stand for the east. The allusions to the fall of Hygelac, and the Finn and Ingeld episodes, serve to link north and west. The association of Sigemund with Heremod, and the (rather artificial) connection of both with Beowulf himself, have a like function, while Offa, the representative of the Angles (the poet's own tribe), though introduced by a *tour de force,* well symbolizes the unity of ancient Germania: in after years both English and Danes claimed him for their own. In these and other ways the poet rises above mere story-telling; he brings before us a whole world, the heroic age of his forefathers and ours. But the greatness of *Beowulf* lies largely if not chiefly in its wording, and here the poet is no innovator; he is rather the master of a traditional style, a mode already old in his day. In the words of M. B. Ruud,[24] *Beowulf* has

a magnificence of language which leaves critic and translator helpless. Indeed, if the poem has a weakness as a work of art, it lies in this all-pervasive artistry. *Beowulf* seldom pierces one with a stab of eloquence straight from a heart on fire—as lesser poems do, even *Maldon*; it carries one along on a great golden stream of poetic rhetoric. . . . It is a great literary tradition at its finest flowering. . . . *Beowulf* may not be one of the half-dozen great poems of the world—I confess I do not know—but for sheer *style,* there are not many works to be put above it.

Waldere   With *Beowulf* we take the two *Waldere* fragments (of 32 and 31 lines respectively). These are recorded on two pieces of vellum, all that is left of an English MS of the late tenth century (167b, Royal library, Copenhagen). The verses are done in a style so broad and leisurely that they presumably made part of a long poem (one of 1000 lines or more, perhaps) [25] in which was celebrated the fight between the hero Waldere and a band of Burgundians led by King Guthere. This fight is known to us from other

---

[24] *MLQ,* II (1941). 138-139.
[25] For a different view, see F. P. Magoun, *MLN,* LIX (1944). 498-499.

sources, notably the tenth-century Latin poem *Waltharius*,[26] from which we learn that it was a fight of one against twelve, not counting the spectator Hagena (though he too was finally drawn in). In *Waldere* as in *Beowulf* the theme is secular, the treatment involved and sophisticated, bookish rather than popular. Both poems, moreover, celebrate events of the Germanic heroic age. The fragments are long enough to reveal that *Waldere* lacks the greatness of *Beowulf*. Its clerical composer, however, had considerable skill in versification, and though he used a German source he was steeped in traditional English poetry sacred and profane. In losing *Waldere* we lost a good poem and a stirring tale.

[26] For an earlier date, see K. Strecker, in *Deutsches Archiv für Geschichte des Mittelalters,* IV (1941). 355-381. Ed. K. Strecker, *Ekkehards Waltharius* (Berlin, 1924). Translated by H. M. Smyser and F. P. Magoun, Jr., in *Connecticut College Monograph No. 1* (Baltimore, 1941), pp. 111-145.

X
Literary Prose

Prose
as an
Art Form
　　All compositions in verse may be reckoned examples (by intention, at least) of literary art. This does not hold for prose compositions. In Old English times, even as now, prose was the normal form of non-literary speech and writing, and of the prose works left to us from the period we limit ourselves to those more or less literary in character. The literary prose of Old English is made up, for the most part, of translations or paraphrases of Latin writings. The English did not cultivate prose as an art form until they became acquainted with Latin literature, which gave them both sources and models for prose works of art. These sources and models, chiefly compositions of Christians though they were, had maintained the traditional great prose genres: history, philosophy, and oratory. In addition, minor genres like the epistle were represented. Everywhere, however, new wine had been poured into the old bottles. Thus, the oration appeared as a sermon. It was this Christianized classical tradition which the Roman missionaries brought to England and which the converts and their sons carried on in Latin and English. Throughout Old English times literary prose remained learned and clerical; for the people, verse continued to be the only natural medium of literary art.

King
Alfred
　　In spite of what we have just said, English literary prose owes its start to an unlearned layman. In the seventh and eighth centuries, the golden age of Old English literary culture, the prose writers composed in Latin only, so far as we know,[1] and it was left for King Alfred (849-899) to promote and, finally, himself to undertake composition in English when, in the last two decades of the ninth century, he tried to build up anew that flourishing civilization which the Danish invasions had brought to wrack and ruin. The writings of Alfred and his men must not be thought of as works of art; whatever literary merit they have is a by-product only. They were written as part of an educational program. Alfred hit upon the simple but revolutionary idea of using the mother tongue rather than Latin as the basic medium of instruction, both in the schools and in adult education.

---

[1] Except for Bede's incomplete translation of the Fourth Gospel, unhappily lost. An Old English *Martyrology* which antedates King Alfred should also be mentioned; ed. G. Herzfeld, *EETS*, 116 (1900). The editor dates the work *c.* 850 and localizes it in Lincolnshire. F. Liebermann, *Archiv*, cv (1900). 87, gives reasons for localization at Lichfield. The treatise on Kentish and other English saints published by Liebermann under the title *Die Heiligen Englands* (Hanover, 1889) seems to be little more than a ninth-century list, later extended by combination with another (non-Kentish) list. The treatise thus comes under the head of mnemonic prose. In its final form it is to be dated *c.* 1030.

Unluckily no English schoolbooks or works of reference existed. The King therefore with characteristic energy set out to fill the gap. He began with the history of the nation. We have no contemporary evidence of his part in compiling the Old English *Annals* (the so-called *Chronicles*) [2] or in preparing the Old English version of Bede's ecclesiastical history,[3] but we may reasonably presume (though we cannot prove) that he had something to do with both these undertakings; certainly the earliest extant form of each goes back to the time of Alfred's literary activity, and each was traditionally associated with Alfred.[4] We are better informed about the Old English versions of two works by Pope Gregory the Great: the *Dialogues* [5] and the *Pastoral Care.*[6] The former was translated for Alfred by his friend Bishop Wærferth of Worcester; the latter Alfred himself turned into English with the help of four scholars whom he names in his preface. Here ends what may be called the earlier period of Alfred's literary career. The later period begins with his translation of the world history of Orosius.[7] Next comes Alfred's major work, from the literary point of view: his translation of the treatise of Boethius on the consolation of philosophy.[8] Toward the end of his life he composed his *Blostman* ("Blossoms"), culled chiefly from the Soliloquies of St. Augustine.[9] The twelfth-century historian William of Malmesbury tells us that Alfred began but did not live to finish a translation of the Psalter,[10] and it has been conjectured that William is referring to the incomplete prose translation (Psalms, 1-50) recorded in the Paris Psalter; unluckily the MS itself throws no light on the identity of the translator.[11] Asser, the biographer of Alfred, tells in some detail, under the year 887, of yet another work: a Handbook which the King in that year began to compile. It seems in fact to have been a commonplace book. Possibly some of the passages entered in this book found place in the *Blostman;* the book as such has not survived.[12]

Gregory

---

[2] Ed. C. Plummer, *Two of the Saxon Chronicles* [A₁ and E] *Parallel, with Supplementary Extracts from the Others* (2v., Oxford, 1892-1899); H. A. Rositzke, *C* text (1940, in Förster's *Beiträge zur englischen Philologie*, xxxiv); E. Classen and F. E. Harmer, *D* text (Manchester, 1926); A. H. Smith, *The Parker Chronicle* (1935); trans. G. N. Garmonsway (1953).

[3] Ed. T. Miller, *EETS*, 95-96 and 110-111; J. Schipper, *Bibl. der ags. Prosa*, iv. See also F. Klaeber, *Anglia*, xxv (1902). 257-315; xxvii (1904). 243-282, 399-435.

[4] According to Gaimar's *Estorie des Engles* (twelfth century), lines 3451ff., Alfred had an English book written, consisting of events and laws, etc.; the reference is evidently to some MS (like the Parker) in which the annals are followed by legal texts. We have two Old English references to Alfred as translator of Bede: (1) in an eleventh-century MS of the Old English translation Alfred is named as translator; (2) Ælfric in his homily on Gregory the Great speaks of Alfred as translator.

[5] Ed. H. Hecht, *Bibl. der ags. Prosa*, v. See also P. N. U. Harting, *Neophilologus*, xxii (1937). 281-302.

[6] Ed. H. Sweet, *EETS*, 45 (Part ii) and 50 (Part i).

[7] Ed. H. Sweet, *EETS*, 79 (Part i: Old English text and Latin original). The second part has never come out.

[8] Ed. W. J. Sedgefield (Oxford, 1899).

[9] Ed. H. L. Hargrove, *Yale Studies in English*, xiii; W. Endter, *Bibl. der ags. Prosa*, xi.

[10] *De Gestis Regum Anglorum*, ii. iv (sec. 123).

[11] Ed. J. W. Bright and R. L. Ramsay, *The West Saxon Psalms* (Boston, 1907); see also H. G. Grattan, *MLR*, iv (1909). 185-189.

[12] An English translation of Æsop's fables is attributed to Alfred by Marie de France in the epilogue of her *Esope* or *Fables* (twelfth century), and Miss Helen Chefneux in her study

Asser

Asser, who wrote in 893, might have been expected to mention any books that Alfred had written or inspired up to that date. He actually mentions only Wærferth's translation of Gregory's *Dialogues,* but some version of the *Annals* must have been known to him, since in his biography he in-

Bede

cludes much annalistic matter up to the year 887. From Asser's silence we are bound to infer that the *Pastoral Care,* and of course all the works of Alfred's later period, were written after 893. The Bede, too, was presumably finished after 893, though quite possibly begun much earlier. It is best described as a revision of the original, made to fit the work into Alfred's educational program. Much was left out, condensed or summarized, while other parts were translated literally, to the sacrifice of English idiom now and again. In boldness of excision the translator reminds one of Alfred, but his literal renderings are less reminiscent of the King, who worked by para-phrase despite a few Latinisms. The other two translations of the earlier

Dialogues, Pastoral Care

period, those from Gregory, show less literalness, but greater fidelity to the texts, since they omit little and add little. Wærferth might be expected to understand his text better than Alfred understood his, but in fact the King does better than the bishop, thanks, no doubt, to the help he got. The works of the later period are marked by great boldness in the treatment of the text Alfred felt free not only to omit but also to insert almost at will. Thus, the

Orosius

geographical chapter in Orosius struck him (rightly enough) as deficient when it came to Germany and Scandinavia. He therefore interpolated the famous account of the voyages of Ohthere and Wulfstan, together with a long and valuable section on Germanic and Slavic tribal geography in the ninth century.[13] In all his writings the King was concerned, not so much to reproduce his originals faithfully as to produce books good for his sub-jects and simple enough for them to understand. Through these books he hoped to give them an education at once practical and liberal. The history of the English nation and of the world, the principles of philosophy and the principles and practice of Christianity, such was the reading-matter to b pondered by English youths and men engaged in learning how to read and write their mother tongue. And in the *Dialogues* of Gregory he even provided edifying escape literature: stories of the wonders and miracle wrought by God and by saintly men of old.[14]

Alfred did his paraphrases in prose. To the *Pastoral Care,* however, he added two passages in verse: one of 16 lines at the beginning (between preface and table of contents) and one of 30 lines at the end. Moreover

---

of the fables depicted on the Bayeux Tapestry (*Romania,* LX [1934]. 1-35, 153-194) makes seem likely that the designer(s) of the tapestry drew on this lost English version of Æsop For the so-called *Proverbs of Alfred* see below, p. 152.

[13] The latest discussion of King Alfred as geographer is that of R. Ekblom, *Studia Neophilo logica,* XIV (1942). 115-144; reviewed by F. Klaeber, *ibid.,* XV. 337-338. See also A. S. C. Ros *The Terfinnas and Beormas of Ohthere* (Leeds, 1940), and K. Malone, *Speculum,* V (1930 139-167 and VIII (1933). 67-78.

[14] Bede's *History* is largely made up of like stories, of course. Alfred himself wrote a brief preface for Wærferth's translation of the *Dialogues,* and the translator added a preface of h own: 27 lines of verse in which he sings the King's praises.

after he had finished his prose rendering of Boethius, he made a verse rendering of most of the metrical parts of this work.[15] For the metres of Boethius, then, we have two Alfredian versions, one in prose and one in *Boethius* verse. The verse rendering depends on the prose, not directly on the Latin metres, and there are indications that when Alfred did the verses his prose rendering had been finished and set aside long enough to grow cold in his mind. Alfred was not a man trained in literary composition, and neither his prose nor his verse merits much praise as such. At times he rose above himself and gave us prose passages worthy of a skilled craftsman, but these passages are the exception, not the rule. His accomplishment stands out more clearly when we consider his work in the large. Though he began to write late in life, and had no tradition of English literary prose to feed on, he managed to overcome many of the ills that beset the beginner, and, in hours snatched from his manifold duties as head of the state and father of his people, he was able to produce a body of writings impressive in quantity, expressive of his personality, and readable enough. Moreover, in his later period, at least, he showed a remarkable independence of his originals. Most important of all, he gave prestige to prose composition in English, and thereby opened the way to the cultivation of important literary genres hitherto neglected.

In the year 891 some compiler, probably a cleric in King Alfred's service, *The* finished a set of annals devoted chiefly to the history of the English from *Old* their settlement in Britain to the year of compilation, though not without *English* record of other events in Britain and elsewhere (the earliest event recorded *Annals* is Julius Caesar's invasion of Britain). The compiler used various sources, such as earlier annalistic matter, genealogies, Bede's *History,* and oral reports. A number of copies of his text seem to have got into circulation; in all likelihood King Alfred had them made and distributed among his bishops (or abbots), with instructions to keep them up to date.[16] Certainly his educational program would require some such distribution, and we know that he so distributed the *Pastoral Care*. None of these original copies of the *Annals* survive, but the seven extant versions all descend in one way or another from the compilation of 891. As time went on, entries were added in various MSS by successive annalists. The A_1 text (CCCC 173) was carried down to 1070; the A_2 text (Otho B xi), to 1001; the *B* text (Tib. A vi), to 977; the *C* text (Tib. B i), to 1086; the *D* text (Tib. B iv), to 1079; the *E* text (Laud 636), to 1154; the *F* text (Dom. A viii), to 1058. The *Annals* thus record contemporary events of the ninth, tenth, eleventh, and twelfth centuries, besides the earlier events which the original compiler set down from various sources. For the historian of England these *Annals* are obviously of the first importance. Here we are concerned with them as literature. One goes to annalistic writing with no high expectations; the form

[15] Preserved in MS Cotton Otho A vi.
[16] Continuations, compiled at some center (presumably Winchester), seem to have been sent out from time to time; but the matter is too intricate for treatment here. The *Old English Annals* are often called less accurately the *Anglo-Saxon Chronicle*.

does not lend itself well to artistic effects. The early annals in particular give us, for the most part, mere lists of events, not narrative accounts, and the annalist for 755, who tried his hand at narration, did a bungling job, though he had a stirring story to tell (that of Cynewulf, Cyneheard, and Osric).[17] The narrative passages grow better in the ninth-century annals; the writers usually express themselves clearly and simply enough, and show some skill in avoiding the monotony so often found in annalistic writing. With the death (in 924) of King Edward the Elder, however, the *Annals* begin to languish, and they do not regain their Alfredian vigor and fullness until the reign of King Æthelred the Redeless (979-1016), when a truly literary historical prose emerges and maintains itself to the end of the Old English period. Evidently a traditional craftsmanship had begun to take shape in the midst of political disaster. Moreover, expertness in prose composition was not peculiar to the later annalists; it marks other writings of the period as well. If Old English poetry flowered in the late seventh and eighth centuries, Old English prose flowered in the late tenth and eleventh. We therefore reckon classical, not the early prose of Alfred and his men, but the late prose of the annalists and of other writers taken up below.[18]

Æthelwold   We have seen that the politically glorious tenth century was marked by a decline in English prose, while Æthelred's calamitous reign and the triumph of the Danes in the eleventh century did not keep English prose from reaching heights of achievement worthy of the name classical. Alfred had laid the foundations on which the classical Old English prose writers built, but it was the monastic reform movement of the tenth century, led in England by Dunstan, Æthelwold, and Oswald,[19] which produced and cherished the builders. Æthelwold himself set going the second or classical period of Old English prose with a translation of the *Rule of St. Benedict*[20] which he made about 960.[21] The extant copies of this work all go back to a text made for nuns, but the original text presumably was made for monks weak in Latin. In a historical appendix, found in one MS only,[22] Æthelwold explains that the translation owed its existence to King Edgar's initiative, and it seems evident that the King in having it made was following the example set by his great-grandfather. Æthelwold goes on to apologize for the translation, which he thought of as a concession to weakness (strict disciplinarian that he was), but the Alfredian tradition proved strong enough to overcome whatever scruples he may have had. Indeed, he did his work in the spirit of Alfred: his version of the *Rule* is a paraphrase, not a literal rendering, and

[17] See F. P. Magoun, *Anglia*, LVII (1933). 361-376, and C. L. Wrenn, *History*, XXV (1940) 208-215.
[18] See C. L. Wrenn, *Trans. Phil. Soc.* for 1933, pp. 65-88.
[19] Dunstan, Archbishop of Canterbury (d. 988); Æthelwold, Bishop of Winchester (d. 984) Oswald, Bishop of Worcester and Archbishop of York (d. 992).
[20] Ed. A. Schröer, *Bibl. der ags. Prosa*, II.
[21] Schröer, p. xviii. But F. Tupper, *MLN*, VIII (1893). 350, dates the translation about 97
[22] Cotton Faustina A x. Old English text and modern rendering in T. O. Cockayn *Leechdoms*, etc., III. 432-444. The appendix may have been composed by 970, though Liebe mann, *Archiv*, CVIII (1902). 375-377, dates it after the death of Edgar in 975.

shows everywhere his concern to make things clear and simple for the reader. The smoothness and general competence of Æthelwold's English may reflect, more or less indirectly, the schooling he got under Dunstan at Glastonbury; certainly he was a man schooled and trained, not a self-taught writer like Alfred.

We come now to the leading prose writer of the period: Ælfric [23] *Ælfric* (*c.* 955-*c.* 1020), sometime pupil of Æthelwold at Winchester and lifelong disciple of his old master. Ælfric's many writings include homilies, pastoral letters, lives of saints, versions of books of the Bible, learned works of various kinds—a whole library to meet practical needs of the Church in his day. We pass over his *Grammar* and *Glossary,* with their pendant the *Colloquy,* in spite of their great cultural interest,[24] and begin with the 120 sermons, in three series of 40 sermons each, which he wrote between the years 990 and 998 [25] while a monk at Winchester or Cernel. The first and second series go by the name *Homiliæ Catholicæ;* the third series is called *Passiones Sanctorum.* These serial titles, however, cannot be taken strictly; saints' lives are included among the homilies, and homilies among the saints' lives. Each sermon was written for use on a suitable day of the Church year; thus, the sermon on Gregory was to be preached on March 12 (the day of that saint). Through his vernacular sermons Ælfric sought to make things easier for the preachers, who could use the discourses which he provided, without having to wrestle with the Latin originals, the meaning of which, in spots at least, those weak in Latin might find it hard to fathom. For sources Ælfric drew on the abundant stock of sermons and other religious writings available in Latin; he made particular use of Gregory, Bede, and Augustine. He treated his sources with great freedom, adapting the material to the needs of English pastor and flock. All three series are marked by good construction and clear, happy expression; as W. P. Ker has said, Ælfric is "the great master of prose in all its forms." [26] The series differ somewhat in style. In the first, alliteration is used now and then to heighten the effect; in the second, this device is used more freely; in the third, many passages are written in a rhythmic alliterative prose which some scholars have wrongly taken for verse and ·even printed as such. Ælfric in his rhythmical effects was following a fashion of his time, found in Latin prose and carried over into vernacular composition.[27] We note also, as we proceed from series to series, a shift of balance: the story looms larger, the mor-

[23] See C. L. White, *Ælfric, . . . (Yale Studies in English,* II). Ed. *Bibl. der ags. Prosa,* I Grein), III (Assmann), IX (Fehr), X (Crawford); *EETS,* 76, 82, 94, 114 (Skeat), 160 Crawford), 213 (Henel). For other editions see *CBEL,* I. 89-92. Miss Dorothy Whitelock, in *1LR,* XXXVIII (1943). 122-124, points out the inadequacy of the evidence for the date of Elfric's death.

[24] Ed. J. Zupitza, *Ælfrics Grammatik und Glossar* (Berlin, 1880); G. N. Garmonsway, *Ælfric's Colloquy* (1939). These works may have grown out of his experiences as teacher of blates at the monastery of Cernel in Dorsetshire (987-989). See above, p. 18.

[25] The first series was finished in 990 or 991; the second, in 992; the third, between 993 nd 998. See K. Sisam, *RES,* VII (1931). 16-18, VIII (1932). 55, 67-68.

[26] *English Literature, Medieval,* p. 55.

[27] G. H. Gerould, *MP,* XXII (1925). 353-366. Cf. also A. Cordier, *L'Allitération latine* Paris, 1939).

alizing commentary smaller. The saints' lives in particular [28] tend to become tales of wonder not unlike the legends of Middle English times.

Alongside the three series of sermons we set, as a fourth major work of Ælfric, the so-called *Heptateuch*, an English version of the first seven books of the Bible. This version seems to have been made in several stages. Genesis was translated in 997 or 998, at the instance of the ealdorman Æthelweard, to whom its epistolary preface is addressed. For the same nobleman, and presumably at about the same time (if not earlier), Ælfric turned Joshua into English. The exact times and occasions of composition cannot be given for the other books of the *Heptateuch*, but the whole was hardly complete by 1005, when Ælfric became Abbot of Eynsham in Oxfordshire. The seventh book, Judges, was not included in the B text (MS Claudius B iv), and though included in the L text (MS Bodley Laud Misc. 509) it is there set off from the rest by a blank page; presumably Judges was first composed as an independent work, or as a fellow of the homilies on other books of the Bible: Kings and Maccabees, incorporated into the third series of sermons; Job, used in the second series; Judith; and Esther. The whole Bible was summarized by Ælfric in a treatise (really two treatises) on the Old and New Testaments written for a certain Sigwerd, and this treatise has been taken for an introduction to the *Heptateuch*, though its place in the MS (Bodley Laud Misc. 509) does not support the theory. Introduction or no, the treatise was composed later than the *Heptateuch* proper; not earlier than 1006, not later than 1012. If we compare Ælfric's *Heptateuch* with the original we find it a volume of selections; large parts of the scriptural text are omitted. This holds least for Genesis, though even here omissions may be noted. In general, Ælfric left out things which he thought unsuitable for an English layman. Incidentally he thereby made his version more readable. Whatever he chose to translate he reproduced faithfully, with due regard to English idiom. He made much use of alliteration and rhythm here as elsewhere. For the latter part of Genesis, and perhaps for Exodus and Leviticus as well, Ælfric had before him an English translation made by somebody else; this translation he seems to have incorporated (in somewhat revised form) into his own version. His procedure here is indicative of the man: he saw no reason to work out a fresh version when one already existed which with a little patching could be made to serve. His sermons mean more to him. Here he was capable of discarding earlier work of his own for the sake of giving more adequate treatment to a theme. Thus, the *Hexameron*, a homily on the Creation, treats more fully a theme which he had already used in the *Catholic Homilies*, and the MS evidence suggests that Ælfric wrote the *Hexameron* to take the place of this earlier creation sermon.[29]

In general, Ælfric's literary activities grew out of practical needs or de

[28] On their form, see D. Bethurum, *SP*, xxix (1932). 515-533.
[29] The name *Hexameron* was traditional; Ælfric presumably got it from Bede. The six parts implied answer to the six days of Creation but Ælfric gives us much not mentioned in the Bible; his chief extra-biblical source was Bede.

mands; here he followed the tradition of Alfred, whose writings he knew. Sometimes Ælfric himself took the initiative in meeting such needs. In other cases he wrote to order: thus, bishops would commission him to prepare pastoral letters for use in their dioceses, and patrons (as we saw above) would ask him for English renderings or summaries of Holy Writ. Whatever the circumstances, his work shows a high level of competence, and often rises to æsthetic heights in its kind. Ælfric's artistic achievement, however, should not make us lose sight of the didactic purpose and effect which, for him, alone gave point to the labor of composition. The things he wrote proved, in fact, so well adapted to the needs of pastoral and monastic instruction that they withstood the cultural collapse brought on by the Norman Conquest, and kept alive till better days the tradition of English devotional prose.

The chief literary contemporary of Ælfric was his superior and friend **Wulfstan** Wulfstan,[30] Bishop of London (996-1002), Bishop of Worcester (1002-1016), and Archbishop of York (1002-1023). He died in 1023. He is best known as a homilist. Indeed his literary fame rests mainly on a single homily composed in the troublous year 1014: the eschatological *Sermo Lupi ad Anglos*.[31] He begins conventionally enough with the statement that "this world is in haste, and it draws nigh to the end." In other words, Doomsday is almost upon us. The evils of the time drive the preacher to his fateful conclusion, evils which he proceeds to particularize in vigorous speech. The English by their sinful ways have called down these evils upon themselves, and unless they repent and turn from wickedness to righteousness they will have every reason to quake before the judgment which is at hand. This powerful and timely sermon, thundered from the pulpit by Wulfstan himself or by some other clerical orator, might well have brought an eleventh-century congregation to sackcloth and ashes. Even today, after more than 900 years, its fiery periods stir the heart. The sermons of Ælfric were written to instruct; those of Wulfstan, to move; both homilists in the process produced works of art unmatched in their respective kinds. Wulfstan has aptly been compared to an Old Testament prophet; certainly he speaks with prophetic eloquence and zeal. The canon of his works remains a problem.[32]

The *Blickling Homilies*,[33] a batch of 19 sermons in a MS of *c.* 970 and **Blickling** named (by modern scholars) after the former home of the MS, antedate the *and* homilies of Ælfric and Wulfstan. Their literary merit is small, and we need **Vercelli** no more than mention them here. The 23 prose pieces of the Vercelli **Homilies** book, a collection made *c.* 1000 if not earlier, are mostly homilies,[34] but include a fragmentary life of St Guthlac.[35]

[30] See A. [S.] Napier, *Wulfstan* (Berlin, 1883); D. Bethurum, *PMLA*, LVII (1942). 916-929.
[31] The best edition is that of D. Whitelock (1939).
[32] But see K. Jost, *Anglia*, LVI (1932). 265-315.
[33] Ed. R. Morris, *EETS*, 58, 63, 73. See also A. E. H. Swaen, *Neophilologus*, xxv (1940). 4-272, and R. Willard, *Univ. of Texas . . . Studies in English*, 1940, pp. 5-28.
[34] Ed. (first half only) M. Förster, *Bibl. der ags. Prosa*, xii.
[35] A fuller text of the prose *Guthlac* is recorded in MS Cotton Vesp. D xxi. Edition, based both texts, by P. Gonser, *Anglistische Forschungen*, xxvii (Heidelberg, 1909).

A number of other homilies and legends have come down to us, singl⟩ and in groups. Some of them still await publication.[36] We do not treat them in this history, but pass on to the gospel translations and other prose works

Gospels The West Saxon version of the four gospels [37] is commonly dated *c.* 100⟨ The translation, idiomatic but faithful to the Vulgate text, bears comparison with the Authorized Version of 1611 in literary quality.[38] The so-calle⟨ Lindisfarne and Rushworth gospels are only glosses, and do not concern u⟨ here. The same may be said of the many glossed texts of the Latin Psalter Such works as the penitentials attributed to Archbishop Egbert of York [3] likewise have little or no literary interest; they are essentially (ecclesiastica⟩ legal texts. The many legal documents of Old English times have alread⟨ been looked at (above, pp. 35-38) for the metrical bits which they incor porate. We omit from this history any consideration of legal prose. Th Handbook of Byrhtferth,[40] and other works of interest to the historian ⟨ science,[41] we likewise omit. The translation of that famous medieval co lection of proverbs known as the *Distichs of Cato* [42] may be worthy ⟨ mention. The most notable piece of late secular prose, however, is the Ol

Apollonius English version of the Apollonius of Tyre story.[43] This romance of classic antiquity, deservedly popular in the Middle Ages, found an English tran lator even though it served for entertainment pure and simple. Unluck⟨ only a fragment of the translation has survived. Its author shows consi erable skill in that difficult art; his version reads well and gives us som idea of what the English literature of entertainment might have becom but for the Norman Conquest. Of less interest are two secular prose piec recorded in the Nowell codex: [44] the Old English version of *Alexander Letter to Aristotle,* and a piece known as *Wonders of the East.* Both the pieces, along with *Apollonius* and many a saint's legend, show a taste f Oriental wonders and adventures, a taste which the crusades were destin to whet.

Summary During the late tenth and eleventh centuries, the classical period of C English prose, many writers were active and much good prose was writt⟨ Homiletic prose in particular reached heights of achievement comparal to the masterpieces of modern times. Historical prose, too, flourished, a⟨

---

[36] On the unpublished homilies of MS CCCC 41, see R. Willard, in Förster's *Beiträge ⟨ englischen Philologie,* xxx (1935). 2.

[37] Ed. J. W. Bright (4v, 1904-1906). On the Vulgate text used by the translator, see Glunz, in Förster's *Beiträge,* ix (1928) and *Kölner anglistische Arbeiten,* xii (1930).

[38] Here may be mentioned the Old English version of the apocryphal gospel of Nicodem Text and discussion by W. H. Hulme in *PMLA,* xiii (1898). 471-515 and *MP,* i (19⟨ 579-614. Ed. E. J. Crawford (Edinburgh, 1927).

[39] Editions: *Poenitentiale* by J. Raith (1933); *Confessionale* by R. Spindler (1934).

[40] Ed. S. J. Crawford, *EETS,* 177 (1929). See also H. Henel, *JEGP,* xli (1942). 427-4 and *Speculum,* xviii (1943). 288-302.

[41] Many texts may be found in O. Cockayne's *Leechdoms, Wort-Cunning, and Star⟨ (3v, Rolls Series, 1864-1866); see also G. Leonhardi, *Bibl. der ags. Prosa,* vi (1905), and⟨ Henel, *EETS,* 213 (1942).

[42] Ed. J. Nehab, *Der altenglische Cato* (Berlin, 1879). See also G. Schleich, *Anglia,* (1880). 383-396.

[43] Ed. J. Zupitza, *Archiv,* xcvii (1896). 17-34. See also P. Goepp, *ELH,* v (1938). 150-⟨

[44] Ed. S. Rypins, *EETS,* 161 (1924).

a beginning was made with scientific prose. Moreover, prose writers even ventured into the realm of fiction, territory hitherto monopolized by verse. Had this rapid development kept up, the twelfth and thirteenth centuries might have been as glorious in English literature as they actually were in Icelandic. But William of Normandy won at Hastings. King Alfred, the noblest Englishman of them all, had laid out the garden of English prose. Ælfric and his fellows brought it to high cultivation, and extended it with new plantings full of promise. The Normans laid it waste, and slew its keepers.[45]

---

[45] A. Brandl sums up the matter thus (*Grundriss*, p. 1133): "In the last phase of Old English culture, creative power was still active in the most diverse fields. In poetry the rise of rime was opening the way to a flowering of song. In prose, a homiletic style of singular force and vigor had grown up, and at the same time story telling made its way in a fullness comparable to the period of the crusades. In science, meager though the achievement, the zeal of the students was worthy of praise, while not only a great man [Ælfric?] but also an organization extending over the whole country provided for popular education. It was no tired, late autumnal culture but a field freshly sown with many promising seeds upon which fell the foreign rule of the Normans like the snows of winter." Less authoritative but of particular interest to Americans is the judgment of Ralph Waldo Emerson (*English Traits* [Boston, 1903], pp. 60-61): "... Twenty thousand thieves landed at Hastings. These founders of the House of Lords were greedy and ferocious dragoons, sons of greedy and ferocious pirates. They were all alike, they took everything they could carry, they burned, harried, violated, tortured and killed, until everything English was brought to the verge of ruin. ..."

BOOK I
The Middle Ages

‿◞◠‿

PART II
The Middle English Period
(1100-1500)

Guide to reference marks
Throughout the text of this book, a point • set beside a page number indicates that references to new critical material will be found under an identical paragraph/page number (set in **boldface**) in the BIBLIOGRAPHICAL SUPPLEMENT.
In the Index, a number preceded by an **S** indicates a paragraph/page number in the BIBLIOGRAPHICAL SUPPLEMENT.

I

General Characteristics of the Period

The Middle English period may be defined chronologically as the period *The Period* from 1100 to 1500. Some scholars prefer to date the beginning from 1150, *Defined* and, so far as literature in English is concerned, there is much to be said for this view. It is not merely because little or nothing in English has come down to us from the first half of the century and what has, such as the *Old English Annals* (*Anglo-Saxon Chronicle*) carried on at Peterborough until 1154, is better thought of as a continuation of what went before, but because the changes in the Old English language, especially the wearing away of inflections, and the reflection of these changes in the orthography reach a point about 1150 which justifies our setting at this date the boundary between Old and Middle English. When we consider, however, that English literature is rightly to be thought of as the literature written in England,[1] reflecting English life and thought, whether it is written in English or in French or Latin, we may with equal justice begin our present survey with the opening of the twelfth century. The adoption of 1500 as a closing date has only the convenience of a round number to recommend it. However, most of fifteenth-century literature belongs indisputably to the Middle English tradition, and those developments at the end of the century which look forward to the Renaissance of the next are not of a revolutionary character and may be considered as faint stirrings of the new spirit helping to remind us of the complexity characteristic of any period, rightly considered, of literary history.[2]

[1] From the latter part of the fourteenth century on we must include the work of certain Scottish writers.

[2] The most valuable tool for the study of Middle English texts is John E. Wells, *A Manual of the Writings in Middle English, 1050-1400* (New Haven, 1916), with periodic supplements, now nine in number. Vol. 1 of the *CBEL* covers this period. Briefer bibliographical guides are W. L. Renwick and Harold Orton, *The Beginnings of English Literature to Skelton—1509* (1940), and Roger S. Loomis, *Intro. to Medieval Literature, chiefly in England: Reading List and Bibl.* (1939). Indispensable is Carleton Brown's *Register of Middle English Religious and Didactic Verse* (2v, 1916-20; *Bibliographical Soc.*). The second volume, revised and enlarged to include the secular verse, by Carleton Brown and Rossell H. Robbins, has been issued as *An Index of Middle English Verse* (1943; *Index Soc.*). Valuable bibliographical material is presented in Josiah C. Russell, *Dictionary of Writers of Thirteenth Century England* (1936; *Bull. Inst. of Hist. Research*, Special Suppl. No. 3). Additions appear from time to time in the *Bulletin*. Important older works are Thomas Tanner, *Bibliotheca Britannico-Hibernica* (1748), John Pits, *Relationum Historicarum de Rebus Anglicis* (Paris, 1619), John Bale, *Illustrium Majoris Britanniae Scriptorum . . . Summarium* (Ipswich, 1548; enlarged ed., Basle, 1557-9), Bale's *Index Britanniae Scriptorum*, ed. R. L. Poole and Mary Bateson (Oxford, 1902), John Leland, *Commentarii de Scriptoribus Britannicis* (2v, Oxford, 1709), and Thomas Wright, *Biographia Britannica Literaria*, Vol. 11: *Anglo-Norman Period* (1846). — The Middle English period receives extensive treatment in Bernard Ten Brink, *Gesch. der englischen Literatur* (2ed., 2v, 1899-1912; English trans., 3v, 1883-96), suggestive but now somewhat antiquated. The

*The
Norman
Conquest*

   In this period of four hundred years the dominant factor which changed the whole course of Middle English literature, as of English history during the same period, was the Norman Conquest. In 1066 William, the Duke of Normandy and one of the world's great figures, claimed the English throne as the next of kin to Edward the Confessor. He supported his claim by invading England with an army of Norman and French soldiers led by adventurers, ambitious nobles, and the younger sons of many important French families, conquered his rival, Harold, at the Battle of Hastings, and was crowned king. It required four years to stamp out opposition and win complete recognition, four years filled with ruthless campaigns in which he all but wiped out the English nobility. His Norman and French supporters who had made the conquest possible were rewarded with the lands and titles of the English nobles. The result was a new aristocracy in England, an aristocracy almost wholly French. Normans and French filled all important positions in both Church and State. Foreign in nationality and temperament, in tradition and association, they added a new element to the English nation and brought new qualities of mind and character to merge

discussion in J. J. Jusserand, *Histoire littéraire du peuple anglais* (2ed., 2v, 1896-1904) is along more general lines. The English trans. has the title *A Literary History of the English People* (2ed., 3v, 1906-9). Still of importance is A. Brandl, "Mittelenglische Literatur" in H. Paul, *Grundriss der germanischen Philologie*, Bd. ii, Abt. i (1893), pp. 609-718. Wm. H. Schofield's *English Literature from the Norman Conquest to Chaucer* (1906) is readable and well known. There are useful but uneven chapters in the *CHEL* and bibliographies in the *CBEL*. C. S. Baldwin, *Three Medieval Centuries of Literature in England, 1100-1400* (Boston, 1932), P. G. Thomas, *English Literature before Chaucer* (1924), and R. M. Wilson, *Early Middle English Literature* [to 1300] (1939) may be noted. The last best represents the present status of scholarship. Hans Hecht and L. L. Schücking, *Die englische Literatur im Mittelalter* (1927) is slight. W. F. Ker's *English Literature: Medieval* (n.d.) in its brief compass is richly suggestive. Remarkable for its time was Thomas Warton's *History of English Poetry* (1774-81), best consulted in the edition of W. C. Hazlitt (4v, 1871). — For the Old French background the student should consult Gaston Paris's classic, *La Littérature française au moyen âge* (4ed., 1909) or the *Esquisse* translated as *Medieval French Literature* (1903); Karl Voretzsch, *Intro. to the Study of Old French Literature* (1931, from the third German ed.); Urban T. Holmes, *History of Old French Literature . . . to 1300* (2ed, Chapel Hill, 1937); G. Gröber, "Französische Literatur" in Gröber's *Grundriss der romanischen Philologie*, Bd. ii, Abt. (1902), pp. 433-1247; and the monumental *Histoire littéraire de la France* (39v, 1733-1950, in progress). On the Latin literature of the Middle Ages see the references at the end of ch. v. — For the historical background the reader may consult H. W. C. Davis, *England under the Normans and Angevins* (1905), Kenneth H. Vickers, *England in the Later Middle Ages* (1913), George B. Adams, *The History of England from the Norman Conquest to the Death of John (1066-1216)* (1905), T. F. Tout, *The History of England from the Accession of Henry III to the Death of Edward III (1216-1377)* (1905), and C. Oman, *The History of England from the Accession of Richard II to the Death of Richard III (1377-1485)* (1906). Charles Gross, *The Sources and Literature of English History . . . to about 1485* (2ed., 1915) is invaluable. On English life in the Middle Ages the following are of interest: *Medieval England*, ed. H. W. C. Davis (Oxford, 1924); A. Abram, *English Life and Manners in the Later Middle Ages* (1913); L. F. Salzman, *English Life in the Middle Ages* (Oxford, 1926); and the first two volumes of H. D. Traill's *Social England* (rev. ed., 1901-4). For a more general view of the Middle Ages see G. G. Coulton, *Medieval Panorama* (1938); *The Legacy of the Middle Ages*, ed. C. G. Crump and E. F. Jacob (Oxford, 1926); Karl Vossler, *Mediæval Culture*, trans. W. L. Lawton (2v, 1929), with an extensive bibliography by J. E. Spingarn; Henry Osborn Taylor, *The Medieval Mind* (2v, 1911); Henry Adams, *Mont-Saint-Michel and Chartres* (1904); and, for the fullest treatment and widest scope, *The Cambridge Medieval History* (8v, Cambridge, 1911-36). Further references may be found in Louis J. Paetow, *A Guide to the Study of Medieval History* (rev. ed., 1931).

in time with those of the Anglo-Saxon. The practical and enterprising qualities of the Norman, and the French instinct for symmetry and order became part of the English race, and as characteristics of the race were reflected in English literature.

A more immediate consequence of the Norman Conquest was the introduction of French into England as the normal language of the governing class. The new nobility knew no English, and it is unlikely that they made much effort to become acquainted with it. The tradition that William the Conqueror made an unsuccessful attempt to learn the language is not too well founded. On the other hand there is abundant evidence that for at least two hundred years the nobility everywhere used French. We must remember that the conquerors came to England to enrich themselves, not to identify themselves with a people and a national culture which they regarded, with some justice, as less sophisticated than their own. They retained political and property interests in France which required frequent and extended sojourns there. Residence in England was not a matter of choice but of political necessity and financial expediency. Even the small percentage of the English nobles who acknowledged William's claim and retained their estates and titles soon learned French as the language of the class with which their own interests were most closely identified and with which they were mostly associated. The English language naturally continued to be spoken by the mass of the people, but it was the language of the uncultivated. England was thus in the unhappy linguistic situation of a house divided against itself. As to some extent in Belgium today, two languages were in use side by side, one by the upper class, economically and socially, the other by the common people. *The French Language in England*

How long such a situation would have continued if events had not occurred to bring about a change no one can say. Probably in time the weight of numbers would have told and English would once more have become the language of the whole country. But in 1204 England lost Normandy and an important political condition favorable to the maintenance of French in England came to an end. From this date we note the growing tendency for nobles with land in both France and England to divide their possessions geographically among their children and for members of a family to reach a similar agreement among themselves. Finally in 1244 decrees of the King of France and the King of England made it illegal for any one to hold lands in both countries. It is significant that the influx of French words into the English vocabulary assumes really large proportions in the period following 1250, a pretty clear indication that English is coming to be spoken by those accustomed to the use of French. The half century from 1250 to 1300 is the period during which the transition from French to English as the language of the nobility was occurring. By the beginning of the fourteenth century English is for all practical purposes universal. The author of a romance, writing not later than 1325, remarks that everybody now knows *Recovery of English*

Periods of Middle English Literature

English and many a noble can speak no French. From this time on a knowledge of French in England is merely a fashionable accomplishment or a cultural asset.[3]

The linguistic situation here described had an important effect upon the production of literature in the native tongue and determined in no small measure the character of that which was produced at different stages of the Middle English period. It would be wrong to suppose that the Norman Conquest caused a sharp cleavage, cutting off suddenly native production. Rather it altered the course of the native tradition, forced it for a time to run under ground, narrowed the stream. This will be apparent if we examine Middle English literature as a whole, for we will find that it falls into certain well-marked periods.[4] There is first the period running to 1250, the period during which English was the language of only the lower classes. It would be useless to look in it for romances and other types popular at the court. These were being produced in French, the language of the class to which poets looked for patronage. Since writing in English was bound to be without material rewards to the writer, we must look to the clergy for most of what was intended for the common people. It is not surprising, therefore, to find English writings at this date predominantly religious, representing the efforts of those in the Church to instruct the people in Bible story and in the ways of right living. The *Ormulum* (see p. 158) is a typical work of the first period—the Period of Religious Record.[5] When the upper classes begin to adopt English we get a much more varied literature in the native language. The object of English writings becomes entertainment as well as edification. Our earliest romances in English, for example, belong with one exception to the second half of the thirteenth century, and the hundred years from 1250 to 1350 are known as the Period of Religious and Secular Literature. When after 1350 English is once more secure as the language of both the court and the people and there has been sufficient time for the tentative and experimental efforts that seem to precede major literary periods, we reach the high point in Middle English literature. The fifty years from 1350 to 1400, in which Chaucer, Wyclif, Langland, and the *Pearl* poet, not to mention significant but less spectacular figures, appeared, has been called the Period of Great Individual Writers. The remaining hundred years, the fifteenth century, are for a time dominated by the influence of Chaucer and towards the end look forward to the developments which make the sixteenth century one of great literary renaissance. This century may be thought of as the Imitative or Transition Period.

[3] For a full treatment of the relation between French and English in England after the Norman Conquest see the present writer's *History of the English Language* (rev. ed., 1957), chs. v and vi.
[4] These chronological divisions were first suggested by Brandl in his *Mittelenglische Literatur,* noted on p. 110.
[5] The name is meant to suggest that classification is necessarily based on what was recorded in writing and therefore survived. There was doubtless much popular literature—song, ballad, story—which lived only on the lips of the people and the wandering minstrel and which therefore has not come down to us. Cf. p. 209.

The effect on literature of the Norman Conquest as we have so far *Effects of* described it is largely indirect, the consequence of the fact that a new ruling *Norman* class, alien in speech, came into being, interrupting the normal literary de- *Conquest* velopment and temporarily forcing English prose and poetry into the back- *on* ground. But the new influence was not merely negative or entirely bad. *Literature* The Norman conquerors and those who later came in their train brought to England much that was new and stimulating and valuable. They brought with them their Continental tastes and the literature on which those tastes had been formed. French literature in the twelfth century had burst suddenly into flower and was enjoying one of its great periods. It was the leading literature of Europe, rich and varied in theme, polite and urbane in spirit, easy and confident in performance. This literature circulated as freely at the English court as in France. In time it furnished a large body of new material for English poets and gave them new models and standards for imitation and emulation. The new wealth of the Norman nobles attracted French minstrels and poets to the English court and insured liberal rewards for their effort to provide solace or pleasing edification (cf. pp. 135 ff.). The policy of the Conqueror of filling English churches and monasteries with learned Norman bishops and abbots—men like Lanfranc and Gilbert Crispin—however detrimental it was to pastoral needs, gave a needed stimulus to English intellectual life. The close political connection with France, at first through Normandy and later through extensive English possessions in Anjou, Maine, Aquitaine, and Guienne, put an end to any sense of isolation that may have existed and brought England into the stream of Continental thought and culture. The English language was enriched with thousands of French words, becoming a more cosmopolitan and supple medium of literary expression, and the old Teutonic alliterative verse was largely replaced by the French syllabic line, standard all over Europe. We should look upon the Norman Conquest as bringing about the early merging of two great literary traditions, the Teutonic tradition which early England shared with other northern nations and the Romance tradition with its main source in France.

English literature in the period following the Conquest is in three lan- *Literature* guages—Latin, French, and English. Latin, as already in Old English times, *in Three* was not only the language of learning but the vernacular of the learned, *Languages* and the character of such twelfth-century works as Walter Map's *De Nugis Curialium* and Geoffrey of Monmouth's *Historia* attests its use outside the narrower field of scholarship. In French a large body of poetry was written in England or for English patronage and constituted for over two hundred years the literary entertainment of the English court. It is natural for us to take greater interest in the literature written in our own mother tongue and to trace its course as a separate stream. But whatever was written in England, expressing English thought and reflecting English social and intellectual conditions, is rightly to be considered a part of the national literature. For more than half of our period it is possible to distinguish between what was written for the aristocratic class and what was intended for the people merely by the language in which it is written. Even after English had regained its position at court numerous works avow their author's intention of writing for "lewd men," that is, the ignorant. Seldom outside of the Middle Ages is literature quite so class conscious. A great part of Middle English literature, for whatever class intended, must be recognized as derivative, secondary, and imitative. English writers eagerly adopted the themes and fashions of French literature, offering hospitality to the *Song of Roland* and showing a nice impartiality towards heroes of the French national epic. All through the thirteenth and much of the fourteenth centuries the literature of England was constantly indebted to French originals and followed French example. We are here, as always, speaking of what has been preserved. Popular poetry, which must have existed even though it has not come down to us, was surely thoroughly English. But of the productions that took written form a large number derive directly or ultimately from France. Even a British legend like that of King Arthur reached English romance not directly from the Celts but through the French romances of Chrétien de Troyes and his successors. The general character of Middle English literature will be imperfectly apprehended unless we recognize its tri-lingual form, its class distinctions, and its great indebtedness to French sources and models.

Some Character-istics of Medieval Literature

There are other general features of Middle English literature which should be noted, but these are characteristic of all medieval literature. One is what might be called its impersonality. In the first place a great deal of Middle English literature is anonymous. We don't know the names of those who wrote it. It is partly that people were more interested in the poem than in the poet, just as we admire the Lincoln Memorial and marvel at the Empire State Building without making an effort to learn who were the architects. The medieval author was at a disadvantage compared with popular writers today in having no publisher interested in keeping his name before the public. Again, the reproduction of books by hand tended to give them in time a communal character. A text was exposed both to unconscious alteration and conscious change. The medieval scribe was as likely as not to assume the rôle of editor or adapter, so that different manuscripts of a work often differ greatly from one another. Except in the case of a few works of well-known writers a medieval production was subject to the whims of successive generations of scribes. A third consideration tending to give an effect of impersonality to literature was the differing attitude of the Middle Ages towards originality. Originality was not a major requirement of medieval authors. Story material in particular was looked upon as common property and the notion that one could claim property rights in ideas is seldom encountered. To have based one's work on an old and therefore authoritative source was a virtue which led Geoffrey of Monmouth and even greater writers to claim such a source when none existed. It is not surprising that such an attitude raised translation to the level of original creation.[6] The reader must be prepared for a less personal quality in medieval than in modern literature and to find that the original author of a work is often, for us, without a local habitation or a name.

Certain other characteristics distinguish medieval literature as a whole, and in some cases the literature between 1100 and 1500 from that of either earlier or later periods. One such characteristic results from the presence of women in the audience. We have only to notice the difference between *Beowulf* and *Sir Gawain and the Green Knight* to realize the change that takes place in narrative poetry when it passes from the mead-hall to the castle. *Beowulf* is heroic, *Sir Gawain* courtly in tone. In the second place, one is constantly aware in medieval literature of the all-important place of the Church in medieval life. It is often said that men and women looked upon this life mainly as a means to the next. Certainly they lived in much more fear of Hell and its torments and were vitally concerned with the problem of salvation for their souls. Religious writings are, therefore, a large and significant part of medieval literature, not off to one side as in our day, but in the main stream. They bulk large because religion overtopped the common affairs of life as the cathedral dominated the surrounding country. Thirdly, even where religion is not directly concerned, a moral purpose is frequently discernible in literature, openly avowed or tacitly implied as the justification for its existence. John of Salisbury in his *Policraticus* says that all writings serve a practical purpose and this purpose is to convey useful knowledge and promote virtue.[7] In the Middle Ages the literature of knowledge and the literature of power, to use De Quincey's distinction, are often close together if not much the same thing. Lyric poetry passes easily from ecstasy to warning, and in narrative the will to delight is often partner with the will to teach. Finally, it should be noted that much of literature until near the end of the Middle Ages was meant to be listened to rather than read. Until we approach the fifteenth century, literacy was not widespread even among the upper classes and books were expensive. Most people were dependent upon song and recitation, upon the minstrel and the poet reading his work, for their literary recreation. As a result, verse is the normal medium for most forms of literature. Much that would now be written in prose—history, popular instruction, moralizing—was put into verse as the form more easily carried in the memory and more pleasant to listen to.

It remains but to say a word in this chapter about the quality of medieval literature as art. And we must admit at once that judged by modern standards much of medieval literature, Continental as well as English, is infra-literary.[8] This does not mean that there are no great works of the imagination in the Middle Ages. There are some, but poems like the *Divine Comedy* are rare in any age. To admit that most works written between the Fall of Rome and the Renaissance do not claim a place among the

Artistic Quality of Medieval Literature

---

[6] Deschamps addresses a complimentary poem to Chaucer as "grand translateur."
[7] Book VII, chs. 9-11.
[8] The word is F. J. Mather's: cf. *The Bookman* (N. Y.), xxv (1907). 617-619.

world's greatest books is not to deny real interest and importance to the period. To the true humanist every effort of the race to express itself is of interest. The child is father of the man, and in medieval literature there is much of the simplicity of the child. Beauty is not to be denied on the grounds of immaturity, and simplicity itself is not without charm. With Gaston Paris we may recognize that it is not always for us to judge and to prove but to know and to understand. Medieval writing lacks the immediate appeal of the contemporaneous. The human mind grasps more easily the productions of its own day. There are fewer obstacles to understanding. Differences of language and custom will always limit the enjoyment of early literature to the cultivated few. But acquaintance with the past brings understanding, and understanding begets sympathy, appreciation, pleasure. One is privileged in this modern world to waive aside the literature of the Middle Ages, to reason that with life so short and art so long to learn, it is better to snatch the pleasure within easy reach, but such a one will not see later literature in historical perspective and he will miss a body of writings which, sympathetically approached, will be found to contain much of interest, and, as Rossetti observed, "beauties of a kind which can never again exist in art."

II

The Survival of the Native Tradition (1100-1250)

The state of England on the eve of the Norman Conquest is a question *Literary* on which opinion is divided. The older view, that the "history of the Anglo- *Conditions* Saxon from the time of King Alfred to the Norman Conquest is little else *at the* than the history of disorganization, degeneracy, and decay,"[1] has been *Conquest* sharply challenged.[2] No doubt there was political and social slackness, but there was also heroism at Senlac. England was in a transition stage and Old English literature was likewise in transition. We can hardly expect new *Beowulfs* in the eleventh century. The heroic age was past; we do not find new *Iliads* in the Age of Pericles. Old English writers were turning to new themes such as Apollonius and Alexander,[3] themes which they were getting from the Continent and treating in the Continental manner. There is, of course, no way of telling what English literature would have become if it had been allowed to pursue its own course, but its normal development was interrupted by the Conquest. The Normans were not hostile to the native tradition. The decay of literary activity is suffiently explained by the destructive effects of four years of ruthless war, the rapid displacement of English bishops and English abbots in the monasteries, the eviction of the English language and English culture from the place they should have occupied in the national life, and the complete indifference of the new rulers to books in a language which they did not understand. Writing in the native tongue was paralyzed, but, as we shall see, it was not dead.

One indication that interest in the older literature did not die with the *Old* Conquest is the fact that Old English manuscripts continued to be copied. *English* Two of the six MSS of the West Saxons Gospels belong to the twelfth cen- *Survivals* tury and we have twelfth-century copies of King Alfred's *Boethius*, the *Distichs of Cato, the Gospel of Nicodemus*, numerous homilies of Ælfric and others, to mention only a few. Another indication is the fact that the *Old English Annals* were kept up for nearly a hundred years. One manuscript, now lost, was continued in the south of England until 1121 when it was borrowed by Peterborough, possibly to replace a copy destroyed by fire in 1116, and not only copied but carried on there until 1154. Finally there is

---

[1] T. Duffus Hardy, *Descriptive Catalogue of Materials Relating to the History of Great Britain* (3v in 4, 1862-71), II. p. xi. The view was echoed by Gaston Paris, *La Poésie du moyen âge* (Paris, 1885-95), II. 46-7.

[2] Cf. *CHEL*, I. 166; R. R. Darlington, "The Last Phase of Anglo-Saxon History," *History*, XXII (1937). 1-13; R. M. Wilson, *Early Middle English Literature* (1939), pp. 3-22; and above, p. 105.

[3] See above (p. 104) for *Apollonius of Tyre, The Wonders of the East*, etc.

a good bit of evidence that ballads and poems on historical and legendary themes were still being sung in the time of William of Malmesbury (*c.* 1125) and Henry of Huntington (d. 1155). The latter includes translations into Latin of a number of such songs, and William of Malmesbury tells many stories of Athelstan and Edgar and Queen Gunhilda which he says he has learned from *cantilenae* and *nostro adhuc seculo etiam in triviis cantitata.* There were legends of Offa,[4] of Wade, several times alluded to[5] but now known only in Latin epitomes such as Walter Map gives in his *De Nugis Curialium* (cf. p. 146), and of Hereward, the last of which is preserved in a Latin form based, as the author tells us, on an English original. While we must be careful not to attribute literary form to every popular story that has found its way into the chronicles, the lost literature of the period following the Norman Conquest was evidently considerable.[6]

Continuity with the Past

Continuity with the past is likewise evident in some of the earliest texts in Middle English. It can perhaps best be seen in certain miscellaneous collections of religious material. These are made up mostly of prose pieces of varying character and length, rather loosely classified as homilies. Two such collections, the *Lambeth*[7] and *Trinity Homilies,*[8] occur in MSS written around 1200 and on linguistic grounds are thought to have been copied in London.[9] But from mistakes which the scribe makes in the Lambeth MS it is apparent that he was working over older originals and there are indications that his originals were in a dialect further to the south and west. Two of the homilies and part of a third are from Ælfric. The Trinity collection does not betray its dependence upon an older source by mistakes of the scribe, but five of its pieces are also found in the Lambeth MS and the collection is presumably based in like manner on older material. A third group, the *Bodley Homilies,*[10] is almost wholly made up of pieces from Ælfric's homilies and *Lives of Saints,* and from Wulfstan and other Old English homilists, while the fourth collection, the *Vespasian Homilies,*[11] seems to be a commonplace book of extracts and adaptations, mainly from Ælfric. There is much that is interesting from the point of view of legend and popular belief in these homiletic texts—pieces on the Eight Vices, the

[4] The Latin text of the *Lives of the Two Offas* is printed in R. W. Chambers, *Beowulf: An Introduction* (2ed., Cambridge, 1932), pp. 217-243.

[5] Cf. Chaucer, *Merchant's Tale*, E. 1424.

[6] Cf. R. W. Chambers, "The Lost Literature of Medieval England," *Library*, n.s. v (1925). 293-321; R. M. Wilson, "Lost Literature in Old and Middle English, *Leeds Studies in English and Kindred Languages,* II (1933). 14-37; "More Lost Literature in Old and Middle English," *ibid.,* v (1936). 1-49; "More Lost Literature," *ibid.,* VI (1937). 30-49; C. E. Wright, *The Cultivation of Saga in Anglo-Saxon England* (Edinburgh, 1940).

[7] Richard Morris, *Old English Homilies*, First Series (1867-8; EETS, 29 and 34), pp. 1-189.

[8] Richard Morris, *Old English Homilies*, Second Series (1873; EETS, 53).

[9] See H. C. Wyld, "South-Eastern and South-East Midland Dialects in Middle English," *E&S,* VI (1920). 112-145.

[10] Partially edited in A. O. Belfour, *Twelfth Century Homilies in MS Bodley 343* (1909; EETS, 137), and A. S. Napier, *History of the Holy Rood-tree* (1894; EETS, 103).

[11] Rubie D-N. Warner, *Early English Homilies from the Twelfth Century MS Vesp. D. xiv* (1917; EETS, 152). These are not to be confused with the four Kentish homilies in the Cotton MS Vesp. A. XXII. The sources have been fully worked out by Max Förster, "Der Inhalt der altenglischen Handschrift Vespasianus D. XIV," *ESt,* LIV (1920). 46-68.

Eight Virtues, the Seven Holy Sleepers, the Gospel of Nicodemus, the History of the Holy Rood Tree, Signs before Judgment, etc.—but we are interested in them here for the evidence they furnish of the continuity of English prose,[12] a continuity unbroken by the Norman Conquest. Such continuity in verse is less well attested, but appears to some extent in the *Worcester Fragments,* containing among other things an early form of the Body and Soul theme, and the fragment of twenty-five lines of alliterative verse known as *The Grave.*[13] Both of these are conceivably Old English pieces in a twelfth-century form.

In the search for the beginnings of Middle English verse a few short pieces assume importance on account of their age. The earliest, if we disregard the *Curse of Urse,*[14] is *Cnut's Song.* In Book II of the *Liber Eliensis,* which Cnut's is to be dated between 1108 and 1131, we are told that King Cnut, accom- Song panied by Queen Emma and important men of his kingdom, on one occasion making his way by boat to Ely to celebrate the Feast of the Purification, heard the music of the abbey service floating across the water and ordered the boatmen to pull him nearer the church while he drank in the melody. And "he himself expressing with his own lips the joy in his heart, composed a song in English in these words, the beginning of which runs thus":

> Merie sungen ðe muneches binnin Ely
> Ða Cnut ching reu ðer by.
> Roweð, cnites, noer the land
> And here we þes muneches sæng.[15]

The historian tells us that these and the verses that followed were sung even down to his own day publicly in groups (*in choris*) and that the story of their origin was preserved in popular tradition. The passage sounds like an expression of local pride in which an Ely monk called to mind an incident treasured in the monastery. A second local incident is somewhat obscurely represented in the *Here Prophecy,* five lines of verse (*c.* 1191) refer-

---

[12] See the important essay of R. W. Chambers, *On the Continuity of English Prose from Alfred to More and His School* (Oxford, 1932), originally printed in *EETS,* 186.

[13] The Worcester fragments of the *Body and Soul* and the *The Grave* (Bodl. MS 343) are printed in R. Buchholz, *Die Fragmente der Reden der Seele an den Leichnam,* in *Erlanger Beiträge,* VI (Erlangen, 1890). Cf. Louise Dudley, "The Grave," *MP,* XI (1914). 429-442, and Eleanor K. Heningham, "Old English Precursors of *The Worcester Fragments,*" *PMLA,* LV (1940). 291-307.

[14] In the conquest of the west by the Conqueror, Gloucester and Worcester were put under the sheriff Urse of Abetot, who built a castle encroaching on the lands of the monks of Worcester. The monks appealed to the Archbishop, who came and uttered a malediction against the offender, the beginning of which is quoted by William of Malmesbury:

> Hattest þu [art thou called] Urs?
> Have þu Godes kurs.

Unfortunately he gives the rest only in Latin.

[15] Merrily sang the monks within Ely
When Cnut the king rowed thereby.
Row, knights, nearer the land
And let us hear the song of the monks.

ring apparently to a place in Northamptonshire.[16] But the most interesting from a literary point of view are three little poems known as *St. Godric's*

St. Godric *Hymns.*[17] St. Godric, who died in 1170 at the somewhat mature age of a hundred and five, was born in Norfolk and after a career as a peddler, a merchant and ship-owner, and a pilgrim to Rome, Jerusalem, and other holy places, finally settled down as a hermit near Durham. In certain more or less contemporary lives of the saint are preserved the three short poems attributed to him, addressed to the Virgin and to St. Nicholas. His *Hymn to the Virgin* may be quoted for its artless charm and simple piety:

Sainte Marie, Virgine,
Moder Jesu Cristes Nazarene,
Onfo, scild, help þin Godric,   Receive, shield . . . bring him gloriously
Onfang, bring hehlic wið þe in Godes ric.   with thee in God's kingdom.

Sainte Marie, Cristes bur,   bower
Maidenes clenhad, moderes flur,   maiden's purity, flower of mothers
Dilie mine sinne, rixe in min mod,   wipe out . . . rule
Bring me to winne wið self God.   joy

The words fit the liturgical chant to which they are set in the manuscript.[18] *St. Godric's Hymns* are slight in themselves, but they are our earliest examples of the Middle English lyric.

Poema The keynote of English poetry, and indeed of English prose, in the second
Morale half of the twelfth century is struck early in one of the most important and spirited poems of this period, the *Poema Morale*[19] or the *Moral Ode* (*c.* 1170). In some four hundred lines of vigorous seven-stress verse the poet preaches a sermon on the theme, repent before it is too late. His method is suggestive of popular evangelism. He speaks first of his own misspent life and then paints the terrors of Doomsday, the torments of Hell, and the joys of Heaven. The beginning is somewhat disjointed and incoherent, but when the preacher in him begins to speak, the style becomes vivid, straightforward, and eloquent. There is a surprising note of cynicism in the opening lines. Whoever trusts too much in wife or child instead of thinking of himself is in danger of missing salvation. He will soon enough be forgotten by his friends and relatives. Such a mood, however, early gives way before the earnestness with which the author tries to make his points. The rich think to find safety in wall and ditch, but he who sends his treasure to Heaven need have no fear of fire or thief. Each man may purchase Heaven with what he has, the poor man with his penny as surely as the rich with his

[16] See discussion by W. W. Skeat and John W. Hales in *Academy*, xxx (1886). 189-190, 380-381.
[17] Edited by J. Zupitza, "Cantus Beati Godrici," *ESt*, xi (1888), 401-432. See also J. W. Rankin, "The Hymns of St. Godric," *PMLA*, xxxviii (1923). 699-711, and Irene P. McKeehan, "The First Biography of an English Poet," *Univ. of Colorado Studies*, Ser. B 1 (1941). 223-231.
[18] A facsimile of one MS is reproduced as a frontispiece to Saintsbury's *History of English Prosody*, Vol. 1 (1906).
[19] Hans Marcus, *Das Frühmittelenglische "Poema Morale," kritisch herausgegeben . . .* (Leipzig, 1934; *Palaestra*, No. 194).

pound. In the final doom a man's good works will all be known just as the devils have all his misdeeds written down. Repent now! When Death is at the door it is too late to cry for mercy. There is no virtue in hating evil when you can't do evil any more. All the terrors of Hell which the Middle Ages knew from the *Visio Pauli* are described in contrast with the joy which the blessed experience in God's presence. The wicked are enumerated in detail—those who made vows to God and didn't keep them, who led their lives in war and strife, who lied, cheated, persecuted poor men, etc., etc. The poet closes with an exhortation to choose the narrow and difficult road, the road which few follow. The poem is addressed to "simple men and poor" and must stand—as an illustration of matter and purpose—for a number of other twelfth-century pieces which we shall have to mention more briefly.

Similar in theme is a poem of 354 lines that has been named *Sinners, Beware.*[20] It lays the same emphasis on repentance and enforces its plea with a description of the pains of Hell and a warning against the Seven Deadly Sins, directed at various classes from covetous monks and mercenary priests to rich men and proud women. It recalls the horrors of the grave, where the body shall be eaten by worms, and pictures the Judgment Day when the cries of those who would not confess their sins to the priest are contrasted with the happy lot of those whom Christ recognizes as his friends who fed the hungry and clothed the poor. The poem is conventional—all too conventional—in theme, and unfortunately not distinguished in treatment. But it is remarkable in being written in the six-line stanza *aabaab* later often found in the romance and shows how far French verse patterns had penetrated into the English verse tradition by the end of the twelfth century. More flexible and easy is the style of the *Paternoster,*[21] an exposition of the Lord's Prayer in 305 four-stress lines riming in pairs. It is found among the *Lambeth Homilies* (cf. p. 118) and is obviously an intrusion among these prose pieces. But it is homiletic in spirit, explaining the meaning and purpose of each petition, and bidding "Goodmen, listen to me."

Distinct echoes of the *Poema Morale* are found in a group of poems belonging apparently shortly after the turn of the century and associated in two manuscripts.[22] They are unusually interesting, treating familiar themes in a lively and fresh spirit, in verse that shows considerable metrical skill. Most of them run from fifty to a hundred lines in length. *Long Life* serves warning that though we may expect to live long, Death "lurks in our shoes" and strikes suddenly. *An Orison of Our Lady* is a charming expression of devotion to the Virgin, who brought light where Eve brought night. This world will pass away. I have been a fool too long, says the poet. I will mend my ways. Lady, punish me in this life or let me live to correct my

Sinners, Beware

Other Religious Pieces

---

[20] *EETS*, XLIX. 72-83.
[21] *EETS*, XXIX. 55-71.
[22] Cotton Caligula A. IX and Jesus Coll. Oxford 29. In both MSS they occur together and are copied in the same order. The Cotton MS is dated before 1250. They are edited in . Morris, *An Old English Miscellany* (*EETS*, 49), pp. 156-191.

faults. I am sorry for my sins. Mercy, Lady! *Doomsday,* which follows immediately in both MSS, seems to be by the same author. When I think of Doomsday, the poet reflects, full sore I am adread. Fire will consume everything. When angels blow their trumpets the rich who wore fine clothes and rode on palfreys will sing welaway. Christ will speak sweet words to the righteous, but will banish the wicked to Hell. Let us pray our Lady, sweetest of all things, to ask Heaven's King to save us for her sake. The same thought runs through the somewhat longer poem *Death* (264 lines). Hear of one thing, it begins, ye that wear scarlet and pall and sit on your bench: no man can escape death. At the latemost day our bliss is turned to nought. No tongue can tell the pains of Hell. At death the body is sewed in a clout. Then saith the soul with sorry cheer, "Away, thou wretched, foul body,"—and so for the greater part of the poem the soul berates the body with the familiar taunts and accusations of *The Debate between the Body and the Soul.* Finally, in *A Little Sooth Sermon,* there is a deal of plain speaking:

> Herkneþ alle gode men
> 　and stylle sitteþ a-dun,
> And ich ou wile tellen　　　　　　　　　　you
> 　a lutel soþ sermun.

Adam brought us all to grief. He went to Hell. There also will go all backbiters, robbers, thieves, and lechers, and dwell there forever. So will false chapmen, bakers, and brewers, who hold the gallon down low and fill it with froth. All priests' wives shall be damned and those proud young men and women who run to each other in church and market place and speak of clandestine love. They take no thought of Mass and Matins; their paternoster is at home. Robin will take Gill to the ale house, sit and talk and pay for her ale, and she will go with him in the evening shamelessly. But the poet concludes as suddenly as he began, with an appeal to his hearers to forsake their sins. There is something refreshing about the poems in this little group, something that helps us to understand better the secular verse, such as the *Brut* and *The Owl and the Nightingale,* that was occasionally being written at about the same date.

A Good
Orison
of Our
Lady

　　More varied in theme are a few scattered pieces that deserve to be singled out from the body of religious verse that constitutes the most characteristic expression of the poetic impulse before 1250. *A Good Orison of Our Lady* [2] is the work of a poet of the West Midlands writing either, as some think, at the end of the twelfth century or more probably at the beginning of the thirteenth. In it he professes with quiet simplicity his devotion to the Virgin and prays for her protection. He will sing his *lofsong* to her by day and by night. Angels delight to honor her. All who surround her are crowned with golden crowns and Heaven is bright with her presence. He laments his many sins, but says in extenuation that he forsook all that was dear

---

[2] *EETS,* xxxiv. 191-199.

to him and gave himself wholly to her. In the closing lines he voices the hope that "all my friends may be the better today that I have sung to thee this English lay," and he prays "that thou bring the monk to joy that made this song of thee." It is a "song" in the Old English manner. The long lines at the opening, with their irregular flow and alliteration, suggest chanting to the accompaniment of a harp, but though the movement recalls the four-beat rhythm of Old English verse, the alliteration becomes sporadic and the effect of which we are finally most conscious is that of couplets bound together by end-rime. As the monk has here set his love on the Virgin, so in Thomas of Hales' *Love Rune*,[24] a poem of 210 lines written *Thomas* a generation later, a "maid of Christ" is urged to choose as her lover the *of Hales'* Heavenly Bridegroom. Worldly lovers pass: where are Paris and Helen, *Love* Amadas, Idoine, Tristan, Iseult? Christ surpasses them all in beauty and *Rune* riches; even Henry, King of England, is his vassal. His gift to his bride is virginity, most precious of gems. The poet, in fulfilling the maid's request, sends her his poem open and unsealed, with the suggestion that she learn it and sing it and hope that Christ will make her his bride. *The Passion of Our Lord*[25] is an example of the longer, narrative poem, strongly suggestive of the secular romance. In a short prologue the poet says that his tale is not of Charlemagne and his twelve peers but of Christ's passion, which is not a fiction. Its seven-stress lines break into fours and threes with a certain jog-trot swing, but the movement is rapid and the narrative anything but pedestrian with its homely touches, realistic details, and frequent resort to direct discourse. Toward the middle of the century a short poem called *When Holy Church Is under Foot*,[26] with its blaming of simony for the evil state of the Church, shows English verse turned to the frank criticism of contemporary conditions.

The Katherine Group

Up to this point all the writings which we have spoken of, except for several collections of homilies, have been in verse. In some ways the prose of the period is even more remarkable. It consists, in the first place, of five closely related pieces known from the title of one of them as the Katherine Group. They are lives of three women saints—St. Katherine, St. Margaret, and St. Juliana—and two religious treatises, *Hali Meidenhad* and *Sawles Warde*. And in the second place there is that extraordinary work, the *Ancrene Riwle,* closely associated with these but so distinctive as to deserve consideration by itself. It is impossible to assign precise dates to any of them, but general opinion places them either toward the end of the twelfth century or early in the thirteenth.

---

[24] Thomas of Hales was a Franciscan. The Franciscans came to England in 1224. The poem was probably written fairly early in the reign of Henry III (1216-1272); he is most likely the King Henry twice mentioned in it. It is printed in *EETS*, XLIX. 93-99.

[25] *EETS*, XLIX. 37-57 (706 lines).

[26] *EETS*, XLIV. 89; on the date cf. C. G. Child, *Papers in Honor. . . . of Charles Frederick Johnson* (Hartford, 1928), p. 101n.

Exaltation of Virginity

The legends and treatises composing the Katherine Group in all cases but one have as their primary aim the exaltation of virginity. They were all written in the West Midlands, the evidence of dialect pointing to Hereford shire. There are resemblances between some of them that suggest the possibility of common authorship for part of the group. And finally, they are associated in MS tradition: all five occur together in one MS, four appear as a group in another, and three are copied in close proximity in a third. None of them is ever found separately.

All three of the saints' legends tell a story of heroic resistance and ultimate martyrdom in the heroine's determination to preserve her maidenhood.

St. Katherine

St. Katherine [27] may be taken as typical. In ancient Alexandria the holy maiden Katherine one day chides the Emperor for his sacrifices to false gods. Thinking to overcome her scruples by reason, he sends for fifty of his finest scholars. But she overcomes them and they confess themselves powerless before the argument of one supported by the true God. The Emperor has them all burnt and they die the happy death of martyrs. He next tries flattery on Katherine, and the promise of worldly honors. But she replies that nothing "can turn me from the love of my beloved, in whom I believe. He has wedded himself to my virgin state with the ring of true belief ... He is my life and my love, ... my wealth and my joy; nor do I desire anything else." After this she is stripped and beaten and thrown into prison, where she remains for twelve days without food. During this time she is visited by the Queen and the captain of the guard. Both are converted and the captain in turn converts the two hundred knights in his company. Tortures are prepared—four wheels fitted with spikes, turning two by two in opposite directions. At the prayer of the saint God shatters the wheels, killing full four thousand "of that accursed folk" as they stood round about. "There one might have heard the heathen hounds yell and cry and scream on every side, the Christians laugh." The Queen addresses her husband: "Wretched man that thou art, wherefore wilt thou wrestle with the world's ruler? What madness maketh thee, thou bitter baleful beast, to war against Him who created thee and all earthly things? ..." For this affectionate outburst she is tortured and put to death. The captain of the guard suffers a like fate. Katherine is finally beheaded, and miracles accompany her burial.

St. Margaret

It has been necessary to recount the story at some length in order to convey an idea of the subject matter and tone of these legends. *St. Margaret* [28] is very similar in story and treatment although Margaret, unlike Katherine does not court martyrdom. Her struggles are to escape marriage, but she undergoes like torture and suffers the same end. There is the same intemperate language. She rails at her intended husband: "Thou workest the works of thy father, the wicked one, the fiend of Hell. But, thou heathen hound, the High Healer is my help; and if he have granted to thee my body to tear, he will, thou hateful reeve, rid my soul out of thy hands and

[27] E. Einenkel, *The Life of Saint Katherine* (1884; EETS, 80).
[28] Frances M. Mack, *Seinte Marherete* (1934; EETS, 193).

carry it to Heaven." In prison she is swallowed by a dragon, but she has made the sign of the cross, which causes the dragon to burst asunder, and the maiden steps forth unharmed. She is visited by a black devil, but she cows him and beats him and sets her foot upon his rough neck until he cries, "Lady, loose thy foot off my neck!" The differences between the two lives are accounted for by difference of source, but the resemblances are in features and in details that do not occur in the Latin legends which lie behind the English texts. *St. Katherine* and *St. Margaret* are either by the same author or *St. Margaret* was written by some one who knew the *St. Katherine* well.[29]

St. Juliana[30] is also a story of resistance to marriage. There are many marks of resemblance to both of the legends previously mentioned, but the tone is somewhat more restrained and the little touches that unite the *St. Katherine* and the *St. Margaret* are not so apparent here.

St. Juliana

Hali Meidenhad[31] is an extended glorification of virginity in contrast with the baseness and grievous annoyances of marriage. Vehemence and strong conviction make up for the absence of a logical plan. There is little or no progression, but a single idea runs through the whole treatise—that virginity is in every way preferable to marriage. The idea is supported by the constant recurrence of two arguments: virginity is the state most pleasing to God, and marriage is not the happy lot that most people expect to find it. It is particularly in the latter argument that the author is at his best. "Ask even queens, and countesses, and proud ladies about their life. If they acknowledge the truth I will have them for witness that they lick honey off thorns." His picture of fleshly intercourse is so vivid that it shocked his first editor into Latin, for his rendering. It is a sorry picture that he paints of married life—quarrels between husband and wife, the pains of childbirth, the trials of the mother. When she comes in she hears the child scream, sees the cat at the flitch and the hound at the hide; her cake is burning on the hearth and the calf sucks all the milk; the crock spills into the fire and the churl scolds. In the light of such pictures of the married woman's life it is with good reason that the author urges the real or imaginary maiden for whom he writes to choose single blessedness and to think of Christ as her husband. In its wealth of homely illustration, its fondness for the proverbial phrase, and its sustained interest *Hali Meidenhad* is strongly suggestive of the *Ancrene Riwle,* but the uncompromising attitude towards marriage makes one hesitate to attribute it to the same author.

Hali Meidenhad

[29] E. Einenkel, "Über den Verfasser der neuangelsächsischen Legende von Katharina," *Anglia,* v (1882). 91-123, argues that the *St. Katharine* was written first, that the other two legends were by a different author who used the *St. Katharine,* and that *Hali Meidenhad* was written after the *St. Margaret* by still a third author.

[30] S.T.R.O. d'Ardenne, *An Edition of þe Liflade ant te Passiun of Seint Iuliene* (Liége, 1936; *Bibl. de la Faculté de Philos. et Lettres de l'Université de Liége,* LXIV); also O. Cockayne, *The Life of St. Juliana* (1872; EETS, 51). For Cynewulf's treatment of the theme see above, p. 72.

[31] A. F. Colborn, *Hali Meiðhad* (Copenhagen, 1940); also O. Cockayne, *Hali Meidenhad* (1866; EETS. 18). new edition by F. J. Furnivall (1922).

Sawles Warde

The homily called *Sawles Warde* [32] ("The Safeguarding of Soul"), although found in all three MSS with which the Katherine Group is identified, stands somewhat apart in theme and style. It makes only incidental mention of virginity. It is an elaborate allegory of the house, symbolizing the body, whose master is Wit and whose mistress is Will. The precious treasure of this house is the soul, guarded by the four cardinal virtues. Most of the treatise is made up of the discourse of two visitors—Fear, the messenger of death, and Love of Life, messenger of mirth. One describes at length the pains of Hell, the other the joys of Heaven. It is an adaptation of a treatise of Hugh of St. Victor called *De Anima*.

Prose or Verse?

The prose style of the legends in the Katherine Group and of *Hali Meidenhad* is marked by the frequent use of alliteration, and the rhythm of the sentences is such that it can sometimes be read (with much forcing of the accent) as a kind of verse, which has been compared to that of the Old High German poet Otfrid in his *Krist*. [33] But it is a mistake to think of these pieces as anything but prose.

Prominence of the Southwest

It is important to point out that such literary activity in English before 1250 as is surveyed in this chapter is practically confined to the west and south of England. There are also reasons for assigning to the west the *Ancrene Riwle*, which is the subject of the next chapter. Later we shall have occasion to speak of the *Ormulum*, which belongs to the northeast Midlands, the Essex *Vices and Virtues*, and the *Proverbs of Alfred*, which seems to have originated near the southern border of the East Midlands. [34] But of the works so far considered practically all appear to have been written in the West Midlands or within the limits of the late West Saxon kingdom. Two small collections of Kentish sermons [35] lie outside the area, but the rest all belong on the evidence of dialect to the west and south. Were it not for the fact that English was still being written in Essex and Kent and London (*Lambeth* and *Trinity Homilies*) we should be led to believe that a literary tradition in English lived on only where French influence was less felt. As it is, we must attribute its other than sporadic survival to the strength of the Old English culture in the districts which had least felt the devastating effects of the Scandinavian invasions and which had been most directly under the rule of Alfred and his successors.

[32] Edited by R. M. Wilson (Leeds, 1938); also in *EETS*, xxxiv. 245-267.
[33] Cf. Einenkel, *op. cit.*; opposed by Schipper, *History of English Versification* (1910), and others.
[34] All of these belong to the twelfth or the beginning of the thirteenth century, and are thus contemporary with the literature here under consideration.
[35] That in MS Vesp. A. xxii has been mentioned in footnote 11, above. The other, consisting of five short expositions in MS Laud 471, is of little interest except that the texts are translations of French originals, which accompany them in the MS, and show a considerable French element in the vocabulary, a fact which throws an interesting sidelight on the extent to which French words were understood by English listeners at the beginning of the thirteenth century.

III

The Ancrene Riwle

The *Ancrene Riwle* [1] ("Rule for Anchoresses") is the most remarkable prose work in English literature between King Alfred and Malory. To every new reader it comes as a complete surprise that anything with so unpromising a title should have so much interest and charm. Its appeal is not in its subject, since this has lost much of its significance in a materialistic and often skeptical world. But the freshness of its treatment and the personality of its author which shines through every page remain undimmed after the lapse of seven centuries. In two hundred pages of modern print this anonymous treatise offers a complete guide to, and a warm justification of, the anchoress's life. It is carefully planned throughout its eight distinctions or books. Book one is devoted entirely to religious observances and devotional exercises. Then follow books on the five senses as guardians of the heart, the advantages of a life of retirement from the world, the temptations fleshly and spiritual which must be resisted, confession, penitence, and the love of Christ. The eighth and last book gives specific advice on domestic matters—food, clothing, attendants, and a variety of small but important and interesting points.

One circumstance that lends an attractive personal quality to the treatise is the fact that it was not written for an unknown or imaginary audience but was composed at the request of three young women who had apparently long been known to the author. They were sisters in the literal sense of the word. He says, "There is much talk of you, how gentle women you are; for your goodness and nobleness of mind beloved of many; and sisters of one father and of one mother, having in the bloom of your youth, forsaken all the pleasures of the world and become anchoresses." Not only were they young when they entered upon their life of seclusion, but they were still young at the time the book was written, as the general tone implies. The phrase "gentle women," moreover, is no mere allusion to mildness of manner. They were almost certainly connected with a family of some social position and wealth. "I know not any anchoress that with more abundance, or more honor, hath all that is necessary to her than ye three have; our *Composed for Three Sisters*

Their Social Position

---

[1] The only edition at present is that of James Morton, *The Ancren Riwle* (1853) in the Camden Society, Vol. LVII, which contains a translation on opposite pages. The translation can be had separately in the *King's Classics* (now the *Medieval Library*) under the somewhat misleading title *The Nun's Rule* (1905). A new edition of all the MSS is in preparation for the EETS by a group of scholars. In this series two volumes have appeared: *The Latin Text of the Ancrene Riwle*, ed. Charlotte D'Evelyn (1944; EETS, 216), and *The French Text of the Ancrene Riwle*, ed. J. A. Herbert (1944; EETS, 219). In the present book the spelling *Ancrene Riwle*, adopted by the EETS, is used.

Lord be thanked for it. For ye take no thought for food or clothing, neither for yourself nor for your maidens. Each of you hath from one friend all that she requireth; nor need that maiden seek either bread, or that which is eaten with bread, further than at his hall." They were permitted two servants. Their education suggests that of the upper class. The author quotes Latin at the very beginning without translation, although in general his practice is to translate or paraphrase his Latin citations, and the young women are advised to read either in French or English. Always the author seems anxious not to overtax their endurance and he urges them strongly not to take any vows: "for, whoso undertaketh any thing, and promises to God to do it as his command, binds herself thereto, and sinneth mortally in breaking it, if she break it wilfully and intentionally. If, however, she does not vow it, she may, nevertheless, do it, and leave it off when she will...." It is as though he realized the possibility that they might not be able to endure the life they had entered upon.[2] Although such advice is not unknown to other treatises of the kind, all this is consonant with the avowal that his rules are not intended "for any but you alone." Such a purpose is not inconsistent with a realization that his book might come into the hands of others and therefore with his speaking occasionally as though he had a wider audience in mind.

Versions in English, Latin, and French   That his treatise attained to this wider circulation is evident from the number of surviving MSS [3] and from the fact that there were versions in Latin and French as well as English.[4] A question has naturally arisen as to the language in which it was originally composed. We may be sure that it was not Latin. The Latin version contains numerous mistakes which are demonstrably due to misinterpreting the English. In the case of the French the evidence of translation is less obvious but is quite decisive.[5] Moreover, manuscripts of the English text were in the late thirteenth and the fourteenth century in the possession of religious houses with strong aristocratic connections, in which French was certainly the more familiar language and which would have preferred a French version if one had been obtainable.[6] It was not unsuitable to private individuals, for it is in many ways an admirable treatise on morals and a universal guide to piety. It is for this reason

[2] It should be remembered, however, that St. Bernard had written in the same vein concerning vows.

[3] Counting complete and fragmentary texts and including adaptations, there are seventeen MSS now known: eleven in English, four in Latin, two in French.

[4] A growing list of quotations and echoes from it is further evidence of its distribution.

[5] G. C. Macaulay, "The Ancren Riwle," *MLR*, IX (1914). 63-78; 145-160; 324-331; 463-474, an article which contains much useful matter, argues for the priority of the French version. His views were partially answered by Dorothy M. E. Dymes, "The Original Language of the *Ancren Riwle*," *E&S*, IX (1924). 31-49.

[6] The earliest MS of the French text dates from the end of the thirteenth or the beginning of the fourteenth century. The translation was probably made at about this time. On the French text in the Trinity MS see the paper of Miss Hope Emily Allen in *Essays and Studies in Honor of Carleton Brown* (1940), pp. 182-219. On the early ownership of the English MSS the researches of Miss Allen will throw much light. As yet her results are only partially available in her communication to the *LTLS*, Feb. 8, 1936, supplementing her discussion in *MLR*, XXVIII (1933). 485-487.

that it was so easily adapted later to the needs of men and the conditions of monastic life.

What is it that distinguishes this book from other devotional treatises and *The* justifies the high position which it occupies in early English literature? It *Author's* is in the final analysis the personality of the author and the extent to which *Personality* that personality colors all his writing. His qualities of mind and temperament are as attractive to us as they must have been to the three young women for whom he wrote. There is, for example, his independence and remarkable freedom from the conventional attitudes of the ordinary religious writer of the Middle Ages. This independence is shown from the very beginning of his book where he replies to a rather orthodox question— "What rule should the three sisters follow?"—in a very unorthodox way. He tells them that the external rule that they follow is a very minor matter compared with the inward rule which imposes on them genuine piety and obedience to the dictates of their conscience. "All may," he says, "and ought to observe one rule concerning purity of heart, that is, a clean unstained conscience... But all men cannot, nor need they, nor ought they to keep the outward rule in the same unvaried manner.... The external rule... ordains fasting, watching, enduring cold, wearing haircloth, and such other hardships as the flesh of many can bear and many cannot. Wherefore, this rule may be changed and varied according to every one's state and circumstances. For some are strong, some are weak, and may very well be excused, and please God with less; some are learned, some are not, and must work the more, and say their prayers at the stated hours in a different manner; some are old and ill-favored, of whom there is less fear; some are young and lively, and have need to be more on their guard. Every anchoress must, therefore, observe the outward rule according to the advice of her confessor, and do obediently whatever he enjoins and commands her, who knows her state and strength. He may modify the outward rule, as prudence may direct, and as he sees that the inward rule may thus be best kept." In like manner he says, "If any ignorant person ask you of what order you are, as ye tell me some do, who strain at the gnat and swallow the fly, answer and say that ye are of the order of Saint James." This is a very novel solution of their problem, for of course there was no order of St. James, but St. James, as he says, defined pure religion as visiting and assisting widows and fatherless children and keeping oneself pure and unstained from the world. "Herein is religion, and not in the wide hood, nor in the black, nor in the white, nor in the gray cowl." This is hardly a position which many in the Middle Ages would have dared to take and this independent attitude runs all through the book.

Equally refreshing is a certain boldness of speech. His reference to the *His* anchoress who is old and ill-favored and who is therefore less likely to be *Candor* tempted will be recalled in the passage already quoted. There are many such instances of candor. He tells his spiritual sisters that they shall take communion only fifteen times a year because "men esteem a thing as less dainty when they have it often." In advising them to spend some of their time in reading, he says, "Often, dear sisters, ye ought to pray less, that ye may read more. Reading is good prayer. Reading teacheth how, and for what, we ought to pray." He is sometimes blunt. In recommending silence he contrasts Eve's willingness to carry on a conversation with the Devil with Mary's modest demeanor at the Annunciation, and he concludes, "Do you, my dear sisters, imitate Our Lady, and not the cackling Eve." He shows a wholesome disrespect for the Devil, calls him "the old ape" and elsewhere says "he is such an old fool." Perhaps the most striking instances of his readiness to say what comes to mind are his allusions to clerical lapses concerning which reticence was more commonly the order of the day—that is, where we do not have to do with the avowed satirist or reformer. In treating of confession he directs the anchoress to be specific as to the person with whom she committed a sin. "Sir, it was with such a man; and then name him—a monk, a priest, or clerk, and of such an order, a married man, an innocent creature, a woman." There is something startling about the order which he adopts in this enumeration. At confession, he says, "let there be a third person present. . . . Some unhappy creature, when she said that she was at confession, has confessed herself strangely." He can even become ironical on occasion about his professional brethren. "Bathsheba, by unclothing herself in David's sight, caused him to sin with her, though he was so holy a king and God's prophet: and now, a feeble man comes forward and esteems himself highly if he have a wide hood and a close cope, and would see young anchoresses, and must needs look, as if he were of stone, how their fairness pleases him, who have not their complexion sunburnt, and saith that they may look confidently upon holy men, yea, especially such as he is, because of his wide sleeves." We cannot help being drawn to a man who is so free from restraint and whose honesty gives him the courage to be so outspoken.

Descriptive and Narrative Gifts

The author's knowledge of human nature is not the least of his qualifications for writing such a book as he has written, and it results in a number of excursions which anticipate the "characters" of Nicholas Breton and of Overbury.

The greedy glutton is the devil's purveyor; for he always haunts the cellar or the kitchen. His heart is in the dishes; all his thought is of the tablecloth; his life is in the tun, his soul in the pitcher. He cometh into the presence of his Lord besmutted and besmeared, with a dish in one hand, and a bowl in the other. He talks much incoherently, and staggereth like a drunken man who seemeth about to fall, looks at his great belly, and the devil laughs till he bursts.

His description of flatterers and his picture of the backbiter are masterly and have often been quoted. Perhaps less familiar is his vignette of the ways of the seducer:

No seduction is so perfidious as that which is in a plaintive strain; as if one spoke thus: "I would rather suffer death, than indulge an impure thought with regard to you; but had I sworn it, I could not help loving you; and yet I am grieved that you know it. But yet forgive me that I have told you of it; and, though I should go mad, thou shalt never after this know how it is with me." And she forgives him, because he speaks thus fair, and then they talk of other matters. But 'the eye is ever towards the sheltering wood, wherein is that I love.' The heart is ever upon what was said before; and still, when he is gone, she often revolves such words in her thoughts, when she ought to attend diligently to something else. He afterwards seeketh an opportunity to break his promise, and swears that necessity forces him to do it; and thus the evil grows, the longer the worse; for no enmity is so bad as false friendship. An enemy who seems a friend is of all traitors the most treacherous.

In a similar vein is his description of how the newly-wed husband breaks in a wife—in the medieval fashion—but there is not space for all the delightful passages in a work from which there is so much one could quote.

No analysis of the qualities which stand out in the *Ancrene Riwle* and *His* make it so attractive would be adequate which did not lay particular stress *Style* on the incidental features of its style—its proverbial quality, its bestiary allusions, its familiar illustrations from everyday life, its homespun metaphors, its humor. The author is very fond of proverbial wisdom. "Thus often, as is said, of little waxeth mickle"; "the dog enters gladly where he finds an open door"; "the cock is brave on his own dunghill." He has a rich fund of animal lore which he uses to point his moral—the pelican who pierces her own breast, the eagle who "deposits in his nest a precious stone which is called agate" and which keeps off poisonous things, the thievish fox and his cunning. Perhaps his most attractive illustrations are drawn from his own observation of the life about him. "Reflect again thus: that if a child stumble against any thing, or hurt himself, men beat the thing that he hurteth himself upon, and the child is well pleased, and forgetteth all his hurt, and stoppeth his tears." In another place he says, "Our Lord, when He suffereth us to be tempted, playeth with us, as the mother with her young darling: she flies from him, and hides herself, and lets him sit alone, and look anxiously around, and call Dame! dame! and weep a while, and then leapeth forth laughing, with outspread arms, and embraceth and kisseth him, and wipeth his eyes." If all his illustrations cannot have this same kind of charm, they nevertheless have the appeal of homely and familiar things. "A small patch may greatly disfigure a whole garment." "Our Lord doth to us as men do to a bad debtor; he accepteth less than we owe him, and yet is well satisfied." "When greedy dogs stand before the board, is there not need of a rod?" "A man ties a knot upon his belt, that he may be reminded of anything." Sometimes his figures have the simple beauty of the Bible: "All who are in heaven shall be as swift as man's thought now is, and as the sunbeam that darts from east to west, and as the eye openeth and shutteth." He has a beautiful symbol for the Crucifixion: "The true sun in the morning-tide ascended up on the high cross for the purpose of diffusing the warm rays of his love over all." But with all the high seriousness that is never absent from his purpose, he can be whimsical on occasion, as when he remarks that confession erases sin and gives the Devil less writing to do! And we could not miss the dry humor of a man who, in an earnest warning against the temptations of the flesh, can say, "The old woman spoke very truly, when with a single straw all her house caught fire, that 'much cometh of little.' "

Book VIII   The section which seems to have been least regarded in the Middle Ages— it is sometimes missing in the MSS—is the eighth book. But to the modern reader it often has the greatest appeal. It is the book in which the author gathers together his instructions covering the sisters' physical needs. It is here that we catch a glimpse of the actual life of the anchoress. As we would expect, he shows here the same moderation and the same liberal attitude in matters of food and dress as he displays on spiritual issues, but he touches on many details and these not only give the book its completeness but are the chief reason that it interests so much the modern reader. The little things are often the most interesting. "Wear no iron, nor haircloth, nor hedgehog-skins; ... do not with holly nor with briars cause yourselves to bleed without leave of your confessor." "In summer ye are at liberty to go and sit barefoot." "Ye shall eat no flesh nor lard except in great sickness ... and accustom yourselves to little drink. Nevertheless, dear sisters, your meat and your drink have seemed to me less than I would have it. Fast no day upon bread and water, except ye have leave. There are anchoresses who make their meals with friends outside the convent. That is too much friend- ship, because, of all orders, then is it most ungenial, and most contrary to the order of the anchoress, who is quite dead to the world. We have often heard it said that dead men speak with living men; but that they eat with living men, I have never yet found." The anchoress must not make purses to give her friends, or become a schoolmistress. She must not keep cattle. "For then she must think of the cow's fodder, and of the herdsman's hire, flatter the hayward, defend herself when her cattle is shut up in the pinfold, and moreover pay the damage. Christ knoweth, it is an odious thing when people in the town complain of anchoresses' cattle." The behavior of the servants is considered at some length. They should not "munch fruit or anything else between meals." The one who goes out on errands, "let her be very plain, or of sufficient age." No matter in this section is too small for his notice, and for this we can only rejoice.

Identity   We may now ask when and by whom this remarkable book was written.
of the   And the answer is not easy. Our earliest manuscripts of the work were
Three   written when the first quarter of the thirteenth century was already past—
Sisters   1230 is a rough approximation to their date. But they are not the original;
they are copies in some cases two or more removes from the author's auto- graph. How long before was the original written?

In 1918 Miss Hope Emily Allen, in an article of great importance,[7] directed attention to the granting, sometime between 1127 and 1134, of

---

[7] Hope Emily Allen, "The Origin of the *Ancren Riwle*," *PMLA*, XXXIII (1918). 474-546. See also the same author's "On the Author of the *Ancren Riwle*," *PMLA*, XLIV (1929). 635-680.

Kilburn priory as a hermitage to "tribus puellis, Emmae, videlicet, et Gunildae et Cristinae"—i.e., to three unmarried women named Emma, Gunhilda, and Christina—by the abbot and convent of Westminster. Kilburn priory was in Hampstead, then about five miles outside of London and now a part of greater London. A later tradition at Westminster tells us that the beneficiaries of the grant had been maids-in-waiting (*domicellae camerae*) of Queen Maud, wife of Henry I. Many of the circumstances of the three sisters in the *Ancrene Riwle* fit the facts which can be learned about the Kilburn foundation. In a subsequent paper [8] Miss Allen proposed to identify the Emma, Gunhilda, and Christina of the Kilburn grant with three daughters of a certain Deorman, who gave lands, with the consent of their brother Ordgar, to Westminster abbey on condition that they should enjoy the full "society" of the church. The grant is allowed in a royal writ of Henry I. Their names are not mentioned in the writ and their identity with the recluses rests merely upon what Miss Allen calls "the extreme rarity of medieval trios of devout women."

If the double hypothesis here suggested should prove to be true, it would *Miss* clear up a number of questions. It would, of course, identify the three *Allen's* sisters for whom the *Ancrene Riwle* was written. The Deormans were a *Hypo-* prominent and aristocratic Anglo-Saxon or Anglo-Danish family. The Kil- *thesis: Its* burn recluses have English or Scandinavian names. If they were Deorman's *Importance* daughters and were also the sisters of the *Ancrene Riwle* we could under- stand why this work, composed for women of gentle or noble blood, should have been written in English at a time when the language of the English court was French. And it would strongly suggest that the author was Godwin, hermit of Kilburn, who was the master in charge of the Kilburn recluses.

It must be admitted, however, that the acceptance of this very attractive *Certain* hypothesis presents certain difficulties. It would compel us to date the *Difficulties* *Ancrene Riwle* not later than *c.* 1140, and this is rather early. Certain parts of Book VI seem to be based upon the *Sententiae Exceptae* of Geoffrey of Auxerre, a work which must apparently be dated after 1153.[9] If so, it is hard to see how the three sisters of the *Ancrene Riwle* could have been treated as still young at a date subsequent to this, if they had once been in attendance upon Queen Maud, who died in 1118. A second objection is the fact that the earliest associations of the *Ancrene Riwle* are with the west. Practically all the earliest MSS are in the West Midland dialect and several of them have been convincingly assigned to Hereford and Worcestershire, the district with which the Katherine Group is associated on similar linguis- tic grounds. When we consider the close association, in theme, manuscript

---

[8] "The Three Daughters of Deorman," *PMLA*, L (1935). 899-902.

[9] R. W. Chambers, "Recent Research upon the *Ancren Riwle*," *RES*, I (1925). 4-23. Beatrice White, "The Date of the *Ancrene Riwle*," *MLR*, XL (1945). 206-207, argues that the reference in Book VII to Christ nailed to the Cross with one foot on top of the other suggests a date not earlier than 1200, and Morton W. Bloomfield believes that the treatment of the Deadly Sins can hardly be earlier than the beginning of the thirteenth century (*The Seven Deadly Sins,* East Lansing, 1952, p. 148).

tradition,[10] and allusion,[11] of the *Ancrene Riwle* with the Katherine Group one feels that any evidence that would place its composition in the neighborhood of London, or indeed, anywhere but in the west, and at a date far removed from 1200, must be very clear. The origin of the *Ancrene Riwle* is admittedly still an open question.[12]

The
Author
We are accordingly thrown back upon the text itself for our knowledge of the author. From what has already been said and from many other indications scattered through his work, it is apparent that he was a man of maturity, both in judgment and in years. His position was such as to put him beyond the fear of criticism or rebuke. He was probably no obscure priest. He was a man of sound common sense, moderate and reasonable, never extreme in his views or fanatical. His only obsession seems to have been his abhorrence and fear of sensual indulgence. He was completely candid and free from any trace of hypocrisy. Without being of the world, he was not remote from it or ignorant of its ways. Above all, he was a kindly, benevolent spirit, one in whom a genuinely large nature was united with a becoming modesty and true simplicity of soul.[13]

10 All three MSS in which the pieces composing the Katherine Group are found also contain the *Ancrene Riwle*.

11 The *Ancrene Riwle* alludes to "the devil Ruffin, Belial's brother, in our English book of St. Margaret," and one can hardly doubt that this is the *St. Margaret* of the Katherine Group. The statement "Concerning those joys [of Heaven] ye have something written in another place" looks like a reference to *Sawles Warde*, another text of the Katherine Group, although this cannot be proved.

12 No one is more open-minded about it than Miss Allen. A good bit of discussion has grown out of her original paper. In addition to the articles cited in the preceding notes, a few further references may be given. Vincent McNabb, "The Authorship of the *Ancren Riwle*," *MLR*, xi (1916). 1-8; "Further Light on the *Ancren Riwle*," *MLR*, xv (1920). 406-409; H. E. Allen, "The *Ancren Riwle* and Kilburn Priory," *MLR*, xvi (1921). 316-322; G. G. Coulton, "The Authorship of *Ancren Riwle*," *MLR*, xvii (1922). 66-69; H. E. Allen, "On the Author of the *Ancren Riwle*," *PMLA*, xliv (1929). 635-680; J. R. R. Tolkien, "Ancrene Wisse and Hali Meiðhad," *E&S*, xiv (1929). 104-126. Father McNabb's later articles have not added anything of significance to his previous arguments.

13 Four pieces of impassioned prose are found individually in MSS containing the *Ancrene Riwle*. The finest of them, *The Wooing of Our Lord*, is in a MS which contains some of the Katherine Group as well. It is a lyrical address to Christ in terms of passionate endearment, and may have been written by a woman. Cf. E. Einenkel, "Eine englische Schriftstellerin aus dem Anfange des 12. Jahrhunderts," *Anglia*, v (1882). 265-282, whose dating of the text is hardly consonant with his opinion that it was written by one of the anchoresses of the *Ancrene Riwle*. Two of the other pieces, *An Orison of Our Lord* and *A Lovesong of Our Lord*, express similar emotions. All contain at times phrases echoing now the *Ancrene Riwle*, now *Hali Meidenhad* and *St. Margaret*. The fourth piece, *A Lovesong of Our Lady*, addresses the Virgin in terms of equal affection. All four are printed in *EETS*. 34.

IV
Anglo-Norman Literature[1]

In an age when the song and recitation of the minstrel were the almost *French* universal entertainment of the upper classes at meals and in the evening *Literature* and indeed at all times when they could not find their recreation out of *in England* doors, literature was well-nigh indispensable. Since, as we have already seen, the language of the higher classes for more than two hundred years after the Norman Conquest was either wholly or mainly French, any literature that would be intelligible to them would have to be in that language. Naturally the whole body of French literature was at their disposal, but a nation seldom remains for any length of time solely dependent upon foreign sources even for its pleasure. It is not surprising, therefore, to find early in the twelfth century French poets in England, attracted no doubt by an aristocracy freely spending its newly acquired wealth. During the twelfth and thirteenth centuries much that is important in Old French literature was written in England. The dialect in which it was written is known as Anglo-Norman, and this body of writings as Anglo-Norman literature.

Patronage is the life blood of court poets. Where there is generous pa- *Courtly* tronage there is sure to be literature. The Conqueror himself is said to have *Patrons* been indifferent to poets; he may well have been completely occupied with the practical matters of conquest and administration. His successor, William Rufus, was without soul or intellect. But with the accession in the year 1100 of Henry I, the Conqueror's youngest son, literary activity at the court makes its appearance. It is probably not so much the result of his own encouragement—the nickname Beauclerc, which he enjoyed, seems not to have been wholly deserved—as of the fact that he was twice married, both times to women of literary tastes. His first wife Matilda (Queen Maud), though English born, seems to have cultivated French poetry with enthusiasm. The poet Guy of Amiens was her almoner. "Her generosity becoming universally known," says William of Malmesbury, "crowds of scholars, equally famed for verse and for singing, came over." Adelaide

---

[1] For a readable and admirably clear survey of the more important writings in Anglo-Norman see E. Walberg, *Quelques aspects de la littérature anglo-normande* (Paris, 1936); for a comprehensive list of Anglo-Norman texts, with bibliographical annotations, J. Vising, *Anglo-Norman Language & Literature* (London, 1923); and for a suggestive analysis of the Norman character, Gaston Paris, *La Littérature normande avant l'annexion* (Paris, 1899). Those who wish to savor the more important Anglo-Norman texts mentioned in this chapter will often find selections in Paget Toynbee, *Specimens of Old French* (Oxford, 1892), P. Studer and E. Waters, *Historical French Reader* (Oxford, 1924), and in the *Chrestomathies* of Bartsch, Constans, etc. The publications of the *Anglo-Norman Text Society* (since 1939) are making available a number of longer texts.

of Louvain, Henry's second wife, whom he married in 1121, is even better known as a patron. She had a poet named David who composed a rimed history of her husband's achievements, which is lost. We know of it through Gaimar, who boasts that he knew more tales than David ever knew or than Adelaide had in books. For her Philippe de Thaün wrote his *Bestiaire* (*infra*) and Benedeit his *Voyage de St. Brendan* (p. 139). Nor were Henry's queens the only patrons of letters at his court. Gaimar's *Estorie des Engles* is dedicated to "Custance la gentil," wife of Ralph Fitz Gilbert, while Samson de Nanteuil translated the *Proverbs of Solomon* into French verse for Adelaide de Condé. During the troubled years of Stephen's reign and his contest with Matilda poetry seems to have suffered a decline, although during this period Robert, Earl of Gloucester, the natural son of Henry I and one of the greatest patrons of letters in England, was generous in his encouragement of scholars and literary men. With the accession of Henry II and his queen, the famous Eleanor of Aquitaine, the English court became a veritable center of scholarly and literary activity. Henry II's own amazing energy was not confined to judicial reform and administrative reorganization, for which history remembers him, but extended over a wide range of intellectual interests. More than a score of books bear dedications to him, from Adelard of Bath's treatise *On the Astrolabe* to the *Lais* of Marie de France.[2] Eleanor is frequently mentioned in the verses of the troubadours and it was to her that Wace presented his *Roman de Brut*. It was under such auspices that Anglo-Norman literature had its beginnings. Its continuation in the century that follows was made possible by similar encouragement and support from the aristocratic classes.

Character of Anglo-Norman Literature

The Norman temperament was essentially practical. Neither romantic sentiment, nor mysticism, nor lyric cry have much part in the literature of Normandy or Norman England. But curiosity, it would seem, needed constantly to be gratified, and themes of a religious or moral nature are very numerous and imply a wide appeal. Viewed as a whole, Anglo-Norman literature is prevailingly moral and edifying, and relatively 'poor in works frankly romantic and fictional. This is well illustrated in the poems of the earliest Anglo-Norman poet known to us, Philippe de Thaün. His first work was a *Comput* (before 1120), a verse treatise on the calendar and the ways of determining the movable festivals of the Church, to which he added certain symbolical interpretations. His *Bestiary* is a type of poem about which we shall have more to say later, in which highly fanciful characteristics of animals are made the basis of a rather forced moral. He

Philippe de Thaün

---

[2] C. H. Haskins, "Henry II as a Patron of Literature," *Essays in Medieval History presented to Thomas Frederick Tout* (Manchester, 1925), pp. 71-77. On the reign of Henry II as an age of literary activity see William Stubbs, "Learning and Literature at the Court of Henry II," *Seventeen Lectures on Medieval and Modern History* (3ed., Oxford, 1900), chs. VI and VII, and on the general subject of patronage, Karl J. Holzknecht, *Literary Patronage in the Middle Ages* (Philadelphia, 1923). See also Josiah C. Russell, "The English Court as an Intellectual Center (1199-1227)," in *Three Short Studies* (Colorado Springs, 1927; *Colorado College Pub.,* Gen. Ser. No. 148), pp. 60-69. For Custance la gentil and her husband see Alex. Bell, "Gaimar's Patron: Raul le fiz Gilebert," *N&Q*, 12 Ser., VIII. 104.

composed also a *Lapidary*, if not several, dealing with the characteristics and virtues of precious stones.[3] There are numerous other lapidaries in Anglo-Norman,[4] all of which go back to an eleventh-century Latin poem called *De Gemmis*, by Marbode, Bishop of Rennes, which enjoyed an immense vogue throughout the Middle Ages. Of similar didactic aim are the *Distichs of Cato*, translated into Anglo-Norman no less than three times, and a rather uninspired poem of 3000 lines called *La Petite Philosophie*,[5] a compendium of geography and cosmography.

There is a grain of truth in the statement that an uninteresting biography has never been written, and the English court seems early to have been attracted by this type of narrative. The lost poem of David on the achievements of Henry I has already been mentioned. Although Henry II at times initiated literary work, we may be quite sure he did not order the *Vie de Saint Thomas le Martyr*,[6] which was written shortly after the murder, by Garnier (more properly Guernes), a clerk of Pont-Sainte-Maxence, who came to England in 1174 expressly to collect his material on the spot and finish his poem. About 1170 Denis Piramus composed *La Vie Seint Edmund le Rei* in more than 4000 lines of eight-syllable verse.[7] At the time he was probably a monk of Bury St. Edmunds, though his earlier life had been spent, as he tells us, amidst the follies of the court, where he had written "serventeis, chanceunettes, rimes, saluz entre les drues e les drus." In the thirteenth century, at a date now generally thought to be about 1250 or shortly thereafter a life of the famous archbishop was written, apparently by no less a person than the celebrated chronicler Matthew Paris.[8] At approximately the same time (*c.* 1245) Henry of Avranches wrote *La Estorie de Seint Aedward le Rei* in 4680 lines and dedicated it to the Queen, for which (and a life of St. George) he received £10 from the Exchequer.[9] The most remarkable of Anglo-Norman biographies is the anonymous *Histoire de Guillaume le Maréchal*,[10] the celebrated Earl of Pembroke, running to some 19,000 lines. It was written at the command of the Earl's son and is not only important for its historical accuracy but is remarkable for its lifelike picture and vivid narrative.

Religious and Secular Biography

[3] Philippe de Thaün's poems may be read in E. Mall, *Li Cumpoz Philipe de Thaün* (Strassburg, 1873), E. Walberg, *Le Bestiaire de Philippe de Thaün* (Lund, 1900), and Studer and Evans (as below), pp. 201-259.

[4] Paul Studer and Joan Evans, *Anglo-Norman Lapidaries* (Paris, 1924).

[5] Wm. H. Trethewey, *La Petite Philosophie, An Anglo-Norman Poem of the Thirteenth Century* (Oxford, 1939; Anglo-Norman Text Soc., No. 1).

[6] Ed. E. Walberg (Lund, 1922; and again, 1936, in *CFMA*, 77). For another Anglo-Norman life of Becket see *La Vie de Thomas Becket par Beneit, poème anglo-normand du XIIe siècle*, ed. Börje Schlyter (Lund, 1941; Études Romanes de Lund, IV).

[7] The best edition is that of Hilding Kjellman (Göteborg, 1935).

[8] A. T. Baker, "La Vie de Saint Edmond . . . ", *Romania*, LV (1929). 332-381. It was dedicated to Isabelle of Arundel. The MS in which the life is found, the property of the Duke of Portland at Walbeck Abbey, contains thirteen Anglo-French saints' lives. For list, with the places where they have been printed, see A. T. Baker in *Romania*, LXVI (1940). 49n.

[9] Cf. J. C. Russell, *MP*, XXVIII (1931). 267. The text is in H. R. Luard, *Lives of Edward the Confessor* (London, 1858; Rolls Series). For Henry of Avranches see below, p. 149.

[10] Ed. Paul Meyer in the *Société de l'histoire de France* (3v, Paris, 1891-1901); see also Meyer's discussion in *Romania*, XI (1882). 22-74. On the subject of the poem see Sidney Painter, *William Marshall* (Baltimore, 1933).

Historical
Themes

It was in works of history that Anglo-Norman writers scored their greatest success, surpassing in both Latin and French the productions on the Continent at the same period. It is not difficult to understand the popularity of historical subjects at the English court. The conquerors had secured control of a new country, and pride in their achievement stimulated a natural desire to know more about the land over which they had become the rulers. Perhaps they also enjoyed the feeling that this land had had as illustrious a past as that of the kings of France and that their own record was worthy of regard. At any rate it is the history of England and of Normandy, not of Europe or antiquity, that they were interested in. About 1150 Geoffrey

Gaimar

Gaimar, attached in some way to Ralph Fitz Gilbert of Lincolnshire, wrote for "dame Custance," his wife, a verse chronicle in two parts. The first was an *Histoire des Bretons,* that is, of the Celts in Britain, and was a working over in French of Geoffrey of Monmouth's *Historia Regum Britanniae* (see below, p. 168). It is now lost and we know about it only from the opening lines of the second part. This was the *Estorie des Engles.*[11] It consists of some 6500 lines and except for about 800 lines at the beginning, which tell the story of Havelok, later to be made the subject of an admirable English romance, it is a history of the English based on the *Old English Annals* with a few added episodes. Gaimar is not a gifted writer. His narrative, except on rather rare occasions, does not rise above the factual and commonplace. When he can escape from the impediments of fact and tell a story, as in the Havelok and one or two other episodes, interest is better sustained. But he betrays no marks of individuality, shows no prejudices, enthusiasms, or opinions. He treats conqueror and conquered alike, so that we cannot tell whether he was of Norman or Saxon descent. Most serious of all, he lacks the imaginative eye for vivid detail which his contemporary Wace has, and his work was valued only when it presented material not otherwise available in French. This is doubtless the reason that in all manuscripts Gaimar's first part is replaced by Wace's *Roman de Brut,* which covered the same ground.[12] There were several other adaptations of Geoffrey

---

[11] Ed. T. D. Hardy and C. T. Martin (2v, 1888-89; Rolls Ser.). For the Havelok episode see Alex. Bell, *Le Lai d'Haveloc and Gaimar's Haveloc Episode* (Manchester, 1925; *Pub. Univ. Manchester, French Ser.,* IV). On Gaimar cf. Alex. Bell, "Maistre Geffrei Gaimar," *MA,* VII (1938). 184-198.

[12] The *Roman de Brut,* since it occupies a place in the development of the Arthurian legend, will be touched on in chapter VIII, below. Wace was a Norman, who spent his early life at Caen and his last years as a prebendary of Bayeux; he does not belong, strictly speaking, to Anglo-Norman literature. But his *Roman de Brut,* on the testimony of Layamon, was presented to Queen Eleanor, and his second long poem, the *Roman de Rou,* a history of the dukes of Normandy, was begun about 1160 under the patronage of Henry II. Unfortunately he was not allowed to finish this undertaking; for some reason Henry replaced him, after he had written more than 11,000 lines, by a Maistre Beneeit, whom some identify with Benoît de Sainte-More. In addition to the two long poems just mentioned he wrote lives in verse of St. Nicholas, St. George, and St. Margaret, and a poem of 1804 lines on *La Conception Nostre Dame.* The last named enjoyed considerable popularity and found its way eventually into the *Cursor Mundi.* Wace is thought to have died shortly after 1174, at the age of seventy or more. The *Roman de Rou* is edited by H. Andresen (2v, Heilbronn, 1877-79). The latest edition of the *Vie de saint Nicholas* is that of E. Ronsjö (Lund, 1942; *Études romanes de Lund,* V). For the *Sainte Marguerite* see the edition of Eliz. A. Francis (Paris, 1932; *CFMA,* 71). The *Saint George* and the *Conception* are in V. Luzarche, *La Vie de la Vierge Marie* (Tours, 1859).

of Monmouth in Anglo-Norman which need not be mentioned. Of more importance is the fact that recent events were recorded in the same manner as the older history. In 1173 Henry's sons, supported by the Scottish king, revolted against their father. The following year Henry's forces took the Scottish king prisoner in Northumberland and put an end to the revolt. The events of this campaign were witnessed by Jordan Fantosme, who had been a pupil in Paris of the celebrated Gilbert de la Porée and was later secretary to Henry of Blois, Bishop of Winchester. His *Chronicle* of 2000 lines gives an account, full of picturesque detail, of the events of this campaign. Slightly later (*c.* 1225) we have an anonymous account, written in retrospect, of Henry II's conquest of Ireland. As late as the fourteeenth century verse history is still occasionally written in French, although such matter is now more commonly in prose. Peter Langtoft's *Chronicle* [13] covers the period from the destruction of Troy to 1307 in 10,000 lines, and was early translated into English by Robert of Brunne (cf. p. 204).

The body of Anglo-Norman religious literature of every sort is very large. *Religious* Mention has been made above of Samson de Nanteuil's translation into *Subjects* nearly 12,000 lines of verse of the *Proverbs of Solomon* (*c.* 1140). Early in the twelfth century the Psalter was twice turned into French, as were other parts of the Bible later in the century. At the end of the century a poet named Chardry versified the legends of *Barlaam and Josaphat* and the *Seven Sleepers,* and debated various moral questions in the *Petit Plet,* the three making a total of more than 6500 lines.[14] A great number of saints' lives appeared throughout the twelfth and thirteenth centuries. We have mentioned for their biographical interest those of Edward the Confessor, Thomas à Becket, and Edmund, Archbishop of Canterbury. Similar in character but of special interest is the *Voyage of St. Brendan* [15] *(1121) by an unknown Benedeit, mentioned above as one of the works dedicated to Queen Adelaide. It tells the story, first found in the Latin *Navigatio Sancti Brendani,* of an Irish abbot named Brendan and some monks who accompany him on a quest in search of the other world. In the course of their seven-year journey they witness many marvels and are eventually rewarded by a vision of paradise. It is notable as the first introduction into popular literature in England of the Celtic spirit of the marvelous.[16] In the first half of the thirteenth century, the celebrated Bishop of Lincoln, Robert Grosseteste (d. 1253), wrote *Grosseteste* an allegorical poem which he called *Le Château d'Amour.*[17] It ranges all

[13] Edited by Thomas Wright (1866-68) for the Rolls Series.
[14] All three were edited by John Koch in the *Altfranzösische Bibliothek,* Vol. 1 (Heilbronn, 1879). Josophat, the son of a Hindu king, is converted to Christianity by the hermit Barlaam. The *Seven Sleepers* is the story of seven youths who slept for 362 years and awoke in the reign of Theodosius.
[15] E. G. R. Waters, *The Anglo-Norman Voyage of St. Brendan by Benedeit* (Oxford, 1928).
[16] Cf. Walberg, *Quelques aspects,* p. 90.
[17] Edited by J. Murray (Paris, 1918). For two Middle English translations see *EETS,* 98, pp. 355-394 and 407-442, and for the former of these the earlier editions of R. F. Weymouth (1864; *Philol. Soc.*) and J. O. Halliwell (1849). On the allegory of the castle in medieval literature see Roberta D. Cornelius, *The Figurative Castle* (Bryn Mawr, 1930).

the way from a debate of the Four Daughters of God,[18] after which Christ
descends from Heaven into a castle which is the body of the Virgin Mary,
to a discussion of the attributes of Christ and His final judgment of the
world, distributing to each according to his deserts the joys of Heaven and
the pains of Hell.

Robert of
Gretham

Several works of great length and encyclopedic character, dating from
the middle of the thirteenth century, are still unedited. Robert of Gretham's
Miroir or *Les Évangiles des Domnées*[19] (more than 20,000 lines) translates
the Sunday gospels with explanations of their meaning. The same author
seems to have written a second long poem called the *Corset,* a compendium
of popular theology. The poems are dedicated to an unidentified Alain and
his wife, to whom Robert served as chaplain. Of similar scope is the *Lum-*

Peter of
Peckham

ière as Lais[20] (14,000 lines) of Peter of Peckham, adapted in part from
the *Elucidarium* of Honorius of Autun (or Augustodunensis), and the
Manual des Péchés[21] (11,000 lines) by William of Wadington (?), which
was translated into English in Robert of Brunne's *Handlyng Synne* (cf. p.
204). Around the turn of the fourteenth century Nicole Bozon, a Franciscan,
composed a miscellaneous collection of *Contes Moralisés*[22] and wrote a
number of other works in both prose and verse, not all of which have been
identified.[23]

Anglo-
Norman
Romances

Although religious literature and works intended to convey useful knowledge constitute the largest part of Anglo-Norman literature, there is also
a fair number of pieces in which no other end is contemplated than entertainment. These are, as is to be expected, mostly romances, although some

[18] The standard treatment of the allegory is Hope Traver, *The Four Daughters of God*
(Philadelphia, 1907).

[19] Unpublished, but there are considerable extracts in Marion Y. H. Aitken, *Étude sur le
Miroir ou les Évangiles des domnées de Robert de Gretham* (Paris, 1922).

[20] This has not been printed; in one MS it is dated 1267. For an account of the author,
MSS, sources, etc., see M. Dominica Legge, "Pierre de Peckham and His *Lumiere as Lais*,"
MLR, xxiv (1929). 37-47; 153-171. Peckham (the name occurs also as Pecchame and
Feccham) is the author also of a *Vie de Saint Richard,* written *c.* 1270 for the Countess of
Arundel (ed. A. T. Baker, *Revue des langues romanes*, LIII (1910). 245-396), and *Le Secré
de Secrez* (2383 lines), written sometime after the *Lumière as Lais.* It is edited by Oliver
A. Beckerlegge (Oxford, 1944; Anglo-Norman Text Soc., No. 5). The latter is a version of
the *Secreta Secretorum,* of which there were three in Anglo-Norman and several in Continental
French. For English versions see below, pp. 296 and 302 (*Dicts and Sayings of the Philosophers*).

[21] This has been printed in somewhat incomplete form by F. J. Furnivall in his edition of
the *Handlyng Synne* (1901-3; EETS, 119 and 123). See E. J. Arnould, *Le Manuel des Péchés:
Étude de littérature religieuse anglo-normande* (XIIIᵉ siècle) (Paris, 1940), and D. W. Robertson,
Jr., "The *Manuel de Péchés* and an English Episcopal Decree," *MLN*, LX (1945). 439-447.

[22] Edited by L. T. Smith and P. Meyer for the *Société des anciens textes français* (1889).
For the fullest treatment of Bozon see *Hist. Litt.,* xxxvi. 400-424, which should be supplemented
by Sister M. Amelia, "Nicholas Bozon," *Speculum,* xv (1940). 444-453, and the important
Introduction to Johan Vising, *Deux poèmes de Nicholas Bozon* (Göteborg, 1919). Vising has
also edited *La Plainte d'Amour* (Göteborg, 1905-7), probably by Bozon. A. C. Thorn has edited
Les Proverbes de bon enseignement (Lund, 1921; Lunds Univ. Årsskrift, N.F., Avd. 1, Bd. 17,
Nr. 4; another text, from the Vernon MS, is in *EETS*, 117, pp. 522-553) and Mary R.
Learned has edited "Saints' Lives Attributed to Nicholas Bozon," *Franciscan Stud.,* xxv
(1944). 79-88, 171-178, 267-271.

[23] It should be mentioned here that the religious drama is represented by the twelfth-
century Anglo-Norman *Adam* (see p. 276), a *Resurrection* of the early thirteenth century (ed.
Jean G. Wright for *CFMA* in 1931), and a recently discovered text (see T. A. Jenkins and
J. M. Manly, "La Seinte Resureccion," Oxford, 1943; Anglo-Norman Text Soc., IV).

fabliaux and an occasional satirical piece like *Le Jongleur d'Ely* give us a welcome glimpse of the English court in its lighter moments. Mention has been made above of the nearly 800 lines devoted to the story of Havelok the Dane at the beginning of Gaimar's *Estorie des Engles*. The same story in slightly longer form is told separately as a lay by an anonymous poet writing about 1130-40. It shows us the interest which the ruling class took in whatever was thought to concern the earlier history of the island, whether English, Danish, or Celtic. Among several other Anglo-Norman lays, *Amis and Amiloun* enjoyed perhaps the greatest popularity in the Middle Ages as a story of friendship put to a very great test. It should be remembered that the supreme author of such short romantic poems, Marie de France, lived at the English court and translated another of her works, a collection of fables, from English, as she herself tells us. The earliest and most famous and in some ways the best of the longer French romances written in England is the *Tristan* of Thomas, composed about 1170. It is one of the two earliest representatives of the lost French romance from which all subsequent treatments of the Tristan and Iseult story in literature descend. Sometime before the end of the century another Anglo-Frenchman, Robert de Boron,[24] wrote at least two romances on Arthurian themes, *Joseph d'Arimathie* or the *Estoire du Graal*, which in the four thousand lines that are preserved tells the story of the origin of the Holy Grail, and *Merlin*, of which only 400 lines have come down to us. About 1180 another poet named Thomas, who cannot be identified with the author of the *Tristan*, told the story of *Horn*, better known to modern readers in the English romance *King Horn* (cf. p. 175). Two long romances on pseudo-classical themes are the work of Hugh of Rutland. One, *Ipomedon* (*c.* 1185), resembles the story of Guy of Warwick in the hero's efforts to prove himself worthy of the lady he loves. The other, *Protheselaus* (*c.* 1190), relates the quarrel of two brothers, sons of Ipomedon, and their subsequent reconciliation. Each of these romances is more than 10,000 lines long. Of similar length and approximately the same date is Thomas of Kent's *Roman de Toute Chevalerie*, a story of Alexander the Great, while the longest of all the Anglo-Norman romances, the anonymous *Waldef* (22,000 lines) of the end of the twelfth century, relates the tragic struggle of an English king to regain his throne, and the avenging of his death by his sons.[25] Both the *Roman de Toute Chevalerie* and the *Waldef* still remain in manuscript. A romance of *Fouke Fitz Warin* in verse exists only in a later prose redaction.[26] It would seem that the writing of romances in French died out in England with the spread of English to the upper classes in the thirteenth century. Two, however, were produced in the first half of the century on subjects which were destined to enjoy

---

[24] There are those who believe that he was not an Englishman. See the discussion of W. A. Nitze in the *Manly Anniversary Studies* (Chicago, 1923), pp. 300-314. For a more acceptable position see the same author's "The Home of Robert de Boron," *MP*, XL (1942). 113-116.
[25] The Latin *Waldef* has been edited by R. Imelmann, *Johannes Bramis' Historia Regis Waldei* (Bonn, 1912; *Bonner Studien*, IV).
[26] The prose version is edited by Louis Brandin (Paris, 1930; *CFMA*, 63).

the greatest popularity when they were later treated in English—*Gui de Warewic* and *Boeve de Haumtone*. Some others probably once existed but are now lost, such as a *Richard Cœur de Lion* which is several times referred to in the English romance of that name.[27]

Anglo-Norman literature had passed its crest by about 1250,[28] although in diminishing amounts works in French continued to be written in England until the end of the fourteenth century. Even John Gower, who holds a modest but respectable place in English poetry, could write as late as 1376 one of his long poems, the *Mirour de l'Omme* (30,000 lines), in French.[29] Slightly more than four hundred texts, ranging from short lyrics to pieces of staggering length, are known today and testify to the place which French once held in the culture of the English upper classes.

[27] The romances mentioned in this paragraph will be found in the following editions: E. Kölbing, *Amis and Amiloun* (Heilbronn, 1884); J. Bédier, *Le Roman de Tristan par Thomas* (2v, Paris, 1903-5; *SATF*); for an English translation see R. S. Loomis, *The Romance of Tristram and Ysolt by Thomas of Britain* (1931); W. A. Nitze, *Robert de Boron: Le Roman de l'Estoire dou Graal* (Paris, 1927; *CFMA*, 57), containing also the fragment of the *Merlin*; earlier edition by F. Michel (Bordeaux, 1841); R. Brede and E. M. Stengel, *Das anglonormannische Lied vom wackern Ritter Horn* (Marburg, 1883; *Ausgaben und Abhandlungen*, VIII); E. Kölbing and E. Koschwitz, *Ipomedon* (Breslau, 1889); F. Kluckow, *Hue de Rotelande: Protheselaus* (Göttingen, 1924); A. Ewert, *Gui de Warewic* (2v, Paris, 1932-3; *CFMA*, 74-75; A. Stimming, *Der anglonormannische Boeve de Haumtone* (Halle, 1899).

[28] Walter of Bibbesworth, the author of two whimsical poems, is the author of a famous *Traité* (1240-50) written to teach French to the children of Dionysia de Munchensy. On the poems (now BM Add. MS 46919, formerly Phillipps MS 8336) see Miss Legge's *Anglo-Norman Literature*, pp. 348-9, on the *Traité* Alexander Bell, "Notes on Walter de Bibbesworth's Treatise," *PQ*, XLI (1962). 361-372, and Albert C. Baugh, "The Date of Walter of Bibbesworth's *Traité*," *Festschrift für Walther Fischer* (Heidelberg, 1959), pp. 21-33.

[29] A list of books owned by Richard II contains mostly romances in French. Cf. Edith Rickert, "King Richard II's Books," *Library*, n. s. XIII (1932). 144-147.

V

Early Latin Writers

In any age up to the Renaissance, the Latin literature of Europe is the *A Measure of Intellectual Life* measure of its intellectual life. In a day when all books which made a pretense to learning were written in Latin, such books are a barometer recording by their number and importance the advances, the retrogressions, or the periods of hesitation in European civilization. But while Latin is the language of learning, not all books written in it are necessarily learned. Learned men have their moments of leisure. All through the Middle Ages important positions in the government and at court were filled by bishops and clerks trained for the church, men whose progress through the schools or the university had by a process of natural selection marked them as possessed of the intellectual grasp and learning needed in dealing with the problems of government and the State. Such men, though churchmen, were more occupied with worldly than religious matters and in some cases their natural inclinations were anything but pious. It would be a mistake to think that their reading—done in Latin with the ease that comes of long habit— was exclusively edifying. Hence such Latin books as the *De Nugis Curialium*, the *Speculum Stultorum*, the *Otia Imperialia,* and the mass of light, satirical, and scurrilous verse that we know as Goliardic poetry.

Since the Latin language was international, the Latin writings of any *Twelfth-* particular country are also a measure of the extent to which that country *Century* participates in the general progress that is being made. There was a time, *Renais-* in the eighth century, when England led the world in learning, when at *sance* the beginning Bede was writing and at the end Charlemagne was forced to bring Alcuin from York to direct the intellectual reforms which he was bent on in France. And there was also a time a century later when King Alfred could lament that "there were very few on this side of the Humber who could ... translate a letter from Latin into English." Fortunately the Benedictine Reform [1] and the Norman Conquest had brought improvement. However limited were the Conqueror's own bookish interests, he had a respect for learning and filled the English churches and monasteries with learned bishops and abbots and monks. As a result, a generation later England was ready to participate in the general awakening that was taking place in Europe. The twelfth century is one of those periods in history in which many things have their beginnings and in which there is both substantial achievement and promise of greater achievement to come. It was

[1] See above, p. 100.

the century in which the great cathedrals of Europe were begun. It was the century of the troubadours and of Chrétien de Troyes. It witnessed the rapid development of scholastic philosophy with William of Champeaux, Abelard, and Peter Lombard, preparing the way for the great Schoolmen of the thirteenth century, Albertus Magnus, Thomas Aquinas, and Duns Scotus. And it saw the founding of the universities, above all of Paris, but also of Bologna and Oxford and, towards the end of the century, Cambridge. What the University of Paris alone meant to the intellectual life of the Middle Ages can hardly be estimated. Everywhere there are signs of quickened intellect and new life. It is not without reason that we have come to speak of a Twelfth-Century Renaissance,[2] and in the Latin literature and learning of this century England has a full share.

John of Salisbury From the large number of Latin writers of England in the twelfth and thirteenth centuries a few names stand out in bold relief. Of these the earliest is that of John of Salisbury. His experience is typical of many for whom a career in the Church was equivalent to a position in public life, whether assumed willingly or, as in his case, against inclination. He was born about 1120, and studied for twelve years in Paris and at Chartres under such teachers as Abelard and William of Conches. Chartres was a center of literary and humanistic studies, and John of Salisbury owes his wide acquaintance with classical poets to the tradition which the famous Bernard established there. On his return to England in 1154, after some years in the service of the Pope, he became secretary to the Archbishop of Canterbury, Theobald, and later held the same office under Becket, whose cause he supported and whose exile he shared. The last four years of his life he spent as Bishop of Chartres, where he died in 1180. His two principal works are the *Policraticus* and the *Metalogicon*,[3] both finished in 1159 and dedicated to Thomas à Becket, then chancellor to Henry II. The latter is a defense of logic and apart from an interesting section on the author's student years in France is of value chiefly for its account of scholastic studies in his day. The *Policraticus* is of wider interest.

The Policraticus The *Policraticus* (Statesman's Book), whether conceived as a whole from the beginning or growing under the author's hand, is the embodiment of a large purpose which must have been in his mind whether he had formulated it consciously or not. For the work is nothing less than a treatise on the good life, which, since we live in an organized society, involves a consideration of the welfare of the State. With all its essay-like informality in the individual chapters, it hangs together in a fairly logical way. While John addresses

---

[2] C. H. Haskins, *The Renaissance of the Twelfth Century* (Cambridge, Mass., 1927); G. M. Paré, et. al., *La Renaissance du XIIe siècle: les écoles et l'enseignement* (Paris, 1933).
[3] Critical editions of the *Policraticus* and the *Metalogicon* have been published by C. C. J. Webb (Oxford, 1909 and 1929). The *Policraticus* can now all be read in translation, part of it in John Dickinson, *The Statesman's Book of John of Salisbury* (1927), the remainder in Joseph B. Pike, *Frivolities of Courtiers and Footprints of Philosophers* (Minneapolis, 1938). C. C. J. Webb's *John of Salisbury* (1932) is popular but authoritative. Good brief accounts will be found in Helen Waddell, "John of Salisbury," *E&S*, XIII (1928). 28-51, and R. L. Poole, *Illustrations of Medieval Thought* (2ed., 1920), ch. VII.

himself to the chancellor of England, he has in mind the whole governing class as well as that intangible entity, posterity. He begins by attempting to clear away the habits and practices which he considers unworthy, or foolish, or actually immoral, and which are not always recognized as such, particularly when they occur where they do the most harm—at the court and in high places. And so he condemns hunting, gaming, actors and mimics, magic and astrology, and the things inimical to the public welfare—pride, concupiscence, flattery, especially as a vicious means of advancement. All this occupies the first three books. In the next three he considers the proper functioning of the State—the character and conduct of the prince and his relation to the law, the commonwealth and its members, the administration of justice, the behavior of its armed forces, the cohesion of its parts. And in the concluding books he turns successively to the things which his own studies have shown to be important, first to the intellectual and ethical principles "which have in view the health of body and soul," and hence to the efforts of philosophers to attain wisdom and truth; and lastly to those private virtues on which all happiness ultimately depends—modesty, moderation, sobriety, and the like—all of which leads to the conclusion that the happy man is he who fears God and frames his life accordingly. There are sometimes long digressions which tend to obscure the plan, but it is impossible not to sense the larger purpose which throughout animates this really lengthy work.

John of Salisbury is not a profound or original thinker, a philosopher *His* who builds a new system or tears down old ones. He is content not to be *Character* dogmatic on matters about which a wise man may well confess doubt, and he specifically disclaims originality. But he expresses his convictions boldly, even to justifying the putting to death of tyrants, and he quotes a conversation which he had with Pope Adrian IV in which he assuredly did not mince words on the corruption of Rome and the papal court. His weakness is the result of the very circumstance to which he owes much of his strength —the twelve years which he spent in study at Paris and Chartres. He has read everything and he quotes endlessly—Horace and Virgil, Juvenal, Ovid, Terence, and the whole range of Latin writers, pagan and Christian, until at times present reality is lost in the wealth of historical example. There is enough of himself on every page, however, to dominate the thought, so that interest does not flag. Student and moralist, he has been forced to spend his life with kings and chancellors, archbishops and popes. He has seen the shortcomings not so much of Church and State as of prelates and statesmen, and being a man of convictions he sets down his philosophy of life for the benefit of those among whom it may do some good.

Walter Map (*c.* 1140-*c.* 1209) needed a Boswell. Like Johnson he was a *Walter* greater talker than writer; he was noted for his witty conversation and his *Map* good stories. His life would have made a fascinating biography, beginning with his student years in Paris and continuing with his experiences as a clerk in the king's household and as an itinerant justice, and ending with his death as Archdeacon of Oxford. He was a favorite of Henry II, traveled with him, met scores of interesting people, and saw Rome as a delegate to the third Lateran Council. He passed in the Middle Ages as the author of some of the most famous of the Goliardic poems; he may have written verses of this sort in his early days. A persistent and early tradition credits him with the authorship of the prose *Lancelot* and other Arthurian romances, a tradition that cannot be accepted in any literal sense. His one extant book, *De Nugis Curialium* [4] ("Courtiers' Trifles"), passed completely unnoticed in the Middle Ages and survives in a single manuscript copied two hundred years after it was written. It is a collection of stories, historical anecdotes, scraps of folklore, witty remarks and amusing incidents, occasionally bits of satire and denunciation, without order or plan, written down between 1181 and 1193.[5] A somewhat comparable book is the *Otia Imperialia* of Gervase of Tilbury, who chose England for his birth and death but lived most of his life abroad. It is a veritable Book of Knowledge into which the author put all the interesting things he knew about the earth and its history, with a collection of wonders thrown in for good measure. It was written in 1211 for the entertainment and (we may suspect) the edification of the Emperor Otto IV.

Gervase of Tilbury

Another interesting personality of Henry II's reign, Giraldus Cambrensis,[6] was like his friend Walter Map a Welshman and a cleric, but there the resemblance ends. For whereas Map was possessed of an amiable indolence and acquired numerous preferments, Giraldus had the zeal of a reformer, loved a fight, and was always willing to excommunicate his opponent. He spent the best years of his life in an unsuccessful effort to become Bishop of St. David's and raise the see to metropolitan rank in Wales, the equal of Canterbury and York. He is commonly classed as an historian and indeed he wrote a *Topography of Ireland*, the *Conquest of Ireland*, an *Itinerary of Wales*, based on his journey through Wales with Archbishop Baldwin to preach the Third Crusade, a *Description of Wales*,[7] and other more strictly historical works. For he was a voluminous writer, whose extant writings fill eight volumes in the Rolls Series. But among them are a number of pieces of a more general character, including two which are in the

Giraldus Cambrensis

[4] Edited by M. R. James (Oxford, 1914) and earlier by Thomas Wright for the Camden Soc. (1850); trans. by F. Tupper and M. B. Ogle (1924) and by M. R. James (1923); *Cymmrodorion Record Ser.*, No. IX).

[5] James Hinton, "Walter Map's *De Nugis Curialium*: Its Plan and Composition," *PMLA*, XXXII (1917). 81-132.

[6] Also known as Gerald de Barri. His dates are *c.* 1146-1220. He spent, as he tells us himself, three periods of several years in study at Paris and shows wide acquaintance with classical literature. He served as archdeacon of Mynyw. (St. David's) and in other ecclesiastical capacities. He was elected Bishop of St. David's in 1198, but in spite of three trips to Rome could not overcome the influence of the Archbishop of Canterbury and the King's natural fears. The election was not confirmed, and he retired gracefully from the field. For an excellent treatment of Gerald see the lecture of F. M. Powicke, "Gerald of Wales," *Bull. John Rylands Library*, XII (1928). 389-410, reprinted in *Christian Life in the Middle Ages and Other Essays* (Oxford, 1935).

[7] A translation of these four works is in the Bohn library, *The Historical Works of Giraldus Cambrensis*, ed. Thomas Wright, and the two on Wales are available in the Everyman's Library.

nature of an autobiography,[8] and even in the works which have an importance for the historian there is so much incidental anecdote and observation, popular tradition, legend, and folklore that they have considerable appeal to the general reader. His narrative is always swift and vigorous, full of the unexpected, lively, never hampered by moderation or restraint. Even his outrageous egotism is so frank as to disarm criticism.

The name of one other Welshman should be found with those of Walter *Geoffrey* Map and Giraldus Cambrensis in this place, that of Geoffrey of Monmouth. *of* But since his *History of the Kings of Britain* (1137) and his verse life of *Monmouth* Merlin (*Vita Merlini*) owe their interest chiefly to their connection with Arthurian romance, consideration of them will be postponed until chapter VIII, where they may be given their proper place in the development of the Arthurian legend.

We have already seen in the preceding chapter how widespread was the *Chroniclers* interest in history among the new rulers of England after the Norman Conquest and how that interest was satisfied by Anglo-Norman poets for those who could not read Latin. The same interest gives us a long series of chronicles and histories in Latin unequaled in any other country of Europe. We cannot speak here of the many monastic annals compiled at religious houses and concerned mainly with local affairs. These belong with a few notable exceptions to the middle and south of England and tend to disappear after 1300. The more ambitious chronicle commonly begins with the Anglo-Saxons, or at times with the creation of the world, and comes down to the writer's own day. Thus Simeon of Durham [9] covers the period from 616 to 1130, and Florence of Worcester, whose *Chronicon ex Chronicis* is a rather bare record of events, begins with the time of Julius Caesar and continues to within a year or so of his own death in 1118. Ordericus Vitalis, the son of a Norman father and an English mother, compiled between 1130 and 1141 an *Historia Ecclesiastica* from Creation to the time of writing, an interesting and valuable source for the period beginning with the Norman Conquest. Two writers stand out for their literary interest. William of Malmesbury, whose *Gesta Regum Anglorum* (449-1128) is the most ambitious of his several undertakings, treats the writing of history as an art. He is careful to differentiate his work from that of the mere chronicler, and justifies an occasional digression on the score of variety and interest. Henry of Huntingdon, whose value to the historian is rather slight, inserts in the form of

---

[8] *De Rebus a se Gestis* and *De Jure et Statu Meneuensis Ecclesiae* (Vols. I and III of the edition in the Rolls Series). These have been translated by H. E. Butler, *The Autobiography of Giraldus Cambrensis* (1937), except for a portion of the latter which has no autobiographical interest. The *Speculum Ecclesiae*, one of the pieces of more general character referred to in the text, has not been translated. It is a collection of satirical and often scurrilous sketches of unworthy clerics.

[9] All of the works mentioned will be found edited in the Rolls Series. For a full list of the English chroniclers and an appraisal of their historical importance see Charles Gross, *Sources and Literature of English History . . . to . . . 1485* (2ed., 1915), pp. 326-399. English translations of the more important are included in the Bohn Library, the Church Historians of England, the Everyman's Library, etc. On the origins of the medieval chronicle see R. L. Poole, *Chronicles and Annals: A Brief Outline of Their Origin and Growth* (1926).

Latin translation many ballads and popular traditions which he heard among the people, and these do much to make up for his rather brief and matter-of-fact style. Of special importance for the reign of Henry II are William of Newburgh's *Historia Rerum Anglicarum* (to 1197), the work of a careful student with many of the ideals of the modern scholar, the *Gesta Regis Henrici Secundi* ascribed to Benedict of Peterborough and possibly the work of Richard Fitz-Neal, author of the famous *Dialogus de Scaccario* ("Dialogue of the Exchequer"), and the *Chronica* of Roger Hoveden whose work is of greatest value for the closing decade of the twelfth century. It may be said of all these writers that for the past they merely compile or slavishly copy from earlier sources and that they become interesting and assume importance when they reach the period of which they have personal knowledge.

In the thirteenth century one school of historians stands out above all others, the chroniclers who wrote at the great monastery of St. Albans. Situated only twenty miles from London on one of the main highways, the abbey was a convenient stopping place for travelers the first night out of the city, and frequently had as guests the king and other magnates of the realm. In the days when most current events were known by direct report this gave the abbey a unique advantage in the gathering of historical material. The greatest of the St. Albans chroniclers was Matthew Paris, who seems to have been as gifted as an illuminator and worker in gold and silver as he was as an historian. His principal work, the *Chronica Majora*,[10] incorporates that of his predecessors John of Cella and Roger of Wendover and continues to the year 1259. It is a vivid and colorful narrative. His history was continued by a fellow monk, William Rishanger (to 1306), and by others down to Thomas Walsingham, who closes the series in 1422. In the first half of the fourteenth century a monk of Chester abbey, Ranulf Higden, compiled a universal history called the *Polychronicon,* extending from the beginning of the world to 1327, which was continued by others to 1357 and enjoyed an enormous popularity in the century following. It would not be possible to omit mention of the "Chronicle" of Jocelyn de Brakelond,[11] though it is not a chronicle in the usual sense. It is really a life of the abbot Samson and an account of his efforts to restore discipline and a business-like conduct of affairs in the great Benedictine monastery of Bury St. Edmunds. It is charming in its frankness, sincerity, and occasional touches of shrewd humor. Its picture of laxity, petty politics, the self-seeking of unscrupulous monks, and the sympathetic portrait of abbot Samson leave with one an indelible impression of what sometimes went on in a great monastic house. The story is familiar to all readers of Carlyle's *Past and Present.*

St. Albans

Matthew Paris

Jocelyn de Brakelond

---

[10] Edited in the Rolls Series (1872-83). His *Historia Minor* is an abridgment with additions (1067-1253). He is also the author of *Vitae Abbatum S. Albani,* various saints' lives, etc.

[11] Edited by J. G. Rokewode (1840; Camden Soc., Vol. 13). It may be read in English in the translation of L. C. Jane *The Chronicle of Jocelin of Brakelond* (1907). It was written in 1202 and covers the years 1173-1202.

In the Latin literature of England in the Middle Ages the prose is of *Latin* much greater significance than the verse. Nevertheless a good bit of verse *Verse* was written, ranging from the serious epic to the light, the satirical, and at times the highly indecorous. Joseph of Exeter, who accompanied Archbishop Baldwin on the Third Crusade,[12] composed an epic in six books known as the *De Bello Trojano* (c. 1184) in the manner of Virgil. It is a more than respectable performance, but unfortunately, so far as modern readers are concerned, has run into fatal competition since the Renaissance with a certain Greek poem. If Joseph of Exeter falls somewhat short of his model, Virgil, it is a still farther cry from Horace to the *Nova Poetria*[13] of Geoffrey de Vinsauf, an interesting mixture of classical precept and medieval practice. A delightfully amusing satire on ambitious monks is Nigel Wireker's *Speculum Stultorum*[14] (c. 1180), a mirror in which fools may see themselves as the ass Burnellus, who thought his tail was too short. His adventures with the doctors of Salerno, his years of study at the University of Paris, at the end of which he is still only able to say *ya*, his determination to found a new kind of monastery where every monk may have a mistress, are related with much more than mere humor. Finally, there is the large body of strongly rhythmical verse, by turns trivial, amorous, scurrilous, and coarse, written by university students sowing their wild oats or by *scholares vagantes* who have quit the academic life permanently or temporarily and taken to the road. Although we must discard the attribution of much of this verse to Walter Map, Englishmen seem to have had a share in its pro- *Goliardic* duction.[15] It is the poetry of the bohemian life and the tavern. It shows no *Verse* respect for rank or authority, makes light of death, has no concern for the future either in this world or the next. It is the flaunted gaiety of the socially declassed, the voice of defiant nonchalance in rags.

[12] He celebrated the expedition in a Latin poem called the *Antiocheis*, of which only a few lines remain.

[13] Text in E. Faral, *Les Arts poétiques du XII* et du XIII* siècle* (1923).

[14] In Thomas Wright, *Anglo-Latin Satirical Poets* (2v, 1872; Rolls Ser.). On Wireker see the articles of John H. Mozley: "On the Text of the *Speculum Stultorum*," *Speculum*, IV (1929). 430-442; V (1930). 251-263; "The Unprinted Poems of Nigel Wireker," *Speculum*, VII (1932). 398-423; "Nigel Wireker or Wetekre," *MLR*, XXVII (1932). 314-317. As an example of the occasional poet, who in this case was not English but spent a number of years in England and wrote much for English patrons, see J. C. Russell, "Master Henry of Avranches as an International Poet," *Speculum*, III (1928). 34-63. For the large body of Latin political verse consult the collections of Thomas Wright noted on p. 222.

[15] Such verse is known as Goliardic poetry from the fact that a certain Golias, called *episcopus* or *pontifex*, who has numerous children or disciples, is frequently mentioned as the author and progenitor of it. The authorship of some of the poems is concealed under the names Primas and Archipoeta. An Englishman credited with others, Serlo of Wilton, is mentioned among the acquaintances of both Walter Map and Giraldus Cambrensis. A number of texts are printed in Thomas Wright, *The Latin Poems Commonly Attributed to Walter Mapes* (1841; Camden Soc., Vol. 16). Further references will be found, together with a valuable introduction summarizing the results of modern scholarship, in Olga Dobiache-Rojdestvensky, *Les Poésies des goliards* (1931). See also Helen Waddell, *The Wandering Scholars* (1927), P. S. Allen, *The Romanesque Lyric* (1928), the same author's *Medieval Latin Lyrics* (1931), and F. J. E. Raby, *A History of Secular Latin Poetry* (2v, Oxford, 1934). Howard Mumford Jones contributed translations to Allen's earlier volume; other translations will be found in John Addington Symonds, *Wine, Women, and Song: Medieval Latin Students' Songs* (1884) and Helen Waddell, *Mediæval Lyrics* (1929).

Variety of the Latin Literature   Space forbids the proper consideration of much more that is important in the Latin literature of England. We can only hint at its variety. Scientific interests are represented by Alexander Neckham (1157-1217), whose *De Naturis Rerum*,[16] like Bartholomeus Anglicus's *De Proprietatibus Rerum* (c. 1230-50), ranges over the whole field of physical and natural science. Not content with Western scholarship, Adelard of Bath [17] traveled to Greece and Asia Minor in search of Arabic learning, and Daniel Morley went from Paris to Toledo gathering Arabic teachings on earthly and heavenly bodies (*De Naturis Inferiorum et Superiorum*). One of the greatest of medieval scientists, Roger Bacon (c. 1214-1294), who is also one of the few Englishmen who knew Greek in his century, covered in his *Opus Majus* not only mathematics and the sciences, but grammar, logic, and moral philosophy, experimenting with the microscope and pointing the way to the inductive methods of modern research.[18]

In the Middle Ages as now, each man wrote about the thing that interested him. Ralph de Glanville, appointed Chief Justiciar of England in 1180, produced a treatise invaluable for the historian, *De Legibus et Consuetudinibus Regni Angliae*. Osbern (fl., 1090), a monk of Christ Church, Canterbury, was given to translating saints' lives from Old English. Ailred of Rievaulx (c. 1109-1166), abbot of the Cistercian monastery of that name in Yorkshire, composed a rule for recluses and a number of works on religious and historical subjects. The great Bishop of Lincoln, Robert Grosseteste (c. 1175-1253) translated Aristotle's *Ethics* and wrote so extensively on science, mathematics, religion, etc. that the list of his works fills twenty-five closely printed pages.[19] An Englishman of the thirteenth century is supposed to have compiled that widespread collection of stories with a moral, the *Gesta Romanorum*,[20] at the same time that Odo of Cheriton (1247) was producing his Latin fables and his sermons on the Sunday gospels. In the fourteenth century Richard of Bury, Bishop of Durham (1287-1345), an indefatigable if sometimes unscrupulous book collector, expressed his love of books in a delightful treatise, the *Philobiblon*.[21] And, lest the preachers should be entirely neglected, room may be found for the mention of the *Summa Praedicantium* of John Bromyard (c. 1390), full of good stories and apposite illustrations.

[16] Edited by Thomas Wright for the Rolls Series (1863). On the general subject of medieval science see Lynn Thorndike, *A History of Magic and Experimental Science* (6v, 1923-41), and C. H. Haskins, *Studies in the History of Mediæval Science* (Cambridge, Mass., 1924).

[17] His *De Eodem et Diverso* was written about 1116. His other writings include *Questiones Naturales* and treatises on the abacus and the astrolabe.

[18] The *Opus Majus* has been translated by Robert B. Burke (2v, Philadelphia, 1928). His other writings include the *Opus Minus*, *Opus Tertium*, a *Compendium Philosophiae*, a Greek grammar, works on alchemy, etc.

[19] See F. S. Stevenson, *Robert Grosseteste* (1899) and S. Harrison Thomson, *The Writings of Robert Grosseteste, Bishop of Lincoln, 1235-1253* (Cambridge, 1940).

[20] An English translation is available in the Bohn Library (1877).

[21] Text and translation by E. C. Thomas (1888); translation separately (1902) in the King's Classics and now in the Medieval Library. In a number of MSS the work is attributed to Thomas Holkot.

An adequate survey of the medieval Latin literature of England would require a large volume. It is the purpose of the present chapter merely to suggest its wealth and variety and thus reveal the more intellectual side of English culture in the Middle Ages.[22]

[22] The student who wishes to pursue the subject further may consult the monumental work of Max Manitius, *Geschichte der lateinischen Literatur des Mittelalters* (3v, 1911-31), which unfortunately only reaches to the end of the twelfth century; Adolf Ebert, *Histoire générale de la littérature du moyen âge en occident*, trans. by J. Aymeric and J. Condamin (3v, 1883-89, superior to the German edition); F. J. E. Raby, *A History of Christian-Latin Poetry* (Oxford, 1927) and *A History of Secular Latin Poetry* (2ed, 2v, Oxford, 1957).

VI
Wit and Wisdom

In two previous chapters [1] we traced the survival of the Old English literary tradition in its most prevalent form, religious pieces in prose and verse. It is now necessary to note its appearance also in three works not of a religious nature, the *Proverbs of Alfred, The Owl and the Nightingale,* and Layamon's *Brut.* The first two of these we shall consider in the present chapter. Layamon's *Brut* we shall merely recognize as belonging with them in time and secular character, but we shall postpone the further consideration of it until chapter VIII, where we can better indicate its place in the development of the Arthurian legend. There is the more reason for this since in spite of being written in English and being in verse and style the heir of Old English poetry, it derives its subject matter from a French source.

Proverbs of Alfred The *Proverbs of Alfred* belongs to a very old type of didactic literature. There seems to be something perennial in the desire to hear universal truths even when they are so obvious as to be truisms. Nowadays the proverb is generally short and pithy, "the wisdom of many and the wit of one," as Lord Russell expressed it, and is thus justified by its cleverness•and quotable quality. But there is apparently an equal disposition to treasure bits of homely wisdom distilled from experience, especially when clothed with authority, associated with the name of one who is reputed wise. It is this that accounts for the popularity of the sayings of "Poor Richard" in colonial America. In literature the proverb may also be a short discourse offering moral guidance or practical advice as in the Proverbs of Solomon, and it is this form which the *Proverbs of Alfred* takes. There is no reason to suppose that King Alfred is in any way responsible for the observations here attributed to him, but his reputation for wisdom was traditional and his name, like that of King Solomon, carried conviction to the average Englishman in the centuries following his death.

Their Character Bad luck has pursued this interesting Middle English text. What appears to have been the oldest and best MS [2] was mostly consumed in the fire that destroyed a part of the Cotton collection and damaged the Beowulf codex. Our next oldest text is also fragmentary [3] and a third MS was lost for thirty years. In its fullest form the *Proverbs of Alfred* consists of about thirty-five

---

[1] Chs. II and III.

[2] Brief extracts are preserved and recently three leaves have been identified and printed by N. R. Ker in *MA*, v (1936). 115-120.

[3] Discovered and published by Carleton Brown in *MLR*, xxi (1926). 250-260.

sayings amounting to a little more than 600 lines.[4] The precepts fall into three easily distinguished groups. In the initial group, consisting of the first eleven sayings, the advice is general or concerned with matters of public interest: a king should be learned and wise; earl and atheling should rule justly; wealth without wisdom is of little value; it is transitory and often the cause of a man's undoing; life itself is uncertain. In the middle group (sayings 12-29), the largest and most interesting section, the precepts concern personal conduct. There is advice on choosing a wife: choose her not for her face or her possessions—you may regret your choice the rest of your life. There are rather cynical warnings against failing to rule one's wife firmly, listening to her counsel, telling her too much of your business— "woman is word-mad." Other teachings concern friendship, sparing the rod, excessive drinking, misplaced confidence—believe not every man, confide not too much in others; a fair apple is often bitter inside. The suggestions are sometimes picturesquely and effectively expressed. Instead of telling every one of your sorrow

> Seie it þine sadel boȝe
> & rid te singinde

—tell it to thy saddle-bow and ride singing away. Much of this section and the next anticipates the advice of Polonius to Laertes. The last group of precepts is addressed to "my son so dear," resembling in this respect some of the proverbs of Solomon, and is of the familiar type of parental advice. It has to do chiefly with choosing one's companions, especially whom to avoid. Give the drunken man the road, cherish the old man's counsel, and the like. There is at the end a curious warning not to choose for a companion the little man, the "long" man, or the red-haired man.

The reputation of Alfred's proverbial sayings was already well established in the twelfth century. They are referred to in the twelfth-century part of the *Annals of Winchester* and mentioned by Ailred of Rievaulx, who died in 1166. But we cannot be sure that these allusions are to the *Proverbs* in written form, since in all likelihood such sayings circulated freely in oral tradition. In *The Owl and the Nightingale,* discussed below, in which *Dissemina-* proverbs are often quoted, eleven are specifically attributed to Alfred, but *tion* only three of these are found in the existing collection. Nevertheless it is almost certain that the literary form in which we have them goes back to

[4] The most recent edition is that of Helen P. South, *The Proverbs of Alfred Studied in the Light of the Recently Discovered Maidstone Manuscript* (1931). Valuable also is the edition of E. Borgström (Lund, 1908) for its complete texts of the Trinity and Jesus MSS and its critical apparatus. For a detailed study of the various versions and their relation see O. S. A. Arngart, *The Proverbs of Alfred: 1. A Study of the Texts* (Lund, 1942). A slightly later collection is known as the *Proverbs of Hendyng.* Editions from different MSS will be found in Thomas Wright and J. O. Halliwell, *Reliquiae Antiquae* (1841-43), I. 109-116; K. Böddeker, *Altenglische Dichtungen des MS Harl. 2253* (Berlin, 1878), pp. 285-300; H. Varnhagen, in *Anglia,* IV (1881). 182-200; G. Schleich, "Die Sprichwörter Hendings und die Proverbis of Wisdom," *Anglia,* LI (1927). 220-277 (a critical text). S. Singer, "Die Sprichwörter Hendings," *Studia Neophil.,* XIV (1942), 31-52, offers a commentary and a reconsideration of the manuscripts. Modern renderings of both collections are in Jessie L. Weston, *The Chief Middle-English Poets* (Boston, 1914). For the gnomic poems of Old English see above, p. 43.

the twelfth century. The Cotton MS was written early in the thirteenth century and it is not the parent version. The language is more easily thought of as that of the twelfth than of the thirteenth century. The metrical form is essentially that of the Old English alliterative verse, much relaxed and threatening at any moment to break into three-stress lines, occasionally bound together into pairs by rime. The collection was probably put together in Sussex. As a work of literature the *Proverbs of Alfred* is interesting not only in its own right, but as an example of popular English tradition more secular than religious in its content.

The existence of such a work in the twelfth century causes no surprise. Though not religious, except incidentally, it has its roots in folk wisdom **The Owl** and it traces its authority to an Old English king. But *The Owl and the* **and the** *Nightingale* [5] is another story. Written not far from the year 1200, it is a **Nightingale** truly amazing phenomenon in Middle English literature.

It is cast in the form of a debate, a heated argument between the two birds. The literary debate, very popular in the Middle Ages, is a form that is likely to flourish in a period of intellectual immaturity. It represents argument for the sake of argument, disagreement not through conviction but for the sake of matching wits. It is as though the individual has just discovered that he has a mind and enjoys the exercise of his new-found capacity. As we grow older and more polite we avoid arguments, and since nations and civilizations are somewhat like individuals, the artificial disputation has largely disappeared from our literature. The origin of the form has been traced back to the classical eclogue of Theocritus and Virgil,[6] which sometimes portrays a contest of skill between two shepherds. In the Middle Ages there are well-known examples as early as the eighth century. *Literary* A *Conflictus Veris et Hiemis* is attributed to Alcuin and in the ninth cen- *Debate* tury Sedulius Scotus composed *De Rosae Liliique Certamine.* Thereafter examples multiply and we get disputes between water and wine, the heart and the eye, youth and age, Phillis and Flora, Ganymede and Helen—academic, moral, witty, sometimes obscene. One of the most famous English examples is the *Debate between the Body and the Soul,* which will be discussed in the next chapter. The conventions of the type can be seen through the variety of subject matter and treatment. There is generally an opening describing the setting and the occasion for the debate or the circumstances under which the poet witnesses or overhears it. The debate itself follows in the form of actual dialogue, and a decision may or may not be rendered at the end. Often, as in *The Owl and the Nightingale,* the poet professes to be ignorant of the result.

In the present instance the author comes upon the two birds in a secluded

---

[5] The best-known editions are those of J. E. Wells (1907, revised 1909; *Belles Lettres Ser.*), W. Gadow (1909; *Palaestra,* LXV), J. W. H. Atkins, with translation (1922), and J. H. G. Grattan and G. F. H. Sykes (1935; *EETSS,* 119).

[6] Cf. J. H. Hanford, "Classical Eclogue and Mediæval Debate," *Romanic Rev.,* II (1911). 16-31, 129-143.

spot in an unnamed valley. The Nightingale is perched in a thick hedge, safe from her opponent's claws, while the Owl occupies an old tree-stump. The Nightingale is the aggressor and provokes the argument by open insults. "Monster," she says, "fly away! I am the worse for seeing thee. Thy ugliness spoils my song. When I hear thy foul howling I would rather spit than sing!" The Owl waits until evening to reply, and although she is ready to burst with rage, she controls herself very well. The Nightingale, she says, wrongs her time and again. If once she would come out into the open, she would sing another tune. This, of course, the Nightingale declines to do, and instead continues to revile her opponent. "Thou art loathsome to behold.... Thy body is short, thy neck is small, thy head is greater than all the rest of thee." In this vein she accuses the Owl of unclean habits, raising a filthy brood that defiles its own nest, and being in general a symbol of all that is worthless, after which she breaks out into melodious song. The Owl listens perforce, puffed out and swollen "as if she had swallowed a frog." After a while the Nightingale, quite unreasonably, proposes that they stop their useless squabbling and proceed in a decent and orderly manner to argue their case before a suitable judge. The Owl agrees, but the Nightingale's tone does not undergo any noticeable change. The dispute turns upon the respective merits of their singing, but breaks over constantly into personalities and mutual abuse. Neither can see that the other serves any useful purpose. The Owl accuses the Nightingale of singing amatory songs and of enticing men and women to sin. The Nightingale retorts that the Owl is a bird of ill omen, whose song is ever of sorrow and misfortune. In the end the birds set out to lay their case before the judge—the Owl says she can repeat every word from beginning to end—but the poet disclaims knowledge of the outcome.

It would seem that so delightful and lively a poem might be allowed to stand as an example of the bird fable, as a story told for its own sake, without our seeking to find in it a hidden meaning which isn't there. But the impulse to read allegorical significance into early works of literature, from which even the *Beowulf* has not escaped, has been at work also on *The Owl and the Nightingale*. The poem has been interpreted as symbolizing the antagonism between pleasure and asceticism, gaiety and gravity, art and philosophy, the minstrel and the preacher. Most recently it has been viewed as a conflict between the ideals of the newer love poetry of courtly origin and the religious, didactic poetry so prominent in medieval verse. A plausible case can be made out for all these interpretations and it is a pleasant exercise for one's ingenuity, but there is no necessity for seeing in the poem anything more than a lively altercation between two birds, with the poet's skill sufficiently revealed in the matching of wits, the thrust and parry of the opponents, the shrewd observation and homely wisdom for which the argument gives constant occasion. Its popularity is not easy to estimate. It survives in only two manuscripts, but there is record of a third and possibly also of a version in French which belonged in the fourteenth century to the abbey

Not an Allegory

of Titchfield in Hampshire.[7] This is not far from the region in which, on the evidence of dialect and allusions, the poem was probably written. It is interesting to note that the two MSS in which it is preserved today are those in which many of the religious poems discussed above [8] as evidence of the survival of the native tradition have likewise come down to us. That the poem is of English inspiration appears likely not only from the general tone and the frequent citation of English proverbs, many of them attributed to Alfred, but from the fact that no source has been found for the debate as a whole. The author was familiar with the matter found in books on natural history, but the theme and conduct of the poem seem to have been largely his own invention.

Date

It seems rather likely that the poem was written during the twelfth century, although the attempt to fix upon a more precise date has led to sharp differences of opinion. The earlier of the two MSS in which it exists is assigned on paleographical grounds to the first half of the thirteenth century. It contains an Anglo-Norman chronicle which stops at 1216 and the rest of the page is left blank, contrary to the usual practice of the scribe, as if with an eye to its possible continuation.[9] The MS was most likely written at about this time. The extant texts of *The Owl and the Nightingale,* however, go back to an earlier copy, which was itself not the author's original. Allowing for a reasonable time to permit of these stages in its transmission, we may venture to assign the poem to a date before 1200. More precise dating depends upon the interpretation placed upon certain allusions in the text. Near the middle of the poem there is reference to an incident that happened in the time of King Henry, and the mention of the king prompts the poet to say "Jesus his soule do merci!" The king alluded to can hardly be other than Henry II, who died in 1189, and if the natural interpretation is placed upon these words and we infer that the king is dead, we must date the poem after, but perhaps not long after 1189.[10] A seemingly pregnant allusion to "this peace" has been connected with a proclamation of 1195.[11] An allusion to a papal mission to the north is less clear, and has been interpreted in various ways. On the whole, a date in the closing years of the

[7] See R. M. Wilson, "More Lost Literature, II," *Leeds Studies,* VI. 31-32.
[8] Ch. II.
[9] Although, as J. E. Wells has pointed out (*MLN,* XLVIII. 515-519), the blank half page comes at the end of a gathering, this is still the most natural interpretation.
[10] Some scholars who interpret other allusions as referring to an earlier date seek to show that the expression might have been used of a living person. See, for example, Henry B. Hinckley, "The Date, Author, and Sources of the *Owl and the Nightingale,*" *PMLA,* XLIV (1929). 329-359, and Kathryn Huganir, *The Owl and the Nightingale: Sources, Date, Author* (Philadelphia, 1931). Arguments against such an interpretation are presented by Frederick Tupper, "The Date and Historical Background of *The Owl and the Nightingale,*" *PMLA,* XLIX (1934). 406-427, and J. W. H. Atkins, "A Note on the Owl and the Nightingale," *MLR,* XXXV (1940). 55-56. For additional discussion by these and other scholars see the bibliographies mentioned on p. 109.
[11] J. Hall, *Selections from Early Middle English,* II. 566, notes the peace maintained by the Justiciar Hubert Walter during Richard I's absence in 1194-98, and Frederick Tupper, in the article referred to above, calls attention to the *Edictum Regium* of 1195 "requiring every man above the age of fifteen years to take an oath that he would do all that in him lay for the preservation of the King's Peace."

twelfth century would seem to agree best with the present state of our knowledge.

Naturally the authorship of such a poem is a matter of considerable in- *Authorship* terest. Near the beginning of the debate the birds agree to refer their differences to "Master Nicholas of Guildford," who is praised by the Nightingale as wise and prudent and an enemy of vice, one who has moreover insight in matters of song. The Owl remarks that he was rather passionate in days gone by and fond of the nightingales, but his ardor is now cooled and she will trust his judgment. Again at the very end of the poem his name is introduced with obvious explicitness and his place of residence is carefully specified as at Portisham, in Dorsetshire. He is shamefully neglected by the bishops, who bestow livings on their own kin, even on children, while passing him by. He has but one dwelling, whereas it would be for their own good if he were always at their service with livings in several places. He delivers many right judgments and much wisdom "through his mouth and through his hand," whereby things are better even as far away as Scotland. The most natural explanation of these passages is that the author was taking the opportunity to call attention to himself, and we should therefore seek to identify this Nicholas of Guildford. Various persons have been proposed, but none of them possesses all the qualifications for a completely satisfactory identification.[12] Whoever he was, he was a man of considerable learning, of an age to have left the wildness of youth behind him, a cleric living at the time he wrote the poem in the Dorset town of Portisham.[13]

The Owl and the Nightingale would have been a remarkable poem at any date, even in the time of Chaucer. It would cause perhaps less surprise about the year 1200 if it had been written in French. But the only thing French about it is the four-stress couplet in which it is cast. For a poem of 1704 lines to be written at this date in English on a secular theme, when almost everything that we have in English verse is either religious or didactic, is what seems so extraordinary. One remembers as comparable only occasional passages in Layamon's *Brut*. Its charm lies in its naturalness and freshness, the frankness with which the birds bring their accusations against each other, the liveliness and skill with which they meet each charge. They are very human in their emotions and their reasoning, but they never cease to be birds, each revealing the characteristics which are associated with its species in the popular mind. The poem is without a dull moment; it is a superb *jeu d'esprit*, the clearest proof that the English poetic impulse, in districts sufficiently removed from the court, survived the Norman Conquest.

---

[12] Gadow equates him with one of that name found in documents of the diocese of Salisbury in 1209 and 1220, but there is nothing to connect this man with Portisham. Miss Huganir suggests a certain Nicholas, son of Thorwald, who served as an itinerant judge in certain counties between 1179 and 1182. Nothing connects him, however, with either Guildford or Portisham.

[13] A note in the MS indicates that a song once in the volume was the work of a *John* of Guildford, but it is not necessary to believe that he was therefore the author of the present poem.

VII

For Their Soul's Need

In the period before 1250, when the popular literature intended for the upper class was almost certain to be in French, there is no more typical example of the writing produced for the religious instruction and moral guidance of the mass of the people than the *Ormulum*. Some of the most interesting and characteristic works of the period to be written in English were composed, as the author of this long poem tells us, to be read to the folk "for their soul's need."

The *Ormulum* [1] is a poem which, if it had been preserved in its entirety, *Ormulum* would have reached the amazing length of 150,000 lines. We have, however, only about an eighth of it, some 20,000 short verses. As the author tells us in his preface,

> Þiss boc iss nemmnedd Orrmulum
> Forrþi þatt Orrm itt wrohhte,
> & itt is wrohht off quaþþrigan,
> Off Goddspellbokess fowwre.[2]

It would seem that Orm combined the ending of the Latin word *speculum*, so familiar in titles of medieval books (*Speculum Historiale, Speculum Vitae*, etc.), with his own name. It is possible that he was conscious of the diminutive force of the ending and was suggesting modestly that his effort should be thought of as "the little book of Orm." If so, it is the only evidence in the entire work that he had a sense of humor, for it would have filled ten volumes of modern print.

The name Orm (or Ormin) is Scandinavian. In the dedication addressed to Walter, his brother, Orm says that they were both members of the same religious order, the order of Augustinian canons. Attempts to identify him have not been successful,[3] but from his dialect it would seem that he lived in the northeast Midlands, possibly in northern Lincolnshire, and wrote about the year 1200. His laborious task was carried out at his brother's bidding and now that he has finished it he asks him to examine every verse and see that it contains nothing contrary to true belief. Conscious of his

---

[1] Ed. R. M. White (2v, Oxford, 1852) and Robert Holt (2v, Oxford, 1878).

[2] This book is named *Ormulum*
Because Orm wrought it,
And it is wrought of the *quadriga*
Of the four books of the gospel.

[3] For conjectures see Henry Bradley, "Where Was the *Ormulum* Written?" *Athenaeum*, May 19, 1906, p. 609, and James Wilson, *ibid.*, July 28, 1906, p. 104.

own rectitude he scorns detractors and rests confident that he will have earned his reward in Heaven.

What is the *Ormulum*? The author tells us that he has attempted with *Its* the little wit that the Lord has lent him—unfortunately not an understate- *Purpose* ment—to explain to ignorant folk most of the gospels that are read in the Mass throughout the year. From the list of Latin texts drawn up at the beginning as a kind of table of contents it is apparent that he went beyond the gospels and included also a number of excerpts from the Acts of the Apostles. His method is to begin with a paraphrase of the biblical passage and then to explain it in an extended exposition:

> Icc hafe sammnedd o þiss boc
> Þa Goddspelless neh alle,
> Þatt sinndenn o þe messeboc
> Inn all þe ȝer att messe.
> & aȝȝ affterr þe Goddspell stannt
> Þatt tatt te Goddspell meneþþ,
> Þatt mann birrþ spellenn to þe follc
> Off þeȝȝre sawle nede.

From this statement it might be inferred that the poet follows the missal and explains the gospel narratives as they occur day by day. This, however, is not what he does. He has reassembled the texts in a chronological arrangement, giving us the life of Christ in a series of episodes with homiletic interpolations. He has at times supplied links implying that his work was to be read consecutively and not in sections according to the gospel of the day. Where he found the materials for his explanations is still largely an unsolved problem.[4]

It must be admitted that in literary value the *Ormulum* approaches what *Its Value* the physicist calls the absolute zero. It is very tedious. Orm was careful not to overestimate the intelligence of his hearers, and he explains the obvious at painful length. He is a master of the art of writing without making the thought advance. He repeats himself shamelessly without so much as varying the phrase. He would have made a good pedagogue. Yet, paradoxically, the *Ormulum* is not without interest. In the first place, as a document in English cultural history it shows with what plain fare any literary taste of the humble classes might have to be satisfied when they were dependent for their books on the benevolent zeal of the pious. One can only hope that an abundant oral literature, though unrecorded, supplied what was missing from a well-balanced diet. In the second place, the *Ormulum* is not without interest as a revelation of human personality, for there *is* a personality be-

---

[4] The latest attempt at a solution is in H. C. Matthes, *Die Einheitlichkeit des Ormulum* (Heidelberg, 1933), where it is suggested that Orm used a *Biblia cum Glossis*, i.e., a text of the Bible provided with the interlinear gloss of Anselm of Laon (or more probably Peter Lombard) and the marginal commentary or *Glossa Ordinaria* commonly attributed to Walafrid Strabo. The present writer's objections to this theory are stated in *JEGP*, xxxvi (1937). 263-268. Cf. also Matthes' supplementary discussion, "Quellenauswertung und Quellenberufung im *Orrmulum*," *Anglia*, LIX (1935). 303-318.

hind it. It comes out most clearly in the dedication and the preface, but is apparent throughout the work. It is that of a completely serious nature, pursuing its laborious task with unswerving devotion and entire conviction. Orm is never in doubt about the importance of his mission. His zeal never flags. He is meticulous about little things, determined to be clear even to the dullest mind, for souls are at stake. He devises a new system of spelling,[5] thereby becoming our first spelling reformer, and admonishes future copyists always to write consonants twice where they are doubled in his copy: "otherwise they may not write rightly the word." He was obviously a "fussy" person, one that we might not enjoy living with, but distinctive. We would be touched by his piety and unselfishness, wearied by his prolixity, irritated by his insistence upon little things of no importance, but we would remember him. The reward which he deserved and confidently looked forward to in the next world is doubtless his, but the hope that his book would be often copied and widely read was never realized. What survives is apparently a fragment of his own holograph manuscript.

Vices and Virtues

At about the same date as the *Ormulum* an anonymous treatise in prose was written in the East Midland area, probably in Essex. It has been given the name *Vices and Virtues*,[6] since the beginning is a soul's confession of its sins and the remainder an extended discourse by Reason on a wide variety of virtues. The treatise is cast in a slight framework of dialogue which amounts to little more than an occasional request by the soul for further instruction from Reason. Each vice or virtue is treated as a separate item without much attempt at continuity or strict sequence. Yet the occasional instances in which the preacher passes from the general to concrete and particular illustrations of his teaching, or drops a remark which hints at contemporary conditions, save the work from the dullness to which its commonplace matter and workaday style would predispose it. Once in a long while the author surprises us with a striking thought or picturesque phrase, as when he remarks that it is "a great wrath of God that man is so blind that he goes to Hell laughing." But in general he presents his matter plainly and soberly, in a manner consistent with his aim, expressed at the close through the mouth of Reason: "Dear soul, I have made this little writ with sore toil ... in order to instruct thee, to warn thee, and to help thee and to save thee."

Genesis and Exodus

Serving the soul's need in another way is the biblical paraphrase of *Genesis and Exodus*[7] written in its present form about 1250 in Norfolk, although probably originating somewhat farther north. It consists of slightly more than 4000 lines in fairly regular four-stress couplets. The author has great faith in human nature:

[5] The *Ormulum* is of the greatest value to the Middle English philologist in indicating for us the quantity of the vowels in the many words which it contains.
[6] Ed. F. Holthausen (London, 1888-1921; *EETS*, 89 and 159).
[7] Ed. Richard Morris (London, 1865; *EETS*, 7). The suggestion of Ten Brink that the *Exodus* might be by a different author is disposed of by A. Fritzsche, "Ist die altenglische Story of Genesis and Exodus das Werk eines Verfassers?" *Anglia*, v (1882). 43-90.

Cristene men ogen ben so fagen
So fueles arn quan he it sen dagen,
Ðan man hem telled soðe tale
Wid londes speche and wordes smale
Of blisses dune, of sorwes dale.[8]

And so he begins to tell the story of Genesis with many an interesting detail. The Devil was created on Sunday and "fell out" on Monday. Adam was made "in Damascus field." While God created woman Adam slept and saw in a dream much that should be hereafter. The woman's first name was Issa; after she brought us to woe Adam named her Eve. Abel was a hundred years old when Cain slew him. Such legendary matter is most prevalent in the first five hundred lines. The *Exodus* is more selective and considerably shorter than the *Genesis*. It is concerned mainly with the life of Moses. "Out of Latin," says the poet, "this song is drawn," and it is clear that he drew upon more than the Bible. He certainly used the *Historia Scholastica* of Peter Comestor and we may feel fairly sure that he used it at first hand.[9] It is equally certain that in the earlier pages he had other sources as well, possibly one of the biblical paraphrases in French verse. *Genesis and Exodus* lacks the poetical quality, the richness of phrase and emotional force, of the Old English *Genesis* and other Old English biblical poetry, but it tells its story clearly and easily, and by a judicious selection of incidents offers a pleasantly versified survey of early Old Testament history.

Written in the same dialect and at about the same time is the Middle English representative of a popular medieval type, the *Bestiary*.[10] The poem, some 800 short lines, is made up of descriptions more or less fabulous of the lion, eagle, serpent, ant, hart, fox, spider, whale, mermaid, elephant, turtle-dove, panther, and the culver or dove, followed in each case by a Christian application or moral. The *Bestiary* is associated in our minds with popular science, and doubtless it was for its natural history that it enjoyed its great popularity. But in plan and intention it was a work of religious and moral edification and should be so thought of. The fictitious natural history is adopted for the sake of the moral. *The Bestiary*

Cethegrandë [whale] is a fiṡ [fish]
Ðe moste ðat in water is.

When the sea is stormy it comes to the surface. Sailors, thinking it is an island, take refuge on its back and build a fire. When the whale eventually feels the heat, it dives to the bottom, carrying all its too trusting victims

---

[8] Christian men ought to be as fain
As birds are when they see it become day,
When man tells them a true tale
With native speech and words small,
Of bliss's down [upland], of sorrow's dale.

[9] Cf. Fritzsche, *op. cit.*, p. 48.

[10] Edited several times but most accessible in Richard Morris, *An Old English Miscellany* (London, 1872; EETS, 49) and Joseph Hall, *Selections from Early Middle English* (Oxford, 1920). See also above, p. 136.

to destruction. It symbolizes the devil and his wiles. The serpent when old fasts until its skin grows loose about it; then it strips off its covering by crawling through a stone with a hole in it. Man by fasting and penance should in like manner free himself from the sins in which he has become enveloped. The elephant is made to illustrate all Christian history. It falls, like man, because of a tree; it cannot be raised by its fellows until one young elephant (like Christ) effects its release. The English poem is a free rendering of the Latin *Physiologus* of Theobaldus, an eleventh-century abbot, it is thought, of Monte Cassino. But all medieval bestiaries go back ultimately to a Greek text of the fourth century written in Alexandria, or, more probably, in Caesarea in Palestine,[11] and translated into Syriac, Armenian, and most of the European languages. The influence of the *Physiologus* on medieval art was widespread, and allusions to bestiary material are frequent in literature down to the Age of Elizabeth, when Lyly made unnatural natural history a feature of Euphuistic style.[12]

A religious theme which enjoyed equal popularity throughout Europe in the Middle Ages was the story of Christ's descent into Hell to release the souls of those who had lived worthily and died before His coming. The *Harrowing of Hell*[13] in Middle English verse was written about 1250. It is based on the apocryphal *Gospel of Nicodemus*,[14] which contributed not only this striking episode to literature but is largely responsible for the popularity of such legends as that of Longinus, who pierced Christ's side with his spear and was cured of blindness by the blood which fell on his eyes, of St. Veronica and her handkerchief, of Seth's mission to Paradise for the oil of mercy, of Antichrist, and other characters and incidents. The framework of the *Harrowing of Hell* is narrative, but after a forty-line introduction the account proceeds entirely by means of dialogue in which Adam and Eve, Abraham, David, John the Baptist, and Moses call confidently upon Christ and in each case have their claims acknowledged. The form of the text renders it suitable for dramatic presentation, but there is no evidence that it was ever so produced.

The Harrowing of Hell

The liveliest of the early religious and admonitory works considered in this chapter is a spirited debate known as the *Disputisoun between the Body and the Soul*.[15] The poet, lying in bed on a winter night, sees a man

The Body and Soul

[11] See Max Wellman, *Der Physiologus* (Leipzig, 1930). The standard earlier authority is Fr. Lauchert, *Geschichte des Physiologus* (Strassburg, 1889); Lauchert is also the author of the article in the *Catholic Encyclopedia*.
[12] Cf. John Lyly, *Works*, ed. R. W. Bond (3v, Oxford, 1902); intro., I. 131-134.
[13] The text is edited from all MSS by William H. Hulme, *The Middle-English Harrowing of Hell and Gospel of Nicodemus* (London, 1907; EETSES, 100). For the development of the legend see Hulme's introduction and J. Monnier, *La Descente aux Enfers* (Paris, 1905). On the popularity of the theme in drama see Karl Young, *The Drama of the Medieval Church* (Oxford, 1933), I. 149-177, and the works mentioned on p. 561.
[14] The Latin *Gospel of Nicodemus* consists of two parts, the *Acta Pilati* (fourth century) and the *Descensus Christi ad Inferos* (second or third century). The text is in C. Tischendorf, *Evangelia Apocrypha* (Leipzig, 1876), English translation in M. R. James, *The Apocryphal New Testament* (Oxford, 1924). Versions in Middle English verse (c. 1300-1325) and prose exist, the verse texts being edited by Hulme, as above.
[15] Four of the seven manuscripts of the text are printed by W. Linow, *Þe Desputisoun bitwen þe Bodi and þe Soule* (Erlangen, 1889; *Erlanger Beiträge*, 1).

velous vision—the body of a proud knight lying on a bier. As the soul of the dead man is about to depart, it pauses and beholds the body from which it has just come. "Woe worth thy flesh, thy foul blood!" it says, and proceeds to taunt the Body truculently. Where now are its castles and towers, its rich clothes, its fine horses, its cunning cooks, through whose skill it made its foul flesh to swell? Now both Body and Soul shall suffer the pains of Hell. The Body retorts that it was the Soul's business to keep it from evil. But this simple exculpation does not suffice. "Body, be still!" says the Soul. "Who taught thee all this wit?" Both of us shall answer for our misspent life at Doomsday. Thou hast paid no heed to God. Now thou art loathsome to see: no lady would kiss thee: thy friends would flee if they saw thee coming down the street. The Body's rejoinder is that it did nothing without the Soul, that it would have been better off without a soul, like a dumb beast conscious of no hereafter. The Soul denies that it had any influence over the Body after its childhood, and the Body argues that more strict discipline in youth would have saved it. After this the Soul weeps and reiterates its charges of the Body's wilful ways. Finally the Body laments its past life, but as the Soul says, it is too late. Repentance is futile after death. And now the Soul may linger no longer. The fiends of Hell are heard crying exultantly as they come to fetch it away. There is a terrifying description of the tortures inflicted by the devils as they fall upon the unhappy Soul, and the dreamer awakes in a cold sweat because of the scene which he has witnessed.

The origin of this lively conception has been traced back to the Eastern *Its* church,[16] to a sermon, or sermons, of the *memento mori* type in which a *Origin* reminder of death is used as an inducement to virtue, and the admonition is pointed by an *exemplum* portraying the death of a sinful man amid the reproaches of the departing soul. There were apparently two types of this sermon: one a fairly common type in which only the soul speaks, and the other a type of which the only example yet known consists of some fragments embedded in an Irish homily of the *Leabhar Breac,* in which the body speaks in reply. The first may be considered the prototype of those Body and Soul texts in which the Soul addresses the Body, but the Body does not reply.[17] The second type is presumably the ancestor of the debates between the Body and Soul. The earliest literary treatment of the debate type is a long Latin poem of the twelfth century, the importance of which has only recently been demonstrated.[18] It is the source of a number of subsequent treatments in Latin, French, Spanish, etc. In spite of considerable merit, the poem is lacking in that lively interchange of accusation and rejoinder necessary to the true debate. This defect was supplied by a thirteenth-

[16] On the beginnings of the legend see Th. Batiouchkof, "Le Débat de l'ame et du corps," *Romania,* xx (1891). 1-55; 513-578, and Louise Dudley, *The Egyptian Elements in the Legend of the Body and Soul* (Baltimore, 1911).
[17] Such as the Old English *Address of the Soul to the Body* (see above, p. 81) and the early Middle English text preserved in the *Worcester Fragments* (see p. 82).
[18] Eleanor Kellogg Heningham. *An Early Latin Debate of the Body and Soul* (1939).

century poem, the *Conflictus Corporis et Animae,* which may well have been the work of Bishop Grosseteste.[19] In this Latin form the Body and Soul theme attained its widest circulation,[20] and it is from this text that the Middle English poem derives.

Nearly all these works of religious edification or moral exhortation of the thirteenth century may be considered as patterns for later writings of a similar kind. The *Ormulum,* for example, may be compared with the *Northern Homily Cycle* (p. 205), the *Genesis and Exodus* with the earlier part of the *Cursor Mundi* (p. 206), the *Vices and Virtues* with *Handlyng Synne* (p. 204) or the *Parson's Tale.* Occasionally they inspired direct imitation as when an unknown poet modeled after the debate of the *Body and Soul* a similar dialogue between the *Body and the Worms.*[21] Always the motive is the same: each poet is writing for the people something "for their soul's need."

[19] See Hans Walther, *Das Streitgedicht in der lateinischen Literatur des Mittelalters* (Munich, 1920), pp. 70 ff.

[20] There are 132 MSS extant. The poem is often called the *Visio Philiberti.* Entering into the Body and Soul poems and many other religious works involving legends of Heaven and Hell are elements which received wide circulation in the Middle Ages through the apocryphal *Visio Pauli.* On this important text see Theodore Silverstein, *Visio Sancti Pauli: The History of the Apocalypse in Latin together with Nine Texts* (London, 1935; *Studies and Documents,* ed. K. and S. Lake, Vol. IV).

[21] Edited by Karl Brunner, *Archiv,* CLXVII (1935). 29-35.

VIII
The Arthurian Legend to Layamon

The most popular theme which later English poetry derived from medieval *The* legend is the story of King Arthur, his wife, Guinevere, and the celebrated *Arthurian* knights—Lancelot, Gawain, Perceval of Grail fame, and many others— *Legend* associated with his court.[1] The origin of many of the stories which came eventually to make up this complex body of material is obscure and we cannot even be certain that an historical figure lies behind the character of Arthur himself. In the present chapter we shall consider the development of the legend up to Layamon, the point at which it first makes its appearance in English, reserving our treatment of the romances concerned with this matter for a later chapter.

It is universally acknowledged that the story of Arthur belongs to Celtic *Of Celtic* tradition and that it originated with the particular branch of the Celts settled *Origin* in Wales and Cornwall. It seems to have remained largely a matter of local interest until the twelfth, or as some believe, the eleventh century. It achieved European circulation and renown with the publication of the *Historia Regum Britanniae* (1137) of Geoffrey of Monmouth and the Arthurian romances of the greatest of French writers of romance, Chrétien de Troyes (fl. 1160-90).[2] On these simple facts there is general agreement,

[1] The first comprehensive work on the Arthurian legend was J. D. Bruce, *The Evolution of Arthurian Romance ... to ... 1300* (2v, Baltimore and Göttingen, 1923; rptd. with supplement to bibliography by A. Hilka, 1928; *Hesperia*, Ergänzungsreihe, VIII-IX). The subsequent bibliography may be found in *Arthurian Bibliography*, Vol. I (1922-29), Vol. II (1930-35) compiled by John J. Parry and Margaret Schlauch for the MLA (1931, 1936), and continued for subsequent years in *MLQ*. E. K. Chambers, *Arthur of Britain* (1927) is a brief but stimulating treatment. For the earliest materials see Robert H. Fletcher, *The Arthurian Material in the Chronicles* (1906; *Harvard Studies & Notes in Phil. & Lit.*, X). Edmund Faral's discussion of this material, *La Légende Arthurienne* (3v, Paris, 1929), has a strong anti-Celtic bias. On the French Arthurian romances the article of Gaston Paris, "Romans en vers du cycle de la Table Ronde," *Hist. Litt. de la France*, xxx (1888), 1-270, is indispensable.

[2] Chrétien de Troyes is the author of the earliest Arthurian romances that have come down to us: *Erec et Enide, Cligés, Lancelot* (or *Le Conte de la Charette*), *Yvain*, and *Perceval*, or *Le Conte du Graal*. In addition, he mentions a poem on King Marc and Iseult which has not survived but which must have been concerned with at least a part of the Tristan and Iseult story. The extant romances of Chrétien were written in the order named, but they cannot be dated more precisely than c. 1160-1190. (For an attempt to push the earlier date forward somewhat, see F. E. Guyer, in *MP*, xxvi (1929). 257-277.) The standard editions of *Erec, Cligés, Lancelot,* and *Yvain* are those of Wendelin Foerster (Halle, 1884-). These romances have been translated into English by W. W. Comfort for the Everyman's Library (1913). The *Conte du Graal* was left unfinished at Chrétien's death (about 10,000 lines) and continued by a succession of continuators to a length of 60,000 lines. The text of Chrétien's portion is now available in Alfons Hilka, *Der Percevalroman* (Halle, 1932), replacing the very scarce edition of C. Potvin (6v, Mons, 1865-71). For a bibliography of Chrétien scholarship see John Reinhard, "Chrétien de Troyes: A Bibliographical Essay," *Essays and Studies in English and Compar. Lit.* (Ann Arbor, Mich., 1932), pp. 195-231, and Wilhelm Kellermann, "Wege

but on a number of other important questions scholarly opinion is sharply divided. How fully developed were Arthurian stories in Celtic literature? How much did Chrétien and other French poets owe to Celtic sources? Were there Arthurian romances in French before Chrétien? Was Arthur an historical figure? Did Geoffrey of Monmouth have an ancient book in the British tongue, as he maintained, even though his own work is demonstrably more than a translation of such a volume?

Celticists and Inventionists

On the first three of these questions scholars split sharply into two schools, the Celticists and the inventionists. The former are strongly impressed by the many parallels between the romances of Chrétien and of other medieval poets on the one hand and Celtic stories, folk-tales, and popular traditions on the other.[3] They believe that the writers of French romances derived an important part of their material from Welsh and Breton tradition, either written or oral. The opponents of this view, however, feel that the indebtedness of French authors to Celtic sources has been overstressed. They insist that Chrétien and his contemporaries were not folklorists but poets possessed with creative imagination, and that they enjoyed the same privilege of inventing their stories as do modern poets. It may be questioned whether what we know of the ways of medieval poets in other fields than Arthurian legend justifies the belief that they habitually exercised this privilege, but at least the position of the inventionists has the virtue of simplicity: what cannot be traced to a source fairly close at hand can be credited to the invention of the poet.

Scarcity of Welsh Texts

It must be admitted that the Celticists have sometimes pushed their quest for parallels pretty far, but the proper presentation of their point of view is rendered difficult by the paucity of Welsh and Breton literature that ha come down to us from early times. For Brittany there are no literary text from the Middle Ages. What survives from the Welsh literature of thi period is mainly contained in four manuscripts that fill two moderate-size volumes of modern print.[4] If the surviving Welsh literature were in an way comparable in richness to that of Ireland, where geographical and po litical separation permitted an unbroken continuity of language and literar tradition, many problems of Arthurian origins which must continue t trouble us would be readily settled. As it is, recourse must be had constantl to Irish literature. Since the Welsh and the Irish are merely differer branches of the same ethnic and linguistic stock, it is to be assumed tha they preserved many traditions in common and may well have influence each other. Although Irish literature does not know Arthur, we find man parallels in incident and motif with Arthurian romance, which give us som

---

und Ziele der neuen Chrestien de Troyes-Forschung," *Germ-Rom. Monatsschrift*, XXIII (1935 204-228.
    [3] For examples of this view see the studies of Arthur C. L. Brown, particularly *Iwain: Study in the Origins of Arthurian Romance* (Boston, 1903; *Harvard Studies & Notes Phil. & Lit.*, VIII.) and "The Round Table before Wace," *ibid.*, VII (1900). 183-205. A mo extreme position is taken by Roger S. Loomis, *Celtic Myth and Arthurian Romance* (192
    [4] W. F. Skene, *Four Ancient Books of Wales* (2v, Edinburgh, 1868).

idea of what we might expect in Welsh literature if it had been preserved in equal fullness. However, the existence among the *Mabinogion* [5] of a *The* Welsh story like *Kulhwch and Olwen* with its obviously primitive features *Mabinogion* is an indication that a well-developed body of Arthurian narrative existed among the Welsh before such stories appear in French literature in the work of Chrétien de Troyes.

With the poems of Chrétien French romances of Arthurian theme reached *Were* their highest perfection in the Middle Ages. But these poems are also the *There* earliest Arthurian romances that have come down to us, and therefore some *Arthurian* students are disposed to credit Chrétien with the creation of the type. This *Romances* is somewhat as if the author of *Hamlet* had been the inventor of English *before* tragedy, or at least of the revenge play It is not usual for new literary types *Chrétien?* to spring fully formed from the head of Jove, and such a method of accounting for *Hamlet* would not carry full conviction even if we could not trace the development of English drama back through the *Spanish Tragedy* and *Gorboduc* to the *Quem quaeritis* (see chapter XIX). It is some such difficulty as this that many scholars find with the view that Chrétien was the creator of Arthurian romance. And, indeed, there is some evidence at least that Arthurian stories that could not have come from Geoffrey of Monmouth were known on the Continent at least by the time Chrétien was writing and probably as early as the close of the previous century. This is not the place to go into the evidence, which Pio Rajna called attention to,[6] of Italians who had been named after Arthur and Gawain before 1100, or the implications of the Arthurian sculpture on the cathedral at Modena in northern Italy, which some scholars date 1099-1106 and others put after the middle of the twelfth century.[7] It is enough for us here to recognize that there are many uncertainties in the early history of the Arthurian legend, many questions on which it is ill-advised to be too dogmatic.

If Arthur played a part in actual history, it was as a leader of the Celts *Arthur* in their resistance to the Teutonic invaders at the beginning of the sixth century. The name is Roman (*Artorius*) and suggests a Roman family settled in Britain. We know of a Roman military man who held a high com-

---

[5] The *Mabinogion* has become almost an English classic in the translation of Lady Charlotte Guest, which has often been reprinted. A critical edition of the Welsh text with scholarly apparatus and a more literal, French translation will be found in J. Loth, *Les Mabinogion* 2ed., 2v, Paris, 1913).

[6] Pio Rajna, "Gli eroi brettoni nell' onomastica italiana del secolo XII," *Romania*, XVII (888). 161-185, 355-365.

[7] The bibliography of this controversy has become too extensive to record here. The arguments for an early date are presented (with excellent plates) by Roger S. Loomis in "The Date, Source, and Subject of the Arthurian Sculpture at Modena," *Medieval Studies in Memory of Gertrude Schoepperle Loomis* (Paris, 1927), pp. 209-228, and "La Légende archéologique la cathédrale de Modène," *Gaz. des Beaux-Arts*, XVIII (1928). 109-122. The most recent attacks on an early date are Leonardo Olschki, "La Cattedrale di Modena e il suo rilievo arturiano," *Archivum Romanicum*, XIX (1935). 145-182, and G. H. Gerould, "Arthurian romance and the Date of the Relief at Modena," *Speculum*, X (1935). 355-376, to which Professor Loomis has replied in "The Modena Sculpture and Arthurian Romance," *Studi Medievali*, n.s. IX (1936). 1-17, and "Geoffrey of Monmouth and the Modena Archivolt," *Speculum*, XIII (1938). 221-231. From these articles the previous scholarship on the question can be assembled.

mand in the island in the third century,[8] and who might have left numerous descendants in a profession which was traditional in Roman families. There is no mention of Arthur in any contemporary record, and we cannot but consider it strange that Gildas,[9] who mentions the battle of Mount Badon— in later accounts Arthur's most famous battle—makes no mention of Arthur, but names Ambrosius Aurelianus as the distinguished Roman leader of the Celtic forces. The earliest explicit mention of the Arthur of later romance is

Nennius in a compilation of around 800 known as the *Historia Brittonum*, by Nennius.[10] Here Arthur receives a paragraph and is said to have been twelve times chosen as the leader of the Celts and to have been victorious in twelve great battles. In the last of these, the battle of Mount Badon, he is credited with killing 960 of the enemy single-handed. It is clear that in Nennius Arthur has already become the object of legendary exaggeration, but it is interesting to observe that Nennius describes him as *dux bellorum,* not as a king, and explicitly says that there were many more noble in rank than he. This seems to ring true, and in spite of the lack of trustworthy evidence, most scholars are disposed to agree with Oman when he says, "I . . . incline to think that a real figure lurks beneath the tale of the *Historia Brittonum.*"

It would be interesting to pause over the bits of Arthurian material in the *Annales Cambriae* (*c.* 954),[11] in the *Chronicle of Mont St. Michel* (after 1056) in which Arthur is called "Rex Britannorum," in the lives of certain Welsh saints,[12] the miracle reported by Herman of Tournai some time after 1113,[13] and the testimony of William of Malmesbury to the existence of popular traditions concerning Arthur in his *Gesta Regum Anglorum* (1125) since this is the work of an Englishman. None of these texts throw any light on the historical character of Arthur, but they would bear witness to his growing popularity and the existence of numerous legends about him as well as about Gawain, Kai, Bedevere, and others associated with him. We must, however, turn at once to the most important work in the earlier history of this legend.

Geoffrey of Monmouth Geoffrey of Monmouth (*c.* 1100-*c.* 1155) was born and reared in Wales, though possibly of Breton stock,[14] and, like Sir Walter Scott later, must have been saturated from childhood with the folk tales and traditions of the story-

[8] Cf. the art. "Artorius" in Pauly-Wissowa, *Real-Encyclopädie*, Charles Oman, *England before the Norman Conquest* (1910), p. 211, Kemp Malone, "Artorius," *MP.* XXII (1925) 367-374, and R. G. Collingwood and J. N. L. Myres, *Roman Britain and the English Settlement* (Oxford, 1936), pp. 320-324.

[9] The *De Excidio et Conquestu Britanniae* (written about 545) gives after a fashion an account of the history of Britain (first twenty-six chapters) but the greater part of the treatise is an attack upon certain rulers in Gildas's own day, the policy of forming an alliance with the Teutons, and the vices of the British people which have brought their present misfortune upon them. He also makes no mention of Constantine, Germanus, Hengist, and others whom he might be expected to refer to. The standard edition is that of Mommsen in the *Mon. Germ. Hist.* (1898). There is a translation in John A. Giles, *Six Old English Chronicles* (1848).

[10] The standard editions are those of Mommsen, *op. cit.,* and Ferdinand Lot, *Nennius et l'Historia Brittonum* (Paris, 1934). Translation also in Giles.

[11] On these matters see Bruce, and other works mentioned in the footnote on p. 165.

[12] Cf. the most recent examination of these texts by J. S. P. Tatlock, "The Dates of the Arthurian Saints' Legends," *Speculum*, XIV (1939). 345-365.

[13] See E. Faral, "Un des plus anciens textes relatifs à Arthur," *Arthuriana*, I (1929). 21-29

[14] See Sir John Edward Lloyd, "Geoffrey of Monmouth," *EHR*, LVII (1942). 460-468.

loving Celts. From the age of about thirty he was living as a canon at Oxford, and, having friends like Walter the Archdeacon and Robert de Chesney, must have looked forward in like manner to a career in the Church. Whether obeying an innate urge or acting with an eye to promotion, he produced a book ostensibly recording the early history of Britain, the *Historia Regum Britanniae* (1137).[15] It is full of legendary matter that has found its way into later English literature—stories of Locrine, Lear, Gorboduc, Cymbeline, and the like. What is more important, it reaches by the middle of Book VI the figures of Uther Pendragon and Merlin, and continues with Arthurian matters to the end of the work. In all about two-fifths of a sizable volume are devoted to the doings of King Arthur.[16] We get the story of his birth and Merlin's share in the affair between Uther and Ygerne. Upon Uther's death, Arthur becomes king, subdues the Picts and Scots, conquers Ireland, Iceland, Norway, Dacia, Aquitaine, and Gaul, with of course the help of Gawain and other loyal supporters. There is an excellent account of his single combat with Frollo, governor of Gaul. He celebrates his victories with a magnificent court and coronation ceremony attended by princes from all over western Europe. In the midst of the revelry Rome demands tribute of the Britons, a demand which is not only scornfully rejected but which leads Arthur to determine on the conquest of the imperial city. He commits the government and Queen Guanhumara to his nephew Mordred and sails for the Continent, only to be recalled by his nephew's treason and his wife's disloyalty. There is an account of Guinevere's flight to a nunnery, the defeat of Mordred, and the carrying of the mortally wounded Arthur to Avalon. Here is the full framework of the story so well known to us in later times. In it Arthur occupies the center of the stage and has not yet been thrust into the background by the adventures of his famous followers. He is represented as a great warrior, conquering all the better known parts of the world, rather than as a fairy king holding sway over a realm not too clearly defined.

In the dedication and in three other places in the volume Geoffrey claims as his authority a certain ancient book in the British tongue—that is, in Welsh or Breton—which he was given by his friend Walter, Archdeacon of Oxford. This book, he says, related in due sequence and in stories of exceeding beauty the whole history of the island from Brutus, the first king of the Britains, down to Cadwallader, the son of Cadwallo. All he has had to do is to turn it into simple and unadorned Latin. This modest avowal is not to be taken too seriously. No such book is known and in his later references to it the author, it strikes us, "doth protest too much." It is hard to reconcile his close paraphrases and direct borrowings from Gildas, Nennius, Bede, Livy, and even Virgil, with the idea of a simple translation of a Celtic book, to say nothing of the appearance, thinly disguised, of numerous incidents

His Avowed Source

[15] The text is conveniently available in Acton Griscom, *The Historia Regum Britanniae of Geoffrey of Monmouth* (London, 1929) and Edmond Faral, *La Légende Arthurienne* (3v, Paris, 1929).

[16] Geoffrey of Monmouth is possibly the author also of a Latin poem of 1529 lines on the life of Merlin. Text and translation will be found in J. J. Parry, *The Vita Merlini* (Urbana, 1925).

in recent history transferred to ancient times. Geoffrey's *Historia* is a mixture of matter drawn from previous books, the products of his own free invention, and probably a large element of legendary lore. It would not have done to admit that what purported to be a serious history was partly fiction and partly a synthesis of old wives' tales.[17]

The popularity of Geoffrey's history, whatever some of his contemporaries thought of its validity, was very great,[18] but its enjoyment was naturally limited to those who could read Latin. For a large number of men and women at the court it would have remained a closed book if it had not been translated. Several translations, indeed, soon appeared in French verse, among them one by Geoffrey Gaimar, another by Wace. Gaimar's version is lost,[19] no doubt a victim of neglect after the appearance of Wace's more brilliant rendering, the *Roman de Brut* (1155).[20] Wace was a Norman poet (*c.* 1100-*c.* 1175) who wrote under English patronage.[21] In his 15,000 lines he converted Geoffrey's dignified prose narrative into a lively and vigorous story. Geoffrey was ostensibly writing history; Wace was writing a poem. He paints vivid pictures, dramatizes important incidents, gives expression to his personal feelings, and never seems to forget the audience he is aiming to please. He makes a few interesting additions to his source, and mentions three times the Round Table in a manner which suggests that it was already familiar to his audience. Yet these are the earliest references to it in literature. It is apparent that he was familiar with Arthurian traditions apart from what he found in Geoffrey of Monmouth.[22]

Wace

The Arthurian story makes its first appearance in English in the work of a humble priest living on the banks of the Severn in Worcestershire. As he tells us in the preface to his work, his name was Layamon [23] and he was attached to the church at Ernley (Arley Regis), near Radstone. While enjoying this quiet life of a clerk, he says, it came into his mind to write about

Layamon's Brut

[17] On Geoffrey of Monmouth's literary practices see Vol. II of Faral, who minimizes, however, the elements that may have come from popular tradition.

[18] This is evident from the more than 200 manuscripts still extant. Alfred of Beverley, writing about 1150, says it was such a common subject of conversation that any one who did not know its stories was considered a fool. A part of its popularity may have been due to the satisfaction it gave the Anglo-French court to point to something in the past history of Britain comparable to Charlemagne and his peers in France. See G. H. Gerould, "King Arthur and Politics," *Speculum*, II (1927). 33-51.

[19] On Gaimar see above, p. 138. A text known as the Münchener *Brut* has sometimes been thought a fragment of Gaimar's version, but there are objections to this view. See the discussion by Alexander Bell, "The Munich *Brut* and the *Estoire des Bretuns*," MLR, XXXIV (1939) 321-354.

[20] Edited by Le Roux de Lincy (2v, Rouen, 1836-38). A new edition has now appeared in the SATF, edited by Ivor Arnold (2v, Paris, 1938-40).

[21] Layamon tells us that Wace dedicated the *Roman de Brut* to Eleanor of Aquitaine, and it was for her husband, Henry II, that he began a poem of similar character on the history of Normandy, the *Roman de Rou* (Rollo). See above, p. 138.

[22] See also Margaret Houck, *The Sources of the Roman de Brut of Wace* (Berkeley, 1941 *Univ. of Calif. Pub. in English*, Vol. V, No. 2).

[23] Properly Laȝamon. The spelling *Layamon* is a concession to printers' fonts sanctioned by usage. The guttural spirant was vocalized in the twelfth century to form a diphthong *au* often written *aw*. Consequently some scholars prefer the modernization Lawman. The only edition of Layamon's *Brut* is that of Sir Frederic Madden (3v, 1847), where the two texts are printed in parallel. See also N. Bøgholm, *The Layamon Texts: A Linguistical Investigatio* (Copenhagen, 1944; *Travaux du cercle linguistique de Copenhague*, III).

the noble deeds of the English, and with this purpose in view he traveled about in search of books on the subject. The three that he acquired were Bede's *Ecclesiastical History* in the Old English translation inspired by King Alfred; the Latin text of this, which he does not seem to have fully recognized; and the work of a French clerk named Wace ("how he could write!"). He set out to condense these three works into a single narrative, but it is clear that he soon found himself so completely under the spell of Wace that he put the other two aside and devoted himself to turning the *Roman de Brut* into English. Allusions in his poem show that he was writing after the death of Henry II (1189) and probably just before King John forbade the payment of Peter's pence in May, 1206. It is customary, therefore, to assign Layamon's *Brut* to the year 1205.

The English poem is twice the length of the French. The difference is due mainly to a certain leisurely manner that seems to characterize Layamon. He adds to an idea already adequately expressed a line of explanation or supplement; he sometimes repeats himself in only slightly different words. He did not aim at terseness or compression. To a slight extent the difference in length is due to new materials which he introduced. These are not numerous but have a certain significance. They include such things as the gifts which the elves conferred upon Arthur at birth, the description of his armor—its magic properties or fabrication by supernatural smiths—the dream in which he received warning of Mordred's treason, and added circumstances in the account of the passing of Arthur. But the longest and most interesting addition which Layamon makes is the story of the creation of the Round Table—describing the fighting that broke out at a Christmas feast over precedence at table, and telling how some time later when the king was journeying in Cornwall a skilful craftsman in wood offered to fashion him a table at which sixteen hundred or more could sit without discrimination yet which could be folded up and carried about from place to place. An attempt has often been made in the past to account for these additional features by suggesting that Layamon may have had a version of the *Roman de Brut* fuller in certain respects than that available in the edition of Le Roux de Lincy—in other words, an expanded Wace. But the recent publication of a new text based upon all the extant manuscripts does not support this view, and we must continue to suppose that Layamon, like Wace, was familiar with Arthurian traditions, oral or written, not found in his immediate source.

In spite of the fact that he was translating from a French source Layamon is a thoroughly English poet. He had apparently been brought up on the Old English alliterative verse and his own lines are so clearly in this tradition that about half of them can be scanned by Old English standards. He makes frequent use of rime, however, as an additional ornament. The tradition which he represents is apparently a late one which has left behind some of the older practices and acquired certain new habits in their place.[24]

Layamon's Additions

Its English Character

[24] See J. S. P. Tatlock. "Laȝamon's Poetic Style and Its Relations," *Manly Anniversary Studies* (Chicago, 1923), pp. 3-11.

Nevertheless it is still English. His vocabulary is remarkable for the small number of French words in it, particularly in view of the fact that he was translating from a French poem. But it is in those less tangible qualities of tone and spirit that he is perhaps most English of all.[25] In scores of little touches he adds to or alters a scene, an image, or an idea, until it appears something quite different from what it was in Wace. He has an eye for

Layamon the Poet

nature and outdoor life, the sea and the sky. Arrows fly as thick as hail; a cornered warrior is compared to a wild boar at bay; Childeric pursued by Arthur is likened to a fox with the dogs following close on his trail, seeking his hole only to be trapped. These are images drawn from his own observation, but he seems to be equally at home, at least in imagination, in describing animated scenes of feasting and revelry in hall and palace or the very different activities of war and the battlefield. Layamon is more than a translator; he is a poet and his effects are the effects of conscious art.

This is the first and also for quite a while the last appearance of King Arthur in English. When he again returns to the island of his birth it will be after a considerable sojourn in France, a sojourn which has profoundly altered his character.

[25] See Henry Cecil Wyld, "Laȝamon as an English Poet," *RES*, vi (1930). 1-30.

IX
The Romance: I

To most people today the word *romance* [1] suggests a love story, and be- *Definition*
cause some medieval romances involve famous love stories—such as those
of Lancelot and Guinevere, Tristan and Iseult, Floris and Blancheflour—
they assume that a love interest is a necessary ingredient in the romance of
the Middle Ages. This is not strictly true. One has only to think of the romances of Alexander, Richard the Lion-Hearted, and many lesser figures
to realize that medieval romance could get along very well with little or no
love element. The basic material is knightly activity and adventure, and we
may best put the emphasis in the right place if we define the medieval romances as a story of adventure—fictitious and frequently marvelous or supernatural—in verse or prose. Except for the few romances in which a love
story is the main feature, [2] love, if it enters into the narrative at all, is either
subordinated to the adventure (*Erec, Yvain*), or is incidental, as when a
Saracen princess conceives a desperate passion for the hero (*Bevis of Hampton*), or is used as a motivating force, an excuse for the adventures of the
hero (*Guy of Warwick*). It may be added that the earlier romances are in
verse; those in prose are generally late. The former ordinarily range in length
from one thousand to six thousand lines, with occasional productions running to nearly double this limit. The commonest metres are the eight-
syllable couplet and a variety of tail-rime stanzas (*aabccb, aaabcccb,* and
twelve-line stanzas of more elaborate pattern).

The romance in verse, in so far as it tends to be a narrative of heroic *Character-*
adventure, has some things in common with the epic. [3] But it has less unity of *istics*
action and the characters are not so well defined. Although occasional romances have a simple and skilfully managed plot, many are little more than

[1] The word *romance* comes from a Latin adverb *romanice,* meaning "in the Roman manner"
(*loqui romanice,* to speak in the Roman manner, i.e., speak colloquial Latin). In time, with
the change of Vulgar Latin into the various Romance languages, it came to mean more
particularly French, and then something written in French, especially something translated
from Latin. Samson de Nanteuil calls his metrical translation of the *Proverbs of Solomon* a
romance. As was natural, however, the word came gradually to designate the most popular type
of French poem and hence a poem of this type in any language. See Reinald Hoops, *Der
Begriff 'Romance' in der mittelenglischen und frühneuenglischen Literatur* (Heidelberg, 1929;
Anglistische Forschungen, No. 68).
[2] The type is better represented in France, where courtly love enjoyed greater vogue. For a
treatment of these see Sarah F. Barrow, *The Medieval Society Romances* (1924; *Columbia Univ.
Studies in English and Compar. Lit.,* No. 34).
[3] For an interesting paper suggesting that romance is transplanted epic, which has undergone
a kind of sea-change in the passage, see N. E. Griffin, "The Definition of Romance," *PMLA,*
xxxviii (1923). 50-70. For a stimulating discussion of the whole subject see W. P. Ker, *Epic
and Romance* (2ed., 1908).

a loose succession of incidents strung on a biographical thread. The characters of medieval romance are poorly differentiated. They are types rather
than individuals. The hero conforms to a pattern, that of the ideal knight,
and within the pattern there is little room for individual variation. Lancelot,
Tristan, Gawain—they are hardly distinguishable, although we can occasionally recognize Lancelot by catching a glimpse of Guinevere in the
background, or Tristan if he is contriving a secret meeting with Iseult.
Since the romance deals for the most part with types and the hero is himself
an idealized type, the action likewise does not admit of great variety. There
is only one way in which a knight may prove himself worthy to be the hero
of the story and that is by showing himself superior to other knights. Now
the ways in which one may dispose of an opponent in tournament or battle
are limited, and it is therefore not surprising that the poet occasionally foists
in a giant or a dragon to lend variety to his hero's adventures. Yet in spite
of the obvious weaknesses of the genre—weakness in plot, faintness of characterization, sameness of incident—it is surprising how interesting the individual romance, taken by itself, contrives to be.[4]

*An
Aristocratic
Genre*

The romance in its beginning was an aristocratic type appealing to the
tastes of the upper class. As long as French remained the normal language
of the English ruling classes the romances that circulated in England were
French and those written in England were written in French. This means
that romances in English are not to be expected until English begins to displace French as the language of polite society, that is, until the middle of
the thirteenth century. There is only one English romance that can be dated
with certainty earlier than 1250. Unfortunately by this time the romance in
France, and indeed in Europe generally, had passed its prime. The great
creative period of medieval romance was the twelfth century,[5] and the beginning of the thirteenth. By the end of the latter century the type begins
to deteriorate. Poets, chewing over the old straw, are driven to desperate
measures to make it seem more palatable. Overstraining after effect replaces
the easy confidence of a Chrétien de Troyes or Gottfried von Strassburg.
Most of our English romances belong to the fourteenth century and nearly
all of them are translations or adaptations from French originals. Yet while
they seldom come up to the level of medieval romance at its best, it must
not be thought that they are quite what readers of Chaucer might infer
from *Sir Thopas.*

*English
Romances
Late*

*The
"Matters"
of
Medieval
Romance*

While medieval romance was at the height of its popularity a Continental
poet, Jean Bodel, wrote in his *Chanson des Saisnes:*

N'en sont que trois materes a nul home entendant
De France, et de Bretaigne, et de Rome la grant

---

[4] Years from now any one curious about our current mystery stories will probably find in
them a similar tendency to run to type, yet the individual story manages to be interesting.
[5] The romance is a product of the twelfth century, along with the troubadour lyric, the
great cathedrals, scholastic philosophy, and other evidences of the creative mind at work in
this renaissance period. See Haskins, as above.

It has been customary ever since to speak of medieval romance under these headings—the Matter of Rome, by which is meant romances based on classical history and legend, the Matter of France, meaning stories of Charlemagne and his peers, and the Matter of Britain or the Arthurian cycle. This is a fairly adequate statement of aristocratic taste on the Continent, but it needs to be supplemented in one direction for England. It leaves out of account a group of romances of great interest. These are the romances concerned with native English heroes or with a figure like Havelok the Dane, whose fortunes are tied up with England and whose principal adventures take place in the island. Later it would have been necessary for a comprehensive classification to take cognizance of many romances of Eastern and other exotic themes.

i. The Matter of England

It is possible to suppose that when the English language spread to the upper class it was adopted first by those whose interests were less closely bound up with the Continent and who were more ready to identify themselves with the people among whom they lived. And it may equally well be that having come to look upon England as their country of first allegiance they were interested in stories about English worthies. At all events, we cannot help noticing that most of the romances, and certainly the most popular, written in English before 1300 were concerned with English subjects and that only after 1300 do we find stories of the Charlemagne and Arthurian cycles or of classical legend being adapted for a public that now preferred its entertainment in English rather than in French.[6]

The two earliest of these romances, it would seem, are *King Horn* and *Havelok the Dane*. The former has often been placed as far back as 1225, but the basis for so early a date is very questionable. We must distinguish here, as in the case of *Havelok*, between the underlying legend and the romance in its English form. A more conservative date about 1250 for the English versions of both stories seems safer. *King Horn*[7] relates the adventures of a prince who is driven out of his country by pagan invaders, but in the end wins back his possessions and throne—the so-called exile and return motif. During the hero's youth his father's kingdom of Suddene (in southwestern Scotland) is invaded by people called Saracens in the poem, but apparently Scandinavians. With a dozen companions he is set adrift in a boat which carries him to the Mull of Galloway.[8] Here he is loved by

King Horn

[6] The only exceptions to this generalization are *Floris and Blancheflour*, of the first half of the thirteenth century, and *Arthur and Merlin* and *King Alisaunder*, which may have been written shortly before 1300.

[7] Editions by J. Hall (Oxford, 1901), G. H. McKnight (1901; EETS, 14), and T. Wissmann (Strassburg, 1881; Quellen u. Forschungen, XLV). The text of this and a number of other romances discussed in the present chapter can be read conveniently in W. H. French and C. B. Hale, *Middle English Metrical Romances* (1930). For an excellent discussion of the date, versions, etc., of *King Horn* see Laura Hibbard, *Mediæval Romance in England* (1924), pp. 83-102. See also W. H. French, *Essays on King Horn* (Ithaca, 1940).

[8] The most convincing attempt to explain the hitherto baffling geography of the romance is that of Walter Oliver, "*King Horn* and Suddene," *PMLA*, XLVI (1931). 102-114. In this con-

the king's daughter Rimenhild, but he is forced through the treachery of a companion to leave the country. After the lovers have sworn to remain faithful for the usual seven years he goes to Ireland. He fights valiantly for the Irish king and remains in his service until recalled by a message from Rimenhild. With the help of Irish soldiers he returns in time to prevent her marriage to an unwelcome suitor. The same warriors help him to regain his own kingdom, whereupon he comes back and marries the much harassed but faithful and romantically patient lady. This simple action is built up with enough good fighting, dangers, narrow escapes for Rimenhild, and conduct worthy of both hero and heroine to make it a lively and satisfying tale.[9]

Havelok

The romance of *Havelok*[10] has a somewhat more artfully constructed plot. The heroine is an English princess named Goldborough, left an orphan at the tender age of two. While she is growing up, the country is ruled by a regent named Godrich, who has promised her father not only to preserve the kingdom for her but to marry her to the best, fairest, and strongest man living. Instead he shuts her up in Dover Castle. This constitutes the first part of the story. In part two we make the acquaintance of Havelok, who is in somewhat like fashion the victim of treachery. When his father, the King of Denmark, dies the boy is given over to a trusted councilor named Godard, who rewards the confidence placed in him by arranging with a fisherman named Grim to have Havelok drowned. A luminous mark on the boy's shoulder and a bright light which issues from his mouth, however, tell Grim as plainly as words that he is the royal heir. So the fisherman flees with his family and Havelok to England and settles near the mouth of the Humber at a place afterwards called Grimsby. There with his sons he pursues his occupation of fishing, and Havelok sells his basket of fish like the rest. In time the lad grows big and very strong. When a famine occurs he is unwilling to be a burden on Grim and seeks employment in Lincoln, the nearest large city. He gets a job with the Earl of Lincoln's cook and is a great favorite with everyone.

It is necessary now for the poet to find some way of bringing the hero and

nection cf. the resemblances to the legend of St. Cuthbert pointed out by Irene P. McKeehan, "The Book of the Nativity of St. Cuthbert," *PMLA*, XLVIII (1933). 981-999.

[9] The story is treated in a later English version, *Horn Childe and Maiden Rimnild*, found in the Auchinleck MS (printed in an appendix in Hall and by Caro, below), and in ballads telling the episode of Horn's return to save Rimenhild (*Hind Horn*, Child, No. 17). It was adapted in French by Geoffrey de la Tour Landri and in this form was turned into English prose in the fifteenth-century *King Ponthus and the Fair Sidone* (ed. F. J. Mather, Jr., *PMLA*, XII (1897). 1-150). The origin of the legend and the relation of the versions, English and French, are much disputed questions. In addition to the references given in a previous note see especially T. Wissmann, *King Horn: Untersuchungen* ... (Strassburg, 1876; *Quellen u. Forschungen*, XVI); J. Caro, "Kleine Publikationen aus der Auchinleck-Hs: Horn Childe and Maiden Rimnild," *ESt*, XII (1889). 323-366 (text and study); O. Hartenstein, *Studien zur Hornsage* (Heidelberg, 1902; *Kieler Studien*, IV); W. H. Schofield, "The Story of Horn and Rimenhild," *PMLA*, XVIII (1903). 1-83; Paul Leidig, *Studien zu King Horn* (Borna-Leipzig, 1927); Leslie G. Burgevin, "The Origin and Development of the Saga of King Horn," *Harvard Univ.... Summaries of Theses, 1931*, pp. 212-215.

[10] Edited by W. W. Skeat (revised by K. Sisam, Oxford, 1915), and by F. Holthausen 3ed., Heidelberg, 1928); earlier ed. by Skeat in *EETSES*, 4 (1868).

heroine together. A parliament which Earl Godrich convenes at Lincoln offers a convenient excuse. In the festivities called forth by the occasion Havelok wins a prize and much local fame by putting the stone twelve feet farther than any other man. When Godrich hears of this record-breaking achievement he has an idea. He has sworn to marry Goldborough to the best, fairest, and strongest man in England. He will marry her to Havelok, the kitchen knave! Goldborough is forced to submit to the marriage, outrageous as it seems to her. However, one night as she lies beside Havelok, bewildered and somewhat resentful, she sees the luminous mark on his shoulder and is told by an angel that she is married to a king's son. Filled with joy, she kisses him. This unexpected attention wakes him up from a dream in which he has seen all Denmark and England subject to him. With the help of Grim's three sons he invades Denmark and wins the support of a Danish noble named Ubbe, especially when Ubbe discovers the great light that issues from Havelok's mouth as he sleeps. It is of 107 candlepower. Havelok regains his kingdom, conquers England, and rewards all who have been good to him, especially the Earl of Lincoln's cook. He and Goldborough live a hundred years and have many children. As a final word the poet begs his hearers "to say a paternoster for him that hath made the rime and therefore sat up many nights."

It has seemed well to tell the story of *Havelok* at some length to show that English romances are not all formless and that authors of medieval romance could occasionally construct a good plot. Notwithstanding its naïve elements suggestive of the fairy tale *Havelok the Dane* is a well-planned story. As in *King Horn,* the emphasis is on the adventure. Neither romance has much of the glamour or sophistication of courtly society. In fact *Havelok* is almost democratic in tone. There is respect for honest labor, the hero is *Bourgeois* associated most of the time with common people, and such people and their *Elements* activities play a large part in the story. His great triumph is not in knightly competition but in putting the stone. The charm of his character is not revealed in courtly graces, but in homely and natural virtues—a cheerful, sunny disposition which makes the children and the cook like him, a readiness to accept without question his humble lot as a fisher boy and scullery knave. Though both *King Horn* and *Havelok* are based on earlier French narratives,[11] they seem to reflect the spirit of the English middle class, or to be the work of minstrels little acquainted with the ways of the court.[12] It is among such that we might well look for the authors of romances at a time when the upper class was just beginning to adopt English in numbers. While dating these two romances *c.* 1250, we must allow for minor revisions at least in *Havelok* shortly after 1300.[13]

---

[11] For the French versions see above, pp. 138, 141.

[12] Defects in one of the MSS show that both romances were copied from an original with only twenty lines to a page. Such a book, if 3½x4 inches in size and composed of 120 leaves, would have held *Horn* and *Havelok* and been very convenient for a minstrel.

[13] England is twice described as extending from Roxburgh to Dover, which could hardly be said until Roxburgh became a border fortress in 1296 (J. W. Hales, *Folia Litteraria,* pp.

Guy of
Warwick

Enjoying the widest popularity and longest life accorded to any English romances were two stories written about 1300, *Guy of Warwick* and *Bevis of Hampton*. The former has been preserved in four versions ranging in length from seven to twelve thousand lines.[14] It is very typical of romances in which everything is subordinated to adventure. It consists of the individual encounters of the hero with an endless succession of adversaries. The excuse is love. Felice, daughter of the Earl of Warwick, will not consider marriage with the hero, who is only the son of her father's steward, until he proves his worth in the field. After many victories Guy returns hopefully, only to be told by his sweetheart that she will marry a mere knight only if he is the best knight in the world. Guy's mingled disappointment and unquenchable hope are the incentive for a wide variety of additional combats and adventures, after which the rather difficult mistress is satisfied and the marriage takes place. Here the romance would have had to end and perhaps originally did end. But an excuse was found for continuing it. After a few months of married life Guy's conscience hurts. All his achievements have been for a selfish end, to win the love of Felice. He feels that he should do something for God, fight against the infidel in the cause of the true faith. Accordingly with Felice's consent he sets out on a third series of adventures, and when he returns he has little more than time to withdraw from the world and compose his soul for death. This part of the romance is reminiscent of the crusades, and the spirit of renunciation and humility in which he spends his last days in his lonely cell almost suggests the possibility of a monkish hand in this part of the story.

Its Popularity

By the year 1410 the fame of *Guy of Warwick* had spread even to the Holy Land where the Sultan's lieutenant remarked that they had the story in books in their own language. In England it was published by the earliest English printers and in the Elizabethan period was made into ballads and plays. In the seventeenth century it was told in poems of epic proportions and was also adapted to the tastes and purses of the plebeian citizenry in the form of chapbooks that lasted on into the eighteenth century, when it became the object of antiquarian interest.[15] Such popularity was no doubt due in part to the belief that the romance had an historical foundation. The story is laid in the reign of Athelstan (925-940), the grandson of King Alfred. In the romance Guy returns to England in time to take a leading part in Athelstan's fight with the Danes. Guy's fight in single combat with Colbrand, the Danish champion, was accepted as fact for a long time and was told in a number of chronicles as sober truth—so well did the storyteller

---

30-39). The only Parliament held at Lincoln was in 1300. Such details suggest that the story was brought up to date shortly after the turn of the century.

[14] A French romance of *Gui de Warewic*, earlier than the English, exists in thirteen MSS (ed. Alfred Ewert, 2v, Paris, 1932-33; *CFMA*, 74-75). The English romance, in various versions is edited by J. Zupitza (1875-91; *EETSES*, 25, 26, 42, 49, 59).

[15] See Ronald S. Crane, "The Vogue of *Guy of Warwick* from the Close of the Middle Ages to the Romantic Revival," *PMLA*, xxx (1915). 125-194. The larger aspects of the survival of medieval romance are studied in the same author's dissertation (Univ. of Pennsylvania), on which the above article is in part based.

do his work. Patriotism thus combined with interest in the story to keep the romance alive long after better romances were forgotten.

Equally famous were the adventures of Bevis of Southampton. We have romances, often in several versions, from France, Italy, Scandinavia, and the Netherlands, to say nothing of two in Celtic and several in Slavonic. The story begins with a variant of the Hamlet theme. Bevis's mother plots her husband's death and afterwards marries the murderer. Bevis is sold to foreign merchants, and in time is taken into the service of Ermin, King of the Saracens. Ermin's daughter Josian falls in love with him and most of his adventures grow out of his efforts to maintain his reputation as a Christian knight amidst pagan envy and treachery, or else to defend Josian against her Saracen suitor. In the end marriage and the recovery of his inheritance give him twenty years of happiness before he dies. *Bevis of Hampton* is not a remarkable example of medieval romance. It is made up of stock motifs and episodes—the January and May marriage of Bevis's parents, the child ordered to be put to death but spared through the pity of the servant, the hero sold to heathen merchants, the ubiquitous Saracen princess, fights with giants, wild boars, dragons, the wicked steward who tries to steal the credit for the hero's exploit, as in *Tristan and Iseult*, etc. The articulation of the episodes is loose and inexpert. What gives the romance its chief distinction is its exuberance, its racy, buoyant style, and the spirit of broad humor in which it is written. A thirty-foot giant whom Bevis fights was among his own people so small that everybody picked on him. They called him the dwarf and he was forced to run away. When Bevis fells him and is on the point of cutting off his head, Josian suggests sparing him that he may be her page. When Josian is baptized they decide to baptize the giant too. A special font is constructed, but when the bishop attempts to push him in he leaps out and cries, "Priest, wilt thou drown me? ... I am too big to be Christian." The author wrote with evident gusto, which has not always been appreciated. His learned German editor says, "The strain in which this work is written is serious, even severe." [16]

Richard Cœur de Lion [17] is one instance in which history really furnished hero and a series of adventures adequate and ready to the poet's hand or the purposes of romance. Richard I as a ruler would not have inspired much enthusiasm among the English. He looked upon his office as a means to an end, and spent only six months of his ten-year reign in England. But his adventurous nature, his daring exploits and personal triumphs as the leader of the Third Crusade, his captivity in Germany, the picturesque circumstances of his death, and the magnanimity with which he treated the fanatical warrior whose bolt had struck him were a source of patriotic pride and popular admiration which increased as reality passed into legend. The author of the romance has a general idea of the facts in Richard's life, but

(margin notes: Bevis of Hampton; Richard Cœur de Lion)

[16] Ed. E. Kölbing (1885-94; EETSES, 46, 48, 65). For the Anglo-Norman version see above, p. 142.
[17] Edited from all the MSS by Karl Brunner, *Der mittelenglische Versroman über Richard Löwenherz* (Vienna, 1913; *Wiener Beiträge*, XLII).

he does not hesitate to alter history to suit his purpose. He has Richard's captivity precede the crusade and in order to explain it, has Richard journey as a pilgrim to the Holy Land first. It would seem that his knowledge of history was somewhat sketchy and confused, but he was a storyteller and not a historian, and did not feel called upon to aim at scholarly accuracy. Moreover he introduced legendary elements freely and these are at times the most interesting part of his narrative. Such an element is the episode during Richards captivity in which his captors try to bring about his death by admitting a lion to his cell. He meets the lion with a tremendous kick and as the animal opens its jaws wide in a howl of pain Richard thrusts his arm down the lion's throat, tearing out its heart and various other organs, in fact "all that he found," says the storyteller. Then taking the heart still warm, he goes into the hall, dips it into the salt and eats it before the astonished court. Thus the poet accounts for his nickname, Lion-Hearted. It is a romance of adventure, historical and pseudo-historical. The author refers to his source as French, but the strong English bias and open scorn expressed for the French king put its English origin beyond any doubt. It dates from about 1300.

Athelston   What *Richard Cœur de Lion* does on a large scale the romance of *Athelston* [18] does on a small. In some 800 lines a poet of about 1350 has constructed a purely fictitious story about a king who bore a name famous in Old English history.[19] He has used scraps of history, legend, folklore, and commonplaces of romance. How he has woven together this heterogeneous assortment of ideas will be seen from the footnote below.[20] It will suffice here to remark that by a shameless disregard for historical truth he has devised a well-knit and highly effective plot. The romance has many qualities of the ballad—tags, and repetitions, and commonplaces, to say nothing of the opening in which the four messengers meet on the edge of a wood and with-

[18] Ed. A. M. Trounce, *Athelston: A Middle English Romance* (1933; also 1951; *EETS*, 224).
[19] See the account of the *Battle of Brunanburh*, above, p. 56.
[20] Athelston meets three other messengers and swears blood-brotherhood with them. On this motif see G. H. Gerould, "Social and Historical Reminiscences in the Middle English *Athelston*," *ESt*, xxxvi (1906). 193-208. Upon becoming king he makes his companions respectively, Archbishop of Canterbury, the Earl of Dover, and the Earl of Stane, giving also to the last named his sister in marriage. Believing the jealous representations of Dover, he sends for the Earl of Stane and his family, ostensibly to confer knighthood on the two sons. Instead he throws them into prison, and when the Queen begs him on her knees to give them a hearing he becomes enraged and kicks her, killing his unborn heir. On the kicked Queen see A. C. Baugh, "A Source for the Middle English Romance, *Athelston*," *PMLA*, XLIV (1929) 377-382. The Queen appeals to the Archbishop, who similarly incurs Athelston's anger. But the Archbishop excommunicates the King and puts all England under an interdict. This incident recalls the story of Thomas Becket; see Gerould, as above, and Paul Brown, *The Development of the Legend of Thomas Becket* (Philadelphia, 1930). The King agrees to permit the accused noble and his family to have a trial by ordeal. They must walk over nine red-hot stones. This is the story of Queen Emma and the plow-shares; see L. A. Hibbard, "*Athelston*, a Westminster Legend," *PMLA*, xxxvi (1921). 223-244. As the countess successfully completes her part of the ordeal, she is seized with the pains of childbirth and is delivered of a son. The King, now fully convinced and penitent, adopts the child in place of the heir which his wicked rage had destroyed. The child is said to be Saint Edmund, king and martyr. This last touch is a per version of history amounting to genius. Athelston, the hero of Brunanburh, was succeeded b Edmund. Edmund was a younger brother, however, not a nephew, and Edmund Martyr live a century before!

out explanation proceed to swear blood-brotherhood with one another. It is probably the work of a minstrel, but the humiliation of the king by the power of the Church and the prominence given to moral issues has been cited as evidence that the story was written under ecclesiastical influence.[21]

All these romances, it will be seen, capitalize upon the interest in native figures, real or imaginary. By the time most of them were written the habit of writing romances in English was thoroughly established, and poets were ready to go outside the English circle for their themes.

ii. *The Matter of Rome*

Medieval romances based on classical stories generally had to do with one of four subjects: Alexander the Great, the Trojan war, the siege of Thebes, and the adventures of Æneas. All four were made into long French romances in the twelfth century, and all four had English offspring, but only two enjoyed genuine popularity in England. These were the stories of Alexander and of Troy, with Alexander well out in front.

All popular medieval treatments of Alexander [22] go back ultimately to a *The* romantic biography in Greek prose, written at Alexandria some time before *Legend of* 200 A.D.[23] The author, who is known to modern scholarship as pseudo- *Alexander* Callisthenes, doubtless embodied in his account current legends concerning Alexander's birth designed to make the founder of his native city an Egyptian. This amazing story is one of the two features that insured the popularity of the work in later times. The other is the extended treatment of Alexander's travels, especially in India, with its multitude of strange sights, marvels of nature, and wonderful experiences.[24] Pseudo-Callisthenes was translated into Latin *c.* 300 A.D. by Julius Valerius,[25] and in an abridgement of the ninth century circulated widely.[26] Finally, about 950, the Greek was again translated into Latin by one Leo, Archpresbyter of Naples. This version, generally known as the *Historia de Preliis* [27] (i.e., the wars of Alexander), enjoyed still greater popularity. From one or another of these Latin derivatives of pseudo-Callisthenes a great number of accounts in the vernaculars of western Europe was composed. The oldest is a Provençal poem of the eleventh century by Alberic of Pisançon, of which only a fragment is preserved. It was, however, adapted in French about 1160 in lines of ten syllables, and altered and continued toward the end of the century in twelve-

---

[21] Wells, p. 25.

[22] The most extended treatment of the Alexander legend, Paul Meyer, *Alexandre le Grand dans la littérature française du moyen âge* (Paris, 1886), is now somewhat antiquated. For an excellent brief discussion see the introduction to F. P. Magoun, Jr., *The Gests of King Alexander of Macedon* (Cambridge, Mass., 1929).

[23] Edited (one recension) by W. Kroll, *Historia Alexandri Magni* (Berlin, 1926).

[24] This feature of the story was already known in England in Old English times. See above, p. 104 for a mention of the *Letter of Alexander to Aristotle* and the *Wonders of the East.*

[25] *Res Gestae Alexandri Macedonis,* ed. B. Kübler (Leipzig, 1888).

[26] It is often called the *Zacher Epitome* because it was edited by J. Zacher (Halle, 1867). It was incorporated in condensed form by Vincent of Beauvais in his *Speculum Historiale* (c. 1250).

[27] Ed. F. Pfister, *Der Alexanderroman des Archipresbyters Leo* (Heidelberg, 1913). It is translated in English (omitting Book II) in Margaret Schlauch, *Medieval Narrative* (1928).

syllable verses. This later *Roman d'Alexandre* [28] was the standard form in which the story circulated in French. There was, however, another French poem written in England (*c.* 1280) by Thomas of Kent. It was based on the *Zacher Epitome* and is known as the *Roman de Toute Chevalerie*.[29] From it is derived the best known English romance on the subject, *King Alisaunder*.[30]

King Alisaunder

King Alisaunder runs to 8000 lines (in four-stress couplets). Since it is found in a manuscript of 1330-40 it cannot be later than this and is probably to be dated *c.* 1300. It is divided by the author into two parts. The first tells the story of Nectanebus, the Egyptian king who exercises his magic on Olympias, the wife of Philip of Macedon, and becomes the father of her child, Alexander. It also relates at length Alexander's military exploits, treating with especial fullness his triumph over Darius. The second part deals with Alexander's conquest of India and the multitude of fabulous creatures and terrifying experiences which he met with in the course of his extensive travels. While the romance is clearly intended for oral delivery, as numerous remarks indicate, it is the work of a bookish man. He frequently appeals for authority to his sources. On one occasion, he declines to relate an incident which he finds in his French "geste" because it is contradicted by the scholarship (*lettrure*) on the subject.[31] In another place he supplies a gap in his French source from another work in Latin,[32] and once he speaks of the strange people in Egypt "in *oure* bokes as we findith," where he seems to identify himself with those who have and use books—clerks. Alexander romances in general descend by a literary rather than a popular tradition and nowhere is this better illustrated than in the English *King Alisaunder*.

Alexander A *and* B

The same thing is true of the two fragments of a romance in alliterative verse known as *Alexander A* and *Alexander B*.[33] In the former the author is clearly not dependent upon any previous romance in French. He tells of the ancestry and conquests of Philip of Macedon through 450 lines taken from the Latin of Orosius because, as he remarks, he could not find any book when he began to write that told of Alexander's birth. But apparently he later got hold of a copy of the *Historia de Preliis* and so he plunges at once into the story of Nectanebus. He has hardly described the youthful feats of Alexander when the fragment breaks off. Practically the whole of *Alexander B* (1139 lines) is given over to the exchange of letters between Alexander and Dindimus discussing the Brahmin way of life. The author

[28] Ed. H. Michelant (Stuttgart, 1846) and E. C. Armstrong, *et. al.* (Princeton, 1937; *Elliott Monographs*, Vols. 36 and 37). The popularity of this version is responsible for our still calling the twelve-syllable line an Alexandrine.

[29] Still unpublished. See above, p. 141.

[30] In H. Weber, *Metrical Romances of the Thirteenth, Fourteenth, and Fifteenth Centuries* (Edinburgh, 1810), Vol. I, superseded by ed. of G. V. Smithers (2v, 1952-7; EETS, 227, 237).

[31] Cf. lines 3511-21.

[32] This batail destuted [lacking] is,
In the French, wel y-wis,
Therefore Y have, it to colour,
Borowed of the Latyn autour. (lines 2199-2202.)

[33] The best edition is that of F. P. Magoun, Jr., *The Gests of King Alexander of Macedon* (Cambridge, Mass., 1929), who believes that *B* is a continuation rather than a part of

handles the alliterative line with apparent ease, drops into dialogue when necessary, and tells his story fluently. He wrote in the West Midlands and, as nearly as we can judge, in the middle third of the fourteenth century.[34]

Next to the story of Alexander the most popular subject for romances of classical theme was the fall of Troy, and this in spite of the fact that Homer was completely unknown to western Europe in the Middle Ages. The Middle Ages derived their knowledge of the Troy story from two short prose accounts translated from late Greek. These went under the names of Dares and Dictys respectively.[35] The two accounts are usually found together in medieval manuscripts and although involving some duplication each includes matter not found in the other. The combination gave a fairly complete, if wholly prosaic, account of events from the story of Jason and the Golden Fleece through the particulars of the siege to the return of the Greeks and the death of Ulysses at the hands of his son Telegonus. The first vernacular treatment of this material was the work of a Norman-French poet, Benoît de Sainte-More, whose *Roman de Troie*[36] runs to 30,000 verses. It is a spirited and effective narrative, but not a little of its fame today is due to the elaborate treatment of an episode that here makes its first appearance in literature—the Troilus and Briseida (Cressida) story.[37] A century later Benoît's verse was turned into Latin prose by a Sicilian judge, Guido della Colonna, as the *Historia Destructionis Troiae* (1287).[38] In these two forms the story had a wide circulation and passed into later vernacular versions.

The Roman de Troie

The earliest Troy romance in English is the *Seege of Troye*, a poem of about two thousand lines.[39] There is frequent appeal to the "lordings" to listen and it is obviously intended for minstrel production. It was designed to be recited or read in two installments, for the minstrel pauses just half

Seege of Troye

[34] Other Alexander romances survive. One in alliterative verse of the early fifteenth century is known as *Alexander C*. It runs to nearly 5700 lines and lacks a few leaves at the end. Another preserved in a Cambridge MS is in stanzas of alternate rime (ed. Rosskopf, Erlangen, 1911). A prose romance running to about 100 pages is in the Thornton MS, 1430-40. Two long Scottish poems, written in the fifteenth century are mentioned below (p. 300).

[35] Dares Phrygius, *De Excidio Trojae Historia* (sixth century), and Dictys Cretensis, *Ephemeris de Historia Belli Trojani* (fourth century). Dares and Dictys represent themselves as having fought in their respective armies, Dares on the side of the Trojans and Dictys on the side of the Greeks. Both claims, of course, are fraudulent. They were made to give the authority of eye-witnesses to works written centuries later. See N. E. Griffin, *Dares and Dictys: An Introduction to the Study of Medieval Versions of the Story of Troy* (Baltimore, 1907).

[36] It was written in the second half of the twelfth century, possibly about 1155-60, and dedicated to the English queen, Eleanor of Aquitaine. This is the date arrived at by its modern editor, L. Constans, *Le Roman de Troie, par Benoît de Sainte-Maure* (6v, Paris, 904-12; *SATF*). For a slightly later date (after 1184) see the argument of F. E. Guyer, "The Chronology of the Earliest French Romances," *MP*, xxvi (1929). 257-277.

[37] The love story begins at line 13, 261 and accompanies the main narrative at intervals to the death of Troilus (lines 21, 397 ff). It serves to fill in the uneventful periods of truce and adds an important element of variety to the narrative. It is not thought that Benoît invented his love story, but if he followed an expanded Dares, as some believe, his source has disappeared.

[38] Ed. N. E. Griffin, *Guido de Columnis: Historia Destructionis Troiae* (Cambridge, Mass., 936).

[39] Mary E. Barnicle, *The Seege or Batayle of Troye* (London, 1927; *EETS*, 172). See the valuable study by G. Hofstrand, *The Seege of Troye* (Lund, 1936), and C. H. A. Wager, *The Seege of Troy* (1899), which is still important.

way through for an intermission—"Rest we now a litel pece"—and suggests that the company "fyl þe cuppe and mak ous glad." The original poem from which the existing manuscripts descend was written in the northeast Midlands at the beginning of the fourteenth century and follows the plan of Dares with additions from Benoît and commonplaces of classical tradition. But in order to cover the ground from the adventures of Jason and the Golden Fleece to the destruction of Troy and the triumphant return of the Greeks, it is necessary for the poet to hurry from episode to episode without time to pause for those particulars and details that lend

Other interest to a story. Very different is the *Laud Troy Book*,[40] which covers
Treatments the same ground but was written to be read. Apparently the work of a cleric, it fills more than 18,000 verses of considerable fluency. It is somewhat older than the existing MS and dates from about 1400. To the latter half of the fourteenth century belongs also the *Gest Historiale of the Destruction of Troy,* a poem in 14,000 alliterative verses.[41] It is a product of the Alliterative Revival in the north. The Troy story seems to have enjoyed considerable popularity in Scotland. Extensive fragments of a version attributed to the Scottish poet Barbour have been preserved, imbedded in MSS of Lydgate's *Troy Book.*[42]

Thebes Classical times and the Middle Ages took a strange interest in the un-
and natural story of Œdipus and his marriage to his own mother. When his
Æneas sons quarreled over the right to rule Thebes and the party of Polynices laid siege to the city, the opportunity existed for an epic narrative, comparable to that which described the siege of Troy. The Virgilian epic, the *Thebaid,* by Statius, a Roman poet of the Silver Age, gave western Europe such a treatment. Either the *Thebaid* or an epitome of it was made into a French poem in the twelfth century called the *Roman de Thèbes,* and this in turn became the basis of other romances. The only English poem on the subject was Lydgate's *Siege of Thebes,* discussed below.[43] The story of Æneas is practically unrepresented in English [44] until Caxton translated a French prose romance in his *Eneydos* (1490), although it was available to the English upper classes in the French *Roman d'Eneas.* It is apparent, therefore, that the stories of Alexander and of Troy were the only themes in the Matter of Rome that showed any real vitality in medieval England.

[40] So called because the unique MS in which it is preserved was once in the possession of Archbishop Laud. Edited by J. E. Wülfing (1902-3; *EETS,* 121-122).
[41] *EETS,* 39 and 56 (1869-74).
[42] For Lydgate, see below, p. 296. For treatments in prose see p. 301.
[43] Chaucer's *Knight's Tale* treats an episode loosely attached to the Thebes story. So too are the Anglo-Norman romances *Ipomedon* and *Prothesilaus* mentioned on p. 141.
[44] Chaucer tells the story of Dido in the *House of Fame* and more briefly in the *Legend of Good Women.*

X
The Romance: II

iii. *The Matter of France*

When we turn to the Matter of France we are met by a slight anomaly. Considering the Continental possessions and the long and close association of the English nobility with France, one might expect considerable interest in a body of legends centering in the French court and in important Carolingian families. Instead we find only limited representation of this great collection of stories, and those which are found in English versions seem to be written without special enthusiasm. It would appear that the political rivalry between the two countries which had developed by the time romances in any number were being written in English had dampened the interest in material which centered in the doings of French personages. In any case the national appeal which such stories had in France was lacking in England.

The French *chansons de geste*, which included more than one hundred poems, were recognized not long after 1200 as falling into three general groups.[1] The most famous is the *geste du roi*, the epics more or less directly connected with Charlemagne, in many of which he appears as the champion of Christendom in wars against the infidel. Of these the best known is the *Chanson de Roland*. A second group is concerned with his struggles with his vassals. The epics of this group constitute the *geste de Doon de Mayence,* so called from the supposed ancestor of the rebels. The third concerns the adventures and conquests of William of Orange and members of his family. This group likewise takes its name from the legendary progenitor of the family and is known as the *geste de Garin de Monglane.* While each of these branches of the French epic has many points of interest, not all are represented in English. Indeed the only Charlemagne romances that have come to us in English verse belong to the cycle of the king, the *geste du roi*.[2]

Chanson de Geste

---

[1] The classification is that of Bertran de Bar-sur-Aube, the author of two such poems, *Girart de Vienne* and *Aymeri de Narbonne*. In the former (after 1205) he says:
> N'ot que trois gestes en France la garnie . . .
> Du roy de France est la plus seignorie,
> Et l'autre. apres, bien est droiz qui jeu die,
> Fu de Doon a la barbe florie,
> Cil de Maience qui molt ot baronnie . . .
> La tierce geste, qui molt fist a prisier,
> Fu de Garin de Monglenne au vis fier. (lines 11-47.)

[2] This is not the place to enter into the vexed question of the origin of the French epic. The most popular explanation in recent years is that of Joseph Bédier, *Les Légendes épiques*

185

Song of
Roland

Among these the Middle English *Song of Roland*[3] stands somewhat apart. Preserved in a single MS, it tells the famous story of Roland's last stand in 1049 four-stress lines rimed in couplets. When it breaks off Roland is just about to blow the blast on his horn that will summon Charlemagne. In spite of its rough versification and many careless rimes it manages a monotonous succession of individual combats with vigor and considerable variety. The poem naturally suffers by comparison with the great French epic on which it is based, but it does not entirely deserve the harsh words which it usually receives. Except for the late *Rauf Coilyear* ("Ralph the Collier"),[4] in which Charlemagne *incognito* is entertained by a peasant, with humorous consequences, the remaining Charlemagne romances fall into two classes, a Ferumbras group and an Otuel group.

The
Ferumbras
Group

The Ferumbras group treats the incidents found in two French *chansons de geste,* the *Destruction de Rome* and *Fierabras,* which in versions differing but slightly from those that are preserved seem to be the direct sources of the English romances. *The Sowdone* [i.e., Sultan] *of Babylone*[5] tells first how Laban (usually Balan) with the help of his son Ferumbras, sacks Rome, gets possession of the cross, the crown of thorns, and the nails of the Crucifixion, and sends them to Spain. The second part covers rapidly the incidents more fully treated in *Sir Ferumbras.*[6] Here Charlemagne's army, having come to Spain to punish the Saracens and recover the sacred relics, is met by Ferumbras, a formidable knight twenty feet tall. He is conquered in single combat by Oliver and becomes Christian, thereafter fighting on the Christian side. Oliver, on his way back to camp, is taken captive by a

(4v, Paris, 1908-13; 2ed., 1914-21). Recognizing in many of the *chansons de geste* the prominent notice taken of churches and monasteries along the great pilgrim routes of the Middle Ages, he suggested that these churches furnished the jongleurs with historical facts and traditions to be worked up into poems. In this way any claim to prominence which a church had because of the historic importance of its founder, the possession of the tomb or relics of a heroic figure, or the like, would be enhanced and more widely disseminated. The acceptance of this theory as a comprehensive explanation of the origin of the *chanson de geste* is not unattended by difficulties, although as a method of accounting for individual poems it is at times very convincing. Various critiques and correctives of Bédier's views are contained in the articles of F. Lot. For a bibliography and summary of Lot's position see E. J. Healy, "The Views of Ferdinand Lot on the Origins of the Old French Epic," *SP,* xxxvi (1939). 433-465. The older work of Léon Gautier, *Les Épopées françaises* (4v, 2ed, Paris, 1878-82) is still of value as a descriptive survey. For an excellent brief account of the many theories of the origin of the Old French epic see K. Voretzsch, *Introduction to the Study of Old French Literature* (Eng. trans., 1931), pp. 89-99.

[3] Edited by S. J. Herrtage (1880; EETSES, 35).

[4] Written in Scotland *c.* 1475 or slightly before. Edited by S. J. Herrtage (1882; *EETSES* 39); William H. Browne (Baltimore, 1903). See also H. M. Smyser, "*The Taill of Rauf Coilyear* and Its Sources," *Harvard Studies & Notes in Phil. & Lit.,* xiv (1932). 135-150.

[5] Edited by Emil Hausknecht (1881; *EETSES,* 38). It is in quatrains of alternate three- and four-stress verses. For a discussion of its source see the careful study of H. M. Smyser, "The Sowdon of Babylon and Its Author," *Harvard Studies & Notes in Phil. & Lit.,* xiii (1931). 185-218, supplemented and corrected by the same author's "A New Manuscript of the *Destruction de Rome* and *Fierabras,*" *ibid.,* xiv (1932). 339-349.

[6] Known as the Ashmole version to distinguish it from that in the Fillingham MS. The edition in *EETSES,* 34 is printed in long lines which disguise its true metrical form. It is really in 10,540 verses, of which the first 6820 are in quatrains (*abab*), the last 3720 in romance sixes (*aab ccb*). Fragments of the author's original draft are preserved, written on the back of two documents belonging to the diocese of Exeter at the end of the fourteenth century. The romance was apparently composed at about the same time and place.

Saracen force, and the greater part of the story grows out of his capture and the circumstance that the Sultan's beautiful daughter, Floripas, is in love with another of Charlemagne's knights, Guy of Burgundy. Her determined and resourceful personality plays a large part in the ultimate victory of the Christians and the recovery of the relics. Needless to say, she receives her reward in marriage to Guy, after being duly baptized. It is a pity that the unique manuscript in which *Sir Ferumbras* is preserved has lost a leaf or two at the beginning and end, for it is much the best of the English Charlemagne romances. The author was a conscious artist and took obvious pains with his work. It is full of effective scenes and nice touches. Incidentally it is almost the only case in which any part of an English romance has come down in the author's autograph. By comparison the recently recovered Fillingham *Firumbras*[7] seems lacking in distinction. The same incidents are treated more briefly by one who seems to be telling a story without being a storyteller.

The Otuel group consists of five romances. *Roland and Vernagu*,[8] in *The* tail-rime stanzas, is full of wild statements and childish exaggeration. *Otuel* The earliest part relates the circumstances under which Charlemagne *Group* comes to the aid of the Patriarch of Jerusalem and receives the crown of thorns, the arm of St. Simeon, Our Lady's smock, and many other relics. His invasion of Spain is like a triumphal march, after his prayers have caused the walls of one or two stubborn cities to fall. The romance takes its name from the latter part in which his douzepers are challenged by a forty-foot Saracen named Vernagu. After Ogier and several other paladins who undertake to fight him are picked up by Vernagu and carried off under his arm to prison, Roland disposes of him although he barely escapes the same ignominious treatment. The romance is incomplete, and as it breaks off amid the general rejoicing, it seems to be about to proceed to the story of Otuel which we have in other Middle English versions. *The Sege of Melayne*[9] (Milan) may have been intended to form another introduction to the Otuel story, although nothing corresponding to it in French literature is known. It relates a very unhistorical incident but tells its story well. Its most significant feature is the character of Archbishop Turpin, who abandons his priestly robes and conducts himself with great credit on the battlefield.

Three romances tell the story of Otuel proper. His reason for challenging Roland is partly the fact that Vernagu, whom Roland had killed, was his uncle. They all tell the same story with slight variations. Otuel in the midst of his single combat with Roland is converted to Christianity when the

---

[7] So called from the owner of the MS at the beginning of the nineteenth century. Lost for hundred years, it was acquired by the British Museum in 1907 (Add. MS 37, 492). Edited Mary I. O'Sullivan (1935; EETS, 198).

[8] EETSES, 39. See Ronald N. Walpole, *Charlemagne and Roland: A Study of the Source Two Middle English Metrical Romances*, Roland and Vernagu *and* Otuel and Roland Berkeley and Los Angeles, 1944; *Univ. of Calif. Pub. in Mod. Phil.*, xxi, No. 6).

[9] EETSES, 35. It is in twelve-line tail-rime stanzas of the late fourteenth century. The dialect of the original was northern, though it is preserved in a Midland copy.

Holy Ghost descends in the form of a dove and settles on his helmet. King Charles welcomes him to his company and promises him the hand of his daughter, Belesant. After he has accompanied Charlemagne on his expedition to Spain and contributed his share to the victory of the Christians, he marries Belesant and becomes lord of Lombardy. The oldest version in English is the *Otuel* in four-stress couplets preserved in the Auchinleck MS.[10] It is without much merit. Somewhat better is the *Duke Rowland and Sir Otuell of Spayne* [11] preserved in the same manuscript as the *Sege of Melayne*. It has more minstrel vigor. Like the *Sege of Melayne* it is in tail-rime stanzas and was composed in the north. The third romance, the Fillingham *Otuel and Roland*,[12] is probably a continuation of *Roland and Vernagu* and differs from the other Otuel romances in carrying on the story for another thousand lines with material drawn from Pseudo-Turpin.[13] In brief form the addition recounts Charlemagne's victories over the Saracen Ebrahim and the King of Navarre and concludes with Roland's death at Roncevaux. All three Otuel romances have a number of peculiar features in common and even individual lines or short passages. Although they diverge widely enough to preclude the possibility of mutual dependence, they are probably all based ultimately upon an English romance now lost.

Religious Interest in Charlemagne Romances   The interest in the Charlemagne romance in England seems to have been mainly pietistic—the glorification of the Christian faith. The Fillingham *Otuel* opens with a demand for attention "in the worchype of ihesu cryst," and the *Ferumbras* in the same manuscript ends with a promise of one hundred days' pardon to all who listen to the story "with gode devocyoun." *The Sowdone of Babylone* begins with a homiletic opening, and the rough draft of *Sir Ferumbras* was begun on the back of two ecclesiastical documents. Both Ferumbras and Otuel, the two chief Saracen champions, are converted, and there are many cases of divine intervention. In the *Sege of Melayne* the militant bishop Turpin, although somewhat melodramatic and blustering, is a truly heroic figure and certainly the main character. The subject of the Sultan of Babylon-Ferumbras romances is the loss and recovery of the Crown of Thorns and other sacred relics, supposedly given by Charlemagne to the church of St. Denis. Indeed these romances constitute a kind of Carlovingian counterpart of the Grail theme in Arthurian romance with Roland and Oliver answering to Perceval and Gawain in Chrétien. Judged by both choice of subject and treatment the English Charlemagne

[10] *EETSES,* 39.

[11] *EETSES,* 35.

[12] Ed. Mary I. O'Sullivan, *Firumbras and Otuel and Roland* (as above, note 7). The *Roland and Vernagu* and the *Otuel and Roland* are often given the group title *Charlemagne and Roland.* See the important studies of Ronald N. Walpole, *Charlemagne and Roland: A Study of the Sources of Two Middle English Romances,* Roland and Vernagu *and* Otuel and Roland (Berkeley and Los Angeles, 1944; *Univ. of Calif. Pub. in Mod. Phil.,* Vol. XXI, No. 6, pp 385-452), and H. M. Smyser, "*Charlemagne and Roland* and the Auchinleck MS," *Speculum* XXI (1946). 275-288.

[13] A spurious *Historia Caroli Magni et Rotholandi,* written in the twelfth century and fathered on Archbishop Turpin. The latest edition is that of H. M. Smyser, *The Pseudo-Turpin* (Cambridge, Mass., 1937).

romances seem, with one or two exceptions, to be a group in which the missionary spirit is made to work through minstrel recitation.

iv. *The Matter of Britain*

The development of the Arthurian legend up to its first appearance in English in Layamon's *Brut,* while encumbered with numerous vexed questions, is not without a recognizable continuity.[14] Now, so far as England is concerned, that continuity is broken, for English romances on Arthurian subjects do not begin to appear until about 1300 and in spite of the interval *English* of but a century that divided them from Layamon, they seem to be separated, *Arthurian* generally speaking, by a much wider gulf. The reason is not far to seek. *Romances* Arthurian romance enjoyed its great creative period in the latter part of *Late and* the twelfth century and the beginning of the thirteenth, particularly in *Derivative* France and Germany. It was the period of Chrétien de Troyes, Wolfram von Eschenbach, Gottfried von Strassburg, and others only less great. As the thirteenth century wore on, the impulse lost some of its force. The English Arthurian romances follow later and, since their sources are nearly all French, reflect this earlier development. But to read them without knowing their French background is like seeing a play in which we have missed the second act.[15] It might seem reasonable to expect that the English romances, built on so solid a French foundation, would reach an equally high level. Unfortunately, the great days of medieval romance were past, and English poets, with a few notable exceptions, were unable to recapture the spontaneity and fire of their Continental predecessors.

It is one of the distinctions of Chrétien that he got away from the bio- *Romances* graphical or compendious type of romance found, for example, in the *Roman* *of Arthur* *l'Alexandre* or *Bevis of Hampton* and confined himself to a single episode or closely related group of episodes in his hero's career. Later Arthurian romance generally follows this pattern.[16] There are accordingly almost no English romances which attempt to cover the whole life of Arthur. There is a short poem of 642 lines, probably written in the second half of the fourteenth century, to which the name *Arthur* [17] has been given. It is of slight value and would scarcely deserve mention if it were not the only example of this inclusive type. Elsewhere we have only romances on certain aspects of Arthur's career, or on the adventures of individual knights of the Round Table, or on themes such as the history of the Holy Grail.

[14] See ch. viii. It should be remembered that Layamon's *Brut* is a translation of Wace and therefore represents the state of Arthurian development prior to Chrétien.
[15] For the linguistic conditions that account for the lateness of English romance see above, p. III.
[16] In thirteenth-century France the separate stories were again combined into long composites, this time intended for reading rather than recitation. These were in prose. The best known is the Vulgate Cycle generally attributed in the manuscripts, though quite falsely, to Walter Map. Malory's *Morte Darthur* is an example of such a composite in English.
[17] *EETS,* 2. It is incorporated in a Latin chronicle of the kings of Britain. It traces briefly Arthur's life from birth to death. From the circumstance that the narrator pauses every hundred lines and bids the listener to say a paternoster one must assume a clerical origin.

and Merlin   The early life of Arthur is intimately associated with the figure of Merlin. It was through Merlin's magic that Uther Pendragon gained access to Ygerne the night Arthur was begotten. His advice and supernatural powers are helpful to Arthur on many occasions from the time the young prince pulls the sword from the stone and becomes king until he has emerged successfully from his contests with the rebels at home and his enemies abroad. This phase of Arthurian story is told in a romance of nearly ten thousand lines, called *Arthur and Merlin*, written about 1300.[18] It is not an inspired production; indeed it becomes rather tedious with its endless detail of battles and combats and its particularity concerning the numbers in each army and division and petty band. It is evidently based on a French source—variously referred to as the *Brut*, "the romance," or simply "the book"—apparently in verse and similar in content to the French prose *Merlins*.

Gawain   Gawain's early adventures, largely military, constitute a major element in the romance just spoken of. His various exploits were destined to become the most popular of the subjects from which English poets chose their themes. A dozen romances, many of them short and rather late, attest his continued popularity. The greatest, of course, is *Sir Gawain and the Green Knight*, more fully discussed among the works of the *Pearl* poet.[19] Admirably smooth in style and narrative technique is *Ywain and Gawain*[2] (*c.* 1350), in which Gawain and the hero fight a drawn battle, each ignorant of the other's identity. It is an adaptation of Chrétien's *Yvain* slightly condensed. Further evidence of Gawain's preëminence in popular favor is the fact that his son is made the hero of a romance, *Libeaus Desconus* (The Fair Unknown).[21] In this story Gingelein, the unknown and untried knight, undertakes to free the Queen of Sinadoun from captivity and enchantment. He succeeds, after preliminary encounters with sundry knights and giants, and in the end weds the lady.[22]

Lancelot   Lancelot is the subject of only one English romance, the late-fifteenth-century *Lancelot of the Laik*.[23] It tells of his part in the war between Arthur

[18] Eugen Kölbing, *Arthour and Merlin, nach der Auchinleck-HS, nebst zwei Beilage* (Leipzig, 1890; *Altenglische Bibliothek*, IV).
[19] See below, pp. 236.
[20] Ed. Gustav Schleich, *Ywain and Gawain* (Oppeln, 1887).
[21] Ed. Max Kaluza (Leipzig, 1890; *Altenglische Bibliothek*, v). The source is a French romance closely resembling *Le Bel Inconnu* (ed. G. P. Williams, Paris, 1929; *CFMA*, 38). See further Wm. Schofield, *Studies on the Libeaus Desconus* (Boston, 1895); *Harvard Studies & Notes in Phil. & Lit.*, IV.).
[22] Most of the Gawain romances can be found in Sir Frederic Madden, *Syr Gawayne* (London, 1839; *Bannatyne Club*, LXI). For other editions see Wells and the *CHEL*. These include *The Green Knight*, a fifteenth-century retelling of *Sir Gawain and the Green Knight*, *The Turk and Gawain*, in which a more primitive form of the same story can be recognized. *Sir Gawain and the Carl of Carlisle* which treats the temptation part of the story in a variant form. *The Wedding of Sir Gawain and Dame Ragnell*—there is a modernization by George Brandon Saul (1934)—is a version of the story, so beautifully told by the Wife of Bath, of the knight and the loathly lady. In the *Geste of Sir Gawain* the hero, surprised in his love making, is forced to fight the lady's father and brothers. His reputation for valor and fine courtesy is maintained in *Golagrus and Gawain*, involving an expedition to the Holy Land, his generosity is featured in *The Awntyrs (Adventures) of Arthur*, where an adventure of Gawain is loosely combined with a religious theme better known in *The Trental of St Gregory*.
[23] There are several editions, the most useful being that of W. W. Skeat (1865; *EETS*, 6

and Galiot (Galehault), following the French prose *Lancelot,* and doubtless ended with Guinevere's acceptance of him as her lover, although this part of the text is missing. In spite of some vigorous battle scenes, in which both Gawain and Lancelot distinguish themselves, it is a bookish production with a tedious prologue which is ·not fully redeemed by some interesting Chaucerian echoes, and the story pauses in the middle while Arthur receives with more patience than the reader a seven-hundred-line sermon on the duties of kingship.[24] The author was a Scot who affected certain dialectal traits of Southern English. While this is our sole Lancelot romance so far as title goes, the stanzaic *Morte Arthur* [25] (*c.* 1400) is really concerned chiefly with Lancelot's adventures, his love for the queen, their final parting, and his death. It takes its name from the latter half when the lovers are betrayed by Agravain and Arthur makes war on Lancelot. It is in the midst of this struggle that Arthur is forced by Mordred's treason to return home and later receives his death wound. The narrative is terse and the action rapid. The *Morte Arthur* is the most ballad-like of the longer English romances. It is to be sharply distinguished from the romance of similar title, the alliterative *Morte Arthure* (*c.* 1360).[26] The latter is the story of Arthur's Roman campaign, which in this romance is interrupted by Mordred's treason. Unlike the stanzaic tale, the alliterative *Morte Arthure* makes no mention of Arthur's being carried off by boat to be healed of his wounds. He here dies a mortal's death and is buried at Glastonbury. The romance is found in a MS copied by Robert Thornton *c.* 1430-40, but recent discoveries make it clear that in Thornton's text the original has been altered and shortened.[27] That original was undoubtedly Malory's source for the episode in the *Morte Darthur* (Book v), paraphrased and severely condensed. The alliterative *Morte Arthure* is remarkable for its careful workmanship and artistic elaboration. On various occasions the author lets his pen flow—the farewell scene between Arthur and Guinevere, Arthur's banquet, his fight with the giant, his dream, his final battle—and the result is a fullness of treatment and richness of detail rare in the romances of England. The narrative is that of a vigorous and genuinely gifted poet.

Two of the most popular subjects of the Arthurian cycle in the Middle Ages, the Perceval-Grail theme and the Tristan story, receive but little

Morte Arthur (margin)

Perceval (margin)

[24] On the basis of this passage a date after 1482 has been suggested. See Bertram Vogel, "Secular Politics and the Date of *Lancelot of the Laik*," *SP*, XL (1943). 1-13.

[25] The most accessible editions are those of J. Douglas Bruce (1903; *EETSES*, 88) and Samuel B. Hemingway (Boston, 1912). On the interesting question of the relation of this poem to Books xx and xxi of Malory, see Bruce, "The Middle English Metrical Romance *Le Morte Arthur* (Harleian MS 2252): Its Sources and the Relation to Sir Thomas Malory's *Morte Darthur,*" *Anglia*, XXIII (1900). 67-100.

[26] The best editions are those of E. Brock (1871, *EETS,* 8), Mary M. Banks (1900), and Erik Björkman (Heidelberg, 1915). S. O. Andrew, "The Dialect of *Morte Arthure,*" *RES*, IV (1928). 418-423, argues convincingly that the original dialect was Northwest Midland. On the sources see R. H. Griffith, "Malory, Morte Arthure, and Fierabras," *Anglia*, XXXII (1909). 9-398, and Tania Vorontzoff, "Malory's Story of Arthur's Roman Campaign," *MA*, VI (1937). 99-121. The latter is a corrective to P. Branscheid, "Über die Quellen des stabreimenden Morte Arthure," *Anglia Anzeiger*, VIII (1885). 179-236, meritorious for its day and still useful.

[27] E. V. Gordon and E. Vinaver, "New Light on the Text of the Alliterative *Morte Arthure,*" *MA,* VI (1937). 81-98.

attention from English poets. *Sir Perceval of Gales (Wales)*,[28] in sixteen-line stanzas linked by conscious repetition, tells a part of the story found in Chrétien's *Perceval*. Perceval, reared in the forest in ignorance of knighthood, is here even more the rustic than usual, but shows his ability by killing the Red Knight and other opponents, rescues the Lady Lufamour from her Saracen suitor, and marries her. In the end he is happily reunited with his mother. There is no Grail quest; the Grail is not even mentioned. The English romance preserves the Perceval story in a distinctly primitive form, and although the question has been much discussed, it is doubtful if the poem owes anything to Chrétien's romance or its continuations.[29] The quest of the Holy Grail is not treated in any Middle English romance outside of Malory. But quite early an attempt was made to account for the Grail and its mystical history. This appears in Robert de Boron's *Joseph d'Arimathie* (see p. 141) and in greatly expanded form in the Vulgate *Estoire del Saint Graal*.[30] A brief English romance in 709 alliterative lines, *Joseph of Arimathie*[31] (c. 1350), tells the early part of the story, and a century later a London skinner, Henry Lovelich, told it at great length in a poem which goes by the name of *The History of the Holy Grail*.[32] The story of Tristan and Iseult comes off still worse at the hands of English poets. The only separate treatment of the theme (i.e., outside of Malory) is a northern poem of about 1300 called *Sir Tristrem*.[33] It is written in a curious eleven-line stanza in which most lines have three stresses. The effect of the verse is quite staccato and the narrative is equally so. Although the poet contrives to tell the story in most of its incidents—from the birth of the hero, his adventures at the court of King Mark and in Ireland, his mission to conduct Iseult to be the bride of his uncle, the drinking of the fateful love potion, the many adventures which his clandestine meetings with Iseult lead to, down to the final episode in which he dies—the narrative is generally so abrupt and condensed that without previous knowledge of the story it would in some places hardly be understood and in others would seem poorly motivated. It is seemingly the work of a minstrel telling a tale already familiar to his audience.

The Holy Grail

Tristan

28 J. Campion and F. Holthausen, *Sir Perceval of Gales* (Heidelberg, 1913; *Alt-und Mittelenglische Texte*, No. 5). There is an earlier edition by J. O. Halliwell (1844; *Camden Soc.*). The poem was written in the north Midlands about 1350.

29 The literature is too extensive to be listed here. The student may consult Reginald H. Griffith, *Sir Perceval of Galles: A Study of the Sources of the Legend* (Chicago, 1911) and a series of articles by Arthur C. L. Brown called "The Grail and the English *Sir Perceval*" in *MP*, XVI–XXII (1919–24); opposed by Bruce (I. 309–312) and others.

30 For a discussion of this part of the Vulgate cycle, see Bruce, I. 374–394.

31 W. W. Skeat, *Joseph of Arimathie* (1871; *EETS*, 44).

32 See p. 300.

33 Edited by E. Kölbing, *Die nordische u. die englische Version der Tristansage* (2v, Heilbronn, 1878–82) and by George P. McNeill, *Sir Tristrem* (Edinburgh, 1886; *Scottish Text Soc.*, VIII). Bertram Vogel, "The Dialect of Sir Tristrem," *JEGP*, XL (1941). 538–544, shows that the dialect of the Auchinleck text is prevailingly that of London or the southeast Midlands and not Northern, and suggests that the author was a Londoner who had spent part of his youth in the north. It seems simplest, however, to believe that the numerous instances of *a* for Old English *ā* and occasionally other Northern features are inherited from a Northern original.

English romance contrives to treat most of the major figures and famous themes of Arthurian legend—Merlin and the early life of Arthur, Lancelot, Gawain, the morte d'Arthur, Perceval, the Grail history, Tristan and Iseult. Only the Grail quest is lacking. Nevertheless what remains seems like the chance survival of a few romances, and not always the best, from a much larger number that either died on the lips of the minstrels who chanted them or have perished in the precarious course of manuscript transmission.

v. Non-cycle Romances

There were many romances outside the three "matters" noted by Jean Bodel and the group which we have called the Matter of England. Among them is one of the earliest to be written in English, *Floris and Blaunche-flour,*[34] probably dating from somewhat before 1250. It is an Eastern story with analogues in the *Arabian Nights.* It concerns a king's son who refuses to give up the girl he loves, even after she has been sold to merchants and carried overseas, who finds her in Babylon among the maidens of the Sultan, and eventually is united to her. Although somewhat too brief and condensed in style, it is a charming little love story. *Ipomedon*[35] is an artfully contrived variation of the Guy of Warwick theme—the hero must establish his reputation for prowess before winning his lady's hand. In *The Squire of Low Degree*[36] a simple squire is in love with the King of Hungary's daughter. The lady in this case is favorable to him. She is also faithful to the point of keeping what she supposes is his dead body in her room for seven years. When he reappears alive and suitable explanations have been made the lovers are married with the full approval of the King. *Eger and Grime,*[37] in which the lady will wed only a knight who has never been conquered, won the commendation of even so unpartisan a critic as Lowell. A somewhat different theme appears in *Amis and Amiloun,*[38] the devoted friendship of two men, which does not stop for leprosy or the slaying of the one's children when the other's life is at stake.

A group of romances, often in the twelve-line tail-rime stanza popular in the north,[39] concerns the patiently suffering wife, plotted against, exiled, deprived of her children, but eventually restored to happiness. Such is the matter of *Sir Eglamour*[40] and *Torrent of Portingale,* which closely resemble each other. In *Sir Isumbras,* the husband suffers as well. Sometimes, as in *Oc-tavian,* a wicked mother-in-law brings about the wife's persecution, some-

Floris and Blaunche-flour

Ipomedon

The Squire of Low Degree

Sir Eglamour

---

[34] Most recent edition by A. B. Taylor (Oxford, 1927). The reader will be reminded of the charming French chante-fable, *Aucassin et Nicolete,* of the thirteenth century.
[35] E. Kölbing, *Ipomedon, in drei englischen Bearbeitungen* (Breslau, 1889).
[36] Ed. W. E. Mead (Boston, 1904).
[37] Ed. J. R. Caldwell (Cambridge, Mass., 1933; *Harvard Studies in Compar. Lit.,* IX).
[38] Ed. MacEdward Leach (1937; *EETS,* 203).
[39] A score of romances in this stanza form indicate its vogue at one time. An attempt has been made by A. M. Trounce, "The English Tail-Rhyme Romances," *MA,* I (1932). 87-108, 168-182; II (1933). 34-57, 189-198; III (1934). 30-50, to show that these romances have their source in East Anglia, but the conclusion cannot be accepted.
[40] For editions of the romances mentioned in this section see Wells' *Manual* and Laura A. Hibbard, *The Mediæval Romance in England.*

times a treacherous steward, as in *Sir Triamour*. In *Le Bon Florence of Rome* treachery is manifold and knows no bounds.

William of Palerne   The supernatural enters incidentally into many romances, but in certain stories it is fundamental. *William of Palerne* tells the story of a prince of Spain who has been turned into a werewolf by his stepmother. The werewolf carries off William, the King of Apulia's son, who, when found and brought up by the Emperor, falls in love with the Emperor's daughter. After many adventures William's identity is revealed, the wicked stepmother is forced to return the werewolf to his rightful form, and the story ends in marriages all around.[41] The twelve-thousand line *Partonope of Blois*[42] is a fairy-mistress story in which Partonope's love for the mysterious Melior is twice interrupted when he disobeys her instructions and breaks the spell, but in which of course he eventually marries her. In the romance of *Partenay*[43] (or *Melusine*) the hero is not so fortunate. He marries a fairy of great beauty, promising not to disturb her on Saturdays, and is supremely happy until one Saturday he spies on her and finds that on this day she is a serpent from the waist down. He is forgiven the first time but when he repeats his offense he loses her forever. The brief alliterative romance, the *Chevelere Assigne*,[44] less than four hundred lines long, is the only treatment of the swan-knight story in English verse.

Minor Romances   A few minor romances are interesting for special reasons. The *Tale of Gamelin* is found in a number of manuscripts of the *Canterbury Tales*, generally assigned to the Cook, and was probably among Chaucer's papers waiting to be worked up for one of the pilgrims. It is the story of the ill-treated younger brother which was to find its way into *As You Like It*. *Sir Degrevant* concerns a vassal wronged by his overlord, who marries the daughter and not only recovers his own but inherits his overlord's lands. It suggests the usurer plot in Elizabethan drama. *Generides*, of which we have a version in couplets and a second in rime royal, is an interesting compound of stock features—wicked steward, exiled king, faithless wife, lovers separated and estranged. In the end Clarionas comes like Iseult to cure Generides and the lovers are married.[45]

Romances of Didactic Intent   Certain romances, finally, seem to have been composed with a clearly didactic intent. *Sir Amadas* exemplifies courtesy, generosity, pledges kept at great sacrifice, and the like. *Sir Amadas* has exhausted his estate in entertainment and liberality, even giving his last forty pounds to pay off the debts of a dead knight and permit the burial of the body. When he later marries a princess and regains his former prosperity it is through the help of the soul of the grateful dead. *Sir Cleges* turns on a familiar folk motif.

---

[41] For an interesting discussion of the story's reflection of actual people see Irene P. McKeehan, "Guillaume de Palerne: A Medieval 'Best Seller'," *PMLA*, XLI (1926). 785-809.
[42] Ed. A. T. Bödtker (1912; *EETSES*, 109).
[43] Ed. W. W. Skeat (1866; *EETS*, 22).
[44] Ed. Henry H. Gibbs (1868; *EETSES*, 6).
[45] Sometimes classed with the romance is *The Seven Sages of Rome*, known in the East as the *Book of Sindibad*. It is a collection of framed tales and exists in three different Middle English versions. Ed. Killis Campbell (Boston, 1907); Karl Brunner (1933; *EETS*, 191).

The hero, forced to share any reward he receives with grasping officials, asks for twelve strokes.[46] A didactic purpose is obvious in *The King of Tars*. A Christian princess married to a heathen sultan gives birth to a formless lump of flesh. After the heathen gods have proved powerless, baptism changes the monstrosity to a handsome boy.[47] In *Titus and Vespasian* [48] (*c.* 1400) we have a thoroughly religious romance with its stories of the life of Christ, Pilate, Judas, and others woven into the miraculous cure of Vespasian from leprosy through the agency of St. Veronica's handkerchief and his own belief in Christ. The shorter and perhaps slightly earlier *Siege of Jerusalem*,[49] in alliterative verse, is similar in matter, but the poet's main interest is in the description of the battle. In stories such as these two it is difficult to say where romance ends and religious legend begins.[50]

vi. *The Breton Lay and the Fabliau*

Most medieval romances were too long to be recited at one sitting and some of them are furnished with convenient stopping points at intervals in the story. It is obvious, however, that short narratives suitable for a brief recitation, capable like the modern short story of being read or heard in complete form at one time, would be composed. Certain romances just considered, such as *Sir Cleges* and *Sir Eglamour,* are of suitable length for a single recitation and do not differ in subject matter and treatment from some of the stories discussed in the present section. They could well be included here. But it has become customary to segregate a small number of such short pieces and give them, with not too much warrant, the distinctive name of *Breton lays.*

It would seem that at one time the Bretons had a reputation for storytelling, a reputation which may owe much of its currency in the later Middle Ages to Marie de France. It is conceivable that their shorter tales were distinguished by a particular musical form, that they showed a predilection for love and the supernatural in subject matter, and that many of them had their setting in Brittany. But by the time such tales were written in English, that is, in the fourteenth century, references to the lays of the Bretons seem to be a mere convention. They are always spoken of as belonging to the rather distant past. Thus, when Chaucer's Franklin begins to tell one of them he says:

The Breton Lay (margin note)

[46] See John R. Reinhard, "Strokes Shared," *Jour. Amer. Folk-Lore*, xxxvi (1923). 380-400.
[47] See Lillian H. Hornstein, "A Folklore Theme in *The King of Tars*," *PQ*, xx (1941). 82-87; "The Historical Background of *The King of Tars*," *Speculum*, xvi (1941). 404-414; "New Analogues to the *King of Tars*," *MLR*, xxxvi (1941). 433-442. The valuable discussion of Robert J. Geist, "On the Genesis of *The King of Tars*," *JEGP*, xlii (1943). 260-268, should also be consulted.
[48] Ed. J. A. Herbert (1905; *Roxburghe Club*).
[49] Ed. G. Steffler (Emden, 1891), and E. Kölbing and Mabel Day (1932; *EETS*, 188).
[50] On the relation between saint's legend and romance see Irene P. McKeehan, "Some Relationships between the Legends of British Saints and Medieval Romance," [Univ. of Chicago] *Abstracts of Theses*, Humanistic Ser., ii (1926). 383-391, and the portion printed in full as "St. Edmund of East Anglia: The Development of a Romantic Legend," *Univ. of Colorado Studies*, xv (1925). 13-74.

> Thise olde gentil Britouns in hir dayes
> Of diverse adventures maden layes,
> Rymeyed in hir firste Briton tonge;
> Whiche layes with hir instrumentz they songe,
> Or elles redden hem for hir plesaunce. . . .

This is similar to the opening lines of *Sir Orfeo*, a passage which is also found at the beginning of the *Lay le Freine*, where we are told:

> In Brytayn þis layes arne y-wryte,
> Furst y-founde and forþe y-gete. . . .
>
> When þey myght owher [anywhere] heryn
> Of adventurës þat þer weryn,
> Þey toke her harpys wiþ game,
> Maden layes and ȝaf it name.

The same passage tells us that Breton lays may treat of almost any subject—weal or woe, joy and mirth, treachery and guile, even jests and ribaldry; some, it says, are of faëry, but most are about love. Certainly there is nothing distinctive in the subject or treatment of the so-called Breton lays in English, and whether a given short romance is classed as a Breton lay or not depends mainly on whether it says it is one (e.g., *The Earl of Toulouse, Sir Orfeo, Lay le Freine*), or has its scene laid in Brittany (*Sir Degarë*), or contains a passing reference to Brittany (*Sir Launfal*), or tells a story found among the *lais* of Marie de France. Doubtless reference to the Bretons was often no more than a trick of the poet to lend authority or the charm of age to his story.

Emare

We can but glance in passing at the delightful little English poems which constitute the group. *Emare* [51] is a supreme instance of a story made up of the commonplaces of romance. There is not a novel character or situation in it. To list its episodes is to begin a motif-index of medieval romance—the emperor who wishes to marry his own daughter, the heroine set adrift in a boat, in this case twice, the wicked mother-in-law who not only opposes her son's marriage but by a substitution of letters brings about the unhappy bride's exile, pilgrimages to Rome with their chain of coincidences bringing about final recognition and reunion. It must not be supposed, however, that the story is without charm. Emare herself is very beautiful, and bears her sufferings with so much sweetness and patience that she wins our hearts. The king, her husband, loves her so loyally and behaves so honorably that we rejoice with him when his wife and child are at long last restored. *Emare* is classed as a Breton lay because the poet says it is one. Chaucer's Constance story told by the Man of Law, which is very similar, is not. *Sir Degarë* [52] is also made up of familiar features—the king who will marry his daughter

Sir
Degare

[51] Ed. A. B. Gough (Heidelberg, 1901), Edith Rickert (1908; *EETSES*, 99), and in French and Hale's *Middle English Metrical Romances*.

[52] Ed. David Laing (1849; *Abbotsford Club*), and in French and Hale, *op. cit.* A later text is in Hales and Furnivall's edition of the Percy Folio, Vol. III. See also George P. Faust, *Sir Degare: A Study of the Texts and Narrative Structure* (1935; *Princeton Studies in English*, 11)

only to one who overcomes him in battle, the daughter forced to yield to an unknown knight in the forest, the child left on a hermit's step, the youth who nearly marries his own mother but recognizes her through a pair of gloves that will fit no one else, the son who discovers his father through a sword with a missing piece. The scene is Little Britain, but this is the only thing that makes it a Breton lay.

Two of the English lays derive ultimately from *lais* of Marie de France. The *Lay le Freine*,[53] so named, as the English poet tells us, because *freine* in French means ash-tree, tells the story of an infant abandoned in a hollow ash, who later wins a husband and her parents back through one turn of Fortune's wheel. *Sir Landeval* [54] is about a knight who enjoys the love of a fairy mistress as long as he refrains from any mention of her, who breaks the covenant and loses her, but, since there are extenuating circumstances, recovers her favor. *Sir Landeval* was elaborated by Thomas of Chester in his *Sir Launfal*,[55] without always being improved in the process. *Sir Orfeo* [56] retells the classical story of Orpheus and Eurydice with medieval modifications. *Sir Gowther*,[57] telling the legend of Robert the Devil, is not without its didactic intent; indeed one manuscript ends with the words, "Explicit Vita Sancti." *The Earl of Toulouse* [58] is the story of a vassal persecuted by the Emperor; in the end he not only wins justice but marries the Emperor's beautiful widow. It resembles in a number of ways the story of *Sir Degrevant* (see above), but because the author of *The Earl of Toulouse* says he got it from "a lay of Bretayn" the latter is included among Breton lays.

The edifying element found in some of the lays becomes the chief feature of another type of short narrative, the miracle of the Virgin. The miracle of the Virgin is a kind of *conte dévot* or pious tale in which devotion to the Virgin wins her intercession. Thus, the nun who has run away from her convent and has returned repentant after a period of worldly life finds her absence unnoticed. Because she had venerated the Virgin from the days when she was a young novice, her place has been supplied and her duties have been performed by the Mother of Christ. Readers are familiar with the story in John Davidson's *Ballad of a Nun* and in the dramatic production *The Miracle*, in which Lady Diana Manners appeared in the rôle of the Virgin. In another widely distributed example a harlot is induced to pray. She prays in a chapel dedicated to the Virgin and at her death is assured of salvation. The tale told by Chaucer's Prioress is another well-known example of the type. A small collection of these stories is found in the *South English Legendary*. A more important group of forty-two apparently once formed part of the famous Vernon manuscript, but in the present mutilated condition of the codex only nine are preserved. Finally, not to mention

Marginal notes: Le Freine — Sir Landeval — Other Lays — Miracles of the Virgin

---

[53] Ed. H. Weber, *Metrical Romances*, Vol. 1, and H. Varnhagen, *Anglia*, III (1880), 415-423.
[54] Ed. G. L. Kittredge, *Amer. Jour. Phil.*, x (1889). 1-33, and Rudolf Zimmermann (Köningsberg, 1900).
[55] Most conveniently available in French and Hale, *op. cit.*
[56] In French and Hale, *op. cit.*
[57] Ed. Karl Breul (Oppeln, 1886).
[58] In French and Hale, *op. cit.*

scattered examples, there is a collection of eighteen in a Phillipps manu‚ script now in the British Museum. These collections, which are all in verse, extend from the thirteenth to the fifteenth century, but the type is dateless and examples in English may well have existed as early as the twelfth century.[59]

The *fabliau*   One other form of narrative poem in Middle English must be mentioned here, and its aim was simply to entertain. The fabliau, like the lay and the miracle of the Virgin, is short, but there the resemblance stops. It is a humorous story, generally ribald or at least unconventional, told in verse with conscious literary art. In the Middle Ages it enjoyed its greatest vogue in France,[60] but turned into prose it forms an important element in such collections of tales as we have in Boccaccio's *Decameron* and their derivatives in all the languages of Europe. It is in no sense biographical and seeks its effect in the rapid succession of events forming a single episode. Its humor is not that of the jest, nor does it depend on a play on words, but is the humor of situation, rooted in human nature. It has a special fondness for wives who trick their husbands, and individuals whose greed or gullibility makes them fair game for the cleverness of rogues.

Examples *in Chaucer*   In English the type is best represented by a half dozen stories in Chaucer's *Canterbury Tales,* those told by the Miller, the Reeve, the Friar, the Summoner, the Merchant, and the Shipman. The Cook's tale would undoubtedly have been of the type if he had gone on. That Chaucer was aware of the effect which such of his tales would have upon some readers is evident in his warning just before beginning the *Miller's Tale:*

> And therefore, whoso list it nat yheere,
> Turne over the leef and ches another tale.

Dame *Sirith*   Before Chaucer the only true fabliau in English is *Dame Sirith* [61] (*c.* 1250), turning on a trick by which Dame Sirith, a hypocritical bawd, succeeds in terrifying a young wife named Margeri into accepting as a lover the clerk Wilekin. The plot outrages probability, but the tale is skilfully told with much natural dialogue. There are a few post-Chaucerian pieces such as *The*

---

[59] The basic work on the miracles of the Virgin is A. Mussafia, *Studien zu den mittelalterlichen Marienlegenden* (5 parts, Vienna, 1887-98; *Sitzungsberichte der kgl. Akad. der Wissenschaften,* Philos.-hist. Classe, CXIII-CXXXIX). Much important material on collections in Latin, French, and English will be found in H. L. D. Ward, *Catalogue of Romances . . . in the British Museum,* II (1893). 586-740. A list of Latin miracles running to nearly 1800 items has been published by Father Poncelet in *Analecta Bollandiana,* XXI (1902). 241-360. One of the best known collections in the Middle Ages was that of Johannes Herolt, which can be read in the translation of C. C. S. Bland (1928), with an excellent short Introduction by Eileen Power. G. G. Coulton, *Five Centuries of Religion,* I (Cambridge, 1923). 501-516, offers a brief discussion with examples. Ruth W. Tryon, "Miracles of Our Lady in Middle English Verse," *PMLA,* XXXVIII (1923). 308-388, publishes a number of hitherto unprinted texts.

[60] The standard work on the subject is J. Bédier, *Les Fabliaux* (4ed., Paris, 1925). For the fabliau in English see the introduction to George H. McKnight, *Middle English Humorous Tales in Verse* (Boston, 1913), H. S. Canby, "The English Fabliau," *PMLA,* XXI (1906). 200-214, and W. M. Hart, "The Fabliau and Popular Literature," *PMLA,* XXIII (1908). 329-374.

[61] In McKnight, as above, and for discussion see Edward Schröder, "*Dame Sirith,*" *Nachrichten aus der neueren Philologie und Literaturgeschichte,* I (1937). 179-202 (*Gesellschaft der Wissenschaften zu Göttingen*).

Wright's Chaste Wife [62] and *The Prioress and Her Three Suitors*,[63] but they do not merit treatment here. When we consider that nearly one hundred and fifty specimens of the fabliau are found in Old French, we can only believe that these realistic episodes from everyday life ran counter to the more puritan spirit in England and were less often committed to writing than allowed to die on the lips of minstrels and other purveyors of backstairs entertainment.[64]

[62] Edited by Furnivall, *EETS*, 12.
[63] Ed. Johannes Prinz, *A Tale of a Prioress and Her Three Wooers* (Berlin, 1911; *Literarhistorische Forschungen*, 47), and J. O. Halliwell, *Minor Poems of ... Lydgate* (1840; *Percy Soc.*, 11), pp. 107-117.
[64] A number of stories found in the French fabliaux occur in the English ballads.

XI
The Omnibus of Religion

Ignorance among the Lower Clergy

In 1222 the Bishop of Salisbury ordered an examination of the priests in seventeen of his parishes. The examination was a simple one, based on the words, *Te igitur clementissime Pater ... rogamus* ("we therefore beseech thee, most merciful Father"). These words open the first prayer in the Canon of the Mass, the most solemn and at the same time an invariable part of the service. Five could not tell the case of *te* or identify the governing verb. Some of the others refused to answer. The incident is unfortunately not an isolated case. The ignorance of parish priests was frequently appalling, especially in country parishes remote from towns and larger centers. In the register of William of Wykeham, Bishop of Winchester, it is more than once recorded that a priest was made to take oath that within one year he would learn the Creed, the Ten Commandments, the Seven Deadly Sins, etc. under penalty of being fined forty shillings. In the light of such cases we need not be surprised at frequent complaints that the simplest spiritual needs of the people were not being cared for.[1]

The Coming of the Friars

When an evil is clearly recognized the remedy is often not far off. At the beginning of the thirteenth century St. Francis and St. Dominic conceived almost at the same time the idea of carrying religion directly to the people, without the organization of churches and religious houses. St. Francis was filled with the need for embracing poverty and ministering to the poor, St. Dominic with the necessity of combating heresy. With incredible rapidity they gained followers and soon the Friars Minor and the Friars Preachers had spread over many parts of Europe. The Dominicans reached England in 1221 and the Franciscans in 1224. Though learning was in the beginning more necessary to the Preachers than to the Minorites, both orders soon found it necessary to the successful prosecution of their work. The friars were in time to become famous for learning and for works in which that learning was adapted to the spiritual needs of the people.

Their Emphasis on Preaching

While the activities of the friars were greatest among the depressed classes in the poorer quarters and on the edges of large cities, there were few localities that did not come under their influence. So great was the stress which they laid upon preaching that they even curtailed the rest of the service to save more time for the sermon. It was their method of bringing home the teachings of Christ and enforcing his precepts with the vividness of direct speech. Some friars traveled from place to place, preaching in parish

---

[1] For a brief statement of the facts see G. G. Coulton, *Medieval Panorama* (1938), pp. 156-160, or Margaret Deanesly, *The Lollard Bible* (1920), pp. 193-195.

churches, the churchyard, the market-place, and the crossroads; others preached regularly in their own churches—which in the course of time they established—on Sundays and festivals and on rainy days, when, as Pecock tells us, great numbers were wont to come to the friars' churches.[2] One reason for their popularity was their concern with basic social and moral questions. Another was undoubtedly the skill with which they adapted themselves to their audience, generously sprinkling their discourse with anecdote and illustration and even adopting devices learned from the minstrels. There is little doubt that they sometimes preached in verse. Wyclif accuses them of corrupting the word of God, "some by riming and others by preaching poems and fables." [3]

The success of the friars was naturally a shock to the regular clergy, *Their* arousing bitterness in some but warm admiration in others. It is not necessary *Influence* to suppose that nothing would ever have been done for the people without the stimulus of the mendicants,[4] but the action soon to be taken may well have owed something to the example of the friars. Robert Grosseteste, lecturer to the Franciscans at Oxford and one who, though not belonging to the order himself, expressed the desire to have about him at all times members of the order, issued a set of Constitutions shortly after he became Bishop of Lincoln, requiring the clergy in his diocese to know and to teach the people in their mother tongue the Decalogue, the Seven Deadly Sins, the Seven Sacraments, and the Creed. A few years later his example was followed by the Bishop of Worcester,[5] while in 1246 the Bishop of Chichester set up a similar though simpler requirement that the laity be taught the Paternoster, Creed, and Ave. These efforts toward reform were inspired by the activities of Innocent III and the decrees of the fourth Lateran Council (1215-16), soon reaffirmed by the Council of Oxford called by Stephen Langton in 1222. But the injunctions of individual bishops were of direct force only in their own dioceses. In 1281 a regulation of national scope was

[2] See A. G. Little, "Popular Preaching," in *Studies in English Franciscan History* (Manchester, 1917), and the two books of G. R. Owst, *Preaching in Medieval England* (Cambridge, 1926) and *Literature and Pulpit in Medieval England* (Cambridge, 1933). On the friars' sermons see Horace G. Pfander, *The Popular Sermon of the Medieval Friar in England* (1937).

[3] See the references gathered by Deanesly, *Lollard Bible*, p. 148n.

[4] Edmund Rich, Archbishop of Canterbury (1234-40) in the *Merure de Seinte Eglise* (*Speculum Ecclesiae*), written toward the end of his life, discusses the Seven Deadly Sins, Seven Virtues, Seven Gifts of the Holy Ghost, Ten Commandments, Twelve Articles of the Faith, Seven Sacraments, Seven Works of Mercy, and the Seven Petitions of the Pater Noster. This is the standard list of subjects for popular instruction, but there is no indication that it was intended for the people. The Latin text can be had only in early editions. The French text has been edited by Harry W. Robbins (Lewisburg, Pa., 1925). A Middle English translation is printed in C. Horstman, *Yorkshire Writers*, I (1895), and a modernized version has been published by Francesca M. Steele (1905).

[5] C. R. Cheney, *English Synodalia of the Thirteenth Century* (Oxford, 1941), proposes a date for Grosseteste's statutes after the synod held at Worcester, but the evidence is not convincing. Grosseteste's *Templum Domini*, a treatise on the Virtues and Vices, Articles of the Faith, Ten Commandments, and Sacraments, exists in more than sixty manuscripts but has not been printed. An English poem of the same name has been published by Roberta D. Cornelius, *The Figurative Castle* (Bryn Mawr, 1930), pp. 91-112. It shows some resemblance to the first half of Grosseteste's treatise, but the indebtedness has been questioned. For Grosseteste's *Château d'Amour*, which includes brief treatments of the Ten Commandments, Creed, Seven Sacraments, Seven Gifts of the Holy Ghost, etc., see above p. 139.

Archbishop Peckham's Constitutions (1281)

adopted. John Peckham, a Franciscan friar, almost immediately upon becoming Archbishop of Canterbury called a general council at Lambeth and issued the famous Constitutions of Lambeth. They begin with a preamble which asserts that "the ignorance of priests casts the people into the pit of error" and then proceeds:

> As a remedy for this peril we expressly command that four times a year, that is, once in each quarter of the year, upon one or more holy days each priest having charge of the people, either personally or through some one else, shall explain to the people in their mother tongue, without any fantastic subtlety, the fourteen articles of the faith, the ten commandments of the decalogue, the two precepts of the gospels [love of God and love of man], the seven works of mercy, the seven deadly sins with their offspring, the seven cardinal virtues, and the seven sacraments of grace. And lest any one on account of ignorance excuse himself from the aforesaid things, which all ministers of the church are bound to know, we touch upon them here in a brief summary.

A series of paragraphs on the topics mentioned carries out the promise of the last sentence. Peckham's Constitutions were constantly referred to for upwards of two hundred years and were followed by a succession of pronouncements from bishops in various parts of England reaffirming them in spirit and often in identical words.[6] They remained the authoritative outline of doctrine upon which the people were supposed to be instructed until the end of the Middle Ages.

Manuals and Treatises in Latin and French

This basic body of theological teaching was already old long before Peckham's time, but now that he had provided for its regular presentation to the people it was soon embodied in a number of works intended for the common people or for those priests who were in need of simple manuals or ready-made discourses suitable for oral presentation. Authoritative sources upon which the authors of such popular treatises could draw were not lacking. There were especially two great works which became the parents of a numerous offspring, the huge compilation of Raymond of Pennafort called the *Summa Casuum Poenitentiae* (*c.* 1235) and the twin treatises of Guillaume de Perrault, the *Summa de Vitiis* and *Summa de Virtutibus* (before 1261). From these and other sources Friar Lorens, the confessor of Philip the Third, compiled in 1279 a treatise called the *Somme des Vices et Vertus,* commonly known as the *Somme le Roi,* which circulated widely. An analogous work, and in parts identical, went by the name of *Miroir du Monde.* Both the *Somme le Roi* and the *Miroir du Monde* became in turn the parents of numerous works in French and English. The interdependence of the many treatises in which the Ten Commandments, the Twelve Articles of the Faith (Apostles' Creed), the Seven Deadly Sins,

---

[6] See J. L. Peckham, *Archbishop Peckham as a Religious Educator* (1934; *Yale Stud. in Religion,* No. 7), pp. 83-96. The movement for the reformation of the clergy and for the instruction of the people in essential doctrine is traced in ch. 1 of E. J. Arnould, *Le* Manual des Péchés: *Étude de littérature religieuse anglo-normande* (xiii⁰ siècle) (Paris, 1940), which appeared during the Second World War and reached this country too late to be utilized in the writing of this chapter.

the Four Cardinal and Three Theological Virtues, the Seven Sacraments, the Paternoster, the Seven Gifts of the Holy Ghost, and often other doctrinal matters were covered makes it difficult and often impossible to tell where a given English work owes its chief debt. Chaucer's *Parson's Tale* is an excellent case in point.

The English works [7] range all the way from simple and unpretentious *In English* manuals to highly ingenious and sometimes quite fanciful allegories. The earlier ones are often in verse. Thus, when John Thoresby, Archbishop of York, published in 1357 an explanation in Latin of the points prescribed by Peckham, known in modern times as the *Lay Folks' Catechism*,[8] he issued at the same time a somewhat expanded version in English. The crude verse of the English was the work of John Gaytryge, a monk of St. Mary's abbey, York; it is commonly known as *Dan John Gaytryge's Sermon*. A little later *John* a still longer version, likewise in verse, was prepared by John Wyclif or one *Gaytryge* of his followers.[9] At the beginning of the fifteen century a canon regular of Lilleshall in Shropshire, John Mirk by name, wrote a manual of *Instructions for Parish Priests*.[10] He likens many priests to the blind leading the blind,

> Wharefore þou preste curatoure . . .
> ʒef thou be not grete clerk,
> Loke thow most on thys werk.

He includes some general instructions on the duties of a parish priest, with specific directions on the form of baptism, the method of hearing confession, and the like, but parts of his text were intended to be taught to the people, and this doubtless was one reason for his writing the whole in verse. For priests who could manage the Latin a much fuller treatment was provided in the *Speculum Christiani* (c. 1360). It is the work of an Englishman and *Speculum* covers the usual topics. At least sixty-five extant manuscripts testify to its *Christiani* popularity. It is mentioned here because the whole work was translated into English by a Lollard, doubtless, as the editor notes, for the benefit of the many unlearned Lollard preachers and possibly to provide a manual of devotion for laymen.[11] As an example of the elaborate allegorical method we may cite *Jacob's Well*, a collection of ninety-five sermons or discourses de- *Jacob's* livered to some audience at intervals of a few days (c. 1425). Man is likened *Well* to a well which must be cleansed with the implements used in cleaning wells, protected against pollution through the springs of the senses, etc. It

[7] See on the general subject H. G. Pfander, "Some Medieval Manuals of Religious Instruction in England and Observations on Chaucer's Parson's Tale," *JEGP*, xxxv (1936). 243-258.

[8] An explanation of the Mass and directions for hearing it were provided in English verse about 1300; see *The Lay Folks Mass Book* (1879; EETS, 71). In the following century appeared a book for private devotions known as the *Primer*; see *The Primer or Lay Folks' Prayer Book* (1895; EETS, 105).

[9] All three texts are printed in *EETS*, 118.

[10] Ed. Edward Peacock (1868, rev. ed. 1902; EETS, 31). Most of Mirk's treatise is translated from the second part of William de Pagula's (or Page's) *Oculus Sacerdotis*, one of a number of Latin texts called forth by the same need. Space does not permit the discussion of these here.

[11] Ed. Gustaf Holmstedt (1933; EETS. 182).

is in prose; the preacher must have been able to count on the attention—and the endurance—of his audience. Although each discourse fills only about thirty minutes and for the sake of interest closes with one or two illustrative stories, it is one of the most voluminous treatises of the kind that we have.[12]

Virtue and vice in the abstract are likely to be dull subjects. How interesting a treatise on the Ten Commandments, the Deadly Sins, and the Sacraments can be when these things are brought realistically into relation with **Handlyng** life is seen in the *Handlyng Synne* (1303) of Robert of Brunne.[13] Based on **Synne** ·he Anglo-Norman *Manuel des Péchés* of William of Wadington(?),[14] with many omissions and additions, it is in reality a collection of tales and anecdotes and concrete instances illustrating the vices and weaknesses of man. Holidays are holy days, not to be spent in dancing, wrestling, crowning a beauty queen, haunting taverns, or playing chess when one should be in church. Women should not be proud of their hair, use powder "or other flour to make them whiter of color," or borrow clothes to go to the dance. Miracle plays are forbidden, but one may play the Resurrection in church. Minstrels get their clothes, and their meat and drink, through folly. . . . Seldom do we get such a picture of the details of medieval life. There is not a dull page in the 12,630 lines of the *Handlyng Synne*.

Ayenbite More simply doctrinal are the translations into English of Friar Lorens's **of Inwit** *Somme*. The best known of these today is the *Ayenbite of Inwit* ("Remorse of Conscience")[15] translated in 1340 by Dan Michel of Northgate, who tells us that the manuscript was written with his own hand and belonged to the library of St. Augustine's, Canterbury. As a specimen of the Kentish dialect it is important, but it seems to have had no circulation. Other translations of the *Somme* were made in the course of the next hundred years, and one of these, *The Book of Vices and Virtues*, in the East Midland dialect enjoyed greater popularity, since it has come down to us in several manuscripts.[16] Preserved in more than thirty copies is an adaptation of the *Somme* **Speculum** in verse by William of Nassyngton which went by the name of *Speculum* **Vitae** *Vitae*. Using the Paternoster as the point of departure, it presents the whole body of doctrinal and ethical teaching necessary for laymen in a lively, realistic style which marks the author as a person of considerable literary gifts.[17]

---

[12] Only the first half has been published, edited by Arthur Brandeis (1900; *EETS*, 115). An edition of the rest is promised by G. R. Owst.

[13] I.e., manual of sins. Ed. F. J. Furnivall, with the *Manuel des Péchés* in parallel (1901-3; *EETS*, 119, 123). The author's full name was Robert Mannyng, of Brunne or Bourne (Lincs.). He belonged to the Gilbertine priory at Sempringham, but he was for a time at another Gilbertine house at Sixhills and at Cambridge. His literary activity falls between 1303, when he began the *Handlyng Synne*, and 1338, when he finished a translation of Langtoft's *Chronicle*. The latter forms the second part of his *Story of England*; the first part is based on Wace's *Roman de Brut*. The two parts are edited respectively in the Rolls Ser. (1889) and by T. Hearne (2v, Oxford, 1725). The latest examination of the facts of Robert's life is by Ruth Crosby, "Robert Mannyng of Brunne: A New Biography,"' *PMLA*, LVII (1942). 15-28.

[14] See p. 140.

[15] Ed. Richard Morris (1866; *EETS*, 23).

[16] Ed. W. Nelson Francis (1942; *EETS*, 217).

[17] An adequate account must await the publication of this important text. Only the first 370 lines have been printed (*ESt*, VII. 468-72). The best discussion is that of Hope Emily

Standing somewhat apart from those works which embody in one way or another Peckham's program is a poem which was intended nevertheless to act as a spur to righteousness. It is difficult now to see in its 9624 pedestrian lines how it could ever have become the most popular work of the fourteenth century, but more than a hundred extant manuscripts show that in this respect the *Prick of Conscience* surpassed the *Canterbury Tales, Piers Plowman,* and every other Middle English poem. In a prologue and seven parts it tells of the wretched nature of man, the unstableness of the world, and of death which is inevitable, thus building up to the last four parts which treat of Purgatory, Doomsday, the pains of Hell, and the joys of Heaven. It was long attributed to Richard Rolle, but there is neither external nor internal evidence to justify our continuing to do so.[18]

Although none of the manuals for priests recommend including the Sunday gospel as part of the sermon, the practice was certainly contemplated as early as Orm, and indeed most medieval books of sermons were made up of homilies on the Sunday gospel or epistle. With the spread of popular preaching vernacular collections of such homilies in verse were prepared for delivery either by the author or by others lacking in cunning or industry. They may have been intended for private reading as well. One such collection, the *Northern Homily Cycle* (c. 1300), provides sermons for the Sundays and certain festivals throughout the year, many of them furnished with appropriate exempla. The latest student of this cycle believes it to be the work of a Dominican.[19] Prose collections of similar scope, almost certainly intended to provide ready materials for unlearned priests, are found in the *Festial*[20] of John Mirk, whom we have already mentioned as the author of *Instructions for Parish Priests,* and in an anonymous compilation, also of the fifteenth century, known as the *Speculum Sacerdotale.*[21]

The Prick of Conscience

Northern Homily Cycle

Allen, *Radcliffe Coll. Monographs,* No. 15, pp. 169 ff, and her *"Speculum Vitae:* Addendum," *PMLA,* XXXII (1917). 133-162. We cannot feel sure of the date, the identity of the author, or the immediate source of the poem. The author says he has translated from the Latin of John de Waldeby, but Miss Allen has shown that Waldeby's treatise on the Paternoster is not the source. In our present state of knowledge the closest connection seems to be with Friar Lorens and an English prose *Myrour to Lewde Men and Wymmen,* similar in content and often verbally identical. The *Speculum Vitae* is also one of the sources of *Jacob's Well.*

[18] See Hope Emily Allen, "The Authorship of the *Prick of Conscience," Radcliffe Coll. Monographs,* No. 15, pp. 115-170, and the references under Rolle in ch. XIII. The only edition is that of Richard Morris for the *Philological Society* (1863).

[19] James E. Carver, *The Northern Homily Cycle* (1941), abstract of his N. Y. Univ. diss. He believes it was written between 1295 and 1306, probably before October, 1303. (For his evidence see *MLN,* LIII (1938). 258-261). Only fragmentary texts have been published by John Small, *English Metrical Homilies from Manuscripts of the Fourteenth Century* (Edinburgh, 1862), and C. Horstmann, *Altenglische Legenden* (Heilbronn, 1881), pp. 1-188. A new edition is in preparation by Carver. The sources of the exempla are studied in Gordon H. Gerould, *The North-English Homily Collection: A Study of the Manuscript Relations and of the Sources of the Tales* (1902). The suggestion (*MLN,* XXII. 95-96) that the work was based on Robert of Gretham's *Miroir* has not been substantiated.

[20] Ed. Theodor Erbe (1905; EETSES, 96).

[21] Ed. Edward H. Weatherly (1936; EETS, 200). Space does not permit a discussion of the large body of sermon literature that has been preserved from the fourteenth and fifteenth centuries. For this the reader must be referred to the two books of G. R. Owst mentioned above. A collection of sermons formed at Oxford in the first half of the fifteenth century is edited by Woodburn O. Ross, *Middle English Sermons* (1940; EETS, 209). Although preaching in Latin was confined to sermons for monks and the clergy and scholarly audiences, many

Life of
Christ

The
Passion

Cursor
Mundi

South
English
Legendary

In a day when the Bible was not a familiar book to the layman some form of gospel harmony presenting the life of Christ was an appropriate substitute. The *Stanzaic Life of Christ* is a long fourteenth-century poem, probably by a monk of St. Werburgh's abbey in Chester, who drew his material not from the Bible but from Higden's *Polychronicon* and the *Legenda Aurea*. Apart from exemplifying a type of religious omnibus it derives a certain interest from having been used in the composition of the *Chester Plays*.[22] Even more popular were treatments of the Passion, of which two in Middle English have come down to us. The *Northern Passion* [23] is much superior to the *Southern Passion*, and is found also in Midland and Southern manuscripts. It is based upon an Old French *Passion*, and in an expanded form is sometimes incorporated in the *Northern Homily Cycle*. It was used in certain episodes of both the *York* and the *Towneley Plays*. The *Southern Passion* [24] is always found as part of the *South English Legendary* (discussed below) and seems to have been written for this collection.

An attempt to cover the outstanding events of the Old as well as the New Testament is the northern poem called the *Cursor Mundi*,[25] because, as the author explains, it runs over the whole world. It is one of the longest of the omnibus poems, filling nearly 24,000 lines, with additional pieces at the end. After a prologue in which the author explains his plan and his intention of writing in English for the common people he divides his story into seven ages, beginning with Creation and ending with the Last Judgment. He has drawn his material from various sources, about a fifth from Herman of Valenciennes' *Bible*,[26] other parts from Grosseteste's *Château d'Amour*, Methodius, an Old French legend of the Holy Rood, and the Assumption of the Virgin from a Southern English poem on the subject. What cannot be otherwise accounted for is usually attributed to Peter Comestor (whom he names), but we shall probably find some day other more immediate sources for some of this matter. The work belongs to the last part of the thirteenth century or early in the next.

What goes by the name of the *South English Legendary* [27] could almost be described as a group of similar works having certain parts in common. It is obviously a matter of gradual growth, undergoing modifications and accretions for upwards of a hundred years. Like the *Legenda Aurea*, to which it bears an obvious family likeness,[28] it consists not only of saints'

---

sermons preached in the vernacular are preserved only in Latin. A famous example is John Bromyard's *Summa Predicantium* of the middle of the fourteenth century.

22 See the edition of Frances A. Foster (1926; *EETS*, 166).

23 Ed. Frances A. Foster (1913-16; *EETS*, 145 and 147).

24 Ed. Beatrice Daw Brown (1927; *EETS*, 169).

25 Ed. Richard Morris (1874-78; *EETS*, 57, 59, 62, 66, 68).

26 Lois Borland, "Herman's *Bible* and the *Cursor Mundi*," *SP*, xxx (1933). 427-444.

27 One manuscript that has been printed in full is Laud 108, dating 1280-90. It is edited by C. Horstmann (1887; *EETS*, 87).

28 For a discussion of the possible influence of the *Legenda Aurea* on the English collection see Minnie E. Wells, "The *South English Legendary* in Its Relation to the *Legenda Aurea*," *PMLA*, li (1936). 337-360.

legends but narratives for important seasons in the ecclesiastical year. The many manuscripts in which it was copied differ greatly in the number, choice, and arrangement of items, but it is possible to see, along with the addition of new legends, a gradual expansion of the biblical and apocryphal matter until, in one of its later forms, the whole is divided into a Temporale and a Sanctorale and arranged approximately in accordance with the calendar. Although the earliest manuscript belongs to the end of the thirteenth century, the collection can hardly have been begun before about 1275. There is reason to think that it originally took shape in or near the abbey of Gloucester, and that the original compilation was the work of a Franciscan.[29] Probably many groups and individuals, however, had a hand in it in the course of its development.

It is interesting to note how many of the works discussed in this chapter belong to the north. The *Cursor Mundi,* the *Northern Homily Cycle,* and the *Northern Passion* come to mind immediately. Thoresby was Archbishop of York and John Gaytryge, who translated his *Catechism,* was a monk there. While we no longer need to think of the *Prick of Conscience* as associated with Rolle and Yorkshire, it is nevertheless a northern poem, and the Nassyngton who wrote the *Speculum Vitae* was most likely an advocate in the ecclesiastical court at York. The *Stanzaic Life of Christ* was probably written at Chester, and the *Handlyng Synne* certainly in Lincolnshire. In this list the northeast is especially prominent. We must recognize an active religious ferment in any region which in addition could give birth to Wyclif and the Lollard movement, call forth the great mystics, and produce the most ambitious cycles of biblical plays.[30]

Prominence of the North

[29] See Minnie E. Wells, as above, and her later article, "The Structural Development of the South English Legendary," *JEGP,* XLI (1942). 320-344.

[30] Space does not permit discussion of the collections of exempla for the use of preachers, such as the Latin *Liber Exemplorum* (*c.* 1275), ed. A. G. Little (1908), *Speculum Laicorum* (*c.* 1285), ed. J. T. Welter (Paris, 1914), and *Fasciculus Morum* (*c.* 1320?), still unpublished, or of collections translated in the fifteenth century into English, like the *Gesta Romanorum* (*EETSES,* 33) and the *Alphabet of Tales* (*EETS,* 126-127). See T. F. Crane, introduction to *The Exempla . . . of Jacques de Vitry* (1890; *Folk-Lore Soc. Pub.,* XXVI) and "Mediæval Sermon-Books and Stories and Their Study since 1883," *Proc. Amer. Philos. Soc.,* LVI (1917). 369-402; J. T. Welter, *L'Exemplum dans la littérature religieuse et didactique du moyen âge* (Paris, 1927); and J. H. Mosher, *The Exemplum in the Early Religious and Didactic Literature of England* (1911).

XII

The Lyric[1]

It is a commonplace of literary history that there is little or no lyric in the poetry of the Anglo-Saxons. Such dramatic pieces as the *Seafarer*, the *Husband's Message*, or the *Wife's Lament*, or such elegiac reflections as the *Ruin* are lyrical rather than lyrics. Cædmon's *Hymn*, *Eadwacer*, and *Deor*, the last so fine in its simple unity and directness, come closest perhaps to the lyric in expressing the personal emotion of the poet.[2] But it is evident that Old English poetry found its most natural expression in the epic and in other types of narrative verse.

Likewise the Normans seem to have been without a lyrical bent. If we are to accept Gaston Paris's analysis of the Norman character,[3] the Norman was practical and business-like, earnest rather than gay. At all events, in the lyric of northern France, that is, in the poetry of the trouvères, the Normans seem to have played a very minor part. The same observation holds true for England. In the very considerable body of Anglo-Norman poetry there are few secular lyrics,[4] and it does not seem that Continental specimens were often copied in manuscripts written in England. During the period when French was the predominant language of the upper class it would be useless to look for lyrics of the French courtly type in English. The few lyrical fragments older than the thirteenth century, such as *St. Godric's Hymns* and *Cnut's Song*,[5] are of liturgical and clerical inspiration. When, therefore, English secular lyrics begin to appear about 1250, it is a little difficult to say precisely what are their antecedents.

[1] A convenient introduction to the Middle English lyric is the little volume of *Early English Lyrics* edited by E. K. Chambers and F. Sidgwick (1907) with an essay by Chambers on "Some Aspects of the Mediæval Lyric" and a list of important manuscripts in which the lyrics are found. Carleton Brown's three volumes, *English Lyrics of the XIII*th *Century* (Oxford, 1932), *Religious Lyrics of the XIV*th *Century* (Oxford, 1924), and *Religious Lyrics of the XV*th *Century* (Oxford, 1939), are indispensable collections of texts, as is Richard L. Greene's *The Early English Carols* (1935). Richard Morris, *An Old English Miscellany* (1872; EETS, 49) prints many of the older lyrics, and Thomas Wright and J. O. Halliwell, *Reliquiae Antiquae* (1841-3) includes many isolated texts. Böddeker's edition of poems in MS Harl. 2253 is mentioned below; W. Heuser's *Die-Kildare-Gedichte* (Bonn, 1904; *Bonner Beiträge zur Anglistik*, XIV) and *The Minor Poems of the Vernon MS*, ed. C. Horstmann and F. J. Furnivall (2v, 1892-1901; EETS, 98 and 117) should be noted. On special aspects of the Middle English lyric consult Otto Heider, *Untersuchungen zur mittelenglischen erotischen Lyrik (1250-1300)* (Halle, 1905), Alex. Müller, *Mittelenglische geistliche u. weltliche Lyrik des XIII. Jahrhunderts . . . nach Motiven u. Formen* (Halle, 1910), and the works mentioned in subsequent notes to this chapter.

[2] On all of these pieces see Part I, above.

[3] Gaston Paris, *La Littérature normande avant l'annexion* (912-1204) (Paris, 1899); see especially pp. 19-20 and 39-40.

[4] If the court referred to by Denis Piramus can be assumed to be the English court (see p. 137), there may have been more Anglo-Norman secular lyrics than we know about.

[5] See above, pp. 119-120.

208 •

In considering the origins of the Middle English lyric we must of course *Genesis* distinguish between religious and secular types. The religious lyric belongs *of the* to an ecclesiastical and literary tradition which knows no national bound- *Middle* aries. It is as wide as the Christian faith itself. The secular lyric, on the *English* other hand, could conceivably have roots in the native soil, or in Continental *Lyric* poetry—French or Provençal—or in the secular Latin lyric which is conveniently, if somewhat loosely, characterized by the term Goliardic.

In view of the scarcity just remarked of lyrics in Old English, any *Popular* native impulses that lie behind the Middle English lyric should presumably *Song* be sought in folk and minstrel song. That popular songs, often accompanied by dancing, were sung, especially by women, is sufficiently clear, although specimens of the songs themselves are wholly lacking. The twelfth-century chronicler of the deeds of Hereward the Exile tells us that women and girls sang of him in their ring-dances.[6] While this would suggest a ballad rather than a lyric, a love song is unmistakably referred to in the story told in the same century by Giraldus Cambrensis.[7] A parish priest in Worcestershire, he says, had been kept awake all night by dancers in the churchyard so that in the service the next morning he sang the refrain

Swete lamman dhin are!

(Sweet leman, thy favor!) instead of *Dominus vobiscum*. Such references to popular songs become more numerous in succeeding centuries.

There is no evidence of the direct influence of Provençal poetry upon the *Provençal* English lyric, and little to make such influence probable.[8] But the troubadour *Influence* lyric was widely imitated in northern France and certain conventions which *Negligible* make a sporadic appearance in the English lyric could have reached England by way of French poets. Possible Provençal influence is therefore part of a larger question—how much does the English lyric of the Middle Ages owe to the lyric poetry of France?

To answer this question it is necessary to recall briefly the principal *Old French* types and general characteristics of the Old French lyric.[9] It is customary *Types*

---

[6] *De Gestis Herwardi* (ed. S. H. Miller, Peterborough, 1895, p. 12; *Lestorie des Engles* (1888; Rolls Ser.), II. 344): Mulieres ac puellae de eo in choris canebant.

[7] *Gemma Ecclesiastica* (*Opera*, Rolls Ser., II. 120).

[8] See H. J. Chaytor, *The Troubadours and England* (Cambridge, 1923), especially pp. 20-23 and ch. III. J. Audiau, *Les Troubadours et l'Angleterre* (2ed., 1927), while disposed to believe in the direct imitation of the troubadours in England, admits that "elle se cache le plus souvent sous des réminiscences vagues et presque insaississables" (p. 35). The resemblances pointed out by Elinor Rees, "Provençal Elements in the English Vernacular Lyrics of Manuscript Harley 2253," *Stanford Studies in Lang. and Lit.* (1941), pp. 81-95, are often commonplaces and are found equally in the poetry of the trouvères.

[9] The student should consult Alfred Jeanroy's *Les Origines de la poésie lyrique en France au moyen âge* (3ed., 1925) and the same author's chapter in L. Petit de Julleville, *Histoire de la langue et de la littérature française*, I. 345-404; Gaston Paris, "Les Origines de la poésie lyrique en France au moyen âge," *Jour. des Savants*, 1891-92 (pub. separately, 1892); and the histories of Old French literature mentioned on p. 110. A recent study is Guido Errante, *Lirica romanza del primo secolo: un saggio d'interpretazione* (1943; Columbia Univ. diss.) On the Provençal lyric see A. Jeanroy, *La Poésie lyrique des troubadours* (2v, 1934) or the shorter treatments in H. J. Chaytor, *The Troubadours* (1912) and J. Anglade, *Les Troubadours: leurs vies, leurs œuvres, leur influence* (1908).

to distinguish two groups, the popular and the courtly.[10] The former includes certain of the more objective forms. The *chanson de toile* (also called *chanson d'histoire* or *romance*) tells a story, generally of a young girl having a love affair frowned upon by her parents, languishing for a distant lover, deserted by one to whom she has given her love, etc. We should have to look for analogous themes in English among the ballads, which the *chanson de toile* resembles in the directness and economy with which it tells its story. In the *chanson de la mal mariée* the poet observes a woman rebellious against marriage or lamenting her bondage to a husband she does not love. It is a highly conventional type and is not found in the English lyric. The *aube* (Prov. *alba*) is a lyric in which two lovers who have spent the night in each other's arms are forced to part by the coming of dawn, evident in the growing light, the song of the lark, or the announcement of the watch. They try to explain away the unwelcome signs and voice their annoyance over the interruption of their love. The situation occurs in Chaucer's *Troilus* [11] and is familiar to everyone in *Romeo and Juliet,* in Juliet's

> Wilt thou be gone? It is not yet near day.
> It was the nightingale, and not the lark. ....[12]

Popular in southern France, the *aube* is scarcely found in the north and is quite unknown to the English lyric. Finally, there is the *pastourelle*,[13] a very distinctive type, and in this case one that was more popular among the trouvères than with the troubadours. The poet, usually represented as a knight, comes upon a shepherdess tending her flock in the fields and makes love to her. There is always verbal fencing, ending either in easy success or in disappointment which the poet turns off with cavalier grace. Not more than three specimens have been found in England before 1500, none of them really close to the French type. Thus, so far as the "popular" types of French lyric are concerned, French influence upon the English lyric appears to be negligible.

Among the courtly types of French lyric there are numerous minor varieties, which can be passed over quickly. The *rondet* or dance song, not found in English, follows the form of the modern triolet, and the *ballette,* ancestor of the ballade, does not appear in English until Chaucer introduced it under the influence of fourteenth-century French poets (Machaut, Deschamps,

Popular Types

Courtly Types

---

[10] It may be questioned whether the distinction is well founded. Some scholars hold, however, that the so-called popular types are not dependent on Provençal models. One of the oldest of these, the *rotrouenge,* is omitted from consideration here because there is not sufficient evidence to justify a definition. The term is thought to be used in Old French for any song with a refrain (P. Meyer, *Romania,* xix. 102; Jeanroy, *ibid.,* xxx. 424). In like manner the *reverdie* must be rejected as a distinctive type, although the celebration of the return of spring could well have formed the subject of lyrics in itself besides being the introductory setting for the pastourelle and other forms.

[11] iii. 1415-1533 and 1695-1712.

[12] On poems distantly related to the *aube* found in later English literature see Charles R. Baskervill, "English Songs on the Night Visit," *PMLA,* xxxvi (1921). 565-614.

[13] W. Powell Jones, *The Pastourelle, A Study of the Origins and Tradition of a Lyric Type* (Cambridge. Mass., 1931).

etc.). The *estampie*,[14] *lai, descort*,[15] and *motet*[16] are forms scarcely to be identified in Middle English. The debate types—*tenson* and *jeu parti*—and the personal or political *serventois* (Prov. *sirventes*) can be paralleled, but the poetical debate and the political poem are such natural forms and are found so early in the Latin poetry of the Middle Ages that it is doubtful whether we should credit the English examples to French inspiration. All these types, however, are of secondary importance. The courtly form par excellence of the French lyric was the love song or *chanson d'amour*, the equivalent of the Provençal *canso*.

More than half of all the Old French secular lyrics that have been pre- *The* served are *chansons*. The *chanson* consists generally of five stanzas and an *Chanson* envoy,[17] and the theme is always love. The universality of love as a subject *Courtoise* for poetry would suggest that here, if anywhere, the influence of France on the English lyric could be exerted. The difference, however, between the French and the English love-songs is more basic than the similarity. This difference begins with the very conception of love itself that is revealed in the lyrics of the two countries. The love of the *chanson courtoise* is courtly *and* love, the devotion of the poet to a married woman. The relation is that of *English* vassal and overlord. The lover is enlisted in the service of love. He expects *Love-Songs* the lady to be haughty and capricious; he endures any hardship and suffers all in the desire to make himself worthy of her. Love is for him a cult, and he expresses his devotion in extolling the physical charms, the goodness, and the spiritual excellences of the woman who is to him its major divinity. One would expect this poetry to be full of fire and emotion. It is not. It is cold.[18] The poet analyzes his emotions, theorizes about the cause and effect of love, and finds enjoyment even in the suffering which he endures. The monotony with which the *chansons courtoises* repeat this conventional attitude is the fault with which they are most often charged, and to pass to the English love-lyric is like stepping from make-believe into the real world. Here we have no *Frauendienst* of the knightly class, but feelings natural to two young people between whom there is no social gulf. The English lyric is frank and outspoken. It looks forward to marriage or the intimacies of possession:

> He myhte sayen þat Crist hym seȝe,   regarded
> Þat myhte nyhtes neh hyre leȝe,
> hevene he hevede here.

The poet's affection is for a *burde* "maiden" *in bower*, a *may*, or a *maide*, or his *make*. She is his *sweet leman* or his *sweeting*:

[14] W. O. Streng-Renkonen, *Les Estampies françaises* (Paris, 1931; *CFMA*, 65). Lloyd Hibberd, "Estampie and Stantipes," *Speculum*, XIX (1944). 222-249, is primarily concerned with the music.
[15] A. Jeanroy, L. Brandin, and P. Aubry, *Lais et descorts français du XIII* siècle* (1901).
[16] Originally a musical term, designating a song for several voices with different words for each. See J. B. Beck, *La Musique des troubadours* (1910).
[17] Sometimes six or seven stanzas. The number of lines in the stanza varies greatly.
[18] Jeanroy in L. Petit de Julleville, *Histoire de la langue et de la littérature française*, I. 372.

Blow, northerne wynd,
Sent þou me my suetyng!
Blow, norþerne wynd,
Blou! blou! blou!

He has no reason to conceal her identity: she is Annot, or Alysoun, or "woneþ by west."

Few Early Secular Lyrics In English secular lyrics that have been preserved are not numerous.[19] One of the most lilting of English songs is that in which the poet rejoices over the good fortune that has let him fall in love with Alysoun:

Bytuenë Mersh and Averil,
When spray biginneþ to springe,
Þe lutel foul haþ hire wyl   little bird
On hyre lud to synge   voice
Ich libbe in love-longinge
For semlokest of alle þinge;   seemliest
He may me blisse bringe,   She
Ich am in hire bandoun.   at her disposition
An hendy hap ichabbe y-hent   fortunate chance I have got
Ichot from heuene it is me sent: I know
From alle wymmen mi love is lent   departed
And lyht on Alysoun.   alighted

Alysoun He describes her fair hair, brown eyes, her "middel smal"; no man can tell all her goodness. His only fear is lest someone else should take her from him:

Icham for wowyng al forwake,
Wery so water in wore,   pond (weir)
Lest eny reve me my make.   deprive . . . of
Ychabbe y-ȝerned ȝore.   for a long time
Better is þolien whyle sore   to suffer
Þen mournen evermore.
Geynest under gore,   most gracious
Herkne to my roun.   song
An hendy hap ichabbe y-hent,
Ichot from hevene it is me sent:
From alle wymmen mi love is lent
And lyht on Alysoun.

Love Themes A favorite occupation of the love poet in all times and places is to dwell on his lady's graces. Besides entering incidentally into a number of lyrics, such description makes up the whole of two early lyrics. In one the poet boasts "Ichot a burde in a bour ase beryl so bright" and in five stanzas he compares her successively to gems, flowers, various birds, and even to herbs

---

[19] That more of the secular lyric has possibly been lost than is preserved is suggested by the so-called Rawlinson fragments. These are opening lines and stanzas (possibly in some cases complete little poems) preserved in a single leaf of the early fourteenth century from what may well have been some minstrel's notebook. They are edited by W. Heuser, "Fragmente von unbekannten Spielmannsliedern des 14. Jahrhunderts, aus MS Rawl. D. 913," *Anglia*, xxx (1907). 173-179.

medicinal to the body as she is medicine to his soul. In the other he describes her eyes, her merry mouth, her teeth, in fact her whole appearance. She has lovely "rede lippes ... romaunz forto rede" and even "hire neose ys set as hit wel semeþ." One must not think, however, that medieval poets did not also experience the sorrows of love. In a little thirteenth-century piece despair is expressed in what must be close to the ultimate in condensation:

Foweles in þe frith	woods
Þe fisses in þe flod.	fishes
And I mon waxe wod.	mad
Mulch sorw I walk with	much sorrow
For beste of bon and blod.	

In a lyric in the famous Harleian manuscript,[20] from which some of the above examples have been taken and which preserves most of the small number of pre-Chaucerian love lyrics that have come down to us, the poet complains:

Wiþ longyng y am lad,	
On molde y waxe mad,	earth
A maide marreþ me.	

He protests that he loves her faithfully and will die before his time if she does not show pity:

Levedi, wiþ al my miht	
My love is on þe liht,	
To menske when y may,	honor
Þou rew & red me ryht!	
To deþe þou havest me diht:	
Y deȝe longe er my day,	
Þou leve upon my lay	believe
Treuþe ichave þe plyht	
To don þat ich have hyht	promised
Whil mi lif leste may.	

The sentiments expressed in these poems are those of lovers everywhere; neither in thought or tone are we reminded of the French lyric. A common French convention, however, represents the poet as wandering by the way and coming unexpectedly upon a love adventure,[21] and this convention is reflected in one thirteenth-century lyric in another manuscript:

Nou sprinkes the sprai:	springs
Al for love icche am so seeke	
That slepen I ne mai.	

[20] Harl. 2253, a collection of pieces in French and English, of quite varied character, gathered together about 1340, with greatest probability somewhere in Herefordshire. The English lyrics are all in K. Böddeker, *Altenglische Dichtungen des MS Harl. 2253* (Berlin, 1878). A number of graceful little love poems are found in the works of Chaucer, but they follow a later convention.

[21] For the French type as imitated in English, often at a very great distance, see the excellent study of Helen E. Sandison, *The "Chanson d'Aventure" in Middle English* (Bryn Mawr, 1913).

Als I me rode this endre dai   *other day*
   O mi pleyinge
Seih I hwar a litel mai   *saw*
   Bigan to singge:
   "The clot him clingge!
Wai es him i lovve-longinge   *in*
   Sal libben ai,"   *shall live*
     Nou sprinkes, etc.

Son icche herde that mirie note
Þider I drogh;   *drew*
I fonde hire in an herber swot   *sweet*
   Under a bogh
   With joie inogh.
Son I asked, "Thou mirie mai
   Hwi sinkes-tou ai?"   *singest thou*
     Nou sprinkes the sprai, etc.

Than answerde that maiden swote,
   Midde wordes fewe:
"Mi lemman me haves bi-hot   *promised*
   Of lovve trewe;
   He chaunges a newe.
Ȝiif I mae, it shal him rewe
   Bi this dai!"
     Nou sprinkes, etc.

The Cuckoo Song   The association of love with spring is older than the Middle Ages, but seems to have had less meaning in classical times in the climate of the Mediterranean. In the poetry of more northern countries, however, the return of warm weather was greeted with an enthusiasm which is not always appreciated by the modern reader, who controls his comfort with a thermostat. What is perhaps the best-known lyric in Middle English, the famous *Cuckoo Song* (*c.* 1300), is a simple outburst of joy at the return of Spring:

Sumer is i-cumen in,
   Lhude sing, cuccu!
Groweth sed and bloweth med
   And springth the wde nu.   *woods*
     Sing, cuccu!
Awe bleteth after lomb,   *ewe*
Lhouth after calve cu,   *cow*
bulluc sterteth, bucke verteth;   *leaps up*
   Murie sing, cuccu,
     Cuccu, cuccu!
Wel singes thu, cuccu,
Ne swik thu naver nu!

This delightful song, with all the freshness of popular poetry, is set to music of an elaborate kind [22] with Latin directions for singing by several voices (as a round). As spring brought enjoyment of the out of doors, so winter aroused very different emotions. In the opening stanza of a lyric, of which unfortunately the rest has been cut away in the manuscript, the season is made to symbolize the poet's sorrowful mood over some wrong which he has suffered:

Mirie it is while sumer ilast
 With fugheles song,
Oc nu necheth windes blast   but now nigheth
 And weder strong.
Ej! ej! what this nicht is long,   how . . . long
 And ich wid wel michel wrong
Soregh and murne and fast.   sorrow and mourn

It is to be regretted that we have relatively few secular lyrics preserved. *The Religious Lyric* The great bulk of the Middle English lyric—and its bulk is great—is religious or moral. We should hasten to add, however, that the religious lyrics are almost always touching in their sincerity, often imaginative in conception, and occasionally startle us by their sheer beauty. In spite of the fact that most of them involve some form of appeal to Christ or the Virgin Mary for salvation or intercession, they take a great variety of shapes.[23] If they suffer somewhat from the uniformity of their devotional appeal, we must remember that the piety and religious fervor which produced them are the guarantee of their emotional validity.

The simplest form of lyric addressed to the Virgin is that in which the *Lyrics Addressed to the Virgin* poet sings her praises. She is most often described as the mild mother, Queen of Heaven, angels' bliss.[24] She has come of high kin and is without spot or blemish. Sometimes we hear echoes of the secular love poem: she is "flower of all" and "brightest in bower." "Thy love is ever alike new." Often praise is mingled with prayer as in the charming poem which begins

---

[22] See the account by Dom Anselm Hughes in Grove's *Dictionary of Music and Musicians* (3ed.), where it is described as the oldest known canon, the oldest known six-part composition, etc. A facsimile of the manuscript is reproduced as the frontispiece of Vol. v. The date usually given (*c.* 1240) rests on an untenable inference. Manfred F. Bukofzer, "*Sumer Is Icumen In*": *A Revision* (Berkeley, 1944; Univ. of Calif. Pub. in Music, Vol. II, No. 2), offers strong arguments against so early a date for the music, which he puts about 1310. This seems a little late linguistically for the lyric. See also Carleton Brown, *English Lyrics of the XIII*[th] *Century*, pp. xv ff., for the testimony of Giraldus Cambrensis as to the existence of counterpoint in Wales and Yorkshire *c.* 1190.

[23] Consult F. A. Patterson, *The Middle English Penitential Lyric: A Study and Collection of Early Religious Verse* (1911), Heinrich Corsdress, *Die Motive der mittelenglischen geistlichen Lyrik ... und ihr Verhältnis zur lateinischen Hymnologie des Mittelalters* (Weimar, 1913), and Samuel Singer, *Die religiöse Lyrik des Mittelalters* (Bern, 1933).

[24] Among the poems, mostly doctrinal, of William of Shoreham, vicar of Chart-Sutton in Kent (*c.* 1325) is a graceful little hymn to the Virgin, there attributed to Robert Grosseteste, in which the Virgin is described as the dove of Noah that brought back the olive branch, the bush of Sinai, the temple of Solomon, etc. Shoreham's poems were edited by Thomas Wright for the Percy Soc. (1849) and more recently by M. Konrath (1902; *EETSES*, 86).

Of on that is so fayr and briȝt
velud maris stella
Briȝter than the day is liȝt,
parens et puella,
Ic crie to the, thou se to me,
Levedy, preye thi sone for me
tam pia,
That ic mote come to the,
Maria.

Underlying all such appeals is the thought of the Virgin as the link between God and mankind, a thought which occasionally takes a novel turn:

Thou my sister and mother
And thy son my brother—
Who should then drede?
Who-so haveth the king to brother
And eke the queen to mother
Well ought for to spede.[25]

The Virgin as Subject   Almost all the circumstances of the Virgin's life were the subject of poems. There are poetical accounts of the Annunciation, like the blind John Audelay's [26]

The angel to the vergyn said,
Entreng into here boure,
Fore drede of quakyng of this mayd,
He said, "haile!" with gret honour,
"Haile! be thou quene of maidyns mo,
Lord of heven and erth also. . . ."

Among numerous poems on the Five Joys, one in the Harleian manuscript is interesting for its use of the conventional French opening already illustrated in the secular lyric and now become a matter of meaningless habit:

Ase y me rod this ender day
By grenë wode to sechë play,
Mid herte y thohte al on a may,
Suetest of allë thinge.
Lythe *&* ichou tellë may   listen
Al of that swetë thinge.

"With al mi lif y love that may," the poet says and proceeds to comment on the Annunciation, the Birth of Christ, the Resurrection, the Ascension, and the Virgin's own Assumption into heaven as the moments of greatest joy in her life.

---

[25] In quoting from lyrics, especially of the fifteenth century, I have sometimes slightly modernized the spelling where no harm is done to the metre or rime.
[26] John Audelay (*c.* 1425) was a monk of Haghmond Abbey, near Shrewsbury. He is the author of fifty-five didactic and devotional poems. The best edition is that of Ella K. Whiting, *The Poems of John Audelay* (1931; *EETS,* 184).

Some of the most effective lyrics, both of the Virgin and of Christ, are *Dramatic* those in which the mood is portrayed dramatically, in monologue or dialogue *Lyrics* form. There is a charming dialogue between the Virgin and her Child, beginning

> As I lay upon a night
> Alone in my longing,
> Methought I saw a wonder sight,
> A maiden child rocking.
>
> The maiden would withouten song
> Hir child o sleep bring;
> The child thought she did him wrong,
> And bade his moder sing.
>
> "Sing now, moder," said that child,
> "What me shall befall
> Here-after when I come to eld—
> So don modres all.
>
> "Each a moder truly
> That kan her cradle keep
> Is wont to lullen lovëly
> & singen her child o sleep.
>
> "Swetë moder, fair & fre,
> Sithen that it is so,
> I prayë the that thou lulle me
> & sing somewhat there-to."

In response to this request Mary relates the events from the Annunciation to the birth of the Christ-child, and he continues prophetically with an outline of his own life, ending in his death and resurrection. In the final stanza the poet tells us that the vision came to him on Christmas day:

> Certainly this sight I say,   saw
> This song i herdë sing,
> As I lay this Yules-day
> Alone in my longing.

One of the most beautiful of Middle English lyrics, certainly of those concerning the Virgin, begins:

> Suddenly afraid,
> Half waking, half sleeping,
> And greatly dismayed,
> A woman sat weeping.

It is the Virgin, weeping over the body of Christ:

> With favor in her face far passing my reason,
> And of her sore weeping this was the encheson   cause
> Her son in her lap lay, she said, slain by treason.
> If weeping might ripe be, it seemed then in season.

> "Jhesu!" so she sobbed;
> So her Son was bobbed   beaten
> And of his life robbed,
> Saying these words, as I say thee:
> "Who cannot weep, come learn of me."

Three more stanzas reveal the Virgin's grief, partly in dialogue with the poet, each rising to the same thought—Who cannot weep, come learn of me.[27]

Lyrics to Christ   As with lyrics of the Virgin, so in poems addressed to Christ we have songs of simple praise. A poem taking its theme from the well-known hymn long attributed to St. Bernard, the *Jesu Dulcis Memoria*, begins:

> Ihesu, swete is the love of thee,
> Noon othir thing so swete may be;
> No thing that men may heere ಌ see
> Hath no swetnesse aȝens thee.

and continues as a rosary of fifty stanzas. It is an example of devotion put in the form of meditation. Another lyric of similar intent may have been written by a woman:

> Now I see blostme spring   blossom
> I herde a fuheles song;   bird's
> A swete longing
> Myn herte throughout sprong
> That is of love newe
> That is so swete and trewe
> It gladdeth all my song . . .

The song is of Christ; alas, that I cannot turn all my thought to him and make him my leman! It is an expression of spiritual yearning, and the prayer in the closing stanza begins with the words

> Iesu, leman sweet,
> I send thee this song.

Christ as lover is the theme of the Franciscan Thomas of Hales' *Love Rune* mentioned above (p. 123). Among simple appeals to Christ for help and salvation Richard Caister's *Ihesu, lord, þat madist me* at the beginning of the fifteenth century was deservedly popular, as seventeen manuscripts show.[28]

The most beautiful of the religious lyrics is the *Quia amore langueo,* beginning:

---

[27] On laments of the Virgin see H. Thien, *Über die englischen Marienklagen* (Kiel, 1906) and for their Continental background E. Wechssler, *Die romanischen Marienklagen* (Halle, 1893).

[28] On the author see the Rev. Dundas Harford, "Richard of Caister, and his Metrical Prayer," *Norfolk Archæology*, XVII (1910). 221-244.

In a valey of this restles minde   Quia
    I soughte in mounteine and in mede,   Amore
Trusting a trewe love for to finde.   Langueo
    Upon an hill than I took hede;
    A voice I herde, and neer I yede,
In huge dolour complaininge tho,
    "See, dere soule, how my sides blede,
Quia amore langueo."

The poet comes upon a man wounded and sitting under a tree. It is Christ
—"true love that fals was nevere"—suing for man's soul. She has left him
and is hard to woo, but—

    I wole abide till sche be redy;
        I wole her sue if sche seie nay;

The poem parallels the secular love complaints:

    Fair love, lete us go pleye!
        Apples ben ripe in my gardaine.
    I schal thee clothe in a newe aray;
        Thy mete schall be milk, hony, and wine.
    Fair love, let us go digne!   dine
    Thy sustenaunce is in my crippe, lo!   scrip
        Tarie thou not, my faire spouse mine,
    Quia amore langueo.

He will care for her always:

    Mine owne wife, go not me fro!
        Thy meede is marked whan thou art mort,   dead
    Quia amore langueo.

It is but a step from the devotional lyric to poems of moral reflection and   *Reflective*
admonition. Many of these spring from the thought, sometimes used as a   *and*
refrain, *Timor mortis conturbat me*. They stress the transitoriness of worldly *Admoni-*
pleasures: *tory Poems*

    Wynter wakeneth al my care,
    Nou this levës waxeth bare;
    Ofte y sike & mournë sare   sigh
        When hit cometh in my thoht
    Of this worldes joie—how hit geth al to noht.

Man is but dust. Why should he be proud? This is the theme of the famous
Earth upon Earth, which was often copied and exists in many forms:[29]

    Erthe upon erthe is wonderly wrought
    Erthe upon erthe hath worship of nought
    Erthe upon erthe hath set all his thought
    How erthe upon erthe might be high brought.

[29] Hilda M. R. Murray, *The Middle English Poem, Erthe upon Erthe, printed from Twenty-
four Manuscripts* (1911; EETS, 141).

Similar is the reflection *Ubi sunt qui ante nos fuerunt:*

> Where beth they biforen us weren
> Houndës ladden and havckës beren   led ... hawks bore
> And hadden feld and wode?

Where are those rich ladies in their bower, wearing gold in their hair? They ate and drank and made merry, but in the twinkling of an eye their souls were lost. Where now is that laughter and song?

Lyrics in which the poet reflects on the Passion and Resurrection, and dwells on the sacrifice Christ has made for man are very numerous. Particularly melodious is one beginning:

> Somer is comen *&* winter gon
>   This day biginnith to longe,
> *&* this foulës everichon
>   Joye hem wit songe.
> So stronge kare me bint,   binds
> Al wit joye that is funde
>   In londe,
> Al for a child
> That is so milde
>   Of honde.

Christ is often represented as appealing to man, complaining that man has rejected him, and offering mercy freely to those who will accept it. One such dramatic lyric begins:

> Undo thi dore, my spouse dere,
> Allas! wy stond I loken out here?   locked
>   Fre am I thi make.
> Loke mi lokkes *&* ek my heved
> *&* al my bodi with blod beweved   enveloped
>   For thi sake.
>
> Allas! allas! hevel have I sped   sin
> For senne Iesu is fro me fled,   evil
>   Mi trewe fere.   companion
> With-outen my gate he stant alone,
> Sorfuliche he maket his mone
>   On his manere.

Reflections such as this led one poet to contemplate a baby crying in its crib, sorrowfully:

> Lollai, lollai, litil child, whi wepistou so sore?
> Nedis mostou wepe, hit was iȝarkid the ȝore   prepared for
> Ever to lib in sorow, and sich and mourne evere,   sigh
> As thin eldren did er this, whil hi alives were.   they
>   Lollai, lollai, litil child, child lolai, lullow,
> Into uncuth world icommen so ertow.   unknown

Beasts and birds and fishes in the flood are fortunate when they come into the world, but man is born to sorrow. After five stanzas the poet concludes:

Child, thou nert a pilgrim bot an uncuthe gist	unknown guest
Thi dawes beth itold, thi jurneis beth icast;	days are numbered
Whoder thou salt wend north other est	whether
Deth the sal betide with bitter bale in brest.	shall
Lollai, lollai, litil child, this wo Adam the wroȝt,	
Whan he of the appil ete, and Eve hit him betacht.	handed

A more cheerful note is brought into the fifteenth century by the rapid rise to popularity of the carol [30] associated with Christmas and Epiphany. It is a time of rejoicing: *The Carol*

> Now may we singen as it is
> *Quod puer natus est nobis.*

Often the theme is the simple story of Christ's birth:

> *Make we mery in hall & bowr,*
> *Thys tyme was born owr Savyowr.*

> In this tyme God hath sent
> Hys own Son, to be present,
> To dwell with us in verament,
>   God that ys owr Savyowr.

> In this tyme that ys be-fall,
> A child was born in an ox stall
> ℰ after he dyed for us all,
>   God that ys owr Savyowr.

> In this tyme an angell bryght
> Mete III shepherdis upon a nyght,
> He bade them go anon ryght
>   To God that ys owr Saviowr.

> In thys tyme now pray we
> To hym that dyed for us on tre,
> On us all to have pytee,
>   God that ys owr Saviowr.

But we have also carols celebrating merely the joyful spirit of the season:

> *Make we mery, bothe more & lasse*
> *For now ys the tyme of Crystymas.*

> Lett no man cum in to this hall,
> Grome, page, nor yet marshall,
> But that sum sport he bryng with-all,
>   For now ys the tyme of Cristemas.

---

[30] For an interesting theory concerning the origin of the word see Margit Sahlin, *Étude sur la carole médiévale: l'origine du mot et ses rapports avec l'église* (Uppsala, 1940).

If that he say he can not syng,
Some oder sport then lett hym bryng,
That it may please at this festing,
For now is the time of Cristemas.

If he say he can nowght do,
Then for my love aske him no mo,
But to the stokkes then let hym go,
For now is the time of Cristemas.

Political,
Satirical,
and
Convivial
Songs

Space does not permit more than a passing reference to the political poems which offer editorial comment on current events,[31] or to those comments, often satirical, upon abuses of the time and the weaknesses of an erring humanity.[32] Nor is there need to speak of the shorter poems of Chaucer, whose more important work is treated elsewhere, or of Lydgate who is likewise discussed in another place.[33] It would be pleasant to touch on the small number of humorous, satirical, and convivial songs which appear toward the end of the Middle English period. One answers the question "when to trust a woman" by suggesting, "when nettles in winter bear roses red, and thorns bear figs by nature," when laurels bear cherries, when sparrows build churches, when wrens carry sacks to the mill, and other possibilities equally likely. There is the lament of the man married to a shrewish wife:

All that I may swink or swete,
My wife it will both drink and ete . . .

and the warning to young men not to marry.
A drinking song such as

Tapster, fille another ale.
Anonne have I do.
God sende us good sale;
Avale the stake, avale!　　　　drink down the pledge(?)

---

[31] An example is the *Song of Lewes* written by a sympathizer with Simon de Montfort after his victory in the battle of Lewes (1264). It is directed at the King's brother, Richard, Earl of Cornwall, each stanza ending:

Richard, thah thou be ever trichard [traitor]
Tricchen shalt thou nevermore!

See the edition of C. L. Kingsford (Oxford, 1890). Many political songs have a narrative base, as, for example, those of Laurence Minot concerning incidents between 1333 and 1352. Minot's poems have been often edited; the best edition is that of Joseph Hall (Oxford, 1897). For collections of political songs, in Latin, French, and English, see Thomas Wright, *The Political Songs of England, from the Reign of John to that of Edward II* (1839; *Camden Soc.,* VI); Thomas Wright, *Political Poems and Songs relating to English History . . . from the Accession of Edw. III. to that of Ric. II* (2v, 1859-61; Rolls Ser.); cf. also Livingston Corson, *A Finding List of Political Poems Referring to English Affairs of the XIII and XIV Centuries* (n.d.; Univ. of Penna. diss.).

[32] See for examples the poems in Carleton Brown, *Religious Lyrics of the XIVth Century,* pp. 152 ff., one of which expresses the idea that the world is run by flattery and dissembling, another speaks with mild bitterness of fair-weather friends, etc.

[33] For Richard Rolle, who wrote a small number of lyrics, see ch. XIII. A conscientious but uninspired versifier, James Ryman (c. 1490) has left a large number of devotional poems, which are edited by Zupitza in *Archiv,* LXXXIX (1892). 167-338.

Here is good ale ifounde.
Drinke to me,
And I to thee,
And lette the cuppe go rounde—

reminds us that conviviality has expressed itself in song in practically all
periods of literature.

Most of our early lyrics are anonymous. Some show the same kind of *Authorship*
variations between texts as we find in the ballads and these variants have
apparently arisen in the course of oral transmission.[34] It is natural to attribute
most of the religious pieces to clerkly authorship,[35] but it is not impossible
that some of the secular love songs, too, were written in the shadow of the
church. Jolly Absolon had many brothers, and the spirit of the English
secular lyric finds its closest parallel in the Latin love songs of the *scholares
vagantes*.[36] The earlier Middle English lyrics were intended for the ear
rather than the eye. Many of them are accompanied in the manuscripts by
music,[37] and we should make liberal allowance for the loss which they
suffer in being deprived of their melody. Few popular songs of our own
day, similarly stripped, would stand up so well.

In the later fourteenth century and certainly in the fifteenth the lyric
becomes increasingly literary.[38] From the village green and the great hall it *Late*
passes to the study. Spontaneity at times gives way to the gracefully turned *Tendencies*
conceit. At times the imaginative quality becomes genuinely arresting. The
fifteenth-century poet was unwittingly looking forward to Alan Seeger's
I Have a Rendezvous with Death when he wrote:

Farewell, this world! I take my leave forever!
I am arrested to appear at Goddës face. . . .[39]

Philosophy takes its place beside religion; the poet is as likely to address
Fortune as God:

A! Mercy, Fortune, have pitee on me,
And thynke that thu hast done gretely amysse
To parte asondre them which ought to be
Alwey in one; why hast thu doo thus?
Have I offendyd the? I, nay ywysse!
Then torne thy whele and be my frende agayn,
And send me joy where I am nowe in payn.

[34] See the various texts of the *Alma Redemptoris Mater*, beginning "As I lay upon a night,"
in Greene, pp. 166-7.
[35] For the importance of the Franciscans as authors of the religious lyric see Rossell H.
Robbins, "The Authors of the Middle English Religious Lyrics," *JEGP*, xxxix (1940). 230-238,
and "The Earliest Carols and the Franciscans," *MLN*, liii (1938). 239-245.
[36] For references see p. 149, note 15.
[37] An important collection of facsimiles with transcriptions is in Sir John Stainer's *Early
Bodleian Music* (2v, 1901).
[38] Extensive collections of fifteenth-century lyrics are edited to Bernhard Fehr in *Archiv*,
cvi, cvii, and cix.
[39] Brown, *Religious Lyrics of the XVᵗʰ Century*, p. 236.

And thynke what sorowe is the departyng
Of two trewe hertis lovyng feithfully,
For partyng is the most soroughfull thynge,
To myn entent, that ever yet knewe I.
Therefore, I pray to the right hertely
To turne thy whele and be my frende agayn,
And send me joy where I am now in payn. . . .[40]

With such a lyric as this we look forward to the poetry of the Renaissance.

[40] *Ibid.*, p. 262.

XIII

Richard Rolle and Other Mystics

Mysticism [1] is the most intense form of personal religious experience. In *Definition* Christian mysticism the individual seeks through solitary contemplation to enter into direct communion with God or to attain spiritual union with God. In such union, with its accompanying illumination, the will seems temporarily in abeyance and the individual is in a state of complete though receptive passivity. The experience is by nature transient, and above all, it is ineffable: it cannot be expressed in words or conveyed from one person to another.

The mystic state is not an experience into which one can enter at will. *The Three* When St. Paul said that he was *caught up* to the third heaven, he meant, as *Stages* St. Bernard observed, that he could not have attained such rapture by any strength or toil of his own. One must hear the call of God, after which grace supplies the strength that is lacking in the individual. Once the awakening has taken place, there are three stages, generally speaking, through which the soul must pass. The first is Purgation. "Pure truth is seen only with a pure heart." By sanctity of life, sincere repentance, and an intense desire for holiness the obstacles are removed which stand in the way of the soul's progress. The second stage, known as Illumination, is that in which the mind detaches itself from outer sensations and yields in complete surrender to the will of God. The soul prepares itself, as it were, for union with the Divine Presence. Meditation is the basis of mystical detachment and one who hopes to attain to the highest of the mystical states should, in the words of Rolle, "accustom himself to meditation and devout prayer before he reaches out to the contemplation of heavenly joys." For Rolle, meditation on the Passion seemed the most fitting form which such devotion could take. The final stage, known as Contemplation, is that in which the soul is brought into the presence of God and becomes one with God. It is a state of ecstasy or vision, incapable of being described in words, generally one of the purest and intensest joy. It is in this stage that the individual sometimes sees visions, hears voices, and experiences "those ab-

---

[1] The student of English mysticism can begin with two small but excellent books: Dom David Knowles, *The English Mystics* (1927) and Evelyn Underhill, *The Mystics of the Church* (n.d.). Dom Cuthbert Butler's *Western Mysticism* (1922) contains liberal extracts from St. Augustine, St. Gregory the Great, and St. Bernard. More extended discussions of mysticism re Evelyn Underhill, *Mysticism* (1911), and W. R. Inge, *Christian Mysticism* (1899). See also William James, *The Varieties of Religious Experience* (1902), Lectures xvi and xvii, and Arthur Devine, *A Manual of Mystical Theology* (1903). Francis D. S. Darwin, *The English Medieval Recluse* (1944), gives a general picture of the recluse in a brief and popular form.

normal psychic phenomena which appear so persistently in the history of the mystics."[2] For the mystical experience also yields knowledge and comprehension of spiritual things, truth intuitively perceived. Truth is revealed to the contemplative soul as material things are visible to the bodily eye. The mystic reward is thus not only the personal joy felt in being present in spirit with God, but at times the deeper understanding of spiritual truth.

Necessarily Personal

As we have already observed, mysticism is in the highest degree personal. The contemplative experience must come from within and is a manifestation of divine grace. It is not communicable. One might suppose, therefore, that since mystic exaltation begins and ends with the individual, there would be no occasion for putting it into words. There are several reasons why this is not so. In the first place, the inner light that the mystic attains is felt to be authoritative, and we can understand the impulse to share his insight with others and perhaps lead others to a similar desire for inner illumination. Again, the mystic in the light of his experience may feel that he is in a position to instruct others in the way to contemplative joy. And finally, the mystic is not unlike the poet in his wish to give permanence to the things that he has felt deeply and to give vent to his joy in the outpouring of his emotion. Hence the very considerable body of mystical writing—autobiographical, didactic, lyrical.

The Fourteenth Century

The fourteenth century is the great age of mysticism, not only in England but in other parts of Europe as well.[3] Whether, as has been suggested, it was a reaction against the extremes of scholasticism or a part of the general religious awakening discussed in a previous chapter, it reflects the mystics' dissatisfaction with casual observances and the ordinary forms of worship—"any long psalter unmindfully mumbled in the teeth," as the *Cloud of Unknowing* puts it. Rolle contrasts the fervor of the contemplative with the lukewarm devotion of the monks. Mysticism reflects the craving for a more eager, personal spirituality having its source in the individual. It must not be thought, however, that the flowering of mysticism in the fourteenth century is a sudden phenomenon. Its roots reach back to apostolic times, and the mystical tradition in the west descends from St. Augustine and (Pseudo) Dionysius the Areopagite to the great triumvirate, St. Bernard, Richard of St. Victor, and St. Bonaventura.[4]

[2] Evelyn Underhill, *Mysticism*, p. 319.
[3] In Germany there were Meister Eckhard (d. 1327), John Tauler (d. 1361), and Henry Suso (d. 1365), to mention only the greatest. In Flanders Jan Ruysbroek died in 1381, and in Italy we have Jacopone da Todi (d. 1306), who belongs mostly to the preceding century, and St. Catherine of Siena, who died in 1380.
[4] The mysticism of St. Bernard is found chiefly in his *Sermons on the Canticles* (Eng. trans. 2v, Dublin, 1920), in which the fifteenth sermon is particularly significant; in *The Love of God* (trans. Edmund G. Gardner, 1916; T. L. Connolly, 1937); and in *The Steps of Humility* (ed. and trans. by Geo. B. Burch, Cambridge, Mass., 1940). Richard of St. Victor's masterpiece is the *De Gratia Contemplationis*, commonly known as *Benjamin Major*, in five books. *Benjamin Minor*, a shorter treatise, serves as a kind of introduction to the larger. An English version of the *Benjamin Minor*, dating from the middle of the fourteenth century, is printed in Horstman, *Yorkshire Writers*, I. 162-172. A later version can also be had in Edmund Gardner, *The Cell of Self Knowledge* (1910). The *Four Degrees of Burning Love* has also been translated. Mystical writings form but a small part of St. Bonaventura's works. Most important is the *De Triplici Via*, sometimes known as the *Incendium Amoris* (in Vol. v

English mysticism finds its first formal expression in the writings of *Richard*
Richard Rolle, hermit of Hampole.[5] The account of his awakening some *Rolle*
time in early manhood is best quoted in his own words:

I was sitting forsooth in a chapel and whilst I was delighting in the sweetness
of prayer or meditation, suddenly I felt a merry and unknown heat in me. At
first I was uncertain, doubting from whom it should be. After a long time I
became convinced that it was not of a creature but of my Maker, for more hot
and gladder I found it. . . .

Whilst truly I sat in the same chapel and sang psalms as I might in the
evening before supper, I perceived, as it were, the sounds of readers or rather
singers above me. Whilst also I took heed, praying to heaven with all desire,
suddenly, in what manner I know not, I felt in me the noise of song and was
aware of the most pleasing heavenly melody, which dwelt with me in my mind.
Forsooth my thought was changed to continual mirth of sound and thenceforth
for fullness of inward sweetness I burst out singing what before I said—forsooth
privily and only before my Maker. . . .

Wherefore from the beginning of my changed soul unto the high degree of
Christ's love which, God granting, I was able to attain, in which degree I might
sing the love of God with joyful song, was four years and about three months.[6]

From this time on, his life was spent in the exercise of piety—meditation,
prayer, writing, and giving spiritual comfort to others.

Rolle's more important mystical writings are in Latin.[7] One of the most   *Latin*
significant, the *Melos Amoris,* often called *Melum Contemplativorum* and   *Writings*
also known as the *Book of the Glory and Perfection of the Saints,* has only
lately been published (see Supplement). It is an extensive account of his
mystical joy, written in a highly mannered prose hard to reconcile with the
genuineness and intensity of feeling which it expresses. There are autobiographical passages indicating that his mode of life was not free from

of the standard edition, *Opera Omnia,* Quaracchi, 1882-1902). A work commonly attributed
to him in the Middle Ages, the *Meditationes Vitae Christi,* but not his, had great influence.
A brief section (chs. 74-92) was turned into English by an anonymous follower of Rolle as
The Privity of the Passion (Horstman, I. 198-218), modernized in Geraldine E. Hodgson,
Some Minor Works of Richard Rolle with The Privity of the Passion (1923), and large
portions were Englished by Nicholas Love before 1410 as *The Mirrour of the Blessed Lyf of
Iesu Christ* (ed. Lawrence F. Powell, 1908).

    [5] What we know of Rolle's life, apart from autobiographical allusions in his writings, comes
from the *Office of St. Richard Hermit* compiled in hope of his canonization at the end of the
fourteenth century. It is supposed that he was born about 1300 at Thornton Dale, some forty
miles from York. He was for a time at Oxford, but returned home at eighteen for religious
reasons. Improvising a hermit's dress from his father's rain hood and two of his sister's
kirtles, he went off by himself, leaving his sister convinced that he was mad. He was taken
in by a family named Dalton, where he was given a solitary cell or room, and there composed
some of his earlier works. After he left the Daltons his movements cannot be traced very
definitely, but we may be sure that he pursued a solitary life most of the time. He lived for
a while in the archdeaconry of Richmondshire, but at the end of his life he was at Hampole,
in southwest Yorkshire. It is supposed that his death in September, 1349, was due to the
plague. For a translation of the *Office* see F. M. M. Comper, *The Fire of Love* (1914), pp.
lv-lviii.

    [6] *Incendium Amoris,* ch. xv, adapted from the translation made by Richard Misyn (1435).
    [7] The definitive study of the Rolle canon is Hope Emily Allen, *Writings Ascribed to Richard
Rolle, Hermit of Hampole, and Materials for His Biography* (1927; MLA Monograph Ser.,
II). For a briefer account see the same author's intro. to *English Writings of Richard Rolle,
Hermit of Hampole* (1931) and Frances M. M. Comper, *Life of Richard Rolle* (1929).

criticism and attack. His best known works are the *Incendium Amoris,* written in middle life, and the somewhat later *Emendatio Vitae.*[8] It is from the former of these that we have quoted the account of his initiation into the mystical experience. The *Mending of Life* offers practical advice on the means to grace, through despising the world, embracing poverty, cultivating humility, and the like. The last chapter treats the joys of the contemplative life.

Rolle seems to have acquired disciples and he became in time the spiritual adviser to certain holy women—a nun of Yedingham, one of Hampole, and a recluse named Margaret Kirkby. For them he wrote his three English epistles on the love of God and its attainment through contemplation—*Ego Dormio, Commandment of the Love of God,* and the *Form of Living.* They are among his latest works, and the *Form of Living,* written for Margaret Kirkby, is of the three the most orderly and mature exposition of his views.[9]

Calor, *Canor,* *Dulcor*   For Rolle "joy in þe life of Jhesu" is the keynote of his mysticism, in which the loving contemplation of the Holy Name of Jesus has its part. The tokens of his mystical union were *Calor, Canor,* and *Dulcor*—Heat, which signifies not merely burning love but the physical sensation of warmth; Song, which means that his soul was filled with heavenly music and he responded in spiritual melody; Sweetness, which means a sense of inexpressible joy felt in the soul. The sensuous character of Rolle's contemplative experience together with the fact that it seems to have been present not intermittently but more or less constantly has led some to question his place in the inner circle of mystics. Nevertheless his reputation for piety and the character and extent of his writings make him a figure of the greatest importance in the spiritual revival of the fourteenth century. This is not the same as saying that he occupies a place of equal importance in English literature. His literary reputation until recently has rested in no small measure on a work, the *Prick of Conscience,* which he did not write. His few lyrics have in them more piety than poetry, and his English treatises, though written in competent prose, are less important than his Latin writings. Though his *Meditations on the Passion* has passages of deep feeling expressed with simple fervor, and his translation of the Psalter with its accompanying commentary was widely read until the time of the Reformation, we must conclude that his importance lies mainly in his influence on later mystics and on subsequent religious thought. We miss in his work those personal qualities that endear the author of the *Ancrene Riwle* to us. Great

---

8 These two works are available in English versions, *The Fire of Love . . . and The Mending of Life,* ed. Frances M. M. Comper (1914). Several other modern versions of the *Mending of Life* have been published. G. C. Heseltine, *Selected Works of Richard Rolle, Hermit* (1930) is useful. Most of the texts in Geraldine E. Hodgson's *Some Minor Works of Richard Rolle* (1923) are no longer thought to be by Rolle, but are useful as illustrating English mysticism in the fourteenth century.

9 All three epistles are printed in H. E. Allen, *English Writings of Richard Rolle,* and Horstman, *Yorkshire Writers,* I. 3-71. *The Form of Living* has been published in modernized form by G. E. Hodgson (1910).

before they agreed to a life of continence. For six months after the birth of her first child she was out of her mind, but one day Christ appeared to her and spoke to her and her reason was miraculously restored. It was some time, however, before she abandoned her pride of dress, envy of her neighbors, and other sinful ways. Gradually she began to see visions and to receive other evidences of God's favor.

The spiritual change wrought in her showed itself, after her pilgrimage to Jerusalem, in frequent and abundant weeping. The sight of the crucifix, a good sermon, the taking of communion would cause her to break into tears and utter loud cries, and sometimes writhe on the ground, frequently to the great annoyance of those present. On Corpus Christi day, as the priests bore the sacrament about the town in solemn procession, "she cried, 'I die, I die,' and roared so wonderfully, that people wondered upon her." She takes obvious satisfaction in her wonderful "cryings," noting that on one day she had fourteen. She seems to attach importance to their loudness. She tells us that on one occasion when receiving the sacrament "she cried so loud that it could be heard all about the church, and outside the church," and she records with distressing frequency the occasions on which "she cried and roared," and "wept full boisterously."

Margery Kempe was no recluse. She traveled to London and Canterbury, to Norwich, Lincoln, and York, to Rome and Jerusalem, and Compostella, and, at the age of sixty, to Danzig, Aachen, and other places on the Continent. Nor was she one to hide her light under a bushel. She confessed her sins from childhood to several different confessors and "shewed her manner of living to many a worthy clerk, to worshipful doctors of divinity, both religious men and others of secular habit." She insisted on wearing white, even though it made her conspicuous, and notes without reticence that on one occasion in a church at Leicester "there was so much people that they stood upon stools for to behold her."

Of the quiet sense of oneness with God experienced by other mystics Margery Kempe says little. Instead, she reports at length many conversations with Christ, and mentions other occasions on which she was spoken to by the Virgin Mary, St. Peter, St. Paul, St. Katherine, "or whatever saint in heaven she had devotion to." She appears to have been quite susceptible to the power of suggestion and her experiences often recall those of Rolle, Julian of Norwich, and other mystics whose writings had been read to her, but for valid comparisons one must look to certain women on the Continent, and especially in Germany, at about the same period. Each reader will form his own opinion of Margery's neurotic temperament and of the extent to which her eccentricities and hysterical outbursts were the result of genuine religious feeling. Certainly her boisterous weeping and sobbing, her "roaring" and writhings would not have found favor with the deeply spiritual, albeit outspoken, author of the *Cloud of Unknowing*. But as a human document and for its many glimpses of medieval life the *Book of Margery Kempe* has great interest, and as time goes on will reach a widening circle of readers.

XIV
The Alliterative Revival

In the last few chapters—on the romance, the religious omnibus, the lyric, and the writings of the mystics—we have become increasingly aware of the intense literary activity that marks the whole fourteenth century, an activity that reaches its culmination for most readers today in the great narrative poetry of Chaucer. It is an activity that extends from one end of England to the other, an activity in which London and the court participate to no overwhelming extent but rather share along with many other sections of the country. The widespread distribution of the ferment that was at work is indicated perhaps nowhere more plainly than in the emergence about 1350 of the Old English alliterative tradition after it had lain hidden for nearly two hundred years.

Alliterative Roughly between the years 1350 and 1400 there appeared a score of poems,
Verse ranging from a few hundred lines to several thousand, in a metre which had clearly evolved in an unbroken development from the old four-beat alliterative measure of *Beowulf* and Cynewulf. It is not an antiquarian revival, but the reappearance of a metrical pattern which has undergone considerable change. The line has become in most cases the unit of thought and the alliteration is therefore not so much structural as decorative. With some poets hunting the letter becomes a passion, and the alliteration falls on three syllables in a half-line or is carried through several consecutive lines. Verse of this sort was obviously associated in Chaucer's mind with the north, as is indicated by the well-known words of the Parson:

Associated   But trusteth wel, I am a Southern man,
with the   I can not geste—rum, ram, ruf—by lettre.
North and
West   And most of the poems in the alliterative revival belong to the north and to the northwest Midlands. While one of the most important—*Piers Plowman*—has its origin in the west Midlands, we may think of the alliterative revival as occurring in the north and more particularly the northwest of England.

Three of the earliest poems in the revival, *Alexander A, Alexander B,* and *William of Palerne,* have already been discussed in the chapters on the romance. There we have likewise treated other later romances in alliterative verse, such as *The Wars of Alexander, The Destruction of Troy,* the *Morte Arthure,* and the religious romance *The Destruction of Jerusalem.* It not practicable to include them again here, where as part of the alliterative

232

movement they would be fully entitled to a place.[1] We shall have to be content with this brief reference, and confine ourselves in this and the following chapter to the other classes of alliterative poetry. In the present chapter we shall treat the works of the *Pearl* poet and one or two poems in some ways related to his. In the chapter which follows we shall consider a group of poems concerned with social and ethical questions, of which the most important is the great social document *Piers Plowman*. *The* Pearl *Poet*

Of the many unique manuscripts gathered together in the seventeenth century by the famous antiquary Sir Robert Cotton, among which are the *Beowulf* codex, the two texts of Layamon's *Brut,* the *Ludus Coventriae,* and others only less famous, one is a modest quarto volume known as Nero A x.[2] The contents consist of four alliterative poems in a hand of the end of the fourteenth century. Accompanying the text are twelve illustrations of quite crude workmanship depicting episodes in some of the poems. None of the texts is accompanied by any title, but they have been named, in the order of their occurrence in the manuscript, the *Pearl, Purity* (or *Cleanness*), *Patience,* and *Sir Gawain and the Green Knight.*

The *Pearl*[3] is not only first in the manuscript but shares with the *Gawain* the first place in the interest of modern readers. In a hundred stanzas of twelve lines each,[4] ingeniously linked in groups of five by repetition and a refrain, the poet tells how a lovely pearl, smooth and white, slipped from his hands into the grass and was lost in the ground. In his grief he often visits the spot which covers his pearl, and one August day, lulled by the fragrance of herbs and flowers, he falls asleep on the little mound. There as he slumbers he dreams that he is in another world, a world of crystal cliffs, bright woods, and strands pebbled with precious stones. Such sights make him forget his grief, and he wanders about in sheer delight. Finally he comes upon a stream, clear and sparkling, beyond which he thinks must be Paradise. It is backed by a crystal cliff, at the foot of which sits a child— Pearl

> A gracious maiden full debonaire;
> Glistening white was her robe:
> I knew her well; I had seen her before.

The longer he looks at her the better he knows her. He has an impulse to call her, but seeing her in so strange a place deters him. She is spotless, and her dress is trimmed profusely with pearls. She wears a crown, from beneath which her hair falls loosely on her shoulders. No tongue could fittingly describe the sight:

---

[1] See above, pp. 182 ff. On the later alliterative movement in Scotland see Sir William Craigie, "The Scottish Alliterative Poems," *Proc. Brit. Acad.,* XXVIII (1942). 217-236.

[2] It is reproduced in facsimile in *EETS,* 162.

[3] Edited by Richard Morris (2ed., 1869; *EETS,* 1), Sir Israel Gollancz (1891; 1921), and Charles G. Osgood (1906; *Belles-Lettres Ser.*). A translation is included in Gollancz's edition, and there are modern renderings by G. G. Coulton (1907), Osgood (1907), Sophie Jewett (1908), and Stanley P. Chase (1932).

[4] The rime scheme is *ababababab bcbc.* There are 101 stanzas, but one is considered spurious or was canceled by the author.

So clean was it and clear and pure,
That precious pearl where it was set.

Thus arrayed she comes down to the brink. She was nearer to me, he says, than aunt or niece. Finally she speaks to him and he then addresses her:

O Pearl, quoth I, in pearls bedight,
Art thou my pearl that I have 'plain'd,
Regretted when all alone at night?
Much longing for thee have I restrained
Since into the grass thou didst from me glide.

Grown in stature and in wisdom, she reveals to him her life as spouse of the Heavenly Bridegroom. The dreamer's pearl was not lost when it was put in a coffer so comely as is this gracious garden. Along with thousands of others she shares a most happy lot. When the poet objects that she did nothing to deserve so great a reward, since she "lived not two years in our land" and knew neither her Paternoster nor Creed, she enters upon an elaborate discourse on the part played by merit and grace in salvation and the equality of the saved before God,[5] illustrating her views at length by biblical parables. The poet is finally granted a view of her abode—the New Jerusalem—vividly adapted from the Apocalypse. His effort in trying to cross the stream and reach the heavenly city wakens him from his dream, and he rises from the mound on which he had slumbered, filled with a new spiritual strength.

The Allegory   This beautiful and seemingly transparent allegory has been interpreted in various ways and has led to considerable controversy. The traditional view sees in the poem an elegy in which the poet grieves for the death of a two-year-old daughter and is consoled by her in a vision of a common medieval type. This view was challenged by Schofield in 1904, who denied the autobiographical interpretation and suggested that the poet was merely upholding the virtue of purity under the symbolism of a pearl, with appropriate personification.[6] While his view has not found much favor[7] his example has led others to attempt new explanations and various modifications of the original interpretation. The *Pearl* has been taken as symbolizing the Eucharist[8] and more recently as recording a state of "spiritual dryness" experienced by the poet and not unknown to religious and to mystics.[9] Still

---

[5] The orthodoxy of the poet's views was questioned by Carleton F. Brown, "The Author of *The Pearl* Considered in the Light of His Theological Opinions," *PMLA*, XIX (1904). 115-153, and defended by James Sledd, *MLN*, LV (1940). 381. While his attitude toward grace has been shown to be good doctrine, equality of reward appears to be stressed beyond medieval orthodoxy.

[6] W. H. Schofield, "The Nature and Fabric of *The Pearl*," *PMLA*, XIX (1904). 154-215; "Symbolism, Allegory, and Autobiography in *The Pearl*," *PMLA*, XXIV (1909). 585-675.

[7] Schofield's interpretation was opposed by Osgood (*ed. cit.*) and his objections to an autobiographical interpretation were disposed of by Coulton in *MLR*, II (1907). 39-43.

[8] R. M. Garrett, *The Pearl—An Interpretation* (Seattle, 1918; *Univ. of Wash. Pub. in English*, Vol. IV, No. 1).

[9] Sister M. Madeleva, *Pearl: A Study in Spiritual Dryness* (1925).

others have sought to reconcile the elegiacal and symbolical interpretations.[10] There is symbolism, to be sure, in incidental ways in the poem, and the problems of divine grace and the equality of heavenly rewards constitute the major theme for discussion, but there are too many features which are meaningless on any other assumption than that the poet mourns the loss of a real child.[11] The poem treats certain aspects of salvation in the framework of a personal elegy, employing the medieval conventions of vision and debate. *A Personal Elegy*

Viewed as a personal elegy the *Pearl* is a poem of deep feeling, the poet's grief yielding gradually to resignation and spiritual reconciliation. In its sensuous beauty, its artistic restraint, its skilful manipulation of a complex and difficult metrical pattern, and its imaginatively beautiful descriptions of the garden, the pearl-maiden, and the New Jerusalem, it is in its best parts unsurpassed by anything in Middle English poetry.

In two respects *Purity*,[12] the second poem in the manuscript, resembles the *Pearl*—in its preoccupation with an ethical question and in its predilection for extended paraphrases of biblical incident. For here we have a discourse on purity, showing how impossible it is for one who is unclean to approach God's pure presence, and enforcing the point by the parable of the man without a wedding garment. This and other episodes such as the Fall of Lucifer and the Expulsion from Paradise are merely preliminary, however, to the main purpose, which is to tell the stories of the Flood, the Destruction of Sodom and Gomorrah, and the profanation of the holy vessels in Belshazzar's Feast. The homiletic purpose is plain, and at the end the poet not only reminds us that "upon þrynne wyses" he has showed the sorrow that uncleanness causes our Lord but he closes with a prayer for grace. The stories are vividly told, but the poem suffers by comparison with the *Pearl* through the lack of any framework or artistic motivation. *Purity*

This is also true of its companion piece, *Patience*,[13] which devotes all but the first sixty of its 531 lines to the story of Jonah and the whale. But concentration upon a single subject gives greater unity to the piece, and the poet has allowed his imagination freer rein in embellishing his theme. He shows us the activity in getting under sail, describes vividly the storm at sea, pictures with realistic detail the slimy insides of the whale, and reports dramatically Jonah's conversations with God. God's rebuke of Jonah for his impatience leads the poet to his closing reflection. He who is too hasty in tearing his clothes will often sit sewing them up. Even poverty must be borne with patience, which "is a noble point, though it displease *Patience*

[10] Jefferson B. Fletcher, "The Allegory of the *Pearl*," *JEGP*, xx (1921). 1-21, and René Wellek, "*The Pearl*: An Interpretation of the Middle-English Poem," *Studies in English* (Charles Univ., Prague), iv (1933). 1-33. Both these papers stress the complex character of the symbolism.

[11] For an attempt to identify the child see Oscar Cargill and Margaret Schlauch, "*The Pearl* and Its Jeweler," *PMLA*, xliii (1928). 105-123.

[12] Edited by Richard Morris (2ed., 1869; *EETS*, 1), Robert J. Menner (1920; *Yale Stud. in English*, 61), and Sir Israel Gollancz (1921).

[13] Edited by Richard Morris (as above), Hartley Bateson (Manchester, 1912; 2ed., 1918), and Israel Gollancz (1913).

oft." In both *Purity* and *Patience* the poet's principal indebtedness is to the Bible, and the *Pearl* not only draws its parables from the same source but derives its description of the New Jerusalem from the Apocalypse. Other sources in Tertullian, an eclogue of Boccaccio, and even the *Book of the Knight of La Tour Landry* have been suggested but with the possible exception of Boccaccio's eclogue, must be described as very doubtful. The poet refers once to Jean de Meun and his part of the *Roman de la Rose*, and he has drawn scattered details in *Purity* from Mandeville's *Travels* in their French form. But while the author of these poems was apparently well read, we have not been very successful in tracking down the sources of his inspiration outside of the Scriptures.

There seems to be no reason to doubt that the three poems the *Pearl*, *Purity*, and *Patience* are the work of one man. The fourth poem in the manuscript is of such a different kind that if it were not found in association with the others we might well hesitate to attribute it to the same authorship,

Sir Gawain and the Green Knight

in spite of obvious stylistic resemblances.[14] *Sir Gawain and the Green Knight*[15] is a courtly romance, the finest Arthurian romance in English. Though it exemplifies the knightly virtues of courage and truth, it is in no sense a story told to enforce a moral. It is quite in the spirit of French romance, told for its own sake.

Subject Matter and Treatment

The plot itself is so well known as to need no retelling. The main adventure is the challenge, which Gawain accepts, of an exchange of blows with the Green Knight, in which he beheads the challenger but must submit to the same hazard a year later. With this is combined the adventure at Bercilak's castle, in which Gawain is tempted on three successive mornings by his host's wife and in which his only fault is in concealing the magic girdle which she gives him. Both of these stories are found separately either in Celtic or in Old French romances.[16] They are first found combined in the English poem,[17] and whether we owe the combination to the English poet

[14] Apart from the stylistic features common to all four poems, there are noteworthy parallels between *Sir Gawain and the Green Knight* and *Purity*. It should be remembered, however, that the romance also shows many striking parallels in phrases and lines with the *Wars of Alexander*.

[15] There are older editions by Sir Frederic Madden for the Bannatyne Club (1839) and Richard Morris (1864; EETS, 4); revised by I. Gollancz (1897 and 1912), but the romance is best studied in the edition of J. R. R. Tolkien and E. V. Gordon (1925) or the new edition of Sir Israel Gollancz with introductory essays by Mabel Day and Mary S. Serjeantson (1940; EETS, 210). Modern renderings by Jessie L. Weston (1898), often reprinted, T. H. Banks (1929), G. H. Gerould (1934), etc. are available separately or in anthologies.

[16] The fullest study of the sources of the romance is George L. Kittredge, *A Study of Gawain and the Green Knight* (Cambridge, Mass., 1916). The challenge or beheading game is found in an episode known as *The Champion's Bargain* which closes the Irish romance (at least as old as the eleventh century) of *Fled Bricrend*, or *Bricriu's Feast*. From there it passed into French, where it was embodied independently into four separate romances (the *Livre de Caradoc*, incorporated in the first continuation of Chrétien's *Perceval*, the short thirteenth-century romance *La Mule sanz Frain*, the prose Grail romance known as the *Perlesvaus* in which the adventure is attributed to Lancelot, and another thirteenth-century romance entitled *Gawain et Humbaut* in which the ending has been completely changed). Parallels to the temptation motif are not so close, but in one form or another it is found in the Old French *Ider*, in the late English *Carl of Carlisle*, and elsewhere.

[17] There are many theories accounting for the combination. Kittredge believed that *Sir Gawain and the Green Knight* was based on a lost French romance in which the adventures

or to his source we must grant that it was a happy inspiration which tied the three temptations to the three blows offered Gawain at the Green Chapel and made the wound received from the third blow the result of his concealing the girdle. Accepting the supernatural as a prerogative of medieval story, we have a skilfully contrived plot,[18] a feature always worthy of remark in medieval romance. But it is only one, and that perhaps the least, of the qualities which give this remarkable poem its high place among English romances. From the beginning almost to the end it proceeds by a succession of scenes and situations full of color and movement and vivid detail. We begin with the New Year's feast, the guests exchanging greetings and gifts, the maidens laughing and making mirth till it is time to eat, then washing and seating themselves at tables. Just as the music ceases and the first course has been served the Green Knight enters. He is fully described—stature, appearance, dress, armor, horse, trappings—as he rides straight up to the daïs. And so it goes from episode to episode like a succession of tapestries or medieval illuminations. The descriptions of the seasons as they mark the passing of the year and bring Gawain to the time when he must set out to keep his pledge are no mere literary exercises, and the hunting scenes have all the excitement and lifelikeness of first-hand experience or observation. Striking, too, is the poet's mastery of dialogue, always easy and natural, but particularly skilful in the extended conversations between Gawain and the lady of the castle, as she seeks an opening and he adroitly evades and parries each thrust. Finally, one should remark the dexterous way in which the poet keeps the various actions moving forward simultaneously, passing from the dalliance of the lady to the husband's adventures in the chase and back again to the bed chamber until all parties are brought together naturally at the end of each day. But there is no end of things to exclaim over and we can only hint at the enjoyment to be had from reading and rereading this fine romance.[19]

---

were combined. J. R. Hulbert, "Syr Gawayn and the Grene Knyȝt," *MP*, XIII (1915-16). 433-462, 689-730, believes they were originally joined in a Fairy Mistress story as the conditions which the hero must fulfill. Else von Schaubert, "Der englische Ursprung von *Syr Gawayn and the Grene Knyȝt*," *ESt*, LVII (1923). 330-446, maintains that they were first combined by the English poet. This is also the view of Miss Day in the essay noted above. O. Löhmann, *Die Sage von Gawain und dem grünen Ritter* (Königsberg, 1938), likewise believes in the English origin of the romance, but argues that a Fairy Mistress story has been changed into a test of the hero.

[18] The idea that *Sir Gawain and the Green Knight* is connected in some way with the Order of the Garter is most fully advocated in Isaac Jackson, "*Sir Gawain and the Green Knight* considered as a 'Garter' Poem," *Anglia*, XXXVII (1913). 393-423, and opposed by J. R. Hulbert in the article already referred to (*MP*. XIII, especially pp. 710 ff.).

[19] In the absence of any objective evidence for determining the order of composition it has seemed best to treat the poems in the order in which they occur in the manuscript. *Patience* and *Purity* probably belong together, and since *Purity* has a number of parallels with the *Gawain*, it probably stands closer to the latter. On artistic grounds the *Pearl* and *Gawain* should follow the homiletic pieces, though this is not a safe criterion for pieces unlike in kind. One could argue for an order which would put the *Gawain* first, followed by the *Pearl*, the bereavement in which led the poet to the moral concerns of *Purity* and *Patience*. Such an order would have the advantage of putting *Patience* after *Purity*, to which it is superior in structure and unity.

*The
Author*

All that we know about the author of these four poems is what can be cautiously inferred from his work, and all attempts to identify him with Huchown, Strode, or any other individual have failed. The dialect of the manuscript, which there is no reason to think differs essentially from that of the author, would indicate that he belonged to the northwest Midlands, probably south Lancashire, and this general locality is supported by the landscape and local allusions in the poems. He need not have been a priest in spite of his preoccupation with theological and moral questions, though a position as chaplain in some nobleman's household would make such an interest natural and account for his familiarity with the ways of courtly life. Naturally, however, such knowledge could be otherwise accounted for. His vocabulary contains a large French element which might result from his social status or his acquaintance with French literature. This was certainly considerable. He impresses us as a man of cosmopolitan taste whose horizon was not bounded by the limits of a provincial neighborhood. That he was at once observant and imaginative is apparent. His literary activity coincides roughly with the earlier part of Chaucer's career, and in the absence of more precise information we cannot do better than to date his work *c*. 1375.

St.
Erkenwald

Various other alliterative poems have from time to time been attributed to the *Pearl* poet. Among them the one that has found most supporters is *St. Erkenwald* [20] which attributes to the Old English bishop of this name a miracle not otherwise recorded. When St. Paul's in London was being rebuilt a tomb was uncovered in which was the body of a pagan judge. Since he had always been just in his awards, his body and clothing were still as fresh as at the time of his death. At Erkenwald's bidding the corpse reveals its identity, whereupon the bishop's tears fall on the body, constituting baptism and releasing the soul. Bodily decay at once sets in. The story is told in 352 clear and straightforward verses, but the present writer at least cannot accept the attribution to the *Pearl* poet.

Pistel of
Swete
Susan

Associated with the poems previously discussed is a short piece of twenty-eight tail-rime stanzas, each with thirteen alliterative lines, called the *Pistel of Swete Susan.*[21] It tells the story of Susanna and the Elders from the thirteenth chapter of Daniel (in the Vulgate), with the description of the garden embellished with details drawn from the *Roman de la Rose*. It is told simply and effectively, at times with the deft touches of an artist. When Susanna, allowed to speak to her husband, has avowed her innocence and fidelity to him,

> Ðei toke þe feteres of hire feete,
> And evere he kyssed þat swete:
> "In other world schal we mete."
> Seide he no mare. (lines 257-60)

[20] Edited by Horstmann, *Altenglische Legenden* (1881), Gollancz (1922), and Henry L. Savage (1926; *Yale Stud. in English*, 72).
[21] Edited by Hans Köster, *Huchown's Pistel of Swete Susan* (Strassburg, 1895; *Quellen und Forschungen*, LXXVI).

A passage in Wyntoun's *Orygynale Cronykil* (c. 1420) asserts that the author was Huchown of the Awle Ryale (Royal Court), who is there credited also with the *Gret Gest off Arthure* and the *Awyntyre off Gawane*.[22] The attribution cannot be accepted, but the passage has led some to believe that Huchown was not only the *Pearl* poet but the author of most of the poems in the alliterative revival.[23] Naturally such extravagant claims have not met with much favor. While the six poems discussed in the present chapter are linked together by certain features of subject matter and treatment it seems best to hold to the conservative view which limits the work of the *Pearl* poet to the poems preserved in the famous Cotton manuscript.

[22] He made the *Gret Gest off Arthure*
And the *Awyntyre off Gawane*
The *Pystyll* als off *Swete Swsane*. . . .

The *Gret Gest off Arthure* is believed to be the alliterative *Morte Arthure*, presumably in its fuller form (see ch. x, above). The *Awyntyre off Gawane* is identified by those who believe Huchown to be the *Pearl* poet with *Sir Gawain and the Green Knight*, by others with the *Awntyrs of Arthur* (see p. 190, note 22).

[23] George Neilson, '*Huchown of the Awle Ryale*', the *Alliterative Poet* (Glasgow, 1902), who argues that Huchown is to be identified with the "gude Sir Hew of Eglintoun" mentioned by Dunbar in his *Lament for the Makaris*. In spite of the extravagance of his thesis Neilson's book contains much interesting matter.

XV

Piers Plowman and Other Alliterative Poems

Poems of Social Protest

It is a noteworthy feature of the alliterative revival in the second half of the fourteenth century that a number of poems in the older measure, and among them some of the most important, are poems of social and moral protest.[1] This should not cause surprise when we remember that the period was ushered in by the Black Death with its grave economic and political consequences, that it saw the Peasants' Revolt in 1381, and that Wyclif and the Lollard movement are only another manifestation of the general upheaval which unsettled so many established conditions and beliefs. Nor should it seem altogether strange that much of this social criticism should appear in alliterative verse rather than in the more conventional measure of the court. The criticism is directed at the government which tolerated so many abuses, and like most forms of political opposition came from those outside the group in power. The poems which we shall consider in the present chapter all express the point of view of the common man. They are like voices crying in the wilderness, denouncing evils without seeming so much as to hope for their redress.

Wynnere and Wastoure

The earliest, apparently, is *Wynnere and Wastoure*,[2] dating from about 1352. Allusions in the prologue indicate that it is by a "western man" and in all probability a professional minstrel of the old school, since he complains that the minstrel's calling is not what it once was but is filled with beardless youths who "jangle als a jaye and japes telle." In some five hundred lines the poem presents a dispute between thrift (Winner), representing the merchants, lawyers, the Pope, the four orders of friars [3]—all men of property—and waste represented by a gay young spendthrift who neglects his lands and dovecotes, sells his holdings, and squanders his money on revelry and proud clothes for himself and his wife. In the third and pre-

[1] Social complaint is not unknown to English verse before the period of which we speak, but it is for the most part brief and sporadic. *When Holy Church Is under Foot* has been mentioned above (see p. 123). Two poems in MS Harl. 2253 offer respectively *A Satire on the Consistory Courts* and a *Song of the Husbandman*, the latter a husbandman's complaint that he is taxed and fleeced until he has nothing left. A poem in the Auchinleck MS on *The Evil Times of Edward II* (476 lines) parallels more closely some of the poems discussed in the present chapter, at least in the abuses which it describes. The late fourteenth-century *Sir Penny* treats a theme—money can do anything—found also in Latin and French. Most of these poems are printed in Thomas Wright's *Political Songs of England* (1839; Camden Soc.).
[2] Edited by Sir Israel Gollancz (1920, 1931), and previously for the Roxburghe Club (1897). For further evidence bearing on the date see J. R. Hulbert, "The Problems of Authorship and Date of *Wynnere and Wastoure*," *MP*, XVIII (1920). 31-40; J. M. Steadman, Jr., "The Date of *Winnere and Wastoure*," *MP*, XIX (1921). 211-219; Gardiner Stillwell, "*Wynnere and Wastoure* and the Hundred Years' War," *ELH*, VIII (1941). 241-247.
[3] The meaning of the two hosts and their constituents is not very clear.

sumably last "fitt" the King (Edward III) gives the disputants the surprising advice to go each his own way—Winner to the Pope at Rome, Waster to Cheapside—each to live "in a land where he is loved most." The conclusion of the poem is missing, so that the final attitude of the author is unknown, but he seems to be trying to please both sides and therefore presents his ideas in the familiar debate form.

Parlement of the Thre Ages

Less unified is the *Parlement of the Thre Ages.*[4] Not capable of being exactly dated, it has been associated on rather slight grounds with *Wynnere and Wastoure* and attributed to the same author. This at least is quite doubtful.[5] The *Parlement* in general plan reminds us of *Purity* and *Patience:* the poet puts forward a proposition which offers the excuse for a long narrative illustration. In this case, after a prologue of 103 lines telling how he shot, dressed, and concealed a hart (i.e., he was poaching [6]), he falls asleep. In his dream he sees three men—Youth, aged thirty, gaily dressed in green; Middle Age, sixty years old, in sober gray; and Old Age, in black, described as a decrepit old man of a hundred, mumbling his Creed. In the *parlement* (talk, discussion) which follows each explains his philosophy of life. The young man speaks of his leman, of dancing, chess, hawking by the river. Middle Age deprecates Youth's expensive clothes, the price of which would purchase lands. Old Age assures them they are both foolish. He was once just like them. Now death has stolen upon him, as it has on many another great and proud. This gives the poet his opportunity to relate the experience of some of these, and in the remainder of the poem, more than half of its 665 lines, he gives accounts of each of the Nine Worthies, next of the "wights that were wisest"—Aristotle, Virgil, Solomon, and Merlin—and finally of "the proudest in press that paramours loved"—Amadas and Ydoine, Samson and Delilah, Tristan and Iseult, and others. All these prove that nothing avails against death; and Old Age, urging his companions to confess their sins, goes off with the words, "Death dings on my door; I dare no longer abide." The theme is naturally perennial and such social criticism as occurs in the poem is purely incidental.

Piers Plowman

The greatest of all the alliterative poems of social protest is *Piers Plowman,* or more properly *The Vision of William concerning Piers the Plowman.* Even this longer title is inadequate to describe the poem in its fullest form, for it has come down to us in three very different states.[7] The earliest or *A*-text is rather short (2579 lines) and consists of a prologue and eleven

[4] Edited by Israel Gollancz (1915) and earlier for the Roxburghe Club (1897).

[5] Gollancz's theory of common authorship is opposed by Hulbert (*MP,* XVIII. 31-34) and Steadman (*MP,* XXI. 7-13).

[6] See H. L. Savage, "Notes on the Prologue of the *Parlement of the Thre Ages*" (*JEGP,* XXIX (1930). 74-82), who here and elsewhere has shown how exact was the poet's knowledge of deer hunting and outdoor life.

[7] The three versions were edited separately by W. W. Skeat for the *EETS* (1867-84; texts in Vols. 28, 38, 54, notes and glossary in Vols. 67, 81) and later *en regard* (2v, Oxford, 1886). No one should ever belittle the work of Skeat, who through his tireless labors as an editor did an incalculable service to Middle English scholarship. Nevertheless, more critical editions of all three texts are badly needed, and are in preparation.

Three
Texts

cantos or *passus*.[8] The second or *B*-text is a revision of the first and a continuation amounting to the prologue and twenty passus (7241 lines). The third or *C*-text represents a further revision, sometimes slight but sometimes considerable. It is of about the same length as the *B*-text (it is 7353 lines [9]) but is divided into twenty-three passus. Such repeated revisions of the poem are evidence of its continued popularity, a popularity which is confirmed by the existence today of more than fifty manuscripts. It is therefore worth while to consider in some detail the contents of this remarkable work.

The First
Vision

In its earliest form the poem consists of three successive visions, two of them intimately connected, the third rather incoherent. As the poem opens, the author clad as a hermit is wandering one May morning on the Malvern hills, falls asleep on the bank of a brook, and dreams a marvelous dream. In a wilderness, he knows not where, but doubtless the neighborhood in which he has been wandering, he sees off to the east a tower on a high hill, down in the valley below a dungeon, and in between a "field full of folk"— some plowing, some wearing fine clothes, business men, beggars, pilgrims, hermits, friars of the four orders preaching and often covetous, parish priests hurrying to London, lawyers, bishops, and tradesmen of all kinds. Soon a lady named Holy Church comes down from the cliff and chides the dreamer for sleeping. Doesn't he see all these people so busy in their various ways? Somewhat afraid, he asks her to explain what the scene before him means. She tells him that Truth, who is God, dwells in the tower and that the Father of Falseness (the Devil) inhabits the dungeon. He asks her to teach him how to save his soul. Truth is best, she says, and charity, and especially love of the poor. But he wishes to know more, how he can recognize and thus avoid Falseness. She bids him look on his left. There he sees a woman, richly clad in a scarlet robe and many jewels, the equal of a queen. She is Lady Meed, the symbol both of just reward and of bribery, more often the latter. She is about to be married to False, with the assistance of Guile, Simony, Liar, and other evil characters, until Theology protests. The King thereupon proposes to marry her to Conscience, but Conscience refuses, pointing out many evil practices which Lady Meed is responsible for. Unable to reconcile the two, for bribery and conscience are naturally irreconcilable, the King appeals to Reason, who consents to serve the King if Conscience will be their counselor. At this point the dreamer awakes and the first Vision ends.

Second
Vision

But before he has walked a furlong drowsiness overtakes him and he again dreams. In his second vision, the vision of the Seven Deadly Sins and the search for Truth, he is back with his field full of folk, to whom Conscience is about to preach a sermon. Conscience alludes to the recent pestilences and the destructive wind of Saturday [January 15, 1362], evidences of God's anger at the sins of the people. He calls upon sundry classes and individuals to repent—wasters, Pernel the Courtesan, priests, prelates, etc

[8] A portion of a twelfth passus with a conclusion by John But is found in one MS.
[9] These figures are based upon Skeat's texts. Manly gives *B* as 7242 and *C* as 7357 (*CHEL* II. 3).

His words have the effect of making the various sinners confess their evil ways, repent, and even set out to seek St. Truth. A Palmer whom they meet and whose life has been spent visiting holy places seems a natural person to direct them in their quest. But he fails them miserably, admitting that he never knew a palmer to seek such a saint! It is at this point that a simple plowman named Peter puts forth his head and says he knows the saint very well. Common sense and a clean conscience have acquainted him with St. Truth and he has served him for the last fifteen years. No man is better pay. The way to his court is through Meekness to Conscience and thus on through the Ten Commandments. Grace is warden of the gate. If Grace permits them to enter, they shall see Truth himself in their hearts.

This is another way of saying that to attain to God man must "do well," must lead a worthy life. But what does the poet consider a worthy life? A concrete instance makes it fairly clear: Piers tells the company that before he can go with them and show them the way to Truth he has a half-acre to plow. It is an interesting picture. Some help him to plow, but others sit and drink or pretend to be sick and won't work until Hunger compels them. The whole episode suggests that man should do the task that falls to his lot. The names of Piers' wife and children imply further that the ordinary man at least, besides working in season, should keep out of mischief and mind his own business.

In the eighth passus Truth gives Piers a pardon which is found to contain only two lines

> Et qui bona egerunt, ibunt in vitam eternam;
> Qui vero mala, in ignem eternam.

A priest sniffs at such a pardon, but as the dreamer wakes and reflects on his dream he is convinced that Do-well is worth more at Doomsday than all the pardons of St. Peter's church. The passus concludes with the words *Explicit hic Visio Wilhelmi de Petro de Plowʒman. Eciam incipit Vita de Do-well, Do-bet, et Do-best secundum wyt et resoun.*

The ninth passus accordingly marks a new departure in the poem. The *Third* poet, taking up Piers' quest, roams about a whole summer in search of *Vision* Do-well. Two Franciscan friars tell him that Do-well dwells with them, but he disputes their claim and continues his search. As he rests beside a wood, he again falls asleep and dreams. He soon meets Thought, who is described as a large man like himself. Thought explains that Do-well is when a man is mild of speech, true of tongue, and fair in his dealings. Do-bet, besides practising these virtues, gives to the poor. Do-best bears a bishop's cross. For further information they go to Wit, whose wife is Dame Study, and who sends Piers to her cousin Clergy (learning) and his wife Scripture (book-knowledge). There is much rambling observation and moralizing in these episodes, so that when the dreamer says he is none the nearer for all his walking to knowing what Do-well is, we can only agree with him. As the text breaks off he has asked Scripture to direct him to Kind Wit (Common Sense).

Continuation in the B-text

It is impossible to continue our analysis of the poem as it proceeds in the B-text, partly because the larger plan, the quest of Do-well, Do-bet, and Do-best, is vague and at times completely obscured, partly because the constant digressions, parenthetical discussions, and breaks in continuity show that the author was powerless to resist the impulse to pursue any idea suggested by another idea or even by a word that he happens to use. Mention of the cardinal virtues leads him into a digression on cardinals from Rome. He simply cannot make his thought hew to the line. As a result this part of the poem consists of many dialogues and discourses on truth, poverty, learning, charity, and the like, exemplified in the conduct of figures like Faith and Hope contrasted with Samaritan, or in the friar Flattery, or Haukyn the Active Man. There are some memorable scenes such as the dinner at which a friar, a "doctor on the high daïs," ate his food and drank wine with gluttonous delight, while not four days past he had preached before the Dean of St. Paul's on hunger endured as a penance. There are narratives of the Annunciation, episodes in the life of Christ, visions of the Resurrection and the Harrowing of Hell, which are vigorously related, and there is many a vivid flash of satirical observation which dies away before we have quite discerned what it was meant to illuminate. Read for the individual visions and scenes the poem is genuinely absorbing, but it is the despair of anyone who seeks in it a completely orderly plan or logical development from episode to episode.

Date

When and by whom was this long and intensely earnest poem written? Neither of these questions is easily answered, but a number of topical allusions in the three texts offer a basis for inference concerning the date. The A-text makes reference to a "Southwestern wind on a Saturday at even" (v. 14) which has long been recognized as an allusion to a severe windstorm mentioned in the chronicles as occurring on Saturday, Jan. 15, 1362. This and other allusions to events of the year or two previous have led to a fairly general acceptance of 1362 as the date of the first version. Some allusions can be interpreted, however, as referring to events in the later 'sixties[10] and the composition of the poem may have extended over several years. The B-text likewise presents somewhat conflicting evidence, but a date not long after 1377 seems best to fit the facts. The revision may likewise have extended over a considerable time.[11] The C-text has usually been dated 1393,

[10] Oscar Cargill, "The Date of the A-text of Piers Ploughman," *PMLA*, xLvII (1932). 354-362, argues for 1376, which seems too late; Bernard F. Huppé, "Piers Plowman and the Norman Wars," *PMLA*, LIV (1939). 37-64, suggests 1370-76, probably after 1373; J. A. W. Bennett, "The Date of the A-text of Piers Plowman," *PMLA*, LVIII (1943). 566-572, while dissenting from some of the views expressed in these articles, argues that certain lines in Passus IV must have been written after October, 1367, and before September, 1370.

[11] Bernard F. Huppé, "The Date of the B-text of Piers Plowman," *SP*, xxxvIII (1941). 33-44, argues from a passage in Passus xIx that the poem was not completed until after the autumn of 1378. On the other hand, Miss Mildred E. Marcett's strong case for identifying the "doctour on the heigh dese" with the friar William Jordan (*Uhtred de Boldon, Friar William Jordan, and Piers Plowman*, 1938) suggests a date around 1370 or even slightly earlier for this episode,

as Skeat thought, or 1398, as Jusserand argued. But it has been shown that a date not later than 1387 is suggested by a number of considerations,[12] and we may tentatively accept this year as the *terminus ad quem* for the final form of the poem.

One of the most remarkable things about this series of poems is the mystery that surrounds their authorship. We are accustomed to anonymity in works of medieval literature, especially in the romance, where stories were told and retold, and in religious poems where personal reputation was not the author's main object. It is also true that practically all the poems that make up the alliterative revival are by poets whose names we do not know. Nevertheless it is surprising that in *Piers Plowman,* the three texts of which contain so many seemingly personal revelations, the poet has so completely concealed his identity. For all the poem's popularity, no contemporary reference to the author has come down to us. Even the John But who wrote a conclusion to the *A*-text that is preserved in one manuscript seems not to have known the name of its author, and his statement that "When this work was wrought .... Death dealt him a dint" may be only an inference from the poem's unfinished appearance. Two fifteenth-century notes in manuscripts of the poem [13] are the sole clue to the author's name, and on the strength of their testimony *Piers Plowman* has generally been attributed to William Langland. *Authorship*

On the basis of these notes and of allusions scattered through the three texts of the poem a hypothetical biography would run somewhat as follows. Born about 1332 at Ledbury in Shropshire, the son (possibly illegitimate) of Eustace de la Rokayle, the author was sent to school, perhaps at the priory of Great Malvern, by his father and his friends, and took minor orders. At the age of about thirty he began the first version of *Piers Plowman.* In the course of the work he moved to London, where he lived in Cornhill with his wife Kitte and his daughter Calote, a kind of clerical vagabond earning his bread by means of the *Paternoster, Placebo, Dirige,* the Psalter, and the Seven Penitential Psalms, which he sang for the souls of those who contributed to his support. In the *B*-text he mentions his age as forty-five. The *Hypothetical Biography*

---

and Father A. Gwynn, "The Date of the *B*-text of *Piers Plowman,*" *RES,* xix (1943). 1-24, has gathered other evidence for a date *c.* 1370-72 for Passus xiii-xx, while recognizing that the revision of Passus i-viii must have occurred as late as 1376-7. J. A. W. Bennett, "The Date of the B-text of Piers Plowman," *MA,* xii (1943). 55-64, interprets certain passages as evidence that work on parts of the *B*-text was going on as late as 1377 and possibly in 1379 or even later. Work on the B-text extending over ten years need cause no great surprise.

[12] Sister Mary Aquinas Devlin, "The Date of the *C* Version of Piers the Plowman," [Univ. of Chicago] *Abstracts of Theses,* Humanistic Ser., iv (1928). 317-320.

[13] Ashburnham MS 130, now in the Huntington Library, says simply "Robert or William langland made pers ploughman." The other, Trin. Coll. Dublin MS D. 4. 1, makes an important additional assertion: "Memorandum quod Stacy de Rokayle pater Willielmi de Langlond, qui Stacius fuit generosus, et morabatur in Schypton vnder Whicwode, tenens domini le Spenser in comitatu Oxon, qui predictus Willielmus fecit librum qui vocatur Perys ploughman." In 1559 John Bale in his *Scriptorum Illustrium Maioris Britanniae Catalogus* stated that Langland was born at Cleobury Mortymer in Shropshire. It has been plausibly suggested that this is a scribal error for Ledbury, in which case Langland's birthplace would be the same as that of John Masefield. See Allan H. Bright, *New Light on 'Piers Plowman'* (Oxford, 1928).

C-text would thus belong toward the end of his life. Most of the allusions on which this inferential biography is based are found only in the C-text.

Single or Multiple Authorship It is obvious that the picture here sketched assumes that all three versions of *Piers Plowman* are the work of one man. This assumption was questioned as long ago as 1856, and in 1906 John M. Manly [14] brought the issue clearly to the fore in an article which not only argued that the three texts were by different poets but that the *A*-text itself was not a unit. The prologue and first eight passus, he maintained, were by one man and the remainder of the *A*-text by another, to which John But added a conclusion. According to this hypothesis five different authors had a hand in the poems which go by the name of *Piers Plowman*. Manly's opinion was based upon what he felt to be "differences in language, differences in versification, differences in the use and in the kind of figurative language, and above all by such striking differences in the mental powers and qualities of the authors as make it highly improbable that they can be one and the same person." He further supported his view by the famous theory of a "lost leaf." [15] Manly's theory was at once attacked by Jusserand and others, and the controversy over single or multiple authorship has not yet ended. We cannot follow the course of this controversy here.[16] But however opinion may vary as to the justice of Manly's contention, it cannot be denied that it has enormously stimulated the study of the poem and led to a much better understanding of it. It is hazardous to attempt a statement of present scholarly opinion since it is still strongly divided.[17] It may be said, however, that Manly's belief in differences in language and versification has not been confirmed, and that the treatment of allegorical characters and the use of the Bible are noticeably alike in the three versions.[18] To the present writer it seems that separate authorship for the *A* and *B* texts has not been proved, but that in the C-text the attitude towards the poor, the treatment of ecclesiastics, the preoccupation with theological matters,[19] numerous changes for the

---

14 "The Lost Leaf of *Piers the Plowman*," *MP*, III (1906). 359-366. Manly presented his views more fully in "*Piers the Plowman* and its Sequence," *CHEL*, II. 1-48.

15 In Passus v of the *A*-text Conscience preaches a sermon which leads to confessions by the Seven Deadly Sins. In this series of confessions the sin of Wrath is left out, and between lines 235 and 236 there is a dislocation of sense, the confession of Sloth suddenly changing to that of Robert the Robber. The loss of a leaf at this point would explain the abrupt ending of the confession of Sloth and the absence of a suitable introduction to the character of Robert the Robber. By assuming a manuscript with 30-40 lines to the page Manly shows that this lost leaf could have belonged to the sheet next to the inner sheet of a gathering and that its counterfoil would come where the confession of Wrath should occur, i.e., after the confession of Envy. The confession of Envy, as has often been noticed, closes abruptly. The significance of this demonstration for Manly's theory of multiple authorship lies in the fact that the author of the *B*-text in revising this portion of the poem did not deal with these defects adequately and therefore could not have been the original poet.

16 The earlier articles in the controversy are reprinted in *EETS*, 139. For subsequent bibliography see Wells' *Manual* and its supplements, and Morton W. Bloomfield, "Present State of *Piers Plowman* Studies," *Speculum*, XIV (1939). 215-232.

17 The best statement of the argument for single authorship is that of R. W. Chambers in his preface to Bright's book noted above.

18 Dorothy L. Owen, *Piers Plowman: A Comparison with Some Earlier and Contemporary French Allegories* (1912); M. R. Adams, "The Use of the Vulgate in *Piers Plowman*," *SP*, XXIV (1927). 556-566.

19 See George Sanderlin. "The Character of "Liberum Arbitrium' in the C-text of *Piers Plowman*." *MLN*, LVI (1941). 449-453.

worse in the text,[20] and other considerations raise serious doubts about the authorship of this version.[21] Even in the B-text it cannot be denied that the poet is incapable of steering a straight course, possibly because he has become more deeply involved in his allegory. But until Manly's theory of a lost leaf is more satisfactorily disposed of, his claim for separate authorship of the A, B, and C texts cannot be dismissed.

The greatness of the poem is due almost entirely to the A and B versions. Whatever its shortcomings in design—and these are most apparent in the B continuation—we are in the presence throughout of a powerful imagination, wayward and rhapsodic though it is in the B-text. In the vivid delineation of scenes and the realistic painting of character the poem bears comparison with the best of medieval allegories, with the *Roman de la Rose* or the *Divine Comedy*. Its distinguishing characteristic is its trenchant satire, both in sidelong glance and direct attack. And permeating the whole is the evident sincerity of the author or authors, the deep moral earnestness which compels us to read every line with close attention while insuring our interest up to the very end.

The Poem's Greatness

So popular a poem was naturally not without imitators. A Wyclifite attack on the friars was given the name *Pierce the Ploughman's Creed* [22] (*c.* 1394). The author goes to each of the four orders looking for some one to teach him the Creed, but a Minorite runs down the Carmelites, the Dominicans abuse the Austin friars, and so on. A poor plowman named Piers abuses them all in a long and general condemnation, finally explaining the Creed himself. The poem, which was apparently written in London, is interesting mainly for its outspoken criticism of the mendicant orders.

Pierce the Ploughman's Creed

Another alliterative poem, once attributed to the author of *Piers Plowman*, was published many years ago under the title *Richard the Redeless*.[23] Written after Richard II had been taken prisoner (September, 1399), the poem offers belated advice to the King. It criticizes him for surrounding himself with young and inexperienced advisers who squandered his money and thought only of fashionable clothes, and for filling the country with retainers who wore his livery and oppressed the people. It breaks off, shortly after the beginning of Passus IV, in the midst of an attack on the Parliament of 1398 and its indifference to the public welfare. The poem was known to Nicholas Brigham, a sixteenth-century antiquary, by the title *Mum, Sothsegger* (Hush, Truth-teller). The identification is certain because he quoted the first two lines (in a Latin paraphrase). When accordingly a manuscript turned up in 1928 containing some 1750 lines of a poem made up throughout of a dialogue between Mum and Sothsegger it seemed reason-

Richard the Redeless

Mum and the Sothsegger

[20] See T. D. Hall, "Was 'Langland' the Author of the C-text of *The Vision of Piers Plowman?*" *MLR*, IV (1908). 1-13.
[21] Even Chambers admits that "*C* is probably much interpolated" (*op. cit.*, p. 23).
[22] Edited by W. W. Skeat (1867, 1895; *EETS*, 30) and in a convenient small edition (Oxford, 1906).
[23] Edited originally by Thomas Wright (1838; *Camden Soc.*) and more recently by W. W. Skeat (1873; *EETS*, 54). It is also included in his edition of *Piers Plowman* (2v, Oxford, 1886). But see the following note.

able to assume that the two somehow belonged together. They have now been so published under the title *Mum and the Sothsegger*.[24] An interval must have separated the writing of the two parts since allusions in the new fragment to contemporary events indicate a date for it *c.* 1403-6. The poet suggests that the most valuable member of Henry's household would be a Truth-teller. He fears that the King may be led by selfish counselors. Mum bids him keep quiet. Truth-tellers get no thanks. And he finds out to his sorrow that most of the world follows Mum's policy. Finally a gardener tending his bee-hives encourages him to go on and he will find Truth-teller in man's heart. He is advised to write his book and give a copy to the King, whereupon he launches into his account of the many evils which beset the country. We are conscious of a considerable change of style as we pass from *Richard the Redeless* to the later fragment and there are other difficulties which prevent us from being sure that we are dealing with two parts of the same work, but on any other assumption it is difficult to account for the association of the unusual names Mum and Sothsegger with both poems.

Death and Life

Related more closely to *Wynnere and Wastoure* and to *The Parlement of the Thre Ages* is a poem dating from the end of the fourteenth century but preserved only in a seventeenth-century transcript in the Percy Folio. *Death and Life*[25] relates a vision in which Lady Life, described as very beautiful, disputes with Death, a woman of horrible appearance. Recalling the theme of Old Age's discourse in the *Parlement,* Death boasts of those whom she has struck down from Adam to Lancelot and Gawain and Galahad. But Life tells how Death herself was vanquished, recounting the Resurrection and the Harrowing of Hell, and finally in the character of Eternal Life assures her followers that through baptism and the Creed they need have no fear of Death. There are beautiful passages in the poem testifying to the continuance of the poetical impulse in the north well after the productions of the *Pearl* poet.

The alliterative poems which we have considered in this chapter have much in common. Of them *Piers Plowman* would alone be sufficient to guarantee the major importance of the group. Taken together they are the most significant vernacular expression of English social thought in the Middle Ages.

24 Ed. Mabel Day and Robert Steele (1936; *EETS,* 199).
25 The text is in Vol. III of *Bishop Percy's Folio Manuscript,* ed. Hales and Furnivall, but there are more recent editions by James H. Hanford and John M. Steadman, Jr. in *SP,* xv (1918). 221-294, and by Sir Israel Gollancz (1930). See also Edith Scamman, "The Alliterative Poem: *Death and Life,*" *Radcliffe Coll. Monographs,* No. 15 (1910). 95-113.

XVI

Chaucer: I

Geoffrey Chaucer,[1] the only known son of John Chaucer, a vintner of London, was born about 1340.[2] Of his early life and education we know nothing.[3] The earliest biographical fact of which we are sure is that in April, 1357, he was a page in the household of the Countess of Ulster, wife of the King's son Lionel. The Countess spent the following Christmas at Hatfield in Yorkshire, and at this time Chaucer probably made the acquaintance of John of Gaunt, his lifelong patron and friend, who was among the guests. In 1359 he went to France with the army, where he was taken pris-

[1] The most valuable book for the student to have is *The Complete Works of Geoffrey Chaucer*, ed. F. N. Robinson (Boston, 1933), with its scholarly and bibliographical apparatus. *The Complete Works of Geoffrey Chaucer*, ed. Walter W. Skeat (7v, Oxford, 1894-97) is still of value for its notes and glossary; it is often cited as the *Oxford Chaucer*. The one-volume abridgment (Oxford, 1897) and the Globe Chaucer, ed. Alfred W. Pollard, *et al.* (1898) are not, or but slightly, annotated. The volume of selections from the *Canterbury Tales* edited by John M. Manly (1928) contains an admirable introduction. Special bibliographies are E. P. Hammond, *Chaucer: A Bibliographical Manual* (1908), D. D. Griffith, *A Bibliography of Chaucer, 1908-1924* (Seattle, 1928), W. E. Martin, *A Chaucer Bibliography, 1925-1933* (Durham, N. C., 1935), and Wells' *Manual* with its supplements. For a comprehensive survey of Chaucer's work the following can be recommended: R. K. Root, *The Poetry of Chaucer* (2ed., 1922), R. D. French, *A Chaucer Handbook* (2ed., 1947), and G. L. Kittredge, *Chaucer and His Poetry* (1915). Of interest in various ways are Émile Legouis, *Geoffrey Chaucer* (Paris, 1910; English trans., 1913), A. Brusendorff, *The Chaucer Tradition* (1925), T. R. Lounsbury, *Studies in Chaucer* (3v, 1892), J. L. Lowes, *Geoffrey Chaucer and the Development of His Genius* (1934), J. M. Manly, *Some New Light on Chaucer* (1926), H. R. Patch, *On Rereading Chaucer* (1939), Percy V. D. Shelly, *The Living Chaucer* (Philadelphia, 1940). Among special studies Walter C. Curry, *Chaucer and the Mediæval Sciences* (1926) and Edgar F. Shannon, *Chaucer and the Roman Poets* (Cambridge, Mass., 1929; *Harvard Stud. in Compar. Lit.*, vii) may be mentioned for their wide scope. The publications of the Chaucer Society contain texts, monographs, the *Life Records* compiled by W. D. Selby, F. J. Furnivall, E. A. Bond, and R. E. G. Kirk (index by E. P. Kuhl in *MP*, x. 527-552), and source material. There is a concordance by J. S. P. Tatlock and A. G. Kennedy (Washington, 1927). The allusions to Chaucer are gathered together in C. F. E. Spurgeon, *Five Hundred Years of Chaucer Criticism and Allusion, 1357-1900* (7 parts, 1914-24; *Chaucer Soc.;* also 3v, Cambridge, 1925). — The chronology of Chaucer's writings has been worked out by a long succession of scholars, so that today we may feel that the main lines have been laid down. Of major importance in this work are F. J. Furnivall, *Trial-Forewords* (1871; *Chaucer Soc.*, 2nd Ser., 6) John Koch, *The Chronology of Chaucer's Writings* (1890; *Chaucer Soc.*, 2nd Ser., 27), J. S. P. Tatlock, *The Development and Chronology of Chaucer's Works* (1907; *Chaucer Soc.*, 2nd Ser., 37), and the two articles of J. L. Lowes in *PMLA*, xix (1904). 593-683 and xx (1905). 749-864. For other contributions to the subject the reader must be referred to the bibliographies mentioned earlier in this note.

[2] In 1386 Chaucer testified in the Scrope-Grosvenor trial, a suit over a disputed coat of arms, and gave his age as "forty years and upwards." In the absence of any more precise indication, it seems best to hold to a round number, although some are disposed to put the date a few years later. On the Chaucer family see Alfred A. Kern, *The Ancestry of Chaucer* (Baltimore, 1906).

[3] It has been suggested that he may have gone to school at St. Paul's, but the suggestion rests on nothing more than the fact that in 1358 the schoolmaster bequeathed nearly a hundred books to the school and the collection included many titles which Chaucer was later acquainted with. Cf. Edith Rickert, "Chaucer at School," *MP*, xxix (1932). 257-274.

oner, for in March, 1360, Edward III contributed £16 towards his ransom. After October we know nothing about his life for the next six years, although subsequent events make it likely that at some time during this period he was taken into the King's service. In any case, by 1366 he is already married to a Philippa, one of the damoiselles in the Queen's service, who seems to have been the daughter of Sir Payne Roet and sister of Katherine de Swynford, mistress and later wife of John of Gaunt.[4] In 1367 Chaucer appears as a valet in the King's household and the next year as an esquire. As such he begins to be employed on small missions and from then on his name occurs pretty constantly in the records. Chaucer's early history, as thus seen, is quite normal for one whose parents were able to secure a place for their son in the household of some noble. He was more fortunate than many, however, in being taken into the service of a member of the royal family.

Public Service   From this time on his life is a record of employment in one form or another of public service, rewarded by pensions, grants, and special payments. He is sent abroad frequently on the King's business, sometimes on "secret negotiations," once as a member of the group which tried in 1381 to arrange a marriage between Richard II and the daughter of the King of France. Most of these journeys were to France and the Low Countries, but at least two were to Italy. These are of special importance since they gave him an opportunity to become acquainted with Italian literature, especially with the work of Dante and Boccaccio. The first Italian journey which we can be sure of was in 1372, when he went to Genoa to negotiate a commercial treaty. His business also took him to Florence and from an allusion in the *Clerk's Tale* it is conjectured that he may have been in Padua and met Petrarch.[5] He was gone about six months. The second Italian mission was in 1378. This time he was gone only four months and his business brought him in contact with Barnabo Visconti, lord of Milan, whose death is the subject of a stanza in the *Monk's Tale.*

In 1374 Chaucer received the first of several appointments in the civil service. He was made Controller of the Customs and Subsidy on Wool Skins, and Hides in the port of London, with the usual provision that he should keep the records with his own hand. He was now freed from his attendance upon the King, and went to housekeeping in an apartment above Aldgate. During this period he seems to have enjoyed considerable prosperity, receiving in addition to his salary and the annuities which he and Philippa had, certain wardships and a fine which brought him in sums a

---

4 The relationship is not entirely clear. Katherine was the sole heir of Sir Payne Roet. Moreover Chaucer's relation to John of Gaunt does not seem to have been that of a brother-in-law. Philippa may have been Katherine's sister-in-law, in which case she would have been a Swynford. On the other hand, Thomas Chaucer, who was almost certainly the poet's son, has the Roet arms on his tomb. Philippa seems to have had social connections since she receives a number of grants and honors, in some of which her husband did not share.
5 The argument for the affirmative is presented by J. J. Jusserand, "Did Chaucer Meet Petrarch?" *Nineteenth Century*, xxxix (1896). 993-1005. On this general aspect of Chaucer's life see James R. Hulbert, *Chaucer's Official Life* (Menasha, 1912).

large as £104, the equivalent of twenty or more times that amount today. In 1382 he received the additional appointment of Controller of the Petty Customs with permission to exercise the office by deputy. These positions he resigned or lost in 1386. At this time he gave up his apartment over Aldgate, and perhaps was already living in Kent, for he was appointed a justice of the peace there in 1385 and the next year represented Kent in Parliament.[6] On this occasion he had the uncomfortable experience of seeing his friend John of Gaunt stripped of most of his power. In June of the following year Philippa received the last payment of her pension and it is assumed that shortly after that she died.

In the last dozen years of his life Chaucer's position and financial status *Later* fluctuated. In 1388 he sold his annuity, apparently through necessity. How- *Years* ever, the next year, when Richard asserted his royal prerogative, Chaucer was appointed Clerk of the King's Works, in charge of the repairs and upkeep of the royal residences and other properties. It was a fairly lucrative position and in addition he was given special commissions of a similar nature the following year. In September, 1390, he was robbed three times, twice on the same day, of money belonging to the King. The thieves were caught and Chaucer was forgiven the loss of the money. His loss of the clerkship nine months later does not seem to be connected with the robberies. Although the King gave him a reward of £10 in 1393 and granted him an annuity of £20 the next year, he was apparently in financial difficulty, since he was forced to borrow small sums and in 1398 was sued for debt. From about 1395 he seems to have been attached in some capacity to John of Gaunt's son, Henry of Lancaster, and when Henry was declared king on September 30, 1399, Chaucer sent the well-known *Complaint to his Empty Purse.* Four days later Henry IV responded with an annuity of 40 marks. The poet promptly leased a house in Westminster, but lived to enjoy his new security only a few months. According to a late inscription on his tomb in Westminster abbey, he died October 25, 1400.[7]

From this brief sketch of Chaucer's life we may make certain observations *His* which will be helpful in understanding his character as a poet. In the first *Literary* place he was an active man of affairs and must have had a highly developed *Affiliations* practical side. Poetry was for him not a vocation but an avocation. As the eagle says in the *Hous of Fame,*

> For when thy labour doon al ys,
> And hast mad alle thy rekenynges,
> In stede of reste and newe thynges,
> Thou goost hom to thy hous anoon;
> And, also domb as any stoon,

---

[6] On this period of his life see an illuminating paper by Margaret Galway, "Geoffrey Chaucer, J. P. and M. P.," *MLR,* xxxvi (1941). 1-36.

[7] Lewis, for whom he wrote the *Astrolabe,* and Thomas Chaucer, a prominent member of the government in the early part of the fifteenth century, were probably the poet's children. On the latter see Martin B. Ruud, *Thomas Chaucer* (Minneapolis, 1926) and A. C. Baugh, "Kirk's Life Records of Thomas Chaucer," *PMLA,* xlvii (1932). 461-515.

Thou sittest at another book
Tyl fully daswed ys thy look.... (lines 652-8)

He read and he wrote because he wanted to, because there was something within him, as in every true poet, that impelled him to write. But since writing was a pastime he did not always take it too seriously. In the second place, all his life was spent in association with people at the court and in government circles, people for whom French had been not so long ago more familiar than English and whose tastes were formed on things French. Such an environment is sufficient to account for the fact that Chaucer is completely Continental in his literary affiliations. He is remarkably indifferent to English writings, but the *Roman de la Rose* and the poems of Machaut are his missal and breviary; in Latin Ovid is his bible. His indebtedness to recent and contemporary French poets, including Deschamps and Froissart, and to certain classical authors at either first or second hand is the most noticeable characteristic of his early work and has often led to the designation of it as his French period. With his two journeys to Italy he comes under the influence of Italian poetry, the *Divine Comedy* to some extent but more especially certain poems of Boccaccio. With the *Hous of Fame* begins what is often called his Italian period. He never deserts his first love, French poetry, so full of allegorical love visions and their conventions, but he builds on the old framework with new matter from Italy. It is only relatively late—in certain aspects of the *Troilus* and chiefly in the *Canterbury Tales*—that having learned all he could from his teachers and having won the complete mastery of his art, he dares to strike out on his own with confidence and ease. This phase of his career can only be described as his English period.

The Romance of the Rose

The *Roman de la Rose* was the most popular and influential of all French poems in the Middle Ages, and set a fashion in courtly poetry for two centuries in western Europe.[8] This poem Chaucer tells us he translated, and it is altogether likely that it is one of the ways in which he served his apprenticeship in poetry. The version which has come down to us covers only a part of the original, and though generally printed in editions of Chaucer, is probably not all his work. But there are passages from the *Roman* scattered through his poetry as late as the *Canterbury Tales*.

Book of the Duchess

The earliest of Chaucer's original poems of any length is the *Book of the Duchess*. It is an elegy recording in an unusually graceful way the loss which John of Gaunt suffered in 1369 in the death of his first wife, Blanche. After relating a story which he has been reading, the tragic story of Ceys and Alcyone, the poet falls asleep and dreams that he comes upon a knight dressed in black, sitting sorrowfully beneath a tree in the woods. The

[8] It was begun about 1225 by Guillaume de Lorris as a vision picturing in allegorical form the quest of a lover for his ideal, symbolized by a rose. It ran to only about 4000 lines. Some forty years later it was continued by Jean de Meun in a more realistic and satirical vein with not a little that is frankly didactic, until it reached a length of 18,000 lines. The standard edition of the French text is by E. Langlois (5v, 1914-24; SATF). There is a verse translation in English by F. S. Ellis in the Temple Classics.

stranger recognizes his solicitude and tells him the cause of his grief: he has played a game of chess with Fortune and the goddess has taken his queen. The poet seems not to understand quite what he means and he tells him in detail the story of his love—how he met one day a lady, whom he describes: her beauty, accomplishments, gentle ways, soft speech, goodness. Her name was White. He finally persuaded her to accept his heart and they lived in perfect bliss full many a year. All this he relates sadly and at length. Now he has lost her.

> "Allas, sir, how? what may that be?"
> "She ys ded!" "Nay!" "Yis, be my trouthe!"
> "Is that youre los? Be God, hyt ys routhe!"

The simplicity and restraint of this close, the absence of strained sentiment, show the delicate instinct of the artist. The poem is greatly indebted to Machaut, Froissart, Ovid, and other poets, in fact is a mosaic of passages borrowed or remembered, but the concept and, what is more important, the tone and treatment are Chaucer's own.

It is apparently ten years before we get another long poem from his pen, although we can hardly believe that he wrote nothing in all this time. However, he had been to Italy and he had read Dante's great vision of a journey to the Inferno, to Purgatory, and to Paradise. Such earnestness and tragic grandeur were beyond his power of emulation, but the idea of a journey to regions unknown was one which he could turn to his own purposes. The *Hous of Fame,* generally dated about 1379, is a badly proportioned, *The* Hous incomplete, and utterly delightful poem. It is in three books, with all the of Fame epic machinery of invocations, proems, apostrophes, and the like. In the first book the poet dreams that he is in the temple of Venus, where he reads on the wall and tells at length the story of Dido and Æneas. The episode is pleasantly related but is a digression and is artistically one of the blemishes in the poem. At the end he steps out of doors and sees flying toward him an eagle of great size and shining so brightly that it appears to be of gold. It is obviously of the same family as Dante's eagle in the ninth book of the *Purgatorio.* The eagle seizes him in its claws and immediately soars aloft with him, telling him that Jove means to reward him for his long service to Venus and Cupid by taking him to the house of Fame where he will hear abundant tidings of Love's folk. The second book is wholly taken up with the eagle's flight and is one of the most delightfully humorous episodes in literature, what with the eagle's friendliness and loquacity, and the poet's utter terror. The contrast between the eagle's talkativeness and familiarity—he calls him Geoffrey—and the speechless fright of the poet, who can answer only in monosyllables, "Yes" and "Well" and "Nay", is high comedy. Unfortunately the third book, which describes what the poet saw when the eagle set him down outside of Fame's house, carries us to the point where he is about to hear an announcement from "a man of greet auctoritee" and leaves us still waiting for the expected news. For at this point the poem breaks off. Scholars have interpreted the poem in different ways and taken it perhaps too seriously. Some have seen in it an allegory of the poet's life,[9] others a conventional love vision of a kind for which French literature furnished many models,[10] and still others have tried to solve the mystery of the news which the poet is about to hear. One explanation [11] holds that Chaucer's purpose was to introduce a series of stories as in the *Legend of Good Women* and the *Canterbury Tales*. But it seems likely from an allusion at the beginning of Book Three to "this lytel laste bok" that the poem as we have it is nearly complete and that the announcement was something which Chaucer decided not to write or perhaps later suppressed.

If the *Hous of Fame* was left unfinished, it would be far from the only work which Chaucer began and did not complete. At about this time he

Anelida and Arcite
apparently started what was to be a considerable poem of *Anelida and Arcite*, but after some three hundred lines he abandoned the project. It is a pity that it remains such a fragment, if for no other reason than that it keeps from the full recognition of its worth the beautiful "Complaint" of Anelida, which with its perfect balance of strophe and antistrophe is one of the most finished and charming examples of the type in medieval literature. To this period may also belong some of the shorter pieces such as the *Complaint unto Pity* and *A Complaint to his Lady*.

Parlement of Foules
The *Parlement of Foules* is clearly an occasional poem, but the occasion for which it was written is not so clear. It takes its theme from the popular belief that on St. Valentine's day the birds choose their mates, and it accordingly represents a gathering of birds for that purpose. Dame Nature holds on her hand a formel or female eagle of great beauty and goodness, for whom three royal and noble eagles make their respective pleas. Although Nature advises in favor of the royal suitor, the formel asks and is granted a year in which to make her choice. There is much amusing by-play over the impatience of the lesser birds and the varied opinions that they express, but one cannot escape the thought that the essence of the poem is the competition of the three noble eagles for the hand of the worthy formel. The most commonly accepted interpretation is that the poem celebrates the betrothal of Richard II to Anne of Bohemia, whom he married in January, 1382. The rival suitors according to this theory were Friedrich of Meissen and Charles VI of France.[12] Other interpretations have been suggested,[13]

[9] Sandras, Ten Brink, and early scholars quite generally.
[10] W. O. Sypherd, *Studies in Chaucer's Hous of Fame* (1907; *Chaucer Soc.*, 2nd Ser., 39).
[11] J. M. Manly, "What Is Chaucer's *Hous of Fame?*" *Kittredge Anniversary Papers* (Boston, 1913), pp. 73-81.
[12] The interpretation was proposed by Koch in 1877 and modified by O. F. Emerson, "The Suitors in Chaucer's *Parlement of Foules*," *MP*, VIII (1910-11). 45-62; reprinted in *Chaucer Essays and Studies* (Cleveland, 1929). The objections to it were summed up by J. M. Manly, "What Is the *Parlement of Foules?*" *Festschrift für Lorenz Morsbach* (Halle, 1913; *Studien zur englischen Phil.*, 50), pp. 279-290.
[13] Edith Rickert, "A New Interpretation of the *Parlement of Foules*," *MP*, XVIII (1920), 1-29, identified the formel eagle with Philippa, a daughter of John of Gaunt. More recently Haldeen Braddy, in "*The Parlement of Foules*: A New Proposal," *PMLA*, XLVI (1931). 1007-1019, and in subsequent papers, has suggested a connection with negotiations in 1377 for the marriage of Richard with the princess Marie of France. For parallels to the general situation see Willard E. Farnham, "The Contending Lovers," *PMLA*, XXXV (1920). 247-323.

and if none of them carries complete conviction, the fact need not detract from our enjoyment of the poem as one of Chaucer's smaller but most finished productions.

At about this time, somewhere in the early eighties, Chaucer translated *Boethius* the *Consolation of Philosophy* of Boethius,[14] if we may judge by the fact that its influence is very noticeable in such poems as *Palamon and Arcite* (included in the *Canterbury Tales* as the *Knight's Tale*) and *Troilus and Criseyde,* which were written, it would seem, between 1382 and 1385-6. It is significant as an indication of the range of Chaucer's interests, but as a translation it leaves much to be desired. Chaucer's prose both here and in the *Astrolabe* (1391), and in the prose tales included in the *Canterbury Tales* as well, is formless and undistinguished.

Troilus and Criseyde [15] is at once Chaucer's longest complete poem and *Troilus* his greatest artistic achievement. In some 8000 lines, in stanzas of rime *and* royal, it tells a tragic love story from the time Troilus first sees Criseyde, a *Criseyde* young and beautiful widow whose father, Calchas, has abandoned Troy and gone over to the Greek side, until she proves unfaithful to him, and death puts an end to his suffering. For three skilfully ordered books the story rises steadily to a climax when Troilus, with the aid of Pandarus, his friend and the uncle of Criseyde, having overcome her natural caution and conventional reserve, finally possesses her completely, both body and soul. For three years they are united in a mutual love that could not be more complete. Then in the last two books events move inevitably toward their tragic conclusion. Through an exchange of prisoners Criseyde must go to her father in the Greek camp. She leaves, swearing undying love and fidelity and promising to find some way of returning before ten days are past. But by the time the ten days are up her handsome Greek escort, Diomede, has caused her to change her mind, and within a few months she has given him the brooch which had been Troilus's parting gift to her when she left.

The main features of the story Chaucer took from a poem by Boccaccio called the *Filostrato.*[16] Boccaccio had found the latter part of it in Benoît

[14] Boethius illustrates the medieval conception of tragedy, the fall of a great man from his high estate. In the innermost counsels of the emperor Theodoric, he was accused of disloyalty, thrown into prison, and eventually (524) put to death. The *Consolation of Philosophy* was written in prison, and was so in harmony with Christian teaching on the questions which it discusses that it became one of the most widely read books of the Middle Ages. For the earlier translation due to King Alfred, see above, p. 99. It was later translated by Queen Elizabeth. See Howard R. Patch, *The Tradition of Boethius: A Study of His Importance in Medieval Culture* (1935).

[15] The definitive edition of the poem is that of R. K. Root (Princeton, 1926). Professor Root has settled a long controversy over the date of the poem by identifying a rare astronomical phenomenon mentioned in Book III, which shows that it could not have been finished before May, 1385. Cf. R. K. Root and H. N. Russell, "A Planetary Date for Chaucer's *Troilus*," *PMLA*, XXXIX (1924). 48-63. See also Thomas A. Kirby, *Chaucer's* Troilus: *A Study in Courtly Love* (University, La., 1940; *Louisiana State Univ. Stud.,* No. 39).

[16] As is well known, the story of the Trojan war was familiar to the Middle Ages not through Homer but in two late accounts by Dares Phrygius and Dictys Cretensis. These were made the basis, about 1155, of the French poem by Benoît mentioned in the text. An account in Latin prose, the *Historia Trojana*, was taken from Benoît's poem about 1287 by Guido della Colonna (ed. N. E. Griffin, Cambridge, Mass., 1936; *Mediaeval Acad. of Amer.,* Pub.

Relation to Boccaccio's Filostrato de Sainte-More, who had hit upon the idea of filling out with a love story the lagging intervals between periods of fighting in his *Roman de Troie.* All that part of the story which precedes Criseyde's departure for the Greek camp is due to Boccaccio, and he also created the character of Pandarus. But while Chaucer's indebtedness to the Italian poem is very great, his own contribution is still greater. He has basically altered the character of Pandarus and he has added complexity and mystery to Criseyde until she is much more than Troilus's mistress. Without losing its essential qualities of medieval romance or abandoning the conventions of courtly love, *Troilus and Criseyde* has taken on many of the characteristics of the psychological novel. It should be remembered that less than 2600 lines in Chaucer's poem have their counterparts in Boccaccio.

The Character of Criseyde What gives the story its chief interest and acts as a constant challenge to understanding is the character of Criseyde. She combines the qualities that will always appeal in woman, beauty and mystery. Her behavior is never transparent and we try without complete success to penetrate the mingling of impulses and the complex workings of her mind. In her early defensive attitude toward the advances of Troilus there is probably a mixture of caution and the courtly love tradition which expected the woman to be difficult to approach. She is more interested in her reputation than her virtue. Her ultimate surrender is brought about partly by circumstance, but when she yields it is because she has made her own decision. How much of her emotion is the womanly love of being loved we cannot say, but during the three years that she gives herself to Troilus her affection is genuine and complete. When finally as a result of separation she abandons him for Diomede she reproaches herself, but her love is not the kind that is proof against every storm. Her father was a traitor and an opportunist; she was of a yielding disposition, "slydynge of corage." When in the end she gives Diomede gifts which Troilus had given her, we cannot but admit that she was without depth of feeling. And yet withal, her faults spring from weakness rather than baseness of character, and the poet in pleading that we judge her not too harshly says, "I would excuse her if I could."

The Legend of Good Women The *Legend of Good Women* was begun, according to the prologue, as a penance imposed by Queen Alceste for his offenses against the God of Love in writing the *Troilus* and the *Romance of the Rose,* which speak slightingly of women. Chaucer refers to the work elsewhere as the *Seintes Legende of Cupide,* and it was to be a collection of nineteen stories about women famous for their faithfulness in love. A twentieth and longer legend of Alceste would doubtless have completed the whole. The most interesting part of the poem is the long Prologue, with its frank enjoyment of nature

---

No. 26). Boccaccio adopted from Benoît the love story, keeping only as much of the war and the fighting as he needed for background to the Troilus and Criseyde story. The *Filostrato* can be had most conveniently with an English translation in *The Filostrato of Giovanni Boccaccio* by N. E. Griffin and A. B. Myrick (Philadelphia, 1929), with an excellent introduction on the development of the story. See also Karl Young, *The Origin and Development of the Story of Troilus and Criseyde* (Chaucer Soc., 1908).

and the spring, its amusing picture of the God of Love's anger at the poet, the Queen's generous intercession, the partly gratuitous enumeration of his works, and the penance that is imposed upon him. Some of the legends had been written earlier, but even so, the poem as it has come down to us is unfinished, breaking off in the midst of the ninth legend. It has been suggested that Chaucer found the idea too monotonous. If the suggestion recently made [17] that he was writing the poem for Joan, the widow of the Black Prince, is accepted, we might assume that her death in August, 1385, removed the immediate occasion for writing it. It does not make any easier our understanding the fact that he subjected the Prologue to a very careful revision in 1394; one does not ordinarily devote so much time and labor to the preliminary part of an unfinished work. In any case, if he abandoned the project originally to devote himself to the *Canterbury Tales,* we cannot feel regret, and to this, his last and best-known work, we turn in the next chapter.

[17] Margaret Galway, "Chaucer's Sovereign Lady: A Study of the Prologue to the *Legend* and Related Poems," *MLR*, xxxiii (1938). 145-199. Objection to so early a date, based on Chaucer's supposed use of Deschamps' *Lai de Franchise,* has little force. See Marian Lossing, "The Prologue to the Legend of Good Women and the *Lai de Franchise,*" *SP,* xxxix (1942). 15-35.

XVII
Chaucer: II

The Canterbury Tales

If Chaucer had never written anything more than the works considered in the preceding chapter, he would have been recognized as a great poet, but he would not have been so popular a poet since his popularity today rests in large measure upon the *Canterbury Tales*.[1] Any one who knows anything about Chaucer knows the *Canterbury Tales*. He knows the General Prologue with its wonderful portrait gallery of pilgrims, and he knows at least some of the tales. And he would be willing to admit perhaps that such a work deserves closer acquaintance.

The Framed Tale
It would seem that about 1387 Chaucer, having finished or laid aside the *Legend of Good Women,* conceived the idea of writing a collection of stories of more varied character. He doubtless had on hand some material suitable for his purpose, such as the *Palamon and Arcite,* which in the Prologue to the *Legend of Good Women* he had said was little known, and "the lyf also of Seynt Cecile," mentioned in the same place. The idea of binding a collection of stories together in a framework is a familiar one in literature. It extends from ancient India to Uncle Remus. Chaucer's plan was to relate 120 stories and have them told by a group of pilgrims, thirty in number, journeying from London to Canterbury. Each pilgrim agrees to tell two tales each way. Harry Bailey, the Host of the Tabard Inn, where Chaucer and the other travelers assemble, agrees to go along and act as master of ceremonies. It was an admirable method for bringing together people of various types and different social classes. The group includes a knight and an esquire, his son, professional men like the doctor and the lawyer, a merchant, a shipman, various representatives of the religious orders such as the prioress, the monk, the honest parson, and the friar, a substantial farmer, a miller, a reeve, a London cook, and several craftsmen, not to attempt a complete list. Nearly all are described with such particularity as to suggest that in some cases at least Chaucer was drawing his portraits from individuals in real life.[2] How the suggestion for such a plan came to him, if not from experience, we cannot say. Boccaccio had used a somewhat

---

[1] Full critical apparatus is provided for the study of the *Canterbury Tales* in J. M. Manly and Edith Rickert, *The Text of the Canterbury Tales* (8v, Chicago, 1940). A new collection of *Sources and Analogues of Chaucer's Canterbury Tales* has been prepared by a group of scholars under the editorship of W. F. Bryan and Germaine Dempster (Chicago, 1941).

[2] For one or two plausible identifications and a number of interesting speculations see J. M. Manly, *Some New Light on Chaucer* (1926).

analogous idea in the *Decameron,* a collection of a hundred stories told by *Earlier* ten people of the gentle class who have retired within a palace to escape the *Examples* plague. It is unlikely that Chaucer knew the *Decameron,* since if he had known it he would certainly have made use of it. In any case, Chaucer's plan admits of greater discrepancies among the pilgrims, greater variety in the stories they can appropriately tell, and greater opportunity for incidental adventure. A closer analogy is found in the *Novelle* [3] of Giovanni Sercambi, written about 1374. Here we have actually the device of a pilgrimage, with a leader and by-play among the pilgrims, but the stories are all told by the author. It is unlikely that Chaucer was acquainted with this collection for the same reason as that which we have alleged in the case of the *Decameron.* At present we can best believe that Chaucer's plan for the *Canterbury Tales* was a happy idea of his own.

The plan laid down in the General Prologue was only partially carried *The* out. There are but twenty-four tales, and of these, two are interrupted before *Unfinished* the end and two break off shortly after they get under way. Even before *Character* Chaucer laid aside the work, possibly about 1395, there are indications that *of the* he had altered his original intention. At the beginning of the *Parson's Tale* *Work* the Host says, "Now lakketh us no tales mo than oon," showing that Chaucer then had in mind only one tale from each pilgrim. There are many marks of the unfinished state in which he left the work. In putting his life of St. Cecilia in the mouth of the Second Nun he neglected to make the necessary revision and she accordingly refers to herself as an unworthy *son* of Eve. The Man of Law says he will speak in prose, but instead he tells the story of Constance in well-turned stanzas. The *Shipman's Tale* was apparently written for the Wife of Bath, with the result that this "good felawe" whose beard had been shaken by many a tempest alludes to himself as a woman; and some students have seen equally clear evidence that the *Merchant's Tale* was originally intended for one of the religious pilgrims.[4] Small matters like this are not serious. What is much more troublesome is the fact that we cannot now tell in what order the tales would have ultimately been arranged.

The beginning is clear enough. When the party has ridden a short dis- *The* tance out of town Harry Bailey bids them draw lots and by good luck or *"Groups"* manipulation the lot falls to the Knight to tell the first tale. He relates the story of the love of two friends, Palamon and Arcite, for the same lady. When he finishes, the pilgrims all express enthusiastic approval and the Host, pleased at so good a start, calls upon the Monk to tell the next tale. But the Miller is drunk and unruly and insists on telling his story in spite of all entreaty. His indecent tale is about a carpenter, and when he finishes, the Reeve, who "was of carpenteris craft," takes offense and tells an equally

---

[3] Karl Young, "The Plan of the Canterbury Tales," *Kittredge Anniv. Papers* (Boston, 1913), pp. 405-417, and Robert A. Pratt and Karl Young in *Sources and Analogues,* pp. 1-81.

[4] The present writer believes that the evidence clearly points to the Friar ("The Original Teller of the *Merchant's Tale,*" *MP,* xxxv (1937). 15-26); for a dissenting opinion see Germaine Dempster, *ibid.,* xxxvi (1938). 1-8.

vulgar story about a miller. Chaucer has evidently an eye to contrast and means to offset the seriousness of the Knight's story with these two in a lighter vein. The Cook next exclaims with glee over the Reeve's story and offers to tell a joke about an apprentice in the city. But Chaucer must have felt that three humorous stories in a row would be too many and stopped after fifty lines. Up to this point the sequence of tales is clear; the incompleteness of the Cook's Tale, however, leaves us with no hint as to what was to follow. Other stories are bound together into groups in a similar way, but the arrangement of the groups is not indicated. In some of the stories and links there are occasional allusions to the time of day and to places along the way. These apparently guided scribes or editors, as we should say, of manuscripts, but there is great variation among the early texts. Modern editions usually follow the arrangement of the Ellesmere manuscript or adopt an arrangement of the groups that does least violence to the local allusions. The precise order of all the tales is something which at his death Chaucer himself had not settled.

Dramatic   The *Canterbury Tales* is more than a collection of stories. It is a pageant
Character   of fourteenth-century life, a *comédie humaine,* in which a group of thirty people of various classes act their parts on this mundane stage in such a way as to reveal their private lives and habits, their changing moods as well as their prevailing dispositions, their qualities good and bad. Much of this life is revealed not by the stories they tell but by their behavior along the road and their remarks by the way. Chaucer never lets us forget that the stories in his collection are part of a pilgrimage, incidental to it in fact, and in the links between the tales he accomplishes his end in a variety of ways. Most important is the part played by Harry Bailey, the hearty, boisterous Host, with his frankness, his rough humor, his unconscious profanity which so shocks the Parson, and his good sense. He twits the pilgrims, draws the shy ones out, shows a clumsy deference to those entitled to it, smooths over differences, and keeps the company generally in good spirits. There are, of course, quarrels, and these are used most effectively to introduce some of the stories. The Reeve's resentment of the Miller's tale has been mentioned. A similar feud breaks out later between the Friar and the Summoner and results in the telling by each of them of a story defaming the other's calling. A humorous and realistic touch is given when some story proves tiresome and the speaker is cut short. The effect is particularly ironic when it is Chaucer's own story that the Host objects to, but it is a useful device, too, when the lugubrious tragedies of the Monk threaten to weary the reader as well as the original company. One of the most realistic incidents is that in which the pilgrims are overtaken at Boughton-under-Blee by a Canon and his Yeoman. The Yeoman talks too freely about his master's private affairs and the Canon rides off "for verray sorwe and shame." Whether the Yeoman tells a story because Chaucer noticed that his pilgrims were short one of their thirty or because he saw an opportunity of using in this way his knowledge of the frauds practised by alchemists we shall never

know. In any case, the incident contributes much to our feeling that a minor drama is being unfolded all along the route.

A lesser unity is achieved at least once within the whole by the concentration in a fairly close sequence of several stories which deal in one way or another with the problem of marriage. The question is opened by the Wife of Bath, whose philosophy of life is distinctly earthy. She has had five husbands and is not unwilling to take a sixth. She openly renounces the idea that virginity is to be preferred by all to matrimony. But she is equally frank in describing her former husbands and in telling how she maintained the upper hand over all of them. Her theory, confirmed by practice, has been that happiness in marriage depends on the acceptance of the wife's mastery, and the story she tells of the knight and the loathly lady is meant to illustrate and enforce this view. Any debate that might have been provoked by a doctrine so contrary to medieval notions is prevented by the quarrel between the Friar and the Summoner, which bursts into flame as soon as she has finished, but when each has told his story and cooled his wrath the Host calls on the Clerk for a tale. The tale which he tells is one of a woman's submission to her husband, the story of Patient Griselda, whose patience was finally rewarded with happiness. There is sharp contrast at least between the Wife's and the Clerk's stories. The Merchant next tells the story of January and May, a fabliau about an old man who marries a young wife and is shamefully tricked by her. It introduces a somewhat different marriage problem. The *Squire's Tale* which follows is a fragment of Eastern romance and has nothing to do with marriage, nor has the *Franklin's Tale,* which is a story of generosity and honor put to a severe test. But in the story told by the Franklin the married life of Arviragus and Dorigen is so harmonious and happy, and their relations are governed by such mutual tolerance and forbearance as well as confidence and love, that it is easy to see in it the ideal solution of the marriage relationship. Their vows express this forbearance and in a long aside the Franklin voices the conviction that

> Love wol not been constreynëd by maistrye.
> Whan maistrie comth, the God of Love anon
> Beteth his wynges, and farewel, he is gon!

The "Marriage Group," as the sequence here surveyed is called, is brought to a close with the *Franklin's Tale* and it is thus natural to suppose that the views of the Franklin were those of Chaucer himself.[5]

The So-Called Marriage Group

[5] The existence of a Marriage Group was first suggested by Miss Hammond (*Manual,* p. 256), but the full exposition of the idea is due to Professor Kittredge, in an article called "Chaucer's Discussion of Marriage," *MP,* IX (1912). 435-467. A number of scholars deny a conscious intention on Chaucer's part to present a marriage "group," and point out that various aspects of marriage and "maistrie" in marriage are presented in several other tales as well. Full reference to the scholarly literature on the question will be found in the bibliographies mentioned on p. 249.

*An
Anthology
of
Medieval
Literature*

Viewed merely as a collection of separate pieces, the *Canterbury Tales* in its extent and variety offers a remarkable anthology of medieval literature. The courtly romance is represented well enough by the *Knight's Tale* or the story of Constance told by the Man of Law, not to mention the fragmentary *Squire's Tale,* while we have in *Sir Thopas* a parody of the more popular type of romance, such as *Guy of Warwick* and *Bevis of Hampton.* The *Franklin's Tale* is a Breton lay, with its setting in Brittany, its fidelity of true lovers, and its element of the supernatural or marvelous. The *Physician's Tale* of Virginius and his daughter, whom he kills to save her honor, is the retelling of a classical legend, like many examples in Old French literature and like Chaucer's own "Ceys and Alcyone" in the *Book of the Duchess.* The *Wife of Bath's Tale* is a folk-tale which was often given literary form. The coarser type of story is represented by a quarter of the collection, by the fabliaux of the Miller, Reeve, Merchant, and others. Two widespread religious types appear in the saint's legend (St. Cecilia) told by the Second Nun and in the miracle of the Virgin related so beautifully by the Prioress. The Monk's numerous examples of great men who have fallen from their high estate to misery and death are tragedies, as the Middle Ages understood the word, while the story of the three rogues told by the Pardoner is an exemplum, one of thousands of such stories with which preachers adorned their sermons and pointed a moral. The sermon or didactic treatise, though hardly to be considered a tale in the most liberal sense of the word, is represented by the *Parson's Tale* and by Chaucer's own second attempt, the *Melibeus.* Finally, we have a truly magnificent example of the beast fable, familiar to every one in the Middle Ages through *Reynard the Fox,* in the story of Chauntecleer and Dame Pertelot which the Nun's Priest tells. Without forcing matters we might note that there are even examples of the short lyric in the "Envoy" to the *Clerk's Tale* and the "Invocation to Mary" at the beginning of the *Second Nun's Tale.* The *Canterbury Tales* is a miniature five-foot shelf of medieval literature.

*Chaucer's
Character
as a Poet*

When we look at Chaucer's poetry as a whole and try to comprehend its character in its larger aspects, we must recognize that this character was due partly to his environment, partly to himself—the mysterious combination of hereditary qualities that made him the kind of person he was. Environment made him a court poet. He wrote for the circle in which he lived; therefore we see him as a graceful occasional poet and a teller of tales. The tastes of the court, as we have said, had been formed on French literature [6] and as his environment determined his education and literary background, so he was attracted by, and his literary tastes were almost wholly formed upon, the literature of France and Rome and later of medieval Italy. He scarcely refers to English writings, and when he does it is to parody the romances or to refer somewhat humorously to riming rum-ram-ruf. Of course he was the heir of previous centuries of English civilization and of a language adequate for his purpose, but what he owes to previous English

[6] Cf. the note on Richard II's books on p. 142.

writers is slight in comparison with his debt to French and Latin and Italian books. Others had translated and adapted French works before, but nobody else, either in his own day or before or after his day, so completely transferred to English the whole spirit of polite literature in Europe. This much of his poetic character comes from the accident of environment; the rest comes from himself. Environment could not make him the incomparable storyteller that he was. And environment alone will not account for the largeness and sanity of his mind. It may have taught him to keep his own counsel on political and public questions or to keep his opinions on such matters out of his poetry. But it may be that he was not easily wrought up over issues which at times provoke the quiet laughter of the gods. He was by nature tolerant, gentle, whimsical, good-humored, at all events in his poetry. And he had an incomparable sense of humor. His humor is all-pervasive. It flickers and glows and occasionally flashes like lightning in a summer sky. At times he seems unable to repress it, as when in the *Book of the Duchess,* a poem upon a sad occasion, he offers the God of Sleep the best gift he can think of, a feather bed, if he will make him sleep like Alcyone. But this is only at times. When the occasion really calls for it he can be serious, and he is capable of deep pathos.

Chaucer is sometimes denied the rank of a great poet on the ground that he lacked the higher seriousness, that his poetry is without great themes nobly conceived. It is true that he is not given to lofty and impassioned sentiments. His *Paradise Lost* is but the earthly paradise that Troilus lost, and his *Purgatorio* is generally such as lovers and lesser mortals experience in this life. But no one can deny the dignity and seriousness of the *Troilus* at certain great moments in the poem. We know that he was capable of moral earnestness and deep feeling, and if he chose more often to be cheerful and in general to devote himself to lighter themes, there are some students of medieval literature—and not the least devoted among them—who rest content with his choice.

XVIII

Other Contemporaries of Chaucer

When Chaucer at the close of *Troilus and Criseyde* addressed his book to a fellow poet with the salutation "O moral Gower," he was paying his friend a sincere compliment, little supposing that the adjective would in time acquire a connotation anything but helpful to John Gower's reputation with modern readers. But we have become suspicious of literature aimed at our improvement, and are prepared to be bored by anything to which a moral, or the word *moral,* is attached. Gower is the victim of this prejudice. But it must also be admitted that he suffers by comparison with his greater contemporary. Although the names of Chaucer and Gower were constantly coupled together with equal respect throughout the fifteenth and sixteenth centuries, nowadays we rightly prefer Chaucer's humanity and humor to the unrelieved earnestness of Gower's larger works. Yet modern criticism has sometimes gone too far in dismissing this dignified figure with an impatient shrug.

It is surprising how little we know about a man who was personally known to both Richard II and Henry IV and who has left us a body of poetry that fills four large volumes. He was of a Kentish family, and had considerable wealth, which it is conjectured he made in trade. But if we decline to identify with the poet a John Gower who was connected with some questionable transactions in land, we know him only for his friendship with Chaucer, later strained, as the owner of certain manors in Norfolk and Suffolk, and as a liberal benefactor in his will of churches in Southwark.[1] In his later years he had an apartment in the priory of St. Mary Overy, in Southwark. Late in life (1398) he married Agnes Groundolf, perhaps his second wife. No children are mentioned in his will, which was probated Oct. 24, 1408. He died presumably in that month and was buried in the priory church, now St. Saviour's, where his tomb can still be seen.

The effigy on Gower's tomb shows the poet's head resting on three folio volumes bearing the titles *Speculum Meditantis, Vox Clamantis,* and *Confessio Amantis.* These are his three principal works.[2] Though their titles are

---

[1] In 1393 as an esquire in the service of Henry Earl of Derby he was given a collar. Two months after the Earl became Henry IV he granted (Nov. 21, 1399) "for life to the king's esquire John Gower two pipes of wine of Gascony yearly." *CPR, 1399-1401,* p. 128 and *CCR, 1399-1402,* p. 78. On Dec. 11, 1397 Thomas Caudre, canon in the priory of St. Mary Overy in Southwerke was bound to do or procure no hurt or harm to John Gower; *CCR, 1396-99,* p. 238. Cf. also *CCR, 1402-5,* p. 484.

[2] *The Complete Works of John Gower,* ed. G. C. Macaulay (4v, Oxford, 1899-1902). Cf. George R. Coffman, "John Gower in His Most Significant Role," *Univ. of Colorado Stud.,* Ser. B, Vol. ᴎ, No. 4 (1945). 52-61.

in Latin the poems are in French, Latin, and English respectively. The first, also known as *Speculum Hominis* or *Mirour de l'Omme* (before 1381), consists of some 30,000 lines of French verse. It treats in great detail the Seven Deadly Sins and their "daughters," then in equal fullness the corresponding Virtues, and shows the effects of the conflict between the two groups in all classes of society from Pope and cardinals down to craftsmen and laborers, concluding with a long tribute to the Virgin. The work is carefully planned and in spite of its great length is no more tedious than other works of its kind. It shows general resemblances to treatises like the *Somme le Roi* and the *Miroir du Monde,* but no immediate source has been found.[3] *Mirour de l'Omme*

The *Vox Clamantis,* a Latin poem of 10,000 lines, was written shortly after the Peasants' Revolt in 1381, of which the first third of the poem gives a vivid account. This part may have been a later addition, for the major theme of the poem is a representation, like that in the *Mirour de l'Omme,* of the evils of society—clergy, knighthood, peasantry—and of man as a microcosm in which the sins of the world are abundantly exhibited. Gower has borrowed extensively from previous Latin poets, classical and medieval, but he obviously handles his Latin fluently and forcefully. The *Confessio Amantis* is the work of Gower's later years, when he had come to realize that a didactic intent unrelieved by entertaining features does not win many readers: *Vox Clamantis* *Confessio Amantis*

> Bot for men sein, and soth it is,
> That who that al of wisdom writ
> It dulleth ofte a mannes wit
> To him that schal it aldai rede,
> For thilke cause, if that ye rede,
> I wolde go the middel weie
> And wryte a bok betwen the tweie,
> Somwhat of lust, somwhat of lore. . . .

He will therefore write of Love. He is himself one of Love's unrewarded servants. Venus hears his complaints and bids him confess to her priest, Genius. But a priest hears confessions of sin, and so the scheme of the poem is the Seven Deadly Sins, expounded by the priest, and applied, not always very easily, to the lover's problems. Stories illustrate the various points as they arise. It is obvious that as a framework for a collection of tales, Gower's plan is much inferior to Chaucer's. But to criticize it on this score is quite unfair. It assumes that the framework is an excuse for telling a series of stories, whereas in Gower's case the stories are secondary, a concession to his public. He is still the moralist and preacher; he has not abandoned the didactic purpose, but is attempting to make his teaching more palatable by a liberal use of tales and anecdotes. Under the circumstances it is surprising how well he can tell a story. He is neither dramatic nor humorous

[3] See above, p. 202, and cf. R. Elfreda Fowler, *Une Source française des poèmes de Gower* (Macon, 1905).

His nature was essentially sober, but his narrative is always fluent, generally rapid, and at times marked by genuine grace of both language and metre. The popularity of the *Confessio Amantis* is attested by more than forty extant manuscripts.[4]

Gower as Poet

Gower is not a great poet. He is an earnest man with a message for his times. He is alarmed at the way the world is going. He exhorts the King, preaches to the public. He is for reform within the established order. He is opposed to Lollardry, and the Peasants' Revolt fills him with horror. What more can the serious and thoughtful layman do than try to arouse his contemporaries to action?

Barbour's Bruce

If we look to the north, to Scotland, we meet at this time, in addition to some of the poems in the alliterative revival, the famous work of John Barbour called *The Bruce* (1376),[5] relating in more than 13,000 lines the guerilla warfare between Robert Bruce and the English. The poet is equally stirred by the deeds of Douglas, Bruce's loyal supporter, and indeed closes his poem with Douglas's adventures in Spain, in which he met his death. Barbour was Archdeacon of Aberdeen and died in 1395. He calls his poem a romance, and the style and spirit of the narrative partly justify the designation, but this should not blind us to the fact that Barbour was of a studious nature and a man of wide reading. He meant his work to be taken as history, and in many places his narrative is believed to embody authentic tradition.[6] Barbour's younger contemporary, Andrew of Wyntoun, held *The Bruce* in such regard that he incorporated a portion of it in his *Original Chronicle*.[7]

Andrew of Wyntoun

This, in its 30,000 lines of eight-syllable verse, covers the period from the origin of the world (whence its name) down to the year 1408. In form and matter it belongs with *The Bruce*, although chronologically it falls in the fifteenth century. It was completed shortly after 1420.

Increasing Use of Prose

It is worth a moment's reflection that none of Chaucer's writings in verse leave us with the feeling that they could just as well have been in prose. This is not true of all his contemporaries. The *Mirour de l'Omme* and the *Vox Clamantis* deal largely with subjects for which prose would be appropriate, and the same may be said of Wyntoun's *Chronicle*. As the fourteenth century wears on we notice the greater use of prose, for reasons which become more influential in the fifteenth century and which will be discussed

---

[4] Gower is the author of a series of *Cinkante Balades* of love and a *Traitié* consisting of eighteen additional balades in French for married lovers. Both sequences are among the most graceful of his poems. He also composed other short pieces and a *Chronica Tripertita* in Latin, begun in 1387 and continued at intervals, dealing with events in the later years of Richard's reign.

[5] Edited by W. W. Skeat (4v, 1870-89; EETSES, 11, 21, 29, 55; reprinted in 1894 for the STS, 31-33). On the Scottish literature of the period see T. F. Henderson, *Scottish Vernacular Literature* (3ed., Edinburgh, 1910) and Friedrich Brie, *Die Nationale Literatur Schottlands von den Anfängen bis zur Renaissance* (Halle, 1937).

[6] The contention of J. T. T. Brown, *The Wallace and the Bruce Restudied* (Bonn, 1900; Bonner Beiträge zur Anglistik, vi), that the text as we have it was seriously tampered with by John Ramsay, the copyist, at the end of the fifteenth century, has been resented but not disproved, and has something to recommend it.

[7] The best edition is that of F. J. Amours (6v, Edinburgh, 1903-14; STS, 50, 53, 54, 56, 57, 63).

in the next chapter. Here we are concerned chiefly with the writings of three men, Mandeville, Trevisa, and Wyclif.

The *Travels of Sir John Mandeville* is one of the best-known books of the Middle Ages. Everyone knows about the incredible things he pretends to have seen: the gigantic race with one eye in the middle of the forehead, people with no heads but with eyes in their shoulders, others with great ears hanging to their knees, snails so great that many persons may lodge in their shells, and scores of other marvels. Setting out to write merely a guide-book for those who might be making a pilgrimage to Jerusalem, he gives the usual account of routes, and towns, and places of interest at the more important points. But when this part of his plan is finished he continues with his travels in Egypt, Asia Minor, Persia, India, Cathay or China, and many other places. He professes to have been born at St. Albans, to have left England in 1322, and, after spending years on his vast journey, to have arrived at Liége, where he was persuaded to write down his experiences.[8] The original, composed apparently between 1366 and 1371,[9] was in French, but it was soon translated into Latin and English. There are at least two translations into English, one from the Latin and one from the French original.[10] The earliest English manuscripts are of the beginning of the fifteenth century, but it cannot be doubted that the translations were made soon after the original appeared.

In the last fifty years the sources of Mandeville's *Travels* have been minutely traced, and it is now known that the whole work is a compilation which could have been written without the author's venturing a foot from home. What is more, it has even been thought the work of a Liége physician generally known as John of Burgundy or John with the beard (*ad Barbam*), the author of other works including medical treatises and a lapidary.[11] The

Travels of Sir John Mandeville

[8] References to thirty-four different John Mandevilles in medieval England are gathered together by K. W. Cameron, "A Discovery in *John de Mandevilles,*" *Speculum,* xi (1936). 351-359.

[9] Arpad Steiner, "The Date of Composition of *Mandeville's Travels,*" *Speculum,* ix (1934). 144-147.

[10] The version translated from the French is edited from a Cotton MS by P. Hamelius (2v, 1919-23; *EETS,* 153-154). Previous printed editions of Mandeville are all incomplete until that of A. W. Pollard (in modern spelling, 1900). The Egerton MS, edited by Sir George Warner for the Roxburghe Club (1889) with valuable apparatus, contains a composite text derived in part from one of the versions from French and in part from the version based on the Latin translation. The original French is available only in the Roxburghe volume noted above.

[11] In the fourth part (now lost) of Jean d'Outremeuse's *Myreur des Histoires* a note recorded that on Nov. 12, 1372 there died at Liége a man of distinguished birth who was content to be known as Jean de Bourgogne, called "with the beard." On his deathbed he revealed himself to Jean d'Outremeuse and made him his executor. In his will he called himself John de Mandeville, knight, count of Montfort in England and lord of the Isle of Campdi and of the castle Pérouse. However, having had the misfortune in his country to kill a count who is not named, he undertook to traverse the three parts of the world, coming to Liége in 1343. Having sprung from the nobility, he preferred to keep himself hidden. He was moreover a great naturalist, profound philosopher and astrologer, adding to this an unusual knowledge of physic, seldom being mistaken in a diagnosis. He was buried with the Guillemins. Now, as a fact, there existed down to the French Revolution a tomb in the church of the Guillemins with an epitaph several times independently copied down: Hic iacet nobilis Dominus Joannes de Montevilla Miles, alias dictus ad Barbam. . . . etc., recording that he was born in England, was of the medical profession, and died Feb. 7, 1372. For other considerations complicating the

theory of Hamelius [12] that the author was the Liége poet and chronicler Jean d'Outremeuse rests on rather slender grounds and as yet has not found many adherents.

Trevisa   Less romantic but no less important is the work of John Trevisa. Born in Cornwall, he entered Oxford in 1362, became a fellow of Queen's College, and for more than forty years was vicar of Berkeley and chaplain to three of the Lords Berkeley. His most important translations were made at the command of Thomas, Lord Berkeley, a true patron of learning. Trevisa died in 1402.[13] Apart from his having translated the Bible, a matter still in dispute, his most important works are his translations of Higden's *Polychronicon*,[14] which he finished in 1387, and of the *De Proprietatibus Rerum* of Bartholomew Anglicus,[15] completed in 1398. He is to be credited with the translation of a rule of princes, *De Regimine Principum*, found in a single MS. Among his shorter renderings are the *Gospel of Nicodemus*, the *Dialogus inter Militem et Clericum*, a discussion of the secular power of the Church, and the *Defensio Curatorum*, translated from a sermon of Richard FitzRalph, Archbishop of Armagh, against the friars.[16] Not the least interesting of Trevisa's works are two short, original essays on translation prefixed to the *Polychronicon*, the first justifying translations into the vernacular, the second explaining his method.[17] Trevisa has been accused of wordiness, but his aim was above all to be clear. His prose shows care and a certain amount of conscious artistry, looking forward at times to the balance and alliteration of Euphuism.

Thomas Usk's *Testament of Love* [18] is better known than it deserves to be, because borrowings from *Piers Plowman* and Chaucer's *Troilus* make it

---

problem the reader must be referred to E. B. Nicholson, "John of Burgundy, *alias* Sir John Mandeville," *Academy*, xxv (1884). 261-2; the article of Nicholson and Sir Henry Yule in the *Encyclopaedia Britannica*, eleventh ed.; G. F. Warner in the *DNB*; and the discussions listed in the next note.

[12] P. Hamelius, "The Travels of Sir John Mandeville," *Quar. Rev.*, ccxxvii (1917). 331-352, and the introduction to the *EETS* edition noted above.

[13] The best account of Trevisa's life is in Aaron J. Perry's introduction to three of Trevisa's shorter pieces edited for the *EETS*, 167 (1925). See also the same author's "John Trevisa: A Fourteenth Century Translator," *Manitoba Essays* (1937), pp. 277-289.

[14] See above, p. 148. Trevisa's translation is edited in the Rolls Ser. (9v, 1865-86).

[15] See above, p. 150. Trevisa's translation has not been printed since 1582, but selections (modernized) can be had in Robert Steele, *Mediæval Lore from Bartholomew Anglicus* (1893, and later reprints).

[16] The last two works and a doubtful translation from Methodius are edited by Perry, *op. cit.* A translation of the *De Re Militari* of Vegetius, often attributed to Trevisa, must be given up. Cf. Perry, p. xcvii (and see below, p. 301).

[17] Conveniently reprinted in Alfred W. Pollard, *Fifteenth Century Prose and Verse* (1903), pp. 201-210.

[18] Edited by W. W. Skeat, *Chaucerian and Other Pieces* (Oxford, 1897; *Oxford Chaucer*, Vol. vii). Usk was executed in 1388 after a checkered and seemingly none too honorable political career. Ramona Bressie, "The Date of Thomas Usk's *Testament of Love*," MP, xxvi (1928). 17-29, attributes the allegory to a period of imprisonment covering roughly the first six months of 1385. This seems a little early to allow for the borrowings from *Troilus and Criseyde*. See also the same author's "A Study of Thomas Usk's *Testament of Love* as an Autobiography," [Univ. of Chicago] *Abstracts of Theses*, Humanistic Ser., vii. 517-521. The third book has been traced to St. Anselm's *De Concordia Praescientiae et Praedestinationis*, of which it is in part a translation. See George Sanderlin, "Usk's *Testament of Love* and St. Anselm," *Speculum*, xvii (1942). 69-73.

useful in fixing the dates of these poems. It is a political allegory in prose, *Thomas* written while the author was in prison. In it he treats the cause of his im- *Usk:* prisonment, justifies his conduct, and indicates that he should be released and Testament restored to favor. The allegory is full of obscurities which we can hardly of Love hope to clear up, but even if we could, no great service would be done to English literature.

The most famous writer of English prose at the end of the fourteenth *Wyclif* century was John Wyclif,[19] but it must be confessed that his importance rests more upon his efforts toward social and ecclesiastical reform than on his contributions to literature. Now that we believe he had very little hand in the translation of the Bible that goes by his name, his position in the history of English prose must be judged by his sermons and a number of tracts, expository and controversial, the canon of which is not easy to determine.

Born, as is now thought, about 1328 at Wycliffe in the North Riding of *His Life* Yorkshire, he proceeded to Oxford about 1345 and gradually distinguished himself so that by 1360 he had become Master of Balliol College. During these years he received the usual strict training in scholasticism with its basis in grammar and logic and its emphasis on Aristotle. After further years spent in the study of theology he lectured on the Bible and the *Sentences* of Peter Lombard, a standard textbook of the day. In 1361 he was appointed rector of Fillingham, but resigned his charge in 1368 to accept one nearer Oxford, at Ludgershall. Although he was given leaves to pursue his theological studies, his academic career was prolonged and he did not receive his degree as Doctor of Theology until 1372.

About this time he appears in the service of the king and we may think of him as entering upon the second stage of his career. His opposition to the papal claims on the Crown [20] recommended him to the government, and in 1374 he was rewarded with the rectory of Lutterworth, in Leicestershire, which he held until his death. In this year he was sent to Bruges as a member of a commission to negotiate with representatives of the pope. During the next few years he stated his position at length in two Latin treatises, the *De Dominio Divino* and *De Civili Dominio,* laying down the principle that all temporal lordship is under the overlordship of God, that the condition on which it may be exercised is righteousness, and that if this condition is violated the unrighteous may be deprived of their property. He maintains that the Church has no concern with temporal matters, that the clergy has no right to hold property, and in any case that the civil authority may deprive it of its property if unworthy of the trust. Such views, however acceptable to the State, were bound to bring him into conflict with the rulers of the Church.

As long as Wyclif's departures from orthodoxy were largely confined to

---

[19] The best biography is Herbert B. Workman, *John Wyclif: A Study of the English Medieval Church* (2v, Oxford, 1926).

[20] In 1374 Gregory XI demanded the payment granted by King John in 1213 together with all arrears.

temporal matters he seems not only to have escaped official censure but to have enjoyed a measure of political support. On occasion he was consulted by the king. John of Gaunt, seeing that he might be useful, enlisted him in his service. Consequently when Wyclif was attacked in 1377 by the Church and arraigned before Courtenay, Bishop of London, and when Gregory XI denounced his views and ordered his arrest, he was supported by John of Gaunt and other members of the royal family and suffered only minor inconveniences. But when he began about 1379 to attack such basic beliefs of the Church as the doctrine of transubstantiation he alienated

*His Con-
demnation*

many of his previous supporters, including John of Gaunt. In 1380 he was publicly condemned by a committee of twelve Oxford scholars, and shortly afterwards he left Oxford for good.

The rest of his life, which may be thought of as the third and last phase of his career, was spent at his parish in Lutterworth. There, impaired in health, he continued to defend his views while he gathered together and edited his sermons, organized his writings into an elaborate *Summa,* and directed the flock of "poor priests" who were spreading his ideas over many

*The "Poor
Priests"*

parts of England. In 1382 Courtenay, now archbishop, called a council of forty-four bishops, doctors of theology, and others on whose support he could count—the Blackfriars Synod—and obtained a sweeping condemnation of Wyclifite views. But though Wyclif's followers were hunted down, punished, and forced to recant, Wyclif remained unmolested in his Lutterworth parsonage. Courtenay evidently knew when to stop. During his two remaining years Wyclif suffered a partial paralysis, the result of a stroke. His death occurred on the last day of the year 1384.

*His
Views*

It is not a part of our purpose to discuss here in detail Wyclif's views as set forth most fully in his many Latin writings. Such a discussion belongs to political and social history rather than to literature. We have already mentioned his theory of "dominion" as presented in two basic works about 1375-6.[21] Equally basic is his insistence on the absolute authority of the Bible.[22] Gregory XI's condemnation led him to an examination of the constitution and claims of the Church,[23] which he followed with a similar consideration of the office of the king [24] and the authority of the pope.[25] He felt that material possessions had made the Church worldly. He there-

---

[21] The *De Dominio Divino* and *De Civili Dominio*, like most of Wyclif's Latin writings, have been published by the Wyclif Society.

[22] *De Veritate Sacrae Scripturae* (1378).

[23] *De Ecclesia* (finished late in 1378) asserts that the exercise of religious functions by ecclesiastics depends on their worthiness. He condemns indulgences by the pope, trentals, prayers for the dead, and the like, rejects the cult of the saints, and opposes (more mildly than in his later writings) relics and pilgrimages.

[24] *De Officio Regis* (1378) really concerns the question of Church and State. The king is God's vicar and therefore must rule wisely and justly. He has jurisdiction over the clergy, should see that the clergy perform their functions in a worthy manner, and he is not bound to obey the pope.

[25] *De Potestate Papae* (1379) asserts that the primacy of the pope depends upon character (sanctity) and that he is not necessarily St. Peter's successor. It questions the right of the Romans to determine the succession. The *De Ordine Christiano* is a brief statement of the same position.

fore urged the king to take back the endowments of the Church and restore the clergy to their original poverty. He opposed both the employment of ecclesiastics in secular office and the life of monastic retirement which too often fell away from the spiritual ideal. The function of the clergy, in his opinion, was to minister to the people. For this reason he was at the beginning more sympathetic to the friars, but in the end he found them wanting and attacked them bitterly.

Wyclif's English writings are not always easy to separate from those of *His* his followers.[26] His sermons, which fill two volumes, are for the most part *English* to be accepted as his, but they are generally only two or three pages long *Writings* and were probably prepared for the guidance of his poor priests. Many of his English treatises represent translations and abridgments of his Latin works, and some of these may have been prepared by his followers. Among those that can be attributed to Wyclif himself, some are treatments such as we find elsewhere of the Ten Commandments, The Seven Deadly Sins, and the Seven Works of Mercy. More interesting are the *De Papa* and *The Church and Her Members* in which he puts into English the views already put forward in Latin concerning the authority of the pope, the objection to monastic orders, the lapses of the friars, disendowment, and the like. Two of his English treatises are especially interesting because they deal with social questions and are not adaptations of Latin works. *Of Servants and Lords* was inspired by the Peasants' Revolt. It is a very moderate treatment, insisting on the duty servants owe to their lord as well as the obligation of lords, but discussing in plain terms the many ways in which the poor are wronged. *Wedded Men and Wives* offers wholesome advice on marriage and the rearing of children. Virginity is a higher state than matrimony, but matrimony is holy. He is not at all sure that celibacy is a wise requirement for the priesthood. The whole treatise is a compound of biblical precept and good common sense.

The so-called Wyclif Bible [27] appears to owe little more to Wyclif than *The* the impulse behind it. It was apparently the work of his companions and *Wyclif* helpers. Nicholas of Hereford translated about three-fourths of the Old *Bible* Testament, as we learn from a note in one of the manuscripts. The style is awkward and anything but idiomatic and does not agree with any of the translations which Wyclif gives in his sermons. Apparently it was early felt to be unsatisfactory, and perhaps even before Wyclif's death a revision was undertaken by John Purvey,[28] who assisted Wyclif in his last days at Lutterworth. Although Purvey was aided, as he says, by "many good fellows and cunning," his revision was not completed until about 1395. It is in every way superior to the early version. Not a little of the sentence structure and

---

[26] The principal collections are Thomas Arnold, *Select English Works of John Wyclif* (3v, Oxford, 1869-71), which contains many pieces now rejected from the Wyclif canon, and F. D. Matthew, *The English Works of Wyclif Hitherto Unprinted* (1880; EETS, 74), which likewise includes some doubtful works. A convenient small volume is Herbert E. Winn, *Wyclif: Select English Writings* (1929).

[27] Edited by J. Forshall and Sir F. Madden (4v, Oxford, 1850).

[28] Purvey's part in the translation rests on strong evidence, just short of proof.

an occasional fine phrase have been carried over into the Authorized Version of 1611.

Even though Wyclif may have had no part at all in the actual work of translation, the important step of putting the whole Bible into English for the first time was the result of his attitude toward the Scriptures as the ultimate authority in all questions concerning man's moral and spiritual life. He believed it was the right of simple men to turn to the Bible for "the points that be most needful to salvation." Simple piety was worth more than forms and ritual. His poor priests resembled the early friars in seeking to bring religion home to the common man. Coming from the north where we have seen that so many of the religious movements of the fourteenth century had their beginning, Wyclif sought in a different way what Rolle and the mystics were seeking—to bring a more direct and personal meaning into religious life.[29]

[29] Exemplifying Wyclif's purpose to bring religious instruction to the poor is an anonymous treatise of the late fourteenth century called *Pore Caitiff*. It is found in a large number of MSS, but has been printed only in modernized form and in selections. In addition to treatments of the Paternoster, Creed, etc., it discusses patience, temptation, and other subjects for poor men's spiritual profit. Extracts have been printed in R. Vaughan's *Life of Wycliffe* (1852), pp. 382 ff. See also M. T. Brady, "*The Pore Caitif*: An Introductory Study," *Traditio*, x (1954). 529-548.

XIX
The Beginnings of the Drama

Mimicry and make-believe are well nigh universal human impulses and drama has therefore developed independently at various times and places in the world's history. Among the Greeks it attained high distinction. Among the Romans it was less popular. Conditions in the Roman Empire were politically disturbed, and the populace preferred to shout and cheer at the chariot races and gladiatorial combats of the circus and amphitheatre rather than quietly watch a play. The theatre apparently did not attract the best literary talents in Italy. Plautus and Terence are not comparable to Virgil, Horace, or Livy in other forms of literature, and Seneca's tragedies were closet dramas. The most popular theatrical entertainments were the performances of mimes [1] in which coarse humor and indecency combined to secure at times the attention of the vulgar. The hordes of barbarians pouring into Rome did not help matters. Drama had apparently never developed among the Teutons, and witty dialogue was wasted on the speakers of an unfamiliar tongue. With the rise of Christianity the theatre ran into other difficulties. The Church objected to its associations with paganism, to the fact that in its lower forms it often ridiculed the new religion, and perhaps most of all to the immorality of both performances and performers. With the fall of the Empire, Roman drama disappeared, and for five hundred years only a faint dramatic tradition may have survived, passed on from the mimes to the medieval minstrel.

Disappearance of Roman Drama

It is ironical that the Church, the force that had done most to drive Roman drama out of existence, should have been the institution in which modern drama was to take its rise. For the drama of the Middle Ages is not a continuation of Roman drama but a development from entirely new beginnings in the services of the Church,[2] first in the more solemn service of the Mass and later in the less rigid office of Matins. Theoretically no departure from the text of the missal was permitted in the celebration of Mass, but actually intrusions crept in, at first in the form of musical embellishments at the end of the gradual, to which words were in time added,[3]

Beginnings of Modern Drama in the Church

[1] See H. Reich, *Der Mimus* (2v, Berlin, 1903).

[2] The authoritative work on the liturgical drama is Karl Young, *The Drama of the Medieval Church* (2v, Oxford, 1933), where full references to previous literature are given. For the background of the drama in folk custom and a general survey of dramatic developments see E. K. Chambers, *The Medieval Stage* (2v, Oxford, 1903).

[3] The *gradual* is a chant sung after the epistle of the day, and closes with *alleluia*. The name *sequence* was at first applied to the melody in which the final *a* of *alleluia* was prolonged. Later words were fitted to such melodies and the term *sequence* designated both the words and music. Additions to other parts of the service are called tropes. For the distinction

and later through amplifications woven into various other chants. The latter are called *tropes,* and it is with a trope in the Mass of Easter that we are most concerned.

The Quem quaeritis

The Introit or opening chant began with the words *Resurrexi et adhuc tecum sum.* At about the year 900 we find it prefaced by a trope which the following slightly normalized text exemplifies in its simplest form:

Quem quaeritis in sepulchro, o Christicolae?
Jesum Nazarenum crucifixum, o caelicolae.
Non est hic; surrexit sicut praedixerat;
ite, nuntiate quia surrexit de sepulchro.[4]

These lines are a paraphrase of the dialogue between the angel and the Marys at the tomb of Christ as implied in the Gospel of St. Matthew. As sung antiphonally—i.e., alternately by the two halves of the choir—they constitute merely a dialogued chant. They never became much more as long as they were attached to the Mass. But they are of great importance, for they are the germ out of which modern drama grew.

Development of the Trope

The development of this trope in the Mass never went far enough to be embarrassing to the service, and indeed it could not have grown much without becoming so. The words, however, were equally appropriate to the office of Matins a little earlier in the day, a service with which the *Elevatio Crucis* was in many places associated. When transferred to the end of this office the *Quem quaeritis* underwent a gradual change. Two members of the choir, robed in white to suggest angels, took positions beside the altar, while three others in black represented the Marys. This simple but momentous change [5] introduced the element of impersonation and the result was a miniature opera. Slowly other lines were added. *Who will roll away for us the stone?* the Marys ask, approaching the supposed sepulcher. The angels, after announcing the Resurrection, invite the Marys to *Come and see the place where the Lord was laid,* which they do, and then hold up the linens with suitable words. When the angels bid them carry the news to the disciples they do so, and in some places Peter and John race to the sepulcher (cf. John, 20:4). In certain texts the episode in which Christ appears to Mary Magdalene (cf. John, 20:11-18) occurs. When all of these amplifications are present we have a sizable and highly dramatic ceremony.

So successful an innovation was soon imitated, and a similar ceremony was introduced at Christmas. By a slight change in wording the dialogue be-

---

and for the development of tropes see C. Blume, introduction to *Analecta Hymnica,* LIII, and L. Gautier, *Histoire de la poésie liturgique au moyen âge: les tropes* (Paris, 1886).

[4] Whom seek ye in the sepulchre, O Christians?
Jesus of Nazareth who was crucified, O angels.
He is not here; he has arisen as he foretold;
go, announce that he has arisen from the grave.

The fullest collection of *Quem quaeritis* texts is in Carl Lange, *Die lateinischen Osterfeiern* (Munich, 1887).

[5] It occurs in a few texts of the Introit trope. In time temporary or permanent structures known as Easter sepulchers were constructed for the ceremony.

tween the angels and the Marys could be adapted to the shepherds who **Officium**
came to adore the Christ-child. *Obstetrices* or midwives replace the angels **Pastorum**
as interlocutors, and the result is:

> Quem quaeritis in praesepe, o pastores, dicite.
> Salvatorem Christum Dominum, infantem pannis
> involutum, secundum sermonem angelicum.
> Adest hic parvulus cum Maria matre sua....
> Et nunc euntes dicite quia natus est.[6]

Such a conversation though plausible, is lacking in any biblical authority, differing in this respect from the words spoken at the tomb. It is quite obviously an imitation of the Easter trope, and is known as the *Officium Pastorum*.

The simple little act of worship performed by the shepherds offered only **Officium** limited possibilities for dramatic development. More productive were cer- **Stellae** tain other ceremonies of the Christmas season. On Twelfth Day was cele- brated the coming of the Magi, not only to adore but to bring rich gifts. As kings they were impressive in their costumes of Oriental splendor, but more important was the fact that they had to pass through the kingdom of Herod and be questioned concerning the new-born king whom they were seeking. Herod soon becomes the central figure in the action. Surrounded by a con- siderable retinue of courtiers, scribes, messengers, and soldiers, he symbolizes the tyrant's power jealous of any threat to its supremacy. He dislikes what the Magi tell him, sends for his learned men, is unwillingly convinced that their book contains disturbing prophecies, and in one text throws the book down in a rage. We have thus early the model for the ranting Herod of later drama.[7] From the fact that a star suspended from the roof of the church guided the Magi on their journey the ceremony here described is known as the *Officium Stellae,* the Office of the Star.[8]

Two other developments took place at the Christmas season. One was a **Ordo** natural extension of the *Stella,* showing the slaughter of the innocents by **Rachelis** Herod's soldiers. The children are slain and Rachel, representative of the **and** grieving mothers of Israel, sings her lament in a little duet with conventional **Ordo** *consolatrices.* From the latter circumstance the episode is known as the **Prophe-** *Ordo Rachelis.* The other was the *Ordo Prophetarum,* a ceremony of some **tarum** interest since it originated not in a chant of the choir but in a sermon.[9] In

---

[6] Whom seek ye in the manger, O shepherds, tell us.
Christ our Lord the Savior, an infant wrapped in
swaddling clothes, as the angels say.
Here is the little one with Mary, his mother. . . .
And now go and say that he is born.

[7] Cf. *Hamlet,* III. ii. 16.

[8] In addition to Karl Young, as above, see Heinrich Anz, *Die lateinischen Magierspiele* (Leipzig, 1905).

[9] The development from sermon to dramatic ceremony was first studied by M. Sepet, *Les Prophètes du Christ* (Paris, 1878; also published in installments scattered through the *Bibliothèque de l'Ecole des Chartres,* Vols. XXVIII, XXIX, and XXXVIII), the basic treatment. Karl Young corrects Sepet in detail and adds important texts in his "Ordo Prophetarum," *Trans. Wisconsin Acad.,* XX (1921). 1-82, and in his *Drama of the Medieval Church,* ch. XXI. A translation of

the Middle Ages an attempt to convince unbelievers out of their own mouths, wrongly attributed to St. Augustine and entitled *Contra Judaeos, Paganos, et Arianos,* was frequently read as a *lectio* in the Christmas'·Matins. In one section of this sermon various Old Testament prophets—Isaiah, Jeremiah, Daniel, etc.—are called upon by the preacher to testify to the coming of Christ. When their words are not merely reported but delivered by separate personages appropriately costumed the sermon becomes elementary drama. In time episodes connected with some of the prophets, such as Nebuchadnezzar and Balaam, were represented. It has been claimed that from such episodes sprang the treatment of Old Testament subjects in medieval drama. While this may be doubted, it is apparent that once the impulse towards dramatic representation was abroad, a sermon or any other suitable material could become the stuff out of which drama was made.

From Church to Craft

The amalgamation and elaboration of such dramatic ceremonies within the church in time put a strain upon the services. And what is more, additional episodes tended to develop, if not actually in the office, at least in a transitional stage ending in separation from the church. The birth of Christ, for example, called for some explanation. If Adam and Eve had not fallen, man would not have been in need of redemption. A scene was needed showing the temptation of Eve by Satan in the Garden of Eden. But why did Satan tempt Eve? Out of malice for having been driven out of Heaven. Why was he driven out of Heaven? That also must be told. Finally, the evil brought to the world by man's disobedience can be symbolized by the slaying of Abel by Cain. Such an extension of theme is illustrated in the twelfth-century Anglo-Norman *Adam,* which consists of a long episode, running to nearly 600 lines, on the Fall and Expulsion from Paradise, a shorter treatment of Cain and Abel, and a Prophets play, incomplete.[10] The same episodes sometimes served as an equally suitable introduction to the drama of Easter. Not only would such an extensive action take up much time and interfere with the service proper, but it would tax the resources of the clergy. In some places it was necessary to call in outsiders of good and discreet character to assist in the performance. Realistic elements verging on the humorous crept in. Balaam delivered his prophecy after a little by-play in which he beat his ass and the faithful beast brayed touchingly. In one text Mary Magdalene is shown with her lover, singing a profane song and buying aids to her complexion, before being converted and exchanging the cosmetics for ointment. Such incidents are inappropriate to the solemn ritual of the church. Adequate space for settings and accommo-

Realism and Humor

the pertinent portions of the sermon has been published by Edward N. Stone in the *Univ. of Wash. Pub. in Lang. and Lit.,* Vol. IV, No. 3 (1928).

10 The play is mostly in French with a few liturgical elements in Latin. The stage directions, also in Latin, are remarkably detailed with respect to action, costume, and setting. The most satisfactory edition is that of Paul C. Studer (Manchester, 1918). The play has been twice translated into English: (1) by Sarah F. Barrow and Wm. H. Hulme in *Western Reserve Univ. Bull.,* Vol. XXVIII, No. 8 (1925); (2) by Edward N. Stone in *Univ. of Wash. Pub. in Lang. and Lit.,* IV (1926). 159-193.

dation for the crowds that would want to witness the performances raised other difficulties. And so from choir to nave, and nave to church-porch were natural steps on the way to the public square. Once outside the church the performances gradually broke their liturgical bonds. Latin, the liturgical language, gave way to the vernacular.[11] At the same time the musical rendering yielded to the more realistic spoken word. We must suppose that the laity now participated to an increasing extent while the clergy more and more withdrew until the plays ended up entirely in the hands of the people.

The transition here sketched may be accepted with some confidence in its main outlines, but it must be admitted that we are far from clear about many of its details. While the drama is growing up within the church we can trace its development with fair continuity, although we would gladly know more about the genesis of some of its later and more elaborate texts. *Mystery* When we turn to the large vernacular cycles it is as though something in *Cycles* between had dropped out. For example, we can observe the tendency, already described, for the episodes of liturgical drama to collect in sequences, but there is no sequence of episodes in liturgical drama comparable in scope to the great mystery cycles. At one stage we see the drama in the process of passing out of the church and the control of the clergy. We next see it in the hands of the craft guilds or mysteries and in the control of the civic authorities. The intermediate steps are missing. A factor of considerable importance was probably the establishment in England of the festival of Corpus Christi, but its influence has yet to be defined.[12] We know that Corpus Christi day [13] was generally observed in England from 1318 on, *Corpus* and that by papal decree a procession with five (nondramatic) pageants *Christi* constituted a major feature of the observance. The pageants or tableaux *Day* suggested the need for Corpus Christi by portraying the Fall of Man, then the prophecies, the coming, and the death of Christ, and finally the triumph of Corpus Christi in the Judgment Day. With many additional details this constitutes the subject matter of the mystery cycles, and since Corpus Christi day came to be the most popular date in England for the performance of mystery cycles, it is likely that in scope, time of performance, and the use of movable pageant wagons the mystery cycles owe something to the Corpus Christi procession. One may put it another way by saying that the religious plays emerging from the church took the form in which we know them under the inspiration of the Corpus Christi festival. It is perhaps significant

[11] The transition can be seen in certain texts from England, France, and Germany in which the words of a speech are first sung in Latin and then spoken in the vernacular. In England this stage is illustrated by the Shrewsbury fragments, conveniently available in Adams, *Chief Pre-Shakespearean Dramas* (Boston, 1924), pp. 73-78.

[12] For a discussion of the problem see Hardin Craig, "The Corpus Christi Procession and the Corpus Christi Play," *JEGP*, XIII (1914). 589-602, and M. Pierson, "The Relation of the Corpus Christi Procession to the Corpus Christi Play in England," *Trans. Wisc. Acad.*, XVIII (1915). 110-165.

[13] Corpus Christi day is the Thursday following Trinity Sunday, i.e., a little more than eight weeks after Easter. It falls generally at the end of May or early in June, an ideal time for outdoor performances.

that the second quarter of the fourteenth century seems to have been the period in which they were taking shape.

In spite of their religious content and their association with the festival of Corpus Christi it is important to stress the civic character of the English religious cycles. Where the cycles attained significant size and were performed regularly every year it was because the governing body of the city considered them an asset to be maintained and promoted, just as countless chambers of commerce today seek conventions and promote fairs or other activities that attract visitors and augment local prestige. In the beginning the various pageants must have been distributed to the guilds by mutual agreement or on the decision of the central authority; otherwise it is unlikely that we should find so many crafts giving plays especially appropriate to them.[14] As we read the records of a city like York [15] we see the city council regulating the performances, settling disputes between guilds, imposing fines, reassigning plays, and exercising many other sorts of control. At first the attitude of the guilds is one of pride in performance, and there is rivalry in getting possession of a pageant. Later the plays become a duty, often burdensome upon crafts whose prosperity had declined. But while the burden is sometimes shifted or shared by another guild, the attitude of the city fathers is always that the plays must go on.

Cycles of mystery plays [16] seem to have been a regular feature only in some of the larger towns. Other places were content with an occasional episode, a saint's play, or a performance by a visiting troupe. The evidence for the existence of a cycle is clear for only about a dozen places in England. Of these, London alone is in the south and the few mentions of its plays suggest occasional performances by the parish clerks and not the guilds. The important centers were in the north and the Midlands—York, Wakefield, Beverley, Newcastle-upon-Tyne, Norwich, Coventry, and Chester. The performance was not in all cases on Corpus Christi day, but this was the most usual practice. Naturally the size and scope of the cycles varied greatly in different localities and sometimes at different dates. The York cycle at the height of its development contained as many as fifty-seven pageants. At the other end of the scale stood Worcester, which never seems to have had more than five. Of all this religious drama we are fortunate in having a considerable part preserved. It is rather remarkable that the only important cycle of which no fragment remains seems to be that of Beverley, which contained thirty-eight plays. We have two of the Coventry plays and one each from Norwich and Newcastle; all three of these cycles originally consisted of about a dozen plays.[17] We also have preserved two isolated plays

14 At Newcastle the Noah play was assigned to the shipwrights and other watermen, the Magi to the goldsmiths, the Disputation in the Temple to the lawyers, the Flight into Egypt to the stable keepers, the Last Supper to the bakers, etc. It was so elsewhere.

15 For example, the York Memorandum Book, ed. Maude Sellers (2v, Durham, 1912-15; Surtees Soc., 120, 125).

16 On the English cycles see E. K. Chambers, as above, and Charles M. Gayley, Plays of Our Forefathers (1907).

17 Newcastle may have been slightly larger, but the evidence is not unequivocal. The Coventry cycle almost certainly contained ten plays. The best edition of the extant Coventry

of *Abraham and Isaac* which we cannot localize. They may be fragments of otherwise lost cycles or they may always have been independent. The same may be said of three items in the Digby MS. Of the cycles preserved in full, those of York, Wakefield, and Chester, and the misnamed *Ludus Coventriae,* we shall speak more at length. When we consider that we have a cycle in Cornish which we can use for purposes of comparison we must conclude that time has dealt rather gently with us in the matter of the old English mystery plays, and avoid the mistake of supposing that much of major importance has disappeared without leaving some trace behind.

The most extensive English cycle of which we know was that of York.[18] *The* York In the form in which it has come down to us it consists of forty-eight Plays plays, but the MS dates from about 1475 and the cycle was at one time longer. The plays are first referred to in 1378 and then they are spoken of as "of old time." They cover very fully the whole of biblical history. They begin with the creation of the world and pass successively through the expulsion from Paradise, the killing of Abel, the story of Noah and the flood, of Abraham and Isaac, and of the Israelites in Egypt. In all, eleven plays are devoted to Old Testament matter. Then come the Annunciation and visit to Elizabeth, and the birth of Jesus with the familiar episodes of the shepherds and the Magi up to the slaughter of the innocents. With Play xx we take up the life of Christ—his dispute with the doctors in the temple, his Baptism, Temptation, Transfiguration, encounter with the woman taken in adultery, his raising of Lazarus, and finally his entry into Jerusalem. With the events leading to the Crucifixion the treatment becomes unusually full. Sixteen plays tell the story from the conspiracy to take Jesus, the Last Supper through the accusation and trial, the Crucifixion, the Resurrection, on to the journey to Emmaus and the incredulity of Thomas. The last few pageants portray Christ's Ascension, the death of Mary, her appearance to Thomas, and her Assumption. The whole concludes with the Judgment Day. Allowing for individual omissions and modifications, this may be taken as typical of the scope of the English cycles. It must not be supposed that the York plays reached such a degree of elaboration in one creative effort. It is likely that the original cycle was much smaller. There are evidences that it underwent major revision at two different times, and it is likely that subdivision, amalgamation, and alteration frequently occurred in individual plays as occasion arose. The cycle was not static, but subject to improvement and frequent modification to adapt it to changing conditions among the crafts that produced it. This will account for the great variations in tone, effectiveness, versification, and humor in its different parts.

On the whole it is a dignified and impressive production. Only rarely, as in the case of the *Annunciation,* is the action undramatic, and in certain

plays is that of Hardin Craig, *Two Coventry Corpus Christi Plays* (London, 1902; *EETSES,* 87). The Norwich and Newcastle fragments will be found in O. Waterhouse, *The Non-Cycle Mystery Plays* (London, 1909; *EETSES,* 104). The Digby Plays were edited by F. J. Furnivall (London, 1896; *EETSES,* 70).
[18] *York Plays,* ed. Lucy Toulmin Smith (Oxford, 1885).

episodes it is highly realistic and vigorous. Homely humor enlivens the play of Noah and the flood, in which Noah's wife demurs about entering the ark and prefers to go to town. When she finally yields to persuasion she saves face by complaining that Noah might have told her earlier of his plans, and she expresses her annoyance by giving him a clout over the head. In the play of the shepherds there is much excitement over the appearance of the star, voiced in exclamations of "Wow!" and "Golly!" There is an attempt to differentiate the shepherds. The Second Shepherd thinks the others have something to eat and comes up eagerly. Their gifts are not without a suggestion of amusing simplicity. The First Shepherd presents a brooch hung with a little tin bell and the Second offers two cobb-nuts on a ribbon. Both, simple souls that they were, naïvely express the wish that the new-born King will remember them when he comes into power. The Third Shepherd, on the other hand, offers somewhat apologetically a horn spoon that holds forty peas, and in his simple piety asks no reward. Realism of another kind accompanies the Crucifixion. The four soldiers, as they nail Jesus to the cross, find the cross too large and while they pull and stretch they make comments that are almost too realistic. Again, as they carry the cross up the hill they make much of its weight. One of them must set it down or his back will break; another is out of breath. Finally they set the cross in the mortise and accompany the driving in of the wedges with taunting remarks. While in such scenes we may question the dramatists' taste, we cannot deny them vigor and a lively dramatic sense.

The Towneley Plays   Some forty miles southwest of York lies the town of Wakefield, to which with most probability the cycle known as the *Towneley Plays* [19] is to be assigned. Originally rather small, Wakefield experienced rapid growth in the fifteenth century when heavy taxes in York drove many engaged in the woolen industry to other nearby centers. [20] This circumstance may account for the close relation of the Towneley cycle with the *York Plays* which we shall notice shortly. The cycle is only slightly shorter than that of York. The extant MS, which has lost at least two plays, contains thirty-two pageants treating a range of subjects similar to that indicated in the description of the York cycle. It is even more composite. Three stages are recognized by which it attained its present form. Beginning as a group of plays of simple religious tone, it took over early in the fifteenth century five plays,

[19] So called from the circumstance that the MS (dated *c.* 1460) was long preserved at Towneley Hall in Lancashire. It is now in the Huntington Library in California. The latest edition is that of George England and Alfred W. Pollard (London, 1897; *EETSS,* 71).

[20] See Herbert Heaton, *The Yorkshire Woollen and Worsted Industries* (Oxford, 1920). There is some doubt whether Wakefield had a sufficient number of guilds to produce a cycle as extensive as the *Towneley Plays.* Unfortunately medieval records of Wakefield have almost completely disappeared. It has recently been shown, however, that there were Corpus Christi plays there in 1533 (*LTLS,* March 5, 1925, p. 156). It would seem that Wakefield reached its height as a woolen center some time in the first half of the fifteenth century, after which its woolen trade was on the decline. This would correspond with the period at which on other grounds we know that the Towneley cycle was being expanded and revised. The association of the cycle with Wakefield rests upon a number of clear local allusions in some of the plays.

and possibly more, from the York cycle.[21] Other plays showing York influence were conceivably revised or composed at the same time. Finally in
the reign of Henry VI [22] and probably in the second quarter of the fifteenth
century a writer of great dramatic gifts contributed a number of plays,
mostly in a distinctive nine-line stanza, and touched up several others. It is
the work of this man that gives the *Towneley Plays* their special distinction
in early English drama, and in our ignorance of his name and identity we
refer to him justly as "the Wakefield master."

The work of the Wakefield master is unique in medieval drama. Nowhere   *The*
else do we find such a combination of what we call nowadays "good   *Wakefield*
theatre" with boisterous humor and exuberance of spirit. Satirical sallies   *Master*
and farcical situations burst forth without regard to propriety or convention.
In the *Murder of Abel* this medieval Aristophanes introduces a scene of
rough humor in which Cain and Garcio abuse each other, and he makes
Cain boldly rebellious toward God, who, he says, has given him only sorrow
and woe. To so solemn a play as the *Doomsday* he contributes two broadly
humorous scenes. The devils carry on a lively dialogue alluding to the
unusual amount of evidence they have against women and remark that if
the Judgment Day had not come when it did they would have had to make
Hell larger. Nowhere does his ability appear, however, to better effect than
in the *Second Shepherds' Play*.[23] As a prelude to the adoration he tells the
story of Mak, a notorious sheep-stealer, and his attempt to steal a sheep
from the shepherds by concealing it in a cradle and pretending that it is a
baby to which his wife has just given birth. The theme is a folk-tale [24]
worked up through successive moments of dramatic suspense to a climax
in which the culprit's guilt is dramatically revealed. There is humor of
situation and humor of dialogue and incidental allusion—jibes at shrewish
wives and crying children, taxes and the poor man's lot. The length of the
Mak episode is hopelessly out of proportion to the proper matter of the
play. The *Second Shepherds' Play* as a shepherds' play is an artistic absurdity; as a farce of Mak the sheep-stealer it is the masterpiece of the English religious drama.[25]

Not so much can be said for the third great English cycle which we can   *The*
definitely localize. The *Chester Plays* [26] are rather lacking in dramatic   Chester
Plays

[21] Miss Marie C. Lyle has argued that these plays are the residue of a parent cycle from
which both York and Towneley descend. Cf. *The Original Identity of the York and Towneley
Cycles* (Minneapolis, 1919; *Research Pub. of the Univ. of Minn.* Vol. VIII, No. 3).
[22] See Mendal G. Frampton, "The Date of the Flourishing of the Wakefield Master," *PMLA*,
L (1935). 631-660.
[23] There are two (alternate) plays of the shepherds in the cycle, both by the Wakefield
genius. The first, however, is overshadowed by the second.
[24] See A. S. Cook, "Another Parallel to the Mak Story," *MP*, XIV (1916). 11-15; A. C.
Baugh, "The Mak Story," *MP*, XV (1918). 729-734; B. J. Whiting, "An Analogue to the Mak
Story," *Speculum*, VII (1932). 552; Robert C. Cosbey, "The Mak Story and Its Folklore Analogues," *Speculum*, XX (1945). 310-317.
[25] On the work of the Wakefield master see Millicent Carey, *The Wakefield Group in the
Towneley Cycle* (Baltimore and Göttingen, 1930; *Hesperia, Ergänzungsreihe*, XI).
[26] Ed. Hermann Deimling and Dr. Matthews (2v, 1893-1916; *EETSES*, 62, 115).

quality. As a cycle they are much more of one texture than the York or Towneley plays and that texture is narrative rather than dramatic. This uniformity is the more remarkable when we consider that the plays were performed occasionally as late as 1575.[27] In the sixteenth century they had become the object of antiquarian interest: no less than four extant MSS were copied out between 1591 and 1607, and various traditions concerning their origin were recorded. One of these traditions credits the composition of the cycle to Ranulf Higden in 1328. Higden was a monk of Chester abbey, well known as the author of the *Polychronicon* (cf. p. 148). There is nothing improbable in this attribution. The character of the plays is quite in keeping with what we might expect from such an author. Whoever wrote them originally was a man of cosmopolitan taste, learned but not deep, scholarly rather than popular, with little or no humor and slight ability to project himself into his characters. He may have been familiar with the way similar religious cycles were drawn up in France, for in the curtailed character of the Old Testament matter and in certain features of the treatment the *Chester Plays* resemble the French *mystères* rather than the other English cycles.[28]

The Ludus Coventriae   The last of the four extant cycles presents a number of problems. In the seventeenth century it was wrongly identified with the plays for which Coventry was famous, and the name then attached to the MS has caused it ever since to be known as the *Ludus Coventriae*.[29] The one thing that we can be surest of about this collection is that it has nothing to do with Coventry. Apart from the fact that the two genuine Coventry plays that have been preserved show no resemblance to the corresponding episodes in the *Ludus Coventriae*, we know that the Coventry plays were given on Corpus Christi day (a Thursday) whereas the *Ludus Coventriae*, as we learn from the Banns or Proclamation, was performed on Sunday. From allusions in the text we also know that the plays were given in installments, successive groups being given in successive years. Finally the Proclamation, in advertising the performance, announces that it will be given in "N. towne." This was formerly taken to designate some town whose name began with *N*, but the *N* is more likely to stand for the Latin word *nomen* and to indicate performance by a traveling company which would thus be free to insert any desired name in the announcement at this point. The *Ludus Coventriae* is interesting in many ways, but it is less significant dramatically than the other cycles.

Except for the *Ludus Coventriae* the extant English cycles seem all to

---

[27] On the development of the cycle see a valuable study by F. M. Salter, "The Banns of the Chester Plays," *RES*, xv (1939). 432-457; xvi (1940). 1-17, 137-148, and the joint publication of Salter and W. W. Greg, *The Trial & Flagellation with Other Studies in the Chester Cycle* (1935; *Malone Soc. Studies*).

[28] Albert C. Baugh, "The Chester Plays and French Influence," *Schelling Anniversary Papers* (1923), pp. 35-63.

[29] *Ludus Coventriae*, ed. K. S. Block (1922; *EETSES*, 120). See also a brilliant essay by W. W. Greg in his *Bibliographical and Textual Problems of the English Miracle Cycles* (1914), pp. 108-143.

have been given in a manner peculiar to England.[30] Each episode was per- *Method* formed on a separate stage set on wheels so that it could be drawn from *Perform-* point to point in the city. The stations were designated in advance. At one *ance* time there were as many as fourteen in York and each episode in the cycle had to be repeated fourteen times. Fortunately for the actors, a smaller number generally sufficed. Where the entire cycle was given in one day it was necessary to begin early—at six o'clock in the morning or even earlier. But the crowd was in a holiday mood, pageant wagons and streets were gay with flags and bunting, and the occasion must have been one of the memorable events of the year for many a citizen who lived within reach of a town that boasted of a cycle of Corpus Christi plays.

It must not be supposed that communities less fortunate were without any *Non-Cycl* form of dramatic entertainment. Isolated plays are common enough in the *Plays* fourteenth and fifteenth centuries, though in most cases only the records of their performance have survived. Popular Bible stories such as that of Noah or of Abraham and Isaac were sometimes given by themselves, and many a saint was celebrated in a dramatic representation of his life or martyrdom. Indeed, once the drama is established as a literary form, almost any subject of religious or doctrinal significance might be made into a play. We have a play of *Mary Magdalene,* in which elements of the morality play, which we shall turn to in a moment, are combined with the miracle of her conversion. The Croxton *Play of the Sacrament* dramatizes a widespread story of the torture of the sacred Host by Jews. At York as early as 1378 there was a *Paternoster Play,* and in the fifteenth century a *Creed Play* was sometimes performed in place of the Corpus Christi cycle. The last two have not come down to us. We would gladly know more about them since they may well have been transitional types to the morality play. Clearly there is a tendency to go outside the range of Bible story in the search for variety, and such a search finds its most characteristic expression in the type just mentioned and to which we now turn.

It is not easy to define simply the morality play. From the point of view *The* of the dramatis personae the morality differs from previous drama in dealing *Morality* with personifications of abstract qualities such as Beauty, Strength, Gluttony, *Play* and Peace, or with generalized classes such as Everyman, King, and Bishop. But not all plays concerning such characters are morality plays. In its true form the morality is distinguished by certain characteristic themes treated allegorically. These include such subjects as the summons of Death, the conflict of vices and virtues for supremacy in man's life, and the question of his ultimate fate as debated by the Four Daughters of God. They all seem to center in the problem of man's salvation and the conduct of life as it affects his salvation. The morality is also characterized by a definite purpose or object which it seeks to promote. Whereas the mystery plays were to bring the important facts of the Bible vividly home to the average

[30] Much useful information on the method of performance is gathered together in M. Lyle Spencer, *Corpus Christi Pageants in England* (1911).

man, the morality teaches a lesson about right living—preaches a sermon in dramatic form. We may combine these considerations into a definition by saying that the morality play presents allegorically some object lesson or warning by means of abstract characters or generalized types for man's spiritual good.

The origins of the type are not easily traced. When it appears in our first text it is already fully formed. Earlier possible examples such as the *Paternoster* and *Creed* plays are, as we have seen, lost. The elements which enter into it are common in medieval literature. The allegorical method and admonitory purpose are everywhere in the Middle Ages and its main themes are known in various forms. Thus, the conflict of personified vices and virtues forms the subject of a long Latin poem by the fourth-century poet Prudentius.[31] The summons of Death, bringing home the warning that death strikes often when least expected and is no respecter of persons, was present in the medieval treatments of the Dance of Death, although more familiar to us in Holbein's famous series of woodcuts. The argument of the Four Daughters of God, Mercy and Peace pleading for man's salvation and Righteousness and Truth for his eternal punishment, was a widespread motif, and we have already discussed the *Debate between the Body and Soul* in its Middle English form. But these things represent the ultimate, not the immediate, sources of the morality play. It has been suggested that the medieval sermon was often rather dramatic in character and by others that allegorical figures occasionally occur in the mystery plays. By what process of synthesis, however, these various elements of theme and method were gradually or suddenly combined into the morality play we cannot say.

The earliest play of this type that has come down to us, *The Pride of Life*,[32] dates from about 1400. It is unfortunately incomplete, but a long prologue tells us what to expect, and the five hundred lines that we have are more than half of the play and enable us to judge adequately of its character and quality. A King shows by his boastful speech that he fears nothing—not even Death—and his knights, Fortitude (or Strength) and Sanitas (or Health), assure him that with their help he will live forever. The Queen is not so sure. She reminds him that all men die and that Holy Church bids him think of his end. Her words have little effect and she sends for the Bishop. Although the Bishop preaches a long sermon on the evils of the times—wit is now treachery, love is now lechery, rich men are ruthless, etc.—and urges the King to mend his ways, the King is defiant.

31 The *Psychomachia*, of which the best edition is that of Joannes Bergman (Vienna, 1926; *Corpus Scriptorum Ecclesiasticorum Latinorum*, LXI); English trans. by Mary L. Porter (Raleigh, N. C., 1929; *Meredith College, Raleigh, Quar. Bull.*, Ser. 23, No. 1). On the subject in general see E. N. S. Thompson, *The English Moral Plays* (New Haven, 1910; *Trans. Conn. Acad.*, xiv. 291-414), and W. Roy Mackenzie, *The English Moralities from the Point of View of Allegory* (Boston, 1914).

32 The text of many of the early moralities may be found in A. Brandl, *Quellen des weltlichen Dramas in England vor Shakespeare* (Strassburg, 1898), J. M. Manly, *Specimens of the Pre-Shakespearian Drama* (2v, Boston, 1897), and J. Q. Adams, *Chief Pre-Shakespearean Dramas* (Boston, 1924).

He will try conclusions with Death and sends his messenger, Mirth, to seek him out. The text breaks off in the midst of Mirth's proclamation, but from the prologue we know that Death fought with the King and slew him. Although the arrangement of the dialogue is rather mechanical—in the beginning all speeches are three quatrains long—there are vigorous passages, and the author was not unskilful in the management of the action.

It is interesting that this, the earliest of the English moralities of which any part has come down to us, should have as its theme the summons of Death, the theme of the last and greatest of the medieval moralities, *Everyman.* The fact that its characters are for the most part not abstractions but individuals generalized to represent a class may suggest that we have in *The Pride of Life* something like a transition stage to the more fully developed, abstract type. In subject and treatment its closest affinity is to the scene depicting the death of Herod in the *Ludus Coventriae,* to which the resemblance is rather striking. Like the mystery plays *The Pride of Life* was performed outdoors, as the opening lines with a reference to the weather show, and the audience was a fairly mixed one.

The longest and most comprehensive of the English moralities of the fifteenth century is *The Castle of Perseverance.*[33] It contains over 3600 lines and tells the story of man's career from birth to death and final judgment. We see him, alternately persuaded by his good and bad angels, yielding to the delights of the World. Even after he has been rescued and brought to the Castle of Perseverance with the Seven Virtues as defenders against the forces of the World, the Flesh, and the Devil, he is lured again into sin. We witness his death, the bitter chiding of the Body by the Soul, and his final trial, with the Four Daughters of God arrayed on opposite sides, pleading respectively for mercy and strict justice. Like the *Pride of Life* it was given outdoors and an interesting diagram in the MS shows the arrangement of the playing space. Of very different character is the morality of *Wisdom,* also known as *Mind, Will, and Understanding.*[34] It requires a large cast and calls for elaborate and expensive costuming. The Devil entices Mind, Will, and Understanding from what appears to be the monastic life, but in the end they are recalled and brought to repentance by Wisdom, who is Christ. It can hardly have been intended for a popular audience, and it has been suggested that its purpose was to combat the growing tendency of monks to desert their monasteries.[35] We cannot at present date the play more closely than *c.* 1460. A still stranger production is the play known as *Mankind.*[36] Here we have the framework of the morality adapted to the

(margin notes: The Castle of Perseverance · Wisdom · Mankind*)*

[33] The text is edited by F. J. Furnivall and A. W. Pollard in *The Macro Plays* (1904; EETSES, 91). A facsimile of the MS is included in J. S. Farmer's *Student's Facsimile Series.* For discussion see Walter K. Smart "The *Castle of Perseverance:* Place, Date, and a Source," *Manly Anniversary Studies* (Chicago, 1923), pp. 42-53, where reasons are advanced for assigning the play to Lincolnshire, *c.* 1405.

[34] Also edited in *The Macro Plays,* as above.

[35] See the valuable monograph of Walter K. Smart, *Some English and Latin Sources and Parallels for the Morality of Wisdom* (Menasha, 1912).

[36] Printed among *The Macro Plays,* as above, and in Manly, Adams, etc. For date and locality see W. K. Smart, "Some Notes on *Mankind,*" *MP,* XIV (1916). 45-58; 293-313.

purposes of low comedy. It was performed in an inn-yard and a collection was taken from the spectators at a certain point in the performance. So far as the play has a morality motive at all it is to be found in the character of Mercy who in the beginning urges gratitude to God for man's redemption and stresses his own large part in it, and at the end chides Mankind for paying so little heed to his words. But most of the play is given over to horse-play and coarse humor. Some of the lines are unprintable. As a morality play it is so debased as to be rather a contradiction of the type, but it is valuable as showing the step that had been taken by about 1471 towards the popular stage.

Somewhat later, probably around the turn of the century, we get the
veryman   classic of the English morality plays, *Everyman*.[37] With a fine sense of unity the play avoids any direct representation of Everyman's heedless life and confines itself to the hour in which he receives the summons of Death. Told by the messenger that he must go on a long journey, he pleads in vain for a delay and has only the consolation of knowing that he can ask his more intimate friends to accompany him. But he finds that Fellowship, Kindred, Cousin, and Worldly Goods cannot or will not go with him into the next world. Good Deeds, with whom he has had all too little to do in his lifetime, alone stands by him and descends with him finally into the grave. In its 900 lines *Everyman* conveys its lesson with a simple effectiveness that has been more than once demonstrated by revivals on the modern stage.[38]

The morality play represents a collateral line in the descent of English drama. From the Mak episode to the *Four P's* to *Gammer Gurton's Needle* we perceive a continuity in which the morality forms no essential link and into which it can hardly be fitted. Its place is off to one side. At a point in the development of the drama (about the beginning of the fifteenth century) when the mystery cycles are approaching maturity, it appears as a type of play which does not concern Bible story and which suggests the homily in dramatized form. While it must be considered somehow an offshoot from the main dramatic stem, its origin is far from clear. After a brief career it loses its distinctive character and in the sixteenth century lives only, in much altered form, in the didactic interlude such as *Wealth and Health,* or the moral interlude such as *The Nice Wanton,* or as the medium of religious controversy. Its elements occasionally appear

---

[37] Often edited; an excellent text by W. W. Greg in *Materialien zur Kunde des älteren englischen Dramas,* IV (Louvain, 1904); modernized in Clarence G. Child, *The Second Shepherd's Play, Everyman, and Other Early Plays* (Boston, 1910).

[38] It is a disputed question whether *Everyman* or its exact counterpart, the Dutch play *Elckerlijc,* is the original, but it is almost certain now that the Dutch play is the earlier. The more important discussions of the subject are K. H. De Raaf, *Den Spyeghel der Salicheyt van Elckerlijc* (Groningen, 1897); H. Logeman, *Elckerlijc-Everyman, de Vraag naar de Prioriteit opnieuw onderzocht* (Gand, 1902); J. M. Manly, "Elckerlijc-Everyman: The Question of Priority," *MP,* VIII (1910-11). 269-277; F. A. Wood, "Elckerlijc-Everyman: The Question of Priority," *MP,* VIII (1910-11). 279-302; E. R. Tigg, "Is *Elckerlijc* prior to *Everyman?*" *JEGP,* XXXVIII (1939). 568-596. All except De Raaf (supported by Creizenach, *CHEL,* v. 59n, English ed., p. 53n) argue for the priority of the Dutch play.

in Elizabethan chronicle play, comedy, and tragedy, but otherwise by the time of Shakespeare it drops out of sight until the performance of *Everyman* inspired in the twentieth century a temporary revival in such plays as *The Passing of the Third Floor Back* and *The Servant in the House*.[39]

[39] This revival is treated in Joseph W. Barley, *The Morality Motive in Contemporary English Drama* (Univ. of Penna. diss., Mexico, Mo., 1912).

XX
Ebb Tide

The fifteenth century is commonly dismissed as a dreary and barren waste in the history of English literature. Such a judgment is severe, and results in part from the reader's disappointment when he finds that the high level reached at the end of the fourteenth century in the *Pearl, Sir Gawain and the Green Knight, Piers Plowman,* and the poetry of Chaucer is not maintained in the work of Lydgate, Hoccleve, and their contemporaries. Moreover, the fifteenth century has little new to offer. In many respects it continues the fourteenth, rather than breaking new ground. Its poets appear as followers of Chaucer and Gower, and later of Lydgate, rather than as leaders pointing new directions. It continues to treat the themes and types already current. Thus it shows an unbroken continuity with the past, and for this reason we have considered some of the works of this century along with those of earlier periods, especially in the chapters on the romance, the lyric, and the drama. However, in the drama and in English prose the fifteenth century made significant contributions. We should not forget that it was the century which produced Malory and the *Second Shepherds' Play.*[1]

Nowhere is the fifteenth century more plainly the child of the fourteenth than in its religious writings. Many of these works, except for the tyranny of dates, could be thought of as products of the earlier period. At the beginning of the century two of the three parts of Deguilleville's trilogy[2] were rendered into English. Lydgate made a verse translation of the first in his *Pilgrimage of the Life of Man,*[3] while an anonymous translator turned it into excellent prose.[4] There were still other translations, including one by Skelton now lost. An English prose version of the second, known as *Grace Dieu, or The Pilgrimage of the Soul,* made in 1413, has survived in at least

---

[1] The literary history of the fifteenth century remains to be written, although there are useful chapters in Vol. II of the *CHEL.* In the absence of Professor Wells' long promised bibliography we are dependent upon the *CBEL* and Lena L. Tucker and Allen R. Benham, *A Bibliography of Fifteenth Century Literature* (Seattle, 1928; *Univ. of Wash. Pub. in Lang. and Lit.,* Vol. II, No. 3). F. J. Snell's *The Age of Transition: 1400-1580* (2v, 1905) covers the period rather superficially. G. Gregory Smith, *The Transition Period* (1900; *Periods of European Literature,* ed. Geo. Saintsbury, Vol. IV) gives the European background. Eleanor P. Hammond, *English Verse between Chaucer and Surrey* (Durham, N. C., 1927), offers a selection from the poetry with valuable commentary. W. A. Neilson and K. G. T. Webster, *Chief British Poets of the Fourteenth and Fifteenth Centuries* (Boston, 1916) is a volume of modernizations.

[2] *Le Pèlerinage de la Vie Humaine* (1330-31, revised 1355), *Le Pèlerinage de l'Ame* (between 1330 and 1358), *Le Pèlerinage de Jhesucrist* (1358). All three poems have been edited by J. J. Stürzinger for the Roxburghe Club (1893-97).

[3] See the discussion of Lydgate below.

[4] *The Pilgrimage of the Lyf of the Manhode,* ed. Wm. A. Wright (1869; *Roxburghe Club*).

eight manuscripts,[5] and was printed by Caxton in 1483. These two poems of Deguilleville obviously stem from the *Roman de la Rose* and look forward to Bunyan. *Dives and Pauper* (1405-10) is a long prose treatise in dialogue form. It is a treatment of the Ten Commandments with an extended prologue on poverty and is still unedited.[6] Touching the mystical tradition at one or more removes is Nicholas Love's *Mirrour of the Blessed Lyf of Jesu Christ* (c. 1410),[7] a free translation of parts of the *Meditationes Vitae Christi* doubtfully attributed to St. Bonaventura, from which Rolle had previously drawn. The *Orologium Sapientiae, or The Seven Points of True Wisdom*[8] was translated from the German mystic, Henry Suso, by an unknown chaplain for an unknown "moste worschipful lady." The *Revelations of St. Birgitta*[9] was naturally inspired by the establishment of the Bridgettine order in England in 1415. Legends of the saints continued to be written, although this type of narrative was soon to disappear from English poetry. Osbern Bokenham, "a suffolke man, frere Austyn of the convent of Stokclare" (Stoke Clare), composed a collection of thirteen *Legendys of Hooly Wummen*[10] (c. 1445) running to more than 10,000 lines. *Bokenham* It may be compared with legends in the *South English Legendary,* manuscripts of which continued to be copied throughout the fifteenth century. Into one of them was inserted a new version of the Theophilus legend, the story of the clerk who, like Faustus, sold his soul to the devil, in this case for worldly goods. But unlike Faustus he was saved from carrying out his compact when the Virgin went to Hell and forced Satan to return the charter. This version[11] is in lively six-line stanzas (romance sixes) and with its free use of dialogue reminds us of some of the shorter romances.

We may note also as growing out of the fourteenth century the efforts to *The* defend or expound the doctrines of Wyclif. Best known of these is the *Lollards Apology for Lollard Doctrines,* a lengthy tract at one time attributed to Wyclif himself.[12] In it the author takes up, one by one, thirty points of Lollard belief, which he apparently has been accused of holding, and de-

---

[5] Cf. Ward, *Cat. of Romances,* II. 580-585, and Victor H. Paltsits, "The Petworth Manuscript of *Grace Dieu*. . . ," *Bull. N. Y. Pub. Library,* XXII (1928). 715-720. The Caxton text (with some omissions) will be found in Katherine I. Cust, *The Booke of the Pylgremage of the Sowle* (1859).

[6] There are six MSS and three early printed editions. See H. G. Richardson, "Dives and Pauper," *N&Q,* 11 Ser., IV (1911). 321-323; H. G. Pfander, "Dives et Pauper," *Library,* 4 er., XIV (1933). 299-312; H. G. Richardson, "Dives and Pauper," *ibid.,* XV (1934). 31-37. The Seven Deadly Sins and their contrasting virtues are worked into a fanciful allegory in the *peculum Misericordiae,* printed by Rossell H. Robbins, *PMLA,* LIV (1939). 935-966.

[7] Ed. Lawrence F. Powell (1908). Twenty-three manuscripts attest its popularity, besides he fact that it was printed by Caxton, Pynson, and Wynkyn de Worde (twice).

[8] Ed. K. Horstmann, *Anglia,* x (1888). 323-389.

[9] Ed. W. P. Cumming (1929; *EETS,* 178). To the second quarter of the century is to be ssigned the verse translation of the *Revelations* of Methodius (ed. Charlotte D'Evelyn, *PMLA,* XXIII. 135-203).

[10] Ed. Mary S. Serjeanston (1938: *EETS,* 206). Sister Mary Jeremy, "The English Prose-ranslation of *Legenda Aurea,*" *MLN,* LIX (1944). 181-183, has revived the suggestion that okenham may have been the translator of the prose version preserved in a number of manuripts and used by Caxton along with other sources.

[11] Ed. W. Heuser, *ESt,* XXXII (1903). 1-23.

[12] As by its editor, J. H. Todd (1842; *Camden Soc.,* xx).

fends his views: the pope is not Christ's vicar on earth, it is wrong to sell indulgences, to excommunicate, to encourage the worship of images, etc. Another defense of basic Wyclif doctrines, *The Lanterne of Liȝt* [13] (c. 1410), discusses such matters as the supreme authority of the Bible, the primary importance of preaching, the evil of clerical endowments, and the authority of the pope, considered to be Antichrist. On the whole, the tone of both these tracts is moderate. Certainly they are less belligerent than the *Remonstrance against Romish Corruptions in the Church*,[14] by Wyclif's friend and disciple John Purvey, at the close of the previous century (1395).

Secular Works   When we turn to secular writings we find the fifteenth century likewise carrying on the conventions and traditions of the fourteenth. The use of allegory and the dream-vision as a framework for popular didacticism, a device with a long and distinguished history extending from Martianus Capella and Boethius down, is seen in *The Court of Sapience* [15] (c. 1465). In this poem of some 2300 lines in rime royal we have first a debate between the Four Daughters of God, carried on at length, and then we are taken with the author on a dream journey to the Court of Sapience, where the Seven Liberal Arts are expounded. Thus theological and secular instruction is fitted into a slight allegorical framework. Something like the same purpose lies behind *The Assembly of Gods*,[16] formerly attributed, like the *Court of Sapience*, to Lydgate. Here a dispute among the Gods is followed by a battle between the Seven Deadly Sins and their corresponding virtues, recalling the *Psychomachia* of Prudentius, and leading to an explanation by Doctrine and others of the gradual progress from idolatry to "reconciliation" in New Testament times. The many personages which are introduced do not make easier the task of following the complicated allegory. *Sidrac and Boctus*, by Hugh of Campedene, [17] is a verse translation in over 12,000 lines of the *Fontaine de Toutes Sciences*,[18] offering instruction on a variety of topics—theological, cosmological, sociological, moral, and others—in a dialogue between the sage Sidrac and King Boctus of Bactria. More frankly practical are George Ripley's *Compend of Alchemy* [19] (1471) and the anonymous *Libell* (*Little Book*) *of Englische Policye* [20] (c. 1436), which put into verse quite mundane matters. The former explains the pseudo-scienc

---

[13] Ed. Lilian M. Swinburn (1917; *EETS*, 151).
[14] Ed. J. Forshall (London, 1851).
[15] Ed. Robert Spindler (Leipzig, 1927; *Beiträge zur engl. Phil.*, vi). On the sources see Cu F. Bühler, *The Sources of the Court of Sapience* (Leipzig, 1932) in the same series.
[16] Ed. Oscar L. Triggs (1896; *EETSES*, 69). The movement of the lines, each hurrying to the end, is utterly unlike Lydgate, who loves a caesura and, as Miss Hammond remark seems to think in half-lines. The piece has been dated 1403 and 1420-22. I should put it o stylistic grounds not much earlier than the earliest manuscript, which is not older than 146 [17] See K. Bülbring, "Sidrac in England," *Festschrift für Wendelin Foerster* (Halle, 1902 pp. 443-478. There was also a translation in prose, of which a fragment is preserved.
[18] See *Hist. Litt.*, xxxi (1893). 285-318.
[19] Last printed in Elias Ashmole, *Theatrum Chemicum Britannicum* (1652); extract Hammond, *op. cit.* Ripley wrote much on scientific subjects in Latin (see Tanner, *op. cit.*
[20] Ed. Thomas Wright, *Political Poems* (1859-61), Wilhelm Hertzberg (Leipzig, 1878), a Sir George Warner (Oxford, 1926). Selections in Hammond, *op. cit.* Abridged and moderniz text in W. H. Dunham, Jr. and Stanley Pargellis, *Complaint and Reform in England, 143 1714* (1938), pp. 3-30.

of alchemy to Edward IV in rime royal; the latter deals with foreign trade and what ought to be England's commercial policy.

Social satire of the *Piers Plowman* type is skilfully presented in the little ballad known as *London Lickpenny*.[21] The poet's experiences in London, where he is unable to get any attention at the King's Bench, Common Pleas, or Chancery, and succeeds only in being robbed of his hood, are told in sixteen eight-line stanzas, most of which end in the refrain, "For lacke of money, I may not spede." The Scottish tradition of Barbour is continued in the work of Blind Harry the minstrel, who presents something of a problem. Toward the end of the fifteenth century he appears in the records as receiving small gifts from the king, and ever since this time he has been remembered as the author of the most popular poem in Scotland down to the eighteenth century. The poem, *The Wallace* [22] (*c.* 1475), is an epic of some 11,000 lines recounting the heroic deeds of the Scottish patriot Sir William Wallace, who was finally captured and executed by the English in 1305. The humble origin of Blind Harry and his blindness from birth are facts incompatible with the literary character of the poem, its aureate vocabulary,[23] the extensive topographical knowledge displayed, which is detailed and exact, and above all the many borrowings from other works of English and French literature. It is likely that the poem in its present form owes much to another hand.[24] About 1450 Richard Holland, a priest and follower of the Douglases, wrote *The Buke of the Howlat* (Owl).[25] It is the familiar story of the bird that became overproud of its borrowed plumage, with nice satirical implications in the parts assigned to the various other birds. Any general political allegory, however, which the poem may have had was probably slight and has now lost its meaning.

Throughout the fifteenth century the authority of Chaucer was paramount, although Gower is mentioned with almost equal respect. Lydgate pays tribute to him on numerous occasions, always in the same tone, as

> The noble poete of Breteyne,
> My mayster Chaucer.

The Chaucerians

Hoccleve, whose affection seems to have sprung from personal acquaintance, calls him "maister deere and fadir reverent." That he felt Chaucer's death deeply is apparent from the frequency with which he alludes to it:

> Death, by thi deth, hath harm irreparable
> Unto us doon;

---

[21] Printed in Hammond, pp. 238-239.
[22] Edited by John Jamieson (2v, Edinburgh, 1820) and James Moir (1889; STS, 6-7,17); facsimile, ed. Sir William Craigie (1939). On the writers mentioned in this paragraph see William Geddie, *A Bibliography of Middle Scots Poets* (Edinburgh, 1912; STS, 61); T. F. Henderson, *Scottish Vernacular Literature* (3ed., Edinburgh, 1910).
[23] The excessive use of Latin derivatives, often slightly assimilated. See John C. Mendenhall, *Aureate Terms: A Study in the Literary Diction of the Fifteenth Century* (Lancaster, Pa., 1919).
[24] See the exhaustive examination of the problem by J. T. T. Brown, *The Wallace and The Bruce Restudied* (Bonn, 1900; *Bonner Beiträge zur Anglistik*, VI), where an interesting case is made out for John Ramsay, known to Dunbar as Sir John the Ross. The identification, however, is disputed.
[25] The best edition is in F. J. Amours, *Scottish Alliterative Poems* (1897; STS, 27), pp. 47-81,

and he had his portrait painted in his *Regiment of Princes* "to puise othir men in remembraunce of his persone." Many other writers pay Chaucer lip service [26] or follow his example, albeit at long remove. For the qualities that make Chaucer great are those incapable of imitation. As Lydgate says:

> We may assay forto countrefete
> His gay style but it wyl not be.

Additional Canterbury Tales   It is not easy to follow the Chaucer tradition in the fifteenth century since it takes a variety of forms and ranges from close dependence, in poets like Hoccleve and Henryson, to occasional verbal echoes which merely indicate familiarity with Chaucer's works. Some go so far as to include among the "Chaucerians" any one who wrote in Chaucer's better-known metres, such as the *Troilus* stanza (rime royal). But such influence is doubtless in many cases at second or third hand. In the anonymous *Plowman's Tale* [27] we have a very un-Chaucerian piece arbitrarily attached to the *Canterbury Tales*. It is a Lollard tract in verse form, in which, under the guise of a conversation between a griffon and a pelican, the author launches into a long denunciation of the pope and the clergy—their pride, luxury, greed and the evil practices resulting therefrom, and many other abuses within the Church. Almost every idea expressed can be paralleled in the writings of Wyclif and his followers, but it is not without interest as a tract for the times and its irony is sometimes telling. More successfully fitted to the *Canterbury Tales* is the *Tale of Beryn* [28] with its Prologue detailing the doings of the pilgrims in the cathedral town and especially the ill-starred attempt of the Pardoner to spend the night with Kit the bar-maid. The Prologue has some of Chaucer's realistic vigor, but none at all of his sly humor or happy turn of phrase. The tale is rather long-drawn-out. Besides these attempts to continue the *Canterbury Tales* we should note that Lydgate's *Siege of Thebes,* discussed below, is fitted with a prologue likewise linking it with the return journey.

In the early editions of Chaucer a number of poems by other poets were commonly included. Some of these were considered genuine, others included because they were in Chaucer's manner. Apart from pieces by poets like Lydgate and Hoccleve and Henryson, who will be discussed later, a little sheaf of poems deserves mention. *La Belle Dame sans Mercy* [29] is a translation in 856 lines from Alain Chartier. The translator's preface and the opening of the poem proper, with its garden and gentlefolk and the approach to the conversation between the lover and his lady, are such as Chaucer might have devised, but he never could have carried on the tiresome and long-winded debate in which the lover pleads and the lady repels all his

[26] Caroline F. E. Spurgeon, *Five Hundred Years of Chaucer Criticism and Allusion, 1357-1900* (3v, Cambridge, 1925).
[27] Printed by Skeat in the *Oxford Chaucer*, VII. 147-190. From an allusion in the poem and from other considerations it is apparent that it was written by the author of *Pierce the Ploughman's Creed.*
[28] Ed. F. J. Furnivall and W. G. Stone (1909; *EETSES*, 105).
[29] All the pieces mentioned in this paragraph are printed in Vol. VII of the *Oxford Chaucer.*

pleas for mercy. The author, Sir Richard Ros, about whom little is known except his parentage, does not have much to recommend him but a certain metrical skill. *The Flower and the Leaf* is somewhat lacking in substance. It is little more than a tableau gracefully described,[30] in which one company of knights and ladies representing the Flower gets drenched in a shower and is hospitably given shelter by another company representing the Leaf. The author alludes to herself as a woman, and since this is true also of another poem, *The Assembly of Ladies,* it has been suggested that they are both by the same writer. But since the former is thought to date from about 1450[31] and the latter shows a much later treatment of the final *e,* this is at least doubtful. *The Assembly of Ladies* is not very logically planned. In the usual dream convention the author, along with her four companions and many others, is peremptorily summoned to appear before a lady named Loyaltè, merely to allow each one to present a "bill" complaining of broken promises, disappointment in love, and the like. The poem owes something to Lydgate's *Temple of Glas.* In tone and phrasing the most Chaucerian of all these apocryphal pieces is a little poem of 290 lines called *The Cuckoo and the Nightingale.* In the manuscripts it is just as fittingly called *The Book of Cupid, God of Love,* for it explains that the God of Love has great power over folk, even over the poet, who is "old and unlusty." The body of the poem is a dispute between the two birds over the joys and sorrows of love, recalling at times in setting and circumstances the altercation in the *Owl and the Nightingale.* On the basis of an "Explicit Clanvowe" in the Cambridge MS it has been attributed to Sir Thomas Clanvowe, a friend of Chaucer's friend, Lewis Clifford, and quite possibly known to Chaucer himself.[32] But whatever its authorship the piece has quite enough charm to account for its influence on Milton in his sonnet "To the Nightingale" and for the modernization found among Wordsworth's poems.

In many ways the Scottish Chaucerians were more successful in their efforts than their English contemporaries. In 1406, at the age of eleven, the young King James I of Scotland was captured by the English and for eighteen years was a prisoner in England. He does not seem to have been badly treated and had plenty of leisure in which to acquire the intimate knowledge of Chaucer's poetry which he shows. Upon his release in 1424 he was married to Joan Beaufort, the niece of two of the most powerful magnates in England. The story of his capture and imprisonment, his falling in love at first sight when, like Palamon in the *Knight's Tale,* he caught a glimpse of a surpassingly beautiful lady in the garden below his prison window, and the dream in which he is carried aloft, like Chaucer in the *Hous of Fame,* to the palace of Venus and later is advised by Minerva

The Flower and the Leaf

The Assembly of Ladies

The Cuckoo and the Nightingale

Scottish Chaucerians

---

[30] Dryden, who translated it in his *Fables Ancient and Modern,* thought it was by Chaucer and says, "I was so particularly pleased, both for the invention and the moral, that I cannot under myself from recommending it to the reader."

[31] It must be admitted that the dates of these poems are highly conjectural.

[32] Kittredge (*MP,* I. 13-18) argued for Sir John Clanvowe, who died in 1391. Although Skeat's dating of the poem after 1402 is none too secure, Thomas seems the better candidate.

The Kingis
Quair

—such incidents form the subject of *The Kingis Quair* ("King's Book").[33] Written apparently just before his release, in a language the Chaucerian character of which has been somewhat obscured by Scottish copyists,[34] it makes a very pleasing little romantic story out of facts which are in part at least autobiographical. As its 197 stanzas are those of Chaucer's *Troilus* the form has generally been known since as "rime royal." Later in the century another Scottish poet, Robert Henryson, schoolmaster of Dunfermline,

Robert
Henryson

caught some of the spirit of Chaucer in his *Fables*,[35] where he told such stories as "The Cock and the Fox" and "The Town Mouse and the Country Mouse," adding to each, however, a rather un-Chaucerian "moral." He turned the tale of Orpheus and Eurydice into rime royal and wrote a number of shorter moralizing pieces. His ballad of *Robene and Makyne* has been admired as an early pastoral and considered superior to the *Nut Brown Maid*, a judgment with which many will agree. But the poem which at-

The
Testament
of
Cresseid

taches itself most closely to Chaucer is *The Testament of Cresseid*. In this piece Cresseid, deserted by Diomede, curses the gods and is punished by leprosy. Ashamed to be seen by her friends, she goes to the spittel-house to live among the lepers. The crowning torture which she endures is to be given alms, as one of the beggars, by Troilus, whom Henryson represents as still living and who happens to pass by in a company of knights. Neither recognizes the other at the time, although Troilus is disturbed by a puzzling resemblance to Cresseid and she afterwards learns who he was. In a closing lament Cresseid blames her own unfaithfulness on "lustis lecherous," crying

> Fy! fals Cresseid! O, trew knight Troilus!

The poem presents a grim incident with moving pathos, and shows how less tolerant poet would have concluded Chaucer's great poem.

Charles
d'Orléans

Although the English translations of the poems of Charles d'Orléans contain occasional echoes of Chaucer, he may be mentioned here not so much because he shows the influence of Chaucer as because he is the heir to the French tradition of Deschamps and Froissart which so greatly influenced Chaucer. In the case of Charles d'Orléans this tradition expressed itself wholly in the conventional chanson and ballade of love. In spite of an occasional sentiment or graceful phrase that recaptures one's attention, the poems tend to become tiresome in their repetition of a few stock themes—praise of the lady, appeals for pity, avowal of lifelong service, conventional despair, and the like. Such poetry is something of an anachronism in the second quarter of the fifteenth century.

---

33 The most recent editions are those of Alex. Lawson (1910), W. W. Skeat (1911; ST n.s. 1), and W. Mackay Mackenzie (1939). The date and authorship of the poem have been questioned, but without much success. The most authoritative biography of James I is that E. W. M. Balfour-Melville (1936).
34 Sir William Craigie, "The Language of the *Kingis Quair*," E&S, xxv (1940). 22–
35 The works of Henryson have been edited by G. Gregory Smith (3v, 1906-14; STS, 58, 64), and in one volume by H. Harvey Wood (2ed, Edinburgh, 1958).
36 Ed. Robert Steele (1941; EETS, 215; notes by Robert Steele and Mabel Day, 1946, EE 220).

It has been said that John Lydgate lived thirty years too long for the good of his literary reputation. Be this as it may, it is certain that to the last half of his life belong most of the incredibly voluminous writings which students of literary history know, if only by name, today. He was born in Lydgate, in Suffolk, probably around 1370, and at the age of about fifteen was admitted to the nearby abbey of Bury St. Edmunds. It is suspected that he was sent to study for a time at one of the universities. In any case he was ordained a priest in 1397, after which we know nothing more about him for nearly twenty years. In 1423 he was elected prior of Hatfield Broadoak, in Essex. He soon relinquished the office, certainly by 1430 [37] and possibly in 1425, for about 1426 he was in Paris, and probably remained long enough to have translated a poetical pedigree for the Earl of Warwick, written the *Dance of Macabre,* and begun his translation of Deguilleville, this last at the command of the Earl of Salisbury. From 1434 until he died Lydgate was back at Bury St. Edmunds. The date of his death is uncertain, but it probably occurred in the year 1449.[38]

Lydgate

Among Lydgate's poems, which run to well over 100,000 lines, there are many unsolved problems of chronology, but fortunately his longer pieces can all be dated with some approximation to definiteness. His selection from Aesop's fables and *The Churl and the Bird* [39] were probably written toward the close of the fourteenth century. To the period just after 1400 belong certain pieces in which the influence of Chaucer is very evident— the *Floure of Curtesy,*[40] a valentine poem praising his lady in the courtly love manner, the *Complaint of the Black Knight,*[41] which echoes the situation in Chaucer's *Book of the Duchess,* and the *Temple of Glas,*[42] in which a surpassingly beautiful lady complains to Venus of being separated from her knight, the knight reveals his love sickness, and the lovers are happily united through the favor of the goddess. The last employs the familiar convention of the imaginary dream. Between these poems and the beginning of the *Troy Book* in 1412 stands *Reason and Sensuality,* after the *Troy Book* the *Life of Our Lady. Reason and Sensuality* [43] (c. 1408), in spite of its 7000 lines, still makes rather pleasant reading with its allegory of the poet's meeting with Venus and the journey to the Garden of Pleasure which Guillaume de Lorris had acquainted us with in the *Roman de la Rose.* *The Life of Our Lady* [44] (nearly 6000 lines in rime royal) is now edited. Lydgate's later years were occupied by a series of enormous translations

His Volumi- nous Production

[37] See Georg Fiedler, "Zum Leben Lydgate's," *Anglia,* xv (1893). 389-395.
[38] The best account of his life is that of J. Schick in his edition of the *Temple of Glas* (1891; EETSES, 60), followed not too cautiously by the *DNB.*
[39] Both in *The Minor Poems of John Lydgate,* ed. Henry N. MacCracken, Vol. II (1934; ETS, 192).
[40] *Minor Poems,* II. 410-418.
[41] *Minor Poems,* II. 382-410.
[42] Ed. Schick, as above.
[43] Ed. Ernst Sieper (1901-3; EETSES, 84, 89).
[44] Ed. Joseph A. Lauritis, Ralph A. Klinefelter, and Vernon F. Gallagher (Pittsburgh, 1961; Duquesne Univ. Stud., Philol. Ser., No. 2).

*His
Transla-
tions*

of well-known works. The *Troy Book*[45] (30,117 lines in decasyllabic couplets), rendered from the Latin prose of Guido della Colonna, occupied most of his time from 1412 to 1420. This was followed by the *Siege of Thebes*[46] (1420-22), based on a French prose condensation of the *Roman de Thèbes*. It is provided, as already noted, with a prologue attaching it to the homeward journey of Chaucer's Canterbury pilgrims, and serves as a companion piece to the *Knight's Tale* on the outward journey. Although only 4716 lines, it is still too long for such an occasion. The *Pilgrimage of the Life of Man*[47] (1426-30) fills nearly 24,000 lines in octosyllabic couplets. It renders the first of Deguilleville's three *Pèlerinages* (see p. 288). Finally, the longest of all his works, *The Fall of Princes* (1431-38), is also the most tedious. One can hardly appreciate the taste of an age which endured more than 26,000 lines detailing the tragedies which have befallen the great.[48] It is based on the French prose *Des Cas des Nobles Hommes et Femmes* of Laurent de Premierfait, itself an expansion of Boccaccio's *De Casibus Virorum Illustrium*. At the time of his death Lydgate was at work on the *Secrees of Old Philisoffres*, a translation of the *Secreta Secretorum* attributed in the Middle Ages to Aristotle. It was finished by a disciple, possibly Benedict Burgh.[49]

*Shorter
Pieces*

In addition to his longer works Lydgate's shorter pieces fill two volumes in modern print.[50] He was evidently known as a ready versifier, able to turn out a poem suitable for any occasion, and therefore during most of his life was at the call of any one who chose to command his services. He wrote poems on the occasion of Henry VI's coronation, on Gloucester's marriage, on a royal entry into London, the departure of Thomas Chaucer for the Continent, etc. He composed verses for mummings at Bishopswood, Eltham, Hartford, London, Windsor, and for the mercers and the goldsmiths of London.[51] His lyrics and shorter poems likewise show a certain unmonastic variety. There are, of course, many religious lyrics of the types familiar to us elsewhere—hymns and prayers to the Virgin and Christ, translations of Latin hymns, little sermons in verse, and all varieties of hortatory and devotional poems. They are marked by sincerity, smoothness of metre, and an occasional happy image. Some, like the *God Is Myn Helpere* and *An Holy Medytacion,* are among the best things he wrote. There are

---

[45] Ed. Henry Bergen (1906-35; *EETSES,* 97, 103, 106, 126). On Lydgate's sources see, in addition to Bergen, E. Bagby Atwood, "Some Minor Sources of Lydgate's *Troy Book,*" *SP* xxxv (1938). 25-42.

[46] Ed. Axel Erdmann and Eilert Ekwall (1911-30; *EETSES,* 108, 125).

[47] Ed. F. J. Furnivall and Katharine B. Locock (1899-1904; *EETSES,* 77, 83, 92).

[48] Ed. Henry Bergen (1924-27; *EETSES,* 121-124). He well characterizes it as "a collection gathered throughout the centuries describing the most memorable and crushing blows dealt by fate to the illustrious personages of mythology and history, and written, as the author himself said, with the object of teaching princes the virtue of wisdom and moderation by holding up to them the example of misfortunes provoked by egotism, pride and inordinate ambition."

[49] Ed. Robert Steele (1894; *EETSES,* 66). Other fifteenth-century translations in prose are edited by Steele (1898; *EETSES,* 74). On Benedict Burgh see below, p. 302.

[50] Henry N. MacCracken, *The Minor Poems of John Lydgate* (1911-34; *EETSES,* 107 and *EETS,* 192). The first volume contains a discussion of the Lydgate canon.

[51] These are all printed by MacCracken, as above. On the general type see Robert Withington, *English Pageantry: An Historical Outline* (2v, Cambridge, Mass., 1918-20).

didactic and moralizing pieces ranging from *A Dietary*, giving simple rules for good health, or *Stans Puer ad Mensam*, teaching the rules of courtesy and conduct, to his own *Testament*, which combines moral reflection with interesting autobiographical allusions. Of similar utilitarian aim are admonitory pieces like the *Dance of Macabre* or fables like *The Churl and the Bird* and *Horse, Goose, and Sheep*, with its refrain advising man "For no prerogatif his neyghburghe to dispise." The good monk saw nothing inappropriate in composing an occasional love poem in the courtly tradition, such as *My Lady Dere* or *A Lover's New Year's Gift*, and his muse occasionally takes a humorous and satirical turn as in *Bycorne and Chychevache* and *The Order of Fools*. *Bycorne and Chychevache* presents an amusing picture of a fat and a lean beast, who feed only on patient husbands and wives respectively. Chychevache is distressingly thin; she complains that it is a "dear year" in patient wives. The *Order of Fools* describes a new mendicant order which is made up of all sorts from the sacrilegious and adulterous to the credulous and those who marry an old woman for money. It is not right to think of all these shorter pieces as the work of Lydgate's early years, but it is true that his standing as a poet would have been higher if he had written only these and had not made the interminable translations which constitute the great bulk of his writings.

Some blame for the latter, however, must be shared by the numerous *Poetry* patrons who requested him to make them. The *Life of Our Lady* and the *to Order* *Troy Book* were written at the command of Prince Hal, while the *Fall of Princes* was translated at the desire of Humphrey, Duke of Gloucester, uncle and regent of Henry VI. The Deguilleville was for Thomas de Montacute, Earl of Salisbury. When Henry VI visited the shrine of St. Edmund at Christmas in 1422 Lydgate's abbot commanded him to write the *Legend of St. Edmund and Fremund,* and when the abbot of St. Albans wished his house to be honored in a similar way he turned to the monk of Bury for the *Life of Albon and Amphabel.* Many other shorter pieces were written upon request, such as the mummings, already mentioned, for the mercers and the goldsmiths of London. Lydgate was the most competent literary handy-man available, and we should be expecting too much to hope that all his odd jobs should have been done and his extensive commissions executed with the inspiration of high art.

Strictly contemporary with Lydgate and an even more devoted admirer *Hoccleve* of Chaucer was Thomas Hoccleve (*c.* 1369-*c.* 1450). From the age of nineteen or twenty he spent the better part of forty years as a clerk in the Privy Seal Office. Fortunately he is one of the most autobiographical of English poets. He was given an annuity of £10 in 1399, and on various occasions when it was in arrears (as it often was) he appealed in ballades to those who might expedite its payment. Whatever he received he spent on a merry life, eating and drinking to excess, haunting the tavern, kissing the girls and paying for their refreshment, riding on the river and paying the boatmen lavishly, for the pleasure of being called "master." All this he tells us in *La Male Regle de T. Hoccleve* (*c.* 1406). He promises there to amend his ways. In any case, a few years later he married. For a period of five years he suffered from a nervous breakdown (*c.* 1415-20) and, as he says, was mad. In the *Complaint* and *Dialogue with a Friend,* which really form a single poem of some 800 lines (*c.* 1421-2), he writes at length about his illness and his difficulty in convincing others of his recovery. About 1425 he seems to have been retired on a corrody at the priory of Southwick in Hampshire. He was apparently alive in 1448, but died probably a year or two later.

The Regiment of Princes

The bulk of Hoccleve's verse is not large, and the range is limited.[52] A few autobiographical pieces, a dozen occasional poems, mostly short, an equal number of lyrics to the Virgin and Christ, some of them translations, a couple of tales from the *Gesta Romanorum,* two short translations (*The Letter of Cupid, Learn to Die*), and the *Regiment of Princes* make up his work. Of these the longest (5463 lines) is the *Regiment of Princes* (1412), written for the young prince who was about to become Henry V. It is the usual advice on how to live and rule, put together from the *De Ludo Scachorum* of Jacobus de Cessolis, the *Secreta Secretorum,* and the *De Regimine Principum* of Egidio Colonna, with a long prefatory section (2000 lines) full of personal allusion. Hoccleve does not have Lydgate's fatal fluency, or Gower's social and moral urge. He does not write for the sheer love of writing, and he seldom rises to the level of poetry. Yet his complete frankness, his many personal revelations, and his frequent references to current events make his verse almost always interesting. In poets of the fifteenth century, or indeed of later centuries, this is no small merit.

The Amateurs

About the middle of the century we can distinguish a number of amateurs who hazarded an occasional venture in verse. George Ashby, who lived to be nearly eighty, and who was for "full fourty yere" a clerk of the Signet, left behind him three poems.[53] *A Prisoner's Reflections,* written during an imprisonment in 1463 in the Fleet, is a modest consolation of philosophy in 350 lines of rime royal. His other poems are *The Active Policy of a Prince* (918 lines), written for Edward, Prince of Wales, and a paraphrase of some extracts from the *Liber Philosophorum Moralium Antiquorum.*[54] John Shirley,[55] who died in 1456 at about the age of ninety, is chiefly remembered as the copyist of a number of manuscripts containing the works of Chaucer and Lydgate, but wrote two prologues in verse for books which he compiled. In one of Shirley's manuscripts is preserved the only copy of a poem of 172 lines called *Evidence to Beware and Good Counsel* by "that honurable squier," Richard Sellyng.[56] Two stanzas attributed in manuscripts

---

[52] It is all printed in *Hoccleve's Works* (EETSES, 61, 72, 73).
[53] *George Ashby's Poems,* ed. Mary Bateson (1899; EETSES, 76).
[54] For other translations of the *Dicts and Sayings of the Philosophers* see below, p. 302.
[55] See Otto Gaertner, *John Shirley: Sein Leben und Wirken* (Halle, 1904) and Hammond, *op. cit.* Miss Hammond conjectures that he may have run a bookshop and lending library in London.
[56] See "Richard Sellyng," by the present writer, in *Essays and Studies in Honor of Carleton Brown* (1940), pp. 167-181.

to "Halsham Esquier" have been referred to John Halsham, who died in or before 1415 owning lands in Sussex, Kent, Norfolk and Wilts.[57] None of these poems is intrinsically important, but they are interesting as suggesting the extension of literary activity among those not of the literary profession or the Church.

[57] Helen P. South, "The Question of Halsam," *PMLA*, L (1935). 362-371.

XXI
Looking Forward

Growth of a Reading Public

All through the fifteenth century there is growing evidence of the extension of the reading public.[1] That works were being written to be read through the eye rather than taken in through the ear is apparent not only from the frequency with which reference is made to reading, but from the length of such poems as Lydgate's *Troy Book* and the *Fall of Princes*, which could not conceivably have been intended for minstrel recitation. The industrial development at this period and the growth of a landed gentry were accompanied by more widespread education and the leisure to enjoy it. The new reading public is nowhere more plainly indicated than in the production of certain late romances very different in length and character from those of an earlier period. We have already spoken of the *Gest Historiale of the Destruction of Troy* with its 14,000 long alliterative lines.[2] More extreme cases are the two Gargantuan poems of the London skinner, Henry Lovelich. Written about 1425, the *Merlin*[3] reaches a total of 27,852 four-stress lines when the manuscript breaks off, and the *History of the Holy Grail*[4] runs to nearly 24,000 lines, with an additional section of several thousand missing in the beginning. On a similar scale two treatments of the Alexander legend were written in Scotland—one an anonymous poem completed in 1428 in 11,000 lines,[5] the other a narrative of about 20,000 verses written by Sir Gilbert Hay towards the end of the century.[6]

Prose Romances

Growth of the reading public is also shown by the use of prose for works which would earlier have been written in verse. In this century we witness the beginning of the prose romance.[7] What is apparently the earliest is a prose *Alexander* in the Thornton MS (1430-40),[8] but from about the middle

[1] On this general subject see the articles of H. S. Bennett, "The Author and His Public in the Fourteenth and Fifteenth Centuries," *E&S*, XXIII (1938). 7-24; "Caxton and His Public," *RES*, XIX (1943). 113-119; "Science and Information in English Writings of the Fifteenth Century," *MLR*, XXXIX (1944). 1-8; J. W. Adamson, "The Extent of Literacy in England in the Fifteenth and Sixteenth Centuries: Notes and Conjectures," *Library*, 4 Ser., X 1929). 163-193; C. L. Kingsford, *English Historical Literature in the Fifteenth Century* (1913), and the same author's *Prejudice and Promise in Fifteenth Century England* (1925).

[2] See above, p. 184.

[3] Ed. Ernst A. Kock (1904-32; *EETSES*, 93, 112; *EETS*, 185).

[4] Ed. F. J. Furnivall (1874-78; *EETSES*, 20, 24, 28, 30).

[5] Ed. R. L. Graeme Ritchie (4v, 1921-29; *STS*, n.s. 12, 17, 21, 25). On the controversy over the authorship that has raged for fifty years see Ritchie's intro., where the presentation of the case for Barbour is no more conclusive than previous attempts.

[6] Only selections have been printed; see A. Hermann, *The Forraye of Gadderis; The Vowis* (Berlin, 1900).

[7] Prose romance might have developed from stories like the Old English *Apollonius* (see p. 104), but any such development was cut short by the Norman Conquest.

[8] Ed. J. S. Westlake (1913; *EETS*, 143).

of the century date *Pontus and Sidone* [9] and a very long prose *Merlin*.[10] Of
about the same date are prose condensations of the Troy and Thebes stories
in a Rawlinson MS.[11] With the introduction of printing a number of new
prose romances were produced, all of them taken from French originals.
Caxton translated (1469-71) and printed at Bruges in 1474 or 1475 his
Recuyell of the Historyes of Troye.[12] In England he made and printed translations of *Godeffroy of Boloyne* [13] (1481), the story of the siege of Jerusalem
in the first crusade, deriving ultimately from William of Tyre and familiar
later in Tasso's *Gerusalemme Liberata;* the excellent story of *Paris and
Vienne* (1485); *Charles the Great* [14] (1485), from the French prose *Fierabras; The Foure Sonnes of Aymon* [15] (c. 1489), recounting Charlemagne's
struggle with these valiant nobles; *Blanchardyn and Eglantine* [16] (c. 1489),
a pleasing story reminiscent, in its earlier part, of the Perceval and involving
in the remainder the hero's rescue of his lady from the usual unwelcome
suitor. His *Eneydos* (1490) has been mentioned in a previous chapter.
Malory's great work, which Caxton printed, will be discussed later. Caxton's
practice was followed by his successor Wynkyn de Worde, who set his
apprentice Henry Watson to translating books from the French. One such
is the romance of *Valentine and Orson* [17] printed by him soon after the
turn of the century. Nor did the fashion die with the fifteenth century. About
1525, Sir John Bourchier, Lord Berners, best known for his translation of
Froissart, occupied his leisure at Calais by turning into English the story
of *Huon of Bordeaux*,[18] loosely connected with the Charlemagne cycle.
Many of these prose romances enjoyed considerable popularity throughout
the sixteenth century, were frequently reprinted, exerted their influence on
Spenser and others, and even furnished material for the Elizabethan drama.

The prose romance, however, is only one type in which the translators *Other*
were busy. Translation from the French was, of course, characteristic of the *Prose*
whole Middle English period, at least from the time of Layamon, and we
have already mentioned a number of works turned into English verse in the
fifteenth century, notably in Lydgate's longer poems. At this time several
lesser men were contributing individual pieces to the growing body of
popular books available in the native tongue. John Walton, a canon of
Osney, seems to have succeeded Trevisa as literary purveyor to the Berkeley
family. To him has plausibly been attributed the translation of Vegetius'
De Re Militari made in 1408 for Lord Thomas Berkeley, Trevisa's former

[9] Ed. F. J. Mather, Jr., *PMLA*, XII (1897), pp. l-lxvii, 1-150.
[10] Ed. Henry B. Wheatley (1865-69; EETS, 10, 21, 36) with an introduction by Wm. E. Mead (1899; *EETS*, 112).
[11] The *Sege of Troy* is edited by N. E. Griffin, *PMLA*, XXII (1907). 157-200; both are printed by Friedrich Brie, "Zwei mittelenglische Prosaromane: The Sege of Thebes und The Sege of Troy," *Archiv*, cxxx (1913). 40-52, 269-285.
[12] Ed. H. Oskar Sommer (2v, 1894).
[13] Ed. Mary N. Colvin (1893; EETSES, 64).
[14] Ed. Sidney J. H. Herrtage (2v, 1880-81; EETSES, 36-37).
[15] Ed. Octavia Richardson (2v, 1884-85; EETSES, 44-45).
[16] Ed. Leon Kellner (1890; EETSES, 58).
[17] Ed. Arthur Dickson (1937; EETS, 204).
[18] Ed. S. L. Lee (4v, 1882-87; EETSES, 40, 41, 43, 50).

patron,[19] and in 1410 he certainly translated for Berkeley's daughter Eliza-beth, who was later to marry the Earl of Warwick, Boethius' *Consolation of Philosophy* [20] into eight-line stanzas and rime royal, with much indebted-ness to Chaucer's prose version. Sometime in the earlier part of the century an anonymous translator turned *Palladius on Husbandry* [21] also into rime royal.

East Anglian Patronage

Scrope

Metham

Burgh

But in some ways the most interesting group of poet-translators was that which wrote for a little coterie of East Anglian patrons around the middle of the century.[22] Stephen Scrope (*c.* 1396-1472) translated and presented to his stepfather, Sir John Fastolf, a version in prose of *The Dicts and Sayings of the Philosophers* [23] from the French of Tignonville. There were other translations of the *Dicts,* the best known of which was that of Anthony Wydeville, Earl Rivers (after 1473), printed by Caxton. Scrope also trans-lated from Christine de Pisan *The Epistle of Othea to Hector,*[24] a variety of courtesy book offering instruction to a prince in the form of a hundred stories with spiritual and chivalric applications. Later in the century a second translation was made by Anthony Babyngton.[25] Scrope may have done the translations of *Tulle of Old Age* printed by Caxton [26] and the *Boke of Noblesse,*[27] more often attributed to William Worcester, Fastolf's secretary, who is known to have made a revision of Scrope's *Dicts and Sayings.* An-other Norfolk author, John Metham, in addition to treatises on palmistry and physiognomy, wrote in 1448-9 for Sir Miles Stapleton and his wife a poem of 2200 lines in rime royal called *Amoryus and Cleopes,*[28] a variant of the Pyramus and Thisbe theme loosely associated with the story of Alexander the Great. Stapleton, prominent in Norfolk affairs, was a friend and neighbor of Fastolf. Most of the legends of Osbern Bokenham, already discussed,[29] were written for various ladies in Suffolk, including Katherine Howard, great-grandmother of Henry Howard, Earl of Surrey, and Lady Isabel, wife of Henry Bourchier, later Earl of Essex. For the latter's son Benedict Burgh, mentioned above as the possible continuator of Lydgate's *Secrees of Old Philisoffres,* wrote a verse paraphrase of the *Distichs of Cato,*[30] a miscellaneous body of aphorisms on conduct and morals. Finally

[19] See Mark Science, as below, pp. xlviii-xlix.

[20] Ed. Mark Science (1927; EETS, 170).

[21] Ed. Rev. Barton Lodge (1873-79; EETS, 52, 72).

[22] See Samuel Moore, "Patrons of Letters in Norfolk and Suffolk, c. 1450," PMLA, xxvii (1912). 188-207; xxviii (1913). 79-105.

[23] Ed. Margaret E. Schofield (Phila., 1936), with an introduction containing the best account of Scrope's life, and Curt F. Bühler (1941; EETS, 211), who prints also an anonymous translation and modifications of Scrope's translation.

[24] Ed. G. F. Warner (1904; Roxburghe Club).

[25] Ed. James D. Gordon (Phila., 1942).

[26] Ed. Heinz Susebach (Halle, 1933; Studien zur englischen Philologie, 75).

[27] Ed. J. Gough Nichols (1860; Roxburghe Club).

[28] The Works of John Metham, ed. Hardin Craig (1916; EETS, 132).

[29] See p. 289. To Norfolk apparently belongs the translation of Methodius mentioned above p. 289.

[30] The best edition is that of Max Förster, "Die Burghsche Cato-Paraphrase," Archiv, cxv (1905). 298-323. For Burgh's other works see Max Förster, "Über Benedict Burghs Leben und Werke," Archiv, ci (1898). 29-64.

we may note that William de la Pole, Duke of Suffolk, husband of Alice Chaucer and friend of Charles d'Orléans, besides being a literary patron wrote ballades in French and, if the attribution is sound, a small group of poems in English.[31] The various persons who thus appear as patrons of letters in Norfolk and Suffolk were all well known to the Pastons. Many of them appear in the *Paston Letters*,[32] a collection of letters by and to mem- **Paston** bers of this well-known Norfolk family over a period of three generations **Letters** (1422-1509), which, if not literature, are fascinating for the pictures they give us of life in fifteenth-century England.[33]

The inference lies close at hand that the growth of a landed gentry and **Courtesy** the rising fortunes of the middle class were having a stimulating effect on **Literature** certain types of writing. This inference is borne out by a succession of courtesy books intended for just such classes.[34] There are works belonging to the type known as parental advice, such as Peter Idley's *Instructions to His Son*,[35] the anonymous Scottish *Ratis Raving*,[36] both in verse, and the *Book of the Knight of La Tour-Landry*, written by the French author (1371-72) for his daughters, and twice rendered into English, once about 1450[37] and again by Caxton in 1484. The contemporary *Babees Book*[38] offers more limited instructions on social amenities and the behavior of young people, while John Russell's *Boke of Nurture*, the work of Humphrey, Duke of Gloucester's marshal, deals comprehensively with the whole training for service with a nobleman. Even such a collection as the volume commonly known as the *Book of St. Albans*, containing treatises on hawking and heraldry, and one on hunting by Dame Julians Barnes,[39] shows by its frequent reference to "gentill men" the class to whose interests it appealed.

English prose in the fifteenth century found its most voluminous expres-

[31] See Henry N. MacCracken, "An English Friend of Charles of Orléans," *PMLA*, xxvi (1911). 142-180.
[32] Ed. James Gairdner (6v, 1904).
[33] Although he was not a part of the Norfolk group, mention should be made of John Tiptoft, Earl of Worcester, whose translation of Cicero's *De Amicitia* and Buonaccorso's *De Honestate* were printed by Caxton, and to whom other translations are questionably attributed. He was an enthusiast for the new learning, traveled in Italy buying books, and generously assisted Italian and English scholars. See R. J. Mitchell, *John Tiptoft, 1427-1470* (1938), and H. B. Lathrop, "The Translations of John Tiptoft," *MLN*, xli (1926). 496-501. It would be pleasant to pause over the early humanists—Grey, Gunthorpe, Flemming, and John Free. They are a part of English cultural history, but the importance of humanism for literature came later. See George R. Stephens, *The Knowledge of Greek in England in the Middle Ages* (Phila., 1933), W. F. Schirmer, *Der englische Frühhumanismus* (Leipzig, 1931), and R. Weiss, *Humanism in England during the Fifteenth Century* (Oxford, 1941).
[34] For the different types and a brief sketch of early courtesy literature see ch. 1 of John E. Mason, *Gentlefolk in the Making* (Phila., 1935).
[35] Ed. Charlotte D'Evelyn (1935; *MLA* Monograph Ser., vi).
[36] Ed. J. R. Lumby (1870; *EETS*, 43), and, more recently, R. Girvan (1939; *STS*, 3rd ser., Vol. xi). The title is supposed to mean Rate's raving.
[37] Ed. Thomas Wright (1868, revised 1906; *EETS*, 33).
[38] This and other early courtesy books, including Russell's *Boke of Nurture* are ed. by F. J. Furnivall (1868; *EETS*, 32).
[39] Julians' Barnes was the name of a messuage near St. Albans. Dame Julians was presumably the wife or widow of the country gentleman who owned it. The familiar designation Dame Juliana Berners is an invention of eighteenth-century antiquarians, as is the legend that she was abbess of Sopwell priory. See the introduction to William Blades' edition (1901) and the communications of W. W. Skeat in the *Academy*, lxxv (1908). 87-88, 110-111. Much of the *Book* is based on Twici's *Treatise on Hunting* and other earlier works.

Pecock

sion in the work of Reginald Pecock (*c.* 1395-*c.* 1460). A brilliant career at Oxford recommended him to Humphrey, Duke of Gloucester, who brought him to court and later secured for him the bishopric of St. Asaph. His active and original mind was soon employed on numerous expository and controversial works. *The Reule of Crysten Religioun* [40] (1443) has been well described as "the first book of a *summa theologica.*" The *Donet,*[41] which followed soon afterwards, serves as an introduction to it and, at the same time, a more general guide to the Christian life. The *Poore Mennes Myrrour* is an extract from the first part of the *Donet* prepared for the "persone poorist in haver (possessions) and in witt." His most famous work is a systematic attempt to refute by reason, rather than authority, the views of the Lollards. It is known as the *Repressor of Over Much Blaming of the Clergy* [42] (*c.* 1450). Two other treatises remain, the *Folewer of the Donet* [43] (before 1454), which supplements the *Donet* with an exposition of the more intellectual virtues residing in the reason rather than the will, and *The Book of Faith* [44] (*c.* 1456), which defends the authority of the Church even if it be admitted that she can err. While Pecock's position was, generally speaking, orthodox enough, his daring and often tactless statements played into the hands of his enemies, and he had a genius for alienating even those who might have admired his ability and sympathized with his views. In the end his independence and self-confidence gave his opponents their opportunity and brought about his condemnation. He was forced to recant, or go to the stake, and he spent his closing years confined in Thorney abbey without books or writing materials. Though he escaped the flames, his works nevertheless were burnt, and all six that survive exist in unique manuscripts. Of late his prose style has come in for enthusiastic praise, but sober judgment can hardly acquiesce in too high an estimate of his purely literary importance.

Religious and Secular Works

Pecock's contemporary, William Lichfield, who was associated with him on several occasions, was parson of All Hallows the Great in Thames Street. He was famous as a preacher and left at his death in 1448, as we learn from a contemporary record, 3083 sermons. They have not come down to us, but we have from his hand an interesting version of a portion of the *Ancrene Riwle.*[45] Other writers at the same time were using prose for secular subjects. John Capgrave, an Austin friar of Lynn, when he died in 1464 was at work on a *Chronicle of England,*[46] which reaches the year 1417. That

---

[40] Ed. Wm. Cabell Greet (1927; EETS, 171). On Pecock see V. H. H. Green, *Bishop Reginald Pecock: A Study in Ecclesiastical History and Thought* (Cambridge, 1945).

[41] Ed. Elsie V. Hitchcock (1921; EETS, 156). The name of Donatus, author of the little catechism of Latin grammar (the *Ars Minor*) with which everybody began his study of Latin in the Middle Ages, came to designate a primer or elementary book on any subject.

[42] Ed. C. Babington (2v, 1860; Rolls Ser.).

[43] Ed. Elsie V. Hitchcock (1924; EETS, 164).

[44] Ed. J. L. Morison (Glasgow, 1909), with an excellent essay on Pecock's relation to fifteenth-century thought.

[45] He wrote also a poem called *The Complaint of God to Sinful Man* (EETS, xv. 198-232), preserved in more than a dozen manuscripts.

[46] Ed. F. C. Hingeston (1858; Rolls Ser.). He also wrote in Latin the *Nova Legenda Angliae*, ed. C. Horstmann (2v, Oxford, 1901), and, in English, lives of St. Augustine and Gilbert of Sempringham.

verse, however, was not completely discarded for such purposes is shown by the *Chronicle* of John Hardyng,[47] whose experience in the battle of Agincourt unfortunately did not improve his metrical aim. And we may note that while his best-known work, the *De Laudibus Legum Angliae* (1471), is in Latin, Sir John Fortescue, Chief Justice of the King's Bench, wrote in English *On the Governance of England*,[48] the first work in English on constitutional history, and other shorter pieces.

Of all the books of English fifteenth-century literature the best known is Malory's *Morte Darthur*, not only because it is still often read in its own right but because it has furnished the inspiration for the *Idylls of the King* and numerous other modern treatments of Arthurian story. Gathering together, as it does, the main body of Arthurian legends into one comprehensive narrative, it has enjoyed, except for ɔ brief period in the days of Dryden and Pope, an almost unbroken popularity down to our own time. It is a work which obviously required much leisure to produce. Therefore, the author's closing request to his readers, "Pray for me, while I am on live that God send me good deliverance," is not without meaning when properly understood. For the book, as we now know, was written in prison, where Malory spent the major part of the last twenty years of his life.

Malory: Morte Darthur

It is only in recent years that we have learned the full story of Sir Thomas Malory.[49] The date of his birth is unknown, but he was the son of a Warwickshire gentleman who died in 1433-34. Entering the service of Richard Beauchamp, Earl of Warwick, he was with the "Father of Courtesy" at Calais possibly in 1436. He was knighted before 1442 and served in the Parliament of 1445. By this time he had begun taking the law into his own hands, after the turbulent manner of his day, and was soon launched on a career of violence which led to a variety of felonies and misdemeanors, including assault, extortion, jail breaking, poaching, and a cattle raid. The two most serious offenses of which he was accused were lying in ambush with an armed band to murder Humphrey, Duke of Buckingham, and two attacks on Coombe abbey, in which with a hundred followers he broke down doors, terrorized the monks, and plundered the abbot's chests. For his various offenses he was kept in fairly continuous confinement from about 1451 on, and died, presumably in prison, on March 12, 1471. He was buried near Newgate, in a chapel at the Grey Friars. In view of his life it

Malory's Life

[47] Ed. Henry Ellis (1812). On Hardyng, see C. L. Kingsford, *English Historical Literature in the Fifteenth Century* (Oxford, 1913), ch. VI.

[48] Ed. Charles Plummer (Oxford, 1885). See his *Works,* ed. Lord Clermont (2v, 1869).

[49] Our knowledge goes back to an identification made in 1894 by G. L. Kittredge, most fully presented in "Who Was Sir Thomas Malory?" *Harvard Studies & Notes in Phil. & Lit.,* v (1896). 85-106. A few details were added in 1922 by E. K. Chambers in his *Sir Thomas Malory* (*English Association Pamphlet*, No. 51). These two discussions led to the discovery of four documents, including a very important King's Bench indictment, which became the basis of Edward Hicks, *Sir Thomas Malory, His Turbulent Career* (Cambridge, Mass., 1928). A score of additional records were printed by the present writer in "Documenting Sir Thomas Malory," *Speculum,* VIII (1933). 3-29. A summary of our knowledge up to 1929 is given in an appendix to Eugène Vinaver, *Malory* (Oxford, 1929). See also George L. Kittredge, *Sir Thomas Malory* (Barnstable, privately printed, 1925).

is interesting to contemplate the profession at the close of the *Morte Darthur,*
that he was "the servant of Jesu both day and night."

His
Sources
It is possible that the nearby house of the Grey Friars, which possessed a
considerable library in Malory's day, supplied him with the books which
he needed to solace his dreary hours in Newgate. For the *Morte Darthur*
these books need not have been many. The thirteenth century had seen the
compilation in France of long prose versions of the Arthurian stories, such
as the prose *Tristan* and the cycle known as the Vulgate, or ordinary,
version (made up of the *Estoire del Saint Graal,* a *Merlin* and its continuation,[50] an enormous *Lancelot,* a *Queste del Saint Graal,* and the *Morte Artu*)
or its derivative, the Pseudo-Robert de Boron cycle. Such a collection, perhaps in three or four volumes, was Malory's principal source, although the
precise combination of versions which he based his work on is not found
in any surviving manuscript.[51] It is so, too, with his French *Tristan,* which
must be reconstructed from the characteristics of three different manuscripts
among those we know.[52] Malory made use of the alliterative *Morte Arthure*
in English [53] and possibly of the stanzaic *Morte Arthur.* In general, his
method was to abridge and condense his sources severely, especially by
omitting minor episodes and digressions. The result is a much less discursive
narrative, though it must be admitted that he sometimes left out important
incidents and introduced unnecessary obscurities into his text.

The *Morte Darthur* was printed in 1485 by Caxton, with some misgivings
about its credibility, and all subsequent editions have been hitherto derived
from his.[54] One of the most interesting discoveries of recent years, however, is
that of a manuscript in the Fellows' Library of Winchester College,[55] which
is independent of Caxton's text and closer to Malory's original. It furnishes
further proof of Malory's identity with the Warwickshire knight, renders
more certain his use of the alliterative *Morte Arthure,* and makes it clear
that Caxton condensed his text in many places. One may confidently expect
that its publication will give us Malory's work in a still more acceptable
form.

In spite of obvious defects the *Morte Darthur* is a great book. The older

[50] Known as the *Suite de Merlin* or *Livre d'Artus.*
[51] Malory's *Merlin,* for example, was in part similar to the Huth *Merlin,* edited by Gaston
Paris and J. Ulrich (2v, 1886; *SATF*).
[52] On this subject see Eugène Vinaver, *Le Roman de Tristan et Iseut dans l'œuvre de Thomas*
Malory (Paris, 1925), and the same author's *Malory,* pp. 128-154. The latter is the best general
discussion of Malory's sources, replacing that of H. Oskar Sommer in Vol. III of his edition
of the *Morte Darthur* (1891) and Vida D. Scudder, *Le Morte Darthur of Sir Thomas Malory*
& Its Sources (1917).
[53] See above, p. 191.
[54] The most scholarly edition, but still rather inaccurate, is that of H. Oskar Sommer (3v,
1889-91). An excellent text in modernized spelling is that of A. W. Pollard (2v, 1900). That
in the Everyman's Library (2v, 1906) is also a good modernized reprint of Caxton's text,
and there are of course many other editions and abridgments.
[55] See the communications of W. F. Oakeshott to the London *Times,* Aug. 25, 1934 and to
the *LTLS,* Sept. 27, 1934. The manuscript is more fully discussed by Eugène Vinaver, "Malory's
Morte Darthur in the Light of a Recent Discovery," *Bull. of the John Rylands Library,* xix
(1935). 438-457. A new text of Malory based on this manuscript and Caxton, edited by Professor Vinaver, appeared in 1947 under the title *The Works of Sir Thomas Malory* (2ed, 3v,
Oxford, 1963).

spirit of courtly love was something Malory either did not understand or *Style* found uncongenial. The romantic charm of his original was partly lost on *and* the blunt practical nature which our knowledge of his life suggests. But *Spirit* he had a genuine admiration for knighthood and chivalry, and would have endorsed the words of Caxton in his preface, that the book was offered "to the intent that noble men may see and learn the noble acts of chivalry, the gentle and virtuous deeds that some knights used in those days, by which they came to honor, and how they that were vicious were punished and oft put to shame and rebuke." Malory was himself a man of action and dispatch, and his style suggests such a man. He converted the long and involved periods of his French originals into simple, idiomatic prose. Where his original is diffuse, Malory is terse and forthright. Yet his short, firm sentences, while they give an impression of intentional economy, are seldom abrupt, but flow in a naturally modulated prose rhythm. The style of the *Morte Darthur,* when all is said and done, is Malory's greatest distinction, and it is wholly his own. But he has also preserved for subsequent generations a matchless body of romantic stories which might otherwise have remained the property of the Middle Ages, forgotten by modern poets and readers in the English-speaking world, as they have been forgotten in France.

As a symbol of the spread of English prose in the fifteenth century there is nothing more indicative than the enormous bulk of William Caxton's [56] many translations. A number of these have already been mentioned, but in addition to turning French romances into English he translated, generally from the French, such major works as the *Mirrour of the World* (1481), *Caxton* *The Golden Legend* [57] (1483), *The Royal Book* (1488), besides many titles only less well known.[58] But it is impossible to think of Caxton apart from his services as England's first printer, as the man who in 1476 set up the first printing press in England, who gave the world the *Morte Darthur* and put in print the *Canterbury Tales*. It is as a printer rather than as a writer that he is primarily remembered. He was a business man who, after a successful career in the commercial world, turned to the new method of producing books, and he remains a business man to the end. It is not to

---

[56] Born about 1422 in Kent, he was apprenticed in 1438 to Robert Lange, a London mercer who became Lord Mayor the following year. Caxton was later admitted to the Mercers' Company in 1453. About 1445 (possibly in 1441) he went abroad and lived for thirty years "in the contres of Braband and Flanders, Holland and Zeland." He became in time governor of the Merchant Adventurers at Bruges. In the early seventies he learned the art of printing at Cologne, and printed three books abroad. He seems to have returned to England towards the close of 1476 and set up his press at Westminster. His publishing (and writing) was done in the last twenty years of his life. His death occurred sometime in the year 1491. The best recent account of Caxton's life, with new documents, is that of W. J. B. Crotch in the Introduction to his edition of *The Prologues and Epilogues of William Caxton* (1928; *EETS,* 176). William Blades' *Life and Typography of William Caxton* (2v, 2ed., 1882) is a classic work. See also Seymour de Ricci, *A Census of Caxtons* (1909; *Bibl. Soc., Illustrated Monographs,* No. xv), E. Gordon Duff, *William Caxton* (1905) and, for a popular treatment, Nellie S. Aurner, *Caxton, Mirrour of Fifteenth-Century Letters* (1926).
[57] On Caxton's sources see Pierce Butler, *Legenda Aurea—Légende Dorée—Golden Legend* (Baltimore, 1899), and p. 289, note 10.
[58] See A. T. Byles, "William Caxton as a Man of Letters," *Library,* 4 Ser., xv (1934). 1-25.

be doubted that he was genuinely fond of reading, but as a publisher his approach to literature was practical, and his style has the journeyman quality of one working at his job. He did not have a natural and instinctive sense of form. He seems never to have grasped the function of the sentence as a unit of thought. His ideas, unless controlled by his original, are joined one to another in a loose and at times unending chain, often without logical or syntactical cohesion. Compared with Trevisa, or Malory, or even Pecock, he cannot be said to have advanced the art of English prose. But for making available to English readers the most popular and useful books of his day— a truly noble five-foot shelf—his service to English culture is inestimable.

Popular
Literature

In the preceding pages we have been surveying the writings of the fifteenth century which circulated in manuscripts and printed books. It remains to say something of the considerable body of popular literature which existed for the most part only in the memory of the people and which was passed on from generation to generation by word of mouth. We shall never know how much of this traditional literature there was, for most of the tales and folk songs are probably lost. But there is one type of folk song, the popular ballad, which lived on, and indeed still lives on in Britain and America, and which has been recorded in modern times to the extent of some three hundred examples.[59] One of the ballads is as old as the thirteenth century and some originated as late as the seventeenth, but they were clearly flourishing by the close of the Middle English period and it has become customary in literary histories to treat them there. They may not unfittingly close our discussion of the Middle Ages and serve as one of a number of links establishing continuity with modern times.

The
Ballad

The popular ballad is one type of narrative song with certain clearly marked characteristics which distinguish it from other kinds of poetry. It is composed in simple stanzas, generally of two or four lines, suitable to a recurrent tune. Most commonly the stanza consists of alternate four and three stress lines riming on the second and fourth, as in the opening verse of *Sir Patrick Spens:*

> The king sits in Dumferling toune,
> Drinking the blude-red wine:
> "O whar will I get a guid sailor,
> To sail this ship of mine?"

The story is usually a single episode, the climax of events only briefly sketched or hinted at. "It begins," as Gray said of *Child Maurice,* "in the

[59] The great collection of British ballads is that of F. J. Child, *English and Scottish Popular Ballads* (5v, Boston, 1882-98). An excellent one-volume abridgment is H. C. Sargent and G. L. Kittredge, *English and Scottish Popular Ballads, edited from the Collection of Francis James Child* (Boston, 1904), with an introduction by Kittredge. Among the best discussions of the ballad are F. B. Gummere, *The Popular Ballad* (1907), Gordon H. Gerould, *The Ballad of Tradition* (1932), and, from the Scandinavian point of view, J. C. H. R. Steenstrup, *The Medieval Popular Ballad* (Eng. trans., 1914). Of wider scope and great value is W. J. Entwistle, *European Balladry* (1939). On the folk tale see Stith Thompson, *The Folktale* (1946).

fifth act of the play." Sometimes the story is revealed in a succession of brief scenes. The presentation is thus to a high degree dramatic, and the effect is one of condensation and severe economy. Ballad art is always objective, with no marks of personal authorship and no attempt to analyze or interpret the action or the characters of the story. In many ballads there is a refrain, and a frequent characteristic is the habit of repeating a stanza with slight modifications that advance the story, a device Gummere aptly called incremental repetition. In general the ballad reflects the simple direct approach to a story characteristic of unlettered people, the people who through the centuries have made the ballads what they are when they become known to us.

Most readers of this book will be familiar with some ballads, such as *Edward* and *Barbara Allen,* and will recognize in them the characteristic tendency to tragedy which the ballads as a whole show. A simple dénouement often serves the purpose of such a theme, as when in two stanzas the ladies in *Sir Patrick Spens* sit hopelessly

Tendency to Tragedy

> Waiting for thair ain deir lords,
> For they'll se thame na mair—

or when we are told of *Bonnie James Campbell:*

> Saddled and briddled
> and booted rade he;
> Toom hame cam the saddle,
> but never cam he.

Many of the ballads, like *Edward* mentioned above, concern domestic tragedies of one sort or another. In *Babylon* two out of three sisters are killed by a young outlaw before he learns from the third that he is their brother. *Twa Sisters* is the age-old tragedy of the younger sister preferred to the elder, while *Lord Thomas and Fair Annet* tells the equally old story of the rivalry between wealthy bride and lowly sweetheart. *Child Maurice* is doubly tragic in that the husband, thinking to kill his wife's lover, learns that he has slain her only son. The situation was dramatic enough to be made in the eighteenth century into Home's tragedy of *Douglas.* Outraged propriety leads "the cruel brother" in the ballad of that name to revenge himself on his sister on her marriage day, because she forgot to ask his consent to the marriage:

> She leand her oer the saddle-bow,
> To give him a kiss ere she did go.

> He has taen a knife, baith long and sharp,
> And stabbd that bonny bride to the heart.

Love naturally occupies a prominent place in the ballads, and more often than not it is the sorrow and tragedy of love rather than the happy fulfill-

Love

ment of young hope. Remorse over deserting a sweetheart leads the ballad of *Fair Margaret and Sweet William* to a simple, if obvious, conclusion:

> Fair Margaret dy'd today, today,
>   Sweet William he dy'd the morrow;
> Fair Margaret dy'd for pure true love,
>   Sweet William he dy'd for sorrow.

The lady in *Fair Janet* must be separated from her lover, to whom she had borne a son:

> "O we maun part this love, Willie,
>   That has been lang between;
> There's a French lord coming oer the sea,
>   To wed me wi a ring."

There is a touch of melodrama in the close, when she gets up from child-bed to go through with the wedding but falls dead while dancing with her true love. One of the finest examples of the ballad way of telling a story is *Lord Randal*. Each stanza follows the same formula:

> "O where ha you been, Lord Randal, my son?
> And where ha you been, my handsome young man?"
> "I ha been at the greenwood; mother, mak my bed soon:
> For I'm wearied wi hunting, and fain wad lie down."

Slowly, in spite of his evasive answers, the mother learns that her son has been poisoned by the girl he loves. Jealousy and revenge motivate the tragedy in *Young Waters* and in *Young Hunting*. Not all the love stories, however, end tragically. The daring and loyalty of the lady are sometimes rewarded, as in *Young Beichan* or *The Gay Goshawk*. Even seduction, though sometimes successfully resisted, when carried out does not always end unhappily for either the seducer or the seduced. A third of all the ballads deal with love, and naturally not many of the familiar situations fail of treatment.

Outlaw Life and Other Themes   The ballads reflect, of course, the social conditions of the period and the region that produced many of them. Border feuds find expression in the fine ballad of *Captain Car* and in *Kinmont Willie*, while two of the most famous ballads, *The Battle of Otterburn* and *The Hunting of the Cheviot*, tell in different ways the fight between Percy and Douglas which in one version or the other moved Sir Philip Sidney's heart "more than with a trumpet." There are ballads, too, of outlaw life such as *Johnny Armstrong* and *Adam Bell, Clim of the Clough, and William of Cloudesly*, besides the group concerned with the more famous Robin Hood. The supernatural enters into such ballads as *Thomas Rymer* and *Clerk Colvin*, whose adventure with a mermaid proves his undoing.[60] Sometimes the ballad turns journalistic and reports a local event as in *Bessie Bell and Mary Gray*, or the sixteenth-century *Mary Hamilton*, which records the punishment meted out for a case of child-murder at the court of Mary Queen of Scots. On

[60] See Lowry C. Wimberly, *Folklore in the English & Scottish Ballads* (Chicago, 1928).

rare occasions the theme is a humorous incident, such as the delightful revelation of human nature in *Get Up and Bar the Door*.

Best known probably of all the ballad subjects are Robin Hood and his *Robin* carefree yeomen and their varied adventures in the "merry greenwood." *Hood* His fame was known to the author of *Piers Plowman*, but how much earlier we cannot say. He is the people's counterpart of aristocratic heroes like Sir Gawain. Courteous, ever ready for an adventure, and with a rough and ready sense of humor, he is the champion of the weak and the friend of honest poverty. As an outlaw he is free from the ordinary restraints of law. Though loyal to the king, he helps himself freely to the king's deer, and levies with a clear conscience on knights and barons, bishops and abbots, the silver which he bestows with equal readiness on those who need it. He takes the law into his own hand and deals out rough justice on the spot, as when in *Robin Hood and Allen a Dale* he not only prevents the marriage of Allen's sweetheart to an old man but unites the lovers in a very uncclesi-astical ceremony. He has, of course, the physical virtues which befit the yeoman ideal, such as uncanny skill with the bow and the long staff, though he often meets his match and generously acknowledges the superior strength or craft of his opponent. His life is marked by frequent encounters with the sheriff of Nottingham, and if he generally comes off from them suc-cessfully, not the least reason is his sincere and unfailing devotion to Our Lady. More than thirty ballads, some early and some late, recount his lively adventures. By about 1500, and perhaps earlier, a number of episodes were woven together into a miniature epic printed as *A Gest of Robyn Hode*.[61]

The origin of the ballad is a question on which opinion has gradually *Ballad* shifted.[62] The concept of the folk forming a homogeneous community, *Origins* with a common fund of experience and common responses to whatever affects the community, expressing as a group the emotion felt by all, not only in rhythmic movement and dance, but in words which result in a record of the event celebrated, was widely held a generation ago. *Das Volk dichtet,* it was said, and with certain modern instances of group composition which could be pointed to in the Faroe islands, among Negroes in the southern part of the United States, and elsewhere, it was possible to erect a communal theory for the origin of the ballad. The refrain, which was considered a primitive and essential feature of the earliest ballads, could be sung by the group, while a leader and a few of the more inventive, or more vocal, con-tributed most of the verses. Although it would be rash to deny the possibility that a few of our ballads originated in this way, it cannot be proved, and such an origin is unlikely in the case of most of the English ballads that have been preserved. While ballads are doubtless older than our earliest

---

[61] For the literature of the subject see J. Harris Gable, *Bibliography of Robin Hood* (Lincoln, Neb., 1939; *Univ. of Nebraska Stud. in Lang., Lit., and Crit.*, No. 17).
[62] For the older view see the discussions of Kittredge and Gummere, as above, and F. B. Gummere, "The Ballad and Communal Poetry," *Harvard Studies & Notes in Phil. & Lit.*, v (1896), 41-56, and *The Beginnings of Poetry* (1901). For the argument against the communal theory see Louise Pound, *Poetic Origins and the Ballad* (1921).

recorded specimen, the *Judas* found in a late thirteenth-century manuscript, the English ballads do not reflect so simple a social structure as the communal theory necessarily assumes.

Effects of Oral Transmission
But if the ballads were not written by the people acting as a group, they have certainly been rewritten by them, if we may use the word of people who had seldom learned the use of a pen. In the process of oral transmission over the centuries the ballads that lived in the memories and on the lips of the people have been slowly transformed. The numerous versions that have been collected of some of the more popular ballads show that this transformation has not always been for the better. But there can be little doubt that in other cases the selective memory of the people has sifted the matter of a ballad, dropping out non-essentials and leaving the main features of the incident or story in greater relief. If the ballad is not communal in origin, it is, as has been well said, communal in transmission,[63] and owes some of its most distinctive qualities to the genius of the folk.

Ballad Tunes
No one who has not heard ballads sung can have a just appreciation of their effectiveness. Ballad melodies,[64] as traditional as the words, not only contribute greatly to their appeal but by their slow tempo and leisurely movement allow each stanza to work its influence on the listener. Ballads were never meant to be scanned quickly with the eye. When printed in books they are like museum specimens, interesting and often beautiful, but revealing only a small part of their true character and charm.[65]

[63] See the discussion of G. H. Gerould, "The Making of Ballads," *MP*, xxi (1923). 15-28.
[64] Sigurd B. Hustvedt, *A Melodic Index of Child's Ballad Tunes* (Berkeley, 1936; *Pub. Univ. of Calif. at Los Angeles in Lang. and Lit.*, Vol. i, No. 2), and the music included in many of the works mentioned in the following note.
[65] British ballads are still being sung in America, particularly in communities more or less isolated, by the descendants of English and Scotch-Irish settlers who brought them to this country in the eighteenth century. An excellent collection of such versions, with the music, will be found in Cecil J. Sharp, *English Folk-Songs from the Southern Appalachians* (2ed., 2v, 1932). Arthur K. Davis, Jr., *Traditional Ballads of Virginia* (Cambridge, Mass., 1929), contains 51 ballads in 650 versions. A similar collection is Phillips Barry, Fannie H. Eckstorm, and Mary W. Smyth, *British Ballads from Maine* (New Haven, 1929). Many versions of British and American ballads may be found in Reed Smith, *South Carolina Ballads* (Cambridge, Mass., 1928), with interesting evidence of the communal process, John H. Cox, *Folk-Songs of the South* (Cambridge, Mass., 1925), Arthur P. Hudson, *Folksongs of Mississippi and Their Background* (Chapel Hill, 1936), W. Roy Mackenzie, *The Quest of the Ballad* (Princeton, 1919) and *Ballads and Sea Songs from Nova Scotia* (Cambridge, Mass., 1928), Emelyn E. Gardner and Geraldine J. Chickering, *Ballads and Songs of Southern Michigan* (Ann Arbor, 1939). The student interested in American folk poetry should consult Louise Pound, *American Ballads and Songs* (1922), John A. Lomax, *Cowboy Songs and Other Frontier Ballads* (1910; new ed., 1938), John A. and Alan Lomax, *American Ballads and Folk Songs* (1934) and *Our Singing Country* (1941), Carl Sandburg, *The American Songbag* (1927), Roland P. Gray, *Songs and Ballads of the Maine Lumber Jacks, with Other Songs from Maine* (Cambridge, Mass., 1924), Earl C. Beck, *Songs of the Michigan Lumberjacks* (Ann Arbor, 1941), the delightful volumes of Dorothy Scarborough, *On the Trail of Negro Folk-Song* (1925), and *A Song Catcher in Southern Mountains* (1937), and Newman I. White, *American Negro Folk-Songs* (Cambridge, Mass., 1928). For further references see Alan Lomax and Sidney R. Cowell, *American Folk Song and Folk Lore: A Regional Bibliography* (1942).

BOOK II
The Renaissance

PART I
The Early Tudors
(1485-1558)

I

Links with the Past

The literature of the first Tudor king, Henry VII (1485-1509), was in its main interests retrospective, not forward-looking. Except only in the interlude—where, as we shall see, new viewpoints were being opened up—the writers of this reign offer little promise of the spacious days to come. Instead, their attitude is habitually skeptical of the future and nostalgic toward the past. Satisfactory reasons for this trend of mind are more easily found than is always the case in literary movements. The chief reasons are the Wars of the Roses (1455-1485) and the establishment of the printing-press in England in 1476.

In matters of culture, as in matters of political economy, the chief need after the settlement at Bosworth Field was to rebuild what had been wasted, to renew the links with the past. In this spirit William Caxton [1] (c. 1422-1491) and the three printers who most immediately continued his work—Wynkyn de Worde, Richard Pynson, and Robert Copland—directed their presses. They were not seekers after novelty, but conservators of the old tradition. Caxton's first book, the *Recuyell of the Historyes of Troye* (printed at Bruges, 1475) is a summary of early Greek fable, from the legendary origins of the pagan gods to the fate of the heroes who fought at Troy.[2]

His earliest publication on English soil, *The Dicts or Sayings of the Philosophers,* is an anthology of epigrammatic wisdom, more Arabic in fact than Greek, but ascribed to the Hellenic sages and wholly in the medieval fashion.[3] Caxton printed also a number of the source books of medieval learning—Boethius in 1478, the encyclopedic *Mirrour of the World* in 1481, the *Golden Legend* in 1483, and several of the most popular romances and courtesy books. In procuring Malory's *Morte Darthur* he was seeking less the contemporary classic which he got than the summary of ancient Arthurian fable which that great work likewise constitutes. For poetry his press gave the readers of 1500 Chaucer, Gower, and Lydgate, the poets par excellence of the fourteenth and fifteenth centuries, and also such traditional popular verse as is best typified in *A Gest of Robyn Hode.*[4] The first effect

Conservatism of the Early Printers

Caxton's Books

---

[1] Cf. N. S. Aurner, *Caxton* (1926).
[2] This book had an important history in the next century. It was reprinted three times between 1502 and 1553. Then, with the title changed to *The Ancient History of the Destruction of Troy* and the English slightly modernized by William Fiston, it went through half a dozen more editions, serving as a source for Shakespeare's *Troilus and Cressida.*
[3] For Caxton as a translator see Book. I.
[4] This interesting work was several times printed. The date and printer of the first edition are undetermined; reprints came from the presses of both Wynkyn de Worde and William

of the multiplication of printed books was, therefore, to turn the readers back to the thought and manners of the Middle Ages.

Chronicles of the Past   Nations that have emerged from the shadow of protracted war do not usually face the future with blithe self-confidence. They are more likely to feel dwarfed by the cataclysm behind them and to look back to the elder sages in the spirit in which Dryden later regarded the Elizabethans: "Theirs was the Giant race before the Flood." So the subjects of Henry VII thought of Edward III and Chaucer, even of Lydgate; and a vivid interest in past history is one of the most enduring, as well as most imaginatively stimulating, of all the literary interests of the Tudor period. A chronicle of England, based on the early *Polychronicon,* had been one of the more popular of Caxton's books (1480).[5] *The New Chronicles of England and France*[6] by

Fabyan   Robert Fabyan (d. 1513) was printed by Pynson in 1516 and reprinted with additions three times between that date and 1560, being the first in an august series of Tudor histories which no reading man of the period and few dramatists ever neglected. Fabyan's prose is readably workmanlike and is set off by inserted passages of verse, one of which found its way from his chronicle into Marlowe's *Edward II.*

Tudor statecraft early turned to its advantage the historical curiosity of the time. Cardinal Morton (d. 1500) is credited with originating the official life of Richard III, which depicted the usurper so luridly that he became the favorite villain of the century, both on and off the stage. In 1505 Henry VII commissioned a learned Italian, Polydore Vergil (*c.* 1470-*c.* 1555), to write a grandiose new history of England, which after nearly thirty years of careful research appeared at Basel (1534)[7] with a dedication to Henry VIII. Written in Latin and published (in several editions) abroad, this work affects English literature less directly than do the vernacular histories founded upon it. Of these the first and most distinguished is Edward Hall's

Hall's Chronicle   *Union of the Noble and Illustre Families of Lancaster and York* (1542), which covered the story from Henry IV's accession to that of Henry VII and gave a Tudor bias and heightened dramatic rhetoric to the events it dealt with. Even to the Elizabethans Hall's manner seemed over-stately; but the chroniclers that succeeded—Richard Grafton (1568), Raphael Holinshed (1577), John Stow (1580)—were content to incorporate large sections of his work in their own more extensive volumes. Shakespeare's political philosophy, his verdicts upon historical personages, and to some extent his style, derive from Hall, and through him from Polydore Vergil.[8]

Copland. Modern editions by J. S. Farmer (*Tudor Facsimile Texts,* 1914) and E. and R. Grabhorn (San Francisco, 1932).

[5] It was reprinted in 1482.

[6] This title is from the colophon of the edition of 1516. Fabyan's original title seems to have been "The Concordance of Histories."

[7] *Polydori Vergilii Urbinatis Anglicae Historiae libri xxvi.* A sixteenth-century English translation was edited by Sir H. Ellis for the Camden Society (1844, 1846). See also D. Hay, "The Manuscript of Polydore Vergil's *Anglica Historia,*" *Eng. Hist. Rev.,* LIV (1939). 240-251.

[8] See W. G. Zeeveld, "The Influence of Hall on Shakespeare's English Historical Plays," *ELH,* III (1936). 317-353. The chronicles of Hall, Grafton, and Holinshed were reprinted (1807-1809) in nine large volumes under the editorship of Sir H. Ellis. Stow's popular and

English and French history are in the fourteenth and fifteenth centuries *Froissart* not easily detachable. The chronicle of "unfruitful Fabyan"—as the *Mirror* *and Berners* *for Magistrates* called him—handled events in the two countries in simple alternation. A nicer balance is found in the great work of Jean Froissart, greatly translated about 1520 [9] by John Bourchier, Lord Berners. It is first in the eminent line of Tudor translations, standing as a classic in its own right and as a memorial of the ardor with which the early sixteenth century turned back to the fourteenth. Berners follows close in the footsteps of Caxton in the rendering of Froissart and also in his next translation, that of the French prose romance of *Huon of Bordeaux,*[10] (*c.* 1530) which introduced the English public to Oberon, King of Fairies. Both books proved rich mines for the Elizabethan dramatists. These were followed by Lord Berners' last important work, *The Golden Book of Marcus Aurelius,* translated through a French version from the Spanish of Antonio de Guevara and printed in 1535. Here, for the first time, one observes some concession to the special interests of the Renaissance and an approach, though still hesitant, to the sixteenth-century linguistic habits out of which Euphuism grew.[11]

Though the kingdoms of England and Scotland were distinct, literary *The Scot-* relations were close in the sixteenth century and the dialects of the two *tish School* countries were not divided by the border. The most vigorous English poetry of the generation following Henry VII's accession was written by Scots who had trained themselves in the Chaucerian tradition; and the best of these is William Dunbar [12] (*c.* 1460-*c.* 1520). Freshness, metrical facility, and *William* variety are Dunbar's great merits. In *The Golden Targe,* of about 1503, he *Dunbar,* handles the exacting nine-line stanza of Chaucer's *Womanly Noblesse* and *The Golden* *Anelida and Arcite (aabaabbab)* with real mastery through nearly three *Targe* hundred lines which depict the poet asleep in a May morning on "Flora's mantle," and portray the dream visions of a ship filled with a hundred allegorical ladies and of King Cupid's court, where Reason with his golden shield attempts, though ineffectually, to guard the sleeper from the arrows of love. The conclusion is an invocation to "moral Gower" and "Lydgate laureate," but especially to "reverend Chaucer, rose of rhetors all," concerning whom the poet demands

> Was thou not of our English all the light,
> Surmounting every tongue terrestrial
> Als far as May's morrow does midnight?

---

equently expanded chronicle went through many editions between 1565 and 1632, but has not been edited in modern times.

[9] Printed, 1523-25, by Pynson; ed. W. P. Ker (6v, 1901-3) and reprinted (8v, Oxford, 1927-8).

[10] Edited by S. L. Lee (4v, 1882-87; *EETSES,* 40, 41, 43, 50) and in modernized form by . Steele (1895).

[11] See J. M. Galvez, *Guevara in England* (Berlin, 1916), which includes the text of Berners' olden Book.

[12] See R. A. Taylor, *Dunbar* (1932), and P. H. Nichols, "William Dunbar as a Scottish Lydgatian," *PMLA,* XLVI (1931). 214-224. *The Poems of William Dunbar* are edited by John Small (*Scottish Text Soc.,* 3v, 1893) and in more recent texts by H. B. Baildon (1907) and . M. Mackenzie (Edinburgh, 1932).

For the English as well as the Scottish court Dunbar exercised some of the functions of a poet laureate. In 1501 he accompanied the mission that arranged the marriage of Henry VII's daughter Margaret to James IV of Scotland. On this occasion he wrote for the Lord Mayor of London the delightful ballade in which each stanza ends with the refrain, "London, thou art the flower of cities all," and doubtless the verses "written at Oxinfurde," in which with Caledonian soberness he admonishes the clerks of that university,

> If to your saws your dedes contrair be,
> Your maist accuser salbe your own cunning:
> A perilous sickness is vain prosperity.

The Thistle and the Rose For the royal wedding mentioned above he composed in twenty-seven rimeroyal stanzas the allegory of *The Thistle and the Rose* (dated May 9, 1503), in which Dame Nature marshals all the denizens of her garden and, after awarding the rule of her beasts to the lion and her birds to the eagle, gives the preëminence among plants to the Scottish thistle and the English rose.

Light Poems of Dunbar This is all convincingly, and not too imitatively, Chaucerian or Lydgatian. No less so are Dunbar's satirical and realistic poems. The obscene self-revelation of *The Two Married Women and the Widow* (in unriming alliterative verse) exceeds that of the Wife of Bath. Dunbar knew how to make the most poetically of the devil and the seven deadly sins; and also of the ballad rhythm and the repeated refrain, as in his famous *Lament for the Makers* (printed, 1508):

> He [i.e., Death] has done piteously devour
> The noble Chaucer, of makers flower,
> The monk of Bury, and Gower, all three;
> *Timor mortis conturbat me;*

or in his flippant ballade on the blackamoor girl:

> Long have I made [i.e., rimed] of ladies white;
> Now of one black I will indite,
> That landed forth of the last ships.
> How fain would I descrive perfite [describe perfectly]
> My lady with the mickle lips.

Liveliness is the keynote of all Dunbar's work. Even in his allegories the woods are noisy with the din of birdsong, and the landscape splashed with exuberant color. In *The Golden Targe* "the skies *rang* for *shouting* of the larks," and

> The *crystal* air, the *sapphire* firmament,
> The *ruby* skies of the orient
> Cast *berial* [pale green] beams on *emerald* boughes green . . .
> With *purple, azure, gold* and *gules* gent.

Till we reach Robert Burns we shall hardly find a poet more animated than Dunbar in his dealings with nature and human nature.

Gavin Douglas [13] (1475-1522), son of the famous Earl of Angus known *Gavin*
as "Bell-the-cat" and uncle by marriage of Queen Margaret of Scotland, for *Douglas*
whom Dunbar wrote *The Thistle and the Rose,* was an M.A. of St. Andrews
University and Bishop of Dunkeld. He died in London in 1522. Douglas
is one of the most redundant of poets, but he is a real poet and an allegorist
of remarkable ingenuity. His longest, and apparently earliest, independent
poem, *The Palace of Honor* (1501), fills eighty pages of intricate nine-line   The Palace
stanzas [14] and hardly yields in imaginative merit to any of the other offspring   of Honor
of the *Romance of the Rose.* On a May morning the author enters a garden
of pleasance which Dame Flora has superabundantly decorated. The sun
rises and seems to evoke from nature a hymn of praise so overpowering that
the poet falls fainting and imagines himself in an antithetical place, a bleak
forest by "a hideous flood with grisly fish." Terrified in "this wilderness
abominable and waste," he laments Fortune's inconstancy and creeps for
shelter into a hollow tree, whence he observes the passage of various mythological companies en route to the Palace of Honor: first that of the Queen
of Sapience, Minerva; then Diana and her depleted band of maidens; finally
Venus in a wonderful chariot, with Cupid, Mars, and many lovers. The last
spectacle so moves the concealed poet that he sings a sort of "enueg" or
hymn of hate against inconstant love, Cupid, false Venus, and all their court,
with the result that he is dragged out and threatened with dire punishment
as the first part of the poem ends. In his extremity a new company arrives,
consisting of Muses and poets, from Homer, Virgil, and Ovid to "Great
Kennedy [15] and Dunbar yet undead." Calliope, the epic Muse, secures the
poet's release, and under the guidance of a sweet nymph he makes, in Part
II, a wonderful journey through all the places of classic geography, with
special attention to the fountain of Hippocrene, of which, however, he is
unable to drink a drop by reason of the crowd around it. In Part III he
reaches the Palace of Honor, in the description of which Douglas shows
much vividness and poetic resourcefulness, as he does in his conclusion:
following his guide over a fallen tree that spans the moat of the Palace, the
hero falls into the water and awakes to find himself in the garden in which
the poem opened.

King Heart, in the "Monk's Tale" eight-line stanza, is half as long as *The*   King Heart
Palace of Honor, and seems to be a maturer poem. It is Douglas's *Everyman,*
an allegory of man's life and death. The hero, a young king, dwells, like the
heart in man's body, in his "comely castle strong," served by the five senses
and a countless train of personified impulses. When the lady of a neighboring castle, Dame Plesance, rides by to hunt, her retinue of attendant emotions
captivates the servants of King Heart. This leads to war, in which the king
is wounded by Beauty and imprisoned; but Pity enables him to turn the
tables, and the first canto ends with the mating of the two principals, who

[13] For the text see John Small, *The Poetical Works of Gavin Douglas* (4v, Edinburgh, 1874).
[14] In the first two books the rime scheme is *aabaabbab,* as in Dunbar's *Golden Targe.* In the
third book it is *aabaabbcc.*
[15] Walter Kennedy, antagonist of Dunbar in the famous *Flyting.*

in the course of the story have called upon the services of some one hundred abstract agents. Canto II shows Age arriving, along with Conscience, Disease, and many more. It shows the departure of King Heart's old supporters and concludes with his testament, in which in ballad fashion he remembers his friends and foes. This is a grim piece; it handles one of the tritest allegories without becoming merely ingenious or stereotyped.[16]

Douglas's Translation of Virgil

Douglas's translation of the *Æneid* in riming couplets (1512-1513, printed 1553) was his greatest and most famous labor. Preceded among English renderings only by Caxton's *Eneydos*, towards which Douglas is justly scornful, it has the virtues of accuracy, clearness, and, save for the dialect, readability. Naturally the copious Scot was no man to emulate Virgil's great compactness; he normally requires two lines for each line of the Latin, but the result is seldom incorrect or heavy. This translation was embellished with an original "prologue" before each book, constituting a set of thirteen[17] poems on various subjects, in nine different metres,[18] and amounting in the aggregate to nearly 2500 lines. This is the length of Spenser's *Shepherds' Calendar*, a work which Douglas's prologues suggest in their various concern with moral criticism and natural beauty and with experiments in style and language. The differences that one sees in Spenser's eclogues are mainly the differences that came in with the humanist tradition. The eighth prologue, unreadable today without a glossary, is sheer medievalism; it is a dream vision after Langland's manner, expressed in ultra-alliterative language and woven into very complicated thirteen-line stanzas. On the other hand, the seventh, twelfth, and thirteenth, written in simple couplets, deal with natural description of the seasons of winter, spring, and summer, respectively, and are no unworthy progenitors of James Thomson's *Seasons*. They were long popular in Scotland and established a style.

Sir David Lindsay

The last important poet of this group, Sir David Lindsay[19] (*c.* 1485-1555) has had his fame brightened by Sir Walter Scott.

> In the glances of his eye
> A penetrating, keen, and sly
>   Expression found its home;
> The flash of that satiric rage
> Which, bursting on the early stage,
> Branded the vices of the age,
>   And broke the keys of Rome.

[16] For an admirable discussion of Douglas's allegorical poems see C. S. Lewis, *The Allegory of Love* (Oxford, 1936), pp. 287-292.

[17] Douglas translated not only the twelve books of Virgil, but the thirteenth book added by Mapheus Vegius in the fifteenth century.

[18] Couplets, five-line stanza, six-line stanza, rime royal, two eight-line stanzas, two nine-line stanzas (as in *The Palace of Honor*), thirteen-line stanza.

[19] Lindsay's works have been admirably edited for the Scottish Text Society by Douglas Hamer (4v, 1931-36). See also D. Hamer, "The Bibliography of Sir David Lindsay," *Library* X (1929). 1-35. W. Murison's *Sir David Lyndsay, Poet and Satirist* (Cambridge, 1938) contains a good brief life and estimate.

Still is thy name in high account,
And still thy verse has charms,
Sir David Lindesay of the Mount,
Lord Lion King-at-arms!

Thus he enters Scott's *Marmion*. Born a few years before 1490, Lindsay belongs to a somewhat younger generation than the Scottish poets we have just discussed, but represents many of the same traditions. Appointed "master usher" to the infant king, James V (Scott's Fitz-James), and later engaged in negotiations for his marriage, he addressed to the boy a number of his poems. One, the *Answer to the King's Flyting*, is more graphic than decent; another, *The Complaint and Public Confession of the King's Old Hound called Bagshe*, which has been called "the first dog-poem in English literature," [20] is a moral on court life and has an affinity with the *Twa Dogs* of Burns. *The Dream of Sir David Lindsay*, which has been ascribed to the year 1528, and may be his earliest extant poem, is longer and more important: it rings ingenious changes on the old convention of the dream allegory. Unable to sleep in a snowy January night, Lindsay dresses himself in cloak, hood, double shoes, and mittens and goes out at sunrise. He meets Dame Flora, deprived of all her May sweetness, hears the complaints of the birds, and finds a shelter in a rock, where he thinks to write in rime "some merry matter of Antiquity." He falls asleep. In a vision Remembrance salutes him, and in a passage anticipatory of Sackville's *Induction* takes him to Hell, where he sees popes, emperors, and especially prelates, whose faults are described, and princes, lords, and ladies suffering for their sins. They next visit Purgatory and the Limbo, and ascend through the four elements and the spheres of the seven planets and fixed stars to the crystalline heaven, which is fully described. Remembrance will not permit him to remain there, but at his request she describes the Earth, the Earthly Paradise, and finally the realm of Scotland. When the poet asks how a country so well endowed by nature and so superior in its population can be so poor, she puts the blame chiefly on the princes and governors:

*Lindsay's
Dream*

the negligence
Of our infatuate headis insolent
Is cause of all this realm's indigence.

They meet John the Commonweal,[21] who is everywhere ill treated and sums up his miseries in the proverb: "Woe to the realm that has over-young a king!" Remembrance brings the author back to the rock where he fell asleep. A ship approaching harbor awakes him with its signal cannon, and he adds the "Exhortation to the King's Grace," urging moral conduct upon him.

[20] Hamer, *Works*, IV, p. xxii.
[21] This character has an important part also in Lindsay's play, *A Satire of the Three Estates*. Cf. below, ch. v.

The Complaint of Sir David Lindsay was written a year or two later in happier days. The formal rime royal of the *Dream* is here changed to rather jocular tetrameter, and Lindsay couches his complaint under good-tempered irony.

> Seand [seeing] that I am not regardit,   ·
> Nor with my brether in court rewardit,

he reminds the King (as he had in the earlier poem also) of his unrequited service from the day of the latter's birth and of the bad influence of the self-seekers (headed by the Earl of Angus) who had lately controlled his royal youth:

> They became rich, I you assure,
> But aye the prince remainit poor.

Now these have all been banished and the kingdom is purified:

> So is there naught, I understand,
> Without good order in this land,
> Except the spirituality.

It is time for the King to put the latter in order, and to lend Lindsay "of gold ane thousand pound or tway," which he will repay "when kirkmen yearns no dignity," or at some other highly improbable occasion.

The Testament and Complaint of Our Sovereign Lord's Papingo (1530) is a bird poem which suggests both the *Speak, Parrot!* and the *Philip Sparrow* of Skelton, the one in its political vehemence, the other in pathos. James V's parrot or "papingo," of which Lindsay was the keeper, fell one day from a tree and was mortally wounded. After upbraiding the inconstancy of fortune, she sends a message to the young King, bidding him remember that a ruler, being himself the servant of God, should follow justice and seek good reputation; and another message to the courtiers, bidding them profit by the tragic lessons of Scottish, as well as French and English, history. The last section of the poem is a grim satire on the falsity of churchmen. About the dying parrot three birds of prey assemble: the magpie, the raven, and the kite, representing themselves as a canon regular, a black monk, and a friar respectively. When they challenge her to justify the distrust in which she holds them, the parrot has occasion to discuss at length the Donation of Constantine, whereby the Church has grown rich and sensual, the universal banishment of chastity, the lack of learned preaching, and in general the clerical faults that Lindsay develops with yet more copiousness in his *Satire of the Three Estates*. At the end of a thousand lines the parrot makes her will, dies, and is at once devoured by her false confessors. The introduction of this poem, differentiated from the rest (which is in rime royal) by the use of a nine-line stanza, contains a notable beadroll of poets, beginning as usual with "Chawceir, Goweir, and Lidgate laureate," and paying special honor to Gavin Douglas.

In Sir David Lindsay the unchecked current of medieval poetry flows with hardly a trace of humanist transition into the high tide of the Reformation. This is most impressive in his longest poem, *A Dialogue betwixt Experience and a Courtier of the Miserable Estate of the World*,[22] to which an internal reference allows us to fix the late date of 1553.[23] Here the poetic form and spirit seem to be pure Gower, while the poet's critical ideas are those of John Knox and the Covenanters. The scope is Gothic and enormous, from Creation to Judgment Day, with particular emphasis on the four historical monarchies (Assyria, Persia, Greece, and Rome) and the "fifth monarchy" of the Pope. The verse is mainly the tetrameter couplet of the *Confessio Amantis,* seldom employed since the fourteenth century with such force and freedom. On a May morning the Courtier hears the birds hail the rising of the sun and meets an old man, Experience, who recounts to him the history of the world in a dialogue broken at the important points by "exclamations" and "descriptions" in stanzaic verse. The avowed sources are mainly the masters recognized in Gower's age: Orosius, Diodorus Siculus, Eusebius, Josephus, Boccaccio; but while industriously exploiting their narratives, Lindsay attacks with fury the evils of his own time: idolatry, war, adultery, clerical celibacy, and clerical rapacity.

Lindsay's Dialogue

The effect of this forceful poem is enhanced by contrast. The fulminations at the wickedness of Edinburgh are set against such passages of old-fashioned piety as these from the long description of the Judgment:

> The Fathers of the Auld Testament,
> Quhilk were to God obedient,
> Father Adam shall them convoy,
> With Abell, Seth, Enoch, and Noye [Noah],
> Abraham, with his faithful warks,
> With all the prudent Patriarchs.
> John the Baptist there shall compeir [appear],
> The principal and last messenger,
> Quhilk come but half a year afore
> The coming of that king of glore [glory]. . . .
> Then, with one rair [roar], the earth shall rive,
> And swallow them, both man and wive.
> Then shall those creatures forlorn
> Warie [curse] the hour that they were born,
> With many yammer, yewt [cry], and yell,
> From time they feel the flamis fell
> Upon their tender bodies bite,
> Quhose [Whose] torment shall be infinite; [24]

or this stanza of Lindsay's conclusion, in which the day ends and untainted nature reasserts herself:

[22] Usually known as *The Monarche,* or *Monarchie.*
[23] Line 5301. The colophon dates it 1552.
[24] Lines 5644-53, 5998-6005.

The blissful birdis bounis [betake themselves] to the trees,
And ceases of their heavenly harmonies:
The corncrake in the croft, I hear her cry;
The bat, the owlet, feeble of their eyes,
For their pastime now in the evening flies;
The nightingale, with mirthful melody,
Her natural notis pierceth through the sky,
Till [to] Cynthia makand [making] her observance,
Quhilk on the night does take her dalliance.[25]

Two biographical poems, dating from the latter years of Lindsay's life, deserve attention. The "Tragedy" of Cardinal Beaton, in professed imitation of Boccaccio's *De Casibus Virorum Illustrium*, relates the story of this Scottish counterpart of Wolsey to his murder in 1546 and adds warnings for prelates and princes. It is in rime royal and in the form of monologue by a ghostly visitant, thus anticipating the method of *The Mirror for Magistrates*. In *The History of a Noble and Valiant Squire, William Meldrum*, on the other hand, Lindsay handles the life of a contemporary soldier of fortune, who died in 1550, in the form and manner of the *chanson de geste*. No reformatory ethics or anticlerical satire appears in this attractive, if extended, work. The verse is the tetrameter couplet of *The Lady of the Lake*, and the substance is the pagan doughtiness of the valiant squire, on land and sea, in war and love.

*tephen   Stephen Hawes (1474-1523) had been educated at Oxford and was one of
lawes* the grooms of the chamber to Henry VII, to whom he dedicated, in the nineteenth year of the King's reign (1503-4), *The Example of Virtue* and, in the twenty-first year (1505-6), *The Pastime of Pleasure*.[26] The earlier work, though it stretches out through three hundred stanzas of rime royal verse, is of very slight importance: it is a homiletic tract encased in the thinnest of allegorical shells. *The Pastime of Pleasure* was printed by Wynkyn de Worde in 1509 and again in 1517 in editions rather handsomely adorned with woodcuts and divided, for the benefit of the casual reader, into forty-six chapters. There seems to have been no further demand for it till the beginning of Queen Mary's reign, when three editions were issued in two years (1554, 1555), a testimony, one would suppose, to its reactionary trend. The next printing was in 1831, under the editorship of Robert Southey, and the poem has since been food for the antiquary. In truth, Hawes enters the Renaissance scene rather in the posture of Spenser's Sir Trevisan: his eye was backward cast.

*The Pas-   The title of *The Pastime of Pleasure* raises expectations which it could
ime of* probably not have satisfied in any age, and it suffers from faults that explain
Pleasure the author's clear preference of Lydgate to Chaucer as a model, the medieval faults of all-inclusiveness and verbosity. Hawes's intention seems to have

[25] Lines 6312-20.
[26] Hawes' *Pastime of Pleasure* is well edited by W. E. Mead (1928; EETS, 173). Concerning a slightly later poem by Hawes, *The Comfort of Lovers* (*c.* 1510) see R. D. Cornelius, *The Castell of Pleasure by Wm. Nevill* (1930; EETS, 179), pp. 26-29.

been to give his reader everything that the bygone centuries had to offer. Love allegory is here in the really charming romance of Grand Amour and La Belle Pucelle. Scholastic erudition fills a vast number of pages which treat the trivium and quadrivium, with special attention to the art of rhetoric. Giant-fighting is conspicuous; the hero slays a three-headed giant twelve feet high, then one with seven heads and fifteen feet of stature, and finally a wonderful monster created out of the seven metals by a wicked enchantress. The fabliau element is here in the coarsely amusing episode of Godfrey Gobylive,[27] and the macabre element in the account of the hero's death and the remarks of the Seven Deadly Sins over his "vile carcass," accentuated by two grisly woodcuts.

Opinion concerning this poem is not likely to be fair. The first risk is that it will not be read; it consists of nearly six thousand lines of lame rime royal. The second risk is that those who read it will be beguiled into over-praise by the sense of their own virtue and by the isolated charms of some of its portions. The writer confesses that the wan heroine seems very pleasant, particularly in the courtship scene (lines 1989-2408). The absurd greyhounds, Governance and Grace, who accompany the hero from tower to tower and from giant to giant, grow upon one; and there are passages which delight by their soundly human prosiness, like the stanza at the opening of chapter 33:

> Up I arose and did make me ready,
> For I thought long unto my journey's end;
> My greyhounds leapt on me right merrily,
> To cheer me forward they did condescend;
> And the three ladies, my cheer to amend,
> A goodly breakfast did for me ordain:
> They were right glad the giant was slain.

Passages have sometimes been cited to prove that Hawes was a poet. A work which speaks so largely of love, death, fame, time, and eternity could hardly fail to have some quotable sentiments, and this one has many; but the gems gain part of their effect from the unlikely contexts in which they are discovered, and the limp of Hawes's verse, like Charles Lamb's stammer, gives his good things a slightly illegitimate emphasis. The best practice would be for the modern reader to approach *The Pastime of Pleasure* in the spirit in which the printer recommended it to the reader of 1554, as a poem "containing and treating upon the seven liberal sciences and the whole course of man's life." Thus he would find it a compendious statement of what the Tudor gentleman was supposed to retain out of the mental and moral gatherings of the Middle Ages, and the romantic or humorous gildings would be pleasantly added unto him.

---

[27] In this section of the poem couplets replace the rime royal, and the southern dialect is employed.

II

The New Learning

There is still dispute concerning the processes by which medieval habits of thought were in England supplanted by the newer attitude and discipline to which the terms *Renaissance* and *Humanism* are applied.[1] English humanism was a matter of thought and training more than of spontaneous emotion, of borrowing from Italy, France, and Germany more than of native impulse. The movement affected English literature, narrowly considered, rather slowly and rather indirectly. It came in by two doors: the court and the university.

As early as 1437 an Italian schoolmaster, Tito Livio Frulovisi, was living in England in the service of Humphrey, Duke of Gloucester. He wrote a Latin life of the Duke's brother, Henry V, and left seven Latin plays, in partially classic style, which have been recently edited from the unique manuscript in St. John's College, Cambridge.[2] This is but a typical example. The Wars of the Roses did not quite break the connection with Renaissance Italy,[3] but it was not till after Henry VII's accession in 1485 that humanists appeared significantly at the English court. In this reign Adrian of Castello, Giovanni and Silvestro Gigli were all rewarded with English bishoprics for their public service as Latin orators and letter writers. Pietro Carmeliano was appointed Latin Secretary and dignified with the title of poet laureate. Another "poet laureate," Bernard André, a French scholar from Toulouse, combined courtly duties and the instruction of the King's son with classical lectures at Oxford.[4]

These exponents of the Italian and French Renaissance served the English

---

[1] Neither word appears to have been so used in England till the nineteenth century; but *humanist* began to be employed at the end of the sixteenth for a scholar in worldly learning, usually in direct opposition to *divine*. Only in the eighteenth century did *humanist* commonly have the sense in which we use it: a scholar devoted to the study of Greek and Latin antiquity, either for aesthetic, historical, or theological purposes. Johnson's Dictionary (1755) defines *Humanist* as "a philologer, a grammarian; a term used in the schools of Scotland." For an admirable general discussion see Douglas Bush, *The Renaissance and English Humanism* (Toronto, 1939); also L. E. Elliott-Binns, *England and the New Learning* (1937), and Wallace K. Ferguson, *The Renaissance* (1940). V. de Sola Pinto, *The English Renaissance, 1510-1688* (1938), covers a wide field in brief compass, with excellent historical chapters and useful bibliographies.

[2] C. W. Previté-Orton, *Opera hactenus inedita T. Livii de Frulovisiis de Ferraria* (Cambridge, 1932).

[3] See Elizabeth C. Wright, "Continuity in Fifteenth-Century English Humanism," *PMLA*, LI (1936). 370-376; Roberto Weiss, "Humanism in Oxford," *LTLS*, XXXVI (Jan. 9, 1937). 28, and *Humanism in England during the Fifteenth Century* (Oxford, 1941); A. Hyma, "The Continental Origins of English Humanism," *HLQ*, IV (1940). 1-26.

[4] See William Nelson, "The Scholars of Henry VII," in *John Skelton, Laureate* (1939), pp. 4-39.

court by raising the quality of the official state papers, substituting the language of Cicero for the more barbarous Latin of the Middle Ages, and by producing elegant Latin verses on public occasions. At Oxford humanism bit deeper, concerning itself particularly with the encouragement of Greek learning and the development of sounder methods in the study of philosophy, medicine, and divinity. The eldest of the Oxford humanists was William Grocyn [5] (c. 1446-1519), who seems to have acquired some knowledge of Greek from Cornelio Vitelli at New College, and in 1488, during the last *William* years of Lorenzo the Magnificent, went to Florence for the improvement of *Grocyn* his studies under the matchless Politian. He became the friend and benefactor of Erasmus (1466-1536), who loses no opportunity of praising his learning,[6] but he has bequeathed us no writings except a Latin letter to the famous Venetian printer, Aldus Manutius.[7]

Grocyn's scholarship focused upon theology; he lectured at Oxford on Greek and divinity and at one time held four church livings concurrently, though his generosity to students was so great that he died a poor man.[8] *Thomas* His pupil and lifelong friend, Thomas Linacre (1460-1524), who had been *Linacre* his companion also at Politian's lectures in Florence and was his executor, directed his own studies particularly to medicine. He translated several of the Greek writings of Galen into useful and polished Latin, and won lasting fame by founding the Royal College of Physicians in London, of which he was the first president. Linacre's interest in linguistic scholarship is evidenced by several monographs on Latin grammar, one of which, *Rudimenta Grammatices,*[9] originally composed in English for the use of Princess Mary, was later translated into Latin by the great Scot, George Buchanan. These bring Linacre into close connection with two younger Oxford humanists, John Colet [10] (1466-1519) and William Lyly (c. 1468-1523), the latter Grocyn's godson and grandfather of the.author of *Euphues.*[11]

Colet and Lyly likewise, after absorbing the learning available in Oxford, *John Colet* perfected their scholarship in Italy, Colet studying also in France, and Lyly pressing as far as Rhodes in search of remnants of Greek culture. On his return Colet entered upon a clerical career of great success, first as a lecturer on Pauline theology at Oxford and then as Dean of St. Paul's, London. Having inherited a large fortune from his father, who had been twice Lord

---

[5] See Montagu Burrows, "Memoir of William Grocyn," *Collectanea,* 2nd Series (Oxford, 1890), pp. 332-380.

[6] Erasmus spoke of Grocyn as "holding the first place among the many learned men of Britain," and as "the patron and preceptor of us all."

[7] Aldus printed this in his edition of Linacre's translation of Proclus, 1499.

[8] Grocyn left a library of 105 printed books and 17 manuscripts, mainly theological and classical, of which Linacre made a catalogue.

[9] Linacre had earlier prepared a grammar for the use of Colet's new school, St. Paul's, but Colet declined it as too difficult. Cf. F. Seebohm, *The Oxford Reformers of 1498* (1867), p. 148.

[10] Cf. Sir J. A. R. Marriott, *The Life of John Colet* (1933); Kathleen C. MacKenzie, "John Colet of Oxford," *Dalhousie Rev.,* xxi (1941). 15-28.

[11] For an interesting account of William Lyly and his family see A. Feuillerat, "Une famille d'érudits au XVIe siècle," in *John Lyly* (Cambridge, 1910), pp. 3-24. See also M. B. Stewart, "William Lily's Contribution to Classical Study," *Classical Jour.,* xxxiii (1938). 217-225.

Mayor of London, Colet devoted it to the endowment of St. Paul's School in the center of the city, to serve as a model and seedbed of the new learning (1510). William Lyly was the first headmaster, and John Milton, in later years, was probably the greatest tribute to the efficacy of its education. Colet, Lyly, and Erasmus collaborated on the constitution of the school and also on a new Latin grammar for the pupils, which was to prove the most influential of all English textbooks.[12]

The interplay of influences among these humanists is illustrated in the following account of the genesis of one part of the book:

> The Latin syntax was first drawn up by Lyly, and then sent by Dean Colet to Erasmus for his review, who so far altered it that neither of them afterwards thought he had a right to own it; for which reason it was at first published without any author's name, and only an epistle of Colet prefixed to it, in which his affectionate concern for the success of his new school and great generosity in founding it are finely expressed.[13]

The bibliography of this remarkable book will doubtless never be precisely traced. The earliest edition may date from 1513, the latest from 1858. Sections of it bore different titles, and revisions were made from one generation to another for over three centuries. It was most commonly referred to as Lyly's Grammar, but sometimes as "Paul's Accidence," from the name of the school for which it was first made; later editions called it the Eton Grammar. Almost countless editions can be found, but it is probable that many others were thumbed to pieces without leaving a surviving copy.[14] One of the pedagogical methods employed in the book was to make the rules of grammar unforgettable by concentrating them in mnemonic passages of hexameter, and the opening words of some of these—"as in praesenti," "propria quae maribus," etc.—as well as some of the illustrative classical quotations, became a jargon which Shakespeare and his contemporaries never tired of. The address to his pupils, which Lyly wrote in elegiac couplets as an introduction ("Qui mihi discipulus, puer, es, cupis atque doceri," etc.), was probably the most widely known of all sixteenth-century poems, and it does indeed give a charming picture of what the good Tudor schoolboy was supposed to be. Less pleasant, but no less typical of Renaissance manners, was the grammarians' war that followed. Robert Whittinton of Magdalen College, Oxford, which was also Lyly's college and probably Colet's, had himself published five or six very popular grammatical treatises[15] between 1512 and 1519, and had been designated "laureate in grammar." When Whittinton carried his rivalry to the point of affixing denunciatory Latin

[12] A great wealth of information concerning the sixteenth-century school system in England, springing ultimately from Erasmus and the St. Paul's establishment, will be found in T. W. Baldwin, *William Shakspere's Small Latine & Lesse Greeke* (2v, Urbana, 1944).

[13] John Ward, preface to the edition of 1789, *A Short Introduction of Grammar*, pp. iv, v.

[14] Cf. Rev. Vincent J. Flynn, *The Life and Works of William Lily* (unpublished dissertation, University of Chicago, 1939), and "The Grammatical Writings of William Lily," *Papers of the Bibl. Soc. of America*, xxxvii (1943). 85-113.

[15] These went through so many editions that they make up nearly 140 entries in the Short-Title Catalogue.

verses against Lyly (signed with the pseudonym "Bossus") to the door of
Lyly's own school, William Horman, Vice-Provost of Eton, replied by
attacking Whittinton in a work called *Antibossicon* (1521), which he
dedicated to Lyly. Henry VIII ultimately settled the matter by decreeing
that Lyly's grammar should be the one used in schools.[16]

Grocyn, Linacre, Colet, and Lyly—the "Oxford Reformers" as they have
been called [17]—produced no pure literature, but they produced the matrix
in which it was molded. They were all saintly souls, living abstemious lives,
possessing an incredible ardor for learning and extraordinary powers of
administration. The thing they did was to gather from the tainted luxuriance
of late-Renaissance Florence, in the time of Lorenzo the Magnificent, the
seeds of humanistic piety and develop them into more than their pristine
purity. They wrote little of themselves or of each other; we know them best
by the institutions they created and the pupils, such as More, that they trained
up. But their friend Erasmus, who came to England first in 1497, has immortalized them in his letters. Of the greatest of them, Colet, he has left a
long character sketch [18] (dated 1519) which ranks with the classic brief lives
of Izaak Walton. A sentence of Erasmus, often quoted, is their best epitaph:

> When I listen to my friend Colet, I seem to be listening to Plato himself. Who
> does not admire in Grocyn the perfection of his training? What can be more
> acute, more profound, or more refined, than the judgment of Linacre? What
> has nature ever fashioned softer, or sweeter, or pleasanter than the disposition of
> Thomas More? [19]

And the ironic *Praise of Folly*,[20] which Erasmus wrote at More's house in
1510, is the best expression in literature of the attack that the Oxford
reformers were making upon the medieval system.

The great organizer of the learning that the English humanists had
gathered was Sir Thomas Elyot (*c.* 1490-1548), whom Nashe lauded half a
century later as "a man of famous memory" and as one whose elegance in
adapting the classics "did sever itself from all equals, although Sir Thomas
More with his comical wit at that instant was not altogether idle." [21] Elyot's
first and most important work, "the first fruits of my study," as he called it,
is *The Book Named the Governor*, printed in 1531 with a dedication to King
Henry VIII, whose almost precise coeval Elyot was in date of birth and span
of life. It brought the author immediate and lasting honor; by 1580 it had
gone through eight editions, and within a few months of its appearance
Elyot was named to the high office of ambassador to the Emperor Charles V.
The aim of *The Governor*, the King is told, is "to describe in our vulgar

The

"Oxford
Reformers"

Erasmus

The Praise
of Folly

Sir Thomas
Elyot

The
Governor

---

[16] Cf. Leicester Bradner, *Musae Anglicanae* (1940), pp. 10-19.
[17] Frederic Seebohm's classic book, *The Oxford Reformers of 1498*, deals mainly with Colet,
Erasmus, and More. Though published in 1867, it is still a work of importance.
[18] Translated by J. H. Lupton, *The Lives of Jehan Vitrier and John Colet* (1883).
[19] Letter of Dec. 5, 1499.
[20] Written in Latin with the title *Moriae Encomium*. An English translation by Sir Thomas
Chaloner was printed in 1549. Best modern translation and commentary by H. H. Hudson
(Princeton, 1941).
[21] *Works of Thomas Nashe*, ed. McKerrow, I. 39; III. 317.

tongue the form of a just public weal, which matter I have gathered as well of the sayings of most noble authors (Greeks and Latins) as by mine own experience," and it "treateth of the education of them that hereafter may be deemed worthy to be governors of the public weal under your highness." [22] There could hardly be a better statement of the ideal toward which the English universities since Elyot's time have most commonly aimed: the training of leaders of the nation through the study particularly of ancient history and philosophy. Elyot, so far as is known, had not been educated at either university, but rather, as he says, "continually trained in some daily affairs of the common weal...almost from my childhood,"—that is, in clerical and administrative duties under his father, who held high legal offices in the west of England. To this circumstance may be due the fact that Elyot, almost alone among the scholars of his generation, employed English exclusively in his writings [23] and labored with conscious purpose at the improvement of the then formless vernacular. His occasional translations of Latin verse into ragged rime royal have little merit; but he deserves deep gratitude for his intelligent, and essentially moderate, effort to extend the English vocabulary—"to ornate our language with using words in their proper signification"—and for his creation of a prose style. The speech of a man having authority, he says, should be "compendious, sententious, and delectable." His own style at its best has these qualities beyond any other English prose that had yet been written. A good example is the following paragraph in praise of benevolence:

When I remember what incomparable goodness hath ever proceeded of this virtue, benevolence, merciful God! what sweet flavor feel I piercing my spirits, whereof both my soul and body to my thinking do conceive such recreation, that it seemeth me to be in a paradise, or other semblable place of incomparable delights and pleasures. First I behold the dignity of that virtue, considering that God is thereby chiefly known and honored both of angel and man. As, contrariwise, the devil is hated and reproved both of God and man for his malice, which vice is contrarious and repugnant to benevolence. Wherefore without benevolence may be no God. For God is all goodness, all charity, all love, which wholly be comprehended in the said word benevolence.[24]

Though strongly influenced in its form by certain Continental works, [25] *The Governor* is a highly English book. Its deplores the fact that in the æsthetic arts "Englishmen be inferiors to all other people," and argues that poetry, comedy, and dancing should not be omitted from a good education, though the supreme studies are history and Platonic philosophy. Elyot's manner is a pleasant one. "In every discipline," he says, "example is the best

22 *The Booke Named The Governor*, ed. H. H. S. Croft (1883), p. cxcii (*The Proheme*). Compare D. Bush, "Tudor Humanism and Henry VIII," *Univ. of Toronto Quar.*, VII (1938). 162-177.
23 A letter in Latin, from Elyot to Thomas Cromwell, is printed in Croft, I, pp. cxl-cxli.
24 Croft, II. 92, 93.
25 Giovanni Pontano, *De Principe* (1490); Francesco Patrizi, *De Regno et Regis Institutione* (1518); Erasmus, *Institutio Principis Christiani* (1516).

instructor," and his "accustomed manner" is "to recreate the spirits of the diligent reader with some delectable histories." Usually these are drawn from his wide classical knowledge; but he reinforces his Ciceronian discussion of friendship by adding a translation of Boccaccio's story of Titus and Gisippus, and in the chapter on "Placability" (Book II, chapter 6) he tells, apparently for the first time, the fable of the wild Prince Hal and the courageous Lord Chief Justice, which later became so popular.[26]

No English writer of this time was more imbued with the spirit of Platonic philosophy than Elyot. In three works which followed *The Governor* he employs the form of the Platonic dialogue. The most important of these is called *Of the Knowledge Which Maketh a Wise Man*, with the subtitle, "A disputacion Platonike."[27] It consists of five dialogues which develop in logical sequence the heart of Plato's philosophy: the true nature of wisdom, the qualities of the human soul, and the relation of men, beasts, and God. The speakers are Plato himself and Aristippus, who like Plato had been a pupil of Socrates, but had come to prefer a philosophy of pleasure. The arguments are handled neatly, and with a certain dramatic vividness. In the other two dialogues there is more effort to be amusing and a closer approach to the manner of the interlude. *Pasquil the Plain* (1532) treats of the respective advantages of speech and silence in a discussion between Gnatho, Harpocrates, and Pasquil. Gnatho enters with a New Testament in his hand and a copy of *Troilus and Criseyde* in his pocket. *The Defence of Good Women* [28] (1545) shows Caninius, who "like a cur at women's conditions is always barking," and Candidus arguing this matter and incidentally the superiority of Plato to Aristotle. Zenobia, a noble queen living in retirement, joins in the talk at the end, as a model of her sex and probably as a picture of Katharine of Aragon.

Elyot's Platonic Dialogues

Elyot took a place in the immediate line of humanist endeavor by translating (directly from the Greek) Isocrates' oration to Nicocles (*The Doctrinal of Princes*, 1534) and Plutarch's essay on the education of children (1535?). He translated also a sermon of Saint Cyprian and the *Rules of a Christian Life* of Pico della Mirandola (1534), and produced in 1538 a Latin-English dictionary, the first worthy of the name, which after going through several editions was enlarged by Thomas Cooper [29] and, under the title of "Cooper's Thesaurus," became one of the best known Elizabethan books. Two other works may be regarded as by-products of the immense reading that Elyot did for *The Governor*. The *Bankette* [banquet] *of Sapience* (printed as

Minor Works of Elyot

[26] Cf. Shakespeare, *Henry IV, Part II*, v. ii. 64-121. For other possible borrowings of Shakespeare from Elyot see D. T. Starnes, "Shakespeare and Elyot's *Governour*," *Univ. of Texas Stud. in English*, VII (1927). 112-132; and D. Bush, "*Julius Caesar* and Elyot's *Governour*," *MLN*, LII (1937), pp. 407-408.

[27] Three editions are known, the earliest dated 1533; reprinted in K. Schroeder, *Platonismus in der englischen Renaissance vor und bei Thomas Eliot* (Berlin, 1920; Palaestra, LXXXIII).

[28] The only edition bears this date, but the dialogue was written considerably earlier. It is reprinted in Foster Watson, *Vives and the Renascence Education of Women* (1912), pp. 213-239, and by E. J. Howard (Oxford, Ohio, 1940).

[29] This was the Cooper, Bishop of Winchester, who was so badly handled by the Marprelate writers. See below, ch. VI.

"newly augmented" in 1539) is a collection of wise and moral sayings of the kind the Renaissance adored; it was popular enough to have at least five editions. *The Image of Governance* (1541) illustrates concretely in the life of the good emperor, Alexander Severus, the principles that *The Governor* laid down. Elyot states that he translated it largely from a Greek manuscript by "Eucolpius" which a gentleman of Naples had lent him nine years before. Nothing is known of this source, but it has been lately shown that about a third of the work is taken from the Latin history of Lampridius.[30] The *Image*, like Elyot's other works, was popular, as four surviving editions attest.

The Castle of Health

The most popular of all his works, and, apart from *The Governor*, the most interesting to students today, is *The Castle of Health* (1539), which had no fewer than fifteen editions by 1610.[31] It is a layman's guide to health, and was inveighed against by doctors, for that reason and because it was in English. Elyot's reply is supposed to contain a tribute to Linacre:

Now when I wrate first this book, I was not·all ignorant in physic; for before that I was twenty years old a worshipful physician, and one of the most renowned at that time in England, perceiving me by nature inclined to knowledge, rad unto me the works of Galen of temperaments, natural faculties, the Introduction of Johannicius, with some of the aphorisms of Hippocrates.[32]

The reader will find here a lucid statement of the theory of humors and other medical theories, along with priceless details concerning sixteenth-century dietary and hygiene.

The Absorption of Humanism

A successful effort to adapt humanist learning to the needs of a very wide public was made by William Baldwin [33] in *A Treatise of Moral Philosophy, Containing the Sayings of the Wise* (1548). The dedication to the young Earl of Hertford confesses its elementary nature:

William Baldwin

Forsomuch as it was not of value to be given to any ancient councillor, which are all therein sufficiently seen [skilled] already, I judged it most convenient to be given to some that were younger.

The first book relates the lives of the ancient philosophers, largely on the authority of Diogenes Laertius (2nd century). The second, "of precepts and counsels," classifies their pronouncements on the weightiest subjects; the third, "of proverbs and adages," collects a huge number of more trivial, or at least more varied, sayings, some of which are put into verse; [34] and the fourth book is a collection of elaborate similes which probably had an

---

30 *The Image of Governance,* ed. H. E. Joyce (MS diss., Yale, 1926).

31 The edition of 1541 has been recently reproduced in facsimile (*Scholars' Facsimiles & Reprints,* 1937).

32 Preface, ed. 1541, sig. A IV. Nothing in Elyot's voluminous works is more interesting than the long prefaces which he usually affixed to them. They deserve to be collected and published separately.

33 This was the originator of *The Mirror for Magistrates;* see below, Part II, ch. II. Few facts concerning his life have been discovered.

34 One of them is Surrey's fine translation of Martial, called "The Things that Cause a Quiet Life."

influence upon Meres's *Palladis Tamia* half a century later.[35] Baldwin thus provides both a Story of Philosophy and a manual for the English orator or poet. He owes, and acknowledges, a great debt to the Latin compilations of Erasmus, and in his life of Plutarch pays a high compliment to

the excellent and famous knight, Sir Thomas Elyot, whose good zeal and love both to further good learning and to profit his country appeareth as well thereby [36] as by other many works which he hath pained himself to bring into our language.

The book was expanded by Thomas Palfreyman (*c.* 1556) and by 1651 had been printed in something like thirty editions. [37]

Roger Ascham [38] (1515-1568) was in a sense the last humanist. The move-*Roger* ment which began with Grocyn as an exotic force is in him wholly absorbed *Ascham* into the native culture, and his most famous passage is his fiery diatribe, on moral grounds, against the Italian journeys which had been so essential to the earlier humanism.[39] It was no longer necessary to go to Italy. Nor was it necessary to write in Latin. Though Ascham did so habitually in his letters and poems, and insists that that language or Greek would be easier for him and more "fit for my trade in study," yet in his three most important works he holds it better to "have written this English matter in the English tongue for English men." Ascham's English works cover a span of over twenty years; one belongs to the close of Henry VIII's reign, the second to the final months of Edward VI's, and the third to the first decade of Elizabeth's. They vary in everything except style. *Toxophilus,* the earliest (1545), is a pair of Platonic dialogues on the use of the long bow and the general theme, *mens sana in corpore sano.* The *Report ... of the Affairs and State of Germany* is a philosophical analysis of the factors which during the three years (1550-1553) that Ascham had lived at Charles V's court as secretary to the ambassador had caused the waning of the Emperor's prestige. *The Schoolmaster,*[40] first printed in 1570, is a plan for a more humane and thor-ough system of education. Doctor Johnson said that it "perhaps contains the best advice that was ever given for the study of languages."

No scholar of the time was more learned than Ascham. In loving rivalry with his revered guide, Sir John Cheke (1514-1557), who was also his pre-decessor in the Regius Professorship of Greek, he had at Cambridge fed full on all the familiar and obscure authors. The references in his writings are a complete index to what the sixteenth century knew of Greece and Rome.[41] Yet his English style is markedly simple; it is far less Latinized, for example,

---

[35] As the earlier books and Elyot's *Bankette of Sapience* did on the Ling-Bodenham *Politeuphuia* of 1597. See below, Part II, ch. I.

[36] That is, by Elyot's translation of Plutarch.

[37] See T. W. Camp, *William Baldwin and his Treatise of Moral Philosophy* (Yale diss., unpubl., 1935); E. I. Feasey, "William Baldwin," *MLR,* xx (1925). 407-418.

[38] The original form of the name is "Askham," and it should be so pronounced. A. Katter-feld, *Roger Ascham, sein Leben und seine Werke* (Strassburg, 1879) seems still to be the most copious source of information.

[39] Close of Book I of *The Schoolmaster. English Works of Roger Ascham* (Cambridge, 1904), pp. 223-236.

[40] See G. B. Parks, "The First Draft of Ascham's *Scholemaster,*" *HLQ,* I (1938). 313-327.

[41] Cf. Gertrude Noyes, *A Study of R. Ascham's Literary Citations* (Yale diss., unpubl., 1937).

than that of Elyot.[42] Ascham was one of the first to complain of "strange and inkhorn terms" and of the "indenture [i.e., law book] English" of Hall's Chronicle. The beauty of his own style is in its balance, as in this sentence from his *Report* on the Duke Maurice of Saxony:

He was five years prisoner in this court, where he won such love of all men as the Spaniards now say they would as gladly fight to set him up again as ever they did to pull him down; for they see that he is wise in all his doings, just in all his dealings, lowly to the meanest, princely with the biggest, and exceeding gentle to all; whom no adversity could ever move, nor policy at any time entice, to shrink from God and his word.

Ascham is a master also of graphic detail. His descriptions of St. John's College, Cambridge, in his youth, of the Lady Jane Grey at her Plato, and of his own pupil, Queen Elizabeth, linger in the imaginations of all who love good prose. *Toxophilus* and *The Schoolmaster* both open with a picture which a painter might set on canvas as his evocation of the humanist ideal. In the one it is a gentleman walking in the bright afternoon sunshine, absorbed in reading Plato's *Phaedrus,* while his friends go out with bows and arrows to shoot at the "pricks," or archery targets. In the other it is Sir William Cecil's chamber at Windsor (in December, 1563), where the Queen's greatest statesmen are dining together and passionately disputing the question, how best to make a schoolboy love his books.

The Antiquaries   An important result of the study of classical antiquity by the humanists was to deepen curiosity concerning the ancient life of Britain and to supply investigators with improved techniques. At the same time the religious controversies incident to the Reformation gave polemical significance to the early church history of the island and stimulated researches which led, among other things, to recovery of the ability to read Anglo-Saxon (long an unknown tongue).[43] The term *antiquary* was first borne by John Leland

John Leland   (c. 1506-1552), who, after studying under William Lyly at St. Paul's School, and after a university career at Cambridge, Oxford, and Paris successively, became chaplain and librarian to King Henry VIII. In 1533 he was created "King's Antiquary" and empowered to search for manuscripts and relics of antiquity in all monasteries, convents, and colleges, "to the intent that the monuments of ancient writers ... might be brought out of deadly darkness to lively light." [44] This commission was not unconnected with the plan for suppression of the monasteries which was then going forward. Leland devoted six years (c. 1536-1542) to a painstaking tour of England and Wales, collecting an enormous mass of documents which he was unable to organize, for in 1547 he went insane. His collections, now chiefly in the Bodleian Library and the British Museum, were finally edited in many volumes by Thomas Hearne of Oxford in the early eighteenth century. During his

[42] Ascham pays his homage to Elyot (as who, indeed, did not?): "... I was once in company with Sir Thomas Eliot Knight, which surely for his learning in all kind of knowledge bringeth much worship to all the nobility of England" (*Toxophilus, English Works,* p. 53).
[43] See T. Brooke: "The Renascence of Germanic Studies in England," *PMLA,* XXIX (1914). 135-151; E. N. Adams, *Old English Scholarship in England, 1566-1800* (New Haven, 1917).
[44] Leland, *New Year's Gift,* ed. 1895, p. 33.

lifetime Leland published only a vindication of the historical existence of King Arthur and some Latin poems of note, one of them being an obituary for Sir Thomas Wyatt. [45] A single small pamphlet on his antiquarian labors, which he called *A New Year's Gift to King Henry VIII*, was first printed in 1549, with large intercalations by John Bale (1495-1563), under the title, *The Laborious Journey and Search of John Leylande for England's Antiquities*.

Bale, whose polemical plays require notice elsewhere, was a vehement *John Bale* and even scurrilous partisan of the Reformation. Yet he was an ardent student of the past, and the additions by which he more than quadrupled the length of Leland's *Laborious Journey* contain the most vigorous denunciation of the destruction of old libraries, which accompanied the expropriation of monastic property. He exerted himself to make good the threatened loss by collecting all that could be learned about the earlier English writers. He published the first dictionary of English literature, *Illustrium Maioris Britanniae Scriptorum Summarium*, in 1548, and an enlarged version, *Scriptorum ... Catalogus*, in 1557 and 1559; and left a further manuscript compilation which was edited by R. L. Poole and Mary Bateson in 1902. These are of great use to modern students. [46]

John Stow, the chronicler (c. 1525-1605), was also a diligent collector of *John Stow* antiquities. His *Survey of London* [47] (1598) incorporates material about the city which Stow discovered in William Fitzstephen's twelfth-century life of Thomas à Becket and in many other places; it gives moreover the best account of the city as it was in Shakespeare's time. Stow also copied out in his own handwriting a large part of Leland's papers and later sold this material to the greatest of the Elizabethan antiquaries, William Camden (1551-1623), whose fame rests chiefly upon two mighty works, the *Britannia* (1586) and *Annals* (1615),[48] and upon the fact that he was the teacher of *William* Ben Jonson. Camden had himself been trained at St. Paul's School and at *Camden* Magdalen, Oxford; he became headmaster of the Westminster School and prepared for his pupils there a Greek grammar which ranked with the Latin grammar of Lyly. He was one of the members of the Society of Antiquaries, the earliest English learned academy,[49] which included also on its roll the great library-founder, Sir Robert Cotton. and the great scholar-jurist, John Selden [50] (1584-1654).

[45] Cf. L. Bradner, *Musae Anglicanae* (1940), p. 26. Bale says of Leland: "he had a poetical wit, which I lament, for I judge it one of the chiefest things that caused him to fall besides his right discernings" (Preface to *Laborious Journey*, ed. 1895, pp. 24f).
[46] For Bale's plays and bibliographical references see below, ch. v.
[47] Ed. C. L. Kingsford (2v, Oxford, 1908-27).
[48] Camden's text of both books was in Latin. An English translation of the *Britannia* appeared in 1610, and of the *Annals* in 1625. The most interesting of Camden's works for the general reader is the collection of essays on various subjects (languages, names, money, apparel, etc.) which he published in 1605 under the title, *Remains of a Greater Work Concerning Britain* (reprinted, 1870).
[49] See H. R. Steeves, *Learned Societies and English Literary Scholarship* (1913), ch. II, pp. 5-35.
[50] Selden's *Table Talk*, compiled by the Rev. Richard Milward, his secretary, and first printed in 1689, has been edited by Sir Frederick Pollock (1927).

III

The New World

Thomas
More and
the Utopia

Thomas More (1478-1535) died a martyr and has been made a saint, but his humanism was of the kind that concerned itself more with the expansion of man's possibilities in this world than with the study of the past or thoughts of the world to come. [1] He was fourteen years old when Columbus discovered America, and twenty-nine when Amerigo Vespucci popularized the news of that event. More is known to us by some memorable historical scenes, in which he played noble parts, but the scene that perhaps portrays him best is not historical. It is the scene he has imagined at the opening of the *Utopia,* when his Antwerp friend, Peter Giles, presented to him an alleged companion of Vespucci, one Raphael Hythloday,[2] with the assurance that the latter must be very welcome to More, "for there is no man this day living that can tell you of so many strange and unknown peoples and countries as this man can. And I know well that you be very desirous to hear of such news."

The account of the island of Utopia, in some unknown ocean of the New World, was written in 1515, when More was in Flanders on an embassy for Henry VIII. In the next year he wrote, in London, his account of the discoverer, Hythloday, which became Book 1 of the completed work. The two books of the Utopia are consciously contrasted, and artfully play the old world against the new. In Book 1 Hythloday, who though a voyager by vocation is a humanist by training, tells how much easier is the former's quest: "For nothing is more easy to be found than be barking Scyllas, ravening Celaenos [harpies] and Laestrygonians, devourers of people, and such like great and incredible monsters; but to find citizens ruled by good and wholesome laws, that is an exceeding rare and hard thing." He illustrates from conditions in England, which he had visited in the days of the good Cardinal Morton (d. 1500)—with whom More had served as page in the years before he went to Oxford. There, Hythloday says, he had argued against the savagery of the laws (e.g., hanging for theft), the inordinate greed (e.g., eviction of farmers to increase sheep-herding), nationalistic ambition, selfish war, unjust taxation, and the unequal distribution of property. The handling of these evils is cautious and ironic. They are referred to the reign of Henry VII, not Henry VIII, and to the tongue of Hythloday, not More. When Raphael's hearers rate him as too critical, his

---

[1] See W. Nelson, "Thomas More, Grammarian and Orator," *PMLA,* LVIII (1943). 337-352.
[2] When translated from the Greek, this name yields the meaning, "a recounter of nonsense." Similarly, Utopia means "the place that is not."

reply is always: "If you had been with me in Utopia!" Consequently, in Book II we have a description of a land where there is no private wealth or money, no unemployment or tavern-loitering, and no wars of aggression; where the working day is but six hours long, and "a great multitude of every sort of people, both men and women, go to hear lectures," notably on Greek learning; where gold and precious stones are held in contempt, and complete religious liberty exists, except only for those who deny a divine providence and the immortality of the soul. Again More's conclusion is ironic: *he* cannot agree to all the things Hythloday said, and he must needs confess "that many things be in the Utopian weal public which in our cities I may rather wish for than hope for."

The *Utopia* was written in Latin and circulated throughout Europe. It is a companion piece to the less imaginative and more openly satirical *Praise of Folly*, which More's friend Erasmus had written in his house six years before. The first English translation of the *Utopia* was made by Ralph Robinson, citizen and goldsmith of London (1551), "at the procurement and earnest request of George Tadlowe, citizen and haberdasher of the same city." It has not been surpassed.[3]

Neither *The Praise of Folly* nor the *Utopia* is particularly concerned *More's* with religion. More at no time followed the trend toward reformed doctrine *Religion* that shows itself in most of the other English humanists, e.g., Colet, Cheke, and Ascham; but it was the rise of Lutheranism after 1520 that drove him definitely into the other camp and produced the great mass of controversial writing which filled his later years.[4] His scanty English verse includes a *His English* "merry jest" or quasi-ballad on the terrific beating administered to a police *Verse* sergeant who disguised himself as a friar in order to make an arrest, and some not very distinguished rime royal stanzas on serious subjects, such as the "Lamentation on the Death of Queen Elizabeth"[5] (1503). More important is the prose *History of King Richard III*, dated about 1513, which *His* was written both in English and in Latin. Neither version was completed; *Richard III* the one in English is the more comprehensive and the more significant, since it passed almost unaltered into Holinshed's Chronicle and thus became the direct source of Shakespeare's *Richard III*.[6] More derived most of the vivid details in his life of Richard from Cardinal Morton, who had had a large part in the events described. The effect is that of an eye-witness account, and this is the effect which the best biography aimed at in Henry VIII's

---

[3] Of the many editions of the *Utopia* those by J. H. Lupton (Oxford, 1895) and by G. Sampson and A. Guthkelch (1910) may be recommended. For discussion see R. P. Adams, "The Philosophical Unity of More's *Utopia*," *SP*, xxxviii (1941). 45-65.

[4] Cf. below, ch. vi.

[5] This was the Queen of Henry VII. The poems referred to will be found in *The English Works of Sir Thomas More*, ed. W. E. Campbell and A. W. Reed, Vol. 1 (1931), pp. 327-344, 381-396.

[6] See R. W. Chambers, "The Authorship of the *History of Richard III*," in *English Works* of More cited above, pp. 24-53; L. F. Dean, "Literary Problems in More's *Richard III*," *PMLA*, LVIII (1943). 22-41; and for a work of opposed intention see W. G. Zeeveld, "A Tudor Defense of Richard III," *PMLA*, LV (1940). 946-957.

Roper's Life reign. George Cavendish's *Life of Cardinal Wolsey* is a classic in this style;[7]
of More   the *Life* of More himself by his son-in-law, William Roper (1496-1578), is
              something further: it is one of the most charming books in the world, and
              has been called by R. W. Chambers "probably the most perfect little biog-
              raphy in the English language." [8]

Thomas   Many of the social and political reforms advocated in the *Utopia* are
Starkey's   urged with still more frankness in Thomas Starkey's remarkable *Dialogue*
Dialogue   *between Pole and Lupset* (1535?) [9] and *Exhortation to the People* (1536).
              Though an acute dialectician, Starkey lacks literary grace, and he also
              lacked political prudence in such a degree that he may be counted fortunate
              in quietly dying a short time after he had despatched his dialogue with a
              covering letter to Henry VIII.

One of the king's chaplains, Starkey was also a personal friend of Reginald
Pole and was employed to secure from the latter a public judgment favorable
to Henry in the dispute over his divorce (1535). He optimistically misrepresented Pole's point of view, and was utterly discredited when Pole's unmitigated championship of the papal decision finally appeared (*Pro Ecclesiasticae
Unitatis Defensione*, 1536). Against this inauspicious background he constructed his imaginary conversation between Pole and the late Thomas
Lupset (d. 1532), a friend of More and sometime Reader in Humanity at
Oxford.[10] Both interlocutors are pleasingly presented, but there seems to be
an unconscious irony in the fact that Lupset, a sometimes indiscreet pupil
of Colet and Erasmus, has the timid rôle, while Pole, later Queen Mary's
Archbishop, presents the root-and-branch proposals for democratic change
in church and state. Pole does most of the talking. It is he who asserts that
the monk who retires to the safety of a religious house is less praiseworthy
than "he which in dangerous prosperity, so full of so many occasions of
errors and doing amiss, governeth his mind well and keepeth it upright;"
it is he who advocates taxes on bachelors and marriage of the secular clergy,
as well as translation of the gospel and divine service into the vernacular.
He objects outspokenly to the Pope, "usurping a certain cloaked tyranny
under the pretext of religion," and says to Lupset: "I will not follow the
steps of Luther, whose judgment I esteem very little; and yet he and his

[7] Cavendish was a gentleman usher in Wolsey's household. His manuscript life was first
printed in the nineteenth century.
[8] See E. V. Hitchcock, *Roper's Life of More* (Oxford, 1935). Another early life of More
in English, by Nicholas Harpsfield, has been recently (1932) printed for the first time. Of
the many recent studies of More evoked by the quatercentenary of his death the best is doubtless that of R. W. Chambers, *Thomas More* (1935). See also E. M. G. Routh, *Sir Thomas
More and his Friends* (Oxford, 1934).
[9] The date is not quite certain; see J. A. Gee, *The Life and Works of Thomas Lupset* (New
Haven, 1928), pp. 150-152. The only printed edition of the *Dialogue* is that of J. M. Cowper
(1871; *EETSES*, 12), but see also *Starkey's Life and Letters* (1878; *EETSES*, 32). There is important new material, especially on Starkey's *Exhortation*, in W. G. Zeeveld, "Thomas Starkey
and the Cromwellian Polity," *Jour. of Mod. Hist.*, xv (1943). 177-191.
[10] The conversation may be imagined as taking place in 1529 (Gee, *op. cit.*, p. 153).
Lupset's chief works are *A Treatise of Charity* (1533), *An Exhortation to Young Men* (1535),
and *A Compendious and a very Fruitful Treatise teaching the Way of Dying Well, by the
flower of learned men of his time, Thomas Lupset* (1534). They are broad-minded humanist
tracts and have been well edited by J. A. Gee (*op. cit.*).

disciples be not so wicked and foolish that in all things they err. Heretics be not in all things heretics."

Though Pole, Lupset, and Starkey were all clerics, this dialogue is not a work of religious controversy. It has a hearty, mundane tone, explicit in Pole's rebuke to his companion: "Master Lupset, you speak like a man of the old world and not of this time," and in his definition of felicity as including health, strength, beauty, riches, and virtue of mind, "with all honest and due behaviour both toward God and man," which is certainly more humanist than ascetic, and more sixteenth-century than fifteenth. The real interest of the dialogue is social and political. Like the *Utopia,* but more openly, it advocates elective monarchy. "It is not man," says Pole, "that can make a wise prince of him that lacketh wit by nature, nor make him just that is a tyrant for pleasure. But this is in man's power: to elect and choose him that is both wise and just, and make him a prince, and him that is a tyrant so to depose."[11] It is regrettable that Starkey was not master of a more sprightly style, or capable of restricting himself to less than 75,000 words; but it is impossible to read his dialogue without admiration of its downright merits or without wondering whether Henry VIII did indeed read the manuscript copy that Starkey so heartily and incautiously commended to him.[12]

The chronicle of Tudor poetry, with its fine frenzies and passions, begins and ends with the saga[13] of a noble friendship. Through Wyatt and Surrey, stationed like Pillars of Hercules at the head of the Elizabethan sea, flowed the inspiration. At the other end stand Beaumont and Fletcher, rather parallel figures, through whom the last surges of this tide pass into the lyrically alien reaches of the Stuart period. In each case the consideration paid to higher social rank has attracted the fancy to the younger and shorter-lived of the pair of poets. Surrey and Beaumont each lived about thirty years; Wyatt (1503-1542) lived nearly forty, and Fletcher forty-six. But while Beaumont, by right of his finer and purer poetic spirit, may deserve

The Tudor Lyric

[11] *Dialogue,* ed. Cowper, p. 167. On the next page a rather doubtful concession is made to the reigning king: "Albeit we have now in our days, by the providence of God, such a prince, and of such wisdom, that he may right well and justly be subject to no law ... yet we now ... may not deny but that in our order here is a certain fault, and to the same now devise of some remedy."

[12] The prose literature of social protest in Henry VIII's reign includes the brief but pungent *Supplication for the Beggars* (1529) by Simon Fish, which addresses the king on the greed and immorality of the clergy. Incidentally, Fish questioned the doctrine of purgatory, and thus evoked a reply from Sir Thomas More, *The Supplication of Souls,* which in turn led to the controversy between More and Tyndale. Several other *Supplications,* urging reform of abuses, followed; see Furnivall and Cowper, *Four Supplications, 1529-1553* (1871; EETSES, 13). Henry Brinkelow, a protestant exile who wrote under the name of "Roderick Mors," published two invective tracts: *The Complaint of Roderick Mors* (1542) and *The Lamentation of a Christian against the City of London,* "printed at Jericho in the land of promise" (but actually at London, 1542), and later at Nürnberg. The first addresses the Parliament on the subject of social abuses; the second reprimands the Londoners for their religious laxity. Both are reprinted, (1874; EETSES, 32). See H. O. Taylor, *Thought and Expression in the Sixteenth Century* (1920), II. 50-69.

[13] There is little likelihood of an actual friendship between Wyatt and Surrey, who can have met but seldom.

the precedence granted him over Fletcher, to put Surrey before Wyatt would be a critical distortion.

Sir Thomas Wyatt

The finest part of Sir Thomas Wyatt's work is the part which stands freest of foreign influences. It is a series of lyrics, written for the lute, singularly native in melody and form, and singularly individual in their appeal. Nothing very like these thrilling little songs had appeared before, and nothing very like them followed. There is a suggestion of the lyric manner of Sir Walter Ralegh, and occasionally of Donne; but the poetry that in quality they most resemble is perhaps that which appeared in 1896 in *A Shropshire Lad*. Like Housman, Wyatt "has an unquenchable desire and no hope." [14]

Wyatt's Songs

His singing range is very restricted. The mood of his songs is nearly always that of the stout-hearted but forsaken lover—and a piquancy is added to this theme by the not unlikely rumor that he had been Anne Boleyn's lover before King Henry was. His typical poem is a series of lyric cries, artfully repeated and modulated, and clinched by a refrain at the end of each stanza, e.g.,

> Take heed betime, lest ye be spied; . . .
> Therefore take heed!

> And wilt thou leave me thus?
> Say nay, say nay, for shame! . . .
> Say nay, say nay!

> Disdain me not without desert,
> Nor leave me not so suddenly. . . .
> Disdain me not!

> Blame not my lute, for he must sound
> Of this and that as liketh me. . . .
> Blame not my lute.

In many of these the utterance is perfect, as in the following:

> There was never nothing more me pained,
> Nor nothing more me moved,
> As when my sweetheart her complained
> That ever she me loved.
> Alas the while!

or this:

> Forget not yet the tried intent
> Of such a truth as I have meant,
> My great travail so gladly spent:
> Forget not yet!

or in this last stanza of a song on his liberation:

[14] J. C. Squire, *Essays on Poetry* (1924), p. 155.

Was never bird, tangled in lime,
That brake away in better time
Than I, that rotten boughs did climb
And had no hurt, but scaped free.
Now ha, ha, ha, full well is me,
For I am now at liberty.

Fifty or sixty poems of this sort are Wyatt's chief warrant of immortality; and they show that a new world was opening for poetry, a world in which the microcosm, man, was as a center of interest displacing the macrocosm in which he lived. Wyatt was perhaps the first English poet to adopt consciously the principle previously illustrated only by the anonymous writers of popular song; namely, that the expression of personal feeling in the simplest and briefest form is itself the highest poetry and needs no narrative or allegorical support.

If in these respects Wyatt was following native influences, he also (as *Foreign* Tillyard says [15]) "let the Renaissance into English verse" by importing *Influences* Italian and French forms more largely than any predecessor had done since *on Wyatt* Chaucer. He had lived, on the King's service, in France, Italy, and Spain. The story of his first visit to Italy is entertainingly told in the Wyatt Papers.[16] In 1527 the ambassador, Sir John Russell, as he was being rowed down the Thames encountered Wyatt, and

after salutations was demanded of him whither he went, and had answer: "To Italy, sent by the king." "And I," said Wyatt, "will, if you please, ask leave, get money, and go with you." "No man more welcome," answered the ambassador.

Wyatt returned from Italy, bringing no observable store of the classical learning with which the English humanists had enriched themselves,[17] but bringing new poetic patterns that Dante and Petrarch had made famous. The three Horatian verse epistles, which he wrote about 1536 to his friends Pointz and Brian, against the life at court and the quest of glory, are in *terza rima.* Many of his "epigrams," adapted from Italian and French sources, are in *ottava rima;* and both metres are extensively employed in his *Penitential Psalms.* He wrote a number of imitative *rondeaux*—intricate fifteen-line affairs, and, in particular, he furnished English poetry with one of its most useful implements by writing thirty-two sonnets. Seventeen of these are adaptations of Petrarch. Twenty-eight have the Petrarchan *abbaabba* octave and twenty-six the *cddcee* sestet. In the last three only he experiments with

---

[15] E. M. W. Tillyard, *The Poetry of Sir Thomas Wyatt, A Selection and a Study* (1929), p. 13. This volume contains a generous selection of Wyatt's best poems and an admirable introduction.

[16] Quoted in the *DNB,* article on Wyatt.

[17] Wyatt (who usually signed his name "Wiat") was an M. A. of Cambridge. He had the education of a gentleman, as became the only son of one of Henry VII's most faithful and best rewarded followers and the inheritor of Allington Castle in Kent; but he shows no particular leaning toward classical scholarship. His prose translation of Plutarch's epistle on *The Quiet of Mind* was presented to Katherine of Aragon as a new year's gift (1528) and printed by Pynson. The style is not distinguished.

Wyatt's
Sonnets

the Shakespearean formula, three quatrains and a couplet, and virtually produces it in his thirtieth, which rimes *abab, abab, abab, cc.*[18]

Wyatt's sonnets are in the main hard reading, being disfigured by much "not keeping of accent," which is a particularly hangable offence in a sonneteer.[19] The most charitable explanation is that which Sir E. K. Chambers offers; namely, that they "ought to be regarded as mere exercises in translation or adaptation, roughly jotted down in whatever broken rhythms came readiest to hand, and intended perhaps for subsequent polishing at some time of leisure which never presented itself."[20] How fluent Wyatt can occasionally be is indicated by No. 23, for which, incidentally, no foreign source has been discovered:

> Divers doth use, as I have heard and know,
> When that to change their ladies do begin,
> To moan and wail, and never for to lin [cease],
> Hoping thereby to pease [calm] their painful woe.
> And some there be, that, when it chanceth so
> That women change and hate where love hath been,
> They call them false, and think with words to win
> The hearts of them which otherwhere doth go.
>
> But as for me, though that by chance indeed
> Change hath outworn the favor that I had,
> I will not wail, lament, nor yet be sad,
> Nor call her false that falsely did me feed:
> But let it pass, and think it is of kind [by nature]
> That often-change doth please a woman's mind.

Henry
Howard,
Earl of
Surrey

Henry Howard, Earl of Surrey,[21] (*c.* 1517-1547) was a man of action, of courage, and of sensibility. In 1539 the Dean of Westbury, John Barlow, called him "the most foolish proud boy that is in England,"[22] and if he was a man of subtle thought, Holbein's portraits of him, as well as his own verses, do him injustice. He had a good many of the qualities of Lord Byron, and like Byron early became a romantic figure, moulding the tastes of his readers.

Grace and tenderness of feeling beautify Surrey's work as manly simplicity does that of Wyatt. He tends to be pictorial and discursive where Wyatt is sententious. His stanzas written during the imprisonment he endured at Windsor—apparently for striking a political enemy in the King's Court—

---

[18] The sonnets are referred to by the numbers assigned them in A. K. Foxwell's *Poems of Sir Thomas Wiat* (2v, 1913).

[19] Cf. Ben Jonson on Donne, *Conversations with Drummond.*

[20] E. K. Chambers, *Sir Thomas Wyatt and Some Collected Studies* (1933), p. 122.

[21] Surrey did not live long enough to inherit a peerage, but bore this "courtesy title" as eldest son of the Duke of Norfolk. His life has been sympathetically written by Edwin Casady, *Henry Howard, Earl of Surrey* (1938), and his poems edited by F. M. Padelford, *The Poems of Henry Howard, Earl of Surrey* (rev. ed., 1928). See also J. M. Berdan, *Early Tudor Poetry* (1920), pp. 504-545.

[22] Quoted in a letter from George Constantyne to Thomas Cromwell, *Archaeologia,* XXIII (1831). 62.

are among his best. He recalls in sentimental retrospect and in great detail the occupations and feelings of the boyhood days he had spent at Windsor with the king's son, Richmond, who had become Surrey's brother-in-law, and now was dead:

> The stately sails, the ladies bright of hue,
> The dances short, long tales of great delight
>
> The palm play,[23] where, despoiled [stripped] for the game,
> With dazed eyes oft we by gleams of love
> Have missed the ball and got sight of our dame,
> To bait [attract] her eyes which kept the leads [24] above.
>
> The secret thoughts imparted with such trust,
> The wanton talk, the divers change of play,
> The friendship sworn, each promise kept so just,
> Wherewith we passed the winter nights away.

Equally pleasing are the stanzas on Wyatt's death, one of five poems in which Surrey mentions the elder poet with reverence. This one begins, "W. resteth here, that quick could never rest," and goes on to catalogue Wyatt's good points:

> A head, where wisdom mysteries did frame;
> Whose hammers beat still in that lively brain
> As on a stithy, where that some work of fame
> Was daily wrought to turn to Britain's gain, . . .

This stately tribute must, one would suppose, have been the model for Sir Walter Ralegh's similar epitaph on Sidney forty-five years later.

Like Wyatt, Surrey employed both the *terza rima* and *ottava rima,* though rarely, using the former measure for the most amusing of his poems, the mock-apology he wrote when he and Wyatt's son were charged with breaking windows in a nocturnal frolic in 1543. He explains that his motive was to make the London burghers repent of their hidden sins by simulating a visit of the wrath of God. He used altogether a surprising number of metrical patterns,[25] and his work is almost completely free from rough lines. His artistic innovations are concerned mainly with his use of the sonnet, blank verse, and the "poulter's measure."

Surrey's sonnets are only half as numerous as Wyatt's, but of the fifteen or sixteen credited to him ten have the "Shakespearean" rime scheme, which was thenceforth much the most frequent in the sixteenth century. They are easy and interesting, sometimes judiciously paraphrased from Petrarch, and sometimes based on Surrey's own observation of natural beauty or on incidents in his life. Three of them are tributes to Wyatt, and one an epitaph on the poet's faithful squire, Thomas Clere. The most famous is the one on

Surrey's Sonnets

23 I.e., hand ball, an early variety of tennis.
24 I.e., balconies with floors of lead.
25 Cf. Casady, *op. cit.,* pp. 222-243.

the Lady Geraldine, "From Tuscan came my lady's worthy race," [26] which seems to have been almost solely responsible for the fictitious romance with which Thomas Nashe and other Elizabethans embellished Surrey's story.

Blank verse   Blank verse first appears in English poetry in the version of the fourth book of the *Æneid* which was printed about 1554 with a title-page describing it as "translated into English, and drawn into a straunge metre, by Henry late Earl of Surrey." [27] A few years later (1557) Richard Tottel published another text of this work, along with Surrey's rendering of *Æneid,* Book II, and in his *Miscellany* of the same year added two shorter blank verse poems by Nicholas Grimald. [28] Whether Surrey made use of Gavin Douglas's translation of the *Æneid,* which, though not printed in his lifetime, may have been available in manuscript, is not certain; but that he got the hint for his "strange metre" from Italy, whence strange metres usually came, can hardly be doubted. In 1534 a translation of Virgil's fourth book in the Italian equivalent of blank verse *(versi sciolti)* had appeared, and other books, in-

Surrey's   cluding the second, were in print in Italian by 1540. Surrey's blank verse
Translation is far more compact than Douglas's stanzas. It already possesses force and
of the   variety, but a generation passed before this metre was thoroughly domesti-
Æneid   cated in England. How far its refinement was to go is evident if one compares Surrey's version of *Æneid,* IV. 365 ff.,

> Faithless, forsworn, thy dame ne goddess was,
> Nor Dardanus beginner of thy race,
> But of hard rocks Mount Caucase monstruous
> Bred thee, and teats of tiger gave thee suck,

with Marlowe's:

> Thy mother was no goddess, perjur'd man,
> Nor Dardanus the author of thy stock;
> But thou art sprung from Scythian Caucasus,
> And tigers of Hyrcania gave thee suck. [29]

The verse form to which Surrey was most addicted is the iambic couplet of twelve and fourteen syllables alternately, for which George Gascoigne, in his *Certain Notes of Instruction* (1575) invented a jesting name that has stuck, "Poulter's Measure." It was, Gascoigne says, "the commonest sort of verse which we use nowadays," [30] and, though Wyatt had employed it in a couple of poems, Surrey's example was doubtless responsible for the baleful

---

[26] Geraldine was Elizabeth Fitzgerald, a child of nine when the sonnet was written. Cf. Casady, *op. cit.,* pp. 244-250.

[27] This has been reproduced in facsimile and edited, from the only surviving copy in the library of Mr. Pforzheimer, by Herbert Hartman (Purchase, N. Y., 1933).

[28] Grimald's blank verse poems are likewise translations of Latin hexameter verse, one from Walter of Lille's *Alexandreis,* the other from Beza's *Mors Ciceronis.* For "Tottel's Miscellany," in which the general body of Surrey's and Wyatt's poems was first printed, see below, Part II. ch. I.

[29] Christopher Marlowe, *The Tragedy of Dido Queen of Carthage,* lines 1564-1567 (Act V, sc. I).

[30] *Complete Works of George Gascoigne,* ed. J. W. Cunliffe, I (1907). 472.

luxuriance with which it overspread the Elizabethan song books. The lines *"Poulter's*
could, of course, be split and made to look like lyric; e.g., *Measure"*

> Wrapt in my careless cloak,
> As I walk to and fro,
> I see how love can show what force
> There reigneth in his bow.[31]

But there is a fatal singsong in this measure, and a terrible temptation to
verbosity. Of the eighteen poems—nearly a thousand lines in all—that
Surrey wrote in poulter's measure, about half were translations from *Ecclesiastes* and the *Psalms*. Thence it and its derivative, the straight "fourteener" couplet, completely overran devotional literature; and as exemplified
in the Sternhold and Hopkins metrical psalms (1547, etc.), they had a *Sternhold*
melancholy effect on piety which lasted for centuries.[32] One might say that *and Hop-*
the progress of poesy in the Elizabethan age was largely a matter of dis- *kins*
entangling it from poulter's measure and developing blank verse. The best
and the worst in the prosody of the later sixteenth century both derive
from Surrey.

[31] "Tottel's Miscellany," 26; Padelford, *Poems of Surrey*, p. 78.
[32] Thomas Sternhold preferred the "fourteener" form, i.e., seven feet in each line; but his
version of Psalm xxv is in poulter's measure: "I lift my heart to thee, my God and guide most
just. Now suffer me to take no shame, for in thee do I trust."

IV

Satire

"Better a dumb mouth than a brainless skull," said John Skelton [1] (*c.* 1460-1529); but he heeded the adage very little, if a brainless skull is one which prompts its possessor to speak when silence would be more decorous or more prudent. It is doubtful whether many readers, except the special enemies of Cardinal Wolsey, have derived as much pleasure from Skelton's verse as the poet's manifold endowments and engaging personality qualified him to bestow.[2] He is one of the hardest authors to measure artistically, and it is not even easy to fix his historical position. Chronologically, he is one of the earliest of the Tudor writers, and the mechanism of his verse has more affinity with the fifteenth century than with Wyatt and Surrey; but his satiric spirit links him spiritually with Lindsay and the period of the Reformation, while the earliest literary notice of him, by Caxton in 1490,[3] presents him as a humanist scholar.

Most of Skelton's peculiarities are combined in his *Right Delectable Treatise upon a Goodly Garland or Chaplet of Laurel,* which is his longest poem and one of his latest.[4] It begins in medieval fashion and in the rime royal stanza. Skelton, while a guest of the Countess of Surrey at Sheriff-Hutton Castle, Yorkshire, falls asleep beneath an oak tree and dreams that he hears Pallas Athene and the Queen of Fame arguing concerning him. The queen complains that despite the laurel with which he has been graced,[5] he has become "wonder slack" in poetic production, to which the goddess replies that he is justly cautious,

> For if he gloriously polish his matter,
> Then men will say how he doth but flatter;

[1] The standard text of Skelton is still that of Alexander Dyce (1843), a remarkable piece of scholarship, several times reprinted. A handsome, but incomplete, selection of his poems, slightly edited by Richard Hughes, appeared in a limited edition (1924); and the "complete poems" (modernized), edited by Philip Henderson (1931). Some very illuminating critical interpretation has recently appeared, notably in William Nelson, *John Skelton, Laureate* (1939) and I. A. Gordon, *John Skelton, Poet Laureate* (Melbourne, 1943). See also J. M. Berdan, *Early Tudor Poetry,* pp. 156-205, and L. J. Lloyd, *John Skelton, A Sketch of His Life and Writings* (Oxford, 1938).

[2] Skelton's art has, however, a strong affinity with much of our most recent English verse. See W. H. Auden, "John Skelton", in *The Great Tudors* (1935), and I. A. Gordon, *op. cit.,* ch. XII.

[3] In the preface to *The Boke of Eneydos,* Caxton refers to him as "Master John Skelton, late created poet laureate in the university of Oxenford," and praises his classical learning in the highest terms. See, however, R. L. Dunbabin, "Skelton's Relation to Humanism," *MLR,* XII (1917). 129-137.

[4] Printed in 1523, the year of its composition.

[5] He had been crowned poet laureate, not only at Oxford (see note 3), but also at Louvain and Cambridge.

And if so him fortune to write true and plain,
As some time he must vices remord [rebuke],
Then some will say he hath but little brain,
And how his words with reason will not accord.

Then, in a passage reminiscent of Chaucer's *House of Fame*,[6] Æolus the trumpeter is bidden to summon all the poets in Fame's retinue, who appear to the number of nearly a thousand, led by Phoebus. Gower, Chaucer, and Lydgate are among them, and these, after exchanging courtesies with Skelton, leave him in the guidance of Fame's "registary," Occupation, who with words of praise and assurance leads him to a walled field, with a thousand gates, new and old, by which the poets of the various nations are admitted, while the unworthy aspirants are driven off with gunshot. Within the gate which has engraved on it a capital *A* for "Anglia" Skelton finds a lovely garden where the Muses and Dryads dance, and a building in which the Countess of Surrey is directing her ladies in the embroidery of a coronal of laurel

for Skelton, my clerk,
For to his service I have such regard,
That of our bounty we will him reward.

Skelton then addresses verses of homage to the countess and to each of her ten attendants. He places the laurel upon his head and, once more accompanied by Gower, Chaucer, and Lydgate, presents himself before the Queen of Fame, where Occupation reads—in 350 lines, in which the rime royal is interspersed with "Skeltonics" and even Latin hexameters—the long roll of the author's works. The poem is completed by some Latin lines in laudation of Skelton and in compliment to Henry VIII and Cardinal Wolsey, with the latter of whom he was now, or desired to be, reconciled.

The main fabric of the *Garland of Laurel* is evidently medieval. *The Bowge of Court* (i.e., "court rations") a much earlier poem,[7] is likewise a dream allegory in rime royal; but the dream is here a nightmare. The hazards of one who lives at the court are powerfully imaged in the growing terror of a young man, Dread, who believes himself at sea with a gang of ruffians and awakes at the moment when he is about to leap overboard to escape their malign whisperings.[8] It is doubtless not unbiographical and may supply the lack of recorded fact concerning Skelton's life at court during the first half of Henry VII's reign. In 1498, at an unusually advanced age, he entered the priesthood, and the next year received from Erasmus some, probably quite conventional, praise as the tutor of the young prince, later Henry VIII,

The Bouge of Court

Skelton at Court

[6] See A. S. Cook, "Skelton's *Garland of Laurel* and Chaucer's *House of Fame*," *MLR*, xi (1916). 9-14.
[7] Printed, and probably composed, about 1499. See H. S. Sale, "The Date of Skelton's *Bowge of Court*," *MLN*, lii (1937). 572-574.
[8] The theme may have been slightly suggested by Brant's *Narrenschiff*. See C. H. Herford, *Literary Relations of England and Germany in the Sixteenth Century* (1886), pp. 350-357.

for whom he wrote in 1501 a little Latin manual of conduct called *Speculum Principis.*[9] At some time before 1504 he had been presented to the rectory of Diss in Norfolk, nearly a hundred miles from London.

Skelton at Diss   At Diss Skelton composed some of his most caustic poems,—e.g., *Ware the Hawk,* against a fellow-priest more given to falconry than religion—and also the most endearing and playful of his works, *Philip Sparrow.* This

Philip Sparrow   is in Skeltonic verse,[10] and through most of its length is a dramatic monologue set in the mouth of a Norfolk schoolgirl, Jane Scroop, whose pet sparrow has been killed by a cat. Skelton's uneconomic art here achieves two triumphs: one in his evocation of the various church services for the dead, which one seems to hear intoned as the poem proceeds;[11] and a greater one in the complete picture he gives of a young girl's mind. Jane seems to empty out the whole content of her innocent brain: all the kinds of birds she knows and all the kinds of books, all her sentiments of love, hate, and propriety, and all the vivid trifles she has observed about the slain bird. Toward the end the poet takes over the discourse and shapes it into a eulogy of Jane.

The converse and logical companion piece of this delicate poem is the indelicate *Tunning of Eleanor Rumming,* the only major work of Skelton which could justify Pope's epithet, "beastly."[12] It is divided into seven

Eleanor Rumming   "passus" after the fashion of Langland and has traces of that poet's alliterative rhythm, which indeed must be considered in any full study of the origins of the "Skeltonic" verse.[13] It owes an obvious debt to Chaucer's *Wife of Bath* and a less conspicuous one to the opening of the *Nun's Priest's Tale;* but in following these earlier realists Skelton has bettered the instruction. His biting rimes and prodigious fecundity of detail are nowhere more effective than in this picture of the appalling old ale-wife who dwelt on a hill beside Leatherhead in Surrey, and the abominable hags who came to her shop. It has the actual beastliness of bestial humanity; it marks one limit of Skelton's graphic power, and *Philip Sparrow* marks the other.

Skelton's Lyrics   Skelton is a memorable lyrist. Besides shaping his own peculiar rime into song measure—as in *Woefully Arrayed, The Manner of the World Nowadays,* and some of his outbursts against the Scots[14]—he gave wings also to the grave rime royal, syncopating the lines in *Against a Comely Coistrown* and *Womanhood, Wanton, ye Want,* and lightening it with a refrain in *Lullay, Lullay, Like a Child.*[15]

---

[9] First printed by F. M. Salter, *Speculum,* IX (1934). 25-37.
[10] Lines, usually of two or three accented syllables, arranged in blocks of consecutive rime.
[11] See I. A. Gordon, "Skelton's *Philip Sparrow* and the Roman Service-book," MLR, XXIX (1934). 389-396.
[12] *Epistle to Augustus,* lines 37 f.: "Chaucer's worst ribaldry is learned by rote, And beastly Skelton heads of houses quote."
[13] William Nelson, *op. cit.,* pp. 82-101, has argued the derivation of Skeltonic rime from Latin rimed prose.
[14] His *Ballad of the Scottish King,* on the Battle of Flodden (1513), has been called the earliest printed English ballad. (Reproduced in facsimile by John Ashton, 1882).
[15] Compare also *Garland of Laurel,* lines 836-905.

At the age of sixty, more or less, Skelton focused his satiric powers in *Poems* three long poems, which with increasing vehemence and clarity attack *Against* Cardinal Wolsey and the corruption of the kingdom. These have all been *Wolsey* referred on persuasive evidence to the brief period between the autumn of 1521 and the same season in 1522.[16] *Speak, Parrot!*, in rime royal, cloaks its *Speak,* satire by putting it into the mouth of a parrot who employs scraps of most *Parrot!* of the known languages and also some apparent gibberish. The portion of this poem which the early printers of Skelton published contains no very clear satire of Wolsey, but rather a thorough-going attack upon the new, humanistic system of education. A single manuscript, however, in the British Museum [17] contains nearly two hundred and fifty additional lines, consisting of four postscripts or "envoys," obscurely dated and undoubtedly directed against the cardinal. These, it may be assumed, were intended for the exclusive perusal of the poet's most trusted friends.

In the two poems that so quickly followed the author abandoned rime *Colin* royal like an encumbering garment and bent to his work in hard-hitting *Clout* Skeltonics, "angry Skelton's breathless rimes," as Joseph Hall well termed them.[18] *Colin Clout,* indeed, preserves a thin pretense of impersonality; it is not Skelton who speaks but the typical representative of the proletariat, and the theme announced is the faultiness of all classes:

> And if ye stand in doubt
> Who brought this rime about,
> My name is Colin Clout.
> I purpose to shake out
> All my cunning bag,
>
> . . . .
>
> For, as far as I can see,
> It is wrong with each degree.

But the faults actually stressed are those of the higher clergy, and the particularity with which they are developed is often so great as to make them fit only the Cardinal-Chancellor.

In *Why Come Ye Not to Court?* there is no disguise; after a few pages *Why Come* of warming-up Skelton drives straight at his mark. The king's admiral, "the *Ye Not to* good Earl of Surrey," has defeated the French (July-October, 1522), *Court?*

> But yet they overshoot us
> With crowns and with scutus [i.e., écus, coins];
> With scutis and crowns of gold
> I dread we are bought and sold;
> It is a wonders wark:
> They shoot all at one mark,

---

[16] See W. Nelson, *op. cit.,* pp. 158-190; H. L. R. Edwards and W. Nelson, "The Dating of Skelton's Later Poems," *PMLA,* LIII (1938). 601-622. I. A. Gordon (*John Skelton,* pp. 147f) dates *Colin Clout* 1519-20 and regards it as the earliest of the group.
[17] Harleian 2252.
[18] *Virgidemiarum,* lib. 6, sat. 1, line 76 (1598).

At the Cardinal's hat,
They shoot all at that.
Out of their strong towns
They shoot at him with crowns;
With crowns of gold enblased
They make him so amazed,
And his eyen so dazed,
That he ne see can
To know God nor man.

Thereafter, through a thousand lines the gibes patter upon the "Red Hat" as innumerable and remorseless as hailstones, rising (or perhaps sinking) to such invocations as the following:

He would dry up the streams
Of nine kings' realms,
All rivers and wells,
All waters that swells;
For with us he so mells [meddles]
That within England dwells,
I would he were somewhere else;
For else by and by
He will drink us so dry,
And suck us so nigh,
That men shall scantly
Have penny or halfpenny.
God save his noble grace,
And grant him a place
Endless to dwell
With the devil of hell!

There is no reason for doubting the tradition that this poem was written from the relative security of sanctuary at Westminster. The wonder is that Skelton ever emerged from sanctuary; yet if the dating of recent critics is correct, as it seems to be, he was writing his *Garland of Laurel* from Sherriff-Hutton Castle a few months later in a spirit of great self-complacency "and

Skelton's Reconciliation with Wolsey

calm of mind, all passion spent." He dedicated *The Garland of Laurel* to Wolsey, as has been said, and also his flyting, *The Doughty Duke of Albany*, of the same year, 1523; and in 1528 he produced under the cardinal's formal patronage his *Replication* against the Cambridge heretics. The situation does no great credit perhaps to Skelton's consistency or courage—though neither of these requires defense; but it suggests shrewd broad-mindedness in Wolsey. One might recall the anecdote concerning Pope's lines on "Atticus." "I sent the verses to Mr. Addison," said Pope, "and he used me very civilly ever after." [19]

[19] Skelton had imitators, of course. *Read Me and Be not Wroth,* a long riming satire in dialogue form, appears to be the work of William Roy and Jerome Barlow, abjured Franciscans who were associated with Tyndale on the Continent. Printed in Strassburg, 1528, and in London, 1546, it attacks Wolsey and his hierarchy with a good deal of wit. It is reprinted by E. Arber (*English Reprints*, 1871). Coarser examples of Skeltonizing verse are *Jill of Brentford's*

The blazing originality of Skelton finds no parallel in the other great *Alexander* satirist of the age. Alexander Barclay [20] (*c.* 1475-1552), who decried the *Barclay* heterodoxy of the Rector of Diss and was himself an orthodox priest, likewise followed the old models in style, and for his subjects preferred to recast and amplify Continental works. His first (not positively authenticated) production was a translation in rime royal of a very recent French allegory by Pierre Gringoire, *The Castle of Labor*,[21] of which both Pynson and Wynkyn de Worde printed editions in 1505-1506. He later translated Sallust, a life of St. George, and a Latin poem on the four cardinal virtues by Dominicus Mancinus, the latter under the pleasant title of *The Mirror of Good Manners*.[22] At the command of the Duke of Norfolk—for through his long life Barclay seems never to have lacked important patrons—he compiled an elementary book on French, *The Introductory to Write and to Pronounce French* (1521), which has value today chiefly as a guide to the contemporary pronunciation of English.

Whether Barclay was English or Scotch by origin, and which of the universities, if any, he attended, are still debated questions.[23] He is first heard of far in the southwest of England, at Samuel Taylor Coleridge's birthplace, Ottery St. Mary, near Exeter. In 1508 he was chaplain of the college there, and in that place made his translation of Sebastian Brant's *Ship of Fools,* which Pynson printed the next year. Barclay professes to use three versions of his original: Brant's "in plain and common speech of Doche," another in French, and J. Locher's in Latin elegiacs. It is the last that he mainly depends upon, but he has no notion of translating closely, and frankly says so. He retains Brant's woodcut illustrations, which gave the poem much of its appeal, but often alters the chapter captions and greatly increases the length, so that 310 pages in Brant become 650 in Barclay. The enlargement is partly due to substitution of the rime royal for Brant's compacter tetrameter couplets, but it mainly arises from the fact that Barclay is a more concrete writer than Brant, and is intent upon localizing the fools in England, which he does so effectively that few would have believed his book of foreign origin, had he not so candidly confessed it. When something in Brant is inapplicable to England, he omits it or inserts a *Caveat;* e.g., in the chapter

---

Testament by Robert Copland (ed. F. J. Furnivall, 1871); and a "treatise" on beards by a certain Barnes, which bears the pseudonym of Colin Clout (ed. Furnivall, *EETSES*, 10, 1870). Later political rimes in Skelton's metre (sometimes claiming his authorship) include *Doctor Double-Ale, Vox Populi Vox Dei,* and *A Poor Help.* The first two are Protestant in tone; the last, which dates from the opening of Mary's reign, Catholic. All three are found in W. C. Hazlitt, *Early Popular Poetry,* III (1866). 249-321.

[20] See T. H. Jamieson, *The Ship of Fools* (2v, 1874); B. White, *The Eclogues of Alexander Barclay* (1928; *EETS,* 175); C. H. Herford, *Studies in the Literary Relations of England and Germany,* Ch. VI; J. M. Berdan, *Early Tudor Poetry,* pp. 237-256; R. W. Bond, "Brant's *Das Narrenschiff"* in *Studia Otiosa* (1938), pp. 18-42.

[21] Facsimile, ed. A. W. Pollard (Roxburghe Club, Edinburgh, 1905). Barclay's translation is not to be confused with a long original poem by William Nevill, *The Castle of Pleasure,* printed about 1518.

[22] Reprinted, Spenser Soc. (1885). For the later translation of this poem by Turberville (1568) see below, Part II, ch. I, n. 35.

[23] See W. Nelson, "New Light on Alexander Barclay," *RES,* XIX (1943). 59-61.

"Of night-watchers and beaters of the streets, playing by night on instruments and using like follies, when time is to rest":

> Though I have touched of this enormity
> In English tongue, yet is it not so used
> In this Royalme as it is beyond the sea;
> Yet much we use which ought to be refused.
> Of great night-watching we may not be excused,
> But our watching is in drunken gluttony
> More than in singing or other melody.

He commonly adds an *envoy* of his own ("Barclay to the Fools," or "The Envoy of Barclay") to what he finds in his source, and usually differentiates this by the use of the Monk's Tale stanza. He grows more independent as he proceeds, and at the end of his book diverges very widely from Brant. The printer nobly put up with this copiousness, but not without some alarm, for quite early in the work Barclay summons one group aboard in the following words:

> Come to our ship; our anchors are in-weighed;
> By right and law ye may challenge a stage.
> To you of [i.e., by] Barclay it shall not be denayed,
> Howbeit the charge Pynson hath on me laid,
> With many fools our navy not to charge.

Imitations of The Ship *of Fools*   The anonymous poem, *Cock Lorell's Boat,* seems to be an imitation of *The Ship of Fools.* It exists in a single undated and fragmentary copy of about four hundred lines from the press of Wynkyn de Worde.[24] Cock Lorell receives into his vessel a minutely itemized company of all the reprobates in London.

> Than [i.e., then] Cock weighed anchor and housed [hoisted] his sail,
> And forth he rowëd without fail;
> They sailëd England through and through,
> Village, town, city, and borough.

This piece has a certain rude vigor, but no humor or specific satire. It is referred to, and is itself imitated, in a much longer poem, *The Highway to* *Robert Copland*   *the Spital-house,*[25] written by Robert Copland and published by him about 1535. Here Copland, who introduces himself as one of the interlocutors, receives from the porter of a London hospital a report, sometimes gruesome and sometimes moralistic, on all the different types brought to the institution by disease, crime, or penury. The details are valuable, but the tone is harsh, and the description leaves one uncertain whether the place should be thought of in modern terms as prison, almshouse, or sanatorium. The classifying and satiric method of the *Ship of Fools,* and similar woodcut illustrations, are found in the thirty-nine chapters of *The First Book of the*

24 Reprinted by E. F. Rimbult (Percy Society, 1843).
25 Reprinted in A. V. Judges, *The Elizabethan Underworld* (1930), pp. 1-25. See W. G. Moore, "Robert Copland and his *Hye Way,*" *RES*, VII (1931). 406-418.

Introduction of Knowledge (1542) by the amusing physician-traveler, *Andrew Borde* Andrew Borde [26] (*c.* 1490-1549), in which doggerel descriptions of the various races of men are followed by articles in prose on their countries, manners, currency, and languages.

Shortly after the printing of *The Ship of Fools,* it appears that Barclay *Barclay's* left Devonshire and became a monk at Ely. His *Eclogues,* which are the *Eclogues* earliest in English poetry, were published about 1515 with a prologue explaining that at the age of "forty year save twain" he had had the fortune to find his youth again, that is to discover a little "treatise" that he had compiled long before. This testimony, suggestive of Sir Walter Scott's experience with the manuscript of *Waverley,* is corroborated by topical allusions which indicate that portions of the *Eclogues* were written shortly after 1500,[27] and therefore before the *Ship of Fools,* and other portions very near the date of publication. The verse form is a somewhat stiff but metrical riming couplet, changing to the Monk's Tale eight-line stanza in the "ditties" of Eclogue 4.[28] Barclay acknowledges as his model in this pastoral style a recent humanist poet of Italy to whom Shakespeare also offered tribute,

> the most famous Baptist Mantuan,
> The best of that sort since poets first began.

The fourth and fifth eclogues—on rich men and poets and the citizen and the countryman respectively—are in fact lengthened imitations of the fifth and sixth eclogues of Mantuanus. Barclay's first three eclogues, on the miseries of courtiers, derive their material from the Latin prose of Æneas Silvius (1405-1464), the noted scholar who became Pope Pius II.

Barclay is a master of detail and of homely wisdom. The dialogue between his shepherds is vigorously handled, and often has a tang of the British soil, e.g.,

> But trust me, Corydon, there is diversity
> Between to have riches and riches to have thee;
>
> A small sparkle may kindle love, certain,
> But scantly Severn may quench it clean again;
>
> Our Lord destroyed five cities for outrage;
> Read where for sin He wasted one village.

The most striking passage is the long and horrid description of court table manners in Eclogue 2, which goes far beyond its original in Æneas Silvius;

---

[26] Ed. F. J. Furnivall (1870; *EETSES,* 10). Borde—who sometimes spelled his name Boorde and punningly Latinized it as "Andreas Perforatus"—is also the author of two entertaining medical works in the style of Elyot: *A Dietary of Health* and *The Breviary of Health.* He has been uncertainly credited with compiling several jestbooks, e.g., *The Merry Tales of the Mad Men of Gotham* and *Scoggin's Jests.*

[27] I.e., laments on the deaths of Cardinal Morton and Bishop Alcock of Ely. Both died in 1500. See especially Eclogue 3, lines 457-508.

[28] The longer of these, "The description of the tower of virtue and honor," is an elegy on the death of Sir Edward Howard in 1513.

but Barclay has many pleasant bits as well—e.g., the admirably told fable of God's gifts to Eve's children [29] and the pretty vignettes of winter amusements.[30] He follows his sources, but his work is everywhere "circumstantiated" (as Lamb said of Sidney's sonnets) by references to current English affairs.[31]

John Heywood

John Heywood [32] (*c*. 1497-*c*. 1580), whose wife was Sir Thomas More's niece and whose grandson was John Donne, is one of the most genial and rational of satirists. Neither a humanist nor a reformer by temperament, he was content to be a professional entertainer to three courts, and though forced to a public recantation in the hectic last years of Henry VIII (1544), he neither changed nor stressed unduly his good-natured Catholicism. He wisely avoided trouble during the reign of Edward VI, stood very high in favor under Queen Mary, and early in Elizabeth's reign abandoned England for Catholic Belgium, where he died at a very advanced age.

His Songs

The songs for which he was famous have been ill preserved and are not always well authenticated, but enough exist to give the measure of a very likable personality. The best known is the one on Queen Mary, printed anonymously by Tottel, but said in one version to have been written by Heywood when the princess was eighteen (1534):

> Give place, you ladies, and be gone!
> Boast not yourselves at all;
> For here at hand approacheth one
> Whose face will stain you all.

He seems to have written the earliest version of the willow song that Desdemona sings, with the line,

> For all a green willow is my garland.

His most passionate lyrics are directed at social transgressors, as in this stanza against slanderers:

> Christ cri'th out still,
> "Say good for ill";
> But we say harm for harm.
> Yea, ill for good
> Ill tongues do brood,
> Wrath is in them so warm!

or another against idlers,

> The proud man may be patient,
> The ireful may be liberal,
> The gluttonous may be continent,

---

[29] Eclogue 5, lines 237-396.
[30] *Ibid.*, lines 87-106.
[31] See J. R. Schultz, "The Method of Barclay's Eclogues," *JEGP*, XXXII (1933). 549-571.
[32] See R. de la Bere, *John Heywood: Entertainer* (1937); R. W. Bolwell, *The Life and Works of John Heywood* (1921); J. M. Berdan, *Early Tudor Poetry*, pp. 102-116. For Heywood as a dramatist see below, ch. v.

The covetous may give alms all,
The lecher may to prayer fall:
Each vice bideth *some* good business
Save only idle idleness.

Jollity and good company are what he likes. A dainty song of welcome ends
with the pleasant line,

Your welcome is here your best dish,

and another says,

Man hardly hath a richer thing
Than honest mirth.[33]

Heywood's only extended satire, apart from his plays, is *The Spider and* The Spider
the Fly (1556). It is very extended indeed, for a most trivial incident, the and the Fly
imprisonment of a fly in a cobweb, is developed into a poem in rime royal
which is nearly as long as *Paradise Lost* and nearly as argumentative as *The
Ring and the Book*. The printer of the only edition increased the reader's
trouble by over-lavish use of colons in the most uncalled-for places.[34] Students
who surmount these obstacles find it an amusing and highly intelligent
work. The plot, which culminates in a mass engagement between armies
of flies and spiders, evidently was suggested by the pseudo-Homeric battle
of the frogs and mice, a very popular classic in the sixteenth century; and
it ends, with the death of the spider, in a scene that recalls the close of the
Æneid and has a good deal of dignity. That is, *The Spider and the Fly* is
not simply a mock epic; it is rather, as Heywood called it, a parable, an
allegorical comment on contemporary conditions, developed mainly by
dialogue and debate.[35]

The author's conclusion explains that he had begun the poem more than
twenty years before and had left it unworked at for over nineteen. It seems,
then, that Heywood conceived the plan, and wrote most of the work, about
the time of More's death in 1535, as an outlet for his feelings; but naturally
found it indiscreet to publish till the accession of Mary enabled him to add
the dénouement, in which the servant maid, typifying the Queen herself,
enters with her broom to liberate the imprisoned fly and judicially crush
the spider, who can now be clearly equated with Archbishop Cranmer.[36]
In a general way, the flies represent the simple people of England, who are
Catholic, and the spiders the new wealthy classes, who are Protestant; but
the satire is nowhere bitter and is not primarily religious. Heywood was
humanist enough to love debate and intellectual dexterity for their own

[33] Texts of many songs by Heywood are in the manuscript which contains Redford's play,
Wit and Science. It was edited for the Shakespeare Society by J. O. Halliwell (1848).
[34] The best reprint is that of the Spenser Society (1894) which contains an admirable introduction by A. W. Ward. See also J. Haber, *John Heywood's "The Spider and the Flie"* (Berlin,
1900) which argues for a different date of composition from the one here assumed.
[35] For the possibly direct influence of this poem upon Swift's *Battle of the Books* see J. W.
McCain, Jr., "Swift and Heywood," *N&Q*, CLXVIII (1935). 236-238.
[36] Cranmer was burned at the stake, after a long trial, in March, 1556.

sake. During the first half of the poem, which reads dully today, the disputation is mainly a huge, ingenious parody of the ways of lawyers. The
spider and fly, with their learned counsel (ant and butterfly, respectively),
chop logic interminably, and finally reach the conclusion that everything
is just as it was before. Then the action takes an epic turn with the appearance of armies of flies and spiders, and the Pilgrimage of Grace uprising
(1536) is analyzed with reference to such economic and modern questions
as the effect of rising price levels upon the different classes of society (chapter 44). The spiders are here the capitalists and the flies the laborers. Heywood
is sympathetic to all except the "neuters" in each class, who act not by
conviction but from opportunism (chapter 63). At the end this devout
Catholic welcomes the Queen less as the restorer of the church than as
the creator of order, and puts into her mouth just the sentiment with which
Coleridge closes his *Ancient Mariner:*

> spiders and flies are the creatures of God,
> And all his creatures, in their creation good,
> I know and acknowledge . . .
> I hate neither the spiders' nor the flies' brood,
> I love all, as behoveth maidenly mood.
> All his creatures in an order we must love,
> That orderly use themselves as doth behove.[37]

"Misorder" was the crime of the Reformation in Heywood's view, and
was detrimental to all classes:

> Spiders and flies have lived like as in hell,
> Since new misorder did th' old order expel.

Now, ironically enough at the beginning of the Marian massacres, he sees
order restored and urges clemency even to the memories of such innovators
as Cromwell and Somerset:

> Touching deeds and deaths of those that so past be,
> Let us rather (when memory them to mind calls)
> Lament their false facts [i.e., deeds] than rejoice their foul falls.

Heywood's   In spite of the delightful woodcuts, which make it one of the quaintest
Epigrams   picture books in the world, *The Spider and the Fly* had few readers and
and   no open admirers after the accession of Elizabeth. It was "Heywood the
Proverbs   Epigrammatist" that the later age admired, "who," as Puttenham said,[38]
"for the mirth and quickness of his conceits, more than for any good learning was in him, came to be well benefited by the King" (i.e., Edward VI).
Possibly the good learning that was missed was orthodox Protestant doctrine,
for Heywood was reputed to have studied at Oxford and alludes familiarly
to that university. His are said to be the first epigrams in English, and were

[37] Ch. 95, p. 440. Compare "He prayeth well, who loveth well both man and bird and beast," etc.
[38] *The Art of English Poesy* (1589), ch. 31.

produced by him literally in hundreds.[39] They are not very mirth-provoking —few epigrams are; but they distinguish themselves from most of those that followed by their good temper. The author asserts,

> In all my simple writing never meant I
> To touch any private person displeasantly.

This is true. He is seldom more savage than in the following, which if "displeasant," is certainly redeemed by its pungency and wit:

> 'God is no botcher.' But when God wrought you two,
> God wrought as like a botcher as God might do.[40]

They are the merest trifles, but throw revealing lights upon the London of his day; e.g., its odors:

> But for blemish of a face to look upon,
> I doubt which were best, to have a nose or none.
> Most of our savors are more sour than sweet:
> A nose or no nose, which is now most meet? [41]

or the women's fashions:

> Alas! poor fardingales must lie in the street:
> To house them no door in the city made meet.
> Since at our narrow doors they in cannot win,
> Send them to Oxford, at Broadgates [42] to get in.

Three hundred of Heywood's epigrams, including one quoted above, are based on proverbs. Something in his homely nature warmed to what he called "our common, plain, pithy proverbs old," and he made himself their great exponent and collector. That they could be built into coherent contemporary satire he shows in one of his most ingenious poems, *A Dialogue Containing the Number in Effect of All the Proverbs in the English Tongue, Compact in a Matter Concerning Two Manner of Marriages*, of which four editions appeared between 1546 and 1561.[43] In this grimly realistic piece the author's advice is sought by a young man who has it in his power to marry either an elderly rich widow or a penniless maid. The referee recounts with much liveliness and detail the bleak experiences of his two neighbors, each of whom has been gored on one of the horns of this matrimonial dilemma, and the client resolves to forgo both his opportunities. The poem, which extends to about a hundred pages and has merit both as narrative and as social photography, is so pieced together with current proverbs as to be a mosaic, and it is a chief storehouse for students of the folk wisdom of the age.

[39] Reprinted, Spenser Society (1867).
[40] *Epigrams upon Proverbs*, No. 62.
[41] *The First Hundred of Epigrams*, No. 31, "Of a nose."
[42] I.e., Broadgates Hall. *The Fifth Hundred of Epigrams*, No. 55, "Of fardingales."
[43] Ed. J. S. Farmer (1906).

V

The Interlude

**From
Morality to
Interlude**

The first impression that the student receives in passing from the fifteenth-century morality to the Tudor interlude [1] is one of sudden light. He passes from a species preserved in the scantiest examples to one so copiously illustrated that coherent brief discussion is impossible; from a drama wholly anonymous and (except *Mankind*) unlocalized, to plays heavily charged with London realism and to a large extent written by figures of definite historical importance; from a drama based upon the abstractions of the universal medieval church to one that is above all things topical, mundane, and aristocratic.

**Medwall,
Fulgens and
Lucrece**

At the very outset we meet the first positively known English dramatist in Henry Medwall, chaplain to Cardinal Morton, and the first play to introduce a central love-theme and to provide definite information concerning the place, date, and circumstances of its production. Medwall's *Fulgens and Lucrece*, as A. W. Reed appears to have shown,[2] was first acted in Lambeth Palace at Christmas, 1497, to grace an entertainment for Flemish and Spanish ambassadors. It is divided into two parts, the first presented at the end of the midday dinner, the second later the same evening, and is thus literally a pair of interludes in the feasting. The main plot handles the marriage problem of Lucrece, a Roman heiress, who decides for the suitor of worth but lowly origin against the blue-blooded waster. This theme, without the romantic dénouement, came from a Renaissance dialogue which Caxton had printed in 1481.[3] Medwall adds effective low comedy in the lady's maid and in the servants of the lovers, who, though only algebraically

---

[1] The term *interlude*, of disputed origin, soon after 1500 began to replace the term *moral play* or *morality*, of which type the interlude is the historical successor. Though usually implying abstract figures and ethical symbols, the interlude was not limited to these, and in popular usage the word came to cover any sort of play. Texts (of varying critical value) of most of the interludes mentioned in this chapter will be found in one or another of the following collections: A. Brandl, *Quellen des weltlichen Dramas in England vor Shakespeare* (Strassburg, 1898; *Quellen und Forschungen*, 80); W. Bang, *Materialien zur Kunde des älteren englischen Dramas* (Louvain); J. S. Farmer, *Students' Facsimile Series; Malone Society Reprints*. Some few are also in the Dodsley-Hazlitt *Select Collection of Old English Plays*, J. M. Manly's *Specimens of the Pre-Shaksperean Drama* (2v, 1897), and J. Q. Adams' *Chief Pre-Shakespearean Dramas* (1924). For general discussion see T. Brooke, *The Tudor Drama* (1911), chs. III and IV, and F. S. Boas, *An Introduction to Tudor Drama* (Oxford, 1933).

[2] See *Fulgens and Lucres*, ed. F. S. Boas and A. W. Reed (Oxford, 1926); and A. W. Reed, *Early Tudor Drama* (1926), ch. IV. There is brief discussion in J. K. Lowers, "High Comedy Elements in Medwall's *Fulgens and Lucres*," *ELH*, VIII (1941). 103-106.

[3] This was a translation of Buonaccorso's Ciceronian imitation, *De Nobilitate Controversia* (1428). In Germany, a little after Medwall's time, the same work served as source for Sixt Birck's first play, *De Vera et Falsa Nobilitate*.

358 ·

distinguished as "A" and "B", are already clear forerunners of Shakespeare's Launce and Speed.

Medwall's other play, *Nature,* probably a little earlier in date, is certainly *Medwall's* so in type, for it presents the history of "Man" from childhood to old age, *Nature* his dalliance with the Seven Deadly Sins, and ultimate repentance. It has also the device, which was repeated *ad nauseam* in later interludes, of having the vices masquerade under well sounding pseudonyms, e.g., Pride as "Worship," etc. However, the moral subject is humanistically treated. Nature, the dominating power under God almighty, is an Aristotelian goddess, and she bids Man make the journey of life under the joint guidance of Reason and Sensuality. The latter is necessary to him,

> For if there be in him no manner of feeling,
> Nor no lively quickness, what lord is he?
> A lord made of clouts, or carved out of tree.

His sins result from deserting the *via media,* and his leanings to the side of sensuality are dramatized with pagan and realistic vigor. This play also was performed in two parts, with an indicated interval of about three days between them.

Mundus, the world, has an imposing though slight part in *Nature* as the *The World* rival force to that goddess and leader of the non-philosophical and hence *and the* subversive influences. He appears more prominently in *Mundus et Infans Child and* ("The World and the Child"), printed by Wynkyn de Worde in 1522. The *Related* subject of this anonymous play resembles that of *Nature,* man's adventures *Interludes* along the primrose path from infancy to old age; but progress is marked in its greater compactness, smoother metre, and in the more picturesque development of the London background. Similar qualities are found in another interlude of unknown authorship that Wynkyn printed, *Hick-Scorner,*[4] and in lower degree in *John the Evangelist.* In both the last the realistic adornment has so corroded the moral structure as to leave the plot unintelligible. In the earlier *Interlude of Youth* and the later *Lusty Juventus* contemporary youth seduced by vice is likewise treated, and the waning moral interest is replaced by doctrinal preaching, Catholic in the former and Protestant in the latter.

In *Wit and Science* John Redford, who was a poet and musician of im- *John* portance and teacher of singing in St. Paul's (*c.* 1530), introduced a timely *Redford* adaptation by substituting an educational motive for the original moral purpose of the interlude. He presents the adventures of young Wit, who desires to wed the Lady Science, daughter of Reason and Experience.[5] It is the romance of the humanist mind, the mating of natural ability with learning. To prove his worthiness Wit must make a pilgrimage to Mount

---

[4] *Hick-Scorner* is perhaps the earliest printed English play; see W. W. Greg, "Notes on Some Early Plays," *Library,* xi (1930-31). 44; and *A Bibliography of The English Printed Drama to The Restoration,* 1 (1939). 81.

[5] This plot is derived from the well known fifth-century schoolbook by Martianus Capella. *De Nuptiis Philologiae et Mercurii.*

Parnassus and overcome the giant Tediousness which besets its slopes. Attended by Instruction, Study, and Diligence, he adventures upon the curriculum and suffers all the collegiate discomfitures before he slays the giant and receives his diploma in the person of the lady. Redford has some scenes of amusing but long drawn out farce, some rather neat psychological demonstrations, and, since he had his singing boys at command, some songs of unusual complexity. The play was not printed, but must have had influence, since it was followed by two imitations: *The Marriage of Wit and Science* (*c.* 1569) and *The Marriage of Wit and Wisdom* (*c.* 1579).

John Rastell   John Rastell (*c.* 1475-1536), a lawyer of distinction and member of Parliament, was a man of wide humanist interests and multifarious activities. He set up a printing press about 1515 and printed the only edition of *Fulgens and Lucrece*. He also printed a similar piece, *A New Comedy in English*

Calisto and   *in Manner of an Enterlude,* which, as he gave it no preciser title, has in
Melebea   modern times been named *Calisto and Melebea* from the chief characters. It is largely translated from the famous Spanish "tragicomedy" *Celestina* (1499), or rather from the early sections of that long work, but it rejects the consummation and tragic consequences of the original love story and closes in a way which is artistically unacceptable but entirely in the spirit of the Tudor interludes. At the moment when the clever bawd, Celestina, has persuaded Melebea to listen to Calisto's suit, the girl's father is brought in to relate a nightmare he has had concerning her. Melebea recognizes the warning, interprets the dream:

> The foul pit whereof ye dreamed, which hath
> Destroyed so many, betokeneth vice and sin,
> In which, alas, I had almost fallen in,

and lives happily ever after. Thus a play which gives promise of being an early *Troilus and Cressida* ends with an admonition to virgins and in the last lines is further diverted into an argument that the bringers-up of children should give them good practical educations and the lawgivers concern themselves with remedial rather than punitive legislation. Rastell claims only

The Nature   to be the publisher of this piece, but may have written it. He is more certainly
of the Four   the author of the interlude of *The Nature of the Four Elements,* "declaring
Elements   many proper points of philosophy natural, and of divers strange lands, and of divers strange effects and causes," which is a dramatized lecture on recent discoveries in science and geography, incorporating Rastell's own experiences with some piratical seamen who balked his effort to explore Newfoundland in 1517.[6]

John   Rastell's wife was the sister of Sir Thomas More, and their daughter Joan
Heywood   married John Heywood [7] (*c.* 1497-*c.* 1580). Mores, Rastells, and Heywood

---

[6] See A. W. Reed, *Early Tudor Drama,* p. 12; G. B. Parks, "The Geography of the *Interlud of the Four Elements," PQ,* XVII (1938). 251-262; M. E. Borish, "Source and Intention of The Four Elements," SP,* XXXV (1938). 149-163; E. M. Nugent, "Sources of John Rastell The Nature of the Four Elements," PMLA,* LVII (1942). 74-88.
[7] For Heywood's nondramatic works see the previous chapter.

lived together in great harmony and in an intellectual comradeship which somewhat complicates the distribution of literary property. More was interested in drama and is traditionally reported to have had a hand in the production of interludes, as Rastell had; but Heywood, who from 1519 was employed at court as a musician, was the special playwright of the group and the most gifted of all interlude composers. Seven plays make up the conventional Heywood canon: [8] (1) *Witty and Witless;* (2) *Gentleness and Nobility;* (3) *John-John the Husband, Tib his Wife, and Sir John the Priest;* (4) *The Play of Love;* (5) *The Pardoner and the Friar, the Curate, and Neighbor Pratte;* (6) *The Four P's;* and (7) *The Play of the Weather.*

The Heywood Canon

Heywood was not a dramatic poet; he has no emotional scenes or high-flown descriptions. He was a court entertainer and emphasizes two qualities, liveliness of action and witty dialogue. He commenced at the foot of the dramatic ladder, the two simplest pieces in the list being no more than debates on a set subject. In *Witty and Witless,* which was presented before Henry VIII, and which might be called "The Three J's," James argues a rather thick-headed John into admitting that it is better to be a fool than a wise man; whereupon Jerome enters (replacing James) and forces John to confess the opposite.[9] In *Gentleness and Nobility,* after a merchant and a knight have disputed which is the better gentleman, a plowman comes forward and proves more than a match for them both.[10] *John-John* introduces the method of French farce, and with it much more action and obscenity.[11] There are still but three characters, all social types, the husband, the wife, the priest; but the dramatist can move them separately, not as before in groups of two, and he can make them act out a story in several scenes.

Four characters are employed in the next three plays, with a steady increase in dramatic effectiveness. In *Love* they are set up formally in a sort of psychological parallelogram, and the play between Lover-loved, Lover-not-loved, Neither-lover-nor-loved, and Beloved-not-loving proceeds rather like a chess game. In the *Pardoner and Friar* there is no formality and what debate there is is carried on by dint of shouts and fisticuffs to a most effective conclusion. In the great *Four P's* Heywood handles the same number of

---

[8] J. S. Farmer, *The Dramatic Writings of John Heywood* (1905), offers a careless text. *Weather* and *John-John* are well edited by A. W. Pollard in C. M. Gayley's *Representative English comedies,* Vol. 1 (1903), *The Four P's* in the collections of J. M. Manly and J. Q. Adams cited above, and *The Play of the Weather* by K. W. Cameron (Raleigh, N. C., 1941). For discussion of Heywood's claim to these plays see A. W. Reed, *op. cit.,* ch. v, and H. N. Hillebrand, "On the Authorship of the Interludes attributed to John Heywood," *MP,* XIII (1915). 267-280.

[9] See K. W. Cameron, *The Background of John Heywood's Witty and Witless* (Raleigh, N. C., 1941), which includes a bibliography of Heywood scholarship.

[10] *Gentleness and Nobility* is now commonly ascribed to Rastell's authorship, largely because it contains some close parallels of thought and wording with Rastell's prose works; see Reed, *op. cit.,* pp. 106-112. Perhaps Rastell contributed these portions, or perhaps they are not too close for a son-in-law to have written. The play as a whole seems to be in Heywood's manner, and Rastell does not claim to have written it. His colophon says, "Johēs rastell me fieri fecit," which is just the phrase Caxton used to describe his relation to the *Morte Darthur.*

[11] See K. Young, "The Influence of French Farce upon the Plays of John Heywood," *MP,* II (1904). 97-124.

The Four
P's, The
Play of the
Weather

figures with still more remarkable skill and vivacity. *The Four P's* is his wittiest play; his cleverest is *Weather,* in which he equates the inability of men to agree upon the best weather with their similar incapacity for pronouncing in matters of government and religion. Ten characters are here charmingly activated and contrasted, wisdom and rime royal being the exclusive prerogatives of Jupiter, who is obviously King Henry VIII.

Heywood was immensely interested in the motions of the mind, and not at all in the movements of the heart. His characters are all types, but they owe next to nothing to the morality. The only two "vices" in his plays [12] are that in name merely, and tne only two virtues he emphasizes are tolerance and humor. He developed naturalness in entrances, exits, and stage business beyond anything previously seen in the English theatre, and drilled the wooden lines of the old interludes till in the best parts of *The Four P's* and *Weather* they approach the plasticity of Coleridge's *Christabel.*[13]

The
Political
Interlude:
Skelton's
Magnifi-
cence

Three great literary insurgents—Skelton, Bale, and Sir David Lindsay— shaped the hitherto harmless or gently edifying interlude into an offensive weapon. Skelton's *Magnificence* (*c.* 1516) is the earliest; it has the structure of a moral play, but its teaching is political. A well-meaning and prosperous prince is beguiled into accepting four dissolute councilors, who lead him into evil ways and allow him to be robbed. Adversity overwhelms him, and Poverty reminds him that fortune is unstable. His overthrow is so complete that Despair and Mischief have almost succeeded in bringing him to suicide when Good Hope snatches away the knife and other virtues teach him to recover his state by abandoning wanton excess. The warning was timely in the years that preceded the Field of the Cloth of Gold (1520), but the opposition to Wolsey's influence is as yet more general than particular.[14]

John Bale

John Bale [15] (1495-1563). is Heywood's converse in most things, and next to him the most original writer of interludes. He was an exacerbated, not to say bilious, proponent of the Reformation, and used the stage as a vehicle for propaganda. He translated the famous anti-papal *Pammachius* of the Lutheran Kirchmayer, and turned sections of the Bible story into pious

[12] Merry Report in *Weather* and Neither-lover-nor-loved in *Love.*
[13] There is hardly sufficient evidence to date Heywood's plays with precision, or even to set them in their relative order. For an interesting effort to do so see Wesley Phy, "The Chronology of John Heywood's Plays," *ESt,* LXXIV (1940). 27-41. A stanza at the end of *Witty and Witless* indicates a date not earlier than 1521, when Henry VIII became Defender of the Faith. *John-John, Love, Pardoner and Friar,* and *Weather* were all first printed in 1533, and the tone of the last named play best fits the period when the divorce question was rife (1532-33), as also does a passage (line 636) alluding to the bad harvest of 1527, "How rain hath priced corn within this seven year." The decade, 1522-1532, very likely covered Heywood's entire dramatic activity. He seems to have produced no more interludes after More's imprisonment and death.
[14] R. L. Ramsay's admirable edition (1908; *EETSES,* 98) is still the standard work on *Magnificence.* Facsimile ed., J. S. Farmer, *Tudor Facsimile Texts* (1910). For another play, possibly by Skelton, see G. L. Frost and R. Nash, "*Good Order:* a Morality Fragment," *SP,* XLI (1944). 483-491. Of Skelton's *Nigramansir* (*Necromancer*), of which Thomas Warton (*History of English Poetry,* section 33) saw a copy printed by Wynkyn de Worde in 1504, and of which Warton gives an abstract, nothing more seems to be known.
[15] Texts in J. S. Farmer, *The Dramatic Writings of John Bale* (1907). See W. T. Davies, *A Bibliography of John Bale* (Oxford, 1939), which includes an extensive discussion of Bale's life and work; and J. W. Harris, *John Bale, A Study in the Minor Literature of the Reformation* (Urbana, 1940).

drama in *The Chief Promises of God, John Baptistes Preaching in the Wilderness,* and *The Temptation of Our Lord by Satan.* In his *Comedy Concerning Three Laws, of Nature, Moses, and Christ, Corrupted by the Sodomites, Pharisees, and Papists,* he uses the five-act structure and shows the anger, if not the art, of Aristophanes. All four of these plays are stated on title-page or colophon to have been "compiled in 1538," in which year Bale, who had been ejected from his pulpit for over-vehemence, appears to have been pleading his cause about the country with the help of a company of actors.

Bale's most valuable play, *King John,* was not printed and not known till a century ago, when the text of it was discovered at Ipswich, where the author had passed his latest years. The condition of this manuscript indicates that Bale composed it in the years before Cromwell's fall (in 1540) forced him to take flight to Germany, and returned to the attack, with elaborate amplification of the latter part, after Elizabeth's accession to the crown gave him another opportunity.[16] The text as we have it may have been intended for performance before the Queen when she visited Ipswich in August, 1561. The play is powerfully conceived, on coarse controversial lines, to arouse compassion for afflicted virtue in the persons of Widow England and her blind son Commonalty, and for King John whose courageous efforts to save them are foiled by agents of Rome. "There is no malice to the malice of the clergy," says Bale, and he declares that his purpose is to vindicate a patriot king from the Rome-inspired imputations of Polydore Vergil.[17] The individual characters do not much stand out, being blurred by Bale's quick transitions from allegory to history, for example, from Sedition as a vice to Sedition as a portrait of Stephen Langton; but the dreadful power of a malign foreign ideology over the superstitious and ignorant is set forth with blood-curdling effect. The cure, Bale hints, is in the "new learning," from which Sedition warns John's nobility to flee. "From the new learning!" says Nobility, "Marry, God of heaven save me! I never loved it of a child!" Distressed England is only relieved, after John has been murdered, when Verity enters with Imperial Majesty, and the play ends, in its revised form, with a benediction upon Elizabeth's labors for truth.

During just the period when Bale was writing *King John* his contemporary and fellow-Protestant, Sir David Lindsay, was producing his *Satire of the Three Estates* at the Scottish court.[18] It is a very long play, longer than any form of *Hamlet.* The performance took all day, and it is divided into two parts, with a break between them while "the people make collation." Lindsay had been the King's tutor, as Skelton had been Henry VIII's, and he employs the first part to recall his teachings. A young king, Rex Humanitas, is misled by vices under virtuous pseudonyms. Good Counsel cannot reach him; Verity, bearing a New Testament "in English tongue and printed in

Bale's King John

Lindsay's Satire of the Three Estates

---

[16] See the Malone Society edition of the play, ed. J. H. P. Pafford (Oxford, 1931).
[17] See above, ch. 1.
[18] Acted before James V, Jan. 6, 1540, and elaborated for later performances, 1552, 1554. Text, ed. F. Hall (1869, 1883; *EETS,* 37).

England," is set in the stocks as a malefactress, and is soon joined there by Chastity, who can find no lodging in Scotland. Divine Correction, however, liberates them and rebukes the King, by whose authority a parliament is summoned.

This follows the formula of Medwall's *Nature* and of *Magnificence,* but the second part is highly original. John the Commonweal—Lindsay's pet name for the abused common people of Scotland—indicts his oppressors before the parliament of the three estates, i.e., the lords spiritual, the lords temporal, and the merchants. It is mainly the clergy that he attacks for their faults of greed, ignorance, sloth, and lechery; and one of the high points of the play is reached when John, challenged by spiritual lords to state his faith, simply repeats the Apostles' Creed, and the presiding judge, Correction (who wears angel's wings), remarks,

> Say what ye will, sirs, by St. Anne,
> Methink John ane good Christian man.

Lindsay was a broader man than Bale. The comic divertissements that he inserts are often indescribably vulgar, but they are funny and effectively prove his points. On the other hand, he can be crushingly simple, as in the line,

> Christ Jesus had no property but the gallows,

or in the retraction of the worldly prioress, who confesses that nuns are not necessary,

> But I shall do the best I can,
> And marry some good honest man,
>   And brew good ale and tun.
> Marriage by my opinion,
> It is better religion
>   As [Than] to be friar or nun. (3669-74)

The parliament adopts fifteen acts which are the constitution of the reformed church of Scotland, and then the huge work ends with a sermon by the wise jester, Folly.

Respublica   The views that Bale and Lindsay attacked found dramatic defence in *Respublica,* an interlude constructed on the classical five-act pattern and probably written by Nicholas Udall, who had the special favor of Queen Mary.[19] It was written in 1553, "the first year of the most prosperous reign of our most gracious sovereign, Queen Mary the First," but was not printed till modern times. The fact is that, though termed "a merry interlude," *Respublica* shows little merriment except the underlying jubilation the author feels at the overthrow of the political party which had held power under Edward VI, and the pattern of the play is rather archaic. Five or six years ago (i.e., at the accession of Edward) "People," the English nation, was prosperous; but Conscience and Honesty were drowned "last year"; so Respublica falls under

19 See L. Bradner, "A Test for Udall's Authorship," *MLN,* XLII (1927). 378-380.

the sway of the four Edwardian vices, Avarice, Insolence, Oppression, and Adulation, who call themselves Policy, Authority, Reformation, and Honesty. She and People are saved when the four heavenly virtues of Mercy, Truth, Peace, and Justice arrive with Nemesis and put an end to the malefactors' rule. The most interesting figure is People, who speaks a southwestern dialect described in another interlude [20] as "Cotswold speech." This, on the Elizabethan stage, became the favorite language for countrymen and is affected by Edgar in *King Lear.*

The Interlude in Decay

The interlude never reached again the position it had in Henry VIII's reign. It was properly a courtly and superficial product, not unrelated to the Jacobean masque, and like the latter dependent for much of its effect upon the brilliance of its social setting. It lost its gaiety when it became political, and soon lost its aristocratic clientele. After Bale it became an arena for the debate of current problems, and the unknown authors of *New Custom, Albion Knight, Wealth and Health, Impatient Poverty,* and *The Trial of Treasure* used it to air views which would now find their way into an economic or political quarterly. In its decay, however, it was extremely prolific, and it continued to be produced to the end of Queen Elizabeth's reign side by side with comedies, tragedies, and history plays, with all of which it was more or less contaminated. As the vicious characters came to be centred in a single Vice, whose pranks were mischievous rather than soul-destroying, and as the figures in general tended, like Heywood's, more to the class type than moral personification, many of these interludes approached farce or social comedy; e.g., Ulpian Fulwell's *Like Will to Like* (1568), George Wapull's *The Tide Tarrieth No Man* (1576), Thomas Lupton's *All for Money* (1578), and William Wager's *The Longer Thou Livest, the More Fool Thou Art.*[21] Since the authors were now largely schoolmasters or clergymen writing for bourgeois audiences, many of the later interludes deal with problems of incorrigible children such as the Continental dramatists were handling; e.g., the excellent *Nice Wanton* (1560), Thomas Ingelend's *Disobedient Child,* and George Gascoigne's *Glass of Government* (1577).

Sometimes, as in *The Conflict of Conscience* by Nathaniel Woodes (1581), the interlude is built around a recent event, in this case the religious apostasy of one Francis Spiera.[22] More often a stiffening for the wilted allegory is found by introducing stories from the Bible, classical literature, or even medieval fiction; as in *Godly Queen Hester* (1561), *King Darius* (1565), Lewis Wager's *Life and Repentance of Mary Magdalene* (1566), Thomas Preston's *Cambises, King of Persia* (*c.* 1569), John Pikering's *Interlude of Vice Containing the History of Orestes* (1567), R. B.'s *Appius and Virginia* (1575), John Phillip's *Patient and Meek Grissill* (*c.* 1565), and Thomas Garter's *Most Virtuous and Godly Susanna* (1578).

[20] William Wager's *Enough Is as Good as a Feast,* sig. E 1 (*Huntington Library Facsimile Reprints,* 1920).

[21] Dates in this section are dates of publication, not composition. Undated pieces were printed without date. Further details are given in T. Brooke, *The Tudor Drama,* chs. III and IV.

[22] See C. Wine, "Nathaniel Wood's *Conflict of Conscience,*" *PMLA,* L (1935). 661-678.

A New Interlude for Children to Play Named Jack Juggler (1562) shows how Plautus could be rewritten in the native fashion, while Robert Wilson's *Three Ladies of London* (1584), *Three Lords and Three Ladies of London* (1590), and *Cobbler's Prophecy* (1594),[23] the anonymous *Sir Clyomon and Sir Clamides* (1599), *Common Conditions* (1576), and particularly *A Knack to Know a Knave* (1594) show how the interlude technique accommodated itself to plays of very different character. It was long before Englishmen found it unnatural to speak of any play as an "interlude," and still longer before stock interlude devices, such as evil powers disguising themselves as virtues or debating with angels for man's soul, and the Vice brandishing his dagger of lath or riding to hell on the devil's back,[24] ceased to be generally remembered. Two excellent things persisted in the interlude to the end of its dreary history and did much to keep theatre doors open while a more subtle drama was forming: even the dullest examples of the species are likely to be enlivened with good songs[25] and to offer oases of easily actable clownage.

[23] See K. H. Gatch, *Robert Wilson, Actor and Dramatist* (Yale, diss. unpub., 1928). Another play, *The Pedlar's Prophecy*, printed in 1595 (Malone Soc. reprint, 1914), is not by Wilson and refers to political events of about 1561. See G. L. Kittredge, "The Date of *The Pedlers Prophecie*," *Harvard Studies & Notes in Phil. & Lit.*, XVI (1934). 97-118.

[24] Thus James Howell writes to Sir E. B. in 1635 that he "could be content to see an Anabaptist go to hell on a Brownist's back."

[25] See J. E. Bernard, *The Prosody of the Tudor Interlude* (New Haven, 1939) for the contributions of the interlude to dramatic verse form.

VI

Religious Prose

The only Bible in common use during the middle ages was the Latin *The Bible* "vulgate" text, which had been prepared by St. Jerome about the year 400. *in English* Wyclif's agitation for an English translation which the unlearned people could read was only the reiteration of a desire that had been recognized and partially satisfied in Anglo-Saxon times; but Wyclif antagonized the church authorities, and the association of the idea of an English Bible with Lollardry postponed the licensed production of such a thing for another century and a half.[1] It was Erasmus' great edition of the Greek New Testament (1516), largely prepared at Cambridge, which released the spring. This was a work of infinite labor and great intellectual courage; it offered a text much more authoritative than had previously existed and enriched it with new Latin annotations which piqued men's desire to know and explain what the Bible really meant.

The first to undertake the translation of the Greek Testament into English *William* was William Tyndale[2] (*c.* 1494-1536), a graduate of Oxford, who was *Tyndale* moved by the study of Erasmus to go to Germany in 1524[3] and there devote himself to a task that the clerical authorities in England would in no way permit. In 1526 two editions of Tyndale's version of the New Testament had been smuggled into England and extensively circulated in defiance of a ban which the Bishop of London promptly laid upon them. Many copies were confiscated and burned, and persons responsible for their sale savagely punished. Sir Thomas More entered into an acrimonious pamphlet war with Tyndale,[4] who was driven, a hunted man, through various cities of Germany and the Netherlands. He translated also the five books of Moses and other parts of the Old Testament and issued a number of polemic tracts before he was arrested at Antwerp (May, 1535) and, after a long imprisonment, put to death at Vilvorde near Brussels in October, 1536.

[1] See B. F. Westcott, *A General View of the History of the English Bible*, 3ed., revised by W. A. Wright (1905); C. C. Butterworth, *The Literary Lineage of the King James Bible, 1340-1611* (Philadelphia, 1941).

[2] See J. F. Mozley, *William Tyndale* (1937); S. L. Greenslade, *The Work of William Tindale,* with an Essay on Tindale and the English Language by G. D. Bone (Glasgow, 1938); and an essay on Tyndale in R. W. Chambers, *Man's Unconquerable Mind* (1939), pp. 190-203. The 1534 text of Tyndale's New Testament has been edited by N. H. Wallis, with introduction by Isaac Foot (Cambridge, 1938).

[3] Luther's translation of the New Testament into German appeared in 1522. Tyndale probably visited him and may have received help from him.

[4] See W. E. Campbell, *The Dialogue concerning Tyndale by Sir Thomas More* (1927; reprinted in Vol. II of *English Works of Sir Thomas More*, 1931). More's *Dialogue* was printed in 1529. Tyndale replied in *An Answer unto Sir Thomas More's Dialogue* (1530), and More in *The Confutation of Tyndale's Answer* (1532; second part, 1533).

The fate of Tyndale is marked by a tragic irony. While he was awaiting trial in the Low Countries, the situation of affairs in England reversed itself completely. His most vigorous assailant, Sir Thomas More, became himself a martyr in 1535, and King Henry VIII, from being the persecutor, grew for a time to be the patron of Bible translators. In this year 1535 Miles Coverdale (1488-1568) published the first complete English Bible with a flattering dedication to the King. It was made up of Tyndale's revised version of the New Testament and Pentateuch, essentially unchanged, to which Coverdale added his own translation of the remainder of the Old Testament and the Apocrypha. It was printed, like all of Tyndale's works, on the Continent, but was allowed to circulate without restraint in England. In 1537 another edition of the Tyndale-Coverdale translation, revised by Tyndale's associate, John Rogers, was published with the King's special license; [5] and this was rapidly followed, in April, 1539, by the "Great Bible," revised by Coverdale, sumptuously printed in Paris and provided with a fine pictorial title-page that shows the King handing "Verbum Dei" to his subjects. The second edition of the Great Bible, in 1540, bore a statement on the title-page, "This is the Bible appointed to the use of the churches," and a long preface by the Archbishop of Canterbury (Cranmer), pointing out "what it availeth scripture to be had and read of the lay and vulgar people."

Miles Coverdale

The Great Bible

Seven editions of the Great Bible are recognized by bibliographers before the end of 1541, and there were many reprints. An independent revision of Tyndale and Coverdale by Richard Taverner had also appeared in 1539. The next English Bible was the famous Genevan version, prepared by Protestant exiles during the reign of Mary, one of whom was the indefatigable Coverdale.[6] They issued the New Testament from Geneva in 1557, and in 1560 the entire Bible, with a dedication to Queen Elizabeth, who had succeeded to the throne in the course of their work. This was a scholarly and well edited text; it has been often referred to as the "Breeches Bible" from its rather quaint rendering of Genesis 3:7:

The Geneva Bible

Then the eyes of them both were opened, and they knew that they were naked, and they sewed figtree leaves together and made themselves breeches.

It had practical advantages which served to make it vastly the most popular Bible during the Elizabethan period: it was much smaller in size than the large folios that preceded it, was printed in clear Roman type instead of black letter, inserted for the first time the now familiar numbering of verses in each chapter, added marginal explanatory notes and rather excellent woodcut illustrations and maps. It has been calculated that one hundred and forty editions of the Geneva Testament and Bible were printed. The official Bible for church reading during most of Queen Elizabeth's reign was, however, the Bishops' Bible, prepared by a group of ecclesiastical dignitaries under the

The Bishops' Bible

---

[5] This edition is ascribed to Thomas Matthew, perhaps a fictitious character.
[6] The leader of the group was William Whittingham. See H. Craig, Jr., "The Geneva Bible as a Political Document," *Pacific Hist. Rev.*, VII (1938). 40-49.

direction of the scholarly Archbishop Parker and first issued in 1568. The title-page bears the simple title, *The Holie Bible,* and a large portrait of the Queen. The Catholic English exiles, mainly Oxford and Cambridge scholars who had retired for religion's sake to Douai and Rheims, replied with a translation of their own, based upon the Latin vulgate text and accompanied by notes on doctrinal points. The New Testament in this version was printed at Rheims in 1582, and the entire Bible at Douai in 1609-10. This, naturally, is the Bible which most diverges from the text of *The Douai* Tyndale and Coverdale, though it has often accepted their phrasing, and it *Bible* in turn, in the New Testament at least, had some influence upon the translators of the King James version.[7]

The King James Bible, or Authorized Version, was the accidental result *The King* of a petition submitted to the King immediately after his accession in 1603 *James Bible* by disaffected members of the Church of England, who hoped to secure religious changes along Presbyterian lines. The King summoned a conference of representative leaders at Hampton Court in January, 1604, at which much was discussed but little decided, except that the Bible should be once more revised, the King having, as it appeared, more prejudice against the Genevan version than his bishops had. He appointed fifty-four scholars, of whom we know the names of forty-seven, and these worked in six groups, two groups meeting in Westminster, two in Cambridge, and two in Oxford. They were instructed to be conservative, and they were very intelligently so, but they were thorough. Their Bible, first printed in 1611, is undoubtedly superior to any that had preceded it, and no later translation has seriously challenged its prestige. Writing in 1841, the author of *An Historical Account of the English Versions of the Scriptures*[8] said of it: "If a testimony were needed of the general excellence of this version, an appeal need only be made to the fact that it has maintained its ground for two hundred and thirty years." A century more has now passed, and it still maintains its ground.[9] It would be hard to instance another piece of large collective scholarship so successfully performed; but the primary credit for its greatness rests with Tyndale and Coverdale, and after them with the long series of ardent men, of whom King James's translators were the last, who for eighty years probed and polished its phrases.

Tyndale and Coverdale are not only the originators of the modern English Bible; they are also the greatest literary artists connected with it. Whether they worked together over certain parts of it, as an ancient tradition states, is now doubted, and it is doubtful whether Coverdale had the classical learning of Tyndale; but both of them had a power of style which fixed forevermore the character of our Bible. They had a Homeric power of placing words in simple musical narrative, the effect of which is best expressed in

[7] See Hugh Pope, "A Brief History of the English Version of the New Testament first published at Rheims in 1582," *Library,* xx (1940). 351-376; xxi (1940). 44-77.
[8] Prefixed to *The English Hexapla, Exhibiting the Six Important English Translations of the New Testament Scriptures* (1841), p. 160.
[9] See David Daiches, *The King James Version of the English Bible* (Chicago, 1941).

Thomas Poyntz's account of the way Tyndale used to read what he had translated to his friends in Antwerp:

When the Sunday came, then went he to some merchant's chamber or other, whither came many other merchants, and unto them would he read some one parcel of scripture: the which proceeded so fruitfully, sweetly, and gently from him, much like to the writing of John the Evangelist, that it was a heavenly comfort and joy to the audience to hear him read the scriptures.

Pollard [10] has estimated that the King James version of the New Testament "alike in language, rhythm, and cadence," is fully ninety per cent Tyndale's. Coverdale's renderings of the Old Testament naturally required more change when better Hebrew scholars put them under scrutiny; but Coverdale, too, had the grand style, and his version of the Psalms, employed in the English prayer book, has held its place there unchanged because even the King James version cannot equal it in euphony.[11]

The Book of Common Prayer   The motive which led to the English prayer book was to a large degree the same as that which prompted the translation of the Bible: the desire to make the word of God more widely known. It had been the theory of the medieval Divine Service, or "hours of prayer," that worshipers attending all the devotions, as monks and nuns did, should chant through the entire book of psalms each week and have the entire Bible read once a year—in Latin, of course. This was the basic purpose about which the office had developed; but with the intrusion of new saints' days and many ornamental developments it had come about that comparatively little of the Bible remained in the service. The genius of the English prayer book was Thomas Cranmer (1487-1556), whom Henry VIII had made Archbishop of Canterbury and nature had endowed with the most beautiful prose style of his generation. When it became his duty, on the accession of Edward VI in 1547, to preside over the reconstruction of the liturgy, he returned to its original purpose and so arranged the calendar of services that the psalter should be completed every month, the Old Testament read through once, and the New Testament thrice, each year, the English text of the Great Bible being substituted for the Vulgate.

Thomas Cranmer   Cranmer was a man of compromise and natural timidity. His life included some rather mean episodes and had in it perhaps nothing very noble except his last gesture at the stake. He was surrounded by reformers of much more positive, heroic, and ungainly mold, men like Hooper and Latimer, who would have destroyed every tie between the new English service and the Middle Ages; but Cranmer was an accomplished liturgiologist, incapable of renouncing, capable even of reproducing in a new medium, the beauties which in the Roman breviary had encompassed the primitive devotion. He studied Cardinal Quignon's proposals for reforming the Latin service (1535,

[10] *The Beginning of the New Testament translated by William Tyndale, 1525,* with an introduction by A. W. Pollard (Oxford, 1926), p. xxi.
[11] See H. R. Willoughby, *The Coverdale Psalter and the Quatrocentenary of the Printed English Bible* (Chicago, 1935).

1537) and many Lutheran devotion books, and out of his great gifts for compromise and for style he constructed an order of service in English worthy to be the setting for the English Bible.[12] Hilaire Belloc, who loves neither Cranmer nor his church, has spoken nobly of him as a "jeweler in prose," who, when he has something special to do "constructs with a success only paralleled by the sonnets of Shakespeare":

There is not in all that he has thus left of perfect English one lengthy passage; most of the Collects, which with the isolated phrases of the Litany are his chief triumph, consist in a single sentence—but they are sentences which most men who know the trade would give their eyes to have written. And since that endures which is carved in hard material, they have endured, and given endurance to the fabric—novel and revolutionary in his time, the institution at the root of which he stands—The Church of England.[13]

The two Edwardian prayer books of 1549 and 1552 were put together in a time of violence and bitter religious strife. Over half the nation was infuriated, to the point of armed rebellion, by their substitution for the traditional Latin liturgy; of the rest there seem to have been few (among the leaders, at least) who did not vehemently assail them as a betrayal of Protestant principles. They were Cranmer's almost unaided work, and it is remarkable that work fitted to such a turbulent emergency could have such eternal grace. Note the passage in the communion service in the text of 1549. It is obviously a prayer for that particular year and for this new form of worship so hazardously and quarrelsomely inaugurated:

Almighty and everliving God, which by thy holy apostle hast taught us to make prayers and supplications and to give thanks for all men, we humbly beseech thee most mercifully to receive these our prayers, which we offer unto thy divine majesty, beseeching thee to inspire continually the universal church with the spirit of truth, unity and concord: and grant that all they that do confess thy holy name may agree in the truth of thy holy word and live in unity and godly love. Specially we beseech thee to save and defend thy servant, Edward our king, that under him we may be godly and quietly governed. And grant unto his whole council, and to all that are put in authority under him, that they may truly and indifferently minister justice, to the punishment of wickedness and vice, and to the maintenance of God's true religion and virtue. Give grace, O heavenly Father, to all bishops, pastors, and curates, that they may both by their life and doctrine set forth thy true and lively word and rightly and duly administer thy holy sacraments.

Some of the topical references have now of necessity dropped out, and with them we lose our sense of the compelling occasion; but the remainder has the polish of old ivory and shows what no one at the time would have suspected, that the new English prose could be made to match the sonorous dignity of medieval Latin.

[12] See J. W. Legge, *Cranmer's Liturgical Projects* (1915); F. Procter and W. H. Frere, *A New History of the Book of Common Prayer* (1901). Cranmer's disputations and letters were edited by J. E. Cox in two volumes for the Parker Society (Cambridge, 1844, 1846).
[13] Hilaire Belloc, *Cranmer* (1931), p. 43.

Hugh Latimer [14] (*c.* 1485-1555) was compared to Saul of Tarsus, whom he resembled in his course of life and particularly admired, for, as he says, "Paul was no sitting bishop, but a walking and a preaching bishop." The son of a humble Leicestershire yeoman, whose old-fashioned virtues shine in his son's reminiscences of him, Latimer was brought up at Cambridge in the most zealous orthodoxy, "as obstinate a Papist as any was in England"; but about 1524 he experienced a Pauline conversion at the hands of the Protestant martyr, Thomas Bilney (d. 1531), and thereafter preached the reformed doctrine with a vigor which several times brought him to trial for heresy. It is questionable whether he owed his escape at this period more to his fundamental likableness and shrewd sense or to the growing alienation of Henry VIII from the Pope. The outcome was that the King made him one of his chaplains, and in 1535 Bishop of Worcester. When the reaction came four years later, Latimer renounced his bishopric rather than sign the Catholic "six articles," was silenced as a preacher for almost eight years, and variously imprisoned. Edward VI's accession brought him on the stage again as the great preacher of the day and special director of the young King's conscience. He did not resume his episcopal dignity, but moved like a prophet between Archbishop Cranmer's palace at Lambeth, where he lived as an especial guest, and the royal palace of Whitehall. He was the strongest, simplest, and most honorable of all the English reformers, and crowned his career with the words he spoke at the stake, October 16, 1555:

Be of good comfort, Master Ridley, and play the man: we shall this day light such a candle by God's grace in England as, I trust, shall never be put out.

About forty-five of Latimer's sermons have been in some form preserved. Twenty-seven were collected in an early Elizabethan volume (1562), and fourteen others had been printed in his lifetime; e.g., the fourth sermon "Of the Plough," delivered outside St. Paul's, January 18, 1549, and the seven preached before the King at Westminster in the following Lent. They appear to have been partly extemporal, and the texts depend to some extent upon notes taken by pious listeners; but these texts give us the real quality of Latimer's preaching. The style is very homely and lucid, suited alike to the downright earnestness of the preacher and to the mental capacity of the eleven year old King at Westminster or the outdoor London crowd in Paul's Churchyard. The short sentences are salty with anecdote and vivid figure; such as that of the woman who went to the sermons to sleep, or the country church which Bishop Latimer, arriving for an official visit, found locked up because the people were celebrating Robin Hood's Day, or the following great tribute to the devil:

[14] See R. W. and A. J. Carlyle, *Hugh Latimer* (Boston, 1899). Latimer's sermons are usefully reprinted in Everyman's Library, No. 40, with preface by Canon Beeching. The seven sermons before Edward VI and the sermon of the ploughers are in Arber's series of *English Reprints* (1869). See Elizabeth T. Hastings, "A Sixteenth-Century Manuscript Translation of Latimer's First Sermon before Edward," *PMLA*, LX (1945), pp. 959-1002.

And now I would ask a strange question. Who is the most diligent bishop and prelate in all England, that passeth all the rest in doing his office? I can tell, for I know him, who it is; I know him well. But now I think I see you listing and harkening that I should name him. There is one that passeth all the other, and is the most diligent prelate and preacher in all England. And will ye know who it is? I will tell you. It is the Devil. He is the most diligent preacher of all other. He is never out of his diocese, he is never from his cure; ye shall never find him unoccupied, he is ever in his parish, he keepeth residence at all times. Ye shall never find him out of the way; call for him when you will, he is ever at home, the diligentest preacher in all the realm.[15]

He coins nicknames that stick; e.g., "strawberry preachers" for unpreaching prelates, because like strawberries they come but once a year and are luxuries, not meat. He is a particular master of the ironic question, as when he complains of clergymen in worldly office—"minters," he dubs them. They say they are too busy to preach.

They are otherwise occupied; some in the king's matters, some are ambassadors, some of the Privy Council, some to furnish the courts, some are lords of the Parliament, some are presidents, and some comptrollers of mints. Well, well! Is this their duty? Is this their office? Is this their calling? Should we have ministers of the church to be comptrollers of the mints? Is this a meet office for a priest that hath cure of souls? Is this his charge? I would here ask one question: I would fain know who controlleth the devil at home at his parish, while he controlleth the mint? If the apostles might not leave the office of preaching to be deacons, shall one leave it for minting? [16]

There is something of Jeremiah in him as he inveighs against the selfish vices of his time:

But London was never so ill as it is now. In times past men were full of pity and compassion; but now there is no pity, for in London their brother shall die in the streets for cold, he shall lie sick at their door between stock and stock ... and perish there for hunger.... When I was a scholar in Cambridge myself, I heard very good report of London, and knew many that had relief of the rich men of London, but now I can hear no such good report, and yet I inquire of it and harken for it; but now charity is waxed cold: none helpeth the scholar nor yet the poor.

The sermons of this Lent, 1549, were preached to the sinister accompaniment of the Lord Admiral's catastrophe. He was being attainted and executed as Latimer spoke, and in the last of the series Latimer somberly draws the moral:

He was a covetous man, an horrible covetous man. I would there were no mo in England. He was an ambitious man. I would there were no mo in England. He was a seditious man, a contemner of common prayer. I would there were no mo in England. He is gone. I would he had left none behind him. Remember

15 *The Ploughers,* Arber, p. 29.
16 *Ibid.,* 27.

you, my lords, that you pray in your houses to the better mortification of your flesh.[17]

John Foxe

When Edward VI died, in 1553, and Mary came to the throne, many Protestant zealots avoided the fate of Cranmer and Latimer by fleeing to Lutheran Germany or Calvinist Switzerland, and there hardened their dissent.[18] One of the most turbulent groups gathered in Frankfort under the leadership of Cox, Foxe, and Knox. Richard Cox (1500-1581) later became Bishop of Ely and wrought much woe in that diocese, as he had formerly done in Oxford. John Knox [19] (1505-1572), a Scot, returned from Continental bickerings with Cox to make himself the Presbyterian autocrat of Edinburgh. The worldly career of John Foxe (1516-1587) was much less notable, but his influence on British Puritanism was perhaps the greatest of the three. He returned to England after Elizabeth's accession, but secured no office of prominence or emolument. One of the most paradoxical and admirable things we know of this arch-fabricator of Protestant propaganda is that he retained through life the affection and financial support of the poet Surrey's son, the Duke of Norfolk, whose tutor he had been. When Norfolk was beheaded for Popish treason (1572), Foxe loyally attended him to the scaffold, and the Duke remembered Foxe with an annuity in his will.

While still in Germany, Foxe undertook to implement the Protestant Reformation by an account of Christian martyrdoms. As published at Strassburg in 1554, the book is in Latin,[20] and brings the roll of martyrs only as far as Savonarola; but the events of the next few years in England provided Foxe with much more material and a far bitterer purpose. He started again in English and brought the work up to date in a folio of nearly two thousand double-columned pages, *The Acts and Monuments of the Church* (1563).

Foxe's "Book of Martyrs"

The book was enormously successful, and was further enlarged in later editions, of which three more appeared before Foxe's death. It was familiarly called "The Book of Martyrs," and with its ghoulish pictures and dilated tales of persecution became favorite reading for a large public. In attenuated and modernized form it long continued to hold a darkly significant place in Sunday-school libraries and pious homes.

By classic standards Foxe is no great writer. As a historian he is sometimes contemptible; his psychology is childish, and the invariable bias of his views often diminishes his effects. But his work has the power that strong passion gives writing produced under the immediate shadow of direful events, and his command of documentary and reported detail is unapproached by anything else that has come down from the same period. His accounts of Tyndale and Latimer, for example, contain much which cannot be found elsewhere

[17] *Seventh Sermon Before the King's Majesty*, Arber, pp. 197f. A contemporary preacher of importance was Thomas Lever (1521-1577), three of whose sermons, preached in 1550, are edited by Arber, *English Reprints* (1870).

[18] See Christina H. Garrett, *The Marian Exiles* (Cambridge, 1938).

[19] See E. Muir, *John Knox: Portrait of a Calvinist* (1929); G. R. Preedy, *The Life of John Knox* (1940).

[20] *Commentarii Rerum in Ecclesia Gestarum ... Liber Primus.* See J. F. Mozley, *John Foxe and his Book* (1940). The *Acts and Monuments* is edited by J. Stoughton (8v, 1877).

but bear unmistakable marks of truth. The "Book of Martyrs" did much to keep England Protestant, but it also had a primary and evil part in developing friction between Anglican and Puritan. It suspended the virtues of tolerance and humor, and encouraged the will to martyrdom in any cause that could be made to assume a religious bearing. It was this approved and honored book, much more than the Marprelate tracts, that the bishops would have suppressed if they had had a real understanding of their danger.

Another of the exiled brethren, Thomas Becon (1512-1567) became the great purveyor of popular Puritan piety. His "Works" in three folio volumes were issued by John Day in the years just preceding Shakespeare's birth. His best circulated piece, *The Sick Man's Salve*, was entered in the Stationers' Register in 1558-9 and had at least seventeen editions by 1632. It was bedside literature for vast numbers of good people, and is alluded to by the realistic dramatists. *Thomas Becon*

By 1572 Puritan hostility to the episcopal system, the established prayer book, and ecclesiastical vestments had grown so bitter that an attempt was made through anonymous pamphlets to carry these questions over the heads of the Queen and bishops to the attention of the Parliament and the people at large. An *Admonition to the Parliament* was surreptitiously printed soon after Elizabeth's fourth Parliament assembled (May, 1572). The identity of the printer is still uncertain, but the authors were arrested and imprisoned for a time in Newgate. They were, of course, reforming ministers, John Field (father of the actor-dramatist, Nathan Field) and Thomas Wilcox. Their pamphlet is incisive and well written, dignified, but clearly seditious by the laws of the time. *A Second Admonition to the Parliament* soon followed, also anonymous, but ascribed to Thomas Cartwright (1535-1603), a man of very high repute among the Puritans for life and learning, who had recently lost his professorship of divinity at Cambridge.[21] Bishop Whitgift's two replies to the *Admonitions* (1572, 1574) are not effective, at any rate as literature; but the bishops had the law and the Queen on their side, and the opposition made no great headway till the Armada year of 1588 brought an explosion of the first magnitude. *The Puritan Controversy*

The immediate literary occasion of the Marprelate tracts is trivial enough. Another dull episcopal book had appeared in the course of the Church's embarrassed efforts to keep the Puritan goslings beneath her wing: *A Defence of the Government Established in the Church of England for Ecclesiastical Matters* (1587). It was by John Bridges, the Dean of Salisbury, and was a reply to an anonymous apology for the dissenters (1584).[22] Two well-known Puritans at once replied to Bridges: Dudley Fenner in *A Defence of the Godly Ministers Against the Slanders of Dr. Bridges* (1587), and Hooker's

[21] For text and discussion of these works see W. H. Frere and C. E. Douglas, *Puritan Manifestoes* (1907). For the ampler background consult A. S. Pearson, *Thomas Cartwright and Elizabethan Puritanism* (1925); M. M. Knappen, *Tudor Puritanism* (Chicago, 1939); and, for a still broader and very readable account, Wm. Haller, *The Rise of Puritanism ... from Thomas Cartwright to John Lilburne and John Milton* (1938).

[22] *A Brief and Plain Declaration Concerning the Desires of All Those Faithful Ministers That Have and Do Seek for the Discipline and Reformation of the Church of England.*

antagonist, Walter Travers, in *A Defence of the Ecclesiastical Discipline* (1588).[23] This was quite as usual, but it was strange that Martin Marprelate should in this year of national peril raise his ugly though amusing head. The immediate occasion was neither literary nor doctrinal. Robert Waldegrave, an experienced printer, was loose in the land with certain cases of contraband type and with anger in his heart. Waldegrave had incurred much punishment for issuing unauthorized Puritan polemics. In the uneasy month of April, 1588, his printing house was raided by order of the Star Chamber. The searchers confiscated his press and type, along with the book he was printing, a satirical dialogue against the state of the Church of England by John Udall, the nonconformist preacher at Kingston-on-Thames.[24] Waldegrave went into hiding near Kingston, put together a secret press, and printed another anti-episcopal book by Udall, as well as the *Exhortation unto the Governors and People of Wales* by the redoubtable John Penry, who was Udall's friend and former college companion. Here Waldegrave also printed the first of the pamphlets (*Oh Read over Dr. John Bridges, for It Is a Worthy Work*) claiming the authorship of the "reverend and worthy Martin Marprelate gentleman."

The press was then removed from the dangerous proximity of London to Fawsley House, Northamptonshire, where the second pamphlet, continuing the attack on Bridges, was printed; thence to Coventry, where two more were produced. By this time Waldegrave was exhausted by the perilous and exacting labor, and he made his escape, first, it is said, to La Rochelle, later to Edinburgh, where he was licensed by King James and prospered. A substitute printer was found, the itinerant press moved on, and three more pamphlets came from it before a roadside mishap led to the capture of press and printers near Manchester, August 14, 1589. The last piece of all, *The Protestation of Martin Marprelate,* was, with almost incredible gallantry, printed by accomplices in the plot on a substitute press, after this arrest and while the toils were closing upon them. The enraged prosecutions which followed the capture of Marprelate's agents have given us more detailed information about this secret press than we possess about any comparable episode in Queen Elizabeth's reign.[25] We know with surprising exactness the facts about its manipulation and about the day by day lives of many of the men and women concerned with it during the twelve months of its operation; but the authorities never discovered, and we do not know today, who wrote the pamphlets. They hanged John Penry four years later on another charge; they tried and acquitted Job Throckmorton. Both of these

(margin notes: Martin Marprelate; The Marprelate Press)

---

[23] This is anonymous and has been ascribed also to Penry.

[24] This short dialogue by Udall (*c.* 1560-1592) has a long title: *The State of the Church of England, Laid Open in a Conference between Diotrephes a Bishop, Tertullus a Papist, Demetrius an Usurer, Pandochus an Innkeeper, and Paul a Preacher of the Word of God.* Both it and Udall's slightly later tract referred to above, *A Demonstration of the Truth, etc.,* are reprinted by E. Arber (*English Scholar's Library*, Nos. 5, 9, 1879, 1880). They are venomously bitter against the bishops, but have no touch of Marprelate's amusing buffoonery.

[25] See W. Pierce, *An Historical Introduction to the Marprelate Tracts* (1908) and, for the texts, *The Marprelate Tracts, 1588, 1589* (1911). Pierce's treatment is biased, but very full.

were in the plot to the ears, but whether either was Marprelate we know no more than we know who Junius was two centuries later.[26]

Marprelate anticipates Junius in a number of things. He has the same assurance that he cannot be discovered:

Whosoever Martin is, neither thou, nor any man or woman in England shall know while you live, suspect and trouble as many as you will; and therefore save your money in seeking for him, for it may be he is nearer you than you are ware of. . . . I am alone. No man under heaven is privy, or hath been privy, unto my writings against you. I use the advice of none therein.[27]

Like Junius, he attempts to overawe his victims by the extensiveness of his private knowledge, and threatens further exposure if they pursue him. He pretends also to be the leader of an insuppressible movement:

For the day that you hang Martin, assure yourselves, there will twenty Martins spring in my place.

He had, indeed, most devoted and self-sacrificing associates, but he had no great backing in the Puritan party, for he offended unpardonably against the grave dignity that was the hall mark of their profession. Men like Cartwright were as outraged as Richard Hooker was by the style of dialectic which addressed a learned antagonist as "you sodden-headed ass, you." Moreover, when the first pamphlet was being prepared, Drake was still defending the Channel against the Armada, laden with the common enemies of Puritan and Prelatist. The bishops whom Martin attacks and lampoons were not only Elizabeth's chief agents in maintaining the national morale; the leading ones were members of the privy council. The pamphlets were most foolishly and wickedly ill-timed.

Their racy style has saved them. They evoked a series of replies and imita- *Martin's* tions, which, however, it would be absurd to consider under the classification *Style* of religious prose.[28] Shakespeare, one would think, must have read Marprelate. Their idioms are sometimes strangely alike; as in these passages:

Bishops are cogging and cozening knaves. This priest [i.e., the Bishop of London] went to buffets with his son-in-law for a bloody nose. Well fare, all good tokens.[29]

Then it was not for nothing that my nose fell a-bleeding on Black-Monday last, at six o'clock i' the morning, falling out that year on Ash-Wednesday was four year in the afternoon. (*Merchant of Venice*, II. v. 24f.)

[26] J. Dover Wilson argues for Sir Roger Williams: "Martin Marprelate and Shakespeare's Fluellen: A New Theory of the Authorship of the Marprelate Tracts," *Library*, 3rd ser. III (1912). 113-151, 241-276, 345-374; IV (1913). 92-104. D. J. McGinn emphatically reasserts Penry's authorship in "The Real Martin Marprelate," *PMLA*, LVIII (1943). 84-107.
[27] *Hay Any Work for Cooper?*, ed. Pierce, pp. 220, 246.
[28] See below, Part II, ch. v.
[29] *The Epistle*, Pierce, 77f.

Or compare with the "gracious fooling" in *Twelfth Night* (II. iii) about Pigrogromitus and the Vapians passing the equinoctial of Queubus the close of Martin's *Epistle:*

Given at my castle between two whales, neither four days from Penniless Bench, nor yet at the west end of Shrovetide, but the fourteenth year at the least of the age of Charing Cross, within a year of Midsummer between twelve and twelve of the clock.

Richard
Hooker

God must have seemed very good to Archbishop Whitgift—Caiaphas of Canterbury, as Marprelate called him—when the learned young Master of the Temple begged to be relieved of city duty and assigned to a country parish in order to complete a work on the laws of Anglican church government. Richard Hooker [30] (*c.* 1554-1600) had lately borne off all the honors in a controversy with Walter Travers over subtleties of predestination and justification, and in his personal life he was the very flower and type of that apostolic virtue which the episcopal system was accused of crushing. Accordingly, Hooker was presented to the rectory of Boscombe near Salisbury in 1591, and in 1595 transferred on the Queen's own recommendation to Bishopsbourne in Kent "without any addition," says Walton, "of dignity or profit." The first four books *Of the Laws of Ecclesiastical Polity* were printed in 1593 and the long fifth book in 1597. When Hooker died, the year after Spenser and at the same early age, *his* great work had been completed in eight books; but there is reason to believe that the manuscript of Book VI was tampered with after his death.

Hooker's long preface is frankly addressed to the Puritans, to whom he admits with a quiet irony,

The wonderful zeal and fervor wherewith ye have withstood the received orders of this church was the first thing which caused me to enter into consideration whether (as all your published books and writings peremptorily maintain) every Christian man fearing God stand bound to join with you for the furtherance of that which ye term *the Lord's discipline*. Wherein I must plainly confess unto you that, before I examined your sundry declarations in that behalf, it could not settle in my head to think but that undoubtedly such numbers of otherwise right well affected and most religiously inclined minds had some marvellous reasonable inducements, which led them with so great earnestness that way.

The first book is also introductory, a fundamental assertion of law and order as the *sine qua non* of all worlds and societies. Shakespeare, by intention or otherwise, has summarized its teaching:

---

[30] The best edition of Hooker is still the one edited by the eminent John Keble (6ed., 3V Oxford, 1874). The best life is still that of Izaak Walton, first printed in 1665. There is a separate edition of *Eccl. Polity*, Book VIII, by R. A. Houk (1931) and the entire text is available in two volumes of Everyman's Library. See D. C. Boughner, "Notes on Hooker's Prose," *RES*, xv (1939). 1-7. Valuable new information is supplied by C. J. Sisson, *The Judicious Marriage of Mr. Hooker and the Birth of the Laws of Ecclesiastical Polity* (Cambridge, 1940) and Hardin Craig, "Of the Laws of Ecclesiastical Polity—First Form," *JHI*, v (1944). 91-10

The heavens themselves, the planets, and this centre
Observe degree, priority, and place,
Insisture, course, proportion, season, form,
Office, and custom, in all line of order.

. . . .

Take but degree away, untune that string,
And, hark! what discord follows! [31]

    Against this grave and cosmic background Hooker proceeds in the follow-
ing books to bring to trial each of the dissenters' complaints. He is one of the
subtlest of dialecticians and one of the best humored of debaters, and these
advantages so win upon our sympathy that he perhaps triumphs more than
he should and makes us feel (though Hooker never says so) that the self-
righteousness of men like Cartwright is little better than what he calls "the
scurrilous and more than satirical immodesty of Martinism." A giber might
say that the Church of England had once more been saved by a good prose
style. But the *Ecclesiastical Polity* really triumphs because it is great and sane
and quintessentially attempered to the English mind.[32] So long and controversial a work could hardly have held its place without a great style. Hooker's has
not the brilliance of some of the prose of the next century. It has no great
number of long words, nor any very high proportion of long sentences. It
has no particular mannerisms, beyond a habit of opening sentences with an
inversion: "Choice there is not," "Impossible it was." For the most part
Hooker is content to make his difficult argument simple, lucid, and gracious;
but just often enough he will draw out the stops, and in a breath-taking
sentence show the full power that his pen possessed. These sentences would
be too long to quote, but one should read aloud the ones that begin: "Now if
nature should intermit her course" (i. iii. 2), "And because the greatest part
of men" (i. x. 6), "Concerning Faith" (i. xi. 6), "But that we may at length
conclude" (i. xv. 4). These are all from the first book; I will quote one sentence from Book v, in which he summarizes his defense of the authorized
prayer book (v. xxv. 5):

To him which considereth the grievous and scandalous inconveniences where-
unto they make themselves daily subject, with whom any blind and secret
corner is judged a fit house of common prayer; the manifold confusions which
they fall into where every man's private spirit and gift (as they term it) is the
only bishop that ordaineth him to this ministry; the irksome deformities whereby
through endless and senseless effusions of indigested prayers they oftentimes
disgrace in most unsufferable manner the worthiest part of Christian duty
towards God, who herein are subject to no certain order, but pray both what
and how they list: to him, I say, which weigheth duly all these things the
reasons cannot be obscure, why God doth in public prayer so much respect the
solemnity of places where, the authority and calling of persons by whom, and

---

[31] *Troilus and Cressida* i. iii. 77-137.
[32] See E. N. S. Thompson. "Richard Hooker among the Controversialists," *PQ*, xx (1941).
454-464.

the precise appointment even with what words or sentences his name should be called on amongst his people.

The *Ecclesiastical Polity* is the closest thing in English prose to the *Faerie Queene* of Spenser. Coeval in date and parallel in its national spirit and mediating purpose, it has something of the same sage and serious mellifluence.

BOOK II
The Renaissance

PART II
The Reign of Elizabeth
(1558-1603)

I

The Elizabethan Lyric

The Elizabethan poets [1] to a very great extent·learned their art, and in turn *The* communicated it to their readers, by means of the song collections which is- *Anthologies* sued in a constant stream from "Tottel's Miscellany" in 1557 to Davison's *Poetical Rhapsody* in 1602.[2] So much in demand were they that one or another of them was being published or reprinted in almost every year of this long period. Most of them now touch the fancy chiefly by their charming titles: *A Handful of Pleasant Delights, A Gorgeous Gallery of Gallant Inventions, The Paradise of Dainty Devices, The Phoenix Nest,* etc., but in their time they were read so avidly that perfect copies rank among the very rarest of sixteenth-century books, and we shall never know how many have altogether perished.

Two different strains of poetry furnished the material: on the one hand, the courtly verse which many gentlemen of rank wrote but did not publicly acknowledge; and on the other, the broadside ballad rime which aimed at a somewhat lower and larger class of society.[3] To the first type belongs the *"Tottel's* earliest and most famous of these volumes, the book of *Songs and Sonnets— Miscellany"* known in modern times, from its publisher's name, as "Tottel's Miscellany,"— which gave the world the songs of Surrey and Wyatt, previously unprinted,

[1] The following works will be found useful in connection with matters and authors discussed in Part II (and often in Part III also): E. P. Cheyney, *A History of England from the Defeat of the Armada to the Death of Elizabeth* (2v, 1914-26); *Shakespeare's England,* ed. Sir Sidney Lee and C. T. Onions (2v, Oxford, 1916); Hubert S. Hall, *Society in the Elizabethan Age* (1901); Phoebe Sheavyn, *The Literary Profession in the Elizabethan Age* (Manchester, 1909); M. St. C. Byrne, *Elizabethan Life in Town and Country* (1926); G. B. Harrison, *England in Shakespeare's Day* (1928), and *Elizabethan Journals, 1591-1603* (3v, 1928-33; rev. ed. in one volume, 1939), and *A Jacobean Journal, 1603-1606* (1941); Hardin Craig, *The Enchanted Glass, the Elizabethan Mind in Literature* (1936). Literary histories for the period include George Saintsbury, *A History of Elizabethan Literature* (1887 and many subsequent editions); Thomas Seccombe and J. W. Allen, *The Age of Shakespeare, 1579-1631* (2v, 1903, 6ed., 1914); F. E. Schelling, *English Literature during the Lifetime of Shakespeare* (1910, rev. ed., 1927); E. C. Dunn, *The Literature of Shakespeare's England* (1936).

[2] Admirable editions by H. E. Rollins of most of the books here discussed have been published by the Harvard Univ. Press; viz., *Tottel's Miscellany* (2v, 1928-29); *A Handful of Pleasant Delights* (1924); *A Gorgeous Gallery of Gallant Inventions* (1926); *The Paradise of Dainty Devices* (1927); *The Phoenix Nest* (1931); *England's Helicon* (2v, 1935); *A Poetical Rhapsody* (2v, 1931-32). John Erskine's little book, *The Elizabethan Lyric* (1903), is still a good general guide. Valuable anthologies include F. E. Schelling, *A Book of Elizabethan Lyrics* (1895); J. W. Hebel and H. H. Hudson, *Poetry of the English Renaissance, 1509-1660* (1929); E. K. Chambers, *The Oxford Book of Sixteenth Century Verse* (Oxford, 1932); M. W. Black, *Elizabethan and Seventeenth-Century Lyrics* (Philadelphia, 1938); Roy Lamson and Hallett Smith, *The Golden Hind, an Anthology of Elizabethan Prose and Poetry* (1942).

[3] The two types were less distinct, however, than later; see C. R. Baskervill, *MP,* XXIII (1925). 120. For Skelton's ballad of the Scottish king see above, ch. IV, n.14; and see also J. W. Draper, "An Epitaph upon the Death of King Edward," *JEGP,* XXIX (1930). 370.

and added many poems by Nicholas Grimald, Lord Vaux, and other authors.[4] The ballad poetry is represented in Clement Robinson's collection, *A Handful of Pleasant Delights*, known to us from an edition of 1584, though its first issue probably was in 1566. Here one finds the famous song of "Greensleeves," the ballad of George Mannington (hanged at Cambridge in 1576), and much earlier material. The metres are varied and singable, and in most cases are fitted to a stated air.[5]

The Paradise of Dainty Devices

The *Gorgeous Gallery of Gallant Inventions* is dour in tone and rather monotonous. Only one edition of it (1578) is known to have been printed. Yet *The Paradise of Dainty Devices* (1576), which likewise favors melancholy themes, attained at least ten editions. This influential book was built around the poems that Richard Edwards, master of the Queen's Chapel, had left when he died ten years before. Edwards' May song, his *"amantium irae,"* and his song about music which is quoted in *Romeo and Juliet*,[6] are notable; but many other authors, some thirty in fact, are drawn upon. The selections from Francis Kinwelmarsh and Lord Vaux (one of Tottel's poets also) are among the best. This volume, next to the *Songs and Sonnets*, seems to have had most effect in shaping Shakespeare's first notions of lyric. These early song books are far from being the gay affairs that their titles might suggest. They are marked by a high moral seriousness and a distrust of life; love songs are relatively few and of great sobriety. Poulter's measure and heptameter rime have too much predominance among the metres and give a churchlike air to the compositions written in them. The ballad type of poem too largely takes the form of lament for great men recently deceased. The later years of Henry VIII, reflected in the poems of Wyatt and Surrey, were no very bright period, but in the collections which followed Tottel during the first two decades of Elizabeth's reign one has the measure of a time even less light-hearted and much more bourgeois.

The Phoenix Nest

By the year of Marlowe's death the level of lyric poetry had risen, and in this year (1593) *The Phoenix Nest* was compiled by one "R. S." (perhaps Richard Stapleton) of the Inner Temple, and "built up," as the title-page asserts, "with the most rare and refined works of noblemen, worthy knights, gallant gentlemen, masters of arts, and brave scholars." The social distinction of the book is evident, and for once this is combined with poetical excellence, for *The Phoenix Nest* is one of the most charming productions of its kind. Nearly all the identifiable authors are Oxford men, and the publication may perhaps be connected with Queen Elizabeth's visit to that university the year before. The first thing in the collection is a prose piece vindicating the memory of the Earl of Leicester, late chancellor of Oxford, and this is followed by three elegies on his nephew Sidney (by Matthew Roydon, Ralegh,

---

[4] Almost simultaneously with Tottel's book appeared another collection, *The Court of Venus* (1557-58), of which no complete copy is known.
[5] For further ballad texts of the time see H. E. Rollins, *Old English Ballads, 1553-1625* (Cambridge, 1920).
[6] *Romeo and Juliet*, IV. v. 129-147.

and Dyer,[7] respectively), which were reprinted in 1595 with Spenser's *Astrophel* and are often taken by careless persons to be Spenser's work. Peele, Nicholas Breton, Thomas Lodge, Dr. Eedes of Christ Church, and Thomas Watson, lately revealed as Marlowe's intimate in London, all contributed. The only dissonant note in this group of Oxford poets is the single poem by the Earl of Oxford himself, who was a Cambridge graduate and had been the notorious foe of Sidney. The most valuable pieces in the volume are the lyrics of Ralegh, Lodge, Dyer, and Watson; the longest single poem is *A Dream*, "learnedly set down by a worthy gentleman, a brave scholar, and master of arts in both universities," which is perhaps the work of Dr. William Gager of Christ Church. It consists of sixty rime royal stanzas, and though it attempts a timid approach to Italian eroticism, is much closer to the tone of Sackville's *Induction* and Sir David Lindsay's *Dream*.

There was at Oxford at this time a special cult of Sidney's memory, not *Nicholas* unassociated with pursuit of the patronage of his living sister, the Countess *Breton* of Pembroke; and these things may have something to do with the compilation as well as the title of *The Phoenix Nest*. In the previous year Nicholas Breton, who contributed half a dozen poems to the book, had published at Oxford two long allegories which he inscribed to the Countess, with a secondary dedication to the "gentlemen students and scholars of Oxford": *The Pilgrimage to Paradise, Joined with the Countess of Pembroke's Love.*[8] Together these poems amount to about 2500 lines in the six-line stanza that Breton and his contemporaries particularly affected. They are abstrusely moral and do not belong in a discussion of the lyric anthologies except as their recondite references to the phoenix' nest may be taken as explaining the symbolism of R. S.'s title. In the *Pilgrimage*, Breton says,

> Nor was the labor little for to climb
> The fiery ashes of a phoenix nest;

and in the *Love*,

> O let my soul beseech her sacred rest
> But in the ashes of the phoenix nest.

The phoenix is the symbol of Christ, but also, it would appear, of Sidney, whose merits are reincarnated in his sister.

More germane to the present story are the two anthologies issued by Richard Jones under Breton's popular name: *Britton's Bower of Delights* (1591, 1597) and *The Arbor of Amorous Devices ... by N. B. gent.* (1597).[9] Breton was certainly not the sole author of either volume. He distinctly disclaimed responsibility for the first, except the long opening poem on Sidney's death entitled *Amoris Lachrimae* and "one or two other toys,"

---

[7] On the authorship of this piece, which has been attributed to Fulke Greville also, see R. M. Sargent, *At the Court of Queen Elizabeth* (1935), pp. 211-213.
[8] Reprinted in Vol. 1 of Breton's *Works*, ed. A. B. Grosart (1879).
[9] Both are reproduced in facsimile in *Huntington Library Pub.* with introductions by H. E. Rollins (1933, 1936). There was evidently an edition of the *Arbor* in 1594, but no copy is known to survive.

which, however, is an understatement of his contribution. Ten poems are found in both the collections. There is much charming verse in these little books; they include several delightful lyrics, such as the song Richard Edwards had written for Emily to sing in his lost play of *Palamon and Arcite,* the ditty Bottom had in mind when he sang of

> The ousel-cock so black of hue,
> With orange-tawny bill,[10]

and a ballad with the enchanting refrain,

> Give me leave to love thee, lass,
> Give me leave to love thee;
> Thou seest that I can do no less,
> Then give me leave to love thee,

There are a number of poems on Sidney, one of which contains the fine lines,

> Here lies the flower of chivalry that ever England bred,

and

> He was a Phoenix of a man; I fear there are no mo,

and some quaint acrostical tributes to well-known ladies of Elizabeth's court.

A greater name than Breton's was invoked in 1599 by William Jaggard to advertise the collection that he called *The Passionate Pilgrim, by W. Shakespeare.*[11] Jaggard's purpose was probably to persuade the purchasers of the book that they were obtaining the Shakespearean rarity which Meres had mentioned in 1598 as "his sugared sonnets among his private friends." He does begin with two genuine sonnets from the "dark lady" sequence, which he had somehow secured in manuscript, adds three other Shakespeare items from the recently printed text of *Love's Labor's Lost,* and completes the little volume with pleasant lyrics by Richard Barnfield, Marlowe, Bartholomew Griffin, and other writers. A similar Shakespearean interest attaches
Chester, to Robert Chester's *Love's Martyr* (1601). This is in itself not an anthology,
Love's but a curious mélange of stanzaic poems by Chester, partly Arthurian in
Martyr subject, partly botanical, partly complimentary to his patron, Sir John Salusbury.[12] Appended to it, however, is a group of "poetical essays" on the theme of the turtle (i.e. dove) and phoenix, consisting of remarkable signed poems by "Ignoto," Shakespeare, Marston, Chapman, and Ben Jonson.

The most valuable of all the poetical anthologies is *England's Helicon* (1600), compiled apparently by the printer Nicholas Ling, whose reversed initials (L. N.) sign the preface, and dedicated to John Bodenham, who was the patron of the commonplace books *Politeuphuia*[13] (1597), *Wit's Theatre*

---

10 *A Midsummer Night's Dream,* III. i. 131 f.
11 See edition by J. Q. Adams (*Folger Shakespeare Library Pub.,* 1939).
12 Edited by A. B. Grosart (1878). See also Carleton Brown, *Poems by Sir John Salusbury and Robert Chester* (Bryn Mawr, 1913); and H. E. Rollins, *New Variorum Shakespeare, The Poems* (1938), pp. 559-583.
13 This is derived from Sir Thomas Elyot's *Banquet of Sapience* and William Baldwin's *Treatise of Moral Philosophy.* See above, Part I, ch. II.

(1599), *Belvedere* [14] (1600), and less directly of Meres' *Palladis Tamia, or* England's *Wit's Treasury* (1598). The *Helicon* contains about a hundred and fifty Helicon poems and includes many of the finest lyrics that had appeared from Tottel's Miscellany to Shakespeare. One of Ling's meritorious innovations was to add the authors' names more frequently and more accurately than had previously been the practice; another was to recognize, to the extent of fourteen examples, the lyrics in the song books of Byrd, Dowland, Morley, and Nicholas Yonge. A desire, rather curious in 1600, to specialize in pastoral themes has led to the chief defects of the work: over-representation of the chilly, translated pastorals in Bartholomew Yong's Montemayor (1598), and, what is worse, tampering with the texts of other songs to give them a falsely pastoral color.

Equally well known, though of far less poetic value, is the large compila- England's tion which Robert Allot published later in 1600 under the imitative title, Parnassus *England's Parnassus, or the Choicest Flowers of Our Modern Poets.*[15] Well over two thousand passages of verse are here gathered together under subject headings such as "angels," "temperance," "sorrow," etc. Since the book contains 510 pages and attempts to name the author of each excerpt, and since it covers plays as well as nondramatic poetry, it is a familiar aid to bibliographers. It gives us several poems not otherwise known; but its selections are neither made with taste nor classified with care. The lover of poetry cannot read it and the scholar cannot rely upon it, but neither can safely disregard it.

The last of the Elizabethan lyric anthologies, Davison's *Poetical Rhapsody* A Poetical (1602), has fewer great names associated with it than *England's Helicon,* Rhapsody but in the average quality of its contents is only slightly inferior. It was deservedly popular, and in three new editions (1608, 1611, 1621) maintained the vogue of this essentially Elizabethan type of book till the end of James I's reign. It differs from all the earlier collections in the way its contents are made up. The bulk of the volume consists in the work of three carefully distinguished writers, comprising (1) 40 poems of various types, "sonnets, odes, elegies, and madrigals," composed by the editor, Francis Davison (*c.* 1575-*c.* 1619), son of Queen Elizabeth's ill-treated secretary; (2) 18 similar poems by his young brother, Walter (1581-*c.* 1608); (3) 65 poems, "sonnets, odes, elegies, and other poesies," by "Anomos," whom the editor describes as his dear friend, and of whose contributions he says, "those under the name of Anomos were written... almost twenty years since, when poetry was far from that perfection to which it hath now attained." There are about fifty other poems, arranged either in an introductory group or in a final section of "divers poems of sundry authors,"—both, as Davison says, added by the printer. These additions include, besides further work of the three main contributors, some lovely lyrics by Sidney, Ralegh, Camp-

---

[14] *Belvedere* professes to be a collection of very short poetical passages; but see C. Crawford's discussion of it, *England's Parnassus* (Oxford, 1913), p. xiv f.

[15] This has been admirably edited, as indicated in the note above. See also F. B. Williams, Jr., "Notes on *England's Parnassus*," MLN, LII (1937). 402-405.

ion, Constable, and others. Further poems were added in the later editions, but it is not likely that Davison had much to do with their selection or that they can tell us much about the origin of the book.

The Davisons are pleasant love poets. Walter, the minor brother, who was but eighteen when he wrote, is much given to sonnets of the *Astrophel and Stella* type, though this style was rather *passé* at the time. Francis, too, has nine such sonnets, but gives particular attention to the short madrigal built for musical setting. These poets have the freshness of youth, and something of youth's bad judgment, as when Francis attempts to put down Spenser and set up Samuel Daniel as "prince of English poets," or in his truly unhappy "inscription for the statue of Dido," which Shakespeare must have been smiling at in the "widow Dido" passage of the *Tempest*,[16]

> O most unhappy Dido,
> Unhappy wife and more unhappy Widow!

The great problem of the book is "Anomos." In certain manuscript lists in Francis Davison's handwriting the poems assigned to him in 1602 are credited to an "A. W.", whose initials appear only once in the 1602 edition of the *Rhapsody*. It is unlikely that A. W. stands for "anonymous writers," or that Anomos (as the printer of the 1608 reprint seems to have thought) was an illiteracy for "anonymous." Anomos, which in Greek may mean "unmusical" or "lawless," is most prudently to be regarded as just what Davison says it is, the pseudonym of a single poet, writing some twenty years before the publication of the volume. He was an interesting poet, devoted to Sidney and strongly under the influence of the young Spenser. Like Sidney, Spenser, and Harvey in the years around 1580, he was attracted by the movement to write English poems in classical metres, such as phaleuciacs, hexameters, and sapphics. He had outgrown poulter's measure, but was still very much in the grasp of the *Venus and Adonis* metre, which he used for twenty-five poems, and the Davison brothers for only three. By reducing this stanza to four-foot lines he gets a more lyric movement which serves him well in eight other songs. He was not much of a sonneteer, offering only four specimens where the Davisons have twenty-three; but he had a very fresh and happy vein in the lighter lyrics which he calls odes, and he has one song, "in praise of a beggar's life," which Izaak Walton rightly chose for a special immortality:

> Bright shines the sun: play, beggars, play!
> Here's scraps enough to serve today.

The Song Books   In the preceding pages an effort has been made to avoid the phrase "song book," descriptive though it is of some of the poetical anthologies, in order to reserve the term for books which give us both songs and their music.[17]

---

[16] *Tempest*, II. i. 80 ff.

[17] An excellent brief survey of Elizabethan music by W. Barclay Squire will be found in *Shakespeare's England* (Oxford, 1916), II. 15-49. The great modern authority is E. H. Fellowes, who, besides editing for musicians' use a great many of the song books, has published the following books of more general appeal: *The English Madrigal* (1925); a succinct summary;

Much of the finest Elizabethan lyric, and some of the highest achievements of the Elizabethan mind, are found in the collections that the musicians made for household singing, for the English musicians in this period were, like the poets, the greatest in Europe. The songs now to be very briefly considered are of two kinds: those arranged for polyphonal singing by three to six persons without instrumental accompaniment; and songs, usually solos, accompanied by the lute or other instrument.

A book of the first kind was issued by Wynkyn de Worde in 1530, and another, *Songs of Three, Four, and Five Voices,* by Thomas Whythorne from John Day's press in 1571; but the first great master of this style was William Byrd (1543-1623), the Atlas of English music.[18] Besides composing very great settings for the services of both the Roman and the English church, Byrd published, "for the recreation of all such as delight in music," three volumes (1588, 1589, 1611) of songs grave and gay for private singing, using sometimes psalms and sometimes lyrics from such poets as Sidney, Dyer, Oxford, or other contemporaries. Hardly less preëminent in this field are Byrd's brilliant pupil, Thomas Morley (1558-1603), Thomas Weelkes (*c.* 1575-1623) and John Wilbye (1574-1638). Between them they had by 1609 published a dozen books, each consisting of some twenty or more lyrics set for group singing, and other musicians added vastly to the number. Morley, who at one time was Shakespeare's neighbor in the parish of St. Helen's, Bishopsgate, set his song, "It was a lover and his lass" for the lute,[19] and he wrote also in dialogue form a most attractive textbook of his art, *A Plain and Easy Introduction to Practical Music* (1597).[20]

After the appearance of Nicholas Yonge's *Musica Transalpina* in 1588 these unaccompanied vocal pieces came to be known commonly by the Italian name of madrigals. By their settings the musicians enhanced the loveliness and greatly increased the popularity of the contemporary lyrics, and their books also preserve the texts of many charming songs which have not otherwise survived. One of the showpieces of the type is the collection edited by Morley in 1601, *The Triumphs of Oriana, to Five and Six Voices.* Here twenty-five lyrics in praise of Queen Elizabeth are set to music by nearly the same number of different composers, among whom appears John Milton, the poet's father.[21] Each poem ends with an acclamation of the old Queen:

> Then sang the shepherds and nymphs of Diana:
> Long live fair Oriana!

(margin: William Byrd)

(margin: Thomas Morley)

(margin: Madrigals)

The English Madrigal Composers (Oxford, 1921), a fuller treatment; and *English Madrigal Verse, 1588-1632* (Oxford, 1920), full texts of the lyrics without the music. See also M. C. Boyd, *Elizabethan Music and Musical Criticism* (Philadelphia, 1940).

[18] See E. H. Fellowes, *William Byrd* (Oxford, 1936).

[19] In his *First Book of Airs ... to Sing and Play to the Lute* (1600). It is remarkable that the composers of purely vocal music seem to have used none of Shakespeare's songs. See E. Brennecke, Jr., "Shakespeare's Musical Collaboration with Morley," *PMLA*, LIV (1939). 139-149, and discussion, *ibid.*, pp. 149-152.

[20] Facsimile edition, Shakespeare Association (1937). The form of this book is doubtless imitated from Ascham's *Toxophilus.*

[21] See E. Brennecke, Jr., *John Milton the Elder and His Music* (1938), pp. 44-60.

It is very fine, but the Queen's praise had been quite as beautifully rendered in one of Morley's earlier songs (1593), which begins,

> Blow, shepherds, blow your pipes with gladsome glee resounding,
> See where the fair Eliza comes with love and grace abounding;

and another of Morley's gems, in his collection of 1594, preserves with wonderful fidelity the spirit of Elizabethan merriment:

> Ho! who comes here along with bagpiping and drumming?
> O 'tis the morris dance I see, the morris dance a-coming, . . .

John Dowland   Books of songs for lute accompaniment were quite as numerous, and these give the original texts with less truncation or change than they sometimes suffered when adapted to voices alone. John Dowland's four books of songs and airs for the lute (1597, 1600, 1603, 1612) and Robert Jones's five of about the same dates are admirable lyric anthologies, consisting mainly of songs of unknown authorship. In one of the *Passionate Pilgrim* poems of 1599, "If music and sweet poetry agree," Richard Barnfield parallels Dowland with Spenser:

> Dowland to thee is dear, whose heavenly touch
> Upon the lute doth ravish human sense;
> Spenser to me, whose deep conceit is such
> As, passing all conceit, needs no defence.[22]

Thomas Campion   The most important of the lutenist collections in a literary sense, however, are the five books in which the lyrics of Thomas Campion [23] (1567-1620) were published. Campion was a man of varied abilities: a Cambridge scholar trained in the law, also a doctor of medicine, the author of a large body of excellent Latin verse [24] and of four masques, and a controversialist in prose. Above all he was an understanding lover of Horace and of Catullus, and his genius reached its height in the great body of songs, of which he customarily composed both the words and the music. They are in the best sense pagan and the best of them are remarkable for their freshness and variety. Shakespeare's age produced little that is better than such works of Campion as "I care not for these ladies," "Shall I come, sweet love, to thee?" "Never love unless you can Bear with all the faults of man," and "There is a garden in her face."

Early Elizabethan Lyrists   To return from the songs of Campion to those of the opening of Queen Elizabeth's reign is to convince oneself of the progress that lyric art made in forty years. The poets whose works were collectively published in the two pre-Spenser decades, 1558-1578, do not stand in distinction or power much above the casual contributors to the early anthologies. They had, indeed, learned their art from Tottel's Miscellany and were not very am-

---

[22] This poem had been published by Barnfield in 1598.

[23] See Campion's *Works*, ed. P. Vivian (Oxford, 1909); also A. H. Bullen, *Elizabethans* (1924), pp. 125-152; M. M. Kastendieck, *England's Musical Poet, Thomas Campion* (1938); R. W. Short, "The Metrical Theory and Practice of Thomas Campion," *PMLA*, LIX (1944). 1003-1018.

[24] See L. Bradner, *Musae Anglicanae* (1940), pp. 52-54.

bitious to improve it. Self-consciousness and timidity hang over them; the display of aesthetic emotion in print was regarded as a vulgar act, and if we believe these poets' prefaces, there can hardly have been a time when the artist so trembled before the critic. They hasten to confess that they lack the skill of Chaucer or Surrey or Sackville, and in servile terms beg the protection of some great lord or lady against the Momuses and Zoili ambushed for their destruction. They deprecate novelty and seek respectability for their efforts either by basing them upon accepted classics or by chanting them to hymnlike airs.

Such was Lord Burghley's kinsman, Barnabe Googe (1540-1594), who *Barnabe* after study at both the English universities broadened himself by life in *Googe* France and Spain, returned to shine for some years as a love poet and translator of anti-papal satire, and then passed into the Irish civil service, where he must have known, and probably influenced, Spenser.[25] Googe's *Eglogs, Epitaphs, and Sonnets* [26] were published in 1563, ostensibly by a blundering friend and an over-hasty printer, who, however, did not fail to allow the poet opportunity to add a dedicatory letter explaining "how loath I have been, being of long time earnestly required, to suffer these trifles of mine to come to light." Googe has little lyric power and little variety of form. Whatever he has to say he is usually content to say in the heptameter couplet. He uses it in his version of Palingenius' long *Zodiac of Life* (1560-1565) and in his historically interesting translation of Thomas Kirchmayer's *Regnum Papisticum,* which he entitled *The Popish Kingdom, or Reign of Antichrist* (1570).[27] The same languishing metre suffices him for most of his poems in the volume of 1563, though it is made to look different by splitting each line after the fourth foot.[28] Thus the rhythm is indicated which hymn-writers note as "common measure," e.g., in the long allegorical poem, *Cupido Conquered,* which begins:

> The sweetest time of all the year
> it was whenas the sun
> Had newly entered Gemini,
> and warming heat begun;

[25] See R. Tuve, "Spenser and *The Zodiake of Life," JEGP,* xxxiv (1935). 1-19.
[26] Reprinted, E. Arber, *English Reprints* (1871).
[27] The fourth book alone is reprinted in the New Shakespeare Soc. edition of Stubbes' *Anatomy of Abuses* (1877-9), pp. 323-348.
[28] The same metre is employed throughout the eight long satires on the greed of Londoners, which Edward Hake wrote under the title, *News out of Paul's Churchyard.* First printed about 1567, this monotonous but rather informative indictment of clergy, physicians, merchants, usurers, brokers, etc. exists only in the revised edition of 1579 (ed. C. Edmonds, 1872). Hake claimed little for himself as an author, but he issued a considerable number of pamphlets in prose and verse which enjoyed a vogue because of their timeliness and sound Protestant morality. Besides a translation of one of Erasmus' *Colloquies,* the *Diversoria* (ed. H. de Vocht, *The Earliest English Translations of Erasmus' Colloquia,* Louvain, 1928), they include *A Touchstone for This Time Present* (1574), which among other things contains a versified paraphrase of a Latin book on the bringing up of children. In 1575 he produced, likewise in the divided heptameter couplet, *A Commemoration of the Most Prosperous and Peaceable Reign of Our Gracious and Dear Sovereign Lady Elizabeth;* and he lived long enough to greet King James with a volume of mingled verse and prose, *Of Gold's Kingdom and This Unhelping Age* (1604).

and in the eight eclogues that begin the volume, two of which are versified from the new pastoral prose of Montemayor's *Diana Enamorada* and represent the first impact of that famous work upon English literature.[29] He has no notion of a "sonnet" as a special kind of verse, though his works include two examples of the form.[30] He has a few personal love pleas; epitaphs on a number of warriors and literary men, e.g., Thomas Phaer the translator of Virgil, and Nicholas Grimald; and pleasant addresses to the aged John Bale and the universally admired Richard Edwards. Inspired by his handling of the heptameter, he secures a quasi-classic and pseudo-lyric, but not altogether unagreeable, effect by splitting the lines of ordinary pentameter quatrains at the second foot, as in this invocation to his slowly accomplished translation of Palingenius:

> The labor sweet
>   that I sustained in thee,
> O Palingene,
>   when I took pen in hand,
> Doth grieve me now,
>   as oft as I thee see
> But half hewed out
>   before mine eyes to stand.
>
> But if that God
>   do grant me greater years,
> And take me not
>   from hence before my time,
> The Muses nine,
>   the pleasant singing feres [companions],
> Shall so inflame
>   my mind with lust to rime,
> That, Palingene,
>   I will not leave thee so,
> But finish thee
>   according to my mind.

George Turberville

Descended from an ancient Dorsetshire family, George Turberville[31] (c. 1544-c. 1597) was educated at Winchester and Oxford, but, leaving the university (as Googe had left two) before he graduated, went to one of the Inns of Court in London, where, according to Anthony Wood, "he was much admired for his excellencies in the art of poetry." In 1568 he was sent to Russia as secretary to Thomas Randolph on a mission to secure privileges for English merchants. After his return he served, without distinction, as a captain of militia, committed a homicide in 1573 for which he was duly pardoned, and published verse translations of various Italian *Tragical Tales,* chiefly from Boccaccio (c. 1574), as well as two gentlemanly books in prose:

[29] See T. P. Harrison, "Googe's *Eglogs* and Montemayor's *Diana,*" *Univ. Texas Studies in English,* v (1925). 68-78.
[30] See H. H. Hudson, "Sonnets by Barnabe Googe," *PMLA,* XLVIII (1933). 293-294.
[31] See J. E. Hankins, *The Life and Works of George Turberville* (Lawrence, Kansas, 1940).

The Book of Falconry or Hawking and *The Noble Art of Venery or Hunting* (1575). About this time he married, acquired property in his native county, ceased to write further, and illustrated the elegant inconspicuousness for which the young Pope longed:

> Thus let me live, unseen, unknown,
> Thus unlamented let me die,
> Steal from the world, and not a stone
> Tell where I lie.[32]

It is a typical pattern of early Elizabethan life. After his death, the date and place of which are not recorded, Sir John Harington remembered him with praise:

> When rimes were yet but rude, thy pen endeavored
> To polish barbarism with purer style,[33]

but it is hardly more than a likely guess that he was the "good Harpalus, now woxen aged," to whom Spenser dropped a slight tribute in 1591.[34]

Turberville has an important place as a translator and early writer of blank verse;[35] but his original poetry is all contained in a thick little volume, *Epitaphs, Epigrams, Songs, and Sonnets* (1567), and in a supplement of interesting verse letters and other poems from Russia, entitled *Epitaphs and Sonnets* and dated 1569.[36] He dedicates his love poems to a great lady, Anne Countess of Warwick, and ties them loosely into a vague narrative of the adoration of Timetes ("the estimator") for Pandora, or Pindara. They are too prolix and fall too easily into the jog-trot of poulter's measure, but the poet can sometimes build a terse stanza on a different model; e.g.,

> To Venus do your due, you senses all,
> And to her son, to whom you are in thrall;
> To Cupid bend thy knee and thanks repay,
> That after linger'd suit and long delay
> Hath brought thy ship to shore.[37]

Turberville writes smoothly, but his language lacks variety and he is too much addicted to the common classical references which a university man was supposed to know. In this respect and others the realistic Russian poems offer relief. Notwithstanding both the titles of his collections, he has no true sonnets, but he was profuse of epitaphs on friends deceased, no less than four of whom were drowned at sea. Some of these—e.g., those on

---

[32] Pope, *Ode on Solitude*, c. 1709.

[33] *The Letters and Epigrams of Sir John Harington*, ed. Norman E. McClure (Philadelphia, 1930), p. 164.

[34] See J. E. Hankins, "The Harpalus of Spenser's *Colin Clout*," *MLN*, XLIV (1929). 164-167.

[35] His versions of Ovid's *Heroides* and of Mantuan's eclogues (facsimile, ed. D. Bush, 1937) were printed in 1567 and his Mancinus in 1568. Mantuan and Mancinus had both been previously translated, in very different style, by Barclay; see above, Part I, ch. IV. Six of the *Heroical Epistles* are rendered in blank verse.

[36] In the only extant edition these are attached to the *Tragical Tales* of 1587 (ed. J. P Collier, 1867).

[37] "The lover, hoping assuredly of attaining his purpose," etc.

Richard Edwards, the dramatist,[38] and Arthur Brooke, the author of *Romeus and Juliet*—have historic value; and most of them give a pleasant impression of sincerity, for Turberville, like most of the writers of his generation, seems to have been a man of simple and honest heart. He was on terms of easy friendship with Googe, and his epigrams have a pleasanter quality than is usual with the type. Unlike John Heywood, who devised his own epigrams, Turberville found his themes largely in the Latin collection that Janus Cornarius had issued at Basel in 1529. Many of these came from Sir Thomas More, and a still larger proportion derived ultimately from the Greek Anthology.[39]

George Gascoigne (c. 1539-1577)   The richest collection of early Elizabethan poetry is contained in a volume published anonymously in 1573 under the title, *A Hundreth Sundry Flowers Bound up in One Small Posy.*[40] It purports to be gathered together by one "G. T." (who may be George Turberville) and to be written by "Master F. I. and divers others." The first of the contents is an interesting brief novel in prose, *The Adventures of Master F. J.*,[41] which serves as a setting for fourteen poems of considerable merit. Then follow enough other poems to make an even hundred, twenty-one being specifically assigned to George Gascoigne [42] and the rest to other writers allegedly unknown to the editor. At the moment of publication Gascoigne was abroad on military service in Holland; but early in 1575 he published a new edition entitled *The Posies of George Gascoigne Esquire, Corrected, Perfected, and Augmented by the Author,* in which he made little change except to add a long poem that he had written in Holland, *Dulce Bellum Inexpertis,* and to rearrange the

---

[38] Turberville's volume contains two epitaphs on Edwards, one by Thomas Twine and one by himself.

[39] See H. B. Lathrop, "J. Cornarius's *Selecta Epigrammata Graeca* and the Early English Epigrammatists," *MLN,* XLIII (1928). 223-229. The historian of the English epigram, if any one were to essay that sad task, would have to consider Timothy Kendall's *Flowers of Epigrams* (1577), which are mainly translated or adapted; and also Robert Crowley's very different and earlier *One and Thirty Epigrams* (1550). Crowley (*c.* 1518-1588) was a remarkable minor character, a Puritan printer and preacher, at one time archdeacon of Hereford and vicar of St. Giles Cripplegate in London. He issued the first printed edition of Langland's *Piers Plowman* in 1550, and also printed his own poetical works, which deal with religious and social abuses and are in doggerel verse of considerable ingenuity. The best is *The Fable of Philargyrie, the Great Gigant* [giant] *of Great Britain* (reprint, W. A. Marsden, 1931). A somewhat better poet, closely contemporary with Tuberville, is Thomas Howell, whose *Arbor of Amity* appeared in 1568 and his *New Sonnets and Pretty Pamphlets* soon afterwards. The most interesting poems are perhaps "Jack shows his qualities and great good will to Joan," which is in the southwestern dialect, and "A dialogue touching the matrimonial degree." One is in each volume. In 1581 Howell published another collection of miscellaneous lyrics, *Howell his Devices, for his Own Exercise and his Friends' Pleasure,* with a dedication to Lady Pembroke. All these are reprinted by Grosart, *The Poems of Thomas Howell* (1879), and Howell's *Devises* by Sir W. Raleigh (Oxford, 1906). Still more in Turberville's style is a somewhat later poet, Matthew Grove, whose "pleasant devises, epigrams, songs, and sonnets" are attached to his only book, the verse narrative *History of Pelops and Hippodamia* (1587). Grove usually writes in poulter's measure, and his love verses, though fluent, are commonly dolorous.

[40] Reprinted (incompletely) with Introduction by B. M. Ward (1926).

[41] See below, ch. III.

[42] See *The Works of George Gascoigne,* ed. J. W. Cunliffe (2v, Cambridge, 1907-10); S. A. Tannenbaum, *George Gascoigne, a Concise Bibliography* (1942). A long series of articles on Gascoigne's life and works will be found in *RES,* beginning with Vol. II (1926) and continuing to Vol. XIV (1938). The scholarship is soundly digested and valuable new facts added in C. T. Prouty, *George Gascoigne, Elizabethan Courtier, Soldier, and Poet* (1942).

order of contents, according to a fantastic judgment of their moral value, into "flowers," "herbs," and "weeds." Gascoigne avowed his authorship of the entire volume, nineteen contemporaries contributed commendatory verses on the same assumption, and there seems to be no good reason for doubting it.[43] In fact several poems ascribed to other writers in the earlier version bear definite evidence of his authorship,[44] and they all have an evenness of technique that suggests a single writer.

In his *Notes of Instruction Concerning the Making of Verse*, which is appended to the 1575 volume, Gascoigne admits that contemporary English poetry is written exclusively in iambic measure, and he makes little effort to extend its metrical range. Poulter's measure, the sonnet of three quatrains and couplet, the six-line (quatrain and couplet) stanza, and rime royal are the only forms he uses much, but he uses these with commendable ease and accuracy. This soldier-poet's verse is notably well drilled. The lines march regularly and effectively, with little individual brilliance and without faults of rhythm. Within his limitations, which were the general limitations of his age, Gascoigne is both a fine and an interesting workman; he has two rather effective experiments in sonnet-linking,[45] and the series of poems which he calls his "Memories" shows a high degree of virtuosity in the forms that he exploited. His love poems often have grace, but they bear the yoke of early Elizabethan morality. Though he apologized for their boldness and segregated a number of them among his "Weeds," they are conventional enough, and bear out his remark that "if ever I wrote a line for myself in causes of love, I have written ten for other men." He is best perhaps as a narrator in verse and a social critic. The long amatory woes of *Philomene*, Dan Bartholmew of Bath, and of the Green Knight, show how suspect emotional freedom was to Englishmen who had grown up in the years of religious intolerance. The extended Erasmian opening of *Dulce Bellum Inexpertis* and the still longer *Steel Glass* [46] in blank verse show how the manner of the preacher still clung to the poet. Gascoigne is less self-conscious in the latter part of *Dulce Bellum*, where he is relating his own experiences; and in the vividly bitter narrative of his shipwreck in Holland.[47] His earlier masque for the Montacute weddings includes accounts of the recent capture of Famagusta in Cyprus by the Turks [48] and of the battle of Lepanto (both in 1571).

Gascoigne's literary patron was Lord Grey of Wilton, who less than ten years later was receiving the poetical homages of Spenser. By that time

[43] See W. W. Greg, "A Hundreth Sundry Flowers," *Library*, VII (1926). 269-282; VIII (1927). 123-130; F. T. Bowers, "Notes on Gascoigne's 'A Hundreth Sundrie Floweres' and 'The Posies'," *Harvard Studies & Notes in Phil. & Lit.*, XVI (1934). 13-35.
[44] E.g., Cambridge ed., Vol. I, p. 502, which contains an anagram of his name ("GASCON"); and p. 47, where in the 1573 edition G. G.'s initials twice appear, "the author" being substituted in 1575.
[45] Cambridge ed., p. 388 f., 463 f.
[46] This historically important satire was written late and printed with *Philomene* in 1576.
[47] Cambridge ed., pp. 354-363.
[48] See R. R. Cawley, "George Gascoigne and the Siege of Famagusta," *MLN*, XLIII (1928). 296-300.

Gascoigne was dead. In the two years between his death and the appearance of the *Shepherds' Calendar* poetry passed over a mighty watershed and Gascoigne's work, so broadly representative of the early Elizabethan effort, became only a landmark in the past. Nashe can remember him kindly in 1589 as the one "who first beat the path to that perfection which our best poets have aspired to since his departure," [49] but for Sir John Davies it is the mere height of absurdity in a newfangled youth that he should "praise old George Gascoigne's rimes." [50] Fate was kinder to him than to his less gifted and longer-lived companions: George Whetstone [51] (*c.* 1544-*c.* 1587), who bemoaned him in numerous but uninspired stanzas, *A Remembrance of the Well Employed Life and Godly End of George Gascoigne Esquire;* and Thomas Churchyard (*c.* 1520-1604), who went on lisping the obsolete strains through the music of a greater age.[52]

Thomas Tusser   Thomas Tusser (*c.* 1525-1580), a gentleman of good birth like Gascoigne, and a graduate of Eton and Cambridge, became the laureate of the early Elizabethan farm, as Gascoigne was of the court and camp; and Tusser's verses held their vogue much longer. They are no more for the most part than doggerel directions, covering all the activities of country folk through the year, but their concrete homeliness and vivid sense of time and place give them a natural poetry. Published originally by Richard Tottel (in the year of his famous Miscellany, 1557) under the modest title, *A Hundreth Good Points of Husbandry,* they were later much expanded, embellished with new pictures and a quaint metrical autobiography of Tusser, and thus developed into a countryman's classic which has hardly been out of print from that day to this, except in the unbucolic period of the later eighteenth century.[53]

Robert Southwell   A much younger and essentially greater poet may find mention here, for only chronologically, not at all in spirit, does he belong with the later movement led by Spenser, Sidney, and Marlowe. Robert Southwell [54] (1561-1595), the Jesuit martyr, left a number of devotional works in mannered prose [55] and a priceless apology for his co-religionists, written with fervent simplicity and entitled *An Humble Supplication to Her Majesty* (1595). He left also a long poem in 132 six-line stanzas, *St. Peter's Complaint,*[56] based

---

[49] McKerrow, *Works of Thomas Nashe,* III. 319.

[50] Epigram 22, "In Cyprium."

[51] See Thomas C. Izard, *George Whetstone, Mid-Elizabethan Gentleman of Letters* (1942).

[52] Those who wish to linger over the mild fragrance of this bygone day may find it in *A Posie of Gilloflowers* by Humphrey Gifford, 1580 (Hawthornden Press, 1933). Gifford was a Devonshire schoolmaster of serious temper, using mainly the six-line stanza, but he sometimes shows liveliness, variety, and foreign influence. His most vigorous poem, in irregular long lines, is entitled *For Soldiers.*

[53] Two editions appeared in 1931: *Five Hundred Points of Good Husbandry, with an Introduction by Sir Walter Scott and a Benediction by Rudyard Kipling,* and D. Hartley, *Thomas Tusser . . . his Good Points of Husbandry.*

[54] See A. B. Grosart, *The Complete Poems of Robert Southwell* (1872); C. M. Hood, *The Book of Robert Southwell* (life and a selection of his poems; Oxford, 1926); P. Janelle, *Robert Southwell, the Writer* (Clermont-Ferrand, 1935).

[55] Ed. W. J. Walter (1828).

[56] Concerning an inferior poem in the same metre, doubtfully ascribed to Southwell, see H. J. L. Robbie, "The Authorship of *A Fourfold Meditation,*" *RES,* V (1929). 200-202. Two other long poems in this stanza, strongly influenced by Southwell, are ascribed to Gervase

on an Italian work of similar title and content by Luigi Tansillo. His literary fame rests, however, on his exalted religious lyrics, which were written in prison and published in the year of his execution, partly as a supplement to *St. Peter's Complaint,* and partly in a separate volume, *Maeoniae* (i.e., Lydian Muses).

Southwell had been educated by the Jesuits abroad, at Douai, Paris, and Rome, and he wrote verse in Latin as well as in his native tongue. His English prosody is old-fashioned, suggesting Gascoigne or Turberville. He does not use the sonnet or *ottava rima,* though both must have been familiar to him in Italy; and only seldom ventures beyond the old six-line stanza and the long couplet of six, seven, or eight stresses. The sweet and often mystical fervor which he can put into these hackneyed forms is evidenced in *A Child My Choice:*

Let folly praise that [i.e., what] fancy loves, I praise and love that Child,
Whose heart no thought, whose tongue no word, whose hand no deed defil'd.
I praise Him most, I love Him best, all praise and love is His;
While Him I love; in Him I live, and cannot live amiss;

or in the memorable conclusion of his best known poem, *The Burning Babe,*

With this He vanish'd out of sight, and swiftly shrank away,
And straight I called unto mind that it was Christmas Day.

He has a homely and saintly simplicity that reminds one occasionally of Francis Thompson, as in the fine poem, *Upon the Image of Death:*

The gown that I do use to wear,
The knife wherewith I cut my meat,
And eke the old and ancient chair
Which is my only usual seat:
All these do tell me I must die,
And yet my life amend not I.

As befitted his training, he is fond of gnomic wisdom, which he converts to pious purposes; and in *A Vale of Tears* he rather surprisingly fits his emotion to the well observed scenery of an Alpine valley. Without a tithe of the preciosity and metrical genius of George Herbert, Southwell possessed much of that poet's religious charm; and it is to the credit of his countrymen that, though he died a felon's death, his works, both in prose and verse, long enjoyed in England a wide and reverent esteem.

Markham; viz., *The Tears of the Beloved, or the Lamentations of St. John* (1600), and *Mary Magdalen's Lamentations for the Loss of her Master Jesus* (1601). These are reprinted in Grosart's *Miscellanies of the Fuller Worthies Library* (1871).

II

Verse Narrative

The high esteem in which the early Tudor readers held the moral works of Lydgate has been evident in many of the poems hitherto discussed; but nothing in Lydgate appealed more than the series of tragic histories which he had borrowed from Boccaccio under the title of *The Fall of Princes,* and which the lurid revolutions of Fortune's wheel in the second quarter of the sixteenth century brought back to men's attention with a melancholy immediacy. It is very natural, therefore, that two new editions of Lydgate's *Fall* were printed early in Queen Mary's reign. One was published by Tottel in 1554; the other by the Queen's printer, John Wayland, in 1554 or 1555. Wayland's intention was originally more ambitious, for there exist, in a single copy, a canceled title-page and prefatory note, stating that the book contained, in addition to Lydgate's work, "the fall of all such as since that time were notable in England, diligently collected out of the chronicles," and "penned by the best clerks in such kind of matters that be this day living, not unworthy to be matched with Master Lydgate." However, Queen Mary's chancelor, Stephen Gardiner, prohibited the modern section, which was not permitted to appear till Elizabeth had succeeded to the throne. It was first published in 1559 under the title, *A Mirror for Magistrates,*[1] and, separate henceforth from Lydgate, ran a career perhaps more complex and influential than that of any other Elizabethan book.

The first edition mirrors the instability of fortune and punishment of vice in nineteen historical tales from the century between Richard II's reign and Edward IV's (1377-1483), the reader being constantly reminded that "the only thing which is purposed herein is by example of others' miseries to dissuade all men from all sins and vices." The prose introductions dramatize a scene which must have been reënacted whenever a group of collaborating playwrights later met to plan a history play for the theatre. In this case, William Baldwin,[2] the chief author in question and printer's agent, meets by appointment with George Ferrers (c. 1500-1579) and five other gentlemen in a room where, till nightfall, they turn over the pages of Hall's and Fabyan's Chronicles and prepare their copy for the new book. Each reads

[1] See *The Mirror for Magistrates,* ed. from the original texts by Lily B. Campbell (Cambridge, 1938) and *Parts Added to The Mirror for Magistrates by John Higgins and Thomas Blenerhasset,* ed. Lily B. Campbell (Cambridge, 1946); and, by the same author, *Tudor Conceptions of History and Tragedy in A Mirror for Magistrates* (Berkeley, 1936). On the historical poems treated in this chapter see Homer Nearing, *English Historical Poetry, 1599-1641* (Philadelphia, 1945). *Magistrate* here means what Sir Thomas Elyot meant by *Governor,* a man possessed of great public responsibility.

[2] See above, Part I, ch. II; Eveline I. Feasey, "William Baldwin," *MLR,* xx (1925). 407-418.

for the others' criticism the lives that he has written, and they are reviewed against the chroniclers' narrative. The poems take the form of dramatic monologues, in which the nineteen unfortunates comment upon their lives, usually in the rime royal that was the conventional literary speech of great personages.[3]

The first edition of the *Mirror for Magistrates* has much historic significance, but no poetic value. Any judicious reader would rate its contents from poor to middling. The second edition, in 1563, added eight other lives, and among them one by a new and young writer which strangely outshines all the rest. Thomas Sackville (1536-1608) handles the rime royal as few *Thomas* poets have done since Chaucer, and even Chaucer, though far greater in *Sackville* pure narrative, has left little to equal the *Complaint of Henry Duke of Buckingham* for dark beauty and sustained emotion.

One of the qualities by which Sackville towers over all the other poets of the *Mirror* is his fastidious feeling for words, as in the perfect line,

In dreadful fear amid the dreadful place.[4]

Another is his feeling for the solemn aspects of external nature, e.g.,

Midnight was come, and every vital thing
With sweet sound sleep their weary limbs did rest;
The beasts were still, the little birds that sing
Now sweetly slept beside their mother's breast;
The old and all were shrouded in their nest:
The waters calm, the cruel seas did cease;
The woods, the fields, and all things held their peace.

This passage is from the *Complaint* proper, but Sackville's finest poetry is found rather in the 550 preliminary lines printed in the 1563 text as "The Induction," though the holograph manuscript at Cambridge does not so separate them.[5] Here, quite outside the Lydgatian frame that confined the other contributors to the *Mirror,* Sackville has written a great independent poem that has three parts: the picture of a winter evening; a Dantesque meeting with a tremendous abstraction, Sorrow; and a Virgilian journey to Hell. This is indeed, to quote a judgment no less true than trite, "the best poetry written in the English language between Chaucer and Spenser."[6]

Where the other poets of the *Mirror* sought a moral and a rule for life, Sackville sought and found the uplifting tenderness of tragedy, present for him particularly in the heartbreak he feels at the fate of Troy:

Not worthy Hector, worthiest of them all,
Her hope, her joy! his force is now for nought.
O Troy, Troy, there is no boot but bale.

[3] However, Richard II uses a difficult ten-line stanza, Henry VI an adaptation of poulter's measure, and Edward IV speaks the poem Skelton had written for him in twelve-line stanzas.
[4] *Induction,* line 217.
[5] See M. Hearsey, *The Complaint of Henry Duke of Buckingham* (New Haven, 1936); Fitzroy Pyle, "Thomas Sackville and *A Mirror for Magistrates,"* RES, XIV (1938). 315-321.
[6] G. Saintsbury, *A History of Elizabethan Literature* (1887), p. 11.

The hugy horse within thy walls is brought;
Thy turrets fall, thy knights, that whilom fought
In arms amid the field, are slain in bed,
Thy gods defil'd, and all thy honor dead.

If this recalls Chaucer, as it does, it has also the feel of Shakespeare; and Shakespeare seems close in Sackville's picture of nightfall,

When, lo, the night, with misty mantles spred,
Gan dark the day and dim the azure skies; [7]

or of sleep,

The body's rest, the quiet of the heart,
The travail's ease, the still night's fere [mate] was he,
And of our life in earth the better part;
Reaver of sight, and yet in whom we see
Things oft that tide, and oft that never be;
Without respect esteeming equally
King Croesus' pomp and Irus' poverty; [8]

most of all, however, when the Induction ends with the evocation of the ghost of Buckingham,

Then first came Henry duke of Buckingham ...
Wringing his hands, and Fortune oft doth blame,

for this was the last ghost in the terrifying procession that appeared before Shakespeare's Richard III at Bosworth:

The first was I that help'd thee to the crown;
The last was I that felt thy tyranny.
O, in the battle think on Buckingham!

Churchyard,
Shore's
Wife
One other contribution to the second edition of the *Mirror for Magistrates* reaches a notable, though much lower, poetic level. It is the *chef d'œuvre* of Thomas Churchyard, whose sentimental vein found an apt subject in the story of Jane Shore, the royal mistress. His *Shore's Wife* became highly popular and made her a dependable theme to point a moral or adorn a play down to the time of Nicholas Rowe (1714). Two of Churchyard's lines struck a spark in Marlowe's brain, for he made Jane say of her enticing friends,

They brake the boughs and shak'd the tree by sleight,
And bent the wand that might have grown full straight. [9]

Upon this hint the greater poet spoke (though he was also thinking of Psalm 80: 15) when he wrote the epilogue to *Faustus,*

Cut is the branch that might have grown full straight.

[7] Compare *Hamlet,* I. i. 166.
[8] Compare *Macbeth,* II. ii. 36 ff.
[9] Mirror, ed. Campbell, p. 379. The parallel was noted by Henry Morley and also by A. Thaler, *MLN,* xxxviii (1923). 89-92.

Other editions of the *Mirror* followed to 1587, and John Higgins (1574) and *Later Edi-*
Thomas Blennerhasset (1578) published supplementary series of "tragedies," *tions of the*
which carried the story back to the legendary years of Locrine, Lear, *Mirror*
and King Arthur. The series was not complete till the edition of Richard
Niccols in 1610, "newly enlarged with a last part called *A Winter Night's
Vision*," in which 91 tales appear, the last a long tribute to "England's Eliza."
It is impossible to estimate the effect of all this motley work upon the Elizabethan taste and point of view. At least twenty-five of the sections dramatize
characters conspicuous in Shakespeare's plays, and the relation to other
historical dramas is hardly less close. The same material could, indeed, be
generally found in Holinshed or Hall, but it is questionable whether the
playwrights would have thought of using it so largely, if the *Mirror* had not
already carried it such a long way toward the stage.

The *Mirror for Magistrates* also produced a liking for historical narrative *Imitations*
in verse which stimulated work by some of the best known as well as some *of the*
of the obscurest poets. One of the latter is the author of *Throckmorton's* *Mirror*
Ghost*, preserved in several old manuscripts. In the printed edition [10] it runs
to 229 six-line stanzas of only moderate poetic quality but of much interest,
for it plausibly purports to be written by a nephew of Sir Nicholas Throckmorton (1515-1571), whose ghost visits him to warn him against ambition
by relating his own chequered career. A few minor slips in detail may increase the probability that this is a genuine family document. As a record of
the ups and downs, private hopes and fears, and domestic relations of a
pushing aristocrat, from the close of Henry VIII's reign till well into Elizabeth's, this poem deserves more notice than it has had. Spenser's *Ruins of
Time* shows how a budding genius might treat this type of poetry, and *The
Ghost of Richard III* by Christopher Brooke [11] (1614) shows how it could
be fitted to the systematic character-dissection that Donne and his friends
admired. The author was Donne's intimate, and received commendatory
verses from Chapman, Wither, and Jonson. He writes in the *ottava rima*
stanza that Daniel and Drayton had brought in, and at great length psycho-
analyzes the villain-hero whom Shakespeare's play had made notorious.

William Warner (*c.* 1558-1609) frankly aimed at the reader's amusement *William*
in *Albion's England*, which, first printed in 1586 while the *Mirror* was still *Warner,*
in hot demand, augmented itself through six or seven editions in the next *Albion's*
quarter-century, and, with a "continuance" in 1606, finally reached sixteen *England*
books. Warner writes in "fourteener" couplets, and for his dedicatory
epistles employs a highly Euphuistic prose. The first two books are a compendium of mythology, after the manner of the Troy Books, from the
Flood to Brute, the legendary founder of Britain. Book III begins with the
story of Lear and is closely followed by that of Gorboduc; but before long
Warner gives up serious effort to be historic and becomes a narrator of
pleasant tales. That of Curan, the disguised prince, and the afflicted princess

[10] Ed. J. G. Nichols (Roxburghe Club, 1874).
[11] Ed. J. P. Collier (Shakespeare Soc., 1844).

Argentile (chapter xx) is one of the best and may have suggested to Shakespeare the name of a minor character in *King Lear*.

In the year of Warner's death appeared another very long poem which is still conspicuously in the Elizabethan style: Thomas Heywood's *Troia Britannica, or Great Britain's Troy* (1609). It is in the then fashionable *ottava rima*, but covers much the same material as *Albion's England*, though with a difference of emphasis. Of the seventeen books fifteen poetize the mythological and Trojan events in Caxton's Troy Book, and the last two run over British history from Brute to James I. There is considerable interest in this poem. Nineteen stanzas of the last book recapitulate the incidents of Elizabeth's reign, and modern affairs are often introduced episodically in earlier sections; e.g., the fight of the "Revenge" in Book v, the coronation celebration of James and Anna in Book iv, and Queen Elizabeth's treatment of transgressing maids in Book iii:

> So did our Cynthia chastity prefer,
>   The most admired queen that ever reign'd:
> If any of her virgin train did err,
>   Or with the like offence their honors stain'd,
> From her imperial court she banish'd her,
>   And a perpetual exile she remain'd.

Into Books ix and x Heywood introduced translations (in couplets) of the Ovidian epistles of Paris to Helen and Helen to Paris, which his publisher, Jaggard, impudently stole in order to eke out the scanty poetry of *The Passionate Pilgrim* —a circumstance that has given us one of the pleasantest anecdotes of Shakespeare.

Samuel Daniel [12] (1562-1619) is seldom mentioned without praise, and not often read without weariness. He is naturally bracketed with Drayton. They were of the same age and gentlemanly social order, served the same type of patroness, and in a well-bred way were very conscious of their rivalry. Since both were prolific, industrious, and conventional, it is natural that they produced the same kind of poetry: sonnets, pastorals, occasional verse, and particularly historical poems. Drayton, with more lyric power and more enthusiasm, and much more sense of humor and of fantasy, extended beyond these limits, and he is the better poet. "Well-languaged" [13] Daniel is the more correct and judicial. Indeed, the suavity, clarity, and seemingly modern quality of his verses are always surprising to a reader who comes upon them in an Elizabethan miscellany. His highest feats are the philosophic verse letters, like the famous one to the Countess of Cumberland, beginning,

He that of such a height hath built his mind,

---

[12] *Complete Works*, ed. A. B. Grosart (5v, 1885-96); *Poems and a Defence of Ryme*, ed. A. C. Sprague (Cambridge, Mass., 1930); S. A. Tannenbaum, *Samuel Daniel, a Concise Bibliography* (1942).
[13] The title was conferred upon him by William Browne of Tavistock.

or the discourse between Ulysses and the Siren, which say noble and timeless truths with a Chinese gravity.

Daniel's *Complaint of Rosamond* (1592) gave a new lease of life to the *Mirror for Magistrates* type of poetry by turning it into a mirror for fair ladies. He uses the old device of the ghostly visitant bewailing in rime royal, and admits his debt to *Shore's Wife;* but Daniel endows his damned lady with all the upper-class sensibilities, and by introducing a graceful reference to his own virtuous Delia at the end makes it the kind of poem one could send one's niece with the ingratiating endorsement, "Look here upon this picture, and on this." *The Civil Wars between the Two Houses of Lancaster and York* (1595, 1609) treats in leisurely *ottava rima* verse the stormy period that Shakespeare covers from *Richard II* to *Henry VI*. After eight long books Daniel left it incomplete and turned to history in prose. It has gracious passages; those dealing with Richard II's queen may have offered hints to Shakespeare. One can understand how the Countess of Pembroke, to whom it is dedicated, may have liked its elegiac gentleness, but her brother Sidney would not. It gives an effect of violent actions portrayed in slow motion, and is sometimes a little absurd. *Daniel's Rosamond*

Drayton's devotion to the historical muse was unceasing and in his own day well rewarded, but has done little for his fame.[14] He tried nearly every variation that could be worked out of the *Mirror* type of poem, and was incredibly industrious in the work of revising. *Piers Gaveston* (1593) allows the ghost of that worthy to tell his story in nearly three hundred six-line stanzas. *Matilda* (1594), in avowed rivalry with Daniel's *Rosamond*, Shakespeare's *Lucrece*, and Churchyard's *Jane Shore*, employs rime royal; as does *The Tragical Legend of Robert Duke of Normandy* (1596), which attempts to add attractiveness to the chequered career of William the Conqueror's eldest son by a dream-setting concerned with a contest between Fortune and Fame. *Mortimeriados*[15] (1596) is a sequel to *Gaveston;* the two poems cover the events related in Marlowe's *Edward II,* and do so at considerably greater length, but with less human interest. Before Drayton's collected works appeared in 1619, *Mortimeriados* had been altered from rime royal to *ottava rima,* lengthened, divided into six cantos, and renamed *The Barons' Wars.* One shudders to think of the labor this cost. Practically every rime was changed, and practically every clause reworded; yet at the end the poem remains much the same as before. In the time spent on aesthetically trifling improvements of these popular historical poems Drayton could have turned off many more gems like *Nymphidia;* he could even have carried *Poly-Olbion* into Scotland. However, one may admit that the sixth book of *The Barons' Wars* is a very pleasing and variegated poem, and no doubt the best thing Drayton has done of this sort. *The Legend of Great Cromwell* (1607), *Michael Drayton (1563-1631*

14 See *Works,* Tercentenary Ed., ed. J. W. Hebel (4v, 1931-35; 5th vol., ed. K. Tillotson and B. H. Newdigate, 1941); Oliver Elton, *Michael Drayton, a Critical Study* (1905); B. H. Newdigate, *Michael Drayton and his Circle* (1941).

15 I.e., *Mortimerias* "the story of Mortimer." Following classical precedent, the title-page uses the Greek genitive case.

probably suggested by the play on the subject, "by W. S.", in 1602, shows his afflatus very much reduced.[16]

With characteristic energy Drayton tried another method in *England's Heroical Epistles* (1597-1602), in which the subject matter of the *Mirror* is handled in the fashion of Ovid's *Heroides*. Twelve pairs of famous English lovers, beginning with Henry II and Rosamond and concluding with Lady Jane Grey and Guildford Dudley, write long letters to each other in couplet rime. To us this series seems sadly lacking in variety and heavily overcharged with platitude, but Drayton's readers loved it through six editions.

Romeus
and Juliet

Free romantic invention did not flourish on early Elizabethan soil, doubtless because of the strong inhibitions the poets of that time always confessed. A single remarkable, and very early, example there was in the *Romeus and Juliet* of Arthur Brooke, which Tottel published in 1562.[17] The plot was developed from a prose tale in a recent French collection by Pierre Boisteau or Boaistuau (1559), who had imported it from Italy. Brooke's poem, as is well known, served Shakespeare a generation later for his first significant tragedy, and it is surprising to remind oneself how completely the dramatist's characters and incidents are in the poem. It required genius to discover their value, for they lie buried beneath three thousand lines of venomously verbose poulter's measure. This is the more distressing as the young author, who was drowned the next year and left no other imaginative work, shows in his prefatory sonnets that he could write very like a poet in that form. Poulter's measure may have been a protective device, lest he appear Italianate. His horrid epistle to the reader is clearly protective:

The glorious triumph of the continent man upon the lusts of wanton flesh encourageth men to honest restraint of wild affections; the shameful and wretched ends of such as have yielded their liberty thrall to foul desires teach men to withhold themselves from the headlong fall of loose dishonesty ... And to this end, good Reader, is this tragical matter written, to describe unto thee a couple of unfortunate lovers, thralling themselves to unhonest desire; neglecting the authority and advice of parents and friends; conferring their principal counsels with drunken gossips and superstitious friars ... attempting all adventures of peril for th' attaining of their wished lust; using auricular confession ... abusing the honorable name of lawful marriage to cloak the shame of stolen contracts; finally by all means of unhonest life hasting to most unhappy death.

---

[16] See K. Tillotson, "Michael Drayton as a 'Historian' in the *Legend of Cromwell*," MLR, xxxiv (1939). 186-200. Concerning another long poem of about this same date, *Leicester's Ghost* by Thomas Rogers (c. 1575-1609), see F. B. Williams, Jr., "Thomas Rogers of Bryanston," *Harvard Studies & Notes in Phil. & Lit.*, xvi (1934). 253-267. Drayton's much later *Battle of Agincourt* and *Miseries of Queen Margaret* suffered by being published in the same volume with *Nymphidia* (1627), and the former, a long historical account in 2500 ottava rima lines, has been practically wiped out of literary memory by the poet's more famous *Ballad of Agincourt* (1619).

[17] Ed. J. J. Munro (*Shakespeare Classics*, 1908). Note also Edward Lewicke's uninspired metrical version of a very popular legend in his *Titus and Gisippus* (ed. H. G. Wright, *Tales from the Decameron*, 1937; EETS, 205, pp. 174-216), which was printed in the same year as *Romeus and Juliet*.

The poem itself nowhere suggests this sinister moral. The need to use it as a red herring may explain why nearly all narrative poetry of romantic coloring clung to the respectable themes of English history or classic myth. Though *Romeus and Juliet* was twice reprinted, it was very little imitated.[18]

Elizabethan narrative poets owed much to Virgil, who influenced them *Virgilian* not only in his Latin, but also in the extraordinary variety of taste and metre *Influences* represented through the translations of the *Æneid* by Gavin Douglas, Surrey, Phaer and Twyne, and Stanyhurst. Nicholas Grimald's two set-pieces, *The Death of Zoroas* and *Cicero's Death*,[19] must also have been much studied. Neither is strictly mythological, or even classical in a narrow sense, but they ranked as such, had a key position in Tottel's Miscellany, and, with Surrey's *Æneid,* were the earliest examples in English of the new "strange metre," blank verse.

The poetical anthologies following Tottel have their more lyrical contents *Renderings* interspersed with mythological tales, and half a dozen separate poems based *of Ovid* on Ovid appeared in the 1560's;[20] but the most influential poems of this type, and one might almost add, the most characteristically Elizabethan, were the direct translations of Ovid. Turberville's rendering of the *Heroides* (1567) is careful and intelligent work, particularly interesting because it shows the poet experimenting with three media: poulter's measure, "fourteeners," and blank verse. It went into at least half a dozen editions, but was outdone by Arthur Golding's contemporary version of the *Meta-* *Golding's* *morphoses* (1565, 1567),[21] which is more rugged poetry. The heptameter *Golding's* riming couplet, which Golding uses throughout, has nothing in common *Ovid* with the Latin hexameter except its length of line, and Golding's handling of it does little to conceal its fundamental lack of grace and variety. Nor is it likely that the delicately decadent Ovid ever had a translator more unlike him than this stout Calvinist,[22] whose effort was to force a serious moral interpretation upon the stories of the loves of the gods. It is probable and fortunate that Shakespeare read Ovid also in the original, but Golding's particular influence was very great. For example, from the philosophical verse epistle which Golding added in dedicating his translation to the Earl of Leicester, Shakespeare drew the conception of the "wheel of time" which he employs so brilliantly in his Sonnets,[23] and also the Puritan denunciation

---

[18] In this strain are Turberville's verse translations of ten Italian prose *novelle*, seven by Boccaccio (*Tragical Tales*, 1576?, 1587); and Gascoigne's *Dan Bartholmew of Bath* (1573). Particularly notable are three verse narratives in George Whetstone's *Rock of Regard* (1576). Two of these are rime royal "complaints" in the *Mirror for Magistrates* style, set in the mouths of the wicked Countess of Celant and of Cressida respectively. The third, in riming heptameter, tells a romantic story of Bohemian and Hungarian knights with affinity to the wager plot in *Cymbeline* and, more closely, to the plot of Massinger's play, *The Picture*. Whetstone's chief source is Painter's prose *Palace of Pleasure*.

[19] See L. R. Merrill, *The Life and Poems of Nicholas Grimald* (New Haven, 1925).

[20] See D. Bush, *Mythology and the Renaissance Tradition in English Poetry* (Minneapolis, 1932), pp. 301 ff, and "Classic Myths in English Verse, 1557-1589," *MP*, xxv (1927). 37-47.

[21] Ed. W. H. D. Rouse, *Shakespeare's Ovid* (1904).

[22] See L. T. Golding, *An Elizabethan Puritan* (1937).

[23] See Sidney Lee, "Ovid and Shakespeare's Sonnets," *Elizabethan and Other Essays* (1929), pp. 116-139.

of the theory of transmigration of souls, alluded to when Malvolio is asked, "What is the opinion of Pythagoras concerning wild fowl?" [24] Likewise, in the thirteenth book, it is Golding's railing Ajax and Ulysses, rather than their originals, that suggest Shakespeare's presentation of them in *Troilus and Cressida*.

Imitations of Ovid   It was some time before imitations of Ovid appeared in any number or worthiness. One of the earliest is Gascoigne's *Philomene,* which has an interesting history. He was riming it one day in April, 1562, "riding by the highway between Chelmsford and London," when a shower diverted his thoughts, and fourteen years passed before he completed it. It is a long poem, blending Ovidian narrative with the medieval dream vision, and is a good deal a song of the road, vigorous in narrative and full of bird notes and spring air. Matthew Grove's *Pelops and Hippodamia* (1587) tells a good story in Golding's metre and perhaps suffered from its antique style, *Peele's Tale of Troy*   for it had no success. Peele's *Tale of Troy* (1598) has the quaint flavor that usually attaches to the work of that interesting person. It is unlike any other piece of the time, and the particular occasion for it does not appear. Perhaps it represents an assembling of notes for *The Arraignment of Paris,* which it most likely preceded in date of composition; perhaps it was written on order from some unlearned citizen. In five hundred semi-jocose and negligently riming pentameters Peele digests all that one should know about the Troy business—skilfully, but with a cock of the eye.

Lodge, Scylla's Metamorphosis   Graceful description makes the merit of Lodge's long poem, *Scylla's Metamorphosis* (1589). It uses Ovid only as the nucleus of its story, and to readers who did not yet know Marlowe's or Shakespeare's powers in this style must rightly have seemed a pretty piece of invention. The six-line stanza is well modulated, and the tale moves pleasantly, bringing Glaucus the sea-god up the Thames to exchange sympathy with a modern lover, and later carrying them both (on dolphins for two) back to the waters of Sicily to attend the punishment of the heartless fair. Abraham Fraunce's *Amintas Dale* (1592) attempts to retell the salient tales of the *Metamorphoses* in sixteen examples of English hexameter verse, inset in pastoral prose. It is interesting chiefly as a metrical audacity.

The Heyday of Amatory Verse   The heyday of Elizabethan amatory verse was reached by the year 1594. The sonneteering carnival was at its height; Marlowe's great love poem and Shakespeare's two were out. The air was drowsy with languorous descriptions of fruit, birds, flowers, and the life of the senses. The two long poems of Thomas Edwards, *Cephalus and Procris* and *Narcissus,*[25] show with what copious though unthinking enthusiasm a minor writer could at this time set himself to out-Ovid Ovid. In *Cephalus and Procris* Edwards is more particularly imitating Marlowe, and in the other poem Shakespeare, but both these influences are discernible in either work. The Envoy to *Narcissus* has some notable lines on the late decease of Marlowe and his friend Thomas

[24] *Twelfth Night*, IV. ii. 55; Golding's Epistle, line 26.
[25] Entered Oct. 22, 1593, printed 1595; ed· W. E. Buckley (*Roxburghe Club,* 1882).

Watson (*c.* 1555-1592), whose Latin *Amintae Gaudia* of 1592 [26] was in much the same amorous style:

> Amintas and Leander's gone.
> O dear sons of stately kings,
> Blessed be your nimble throats,
> That so amorously could sing!

Marlowe's empty-headed admirer, Henry Petowe, marks a yet lower descent into day-dreaming absurdity. He had not the brains to be consistently Ovidian or anything else, but he luxuriated in romantic images and could spin well-sounding couplets and sixains. His *Hero and Leander's Further Fortunes* (1598) treats the myth as if it were an Italian novella and gives it a perfectly unclassical happy ending. His *Philochasander and Elanira* (1599) is rather more lyrical than narrative. It seems to have a medieval plot, but handles it most inconsequently.

In 1594 Chapman's *Shadow of Night* [27] clearly sounded the reaction, while Richard Barnfield's *Affectionate Shepherd* of the same year registers with nerveless beauty the full tide of paganism. Barnfield [28] (1574-1627) was a Shropshire lad with enough country background and Oxford training to make him a gourmet in amorous verse. It is the *Venus and Adonis* metre that he uses, and he reproduces the syrupy effect of Shakespeare's stanzas rather charmingly; but there is no real passion in his shepherd Daphnis, and the myth has evaporated in a pleasant wilderness of classical reminiscences, gnomic sayings, and florid garden pictures. For his second poem Barnfield, like Shakespeare, changed to rime royal and moralized more, but he omitted the story entirely, and *The Shepherd's Content,* "or the happiness of a harmless life" is just a plea for *dolce far niente.* In his next two poems, *Cynthia* and *Cassandra* (1595), he retells myths, borrowing the stanza of the former from the *Faerie Queene* and the plot from Peele's *Arraignment of Paris.* It would be wrong to blame his over-lavish borrowings or underrate his charm. He came at an idle moment, and was the idlest poet in it; but he had more worth than such rudderless boats as "J. C.", the author of *Alcilia* (1595), and Anthony Scolaker, the author of *Daiphantus* (1604). He tried to make personal the rich tropical calm that Shakespeare and Marlowe briefly dallied with; but discontent soon found Barnfield also. His two poems of 1598, still in the *Venus and Adonis* stanza, are *The Praise of Money* and *The Complaint of Poetry for the Death of Liberality.* [29]

Richard Barnfield

---

[26] See L. Bradner, *Musae Anglicanae* (1940), pp. 44-51.
[27] See below, Part III, ch. IX.
[28] Barnfield's poems are reprinted in A. H. Bullen, *Some Longer Elizabethan Poems* (1903), pp. 147-270.
[29] Here should be mentioned a mysterious character, William Goddard, who seems to have been a soldier and to have lived for a time in Holland. His *Satirical Dialogue . . . between Alexander the Great and That Truly Woman-hater Diogynes* (ed. J. S. Farmer, 1897) bears no date and claims to have been printed in the Low Countries, but may have been surreptitiously issued in London just after the ban on satire in 1599, to which it makes bitter reference. It is mainly in riming couplets and is largely narrative, Diogenes telling Alexander lewd stories to the discredit of women. The tones of Marlowe and of Marston are curiously intermingled.

There is no paganism, and only a tantalizingly vague thread of story in the famous *Willobie his Avisa*[30] (1594), which exhibits the successful and argumentative virtue of an innkeeper's wife in the country about Cerne Abbas, Dorset. The prefatory verses contain the first literary tribute to Shakespeare's *Lucrece,*

> And Shake-speare paints poor Lucrece' rape;

and it is probable that the "W. S.", who is briefly introduced as an experienced lover and "old player," is the great dramatist.[31] The poem was apparently written by an Oxford student, Henry Willoughby, and it made enough stir through half a dozen editions to indicate that some real scandal may have underlain its now harmless moralizing. Another Oxford student, Peter Coles, or Colse, replied to it in *Penelope's Complaint*[32] (1596), dedicated to Lady Horsey of Dorsetshire. Coles confessed to using "the same style and verse" as *Avisa,*—that is, tetrameter sixains grouped in brief snippets of dialogue; but he brought the subject back to the more conventional Greek legend.

Two years later Robert Tofte offered his *Alba,*[33] "the month's mind of a melancholy lover" (1598), in unshortened *Venus and Adonis* verse. It is more reflective than narrative, and like Tofte's more lyrical sequence, *Laura,* of the previous year, does not lack sweetness; but it is remembered now chiefly for its reference to one of Shakespeare's comedies:

> Love's Labor's Lost! I once did see a play
> Ycleped so, so called to my pain.

Alba resembles Willoughby's *Avisa,* in that it seems to rest on amatory experience of which all the contours have been prudentially blurred in the telling. The poet's mistress leaves him in London and withdraws to a village in northwest England, inferentially Warrington on the Mersey. He fills a hundred pages with complaints of his loneliness and her hard heart. Nothing could show plainer how the hot blood of *Hero and Leander* and *Venus and Adonis* had been cooled; yet Tofte found it proper to add a long apology to God *("Deo optimo, maximo")* in the same metre, which begins:

> With tears in eyes, with drops of blood from heart,
> With scalding sighs from inward grieved soul,
> A convertite from vain love now I part,

Goddard's *A Mastiff-whelp,* "imprinted amongst the Antipodes, and are to be sold where they are to be bought" (1599), and his later *Nest of Wasps* (Dort, 1615; ed. C. H. Wilkinson, Oxford, n.d.) illustrate the transition from cynical amatory narrative to the satirical epigram. The *Moriomachia* ("battle against folly," 1613) and *Philosopher's Satires* (1616; re-issued in 1617 as *Vice's Anatomy*) by Robert Anton of Magdalene College, Cambridge, continue the onslaught, but these are definitely Jacobean and rather in the manner of Joseph Hall.

[30] Ed. G. B. Harrison (1926).

[31] See Leslie Hotson, *I, William Shakespeare* (1938), pp. 53-70; T. Brooke, "Willobie's *Avisa,*" in *Essays in Honor of Albert Feuillerat* (New Haven, 1943), pp. 93-102.

[32] Reprinted by A. B. Grosart, *Occasional Issues,* XI (1880). 159-183.

[33] Reprinted Grosart, *op. cit.*

Whilst for my sins 'fore heaven I do condole.
I know and 'knowledge I have lived wrong,
And wilful sought mine own destruction long.

It is his *Hymn of Heavenly Love.*

Drayton's *Endimion and Phoebe*[34] (1595) has great dignity, like all the other work of that admirable man. There is day-dreaming in it, but "proud Momus," from whom he asks in his epilogue to be defended, could have found little to attack, and with *Venus and Adonis* in view would not have been tempted. The theme is that of Keats's *Endymion,* and the metre is the riming couplet which Marlowe had used and Keats was further to romanti-cize. It is not without profit to compare Drayton's forthright goddess with the high-fantastical deity of the later poet, for two ways of classicizing poetry are clearly distinguished. Impudence, on the other hand, is what marks the last significant mythological poem of the Elizabethan period, John Marston's maiden effort, *The Metamorphosis of Pygmalion's Image*[35] (1598). It is in spirit already beyond the period. Marston has no reverence for the myth, or interest in the story save as it permits him some fleshly sketches and witty comments. There had been nothing so Byronic before as the asides of this disillusioned young man over Pygmalion's plight; e.g.,

> And, therefore, ladies, think that they ne'er love you,
> Who do not unto more than kissing move you.

Essentially, Marston stands at the end of this tradition and annuls it by exposing it to the strain of merry mockery that had come in with Sir John Harington's translation of *Orlando Furioso* in 1591. A few beginners, to be sure, practised their pens by frank imitations of the elder masters. Thus Thomas Middleton, at the age of about nineteen, admires the long laments of Shakespeare's Lucrece, and in *The Ghost of Lucrece*[36] (1600) calls her back to earth in order to provide her with more in the same style. *Salmacis and Hermaphroditus*[37] (1602) is by an imitator of *Hero and Leander,* not impossibly the eighteen-year-old Francis Beaumont. He has admired Marlowe's myth-making propensity and so travesties it that his slight Ovidian plot is nearly lost in a vague *chronique scandaleuse* of the gods. The author is bright and ingenious, but he cannot yet tell a story. William Barksted, who as a boy actor in 1609 performed a part in Jonson's *Epicœne,* issued two years earlier an unpolished tribute to Shakespeare's influence, *Mirrha, the Mother of Adonis* (1607), while a certain H. A. produced a more work-manlike treatment of the same theme in *The Scourge of Venus*[38] (1613). A better poem is *Venus and Anchises (Britain's Ida),* written by young Phineas Fletcher (1582-1650) in imitation of Spenser.[39] It has an intricate

Drayton, Endimion and Phoeb

Marston, Pygmalion Image

---

[34] Ed. Hebel, I. 125-156.
[35] Separately printed, Golden Cockerel Press (1926). See D. Bush, *op. cit.,* pp. 177-180.
[36] Ed. J. Q. Adams (1937).
[37] Ed., *Shakespeare Soc. Papers,* III (1847). 98-126. See D. Bush, *op cit.,* pp. 180-183.
[38] Both these are edited by A. B. Grosart (1876), as well as Barksted's *Hiren, or The Fair Greek* (1611), which versifies a tale that had had considerable vogue on the stage.
[39] Ed. E. Seaton (1926).

Renaissance stanza and the sense of pure harmony which the Spenserians kept after every one else had given it up.

*ilosoph-
l Poetry
As the poetry of sensation reached its mellow maturity in 1593-94 and rapidly waned, there came in a poetry of idea such as had been little in evidence before. Some of the underlying impulse expressed itself in the flood of critical epigrams that filled the later 1590's; some of it prepared the way for the "metaphysicals," and, as illustrated in Ralegh and Chapman, will be discussed in Part III. A very typical *fin de siècle* poet is Sir John *r John
avies* Davies [40] (1569-1626), who had one of the best brains of the century and put it to strange tasks. His epigrams, published with Marlowe's translation of Ovid's *Amores,* are as witty and doubtless as coarse as any. From the group of forty-eight one could organize a remarkably detailed account of the way some men lived. His twenty-four *Hymns of Astraea* (1599), all in the same metre and all acrostically spelling "ELISABETHA REGINA," are a triumph of ingenuity, and do not lack either melody or sense. His long poem, *Orchestra* [41] (1594), in rime royal, is a more exhausting *tour de force.* It starts epically with Antinous inviting Queen Penelope to dance, an excuse for the poet to assemble thirty pages of dancing metaphors out of earth and sea and sky, illustrated by a vast amount of learning and casuistry. Davies' *magnum opus* is the truly impressive philosophical poem, *Nosce Teipsum* (1599), in which he argues the nature of the soul (or perhaps the mind) and its immortality through fifty pages of extremely easy and well phrased quatrains. The subject, it might be thought, is hardly suited either to a professional lawyer or to the trammels of stanzaic verse, but Davies seems little embarrassed by either handicap; and from time to time *Nosce Teipsum* is rediscovered by amateurs who laud it beyond idolatry.

*Daniel's
Musophilus*
There was no Elizabethan poet more concerned with the idea of his future fame than Samuel Daniel. He seems to have posterity constantly in view, with a modest assurance; and posterity, if it has not answered his expectations, has been friendly to him. In *Musophilus* (1599) he builds up the case for the literary man to the length of over a thousand lines, against a worldly man, Philocosmus. What he says is noble. Part of it is said by Milton in *Lycidas;* but Milton was not prolix or apologetic.[42]

Paradise Lost is sometimes loosely thought of as the last Elizabethan long poem, but it would be more exact to give the title to Drayton's earthier,

---

[40] See A. H. Bullen, *Some Longer Elizabethan Poems* (1903), pp. 1-122; A. B. Grosart, *Complete Poems of Sir John Davies* (2v, 1876); facsimile ed., C. Howard (1941). See M. D. Holmes, *The Poet as Philosopher* (Philadelphia, 1921).

[41] Ed. E. M. W. Tillyard (1945).

[42] The tendency to replace poetry of action by poetry of reflection is illustrated by two long poems on the deaths of heroic figures: *The Most Honorable Tragedy of Sir Richard Grinvile Knight,* in *ottava rima,* by Gervase Markham, 1595 (reprinted, E. Arber, 1871); and *Sir Francis Drake, his Honorable Life's Commendation and his Tragical Death's Lamentations* by Charles Fitzgeoffrey, 1596. The latter, though its nearly 300 rime royal stanzas are too lush in style, contains the better poetry. (See *The Poems of Charles Fitzgeoffrey,* ed. A. B. Grosart, 1881). Neither contains much narrative or descriptive matter, though the subjects might naturally have invited such treatment.

longer, and more Renaissance *Poly-Olbion*.[43] Even it hardly falls quite within
the limits; it was, of course, a long time in writing. The first part was not
printed till 1613, and the second part only in 1622; but, as Meres tells us,[44]
it was already well started in 1598, and it is but the homelier and fuller
carrying out of a plan of Spenser's youth. It is a drowsy, frowsy poem like
the *Excursion,* which its admirers never lose their taste for. It runs on in its
hexameter couplets almost as endlessly as one of the English brooks that
it describes, and bears along a silt of disparate facts such as only a Renaissance
mind could assemble. Yet it has a unifying spirit, which is the heroic love
of every British natural object, and a simple method, which is that of
personification. Here we have the marriage of the Isis and Tame and the
Thames and Medway, the orations of the mountains of Wales, the catalogues
of famous captains and British brave sea-voyagers. The poem was finished
in the seventeenth century, but that century could hardly have conceived it,
for it lacked the solidarity of national feeling and the sense of the paganism
of nature. In *Poly-Olbion* not only the streams and hills but the highroads
have their immanent deities, and there is no faith but one, whose prophetess
is the Queen. It is doubtful whether the mythological tendency on its simplest
levels has had such large expression since the early Greeks, or whether
anything more typically Elizabethan has survived.

[43] In Hebel's edition of Drayton, the entire fourth volume (1933) is devoted to *Poly-Olbion*.
See M. Marten, *Draytons "Poly-Olbion" im Rahmen der englischen Renaissance* (Münster, 1934).
The title of the poem means "The Land of Many Blessings," with a pun, of course, on "Albion."
[44] D. C. Allen, *Francis Meres's Treatise "Poetrie,"* (Urbana, 1933), p. 75.

Prose Narrative:[1] I. Lyly and His Predecessors

Books

When Beatrice is alleged to have had her good wit "out of the Hundred Merry Tales," [2] it is implied that she depends upon the most archaic source of inspiration an Elizabethan could well have resorted to. The book in question was printed by John Rastell about 1525 as *A C. Mery Talys,* and was followed a decade later by T. Berthelet's *Tales and Quick Answers, Very Mery and Pleasant to Rede.* In its ultimate form, *Merry Tales, Witty Questions, & Quick Answers* (1567), it contained 113 brief selections of a sportive nature, calculated for a pre-Reformation public.[3] Some are mere jests, some classical anecdotes or *exempla* from such authors as Aulus Gellius, and some are rapidly told fabliaux. Several of them reappeared in Painter's *Palace of Pleasure.* The majority are well told and really witty, and usually there is a shrewd or surprising moral at the end. The tales of the radish root given to King Louis of France and of the man who paid his debt with crying "baa!" [4] are admirable examples of the short story; and there is merit even in so brief a *jeu d'esprit* as the one "Of the Beggar's answer to Master Skelton the poet":

A poor beggar that was foul, black, and loathly to behold, came upon a time unto Master Skelton the poet, and asked him his alms. To whom Master Skelton said: I pray thee, get thee away from me, for thou lookest as though thou camest out of hell. The poor man, perceiving he would give him nothing, answered: Forsooth, sir, ye say truth: I came out of hell. Why diddest thou not tarry still there? quod Master Skelton. Marry, sir, quod the beggar, there is no room for such poor beggars as I am; all is kept for such gentlemen as ye be.

William Bullein d. 1576)

Here, perhaps, belongs William Bullein's strangely vivid *Dialogue against the Fever Pestilence* [5] (1564-5), which, though in the form of a loosely linked series of dialogues between contemporary type-figures, and full of pungent

---

[1] *The English Novel in the Time of Shakespeare* by J. J. Jusserand (1890) is still an attractive introduction to the subject. E. A. Baker, *The History of the English Novel,* Vol. II: *The Elizabethan Age and After* (1929), may be consulted. For bibliography see A. Esdaile, *A List of English Tales and Prose Romances printed before 1740* (1912). R. Pruvost, *Matteo Bandello and Elizabethan Fiction* (Paris, 1937), contains much information.

[2] *Much Ado about Nothing,* II. i. 137.

[3] See for texts W. C. Hazlitt, *Shakespeare's Jest-Books* (3v, 1864), and for the bibliography, which is complicated, consult F. P. Wilson, "The English Jestbooks of the 16. and early 17. Century," *HLQ,* II (1938). 121-158.

[4] This is from the French farce, *Maître Pathelin,* or some congener.

[5] Ed. M. W. and A. H. Bullen (1888; *EETSES,* 52). See A. H. Bullen, *Elizabethans* (1924), pp. 155-181. Little is known of Bullein's life. The more technical parts of his *Dialogue* and his earlier books, *The Government of Health* (1558) and *Bulwark of Defence against All Sickness,* etc. (1562), show that he stood in the medical tradition of Elyot and Borde (see above, Part I, chs. II and IV).

satire against usurers, doctors, lawyers, Scots, Papists, etc., is largely a collection of tall tales within a framing narrative. A wealthy London citizen and his wife, unable to endure the horrors of the 1564 plague, ride into the country in search of safety, accompanied by their man Roger, who has a great supply of folk tales and fables. Beyond Barnet they dine in an inn adorned with emblematic pictures and hear a certain Mendax tell marvelous stories of Cuba (where the cannibals dwell), of Ethiopia, and other singular countries. Later in their journey a storm overtakes them, and in the storm comes Death, bearing the dart of the pestilence which the old citizen has not escaped. Bullein's book, which is by turns both grim and gay, exotic and acridly realistic, was deservedly popular. By 1578 it had been considerably revised and had gone through three editions.

The influence of the fabliau gave place to that of the erotic *novella* in William Painter's great collection of one hundred and one tales, *The Palace of Pleasure*, published in two volumes, 1566, 1567.[6] Painter (*c.* 1525-1594), a Kentish schoolmaster advanced by Ambrose, Earl of Warwick to a post in the national service,[7] inscribed his work to that nobleman, whose countess simultaneously received the dedication of Turberville's poems. Painter's dedicatory epistle informs us that his original purpose had been to prepare a collection of classical tales out of Livy. The first stories are of that general character,[8] and perhaps represent the lost book registered in 1562 under the title of "*The City of Civility*, translated into English by William Painter"; but Livy's "majesty" offered difficulties and Painter turned to the more congenial task of introducing Englishmen to the love stories of Boccaccio, Bandello, Queen Margaret of Navarre, and other modern *novellieri*, by whom, as he tells his reader, "The sad shall be discharged of heaviness, the angry and choleric purged, the pleasant maintained in mirth, the whole [i.e. healthy] furnished with disport, and the sick appaised [i.e. relieved] of grief."

Shakespeare found here the source of *All's Well That Ends Well*, and also, it may be, his first acquaintance with the stories of Lucrece, Coriolanus, Timon of Athens, and Romeo and Juliet. Other dramatists who used this reservoir of plot include Fletcher, Webster, Massinger, Shirley, Thomas Heywood, and, in particular, Marston. Painter's style is good and plain; he has few recondite terms and is mainly concerned to make the reader see the situation; as in this picture of an encouraged lover:

He, that marched not but upon one foot and burned with love, and whose heart leapt for joy and danced for gladness, thought that he had now obtained the top of his felicity and the whole effect of his desire. Suddenly he cast away the despair of his former conceits, objecting [i.e., exposing] himself to the danger wherein

Painter, *The* *Palace of* *Pleasure*

---

[6] Reprinted (Cresset Press, 4v, 1929) with introduction by Hamish Miles. Ten of the tales are in P. Haworth, *An Elizabethan Story-Book* (1928).
[7] Clerk of the ordnance in the Tower of London. Painter was charged with embezzling public property with the connivance of the Earl, but he continued to hold office till his death.
[8] See D. Bush, "The Classical Tales in Painter's *Palace of Pleasure*," *JEGP*, XXIII (1924), 331-341.

he was to be overwhelmed if the lady accepted not his request with good digestion.[9]

In the very year after Painter's first volume appeared with its dedication to the Earl of Warwick, Geoffrey Fenton (*c.* 1539-1608) issued a similar work with a long dedication to Warwick's sister, the Lady Mary Sidney, mother of Sir Philip. Fenton, who later attained knighthood and considerable notoriety as a political agent in Ireland, was at the time only about twenty-eight. His *Tragical Discourses* [10] (1567) consists of thirteen tales of Bandello, translated through the medium of Boisteau and Belleforest's French.

Fenton is not a very pleasing writer. His sentences are heavy with moral clichés and he has a curious disposition to overuse certain favorite words like *glee, humor, haunt, imp,* and the unanglicized French terms he had picked up in Paris. More even than the other writers of *novelle,* he puts long speeches into the mouths of his characters and makes them all speak alike. His choice of tales was praised by the first writer to call critical attention to them, Thomas Warton,[11] who describes his book as "in point of selection and size, perhaps the most capital miscellany of this kind," and indeed they are good tales; but Fenton—aiming perhaps at his patroness, who was a great lady and the particular friend of the Queen—gives them a specialized female interest that goes beyond Bandello and is not pretty. More than Painter, he illustrates the "Italianate" taint which Ascham at just this time was denouncing in the *Schoolmaster;* but the taint, both in the moral and the literary sense, would be less serious if Fenton were franker and more Italian. Belleforest had vitiated Bandello by overlaying his paganism with a moral veneer, and Fenton carries the process further. In his versions of the tales the interpolations and asides on the subject of chastity suggest an unhealthy Puritan obsession and fit very ill with the leering quality of his carnal passages, which are varied and voluptuously illustrated beyond Elizabethan wont. Fenton's style has a good deal of what one finds later in the dramas of Fletcher, the same overwrought morality and fluent emotionalism; as in this speech of Charles Montamin to his sister when demanding of her a more than quixotic sacrifice:

But if your answer put me either in doubt or despair of this means to make even with so true a creditor, assure yourself I will rather abandon both city and country and disclaim the company of all my friends than live amongst you with the name of an unthankful person, or be pointed at of the world not to requite so great a good turn as the delivery and saving of my life.[12]

[9] No. 41, "A Lady Falsely Accused."
[10] Reprinted in "Broadway Translations" series with introduction by R. L. Douglas. Unpublished diss. (Yale), J. Fellheimer, *Geoffrey Fenton, a Study in Elizabethan Translation* (1941).
[11] *History of English Poetry* (1781).
[12] *Ed. cit.,* p. 95. To this date belongs also the only publication of Edmund Tilney (d. 1610), who as Master of the Revels, 1579-1608, was a man of some importance. His collection is dedicated to the Queen and entitled, *A Brief and Pleasant Discourse of Duties in Marriage, called the Flower of Friendship* (1568). In a luxuriantly described spring the author and M.

George Pettie (*c.* 1548-1589) was rather more a gentleman and less a   *Pettie's*
puritan than Fenton. Of his life little is known except that he graduated   Petite
B. A. from Christ Church, Oxford, in 1570, saw military service abroad, and   Palace
was the great-uncle of the Oxford antiquary, Anthony Wood. For the
collection of twelve tales to which his editor gave the punning title, *A Petite
Palace of Pettie his Pleasure* [13] (1576), he took many hints from Painter,
but he ignored the Italian *novelle* which Fenton had rather garishly exploited. Pettie's graver taste turned in one instance to medieval legend (St.
Alexius), and in all the rest to classic myth. He is not, however, a translator,
even in the free way his predecessors in the Elizabethan short story had
been. He brings his myths out of antiquity and covers them over with the
details of sixteenth-century life. Pasiphae is a waiting gentlewoman in King
Minos' court with a suitor, Verecundus, who might be any impressionable
young friend of Philip Sidney; Pygmalion is a gentleman of Piedmont and
doesn't take to sculpture till after three quarters of the tale have recounted
his most unclassical disappointment in Platonic love; Cephalus and Procris
live in the Duke of Venice's court, and though they suffer the fate the myth
assigns, the circumstances are of a very modern kind.

The most interesting thing about Pettie is his manner, which is the most
consciously artificial that had yet appeared in English prose. He uses most
of the tricks of alliteration, antithesis, and simile from alleged natural history
which two years later gave fame to the style of *Euphues.* The resemblance
is often so striking as to make it almost certain that Lyly is his imitator;
e.g.,

as spices, the more they are beaten, the sweeter scent they send forth; or as the
herb camomile, the more it is trodden down, the more it spreadeth abroad; so
virtue and honesty, the more it is spited, the more it sprouteth and
springeth...[14]

for as the bird caught in the lime, or coney in hay [i.e., net], or deer in toil, the
more they strive the faster they stick; so the more diligently she labored to get
out of the labyrinth of love, the more doubtfully was she intricated therein.[15]

Ah, the bravery of these fine girls! the more they are courted, the more they are
coy; the more humbly they are sued unto, the more loftily they look. And if a
man practise them in the way of marriage, good God, what show of shame-

---

Pedro di Juxan walk in fields till noon, then dine at Lady Julia's house, where they meet
Lodovico Vives "and an old gentleman called M. Erasmus." After talk of Boccace and County
Baltizer (Castiglione) they go into a flowery arbor, where Pedro discourses to them of the
nine "herbs" or requisites of a husband in guiding his married life. A continuation deals with
"The office or duty of the married woman."
  [13] Ed. H. Hartman (1938). See M. P. Tilley, *Elizabethan Proverb Lore in Lyly's "Euphues"
and in Pettie's "Petite Palace" with Parallels from Shakespeare* (1926); D. Bush, "Pettie's
Petty Pilfering from Poets," *PQ*, v (1926). 325-329; "The Petite Pallace of Pettie his Pleasure,"
JEGP, xxvii (1928). 162-169; C. J. Vincent, "Pettie and Greene," *MLN*, liv (1939). 105-111;
J. Swart, "Lyly and Pettie," *English Studies*, xxiii (1941). 910-918.
  [14] *Ed. cit.*, p. 29; compare *Euphues*, ed. Bond, p. 191.16 and 196.3, and Shakespeare,
I Henry IV, ii. iv. 447 ff.
  [15] *Ed. cit.*, p. 75.

fastness will they make, what visors of virginity will they put on, what colors of continency will they set forth, what chariness will they make of their chastity! [16]

ange and
lbancke   John Grange's only recorded work is a novelistic *novella, The Golden Aphroditis* [17] (1577), which fills the brief interval between the *Petite Palace* and *Euphues* with an almost biological symmetry and further illustrates the fact that Lyly was more expressive of a movement than of an individual taste. Like Pettie, Grange handles a mythological tale in very modern fashion, but like Lyly he invents his slight plot, which concerns the successful suit of a certain Sir N. O. for the Lady A. O. (Alpha Omega), who is no less than the daughter of the goddess Diana and Endymion. The narrative is interspersed with songs in the manner Greene and Lodge made popular, and the prose is encrusted with proverbial, lapidary, pseudo-classical ornaments borrowed from the borrowers of Pliny and Erasmus.[18] Still more characteristic of the taste for extraneous and plundered adornment is another obscure one-book novelist, Brian Melbancke, whose *Philotimus* (1583) follows *Euphues* in date, but gets its plot mainly from the first story in Pettie's collection and its style from practically any contemporary book that came Melbancke's way.[19]

ascoigne,
dventures
F. J.   The most interesting piece of Elizabethan prose fiction, when viewed as a remote ancestor of the novels of Richardson and Meredith, is the lively sketch of English country-house life by George Gascoigne, which was published in 1573 as *The Adventures of Master F. J.* Though it may owe a little to Pope Pius II's *History of Lucrece and Eurialus,*[20] which had appeared thrice in English translation between 1550 and 1567, it has no similarity to the tales of Painter, Fenton, or Pettie. Where the *novella* usually offers sensational incident and slender characterization, Gascoigne does the reverse. He depicts to the length of 25,000 words the emotions and day-by-day lives of a group of idle gentlefolk in a great house in northern England. There are no exciting or melancholy events. The hero, a guest in the house, fails to reciprocate the affection of the charming daughter of his host, Frances, and instead engages in a clandestine affair with Elinor, the daughter-in-law. When Elinor jilts him for another lover, F. J. quietly takes his leave; Frances remains unwed, virgin, and not too downcast; and Elinor goes on with her

[16] *Ed. cit.*, p. 170. Two slightly later collections of tales are of importance as sources of plays: Henry Wotton's *Courtly Controversy of Cupid's Cautels* (1578), containing five stories translated from French; and Whetstone's *Heptameron of Civil Discourses* (1582).

[17] Reprinted (1939) in *Scholars' Facsimiles and Reprints.* The volume contains also *Grange's Garden,* a collection of short pieces in verse and prose.

[18] See P. W. Long, "From *Troilus* to *Euphues,*" in *Kittredge Anniversary Papers* (1913), pp. 367-376; H. E. Rollins, "John Grange's *The Golden Aphroditis,*" *Harvard Studies & Notes in Phil. & Lit.,* XVI (1934). 177-198. Two somewhat similar prose tales with metrical inserts are found in Whetstone's *Rock of Regard* (1576): "Rinaldo and Giletta" and "The Orchard of Repentance." The former is a complex story of lovers brought into temporary distress by a villain's wiles; the latter has the appearance of being autobiographical.

[19] See H. E. Rollins, "Notes on Brian Melbancke's *Philotimus,*" *SP,* extra series, I (1929). 40-57; "Notes on the Sources of Melbancke's *Philotimus,*" *Harvard Studies & Notes in Phil. & Lit.,* XVIII (1935). 177-198; "Thomas Deloney and Brian Melbancke," *ibid.,* XIX (1936). 219-229; M. P. Tilley, "Further Borrowings from Poems in *Philotimus,*" *SP,* XXVII (1929). 186-204; D. C. Allen, "Melbancke and Gosson," *MLN,* LIV (1939). 111-114.

[20] Reprinted (*Roxburghe Club,* 1873) with John Partridge's *History of Plasidas.*

philanderings. Besides the three chief characters certain others are presented with a good deal of distinctness, and the ordinary occupations of such a group are realistically depicted: games, dancing, tale-telling and verse-making, walks and rides in the park, and sociable little gatherings in bedrooms when some one is indisposed. It has the air of being drawn from life; but when Gascoigne published it under his own name in 1575, he took a number of self-protective steps, adding an apologetic epistle to "the reverend divines" who had suspected scandal in it, changing the scene to Italy, and excising the more immoral passages. The effect was to close a door which had for the nonce been very invitingly opened.[21]

John Lyly [22] (1554-1606) took fewer risks three years later in the first part *John Lyly* of his *Euphues* (1578). Grandson of the famous grammarian, Lyly had been well bred in Kent and carefully educated at Oxford. He was one of the most exquisite persons of his age, and if a hint in the autobiography of his fellow collegian, Simon Forman, has been properly interpreted,[23] the slender narra-   *Euphues:* tive plot of *Euphues* is based upon what actually happened between the   *The Anat-* author, the mayor's daughter of Brackley near Oxford, and John Thorn-   *omy of Wit* borough during Lyly's college days; but this was never admitted in the novel, which from the first set the story in Italy. Nothing could be much simpler than this tale. Euphues, a foppish Athenian, goes to Naples to lead a life of pleasure and there forms an intimate friendship with another young man, Philautus, who introduces him to his fiancée, Lucilla, daughter of "one of the chief governors of the city." Euphues deceitfully alienates Lucilla's affections, whereupon he and Philautus exchange taunting letters; but when the fickle Lucilla discards Euphues for a third suitor, they decide ·to be friends again, and Euphues returns to Athens. There is far less human interest or graphic detail than in Gascoigne's story, which is of nearly the same length; and Lyly is staggeringly moral: nothing in the least risqué occurs.

The book is sub-titled *The Anatomy of Wit* and makes it appeal to the intelligence rather than the emotions or even the conscience. The narrative is but half the work and is followed by a long epistolary essay against love, called "a cooling card for Philautus and all fond lovers"; a paraphrase of Plutarch's tract on the education of children, which Sir Thomas Elyot had translated long before (here called "Euphues and his Ephebus"); a controversial dialogue between Euphues and an easily converted atheist; and

[21] See L. Bradner, "The First English Novel: A Study of George Gascoigne's *Adventures of Master F. J.*," *PMLA*, XLV (1930). 543-552; also P. W. Long, "From *Troilus* to *Euphues*," cited in note 18 above.
[22] R. W. Bond, *Complete Works of John Lyly* (3v, Oxford, 1902); A. Feuillerat, *John Lyly: Contribution à l'histoire de la renaissance en Angleterre* (Cambridge, 1910); S. A. Tannenbaum, *John Lyly, a Concise Bibliography* (1940). The separate edition of *Euphues* by M. W. Croll and H. Clemens (1916) is very useful. Rose Macaulay has a pleasant essay on "Lyly and Sidney" in D. Verschoyle, *The English Novelists* (1936), pp. 33-50. The Euphuistic style, discussed in the works of Bond, Feuillerat, and Croll just cited, is carefully analyzed by C. G. Child, *John Lyly and Euphuism* (Munich, 1894). For a recent interesting theory of its origin see W. Ringler, "The Immediate Source of Euphuism," *PMLA*, LIII (1938). 678-686, and Ringler's introduction to John Rainolds, *Oratio in Laudem Artis Poeticae* (Princeton, 1940). For further discussion of Lyly and his style, see below, ch. VI.
[23] See Feuillerat, *op. cit.*, pp. 274 f.

finally, a set of rhetorical letters "writ by Euphues to his friends." It is a strange amalgam of mercurial wit and very heavy metal. That it was phenomenally popular every one knows; that it could have been is evidence that England in Lyly's time was still far more moved by the humanistic ideals that Ascham stood for than by those of the new Italian school he condemned. Verbal ingenuity, sententiousness, and weighty learning lightly handled were what most appealed to a society painfully conscious of its cultural limitations; and no one quite equalled Lyly in these respects till Bacon, or perhaps till Addison, wrote their essays.[24]

Euphues and His England

The second part, called *Euphues and His England* (1580), has a little more coherence and a still more artful style. Euphues and Philautus embark at Naples, and after eight weeks land at Dover. They visit Canterbury and, traveling Londonwards, pause at the country house of an old man, Fidus, who tells them something of the glory of the Queen and illustrates the laws of monarchy by the domestic economy of his honey bees, as later the Archbishop of Canterbury does in Shakespeare's *Henry V*. He also relates the story of his sad and chaste love for Iffida. Thus adjusted to the moral climate of the island, the visitors reach London and the court, "in the which Euphues took such delight that he accounted all the praises he heard of it before rather to be envious than otherwise, and to be partial in not giving so much as it deserved, and yet to be pardoned because they could not." The impressionable Philautus is devastated by his first sight of an English maid of honor, Camilla, whose chaste perfections strain the utmost powers of Lyly's rhetoric:

...oftentimes delighted to hear discourses of love, but ever desirous to be instructed in learning; somewhat curious to keep her beauty, which made her comely, but more careful to increase her credit, which made her commendable: not adding the length of a hair to courtliness that might detract the breadth of a hair from chastity; in all her talk so pleasant, in all her looks so amiable, so grave modesty joined with so witty mirth, that they that were entangled with her beauty were enforced to prefer her wit before their wills, and they that loved her virtue were compelled to prefer their affections before her wisdom. Whose rare qualities caused so strange events, that the wise were allured to vanity and the wantons to virtue: much like the river in Arabia, which turneth gold to dross and dirt to silver.

After an intolerable amount of soliloquizing, the lovesick wretch betrays his infatuation to Euphues, who, for reasons not clear to a modern reader, rebukes him as savagely as if he were a backsliding Trappist monk; and to Camilla, whose response is unkind in the extreme:

I never looked for a better tale of so ill a face; you say a bad color may make good countenance, but he that conferreth your disordered discourse with your deformed attire may rightly say that he never saw so crabbed a visage, nor heard so crooked a vein.

[24] The immediate popularity of the first part of *Euphues* is illustrated by the rapid appearance of a narrative constructed on the same principle and in imitative style, Stephen Gosson's *Ephemerides* (i.e., Diary) *of Phialo*, which was entered on the Stationers' Register Nov. 7, 1579, and published the same year.

The moral seems to be, to put it mildly, that lovemaking is frowned upon at Queen Elizabeth's court. More soliloquy leads to a visit to Psellus the sorcerer, which brings the distraught lover nothing but seven pages of curious classical lore about herbs and minerals. He therefore writes an ultra-Euphuistic letter, which he delivers, hidden in a pomegranate, on an occasion when Camilla "suddenly complained of an old disease wherewith she many times felt herself grieved, which was an extreme heat in the stomach." The delicate Camilla replies with written discouragement, "stitched into an Italian Petrarch" and delivered by hand at the next social gathering. More letters offer more samples of epistolary grace and are exchanged at delightfully described parties, but Philautus makes no progress in his love. Camilla prefers an English suitor, the noble Surius, and at last, by the advice of the incomparable Euphues and the help of the wise lady Flavia, her Italian worshipper is induced to fix his affections upon a less unattainable object. This result is expedited by a supper party that Flavia gives, at which the guests exhibit, for a prize, their best specimens of courtly discourse. The subject is, of course, love, and the opinions mainly Platonic.

There seems to be no reason why Euphues should ever cease to depict the stately charms of the Elizabethan court, but arbitrarily "serious and weighty affairs of his own," hitherto quite unsuspected, require his return to Athens, "out of England," as he says, "a place in my opinion (if any such may be in the earth) not inferior to a Paradise." For the improvement of the ladies and gentlewomen of Italy he writes what he calls "Euphues' glass for Europe," which in the beginning is a paraphrase of William Harrison's recent description of England,[25] and in the last fifteen pages a portrait of Queen Elizabeth, probably the most elaborately flattering that that much flattered sovereign ever received.

In addition to all the stylistic charms of the *Anatomy of Wit, Euphues and His England* had two allurements that the fashionable public of the day found irresistible. In the first place, it was all transparently about themselves, the scene being London, the characters the highest circle of society, and the time (as numerous dates and allusions reminded them) the very year in which the volume appeared. And, in the second place, Lyly was most careful to depict them, not as they were, but as they would have liked to have themselves regarded. They would have spoken and behaved somewhat like the people in his pages, if they had been infinitely cleverer and a great deal more righteous than they were. It was only much later that the level-headed Drayton found courage to assert that Lyly taught the English to speak and write "all like mere lunatics."[26] Edward Blount's preface to Lyly's *Six Court Comedies* (1632), in a time when under Queen Henrietta Maria all the English court was French, illustrates the influence of *Euphues* with a striking figure:

---

[25] Published with Holinshed's Chronicle (1577).
[26] To Henry Reynolds, "Of Poets and Poesy" (1627).

Our nation are in his debt for a new English which he taught them. *Euphues and his England* began first that language. All our ladies were then his scholars, and that beauty in court which could not parley Euphuism was as little regarded as she which now there speaks not French.

Euphues was silly, but it stood soundly in the moral tradition of Lyly's humanist grandfather, William Lyly the grammarian, and Charles Kingsley's nineteenth-century tribute, though surprising, is in no way undeserved: "as brave, righteous, and pious a book as a man need look into." If Queen Elizabeth's maids of honor, who gave their days and nights to the volumes of Lyly, had emulated the conduct of his characters as assiduously as they strove to imitate his language, the social chronicles of that time would have made far tamer reading.

IV

Prose Narrative: II. Greene and His Followers

In the twentieth century Robert Greene [1] (1560-1592) could hardly have *Greene's* escaped becoming a journalist. He had in remarkable degree the "nose for *Personality* news," the untiring pen, the ability to give the public just what the public wanted. He was the literary chameleon of his age, imitating, often superficially but usually with a certain added charm, anything that his contemporaries had successfully created. There is no more typical Elizabethan than Greene, brought up as he was at Norwich rather poorly and rather puritanically, educated at Cambridge rather broadly than deeply, seasoned by Italian travel, and experienced, on the one hand, in all the squalors of lowest London and, on the other (as his dedications show), in all the arts of social blandishment. These things, plus endless energy and a personal attractiveness that still reflects itself in what he wrote, made him a man of the first note, though as an author he seldom rose above the second rank.

It was impossible for such a man to ignore the popularity of *Euphues,* or *Greene's* fail to see how the formula could be improved by increasing the love interest *Euphuistic* and accelerating the narrative. So, in the ten years that followed the publica- *Romances* tion of Lyly's *Euphues and His England,* Greene turned out a score of little novels, seldom much over a hundred pages in length, which have a great outward variety and a great fundamental sameness. The first part of *Mamillia,* "a mirror or looking-glass for the ladies of England" (entered on the Stationers' Register in October, 1580), tells how Mamillia, daughter of the Duke of Padua, has a virtuous admirer, Florion, and a wily pursuer, Pharicles. Her father proposes to marry her to Pharicles, who, however, is smitten by the beauty of Mamillia's cousin, Publia, and decides to pretend love to both girls, being "a perfect pattern of lovers in these our days." He allows himself to be formally affianced to Mamillia, but exchanges love letters with Publia. When Mamillia hears of his dissembling, he decamps for Sicily. In the second part (entered, 1583) Pharicles has become the friend of Feragus, son of the governor of "Saragossa," capital of Sicily. He rebuffs Clarinda, a proud and wealthy courtesan, who denounces him as a spy, and he is about to be executed when Mamillia arrives, discloses Clarinda's duplicity, and marries him. In the meantime Publia has entered a nunnery and

---

[1] See A. B. Grosart, *Life and Complete Works of Robert Greene* (15v, 1881-6); R. Pruvost, *Robert Greene et ses romans* (Paris, 1938); S. A. Tannenbaum, *Robert Greene, a Concise Bibliography* (1939). A number of the pamphlets by Greene and relating to him are conveniently available in the "Bodley Head Quartos" (1923-4). The novelized life of Greene, *Garland of Bays,* by Gwyn Jones (1938) is of interest and value.

left her fortune to Pharicles. The worthy Florion has been quite forgotten, and so have the author's doubts concerning Pharicles.

The Mirror of Modesty (1584), dedicated to the Countess of Derby, is the story of Susanna, told with a lack of artifice for which Greene apologizes; but *Gwydonius, or The Card of Fancy* (i.e., chart of love), published in the same year and dedicated to the Earl of Oxford, is one of Greene's most elaborate fictions. *Morando, the Tritameron* (i.e., three days) *of Love,* dedicated to the Earl of Arundel, is like *Mamillia* in two parts (1584, 1587), and lays more stress upon the Renaissance taste for philosophic debate. The influence of Castiglione is clear. *Arbasto, the Anatomy of Fortune* (1584) sets the romantic tale within a melancholy frame. The undescribed narrator, visiting Sidon, sees in a hermitage an old archflamen (priest) "pouring forth streams of waterish tears," who plays a "dump" about fortune and then tells his story. He was once Arbasto, King of Denmark, who, while warring against the French king, fell in love with the latter's daughter, Doralicia. She scorned him, but her sister Myrania became enamoured, released him from prison, fled with him to Denmark, and died of a broken heart when she discovered his indifference. Doralicia then repents and offers love, but is rebuffed and she too dies, whereupon Arbasto's subjects revolt and banish him, and he finds content in his hermit's cell.

In *Planetomachia,* dedicated to the Earl of Leicester (1585), the frame is a quarrelsome discussion between the seven Ptolemaic "planets." Venus relates a tragedy, not unlike *Romeo and Juliet,* of two lovers in Ferrara, who are destroyed by the saturnine malignity of the lady's father; and Saturn retorts with a tale of Venus's balefulness. A Homeric theme is developed in *Penelope's Web* (1587), dedicated to the sister countesses of Cumberland and Warwick; and another Homeric subject inspires a balancing romance of the same year, *Euphues his Censure to Philautus* (1587), which is dedicated to the Earl of Essex and "aimeth at the exquisite portraiture of a perfect martialist." The title of this novel has no appropriateness, unless to avow Greene's continued discipleship to Lyly, from whose method he was in fact steadily departing. In *Alcida, or Greene's Metamorphosis,* registered in December, 1588, Ovid is the remote model, and the narrator is ship-wrecked on the island of Taprobane (Ceylon) in the Antarctic seas. In *Perimedes the Blacksmith* (1588) the poor smith and his wife Delia (who were probably borrowed by Peele for his *Old Wives' Tale*) dwell in Memphis respected by the Egyptians for their industry and contentment. Conjugal discourse on the blessings of humble life leads to tales of very romantic quality, from which one would infer that Greene had been reading Ariosto and the *novelle.*

Greene's *Pandosto, the Triumph of Time* (1588) provided Shakespeare with the plot of *The Winter's Tale,* though offering no hint for Autolycus or for the statue scene. It was the most popular of all these romances and remained in common circulation for centuries, in the later editions under the alternative title of *Dorastus and Fawnia.* It is marked by better narrative

Margin note left of third paragraph: Arbasto

Margin note left of final paragraph: Pandosto

shorter soliloquies, and less Euphuism than its predecessors. A certain similarity of plot is found in Greene's *Philomela*, which, though not printed till 1592, had been written earlier. The tale resembles also the "curious impertinent" story of Cervantes,[2] but the handling is less realistic and less bleak than the Spaniard was to give it. It deals with an incredibly chaste, maligned, and ultimately vindicated countess, and contains several of the most charming of Greene's occasional songs. *Menaphon, Camilla's Alarum to Sleeping Euphues*, which appeared in 1589, has nothing to say of Euphues or Camilla, but is distinguished by a long prefatory essay of Thomas Nashe upon the state of contemporary literature,[3] less intelligible now than might be desired, but of considerable importance, as are also Greene's briefer slurs on the *Tamburlaine* type of drama in his own preface to *Perimedes*. *Menaphon*, like *Pandosto* before it, shows that Greene has come under the influence, if not of Sidney's yet unprinted *Arcadia* [4] (which is most likely), certainly of the Greek romances from which the *Arcadia* drew. The scene of *Menaphon* is Arcadia, and its plot, like those of *Pandosto* and *Arcadia*, concerns the working out of a riddling oracle. Pirates, shepherds, disguised royal personages, a Sohrab-and-Rustum combat of father and son, the siege of a castle, Mediterranean voyages, and most complicated lovemaking give this entertaining piece much more the flavor of Sidney than of Lyly. It contains also fourteen of the lyrics with which Greene had learned, with no precedent from Lyly, to idealize his novels.[5]

    Perhaps the last, and perhaps the best, of Greene's Euphuistic romances is *Ciceronis Amor*, or *Tully's Love*, published in 1589, with a dedication to Ferdinando Lord Strange, and eight times reprinted in the next half century. Terentia, daughter of the consul Flaminius, has a heart which Cupid allegedly cannot pierce, though the patrician warrior Lentulus pines for her love. At a dinner at the consul's house, where the poet Archias discourses of jealousy, and verse, both English and Latin, is recited, Lentulus unavailingly addresses Terentia, who finds herself strongly attracted to his low-born friend, the young orator Cicero, while her companion, Flavia, becomes infatuated with Lentulus. Lentulus pines and grows sick. One day Terentia, Flavia, and Cornelia walk to Arpinatum "to take the air." They meet Cicero, whose talk further inflames Terentia's love; then they hear an old shepherd's tale of Coridon and Phyllis, and listen to his pretty ode, "Walking in a Valley Green." The girls fall asleep under a tree, and the loutish Fabius, on sight of the sleeping Terentia, feels the refining touch of love, as in the tale Boccaccio tells, and after him Dryden, of Cymon and Iphigenia. In a scene more suggestive of the courtship of Miles Standish, Cicero pleads with Terentia for Lentulus. Fabius, to forward his suit, puts himself at the head of a band of rioters; Cicero saves the situation by an oration before the senate, and is

Menaphon

Tully's Love

[2] *Don Quixote*, Part I, ch. 33-35 (1605).
[3] See M. Knapp, "A Note on Nashe's Preface to Greene's *Menaphon*," *N&Q*, CLXIV (1933). 8; V. Osterberg and J. D. Wilson, "Nashe's 'Kid in Æsop,'" *RES*, XVIII (1942). 385-394.
[4] For discussion of Sidney's *Arcadia* see ch. VIII, below.
[5] Greene's songs are discussed by Alice Meynell in an essay, "Strictly an Elizabethan Lyrist," ı *The Second Person Singular* (1922).

rewarded with Terentia's hand, while Lentulus marries Flavia and Fabius Cornelia.[6]

Greene's Tricks of Style

Greene's discipleship to Lyly was never very earnest. In the earlier romances he applies Euphuism with a trowel; but his nature lore, instead of being grubbed out of Pliny, must often have been improvised with tongue in cheek; e.g.,

> As he which is wounded of the porcuntine can never be healed unless his wounds be washed with the blood of the same beast; as there is nothing better against the stinging of a snake then to be rubbed with an adder's slough ... For it is unpossible, Valericus, to call the falcon to the lure wherein the pens [i.e., feathers!] of a chameleon are pricked, because she doth deadly detest them; it is hard to train the lion to that trap which savoreth of diagredium [i.e., scammony, a purgative drug], because he loatheth it ...[7]

or

> the violets in America, which in summer yield an odoriferous smell and in winter a most pestilent savor;[8]

and his perversions of classical story are often surprising in one who was master of arts in both the universities. In *Euphues his Censure* Iphigenia is in the Greek camp at Troy, placidly acting as hostess for her father, and in *Mamillia* the reader is asked, what man

> offered to die for his wife as *Admeta* did for her husband *Alcest?* What man ever swallowed burning coals as *Portia* did for *Cato?*[9]

He was amusingly unscrupulous in eking out a later novel with pages stolen from an earlier one.[10] Other faults could be mentioned; but they would not alter the fact that these books, which went through approximately seventy-five editions before 1640 and (as the dedications and commendatory verses show) appealed to the great as well as the obscure, are readable still. Beginning with style, Greene came to depend more upon the inserted *novella* and lyric, and at last, as in *Pandosto, Menaphon,* and *Tully's Love,* upon complexity of story.

That Greene was really ashamed of his romantic tales, as he professed to be, is hardly credible. More unsullied pages are not to be found in any library of love literature, and no critic has disputed the justice of R. B.'s tribute to him in *Greene's Funerals* (1594),[11]

---

[6] An anonymous play, *Every Woman in Her Humor* (1609) follows the plot of this romance. The plot of *Menaphon* is the foundation of another play, *The Thracian Wonder* (1661), ascribed to Webster and Rowley; and the plot of *Philomela* of Davenport's *City Nightcap*.

[7] *Gwydonius*, ed. Grosart, p. 51 f. See D. C. Allen, "Science and Invention in Greene's Prose," *PMLA*, LIII (1938). 1007-1018.

[8] *Op. cit.,* p. 26.

[9] *Mamillia*, Part II, p. 157.

[10] See C. J. Vincent, "Further Repetitions in the Works of Robert Greene," *PQ*, XVIII (1939). 73-77, and articles there cited.

[11] Reprinted, R. B. McKerrow (Stratford-upon-Avon, 1922). See C. Crawford, "Greene Funeralls, 1594, and Nicholas Breton," *SP*, extra ser. I (1929). 1-39.

His gadding muse, although it ran of love,
Yet did he sweetly moralize his songs;
Ne ever gave the looser cause to laugh,
Ne men of judgment for to be offended.

But it is easy to understand that Greene was sick of Euphuistic unreality. *Greene's* The jaundiced eye with which he now regarded the literature of escape *Turn to* helped him to see the possibilities of its converse, the literature of sociological *Realism* realism. As usual, he went with his public, and he was one of the first to exploit in popular writing the social unrest that followed the heroic effort of the Armada years.

A quarter-century before, a country gentleman, Thomas Harman, had *Harman's* published his extraordinary report of the underworld characters he had *Caveat* examined in Kent: *A Caveat or Warning for Common Cursitors, Vulgarly Called Vagabones* (1566); and a well-written dialogue, *A Manifest Detection of Dice-play and Other Practices* (c. 1552), had dealt excellently with the London scene.[12] But Greene's pamphlets were particularly well timed, for the criminal class of London had just been greatly increased by the disbanded soldiers turned adrift after the Drake and Norris expedition of 1589.[13] The *Greene's* first one appeared, and went through three editions,[14] in 1591: *A Notable Cony-Discovery of Cozenage Now Daily Practised by Sundry Lewd Persons Catching Called Cony-Catchers and Crossbiters.* It is dedicated "to the young gentle- *Pamphlets* men, merchants, apprentices, farmers, and plain countrymen," and warns them of the tricks of card-sharpers and swindlers with women. Greene, with his reporter's eye and Bohemian acquaintance, was well equipped for such work, which he makes always vivid, often comic, and sometimes pathetically moving, as in this picture of the fleeced "cony":

Then the barnacle's card comes forth, and strikes such a cold humor unto his heart, that he sits as a man in a trance, not knowing what to do, and sighing while his heart is ready to break, thinking on the money that he hath lost. Perhaps the man is very simple and patient and, whatsoever he thinks, for fear goes his way quiet with his loss, while the cony-catchers laugh and divide the spoil; and being out of the doors, poor man, goes to his lodging with a heavy heart, pensive and sorrowful; but too late, for perhaps his state did depend on that money, and so he, his wife, his children, and his family are brought to extreme misery. . . .

The *Second* and the *Third Part of Cony-Catching* both followed in 1592. One exposes five other kinds of deceit, illustrated by instances that had recently occurred; the other consists of ten picaresque tales, professedly based on notes given to Greene by an elderly justice of the peace. This last year of Greene's life was one of furious industry; it produced three more

[12] Both are reprinted, with Greene's cony-catching pamphlets and related material, by A. V. Judges, *The Elizabethan Underworld* (1930). See F. Aydelotte, *Elizabethan Rogues and Vagabonds* (Oxford, 1913).
[13] See Judges, *op. cit.*, pp. xvii f.
[14] R. Pruvost, *LTLS*, Oct. 6, 1932, p. 716, and the same writer's *Greene et ses romans*, p. 422.

pamphlets of this nature. *A Disputation between a He-Cony-Catcher and a She-Cony-Catcher* begins with the debate between Laurence and Nan, leading practitioners of the two professions, and adds *The Conversion of an English Courtesan*, a brief novel related in the first person, which may be regarded as forecasting Defoe's *Moll Flanders*. *The Black Book's Messenger* is a set of stories of the life and death of Ned Browne, "one of the most notable cutpurses, crossbiters, and cony-catchers that ever lived in England." The *Black Book* itself, which was to be a Who's Who of the cony-catching world, Greene did not apparently live to complete; but he produced a more imaginative book, which is one of his best and may be regarded as his final word of social criticism, *A Quip for an Upstart Courtier*, "or a quaint dispute between Velvet-breeches and Cloth-breeches, wherein is plainly set down the disorders in all estates and trades." It is April in London, the last April of Greene's life. In Chaucerian mood he goes into the fields, falls asleep, and has a fantastic vision in which he sees a monstrous headless creature in velvet breeches striding to meet a similar apparition in cloth breeches. Each is armed, and they are about to fight for their right to "frank tenement" in England, when the author proposes trial of their claims by jury. A great number of type figures now pass, from whom, after discussion of the civic qualities of each, a jury of twenty-four is made up. The foreman is a knight; the last member chosen a poet, described as in one of the Jacobean character books:

A Quip for an Upstart Courtier

> a certain kind of an overworn gentleman, attired in velvet and satin, but it was somewhat dropped and greasy, and boots on his legs, whose soles waxed thin and seemed to complain of their master, which, treading thrift under his feet, had brought them unto that consumption. He walked not as other men, in the common beaten way, but came compassing *circum circa,* as if we had been devils and he would draw a circle about us, and at every third step he looked back as if he were afraid of a baily or a sergeant.

After due deliberation the knight pronounces the jury's verdict in favor of Cloth-breeches and old fashioned simplicity.

Greene's Autobiographical Pamphlets

Greene's revulsion from tales of love, which was doubtless 'aesthetic, though he interpreted it as moral, made itself apparent even before he found an escape in the cony-catching series. It synchronizes with the booksellers' discovery, about 1588, of the mercantile worth of his name in a title. *Greene's Orpharion*, of uncertain date, 1588-1590, represents the narrator, who has "found love to be a labyrinth, a fury, a hell," as visiting all the shrines of Venus in search of relief. Finally, Mercury, disguised as a shepherd, shows him a vision in which Orpheus and Arion (hence the title) tell contrasted tales of the cruelty and nobility of love. The moral is that women have both vanities and virtues, but the vision cures Greene of his infatuation, and the last words are: "I was overtaken with repentance." It is not to question his sincerity to say that he recognized the news value of his own personality and from this time used the pattern of his life as stiffening for his stories. He dedicates *Greene's Mourning Garment* (1590) to the Earl of Cumberland as presenting "the reformation of a second Ovid," and in the conclusion calls it "the first fruits of my new labors and the last farewell to my fond desires." It is a version of the parable of the prodigal son, reflecting Greene's dissoluteness and repentance in the adventures of young Philador of Callipolis.

Greene's Farewell to Folly (1591), "sent to courtiers and scholars as a precedent to warn them from the vain delights that draw youth on to repentance," is a discourse of Florentine ladies and gentlemen, who withdraw to a farm and tell moral tales illustrating three kinds of folly: pride, lust, and drunkenness. The fictional interest is greater and the autobiographical hints more concrete in *Greene's Never Too Late* and its sequel, *Francesco's Fortunes* (1590), of which there were eight editions by the end of 1631. Within one of Greene's pleasant Italian frames it paints the portrait of Francesco, a young Englishman, and his chaste wife Isabel. They elope and after many hardships are pardoned by Isabel's father, a wealthy country gentleman. All then goes well till business takes Francesco to London (Troynovant), where he is seduced and ruined by the loathsome Infida, it being pointed out that "our courtesans of Troynovant are far superior in artificial allurement to them of all the world." By luck the destitute Francesco

> fell in amongst a company of players, who persuaded him to try his wit in writing of comedies, tragedies, or pastorals, and if he could perform anything worth the stage, then they would largely reward him for his pains.

Greene and the Players

So Francesco,

> getting him home to his chamber, writ a comedy which so generally pleased all the audience, that happy were those actors in short time that could get any of his works, he grew so exquisite in that faculty.

A discourse on plays, playmakers, and players is here interjected, after which we learn of Isabel's persecutions in the country, ended, in some delightful pages of wishful thinking, when the successful and repentant Francesco returns and is forgiven.

The story is told more bleakly in the death-bed pamphlet called *Greene's Groatsworth of Wit Bought with a Million of Repentance* [15] (1592). Here the author is Roberto, a disinherited younger son, "a scholar, and married to a proper gentlewoman." The courtesan Lamilia beguiles him and causes him to be cast out of his brother's house; but again he meets an actor, by whose providential advice he becomes

Greene's Groatsworth of Wit

> famoused for an arch-playmaking poet; his purse like the sea some time swelled, anon like the same sea fell to a low ebb: yet seldom he wanted, his labors were so well esteemed.

He leads the dissolute life with which Greene is charged, and this time resists the efforts of his wife to "recall" him. Then Greene becomes frankly autobiographical and ends with the well-known letter to his "fellow scholars about

---

[15] See H. Jenkins, "On the Authenticity of *Greene's Groatsworth of Wit* and *The Repentance of Robert Greene*," *RES*, xi (1935). 28-41.

this city" in which he warns them of "Shake-scene," and with a poignant but evidently retouched letter to his wife, "found with this book after his death." This last letter, in a more authentic version, is printed also in *The Repentance of Robert Greene* (1592), which opens with an earnest avowal of sin that has been compared to Bunyan's *Grace Abounding,* and proceeds to give some facts of his disordered life in a setting that makes it hard to believe in his moral ruin.[16]

Greene's Vision

One more posthumous pamphlet, *Greene's Vision,* "written at the instant of his death," as the title-page claims, must have been composed several years earlier, about the time of *Orpharion.* Worried by the vanity of his writings, Greene falls asleep and dreams that Chaucer and Gower come to him, "grave laureates, the types of England's excellence for poetry." Chaucer comforts him with the example of the *Canterbury Tales,* "broad enough ... and written homely and pleasantly," and tells a ribald story of Tompkins, the wheelwright of Grantchester. Gower, a strict Christian, replies with a pious *exemplum.* Greene decides that Gower is right, renounces love tales (after he has finished *Never Too Late*), and promises the public his *Mourning Garment.* Solomon then appears to confirm his judgment. Actually, one may be sure, no Solomon could have taught Greene to emulate the moral Gower.

Greene's Death

He led a sordid life, no doubt; but the legend of his special depravity rests mainly on his own practice of sensationalized autobiography and on the overheated revilings of Harvey. We may leave him with the reflection that a man who, dying at thirty-two, had pushed a quill pen over as much paper as was covered by his writings can have had no extraordinary leisure for Bacchanalian pleasures. The ultimate cause of Greene's death is more likely to have been overwork than Rhenish wine and pickled herrings.

Greene's Followers:

Many writers imitated Greene, but none of them enjoyed such broad or lasting popularity. One of them, Samuel Rowlands (*c.* 1570-*c.* 1630), prefaces his poem, *'Tis Merry When Gossips Meet* [17] (1602) with a "conference

Rowlands

between a gentleman and a 'prentice" supposed to occur ten years after Greene's death. The scene is a London book stall:

Prentice. What lack you, Gentleman? See a new book, new come forth, sir; buy a new book, sir.

Gentleman. New book, say'st? Faith, I can see no pretty thing come forth to my humor's liking. There are some old books that I have more delight in than your new, if thou couldst help me to them.

Pren. Troth, sir, I think I can show you as many of all sorts as any in London, sir.

16 With these accounts should be compared Gabriel Harvey's contemporary evidence in his *Four Letters ... Especially Touching Robert Greene, and Other Parties by him Abused* (1592, reprinted, "Bodley Head Quartos," II, 1922). Harvey had been made furiously angry by Greene's *Quip for an Upstart Courtier,* and he by no means spares the dead man; but his account brings out the pathos of Greene's end, and it is he rather than Greene's literary executors who seems to give us the actual words of the dying man's message to his wife: "Doll, I charge thee by the love of our youth and by my soul's rest that thou wilt see this man paid, for if he and his wife had not succored me, I had died in the streets." See the following chapter.

17 *The Complete Works of Samuel Rowlands,* Hunterian Club (Glasgow, 1880), Vol. I. The same volume contains *Greene's Ghost Haunting Cony-catchers* (1602).

Gent. Canst help me to all Greene's books in one volume? but I will have them every one, not any lacking.

Pren. Sir, I have the most part of them, but I lack *Cony-Catching* and some half dozen more; but I think I could procure them.

Henry Chettle [18] (*c.* 1560-*c.* 1607), the printer-playwright who published *Chettle* Greene's *Groatsworth of Wit,* issued his own *Kind-heart's Dream* three months later with a famous preface disavowing Greene's attack upon Shakespeare. Interest stops with the preface, for the body of the work is a poor blend of Greene and Nashe and has little narrative worth, except for one good conjuring story. A much better book is *Greene's News both from* *Greene's* *Heaven and Hell* [19] (1593) by B. R., giving a delightful account of the *News* wanderings of Greene's ghost. The author is doubtless Barnabe Riche (*c.* 1540-1617), a retired captain whose industrious pen had already attempted fiction in the two parts of *The Strange and Wonderful Adventures of Don* *Simonides, a Gentleman Spaniard* (1581, 1584) and *The Adventures of* *Brusanus* (1592). These neither deserved, nor have yet obtained, a second *Barnabe* edition; [20] but Riche was far luckier with his collection of eight *novelle,* *Riche* *Riche his Farewell to Military Profession* [21] (1581), the second of which, "Of Apolonius and Silla," was used by Shakespeare, after some purifying, as the basis of *Twelfth Night.* Riche's tales, though "gathered together for the only delight of the courteous gentlewomen both of England and Ireland," have none of the delicacy of Lyly and Greene, and represent an earlier fashion. They are sometimes coarse in a bluff, soldierly way and make no pretension to style, but they have a good deal of narrative vigor.

Greene's *Menaphon* is probably the strongest influence, though Lyly and Sidney have also had an effect, on John Dickenson's *Arisbas* (1594), which is subtitled "Euphues amidst his Slumbers, or Cupid's Journey to Hell." *John* Dickenson,[22] who wrote considerably in Latin as well as English, has filled *Dickenson* out his rather trivial plot with a great variety of occasional poetry, both in the normal English metres and in English hexameters, elegiacs, and sapphics. Arisbas, prince of Cyprus, eloping with Timoclea, is separated from her by a

[18] See H. Jenkins, *The Life and Work of Henry Chettle* (1934).

[19] Ed. R. B. McKerrow (Stratford-upon-Avon, 1922). Another imitator of Greene, identified only as "A," produced *Tell-troth's New-Year's Gift* and *The Passionate Morris* in 1593 (ed. F. J. Furnivall, New Shakspere Soc., 1876). In the former and more interesting of these pamphlets Robin Goodfellow, fresh from Hell, meets Tell-troth near Islington on a frosty morning and discusses the causes of jealousy, which above all other vices fills the infernal regions.

[20] Similar neglect befell Austin Saker's *Narbonus, the Labyrinth of Liberty* (1580) and Anthony Munday's *Zelauto, the Fountain of Fame,* of the same year, in spite of the latter's not unattractive illustrations. Recently Munday's novel has received attention because of a parallel in its third part to the bond story of *The Merchant of Venice.* See F. Brie, *Shakespeare-ahrbuch,* XLIX (1913). 97-122.

[21] Reprinted, Shakespeare Soc. (1846). See D. T. Starnes, "Barnabe Riche's 'Sapho Duke of Mantona': A Study in Elizabethan Story-making," *SP,* XXX (1933). 455-472. A different view of Riche is given by H. J. Webb, "Barnabe Riche, 16th Century Military Critic," *JEGP,* LII (1943). 240-257. Somewhat similar to Riche's *Farewell,* and of the same date, are the seven stories in William Warner's *Pan his Syrinx* (1584, 1597), which are even more nautical and exotic. The first of Warner's tales, *Arbaces,* has a plot resemblance to a Fletcher-Massinger play, *The Sea-Voyage.*

[22] A. B. Grosart, *Prose and Verse by John Dickenson* (1878).

storm, which leaves him stranded in Arcadia, the guest of a friendly shepherd; while Timoclea, after escaping from pirates and finding refuge in another part of Arcadia, is recognized at a shepherd festival and rejoined to Arisbas. In *The Shepherd's Complaint* (*c.* 1596) Dickenson has not enough story to float the heavy concentration of pastoral verse; but his *Greene in Conceipt* (1598) limits itself to a single rather excellent "canzon" and otherwise plods in moral prose through "the tragic history of fair Valeria of London," which Greene's ghost comes from the grave to urge him to complete. Dickenson's narrative style is not equal to his learning or to his poetic capacity. Without precisely imitating any of his models, he produces a self-conscious prose mainly remarkable for its striving after alliteration and pompous adjectives.

Lodge's
Rosalind

The best of Greene's imitators in the romantic tale was Thomas Lodge [23] (*c.* 1558-1625). *Rosalind, Euphues' Golden Legacy* [24] (1590) owes comparatively little except the title to Lyly; indeed, the preliminary matter shows that Lodge, who wrote the book aboard ship, had even forgotten that Lyly's Philautus did *not* win his Camilla. The debt to Greene is clear; but *Rosalind* is a better story than any of Greene's, for Lodge has strengthened it by introducing good masculine material from the pseudo-Chaucerian *Tale of Gamelin,* and the inserted lyrics can vie with Greene's best. Shakespeare, in transforming it into *As You Like It,* added the characters of Touchstone and Jaques, but hardly found it necessary to improve upon the plot. The dénouement and the treatment of Oliver (i.e., Saladyne) are more plausible in the romance than in the play. *Rosalind* was deservedly popular, but it was Lodge's only success in this style. *The History of Forbonius and Prisceria,* appended to his *Alarum against Usurers* (1584), *Euphues' Shadow* (1592), and *A Margarite of America* (1596) are distinctly inferior, and so the public evidently thought, for none of them was able to reach a second edition. Yet

Emanuel
Forde

Emanuel Forde's *Ornatus and Artesia* (*c.* 1595) and *Parismus, Prince of Bohemia* (1598) had a vogue, lasting quite through the seventeenth century, at which today one can only marvel.

Greene's realistic vein was promptly taken up by one who signed himself "Cuthbert Cony-Catcher," in *The Defence of Cony-Catching* (1592), "a confutation of those two injurious pamphlets published by R. G."; and the entertaining Samuel Rowlands, previously mentioned, owed much to him, but the writer who best carried Greene's method into the seventeenth cen-

Thomas
Dekker

tury was Thomas Dekker. In *News from Hell* (1606), expanded the next year into *A Knight's Conjuring,* Dekker is following both Nashe and Greene. In *Jests to Make You Merry* (1607), compiled with the assistance of George Wilkins, and particularly in his justly popular *Bellman of London, Bringing to Light the Most Notorious Villainies* (1608), and its continuation

23 *Complete Works of Thomas Lodge* (4v, Hunterian Club, Glasgow, 1883); N. B. Paradise, *Thomas Lodge: The History of an Elizabethan* (New Haven, 1931); C. J. Sisson, *Thomas Lodge and Other Elizabethans* (Cambridge, Mass., 1933), pp. 1-163; E. A. Tenny, *Thomas Lodge* (Ithaca, N. Y., 1935); S. A. Tannenbaum, *Thomas Lodge: A Concise Bibliography* (1940).
24 Ed. W. W. Greg (Oxford, 2ed., 1931).

Lanthorn and Candle-Light, Dekker gave a renewed vogue to the work of Harman and Greene, putting their realism within a romantic setting in which Euphuism has given place to a much more modern conception of prose harmony.[25] Thus, finally, the idealized vagabonds of Dekker passed into Jonson's masque[26] and Fletcher and Massinger's play.[27]

In the same year (1594) in which Shakespeare dedicated his *Rape of Lucrece* to the Earl of Southampton, that young nobleman received from Thomas Nashe a "fantastical treatise," as the author calls it, a highly seasoned narrative in prose which differs markedly from the rest of Nashe's work and has no very close relationship to anything else in Elizabethan literature. It is regrettable that the vein was not pursued, for the theme, a young Englishman's experiences in seeking Italy, was one of paramount interest for the age.[28] *The Unfortunate Traveler*[29] has no real structure, except that it begins with incidents of a farcical kind and develops into melodrama; but it carries the reader along the main-traveled road of the Elizabethan gallant, through France, Münster, Wittenberg, the Emperor's court, Venice, Florence, and Rome. The narrator is a young page, Jack Wilton, and the supposed time is that halcyon period, the early years of Henry VIII. It is less a novel than a series of tales, gay and sinister, in all of which Wilton has a part; but it points the way from afar to the historical novels of Scott by introducing famous personages like the poet Surrey, Erasmus, More, Luther, and Aretino, in unhistoric and anachronistic relations. Nashe's wit and peculiar brilliance in description make it one of the most readable books of its time.

Thomas Deloney[30] (d. 1600) has even less sense of unified fiction. A silk-weaver by trade and a copious writer of narrative ballads, in his prose books he gave exaggerated pictures of the bourgeois society he knew against pseudo-historic backgrounds. The earliest, *Jack of Newbury* (1597), is set in the same period that Nashe selected for *The Unfortunate Traveler.* Where Nashe begins with life in Henry VIII's camp during the French expedition of 1513, Deloney gives us life among the clothworkers in the Berkshire town of Newbury at the same period. The eleven chapters are separate anecdotes, held together by the figure of the incredibly shrewd and prosperous weaver, John Winchcomb, who marries the widow of his rich employer, equips a company of 250 artisans for war against the Scots in the Flodden campaign (1513), and performs other acts to the greater glory of the English clothworkers, to whom the book is dedicated. In *Thomas*

Quasi-Historical Novels

Nashe, The Unfortunate Traveler

Thomas Deloney

[25] See G. V. Jones, "Greene and Dekker," *LTLS,* June 11, 1925, p. 400, and letter by R. B. McKerrow in next issue (June 18), p. 416. For more on Dekker's prose see next chapter.
[26] *The Gypsies Metamorphosed* (1621).
[27] *Beggars' Bush* (1622).
[28] Something of Jack Wilton's spirit is found in two biographical works: Anthony Munday's *The English-Roman Life,* 1582 (reprinted, "Bodley Head Quartos," XII, 1925); and still more in Thomas Coryate's *Crudities,* 1611 (reprinted, 2v, Glasgow, 1905).
[29] Ed. H. F. B. Brett-Smith (Oxford, 1920), and in R. B. McKerrow, *Works of Thomas Nashe,* Vol. II.
[30] F. O. Mann, *The Works of Thomas Deloney* (Oxford, 1912); A. Chevalley, *Thomas Deloney* (Paris, 1926); Ll. Powys, "Thomas Deloney," *Virginia Quar. Rev.,* IX (1933). 578-594.

of Reading, or the Six Worthy Yeomen of the West, Deloney draws a longer
bow, setting his fifteen stories far back in the reign of Henry I, the Conqueror's son, when (to believe him) the salient fact about English life was
the bourgeois magnificence of Thomas Cole and his cronies, master-weavers
all, who travel like princes through the country at the head of caravans of
fine cloth and enjoy the unlimited admiration of their sovereign. In *The
Gentle Craft* (1597) Deloney treated the shoemakers to the same flattery,
with such effect that Dekker promptly dramatized one tale in *The Shoemakers' Holiday* (1599), and a second part, consisting of eleven more shoemaker stories, was issued.

Deloney's homely tales were so well read that the early editions seem to
have entirely perished; they are known today only in late reprints.[31] It is
not, however, to be supposed that in Deloney prose fiction took a long step
forward, or that anything like what we now call a realistic novel was in
view. What Deloney's popularity indicates is that there was a strong revulsion
in taste from the fantastic aristocracy of Lyly and Greene.[32] As intelligent
readers tired of Euphuism, middle-class reading matter for a moment filled
its place.[33] Such were the stories of Deloney, the old-fashioned romances
that Anthony Munday translated,[34] and a quantity of frank jest books [35]
not much more developed than those mentioned at the opening of the preceding chapter. These works, however, could not long hold the attention
of thinking people, and prose fiction, in a very remarkable degree, faded
from the English intellectual horizon in the seventeenth century.

*The Decline
of Prose
Fiction*

Sidney's *Arcadia* excepted, Elizabethan literature failed to produce any
work of fictional prose comparable in largeness and nobility with its productions in other fields. One reason may be that prose as an aesthetic art
had not yet quite "arrived," and its practitioners were driven to emphasize
its claims by petty prettinesses inconsistent with a major effort. It is also
true that in that age the place in men's minds and education now held by
the more thoughtful novels was occupied by the work of the great historians
and classical translators, such as Holinshed and North, and particularly by
such tales of actual adventure as Richard Hakluyt collected in his *Principal
Navigations, Voyages, and Discoveries of the English Nation* (1589-1600).

[31] E.g., the earliest edition of *Jack of Newbury* known to the *Short-Title Catalogue* is that
of 1619, marked as the eighth printing.
[32] For Deloney's Euphuistic sources, which he sadly misuses, see two articles by H. E.
Rollins, *PMLA*, L (1935). 679-686; LI (1936). 399-406.
[33] One should consult L. B. Wright's comprehensive and authoritative book, *Middle-Class
Culture in Elizabethan England* (Chapel Hill, 1935).
[34] *Palmerin of England*, three parts (c. 1581-1597); *Palmerin d'Oliva* (1588), *Palladine of
England* (1588), *History of Palmendos* (1589), *Gerileon of England* (1592), *Primaleon of
Greece* (1619), *Amadis of Gaul* (1619). See Celeste Turner, *Anthony Munday, an Elizabethan
Man of Letters* (Berkeley, Calif., 1928).
[35] E.g., *Tarlton's News out of Purgatory* (1590) and *Tarlton's Jests* (1609); *The Cobbler
of Canterbury* (1590); *Merry Conceited Jests of George Peele* (1607); Robert Armin, *A Nest
of Ninnies* (1608). Of similar quality are the very popular prose chapbooks dealing with Friar
Bacon, Dr. Faustus, Friar Rush, George-a-Greene, etc. (see W. J. Thoms, *Early English Prose
Romances*, 3v, 1858), which have an affinity with some well-known plays, and Richard
Johnson's *Most Famous History of the Seven Champions of Christendom* (1596), which lasted
far into the eighteenth century and affected the later development of the St. George plays (see
E. K. Chambers, *The English Folk-Play*, Oxford, 1933, pp. 174 ff.).

This is the work which Froude described in a much quoted phrase as "the *Richard* prose epic of the modern English nation." [36] A recent scholar has thus *Hakluyt* analyzed it:

The collection of more than one hundred long narratives is composed by nearly as many hands. Some of these hands were of exceeding skill, like Ralegh's and like Hakluyt's own in his translations. Some were crude and unfinished, like those of many of the sailors who copied their log books ... The romance of action runs through even the most pedestrian account of perils and profits, to reach its height in the naval exploits against Spain and in the exploring of the frozen north. The romance of wonder at the marvels of man and of nature illumines the whole fabric of the work which portrays the epic enterprise of England. [37]

[36] J. A. Froude, "England's Forgotten Worthies," in *Short Studies of Great Subjects*, ed. 1873, p. 361.

[37] G. B. Parks, *Richard Hakluyt and the English Voyages* (1928), pp. 187-199. See also Walter Raleigh, *The English Voyages of the Sixteenth Century* (Glasgow, 1906). Hakluyt's collection is handsomely reprinted (12v, Hakluyt Soc., Glasgow, 1903-5).

<h1 style="text-align: center;">V</h1>

<h2 style="text-align: center;">Miscellaneous Prose</h2>

The Tudor From Sir Thomas Hoby's *Book of the Courtier* (1561) to John Florio's
Translations Montaigne and Philemon Holland's Plutarch (both in 1603) a massive
line of translated classics extends through the Elizabethan period.[1] The
august series began earlier, indeed, with Caxton and Berners, and continued,
though with abated vigor, into the period of James I. Shakespeare was
indebted concretely to each of the three works mentioned, and in still
higher degree to Golding's Ovid (1567) and Bartholomew Yong's Montemayor (1598); his greatest debt is to what stylistically is the greatest translation of all, Sir Thomas North's version of Plutarch's *Lives* (1579). The
series, which reached a higher level in prose than in verse, included some
of the most recent as well as some of the most ancient of the world's great
books—Harington's Ariosto[2] (1591) and Shelton's Cervantes (1612) as
well as Chapman's Homer (1598-1616) and the various late Greek romances.[3] It brought with it an avalanche of plot material and at the same
time schooled the new English prose by discipleship to what had been best
thought and said in the literature of Greece, Rome, France, Italy, and Spain.
Only a peculiarly vigorous national style could have kept its course under
such stress of foreign influence, but the Elizabethan translations are always
more Elizabethan than translated.

Standards The most worrying problem for Elizabethan writers and speakers was
for Prose the problem of domesticating the vast quantity of foreign words which
humanism had introduced, and which made too many authors resemble
the characters in *Love's Labor's Lost* who had "been at a great feast of
languages and stolen the scraps."[4] Lord Berners, in the preface to his
translation of Froissart (1523), illustrates the vice:

> They [i.e., the writers of histories] show, open, manifest, and declare to the
> reader, by example of old antiquity, what we should enquere, desire, and follow,
> and also what we should eschew, avoid, and utterly fly; for when we, being
> unexpert of chances, see, behold, and read the auncient acts, gestes, and deeds,

---

[1] See the two series of *The Tudor Translations*, 1892-1903 (32 vol.), 1924-1927 (12 vol.);
also H. F. B. Brett-Smith and S. Gaselee, *The Loves of Clitophon and Leucippe*, translated by
Wm. Burton, 1597 (Oxford, 1923); C. H. Conley, *The First English Translators of the
Classics* (New Haven, 1927); F. O. Matthiessen, *Translation, an Elizabethan Art* (Cambridge,
Mass., 1931); A. F. Clements, *Tudor Translations, an Anthology* (Oxford, 1940).
[2] See Townsend Rich, *Harington and Ariosto, a Study in Elizabethan Verse Translation*
(New Haven, 1940).
[3] See S. L. Wolff, *The Greek Romances in Elizabethan Prose Fiction* (1912).
[4] For a comprehensive discussion of English linguistic problems in the Renaissance see A. C.
Baugh, *A History of the English Language* (1935), ch. VIII.

how and with what labors, dangers, and perils they were gested and done, they right greatly admonest, ensigne, and teach us how we may lead forth our lives.

The soundest of the humanists—such men as Sir John Cheke and Ascham —were strongest in disapproval of this tendency to false learning and redundancy, urging the removal of all "inkhorn terms"; and the same ascetic spirit informed the influential textbooks of Thomas Wilson (*c.* 1525-1581), "whose discretion," as Barnabe Barnes said, "did redress our English barbarism." [5] Wilson's *Rule of Reason*, which is a manual of logic, went through *Thomas* seven editions between 1551 and 1593, and his *Art of Rhetoric* [6] had eight *Wilson* between 1553 and 1585. Rhetoric is defined by Wilson as the art of the orator, and it is spoken English that he particularly considers. His theory of style is in no wise original, and repeats much that had already been said on the authority of Cicero or other ancients by Leonard Cox *(The Art or Craft of Rhetoric,* 1524, 1532) and Richard Sherry *(A Treatise of the Figures of Grammar and Rhetoric,* 1555); but Wilson was more complete, more amusing, and much more popular.[7] His warnings against inkhorn terms, vulgar ostentation, and other faults of language are enforced by humorous anecdotes and sample letters or speeches, which point to the earliest model-letter book, *The Enemy of Idleness,* by William Fulwood, and so to Breton's beloved *Post with a Mad Packet of Letters* (1602) and, in the course of time, *Pamela.*[8] It would have been unfortunate if the austere ideal of Cheke and Wilson had dominated Elizabethan prose,[9] but this was the least of dangers at that time, and the *Art of Rhetoric* served to buttress a flamboyant generation against the extravagances of Euphuism.

The First Part of the Elementary, Which Entreateth Chiefly of the Right *Richard* Writing of our English Tongue [10] (1582) by Richard Mulcaster (*c.* 1530- *Mulcaster* 1611) is a work of the same tendency and of equal distinction. It is a weighty though doubtless over-philosophical discourse on elementary education by the most famous schoolmaster of the age, who was head of the Merchant Taylors' School in London when Spenser studied there, and later master at St. Paul's. Mulcaster's discussion of the rules for spelling is of importance to students of Elizabethan phonetics, and his book reaches the height of a plain style in the "peroration," which includes a notable defense of English as a literary language:

[5] Prefatory sonnet to Harvey's *Pierce's Supererogation* (Grosart, *Works of Gabriel Harvey,* II. 24).
[6] *Wilson's Art of Rhetorique, 1560,* ed. G. H. Mair (Oxford, 1909).
[7] See R. H. Wagner, "Thomas Wilson's Contributions to Rhetoric," in *Papers in Rhetoric,* ed. D. C. Bryant (St. Louis, 1940), pp. 1-7. On all these writers consult Wm. G. Crane, *Wit and Rhetoric in the Renaissance* (1937); and for Sherry in particular see T. W. Baldwin, *William Shakspere's Small Latine and Lesse Greeke* (Urbana, 1944), II. 35-39.
[8] See K. G. Hornbeak, *The Complete Letter-Writer, 1568-1800* (Northampton, Mass., 1934).
[9] George Pettie replied very effectively in the preface to his translation of Guazzo's *Civil Conversation* (1581).
[10] Ed. E. T. Campagnac (Oxford, 1925). Mulcaster did not publish a second part of his *Elementary,* but in the previous year (1581) had dedicated to Queen Elizabeth a somewhat similar work called *Positions.* For fuller consideration of Mulcaster see A. C. Baugh, *op. cit.,* pp. 250-255; and R. F. Jones, "Richard Mulcaster's View of the English Language," *Washington Univ. Studies,* XIII (1926). 267-303.

I love Rome, but London better; I favor Italy, but England more; I honor the Latin, but I worship the English . . . I do not think that any language, be it whatsoever, is better able to utter all arguments, either with more pith or greater plainness, than our English tongue is, if the English utterer be as skilful in the matter which he is to utter as the foreign utterer is.

The Art of Poetry

Early Elizabethan poetry was not certain of its purposes and led to no criticism [11] that went deeper than George Gascoigne's *Certain Notes of Instruction concerning the Making of Verse or Rime in English* (1575). These "notes," as they truly are, extend to less than ten pages and were written at the request of Master Edouardo Donati, presumably a novice in the art. They are wholly superficial, but have the value which Gascoigne's intelligence and long experience in his craft could give even to trifling observations.

Gascoigne's Notes of Instruction

Latin Metres for English Verse

There was, however, a very fundamental question in the air, critical for the whole future of English poetry, which found expression in the series of letters exchanged between Spenser and Gabriel Harvey in 1579-80.[12] From these it appears that groups of young scholars, including Spenser, Sidney, and Dyer in London and the Harvey brothers at Cambridge, were seriously concerned to follow up a hint of Ascham's [13] and work out a new English prosody on classical quantitative lines.[14] It was the equivalent in aesthetics of the search for the Northwest Passage; much labor and some poetic lives were lost in it. It was no unreasonable revolt against the rudeness of poulter's measure and riding rime, and if poetic miracles had not occurred in the 1580's, it might well have won the day and brought in night. The irony is that the particular miracle-workers, Spenser and Sidney, are so conspicuous in the other camp. William Webbe's attractive *Discourse of English Poetry,* "together with the author's judgment touching the reformation of our English verse" (1586), is mainly notable for its enthusiastic admiration of the "new poet," Spenser, and its not quite consistent faith in the practicability of Latin metres for English poems. Webbe translates two of Virgil's eclogues into English hexameters and puts Spenser's song in the "April"

Webbe

---

[11] The most important texts are assembled in J. Haslewood, *Ancient Critical Essays upon English Poets and Poesy* (2v, 1811, 1815); and G. G. Smith, *Elizabethan Critical Essays* (2v, Oxford, 1904). On the general subject see F. E. Schelling, *Poetic and Verse Criticism of the Reign of Elizabeth* (Philadelphia, 1891; *Univ. of Pennsylvania Ser. in Philology,* etc., Vol. I, No. 1.) For the philosophical background see J. E. Spingarn, *A History of Literary Criticism in the Renaissance* (1899; 5th impression, 1925) and C. S. Baldwin, *Renaissance Literary Theory and Practice* (ed. D. L. Clark, 1939).

[12] *Three Proper and Witty Familiar Letters, Lately Passed between Two University Men* (1580); *Two Other Very Commendable Letters of the Same Men's Writing* (1580). Reprinted in complete editions of Spenser.

[13] "How our English tongue, in avoiding barbarous riming, may as well receive right quantity of syllables and true order of versifying . . . as either Greek or Latin, if a cunning man have it in handling" (*Schoolmaster,* ed. W. A. Wright, 1904, p. 224).

[14] One of Ascham's most earnest followers in the effort to latinize English prosody was the learned, Oxford-bred, and much-traveled Irishman, Richard Stanyhurst (1547-1618), who translated the first four books of the *Æneid* into English hexameter, "a foul, lumbering, boisterous, wallowing measure," as Nashe not unjustly called it (but see the defense of this work in D. van der Haar's edition, Amsterdam, 1933). Stanyhurst was a notable spelling reformer and coiner of new words, and his various prefaces are of interest to students of linguistic reform. He wrote the *Description of Ireland* for Holinshed's *Chronicles* (1577) and continued Edmund Campion's *History of Ireland* (cf. below, ch. IX).

section of the *Shepherds' Calendar* into sapphics. He is forced to break off exhausted, but with his optimism unimpaired, "for in truth," he says,

I am persuaded a little pain-taking might furnish our speech with as much pleasant delight in this kind of verse as any other whatsoever.

The same *ignis fatuus* sixteen years later misled the great lyrist and musician, *Campion* Thomas Campion, in his *Observations in the Art of English Poesy* (1602), *and Daniel* in which he offers unfortunate examples of eight Anglo-Latin metres; and Campion's misguided performance called forth Samuel Daniel's *Defense of Rime* [15] (1603), which, along with Nashe's effective lampooning, for a while laid the ghosts of English iambics, sapphics, hexameters, and the like.

George Puttenham's *Art of English Poesy* [16] (1589) observes a moderate and skeptical, though wistful, attitude toward the metrical innovations from Latin. Puttenham's is the longest, and with the exception of Sidney's the *Puttenham* best, of the Elizabethan manuals of poetry. He handles problems of prosody, as Wilson does those of prose, with scientific method, and discusses recent English poets somewhat more broadly than Webbe. The fourth chapter of Book III, "Of Language," is an acute essay on spoken English, and chapter 24, "Of Decency in Behavior," shows that the enigmatic author was not only a literary critic, but also an accomplished philosopher, courtier, and gentleman. Another such was Sir John Harington, whose *Brief Apology* *Harington* *of Poetry and of the Author,* prefixed to his translation of the *Orlando Furioso* (1591), is a frank and amusing reply to the Puritan critics.[17] Wit and coherent argument are both forbidden by the mechanical form of the twenty-five pages Francis Meres devotes to poetry and poets in his encyclo- *Meres* pedic *Palladis Tamia* [18] (1598), but the richness of his details makes this shoddy work rank in usefulness at the top of all the criticism of the decade.

The Martin Marprelate pamphlets of 1588-89 [19] evoked replies likewise *The Anti-* anonymous and written in the same strain of unmannerly invective. These *Martin* irregular auxiliaries of the established clergy were from some of the best *Tracts* pens in England. *Pap with an Hatchet* [20] (1589) is by Lyly; *An Almond for a Parrot* [21] (1590) may be by Greene; but the author who most delighted in the fray was apparently young Tom Nashe (1567-c. 1601), whose first work, *The Anatomy of Absurdity* [22] (1589), had shown an undiscriminating desire to be witty at the cost of Euphuistic writers, women, hypocrites, bad poets, students, gluttons, and anything else. Nashe's most judicious editor

[15] These are both available in "Bodley Head Quartos," No. XIV (1925).
[16] G. D. Willcock and A. Walker, *The Arte of English Poesie by George Puttenham* (Cambridge, 1936).
[17] Harington was a man of many gifts. See Norman E. McClure, *The Letters and Epigrams of Sir John Harington, together with The Praise of Private Life* (Philadelphia, 1930).
[18] D. C. Allen, *Francis Meres's Treatise "Poetrie"* (Urbana, 1933).
[19] See above, Part I, ch. VI.
[20] Reprinted, Bond, *Works of John Lyly*, III. 389-413.
[21] Reprinted, McKerrow, *Works of Thomas Nashe*, III. 337-376. For extensive evidence favoring Nashe's authorship of this pamphlet see D. J. McGinn, "Nashe's Share in the Marprelate Controversy," *PMLA*, LIX (1944), pp. 952-984.
[22] This was inspired by Stubbes' *Anatomy of Abuses*. See below, and D. C. Allen, "The Anatomy of Absurdity, a Study in Literary Apprenticeship," *SP*, XXXII (1935). 170-177.

finds no particular evidence of his hand in the "Pasquil of England" pamphlets [23] usually attributed to him; but there can be no doubt that he joined with much spirit and with improvement of his invective style in the general hue and cry after Martin, and he may have had a part in the anti-Martin plays which were much referred to, but not preserved.

Nashe and Harvey   Nashe's next acknowledged work, *Pierce Penniless his Supplication to the Devil* (Aug., 1592), shows how much more entertainingly than in the *Anatomy of Absurdity* he could now rail at the contemporary scene.[24] He devises an amusing fable which enables him, among other things, to analyze each of the Seven Deadly Sins; pauses in his treatment of sloth for an interesting defense of plays, and inserts into the section on wrath four pages of colorful abuse on the sons of Harvey, the Saffron Walden ropemaker, one of whom had sneered at Nashe's preface to *Menaphon*.[25] It is quite delightful, for those whose withers are unwrung, and all in the spirit of clean sport. Stopping for breath and punctuation, Nashe invokes his readers:

> Have I not an indifferent pretty vein in spur-galling an ass? If you knew how extemporal it were at this instant, and with what haste it is writ, you would say so. But I would not have you think that all this that is set down here is in good earnest . . . but only to show how for a need I could rail if I were thoroughly fired.[26]

Nashe's liberties were taken at an unlucky time, for the Harvey brothers had just been more than sufficiently spur-galled in Greene's *Quip for an Upstart Courtier* (July, 1592), where a passage that was later canceled had assified them with art and precision.[27] The eldest of the brothers, Spenser's friend Gabriel, whose family affection was as enormous as his vanity, went to London early in September with the idea of prosecuting Greene at law, *Harvey's Four Letters* but arrived just as the latter died. He vented his feelings in the angry *Four Letters and Certain Sonnets, Especially Touching Robert Greene and Other Parties by Him Abused* [28] (dated September 16, 1592), which is largely responsible for the odor of unsanctity that clings about Greene's memory. Naturally, he fulminated against *Pierce Penniless* also, but less vindictively, and in the last letter called upon Nashe to repent and be forgiven.

Nashe's Strange News   Nashe, however, replied in a pamphlet, the very title of which is a lewd jest: *Strange News of the Intercepting Certain Letters and a Convoy of Verses as They Were Going Privily to Victual the Low Countries* (January, 1593). It contains several apologies for Greene, which should be considered,

[23] *A Countercuff Given to Martin Junior by . . . Pasquil of England* (1589), *The First Part of Pasquil's Apology* (1590). See R. B. McKerrow, *Works of Thomas Nashe*, v (1910). 34-65.
[24] For works of Nashe referred to in this section see McKerrow's ed. just cited; for works of Harvey see A. B. Grosart, *Works of Gabriel Harvey* (3v, 1884). Consult also C. Sanders, *Robert Greene and the Harveys* (Bloomington, Ind., 1931).
[25] The offender was not Gabriel, but Richard Harvey, in the Preface to his *Lamb of God* (1590).
[26] Ed. McKerrow, I. 199.
[27] This passage seems to be preserved only in the Huntington Library copy. See G. W. Cole, "Bibliography—A Forecast," in *Papers of Bibl. Soc. of America*, XIV (1920). 7, 8.
[28] Separately reprinted, "Bodley Head Quartos," no. II (1922). See F. R. Johnson, "The First Edition of Gabriel Harvey's *Foure Letters*," *Library*, 4 ser., XV (1934). 212-223.

and makes sad havoc of Harvey's dignity by commenting *seriatim* on his charges. Harvey, though he wielded a wicked pen, was no match for this antagonist. His *Pierce's Supererogation* (1593), or "a new praise of the old ass," shows that his anger had consumed what little humor and discretion he possessed. It is quite unduly long, for it incorporates a hundred pages against *Pap with an Hatchet* that had been written in 1589, and it is indeed the huge ungainly lamentation of a thin-skinned man in a nettle bed. He flaunts the flattering letters of his literary friends as a dog licks its wounds and snaps out in all directions against each of his four bugbears: Nashe, Greene, Lyly, and Doctor Perne of Cambridge. There is, however, plenty of power in Harvey's prose. His long diatribe against Perne is a model of academic venom, and in his anger with Nashe he sometimes pays the perfect tribute to the latter's style, calling him in one place "this brave Columbus of terms," [29] and complaining in another that "his pen is like a spigot." "Nashe, Nashe, Nashe," he cries, *{margin: Harvey, Pierce's Supererogation}*

Vain Nashe, railing Nashe, craking Nashe, bibbing Nashe, baggage Nashe, swaddish Nashe, roguish Nashe, Nashe the belwether of the scribbling flock, the swish-swash of the press, the bum of impudency, the shambles of beastliness, the polecat of Paul's Churchyard, the screech-owl of London, the toadstool of the realm, the scorning-stock of the world, and the horrible confuter of four letters.[30]

A little later in the same year (October, 1593) [31] Harvey's *New Letter of Notable Contents* appeared, a confused work that adds nothing to his reputation. His state of mind is apparent in the ghoulish but incoherent glee with which he welcomes the recent news of Marlowe's death.[32] Nashe should perhaps not have replied, and he was slow to do so. In his *Christ's Tears over Jerusalem* (September, 1593), which is really a moral exhortation to London, he renounces "fantastical satirism," and asks pardon of all his enemies, "even of Master Dr. Harvey"; but as *Pierce's Supererogation* and the *New Letter* came out just after, the second edition of *Christ's Tears* (1594) has a brief but indignant withdrawal of the reconciliation. *The Unfortunate Traveler* (1594) says nothing of Harvey, and it was not till 1596 that smouldering wrath, or perhaps the expostulations of Nashe's friends, caused the latter to give Harvey his quietus in *Have with You to Saffron Walden, or Gabriel Harvey's Hunt Is Up*. It is cruel, crushing, and complete, perhaps the brightest and most pungent of all Nashe's works of raillery. Whether Harvey wrote the *Trimming of Thomas Nashe*, which appeared pseudonymously the next year, is doubtful and unimportant, for it did nothing to retrieve the situation. Nashe turned to dramatic satire, and for collaborating with Ben Jonson in the now lost comedy, *The Isle of Dogs* *{margin: Harvey's New Letter; Nashe, Have with You to Saffron Walden}*

---

[29] "This brave Columbus of terms and this only merchant-venturer of quarrels, that detecteth new Indies of invention" (p. 45).

[30] Ed. Grosart, II. 273.

[31] *Pierce's Supererogation* is dated by Harvey Apr. 27, 1593, but the book was not published at once.

[32] See H. Moore, "Gabriel Harvey's References to Marlowe," *SP*, XXIII (1926). 337-357.

(July, 1597), had to flee to Yarmouth [33] and lie *perdu* among the herring-fishers. He improved the occasion by putting together the pleasant gallimau-

Nashe's Lenten Stuff

fry, *Nashe's Lenten Stuff, or the Praise of the Red Herring* (1599), interesting as an extended, though jocular, attempt to write the history of a municipal corporation and an article of commerce. It was his last work for the censors of printing had had enough of him and Harvey, and extinguished both as literary forces by their decree of June 1, 1599:

> That all Nashe's books and Dr. Harvey's books be taken, wheresoever they may be found, and that none of their books be ever printed hereafter.[34]

This rigor did not long inconvenience Nashe, for he was dead by 1601, and Dekker had a vision of him in the Elysian fields, where

The End of Nashe and Harvey

> Marlowe, Greene, and Peele had got under the shades of a large vine, laughing to see Nashe that was but newly come to their college.[35]

But Harvey lived on in Saffron Walden for thirty years longer, ingloriously mute, in melancholy refutation of the judgment Spenser had written of him before Nashe was known:

> Harvey, thee happy above happiest men
> I read [i.e., esteem], that, sitting like a looker-on
> Of this world's stage, dost note with critic pen
> The sharp dislikes of each condition....[36]

The Marprelate controversy and the quarrel of Harvey and Nashe suppled the joints of English prose almost incredibly. Without such models one could hardly imagine the language of Lyly and Greene being accelerated in less than a generation into the talk of Falstaff or such a gem of vilification as that of Kent on Oswald:

> A knave, a rascal, an eater of broken meats; a base, proud, shallow, beggarly, three-suited, hundred-pound, filthy, worsted-stocking knave; a lily-liver'd, action-taking knave; a whoreson, glass-gazing, super-serviceable, finical rogue ... and the son and heir of a mongrel bitch: one whom I will beat into clamorous whining if thou deniest the least syllable of thy addition.[37]

Thomas Dekker (*c.* 1572-1632) was Nashe's successor as well as Greene's.[38] His *News from Hell, or The Devil's Answer to Pierce Penniless* (1606) is confessedly a sequel to Nashe's *Supplication,* and shows how Dekker has

[33] So Nashe says, but he may have actually retired to Lowestoft, his birthplace, which is less than fifteen miles from Yarmouth.

[34] E. Arber, *Transcript of the Register of the Company of Stationers,* III. 677.

[35] Dekker, *A Knight's Conjuring* (1607).

[36] Spenser's sonnet is dated Dublin, July 18, 1586, and was first printed in Harvey's *Four Letters* (1592).

[37] *King Lear,* II. ii. 15 ff.—Harington's brilliantly Rabelaisian *Metamorphosis of Ajax* (1596) belongs to the same year as Nashe's *chef d'œuvre, Have with You to Saffron Walden,* which probably drew an illustration from it (see McKerrow, *Nashe,* III. 38). Harington is hardly Nashe's inferior in this robust and witty prose; but one of the sequel pieces, *Ulysses upon Ajax,* is merely coarse and is most likely not by Harington. See A. E. M. Kirwood, "The *Metamorphosis of Ajax* and its Sequels," *Library,* 4 ser., XII (1931). 208-34.

[38] See above, ch. IV. Dekker's nondramatic works are edited by A. B. Grosart (5v, 1884-86).

taken over Nashe's vivacity and his knack of working the macabre into social criticism, as in this picture of Charon's ferry:

In a few minutes, therefore, is he come to the bankside of Acheron, where you are not baited by whole kennels of yelping watermen, as you are at Westminster-bridge, and ready to be torn in pieces to have twopence towed out of your purse. No, shipwrights there could hardly live; there's but one boat, and in that one Charon is the only ferryman; so that if a Cales knight [39] should bawl his heart out, he cannot get a pair of oars there to do him grace with "I plied your wor-ship first," but must be glad to go with a sculler. By which means, though the fare be small (for the waterman's wages was at first but a halfpenny, then it came to a penny, 'tis now mended and is grown to three halfpence; for all things wax dear in hell, as well as upon earth, by reason 'tis so populous) yet the gains of it are greater in a quarter than ten western barges get in a year. Ditchet Ferry comes nothing near it.[40]

Dekker was a gentler person than Nashe, and had a suaver style. *The Seven Deadly Sins of London* (1606) follows in a lighter vein Nashe's condemnation of the citizens' vices in the latter part of *Christ's Tears*, whereas Nashe's treatment of the destruction of Jerusalem by Titus, in the earlier part of the same work, finds its parallel in Dekker's versified *Canaan's Calamity* (1618). Dekker is the great chronicler of the London plagues in a series of pamphlets [41] beginning with *The Wonderful Year* (1603), in which, after his wont, narrations of the grimmest horror are interspersed with passages of the purest fantasy and descriptive beauty. His most famous prose work is *The Gull's Hornbook* (1609), which, with an irony too urbane for Nashe, instructs the young gallant from the country how he can make the greatest nuisance of himself through the various occupations of a London day. Chapter VI, "How a Gallant Should Behave Himself in a Playhouse," is perhaps the neatest, for Dekker is always at his best when talking of the stage, and he alludes to it so continually in his prose works that they are a happy hunting ground for students of the drama.[42] *Thomas Dekker*

The Gull's Hornbook

Articulate Puritanism in Elizabeth's reign, in so far as it discussed public morals rather than church government, is closely associated with criticism of the contemporary theatre.[43] The earliest pamphlet of this kind followed by only a year or two the opening of the first two regular playhouses, the Theatre and Curtain in Shoreditch. It is John Northbrooke's *Treatise wherein Dicing, Dancing, Vain Plays or Interludes, with Other Idle Pastimes...Are Reproved* (c. 1577).[44] Quoting broadly from both the pagan classics and the Christian, Northbrooke throws his argument into the form of a dialogue *The Stage and Public Morality*

North-brooke's Treatise

---

[39] I.e., a knight dubbed on the Cadiz expedition of 1596.
[40] Ed. Grosart, II. 117.
[41] F. P. Wilson, *The Plague Pamphlets of Thomas Dekker* (Oxford, 1925).
[42] See W. J. Lawrence, "Dekker's Theatrical Allusiveness," *LTLS*, XXXVI, Jan. 30, 1937, p. 72.
[43] See E. K. Chambers, *The Elizabethan Stage* (Oxford, 1923), IV. 184-259; E. N. S. Thompson, *The Controversy between the Puritans and the Stage* (1903); T. S. Graves, "Notes on Puritanism and the Stage," *SP*, XVIII (1921). 141-169; W. Ringler, "The First Phase of the Elizabethan Attack on the Stage, 1558-1579," *HLQ*, V (1942). 391-418.
[44] Ed. J. P. Collier for the Shakespeare Soc. (1843).

between an old man and a young. The tone is that of a moderate though determined Puritan, and the discussion proceeds through a castigation of contemporary Sabbath-breaking and idleness to condemnation of stage-players and "those places also which are made up and builded for such plays and enterludes, as the *Theatre* and *Curtain* is, and other such like places besides." "God be merciful to this realm of England," the Old Man says,

for we begin to have itching ears and loathe that heavenly manna, as appeareth by their slow and negligent coming unto sermons, and running so fast and so many, continually, unto plays. . . .

Yet he grants that academic and school plays may be permitted, provided that they be free from ribaldry or wanton love, inexpensively staged, infrequent, and not produced for gain but "for learning and utterance' sake, in Latin, and very seldom in English."

Northbrooke's dignified protest was quickly followed, and in a way travestied, by Stephen Gosson's "pleasant invective against poets, pipers, *Gosson, The* players, jesters, and such-like caterpillars of a commonwealth," which he *School of* entitled *The School of Abuse* [45] (1579). Young Master Gosson (1554-1624), *Abuse* who, like Marlowe, was son of a Canterbury tradesman and had been bred at the same excellent school, had been Lyly's contemporary at Oxford, and was Lyly's ape in style. His brief discourse, when stripped of its Euphuistic husk and classical digressions, is to this effect: Gosson has written plays himself; he mentions three by title (all now lost), and states in the first sentence of his address to the reader that they "are daily to be seen upon stages." He has, however, reformed and wishes to tell the world that poetry, piping, and playing "are of great affinity and all three chained in links of abuse." Modern England is a sink of iniquity. *"Experto crede:* I have seen somewhat, and therefore I think I may say the more." "In our assemblies of plays in London," the reader may see "such heaving and shoving, such itching and shouldering to sit by women," that Gosson's soul revolts, though his pen goes on to round out a luscious and very mannered paragraph. Yet he knows that some of the players are very excellent men, and some of the plays presented at the Theatre and at the Belsavage and Bull innyards are admirable, among which is his own *Catiline's Conspiracies,* but "because it is a pig of mine own sow" he will speak the less of it.

These plays are good plays, and sweet plays, and of all plays the best plays, and most to be liked, worthy to be sung of the muses, or set out with the cunning of Roscius himself; yet are they not fit for every man's diet.

Therefore, says Gosson, who was soon to become a parson,

Let us but shut up our ears to poets, pipers and players; pull our feet back from resort to theatres, and turn away our eyes from beholding of vanity, [and] the greatest storm of abuse will be overblown and a fair path trodden to amendment of life.

[45] Reprinted by the Shakespeare Soc. (1841) and by E. Arber (1868). Consult W. Ringler, *Stephen Gosson* (Princeton, 1943).

The frothy stuff, which may have been written to the order of the City authorities, was frothily dedicated to Philip Sidney, and we have Spenser's testimony that the author "was for his labor scorned."[46] Yet it made far more stir than Northbrooke. Another reformed dramatist, probably Anthony Munday, joined in Gosson's crusade, his essay being published, along with a translation of Salvian's attack on the ancient theatre,[47] under the title, *A Second and Third Blast of Retrait* (i.e., retreat) *from Plays and Theatres* (1580). It is in a sincerer style than Gosson's, and harps upon the three most effective arguments of the day: *(a)* the sacrilege of performing plays commonly on Sunday, *(b)* the social dangers arising from the presence of unchaperoned women, and *(c)* the common Elizabethan conviction that wherever a crowd is gathered together for any other purpose than God's service, it is sure to be serving the devil. This writer treats Gosson with marked politeness, but Thomas Lodge replied to him with truculent derision in a pamphlet that has come down to us without title or date,[48] and again in the preface of his moral tract, *An Alarum against Usurers* (1584). Gosson, in his *Plays Confuted in Five Actions*[49] (entered, S. R., 1582), let a spate of alliteration and classical apologue descend upon Lodge, with much mention of an ever-busy devil in the playhouses. Each delighted in calling the other a foolish young man, and it is certain that both were right. The strife was even carried to the stage in a lost allegorical piece at the Theatre (Feb. 23, 1581-2), *The Play of Plays*, which evidently resembled Redford's *Wit and Science* in plot. The whole business looks like a peculiarly trivial "war of the theatres," except as it reveals the deep abiding sense of moral fragility out of which Puritanism grew.

Munday

Lodge

    That sense is much better expressed in a mellower and broader work, Philip Stubbes's *Anatomy of Abuses*[50] (1583), the first part of which is a long dialogue between Spudeus and Philoponus, the zealous and the industrious man. Philoponus has spent seven years in Ailgna,[51] "a pleasant and famous island, immured about with the sea, as it were with a wall,"[52] and proceeds to describe to his friend in most valuable detail the vanity and sinfulness of the islanders. The special reprehension of plays arises out of the discussion of Sabbath-breaking and leads, as in Northbrooke also and in Gosson, to condemnation of such other pagan pleasures as May-games, dancing, cards, bear-baiting, football, and the reading of evil books.

Stubbes, The Anatomy of Abuses

[46] Letter to Harvey, Oct. 16(?), 1579. See W. R. Orwen, "Spenser and Gosson," *MLN*, LII (1937). 574-576.

[47] *De Gubernatione Dei*, Book 6 (5th century, A.D.). *A Second and Third Blast of Retrait* is reprinted by W. C. Hazlitt, *The English Drama and Stage* (1869), pp. 97-154.

[48] Gosson seems to suggest that it was called *Honest Excuses;* the date must be 1579 or 1580. It is reprinted, with the title "A Defence of Poetry, Music, and Stage-Plays," by D. Laing (Shakespeare Soc., 1853). See W. Ringler, "The Source of Lodge's Reply to Gosson," *RES*, xv (1939). 164-71.

[49] Reprinted, W. C. Hazlitt, *op. cit.*, pp. 157-218.

[50] Reprinted with elaborate commentary by F. J. Furnivall (New Shakspere Soc., 1877-79). See also G. C. Taylor, "Another Renaissance Attack on the Stage," (in *Politic Discourses*, trans. by Sir E. Hoby, 1586), *PQ*, ix (1930). 78-81; and works analyzed by Chambers, *Eliz. Stage*, iv, Appendix C.

[51] I.e., Anglia, England (Stubbes spells his place names backwards).

[52] Compare *Richard II*, ii. i. 46 f.

Objection to the public playhouses and the vulgar actors spread in the course of time to the university stage and produced classic results in the debate at Oxford between Dr. William Gager, the Latin dramatist, and
Rainolds and Gager Dr. John Rainolds, one of the most eminent ascetic theologians of the age. It began in a private exchange of letters in 1592. Gager's long defense, which is a model for style and argument, has been only recently printed; [53] Rainolds' much longer attack was published in 1599 with the title: *Th' overthrow of Stage Plays, by the Way of Controversy Betwixt D. Gager and D. Rainoldes.* The interesting William Vaughan (1577-1641), poet, Newfoundland colonist, and devotional writer, published in 1600 *The Golden Grove, Moralized in Three Books,* in one chapter of which he vehemently and categorically denied that stage-plays should be allowed in a Christian commonwealth.[54]

Heywood's Apology for Actors It was very likely the second edition of this work in 1608 that provoked Thomas Heywood's *Apology for Actors* [55] (1612), which is the pinnacle of all this literature. It is one of the most successful *apologias* in the language, and though it opens with a sharp rebuke of "the sundry exclamations of many seditious sectists in this age, who in the fatness and rankness of a peaceable commonwealth grow up like unsavory tufts of grass," it proceeds with an irresistible modesty and common sense. The motive of it is loyalty and it has a double dedication: to a grand old nobleman, the fourth Earl of Worcester, who had been the patron of Heywood's company in Elizabethan years, and to those whom Heywood terms "my good friends and fellows, the city actors." Heywood says that he "could willingly have committed this work to some more able than myself," but there is only one man to whom posterity would more willingly have assigned the task, and that is Shakespeare, who we know was the author's friend, and whom Heywood seems to have resembled, in personality and range of experience, more than any other writer. Heywood was not only an actor and a playwright, but also a university scholar and a gentleman. His replies to the charges against the stage utilize the learning and dialectic he had acquired at Cambridge. Thus, to the argument that Marcus Aurelius had outlawed plays he rejoins:

This Aurelius was a great and sharp reprover, who, because the matrons and ladies of Rome, in scorn of his person, made a play of him, in his time interdicted the use of their theatres . . . Do but peruse the ancient Roman chronicles, and you shall undoubtedly find that from the time of this precise emperor that stately city, whose lofty buildings crowned seven high hills at once and overpeered them all, straightway began to hang the head . . . Marcus Aurelius ended their mirth, which presaged that shortly after should begin their sorrow. He banished their liberty, and immediately followed their bondage.

[53] By K. Young, *Trans. Wisconsin Acad.,* XVIII (1916). 593-638.
[54] 2nd. ed., 1608, ch. 66. Thomas Beard's *Theatre of God's Judgments* (1597), which also contains violent words against actors, had a second edition in 1612. "Vain, idle, wanton pamphlets," as well as plays, are assailed at great length in *Virtue's Commonwealth* (1603), by Henry Crosse (ed. Grosart, 1878, pp. 99-123).
[55] Reprinted, Shakespeare Soc. (1841). Facsimile, ed. R. H. Perkinson (1941: *Scholars Facsimiles & Reprints*).

However, he is not content merely to parry the attacks; the best part of his defense is the full-throated assertion of the social profits the actors' art had conferred on London. Play-acting teaches a man decorum in speech:

not to stare with his eyes, draw awry his mouth, confound his voice in the hollow of his throat, or tear his words hastily betwixt his teeth; neither to buffet his desk like a mad man, nor stand in his place like a lifeless image, demurely plodding, and without any smooth and formal motion. It instructs him to fit his phrases to his action, and his action to his phrase, and his pronunciation to them both.

The plays of London have drawn admiring visitors from all countries, and vastly improved the language:

Our English tongue, which hath been the most harsh, uneven, and broken language of the world, part Dutch, part Irish, Saxon, Scotch, Welsh, and indeed a gallimaffry of many, but perfect in none, is now by this secondary means of playing continually refined, every writer striving in himself to add a new flourish unto it; so that in process, from the most rude and unpolished tongue it is grown to a most perfect and composed language, and many excellent works and elaborate poems writ in the same, that many nations grow enamoured of our tongue, before despised.

They have spread education:

Plays have made the ignorant more apprehensive, taught the unlearned the knowledge of many famous histories, instructed such as cannot read in the discovery of all our English chronicles; and what man have you now of that weak capacity that cannot discourse of any notable thing recorded, even from William the Conqueror, nay, from the landing of Brute, until this day?

But chiefly it is the effects of drama on character that he stresses:

What English blood, seeing [seeth] the person of any bold Englishman presented, and doth not hug his fame and hunny [feel delight] at his valor, pursuing him in his enterprise with his best wishes, and as being rapt in contemplation, offers to him in his heart all prosperous performance, as if the personator were the man personated? so bewitching a thing is lively and well-spirited action that it hath power to new-mould the hearts of the spectators, and fashion them to the shape of any noble and notable attempt.

Heywood's *Apology* is full of such fine and fervid claims. He loved his art as honestly as Ben Jonson did, and he loved his fellow-actors better. Twenty years later, when William Prynne (1600-1669) compiled his enormous *Histrio-Mastix* (1633) in their dispraise, there was doubtless less to be said for either; but in 1612 dramatic art, if not in the very May-morn of its youth, was still

> Ripe for exploits and mighty enterprises,

and the angry reply of one I. G., *A Refutation of the Apology for Actors* (1615), fell very flat.

VI

Elizabethan Comedy

Elizabethan Theatres

The terms *theatre, stage,* and *actor* had in Queen Elizabeth's time no such definite meanings as they have today.[1] Stage architecture and techniques were so rapidly developing that efforts to visualize a typical "Elizabethan stage" are illusory. The theatre might be a schoolroom or college hall, where students performed under the direction of their masters; it might be the social hall of one of the London legal societies (the Inns of Court), or of some great house or palace; it might be the choirboys' concert chamber, or the galleried but roofless "yard" of a carrier's inn, utilized normally for the delivery of produce from the country. When the actors traveled, it might be any place where an audience could be gathered, from a town hall to a barn. The plays mentioned in the next two chapters were acted under the most different conditions and in the most diverse places.

Status of Actors

It is important to recognize the relatively great significance in Shakespeare's age of what we should call amateur or semi-amateur productions, and the special disabilities under which the professional companies worked. The actor was not recognized in the reign of Elizabeth as a bona fide wage-earner, and in a London still governed by the old guild system he had no professional safeguards. He was, moreover, increasingly jeopardized by the predominant Puritan spirit in the City, which, though perhaps not very menacing in the early part of the reign,[2] grew strong enough to suppress acting altogether before the next century was half over. The actors

---

[1] In connection with this chapter and the next the *CBEL,* I. 487 ff., should be consulted. The essential reference books are W. W. Greg, *A Bibliography of the English Printed Drama to the Restoration,* I (1939), Plays to 1616; and E. K. Chambers, *The Elizabethan Stage* (4v, Oxford, 1933). A. Harbage, *Annals of English Drama, 975-1700* (Philadelphia, 1940), and H. W. Wells, *Chronological List of Extant Plays Produced in and about London, 1581-1642* (1940, a supplement to his *Elizabethan and Jacobean Playwrights,* 1939) give tentative chronological lists. J. Q. Adams, *Shakespearean Playhouses* (Boston, 1917) is the standard account of Elizabethan theatres, but may be supplemented by A. H. Thorndike, *Shakespeare's Theatre* (1916; latest impression, 1935) and by three recent studies of great importance: Alfred Harbage, *Shakespeare's Audience* (1941); John C. Adams, *The Globe Playhouse, Its Design and Equipment* (Cambridge, Mass., 1942); and G. F. Reynolds, *The Staging of Elizabethan Plays at the Red Bull Theatre, 1605-1625* (1940). The long dramatic histories of A. W. Ward, F. E. Schelling, and W. Creizenach are still of value. More recent and briefer treatments include T. Brooke, *The Tudor Drama* (Boston, 1911); F. E. Schelling, *Elizabethan Playwrights* (1925); Janet Spens, *Elizabethan Drama* (1922); F. S. Boas, *An Introduction to Tudor Drama* (Oxford, 1933); G. B. Harrison, *Elizabethan Plays and Players* (1940); T. M. Parrott and R. H. Ball, *A Short View of Elizabethan Drama* (1943). The whole development of English comedy is covered by A. H. Thorndike, *English Comedy* (1929), a treatment which may be supplemented by the excellent introductions of C. M. Gayley to the first three volumes of *Representative English Comedies* (1903-1914).

[2] See W. Ringler, "The First Phase of the Elizabethan Attack on the Stage," *HLQ,* v (1942). 391-418.

postponed their doom by two recourses. To avoid the laws against vagabonds *"Public"* they described themselves, more or less fictitiously, as the private servants of *Playhouses* some great lord or of the Queen; and to escape the unfriendly City government they built their public playhouses outside the corporate limits. The earliest of these, the Theatre and Curtain, both erected in 1576-7, were in the unsavory Shoreditch suburb north of the city wall, and were followed by the Fortune (1600) and the Red Bull (*c.* 1605) farther west. The Rose (1587), Swan (*c.* 1595), and Globe (1599), on the other hand, established themselves, like the later Hope (1614), on the south bank of the Thames, just opposite the City, but in the county of Surrey. All these, though with time they grew more spacious and expensive, followed the original innyard structure and featured a roofless auditorium offering standing room only for the rabble and seats in the roofed galleries for patrons who paid more. The chief source of information about the day by day business of an Elizabethan public playhouse is the *Diary,* or account-book, of Philip Henslowe, manager of the Rose and Fortune.[3]

Theatres which were able to intrude within the City proper were called by *"Private"* the palliative name of "private" playhouses. From the first these catered to *Playhouses* a wealthier and smaller clientele, offering seats (and roofing) for all, elaborate music, and artificial lighting. The only such houses during Elizabeth's reign were the one used by the Paul's Boys and the two Blackfriars enterprises, of which the earlier (1576-84) was soon suppressed and the later (*c.* 1600) had great difficulty in opening. In Stuart times, however, the private playhouses rapidly increased, until they became the dominant theatres and passed on their particular conventions, rather than those of the "public" houses, to the Restoration and the modern stage.

It was of great importance in the development of English comedy that *Latin* Plautus, and particularly Terence, had a leading place in the scheme of *Comedy* Renaissance education. An edition of the six comedies of Terence by Pynson *at School* (1495-97) ranks among the English incunabula; a translation of the first comedy, *Andria,* was printed along with the Latin text about 1530; and in 1533 the same dramatist was carved up to make a pedagogical implement in Nicholas Udall's *Flowers for Latin-Speaking, Selected and Gathered out of Terence and the Same Translated into English,* which was later enlarged and frequently reprinted. Alexander Nowell, the great headmaster of Westminster School (1543), required the reading of Terence "for the better learning the true Roman style," and the school regulations of 1561 insisted upon the performance of Latin plays at Christmas. In the year of Shakespeare's birth the Westminster boys produced a comedy of Terence *(Heautontimorumenos)* and one of Plautus *(Miles Gloriosus),* the latter being repeated before Queen Elizabeth, who, as well as four of her nobility,

---

[3] *Henslowe's Diary* is edited by W. W. Greg (2v, 1904-8) and supplemented by *Henslowe Papers* (1907). Further information is found in J. T. Murray, *English Dramatic Companies* (2v, 1910) and in several volumes of collected papers by W. J. Lawrence.

received a complimentary copy of Plautus on the occasion.[4] So it was elsewhere; Tudor schoolboys acted Roman comedy for the improvement of their conversational Latin and thus acquired their ideas of dramatic art. The result was an indoctrination of Plautine and Terentian method that quickly made itself apparent in English plays of academic nature.

The First Regular Comedies

In *Jack Juggler,* "a new interlude for children to play" (printed in 1562), the scene of the two Sosias with which Plautus's *Amphitruo* opens, has been developed into 1200 lines of purely native London farce.[5] This is still an interlude; but in Udall's *Ralph Roister Doister* and William Stevenson's *Gammer Gurton's Needle,* both dating from about the opening of Queen Mary's reign (1553),[6] the Latin five-act comedy suddenly appeared, complete in all its parts and wholly domesticated. It would be hard to find another instance of such immediate acceptance of a foreign art form. In these plays the characters and setting are wholly English, the structure wholly Latin. Each observes precise unity of time and place, and is divided into five acts with rigid care, on the Renaissance principle that a new act begins when the stage is bare and a new scene when a character joins or leaves those who are in conversation. The two plays give contrasting pictures of urban and of country society. *Roister Doister,* which was probably first acted by Queen Mary's Chapel Royal or at Westminster School,[7] depicts middle class life in London. *Gammer Gurton* reeks with the rusticity of the sixteenth-century village; one might call it Stratford-on-Avon and gain a materially better appreciation of the world Shakespeare entered at his birth.

Both plays contain delightful songs; the "Back and side, go bare, go bare," which opens the second act of *Gammer Gurton,* is so irresistible that it has been filched times without number by producers of Shakespearean plays. Naturally, the conventional character types of the Greek and Roman city comedy are most observable in *Roister Doister,* which has a braggart soldier and a parasite, but the leading figure in that play, Dame Christian Custance, is as English as the Wife of Bath. She combines, not unengagingly, an acute sensitiveness about social proprieties and the discipline of servants with a prompt efficiency in boxing the ears of unwise suitors. In *Gammer Gurton's Needle* [8] the plot thickens and the action moves post-haste. Instead of one widow, we here have two, equally honest and upstanding, and still less cramped in the enjoyment of their plebeian temperaments than the city-bred Dame Custance. The causes of war also pass from the abstract to the concrete. Disembodied proprieties do not here inflame the Amazons; they fly to arms

Ralph Roister Doister

Gammer Gurton's Needle

[4] See E. J. L. Scott, "The Westminster Play Accounts of 1564 and 1606," *Athenaeum,* Feb. 14, 1903, p. 220; and T. H. V. Motter, *The School Drama in England* (1929).
[5] See above, Part I, ch. v. A closer adaptation of the *Amphitruo* has been preserved in manuscript (*c.* 1600) with the title, *The Birth of Hercules:* printed by the Malone Soc. (1911). It expands the Latin play considerably and adds a new servant named Dromio (cf. *The Comedy of Errors*).
[6] See T. W. Baldwin and M. C. Linthicum, "The Date of *Ralph Roister Doister,*" *PQ,* VI (1927). 379-395. For arguments for an earlier date see the edition of the play by C. G. Child (1912), pp. 31-42.
[7] The most recent separate editions of *Roister Doister* are those of the Malone Soc. (1935) and G. Scheurweghs (Louvain, 1939).
[8] Ed. H. F. B. Brett-Smith (Oxford, 1920).

ιο redeem a stolen darning-needle or defend a threatened hen-roost. Blood flows, hair flies, the village curate, defender of the virtues and the peace, is cudgelled stiff and stark in pursuance of a remarkable round of duty. The fifth act is an inexpressibly joyous affair, beautifully stage-managed, as the tight-tangled plot is let out reef by reef till the quintessential moment arrives in which the eponymous hero of the piece, Gammer Gurton's Needle, quiescent in the seat of honest Hodge's breeches, brings about the final dénouement.

Nothing about this play is more likely to cause surprise, or is more really significant, than the character of the author and of the audience for whom it was written. It was composed by Master S,[9] M. A. of Christ's College, Cambridge (later the college of Milton), and was acted for the amusement of that demure society. Similarly, *Ralph Roister Doister* was written by an eminent clergyman and scholar, high in favor with both King Edward VI and Queen Mary, successively headmaster of the great schools of Eton and Westminster. When we compare these earliest examples of the classical tendency in English comedy with the charming interludes of John Heywood, a paradox appears. The net result of bringing into the drama the influence of pagan culture was, it would seem, to make it much more moral in the ordinary Christian sense and indescribably less cultivated or refined. To compare Heywood's wit with that of the earliest comedies is like comparing Beau Brummel with a prize-fighter; and yet, whereas Heywood's development of the so-called morality play is frankly immoral, or unmoral in high degree, the Elizabethan imitations of wicked Terence and Plautus are staggeringly righteous. Taken as a class, they are surprisingly inoffensive in their morals, and appallingly vulgar in their social tone. *The Social Tone of Early Elizabethan Comedy*

This is less true, of course, of comic plots borrowed from Italy.[10] One of the earliest modern comedies was *I Suppositi* (i.e., the substitutes or changelings) by Ariosto, acted at Ferrara in 1509. It was in prose,[11] but followed Latin precedent in other structural respects, and was largely built up by a clever combination of plot devices from a comedy by Plautus and another by Terence.[12] George Gascoigne translated this into English prose as *The Supposes,* for presentation at Gray's Inn in 1566, retaining the Italian names and setting; and thus the English stage received the story and the comic figures which are found again as Lucentio, Tranio, Gremio, and the true and false Vincentio in the minor plot of *The Taming of the Shrew.* *Comedies from the Italian* *Gascoigne's Supposes*

A somewhat similar comedy is *The Bugbears,* adapted from A.-F. Grazzini's *La Spiritata* ("The girl possessed by the devil," 1561) and set in Florence. It employs rough riming verse instead of prose and follows the Italian source less closely than *The Supposes* does, but is no less careful *The Bugbears*

---

[9] Identified by Henry Bradley with William Stevenson; see C. M. Gayley, *Representative English Comedies*, I (1912). 197-202. For an opposed view see C. W. Roberts, "The Authorship of *Gammer Gurton's Needle*," PQ, xix (1940). 97-113.
[10] See R. W. Bond, *Early Plays from the Italian* (Oxford, 1911), which contains texts of *Supposes, Bugbears,* and *Misogonus.*
[11] Ariosto later recast the play in verse (1529).
[12] I.e., the *Captivi* and the *Eunuchus.*

about the five-act structure. *The Bugbears* exists in a single manuscript, written, as a note on the last page says, by one John Jeffere, who may be the English adapter or merely the scribe. The date appears to be about the same as that of *The Supposes, c.* 1565, and the company for which it was intended an amateur band of schoolboys. As there is no record of printing or public performance, the fact that the chief intriguing servant is called Biondello, like a parallel character in *The Taming of the Shrew,* must be set down to coincidence. *The Bugbears* has the same type of Greco-Latin comic plot as *Supposes:* children carrying out amorous schemes with the aid of clever servants against the wills of avaricious or doting old men; but it adds a noisier and more farcical element by bringing in imaginary spirits ("bugbears") to haunt the house of the old miser, Amideus, and to be exorcised by a false "astronomer."

Misogonus

There is still more uproarious comedy, more variety, and more realism in another manuscript play, *Misogonus,* which mingles the prodigal son motif with Italian comedy of lost children. The one manuscript is incomplete, and both authorship and sources are doubtful, though a certain Laurentius Bariona has set his name and the date 1577 on the title-page, and a Thomas Richards has signed the prologue.[13] The scene is Italian and the structure classical, but the versification is rough and the general spirit of the piece derives quite as much from the English interlude as from Terence.

Two Italian Gentlemen

Anthony Munday's version of *Il Fedele* (1575) by Luigi Pasqualigo was acted before Queen Elizabeth and printed with the title, *Fedele and Fortunio, the Deceits in Love, or A Pleasant Comedy of Two Italian Gentlemen,* in 1585,[14] several years after a Latin version of the same original had been produced at St. John's, Cambridge.[15] To compare these three plays, respectively Neapolitan, Latin, and English, is to receive an instructive lesson in the variations which the same theme might sustain in being fitted to three different types of hearers. It would seem from Munday's treatment that the Queen's taste was for the braggadocio of Captain Crackstone, who adds malapropism to his other absurdities as *miles gloriosus,* and for lively song. Instrumental music is called for between the acts, which are unified on classic principles, as in the other plays of this group. False enchantment and horseplay add liveliness, but the comedy is essentially a love intrigue on the formula which repeats itself in *The Two Gentlemen of Verona, A Midsummer Night's Dream,* and *Much Ado about Nothing:* two romantic couples, brought into cross purposes by inconstancy or plotting, show how the course of true love never did run smooth, and in the end pair off as in the beginning.

The ancient foundation of the Chapel Royal, which supplied the religious

---

13 See S. A. Tannenbaum, "The Author of *Misogonus,*" in *Shaksperian Scraps* (1933), pp. 129-141.

14 Entered, Stationers' Register, Nov. 12, 1584; reprinted by the Malone Society (1910) with supplement (1933). That Munday was the adapter of this play seems highly probable, but has not yet been fully proved.

15 *Victoria,* by Abraham Fraunce, ed. G. C. Moore Smith (Louvain, 1906).

exercises of the court, included a body of choir boys, fixed at the number *The Chil-* of twelve by a patent of 1526. From an early date these boys were occasionally *dren of the* employed in "disguisings" and other secular entertainments, and in pro- *Chapel* portion to the energy and resourcefulness of the masters who had them in charge they might be drilled to present plays. At several periods during Elizabeth's reign their prestige as an acting company was so great as to challenge that of the best adult professionals and attract the services of the leading dramatists.[16]

William Cornish, who was master of the Chapel Children from 1509 till 1523, produced interludes and pageants at Henry VIII's court with much apparent favor, though the texts have not survived. Cornish's successors, William Crane and Richard Bower, did something to continue the tradi- tion; but it was not till Bower was succeeded by Richard Edwards [17] (1524- *Richard* 1566) in 1561 that a great advance was made. Edwards' only extant play, *Edwards* *Damon and Pythias,* acted before the Queen at Christmas, 1564, introduces several important innovations. The prologue begins, like that of Marlowe's *Tamburlaine,* by informing the audience that the poet has turned his back upon the customary "toying plays," i.e., interludes. It proceeds to develop the Horatian theory of decorum in character types and to define the offered play—in a new phrase which was later to become very famous—as a "tragical comedy." *Damon and Pythias* is in fact the interesting result of a blend of *Damon and* elements from classic comedy and tragedy with certain conventions of Eng- *Pythias* lish farce. The dignified and edifying story, lauding the noblest Elizabethan virtue, self-sacrificing friendship, is the stuff of tragedy, as are the characters of Eubulus, the good councilor, and Dionysius, the tyrant monarch; and this quality is enforced by moral declamations that might have come out of Seneca. But the story has a happy ending and is set in a comic frame which deals with the duel of wits between Aristippus and Carisophus. There is no formal division into acts or scenes, and though the place is confined to Syracuse, the time covers a couple of months, the lapse being rather cleverly concealed by an inserted farce lampooning one of the most currently disliked types of petty swindler, the dishonest coal-dealer. The songs are excellent, as Edwards' reputation would lead one to expect; and everything in the play pleases except the style, which to a modern reader is very heavy. Even this, at a time when blank verse had not yet shown its suitability for comedy, can be justified as an experimental innovation, and it may be best to regard it as riming prose.[18]

A similar tragicomic method was employed with even greater success in *Palamon* Edwards' *Palamon and Arcite,* presented in two parts at Christ Church when *and Arcite* Queen Elizabeth visited Oxford in September, 1566. It was based on Chaucer's *Knight's Tale* and produced with a splendor and an effort at scenic realism hitherto unattempted, but the text is lost, except for a single

[16] See E. K. Chambers, *The Elizabethan Stage* (1923) I. 213-234, II. 8-61; H. N. Hille- brand, *The Child Actors* (Urbana, 1926).
[17] See L. Bradner, *The Life and Poems of Richard Edwards* (New Haven, 1927).
[18] See Bradner, *op. cit.,* pp. 70 f.

song by Emilia out of the second part.[19] This pair of plays, even more than *Gorboduc*, seems to have been the great dramatic triumph of the decade of the 1560's, and Edwards' death a few months later, at the early age of forty-two, was a grievous blow. He and his favored band of Chapel Children stood evidently on the brink of fine achievements; but though the records of the Revels Office [20] suggest sporadic efforts to dramatize romantic themes such as he had handled, fifteen years passed before another writer arose who could give any real impulse to comedy.[21]

Lyly is an excellent illustration of the principle that the need brings forth the man.[22] His delicate and refined talent appeared at the precise middle of Queen Elizabeth's reign, as though in answer to a special demand, to give light to the gentiles and urbanity to those who dwelt in the shadows of boorishness. To understand his popularity and influence it is necessary to remember the social gulf which divided the Elizabethan court from that of Henry VIII. The rich and ripened civilization of the earlier age, brought back to us by Holbein's portraits of courtly gentlefolk, by stories of the Field of the Cloth of Gold, and by the gracious writings of Wyatt and Surrey, More, and the witty, worldly Heywood, came to a violent end. The religious and political fluxes of Henry's last years, and the reactionary reigns of Edward VI and Mary, carried the natural inheritors of this culture, the peers and the aristocrats of the nation, into disgusted obscurity, if not actually along the manifold ways of rebellion and sudden death; and Elizabeth found herself a queen of the bourgeois and Philistines. It was the business folk of London and the country squires who made her queen and kept her so, and it was they who made the literary as well as the historical drama of her reign. Her great men, who molded the spirit of her age—the Cecils, Bacons, Raleghs, Walsinghams, Hattons,—were plain and insular Englishmen with few pretensions to breeding and none to hereditary elegance. They had (to speak broadly) the best wits in Europe and the worst manners, the constitutions of plowmen and the sense of humor that ordinarily goes with that endowment. Finesse, one easily guesses, would not be the most congenial implement for their abilities; but the ambiguous foreign policy of Elizabeth kept them for thirty years in one long battle of finesse, constantly at diplomatic swords' points with the most consummate patterns of French, Spanish, and Venetian courtliness, past masters in the art of polite dissimulation and cunning persiflage. Shakespeare,

[margin: hn Lyly (1554-1606)]

[margin: arly lizabethan ulture]

---

[19] See H. E. Rollins, *RES*, IV (1928). 209f.

[20] See Chambers, *Eliz. Stage*, IV. 144-160; A. Feuillerat, *Documents Relating to the Office of the Revels in the Time of Queen Elizabeth* (Louvain, 1908).

[21] Perhaps the most characteristic plays of this period, 1566-1581, were extravaganzas of chivalrous adventure, with elaborate vice-parts out of the interlude. Such are *Common Conditions* (1576), prepared for a strolling company of six, and *The History of the Two Valiant Knights, Sir Clyomon . . . and Clamydes*, printed 1599 as acted by the Queen's Players. To the same strain belongs the enormously popular but worthless *Mucedorus*, printed 1598.

[22] R. W. Bond, *Works* (Oxford, 1902) Vol. II, III; A. Feuillerat, *John Lyly* (Cambridge, 1910); V. M. Jeffrey, *John Lyly and the Italian Renaissance* (Paris, 1929); G. W. Knight, "Lyly," *RES*, XV (1939). 146-163; S. A. Tannenbaum, *John Lyly, A Concise Bibliography* (1940).

in an early comedy, acknowledges the fascination the blunt English felt
in these brilliant creatures:

> Our court, you know, is haunted
> With a refined traveler of Spain;
> A man in all the world's new fashion planted,
> That hath a mint of phrases in his brain;
> One who the music of his own vain tongue
> Doth ravish like enchanting harmony . . .
> How you delight, my lords, I know not, I;
> But, I protest, I love to hear him lie.[23]

If the common sense and character of the English leaders enabled them
ultimately to win the campaigns, their lack of courtly civilization and social
adroitness brought them many a rankling defeat in the diplomatic skirmishes.
Sharp diseases, it is said, require sharp cures; and if Lyly's cure for English
rusticity of speech and manner seems to us pretty drastic, no true Elizabethan
shrank from kissing the rod and following his instructions to the letter. It
was about 1578 that this young elegant from Magdalen College, Oxford,
appeared in London with his novel of *Euphues,* the Well-bred Man, and
with introductions to Lord Burghley. Encouraged by the enormous vogue
of *Euphues,* Lyly carried his conquering prose into the drama in a series
of seven comedies, beginning with *Campaspe* about 1581 and closing with *Lyly's*
Mother Bombie about 1590. The subjects of these plays vary considerably *Theme*
and the manner undergoes a development toward simpler and more lifelike
dialogue; but through them all, as through *Euphues* also, a single purpose
runs, for, like the Pardoner's in Chaucer, Lyly's theme was "always one, and
ever was." Put in a sentence, his grand text, reiterated and elaborated through
twelve years, was simply this: Radix malorum est *rusticitas.*

For Lyly breeding begins with language, and he furnishes his countrymen *The*
with a ready-made coat of words of many colors, as *précieux* and ridiculous *Euphuistic*
and yet somehow as stately and engaging as the steps of a minuet. Shake- *Style*
speare has not inaccurately characterized the style:

> Taffeta phrases, silken terms precise,
> Three-pil'd hyperboles, spruce affectation,
> Figures pedantical.

Modern analysts have sifted out its various constituents: mock natural history,
classical mythology, fable and anecdote, alliteration, antithesis, and the like.[24]
Here is a full-flavored sample from the prologue of *Campaspe:*

Basil softly touched yieldeth a sweet scent, but chafed in the hand a rank savor:
we fear, even so, that our labors slily glanced on will breed some content, but
examined to the proof small commendation . . . There went two nights to the
begetting of Hercules. Feathers appear not on the phoenix under seven months,

---

[23] *Love's Labor's Lost,* I. i. 161 ff.; v. ii. 407 ff.
[24] See above, ch. III.

and the mulberry is twelve in budding; but our travails are like the hare's, who at one time bringeth forth, nourisheth, and engendreth again; or like the brood of trochilus, whose eggs in the same moment that they are laid become birds.

Lyly's reform began with language, but it did not end there. There is none of his prose comedies which does not deserve the praise a modern scholar has given them: "Clean, dainty, fantastic; written with the thought constantly in mind that boys were to act them." [25] Most loyally he maintained the early Elizabethan tradition of moral comedy, but to moral soundness he added a delicacy which is that of the true gentleman. His figures are not gentlefolk in word alone; he delights to show them performing deeds of tenderness and magnanimity. The theme of *Campaspe* is the renunciation of Alexander the Great, who resigns his claim to the Theban captive when he discovers that she loves Apelles. The two lovesick Lincolnshire maids in *Gallathea* would do credit to a nineteenth-century finishing school by their good breeding. A typical situation is that in *Endimion*, in which the wise old man, Geron, urges Eumenides to secure the relief of his unfortunate friend rather than the happy ending of his own love-suit. Here the quaint stateliness of the words does not conceal the sincerity of this little essay on friendship.[26]

Lyly's chief audience was the Queen, before whom, as the title-pages inform us, *Campaspe, Sapho and Phao, Endimion, Gallathea, Midas,* and *The Woman in the Moon* were all played. His actors were "her majesty's children," i.e., the boys of the Chapel, or the similar boy company of St. Paul's, who under the management of Sebastian Westcote (d. 1582) had acquired an equal repute. His theatres were the Queen's palaces at Greenwich (*Endimion, Gallathea*) or Westminster, or during two brilliant years, 1583 and 1584, the private auditorium at Blackfriars, where, under the patronage of the Earl of Oxford, Lyly was able to present his own plays by means of a combination of the Chapel and Paul's companies.[27] His plays are all comedies and are all classically divided, but he is essentially romantic in his plots and violates the unities of time and place when he likes. All but *The Woman in the Moon* are in prose, and all but *Mother Bombie* have their foundation in classic myth, ingeniously varied and—particularly in *Sapho and Phao, Endimion,* and *Midas*—given a piquant application to contemporary affairs. Yet *Mother Bombie* is really the most classic of his plays and the most stageable; by fixing the scene in contemporary Rochester and foregoing learned ornament he showed for once that he could write good Plautine comedy, just as in *The Woman in the Moon* he showed that he could compose harmonious blank verse. But these novelties in his last two plays were not sufficient to maintain his declining vogue, and this most talented dramatist was crowded off the stage about 1590 by the pentecost of genius that

Lyly's Gentlefolk

Lyly's Stage and Actors

Features of His Plays

[25] G. P. Baker, in Gayley's *Representative English Comedies*, III (1914). 425.
[26] III. iv. 122-141 (ed. Bond, p. 50).
[27] This company was often known as "Oxford's boys," and the Earl of Oxford's contemporary repute as a dramatist may rest upon their productions of Lyly's plays, which were anonymous in the earliest editions.

then appeared.[28] His songs have best kept his memory fresh, but even they,   *His Songs*
in recent times, have been denied him.[29]

We come now to a bad man and a surpassing poet. Of all the dramatic
predecessors of Shakespeare George Peele [30] (1556-1596) is perhaps the only   *George*
unredeemed scapegrace, and he is the only one except Marlowe to whom   *Peele*
the great word, genius, can be seriously applied. He was a product of
London streets and gutters, and, high as his imagination soared, his personal
tastes, character, and fortunes do not seem ever to have risen above them.   *Peele's*
At Oxford he made a considerable reputation as scholar and poet, but his   *Character*
academic prowess did not much avail him after his return to London, where
he appears to have been always on the edge of beggary and never far from
the prospect of jail. He died at the age of forty [31] unwept, unhonored, and
unsung; but by no means forgotten, for a dozen years later, in 1607, appeared a popular book called *The Merry Conceited Jests of George Peele*,
which, it has been said, "perhaps better than any other gives a picture of
the wealth and poverty, the squalor and magnificence of Elizabethan London." [32] Many of the swindles here ascribed to him are without doubt
apocryphal, but one can hardly question the essential justice of the portrait
of this Villon of the sixteenth century.

The scamp's audacity is clear enough in much of his poetry. He was an
outrageous jingo in politics, a fire-eater and mouther of marvelous patriotic
hyperboles. A fleet of privateers or detachment of troops for the Continent
could hardly set sail without a farewell burst of minstrelsy from Peele
who gushed into splendid incoherence over the necessary contemptibleness
of all French and Spaniards. He turned many a relatively honest penny
by impassioned addresses, pageants, and pastorals upon such occasions as
the annual election of a new mayor of London, a ceremonial meeting of
the Knights of the Garter, or the gathering of elderly cavaliers at a tournament or militia show. But Peele's masterpiece of impudence is the unbelievable situation with which he concludes his first play, *The Arraignment of
Paris*, presented before the Queen by the Children of the Chapel. Lyly gave
point to a number of his plays by introducing into the mythological story

[28] For an account of his last days see D. Jones, "John Lyly at St. Bartholomew's," in Sisson,
Thomas Lodge and Other Elizabethans (1933), pp. 363-407; also B. M. Wagner, "Elizabethan
Dramatists," *LTLS*, Sept. 28, 1933.

[29] With unimportant exceptions, the songs were not printed in the quarto editions, but
only in the posthumous collection of *Six Court Comedies* (1632). Hence W. W. Greg ("The
Authorship of the Songs in Lyly's Plays," *MLR*, I (1906). 43-52) and J. R. Moore ("The
Songs in Lyly's Plays," *PMLA*, XLII (1927). 623-640) argue that they were composed later,
perhaps by Dekker. Their authenticity has been more persuasively supported by W. J. Lawrence
("The Problem of Lyly's Songs," *LTLS*, Dec. 20, 1923, p. 894), G. W. Whiting ("Canary
Wine and *Campaspe*," *MLN*, XLV (1930). 148-151), R. W. Bond ("Lyly's Songs," *RES*, VI
(1930). 295-299 and "Addendum," *RES*, VII (1931). 442-447).

[30] *Works*, ed. A. H. Bullen (2v, 1888); Peele's plays have been separately reprinted by the
Malone Society (1906-1913). See P. H. Cheffaud, *George Peele* (Paris, 1913); T. Larsen,
"Bibliography of Writings of George Peele," *MP*, XXXII (1934). 143-156 (and other essays cited
in *CBEL*, I. 527); S. A. Tannenbaum, *George Peele, A Concise Bibliography* (1940); H. M.
Dowling, "The Date and Order of Peele's Plays," *N&Q*, CLXIV (1933). 164-168, 183-185.

[31] For the probable dates of his birth and death see B. M. Wagner, *LTLS*, Sept. 28, 1933,
and K. L. Bates, *MLN*, XXXV (1920). 54.

[32] Sir W. Raleigh, in *Shakespeare's England* (1916), I. 18.

flattering topical allusions to Queen Elizabeth and her courtiers; Peele went farther. His plot takes up the old myth of the quarrel of the three goddesses over the golden ball that is the perquisite of the fairest of all divinities. At the end he makes Diana enter to appease the strife by explaining that the ball belongs to none of the claimants, but to

> a gracious nymph,
> That honors Dian for her chastity,

and who fortunately dwells near by. Immediately, with charming unanimity and fervor, the celestials cry out that the only possible candidate has been discovered, and Diana steps to the royal box and *"delivereth the ball of gold to the queen's own hands,"* while the three Fates come forward with a song and yield up the symbolic distaff, spindle, and knife that typify control over earthly affairs. Even Elizabeth, now fifty years old, seems to have realized that there was less of the sublime than of the ridiculous in such a dénouement, and Master Peele does not appear to have been allowed another opportunity to manifest his appreciation.

Though *The Arraignment of Paris* is quite classically divided, Peele had in general no idea of structure, no common sense or reserve. Reason, order, and consistency simply were not his; but he had in very rare degree some immortal gifts. One was the power of drawing an unearthly beauty out of words, a power that marks him as belonging to a class of poets different from Lyly, Greene, or Kyd; to the class, that is, in which we naturally place Marlowe and Shakespeare. Other gifts are more peculiarly dramatic. His three great plays have an intensity of fancy that enables him to transcend the laws of logic, and they are filled with a kind of dramatic intuition that is the strangest thing about Peele. They are as different as possible in form and subject. *The Arraignment of Paris* is a Greek pastoral, written mainly in varied lyrical measures, though the scant two hundred lines of blank verse it contains are much the loveliest that any one wrote before Marlowe. *David and Bethsabe,* which is post-Marlowe, is a tragedy from the Old Testament, nearly wholly in blank verse; and *The Old Wives' Tale* is an extravaganza of English folklore, mostly in prose.

In *The Arraignment of Paris* Peele sees a vision of pre-Homeric Greece, the simple loveliness of the golden age, where song is the natural speech of men, and the genial gods and shepherds mingle in every view. We are in a world before Homer, in comparison with which the people in the *Iliad* seem sophisticated. The theme is the Trojan shepherd Paris and the consequences of his infidelity to his sweetheart Oenone. How sweetly it is introduced as the happy lovers sit together under a tree upon Mount Ida. Paris proposes a song, and with prophetic irony Oenone replies:

> There is a pretty sonnet, then; we call it "Cupid's curse":
> "They that do change old love for new, pray gods they change for worse!"

David and Bethsabe drops us into a totally different world. It is the effete, voluptuous, Oriental world of King David and his sons, a world of overripe

luxury, of lust and crime and penitence. There are no light lyrics in this
play; the one song is a prayer for the avoidance of sin, set to the sad music
of the Hebrew harp. Read these two plays, and you have the gist of Arnold's
distinction between Hebraism and Hellenism. And on the other hand, the
Old Wives' Tale takes us into the nursery. The text has perhaps been badly
preserved, and it contains incidental satire on Gabriel Harvey and other
adult topics; but the mind behind it is that of a dreamy child who has fed
full on the tales the old wives told about 1570.[33] This is a play which for
few readers can create the necessary suspension of disbelief: it must be seen
on stage.[34]

David and Bethsabe

The Old Wives' Tale

The amount of Greene's work in comedy can be only vaguely estimated.[35]
It was probably much more than can now be definitely assigned to him,
but the main lines of his important influence are clear. In a prosier, but
more imitable, way than Peele he introduced a nostalgic, day-dreaming
element and he developed variety, subordinating form to atmosphere, and
packing each play with such diverse materials that plot outlines become
meaningless. The formula for his best plays, *Friar Bacon and Friar Bungay*
and *James IV*, would be something like this: Take a tangled love story
involving rural scenes; mix with a like amount of fairy-lore or magical
display; flavor with Plautine jokes, interlude devices (e.g., the Vice riding
to hell on the devil's back), and classic reminiscence; color with a dash of
pseudo-history; shake and serve. The fictional source for one of these plays
is a prose *History of Friar Bacon,* for the other a story in Cinthio's *Ecatomiti,*
but neither is more than fitfully traceable among the motley ingredients.[36]
The love story is much the same in both, Prince Edward, Lacy, Elinor, and
Margaret in one play balancing James IV, Eustace, Dorothea, and Ida in
the other. In each, vicious love is repelled by the virtuous heroine, and a
happy conclusion follows, in one play by the renunciation of the prince
(as in Lyly's *Campaspe*), in the other by the penitence of the king.

Robert Greene

Friar Bacon and James IV

Greene was no less cavalier in handling his source in *Orlando Furioso,*
which was played before the Queen and probably suggested by Harington's

[33] See S. L. C. Clapp, "Peele's Use of Folklore in *The Old Wives' Tale," Univ. Texas Studies
in English* (1926), pp. 146-156; G. Jones, "The Intention of Peele's *Old Wives' Tale," Aberystwyth Studies,* VII (1925). 79-93; T. Larsen, "The Date of Peele's *Old Wives' Tale," MP,* XXX
(1932). 23-28.
[34] Peele could hardly be imitated as Lyly and Greene were, but something of his delicate
handling of myth, song, and atmosphere may be found in a group of masquelike plays:
(1) The early *Rare Triumphs of Love and Fortune,* acted before the Queen, 1583, printed 1589;
reprinted, Malone Soc., 1931.
(2) *The Maid's Metamorphosis,* acted by the Children of Paul's, printed 1600 (see S. R. Golding, "The Authorship of *The Maid's Metamorphosis," RES,* II (1926). 270-279).
(3) Nashe's *Summer's Last Will and Testament,* 1600 (McKerrow, *Works of Thomas Nashe,*
III. 227-295).
(4) Ford and Dekker, *The Sun's Darling,* licensed 1624, printed 1656. Probably a revision of
Dekker's lost *Phaeton,* which was bought for the Admiral's men, 1598, and acted at court,
1600.
[35] *Plays and Poems,* ed. J. C. Collins (2v, Oxford, 1905); ed. T. H. Dickinson (Mermaid
Ser.); five of Greene's plays are separately reprinted in the Malone Soc. (1907-1932).
[36] See P. Z. Round, "Greene's Materials for *Friar Bacon and Friar Bungay," MLR,* XXI
(1926). 19-23; R. Hudson, "Greene's *James IV* and Contemporary Allusions to Scotland,"
PMLA, XLVII (1932). 652-667.

Orlando
Furioso

translation.[37] It is romantic comedy, spiced with melodrama and farce, and follows Ariosto at a very great distance. The blank verse, like Greene's blank verse in general, effects such a quick *reductio ad absurdum* of Marlowe's style as to make one think it half malicious. *A Looking-Glass for London and England,* by Thomas Lodge and Greene, is a blend of scriptural history, spectacle, and contemporary social satire, and was very popular.[38] Greene's habit of fictionizing history spread to other plays which are either by him or of his school; e.g., *George a Greene,*[39] revived in 1593 by Sussex's company; *Fair Em,*[40] acted by Strange's men about 1590; and *The Famous Victories*

The School
of Greene

of Henry V,[41] acted by the Queen's men before 1588. These were great standbys of the professional troupes in the years before Henslowe began his diary (February, 1592). Later examples of the species Greene created are Munday's *John a Kent and John a Cumber*[42] (*c.* 1594), *Downfall of Robert Earl of Huntingdon* (1598), and *Sir John Oldcastle*[43] (1599); and the anonymous, but delightful and long beloved *Merry Devil of Edmonton*[44] (*c.* 1603).

Greene and
Shakespeare

Greene's influence was great on Shakespeare's romantic comedies, which are based upon much the same premises and materials; e.g., the nostalgic charm of the next county (Suffolk for Greene, Gloucestershire for Shakespeare); the woodland setting and idyllic atmosphere, where evil, though present in its blackest form, is easily dispelled; the capable and high-spirited heroine, fond of disguising herself as a boy; Oberon and his fairies as factors in a human love story; and the melancholy, worldly humorist (Bohan, Jaques) as a commentator on Utopia.[45]

Henry
Porter's
Two Angry
Women of
Abingdon

To see concretely the progress that comedy made in Elizabeth's reign, it is better to turn from Greene's romantic school to a stricter comic type and compare Henry Porter's *Two Angry Women of Abingdon,*[46] which was acted by the Admiral's men about 1598 and printed in 1599, with *Gammer Gurton's Needle.* They were written nearly half a century apart. Both are

[37] Harington's Ariosto was entered on the Stationers' Register, Feb. 26, 1591. It is not necessary to believe that Greene awaited publication of the book, the progress of which was well known at court. See M. R. Morrison, "Greene's Use of Ariosto in *Orlando Furioso,*" *MLN,* XLIX (1934). 449-451.

[38] See C. R. Baskervill, "A Prompt Copy of *A Looking Glass for London and England,*" *MP,* XXX (1932). 29-51; R. A. Law, "*A Looking Glasse* and the Scriptures," *Univ. Texas Studies in English* (1939), pp. 31-47.

[39] Reprinted, Malone Soc. (1911). See H. D. Sykes, "Robert Greene and *George a Greene,*" *RES,* VII (1931). 129-136.

[40] Reprinted, Malone Soc. (1928); also in the *Shakespeare Apocrypha,* ed. T. Brooke (Oxford, 1908).

[41] This, as well as *George a Greene,* is included in J. Q. Adams' *Chief Pre-Shakespearean Dramas* (1924).

[42] Reprinted from MS, Malone Soc. (1923). See J. W. Ashton, "Revision in Munday's *John a Kent and John a Cumber,*" *MLN,* XLVIII (1933). 531-537.

[43] Reprinted, Malone Soc. (1908); also in the *Shakespeare Apocrypha.* The authors were Munday, Drayton, Wilson, and Hathway.

[44] Another of the "Shakespeare Apocrypha"; ed. J. M. Manly in Gayley, *Representative English Comedies,* II (1913); William A. Abrams (Durham, N. C., 1942).

[45] See P. Reyher, "Greene et Shakespeare," *Revue anglo-américaine,* II (1924). 51-54.

[46] Ed. C. M. Gayley, *Representative English Comedies,* I (1912); Malone Soc. (1913). See R. E. Shear, "New Facts about Henry Porter," *PMLA,* XLII (1927). 641-655; E. H. C. Oliphant, "Who Was Henry Porter?" *PMLA,* XLIII (1928). 572-575; L. Hotson, "The Adventure of the Single Rapier," *Atlantic Monthly,* CXLVIII (1931). 26-31; J. M. Nosworthy, "Notes on Henry Porter," *MLR,* XXXV (1940). 517-521.

admirable pieces, filled with vigorous action and motivated by the suspicious fury of a pair of rustic beldames; but in Porter's play farce has broadened into comedy without becoming in any respect romantic or exotic. The social station of the characters has been raised, the literary medium refined into very competent blank verse and prose, and the fable enlarged to include a love plot and the specialized humor types of Dick Coomes and Nicholas Proverbs. In form Porter's play is a "nocturnal," [47] most of the action taking place at night out of doors, in imitation of *A Midsummer Night's Dream,* which is in several places recalled, though there is here a complete absence of supernatural elements. On the other hand, *Two Angry Women of Abingdon* probably suggested the title [48] and some plot elements in *The Merry Wives of Windsor,* in which play likewise one sees what the *Gammer Gurton* species of village comedy could develop into by the year 1600. The balancing species of city, i.e., London, comedy projected in *Ralph Roister Doister* was only slightly exploited in Queen Elizabeth's reign till Chapman and Jonson began moving in that direction at the end of the century; but before those dramatists had developed their ideas, the type had reappeared in William Haughton's amusing *Englishmen for My Money, or A Woman Will Have Her Will,*[49] which, like Porter's *Angry Women,* is first recorded in Henslowe's Diary in 1598. It has been called the first full-length comedy of London life and holds a significant position in the development of urban realism between Udall's play and Middleton's seventeenth-century comedies of London life.

Haughton, Englishmen for My Money

[47] See W. J. Lawrence, "Shakespeare from a New Angle," *Studies* (Dublin, 1919), pp. 442-455; T. Brooke, "Elizabethan Nocturnal and Infernal Plays," *MLN*, xxxv (1920). 120-121.

[48] See R. B. Sharpe, *The Real War of the Theaters* (1935), p. 106. Besides payment for a non-extant second part of the *Two Angry Women,* Porter received an advance from Henslowe on a play to be called *Two Merry Women of Abingdon* (Feb. 28, 1599), which his death at the hands of John Day (June 7 following) must have interfered with.

[49] See the edition of A. C. Baugh (Philadelphia, 1917).

VII
Elizabethan Tragedy

Though tragic narrative, as illustrated in the *Fall of Princes* and *Mirror for Magistrates,* had a great hold on readers, there was hardly any tradition of tragedy on the English stage when Elizabeth came to the throne.[1] Thus, although Seneca was acted at schools and original tragedies in Latin were produced at the universities—several of which, e.g., Grimald's *Archipropheta* (1547), have great merit—there appears to have been no popular interest in English tragedy till after 1580. Up to that time such tragedies as appeared in the vernacular were exotics, quite unlike in that respect to the early comedies. They could be produced only before élite groups such as the Inns of Court, and, with their emphasis upon musical and spectacular adornment, had somewhat the same limited appeal that grand opera has today.

nfluence   Early Elizabethan tragedy is Senecan tragedy.[2] The fact that Lady Lumley
f Seneca made a prose translation of Euripides' *Iphigeneia at Aulis,* which remained in manuscript till 1909,[3] and that Peele at Oxford translated either the same play or its sequel into English verse argues no direct contact between the English stage and the art of Greece. Nor is it likely that the tragic implications of medieval nondramatic writings, lately well analyzed by Professor Farnham, would have found outlet in the theatres if the remarkable interest in Seneca between 1559 and 1581 had not prepared a channel for it. During these years the entire canon of ten tragedies ascribed to Seneca was translated by different hands, and in 1581 they were published together in an impressive volume.

The   The quality of Seneca's plays may be indicated by a digest of his *Thyestes*
Thyestes which had been printed in Jasper Heywood's translation in 1560, and which perhaps influenced the structure of English tragedy more than any other. If

---

[1] Consult for the general background, in addition to works listed at the head of the previous chapter: A. H. Thorndike, *Tragedy* (1908); M. C. Bradbrook, *Themes and Conventions of Elizabethan Tragedy* (Cambridge, 1935); Willard Farnham, *The Medieval Heritage of Elizabethan Tragedy* (Berkeley, 1936); Theodore Spencer, *Death and Elizabethan Tragedy* (Cambridge, Mass., 1936); L. L. Schücking, *The Baroque Character of the Elizabethan Tragic Hero* (British Academy Shakespeare Lecture, 1938); Hardin Craig, "The Shackling of Accidents, a Study of Elizabethan Tragedy," *PQ,* XIX (1940). 1-19; F. T. Bowers, *Elizabethan Revenge Tragedy, 1578-1642* (Princeton, 1940). E. M. W. Tillyard in *The Elizabethan World Picture* (1943) gives a brief and lucid sketch of the philosophical background of Elizabethan serious thinking.

[2] See J. W. Cunliffe, *Early English Classical Tragedies* (Oxford, 1912); F. L. Lucas, *Seneca and Elizabethan Tragedy* (Cambridge, 1922). The best critical treatment of Seneca's plays is in C. W. Mendell, *Our Seneca* (New Haven, 1941). Howard Baker, *Induction to Tragedy* (Baton Rouge, 1939), doubts the extent of Seneca's influence.

[3] Printed in that year by the Malone Soc.

one ignores the choral chants that divide the "acts," and are Seneca's finest poetical contribution, the content of the play is simply this:

Act. I. Dialogue between the ghost of Tantalus and a fury, telling of the curse upon the house of Atreus.

Act II. Atreus announces to an attendant his intended vengeance upon his brother Thyestes.

Act III. Thyestes and his three sons return from banishment at the invitation of Atreus. Thyestes has lost his previous sense of security. He is greeted by Atreus with a false show of love.

Act IV. A messenger informs the chorus of the sacrifice of Thyestes' sons and the unnatural feast at which their father has been fed upon their bodies. Darkness falls at mid-day.

Act V. Atreus discloses to Thyestes that he has consumed his sons.

There is no final chorus or further act of violence. The play ends with the two men discussing the situation in a lurid quiet.

The earliest English tragedy was written by two members of Parliament *Sackville* and presented before Queen Elizabeth at Whitehall, January 18, 1562, by the *and Norton* gentlemen of the Inner Temple. In the first edition (1565) it is called the Gorboduc *Tragedy of Gorboduc;* in the second (*c.* 1570), which does not materially differ, the *Tragedy of Ferrex and Porrex.* The first three acts are said to be the work of Thomas Norton (1532-1584) and the last two of Thomas Sackville (1536-1608), whose notable contribution to the *Mirror for Magistrates* belongs to the same year as the play; and the division is borne out by stylistic evidence.[4] Both writers employ an admirable blank verse, not before attempted in a drama, and for the choral speeches, which in Senecan fashion separate the acts, they use the six-line stanza (*ababcc*) with occasional variation. There is a heavy embellishment of dumb-shows after the Italian style, and of atmospheric music by violins, cornets, flutes, hautboys, and drums successively. The plot is from a source congenial enough to an author of the *Mirror,* i.e., the ancient history of Britain; and the play is itself a mirror for magistrates, indeed a special warning piece for the young Queen against the dangers of sedition and divided sovereignty. To get this effect *Gorboduc* renounces the classic unities and presents a fifth act which is a dramatic irrelevance, since the important characters are already dead. Politically, the last act is far from irrelevant, for it shows a nightmarish picture of ignorant armies clashing and selfish leaders advancing their claims through fifty years of anarchy. The poetry has here the dark grandeur of Sackville's *Induction,* and the play ends with two great, and greatly anachronistic, orations—respectively sixty-five and a hundred lines in length—in praise of parliamentary government.

It may be assumed that the example of *Gorboduc* inspired the sister society Jocasta of Gray's Inn to produce *Jocasta* four years later (1566). This claims to be translated from Euripides (*Phoenissae*), but like Gascoigne's *Supposes* is

---

[4] See J. E. Gillet, "The Authorship of *Gorboduc," MLN,* xxxi (1916). 377-378; S. A. Small, "The Political Import of the Norton Half of *Gorboduc," PMLA,* xlvi (1931). 641-646; S. R. Wilson, "*Gorboduc* and the Theory of Tyrannicide," *MLR,* xxxiv (1939). 355-366.

borrowed from the Italian, i.e., from Lodovico Dolce's *Giocasta,* which
rather remotely followed a Latin translation of the Greek. It has the five-act
division of Senecan drama, acts one and four being signed by F. Kinwelmarsh, the others by G. Gascoigne. The dumb-shows are even more elaborate than in *Gorboduc,* the blank verse a good deal less harmonious, and the
chorus favors the rime royal instead of the six-line stanza.[5] The spectators of
this play supped full with horrors, but they were edified also by abundant
moral clichés to which the printer called attention by marginal notes and
inverted commas.

Gismond of
Salerne

The Inner Temple replied the next year (1567-8) with a tragedy out of
Boccaccio, *Gismond of Salerne in Love,* written in five acts by five different
gentlemen, one of whom was Christopher Hatton, later Lord Chancellor, and
another Robert Wilmot.[6] It was acted before the Queen at Greenwich.[7] The
five authors have well assimilated their styles and produced a very Senecan,
though romantic, play. Gismond's lover is raised in the social scale to appease
Aristotelian critics: from a varlet he becomes an earl. The unities are all
respected, and pagan coloring is provided by the introduction of Cupid and
Megaera. The chorus, which, as in *Gorboduc* and *Jocasta,* consists of four
persons, is not metrically set off from the other speakers. In the original
version the entire play uses alternate rime with few deviations; but years
later (1591) Wilmot gave himself the pains of recasting most of it as blank
verse, adding the dumb-show descriptions, increasing the realistic stage-
effects, and changing the title to *The Tragedy of Tancred and Gismund.*[8]

The Mis-
fortunes of
Arthur

This would indicate that such taste as there was for courtly Senecan tragedy
did not alter very much in a quarter century; and the same thing is shown
in the *Misfortunes of Arthur,* which the Gray's Inn gentlemen acted before
the Queen at Greenwich on February 28, 1588. Francis Bacon had a hand in
it, and Thomas Hughes seems to have been the chief author. Six others
assisted, but they made no improvement upon *Gorboduc.* The blank verse
is less good, the dumb-shows less ingenious, and the choral interludes duller.
The dependence on Seneca is a good deal closer, both in the number of
borrowed lines and in structure. Indeed, the tale of Arthur is here not much
more than a blend of the *Thyestes* and *Oedipus* stories. One might have
expected more English application in the year after Mary Queen of Scots was
beheaded and while the Spanish Armada was preparing to sail.[9] It was still
true that Senecan tragedy could be produced only when it could draw upon
the amateur ambitions of the Inns of Court and count on the Queen's Palace
for a theatre.

[5] The last chorus is a sonnet, similar in form to the one that begins *Romeo and Juliet.*
[6] It is probable that the Inner Temple had previously produced an Italianate tragedy on
the story of Romeo and Juliet at Christmas, 1561, for Arthur Brooke mentions such a play in
his preface to *Romeus and Juliet* (1562). See Cunliffe, *op. cit.,* p. lxxxvii.
[7] See "Sonnet of the Queen's Maids," Cunliffe, *op. cit.,* p. 163.
[8] This text is reprinted, Malone Soc. (1915). See D. Klein, "According to the Decorum of
These Daies," *PMLA,* xxxiii (1918). 244-268; John Murray, "*Tancred and Gismund,*" *RES,*
xiv (1938). 385-395.
[9] See E. H. Waller, "A Possible Interpretation of *The Misfortunes of Arthur,*" *JEGP,* xxiv
(1925). 219-245.

It was Thomas Kyd [10] (1558-1594), and a little after him the subtler, nobler *Thomas* Marlowe, who succeeded around 1585 [11] in producing an English adaptation *Kyd* of Latin tragedy that not only gained the approval of the people as a whole, but aroused an excited enthusiasm such as no other productions of the English theatre have quite equaled. Kyd was no poet, though he can write tolerable blank verse, but as a deviser of stage tricks and a master of the art of giving his audiences the sort of thrills that will most powerfully agitate their spines he has had very few superiors. In his most famous play, *The Spanish Tragedy*, The Span- he takes as a foundation three conventional devices which the stilted earlier ish Tragedy writers had borrowed from Seneca. One was the ghost, another the theme of revenge for the murder of a relative (Kyd makes it the revenge of old Hiero- nimo for the murder of his son), and the third was a liberal use of stage declamation and soliloquy. These he proceeded to aerate and enliven by inventing a whole bagful of novel applications. We can list only the most striking:

1. He discards the antique story taken from classic mythology or legendary British history, and gives his spectators a piping hot play of modern love and war. His setting is Spain, a country quite uniquely interesting to Kyd's countrymen at this time. His plot is imaginary, but it is supposed to arise out of the consequences of the battle of Alcantara, fought as recently as 1580.

2. The Elizabethans liked complexity in their stories, and the Senecan plays had been unbearably monotonous in plot. Kyd evolves a perfect wilder- ness of subplots, with enough hair-raising tricks and turns to make the fortune of a detective novelist.

3. The Elizabethans liked queer people, and the characters of the earlier tragedies, heroes and villains alike, had a distressing tendency to talk like members of Parliament. Kyd gives his characters lurid psychological twists of mind. Hieronimo, the hero, is obscurely mad; Lorenzo, his antagonist, is an embodiment of Machiavellian cunning and ruthlessness; Viluppo is a blue-print for all the heavy villains of nineteenth-century melodrama; Bel- Imperia is that ever new and dreaded portent, the "new" woman, who flouts the mores with a lethal charm.

4. Kyd invents stage business in unbelievable quantities. The Senecan play was notoriously weak in this respect, most of the interesting things taking place behind the scenes and being reported to the audience in a communiqué by a professional bore called the *nuntius* or messenger. The *nuntius* finds no place with Kyd. Of murders and suicides on the stage *The Spanish Tragedy* offers eight, cleverly spaced and diversified, besides the spectacle of a public hanging, the running lunatic of an elderly gentlewoman, the biting out of a gentleman's tongue, and other devices to prevent tedious-

[10] F. S. Boas, *The Works of Thomas Kyd* (Oxford, 1901); C. Crawford, *A Concordance to the Works of Thomas Kyd* (Louvain, 1906-10); J. de Smet, *Thomas Kyd, l'homme, l'œuvre, le milieu* (Brussels, 1925); P. W. Biesterfeldt, *Die dramatische Technik Thomas Kyds* (Halle, 1936).
[11] See T. W. Baldwin, "On the Chronology of Thomas Kyd's Works," *MLN*, XL (1925). 343-349; and "Thomas Kyd's Early Company Connections," *PQ*, VI (1927). 311-313.

ness. Kyd devised the arrangement of the play within the play, which Shakespeare found so useful; and in two separate scenes of the *Spanish Tragedy* [12] he gets a novel three-ring-circus effect by having certain characters discuss their intimate affairs while others look on from without, and Revenge and Andrea gaze down upon the whole—the spectators, of course, diverting themselves with the emotions of all three groups at once.

Finally, Kyd invented a ranting style of verse admirably fitted to the robustious personality of Edward Alleyn and to the acoustics of an open-air, theatre. It drew the very souls out of the groundlings and became as popular with the apprentices of London as Euphuism was with the courtly classes:

> O eyes, no eyes, but fountains fraught with tears!
> O life, no life, but lively form of death!

Dozens of such morsels of Kydian phrase were bawled about the streets and quoted in popular literature for fifty years. Naturally, the play made the fortunes of the actors. Long after Kyd's unhappy death it was being revised and expanded and revised again: [13] as a stage play it simply would not die, though all the men of taste condemned it. At least ten printed editions are known before 1634, and some have disappeared. We may imagine that many of the plain people of London never enjoyed a more perfect moment than when they had got themselves standing room in Henslowe's theatre and were wafted into Elysium by the famous opening words of Don Andrea's ghost:

> When this eternal substance of my soul
> Did live imprisoned in my wanton flesh . . .
> I was a courtier in the Spanish court.

Other Plays by Kyd　　The rest of Kyd's short life seems to have been mainly spent in exploiting the success of *The Spanish Tragedy*. There was a now lost *Spanish Comedy* or *Don Horatio,* that was being produced by Henslowe in 1592. This was probably by Kyd and may have had a connection with *The First Part of Jeronimo* (1605) by a later hand, which gives the antecedent history and explains how Andrea came to be a ghost. The latter is a flat play, but was enough in demand in 1604 to cause a quarrel between Shakespeare's company and the Children of the Revels over the stage rights. In *Soliman and Perseda* Kyd has expanded into a five-act tragedy the story he had used for the inserted play which brings the *Spanish Tragedy* to its catastrophe, adding an induction-choral framework and a braggart soldier, Basilisco, whom Shakespeare appears to have found amusing. [14] The little we know of the lost play of

---

12 II. iv., IV. iv.
13 On the vexed subject of the extraordinary additions (not by Kyd) which first appeared in the quarto of 1602, see the introduction to the Malone Soc. edition of this text; the Oxford *Jonson,* II. 238-241; H. W. Crundell, *N&Q,* CLXIV (1933). 147-149, CLXVI (1935). 246; L. L. Schücking, *Die Zusätze zur Spanish Tragedy* (Leipzig, 1938) and *LTLS,* June 12, 19, 26, July 17, 1937 (pp. 442, 464, 480, 528).
14 See *King John* I. i. 244. Compare also *Soliman and Perseda* I. iii. 51 f. and *Merchant of Venice* II. i. 25 f., and see S. C. Chew, *The Crescent and the Rose* (1937), p. 254.

Hamlet which preceded Shakespeare's indicates that it was Kyd's work:[15] *The Old* a "Danish tragedy" intentionally conceived as a sort of obverse of the *Hamlet Spanish Tragedy,* and marked by the same faults and showy brilliances as the earlier play. Similarities remain even when Kyd's extant play is compared with Shakespeare's. Each has an amiable Horatio, whose name sounds somewhat strangely in Denmark. One concerns a father's vengeance and the other a son's; in each case justice is retarded by the mental state of the avenger, and questions arise of internal vs. external difficulties. In each there is a ghost returned from the dead to spur revenge, a lady driven mad, and a play within the play to forward the avenger's purpose. Each, in the measure of the author's ability, highlights soliloquy, and blends a profound Senecan melancholy with the frankest sensationalism.

Paradoxically enough, Kyd appears also as one of the earliest apostles of *French* the French school of Senecan tragedy fathered by Robert Garnier[16] (1534- *Seneca* 1590). Garnier had carried to a very high point a conception of drama quite antipodal to that of the *Spanish Tragedy:* in it the lyric and reflective beauties of Seneca were delicately enhanced and all the brutality of plot purged away. In the year of Garnier's death the Countess of Pembroke translated his *Marc-Antoine* into accurate but dull English blank verse. This was printed in 1592 and two years later Kyd joined the movement with his *Cornelia,* translated *Kyd's* from another of Garnier's plays and dedicated to the Countess of Sussex. A *Cornelia* quieter drama could hardly be imagined. Act I consists of a single speech by Cicero (158 lines) and nine stanzas of lamentation on the miseries of civil war by the chorus. In Act II Cicero talks with Cornelia, the sorrowing widow of Pompey the Great, dissuading her from suicide, and the chorus sings of the mutability of human affairs. In Act III Cornelia talks with the chorus and with Pompey's servant Philip, and Cicero makes another philosophical oration. In Act IV Cassius and Decimus Brutus discourse in one scene, Caesar and Mark Antony in another. In Act V a messenger arrives to inform Cornelia that her father, Scipio, has been forced to slay himself. Cornelia makes it clear that the times are very bad, but that she must live, "(though life she hateth)," to make the tombs and mourn upon the hearses of her illustrious dead.

Nothing was less suited to Kyd's peculiar talents than this type of closet drama, to which he can hardly have been drawn by anything except the hope of recommending himself to its influential patronesses. The thing fitted the feminine nature of Samuel Daniel much better, and the latter's *Cleopatra,* *Daniel's* an original play on Garnier's formula, is the best work of the school. It first *Cleopatra* appeared in the same year as Kyd's *Cornelia* (1594), with a flattering inscription to Lady Pembroke, but was much revised later. Daniel employs riming verse (mainly quatrains) in the dialogue; his choruses are as charming as are Garnier's, and his lack of action as complete. The first act consists of a

[15] See C. M. Lewis, *The Genesis of Hamlet* (1907); H. D. Gray, "Reconstruction of a Lost Play," *PQ,* VII (1928). 254-274.
[16] See A. M. Witherspoon, *The Influence of Robert Garnier on Elizabethan Drama* (New Haven, 1924).

single long monologue by Cleopatra (196 lines), with comment by chorus, and the catastrophe is related by the *nuntius* in Act v at still greater length. Daniel's second classical play, *Philotas* (1605), which centers on a trial some of the same purple patches that Shakespeare later wove into his very different fabric. In the edition of 1607, which was the seventh to appear, *Cleopatra* has been recast into something more closely resembling the Anglo-Saxon conception of a play. The changes are probably due to the influence of Daniel's second Plutarchan play, *Philotas* (1605), which centers on a trial for high treason and has for its hero a vain and foolish soldier-favorite of Alexander the Great, who (though Daniel denied it) [17] greatly resembles the unfortunate Earl of Essex. This play, unlike the original *Cleopatra,* was mtended for the actual stage and has more animation, though it is still questionable whether actors could have learned some of the long speeches or auditors endured them. The chorus, *nuntius,* and riming verse continue to be characteristic features.

Samuel Brandon's *Tragicomedy of the Virtuous Octavia* [18] (1598) imitates the *Cleopatra* of Daniel in metre, but does not approach it in excellence. It likewise follows North's version of the Life of Antony, but Antony does not himself appear, nor does Cleopatra. Antony's virtuous and forsaken wife is almost the only important figure in a play which even more than *Cornelia* and *Cleopatra* emphasizes the special distaff interest of this school. Brandon appended a pair of Ovidian epistles, from Octavia to Antony and from Antony to Octavia, written like the choruses of his play in a lax ballad metre. Another imitator of Daniel was a lady of rank, Elizabeth, the wife of Sir Henry Cary and mother of the famous Lord Falkland of the civil wars. Her tragedy of *Mariam, the Fair Queen of Jewry,*[19] printed in 1613, may be the earliest play composed (as distinguished from translated) by an English-woman. She took out of Josephus's history of the Jews one of the great stories of the world,[20] and by setting the day of action just after the battle of Actium brought it into connection with the familiar Antony and Cleopatra material. She attempts to write with cautious classic elegance, but this style is not suited to the amount of romantic excitement she wished to introduce.

On the accession of James I Daniel became a favorite at court and gave up tragedy for masques and pastoral comedies of no great importance.[21] The chief Jacobean continuators of the Garnier type of tragedy were two grave philosophical poets, Sidney's friend, Fulke Greville [22] and King James's Scottish friend, Sir William Alexander [23] (c. 1567-1640). The latter's four

---

[17] In his "apology" for *Philotas* Daniel asserts that three acts of the play had been written before the Essex uprising of 1601.

[18] Reprinted, Malone Soc., 1910.

[19] Reprinted, Malone Soc., 1914.

[20] See M. J. Valency, *The Tragedies of Herod and Mariamne* (1940).

[21] I.e., *The Vision of the Twelve Goddesses* (1604); *The Queen's Arcadia* (1605); *Tethys' Festival* (1610); *Hymen's Triumph* (1615).

[22] See below, Part III, ch. VI.

[23] See L. E. Kastner and H. B. Charlton, *Sir William Alexander, Earl of Stirling: the Dramatic Works* (Manchester, 1921) which has a very notable introduction; T. H. McGrail, *Sir William Alexander, First Earl of Stirling* (Edinburgh, 1940).

Monarchic Tragedies (1603-1607) deal with four great crises of the ancient world, beginning with the *Tragedy of Croesus* and ending with that of Julius Caesar. They employ the chorus and the alternately riming verse which had become conventional in this sort of drama. Occasionally they introduce a ghost or a classical goddess to open the play, but they pay no close attention to the unities and are overlong. They justly challenge our respectful considera- tion, but more by the political wisdom they contain than by any dramatic pleasure they impart. *Sir Wm. Alexander, Monarchic Tragedies*

The first part of Marlowe's *Tamburlaine* created in all sorts of writers a desire to emulate its success, and at the same time confused their notions of tragedy. One of the feeblest imitations is *The Wars of Cyrus,* printed in 1594 as played by the Children of the Chapel, though the date of such performance is a mystery. It is a happy romantic narrative, to which gravity is added by two deaths at the end. The ultimate source is Xenophon's *Cyropaedia,* to which a very popular tale in Painter's *Palace of Pleasure* [24] had given cur- rency. One of the most fulsome imitations of *Tamburlaine* is *The Comical History of Alphonsus, King of Aragon,* published in 1599 as by "R. G." If Greene wrote it, it was Greene at his worst. Nothing comical appears except the stylistic excess and the happy ending, in which the vainglorious hero, after conquering the Great Turk and other sovereigns, marries his disdainful captive. There is a good deal of killing on the stage and a great deal of magic. Venus is the introducer of each act, and the story is presented as the work of Calliope, the muse of epic poetry, rather than of the tragic muse, Melpo- mene. *Popular English Tragedy*

The Battle of Alcazar, surviving only in a bad text (1594), bears no author's name, but can be accepted as the work of Peele, whose chaotic notions of structure and occasional grandeurs of style [25] are both apparent. It was evi- dently admired in its day and was rather frequently quoted. The *Spanish Tragedy* may have suggested the idea of dramatizing the battle of Alcazar (1578) and the death of Sebastian of Portugal, but *Tamburlaine,* which is mentioned in the text, no doubt inspired the hazy background of warring Moorish kings. The chief villain is the terrible Negro, Muly Mahamet, who has a beloved wife (Calipolis) and son; and they in turn laid down the specifications for Aaron in *Titus Andronicus.* Peele's spirit was too eclectic and impatient for Senecan restraint, but he keeps a hint of the pseudo-Roman method in the presenter who introduces each act and in the three ghosts and numerous dumb-shows.[26] *The Battle of Alcazar*

[24] No. xi, "King Cyrus and the Lady Panthea." The play is reproduced by J. S. Farmer, *Tudor Facsimile Texts* (1911); and has been carefully edited by J. P. Brawner (Urbana, 1942).
[25] E.g., the praise of Queen Elizabeth, Malone Soc. ed., lines 724 ff., and the last speech of Stukeley, lines 1454 ff.
[26] A somewhat similar method and theme appear in *Alarum for London, or the Siege of Antwerp* (1602), acted by Shakespeare's company and entered for publication in 1600. It is based on a pamphlet by Gascoigne and treats the sack of Antwerp by the Spaniards in 1576, with emphasis on the heroic deeds and death of two English officers Reprinted. Malone Soc., 1913.

Turkish history of the early sixteenth century is weirdly dramatized in *Selimus* [27] (1594), written by some one who fancied himself as a poet but had no notion of playmaking. There is evidence connecting this piece with Greene, but it is not strong enough to overcome the incredulity produced by the general nature of the work. [28] *Selimus* is clearly a derivative of *Tamburlaine* and has some close parallels with the pseudo-Shakespearean *Locrine* (1595), a sultry tragedy of love and war in ancient Britain, in which Ate and a dumb-show introduce each act and various ghosts enliven the proceedings.

Lodge's *Wounds of Civil War* [29] (1594) carries the Tamburlaine motif into Roman history, presenting Sulla as a young conqueror who rides in triumph, but blending this conception, it would seem, with reminiscence of the treatment of war in the *Henry VI* plays, which perhaps first opened the eyes of hard-pressed playwrights to the wealth of gory incident in the English chronicles. [30] Henslowe's Diary shows how largely such material was used in plays which have not survived. Existing tragedies of this kind include the *Troublesome Reign of John King of England* [31] (1591), in two parts, and the effective *True Tragedy of Richard III* [32] (1594), besides plays of less clearly tragic import, such as Peele's *Edward I* [33] (1593) and the anonymous *Edward III* [34] (1596), in which there are some good reasons for seeing Shakespeare's hand. It was natural and easy to frame tragedies also out of the lives of well known English statesmen; e.g., the manuscript plays of "Woodstock" or Thomas, Duke of Gloucester [35] and of Sir Thomas More; [36] *Sir John Oldcastle* [37] (1600), *Thomas Lord Cromwell* [38] (1602); and even, on a lower social level, *Jack Straw* [39] (1593) and *Captain Thomas Stukeley* [40] (1605).

English Chronicle Plays

The interest in chronicle history may be credited also with shaping a bourgeois tragedy which was one of the most vital Elizabethan types. Forecasts of this are perhaps found in such interlude developments as John Phillip's *Patient and Meek Grissill* [41] (c. 1565), Thomas Garter's *Virtuous*

Bourgeois Tragedy

[27] Reprinted, Malone Soc., 1909.
[28] There is a great deal of elaborate stanzaic verse and emphasis on the favorite themes of abdication and mutilation. *Tamburlaine* is directly alluded to in lines 2345 and 2439.
[29] Reprinted, Malone Soc., 1910.
[30] See F. E. Schelling, *The English Chronicle Play* (1902).
[31] Reprinted in "Shakespeare Classics," ed. F. J. Furnivall and J. Munro (1913); also in the Furness Variorum Shakespeare *King John* (1919).
[32] Reprinted, Malone Soc., 1929.
[33] Reprinted, Malone Soc., 1911.
[34] Reprinted, *Shakespeare Apocrypha* (1908).
[35] Malone Soc., 1929.
[36] On the question of Shakespeare's part in this play see the edition by W. W. Greg (Malone Soc., 1911), Sir E. M. Thompson, *Shakespeare's Handwriting* (Oxford, 1916), A. W. Pollard, *et al.*, *Shakespeare's Hand in the Play of Sir Thomas More* (Cambridge, 1923), E. K. Chambers, *William Shakespeare* (2v, Oxford, 1930), I. 499-515, and R. W. Chambers, "Some Sequences of Thought in Shakespeare and in the 147 Lines of *Sir Thomas More*," *MLR*, xxvi (1931). 251-280.
[37] Malone Soc., 1908; *Shakespeare Apocrypha* (1908).
[38] *Shakespeare Apocrypha* (1908).
[39] *Tudor Facsimile Texts*, ed. J. S. Farmer (1911).
[40] *Tudor Facsimile Texts*, ed. J. S. Farmer (1911); J. Q. Adams, "Captaine Thomas Stukeley," *JEGP*, xv (1916). 1-23.
[41] Reprinted, Malone Soc., 1909.

and Godly Susanna [42] (1578), and particularly in George Whetstone's *Promos and Cassandra* [43] (1578), which handles the same theme as Shakespeare's *Measure for Measure.* In all these plays there are "happy" endings and rough clownage, but the main problem is domestic and deeply serious. The first unmitigated tragedy of ordinary life is *Arden of Feversham* [44] (1592) dramatized from Holinshed's account of the murder of a leading citizen of Faversham in Kent in 1551. The play is an *Agamemnon* of middle-class English life, very faultily constructed, but extremely vivid in its picture of manners and customs. Alice Arden, the best drawn character, is not quite unworthy to be mentioned with Clytemnestra, and Mosby, her lover, fairly fills the rôle of Aegisthus; but there is no thought of classic parallels in this bleak transcript of sordid acts and feelings. The catastrophe is not artistically developed, but the situations evoke at times a very striking poetry and at other times unusually graphic vignettes of Tudor life. The only other extant play of the type comparable with *Arden* is *A Warning for Fair Women* (1599), based upon a similar *crime passionnel.*[45] It was acted by Shakespeare's company, and probably at the new Globe theatre which was opened in the spring or summer of 1599. The unknown author was master of a remarkable plain and easy style, both in blank verse and prose. He justly calls his work a "true and home-born tragedy": it leaves a rather horribly convincing impression of the London middle-class, smug, purse-proud, and sensual, steadily pushing themselves up amid brutal crime and yet more brutal punishment.

Of the same nature is the realistic portion of Robert Yarington's (?) *Two Lamentable Tragedies* [46] (1601, but written earlier), dealing with the murder of another London merchant in 1594; and the type persisted as late as 1624 in a lost work, *The Late Murder in Whitechapel,*[47] in which four very considerable dramatists—Dekker, Rowley, Ford, and Webster—combined their talents. *Page of Plymouth,* for which Henslowe paid Dekker and Jonson in 1599, depicted an adulterous murder in the west, perpetrated in 1591; and *A Yorkshire Tragedy* [48] (1608), "written by W. Shakespeare," as the title-page alleged, and undoubtedly acted by his company at the Globe, deals with a northern crime of 1605. Shakespeare can hardly be held responsible for much of the language of this ephemeral piece, but it seems to have

(margin note: Arden of Feversham)

---

[42] Reprinted, Malone Soc., 1937.
[43] *Tudor Facsimile Texts,* ed. J. S. Farmer (1910). Whetstone's play is in two parts, like *Tamburlaine,* and was published by the same stationer, Richard Jones, who entered both pairs of plays on the Stationers' Register with the identical description, "two comical discourses." The title-page of *Tamburlaine* changed this to "two tragical discourses."
[44] Reprinted, *Shakespeare Apocrypha.* See H. D. Sykes, *Sidelights on Shakespeare* (Stratford-upon-Avon, 1919), pp. 48-76 (arguing for Kyd's authorship).
[45] J. S. Farmer, *Tudor Facsimile Texts* (1912). The subject is the murder of George Saunders of London in 1573. See J. Q. Adams, "The Authorship of *A Warning for Fair Women,*" *PMLA,* XXVIII (1913). 594-620.
[46] Ed. J. S. Farmer, *Tudor Facsimile Texts,* 1913. R. A. Law, "Yarington's *Two Lamentable Tragedies,*" *MLR,* V (1910). 167-177, and the introduction to William Haughton's *Englishmen for My Money,* ed. A. C. Baugh (Phila., 1917), pp. 48-60.
[47] See C. J. Sisson, *Lost Plays of Shakespeare's Age* (Cambridge, 1936), pp. 80-124.
[48] Reprinted, *Shakespeare Apocrypha* (1908).

provided him with an effective episode in *King Lear*,[49] and his great early Jacobean tragedies—*Othello, Lear, Macbeth*—are, for one thing, transmutations of the Elizabethan tragedy of domestic crime.

There was also a return at about the time of Shakespeare's *Julius Caesar* (1599) and Jonson's *Sejanus* (1603) to the imperial Roman subjects by writers unconnected with the Senecan school. The fine play, *Caesar's Revenge*[50] (1606), "privately acted by the students of Trinity College in Oxford," has Discord to introduce each act and makes a good deal of Caesar's ghost; but it lacks the chorus, which the Senecans so prized, and instead of restricting the action to a day, covers the whole six years from Pharsalia to Philippi. In the next year (1607) was printed *The Tragical Life and Death of Claudius Tiberius Nero*[51] (i.e., the emperor Tiberius), likewise by a young man of one of the universities. It is very long and very violent, and deals with the same historical period as Jonson's *Sejanus*. Equally anonymous, and of greater merit, is *The Tragedy of Nero* (i.e., the emperor Nero), which was not printed till 1624.[52]

The scene was transferred to Germany and the horror intensified in two hectic revenge plays: Henry Chettle's *Tragedy of Hoffman*, "or a revenge for a father,"[53] mentioned in Henslowe's Diary in 1602; and *The Tragedy of Alphonsus, Emperor of Germany*,[54] not printed till 1654, though its first form may have antedated 1600. Italy became the scene in Marston's *Antonio's Revenge*[55] (1602), acted by the children of Paul's, and in two powerful plays printed in 1607 as previously acted by Shakespeare's company: *The Devil's Charter*[56] by Barnabe Barnes and *The Revenger's Tragedy*[57] by Cyril Tourneur. The Turk came back in John Mason's tragedy of that title (1610),[58] and the monstrous Moor against a Spanish background in *Lust's Dominion*,[59] which the only surviving text (1657) states to have been "written by Christofer Marloe, Gent."

The uncertainties of authorship, date, and text are so great in most of these plays as to baffle intelligent discussion. They may be said to represent the position of tragedy, except in the hands of the greatest masters, at the

---

[49] See T. Brooke, *"King Lear* and *A Yorkshire Tragedy,"* MLN, xxvii (1912). 62.
[50] Reprinted, Malone Soc., 1911.
[51] Reprinted, Malone Soc., 1915.
[52] Reprinted, *"Nero"* & *Other Plays*, Mermaid Series, n. d.
[53] Ed. J. S. Farmer, *Tudor Facsimile Texts* (1913); see H. Jenkins, *The Life and Work of Henry Chettle* (1934), pp. 71-108. *The Death of Robert Earl of Huntington*, by Munday and Chettle, 1598, grafts the same horrid sort of tragedy upon the Robin Hood legend.
[54] Ed. H. F. Schwarz (1913), and T. M. Parrott, *Tragedies of George Chapman* (1910), pp. 401-471, 683-720.
[55] Reprinted, Malone Soc., 1922.
[56] Ed. R. B. McKerrow (Louvain, 1904).
[57] See A. Nicoll, *Works of Cyril Tourneur* (1929) and below, Part iii, ch. iii.
[58] Ed. J. Q. Adams (Louvain, 1913). There was a new edition of Mason's play in 1632, perhaps called forth by the posthumous publication of the two still more lurid Oxford tragedies of Thomas Goffe (1591-1629): *The Raging Turk, or Baiazet the Second* (1631) and *The Courageous Turk, or Amurath the First* (1632). For the best account of all these Turkish plays see S. C. Chew, *The Crescent and the Rose* (1937), ch. xi.
[59] Ed. J. L. G. Brereton (Louvain, 1931).

close of the Elizabethan period. What they most possess is robust violence and great popular appeal, qualities very unlike those of the Senecan imitations from which they grew. Their chief lesson for the critic is that he should not be too much surprised, or speak of sudden and unheralded decadence, when he passes from the sober tragedy of Shakespeare, Jonson, and Chapman to the vehemence of Webster and of Ford.

VIII

Sidney and the Sonneteers

No student of English literature need apologize for devoting a considerable part of his attention to the more personal and social aspects of Sir Philip Sidney [1] (1554-1586). In three directions, to be sure, Sidney's actual achievement ranks him among the very highest of the Elizabethan writers. None but Shakespeare and Spenser produced a finer sonnet sequence. None but Ben Jonson surpassed him as a literary critic. None of the writers of his age approached his influence in the field of prose romance. Yet if *Astrophel and Stella*, the *Defense of Poesy*, and the *Arcadia* had never been published, we should still have to regard Sidney as a cultural landmark. Seconded by his sister, he created through his personal efforts and his personal charm a new artistic atmosphere more stimulating than any other that then existed. Together—or more strictly in succession, for the Countess of Pembroke (1561-1621) was but twenty-five when her brother died—they first produced what in the highest sense may be called the academic spirit in English letters.

In an unusual degree Sidney's personality and influence were affected by his environment and by the circumstances of his worldly position. His character was unusually serious and consistent, but the conditions under which he lived his life were extraordinarily fickle and perplexing. The fantastic lights and shadows of his fortune, playing over the high-spirited constancy of his disposition, ripened his romantic genius and gave him the unique place that he held among his contemporaries and yet holds with us. The grandson of a duke, godson of a king, nephew to four earls, brother-in-law of an earl, brother of an earl, and uncle to three earls, he was himself, through nearly all his life, an untitled commoner. Throughout his life he was poor, yet within easy expectation of huge wealth. A special favorite of the Queen and of the most powerful peers, he was without public influence and frequently deprived of ordinary personal liberty. Had he lived two years longer, he might have become Earl of Leicester, as his brother Robert later did; but the only title which he in fact received, that of knight, was granted for the sorriest of possible reasons and brought him neither commendation nor reward. The grotesque alternations of fate manifested in his own family

---

[1] A. Feuillerat, *The Complete Works of Sir Philip Sidney* (4v, Cambridge, 1912-1926). The best lives are: M. W. Wallace, *The Life of Sir Philip Sidney* (Cambridge, 1915); M. Wilson, *Sir Philip Sidney* (1931); A. H. Bill, *Astrophel* (1937). New manuscript material regarding Sidney is available in V. B. Heltzel and H. H. Hudson, *Nobilis . . . and Lessus Lugubris by Thomas Moffet* (San Marino, Calif., 1940). Sidney's prose works are discussed in K. O. Myrick, *Sir Philip Sidney as a Literary Craftsman* (Cambridge, Mass., 1935). Fuller references in S. A. Tannenbaum, *Sir Philip Sidney, A Concise Bibliography* (1941).

strengthened his romanticism, his sense of the strangeness of life; the uncertainties and disappointments of his own career heightened in him that democratic independence of mind which makes romanticism potent. Had he been less brilliantly connected or had he himself held a more splendid position, his impact upon literature would probably have been smaller. Master Philip Sidney could befriend Spenser without patronage; the heir presumptive of the Earl of Leicester could practise innovation without suspicion of demagoguery, and get a hearing for his innovations.

Sidney's immense influence was based first upon his open-mindedness, his democratic attitude, and second upon his sincere and eager fancy. These are the qualities in his work also which made it a gospel of romanticism. His open-mindedness brought him acquaintance with very diverse friends *His Friend* and made his brain hospitable to notions sometimes rather alien to his real tastes and convictions. Two groups of literary friends have left traces on his work and on the history of the period. One gathered at Leicester House in London during 1579 and 1580 and was called by Spenser—perhaps only jokingly—the "Areopagus." To this belonged Sidney and Edward Dyer (later Sir Edward), Spenser, and others. What we know of it we learn from the letters that passed between Spenser and Gabriel Harvey of Cambridge at the time. It appears from them that "some use of familiarity" existed between Spenser and Sidney, and that those two arch-romantics were employing much of their leisure in the futile and unromantic attempt to fit English poetry to classical metres. Spenser's interest in the projected reform in prosody may be assumed to have been short-lived; it was probably imbibed at Cambridge from Harvey. That Sidney's interest was serious is evidenced by the large mass of classicizing verse which he introduced into his *Arcadia*.[2]

The second group of literary friends by whom Sidney's work was affected *Wilton* is that which met at Wilton, the country house of his sister Mary, the *House* Countess of Pembroke. Here also his romanticism would seem to have developed among ideas predominantly unromantic. The Lady Mary's literary taste appears to have had little in common with Philip's, except that it was fervent and generous. Her claim to recognition as an author rests upon her *Antony,* a translation made four years after Sidney's death, from the French of Robert Garnier.[3] The Elizabethan era has little to show that is less romantic in tone or conception. In the works of others which she inspired—the *Cleopatra* of Daniel, *Cornelia* of Kyd, the *Countess of Pembroke's Ivy-church* and *Countess of Pembroke's Emanuel* by Abraham Fraunce [4]—the neo-classical spirit is equally rampant. For Mary, we may infer, rules were the essence of literature; by Philip they were certainly

---

[2] See G. D. Willcock, "Passing Pitefull Hexameters: A Study of Quantity and Accent in English Renaissance Verse," *MLR*, XXIX (1934). 1-19.

[3] Cf. the preceding chapter, and consult Frances B. Young, *Mary Sidney, Countess of Pembroke* (1912), and F. E. Schelling, "Sidney's Sister, Pembroke's Mother," *Johns Hopkins Alumni Mag.*, XII (1923). 3-23; reprinted in *Shakespeare and "Demi-Science"* (Philadelphia, 1927), pp. 100-125.

[4] Both Fraunce's works are in "English hexameters."

respected, but they must largely have appealed to him as material for debate or as points of departure for individual inspiration.

Friendly debate there probably was in plenty at Wilton, and inspiration there must have been; for Sidney's sojourn produced his most conspicuously romantic work, the first *Arcadia,* and most likely also his Shelleyan *Defense of Poesy.* From the dedication of the former it may be fair to conjecture that the author felt something more than ordinary diffidence before his young sister's judgment on his novel—the diffidence which the inspired experimentalist usually feels before the judgment of an esteemed reader who lives fortified by rules and standards:

Here now have you (most dear, and most worthy to be most dear, lady) this idle work of mine; which I fear, like the spider's web, will be thought fitter to be swept away than worn to any other purpose ... Now it is done only for you, only to you: if you keep it to yourself, or to such friends who will weigh errors in the balance of good will, I hope for the father's sake it will be pardoned, perchance made much of, though in itself it have deformities. For, indeed, for severer eyes it is not, being but a trifle, and that triflingly handled. Your dear self can best witness the manner, being done in loose sheets of paper, most of it in your presence, the rest by sheets sent unto you as fast as they were done. ...

he Old
rcadia

This was written about 1581 for what is now known as the "Old *Arcadia,*" *The Countess of Pembroke's Arcadia* in its original sense, a work which till 1926 had only been printed in bowdlerized and very incomplete form.[5] It will be better to speak of this admirable story separately, for nothing but confusion has ever resulted from the attempt to criticize it in conjunction with the unfinished enlargement that Sidney later undertook. It may be reasonably supposed that his original purpose was to devise a light pastoral tale beautified with rustic verse after the fashion of Sannazaro's Italian *Arcadia* (1504); but Sidney's spirit was of a more virile cast, and from the start his story showed less similarity to Sannazaro than to the wilder, earlier fictions of Heliodorus and Achilles Tatius.[6] His first *Arcadia,* surviving in half a dozen manuscript copies, is divided into five books or "acts," separated by lengthy intercalations termed "eclogues," which are partly verse (both conventional and quantitative) and partly prose, partly narrative and partly lyrical. The main story, handled in the "acts," has much the quality and structure of one of the tragicomedies which Sidney's namesake, Philip Massinger, later wrote for the seventeenth-century stage. The author appeals first of all to his reader's curiosity. Mystery, variety, suspense, and thrilling episode are the tools he works with. The story begins with disguise, the disguise of the princes Pyrocles and Musidorus; and with mystery, the strangely retired and fearful life led by King Basilius and his family; and

---

[5] See R. W. Zandvoort *Sidney's Arcadia: A Comparison between the Two Versions* (Amsterdam, 1929); M. S. Goldman, *Sir Philip Sidney and the Arcadia* (Urbana, 1934); A. G. D. Wiles, "Parallel Analyses of the Two Versions of Sidney's *Arcadia,*" *SP,* xxxix (1942). 167-206.

[6] See S. L. Wolff, *The Greek Romances in Elizabethan Fiction* (1912). For the influence of the Spanish *Diana* (1559-64) see T. P. Harrison, "A Source of Sidney's *Arcadia,*" *Univ. Texas Studies in English,* vi (1926). 53-71; H. Genouy, *L'Arcadia de Sidney dans ses rapports avec l'Arcadia de Sannazaro et la Diana de Montemayor* (Montpellier, 1928).

it culminates like a modern detective story in the rational but quite unguessable solution of a portentous series of suspected crimes.

The first act is brought to a rousing finish by the incursion of a lion and she-bear upon the pastoral entertainments, to be slain in the nick of time by the two heroes. Act II likewise rises to a climax in which the heroes save the king's party from the attack of a rather French-Revolutionary mob upon their rustic lodges. In Act III the lovers have made such progress that Musidorus is able to flee with Pamela toward the seacoast, while Pyrocles, tricking his prospective father- and mother-in-law into a nocturnal meeting with each other, consummates his own love with Philoclea. Act IV brings in the reversal of fortune. It opens with comic relief, in an exceedingly funny account of the discomfiture of Pamela's guard Dametas and his foolish wife and daughter; and passes into melodrama when Basilius drinks a love philtre which his wife Gynecia had intended for Pyrocles, and falls seemingly dead. General Philanax arrives with troops, Pamela and Musidorus are intercepted and brought back captive, and the entire body of lovers put into prison under charges of rape, murder, and treason. Act V opens, like the last act of *Gorboduc,* with discussion of "the dangerous division of men's minds" upon the death of a sovereign. Then appears as *deus ex machina* King Evarchus of Macedon, father of Pyrocles, who presides at a trial full of dramatic tension and noble oratory. The just Evarchus is being obliged to condemn his son and nephew to death when Basilius, recovering from the effects of the potion, is able to procure the happiness of all, and at the same time justify the enigmatic oracle with which the story commenced.

The Old *Arcadia* was plotted as a love trifle for the amusement of the fair and worthy ladies who are in the beginning being constantly invoked; but it was executed in a very masculine spirit. In the portions which Lady Pembroke permitted to be printed in 1593 she has palliated the male forthrightness of several situations;[7] and though this is the strongest and most ingenious love story that any Elizabethan prose writer created, the core of Sidney's thinking is not love but practical psychology, ethics, and politics. The style is smooth and usually simple, depending little upon the alliterative and figurative ornaments that were Lyly's mainstay. It is chiefly marked by the philosophical comments Sidney adds upon the ways men's minds are moved. It is people that interest Sidney, not merely emotions, and his gallery is large, even in the original *Arcadia.* The clownish figures, though caricatures, are outlined with vigor and true humor,[8] and the women are at least courageously attempted; but the main effort goes to probing the minds of gentlemen. In the great trial scene that closes the book attention is focused on four chivalrous characters, who all place duty above self-advan-

[7] K. T. Rowe, "The Countess of Pembroke's Editorship of the *Arcadia," PMLA,* LIV (1939). 122-138, argues that Sidney made these changes.
[8] Similar farcical characters, Lalus and Rombus, in Sidney's masque, *The Lady of May* (1578), appear to be prototypes of Don Armado and Holofernes in *Love's Labor's Lost.*

tage and by the power and subtlety of their speeches bring the melodramatic situation near to real tragedy.[9]

Presumably, Sidney was impelled to rewrite the *Arcadia* by the classical and neo-classical studies that he made for his *Defense of Poesy*. His sister and her coterie may have moved him in the same direction. The later *Arcadia* is an attempt to turn a romance into a prose epic which should have the unified complexity and the dignity that the Renaissance Aristotelians demanded.[10] The style is heightened,[11] and the narrative, instead of starting at the beginning (i.e., with the oracle of Basilius), opens in more or less Virgilian fashion with an unexplained shipwreck. The earlier adventures of the heroes in Asia Minor, which had been narrated in the supplementary "eclogues" of the Old *Arcadia,* are woven into the main story of the New. Most important of all, the epic dignity of warfare is imposed upon the pastoral plot by the creation of entirely new characters and incidents more akin to *Amadis of Gaul* and the *Morte Darthur* than to anything in the Old *Arcadia.*[12]

None of these changes was really dissonant from Sidney's taste, and they have been made with great brilliance. The Old *Arcadia* has been taken apart like a watch, its individual movements polished and then fitted into the new structure, often in quite dissimilar positions and amid a vast amount of new material. The third book is altogether new and entirely epical in tone. Here the heroines are kidnapped and imprisoned in a castle by their wicked aunt Cecropia and her knightly son Amphialus, characters unknown to the earlier version. The perils of the captives, and the daring deeds of the besiegers and defenders alike, fill this book with a high and varied excitement. Some of Sidney's finest writing is here; for example, the story of the deaths of Argalus and Parthenia and the noble prayer of Pamela,[13] which in the *Eikon Basilike* was credited to King Charles I. It is clear, however, that the New *Arcadia* was being carried entirely out of touch with the Old, and it seems doubtful whether Sidney could have brought it to any consistent conclusion. At any rate, it breaks off near the end (we may presume) of Book III, in the midst of a most furious single combat between Anaxius and Pyrocles, and in the middle of a sentence. Earlier *lacunae* show that the text had not received Sidney's final revision; but the effort at sonorous style, especially at the crises of action, is much greater than in the Old *Arcadia*. One such, pitched in the key of wonder, is the passage that Scott copied in *Ivanhoe,* the arrival of the mysterious Black Knight (Musidorus) before the besieged castle:

[9] See W. D. Briggs, "Political Ideas in Sidney's *Arcadia,*" *SP,* xxviii (1931). 137-161; xxix (1932). 534-542.

[10] See E. A. Greenlaw, "Sidney's *Arcadia* as an Example of Elizabethan Allegory," *Kittredge Anniversary Papers* (1913), pp. 327-337; "The Captivity Episode in Sidney's *Arcadia,*" *Manly Anniversary Studies* (Chicago, 1923), pp. 54-63; Myrick, *op. cit.,* pp. 110-193; J. H. Hanford and S. R. Watson, "Personal Allegory in the *Arcadia,*" *MP* xxxii (1934). 1-10.

[11] See W. Clemen, *Shakespeare's Bilder* (Bonn, 1936), pp. 317-322; S. Harkness, "The Prose Style of Sir Philip Sidney," *Univ. Wis. Stud. in Lang. and Lit.,* ii (1918). 57-76.

[12] See M. S. Goldman, *op. cit.,* pp. 186-210.

[13] Ed. Feuillerat, p. 382.

But Philanax his men, as if with the loss of Philanax they had lost the fountain of their valor, had their courages so dried up in fear that they began to set honor at their backs ... when into the press comes (as hard as his horse, more afraid of the spur than the sword, could carry him) a knight in armor as dark as blackness could make it, followed by none and adorned by nothing ... But virtue quickly made him known, and admiration bred him such authority, that though they of whose side he came knew him not, yet they all knew it was fit to obey him ... For, taking part with the besiegers, he made the Amphialians' blood serve for a caparison to his horse and a decking to his armor. His arm no oftener gave blows than the blows gave wounds, than the wounds gave deaths; so terrible was his force, and yet was his quickness more forcible than his force, and his judgment more quick than his quickness.[14]

A specimen of subtler writing is the delicate analysis of the stages by which Philoclea fell in love, which has been developed out of something much less detailed in the earlier version:

For after that Zelmane [i.e., Pyrocles in female disguise] had a while lived in the lodge with her, and that her only being a noble stranger had bred a kind of heedful attention, her coming to that lonely place (where she had nobody but her parents) a willingness of conversation, her wit and behavior a liking and silent admiration; at length the excellency of her natural gifts, joined with the extreme shows she made of most devout honoring Philoclea (carrying thus in one person the only two bands of good will, loveliness and lovingness) brought forth in her heart a yielding to a most friendly affection; which, when it had gotten so full possession of the keys of her mind that it would receive no message from her senses without that affection were the interpreter, then straight grew an exceeding delight still to be with her, with an unmeasurable liking of all that Zelmane did: matters being so turned in her that, where at first liking her manners did breed good will, now good will became the chief cause of liking her manners; so that within a while Zelmane was not prized for her demeanor, but the demeanor was prized because it was Zelmane's.[15]

The characteristics which make the *Defense of Poesy*[16] a great piece of criticism, and which at the same time note it as a romantic work, for all its dependence on neo-classic learning, are, first, its vindication of the spirit of poetry as opposed to details of form or content; and, second, its democratic attitude—that is, its sweet reasonableness, its approval of what is genuine and impressive even where not justifiable by rules of art.[17] There is nothing iconoclastic in Sidney's attitude toward rules. He treats them with respect and is willing to accept their validity where, as in the drama

The Defense of Poesy

[14] Ed. Feuillerat, p. 391 f.
[15] Ed. Feuillerat, p. 169; compare Old *Arcadia*, p. 93, lines 11-15. The most important derivative of the *Arcadia* is the *Argenis* of the Franco-Scot John Barclay (1582-1621), in five long books, which achieved great popularity by combining knightly (Sicilian) romance and political allegory. Written in Latin and first printed at Paris in 1621, it was speedily translated into English (e.g., by Ben Jonson in a non-extant version (1623), and by Kingsmill Long in 1625) as into many other vernaculars; but it hardly belongs to English literature.
[16] Two editions were printed in 1595, one with the title here used, the other with the title, *An Apology for Poetry.*
[17] See Irene Samuel, "The Influence of Plato on Sir Philip Sidney's *Defense of Poesy*," *MLQ,* 1 (1940). 383-391.

before 1580, violations had not justified themselves. But his fundamental position is a protest against dogma; it was dogmatic Puritanism, as embodied in Gosson's *School of Abuse*,[18] which occasioned the writing of the essay, if we may believe Spenser [19] and the bibliographical evidence in the case.

Sidney begins his defense of poetry by championing the superiority of imagination over fact. The poet, he says, is a finer influence than the historian, the philosopher, or the mathematician, because more truly than they he creates; because he does not simply analyze nature, but transcends her; because his end is less narrow and more ideal. Sidney's breadth of literary sympathy and his predominating romanticism are evidenced by the works which he selects for praise: Chaucer's *Troilus and Criseyde*, the *Mirror for Magistrates*, Surrey (i.e., Tottel's Miscellany), *Gorboduc*, the *Shepherds' Calendar*, and the ballad of Percy and Douglas. The judicious Hallam has a remark on Sidney in relation to the literature of his time, which has been echoed in a mistaken sense, as if his critical taste had been out of harmony with the true current of the age. "It is amusing to reflect," says Hallam,

that this contemptuous reprehension of the English theatre (and he had spoken in as disparaging terms of our general poetry) came from the pen of Sidney, when Shakespeare had just arrived at manhood. Had he not been so prematurely cut off, what would have been the transports of that noble spirit, which the ballad of Chevy Chase could "stir as with the sound of a trumpet," in reading the *Faery Queen* or *Othello!* [20]

It is not the smallest proof of the fidelity of Sidney's *Defense* to the spirit of Elizabethan romanticism, that its temper seems so just to us who read it in the light of the literature that was to follow. No harder task for a critic could well be imagined than that which Sidney accomplished: to write at the moment of Elizabethan dawn a sketch of the function and powers of poetry which Shakespeare, Spenser, and Marlowe should not render obsolete. Though there are in his essay some generalities, orthodox in 1580, which Sidney would certainly have abandoned in 1600, there can be no question that he was inwardly adjusted to the romantic noontide he was not to see. Of the *Cambises* vein in tragedy he thought as Shakespeare thought. Let us remember to his honor that in judging the best tragedy of his lifetime, *Gorboduc*, which he praised as "climbing to the height of Seneca his style," he did not seek to fill the loftier niches reserved for *Doctor Faustus* and *Othello;* and that in his mingled praise and blame for the *Shepherds' Calendar* he seemed to sense the greater splendor of the *Faerie Queene*.

Sidney's poetical works fill three volumes in Grosart's edition. Their variety is as great as their quantity. They comprise nearly a hundred and fifty sonnets, many songs for musical setting, pastoral narratives and dia-

[18] See above, ch. v.
[19] Spenser's letter to Harvey, Oct. 5, 1579, mentions Sidney's "scorn" of the *School of Abuse*. See J. S. P. Tatlock, "Bernardo Tasso and Sidney," *Italica*, xii (1935). 74-80.
[20] Henry Hallam, *Introduction to the Literature of Europe*, Part ii., ch. vi.

logues, epithalamia and other occasional verse, translations of French and Latin poetry, and metrical versions of the psalms of David. They illustrate all the different forms of the sonnet and all the chief metres employed in English and in Latin versification. The *Astrophel and Stella* sequence— Astrophel one hundred and eight sonnets and eleven songs—contains about a third and Stella of Sidney's extant poetry, and the metrical insertions in the *Arcadia* another third. It was *Astrophel and Stella,* apparently, that the Elizabethans mainly thought of in connection with Sidney's name; and it is as the author of *Astrophel and Stella* that posterity also best remembers him.

Like the other major works of this frequently interrupted courtier, *Astrophel and Stella* may have been written over a number of years; but the mastery of the Petrarchan sonnet structure which it displays indicates that it is later than the fifteen sonnets in the Old *Arcadia,*[21] and most of it was probably composed between the marriage of Penelope Devereux to Lord Rich in the autumn of 1581 [22] and that of Sidney to Frances Walsingham two years later. Though these poems are, almost without exception, superb in form, nothing could be much more misguided than the effort to interpret them as merely formal exercises. The autobiographical sincerity asserted in many of them is evident in nearly all; not to recognize it disqualifies the critic.[23] They report the feeling of an earnest and emotionally-delayed youth for a young girl with whom he had almost contracted a marriage of convenience in her childhood and with whom he had been on matter-of-course relations by reason of her mother's marriage to his uncle. Sidney seems to have looked in his heart only after she was betrothed to another. Penelope apparently escaped seduction, having another lover to whom she was more faithful than to her husband; but she came near enough to it to set in motion all the pulses of Sidney's being, and his sonnets, with the interspersed songs that punctuate and interpret them, form one of the greatest love poems in the language, as flawless in its psychology as in its rhythms. It is, as Hazlitt called *Romeo and Juliet,* the story of Hamlet in love. But though love, entirely real and essentially noble, is the dominant theme, *Astrophel and Stella* is no more than the *Arcadia* simply a narrative of love. The adjectives that Lamb [24] applies to it, "full, material, and circumstantiated," have not been improved upon. This late, tormenting, and unsatisfied passion becomes the master light that reveals the depths of a

---

[21] Nine of these are in the Shakespearean form, which is not used at all in *Astrophel and Stella* proper, though it does occur in the fine supplementary sonnet, "Leave me, O love, which reachest but to dust" (No. 110), first found in the folio of 1598. See R. G. Whigam and O. F. Emerson, "Sonnet Structure in Sidney's *Astrophel and Stella,*" SP, XVIII (1921). 347-352.

[22] See L. C. John, "The Date of the Marriage of Penelope Devereux," *PMLA,* XLIX (1934). 961-962.

[23] See H. H. Hudson, "Penelope Devereux as Sidney's Stella," *Huntington Library Bull.,* no. 7 (1935), pp. 89-129; J. M. Purcell, *Sidney's Stella* (1934); T. H. Banks, "*Astrophel and Stella* Reconsidered," *PMLA,* L (1935). 403-412; W. G. Friedrich, "The Stella of Astrophel," *ELH,* III (1936). 114-139; D. E. Baughan, "Sir Philip Sidney and the Matchmakers," *MLR,* XXXIII (1938). 506-519.

[24] "Some Sonnets of Sir Philip Sydney," in *Last Essays of Elia.*

character not primarily amorous, but living in a world of men and great deeds.

The underlining of the genuine rather than the fashionable is what gives these poems their closest affinity with the *Arcadia* and the *Defense of Poesy*. The sonnet to the moon, one of Lamb's three special favorites, is an instructive example of straightforward realism, as opposed to the classical formalism of much Elizabethan verse. It would not be easy to find a contemporary invocation to the orb of night which refrains from calling her Cynthia, or which so honestly restricts itself to thoughts of the actual moon and the actual poet. Sidney's address should be compared with Jonson's beautiful apostrophe in the classical spirit to the "Queen and huntress, chaste and fair,...goddess excellently bright." The contrast shows how ornate classic art can often be, and how pure romantic art.

The Vogue *of the Son-* *net after* *Sidney*

The sonnet of fourteen lines, based on Petrarch or his Italian and French imitators, was conspicuous in Tottel's Miscellany (1557), but it evidently lost favor and its name was transferred to other types of short lyric. After Tottel, the true sonnet is not often found in the anthologies until the appearance of the *Phoenix Nest* (1593), which contains fifteen examples, mainly of the Shakespearean or Surreyesque kind. It was Marlowe's friend,

Watson's *Hecatom-* *pathia*

Thomas Watson (*c.* 1557-1592) who recalled the sonnet to the attention of English readers in his *Hecatompathia* (1582), published at just the time when Sidney was composing his own sequence; and the great vogue began when *Astrophel and Stella* was printed, in three editions, in 1591, the first prefaced by Thomas Nashe.[25]

Daniel's *Delia*

The first to follow was Samuel Daniel with his *Delia* (1592). Daniel was the protégé and neighbor of Lady Pembroke, to whom his sequence was dedicated. Twenty-eight of his sonnets—that is, about half—had indeed appeared in 1591 as a supplement to Newman's edition of *Astrophel and Stella*. Daniel is a smooth writer, though too much given to bad rimes and strange new words. His best, as well as best-known, sonnet is No. 49, "Carecharmer sleep, son of the sable night." He uses almost exclusively the easy Shakespearean form and borrows his ideas copiously from Desportes and other Continental poets. His worst fault is prolixity, which gives a dreadful pertinence to the line that closes his last sonnet:

> I say no more. I fear I said too much.

Constable's *Diana*

Henry Constable's *Diana* favors the rime-scheme that Sidney used most: *abbaabba cdcdee*. As first printed in 1592, it contained but twenty-three poems, which the publisher two years later increased to seventy-seven by adding sonnets of Sidney and other unnamed poets. Fantastic conceit is Constable's worst enemy.

[25] Sidney Lee, *Elizabethan Sonnets* (2v, n.d.); J. G. Scott, *Les sonnets élisabéthains* (Paris, 1929); L. C. John, *The Elizabethan Sonnet Sequences* (1938). L. E. Pearson, *Elizabethan Love Conventions* (Berkeley, 1938) is pertinent to this topic. Nearly all the sequences mentioned here will be found in Lee's collection; *Emaricdulfe* and Rogers' *Celestial Elegies*, however, are in *A Lamport Garland*, ed. C. Edmonds (*Roxburghe Club*, 1881).

The next year, 1593, brought out a posthumous volume by Watson, *The Barnes,* *Tears of Fancy,* which has technical skill but lacks emotion; and also the *Fletcher,* *Parthenophil and Parthenophe* of Barnabe Barnes, *Licia* by Giles Fletcher *Lodge* (the elder), and *Phyllis* by Thomas Lodge. The best of these is Fletcher, who is fluent and intelligible. Lodge, who was writing during a sea-voyage, is the most servile in his imitations, though here as elsewhere he shows abundant sweetness. Barnes, a north-countryman with a weakness for un- couth words, is the most *outré* as well as the most varied and copious.[26] His 66th sonnet, "Ah, sweet content, where is thy mild abode?", and Fletcher's 28th, on the ravages of time, are admirable treatments of obvious themes.

In 1594 the son of the Earl of Northumberland, William Percy, published *Percy's* his thin collection, *Cœlia,* consisting of twenty sonnets evoked by the ex- *Cœlia* ample of Barnes, who was the friend of the author. It shares Barnes' harsh vocabulary, but lacks his merits. This and the worthless and anonymous *Zepheria* of the same year were quite eclipsed by Drayton's *Idea,* which *Drayton's* seeks variety and scoffs at the sonneteering epidemic even while submitting *Idea* to it; e.g.,

> Think'st thou my wit shall keep the packhorse way
> That every dudgeon low invention goes?
> Since sonnets thus in bundles are impress'd
> And every drudge doth dull our satiate ear,
> Think'st thou my love shall in those rags be dress'd
> That every dowdy, every trull, doth wear? [27]

Drayton is lively and interesting, and though he quite lacks Sidney's depth, he has something of Sidney's directness. The two sonnets on his native Warwickshire stream, the Ankor (Nos. 32, 53), seem to prelude the *Poly-Olbion,* and a later sonnet (No. 47), on Drayton's triumphs in the theatre, is a charming vignette. As first printed in 1594, *Idea* consisted of fifty-two sonnets with a good many different rime-schemes; but the poet kept altering his collection in subsequent editions, and his best beloved example, "Since there's no help, come let us kiss and part," first appeared in the final recension of 1619.

The year 1595 saw the publication of Spenser's *Amoretti* and Chapman's *Chapman's* metaphysical sequence, *A Coronet for his Mistress Philosophy.* Shakespeare's *Sequence* sonnets, too, though not printed, were probably written by this time; and an unidentified E. C. Esq. produced a sequence of forty, *Emaricdulfe,* good *E. C.,* Emar- metrically and of better than average literary quality. This was the height icdulfe, of the movement, which then very rapidly dwindled. The collections that *1595* appeared the next year, 1596, were by young men who were merely following the fashion: *Fidessa* by Bartholomew Griffin, *Diella* by Richard Lynch, and

---

[26] See M. Eccles, "Barnabe Barnes," in C. J. Sisson, *Thomas Lodge and Other Elizabethans* (1933), pp. 165-241. In 1595 Barnes published a hundred religious sonnets, *A Divine Century of Spiritual Sonnets,* almost all in Sidney's usual rime-scheme.
[27] No. 31, first printed in the edition of 1599.

Chloris by William Smith. Robert Tofte's *Laura* (1597) avoids the too familiar quatorzain for stanzas of twelve and ten lines alternately; Thomas Rogers devotes his *Celestial Elegies* (1598) to funeral lamentation rather than love.[28]

Shake-
speare's
Sonnets

The belated publication of Shakespeare's sonnets in 1609 almost certainly happened without his knowledge or approval; presumably the circulation "among his private friends" reported in 1598 was all that he intended. Of all the Elizabethan sonnet sequences Shakespeare's is the least typical.[29] It celebrates not the idealized love of an idealized mistress but the affection of an older man for a gilded and wayward youth. Even the 25 sonnets addressed to a dark lady express repulsion as well as fascination. On the showing of the sonnets Shakespeare's experience of love and friendship was turbid and disheartening. They abound in meditations on estrangement, failure, and death. They bewail the poet's outcast state, death's dateless night, the anxieties of separation, time's giving and taking away, even world-weariness. The conclusion, however, is triumphant—an uncompromising affirmation of the transcendence of love. The later sonnets (100-126) assert and reassert that love, and love alone, withstands the onslaught of time, eternal amidst the world's ruin and decay.

As sheer poetry they have been variously judged. Even in the twentieth century, when their reputation stands high, they have been described as "seldom perfect." It is true that they often end in a minor key; the final couplet, commonly a hyperbolical statement of unstinted admiration, sometimes even of servile devotion, often seems almost an afterthought. Some of the sonnets are obstinately private and elusive, and some are conceits, exercises in reaching old conclusions by new ways. But the happiest of them reach the old conclusions through series of metaphors of incomparable suggestive power. The style, somewhat surprisingly in view of all the auguries, is rich, not gaudy; it is largely free from the ingenuities of the early plays and from the dense figurativeness of the later. The control of tone and texture is superb. The passions of the poet are much less stormy than those of the characters of his plays, but they are expressed with the same power.

There is no saying how many Elizabethan sonnets followed in the wake of *Astrophel and Stella*. A couple of thousand, at least, have survived.

28 The sonnets of Henry Lok, or Locke, 1597 (ed. A. B. Grosart, 1871) are a prodigious monument of technical skill, and unfortunately they are little else. There are nearly four hundred of them, usually on moral and biblical themes, and assembled in centuries under such titles as *Sonnets of Christian Passions* and *Sonnets of a Feeling Conscience*.

29 The latest edition, by H. E. Rollins (*New Variorum Shakespeare*, 2v, 1944), resumes earlier scholarship and criticism and is the best guide to the enormous literature on the subject. Much of it is inspired by the hope of identifying the persons whom the sonnets mention—the fair youth to whom most of them are addressed, the dark lady of sonnets 127-152, and the rival poet. A clue to the identity of the fair youth has been seen in the publisher's dedication to "the onlie begetter of these insuing sonnets Mr. W. H." As the initials fit, at least after a fashion, two noblemen otherwise known to have patronized Shakespeare (Henry Wriothesley, Earl of Southampton, and William Herbert, Earl of Pembroke), each is backed by an impressive number of advocates (see below, p. 526). A persistent suspicion that the order in which the sonnets were published is not the order in which they were written or intended to be read has led to many attempts to rearrange them (see Rollins, II. 74-116).

IX

Edmund Spenser

When the sap seems to have gone out of poetry and the patterns of life   *"The New*
have grown too stereotyped, a new writer will sometimes appear like   *Poet"*
heaven's benediction with the demand for homelier things and a truer
poetic language. *Lyrical Ballads* in 1798 and *A Shropshire Lad* in 1896 were
literary events of the same kind as *The Shepherds' Calendar* [1] in 1579.
Spenser [2] also aimed at fresher cadences, ballad simplicity, and a new social
philosophy. He did not, any more than Wordsworth in 1798, stand quite   The
alone, though for some years readers referred to him only as "the new   Shepherds'
poet," or by his modest pseudonyms, Colin Clout and "Immerito." The   Calendar
twelve eclogues with which he made his début are addressed to Philip   *(1579)*
Sidney in the most charming of all Spenser's famous Dedications:

> Go, little book: thyself present,
> As child whose parent is unkent,
> To him that is the president
> Of noblesse and of chivalry.
> And if that Envy bark at thee,
> As sure it will, for succor flee
> Under the shadow of his wing;
> And asked, who thee forth did bring,
> A shepherd's swain, say, did thee sing,
> All as his straying flock he fed;
> And when his honor has thee read,
> Crave pardon for thy hardihead....
> And when thou art past jeopardy,
> Come tell me what was said of me,
> And I will send more after thee.

[1] See edition by C. H. Herford (1895, 1914); R. B. Botting, "The Composition of the
Shepheardes Calender," *PMLA*, L (1935). 423-34; M. Parmenter, "Spenser's Twelve Aeglogues
Proportionable to the Twelve Monethes," *ELH*, III (1936). 190-217; J. B. Fletcher, "The
Puritan Argument in Spenser," *PMLA*, LVIII (1943). 634-648.
[2] Works, Variorum Edition, ed. E. A. Greenlaw, F. M. Padelford, C. G. Osgood, R. Heffner,
and others (in progress; 8 vols. to date; Baltimore, 1933-); *Poetical Works*, ed. R. E. N. Dodge
(1908); *Minor Poems*, ed. E. de Selincourt (Oxford, 1910). The editions of the minor poems
(with individual titles) by W. L. Renwick (3v, 1928-1930) contain valuable notes. The best
biography, incorporating facts recently discovered, is A. C. Judson, *The Life of Edmund Spenser*
(1945), supplementary to the Variorum. — F. I. Carpenter, *A Reference Guide to Edmund
Spenser* (Chicago, 1923); D. F. Atkinson, *Edmund Spenser, a Bibliographical Supplement*
(Baltimore, 1937); F. R. Johnson, *A Critical Bibliography of the Works of Edmund Spenser
printed before 1700* (Baltimore, 1933), C. G. Osgood, *Concordance* (Washington, 1915); C.
H. Whitman, *Subject Index to the Poems* (New Haven, 1918). For general criticism see H. S.
V. Jones, *A Spenser Handbook* (1930); W. L. Renwick, *Edmund Spenser, an Essay on Renais-
sance Poetry* (1925); B. E. C. Davis, *Edmund Spenser, a Critical Study* (1933); M. Y. Hughes,
Virgil and Spenser (Berkeley, 1929); C. S. Lewis, *The Allegory of Love* (Oxford, 1936).

E. K., who was probably his Cambridge friend Edward Kirke, provided the poems with explanatory notes and a critical introduction in the form of an open letter to Gabriel Harvey. A young man's verses have not often been equipped on first appearance with such a panoply of scholarship.[3]

Spenser's schoolboy labors, ten years before, in translating Petrarch and du Bellay for Van der Noodt's *Theatre* (1569) would have been enough to call his attention to foreign vernaculars, and he had had a thorough grounding in the classics. His last two eclogues are imitations of Clement Marot; the eighth follows Virgil in theme and Petrarch in form. Elsewhere he adapts the ancient Greek pastoral of Bion or Theocritus and the modern Latin satire of Mantuanus, whom Barclay and Turberville had been translating. But behind the remarkable variety, both in matter and metre, which is one of the especial tokens of promise in *The Shepherds' Calendar*, lies the fundamental assertion that the only way for the poetry of Spenser's time is the way of Chaucer, who is exalted as Tityrus, "the god of shepherds,"

> Who taught me, homely as I can, to make.
> He, whilst he lived, was the sovereign head
> Of shepherds all that bene with love ytake; [4]

and he is (as Spenser was later to phrase it) the "well of English undefiled." [5] This prime purpose of the work, to rid poetic diction of foreign encumbrance and restore Chaucerian vigor and simplicity, is again stated with Wordsworthian doggedness in E. K.'s Epistle:

For in my opinion it is one special praise, of many which are due to this poet [i.e., Spenser], that he hath labored to restore, as to their rightful heritage, such good and natural English words as have been long time out of use and almost clean disherited. Which is the only cause that our mother tongue, which truly of itself is both full enough for prose and stately enough for verse, hath long time been counted most bare and barren of both.

Spenser's *Education* The Shepherds' Calendar* is a turning point for Elizabethan poetry. It is the first landmark in Spenser's career. He was twenty-seven years old. Born in London and educated under Mulcaster at the Merchant Taylors' School, he had lived for seven years at Cambridge in Pembroke Hall, which had a strong tradition of Calvinism. Ridley, the martyr, had been Master there, and had been succeeded by Edmund Grindal (Spenser's "Algrind"), whom Queen Elizabeth later suspended from the archbishopric of Canterbury for his too Puritan leanings. When Spenser matriculated, in 1569, Grindal had given place to John Young, a cleric of the same stripe.[6] It is clear that the poet imbibed the sympathies of the place, and these sympathies appear in *The Shepherds' Calendar*. On receiving his M. A. in 1576, he lived for a

---

[3] See D. T. Starnes, "E. K.'s Classical Allusions Reconsidered," *SP*, XXXIX (1942). 143-159.
[4] *June*, 81 ff.
[5] *Faerie Queene*, IV. ii. st. 32.
[6] See P. W. Long, "Spenser and the Bishop of Rochester," *PMLA*, XXXI (1916). 713-735; A. C. Judson, "A Biographical Sketch of John Young," *Indiana Univ. Stud.* XXI (1934); L. Bradner, "An Allusion to Bromley in the *Shepherds' Calendar*," *MLN*, XLIX (1934). 443-445.

period in the north of England, and then or later fell in love with the *His First* Rosalind of the poem, who, though Colin Clout is represented as languishing *Marriage* hopelessly for her, is thought by some to have become Edmund Spenser's wife shortly before his verses were printed.[7]

When *The Shepherds' Calendar* was being written, Spenser had returned to the south, and was "the southern shepherd's boy," that is, secretary to Young, his old college Master, now Bishop of Rochester, whom he praises as "Roffyn" in the September eclogue. By the time the poems were published, *His Politics* however, late in 1579, he had passed into the service of the Earl of Leicester, the·political leader of the more Protestant part of the nation; and, as the letters which he exchanged with Harvey at this time show, he was at home in Leicester House, London, which may be described as the great Conservative Club of the metropolis, and was expecting to be sent abroad on a mission for Leicester. National, literary, and ecclesiastic convictions merge in *The Shepherds' Calendar* in a consistent pattern from which the later Spenser did not depart. He stands for an ultra-English poetry as incarnated in Chaucer, for low-church theology as represented by Grindal and Young against the high-church formalism of John Aylmer, Bishop of London (the "Morrell" of the July eclogue), and (as yet by implication chiefly) for Leicester's policy of suspicion toward French entanglements. The minor note of melancholy withdrawal, which generally marks Spenser's poetry and probably hampered him as a political agent, is strong in the "plaintive" group of eclogues dealing with Colin Clout (Nos. 1, 6, 11, 12). His matchless musical powers, hampered by the archaism of many eclogues, appear chiefly in the song on Queen Elizabeth in *April* and the lines on poetic inspiration in *October,* some of which Ben Jonson had by heart. The breadth and immediacy of its intellectual basis and the variety of effects and rhythms obtained are what most call attention to this work.

Hardly half a year·had elapsed from the publication of *The Shepherds' Calendar* when Spenser's course was diverted by his appointment as secretary to the new governor of Ireland, Lord Grey of Wilton. To call this a penalty for his interference in courtly politics is to ignore Elizabethan, and most other, conceptions of reward and punishment. The post was highly· honorable in itself, and led to further emoluments and advancement; but the life of an administrator in Ireland was arduous and checked for ten years the output of Spenser's poetry.[8] He had begun the *Faerie Queene* before he left England in August, 1580, but it was not till late in 1589 that he was able to return and find a printer for the first three books, which appeared in 1590. This, the earliest publication to bear Spenser's name, he boldly dedicated to Queen Elizabeth, who rewarded him, signally enough, by the grant of a pension of fifty pounds a year. The publisher, William Ponsonby, was soon impelled to seek out more of Spenser's work, and during 1591

[7] For various views see M. Eccles, "Spenser's First Marriage," *LTLS*, Dec. 31, 1931, p. 1053; T. H. Banks, "Spenser's Rosalind: A Conjecture," *PMLA*, LII (1937). 335-337; D. Hamer, "Spenser's Marriage," *RES*, VII (1931). 271-290.

[8] See R. Jenkins, "Spenser: The Uncertain Years, 1584-1589," *PMLA*, LIII (1938). 350-62.

Daphnaida   issued two volumes of his minor poems. *Daphnaida,*[9] which in the preface is dated January 1, 1591, is a long ceremonious elegy on the recent death of a lady of rank, notable for its lovely metrical structure (an original adaptation of rime royal) and delicate balance of parts. It is reminiscent of Chaucer's *Book of the Duchess,* and may be regarded as Spenser's most consummate tribute to medieval art and to his great predecessor.

Complaints   The other volume is of much more mixed character, and is entitled *Complaints, containing Sundry Small Poems of the World's Vanity.*[10] Ponsonby claims to have made the collection, but it is evident that the poet helped him, for the book is in four parts with separate title-pages (the first three dated 1591, the fourth 1590), and each part has a signed dedication from Spenser to a lady of the court, viz. the Countess of Pembroke, and the three titled sisters of the Althorpe Spencer family with whom the poet avowed relationship. In studying this volume one studies the development of Spenser's style from his earliest beginnings to full maturity. The *Visions of Bellay, Visions of Petrarch, Visions of the World's Vanity,* and *Ruins of Rome,* all in sonnet form, are either recastings of his very youthful contribution to the Van der Noodt *Theatre* of 1569 or else exercises in the same direction, showing discipleship to the French Pléiade and the cult of emblem poetry. Also early is the paraphrase of the Virgilian *Culex,* entitled *Virgil's Gnat,* which is in fluent and melodious *ottava rima,* but is chiefly important for the introductory sonnet to Leicester in which Spenser seems to reprimand that nobleman for his part in the obscure business that led to the poet's transfer from Leicester House to Ireland in 1580. Of more uncertain date is the formalized *Tears of the Muses,* probably suggested by Gabriel Harvey's Latin *Musarum Lachrimae* of 1578, and lamenting the decay of art, learning, and virtue. The sentiments are such as Spenser or most other Elizabethans would have subscribed to in any fit of depression, and the supposedly topical allusions have not proved helpful.

Ruins of Time   The first poem in the book, *The Ruins of Time,* is much more significant. Addressed to the Countess of Pembroke and provided with a neo-mythological introduction out of Camden's *Britannia* (1586) and two concluding series of poetical "visions," this remarkably skilful and fervent poem condoles with her on the loss of various relatives, particularly her brother Sidney and her uncles of Leicester and Warwick. The major part of it must have been, and probably all of it was, written shortly before publication. It is not an easy type in which to achieve immortality; but it is marked by Spenser's endearing fineness of feeling, and his handling of the rime royal admits bursts of the verbal orchestration in which he is with Milton; as in this stanza to Sidney in heaven:

[9] Ed. W. L. Renwick, *Daphnaida and Other Poems* (1929), including also *Colin Clout's Come Home Again, Astrophel, Amoretti, Epithalamion, Four Hymns, Prothalamion.* See H. E. Sandison, "Arthur Gorges, Spenser's Alcyon and Raleigh's Friend," *PMLA,* XLIII (1928), 645-674.
[10] Ed. W. L. Renwick (1928). See H. Stein, *Studies in Spenser's Complaints* (1934).

But now more happy thou, and wretched we,
Which want the wonted sweetness of thy voice,
Whiles thou now in Elysian fields so free
With Orpheus and with Linus, and the choice
Of all that ever did in rimes rejoice,
Conversest, and dost hear their heavenly lays,
And they hear thine, and thine do better praise.[11]

There is an undercurrent, however, of the contemptuous anger that rankled in him during the year 1590, while he was prosecuting his claim for reward at court; and this emerges in one most tactless stanza against Burghley, the great Lord Treasurer, who is said to have protested to the queen that fifty pounds a year was too much for a song:

O grief of griefs! O gall of all good hearts!
To see that virtue should despised be
Of him that first was rais'd for virtuous parts,
And now, broad-spreading like an aged tree,
Lets none shoot up that nigh him planted be.
O let the man of whom the Muse is scorned,
Nor alive, nor dead, be of the Muse adorned.[12]

There may be a more sustained allusiveness in another of the great poems **Muiopotmos** in *Complaints;* namely, *Muiopotmos, or the Fate of the Butterfly.* It is in the ironic Italian metre of *Virgil's Gnat, ottava rima,* and opens like a mock-heroic parable:

I sing of deadly dolorous debate,
Stirr'd up through wrathful Nemesis' despite
Betwixt two mighty ones of great estate,
Drawn into arms and proof of mortal fight
Through proud ambition and heartswelling hate,
Whilst neither could the other's greater might
And 'sdainful scorn endure; that from small jar
Their wraths at length broke into open war.

But the story seems to have suffered truncation at some time, perhaps in the process of being turned into a fit offering for Lady Carey, and no satisfactory elucidation is available. It may be Spenser's semi-playful warning to his friend Ralegh to beware of the web that the Cecil spider wove.[13] It needs no such exegesis; for as it stands it is one of the most delightful of poetic fantasies, dealing with matters in which Spenser's genius was always at home: the re-weaving of old myths and the daintiness of insects, formal gardens, and fine needle-work.

---

[11] Lines 330 ff.
[12] Lines 449 ff.
[13] See J. M. Lyons, "Spenser's *Muiopotmos* as an Allegory," *PMLA,* xxxi (1916). 90-113; I. J. C. Grierson, "Spenser's *Muiopotmos," MLR,* xvii (1922). 409-411. The number of variant interpretations of this poem is nearly infinite.

Mother
Hubbard's
Tale

The greatest poem in *Complaints* and the longest is *Mother Hubbard's Tale,* Spenser's only ambitious effort in heroic couplets. Here there is no doubt of the satiric intention; and if, as is commonly believed, the last third of the poem was written ten years after the rest, the joining has been so skilfully done as to leave few stylistic traces. One must assume that the sections which seem to allude to conditions in 1580 were pretty thoroughly recast in 1590. The tale is really four tales of the malefactions of a fox and an ape, who in the first three live disguised in the world of men, but in the last inhabit a beast-world. The satire rises through four levels, in which Spenser successively attacks agricultural, clerical, social, and finally imperial mores. The narrative is in each case interesting and ironic. The picture of life at court in the third part contains a great set passage on "the brave courtier"[14] which may be regarded as a statement of the general Renaissance doctrine of the gentleman, or as an unlabeled character sketch of Sir Philip Sidney in particular; and this part ends with an arraignment of the servile and stultifying conditions of Elizabethan court favor, expressed in the strongest couplet verse written by any Englishman before Dryden:

> So pitiful a thing is suitor's state . . .
> Full little knowest thou that hast not tried,
> What hell it is in suing long to bide:
> To lose good days that might be better spent,
> To waste long nights in pensive discontent;
> To speed to-day, to be put back to-morrow;
> To feed on hope, to pine with fear and sorrow;
> To have thy prince's grace, yet want her peers';
> To have thy asking, yet wait many years;
> To fret thy soul with crosses and with cares,
> To eat thy heart through comfortless despairs:
> To fawn, to crouch, to wait, to ride, to run,
> To spend, to give, to want, to be undone.[15]

In the last tale (lines 938-1384) the fox becomes a quite obvious symbol of Burghley's imperiousness, avarice, and nepotism. It is not surprising that, for this and other imprudences, the *Complaints* volume was "called in" or suppressed, and that Spenser did not adventure further along this congenial but most dangerous path.[16]

Colin
Clout's
Come
Home
Again

His next poem is in very different tone, and is, after the *Epithalamion,* his most attractive work. Though not printed till 1595, it is prefaced by a letter to Ralegh, dated from the poet's Irish home, Kilcolman Castle, December 27, 1591. It is his acknowledgment of thanks to Sir Walter, who had been his sponsor in the momentous English journey of 1589-90. The author

---

[14] Lines 717-793.
[15] Lines 891-914.
[16] See Brice Harris, "The Ape in *Mother Hubberds Tale," HLQ,* IV (1941). 191-203. There were few imitations of *Mother Hubbard's Tale.* Perhaps *The Flea* (1605) by Peter Woodhouse (Grosart, *Occasional Issues,* III, 1877) may be so regarded. It is likewise in riming couplets and handles a debate between an elephant and a flea, but its political purpose is not easily discernible.

of the *Faerie Queene* here lays off his singing robes and reverts to the humble character of Colin Clout, safe in Ireland again among his shepherd mates, to whom he describes the great things and persons he has seen. The instinct for form, which seldom fails Spenser, has chosen for *Colin Clout's Come Home Again* a pentameter quatrain of rustic type and language in keeping with it. The rimes never obtrude and the rime-scheme is visible only to the consciously searching eye. As often as not, one stanza flows without a break into the next, and the flow is so easy that perhaps the author himself did not observe that his second stanza contains but three lines. Primarily, his purpose is to pay his compliments to Ralegh, the "Shepherd of the Ocean," whose meeting with Spenser in Munster, companionship on the voyage, and patronage at court are delightfully narrated. But he also thanks the queen for her favors to him in three passages of skilful adulation,[17] and offers handsome tributes to the courtly poets and court ladies he had met. The pastoral note is admirably sustained, better perhaps than in *Lycidas,* and *Colin Clout's Come Home Again* is equally important as poetic auto- biography, though far less sublime than Milton's pastoral. It gives the impression that Spenser was now happy in Ireland and had honestly abjured the enticements of courtly ambition. It ends in philosophic mood, with a Platonic praise of true love and a reassertion of Colin's loyalty to the loved and lost Rosalind.

Spenser's *Astrophel,* printed in the same volume as *Colin Clout's Come Home Again,* is the first of a group of poems by various authors on Sidney's death. Though published later, it was most likely composed earlier than Shakespeare's *Venus and Adonis,* but is in the same stanza and figuratively represents Sir Philip's wound as caused, like Adonis's, by a tusked beast.   *Astrophel*

The poignant disquisition on love and the sentimental memories of Rosa- lind with which *Colin Clout's Come Home Again* concludes suggest that the poet's homecoming, pleasant as it evidently was for him, was not unmarred by loneliness. A year later he knew that he was enamoured of an English girl, Elizabeth Boyle,[18] who had come to Ireland with her brother and settled near Youghal on the coast, some thirty miles from Kilcolman. The account of the wooing and marriage in *Amoretti* and *Epithalamion,* published together early in 1595, has the same autobiographical forthrightness as *Colin Clout's Come Home Again,* and, of course, much greater depth of feeling. The courtship was not easy. Suing, in any sense, was hard for Spenser; the girl was proud and much his junior, and her family seem to have had considerable ambitions for her. The fourth sonnet of the *Amoretti* is dated by internal evidence January 1, 1593. In the nineteenth "the merry cuckoo, messenger of spring," has commenced to sing; in the twenty-second Lent has begun. The sixtieth sonnet notes that the poet has been in love a year; the sixty-second speaks of New Year, 1594, the sixty-   *Elizabeth Boyle*   *Amoretti*

[17] Lines 233-263, 332-351, 590-647.
[18] See W. H. Welply, "Spenser and Elizabeth Boyle," *LTLS,* May 24, 1923, pp. 355, 356; and R. Heffner, "Edmund Spenser's Family," *HLQ,* II (1938). 79-84.

eighth of Easter, and the seventieth of May Day. The marriage took place on St. Barnaby's Day, June 11, which by the Old Style calendar was the longest of the year.

In all these sonnets except the eighth, which is of the usual "Shakespearean" kind, Spenser employs his special form of linked quatrains, *ababbcbccdcdee,* which he had already used in the *Visions of the World's Vanity* and the Dedication to *Virgil's Gnat.* As regards content, the sequence divides into three unequal parts: Sonnets 1-62, dealing with unrequited love; Sonnets 63-84, dealing with the lovers' happiness; and Sonnets 85-88, dealing with the lovers' brief separation, before their marriage. The last section includes also four little lyrics on Cupid, in the manner of the Greek Anthology, which are merely finger-exercises or preludes to the great *crescendo* of *Epithalamion.*

It is naturally the second group that matters most. The first sixty-two sonnets all report a negative result, and the experience of an unencouraged lover is capable of so little variation as to forbid surprise at the discovery that many of Spenser's ideas have been expressed before.[19] They have not often been so resourcefully illustrated. It is interesting in this group to study the poet's dabbling with the metaphysical conceit, commonly defined as a phase of the reaction against him; and, quite apart from content, admiration is extorted by the Gothic lightness of structure in such a sonnet as No. 56, which in form parallels Shakespeare's No. 73: "That time of year thou mayst in me behold."

No. 64 records the first kiss, and the twenty that follow this have such a grounding in actual incident and true emotion as makes them equal to the best of Sidney's. Some of these—the prayer for Easter Day (68), the one on the girl's needlework (71) and her Christian name (74), for example—need but to be mentioned. A less outstanding instance (67), dealing with the climax of the courtship, deserves quotation, because so few poets and lovers have been able to write so like a gentleman:

> Like as a huntsman after weary chase,
> Seeing the game from him escapt away,
> Sits down to rest him in some shady place,
> With panting hounds beguiled of their prey.
> So, after long pursuit and vain assay,
> When I all weary had the chase forsook,
> The gentle deer return'd the selfsame way,
> Thinking to quench her thirst at the next brook.
> There she, beholding me with milder look,
> Sought not to fly, but fearless still did bide,
> Till I in hand her yet half-trembling took,
> And with her own good will her firmly tied.
> Strange thing, me seem'd, to see a beast so wild
> So goodly won, with her own will beguil'd.

[19] See J. G. Scott, "The Sources of Spenser's *Amoretti,*" *MLR,* xxii (1927). 189-195; E. Casady, "The Neo-Platonic Ladder in Spenser's *Amoretti,*" *PQ,* xx (1941). 284-295.

Spenser's marriage, when finally arranged, was hurriedly performed.
The *Epithalamion* [20] is his gift to his bride and to himself. "I unto myself
alone will sing," says he; but the song has been his most universal passport
to posterity. The *Faerie Queene* is not always or in all respects admired,
but the superiority of the *Epithalamion* to everything else in its class would
hardly be disputed. It differs from the other marriage hymns in its larger
melodic range, for Spenser has here used the total resources of his musical
power. It differs also in its broader humanity, for in its twenty-three strophes
some twenty hours of an Irish day are registered with a vividness that never
fades. Perhaps it differs most of all in striking the nearly unattainable line
between too hot and too cold. Flesh has just its proper place, and Platonism
also. It may seem trifling praise to say that, whatever codes of conduct come
and go, the *Epithalamion* is always in good taste, but that can be said of
few other marriage odes.

The *Prothalamion* is one of the casual results of Spenser's visit to London
in 1596 to see Books IV-VI of the *Faerie Queene* through the press. *Epi-*
thalamion had been printed the year before; and it is evident that the Earl
of Worcester, who had to provide a state wedding for his two daughters, the
Ladies Elizabeth and Katherine Somerset, took advantage of the poet's
presence at court to commission him to write a marriage poem like the other
for this occasion. The earl got extraordinary value for his money. He got
an extremely great poem, less than half the length of *Epithalamion,* but
even more exquisitely proportioned. However, the emotion of the earlier
work could not be reproduced, and Spenser made no slightest effort to do
so. The brides are pretty lay-figures, likened to white swans, and are only
individualized in one mediocre pun on their family name: "Yet were they
bred of *Summer's-heat,* they say." The bridegrooms barely rate a mention
in the last stanza. What the wise poet and the foolish courtier does is to
express his own emotion at being again in London, walking beside the
Thames. The spousal interest is delicately dismissed in the opening lines,
in which Spenser airs once more his long-standing grievance against courts:

> Calm was the day . . .
> When I, whom sullen care,
> Through discontent of my long fruitless stay
> In prince's court, and expectation vain
> Of idle hopes, which still do fly away
> Like empty shadows, did afflict my brain,[21]
> Walk'd forth to ease my pain
> Along the shores of silver-streaming Thames.

At the close, in the lines that everyone remembers best, he lingers over his
associations with "merry London, my most kindly nurse," and with the
dead Leicester and the living Essex. It was hardly possible for Spenser to

---

[20] Ed. C. Van Winkle (1926).
[21] The meaning is: "I whose brain sullen care . . . afflicted."

The Four
Hymns

be ungraceful, and the pretty symbolism of the brides-elect is charmingly brought in; but it has never been much more than floral background.

The *Four Hymns,*[22] prefaced by an interesting letter to the Countesses of Cumberland and Warwick which Spenser dated from Greenwich (where the court was) on September 1, 1596, were printed in the same year and are one of the latest publications of his lifetime. In them he attempts a formal statement of the idealistic philosophy, of pagan-Christian blend and neo-Platonic pattern, which is suffused over the whole of the *Faerie Queene.* They are more poetic than systematic. The letter explains that the first two poems, on the pagan theory of love and beauty, had been written "in the greener times of my youth," but when one of the sister-countesses had urged him to suppress them, he had been unable to do so by reason of the number of manuscript copies in circulation, and so resolved

at least to amend and by way of retractation to reform them, making instead of those two hymns of earthly or natural love and beauty two others of heavenly and celestial.

This retraction sounds like the one in which Chaucer disavows his book of Troilus and the *Canterbury Tales,* and may have been suggested by it. Spenser had less cause to renounce the morality of the two earlier hymns, and if he had indeed outgrown them, he would not have inserted a re-capitulation of the *Hymn in Honor of Love* in *Colin Clout's Come Home Again* [23] or concerned himself with such lovely heresies as the Garden of Adonis passage in the *Faerie Queene.*[24] The probability is that, having at no very "green" period written these two digests of Platonism and wishing to publish them, he apprehended that his pious patronesses might not be edified by such reverent treatment of pagan gods and philosophers, and so added the Christian counterparts to float, not submerge them.[25]

The four Hymns are in particularly delicate and accomplished rime royal, which is made to lend itself perfectly to abstruse exposition. The first two, not very clearly distinguished in content, start from the notion that love is born of beauty as Cupid was of Venus, develop the conception of love as the prime creative force (as in Plato's *Symposium*), and then pass, in the *Hymn to Beauty,* to the demonstration of man's moral progress through the love of beauty at its successive levels. In the *Hymn of Heavenly Love,* Christ replaces Cupid as creative love, and in this poem, the least successful of the four, becomes a rationalization of the Fall and Redemption, a sort of *Paradise Lost* in little. In *Heavenly Beauty* the Platonic ladder is set up against the edifice of Christian theology, and the Platonic "idea" is identified

---

[22] Ed. L. Winstanley (Cambridge, 1930). See R. W. Lee, "Castiglione's Influence on Spenser's Early Hymns," *PQ,* vii (1928). 65-77.

[23] Lines 835-894.

[24] Book iii, canto vi. See J. W. Bennett, "Spenser's Garden of Adonis Revisited," *JEGP,* xli (1942). 53-78, and discussion, *ibid.,* pp. 492-9.

[25] See J. W. Bennett, "The Theme of Spenser's *Foure Hymnes,*" *SP,* xxviii (1931). 18-57, and "*Addenda,*" *SP,* xxxii (1935). 131-157; F. M. Padelford, "Spenser's *Foure Hymnes,* a Resurvey," *SP,* xxix (1932). 207-252.

with the ineffable presence of God, which the soul inspired by heavenly beauty climbs to through gradual apprehension of His various works (lines 127-133).

Spenser retracted nothing in the later Hymns, which are essentially as Greek as the earlier ones, and not much hampered by the new medium into which the doctrine has been translated. "For all that's good is beautiful and fair"[26] is the kernel of his thought, and the grand summary at the close of *Heavenly Beauty* (lines 267-87) is as frank neo-Platonism, or rather, as pure Platonism, as anything in the earlier pair. The conception of love and beauty as a gradual infusion is one of the points that distinguish Spenser from that other Hellenist, Marlowe, who stressed intuitive genius. In the second Hymn he categorically denies the Dead Shepherd's yet unpublished cliché:

> For all that like the beauty which they see
> Straight do not love; for love is not so light
> As straight to burn at first beholder's sight.[27]

Spenser's chief prose work, *A View of the Present State of Ireland,* was provisionally entered for publication on April 14, 1598, and was probably composed while the author was in England in 1596.[28] A number of manuscript copies circulated, but it was not printed till long after (1633), when Sir James Ware brought it out in conjunction with the briefer *History of Ireland* written in 1571 by Edmund Campion, the Jesuit martyr.[29] Spenser's treatise, containing over 60,000 words, is a well-planned dialogue on Irish laws, customs, and military government. In the character of Irenius, who is represented as having recently arrived from Ireland, he gives his own opinions, which are well ventilated and interpreted by the intelligent interlocutor, Eudoxus. The latter has plenty to say and does not merely serve, as the second speaker does in too many "Platonic" discourses, as the means of dividing a long disquisition into its component parts. The prose style is very fine, simple in syntax and vocabulary, but with a periodic roll that marks it for the prose of a poet; as in Irenius's condemnation of the social influence of the Irish bards:

The View of Ireland

It is most true that such poets as in their writings do labor to better the manners of men, and through the sweet bait of their numbers to steal into young spirits a desire of honor and virtue, are worthy to be had in great respect. But these Irish bards are for the most part of another mind, and so far from instructing young men in moral discipline, that they themselves do more deserve to be sharply disciplined; for they seldom use to choose unto themselves the doings of good men for the ornaments of their poems, but whomsoever they find to be most licentious of life, most bold and lawless in his doings, most dangerous

---

[26] *Hymn of Heavenly Beauty*, line 133.
[27] Lines 208-210.
[28] Ed. W. L. Renwick (1934). See R. B. Gottfried, "The Date of Spenser's *View,*" *MLN,* LII (1937). 176-180; "Spenser as an Historian in Prose," *Trans. Wis. Acad.,* xxx (1938). 317-330; "Irish Geography in Spenser's *View,*" *ELH,* vi (1939). 114-137; R. Heffner, "Spenser's *View of Ireland:* Some Observations," *MLQ,* iii (1942). 507-515.
[29] Ed. R. B. Gottfried (*Scholars' Facsimiles and Reprints,* 1940).

and desperate in all parts of disobedience and rebellious disposition, him they set up and glorify in their rimes, him they praise to the people, and to young men make an example to follow.

Two-thirds of the essay express the sympathetic interest with which Spenser had studied the antiquities, art, and customs of the island; [30] but critics, with the *mauvaise honte* that always afflicts Anglo-Saxons when discipline for Ireland is in question, have habitually condemned the brutality of the *View*. The poet defends in the most downright way the severe practices of his old chief, Lord Grey, and asserts that present reform, must be "by the sword," promising that it can be achieved by 11,000 soldiers in a year and a half. He advocates group removal of disloyal population to another part of the country and systematic starvation to check outlaws. He proposes mercy for the mean and submissive, but none for the great rebels like Tyrone. He deplores the Queen's soft-heartedness and the irresolution of many of her governors, and waxes angry over the contrast between the self-sacrifice of the Popish priests and the hedonism of many Protestant pastors:

It is great wonder to see the odds which is between the zeal of Popish priests and the ministers of the gospel; for they spare not to come out of Spain, from Rome, and from Rheims, by long toil and dangerous travel hither, where they know peril of death awaiteth them, and no reward nor riches is to be found, only to draw the people to the Church of Rome; whereas some of our idle ministers, having a way for credit and estimation thereby opened unto them, and having the livings of the country offered them without pains and without peril, will neither for the same, nor for any love of God, nor zeal of religion, nor for all the good they might do by winning of so many souls to God, be drawn forth from their warm nests and their sweet loves' side to look out into God's harvest, which is even ready for the sickle, and all the fields yellow long ago. Doubtless those good old godly Fathers will (I fear me) rise up in the Day of Judgment to condemn them.

Those who cleave to the conception of the "gentle Spenser" are pained by these views, and do not admit the right of a man residing on a volcano to resent the encouragement of its activities. Four months after his book had been ineffectively registered in London, "upon condition that he get further authority before it be printed," Tyrone struck again. All Munster rose in unexpected tumult. Kilcolman was destroyed, and very likely some important portions of the *Faerie Queene;* but the *View of the Present State of Ireland* was signally vindicated. Spenser, now Sheriff of Cork, was sent to London in December, 1598, with official despatches concerning the revolt. There, apparently in the last month of his life, he wrote the "Brief Note of Ireland," which is an appeal on behalf of the sufferers from the insurrection.[31] He minces no words, demanding that the Queen protect and

Revolt in Ireland

---

[30] For the possible influence of Irish poetry on Spenser's own see P. Henley, *Spenser in Ireland* (Cork, 1928).
[31] A. B. Grosart, *Works of Spenser* (1884), I. 537-555.

avenge her subjects, openly declaring his doubts of her "wonted merciful mind"; and ends with a logical *précis:* "Certain points to be considered of in the recovery of the realm of Ireland." This paper, first printed by Grosart, was unknown to Landor when he wrote the imaginary conversation between Essex and Spenser, portraying the latter as a broken and despondent man.

Spenser died at Westminster, January 13, 1599, doubtless a victim of the *Spenser's* tensions he had been under.[32] He was about forty-seven years old, and quite *Death* at the height of his career both as poet and as public official. His sons, whom he had given the pioneering names of Sylvanus and Peregrine, returned to his Irish estates, which Spenser's works show that he loved quite as much as he feared, and they populated that country with his posterity. In time these doubtless became undistinguished, for nothing is less like the Sheriff of Cork and delineator of Prince Arthur than the epitaph of one of them:

Here lies the body of Edmond Spenser, great-great-grandson of the poet Spenser. Unfortunate from his cradle to his grave.[33]

[32] See W. I. Zeitler, "The Date of Spenser's Death," *MLN*, XLIII (1928). 322-324; R. Heffner, "Did Spenser Die in Poverty?" *MLN*, XLVIII (1933). 221-226; J. W. Bennett, "Did Spenser Starve?" *MLN*, LII (1937). 400-401.
[33] Kilcolman was sold in 1736 for the debts of Spenser's great-grandson; see H. Wood, "Spenser's Great-grandson," *LTLS*, Feb. 14, 1929.

X

The Faerie Queene: The Spenserians

Form and
Purpose
of the
Faerie
Queene

The opalescent and kaleidoscopic quality in the *Faerie Queene,* which is the delight of the sympathetic reader and despair of the critic, is not solely due to its allegorical character or to the variety of models that Spenser drew from: Ariosto, Chaucer, Malory, etc.[1] It results also from important changes in the poet's purpose, particularly during the ten-year period in which the first three books were incubating. The letters that passed between Spenser and Harvey show that in April, 1580, he had already submitted a considerable section of the work for his friend's criticism. At this time he was attempting

The Early
Plan

to emulate or "overgo" the *Orlando Furioso,*[2] and Harvey's judgment was wholly unfavorable. Probably the *Faerie Queene* was never greatly to the latter's taste, for the commendatory verses he wrote for the edition of 1590 are not fervent; but something more than critical distrust may have lain behind the urgency with which, in 1580, he bade his protégé desist. The young man seems to have been contemplating propagandist poetry of the most flagrant kind, in which Leicester, typified as Prince Arthur, should achieve Gloriana by his matchless exploits, and then, ruling as *King* Arthur, should with her lead Fairyland to triumph over the Paynim King (Philip II) in the Armageddon that every one foresaw. This is the apparent promise of the vision Arthur has (I. ix. st. 13, 14) and the purpose of Una's advice to the Queen to make the most of her opportunity (st. 16.):

> O happy Queen of Fairies, that hast found,
> 'Mongst many, one that with his prowess may
> Defend thine honor and thy foes confound!
> True loves are often sown, but seldom grow on ground.

So ardent does Spenser become in anticipation of the international theme that the fight of the Red Cross Knight with the dragon seems secondary to him, and he prays his muse to reserve her strength for the greater subject (I. xi. 7):

---

[1] Consult *Faerie Queene,* Variorum Ed.; J. Spens, *Spenser's Faerie Queene: An Interpretation* (1934); E. Greenlaw, *Studies in Spenser's Historical Allegory* (Baltimore, 1932); C. B. Millican, *Spenser and the Table Round* (Cambridge, Mass., 1932); J. H. Walter, "The Faerie Queene, Alterations and Structure," *MLR,* XXXVI (1941). 37-58; "Further Notes," *MLR,* XXXVIII (1943). 1-10; and especially J. W. Bennett, *The Evolution of the Faerie Queene* (Chicago, 1942).

[2] See R. E. N. Dodge, "Spenser's Imitations from Ariosto," *PMLA,* XII (1897). 151-204, with supplement by the same, *PMLA,* XXXV (1920). 91-92, and by A. H. Gilbert, *PMLA,* XXXIV (1919). 225-232; S. J. McMurphy, "Spenser's Use of Ariosto for Allegory," *Univ. Washington Pub.,* II (1924). 1-54.

> Fair goddess, lay that furious fit aside,
> Till I of war and bloody Mars do sing,
> And Briton fields with Saracen blood be-dyed,
> 'Twixt that great Faery Queen and Paynim King,
> That with their horror heaven and earth did ring,
> A work of labor long and endless praise:
> But now a while let down that haughty string,
> And to my tunes thy second tenor raise,
> That I this man of God his godly arms may blaze.

And the muse cannot but be thinking of the Armada beacons of 1588 in her description of the dragon's eyes (st. 14).

Leicester's prospect of becoming king-consort had really dwindled to nothing by 1580; and when he died in 1588 a great deal of recasting must have been done, of which a trace remains in the curious obituary lines tacked to the end of the first mention of Prince Arthur and his armor (I. vii. st. 36):

> But when he died, the Fairy Queen it brought
> To Fairyland, where yet it may be seen, if sought.

Meantime, Spenser's growing acquaintance with Tasso, whose *Jerusalem Delivered* was first published in 1581, besides lending him inspiration for specific passages,[3] must have deepened the moral and crusading element in *Ralegh's* the *Faerie Queene*. His poem was probably in a complete welter when *Influence* Ralegh arrived in Ireland, and it might never have been printed, if that magnetic person had not talked poetry with Spenser and enlisted him in his own scheme to assail court favor and the Queen's vanity once more.

The open letter to Ralegh on the poem's "whole intention," which was *The Letter* added (Jan. 23, 1590) as the first three books were going through the press, *to Ralegh* is not to be taken too literally. It was prepared for the occasion, and like any author's preface makes the design appear much more logical and complete than it was. It exaggerates the Aristotelian element, which is mainly to be found in Book II, and changes Arthur from a political-campaign portrait of Leicester as Protestant leader and king-to-be into "Magnificence," the philosophical summation of all Aristotle's virtues, private and public. It is easy to be ambitious in a preface, and Spenser rapidly sketches a plan to develop the three books he has written into a twelve-book epic, with an airy promise that, on proper encouragement, he will write twelve further books on the political virtues. One need not worry over the fact that this plan contains several basic inconsistencies, and fits Book I much better than Books II and III. It was camouflage, and Spenser, in proceeding with his work, seems to have paid little attention to it, or indeed to Aristotle. John Florio ignored it, and still saw in the first half of the *Faerie Queene* Spenser's quixotic loyalty to the dead Leicester. In dedicating his own *Second Fruits*

---

[3] See H. H. Blanchard, "Imitations from Tasso in the *Faerie Queene*," *SP*, XXII (1925). 198-221; C. B. Beall, "A Tasso Imitation in Spenser," *MLQ*, III (1942). 559-560.

the next year (1591) Florio mentioned the great earl, whom "every miscreant Myrmidon dare strike, being dead," and continued:

But nor I nor this place may half suffice for his praise, which the sweetest singer of all our western shepherds hath so exquisitely depainted that ... I account him thrice-fortunate in having such a herald of his virtues as Spenser. Courteous Lord, courteous Spenser! I know not which hath purchased more fame: either he in deserving so well of so famous a scholar, or so famous a scholar in being so thankful without hope of requital to so famous a lord.[4]

The Allegory

The "continued allegory or dark conceit," as Spenser calls it—that is, the politico-theological purpose of the poem—is now too confused for lucid interpretation. It is one of the effective elements in its rich texture, and is not to be ignored, but the threads cannot be clearly followed. The letter to Ralegh stresses two other elements that more immediately recommended the work at the time, and that are indeed among its salient beauties; namely, its ethical motive, "to fashion a gentleman or noble person in virtuous and gentle discipline," and its intention to praise Queen Elizabeth through Gloriana and Belphoebe, in her two embodiments as monarch and as woman.

Spenser's Ethics

Spenser is preëminently a moral poet. His disapproval, in the passage previously quoted, of the laudation of outlaw heroes by the Irish bards is fundamental. The object of his own poem is to make vice ugly and virtue attractive. No other poet has painted with more terrible truth the images of Despair, Slander, Care, Envy, and Detraction, the Blatant Beast of Scandal, and the brazen dragon of Sin. These are academic abstractions to nobody who has come to grips with life. To Spenser and the men of his age, to all the noble spirits to whom since the *Faerie Queene* has been an inspiration next only to the Bible and Shakespeare, these things have counted among the most significant forces in the world. And, on the other hand, nothing in all his poetry is more stirring than the great *catena* of passages, the

> goodly golden chain, wherewith yfere
> The virtues linked are in lovely wise,

that gives emotional unity to the book and describes the moral weapons with which his warriors fight: generosity, for example, in the passage just referred to (I. ix. 1), or "simple truth and blameless chastity" (IV. viii. 30), or aid to the weak (V. ii. 1): .

> Nought is more honorable to a knight,
> Ne better doth beseem brave chivalry,
> Than to defend the feeble in their right,
> And wrong redress in such as wend awry;

[4] A century later, Dryden, in his *Essay on Satire* (1693), had the same understanding of the poem's original purpose, though he mistakenly equated Arthur with Sidney rather than Leicester: "But Prince Arthur, or his chief patron, Sir Philip Sidney, whom he intended to make happy by the marriage of his Gloriana, dying before him, deprived the poet both of means and spirit to accomplish his design." See, however, Mrs. Bennett's different interpretation in *The Evolution of the Faerie Queene*, pp. 80-100.

or the power of justice (v. xi. 1), or self-control (ii. v. 15, vi. i. 41), or courtesy (vi. ii. 1):

> What virtue is so fitting for a knight,
> Or for a lady whom a knight should love,
> As courtesy, to bear themselves aright
> To all of each degree, as doth behove?

or concord (which Shakespeare calls "degree"), that most worshipped safeguard of nations and families, "Mother of blessed peace and friendship true" (iv. x. 34, 35):

> By her the heaven is in his course contained,
> And all the world in state unmoved stands,
> As their Almighty Maker first ordained,
> And bound them with inviolable bands.

The praise of Elizabeth is a lower thing, but where was mortal ever so *Praise of* sweetly praised? It, too, gilds and unifies the poem, and better than anything *the Queen* else that has survived illustrates the influence that this strange woman had in all the mighty labors which "live with the eternity of her fame."

It might be hard to say who originated the idea that the *Faerie Queene* is *The Story* dull. It was a late idea which few readers in the sixteenth or seventeenth century would have understood, but Macaulay gave it currency by a careless excursus in his essay on Bunyan:

Nay, even Spenser himself, though assuredly one of the greatest poets that ever lived, could not succeed in the attempt to make allegory interesting. . . . One unpardonable fault, the fault of tediousness, pervades the whole of the *Faerie Queene*.[5]

Allegory, forsooth! If the *Faerie Queene* is allegorical, so in their different ways are *Hamlet* and *Tom Jones* and the Book of Job; so is all great fiction and most poetry. Spenser's fairyland is no mystic fantasy, but a true picture of the democracy of life. His men and women pursue their careers through ever fresh and apparently unpremeditated incidents, resisting or yielding to the natural temptations they encounter, performing their heroisms and their meannesses; lost sometimes for long series of cantos to the reader, but always reappearing in the natural progress of events, never hurried on to forced conclusions, always advancing from task to task in the simple human way. While life lasts, interest continues and duty drives. The Red Cross Knight accomplishes early his great devoir. He slays the dragon and wins his lady, but wedding bells do not sweep him off the stage. The later books see him again and again, following his godly course, bearing modestly his laurels, aiding his friends, resisting his foes, and losing little of his interest although he never again has a central position.

[5] See H. C. Notcutt, "The *Faerie Queene* and its Critics," *E&S*, xii (1926). 63-86.

For variety of character and incident and even for skill of structure the *Faerie Queene* is remarkable in the world's fiction; but these merits appear least in the first two books, which, despite their more colorful style [6] and the brilliance of individual scenes, lack the fluidity of movement and economy of effect that Spenser grew to. If one compares the description of Lucifera's "coach" in I. iv. 16-37 with the procession of seasons in the second Mutability canto (VII. vii. 28-46), one sees how much more is done with nineteen stanzas in the later passage than with twenty-two in the earlier.

The third book is a good example of the poet's method. It is entitled the book of Chastity, and concerns itself almost wholly with the aspect of life involved in the consideration of that virtue and its opposite. The first three cantos and the last two deal chiefly with the exploits of Britomart, the titular heroine of the book, but in none of the intermediate seven cantos is she the main figure. Thus the beautiful legend of Britomart is thrown round the book like the hoops about a bulging cask. But Britomart is for Spenser more than a symbol of chastity, and her destiny carries her beyond the limits of the book to which she gives her name. So chastity is too manifold in its human variations to be the embellishment of a single individual. It reveals itself in the third book in many types of women: in the knightly Britomart, seeking with passionate longing the just Sir Artegal; and quite differently in the huntress Belphoebe, vowed to Diana and immune from human love, yet softly human in her ministrations to the wounded squire, and human also in the pique she feels when Timias shows sentiment for another maid. Again chastity is glorified in the virgin wife Amoret, kidnaped on her wedding day and resisting the superhuman torments and temptations of her captor; and once more in Florimel, the charming lady of the court, whose pretty story shoots like a gold thread through all the rainbow colors of the third, fourth, and fifth books as she braves the terrors of forest and sea to save her reluctant lover Marinel.

It is no lotus-land that Spenser creates. With all the lovely virtue there is little oversweetness in his poem. The woods are full of loathly foresters, the sea has its lewd fishermen, and knightly armor often hides the poltroon and deceiver. In two cantos of Book III, with Italianesque realism, he sets off his pictures of chastity by the unchaste story of the gay Lothario, Sir Paridel, the jealous Malbecco, and the wanton Hellenore. They fill in the picture of life, and the greatness of the book shows in this, that Paridel and Hellenore seem as genuinely native to the story, as thoroughly entitled to their existence, as Britomart herself.

So, then, the poem moves, one of the truest Human Comedies and one of the most beautiful. Still beginning, never ending, character is added to character, incident to incident, as our motley life flows past the windows of Kilcolman Castle. Here, if ever, is art concealing art; every episode seems to

---

[6] See J. V. Fletcher, "Some Observations on the Changing Style of the *Faerie Queene*," SP, XXXI (1934). 152-159.

grow to its perfection as inconspicuously as if the sun and rain of heaven fostered it, and one caught by the witchery of this narrative may at times be tempted to blaspheme against the other great gods of Parnassus. Even Chaucer's art may look puerile, and beside the tidal flow of Spenser even the great dramatist's method, with its spotlights and overhaste, may sometimes seem like tinsel against moonlight.

Spenser, of course, has his conventions, as the artist must; but they are conventions that enlarge instead of cramping. Fairyland is one.[7] His charac- ters are fairies, Britons, Moslems, dwarfs, enchanters, savage men—all the masques the heart of man can wear; but the masques never conceal the real men and women. They impress us as beautiful externals, as so many gorgeous costumes of the soul. Another convention is the knightly quest, which enabled him to bring his story out of doors into the Irish plains and forests.[8] The paths of Fairyland are the main-traveled roads of Elizabethan Ireland, and the descriptions are some of the best in English poetry; as of Una meet- ing the girl with the pot of water on the grassy path beneath the mountain (i. iii. 10-12), or Florimel coming at nightfall to the witch's dwelling "in a gloomy hollow glen" (iii. vii. 4-6), or old Meliboee entertaining Calidore in his "cottage clad with loam" (vi. ix. 16-17). The poem is notably full of hunting scenes and of dogs—from bull-baiting mastiffs (ii. viii. 42; vi. vii. 47) to the scavenger hounds by the roadside (vi. xi. 17)—and, above all, of the small things of nature, the gnats and flies and little birds, in which Spenser had a special interest. *Spenser's Conventions*

Ben Jonson, who was a professed grammarian and classicist, resented Spenser's archaisms and asserted that he "writ no language." [9] The proper reply is that if Spenser had written the *Faerie Queene* in Esperanto and therein achieved the expressiveness the poem has, Esperanto would be a very great poetic language. But Spenser did not write Esperanto; he wrote, in all his works except the *Shepherds' Calendar* and the *Faerie Queene* (where his design required archaism), the very purest of pure English. He is the arch-priest of the movement against the inkhorn terms which were corrupt- ing as well as enlarging the Renaissance vocabulary. It was one of the passions of his life, which he may have imbibed at the Merchant Taylors' School from Mulcaster,[10] to keep his English undefiled. Yet the stock of words had undoubtedly grown trite and flat in the sixteenth century, and was inadequate to the expanding range of ideas. Where others supplied deficiencies by importations from the classics and modern foreign tongues, Spenser proposed to dig deeper into the native stores. The *Shepherds' Calendar* offers a series of experiments to this end. It is open to any critic to regret that Spenser did *Spenser's Language*

---

[7] See Isabel E. Rathborne, *The Meaning of Spenser's Fairyland* (1937).
[8] See M. M. Gray, "The Influence of Spenser's Irish Experiences on the *Faerie Queene*," *RES*, vi (1930). 413-428.
[9] "Spenser in affecting the ancients writ no language. Yet I would have him read for his matter" (*Discoveries*).
[10] See ch. v, above, and C. B. Millican, "Note on Mulcaster and Spenser," *ELH*, vi (1939). 214-216.

not possess a modern professor's equipment in Middle English, but it is hardly possible to deny that his idea was sound.[11]

The archaisms in the *Faerie Queene* make little trouble. There is no page of the poem that is not easier for a child to understand than a page of *Paradise Lost*. Yet the archaic flavor is strongly present, and two practical reasons for it may be suggested. It is needed to fit the language to the antique atmosphere of the story. Milton raised the style of his epic by Latinism; Spenser secured a like effect, in a way better suited to his theme and temper, by reminiscence of Chaucer. Neither poem would be tolerable in Basic English. Spenser, moreover, had a problem which Milton quite escaped: the bondage of rime. The stanza he had committed himself to necessitated four-fold, treble, and double riming almost *ad infinitum;* and his stock of rime-words would have become hopelessly tedious within a single book, if he had not freshened it with new coinages. The most sufficient statement about the language of the *Faerie Queene* was made, very briefly and long ago, by Barrett Wendell: [12]

You may despair as much as you like over the pre-Quixotic intricacies of its tenuous plot; you may lose your way, again and again, in futile efforts to follow the invisible thread of its allegories; you may lay the book down, more than once or twice, dazed for the moment with the sweetness of its melody; but you may search it almost in vain for the page, for the stanza, even for the line, which is not alive to this day with the very soul of Elizabethan music. Such mastery of language, turning into deathless beauty words and phrases which had seemed fit only for humdrum use, English had never before approached; and that mastery has never been surpassed. Indeed, one can hardly imagine that it ever will be.

Spenser's
Imitators:
1. Drayton

Nothing in Elizabethan literature, perhaps nothing until Byron's time, equaled the over-night fame of the *Faerie Queene*.[13] Spenser became at once "the only living Homer" and the supreme literary celebrity of the age. One of his earliest imitators is Richard Barnfield,[14] but Michael Drayton was as early and of more significance. The latter's elegy to Henry Reynolds contains the well-known tribute to the "grave moral Spenser,"

> Than whom I am persuaded there was none,
> Since the blind bard his *Iliads* up did make,

[11] See E. F. Pope, "Renaissance Criticism and the Diction of the *Faerie Queene*," *PMLA*, xli (1926). 575-619; B. R. McElderry, "Archaism and Innovation in Spenser's Poetic Diction," *PMLA*, xlvii (1932). 144-170; F. M. Padelford, "Aspects of Spenser's Vocabulary," *PQ*, xx (1941). 279-283. Also W. L. Renwick, "The Critical Origins of Spenser's Diction," *MLR*, xvii (1922). 1-16, and H. C. Wyld, "Spenser's Diction and Style in Relation to Those of Later English Poetry," in *A Grammatical Miscellany offered to Otto Jespersen* (Copenhagen, 1930, pp. 147-165).

[12] *The Temper of the Seventeenth Century in English Literature* (1904), p. 25.

[13] See H. E. Cory, "The Golden Age of the Spenserian Pastoral," *PMLA*, xxv (1910). 241-267; and "Spenser, the School of the Fletchers, and Milton," *Univ. California Pub. in Mod. Phil.*, ii (1912). 311-373. *Godfrey of Bulloigne*, a fine translation of Tasso's *Jerusalem Delivered* by Edward Fairfax (d. 1635), was published in 1599-1600, just after Spenser's death, and owes much to his example.

[14] See above, ch. ii.

> Fitter a task like that to undertake,
> To set down boldly, bravely to invent,
> In all high knowledge surely excellent.

It was Spenser's pastorals that Drayton, writing under the pseudonym of "Rowland," began by echoing in *The Shepherd's Garland* (1593), a group of nine eclogues prefaced [15] by the statement:

Master Edmund Spenser had done enough for the immortality of his name, had he only given us his *Shepherds' Calendar*, a masterpiece if any . . . Spenser is the prime pastoralist of England. My pastorals hold upon a new strain, must speak for themselves.

It is true that Drayton's discipleship, though marked, is not slavish; and Spenser seems to have acknowledged the newcomer's promise by placing him at the end of a list of poets in *Colin Clout's Come Home Again:*

> And there, though last not least, is Aetion;
> A gentler shepherd may nowhere be found,
> Whose muse, full of high thoughts' invention,
> Doth like himself heroically sound.[16]

In his two finest odes, *To the Virginian Voyage* and the *Ballad of Agincourt,* Drayton repeats Spenser's note of romantic patriotism, as he does in *Poly-Olbion;* and he follows him again in his four long mythological or sylvan poems: *Nymphidia, The Quest of Cynthia, The Shepherd's Sirena,* and *The Muses' Elysium.* In the *Nymphidia,* which is probably Drayton's most charming work, he accomplishes the remarkable feat of imitating Chaucer, Shakespeare, and Spenser, all three, without loss to the poem's individuality. The mock-heroic manner is from the *Rime of Sir Thopas,* the fairy lore from *A Midsummer Night's Dream,* and the narrative method from the *Faerie Queene.* Yet the poem is wholly Drayton's and is one of the most individual in English literature.

William Basse [17] (*c.* 1583-*c.* 1653), who lived a long life in the delightful country about Thame in Oxfordshire, claims to be "Colin's loved boy," and asserts that Spenser

2. Basse

> his pipe into my bosom flung,
> And said: Though Colin ne'er shall be surpass'd,
> Be while thou liv'st as like him as thou maist.[18]

He is not much like him; but in *Three Pastoral Elegies,* printed in 1602, and nine *Pastorals,* written about 1616 and prepared for publication in 1653, but not printed, he obviously follows the *Shepherds' Calendar,* calling himself "Coliden" in the latter collection and anticipating Gay by making it a shepherd's week. His rustic verse flows pleasantly along, with much compli-

---

[15] In the later edition (1619), in which an additional eclogue is included.
[16] Lines 444-447. It should be said that the reference to Drayton is not certain, though plausible.
[17] *The Poetical Works of William Basse,* ed. R. W. Bond (1893).
[18] Ed. Bond, pp. 73-74.

mentary allusion to the great persons he knew, one of whom, Poemenarcha, or the shepherds' queen, is the famous Countess of Pembroke, who died in 1621. Basse's most familiar poem is his epitaph on Shakespeare:

> Renowned Spenser, lie a thought more nigh
> To learned Chaucer, and rare Beaumont, lie
> A little nearer Spenser, to make room
> For Shakespeare in your threefold-fourfold tomb. . . .

This appeared in the 1640 edition of Shakespeare's poems. Though not printed in the Folio of 1623, it was evidently in manuscript circulation, since Jonson alludes to it in the opening lines of the great poem he contributed to that volume:

> My Shakespeare, rise! I will not lodge thee by
> Chaucer or Spenser, or bid Beaumont lie
> A little further to make thee a room.

3. Phineas and Giles Fletcher

The two Cambridge poets, Phineas and Giles Fletcher,[19] sons of Dr. Giles Fletcher, the poet-ambassador,[20] and first cousins of the dramatist, lapped up Spenser in their tenderest years and spent the rest of their lives playing with his cadences and his ideas. When Milton went to Cambridge, their works, in print or manuscript, were much in vogue, and they undoubtedly influenced him both in his conception of Spenser and in his own poems. Today the interest of the Fletchers is largely a matter of their close relation with the great poet from whom they borrowed and the otherwise great one to whom they lent. On the whole their discipleship was a disservice to Spenser, for they ran his morality into the ground, and so over-refined his melodies that a reaction toward the ruggedness of Jonson and Donne became imperative.

The two brothers made their first poetical appearance in the Cambridge miscellany, *Sorrow's Joy* (1603), issued to commemorate the emotions of the university on the death of Queen Elizabeth and the accession of James I. Though very young, they are already confirmed Spenserians, Giles' poem being in an eight-line adaptation of the *Faerie Queene* stanza (*ababbccC*), while Phineas tries something like the stanza of Spenser's marriage odes. The older and more productive brother, Phineas [21] (1582-1650), wrote about 1611 a Latin hexameter poem on the recent Gunpowder Plot of 1605, *Locustae, vel Pietas Jesuitica,* a work of much Miltonic interest. When printed in 1627, it was provided with an expanded English paraphrase, *The Locusts,* or *Apollyonists,* in five cantos and in a variation of the *Faerie Queene* stanza: *ababababccC*. In his *Purple Island, or the Isle of Man* [22] (1633) which moved

[19] F. S. Boas, *The Poetical Works of Giles Fletcher and Phineas Fletcher* (2v, Cambridge, 1908-9).
[20] See ch. VIII, above and L. Bradner, *Musae Anglicanae,* pp. 38-39, 56-57.
[21] See A. B. Langdale, *Phineas Fletcher, Man of Letters, Science, and Divinity* (1937).
[22] See A. G. Pohlman, "*The Purple Island* by Phineas Fletcher: A Seventeenth Century Layman's Poetical Conception of the Human Body," *Johns Hopkins Hospital Bull.,* XXVIII (1907). 1-12.

Francis Quarles to dub Phineas "the Spenser of this age," he combines the *Shepherds' Calendar* pastoral convention of singing shepherd boys with an enormous extension of the anatomical and psychical allegory of the *Faerie Queene* II. ix. and I. x. ending in one of the most mystifying and protracted of all allegorical dragon-fights. It is as long as a book of the *Faerie Queene,* is similarly divided into twelve cantos, and uses a derivative stanza form: *ababccC.* It is generously sprinkled with poetic beauties, and is so rich in learning, mental ingenuity, and moral soundness that its unreadability must be deeply deplored. In *Britain's Ida, or Venus and Anchises,*[23] a work of earlier youth and greater warmth, and much more brevity, there was so much suggestion of Spenser as to encourage Thomas Walkley to publish it, in 1628, as his work; but a careful reader will hardly forgive Walkley. In his seven *Piscatory Eclogues* (1633) Phineas follows the Italian Sannazaro (1458-1530) in substituting fishermen for the Spenserian shepherds, as he does also in his "piscatory" play, *Sicelides,* acted at King's College, Cambridge, and printed in 1631. The play is in riming verse and prose, the eclogues in various intricate metres, but they seldom lack the closing alexandrine, which in the work of the Fletchers begins to justify its epithet of "needless."

The only important poem of Giles Fletcher, the younger (*c.* 1585-1623), is *Christ's Victory and Triumph,* printed at Cambridge in 1610. It is in the same eight-line stanza which he used in his contribution to *Sorrow's Joy,* and which his brother employed in *Britain's Ida* and here and there in the *Piscatory Eclogues: ababbccC.* It is in four books, and must have delighted the young Milton, for here the sacred lyre is struck with lovely resonance. The first book, *Christ's Victory in Heaven,* is the debate between Mercy and Justice over the redemption of man; the second, *Christ's Victory on Earth,* is the Temptation in the wilderness, the theme of *Paradise Regained.* The third book, *Christ's Triumph over Death,* deals with the Crucifixion, and the last, *His Triumph after Death,* with the Resurrection. Into the last are woven the praises of James I as the prince of peace and of Phineas Fletcher's *Purple Island,* which, though not printed till twenty-three years later, was apparently already finished. In Giles Fletcher, even more than in his brother, the sweetness of Spenser is developed into a sedative so potent that, without the prose gloss that the margins provide, it would be very hard to attend to his argument.

The Fletchers gave a religious turn to Spenser's ethical teaching, and they had many followers. Thomas Robinson's *Life and Death of Mary Magdalene*[24] (*c.* 1620) is in Giles Fletcher's metre, and spices its sanctimonious narrative, not unpleasingly, with conceits and luscious imagery. The Cambridge philosopher, Henry More (1614-1687), employed the years of most violent national strife in setting down in Spenserian stanzas his long and subtle monograph on Christian Neoplatonism, *Psychozoia, or the Life of the* Followers of the Fletchers: Robinson

Henry More

[23] See above, Part II, ch. II.
[24] Ed. H. O. Sommer (1899: *EETSES,* 78).

Joseph
Beaumont

Soul,[25] printed in 1642, and in elaborated form in 1647. There is more memorable poetry, but also much more length, in the twenty-four cantos of another work of somewhat similar date, but different doctrinal purpose: *Psyche, or Love's Mystery,* "displaying the intercourse betwixt Christ and the soul," by Joseph Beaumont[26] (1616-1699). Written in the lighter six-line stanza of *Venus and Adonis,* this enormous work, "the longest poem in the language," moves with surprising ease through the three realms of scriptural history, allegory, metaphysics, and contains passages of great imaginative vigor, as does also the large body of Beaumont's religious minor poems,[27] which mark him as no unworthy member of the lyrical school of George Herbert.

4. William
Browne

William Browne of Tavistock in Devon[28] (*c.* 1590-*c.* 1645) is a link between Spenser and Keats, as the Fletchers are between Spenser and Milton. His bright and tuneful eclogues, published in 1614 as *The Shepherd's Pipe,* associate him not only with Spenser and Drayton, but with his immediate friends and fellow-rimers, Wither, Christopher Brooke, and John Davies of Hereford, as well. He wrote also a masque on the theme of Circe and Ulysses (1614) for the Inner Temple, of which he was a member, a couple of dozen good sonnets in Shakespearean form, some admirable songs, a humorous lyric (*Lydford Journey*) which is one of the best of its kind, and much occasional verse. His long elegy on the Countess of Pembroke, "Time hath a long course run since thou wert clay," is a fine example of the conceit-laden poetry that Donne transfigured; and the famous epitaph on the same lady, "Underneath this sable hearse," if by him, as good manuscript authority asserts, shows that he could at times equal Jonson.

He admired Drayton, whose fairy-lore he sometimes imitated, and idolized Spenser, who has been better praised by few poets.[29] Browne was wise enough not to meddle with the Spenserian stanza. His largest and most characteristic, and most Spenserian work is *Britannia's Pastorals* (1613-16, and a third book left incomplete in MS), begun before the age of twenty, for which he uses the fluent and honey-sweet couplets that Keats returned to in *Endymion.*[30] He quite lacks Spenser's ability to tell a story and allows his pretty tales of Marina and the other nymphs and shepherds to grow pale from inanition and to become rather hopelessly entangled; but his Devonshire memories and landscapes are full of nostalgic passion and of color. Browne is distinctly a backward-looking bard. In his view the good days

---

[25] See G. Bullough, *Philosophical Poems of Henry More* (Manchester, 1931).

[26] A. B. Grosart, *The Complete Poems of Dr. Joseph Beaumont* (2v, 1880). *Psyche* was published in 20 cantos in 1648, but was enlarged and altered in the posthumous edition of 1702.

[27] See E. Robinson, *The Minor Poems of Joseph Beaumont, D.D.* (1914). For Robert Aylett (*c.* 1583-1655), another Spenserian moralist of great productivity, see the admirable account of F. M. Padelford, *Huntington Library Bull.,* No. 10 (1936). 1-48.

[28] See G. Goodwin, *The Poems of William Browne of Tavistock* (2v, 1893); F. W. Moorman, *William Browne* (Strassburg, 1898).

[29] E.g., *ed. cit.,* I. 222, 225; II. 51.

[30] In the last canto (Book III, second song) he changes to *ottava rima.* For relation of the early editions see G. Tillotson, "Towards a Text of Browne's *Britannia's Pastorals,*" *Library,* XI (1930). 193-202.

for poets and for common men have passed. Sometimes his charming muse grows acidulous and speaks like his friend Wither's in satire of the present age, but much oftener it takes the quiet road to fairyland and the idealized banks of the Tavy.[31]

[31] Another west-country Spenserian of humbler pretensions was John Dennys, a Gloucestershire gentleman who died in 1609, leaving one long poem in *ottava rima* verse: *The Secrets of Angling, Teaching the Choicest Tools, Baits, and Seasons for the Taking of any Fish in Pond or River.* This was printed in 1613 and had reached its fourth edition in 1652 (reprint, with introduction by Thomas Westwood, 1883), besides being recast in prose in several agricultural manuals. It was naturally known, and was quoted from, by Izaak Walton. Dennys shows skill in linking his humble subject to the aspiring verse form, and he is occasionally lifted by Spenserian reminiscence into a higher air; e.g., in his last stanza, which is an echo of the close of the *Faerie Queene*, Book I.

XI

Christopher Marlowe

Literary history has singularly vindicated itself in the study of Christopher Marlowe [1] (1564-1593). At the beginning of the nineteenth century his works were almost wholly unread and his name was hardly known.[2] The Romantic critics recovered his fame and raised him to a dizzy eminence as the special forerunner of Shakespeare, but as late as 1900 scarcely anything was known of the man, except that he was born, the son of a Canterbury shoemaker, in February, 1564, educated at Cambridge, and slain in 1593 in a tavern brawl. Only during the last generation have the researches of scholars, both laborious and brilliant, thrown such lucky light upon the facts of Marlowe's life that it is now fairly possible to estimate the personality which moulded his extraordinary and exciting poetry, and which his literary contemporaries hailed by such terms as "translunary" and "divine." Souls of poets dead and gone continue to speak to the world by two voices: by their achievements and their character. These are never altogether distinct, yet never wholly merge; and it will be useful to consider in both aspects the impression which Marlowe leaves.

Marlowe's Achievements

The Mighty Line

It was Ben Jonson who characterized with immortal felicity the first of the Cambridge scholar's achievements: "Marlowe's mighty line." [3] Unriming decasyllables had been written before him by several sixteenth-century Englishmen: by the Earl of Surrey and Nicholas Grimald, by Sackville and Norton in *Gorboduc*, by Gascoigne in *The Steel Glass,* by Turberville, by Peele in *The Arraignment of Paris,* by the youthful Spenser, and probably by Kyd. Various, and yet similar, purposes seem to have prompted these innovators: the desire to approximate the Virgilian hexameter or the *senarius* of Seneca, the desire for a prose-like (Horatian) vehicle of contemporary satire in Gascoigne, the effort at Ciceronian eloquence in the play of Peele. They were all rather exotic ambitions, and except in Peele's few

---

[1] *The Works of Christopher Marlowe* (Oxford, 1910; references are to this edition); *The Works and Life of Christopher Marlowe,* general editor R. H. Case (6v, 1930-33); U. M. Ellis-Fermor, *Christopher Marlowe* (1927); John Bakeless, *Christopher Marlowe, the Man in His Time* (1937) and *The Tragical History of Christopher Marlowe* (2v, Cambridge, Mass., 1942); F. S. Boas, *Marlowe and his Circle* (Oxford, 1929) and *Christopher Marlowe* (Oxford, 1940); F. C. Owlett, "The Eulogy of Marlowe," *Poetry Rev.,* xxvi (1935). 5-18, 127-138; Marion B. Smith, *Marlowe's Imagery and the Marlowe Canon* (Philadelphia, 1940); P. H. Kocher, *Christopher Marlowe: A Study of His Thought, Learning, and Character* (1946); S. A. Tannenbaum, *Christopher Marlowe: A Concise Bibliography* (1937).

[2] See T. Brooke, "The Reputation of Christopher Marlowe," *Trans. Conn. Acad. of Arts and Sciences,* xxv (1922). 347-408.

[3] See T. S. Eliot, "Notes on the Blank Verse of Christopher Marlowe," in *The Sacred Wood* (1928), pp. 86-94; T. Brooke, "Marlowe's Versification and Style," *SP,* xix (1922). 186-205.

lines they produced exotic effects. It was Marlowe who changed the sow's ear into the silken purse. When he employed it, blank verse became at once what Shakespeare, Milton, and so many others have shown that it can hardly cease to be, the most expressive and the grandest of English metres.

Few poets have equaled the ability that Marlowe possessed of condensing an entire lyric into a single verse. In *Tamburlaine* and *Faustus* particularly, there are lines that glitter and writhe like burnished serpents; e.g.,

> For Tamburlaine, the scourge of God, must die (*2 Tamb.*, 4641),
> I'll burn my books! Ah, Mephistophilis! (*Faustus*, 1477),
> But stay a while! let me be king till night! (*Edw. II.*, 2045),
> O girl! O gold! O beauty! O my bliss! (*Jew of Malta*, 695).

In ten syllables Marlowe can reveal the wild beauty of a yearning soul:

> Was this the face that launch'd a thousand ships? (*Faustus*, 1328),
> And ride in triumph through Persepolis (*1 Tamb.*, 754),
> Still climbing after knowledge infinite (*1 Tamb.*, 875).

He can lay bare a mind in the moment of irrevocable decision:

> A God is not so glorious as a king (*1 Tamb.*, 762),
> And all is dross that is not Helena (*Faustus*, 1334);

or sum up with a divine finality one of the great truths of human experience:

> And where Hell is, there must we ever be (*Faustus*, 555),
> Cut is the branch that might have grown full straight (*Faustus*, 1478).

Marlowe's second achievement was in teaching the drama what Spenser *Marlowe's* was teaching verse fiction, the meaning of romance. As the first great roman- *Roman-* tic dramatist Marlowe taught the difference between living and life. Previous *ticism* writers had dealt with the externals of living: restless living, as in the lover's pains of Wyatt and Surrey; fashionable living, as in Lyly; foolish living, as in Gascoigne's satires; evil living, as in Greene. The caustic radiance of Marlowe's mind burned through these externalities and revealed the protoplasmic life within. Smug questions grow impossible. Does Tamburlaine live well or ill? Does Faustus live wisely or unwisely? Does Barabas act justly or unjustly? As well ask whether a mountain ought to tower in sterile grandeur above the pleasant useful meadows, or whether the ocean has a right to roar. Life's the thing, not how, or where, or why one lives. In some of the most dynamic lines that ever accompanied the apparition of new-born Athene Marlowe spoke the message of romance:

> From jigging veins of riming mother-wits,
> And such conceits as clownage keeps in pay,
> We'll lead you to the stately tent of war.

The time of homily and dalliance is past; the age of vision is at hand. From this moment the great crusade is on. Excelsior is the motto of every man. The

votaries of life burst their manacles, and, in the words of the last of Marlowe's
Stuart followers,

> O'er bog or steep, through strait, rough, dense or rare,
> With head, hands, wings, or feet [4]

pursue their way. The avenues through which the chase proceeds are as
numerous as the lives of men: regal ambition, knowledge, the sacred hunger
for gold, the thirst for friendship, or the consuming fire of love. These are
the topics of Marlowe's chief plays; but always there is life ahead, life which

> Wills us to wear ourselves and never rest (*1 Tamb.*, 877),

and makes of us all crusading knights,

> That in conceit bear empires on our spears,
> Affecting thoughts coequal with the clouds (*1 Tamb.*, 260 f.).

It was Milton again who put into the mouth of his most romantic and
Marlowesque figure the proper comment upon the careers of Tamburlaine
and Faustus, Guise, Barabas, and Mortimer:

> That strife
> Was not inglorious, though the event was dire.[5]

Writing before the romantic achievement of either Spenser or Marlowe
was performed, Sir Philip Sidney spoke golden words of one of the finest
poems of martial romance then audible to English ears:

Certainly, I must confess mine own barbarousness. I never heard the old song
of Percy and Douglas that I found not my heart moved more than with a
trumpet: and yet it is sung but by some blind crowder, with no rougher voice
than rude style.

When the blind crowder (fiddler) was supplanted by Marlowe, "the Muses'
darling," as Peele called him, and the rude style became the mighty line,
the ideal poet described by Sidney stood confessed:

He cometh to you with words set in delightful proportion . . . and with a tale,
forsooth, he cometh unto you, with a tale which holdeth children from play
and old men from the chimney corner.[6]

Marlowe's Dramatic Sense

For three and a half centuries Marlowe's works have done no less.

Marlowe's third great achievement was the discovery of the secret of
dramatic action. It seems usual to think of this poet as a great lyrist who by
pure chance blundered upon the drama in his search for a means of self-
expression. Blunders of this kind hardly happen to men of genius, and
certainly nothing of the sort happened to Marlowe. Few men can ever have
possessed a surer native sense of dramatic values. It seems clear, as far as
contemporary tributes and allusions permit us to judge, that even the first

---

[4] *Paradise Lost*, II. 948 f.
[5] *Paradise Lost*, I. 623 f.
[6] *Defense of Poesy*, ed. Feuillerat, p. 24, 20.

play, *Tamburlaine,* owed its sweeping success not so much to the splendid poetry of its lines or the romantic wonder of its story as to the brilliance of its dramatic effects. The instinct for dramatic situation is everywhere apparent, and it was this instinct to which the greatest succeeding dramatists did homage. It is not merely in the portrayal of the chief figure that Marlowe's dramatic eye appears. The essential playwright is revealed in the very first speech, in those five lines of Mycetes which at once tear the veil from before the gorgeous impotence of the Persian throne:

> Brother Cosroe, I find myself aggrieved,
> Yet insufficient to express the same. . . .

The first part of *Tamburlaine* exhibits a certainty of purpose and method hardly less extraordinary in a young author's work than that expressed in the astounding prologue. The first act pictures the blossoming of the hero's innate ambition under the stimulation of Zenocrate's beauty and the threat of the thousand horsemen of Theridamas. This act ends with the establishment of the moral ascendancy of the shepherd over, first, his intended captor, and, second, his destined bride. The second act shows this transmuted into actual accomplishment, as the shepherd's imagination is fired by the picture of the royal conqueror riding in triumph through Persepolis; and the act concludes with a magnificent finale, as the hero takes the Persian crown and sets it, Napoleon-like, upon his own head. The opening of the third act introduces the vainglorious and mighty Bajazet, most redoubtable of the Scythian's foes, threatening vast ruin to the upstart; and this act rises rapidly to the crisis of the play, the battle of Ankara. When the act ends, the new king of Persia is the supreme ruler of all Asia. The fourth act is a structural masterpiece. The conqueror has apparently reached the height of his career. Is not his boasted fortune now preparing to forsake him? The first scene shows a storm gathering in far off Egypt. The Soldan summons his hordes:

> Awake, ye men of Memphis! hear the clang
> Of Scythian trumpets; hear the basilisks
> That, roaring, shake Damascus' turrets down!

The third scene shows Egypt and Arabia on the march, apparently irresistible, and confident of victory. And while the storm-clouds gather, Tamburlaine, careless of the future, vaunts himself in the height of tragic *hybris.* He joys in the humiliations of the captive Bajazet and Zabina, blind to their sufferings, reckless of their curses and prayers for vengeance. The whole act is, as a fourth act should be, a breathless lull of suspense; and in the last lines the hero makes a yet more wanton demand of fortune:

> We mean to travel to th' antarctic pole,
> Conquering the people underneath our feet,
> And be renown'd as never emperors were.

Whom the gods wish to ruin, one remembers, they first make mad. In the fifth act the clouds darken, suspense thickens. "Still doth this man, or rather god, of war" batter at the walls of Damascus, regardless of the brewing storm. The virgins move him not. By their slaughter he vindicates his tragic consistency and throws another gauntlet into the teeth of Nemesis. Then, lest tragic pity be lost to sight in all this accumulation of tragic fear, the stage is cleared, and the man of war exposes in one of the grandest soliloquies the heart of the lover, the soul of the idealist:

> Ah, fair Zenocrate! divine Zenocrate! . . .
> What is beauty, saith my sufferings, then?
> If all the pens that ever poets held. . . .

There follow the deaths of Bajazet and Zabina, another weight in the scale of Nemesis. Does not the fate of Tamburlaine now totter in the balance? So Zenocrate thinks, as she wrestles in prayer for the life of her lover:

> Ah, Tamburlaine, my love, sweet Tamburlaine,
> That fight'st for sceptres and for slippery crowns,
> Behold the Turk and his great emperess!
> Thou that in conduct of thy happy stars
> Sleep'st every night with conquest on thy brows,
> And yet would'st shun the wavering turns of war . . .
> Behold the Turk and his great emperess!
> Ah, mighty Jove and holy Mahomet,
> Pardon my love!

At this point the blow, hanging in the air during two acts, falls at last. Enter Philemus to announce:

> Madam, your father and the Arabian king . . . come now,
> Ready for battle 'gainst my lord the king.

If all this is not dramatic, what is drama? But drama having had its say, romance may claim a hearing. They sound to the battle, and Tamburlaine enjoys the victory, and so, after two pages of reconciliation, the tragedy closes on the Greek note: pity and terror, followed by serenity and clothed in beauty infinite. So much for the least mature of Marlowe's greater plays. From later practice he learned much concerning the mechanics of stage presentation, but he was indeed a dramatist born.

Such, then, were the three great achievements of Marlowe's six years. He let drop upon an astonished world what Alfred Noyes has called Marlowe's "eagle's feather of blank verse"; [7] he, along with Spenser and with Sidney, planted in modern England the magic flower of romance and enriched for centuries the soil in which it grows; finally, he taught the English tragic stage more than it learned from any other man except Shakespeare, who was the greatest of Marlowe's debtors and continuators.

Marlowe's Character Of the man himself, the storehouse of this energy, we have learned a great deal, as everybody knows, in the last twenty years, [8] and each accretion

---

[7] *Tales of the Mermaid Tavern* (1913), p. 28 ("A Coiner of Angels").

[8] See especially J. L. Hotson, *The Death of Christopher Marlowe* (1925) and M. Eccles, *Christopher Marlowe in London* (1934).

of knowledge has on the whole tended to raise his status, if only by disproving slanders with which modern fiction and ancient polemics had darkened him. Laying the gratuitous imaginings aside, we may consider the qualities of his personality which are most clearly mirrored in his writings. First, then, he was, like Spenser, a scholar, one of the truest of his time. He loved learning deeply and hated ignorance. Few English poets—perhaps none but Spenser, Milton, and Browning—have so well vindicated the literary uses of academic knowledge. Marlowe is never more the poet than when he is most the scholar: in the address to Helen in *Faustus* or in Tamburlaine's comparison of Zenocrate to the heroines of classical literature;[9] in Æneas's story of the wooden horse,[10] or in the numberless passages that give perpetual value to the sixteenth-century accomplishment in geography,[11] astronomy, and philosophy. His scholarship gave him his remarkable sense of form, form in the single line, in the scene, and in the play as a whole; and the sense of form was precisely the rarest and most needed of virtues in Elizabethan poetry. His scholarship gave him the scholar's passion for truth, for fair play in intellectual disputes. In an age of bigotry his was one of the few voices raised in defence of alien races and alien creeds. Better a true Turk, he says, or a consistent Jew, than a faithless and time-serving Christian. One needs but little acquaintance with religious controversy to understand why the Prelatists and Puritans alike flinched before this reasoning and drowned the logic of the poet with cries of "libertine" and "atheist." Marlowe may, in certain senses, have been both,[12] but the clamor must have appeared silly, even to contemporaries, in view of the tremendous close of *Tamburlaine* and the whole mighty lesson of *Faustus,* in view of the deep earnestness of every word Marlowe wrote.

His Scholarship

So much for Marlowe's intellectual character. His personal character reveals itself no less vividly. In the first place, he held himself high, and though plying a vulgar trade, refused to be vulgarized. Not even from his Puritan defamers do we hear concerning him stories of such low associations as cling to the memory of Greene and Peele. To his familiars he was Kit Marlowe. Such were his fellow-scholar Nashe, the poet Watson, the grave and learned Chapman, and Sir Walter Ralegh himself;[13] but the company of his friends seems to have been as small as it was select. The printer of *Tamburlaine,* dedicating the two plays to the Gentlemen-Readers in 1590, allows himself none of the usual liberties. He is but a tradesman presenting one gentleman to others:

His Personal Character

---

9 2 *Tamburlaine,* 3054 ff.
10 *Dido,* 477 ff.
11 See Ethel Seaton, "Marlowe's Map," *E&S,* x (1924). 13-35.
12 See H. W. Herrington, "Christopher Marlowe, Rationalist," *Essays in Memory of Barrett Wendell* (Cambridge, Mass., 1926), pp. 119-152; M. Eccles, "Marlowe in Kentish Tradition," *N&Q,* CLXIX (1935). 20-23, 39-41, 58-61; P. H. Kocher, "The Development of Marlowe's Character," *PQ,* XVII (1938). 331-350, and "Marlowe's Atheist Lecture," *JEGP,* XXXIX (1940). 98-106.
13 Kyd, in his letter to Puckering, mentions as special friends of Marlowe "Harriot, Warner, Roydon, and some stationers [book-publishers] in Paul's Churchyard." These also were no mean company.

Great folly were it in me to commend unto your wisdoms either the eloquence of the author or the worthiness of the matter itself.

Thomas Heywood, introducing the 1633 edition of the *Jew of Malta,* refers ceremoniously to this work "by so worthy an author as Master Marlowe," and the most gentlemanly of the publishers of the time, Edward Blount, writes a dedication of *Hero and Leander* to Sir Thomas Walsingham which, considering the dignity of the person addressed, indicates that Marlowe's friends did not feel that he had left a wounded name:

Sir, we think not ourselves discharged of the duty we owe to our friend, when we have brought the breathless body to the earth; for albeit the eye there taketh his ever-farewell of that beloved object, yet the impression of the man that hath been dear unto us, living an after-life in our memory, there putteth us in mind of farther obsequies due unto the deceased . . . I suppose myself executor to the unhappily deceased author of this poem, upon whom knowing that in his life-time you bestowed many kind favors, entertaining the parts of reckoning and worth which you found in him with good countenance and liberal affection: I cannot but see so far into the will of him dead that whatsoever issue of his brain should chance to come abroad, that the first breath it should take might be the gentle air of your liking: for since his self had been accustomed there-unto, it would prove more agreeable and thriving to his right children than any other foster countenance whatsoever. . . . Of a double duty, the one to your-self, the other to the deceased, I present the same to your most favorable allow-ance. . . .

This was written five years after Marlowe's death, and scandalous tongues were wagging. In the circumstances it is not the language a reputable pub-lisher would use in coupling a great living name with the name of a dead atheist and profligate. "Slain by a bawdy serving man, a rival of his in his lewd love," Meres wrote of Marlowe in this same year 1598, [14] basing his statement upon that of a Puritan pamphleteer, Thomas Beard, who based his on hearsay. Factually, the charge has been disproved by Mr. Hotson's discovery of the death record; more fundamentally, it is disproved by *Hero and Leander.* The subject of this fragment, the last thing Marlowe did, is one of the most beautifully sensuous stories in all the pagan literature of Greece, and the treatment Marlowe gives it is one of the purest things in Elizabethan poetry. In what he wrote there is not an obscene word or a degenerate suggestion; everywhere he sees the marriage of true minds, the cleanliness of ocean-dewy limbs and childlike souls. Even in the verse there seems to be a kind of reticence. The narrative is masculine and straightfor-ward beyond any other of its genre and age,[15] but in Marlowe's couplets there is no fluent and suggestive ease; there is, on the contrary, a sweet hesitancy, not otherwise characteristic of the poet, which cools instead of

Hero and Leander

---

[14] See D. C. Allen, "Meres and the Death of Marlowe," *LTLS,* Feb. 5, 1932, p. 70.
[15] See D. Bush, "The Influence of Marlowe's *Hero and Leander* on Early Mythological Poems," *MLN.* XLII (1927). 211-217.

inflaming the mind. And everywhere there is moral poise; everywhere there are grave and tender observations, as of a soul firm fastened in its roots:

> For faithful love will never turn to hate.

> It lies not in our power to love or hate,
> For will in us is overrul'd by fate.
> Where both deliberate, the love is slight;
> Who ever lov'd that lov'd not at first sight?

> My words shall be as spotless as my youth,
> Full of simplicity and naked truth.

> Sweet are the kisses, the embracements sweet,
> When like desires and affections meet;
> For from the earth to heaven is Cupid rais'd
> When fancy is in equal balance peis'd [i.e., weighed].

> Love is too full of faith, too credulous,
> With folly and false hope deluding us.

> Love is not full of pity, as men say,
> But deaf and cruel where he means to prey.[16]

It is unfashionable but just to assert the abstention from impure suggestion in all Marlowe's original work. How else explain the stress upon the chastity of his remorseless Scythian conqueror, and the refusal in the case of the great sensualist, Faustus, and the degenerate Edward II, to dwell upon any sensual detail; or the splendid candor which makes the lines to Helen a veritable hymn, and the flowerlike grace of the Passionate Shepherd's proposal, "Come live with me and be my love," which might have been so robust? How else explain the tender treatment of Abigail and the tenderer care to extenuate the sin of Isabella?

Marlowe's first play seems to be *Dido, Queen of Carthage,* though nothing is known of it till the year after his death, when it was published as by Marlowe and Nashe. It is a reverent but rather bold version, in five acts and in blank verse, of the first, second, and fourth books of Virgil's *Æneid.* The company to which it is assigned on the title-page, the Children of the Chapel, is not one with which Marlowe is known to have had any contact otherwise, and the probability is that the play was written at Cambridge before his London career began. It is mainly notable for the poignant treatment of Dido's love and for the anticipation in many lines of more famous passages in later plays. *Marlowe's Development as a Dramatist*

The first part of *Tamburlaine* was probably also drafted, if not written, before Marlowe left Cambridge in 1587. References to it forbid placing it much later, and it shows no special familiarity with the London stage. As in *Dido,* the classical influence is strong. Though based upon the career of the famous Timur, who was a contemporary of Chaucer, the Persia Marlowe *Tamburlaine*

---

[16] *Hero and Leander,* 1st Sestiad, 128, 167 f., 207 f.; 2nd Sestiad 29-32, 221 f., 287 f. See D. Bush, "Notes on Marlowe's *Hero and Leander,*" *PMLA,* XLIV (1929). 760-764.

imagines is the Persia of Herodotus and Xenophon; and the Platonic element in the play's philosophy is conspicuous.[17] The other chief external influences are the legends of the heroic outlaw, e.g., Robin Hood, and the work of Spenser. Though the *Faerie Queene* had not been published, it is evident that Marlowe was very familiar with at least the seventh and eighth cantos of Book I. Passages from them are embroidered upon both parts of Tamburlaine, and hang there as a gracious link between two poets who had not very much in common and, quite possibly, never met.[18]

It may have been only accident that caused *Tamburlaine* to fall into the hands of Edward Alleyn, the all-dominating chief actor of the Admiral's company; but the affinity between the rôle and the player was so perfect that a second part was at once required and Marlowe was committed to one-man plays.[19] His own mind, certainly, ran in that direction, for the insolence of youth was fervent in him. "No one," it has been said, "has ever expressed so well a young man's emotion at the new consciousness of what a world there is, all before him." [20] *Tamburlaine* is a hymn to intellectual beauty, a paean on the superiority of mind over matter. Marlowe was a Carlylean before Carlyle, and summed up the doctrine of the "hero" or superman in his Scythian shepherd's words, "I, thus conceiving, . . .

> Shall give the world to note, for all my birth,
> That virtue solely is the sum of glory,
> And fashions men with true nobility,[21]

virtue being that virile soul-stuff that enables the great man to focus all his energies upon a single goal, a "perfect bliss and sole felicity." For Tamburlaine the goal happens to be "the sweet fruition of an earthly crown." [22] For Faustus it is the superhuman knowledge which is the ultimate in power. " 'Tis Magic, magic, that hath ravish'd me," Faustus says; and for Barabas it is the power, beauty, and romance of wealth. But all these characters are off the same block, and their great speeches are sometimes almost interchangeable; as where Faustus visualizes his desire in terms of "huge argosies," gold, and orient pearl,[23] or Barabas speaks of himself as a warrior,

> That in a field amidst his enemies
> Doth see his soldiers slain, himself disarm'd.[24]

---

[17] See W. Thorp, "The Ethical Problem in Marlowe's *Tamburlaine*," *JEGP*, XXIX (1930). 385-89; R. W. Battenhouse, *Marlowe's Tamburlaine, a Study in Renaissance Moral Philosophy* (Nashville, 1941).

[18] See G. Schoeneich, *Der litterarische Einfluss Spensers auf Marlowe* (Halle, 1907); C. Crawford, *Collectanea* I (1906). 47-100; and for a divergent opinion T. W. Baldwin, "The Genesis of Some Passages Which Spenser Borrowed from Marlowe," *ELH*, IX (1942). 157-87.

[19] See Helen L. Gardner, "The Second Part of *Tamburlaine the Great*," *MLR*, XXXVII (1942). 18-24.

[20] E. T. McLaughlin, edition of *Edward II* (1894), p. 169.

[21] *I Tamburlaine*, 1964 ff.

[22] *I Tamburlaine*, 879 f.

[23] *Doctor Faustus*, 110 ff., 159 ff.

[24] *Jew of Malta*, 436 f.

Doctor Faustus and *The Rich Jew of Malta* are both preserved in imperfect
texts, and so, in perhaps even more deplorable degree, is the *Massacre at*
Paris,[25] which centers attention upon the villain-hero Guise and is likely to
seem to the reader mainly a matter of a few fine soliloquies, though (as is
always the way in Marlowe) the driving purpose comes out better in the
acting.

Marlowe was the first man to elicit the poetry in the Faust legend,[26]
translating the quest of swinish pleasures which the Faustbook (1587)
pictured into a quest of intellectual power. In the earlier, briefer, and better
of the two bad versions which have survived, the outlines of an original five-
act tragedy can be traced, but as the text stands it divides into three parts: a
grand opening, dealing with the signing of the bond, and a magnificent
conclusion, which are bound together by a series of discontinuous and sometimes prosaic interludes.[27] It would seem that the poet is here attempting an
interesting dramatic experiment, attempting, that is, to give stage plausibility
to the passage of a great deal of time (twenty-four years) between the opening and close of the play. On the stage, indeed, the effect is felt, even in our
truncated text, but the reader is likely to pass from the poetry of the opening
to that of the close too impatiently to observe it.

Criticism of the *Jew of Malta,* extant only in a single very late quarto
(1633), is like the restoration of a badly repainted masterpiece, and requires
both delicacy and diffidence. It was apparently the most steadily popular of
all Marlowe's plays, but has been outrageously overlaid with alien grotes-
query, particularly in the third and fourth acts. The genuine parts are
remarkable for their effective stage business and melodious blank verse. The
first two acts, said Hallam, "are more vigorously conceived, both as to
character and circumstance, than any other Elizabethan play, except those of
Shakespeare;"[28] and Swinburne judged that "in the blank verse of Milton
alone . . . has the glory or the melody of passages in the opening soliloquy of
Barabas been possibly surpassed."[29] It was another dramatic experiment,
aiming to present history-in-the-making as suggested by rumors concerning
a contemporary Jew, in Constantinople, David Passi, and a Turkish attack on
Malta, which, though excitedly discussed in the early part of 1591, did not
actually take place.[30]

---

[25] Ed. Malone Soc. (1928). See J. Q. Adams, "The *Massacre at Paris* Leaf," *Library,* xiv
(1934). 447-469.
[26] See P. M. Palmer and R. P. More, *Sources of the Faust Tradition from Simon Magus to
Lessing* (1936); B. D. Brown, "Marlowe, Faustus, and Simon Magus," *PMLA,* liv (1939).
82-121; P. H. Kocher, "The English Faust Book and the Date of Marlowe's *Faustus,*" *MLN,*
lv (1940). 95-101, and "The Early Date for Marlowe's *Faustus,*" *MLN,* lviii (1943). 539-
542; Leo Kirschbaum, "Marlowe's *Faustus:* A Reconsideration," *RES,* xix (1943). 225-241.
[27] See an important article by P. H. Kocher, "Nashe's Authorship of the Prose Scenes in
Faustus," *MLQ,* iii (1942). 17-40.
[28] Henry Hallam, *Introduction to the Literature of Europe,* ed. 1864, ii. 270.
[29] Article on Marlowe in the *Encyclopedia Britannica.*
[30] See T. Brooke, "The Prototype of Marlowe's Jew of Malta," *LTLS,* June 8, 1922, p. 380;
E. Seaton, "Fresh Sources for Marlowe," *RES,* v (1929). 385-401.

Marlowe's last play, *Edward II*,[31] is very unlike the rest. It is not at all a one-man drama, and though it contains great poetry, it is not poetic drama in the sense in which Marlowe's other plays are. The change is to be attributed both to growing experience and to the fact that Marlowe was now dissociated from Alleyn, probably by reason of the merging of the Lord Admiral's and Lord Strange's men in 1591. *Edward II* was produced by a less distinguished company, the Earl of Pembroke's, which also acted the early versions of the second and third parts of *Henry VI*. In *Edward II* there is little declamation and much brilliant stage action. The dialogue is nearly three times as rapid as in *Tamburlaine;* the whole emphasis is upon the business of the theatre, and it is quite certain that in writing this play Marlowe did not have the reader in mind. Readers have resented this and deplored the lack of interest. It is not recorded that spectators ever have, and it seems sounder to stand with Lamb[32] in admiring the extraordinary dramaturgy of (for example) the death scene than with those who find poetry lacking in the many sinewy and frugal speeches.

[31] Ed. W. D. Briggs (1914); Malone Soc. (1925). See J. M. Berdan, "Marlowe's *Edward II*," *PQ*, III (1924). 197-207; L. J. Mills, "The Meaning of *Edward II*," *MP*, XXXII (1934). 11-31.
[32] Charles Lamb, *Specimens of the English Dramatic Poets* (1808).

XII

Shakespeare to 1603

William Shakespeare [1] (1564-1616) was born, in the sixth year of Queen *The* Elizabeth's reign, at Stratford-on-Avon, Warwickshire, in the rural centre of *Stratford* England, rich in legend and in associations with leading events and characters *Setting* of the Wars of the Roses. He was baptized in Stratford Trinity Church, April 26, 1564, and buried there fifty-two years later. The precise date of his birth is unrecorded, but tradition fixes it on St. George's Day (April 23), which was also the date on which he died in 1616. In the poet's time Stratford was a thriving market town, situated on a well-traveled thoroughfare of Roman origin between the Cotswold Hills, which were famous in the annals of country sport, and the still timbered "forest of Arden" to the north. There was a considerable Welsh element in the population, drawn from the Severn country farther west. Otherwise the local types that were most familiar were the agricultural "clowns" or farmhands, the constables, schoolmasters, parsons, and "mechanical" tradesmen, and the country gentry, who lived on

[1] This note is necessarily limited to some of the most important modern biographical and critical works on Shakespeare and to some standard works of reference. See W. Ebisch and L. L. Schücking, *A Shakespeare Bibliography* (Oxford, 1931) and *Supplement* (Oxford, 1937). — E. K. Chambers, *William Shakespeare* (2v, Oxford, 1930), indispensable; abridgment by C. Williams (Oxford, 1933). J. Q. Adams, *A Life of William Shakespeare* (1923); T. Brooke, *Shakespeare of Stratford* (New Haven, 1926); T. Alexander, *Shakespeare's Life and Art* (1939); E. I. Fripp, *Shakespeare, Man and Artist* (2v, Oxford, 1938); Hazelton Spencer, *The Art and Life of William Shakespeare* (1940); W. Raleigh, *Shakespeare* (EML Series, 1907); H. C. Bartlett, *Mr. William Shakespeare* (New Haven, 1922); G. B. Harrison, *Shakespeare under Elizabeth* (1933); E. K. Chambers, *Shakespeare, a Survey* (1926). Many aspects of Shakespearean scholarship are considered in H. Granville-Barker, G. B. Harrison, and others, *A Companion to Shakespeare Studies* (1934). B. R. Lewis, *The Shakespeare Documents* (2v, Stanford University, 1941) assembles a vast amount of more or less pertinent material. General surveys primarily critical rather than biographical include J. M. Murry, *Shakespeare* (1936); Mark Van Doren, *Shakespeare* (1939); J. D. Wilson, *The Essential Shakespeare* (1932); H. Granville-Barker, *Prefaces to Shakespeare* (three series, 1927-1936); G. W. Knight, *The Wheel of Fire* (Oxford, 1930) and later volumes; M. R. Ridley, *Shakespeare's Plays, a Commentary* (1937). Theodore Spencer, *Shakespeare and the Nature of Man* (1942) interprets the plays in terms of the Renaissance concept of the "world order." Special topics are considered in E. E. Stoll, *Shakespeare Studies* (1927), *Art and Artifice in Shakespeare* (Cambridge, 1933), and other volumes; C. F. E. Spurgeon, *Shakespeare's Imagery and What It Tells Us* (1935); A. C. Sprague, *Shakespeare and the Audience* (1935), on the technique of exposition, and *Shakespeare and the Actors* (1944), on stage business; O. J. Campbell, *Shakespeare's Satire* (1943); T. W. Baldwin, *The Organization and Personnel of the Shakespearean Company* (Princeton, 1927). — H. C. Bartlett and A. W. Pollard, *A Census of Shakespeare's Plays in Quarto, 1594-1709* (New Haven, 1916; rev. ed., 1939); J. J. Munro, *The Shakespeare Allusion-Book* (2v, 1909), revised ed. (2v, 1932), supplemented by other collections of early allusions; W. Franz, *Die Sprache Shakespeares in Vers und Prosa* (Halle, 1939); G. S. Gordon, *Shakespeare's English* (Oxford, 1928; S. P. E. Tract, no. 29); C. T. Onions, *A Shakespeare Glossary* (Oxford, 1911); J. Bartlett, *Concordance* (1906); annual bibliographies appear in *SAB*. Other important specialized studies are cited in later notes.

their estates but did their business in Stratford. These are among the types that Shakespeare portrays with the greatest clearness and affection.[2]

arentage
d Educa-
on
The poet's parents, John Shakespeare and Mary Arden, were both from the adjacent country and, particularly his mother, had valid claims to gentility. His father prospered at the local industry of glove-making and also attained the highest municipal offices in the town, but by the time Shakespeare was growing up he had met reverses in consequence of law-suits and a too sanguine temperament. The young William, eldest son of the family, attended the Stratford Grammar School,[3] which had an excellent reputation and rather distinguished teachers. There is even a possibility, but no definite proof, that he may have had a term or two at Oxford.[4] However, his hasty marriage at the age of eighteen to Anne Hathaway of Shottery village, on the outskirts of Stratford, and the birth of his three children within the next three years certainly put an end to his regular schooling. There is no evidence how or where he lived during the next half-dozen years. The seventeenth-century tradition, reported by Aubrey from Beeston, that he had been "in his younger years a schoolmaster in the country" is one of the oldest and most plausible, for there is much about schools in Shakespeare and it usually suggests the teacher's rather than the pupil's point of view.

ife in
ondon
Before long, evidently, Shakespeare followed the procession of talent to London and gave himself to the rapidly expanding vocation of the stage. By 1592, when Greene singled him out for spiteful notice,[5] he had obviously attained some prominence as an actor and playwright, while Chettle's apology of the same year shows that he had become the esteemed protégé of "divers of worship," i.e., persons of high social standing, and was favorably known for the qualities of geniality and good breeding which Elizabethans described by the word *gentle,* and which are the traits most noted in the contemporary mentions of him. Before 1594, by means now wholly unknown, he had established a friendship with the young Earl of Southampton, to whom he dedicated his two long poems, and to whom he addressed, probably between 1593 and 1597, the bulk of his sonnets. His purely literary ambition appears to have been soon crowded out by increasing theatrical business. He was one of the principal actors in the Lord Chamberlain's Company till 1603, though probably a dignified rather than highly gifted performer, and he was one of the seven partners in the building of the Globe Theatre in 1599. When James I took the Chamberlain's Men under his personal patronage in 1603, Shakespeare shared largely in the mounting prestige and prosperity of the company and had a modest place at court. His ties with

---

[2] For the Stratford background see E. I. Fripp, *Shakespeare's Stratford* (Oxford, 1928); Oliver Baker, *In Shakespeare's Warwickshire and the Unknown Years* (1937); and D. H. Madden, *The Diary of Master William Silence* (1897).

[3] For the educational methods at the earliest levels see T. W. Baldwin, *William Shakspere's Petty School* (Urbana, 1943) and *William Shakspere's Small Latine & Lesse Greeke* (2v, Urbana, 1944); also David Brown, "What Shakspere Learned at School," *Bucknell Univ. Stud.,* I (1941). 1-20.

[4] This idea is developed by J. S. Smart, *Shakespeare Truth and Tradition* (1928), pp. 175-182.

[5] See above, Part II, ch. IV.

Stratford, however, remained close. The only private letter to him that has survived shows him acting in 1598 as the London friend of the Stratford corporation. He invested his wealth largely in Stratford property and in 1597 *Retiremen* bought "New Place," one of the great houses of the town, which about 1610 became his chief residence and the home of his family. *The Quart*

Shakespeare's first published play was *Titus Andronicus,* printed anony- *Editions* mously in 1594 [6] and followed within about a month by a bad text of *Henry VI, Part II,* likewise anonymous and of still disputed authorship. Sixteen other plays were published in his lifetime in separate "quarto" form.[7] From 1598 on, his name is usually played up on title-pages and in stationers' entries in such a way as to show that it had a high sales value; but there is not much indication that Shakespeare himself authorized or approved any of these publications, except perhaps the second editions of *Romeo and Juliet* and *Hamlet,* issued to curtail the circulation of earlier corrupt texts. The "bad quartos" include also the first editions of *Henry V,* *The Merry Wives of Windsor, Pericles,* and the third part of *Henry VI.* Theories of their origin vary. Stenographic reporting, "memorial reconstruction" (i.e., efforts by actors to put a play together from memory), and the use of "foul papers" (i.e., unrevised first drafts) have all been suggested. These bad quartos should be distinguished from the "good quartos," which, whether published with the author's consent or not, rest on authentic texts, sometimes fuller than those of the Folio, but the line of demarcation is not precise.[8]

In 1619, three years after Shakespeare's death, ten plays by, or ascribed to, him were published by Thomas Pavier without authority, some with protective pre-datings. Soon afterwards Shakespeare's actor-colleagues, John Heminge and Henry Condell, undertook the editing of his complete dramatic works with the backing of Ben Jonson, who had published his own *Works*

---

[6] Facsimile, ed. J. Q. Adams (Folger Shakespeare Library, 1937).
[7] The original quarto editions were facsimiled under the direction of F. J. Furnivall (43v, 1880-9), but this reproduction is not always reliable. A new series has been begun by the Shakespeare Assoc. and Sidgwick & Jackson of London, of which five volumes have appeared to date. The 1603 and the 1604 *Hamlet* have been reproduced by the Huntington Library (1931, 1938), and the Sonnets in several facsimiles (1905, 1925, 1926). The first folio has been facsimiled by the Clarendon Press, Oxford (ed. S. Lee, 1902) and by Methuen & Co. (1910); the other three folios also by Methuen & Co. (1904-9). The editions most valuable for their annotations and other apparatus are the so-called (third) Variorum, ed. J. Boswell (21v, 1821); the Cambridge, ed. W. G. Clark, J. Glover, and W. A. Wright (9v, 1863-6; revised ed., 1891-3); the *New Variorum,* ed. H. H. Furness, his son, and others, in which 21 plays, the poems, and sonnets have now appeared (Philadelphia, 1871-   ); and the *Arden,* general editors W. J. Craig and R. H. Case (39v, 1899-1924). Convenient editions in small volumes, with less elaborate annotation, include the *Tudor Shakespeare,* ed. W. A. Neilson and A. H. Thorndike (40v, 1911-13, new issue 1922, 1941); *Yale Shakespeare,* ed. T. Brooke, W. L. Cross, W. H. Durham (40v, 1918-28); *New Temple Shakespeare,* ed. M. R. Ridley (39v, 1934-6). The following editions of selected plays, primarily school texts, are also useful: the Clarendon Press series, ed. W. A. Wright (10v, Oxford, 1868-83), and the series ed. G. L. Kittredge (16v, Boston, 1939-46). The best texts currently available in one volume containing all the plays and poems are those ed. W. A. Neilson (Boston, 1906; rev. ed., 1942) and G. L. Kittredge (Boston, 1936).
[8] See A. W. Pollard, *Shakespeare Folios and Quartos* (1909) and *Shakespeare's Fight with the Pirates* (Cambridge, 1917; 2ed., 1920); L. Kirschbaum, "A Census of Bad Quartos," *RES,* XIV (1938). 1-24.

in 1616. Difficulties involving publishers' rights, mislaid manuscripts, and rival demands upon William Jaggard's printing press caused delay, and the great First Folio edition did not appear till 1623.[9] It is a large and sumptuous volume, betraying indeed many evidences of the confusions amid which it had been compiled, but essentially well printed. It is our only source for eighteen of the plays, and for all the rest except *Pericles,* which the Folio omitted, it offers texts that, if not invariably better than the corresponding quarto texts, are always of capital importance.[10]

The posthumous life of Shakespeare, as expressed in the influence of his work on the intelligence of later generations, has been the most active of which we have record. Many of the most significant writers of the last three centuries have found channels for their own thought in criticizing Shakespeare.[11] This is notably true, for example, of Pope, Samuel Johnson, Coleridge, Lamb, Hazlitt, Swinburne, Walt Whitman, and Shaw, and in foreign countries of Voltaire and Victor Hugo, Lessing, Schlegel, Goethe, Croce, and many others. The results are often of the highest literary value, but are sometimes more important in the aesthetic history of the writers' own ages than they are for Shakespeare absolutely considered. In the end of the

eighteenth century and the beginning of the nineteenth the Shakespearean interest effervesced into a movement known as "Shakespeare idolatry."[12] This romantic fallacy, that Shakespeare was superhuman and could do nothing wrong, began working itself out, less than a century ago, in a wilderness of attempts to postulate some more suitable author for the immortal works than the humble "man of Stratford." Centering at first on Francis Bacon as a more learned, more conspicuous, and allegedly wiser pundit, the "heterodox" school has now so ramified that there are few eminent Elizabethans left (except, strangely, the other great poets) for whom some one has not built up a specious claim to Shakespeare's crown. Many very unlikely candidates have been chosen, on the principle, apparently, that any stick will do to beat the Stratfordian dogma; and the net profit from all this ingenious and sometimes brilliant labor is very small.

A scientific attitude asserted itself in the later nineteenth century in connection with the New Shakespeare Society under the direction of F. J. Furnivall. This worked out the well-known metrical tests and in other ways laid the ground for more precise study,[13] and it has been followed during the last forty years by the "new bibliography," illustrated in the often very illuminating work of W. W. Greg, A. W. Pollard, R. B. McKerrow, and J. Dover Wilson. Over-enthusiastic members of this school have sometimes carried research into blind alleys and introduced untenable emendations into the

---

[9] See M. H. Spielman, J. D. Wilson, and others, *Studies in the First Folio* (Oxford, 1924); E. E. Willoughby, *The Printing of the First Folio of Shakespeare* (Oxford, 1932), and *A Printer of Shakespeare: The Books and Times of William Jaggard* (1934).

[10] See R. B. McKerrow, *Prolegomena for the Oxford Shakespeare: A Study in Editorial Method* (Oxford, 1939); and W. W. Greg, *The Editorial Problem in Shakespeare* (Oxford, 1942).

[11] See Augustus Ralli, *A History of Shakespearian Criticism* (2v, Oxford, 1932).

[12] See R. W. Babcock, *The Genesis of Shakespeare Idolatry, 1766-1799* (Chapel Hill, 1931).

[13] See *Transactions of the New Shakspere Society* (1874-92).

text, but a brilliant advance has been made in explaining the conditions under which Shakespeare's manuscripts were prepared and printed.[14]

Had Shakespeare died when Queen Elizabeth did, in his thirty-ninth year, he would still have had ten years more than Marlowe, and would still no doubt rank as England's greatest dramatist; but his reputation for original genius would not be exceptionally high. He would, to be sure, have left one play, *Hamlet,* as Marlowe left *Edward II,* to puzzle critics by its difference from what preceded and provoke unanswerable questions about the new path into which he would seem to have turned. The best way to bring into *The Devel-* focus the multifold activities of his first dozen years is to view them as efforts *opment of* to acquire the various "skills" of his profession. Shakespeare was unlike his *Shake-* own characterization of Cicero [15] in that *he* would always follow what other *speare's* men began, and Pope's appraisal of him, if restricted to his Elizabethan *Style* period, is not very inaccurate:

> For gain, not glory, wing'd his roving flight,
> And grew immortal in his own despite.[16]

The broadest single fact about his poems and early plays is that he is following the lines of least resistance and going with the crowd, both in choice of materials and in workmanship. *Venus and Adonis* and *Lucrece* deal with the kind of classical story which had the greatest popular appeal at the time, and are written in the two stanza-forms most conventional in such work. His sonnets differ from their only worthy competitors, those of Sidney and Spenser, in being composed in the form that was the commonest and the easiest to write.

It is hardly possible to say whether he began as a dramatist by imitating *His Imita-* Plautus in *The Comedy of Errors,* or Munday and Greene in *The Two tions* *Gentlemen of Verona,*[17] or Lyly in *Love's Labor's Lost,* or Peele and Marlowe in *Henry VI.* He imitated them all, and in each case seems mainly concerned to turn out a workmanlike product along lines which the public taste had already approved. He shows at this time no prepossessions concerning metre. The broken-backed rimes of the interludes (particularly frequent in the *Comedy of Errors*), prose, pentameter couplets, blank verse, and the six-line (*ababcc*) stanza, which *Venus and Adonis* and the writing of the sonnets had made second nature for him—all mix themselves in his earliest plays in an anarchy for which it would usually be absurd to seek any special purpose. His main ambition was to learn how to write, and he was willing to adapt himself, humbly enough, to any models that were then in vogue.

The development of his style can be most clearly traced in the succession

[14] Examples are W. W. Greg, *The Merry Wives of Windsor, 1602* (Oxford, 1910); A. W. Pollard, *Richard II* (1916); P. Alexander, *Shakespeare's Henry VI and Richard III* (Cambridge, 1929); D. L. Patrick, *The Textual History of Richard III* (Stanford Univ., 1936); G. I. Duthie, *The Bad Quarto of Hamlet* (Cambridge, 1941); and *The New Cambridge Shakespeare,* ed. Sir A. Quiller-Couch and J. Dover Wilson (Cambridge, 1921-   ).
[15] *Julius Caesar,* II. i. 151.
[16] *Epistle to Augustus,* 71 f.
[17] See J. Spens, *An Essay on Shakespeare's Relation to Tradition* (Oxford, 1916).

*he History
*lays

of his history plays. They are the most numerous group in his early period, and one need seek no other reasons for this than simply that they were the most popular type of drama in the 1590's and intrinsically the least difficult to construct. In all the three plays of *Henry VI* he is expanding earlier pieces,[18] with great deference to his predecessors, but displaying in his additions the two points of view which in the beginning were his most notable peculiarities: the sweet and lugubrious sentimentality which drugs his poems, and the humorous understanding of simple stupid men, which is perhaps the only common denominator between the three earliest comedies.

King John is in a way the converse of *Henry VI*, for here, instead of enlarging, he is contracting the work of a predecessor, making two plays into one. Again he shows extreme respect for his model, hardly deviating in plot or in the roll of characters; but stylistically he is now independent, for his recension borrows only a line or two from the *Troublesome Reign*. There could hardly be clearer evidence that Shakespeare's interest is at this point in style, not in structure or philosophy. The play lives for the two qualities already mentioned: the sentimentalism of Constance and Arthur, and the salty earthiness of Falconbridge.

Richard III and *Richard II*, which are probably earlier than *John*, devote themselves to the imitation of Marlowe. Contrary to his whole mature practice, Shakespeare here abjures prose and song, and concentrates on recapturing Marlowe's great blank verse harmonies. These plays were, with *Romeo and Juliet*, his first outstanding successes. They are not alike in tone, for *Richard II* is greatly influenced by *Edward II;* but in style it is the earlier work of Marlowe that dominates both. Both are in less degree solutions of dramatic conflicts than vehicles, such as *Tamburlaine* had been, for splendid declamation. For pure eloquence *Richard II* could hardly be surpassed, but the *Henry IV* plays show a broader mastery, and more of that ability to make the characters speak like persons in real life which was one of Shakespeare's greatest accomplishments in style.[19] In *Henry IV* prose, in the scenes dealing with Falstaff, has a more important function than in any previous Shakespearean play. *Henry V*, which followed, dates from the time of the opening of the Globe Theatre (summer of 1599), and may well have been written for this occasion. It has the appearance of an occasional piece, emphasizing display and variety of interest, and is extremely skilful in handling all the elements that make for broad public appeal. Thereafter Shakespeare abandoned the history play, returning to it only in another show-piece at the very end of his life, *Henry VIII* (1613).

His Devel-
opment in
Comedy

Shakespeare's comedies,[20] though they, of course, illustrate the general improvement of his style during the decade from 1590 to 1600, show no such constant progress as the histories. They are, indeed, remarkably heterogeneous

---

[18] For a contrary view see P. Alexander, *Shakespeare's Henry VI and Richard III* (Cambridge, 1929), and E. M. W. Tillyard, *Shakespeare's History Plays* (1944).

[19] See Madeleine Doran, "Imagery in *Richard II* and in *Henry IV*," *MLR*, xxxvii (1942), 113-122; J. D. Wilson, *The Fortunes of Falstaff* (1943).

[20] See H. B. Charlton, *Shakespearian Comedy* (1938).

in pattern. The three earliest, unlike in theme and feeling as they were, were followed by *A Midsummer-Night's Dream* and *The Merchant of Venice,* which, though not like each other, both resemble the *Two Gentlemen of Verona* at various points. These later plays are of somewhat uncertain date. They were, however, in existence in 1598, when Meres listed both among Shakespeare's works, and both were published in 1600. Though they now rank among the most valued plays, they do not seem to have been particularly popular in their own time; nor have they very much in common with his later comedies. *A Midsummer-Night's Dream* probably got a hint for its fairy element from Greene's *James IV,* and its Athenian background from Chaucer's *Knight's Tale* and Plutarch's *Life of Theseus,* whereas the plot of the lovers is a more succinct rehandling of the main theme of *Two Gentlemen of Verona.* It seems to have been written, or at least recast, for a state wedding, and is the most lyrical of all the plays. It has little real resemblance to any of the rest, unless perhaps to the much later *Tempest,* which was likewise adapted to celebrate a royal wedding. *The Merchant of Venice,* on the other hand, is one of the gravest of comedies, and capable of being misread as a tragedy. It is, likewise, a play of motley ingredients and Gothic atmosphere, and has no particular congener in the Shakespeare canon.

Bibliographical evidence coincides with evidence of other kinds to show that by 1598 Shakespeare had, however unwittingly and unmethodically, attained name and fame. Two natural consequences of success—pressure towards over-production and a certain slackening of creative energy—may perhaps be observed in other comedies of the decade. *The Taming of the Shrew* is hard to date. Shakespeare may have been employed in fitting it to the stage since 1594, when some such play appears in the repertory of his company. The text printed in the Folio of 1623 presents an admirable farce, considerably superior to the *Comedy of Errors,* but not very suggestive of Shakespeare's unaided work.[21] The other farce, *The Merry Wives of Windsor,* which seems to be an offshoot of *Henry V,* belongs to the latter part of 1599 or 1600, and the tradition that it was written in great haste is easily credible. Admitting its limitations and the many textual problems it obtrudes,[22] one must yet rate it one of the best farces in the world. It was Shakespeare's last effort in this genre.

The Farces

The period from the middle of 1599 to 1601, that is, from Essex's departure to Ireland till his ill-omened insurrection, shows Shakespeare's career traversing a kind of plateau. It was in general a period of suspended activity and indecision. The three great comedies of these years seem in their very titles to express a sort of carelessness: *Much Ado about Nothing, As You Like*

The Essex Period

[21] Three recent papers by R. A. Houk should be consulted: "The Integrity of Shakespeare's *The Taming of the Shrew,*" *JEGP,* xxxix (1940). 222-229; "The Evolution of *The Taming of the Shrew,*" *PMLA* lvii (1942). 1009-1038; "Strata in *The Taming of the Shrew,*" *SP,* xxxix (1942). 291-302. Also G. L. Duthie, "*The Taming of a Shrew* and *The Taming of the Shrew,*" *RES,* xix (1943). 337-356.
[22] See W. W. Greg's edition (Oxford, 1910); and, for a very fanciful interpretation, J. Crofts, *Shakespeare and the Post Horses* (Bristol, 1937).

It, and *What You Will* (i.e., *Twelfth Night*). Carelessness has seldom been so fruitful of delight. They are escapes from thinking, anodynes against worry, inclining heavily to prose in their style, and in their themes savoring more of the world of pleasant fancy than the world of strong imagination. Their mastery of form and balance of social judgment are superb—and in these respects the latest, *Twelfth Night,* is the most perfect. They mark a gracious interlude in Shakespeare's progress, a halcyon period when he was aware of his matured powers and as yet unwilling to urge them to new tasks.

Thus, by the end of Queen Elizabeth's reign, Shakespeare had brought his writing of English history plays to a close, having developed that type to the limit of its artistic possibilities; while in comedy he was floating in dead water, exploiting his elegant connoisseurship and for the moment content to take his profits as a public entertainer. As a nondramatic poet he had quite shot his bolt. *Venus and Adonis* and *Lucrece* had no successors from his hand; and the great series of sonnets—if written to, or apropos of, Lord Southampton, as the present writer thinks they certainly were—can scarcely be later than 1597.[23] Only in tragedy is there any close link between Shakespeare in Elizabeth's reign and in King James's.

Tragedy   Apart from the history plays, Shakespeare's known output in tragedy before 1603 consists of but four plays, separated from each other by considerable intervals of time and very remarkable differences of manner. All four, however, belong to the revenge or vendetta type of play familiar in Seneca, and they all owe more to Kyd than to Marlowe. There is no good

Titus Andronicus reason for denying *Titus Andronicus* to Shakespeare.[24] One should hardly wish to do so, for it is a brilliant specimen of its repulsive kind. Harmoniously worded and very well constructed, it holds the interest of any reader who will read it, and even on the modern stage is almost lethally effective. It is the only representative of the tragedy of blood, except *Richard III,* which can fairly challenge the supremacy of Kyd's *Spanish Tragedy.* Like that play, and like *Hamlet,* it makes good use of quasi-insanity, and in Act v, scene ii, has a movement cleverly varied from Kyd's play-within-the-play. It is, on the whole, closer to Seneca than the *Spanish Tragedy* is, and borrows its culminating horror, the banquet of human flesh, direct from the *Thyestes.*

Romeo and Juliet *Romeo and Juliet* is so different that one easily overlooks its Senecan affinities; for here Shakespeare stresses not the horror but the pity of it, and writes, as it were, a Senecan play to end Senecan plays. But one should not overlook the vendetta spirit and Tybalt as the evil genius of the piece, marking Verona as a kind of counterpart of the Senecan Thebes. That we do so is due to the characteristic in Shakespeare that so often allows his interest in persons to drive a play athwart its normal course. As with Shylock and Falstaff, there occurred an unleashing of romantic sympathy for Romeo and Juliet which threatened at every moment to turn the drama

23 See editions of the sonnets by T. Brooke (1936), H. E. Rollins, (2v, Philadelphia, 1944; *New Variorum* ed.), and R. M. Alden (Boston, 1916).
24 See H. T. Price, "The Authorship of *Titus Andronicus,*" *JEGP,* XLII (1943). 55-81.

into tragicomedy. What uninformed reader of the first four acts could expect a tragic conclusion? It is this swirling conflict of intuitive sympathy with predetermined form that hollows out the deepest reaches of Shakespeare's art. It would be foolish, however, to ignore the tragic pattern and regard the play merely as a story of young lovers who met astonishingly bad luck. The broader tragic theme, stated in the prefatory sonnet, is a main constituent of the play's success, which was from the first enormous. It was perhaps the earliest of Shakespeare's great triumphs, and in its first form may even be as early as 1591.[25] One may wonder that he never wrote another tragedy like it. This is perhaps the key to Shakespeare's remarkable originality and development, that, while imitating others so easily, he so resolutely forbore to imitate his own best things.

The next tragedy, after a number of years, was *Julius Caesar,* which was Julius produced at the Globe in the autumn of 1599, immediately after *Henry V*.[26] Caesar Mechanically, these two plays are much alike, and they exhibit the culmination of Shakespeare's middle style. The language of the stage could not be more crystal clear or more simply eloquent, and the dramatic ideas could not be more intelligibly and interestingly presented, or better chosen to fit the tastes of the average man. As a writer for the million, Shakespeare had in these plays reached the top of his career, and the million have never failed to delight in them. *Julius Caesar* can still be called a Senecan tragedy, complete with ghost and revenge-motif; but it is given a bias-movement by the character of Brutus, which evidently bothered Shakespeare as he turned his attention from Holinshed's boldly two-dimensional sketches to Plutarch's more ambiguous figures. For the understanding of the average playgoer he allows Brutus to remain the idealistic hero that Plutarch called him; but he had inward doubts which a careful and repeated reader of the play begins to share; while Cassius, so clearly slated for the villain's part, refuses to maintain that status and ends by robbing his colleague of much of our sympathy.

Brutus in *Julius Caesar,* though a fine and effective stage type, is not a thoroughly harmonized portrait. He is a preliminary drawing for Shakespeare's Hamlet, who has many of the same difficulties to face and is of similar mental fiber. It is perhaps not too rash to assume that the unresolved doubts which half appear in the stage-character of Brutus drove Shakespeare to attempts at deeper introspection, and so to higher and somewhat extra-dramatic triumphs. Shakespeare's standard play is *Hamlet*.[27] In some ways

---

[25] See H. B. Charlton, *"Romeo and Juliet* as an Experimental Tragedy" (British Academy Shakespeare lecture, 1939); T. Brooke, "Shakespeare Remembers his Youth in Stratford," *Essays and Studies in Honor of Carleton Brown* (1940). 253-256; H. R. Walley, "Shakespeare's Debt to Marlowe in *Romeo and Juliet," PQ,* xxi (1942). 257-267.

[26] See H. Granville-Barker, "From *Henry V* to *Hamlet"* (British Academy Shakespeare lecture, 1925).

[27] A small shelf of works bearing on *Hamlet* might include the following: A. A. Raven, *A Hamlet Bibliography and Reference Guide* (Chicago, 1936); J. Schick, *Corpus Hamleticum: Hamlet in Sage und Dichtung, Kunst und Musik* (Leipzig, 1938); *Hamlet,* ed. J. Q. Adams (Boston, 1929); T. M. Parrott and H. Craig, *The Tragedy of Hamlet: A Critical Edition of the Second Quarto* (Princeton, 1938); E. E. Stoll, *Hamlet, an Historical and Comparative Study*

this strange refashioning of an old melodrama has fixed itself in the minds of all sorts of people as both the truest mirror of Shakespeare's personality and the ripest production of English literary art. The man in the street, the professional actor, the poet, and the philosopher all agree in this truism. Hardly any other critical dogma about Shakespeare is so universally accepted, and yet the wisest of the play's critics have not been able to explain very clearly why this should be so. They can only agree that the charm and value of *Hamlet* are mysteriously incorporated in the personality of the hero—"the best part, I believe, that ever man acted," as Pepys was saying in 1668—so that, though the tragedy contains many other brilliant characters and abounds in violent action, the proverbial *"Hamlet* without the character of Hamlet" has become the classic way of describing a literary vacuum. Hamlet's individuality suffuses the entire play, giving a special reality and poignancy to all the parts.

To sketch the development of the Hamlet story is to trace the long evolution of an ideal of the human mind. Out of a tangle of Norse pagan myth Saxo Grammaticus produced his character of Amleth, the grim and purposeful avenger of his father's murder. This story, through the French version of Belleforest, had before 1589 been made into an English play by a bold and vigorous adapter, presumably Kyd, who evidently (though his version has not been preserved intact) overlaid the realistic paganism of the North with supernatural paganism from Greece and Rome, introducing the ghost and other Senecan machinery and changing the crafty assumption of idiocy in Saxo's hero into neurotic brainsickness. Shakespeare may have been acting in this play in 1594, when we know that the Chamberlain's Company had an interest in it, and he may already have begun revising it.[28] When his revision was complete, as it first appears in the quarto of 1604, the theme had been altered more than it is quite easy to realize. *Hamlet* was really no longer a play of revenge; it was a play of life and death and of man's ambiguous relation to them both. It was the passionate protest of a keen and honest thinker against the inescapable sophistications of thought, which make everything *seem* and yet can give no assurance that anything is absolutely true. Hamlet enters the play expostulating against the hypocrisy of appearances. "A little more than kin and less than kind"; "Seems, madam! nay, it is; I know not 'seems.'" The keynote of his tragedy, the most profound and melancholy saying in the play, is the cry forced from him as the crisis approaches: "There is nothing either good or bad but thinking makes it so."

(Minneapolis, 1919), and *Hamlet the Man* (English Assoc., pamphlet 91, 1935); A. J. A. Waldock, *Hamlet, a Study in Critical Method* (Cambridge, 1931); J. D. Wilson, *The Manuscripts of Shakespeare's Hamlet and the Problems of its Transmission* (2v, Cambridge, 1934), and *What Happens in Hamlet* (Cambridge, 1935, 2ed., 1937); L. L. Schücking, *Der Sinn des Hamlet* (Leipzig, 1935; English trans., *The Meaning of Hamlet*, Oxford, 1937); W. W. Lawrence, "Hamlet and the Mouse Trap," *PMLA*, LIV (1940). 709-735; J. E. Hankins, *The Character of Hamlet and other Essays* (Chapel Hill, 1941); C. S. Lewis, *Hamlet, the Prince or the Poem?* (Brit. Acad. Shakespeare lecture, 1942).
28 See C. M. Lewis, *The Genesis of Hamlet* (1907).

Thus for Shakespeare, at this period of devastating clarity, man stands between life and death as between two worlds, both of which elude his grasp and leave him nothing but the chimeras of thought. In the soliloquy, "To be or not to be," Hamlet hesitates to slay himself, for, after all, death may be worse than life. In the beautifully contrasted soliloquy, "Now might I do it pat," he hesitates to slay Claudius, for life may be worse than death. Certitude is a boon enjoyed only by paltry minds: by the parrot actor who feels the fiction of Hecuba's woes like fact, or the undiscriminating Fortinbras who puts all to stake "even for an eggshell." Straws though these are, Hamlet grasps eagerly at them, and for brief moments imagines they will support him in the quicksands of thought. They can, of course, do nothing for one who, while feeling so exquisitely "what a piece of work is a man," must yet confess, "man delights not me." To spare Claudius and slay Polonius, devise death for Rosencrantz and Guildenstern, and walk open-eyed himself into his fate: to him these things are alike indifferent, for death and life are to him equally unreal.

One sees, then, how Shakespeare has lived himself into Hamlet till he produced—probably not in one writing, but after many—a perfect tabernacle for the questioning modern brain. The avenging prince of Saxo's chronicle lived in a dark but entirely material world, and was plain as a pikestaff in his response to its challenge. The hero of Kyd lived among ancient ghosts and nightmares, and struggled with internal rather than external obstacles to action. Shakespeare's Hamlet is a harmony and vastly subtler evolution of them both: he brings the uncompromising mentality of the Norse Amleth into the crepuscular world of Kyd. In his psychology the external and internal are wholly blended. Thought, with its illusions and illuminations, is the only great reality; under its force the so-called facts of material and moral life are dissipated into impalpable fog.

Hamlet, which in Shakespeare's mature version seems to date from about 1601, and may owe a good deal to the appalling tragedy of Essex in that year, is a play of far greater philosophical density than anything that had preceded it. The Elizabethan Shakespeare had acquired an unrivalled skill in playcraft and a style yet more unequaled; but, except in his greatest sonnets, he had hitherto hardly scratched the surface of his mind. He had done his worldly task and ta'en his wages; and when Elizabeth died, he faced the new era, as one might say, with only *Hamlet* in his scrip.[29]

[29] Certain passages in the preceding paragraphs are quoted from *Shakespeare's Principal Plays* (1935), pp. 48-68, which discusses the early plays more fully than is here possible.

BOOK II
The Renaissance

~∾~

PART III
The Early Stuarts and the Commonwealth
(1603-1660)

I

Shakespeare under James

Horatio's farewell to the dying Hamlet,

> Good night, sweet prince,
> And flights of angels sing thee to thy rest,

was explained by Malone as an allusion to the somewhat similar words with which the Earl of Essex went to his death on February 25, 1601: "When my life and body shall part, send Thy blessed angels, which may receive my soul and convey it to the joys of heaven." This is not impossible; and though skepticism is recommended toward most modern attempts to read politics into Shakespeare, there is every reason to suppose that the death of the young and romantic Essex, involving also Southampton's peril and disgrace, was a more important dividing line in the dramatist's progress than the death of the old Queen twenty-five months later. Essex's attempted uprising may have been a puny thing, but it marked with ghastly conspicuousness the breach of all the loyalties which the poet, and indeed his whole generation, had held unassailable. *Shakespeare and Essex*

Shakespeare's Elizabethan period really ended with the sunny comedies, of which *Twelfth Night* is the last, and the questioning spirit which we may call Jacobean is strong in the play that most immediately followed *Hamlet,* that is, *Troilus and Cressida*. This was registered for publication, February 7, 1603, a few weeks before Elizabeth's death, and is most naturally grouped with the "problem comedies," *Measure for Measure* and *All's Well that Ends Well*.[1] Like *Hamlet, Troilus and Cressida* is a very long play, crammed with poetry and social discontent. The dramatic structure is baffling, and the concluding scenes, though not unshakespearean in style, are so scamped as to be ineffective. In the form in which it survives it was probably not intended for public production; but as the poet's grieved and angry analysis of the disintegration of a heroic age it is quite priceless, and in its best parts it reaches Shakespeare's highest poetic plane.[2] To about the same period and spirit may be assigned the revision of *All's Well that Ends Well,* which is composed in two very different styles. In its first version it may have been the *Love's Labor's Won* that Meres mentions in 1598. Helena, the chief character, is one of the exuberant Elizabethan heroines, *The "Dark Comedies"* *Troilus and Cressida*

---

[1] See W. W. Lawrence, *Shakespeare's Problem Comedies* (1931).
[2] See O. J. Campbell, *Comicall Satyre and Shakespeare's Troilus and Cressida* (San Marino, 1938); and for different views, T. Brooke, "Shakespeare's Study in Culture and Anarchy," *Yale Rev.,* XVII (1928). 571-577, and W. W. Lawrence, "Troilus, Cressida and Thersites," *MLR,* XXXVII (1942). 422-437.

capable of anything except failure and the failure to please. She stoops to conquer with the same irresistible and unreal grace as Rosalind and Viola; but the unpleasant figures of Bertram and Parolles are developed in the later style of social irony and disgust. They belong in a different world from Helena's, and often speak a language that varies as much in its cynicism as in its metrical form from that of the romantic passages. One of the more notable things about the play is the loving care with which Shakespeare has idealized the elderly characters of the king, the countess, and Lord Lafeu. His sources gave him nothing here, and for the purposes of the plot these persons need no such emphasis. They seem to be there to harp upon and to illustrate the virtues of the older time, and to weight the author's denunciation of modern profligacy.

Measure for Measure, acted at court December 26, 1604, was certainly written for King James, who is incidentally flattered in the person of the duke. It is one of Shakespeare's most sociological plays, along with *King Lear* and *Timon of Athens,* which in this respect it resembles; and in the relevance of its theme it is the most contemporary. A recent writer has called it, of all the plays, "the one which bears in it most clearly and unmistakably the impress of Shakespeare's mind and outlook." [3] Its heroine, Isabella, is very beautifully depicted, but it is not a play of love. The problems it deals with are those of city government and of the police court, and its main lesson points the need for sincerity and common sense in public affairs. It is less angry and more seemingly mature than the other dark comedies, offering a more constructive criticism of the new life and carrying psychological analysis in the chief figure, Angelo, almost as far inward as *Hamlet* had done. [4]

The satirical and contemptuous attitude was not normal with Shakespeare; and though in the dark comedies just mentioned he went for a time with the crowd, as he had so often done, the great effect upon him of the Jacobean disillusionment was to induce reflections upon the nature of evil which crystalized into a nobler and deeper poetry than he had yet written. The Elizabethan Shakespeare had not seriously believed in villainy. Richard the Third and even Aaron the Moor tug strongly at our sympathies, and keep their atrocities at so grand a pitch that average human experience hardly resents them. The villains of *The Merchant of Venice* and *Julius Caesar,* Shylock and Cassius, rather turn the tables on their author, as every one has noted; and if Falstaff was intended for the villain of *Henry IV,* he also very gloriously missed his cue. The villains of the high comedies, Don John, Oliver, and Duke Frederick, are bad-tempered dyspeptics whom Shakespeare pushes hither and yon through his plots but denies any real attention. Even

---

[3] C. F. E. Spurgeon, *Shakespeare's Imagery* (1935), p. 290. The essay on *Measure for Measure* in Walter Pater's *Appreciations* (1889) is one of the first serious discussions of the play and still deserves attention.

[4] For a somewhat divergent view, brilliantly developed, see R. W. Chambers, *The Jacobean Shakespeare and "Measure for Measure"* (British Academy Shakespeare lecture, 1938).

Claudius, though capable of the blackest deeds when sufficiently pressed, is a finer fellow than his nephew would like to believe.

The three great tragedies of *Othello, Lear,* and *Macbeth*[5] stand very close *The Great* together, and apart from everything which preceded, in their assertion that *Tragic* the world is full of inscrutable and absorbingly interesting evil. They are *Triad* essentially different from *Hamlet* and from the group of dark comedies: from the latter in that there is nothing in them (unless here and there in *King Lear*) of the satirist, the man who hates the world he lives in and attacks the individuals he dislikes; and from *Hamlet* in that the evil they deal with is wholly objective, not largely a matter of subjective maladjustment to one's environment. There is no suspicion of pique in these plays. For Shakespeare and for his company the advent of King James was unmixed good fortune.[6] He was never happier in a worldly way, few dramatists have ever been, than when, as the laureled favorite of the new court and the idol of playgoers, he sat down to wrestle with the dark work which Lear proposes and which in essence continues through the three plays:

Let them anatomize Regan; see what breeds about her heart. Is there any cause in nature that makes these hard hearts?

It is the most elusive of problems, and Shakespeare has made it more tractable in each of the plays by studying it in almost over-simplified human types. *Lear* and *Macbeth* are placed in very ancient times, not from historic interest, for both plays are crowded with contemporary allusion, but in order to get the characters reduced to their most primitive essentials. *Othello* secures a like effect by presenting its domestic tragedy against a background of war, which likewise pares life down to fundamentals.

Othello, which the young Macaulay called "perhaps the greatest work in Othello the world,"[7] comes near to meriting that daring superlative. For one thing, it is, with the possible exception of *Romeo and Juliet,* the most drenched in poetry of all the plays—if we understand the greatest poetry to be that which voices the most compelling emotions in the most irresistible and bewitching language.[8] The music of the great speeches of Othello and Desdemona is the loveliest in the whole Shakespearean symphony, and these two characters, the most unsophisticated of his creatures, take precedence—not intellectually, but emotionally—over all the men and women in the plays,

> Adam, the goodliest man of men since born
> His sons, the fairest of her daughters Eve.

[5] The most complete interpretation of these plays is still that of A. C. Bradley, *Shakespearean Tragedy* (2ed., 1905). See also Allardyce Nicoll, *Studies in Shakespeare* (1927), six lectures on Shakespearean tragedy. The commentary in the separate editions of J. Q. Adams is very helpful. The contemporary psychological background is covered by L. B. Campbell, *Shakespeare's Tragic Heroes, Slaves of Passion* (Cambridge, 1930).

[6] See C. J. Sisson, *The Mythical Sorrows of Shakespeare* (British Academy Shakespeare lecture, 1934).

[7] T. B. Macaulay in *Knight's Quarterly Magazine* (Jan., 1824, p. 219). See E. E. Stoll, *Othello, an Historical and Comparative Study* (Minneapolis, 1913).

[8] See G. Wilson Knight, "The *Othello* Music," in *The Wheel of Fire* (Oxford, 1930), pp. 107-131,

So one thinks of Othello and Desdemona in the gallery of Shakespeare's figures. Milton's words remind us that Paradise was tenanted by Adam, Eve, and the Devil. The Satan of *Othello*, Iago, is also a character of Miltonic proportions, romantically and sympathetically conceived: a blindly wandering spirit whose evil is the perversion of potentialities for good, whose psychoses are those of a mischievous boy, forever subject to rash urges and unwitting of consequences. He is Shakespeare's greatest and most likable villain, but the impression he makes has been somewhat distorted by two misleading phrases of great critics: Coleridge's "motive-hunting of a motiveless malignity," and Bradley's "deadly coldness." If we cannot share Shakespeare's intellectual sympathy with Iago and his sense of the pity of Iago's case, we shall dislike the plot of the play and underrate the hero and heroine.[9] *Othello* is, finally, the most perfectly constructed of all the tragedies, the most classic and harmoniously molded work of art. Its dramatic method is the highest exemplification of what is meant in Sir William Watson's tribute to the poet,

> How welcome, after gong and cymbal's din,
> The continuity, the long, slow slope,
> And vast curves of the gradual violin.[10]

This is not quite to say that *Othello* is Shakespeare's greatest tragedy. Of no one tragedy can that be said. Othello lacks the supreme intellectuality and intimate revelation of the author's self which *Hamlet* offers; it lacks the tremendous world-criticism and cosmic sweep of *Lear* and *Macbeth*. But it is (with *Antony and Cleopatra*) the most richly human, and in the Greek sense the most beautiful of them all.

Othello was performed at court, November 1, 1604. *King Lear* and *Macbeth* followed in quick succession. It is not quite certain which of the two is earlier; both must have been in existence by the end of 1606, though external evidence seems to be lacking in the case of *Macbeth*. *Lear* is a study of private King Lear selfishness; *Macbeth* of ambition, that is, public selfishness. In *Lear*[11] the theme is bourgeois, in spite of the rank of the protagonists; the vices portrayed are mean and the virtues homely. The simplification is extreme; men and women have been stripped of the vestments of culture and even of their formal Christianity. Lear is a barbarian, worshiping sun, moon, stars, and pagan gods.[12] The springs of conduct are laid starkly bare, and the Browningesque moral, "It's wiser being good than bad," is cut deeply into this monolithic play. It asserts the self-destroying nature of sin and

    [9] See T. Brooke, "The Romantic Iago," *Yale Rev.*, VII (1918). 349-359; E. E. Stoll, *Shakespeare and Other Masters* (Cambridge, Mass., 1940), chs. V-VII.
    [10] Epigram, "After Reading *Tamburlaine the Great.*"
    [11] See S. A. Tannenbaum, *Shakespeare's "King Lear": A Concise Bibliography* (1940); and note two important recent papers by W. W. Greg: *The Variants in the First Quarto of King Lear* (Bibl. Soc., 1940); "Time, Place, and Politics in *King Lear*," *MLR*, XXXV (1940). 431-446.
    [12] For the relation of the play to its sources see R. W. Chambers, *"King Lear"* (Glasgow, 1940; W. P. Ker Memorial Lecture); W. W. Greg, "The Date of *King Lear* and Shakespeare's Use of Earlier Versions of the Story," *Library*, XX (1940). 377-400.

the world-regenerating power of such naïve virtue as is pictured in Kent, Albany, Cordelia, and Edgar.

Almost equally primitive in its setting, Macbeth [13] is a study of two char- **Macbeth** acters, whose finest quality, their mutual love, becomes under evil ambition the means of their ruin. Nothing in Shakespeare is more poignant than the interplay of influence between Macbeth and his wife. Without the other, neither would have sinned; for Macbeth's exorbitant ambition has plenty of natural checks and balances, and her urgency in crime is so wholly altruistic and so uncomprehending as to be almost virtuous. And hardly anything in Shakespeare is so just and delicate as the chiastic movement of their two minds under the stress of sin. Macbeth, having by the first murder violated his imaginative controls, finds his imagination atrophy and die, till in the awful soliloquy, "Tomorrow, and tomorrow, and tomorrow," his mind is as empty as a lunar landscape; whereas Lady Macbeth, giving the dare to the imaginative bugbears she has never felt ("A little water clears us of this ˙deed"), is bedeviled to death by the new fancies that are her penalty. No more than in *King Lear* is there any Christian feeling in *Macbeth*.[14] In both plays Shakespeare is studying minds cleaned, like laboratory specimens, of everything extrinsic. This, perhaps, is what gives them their universal power and makes them seem so much like Aeschylus.

It would appear that, while writing *Macbeth,* Shakespeare was meditating another Roman tragedy out of Plutarch which should be the sequel to *Julius Caesar*. Macbeth's mind is strangely occupied with the story of Mark Antony. In III. i. he rather forcedly compares Banquo and himself to Octavius and Antony; in v. viii. he speaks of playing "the Roman fool" and dying on his own sword; and Banquo, in the scene with the witches (I. iii. 84 f.), uses words,

> have we eaten on the insane root
> That takes the reason prisoner?

which have very little meaning for persons who have not read Plutarch's account of Antony's Parthian campaign.[15] *Antony and Cleopatra* was reg- **Antony and** istered for publication on May 20, 1608, nearly nine years after the date of **Cleopatra** *Julius Caesar*. That play had ended with the battle of Philippi in 42 B.C.; this one proceeds with the story from Fulvia's death in 40 B.C. to that of Cleopatra in 30.[16] Historically, it is a much looser play than its predecessor, just as the second part of *Henry IV* is looser than the first; but psychologically it is far more intense. The characters are older, hard-bitten veterans and sophisticates, who in the decade (more or less) since Philippi have definitely entered middle age. The important ones are of the age of Shakespeare

[13] See S. A. Tannenbaum, *Shakespeare's "Macbeth": A Concise Bibliography* (1939); E. E. Stoll, "Source and Motive in *Macbeth* and *Othello*," *RES*, XIX (1943). 25-32; A. N. Stunz, "The Date of *Macbeth*," *ELH*, IX (1942). 95-105.
[14] For the supernatural atmosphere see W. C. Curry, *Shakespeare's Philosophical Patterns* (Baton Rouge, 1937).
[15] See *Shakespeare's Plutarch* (Shakespeare Classics, 1909), II. 72 f.
[16] For this play as well as *Coriolanus* see M. W. MacCallum, *Shakespeare's Roman Plays and Their Background* (1910); and G. Wilson Knight, *The Imperial Theme* (Oxford, 1931).

himself, who is now mature enough to appreciate Plutarch as he had not fully done in *Julius Caesar,* and who uses him with a superb mastery.

The influence of *Macbeth* is strong in *Antony and Cleopatra.* Here also, and even more distinctly than in *Macbeth,* the tragedy is two-fold, treating the fate of a devoted pair so opposite in mind and temperament that each brings out the best in the other only at the cost of ruin. To make this clear, Shakespeare has ventured his very boldest experiment in structure, for he has written two conclusions into *Antony and Cleopatra.* The fourth act is Antony's catastrophe, the fifth act Cleopatra's. To maintain this doubled tension was perhaps the hardest task his creative energy ever undertook. By all reason the fifth act should be an anticlimax; by all experience it is not. There is really no fourth act in the play, to build up for the great *finales,* and the middle portion is therefore so broken and synoptic that the modern stage can hardly attempt it. Here Shakespeare was obliged to construct with fragments, making lines do the work of scenes, and his genius responded extraordinarily to the challenge. A short speech of Cleopatra illustrates:

> O my lord, my lord,
> Forgive my fearful sails! I little thought
> You would have followèd (III. xi. 54-56).

There is no more, but this tells all. Cleopatra entered the play demanding a measure of Antony's love; the first line she speaks is,

> If it be love indeed, tell me how much.

At Actium she found an opportunity for the test, and the test, though costly beyond almost anything in history, was successful. From this point Cleopatra's temperament changes and she grows gentle; from this point she is a satisfied woman. Whole acts have been written about less; but Shakespeare has achieved a brilliant economy by applying the wisdom of the Wife of Bath to one of the puzzles of classical history. The lovers' progress, from Romeo and Juliet, the victims of chance, to Troilus and Cressida, the victims of environment, and so to Antony and Cleopatra, the victims of their own character, shows the upward climb of Shakespeare's art. *Antony and Cleopatra* is the greatest of these great plays. It is a play of such compacted power and understanding that one can hardly admit that Shakespeare wrote any greater.

Coriolanus   In *Coriolanus* he turns back from the lush civilization of the Augustan age to the infancy of the Roman republic and to the primitive types which particularly attracted his analysis. *Coriolanus,* which is of about the same date as *Antony and Cleopatra* (1607-8) and likewise based on Plutarch, deals with a large and simple hero conceived on the lines of Othello, Lear, and Macbeth. He might be an African chief or a robber captain. His generous and childish nature is wholly dominated by pride, and his mother and wife are framed in the same proportions. It is evident that they have no chance of survival in a complex society; progress rests with the mean little people, the Siciniuses and Brutuses, and with the horrid mob who demand betterment of their condition. *Coriolanus* is one of the most political of Shakespeare's plays. Hazlitt has described it as the creed of an arch-aristocrat, and so it is, if one judges by poetic sympathies; but it is no play on which to base a reasoned defense of oligarchy. Probably the poet wrote into it his nostalgia for the heroes of his youth, the colorful, useless, and totally extinct barons of the Wars of the Roses, and perhaps he thought of Sir Walter Ralegh; but his obvious purpose in selecting the subject was the same as in *Othello, Lear,* and *Macbeth:* to find an uncomplicated specimen for his psychological analysis. ·

Another play, *Timon of Athens,* belongs in this category, a play only partly Shakespeare's and of uncertain date. Stylistically, so far as Shakespeare's part goes, it most suggests *King Lear,* and it is animated by the same bitter wrath against ingratitude. Timon's story has been interpreted as a parable of the fate of Essex,[17] and, from the point of view of an adherent of Essex, there is a similarity between them. On the other hand, the theme seems to have come to Shakespeare's notice in Plutarch's Life of Antony, and is not very likely to have been worked up thence until *Antony and Cleopatra* was finished. Moreover, there is plausibility in Sir Edmund Chambers' suggestion [18] that the incompleteness of the play might be due to a physical breakdown (not recorded), which could have cut short the poet's tragic period and put an end for evermore to these strenuous analyses of the human mind.

Timon of Athens

Pericles, Prince of Tyre, was entered on the Stationers' Register the same day as *Antony and Cleopatra* (May 20, 1608), but it is marked by a later style and might naturally have followed the hypothetical illness just referred to.[19] It is Shakespeare's only from the third act on, and no reason can be imagined for allowing the author of the first two acts to do what he did, except that Shakespeare's services and advice were unprocurable at the time. The story is from Gower's *Confessio Amantis* and is an outgrowth of the travelogue-and-missing-persons literature of the Alexandrian Greek romances. Shakespeare's part begins with the announcement of Marina's birth, and his contribution was primarily the creation of a new type of heroine, gentler, less self-confident, and more childish-seeming than those in his earlier comedies. To the disgust of Ben Jonson (whose proclaimed contempt may have caused the exclusion of *Pericles* from the Shakespeare Folio), this ill-constructed play had an outstanding and long success, for the Jacobeans were well convinced that they were a coarse generation, and they found the same zest the dark ages did in virgin saints.

The Last Plays

Pericles

Such figures, drawn from a paternal or even grandfatherly point of view, and suffused with the enchantment of distance, appear in all the later plays

[17] See Dixon Wecter, "Shakespeare's Purpose in *Timon of Athens,*" *PMLA,* XLIII (1928). 701-721.

[18] *William Shakespeare,* I. 86.

[19] See, however, T. S. Graves, "On the Date and Significance of *Pericles,*" *MP,* XIII (1916). 177-188.

Cymbeline, The Winter's Tale, and *The Tempest.*[20] There is a half-holiday atmosphere about the entire group, a valedictory note, as of a virtuoso displaying his skill for his own delight. They are all *tours de force,* special exercises in difficult technique. *Cymbeline* practises the utmost intricacy in tying and resolving a complex plot. *The Tempest* performs the gratuitous feat of limiting a highly unreal fable to the strictest unity of time, place, and action. *The Winter's Tale* takes two half-plays, one a realistic tragedy, the other an idyllic pastoral, and glues them together with a Chorus and the lapse of sixteen years. There are critics who will condemn one of these plays and laud the others;[21] but the spirit and essential genius are the same in all, and each in its particular way is unique. They are plays of light touch and easy mastery, but they should not be called plays of easy optimism. Shakespeare wrote nothing after the opening of the seventeenth century which ignores or palliates the evil in the world. The brothel scenes in *Pericles* and the workings of Leontes' jealousy in *The Winter's Tale* are as foul as anything he has pictured; the bad characters in *Cymbeline* and *The Tempest* are fully as unforgivable and as unforgiven as any earlier reprobates. If Cloten and his mother, or Antonio and Sebastian, seem relatively inconsiderable factors in the final balance which these last plays present, that is in no way at variance with Shakespeare's philosophy in the so-called tragic period. He never wrote anything so dark or cynical as to hide his pious faith that the good elements in life are enduring and constructive, while the evil must by their own nature reform themselves or perish.

The wheel of Shakespeare's art came full circle and left no broken arc. Though he died at fifty-two, his life is one of the completest of which record remains. The last plays show his mind returning, as his body returned, to the pastoral and richly storied country out of which it had come. He had four or five years of ease at Stratford, varied, so far as we know, only by the rather minor help he gave his pupil Fletcher in some dramatic spectacles for the Globe: *The Two Noble Kinsmen,*[22] which attempted to bring on the stage the chivalrous magnificence of Chaucer's longest Canterbury Tale; and the great pageant of *Henry VIII,* which, ending in the elaborate show of Queen Elizabeth's baptism, was thereby also a contribution to the current rejoicings over the marriage of her namesake, the Princess Elizabeth (1613). It was fitting that the "chambers" or small cannon, which had added to the joyous clamor of *Henry V* when the Globe was new, should be employed again in *Henry VIII;* and it was rather fitting that on this occasion (June 29, 1613) one of them should misfire and reduce to ashes the shell out of which the genius of Shakespeare was departing.

[20] See E. M. W. Tillyard, *Shakespeare's Last Plays* (1938); E. E. Stoll, *Shakespeare and Other Masters* (1940), ch. VIII; Theodore Spencer, "Appearance and Reality in Shakespeare's Last Plays," *MP,* XXXIX (1942). 265-274.
[21] E.g., F. R. Leavis, "The Criticism of Shakespeare's Latest Plays," *Scrutiny,* X (1942). 339-345.
[22] See Theodore Spencer, *"The Two Noble Kinsmen,"* MP, XXXVI (1939). 255-276.

II

Jacobean Drama: I. Dramatists of the Old School[1]

Thomas Dekker [2] (*c.* 1572-1632) wrote under the influence of Marlowe *Dekker* and Shakespeare; echoes of both can be found almost everywhere in his work, but he was a looser technician and in his total effect is more likely to recall Greene. *Old Fortunatus,* based upon much the same sort of German folklore as *Doctor Faustus* and full of Marlovian allusions, does not quite reach tragic intensity, and ends by being an improvement on Greene's *Orlando Furioso.*[3] The *Shoemakers' Holiday,* though it imitates *Romeo and Juliet* [4] and contains little hints at *Henry V,* which was being played at the Globe when it went on at the Rose, has more of the pleasant homeliness and romantic variety of *Friar Bacon and Friar Bungay,* from which it borrows the name of its hero, Lacy, and the idea of a disguised noble wooing a socially unsuitable sweetheart.

Dekker is first heard of in 1598, in the service of Marlowe's old company, the Lord Admiral's, for whom, according to Henslowe's Diary, he wrote ten plays and collaborated in about thirty in the period from 1598 to 1602. In the second year, 1599, he reached the peak of his production with the two plays just mentioned, *Old Fortunatus* and *The Shoemakers' Holiday,* both of which were acted at Queen Elizabeth's court during the Christmas season of that year. Thereafter, though he lived for an entire generation longer, he never did anything better or essentially different. Romance and realism are never separate in Dekker. He loved the fairy tale and loved the streets of London, and he mingled the two in most of his plays in a manner to recall the less categorical days of Peele and Greene. His wildest

---

[1] See W. W. Greg, *A Bibliography of the English Printed Drama to the Restoration,* Vol. I. plays to 1616 (1939) and for plays printed after 1616, Greg's *List of English Plays written before 1643 and printed before 1700* (1900); G. E. Bentley, *The Jacobean and Caroline Stage* (2v, Oxford, 1941-   ); U. M. Ellis-Fermor, *The Jacobean Drama* (1936); H. W. Wells, *Elizabethan and Jacobean Playwrights* (1939); Gamaliel Bradford, *Elizabethan Women* (Cambridge, Mass., 1936). There is still value in J. R. Lowell, *The Old English Dramatists* (1893) and A. C. Swinburne, *The Age of Shakespeare* (1908). T. S. Eliot, *Elizabethan Essays* (1934) contains brief reviews of Jonson, Middleton, Heywood, Tourneur, Ford, Massinger, and Marston (besides Marlowe and Shakespeare).

[2] R. H. Shepherd, *The Dramatic Works of Thomas Dekker* (4v, 1873); five plays are reprinted in the Mermaid Series with introduction by E. Rhys; criticism in M. L. Hunt, *Thomas Dekker* (1911); A. H. Bullen, *Elizabethans* (1924), pp. 73-94; K. L. Gregg, *Thomas Dekker, a Study in Economic and Social Backgrounds* (Seattle, 1924). See S. A. Tannenbaum, *Thomas Dekker: A Concise Bibliography* (1939).

[3] Dekker's devil-play, *If It Be Not Good, the Devil Is in It* (1612), uses the Friar Rush legend, as well as much other diabolical machinery, including Guy Fawkes; but it is too incoherent to be entertaining. The same disorderliness appears in a later tragicomedy, *Match Me in London* (1631), a play the present writer cannot praise.

[4] See R. A. Law, "*The Shoemakers' Holiday* and *Romeo and Juliet,*" *SP,* xxi (1924). 356-361.

piecework was done for an occasion, in 1601, when he grafted some very delightful scenes satirizing Ben Jonson upon an unfinished romantic tragedy of William Rufus and called it *Satiromastix,* in order that Shakespeare's company and the Children of Paul's might have a quick answer to Jonson's *Poetaster.*

By Jonson's standards Dekker was a primitive playwright; "a very simple honest fellow," the former called him, and "a dresser of plays about the town here." [5] But his art is so deeply rooted in poetry that it has the quality of other primitive things, the ability to survive and flourish amid conditions that would kill a more specialized type. Dekker throve even on collaboration. Much of his best work is in plays he did with men quite unlike himself: in *Patient Grissell* (1600) with Chettle and Haughton, in three plays with Webster,[6] in *The Roaring Girl* (1611) with Middleton, *The Virgin Martyr* (c. 1620) with Massinger, *The Sun's Darling* (1624) with Ford, *The Witch of Edmonton* (c. 1622) with Ford and William Rowley, and the lost play which must have resembled the last named, *The Late Murder in White-chapel* (1624) with Ford, Rowley, and Webster.[7] Dekker's function in all these is to keep a current of the older poetry flowing into the new dramaturgy.[8] He may have had Middleton's assistance, though slightly, in the first of the two great plays of *The Honest Whore* (1604-1608). The theme is the romantic one of the converted courtesan, ultra-romantically presented on a background of starkest realism. The scene is Milan, but the subject, of course, is London. One play ends at Bedlam, the other at Bridewell, and both end happily. The second part, supposed to occur years later, might be thought an inferior sequel, if the introduction of a new figure, Bellafront's father, did not do for it what the introduction of Justice Shallow does for the second part of *Henry IV.* The character and shop of Candido, the linendraper, are as good London realism as the shop and character of Simon Eyre in *The Shoemakers' Holiday;* and Candido's well known speech at the end of Part I of *The Honest Whore* is quintessential Dekker. A dramatist's personality is often miniatured in his treatment of the virtue he most esteems. For Marlowe this virtue was intelligence, for Shakespeare mercy, for Chapman justice. For Dekker, who was in and out of debtor's prison all his life, the great virtue is the one of which Candido speaks:

> Patience, my lord! why, 'tis the soul of peace;
> Of all the virtues, 'tis nearest kin to Heaven.
> It makes men look like gods. The best of men
> That e'er wore earth about him, was a sufferer,
> A soft, meek, patient, humble, tranquil spirit,
> The first true gentleman that ever breathed.

(margin note) s Primi- e Art

[5] *Poetaster,* III. iv. 320 f.
[6] See later in this chapter.
[7] See C. J. Sisson, *Lost Plays of Shakespeare's Age* (Cambridge, 1936), pp. 80-124.
[8] See G. F. Reynolds, "Aims of a Popular Elizabethan Dramatist," *PQ,* xx (1941). 340-344.

Dekker spent all his life in London. No Londoner was ever more like *The Qua* Charles Lamb, and Lamb, of course, has known how to praise him.[9] But *of His* there is a peculiarity about Dekker's London realism, when compared with *Realism* Jonson's or Middleton's, which suggests a query. The name Dekker, or in Henslowe's spelling Dickers and Deckers, seems hardly English and may be Dutch, and there may be a connection between the dramatist and Father John Dekkers (1560-1619), who was born at Hazebrouck in Flanders and educated at Douai, where he met the martyr poet, Robert Southwell, whose life he later wrote in Latin.[10] However this be, there is something in Dekker's inveterate interest in dialect, Irish, Welsh, French, Spanish, thieves' Latin, and particularly Dutch, which may reflect a foreign background, and his pictures of London are unique in their longer focus. Such scenes as the best, for instance, in *The Shoemakers' Holiday*—early morning in Tower street (II. iii), Eyre's election to the shrievalty (III. iv), the party at Old Ford (III. v), Jane in the sempster's shop (IV. i), Firk outwitting Oatley and Lincoln (IV. v), the "stir" outside St. Faith's (v. ii), and the pancake feast at Leadenhall (v. iv)—are as admirable in their special functions as those of Dekker's competitors; but Dekker's scenes have a general value also as picturing aspects of London life through the ages. His eye, as a partly foreign eye often does, sees the continuing characteristics, where the strictly native observer is concerned with the affairs of the moment. A reader of Dekker will be reminded of Chaucer and Dickens almost as often as of Jonson and Middleton, and this is a tribute to his selective art.

With Dekker and Shakespeare, Thomas Heywood [11] (c. 1570-1641) is one *Thomas* of the three main props of the bridge by which the drama of Marlowe *Heywood* communicates with that of Jonson. He was proverbially productive and refers in one of his prefaces to 220 plays in which he had "either an entire hand or at the least a main finger." [12] About ten per cent of this number survive, though by no effort of Heywood, who takes pride in the fact that his plays "are not exposed unto the world in volumes, to bear the title of works," [13] and elsewhere [14] declares, "It hath been no custom in me of all other men ... to commit my plays to the press." He remained faithful to

[9] In *Specimens of English Dramatic Poets* (1808).
[10] *Catholic Record Society*, v (1908). 294. This might explain Dekker's indictment as a recusant in 1626 (see F. P. Wilson, "Three Notes on Thomas Dekker," *MLR*, xv (1920). 82-85). Though his allegorized drama on Queen Elizabeth, *The Whore of Babylon* (1607), might argue against his being a Catholic, he was certainly not a Puritan or an unbeliever.
[11] R. H. Shepherd, *The Dramatic Works of Thomas Heywood* (6v, 1874); five plays are reprinted in the Mermaid Series with introduction by J. A. Symonds. Consult A. M. Clark, *A Bibliography of Thomas Heywood* (Oxford, 1927); S. A. Tannenbaum, *T. Heywood: A Concise Bibliography* (1939); A. M. Clark, *Thomas Heywood, Playwright and Miscellanist* (Oxford, 1931); Otelia Cromwell, *Thomas Heywood, a Study in the Elizabethan Drama of Everyday Life* (New Haven, 1928).
[12] *The English Traveller.* The following anonymous plays have in recent times been suggested as additions to the Heywood canon: *How a Man May Choose a Good Wife from a Bad*, 1602 (see J. Q. Adams, *ESt*, xlv (1912). 30-44); *No-body and Some-body*, 1606; *The Fair Maid of the Exchange*, 1607 (see L. A. Hibbard, *MP*, vii (1909). 383-394); P. Aronstein, *ESt*, xlv (1912). 45-60); *A Warning for Fair Women*, 1599 (see J. Q. Adams, *PMLA*, xxviii (1913). 594-620); *Captain Thomas Stukeley*, 1605 (see J. Q. Adams, *JEGP*, xv (1916). 1-23).
[13] *The English Traveller*, Preface.
[14] *The Rape of Lucrece*, Preface.

the acting company of which he was a member, for which he wrote most of his dramas, and beyond which he seems to have desired no fame. This company, known as the Earl of Worcester's, and after James's accession as the Queen's, was the least distinguished of the three that regularly performed in London, and had a rather low-class clientele. Heywood, a gentleman of a good Lincolnshire family [15] and a graduate of Cambridge, devoted himself very honorably to giving his audience what it needed. He is seldom highly poetic, as Dekker is, but seldom writes beneath his subject. In a very high degree he is clear and emotionally sound. He did not aim at being readable, but is; and his plays well justify the Horatian motto which often appeared on their title-pages, *Aut prodesse solent, aut delectare*.[16] They are seldom strict tragedies or strict comedies, and few of them meet the definition of tragicomedy. They tend to be slices of life and cross-sections of history. Four types may perhaps be distinguished:

(*a*) Classical plays. "The Four Ages" is a panorama of Greek myth, organized into five plays, the *Golden Age, Silver Age, Brazen Age,* and two parts of the *Iron Age.* In the first three Homer appears as introducer, but the chief source is Caxton's Troy Book in the edition of 1596, which offered a corpus of the legends, from the earliest tales of the gods (*Golden Age*) to the stories of the fates of the warriors who had fought at Troy (*2 Iron Age*).[17] Heywood dramatizes this mass with vigor and variety, in many forms of verse, sometimes imitating Marlowe and Shakespeare, sometimes satisfying himself with merely workmanlike dialogue. The relation between the first part of the *Iron Age* and *Troilus and Cressida* is very interesting, particularly in the character of Thersites; and in the last act of the second part there is a situation clearly borrowed from *Hamlet* (III. iv), where Agamemnon's ghost appears to Orestes while invisible to the latter's mother. Heywood's purpose in these plays, as he stated it, was

> to unlock the casket long time shut,
> Of which none but the learned keep the key,[18]

and he reminds his readers that "these were the plays often (and not with the least applause) publicly acted by two companies upon one stage at once." [19] Dr. Adams [20] has interpreted these words to mean that Shakespeare's company coöperated with Heywood's in "a philanthropic attempt to popularize Greek culture among the middle classes of London"; and it is likely enough, for the friendly relations of the two dramatists are well established, and the presentation of the "Four Ages" would have strained the resources of Heywood's troupe.

15 See K. L. Bates, "A Conjecture as to Thomas Heywood's Family," *JEGP*, XII (1913). 1-17.
16 *Ars poetica*, line 333: "Aut prodesse volunt aut delectare poetae."
17 See J. S. P. Tatlock, "The Siege of Troy in Elizabethan Literature, especially in Shakespeare and Heywood," *PMLA*, XXX (1915). 673-770; R. G. Martin, "Notes on Thomas Heywood's *Ages*," *MLN*, XXXIII (1918). 23-29.
18 Prologue to *The Silver Age*.
19 Preface to *The Iron Age*, Part One. "Not with the least applause" means with very considerable applause.
20 J. Q. Adams, "Shakespeare, Heywood, and the Classics," *MLN*, XXXIV (1919). 336-339.

Early Roman history out of Livy is treated in similar manner in Hey- *Heywood's* wood's *Rape of Lucrece* (1608). The title was nearly inevitable in view of *Roman* the popularity of Shakespeare's poem, but the story of Lucrece is only one *Plays* in a series of episodes, beginning with the usurpation of Tarquin the Proud and murder of Servius, and running through the exploits of Horatius at the bridge and of Mutius Scaevola, to close with the deaths of Sextus Tarquin and Brutus in single combat and the establishment of the Roman republic. Lucrece is not very sympathetically portrayed, the author's chief interest being in the patriot Brutus and his amusing co-conspirator Valerius, whose highly anachronistic songs did most to account for the play's great success. These songs are nearly as numerous, varied, and excellent as those in *The Beggar's Opera*, and if added to the ones Heywood wrote for the "Four Ages" would make a remarkable anthology. In *Appius and Virginia* (printed in 1654 as by Webster alone) [21] we have probably another example of Heywood's desire to make Livy palatable on the stage. In *The Captives* [22] (c. 1624) he has tried his hand at modernizing a comedy of Plautus, the *Rudens*. This, of course, was something that Chapman and Jonson had already done with all the prestige of their learning; but Heywood's is no humor play or satire. It romanticizes the theme simply, and in so far as it resembles those other writers resembles Jonson in his very early *Case Is Altered*.

(b) English history.[23] The two parts of *King Edward the Fourth* (1599), *Heywood's* published in six editions without Heywood's name, are, though early, good *Treatment* examples of his method, and they explain well what Lamb meant in calling *of English* him a "prose Shakespeare." The material covered overlaps that of Shake- *History* speare's *Richard III* to a considerable extent and many of the same characters appear; but where the latter fixes upon the melodramatic and tragic aspects of history, Heywood's genial plays give us the bourgeois and episodic elements in the same life. It is a tribute to the untrammeled Elizabethan art that the same sources could be so effectively employed in such different directions. Heywood's two plays on Queen Elizabeth, which he labeled *If You Know Not Me, You Know Nobody* (1605), have the same homely quality. The first part,[24] based very closely on Foxe's *Book of Martyrs*, is a sentimental record of Elizabeth's dangers and privations during Mary's reign. The second part does what Heywood dearly loves to do: it pictures, by means of a large group of bourgeois or humble characters, the day-by-day life of England in the great queen's reign. A much later play, *Dick of*

---

[21] Against the prevailing view that this play is mainly Heywood's, see H. D. Sykes, "Webster's *Appius and Virginia*," in *Sidelights on Elizabethan Drama* (1924), pp. 108-139; and on the other side A. M. Clark, "The Authorship of *Appius and Virginia*," *MLR*, XVI (1921). 1-17.
[22] Ed. A. C. Judson (New Haven, 1921). See A. H. Gilbert, "Thomas Heywood's Debt to Plautus," *JEGP*, XII (1913). 593-611.
[23] See L. B. Wright, "Heywood and the Popularizing of History," *MLN*, XLIII (1928). 287-293, and *Middle-class Culture in Elizabethan England* (Chapel Hill, 1935), pp. 603-654.
[24] See Mary I. Fry, "*The Troubles of Queene Elizabeth*," *Huntington Library Bull.*, no. 2 (1931), pp. 172-176; and G. N. Giordano-Orsini, "Thomas Heywood's Play on *The Troubles of Queen Elizabeth*," *Library*, XV (1933). 313-338.

Devonshire,[25] follows in more romantic fashion the exploits of Richard Peeke of Tavistock as recorded in his *Three to One* (1626).

Heywood's Dramatic Romances

(*c*) Romances. Recent English history lends a stiffening also to the two parts of the *Fair Maid of the West*, first printed in 1631 but acted much earlier, and to *Fortune by Land and Sea* by Heywood and William Rowley (not printed till 1655). They are among Heywood's most attractive works. Basing one on Essex's "Island Voyage," which started from Plymouth in 1597, and the other on the capture of the pirates Purser and Clinton in 1583, he contrives in each case a tissue of wild adventure involving excellently handled sea-fights, duels, Moroccan kings, tavern bullies, and hard-souled villains, all leading to happy conclusions and the greater glory of his heroines, Bess Bridges and Anne Harding, who, though wholly unreal, are among the most charming women of minor Elizabethan drama. *The Four Prentices of London*, one of Heywood's earliest plays, though not printed till 1615, is a mere foretaste of this style, the use of history being blatantly absurd, and the only purpose of the play that which it achieved, of flattering the lighter-brained members of the livery companies. There is as much romance and more dignity in two pleasant later plays, *A Challenge for Beauty* (1636) and *The Royal King and Loyal Subject* (1637). Each has the distinct double plot that Heywood loved and the fundamental assumption of the superiority of Englishmen in honor, valor, and generosity. The heroine of the *Challenge* resembles Shakespeare's Imogen in situation and somewhat in character; the Lady Mary Audley, the loyal true-love in the less conspicuous plot of the *Royal King*, is another of Heywood's memorable women. In *A Maidenhead Well Lost* (1634) Heywood uses a title that might suggest Middleton for a play as innocent (almost) as *Cinderella*, and nearly as full of the fairy-tale atmosphere. The last words of the foiled Iago of this not very powerful piece are:

> Who would strive
> To be a villain, when the good thus thrive!

Heywood's Realism

(*d*) Bourgeois realism. Most of the plays in the two preceding groups contain scenes of literal realism which give ballast and humanity to Heywood's high-flying romance. His best plays are those in which he most restricts himself to the local scene. The cleverest, though in some ways the most uncharacteristic, is *The Wise-Woman of Hogsdon* (1638), which limits its action to London and its theme to the inconstancy of young men. Nothing more effective could well be found than the gambling scene with which this play opens or the intricate and exciting dénouement with which it closes. The whole comedy, indeed, which is mainly in prose, is superbly plotted; but, without being at all bitter, it lacks the heart interest one expects in Heywood.

[25] First printed in Bullen's *Collection of Old English Plays*, vol. II (1883). See J. B. Rowe, "Richard Peeke of Tavistock, his *Three to One*," *Devon Notes and Queries*, III, Part 2 (Exeter, 1905).

The fact is, Heywood's heart was no more than Shakespeare's in London, and his best play is an earlier one, *A Woman Killed with Kindness,* which he set in the grim land that the balladists knew as "the north countree," and shaped more tragically than was his wont. Since Henslowe's final payment for it was made on March 6, 1603, it may rank as the last great play of Queen Elizabeth's reign. It came three years after Dekker's *Shoemakers' Holiday* and a year and a half before *Othello,* with both of which it has interesting relationships. The three works illustrate the best that was being offered to the public by the three chief dramatic companies of the day. The double-barreled plot of the *Woman Killed with Kindness* is based on three stories in Painter's *Palace of Pleasure,*[26] but essential unity and importance are achieved by the authenticity of the realism. One will hardly find in any play more data about the amusements of an Elizabethan country household, the dancing, hunting, hawking, cards, etc.; nor a more exact picture of the evils of that life, the unbridled passions, wild extravagance, the heartless usurers, harsh laws and prisons, and the dangers of casual travel. From all this emerge the characters of Frankford, the perfect gentleman, and Susan Mountford, the ideal sister, and the almost incomparable rustic servants. Heywood's heart was certainly in this play, dealing more than any of his others with the virtue of loyalty, which for him was what Spenser called chastity,

> That highest virtue, far above the rest.

He illustrated it in his life and in many of his writings, but *A Woman Killed with Kindness* is a perfect symphony on loyalty in the various relations of husband and wife, sister and brother, host and guest, master and servant.[27]

In a later and rather strangely titled play, *The English Traveller* (1633), Heywood returned to the same theme with an angrier arraignment of marital disloyalty and false friendship. The hero, young Geraldine, is almost as finely conceived as Frankford, but the erring characters are villainous hypocrites, as they had not been in *A Woman Killed with Kindness,* and the secondary plot, out of Plautus's *Mostellaria,* lacks the harmony with the main theme that Heywood was usually able to provide.

John Webster[28] (*c.* 1580-1638) was no traditionalist, as Dekker and Heywood were, and cannot be grouped with them without some blurring of his uniqueness; but he cannot be classed, either, with the more typical Jacobeans. He was neither a satirist, a defeatist, nor an escapist, and the tone of his greatest works allies him more closely with Shakespeare and

John Webster

[26] See R. G. Martin, "A New Source for *A Woman Killed with Kindness,*" *ESt,* XLIII (1910). 229-233.

[27] See H. D. Smith, "*A Woman Killed with Kindness,*" *PMLA,* LIII (1938). 138-147. Many of the special merits of this play are found also in a later north-country drama, *The Late Lancashire Witches* (1634), ascribed to Heywood and Richard Brome. See C. E. Andrews, "The Authorship of *The Late Lancashire Witches,*" *MLN,* XXVIII (1913). 183-166; R. G. Martin, "Is *The Late Lancashire Witches* a Revision?" *MP,* XIII (1915). 253-265.

[28] See F. L. Lucas, *Complete Works of John Webster* (4v, 1927); E. E. Stoll, *John Webster* (Cambridge, Mass., 1905); Rupert Brooke, *John Webster and the Elizabethan Drama* (1916).

Marlowe than with any of his more exact contemporaries. The record of his life is almost non-existent and the bibliography of his writings exceptionally obscure and fragmentary; two strange facts, since his prefaces indicate that hardly even Jonson had a serener confidence in the merits of his work, and the emphasis the publishers gave his name on title-pages is equal to that they gave to Shakespeare's. The complimentary verses which Middleton, Rowley, and Ford all wrote for *The Duchess of Malfi* are a rare tribute to great (and it would appear, broadly recognized) achievement.

Webster is first mentioned in Henslowe's Diary in 1602 as author of various plays which have now disappeared. One of them, *Lady Jane* (viz., Grey), can probably be traced in *Sir Thomas Wyat*, printed in 1607 as by Dekker and Webster. It is a loose chronicle play, in casual verse and prose, and is most akin to the first part of Heywood's *If You Know Not Me*, which it likewise resembles in being preserved in a very faulty text.[29] In 1604 Webster wrote for Shakespeare's company the famous induction to Marston's *Malcontent*, which, unfortunately brief as it is, gives a priceless view of what went on during a performance at the Globe. About the same time he collaborated with Dekker again in two city comedies for the Children of Paul's, *Westward Ho!* and *Northward Ho!* The former received a notable accolade from Ben Jonson in the prologue to the oppositely-named *Eastward Ho!*

For that was good, and better cannot be.

They are lively and well-plotted pieces, both in prose and both dealing with the amorous amusements of London wives. It is naturally impossible to recognize in them the later Webster, but they do not appear to be overwhelmingly Dekker's work.[30] They are quite devoid of the caustic satire which was the fashion of the day, and, though the language and situations are pungent enough, the moral in both plays is the unfashionable one that the citizens' wives are a good deal better than their reputations. The loss of Webster's play of *Guise* is much to be deplored. He evidently thought well of it, bracketing it with *The White Devil* and *The Duchess of Malfi* in the dedication of his *Devil's Law-Case*. It was most likely founded on Marlowe's *Massacre at Paris* and would probably emphasize the Marlovian strain in Webster. His fame rests now almost wholly upon the two tragedies just mentioned, which are like no other plays of the period.

The White Devil

The White Devil was acted by the Queen's company (Heywood's) and printed in 1612. It concerns the rather recent case of Vittoria Accoramboni, Duchess of Bracciano, who lived from 1557 to 1585. By following the available accounts of her brief and stormy life Webster could have produced a much more plausible tragedy than the one he wrote;[31] but Webster is never plausible, and when he varies from his sources usually does so in order to

[29] See M. F. Martin, "*If You Know Not Me You Know Nobody* and *The History of Sir Thomas Wyat*," *Library*, XIII (1932). 272-281; W. L. Halstead, "Note on the Text of . . . *Sir Thomas Wyatt*," *MLN*, LIV (1939). 585-589.

[30] See F. E. Pierce, *The Collaboration of Webster and Dekker* (1909).

[31] See B. Colonna, *La nipote di Sisto V: il dramma di Vittoria Accoramboni* (Milan, 1936), and Lucas's historical introduction, *Works of Webster*. I. 70-90.

emphasize the brutal irrationality of life, and thus increases his constructional difficulties. Vittoria in his play is neither white nor a devil. Her
complicity in her husband's murder, though morally certain, is not avowed,
and in the great scene of Act III, in which she is arraigned before Cardinal
Monticelso and the embarrassed ambassadors, Webster allows her all the
honors of the conflict. It is a scene that John Fletcher may be thought to
have done well to copy a year or two later, when he wrote Katharine of
Aragon's defense of herself before Cardinals Wolsey and Campeius.[32] Vittoria has a brother, Flamineo, who is one of the most bloodcurdlingly real
villains in English drama, and a mother, Cornelia, who is one of its most
pathetic creations, a kind of ancient Ophelia. Webster works with terror
and pity, undiluted, and in copious outpourings. He employs ghosts and
horrid dumbshows after the manner of the early Senecans, and has many
of the grisliest stage deaths in literature. Isabella dies by kissing a poisoned
picture of her husband, Camillo's neck is broken by his companions while
vaulting, Brachiano is killed by a poisoned helmet (the pain driving him
mad), Marcello is without warning run through the body by his brother
in their mother's presence; Vittoria, Zanche, and Flamineo are all stabbed
after a scene in which Flamineo has most horridly pretended to be shot
with pistols. The deaths pile up so lawlessly that one is tempted to retort
upon the author the last question in the play:

> By what authority have you committed
> This massacre?

But between these are small and moving voices that protest and point the
pity of it; for instance, the boy Giovanni's talk with his uncle (III. ii) and
Cornelia's mad song (v. i),

> Call for the robin redbreast and the wren,
> Since o'er shady groves they hover,
> And with leaves and flowers do cover
> The friendless bodies of unburied men.

The Duchess of Malfi, which was acted by Shakespeare's company about
1613 and revised a little later, is a better play because, along with as much
terror, it has more pity, and so gives Webster's view of life in better balance.
The plot, derived from Bandello through Painter and based on very early
sixteenth-century history, has been made as absurd as possible. The duchess,
contracting a marriage of love with her honest and knightly master of the
household, must keep it secret from her two domineering brothers, who have
planted a super-spy, Bosola, in her palace to inform them of just such matters.
An average detective would do Bosola's business in a day, but in this play
the obvious is never discernible. Years pass, while Bosola pries and plots.
Children are born and almost grow to maturity in the way Sidney deplored,
before the wicked brothers find a motive for their cruelty. The fourth act

*The
Duchess
of Malfi*

---

[32] *Henry VIII*, III. i. Fletcher's additions to Holinshed's account may be presumed to come
from Webster.

is wholly devoted to the duchess's death, and may well be the greatest death scene in Elizabethan literature. The fifth act, which presents six deaths more, should be an anticlimax, but is kept aloft by Webster's mastery of the macabre.

The business of Webster's plays almost carries one back to the work of Kyd, but his strange art is far more intelligent. His style is curiously un-rhythmic, except in the songs which crash in, like the trumpets of doom, upon the cacophonies of mundane speech. His dialogue is often patched with sayings from Sidney, Montaigne, or Donne, which he had stored in his note-books,[33] and he sometimes introduces formal "characters" such as he was writing for the Overbury collection.[34] His view of life is Elizabethan rather than Jacobean in the sharp distinction he maintains between good and bad and the straightforwardness with which he faces death and horror. He is one of the most romantic of dramatists. Life, he teaches, is a labyrinth. "Wish me good speed," says the Duchess near the beginning of her play,

> For I am going into a wilderness,
> Where I shall find nor path nor friendly clue
> To be my guide.

The only constant is death, up to which he leads his characters relentlessly, and dismisses them under the glare of death's great illumination. He makes no theological assertions, but the reading of him is a kind of religious ex-perience, and if any affinity for him must be sought among the Stuart writers, it will be found in such mystic poets as Herbert and Vaughan. Webster, too, seems constantly to be whispering,

> Dear, beauteous death, the jewel of the just,
> Shining nowhere but in the dark,
> What mysteries do lie beyond thy dust,
> Could man outlook that mark! [35]

No one, however, is more like him than Shakespeare in the latter's darkest moods, and the play that most resembles Webster's two tragedies is *King Lear*. Lear says something very like "I am Duchess of Malfi still," [36] and Gloster parallels Bosola's cosmic despair,

> We are merely the stars' tennis-balls, struck and bandied
> Which way please them.[37]

Webster's most famous line,

> Cover her face; mine eyes dazzle; she died young,

may have had its cue in *King Lear*, v. iii. 242; and perhaps only Shakespeare can bedew his horror with such appeals to simple pity as the Duchess's

[33] See C. Crawford, *Collectanea*, I. 20-46, II. 1-63 (Stratford-upon-Avon, 1906, 1907).
[34] E.g., *White Devil*, III. ii. 82-85 (*ed.* Lucas); *Duchess of Malfi*, I. i. 157-166.
[35] Henry Vaughan, "They are all gone into the world of light."
[36] *King Lear*, IV. vi. 110, "Ay, every inch a king!"
[37] See *King Lear*, IV. i. 36 f.

I pray thee, look thou giv'st my little boy
Some syrup for his cold, and let the girl
Say her prayers ere she sleep.

Webster's two later plays, *The Devil's Law-Case* (1623) and *A Cure for a Cuckold* (printed 1661)—the latter in unfortunate collaboration with Rowley—must be briefly dismissed; not because they are altogether inferior, but because Webster is here attempting tragicomedy and finds that medium too light for his hand. The chief figure of the *Law-Case*, Romelio, the wealthy merchant of Naples, who in one scene disguised as a Jew, is a not unworthy imitation of Marlowe's Barabas, and his mother and sister belong with Webster's greatest women. The long court scene (IV. ii), which occupies a fifth of the play, is comparable with the one in *The White Devil*, and some of Webster's most characteristic lines are in this play, as well as one of his greatest songs,

> Courts adieu, and all delights,
> All bewitching appetites! ·
> Sweetest breath and clearest eye,
> Like perfumes, go out and die.

III

Jacobean Drama: II. The Satiric Group

As the sixteenth century was closing, England found herself afflicted with a sharp seizure of class consciousness and social discontent. The great ardors and endurances of the Spanish war were now past and the piper was to pay. The distribution of wealth had got seriously out of balance; and Gloriana had been reigning forty years, which was too long for a sovereign who refused to make any concessions to the passage of time. The world looked very black to politicians, to gentlefolk of moderate means, and particularly to young people with careers to find.[1]

The Cam-bridge Plays   The spirit of the age is expressed in a burst of quarrelsome and rebellious English plays acted by students of Cambridge in temporary contravention of their habit of Latin drama.[2] *Club Law,*[3] produced at Clare Hall about 1599, is a dramatic lampoon on the mayor of Cambridge and other well-known members of the town. Fuller relates that the cruelty was increased by inviting the persons attacked, with their wives, and forcing them to sit the performance through. Town and gown relations were such that the malefactors, by collusion of the college authorities and their government patrons, escaped punishment. The play is in undistinguished prose, and the author is unknown.[4] It is lively, completely partisan, and of course realistic, charged with the same spirit that in London was sharpening courtiers' pens against the citizens.

The "Parnassus" Group   The *Parnassus* trilogy[5] (*c.* 1598-1602), acted in St. John's College, is more broadly critical and more ambitious in a literary way, though the short first part, *The Pilgrimage to Parnassus,* claims to have been written in "three days' study." This is mainly a verse allegory, and has lines echoing Marlowe's *Hero and Leander,* first printed (so far as known) in 1598. Old Consiliadorus sends two hopeful boys, Philomusus and Studioso, to college, that is, on the pilgrimage to Parnassus. They journey over the appalling countries

---

[1] See L. C. Knights, *Drama and Society in the Age of Jonson* (1937).

[2] When the great plague of 1592-3 suspended productions in London, the Cambridge authorities were asked to provide an English comedy for the Queen's amusement. They replied: "English comedies, for that we never used any, we presently have none." See G. C. Moore Smith, *College Plays Performed in the University of Cambridge* (Cambridge, 1923); and, for a broader view, F. S. Boas, *University Drama in the Tudor Age* (Oxford, 1914).

[3] Ed. G. C. Moore Smith (Cambridge, 1907).

[4] There is an unverifiable tradition that he was George Ruggle, author of the famous Latin comedy, *Ignoramus,* performed before King James in 1615.

[5] See W. D. Macray, *The Pilgrimage to Parnassus, with Two Parts of the Return from Parnassus* (Oxford, 1886); W. J. Lawrence, "The Date of 'The Return from Parnassus, Part II,'" *MLR,* xiv (1919). 324. J. B. Leishman, "The Text of the Parnassus Plays," *RES,* xviii (1942). 395-412.

known as Logic, Dialectic, Rhetoric, etc., meeting various collegiate types: Madido the drunkard, Stupido the Puritan, Amoretto the lover, Ingenioso the literary man. In four years they have reached the foot of Parnassus, i.e., taken the B. A. degree.

The prologue to the second play (*I Return from Parnassus*) [6] informs us that the author, whose name has something to do with Cheshire, has been disciplined for the first part. Seven years have now elapsed, and the pilgrims, having attained their M. A.'s, are facing with great misgivings the necessity of entering the world. Ingenioso, who displays characteristics of Robert Greene and perhaps of Nashe, has found beggarly employment with the printers and the miserly patrons of poetry; Luxurioso falls heir to the trade of the "great-nosed balladmaker," William Elderton, lately deceased (*c.* 1592); Philomusus and Studioso, leaving debts behind them in the Cambridge shops, labor for a while as sexton and male-governess respectively, but are soon dismissed from even those low posts. Consiliadorus points the moral:

> Henceforth let none be sent by careful sires,
> Nor sons nor kindred, to Parnassus hill,
> Since wayward fortune thus rewards our cost
> With discontent, their pains with poverty.
> Mechanic arts may smile, their followers laugh,
> But liberal arts bewail their destiny.

The end is angry despair, and an ironic appeal to the whole body of the university,

> Whatever scholars discontented be,
> Let none but them give us a *Plaudite!*

In the third play, subtitled *The Scourge of Simony,* they are in London, saying, "Fain would I have a living, if I could tell how to come by it;" to which ironic Echo replies, "Buy it!" They discover that church livings are sold to illiterate boors and that scholarship has no market value. In one scene we have Ingenioso haggling with Danter, the piratical publisher of *Romeo and Juliet,* for obscene pamphlets, the only literature that will sell; while Philomusus and Studioso are driven to consider "the basest trade" and make overtures to the patronizing actors, Kempe and Burbage. The interview, however, revolts them, and at the close of this singularly bitter piece they set off for Kent to keep sheep.

Too acute interest in contemporary letters is usually a bad symptom in a university, and the contemporaneity of the literary references in these plays is excessive. In one scene Ingenioso reads from a copy of Bodenham's *Belvedere* hot from the press.[7] To us the scene is arousing, for he reads a list of names beginning with Edmund Spenser and ending with Kit Marlowe. The comment elicited is the only bit of warm youthful enthusiasm in the plays; but Ingenioso and his friends knew all too well that their predecessors,

---

[6] Prologue, line 11. The ascription to John Day is unlikely; see Boas, *op. cit.,* p. 332, note.
[7] Published late in 1600. See above, Part II, ch. I.

Greene, Marlowe, Nashe, and the rest, had left their bones on the shoals against which they were being driven. Even Spenser, who had the highest abilities and the brightest prospects, had now just died—as gossips said, for lack of bread.

Chapman *and Jonson*

George Chapman [8] (1559-1634) was some five years older than Shakespeare and Marlowe, and had been the personal friend of the latter, whose *Hero and Leander* he continued in his own very different fashion. Yet he did not publicly appear as a poet till 1594 or as a playwright till 1596. His initiation in drama came by writing for the Admiral's company under the direction of that illiterate apostle of quick returns, Philip Henslowe, and Chapman was thus brought into contact with Jonson, who was likewise in Henslowe's employ. It is not now possible to say which was the directing influence, though Chapman was the elder by over a dozen years; but it is certain that the ideas mutually struck out by these two abnormally learned and ethical minds gave great effect to a change the times were calling for. Chapman and Jonson recognized that the chronicle and romantic types of drama were passé, and they set out together to make the theatre more realistic while making it more classic.

Chapman's *Comedies*

The Blind Beggar of Alexandria

Chapman's first surviving comedy, *The Blind Beggar of Alexandria*, produced at the Rose in February, 1596, was phenomenally popular. There is a great deal of Marlowe in this flippant but amusing play. The hero is a conquering Tamburlaine, "yet but a shepherd's son at Memphis born." He is also a great lover like Faustus, and a master of craft and multiple disguise like the Jew of Malta. There are some quite lovely Marlovian echoes, and also some lines of rank burlesque, like

And stern Bebritius of Bebritia.

The public evidently delighted in the lively mixture of moods and the complete cynicism with which the women are handled. The text has probably been a good deal corrupted, but at its best the *Blind Beggar* cannot have been much more than a clever skit, an overture to the new fashion.[9]

A Humor-ous Day's Mirth

Early in the next year Chapman's *Comedy of Humors* was produced.[10] Here, some fifteen months before Jonson's more famous comedy, one finds the "humor" theory in considerable development. The action takes place between morning and evening of a single day at the French court, which always had a peculiar interest for Chapman. Lemot, "minion" of the king, has the humor of Jonson's Knowell and Wellbred for collecting and exhibiting gulls. He devises the situations which bring the Puritan lady, the old man with the young wife, the old woman with the young husband, the father suspicious of his young daughter, the wealthy fop, and ultimately even

[8] See *Chapman's Comedies*, ed. T. M. Parrott (1914); A. C. Swinburne, *George Chapman, a Critical Essay* (1875); A. H. Bullen, *Elizabethans* (1924), pp. 49-69; S. A. Tannenbaum, *George Chapman: A Concise Bibliography* (1938).

[9] The popularity of Chapman's *Blind Beggar* produced other disguise plays; e.g., the anonymous *Look about You*, printed 1600, "as it was lately played by" the Admiral's company; and *The Blind Beggar of Bednall Green*, by Chettle and Day (1600).

[10] Printed in 1599 under the title, *An Humorous Day's Mirth*.

the King and Queen of France, in great excitement to Verone's ordinary or inn, whence, we are to suppose, all depart more wise, and with no harm done. As in *Every Man in His Humor*, there is just a trace of true romance in the love of Martia and the melancholy and poetic Lord Dowsecer. Chapman had great dramatic gifts, apart from his superlative intellectual and poetic equipment; but he was not a very good playwright, as compared with Jonson, because he did not stop to develop the new veins he opened. He seems to have been more interested in showing what the drama could do than in doing it, and in this he reflects the restlessness of the age. His next comedy, *All Fools*, acted at the Rose in 1599 and later at Blackfriars, shows how All Fools Terentian plots should be adapted to the modern stage. The intriguing slave has been elevated into a gentleman, Rinaldo, who stands rather outside of the action and, like Lemot, controls the movements of the rest. There is little use of the humor idea. Indeed, the stress is almost wholly on plot, which is so very intricate that a reader finds it hard to follow, though intelligent actors could make it exceedingly diverting.

At this point Chapman found it possible to transfer his plays from the Admiral's company to the boy company of the Children of the Chapel, which opened at Blackfriars in 1600, and for which he wrote all his remaining comedies and most of his tragedies. Doubtless he was attracted by their patrician audience, fashionable and receptive of new ideas; but it is to be remembered in behalf of Chapman and the other dramatists who wrote habitually for the boy companies that service with them had also its drawbacks. The boys could memorize anything and could often get safely by with innovations and innuendoes which would have endangered the public players; but they could not be trusted for deeply emotional effects. Therefore, when one finds *Sir Giles Goosecap*,[11] which was probably his first play at Blackfriars, rather thin, this may indicate a falling off in dramatic *élan*, or may merely mean the exercise of good judgment.[12] The main story is that of Chaucer's *Troilus and Criseyde*,[13] denuded of passion and candor and transferred to Elizabethan polite society. There is much charming verse in this part of the play, and the poet-lover, Clarence, talks a good deal like Chapman himself. The title comes from the name of one of the numerous humor characters that enlarge the piece. Some especially personal matter relating to the drunken Lady Furnifall appears to have been excised in the printed edition.

May-day, which like *Sir Giles Goosecap* may have been writen in 1602, is an exercise in modern Italian comedy, doing for the *Alessandro* of A. Piccolomini (c. 1545) more or less what *All Fools* had done for Terence's *Heautontimorumenos*. It is brisk, gay, and inoffensive. The next two plays, *The Gentleman-Usher* (c. 1603) and *Monsieur d'Olive* (c. 1604), are perhaps Chapman's most attractive comedies. Each takes its name from an elaborate

---

[11] Printed in 1606 without Chapman's name, but certainly by him.
[12] Professor Parrott (*op. cit.*, p. 893) suggests that here Chapman was making a special effort to imitate Jonson.
[13] See G. L. Kittredge, "Notes on Elizabethan Plays," *JEGP*, II (1898). 10-13.

The Gentle-man-Usher and Monsieur d'Olive

humor character. Bassiolo, the gentleman-usher, is indeed an important instrument in the romantic main-plot of the earlier play, but d'Olive, a satire on the new ambassadors King James was sending abroad, is almost unrelated to the serious action. These two plays illustrate the lack of integration of which Chapman is often guilty. In *The Gentleman-Usher* the interest hardly begins till the third act, after which it builds up in a melodramatic manner. In *Monsieur d'Olive,* on the other hand, the opening acts are brilliant in vigor and economy, though they deal with Platonic love and other amorous exaltations à la française, but the action seems to run down in Act IV, and Act V has the effect of a gratuitous addition in another key.

The Widow's Tears

There could hardly be a greater contrast, within the work of a single comic writer and within a couple of years at most, than that between *Monsieur d'Olive* and Chapman's next and last comedy, *The Widow's Tears* (c. 1605).[14] *D'Olive* is remarkable for the pleasant people it presents. The ladies and gentlemen of the main plot are without exception high-minded and engaging; and d'Olive himself, though satirical in intention and genuinely comic, has a Falstaffian robustness that endears him and a harmlessness that is by no means Falstaff's. There are really no pleasant people in *The Widow's Tears,* and the story, that of the Ephesian widow in Petronius, is one of the most cynical in literature. "Bitter" was one of the most popular adjectives of the day; Chapman's characters are fond of throwing it at each other, even in plays which are not bitter. In *The Widow's Tears*—moved by a desire to be in fashion, or by some special disgust with widows, or merely by his propensity to try new things—Chapman has written a play that is entirely bitter. Its tone has been fairly likened to Wycherley's, for the light misogyny of *The Blind Beggar of Alexandria* is here developed past joking. The women are whited sepulchres, and the men are interesting only as the means or discoverers of their lust. The drama is powerfully plotted, and Tharsalio, the intriguer, who here has a large personal interest in the action he contrives, is a character of great force. One must admire the art by which the entire play, harsh as it is, is kept within the true bounds of comedy. It is contemporary with Chapman's earliest tragedies, but it makes no appeal to pity or fear, and is quite without either tragic or tragicomic elements.

Chapman's Tragedies

Bussy d'Ambois,[15] published in 1607 as acted by the Paul's children, is *Tamburlaine* twenty years after. The very first speech, a soliloquy by the hero, contains one of the finest of the great Homeric similes with which Chapman weights his tragedies, and the moral of it is,

> We must to Virtue for her guide resort,
> Or we shall shipwreck in our safest port.

It is the same Virtue in which Tamburlaine had seen the sum of glory, which fashions men with true nobility. Boundless self-confidence and self-assertiveness are its marks, and in these things Bussy resembles Tamburlaine, as well

---

[14] Chapman's joint-work, with Jonson and Marston, in *Eastward Ho!* probably intervened.
[15] See C. E. Engel, "Les sources du Bussy d'Amboise de Chapman," *RLC,* XII (1932). 587-595; R. G. Howarth, "The Date of *Bussy d'Ambois,*" *N&Q,* CLXXVII (1939). 25.

as in the great poetic energy of his speeches. The greatest difference between the two plays is in the constrictedness of the latter. Tamburlaine was a vague and heroic world-conqueror, Bussy a recent French soldier of fortune of no very special achievement, born ten years before Chapman and murdered at the age of thirty. While Tamburlaine scourges kingdoms with his conquering sword, Bussy domineers over a peculiarly ignoble group of courtiers and is assassinated by the husband of the lady he has seduced. The earth-shaking vaunts of *Tamburlaine* and occult agencies of *Dr. Faustus* often seem absurd in *Bussy;* but Chapman strengthens his play by Senecan devices such as the wonderful use of the *nuntius* in II. i, and by large draughts of Stoic philosophy. He also borrows some hints from the comedy of humors. Bussy, Monsieur, and Guise are in some respects humor characters; and some of the early scenes, e.g., the talk between Bussy and Maffé (I. i) and Bussy's introduction to the court (I. ii), are more like comedy than tragedy. Altogether, *Bussy d'Ambois* is a successful transfer of Elizabethan romanticism into the lower key and narrower range of the new age. It was very popular and its vogue lasted well into the Restoration period. Historically, it is significant as marking a half-way stage between the heroic drama of Marlowe and the heroic, "love-and-honor" drama of Dryden.

Chapman's tragedies [16] are all studies of political decay, swan-songs of Renaissance individualism. They all deal, like the fifth book of the *Faerie Queene,* with a world that Astraea, the goddess of justice, has abandoned; and five of the six get their material from France, which in the later sixteenth century was par excellence the country of civil strife and eccentric personalities. In the two parts of *The Conspiracy and Tragedy of Charles Duke of Byron* (1608) Chapman deals with an even more recent figure than Bussy d'Ambois, and a much more important one. Hardly any Frenchman except Henry of Navarre was better known in England than the Duke of Biron (1562-1602), and Chapman's double-tragedy, based closely upon an English book that had just appeared (Edward Grimestone's *General Inventory of the History of France,* 1607), concentrates on these two figures. Henry is very sympathetically presented, but his ambassador in London naturally objected to some of the realism, and both parts have been badly curtailed. Byron is, like Tamburlaine and Bussy, an aspiring giant, but aspiration is no longer the law of nature; it is a fatal sin against the classic concept of the balanced personality. There is some grand poetry in *Byron;* for example, the hero's famous apostrophe in the viking mood: [17]

> Give me a spirit that on this life's rough sea
> Loves t' have his sails fill'd with a lusty wind,
> Even till his sail-yards tremble, his masts crack,

Bussy d'Ambois

The Byron Plays

---

[16] *Chapman's Tragedies,* ed. T. M. Parrott (1910). See A. S. Ferguson, "The Plays of George Chapman," *MLR,* XIII (1918). 1-24; XV (1920). 223-239; J. Spens, "Chapman's Ethical Thought," *E&S,* XI (1925). 145-169; H. Craig, "Ethics in the Jacobean Drama: the Case of Chapman," and C. W. Kennedy, "Political Theory in the Plays of George Chapman," in *Parrott Presentation Volume* (1935), pp. 25-46, 73-86.

[17] *Byron's Conspiracy,* III. iii. 135 ff.

And his rapt ship run on her side so low
That she drinks water, and her keel plows air.
There is no danger to a man that knows
What life and death is . . .

and it develops more clearly than any of Chapman's other plays the idea
Shakespeare is so fond of, overthrow of an essentially noble character by a
fault which is complementary to its virtue.

The Revenge of Bussy

The Revenge of Bussy d'Ambois, written after the Byron plays and first
printed in 1613, is less a sequel to the original *Bussy* than a development of
the political philosophy of *Byron.* The hero, Bussy's brother and avenger,
Clermont d'Ambois, is an entirely fictitious figure invented by Chapman as
an example of the Stoic or "Senecal man," adequate to every situation and
armed against all the chances of life.

> Come fair or foul, whatever chance can fall,
> Fix'd in himself, he still is one to all.

This is the ideal type Chapman, and Jonson too, set up in reprobation of the
vain and unbalanced humor figures they found their world producing.[18]

Chabot

The Tragedy of Chabot Admiral of France, first printed in 1639 as by
Chapman and Shirley,[19] and based on an episode at the court of Francis I
(c. 1540), has been interestingly interpreted as a political parable applicable
to the English court of James I about 1615-21.[20] By this reading, Chabot, the
king's noble servant who is injured by calumny, is the disgraced favorite
Somerset, and the vindictive Lord Chancellor is Francis Bacon. Chapman's
sympathy with Somerset is certain, and the parallelism of figures and events
is undoubtedly striking. Such a purpose may account for the sentimental
strain in the play, which deals, like *Byron,* with the relation of king and
subject, and, like the *Revenge of Bussy,* with the ideals of ethical justice. In

Caesar and Pompey

The Tragedy of Caesar and Pompey, printed 1631, Chapman undisguisedly
upholds the thesis that "only a just man is a free man." Setting out to show
the righteousness of the Stoic Cato in contrast with the ambition of Caesar
and of Pompey, he becomes sympathetic with both the others and makes all
three mouthpieces of Stoic doctrine. Despite the title, however, Cato is the
hero, the Senecal man courageous enough not to seek his ends by violence;
and the scenes dealing with Cato's death make an interesting comparison
with Addison's *Cato.*

Ben Jonson [21] (1572-1637) entered the English theatre like a scourge and

---

[18] See R. H. Perkinson, "Nature and the Tragic Hero in Chapman's Bussy Plays," *MLQ,* III
(1942). 263-285.
[19] Shirley's part probably consists in alterations and additions not germane to the original
work.
[20] See N. D. Solve, *Stuart Politics in Chapman's Tragedy of Chabot* (Ann Arbor, 1928).
[21] The standard edition is that of C. H. Herford and P. and E. Simpson (7v, Oxford, 1925,
in progress), superseding the Gifford-Cunningham edition (9v, 1875). See S. A. Tannenbaum,
Ben Jonson: A Concise Bibliography (1938); J. F. Bradley and J. Q. Adams, *The Jonson Allusion
Book, 1597-1700* (New Haven, 1922), and G. E. Bentley, *Shakespeare and Jonson: Their
Reputations in the Seventeenth Century Compared* (2v, Chicago, 1945); M. Castelain, *Ben Jonson,
l'homme et l'œuvre* (Paris, 1907); C. R. Baskervill, *English Elements in Jonson's Early Comedy*

for some time was regarded as an affliction. The first play with which his *Ben* name can be connected is a lost comedy, *The Isle of Dogs* (1597), in which *Jonson* he collaborated with Nashe. Its satire so incensed the authorities that they commanded the closing of all playhouses, and imprisoned Jonson and two of the other actors in the Marshalsea.[22] At this time Ben was both actor and playwright,[23] and he seems to have disposed of his works as best he could among the different companies. *The Isle of Dogs* was not produced at Henslowe's theatre, but Henslowe was enough his friend to lend him £4 toward the cost of imprisonment, and on the following December 3 advanced him twenty shillings on the plot of a play he was to finish by Christmas. Jonson failed to complete the assignment, and a year later Chapman was being paid for work on a tragedy of "Benjamin's plot."

By 1598 Jonson had written *The Case Is Altered* for the Chapel Children, a comedy comparable with Chapman's *All Fools,* though more romantic in tone and less expertly worked out. He takes Plautus for his model, where Chapman used Terence, and similarly develops the classic themes into a comedy of modern Italy. To this early period may also belong the original form of *A Tale of a Tub,* which exists only as Jonson revised it much later. His fame began with the first play by him that the Chamberlain's company acted, *Every Man in His Humor.* Tradition, reported by Rowe in 1709, states *Every Man* that Shakespeare's personal intervention induced the company to accept this *in His* play. Certainly Shakespeare acted a part in it when it was produced, about *Humor* September, 1598, and it quickly became one of the great successes of the day. As the text then stood, it was superficially another Italian comedy, set in Florence and concerned with the classic devices of the duel of wits between father and son and the stratagems of an intriguing slave; but behind this there was a keen analysis of contemporary English society which came more sharply into focus when Jonson revised the play for his Folio of 1616, giving the characters English names and introducing a vast apparatus of pungent London allusion. Essentially, it is the arraignment of an era bent on acquiring fashionable prestige at small cost. The absurd quest of gentlemanliness is lashed in a diversity of one-track "humor" characters. The country cousin, Stephen, thinks he can rate as a gentleman by studying a book about hawking, and the city youth, Matthew, seeks the same end by pretending to be a poet. The coward Bobadill wins temporary respect by boasts about his fencing, and by the elegance with which he swears and takes tobacco. The most intelligent of the young men, Knowell and Wellbred, make an avocation of exploiting the fools they meet for the gratification of their own vanity. The public, sick of the insincerities of the time, welcomed Jonson's

---

(Austin, 1911); Elisabeth Woodbridge, *Studies in Jonson's Comedy* (1898); Esther C. Dunn, *Ben Jonson's Art* (Northampton, Mass., 1925). The best recent biographies, in addition to the account in Herford-Simpson, are G. Gregory Smith, *Ben Jonson* (*EML Series,* 1919); Eric Linklater, *Ben Jonson and King James* (1931); John Palmer, *Ben Jonson* (1934). Copiously annotated texts of the various plays are available in the *Yale Studies in English* (general editor A. S. Cook, 14v, 1903-1926).

[22] Jonson's imprisonment lasted from July till October, 1597.
[23] See F. T. Bowers, "Ben Jonson the Actor," *SP*, xxxiv (1937). 392-406.

satire with delight, and the liveliest commentator of the day, Samuel Row-lands, was soon urging all poets to follow his lead:

> Good honest poets, let me crave a boon:
> That you would write, I do not care how soon,
> Against the bastard humors hourly bred
> In every mad-brain'd, wit-worn, giddy head.
> At such gross follies do not sit and wink;
> Belabor these same gulls with pen and ink! [24]

Every Man out of His Humor

Every Man out of His Humor was acted at the Globe the next year (1599), and Jonson was so proud of it that he rushed it into print in 1600 with a signed dedication to the gentlemen of the Inns of Court, the arbiters of elegance of the day. This play has been explained as an effort to employ the stage as a vehicle for the type of caustic satire which the censors of the press were prohibiting,[25] and certainly it belongs to the same literary movement that produced the satires of Hall and Marston; but it is probably enough to say that Jonson was so delighted with the success of his new technique in *Every Man In* that in the second play he came close to running it to death. There is nothing like a dramatic plot in *Every Man Out;* it consists of dramatic episodes and acute psychological generalizations. The characters still have Italian names, but do not live in Italy. They inhabit the "Fortunate Island," which in the obvious language of irony means England. Ten or twelve social misfits exhibit their egotistic folly through four acts, and in the fast-moving fifth each is by the logic of events kicked "out of his humor," that is, into a more normal state of mind. The printed text is prefaced by a clever list of "the characters of the persons," in which each is neatly impaled, like the insects in an entomologist's collection; and there is an inordinately heavy mass of running commentary, four persons being used to emphasize the author's views or show the wisdom of his method.

Cynthia's Revels

We do not know what Shakespeare thought of *Every Man out of His Humor,* but it is safe to infer that his company did not find it rewarding, for several years passed before they again acted a play by Jonson. His next, *Cynthia's Revels* (1600), was sold to the boys of the Queen's Chapel. It is a slighter piece, but even more aggressive, and in a number of respects forecasts Jonson's development.[26] It ends in an authentic masque, and includes the loveliest song that he yet had written: "Queen and huntress, chaste and fair." In the elaborately satiric definitions of courtier types it goes beyond *Every Man Out* and prepares for the "characters" of Overbury and Earle. It is a last dramatic tribute to the aged Queen, who, as in Lyly, is pictured in Cynthia; but through the stately grace of the allegory tramps the burly figure of the author, originally called Criticus, but in the 1616 text magnified into

[24] Epigram "To Poets" in *The Letting of Humor's Blood in the Head-Vein* (1600).
[25] See O. J. Campbell, *Comicall Satyre and Shakespeare's Troilus and Cressida* (San Marino, 1938), pp. 1-81.
[26] See E. W. Talbert, "The Classical Mythology and the Structure of *Cynthia's Revels,*" *PQ,* xxii (1943). 193-210; A. H. Gilbert, "The Function of the Masques in *Cynthia's Revels,*" *PQ.* xxii (1943). 211-230.

Crites, the Judge. He is the man who is always right, receives the Queen's ecstatic praise for his poetry and wisdom, and at the end writes himself Cynthia's warrant to purge society, along with his chosen companion, Arete, or Virtue:

> Dear Arete and Crites, to you two
> We give the charge: impose what pains you please;
> Th' incurable cut off, the rest reform.

Such bumptiousness was intolerable, and Jonson was angrily laughed at. Even his admirer, Marston, seems to have gibed at him a little in the revised anti-war play, *Histriomastix,* in *Jack Drum's Entertainment,* and elsewhere. Jonson's reply was *Poetaster* (1601), which begins with Envy hopefully rising *Poetaster* "to damn the author," but trodden underfoot by the mailed prologue of the piece. If not one of the greatest plays, *Poetaster* is one of the most amusing. The scene is Rome in the reign of Augustus, and the chief characters are the great poets of that age, their patrons and enemies. Jonson arrogates to himself the character of Horace and belauds him plentifully, while excoriating Marston as the poetaster, Crispinus. But during the fifteen weeks that he spent in composition Jonson must have talked, and his intended victims were ready for him. Dekker's more rapid pen was enlisted, and his *Satiromastix, or the Untrussing of the Humorous Poet,* must have been on the stage almost as soon as *Poetaster.* One appeared at Blackfriars, the other both at the Globe *The War of* and at Paul's. Jonson evidently knew of Dekker's commission in time to add *the Theatres* him as a subsidiary poetaster (Demetrius) and to work in some diverting calumny of the Globe company in Histrio.[27] Ben himself offered a broader target for ridicule than did the poetasters, and Dekker, with no virulence, has taken good advantage of it. His play is a mine of information on Jonson as his contemporaries knew him in 1601. His slowness in composition, self-esteem, his career as bricklayer and barnstorming actor, his poverty and sycophancy to the great, his killing of a player and escape from Tyburn by his "neck-verse," his "parboiled face," that looked "for all the world like a *Dekker's* rotten russet apple when 'tis bruised," and his habit of epigramming his *Satiromastix* friends are all set down with the precision of a master realist. The two play-houses that gave Dekker's play must have been well filled, and a printed text of *Satiromastix* was immediately in demand.

Jonson recognized the glassiness of the house he lived in, and for a time *Jonson's* withheld his stones. In a dignified "apologetical dialogue" to *Poetaster* he *Roman* withdrew from the stage war and devoted himself to classic tragedy. In this *Plays* he is in amusing contrast with Dick Steele, who, having given umbrage to his army friends by the seriousness of *The Christian Hero,* turned to comedy to retrieve his popularity.[28] Jonson rescued himself by *Sejanus* (1603), a historical play of ponderous ethics and meticulous scholarship. It

---

[27] A slightly different conjecture of the situation is given by Herford and Simpson, *op. cit.,* I. 27-29. Earlier and more elaborate discussion in J. H. Penniman, *The War of the Theatres* (1897), and R. A. Small, *The Stage-Quarrel between Jonson and the So-called Poetasters* (1899).
[28] See *Mr. Steele's Apology for Himself and His Writings* (1714), p. 102.

has the kind of greatness that Chapman's later tragedies have. Chapman, as well as Marston, wrote commendatory verses for the first quarto in 1605, and Chapman may indeed have had a part in composing the stage version. Shakespeare's company produced it, as they later did Jonson's other Roman tragedy of *Catiline's Conspiracy* (1611), and Shakespeare himself, now on the point of retiring as an actor, performed a part in *Sejanus*. The war of the theatres was quite over.

 Jonson's training as a comic realist served him well in *Sejanus,* which gives an impressively real view of imperial Rome and develops the great figures as enlarged and darkened humor characters. It is an important play, but most important for what it led to, for it led to *Volpone, the Fox* (1606). This magnificent if rather dreadful comedy, acted by Shakespeare's company,

Volpone which had now become the King's, is supposed to take place in modern Venice; but its treatment of the theme of greed comes from Jonson's study of the enormities of ancient Rome. The character symbolism peculiar to humor comedy is here intensified by imitating the method of the beast-fable, which taught how human types could be caricatured by representing them as animals.[29] The chief villain is, as usual, called the fox; his agent is the fly (Mosca), and his dupes are the birds of prey, crow, vulture, and raven. The technical perfection of the plot is a little marred, but the human appeal a good deal increased, by the addition of three English types: Peregrine (the falcon), Sir Pol (the talkative parrot), and the latter's extraordinarily British and modern wife.

 Very good judges have thought *Volpone* the finest of Jonson's plays. Dryden gave the palm to his next production, *The Silent Woman* (1609), which verges upon farce, as *Volpone* does upon tragedy. Either of them—so wonderfully are they articulated and so amazingly lifelike—might doubtless assure Jonson's place as the greatest satiric dramatist England has produced; but they are both surpassed by his third crowning play, *The Alchemist* (1610), which in tone strikes an exact center between the other two, and

The Al-
chemist which has an even more perfect economy. In *The Alchemist,* it may be said, every word and gesture counts in the final effect. The fusion of classic method and English scene is here complete and could go no further. The place is not only London; it is the fashionable Blackfriars quarter where Jonson lived, and from which he had signed the dedication of *Volpone.* Everything occurs either inside Lovewit's house or before the door. The time is during the plague of 1610, which was raging as Jonson wrote, and it is not longer than the actual time the actors are on the stage. A single spring moves all the characters, the desire to get something for nothing. Three of the twelve dramatis personae are knaves; seven are dupes, representing five classes of people one would expect to see at Blackfriars: the young, professional law clerk, the luxury merchant dealing in tobacco and other courtly wares, the pleasure-loving knight, the two Puritan preachers, and the wealthy young man up from the country with his sister. The remaining characters, Surly

---

[29] See H. Levin, "Jonson's Metempsychosis," *PQ*, xxii (1943). 231-239.

and Lovewit, are neither quite knave nor quite dupe, but potentially both, as the action reveals. Such was Jonson's picture of his neighbors, presented without romance and quite without poetic justice, but also without bitterness. It lacks the harshness of *Volpone* and enforces its moral with a more cleansing laughter.

Such precision could hardly be repeated without growing stale, and Jonson's later comedies are in some sense inferior. His comic art was a very jealous mistress, and from it he was more and more distracted by his famous masques which from 1610 demanded an increasing amount of his attention.[30] Two very important plays were, however, produced: *Bartholomew Fair* in 1614 and *The Staple of News* in 1626. The former is the complement of *The* *Jonson's* *Alchemist,* a picture of the other side of London, where the lower classes *Later Plays* congregate at Smithfield during the famous August fair. It takes a larger canvas and many more characters, but Jonson finds much the same people there and the same vices. The characterization and satiric brilliance can hardly be said to be inferior to anything he had done, but the structure is less neat. The scenes in *The Staple of News* that ridicule the impostures of the new business of journalism are equally fine. "No man," said Swinburne, not unwisely, "can know anything worth knowing of Ben Jonson who has not studied and digested the text of *Every Man in His Humor, The Fox, The Alchemist,* and *The Staple of News;* but any man who has may be said to know him well."[31] *The Devil Is an Ass* (1616) and *The New Inn* (1629) are on a lower plane, but they have more romantic charm than anything Jonson had written in drama since *The Case Is Altered.* As he grew older and sadder, and his classic certitude relaxed, he became in some ways more Elizabethan, and he gave best expression to this side of himself in the beautiful fragment of pastoral drama that he left uncompleted, *The Sad Shepherd.*

John Marston[32] (1576-1634) has been called "a screech-owl among the *John* singing birds."[33] He resembles John Donne a good deal, though scarcely in *Marston* genius. The son and heir-apparent of John Marston of Coventry, Esq., who was also a distinguished lawyer of London, he was educated at Brasenose College, Oxford, and early admitted to the Middle Temple, where it was expected that he would prepare for the bar. His father's will leaves his law books "to my said son, whom I hoped would have profited by them in the study of the law, but man proposeth and God disposeth."[34] Like many of the young Templars, and like Ovid in Jonson's *Poetaster,* Marston preferred

[30] Jonson's masques and entertainments are best studied in Vol. vii of the Herford-Simpson *Ben Jonson* (Oxford, 1941). For valuable discussion and many illustrations see A. Nicoll, *Stuart Masques and the Renaissance Stage* (1937).

[31] A. C. Swinburne, *A Study of Ben Jonson* (1889), p. 74.

[32] *The Plays of John Marston,* ed. H. H. Wood (3v, Edinburgh, 1934-1938); *Works,* ed. A. H. Bullen (3v, 1887). See A. C. Swinburne, *The Age of Shakespeare* (1908), pp. 112-149; T. Spencer, "John Marston," *Criterion,* xiii (1934). 581-599.

[33] L. Lockert, "Marston, Webster, and the Decline of the Elizabethan Drama," *Sewanee Rev.,* xxvii (1919). 62-81.

[34] R. E. Brettle, "John Marston, Dramatist: Some New Facts about His Life," *MLR,* xxii (1927). 7-14; "John Marston ... at Oxford," *RES,* iii (1927). 398-405.

to write flamboyant and cynical verse. He fell strongly under the influence of Jonson, with whom he quarreled, violently but briefly. Playwriting was but an episode in the career of this fashionable youth; his plays all belong to a half-dozen years at the opening of the seventeenth century. At a rather late age he turned to the church, was ordained in 1609, married the daughter of an eminent clergyman, and for most of the rest of his life held a good living in Hampshire. More than most of the genteel writers he scoffed at literary fame, and seems to have been really offended by the publication of his collected plays in 1633. When he died, the next year, he was interred in the choir of the Temple Church, and the Lancaster Herald enrolled his lineage and clerical dignity, but not his repute as a dramatist, in the Office of Arms.

Marston's Early Plays   Marston wrote for the fashionable class and employed only the boys' companies to give his plays—first that of Paul's and later the Queen's Revels children at Blackfriars, in which latter company he had a substantial financial investment. *Jack Drum's Entertainment* (1600) is a boisterous farce, mainly interesting today for the probable ridicule of Jonson as Brabant Sr. The next year Paul's produced a more famous pair of plays: *Antonio and Mellida* and *Antonio's Revenge,* both printed in 1602.[35] Marston likes the conventional Italian setting, using it in these plays and four others, but he handles it with a grim and acrid realism. Feliche, "an honest bitter courtier" in *Antonio and Mellida,* resembles Jonson's Asper in *Every Man Out,* and the play concludes with an armed epilogue jesting at the armed prologue in *Poetaster.* Marston's play is a more melodramatic *Romeo and Juliet* with a happy ending; its strangely matched sequel rather follows *Hamlet* and from start to finish is crammed with ghosts and corpses.[36] Much lighter fare is offered in Marston's *What You Will,* which, though not printed till 1607,[37] was probably composed no later than 1602. The borrowed Italian plot is here very pleasantly handled, but it is overladen with irrelevant by-action relating apparently to the war of the theatres. Quadratus and Lampatho Doria, who quarrel a good deal, may to contemporaries have seemed lively portraits of Marston and Jonson, but posterity has found it hard to equate them with their originals.

The Mal-content and The Fawn   In *The Malcontent* (1604) and *Parasitaster, or the Fawn* (1606) Marston builds his plot around the figure of an Italian duke in disguise. Malevole in the former play wins the confidence of all by vociferous and unremitting acerbity,[38] while the "Fawn" attains the same end by universal geniality. Both

---

[35] Reprinted for the Malone Society (1921). See D. J. McGinn, "A New Date for *Antonio's Revenge,*" *PMLA,* LIII (1938). 129-137.

[36] In the most important matters Marston is guided by Jonson, but no writer of the time is more full of allusions to Shakespeare's plays.

[37] This play was published by Thomas Thorpe, who issued Jonson's *Volpone* in the same year and Shakespeare's sonnets two years later. Thorpe, whose talent seemed to lie in securing inaccessible manuscripts, was also instrumental in publishing *The Malcontent* (1604), *Eastward Ho!* (1605), and *Histriomastix* (1610). The last is probably a revision by Marston of an earlier play.

[38] This very popular play set, or at least confirmed, a fashion for querulousness as a mark of aristocratic behavior. See E. E. Stoll, "Shakespeare, Marston, and the Malcontent Type," *MP,* III (1906). 281-303; "The Date of *The Malcontent:* A Rejoinder," *RES,* XI (1935). 42-50.

are intricately plotted comedies exposing the manifold follies that abound in courts. Marston dedicated *The Malcontent* to the now reconciled Jonson, and in the epilogue repeated his humble admiration of the great man

> To whose desertful lamps [39] pleased fates impart
> Art above nature, judgment above art.

In 1605 he joined with Jonson and Chapman in producing one of the most excellent of all London comedies, *Eastward Ho!*, in which Marston's pen seems to have been the most active and the wickedest.[40] His own *Dutch Courtesan*, likewise printed in 1605, is hardly inferior; it is a play of the most astounding high spirits, carrying knavery to the limits of laughter and the edge of tragedy. The ghoulishness that Marston often affected and the extraordinary bursts of violent language for which he was famous are conspicuous in *The Wonder of Women, or the Tragedy of Sophonisba* (1606), a play of undoubted force and fine feeling, but written, as one may suspect from the prefatory epistle and the style, to show how different a classical tragedy might be from *Sejanus*.[41]

The Dutch Courtesan

Sophonisba

Marston's most violent characteristics, as displayed in his satires and *Antonio's Revenge*, were adopted and surpassed by the mysterious Cyril Tourneur [42] (*c.* 1580-1626) who first appears in 1600 as the author of a poetically expressed but obscure political parable in rime royal, *The Transformed Metamorphosis*.[43] His position in history depends upon two plays: *The Revenger's Tragedy*, printed in 1607 as acted by the King's company, and *The Atheist's Tragedy*, printed in 1611 "as in divers places it hath often been acted." There was but a single edition of each play, and the vague publisher's statement just quoted is the nearest thing to evidence that Tourneur enjoyed any repute at all in his own time. His fame is the gift of nineteenth-century romanticism, and was erected into an article of faith by Swinburne's essay, which speaks extravagantly of Tourneur's "unique and incomparable genius." [44] Tourneur is not a satirist or a realist to the extent that Marston is, and his idea of tragedy is not much subtler than that presented in *Titus*

Cyril Tourneur

---

[39] With reference, probably, to Jonson's well-known consumption of midnight oil. In *What You Will* Lampatho Doria is less flatteringly called "Lamp."

[40] See J. Q. Adams, "*Eastward Ho!* and Its Satire against the Scots," *SP*, xxviii (1931). 689-701; R. E. Brettle, "*Eastward Ho!*, 1605," *Library*, ix (1928). 287-304; P. Simpson, "The Problem of Authorship of *Eastward Ho!*," *PMLA*, lix (1944). 715-725.

[41] Marston also left a tragedy, *The Insatiate Countess* (printed 1613), based on stories in Painter. William Barksted seems to have had a hand in it. Marston's comedies had a close but worthless imitator in another member of the Middle Temple, Edward Sharpham (1576-1608), author of *The Fleire* (1607) and *Cupid's Whirligig* (1607).

[42] A. Nicoll, *The Works of Cyril Tourneur* (Fanfrolico Press, 1930). See L. Lockert, "The Greatest of Elizabethan Melodramas," *Parrott Presentation Vol.* (1935), pp. 103-126; E. M. Waith, "The Ascription of Speeches in *The Revenger's Tragedy*," *MLN*, lvii (1942). 119-121.

[43] See K. N. Cameron, "Cyril Tourneur and *The Transformed Metamorphosis*," *RES*, xvi (1940). 1-7.

[44] *The Age of Shakespeare* (1908), pp. 262-289. Recent efforts to ascribe *The Revenger's Tragedy* to another author seem ill warranted. See, however, E. H. C. Oliphant, "The Authorship of *The Revenger's Tragedy*," *SP*, xxiii (1926). 157-168; W. D. Dunkel (same title), *PMLA*, xlvi (1931). 781-785; U. M. Ellis-Fermor, "The Imagery of *The Revenger's Tragedy* and *The Atheist's Tragedy*," *MLR*, xxx (1935). 289-301.

Andronicus; but he had a real gift for invective, and while exhibiting beastly figures in the perpetration of ill-motivated atrocities he was able to shroud his stage in the miasma of bitter world-weariness which was one of the symptoms of the Jacobean reaction. He is perhaps the most striking dramatist in this particular genre; but it was a low and transient type of art, and it is not strange that the earlier play, *The Revenger's Tragedy,* is more effective than its successor. This kind of thing, as *The Spanish Tragedy* also shows, is often done best when done for the first time.

Thomas Middleton

Thomas Middleton [45] (1580-1627) is the complete Jacobean. His earliest dramatic attempts were made for Henslowe during the last year of Queen Elizabeth's life, but his known plays all fall within King James's reign (1603-1625) and fill it to the very end. He is as typical of Jacobean realism as Fletcher is of its romance. Judgment was the merit that Middleton most regarded, and the best way of describing his plays is perhaps to say that they have a spirit the Lord Chancellor Bacon would have esteemed. The author of the preface to the posthumous (1640) edition of *A Mad World, My Masters,* one of Middleton's early plays, strikes the right critical note:

> Here is no bombasted or fustian stuff, but every line weighed as with a balance, and every sentence placed with judgment and deliberation.

Middleton writes in a time of dubiety, and in the text of this same play expresses the uncertainties of his actors in terms which might be generalized to fit the whole structure of society:

> They were never more uncertain in their lives, now up and now down. They know not when to play, where to play, nor what to play: not when to play, for fearful fools; [46] where to play, for puritan fools; nor what to play, for critical fools.

He could have said as much for playwrights, and does suggest it in his preface to the excellent comedy he wrote with Dekker, *The Roaring Girl* (1611):

> The fashion of play-making I can properly compare to nothing so naturally as the alteration in apparel; for in the time of the great crop-doublet your huge bombasted plays, quilted with mighty words to lean purpose, were only then in fashion; and as the doublet fell, neater inventions began to set up. Now, in the time of spruceness, our plays follow the niceness of our garments: single plots, quaint conceits, lecherous jests dressed up in hanging sleeves; and such are fit for the times and the termers.[47]

As might be inferred, Middleton had no clear-cut convictions about dramat-

---

[45] *Works,* ed. A. H. Bullen (8v, 1885-6). Ten plays are printed in the Mermaid Series, with introduction by A. C. Swinburne, and R. C. Bald has added an excellent edition of *Hengist, King of Kent* (1938). See M. Eccles, "Middleton's Birth and Education," *RES,* vii (1931). 431-441; R. C. Bald, "The Chronology of Middleton's Plays," *MLR,* xxxii (1937). 33-43; T. S. Eliot, *For Lancelot Andrewes* (1928), pp. 100-116, revised in *Elizabethan Essays* (1934); G. Bradford, "The Women of Middleton and Webster," *Sewanee Rev.,* xxix (1921). 14-29, reprinted in *Elizabethan Women* (1936), ch. vi.

[46] I.e., fearful of the plague.

[47] See H. B. Bullock, "Thomas Middleton and the Fashion in Playmaking," *PMLA,* (1927). 766-776.

ic structure, such as Jonson and Chapman had, and no very individualized poetic style. He seems to have had no close theatrical connections either. His plays were simply performed by all the theatrical companies there were, adult or boy, good, bad, or indifferent, as chance might in each case dictate. He is altogether an ambiguous person. By birth a Londoner; by education an alumnus of Queen's College, Oxford; by descent the son of a citizen and bricklayer, who, however, bore the arms of a Westmorland family and had connections of some rank, Middleton remained a citizen, and from 1620 till his death served as City Chronologer, i.e. laureate for the Lord Mayor and corporation.[48] One of the things that mark him is his emphatic lack of interest in the king and court. He has no cavalier propensities. This is one of the many differences that appear when his comedy, *A Trick to Catch the Old One* (1608), is compared with the play Massinger made out of it, *A New Way to Pay Old Debts*. He satirizes Puritans, university men, doctors, usurers, citizens' wives, and country squires, always acutely and often obscenely. He hardly cares at all for heroes, villains, or ghosts; his interest, indeed, is not romantic, but psychiatric. Primarily it is an interest in the "under-dog," in the man or woman with a complex; and something of this he says in his preface to *The Roaring Girl,* the play about the notorious Moll Frith:

Worse things, I must needs confess, the world has taxed her for than has been written of her; but 'tis the excellency of a writer to leave things better than he finds 'em; though some obscene fellow, that cares not what he writes against others... though such a one would have ripped up the most nasty vice that ever hell belched forth, and presented it to a modest assembly, yet we rather wish in such discoveries, where reputation lies bleeding, a slackness of truth than fulness of slander.

This is the spirit behind the enormously enlarging tragedies, *Women, Beware Women* and *The Changeling*. Middleton received the story of de Flores and Beatrice-Joanna from a Puritan homilist's book [49] as an ultimate example of lechery and blood-lust. He palliates nothing, analyzes everything, and dismisses all with only a single moral: Judge not, that ye be not judged. _{The Changeling}

Middleton stands with Jonson as a supreme dramatic realist, but two methods could hardly be more different. Jonson organizes microscopically, and attains a perfection of structure impossible even for himself to abide by. Jonson was never for a moment doubtful about labeling the knaves and fools in his dramatic world or any other. Middleton's plays are case histories, put together in whatever way the data accumulate.[50] His judgments are never final, and his characters are seldom damned. There is just one superlative that can be bestowed on Middleton: no artist of his time equals him in the un-Jonsonian ability to hold his hands off his people. Laisser-faire is the

---

[48] Jonson succeeded him in this post.
[49] John Reynolds, *The Triumphs of God's Revenge against ... Murther* (1621).
[50] See W. D. Dunkel, *The Dramatic Technique of Thomas Middleton in His Comedies of London Life* (Chicago, 1925); R. C. Bald, "The Sources of Middleton's City Comedies," *JEGP*, XXXIII (1934). 373-387.

true source of his power. Even sympathy must be kept under, as he reminds the audience in the last words of *The Changeling*.

> All we can do to comfort one another,
> To stay a brother's sorrow for a brother,
> To dry a child from the kind father's eyes,
> Is to no purpose: it rather multiplies.

William Rowley

It may be considered lucky that so idiosyncratic an artist had often at his elbow a real man of the theatre. William Rowley (*c.* 1585-1626) was a farcical actor of repute, playing fat-clown parts, and he had also a pretty skill in producing popular plays.[51] The three or four he composed alone—e.g., *All's Lost by Lust* and *A Shoemaker a Gentleman*—show ability both in melodrama and in low comedy.[52] He collaborated with many of the leading dramatists: with Heywood in *Fortune by Land and Sea*, Ford and Dekker in *The Witch of Edmonton*, Webster in *A Cure for a Cuckold;* and particularly with Middleton, during the latter part of their careers, in some of the best plays of the Middleton canon: *A Fair Quarrel* (1617), *The Changeling* (1622), and *The Spanish Gipsy* (1622). His hearty touch and his eye on the box-office did no harm, but his blank verse must not be mistaken for Middleton's. The first scene of *The Changeling*, which Rowley wrote, contains such wretched lines as

> Fates, do your worst, I'll please myself with sight
> Of her at all opportunities,

and

> Or follow'd him in fate, had not the late league
> Prevented me.

"You can't tamper with life" was Middleton's principle. Just once, at the close of his work, he came into the open and expressed himself as a partisan. It was an occasion when practically all London, court and city alike, joined with him in rejoicings over the failure of Prince Charles's Spanish match.

A Game at Chess

A Game at Chess[53] (1624) is based on fugitive pamphlets that in the play are held together by dramatic symbolism and by inserted episodes more outspoken and also more sentimental than had been Middleton's way. The allegory, through which the contemporary figures and plots in an intricate game of international politics are represented by movements of players on a

[51] Rowley was also the author of a prose skit, *A Search for Money, or the Lamentable Complaint for the Loss of the Wandering Knight, Monsieur l'Argent* (1609; reprinted, Percy Soc., II, 1840), which, though long drawn out, has some liveliness and realistic value. It deals with the current depression of trade and comes to the uncomforting conclusion that ready money, invisible both in London and in the country, has been locked up in hell and will never again be allowed to circulate.

[52] See C. W. Stork's edition of *All's Lost by Lust* (Philadelphia, 1910); P. G. Wiggin, *An Inquiry into the Authorship of the Middleton-Rowley Plays* (Boston, 1897); A. Symons, "Middleton and Rowley," in *Studies in the Elizabethan Drama* (1919), pp. 211-261; W. D. Dunkel, "Did not Rowley Merely Revise Middleton?" *PMLA*, XLVIII (1933), 799-805.

[53] Ed. R. C. Bald (Cambridge, 1929). See B. M. Wagner, "New Allusions to *A Game at Chess*," *PMLA*, XLIV (1929), 827-834; J. R. Moore, "The Contemporary Significance of Middleton's *Game at Chesse*," *PMLA*, L (1935), 761-768.

chess-board, is too complex to be easily followed by modern readers; but on a stage in which each pawn had human proportions, and before an audience that recognized each detail, the effect was unparalleled. The Globe Theatre seems never to have been so crowded, till the Spanish ambassador forced it to be closed; and copies of the text, printed or manuscript, could not be multiplied fast enough. Rowley had no share in the writing, but played the great burlesque part of the Fat Bishop.[54] Within a year or two, he, Middleton, and King James all died, and an era had ended.

On the periphery of drama lie forms of semi-dramatic spectacle and enter- *Semi-* tainment, aristocratic or popular, of which the most important is the masque. *dramatic* The origins of such festivities have been sought deep in the past, in folk- *Forms* customs and fertility rites. Whatever the validity of such speculations, there are records of "mummings" and "disguisings" at the English court from the period of Edward III. In the fifteenth century there were "royal entries" into London and other cities and analogous pageants for the reception of distinguished personages. These were stationary or processional, more or less allegorical in theme, accompanied by music, and either pantomimic or with dialogue, though speech was quite subordinate to spectacle. The term *mumming* is significant. Of festivities at court there are abundant records from the time of Henry VIII. The central feature of some entertainments was a dance in which the maskers, noblemen and gentlemen (and on a famous occasion King Henry himself), chose partners from among the spectators. This intermingling of actors and guests, "after the manner of Italy" (if the much discussed phrase is to be so interpreted), became an established convention; a vestige of it is discernible in *Comus*. During the reign of Elizabeth we find such comparatively simple and rudimentary forms as Sir Philip Sidney's charming *The Lady of May* (1578), an open-air entertainment for the reception of royalty; but these affairs could be elaborate and costly, as when the Earl of Leicester received Elizabeth at Kenilworth. At court the Queen discouraged lavish expense. The fashion influenced some plays, notably Peele's *Arraignment of Paris,* and into other plays short masques are introduced. In episodes of *The Faerie Queene* the atmosphere and stately splendor of processional spectacle are evoked. But the form came to its full flowering at the extravagant court of James I and it lasted through the reign of Charles I. The modern reader, who has before him only the prose synopses of the action and dry descriptions of the scenes and costumes and movement to supplement the texts, must reconstruct in his imagination the gorgeousness of these occasions. Other masques, probably not so costly, were produced at the Inns of Court.

The first fully developed court masque is Samuel Daniel's *Vision of the* *The* *Twelve Goddesses* (1604), which celebrates allegorically the blessings be- *Masque* stowed upon England by the new monarch. Among other poets who de- signed masques and supplied the accompanying speeches and dialogue were

---

[54] See R. C. Bald in *LTLS*, Feb. 6, 1930, p. 102.

George Chapman, Francis Beaumont, Thomas Campion, and (at a later date) James Shirley. But it was Ben Jonson who fully exploited the possibilities for poetry inherent in the genre. Space is wanting to name here all his masques and entertainments (see the texts in the *Oxford Jonson*, Volume VII, and the introductions to each in *ibid.*, II, 249-334); but there may be singled out for bare mention those great creations, *The Masque of Blackness* (1605) and *The Masque of Queens* (1609), and the charming hymeneal masque for Lord Haddington (1608), which, because Jonson gave it no title, Gifford called *The Hue and Cry after Cupid*. Jonson, elaborating upon the clownish "antics" of earlier spectacles, developed the grotesque and often coarsely humorous "antimasque" which ushers in, and serves as a foil to, the authentic masque with all its dignity and magnificence. He made abundant use—sometimes ponderous use but often exquisitely graceful and fanciful—of classical mythology, English country life, folklore and superstition, far-fetched travelers' tales, and other materials drawn from his prodigious learning; he employed also his eloquence and his lyric gift. Weight and gravity might be added to delicacy and grace, so that in his hands the masque sometimes became the vehicle for satire and social criticism and bold topical allusion, and for moral exhortation—thus pointing the way to *Comus*. The basic patterns and the poetry were worthy to be wedded to the elements of spectacle designed by the great architect Inigo Jones, first the poet's partner and afterwards his rival for acclaim, who was responsible for the ornate settings, the ingenious machinery, and the elaborate baroque costumes.

Of various subsidiary forms, some of them provincial and rustic, there is room to mention only the annual shows in London at the inauguration of the Lord Mayor. These were professional, allegorical, and topical in character. Among the dramatists who designed them and supplied the texts were George Peele and Thomas Middleton.[55]

[55] For the student of various kinds of entertainments John Nichols, *Progresses ... of Queen Elizabeth* (3v, 1823) and *Progresses ... of King James I* (4v, 1828) are still indispensable. There is an abundance of archivistic material in Albert Feuillerat, *Documents relating to the Office of the Revels at Court in the Time of Edward VI and Queen Mary* (Louvain, 1914) and idem, *Queen Elizabeth* (Louvain, 1908). See also R. Brotanek, *Die Englischen Maskenspiele* (Vienna and Leipzig, 1902); W. W. Greg, *A List of Masques, Pageants, &c* (1902); Robert Withington, *English Pageantry* (2v, Cambridge, Mass., 1918-1920); Percy Simpson and C. F. Bell, *Designs by Inigo Jones for Masques and Plays at Court* (Oxford, 1924); Allardyce Nicoll, *Stuart Masques and the Renaissance Stage* (1937). The Continental, ritualistic, and folklore backgrounds are explored in Enid Welsford, *The Court Masque* (Cambridge, 1927). On the annual civic shows see F. W. Fairholt, *Lord Mayor's Pageants* (1843-1844), and, for antecedent developments, Robert Withington, *English Pageantry: An Historical Outline* (2v, Cambridge, Mass., 1918-20).

IV

Jacobean Drama: III. The Romantic Playwrights

If the more than twenty plays which John Day [1] (*c.* 1574-1640), in conjunc- *John Day* tion with other writers, prepared for Henslowe between 1598 and 1603 had survived, he would probably appear as just another competent hack-dramatist working along stereotyped lines. There was, however, a genuine vein of dreamy poetry in Day and a disposition to seek strange worlds, though these qualities show themselves fitfully, and in unstable combination with the bright social patter which was Day's other chief gift. *The Travels of the Three English Brothers* (1607), by Day, William Rowley, and George Wilkins, exaggerates the actual adventures of the three Sherleys in the East and makes its appeal to lovers of the exotic.[2] It is a lower-middle-class play for the Red Bull audience, and is artistically not much superior to Heywood's *Four Prentices of London.* Day's *Isle of Gulls* (1606) seeks to put Sidney's *Arcadia* on the stage, but neither faithfully nor with much clearness of narrative. *Law Tricks, or Who Would Have Thought It?* (1608) has a lively intrigue complicated by the escape of a duke's daughter from Turkish marauders and a dénouement that makes use of the potion business of *Romeo and Juliet.* The third and best of these comedies, all acted by the Children of the Revels, is *Humor out of Breath* [3] (1608), which presents the pretty, fantastic story of an usurping and a banished duke of Mantua and their six children, who pair off preposterously in treble matrimony. Day uses a great amount of riming verse, and likes scenes of pastoral disguise as well as scenes of daring wit. He may have begun *Humor out of Breath* with the intention of writing a humor comedy. The principal young man is named Aspero, and on his first appearance suggests Jonson's Asper (in *Every Man Out*), if not Jonson himself, but he early loses his humor and becomes a guide into the land of romantic adventure.

Day's finest work is not a play, but *The Parliament of Bees*, extant in a *Day's Parliament of Bees* quarto of 1641 and also in a less carefully revised manuscript.[4] It consists of twelve little scenes, or "characters," as he calls them, in couplet verse, picturing a variety of human types and situations by means of bees. Nothing much daintier has come to us from the seventeenth century. Day had the rare

---

[1] See A. H. Bullen, *The Works of John Day* (1881). *The Parliament of Bees* and *Humor out of Breath* (ed. A. Symons) are in the Mermaid Series volume, *Nero and Other Plays.*
[2] See S. C. Chew, *The Crescent and the Rose* (1937), pp. 504-509, and "Islam and England during the Renaissance," *Moslem World*, xxxi (1941). 371-399.
[3] See M. E. Borish, "John Day's *Humor out of Breath*," *Harvard Studies & Notes in Phil. & Lit.*, xvi (1934). 1-11.
[4] See S. R. Golding, "*The Parliament of Bees*," *RES*, iii (1927). 280-304.

ability to improve his own work, and in most of these scenes has simply translated bits of normal drama into the world of bees and thus salvaged them for immortality.[5] In the last two "characters" Oberon and his fairies are brought in, and the poetic medium is quickened into tetrameter.

Francis
Beaumont

No more amiable personality than that of Francis Beaumont[6] (*c.* 1584-1616) has recorded itself in English plays. He was the most original, the sanest, and probably the wittiest of the cavalier dramatists. Born into a higher rank of the county aristocracy than Marston, he followed the same course a scant decade later, through Oxford and the Inns of Court[7] to the theatres of the boys' companies, and he came under Ben Jonson's influence at the period when Jonson was first displaying his full greatness. Beaumont was one of the earliest and truest of the "Sons of Ben," and his first play, *The Woman-Hater* (1607), is Jonsonian comedy sentimentalized. The clever bipartite plot occupies a single day and goes up and down the street of a little Italian city, from the duke's palace at one end to the bagnio at the other. Gondarino, the woman-hater, and Lazarillo, the glutton, are humor characters in boyish exaggeration; and there is witty satire at the expense of the new-made favorites at court and the political informers, who since the Gunpowder Plot of November, 1605, had been blighting England.[8] Essentially, however, *The Woman-Hater* is a romantic play about pleasant, well-bred people. In the Prologue Beaumont explains his attitude:

The
Woman-
Hater

I dare not call it comedy or tragedy; 'tis perfectly neither. A play it is which was meant to make you laugh ... Some things in it you may meet with which are out of the common road. A duke there is, and the scene lies in Italy, as those two things lightly we never miss. But you shall not find in it the ordinary and overworn trade of jesting at lords and courtiers and citizens, without taxation of any particular or new vice by them found out, but at the persons of them. Such he that made this thinks vile, and for his own part vows that he did never think but that a lord-born might be a wise man, and a courtier an honest man.

When Beaumont began to write, the newest literary taste was that for Spanish fiction, brought in by the social prominence of the Spanish embassy at King James's court as much as by its own outstanding merit and the current lack of such an art in England. One of the main characters in *The Woman-Hater* is a variation of the famous Lazarillo de Tormes; and in Beaumont's next play, *The Knight of the Burning Pestle,* there is undoubted reference to *Don Quixote,* though it is unlikely that the dramatist had actually read Cervantes' novel, the first part of which had been printed in Spain in 1605 and in Brussels in 1607. The play was probably produced by the children at Blackfriars about 1608. If it is not the greatest dramatic burlesque in English, it is certainly the most genuinely mirth-provoking and the most

The Knight
of the
Burning
Pestle

---

[5] The plays drawn upon are *The Wonder of a Kingdom* (1636) and *The Noble Soldier* (1634), in which Day seems to have collaborated with Dekker and Samuel Rowley respectively.
[6] See C. M. Gayley, *Beaumont the Dramatist* (1914), and references under Fletcher, below.
[7] Beaumont left Oxford very young, without a degree, and entered the Inner Temple in 1600.
[8] See A. W. Upton, "Allusions to James I and his Court in Marston's *Fawn* and Beaumont's *Woman-Hater,*" PMLA. XLIV (1929). 1048-1065.

genial. It gives a cavalier aristocrat's view of the London middle class. Their purse-proud boisterousness, social inexperience, appalling aesthetic tastes, and passion for civic entertainments are uproariously ridiculed, without the least reflection upon their lives or characters. The humor is more extravagant, but much more kindly, than that in *Eastward Ho!* The citizens are pictured without rancor and without damaging contrast with cavalier types. If there is a cavalier type in this play, it must be old Master Merrythought, the red-nosed, ballad-singing reprobate, who is one of the most delightful progenitors of Mr. Micawber.

One cannot say just when Beaumont and John Fletcher (1579-1625) began *Beaumont* to work together. Slight traces of Fletcher's hand have been found in the *and Fletcher* two Beaumont plays just discussed. It is certain that by 1610 the two drama- tists were collaborating in plays which established forever the prestige of this famous partnership.[9] *The Maid's Tragedy,* which is rather sentimental than tragic, and the tragicomedies *Philaster* and *A King and No King* [10] stand at the head of their performance. In all these the guiding hand is Beaumont's, and the great majority of the lines are in his style. The desire for escape is the chief characteristic. The plots are freely invented and set in strange places; Rhodes, Messina, and Armenia, where young patricians find themselves crushed under the coarse burdens of the world and battle for a better life. Beaumont is the great delineator of these febrile types, whom love, honor, and friendship drive to ecstatic pain, and sometimes to suicide. They are often strongly reminiscent of characters in Shakespeare's later plays, but are markedly more fragile.[11] They are defeated by the grossness that surrounds them and frequently talk like disciples of Rousseau, as when Philaster exclaims:

> Oh that I had been nourish'd in these woods
> With milk of goats and acorns, and not known
> The right of crowns nor the dissembling trains
> Of women's looks; but digg'd myself a cave,
> Where I, my fire, my cattle, and my bed
> Might have been shut together in one shed! (*Philaster,* IV, ii).

Beaumont's style is beautifully suited to these themes. It is in structure and emotional effect much like the style of Shakespeare's last plays, rich in run-on lines and very sweetly modulated. It tends to elegiac and epigrammatic neat-

[9] See S. A. Tannenbaum, *Beaumont and Fletcher: A Concise Bibliography* (1938). The complete text is in *The Works of Francis Beaumont and John Fletcher* (10v, Cambridge, 1905- 1912); critical text with valuable commentary in the incomplete Variorum ed. (4v, twenty plays only, 1904-1913). The best general guide is E. H. C. Oliphant, *The Plays of Beaumont and Fletcher* (New Haven, 1927), with supplement, "Some Additional Notes," *PQ,* IX (1930). 7-22. Consult also R. C. Bald, *Bibliographical Studies in the Beaumont and Fletcher Folio of 1647* (Bibl. Soc., 1938), and B. Maxwell, *Studies in Beaumont, Fletcher, and Massinger* (Chapel Hill, 1939).
[10] See A. Mizener, "The High Design of *A King and No King,*" *MP,* XXXVIII (1940). 133-154.
[11] See D. M. McKeithan, *The Debt to Shakespeare in the Beaumont-and-Fletcher Plays* (Austin, 1938); but see also A. H. Thorndike, *The Influence of Beaumont and Fletcher on Shakspere* (Worcester, Mass., 1901).

ness, and, without being at all stilted or verbose, strikes one as being the veritable language of ladies and gentlemen such as society has not yet quite succeeded in developing.

The Scorn-
ful Lady

An even more popular play of slightly later date, *The Scornful Lady,* has a preponderance of Fletcher in it and is much more mundane, being a strict comedy of London life. It introduces some very famous humor characters in Abigail, the "waiting gentlewoman," Sir Roger the curate, and Morecraft the usurer; but the main interest is love in high life, fantastically considered, and the chief action resolves itself into a duel of the sexes, represented by the ingenious Loveless and the quite unnamed "Lady," who (till the fifth act) outguesses him. This is the theme that Fletcher very successfully returned to in his later *Wild Goose Chase,* and then passed on to Congreve. It is not in Beaumont's spirit, and the latter's contribution may not be very much more than the long opening scene and the second scene of Act v.

Fletcher
without
Beaumont

Beaumont's life as a playwright was shorter than Marston's. In 1612 or 1613 he married and retired from London to live the short remainder of his life as a landed aristocrat in Kent, leaving Fletcher to bear the chief responsibility for the colossal "Beaumont-Fletcher" output, which ultimately amounted to over fifty plays. In nearly all these Fletcher had a considerable part, and in something like a third of the number his is the only hand that has been clearly detected. It is an easy hand to detect, for Fletcher early developed an individual type of blank verse, marked by an enormous proportion (*c.* 90 percent) of end-stopped lines and an unprecedented number (*c.* 70 percent) of double or treble endings. His use of words is very diffuse, where Beaumont prided himself on being laconic. Fletcher makes his blank verse so conversational that his plays have no need of prose and are perhaps the most readable of all verse dramas. The earliest is probably *The Faithful Shepherdess,* a pastoral after the general fashion of such Italian works as Guarini's *Pastor Fido* and Cinthio's *Egle.*[12] Fletcher's preface to it contains his well-known definition of the new type of play that became so closely linked with his name.

The
Faithful
Shepherdess

A tragicomedy is not so called in respect of mirth and killing, but in respect it wants deaths, which is enough to make it no tragedy, yet brings some near it, which is enough to make it no comedy.

It was acted by one of the boys' companies about 1608, but, like *The Knight of the Burning Pestle,* was so novel in method that it failed on the stage, and was immediately after printed with commendatory verses by Beaumont, Chapman, and Jonson. Fletcher's style is still immature in this lusciously romantic piece, but his graceful fluency is already conspicuous, and one recognizes in passages like the Priest of Pan's riming hymn in Act ii the origin of the "pretty paganism" of Keats's *Endymion.*

[12] See V. M. Jeffery, "Italian Influence in Fletcher's *Faithful Shepherdess,*" MLR, xxi (1926). 147-158; W. W. Greg, *Pastoral Poetry and Pastoral Drama* (1906), pp. 264-282.

More normal Fletcherian tragicomedy [13] is contained in *The Loyal Sub-*   *Fletcher's*
ject,[14] *A Wife for a Month*, and *The Mad Lover*, all marked by great ex-   *Tragi-*
travagance of plot; and this sort of thing is still more charmingly done in   *comedy*
Women Pleased (on the theme, in part, of Chaucer's *Wife of Bath's Tale*);
in *The Humorous Lieutenant*, which combines scenes of excruciating comic-
ality with an elevated Oriental plot suggestive of *A King and No King;*
and in *The Chances*, based on one of Cervantes' *Exemplary Novels* first
published in 1613. Another of these tales was used in *Love's Pilgrimage*
(which may not be entirely Fletcher's); and his remarkably close contact
with contemporary Spain appears again in *The Pilgrim*, founded on Lope
de Vega's play of the same title. Best of all, possibly, is *The Island Princess*,
the exotic and exciting play that Fletcher constructed, about 1622, from
Argensola's Spanish history of the conquest of the Molucca Islands (1609).
The literature of escape could hardly go farther, and Milton remembered
to great effect the languorous odors with which Fletcher suffuses his islands
of Ternate and Tidore:

> We are arriv'd among the blessed islands,
> Where every wind that rises blows perfumes,
> And every breath of air is like an incense.[15]

The rather vague borderline between tragicomedy and pure comedy may
be thought to be crossed in the early *Monsieur Thomas* (based on Part two
of d'Urfé's French novel, *Astrée*, 1610), which is very uproarious and
also very sentimental; and in the masterly dramatization of another of
Cervantes' *novelas*, *Rule a Wife and Have a Wife*, which is one of Fletcher's
last and best plays. Lighter comic work—often very light and very broad,
but seldom unlaughable—is found in *Wit without Money* and in Fletcher's
sequel or counterpart to *The Taming of the Shrew*, which he called *The
Woman's Prize, or The Tamer Tamed*, and which may be one of his very
earliest plays. At the opposite emotional pole from these stand another early
play, *Cupid's Revenge* (a melodrama derived from two stories in Sidney's
Arcadia), and two early tragedies of great sentimental power, in plot Roman
and British-Roman respectively, *Valentinian* and *Bonduca*.

Fletcher knew the remedy for a tired and distrustful world, which was
not to satirize but divert it. His plays are artificially flavored, and the
condiments he uses most are variety and vehemence. To be sure, the variety
is somewhat superficial, and the vehemence may be specious. These are less
deeply poetic qualities than Beaumont's vibrant idealism and gnomic grace,
but they have never lost their attractiveness for average humanity. The
reading of Fletcher is like a long voyage through a tropical archipelago.

---

[13] For careful discussion see E. M. Waith, "Characterization in John Fletcher's Tragicomedies,"
RES, XIX (1943). 141-164; and on the general type see F. H. Ristine, *English Tragicomedy*
(1910).
[14] The plays mentioned in this paragraph are not listed in chronological order. Modern
criticism has been much more successful in apportioning the authorship of the Beaumont-
Fletcher-Massinger plays than in determining their dates. A list in approximate chronological
order is given in *CHEL*, VI. 155-159.
[15] *The Island Princess*, I. iii. Compare *Paradise Lost*, II. 636 ff., IV. 159 ff.

The air is sultry and tempestuous, the landscapes are over-florid; but no one forgets the experience, though most of the details—except the magnificent songs [16] and the electric scenes of tension—will soon fade from memory. Fletcher was with Chapman and Shakespeare in the small list of men whom Ben Jonson professed to love, and he was chosen to be Shakespeare's official successor at the new Globe of 1613. Beginning as a writer for the boys' companies, he soon rose to the service of the King's Men, and after collaborating with their leading poet in *Henry VIII* and *The Two Noble Kinsmen* [17] continued as the chief dramatist for that premier company till his death in the plague of 1625. Among all the playwrights of the day no more practical substitute for Shakespeare could have been found. Fletcher kept his two theatres of the Globe and Blackfriars very prosperous, and to contemporary critics it was not always as evident as it should have been that they had suffered a great loss in the exchange they had made. Even the exquisite poet, Henry Vaughan, concludes his lines "Upon Mr. Fletcher's Plays" (1647) with the words:

> This or that age may write, but never see
> A wit that dares run parallel with thee.
> True, BEN must live; but bate him, and thou hast
> Undone all future wits and matched the past.

For about a dozen years Fletcher provided the King's company with three or four plays per annum; and in this Herculean task he received occasional assistance from a number of other dramatists, such as William Rowley, Nathan Field, and even Jonson. Some of the most interesting plays —e.g., *The Knight of Malta, The Bloody Brother,* and *The Fair Maid of the Inn*—offer very difficult problems of multiple authorship. Fletcher's great associate, however, during his latter years was Philip Massinger, who combined with him in more than a dozen plays before 1623. They include many of the best in the Fletcher canon: the tragedies of *Thierry and Theodoret, Barnavelt, The False One, The Prophetess, The Double Marriage,* and *The Lover's Progress;* and, among the tragicomedies, *The Little French Lawyer, Beggars' Bush, The Custom of the Country, The Spanish Curate, The Sea-voyage,* and *The Elder Brother.* It is to be remarked that these are mixed plays. Of the tragedies, only *Barnavelt,* out of contemporary Dutch history, and *Thierry and Theodoret,* from an ancient French chronicle, have much tragic feeling, though they all contain violent deaths. The tragicomedies are wonderful blends of farce and high romance. Among the most interesting of them all are *The False One,* which handles much the same subject as Shaw's *Caesar and Cleopatra,* and *The Sea-voyage,* which is a pendant to *The Island Princess,* dealing with adventures amid the farthest seas. *The Little French Lawyer* and *The Spanish Curate* have some of the most rollick-

Fletcher and Massinger

---

[16] See E. H. Fellowes, *Songs and Lyrics from the Plays of Beaumont and Fletcher* (1928); E. S. Lindsay, "The Music of the Songs in Fletcher's Plays," *SP,* xxi (1924). 325-356, and "The Original Music for Beaumont's Play, *The Knight of the Burning Pestle,*" *SP,* xxvi (1929). 425-443.
[17] See Theodore Spencer, "*The Two Noble Kinsmen,*" *MP,* xxxvi (1939). 255-276.

ing scenes in dramatic literature; but perhaps the best play of the group is *Beggars' Bush*, which, without servile imitation, contrives to combine the main romantic interests in *As You Like It* and *The Merchant of Venice* with the vagrant comedy in Jonson's *Masque of the Metamorphosed Gipsies* (1621).

Massinger's contribution to the "Beaumont-Fletcher" Folios is in bulk very considerably larger than Beaumont's; but in the plays he wrote with Fletcher Massinger was never the controlling partner, and this may have something to do with the fact that Massinger withdrew from participation and took service with another company a couple of years before Fletcher's death. It is Fletcher who gives these plays their characteristic flavor, which is not very different from that of his unaided work. It is usually he who handles the great scenes of climax or boisterous nonsense, and who conceives the most original characters, while Massinger, who is one of the world's finest dramatic technicians, attends usefully to the openings and closes and the general coherence.[18]

[18] See M. Chelli, *Étude sur la collaboration de Massinger avec Fletcher et son groupe* (Paris, 1926).

V
Caroline Drama, 1625-1642

   Philip Massinger [1] (1583-1640) was born at Salisbury, a few miles from the Earl of Pembroke's Wilton House, and was most likely given his Christian name in compliment to the Earl's brother-in-law, Sir Philip Sidney. His father was a man of standing, fellow of Merton College, Oxford, Member of Parliament, and confidential agent of the Herbert family.[2] These influences have affected much of the son's literary work, as was long ago pointed out by the historian, S. R. Gardiner:

> In many of Massinger's plays we have a treatment of the politics of the day so plain and transparent, that any one who possesses only a slight acquaintance with the history of the reigns of the first two Stuarts can read it at a glance.[3]

   Massinger's loyalty is to the old aristocracy as against both royal absolutism and the ambition of courtly parvenus. One of his earlier plays, *The Bondman* [4] (1623), which is dedicated to Philip, Earl of Montgomery, satirizes the amateur-admiral Buckingham, the young and powerful favorite of King James. *The Great Duke of Florence* [5] (1627), written soon after the death of James, seems to present Buckingham less rancorously in his relation to both the old and the new king. Two later plays, *Believe as You List* [6] (1631) and *The Maid of Honor* [7] (1632?), introduce propaganda in behalf of King Charles's unfortunate brother-in-law, the Elector Frederick, who was one of the outstanding victims of Spanish diplomacy and the Thirty Years' War (1618-1648).

   The core of seriousness in Massinger shows itself also in his attitude to religion. He collaborated with Dekker in *The Virgin-Martyr,* an essentially Catholic tragedy of St. Dorothea. In his *Renegado* [8] (1624) the noblest character is a Jesuit priest; and in *The Maid of Honor* the heroine, Camiola, resolves the play by a course unusual on the English stage, that of entering

---

[1] Gifford's edition of Massinger appeared first in 1805 and was reprinted by F. Cunningham (1868, etc.). Ten plays are in the Mermaid Series, ed. A. Symons. There is no modern collected edition, but most of the plays have been elaborately edited as indicated below. See S. A. Tannenbaum, *Philip Massinger: A Concise Bibliography* (1938); A. H. Cruickshank, *Philip Massinger* (Oxford, 1920); M. Chelli, *Le Drame de Massinger* (Paris, 1924); B. T. Spencer, "Philip Massinger," in *Seventeenth Century Studies,* ed. R. Shafer (1933), pp. 3-119.
[2] See M. Eccles, "Arthur Massinger," *LTLS,* July 16, 1931, p. 564.
[3] "The Political Element in Massinger," *Trans. New Shakspere Soc.,* 1875-6, pp. 314-331.
[4] Ed. B. T. Spencer (Princeton, 1932).
[5] Ed. J. M. Stochholm (Baltimore, 1933).
[6] Reprinted, Malone Soc. (1927).
[7] Ed. E. A. W. Bryne (1927).
[8] See W. G. Rice, "The Sources of Massinger's *The Renegado," PQ,* XI (1932). 65-75.

a nunnery. His style, always suave and lucid, is often over-rhetorical, and his characters commonly lack the vitality that Fletcher could give. His forte is dramatic structure, and here very few seventeenth-century playwrights could equal him. *The Duke of Milan*[9] (*c.* 1621), a transplanting of the Herod and Mariamne story to sixteenth-century Italy with many grafts from *Othello,* and *The Unnatural Combat*[10] on a Cenci-like theme of horror, are deftly planned, but melodramatic. *The Roman Actor*[11] (1626), which he termed "the most perfect birth of my Minerva," is indeed a noble tragedy in solemn sort; but it is in comedy that Massinger most escapes from the mechanical and drab excellence which is his weakness. His serious nature seemed to require the fillip that comedy gave, and it is his comedy that best justifies the very high tributes which modern critics have paid him: "next to Shakespeare as a dramatist pure and simple,"[12] and "our first conscious producer of modern literary comedy."[13]

Massinger's finest comedies are two on contemporary English themes: *A New Way to Pay Old Debts*[14] (1626) and *The City Madam*[15] (1632). The first is made on the formula of Middleton's *A Trick to Catch the Old One.* Massinger's play is twenty years the later, and may well appear two centuries later, so expertly has it been modernized. He builds it around the actual figure of Sir Giles Mompesson[16] (1584-1651), a notorious extortioner of the day and protégé of Buckingham, who had been unmasked and convicted in 1621. Massinger has enlarged him into the terrific Sir Giles Overreach, who has the lineaments of the modern city boss, keeping out of office himself (unlike Mompesson)—"in being out of office I am out of danger," he says—and executing his sinister schemes by means of venal judges and slavish henchmen. The wild young realistic rogue of Middleton's intrigue comedy is replaced by a new type of hero in Wellborn, the good-hearted spendthrift, who in his own character and in such descendants as Charles Surface of *The School for Scandal* became the idol of the eighteenth-century stage. Middleton's realistic plotting is replaced by a romantic trick that is the pivot on which Massinger makes his whole play revolve. It is but a whisper in the closing lines of Act I, seen but not heard by the spectators, whereby Lady Allworth endows Wellborn with that most priceless of modern boons: credit. The cataclysmic dénouement, which seems generations more recent than that of Jonson's *Alchemist,* is engineered by recourse to modern chemistry. From the opening scene to the last this

(margin) A New Way to Pay Old Debts.

---

[9] Ed. T. W. Baldwin (Lancaster, Pa., 1918). In this connection bare mention may be made of Robert Gomersall's Oxford play, *The Tragedy of Lodovick Sforza, Duke of Milan* (1628; ed. B. R. Pearn, Louvain, 1933), which keeps much closer to history than Massinger does.

[10] Ed. R. S. Telfer (Princeton, 1932).

[11] Ed. W. M. Sandidge (Princeton, 1929).

[12] Cruickshank, *op. cit.,* p. 123.

[13] C. M. Gayley, *Representative English Comedies,* III (1914), p. lxxxix. Note also William Archer's high tribute to Massinger in *The Old Drama and the New* (1929), pp. 100 ff.

[14] Ed. A. H. Cruickshank (Oxford, 1926).

[15] Ed. Rudolf Kirk (Princeton, 1934).

[16] See R. H. Ball, "Sir Giles Mompesson and Sir Giles Overreach," in *Parrott Presentation Vol.* (1935), pp. 277-287, and *The Amazing Career of Sir Giles Overreach* (Princeton, 1939).

play moves with enormous power. Massinger's *vis comica* is as pulverizing as Jonson's is in *Volpone*, though far less human; and as Edmund Kean played *A New Way to Pay Old Debts* in the early nineteenth century, the effects seem to have exceeded anything that can be expected or desired of comedy:

> In the famous scene in the fifth act the power of Kean's acting was so intense that women in the audience shrieked with terror and Lord Byron was seized with a convulsive fit. That experienced actress, Mrs. Glover, fainted on the stage, Mrs. Horn staggered to a chair and wept aloud; while Munden, who played Marrall, stood so transfixed with terror that he had to be removed from the stage.[17]

'he City
tadam

Kean likewise revived *The City Madam* under the title of *Riches,* and John Keats reviewed the performance with approval in *The Champion* newspaper (December 21, 1817). Here Massinger seems to have set himself the task of modernizing another great comedy of the previous age, *Eastward Ho!* Again he adds a Dickens-like super-monster in Luke Frugal, the hypocrite, who has the same malign brilliance as Overreach. The plot concerns the troubles of a sober and wealthy citizen, Sir John Frugal, with his pampered wife and daughters. It is the situation of *Eastward Ho!,* but here both daughters are perverse and both apprentices riotous. Even the Virginian interest of *Eastward Ho!* is paralleled in a scene of most caustic cynicism, in which Luke, newly come into the family wealth, bargains with some pretended Indian chiefs over the sale of his undesired sister-in-law and nieces for export. Massinger, said Arthur Symons, "is the late twilight of the long and splendid day of which Marlowe was the dawn." The twilight came on robed in solemn clouds of rhetorical tragedy and brilliant coruscations of comic lightning, but what Hamlet called the modesty of nature had largely disappeared from view.

ohn Ford

John Ford[18] (1586-c. 1655), whose name often appears characteristically anagrammatized on his title-pages as *Fide honor* (by faith, honor), was the greatest dramatist of the reign of Charles I. He had collaborated with Dekker in various earlier plays, mainly lost. One of these, still surviving, is *The Sun's Darling* (1624), a "choral masque" which contains passages of very great beauty. The eight plays[19] that are Ford's unaided work all probably belong to the reign of Charles; none can have been written much before the author's fortieth year. Four are comedies or tragicomedies, and would be of little interest but for their connection with his four transcendent trag-

---

[17] John Parker, quoted in Cruickshank's ed., p. 129.

[18] Gifford's edition of Ford, revised by A. Dyce (1869), is of lasting importance. A more scientific text is offered by W. Bang and H. de Vocht (Louvain, 1908-1927; with text of *The Queen,* ed. W. Bang, Louvain, 1905). Five plays are in the Mermaid Series volume, with introduction by Havelock Ellis. The best commentaries are M. J. Sargeaunt, *John Ford* (Oxford, 1935), and G. T. Sensabaugh, *The Tragic Muse of John Ford* (1945).

[19] This number includes *The Queen, or the Excellency of her Sex* (1653), which internal evidence alone assigns to Ford. See H. D. Sykes, "John Ford's Posthumous Play, *The Queen,*" in *Sidelights on Elizabethan Drama* (Oxford, 1924), pp. 173-182; and *ibid.,* pp. 183-199, for assertion of Ford's (unlikely) authorship of *The Spanish Gipsy.* For further addition to the Ford canon see A. Harbage, "Elizabethan-Restoration Palimpsest," *MLR,* xxxv (1940). 287-319, and G. T. Sensabaugh, "Another Play by John Ford," *MLQ,* iii (1942). 595-601.

edies. Ford is like no one but Webster, although, with great similarities, these two have also great differences. *The Broken Heart* was acted by the *Ford and* King's Men at Blackfriars sixteen or eighteen years after the same company *Webster* had performed *The Duchess of Malfi*. Both poets are remarkable for their portraits of suffering women. Both are great dirge-writers, though not otherwise given to song. Neither finds much place for comedy in his serious plays. Ford's prologue to *The Broken Heart* overtly abjures such matter;

> The title lends no expectation here
> Of apish laughter, or of some lame jeer
> At place or persons;

and indeed his attempts at comic relief are almost always failures. Like Webster, but less frequently, Ford uses melodramatic devices to deepen his psychological effects. The mechanical chair in *The Broken Heart* and the entrance of Giovanni in *'Tis Pity* with Annabella's heart on his dagger are in the Websterian tradition. The great difference between these writers is in their tone and style. Webster's method is unnaturally violent, Ford's unnaturally quiet. To pass from one to the other is almost like passing from a train-wreck to the incurable ward of a hospital. The lines of Webster which burn themselves unforgettably into our minds—"I am Duchess of Malfi still," etc.—are followed in Ford by bleak and anguished whispers. There is hardly a detachable line in the beautifully intricated fabric of his dramas. This is partly the result of twenty years more of disillusion, and it may partly be the influence of Beaumont, whose marmoreal style Ford seems to have taken as a model.

Ford is, in a noble sense, a psychopathic dramatist, dealing with the pathology of love and honor. In 1621 Robert Burton's *Anatomy of Melancholy* appeared, and Ford's first published play, *The Lover's Melancholy* (1629), relies very frequently upon this great work. He borrowed from *Ford's Psy-* it heavily in the psychology of three of his tragedies as well.[20] *'Tis Pity* *chopathic* *She's a Whore* is a study of romantic incest, *Love's Sacrifice* of moral *Tragedies* (though not actual) adultery, and *The Broken Heart* of various erotic frustrations. Just as in Middleton, there are hardly any bad people in Ford. His characters are their own worst enemies, and are destroyed by psychoses that arise out of generous natures. They are inevitably destroyed, for civilized man is always too weak in this dramatist to cope with the emotional wilderness into which he has wandered. One of Ford's most pathetic, though possibly unconscious, tricks is to recall the days when men and women were stronger: to cast the estimable duke of *Love's Sacrifice* in the role of Othello; to make the old buffoon, Mauruccio, chant,

> Thus do we march to honor's haven of bliss,
> To ride in triumph through Persepolis! (*Love's Sacrifice*, II. i),

---

[20] See S. B. Ewing, *Burtonian Melancholy in the Plays of John Ford* (Princeton, 1940); also G. F. Sensabaugh, "John Ford and Platonic Love in the Court," *SP*, xxxvi (1939). 206-226, and "John Ford and Elizabethan Tragedy," *PQ*, xx (1941). 442-453.

and make Giovanni in *'Tis Pity* speak for a moment like Fauṣtus,

> Let poring book-men dream of other worlds;
> My world and all of happiness is here,
> And I 'ld not change it for the best to come:
> A life of pleasure is elysium! (v. iii),

or like Tamburlaine,

> why, I hold fate
> Clasp'd in my fist, and could command the course
> .Of time's eternal motion (v. v).

Except when he tries to write comedy, Ford is one of the most refined of dramatists, both in the delicacy of his constructive methods and the essential decency of his probings into disordered soul-states. The gallery of broken hearts in his well-named and well-set Spartan tragedy, where one sees character after character enduring the unendurable till he quietly collapses, is perhaps the best monument of Ford's sympathetic and pessimistic art.

The Broken Heart

In the year after Burton's *Anatomy* another psychological masterpiece was published, Francis Bacon's *History of the Reign of King Henry VII* (1622); and in this Ford found the motive for his fourth tragedy, *Perkin Warbeck*,[21] which was acted by Queen Henrietta Maria's company and printed in 1634. For a generation there had hardly been a great English history play, and since Marlowe's *Edward II* there had been none of this quietly analytical character.

Perkin Warbeck

> Studies have of this nature been of late
> So out of fashion, so unfollowed,

Ford apologized in his prologue. To him Perkin offered an irresistibly attractive subject: the sincere and generous impostor, "a king and no king" in the deepest sense. The famous Beaumont-Fletcher play of that title doubtless gave suggestions, just as another aspect of the same play, the incest motive, must have influenced *'Tis Pity*. But in Bacon's analysis of the minds of Perkin and his adversary, the astute Henry VII, Ford found incitement to the subtle character work in which he excelled. The noble personalities of Perkin and his wife, her father, and her discarded lover Dalyell are exquisitely developed, and the two kings, James of Scotland and Henry of England, are wonderfully just studies. The language, which, as Hartley Coleridge said, in all Ford's plays "is as clear as the stars on a frosty night," [22] is nowhere lovelier or more completely subjected to its dramatic purpose; for instance, in Perkin's farewell to Katherine (iii. ii), in which, as so often, the sense of tragic futility is emphasized by an ironic after-echo of Marlowe:

[21] Ford also used a more prosaic source, Thomas Gainsford's *True and Wonderful History of Perkin Warbeck* (1618). See J. L. G. Brereton, "The Sources of Ford's *Perkin Warbeck*," *Anglia*, xxxiv (1911). 194-234, and M. C. Struble's edition of the play (Seattle, 1926). See also Lawrence Babb, "Abnormal Psychology in John Ford's *Perkin Warbeck*," MLN, li (1936). 234-237.
[22] Introduction to *Works of Massinger and Ford* (1840), p. xlv, note.

If thou hear'st
A truth of my sad ending by the hand
Of some unnatural subject, thou withal
Shalt hear how I died worthy of my right
By falling like a king; and in the close,
Which my last breath shall sound, thy name, thou fairest,
Shall sing a requiem to my soul, unwilling
Only of greater glory, 'cause divided
From such a heaven on earth as life with thee.
But these are chimes for funerals: my business
Attends on fortune of a sprightlier trump;
For love and majesty are reconcil'd,
And vow to crown thee empress of the west.

The greatness of *Perkin Warbeck* needs to be dwelt on, lest hasty readers of Ford get the idea that his effects are simply the consequence of lurid or unhealthy subjects.

The example of Jonson's great plays can be traced in most of the later *The School* dramatists. It is often strong in Beaumont, Fletcher, and Massinger, though *of Jonson* all those writers tended more toward escape and romance than Jonson ordinarily did. The first of his immediate heirs is Nathan Field [23] (1587-1620), who as a boy had been "taken up" or kidnaped for the Chapel *Nathan* Children in time to act important parts in *Cynthia's Revels* and *Poetaster*. *Field* Jonson read Horace and Martial with him, and doubtless helped to undo whatever Puritan inheritance Nat might have received from his father, the Reverend John Field, who had been much the same sort of play-hater as Ben's own parent. When Field grew up, he joined the adult actors and was accounted second only to Burbage. Around 1612 he produced two lewd London comedies,[24] *A Woman Is a Weathercock* and *Amends for Ladies,* both acted by the boys' companies. Later he collaborated with Massinger in a fine tragedy, *The Fatal Dowry* [25] (*c.* 1618), and had a hand in certain Beaumont-Fletcher plays; e.g., *The Knight of Malta* and *Four Plays in One.* Field naturally knew the stage, and he molded his structure, though not his moral philosophy, upon Jonson's. He is adept at bright dialogue, brisk action, and clever disguise. His prose is lively and idiomatic; but his humor characters, though very varied, are superficial, and his verse is uninspired.

Richard Brome [26] (*c.* 1590-*c.* 1652) is first mentioned in the introduction to *Richard* Jonson's *Bartholomew Fair* (1614), where he is alluded to familiarly as *Brome* the "man" or personal servant of the author, who attended to his education, as was his wont. Jonson's patronage may account for the fact that Brome became the friend of Dekker, Fletcher, Ford, and Shirley; and in 1623 he

[23] See R. F. Brinkley, *Nathan Field, the Actor-Playwright* (New Haven, 1928).
[24] Reprinted in a Mermaid Series volume, *Nero and Other Plays,* with introduction by A. W. Verity.
[25] Ed. C. L. Lockert (Lancaster, Pa., 1918).
[26] *Works of Richard Brome* (3v, 1873). See C. E. Andrews, *Richard Brome, a Study of His Life and Works* (1913).

had written a comedy, licensed but now lost, in collaboration with Jonson's son, Benjamin Jr. His name appears with Dekker's on the title-page of the interesting *Late Lancashire Witches* (1634), and he has claim to fifteen extant plays of his own, which are about as full of Jonsonian qualities as the plays of a mediocre dramatist could be.[27] Most of them are humor or intrigue comedies. They retained their popularity into the Restoration age and are still instructive as pictures of manners, and, though coarse-grained, are readable. *The Antipodes*[28] (1638) is a clever *tour de force* in which young Peregrine's bookish humor for travel-literature and various other humors are cured by a pretended voyage to the antipodes. There was a strain of romance in Brome, which rather increased in his later work. His best play is his last and his most romantic, *A Jovial Crew, or The Merry Beggars* (1641), which was acted very shortly before the closing of the theatres. It is, as the prologue well describes it, a play

> Of fortune-tellers, damsels and their squires,
> Expos'd to strange adventures through the briars
> Of love and fate,

a play that still retains a great deal of Jonson, but is most suggestive of the Jonson of *The Metamorphosed Gipsies, The Sad Shepherd,* and the better scenes of *The New Inn.*

Shakerley Marmion

Shakerley Marmion[29] (1602-1639), an impoverished member of a distinguished family, after taking his M. A. at Oxford in 1624 and soldiering for a while in the Low Countries, pushed his literary fortunes with some success, but died prematurely as a result of service in the troop of horse which his friend, Sir John Suckling, raised for the campaign against the Scots that preluded the Civil Wars. He left a fine mythological poem, *Cupid and Psyche*[30] (1637) and three comedies of merit: *Holland's Leaguer* (1632), *A Fine Companion* (1633), and *The Antiquary* (c. 1635). They are amusingly written, with considerable display of classical learning and much Jonsonian reminiscence. The humors of the coward Captain Whibble (an imitation of Bobadill) in *A Fine Companion* and of the antiquary in the play of that name were long appreciated. Marmion will leave the modern reader with a favorable impression of his talents and of the cavalier society he wrote for. His first play is sordid enough in parts, but his sense of humor is true and his language graceful.

Thomas Nabbes[31] (c. 1605-c. 1641), a Worcestershire man of lowly origin, who matriculated at Exeter College, Oxford, in 1621 at the age of sixteen,

---

[27] For possible additions to the Brome canon see A. Harbage, "Elizabethan-Restoration Palimpsest," *MLR*, XXXV (1940). 304-309.

[28] Ed. G. P. Baker in Gayley, *Representative English Comedies*, III (1914).

[29] Marmion's *Dramatic Works* have been edited by J. Maidment and W. H. Logan (2v, 1875).

[30] Ed. G. Saintsbury, *Caroline Poets,* II (Oxford, 1906), pp. 1-60, and more recently by Alice Jones Nearing, *Cupid and Psyche, by Shakerly Marmion—A Critical Edition: with an Account of Marmion's Life and Works* (Philadelphia, 1944). See S. Maxwell, "An Addition to the First Idyl of Moschus," *AJP*, LXIV (1943). 435-439.

[31] See A. H. Bullen, *The Works of Thomas Nabbes* (2v, 1887); and for discussion, C. Moore, *The Dramatic Works of Thomas Nabbes* (Menasha, Wis., 1918).

left a half-dozen plays of different sorts and a few bits of occasional verse, *Thomas* but hardly any other record of his existence. He is inferior to Marmion as *Nabbes* a poet and to Brome as a dramatist, but he had ambition and a creditable desire to bear the Jonsonian torch into various fields. His long "moral masque," *Microcosmos* (1637), is only historically interesting, because of the new elaborateness of its stage effects and the effort to inflate Jonson's masque technique into something suggestive of the old morality play. His tragedy of *Hannibal and Scipio* (1635), introducing the popular figure of Sophonisba, covers so long a stretch of time and place that it falls apart between the acts and amounts virtually to a classical pageant; and his attempt at melodrama, *The Bride* (1638), is feebly constructed and very flatly written. It was in two earlier London comedies—*Covent Garden,* acted in 1632 and dedicated to Suckling, and *Tottenham Court,* acted in 1633—that Nabbes did his best work.[32] They tell a good deal of the life of the time and are amusing illustrations of the zeal with which the Caroline public served God and Mammon. Nabbes's good characters are prigs of the stamp that returned into vogue in the sentimental comedy of Queen Anne's age, while his plots teeter on the brink of Restoration licentiousness.

James Shirley [33] (1596-1666), though a very imitative dramatist, cannot, *James* like those just discussed, be accounted for as simply a follower of Jonson. *Shirley* There are thirty-one extant plays by Shirley, more than by any contemporary except Fletcher and Shakespeare. Had not a famous act of Parliament in 1642 cut off his productivity at its height, there might have been many more, for Shirley was giving his public precisely what they wanted. It was a more limited public than Shakespeare's, confined practically to the royal court and the élite of like-minded cavaliers who patronized the private playhouses. The King's Company now depended upon their intimate performances at Blackfriars, and their great public theatre, the Globe on the Bankside, had lost caste. When some occasion required them to produce Shirley's *The Doubtful Heir* (1640) at the Globe, the dramatist wrote a prologue that is informingly contemptuous of middle-class taste:

> All that the Prologue comes for is to say,
> Our author did not calculate this play
> For this meridian. The Bankside, he knows,
> Is far more skilful at the ebbs and flows
> Of water than of wit . . .
> No clown, no squibs, no devil in 't! Oh, now,
> You squirrels that want nuts, what will you do?
> Pray, do not crack the benches, and we may
> Hereafter fit *your* palates with a play.

[32] These two comedies and others by Marmion, Brome, and Shirley are discussed by Theodore Miles, "Place-Realism in a Group of Caroline Plays," *RES,* xviii (1942). 428-440.

[33] Shirley's *Dramatic Works and Poems* were edited by A. Dyce (6v, 1833). For discussion see A. H. Nason, *James Shirley, Dramatist, a Biographical and Critical Study* (1915); H. T. Parlin, *A Study in Shirley's Comedies of London Life* (Austin, 1914); R. S. Forsythe, *The Relations of Shirley's Plays to the Elizabethan Drama* (1914); A. C. Baugh, "Some New Facts about Shirley," *MLR,* xvii (1922). 228-235, and "Further Facts about James Shirley," *RES,* vii (1931). 62-66.

But you that can contract yourselves, and sit
As you were now in the Blackfriars pit,
And will not deaf us with lewd noise and tongues,
Because we have no heart to break our lungs,
Will pardon our vast stage and not disgrace
This play, meant for *your* persons, not the place.

King Charles took a personal interest in Shirley and collaborated more or less in his play, *The Gamester* (1633), of which, according to the well-known anecdote, the King later reported, "it was the best play he had seen for seven years." When the Earl of Strafford was maintaining viceregal pomp in Ireland (1636-1640), Shirley was brought to Dublin to advance the court prestige there,[34] his plays being, of course, produced in London also.

Under Sir Henry Herbert, Master of the Revels since 1623, the censorship of plays had become almost a matter of court protocol,[35] and Shirley was the writer who best satisfied Herbert's ideals, as he testified in his words concerning *The Young Admiral* (1633):

The comedy called *The Young Admiral,* being free from oaths, profaneness, or obsceneness, hath given me much delight and satisfaction in the reading, and may serve for a pattern to other poets, not only for the bettering of manners and language, but for the improvement of the quality [profession], which hath received some brushings of late.[36] When Mr. Shirley hath read this approbation, I know it will encourage him to pursue this beneficial and cleanly way of poetry; and when other poets hear and see his good success, I am confident they will imitate the original for their own credit, and make such copies in this harmless way as shall speak them masters in their art, at the first sight, to all judicious spectators . . . I have entered this allowance for direction to my successor, and for example to all poets that shall write after the date hereof.

Shirley was in truth a gentleman and a poet. Educated at Spenser's old school, the Merchant Taylors', and at both Oxford and Cambridge, he took Anglican orders and became headmaster of the grammar school at St. Albans, but was converted to Roman Catholicism and in 1625 set up as a playwright in London. He wrote almost every type of play except the chronicle history; masques, comedies, tragicomedies, and tragedies dropped with equal ease from his fluent pen. Except in fecundity, however, he is dwarfed by the "giant race" that stands behind him. He has been likened to the inheritor of an exhausted mine, and the reader of his well-bred and gracious dramas is likely to be haunted by echoes. His fine tragedy, *The Cardinal* (1641), for example, though doubtless independently suggested by the contemporary career of Richelieu in France, reminds one, to its cost, of *The Duchess of Malfi;* and another fine tragedy, *The Traitor* (1631), comes into disadvantageous comparison with *The Revenger's Tragedy* of Tourneur. His tragicomedies, though usually entertaining and noble in sentiment, are too

---

[34] See Allan H. Stevenson, "James Shirley and the Actors at the First Irish Theater," *MP*, XL (1942). 147-160.
[35] See J. Q. Adams, *The Dramatic Records of Sir Henry Herbert* (1917).
[36] Particularly from the *Histrio-Mastix* of William Prynne, published in this year 1633.

mild and too loosely constructed to hold the attention after the best work of Fletcher and Massinger, as any one will note who will read *The Coronation* (1635), which, though by Shirley, was printed in 1640 as "written by John Fletcher, Gent.," and included in the Beaumont-Fletcher Folio of 1679.

Shirley is most successful, on the whole, in pure comedy; and here, for all his sobriety and rectitude, his place is with the Restoration writers. The mock-trial scene between Depazzi and his servant Rogero in *The Traitor* (III. i) is entirely delightful. *The Lady of Pleasure* (1635) is really Restoration comedy in every respect except its date and possibly its scant modicum of social restraint. A still earlier comedy, *The Witty Fair One* (1628), has distinct forebodings of Wycherley, even to a character named Manly; while its chief figures, Aimwell and Fowler, resemble the errant heroes of Farquhar's *Beaux' Stratagem,* in more than name. The flatness that one observes in Shirley's serious work is hardly felt in his songs.[37] In this respect the old drama retained a high degree of freshness to the very end. *The Triumph of Peace,* which Shirley wrote and Inigo Jones produced in 1634, the year of *Comus,* is the most ingenious and elaborate, and not the least harmonious, of its kind; and for a later masque, *The Contention of Ajax and Ulysses,* Shirley wrote the surpassingly noble and prophetic lines that are the finest elegy on this doomed society:

> The glories of our blood and state
>   Are shadows, not substantial things.
> There is no armor against fate,
>   Death lays his icy hand on kings.
>   Sceptre and crown
>   Must tumble down,
> And in the dust be equal made
> With the poor crooked scythe and spade....
>
> The garlands wither on your brow;
>   Then boast no more your mighty deeds.
> Upon Death's purple altar now
>   See where the victor-victim bleeds.
>   Your heads must come
>   To the cold tomb.
> Only the actions of the just
> Smell sweet and blossom in their dust.

Along with Shirley should be mentioned two heterogeneous dramatists of fair productivity and some poetic grace, Robert Davenport[38] and Henry Glapthorne.[39] Davenport is first mentioned in 1624 in licensing entries by Herbert, his best-known play, *The City Nightcap,* being one of those presented in that year. His tragedy, *King John and Matilda,* harks back to the

Davenport and Glapthorne

---

[37] See *The Poems of James Shirley,* ed. Ray L. Armstrong (1941).
[38] See A. H. Bullen, *The Works of Robert Davenport* (1890).
[39] See *The Plays and Poems of Henry Glapthorne,* ed. J. Pearson (2v, 1874).

Robert, Earl of Huntingdon plays of Chettle and Munday in its theme and is rather old-fashioned in its treatment. His *New Trick to Cheat the Devil*, which was printed in 1639, ranks with Glapthorne's *The Hollander*, written in 1635, and *Wit in a Constable*, written in 1639, among the better examples of late Caroline comedy. Glapthorne's tragedy, *Argalus and Parthenia*, is weakly dramatized out of the *Arcadia*, and his tragicomedy, *The Lady's Privilege*, with an aristocratic Genoese setting, carries the love-and-honor theme to absurd lengths. Perhaps his most interesting play is the tragedy, *Albertus Wallenstein*, acted in 1639 and based on the atrocity which had occurred at Eger five years before. It is by no means equal to Schiller, the love scenes being unreal and the treatment of history cheaply sensational, but it contains a good variant of the humorous soldier type in Colonel Newman.

Jonson was imitated by his friend and patron, the Earl of Newcastle, in *The Variety* (*c.* 1639) and *The Country Captain*, probably with the assistance of Shirley; and by Thomas Killigrew (1612-1683) in a similar comedy of intrigue, *The Parson's Wedding*. Both these writers are interesting links between the Caroline stage and that of the Restoration. In the same style, but of a better quality, are *The Ordinary* (*c.* 1635) by Jonson's "son," William Cartwright, and *The City Match* by Jasper Mayne, both written by clerics of Christ Church, Oxford, and members of Charles I's entourage; while at the very end of the period young Abraham Cowley appeared briefly and thinly as a comic writer with his *Guardian* (1642). Nearly all the plays mentioned here were performed before the King and Queen as well as at the private playhouses, and the connection between the theatre and court was so close at this time that the personal tastes of the sovereigns had unusual influence on dramatic developments.[40] The taste of Charles I's consort, Henrietta Maria, for histrionic pleasures gave wicked point to Prynne's *Histrio-Mastix* in 1633, when she herself acted in Walter Montague's insipid pastoral, *The Shepherd's Paradise*. She seems to have cared most for song, Arcadianism, Platonic love, and wild adventure; and there quickly arose a body of amateur dramatists eager to provide these things. No great plays resulted, but the general course of development was affected in at least two ways: in the spread of critical prejudice against "low" characters and situations, and the introduction of more elaborate scenery and costuming than the ordinary stage had hitherto employed. The professional playwrights soon found their amateur rivals a nuisance, and Brome in his *Court Beggar*, as early as 1632, sardonically proposes

Drama at the Court

> That no plays may be admitted to the stage but of their making who profess or endeavor to live by the quality: that no courtiers, divines, students at law, lawyers' clerks, tradesmen or prentices be allowed to write 'em; nor the works of any lay-poet whatsoever to be received to the stage, though freely given unto the actors, nay, though any such poet should give a sum of money with his play.

[40] The subject and the various dramatists concerned are very well treated by Alfred Harbage, *Cavalier Drama* (1936). The texts of many of the plays are to be found (badly edited) in the Hazlitt-Dodsley *Select Collection of Old English Plays* (15v, 1874-76).

The visit of the King and Queen to Oxford in August, 1636, brought the courtly drama into special prominence, William Strode's *Floating Island* and William Cartwright's *Royal Slave* being presented on that occasion with immense pomp and notoriety. Strode is a lyric poet of some worth,[41] but his allegorical drama was too insubstantial for even the Queen's taste. The tragicomedy of *The Royal Slave*, however, dealing with noble Greeks and Persians, was a great and lasting success. It was equipped with gorgeous Persian costumes and eight "appearances" or pictorial scene-sets that became the talk of the fashionable world.[42]

The most important of this group of dramatists was William Davenant (1606-1668),[43] who, besides producing a number of moderately successful plays in the Shirley vein, captured fame by his tendentious court plays, *Love and Honour* (1634) and *The Platonic Lovers* (1635). He was closely paralleled by Thomas Killigrew[44] in *The Prisoners, Claricilla*, and *The Princess* (c. 1635-36), and by Lodowick Carlell (1602-1675) in *The Deserving Favorite* (1629), *Arviragus and Philicia* (1636), and *The Passionate Lovers* (1638). These three writers, with whom other courtiers like Sir John Suckling[45] and Sir William Berkeley should be associated, lived to profit by their cavalier loyalty and grace the Restoration stage. William Habington's *Queen of Aragon*, acted at court in 1640 and later at Blackfriars, is one of the best of this numerous category. Its offers the perfect tribute to the Queen in its central character, who is the worthy object of universal love, and in her lovers presents valiant gentlemen of astonishing magnanimity. The verse is good, the plot interesting, and the dénouement both unexpected and sentimental.[46]

The plays of the five years that followed Jonson's death in 1637 were not lacking in a kind of merit, and certainly not in quantity, but they were severely limited in scope and bore the mark of intellectual death. On literary grounds there can be no complaint against the drastic act of the Puritan Parliament, September 2, 1642:

> Whereas ... the distracted estate of England, threatened with a cloud of blood by a civil war call[s] for all possible means to appease and avert the wrath of God ... it is therefore thought fit and ordained by the Lords and Commons in this Parliament assembled that, while these said causes and set times of humiliation do continue, public stage-plays shall cease and be forborne.

It brought to a formal close the richest flowering of English drama, which had lasted for a time rather shorter than the period from the first play of Aeschylus to the last of Euripides, and which has had no other parallel.[47]

Davenant and Killigrew

The Closing of the Theatres

[41] See Bertram Dobell, *The Poetical Works of William Strode, 1600-1645* (1907).

[42] Cartwright's *Comedies, Tragi-Comedies with Other Poems* were posthumously published in 1651. See below, ch. XI.

[43] See A. Harbage, *Sir William Davenant, Poet Venturer* (Philadelphia, 1935); A. H. Nethercot, *Sir William Davenant* (Chicago, 1938).

[44] See A. Harbage, *Thomas Killigrew, Cavalier Dramatist* (Philadelphia, 1930).

[45] See below, ch. XI. Suckling died in 1642, and Berkeley (d. 1677) left but one play, *The Lost Lady* (1638).

[46] For Habington's nondramatic work see below, ch. XII.

[47] See L. M. Watt, *Attic and Elizabethan Tragedy* (1908).

VI

Seventeenth-Century Prose: I. Bacon and the Prose of Utility

To suppose that all prose writers of the early seventeenth century wrote like Sir Thomas Browne and Milton would be an instance of *pseudodoxia epidemica*.[1] The writers considered in the present chapter were reacting against the mannered, ornamented style of Lyly and Sidney. They formed their prose into an instrument of greater utility and precision and achieved no special elegance, with the exception of some of the Bible-translators, Ben Jonson, and Bacon, all of whom were capable of turning austerity itself into a garment of beauty. One of the features of the change from the Tudor to the Stuart period is that prose advanced itself into a number of provinces of literature where verse had previously ruled. Thus the prose "character" succeeded to the poetical satire and epigram, the essay to the eclogue; and in the work of such long-lived and prolific writers as Nicholas Breton, Dekker, and Heywood it is roughly true that their Elizabethan output is predominantly verse and their Jacobean output mainly prose. Dekker's *Bellman of London* (1608), *Gull's Hornbook* (1609), and his series of plague pamphlets, Heywood's *Apology for Actors* (1612) and *Gunaikeion* (1624) show the shift to realism and social analysis, though Dekker and Heywood remained at heart Elizabethan.[2]

Letter Writers   The expansion of literary and semi-literary prose in the seventeenth century is well illustrated by the personal letters that have survived. There are doubtless no better letters from the previous age than those of Shakespeare's close contemporary, Philip Gawdy[3] (1562-1617), the great majority of which date from Queen Elizabeth's reign. Gawdy was well-connected and intelligent, he had some humor, and he had interesting experiences, which included reasonable intimacy with the Queen and her court, member-

---

[1] For generous and well selected examples of seventeenth-century prose through its entire range, see R. P. T. Coffin and A. M. Witherspoon, *A Book of 17th Century Prose* (1929), which has an admirable introduction, and Cecil A. Moore and Douglas Bush, *English Prose, 1600-1660* (1930). The history of the early part of the century is covered by David Mathew, *The Jacobean Age* (1938), and the intellectual movements by Basil Willey, *The Seventeenth Century Background: Studies in the Thought of the Age in relation to Poetry and Religion* (1934). See also Douglas Bush, *English Literature in the Earlier Seventeenth Century, 1600-1660* (Oxford, 1945). ·

[2] See M. L. Hunt, *Thomas Dekker, a Study* (1911), ch. VII; A. M. Clark, *Thomas Heywood, Playwright and Miscellanist* (Oxford, 1931), ch. V.

[3] See *Letters of Philip Gawdy of West Harling, Norfolk, and of London to Various Members of his Family, 1579-1616*, ed. I. H. Jeayes (Roxburghe Club, 1906). For discussion of the letters of Richard Brakenbury, dating from the same period, see L. C. John, "Elizabethan Letter-writer," *PQ*, XXIV (1945). 106-113.

ship in the House of Commons, and service with Sir Richard Grenville on
the last voyage of the *Revenge* with its aftermath of captivity in Portugal. *Philip*
The preservation of his correspondence is a blessing, but perusal of it shows *Gawdy*
how wholly practical Gawdy's idea of a letter is. He seems restricted to four
stereotyped themes; viz., (1) expression of humble duty toward those who
might do him worldly good; (2) pushing of legal and courtly suits; (3)
transmission of London rumors about politics, high society, and the outer
world to his news-starved rural relatives; (4) the everlasting concern of
discovering in the city and shipping home by carrier all the exotic articles
that Elizabethan gentlefolk required—"sending down my father's foot-
cloth," or his plumtrees, for Elizabethan country-dwellers went to London
even for trees. Any reader will note the advance in literary value in the
charming letters that Serjeant John Hoskyns wrote from London to his
wife and daughter-in-law in the West between 1601 and 1629.[4] Hoskyns, to *John*
be sure, was a wit, and a little of a poet in both English and Latin; but the *Hoskyns*
change is largely due to the spread of peace and peaceful traffic in James's
reign and to the diffusion of intelligence that resulted. The change is.
most marked, of course, in the 479 letters of the prince of letter-writers of *John Cham*
the age, John Chamberlain [5] (1554-1628). Chamberlain was born before *berlain*
Gawdy, but his earliest extant letter is dated June 11, 1597, and it is hardly
possible that letters of their quality could or would have been written at an
earlier period.[6]

King James I of England (1566-1625), like his ancestor, James I of Scot- *King*
land, fancied himself as a poet and had literary ambitions for his country. *James's*
It is possible that if fate had not brought him to the thrones of both kingdoms, *English*
the Scottish literary language might have become as different from English as
Portuguese is from Spanish. Such was James's evident desire during thirty-
six years of his life. Amid the turmoil of his Scottish reign he had visions of
Edinburgh as a new Athens and of himself, like the King of Navarre in
Shakespeare's play, erecting there a little academe with Alexander Mont-
gomerie [7] as his chief guide, colleague, and Berowne. He wrote a consider-

[4] See L. B. Osborn, *The Life, Letters, and Writings of John Hoskyns, 1566-1638* (New
Haven, 1937). Hoskyns, a member of the Middle Temple, London, and like Gawdy a member of Parliament, was a friend of both Jonson and Donne, with the latter of whom he had
been contemporary at New College, Oxford. He left, besides his verses and letters, an important
rhetorical work, *Directions for Speech and Style*, edited by Miss Osborn, *op. cit.*, and separately
by H. H. Hudson (Princeton, 1935).

[5] See *The Letters of John Chamberlain*, edited with an introduction by N. E. McClure (2v,
Philadelphia, American Philosophical Soc., 1939).

[6] Other important collections of seventeenth-century letters are those of the Sidney family,
edited by Arthur Collins (2v, 1746) as *Letters and Memorials of State;* those of Sir Tobie
Matthew (1577-1655), printed as *A Collection of Letters* (1660; see A. H. Mathew and A.
Calthrop, *The Life of Sir Tobie Matthew, Bacon's Alter Ego*, 1907); those of Sir Henry Wotton
(1568-1639; ed. L. P. Smith, 2v, Oxford, 1907); and *The Oxinden Letters, 1607-1642*, ed.
Dorothy Gardiner (1933).

[7] Montgomerie (*c.* 1556-*c.* 1610) was the chief Scottish poet between Sir David Lindsay and
Drummond of Hawthornden. His *Poems* are edited by George Stevenson (*Scottish Text Soc.*,
1910). He was a close companion of the young King, and besides his long poem, *The Cherry
and the Slae* (ed. H. H. Wood, 1937), wrote sonnets with the same Spenserian rime scheme
that James habitually employed.

able amount of more than capable verse in his native dialect [8] and promulgated, at the age of eighteen, *The Reulis and Cautelis to Be Observit and Eschewit in Scottis Poesie.* His *Demonology, in Form of a Dialogue* [9] (1597) and his most important prose work, the *Basilikon Doron* (King's Gift) addressed to his infant son (1599), are in less vehement Scots; but *A Counterblast to Tobacco* (1604), with which he surprisingly saluted his London subjects in the year of his arrival in that city, is in careful Southern English, as are his political writings of this period.[10]

The King's prose style is not a bad one, as can be seen from the following passage of the *Counterblast* ridiculing the alleged virtues of tobacco:

> It cures the gout in the feet, and (which is miraculous) in that very instant when the smoke thereof, as light, flies up into the head, the virtue thereof, as heavy, runs down to the little toe. It helps all sorts of agues. It makes a man sober that was drunk. It refreshes a weary man, and yet makes a man hungry. Being taken when they go to bed, it makes one sleep soundly, and yet being taken when a man is sleepy and drowsy, it will, as they say, awake his brain and quicken his under standing.... Here in England it is refined, and will not deign to cure here any other than cleanly and gentlemanly diseases. O omnipotent power of *Tobacco!*

He is not without humor or argumentative subtlety, but his taste is for a plain style, weighty with learning, but unencumbered with Renaissance ornament.[11] In the *Basilikon Doron* he bids his son, "Use a natural and plain form not fairded [painted] with artifice," and a modern biographer characterizes his way of writing as "that style which, shrewd and effective enough ... rises nowhere to any greatness of imagination or any sudden passion of spiritual truth." [12] Such in fact was the predominant character of English prose during his reign. It is the style of the great translations of this era and transcends itself in the Bible of 1611, through which King James's name has a place in the history of the language with Shakespeare's and with Bacon's.

The Translators   It is instructive to compare the most prized of the great Elizabethan versions of the classics, North's version of Plutarch's *Parallel Lives* (1579), with the translation of Plutarch's *Morals* that Philemon Holland (1552-1637) published in 1603. Holland's materials are more realistic and, one may say, sociological, and his style, though it flows majestically enough, quite avoids

---

[8] I.e., *The Essays of a Prentice in the Divine Art of Poesy* (Edinburgh, 1684); *His Majesty's Poetical Exercises* (Edinburgh, 1591). See A. F. Westcott, *New Poems by James I of England* (1911), which has a valuable introduction.

[9] King James's *Demonology* is a now out-dated argument for the existence of demons, witches, and the like, written in reply to the skeptical and remarkably broad-minded *Discovery of Witchcraft* (1584) by Reginald Scot (c. 1538-1599). Scot's fine and readable book is reprinted with an Introduction by Montagu Summers (1930).

[10] See C. H. McIlwain, *The Political Works of James I* (Cambridge, Mass., 1918); C. J. Sisson, "King James I of England as Poet and Political Writer," in *Seventeenth Century Studies presented to Sir Herbert Grierson* (Oxford, 1938), pp. 47-63; D. H. Wilson, "James I and his Literary Assistants," *HLQ*, viii (1944). 35-57.

[11] His attitude is well expressed in a sonnet to his friend and compatriot, Sir William Alexander (see above, Part ii, ch. vii), rebuking him for writing "harsh verses after the English fashion," i.e., in the metaphysical style. See Westcott, *op. cit.*, pp. 37 f., lxxxix, xc.

[12] Charles Williams, *James I* (1934), p. 145.

the clang and the romantic idiosyncrasies of North.[13] The King James Bible (1611) is the perfect and final thing it is because of the genius its translators showed for compromise and lucidity. It would need a volume to do it justice, but comparison of any single chapter with its counterpart in the Bishops' Bible of 1572 will show the new grace of unambiguous suavity that Jacobean prose had created.[14]

Jonson's remarkable little book, *Timber*, printed posthumously,[15] is an *Ben* informing example of the way seventeenth-century prose shaped itself upon *Jonson's* the classics. It consists to a very great extent of paraphrases or actual trans- Discoveries lations of passages which Jonson found in Seneca the elder, Quintilian, and other favorite Latin authors.[16] There is no evidence that he intended to publish it, and certainly none that he intended to conceal his borrowings. What the book shows is that he has set himself to express his judgments of modern matters in English sentences of completely Roman compactness and economy. He has greatly succeeded, often improving upon the concise-ness of his models. The fact that the following dictum on style owes its idea and most of its words to the Latin of Vives hardly makes it less Jonson-ian or less perfect an example of English structure:

The congruent and harmonious fitting of parts in a sentence hath almost the fastening and force of knitting and connection; as in stones well squared, which will rise strong a great way without mortar. Periods are beautiful when they are not too long; for so they have their strength too, as in a pike or javelin.

And it would be rather absurd to discount Jonson's perfect tributes to Shakespeare and Bacon because his care was to build into them many of the phrases Seneca had used of other men. Bacon would have known how to value these words about himself:

No man ever spake more neatly, more pressly [concisely], more weightily, or suffered less emptiness, less idleness, in what he uttered. No member of his speech but consisted of his own graces . . . The fear of every man that heard him was lest he should make an end.

This was to praise him after the high Roman fashion, and it is this frugal Latin style that Bacon also illuminates.[17]

---

[13] Besides the *Morals*, which is dedicated to King James, Holland translated Livy (1600), Pliny (1601), Suetonius (1606), Ammianus Marcellinus (1609), and Xenophon's *Cryopaedia* (1632). See H. B. Lathrop, *Translations from the Classics into English, 1477-1620* (Madison, Wis., 1933); H. Silvette, *Catalogue of the Works of Philemon Holland, 1600-1940* (Char-lottesville, 1940).

[14] See B. F. Westcott, *A General View of the History of the English Bible* (3ed., 1905), pp. 255-278; and the references in Part I, ch. VI, above.

[15] The title in the first edition is: *Timber: or Discoveries Made upon Men and Matter, as They Have Flowed out of His Daily Reading* (1641). See M. Castelain, *Ben Jonson, Discoveries, a Critical Edition* (Paris, 1906); F. E. Schelling's earlier ed. (Boston, 1892); and Herford and Simpson, *Ben Jonson*, II. 437-451 (Oxford, 1925).

[16] See J. E. Spingarn, "The Sources of Ben Jonson's *Discoveries*," MP, II (1905). 451-460; P. Simpson, "*Tanquam Explorator*: Jonson's Method in the *Discoveries*," MLR, II (1907). 201-210.

[17] Henry Peacham's curious medley, *The Complete Gentleman* (1622; ed. G. S. Gordon, Oxford, 1906), may be mentioned here. Peacham (1576-c. 1644) was a schoolmaster, traveler, draftsman, painter, angler, antiquary, and something of a herald. All these interests assert

The essays of Francis Bacon [18] (1561-1626) are the best picture of his mind. They include some of his earliest and some of his latest writing, and were worked at during the whole of his active life. The term *essay* was, of course, borrowed from Montaigne, whose *Essais* had appeared in France in 1580 and 1588 and were published in John Florio's English translation in 1603.[19] They had been promptly imitated by Sir William Cornwallis, whose collections, printed in 1600, 1610, and 1616 deserve a place in the history of the type.[20]

Bacon's
Essays

Bacon adheres throughout to Montaigne's conception of the essay as something more economical and less dogmatic than the quasi-Platonic dialogue, as represented by Spenser's *View of Ireland,* or the formal discourse as seen in Sidney's *Defense of Poesy;* but in one important respect his essays are totally unlike Montaigne's. Where the French writer, one of the most charming egoists in literature, is mainly concerned with his individual opinions, Bacon is concerned mainly with the type of reader he is addressing. This is not at all the average human being. Bacon has nothing to say to women, or tradesmen, or artists, or professional scholars, or gentlemen of leisure like Montaigne. He is writing for the young men of his own class and tradition, the Elizabethan or Jacobean youth of strenuous ambition and large opportunity, intent upon the completest self-realization in public life. He does not tell these readers how to be more happy, more attractive, or even more moral; he tells them how to be more efficient, for he assumes as naturally as Cecil Rhodes did that any chosen student would "esteem the performance of public duty his highest aim." This is true whether he writes of travel or friendship, discourse, gardens, marriage and single life, or

themselves in his little book without blending. He is factual and somewhat pompous, but has a redeeming store of anecdotes. His work was popular, and his title very likely suggested that of Walton's classic. See D. T. Starnes, *"Elyot's Governour* and Peacham's *Compleat Gentleman,"* *MLR,* XXII (1927). 319-322; and, for a comprehensive account of courtesy literature, John Mason, *Gentle Folk in the Making* (Philadelphia, 1935).

[18] The standard edition of Bacon is that of J. Spedding, R. L. Ellis, and D. D. Heath (14v, 1857-74). This includes *The Letters and the Life of Francis Bacon* by Spedding (7v, 1861-74), of which *The Life and Times of Francis Bacon* (2v, 1878) is an abridgment. Spedding's work is in some respects not likely to be superseded. Modern lives include *Sir Francis Bacon, the First Modern Mind* (1930) by "Byron Steel" (a brief and readable sketch); M. Sturt, *Francis Bacon* (1932); C. Williams, *Bacon* (1933). Useful criticism of Bacon and related writers will be found in W. G. Crane's *Wit and Rhetoric in the Renaissance* (1937), ch. x, "The Essay and the Character," pp. 132-161. See also E. N. S. Thompson, *The Seventeenth-Century English Essay* (Iowa City, 1926).

[19] See J. Zeitlin, "The Development of Bacon's Essays, with Special Reference to the Question of Montaigne's Influence upon Them," *JEGP,* XXVII (1928). 496-519.

[20] Though a number of Cornwallis's essays have the same titles as Bacon's there is little other similarity. The best known perhaps is the long one, in the 1616 collection, on *The Praise of King Richard III,* Cornwallis's claim to which has been recently questioned; see W. G. Zeeveld, "A Tudor Defense of Richard III," *PMLA,* LV (1940). 946-957. Sir William had a leaning toward flippancy and paradox, but could not often make them amusing. See W. L. MacDonald, "The Earliest English Essayists," *ESt,* LXIV (1929). 20-52; and P. B. Whitt, "New Light on Sir William Cornwallis the Essayist," *RES,* VII (1932). 155-169. Don C. Allen has edited the *Essayes* (Baltimore, 1946). Another early essayist is Robert Johnson (the reputed author also of two of the earliest books on the Virginia Colony: *Nova Britannia,* 1609, and *The New Life of Virginea,* 1612). Johnson's *Essaies, or rather Imperfect Offers* (1601) had four editions by 1638. He was followed by Daniel Tuvill ("D. T."), whose two series, *Essaies Politicke and Morall* (1608) and *Essaies Morall and Theologicall* (1609), are heavily ethical and rather overweighted with allusions to Tacitus and other historians.

adversity; and the austere creed, which he nowhere deigns to argue or expound, gives them all a coherence and a certain uplift. Of moral integrity Bacon possessed little enough. His callous ingratitude to his patron Essex and his malfeasance in office can hardly be condoned. Pope has described him as "the wisest, brightest, meanest of mankind," [21] and Macaulay as the man "whom the wise Queen Elizabeth distrusted and the foolish King James honored and advanced." In private life he was self-centered, to say the best of him, and his literary work is entirely incompatible with that of such men as Shakespeare and Spenser; but he possessed a remarkable intellectual integrity, a luminosity of mental truth, which gives his best work a tonic and exhilarating, though quite unwarming, glow.

The stylistic development in the *Essays* is very interesting. The first edition in 1597, contained ten, totaling about six thousand words, a scant hour's reading; the final edition of 1625 contained fifty-nine. There was no recasting or change of fundamental opinion, but the sentences were polished and statements were made more concrete by citation of examples, illustrative anecdotes, and quotations; and naturally the conception of an essay grows larger. Three essays on related subjects show the development. The one entitled *Of Expense*, in its 1597 form, contains about 240 words; it is literally an *essai*, a mere collection of general statements in aphoristic form. As later elaborated, the same essay has over 400 words, the added matter being four observations from worldly experience. The essay *Of Riches*, first printed in 1612 and later expanded, is more ambitious, consisting of an analytical discussion in about 1100 words of (*a*) the value of riches, (*b*) means of attainment, (*c*) their uses. Finally, *Of Usury*, first found in the 1625 edition, is a formal and carefully argued little treatise on an economic problem.[22] It is to be observed that nearly all the essays which directly treat of public life (*Great Place, Nobility, Empire, Counsel, Wisdom for a Man's Self, Seeming Wise, True Greatness of Kingdoms and Estates, Ambition*, and *Judicature*) first appeared in the middle group of essays, dated between 1607 and 1612. At this time Bacon was within sight of his own goal, after years of waiting. In 1607 he became Solicitor General, in 1613 Attorney General, in 1618 Lord Chancellor and Baron Verulam.

In the *Essays* Bacon says very little of scholarship, though that was one of the main passions of his life. He made amends in the *Advancement of Learning* (1605), which is very likely the noblest tract on education ever written by an Englishman.[23] It is addressed as a kind of coronation gift to the new king, James, and is written in a somewhat richer style than the *Essays*. The first book deals with the praise of knowledge, challenging the

Bacon's Advancement of Learning

---

[21] *An Essay on Man*, IV. 282.

[22] In the 1625 edition for the first time, the simple title, *Essays* is expanded into *Essays, or Counsels, Civil and Moral*.

[23] See R. S. Crane, "The Relation of Bacon's Essays to his Program for the Advancement of Learning," in *Schelling Anniversary Papers* (1928), pp. 87-105, the same author's introduction to *The English Familiar Essay*, ed. W. F. Bryan and R. S. Crane (Boston, 1916), and the first two essays in *Seventeenth Century Studies Presented to Sir Herbert Grierson* (Oxford, 1938): G. Bullough, "Bacon and the Defence of Learning," and R. Metz, "Bacon's Part in the Intellectual Movement of His Time."

various prejudices and errors which discredit it in popular opinion, and rising to heights of eloquence suggestive of the great passages in Milton's *Areopagitica*. The second book is a survey of learning, analytical, encyclo-pedic, and inductive in method, laying broad and deep foundations for a **The New** national culture. *The New Atlantis*, left unfinished at Bacon's death and **Atlantis** published in 1627, is a romantic and imaginative complement to the *Advancement of Learning*. In the manner of More's *Utopia* he describes a fictitious land where his principles of collaborative research have been put into effect in a great agricultural and mechanical experiment station called Solomon's House. Out of this book came much of the inspiration for the Royal Society a generation later.[24]

The   Another work of romantic cast and great charm is *The Wisdom of the*
Wisdom *Ancients* (1619), dedicated to Bacon's "foster mother," the University of
of the Cambridge. Here he resorted to the Renaissance fashion of symbolical in-
Ancients terpretation of classic myths to develop many of the same thoughts which appear in the *Essays*. This was one of the works which Shelley had in mind when he asserted, "Lord Bacon was a poet." The section on "Pan, or Nature" has a passage that anticipates the findings of modern biology:

> This biform figure also represents the participation of one species with another: for there appear to be no simple natures, but all participate or consist of two: thus man has somewhat of the brute, the brute somewhat of the plant, the plant somewhat of the mineral; so that all natural bodies have really two faces, or consist of a superior and an inferior species.

The   *The History of the Reign of King Henry VII* (1622) is a landmark in
History of historical writing and a reflection of the psychological curiosity of the early
Henry VII seventeenth century. Essentially a study of the mind and character of a man whose unheroic, inflexible, and efficient personality resembled Bacon's own, it is attempted on a scale, and with a mental subtlety, and in an English style that no previous chronicler had approached. It has some kinship with the "character" writings, Burton, and Walton's lives, but very little with the histories composed in Queen Elizabeth's reign. Bacon's small concern for institutional and sociological matters is apparent in one sentence:

> This year also the king called his Parliament, where many laws were made of a more private and vulgar nature than ought to detain the reader of an history.

Robert
Burton,   With no pretension of style or novelty of subject matter, and no real
The Anat- coherence of argument or narrative, *The Anatomy of Melancholy* (1621)
omy of by a lonely and cross-grained scholar, Robert Burton [25] (1577-1640), became
Melancholy

---

[24] James Harrington's *Oceana* (1656), written in opposition to Hobbes's *Leviathan*, likewise deals with the ideal commonwealth, though superficially. It is a work of considerable political, but no great literary, importance. See R. Koebner, "*Oceana*," *ESt*, LXVIII (1934). 358-396.

[25] Modern editions of *The Anatomy of Melancholy* include those of F. Dell and P. Jordan-Smith (2v, 1927; condensed reissue in one volume, 1929); H. Jackson (3v, 1932; Everyman's Library). Vol. I, Part 3, pp. 155-246, of the Oxford Bibliographical Society's *Proceedings and Papers* (1926) is devoted to Burton. See also P. Jordan-Smith, *Bibliographia Burtoniana, s Study of Robert Burton's "The Anatomy of Melancholy"* (Stanford Univ., 1931).

one of the most popular works of its age and one of the world's great books. It came from the same Oxford background out of which, a little over forty years before, had come *Euphues, the Anatomy of Wit,* and Burton's volume might as well have borne Lyly's title as its own. The only thing either book proves is the social value of a broad classical education. The difference between them measures the change produced by a generation of "malcontent" literature. Lyly has in mind the easy successes of the "brave courtier" of Spenserian tradition; Burton begins with a passage strikingly like Hamlet's melancholy speech, "What a piece of work is a man!" Though draped over an intricate framework of "partitions," "sections," "members," and "sub-sections," imitating the scientific parlance of the day, *The Anatomy of Melancholy* can most simply be regarded as a great collection of essays on man's dissatisfaction with the world and ways to mitigate it. Bacon is the most obvious model for the studiously plain style and the habit of continually starting from a Latin quotation or classical anecdote. The subsections on the nature of spirits (i. 2. i. 2), on "love of learning or overmuch study" (i. 2. 3. 15), the "digression of the air" (ii. 2. 3), and the one on marriage and single life (iii. 2. 5. 5) are among the best examples of the essay of whimsical learning, long drawn out.

Burton bettered Bacon's instruction by vastly multiplying the learned allusions and adding to their effectiveness by his amusing translations, and by often lowering his style into a serio-comic monologue, which became a delight and pattern for both Sterne and Lamb. The book opens dully enough with a long letter of the feigned author, Democritus Junior, to the reader and a restatement of the old psychology, treated previously by Sir Thomas Elyot [26] and so many others; but it grows steadily in interest. The third, and last, "partition" on love-melancholy and religious melancholy becomes, among other things, a digest of the best stories in the world, from the Alexandrian Greek romancers like Achilles Tatius (whom Burton's brother William had translated) [27] to the works of such moderns as Spenser, Marlowe, Jonson, and Shakespeare, "an elegant poet of ours." If all the Elizabethan literature were lost, it would be possible to put together a fairly good account of the chief writers from Burton's quotations and allusions. [28] *The Anatomy of Melancholy* has, moreover, been a perfect arsenal for poets in search of plots. To mention just two examples, Ford, a few years after the book was published, found there the source of his early play, *The Lover's Melancholy* (1629); [29] and two centuries later Keats found the source of *Lamia.*

Burton was a clergyman and held livings at different times in various counties of England; but from his election as "student" of Christ Church in 1599 till his death there forty years later his chief residence was his

[26] See above, Part i, ch. ii.
[27] Printed in 1597; ed. S. Gaselee and H. F. B. Brett-Smith (Oxford, 1923).
[28] See H. J. Gottlieb, *Robert Burton's Knowledge of English Poetry* (1937).
[29] See G. F. Sensabaugh, "Burton's Influence on Ford's *The Lover's Melancholy,*" *SP,* xxxiii (1936). 545-571.

bachelor quarters in that college. It was the fellows' talk in the common room and the racier badinage of the Oxford bargemen on the Isis that developed his views of life and humor, and he drew heavily upon the books at the Bodleian for his recondite knowledge. He published nothing except the *Anatomy*,[30] which made a fortune for its Oxford printer, but hardly affected the placid life of Burton, who was buried three centuries ago in the Christ Church Cathedral, with a punning Latin epitaph that he would have appreciated.[31]

Thomas Fuller

Thomas Fuller [32] (1608-1661), was born in the same year as Milton, and in the same village as Dryden—Aldwinkle in Northamptonshire, where his father was rector of one of the parishes. He was nearly a quarter-century older than Dryden, and his very slight career as a poet ends, in merit as in time, in a *Panegyric on His Majesty's Happy Return*, 1660, at about the point where Dryden's begins.[33] Yet Dryden is the man of the seventeenth century whom Fuller most resembles. They are alike in their engagingly broad humanity, tolerance, and common sense. Whereas Dryden is vastly more the poet, Fuller is somewhat more the wit and social critic. Receiving his M. A. degree at Cambridge at the early age of twenty, Fuller entered the church and became one of the most popular preachers of his time, as well as one of the most popular writers. His first characteristic publication was *The History of the Holy War* (1639). Unlike Bunyan's allegory of similar title,[34] this is a straightforward chronicle of events in Palestine during the Crusades; it is a learned and exact book, but is already marked by Fuller's mannerisms. Thus he explains the failure of maps to show all the places mentioned (Book II, chapter 2): "for some of them were such poor places, that they were ashamed to appear in a map, and fall so much under a Geographer's notice that they fall not under it;" or, with reference to the quarrel between Richard I and the French king, he remarks (Book III, chapter 6): "The best way to keep great princes together is to keep them asunder, accommodating their business by ambassadors, lest the meeting

[30] Burton wrote an amusing Latin comedy, *Philosophaster*, acted at Christ Church in 1617. It was first printed in 1862, and again, with an English transl., by P. Jordan-Smith (Stanford Univ., 1931).

[31] Among the most influential writers of argumentative prose in this period were two friends of Lucius Cary, Lord Falkland: the "ever memorable" John Hales (1584-1656) and William Chillingworth (1602-1644). Both are masters of lucid English, marked by learning and good sense, and strong without adornment. Hales, an Oxford don who retired to spend most of his long life as a schoolmaster at Eton, and who is famous as one of the early encomiasts of Shakespeare, is the more readable today. See his *Golden Remains* (published in 1659) and his *Works*, ed. D. Dalrymple (3v, Glasgow, 1765). Chillingworth's *The Religion of Protestants a Safe Way to Salvation* (1638) went through many editions and was long a bulwark of Anglican theology.

[32] Charles Lamb's *Specimens from the Writings of Fuller the Church Historian* (1811) began the appreciation of Fuller in the nineteenth century. S. Gibson's *Bibliography of Thomas Fuller* (Oxford, 1934) is excellent. See also E. N. S. Thompson, "A Representative Man of Letters," in *Literary Bypaths of the Renaissance* (New Haven, 1924), pp. 173-183.

[33] Compare Dryden's *Astraea Redux* (1660) and *Panegyric* on Charles II's coronation (1661). Fuller's first published work was *David's Heinous Sin, Hearty Repentance, Heavy Punishment* (1631), a long poem in an unmusical alteration of rime royal. The method is rather like that of Quarles's biblical poems, and the theme happens to cover the same incidents as Peele's play, *David and Bethsabe*. Fuller's poems were reprinted by A. B. Grosart (1868).

[34] *The Holy War* (1682).

of their own persons part their affections." It is easy to understand that Fuller's style pained lovers of clerical dignity and prose decorum in his own day as much as it later pleased Charles Lamb. It certainly made his books sell, large in size and antiquarian in content though they mainly are.[35]

Fuller's next book was *The Holy and Profane States*[36] (1642), a miscellany which contains, among other things, about three dozen short sketches or "characters" of ideal social types; e.g., the good wife, the good husband, the good parent, the good child, the constant virgin, the good schoolmaster, the true gentleman. Illustrative brief biographies are appended to many of these; thus, "the faithful minister" is followed by the life of Fuller's favorite theologian, Mr. Perkins, and "the good sea-captain" by that of Sir Francis Drake. Book III varies in consisting entirely of essays, strongly influenced by Bacon's and in some cases on the same subjects; e.g., "Of Travelling," "Of Building," "Of Plantations," "Of Marriage," "Of Fame";[37] and the last (fifth) book balances the previous good characters with "profane" ones; e.g., "The Witch" and "The Atheist," with appropriate lives of the Witch of Endor, Joan of Arc, and Caesar Borgia. For the edification of his readers Fuller has here drawn upon the four most currently popular types of light prose: the essay, "character," short biography, and courtesy or etiquette book. So much moral improvement combined with so much actual readability seldom fails to sell a volume, and this one was very successful. Its appearance, however, coincided with the outbreak of war between Charles I and the Parliament, and Fuller's royalist leanings forced him to forsake his distinguished post of "lecturer" at the Savoy in London and join Charles's court at Oxford. He was by no means a rabid Cavalier, but was a sincere one, and as chaplain went through a campaign with the unsuccessful royalist troops in the west. After their defeat he retired to Exeter and there printed his *Good Thoughts in Bad Times* (1645), which was followed by *Good Thoughts in Worse Times* (1647), and finally, when Charles II was restored, by *Mixed Contemplations in Better Times* (1660).

Brevity and variety are the soul of Fuller's wit. The books just mentioned consist of very brief essays, grouped under such headings as "personal meditations," "Scripture observations," or "historical applications." They commonly begin with an anecdote, and even when most dolorous in subject, are likely to be brightened by Fuller's characteristic witticisms and by sallies of cheerful common sense. They may be regarded as skeleton outlines of the sermons Fuller did not preach, for he lost his clerical appointments at the triumph of the Commonwealth. Later his friend the Earl of Carlisle

The Holy and Profane States

Fuller's Good Thoughts

[35] The Palestinian interest was continued in one of Fuller's handsomest books, *A Pisgah-Sight of Palestine and the Confines Thereof, with the History of the Old and New Testament* (1650).
[36] See W. E. Houghton, *The Formation of Thomas Fuller's Holy and Profane States*, (Cambridge, Mass., 1938); *Thomas Fuller's the Holy State and the Profane State*, edited by M. G. Walten (1938). This work has two title-pages, *The Holy State*, applying to Books I-IV, and *The Profane State*, applying to Book V. In addition to the works discussed above, Fuller published many sermons, e.g. *Joseph's Parti-Colored Coat* (1640).
[37] See D. F. Beckingham, "Parallel Passages in Bacon and Fuller," *RES*, XIII (1937), 449-453.

appointed him curate of Waltham; but Fuller was able to support himself by his busy pen, and he is said to have been the first English writer to do so. In 1655 his great *Church History* was printed, followed by the *History of the University of Cambridge* and by *The Appeal of Injured Innocence* (1659), Fuller's charming *apologia* addressed to Dr. Peter Heylin, who had animadverted upon alleged errors and improprieties in the *Church History*.

The Church History

In 1660 Fuller was among the loyalists sent to Holland to prepare the restoration of Charles II. The King made him his chaplain and destined him for a bishopric; but he died the next year, at the early age of fifty-three, before he could receive that dignity or see the publication of his greatest work, *The History of the Worthies of England* (1662).[38] This book, arranged alphabetically by counties, is a mine of antiquarian learning indispensable to students at the present day; but Fuller's learning is always worn lightly, and the mass of data he has compiled about each county—from natural commodities, wonders, proverbs, buildings and manufactures, through notabilia about its most eminent men and women, to the quaint and witty "farewell" with which he always takes his leave—is so engrossing that a busy man can approach it only with peril. It is here that one finds the famous tale of the "wit combats" between Shakespeare and Ben Jonson (Warwickshire, Writers) and the true story of the Vicar of Bray (Berkshire, Proverbs).

Fuller's Worthies of England

Richard Baxter [39] (1615-1691) was for the general body of devout Puritans much what Fuller was for the devout members of the other party. Like Fuller, he suffered for his convictions with courage and dignity, and professed the faith that was in him without rancor. He was equally voluminous, though within a narrower range. Most of his work dates from after Fuller's death, and after his own preaching had been stopped by the Uniformity Act of 1662; but while still a young man and chaplain in the Parliamentary army, he had written his most popular book of devotion, *The Saints' Everlasting Rest* (printed in 1650). It presents, as Bunyan was to do a little later, the milder and sweeter side of Puritanism, in a style marked by short exclamatory sentences, rhetorical questions, and constant appeals to the reader's better nature. Baxter was a firm believer in hell fire, and could do justice to it; e.g.—

Richard Baxter

The Saints' Everlasting Rest

> The principal author of hell-torments is God himself. As it was no less than God whom sinners had offended, so it is no less than God who will punish them for their offences. He hath prepared those torments for his enemies. His continued anger will still be devouring them. His breath of indignation will kindle the flames. His wrath will be an intolerable burden to their souls. If it were but a creature they had to do with, they might better bear it. Woe to him that falls under the strokes of the Almighty! (ch. vi, ii. 1)

But he labors more to paint the ineffable joys of the "everlasting rest" in heaven and the happiness of an innocent soul. "Avoid frequent disputes

[38] Ed. P. A. Nuttall (3v, 1840).

[39] See F. J. Powicke, *A Life of the Reverend Richard Baxter* (1924); A. R. Ladell, *Richard Baxter, Puritan and Mystic* (1925).

about lesser truths," he advises, "and .a religion that lies only in opinions. They are usually least acquainted with a heavenly life, who are violent disputers about the circumstantials of religion" (ch. xii, i. 4).

And oh, the sinful folly of many of the saints, who drench their spirits in continual sadness, and waste their days in complaints and groans, and so make themselves, both in body and mind, unfit for this sweet and heavenly work! (ch. xii, ii. 7).

The very act of loving God in Christ is inexpressibly sweet. The soul that is best furnished with grace, when it is not in action, is like a lute well stringed and tuned, which while it lieth still maketh no more music than a common piece of wood; but when it is handled by a skilful musician, the melody is delightful. Some degree of comfort follows every good action, as heat accompanies fire, and as beams and influence issue from the sun (ch. viii, 2).

A similar tone of moderate nonconformity and plain speaking informs *The* most of the work of the group of "Cambridge Platonists,"[40] of whom the *Cambridg* chief are: Benjamin Whichcote (1609-1683), Henry More (1614-1687), John *Platonists* Smith (1616-1652), Ralph Cudworth (1617-1688), and Nathanael Culverwel (1618-1651). They drew from deeper philosophical sources than Baxter, who was self-educated. The most learned productions of Cudworth and, in prose, of More date from after 1660. The most interesting stylist is Culverwel, but the most characteristic single work by any of the group may perhaps be the applauded sermon[41] which Cudworth preached before the House of Commons, March 31, 1647, in behalf of broadmindedness and inward piety. It is logical, non-sectarian, and bold, working by homely figures such as the one with which on the last page Cudworth sums up his plea:

Tin or lead, or any other baser metal, if it be cast into never so good a mould, and made up into never so elegant a figure; yet it is but tin or lead still: it is the same metal that it was before. And if we be moulded into never so good a form of outward government, unless we new-mould our hearts within too, we are but a little better than we were before.

The resemblance of this erudite and earnest band to the Oxford group, which revolved about Colet a century and a half earlier, is often striking.

[40] See F. J. Powicke, *The Cambridge Platonists* (Cambridge, Mass., 1926); E. T. Campagnac, *The Cambridge Platonists* (selections from Whichcote, Smith, and Culverwel, Oxford, 1901).
[41] Reproduced by the Facsimile Text Society (1930).

Seventeenth-Century Prose: II. Character Books.
Autobiography. Walton.

Here is no bombasted or fustian stuff, but every line weighed as with a balance
and every sentence placed with judgment and deliberation.

he Char- These words, written about a play of Middleton's and already quoted,
ter Books express also the artistic aim and describe the chief literary merit of the
seventeenth-century "character books"; [1] and they are particularly appropriate
seph Hall if one compares the first such book, Joseph Hall's *Characters of Virtues and
Vices* (1608), with the same writer's earlier *Virgidemiae* [2] (1597) which is
fustian stuff of the most arrant kind. Hall's model was the *Ethical Characters*
of Theophrastus (372-287 B.C.), describing in brief and caustic prose some
thirty unpleasant Athenian civic types. Hall, who has about the same number of sketches, divided them into good and bad examples; e.g., the wise
man, the honest man, the true friend, in contrast with the malcontent, the
flatterer, and the unthrift; and he intensified the moral note. It is not unlikely
that his immediate inspiration was found in the incidental character sketches
that Ben Jonson had introduced into *Every Man out of His Humor* (1599)
and *Cynthia's Revels* (1600).

The only state of mind which would account for the immense popularity
enjoyed by this species of writing is an exaggerated intensity of social consciousness and a temporary suspension of the taste for fiction; but the "character" owed the beginning of its special vogue to a purely accidental cause. Hall's
he characters met with no particular acclaim; [3] it was the next collection, linked
Overbury" with the name of Sir Thomas Overbury, that aroused the public interest.
haracters Overbury had died a mysterious death in the Tower, September 15, 1613, and
early in the next year a publisher brought out his didactic poem, *A Wife*. It
is written dully enough in the six-line *Venus and Adonis* stanza, but another

---

[1] See E. N. S. Thompson, "Character Books," in *Literary Bypaths of the Renaissance* (New
Haven, 1924), pp. 1-27; G. Murphy, *A Cabinet of Characters* (Oxford, 1925); R. Aldington,
A Book of "Characters" (Broadway Translations, n.d.); G. Murphy, *A Bibliography of English
Character-Books* (Bibl. Soc., Oxford, 1925).

[2] This consists of six books of satires in riming verse. The title, which means "a bunch of
switches," is usually quoted, as the title-page prints it, in the genitive case, *Virgidemiarum*.

[3] They had, however, a considerable success in French translation. An interesting transitional
work, worth mentioning here, is *The Curtain-drawer of the World* (1612) by William Parkes,
in which a mannered and sententious prose alternates with forceful satiric verse. Parkes introduces prose characters of such types as the usurer, the lawyer, the courtier, the countryman,
the citizen, the physician, and the harlot to give point to his arraignment of contemporary
vice. His verse contains some interesting echoes of *Hamlet*, and the concluding tetrameter
couplets which he puts into the mouth of Death have real vigor. (Reprinted Grosart, *Occasional
Issues*, III, 1876.)

edition was immediately called for,[4] and this was amplified by twenty-two prose characters ascribed to Overbury "and other learned gentlemen his friends." The Preface to the Reader of this edition is dated May 16, 1614. By August 24 four more editions had appeared, and fourteen others were issued in the next half-century. As the printings multiplied, the number of characters was gradually increased to a total of eighty-three, the work of many unnamed writers, among whom John Donne and the dramatists Dekker and Webster are recognizable.[5] The "Overbury" characters are even shorter than those of Hall; few of them extend to much more than three hundred words. They introduce characters of women as well as men and make no formal division between good and bad, thus achieving greater naturalness and a more pleasing diversity. Good writing went into them, and two of those which are most probably ascribed to Webster, "A Fair and Happy Milkmaid" and "A Franklin" (i.e., country squire), have retained their charm.[6]

The phenomenal popularity of this collection naturally invited competition. A certain John Stephens was early in the field with *Satirical Essays, Characters, and Others* (1615), and those indefatigable pen-pushers, Nicholas Breton [7] (1545-1626) and Richard Brathwait [8] (1588-1673), played further variations upon the new type. A young gentleman at Gray's Inn, Geoffrey Minshull (*c.* 1594-1668), when sent to King's Bench Prison for debt, improved his leisure there by writing his lively if rather vapid *Essays and Characters of a Prison and Prisoners* [9] (1618). Among character-sequences almost as numerous as sonnet-sequences had been, the *Microcosmography* [10] (1628) of John Earle (*c.* 1601-1665) achieved an easy fame (1628). "Some very witty and sharp discourses," says Clarendon, "being published in print without his consent, though known to be his, he grew suddenly into a very general esteem with all men." The esteem has lasted, for Earle is the most attractive of the character writers. He has an individual point of view. Being for nearly twenty years a fellow of Merton College, Oxford, he takes many of his best subjects from college life: a young raw preacher, an old college butler, a downright scholar, a young gentleman of the university, a plodding student, an university don, and so forth. There are only two characters of women among the seventy-eight to which his collection ultimately reached, but he sometimes writes the character of an inanimate object, as of a tavern, which

Earle's Microcosmography

---

[4] A sprightlier imitation, in the same stanza, appeared in 1617 from the pen of Samuel Rowlands: *The Bride* (ed. A. C. Potter, Boston, 1905).

[5] See W. J. Paylor, *The Overburian Characters* (Oxford, 1936).

[6] See F. L. Lucas, *The Complete Works of John Webster* (1928), iv. 5-61.

[7] *Characters upon Essays, Moral and Divine* (with dedication to Bacon, 1615); *The Good and the Bad, or Descriptions of the Worthies and Unworthies of this Age* (1616).

[8] *Essays upon the Five Senses* (1620); *Whimzies* (1631). See M. W. Black, *Richard Brathwait, an Account of his Life and Works* (Philadelphia, 1928). Brathwait's curious book *Barnabee's Journal* (*c.* 1634), called also *Barnabee's Journey*, has constantly been "rediscovered"; the latest reprint appeared in 1933.

[9] Reprinted, 150 copies, Edinburgh, 1821.

[10] The most recent edition is that of H. Osborne (1933). That of P. Bliss (1811) is in a manner of speaking standard; that of A. S. West (Cambridge, 1897) is good.

is a degree, or (if you will) a pair of stairs above an alehouse, where men are drunk with more credit and apology.... It is the common consumption of the afternoon and the murderer or maker-away of a rainy day.... A house of sin you may call it, but not a house of darkness, for the candles are never out, and it is like those countries far in the north where it is as clear at midnight as at midday.

Earle has a neat epigrammatic style which, if he had lived a century later, would have been called Addisonian; and he has real and abundant wit, which grows sharp whenever he attacks insincerity. A pretender to learning, he says, "is one that would make others more fools than himself; for though he know nothing, he would not have the world know so much." There is the true satirist's indignation in his conclusion to "a forward bold man":

Thus preferment at last stumbles on him because he is still in the way. His companions, that flouted him before, now envy him, when they see him come ready for scarlet,[11] whilst themselves lie musty in their old clothes and colleges.

Earle's masterpiece, however, is in another spirit; it is the first character in his book, "A child," and has in it much both of Wordsworth and of George Herbert:

... His hardest labor is his tongue, as if he were loath to use so deceitful an organ; and he is best company with it when he can but prattle. We laugh at his foolish sports, but his game is our earnest; and his drums, rattles, and hobby-horses but the emblems and mocking of man's business. His father hath writ him as his own little story, wherein he reads those days of his life that he cannot remember, and sighs to see what innocence he has outlived. The elder he grows, he is a stair lower from God, and like his first father much worse in his breeches... Could he put off his body with his little coat, he had got eternity without a burthen, and exchanged but one heaven for another.

The *Microcosmography* was very popular, and drew Earle from Oxford to the court, where he became chaplain to the Lord Chamberlain. (the Earl of Pembroke), tutor to the Prince of Wales, and an adviser of Charles I. He was one of the most respected and moderate clergymen of his time, remained true to the royal cause, and after the Restoration became successively Dean of Westminster, Bishop of Worcester, and Bishop of Salisbury.

Numerous books of characters followed the *Microcosmography*,[12] notably the large collection that Samuel Butler wrote after the Restoration; but Earle best illustrates the courtly charm of the species and shows its underlying affinity with the *Tatler* and *Spectator* essays, many of which are far closer to his work than to Bacon's. An important development resulted when the art

---

[11] I.e., the garb of a doctor or judge.

[12] The *Character of the Low Countries* by Owen Feltham (1602?-1668) is an extended example of the local "character," based on actual observations in Holland. This was not printed till 1652, but was written long before. Feltham's *Resolves*, which passed through eight editions between 1623 and 1636 and enjoyed a certain vogue in the nineteenth century, can be best described as a collection of short essays written in the style of the character books. See F. S. Tupper, "New Facts regarding Owen Feltham," *MLN*, LIV (1939). 199-201.

of the fictitious or generic character was applied to the portraiture of historical figures, as in Sir Robert Naunton's *Observations on the Late Queen, Her Times, and Favorites,* written originally about 1630. In the hands of Edward Hyde, Earl of Clarendon (1609-1674), and under the sharpened focus of the civil wars, this type of writing was touched with genius, as in his famous characters of Lord Falkland, Charles I, and John Hampden. These immortal and remarkably impartial estimates of Hyde's contemporary friends and foes were composed in large part in 1646-1648, though not published till after incorporation twenty-five years later in his *History of the Rebellion and Civil Wars.*[18]

Some time after 1610, as the cult of the "character" was developing, an *Autobiog-* isolated survivor from Elizabethan times, Fulke Greville, Lord Brooke (1554- *raphy* 1628), wrote a famous prose work which, though strongly reminiscent of the earlier era, has some affinity also with the spirit of Overbury and Earle. When printed much later, and long after Greville's death,[14] the publisher entitled it *The Life of the Renowned Sir Philip Sidney, with the True Interest of Eng-* *Greville's* *land as It Then Stood...Together with a Short Account of the Maxims and* *"Life" of* *Policies Used by Queen Elizabeth in Her Government,* along with a great *Sidney* deal more, for the title-page is one of the longest that has been employed to introduce a pamphlet of 40,000 words. Greville called it simply "A Dedication," intending it as a consecration of his own poems to the memory of his famous friend. It is not properly a biography of Sidney and tells few facts, though as he and Greville had been intimate companions from the age of ten, it contains some precious anecdotes. It is rather an extended "character" of Sidney, seen through the mist of a quarter-century as the true patriot or ideal gentleman, and of Elizabeth as the wise queen. More fundamentally, it is Greville's political and intellectual autobiography, expressed in his judgments of the persons who had most influenced him, and of the literary works in which he had attempted to set down his own principles. It is the expansive development of that view of himself which he condensed in his famous epitaph: "Fulke Greville, Servant to Queen Elizabeth, Councillor to King James, and Friend to Sir Philip Sidney." Greville's prose style retains the resonance of the Elizabethans and has little of the spruce self-consciousness of the character writers. Splendid sentences abound, but they tend to be over long for their syntactical frame and hence obscure, a single sentence frequently filling a paragraph of two hundred words. In this respect Greville is a link between the style of the *Arcadia* and that of Jeremy Taylor.

Greville's poems, to which the work just discussed was to serve as introduction, are of various and not easily ascertainable dates, having been much

[18] See D. Nichol Smith, *Characters from the Histories and Memoirs of the Seventeenth Century* (Oxford, 1918); and the discussion of Clarendon in Sir Charles Firth's *Essays, Historical and Literary* (Oxford, 1938), pp. 1-33.

[14] In 1652, with a Dedication to the Countess of Sunderland, Waller's "Sacharissa." See *Sir Fulke Greville's Life of Sir Philip Sidney,* with an introduction by Nowell Smith (Oxford 1907).

revised in the course of his long life.[15] He wrote three closet dramas, of which one, on Antony and Cleopatra, was prudentially burned by the poet about the time of the Essex uprising (1601). The surviving ones, *Mustapha* (printed in 1609) and *Alaham,* both existing in several versions, are Senecan tragedies based upon atrocities of the past century in Turkey and Persia respectively. They are important mainly for the author's wrestlings in long choruses and soliloquies with the dark problems of statecraft and human malignity.[16]

Greville's lyrics, entitled *Caelica,* (which his *Dedication* does not mention) are the earliest and, on the whole, the least successful of his writings; for though he had great intelligence and metrical ability, he had little warmth of emotion. They consist of 109 poems, called sonnets, though less than half are actually in that form. Most of them appear to have been composed before Sidney's death in 1586.[17] More really significant are his long philosophical poems or "treatises" in six-line stanzas occasionally interspersed with *ottava rima.* Three of these, on *Human Learning, Fame and Honor,* and *Wars,* were first printed with the plays and *Caelica* in 1633; two others, on *Monarchy* and *Religion,* were brought to light in 1670. The longest and most closely argued is the *Treatise of Monarchy,* in fifteen sections and 664 stanzas; the best poetically is perhaps the first, which attacks the whole problem of knowledge in obvious relation to Bacon's *Advancement of Learning,* though from a much more skeptical point of view. Here one finds lines of pungent satire,

> Then what is our high-prais'd philosophy
> But books of poesy in prose compil'd? (st. 29),

and of brilliant finish,

> The artless use bears down the useless arts (st. 69).

One fine figure, directed against the "instrumental" arts, i.e., grammar, logic, etc., seems an ironic judgment on Greville's own career,

> I say, who too long in their cobwebs lurks,
> Doth like him that buys tools, but never works (st. 102).

Beginning in acrid disillusion over man's efforts to know, this poem works round to a happier view, and toward the end achieves some stanzas of great sweetness and felicity; e.g.,

> The chief use, then, in man of that he knows
> Is his painstaking for the good of all;
> Not fleshly weeping for our own-made woes,
> Not laughing from a melancholy gall,
> Not hating from a soul that overflows
> With bitterness breath'd out from inward thrall:
> But sweetly rather to ease, loose, or bind,
> As need requires, this frail, fall'n humankind (st. 143).

---

[15] The editor of his *Remains* in 1670 explains: "When he grew old, he revised the poems and treatises he had writ long before."

[16] *Poems and Dramas of Fulke Greville, first Lord Brooke,* ed. G. Bullough (2v, 1939); see M. W. Croll, *The Works of Fulke Greville* (Philadelphia, 1903); A. H. Bullen, *Elizabethans* (1924), pp. 195-206; U. Ellis-Fermor, *The Jacobean Drama* (1936), pp. 191-200.

[17] See Wm. Frost, *Fulke Greville's "Caelica," an Evaluation* (Brattleboro, Vt., 1942).

Edward, Baron Herbert of Cherbury (1583-1648), George Herbert's eldest *Lord Her-* brother, has some importance as a poet [18] and more as a philosopher, but he *bert of* chiefly lives today by his autobiography,[19] which hardly presents him at all *Cherbury* in those two aspects, but makes a great deal of him as a swashbuckler and lover. His actual life was not heroic and not even very romantic, but he had many experiences and knew well how to put himself into the center of every picture. His martial encounters do not seem to have been very deadly, but his stories of the quarrels with Lord de Walden and Sir John Ayres are in the best Dumas style and make him appear a second Cellini, or perhaps a second Falstaff. Witness this episode, when he finds Sir Thomas Somerset "with eleven or twelve more" intent upon his bodily injury:

I, running hereupon amongst them, put by some of their thrusts, and making towards him in particular, put by a thrust of his, and had certainly run him through, but that one Lieutenant Prichard, at that instant taking me by the shoulder, turned me aside; but I, recovering myself again, ran at him a second time, which he perceiving retired himself with the company to the tents, which were near, though not so fast but I hurt one Proger and some others also that were with him. But they being all at last got within the tents, I finding now nothing else to be done, got to my horse again, having received only a slight hurt on the outside of my ribs and two thrusts, the one through the skirts of my doublet and the other through my breeches, and about eighteen nicks upon my sword and hilt.

Herbert's style is easy and very readable, and few writers can better tell an anecdote. This, he says, occurred when he was ambassador in France:

It fell out one day that the Prince of Condé coming to my house, some speech happened concerning the King, my master, in whom, though he acknowledged much learning, knowledge, clemency, and divers other virtues, yet he said he had heard that the King was much given to cursing. I answered that it was out of his gentleness; but the Prince demanding how cursing could be a gentleness, I replied: "Yes, for though he could punish men himself, yet he left them to God to punish"; which defence of the King my master was afterwards much celebrated in the French court.

Though he wrote only for his immediate posterity—and indeed the *Life* was not known to the public till Horace Walpole discovered and printed it in 1764—Herbert had a good deal of the showman's art in displaying his wares. A rather trivial accident at the French court is thus advertised:

All which passage I have thought fit to set down, the accident above-mentioned being so strange that it can hardly be paralleled,

and some details about his person begin with the words:

---

[18] Lord Herbert's poems, which were influenced by Donne's, have been most scrupulously edited by G. C. Moore Smith (Oxford, 1923).
[19] Edited with introduction, notes, appendices, and a continuation of the life, by Sidney Lee (1886, etc.). See R. I. Aaron, "The 'Autobiography' of Edward, first Lord Herbert of Cherbury: the Original Manuscript Material," *MLR*, xxxvi (1941). 184-194; and Basil Willey, "Lord Herbert of Cherbury, a Spiritual Quixote of the Seventeenth Century," in *E&S*, xxvii (1942). 22-29.

I shall relate now some things concerning myself which, though they may seem scarce credible, yet, before God, are true.

One of the most artistic things about this amusing work is that Herbert had the dramatic sense to let it break off in 1624, at the close of his ambassadorship to France, which was the highest post he reached. He closes with a well-related miracle that God vouchsafed him in regarding the publication in the same year of his most important philosophical work, *De Veritate*.[20] Of this virtue he says many fine and original things in the Latin treatise, but he did not overwork it in the autobiography.

Sir Kenelm Digby [21] (1603-1665), the third in the series of great seventeenth-century gentlemen who adorned three successive generations, is likewise a man of fashion, poet, philosopher, and autobiographer. The height of Digby's slight performance as a poet is reached in a charming sonnet,

> Like as smells or odors of delight
> Are not decreas'd by smelling of their scent.[22]

He was one of the truest lovers of Spenser in his age. The short essay *Concerning Spencer,* "that I wrote at Mr. May his desire," is as notable a tribute to that poet's powers of mind as can be found in the same compass; and he wrote also "the earliest learned commentary on Spenser," [23] a twenty-five page brochure (1643) on the twenty-second stanza in the ninth canto of the second book of *The Faerie Queene.* He was one of the earliest readers of Sir Thomas Browne and wrote perhaps the earliest printed criticism of *Religio Medici* in his *Observations* on that work (1643).[24] This, though written with liveliness and courtesy, is contentious and abstruse; and Digby aspired to even more arduous philosophical laurels in the *Two Treatises* (1645), aggregating nearly six hundred pages, "in the one of which the nature of bodies, in the other the nature of man's soul, is looked into in way of discovery of the immortality of reasonable souls." They are dedicated to his son Kenelm as a counterpoise against "the calamity of this time."

His quasi-autobiography, to which he gave the title, "Loose Fantasies," and its first publisher (in 1827) the discreeter name of *Private Memoirs,* was

---

[20] See *De Veritate by Edward, Lord Herbert of Cherbury,* translated with an introduction by M. H. Carré (Bristol, 1937). Herbert wrote also a long history of *The Life and Reign of King Henry VIII;* and in Latin a theological work which in title and somewhat in attitude anticipates Dryden: *De Religione Laici.* The last has been edited and translated, with a discussion of Herbert's philosophy and a comprehensive bibliography, by H. R. Hutcheson (New Haven, 1944).

[21] See E. W. Bligh, *Sir Kenelm Digby and his Venetia* (1932), an amusing account with some new material; and J. F. Fulton, *Sir Kenelm Digby, Writer, Bibliophile, and Protagonist of William Harvey* (1937).

[22] See H. A. Bright, *Poems from Sir Kenelm Digby's Papers* (1877).

[23] See, however, C. Camden, "The Architecture of Spenser's 'House of Alma,'" *MLN,* LVIII (1943). 262-265.

[24] Written in great haste in December, 1642, while Digby was imprisoned in Winchester House for royalist activities against the Parliament. The weird adventures and hairbreadth escapes for which Sir Kenelm was famous began almost with his birth. The heir of a wealthy Catholic family in the north, he was not three years old when his father, Sir Everard Digby, was executed for complicity in the Gunpowder Plot against James I. The objections to *Religio Medici* in his *Observations* are those of a devout and philosophical Catholic.

written in earlier happier days, at the age of twenty-five, while the author was commanding a marauding expedition in the Mediterranean. The background suggests the *Adventures of a Younger Son* of Byron's friend Trelawny, whom Digby resembled in some respects. His narrative is a considerably altered version of his love for Venetia Stanley, who after extraordinary experiences had become his wife three years before. It may have been the Greek environment in which he wrote that prompted him to disguise his memoirs as a tale like Sidney's *Arcadia* or the Alexandrian romances. The names are fictitious, Digby appearing as Theagenes,[25] and Venetia, doubtless in memory of Sidney's famous love, as Stelliana. Other characters are not so certainly identifiable; but in spite of its classical names and locale, the book is important as social history, while also interesting as a gesture in the direc- tion of prose fiction at a period when the production of such work was in strange eclipse.

Very unlike the preceding autobiographical works, all of which crept belatedly and with small notice into print, is the *Eikon Basilike* (King's Image), or "the portraiture of his sacred majesty in his solitudes and suffer- ings." This was printed at the time of Charles I's execution, early in 1649, and purports to be the King's spiritual autobiography, that is, his reflections and prayers upon the later events of his unhappy reign and his advice to his son.[26] It made an enormous sensation. Innumerable editions came out; John Earle, the author of *Microcosmography,* translated it into Latin and Milton replied harshly to it in his *Eikonoklastes* (Image-breaker). Attempts to prove it a forgery by Dr. John Gauden made it a mystery hotly debated for over two centuries. Dr. Gauden charged himself with the fraud, and was rewarded after the Restoration with two bishoprics. The mystery cannot be said to be yet finally solved, but on literary grounds there is no very good reason to doubt the King's essential authorship. The *Eikon* is not a great piece of prose, being pietistic, self-exculpatory, and conventional, but it sounds sincere and expresses the ideas that Charles 1 held. If it is an out and out forgery, the author must have been a much cleverer person than the King was, to mimic him so well, and Dr. Gauden was hardly that.

A self-educated shopkeeper of London, Izaak Walton [27] (1593-1683), was raised to intimate friendship with many of the most eminent persons of his day by the simple goodness of his heart and the natural charm of his conver- sation. These same two qualities ·have helped to make him one of the most

Eikon Basilike

Izaak Walton

---

[25] The name of the hero of the *Aethiopian History* of Heliodorus.

[26] The title may have been suggested by the *Basilikon Doron* of Charles's father, which has in part a similar purpose. See the preceding chapter. For a very full discussion of certain aspects of the *Eikon Basilike* and of Milton's relation to it, see S. B. Liljegren, *Studies in Milton* (Lund, 1918), pp. 37-160.

[27] See G. L. Keynes, *The Compleat Walton* (1929). The Lives have been printed with an intro. by G. Saintsbury (Oxford, 1927); see J. E. Butt, *A Bibliography of Izaak Walton's Lives* (1930; *Proc. Oxford Bibl. Soc.,* 11). Among the nearly innumerable editions of *The Complete Angler,* that of R. B. Marston (2v, 1888) is one of the most useful. See P. Oliver, *A New Chronicle of The Complete Angler* (1936), which records that this work was printed five times in the seventeenth century, ten times in the eighteenth, 164 times in the nineteenth, and about 100 times in the first third of the twentieth; and for further details T. Brooke, "The Lambert Walton-Cotton Collection," *Yale Univ. Lib. Gazette.* XVII (1943). 61-65.

beloved English writers. "When I sometimes look back upon my education and mean abilities," he wrote after he had become famous, "it is not without some little wonder at myself, that I am come to be publicly in print."

His beginning was altogether accidental. As a devout member of Dr. Donne's London parish of St. Dunstan's, Walton became, in his own words, "the poorest, the meanest, of all his friends," and through Donne, no doubt, the friend also of the great Dean's lifelong intimate, Sir Henry Wotton, Provost of Eton.[28] On Donne's death Wotton undertook to write his biography and commissioned Walton to collect data for the work, but died himself in 1639 before effecting it. So, lest the great edition of Donne's sermons in 1640 be left to appear without any introduction, Walton attempted the task with such success that, though two good men were never more unlike, his *Life* became almost a *sine qua non* for every subsequent edition of Donne's prose or poetry. An equally brief and luminous life of Wotton naturally followed. A short passage from this will illustrate Walton's simple style; it is the passage that later suggested Gray's *Ode on a Distant Prospect of Eton College.* Walton imagines Sir Henry speaking, after returning when an old man, from a visit to the school of his boyhood:

Walton's Lives

...my now being in that school, and seeing that very place where I sat when I was a boy, occasioned me to remember those very thoughts of my youth which then possessed me: sweet thoughts indeed, that promised my growing years numerous pleasures without mixtures of cares ... But age and experience have taught me that those were but empty hopes ... Nevertheless, I saw there a succession of boys using the same recreations, and, questionless, possessed with the same thoughts that then possessed me. Thus one generation succeeds another, both in their lives, recreations, hopes, fears, and death.

Walton in retirement attended to his angling. "I lay quiet twenty years," he says, "without a thought of either troubling myself or others by any new engagement in this kind, for I thought I knew my unfitness." But at last a great church dignitary—Gilbert Sheldon, in fact, later the Archbishop of Canterbury—constrained the simple soul to write the life of Richard Hooker in order to set right the "many dangerous mistakes" in Bishop Gauden's [29] biography of that great Elizabethan. This is the only case in which Walton stepped out of his own time to describe a man whom he had not seen, but none of the lives is better than that of Hooker, whose humble character and plain religion made an appeal to Walton that he has immortally transmitted. He later added (1670), as "a free-will offering" and "chiefly to please myself," the life of George Herbert, whom Walton infinitely admired though he had not enjoyed his personal friendship; and, at the surprising age of eighty-five, a life of Bishop Sanderson of Lincoln, whom Walton had known in the days of the Puritan persecutions.

[28] Sir Henry Wotton (1568-1639) was, among many other things, a minor poet of considerable charm, whose extant verses will be found in J. Hannah, *The Courtly Poets from Wotton to Montrose* (1870). See also L. P. Smith, *Life and Letters of Sir Henry Wotton* (2v, Oxford, 1907).

[29] The alleged author of *Eikon Basilike;* see above.

The Complete Angler, or the Contemplative Man's Recreation,[30] was   The Com-
printed in 1653, in the long interval between the first two and the last three   plete Angle
of Walton's *Lives*. The date is important, for it was the period of fullest
triumph of the Puritan cause, which Walton loathed. In the *Life of Sanderson* he says:

> When I look back upon the ruin of families, the bloodshed, the decay of common
> honesty, and how the former piety and plain dealing of this now sinful nation
> is turned into cruelty and cunning, I praise God that he prevented me from
> being of that party which helped to bring in this Covenant and those sad con-
> fusions that have followed it.

It is the unmentioned background of senseless war and triumphant evil that
gives *The Complete Angler* the otherworldliness which it rather strangely
shares with the *Pilgrim's Progress*. Walton was as unlike Bunyan as possible
in everything except his piety and his distress. He was neither a mystic nor a
preacher, and had no recourse except to make his humble best of God's lovely
world. So the book opens with a kind of *Magnificat* in which all the creatures
of earth and air and water bless the Lord, praise him and magnify him
forever. The form is loosely that of the dialogue, as in Ascham's *Toxophilus*.
Three plain men,[31] fond respectively of birds, dogs, and fish, turn their backs
upon the city and trudge out Tottenham Court Road into the fields, where
for five days they endure the showers without grumbling and meet only the
simplest and kindliest folk: milkmaids, hostesses of inns, and fellow anglers.
There is a great deal about catching fish and cooking them that anglers think
important, and much misinformation out of Walton's broad but unsystematic
reading; but the preservative element is the nostalgia which a saddened man
of sixty felt for a fairer age that had passed away. The fisherman can forget
politics and recover his innocence. "No life, my honest scholar," says Piscator,

> no life so happy and so pleasant as the life of a well-governed angler; for when
> the lawyer is swallowed up with business, and the statesman is preventing or
> contriving plots, then we sit on cowslip banks, hear the birds sing, and possess
> ourselves in as much quietness as these silent silver streams, which we now see
> glide so quietly by us. Indeed, my good scholar, we may say of angling, as Dr.
> Boteler said of strawberries, "Doubtless God could have made a better berry, but
> doubtless God never did"; and so, if I might be judge, God never did make a
> more calm, quiet, innocent recreation than angling.

In Walton's fancy the quiet rivers still echo with the songs that Marlowe
and Sir Walter Ralegh sang so long ago. The whole book is haunted by the
Elizabethans, whose names are fragrant to him: Frank Davison and Chalkhill, Michael Drayton and Phineas Fletcher; and their nature poetry was
never more charming than in the bucolic setting in which he repeats it. He
omits nothing, one might say, appropriate to his effect, except that song of

[30] James Russell Lowell wrote a charming and witty introduction to the Boston edition of
1889.
[31] In the first edition there are but two, Piscator and Viator. Walton's contemporary popularity gave him opportunity to expand his works considerably, a thing he did with skill and
judgment.

Shakespeare's fool which seems to embody the soul of the Waltonian philosophy,

> He that has and a little tiny wit,
> With hey, ho, the wind and the rain,
> Must make content with his fortunes fit,
> Though the rain it raineth every day.

VIII
Seventeenth-Century Prose: III. The Baroque Glory

The Jacobean tendency to simplicity and sententiousness in prose, eminently illustrated in Bacon and the character writers, was a revulsion from Elizabethan Gothicism and a long step toward the taste of the age of Queen Anne. But the revulsion was never complete, and before James I died (1625) the temporarily arrested Gothic taste had come surging back to create a mingled style which can best be called "baroque" [1] and which, in the dizzy intensities it attained, has never been equaled. Donne's prose is the best illustration of this ferment. *The Baroque Style*

A recent writer has remarked that Donne's preaching "shows all the symptoms of fever." [2] He was the outstanding preacher of his day, and his sermons,[3] of which over 160 have been preserved, fascinated his auditors (as they do the readers still) by silhouetting in darkest horror all the unresolved conflicts of his soul. They are compact of fear, egoism, poetry, and a kind of moral exhibitionism in which the sublime and the loathsome are inextricably confused, as they are also in the awfully symbolic portrait that shows him wearing a prematurely assumed shroud. Worms, putrefaction, and the fear of death and judgment are perpetually in the foreground of his thought. The sins of his youth become the baroque ornaments of his pious eloquence. Thus he speaks to God in one of the remarkable *Devotions upon Emergent Occasions* (1624) which chart the movements of his mind during an almost fatal illness: *John Donne (1572-1631)*

If I accuse myself of original sin, wilt thou ask me if I know what original sin is? I know not enough of it to satisfy others, but I know enough to condemn myself, and to solicit thee. If I confess to thee the sins of my youth, wilt thou

---

[1] *Baroque* as here used describes work in which the Gothic elements listed by Ruskin—e.g., savageness, changefulness, grotesqueness, redundance—develop out of a fundamentally classic pattern. See M. W. Croll, "The Baroque Style in Prose," *Studies ... in Honor of Frederick Klaeber* (1929), and also G. Saintsbury, *A History of English Prose Rhythm* (1912), pp. 168-200.

[2] H. I'A. Fausset, *John Donne, a Study in Discord* (1924), p. 278. On Elizabethan sermon literature see Alan F. Herr, *The Elizabethan Sermon: A Survey and a Bibliography* (Philadelphia, 1940).

[3] E. M. Simpson, *A Study of the Prose Works of John Donne* (Oxford, 1924) is very useful. Excellently selected passages from the sermons have been edited with an essay by L. P. Smith (Oxford, 1919); and the *Devotions upon Emergent Occasions* and *Death's Duel* (Donne's last sermon) by W. H. Draper (Abbey Classics, xx). A sympathetic treatment of Donne's religion will be found in R. W. Battenhouse, "The Grounds of Religious Toleration in the Thought of John Donne," *Church History*, xi (1942). 217-248. For further bibliography see n. 27 in the chapter following.

ask me if I know what those sins were? I know them not so well as to name them all, nor am sure to live hours enough to name them all (for I did them then faster than I can speak them now, when everything that I did conduced to some sin), but I know them so well as to know that nothing but thy mercy is so infinite as they.

Man is a worm, and destined to be worms' meat, he constantly preaches, sometimes in language of torrid terror that builds up like a thunder-storm:

That God should let my soul fall out of his hand into a bottomless pit, and roll an unremovable stone upon it, and leave it to that which it finds there (and it shall find that there which it never imagined till it came thither), and never think more of that soul, never have more to do with it; that of that providence of God, that studies the life of every weed, and worm, and ant, and spider, and toad, and viper, there should never, never any beam flow out upon me . . . (Sermon lxxvi).

The sentence rolls on through one majestic "that" clause after another to the length of five hundred words. And, on the other hand, he can annihilate hope with a single flash of cynical scorn, as

I would not make man worse than he is, nor his condition more miserable than it is. But could I though I would? (*Devotions*, xiv).

Donne's unexpectedness is a large element in his grotesque but moving art. His metaphors are among the most brilliant in our literature; he takes them largely from sea-faring or maps or the courses of the stars, but he can draw a figure of marvelous vividness and precision out of so dry a subject as syntax:

If we consider eternity, into that time never entered; eternity is not an everlasting flux of time, but time is a short parenthesis in a long period; [4] and eternity had been the same as it is, though time had never been.

He sees antitheses and incongruities on all sides. Puns and bitter jokes sometimes break the flow of his most sonorous sentences:

A man that is not afraid of a lion is afraid of a cat; not afraid of starving, and yet is afraid of some joint of meat at the table presented to feed him; not afraid of the sound of drums and trumpets and shot and those which they seek to drown, the last cries of men, and is afraid of some particular harmonious instrument; so much afraid as that with any of these the enemy might drive this man, otherwise valiant enough, out of the field. [5]

In his youth he had written a number of brief flippancies of much cleverness and little weight called *Paradoxes and Problems,* and in his later work his tormented brain circled about the great paradox that a creature with

---

[4] That is, sentence or paragraph. Sir Thomas Browne is probably imitating this when he says at the close of *Christian Morals:* "The created world is but a small parenthesis in eternity."
[5] Compare Shylock's speech, *Merchant of Venice,* iv. i. 47-58.

man's frailties should be immortal. Bacon took pride in the idea,[6] but it terrified Donne and whipped the texture of his sermons into cloudy phosphorescence.[7]

Three or four years after Donne's death a young doctor of thirty, as yet very far from knighthood or other fame, was writing a book which is as brilliant an example of baroque prose as any of the great dean's sermons. In tone and quality of thought it is so different as almost to seem a conscious plea against Donne's dark theology; but this is not likely, for little of the latter, except the *Devotions upon Emergent Occasions,* was yet in print, and Thomas Browne [8] (1605-1682) had had little or no opportunity to hear Donne preach. He had been born in London, but educated, classically and copiously, at Winchester and Oxford, after which he spent several years in medical studies at Montpellier, Padua, and Leyden, receiving his M.D. degree from the last university in 1634. His first book, *Religio Medici* (A Doctor's Religion), written in a Yorkshire village, was the product of the vacant period after his return to England and before he settled into active practice. In 1637 he established himself in Norwich, and spent the rest of his long life as a provincial doctor there. *Sir Thomas Browne*

Religio Medici

Religio Medici is the author's private journal in which he attempts to read his own mind; it was not printed till 1642, and then in an unauthorized text. Had Browne been writing today, he would probably have aired his views on scientific and social theory, but in the seventeenth century theology was the natural field for self-appraisement. He begins by declaring that, though a physician, he is a Christian and a member of the Church of England, not intolerant, however, of other faiths, and has a temperament sympathetic to superstition. He subscribes to the articles of his church, but reserves his right of judgment on other points, deplores quarrels over religion, and avoids them. There must always be heretics, he thinks, and, becoming reminiscential, confesses three heresies that he formerly held but outgrew. "I love to lose myself in a mystery," he says, "to pursue my reason to an *O altitudo!"* [9] He sets down his thoughts about eternity and divine wisdom, and declares that men *should* inquire into God's works and the causes of things: " 'tis the debt of our reason we owe unto God, and the homage we pay for not being beasts." This leads him to the wonders of natural history and to the assertion that God has given us two books, the Bible and the book of Nature, "that universal and public manuscript that lies expans'd unto the eyes of all: those that never

[6] E.g., in the opening of the essay on Adversity.

[7] A contemporary preacher of equal influence and learning, but quieter and more orderly in manner, was Bishop Lancelot Andrewes (1555-1626). See T. S. Eliot, *For Lancelot Andrewes* (1929), pp. 13-48. Andrewes' *96 Sermons* are reprinted in 5v, Oxford and London, 1874-78, and selections from them (160 pp.) in an undated pamphlet of the S.P.C.K.

[8] The best edition is *The Works of Sir Thomas Browne,* edited by G. L. Keynes (6v, 1928-1931), who has also prepared *A Bibliography of Sir Thomas Browne* (Cambridge, 1924). See also Edmund Gosse, *Sir Thomas Browne* (EML Series, 1905); O. Leroy, *Le Chevalier Thomas Browne, sa vie, sa pensée et son art* (Paris, 1931); and R. R. Cawley, "Sir Thomas Browne and His Reading," *PMLA,* XLVIII (1933). 426-470.

[9] A quotation from the Latin text of Rom. XI: 33, "O the depth of the riches both of the wisdom and knowledge of God!"

saw Him in the one have discovered Him in the other." Observation of nature's unlovelier creatures draws from him the remark:

I cannot tell by what logic we call a toad, a bear, or an elephant ugly . . . There is no deformity but in monstrosity, wherein, notwithstanding, there is a kind of beauty, Nature so ingeniously contriving the irregular parts as they become sometimes more remarkable than the principal fabric.

He proceeds to say that he has "always endeavored to compose those feuds and angry dissensions" which arise among the three forces in our minds, faith, reason, and passion:

As Reason is a rebel unto Faith, so Passion unto Reason: as the propositions of Faith seem absurd unto Reason, so the theorems of Reason unto Passion, and both unto Reason.

He illustrates this by a discussion of scientific explanations of biblical miracles. There are too many doctrinal books and the mind is clouded by them, "for obstinacy in a bad cause is but constancy in a good," and "persecution is a bad and indirect way to plant religion." Martyrs may be false as well as true. Browne himself believes in miracles, witches, and spirits, sees five biological levels in human life, from the prenatal embryo to the liberated soul, and has a low opinion of the body, which he deprecates in a figure as fantastically impressive as one of Donne's:

Nay, further, we are what we all abhor, *Anthropophagi* and cannibals, devourers not only of men but of ourselves, and that not in an allegory but a positive truth: for all this mass of flesh which we behold came in at our mouths; this frame we look upon hath been upon our trenchers; in brief, we have devoured ourselves.

Unlike Donne, he has no fear of death and argues against long life:

Were there any hopes to outlive vice, or a point to be superannuated from sin, it were worthy our knees to implore the days of Methuselah. But age doth not rectify, but incurvate, our natures, turning bad dispositions into worser habits, and (like diseases) brings on incurable vices; for every day as we grow weaker in age, we grow stronger in sin, and the number of our days doth but make our sins innumerable—

going on with words that recall the reasoning of Despair in Spenser.[10] He concludes the first book with a survey of eschatology, "the four last things," death, judgment, heaven, and hell, and argues against narrow views, sometimes in the enlightened spirit of Marlowe's Mephistophilis:

Men speak too popularly who place it in those flaming mountains which to grosser apprehensions represent Hell. The heart of man is the place the devils dwell in. I feel sometimes a hell within myself: Lucifer keeps his court in my breast, Legion is revived in me.

[10] *Faerie Queene*, I. ix. st. 43-46.

Upon the hell-fire school Browne turns a debonair back:

I thank God, and with joy I mention it: I was never afraid of Hell, nor never grew pale at the description of that place. I have so fixed my contemplations on Heaven that I have almost forgot the idea of Hell, and am afraid rather to lose the joys of the one than endure the misery of the other ... I am confident and fully persuaded, yet dare not take my oath, of my salvation. I am as it were sure, and do believe without all doubt, that there is such a city as Constantinople; yet for me to take my oath thereon were a kind of perjury, because I hold no infallible warrant from my own sense to confirm me in the certainty thereof.

The second part of *Religio Medici,* much shorter than the first, deals wholly with the virtue Browne most advocates, charity. It is less analytical and even more naïvely personal than the first part, and contains a high proportion of his most memorable and sonorous sentences. The opening paragraph is an excellent example of his manner, as is also this passage near the middle of the book·

There is, I think, no man that apprehends his own miseries less than myself, and no man that so nearly apprehends another's. I could lose an arm without a tear, and with few groans, methinks, be quartered into pieces; yet can I weep most seriously at a play, and receive with true passion the counterfeit grief of those known and professed impostures.

It is likely that Dr. Browne, in all his estimable career, never prescribed a better medicine than when he wrote *Religio Medici.* The world was sick of horrors, on the brink of civil war, and in the throes of a harsh theology. The book is a prophylactic against totalitarian damnation, and the world took it to its heart. To be sure, it is written in a style and with a frank display of ingenuous personality that would sell any book, but its curative value was what carried it through Europe. There were nine English editions before 1660, and five in Latin. Before Browne's death it had been translated also into Dutch, French, and German. In December, 1642, before the acknowledged text had appeared, the Earl of Dorset recommended the book to Sir Kenelm Digby, who read it all night long and dashed off his *Observations* upon it. Browne thought these unfair in their dialectic (as they are), but they contain a perfect tribute to the personality that the *Religio Medici* reveals: "Assuredly, he is the owner of a solid head and of a strong generous heart."[11]

"Vulgar Errors"

Browne's longest work is the *Pseudodoxia Epidemica, or Enquiries into Very Many Received Tenets and Commonly Presumed Truths,*[12] which appeared in a folio volume in 1646 and reached its sixth edition in 1672. The suggestion may have come from Bacon, who in his *Advancement of Learning* noted the lack of such a book, but the only real counterpart is Burton's

---

[11] Browne's *Christian Morals,* a set of moral admonitions of much later date than *Religio Medici* and less interest, was the occasion of Samuel Johnson's life of the author (1756). Both have been edited by S. C. Roberts (Cambridge, 1927).

[12] Commonly known as *Vulgar Errors.*

Anatomy of Melancholy. It would not be easy to instance another work of equal size and equally miscellaneous and detailed scholarship which has so attracted and retained readers as these two. Browne was now a far busier man than Burton ever was, and he complains that the *Pseudodoxia* has had to be "composed by snatches of time" in such "medical vacations" as he has had, though, he confesses, "a work of this nature is not to be performed upon one leg, and should smell of oil, if duly and deservedly handled." It does smell of oil, however, though never pedantically. The spread of subject matter is enormous and enables the author to utilize not only the quasi-scientific data compiled by Aristotle, Pliny, and their learned followers, but also the impressively large amount of accurate observation he had himself made into botany, natural history, and medicine. Book 1 is an introduction, dealing with the psychological causes of error, very cogent in the main, but concluding with the argument that the endeavors of Satan are "the last and great promoter of false opinions." The remaining six books classify errors concerning mineral and vegetable bodies, animals, man, misrepresentations in pictures, etc., geography, and history. It is a work which only the privileged few can read in full; but it can be read with amusement in any part, and referred to with profit in connection with almost any strange belief about nature or history. Indeed, Browne has here confuted dozens of false ideas which some educated persons have even today not thought of questioning. The style is less conscious than that of *Religio Medici,* its chief marks being the author's growing taste for elaborately periodic sentences and the high proportion of Latin words in his vocabulary. Browne, indeed, apologizes for the last and wittily shows his recognition of this tendency in the language:

And indeed, if elegancy still proceedeth, and English pens maintain that stream we have of late observed to flow from many, we shall within few years be fain to learn Latin to understand English, and a work will prove of equal facility in either.[13]

Jrn-Burial   Emphasis on style is more conspicuous in the two shorter works which followed: *Hydriotaphia, or Urn-Burial,* and *The Garden of Cyrus,* printed together in 1658. The latter is almost purely a monument to style and erudition, and can be recommended only to those who will accept those qualities as their own justification. *Urn-Burial,* in part a scientific report on forty or fifty Roman funeral urns recently exhumed near Norwich, becomes a disquisition on burial customs in general,[14] and in its last, most famous, chapter

[13] Prefatory epistle "To the Reader." It is to be noted that Browne's personal letters, of which a great many have been preserved, hardly show any trace of his peculiar style.

[14] Accident curiously repaid the macabre fascination which Browne here imparts to bones and burials. In 1840 his coffin was opened, and his skull (which is very remarkable craniologically) was stolen and sold by the sexton of the Norwich church in which he is buried. At the same time the skull of Ben Jonson was suffering extraordinary vicissitudes in Westminster Abbey (see J. Q. Adams, "The Bones of Ben Jonson," *SP,* XVI (1919). 289-302). Thus two of the most eminent heads of the seventeenth century experienced posthumous adventures in the nineteenth. It is not altogether certain where Jonson's is at present; Browne's was reinterred as late as 1922.

is a prose poem on death of perhaps unequaled verbal harmony.[15] A historian of the English essay has said:

Flawlessness is even more rare in prose than it is in verse, and if all the pieces were collected which a reasonable criticism could praise wholly without reserve, they would make only a very small volume. But an extraordinary proportion would come from *Urn-Burial*, a proportion higher than any other work of equal length would yield.[16]

The mild Anglican theology of Jeremy Taylor [17] (1613-1667) is probably *Jeremy* more respected today than admired or studied; [18] it is by his language that he *Taylor* lives. In the ninety-first *Idler* paper Dr. Johnson paid a compliment to the great preachers, of whom Taylor is perhaps the greatest:

Our own language has, from the Reformation to the present time, been chiefly dignified and adorned by the works of our divines, who, considered as commentators, controvertists, and preachers, have undoubtedly left all other nations far behind them.

Coleridge, grouping him with Hooker, Bacon, and Milton, gives them all just praise:

In all these the language is dignified but plain, genuine English, although elevated and brightened by superiority of intellect in the writer. Individual words themselves are always used by them in their precise meaning, without either affectation or slipslop.... The words are selected because they are the most appropriate, regard being had to the dignity of the total impression, and no merely big phrases are used where plain ones would have sufficed, even in the most learned of their works.[19]

Taylor's place is with the baroque writers, but it is in the quiet center rather than the excited fringes of the movement. His works, enormous in bulk, are all devout, though they cover a wide range, from *The Liberty of Prophesying* (1647), an elaborately argued treatise on religious toleration, and the *Ductor Dubitantium* (1660), which embraces two encyclopaedic volumes of "cases of conscience," to *A Discourse of the Nature, Offices and Measures of Friendship, with Rules of Conducting It* (1657), which is a good-natured reply to Mrs. Katharine Philips ("the matchless Orinda") concerning her Platonic salon.

[15] See N. R. Tempest, "Rhythm in the Prose of Sir Thomas Browne," *RES*, III (1924). 308-318; E. L. Parker, "The *cursus* in Sir Thomas Browne," *PMLA*, LIII (1938). 1037-1053; J. M. Cline, "Hydriotaphia," in *Five Studies in Literature* (Berkeley, 1940), pp. 73-100.
[16] Hugh Walker, *The English Essay and Essayists* (1928), p. 79. Browne's influence upon the 19th century romanticists is well known; see Leroy, *op. cit.*, 301-313, and J. S. Iseman, *A Perfect Sympathy: Charles Lamb and Sir Thomas Browne* (Cambridge, Mass., 1937).
[17] L. Pearsall Smith's *Selected Passages from the Sermons and Writings of Jeremy Taylor* (Oxford, 1930) includes an excellent introduction and a fine bibliography. See also Edmund Gosse, *Jeremy Taylor* (EML Series, 1904); W. J. Brown, *Jeremy Taylor* (1925).
[18] See, however, C. J. Stranks, "Jeremy Taylor," *Church Quar. Rev.*, CXXXI (1940). 31-62.
[19] *Coleridge's Miscellaneous Criticism*, ed. T. M. Raysor (1936), pp. 216f.

Taylor's extraordinary abilities were early discovered by Archbishop Laud, who transplanted him from Cambridge to Oxford and made it possible for him to become Chaplain-in-ordinary to Charles I. His earliest publication is a sermon dedicated to the Archbishop and delivered at St. Mary's, Oxford, in 1638 on the anniversary of the Gunpowder Plot (November 5). The ruin of the King's cause was the ruin also of Taylor's hopes. After a period of imprisonment by the Parliamentary forces he found occupation as a teacher in South Wales, and had the happy chance to win the affection of a great royalist nobleman, Richard Vaughan, Earl of Carbery.[20] His funeral sermon on Lady Carbery, who died in October, 1650, is one of his most beautiful and moving productions. To her husband he dedicated his two most famous books, *The Rule and Exercises of Holy Living* (1650) and *The Rule and Exercises of Holy Dying* (1651).

In the eighteenth century he was dubbed "the Shakespeare of divines," and in the nineteenth Lamb, Coleridge, and Hazlitt sometimes ranked his genius absurdly high, with the result that he has since been overrated and underread. His style is not always great, or even easily readable, though always clear; but when he is deeply moved his mighty sentences unroll themselves like a work of nature—like a sunrise or the incoming of a tide,

> such a tide as moving seems asleep,
> Too full for sound and foam.

Their connectives are hardly noted, and often are omitted. They flow along in successive waves of parallel clauses, each series moving abreast with incomparable smoothness, till all finally give place to the figure for which all have been preparing:

And though her account to God was made up of nothing but small parcels, little passions and angry words and trifling discontents, which are the alloys of the piety of the most holy persons, yet she was early at her repentance; and toward the latter end of her days grew so fast in religion as if she had had a revelation of her approaching end, and therefore that she must go a great way in a little time: her discourses more full of religion, her prayers more frequent, her charity increasing, her forgiveness more forward, her friendships more communicative, her passion more under discipline; and so she trimmed her lamp, not thinking her night was so near, but that it might shine also in the daytime, in the temple and before the altar of incense (Smith, *op. cit.*, p. 23).

Taylor loved this world, and it is a great part of his praise that he let the brightness of its light and the freshness of its streams and breezes flow across his pages. The great sentence in *Holy Dying*, in which he compares man's life to the progress of the sun,

But as when the sun approaches towards the gates of the morning, he first opens a little eye of heaven, ... (Smith, *op. cit.*, p. 42),

---

20 The earl's residence was at Golden Grove, Carmarthenshire. Hence the title of Taylor's book of prayers, *The Golden Grove* (1655), and his chief collections of sermons: *XXVIII Sermons Preached at Golden Grove* (1651) and *XXV Sermons Preached at Golden Grove* (1653).

is almost too famous for further quotation. The lively pathos with which the worm is treated in the following passage is no more admirable than the literary skill with which she is brought in at the opening and the close:

For as a worm creeping with her belly on the ground, with her portion of Adam's curse, lifts up its head to partake a little of the blessings of the air, and opens the junctures of her imperfect body, and curls her little rings into knots and combinations, drawing up her tail to a neighborhood of the head's pleasure and motion; but still it must return to abide the fate of its own nature, and dwell and sleep upon the dust: so are the hopes of a mortal man; he opens his eyes and looks upon fine things at distance, and shuts them again with weakness, because they are too glorious to behold; and the man rejoices because he hopes fine things are staying for him, but his heart aches because he knows there are a thousand ways to fail and miss of those glories, and though he hopes yet he enjoys not; he longs but he possesses not, and must be content with his portion of dust; and being *a worm and no man,* must lie down in this portion before he can receive the end of his hopes, the salvation of his soul in the resurrection of the dead.[21]

Taylor's fluidity and touches of natural color usually give an effect of gentleness, but when angry he can coil his sinuous clauses about an opponent like twisting wire, as in this outburst against the Puritans in 1655:

But now, instead of this excellency of condition and constitution of religion, the people are fallen under the harrows and saws of impertinent and ignorant preachers, who think all religion is a sermon and all sermons ought to be libels against truth and old governors, and expound chapters that the meaning may never be understood, and pray that they may be thought able to talk, but not to hold their peace, they casting not to obtain anything but wealth and victory, power and plunder; and the people have reaped the fruits apt to grow upon such crabstocks: they grow idle and false, hypocrites and careless, they deny themselves nothing that is pleasant, they despise religion, forget government, and some never think of heaven; and they that do, think to go thither in such paths which all the ages of the church did give men warning of, lest they should that way go to the devil.[22]

It is not easy to place the amusing Welshman, James Howell (1594-1666), *James* whose work is in several different styles. He knew a great deal of the real *Howell* world and in mental attitude is more akin to Samuel Pepys than to Sir Thomas Browne or Jeremy Taylor, but he had a vein of Celtic fancy which he could open at will. In early youth he had the opportunity of traveling extensively on the Continent on business connected with the manufacture of glass. Somewhat later he obtained diplomatic employment and did further travel, being in Madrid when Prince Charles and the Duke of Buckingham paid their famous visit to the Spanish court in 1623. He came to be one of the clerks of the Privy Council and dedicated his most interesting book, the *Epistolae Ho-Elianae* (1645), to Charles I. These letters, though not too

[21] Funeral sermon for the Archbishop of Armagh, 1663 (L. P. Smith, *op. cit.,* 40).
[22] Preface to *The Golden Grove* (L. P. Smith, *op. cit.,* 31).

precise about dates and facts, are based upon Howell's observations and have considerable narrative value as well as charm.[23]

His career as a professional writer began very late, but once started, the flow of his publications was incessant. His first book was *Dodona's Grove, or the Vocal Forest* (1640), with a second part in 1650. Here the gossipy clerk in Howell is controlled by the dreamy Celt, who "deeming it a flat and vulgar task to compile a plain downright story ... hath under hieroglyphics, allegories, and emblems endeavored to diversify and enrich the matter." [24] That is, he tells the story of his own time in fantastic but easily penetrated symbolism, countries being represented by forests and individuals by trees. In his *Therologia, or the Parley of the Beasts* (1660), he employs animal symbolism instead:

> Trees spake before, now the same strength of art
> Makes beasts to con the alphabet by heart.

These books were popular in their day. They were accompanied by a multitude of more frankly political or geographical pamphlets, including a "survey" of Venice and *A Perfect Description of the People and Country of Scotland* (1649), which is as vitriolic as any Cavalier could desire. More interesting to us is his *Instructions for Foreign Travel*, first printed in 1642 and later expanded. It is the earliest guide book in English, and carefully leads the reader, who is imagined as a young college graduate, through France, Spain, and Italy, and back to the Inns of Court in London. Howell had had all these experiences and is able to give much valuable information about customs and languages, interlarded with fervent warnings against papist and puritanical error. He was dependent upon his pen for his support and had to make thrifty use of his ideas. It is amusing to observe how often a point plainly stated in the letters is repeated with embellishment in *Dodona's Grove* and further expanded in the *Instructions*, where Howell often attempts the higher reaches of rhetoric. By the exacting standards of his age he is not a great writer of formal prose, but he can sometimes reach a high level, as in this sentence on the idea which Bishop Berkeley was later to immortalize in the line, "Westward the course of empire takes its way":

And as all other things by a kind of secret instinct of nature follow the motion of the sun, so it is observed that the arts and sciences, which are the greatest helps to civility, and all moral endowments as well as intellectual, have wheeled about and travelled in a kind of concomitant motion with that great luminary of heaven: they builded first amongst the Brahmins and Gymnosophists in India, then they blossomed amongst the Chaldeans and priests of Egypt, whence they came down the Nile and crossed over to Greece, and there they may be said to have borne ripe fruit, having taken such firm rooting and making so long a plantation in Athens and elsewhere: afterwards they found the way to Italy, and thence they clammered over the Alpian hills to visit Germany and France, whence

23 See *The Familiar Letters of James Howell*, with an introduction by Agnes Repplier (2v, 1908). There is a brief selection, *Certain Letters of James Howell*, ed. Guy Holt (1928).
24 Second part, 1650, p. 7.

the Britons with other north-west nations of the lower world fetched them over; and it is not improbable that the next flight they will make will be to the savages of the new discovered world, and so turn round and by this circular perambulation visit the Levantines again.[25]

[25] *Instructions for Foreign Travel,* section 1 (ed. E. Arber, *English Reprints,* p. 14).—With Howell's *Instructions* may be associated the principal narratives of travel of the earlier Stuart period. Samuel Purchas (1577?-1626) continued the work of Richard Hakluyt, compiling from materials in manuscript or already published separately his huge *Hakluytus Posthumus or Purchas His Pilgrims* (4v, 1625; reprinted, 20v, Glasgow, 1905-1907). A representative selection is in *Narratives from Purchas His Pilgrims,* ed. H. G. Rawlinson (1931). Thomas Coryate (1577?-1617), a genial eccentric, told of his experiences through the length and breadth of Europe in the much ridiculed but lively and informative *Coryats Crudities Hastily Gobbled up in Five Months Travels* (1611; reprinted, 2v, Glasgow, 1905). William Lithgow, an ill-tempered but courageous Scot, expanded an earlier account of his travels into *A Total Discourse of Rare Adventures and Painful Peregrinations* (1632; reprinted, Glasgow, 1906). The *Itinerary* of Fynes Moryson (1566-1630) was originally written in Latin; parts were translated by the author and published in 1617; other portions of the translation were first published much later; see especially *Shakespeare's Europe: Unpublished Chapters of Fynes Moryson's Itinerary,* ed. Charles Hughes (1903). For George Sandys' *Relation of a Journey* (1615) see ch. x, note 9, below. Covering much the same ground as Sandys' narrative is *A Voyage into the Levant* (1636) by Sir Henry Blount (1602-1682). Sir Thomas Herbert (1606-1682) ventured even further afield and told his story in *Some Years Travels* (1634) which he expanded and spoiled with tedious moralizing in later editions; the best of the original matter is in his *Travels in Persia,* ed. Sir William Foster (1928). American exploration and colonization have their share of interest in the *True Travels, Adventures, and Observations* (1630) by Captain John Smith (1580-1631), a man famous in the history and legend of English expansion overseas. See his *Travels and Works,* ed. A. G. Bradley (2v, 1910). Other travel-narratives of the period will be found reprinted, or printed for the first time, in the *Publications* of the Hakluyt Society, in the Broadway Travellers Series, and in the Argonaut Press Series. See further S. C. Chew, *The Crescent and the Rose* (1937), ch. 1 and *passim;* R. R. Cawley, *The Voyagers and Elizabethan Drama* (Boston, 1938) and *Unpathed Waters* (Princeton, 1940); Boies Penrose, *Urbane Travelers, 1591-1635* (Philadelphia, 1942).

IX

Seventeenth-Century Poetry: I. The Olympians

*he End
f the
Renaissance*

When the Renaissance ended in England is even harder to say than it is to say what it was, but the death of Spenser in 1599 is a convenient date. The removal of the last and greatest of the humanist poets happened at a time when for political and social reasons the Elizabethan spirit, which was synthetic and unifying, had given place to the spirit of the seventeenth cen·tury, which was analytical and disruptive. The strength of the insurgent movement is indicated by the popularity in the later 1590's of satire and epigram, evidenced by the work of Hall, Harington, Marston, Bastard, the two Davies', and many others; [1] and still more by the repressive efforts of the authorities, who in 1599 issued a categorical anathema against such writing.[2]

Whether, as some recent investigators have assumed, there was in any formal sense a School of Night, consisting of Ralegh, Marlowe, Chapman, the mathematician Harriot and others, and dedicated to the study of dark and prohibited subjects, may perhaps be doubted; [3] but it is certain that these men knew each other well and were moved by a spirit more rebellious and questioning than that of the true Elizabethans. The poetry of the first half of the seventeenth century, unsurpassed in certain aspects, takes its origin from the work of the four great personalities discussed in this chapter. After them it splits into two bodies: on the one hand, the great variety of often exquisite singers thrown by the currents of change and war into one or another of the opposing parties; on the other hand, the lonely, single, and indivisible phenomenon of Milton.

Sir Walter Ralegh [4] (c. 1552-1618), the friend of Spenser and of Marlowe,

---

[1] E.g., Joseph Hall, *Virgidemiarum Six Books* (1597); John Marston, *The Scourge of Villainy* (1598); Thomas Bastard, *Chrestoleros* (1598); see A. B. Grosart, *The Poems English and Latin of the Rev. Thomas Bastard* (*Occasional Issues*, XII, 1880); Sir John Davies, *Epigrams* (printed with Marlowe's elegies in several undated editions); Edward Guilpin, *Skialetheia, or a Shadow of Truth* (1598; facsimile ed., Oxford, 1931); John Weever, *Epigrams in the Oldest Cut and Newest Fashion* (1599, ed. R. B. McKerrow, 1911). On the above consult A. Davenport, "The Quarrel of the Satirists," *MLR*, XXXVII (1942). 123-130. For Sir John Harington's epigrams, which were printed later, see the edition of N. E. McClure (Philadelphia, 1926).

[2] For the text of this see, under date of June 1, 1599, *Stationers' Register*, ed. Arber, III. 316. Cf. O. J. Campbell, *Comicall Satyre and Shakespeare's "Troilus and Cressida"* (San Marino, 1938), ch. I.

[3] Cf. M. C. Bradbrook, *The School of Night, a Study in the Literary Relationships of Sir Walter Ralegh* (Cambridge, 1936).

[4] See *The Poems of Sir Walter Ralegh*, edited by A. M. C. Latham (1929); E. K. Chambers, "The Disenchantment of the Elizabethans," in *Sir Thomas Wyatt and Some Collected Studies* (1933); E. C. Dunn, "Ralegh and the 'New' Poetry," in *The Literature of Shakespeare's England* (1936), pp. 140-163; T. Brooke, "Sir Walter Ralegh as Poet and Philosopher," *ELH*, V (1938). 93-112. There is a useful selection from his prose, ed. G. E. Hadow (Oxford, 1926). The lives of Ralegh by Milton Waldman (1928) and Edward Thompson (New Haven, 1926) are modern and well written.

may be said to have started the movement which led away from them. His *Sir*
poetry was never really published, and can now be only scantily and doubt- *Walter*
fully recovered, but the best of it bears the impress of his great personality *Ralegh*
hardly less than do his other achievements. As a man of the court and a man
of the wide world, he caught nuances of the impending change, and his acrid,
questioning, close-packed lyrics, which the *Art of English Poesy* (1589)
described as "most lofty, insolent, and passionate," have in them more of the
seventeenth century than of the Renaissance. His longest extant poem, *The
Eleventh and Last Book of the Ocean to Cynthia,* is probably but a fragment
of the entire work [5] and badly lacks revision; but it is the most poignant valedictory that we have of the Elizabethan age, and is electrically charged with
the macabre power of the Jacobeans.

Ralegh's prose, which is much better preserved than his poetry, and was
probably more carefully written, is of supreme grandeur, whether its purpose
be, as in *The Truth of the Fight about the Isles of Azores* (1591), occasional
and propagandist, or, as in *The History of the World* (1614), meditative and
moral. Both in time and in merit Ralegh belongs among the first writers of
impassioned English prose.[6]

Bacon stated the aesthetic position of Chapman very well when he wrote, *George*
"There is no excellent beauty that hath not some strangeness in the propor- *Chapman*
tion." [7] This strange and most Olympian poet was five years older than *(1559-1634*
Shakespeare or Marlowe, but he gave no hint of his powers till 1594, when
his two sonorous "hymns" appeared in a volume called *The Shadow of
Night.*[8] The only clear things about these invocations, addressed to Night
and to her luminary, the Moon, are that they are deep and rousing poetry of
a new kind, and that they are not written for the general public, but for a
group of adepts or initiates. The preface, which is an open letter to Matthew
Roydon,[9] indicates that three noblemen—Derby, Northumberland, and the
"heir of Hunsdon" [10]—were in some degree sympathetic to Chapman's
crusade. Though certainly obscure, these poems are the reverse of obscurant-
ist. The argument seems to be that the world is degenerate and unjust. Light *The*
typifies the rule of organized society, the tyranny of shallow brains and daily *Shadow*
routine, which is worse than unorganized chaos, while Night represents the *of Night*
regenerative principles, "silence, study, ease, and sleep." Of her Chapman
says, "To thy black shades and desolation I consecrate my life," and in a
passage of dark splendor he summons to their task all the enemies of the
obvious:

[5] See, however, A. M. Buchan, "Ralegh's *Cynthia*—Facts or Legends," *MLQ*, I (1940). 461-
474.
[6] See E. A. Strathmann, *"The History of the World* and Ralegh's Skepticism," *HLQ*, III
(1940). 265-287; and "Sir Walter Ralegh on Natural Philosophy," *MLQ*, I (1940). 49-61.
[7] In the essay, "Of Beauty." See *Poems of George Chapman,* ed. P. B. Bartlett (1941).
[8] See R. W. Battenhouse, "Chapman's *The Shadow of Night,* an Interpretation," *SP*, XXXVIII
(1941). 584-608.
[9] Roydon was a poet whose contemporary fame was out of proportion to the unimportant
remnants of his work that survive.
[10] Presumably George Carey, who became Baron Hunsdon in 1596, and as Lord Chamberlain
(1597-1603) was the patron of Shakespeare's company.

All you possess'd with indepressed spirits,
Endued with nimble and aspiring wits,
Come, consecrate with me to sacred Night
Your whole endeavors and detest the light.
Sweet Peace's richest crown is made of stars,
Most certain guides of honor'd mariners:
No pen can anything eternal write,
That is not steep'd in humor of the Night.

Here one seems to pass as on a bridge from the luminosity of Marlowe to the twilight of Donne. The idea expressed, the artist's endless duty to reach after the ungraspable, is much the same as in Marlowe's "If all the pens that ever poets held"; but the expression, as usually in Chapman, is an anticipation of the manner of the so-called "metaphysicals." Each of these Hymns is provided with a prose "Gloss" such as accompanied *The Shepherds' Calendar*. The glosses do not much assist the modern reader, but signalize the propagandist purpose of the work.

Ovid's Banquet of Sense — Chapman's next poem, *Ovid's Banquet of Sense* (1595), is also prefaced by a letter to Roydon, in which he again states his attitude:

The profane multitude I hate, and only consecrate my strange poems to those searching spirits, whom learning hath made noble and nobility sacred ... Obscurity, in affectation of words and indigested conceits, is pedantical and childish; but where it shroudeth itself in the heart of his [i.e., its] subject, uttered with fitness of figure and expressive epithets, with that darkness will I still labor to be shadowed.

The purpose in this long narrative poem and in two shorter ones, *A Coronet for His Mistress Philosophy* and *The Amorous Zodiac*, is the purpose one observes in Donne's lyrics: to effect an intellectualizing of amatory verse. The handling of metre is masterful and varied,[11] and the poet's control of his matter is never in doubt; but these poems do not greatly engage the reader's interest.

There is rugged force and deep consciousness of intent in Chapman. As Swinburne said of his translations from the Greek: "No poet was ever less of a Greek in style or spirit. He enters the serene temples and handles the holy vessels of Hellenic art with the stride and the grasp of a high-handed and high-minded barbarian." [12] He must have appeared among the poeticules of Henslowe's play-patching factory as a Triton of the minnows, or as one of Spenser's "sea-shouldering whales." He was, by all the evidence, the rival poet to whose strange powers Shakespeare's *Sonnets* pay such tribute, and

[11] In *Ovid's Banquet* he employs a difficult nine-line stanza, riming *ababcbcdd;* in the *Coronet*, the Shakespearean sonnet with a notable number of feminine endings; in the *Amorous Zodiac*, a six-line stanza, *aabccb*.

[12] *Essay on the Poetical and Dramatic Works of George Chapman* (1875). The publication of Chapman's translation of Homer began in 1598 with *Seauen Bookes of the Iliades of Homere, Prince of Poets*, continued at intervals in other volumes, and culminated in *The Whole Works of Homer* (1616). The translation is edited in Vol. III of *The Works of George Chapman*, ed. R. H. Shepherd (3v, 1874-75), and can be had in other modern reprints such as the Temple Classics (4v, 1909).

he was the only Elizabethan poet who could meet Ben Jonson on his own learned ground and answer the latter's dogmatism with unperturbed "invective":

> Great, learned, witty Ben, be pleased to light
> The world with that three-forked fire; nor fright
> All us, thy sublearn'd, with Luciferous boast
> That thou art *most* great, *most* learn'd, witty *most*
> Of all the kingdom, nay of all the earth! [13]

Jonson loved him, as he told Drummond; Donne borrowed from him; and Webster, when he drew up in the preface to *The White Devil* (1612) the list of his most admired colleagues, put Chapman first: "For mine own part, I have ever truly cherished my good opinion of other men's worthy labors, especially of that full and heightened style of Master Chapman..." To the end, however, he remained hard to understand, and the wonderful, Jove-like, portrait of him in old age bears the perfect motto, *Monscium evasi diem,* (I shunned the blabbing day). His command of figurative language is a great part of his style. Often it is baroque and rudely powerful; but many times also the long simile that he borrowed from Homer will light up dark places in his moody plays or irradiate for a moment even so obscure a poem as the *Hymnus in Cynthiam:* ·

> As when a flock of school-boys, whom their mistress
> Held closely to their books, gets leave to sport,
> And then like toil-freed [14] deer, in headlong sort,
> With shouts and shrieks they hurry from the school:
> Some strow the woods, some swim the silver pool;
> All as they list to several pastimes fall,
> To feed their famish'd wantonness withal.

"In his merry humor," Drummond records of Ben Jonson, "he was wont to name himself The Poet." [15] Jonson was not the greatest of Elizabethan, or even of Jacobean, poets, and he knew it. He esteemed Donne the first poet in the world in some things, and his appreciation of Shakespeare is the most just and generous that we have from any writer of the age. But, as even those who began by abominating his bravado came to understand, Jonson is The Poet, the norm and center for the measurement of his fellows. He is so normal that, apart from the outstanding lyrics and plays, we do not easily recognize his greatness; but the greatness is in almost every line he wrote. The average line of Jonson, read, re-read, memorized, and lived with, will

Ben Jonson (1572-1637)

[13] *An Invective written by Mr. George Chapman against Mr. Ben Jonson.*
[14] I.e., freed from a snare.
[15] William Drummond's *Conversations with Jonson.* The standard edition of Jonson is that of Herford and Simpson, of which Vol. VII (Oxford, 1941) contains his masques. The best separate edition of his non-dramatic poetry is *The Poems of Ben Jonson,* ed. B. H. Newdigate (Oxford, 1936); a convenient small volume is *Songs and Lyrics by Ben Jonson* (Shakespeare Head Quartos, VIII, Oxford, 1937). Biographical writers have been much attracted to Jonson and have found it nearly impossible to make his life uninteresting. See S. A. Tannenbaum's *Concise Bibliography* (1938) and other works cited above, Part III, ch. III, n. 21, and also M. Eccles, "Jonson's Marriage," *RES,* XII (1936). 257-272.

assay higher and wear better than the more striking lines of easier poets. For him poetry *was* the criticism of life, and criticism could be no easy thing for author or for reader:

> For though the Poet's matter Nature be,
> His Art doth give the fashion; and that he,
> Who casts to write a living line, must sweat,
> .... and strike the second heat
> Upon the Muses' anvil.[16]

The reader of the *Epigrams, Forest,* and *Under-wood* [17] may be at first repelled by the products of this sweating Titan, who hammered his verses into their hard and shining felicity; but let him try the quality of the metal and workmanship, and most other men's poetry is likely to seem paltry. Even when Jonson is writing flattery to the fashionables of the court, he writes with his whole thinking mind and with proud assertion of the dignity of thought; as thus to the Countess of Rutland (*Forest,* xii):

> Beauty, I know, is good, and blood is more;
> Riches thought most: but, Madame, think what store
> The world hath seen which all these had in trust,
> And now lie lost in their forgotten dust.
> It is the Muse alone can raise to heaven,
> And at her strong arm's end hold up, and even,
> The souls she loves;

or thus to the Earl of Dorset:

> Yet we must more than move still, or go on:
> We must accomplish. 'Tis the last key-stone
> That makes the arch. The rest that there were put
> Are nothing till *that* comes to bind and shut.
> Then stands it a triumphal mark! then men
> Observe the strength, the height, the why, and when,
> It was erected; and still walking under
> Meet some new matter to look up and wonder!

Or note how Jonson can make his reason sing in this discussion of two ways of love, and note how subtly the almost over-sweetness of the melody is curbed by the run-on verses and occasionally inexact rimes:

> The thing they here call love is blind desire,
> Arm'd with bow, shafts, and fire;
> Inconstant like the sea, of whence 'tis born,
> Rough, swelling, like a storm:
> With whom sails, rides on a surge of fear,
> And boils, as if he were

---

[16] *To the Memory of My Beloved, the Author, Mr. William Shakespeare, and What He Hath Left Us.*

[17] Jonson's miscellaneous poems were grouped under these headings in the Folio edition of his *Works* (1616).

In a continual tempest. Now true love
    No such effects doth prove;
That is an essence far more gentle, fine,
    Pure, perfect, nay divine;
It is a golden chain let down from heaven,
    Whose links are bright and even,
That falls like sleep on lovers and combines
    The soft and sweetest minds
In equal knots. This bears no brands nor darts
    To murther different hearts,
But in a calm and godlike unity
    Preserves community;

or in this loveliest of definitions of truth:

    Truth is the trial of itself
        And needs no other touch;
    And purer than the purest gold,
        Refine it ne'er so much.
    It is the life and light of love,
        That sun that ever shineth,
    And spirit of that special grace,
        That faith and love defineth.

There is an Augustan urbanity in many of Jonson's smaller poems which none of his contemporaries could equal; for instance, in his verse letters to Donne and Drayton, and to the "one that asked to be sealed of the Tribe of Ben," in the 101st *Epigram,* inviting a friend to supper; [18] and particularly in the second and third poems of *The Forest,* which show how much manners had improved in the century since Barclay's *Satires.*[19]

No one in his age could more tenderly express true sorrow. The epitaph "on my first daughter" (*Epigram xxii*) is a noble thing, and the lines on his dead son (*Epigram xlv*) are nobler still:

Farewell, thou child of my right hand and joy!

  . . . .

Rest in soft peace, and, ask'd, say here doth lie
Ben Jonson his best piece of poetry.

It was Jonson who wrote the exquisite stanzas on the dead boy actor, Salathiel (or Salomon) [20] Pavy (*Epigram cxx*), which perhaps no other writer of the time could or would have written, and the epitaph on the girl, "Elizabeth, L. H.", which has the lines,

    Underneath this stone doth lie
    As much beauty as could die.[21]

[18] This can be well compared with Milton's sonnet to Mr. Lawrence (1656).

[19] Cf. above, Part I, ch. IV.

[20] See G. E. Bentley, "A Good Name Lost. Ben Jonson's Lament for S. P.," *LTLS,* May 30, 1942, p. 276.

[21] *Epigram cxxiv.* Newdigate suggests that the initials stand for Lady Hatton, but she was still living when the epigram was published. Jonson complimented her in a lyric in the masque of *The Gypsies Metamorphosed* (1621).

This, probably, even more than the now better-known lyrist of the song
books, was the Jonson whom his juniors accepted as their unapproachable
leader. He had a sting, of course, but in his nondramatic works employed
it less often and less effectively than is supposed. He did not regard himself
as a love poet. He had attempted, he says in the first poem of *The Forest*,
but the god of love fled him,

> and again
> Into my rimes could ne'er be got
> By any art. Then wonder not
> That, since, my numbers are so cold,
> When Love is fled and I grow old.

He admits his "mountain belly" and his "rocky face," and a weight but two
pounds less than that attributed in later times to the corpulent Prince Regent.[22] But love songs were demanded by the Jacobeans, in their plays and
in the masques which Jonson's art received as ephemeral trifles and made
immortal.

> The unwieldy elephant,
> To make them mirth, used all his might, and wreathed
> His lithe proboscis.[23]

Out of materials no less diverse than his learning he fabricated songs which
are as purely Elizabethan and as living today as anything their age produced.
One of the earliest is the stately hymn to Queen Elizabeth in *Cynthia's
Revels* (1600), perhaps the most classically perfect lyric in English: "Queen
and huntress, chaste and fair." Into the climactic scene of *Volpone* he introduced one of his marvelous adaptations of Catullus,

> Come, my Celia, let us prove,
> While we can the sports of love;
> Time will not be ours for ever.
>
> .   .   .   .
>
> Suns that set may rise again;
> But if once we lose this light,
> 'Tis with us perpetual night.

He bewitched some passages of Greek prose into the cadences of "Drink
to me only with thine eyes," and put into a lover's mouth in *The Devil Is an
Ass* (1616) a stanza which his "tribe" seem to have taken (and well they
might) as their particular model of lyric excellence,

> Have you seen but a bright lily grow,
>   Before rude hands have touch'd it?
> Have you mark'd but the fall of the snow,
>   Before the soil hath smutch'd it?

---

[22] *Under-wood*, "To Mr. Arthur Squib" (Newdigate, p. 167), "Full twenty stone, of which
I lack two pound," i.e., 278 lbs. Cf. Byron, "Though Ireland starve, great George weighs
twenty stone" (*Don Juan*, VIII, st. 126).
[23] *Paradise Lost*, IV. 345 f.

The lyric richness of Jonson's masques is enormous. In these one-night *The Songs* spectacles, which Bacon called "but toys," he buried gems of song now *in Jonson's* seldom uncovered. They range from the Skeltonic and ribald ditties of *The* *Masques* *Gypsies Metamorphosed* to the organ notes with which descending Pallas addressed the court in the year when Overbury's murderers were being brought to trial: [24]

> Look, look, rejoice and wonder
>   That you, offending mortals, are
>   (For all your crimes) so much the care
> Of him that bears the thunder.
>
> Jove can endure no longer,
>   Your great ones should your less invade;
>   Or that your weak, though bad, be made
> A prey unto the stronger.

Jonson was the pattern for the Restoration singers, and has been well *Influence* described as the real father of the Augustan Age; [25] but his influence was *of Jonson's* broader than this, for he was master also in his odes of an intricate and *Lyrics* entrancing music which hardly reappears in English poetry before the nineteenth century. If one seeks a "source" for the stanza and mood of Wordsworth's immortality ode, one will scarcely find it, tracing back, till one comes to such a stanza as this in Jonson:

> It is not growing like a tree
> In bulk doth make man better be,
> Or standing long an oak, three hundred year,
> To fall a log at last, dry, bald, and sere.
>   A lily of a day
>   Is fairer far in May:
> Although it fall and die that night,
> It was the plant and flower of light.
>   In small proportions we just beauties see,
>   And in short measures life may perfect be.[26]

Ben Jonson was not the greatest poet of his time, no doubt; but under the impact of his colossal mind and art critics have, in every succeeding age, found this hard to believe.

Few men can ever have had as much poetry within them as John Donne [27]

[24] *The Golden Age Restored* (1615).
[25] F. E. Schelling, "Ben Jonson and the Classical School," *PMLA,* XIII (1898). 221-249; reprinted in *Shakespeare and Demi-Science* (Philadelphia, 1927).
[26] Ode to Cary and Morison in *Under-wood,* Newdigate, p. 180.
[27] Concerning Donne there has been a great deal of literature and of dogma recently. See Geoffrey Keynes, *A Bibliography of Dr. John Donne* (2ed., Cambridge, 1932); William White, *John Donne since 1900: A Bibliography of Periodical Articles* (Boston, 1942). The standard edition of Donne's poems is that of Sir Herbert Grierson (2v, Oxford, 1912; new ed., abridged in one vol., 1929). *The Complete Poems of John Donne,* ed. R. E. Bennett (Chicago, 1942) contains new material. *John Donne: Complete Poetry and Selected Prose,* ed. John Hayward (1930), is a convenient volume; and F. W. Payne's *John Donne and his Poetry* (1926) is a useful brief introduction to the poet. Much information is contained in *A Garland for John Donne,* ed. Theodore Spencer (1931), and in T. Spencer and Mark Van Doren, *Studies in*

John Donne (1572-1631), or suffered as much obstruction in expressing it. In his work the Pierian flood is no clear spring; it is more like a Yellowstone geyser: over-heated, turbid, explosive, and far from pure. He might almost have been a Dante; but he lived in the reign of James I and was a hanger-on in one of the most flippant coteries of modern times. So was Ben Jonson; but Jonson, with less, doubtless, of the divine spark, had a sturdier nature, and he found anchorage in the verities of art. Donne never did. Some grand lines in his third *Satire* justify the man who seeks by indirections to find directions out:

> On a huge hill,
> Cragged and steep, Truth stands, and he that will
> Reach her, about must, and about must go,
> And what the hill's suddenness resists, win so;
> Yet strive so that before age, death's twilight,
> Thy soul rest, for none can work in that night.

Such was Donne's method, but, in his secular poems at least, he seldom won to the highest truth or to his soul's rest. He committed unpardonable sins against both the "centers," as he calls them, of his intellectual being: his reason and his faith. The poem just alluded to, the elegy on the death of Prince Henry in 1612, contains a few noble lines—like those that estimate the moral value of thoughts about the dead prince, which are

> Our soul's best baiting, and mid-period,
> In her long journey of considering God;

but it also exemplifies the faults which the student of Donne must begin by learning to discount. According to Drummond, Donne told Jonson that he wrote this piece "to match Sir Edward Herbert [28] in obscureness." Grierson adds: "The obscurity of the poem is not so obvious as its tasteless extravagance." [29] The two qualities, however, bud from a single root; so forceful a thinker would not be so often obscure, if he were not striving to write with more apparent emphasis than he feels. When Donne's patroness, the Countess of Bedford, lost by death a female cousin to whom she had been much attached, the poet addressed the countess in another tasteless and obscure poem which begins

---

Metaphysical Poetry (1939). Consult also G. Williamson, *The Donne Tradition* (Cambridge, Mass., 1930); C. M. Coffin, *John Donne and the New Philosophy* (1937); J. B. Douds, "Donne's Technique of Dissonance," *PMLA*, LII (1937). 1051-1061; and A. R. Benham, "The Myth of John Donne the Rake," *PQ*, xx (1941). 465-473. The *Life and Letters* of Donne by Edmund Gosse (2v, 1899) is still of use. The following works, dealing with Donne and kindred poets, should be consulted: J. F. Bennett, *Four Metaphysical Poets: Donne, Herbert, Vaughan, Crashaw* (Cambridge, 1934), J. B. Leishman, *The Metaphysical Poets: Donne, Herbert, Vaughan, Traherne* (Oxford, 1934), and H. C. White, *Metaphysical Poets* (1936). Special aspects are treated in R. C. Bald, *Donne's Influence in English Literature* (Morpeth, 1932); M. A. Rugoff, *Donne's Imagery* (1939); W. R. Moses, *The Metaphysical Conceit in the Poems of John Donne* (Nashville, 1941); R. L. Sharp, *From Donne to Dryden, the Revolt against Metaphysical Poetry* (Chapel Hill, 1940).
[28] George Herbert's brother, later Lord Herbert of Cherbury; see ch. vi, above.
[29] Grierson, *op. cit.*, II. 205.

You that are she and you, that's double she,
In her dead face half of yourself shall see.

The meaning can be made out, but the satisfaction of his mental ingenuity in so doing is the only reward the reader will receive. It was, for the circle to which Donne addressed these words, enough.

In the fourth act of *Cynthia's Revels* (written in 1600) Jonson portrays a group of just such courtly ladies and gentlemen as were the usual recipients of Donne's poetical epistles, amusing themselves with games of verbal dexterity. One of the games is "Substantives and Adjectives," in which the players ingeniously fit the adjectives "odoriferous," "popular," "humble," "white-livered," "barbarous," "Pythagorical," and "well-spoken," to the substantive, which happens to be "breeches." Often Donne's "wit" and "conceits" have only a purpose of this kind, though elaborated with such more than Jonsonian subtlety as to tempt one to think them seriously oracular. A sentence near the beginning of the fifth *Satire* reads:

If all things be in all,
As I think, since all, which were, are, and shall
Be, be made of the same elements:
Each thing, each thing implies or represents.

It is surprising to discover that this makes sense and is part of a clever, if rather ribald, attack on the court; but the only reasons for such style—at least till it had grown a habit—are to make it appear more thoughtful than it is, and to give the reader a quite unpoetic amusement in untangling it.

Donne's sins against faith are more serious than those against reason, for they mar greater poems. The wonderful *Songs and Sonnets*—fifty-five uncut gems as unique, in their different way, as Browning's fifty *Men and Women* —raise inevitable questions about the literary integrity of the author. The first of these poems, *The Good-Morrow*, lauds pagan love as the be-all and end-all of existence. The next two, "Go and catch a falling star" and *Woman's Constancy*, are as crassly cynical as they are brilliant in wit. The fourth, "I have done one braver thing," is a Paul-and-Virginia pastel. The fifth, "Busy old fool, unruly Sun!" returns magnificently to amorous paganism; and the next is *The Indifferent*, with its astringent motto, "I can love *any*, so she be not true." No theory of dramatic purpose or different dates will account artistically for this emotional welter. Donne was the sort of man whose purest depths could not be stirred without bringing up also a good deal of obscenity and inconsequence. They are all dumped together, often in the same poem, as in *The Relic*, which opens with two solemn lines,

Donne's Songs and Sonnets

When my grave is broke up again,
Some second guest to entertain;

then plummets into the mire in a parenthesis,

(For graves have learn'd that womanhead,
To be to more than one a bed)

and at once mounts to the zenith:

> And he that digs it spies
> A bracelet of bright hair about the bone.

In the third (and last) stanza the poet moralizes:

> First, we lov'd well and faithfully,
> Yet knew not what we lov'd, nor why.
> Difference of sex no more we knew
> Than our guardian angels do.

Donne's Anniversaries

This innocence does not sit well. If Donne's guardian angel learned as much of sex as the author of the *Songs and Sonnets* knew, his fittest comment would have been that of the devil Pug,[30] who visited the London drawing-rooms: "You talk of a university! Why, hell is a grammar-school to this!"

The accent that Donne deserved hanging for not keeping is as much mental as metrical.[31] His bursts of energy and insight lack sustaining poetic faith, and after them he falls back frequently upon verbal jugglery, which is not poetry, but charmed the ingenious in its own day and does so even now. The *Anniversaries* in memory of Elizabeth Drury (1611, 1612), the only extensive body of Donne's poetry printed in his lifetime, had enormous influence. If these poems (three in all, aggregating 1100 lines) are not quite, as Jonson called them, "profane and full of blasphemies,"[32] they are at least poetically untruthful, whether as records of what the death of the fifteen-year-old daughter of one of the wealthiest men in England signified for Donne, or as statements of a cosmic pessimism on the theme, "How ugly a monster the world is!"[33] Less frequently here than in the *Songs and Sonnets* the great lines blaze, but their occasional brilliance is hardly less; e.g., in the passage on Judgment Day,

> These hymns, thy issue, may increase so long
> As till God's great *Venite* change the song,

or the metaphor for death:

> Think, then, my soul, that death is but a groom,
> Who brings a taper to the outward room,
> Whence thou spyest first a little glimmering light,
> And after brings it nearer to thy sight.

Donne was never incapable of these glories. Even the unctuous direct flattery of little Elizabeth will sometimes be purged by a flamelike couplet:

> Whose twilights were more clear than our midday,
> Who dreamt devoutlier than most use to pray;

and even the "ingenious, tasteless poem" (as Grierson calls it) which Donne found it profitable to write on the death of his patroness's brother, Lord

---

[30] In Jonson's play, *The Devil Is an Ass* (1616), IV. i.

[31] Drummond reports Jonson to have said "that Donne for not keeping of accent deserved hanging." For a reply to this criticism see Arnold Stein, "Donne's Prosody," *PMLA,* LIX (1944). 373-397.

[32] Conversations with Drummond.

[33] *Anatomy of the World,* line 326.

Harington, in 1614 deviates happily into telling how a prisoner, sentenced to execution the next morning,

> Doth practice dying by a little sleep;

or more dialectically, how an angel descends, faster than thought, from heaven to earth; or more baroquely, how God on the last day reassembles the perfect bodies of two cannibals, one of whom has consumed the other. What this most metaphysical of poets chiefly lacked was a little real philosophy, an ability to come to terms with his world and trust his own reason and his faith—in fact, what Wordsworth called natural piety, and what Shakespeare, Milton, and Spenser in such great measure possessed. It may be an error to regard Donne as an anti-Spenser. In some aspects he appears almost as a Spenser *manqué:* for example, in the unfinished but interesting *Progress of the Soul,*[34] on the theme of metempsychosis, for which he invented a narrative, ten-line stanza, ending like Spenser's stanza in an alexandrine, and in which he displays unsuspected vivacity as a story-teller; and particularly in his three epithalamia, of which the best is the earliest and the one that most closely follows the Spenserian model in handling the refrain and interlinked rimes.[35] One might imagine the young Donne offering these pieces to the scrutiny of Spenser, and Spenser replying: "Master Donne, you will never be a poet." In which hypothetical case the elder poet would have been wrong, but not indefensibly so.

It was probably Donne's repute as a preacher that won disproportionate attention for his religious poetry, which in bulk amounts to little more than an eighth of his total verse, and, with two or three great exceptions, is less important than George Herbert's. Donne's "holy" *Sonnets* number twenty-six, with two others which are dedicatory. Composed over a period of many years, both before and after his ordination in 1615, they vary greatly in value, but very little in the technical form, which (in distinction from Herbert's sonnets) is always the Petrarchan.[36] They show little piety and are remarkably egocentric, dealing mainly with Donne's two phobias: his sense of personal unworthiness and the terrors of Judgment Day. Some of the conceits are as astonishing as those in the *Songs and Sonnets.*[37] One of these sonnets, No. VII of the second series, rises easily above all the rest: *Donne's Religious Poems*

> At the round earth's imagin'd corners blow
> Your trumpets, Angels! and arise, arise
> From death, you numberless infinities
> Of souls, and to your scatter'd bodies go.

Next to this, probably, ranks No. x:

[34] Not to be confused with the Second Anniversary on Elizabeth Drury, which was given the same title. The fragment referred to is a much earlier poem.
[35] *Epithalamion Made at Lincoln's Inn*, Grierson, I. 141-144.
[36] The dedicatory Sonnet to Mrs. Herbert follows the Shakespearean form. These are, of course, true sonnets, as the earlier *Songs and Sonnets* were not. For discussion see H. I'A. Fausset, *The Holy Sonnets of John Donne* (1938).
[37] Note, for example, the last four lines of Sonnet XVIII.

> Death, be not proud, though some have called thee
> Mighty and dreadful, for thou art not so,

which invites comparison with Shakespeare's No. CXLVI:

> Poor soul, the centre of my sinful earth.

The Litany, written while Donne was still a layman (*c.* 1609), is a series of petitions, effectively set in a metrical form that can be illustrated by the most characteristic stanza:

> When senses, which thy soldiers are,
>   We arm against thee, and they fight for sin;
> When want, sent but to tame, doth war
> And work despair a breach to enter in;
>   When plenty, God's image and seal,
>   Makes us idolatrous,
>   And love it, not him whom it should reveal;
>   When we are mov'd to seem religious
>   Only to vent wit: Lord deliver us!

There is a certain interest in the subtlety of *The Cross* and *Riding Westward;* but it would not be necessary to say more of Donne as a religious poet if he had not, when on the point of death, transcended himself in a "hymn" which at last fuses into harmony the strange riches of his tortured mind. It is, of course, the *Hymn to God, My God, in My Sickness,* which begins thus:

> Since I am coming to that holy room,
>   Where, with Thy choir of saints for evermore,
> I shall be made Thy music: as I come,
>   I tune the instrument here at the door,
>   And what I must do then think here before.
> Whilst my physicians by their love are grown
>   Cosmographers, and I their map, who lie
> Flat on this bed, that by them may be shown
>   That this is my South-west discovery
>   *Per fretum febris,* by these straights to die.

Had Donne written often thus—as Dr. Jonson said of Gray—"it had been vain to blame and useless to praise him."

X

Seventeenth-Century Poetry: II. The Moral Tradition

The extent to which poetry,[1] at about the time of *Hamlet,* was being *John Davies* sicklied o'er with the pale cast of thought is evident in the works of John *of Hereford* Davies of Hereford [2] (1565-1618). At the close of the long sonnet sequence in his *Wit's Pilgrimage* (1605), he says:

> Thus far may speculation help a wit,
> Unapt to love, to write of love's estate.

This amiable but most verbose Welshman acquired prestige and a remarkable acquaintance with the nobility through his prowess as a writing-master in an age when handwriting was an art. His first poetical publications— *Mirum in Modum,* or "a glimpse of God's glory and the soul's shape" (1602), and *Microcosmos* (1603), the latter with elaborate dedications to the new royal family—show Davies' "speculation" flowing almost endlessly through moral, metaphysical, and psychological channels,[3] with a digression in *Microcosmos* into the historical field popularized by Daniel and Drayton. *The Holy Rood, or Christ's Cross* (1609) is another religious-metaphysical work. Davies, who is ingenious but genuinely pious, prefers intricate patterns both for his rimes and his thoughts. He has little wit, and his collection of epigrams, *The Scourge of Folly* (1611), is by no means his best work, though the reference it contains to Shakespeare and other contemporaries has made it his best known.[4]

---

[1] Several of the anthologies and critical works cited for Part II, ch. I cover also the field of the present chapter and the next two. To them should be added H. J. Massingham, *A Treasury of Seventeenth-Century Poetry* (1919); A. C. Judson, *Seventeenth-Century Lyrics* (Chicago, 1927); H. J. C. Grierson and G. Bullough, *The Oxford Book of Seventeenth Century Verse* (Oxford, 1934); Norman Ault, *Seventeenth-Century Lyrics* (1928) and *A Treasury of Unfamiliar Lyrics* (1938); and L. B. Marshall, *Rare Poems of the Seventeenth Century* (Cambridge, 1936).

[2] *Complete Works,* ed. A. B. Grosart (2v, 1878).

[3] He seems indebted to *The French Academy* (Part II, 1594), translated from P. de la Primaudaye. See R. L. Anderson, "A French Source for John Davies of Hereford's System of Psychology," *PQ,* VI (1927). 57-66.

[4] Tolerable reformatory verse, sometimes enlivened by details of social conduct, is found in John Lane's *Tom Tell-troth's Message* (1600; ed. F. J. Furnivall, *New Shakspere Soc.,* 1876), and in Henry Hutton's *Folly's Anatomy* (1619; ed. E. F. Rimbault, *Percy Soc.,* 1842). Christopher Lever's two long poems in easy rime royal, *A Crucifix* and *Queen Elizabeth's Tears* (both printed in 1607; repr. A. B. Grosart, *Fuller Worthies Library,* III, 1872), deserve respect. The former is moral psychoanalysis, the latter a descant on Elizabeth's troubles under Queen Mary. There is less morality and more interest in the anonymous *Pasquil's Nightcap* (1612), published by the enterprising Thomas Thorpe and sometimes ascribed to Nicholas Breton, and in its companion piece, *Pasquil's Palinodia* (1619), which may be by William Fennor.

Ethical poetry in England received a great impulse from the work of the French Huguenot soldier-poet, Guillaume de Salluste, Seigneur du Bartas (1544-1590), whose "heavenly muse" Spenser had been quick to praise.[5] Sidney began a translation, now lost; King James—then James VI of Scotland—published versions of Du Bartas; and numerous other interpreters in English and Latin sprang up, all of whom were eclipsed by Joshua Sylvester (1563-1618), a plain Kentishman whose career as a woolmerchant and translator somewhat resembles that of Caxton. Sylvester has independent merit as sonneteer and lyrist, but his name lives by reason of his free and homely rendering of Du Bartas' *Divine Weeks and Works,* first printed in full in 1605 and many times reprinted during the following half-century.[6] The young Milton must have known and liked this book, which covers much the same material as *Paradise Lost,* though in a style so different as to preclude serious comparisons.[7] Sylvester has no dignity at all. Like his original, he is often tedious and sometimes flat, but as a whole his version still deserves to rank among the most readable of long poems and liveliest of seventeenth-century translations. In manner he probably derived something from Harington's version of Ariosto (1591). He abounds in colloquialisms, quaint realistic digressions, and polysyllabic rimes that seem to be jesting at sublimity; but Dryden[8] was too severe in his rebuke of Sylvester's description of the powers of winter,

> To crystallize the Baltic ocean,
> To glaze the lakes, and bridle up the floods,
> And periwig with wool the bald-pate woods.

If this be abominable fustian, as Dryden says, it is yet rather charming. Sylvester never wanted the natural touch. When Eve has made Adam a garment of feathers, the following scene occurs. How domestic and untranslated it seems!

> "Sweetheart," quoth she, and then she kisseth him,
> "My love, my life, my bliss, my joy, my gem,
> My soul's dear soul, take in good part, I pray thee,
> This pretty present that I gladly give thee."
> "Thanks, my dear all," quoth Adam then, "for this";
> And with three kisses he requites her kiss.

One deals with lechery, the other with drunkenness. Both employ the same eight-line stanza (*ababccdd*) and are reprinted in Grosart's *Occasional Issues,* IV (1877). John Andrewes' attempt to combine satire and religion in *The Anatomy of Baseness* (1615; ed. Grosart, *Fuller Worthies Library,* II, 1871) is a work of no distinction; nor are the moral poems of Gervase Markham, e.g., *The Poem of Poems, or Sion's House* (1596). However, Charles Fitzgeffrey's swan song, *The Blessed Birthday* (Oxford, 1634), in admirable couplet verse, is better poetry than his much earlier elegy on Drake (see above, Part II, ch. II, n. 42).

[5] In the *Envoy* to *The Ruins of Time.*

[6] See A. B. Grosart, *Complete Works of Joshuah Sylvester* (2v, 1880); and a convenient abridgment by T. W. Haight, *The Divine Weeks of Josuah Sylvester* (Waukesha, Wis., 1908).

[7] See G. C. Taylor, *Milton's Use of Du Bartas* (Cambridge, Mass., 1934).

[8] In the dedication of *The Spanish Friar* (1681).

Then on he puts his painted garment new,
And peacock-like himself doth often view,
Looks on his shadow, and in proud amaze
Admires the hand that had the art to cause
So many several parts to meet in one,
To fashion thus the quaint mandilion.[9]

George Wither [10] (1588-1667), whose long life extended from the defeat *George* of the Armada to the Great Fire of London, was a manly poet and in- *Wither* telligent social critic. Though by birth a member of the Hampshire county aristocracy and in youth a fervent subject of King James, he gravitated toward Puritanism and became in the end one of the chief writers of that party and a major in the Parliamentary army. His poems give a clear picture of what an honest man in this position saw and felt. The great hindrance to his fame is his unfortunate prolixity, which causes his *Juvenilia* alone (first collected in 1622) to fill 939 pages in the Spenser Society edition.

After two years at Oxford, of which he gives an excellent account,[11] but where, as he says elsewhere, "ungentle Fate allowed me not to be a Graduate," he pursued the study of law in London and developed a sincere loathing for the vices of the court and city. Two of his first publications, however, were of courtly type: *Prince Henry's Obsequies* (1612), consisting mainly of forty-six adequate sonnets of Shakespearean form, and *Epithalamia* on the marriage in 1613 of the Princess Elizabeth, who was the patroness of both him and Quarles. But in *Abuses Stript and Whipt*, which went through four editions in 1613, the moralist appeared. "Here," he says,

I will teach my rough satiric rimes
To be as mad and idle as the times.

This long work in very fluent riming couplets is divided into two "books." The sixteen satires in Book i, though strong in denunciation of the various passions that deprave man, are safely general. The most interesting passage is the well-told anecdote of the man marooned on a piece of floating ice

---

[9] Grosart, i. 124. (A mandilion is a loose coat.) Compare the French original in *Works of Du Bartas,* ed. Holmes, Lyons, and Linker, iii (1940). 78. Another pious poet and influential translator, who wrote under the special favor of Charles I, is George Sandys (1578-1644), praised by Dryden as "the best versifier of the former age" and by Fuller as "spriteful, vigorous, and masculine." His chastened version of Ovid's *Metamorphoses,* printed in 1626, was largely prepared while Sandys was holding the post of Treasurer with the new Virginia Company in Jamestown, and has been noted as the first literary work of the English settlers in America (See R. B. Davis, "Early Editions of George Sandys's *Ovid,"* *Papers, Bibl. Soc. of America,* xxxv (1941). 255-276). It is in graceful and not unforceful riming couplets, as are Sandys' long paraphrase of the Book of Job (1638) and his copiously annotated translation of Grotius' Latin tragedy, *Christ's Passion* (1640). His most praised work was his paraphrase of the Psalms of David (1636), in a variety of metres, for which Henry Lawes wrote music. Most interesting to modern readers is a much earlier work in prose, *A Relation of a Journey begun An. Dom. 1610* (publ., 1615), which records the author's observations in Italy, Greece, and the Orient. See S. C. Chew, *The Crescent and the Rose* (1937), pp. 41, etc.

[10] There is no convenient modern edition of Wither. References are to the Spenser Society edition (1871-1883). Cf. J. M. French, "Four Scarce Poems of George Wither," *Huntington Library Bull.,* ii (1931). 91-121; and, for a pleasant appraisal of the poet Charles Lamb's essay "On the Poetical Works of George Wither."

[11] In the prefatory poem called "The Occasion of This Work," Spenser Soc. ed., pp. 29 f.

during the recent "hard frost" and almost sucked into the vortex at London Bridge. Book II, "Of the Vanity, Inconstancy, Weakness and Presumption of Men," is more circumstantial. Wither defied the nobles of the court:

> I'll tell the ills you do,
> And put my name for witness thereunto.
> Then 'tis but fetching me *ad Magistratum*,
> And laying to me *Scandalum Magnatum*.

He proceeds to use strong language of the new knights, vain preachers, dishonest lawyers, of the universities, where

> Fair colleges are full of foul abuses,

and of contemporary effeminacy. Near the end there is a rousing invitation to arms and denunciation of the truce with Spain. Though this thorough-going criticism is somewhat qualified by an ironic laudation of the Earl of Salisbury ("that great mighty peer that died lately") and warm praise of contemporary drama and modern poets,[12] it is not altogether surprising that the poet was incarcerated for several months in the Marshalsea prison. He seems to have been far from disheartened by that outcome; for he employed the hours of his captivity in penning a long satire dedicated to King James[13] and, what is more important, *The Shepherd's Hunting*, "being certain eclogues written during the time of the author's imprisonment in the Marshalsea" (1615). In these five pastorals Wither, under the name of Philarete (lover of virtue), allegorically justifies the *Abuses Stript and Whipt* in discourse with his friend Willy (William Browne of Tavistock)[14] and other shepherds. It is the poet's *apologia*, remarkably light-hearted for a prisoner. The pentameter couplets are in places varied by tetrameter and interspersed with lyrics.

Wither's next work, *Fidelia* (1615) is a long "elegiacal epistle," that is, an Ovidian verse letter of complaint from the heroine to her "unconstant friend," prettier but more diffuse than the similar works of Daniel and Drayton. The pastoral note is continued, very pleasingly indeed, in *Fair-Virtue, The Mistress of Philarete* (1622), which contains the choicest of Wither's lyrics.[15] In the previous year (1621) Wither had returned to satire in pentameter couplets and had also paved the way for his emblem poetry by publishing *Wither's Motto: nec habeo, nec careo, nec curo* ("Neither Have I, nor Want I, nor Care I"). The handsome pictorial title-page visualizes the motto and is explained in a poem on the facing page, while the main work develops in over two thousand lines the attitude to life that is thus

---

[12] Spenser Soc. ed., pp. 289-293.

[13] It is subscribed, "Your Majesty's most loyal subject, and yet prisoner in the Marshalsey." Cf. J. M. French, "George Wither in Prison," *PMLA*, XLV (1930). 959-966.

[14] Wither, under the name of Roget, had contributed to Browne's collection of eclogues, *The Shepherd's Pipe* (1614). Richard Brathwait (1588-1673) imitated Wither both in satire and in pastoral; e.g., in Brathwait's *A Strappado for the Devil* (1615) and *Nature's Embassy* (1621).

[15] The best known of them, "Shall I wasting in despair," is found here, but had also appeared previously as an addition to the 1619 edition of *Fidelia*.

summarized. Thirty thousand copies are said to have been at once sold, and Wither was again for a short time in the Marshalsea.

These are what Wither called his *Juvenilia*. Of the eighty-six works which by his own account in 1660 [16] he had composed the only others that require notice are his *Collection of Emblems, Ancient and Modern*, which appeared in the same year as Quarles's *Emblems* [17] (1635), and his enormous verse narrative of the London plague of 1625, entitled *Britain's Remembrancer* [18] (1628). Wither remained voluntarily in London through the plague, and in Canto 3 rehearses the motives which led him to do so. His eye-witness account is of real value.[19]

Born of a good family in Essex and educated at Christ's College in Cam- *Francis* bridge, Francis Quarles [20] (1592-1644) became vehemently royalist in sym- *Quarles* pathy, whereas Wither, with a similar social background, was Parliamentarian. Both began their poetic careers as protégés of James I's daughter, the Princess Elizabeth. Quarles almost rivaled Wither in copiousness, and equalled him in popularity. His themes are strikingly unlike those usually associated with the Cavalier writers, for which a reason may be found in his service, between 1620 and 1629, as secretary to Archbishop Ussher, famous for his effort to fix the precise chronology of events in the Old Testament.

Quarles's first poem, *A Feast for Worms, Set Forth in a Poem of the History of Jonah* (1620), was followed by similar biblical narratives in pentameter couplets: *Hadassa, or the History of Queen Ester; Job Militant;* and *The History of Samson*. The inspiration is from Du Bartas, and the method is to interpolate pious "meditations" between brief sections of narrative, whereby each poem is drawn out to very considerable length. *Sion's Elegies* (1624) is a poetical paraphrase of the prophet Jeremiah, and *Sion's Sonnets* (1625), in couplets like the rest, is a version of the Song of Solomon. *Divine Fancies* (1632) contains four books of moral epigrams, many biblical, but many also dealing with contemporary social conditions in the spirit of Wither's satire.[21] In *Argalus and Parthenia* (1629) he turned for inspiration to Sidney's *Arcadia* and attained equal popularity.

In 1635, the year of publication also of Wither's different book of similar title, Quarles produced his most permanently popular work, the *Emblems,* which has been called the most popular book of verse in the seventeenth

[16] In his *Fides Anglicana* of that year.
[17] Wither's emblem book is a very handsome volume, though it quite failed to achieve the popularity of Quarles's. Each emblem in the former is a circular picture illustrating a Latin adage which is engraved around it. The text, in quatrains or couplets, develops the idea with Wither's customary fullness.
[18] A manuscript of the first two cantos, entitled *The History of the Pestilence*, was printed for the first time in 1932 by J. M. French.
[19] John Taylor, the "Water-poet," (see below, n. 25) dealt with the same calamity in *The Fearful Summer* (Oxford, 1625).
[20] The works of Quarles are available in a very annoying edition prepared by A. B. Grosart (3v, 1880). See A. H. Nethercot, "The Literary Legend of Francis Quarles," *MP*, xx (1923). 225-240.
[21] For what is known of Thomas Bancroft (*c.* 1596-1658), a moral epigrammatist and imitator of Quarles, see Wm. Charvat, "Thomas Bancroft," *PMLA*, xlvii (1932). 753-758.

century,[22] and which from that time to this has gone through something like fifty editions. Each of the five books contains fifteen "emblems" or symbolic pictures, interpreted in verse of various patterns but great piety and simplicity. It has been shown [23] that Quarles owed a great deal stylistically to Sylvester's translation of Du Bartas (1592-1605) and to Phineas Fletcher, and that most of the pictures are redrawings of those which had previously appeared in two Jesuit books of piety. The thing was not new.[24] Jonson's two poems interpreting the pictorial title-pages of Ralegh's *History of the World* (1614) and Coryat's *Crudities* (1611) are excellent examples of the type, but Quarles's gift of quaint, sententious morality made his work a religious classic, particularly among the Puritans, whom he detested. Horace Walpole's quip is well known, "Milton was forced to wait till the world had done admiring Quarles"; but in fact the admiration continued into the late nineteenth century.

Quarles's prose style is notably effective and highly epigrammatic. His *Enchyridion* (1640) and *Observations concerning Princes and States, upon Peace and War* (1642) are made up of brief counsels, moral in the first work and political in the second. They are usually less than ten lines long, and have a sprightliness that makes them still agreeable. The later prose works, *Judgment and Mercy for Afflicted Souls* (1646) and *The Profest Royalist* (1645), attack Puritan preciseness and intolerance. One of the weapons Quarles uses best is humor, and few things of the period are more amusing in small compass than the sections of *Judgment and Mercy* headed "The Drunkard's Jubilee" and "The Swearer's Apology." [25]

George Herbert's mother was among John Donne's most honored friends, and minor evidences are many that Donne's poems—though the vast majority of them were not yet in print [26]—were familiar to Herbert. Yet George Herbert [27] (1593-1633) is not a follower of Donne; he is not a follower of

[22] F. E. Schelling, "Devotional Poetry," in *Shakespeare and Demi-Science* (Philadelphia, 1927).

[23] G. S. Haight, "The Sources of Quarles's *Emblems*," *Library*, XVI (1936). 188-209; also "The Publication of Quarles' *Emblems*," *ibid.*, XV (1934). 97-109.

[24] Geffrey Whitney's *A Choice of Emblems and Other Devices* (Leyden, 1586), and Spenser's *Vision* poems are interesting precursors. On the Continent the vogue of emblem literature goes back to the 1530's. For a pleasant introduction to the subject see E. N. S. Thompson, *Literary Bypaths of the Renaissance* (New Haven, 1924). See also M. Praz, *Studies in Seventeenth-Century Imagery* (1939).

[25] Grosart's ed., I. 73, 75. Another very prolific and entertaining writer in verse and prose is John Taylor (1580-1653), the self-styled "Water-Poet," who after some service in the navy maintained himself as a waterman on the Thames and as a journalistic pamphleteer. His *Works,* "being sixty and three in number," were collected in a folio volume in 1630. They include his *Urania,* a moral poem in 86 *ottava rima* stanzas; *The Sculler* (anti-Romanist and other epigrams, 1612); a great variety of flytings against Thomas Coryat of the *Crudities* (1611); and *Taylor's Motto,* a take-off on Wither's poem of like title and date, with the motto reversed ("Et habeo, et careo, et curo"), 1621. Among the most amusing of Taylor's prose writings are *The Penniless Pilgrimage* (1618), which contains material on Ben Jonson's foot-journey to Scotland in the same year; and *The Praise, Antiquity, and Commodity of Beggary, Beggars, and Begging* (1621).

[26] The earliest collected edition appeared in 1633, the year of Herbert's death.

[27] Herbert belonged to one of the great families of England and Wales. His eldest brother was the Baron Herbert of Cherbury (see above, ch. VII). Another brother, Sir Henry Herbert, was Master of the Revels at court during three reigns. The Earls of Pembroke and Montgomery (the "incomparable brethren" of the Shakespeare Folio) bore the same family name and were

any one. For a proper parallel to his glowing art, infinitely varied in decoration and uniquely personal in theme, one must go back to the art of the Old French troubadours. Herbert was God's troubadour, and devoted himself as proudly and solely to singing his emotions toward the Almighty as did any Provençal singer to the service of his lady. The comparison sounds bizarre, but justifies itself. Herbert's adoration is not in the usual sense holy or humble; it takes small account of the rest of the world, but is intensely individual, addressed to a personal and patrician God, who is capable of appreciating the special sacrifices his high-born servant makes, and of understanding the most exquisite delicacies of technique. The intricacies of Herbert's poems in thought and melody approach those of the Provençal poets. His 169 poems are in something like 140 different stanzaic patterns, of which 116 are employed but once.[28] The pictorial *Easter Wings* and *Altar,* and the poem on Trinity Sunday in three stanzas of three lines each, are gross examples of this poet's facility in devising a special rhythmic form for every emotion. The adjustment is sometimes infinitely delicate, observable only after frequent reading; and with this go a balance and unity of thought-content in which few lyric poets have equaled Herbert.

Yet Herbert's art conceals itself. He abjures sonorousness and affects homeliness of language, and his emotional intensity is so great that his poems often seem simple or even naïve. Note the second stanza of his *Mortification:*

> When boys go first to bed,
> They step into their voluntary graves.
> Sleep binds them fast; only their breath
> Makes them not dead.
> Successive nights, like rolling waves,
> Convey them quickly who are bound for death;

and one from *The Holy Communion:*

> For sure, when Adam did not know
> To sin, or sin to smother [i.e., conceal],
> He might to heav'n from Paradise go
> As from one room t' another;

or the insurpassable ode on *Virtue,* which begins:

> Sweet day, so cool, so calm, so bright,
> The bridal of the earth and sky:
> The dew shall weep thy fall to-night,
> For thou must die.

---

third cousins. Our poet, educated at Westminster School and Trinity College, Cambridge, was for eight years Public Orator of the University, but gave up a career of courtly promise to enter the church in 1630. His poetry was written chiefly during the three years of his rectorship at Bemerton, near Salisbury, and during the period of indecision that preceded his ordination. The edition of G. H. Palmer, *The English Works of George Herbert* (3v, 1905) is of great critical value, but for practical use is superseded by the one-volume *Works of George Herbert,* ed. F. E. Hutchinson (Oxford, 1941). See also R. Freeman, "George Herbert and the Emblem Books," *RES,* xvii (1941). 150-165.

[28] Cf. Palmer, *op. cit.,* i. 123-167, "The Style and Technique"; A. McH. Hayes, "Counterpoint in Herbert," *SP,* xxxv (1938). 43-60.

Herbert's poetry is entirely religious. In one of his earliest works he addresses God and asks,

> Doth Poetry
> Wear Venus' livery, only serve her turn?
> Why are not sonnets made of Thee, and lays
>   Upon Thine altar burnt? Cannot Thy love
> Heighten a spirit to sound out Thy praise
>   As well as any she? Cannot Thy dove
> Outstrip their Cupid easily in flight?

He proved that it could. Under the appearance of simplicity which rewards the attainment of the perfect expression, Herbert is the subtlest lyrist of his generation. *The Dawning* is an *aubade* such as the medieval lover sang, but on the theme of Easter morning:

> Awake, sad heart, whom sorrow ever drowns!
>   Take up thine eyes which feed on earth;
> Unfold thy forehead gather'd into frowns.
>   Thy Saviour comes, and with him mirth.
>   Awake, awake!
> And with a thankful heart his comforts take.
> But thou dost still lament, and pine, and cry,
> And feel his death, but not his victory.

This poem ends in a famous conceit,

> Christ left his grave-clothes that we might, when grief
> Draws tears or blood, not want an handkerchief,

but conceits are not common in Herbert. He can be baroque, as in *The Bag*, which likens Christ's pierced side to a mail-bag for carrying letters to heaven, or *Doomsday*, which is a mad dance of the bones gathering themselves together for the final judgment. He can be as frank toward God as any lover to his lady: blaming himself in *Unkindness*,

> I would not use a friend as I use Thee;

boldly complaining in *Affliction*,

> Now I am here, what Thou wilt do with me
>   None of my books will show.
> I read, and sigh, and wish I were a tree,
>   For sure then I should grow
>   To fruit or shade. At least some bird would trust
>   Her household to me, and I should be just.
> Yet, though Thou troublest me, I must be meek;

or rising to a proud equality in *Bitter-Sweet*, which is as superb a piece of poetry as was ever compressed into eight short lines,

Ah, my dear angry Lord!
Since Thou dost love, yet strike,
Cast down, yet help afford:
Sure I will do the like.
I will complain, yet praise,
I will bewail, approve:
And all my sour-sweet days
I will lament, and love.

Herbert is not often doctrinal, but *The British Church* is one of the love-liest things that has been written since Horace on the *via media*. He is not often broadly ethical, but his *Constancy*, which begins,

Who is the honest man?
He that doth still and strongly good pursue,
To God, his neighbor, and himself most true.
Whom neither force nor fawning can
Unpin or wrench from giving all their due,

is as great a poem as Wordsworth's *Happy Warrior*, which it much re-sembles.[29] He is not frequently mystical or allegorical, but *Love Unknown, The Collar,* and *The Pulley* are among the finest short poems of their type. Similar and not inferior is *The Pilgrimage*, which in its thirty-six lines anticipates both Bunyan and Browning's *Childe Roland*. In the last stanza the wanderer, passing through gloom and disillusionment, perceives that

My hill was further. So I flung away,
Yet heard a cry
Just as I went: *None goes that way
And lives!* If that be all, said I,
After so foul a journey death is fair,
And but a chair [30]

"Sweet" and "bright" seem to have been Herbert's favorite adjectives. In many of his poems the qualities these words imply may be overcast by the vehemence and conciseness of his lyric art. One of his latest poems, *The Flower*, from which the first and last two stanzas may be quoted, does them justice:

How fresh, O Lord, how sweet and clean
Are thy returns! Ev'n as the flowers in spring,
To which, besides their own demesne,[31]
The late-past frosts tributes of pleasure bring.
Grief melts away
Like snow in May,
As if there were no such cold thing. . . .

[29] Cf. T. T. Stenberg, "Wordsworth's *Happy Warrior* and Herbert's *Constancy*," *MLN*, XL (1925). 252-253.
[30] I.e., a sedan-chair for easy travel (one of the earliest uses of the word in this sense).
[31] I.e., the forces which naturally belong to spring.

And now in age I bud again,
After so many deaths I live and write;
I once more smell the dew and rain,
And relish versing. O my only light,
    It cannot be
    That I am he
On whom Thy tempests fell all night.

These are Thy wonders, Lord of love,
To make us see we are but flowers that glide;
    Which when we once can find and prove,
Thou hast a garden for us where to bide.
    Who would be more,
    Swelling through store,[32]
Forfeit their Paradise by their pride.

Discussion of George Herbert leads inevitably to the quoting of endless excerpts out of an endless variety. Excerpts cannot worthily illustrate a poet whose chief merits include unity and structural balance, and who never used a word too much; but they may suggest the loss those readers suffer who ignore Herbert in the belief that religious poetry is monotonous in theme or thin emotionally. Herbert's English poems were first printed, under the title of *The Temple, Sacred Poems and Private Ejaculations,* in 1633, a few months after his death. The volume was at once popular and reached its fifth edition in 1638.[33] He left also some Latin poems of importance,[34] and, in fine English prose, a manual of the clerical life called *A Priest to the Temple* (first printed in 1652), that gives an admirable picture of the mind in which the poems grew.

Richard Crashaw, Steps to the Temple   Like Herrick, Richard Crashaw [35] (1612-1649) is essentially the poet of one book.[36] *Steps to the Temple, with Other Delights of the Muses* was printed in 1646, two years before the *Hesperides,* and like that volume contains two parts, one secular and one religious. But it is the religious pieces of Crashaw which have priority and chief importance, and the title is an act of homage to Herbert's *Temple. The Weeper* (St. Mary Magdalene), *The Tear, Sancta Maria Dolorum,* and other stanzaic poems on religious subjects are as full of conceited language as of pious fervor.[37] *The Name of*

[32] I.e., "proud through prosperity" (Palmer).
[33] Donne's poems, first printed in the same year as Herbert's, reached a third edition only in 1639.
[34] Cf. L. Bradner, *Musae Anglicanae* (1940), pp. 96-97.
[35] The best edition is L. C. Martin, *The Poems, English, Latin, and Greek, of Richard Crashaw* (Oxford, 1927). See R. C. Wallerstein, *Richard Crashaw, a Study in Style and Poetic Development* (Madison, Wis., 1935); the two chapters on Crashaw in H. C. White, *The Metaphysical Poets* (1936), pp. 202-258; and Austin Warren, *Richard Crashaw, a Study in Baroque Sensibility* (Baton Rouge, 1939).
[36] For his Latin epigrams, published in 1634, see L. Bradner, *Musae Anglicanae,* pp. 92-96; and A. Warren, "Crashaw's *Epigrammata Sacra,*" *JEGP,* XXXIII (1934). 233-239.
[37] The nineteenth stanza of *The Weeper* likens the eyes of the weeping Magdalene to
Two walking baths, two weeping motions,
Portable and compendious oceans.

Jesus is an unusually fine example of the pseudo-Pindaric ode that Cowley was at this time introducing into the language; and the *Hymn of the Nativity, Sung by the Shepherds,* is quaint and lovely, a remarkable blend of childlike piety and the pastoral convention. The best of the collection are the poems addressed to Saint Teresa, the new Spanish saint (canonized, 1622) by whom Crashaw had been inspired even before he gave up Protestantism. The *Hymn* to her, in notably free tetrameter couplets and language so plain as to be astonishing when compared with that of *The Weeper,* was acknowledged by Coleridge as one of the sources for the second part of *Christabel.* Sometimes its simple vigor reminds one (for thus apparent extremes meet) of the poetry of Bunyan; e.g.,

> Since 'tis not to be had at home,
> She 'll travel to a martyrdom.
> No home for her, confesses she,
> But where she may a martyr be.

On the other hand, *The Flaming Heart,* on St. Teresa's book and picture, illustrates in short compass both the verbal ingenuity and the sublimity of which Crashaw was capable. The last section brings together such disparate lines as these:

> O sweet incendiary! show here thy art
> Upon this carcass of a hard cold heart....
> O thou undaunted daughter of desires!
> By all thy dower of lights and fires;
> By all the eagle in thee, all the dove;
> By all thy lives and deaths of love;
> By thy large draughts of intellectual day
> And by thy thirsts of love more large than they....

Crashaw's more secular poems, sub-titled *The Delights of the Muses,* include a number of translations from the classics and epitaphs on friends deceased (especially William Herries, d. 1631, for whom four laments were written); three graceful elegies inspired by the legend of Saint Alexias; a long panegyric addressed to Queen Henrietta Maria "upon her numerous progeny"; and two poems inspired by his friendship for Cowley, whose contemporary at Cambridge he had been. The outstanding items of the collection, however, are *Music's Duel,* on the well-known theme of the contest between the lute player and the nightingale, in which Crashaw displays both his command of pathos and his proficiency in music; and the *Wishes to His Supposed Mistress,* addressed to one he doubtless never knew,

---

On the other hand, the ninth stanza has an exquisite reminiscence of Othello's last speech,

> There is no need at all
> That the balsam-sweating bough
> So coyly should let fall
> His med'cinable tears.

Whoe'er she be,
That not impossible she,
That shall command my heart and me,

to whom he wishes, among many other noble things,

Life that dares send
A challenge to his end,
And when it comes say, Welcome, friend!

Crashaw, though in some of his poems diffuse and over-ridden with conceits, was as pure a poet as his age can show. Less ingenious than Cowley, he had a richer and deeper nature and by honest faith traversed the whole range of Christian belief. Born the son of a Puritan divine, he was expelled (like Cowley) from Cambridge as an Anglican, and ended his life a convert to Rome. Cowley's tribute to him is one of the sincerest things that Cowley wrote:

Poet and Saint! to thee alone are given
The two most sacred names of earth and heaven. . . .
And I myself a Catholic will be,
So far at least, great saint, to pray to thee.

Henry
Vaughan

Henry Vaughan [38] (c. 1622-1695), the Silurist (i.e., South Welshman), as he describes himself on the title-pages of his works, came of an important family, and was probably educated at Jesus College, Oxford, as his twin brother Thomas was. Little is known of his life except that he saw some service on the king's side in the civil wars,[39] became a country doctor, dwelling "in retirement" at his native place of Newton, Brecknockshire, on the Usk River, married twice, and was buried at the age of seventy-three. His fame was small in his own day, and he was not discovered by posterity (to whom in a Latin poem he had appealed) until 1847.[40]

Vaughan's secular verse, represented by a small volume of *Poems* in 1646 and another called *Olor Iscanus* (The Swan of Usk) in 1651, is not of great distinction.[41] It consists of translations from the Latin (with a few original Latin poems), love verses, occasional verses to friends, elegies, and an agreeable laudation of his native river, the Usk. It was the discovery of George Herbert's *Temple* that turned Vaughan's thoughts to religion and made him a poet of importance. The preface which he wrote in 1654 for the second edition of his *Silex Scintillans* (Fire from the Flint) is a strong protest against frivolous verse. "The first," he says, "that with any effectual success

[38] The best edition is *The Works of Henry Vaughan*, ed. L. C. Martin (2v, Oxford, 1914). The edition by E. K. Chambers, with introduction by H. C. Beeching (1896), is still useful. See also E. Blunden, *On the Poems of Henry Vaughan* (1927); two excellent chapters on Vaughan in H. C. White, *The Metaphysical Poets* (1936); and the earlier essay of L. I. Guiney in *A Little English Gallery* (1894), pp. 53-118.

[39] See E. L. Marilla, "Henry Vaughan and the Civil War," *JEGP*, XLI (1942). 514-526.

[40] The first modern edition of his poetry appeared in that year, but it is known that Wordsworth possessed and used an early copy of *Silex Scintillans*. See M. Y. Hughes, "The Theme of Pre-existence and Infancy in *The Retreate*," *PQ*, xx (1941). 484-500.

[41] See H. R. Walley, "The Strange Case of *Olor Iscanus*," *RES*, XVIII (1942). 27-37.

attempted a diversion of this foul and overflowing stream, was the blessed man, Mr. George Herbert, whose holy life and verse gained many pious converts, of whom I am the least." The indebtedness of Vaughan to his fellow-Welshman is continually evident in *Silex Scintillans*,[42] and the younger poet often so recaptured Herbert's tone and attitude that if the poems were removed from their respective volumes, it would in many cases be a most delicate task to reassign them. There are now critics who regard Vaughan as the greater poet. Where he and Herbert are strongly distinguishable, it is by a certain romantic heightening in the later writer: he has more mysticism, a somewhat warmer feeling for nature,[43] and a looser logical structure. It is the difference one sees in architecture between the primitive Gothic and the Decorated styles. The three best poems by Vaughan are three that parallel Herbert least closely: *The Retreat, The World*, and "They are all gone into the world of light." Here the Celtic magic in his nature transcends all else, and he leads us into a realm that is almost wholly intuitive. On these three poems, and two or three others [44] that resemble them, Vaughan's fame mainly and securely rests.

Thomas Traherne [45] (*c.* 1636-1674) had the soul of a poet, but not the art. To say this is to imply that he has been sometimes overrated; nor is that surprising. The romantic story of the discovery and publication of a manuscript of his previously unknown poems as late as 1903, and of another, partly different, manuscript collection in 1910, gave him the conspicuousness of a new comet; and beyond this, the mere existence of a poet of his peculiar quality in the reign of Charles II is a piquant paradox. Like Herbert and Vaughan he was of Welsh origin. The known facts of his life are that he was born in or near Hereford and educated at Oxford, where he entered Brasenose College in 1653 and between 1656 and 1669 took three degrees; that he became a clergyman, was appointed chaplain to Sir Orlando Bridgman, Keeper of the Seals in the Restoration (1667-1672), and died in October, 1674, before he had attained the age of forty. He has been compared with Walt Whitman, and though there is no similarity in subject matter or in bulk of personality, there is some resemblance to the American poet in Traherne's intense self-consciousness, his passion for exclamatory apostrophes and long lists of vaguely related objects, and his formlessness.

To speak of Traherne's philosophy in relation to his poems is rather a misuse of the term. Few poets have been less philosophic, except on the Wordsworthian assumption that the best philosopher is a child; just as few poems are more unthinking than the four to which Traherne gave the

Thomas Traherne

---

[42] The subtitle of *Silex Scintillans*, "Sacred Poems and Private Ejaculations," is also the subtitle of *The Temple*.

[43] See A. C. Judson, "Henry Vaughan as a Nature Poet," *PMLA*, XLII (1927). 146-156.

[44] E.g., *Religion* (Martin, p. 404); "And do they so? have they a sense?" (Martin, p. 432).

[45] The best edition of his poems is *The Poetical Works of Thomas Traherne*, ed. G. I. Wade, (1932). See also his *Centuries of Meditations* ed. B. Dobell (1908); the chapter on Traherne in H. C. White, *The Metaphysical Poets* (1936), pp. 315-374; E. N. S. Thompson, "The Philosophy of Thomas Traherne," *PQ*, VIII (1929). 97-112.

title, *Thoughts*. His attractiveness lies largely in the fact that he retained
into adult years a child's-eye view of the world and of God, as in *The Vision:*

> To see His endless treasures
> Made all my own, myself the end
> Of all His labors! 'Tis the life of pleasures,
> To see myself His friend!

His best poems—and they are very charming—are those which, like *Poverty,
Wonder, The World,* and *Innocence,* most simply express the mind of a
child; but he had a very narrow range, little sense of euphony, and a rather
prosaic vocabulary. The lovely rhythms and subtle thought of Herbert and
Vaughan are sadly flattened in many of his efforts. An extreme example
of what could happen to this kind of verse is the stanza in which his
surviving brother Philip dedicated the manuscript called *Poems of Felicity:*

> To God, my sov'reign Lord,
> My heart and hand accord
> These holy first-fruits of a pious mind
> To dedicate.
> At any rate
> I can't be so injurious or unkind
> To the memory of my brother
> As to devote to any other
> These sacred relics he hath left behind;

but Thomas, the poet, could too often approach this nadir, as in the first
stanza of *Love*. Much of his verse is, in spite of the rime, only measured
prose, and Traherne is probably at his best in the professedly prose sketches
of a child's mentality which are found in his *Centuries of Meditations.*

XI

Seventeenth-Century Poetry: III. The Academic
and Courtly Tradition

Secular poetry during the reigns of James I and Charles I lay in the Corbett, shadow of Spenser, Jonson, and Donne; but the lyric undergrowth was King, and very dense. Two bishops, who passed (with a ten-year interval between Other them) through Westminster School and Christ Church, Oxford, and so Minor into the higher order of clergy, illustrate pleasantly the upper-class taste Lyrists of the day. Richard Corbett[1] (1582-1635), successively, Bishop of Oxford and of Norwich, had a humorous bent best carried out in his longest poem, *Iter Boreale,* which describes the journey of "four clerks of Oxford" to the north of England in a certain month of August (*c.* 1620). Henry King[2] (1592-1669), Bishop of Chichester, the close friend both of Jonson and of Donne, owed most discipleship to the former. He wrote on some of the same occasions as Corbett, but had a larger range and a better singing voice. His elegy on the execution of Sir Walter Ralegh in 1618 is a fine example of controlled indignation:

> I will not weep, for 'twere as great a sin
> To shed a tear for thee, as to have been
> An actor in thy death . . . ;

[1] Corbett's poems were published posthumously in 1647, and again in 1807 (4th ed.); see J. E. V. Crofts, "A Life of Bishop Corbett," in *E&S,* x (1924). 61-96. Corbett has been conjecturally identified with the "R. C." whose initials are affixed to the fine series of riming satires called *The Time's Whistle* and other poems, composed about 1615, but first printed by J. M. Cowper (1871; *EETS,* 48). They would considerably enlarge his fame.

[2] See *Poems, Elegies, Paradoxes, and Sonnets* (1657), reprinted by G. Saintsbury, *Caroline Poets,* iii (Oxford, 1921). 161-273, and by J. Sparrow (1925). Consult L. Mason, "The Life and Works of Henry King, D.D." *Trans. Conn. Acad.,* xviii (1913). 225-289. With Corbett and King may be grouped the Leicestershire clergyman, Thomas Pestell (1585-1667), whose long life overlapped theirs and whose subjects are often similar (see Hannah Buchan, *The Poems of Thomas Pestell,* Oxford, 1940); and a more important poet, Sir John Beaumont (1583-1627), the dramatist's older brother, who wrote copiously in both secular and religious strains (see A. B. Grosart, *The Poems of Sir John Beaumont, Bart.,* 1869). Beaumont's first published poem, *The Metamorphosis of Tabacco* (1602), is a long encomium of the weed, embellished with mythology, geography, and dubious medicine, and antithetical at all points to James I's famous *Counterblast* of two years later. Equally discursive and ill-constructed is Beaumont's long political poem, *Bosworth Field,* dealing with the events of a single day. The last may be grouped with the still more conventional poetical narratives of Charles Aleyn (or Allen): *The Battles of Crescey and Poictiers* (1631) and *The History of Henry VII . . . with That Famed Battle . . . upon Redmoore near Bosworth* (1638). For Beaumont's still longer moral poem, *The Crown of Thorns,* see B. H. Newdigate, "Sir John Beaumont's 'The Crowne of Thornes,'" *RES,* xviii (1942). 284-290. Beaumont and Aleyn were both confessed disciples of Drayton. The former wrote mainly in the heroic couplet, which he employed with ease and sometimes with striking skill. His verses, "To his Late Majesty concerning the True Form of English Poetry," anticipate the ideas and technique of Pope's *Essay on Criticism.* His entertainment, *The Theatre of Apollo* (1625), is edited by W. W. Greg (1926).

and nothing could be more gracefully phrased than this couplet from his epitaph on the Earl of Dorset:

> One high in fair opinion, rich in praise,
> And full of all we could have wish'd, but days.

A later group comprises Thomas Stanley (1625-1678); William Hammond (1614-1680), Stanley's uncle; John Hall (1627-1656), Stanley's protégé;[3] and Sir Edward Sherburne (1618-1702), his lifelong friend. They represent a wide variety of poetic virtuosity, and Stanley, like Sherburne, shows an interesting study of Continental writers.[4] Stanley is doubtless the finest lyrist of the group, but Hall also has much charm.

The absence of notable prose fiction in this period is slightly compensated, and perhaps also explained, by a considerable number of long romances in *Minor Nar-* verse: Nathaniel Whiting's *Pleasant History of Albino and Bellama* (1638), *rative Poets* Sir Francis Kynaston's *Leoline and Sydanis* (1642), William Bosworth's *Chaste and Lost Lovers*, or *Arcadius and Sepha* (1651), Edward Benlowes' *Theophila*, or *Love's Sacrifice* (1652), William Chamberlayne's *Pharonnida* (1659), and John Chalkhill's incomplete *Thealma and Clearchus*, which Izaak Walton first published in 1683.[5] Whiting exhibits Italian influence, and Kynaston (who had translated the first two books of *Troilus and Criseyde* into remarkably ingenious Latin rime royal, 1635) shows traces of Chaucer. Of Bosworth his posthumous editor says: "The strength of his fancy and the shadowing of it in words he taketh from Mr. Marlow in his *Hero and Leander.*"[6] The raciest of these writers is Whiting; the most religious Benlowes, who employs a bizarre three-line stanza, and has not enough story to make even a passable allegory. The most poetic of them is Chamberlayne, who is also, unfortunately, the most obscure.[7] There are strikingly good passages in nearly all these elongated works; but any of them, if read in full, will show how curiously the pattern of straightforward narrative has been corroded by pseudo-Spenserian complication and wilful absurdity. The longest, perhaps the most desultory and wilful, and yet the most interesting of all these long narratives is *The New Metamorphosis* by "J. M." (perhaps Gervase Markham), preserved only in manuscript in the British Museum.[8] It is in twenty-four books of heroic couplet verse, which took the author about fifteen years to compose (1600-1615). It is a mine of

---

[3] Stanley, Hammond, and Hall are all reprinted by Saintsbury, *Caroline Poets*, II. 177-225, 483-520, III. 95-189. See also *Thomas Stanley, His Original Lyrics Complete*, ed. L. I. Guiney (Hull, 1907).

[4] See Mario Praz, "Stanley, Sherburne, and Ayres as Translators and Imitators of Italian, Spanish, and French Poets," *MLR*, xx (1925). 280-294.

[5] All these are reprinted by Saintsbury, *op. cit.*

[6] Kynaston's *Cynthiades*, appended to *Leoline and Sydanis*, contains some excellent love songs. Bosworth's long amatory lament, *Hinc Lachrimae*, has only the merit of fluency. The *Poems Divine and Humane* (1641) of Thomas Beedome are of better quality and contain some pretty lines (selection, with introduction by F. Meynell, Nonesuch Press, 1928).

[7] Chamberlayne was also the author of *Love's Victory*, a melodramatic tragicomedy of small worth, which was never acted, but was printed in 1658 (ed. C. K. Meschter, Bethlehem, Pa., 1914).

[8] See J. H. H. Lyon, *A Study of The Newe Metamorphosis* (1919).

contemporary reference and a wilderness of fantastic plot. To conclude with another early example, *Dolarny's Primrose* by John Raynolds [9] (1606), described as "the first part of the passionate hermit," is more moral and much shorter, but hardly less arbitrary in its narrative method. A striking plagiarism from *Hamlet* gets it occasional mention.

Drummond, "unlike most poets," as one of his nineteenth-century biographers remarks, "appears to have left considerable property." [10] Coming of age soon after the union of Scotland and England in 1603 and succeeding his father (who had been gentleman usher to King James) in the possession of the landed estate of Hawthornden, seven miles from Edinburgh, in 1610, William Drummond (1585-1649) was privileged to devote over forty years to learned and literary leisure, broken only by periods of residence on the continent and to some extent at the end by the troubles of civil war. He was Master of Arts of Edinburgh University and the master of many tongues, and was one of the earliest Scots to employ the London literary dialect exclusively in his writings. His life contains few incidents of note except the sudden death of his fiancée, Mary Cunningham. This, and the influence of the Continental sonneteers, engendered a gentle melancholy. Some twenty years later (1632) he married a lady described (perhaps untruly) as "the daughter of a minister by one whose sire was a shepherd" and had by her five sons and four daughters.

William Drummond of Hawthornden

Drummond has a secure place in the history of the English sonnet between Shakespeare and Milton. He did not, like the latter poet, write too few; about a hundred and fifty have been preserved, many mournfully amatory, many religious, and a considerable number complimentary of persons and occasions. He owes much to Sidney and to sixteenth-century French and Italian sonneteers, but his general idea seems to have been to write like Petrarch, whom he followed in the practice of interspersing *canzoni* [11] (and also madrigals) among his sonnets. The latter show obvious facility, but the ideas are usually trite, being very frequently borrowed from Italian and French originals; [12] and Drummond found it difficult to adhere for long to any single type of rime sequence. Most of his sonnets are strictly neither Petrarchan nor Shakespearean. As good as any perhaps, and very pleasing, are the one *For the Baptist,*

Drummond's Sonnets

> The last and greatest herald of heaven's king,

and the one (imitated from Cardinal Bembo) in praise of rustic solitude,

> Dear wood, and you, sweet solitary place,
> Where from the vulgar I estranged live.

[9] Ed. A. B. Grosart (1880).

[10] Drummond's *Poetical Works*, ed. W. B. Turnbull (1890 ed.), p. viii.

[11] Called by him "Songs." They have been regarded as anticipating the pseudo-Pindaric odes introduced by Cowley.

[12] See for a full discussion the introduction to the best edition of Drummond: L. E. Kastner, *The Poetical Works of Wm. Drummond of Hawthornden, with "A Cypresse Grove"* (2v, Manchester, 1913); also A. Joly, *William Drummond de Hawthornden, aperçu d'ensemble sur la vie et l'œuvre du poète* (Lille, 1934), ch. II; R. C. Wallerstein, "The Style of Drummond of Hawthornden," *PMLA*, XLVIII (1933). 1090-1107.

Drummond's earliest published poem was an offering on the much lamented death of Prince Henry, *Tears on the Death of Meliades* (1613), in about a hundred riming couplets and a concluding sonnet. This was followed in 1616 by a larger volume, *Poems: Amorous, Funeral, Divine, Pastoral, in Sonnets, Songs, Sextains, Madrigals;*[13] and in 1623 by another collection, *Flowers of Sion, or Spiritual Poems.* As the laird of Hawthornden, Drummond was an acknowledged leader in the literary life of Edinburgh, and on the return of King James to that city in 1617, he wrote the panegyric,

*orth
*easting

Forth Feasting, in which the Firth of Forth addresses the monarch at length on the subject of the latter's royal virtues and wisdom. The technical precision of these verses, and almost exclusive use of the "closed" couplet, have caused them to be remarked as among the prototypes of Pope's metre. As is Drummond's way, the poem ranges over large tracts of mythology, history, and geography, and he finds occasion to pause over the recent transplantation of the royal prestige to the new world in the naming of Jamestown and the James River. *Forth Feasting* is a colorful, though necessarily fulsome, poem, superior to the highly mythological tributes that Drummond devised for the next king, Charles I, when he came to Edinburgh in 1633. Both these royal visits are overshadowed by the visit of Ben Jonson in 1618. At the end of his famous pedestrian progress from London to Edinburgh Ben spent a couple of weeks at Hawthornden as guest of Drummond, who, though not moved to poetry on the occasion, did a better thing in recording the literary opinions and a large number of personal anecdotes of the stranger.[14] Rough

*The Conver-
sations with
Jonson*

and often tantalizingly incomplete, Drummond's jottings yet give us our clearest and most unbiassed view of Jonson's rugged, rational, ultra-English personality.

Drummond produced one piece of fine prose, as different as possible from the crabbed terseness of his summaries of Jonson's talk. *The Cypress Grove,* published with the *Flowers of Sion* in 1623, is a rather Platonic discourse of about fifty pages on death, the soul, and the future life, suggestive, but in a quieter key, of Browne's *Religio Medici* and *Urn Burial.*

*Drum-
mond's
Prose
Style*

It has a mannered style, rich in figure and in unacknowledged quotation from earlier philosophers,[15] but there is not much excess; the reasoning (considering the subject) is shrewd, and the balance of the sentences is excellent, as in this typical one:

Applause whilst thou livest serveth but to make thee that fair mark against which envy and malice direct their arrows, and when thou art wounded, all eyes are turned towards thee (like the sun, which is most gazed on in an eclipse), not for pity or praise, but detraction.

[13] There is an earlier, less complete edition, without date, assigned by Kastner to *c.* 1614.
[14] These Conversations have been edited separately by R. F. Patterson (1923), and in Vol. 1 of the Oxford Jonson (1925). The attack on the authenticity of the manuscript by C. L. Stainer in *Jonson and Drummond: Their Conversations* (Oxford, 1925) is not effective.
[15] Including Bacon, Montaigne, and Donne. Cf. G. S. Greene, "Drummond's Borrowing from Donne," *PQ,* XI (1932). 26-38; M. A. Rugoff, "Drummond's Debt to Donne," *PQ,* XVI (1937). 85-88.

It might be asserted that Drummond's prose style is better than his poetic, at least in his sonnets. The latter are too full of exclamation; e.g.,

> O woful life! Life? No, but living death,
> Frail boat of crystal in a rocky sea,

and often carry inversion to such a point that one may doubt whether the southern English he employs was perfectly idiomatic to him. Yet a passage from the late *Entertainment of King Charles* (1633) will show again how very good his couplets (and how bad his political judgment) could be:

> A Prince all gracious, affable, divine,
> Meek, wise, just, valiant, whose radiant shine
> Of virtues (like the stars about the pole
> Gilding the night) enlight'neth every soul
> Your scepter sways; a Prince born in this age,
> To guard the innocents from tyrants' rage,
> To make peace prosper, justice to reflower
> In desert hamlet as in lordly bower;
> A Prince that, though of none he stand in awe,
> Yet first subjects himself to his own law;
> Who joys in good, and still, as right directs,
> His greatness measures by his good effects;
> His people's pedestal, who rising high
> To grace his throne, makes Scotland's name to fly
> On halcyon's wings (her glory which restores)
> Beyond the ocean to Columbus' shores [i.e., to Nova Scotia].[16]

Most of the poets treated in this chapter, if not all, could be properly *The Tribe* assigned to the "Tribe of Ben" as drawing from Jonson their chief guidance *of Ben* in poetry; and the same is true of Beaumont, Fletcher, Richard Brome, and numerous others.[17] There was, of course, no ritual by which one became a "Son," though Jonson and others sometimes wrote jestingly as if there were. In so centrifugal a time, moreover, even those who bore the same banner were often found moving in different directions, and it may be sufficient to illustrate the pervasive influence of Ben by two examples from the two universities.

The Cambridge wit and dramatist, Thomas Randolph [18] (1605-1635), who

16 Kastner, II. 120. "In 1621 Sir Wm. Alexander obtained a grant of the whole peninsula and it was named in the patent Nova Scotia instead of Acadia" (*Ency. Brit.*). Alexander (*c.* 1567-1640; see above, Part II, ch. VII), the friend of Drummond, was himself author of a sequence of sonnets and other poems, entitled *Aurora* (1604), and various later works. For specimens of these and of the poems of Sir Robert Aytoun (1570-1638) see G. Eyre-Todd, *Scottish Poetry of the Seventeenth Century* (Glasgow, 1895). Another Scottish poet, contemporary with Drummond, deserves brief mention: Patrick Hannay of Sorby in Galloway. Little is known of his life; but he wrote some acceptable elegies, sonnets, and songs, and two long narratives in stanzaic verse, *Philomela* and *Sheretine and Mariana* (reprinted by Saintsbury, *Caroline Poets*, I (1905). 615-726).
17 See K. A. McEuen, *Classical Influence upon the Tribe of Ben* (Cedar Rapids, Iowa, 1940).
18 Convenient editions are J. J. Parry, *The Poems and Amyntas of Thomas Randolph*, (1917), and G. Thorn-Drury, *The Poems of Thomas Randolph* (1929). See also C. L. Day, "New Poems by Randolph," *RES*, VIII (1932). 29-36, and G. C. Moore Smith, *Thomas Randolph* (Warton Lecture on English Poetry, 1927).

Thomas   like Marlowe died before he reached the age of thirty, was one of the clever-
Randolph est of Jonson's disciples. Pleasant anecdotes are recorded of their relationship,
and one of Randolph's best poems is his *Gratulatory to Mr. Ben Johnson
for His Adopting Him to Be His Son,* which begins,

> I was not born to Helicon, nor dare
> Presume to think myself a Muse's heir.
> I have no title to Parnassus hill,
> Nor any acre of it by the will
> Of a dead ancestor, nor could I be
> Aught but a tenant unto Poetry.
> But thy adoption quits me of all fear,
> And makes me challenge a child's portion there.
> I am akin to heroes, being thine,
> And part of my alliance is divine.

He wrote also a loyal reply to Jonson's ode, "Come, leave the loathèd stage,"
and a long *Eclogue to Mr. Johnson,* in which, in the person of the young
shepherd Damon, he discusses with his master Tityrus (Jonson) the dis-
illusionments of a poet's life.[19]

Randolph wrote few songs, but had a facile hand for the elegies, epithalamia, and translations of classic gems in which the age delighted. He
especially affected the pastoral, sometimes for the sake of voluptuous detail,
as in *A Pastoral Courtship,* and sometimes as a means of satire, as in the
clever *Eclogue Occasioned by Two Doctors Disputing upon Predestination.*
There is a forecast of Burns in the naughty wit of this parody, which begins
with Tityrus challenging Alexis to explain the difference between his twin
lambs,

> Th' one black as jet, the other white as snow:
> Say, in just providence how could it be so?

Randolph's five plays were in some demand in the seventeenth century, as
the list of editions shows.[20] The first, *Aristippus, or the Jovial Philosopher*
(1630), was a Cambridge entertainment; the last, *Amyntas, or the Impossible
Dowry,* a full-dress pastoral in five acts, performed before the King and
Queen at Whitehall. The author's wit and ingenuity are more apparent in
them than any dramatic power.

The poet-dramatist-preacher, William Cartwright [21] (1611-1643), of whom
Jonson said, "My son Cartwright writes all like a man," has not impressed

---

[19] The jocular poem on the loss of Randolph's finger, written by William Hemming, contains many interesting references to contemporary poets; see J. J. Parry, "A 17th Century
Gallery of Poets," *JEGP,* xix (1920). 1-8.

[20] See G. C. Moore Smith, "The Canon of Randolph's Dramatic Works," *RES,* i (1925).
309-323. *The Drinking Academy,* first printed in 1930 (ed. S. A. Tannenbaum and H. E.
Rollins), has been recently added to Randolph's plays. See G. C. Moore Smith's attempt to
ascribe it to Robert Baron, *RES,* vi (1930). 476-483, and Professor Rollins' reply in *PMLA,*
xlvi (1931). 786-801.

[21] See R. C. Goffin, *The Life and Poems of William Cartwright* (Cambridge, 1918); and
for bibliography, G. B. Evans, "Comedies, Tragi-Comedies, with Other Poems. By Mr. William
Cartwright (1651): a Bibliographical Study," *Library* xxiii (1942). 12-22; and J. P. Danton,
"William Cartwright and his Comedies . . . 1651," *Library Quar.,* xii (1942). 438-456.

posterity as a virile force, but he bewitched his contemporaries by his charm *William* and promise. The latter half of his short life was spent at Oxford, and when *Cartwright* he died of fever in the second year of the civil war, King Charles, whose court was then in the city, wore personal mourning for him. Like Randolph, he wrote several plays, as well as a rather thin offering of occasional verse. The poetical form that he uses most is the Jonsonian verse letter or meditation in couplets. He is too often concerned with royal deaths and weddings or compliments to Oxford dignitaries; but he reaches a high level in his elegy on Sir Bevil Greville, the cavalier hero, and in the poem on Jonson himself, which he contributed to *Jonsonus Virbius* in 1638, and which contains the source of Denham's most famous distich in *Cooper's Hill*. Cartwright can occasionally write a warm and unclerical love lyric; and in one delightful poem, *Corinna's Tomb,* which is suggestive of William Collins, he strikes a note of fantasy concerning external nature that was not usual in his time.[22]

Thomas Carew's poems are better known than his life, which seems to *Thomas* have begun about 1595 and to have ended obscurely before the outbreak of *Carew* the civil wars in 1642. He had the favor of Charles I, whose "sewer in ordinary" he was, and in coöperation with Inigo Jones he wrote an amusing masque, *Coelum Britannicum,* for presentation at Whitehall in 1634, the year of *Comus*.[23] Henry Lawes wrote music for both masques. Carew's friends were mainly members of the "Cavalier School" of poets (e.g., Lovelace, Suckling, Davenant) and of the court party, and his reputation was not high even in those indulgent circles. But he appears to have given his poems a care that he did not bestow upon his conduct. The light lyrics beginning, "He that loves a rosy cheek," "Ask me no more where Jove bestows," and "Come, Celia, fix thine eyes on mine," are exceptionally well executed, though they tell us little of Carew as a lover.

Like other dissolute poets, he is prolific of good advice to young girls; and, at the other extreme, he develops with a good deal of art the physical paganism of some of the Elizabethans.[24] His range is pleasantly extended in two charming and detailed poems on country hospitality, *To Saxham,* and *To my Friend G. N. from Wrest;* and he shows more than respectable critical powers in his well reasoned poems to Aurelian Townsend and Ben Jonson. Of the same thoughtful quality is his fine *Elegy on the Death of Dr. Donne,* of whom he says,

> Here lies a king that ruled as he thought fit
> The universal monarchy of wit.

[22] One of the noblest and most notable of Jonson's "sons," Lucius Cary, Viscount Falkland (1610-1643), is relatively unimportant as a poet (see the edition of A. B. Grosart, 1871); but his long *Eclogue on the Death of Ben Johnson,* in which he pays tribute to the "ethic lectures of his comedies" and to Jonson's character, is a fine piece.

[23] Carew's masque was printed in the year of its presentation, 1634. His poems appeared in 1640 and again in 1642. There is no recent edition, but the following are still serviceable: J. W. Ebsworth, *The Poems and Masque of Thomas Carew* (1893); Arthur Vincent, *Poems of Thomas Carew* (1899).

[24] E.g., in *A Rapture, The Second Rapture, The Compliment.*

The giants, Jonson and Donne, were revered by Carew. One was the man "greater than all men else," the other the poet "worth all that went before." He borrowed from them to the extent in which a poet of his powers could: from Jonson the great lesson of classic polish, and from Donne a sense of the exciting power of a figure. The result is sometimes rather fine; e.g.,

> I am the dial's hand, still walking round,
> You are the compass; and I never sound
> Beyond your circle, neither can I show
> Aught but what first expressed is in you.
> (*To Celia, upon Love's Ubiquity*)

> Strew all the pavements where he treads
> With loyal hearts or rebels' heads;
> But, Bifront,[25] open thou no more
> In his blest reign the temple door.
> (*A New Year's Gift to the King*)

Sometimes it was quite absurd:

> So, though a virgin, yet a bride
> To every grace, she justified
> A chaste polygamy, and died.
> (*Maria Wentworth*)

Sir John Suckling

Though the most short-lived, Sir John Suckling [26] (1609-1642) is probably the most typical of the group of court poets, including Carew, Lovelace, Denham, Davenant, and Waller, who flourished in the reign of Charles I. The son of a wealthy state official, he was educated at Trinity College, Cambridge, traveled abroad, saw some military service in Germany under Gustavus Adolphus, and returned in 1632 to become, in the words of his friend Davenant, "famous at court for his accomplishments and ready, sparkling wit." He became notorious also for gambling and dissipation.[27] In 1639 he took part in the King's inglorious expedition against the Scots, and two years later, while sitting as a member in the Long Parliament, entered into a conspiracy with other royalists to secure the Earl of Strafford's escape from the Tower. When this plot, similar to the one in which Waller was implicated a couple of years later, was discovered, Suckling fled to France and put an end to his life, it was said, by poison.

Of all the "Cavalier" group Suckling had the most interesting mind and the largest potentialities for poetry. He had a sense of humor, as is shown in the overrated *Session of the Poets* and the truly delightful *Ballad upon a Wedding,* and a somewhat Byronic gift of social criticism; and he was able to write cogently in prose; e.g., in his political letter to Henry Jermyn (1641).

---

[25] I.e., Janus, whose temple doors were opened in time of war, closed in peace.
[26] The best edition is A. H. Thompson, *The Works of Sir John Suckling in Prose and Verse* (1910).
[27] See F. O. Henderson, "Traditions of Précieux and Libertin in Suckling's Poetry," *ELH*, IV (1937). 274-298.

But his potentialities were mainly unrealized. His four plays—*Aglaura, The Goblins, Brennoralt,* and *The Sad One*—are arid and ill-constructed, too full of melodramatic contrivances and undeveloped characters, and are written in the loosest of blank verse. Their only interest today is in the wealth of literary allusion they contain to Shakespeare and other earlier poets.

Much of Suckling's lyric verse is unpolished; he appears to have prided himself upon his quickness of composition, and he did not feel deeply the passions of love and loyalty. His best verses are the lightest:

> Out upon it, I have loved
> Three whole days together,
> And am like to love three more,
> If it prove fair weather;

or the famous song from *Aglaura,*

> Why so pale and wan, fond lover,
> Prithee, why so pale?

Yet, though there was little faith in him and little warmth, Suckling usually has something to say, and he can sometimes phrase a fine romantic line, such as

> Heaven were not heaven if we knew what it were.[28]

Though he called Donne the "great lord" of "pure wit," [29] Suckling rarely attempts conceits, and he is also notably free from mythological adornment. There is hardly a purer English style in the seventeenth century than Suckling's, and there are few better personal letters of the period than the forty or fifty of his that have been preserved.

Five years younger than Milton and as much older than Cowley, John *John* Cleveland[30] (1613-1658) was educated at Milton's college (Christ's, Cam- *Cleveland* bridge), and on being elected to a fellowship at St. John's in 1634 acquired considerable repute about the university as a wit and poet. He contributed verses in 1638 both to the memorial for Edward King in which *Lycidas* appeared and to the volume in memory of Ben Jonson, *Jonsonus Virbius.* After the outbreak of civil war in 1642 he followed the royalist court to Oxford and served the king both in the field and by satire in prose and verse. His writing is rough and makes little appeal to the reader today, though at the time it had great vogue. *The Rebel Scot* (1644) was his best known piece and can be illustrated by four lines:

> Had Cain been Scot, God would have changed his doom;
> Not forced him wander, but confined him home.
> Like Jews they spread and as infection fly,
> As if the Devil had ubiquity!

[28] *Against Fruition.*
[29] *To My Friend Will Davenant, on His Other Poems.*
[30] *The Poems of John Cleveland,* ed. John M. Berdan (1903); G. Saintsbury, *Minor Poets of the Caroline Period,* III (1921). 1-94. See S. V. Gapp, "Notes on John Cleveland," *PMLA,* XLVI (1931). 1075-1086.

Only once, in *The General Eclipse,* written after the ruinous defeat at Naseby (1645) and the flight of King and Queen, does something of the pathos and poetry of the lost cause enter his verse:

> Ladies that gild the glittering noon
>   And by reflection mend his ray,
> Whose beauty makes the sprightly sun
>   To dance as upon Easter-day,
>   What are you now the Queen's away? . . .
>
> As an obstructed fountain's head
>   Cuts the entail off from the streams
> And brooks are disinherited,
>   Honor and beauty are but dreams
>   Since Charles and Mary lost their beams!

The figure in the last stanza exemplifies the imagery by which Cleveland's earlier love poetry also is rather marred than adorned. He is as fond as Cowley of "conceits," and uses them less intelligently. In *To Julia to Expedite Her Promise* he admonishes the lady by a parallel with the two calendars,

> Your sex lives faster than the males,
>   As if, to measure age's span,
> The sober Julian were the account of man
>   Whilst you live by the fleet Gregorian.

As the difference amounts to something like three days in four centuries, the terms *sober* and *fleet* are not really impressive.

Richard Lovelace

Richard Lovelace (1618-c. 1657) is remembered for his beautiful Cavalier face and name, his military virtues, and for two stirring songs which rise high above the level of his chaste and copious, but not otherwise remarkable verse.[31] Twice—in writing to Lucasta on going to the wars ("Tell me not, sweet, I am unkind"), and to Althaea from prison ("When love with unconfined wings")—the circumstances of his chivalrous life provided him with a perfect poetic opportunity. Lovelace's other songs, though highly praised by his friends and set to music by some of the most eminent composers of his day, lack real vigor; and his many poems in pentameter couplet lack compactness of thought and variety of rhythm. His pastoral, *Amarantha,* is obscure and over-long, and his efforts at humor are not very merry. Lovelace is no nature poet, but a variety is lent to his repertory by his poems on the grasshopper, the fly, the ant, the snail, the falcon, and the toad and spider, which suggest that in a quieter time his talents might have deepened. The prettiest of all his lesser works is the "sonnet" on Elinda's glove,

> Thou Snowy farm with thy five tenements. . . .

[31] The poems of Lovelace appeared first in two small volumes: *Lucasta* (1649) and *Lucasta, Posthumous Poems* (1659). See *The Poems of Richard Lovelace,* ed. C. H. Wilkinson (Oxford, 1930): C. H. Hartmann, *The Cavalier Spirit and Its Influence on the Life and Work of Richard Lovelace* (1925); A. C. Judson, "Who was Lucasta?" *MP,* xxiii (1925). 77-82.

With Lovelace may be linked two other Cavalier poets of rather slender *Sidney* performance but fragrant memory. Sidney Godolphin [32] (1610-1643), killed *Godolphin* in a cavalry charge at Chagford, Devonshire, was of a distinguished Cornish family. He had studied in Oxford, sat in Parliament, and known Jonson, Donne, and Hobbes. On the first two he wrote notable obituary poems, interesting for their justice and for the way in which in each case Godolphin falls into the style of the poet he is celebrating. Hobbes, in turn, wrote Godolphin's praise in the dedication of his *Leviathan* (1651) to the poet's brother. Godolphin's love poems, one or two of which are exquisite (e.g., "Chloris, it is not thy disdain"), have the gentle manliness of Lovelace's with less finish. His longest work is a translation, in flowing couplets, of the fourth book of the *Æneid,* in which Waller also had a hand.

The noble Marquis of Montrose [33] (1612-1650), hero and martyr of the *Montrose* royalist party in Scotland, left a few poems which have in them the headlong and heedless passion of the cause he served. Four lines out of a rambling series of "Love Verses" have made his literary fortune:

> He either fears his fate too much,
> Or his deserts are small,
> Who dares not put it to the touch
> To gain or lose it all.

The son of a well-to-do London goldsmith, Robert Herrick [34] (1591-1674) *Robert* took two degrees at Cambridge and formed his poetic style by study of *Herrick* the classic lyrists [35] and contact with Ben Jonson, then in his prime, whom he called "Saint Ben" and the best of poets. After some experience of court and military life he took orders, at nearly as late an age as Donne, and was presented to the rectory of Dean Prior in Devonshire, of which he says:

> More discontents I never had
> Since I was born than here....
> Yet justly too I must confess
> I ne'er invented such
> Ennobled numbers for the press
> Than where I loath'd so much.[36]

He was ejected from his living by the Puritan government in 1647, restored in 1662, and ultimately buried at Dean Prior at the age of eighty-three. There is little evidence that he affected his contemporaries in any degree. A single poem, *King Oberon's Feast,* was printed anonymously in a fairy miscellany in 1635, and three others in the 1640 edition of Shakespeare's *Poems.* "The Several Poems written by Master Robert Herrick," entered on the Stationers'

---

[32] See W. Dighton, *The Poems of Sidney Godolphin* (Oxford, 1931).

[33] See J. L. Weir, *Poems of James Graham, Marquis of Montrose* (1938).

[34] See F. W. Moorman, *Robert Herrick, a Biographical and Critical Study* (1910); *Poetical Works of Robert Herrick* (Oxford, 1915, 1935); F. Delattre, *Robert Herrick* (Paris, 1912).

[35] See Pauline Aiken, *The Influence of the Latin Elegists on English Lyric Poetry, 1600-1650, with Particular Reference to the Works of Robert Herrick* (1932); G. G. Loane, "Herrick's Sources," *N&Q,* CLXXVIII (1940). 224-225.

[36] *Discontents in Devon.*

Register, April 29, 1640, remained unprinted [37] till the appearance in 1648 of Herrick's only book, *Hesperides: or the Works both Humane and Divine of Robert Herrick Esq.,*[38] and the fame of this now precious volume was a growth of the nineteenth century.

Herrick is the delight and justification of the anthologist. Some twenty easily selected lyrics have made him immortal; the rest are not so much inferior as repetitive of his themes. He is the poet of strawberries and cream, of fairy lore and rustic customs, of girls delineated like flowers and flowers mythologized into girls; as in *To Carnations, a Song:*

> Stay while ye will, or go,
> And leave no scent behind ye:
> Yet trust me, I shall know
> The place where I may find ye.
>
> Within my Lucia's cheek
> (Whose livery ye wear)
> Play ye at hide or seek,
> I'm sure to find ye there.

Corinna's Going a-Maying is one of the most successful poems ever written in immortalizing a mood and depicting a contemporary scene, and its last stanza is unsurpassable in expression. These themes might cloy if Herrick were not a perfect craftsman and a brilliant ironist. Praising pagan love and pastoral beauty as he does, he seldom lets the reader forget that he is a gray-headed parson, who hates the country and abhors matrimony:

> Before I went
> To banishment
> Into the loathed West,
> I co'd rehearse
> A lyric verse,
> And speak it with the best.
>
> But Time (Ay me!)
> Has laid, I see,
> My Organ fast asleep,
> And turn'd my voice
> Into the noise
> Of those that sit and weep;

or (*To Perilla*)

> Age calls me hence, and my gray hairs bid come,
> And haste away to mine eternal home,

or more jauntily,

· [37] Delattre, p. 98, suggests a reason for the suspension of publication.

[38] The "pious pieces" in this volume are introduced by a special title-page calling them *His Noble Numbers* and bearing date 1647.

> A bachelor I will
> Live as I have liv'd still,
> And never take a wife
> To crucify my life,

and

> Love he that will; it best likes me
> To have my neck from love's yoke free,

and (in *To his Tomb-maker*)

> Go I must; when I am gone,
> Write but this upon my stone:
> Chaste I liv'd, without a wife,
> That's the story of my life.
> Strewings need none: every flower
> Is in this word, Bachelor;

and finally, in *To All Young Men That Love,*

> I could wish you all, who love,
> That ye could your thoughts remove
> From your mistresses, and be
> Wisely wanton (like to me).

By the time Herrick's volume was printed, with a dedication to Charles, Prince of Wales, the author was nearly sixty years old and the Cavalier cause was lost. Even the earliest poems in the collection speak of the poet's age, and it is not likely that it contains much unrevised youthful work. When viewed as the mature and consistent reflection of a man's mind, these usually delicious poems do not warrant us in assigning Herrick a very high place among clerical types. His satirical epigrams include some of the most brutal of their kind. He was neither a romantic idealist nor a believer in the golden mean, and his definition of beauty is a true measure of the man:

> Beauty no other thing is than a beam
> Flash'd out between the Middle and Extreme,

that is, in the ironic middle ground between stoicism and enthusiasm.

But he had moments of lyric ecstasy in contemplating the flower-like beauties of earth or daydreaming of the supernatural; e.g., in *The Hag:*

> The Hag is astride,
> This night for to ride,
> The Devil and she together:
> Through thick and through thin,
> Now out and then in,
> Though ne'er so foul be the weather.

And many times he achieves the calm perfection of Horace or Catullus, as in *To Sappho:*

Let us now take time and play,
Love, and live here while we may;
Drink rich wine, and make good cheer,
While we have our being here:
For once dead, and laid i' th' grave,
No return from thence we have.

XII

Seventeenth-Century Poetry: IV. Links with the Restoration

The poets who carried the torch across the interregnum that divided Charles I's kingdom from Charles II's were mainly a conservative group lacking in the ardors for court or creed that marked most of those considered in the last two chapters. Of such, though he did not live to see the Restoration, was William Habington (1605-1654), a Catholic gentleman of quality *William* closely contemporary with Waller and rather like him in spirit.[1] Had his life *Habington* and creative ambition continued, Habington could have been expected to make the progress Waller did through a mild Cromwellianism to a sane acceptance of the Restoration ideal, but the literary work that he left includes only one volume of poetry and one play,[2] both completed by 1640 and both rather excellent in their kind. His *Castara*, printed in 1634 and twice expanded, was composed in honor of Lord Powis's daughter, Lucy Herbert, whom Habington married in the interval between Part I and Part II of the collection. His poetical name for himself is "Araphil" (i.e., Castaraphil), in imitation of Sidney's Astrophel.

Habington is a likable person, who decries "writing wanton and profane" and altogether avoids it, showing indeed an excessive respect for his lady and her high-born relatives; but he can write well of good food and drink and introduces interesting topical allusions. One of his best poems is *Love's Anniversary* in the second part, which shows genuine and fine feeling. The one that immediately precedes this, *In Praise of the City Life in the Long Vacation*, is descriptive, and almost equally good. He generally employs the riming couplet and prefers the "open" variety. His shorter poems are commonly sets of seven couplets, which he would have called sonnets. *Castara* also includes, in its final version, four prose "characters": *A Mistress, A Wife, A Friend, A Holy Man*. The third part, first printed in 1640, has a larger proportion of song measures such as Waller used, in which, however, the subject is either ethical or religious.

Abraham Cowley[3] (1618-1667) was a lover of quiet in an unquiet age, a

---

[1] See a note on Habington by J. M. Nosworthy, *LTLS*, June 5, 1937, p. 428. *Castara* was reprinted by E. Arber (1870).

[2] For this play, *The Queen of Aragon*, see above, ch. v.

[3] For Cowley's life and literary importance see A. H. Nethercot, *Abraham Cowley, The Muse's Hannibal* (Oxford, 1931); and J. Loiseau, *Abraham Cowley, sa vie, son œuvre* (Paris, 1931). A good selected edition of his poems is *"The Mistress," with other select Poems of*

man of moderate opinions and abilities led into rather absurd postures by the violence of his environment. The posthumous son of a London stationer (bookdealer), he received a sound classical education at Westminster School and earned a fellowship at Trinity College, Cambridge, just in time to be dispossessed by the Puritan commissioners in April, 1644. Following his friends to the King's headquarters at Oxford, and later to the royalist center at Paris, he was involved in various sorts of secret service, which he performed so half-heartedly, or at least so unsuccessfully, that he was imprisoned by Cromwell as a spy and suspected by Charles II as a turncoat. In politics, however, as in poetry, he was a sincere man, and was as consistent as conditions and his mild nature permitted him to be. At the end he turned to the study of medicine and botany, living in the country, and composing the personal essays in English and the Latin poems on plants and flowers [4] which are among the most charming of all his works.

Cowley was one of the most precocious of English poets—he produced a successful volume of verse when fifteen; [5] and he was one of the most versatile and inventive in style. It is his misfortune that a large part of his work invites comparison with Donne and another part with Milton. His elegy on his Cambridge friend, William Hervey, a really noble and significant ode, [6] was written (1642) five years after *Lycidas,* and his incomplete biblical epic, *Davideis,* was published ten years before *Paradise Lost.* The *Davideis* once had readers, but its monotonous and self-conscious couplets could not long hold their attention. "Nothing," says Dr. Johnson, "can be more disgusting than a narrative spangled with conceits, and conceits are all that the *Davideis* supplies." It undoubtedly supplied certain hints to Milton, but it also supplied him with a justification for the vigorous words he used in explaining why *Paradise Lost* does not rime.

The Mistress, or Several Copies of Love-Verses (1647) contains nearly a hundred poems in various lyrical measures and very different moods. It purports to tell Cowley's sufferings through some three years at the hands of an unnamed lady of higher rank than his. Her friends oppose, and she does not admit his suit. At times he is so frank as to own that he does not wish her to; at other times he indulges in invectives against the inconstancy and venality of women, "the sex that's worst," and in rhetorical displays of his lacerated heart. History informs us that Cowley never married. *The Mistress* offers many reasons for the fact, most of them inconsistent with each other. An inserted dialogue dramatizing a successful love adventure [7] and a par-

---

Abraham Cowley, edited by John Sparrow (Nonesuch Press, 1926). His English works are printed complete by A. R. Waller (2v, Cambridge, 1905-6). Dr. Johnson's study of Cowley in his *Lives of the Most Eminent English Poets* (1779) has in many respects not been surpassed.

[4] For discussion of his extensive poetical writings in Latin see L. Bradner, *Musae Anglicanae* (1940), pp. 118-122.

[5] *Poetical Blossoms* (1633). It has been suggested that Cowley's precocity inspired Milton's reference to "some more timely-happy spirits" in the sonnet on his twenty-third year.

[6] This is written in nineteen 8-line stanzas of beautiful pattern. The language, though formal, shows true feeling and contains few "conceits."

[7] Camb. ed., pp. 147-148.

ticularly pretty eulogy of country life (*The Wish*) seem to have no connection with the rest of the sequence, if indeed that term can at all be applied to poems so slenderly connected.

Though Cowley followed Donne in the style of *The Mistress*, he followed him at a much greater distance than was formerly supposed, and his claim to the term *metaphysical* is rather shallow. Sometimes he begins a poem with a line that has the startling quality of Donne's openings, e.g.,

> For Heaven's sake, what d' you mean to do?

or

> By Heaven, I'll tell her boldly that 'tis she.

And sometimes he will develop an intricate metaphor, as that life and love represent double time, respectively short and long, like the double revolution of the sun,[8] while hope and fear are day and night; or he likens the lover's inconstancy to the vibration of a magnetic needle before it fixes on the true north;[9] or argues that as the substance of the body reproduces itself every five years, continued love of the same woman would be incest.[10] But these things are not the fabric of Cowley's thinking, as they are of Donne's; they are occasional ornaments, consciously selected and quite clearly worked out. Cowley's natural taste is more for plays on words:

> What lover can like me complain,
> Who first lov'd *vainly*, next *in vain*;[11]

> 'Tis Hope is the most hopeless thing of all;[12]

and for neat similes from the natural or mythological world. Cowley's best poetry has more kinship with Pope's than with Donne's. It has precision of thought and metre, an excellence in small things, and a gay pessimism, which make *The Mistress* still good reading and *The Chronicle* and *Anacreontics* delightful. The grace and zest which Cowley was able to combine in his renderings of Anacreon may be illustrated in a quatrain:

> A mighty pain to love it is,
> And 'tis a pain that pain to miss;
> But of all pains the greatest pain
> It is to love, but love in vain.

The sections on the grasshopper and the swallow in the same series (Nos. x and xi) are fresh enough to recall Leigh Hunt and Keats, for this was a kind of miniature poetry at which Cowley was deft both in English and Latin.

On the other hand, a considerable part of Cowley's early reputation and influence derived from the fifteen *Pindaric Odes*, in which he retained rime

---

[8] *Love and Life, ed. cit.*, p. 91. Cowley follows the Ptolemaic theory.
[9] *Resolved to be Beloved*, p. 96.
[10] *Inconstancy*, p. 74.
[11] *The Vain Love*, p. 82.
[12] *Against Hope*, p. 109.

but otherwise approximated to what is now known as free verse. Two of these poems are paraphrases of two odes of Pindar; others deal with subjects selected by the poet, in some cases ethical or religious, in others political or commendatory of living men, e.g., the philosopher Hobbes and the physician Dr. Charles Scarburgh. No effort was made to reproduce the actual structure of the odes of Pindar or to supply an equivalent, and the "pseudo-Pindaric," as it came to be called, offered little outlet for Cowley's best powers. However, the form, recommended by his name, became very popular, since it looks dignified and is easy to write; and in Cowley's imitators it grew to be a nuisance, until Dr. Johnson stamped it out with a sentence. "All the boys and girls," he said, "caught the pleasing fashion, and they who could do nothing else could write like Pindar." [13]

The poetry of Andrew Marvell [14] (1621-1678), though not very copious, is of a memorable intellectual quality and of great range. Poems like *The Coronet* and *On a Drop of Dew* show his cleverness in building fluent rhythmic patterns in the service of moral conceits which verge on emblem poetry. Few poets except Crashaw have made so much of tears; note his *Mourning* and *Eyes and Tears*. The latter rises to these dubious heights:

> Ope, then, mine eyes, your double sluice,
> And practise so your noblest use.
> For others too can see or sleep,
> But only human eyes can weep.

He is a poet of the virginal pleasures of earth, described with almost fantastic subtlety, as in these lines on the joy he feels in a garden:

> The mind, that ocean where each kind
> Does straight its own resemblance find;
> Yet it creates, transcending these,
> Far other worlds and other seas,
> Annihilating all that's made
> To a green thought in a green shade.[15]

In his greatest poem, *To His Coy Mistress,* he raised the conceit to a glory which Donne never surpassed and gave mystic grandeur to the simple theme of Herrick's "Gather ye rosebuds while ye may":

[13] Alexander Brome (1620-1666) falls under the shadow of Cowley, whom he resembled in his main poetic qualities and in the outline of his life. A friend of Canary wine and an enemy of Roundheads, this trooper-lawyer was a voluble but not very ardent lover, and like Cowley was fond of complex rhythms. He had a reputation for Anacreontic joviality and wrote one comedy, *The Cunning Lovers* (1654), besides various volumes of verse (*Poems upon Several Occasions*, 1660; *Songs and Other Poems*, 1661, etc.) which, though printed after the Restoration, had been in large part written before. There is a modern selection, *Songs and Poems* (Louisville, 1924).

[14] See H. M. Margoliouth's edition of the poems and letters (2v, Oxford, 1927). See also A. Birrell, *Andrew Marvell* (EML Ser., 1905); Pierre Legouis, *André Marvell, poète, puritain, patriote* (Paris, 1928); V. Sackville-West, *Andrew Marvell* (1929); M. C. Bradbrook and M. G. Lloyd Thomas, *Andrew Marvell* (Cambridge, 1940); *Andrew Marvell, Tercentenary Tributes*, ed. W. H. Bagguley (Oxford, 1922).

[15] *The Garden.* Compare *The Nymph Complaining for the Death of Her Fawn;* and see M. C. Bradbrook, "Marvell and the Poetry of Rural Solitude," *RES*, XVII (1941). 37-46.

Had we but world enough, and time,
This coyness, Lady, were no crime. . . .
But at my back I always hear
Time's winged chariot hurrying near;
And yonder all before us lie
Deserts of vast eternity.

One who reads the intervening lines will read as fine an example as English poetry can show of wit blended with imagination; and the couplet with which the next movement of the poem ends is the perfection of tragic whimsicality:

The grave's a fine and private place,
But none, I think, do there embrace.

The son of a clergyman of moderate Puritan principles, Marvell was in politics a Parliamentarian. He sat, during the last twenty years of his life, as Member of Parliament for his native town, Hull in Yorkshire; and in 1657 became Milton's colleague in the Latin Secretaryship. His destiny, both in poetry and in politics, may have been determined by his appointment about 1650 as tutor to the daughter of the great Lord Fairfax, at whose house he lived for several years, writing in his patron's honor one of his longest poems, *Upon Appleton House,* and another, *Upon the Hill and Grove at Billborow.* These are interesting examples of local poetry, composed in what impresses us as an eighteenth-century style. To the same years at Appleton House (in Yorkshire) probably belongs most of Marvell's bucolic verse, which is best exemplified in the very charming *Mower* poems.

Much of Marvell's finest poetry deals with Oliver Cromwell, who has *Marvell or* received no juster tributes. In the *Horatian Ode upon Cromwell's Return Cromwell from Ireland* (1650) he invented a unique metre no less grave and epical than its subject; and it is typical of the candor of Marvell's political verse that the most praised lines are those on King Charles I:

He nothing common did or mean
Upon that memorable scene;
    But with his keener eye
    The axe's edge did try,

Nor call'd the gods with vulgar spite
To vindicate his helpless right,
    But bow'd his comely head
    Down as upon a bed.

In three later poems (*The First Anniversary of the Government under his Highness the Lord Protector, The Victory Obtained by Blake over the Spaniards,* and *The Death of his Highness the Lord Protector*) Marvell appraises Cromwell's government and personality in heroic couplets which, for finish and argumentative skill, have little to learn from Dryden. Dryden is likewise anticipated in two satires: *Fleckno, an English Priest at Rome*

and *The Character of Holland;* and not infrequently Marvell's couplets
seem to go beyond Dryden and find their affinities in Pope; e.g.,

> Unhappy princes, ignorantly bred,
> By malice some, by error more misled; [16]

> The object strange in him no terror mov'd:
> He wonder'd first, then pity'd, then he lov'd: [17]

or the brilliant simile with which the *First Anniversary* opens:

> Like the vain curlings of the wat'ry maze,
> Which in smooth streams a sinking weight does raise,
> So man, declining always, disappears
> In the weak circles of increasing years;
> And his short tumults of themselves compose,
> While flowing Time above his head does close.

Marvell, the friend of Milton, has very little that is Miltonic in his style.
Perhaps a slight suggestion of the young Milton may be found in the beautiful
lines on the Pilgrim Fathers, "Where the remote Bermudas ride," but it is
not close. He is a minor poet, but his few best poems are unsurpassed.

Edmund Waller [18] (1606-1687) lived over eighty years, in great worldly
and social felicity, and wrote poetry for more than sixty. He was moderate
in all things, and most moderate in his output, which hardly averaged above
four or five pages of verse a year. He polished everything he touched to such
effect that Pope admitted he was "smooth" and "sweet," [19] and the editor of
his poems in 1690 (Francis Atterbury) made for him the egregious claim that
"he was, indeed, the parent of English verse, and the first that showed us
our tongue had beauty and numbers in it." He produced a few charmingly
modulated songs; e.g., *To Phyllis* ("Phyllis, why should we delay"), *On a
Girdle,* and *Go, Lovely Rose,* in the last of which the sense and fragrance of
Jonson's "I sent thee late a rosy wreath" and Herrick's "Gather ye rosebuds"
are subtly blended. His avowed devotion to "Sacharissa" is not well authenticated, either in history or by his verse. One of his largest efforts was a brief
mock-epic, *The Battle of the Summer Islands,* on an ineffectual attempt by
the Bermudians to capture two stranded whales. A Member of Parliament
from his sixteenth year and a cherished companion in all the courts there
were, he produced acceptable panegyrics successively on Charles I, Oliver
Cromwell, Charles II, and the Prince of Orange.

Though by 1660 Waller had reached an age at which most poets have
ceased to write, half of his extant verse belongs to the Restoration period, and
he is more typical of that era than of the stormier one that preceded. His

[16] Cf. *An Essay on Criticism,* 612 f.,
> The bookful blockhead, ignorantly read,
> With loads of learned lumber in his head.
[17] Cf. *Essay on Man,* II. 217 ff.
[18] *The Poems of Edmund Waller,* ed. G. Thorn Drury (2v, 1905).
[19] *Epistle to Augustus,* line 267; *Essay on Criticism,* line 361.

favorite metre is the closed pentameter couplet, and he excels, as Pope did, in witty compliment; as in his New Year's verses to Lady Morton,

> Madam, new years may well expect to find
> Welcome from you, to whom they are so kind;

or his lines on the British navy,

> Others may use the ocean as their road,
> Only the English make it their abode; ·

or those on Lady Dorothy Sidney's (Sacharissa's) picture, which praise her above the heroines of her great-uncle's *Arcadia,*

> This glorious piece transcends what he could think,
> So much his blood is nobler than his ink.

There is not much variety in Waller, and there is little growth. The famous "last verses" in his book hardly vary in style, though they do in strength, from those he wrote for Charles I before he was twenty.[20]

More distinctly even than Waller, Sir William Davenant [21] (1606-1668) and Sir John Denham [22] (1615-1669) belong to the Restoration period, though their most characteristic work was done before 1660. Both were loyal Cavaliers and friends of Charles I. Denham produced a tragedy in indifferent blank verse for the Blackfriars, *The Sophy* (1642), on lurid treacheries at the Persian court. [23] Davenant, who had considerable talent for comedy, did a number of more or less Fletcherian plays such as *The Wits* (1634), and several others, such as *Love and Honour* (1635) and *The Platonic Lovers* (1636), which touch upon the Platonic love theme that Queen Henrietta Maria delighted in. *Davenant and Denham*

In 1642 Denham's most famous poem, *Cooper's Hill,* was published, a desultory work of over three hundred lines in loosely flowing couplets, in which the author finds it possible to do justice to the neighboring places of interest—St. Paul's Cathedral, Windsor Castle, Runnymede—and their historical associations, to pay pleasant compliments to the poet Waller and King Charles, and describe a stag hunt with much detail. The hunt is far more like the hunting scenes in Pope's *Windsor Forest* (which *Cooper's Hill* *Denham's Cooper's Hill*

---

[20] Somewhat in the style of Waller are the poems (written about 1650) of Patrick Carey, brother of the famous Lord Falkland, which were introduced to the public in 1819 by (Sir) Walter Scott under the title of *Trivial Poems and Triolets* (reprinted by Saintsbury in *Caroline Poets,* II. 445-482). They are mainly dashing cavalier ditties asserting his independence in love; but they include also (for Carey had been a Roman Catholic abbé and had recanted) some religious pieces of simple feeling and fine rhythm.

[21] There is no satisfactory modern edition of Davenant. For discussion see A. Harbage, *Sir William Davenant, Poet Venturer* (Philadelphia, 1935); A. H. Nethercot, *Sir William Davenant, Poet-Laureate and Playwright-Manager* (Chicago, 1938); and C. M. Dowlin, *Sir William Davenant's Gondibert, Its Preface and Hobbes's Answer: A Study in English Neo-classicism* (Philadelphia, 1934).

[22] Denham is handsomely provided for in *The Poetical Works of Sir John Denham,* ed. T. H. Banks (New Haven, 1928).

[23] Robert Baron's tragedy, *Mirza,* on the same theme, appeared in 1647. Baron (1630-1658), a member of Gray's Inn, plagiarist of Milton, and friend of James Howell, published in 1647 *The Cyprian Academy,* a romantic narrative in inflated prose with large insertions of song and masque, and in 1650 *Pocula Castalia* which includes *Fortune's Tennis-Ball* (a romance in *Venus and Adonis* stanza) and *Eliza* (love poems).

resembles in many respects) than like the panther hunt in Chapman's *Hymn to Cynthia,* though Chapman was very recently dead when Denham wrote, while Pope was not to be born for another half century. The most notable lines are those which, while describing the Thames, came to be accepted as the classical description also of that new ideal of restraint that was replacing the "barbarism" of the Elizabethans:

> O could I flow like thee, and make thy stream
> My great example, as it is my theme:
> Though deep yet clear, though gentle yet not dull,
> Strong without rage, without o'erflowing full!

Davenant's Gondibert

Davenant's unfinished *Gondibert* (1651) is another work of which the significance depends upon what came after. It hardly connects at any point with earlier English poetry, but is an important landmark in neo-classic art. It was to be an epic on a very modern plan, presenting love and ambition in their highest forms. The verse is in quatrains as best fitted for singing, and the structure was to parallel that of a ·Fletcherian tragicomedy, with five books divided into half a dozen cantos each, after the analogy of acts and scenes. The characters and actions were to illustrate classic notions of poetic justice and ethical grandeur. "I intended in this poem," Davenant says,[24] "to strip Nature naked and clothe her again in the perfect shape of Virtue." However, instead of completing the work at leisure in America, whither he was going in the interests of the exiled Charles II, the poet found himself in prison on the Isle of Wight under indictment for high treason against the Commonwealth, and in that emergency published the first two books with commendatory verses by Waller and Cowley.[25] The long critical preface, reinforced by an "Answer" from Thomas Hobbes the philosopher, was so important a part of the design that it was published separately in 1650, a year before the poem itself.

[24] In his "Postscript" to the edition of 1651.
[25] Book Three was written during the poet's imprisonment and included in later editions, except the "seventh and last canto," which has been very recently recovered. See J. G. Mc-Manaway, "The 'Lost' Canto of *Gondibert,*" *MLQ,* 1 (1940). 63-78.

XIII

Milton, "The Last Elizabethan"

Dr. Johnson called John Milton,[1] (1608-1674) with some justification, "an acrimonious and surly republican," and added that "scarcely any man ever wrote so much and praised so few."[2] Wordsworth contradicted such censure by saying that his soul was like a star and dwelt apart, and that he was "pure as the naked heavens, majestic, free";[3] but it is hard to avoid the impression that this tough-minded Galahad was, except in the halcyon period of his Italian journey, an unclubable man. It is no uncommon phenomenon for critics to allow a coolness toward Milton's personality to warp their judgment of his work, to the ultimate and very mortifying confusion of the critics.[4] Time may still further alienate contemporary taste from Milton's temperament and from the subject matter of his writings; but, while poetry is poetry, time is not apt to change the perception a normal reader has of coming into a priceless and inalienable possession. Milton's poetry is as arrogantly supreme as his archangel, and to those who question it needs to reply only: "Not to know me argues yourselves unknown."

In 1645, at the height of the civil wars and in Milton's thirty-seventh year, the first collection of his poems appeared.[5] It is a small volume, for which the

---

[1] The most complete edition is *The Works of John Milton* (Columbia ed., 18v, 1931-38, with three supplements and Index, 2v, 1940); abridgment in one vol., *The Student's Milton* (poetry and most important prose), ed. F. A. Patterson (1933). *The Complete Poetical Works*, ed. W. V. Moody (new ed., 1924) is still useful, as is Sir H. J. C. Grierson's ed. (2v, 1925). Other valuable texts include: *Paradise Lost, Paradise Regained, Minor Poems, and Samson Agonistes*, ed. M. Y. Hughes (2v, 1937); *Poetical Works*, ed. H. C. Beeching (Oxford, 1938); *Complete Poetry and Selected Prose*, ed. E. H. Visiak (1938). *A Milton Handbook* by J. H. Hanford (4ed., 1946) is admirable. Reference books include: E. N. S. Thompson, *John Milton, Topical Bibliography* (New Haven, 1916); D. H. Stevens, *Reference Guide to Milton from 1800 to the Present Day* (Chicago, 1930); H. F. Fletcher, *Contributions to a Milton Bibliography 1800-1930* (Urbana, 1931); J. Bradshaw, *A Concordance to the Poetical Works of John Milton* (1894); Lane Cooper, *A Concordance of the Latin, Greek, and Italian Poems of John Milton* (Halle a. S., 1923); L. E. Lockwood, *Lexicon of the English Poetical Works of John Milton* (1907); A. H. Gilbert, *A Geographical Dictionary of Milton* (New Haven, 1919); C. G. Osgood, *The Classical Mythology of Milton's English Poems* (new ed., Oxford, 1925); G. Sherburn, "The Early Popularity of Milton's Minor Poems," *MP*, XVII (1919-20). 259-278, 515-540; R. D. Havens, *The Influence of Milton on English Poetry* (Cambridge, Mass., 1922); Robert Bridges, *Milton's Prosody* (Oxford, 1921). The *Life of John Milton* by David Masson (7v, 1858-1881, with Index, 1894) is a venerable and imposing monument. *Milton* by Walter Raleigh (1900) is still one of the best introductions to the poet; and Rose Macaulay's briefer sketch, *Milton* (1935), is to be commended. Fuller discussion in E. M. W. Tillyard, *Milton* (1930), and *The Miltonic Setting* (Cambridge, 1938); and in Hilaire Belloc, *Milton* (1935).

[2] In *Lives of the Most Eminent English Poets* (1779).

[3] Sonnet, *London, 1802*.

[4] See L. P. Smith, *Milton and his Modern Critics* (1941); Douglas Bush, *"Paradise Lost" in Our Time* (Ithaca, 1945).

[5] *Poems of Mr. John Milton, both English and Latin*, facsimile edition (Douglas Replicas, 1924).

publisher, Moseley, found a very fit description: "as true a birth as the muses have brought forth since our famous Spenser wrote." In his early poetry Milton turned as naturally to Spenser for inspiration as Spenser had to Chaucer. The intervening Spenserians moved him to little except some technical experiments,—as to try abbreviated variations of the nine-line stanza like the Fletcher brothers, or, like Browne of Tavistock, test the powers of the short couplet. The intervening anti-Spenserians of Donne's school moved him to hardly anything except an occasional slur on

> those new-fangled toys and trimming slight,
> Which takes our late fantastics with delight.[6]

Milton was an accomplished poet at seventeen, as is proved by the charming elegy for his niece, *On the Death of a Fair Infant:*

> O fairest flower, no sooner blown but blasted,
> Soft silken primrose fading timelessly.

It may suggest Keats more than Spenser,[7] but it is quite lovely, and is most Miltonic in the last stanza, which shows the poet already brooding on immortality. He bids his bereaved sister accept God's visitation with patience:

> This if thou do, he will an offspring give
> That till the world's last end shall make thy name to live,

such a child, that is, as Milton was; but his sister's next son was only Edward Phillips. The stanza is rime royal, Spenserized by substitution of an alexandrine in the seventh line. The same stanza is employed in the unfinished and unpromising ode on *The Passion* (1630) and in the introductory movement of the great ode *On the Morning of Christ's Nativity,* composed about Christmas, 1629, just after Milton's twenty-first birthday. The "hymn," of which this ode mainly consists, may seem less Spenserian, and indeed less Miltonic, for its religious spirit is as much Catholic as Puritan, and it has a naïve sensibility which may reflect the influence of Milton's Italian studies; but it is one of the most perfect poems in literature.[8] Since Spenser's *Epithalamion* there had been nothing that for sustained grace of rime and rhythm could well compare with these twenty-seven eight-line stanzas on the pattern, $a_3a_3b_5c_3c_3b_5d_4d_6$:

> The lonely mountains o'er,
> And the resounding shore,
> A voice of weeping heard and loud lament;
> From haunted spring and dale,
> Edged with poplar pale,
> The parting Genius is with sighing sent;

[6] *At a Vacation Exercise.* See G. R. Potter, "Milton's Early Poems, the School of Donne, and the Elizabethan Sonneteers," *PQ,* vi (1927). 396-400.

[7] The actual inspiration, as Tillyard notes, may have been the tenth poem in *The Passionate Pilgrim,* which in Milton's time was assumed to be Shakespeare's.

[8] See A. S. Cook, "Notes on Milton's Ode on the Morning of Christ's Nativity," *Trans. Conn. Acad.,* xv (1909). 307-368; Arthur Barker, "The Pattern of Milton's *Nativity Ode.*" *Univ. of Toronto Quar.,* x (1941). 167-181.

With flower-inwoven tresses torn
The Nymphs in twilight shade of tangled thickets mourn.

Three later and much briefer poems with religious application—*At a Solemn Music, On Time,* and *Upon the Circumcision*—show him developing his organ music in long sentences which, though still intricately rimed, foreshadow the verse paragraphs of *Paradise Lost.* At the same time he was essaying more staccato effects in the fine couplets on Shakespeare, "What needs my Shakespeare for his honor'd bones" (1630), which, being printed in the Second Folio two years later, was the first of Milton's English poems to be published.[9]

The two poems on the death of old Hobson (1631), a well-known Cambridge figure, do not fail of the rudimentary wit they attempt, but in Milton's career they are only curiosities.[10] More significant is the ambitious epitaph on the Marchioness of Winchester (1631), for the tetrameter verse in which it is composed looks like practice work for *L'Allegro* and *Il Penseroso.* There is not a great deal to indicate whether these latter two suavely brilliant poems were written before Milton left Cambridge in 1632 or during the following years, which he spent at his father's country house at Horton near Stoke Poges.[11] Various "sources" for the pair have been suggested.[12] Milton is likely, for example, to have had in mind Burton's riming introduction to the *Anatomy of Melancholy,* published in the previous decade (1621); but his primary model was doubtless the companion poems, by Marlowe and Ralegh respectively, which he could have known in the *Passionate Pilgrim* volume of 1612 as well as from commonplace books. Marlowe's lyric concludes,

> And if these pleasures may thee move,
> Then live with me and be my love;

and Ralegh's,

> These pretty pleasures might me move
> To live with thee and be thy love.

Milton's endings seem to echo them; but it is characteristic that he puts himself in the place of the passionate shepherd's nymph, and fancies himself wooed by two ways of life.

The two poems are most artfully balanced and contrasted. Each opens with a ten-line strophe, riming $a_3b_5b_3a_5c_3d_5d_3e_5e_3c_5$; and then passes into tetrameter couplets, in which iambic and trochaic rhythms are restfully in-

(margin: L'Allegro and Il Penseroso)

---

[9] See H. W. Garrod, "Milton's Lines on Shakespeare," *E&S,* xii (1926). 1-23.
[10] See W. R. Parker, "Milton's Hobson Poems," *MLR,* xxxi (1936). 395-402; G. B. Evans, "Two New Manuscript Versions of Milton's Hobson Poems," *MLN,* lvii (1942). 192-194, and "Milton and the Hobson Poems," *MLQ,* iv (1943). 281-290.
[11] On these poems see Tillyard, *The Miltonic Setting,* pp. 1-28; and S. R. Watson, "Milton's Ideal Day; Its Development as a Pastoral Theme," *PMLA,* lvii (1942). 404-420.
[12] See J. L. Lowes, *"L'Allegro* and *The Passionate Shepherd,"* *MLR,* vi (1911). 206-209; S. F. Damon, "Milton and Marston," *PMLA,* xlii (1927). 873-874, and A. Thaler, *PMLA,* xliii (1928). 569-570; Lawrence Babb, "The Background of *Il Penseroso," SP,* xxxvii (1940). 257-273.

termingled—though there are, as is proper, twice as many of the lighter trochaic lines in the poem addressed to Mirth as in the other. There is little extended nature description or autobiographical detail in *L'Allegro* and *Il Penseroso*. The great merits of these poems are curiously like those of the famous *Elegy* of that other London scrivener's son, Thomas Gray, who, if he had lived a century earlier, would have been Milton's near neighbor in Buckinghamshire. Milton lacks the special "graveyard" interest and strain of sentimentality; his vignettes are sharper, but, like Gray's, they express the reflections of a bookish man in pastoral scenery with a supreme felicity. Marvell may sometimes have approached perfection in this genre, but few others, surely, in English poetry.

he Lawes   From his boyhood in London, Milton had been a friend of the talented
rothers   brothers, Henry and William Lawes, now prominent musicians and gentle-
men of the King's Chapel. The elder and more eminent brother, Henry,[13] was also music-tutor in the family of the Earl of Bridgewater; and it was probably through this connection that Milton was brought to attempt the
rcades   masque in *Arcades,* or "The Arcadians," which has interesting associations. It was written soon after the poet had left Cambridge, and was presented in honor of the Countess Dowager of Derby, the matriarch of the numerous and powerful family to which Lord Bridgewater belonged. This great lady was the last survivor of the three sisters with whom Spenser had claimed kinship,

> The honor of the noble family,
> Of which I meanest boast myself to be.[14]

As Lady Strange, Spenser had made her patroness of his *Tears of the Muses,* and as Amaryllis he had praised her in *Colin Clout's Come Home Again.* Now, twice widowed and a septuagenarian, she still resided at Harefield, ten miles or so from Horton, where she had been mistress for thirty years and had entertained Queen Elizabeth in 1602. Milton's contribution to the open-air pageant which the old lady's family produced for her amusement is in the spirit of this history. *Arcades* is not a Stuart masque but an Elizabethan "entertainment," such as the Virgin Queen had been habitually greeted with in her progresses. It is very short, consisting merely of fifty-eight lines of mythologizing compliment spoken by the "Genius of the Wood" and three delightful songs, of which the last,

> Nymphs and shepherds, dance no more
> By sandy Ladon's lilied banks,

evokes the whole wistful beauty of the Greek pastoral.

Shortly after this, the Earl of Bridgewater, who had married the Countess of Derby's daughter and was besides her stepson, took up his residence at
'omus   Ludlow Castle, Shropshire, as Lord President of Wales, and there *Comus* was presented, September 29, 1634. As in *Arcades,* Milton supplied the words

---

[13] See W. M. Evans, *Henry Lawes, Musician and Friend of Poets* (1941).
[14] *Colin Clout's Come Home Again,* lines 537 f.

and Henry Lawes the music.[15] Lawes also played the part of the Attendant Spirit, while the two brothers and the lady in the piece were acted by the three youthful children of the earl, grandchildren of the lady of *Arcades*. *Comus* is Milton's first poem in blank verse. It is, indeed, the only thing of any importance that he wrote in that form before *Paradise Lost;* but his mastery is apparent in the first sentence,

> Before the starry threshold of Jove's court
> My mansion is, . . .

which in eleven lines sweeps the hearer from heaven to earth and back again, and in referring to "the crown that Virtue gives" sets the theme not only for this poem but for most of what Milton wrote later.[16] Virtue is, in truth, the theme of *Comus;* not chastity merely, and not the "fugitive and cloistered virtue," which Milton cannot praise, "unexercised and unbreathed, that never sallies out and sees her adversary"; [17] but something closer to the Virtue which, as Marlowe's Tamburlaine had said,

> solely is the sum of glory,
> And fashions men with true nobility,[18]

the dynamic Virtue that, in Milton's words,

> could see to do what Virtue would,
> By her own radiant light, though sun and moon
> Were in the flat sea sunk,[19]

and which

> may be assail'd, but never hurt,
> Surpris'd by unjust force, but not enthrall'd;
> Yea, even that which Mischief meant most harm
> Shall in the happy trial prove most glory.[20]

In it, as is declared in the poem's closing words, are summed up human freedom, aspiration, and security:

> Mortals that would follow me,
> Love Virtue; she alone is free;
> She can teach you how to climb
> Higher than the sphery chime:
> Or if Virtue feeble were,
> Heaven itself would stoop to her.

Comus is a true enough masque. It combines in pleasing balance the usual elements of personal compliment, classic story, and opulent song; it provides

[15] There is a handsome edition, with the music: *The Mask of Comus*, ed. E. H. Visiak (Nonesuch Press, 1938).
[16] See A. S. P. Woodhouse, "The Argument of Milton's *Comus*," *Univ. of Toronto Quar.*, XI (1941). 46-71; E. M. W. Tillyard, "The Action of *Comus*," *E&S*, XXVIII (1943). 22-37.
[17] *Areopagitica* (1644).
[18] See above, Part II, ch. XI.
[19] *Comus*, lines 373 ff.
[20] *Comus*, lines 589 ff.

for the "measure" or main dance and for elaborate scenic spectacle, and has moments of dramatic tension. But it must have been very surprising to those who came to it with minds attuned either to Prynne's recent moral castigation of the masques or to Bacon's condescending words, "These things are but toys."

ycidas   Milton, in his early poems, was a perfectionist beyond almost any other English writer except Gray. When called upon for a contribution to the memorial volume in honor of his college friend, Edward King, who had been drowned in the Irish Sea in August, 1637, he still thought of himself, though near the end of his twenty-ninth year, as an uncouth (i.e., untaught) swain, "warbling his Doric lay," a phrase which means much the same as the "native woodnotes wild" that he imputed to Shakespeare. The incomparable *Lycidas*, "probably the most perfect piece of pure literature in existence," [21] opens with an apology for the poet's immaturity which is as sincerely humble as it is obviously unnecessary:

> Yet once more, O ye laurels . . .
> I come to pluck your berries harsh and crude,
> And with forc'd fingers rude
> Shatter your leaves before the mellowing year.

Lycidas almost eludes criticism. It was possible for Dr. Johnson to miss its beauties altogether, and it is very common for its beauties to drive commentators into wholly uncritical ecstasies. Milton's own appraisal is sound, though phrased too self-depreciatingly,

> He touch'd the tender stops of various quills; [22]

that is, he handled, in a tentative manner, a number of styles. The voice of St. Peter, thundering against King's self-indulgent fellow-clerics (lines 108-131), is very different from that of the Sicilian Muse, piping the purest pagan pastoralism (132-151); and both are unlike the voice in which Milton questions his own destiny (64-84), or the other voice, by no means too conventional or too restrained, in which at the opening and the close he testifies to his friendship with King and to the pathos of the latter's premature end.

Though an astonishingly short poem to hold all the electric charges that it contains—it has 193 lines—*Lycidas* was over long in comparison with the other contributions to the anthology for which it was written. Milton has expressed his feelings in four or five movements, not, as he recognized himself, very logically connected. They are, however, fundamentally connected by the underlying theme, *Ars longa, vita brevis,* and develop the emotion of the sonnet on his twenty-third year. That sonnet had been written at the close of his long training at Cambridge; *Lycidas* was written five or six years

---

[21] Arthur Machen, *The Hill of Dreams* (*Works*, 1923, III. 127). See J. C. Ransom, "A Poem almost Anonymous" in *The World's Body* (1938), pp. 1-28; T. P. Harrison, *The Pastoral Elegy* (Austin, 1939). For the poet's original version see F. A. Patterson, *The Cambridge Manuscript of John Milton's Lycidas and Some of the Other Poems, Reproduced from the Collotype Facsimile* (Facsimile Text Soc., 1933).

[22] *Lycidas,* line 188.

later, near the close of his further training at Horton. His spring is still late, his destiny uncertain, and King's untimely death forces angry questions from him, concerning

> The lyf so short, the craft so long to lerne;
> Th' assay so hard, so sharp the conquering.[23]

The "blind mouths" at whom St. Peter rails

> Creep, and intrude, and climb into the fold,

and are content; while the unrecovered bones of King, who had shared Milton's ascetic discipline, are the plaything of life's accidents, hurled beyond the stormy Hebrides, or otherwise into nullity. "Alas, what boots it?" he asks of his own life.

> Were it not better done, as others use,
> To sport with Amaryllis in the shade?

The elegy, like the sonnet, is the outcry of one spur-galled by Fame, which he can call by no better title than "that last infirmity of noble mind," and can hope for nowhere but in heaven. It is no easy thing to make oneself the last of the giant race. Nothing would satisfy Milton but to be a Spenser, and nothing that his age created seemed to be above the stature of a Marvell. This is the heart-breaking truth of *Lycidas*. The Spenserian trumpet is at last in his hand, perfect in every varied cadence and learned grace—the soul-animating strains await his call—and life has given him no will to blow it.

Milton's nineteen [24] English sonnets, supplemented by five others and a canzone in Italian, have an importance out of all proportion to their number. Scattered thinly over nearly thirty years of his life, they give the most consecutive record of his poetic feeling, from the fragile love-longing of the first one, *To the Nightingale* (c. 1630), to the august vision of his deceased wife in 1658. If his sonnets are to be compared with any earlier ones in English, it must be with Sidney's; but the connection is not close. The movement Sidney started had faded out, and Milton kindled the lamp afresh at Italian fires. It may be guessed that his school-companion, Charles Diodati, was the cause of his special Italian interests, and probably the means of his acquaintance with the Italian girl, a certain Emilia, to whom he wrote the six poems in her own tongue that exhibit a remarkable ease and correctness. They develop very pleasantly the amorous note of the "nightingale" sonnet and probably followed it closely in date.

The sonnet on his three-and-twentieth year, written most likely after he had become twenty-four (December 9, 1632),[25] introduces a sober note which

Milton's Sonnets

[23] Chaucer, *The Parlement of Foules.*

[24] One is the "caudate" or tailed sonnet, "Because you have thrown off your prelate lord." The best edition of Milton's sonnets is that of J. S. Smart (Glasgow, 1921). See J. H. Hanford, "The Arrangement and Dates of Milton's Sonnets," *MP*, XVIII (1921). 475-483.

[25] See W. R. Parker, "Some Problems in the Chronology of Milton's Early Poems," *RES*, XI (1935). 276-283.

thereafter is seldom absent. Those to the "Captain, or colonel, or knight-in-arms" (1642) and to the unknown young lady who had chosen "the better part with Mary and with Ruth"; the friendly ones to the Lady Margaret Ley, Harry Lawes, Edward Lawrence, and Cyriac Skinner, and the obituary on another old friend, Mrs. Katherine Thomason, show Milton in more genial mood than anything else that he wrote after Diodati's death; but there is deep gravity in all these, for Milton did not lightly turn to sonneting. For the rest, indignation over the abuse of his divorce pamphlets, the massacre in Piedmont, his blindness, the loneliness that followed the loss of his most beloved wife,[26] and four great political crises lighted the slow fires in which they were annealed. All are strictly Italian in form, more in the sixteenth-century style of Tasso and Giovanni della Casa than in the earlier style of Petrarch. In only one of the English sonnets, that addressed to Cromwell, does the sestet conclude with a couplet, though three of the Italian ones have this ending. In just half, the sense is carried on vigorously from octave to sestet without appreciable pause, and this half includes the four most famous examples: "Cromwell, our chief of men," "Avenge, O Lord," "When I consider how my light is spent," and "Methought I saw my late espoused saint." This feature, though not according to the Petrarchan plan, is neither an innovation nor a blemish. Milton would have been less Milton, if he had not seen the value of such *enjambement*. The nineteen sonnets are like a hoard of ancient coins, few and precious. They are deeply, but frugally, incised, heavy with significance and intrinsic worth, and for all posterity they bear a Caesarian superscription.

[26] On the question which wife this was, see W. R. Parker, "Milton's Last Sonnet," *RES*, XXI (1945). 235-238.

XIV
Milton's Latin Poems and Prose Works

The technique of Milton's Latin poems,[1] like that of his sonnets, has always been most highly praised by those, from Dr. Johnson to Professor Rand,[2] who have best understood the history and aims of the medium in which he worked. "In all the Latin poems of Milton," said Macaulay,[3] "the artificial manner indispensable to such works is admirably preserved, while at the same time his genius gives to them a peculiar charm, an air of nobleness and freedom, which distinguishes them from all other writings of the same class." Classic as his language is, Milton was not merely attempting replicas of antique correctness. He was also competing with such impressive modern rivals as George Buchanan (1506-1582), with men, that is, who had found Latin verse the most practical conveyor of their most earnest thought. When he had persuaded himself, as he tells us in the *Reason of Church Government* (1641), that "I might perhaps leave something so written to aftertimes as they should not willingly let it die," it was to Latin, and the world-audience that Latin then commanded, that he mainly addressed his efforts. Only slowly, "long choosing and beginning late," did he realize that "it would be hard to arrive at the second rank among the Latins," and so resolve "to fix all the industry and art I could unite to the adorning of my native tongue."

Milton's Latin Poems

When Milton published his Latin poems in the volume of 1645, he divided them, in accordance with a pedantic convention of his time, into two books distinguished only by the metres employed; that is, a book of "elegies" in the Ovidian couplet, and another book of *"silvae"* in other forms. This separation must be disregarded by those who wish to study them either chronologically or in relation to subject matter. His earliest extant Latin verses date from the period of his residence at Cambridge (1625-1632), and some are, like his *Prolusions* in Latin prose,[4] incidental to his regular studies. The short epitaph on the university "Bedell" (*Elegy* ii, 1626) is little more than a more learned parallel to the English verses on Hobson which he was writing about the same time. The contemporary poems on the deaths of Launcelot

---

[1] The text, often with a prose translation, is found in most editions of Milton's poetry. See previous chapter, note 1, and also W. MacKellar, *The Latin Poems of John Milton* (New Haven, 1930); L. Bradner, *Musae Anglicanae* (1940), pp. 111-118; G. B. A. Fletcher, "Milton's Latin Poems," *MP*, xxxvii (1940). 343-350; F. R. B. Godolphin, "Notes on the Technique of Milton's Latin Elegies," *MP*, xxxvii (1940). 351-356. The Latin poems have been translated into English verse by William Cowper (1808) and by Walter Skeat, *Milton's Lament for Damon and His Other Latin Poems* (1935).

[2] See E. K. Rand, "Milton in Rustication," *SP*, xix (1922). 109-135.

[3] Essay on Milton (1825).

[4] See P. B. and E. M. W. Tillyard, *Milton: Private Correspondence and Academic Exercises, translated from the Latin* (Cambridge, 1932).

Andrewes, Bishop of Winchester (*Elegy* iii), the Bishop of Ely (*Silvae* iii), and the Vice-Chancellor of Cambridge (*Silvae* i), cleverly suited to the professions of their subjects and most adroitly phrased, belong with the English lines on the death of the Marchioness of Winchester. The longer epic piece on the Fifth of November (*Silvae* ii, 1626), in 226 hexameters, follows an already established tradition of celebrating the frustration of the Gunpowder Plot of 1605 in Latin verse. Phineas Fletcher's *Locustae,* on the same subject and in similar style, though not printed till 1627, had been circulating in manuscript for some fifteen years.[5] It is characteristic of the young Milton that he secures his dénouement by the combined efforts of the Christian God and the Virgilian deity, Fama. Five brief epigrams in elegiac verse have dropped like chips about this larger work. They combine allusions to the death of James I in 1625 with remembrances of his escape from the gunpowder treason.

Formal university occasions produced the eloquent hexameter declamation, "That Nature is not subject to old age," [6] which smacks of Lucretius and effectively contrasts the pagan and Christian ideas of the fate of the universe, and also produced a sort of dramatic monologue in iambic trimeter,[7] in which the poet imagines Aristotle ridiculing the Platonic conception of the "archetype" or perfect man. But no formal occasion produced the fine fifth elegy, *On the Coming of Spring,* written at the age of twenty during Milton's fourth year at Cambridge (1629). Linking wistful thoughts of love with a charming susceptibility to vernal impulses, this poem is in mood like the sonnet to the nightingale and the brief English *Song on May Morning,* but it is ten times as long, and is Milton's prettiest piece of paganism. Less mature and more mawkish is the other May poem, written the year before, but printed at the end of the series of elegies (*Elegy* vii), which records a fit of boyish love for a girl he has seen but once. It is reassuring to know that Milton could be very young, and the poem has had more than its meed of praise. Nothing in it is more sophomoric than the postscript, which announces that the author's Socratic studies at the university have now made him immune to such follies.

The rest of Milton's Latin poems are, with hardly an exception, tributes of friendship or attempts at self-analysis. They have a direct personal quality which only rarely breaks through the Olympian grandeur of his English poetry. Chief of all his friends was Charles Diodati, his Anglo-Italian schoolmate at St. Paul's, who has the place in Milton's life that Richard West has in Gray's. When Milton, like Gray, went to Cambridge, Diodati, like West, had chosen Oxford, and the correspondence between them produced the richest outpouring that we have of the young poet's private thoughts. The first of the Elegies was written to Diodati during Milton's second year at Cambridge. It was written, however, from his father's house in London, to which he had been "sent down" or rusticated in consequence of some infrac-

[5] See above, Part ii, ch. x; and L. Bradner, *op. cit.,* pp. 69-71.
[6] *Silvae* iv (1628?): *Naturam Non Pati Senium.*
[7] *Silvae* v: *De Idea Platonica quemadmodum Aristoteles Intellexit.*

tion of college discipline, presumed to have been a disagreement with his tutor. It is a delightful poem, thoroughly undergraduate. He speaks with a touch of braggadocio of his disregard for Cambridge and his pleasure at being in London, of his joy in quiet reading and (as in *L'Allegro*) in playgoing; then launches into a long praise of the London girls, and ends by saying that he is about to return to college. The next extant verse letter to Diodati was written several years later, in the Christmas season of 1629. It was printed as the sixth elegy, and is contemporary with the ode *On the Morning of Christ's Nativity,* to which it makes important reference in its closing lines. In this very illuminating poem, written just after Milton had passed his twenty-first birthday, we see him poised between the lighter and the severer muse. Taking his hint from the letter of Diodati to which he is replying, he begins by generously praising the poetry of sensuous emotion, such as his own May poems were; and then, in words that have been often quoted (lines 55 ff.), he takes his stand with the epic moralists who have scorned delights and lived laborious days. One of the Italian sonnets is addressed to Diodati, and two letters in Latin prose have survived out of the probably large correspondence between them, but nothing else on Milton's side till Diodati's early death evoked the *Epitaphium Damonis.*

Diodati died at London in August, 1638, just a year after Edward King; but Milton was then in Florence, and he did not put his sorrow into words till two years later, when he had returned to the sights they had known together. A reversed parallel occurred, long after, when Arthur Hugh Clough died in Florence (1864) and in the course of time Arnold wrote his *Thyrsis,* the poem which the *Epitaphium Damonis* ("The Lament for Damon") most resembles. This is almost the barest of Milton's poems, and is more Greek in spirit than Latin. There is a marked avoidance of the mythological ornament that Milton uses with such luxuriant grace elsewhere, and the pastoral convention seems to be maintained with difficulty; chiefly, one might say, through the oft repeated refrain by which, in the fashion of Theocritus and Moschus, he divides the moods of grief,

Epitaphiu Damonis

> Ite domum, impasti; domino iam non vacat, agni.
>
> Go, go, my lambs, untended homeward fare;
> My thoughts are all now due to other care.[8]

The reality of Milton's loss and the genuineness of his sorrow are unquestionable. It is dry sorrow, sometimes expressed in words of Arnoldian bitterness; e.g.,

> We men, Fate-driven, endure a sterner life:
> Minds all estrangement, hearts distract with strife.
> Scarce, haply, shalt thou find,
> E'en out of thousands, one true kindred mind.

[8] Cowper's translation.

> Or if thy vows from Chance win late relief,
> Some day, some hour unween'd of, shall betide
> To snatch him from thy side,
> Leaving thee agelong, nay, eternal, grief.[9]

With the exception of the early poem on the Fifth of November, this is the longest of Milton's Latin poems. Toward the end (lines 162 ff.), he outlines briefly the contents of a Latin epic from early British history which he has been meditating; and, as if such projects were distasteful without Diodati, says that he will abandon poetry, or content himself to write in a language which will confine his fame to his native island, for "omnia non licet uni," one man cannot do all things. Rather curiously, the final picture of Damon's reception into heaven is introduced by the most highly colored passage in the poem, a description of the two ornate "cups" which Milton had received from the Marquis Manso.[10]

The finely self-portraying poem to his father (*Silvae* vi) has not been certainly dated, but seems to belong to the latter rather than the earlier part

,d Patrem

of the Horton period (1632-1638). It presents a much more confirmed mind than the sonnet on his twenty-third year and acknowledges opportunities for culture in excess of a college education. It shows also that any desire the elder Milton had to see his son follow him into the legal profession had been definitely given up. The subject is Milton's choice of a poet's life, which he now regards as final, and the purpose is to thank his father for extraordinary generosity and to disabuse his mind of doubts which the poet in no way shares. He is modest, affectionate, and respectful; but he sees immortality in no too distant prospect. One would say that *Comus*, if not *Lycidas*, was behind him when he wrote. Whatever the respective dates, *Ad Patrem* is a more assured poem than *Lycidas*.

Of the complimentary poems written by Milton during his Italian journey

1ilton's
Compli-
nentary
oems

of 1638-39, the one to the Roman poet, Salsilli,[11] is content to be semi-humorous, and is designedly written in the ungainly *scazontes*, or "limping" trimeter. Salsilli was ill, and Renaissance etiquette prescribed light verse from his literary friends during convalescence. The three epigrams to the Roman singer, Leonora Baroni, express the proper adulation of a music-lover for a *diva*. The poem to Manso, the venerable Marquis of Villa,[12]

1ansus

though also full of flattery (for Milton had much kindness to repay), is of noble quality. "Never before," Macaulay said of it, "were such marked originality and such exquisite mimicry found together." Milton recalls that Manso had been the loyal friend and patron of two great poets, Tasso and Marini; and this leads him to assert the claim of the Britons to have been also worshippers of Apollo in ages past, and his own expectation of writing a poem on the wars of King Arthur. When Milton gave his mind to it, he

---

[9] Lines 106-111, Skeat's translation.
[10] See M. de Filippis, "Milton and Manso: Cups or Books?" *PMLA*, LI (1936). 745-756; D. C. Dorian, "Milton's *Epitaphium Damonis*, lines 181-197," *PMLA*, LIV (1939). 612-613.
[11] *Silvae* VII.
[12] *Silvae* VIII.

could excel most poets in the arts of complaisance. With these adult examples might be compared the boyishly affectionate letter (*Elegy* iv) written at the age of eighteen to his former tutor, Thomas Young; [13] and the last of all his Latin poems, the Pindaresque ode, both grave and gay in mood, which he addressed in 1647 to the Librarian of the Bodleian, John Rouse, when making a wartime gift of his published works to his second university of Oxford.

Milton's verse is small in amount, when compared with that of the other greatest English poets. Chaucer, Spenser, Shakespeare, Wordsworth, Tennyson, and Browning, for example, have all left a great deal more; but no supreme poet, perhaps, except Goethe has left so much or such important prose.[14] It is in Latin and in English, according as he was addressing himself to international or to native readers, and it touches all the themes and emotions which moved him deeply. There is no light prose in Milton. It is the prose of a classical humanist, and the question it raises for modern readers is the question of decorum. It ranges constantly from earth to heaven, from violent and vulgar invective to passages of truly poetical loftiness. It is continually passing above or below the narrow scope of our polite writers, but to call it rude, or allege that in Milton "a useful art had not learned to be also fine," is to apply irrelevant standards. Prose was never in low esteem with the Renaissance scholars in whose tradition Milton wrote.[15] They were apt to set Cicero and Demosthenes not far below Virgil and Homer as artists, and would seldom admit that poetry was necessarily verse-writing. The Bible, which was the book of books, offered a vast gradation of styles. Milton used them all in his prose, and perhaps extended the lower reaches; but in nearly all his English pamphlets, and most frequently in *Areopagitica* (1644), he would soar, when fit emotion warmed him, into starry symphonies which an admirer of literary art would no more wish to be expressed in verse than he would wish *Paradise Lost* written in the metre of *Lycidas*.

In a famous autobiographical digression in one of his earliest controversial pieces,[16] Milton admits that in such writing he has "the use, as I may account it, but of my left hand," and speaks of himself as "sitting here below in the cool element of prose." But his left hand quickly acquired all the

Milton's Prose

---

[13] See W. R. Parker, "Milton and Thomas Young, 1620-1628," *MLN*, LIII (1938). 399-407.

[14] *The Prose Works of John Milton* have been edited by J. A. St. John (5v, 1848-1853); convenient selections by Henry Morley (1889) and M. W. Wallace (World's Classics, 1925), the latter with an excellent introduction. See also E. N. S. Thompson, "The True Bearing of Milton's Prose" in *Essays on Milton* (New Haven, 1914, ch. III), and "Milton's Prose Style," *PQ*, XIV (1935). 1-15; and for historical background D. M. Wolfe, *Milton in the Puritan Revolution* (1941); and M. Y. Hughes, "Milton as a Revolutionary," *ELH*, X (1943). 87-116. The following recent works bear helpfully upon Milton's life and political standing: J. S. Diekhoff, *Milton on Himself* (1939), and "Critical Activity of the Poetic Mind: John Milton," *PMLA*, LV (1940). 748-772; J. M. French, *Milton in Chancery, New Chapters in the Lives of the Poet and his Father* (1939); W. R. Parker, *Milton's Contemporary Reputation . . . with a Tentative List of Printed Allusions to Milton, 1641-1674*, etc. (Columbus, O., 1940); J. M. French, "That Late Villain Milton," *PMLA*, LV (1940). 102-115; Z. S. Fink, *The Classical Republicans* (Evanston, 1945; *Northwestern Univ. Stud. in the Humanities*, IX).

[15] See J. H. Hanford, "Milton and the Return to Humanism," *SP*, XVI (1919). 126-147.

[16] *The Reason of Church Government*, Book II (Wallace, *ed. cit.*, p. 109).

rather horrid skills of contemporary polemic, and his prose was very seldom cool. The remarkable last paragraph of another early pamphlet [17] shows how easily he can combine sinuous majesty of style and real exaltation of spirit with sentiments which we should hardly judge appropriate,—wishing and solemnly asserting that ambitious prelates of Laud's type "after a shameful end in this life (which God grant them) shall be thrown down eternally into the darkest and deepest gulf of hell ..." So Dante might have written, but on the previous page there is a sentence that more suggests Sir Walter Ralegh:

That we may still remember in our solemn thanksgivings, how for us the northern ocean, even to the frozen Thule, was scattered with the proud shipwrecks of the Spanish Armada, and the very maw of hell ransacked, and made to give up her concealed destruction, ere she could vent it in that horrible and damned blast.

As Milton's early feelings are best known to us through his Latin poems, so his mature personality is most fully presented in his prose. The four tracts on divorce (1643-1645), though immediately occasioned by his unsatisfactory experience with his ill-chosen first wife, Mary Powell, are very ably reasoned and contain some of his most sympathetic writing. There is something pitiful in the ardor with which he pleads for a more than physical basis of matrimony and a more liberal interpretation of ecclesiastical law:

Was our Saviour so mild and so favorable to the weakness of a single man, and is he turned on the sudden so rigorous and inexorable to the distresses and extremities of an ill-wedded man? Did he so graciously give leave to change the better single life for the worse married life? Did he open so to us this hazardous and accidental door of marriage to shut upon us like the gate of death, without retracting or returning ... ? [18]

The divorce pamphlets and the great *Areopagitica*, "for the liberty of unlicensed printing," of the same period made Milton a marked man with many calumniators, but had little effect upon the opinions of the Parliament to which they were addressed. He replied to his enemies in his three least dignified sonnets, accepted the submission of his wife, and during three or four years devoted himself to the intense studies that resulted in his imposing *History of Britain* [19] and his enormous Latin treatise on *Christian Doctrine.*[20] The arraignment of Charles I brought him once more before the public with one of his best argued and quietest, though boldest, pamphlets, *The Tenure of Kings and Magistrates,*[21] in which from the proposition that "All men were naturally born free" he develops the principle of the social contract and the corollary that subjects are justified in putting an unworthy

---

[17] *Of Reformation Touching Church-discipline.*
[18] *The Doctrine and Discipline of Divorce* (1645), Book II, ch. 9.
[19] See J. M. French, "Milton as a Historian," *PMLA*, L (1935). 469-479.
[20] See J. H. Hanford, "The Date of Milton's *De Doctrina Christiana,*" *SP*, XVII (1920). 309-319; Arthur Sewell, *A Study of Milton's Christian Doctrine* (Oxford, 1939); Maurice Kelley, *This Great Argument, a Study of Milton's De Doctrina Christiana as a Gloss upon Paradise Lost* (Princeton, 1941).
[21] Ed. W. T. Allison (1911).

king to death.[22] He closes with an attack upon the Presbyterians, who, after warring against King Charles and imprisoning him, were now opposing his trial by Parliament.

Parliament was grateful for this justification, which happened to appear in print just after the king's execution (February, 1649), and Milton in the next month was appointed Secretary for Foreign Tongues in the Council of State. This gave him charge of the government's foreign correspondence a.id made him the official apologist of the Commonwealth régime. In *Eikonoklastes* ("Image-breaker") he fell with partisan fury upon the *Eikon Basilike* ("King's Image"), allegedly the pious work of the now beheaded Charles, which sentimental reaction was investing with a dangerous popularity.[23] When the cause of the martyred king and his exiled son found advocates abroad, he turned to Latin, and without repining sacrificed the sight of his over-strained eyes [24] in preparing his laborious and almost medievally violent *Defense of the English People* (1651) against the learned and abusive Salmasius. His *Second Defense* (1654) is of similar nature. The excellence of its Latin gilded the arguments and barbed the personalities it contained; but it contains a justification of Milton's own career and a laudation of Cromwell and his supporters that would be resplendent in any language.

Other pamphlets in English were called forth by the political uncertainties that followed Cromwell's death in 1658. The last and most impressive was issued in several editions in the spring of 1660, when the return of the Stuarts was becoming more and more inevitable. Its title was a challenge: *The Ready and Easy Way to Establish a Free Commonwealth, and the Excellence Thereof Compared with the Inconveniences and Dangers of Readmitting Kingship in This Nation.*[25] Milton knew how the nation was tending and spoke bold words against "this noxious humor of returning to bondage," justifying the treatment Charles I had received and begging his countrymen not to be less steadfast for liberty than the Dutch. If they allow king and bishops to return, he says,

we may be forced perhaps to fight over again all that we have fought, and spend over again all that we have spent, but are never like to attain thus far as we are now advanced to the recovery of our freedom, never to have it in possession as we now have it, never to be vouchsafed hereafter the like mercies and signal assistances from Heaven in our cause, if by our ingrateful backsliding we make these fruitless.

"Now is the opportunity," he cried in desperate appeal, "now the very season, wherein we may obtain a Free Commonwealth, and establish it

---

[22] "These were not new and revolutionary conceptions, but rather represented the continuity of the normal principles of the political theory of the Middle Ages" (A. J. Carlyle, *Political Liberty*, Oxford, 1941, p. 119). See also W. Haller, "Before *Areopagitica*," *PMLA*, XLII (1927). 875-900.

[23] See W. L. Loewenhaubt, "The Writing of Milton's *Eikonoklastes*," *SP*, XX (1923). 28-51; J. S. Smart, "Milton and the King's Prayer," *RES*, I (1925). 385-391.

[24] See J. M. French, "The Date of Milton's Blindness," *PQ*, XV (1936). 93-94.

[25] Ed. E. M. Clark (New Haven, 1915).

forever in the land without difficulty or much delay." Yet the ink was hardly dry on the last issue of the pamphlet, when Charles II was brought back with uproarious plaudits and Milton became a hunted man. He was now the most conspicuous surviving enemy of the Restoration, and it is not wholly clear why he did not suffer a traitor's or a regicide's fate. He had loyal friends like Marvell, who interceded for him, and he had a name "of which all Europe talked from side to side," [26] and that was a consideration of importance to Charles II's government. At any rate, fourteen more years of unobstructed life were granted him; and neither friends nor enemies nor himself could have forecast the value of those years.

[26] Second sonnet to Cyriac Skinner, line 12 (slightly altered).

XV
Milton in the Restoration

Shakespeare died at fifty-two. At the same age Milton, as a poet, was reborn; and for fourteen years more his renewed but unreconstructed genius projected itself like a Gulf Stream through the incongruous currents of the Restoration.[1] According to Aubrey,[2] he began the writing of *Paradise Lost* "about two years before the king came in," which would be shortly before Oliver Cromwell's death in September, 1658. It is not likely, though, that much was put on paper before the final, and to Milton catastrophic, settlement of 1660. The early books are too much permeated with the sense of a dire foregone decision and with the need to justify the ways of God to men to have sprung out of the chequered hopes and fears, and the immediate political urgencies, of the closing years of the Commonwealth. Milton's prose shows that at this time he was too intent upon the lost cause for which he was himself battling to have had much leisure for Satan's, and a Restoration background seems clearly implied by the vivid lines about Belial in Book 1:[3]

> In courts and palaces he also reigns,
> And in luxurious cities, where the noise
> Of riot ascends above their loftiest towers,
> And injury and outrage; and, when night
> Darkens the streets, then wander forth the sons
> Of Belial, flown with insolence and wine.

Paradise Lost, first printed in 1667, took final form between the Restoration (May, 1660) and the Great Plague of 1665,[4] but it grew from soil that had been long since prepared. Even so far back as the Italian journey of 1639 Milton had seriously dedicated himself, as the Latin poems show, to the

[Right margin notes: Paradise Lost; The Date]

---

[1] See, in addition to works cited at opening of ch. XIII, E. Greenlaw, "Spenser's Influence on *Paradise Lost,*" SP, XVII (1920). 320-359; H. Darbishire, *The Manuscript of Paradise Lost, Book* 1 (Oxford, 1931); H. J. C. Grierson, *Milton and Wordsworth, Poets and Prophets* (Cambridge, 1937); G. W. Whiting, *Milton's Literary Milieu* (Chapel Hill, 1939); E. E. Stoll, "Milton, Puritan of the Seventeenth Century" in *Poets and Playwrights* (Minneapolis, 1930), pp. 241-295, and "Milton a Romantic," RES, VIII (1932). 1-12; Douglas Bush, *The Renaissance and English Humanism* (Toronto, 1939), ch. IV; Grant McColley, *Paradise Lost, an Account of Its Growth and Major Origins* (Chicago, 1940); Z. S. Fink, "The Political Implications of *Paradise Regained,*" JEGP, XL (1941). 482-488; C. S. Lewis, *A Preface to 'Paradise Lost'* (Oxford, 1942); Douglas Bush, *'Paradise Lost' in Our Time* (Ithaca, 1945).

[2] H. Darbishire, *The Early Lives of Milton* (1932), p. 13.

[3] Lines 497-502.

[4] G. McColley, *op. cit.,* pp. 294-325, argues that the poem was written inconsecutively during the years 1652-1663.

idea of a great national epic;[5] but his ponderings during the next few years led him to prefer the plan of a biblical play, and by 1642 he had outlined for himself in considerable detail a tragedy on *Adam Unparadised.* Circumstances thwarted this design; and it is easy to surmise that when he returned to the subject, just as the theatres were licentiously reopening, the notion of drama, even closet drama, would have been distasteful. He laid it by in his patient and retentive brain, and framed his poem again on epic lines. Comparison with the *Adam Unparadised* outline shows that he had not intended to make so much of the cosmic and demonic interests. In particular he had not intended to make so much of Satan; but in the first books of *Paradise Lost* Satan became the glorious scapegoat to bear away Milton's own sin of impatience with the Lord, or in the jargon of psychology to "sublimate" his outraged sense of justice and the repinings of his injured pride. Satan, of course, is not Milton, and in a total view he is not the hero of the poem; but at the beginning he is the "agonist," who struggles as Milton had been struggling and reacts as nature tempted Milton to react. Professor Saurat, who says that "the hero of *Paradise Lost* is Milton himself," [6] shows how the poet contends at every step against this objectivation of his own rebelliousness; and there can be no doubt that the externalizing of his inner strife did him good. He might have said with Wordsworth,

> A timely utterance gave that thought·relief,
> And I again am strong.[7]

He might have said this at the end of the second book, for after that point the sorrows of Satan interest him much less, and his sympathies are on the side of the angels. The third book, opening with one of the most beautiful passages in his poetry, is transitional, carrying the reader, by way of heaven and the new-created universe, to the earthly paradise in which Adam and Eve dwell. This last is the real scene of Milton's poem; of the remaining books seven take place here solely, and the other two in great part. In all the last nine books the interest in Adam and Eve is paramount; even in the episodic Books v to viii, which consist mainly of Raphael's discourse to the happy pair. They are, as Milton intended them to be, the chief figures of the epic, and they are astonishingly real. One can dislike Adam for much the same reasons for which one may dislike John Milton, and charge him with being an over-sexed and priggish Puritan. One may even dislike Eve, for the reason that Milton was, as Sir Herbert Grierson has said,[8] "a sore, angry, intolerant, and arrogant critic of women"; but one cannot escape the moving poignancy of the characterization or fail to note that Milton has applied to Eve a great many of the most winning

The margin notes: The Function of Satan · The Scene of Paradise Lost · Adam and Eve

---

[5] See P. F. Jones, "Milton and the Epic Subject from British History," *PMLA,* xlii (1927). 901-909; R. F. Brinkley, *Arthurian Legend in the Seventeenth Century* (Baltimore, 1932), pp. 126-141.

[6] *Milton, Man and Thinker* (1925), p. 220.

[7] *Ode on Intimations of Immortality.*

[8] *Cross Currents in English Literature of the Seventeenth Century* (1929), p. 155.

words that men have ever used of women or put into their mouths.[9] On this plane *Paradise Lost* is a religious romance, not altogether unlike *The Pilgrim's Progress*, with which through many generations it shared the affections of the humbly pious.[10] On another plane, and particularly in the scenes in heaven, it is a philosophy of religion, asserting man's freedom of will and ultimate responsibility for his acts. As recent critics have been pointing out, it integrates elements from the mystical Jewish *Cabbala* into a remarkably bold and consistent exposition of Christian materialism.[11]

The fact remains that the first two books of *Paradise Lost*, though hardly *The First* more than a colossal prelude in the total economy of the poem, are the part *Two Book* that most delights the modern reader. They are the most dramatically conceived, as if the poet, having long weighed the subject as a play, only slowly adopted the narrator's attitude; [12] and they are the richest part in a literary sense. Milton's heaven seems to us unfurnished, an echoing gallery of pure theological reason; and it could hardly be otherwise in the work of a poet who held God the Father to be wholly unknowable and indescribable. The cool delightfulness of the earthly paradise is largely vegetable, a matter of plants and flowers and charming landscapes; but in Milton's hell the human spirit is at home, for there, by skilful use of simile and anticipatory allusion, he undid his corded bales of worldwide learning, from the giant brood of Phlegra and the Pygmean race beyond the Indian mount to the sea-beast Leviathan slumbering on the Norway foam and the Tuscan artist with his optic glass. These passages are, as everybody knows, one of the peculiar glories of *Paradise Lost*.[13] There is little opportunity for them in the scenes in heaven, and in the later books they are likely to fall into the form of grandiose geographical surveys,[14] where Milton's muse follows the course of Marlowe's in *Tamburlaine;* but in the first two books they are poured out with such a lavish hand that they resemble the jewels in which Barabas counts his wealth:

> Bags of fiery opals, sapphires, amethysts,
> Jacinths, hard topaz, grass-green emeralds,
> Beauteous rubies, sparkling diamonds,
> And seld-seen costly stones of so great price.[15]

By identifying the fallen followers of Satan with the divinities of pagan mythology, Milton found other means of vitalizing the first two books of *Paradise Lost* through contact with the recondite fulness of his reading; but in the most dramatic scene of all, the great council in Pandemonium,

[9] E.g., Books IV. 639-656; VIII. 500-510; IX. 309-314, 445-467; X. 914-936.

[10] See E. N. S. Thompson, "For *Paradise Lost*, XI-XII," *PQ*, XXII (1943). 376-382.

[11] See D. Saurat, *Milton et le matérialisme chrétien en Angleterre* (Paris, 1928); M. H. Nicolson, "Milton and the *Conjectura Cabbalistica*," *PQ*, VI (1927). 1-18; H. F. Fletcher, *Milton's Rabbinical Readings* (Urbana, 1930); C. C. Green, "The Paradox of the Fall in *Paradise Lost*," *MLN*, LIII (1938). 557-571; A. H. Gilbert, "The Theological Basis of Satan's Rebellion and the Function of Abdiel in *Paradise Lost*," *MP*, XL (1942). 19-42.

[12] See J. H. Hanford, "The Dramatic Element in *Paradise Lost*," *SP*, XIV (1917). 178-195.

[13] See W. Raleigh, *Milton* (1900), ch. VI.

[14] E.g., Books III. 431-439; IV. 268-284; IX. 76-82; X. 431-436; XI. 385-411; XII. 135-146.

[15] *The Jew of Malta*, lines 25-28.

he seems to be drawing, not on learning, but on living experience. The authentic tones of real men, arguing a question of intensest actuality, are heard in the wonderfully contrasted speeches of Moloch, Belial, and Mammon. Reading Moloch's jolting and fanatical words,

> My sentence is for open war; of wiles,
> More unexpert, I boast not, . . .

one may fancy that Milton had before his mind's eye Thomas Harrison, the regicide, the first victim of the Restoration, of whom Pepys wrote on October 13, 1660:

> I went out to Charing Cross, to see Major-General Harrison hanged, drawn, and quartered, which was done there, he looking as cheerful as any man could do in that condition. . . . It is said that he said that he was sure to come shortly at the right hand of Christ to judge them that now had judged him, and that his wife do expect his coming again.

And reading the masterly tergiversation with which Belial replies, one assumes that Milton was thinking, as in 1659-60 every one in England was thinking, of General Monck, the "hero of the Restoration," whom Charles II rewarded with the Dukedom of Albermarle, and of whom a biographer has said:

> The course of astonishing dissimulation which Monck steadily pursued from the time of his first declaration in Scotland to that of the Restoration is such as to defy all ordinary perfidy, and to rouse every sense of common honesty in array against the admiration which is due to his dexterity.[16]

Milton's own comment on Monck's career might have been,

> For neither man nor angel can discern
> Hypocrisy, the only evil that walks
> Invisible, except to God alone.[17]

If this seems fanciful, there can surely be little doubt whom Milton had in mind when he pictured Beëlzebub, rising to control the stampeded council:

>   with grave
> Aspect he rose, and in his rising seem'd
> A pillar of state; deep on his front engraven
> Deliberation sat and public care;
> And princely counsel in his face yet shone,
> Majestic though in ruin: sage he stood,
> With Atlantean shoulders fit to bear
> The weight of mightiest monarchies; his look
> Drew audience and attention still as night
> Or summer's noontide air, while thus he spake.

---

[16] J. Stuart Wortley, quoted by O. Warner, *Hero of the Restoration* (1936), p. 162.
[17] Book iii. 682 ff. The idea has been traced to Thomas Aquinas (McColley, *op. cit.*, p. 136).

Aut Cromwell aut diabolus! The advantage Milton had in this scene was that, beyond almost any other great poet, he had been a part of such events. "The man hath seen some majesty, and should know." To which any Cromwellian might have replied,

> Hath he seen majesty? Isis else defend,
> And serving you so long! [18]

Nothing went to waste in Milton: neither the years expended on "all such reading as was never read," both sacred and profane; nor the years devoted to political business and controversy. The incredible naïveté and idealistic folly of his first marriage saved our "Grand Parents" from being lay figures. Milton's Eve is the artistic legacy of all the pain that Mary Powell inflicted. Hate, shame, adoration, and womanliness have hardly been blended with a more dizzying effect since Catullus wrote his *odi et amo*. Milton's blindness helped too. Light and dark are the warp and woof of which *Paradise Lost* is woven. References to light are innumerable and always exciting, from the

> Bright effluence of bright essence increate,

The Effects of Blindnes

which is God, through such tender subtleties as "the sweet approach of even or morn," to the "darkness visible" of hell, and also of Milton's sight-reproductive imagination. The poem develops as a series of great ocular prospects,[19] marvelously selective and exact, the work of a mind that has hoarded and furbished up all its visual recollections.

The superlative exquisiteness of rhythm and rhetoric in *Paradise Lost* must come from the same cause. In these respects *Comus* and *Lycidas* might have seemed to reach the zenith of art; but every reader knows that *Paradise Lost* has something more, in the varied contours of the long wave-like sentences, the vivid marquetry of the Latinisms let into the English style to brighten or to strengthen, and in the perfect matching of the figurative allusions. It is what makes *Paradise Lost* the greatest English classic, and it comes (humanly speaking) from the enforced patience of the blind man, rolling each twenty lines or so over the buffers of his most exigent taste till they acquired the polish of pebbles by the seashore. Perhaps it is a comforting thought that the special merits of *Paradise Lost* are not likely to be paralleled, because another poet, equally endowed, is not likely to be called on to pay the dreadful cost.

Paradise Regained, first printed in 1671, four years after *Paradise Lost,* has been always overshadowed by the greater work, though Milton, as his nephew remembered, "could not bear with patience any such thing" as the suggestion of its inferiority.[20] It is not an epic, being merely a semi-dramatic account, in four short books, of the commencement of Christ's ministry; and instead of opening like *Paradise Lost* in a blaze of glory, it

Paradise Regained

[18] *Antony and Cleopatra*, III. iii. 42 ff.
[19] See M. H. Nicolson, "Milton and the Telescope," *ELH*, II (1935). 1-32.
[20] See H. Darbishire, *The Early Lives of Milton* (1932), p. 75.

begins on the lowest key and reserves most of its magnificence for the last book. It contains many of the quietest lines that Milton wrote, and a few which are actually unmusical; [21] but when it soars, it reaches heights that have not often been equalled; e.g., (II. 355 ff.),

> Nymphs of Diana's train, and Naiades
> With fruits and flowers from Amalthea's horn,
> And ladies of th' Hesperides, that seem'd
> Fairer than feign'd of old, or fabled since
> Of fairy damsels met in forest wide
> By knights of Logres, or of Lyonesse,
> Lancelot, or Pelleas or Pellenore.

Yet this passage, which so gracefully blends Ovid and Malory, and the similar one (III. 337-343) that pays tribute to Boiardo and Ariosto are broadly characteristic only as they join with other indications of the resurgence of youthful feeling in this poem—an aspect which critics seem strangely to have ignored.

The Style   The style is more Homeric tnan that of *Paradise Lost,* as in the repeated narrative clichés; e.g.,

> To whom our Saviour calmly thus replied (III. 43),
> To whom the Tempter murmuring thus replied (III. 108),
> To whom our Saviour answer thus return'd (III. 181);

and in the precise classical similes; e.g. (IV. 15 ff.),

> Or as a swarm of flies in vintage time,
> About the wine-press when sweet must is pour'd,
> Beat off, returns as oft with humming sound;
> Or surging waves against a solid rock,
> Though all to shivers dash'd, th' assault renew,
> Vain batt'ry, and in froth or bubbles end.

There is the feeling of Homer also, though reinforced by the Elizabethan poets, in the description of dawn (IV. 426 ff.),

> Thus pass'd the night so foul, till morning fair
> Came forth with pilgrim steps in amice gray;
> Who with her radiant finger still'd the war
> Of thunder, chas'd the clouds, and laid the winds
> And grisly spectres, which the fiend had rais'd.

The poem is essentially a debate between Christ and Satan, neither of whom is very similar to the corresponding figure in *Paradise Lost.* Satan has here, as in the Book of Job (which in several ways served Milton as a model), rather come to terms with God and been accepted as the allowed leader of the divine Opposition. The young Christ of *Paradise Regained,* though somewhat ungenial toward the Fiend, is the most charming figure in the poem. His divinity (after Milton's manner) is not greatly stressed; but his heroic humanity, ardor, and clear-eyed courage make him the perfect ex-

[21] E.g., Books I. 302, II. 243, IV. 597.

emplar of that ideal of magnanimity through renunciation of the world which was one of the most cherished philosophies of the time.[22] Galahad was in the tradition, and hardly less the young John Milton, so valiantly fastidious, who seems to speak for himself in Christ's words (I. 201 ff.):

> When I was yet a child, no childish play
> To me was pleasing; all my mind was set
> Serious to learn and know, and thence to do
> What might be public good; myself I thought
> Born to that end, born to promote all truth,
> All righteous things. . . . . .
> These growing thoughts my mother soon perceiving
> By words at times cast forth, inly rejoic'd
> And said to me apart: High are thy thoughts,
> O son, but nourish them and let them soar
> To what highth sacred virtue and true worth
> Can raise them, though above example high.

In such passages Horton is recalled as much as Nazareth, and the bruised poet seems to be finding a sweet solace in lingering over the ideals of his youth. The most loftily sustained portion of the whole poem, the first half of Book IV, shows Satan offering a temptation not specified in the Gospel narrative, and aimed rather, it might appear, at the "Lady of Christ's" than the Man of Galilee. It contains the most vivid and winning picture ever drawn in so many English words of "the glory that was Greece and the grandeur that was Rome." Of course, Christ, who will not accept bread at the tempter's hand, cannot accept from him a classical education; but there stand, all incorruptible and undefeated, the lines of radiant and rejoicing humanism: *Christ and Milton*

> The city which thou seest no other deem
> Than great and glorious Rome, queen of the earth, . . .

and

> Behold,
> Where on the Aegean shore a city stands,
> Built nobly — pure the air and light the soil —
> Athens, the eye of Greece, mother of arts
> And eloquence . . . ,

strangely palpitating raptures for a man of sixty.

Paradise Regained and *Samson Agonistes* were given to the world together in the volume of 1671, but the former is best explained as an interval-piece, thrown off during the transfer of Milton's attention from the great epic that had appeared in 1667 to the great tragedy in which his poetry found its completion. *Paradise Regained* is less intense than either, less titanic, and it mediates between the epic and the dramatic point of view. *Samson Agonistes*, on the other hand, shows Milton using all his strength, and the *Samson Agonistes*

22 See M. Y. Hughes, "The Christ of *Paradise Regained* and the Renaissance Heroic Tradition," *SP*, xxxv (1938). 254-277, and note by E. M. W. Tillyard, xxxvi (1939). 247-252; also T. H. Banks, "The Banquet Scene in *Paradise Regained*," *PMLA*, lv (1940). 773-776.

accumulated reflections of a lifetime, as at long last he came back to his old project of a sacred tragedy.[23] It is his most flawless single work of art, in which he openly challenges comparison with Aeschylus, Sophocles, and Euripides, "the three tragic poets unequaled yet by any," and in which he comes near to making his challenge good.[24]

As in the slighter but similar case of Milton's adoption of the Italian sonnet, criticism has seldom done justice to *Samson Agonistes,* because few critics have combined learning and imagination in a degree sufficient to understand the author's problem. Structurally, Milton's play reproduces with extraordinary precision the form of a Greek tragedy as Aristotle conceived it, and the parallel with the *Oedipus at Colonus* of Sophocles is in some details very close indeed; but the poet's mind was too fully permeated with Hellenic drama for his *Samson* to be explainable as imitation of specific plays or of a particular dramatist. His spiritual affinity is closest with Aeschylus, the strictest and sternest of the Athenian playwrights. Like Aeschylus he greatly magnifies the importance of the hero and of the chorus, who between them speak two-thirds of the lines, and like him limits the speaking characters to two in any scene. The unity and gravity of the play are also Aeschylean, but the play as a whole is not Aeschylean; it is Greek.

These things, however, wonderful and even unique though they are in a modern poem, would not make *Samson Agonistes* a vital English tragedy without the religious tone, which is not archaic but of the seventeenth century, and without the individuality of Samson's character, which is deeply Miltonic.[25] Like Milton, Samson is a dedicated soul,

> a person rais'd
> With strength sufficient and command from Heav'n
> To free my country.

Like Milton he has been embittered by an unwise marriage, has suffered blindness, and been delivered into the hands of godless enemies; and like Milton he is grappling humbly with the problem of God's justice and the question, "Doth God exact day-labor, light denied?" This is distinctively a poem of old age, and for Milton curiously unadorned. It has little excitement, and discloses its subtle beauties only after repeated readings, for they depend on delicate psychological strains and stresses. It belongs with nothing in the Elizabethan or the Restoration age. In theme it is wholly Hebraic, in structure wholly Greek; and in effect it is the most autobiographical and (though Christ is never mentioned) the most movingly Christian thing that Milton wrote—at least since the early ode *On the Morning of Christ's Nativity.*

[23] See E. M. Clark, "Milton's Earlier Samson," Univ. of Texas *Studies in English,* VII (1927). 144-154.

[24] For an admirable and very full treatment of this subject, see W. R. Parker, *Milton's Debt to Greek Tragedy in Samson Agonistes* (Baltimore, 1937); also G. L. Finney, "Chorus in Samson Agonistes," PMLA, LVIII (1943). 649-664.

[25] See J. H. Hanford, "*Samson Agonistes* and Milton in Old Age," Univ. of Michigan *Studies in Shakespeare, Milton, and Donne* (1925), pp. 167-189.

BOOK III

The Restoration and Eighteenth Century (1660-1789)

⌁

PART I

The Rise of Classicism

Guide to reference marks
Throughout the text of this book, a point ·● set beside a page number indicates that references to new critical material will be found under an identical paragraph/page number (set in **boldface**) in the BIBLIOGRAPHICAL SUPPLEMENT.

In the Index, a number preceded by an **S** indicates a paragraph/page number in the BIBLIOGRAPHICAL SUPPLEMENT.

I

The Spirit of the Restoration

In May, 1660, invited by Parliament, King Charles II returned from exile, and the Restoration of monarchy in England became a fact.[1] Amidst the spontaneous outbursts of joy, poets and others were not slow in asserting a parallel between this Restoration and the imperial establishment, after civil wars, of Octavius Augustus Caesar in Rome (31 B.C.). This attitude of mind is implicit in the title of Dryden's poem, *Astræa Redux,* composed for the occasion, and explicit in the concluding lines of the effort:

Neo-Augustanism

> Oh Happy Age! Oh times like those alone,
> By Fate reserv'd for great *Augustus'* Throne!
> When the joint growth of Arms and Arts forshew
> The World a Monarch, and that Monarch *You.*

The author (Francis Atterbury?) of the preface to *The Second Part of Mr. Waller's Poems* (1690) more magisterially says, "I question whether in *Charles* the Second's Reign, *English* did not come to its full perfection; and whether it has not had its *Augustan Age,* as well as the *Latin.*" This neo-Augustanism, so promptly recognized and acclaimed, we call neo-classicism. It implies a veneration for the Roman classics, thought, and way of life. It values highly a noble Roman tone. The stately enthusiasm of the time Dryden caught in retrospect as he penned his *Threnodia Augustalis* (1685):

> Men met each other with erected look,
> The steps were higher that they took;
> Friends to congratulate their friends made haste,
> And long-inveterate foes saluted as they pass'd.

The dignity and stateliness outlived the enthusiasm. The new Augustus, Charles II, proved to be both lazy and lecherous, and in spite of his undoubted wit and intelligence (seldom has an English monarch been personally friendly to so many distinguished intellectuals!) disillusionment soon attended his reign. In 1667 Samuel Pepys summed up this attitude:

[1] For general aids on the history of the literature of this period consult A. Beljame, *Le Public et les hommes de lettres en Angleterre, 1660-1744* (Paris, 1881); Richard Garnett, *The Age of Dryden* (1903); Sir Herbert Grierson, *Cross Currents in English Literature of the XVIIth Century* (1929); Sherard Vines, *The Course of English Classicism* (1930); Louis Cazamian, "Modern Times 1660-1932," in *A History of English Literature* (translated from the French [Paris, 1924] in 1927, rev. ed., 1935). — For general bibliographies see Robert Watt, *Bibliotheca Britannica; or, a General Index to British and Foreign Literature* (4v, Edinburgh, 1824); *Annual Bibliography of English Language and Literature,* edited for the MHRA (Cambridge, 1921-   ); Ronald S. Crane, Louis I. Bredvold, Richmond P. Bond, Allen T. Hazen, Arthur Friedman, and Louis A. Landa (successively), "English Literature of the Restoration and Eighteenth Century: A Current Bibliography," annually since 1926 in *PQ*

It is strange how . . . every body do now-a-days reflect upon Oliver, and commend him, what brave things he did, and made all the neighbour princes fear him; while here a prince, come in with all the love and prayers and good liking of his people, who have given greater signs of loyalty and willingness to serve him with their estates than ever was done by any people, hath lost all so soon, that it is a miracle what way a man could devise to lose so much in so little time.

*he Court
nd French
fluence*

Charles and his court had brought back from their Continental exile a love of French wit, gallantry, elegance, and artistic deftness. Doubtless Virgil, Horace, Cicero, Ovid, and Juvenal meant more to the literate English gentle-man of the period than did his French contemporaries, Descartes, Molière, Corneille, and Boileau—though it would be wrong to underestimate the French influence.[2] But the necessary social, economic, and religious readjust-ments crowded in upon the minds of men: their realistic, common-sense, and at times even cynical evaluation of life was at wide variance from Roman stateliness and French refinement. The spirit of the age was far from unified; and in reaction against its complexity Restoration intellectuals thirsted for a rational simplification of their existence. To understand their divergent efforts to reduce confusion to a lucid simplicity it is necessary to have some awareness of their thinking in the fields of science, religion, and politics, as well as their tendencies in the arts.[3]

*'he In-
uence of
cience*

In science the most important work was done by men connected with the Royal Society of London.[4] This organization emerged in 1660, or shortly thereafter, from groups meeting earlier in London at Gresham College or in Oxford at Wadham. Its technical achievements lie chiefly, but by no means exclusively, in the field of mathematics as applied to the motion of the heavenly bodies. For our purposes it cannot too constantly be remembered that the leading fellows of the Society were devoutly religious men: the work of Robert Boyle (1627-91) in chemistry, of John Ray (1627-1705) in other natural sciences, of Sir Isaac Newton [5] (1642-1727) in mathe-

for April; *CBEL*, esp. Vol. II. — For detailed political histories of the Restoration period see Lord Macaulay's *History of England from the Accession of James II* (5v, 1849-61; ed. Sir Charles H. Firth, 6v, 1913-15); George M. Trevelyan, *England under the Stuarts* (1904 ff.); David Ogg, *England in the Reign of Charles II* (2v, Oxford, 1934); and George N. Clark, *The Later Stuarts, 1660-1714* (1934). Among the shorter, one-volume histories of England may be recommended those by Arthur L. Cross (1914) and by George M. Trevelyan (1926). For bibliography see Godfrey Davies (ed.), *Bibliography of British History: Stuart Period, 1603-1714* (Oxford, 1928).

[2] L. Charlanne, *L'Influence française en Angleterre au XVIIe siècle* (Paris, 1906).

[3] For general treatments of this field see Basil Willey, *The Seventeenth Century Background* (1934) and Preserved Smith, *A History of Modern Culture*, Vol. II, "The Enlightenment" (1934). On the more specialized theme of the thirst for simplification see Richard F. Jones, "The Moral Sense of Simplicity," *Studies in Honor of Frederick W. Shipley* (St. Louis, 1942), pp. 265-287.

[4] Important early accounts of the Royal Society are found in Thomas Sprat, *A History of the Royal Society* (1667) and in Joseph Glanvill, *Plus Ultra* (1668). More recently we have Henry B. Wheatley, *The Early History of the Royal Society* (1905) and Sir W. Huggins, *The Royal Society* (1906). Richard F. Jones in his *Ancients and Moderns* (St. Louis, 1936) analyzes the intellectual background of science. Very illuminating also are Edwin A. Burtt's *Metaphysical Foundations of Modern Physical Science* (1925) and Sir Henry Lyons's *The Royal Society, 1660-1940* (Cambridge, 1944).

[5] Sir Isaac was a fellow of the Royal Society after 1671 and President from 1703 until his death in 1727. His *Principia* appeared in 1687.

matics and astronomy—all was designed to support religious orthodoxy, and had no subversive or eccentric ends in view. Great as were their known scientific achievements, for us their significance lies rather in their ability to popularize certain methods of thinking and writing. The motto of the Society, *nullius in verba*—"on the word of no one"—is a direct challenge to historians who, however wrongly, regard English neo-classicism as an appeal to the ancients as authorities. The Royal Society was experimental and empirical in method; assent to a proposition had to be suspended until the evidence was examined. They shunned purely a priori reasoning, and preached the necessity of having a hesitant or "open" mind. Frequently this attitude approached skepticism as method if not as ultimate end. The indirect influence of the Society through the Boyle lectures, founded in 1692 by Robert Boyle's will, "to prove the truth of the Christian Religion," was great in furthering the "physico-theology" that was the answering challenge of the orthodox to certain types of deists. In general, the Society purposed to substitute experiment for disputation as a road to truth. Eventually their method would transfer attention from the pursuit of humane learning to the study of things, but at the start that was far from the intention of scientists, who at times disparaged Aristotle as a student of nature, but were seldom hostile to his efforts as a moralist or a literary critic. They tended to believe in the progress of man through the illumination of the new science; and this idea of progress was gradually to preoccupy later generations.[6]

It has been regarded as significant of the practical and perhaps even materialistic bent of the English mind that while seventeenth-century France created in its celebrated Académie Française (1635) a literary foundation, England organized a society for scientific research. The Royal Society, however, concerned itself with more than scientific experimentation. The inclusiveness of its conception of science perhaps forestalled efforts to establish an academy. It had as fellows many literary men who had slight interest in science, and it actively promoted the study and reform of English prose style, and like the French Academy was eager to improve and fix standards in language. Late in 1664 it appointed, "for improving the English language," a committee that included, among others, Dryden, Evelyn, Waller, and Sprat. Meetings of this committee were held with such other literati present as Cowley, Villiers, Duke of Buckingham, and "Matt" Clifford. Because of the death of Cowley and the interruption caused by the plague of 1665, the committee, so Evelyn wrote in 1689, "crumbled away and came to nothing." The statement is ·not perfectly accurate; for though the committee seems never to have reported formally to the Society, its ideals of style became of very great importance.[7] In a well-known passage in his *History of the Royal Society* (1667) Bishop Sprat has summarized these ideals:

Science and
English
Prose

[6] The origin and history of *The Idea of Progress* can be found treated in the book of that title by an ardent believer in the idea, John B. Bury (1920; 1932).

[7] Richard F. Jones, "Science and English Prose Style in the Third Quarter of the Seventeenth Century," *PMLA*, xlv (1930). 977-1009; significantly reviewed in *PQ*, x (1931). 184-186.

They [the Society] have therefore been most rigorous in putting in execution the only Remedy that can be found for this *extravagance,* and that has been a constant Resolution to reject all amplifications, digressions, and swellings of style; to return back to the primitive purity and shortness, when men deliver'd so many *things* almost in an equal number of *words.* They have exacted from all their members a close, naked, natural way of speaking, positive expressions, clear senses, a native easiness, bringing all things as near the Mathematical plainness as they can, and preferring the language of Artizans, Countrymen, and Merchants, before that of Wits or Scholars.

These ideals, obviously essential to scientific exposition, were reinforced by the conversational tradition of elegant French prose, and became outside scientific circles a part of the reaction from baroque magnificence to neo-Palladian simplicity. Hobbes, who interestingly enough was not approved by the Royal Society, worked "non ut floride sed ut Latine posset scribere"; and Glanvill, who was converted to the stylistic ideals of the Society, urged upon parsons the quality of *plainness* as opposed "First, to *hard words;* Secondly, to *deep* and *mysterious notions;* Thirdly, to *affected Rhetorications;* and Fourthly, to *Phantastical Phrases."*

enteel
olerance
    Under the influence of the new science, then, the useful and the plain were replacing the ornate, the rich, the complex. At first sight it may seem strange that a similar tendency to simplification can be traced in the religious thinking of the time. Certainly religious controversy—"polemical divinity" it was called—was a chief product of the fecund printing press; but gentlemen were becoming bored by such zeal. The religion of all true gentlemen was ideally something that no true gentleman ever argued about: argument might be left to the parsons! As ambassador to Holland Sir William Temple admired the effects of toleration in that country, and in his *Observations upon the United Provinces* (1673) he remarks concerning Dutch composure in religious controversy:

They argue without interest or anger; They differ without enmity or scorn, And They agree without confederacy. Men live together like Citizens of the World, associated by the common ties of Humanity.... The Power of Religion among them, where it is, lies in every Man's heart....

In England this beatific condition seemed more than a channel-crossing distant; but remotely the ideal was perceived and valued as the coil of varied controversy incessantly renewed itself at home. Weary of disputation and eager for a simplified, reasonable creed Dryden could write:

Faith is not built on disquisitions vain;
The things we *must* believe are *few* and *plain.*

But no great number of Englishmen followed Dryden's search for "unsuspected ancients" to serve as authoritative sanctions in faith. The age was prejudiced against any *ipse dixit* authority.
    There were complicated positions taken.[8] The Catholics, disliked largely

[8] Louis I. Bredvold in his *Intellectual Milieu of John Dryden* (Ann Arbor, 1934) gives an admirable picture of this confusion.

for political rather than doctrinal reasons, were at times willing even to *Religious*
undermine the authority of Scripture, since by so doing they undermined *Animositie*
the chief orthodox basis for Protestant faith. The Puritans were still assailing
Anglicans on questions of church government; but many dissenters and
Anglicans, both largely Calvinists, would unite against the rising tide of
Arminianism. In the forefront of its 1629 Protestation the House of Commons had asserted: "Whosoever shall bring in innovation of religion, or
by favour or countenance seek to extend or introduce popery or Arminianism, or other opinion disagreeing from the true and orthodox Church,
shall be reputed a capital enemy to this kingdom and commonwealth." [9]
At the end of the century a kindlier attitude towards practical moral sanctions as opposed to the Calvinist covenant of grace would have made such
a protest impossible.[10] The blood and tears of war, controversy, and political
intrigue had led gradually to a practical, if not always a reasoned, spirit
of toleration.

To civic life the great contribution of "the people called Quakers" was
doubtless their insistent belief in religious toleration.[11] Their contribution
to religious life was their mystical emphasis on experience—on the·life of
God in the soul of man. To them religion ideally was a pleasant psychological *The*
state rather than a terror-stricken argument. An astonishing number of *Quakers*
journals, autobiographies, and histories, some of them by hardly literate *and Reasor*
authors, testify to the zeal of the Friends in promoting religious experience.
Most notable among these would be the *Journal* (1694) of the first great
Quaker, George Fox (1624-1691), for which William Penn (1644-1718)
wrote an important introduction. Penn was no skilful writer, but his *No
Cross No Crown* (1669) and especially his *Some Fruits of Solitude* (1693)
are effectively simple and fervent. The theologian of the Society of
Friends was Robert Barclay (1648-1690), whose *Apology for the True
Christian Divinity* (1678) represents Quaker logic at its best. The mystical
sense of divine immanence, however, was more valued by Friends than was
reasoned theology. In this matter their position was sharply at variance from
that of seventeenth-century Protestants and Catholics, who could agree in
basing faith on reason. Strong in their concept of "the light of reason,"
which the orthodox insisted was uniform and universal, both Protestants
and Catholics were bitterly scornful of the "inner" or private light so valued
by the Quakers and by some other sects—and called by their enemies "enthusiasm." Subjectivity was antithetical to the ideal of constant and universal
reason.

The most effective voice raised in favor of the sanction of common ex- *Locke and*
perience as opposed to the vagaries of "enthusiasm" was that of John Locke *Empiricism*
(1632-1704). His most important work—perhaps the most important in

[9] Godfrey Davies, "Arminian vs. Puritan," *Huntington Library Bull.*, v (1934). 157-179.
Here p. 172 is quoted.
[10] Harry G. Plum, *Restoration Puritanism: A Study in the Growth of English Liberty* (Chapel
Hill, 1943).
[11] Luella M. Wright, *The Literary Life of the Early Friends, 1650-1725* (1932).

English philosophy—was his *Essay concerning Human Understanding* (1690). In the first three books of this work Locke strove to demolish the theory of innate ideas, to define the true nature of ideas, and to explain the relation of language to thought. Finally, in the last and most important book, he developed his theory of knowledge—as coming only from sense experience and from reflection upon that experience. His ability to write with clarity and order as well as his use of the methods of the New Science in philosophical thinking made him the great empirical rationalist of modern philosophy and (unintentionally) the father of much skeptical thinking in the century to follow. He demonstrated the need of an historical revelation of religion; but his psychological approach to the relation of reason to faith (Book IV, chapter XVIII) ultimately weakened reason and strangled faith. His method in the *Essay* and in *The Reasonableness of Christianity* (1695) was seized upon by the deist John Toland, whose *Christianity Not Mysterious* (1696) showed, according to its title-page, "that there is nothing in the Gospel contrary to reason, nor above it, and that no Christian doctrine can be properly called a mystery." Thus while aimed against the subjective enthusiasts, Locke's rationalism unintentionally played into the hands of the great enemy on the other flank, the deists. Locke's influence on deistic thinking, on psychology, and on the new field to be called epistemology, was to be enormous throughout the eighteenth century.[12]

The Deists   Apart from the Quakers, the deists were perhaps the chief religious novelty in the period, and all the professed Christian sects disparaged the deist position. The divergences between the "natural religion" of the deists and the "revealed religion" of their opponents are not always easy to establish. The orthodox Christians asserted that the deists denied the historical revelation made through Jesus Christ and recorded in the Holy Scriptures, and believed only in a revelation seen by human reason in God's created universe. In general the deists certainly stressed their belief in the Creation, the "Book of Nature," as evidently God's handiwork and thus a revelation of Himself. They said little about the Scriptures. John Toland and some others, to be sure, openly attacked the integrity of the Bible. Privately, many deists regarded the historical aspects of the biblical revelation with suspicion; overtly, they annoyed orthodox scientists by stealing and perhaps misapplying some of their thunder. John Ray's book, *The Wisdom of God Manifested in the Works of the Creation* (1691) had a title that might please some deists as much as it clearly did the orthodox "physico-theologians" of the Royal Society. The deists glorified reason, but frequently identified it with common sense or the almost intuitional "light of reason." They could find attributes of deity manifested in the works of the Creation or revealed axiomatically in the minds of all men. They questioned the worth of a local revelation, long past, and stressed the universal

---

12 S. G. Hefelbower gives a useful, if simplified, account in his *Relation of John Locke to Deism* (Chicago, 1918). On the less tangible matter of Locke and literature see Kenneth Mac-Lean's *John Locke and English Literature of the Eighteenth Century* (New Haven, 1936).

religious perceptions or intuitions of men. As Professor Lovejoy states the deist's position:

Precisely this was the ostensible procedure of Herbert of Cherbury. *Summa veritatis norma est consensus universalis;* true religion consists solely of *notitiae communes,* things that everybody knows; and to judge how far a "particular faith" coincides with this norm you must ask, among other things, whether any of its articles "be not controverted among foreign nations, among whom other faiths are received." Thus alone is to be determined the doctrine of the *Ecclesia vere catholica sive universalis,* the only church *quae errare non potest,* because it alone utters the judgment of all mankind with respect to those truths of which they have self-evident knowledge by the light of nature. As Voltaire said, "Sans doute [Dieu] a parlé; mais c'est à l'Univers."

The spectrum of religious opinion would thus range from this belief in a universal, uniform perception of truth through the light of reason to a belief in private revelations of an·inner light, which was purely individual; it would range from the argumentative theologians, such as the Cambridge Platonists, to the quietism of the Quaker or the intellectual libertinism of the fine gentleman, such as Sir William Temple. The Anglicans, torn by divergences among themselves, had to oppose Catholics, deists, and dissenters of many different stripes. The perplexed mind sought various ways out of this confusion, ways including rational simplifications, pure fideism, and, at the other extreme, many types of skepticism. Such escapes frequently tended to undermine the prestige of "polemical divines" and of rational theology itself, and thus aided anti-rational tendencies destined remotely to eventuate in sentimentalism or evangelicalism.

In the field of politics there was similar confusion. A strong and perhaps even pharisaical satisfaction was felt that the English, unlike their neighbors, the French, were not "born to serve" an absolute monarch like Louis XIV. *Political* Yet absolutism and divine right were strongly defended in the *Patriarcha Contro-* (1680) and other popular writings of Sir Robert Filmer, who died in 1653. *versies* Divinely constituted authority was Filmer's refuge from the confusion of conflicting parties, and of parliaments divided against themselves. Thomas Hobbes's *Leviathan* (1651) substituted for the divine sanction of sovereignty a materialistic absolutism based on an original compact that irrevocably delegated to one person power over the governed. Far from granting any religious or ecclesiastical sanction for sovereignty Hobbes made the Church entirely the creature of the monarch. His absolutism, his materialism, and his anti-clericalism—which seemed to go to the length of atheism—as well as his irritatingly systematic thinking, made Hobbes's doctrines the object of loud and continual anathemas throughout the period, and yet the fundamental purpose of his work was, again, the gratification of a love (quite a selfish love in Hobbes's psychology) for a settled peace.

In a period when Parliament was establishing its control over the throne by inviting Charles II to return and William and Mary to displace James II, absolutism might too readily be thought a dead issue. It was, however, the accession of James II, coupled with Continental set-backs to liberty [13] that stimulated John Locke to publish his great works, some of which were of supreme political importance. His views had long been formed, but, appearing at the troubled moment of the Revolution of 1688, they were its cogent defense. A protégé of the great Earl of Shaftesbury, Locke was an intellectual Whig. He had long been for toleration in religion; and his *Two Treatises of Government* (1690) was the best answer to the absolutism of Filmer and Hobbes. Locke's influence on constitutional theories both in England and America was destined to be enormous. He emphatically gave the legislative branch of government supreme power. The authority of the governor, he said, derived solely from the consent of the governed, and the bound of his power was the welfare of those governed by him. *Salus populi suprema lex.* Government thus became in some sense a matter of expediency, and expediency might determine policy—as it did in Locke's denial of toleration to Catholics while extending it to dissenters.

Any political expediency in Locke was only a faint effect of what went on in the actual politics of his day. The laziness of Charles II had allowed the rise of government by cabinet ministers to become remarkable, and in

the heat of the sensational Popish Plot (1678) there had emerged the troublesome and irrational party labels, *Whig* and *Tory.* The Whigs claimed to protect the liberties of the subject, and they certainly attempted to help the dissenters; the Tories, likely to be ardent Churchmen, professed a devotion to royal prerogative and to the legitimate line of succession to the throne. The Tories, with some injustice, accused the Whigs of being republicans, disciples of Oliver, the late Protector; the Whigs retaliated more unjustly after 1688 by calling the Tories Jacobites, that is, supporters of the deposed James II. The necessity of a Protestant succession had provoked endless controversy, even reviving notions of divine right which had to be abandoned upon the accession of William and Mary as joint rulers. The principle of allegiance and the meaning of oaths of allegiance were topics of bitter dispute when, led by Sancroft, Archbishop of Canterbury, many clerics refused to violate their allegiance already sworn to James II by taking the required oaths of allegiance to the new rulers. Such Jacobites were called non-jurors; and they included eminent literary scholars like George Hickes (1642-1715) and Thomas Hearne (1678-1735), and the essayist and critic Jeremy Collier (1650-1726). Hickes and Collier in turn succeeded Sancroft as head of the Jacobite episcopacy: Collier at times signed himself as "Primus Anglo-Britanniae Episcopus."

All this troubled activity of political, religious, and scientific unrest was,

---

[13] "Europe in 1685 was passing through a political and religious crisis such as she had not passed through since 1588. In February of that year James II had declared himself a Catholic. In June, on the death of its Elector, the Palatinate passed into the hands of the Catholic family of Neubourg. In October Louis XIV revoked the Edict of Nantes; and in December the Duke of Savoy withdrew his grant of toleration to the Vaudois. On every side the Reformation and liberty seemed threatened as never before." — C. H. Driver, "John Locke," in *The Social and Political Ideas of Some English Thinkers of the Augustan Age,* ed. F. J. C. Hearnshaw (1928), p. 85.

of course, primarily the concern of the upper classes, especially of university men. Normally, after a period of varying length spent at either university, the young gentleman traveled on the Continent, and then returned to an active life in London or to a retired life in the country. The citizen and the country squire are outstanding types of the period, frequently burlesqued in comedy or in fiction. Men like John Evelyn and Sir William Temple loved the country and viewed eventual retirement there as a desired goal. Men like Samuel Pepys loved London and the amusements it and its environs afforded. As a whole, England must have presented an almost entirely rural aspect. London, to be sure, was the completely dominant metropolis, and contained somewhat less than two-thirds of a million inhabitants—which would be about one-tenth of the whole country's population. Norwich and Bristol had each perhaps 30,000 inhabitants, and York and Exeter had hardly more than 10,000. The great Midland manufacturing towns, already growing, would not be large for more than a century.[14] For the rest the country was sprinkled with small towns, villages, and country seats of gentlemen or noblemen. If we believe Macaulay (and it is not *Social* necessary to give him complete credence), the country squire of this period *Conditions* was practically illiterate. In the Restoration comedies, on the other hand, a valet may be presented as about the most intelligent person in the play. Such pictures are not to be trusted. The classes at times were curiously scrambled. One recalls Pepys's sister Pall, who became briefly a member of his household, "not as a sister but as a servant" who did not sit at table with the family. Pall grew proud and idle, however, and had to be sent back to the country. Unprivileged countryfolk frequently looked on London as a heavenly city; and it is certain that if the population of the island was rural, the arts were very largely urban. In the literature of the period class demarcations were especially strong. Restoration comedy was for courtiers and (perhaps) for rising citizens of London; Bunyan, on the other hand, was for the semi-literate dissenter, and he made his way very slowly towards a just recognition outside of his own class. He was, however, evidently read by other classes, as were the chapbooks of the period, which correspond roughly to the pulp fiction of the present day, to which in many respects they are greatly superior. Naturally, different classes—whether the class distinction is based on social position, on religious bias, or on a town or country background—had different tastes. It is, however, probably wrong to assume rigid demarcations in taste: the population was shifting from class to class, as the career of Pepys amply shows. Prudent Quakers and able dissenters were acquiring fortunes in trade, and were forming a new aristocracy, for which the Civil Wars and other causes had made room. New monarchs had new favorites to reward, and thus the nobility itself was being reconstituted towards the end of the century. In the first edition of Arthur

[14] J. N. L. Baker, "England in the Seventeenth Century," in *An Historical Geography of England before 1800,* ed. Henry C. Darby (Cambridge, 1936), pp. 435-443 on "The Population of England."

Collins's *Peerage* (1709) twenty-one dukes are listed as living: of these only four represented ducal creations antedating 1660.

New dignities, whether of title or of wealth, encouraged new ways of life and renewed respect for Augustan decorum and for the arts of conspicuous consumption. Like the newly created duke, the wealthy citizen or the country squire developed an interest in the beauty of his house— his physical refuge from the turmoil of the day.[15] Of the care bestowed upon country seats Defoe in his *Compleat English Gentleman* (written *c.* 1730) remarks, "Nothing is forgotten to improve the estate, nothing entirely neglected but the heir." Macaulay, who like Defoe had a prejudice against country squires as Tories, in chapter III of his *History* has given a not too kind account of these squires and their homes; but in spite of such opinion and in spite of more real jocose remarks in Restoration comedies slurring country life, the weight of evidence indicates that the gentry and nobility of the time were proud of their country seats and spent large sums on remodeling old Gothic mansions into classical houses. Magnificent palaces such as Longleat and Chatsworth were being built, and the French-Italian axial garden was already becoming a frequent pattern in landscaping before the end of the century. Restoration houses and gardens were pictured in large numbers in extensive works such as James Beeverell's *Délices de la Grand' Bretagne et de l'Irlande* (1707) and Johannes Kip's *Britannia Illustrata* (1707-8). These elaborate productions were the result of pride as well as a cause of increasing pride in domestic architecture and landscaping in the eighteenth century. In the seventeenth century the best English architectural tradition was the Palladian style used by Inigo Jones (d. 1652). The greatest Restoration architect was Sir Christopher Wren (1632-1723), who in a more ornate style labored chiefly on public buildings; and these, from the Sheldonian Theatre in Oxford to the City churches and St. Paul's Cathedral in London, show Italian classicism at its English best.[16] Such of these edifices as now remain after troubled years constitute the best English monuments of architectural Augustanism. The most exquisite details in many Wren interiors are secured by the unbelievably delicate and elaborate wood-carving that is a feature of this late baroque period. The carvings of Grinling Gibbons (1648-1720) are the supreme achievement in this art. Painting in the Restoration period was inferior: Van Dyck, the most distinguished Continental painter working in England during the early century, was dead; and the visiting successors were Sir Peter Lely (1618-1680) and Sir Godfrey Kneller (1646-1723).

> Lely on animated canvas stole
> The sleepy eye, that spoke the melting soul—

---

[15] The authoritative work on this problem is that of Beverley Sprague Allen, *Tides in English Taste (1619-1800): A Background for the Study of Literature* (2v, Cambridge, Mass., 1937).
[16] Sir Reginald Blomfield, *A History of Renaissance Architecture in England, 1500-1800* (2v, 1897), J. A. Gotch, *The English Home from Charles I to George IV* (1918), and Henry A. Tipping, *English Homes, Period IV (1649-1714)* (2v, 1920-28).

ately
omes Are
uilt

such was Pope's verdict on an art that he understood and practised. In childhood Pope inherited from his aunt the painting implements of her husband, Samuel Cooper (1609-72), perhaps the most notable of the skilful miniaturists of the time.

Of the fine arts music was practised with the most distinction. The keen *Music* eye of Samuel Pepys, watching at the waterside as citizens removed their goods by boat during the great London fire, on September 2, 1666, "observed that hardly one lighter or boat in three...but there was a pair of Virginalls [a sort of spinet] in it." Pepys himself, with his collection of viols, his harpsichord, and his flageolet, was passionately fond of music, and was not merely a performer but also a pleasing composer of songs. To contradict facile assertions of emotional deficiencies and artificialities of the period it may be well to quote Pepys's account of some incidental music for Massinger's *Virgin Martyr,* which he heard on February 27, 1667-8:

That which did please me beyond any thing in the whole world was the wind-musique when the angel comes down, which is so sweet that it ravished me, and indeed, in a word, did wrap up my soul so that it made me really sick, just as I have formerly been when in love with my wife; that neither then, nor all the evening going home, and at home, I was able to think of anything, but remained all night transported, so as I could not believe that ever any musick hath that real command over the soul of a man as this did upon me: and makes me resolve to practice wind-musick, and to make my wife do the like.

Music was the Londoner's diversion at home as well as his delight in the theatre. Pepys was a friend of the composers Matthew Locke (1630?-1677) and Henry Purcell (1658?-1695), the last named one of the greatest England has yet produced. His opera *Dido and Aeneas* (*c.* 1690), with Dido's poignant final air, "When I am laid in earth," reinforces the impression made by Pepys's reaction to music—that Restoration lovers of music were far from emotionally callous. Others of the Purcell family were musicians of note; but the introduction of Italian opera rapidly undermined the English musical tradition, and early in the eighteenth century and thereafter London was largely an El Dorado for the best Continental artists, most of whom could be heard there.

These, then, are the principal intellectual and artistic interests of Restoration England. Of the literary achievements the ensuing chapters will attempt to tell the story.

II
Literary Criticism of the Restoration

In the mid-seventeenth century English literary criticism was formulating neo-classical dogma out of ideas long current in Italy and France, and familiar earlier in English academic circles and in such groups as those presided over by Ben Jonson and by "Sidney's sister, Pembroke's mother." The doctrines were marked primarily by traditionalism and secondarily by a common-sense rationalism.[1] Naturally, in view of the great influence of Aristotle, Horace, Cicero, and Quintilian, as well as of Castelvetro, Scaliger, and, later, Boileau, the doctrines have been regarded as not native to English thinking. Although many of the dogmas imported from the Continent were never completely accepted in England, the common-sense aspect of neo-classicism easily domesticated itself. To follow the distinguished methods of the best ancients, that is, to follow "the rules" deduced by common sense from ancient procedure, seemed obviously practical. It was the function of critics to establish these laws for authors and to administer them with equity as judges. But the ancients when fantastic or parochial in habit might properly be disregarded, and no really eminent English critic ever wholeheartedly accepted all the French rules, the "foreign laws" (as Pope called them), laid down for the art of poetry. On the other hand, few were the critics of the period 1650-1750 who did not pay excessive attention to these rules.

The methods of these traditionalist critics were in general analytical or rhetorical. Aristotle, as interpreted by Renaissance commentators, gave doctrines for analytical critics, while Horace, Cicero, and Quintilian (and their disciples) largely originated the rhetorical tradition, which regarded poetry

Tradition-alism and rationalism [margin note]

Analysis and rhetoric [margin note]

---

[1] Perhaps the best single source of information about Restoration criticism is Joel E. Spingarn's *Critical Essays of the Seventeenth Century* (3v, Oxford, 1908-9) with its excellent introduction, texts, and notes. — For general discussions: F. E. Schelling, "Ben Jonson and the Classical School," *PMLA*, XIII (1898). 221-249; reprinted in *Shakespeare and Demi-Science* (Philadelphia, 1927); George Saintsbury, *A History of Criticism* (3v, Edinburgh, 1900-4); W. G. Howard, "Ut Pictura Poesis," *PMLA*, XXIV (1909). 40-123; James E. Routh, *The Rise of Classical English Criticism to the Death of Dryden* (New Orleans, 1915); Donald L. Clark, *Rhetoric and Poetry in the Renaissance* (1922); P. S. Wood, "Native Elements in English Neo-Classicism," *MP*, XXIV (1926). 201-208; René Bray, *La Formation de la doctrine classique en France* (Paris, 1927); P. S. Wood, "The Opposition to Neo-Classicism in England, 1660-1700," *PMLA*, XLIII (1928). 182-197; Marvin T. Herrick, *The Poetics of Aristotle in England* (New Haven, 1930); Arthur O. Lovejoy, "The Parallel of Deism and Classicism," *MP*, XXIX (1932). 281-299; Louis I. Bredvold, "The Tendency towards Platonism in Neo-Classical Esthetics," *ELH*, I (1934). 91-119; Ronald S. Crane, "Neo-Classical Criticism," in *Dictionary of World Literature*, ed. Joseph T. Shipley (1943), pp. 193-203. — For bibliographical aids see *CBEL*, II. 3-31 and John W. Draper, *Eighteenth Century English Aesthetics: A Bibliography* (Heidelberg, 1931).

as a superior refinement on the persuasive arts of oratory. The analytical and rhetorical methods were mutually helpful, and in some ways mutually destructive. Aristotle focused attention on the nature of poetry as existent in certain forms, notably epic and tragedy. He gave a method for analyzing poems of these types. He did not stress either the genetics or the effectiveness of poetry, but concentrated on its component parts and its structural principles. The rhetorical tradition, deriving strength from the fact that in the schools poetry was taught as a sub-topic under rhetoric, stressed creative processes and methods of affecting the mind of a reader. Neoclassical poetry was essentially rhetorical in that it spoke to an audience and attempted to move or to modify the mental state of its audience. Normally it did not, like later, romantic poetry, tend to be soliloquy. The composition of an oration from Greek times had been viewed under three aspects: *invention,* or the finding of material; *disposition,* or the arrangement of material; and *eloquence,* or the embodying of matter in fit style. As applied to the composition of poetry the first of these three aspects of creation was not necessarily cold-blooded. The prologue of the most epical of Shakespeare's plays, *Henry V,* begins,

> O for a Muse of fire, that would ascend
> The brightest heaven of invention;

and usually—but not always—in neo-classical criticism invention is not mere ingenuity but is associated with fire and elevation. It is a favorite word with Dryden; and for most English critics before 1750 it carried a meaning at times approaching that of the term so popular and so undefined in romantic criticism, "creative imagination." From rhetorical theory also, as well as from Bacon, Hobbes, and other psychological writers, the poet learned that to affect his readers he must through his own imaginative deftness appeal to "the passions" (as emotions were termed) of his reader. The principles of criticism changed less in the seventeenth century than the abilities of poets, but in the case of both critics and poets what change there was tended towards admiration of simplicity, sound sense, and propriety, and away from fantasy or anything like imaginative eccentricity. The poet was to sing in perfect full tone; he was not to try for "original" or individual tonal effects.

Before proceeding to discuss the major critics of the period it may be well to mention certain recurring topics sometimes regarded as subjects of universal agreement. While it is true that the belief, current at that time, *The Purpose of Poets* in the uniformity of human reason led critics to announce principles as if axiomatically self-evident, hardly more unanimity was evident in this period than in most ages. There was widespread agreement in the Horatian dogma that poets wished to profit or to please.

> Aut prodesse volunt aut delectare poetae,

Horace had written, and the moderns approved the dictum. Most, to be sure, assumed (as did Horace himself) that the best poetry afforded *both* delight and moral instruction, delight being the immediate and instruction the ultimate end. In 1668 Dryden evoked dissent from Shadwell by saying that "delight is the chief, if not the only, end of poesy: instruction can be admitted but in the second place, for poesy only instructs as it delights." Rymer believed in pleasure alone as object, but he stressed moral instruction as inherent in the higher sorts of poetry. Most critics seem to have regarded instruction as the ultimate end of the art, and poetry in practice frequently became a sort of wisdom-writing. Ten-syllable aphorisms, or even *pensées* in the general fashion of Pascal's, were features in the writing of most authors from Dryden to Blake.

Theories of Imitation   Imitation was the accepted method of poetry, but there was no uniformly accepted meaning attached to the term itself. To Aristotle poetic *mimesis,* badly translated into Latin as *imitatio,* had meant the representation of the actions of men. To Renaissance critics it had meant at times the imitation of one's predecessors, especially ancient classical authors. Its materials were the actions or manners of men, and the process of representation involved two things: depiction of an action and of an implicit principle of action. Critics of the epic, such as René Le Bossu,[2] thought a poet first selected a principle of action or a passion (disunity due to the wrath of Achilles, for example), and then wove a fable to illustrate it. The criteria of imitation were verisimilitude and decorum, and both might refer either to the action itself or to the principle of the action. Other criteria, much appealed to, were Truth, Reason, and Nature—terms used practically as synonyms representing a not too well-defined ultimate of excellence. Poetic mimesis might be idealistic and portray men not as they are but rather as they ought to be. There was no idea that the poet should attempt photographic realism. "Holding the mirror up to nature" might perfectly apply to the art of the actor, but it was less apt with reference to the more intellectual and ideal art of the poet. The meaning of human action as portrayed rather than the appearance of it was what appealed to poets with an abstractionist and moral bias. A further concept, expressed in the phrase *la belle nature,* involved a nature purged of its worthless or trivial dross and in a sense pre-fabricated and tested by the experience of (usually) the ancients. It was in this sense, according to Pope, that the young Virgil found Nature and Homer "the same." [3] Homer was in fact preferable to nature because he had supposedly sloughed off the crudeness of all but *la belle nature.*

The Rules   The criterion of art later most deplored by romantic critics was the rules. Admiration of one's predecessors made one a traditionalist, and critics attempted to judge the intelligence and tact of a poet's imitation by deducing general rules or "methodizing" the tradition followed. One might, at one's peril, depart from the rules; but if the departure did not surprise, delight,

---

[2] René Le Bossu's *Treatise of the Epick Poem* appeared in French in 1675, and was englished by "W. J." in 1695. It became the standard work on the epic, and in 1719 was reprinted. For a recent and thorough treatment of these matters see Hugh T. Swedenberg, Jr., *The Theory of the Epic in England, 1650-1800* (Berkeley, 1944).

[3] *Essay on Criticism,* line 135.

and enrich the tradition, it was likely to be bitterly condemned. The rules varied greatly in nature, but they prescribed, sometimes minutely, the procedure proper for each of the poetic genres. The fundamental trouble with "rules critics," apart from their less accountable absurdities, was summarized later by Dr. Johnson: they judged by principles and not by perceptions. They did not ask what was in a poem, but told what had to be in such a poem if it fulfilled traditional prerequisites. Such critics were early the objects of ridicule. Professor Spingarn found a French critic, the Chevalier de Méré, remarking: "I have noticed that those who lay the most stress on rules have little taste; and yet it is good taste which alone can create good rules."[4] Perception was bound to have its innings, and taste was to become by the turn of the century a word of power. It could modify the rules or defy analysis by insisting on the indefinable grace, the *je ne sais quoi,* as an eminent French critic, the Père Bouhours, called it in a famous essay.[5]

Traditionalist criticism worked through the various genres that French critics had deduced from the classics. Aristotle had hardly treated, in his fragmentary *Poetics,* more than the epic and tragedy; but by the middle of *The Genres* the seventeenth century the accepted genres had been both defined and evaluated. In 1704 John Dennis stated the net results with commendable bluntness:

1. The greater Poetry is an Art by which a Poet justly and reasonably excites great Passion, that he may please and instruct; and comprehends Epick, Tragick, and the greater Lyrick Poetry [i.e., the Pindaric ode].
2. The less Poetry is an Art by which a Poet excites less Passion for the foremention'd Ends; and includes in it Comedy and Satire, and the little Ode, and Elegiack and Pastoral Poems.[6]

The types Dennis lists, it should be noted, are arranged in order of descending importance. In the dedication of his *Aeneis* Dryden had remarked, "A Heroic Poem, truly such, is undoubtedly the greatest work which the soul of man is capable to perform." In the words "truly such" Dryden nods amicably to the traditionalism of his day, to the rules of the epic. But such a nod is not mere pedantry. On Dryden's opinion, his editor, W. P. Ker, comments:

The 'Heroic Poem' is not commonly mentioned in histories of Europe as a matter of serious interest: yet from the days of Petrarch and Boccaccio to those of

---

[4] Spingarn, *op. cit.,* I, p. xcv.

[5] In *Spectator* No. 62 Addison characterized Dominique Bouhours (d. 1702) as "the most penetrating of all the French critics." In his beautifully written *Entretiens d'Ariste et d'Eugène* (1671), ed. René Radouant (Paris, 1920), occur two essays at least, "Le Bel esprit," and "Le Je ne sais quoi," which are often echoed by English authors. In "Le Bel esprit" Bouhours describes wit as *un corps solide qui brille,* and this concept of wit is much quoted. In 1688 Dryden translated Bouhours' *Life of St. Francis Xavier,* and his *Manière de bien penser dans les ouvrages d'esprit* (1687) was translated into English in 1705 and 1728. On the history of this doctrine see Samuel H. Monk, "A Grace beyond the Reach of Art," *JHI,* v (1944). 131-150.

[6] "The Grounds of Criticism in Poetry," in *The Critical Works of John Dennis,* ed. Edward N. Hooker (2v, Baltimore, 1939-43), I. 338. With Dennis's ranking of the genres other critics would tend to agree. Possibly they would not make the excitement of passion the sole criterion for this ranking.

Dr. Johnson, and more especially from the sixteenth century onward, it was a subject that engaged some of the strongest intellects in the world (among them, Hobbes, Gibbon, and Hume); it was studied and discussed as fully and with as much thought as any of the problems by which the face of the world was changed in those centuries. There might be difference of opinion about the essence of the Heroic Poem or the Tragedy, but there was no doubt about their value. Truth about them was ascertainable, and truth about them was necessary to the intellect of man, for they were the noblest things belonging to him.[7]

It was in this lofty Augustan mood that critics at their best accepted the doctrines of neo-classical traditionalism. At their best they never in theory seriously disparaged the imaginative and emotional aspects of literary art; but they did subject these mercurial factors to the rigorous control of judgment. No critic is constantly at his best, and Restoration critics at times made the subjection of imagination to judgment excessive,[8] and at times were too moralistic or too much devoted to a prosaic common-sense attitude towards life. With the rules that concerned unity in structure and plainness in poetic style they struggled not very effectually. Unity is a late and perhaps a rare aesthetic quality, and the problem of appropriate decoration in style is as thorny as that of morals in art. We shall get further light on some of these problems if we examine individually some of Dryden's contemporaries —as well as Dryden himself, who has been called "the first great modern critic."

imagination nd Judgent

avenant s Critic

An early outburst of neo-classical pronouncement occurred in the prose discourses that preceded (1650) Davenant's *Gondibert* on its first appearance. Davenant[9] wrote a long prefatory epistle to his friend Thomas Hobbes,[10] which is in a sense a "defense of poetry" as well as of his own dull epic; and Hobbes contributed a friendly "Answer" to this prefatory epistle. It is significant that the focus of attention here, as in Cowley's critical writing,

[7] *Essays of John Dryden* (2v, Oxford, 1900), I, p. xvi.

[8] On control of the imagination by judgment see George Williamson, "The Restoration Revolt against Enthusiasm," *SP*, xxx (1933). 571-603, and two articles by Donald F. Bond: " 'Distrust' of the Imagination in English Neo-classicism," *PQ*, XIV (1935). 54-69, and "The Neo-classical Psychology of the Imagination," *ELH*, IV (1937). 245-264.

[9] For Davenant's career and works, see below, ch. v, n. 5. The present account of the critical writing of Davenant and Hobbes may be thought to undervalue their work. For other accounts see Spingarn, *op. cit.*, and Cornell M. Dowlin, *Sir William Davenant's Gondibert, its Preface and Hobbes's Answer* (Philadelphia, 1934), and Clarence D. Thorpe, *The Aesthetic Theory of Thomas Hobbes* (Ann Arbor, 1940).

[10] Thomas Hobbes (1588-1679) was born at Malmesbury, the son of a clergyman. After attending local schools from the age of four and learning Latin and Greek at six, he in 1603 entered Magdalen Hall, Oxford, and was graduated in 1608. For most of the rest of his life he was practically a member of the Cavendish family, since he served as tutor and companion to both the second and the third Earls. On his Continental travels Hobbes made many friends— among them, Gassendi and Galileo. Among his English friends were Bacon, Harvey, Selden, Cowley, Waller, Davenant, and Ben Jonson. His enemies were equally numerous: he was among the first to flee to Paris after the Long Parliament met in 1640; and after the publication of *Leviathan* (1651), fearful of French charges of atheism, he returned to England. Here too he underwent this accusation, and his replies as well as his mathematical controversies with Seth Ward, John Wallis, and Robert Boyle, extended over decades. From Clarendon and the church party he was protected by Charles II, who in Paris had been his pupil in mathematics, and who granted him a pension of £100. After a long and disputatious career Hobbes in 1675 retired to the Cavendish country estates at Chatsworth and Hardwick. He died at the age of ninety-one. — *Opera philosophica quae Latine scripsit* (Amsterdam, 1668); ed. Sir William Molesworth (5v, 1839-45); *The English Works*, ed. Sir William Molesworth (11v, 1839-45).

was the epic. In Davenant's opinion "Heroick Poesie...yeelds not to any other humane work"; and the philosophical Hobbes, agreeing, undermined his integrity as critic by such enthusiastic praise of *Gondibert* as "I never yet saw Poem that had so much shape of Art, health of Morality, and vigour and beauty of Expression as this of yours." These were doubtless the qualities that Hobbes and his age felt should exist in great poetry. Davenant found the function of "heroic" poets comparable to that of divines, generals, statesmen, and lawgivers as an aid to "government"; that is, to the control of manners and morals. "And as Poesy is the best Expositor of Nature, Nature being misterious to such as use not to consider, so Nature is the best Interpreter of God, and more cannot be said of Religion."

The apparent nobility of these ideas can be overvalued. Hobbes's "Answer" asserts a high intellectual concept of poetry when he says "That which giveth a Poem the true and natural Colour consisteth in two things, which are, *To know well,* that is, to have images of nature in the memory distinct and clear, and *To know much.*" *To know well* is the basis of decorum; *The* *to know much* is the source of delightful variety resulting from the well- *"Answer"* stored mind. But this high level is not maintained: an unimaginative, *of Hobbes* matter-of-fact disapproval of scenes that take us into fantastic localities, "even into Heaven and Hell...where Nature never comes," shows the really pedestrian concepts involved. The criterion of "truth" is invoked, and Davenant prefers truth of passion (fiction?) to truth of fact: the poet is not bound as is the historian, but he must remain within the limits of the probable. Hobbes dissents "from those that think the Beauty of a Poem consisteth in the exorbitancy of the fiction. For as truth is the bound of Historical, so the Resemblance of truth is the utmost limit of Poeticall Liberty." Thus in critical theory romantic "exorbitancy" was making its exit. A little more than a century later Richard Hurd at the end of his *Letters on Chivalry and Romance* (1762) summed up the results and indicated a counter-change in remarking: "What we have gotten by this revolution, you will say, is a great deal of good sense. What we have lost, is a world of fine fabling."

Few writers have acquired so much reputation in the field of criticism *Hobbes a* on so little bulk of critical writing as has Thomas Hobbes. His philosophical *Rhetorical* thinking was doubtless of great negative influence in the period: it spurred *Critic* all the other major thinkers of England to antagonism. In criticism his influence is less clear. His "Answer" to Davenant's preface, his own preface to his translation of the *Odyssey* (1675), and a few pages in his philosophical writings have caused him to be regarded as the father of neo-classical rationalistic aesthetics, and more recently as a forerunner of modern psychological theory concerning poetic creation. A true rhetorician, Hobbes regarded poetry as a means of modifying the minds of others: he studied the task as a psychological problem. "Invention" is an imaginative process; "disposition" is stressed as judgment, and "eloquence" is associated with certain ornamental functions of "fancy." His terminology is shifting, but his description of the creative process is not with all his meanings essentially novel. "Wit"—a valued faculty—consists of *"Celerity of Imagining,* (that is, swift succession of one thought to another;) and *steddy direction* to some approved end." "A good wit" is called "a good fancy." "But," he says, "without Steddiness, and Direction to some End, a great Fancy is one kind of Madnesse." Wit associates and combines; judgment discerns and differentiates. It is Hobbes's insistence on control in art, on judgment as a check to exorbitancy of fancy, that is his chief contribution to the aesthetics of his day.

The most valuable criticism of the period was that written by John Dryden.[11] The high excellence of his critical writing derives, first, from a mental incisiveness that led him at times with inspired directness to the heart of a problem and, secondly, from an unusually catholic sensitiveness to the merits of several divergent literary traditions. Amongst these traditions his mind has seemed to some merely blown about by various winds of doctrine inconsistently. The truth is that he is almost phenomenally able to see merits in all literary camps.

There is also the problem of development; for Dryden was writing criticism (chiefly in prefaces, there being at the time no other well established vehicles of criticism, except perhaps pamphlets) at frequent intervals throughout a career of almost forty years, and one might expect changes in his position. The temptation is to exaggerate a progressive detachment from Elizabethan "romanticism" in favor of neo-classical "orthodoxy." It is doubtful if any orthodox and tangible neo-classical *credo* was ever widely held; certainly Dryden is no consistent adherent to any such formulated doctrine. His prefaces are, at first sight, preoccupied with transitory, even topical, matters, and this fact makes it difficult to trace development surely, and makes it wise to focus on the aesthetic values basic in his thinking.

His fundamental skeptical independence in dogmatizing is perhaps best seen in his masterpiece in critical writing, the early *Essay of Dramatic Poesy,* written in 1665 and published in 1668, as a part of his argument with his brother-in-law, Sir Robert Howard, over the advisability of writing plays in rime. In form it is a Ciceronian dialogue; the four speakers present diverse points of view, for most of which Dryden felt both sympathy and reservation. The first speaker, Crites, defends the ancients (for whom Dryden has great

Dryden's critical merit

His Development

Of Dramatic Poesy

---

11 For Dryden's career see below, ch. III, esp. n. 2. The best of his critical writings are all in *Essays of John Dryden,* ed. W. P. Ker (2v, Oxford, 1900), and Professor Ker's introduction is still the best brief commentary. Other commentaries include: P. H. Frye, "Dryden and the Critical Canons of the Eighteenth Century," *Nebraska Univ. Stud.,* VII (1907). 1-39; John H. Smith, "Dryden's Critical Temper," *Washington Univ. Stud., Humanistic Series,* XII (1925). 201-220; O. F. Emerson, "John Dryden and a British Academy," *Proceedings of the British Academy,* X (1921). 45-58; F. G. Walcott, "John Dryden's Answer to Thomas Rymer's *The Tragedies of the Last Age,"* PQ, XV (1936). 194-214; J. O. Eidson, "Dryden's Criticism of Shakespeare," *SP,* XXXIII (1936). 273-280; Pierre Legouis, "Corneille and Dryden as Dramatic Critics," in *Seventeenth Century Studies Presented to Sir Herbert Grierson* (Oxford, 1938), pp. 269-291; Guy Montgomery, "Dryden and the Battle of the Books," *Essays and Studies by Members of the English Department, University of California, Univ. of Calif. Pub. in English,* XIV (1943). 57-72; Hoyt Trowbridge, "Dryden's *Essay on the Dramatic Poetry of the Last Age,"* PQ, XXII (1943). 240-250.

admiration); Eugenius, who like Dryden believes in progress in the arts, defends the superiority of contemporary English drama; Lisideius prefers French drama to English and prefers Elizabethan drama to that of the early Restoration period; and Neander, who most nearly is Dryden himself among the speakers, finally defends the English as opposed to the French, gives a glowing account of Jonson, Beaumont and Fletcher, and Shakespeare, but defends the recent use of rime in plays.

Here, and usually, Dryden believes in progress and modernity. He objects to the triteness of Roman comic plots, their faulty moral instruction, their weak wit, and their lack of warmth in love scenes; he praises their excellent contrivance of situation, their structural regularity—which the French imitate but which, he thinks, may easily lead to thinness of action. Irregularity in structure may contribute invaluable variety, but the paths of irregularity are difficult. One of Dryden's triumphant sentences is: "Now what, I beseech you, is more easy than to write a regular French play, or more difficult than write an irregular English one, like those of Fletcher, or of Shakespeare?" He can respect and even overvalue French rules, but he feels that the French are "too strictly tied up" with these formalistic matters; so he loyally asserts that "in most of the irregular plays of Shakespeare or Fletcher ... there is a more masculine fancy and greater spirit in the writing, than there is in any of the French." Dryden is relatively consistent, if somewhat prejudiced, in his evaluation of French drama; his notion of progress led him at times to overvalue his own age as compared with Elizabethan drama, notably in his Epilogue to the Second Part of *The Conquest of Granada* and in the prose "Defence" of the Epilogue (1672), where he asserts that the Elizabethans— often actually "low"—failed to produce polite or courtly dialogue because they were not, like the Restoration comic writers, frequenters of the best school of manners, the court! Normally he recognizes the merits as well as the defects of the Elizabethans. He sums up in his preface to the *Examen Poeticum* (1693), where he exclaims: "Peace be to the venerable shades of Shakespeare and Ben Johnson! none of the living will presume to have any competition with them; as they were our predecessors, so they were our masters."

Dryden swerved from minor positions, such as the use of rime in plays or rant in his heroic dramas; but he is reputably constant in his catholic appreciation of naturalness, "refined" wit, structural neatness (and such rules as conduce to it) as well as of variety (disparaging such rules as constrict genius), of "bold strokes," and of "masculine fancy." These last two values he admires in the Elizabethans, though at times excessively aware of the incorrectness found with them. "Shakespeare," he says, "who many times has written better than any poet, in any language ... is the very Janus of poets; he wears almost everywhere two faces; and you have scarce begun to admire the one, ere you despise the other." Similarly Dryden finds many faults among ancient writers, but yet holds them to be the best teachers for moderns. He believes in a spirited and emulous imitation of Nature as shown

Dryden's Consistenc[y]

by the ancients, but abhors a constricted imitation—"all that is dull, insipid, languishing, and without sinews." He ranges himself among the Aristotelians in his "Grounds of Criticism in Tragedy" (1679), and urges classical restraint in diction in his dedication to *The Spanish Friar* (1681). Both these works are influenced by Thomas Rymer's *Tragedies of the Last Age Consider'd* (1678)—a work to which Dryden planned a reply,[12] and by which he was considerably influenced. In the last decade of his career such prefaces as those to his translations of Juvenal (1693) and Virgil (1697) naturally stress classical topics; but even in the first extreme phase of Rymer's influence— seen in the dedication to *The Spanish Friar*—we find Dryden declaring firmly for tragicomedy as opposed to pure genres, and in one of his last dedications (to his *Aeneis*, 1697) he exclaims, "Let the French and Italians value themselves on their regularity; strength and elevation are our standard." Throughout his career he is likely to be boldly independent.

On such topics as the heroic poem or wit or such a neo-classical ultimate as "Nature," Dryden's thought is always vital and incisive; but a great deal of his impressiveness derives from his directness and pungency of expression. He seasons his assertions with apt and illuminating metaphor or with a summarizing aphorism. Of tragicomedy he concludes: "the feast is too dull and solemn without the fiddles," and his glowing remarks about Shakespeare ("he needed not the spectacles of books to read Nature") and Chaucer ("here is God's plenty") are known examples. Of Ben Jonson's indebtedness to the ancients he says, "You track him everywhere in their snow"; of Jonson's borrowings: "He invades authors like a monarch; and what would be theft in other poets, is only victory in him." A final apt metaphor in the preface to his *Evening's Love* (1671) expresses neatly the neo-classical concept of emulous imitation:

> But in general, the employment of a poet is like that of a curious gunsmith, or watchmaker: the iron or silver is not his own; but they are the least part of that which gives the value: the price lies wholly in the workmanship. And he who works dully on a story, without moving laughter in a comedy, or raising concernment in a serious play, is no more to be accounted a good poet, than a gunsmith of the Minories is to be compared with the best workman of the town.

Obviously Dryden understands not merely poetic expression but also what he himself calls "the other harmony of prose." The frequency with which his phrases turn up in later authors, indicates a considerable and appropriate amount of influence.

Apart from Dryden the most notable critic of the Restoration period was probably Thomas Rymer [13] (1641-1713), who, trained for the bar and per-

His Prose Style [margin note]

---

12 See Hugh Macdonald, *John Dryden, a Bibliography* (Oxford, 1939), p. 179, and James M. Osborn, *John Dryden* (1940), pp. 267-269 ("Dryden's 'Heads of an Answer to Rymer' ").

13 Thomas Rymer (1641-1713), son of a prominent Roundhead who in 1664 was executed after a Presbyterian uprising, was himself a consistent royalist. He attended loyal schools, including Sidney-Sussex College, Cambridge, where, however, he took no degree. A member of Gray's Inn, he was called to the bar in 1673; but thereafter for a time devoted himself to literature rather than to law. He acquired a great and deserved reputation for learning, and in 1692 was appointed historiographer royal, in 1693 editor of diplomatic documents and treaties.

suaded that of all the "Noble Exercises of Humane Understanding.... *Thomas*
Experimental Philosophy is the most noble, beneficial, and satisfactory," *Rymer*
became in criticism the standard-bearer of unimaginative neo-classical rationalism. Rymer had a deservedly great reputation as a historical antiquarian; his *Foedera* (1704-35 in 20 volumes), an enormous collection of
English state papers from the Middle Ages down to 1654, is still a major
landmark in the development of English historical studies. His achievement
as a critic has been from the start debatable. His translation (1674) of René
Rapin's *Reflections on Aristotle's Treatise of Poesie* indicates his regard both
for Aristotle and for French criticism. In his preface to this work he exhibits
his predilection for "exquisite sense" rather than "variety of matter," for neat,
unified plotting rather than for Elizabethan richness or humanity, and for
judgment rather than fancy. In his *Tragedies of the Last Age Consider'd*
he tersely announces, "Common sense suffices," and while this principle is
unimaginatively prominent, an austere sense of decorum is rather what
causes him in this work to castigate three plays of Beaumont and Fletcher.
In 1692 he published *A Short View of Tragedy* (dated 1693), one section of
which contains his notorious attack on *Othello*. His opinions of Shakespeare
seem generally, and justly, to have been regarded by his contemporaries as
extremely severe;[14] his obviously great learning was, however, widely
respected. He had an unusual knowledge of Greek tragedy, and the *Short
View* shows an astonishing diversity of reading. In his *Essay concerning
Critical and Curious Learning* (1698) he involved himself in the controversy
between Sir William Temple and the wits of Christ Church, Oxford, over
ancient and modern learning. Here he neatly states the nature of his adherence to Aristotle, of whom he was perhaps the most bigoted follower in his
day:

Using as model his friend Leibniz's *Codex Juris Gentium Diplomaticus* (1693), he labored for
the rest of his life, often at his own expense, on the arduous undertaking that is his real
monument, his *Foedera*. — *Reflections on Aristotle's Treatise of Poesie by R. Rapin* (translated
by Rymer, 1674); *Edgar, an Heroick Tragedy* (1678); *The Tragedies of the Last Age Consider'd
and Examin'd by the Practice of the Ancients and by the Common Sense of All Ages, in a
Letter to Fleetwood Shepheard, Esq.* (1678); *A Short View of Tragedy: It's Original, Excellency,
and Corruption, with Some Reflections on Shakespear, and Other Practitioners for the Stage*
(1693); *An Essay concerning Critical and Curious Learning: In which are Contained Some
Short Reflections on the Controversie betwixt Sir William Temple and Mr. Wotton; and that
betwixt Dr. Bentley and Mr. Boyl. By T. R.* (1698) [ascribed to Rymer]; *A Vindication of
an Essay concerning Critical and Curious Learning ... by the Author of the Essay* (1698);
Foedera (15v, 1704-13; Vols. XVI-XX [in part by Robert Sanderson], 1715-35). — Sir T. Duffus
Hardy, "Memoir," in Vol. I of his *Syllabus of the Foedera* (1869); A. Hofherr, *Thomas Rymers
Dramatische Kritik* (Heidelberg, 1908); G. B. Dutton, "The French Aristotelian Formalists and
Thomas Rymer," *PMLA*, XXIX (1914). 152-188.

[14] The work attracted great attention. It is reviewed in P. Motteux's *Gentleman's Journal* for
December, 1692 (p. 15), and in Richard Wolley's *Compleat Library* for the same month (pp.
58-66) the work gets a long summary—which omits the whole section on *Othello*. John Dennis's
Impartial Critick (1693) is a spirited reply. Samuel Butler's lines "Upon Critics who Judge of
Modern Plays Precisely by the Rules of the Antients" (Spingarn, *Critical Essays*, II. 278-281) is
a reply to *The Tragedies of the Last Age Consider'd*, and a reply to the *Short View* is addressed
to Dryden, presumably by Charles Gildon, under the title of "Some Reflections on Mr. Rymer's
Short View," in *Miscellaneous Letters* (1694), pp. 64-118. Concerning Dryden's reaction to this
earlier work see Fred G. Walcott in *PQ*, xv (1936). 194-214. Shakespeare was not without
friends!

Critical Learning, in the Modern Acception, is commonly taken for a thorough Understanding of Classick Authors, and an Exact Knowledge of those Rules, by which Men judge and determine nicely of all the finer Parts and Branches of Humane Literature. *Aristotle* was the first that drew these Rules up into Compass, and made Criticism an Art; and the Philosopher took such Care to form his Precepts upon the Practice of the best Writers, and to reduce them withal to the severest Test of Nature and Reason; that he scarcely left any thing for succeeding Ages to do. . . . But in short, he is esteemed a good Critick, who can distinguish the Beauties and Excellencies of an Author; and discover likewise his Failures and Imperfections. When he makes his Judgment of a Book; he takes it in pieces, and considers the whole Structure and Oeconomy of it.

Rymer was analytical: he took tragedies to "pieces"; he is also especially to be noted as a "verbal critic," meticulous and unimaginative in reducing poetic language to "common sense." His devotion to the rules plus an exaggerated evaluation of probability and decorum and an insensitiveness to the richness of human nature in the Elizabethan drama subverted his great learning and his keen sense of the importance of design or plotting in both epic and tragedy. He resented the tendency to regard the "monstrous irregularities" of Shakespeare as "shining beauties." "Good Conduct in War," he pontificates, "is no hindrance to the boldest Undertakings. . . . And a due observation of critical rules, that is, a strict attendance to the rules of nature and reason, can never impede or clog an author's fancy." Here Rymer differs from Dryden and other critics of the time; but it is observable that even for him reason and nature were higher than Aristotle.

Rymer was consistently of the party of the ancients, and thus naturally an ally of Sir William Temple in the campaign against modern writers that arose from Sir William's championing of antiquity in his *Essay upon the Ancient and Modern Learning* (1690). Sir William was a widely but superficially read statesman and man of the world, whose essay, if it had not annoyed certain scholars (William Wotton and Richard Bentley) by its faulty dating of Aesop's *Fables* and the *Epistles* of Phalaris, might have been praised and neglected for its suave and cadenced periods. After Temple's secretary, a young man named Jonathan Swift, reduced the controversy to acrid laughter in his *Battle of the Books* (1704), this essay was less regarded than another, *Of Poetry,* published in the same volume with it. Here Temple is the elegant amateur rather than the pedantic Aristotelian, but he is on the whole very much of his own day. Poetry has something in it "too libertine to be confined to so many rules" as the modern French critics invent; Sir William will content himself with the easier prescriptions of Aristotle and Horace, neglecting their commentators. Yet he agrees that to "the heat of invention and liveliness of wit" poetry must add "the coldness of good sense and soundness of judgment." In three other respects he is significant: (1) The earliest poets were thought to be the best; nature decays; and civilization knows cyclic change, but not progress. Dryden and many contemporaries did not agree here, and Temple's denial of the idea of progress did not deter

Temple and the ancients

others from espousing it. (2) On the basis of the old psychology that regarded heat as precondition for imagination and cold as fostering judgment Temple popularized the idea that genius depended in part on climate. This became a favorite eighteenth-century idea, and encouraged a tendency to think in relative rather than absolute terms. (3) Temple's polished amateurism promoted an aristocratic pose on the part of poets. This was perhaps inherent in the central concept of Augustanism, but it developed the belief that poetry was the most elegant of leisurely and genteel employments: its function was to amuse. So naturally Temple concluded his essay *Of Poetry* with the famous sentence that so well illustrates his pleasingly rhythmical style:

When all is done, Human Life is, at the greatest and the best, but like a froward Child, that must be Play'd with and Humor'd a little to keep it quiet till it falls asleep, and then the Care is over.

In the last two decades of the seventeenth century, verse was increasingly *Criticism* used as a vehicle for criticism in the Horatian tradition. The Earl of Ros- *in Verse* common published a metrical translation of Horace's *Art of Poetry* (1680), and a year later John Oldham also printed a modernized adaptation of the poem. In 1682 John Sheffield (later Duke of Buckinghamshire) published a metrical *Essay upon Poetry*, and in 1683 Sir William Soames and Dryden helped popularize Boileau's recent *Art Poétique* (1674) by an English translation. In 1684 Roscommon brought out his *Essay on Translated Verse*, and other poets followed with various satirical or didactic poems concerned with criticism. In 1700 Sir Richard Blackmore published his *Satyr against Wit*, and his admirer Samuel Wesley (1662-1735), the father of the founder of Methodism, brought out *An Epistle to a Friend concerning Poetry*. Somewhat more interesting was the *Essay upon Unnatural Flights in Poetry*, which, with elaborate prose annotations, "Granville the polite" (Lord Lansdowne) published in 1701. The path was open and well trodden that was to lead to Pope's *Essay on Criticism*. The critic was tied down to decorum, to the natural, to pedestrian common sense. The fantastic was "out"!

III

The Poetry of Dryden

Taste in poetry has changed so extremely in the last century and a half that for many persons John Dryden and his school are practically unreadable. For the intelligent student of poetry this is not true. Dryden is one of the most significant figures in the history of English verse; for he perhaps more than any other single person formulated a method for poetry that has appealed to disciples (some of them, to be sure, only metrical imitators) as different as Pope, Gray, Churchill, Byron, Keats, and T. S. Eliot; a method that for two generations after his death dominated English verse. Dryden's way was not that of the sensuous romantic, "tremblingly alive all o'er," unlocking his heart of hearts for the public to see; it is rather an impersonal, almost editorial, criticism of life. Much of the time it hardly seems to be "the language of the emotions," and seldom is it merely that of the senses. It is a method that conceives of poetry as intellectual utterance emotionally or imaginatively suffused so as to persuade a public "audience." It is, in short, the poetry of eloquence, which, in spite of John Stuart Mill and his followers, is not merely a reputable but an essential method for poets living as Dryden did in times of public emergency. His poetry is "occasional"; and the occasions which it celebrates are public and important—or were in his day. As time passes, however, the importance of occasions fades; the obvious journalistic character of such poetry requires annotation, and annotation is insufferable tedium to later casual readers of verse.

Basically, the school of Dryden is devoted to a belief in *control* as essential to art, to a disbelief in "unpremeditated art." One's imagination was controlled by the procedure of the ancients and by thinking in terms of genres. Accidentally, the school is devoted to translation and to satire; but Dryden—and Pope as well—realized that satire and didactic verse were "low" genres; and each aspired to produce an epic—to Dryden's mind "undoubtedly the greatest work which the soul of man is capable to perform." But the need to gratify patrons, to defend "sacred truth," and to make a living, compelled both Dryden and Pope to inhabit, in Swift's phrase, "the lowlands of Parnassus." Both poets made excellent translations of the greatest epics; but their own epics were never written.

The love of control operated also in the field of metrics, and the closed heroic couplet became the favored metre for Dryden and his followers. One must remember, however, that Dryden excelled all other English poets in the Cowleyan Pindaric, and that the stanza forms used for songs in his plays are both neat and varied. But the bulk of his work was in the couplet, which, though he did not invent, he did in a sense perfect. His chief predecessors in the evolution of the closed couplet as the container for Augustan wit were Ben Jonson, Waller, Denham, and Sandys.[1] Early prosodists to theorize the form were the author of *The Arte of English Poesie* (1589), usually ascribed to George Puttenham, and the author of an essay signed "J. D." in Joshua Poole's *English Parnassus* (1657). Such influences in addition to closing the couplet tended to make verse accent coincide with that of speech, to regulate the placing of the caesura, and to further the frequent use of rhetorical devices of various sorts. Dominated by an ideal of correctness, these tendencies resulted in verse notable for deft artifice and for mechanical perfection. Variety in metrical effect was a quality that Dryden achieved by a frequent use of triplets and of Alexandrines to break the monotony. Along with these metrical mannerisms came attendant rhetorical habits, such as parallelism, balance, antithesis, repetition, and other similar patterns. Aphoristic lines were much favored, especially such as involved epigrammatic surprise. From the early century's love of conceits Dryden derived a habit of illustrative and at times decorative tropes that are a feature of his method. The poetic vocabulary was rigidly restricted by excluding neologisms, archaisms, "low" words, or technical words. To the modern reader the use of Latinate words or idioms and the constant repetition of a few much used epithets—*sad, murmuring, alternate, trembling,* etc.—as well as the love of adjectives ending in *-y* (*wavy, paly,* for example) seem unfortunate mannerisms. They occur more commonly in the second-flight poets of the period than in Dryden.

A curious combination of frequently prosaic matter and a vigorous and lofty manner—of journalistic material in Augustan form—marks much of Dryden's work.[2] At times these two elements are beautifully fused, but in

[1] See George Williamson, "The Rhetorical Pattern of Neo-classical Wit," *MP*, xxxiii (1935). 55-81; and Ruth Wallerstein, "The Development of the Rhetoric and Metre of the Heroic Couplet, especially in 1625-1645," *PMLA*, L (1935). 166-209.

[2] John Dryden (1631-1700) was born in Northamptonshire and was reared there in a Puritan family environment. He was sent (*c.* 1644) to Westminster School, which, under the celebrated headmaster, Dr. Busby, gave the best secondary education and the fiercest floggings that England then afforded its young aristocrats. From Trinity College, Cambridge, he was graduated B.A. in 1654, and before 1660 he was settled in London. After other employment he turned to writing, lodged with his publisher, was elected to the Royal Society (1662), married above his station, and turned playwright to make money. From 1663 to 1678 he averaged something like a play a year, pausing hardly at all when in 1671 powerful wits burlesqued him in *The Rehearsal*. He achieved great fame and won official recognitions, some of them lucrative. Theatrical and political animosities caused him (as well as the rest of the nation) no end of trouble, and in December 1679 he was set upon and beaten for a satire written by another. He himself turned increasingly to satire, attacking enemies of the King as well as personal foes. Attacks on him grew more numerous when, soon after the accession of the Catholic James II in 1685, he became a Catholic. The sincerity of his conversion has been questioned, but without sure reason. After the Revolution of 1688 he lost, as a Catholic, the laureateship and all his other places, and was forced in old age to turn again to his pen for a livelihood. — *Works*, ed. Sir Walter Scott and George Saintsbury (18v, Edinburgh, 1882-92); *Essays*, ed. W. P. Ker (2v, Oxford, 1900; 1926); *Poetical Works*, ed. George R. Noyes (Boston, 1908); *Poems*, ed. John Sargeaunt (1910, 1935); *Poetry and Prose*, ed. David Nichol Smith (1925); *Dramatic Works*, ed. Montague Summers (6v, 1931-32); *The Best of Dryden*, ed. Louis I. Bredvold (1933); *The Letters of John Dryden, with Letters Addressed to Him*, ed. Charles E. Ward (Durham, N. C., 1942). — Hugh Macdonald, *John Dryden: a Bibliography* (Oxford, 1939); reviewed by James M. Osborn, *MP*, xxxix (1941-2). 69-98, 197-212, 313-319. — Samuel Johnson, *Lives of the Poets,*

Dryden's Early Poems

his early poems their incongruity shrieks at one. While still a schoolboy at Westminster, for example, he contributed lines *Upon the Death of Lord Hastings* (a fellow student), remarkable for their grotesquely ingenious conceits about smallpox; and possibly at Cambridge he composed (but did not print) harmlessly flirtatious verses to Honor Dryden, his cousin. In 1659 with Waller and Sprat he published *Three Poems* upon the death of Cromwell. Dryden's effort was entitled *Heroique Stanzas Consecrated to the Glorious Memory of his most Serene and Renowned Highnesse Oliver Late Lord Protector*...and years later these were more than once reprinted by Dryden's enemies to discredit him politically. A cousin of Dryden's had been among the judges who tried King Charles I, and one line (48) of Dryden's heroics was perversely supposed to imply approval of the regicide. When the sky changed a year and a half later, Dryden, like many another, was eager to celebrate the restoration of the monarchy. This he did finely in his poem *Astræa Redux* (1660), a poem which later led enemies to remind him of his celerity in tergiversation. In an epistle of the same date *To Sir Robert Howard* (whose sister in 1663 became Dryden's wife) is a couplet that sums up, doubtless, the attitude of both Dryden and the nation:

> All will at length in this opinion rest:
> "A sober prince's government is best."

The success of *Astræa Redux* as a poem on a "heroic" public occasion was followed by a panegyric on the coronation of Charles II entitled *To his Sacred Majesty,* and presently Dryden, after his speedy success as a playwright was assured, became a hopeful courtier, graciously regarded by royalty itself. This panegyric is ingenious wit-writing, with half-fused conceits and encrustations of imagery: it was good business but not very good poetry. His epistle addressed *To Dr. Charleton* (1663) about Stonehenge is of more interest since it shows Dryden's attitude towards the new science as opposed to ancient science, and because it was not merely another poem addressed to a great personage in the hope of possible rewards in patronage.

In the last poem of this early group, *Annus Mirabilis* (the wonders of the year 1666) Dryden is also glowingly eulogistic of the Royal Society, in which he obviously had some faith and interest even if he never paid his dues. The poem, descriptive of the naval war against the Dutch and also of the great

Annus Mirabilis

fire of London (2-6 September 1666), again makes use of the heroic quatrain, which in his preface Dryden judges to be "more noble, and of greater dignity, both for the sound and number, than any other verse in use amongst us"— and which he does not use again! He regards his matter as historical rather than epic, but insists on the lofty heroic quality of the events, and he makes

ed. G. B. Hill (1905); George Saintsbury, *Dryden* (1881); A. W. Verrall, *Lectures on Dryden* (Cambridge, 1914); Mark VanDoren, *The Poetry of John Dryden* (1920; rev. 1945); Allardyce Nicoll, *Dryden and his Poetry* (1923); T. S. Eliot, *Homage to John Dryden* (1924); T. S. Eliot, *John Dryden: the Poet, the Dramatist, the Critic* (1932); Louis I. Bredvold, *The Intellectual Milieu of John Dryden* (Ann Arbor, 1934); James M. Osborn, *John Dryden: Some Biographical Facts and Problems* (1940). On Dryden's principal plays see Part I, ch. v; on his chief prefatory essays see above, ch. II.

them majestic both by the sound of the verse and by the use of grandiose imagery:

> Then, we upon our globe's last verge shall go,
> And view the ocean leaning on the sky:
> From thence our rolling neighbors we shall know,
> And on the lunar world securely pry.

The poem as a whole is less interesting than its preface, which illuminates Dryden's notion of poetic imagination:

The composition of all poems is, or ought to be, of wit; and wit in the poet . . . is no other than the faculty of imagination in the writer, which, like a nimble spaniel, beats over and ranges thro' the field of memory, till it springs the quarry it hunted after. . . . But to proceed . . . to the proper wit of an heroic or historical poem, I judge it chiefly to consist in the delightful imaging of persons, actions, passions, or things.

The spaniel is active and self-consciously industrious, but if Dr. Johnson justly condemned those who "lay on the watch for novelty," Dryden's nimble faculty seems to deserve a similar censure. Conscious effort is perhaps over-valued here. For one of his school Dryden is in this poem at times daringly descriptive; but generally in description he lacks vivid, specific detail, and so misses delight.

With *Annus Mirabilis* Dryden's first poetical period terminates. He had already gone over to the definitely lucrative career of popular dramatist. Between 1663 and 1681 he produced nearly a score of plays, which aided both his fortune and his reputation. In 1668 he was made poet laureate and in 1670 historiographer royal. A second poetic period, far more distinguished for its non-dramatic poems, falls in the years 1681-87. These years, lurid with political and religious controversy (especially with regard to the succession *Satire* to the throne of England) and ending in the expulsion of the Catholic King James II in 1688, saw Dryden turning brilliantly to political satire and religious argument in verse as well as to translation and to lyric poetry.

The great political satires include *Absalom and Achitophel, The Medal,* *Absalom* and *Mac Flecknoe,* a literary satire born of politics. Somewhat lacking in *and* structure and overweighted with prolonged "scolding," these pieces are all *Achitophel* magnificent in their vigorous dignity, their boisterous vituperation, and their incisive satirical portraiture. After the excitement of the Popish Plot (1678) there had been repeated attempts to force a bill through Parliament excluding Catholics (and thus the legitimate heir, the Duke of York) from the throne of England. The villain in these attempts was the Whig leader, the Earl of Shaftesbury, who in the summer of 1681 was under arrest charged with high treason.[3] At the suggestion of the King, *Absalom and Achitophel* was written and its publication timed to fall just a week before Shaftesbury's fruitless arraignment. The poem makes use of biblical story to suggest how Achitophel (Shaftesbury) is tempting to rebellion Absalom (the Duke of Monmouth,

---

[3] Ruth Wallerstein, "To Madness Near Allied: Shaftesbury and His Place in the Design and Thought of *Absalom and Achitophel," Huntington Library Quar.,* VI (1943). 445-471.

illegitimate son of Charles II and the Whig candidate to succeed his father). Since Monmouth had not yet rebelled, the poem lacks action, but not tenseness. It consists largely of satirical portraits and of eloquent argumentative speeches in Dryden's epical style. Satirical portraits, or characters, were a favorite device of the day, but no one has ever surpassed Dryden's work in this art. Most of the portraits are enlivened merely by political animus; the famous character of Zimri, however, is further spiced by personal pique, for Villiers, Duke of Buckingham, who is Zimri, had satirized Dryden as "Bayes" in the dramatic burlesque *The Rehearsal* (1671). The lines on Zimri—

> A man so various, that he seem'd to be
> Not one, but all mankind's epitome—

are certainly among the most telling ever written in the vein of personal satire.

The Medal
and Mac
Flecknoe

Four months after this successful party piece Dryden published *The Medal* (March, 1682), another satire on Shaftesbury, whose followers upon his release from the charge of treason had cast a commemorative medal in honor of his triumph. The poem, less brilliant than its predecessor, gains force from being centered on a single person, but it lacks the edge of the earlier poem. It was answered, but not in kind, two months after its appearance by a scurrilous and gossipy retort, *The Medal of John Bayes,* probably from the pen of Thomas Shadwell. This dramatist, formerly a close friend, was now among the most venomous of Dryden's many personal and political enemies. In turn, a few months later, Dryden's opinions concerning Shadwell were published twice; first in *Mac Flecknoe,* apparently written in 1678, and secondly in passages inserted by Dryden in Nahum Tate's *Second Part of Absalom and Achitophel.* In his treatment of Shadwell Dryden drops at times his heroics and becomes roundly but still incisively abusive. His picture of Og (Shadwell) in Tate's poem begins:

> Now stop your noses, readers, all and some,
> For here's a tun of midnight work to come,
> Og, from a treason-tavern rolling home.
> Round as a globe, and liquor'd ev'ry chink,
> Goodly and great he sails behind his link.
> With all this bulk there's nothing lost in Og,
> For ev'ry inch that is not fool is rogue:
> A monstrous mass of foul corrupted matter,
> As all the devils had spew'd to make the batter. . . .
> The midwife laid her hand on his thick skull,
> With this prophetic blessing: *Be thou dull!*

The last three words here quoted echo the theme of the earlier *Mac Flecknoe,* certainly one of Dryden's most effective and most influential poems. *Mac Flecknoe* appeared anonymously, but was acknowledged by Dryden in 1693. About 1678, upon the decease of a secular priest, Richard Flecknoe, known as a bad versifier, it had occurred to Dryden to nominate Shadwell successor to the throne of Nonsense. Flecknoe, who

> In prose and verse, was own'd, without dispute,
> Thro' all the realms of *Nonsense,* absolute —

chooses Shadwell to succeed him as the perfect nadir of genius:

> The rest to some faint meaning make pretense,
> But Sh—— never deviates into sense.
> Some beams of wit on other souls may fall,
> Strike thro', and make a lucid interval;
> But Sh——'s genuine night admits no ray,
> His rising fogs prevail upon the day.

Satire on dullness of authors here reaches that high plateau of caustic and relentless phrasing, the other boundary of which might be Pope's *Dunciad*—a poem clearly much indebted to *Mac Flecknoe,* as were the works of other poets and even dramatists, Henry Fielding among them. The *genus irritabile vatum* were embattled over matters of their art with an ardor that hardly can be seen in any other period. For Dryden these excursions into political and personal satire brought a swift and abundant harvest of scurrilous abuse—and doubtless a considerable respect from intelligent and from Tory readers.

The Roman gravity and intellectual quality of Dryden's art, evident in these keen satires, are even more evident in the two great poems that concern his religion. The first of these, *Religio Laici,* published late in 1682, was occasioned by a translation from the French of Father Simon's *Critical History of the Old Testament* earlier in the year. The *Critical History* was a sensational and learned attack on the textual integrity of the Bible, the "one sacred book" of Protestants, and an assertion of ecclesiastical authority or infallibility as the only sure guide to faith. The book would have come to Dryden's attention partly because translated by a young friend, Henry Dickinson, and partly because of Dryden's skeptical interest in theological arguments on faith. In his political poems Dryden had, like a good Tory, tied up with a strong principle of authority in government. Certainly in 1682 he was no Catholic apologist, but he is obviously respectful of authority in religion—which in spite of Father Simon he still places in the Scriptures. He rejects the reason and the universality claimed by the deists; he rejects the Catholic claim of infallibility as preferable to textually faulty Scriptures, and he shrewdly argues that infallibility, if operative, ought to emend and explicate such texts easily—though "no council dare pretend to do" such a thing! While longing for an "omniscient church" and asserting that

> In doubtful questions 'tis the safest way
> To learn what unsuspected ancients say,

he professes himself a good Anglican and a believer perhaps in the light of reason but not in the rationalizing divines, a believer whose compromise is built on the typical principle: "common quiet is mankind's concern." The

Religious Poems: Religio Laici

poem is earnest and smooth in tone. It has less of wit and less of encrusted imagery than almost any other poem of equal length that Dryden wrote. His conclusion is, therefore, very significant:

And this unpolish'd, rugged verse, I chose;
As fittest for discourse, and nearest prose.

Nowadays probably any aesthetician would think this poem, as executed, essentially unpoetical. To Dryden evidently there was no impassable gulf between eloquent prose and poetry. In stating "sacred truth" he was writing *discourse,* and yet the use of metre and a grave dignity of more than prosaic utterance he deemed appropriate. To realize this is essential in understanding both Dryden and the neo-classical tradition. But the adagio movement of the opening lines of the poem is grand poetry, according to any tradition.

The Hind nd the 'anther

In the months following the accession of the Catholic King James II (1685), Dryden like many others became a Roman Catholic. This act has been regarded as gross time-serving, and it has been defended as a natural development of Dryden's earlier quest for "unsuspected ancients" and an "omniscient" or infallible church. It is undisputed that he remained from 1686 to his death a devout Catholic and that as such in 1688 he lost all of his "places" given by Charles II or James II. In 1687 he argued his change of faith in *The Hind and the Panther*. This curious blend of animal fable and religious controversy illustrates Dryden's aesthetic courage rather than his tact. The Milk-white Hind is the Roman Church; the Panther is the Anglican Church, and the various dissenting sects are symbolized also in animal shapes. The First Part characterizes all these allegorical persons with discursive reflections on the problems each presents. At the end of the section the Lion (the King) commands the fiercer beasts to allow the timid Hind to approach the watering place—an allegory of the recent Declaration of Indulgence (April, 1687); and it is this act that thereafter lessens the Hind's timidity. The Second Part is a controversial dialogue between the Hind and the Panther as they stroll together towards the Hind's "lonely cell," a dialogue which covers somewhat the same intellectual issues as *Religio Laici*. In Part Three the argument lasts most of the night, and centers now on more pragmatic English points of controversy. Here the Panther relates the story of the Swallows who were destroyed because they followed the ill counsels of the Martins (the extremists in the Roman clergy, whose influence on James II Dryden perhaps feared), and the Hind retorts with the fable of the Buzzard (Bishop Burnet), which shows the savageness of the extreme Anglican party.

This poem might have been as quaintly amusing as such a medieval *débat* as *The Owl and the Nightingale,* but Dryden was somewhat too earnest in his polemics for that. Arguments between allegorical animals have been frequent in literature, and the absurdity of Dryden's fundamental fable has been too easily ridiculed ever since the early spoofing indulged in by those two young wits, Charles Montagu, Earl of Halifax (1661-1715) and Matthew Prior, in *The Hind and the Panther Transvers'd to the Story of the Country-*

Mouse and the City-Mouse (1687). Doubtless there are at times absurdities; but these are so extremely superficial (or possibly so extremely fundamental) that they do not matter much. The poem has a rich diversity, a complex variety beyond Dryden's imaginative habit. Pope was right, also, in thinking the poem showed at its best the poet's marvelous command of the couplet. The quiet but mannered ease of the opening lines is perfectly melodic:

> A milk-white Hind, immortal and unchang'd,
> Fed on the lawns,[4] and in the forest rang'd;
> Without unspotted, innocent within,
> She fear'd no danger, for she knew no sin.

Shortly, a plain passage on "private reason" is followed by a piece of autobiography unusual in itself and in its devout and passionate appeal:

> Thy throne is darkness in th' abyss of light,
> A blaze of glory that forbids the sight.
> O teach me to believe thee thus conceal'd,
> And search no farther than thyself reveal'd;
> But her alone for my director take,
> Whom thou hast promis'd never to forsake!
> My thoughtless youth was wing'd with vain desires,
> My manhood, long misled by wand'ring fires,
> Follow'd false lights; and, when their glimpse was gone,
> My pride struck out new sparkles of her own.
> Such was I, such by nature still I am;
> Be thine the glory, and be mine the shame.
> Good life be now my task: my doubts are done.

In general in the poem the metrical effects subconsciously are fitted to the mood; the "panic fright" of the huddled sparrows, for example, produces a twittering hesitancy of caesuras and verbal re-echoings that overflow from the couplet to a triplet:

> Night came, but unattended with repose;
> Alone she came, no sleep their eyes to close:
> Alone, and black she came; no friendly stars arose.

The poem is nowadays for poets rather than for theological polemics; it is one of Dryden's most impressive attempts at fusing disparate elements. Here he worked (like his misguided Martin)

> Till grosser atoms, tumbling in the stream
> Of fancy, madly met, and clubb'd into a dream.

Possibly *clubb'd* is a more exact metaphor than *fused;* but even if a conglomerate, the work certainly elevates the author far above the status of a mere "inaugurator of an age of prose and reason."

Dryden was also a lyric poet of considerable ability. His comedies and

---

[4] A *lawn* in Dryden's day was a grassy open space between woods.

Miscellanies are sprinkled with deftly turned witty songs in the Cavalier tradition. Love is the favored theme, and Restoration love is likely to be stereotyped in cynical, physical, or artificially coquettish detail. When Dryden recounts the amorous play of "Fair Iris and her Swain" he elegantly leers both at the lovers and at his readers. The metres are very apt and nimble, Dryden being curiously expert in triple rhythms. His "Sea Fight" in *Amboyna* approaches roughly the rhythms of free verse. In Dryden's day, however, a song was less valued as poetry than was "the greater lyric," by which term was meant the Cowleyan Pindaric, a rimed poem of irregular verses arranged in strophes of no fixed structure. In this form the cult of irregularity, sublimity, and enthusiasm was to express itself for many a year. Against the irregularity protest was to rise, notably in Congreve's *Ode on the Victorious Progress of Her Majesty's Arms* (1706), the prefatory "Discourse" of which condemned Cowley's simplification of the true Pindaric. Yet the Cowleyan form was long popular, and Dryden contributed much to its vogue by his poems of the type.

Two of these, the *Threnodia Augustalis* (1685), in memory of Charles II, and the ode *To the Pious Memory of Mrs. Anne Killigrew* (1686) are dignified and restrained threnodies. In the latter poem Dryden expresses loud repentance for his part in augmenting the "fat pollutions" of the stage. Three other odes were libretti set to music. That *On the Death of Mr. Henry Purcell* is perhaps adequate for the commemoration of the loss of England's greatest composer. The two written for the Musical Society's celebrations of St. Cecilia's day are among Dryden's noblest efforts. The first strophe of the *Song for St. Cecilia's Day*, set by Draghi in 1687, begins and ends with full rich-toned majesty:

> From harmony, from heav'nly harmony
> This universal frame began:
> From harmony to harmony
> Thro' all the compass of the notes it ran,
> The diapason closing full in Man.

There is nothing superior to this in the more famous ode, *Alexander's Feast* (1697), which after two less distinguished musical settings gained added glory when Handel in 1736 composed for it a magnificent score. The effectiveness of the poem, however, is not dependent on musical setting. It has a neatly handled story; it has spirit; and its movement is direct, varied, and speedy as in much of Dryden's best work. It partakes perhaps of the theatrical and he obviously ingenious; it furthermore lacks the gravity of Dryden's best work; but its effectiveness is indubitable, and it remains not Dryden's best but certainly his most popular poem. There is something to be said for a poetic art and a manner of life that enable a poet to produce his most vigorous and attractive lyric at the age of sixty-six.

With the accession of William and Mary, naturally, Dryden lost his pension and the laureateship. The latter went to the "true blue" poet Tom Shadwell! Now, as he was entering old age, Dryden again had to write for a living.

He got a half dozen dramatic pieces staged, but he had lost touch with *Transla-* audiences and had a personal "loathing" for such employment. His main *tions* resource became translation both in verse and prose. In 1684 he had begun editing for Jacob Tonson a series of volumes of miscellanies "by the Most Eminent Hands." In these he collected his original poems and published many translations. As early as 1680 he had made notable contributions to a translation of *Ovid's Epistles* done "by Several Hands"; in the second miscellany, *Sylvae* (1685), he attempted Lucretius with distinction and also Theocritus and some small pieces of Horace; but his major classical translations were those of Juvenal and Persius (1693) and the tremendous task of doing Virgil into English (1697). The *Æneid* was for Dryden a most lucrative and a most distinguished venture in translation.[5] In prose meanwhile he did various translations from the French and from the classics did at least prefatory sections for versions of Plutarch's *Lives* (1683), Polybius (1693), Tacitus (1698), and Lucian (1711). He was in all this drudgery industrious, conscientious, and, thanks to long practice, usually apt, elegant, vigorous, and spirited in his renditions.

Along with these noble pot-boiling efforts Dryden found time to make modern English versions of a variety of poetic narratives, which shortly before his death in 1700 he published as *Fables Ancient and Modern.*[6] These *Dryden's* include the First Book of the *Iliad,* eight tales from Ovid, three from *Fables* Chaucer, and three from Boccaccio, as well as other non-narrative poems. Throughout the eighteenth century the *Fables* were apparently the most popular of Dryden's poems. Doubtless there was more about Chaucer than metre that Dryden did not comprehend as he should: simplicity, lightness are traits in which Dryden was comparatively deficient; but it is clear that he had a warm and keen appreciation of Chaucer's humanity. With Ovid he is excellent, and Boccaccio suits his genius well. It is a pity that Dryden did so little narrative verse; for his speed and his dramatic gift shown here are most suitable for such work. For a poet of almost seventy years the vitality is astonishing.

All this must have made a very busy old age, and yet the work seems not to have kept Dryden from his normal coffee-house pleasures. The tradition is that he wrote mornings, dined at home, and spent the afternoon and early *Dryden's* evening at Will's Coffee-house, where he had his "winter seat" near the fire *Last* and his "summer seat" in the balcony. In 1682 Shadwell had given an ill natured picture of this life in *The Medal of John Bayes:*

You who would know him better, go to the Coffee-house (where he ma˅ ˅e said
almost to inhabit) and you shall find him holding forth to half a˅˅re young
fellows, (who clap him on the back, spit in his mouth, and loo˅˅l on upon the
Whiggs, as they call 'em) puft up, and swelling with their˅˅ise: and the great
Subject of his Discourse shall be of himself, and his P˅˅y; What Diet he uses
for *Epick* what for *Comick;* what course he is in for ˅bel, and what for *Tragedy.*

[5] See J. McG. Bottkol, "Dryden's Latin Scholarship," *MP,* XL (1943). 241-254.
[6] Herbert G. Wright, "Some Sidelights on the Re˅˅tation and Influence of Dryden's Fables," *RES,* XXI (1945). 23-37.

Thus in the company of such friends as Wycherley, Dennis, Southerne, Garth, Walsh, Lockier, Granville, Congreve, and others, Dryden passed the evening of his days. Diet apart, the talk might well have been the best since the days of Ben Jonson at the Mermaid. Enemies Dryden had, but when the virulent Whig, Bishop Burnet (the Buzzard in *The Hind and the Panther*), called Dryden in print "a monster of immodesty and impurity of all sorts," Dryden's remaining friends almost to a man went on record as giving the lie direct to the Bishop. To them Dryden was modesty and kindness itself. There is even an (improbable) anecdote to the effect that on one occasion he gave a very small lad named Alexander Pope a shilling for a boyish effort in translation. *Virgilium tantum vidi* was Pope's later reverent comment concerning the poet who was of all others Pope's master as well as the master of the Restoration period.

IV

Minor Poets of the Restoration

The greater poets of the Restoration period clearly were John Milton and John Dryden. These men represent two developments at the end of the Renaissance. Milton preserved the elevation and glowing richness of the *Higher and* humanist intellect, while Dryden developed in the realistic, critical, and *Lower* skeptical tradition initiated in part by Montaigne. Milton in his post-restora- *Genres* tion poems thought and worked in terms of the higher genres, epic and tragedy, and he thus achieved the acme of English neo-classical distinction.[1] Dryden worked in inferior genres, and the lesser poets in general followed Dryden in this respect. At the end of the century, to be sure, Sir Richard Blackmore (*c.* 1655-1729) was pouring forth interminable epic strains; but these were not highly regarded. The most acclaimed poems, apart from Milton's, were in general satirical or didactic. There was, of course, much writing and singing of popular political songs and ballads as well as songs of love and drinking; but these were regarded much of the time as non-literary. Normally poems in these lower genres were written in a familiar, facetious, and at times even a vulgar or actually indecent tone: the dignity of Augustanism tended to be slighted, but it was still valued for nobler efforts.

The most eminent of these lesser poets—for very different reasons—were Samuel Butler and John Wilmot, Earl of Rochester. These men were poets of distinction and permanent interest. We may well discuss Butler [2] first

---

[1] For the influence of Milton in the period see Raymond D. Havens, *The Influence of Milton on English Poetry* (Cambridge, Mass., 1922).

[2] Samuel Butler (1612/13-1680) was born the son of a well-to-do Worcestershire yeoman, who valued books and learning. The son was educated at King's School, Worcester, and possibly later became a member of Gray's Inn. He was in 1661 steward of Ludlow Castle for the Earl of Carbery, Lord President of Wales. Except for the first two parts of *Hudibras* most of his writing was done after 1667. His "characters," published in 1759, were composed between 1667 and 1669. He was secretary to George Villiers, Duke of Buckingham, for all or part of the time when his grace was Chancellor of the University of Cambridge (1671-4). Anthony Wood asserts that Butler helped write *The Rehearsal*. The popularity of Part III of *Hudibras* (1678) caused the King to give Butler £100 and to order an annual pension of that sum paid to him. Among the poet's friends were Thomas Hobbes, John Cleveland the poet, Samuel Cooper the miniaturist, and Sir William Davenant; surviving him were such other friends as John Aubrey, Tom Shadwell, and Dr. Charles Davenant the economist. Butler's traditional poverty has probably been exaggerated. Many of the above details are taken from the careful article by E. S. de Beer, "The Later Life of Samuel Butler," *RES*, IV (1928). 159-166. Another good source for Butler's family and early life is René Lamar, "Du Nouveau sur l'auteur d'*Hudibras*," *Revue Anglo-Américaine*, I (1924). 213-227. — *Poetical Works*, ed. Reginald B. Johnson (2v, 1893); *Collected Works* (3v [I and II, ed. A. R. Waller; III, ed. René Lamar], 1905, 1908, 1928). — *Lord Roos His Answer to the Marquess of Dorchester's Letter* (1660; see *LTLS*, March 21, 1936, p. 244); *Hudibras*, Part I (1663); *Hudibras*, Part II (1664); *To the Memory of ... Du-Vall* (1671); *Two Letters* (1672); "Heroical Epistle of Hudibras to Sidrophel," in *Hudibras*, Parts I and II (1674); *Hudibras*, Part III (1678). — Samuel Johnson, *Lives of the Poets* (1779), ed. George Birkbeck Hill (1905); Hardin Craig, "*Hudibras, Part I*, and the Politics of 1647,"

and the practical and journalistic poetry of the day, and later turn to Rochester and the court poets.

Butler's contemporary reputation was almost exclusively based on *Hudibras*,[3] since most of his other works were first published in 1759 long after his death, and *Hudibras* is still his major work. A friend and contemporary in 1663 called Part I of the poem "the most admired piece of drollery that ever came forth," and this was a common verdict. A drollery was an attack—or a miscellany largely filled with attacks—on Puritans. The completed poem consists of three parts each containing three cantos, with *An Heroical Epistle of Hudibras to Sidrophel* appended to Part II and two epistles added at the very end of the poem. Ostensibly *Hudibras* is a mock-heroic, and as anti-heroes Butler presented a Presbyterian colonel and knight, named Hudibras, and Ralpho, an Independent in religion, who is the knight's squire. The two remotely resemble Don Quixote and Sancho Panza, but their arguments over theology and church government are more vituperative than the chivalry of Cervantes' hero would have allowed. The action is less amusing now in its loose episodic flow than it was in its own day. Part I, starting slowly, tells how Hudibras and Ralpho tried to stop a bear-baiting in a "western" town. They win the first battle, but in a later encounter Hudibras and Ralpho lose and are imprisoned in place of their foes. Meanwhile, Hudibras has fallen in love with a widow's jointure-land, and so also with the widow. In Parts II and III we have his fruitless adventures in trying to win the widow. In one striking episode he visits a Rosicrucian prognosticator, Sidrophel—a visit that ends in a battle disastrous to second-sight.

The purpose of the whole is obviously satirical, and the action simply a loose thread upon which arguments, reflections, and caustic portraits are strung. Recently there has come to light an important account of the poem in a letter written by Butler in 1663, to accompany a copy of *Hudibras, Part I,* that he was sending to a friend in India. Of his poem he says:

It was written not long before the time when I had first the honor to be acquainted with you, and Hudibras, whose name it bears, was a West Country knight, then a Colonel in the Parliament army, and a committee man, with whom I became acquainted lodging in the same house with him in Holborn. I found his humor so pleasant that, I know not how, I fell into the way of scribbling, which I was never guilty of before nor since. I did my endeavor to render his character as like as I could, which all that know him say is so right that they found him out by it at the first view. For his esquire Ralpho, he was his clerk and an Independent, between whom and the knight there fell out such perpetual disputes about religion as you will find up and down in the book for as near as I could set down their very words. As for the story, I had it from the

Manly Anniversary Studies (Chicago, 1923), pp. 145-155; Jan Veldkamp, *Samuel Butler* (Hilversum, 1923); Beverley Chew, "Some Notes on the Three Parts of Hudibras" [bibliographical], *Essays & Verses about Books* (1926), pp. 65-97; J. T. Curtiss, "Butler's Sidrophel," *PMLA,* XLIV (1929). 1066-1078; Dan Gibson, "Samuel Butler," *Seventeenth Century Studies by Members of the Graduate School, University of Cincinnati,* ed. Robert Shafer (Princeton, 1933), pp. 279-335; Ricardo Quintana, "The Butler-Oxenden Correspondence," *MLN,* XLVIII (1933). 1-11.
[3] Only the ignorant fail to pronounce the final *s* in the name of this very English hero!

knight's own mouth, and is so far from being feigned that it is upon record; for there was a suit of law upon it between the knight and the fiddler, in which the knight was overthrown to his great shame and discontent, for which he left the country and came up to settle at London. The other persons, as Orsin a bearward, Talgot a Butcher, Magnano a Tinker, Cerdon a Cobbler, Colon a Clown etc., are such as commonly make up bear-baitings, though some curious wits pretend to discover certain persons of quality with whom they say those characters agree; but since I do not know who they are, I cannot tell you till I see their commentaries, but am content (since I cannot help it) that everyman should make what applications he pleases of it, either to himself or others. But I assure you my chief design was only to give the world a just account of the ridiculous folly and knavery of the Presbyterian and Independent factions then in power and whether I have performed it well or no I cannot tell, only I have had the good fortune to have it generally esteemed so, especially by the King and the best of his subjects. It had the ill fortune to be printed when I was absent from this town, whereby many mistakes were committed, but I have corrected this book which you will receive myself, with which, Sir, I send you the best wishes and real affections of / Your humble and faithful / Servant Sam: Butler.[4]

From the letter we infer that from the start readers made personal applications of the characters and probably allegorical interpretations of the action. Of this last matter Butler says nothing; of his persons, Hudibras and Ralpho are thus from life, and they come to London from the "West Country" after discomfiture probably resembling that recounted in Part 1 of *Hudibras*. Butler somewhat coyly deprecates identification of minor persons of the story with actual people. Sir Samuel Luke, commonly regarded as the prototype of Hudibras, was from Bedfordshire and not from a western county. Neither the story nor the depiction of actual persons, however, was Butler's "chief design." That was to expose "the ridiculous folly and knavery" of Puritans.

His usual methods are burlesque, through distortion, and travesty, through vulgarization. There are long grotesque "characters" of all the persons involved; there is author's comment by way of analysis or history; and there are interminable violent disputes between Hudibras and Ralpho, Hudibras and Sidrophel—or any other opponent who offers. The knight was, we are told, *Butler's Methods*

> in Logic a great critic,
> Profoundly skill'd in Analytic;
> He could distinguish, and divide
> A hair 'twixt south and south-west side;
> On either which he would dispute,
> Confute, change hands, and still confute;
> He'd undertake to prove by force
> Of argument a man's no horse;
> He'd prove a buzzard is no fowl,
> And that a Lord may be an owl; ...
> All this by syllogism, true
> In mood and figure, he would do.

[4] Modernized from Quintana's text, *MLN*, xlviii (1933). 4.

He was also skilled in the pedantries (not the practical aspects) of rhetoric, mathematics, philosophy, and "school-divinity." The famous lines on his religion show the vigor of Butler's animus:

> For his Religion it was fit
> To match his learning and his wit:
> 'Twas Presbyterian true blue,
> For he was of that stubborn crew
> Of errant saints, whom all men grant
> To be the true Church *Militant:*
> Such as do build their faith upon
> The holy text of pike and gun;
> Decide all controversies by
> Infallible artillery;
> And prove their doctrine orthodox
> By apostolic blows and knocks;
> Call fire and sword and desolation,
> A godly-thorough-Reformation,
> Which always must be carry'd on,
> And still be doing, never done:
> As if Religion were intended
> For nothing else but to be mended.

The burlesque also has objects other than Puritanism. Chivalry, as in *Don Quixote,* and heroism, as in Scarron, are disparaged. The fighting always is far from decorous, and intellectual combat is similarly made cheap. Butler abhors logic-chopping, and is so skeptical by nature that he can doubt the sincerity of conviction through argument. In one passage he asks,

> *What makes all doctrines plain and clear?*
> About two hundred pounds a year.
> *And that which was prov'd true before,*
> *Prove false again?* — Two hundred more.

One of his more significant poems, it may be noted, is an unfinished *Satire in Two Parts upon the Imperfections and Abuse of Human Learning.*

efects of udibras   The defects of *Hudibras* are obvious. It lacks structure, and is only a series of desultory, drifting—and brilliant—passages. In these passages, furthermore, Butler is too leisurely: he spins a dozen couplets where a better artist would have made one do. Forty lines devoted to describing Hudibras's beard have been rightly thought excessive, and there are many such dilated descriptions. The truth was that in the period 1663-78 almost anything was good for a laugh against Puritans, and Butler had no need to restrain himself. Again, Butler is often guilty of bad taste. Admittedly, he has the art of making bad taste amusing, but he goes too far—for example, in the "nasty pickle" that makes Hudibras and Ralpho offensive in the end of II, ii, where he is enforcing the obvious moral:

> That man is sure to lose,
> That fouls his hands with dirty foes.

His taste for unsavory realism persists when he turns to burlesquing the arts of poetry, meretricious or otherwise. Here he maintains a vulgar, anti-heroic, anti-poetic attitude towards his material. He loves to cheapen poetic "imagery":

> The sun had long since, in the lap
> Of Thetis, taken out his nap,
> And like a lobster boil'd, the morn
> From black to red began to turn.

Since Chaucer's day at least this sort of thing has been good fun, though the lobster is doubtless a bold stroke. So likewise Butler burlesques the So-have-I-seen tropes so popular at the time, and he ends passages with aphoristic bits of wisdom much as playwrights punctuated passages with a couplet. His fights mix the grotesque with the mock-heroic. Obviously vulgar brawls, they are called combats or conquests and treated in lofty terms. Most obviously he burlesques poetic arts in his rhythms and double rimes. The jolting effects of his octosyllabic couplets underline the awkwardness of the actions—whether physical or intellectual. Sober folk, like Joseph Addison,[5] would prefer neater rhythms and less screaming rimes; but Addison confesses that "the generality of his [Butler's] readers are so wonderfully pleased with the double rhymes" that they will not approve Mr. Spectator's opinion.

The power of the burlesque lies precisely in these externals, just as the subtlety of it lies in the allusiveness of the text. Clearly the cheap format of the early editions of *Hudibras* Part i indicates that it pleased not only Charles II and the court but "the generality of readers" also. It had a proletarian action; but it had also an appeal to bookish men. It glances at chapbook *The Appeal* stories and at Homer and Virgil as well. It mocks the pedantries of the *of Hudibras* schools, the absurdity of astrology and the new science, and the irrationality of synods and of the "inward light." Butler was a very learned man, and the whole scope of his reading is drawn upon for themes, famous passages, or methods of thinking and writing that might aid his burlesque. He has a remarkable gift for portraiture. The schools of Dutch realism and French travesty meet in his work, which anticipates and rivals the graphic art of his later illustrator, William Hogarth. His favorite classical satirist was Juvenal; but he owed fully as much in theme and method to such moderns as Rabelais, Cervantes, and Scarron. Among English poets he is less a buffoon than he is a jester such as Shakespeare might have created in his later plays.

Butler's intellectual quality, if not his full genius, is seen also in his other works which largely lack the grotesqueness of *Hudibras*. *The Elephant in the Moon*, a facetious satire on Sir Paul Neale, and the *Satire on the Royal* *Butler's* *Society* both show his unsympathetic attitude towards the new learning. *Intellectual* Butler is that contradiction, the complete skeptic combined with the com- *Quality* plete conservative. He hated silly new mechanical ways of doing things. Hudibras,

⁵ *Spectator*, No. 249.

> by geometric scale,
> Could take the size of pots of ale;
> Resolve by sines and tangents straight,
> If bread or butter wanted weight;
> And wisely tell what hour o' th' day
> The clock does strike, by algebra.

One suspects that Gulliver's Laputan tailor had had hints of his trade from Hudibras. Butler and his knight lived in days obsessed with the need of progress—

> No sow-gelder did blow his horn
> To geld a cat, but cry'd Reform.

Self-consciously pious folk nasally intoned new doctrines—

> As if Religion were intended
> For nothing else but to be mended.

Butler was loudly contemptuous of all new doctrine; he even contemned human reason itself because of all these unstable aberrations. At a high point in the satire on Hudibras's mind we are told

> He understood b' implicit faith,
> Whatever Skeptic could inquire for;
> For every *why* he had a *wherefore*.

For such intellectual self-sufficiency Butler's contempt was unbounded. He was on the losing side: the idea of progress through science and a complete trust in human powers was to triumph: his lot was to go down fighting scurrilously. He stimulated many to imitate the surfaces of his work; the cast of his mind was less frequently copied. As a whole he is a unique figure, an intellectual in the burlesque tradition. John Dennis in writing an epitaph for Butler summed it up well:

> He was a whole species of poets in one:
> Admirable in a manner
> In which no one else has been tolerable. . . .

Butler, it is true, had no worthy, avowed disciple. Tom D'Urfey, Ned Ward, Tom Brown, and nameless writers in miscellanies emulated his less desirable traits, but lacking the intellectual quality of his substance, merely vulgarized his manner. Charles Cotton's *Scarronides: or, Virgile Travestie* (1664) perhaps owed some of its great popularity to the vogue of *Hudibras,* but *Scarronides* owed none of its nature to Butler. In formal satire as distinguished from travesty or burlesque the more reputable tradition—formal, Augustan, or neo-classical—swept over and past Samuel Butler.[6]

In this formal tradition appears the work of John Oldham,[7] who followed

---

[6] Butler and Oldham (and later satirists) are well placed in their satirical tradition by C. W. Previté-Orton in his *Political Satire in English Poetry* (Cambridge, 1910).

[7] John Oldham (1653-1683), son of a Gloucestershire nonconformist clergyman, was educated at home, at Tetbury Grammar School, and (1670-74) at St. Edmund Hall, Oxford. Upon graduation he returned to Gloucestershire, probably to teach, and in 1676 became usher at Croydon School, the headmaster of which was a relative of Oldham's college friend, Charles

Andrew Marvell (better known for his non-satirical work) and perhaps *Formal* slightly anticipated Dryden's satires—though of course Dryden's reputation *Satire:* as poet was quite established before Oldham began to publish in 1677. A *John* half-dozen years make up the period in which Oldham was publishing; and *Oldham* since these years were those of the excitement over the Popish Plot, Oldham was naturally led into political satire. He was the foremost and most furious of those who fought on the side of Titus Oates and the Whigs. His *Satyrs upon the Jesuits* (1681), avoiding mock-heroic narrative, made use of a dramatic monologue that gives high heroic eloquence but unfortunately lacks variety and change of pace in its vituperation. With these satires he printed a Pindaric "Ode," already published under the lurid title *A Satyr against Vertue* (1679). Here we meet that dangerous quality irony, which while pretending to glorify vice actually scourges rakes who glory in their viciousness. Oldham's purpose seems not to have been understood by all, and indeed when he ironically curses virtuous fools,

> Who think to fetter free-born souls,
> And tie 'em to dull morality, and rules —

he is expressing a love of freedom which elsewhere in his work is not ironical. He abhorred the servitude of teaching school, and declined the too menial office of chaplain to the Earl of Kingston; he was too proud to dedicate poems fulsomely for a price, as his friend Dryden practically did. In the satire *Addressed to a Friend that is about to Leave the University and Come Abroad in the World,* Oldham affirms this love of freedom eloquently in the inserted fable of the wolf that wanted food but would not endure the indignity of collar and chain put upon the civilized and well-fed Towzer. It is the furious sweep of Oldham's satiric rage that is most impressive, but this fable, and other passages that might seem autobiographical, have a charm that is more amiable. Although his Pindaric odes have more fervor and imagination than the average of his day, and although in *The Careless Good Fellow* he shows ability to turn out a jolly, fiery drinking song, his true medium is the closed heroic couplet, which he uses with an abruptness and ruggedness of rhythm that are individual and sincere but not always pleasantly smooth. Dryden's touching lines *To the Memory of Mr. Oldham* are

---

Morwent, upon whose death Oldham had composed an early ode. Because of poems circulated in manuscript the Earl of Rochester is said to have visited Oldham at Croydon, and here also was written the ode *Upon the Marriage of the Prince of Orange with the Lady Mary* (1677), which won no recognition. In the years 1679-81 he was tutor to a young gentleman, and in 1681, "set up for a wit" in London. His *Satyrs upon the Jesuits* (1681) was a great success; but presently Oldham had again to become a tutor. At the end of his life he enjoyed the patronage of the young Earl of Kingston; he died of smallpox at Kingston's seat, Holme Pierrepont in Nottingham. — Oldham's *Works* were first collected in 1684, and were reprinted several times down to 1722. His *Compositions in Prose and Verse* were edited by E. Thompson (1770) and his *Poetical Works* by R. Bell (1854, 1871); *Some New Pieces* by him appeared in 1681; *Poems and Translations* in 1683, and *Remains . . . in Verse and Prose* in 1684. — See H. F. Brooks, "A Bibliography of John Oldham," *Oxford Bibliographical Soc. Proc.*, v (1936). 1-38 (with a biographical and critical introduction); Weldon M. Williams, "The Genesis of John Oldham's *Satyrs upon the Jesuits*," PMLA, LVIII (1943). 958-970; W. M. Williams, "The Influence of Ben Jonson's *Catiline* upon John Oldham's *Satyrs upon the Jesuits*," *ELH*, XI (1944). 38-62.

Oldham's most enduring monument: they show how the finished, mellow artist in couplet-making viewed an able apprentice:

> Farewell, too little and too lately known,
> Whom I began to think and call my own:
> For sure our souls were near allied, and thine
> Cast in the same poetic mold with mine. . . .
> O early ripe! to thy abundant store
> What could advancing age have added more?
> It might (what nature never gives the young)
> Have taught the numbers of thy native tongue.
> But satire needs not those, and wit will shine
> Thro' the harsh cadence of a rugged line.

Court Poets   Butler and Oldham were almost "professional" poets whom the court condescended to patronize. The chief court poets, the last of the cavalier breed, were Rochester, Sedley, Dorset, and, apart from this group of rakes, Charles Cotton. In this group (but not as lyrists) would come also John Sheffield, Earl of Mulgrave (and later Duke of Buckinghamshire) and Wentworth Dillon, Earl of Roscommon. The most notable and the most notorious of all these was the young Earl of Rochester.[8] If one could blot out his mad debaucheries and the corollary obscene poems, Rochester's more reputable verse would give him a very high place in English poetry. On paper his personality seems brilliant but unlovely. He was a patron of at least a half-dozen poets, on most of whom he turned maliciously after some friendly gestures. He was thought to have embraced the dangerous doctrines of Hobbes; and indeed he was a skeptic, a materialist, a selfish pleasure-loving sensationalist, who doubtless aped the self-love of which Hobbes was regarded as the apostle. He was a young nobleman of sensual appetites so strong that his health was early ruined, and upon his death, aged thirty-three, he became not only the symbol of the grossest debaucheries the time could devise but also a black warning to youthful lords, through the pamphlet

---

[8] John Wilmot, second Earl of Rochester (1647-1680), was born at Ditchley, Oxfordshire, and at the age of eleven he succeeded his father to the earldom. At Wadham College (1660-61) he began writing verse. He traveled in France and Italy, returned to England in 1664, and fought in the war against the Dutch in 1665. Back in London he became intimate with Sedley, Dorset, and Villiers, Duke of Buckingham; and, despite his youth, he speedily became somehow the most notorious of this group of rakes. He rapidly became famous also as a wit and satirist, and he was briefly a fickle patron to several poets, including Dryden. — *Poems on Several Occasions, by the Rt. Hon. the E. of R.* (Antwerpen [i.e., London], 1680); *Poems . . . with Valentinian* (ed. by Rochester's friends; the preface is by Rymer, 1691); *Miscellaneous Works,* with Memoirs by Mons. St. Évremond (1707, etc., esp. 1731, 1939); *Collected Works,* ed. John Hayward (1926); *Poetical Works,* ed. Quilter Johns (1933). — *A Satyr against Mankind* (1675); *The Enjoyment* (1679); *A Letter to Dr. Burnet* (1680); *Upon Nothing* (1711); *Valentinian* (1685); *Familiar Letters* (2v, 1697); *The Rochester-Savile Letters,* ed. John H. Wilson (Columbus, Ohio, 1941). — T. Longueville, *Rochester and other Literary Rakes* (1902); J. Prinz, *John Wilmot, Earl of Rochester* (Leipzig, 1927); V. de Sola Pinto, *Rochester* (1935); Charles Williams, *Rochester* (1935); S. F. Crocker, "Rochester's *Satire against Mankind:* a Study of Certain Aspects of the Background," *West Virginia Univ. Stud., Philological Papers,* II (1937). 57-73; Kenneth B. Murdock, " 'A Very Profane Wit,' " in *The Sun at Noon* (1939), pp. 269-306; 317-318. An excellent text in which to read the worth-while poems by Rochester is the attractive volume called *A Satire against Mankind & Other Poems by John Wilmot Earl of Rochester,* edited by Harry Levin with an introductory essay (Norfolk, Conn., 1942).

on his death-bed repentance by Bishop Burnet, who had saved his soul but perhaps darkened his reputation.

As poet Rochester was primarily a vigorous and mordant satirist in the fields of philosophy, literature, manners, and politics. In the first of these fields fall two of his best works, the *Satyr against Mankind* (1675) and the lines *Upon Nothing. A Satyr against Mankind* attacks both man and man's reasoning powers. It begins impetuously: *The Earl of Rochester*

> Were I, who to my cost already am
> One of those strange, prodigious Creatures *Man,*
> A Spirit free, to choose for my own share
> What sort of Flesh and Blood I pleased to wear,
> I'd be a Dog, a Monkey or a Bear,
> Or any thing, but that vain Animal,
> Who is so proud of being rational.

If this seems extreme or childish misanthropy, one must recall the fact that complacent praise of the nobility and even the divinity of Reason had been common in the earlier Renaissance; and one may also perceive, as Rochester did, that human reason had hardly kept England from shipwreck during much of the thirty years of Rochester's life. Such anti-rationalist utterance was common in the critical revulsion of the later Renaissance. Rochester had found a general suggestion for the form of his poem in Boileau's eighth satire; but the skepticism of all reason (Boileau satirizes the *abuses* of reason) comes from Montaigne and others[9] rather than from Boileau. The attitude is common in English before 1675, but it was nowhere (before Swift's time) stated with such burning energy as here. *Upon Nothing,* which Dr. Johnson thought his lordship's "strongest effort," excels in its ingenious and brilliant playfulness and cynicism. The Stoics held that all creation was derived from an original universal Something. Rochester ironically asserts the precedence of Nothing:

> Ere Time and Place were, Time and Place were not,
> When primitive Nothing Something straight begot,
> Then all proceeded from the great united — What.

The poem is an exceedingly clever witticism at the expense of metaphysics, or at least of Stoic metaphysics. The implications are skeptical to a degree that Dr. Johnson perhaps did not perceive. Rochester is no great thinker, but he is an intellectual. If in these two poems he aims paradox and witticism against sober philosophy and reason, he does it with an intense impulsion that suggests an intellect capable of changing its direction radically and turning towards faith.

Rochester's most important piece of literary satire is his *Allusion to Horace's 10th Satyr of the First Book.* This hasty and unpolished piece is personal satire rather than literary criticism. It is simply an episode in the running battle his lordship was carrying on with many poets, from Dryden *Literary Quarrels*

[9] See S. F. Crocker, *op. cit.*

to the negligible Sir Carr Scrope (1649-80). The rugged opening lines and other passages indicate his recurring and not very valid attitude towards Dryden, who seems to glance back at Rochester in his preface to *All for Love* (1678). Sir Carr Scrope and Otway, among others, replied to Rochester's *Allusion,* and Rochester retorted most abusively on Sir Carr in *An Answer to the Defence of Satyr.* In these poetic essays in literary criticism there was little intellectual or critical merit. Shortly thereafter Roscommon in 1680 translated Horace's *Art of Poetry,* and in 1684 he published his *Essay on Translated Verse;* Mulgrave (John Sheffield) in 1682 brought out his *Essay upon Poetry:* these poems show something as to the climate of literary opinion in its cooler moments. Rochester's *Allusion* and *Tryal of the Poets,* and Mulgrave's *Essay upon Satyr* (not to mention Scrope's *Defence of Satyr*) may make spicier reading, but their chief importance is to indicate the extreme irascibility of the *genus irritabile vatum* whose flowery ease on occasion became vitriolic.

Rochester as the scourge of manners is hardly wiser than Rochester the critic of poets; but he is here more equable and perceptive. In *A Letter from Artemisa in the Town to Cloe in the Country* he has more smooth elegance of finish than in other satires and a more dramatic power of depicting society. *Tunbridge Wells* also has remarkable realism; but these

Social and Political Satire

two pieces and most of his social satires tend to deal with the love-life of Restoration "quality," and they are consequently crude in matter and usually hasty and unpolished in manner. The political satires, closely related to the social, are remarkable for their blunt and obscene attacks on the King (Charles II) and his mistresses and advisers. The Marquis of Halifax (Savile) has left us an unflattering account of the monarch's love of filthy wit in conversation, and Rochester evidently was a master here. For the gross indecorums of these satires Rochester was more than once banished from the court, but was speedily pardoned. One must assume that the Merry Monarch, like King Lear, affected the wit of a "bitter fool," who was a pestilent gall, outstanding for his daring and insight. How else shall we explain his tolerance of Rochester's epigrammatic epitaph?

> Here lies a Great and Mighty King
> Whose Promise none relies on,
> Who never said a Foolish Thing
> Nor ever did a Wise One.

At times, as in *The Commons Petition to King Charles II,* Rochester's wit must have been of welcome service; and in such poems as *The History of Insipids (The Restoration)* his personal attacks on royal advisers were perhaps ostensibly disinterested.

In most of these satires Rochester uses the heroic couplet with so natural a rough vigor and resonance that he takes his place high among the users of this metre, the tune of which a century after his death every warbler was to have learned by heart and to have made tediously commonplace. For

Rochester the couplet is a flexible and exciting vehicle. He must also be set down as a notable writer of songs in an age when, as Mulgrave thought,

> Without his Song no Fop is to be found.

He might well have included Rochester (said by some to be the prototype *Rochester's* of his friend Etherege's Dorimant) and all the flowery courtiers with the *Songs* fops. No one can read Rochester's satires without a sense of his gifts of phrasing, and these served him well also in his songs. But in the satires phrasing is heightened by fiery, spontaneous scorn; and in Rochester's songs, which are chiefly amorous, there is no parallel poetic or sexual fury behind the phrases. He gives us graceful and effective approximations of passion, and shows that he is a wit who cleverly counterfeits. In his very pretty *Strephon and Daphne* he gives his frank philosophy of love:

> Love, like other little Boys,
> Cries for Hearts, as they for Toys:
> Which, when gain'd, in Childish Play,
> Wantonly are thrown away.

At times he seems less like the hard Dorimant. In briefer songs such as *My dear Mistress has a Heart* and in *Love and Life* he shows at least a beautifully firm finish that few lyrists of his day could equal. *Love and Life,* like many cavalier songs, begins with a perfect stanza:

> All my past Life is mine no more,
>   The flying Hours are gone:
> Like Transitory Dreams giv'n o'er,
> Whose Images are kept in store
>   By Memory alone.

One must confess, however, that the poet seems as much like his metrically boisterous self in such a satirical song as that beginning

> Room, room, for a Blade of the Town
>   That takes Delight in Roaring,
> Who all Day long rambles up and down,
>   And at Night in the Street lies Snoaring.

It was insight, impulsive vigor, and an appearance of blunt, unflattering honesty that gave this rake of a lord the charms he must have had to counteract his selfishness or his utter lack of idealistic illusion, and make him an admired type of his time as well as a dominant storm-center in his bleak, brief day.

Sir Charles Sedley [10] (1639?-1701) was admired by Rochester as a fellow *Sir Charles* rake and poet, perhaps chiefly because of his indecorous pranks—notorious *Sedley* before Rochester dawned upon the Town. Sedley was the author of three plays and some satirical poems, but what Rochester and posterity have

[10] V. de Sola Pinto has ably edited *The Poetical and Dramatic Works of Sir Charles Sedley* (2v, 1928), including "A Bibliography of Works by or Ascribed to Sir Charles Sedley" (II. 235-261); and has written an excellent life called *Sir Charles Sedley* (1927).

agreed in praising is his songs. These are love poems of at least two types. The first is pleading, ingratiating, and yet witty, solicitation, seen charmingly in the song beginning

> Not, Celia, that I juster am,
>   Or better than the rest,
> For I would change each hour like them,
>   Were not my heart at rest —

and seen at its best in the rich, almost Elizabethan, melody and fancy of

> Love still has something of the sea,
>   From whence his mother rose;
> No time his slaves from doubt can free
>   Nor give their thoughts repose!

His second type of love lyric is the playful, almost satiric, song, such as that *To a Devout Young Gentlewoman,* who is overacting her piety and is told,

> 'Tis early to begin to fear
>   The devil at fifteen.

Another poem, addressed, let us hope, to an older Phillis, opens with the gay protestation—

> Phillis is my only joy,
>   Faithless as the winds or seas.

Such pieces establish Sedley as one of the best gay lyric poets in his century.

The Earl of Dorset (1638-1706) Charles Sackville,[11] Lord Buckhurst—after 1677 Earl of Dorset—tends to be caustic rather than playful in his songs. His friend Rochester described him as a pointed satirist, "the best Good Man with the worst-natur'd Muse." He wrote relatively few satirical poems but several are tinged with satire. His lines on *The British Princes* of Edward Howard were profusely abusive and his stanzas *On the Countess of Dorchester* ("Dorinda") are strong but unpleasant in their epigrammatic sting. His one famous song is that which is wrongly captioned "Written at Sea, in the first Dutch War, 1665, the night before an Engagement." The rollicking stanzas of this poem are all that remain of Dorset's once very great reputation:

> To all you ladies now at land
>   We men at sea indite;
> But first wou'd have you understand
>   How hard it is to write;
> The Muses now, and Neptune too,
> We must implore to write to you,
>   With a fa, la, la, la, la.

11 Dorset's poems will be found in the collections of English poets made by Samuel Johnson (Vol. xi, 1779), Robert Anderson (Vol. vi, 1795), and Alexander Chalmers (Vol. viii, 1810). They were first collected in *The Works of Rochester, Roscommon, Dorset,* etc. (2v, 1714). For comments on the canon of his works see *MLN,* xlvii (1932). 454-461 (by H. A. Bagley) and l (1935). 457-459 (by R. G. Howarth); Brice Harris, *Charles Sackville Sixth Earl of Dorset* (Urbana, 1940; *Univ. of Illinois Studies in Lang. and Lit.* xxvi).

The last of these cavalier lyrists to achieve a reputation as such was Charles Cotton [12] (1630-1687). In his own lifetime his moderate fame was based on his burlesques, especially *Scarronides,* on his translations, the most notable of which was his excellent version of Montaigne's *Essays,* and on his treatise on fly-fishing, thought worthy in 1676 to be added to his friend Izaak Walton's *Compleat Angler* as Part II. But since the praise of Words- worth, Coleridge, and Lamb made famous the nature lyrics of Cotton, pub- lished first in 1689 as *Poems on Several Occasions,* his delicately simple artistry in lyric poetry has been much admired. He was no court poet, but was in some sense a disciple of Herrick and Carew. His Staffordshire estates were encumbered with debts, but he loved the country and frequented London probably as a publishing center. Instead of cultivating rakish aristo- crats, he made friends of more modest geniuses in verse, but chiefly Izaak Walton (1593-1683), whom he called "my most worthy father and friend." Wordsworth and his group admired the simplicity and profusion of *The Retirement* and *The Ode to Winter.* In the former poem Cotton has escaped from the Town and relaxes in his native environment—particularly praising his river, the silver Dove. He is surprisingly fond of describing storms, espe- cially at sea, perhaps as a result of his voyage to Ireland as a captain in the army (1670?), on which occasion he barely escaped shipwreck. His four sets of quatrains for Morning, Noon, Evening, and Night are at once exquisite in their natural reality and in their fancy. Watching the sheep coming to fold at sunset he describes the shadows:

Charles Cotton

> A very little, little flock
> Shades thrice the ground that it would stock;
> Whilst the small stripling foilowing them,
> Appears a mighty Polypheme.

His love poems, natural and genuine, and his other verses are influenced frequently by French lyrists of the century, and while he produces charming effects in these imitations and translations, the country details of his de- scriptive poems are what one values most.

It remains to add something concerning a device used in the publication of short poems, a device not invented in the Restoration period but one greatly popularized then. This was the method of combining a few poems by each of several authors to make a single volume, called a "miscellany." [13] It was more frequently a publisher's device than it was an author's trick,

Miscellanie and Song Books

---

[12] Cotton's *Genuine Works* (1715); *Poems,* ed. J. Beresford (1923); *Poems* [selected] (illus- trated by Lovat Fraser, 1925). — *The Compleat Gamester* (1674); *The Morall Philosophy of the Stoicks* (transl. from Guillaume Du Vair, 1664); *Scarronides* (2v, 1664-5); *Horace* (transl. from Corneille, 1671); *Burlesque upon Burlesque* (1675); *Essays of Montaigne* (transl. 3v, 1685). — Charles J. Sembower, *The Life and Poetry of Charles Cotton* (1911); J. Beresford, "The Poetry of Charles Cotton," *London Mercury,* v (1921). 57-69; Gerald G. P. Heywood, *Charles Cotton and his River* (Manchester, 1928).

[13] Bibliographies of miscellanies exist as follows: Arthur E. Case, *A Bibliography of English Poetical Miscellanies, 1521-1750* (Bibliographical Soc., Oxford, 1935), and Norman Ault, for the years 1660-1800, in *CBEL,* II. 173-256.

though it enabled satirists and modest poets to appear anonymously and thus to escape a certain amount of personal censure. The most reputable series of miscellany volumes were those published in 1684 and thereafter by the bookseller Jacob Tonson with the advice and aid of John Dryden.[14] These were advertised at times as "published by Mr. Dryden," and they were popularly referred to (even the additions published after the poet's death) as "Dryden's Miscellanies." The series ran to Volume VI (1709), and had no consistent uniformity of title-page. In contrast to these, the least dignified of the miscellanies was a type called *drollery*,[15] which may be said to exist from the time (1655) when "H. H." published the *Musarum Deliciae* of Sir John Mennes and Dr. James Smith to the *Merry Drollery Compleat* (1691). A drollery might contain first-rate poetry, but normally it specialized in printing fugitive manuscript pieces or reprinting broadsides and ballads that attacked the Puritans scoffingly and indecently. Of somewhat more dignity is a series of miscellanies called *Poems on Affairs of State*, which are dominantly but not exclusively political.[16] Begun in 1689, these by 1707 had increased to four volumes with the contents varying somewhat in successive editions. The announced purpose of these volumes was "to remove those pernicious Principles which lead us directly to Slavery." Here James II and the Catholic party replace the Puritans as undesirables. Still another development of this general sort was the songbook.[17] Such very numerous collections, frequently with tunes included, were enormously popular. They unfortunately tended to separate lyrics, the words of songs, from other types of poetry, and then to subordinate lyrics to music. The most notable publishers of popular songs in the period were John Playford and his son Henry. By all odds the most prolific and successful song writer was Tom D'Urfey (1653-1723), author of loyalist satires, of many plays, and of some very bad Pindaric odes, but chiefly a song writer.[18] D'Urfey summed up his own vogue in his stammering remark (recorded or invented by Tom Brown): "The Town may da-da-damn me for a Poet, but they si-si-sing my Songs for all that."

All these types of miscellanies are storehouses for preserving fugitive pieces, and because of the danger in avowing authorship of any spicy political writing the ascriptions of authorship given in these volumes should command very skeptical respect. The publication of poems in miscellany volumes (frequently mixed with short prose pieces) continued to be popular through-

[14] See Hugh Macdonald, *John Dryden, a Bibliography* (Oxford, 1939), pp. 67-83. Also R. D. Havens, "Changing Taste in the Eighteenth Century: A Study of Dryden's and Dodsley's Miscellanies," *PMLA*, XLIV (1929). 501-536.

[15] Harvard University has an unpublished dissertation by Courtney D. C. Smith on *The Seventeenth-century Drolleries* (1943).

[16] Macdonald, *John Dryden, a Bibliography*, pp. 316-322.

[17] Cyrus L. Day and Eleanore B. Murrie, "English Song-Books, 1651-1702, and their Publishers," *Library*, XVI (1936). 355-401.

[18] Cyrus L. Day, *The Songs of Thomas D'Urfey* (Cambridge, Mass., 1933); Willard Thorp, *Songs from the Restoration Theater* (Princeton, 1934). For an excellent bibliography see Cyrus L. Day and Eleanore B. Murrie, *English Song-Books, 1651-1702: A Bibliography with a First-Line Index of Songs* (1940).

out the eighteenth century, and it has been used to the present day. It is, however, especially notable as a popular Augustan device, which in ultimate effect complicates the establishment of the canon of an author's work, and makes difficult the study of the history of short poems. The popularity of a poem or type of poem cannot be inferred from its appearance in a single miscellany; but if reprinted in several its popularity must be assumed.

V

Restoration Drama: I. Heroic Plays and Tragedies

Restoration drama [1] has been regarded as both the glory and the shame of the period. The comedies handle wit, satire, and neat situation in a manner hardly surpassed elsewhere in English drama; but they are notoriously deficient in moral decency, though very sensitive to a superficial norm in manners. In the more serious plays produced shortly after the Restoration there is an artificial declamatory elevation which, joined with bustling action and elaborate spectacle, for some years dazzled audiences. Later this "heroic" type of play yielded to dramas of pathos and domestic sentimentality. The conditions of the theatre that fostered these serious plays and the nature of the plays themselves will be the subject of the present chapter. [2] The comedies will be reserved for the next chapter, although it must be noted that few dramatists specialized either in comedy or tragedy. They thought, however, in terms of genres, and we may well follow their example.

Officially the theatres of London had been closed from the autumn of 1642 until after the Restoration of Charles II. Actually, there were, in Cromwell's time, dramatic performances in the houses of noblemen and even privately among cultivated Puritans. The lower classes, too, still delighted in "mummings," rope-dances, acrobatic acts, and drolls—which last were farcical fragments of plays. [3] At least one of the more proletarian Elizabethan playhouses, the Red Bull, was not dismantled by the Puritans, and was

[1] In the chapters on the drama that cover dramatic history from 1660 to 1789 the dates of plays given in the footnotes are supposed always to be dates of publication. In the text of these chapters the dates of first performances, when known, are given.

[2] General materials on the drama of this period may be found in Allardyce Nicoll, *A History of Restoration Drama, 1660-1700* (Cambridge, 1923; 2d ed., 1928). This is the standard history. Other histories are D. E. Baker, Isaac Reed, and Stephen Jones, *Biographia Dramatica; or, a Companion to the Playhouse* (3v, 1812; a dictionary of [a] playwrights and [b] plays); J. Genest, *Some Account of the English Stage* (10v, Bath, 1832; still exceedingly useful for details about minor plays or about actors and acting); Sir Adolphus W. Ward, *A History of English Dramatic Literature to the Death of Queen Anne* (3v, 1899); Ashley H. Thorndike, *Tragedy* (Boston, 1908); George H. Nettleton, *English Drama of the Restoration and Eighteenth Century* (1914; a readable and reliable brief survey); Bonamy Dobrée, *Restoration Tragedy* (Oxford, 1929; useful for history and criticism). For the influences of the drama of the earlier seventeenth century on Restoration playwrights see Alfred Harbage, *Cavalier Drama* (Philadelphia, 1936). On the theatres of the time see the authoritative studies of Eleanore Boswell, *The Restoration Court Stage* (Cambridge, Mass., 1932) and Leslie Hotson, *The Commonwealth and Restoration Stage* (Cambridge, Mass., 1928). Three books by Montague Summers are useful, if used with caution: *A Bibliography of the Restoration Drama* (1935), *The Restoration Theatre* (1934), *The Playhouse of Pepys* (1935). Very useful is Alfred Harbage's *Annals of the English Drama, 975-1700: An Analytical Record of All Plays, Extant and Lost, Chronologically Arranged* (Philadelphia, 1940).

[3] Hyder E. Rollins, "A Contribution to the History of English Commonwealth Drama," *SP*, XVIII (1921). 267-333.

used briefly after the Restoration, and frequently during the interregnum. In 1673 Francis Kirkman recorded his memories of plebeian performances there in the forbidden period: "I have seen the Red Bull Play-House, which was a large one, so full, that as many went back for want of room as had entered; and as meanly as you may now think of these Drols, they were then Acted by the best Comedians then and now in being." [4] Although the tradition of legitimate drama was mangled rather than killed, evidently the proletarian taste for farce and bustle endured along with a taste for poetic drama.

But Puritanism had worked so well—aided doubtless by the repellent neurotic sensationalism of Jacobean drama—that after the Restoration the *Puritan* theatre was not the popular institution it had been in 1600. At the beginning *and Court* of the century London could support a half-dozen playhouses; after 1660, *Influences* if we shut our eyes to two or three years of free-for-all competition in producing plays, only two theatres maintained a struggling existence, and for the period 1682-95 only one continued regular seasons. Such conditions prevailed in spite of a considerable royal patronage. In the summer of 1660 the King issued "patents" to his friends Sir William Davenant [5] and Thomas Killigrew, which gave them a virtual monopoly in organizing companies of actors and producing plays. Killigrew's company became known as the King's players, and after 1674 they were housed in the Theatre Royal in Drury Lane. Of Davenant's company the King's brother, the Duke of York (later James II), was patron, and it acted after 1671 in a new theatre in Dorset Garden. The very predominance of court influence and courtier management tended perhaps to diminish the appeal of the theatre to the merchant classes. The wealthy citizen of London and his wife were in fact frequently objects of mirth in the comedies of the time; yet it is not altogether clear that the ridicule was offensive to this ambitious and rising social class.

But the citizens were morally respectable—or tended to be; and the theatre

[4] *The Wits,* ed. John J. Elson (Ithaca, N. Y., 1932), p. 268; see also Charles R. Baskervill, *The Elizabethan Jig* (Chicago, 1929), p. 122.

[5] Sir William Davenant (1606-1668), the son of a tavern-keeper, was born at Oxford, and about 1620-21 he was a member of Lincoln College, Oxford. He was for a few years in the service of the Duchess of Richmond and later of Fulke Greville, Lord Brooke. At court he became acquainted with Endymion Porter, Henry Jermyn, and others of influence, and rapidly gained favor as poet and dramatist until in 1638 he succeeded Ben Jonson as poet laureate. An active royalist during the Civil War, he was knighted at the siege of Gloucester (1643). With the court he withdrew to France after the defeat of the royal army, and it was there that he began *Gondibert* and first published the *Discourse on Gondibert* with Hobbes's *Answer* (1650). Sailing for America on a royal mission (1650), he was captured and imprisoned in the Tower. Freed in 1654, Davenant devoted himself to tactful dramatic productions and, after 1660, to the management of his ("the Duke's") company of comedians. As a writer for the stage his real achievement was operatic—in his *Siege of Rhodes* (acted first in 1656) and in his operatic adaptations of Shakespeare's *Tempest* and *Macbeth.* — *Works* (1673); *Dramatic Works,* ed. J. Maidment and W. H. Logan (5v, Edinburgh, 1872-4); *Love and Honour and The Siege of Rhodes,* ed. James W. Tupper (Boston, 1909). — Hazelton Spencer, *Shakespeare Improved* (Cambridge, Mass., 1927); Leslie Hotson, *The Commonwealth and Restoration Stage* (Cambridge, Mass., 1928); Alfred Harbage, *Thomas Killigrew* (Philadelphia, 1930); Friederich Laig, *Englische und Französische Elemente in Sir William Davenants Dramatischer Kunst* (Emsdetten, 1934); Alfred Harbage, *Sir William Davenant* (Philadelphia, 1935); Arthur H. Nethercot, *Sir William D'Avenant* (Chicago, 1938).

tended in the other direction! It was a shock, for example, when after 1660, in imitation of the French theatre, women, and not boys, played female *he Players* rôles on the English stage. The actresses were often the avowed mistresses of noblemen or even of royalty itself. It is perhaps natural that, if we except Thomas Betterton (1635?-1710), the period produced no great histrionic geniuses. Preëminent among his fellow actors Betterton created most of the "heavy" heroic rôles of the period and acted comedy parts as well. He was a most important link in a Shakespearean acting tradition in so far as any such tradition survived the interregnum. Michael Mohun in Killigrew's company was the corresponding tragedian: he had acted before 1642. Later Mrs. Barry and Mrs. Bracegirdle were important actresses. Edward Kynaston had a long and significant career that began by his playing female parts: "the loveliest lady that ever I saw in my life," was the verdict of that connoisseur in ladies, Samuel Pepys. Kynaston's later career was devoted to dignified paternal rôles. Among the popular performers were several excellent low comedians: John Lacy, Cave Underhill, James Nokes, Thomas Doggett, and Joe Haynes—the last famous as a practical jester and clown, especially in "stunt" prologues and epilogues. It is this last type of actor that chiefly shows that sophisticated courtiers were not the only audience towards whom appeal was directed.

he Theatres   The theatres themselves are a development from the private theatres of the Elizabethan age—a rectangular roofed-in hall with a proscenium arch framing the back stage but not framing the wide apron that still projected well into the pit. Davenant featured elaborate scenery, back drops with side flats that slid in grooves, thus opening or closing to change scenes on occasion. Machines, enabling Jupiter to descend in a cloud or aiding spirits, sylphs, or fairies to float through the air, were most elaborate, and "made" many a very popular play or opera. Because of these complicated machines it became increasingly desirable to exclude spectators from the stage. The audience, frequently inattentive and noisy, was not seldom even turbulent. On benches in the pit sat the aristocratic sparks and "ladies of the town." Pinchwife in *The Country Wife* (Act II, Scene 1) made his Margery sit in a box, though she, to his horror, liked the gaily dressed pit. "We sat amongst ugly people," she says. "He would not let me come near the gentry, who sat under us, so that I could not see 'em. He told me, none but naughty women sat there, whom they toused and moused. But I would have ventured, for all that." Pepys, who was almost as jealous as Pinchwife, preferred for many reasons to go to the theatre without his Elizabeth, yet he normally took her to the pit. On October 19, 1667, they went to the première of Lord Orrery's *Black Prince*—

where, though we came by two o'clock, yet there was no room in the pit, but we were forced to go into one of the upper boxes, at 4s. a piece, which is the first time I ever sat in a box in my life. And in the same box came, by and by, behind me, my Lord Barkeley and his lady, but I did not turn my face to them to be known, so that I was excused from giving them my seat; and this pleasure

I had, that from this place the scenes do appear very fine indeed, and much better than in the pit.

The scenes, the music, the "naughty women" in the audience were features as well as the plays themselves. On the stage the chief early developments were operas and heroic plays. Early operas were promoted and at times written by Sir William Davenant, the patentee. Sir William had written masques and romantic plays for fifteen years before the theatres were closed, and had been made governor of the Cockpit company of actors in 1639. During the interregnum he had evaded restrictions by producing operas and entertainments—not technically plays.[6] The most significant of these was *The Siege of Rhodes,* which was performed in various states and finally, in two parts, in 1661. This opera ("the story sung in Recitative Musick") derives dramatically from romances such as Beaumont and Fletcher had popularized.[7] A literary origin is seen in its relation to the heroic poem: it strives for epic elevation. It anticipates neo-classical conventions in its use of balancing characters and situations. Solyman the Magnificent, a sultan, contrasts with Alphonso, a Christian hero, and there is similar balance between the sultaness and Alphonso's wife. There are long moments of self-communings and arguments over "costly scruples" and typical psychological perplexities, such as the difficulty of reconciling love and honor [8]—all of which were soon to be stereotyped in the so-called ."heroic play." *The Beginnings of Opera*

Under Davenant's influence developed both the heroic play and the English opera.[9] Foreign opera was perhaps first heard in England during this period. Perrin's *Ariadne* was heard in French at the Theatre Royal in 1674, and Italian singers performed at court. English opera usually eschewed the new recitative style and interspersed spoken lines with song. Although the appeal of opera derived from the music and spectacular mechanical effects, it is notable that some of the most popular English operas were adapted from Shakespeare: *Macbeth* by Davenant in 1673; *The Tempest* by Davenant and Dryden in 1667, and, more successfully, by Shadwell in 1674; and *The Fairy Queen,* adapted by Settle from *Midsummer Night's Dream* in 1692, with music by Henry Purcell. In general the operas lack literary importance: Nahum Tate's libretto for Purcell's beautifully set *Dido and Aeneas* (1689), for example, has no value apart from what the composer gave it in his rare music.

Davenant's other foster child, the heroic play,[10] is also in some sense a cultural phenomenon rather than a literary achievement, even though Dryden himself enjoyed writing such plays. Dryden, in fact, is not only the chief playwright in this type but also the principal contemporary com- *The Heroic Play*

---

[6] See Alfred Harbage, *Sir William Davenant* (Philadelphia, 1935).
[7] A complete survey of such influence on the Restoration drama is given by Arthur C. Sprague in his *Beaumont and Fletcher on the Restoration Stage* (Cambridge, Mass., 1926).
[8] *Love and Honour* was the title of an early play by Davenant, acted in 1634 and published in 1649; ed. J. W. Tupper, as noted above.
[9] Edward J. Dent, *Foundations of English Opera* (Cambridge, 1928).
[10] For discussions of the heroic play see the books and articles listed in *CBEL,* II. 396, and Alfred Harbage, *Cavalier Drama* (Philadelphia, 1936), pp. 48-71.

mentator on it. In his essay *Of Heroic Plays,* prefixed to *The Conquest of Granada* (1672), he analyzes and defends the type; in the prefaces to *All for Love* (1678) and *The Spanish Friar* (1681) he recants. Davenant he regarded as the father of the type, though he recognized it as a development both of the Elizabethan tradition and of the tradition "of Corneille and some French poets." He also recognized the influence of Ariosto and the heroic poem, observing that "an heroic play ought to be an imitation, in little, of an heroic poem; and, consequently, that Love and Valour ought to be the subject of it." This observation in part accounts for the more than Augustan elevation that makes much of the dialogue in these plays frankly ridiculous. Dryden thought Davenant's plays lacked this elevation as well as the fullness of plot and variety of characters desirable.

In a period of somewhat more than a decade (1664-77 are Professor Nicoll's dates) these qualities were achieved by a group of authors, many of whom elected to write their heroic tragedies in rime. This habit, reintroduced from France and favored by Charles II, was taken up by Roger Boyle, Earl of Orrery (1621-1679), who among the first writers of heroic tragedy exercised considerable influence.[11] He used English materials in two historical plays, *Henry V* (1664) and *The Black Prince* (1667), but cast them in the form of French tragedy and used the popular device of antithetical emotions to tear the souls of his persons between the conflicting duties due to a mistress and to a friend or between love and filial piety. In *The General* (1664) the hero is torn between love and honor, and the emotional conflicts in *Mustapha* (1665), perhaps his most typical play, are exceedingly complex. The political and domestic intrigues of an Oriental royal family seen in swiftly shifting situation and heard in lofty, declamatory rhetoric characterize the work. Orrery uses a strong but artificial style. The love of antithetical wit causes one character, wishing to convey the idea that the sultaness will be merciful, to say:

> Madam, she will not now by one mean act,
> A future stain on her past fame contact.

The play contains much luridly Machiavellian action, much heroic artifice, and some heroic pathos in the death of Mustapha.

But some months before Orrery's first play was acted in London,[12] Dryden, collaborating with his saturnine brother-in-law, Sir Robert Howard, had in January, 1664, produced *The Indian Queen,* and for more than a decade thereafter Dryden was the master-author of heroic plays.[13] In *The Indian*

Side notes: 'he Earl of)rrery; The Indian Queen

11 *The Dramatic Works of Roger Boyle, Earl of Orrery,* ed. William S. Clark (2v, Cambridge, Mass., 1937), contains texts, a bibliography, and a long historical preface.
12 It had been acted in Dublin at least as early as 1662.
13 *Works,* ed. Sir Walter Scott and George Saintsbury (18v, 1882-92); *Dramatic Works,* ed. Montague Summers (6v, 1931-2); *Selected Dramas,* ed. George R. Noyes (Chicago, 1910). There is no really satisfactory edition of all Dryden's plays. — G. R. Noyes, introduction to *Selected Dramas;* M. Sherwood, *Dryden's Dramatic Theory and Practice* (Boston, 1898); Allardyce Nicoll, *Dryden as an Adapter of Shakespeare* (Shakespeare Association, 1922); B. J. Pendlebury, *Dryden's Heroic Plays* (1923); Cecil V. Deane, *Dramatic Theory and the Rhymed Heroic Play* (1931); H. Granville-Barker, "Wycherley and Dryden," in *On Dramatic Method*

Queen love and valor, the prescribed motives,[14] are the conflicting forces. Montezuma, the general of the Inca's forces, defeats the Mexicans, and wishes the hand· of the Inca's daughter, Orazia, as his reward. Not being of royal blood he is deemed ineligible; but at the end of the play it turns out that he is the son of the true (exiled) Queen of Mexico; and hence these two lovers, who throughout the play have both been persecuted by unwanted proffers of affection, noble or lustful, are finally made happy. Evil characters obligingly commit suicide. It is notable that Montezuma, stung when the Inca refuses to give him Orazia, changes sides, and fights for the Mexicans: such a change of allegiance, used more than once in Dryden's later plays, is here fairly plausible. The characters are familiar types: Acacis, the young Mexican idealist, noble, though a prisoner of war ("Virtue is calm in him but rough in me," says Montezuma); Traxalla, the villain-general, whose fame is shaded by Montezuma's and whose love is lust; Zempoalla and Amexia, rival and contrasting queens of Mexico—all these types were soon to be familiar in later heroic plays: the emperor of a remote land, the ever-victorious hero, with a "swelled mind," the rival villain, the dazzlingly virtuous heroine, and the pseudo-royal villainess are all here. A conjuring scene, aerial spirits, and other masque-like, romantic elements, aid the spectacle, which, for the rest,· consists of minds audibly and rhetorically torn by emotion or by "cruel circumstance." It was natural that the great success of this play, Howard's third and Dryden's second, should encourage Dryden to bring on a sequel, *The Indian Emperor,* a year later. This very popular play added no technical developments to the type; it used advantageously the richly exotic scenery painted for *The Indian Queen.*

During the next four years Dryden produced three comedies, but in 1669 he returned to the heroic play in producing *Tyrannick Love, or, The Royal Martyr,* with significant modifications of the type. The plot introduces us to the tyrant Maximin as protagonist and ranter. There is no villainess; and St. Catharine of Alexandria (as "captive queen") introduces an element of Christian apologetics, later more significant in Dryden's nondramatic poetry. St. Catharine gives certain scenes a more intellectual quality than is found in other heroic plays, and her threatened tortures add a new gruesomeness. Porphyrius, the worthy general, who is the only possible hero in the play, hardly rants at all. Maximin's rages are at times super-imperial; he dies contemning the gods— Tyrannick Love

> And after thee I go
> Revenging still, and following ev'n to the other world my blow;
> And shoving back this earth on which I sit,
> I'll mount, and scatter all the Gods I hit.

(1931); Ned B. Allen, *The Sources of Dryden's Comedies* (Ann Arbor, 1935); Mildred E. Hartsock, "Dryden's Plays: A Study in Ideas," *Seventeenth Century Studies, Second Series, by Members of the Graduate School, Univ. of Cincinnati,* ed. Robert Shafer (Princeton, 1937), pp. 71-176; D. W. Jefferson, "The Significance of Dryden's Heroic Plays," *Proceedings of the Leeds Phil. and Lit. Soc.,* v (1940). 125-139.

[14] Prescribed, that is, in Dryden's later essay "Of Heroic Plays," *Essays of Dryden,* ed. W. P. Ker (1900), I. 148-159.

The play is an amazing fusion of complicated rant, love, rationalistic argu-
fying, with, finally, an amusing epilogue spoken by no less a personage than
the King's "Protestant whore," Mrs. Nell Gwyn, who played the emperor's
daughter, Valeria. She ends with the lines:

> As for my epitaph when I am gone,
> I'll trust no poet, but will write my own: —
> Here Nelly lies, who, though she lived a slattern,
> Yet died a princess, acting in S. Catharine.

**The Con-
quest of
Granada**   Thrilling as the final rants of Maximin were (the play ran for fourteen
days), they were less varied and effective than the poetical rhetoric of Dryden's most elaborate heroic play, *The Conquest of Granada,* a play in two
parts (1670, 1671) filling ten highly complicated acts. The moral instruction
seems to be that a nation divided against itself, as were the Moors in Granada,
is easy prey for armies led by a supernaturally effective general such as
Almanzor, who is Dryden's loudest realization of a full-blown hero. The
characters and their complications in love are for the most part familiar.
Boabdelin, the weak ruler of Granada, is betrothed to the lovely Almahide
(Nell Gwyn again), but obviously her ultimate destiny is the arms of
Almanzor. Contrasting with Almahide is the beauteous serpent Lyndaraxa,
of whom one of her male victims, the king's brother, remarks:

> Her tears, her smiles, her very look's a net.
> Her voice is like a Siren's of the land;
> And bloody hearts lie panting in her hand.

This fair creature and her plotting brother are responsible for most of the
villainy in the play. A contrasting and sweetly different couple are Ozmyn
and Benzayda, who illustrate the sentimental appeal of innocent, simple,
idyllic love and the painful contest between love and filial duty.

**The Char-
acter of
Almanzor**   The character of Almanzor and the poetry in which it is expressed are
most remarkable. It is true that Almanzor is frequently absurd: he changes
sides in the wars until he makes one dizzy, and his titanic rants are grotesque.
But, curiously enough, they have a basis in reason and are at the same time
thoroughly romantic. The king's brother sketches the character briefly:

> Vast is his courage, boundless is his mind,
> Rough as a storm, and humorous as wind:
> Honor's the only idol of his eyes;
> The charms of beauty like a pest he flies;
> And, rais'd by valor from a birth unknown,
> Acknowledges no pow'r above his own.

When condemned to death by the king he remarks:

> No man has more contempt than I of breath,
> But whence hast thou the right to give me death?
> Obey'd as sovereign by thy subjects be,
> But know that I alone am king of me.

I am as free as nature first made man,
Ere the base laws of servitude began,
When wild in woods the noble savage ran. . . .
If thou pretend'st to be a prince like me,
Blame not an act which should thy pattern be.
I saw th' oppress'd, and thought it did belong
To a king's office to redress the wrong:
I brought that succor which thou ought'st to bring,
And so, in nature, am thy subjects' king.

When the king, unmoved by this reasoning, orders the guards to execute Almanzor "instantly," the hero replies—

Stand off; I have not leisure yet to die.

Clearly, such a man has something!

The audience's delight in this play was probably not diminished by the burlesque *Rehearsal*[15] (1671), which, composed much earlier to ridicule Sir Robert Howard and Davenant, was now remade as an attack on Dryden (Bayes, in the play) and heroic plays. The ingenious and biting satire, based on a common-sense reaction to the excesses of Almanzor and his sort, seems not immediately to have affected Dryden's reputation or the popularity of the plays satirized. At any rate in 1675 Dryden produced another (his last) rimed heroic play, *Aureng-Zebe,* which followed closely the pattern of the earlier plays in its stock characters, its multiplication of love-complications, with villainy defeated and the two reputable lovers left to live while carnage and madness remove most of the other principals. Indamora, the captive queen of this play, is pursued by three unwanted lovers in addition to the hero: in no other play has Dryden more ingeniously tortured his love affairs. There is here less of rant; the poetry is frequently reflective in substance and more sinuous in its rhythms. Aureng-Zebe's meditations at times are quiet even to melancholy:

Aureng-Zebe and Dramatic Adaptation

When I consider life, 'tis all a cheat;
Yet, fooled with hope, men favor the deceit,
Trust on, and think to-morrow will repay.
To-morrow's falser than the former day —
Lies worse, and, while it says we shall be blest
With some new joys, cuts off what we possessed.
Strange cozenage!

Such a passage indicates the mastery Dryden has achieved in adapting the rimed couplet to dramatic verse; yet this was his last play in rime to be

15 *The Rehearsal,* written by George Villiers, Duke of Buckingham, with the aid of Thomas Sprat, Martin Clifford, Samuel Butler, and perhaps others, invents the device, used later delightfully by Fielding and Sheridan, of having friends of the playwright (Bayes) attend the rehearsal of his play: the rehearsal goes badly; the play itself is absurd, as are the author's explications of it, and the comments of the "friends" add savor in caustic wit. — See the ed. of Montague Summers (Stratford-on-Avon, 1914). Dane F. Smith in his *Plays about the Theatre in England* (1936) comments on the play. According to Emmett L. Avery, "The Stage Popularity of *The Rehearsal,* 1671-1777," *Research Studies of the State College of Washington,* VII (1939). 201-204, there were 291 performances of the play in the period studied. The most popular eighteenth-century portrayers of Bayes were Estcourt, the two Cibbers, and David Garrick.

acted. He did, to be sure, with Milton's permission, base a rimed opera, *The State of Innocence* (1677), on *Paradise Lost;* but this was not performed. Others continued to use the couplet, and it is conceivable that Dryden abandoned rime and ranting heroism together when he found that inferiors (notably Settle) could prove rivals in such a field.[16] Even in his later tragedies, however, Dryden could not escape the epic-heroic elevation that dominated much of his nondramatic work. His tragedies suffer from the fact that they remind us of better things. His adaptations of Shakespeare, *All for Love* (1677) from *Antony and Cleopatra,* and his *Troilus and Cressida* (1679), unlike Tate's popular reworking of *King Lear,* do remain tragedies; but their humanity is artificialized in heroic terms—Troilus and Antony are cousins or brothers of Almanzor and Aureng-Zebe, and Cleopatra much resembles a captive queen in her worries. Yet *All for Love* remains the best of the plays that pour Elizabethan material into neo-classic French molds. Its blank verse is noble, its unity effective; if Shakespeare had never written, it would seem one of the most impressive monuments in English drama. It remains, in fact, from a literary point of view, the most dignified English tragedy in the tradition of the three unities. Dryden's last plays— *Cleomenes* (1692) and *Love Triumphant* (1694)—had little success.

An unfortunate episode in Dryden's career as heroic playwright was the animosity resulting from the great success of *The Empress of Morocco* (1673), the second play of young Elkanah Settle.[17] This was twice successfully acted at court, and was then presented publicly in London. Its success was engineered (at least aided) by noblemen who had been Dryden's patrons, and the success seemed a deliberate challenge to Dryden's fame. The play is hardly more absurd than some of Dryden's, but its plotting, which concerns the successful intrigues of a wicked empress and her lover against her son, is less well knit than Dryden's work, and its poetry is obviously inferior. Its theatrical merit lay in its highly spectacular scenic effects. Dryden and his friends of the moment, Crowne and Shadwell, attacked the absurdities of the play; Settle retorted in kind on *The Conquest of Granada,* and much controversy resulted. Between 1671 and 1718 Settle was to produce almost a score of plays; but from this career of almost unequaled length, he emerges with the reputation of having been scorned by both Dryden and Pope—as well as by lesser authors.

[16] Professor Nicoll (*Restoration Drama,* p. 90) tells us that from 1660-70 there were 18 new plays in the couplet; from 1670-80, 24; in the next decade he found only one; in the last decade of the century, only 4; and in the early eighteenth century, 6.

[17] Elkanah Settle (1648-1724), born at Dunstable, entered Trinity College, Oxford in 1666, but soon left without a degree, and proceeded to London. His first tragedy, *Cambyses* (1671), met with considerable success and for some years his plays were popular. An artificially created rivalry with Dryden led to scurrilous attacks and replies. In 1691 Settle was appointed City Poet, and as such produced the annual pageants for the Lord Mayor's Day. In a long and poverty-stricken old age he did hack work of various sorts. He even wrote drolls for Bartholomew Fair and, according to legend, acted in them. About 1718 he secured admission to the Charterhouse, and he died there in 1724. — His plays are listed in Nicoll's *Restoration Drama.* A biography has been written by Frank C. Brown, *Elkanah Settle* (Chicago, 1910), and Roswell G. Ham has treated the quarrel with Dryden in "Dryden vs. Settle," *MP,* xxv (1928). 409-416.

The chief tragic writers of the period were Lee, Otway, and Southerne. John Banks, with seven or eight tragedies, and Crowne, with eleven, are definitely inferior to these three.[18] All these men are influenced by the *Tragedy* heroic play, by Elizabethan tragedy (especially by the "tragedy of blood"), and by the French tradition formulated from Aristotle and Seneca in the early part of the seventeenth century. Corneille, whose plays date 1629-74, was negligent of the rules, and Racine, whose plays date 1664-91, triumphed by means of the rules: both these great tragic poets exercised much influence in England. Their tradition, allowing nothing to be accidental, neglected external action in favor of portraying the passions or states of mind of heroic personages. This necessitated the use of narrative relations for events off-stage, and extreme focus of action on a final fateful day. All tragedies of this sort might begin on the note sounded early in Lee's *Rival Queens,* "The morning rises black"; and so many did begin in this fashion that the device was easily burlesqued. The persons devote much time to rhetorical displays of feeling and are likely to get casuistically involved in stating moderately simple reactions.

Nathaniel Lee [19] was one of the few specialized dramatists of the period. *Nat Lee* Between 1674 and 1684 he produced eleven tragedies and no comedies. In two additional tragedies, *Oedipus* (1678) and *The Duke of Guise* (1682), he collaborated with Dryden. Nine of these plays were based on stories about Greeks or Romans, some of them found, however, in the French romances of Lee's day. Since Lee mentions Shakespeare, Fletcher, and Jonson in his prefaces, one must conclude that he was consciously attentive to diverse traditions. Like Dryden, his friend, he tried to fuse the Elizabethan idiom with that of French tragedy and French heroic romance. Love was his theme, and in Langbaine's opinion, "His Muse indeed seem'd destin'd for the Diversion of the Fair Sex; so soft and passionately moving are his scenes of Love written." [20] Three of his plays were dedicated to royal mistresses, and *Mithridates* he himself calls a lady's play. It was one of his best. In the crucial years after 1678 he naturally wavered into political innuendo, and one of his very best plays, *Lucius Junius Brutus* (1680), was banned after three performances. Over others he had trouble with the censor.

[18] For John Crowne (1640?-1712?) see Arthur F. White, *John Crowne* (Cleveland, 1922), and for John Banks (*c.* 1652-1706) our best account is the Introduction to Thomas M. H. Blair's edition of Banks's *Unhappy Favourite* (1939).
[19] Nathaniel Lee (*c.* 1649-1692), the son of a clergyman, was educated at Westminster School and at Trinity College, Cambridge (1665-68). Leaving Cambridge, Lee went to London, and in spite of poverty speedily moved in fashionable society. He tried acting, but after a few months abandoned it for the writing of tragedies, at which he was highly successful. His intemperate habits became extreme, and in 1684 his mind failed completely. He was confined in Bedlam for five years (1684-89) and died in 1692. — *Works* (1694; 2v, 1713; 3v, 1734); *Nero* (1675); *Sophonisba* (1675); *Gloriana* (1676); *The Rival Queens, or the Death of Alexander the Great* (1677); *Mithridates* (1678); *Oedipus* (with Dryden, 1679); *Caesar Borgia* (1680); *Theodosius* (1680); *Lucius Junius Brutus* (1681); *The Duke of Guise* (1683); *Constantine the Great* (1684); *The Princess of Cleve* (1689); *The Massacre of Paris* (1689). — Bonamy Dobrée, *Restoration Tragedy* (Oxford, 1929); R. G. Ham, *Otway and Lee* (New Haven, 1931); W. B. VanLennep, "Nathaniel Lee," *Harvard Summaries of Theses* (Cambridge, Mass., 1935), pp. 337-341.
[20] Gerard Langbaine, *An Account of the English Dramatick Poets* (Oxford, 1691), p. 321.

In the essential nature of his tragedies Lee seems an apt illustration of his friend's dictum, "Great wits are sure to madness near allied"; for in his work tragic rant and imagery seem tainted with wildness and confusion. His first tragedy, *Nero,* dealt with the gruesome crimes of that emperor's day; almost his last was based on Mme de Lafayette's *Princesse de Clèves;* and Lee turns her picture of the French court into something almost as distasteful as *Nero.* In Lee the heroic recovered a sort of Jacobean decadence. Certainly he lacked control in his flights. In his dedication to *Theodosius* he says: "It has been often observed against me, That I abound in ungovern'd Fancy; but, I hope, the World will pardon the Sallies of Youth: Age, Despondence, and Dulness come too fast of themselves." And in the dedication to *Lucius Junius Brutus* he thinks a critic of such a story must be a Longinus "or nothing." Sublime flights were his objective; "furious fustian and turgid rants" were his achievement, so Cibber thought; and Cibber gave the added ungenerous opinion that only the dignity of Betterton's utterance as Alexander in *The Rival Queens* could have kept the play on the stage for so many succeeding years. It is easier to make a long list of Lee's faults than to perceive his merits steadily. His characters do rage rather than speak; situations change with absurd rapidity; at times motivation of important deeds is sadly deficient; and there is an almost unvarying high emotional tension. His Alexander, so Crowne thought, was "continually on the fret"; and the observation applies to many of his leading persons. But on the stage the plays had great effect. The fluency and speed of action, the torrent of violent imagery, the introduction of gruesome tableaux, and the fact that the stories of his plays have a strong, crude fascination account for much. His poetic gift, above all, might often make a minor Elizabethan envy him. There is also, along with the impetuosity of it all, a quiet sentimentality, an exaggerated stress on more or less innocent tears and pathos that was in effect somewhat akin to the lachrymose comedies soon to be in vogue.

Otway [21] in his brief career (1675-1683) strengthens the tendency remarked in Lee to develop away from heroics towards sentimental pathos. His first play, the typically heroic *Alcibiades* done in rime, apparently had no great success; but his second, *Don Carlos,* was a great hit, and remained one of his most popular works. Though written in rime and in the fast staling heroic conventions—such as making a tyrant father and his son rivals in

Thomas Otway

---

[21] Thomas Otway (1652-1685), born in Sussex, was educated at Winchester (1665-68) and Christ Church, Oxford (1669-71). In 1671 he left for London, where he first attempted acting (with little success) and soon devoted himself to writing plays under the not very rewarding patronage of the Earl of Rochester. In 1678 he was in Flanders as an army officer; but he returned to London the following year with pockets still empty. The remaining five years of his career as distinguished writer were spent in dissipation and extreme destitution. — *Works* (1692; 2v, 1712); *Complete Works,* ed. Montague Summers (3v, 1926); *Works,* ed. J. C. Ghosh [the best edition] (2v, Oxford, 1932). *Alcibiades* (1675); *Don Carlos* (1676); *Titus and Berenice* (1677); *Friendship in Fashion* (1678); *The History and Fall of Caius Marius* (1680); *The Orphan* (1680); *The Poet's Complaint of his Muse* (1680); *The Souldier's Fortune* (1681); *Venice Preserv'd* (1682); *The Atheist* (1684); *Windsor Castle* (1685). — Otway's *Orphan and Venice Preserv'd,* ed. Charles F. McClumpha (Boston, 1908), an edition with critical and historical comment; Roswell G. Ham, *Otway and Lee* (New Haven, 1931).

love and using a scorned lady (the Duchess of Eboli) as a plotting villainess —the play excelled because Otway treated his exalted personages as if they were human. In his dialogue they spoke the natural language of the heart more nearly than their type predecessors, and with a literary flavoring borrowed, as in the case of Lee, from Shakespeare. Like others of his day Otway could also adapt from the French, and in 1676 he brought out two short pieces, *Titus and Berenice,* based on Racine's *Bérénice* (1670), and a long-popular farce afterpiece, *The Cheats of Scapin,* from Molière. In 1679 he tried to blend two traditions by fusing the story of *Romeo and Juliet* with episodes from Roman history in his *Caius Marius,* a tragedy that had much popularity. He kept his Sulpitius (Mercutio) alive to the end, and expanded and diluted his pathos by having Lavinia (Juliet) revive in the tomb before Young Marius (Romeo) died. Naturally the play is far from being true Shakespeare; but in its day it had popularity.

The Orphan and *Venice Preserv'd,* however, both had and deserved a far greater esteem than these earlier plays. As a domestic tragedy *The Orphan* admirably suited Otway's gifts for pervasive pathos. Twin brothers, Castalio and Polydore, "both of nature mild and full of sweetness," are rivals for the love of Monimia. Castalio, somewhat too considerate of his brother's probable pain in losing Monimia, is married to her secretly; but the lustful Polydore, unaware of the marriage, overhears the nocturnal plans of the newly wedded couple, and, thinking what he hears is merely an agreement for an illicit assignation, contrives in the darkness to substitute himself for his brother in the marriage bed. The last two acts are a protracted expiation of this crime through successive suicides. The rôle of Monimia was written for Mrs. Barry, with whom Otway had fallen hopelessly in love; she was another's; but the pathos of Otway's heart was transferred to Monimia's lips and made the rôle infallible for any audience's tears for many decades.

Venice Preserv'd, or a Plot Discover'd is similarly focused on pathos. It has two added sources of interest: certain indecent comic scenes and a topical political aspect. The corruptness of the Venetian senate, symbolized in the animalism of Antonio—thought comic in 1681 as a satire on the Earl of Shaftesbury—stimulates patriots to a rebellious plot. Jaffeir, the harmless tragic hero, has (like Othello) by marriage robbed another senator, Priuli, of his daughter Belvidera, and is scorned by her father. Hence he falls into the conspiracy, which ultimately costs him his friendship with Pierre and his own and his wife's honor—and of course their lives. Torn by divergent loyalties (that sworn to his bosom companion, Pierre, and that pledged to his wife Belvidera) Jaffeir finds himself in one tense dramatic situation after another until on the scaffold itself he first, in order to save his friend from the tortures, stabs Pierre and then himself. Belvidera goes mad—

> Say not a word of this to my old father,
> Murmuring streams, soft shades, and springing flowers,
> Lutes, Laurells, Seas of Milk, and ships of Amber.

The Orphan (margin note)

Venice Preserv'd (margin note)

With these words, often quoted in the century to follow, her reason leaves her, and soon she dies, haunted in her last moments by the ghosts of Jaffeir and Pierre. The contemporary popularity of this tragedy was in part due to the atmosphere of plotting and counter-plotting that enveloped the last years of Charles II. Otway's attitude expresses a serious condemnation of cabals and plots in a tone that gave the play dignity. But the fact that it has been revived oftener than any English non-Shakespearean tragedy is due, not to political purpose but to its powerful emotional appeal. The play was, in the admirable remark of Dr. Johnson, the work "of one who conceived forcibly and drew originally by consulting nature in his own breast." It may be recalled that in 1756 Joseph Warton in "grading" the English poets placed Otway among the best "sublime and pathetic poets," and ranked him with Lee, behind only Spenser, Shakespeare, and Milton. If six years later, in reprinting the dedication of his *Essay on the Writings and Genius of Pope,* Warton omitted all mention of Otway and Lee in his rankings, the omission is probably due to the disagreement of friendly critics as to the proper placing of these writers rather than to any sudden decline of esteem.

Thomas
Southerne   The charming actress Mrs. Barry, who inspired and created the distressed innocence of Monimia and Belvidera, found a third rôle of great popular appeal in the Isabella of Thomas Southerne's *Fatal Marriage* (1694).[22] Here Southerne avoided the political objectives that limited the popularity of his first serious play, *The Loyal Brother* (1682), and made a notable addition to the tradition of bourgeois tragedy. Although his gifts for comedy more than equaled those for tragedy, he is perhaps best known by *The Fatal Marriage* and by *Oroonoko* (1695). Both these plays are tragicomedies in the sense that a serious story of tragic ending is sandwiched in (and not too smoothly) with an independent comic plot. The serious plots came from short stories by Mrs. Aphra Behn,[23] as Southerne himself tells us; and they emphasize the progress of the last decade of the century through pathos towards sentimentalism. The "passionate distress" of Isabella—innocently wedded to two husbands, one of whom returns after seven years of supposed death—and the more philosophical, as well as more brutal, woes of "the royal slave", Oroonoko, are still moving. There is nothing bourgeois about Oroonoko and his spotless Imoinda—except their appeal! Evidently before 1700 the enslaved "noble savage" or noble exotic greatly attracted English lovers of liberty. Southerne's tragic idiom is most uneven; at times

22 Thomas Southerne (1660-1746) was born in Dublin, the son of a prosperous brewer. After attending Trinity College, Dublin, he went to London and entered the Middle Temple, which seems to have been a cradle for dramatists. He left the Temple, probably about 1682, and, except for a brief career as an army officer (1685-88), devoted himself to dramatic writing. After 1700 he wrote little, but lived quietly in London for the most part. — *Works* (2v, 1713); *Plays* (3v, 1774); *The Loyal Brother* (1682); *The Disappointment* (1684); *Sir Anthony Love* (1691); *The Wives Excuse* (1692); *The Maid's Last Prayer* (1693); *The Fatal Marriage* (1694); *Oroonoko* (1696); *The Fate of Capua* (1700); *The Spartan Dame* (with John Stafford, 1719); *Money the Mistress* (1726). — John W. Dodds, *Thomas Southerne, Dramatist* (New Haven, 1933).
23 On Mrs. Behn's novels see below, Part I, ch. VIII, n. 20.

high and dignified passion is coupled with awkward pedestrian phrasing. His sense of structure is a violent return to early Elizabethan love of variety: the French unities have slight influence here.

Southerne, therefore, is a sort of milestone by which to measure development in tragedy. His deficient sense of structure is exceptional; and the shifting taste of the time is signalized in the fact that Congreve's *Mourning Bride,* one of the most popular of neo-classical "unified" tragedies, was staged in 1697 about a year after *Oroonoko.* But clearly in Otway, Lee, and Southerne the English tradition preserved itself and moved away from the heroics encouraged by French romances and by Dryden's successes, towards a love of strained and intense pathos, based upon private, family emotions akin to those most played upon by sentimentalists. Southerne as well as Lee and Otway made use of ancient classical stories; all of them were influenced by French drama, and all were more concerned with situations that depicted and appealed to the passions than they were with nice motivation of character or with neat construction of unified plots. The popularity of tragic actresses and the increasing number of ladies in the audience encouraged the use of sentimental distress as the vital force in their plays. Other circumstances will further motivate a somewhat similar development in comedy.

VI

Restoration Drama: II. Comedy

Blending Traditions

Diverse elements went to the making of Restoration comedy.[1] When the theatres were reopened in 1660, Davenant's company revived plays of Beaumont and Fletcher, Shakespeare, and less famous Elizabethans, but no Ben Jonson. Killigrew controlled Jonson, of whose plays he used seven. The critics praised chiefly Jonson,[2] Beaumont and Fletcher,[3] and Shakespeare—the last of whom had much influence on tragedy but less on comedy. Jonson contributed a popular type of low comedy, and his method of characterization by means of humors was common throughout the whole century. Idealistic romanticism was "out" in comedy; in its place appeared a somewhat skeptical attitude towards life, derived perhaps from the romances of Beaumont and Fletcher and from such realistic intrigues as those in Fletcher's *Wild-Goose Chase* and *The Chances*—which last the Duke of Buckingham, in February, 1667, made into a very typical Restoration comedy. Writers like Middleton and Shirley showed the way to knotted intrigues and to local color within the environs of London. For plot materials and for a sense of the comedy inherent in social aberration Molière was enormously influential on all the English comic writers of the period.[4] Spanish comedy, too, encouraged bustling plots, and the Spanish *novelas* furnished tricks of intrigue for many plays. Plautus and Terence had long since been absorbed into both the English and the French comic traditions; but in their own right the Romans still had direct influence.

All these elements unite; but something is added to give the true Restora-

---

[1] General references to books and articles on Restoration drama will be found above, ch. v, n. 2. To these may be added the following that deal more specifically with comedy: Charles Lamb, "On the Artificial Comedy of the Last Century" (1822; in "Elia," *Works*, ed. Thomas Hutchinson, Oxford, 1908, I. 648-656); Thomas Babington (Lord) Macaulay, "The Dramatic Works of Wycherley, Congreve, Vanbrugh, and Farquhar," *Edinburgh Review*, LXXII (1841). 490-528; reprinted among his "Critical Essays," see *Complete Writings* (Boston, 1900), XV. 47-100; John Palmer, *The Comedy of Manners* (1913); Bonamy Dobrée, *Restoration Comedy* (Oxford, 1924); Henry T. E. Perry, *The Comic Spirit in Restoration Drama* (1925); Kathleen M. Lynch, *The Social Mode of Restoration Comedy* (1926); Gellert S. Alleman, *Matrimonial Law and the Materials of Restoration Comedy* (Wallingford, Penn., 1942); Clarence S. Paine, *The Comedy of Manners (1660-1700): A Reference Guide to the Comedy of the Restoration* (Boston, 1941); and Elizabeth L. Mignon, *Crabbed Age and Youth: The Old Men and Women in the Restoration Comedy of Manners* (Durham, N. C., 1947).

[2] Gerald E. Bentley, *Shakespeare and Jonson: Their Reputations in the Seventeenth Century Compared* (2v, Chicago, 1945).

[3] Arthur C. Sprague, *Beaumont and Fletcher on the Restoration Stage* (Cambridge, Mass., 1926).

[4] J. E. Gillet, *Molière en Angleterre, 1660-70* (Bruxelles and Paris, 1913), and Dudley H. Miles, *The Influence of Molière on Restoration Comedy* (1910); and John Wilcox, *The Relation of Molière to Restoration Comedy* (1938).

tion flavor. Although dramatists and critics alike agreed that moral in- *Court* struction, through social criticism, was the aim of literature, and that comedy *Influence* was a corrective of vices and follies, undoubtedly laughter or entertainment, and not moral improvement, was the true objective of Restoration comedy. The manners of the court were highly corrupt, and the comedy that the court patronized was unblushing, hard, cynical, and immoral. Among the notable playwrights Dryden, Sedley, Etherege, Wycherley, Congreve, and Vanbrugh were men of fashion or courtiers; and the less aristocratic writers, such as Otway and Mrs. Behn, were as crudely indecent as the courtiers. No French play was adapted into English in this period without a notable increment of grossness. The element of idealism was replaced by a cynical and frequently explicit denial or at least a disregard of healthy values.

Perhaps because of the corruptness of court circles, perhaps because of a *The Social* more general extreme revulsion against all Puritanism, it was good business *Mode of* to present on the stage shamelessly emancipated people. But the real source *Comedy* of comic effect concerns manners rather than morals. It was thought generally that there was or should be an explicit pattern of conduct or decorum for every station in life: for the monarch and for the beggar, for the gentleman and for his valet, for the fine lady and for the bawd. If like Congreve's Witwoud (*The Way of the World*) one pretended to a pattern for which one was unqualified (in this case the dullard pretending to wit), one was comic; if like many boorish country squires one pretended to be a gentleman, one's manner of pretending might be comic. Sir Fopling Flutter, like all the fops that he begot in later plays, was not a gentleman, but a gentleman *manqué*. He was as sure of his exquisite quality as is the drunkard of his dignity of bearing; but at every point he missed the true pattern, with complete unawareness of the fact. As for the ladies—all at heart engrossed in a man-hunt but always industrious to conceal the fact—their hypocritical coyness as well as their not infrequent sudden blunt remarks about sexual appetites seemed comical. Whatever is shocking is a deviation from pattern: some shocks are painful; some that are painful to us were comical to the Restoration. Nowadays it is wise to regret the grossness of situation and of repartee in these comedies and to try to recapture the fine sense of social protocol that made any unconscious singing off key—violating the pattern —amusing.

Elizabethan comedy had been an imaginative representation of men liv- *Portrayal* ing; Restoration comedy is rather an anatomy of life, not more a repre- *by* sentation than a commentary on life and on various social schematisms. *Analysis* The persons frequently are not so much men as specialized humors in Jonson's fashion. They are specialized in type or function: the inelegant country squire, the rake as hero, the male bawd (Otway's Sir Jolly Jumble and Vanbrugh's Old Coupler), the furious rejected mistress—there is no end to the obvious "type" characters habitually used. The dramatists also are conscious of class patterns. Etherege's *Comical Revenge* has four plots: a noble plot (presented in rime) concerning the loves of Lord Bevill's daughters; a genteel plot that presents Sir Frederick's wooing of his widow; a low comedy plot in the gulling of the Cromwellian knight, Sir Nicholas Culley; and lastly a servant plot involving the discomfiture of the valet, Dufoy. Comic implications arising from patterns of social class are common. There are schematic motivations of intrigue: the younger brother or spend-thrift heir must trick a frugal father out of necessary funds; the neglected wife must reclaim her husband's attentions by making him jealous (jealousy is, as Mrs. Loveit in *The Man of Mode* remarks, "the strongest Cordial we can give to dying Love"); most common of all intrigues are the varying devices for disentangling oneself from a love affair or for indemnifying oneself against the boredom of matrimony. The married state is loudly and commonly made a subject for uncomplimentary laughter. Thus one concludes that Restoration comedy is rather less a representation of life than it is a commentary upon manners.

Comic Techniques Used   The techniques involved have in part been hinted. Plots are double or triple; seldom is there perfect unity of action. The unities of time and place are vaguely observed and always strongly influential. Romantic plots may be in rime; most of the comedies are in prose, and are realistic rather than romantic or idealistic. Repartee is much valued, and frequently plot is neglected for discussion of proper conditions for marital happiness, of cuckoldry, and, very commonly, of the nature of wit. In such "conversations" Congreve is the supreme artist. Pepys found no wit in Etherege's first play, and Pope thought Farquhar's dialogue pert and low; yet to an unpractised reader Etherege and Farquhar may now pass as artists in dialogue; to a more experienced reader the superiority of Congreve in finished, formal precision and in brilliant marksmanship will be apparent. There was no steady development towards this perfection of witty comedy: Congreve was a supreme moment in a period remarkable for its gift at repartee. The two outstanding "moments" in Restoration comedy, so far as chronology goes, are found in the years 1668-76 and 1693-1707.

The Early Comedies of Manners   It is natural that the years 1660-1667 should be marked by the revival of old plays and experimentation in the new plays. Of these early efforts Sir Robert Howard's political comedy *The Committee* (1662) had decided topical appeal, and Sir Samuel Tuke's adaptation from the Spanish of *The Adventures of Five Hours* (1663) was a contrasting type of happily ending drama of romantic intrigue. Dryden, not too highly endowed for comedy, began his dramatic career with his *Wild Gallant* (1663), a play of Jonsonian humors and confused intrigue, in which Isabelle's campaign for a husband is the lively driving force. In *Sir Martin Mar-all* (1667) he borrows his material from Molière without borrowing much sparkle of wit. These plays were prophetic of Dryden's tendency to concentrate in comedies on plot-intrigue rather than on "manners." Etherege's first play shows little more tendency towards the typical comedy of manners. His *Comical Revenge* (1664) has a lightness of touch that is promising, but in plot and character-ization Etherege will soon do better. The Duke of Buckingham's reshaping of Fletcher's *Chances* (1667) gave indication of the callous morality, the astonishing gift of manipulating situation swiftly, and the keen, shameless facetiousness of dialogue that was to characterize the true Restoration comedy, and yet this play is fully as Jacobean as it is Restoration in method.

The year 1668 saw several new comedies of some distinction, and the eight years following include the best early achievements in genuine Restoration comedy. The period saw Dryden's reputation increased by heroic plays rather than by comedies, though *Marriage à la Mode* (1671) is one of his best. *The Assignation* (1672) is negligible. *Marriage à la Mode* deals with typical material, but in an independent fashion. The intrigue is romantic rather than cynical in tone: Dryden has a sympathetic interest in his flirtatious couples and lacks the aloofness of Etherege and Congreve. Melantha's passion for French words is most innocently amusing, and the casual comments on the wit of polite conversation are admirably comic.

But these eight years saw more significant developments in the work of Etherege, Wycherley, and Shadwell. Of this trio Etherege and Wycherley were courtiers and wrote respectively only three and four plays. Shadwell in a long career produced eighteen. The work of these three is significantly different.

Etherege's *Comical Revenge* (1664) coming at a period when new comedies were rare, had perhaps undeserved success.[5] *She Wou'd if She Cou'd* (1668) came in a season that offered competition, and being badly acted at first was ill received. Later the play achieved popularity. Shadwell in the preface to his third play, *The Humorists* (1670), called *She Wou'd* "the best comedy that has been written since the Restoration of the Stage," —an interesting opinion from one who in his Preface to *The Sullen Lovers* (1668) had abused the witty, impudent lechery of current plays that lacked humorous Jonsonian characters. In Lady Cockwood, however, Etherege had come as near to a humorous personage as he ever did, and possibly she appealed to Shadwell. Etherege's characters here are rationally defined rather than imaginatively created: of two country knights Sir Oliver Cockwood has a hypocritical wife who seeks adventure, and Sir Joslin Jolley has two young kinswomen—Ariana, sly and pretty, and Gatty, wild and witty —who are pursued by "two honest gentlemen of the town," and are finally wedded to them. The plotting is not too deft, but the light conversation is charming. Contemporary versifiers who said Etherege had "writ two

New Achieve-ments

She Wou'd if She Cou'd

---

⁵ Sir George Etherege (*c.* 1635-1691) came of a genteel family of Berkshire. His father died in France (1649), and the son was reared by his grandfather. As a young man he traveled abroad, and for a time studied law. After 1664 he was a man about town who occasionally wrote a witty comedy; after 1668 he had an intermittent career as diplomat. He was secretary to the Ambassador in Constantinople (1668-71), and returned to marry a fortune and to be knighted. He was James II's envoy to the Diet of Ratisbon (1685-89), from which place he wrote the letters preserved in his *Letterbook* (ed. Sybil Rosenfeld, Oxford, 1928). As a Jacobite he lived in France and died in Paris. — *Works*, ed. A. W. Verity (1888); ed. H. F. B. Brett-Smith (2v, Oxford, 1927). For biographical materials see Sybil Rosenfeld, "Sir George Etherege in Ratisbon," *RES*, x (1934). 177-189; and especially Dorothy Foster, "Sir George Etherege," *LTLS*, May 31, 1928, p. 412, and *RES*, viii (1932). 458-459, where several other contributions by Miss Foster are referred to. Critical and historical comment is found in the introduction to Mr. Brett-Smith's excellent edition.

Talking Plays without one Plot," were perhaps wrong: there were numerous episodic intrigues, though these, particularly in his first play, were not too well fused. "A single intrigue in love," he causes a gentleman to say in *She Wou'd*, "is as dull as a single plot in a play." In this second play all the persons are "dancers on the ropes," a fall from which would mean an awkward betrayal of intrigue. They make use of a dialogue that is easy, airy, and witty, and its cool finish together with the relaxed, objective attitude of the author towards his material—a cavalier detachment from emotion—gave the true Etherege savor, characteristic of the best in the period.

The Man of Mode   Of Etherege's three comedies the third, *The Man of Mode, or Sir Fopling Flutter* (1676), has caused most comment, and is doubtless the best. The plot is basically unified, being the rake Dorimant's progress in his amours. It is, in fact, summarized by his remark (1. i. 200): "Next to the coming to a good understanding with a new Mistress, I love a quarrel with an old one." Modern readers find Dorimant cruel to Mrs. Loveit and Bellinda, but the scenes involving these ladies doubtless were comic to a generation that had no sympathy for ladies who took their light loves seriously. The scene that shows us Dorimant in his dressing gown and Bellinda just ready to leave after their first assignation is in implication most gross; but in its action— with the valet "tying up linen"—doubtless provoked laughter. The better parts of the play are really a succession of episodic scenes that are delightfully comic and most skilfully written. Loveit's rages, Old Bellair's fumbling advances to Emilia, the dissembling love scene of Young Bellair and Harriet, the first appearance of the overdressed Sir Fopling—tactfully referred to in Act III—Lady Woodvill's first meeting with Dorimant in the Mall, Sir Fopling's adventures there with Loveit: all these are handled with a keen sense of the comic. The trick of using a not too important plot to support a succession of such scenes was to teach Congreve much. Dorimant apparently became in theatrical circles the accepted type of fine gentleman of the Restoration, and one of the central objectives of Richard Steele's *Conscious Lovers* (1723) was the desire to correct that acceptance. Dorimant was certainly far from the sentimental ideal, and Etherege himself evidently had qualms about his hero; for he left him on probation with Harriet as the play ended.

William Wycherley [6] probably learned little from Etherege's cynical avoid-

[6] William Wycherley (1641-1716) was born at Clive near Shrewsbury. At about the age of fifteen he was sent to France, where he frequented refined circles and where he became a Catholic. In 1660 he was briefly at Oxford; presently he was in London in the Inner Temple. His first play, acted in 1671, gained him the intimacy of a royal mistress, the Duchess of Cleveland, through whose interest he secured a commission in a foot regiment (1672). His marriage with the Countess of Drogheda (1679 or 1680) displeased Charles II, who had just offered him the tutorship of his son, the Duke of Richmond. Because of debts Wycherley was for some time in Fleet Prison; but he was released by the proceeds of a benefit performance at Whitehall (December 14, 1685) of his *Plain Dealer*. After 1704 he formed a friendship with young Alexander Pope, who, somewhat too zealously, revised many of Wycherley's later verses. On his deathbed Wycherley married again, ostensibly in order to prevent his property from passing to his nephew. — *Miscellany Poems* (1704); *Posthumous Works* (Vol. I, ed. Theobald, 1728; Vol. II, ed. Pope, 1729); *Plays*, ed. William C. Ward (1888); *Complete Works*, ed. Montague

ance of genuine emotion or from his use of successive light satirical vignettes *Wycherley* of polite society—which would impede more engrossing plots—or from his *Independ-* flexible empty dialogue. After his first play, Etherege's art in the transcrip- *ence* tion of life as he actually saw it about him was probably characteristic of the moment rather than a clear case of pioneering: he transcribed life, but he lacked philosophy. To him life was a frivolous game, and to become emotionally engrossed therein was perhaps slightly vulgar. Between *She Wou'd if She Cou'd* and *The Man of Mode* Wycherley produced three of his four plays, and these took a graver view of life, and offered more in the way of commentary on life.

His first play, *Love in a Wood* (1671) was like *The Comical Revenge* Love in in that it presented a series of love intrigues as seen in different classes of a Wood society; but Wycherley focused more on citizens and less on the life of fashion. Alderman Gripe, a hypocritical Puritan, ultimately marries a wench; he is a perfectly Jonsonian comic figure. Lady Flippant, his sister, is the amorous widow whose eager quest for a husband was to be reproduced in many later spinsters. Dapperwit, a fop of wit, as the later Sir Fopling Flutter was to be the fop of mode or dress, gets Gripe's daughter for his wife, but, being a fool, justly misses getting her fortune. Ranger, a moderately uninteresting man about town, temporarily forsakes his mistress Lydia in order, apparently, to complicate the course of true love for the romantic (almost sentimental) couple, Valentine and Christina, who hardly come from the same realistic world as do the other persons. The sardonic philosophy of the play seems to be that in the scale of being every one is someone else's cully or dupe. "Every wit has his cully, as every squire his led captain"; but "the best wits of the town are but cullies themselves ...to sempstresses and bawds." Among set conversations in the play that between Lydia and Dapperwit concerning wit is very striking, and this foppish poet is throughout the play a rich study in "false wit"—anticipating Congreve's more casually conceived Witwoud.

The Gentleman Dancing-Master (1672) is the simplest and least sardonic The of Wycherley's plays. It concentrates on a single intrigue, that of Hippolita, Gentleman who, to avoid marriage with a frenchified fop, finds herself a true gentleman Dancing- who poses as her dancing-master and finally becomes her husband. Subordi- Master nate intrigues are almost completely lacking. The comedy arises from the fact that the fop, though English, burlesques French manners, by being more French than the French, while Hippolita's father (an English merchant) is more Spanish than a grandee. Mrs. Caution, as the suspicious aunt and critical sister, is an admirably comic person. The scenes in which Mr. Gerrard, who "can't dance a step" or play the violin, is compelled to show

Summers (4v, 1924); *Epistles to the King and Duke* (1683); *On his Grace the Duke of Marlborough* (1707). — Charles Perromat, *William Wycherley, sa vie—son œuvre* (Paris, 1921); George B. Churchill, "The Originality of Wycherley," *Schelling Anniversary Papers* (1923), pp. 65-85; Willard Connely, *Brawny Wycherley* (1930); H. P. Vincent, "The Date of Wycherley's Birth," *LTLS*, March 3, 1932, p. 155, and "The Death of William Wycherley," *Harvard Studies & Notes in Phil. & Lit.*, xv (1933). 219-242 (a new explanation of the deathbed marriage).

Hippolita the steps of the coranto in the presence of suspicious relatives must have been uproarious farce. Though Wycherley's gayest and slightest piece, its lack of satiric direction and of multiplicity of intrigue caused it to be perhaps undervalued.

The Country Wife

His third play, *The Country Wife* (1675), has recently been thought his best. It involves two intrigues. The first is that by which Horner, recently returned from France in a condition deceitfully described as "bad as an eunuch," practises promiscuous cuckolding and, chiefly, wins the favor of the Country Wife (Margery) whom the superannuated sensualist, Pinchwife, has married. Pinchwife, by temperament and experience made suspicious and jealous, has had to come to London to marry his sister Alithea to the fop Sparkish. The more polite but less distinguished intrigue of the play concerns her ultimate gulling of Sparkish and marrying with Harcourt. The broad indecency of the leading farcical situation—the alleged impotence of Horner—dominates the play, which is a whimsical gulling of cuckolds, and especially of the distasteful Pinchwife. Margery's country frankness continually punctures the polite duplicity of London social pretense, most notably at the end when she insists on Horner's physical integrity until she finds she can't be rid of her "musty husband," and so will—"since you'll have me tell more lies"—acquiesce in politeness. The central device of the play is doubtless highly indecent: Wycherley's manipulation of it is brilliant. It is notable also that here, as in *Love in a Wood,* he makes his spectators partisans in condemning selfish, pretentious, or hypocritical persons (Pinchwife, Sparkish) and enjoying their discomfiture.

The Plain Dealer

This trick becomes central in his last play, *The Plain Dealer* (1676), which in his own day was thought his finest achievement. Manly, the Plain Dealer, has been robbed and wronged by his mistress Olivia and his closest friend, Vernish. He is aided throughout his misfortunes by the virtuous and lovely Fidelia, who has long followed him disguised as a man. From Racine's *Les Plaideurs* (1668) Wycherley has derived the fantastic litigious Widow Blackacre, who is gulled by Freeman. The play is most sardonic. Manly, derived in part from Molière's *Misanthrope* (1666), rivals the railing malcontents of Elizabethan drama in bleak bitterness. But, on the other hand, Manly anticipates some of the traits of the eighteenth-century good man or benevolist: he is easily gulled and is honest in the extreme, but his tone is misanthropic rather than benevolent. In all his plays, except the second, Wycherley exposes the absurdities of mere pretenders to wit and lashes the hypocrisies of mankind: he paints a dark picture of the men and women of his age. Lacking the aloofness and unconcern of Etherege and Congreve, he is vehement in scorning the backbiting of Dapperwit, the hypocrisy of Alderman Gripe, and the falseness of Olivia. On the other side, in Christina, Hippolita, and Fidelia, he presents more virtuous charm than one can find in the other leading comedies of the time. His scenes are laid in general in the homes of citizens or in the lodgings of impecunious young gentlemen, or in eating houses or other places of recreation. For a man educated in

France he surprisingly lacks aristocratic tone and a regard for modishness. Evidently he did not respect the class in which he moved; probably he did not even respect certain aspects of his own character, and so was not unwilling to expose blackly those who might seem to themselves and to others better than himself. In any case he never wrote without both imaginative and intellectual conviction. If he could have been as refined and easy as he was penetrating and amusing, he might well have been the foremost among English comic writers. One can disregard the prejudice and squeamishness of Macaulay and other Victorians towards Wycherley as a moralist, and yet his pictures of "real life" are, as such, most repugnant.

After 1677 Etherege and Wycherley wrote no more for the stage, and *Shadwell* Dryden produced little comedy of importance except his *Spanish Friar* (1680). In the years 1677-92, furthermore, hardly a single new comic playwright of distinction appeared: these years were a plateau of mediocrity, except perhaps for the work of Thomas Shadwell.[7] During the years of Etherege and Wycherley, Shadwell had produced nine plays and by 1692 his total was eighteen. In the preface to his first play, *The Sullen Lovers* (1668), he had announced his program: he was against the frivolities of wit or repartee, against the love-and-honor clichés, and against the use of either romantic or modishly disreputable lovers; he adhered to the school of Ben Jonson, the comedy of humors. Yet he admired Etherege and at times almost equaled Wycherley in brutality or vulgarity. In his prefaces, prologues, and epilogues he frequently wrote of dramatic art, and was more explicitly concerned with obeying the rules than were the witty comic writers of the time. He pictures the bourgeoisie vividly and amusingly, and more than other dramatists preceding Farquhar lays his scenes in the country, though what he shows us there (as in *Epsom Wells*) are Londoners on a holiday. He was a professional dramatist rather than a gentleman who wrote a few plays. The frankly coarse and low material typical of Jonsonian comedy was less acceptable by 1680 than it had been in 1608, and although Shadwell succeeded with audiences, he did not win too much critical esteem. This failure has been blamed on Dryden's animosity, perhaps too exclusively.

Among his early works *The Sullen Lovers,* a satire on the Howard family of wits, was very successful, as was the more vulgar *Epsom Wells* (1672). In *The Virtuoso* (1676) he had fun with the supposed absurdities of the new science with its strange experiments and its love of theory—as seen in Sir Nicholas Gimcrack's devotion to "the speculative part of swimming" and

---

[7] Thomas Shadwell (*c.* 1642-1692) was born at Santon Hall, Norfolk, and educated in Bury St. Edmunds, Caius College, Cambridge (1656-58), and the Middle Temple. After some travel abroad he devoted himself to literature, and after 1668 for fifteen years produced a new play almost every year. In 1682 began his feud with Dryden, whom at the Revolution of 1688 he had the pleasure to succeed as poet laureate and historiographer royal. — *Dramatick Works* (4v, 1720); *Complete Works,* ed. Montague Summers (5v, 1927). In addition to the plays mentioned here in the text Shadwell wrote *The Royal Shepherdess* (1669); *The Humorists* (1671); *The Miser* (1672); *Psyche* (1675); *The Libertine* (1676); *The History of Timon of Athens* (1678); *A True Widow* (1679); *The Woman-Captain* (1680); *The Medal of John Bayes* (1682); *A Lenten Prologue* (1683); *The Scowrers* (1691); *The Volunteers* (1693). See Albert S. Borgman, *Thomas Shadwell* (1928).

other such picturesque vagaries. The preface to this play condemned false uses of humor in a way that touched more than one contemporary. Naturally in the years after the Popish Plot, Shadwell as a "true blue" Whig won partisan popularity with two political comedies, *The Lancashire Witches* (1681) and *The Amorous Bigotte* (1690). Of his later plays *The Squire of Alsatia* (1688) and *Bury Fair* (1689) are the best. Alsatia was a low section of London, and in its environment Shadwell developed a discussion as to the best way of rearing a son. The contrasting pairs of fathers and sons were as old as the *Adelphi* of Terence; but they came to new life, commonly sentimentalized, in later generations. *The Squire of Alsatia* was enormously popular in its first run, having, one suspects, in parts the appeal of a gangster play of our days.

hra Behn   Apart from the work of Shadwell these middle years (1677-92) saw the continuation of the work of other professional playwrights. Mrs. Aphra Behn's productive career began in 1670 (before Wycherley's), and her last play (1696) was her nineteenth.[8] Only one of these nineteen (*Abdelazer,* 1676) was a tragedy. Much under the influence of Spanish novels, she wrote stories herself and comedies of adventurous intrigue derived from Spanish *novelas.* Typical would be *The Dutch Lover* (1673) and *The Rover,* a play in two parts (1677, 1681). Disguisings, farce elements, and even characters from the *commedia dell' arte* (Harlequin and Scaramouch in *The Rover,* Part II) are used in her plays. Naturally she also included political hits, as, for example, in *The City Heiress* (1682). In character Mrs. Behn was definitely emancipated; and her compliance with the taste of the time, together with the prime fact that her plays came from a woman's pen, gave her a reputation for shocking indecencies as a dramatist. She simply tried to write like the men, whom she in no way surpassed.

venscroft   Edward Ravenscroft (c. 1650-1697) between 1672 and the end of the century produced a dozen plays, about half of them in this middle period. For invention, which he lacked, he substituted adaptation, especially from the French, or even plagiarism. His first plays, *The Citizen Turn'd Gentleman* (1672) and *The Careless Lovers* (1673), were synthesized from Molière in a fashion such as to stress the bustle of situation and even farce and to minimize characterization or wit. He borrowed from the Spanish also, and in *Scaramouch a Philosopher* (1677) he made for the Drury Lane Company an adaptation from Molière's *Scapin* six months after Otway had brought out his very popular *Cheats of Scapin* at the other house. In general Ravenscroft was more competent in farce than in anything subtle enough to be called comedy.

From this middle period of mediocrity (1677-92) we pass to the final brilliant outburst of comedies composed in the Restoration spirit by Congreve, Vanbrugh, and Farquhar, and staged in the years 1693-1707. Chronologically these men—who were small boys when the last plays of Etherege

8 For the life of Aphra Behn (1640-1689) see Part I, ch. VIII. n. 20. A list of her plays will be found in Allardyce Nicoll's *History of Restoration Drama*, pp. 352-353, and in *CBEL*, II. 417-418.

and Wycherley were first produced—hardly belong to the Restoration; but
that they are in the spirit of the Restoration can be seen by examining their
plays and observing the steadiness with which they persevered in that spirit
in spite of a notably rising tide of moral criticism. The focal work in this
attack on the theatre was that of the non-juror, Jeremy Collier, who in 1698
published *A Short View of the Immorality and Profaneness of the English
Stage.*[9] Collier's chief victims were Dryden, Wycherley, Congreve, Vanbrugh,
D'Urfey, and Otway (*The Orphan*). What he most objected to was the use
of profanity in stage dialogue and the unfavorable portrayals of clergymen;
but he also held (chapter IV) that the popular plays of the time encouraged
immorality. He urged, in orthodox neo-classical fashion, that comedy should
correct vice and not promote it. His work attracted more attention than any
other single book or pamphlet; but it is notable that Shadwell in the preface
of his first play (1668) had criticized the morals of comedy, and Dryden in
his *Ode to Mrs. Anne Killigrew* (1686) had admitted gross faults. Both these
dramatists, however, were obvious offenders. The newly founded Society for
the Reformation of Manners had denounced the theatre before Collier's book
appeared, and its members very likely were behind the practical attempts
at censorship made through presentments to the Grand Jury or through the
arrests of actors or through orders from the long-suffering Lord Chamberlain.
The controversy lasted long, and Collier's reforms were still agitated by his
friend and fellow non-juror Richard Russell in *The Grub-street Journal*
(1730-37). Independent playwrights continued to produce "unreformed"
plays, but certain professional playwrights, Colley Cibber, for example, had
begun to produce dramas ostensibly less offensive. Cibber was a shrewd
producer rather than a sincere moralist, as we shall see later—at least no one
in his own day took his moralizing seriously.

William Congreve [10] was definitely among the unregenerate. Doubtless he

[9] The standard work on the Collier controversy is that by Joseph W. Krutch, *Comedy and
Conscience after the Restoration* (1924). See also Sister Rose Anthony's *The Jeremy Collier
Stage Controversy* (Milwaukee, 1937). A brief list of documents in the controversy is found in
the *CBEL*, II. 400-402.

[10] William Congreve (1670-1729) was born at Bardsey, Yorkshire; but his childhood was
spent in Ireland, where his father's military service took the family. He studied at Kilkenny
School (with Jonathan Swift), and attended Trinity College, Dublin. In London he was admitted to the Middle Temple in 1691, but he had little interest in the law, and began a
gentlemanly career as author. He produced four comedies and one tragedy, the first two for
Drury Lane and the last three for Betterton's company in the new theatre in Lincoln's Inn
Fields. He replied to Jeremy Collier's attack on his plays, but after the cool reception of *The
Way of the World* (1700) he wrote virtually nothing for the theatre. He held various government sinecures, and lived politely with many friends and practically no enemies. Much time
during his later years he spent with Henrietta, Duchess of Marlborough, to whom he be-
queathed the bulk of his estate, apparently with a private understanding that the Duchess was
in turn to bequeath it, as she did, to her (and possibly Congreve's) daughter, Lady Mary
Godolphin. — *Works* (3v, 1710); *Complete Works,* ed. Montague Summers (4v, 1923); *Comedies,* ed. Bonamy Dobrée (Oxford, 1925); *The Mourning Bride* (and other works), ed. Bonamy
Dobrée (Oxford, 1928); *Works,* ed. F. W. Bateson (1930); *Incognita* (1692; ed. H. F. B. Brett-
Smith, 1922); *The Mourning Muse of Alexis* (1695); *A Pindarique Ode to the King* (1695);
Letters upon Several Occasions [some by Congreve], ed. John Dennis (1696); *The Birth of the
Muse* (1698); *Amendments of Mr. Collier's False and Imperfect Citations* (1698); *The Judge-
ment of Paris* (1701); *A Hymn to Harmony* (1703); *The Tears of Amaryllis* (1703); *A Pindar-
ique Ode on the Victorious Progress of Her Majesties Arms* [with a prefatory "Discourse of the
Pindarique Ode"] (1706); *An Impossible Thing* (1720); *A Letter . . . to the Viscount Cobham*

was shocked and annoyed to find his work rather ineptly attacked by Collier. Congreve regarded himself as a reformer of the stage; and that he was so regarded by others is evident from the fact that he (with Vanbrugh, another sinner) was chosen to direct the new theatre in the Haymarket, which was opened in 1705 and was supposedly devoted to theatrical uplift. Early in his career Congreve had been praised by Dryden and Southerne, who helped get his first play produced, and by Addison, Swift, and doubtless many others. But his reform was concerned with the technique of drama—its wit, its structure, its dialogue. Perhaps because he .became aware that his sort of reform did not catch on, perhaps because he did not care to compete with less genteel, less acute playwrights, he ceased from writing for the stage at the age of thirty. His prefaces, as well as Swift's rimed epistle to him, indicate that Congreve felt superior to his audiences. Far be it from him to cut blocks with a razor! So he became an elegant minor poet, a gouty man about town, and the gallant of a wealthy duchess. If there was something of the snob in Congreve, he was still an amiable snob, one of the best liked of literary men during a period of nearly forty years (1692-1729), in which very few wits were generally beloved.

Clearly Congreve was a formalist, a technician, a man of artistic rather than moral conscience. He learned much from such predecessors as Etherege, Wycherley, Shadwell, and Molière. That his characters were subtler than Etherege's can be seen by comparing his gentlemen, Vainlove and Mirabell, with the celebrated Dorimant. Congreve's heroes do not love a quarrel with a cast mistress, do not condescend to berate their servants, and are not vain of their inconstancy in love—though they are inconstant. He has, again, none of Wycherley's vehemence, and yet the actions of his plays, especially of the *Double Dealer,* are far from being inherently comic. " 'Tis but the way of the world" might have been said of any of his sophisticated characters in any of his plays, and the way of the world evidently is not a pretty way. With the superficialities of the world, however, the comic writer may safely and amusingly play. "There are," he recognizes, like a true neo-classicist, "Crimes too daring and too horrid for Comedy. But the Vices most frequent, and which are the common Practice of the looser sort of Livers, are the subject Matter of Comedy." So among the affectations and follies of men Congreve works, leaving more serious matters to be corrected by the courts ecclesiastical or civil. "Unmasking," wrote his friend Swift, almost at the same moment when Congreve was defending his plays against Collier, "I think, has never been allowed fair usage, either in the world or the playhouse." But the unmasking of follies is Congreve's forte.

Congreve's highest excellences are not seen in his plots, although he pays more attention to the three unities than his contemporaries did. In the important unity of action this statement is perhaps contradicted by his first play,

---

(1729). — George Meredith, *An Essay on Comedy* (1877; 1897); Edmund Gosse, *A Life of William Congreve* (1888; rev. 1924); D. C. Taylor, *William Congreve* (Oxford, 1931); John C. Hodges, *William Congreve the Man* (1941).

The Old Bachelor (1693), which like Etherege's *Comical Revenge* involves a series of intrigues on different social levels. Neatly blended with the one that gives the play its name is the gulling of Sir Joseph Wittol (a fool who has offended Vainlove) by marrying him to a common woman after Heartwell, the old bachelor and misogynist, has hardly been saved from her charms. Meanwhile Bellmour, in love with Bellinda, takes time off to disguise himself as the fanatic preacher Tribulation Spintext and thus to cuckold the Puritan banker Fondlewife. Vainlove has a relatively easy time in winning the one honorable woman in the cast, Araminta. The play was an enormous success, and the reputation of the young playwright seemed assured. Later in the same year, however, his second play, *The Double Dealer* (1693), failed. This failure is hardly accountable. The plot is far more unified, being merely the struggle of Mellefont against the jealous Lady Touchwood and the Iago-like Maskwell to win his charming Cynthia. There are thrilling episodes, but no divergent intrigues as in the first play. The darkness of the villainy makes the play hardly more than tragicomic, and possibly this fact explains its cool reception. *Love for Love* (April, 1695) was long the most popular of Congreve's plays. The plot here tells how Valentine, at odds with a critical father, is likely to lose his estate to a sea-going younger brother and thus miss getting his beloved heiress, Angelica. The intrigue is deftly suspensive, turning largely on the ultimate triumph of the intelligent younger couple over a star-crazed uncle and an unnatural father, with, in the last act, a masked marriage that tricks the fop Tattle into wedding the blemished Mrs. Frail instead of the expected Angelica. This plot is, in comic effect, Congreve's best. In *The Way of the World* (1700), his best comedy, he had an excellent plot but treated it negligently: he had too much love of topical conversation to waste time in telling the story of how Mirabell evadés the malicious plotting of Lady Wishfort, Mrs. Marwood, and her lover Fainall, and persuades the aloof but charming Millamant to marry him. Obviously all these plots are conventional: we have a comedy, not of love, but of the love-chase. Financial reverses, irate fathers, jealous cast mistresses (particularly coquettish aunts of the pursued lady), are the chief obstacles to success, and legal documents, signed or unsigned, disguisings, and masked marriages that involve mistaken identities, are frequent episodes. It is the same old deck of cards, but Congreve does clever tricks with them.

His characters likewise tend to be conventional. Frequently he gives us *His* relatively flat, two-dimensional persons; but at other times his imagination *Characters* works more vividly than we realize. In Act II of *The Way of the World* Mirabell, talking to Mrs. Fainall about her husband, remarks, "When you are weary of him you know your remedy." The significance of the remark is apparent only at the final discovery in Act v that before marrying Fainall the lady had with remarkable prescience deeded her whole estate in trust to Mirabell. She would never have done that to Dorimant: the Congreve gentleman can be trusted. His top ladies—the virtuous heroine of each play—are not finely imagined. Millamant alone has color and charm, and Millamant above the other three heroines is the clear victim of affectation: the thought of a husband is too, too tedious! In her case it is perhaps Congreve's wit rather than her charm that is truly vivid. Her entry (Act II) in full sail with "a shoal of fools for tenders" is unsurpassable, as is her capitulation to Mirabell at the end. Early in the play Mirabell and Fainall talk of her, and when Fainall opines that she has wit, Mirabell replies: "She has beauty enough to make any man think so, and complaisance enough not to contradict him who shall tell her so." Yet he goes on to say that even her affectations make her more agreeable. The passage is in Congreve's finest vein.

In general, however, it is the incidental or inferior persons that Congreve best delineates. His second gentlemen are negligible plot-ridden sketches; his villains and scorned ladies (except perhaps Lady Wishfort) are melodramatic creatures who belong in heroic plays; but his valets, his gulls, and his fops—who are literary and not, like Sir Fopling Flutter, addicted to overdressing merely—are likely to be superbly conceived. His one worthy country squire, Sir Wilfull Witwoud, is much underrated as a character. Sir Wilfull's eagerness to get his boots off in the drawing-room or to get at his sack, and his lack of eagerness to get at his wooing are all broadly yet finely turned. When critics talk of Congreve's artifice and elegance, they should recall this roistering drunken squire, who nevertheless so pleases Congreve that he is made before the end of the play a friend and ally to Millamant—far more acceptable than his affected, foppish brother. The dramatist's portraits of the gentleman's gentleman are original and unexpected. The admirable Waitwell can disguise himself as Sir Rowland and come a-wooing Lady Wishfort most genteelly. Of his lawfully wedded wife—another of Mirabell's thoughtful precautions to protect Lady Wishfort—Waitwell can say with Jeeves-like dignity: "With submission, we have indeed been solacing in lawful delights; but still with an eye to business, sir. I have instructed her as well as I could." But if Waitwell is prophetic of the Victorian butler, Jeremy of *Love for Love* surpasses prophecy. Watch him in Act v as he underlines the contrast between himself and his "betters":

Jeremy. Sir, I have the seeds of rhetoric and oratory in my head; I have been at Cambridge.
Tattle. Ay! 'tis well enough for a servant to be bred at a university: but the education is a little too pedantic for a gentleman. I hope you are secret in your nature, private, close, ha?
Jer. O sir, for that, sir, 'tis my chief talent: I'm as secret as the head of Nilus.
Tat. Ay! who is he, though? a privy counsellor?
Jer. [Aside] O ignorance! — [Aloud.] A cunning Egyptian, sir, that with his arms would overrun the country: yet nobody could ever find out his headquarters.
Tat. Close dog! a good whoremaster, I warrant him. . . .

His Wit   Such a passage illuminates Congreve's unrealistic but amusing characterizations, also his gifts in wit, and above all his eagerness to take time out, even in a final act, for superfluous verbal by-play. It is from these incidental passages, which overlay his plots always, that Congreve's rather sorry and not very comic stories gain life and sparkle. These superadded social vignettes are the quintessence of Congreve's genius. He dabbles incessantly in witticism, sometimes antithetical in structure, sometimes pungent in repartee, usually deftly humorous in its implications. If in the scale of being there had to be a maidservant called Mincing, she would inevitably announce dinner as Congreve makes her: "Mem, I am come to acquaint your la'ship that dinner is impatient." And her la'ship, who has "a mortal terror at the apprehension of offending against decorums," bravely trusts that "Sir Rowland" will not think her "prone to any iteration of nuptials." Verbal wit was perhaps Congreve's highest value, and apparently it was that of all his gentleman fools (not of his servants), who aspire to wit but for whom it is, as Swift said, "the lost language." For Congreve words danced with stately precision or with gay levity; no English dramatic writer has surpassed him in cool intellectual mastery of diction. He was perhaps too subtle for his own good.

For comedy, as we shall see in the work of Vanbrugh and Farquhar, was tending in another direction, somewhat cheaper, which stressed story element and social "problems" that became a serious interest rather than a cause for brilliant witticism.

Vanbrugh [11] was concerned in somewhat less than a dozen plays, practically all of which were translated or adapted from contemporary French comedies. His career was that of a man who had the interests of good theatre at heart but who lacked either inventiveness or leisure—and it was certainly the latter of these—for the composition of original dramas. *The Pilgrim* (1700) was a reworking of Fletcher; *Aesop* (1696-7) was adapted from Boursault; *The False Friend* (1702) came from Le Sage, who had it from the Spanish; *The Country House* (1703) and *The Confederacy* (1705) were racy translations from Dancourt; while *Squire Trelooby* (1704, in collaboration with Congreve and Walsh), *The Mistake* (1705), and *The Cuckold in Conceit* (1707) were from Molière. Of these the earlier ones had in general the greatest popularity. Of his two original plays both he and the public justly thought more highly of *The Relapse* (1696) than of *The Provok'd Wife* (1697). After Vanbrugh's death Colley Cibber in 1728 completed the fragmentary *Journey to London*, which as *The Provok'd Husband* was acted with great success in spite of the fact that Cibber's verbal ineptitudes both in his preface and in the dialogue caused considerable mirth among critics.

Vanbrugh's first play, *The Relapse*, also had an accidental connection with

Sir John Vanbrugh

[11] Sir John Vanbrugh (1664-1726) was born in London, the grandson of a Flemish merchant, a refugee from the persecutions of the Duke of Alva. Little is known of his early life except that he was for two years in France (1683-85), where he became interested in architecture. He was for some years in the army, and divided his later career between writing and architecture. He was made Comptroller of the Royal Works in 1702, and thereafter he built Castle Howard for the Earl of Carlisle and Blenheim Palace for the Duke of Marlborough. He also designed the Haymarket Theatre, of which he was manager for two years. He was knighted in 1714. — *Plays* (2v, 1719); *Complete Works*, ed. Bonamy Dobrée and Geoffrey Webb (4v, 1927-28). — G. H. Lovegrove, *The Life, Work, and Influence of Sir John Vanbrugh* (1902); John C. Hodges, "The Authorship of *Squire Trelooby*," *RES*, IV (1928). 404-413; Paul Mueschke and Jeannette Fleisher, "A Re-Evaluation of Vanbrugh," *PMLA*, XLIX (1934). 848-889; Laurence Whistler, *Sir John Vanbrugh* (1938).

e
lapse

Cibber, whose first play, *Love's Last Shift,* had been very successful at the beginning of 1696. *The Relapse* was a somewhat cynical sequel to Cibber's comedy. Cibber had shown a debauched and faithless husband, Loveless, reclaimed by the beauty of virtue as seen in Amanda, his wife, whom he failed to recognize after eight years of separation, but whose faithfulness in love most improbably restored him to constancy. This sentimental device of reforming dissolute characters with sudden facility in the last act was popular: it gave the lie to those who thought the stage negligent of morality. But it did not convince Vanbrugh, who taking much the same cast, constructed his *Relapse* to show Loveless's later instability after reform, and to subject the virtuous Amanda to extreme temptation by Worthy. Amanda's virtue survives the test in a crucial scene designed to excite the inflammable spectators by its nearness to a rape and to content the sentimental by the triumph of virtue. In replying to Collier, Vanbrugh alleged speciously that the play was a dramatic discussion of the text "Lead us not into temptation." The subplot shows Young Fashion tricking his elder brother (Sir Novelty, now Lord Foppington) out of his bride, Miss Hoyden, by the aid of Coupler, with whom Young Fashion has made a bargain unmentionable, and unmentioned by Collier and later critics. A chaplain named Bull gave just offense to respecters of the priesthood. Both *The Relapse* and *The Provok'd Wife* are specious and cynical. Marriage, to be sure, is not so much the dull clog as it is a mordant problem. Loveless and Sir John Brute are completely culpable and disgusting as husbands.

*anbrugh's
cial
oblems*

Vanbrugh has a concern with social problems, which he poses only to jeer at them. He does show the tendency of the day to depend on story rather than on witty dialogue, and his characters, while never completely realized, have more human interest than do the persons of the greater plays that preceded his. In dialogue he lacked the chiseled precision and acuteness of Congreve. There was not, as Cibber remarked, "the least Smell of the Lamp in it"; and Cibber adds the opinion of "all the Actors of [his] Time, that the Style of no Author whatsoever gave their Memory less trouble than that of Sir John Vanbrugh." One suspects that whereas the actors had to memorize Congreve's lines exactly, a slip in a speech from Sir John's pen mattered less. As the architect, part-owner, and briefly as manager of the new theatre in the Haymarket, he represented still the aristocratic tradition in the drama, and quite apart from his plays was an influential figure in theatrical affairs.

Farquhar,[12] the last notable figure in the Restoration tradition, really

---

[12] George Farquhar (1677?-1707) was born in north Ireland, the son of a clergyman, and completed his education with a year at Trinity College, Dublin (1694-5). After working for a short time as a corrector for the press of a bookseller, he became an actor, but upon his arrival in London (c. 1697) he devoted himself to writing comedies. In 1703 he married a young lady who had given herself out to be a fortune but who was not. Farquhar, in spite of the trick and of his own penniless state, harbored no resentment. He died in poverty just after the success of his last play. — *Comedies* (1710); *Works* (2v, 1711); *Dramatic Works,* ed. A. C. Ewald (2v, 1892); *Complete Works,* ed. C. A. Stonehill (2v, 1930). *The Adventures of Covent Garden* (1699); *Sir Harry Wildair* (1701); *Familiar and Courtly Letters* (2v, 1700-1); *The Inconstant* (1702); *Love and Business in a Collection of Occasional Verse and Epistolary Prose. A Discourse likewise upon Comedy* (1702); *The Stage-Coach* (1704); *Barcellona: a Poem* (1710). — William Archer, *George Farquhar,* ed. for the Mermaid Series with an ex-

belongs to the eighteenth century. In the years 1698-1707 he produced seven *George* comedies and a farce afterpiece; and this brief career of a highly gifted young *Farquhar* dramatist (he died aged 29) indicates definitely a transitional trend. Farquhar observes in the preface to his least popular play, *The Twin Rivals*, that "A play without a beau, cully, cuckold, or coquette, is as poor an entertainment to some palates, as their Sunday's dinner would be without beef and pudding." Normally, though somewhat influenced by Collier's protest, he tried to give his audience its favored fare, but with a difference. He does not picture his drawing-room characters merely as such; his gentlemen are more human, have more red corpuscles, and are less mere illustrations of the manners of the day than were the gentlefolk of his wittier predecessors. The fact that many of his characters are less modish than those of his predecessors is perhaps referable to the example of Shadwell: certainly the bawds, midwives, constables, citizens, and soldiers that made brief appearances in other plays are here given considerable scenes and organic rôles. The element of story is stressed; only in *The Recruiting Officer* do we get scenes that approach the satirical episodes or conversations so common in Wycherley and Congreve; and in Farquhar's hands such scenes either verge on farce or aid the plot. Like Shadwell he occasionally leaves the City, and gives us a breath of country air—that of Shrewsbury in *The Recruiting Officer* and Lichfield in *The Beaux' Stratagem.*

Even in his short career something of development in skill appears. His first play, *Love and a Bottle* (1698), and his fifth, *The Twin Rivals* (1702), were from the start regarded as inferior, very likely because of their lack of *New* modish elegance. In *The Twin Rivals*, where a younger, deformed brother *Norms of* intrigues to steal his virtuous (elder) twin's title and estate, we see senti- *Conduct* mental elements elbowing and joining hands with the cynically comic tradition. For elegance Farquhar substitutes naturalness as the desideratum in manners. One of his ladies, Aurelia, here says, "I take good manners to be nothing but a natural desire to be easy and agreeable to whatever conversation we fall into"; and this principle she thinks as fitting for a porter as for a duke. Her friend Constance, similarly, believing her lover dead, remarks, "I have no rule nor method for my grief.... I am content with the slight ·mourning of a broken heart." Even more clearly sentimental is the surprising dénouement of the second plot of the play. Richmore, a wealthy fine gentleman, is in the nick of time (Farquhar uses the situation more than once) prevented from raping Aurelia by the intervention of Trueman, who proceeds to reproach Richmore with the wrongs done to another lady, Clelia. A quarter of an hour after his failure with Aurelia, much impressed by Trueman's eloquence, Richmore suddenly announces, "Your youthful virtue warms my breast, and melts it into tenderness"—and forthwith agrees to marry the wronged Clelia! This reform through melting tenderness might be pure Cibber!

---

cellent introduction (1906); J. R. Sutherland, "New Light on George Farquhar," *LTLS*, March 6, 1937, p. 171.

But while sentimental tendencies in comedy led Farquhar to an increased and sincere sympathy with his characters as well as to increased insistence on the story element as compared with social satire, his true and skilful gifts for comedy and his lack of any excessive love for moral instruction kept him most of the time within the Restoration tradition. This allegiance can be seen in his three most popular comedies. His second play, *The Constant Couple* (1699), was very successful, probably because of its varied and bustling action rather than because the dubious virtue of the long-separated couple is ultimately rewarded. Gentlemen in Farquhar's plays fall to fisticuffs much more readily than in Etherege or Congreve; Sir Harry Wildair, perhaps Farquhar's most attractive gentleman, and Colonel Standard both have occasion in this play to beat scorned lovers, and such physical activities are common in Farquhar's plays. Lady Lurewell undergoes a reform towards the end, which, however, is well motivated. The success of the rôle of Sir Harry led to a sequel called *Sir Harry Wildair* (1701), which at the time was successful but is clearly inferior to *The Recruiting Officer* (1706) and *The Beaux' Stratagem* (1707).

he Army
ppears

In *The Recruiting Officer* Farquhar is on sure ground. The disbanded officer (Colonel Standard) had been a familiar figure since Otway's days, and now in Serjeant Kite, recruiting at Shrewsbury, masquerading à la Rochester as a fortune-teller, and serving as pimp for his master Captain Plume, Farquhar gave the stage its most richly comic soldier. A comparison of the rôle of Sylvia with that of Wycherley's Fidelia (both following their lovers disguised as men) will indicate how little there is to choose morally between the two writers. This play hardly classes as high comedy, but in richness of effect and diversity of action, all well fused, it is certainly superior to anything by Shadwell, of whom it remotely reminds one.

lis Last
uccess

The Beaux' Stratagem, which with *The Constant Couple* and *The Recruiting Officer* kept the English stage as well as almost any English comedies have done, tells its story with ease and high spirits. The fortune-hunters, Archer and Aimwell, win our sympathies and keep them; their success, though somewhat accidental, is most pleasing. Lady Bountiful with relatively few lines lives perfectly as a type, and so do other minor persons. The drunken Squire Sullen is shown with brutal vividness, essential, perhaps, to justify the concluding divorce. This formal separation might not have been necessary in Etherege's circle. Times have changed, however, and even in Farquhar's plays one sees a substitution of human interest and somewhat vulgar "character" for the witty, depraved aristocrats of the earlier Restoration. Pope's often quoted line, "What pert, low dialogue has Farquhar writ," contains an element of truth if we remember that he spoke as the close friend of Wycherley and Congreve. Farquhar's scenes are socially (not morally) lower than those of his predecessors—Shadwell excepted; and the lack of attention to rigid social decorum might seem in 1737 to make for something like pertness. But, even if partly just, Pope's line neglects the vivid liveliness, the eager, easy flow of situation, and the true *vis comica* that sets Farquhar apart from and above his actual contemporaries, Cibber and Steele. If there had been more Farquhars or if this one had lived to write more plays, the acceleration towards decline in English comedy might have been arrested. A great decline in comic wit had already taken place when the audiences failed to appreciate *The Way of the World*.

VII

Patterns in Historical Writing

Preoccupation with the Present Moment

Not all the comedy of the Restoration was played on the stage. Life itself was dazzling and theatrical; it might be a merry farce, but it inclined to a serious realization that destiny—whether honor, love, fortune, Heaven, or Hell—depended on manipulation of the present moment. This preoccupation with immediacy results in the common use of Restoration daily life as material for literature and in frequent attempts to elevate this daily life to an ancient Augustan level or at least to draw moral education from it. History, as Bacon and most analysts of the seventeenth century agreed, included three patterns: chronicles, lives, and narrations. The century was so much in love with diary-writing that Bacon might almost have added it as a pattern: doubtless it is included under lives. Diarists of necessity deal with contemporary material; but at this time biographers and even narrative historians in general limit themselves to the familiar matter of their own day. They are obsessed by the present moment either as a delight or as a warning—sometimes as both.

Pepys's Diary

The instinct to live for the moment lyrically and at the same time prudently is seen nowhere better than in the *Diary* of Samuel Pepys [1] (1633-1703). Since the *Diary* is written in Thomas Shelton's system of shorthand, what we have is a transcript improved by successive editors. We are at least one remove from Pepys himself, but the *Diary* is so intimate that we feel closer to Pepys than we do to almost any man who has ever written. The *Diary* covers the years 1660-69, and gives a beautifully detailed account of stirring public events—the return of King Charles, his coronation, the plague of 1665, the London fire of 1666, and the Dutch wars. For its period it pictures also, and most vividly, private life in London and in an average well-to-do house-

---

[1] Pepys's *Diary* has been edited as *Memoirs of Samuel Pepys*, ed. Lord Braybrooke (2v, 1825; 5v, 1828; 5v, 1848-9); as *Diary and Correspondence*, ed. Lord Braybrooke and Mynors Bright (6v, 1875-9); as *Diary*, ed. Henry B. Wheatley (10v, 1893-9). His other published writings include *Memoires Relating to the State of the Royal Navy* (1690), ed. J. R. Tanner (1906); *Private Correspondence and Miscellaneous Papers*, ed. Joseph R. Tanner (2v, 1926); *Further Correspondence*, ed. Joseph R. Tanner (1929); *Letters and Second Diary*, ed. R. G. Howarth (1932); *Shorthand Letters*, ed. Edwin Chappell (Cambridge, 1933); *The Tangier Papers of Samuel Pepys*. ed. Edwin Chappell (1935). A new and unabridged transcript of the *Diary*, to be edited by William Matthews and Robert Latham is eagerly awaited.—Among biographical aids the following are the best: Henry B. Wheatley, *Samuel Pepys and the World He Lived In* (2d ed., 1880); *Occasional Papers Read by Members at Meetings of the Samuel Pepys Club* (2v, 1917-25); Joseph R. Tanner, *Samuel Pepys and the Royal Navy* (Cambridge, 1920); Joseph R. Tanner, *Mr. Pepys: An Introduction to the Diary* (1925); Arthur, Lord Ponsonby, *Samuel Pepys* (1928); John Drinkwater, *Pepys: His Life and Character* (1930); Clara Marburg, *Mr. Pepys and Mr. Evelyn* (Philadelphia, 1935); Arthur Bryant, *Samuel Pepys* (3v, Cambridge, 1933-38).

hold. In richness and humaneness of detail it is hardly rivaled elsewhere in literature.

Pepys was born and passed most of his life in London. His father was a *His* tailor, and the family was sound but modest stock from Huntingdonshire. *Career* Samuel was educated at St. Paul's School, and at Trinity Hall and Magdalene College, Cambridge. At the age of twenty-two he had made a mad love-match with a penniless French beauty, Elizabeth St. Michel; hence he needed, as he got, considerable help from his fortunate cousin, Edward Montagu, who had been a trusted servant of Cromwell in the Admiralty, and who now as Admiral, with cousin Pepys in attendance, brought King Charles over from Holland in May, 1660. Montagu was shortly thereafter created Earl of Sandwich, and he was long to remain Pepys's "Lord" and patron. He got Pepys made Clerk of the Acts in the Navy Office and got him other places as well. Pepys throughout his active life was practically always in the service of the navy, although his career was interrupted dangerously during the uproar over the Popish Plot, when his life was in jeopardy, and he was briefly in 1679 imprisoned in the Tower. In 1683 he accompanied Lord Dartmouth to Tangier, aided in its demolition, and wrote a valuable and interesting journal of the voyage. In 1684 he was President of the Royal Society, and from 1684 to 1689 he was again Secretary of the Admiralty. After the Revolution of 1688 he lived in retirement in "paradisial Clapham," as Evelyn called it. If his devotion to James II now kept him from public employment, his active civic interest still showed itself with regard to Christ's Hospital [2] and possibly other institutions.

The first entry in his *Diary* was dated January 1, 1660—when Pepys was twenty-seven years old. He wrote, one may guess, purely for the pleasure of rehearsing briefly and secretly the joys of the day: there is no evidence that he later reread what he had written or that he ever revised it. Certainly, at the time of writing, the idea of publication would have horrified him. When he died, he left his papers, his books, and his extensive collections of prints, ballads, and broadsides, to go to his college, Magdalene, Cambridge; and there his six volumes of shorthand remained substantially unregarded until John Evelyn's *Diary*, published in 1818, called attention to Evelyn's friend, Pepys. Presently an undergraduate named John Smith was employed to decipher Pepys's shorthand, and in 1825 a much abbreviated edition of the *Diary* was first published.[3]

A year after he began his *Diary* Pepys could set down in his annual sum- *Pepys's Joy* mary of the state of his affairs: "Myself in constant good health, and in a *in His* most handsome and thriving condition. Blessed be Almighty God for it." *Possessions* His cousin had placed him well. The house provided for the Clerk of the Acts was already his pride and joy: life seemed aglow with dignity, prosperity, and delight. He came to feel an exquisite pleasure in his possessions—his

[2] Rudolph Kirk, *Mr. Pepys upon the State of Christ-Hospital* (Philadelphia, 1935).
[3] For a history of the text see Arthur Bryant's *Samuel Pepys, the Man in the Making*, pp. 392-393. This book is the first volume of what is by all odds the most readable and detailed account of Pepys.

books, his bookcases, the hangings in his best room, the dinners he gave, with "all things mighty noble; and to my great content." He loved his beautiful wife passionately, and after her death he had her bust placed in St. Olave's Church, where it was in full view from Pepys's pew. Meanwhile he was madly jealous of Pembleton, her dancing-master, and was at the same sad moment frankly conscious of his own failings in his amours with numerous other ladies.

is Slavery the ·nses Another man in another age might have made a grimy record out of this diary. Pepys was eager for financial gain, and if his pleasure in his increase of goods had not been so naïve and unalloyed, it might have seemed tedious or even grasping. Then too, he was eager to gratify promiscuously his love of fondling pretty women ("God forgive me," he writes, "I had a mind to something more."); and his frank revelations of these flirtations or infidelities, which might have been repellent, are uniformly amusing and at times even comic. Witness, for example, his attempts in St. Dunstan's Church, August 18, 1667:

turned into St. Dunstan's Church, where I heard an able sermon of the minister of the place; and stood by a pretty, modest maid, whom I did labour to take by the hand and the body; but she would not, but got further and further from me; and, at last, I could perceive her to take pins out of her pocket to prick me if I should touch her again — which seeing I did forbear, and was glad I did spy her design. And then I fell to gaze upon another pretty maid in a pew close to me, and she on me; and I did go about to take her by the hand, which she suffered a little and then withdrew. So the sermon ended, and the church broke up, and my amours ended also. . . .

"A strange slavery that I stand in to beauty," he had earlier confessed, "that I value nothing near it." Even in his grosser moments there is a shamefastness or even delicacy that marks him as a connoisseur in sensation, one almost unaware of the tawdry side of experience. Another man, for example, after riding all day in the mud would have been annoyed at night to have his sleep broken; but Pepys in full sense of comfort was pleased to be made conscious of that comfort. He records:

I never did pass a night with more epicurism of sleep; there being now and then a noise of people stirring that waked me, and then it was a very rainy night, and then I was a little weary, that what between waking and then sleeping again, one after another, I never had so much content in all my life. . . .

He savored the bouquet of all experience, from sleep to the ecstasy that he felt for the woodwind music in Massinger's *Virgin Martyr*. Among the arts music was his favorite,[4] and in his household a servant with musical gifts was at once a companion and a pupil. Pepys himself composed at least four songs, and he performed on the viols, the flageolet, and the harpsichord at least. At home music was a frequent pleasure. In the Christmas season (January 3, 1666) he records:

[1] See Sir J. F. Bridge, *Samuel Pepys, Lover of Musique* (1903).

So home, and find all my good company I had bespoke.... and good musique we had, and, among other things, Mrs. Coleman sang my words I set of "Beauty retire," and I think it is a good song, and they praise it mightily. Then to dancing and supper, and mighty merry till Mr. Rolt come in, whose pain of the tooth-ake made him no company, and spoilt ours; so he away, and then my wife's teeth fell of akeing, and she to bed. So forced to break up all with a good song, and so to bed.

Abroad he frequented James Harrington's Rota Club or intellectual society wherever found. The theatre he enjoyed and disparaged by turns; occasionally he swore to stay away entirely, but in a few weeks or months there he would be again.

Pepys's "epicurism" in all the life of sensation easily blinds a reader of the *His Public* *Diary* to the fact that he was a hard-working Clerk and an able servant to *Service* the Royal Navy—one of the very ablest in its history. He put in long hours in the office, scrutinized expenditures watchfully, studied the history of the navy, meddled in rope making and in naval architecture, and became truly an expert administrator. When thirty-two he was made Treasurer of Tangier, a crown possession in the affairs of which he was to have for years an important part. In the same year he was elected to the Royal Society. During the plague of 1665 Pepys remained at his post trying to keep the fleet supplied and active against the Dutch. The King himself, after the terror was over, thanked Pepys: "I do give you thanks for your good service all this year, and I assure you I am very sensible of it." For long years Pepys was to render better and better service. He was to be twice Secretary of the Admiralty Commission, was to be historian of its activities for the decade 1679-88 in his *Memoires Relating to the State of the Royal Navy* (1690), and according to his recent brilliant biographer, Bryant, he was largely responsible for England's naval tradition in modern times.

The appeal of his *Diary*, then, lies not in the fact that Pepys had a petty, *The Nature* gossip-loving mind: he was not that kind of man. It lies in the fact that *of the Diary* Pepys, Puritan bred though he was, coupled with a tremendous business efficiency a ready capacity for delight in all aspects of life—feminine beauty, food, music, architecture, the playhouse, and a cultivated home life. Along with stirring pictures of public events he gives a vivid self-betrayal of his own weakness and strength; above all he shows as no one else ever has shown in complete detail how everyday life may be lived both prudently and glowingly.

The publication of Pepys's *Diary*, it has been noted, was due to the earlier publication (1818) of the parallel work of John Evelyn, who had mentioned Pepys many times.[5] Evelyn has none of the tantalizing charm of Pepys, but

[5] John Evelyn (1620-1706) was born at Wotton (Sussex); he studied (1637-40) both at Oxford and in the Middle Temple. During the troubled forties he spent much time on the Continent, but in 1647 he returned to England, and in 1652 took up residence at Sayes Court, Deptford. He laid plans with Robert Boyle for founding the Royal Society, and in 1659, less successfully, planned with Col. Herbert Morley for the Restoration of the monarchy. In 1653 he had begun to lay out his famous garden at Sayes Court—later ruined by his tenant, Peter

on a more sober level he shared many of Pepys's interests. Pepys was a servant of the court; Evelyn—a product of the squirearchy that Macaulay so abused—was rather a member of the court, one with a zeal for improving and beautifying the life of his day. A sane and reputable virtuoso and projector, he was diversely engrossed in gardening, in city-planning (for London after the fire), in numismatics, in forestry, and in experimental science.

His works, in general, are directed to specific practical purposes. Among them *Fumifugium* (1661) was directed against the smoke nuisance of London (in 1661!), *Sculptura* (1662) described the new method of mezzotint engraving, soon to be perfected and known as "the English method," and *Sylva* (1664) urged the necessity of reforestation in England, and was his most regarded work in his day. He wrote a few poems, translated the First Book of Lucretius (1656), and entered the field of social morals in *Liberty and Servitude* (1649); in *A Character of England* (1659), which attempted to engraft French politeness on the less refined English stock; and in *Publick Employment and an Active Life preferred to Solitude* (1667), where he broaches again the subject treated by Cowley, Sir George Mackenzie, and many others. His most praised work in recent times is *The Life of Mrs. Godolphin*,[6] a private memorial (first published in 1847) of a saintly Maid of Honor, Margaret Blagge, who married Sidney Godolphin and died in 1678 at the age of twenty-five. She was the Pamela of her age and was renowned as such. When Crowne's *Calisto, or the Chaste Nimph* was to be presented at court in 1674, Mrs. Blagge (as she was called even after her marriage) was commanded both by the King and by the Duke of York to return to court and appear as the chaste heroine—which she did "to admiration . . . covered with jewels." The Platonic passion felt by Evelyn and this young woman for each other is a phenomenon reverentially recorded by her biographer.

Apart from writing, Evelyn had a dignified and active interest in the repair or improvement of practically everything from Old St. Paul's[7] to the English garden and even to the English language. He was a charter member of the Royal Society and continued as a devoted fellow and councilor throughout his career. On two occasions the presidency of the Society might have

---

the Great of Russia. In 1694 Evelyn removed to the family seat at Wotton, and he died there in 1706. — *Miscellaneous Works,* ed. William Upcott (1825). Evelyn's *Diary* has been printed from the transcript of William Bray by editors who have selected different passages to publish. A complete edition by E. S. de Beer is in prospect. The four differing texts available are (*a*) ed. William Bray (2v, 1818); (*b*) 2v, 1819, and in the Chandos Classics [1879?]; (*c*) 5v, 1827; ed. Henry B. Wheatley (4v, 1879, 1906); (*d*) ed. John Forster (4v, 1850-52); ed. Austin Dobson (3v, 1906; Globe ed., 1908; Everyman's Library, 2v, n. d.). See *CBEL*, II. 830. — E. Gordon Craig, "John Evelyn and the Theatre," in *Books and Theatres* (1925), pp. 1-68; Arthur, Lord Ponsonby, *John Evelyn* (1933); Clara Marburg, *Mr. Pepys and Mr. Evelyn* (Philadelphia, 1935); Geoffrey Keynes, *John Evelyn: A Study in Bibliophily and a Bibliography of his Writings* (Cambridge, 1937).
   [6] Ed. Samuel Wilberforce (1847); ed. Harriet Sampson (Oxford, 1939).
   [7] See Evelyn's "Londinium Redivivum, or London Restored," in *Jour. Royal Inst. Brit. Architects,* XXVII (1919-20). 467-470; ed. E. S. de Beer as *London Revived. Considerations for its Rebuilding in 1666* (Oxford, 1938).

been his if he had wished.[8] His distinction was not that of a public official, although he was a member of various commissions. During the Dutch wars he impoverished himself as a member of the Commission for the Sick and Wounded. The highest civic office that he achieved was to be briefly one of three commissioners to execute the office of Privy Seal. His true rôle was that of a model country gentleman actuated by the widest and most intelligent "public spirit."

His *Diary* covers more time, but is less revealing, than that of Pepys. It lacks the "confessions" aspect of Pepys's work. If Evelyn was guilty of indiscretion (and one may doubt it), he was not so indiscreet as to record the fact. His *Diary* tends to become a history of his own times, and as such is invaluable because of its balance and sobriety. Much of the first third of it deals with his travels or residence on the Continent during the Commonwealth, at which time he was acquainted with Waller, Hobbes, Denham, Hyde (later Earl of Clarendon), and other royalists.[9] Here also in 1647 he found an estimable if very youthful bride. The richest section of the *Diary* is that dealing with his life at Sayes Court and in London between the years 1652 and 1694. At this last date he retired to his birthplace Wotton, where the remainder of his life was passed. The latest entries in the *Diary* are for January, 1706, a month before Evelyn's death. It was the quiet harmony of this rural existence that he really loved. In a letter to another fellow of the Royal Society, John Beale (July 11, 1679), Evelyn had lamented that for ten years he had been in "perpetual motion, and hardly two months in a year at my own habitation." From Wotton at the age of seventy-seven he wrote to another friend concerning life there:

Evelyn's Diary

We have here a very convenient apartment of five rooms together, besides a pretty closet, which we have furnished with the spoils of Sayes Court, and is the raree-show of the whole neighborhood, and in truth we live easy as to all domestic cares. Wednesday and Saturday nights we call Lecture Nights, when my Wife and myself take our turns to read the packets of all the news sent constantly from London, which serves us for discourse till fresh news comes; and so you have the history of an old man and his no young companion, whose society I have enjoyed more to my satisfaction these three years here, than in almost fifty before, but am now every day trussing up to be gone, I hope to a better place.[10]

Preoccupation with London newspapers—appearing with new liberty since 1695—with his comfortable household, and with the Heavenly City—for his

---

[8] Margaret Denny, "The Early Program of the Royal Society and John Evelyn," *MLQ*, I (1940). 481-497. On Evelyn's connection with the project of an Academy in England see J. E. Spingarn, *Critical Essays of the Seventeenth Century* (1908), II. 337-338; B. S. Monroe, "An English Academy," *MP*, VIII (1910). 107-122; and Edmund Freeman, "A Proposal for an English Academy in 1660," *MLR*, XIX (1924). 291-300.

[9] Evelyn was ambitious to seem to be *the* man to bring about the Restoration and was later envious of General Monck. See E. S. de Beer, "Evelyn and Colonel Herbert Morley in 1659 and 1660," *Sussex Archaeological Collections*, LXXVIII (1937). 177-183, and Arthur H. Nethercot in *HLQ*, I (1938). 439-446.

[10] Letter to Dr. Bohun, January 18, 1697, in the *Diary* (ed. Austin Dobson, 1906), I, pp. lxi-lxii.

journey to which he was "every day trussing up"—these three interests form a trinity quite typical of the better aspects of the Restoration.

Minor Diaries   There were many other diaries kept in this general period,[11] but either they are of little vividness or importance, or else they are specialized in their interest and lack literary quality. For Parliamentary history *The Journal of Sir Simonds D'Ewes,* which "from the beginning of the Long Parliament to the opening of the Trial of the Earl of Strafford" was published in 1933,[12] has great importance—as has also *The Diary of Thomas Burton* (1828) covering the doings of Parliament from 1656-59. Narcissus Luttrell's *Brief Historical Relation of State Affairs* (1678-1714), published in 1857, is compiled frequently from newsletters such as Evelyn and his wife read at Wotton. Luttrell was not always an eye-witness, but his work has some historical value as coming from a notable scholar and collector of pamphlets, ballads, and broadsides. With him we pass to the field of *materiel*—to the work of men who felt it a duty to assemble and preserve data from which history could be written. Such men were numerous. Sir William Dugdale (1605-86) wrote an autobiography as well as important historical works. His son-in-law, Elias Ashmole (1617-92), founder of the Ashmolean Museum, kept a diary, published as his *Memoirs* (1717), and produced an antiquarian history, *The Institution of . . . the Order of the Garter* (1672). Sir Roger Manley (1626?-1688) produced various works of contemporary history, and Sir Paul Rycaut (1628-1700) capitalized on his knowledge of the recent history of the eastern Mediterranean countries. The ecclesiastical historian, John Strype (1643-1737), was also a great collector of facts; but he, like most of these persons here enumerated, lacked literary and philosophical quality. One aimed, it seems, to collect data that might make history full and accurate or might at least enable one to support a controversial position in historical writing.

There were, however, two men in this period who achieved some quality of distinction other than the merely factual in their historical writing—the first Earl of Clarendon and Gilbert Burnet, Bishop of Salisbury.

The Earl of Clarendon   Edward Hyde (1609-1674), created first Earl of Clarendon in 1661, was one of the most distinguished statesmen of the mid-seventeenth century. He derived his education from Oxford, from the Middle Temple, and from companionship with such scholars and literati as Ben Jonson, John Selden, John Hales, Edmund Waller, and Lord Falkland. He was early engaged in politics, and the keynote to his whole career was respect for constitutional monarchy and for the Church, positions which led to a firm adherence to the royalist cause. He was Chancellor of the Exchequer in 1643, and in 1645 became one of the guardians of the Prince of Wales (Charles II). While hiding with the Prince in the Scilly Islands in 1646, he first conceived the idea of his *History.* At the Restoration his influence as Lord Chancellor was enormous; but he had many enemies in Parliament and at court (where,

---

[11] Arthur, Lord Ponsonby in his *English Diaries* (1923) lists and reviews some thirty diaries of the seventeenth century. His *More English Diaries* (1927) adds a half-dozen others. His lists are not complete.

[12] Ed. Wallace Notestein (New Haven, 1933).

Evelyn records, he was "an eye-sore" to the mistresses and revelers), and in 1667 he was dismissed from office and exiled to France. In France he finished his *History*, did some other writing, and there he died in 1674.[13]

Clarendon's *History of the Rebellion* is certainly the noblest example of formal historical writing in the period. Covering the years of strife between Charles I and the Parliament and ending with the Restoration—years during which Clarendon as a royal councilor played a most important part, the sixteen books of the *History* deal with highly controversial matter. Originally it was conceived as a defense of the constitutional royalists who advised Charles I and as a source of counsel for royal action. It was not designed for contemporary publication. Additional material for it, as the project grew, was drawn from the *Life* of himself that Clarendon composed (1668-70) during his exile. The last books of the *History* also were written in France in 1671-2.[14] In reliability the work varies greatly according as the original sources were or were not at hand. The materials from the *Life* are least trustworthy, and Book IX is the most respected section of the work. The object—self-defense, defense of constitutional monarchy, of the crown, and of royal advisers—did not always make for unbiased presentation; and the facts that composition was spread over a period of about thirty years and that Clarendon was constantly distracted from this task by his public employments make the distinguished result somewhat surprising.

The distinction of the *History* depends largely on its neo-classical ideals. It is a formal, elaborate piece of architecture. It led one, so Evelyn wrote to Pepys, "by the courts, avenues, and porches into the fabric." In spite of its imperfections it was and is a noble structure. Much solid merit resides in its expert insight into constitutional problems; much in its clear, forward-moving narrative strength; but its chief delight is its many "characters."[15] To recreate "the eminency and virtue" of leading personages (and such men rather than political issues Clarendon chose to regard as the cause of the Civil Wars) was as much "the true end of history" as the recording of counsels and actions. The author's evident moderation in these characters is perhaps due to his tolerance of human nature in general. In his essay *Of Human Nature* (1668) he concluded that "nature is as much the creation of

Clarendon History [margin note]

---

[13] From 1660-67 Clarendon served ably as Chancellor of Oxford University, and worthy memorials of him still remain, notably the distinguished Clarendon Press. Through the marriage (1660) of his daughter Anne to the Duke of York (later James II), he became the grandfather of Queen Mary II and Queen Anne. He bequeathed his manuscripts to the University, which in 1702-4 published *The History of the Rebellion and Civil Wars in England* in three volumes. The best modern edition is that of W. D. Macray (6v, Oxford, 1888). *The Life of Edward, Earl of Clarendon* appeared in 1759, and was reprinted from the MS in 1857 (2v). See also Thomas H. Lister, *Life and Administration of Edward, First Earl of Clarendon* (3v, 1837-38); *Calendar of the Clarendon State Papers Preserved in the Bodleian Library*, ed. O. Ogle, W. H. Bliss, W. D. Macray, and F. J. Routledge (1872-1932); Sir Charles H. Firth, "Clarendon's *History of the Rebellion*," *EHR*, XIX (1904). 26-54, 246-262, 464-483; Sir Henry Craik, *Life of Edward, Earl of Clarendon* (2v, 1911).

[14] On the composition of the *History* see Sir Charles H. Firth's articles in *EHR*, as cited above.

[15] Many of the best of these are reprinted, with admirable comment, in D. Nichol Smith's *Characters from the Histories and Memoirs of the Seventeenth Century, with an Essay on the Character* (Oxford, 1918).

God as grace is; and it is his bounty that he created nature in that integrity, and hath since restored it to that innocence, or annexed that innocence to it, if it be not maliciously ravished, or let loose, from it." And so his lordship could reprehend Pym's "power of doing shrewd turns" in masterly understatement, and could similarly regret "some unpopular natural infirmities" on the part of Archbishop Laud.[16] In commendation Clarendon was no less even-tempered. His portraiture of his intimate friend, Lord Falkland,[17] is his most glowing work; but he treats the merits of an opponent, John Hampden for instance, with dignity and high respect. His contemporaries are conceived as successors and fellows of the great heroes portrayed by Sallust, Tacitus, or Plutarch. The style lacks the crispness and brevity of the "new prose" of his day, but it is stately, easy, and flowing. Although the sentences are neither so varied, so settled, nor so finely chiseled as those of Gibbon were to be a century later, their effect is true Roman.

Gilbert Burnet

Definitely less of this nobility is seen slightly later in the historical work of Gilbert Burnet,[18] who also writes of his own times and of his own cause— the cause being in his case Protestantism as embodied in latitudinarian Anglicanism. Burnet, a downright, hard-headed Scot, stood in the relation of guide and counselor to William and Mary, as Clarendon had done to Charles II. To the merry monarch himself, however, on January 29, 1680, Burnet had addressed an astonishing letter—which King Charles burned and forgave—urging upon the King the necessity of a change of heart and of manners: "And now, Sir," he remarks, "... suffer me ... to tell you that all the distrust your people have of you, all the necessities you are now in, all the indignation of Heaven that is on you, and appears in the defeating of all your counsels, flow from this, that you have not feared nor served God, but have given yourself up to so many sinful pleasures." There was nothing delicate or fine about Burnet; but his assurance, obnoxious as it was to many, was courageous and at times tolerant. He was a power in battles for the material well-being of the Church during the reigns of William and Mary and of Queen Anne; but he was cordially detested by all High Church Tories. Gross materialism is a charge that these antagonists often brought against him. If he congratulated the anti-Romanist Whig clergy on being "a wall for their church and country," the Tories would sneer, as Jonathan

---

16 As antithetical to the point of view of eighteenth-century sentimentalism it is notable that a chief "infirmity" was that Laud "believed innocence of heart, and integrity of manners, was a guard strong enough to secure any man in his voyage through this world."

17 On Viscount Falkland see Kenneth B. Murdock, *The Sun at Noon* (1939), pp. 1-38.

18 Gilbert Burnet (1643-1715) was born in Edinburgh. A precocious student, he entered Marischall College at the age of ten, and was graduated M.A. in 1657. After the Restoration he mediated between the Crown and the Presbyterians, and in 1673 he became a royal chaplain. His strictures on court life and royal morals made him at times unpopular in court circles, and at the accession of James II he retired to the Continent, where he soon became a close and influential adviser to William of Orange. In 1689 he became Bishop of Salisbury and leader of the Whiggish latitudinarians in the Church. One of the more learned men of his day, he was very active in political and religious writing, strongly anti-Catholic in bias and opportunist in method. — The best *Life* of Burnet is that by T. E. S. Clarke and H. C. Foxcroft (Cambridge, 1907).

Swift did, "A south wall, I suppose, for all the best fruit of the church and country to be nailed on."

From his great mass of miscellaneous writing, chiefly controversial and religious but in part scientific, a few historical works demand attention here, not for their complete trustworthiness but because of an advance at times in method. In 1677 after some years of delay he published his *Memoirs of the* *His* *Lives and Actions of James and William, Dukes of Hamilton*. This work, *Histories* really a continuation [19] of John Spottiswoode's *History of the Church of Scotland* (1655), was based on documents, many of which were printed in the text or at the end of the volume—a procedure not usual at the time in such works but necessary in the case of controversial history. In 1679 appeared Part I of Burnet's *History of the Reformation of the Church in England,*[20] designed both as honest history and as a blast against the papist writers, who were just then agog over a recent French translation of Nicholas Sanders's (d. 1581) *English Schism*. Although an atmosphere of Popish Plots hardly made for unbiased production of such a work, Burnet had done much research on the subject, even advertising in modern fashion in the *London Gazette* (January 1, 1680) for documentary aids, and he was doubtless unaware of any blameworthy prejudice. By the Whig faction and by Low Churchmen the work was highly approved. It marked in some ways a change in the methods of historical writing. Burnet was aware that modern history could not be written in the manner of the ancients with one's eye chiefly on personal and moral lessons of heroic behavior. For him history lost its large or educational function and adopted a precise and limited controversial objective. Evidence both as to conduct and as to analysis of issues became thus indispensable, and factual research was imperative. Here Burnet shows awareness of the antiquarian tendencies arising in the scholarship of his day.

Just as in his *Reformation* Burnet patterned after Paolo Sarpi and Sleidan rather than after the ancients, so in his most important work, the *History of His Own Time* (begun in 1683),[21] his master was the great Frenchman Thuanus (De Thou). Though the work is self-effacing, it partakes at times of the quality of a diary or a collection of *ana* or of anecdotes. As a high-class gossip, Burnet recorded the sources of his tales frequently, and wrote more commonly with credibility than one might at first expect. His memory was prodigious. He was rash and crude in style and method, and here, as in his "characters," he fell far short of Clarendon. His greatest value arises where Clarendon ceased, and for the last quarter of the century he gave an invaluable, if prejudiced, record. The epilogue to the *History* and his *Some Passages of the Life and Death of the . . . Earl of Rochester* (whose notable deathbed repentance Burnet witnessed and here in 1680 recorded) have been praised as well written. In general his style, rapid, easy, and careless, is undistin-

---

[19] So printed in the fourth ed. of Spotiswood (1677) and similarly reprinted, Oxford, 1852.
[20] Part II appeared in 1681; Part III in 1714. Ed. N. Pocock (7v, Oxford, 1865).
[21] *Bishop Burnet's History of His Own Time* (2v, 1724-34; 4v, 1753); ed. M. J. Routh (7v, Oxford, 1823); ed. O. Airy (Vols. I and II only, Oxford, 1897-1900).

guished. One need not go so far as his inveterate enemy, Jonathan Swift, who was constantly jibing at "that peculiar manner of expressing himself, which the poverty of our language compels me to call [his] style." Swift's best quip was his note on Burnet's remark that *Paradise Lost* "was esteemed the beautifullest and perfectest poem that ever was writ, at least in *our* language." In the margin Swift here wrote: "A mistake, for it is in *English.*" Rapier work, elegance, or polish was not Burnet's forte.

iography nd Auto- iography

In the Restoration period history as a type of writing was obviously close to biography and autobiography. Clarendon's *Life* was in part merged with his *History*. Distinguished personages as varied in character and interest as Margaret Cavendish, Duchess of Newcastle, Sir Simonds D'Ewes, and Richard Baxter, wrote autobiographies, and in general this method of self-record is either designed to adumbrate history or, as in the case of Baxter and many other Puritans, to reveal the dangers and triumphs of the spiritual life. Its techniques are variable and unsettled.[22] The word *biography* was new in English at this time, and its intention varies from the private document meant for no circulation, at least outside the family itself, to the public biographical eulogy of a funeral sermon, or to formal biography as generally practised. The best examples are those that blend public with private history, and this can be tactfully done by an intelligent but adoring wife. Margaret Cavendish, Duchess of Newcastle, wrote her own life and that of her husband the Duke.[23] His Grace's life was published in folio in 1667 while he was still alive, and the autobiography of the Duchess herself had appeared much earlier. Such publication, like much else about this learned and literary lady, was unusual. Lady Fanshawe [24] was more in accord with tradition; for in portraying the unblemished worth of her Sir Richard, who in public life met poverty with distinction and the vicissitudes of travel with high courage, she wrote only for the private instruction of her son. Similarly Mrs. Lucy Hutchinson in her clean-cut *Memoirs of Colonel Hutchinson* [25] was erecting a private family memorial to her "murdered" husband, but with a consciousness that some day the defense of a regicide would not be scorned. She writes his *Memoirs* in the third person, and with an objectivity more apparent than real. She stresses the public career of her husband and hence seems to write history; but she writes with a tactfully managed personal interest in what she does. She has an admirable reserved sense of appropriate detail, and is vivid without being trivial or intimate. The argument over what gave significance to small details was already under way.

22 Ch. IV of Waldo H. Dunn's *English Biography* (1916) deals with the period 1500-1700. A fuller treatment is found in Donald A. Stauffer's *English Biography before 1700* (Cambridge, Mass., 1930).

23 The Duchess of Newcastle's sketch of her own life appeared first in Book XI of her *Nature's Pictures Drawn by Fancie's Pencil to the Life* (1655). Her life of her husband was entitled (in part) *The Life of the Thrice Noble, High and Puissant Prince William Cavendishe, Duke, Marquess, and Earl of Newcastle . . .* (1667); ed. Sir Charles H. Firth (1886); in Everyman's Library (1915).

24 Anne, Lady Fanshawe's *Memoirs* (written in 1676) were first printed in 1829; they were reëdited from the MS in 1907.

25 First printed in 1806; well edited by Sir Charles H. Firth (1906). Mrs. Hutchinson's fragment of autobiography is printed with the *Memoirs*.

Burnet condemned trivialities; Dryden in his *Life of Plutarch* was keen for them. Richard Baxter in the beautiful *Breviate of the Life of Margaret Baxter* (1681) [26] memorializes his wife's passion for spirituality, suppresses practically all details of her virtuous "creature" love for himself, and yet contrives to create an atmosphere of passionate intimacy. Effects and techniques must vary when the life deals with public affairs or when it is concerned with spiritual experience. Except as a stimulus to spirituality it would have been indecorous to publish a life of Margaret Baxter only twenty years after her death. The Puritan fervor of the *Breviate* parallels interestingly the *Life*, hardly more worldly than the *Breviate*, in which the Maid of Honor Margaret Blagge (Mrs. Godolphin) was beatified by Evelyn.

However varied the techniques of biography may be, the purposes sought *Short Lives* are usually obvious. It may have historical, spiritual, or ethical interest, or it may, as in the case of "rogue" biographies, be largely mere entertainment. A significant and rather novel development in the period is the prefatory biography that introduces the reader to an author's work and that tends to get collected into something that by the end of the century takes on the likeness of a specialized biographical dictionary. The best of these brief independent or prefatory lives are doubtless those of Richard Hooker (1665) and of George Herbert (1670), both written by Izaak Walton. On a more mundane level Bishop Thomas Sprat's *Life* of Abraham Cowley (prefixed to Cowley's *Works* in 1668) represents an obvious confusion of biography with literary criticism, but is one of the best of the prefatory lives of the time.

Collections of lives perhaps are the distinctive development in biography *Collections* during this half century. Most such collections have a less natural and more *of Biogra-* specialized field than Thomas Fuller's *History of the Worthies of England phies* (1662), which in wit and incisiveness equals anything that was soon to follow. At the opposite extreme is Thomas Pope Blount's imitation of Continental "polyhistors" in his *Censura Celebriorum Authorum* (1690) in which he compiles biographical data for the history of scholarship throughout Europe. He writes in Latin for a European audience, but the interest is thinly antiquarian. Chiefly in all these collections it is the clergy, especially the nonconformist saints, who are treated. Samuel Clarke (1599-1683) had issued in 1650 his *Marrow of Ecclesiastical History*, a farrago of lives of Puritan clergymen, Christian rulers, and "Christians of Inferiour Rank"; he followed this with *A General Martyrologie* (1651). *A Loyall Martyrology* (1662) was produced by William Winstanley (1628?-1698), who in 1687 brought out a thin and not very valuable volume of *Lives of the Most Famous English Poets*. Other collections of literary biographies were *Theatrum Poetarum* (1675) by Milton's nephew, Edward Phillips,

---

[26] Reprinted in 1826 (as *Memoirs...*) and in 1928 by John T. Wilkinson, *Richard Baxter and Margaret Charlton, a Puritan Love Story. The Reliquiae Baxterianae: or, Mr. Richard Baxter's Narrative of the Most Memorable Passages of his Life and Times* was first published in 1696. A useful abridgment under the title *The Autobiography of Richard Baxter* (ed. J. M. Lloyd Thomas) appeared in 1925 (and in Everyman's Library [1931]).

and Gerard Langbaine's *Account of the English Dramatick Poets* (1691), revised in 1699 by Gildon as *Lives and Characters of the English Dramatick Poets*. All of these were very humble but not quite despicable beginnings in the field of literature. Here the outstanding achievement was that of Anthony Wood (1632-1695) in his two volumes of *Athenae Oxonienses: An Exact History of all the Writers and Bishops who have had their Education in ... Oxford from 1500, to the End of the Year 1690*. These volumes (1691-2) were the results of much antiquarian research, in which Wood was indefatigable.[27] Ill-natured and ill-considered statements made his work obnoxious to Oxford, and certain pages accusing the late Chancellor Clarendon of selling offices caused a lawsuit. When Wood was found guilty, his expulsion from the University resulted. The "evidence" against Clarendon came really from notes supplied by an assistant antiquary, John Aubrey (1626-1697), who was as relaxed and amiable as Wood was intense and quarrelsome. Both men had been inspired to antiquarianism by Dugdale's *Warwickshire* (1656). Wood's early ambition was to do a similar history for Oxfordshire, and Aubrey worked to the same end for Wiltshire. But Aubrey's lack of method kept him from achievement of his goal. His collections made over a period of twenty-five years largely for Wood's *Athenae* were edited as *Brief Lives* in 1898. They display the collecting of anecdotes at its best. The trivial details are delightful gossip and yet apparently maintain a high degree of truthfulness. Here as in Pepys and in other witty writers of the period we have the amused observer of life setting down details that delight both the antiquarian and the gossip. The taste of the age, as of all ages, was described by Dryden in remarks concerning intimate biography in his *Life of Plutarch* (1683):

You may behold a *Scipio* and a *Lelius* gathering Cockle-shells on the shore, *Augustus* playing at bounding stones with *Boyes;* and *Agesilaus* riding on a Hobby-horse among his Children. The Pageantry of Life is taken away; you see the poor reasonable Animal, as naked as ever nature made him; are made acquainted with his passions and his follies, and find the *Demy-God* a *Man.*

Aubrey is highly successful in this unbuttoned style, just as Clarendon and others had charmed by a reverse process, in which the men of their day became if not demigods at least heroes of Augustan stature.

27 Extensive and fascinating autobiographical materials were edited by the Rev. Andrew Clark for the Oxford Historical Society from Wood's papers under the title *The Life and Times of Anthony Wood ... described by Himself, Collected from his Diaries and Other Papers* (5v, 1891-1900).

VIII
Types of Prose Fiction

It is notable that in a period when aristocratic playwrights excelled, writers *Fiction for* of fictitious narrative at the same social level were practically non-existent *Various* or lacking in merit. The only English writer of prose fiction to achieve *Classes* permanent distinction as such in this period was the "mechanick" preacher John Bunyan; and for his work the court circles, so influential in the drama, had naturally no regard. Courtly fiction of the moment was imported, and came largely from France, the home of the elegant refinement that was then so highly regarded. One must not assume that fiction was rigidly specialized for class consumption; but clearly there were types of fiction devised for aristocratic, for pious, or for popular lower-class readers. But an aristocrat might be pious, and probably all classes, and not merely the less learned, read chapbooks on occasion. There is a specialization; but it cannot be rigidly asserted.[1]

The lofty French romances by D'Urfé, Gomberville, Mlle de Scudéry, *French* and La Calprenède had undoubtedly a considerable polite vogue. Enormously *Romances* long (eight or ten volumes is a fair average), tediously complicated, and loosely organized, one of these romances was a fiction library in itself. The stories were an escape from the vulgarities of a court where the King fondled his mistresses in public, and where one of them (Castlemaine), doubtless *toute ereintée,* drove in Hyde Park and "lay impudently upon her back in her coach asleep, with her mouth open." [2] The escape, however, was to a world of aristocratic artificiality, a world where the protocol of elegant love or of heroism totally replaced average human behavior. Because of escapism or some other appeal most of the more popular French romances found English translators and readers. La Calprenède's *Cassandra* was englished in part in 1652 and completely translated by Sir Charles Cotterell in 1667, and abridged by other hands in 1703. His *Cleopatra* was gracefully translated by R. Loveday and others (1652-59), and versions of *Pharamond*

---

[1] For bibliographies of Restoration fiction see *CBEL*, II. 488-495, 529-535, and Arundell Esdaile, *A List of English Tales and Prose Romances Printed before 1740* (The Bibliographical Society, 1912). For the French fiction of the time see Ralph C. Williams, *A Bibliography of the Seventeenth-Century Novel in France* (1931). The largest history is Ernest A. Baker's *History of the English Novel,* Vol. III (1929). John C. Dunlop's *History of Prose Fiction* (3v, Edinburgh, 1814; 2v, 1906) summarizes several seventeenth-century romances. Frank W. Chandler's *Literature of Roguery* (2v, 1907) is excellent in its field, as is Charlotte E. Morgan's *Rise of the Novel of Manners* (1911). On French influence in fiction Thomas P. Haviland's *"Roman de Longue Haleine" on English Soil* (Philadelphia, 1931) is useful. For shorter general histories of the English novel, which naturally devote little space to this period, see below, Part II, ch. x, n. 1.

[2] *The Diary of Samuel Pepys* for March 19, 1665.

were made by John Davies (1662) and by John Phillips (1677). Mlle de Scudéry's *Ibrahim* appeared in English (by Henry Cogan) in 1652 and in 1674; and of others from her pen there appeared *Artamenes, or the Grand Cyrus* (translated by "F. G.", 1653-55 in five folio volumes), *Clelia* (translated by John Davies and George Havers, 1655-61, in five volumes), and *Almahide* ("done into English by J. Phillips, Gent." in 1677). There were other similar but less gigantic French works that had a vogue in England —notably the semi-historical stories of Mme de Lafayette.

That the vogue of these romances was immediate, widespread, and enduring cannot be doubted. The heroic plays of the time frequently made use of materials from these epics in prose. Gallant letter writers bandied about the names of the heroes and heroines familiarly. Dorothy Osborne, later wife of Sir William Temple, in her *Letters* was continually discussing the characters of these romances, and poor Mrs. Pepys by ineptly retelling tedious episodes from *The Grand Cyrus* brought wrath to her husband and then tears to herself. Horace Walpole, born in 1717, as a child lived with these romances, and the same was evidently true of the American-born Charlotte Lennox, author of *The Female Quixote* (1752). The nature of the influence of these stories on eighteenth-century fiction is fairly obvious: they encouraged an artificial idealism in decorum, emotional scenes ornamented with *beaux sentiments,* and ·perhaps the concept of prose fiction as related to the heroic poem, as the "epic in prose." It is also true that some of the eighteenth-century *romans à clef* (or "scandal chronicles") owe their romantic veneer to this tradition.

English romance diverges somewhat from the French pattern. John Reynolds's *Flower of Fidelitie* (1650) and John Crowne's *Pandion and Amphigenia* (1665) are greatly, if ineptly, indebted to Sidney's *Arcadia;* and the anonymous *Eromena* (1683) draws its substance from William Chamberlayne's *Pharonnida* (1659): Roger Boyle's *Parthenissa* (1654-69; 1676) is the most pretentious and tedious example of the French pattern. An earlier independent and intellectual tradition is seen following somewhat after Bacon's *New Atlantis* and John Barclay's *Argenis.* Such works furthered philosophical or educational romance. *Aretina* (Edinburgh, 1660), by Sir George Mackenzie, later known as the "bloody advocate" of covenanting persecution, rejoices in the sub-title of "the serious romance," and shows that its author was rather essayist than story-teller. In 1666 Margaret Cavendish, the learned Duchess of Newcastle, published her imitation of Lucian, *The Blazing World,* as an appendage to her *Observations upon Experimental Philosophy.* The story seems an appalling confusion of episode with no clear philosophy emerging.[3] This love for serious romancing is seen also in the religious effort of the Rev. Nathaniel Ingelo (1621?-1683), *Bentivolio and Urania* (1660-64), which went through four editions by 1682, possibly aided by the fact that the title-page advertises that "all the Obscure Words

English Romances

---

[3] See Henry Ten Eyck Perry, *The First Duchess of Newcastle and Her Husband* (Boston, 1918), pp. 252-258, for a summary of the story.

throughout the Book are interpreted in the Margin." Evidently the religious counsels so lavishly inserted are directed towards the less literate of the sexes! Even in heavily didactic romances English authors were inferior at the *Philo-* time to those on the Continent. As the secularization of thought increased, *sophical* there was great interest in how far human reason aided only by "the light *Romances* of nature" could go. Speculatists in these fields found comfort in the accounts of self-taught philosophers such as the medieval Arabic *Hai Ebn Yokdan* by Abi Jaafar Ebn Tophail and its Spanish imitation, Gracian's *Critick*. The Arabic work, translated into Latin by the Rev. Edward Pococke in 1671, was made English in 1674, again in 1686, and again in 1708. Yokdan, exposed new born in a desert island, grows up in solitude, and through contemplation and observation alone arrives at a sophisticated grasp of divine essence and other similar metaphysical concepts. Gracian's romance was made English by Sir Paul Rycaut (1681). His autodidact, Andrenio, is brought up by animals in an underground den: when adult he is suddenly projected by an earthquake to the surface of his desert island (St. Helena), where he meets "the experienced naufrage" Critilo. Their travels and comments on society seen in the light of nature make up the volume. A less exotic educational romance that had later influence was the Abbé Fénelon's *Adventures of Telemachus,* first translated in 1699-1700 and reprinted thereafter many times. A perfect specimen of neo-classicism, written in the tradition of Xenophon's *Cyropaedia* for the edification of the French dauphin, this work stimulated simplified benevolist thinking, and, with its obvious Homeric echoes, increased an awareness that epics might be written in prose. But neither this nor any of the works just mentioned has much relation to skilful narrative art.

Another aspect of polite fiction that has French affiliations is the use of private letters for stcry-telling.[4] Letters in the tradition of Pliny the Younger relate to the essay rather than to narrative fiction—such letters, for example, as the curious *CCXI Sociable Letters* (1664) by the Duchess of Newcastle. *Epistolary* These, however, as well as the translation of the witty epistles of Balzac *Narratives* and Voiture, indicate that the English were learning from abroad in part that the personal letter might possibly be an elegant literary composition. Three types which thus early began to influence fiction were the news letter, the travel letter, and the love letter. In such miscellanies as Charles Gildon's *Post Boy Rob'd of his Mail* (1692-93) letters that tell gossiping episodes are found, and in Tom Brown's popular *Adventures of Lindamira* (1702) this use of letters is full fledged.[5] The travel letter, popularized by the Italian G. P. Marana, whose *Letters Writ by a Turkish Spy* were made English in 1687,[6] may be at times narratives and at times essays in social criticism. A very popular translation of travel letters was Mme d'Aulnoy's

[4] See Helen Sard Hughes, "English Epistolary Fiction before *Pamela," Manly Anniversary Studies* (Chicago, 1923), pp. 156-169, and also Godfrey F. Singer, *The Epistolary Novel* (Philadelphia, 1933).
[5] Benjamin Boyce, *Tom Brown of Facetious Memory* (Cambridge, Mass., 1939), pp. 103-108.
[6] 7v, 1687; Vol. vIII, 1694. A discussion of the authorship that is illuminating is found in *DNB* under Robert Midgley (1655?-1723).

Ingenious and Diverting Letters of the Lady ——'s Travels into Spain (1691-92), of which a reprint in 1708 called itself the "eighth edition." More romantic, normally, were the love letters. The vogue of these for narrative —known in France for a century—became notable in England after Sir Roger L'Estrange translated *Five Love-Letters from a Nun to a Cavalier* and *Seven Portuguese Letters* (1678-81). In this vein English genius can show Mrs. Aphra Behn's *Love Letters between a Nobleman and his Sister* (1684), which went through many editions, and Mrs. Mary Manley's *Letters* (1696), which like others in this kind tend to make love lurid rather than tender.[7] Here we find at times a sentimental tone and at times the cynical mood of Restoration gentlefolk.

Less depraved but equally bleak is the rogue literature of the time. This appealed to readers who, had no great concern with elegance or decorum as they read. A most popular series of crime stories by a merchant named John Reynolds, first published in 1621 as *The Triumphs of God's Revenge against the Crying and Execrable Sin of Murther in Thirty Severall Tragicall Histories,* went through several editions, and was augmented for Restoration readers by ten histories showing "God's Revenge against the Abominable Sin of Adultery" (1679). The popularity of this pious work lasted into the nineteenth century. Lives of rogues from Elizabethan times down had been written with the pretense of warning one against roguery, with the object of exposing the tricks of rogues, or with the actual object of thrilling readers by the sensationalism of crime. Crimes so notorious as to need no embroidering easily expanded from the pamphlet or chapbook state into something approaching fiction. The career, for example, of Mary Moders or Carleton, "the German Princess" from Canterbury, became the subject of many narratives both before and after she was hanged in 1673.[8] The best of these, by Francis Kirkman, was called *The Counterfeit Lady Unveiled. Being a Full Account of the Birth, Life, Most Remarkable Actions, and Untimely Death of that Famous Cheat Mary Carleton, Known by the Name of the German Princess* (1673). Richard Head and Kirkman collaborated on the most extensive of these fictitious biographies—*The English Rogue Described in the Life of Meriton Latroon.*[9] This is neither very English nor very original; for the authors showed as much familiarity with their printed predecessors as they did with actual rogues. The book is earthy and indecent, but it lacks the satiric edge, the variety, and the lightness of touch that characterize the best picaresque fiction; and its undoubted popularity must have been among "non-literary" readers. A more interesting phenomenon

[7] Notable also are the uses of the letter form in the nondramatic writing of George Farquhar, especially his *Love and Business in a Collection of Occasionary Verse and Epistolary Prose* (1702).

[8] Ernest Bernbaum, *The Mary Carleton Narratives, 1663-1673* (Cambridge, Mass., 1914).

[9] Part I (the best part, 1665) is by Head; Part II (1668) is a continuation by Kirkman, and Parts III and IV (1671) were done in collaboration; Part V, very brief, is of undetermined authorship.—*CBEL.* Very little is known about the lives of these men, who seem to have been employed by booksellers or publishers. Kirkman did various translations, and Head did miscellaneous writing. Details about Kirkman have been deduced from his *Unlucky Citizen* (1673) R. C. Bald, "Francis Kirkman, Bookseller and Author," *MP,* XLI (1943). 17-32.

is Head's *Life and Death of Mother Shipton* (1667), which creates a biography for a presumably mythical prophetess or witch supposed to have lived in Yorkshire in the sixteenth century. Head did other books about rogues, and his *Floating Island* (1673) is an ingenious combination of the imaginary voyage with an exposé of London localities such as presently were to be associated with such writing as Ned Ward's *London Spy*.[10] Fictional counterparts of actual, if "tall," tales of voyages were frequent at the time. Henry Nevile's brief *Isle of Pines* (1668) anticipates the flat objectivity of *Crusoe* and *Gulliver*, and has its own philosophical view of man's natural ability to create both a population and an organized Christian society on a desert island.

The one man of high narrative genius to win permanent fame in this period was John Bunyan.[11] This enthusiastic tinker and "mechanick" preacher made certain proletarian narrative forms into vehicles for spiritual instruction. His first important work of this sort is *Grace Abounding* (1666), an autobiography focused on his conversion and early career as preacher. It is one of a common type of "fanatic" autobiographies,[12] and its chief interest lies in the fact that it concerns the author of more significant works. We learn from it that Bunyan came "of a low and inconsiderable generation," but yet that, as he says, "it pleased God to put it into their [his parents'] hearts to put me to school, to learn me both to read and write." All this small learning, however, he neglected and almost lost: his career, he insists, was "a miracle of precious grace," and no achievement is to be credited to man's instruction or ability. He became early "the very ringleader of all the youth

John Bunyan

---

10 See below, Part I, ch. IX, n. 20.

11 John Bunyan (1628-1688) was born at Elstow, Bedfordshire, the son of a tinker. He attended school briefly either at the Bedford Grammar School or at Elstow. He was early set to learn his father's trade. Shortly after his mother's death in 1644 he was for two and a half years in the Parliamentary army, but probably saw no real action. He married about 1648 or 1649, and continued his work as a tinker. The next years were those of spiritual conflict. After the death of his wife (c. 1656), Bunyan began preaching throughout the region. He married again about 1659, and in the following year was imprisoned as an unlicensed preacher. Almost the whole of the next twelve years was spent in prison, where he continually reread and studied the Bible and Foxe's *Book of Martyrs*, as well as other Puritan literature. During his imprisonment he produced books and tracts with rapidity. He continued these labors in prison or out, and until his death preached widely, especially in or about London in his later years. — *Works of that Eminent Servant of Christ, Mr. John Bunyan* (Vol. 1 [all printed], 1692; 2v, 1736-7; 6v, Edinburgh, 1769); ed. George Offor (3v, 1852); ed. H. Stebbing (4v, 1859); *Some Gospel Truths Opened* (1656); *A Few Sighs from Hell* (1658); *Profitable Meditations* ([1661?]; 1862); *The Holy City* (1665); *Grace Abounding* (1666; 1680; 1879; 1888; 1897; Everyman's Library, 1928); *The Pilgrim's Progress* (Part I, 1678; Part II, 1684); ed. R. Southey (1830); ed. George Offor (1856); ed. Charles Kingsley (1860); ed. E. Venables (1866); ed. John Brown (1887); ed. C. H. Firth (1898); ed. James B. Wharey (Oxford, 1928); *The Life and Death of Mr. Badman* (1680); ed. J. A. Froude (1900); ed. John Brown (Cambridge, 1905); ed. G. B. Harrison (1928); *The Holy War* (1682); ed. John Brown (1887 and [Cambridge], 1905); ed. M. Peacock (Oxford, 1892); *A Discourse upon the Pharisee and the Publicane* (1685; 5th ed. 1703); *A Book for Boys and Girls* (1686); ed. E. S. Buchanan (1928); *The Heavenly Footman* (1698). — G. B. Cheever, *Lectures on the Pilgrim's Progress* (1828); Robert Southey, *Life of Bunyan* (1830); J. A. Froude, *Bunyan* (1880); John Brown, *John Bunyan: his Life, Times, and Work* (1885; revised by Frank M. Harrison, 1928—the standard life); James B. Wharey, *Sources of Bunyan's Allegories* (Baltimore, 1904); John Kelman, *The Road, a Study of Pilgrim's Progress* (2v, n.d. [1912?]); G. B. Harrison, *John Bunyan: A Study in Personality* (1928); William Y. Tindall, *John Bunyan, Mechanick Preacher* (1934). — Frank M. Harrison, *A Bibliography of the Works of John Bunyan* (Bibliographical Soc., 1932).

12 See Tindall, pp. 22-41.

that kept me company, in all manner of vice and ungodliness." His worst specific vices were cursing, swearing, lying, dancing, and furtive ringing of the church bell. He married a poor but God-fearing wife—"not having so much household stuff as a dish or spoon between us both, yet she had for her part, *The Plain Man's Pathway to Heaven* and *The Practice of Piety*, which her father had left her when he died." These two books, especially the former, by Arthur Dent, proved a useful dowry. "The Plain Man's Pathway to Heaven" was clearly the ideal title for more than one work by Bunyan himself. His spiritual struggles now began, and as they protracted themselves, these pages of torment and ultimate triumph are studded with significant use of similitude and allegory.

And truly I did now feel myself to sink into a gulf, as a house whose foundation is destroyed: I did liken myself in this condition unto the case of a child that was fallen into a mill-pit, who, though it could make some shift to scramble and sprawl in the water, yet, because it could find hold neither for hand nor foot, therefore at last it must die in that condition.

Even earlier he had a vision of the good Christians of Bedford "as if they were on the sunny side of some high mountain, there refreshing themselves with the pleasant beams of the sun, while I was shivering and shrinking in the cold. . . . Methought also between me and them I saw a wall that did compass about this mountain. Now through this wall my soul did greatly desire to pass." After much search and effort he finds a straight and narrow passage in the wall "and so was comforted with the light and heat of their sun." Such passages are prophetic of better things in later works, especially in his *Pilgrim's Progress*.[18]

ilgrim's rogress   This great book is one of the several masterpieces by various authors written in prison. Bunyan's obstinate vocation to preach—by God's invitation but not by that of any bishop—had caused his arrest in 1660 and his imprisonment for almost twelve years thereafter. During this first imprisonment he wrote *Grace Abounding* and lesser works. For three years, 1672-5, he was "enlarged"; but for six months in 1675 he was again imprisoned for preaching, and during this six months in the bridge-house at Bedford, he composed *Pilgrim's Progress*—again a work about "The Plain Man's Pathway to Heaven"—here an "actual" but allegorical journey from the City of Destruction to the Heavenly Gates. He begins:

As I walk'd through the wilderness of this world, I lighted on a certain place, where was a Den; and I laid me down in that place to sleep: and as I slept I dreamed a Dream. I dreamed, and behold *I saw a man cloathed with Rags, standing in a certain place, with his face from his own House, a Book in his hand, and a great burden upon his back*. I looked, and saw him open the Book, and read therein; and as he read, he wept and trembled: and not being able longer to contain, he brake out with a lamentable cry; saying, *what shall I do?*

18 The most scholarly text of *Pilgrim's Progress* is that of James B. Wharey (Oxford, 1928).

And when the reader hears this cry, he joins his lot with that of the man in rags, and begins the perilous journey.

For Bunyan, a born story-teller, takes us with him. At sight we learn to distrust Mr. Worldly Wiseman and any other who may "look like a Gentleman"; we rejoice when Christian loses his burden; we tremble as we pass the lions in the way; we suffer with Faithful; we are terrified by Giant Despair; we thank God for Hopeful as we swim the dark river, and are perhaps a trifle complacent in assuring ourselves that the fate of Ignorance will never be ours. The episodes are all naturally and thrillingly suspensive, and Bunyan makes them real for us by adding a very pretty sense of landscape surroundings. He is also a natural allegorist, as the "mechanick" preachers of his day were wont to be. We have seen some of his earlier similitudes in *Grace Abounding*. In his prefatory jolting couplets for *Pilgrim's Progress* he tells us

> By metaphors I speak; Was not Gods Laws,
> His Gospel-Laws, in older time held forth
> By Types, Shadows and Metaphors?

His defensive tone is interesting; his insistence on "my method" is natural. No writer of his sort has ever made abstractions live more readily. Christian himself is both universal and yet a peasant from Bedfordshire; Mr. Worldly Wiseman and Talkative we have often met, and Mrs. Diffidence's bolster lecture to her giant husband seems quite wifely and natural. The allegory is consistently ingenious but is not forced in its ingenuity, as is that at times in *The Holy War*. The real appeal of the allegory depends on our sympathy for Christian and on the weighty implications of each dramatic episode and of the action as a whole.

Ingenuity is frequently displayed in presenting doctrinal points. Bunyan tolerates no loose thinking or lack of thought about salvation. Doctrine explains the tragic fate of that "brisk lad Ignorance" (from the country of Conceit!), who is a "good liver," and advises his fellow travelers, "follow the Religion of your Country, and I will follow the Religion of mine." Such counsel will never do; and the last word of Christian's vision concerns the fate of Ignorance and makes the highly disquieting comment: "I saw that there was a way to Hell, even from the Gates of Heaven." Theology apart, the story introduces much deft social satire. "Vanity Fair" is the best known example of this, but it is pervasive. "Fine-spoken" men are reproved in Flatterer and Atheist, and above all in Mr. By-ends of the wealthy town of Fair-speech with his precious family connections—among whom one might expect to find the celebrated Vicar of Bray. His wife, "Lady Faining's daughter ... is arrived at such a pitch of Breeding, that she knows how to carry it to all, even to Prince and Peasant." This couple is "always most zealous when Religion goes in his Silver Slippers." By-ends has been thought a possible caricature of an opponent of Bunyan's, Edward Fowler, the latitudinarian Bishop of Gloucester; possibly also he is another victim of the author's prejudice against the world of fashion or of time-servers. These

The Doctrine Involved

are all minor merits in a story which is a masterpiece because of its gripping and basic character. We need not agree with Christian's theological technicalities; but we must share the acute agony expressed in his first lamentable cry in his search for peace and quiet of mind—"*What shall I do?*"

Mr. Badman

Bunyan's next important narrative is an example of aesthetic backsliding. *The Life and Death of Mr. Badman Presented to the World in a Familiar Dialogue between Mr. Wiseman and Mr. Attentive* (1680) is a warning "that wickedness like a flood is like to drown our English world." So Wiseman tells his friend the story of a reprobate child who became a bad apprentice, a fraudulent business man, a painted sepulchre as a husband, and a hypocrite as a Christian. At death "His sins and his hope went with him to the Gate, but there his hope left him, because it dyed there; but his sins went in with him, to be a worm to gnaw him in his conscience for ever and ever." Mr. Badman, though remotely allied to the rogues of the picar-esque world,[14] is only a little more interesting as a rogue than as a subject for moralizing. The tedious dialogue, patterned after the method of *The Plain Man's Pathway to Heaven,* is drawn away from Mr. Badman by incessant preaching and by parallel episodic stories—borrowed at times from contemporary works such as Samuel Clarke's *Mirrour or Looking-Glass Both for Saints and Sinners* (1646). These stories are interesting, and they are surprising in that Bunyan superstitiously accepts them as veracious. One is the story of Dorothy Mately, "Swearer, and Curser, and Lier, and Thief," who on March 23, 1660, denied stealing twopence, and exclaimed "*That the ground might swallow her up if she had them.*" The ground promptly obliged, and when later Dorothy was "digged up," she had the pennies in her pocket. One gets many details of local manners—including the fashion in which Dr. Freeman ("who was more than an ordinary Doctor") attempted to exorcise a possessed ale-house keeper. But more than once the reader agrees with Mr. Attentive, who says, "These are sad storyes, tell no more of them now." These sad stories, nevertheless, are now the most interesting bits in the book.

The Holy War

By the time Bunyan wrote his work that ranks highest after *Pilgrim's Progress,* namely *The Holy War* (1682), he was somewhat conscious of literary success among the faithful; and this book is definitely more complex and subtle in thought and allegory than any of his other works. It narrates the warfare "made by Shaddai upon Diabolus, for the regaining of the Metropolis of the World, or the losing and the taking again of Mansoul." Here again, remotely after the method of a narrated morality-play,[15] we have the theme of the salvation of the soul allegorically treated. But Bunyan's Mansoul is not a person but a town—so curious, so commodious, so advantageous that "there is not its equal under the whole Heaven." The allegory tends to be political rather than personal in emphasis, and we have

---

[14] Professor G. B. Harrison in his *John Bunyan: A Study in Personality,* pp. 161-162, suggests shrewdly that possibly Badman is allied to certain citizens of Bedford.
[15] The greatest indebtedness yet traced is to Richard Bernard's *Isle of Man* (1626). See James B. Wharey, *A Study of the Sources of Bunyan's Allegories* (Baltimore, 1904).

no such sympathy for this town divided against itself as we had for the torn mind of the man Christian. The story is one of kings, princes, and great leaders; it deals in technical and "ensnaring propositions." The posie for its title-page (as for that of *Pilgrim's Progress*) was the text from Hos. 12:10, "I have used similitudes"; and the critical reader is tempted to exclaim, "Too many of them!" Apart from the allegory of the psychology of conversion, we have the allied biblical account of man's fall and redemption. At times the political chicanery detailed shadows forth the evils of Bunyan's own days when nonconformist saints were persecuted.[16] There is also, it has been urged, a consciousness of the biblical story as reshaped by the millenarian Fifth Monarchy men in Bunyan's day. Sometimes these different levels of allegory clash, but not more commonly than is usual in such works.

If in general we have here the same bag of tricks that were so effective in *Pilgrim's Progress,* it is still a good bag, and the tricks still dazzle. One *Its In-* may weary slightly of the tumults of wars, the marshaling of forces, the *genuity* "ensnaring propositions" for armistices, and the trials of war criminals; one may feel that Bunyan should have stayed in Bedfordshire; but one must at least recognize that Bunyan knows "the methods of godliness" and is satirically caustic about those who do not. His daring directness is amazing. He lets that worthy gentleman Mr. Godlyfear remark of Emanuel, "If that is not a sign of his anger, I am not acquainted with the methods of Godliness"; and at the triumph after the first conquest of Mansoul from Diabolus, Bunyan tells us, "Now after the feast was over, *Emanuel* was for entertaining the Town of *Mansoul* with some curious riddles of secrets." This entertainment consisted of a reading and exegesis of the Holy Scriptures! Such passages are mildly breath-taking, and might lead one to doubt if a mind of such simple directness could be caustic. The careers of the "tatling Diabolonian gentleman" Mr. Carnal Security and of the devil's General, Incredulity, and also of the Election-doubters (the bodyguard of Diabolus) show that we need not fear for any naïveté in Bunyan's thinking. Places of residence are neatly devised: "In *All-base*-lane, at a house next door to the Sign of the *Conscience seared with an hot iron.*" The trial scenes are numerous; but many of them—for example, that of Mr. Falsepeace, who tries to deny his name—are masterly in execution. The vivid moral psychology is still excellent: "Now there was an old man in the Town, and his name was Mr. *Good-deed*. A man that bare only the name, but had nothing of the nature of the thing." (On this favorite theme the Arminian Henry Fielding was not more deft than the old Calvinist Bunyan.) Old Good-deed is no satisfactory petitioner for mercy: "nor can a thousand of old *Good-deeds* save *Mansoul*." If *The Holy War* is nowadays less gripping than *Pilgrim's Progress* the explanation is probably that it is less psychological than social, that theological and political controversies intrude more obviously into the later book, and also that by the accident of history the application of military symbolism to religion is now definitely

[16] See ch. xiv of John Brown's *John Bunyan* on " 'Mansoul' and the Bedford Corporation." See also Tindall, *John Bunyan,* pp. 149-150.

out of vogue. But *The Holy War* is as typical of its age as is its remote cousin *Paradise Lost* or its nearer kin, Bunyan's greatest book.

Christiana's
Pilgrimage

The same year *The Holy War* was published saw the appearance of an unauthorized continuation of *Pilgrim's Progress* by "T. S.," one Thomas Sherman. This event encouraged Bunyan to do his own continuing, and indeed it is clear from the early conversations of Christian with Mr. Worldly Wiseman and with Charity that something had to be done for Christian's wife and family. Hence in 1684 appeared the second part of *Pilgrim's Progress,* narrating the journey of the now aged Christiana and her children. The situation is a little awkward; for hardly have the pilgrims left the wicket gate behind before Christiana and her maid Mercy are attacked by two ruffians; and as their Reliever tells them, he marveled, "being ye knew that ye were but weak Women, that you petitioned not the Lord ... for a Conductor." Such a personage is presently forthcoming. He is Mr. Great-heart, and the pilgrimage speedily becomes his story. He kills giants, scoring a tremendous victory at Doubting Castle, and he offers much good counsel. In Bunyan's mind conversion for women and children apparently lacked the tense terrors that Christian experienced, but required rather more in the way of spiritual instruction. The result is the diminished interest that one normally finds in continuations; and yet this second part is very pleasant reading. There is more homeliness in it. Mercy picks up an unsatisfactory beau in Mr. Brisk, and young Matthew picks up the gripes and undergoes a symbolic purgation. Vanity Fair is reputedly "far more moderate" than in the good old days when Faithful fell its victim, and we are continually delighted to find reminiscences of Christian extant along the way. It is more placid than the first part of the story, but it is pleasingly placid.

Bunyan had no notable successors in his own kind. He was simply an outstanding narrative genius whose truest significance is spiritual rather than literary. The travel story, the rogue biography, the allegory will all find new life presently in the works of Defoe and Swift, among others; but the fervid spiritual glow will not be there. Bunyan made some use of proletarian or Puritan patterns in narrative, but he had far less influence on proletarian fiction than did even the French romances.

The Short
Story or
"Novel"

It remains to speak of one genre, the relatively short narrative called in Continental fashion, until well on in the eighteenth century, the novel. This type of short story had a steady continuing influence easily neglected.[17] That it was a recognized prose type is seen from the preface to Congreve's one attempt, *Incognita* (1692), where we are told, after an account of the nature of romances:

Novels are of a more familiar nature; Come near us, and represent to us Intrigues in practice, delight us with Accidents and odd Events, but not such as are wholly unusual or unprecedented, such which not being so distant from our Belief bring

---

[17] A few of these works are available for convenient reading in the Everyman's Library *Shorter Novels,* Volume II: *Jacobean and Restoration* [*Ornatus and Artesia, Oroonoko, The Isle of Pines,* and *Incognita*].

also the pleasure nearer us. Romances give more of Wonder, Novels more Delight.[18]

Pamela in its day was justly called "a dilated novel"; for it, like the genre Congreve describes, deals in "familiar matter" of its day. The short novel is the true source from which the later long novel emerges. In the Elizabethan period novels came chiefly from Italy; in the seventeenth century, England imported rather from Spain. The novels inserted in *Don Quixote* gave great pleasure and Cervantes' *Novelas Exemplares* were popularly known even before James Mabbe translated six of them in 1640. From Fletcher to Crowne many dramatists had taken plots from these stories. Mabbe's version was reissued in 1654, and in 1687 Sir Roger L'Estrange translated five of these tales with five others from Solorzano and called them *The Spanish Decameron*. There were many other "novels" also in vogue. Most prose stories in chapbook form would serve as novels even if they were merely unified episodes taken from the more fantastic romances. For Michaelmas Term, 1681, *The Term Catalogues* give a typical list of such publications:

The Fair Extravagant .... An English Novel.
The unequal Match, or The Life of Mary of Anjou, Queen of Majorca. An Historical Novel.
The Jealous Gentleman of Estramadure: out of Cervantes Saavedra his Novels.
The Lovely Polander. A Novel.[19]

At least a half dozen other novels were listed for the same Term, all of which sold for a shilling. Peter Motteux's periodical *The Gentleman's Journal* (1692-4) contained numerous excellent stories, and in 1700 appeared *A Collection of Pleasant Novels* (2v), which included the perennially popular "Secret History of Queen Elizabeth and the Earl of Essex," "The Happy Slave" (from the French of Brémond), and, among others, Congreve's *Incognita*.

The most praised and condemned single writer of such novels was doubtless Mrs. Aphra Behn,[20] who produced something less than a dozen of *Aphra Behn*

18 *Incognita: or, Love and Duty Reconcil'd. A Novel* (1692); ed. Bonamy Dobrée (Oxford, 1928). See ed. Dobrée, p. 5.

19 *The Term Catalogues* (ed. Edward Arber, 1903), I. 461. That these works had to compete with "truth" that was as thrilling as fiction can be seen by examining the next two items listed; (1) *The Life and Death of Capt. William Bedloe, one of the Chief Discoverers of the Horrid Popish Plot*, and (2) *Memoires of the Life and Death of Sir Edmond Bury Godfrey*. The mystery of the Godfrey murder (1678) was more thrilling than any novel could be—and still is! See Arthur Bryant, *Samuel Pepys*, Vol. II.

20 Aphra Behn (1640-1689), very likely the daughter of John Amis of Wye, near Canterbury, had a certainly obscure and probably indecorous early career. The most debated episodes are, first, her experiences in Surinam as (so she said) the daughter of the deputy-governor select who died on the voyage out and, secondly, the romantic aspects of her career in Antwerp in 1666. If she was ever in Surinam, it was not as the viceroy's daughter but in some dubious rôle such as that of mistress of William Scot, son of the regicide Thomas Scot. Her efforts in Antwerp in 1666 seem to have been directed towards selling information to the English government in the hope of making a livelihood and of getting a pardon for her lover, William Scot, from whom as an employee of the Dutch government at the Hague the information came. The spies and lovers in their correspondence signed themselves respectively Astrea and Celadon. Apparently they had used these names in Surinam. From Holland she returned to England, without her Scot, in 1667. Her literary career began thereafter, so far as we know. — *The*

these short stories as well as her *Love Letters between a Nobleman and his Sister*. She was even better known as a playwright. Ladies guilty of frailty sometimes enjoy narrating the adventures of others, and much perhaps must be forgiven Mrs. Behn. Her own "Life," as written soon after her death, is a highly interesting piece of fiction based on the speciously autobiographical passages in some of her stories, which, after the manner of her day, she desired to pass off as "true." "The History of the Life and Memoirs of Mrs. Behn, Written by one of the Fair Sex" was published by Charles Gildon in her *Histories and Novels* (1696). For over two centuries this life was generally accepted as sober truth, but recently, thanks to the studies of Professor Ernest Bernbaum,[21] it has come to be regarded as colored much by fiction. It romanticizes her supposed life in Surinam, where she associated on friendly terms, she says, with Oroonoko and Imoinda, who are immortalized in her most famous novel, *Oroonoko; or, The Royal Slave* (1688). About the same time that the "Life" takes Mrs. Behn to Surinam, it also places her in London where she marries a Dutch merchant, becomes a widow, and serves in Antwerp as a secret agent during the Dutch War. It is certain that in 1666 she performed something like this last function. Her career after 1670 was English and was notable as both amatory and literary.

Only the latter aspect concerns us here. Mrs. Behn had been publishing plays for about thirteen years before she is known to have printed any prose fiction. Her *Love Letters between a Nobleman and his Sister* (1684) was apparently very popular; but such work was not so lucrative as playwriting. In 1688 her best stories were published in a volume called *Three Histories, viz. Oroonoko, The Fair Jilt, and Agnes de Castro*. Some of her earliest written tales were apparently first printed in the second collected edition of her *Histories and Novels* (1697). In general her stories are marked by lively intrigues—chiefly amorous—handled without too much tact or care, but still lively and interesting. Action is delayed by slow, vague beginnings, and interest is not heightened by her lack of warm or incisive insight into motives. She makes a great display of casual devices to authenticate material; but it is wise to view such devices as art rather than truth. *The Fair Jilt* doubtless has a relation to her adventures as a spy in Holland, but it is unwise to assume much autobiography here: the story is ill-shaped and as usual combines realistic material with pure story-book stuff. Just

---

Histories and Novels ... in one volume (1696); *Three Histories* (1688); *Plays, Histories, and Novels* (6v, 1871); *Works*, ed. Montague Summers (6v, 1915); *Novels* ... with an introduction by Ernest A. Baker (1913). Concerning her plays, see above, ch. VI, n. 8.

[21] Ernest Bernbaum, "Mrs. Behn's *Oroonoko*," *Anniversary Papers by Colleagues and Pupils of George Lyman Kittredge* (1913), pp. 419-433; and by the same author, "Mrs. Behn's Biography a Fiction," *PMLA*, XXVIII (1913). 432-453. Professor Bernbaum perhaps argued too strongly that Mrs. Behn never saw Surinam, but he made out a very plausible case. The only person to damage that case is Harrison Gray Platt, Jr., who in *PMLA*, XLIX (1934). 544-559, gave evidence coupled with clever guessing that makes it possible that she was there as Scot's mistress. Montague Summers (*The Works of Aphra Behn* [1915], I, pp. xv-lxi) and V. Sackville-West (*Aphra Behn*, 1927) add little beyond their personal opinions concerning Mrs. Behn's life.

when one decides that Mrs. Behn must have witnessed the decapitation of
some Dutch gentleman, the criminal in her story (*Prince Tarquin*), after
having been struck a supposedly fatal blow by the sword of the headsman,
makes an escape—and a recovery! Oroonoko also survives wounds that
would have been fatal to anyone but that superman. Mrs. Behn, however,
does frequently achieve an admirable illusion of reality, though she clearly
has no high sense of duty to truthfulness or even to plausibility, unless one
compares her work with the supernatural episodes of romance.

She treats her material usually in a somewhat hard mood that gives way
at times to sentimentalism. One has little sympathy for most of her persons
—Miranda "the fair jilt," Ardelia (in *The Nun: or, the Perjur'd Beauty*),
or any of the people in *The King of Bantam*. We are eager for the success of
few of her protagonists: we simply watch the puppets. This is, however, not
always the case. *Agnes de Castro*, a translation from Mlle de Brillac, does
have our sympathy; and it goes out even more strongly to the princely
African lovers Oroonoko and Imoinda. As a brief and new romantic story
Oroonoko is an astonishing masterpiece. For years, as in Davenant's *Cruelty
of the Spaniards in Peru* (1658), there had been works idealizing aboriginal
human nature as contrasted with gold-thirsty Christians. Mrs. Behn boldly
takes as her hero a beautiful and powerful Negro slave whose mind is as
noble as his body—and she makes and keeps him impressive to the end.
It is easy to point out flaws in this brief tragic romance, but Mrs. Behn by
some accident of genius has made real for us the noble aborigine as no one
else had done. It is a great achievement in a period in which idealized persons are practically always artificial. It makes one realize that while the prose
fiction of the Restoration is as a whole neither important nor greatly significant, a period that produced masterpieces as diverse as those of the righteous
Bunyan and the unrighteous Mrs. Behn has much to its credit.

IX

The Essay and Allied Forms

Discursive-
ness of the
Essay

In the years 1660-1700 the essay developed slowly and chiefly in relation to allied types of writing.[1] Before *The Spectator,* and even afterwards, the term *essay* was so little defined that it might imply verse as well as prose, though prose was its normal vehicle. It was essentially tentative and discursive; and these qualities of mind were frequently inhibited in a period concerned, on the one hand, with dynamic thinking and controversial or hortatory writing and, on the other hand, with a realistic and scientific regard for definition as the objective in thought. Neither the neo-Augustan thirst for nobility of manner nor the scientific appetite for practical, rigid plainness of enunciation furthered the easy informality that is the soul of essay writing. The discursive play of reason—*discursive,* so their dictionaries said, meant "running to and fro"—was in this sensible era either somewhat neglected or was elevated by ingenious fancy into verse. The essay, furthermore, was hardly a classical form, though in Theophrastus, Cicero, Pliny the Younger, Lucian, and in the Socratic dialogue, one had allied forms that tempted imitators, and led Restoration authors somewhat out of the tradition of the essay if it be narrowly defined.

Essay
Traditions

The essay, therefore, developed chiefly in relation to such types as the "character," the dialogue, the prose epistle, the pamphlet, and the "news-mongering" periodical—the last of which in the century to follow engrossed the form. The essay traditions established earlier in the seventeenth century were sound yet lacking in singleness. Authors with a passion for definition followed in the wake of Bacon and Feltham. That explicit schoolmaster Ralph Johnson, in his *Scholar's Guide from the Accidence to the University* (1665), described the essay as "a short discourse about any virtue, vice, or other commonplace." And the sixth and last of his "rules for making it" is: "In larger and compleat Essays (such as Bacon's, Feltham's, &c.) we must labour compendiously to express the whole nature of, with all observables about our subject." The Bacon-Feltham tradition (if it is a single tradition) with its emphasis on virtues, vices, and other truisms perpetuates itself best in the more limited "character," and less eminently in such essays as derive from accumulations in the author's commonplace-book. Outside

---

[1] In Hugh Walker's *The English Essay and Essayists* (1928) part of ch. IV deals with Restoration authors. For the end of the century Walter Graham's *English Literary Periodicals* (1930) is valuable in its more specialized field. The best survey of the essay for this whole period is E. N. S. Thompson's *Seventeenth-Century English Essay* (Iowa City, 1926; *Univ. of Iowa Humanistic Studies,* III, iii).

its allied type, the character, this Baconian essay tradition is less influential than the work of Montaigne.

The chief disciples of the great French father of the essay in this period were Abraham Cowley [2] (1618-1667) and Sir William Temple. In the last years of his life, Cowley, then in his middle forties, and somewhat disappointed with his lack of monetary success, withdrew himself from "the tumult and business of the world," and produced, among other works, eleven essays all in the personal vein of Montaigne, whom he quotes at least twice. He captures the truly discursive method of his master—frankly personal, frequently autobiographical, quoting aptly from the ancients as well as from the moderns, and making use of anecdote, witticism, and aphoristic moralizing. Called essays "in verse and prose," they embody considerable blocks of poetry translated or original. They deal with virtues and vices—liberty, solitude, obscurity, greatness, and avarice—but frequently from a definitely personal point of view. In the most prized of his essays, *Of Myself*, as well as in *The Danger of Procrastination* (significantly called "A Letter to Mr. S. L.") he is overtly autobiographical. In this last essay he speaks with frank informality concerning his design for a retired life: *Cowley's Essays*

> But there's no fooling with life, when it is once turned beyond forty. The seeking for a fortune then, is but a desperate after-game; 'tis a hundred to one, if a man fling two sixes and recover all; especially if his hand be no luckier than mine.

Cowley's prose truly marks a development away from the somewhat cumbrous splendor of earlier rhetoric towards the simpler, plainer, and more exact manner which the Royal Society, with his aid, was formulating. We seem to hear Cowley *speaking* simply and directly in a fluid, not a rigid, style. Another more elaborate sentence, dating probably 1664, begins *The Garden*, which he addressed to Evelyn in return for the dedication to himself of Evelyn's *Kalendarium Hortense:*

> I never had any other desire so strong and so like to covetousness, as that one which I have had always, that I might be master at last of a small house and large garden, with very moderate conveniences joined to them, and there dedicate the remainder of my life only to the culture of them, and study of nature. . . . And there (with no design beyond my wall) whole and entire to lie in no unactive ease, and no unglorious poverty.

Here Cowley states as his own an ambition that was almost universal among Englishmen of his day, and does it in a style that is easy and far removed from the terse staccato that Bacon had fitted to the essay. Cowley is an independent artist, sensitive enough to stylistic values so that he is a natural eclectic as well as a literary proponent of the new "scientific" ideals in expression. One can make out a case for development in Cowley by going

[2] Cowley's poetry, largely antedating 1660, was very influential after that date, especially his imitations of Pindar, which encouraged poetic strivings after "the sublime." He was also admired for his Anacreontics and for the love poems in *The Mistress* (1647). See Arthur H. Nethercot, *Abraham Cowley. The Muse's Hannibal* (Oxford, 1931).

back to his *Discourse by Way of Vision concerning the Government of
Oliver Cromwell* (1661) and citing the elaborate Ciceronian parallelisms
put into the mouth of "the north west principality" in the character of
Cromwell. The passage appealed to David Hume, who quoted it in his
History of England;[3] but it is less Cowley's own voice than it is his notion
of an idiom proper for the angel of destruction. Cowley wrote with flexibility, frankness, and ease; and his style, personal as it is, was an admirable
example for such as could escape the formal and artificial nobility of the
period or the terse, aphoristic manner that also claimed admirers. Cowley's
prose, like Dryden's, is almost wholly "modern" in style.

*Sir
William
Temple*

The most approved essayist of these years was doubtless Sir William Temple,[4] who, both before and after his retirement (1681) from a distinguished
political career, wrote with elegance, charm, factual negligence, and intellectual insight. His writings dealt either with affairs of state or with his
personal reflections on the employments and delights of the contemplative
life. To the first field are devoted his longer works, such as his *Observations
upon the United Provinces of the Netherlands* (1673), his *Essay upon the
Advancement of Trade in Ireland* (1673), his *Memoirs of what Past in
Christendom from 1672 to 1679* (1692), and his *Introduction to the History
of England* (1695), and, among his shorter works, such pieces as his essays
On the Original and Nature of Government and *Of Popular Discontents.*
His personal reflections or wisdom of life are expressed in such essays as
those *Upon the Gardens of Epicurus* and *Of Health and Long Life;* but all
his prose is marked strongly by his personality.

[3] Hume's *History of England,* ch. LXI, in ed. of 1786 and thereafter. Cf. Cowley's *Essays,
Plays and Sundry Verses,* ed. A. R. Waller (Cambridge, 1906), pp. 347-348.
[4] Sir William Temple (1628-1699) was born in London, and at the age of sixteen he entered
Emmanuel College, Cambridge, where he was for a time the pupil of Ralph Cudworth. He left
without taking a degree, traveled abroad, and in France (1648) met Dorothy Osborne, her
father, and her brother. A courtship began, but the Osbornes as ardent royalists opposed the
match. The letters of Dorothy Osborne to Temple form one of the most famous Restoration
correspondences. In 1654 the two were married. After eight years in Ireland, where Temple
was prominent in the Irish parliament, they returned to England, and settled at Sheen. During
the years following Temple served on diplomatic missions, drafted the Triple Alliance of 1668
between England, Holland, and Sweden, and became (1668) ambassador to the Hague. He
returned to England in 1670, but was again at the Hague in 1674, where he brought about
the marriage of William of Orange and the Princess Mary. Thereafter he twice declined to become Secretary of State, and in 1681 he retired from public life, and before 1689 removed
from Sheen to his new home Moor Park (Surrey). — *Works* (2v, 1720; 4v, 1814); *Essays,* ed.
J. A. Nicklin (1911); *Early Essays and Romances,* ed. G. C. Moore Smith (1930); *Poems*
[1670]; *Observations upon the ... Netherlands* (1673); ed. G. N. Clarke (Cambridge, 1932);
Essay upon ... Trade in Ireland (Dublin, 1673); *Miscellanea: the First Part* (1680); *Miscellanea: the Second Part* (1690); *Memoirs of ... 1672 to 1679* (1692); *An Essay upon Taxes*
(1693); *An Introduction to the History of England* (1695); *Letters ... to the Earl of Arling-
ton and Sir John Trevor* (1699); *Letters* (3v, published by Jonathan Swift, 1700-1703); *Select
Letters* (1701); *Miscellanea: the Third Part* (published by Jonathan Swift, 1701); *Memoirs:
Part Three* [1679-81] (published by Jonathan Swift, 1709). — Abel Boyer, *Memoirs* (1714);
Martha (Lady) Giffard, *The Life and Character of Sir William Temple* (1728); Thomas P.
Courtenay, *Memoirs of the Life, Works, and Correspondence of Sir William Temple* (2v,
1836); *Essays on Ancient and Modern Learning and on Poetry,* ed. Joel E. Spingarn (Oxford,
1909); Albert F. Sieveking, *Sir William Temple upon the Gardens of Epicurus, with Other
XVIIth Century Garden Essays* (1908); Dorothy Osborne Temple, *The Letters of ... to Sir
William Temple,* ed. Edward A. Parry (1901); in Everyman's Library [1932]; ed. G. C.
Moore Smith (Oxford, 1928); Clara Marburg, *Sir William Temple* (New Haven, 1932);
Homer E. Woodbridge, *Sir William Temple* (1940).

His character, thus revealed, is that of a nobly self-indulgent Epicurean, too elegantly cool to be a lively partisan in the scurrilous politics of the eighties, too skeptical to believe in the scientific advances of the Royal Society or the intellectual subtleties of controversial divines such as the Cambridge Platonists, whom he had experienced as an undergraduate. Montaigne and such interpreters of Epicurus as Gassendi, Dr. Walter Charleton, and Saint-Évremond were his masters; his delight in his own reveries and in his modest possessions was his *summum bonum.* It is of course easy to exaggerate the completeness of his retirement. He declined public office after 1681; but King William evidently came to Sheen and to Moor Park for advice, and two of Temple's longer works, his *Memoirs ...from 1672 to 1679* and his *Introduction to the History of England,* were designed, so it has been shrewdly urged,[5] to increase the popularity of the Dutch King William. During most of the last decade of Temple's life Jonathan Swift was his secretary, and Swift's poem *To Congreve* as well as his mission from Temple to the King in 1693 shows that both secretary and patron had keen interest in what went on in London. But the rôle voluntarily assumed by Temple was sincerely motivated by his maxim that "A man, in public affairs, is like one at sea; never in his own disposal, but in that of winds and tides." Fundamentally Temple distrusted his own motive power and his ability to steer a course in a filthy sea. "Does anything," he asks, "look more desirable than to be able to go just one's own pace and way?" Once when young "and in some idle company," he and his friends all told their three dearest wishes. "Mine," he confides, "were health and peace, and fair weather." Such wishes sufficiently indicate the relaxed and pleasure-loving attitude of his later life as expressed in such typical essays as *Of Health and Long Life* and *Upon the Gardens of Epicurus.* In this gardening essay his description of Moor Park (Hertfordshire),[6] where he had spent his honeymoon long ago, is a typically attractive passage and one so famous in its day that it was echoed by Alexander Pope in his *Epistle to the Earl of Burlington* and so famous that for generations it influenced the development of the English garden.

Everyone from Swift and Pope to Goldsmith and Johnson commended Temple as a stylist. He "was the first writer who gave cadence to English prose," said Johnson, who professed to have formed his own style on Temple's. Certainly Temple had great significance as the leading exponent of easy dignity and rhythm: his influence here is undoubted. But in spite of the unkind remarks Macaulay and others have made about his intellectual quality, it seems right to believe that Temple's highest function was to be, like Rousseau or H. G. Wells, a barometer and a weather vane. He was for the following age an intellectual nerve-center but by no means a storm-center. Not a powerful or original thinker and not a writer scrupulously *His Style and His Ideas*

---

[5] By Professor H. E. Woodbridge, *Sir William Temple,* pp. 259-261.

[6] Not the seat in Surrey, where his later years were passed, and which he named Moor Park in memory of the earlier experience. The two places are often confused by writers about Temple.

accurate about his facts when he tried to display his learning, Temple never-theless anticipated and contradicted by turns important tendencies in the thought of his time. In his *Original and Nature of Government* and later in essays such as *Of Health and Long Life* and *Upon the Gardens of Epicurus,* he glorified the state of nature and "the first and most simple ages" long before Rousseau was to do so. He enunciated well the patriarchal origin of society, and was an early proponent in English of the notion that climate determines national character; that artistic achievement may depend on accidents of climate and cultural milieu. By now, let us hope, it is clear that the important thing about his factually superficial essay *Upon Ancient and Modern Learning* is not that it begot first a controversy with Wotton and Bentley and finally occasioned Swift's *Tale of a Tub,* but rather that it was a classical denial of the idea of progress at the very moment when that idea was in England gaining its first momentum. Temple believed in cyclic change but not in progress, and although his historical data were not accurately presented in proof of his position (such "proof" would have been difficult!), the position itself is still an inevitably recurrent classic attitude towards the problem of change. So it is with many of his ideas: they may be superficially stated but they are ingratiatingly stated, and they are ideas that have haunted the mind of man in many ages. Temple's undoubted in-tellectual appeal was not due to his logic or to his learning, but rather to his sensitiveness to human tendency in thinking. He is most influential, perhaps, in *The Gardens of Epicurus* and elsewhere when stating his love of retirement, his delight in his fruits, his flowers, and his bowling green —all of which made evident the superiority of his manner of life to that amidst the smell and smoke of the political battle. More than one dis-appointed statesman was to learn that lesson from him. It has universal appeal. To sum up, his repute lies in his style, his gifts as literary critic,[7] and his gracious and respectable Epicureanism. He is still the most readable of the essayists of his age.

If Temple leaned to an Epicurean philosophy of life, there were other *Religious* writers who affected other schools of thought. Their courageous and dynamic *and Philo-* thinking usually promotes either of two interests, religion or politics. In *sophical* form their work overflows the limits proper for an essay and becomes more *Essays* like a moral monograph or treatise in size. In the case of Sir George Mac-kenzie[8] (1636-1691), for example, this is true not only of such youthful pieces as his *Religio Stoici, the Virtuoso or Stoick* (Edinburgh, 1663) and his *Moral Gallantry* (1667), but also of his last works, *The Moral History of Frugality* (1691) and *Reason, an Essay* (1690). It is perhaps less charac-teristic of the Rev. Anthony Horneck's (1641-1697) *Happy Ascetick* (1681), but only because he breaks up his exhortations into a score of pious "exer-cises." John Norris of Bemerton (1657-1711), called the last of the Cambridge

---

[7] For an account of Temple's critical essays see above, ch. II.
[8] Andrew Lang, *Sir George Mackenzie* (1909); F. S. Ferguson, "A Bibliography of the Works of Sir George Mackenzie, Lord Advocate, Founder of the Advocates Library," *Edin-burgh Bibl. Soc. Trans.,* 1 (1936). 1-60.

Platonists, in his *Miscellanies* (1687) shows more diversity, presenting in conventional form brief essays *Of the Advantages of Thinking* or *Of Solitude,* and other longer essays divided into sections, a series of *Contemplations,* and essays in the form of rather long letters to friends—on, for example, *An Idea of Happiness* or *An Account of Plato's Ideas, and of Platonic Love.* Since the days of James Howell many essays had assumed letter form. Jeremy Collier, remembered for his attack on the stage, brought out (1694-1709) four volumes of *Essays upon Several Moral Subjects* concerning the usual topics, most of which are treated in dialogues of varying lengths.

More important so far as substance goes were the works—treatises rather *Glanvill* than essays—of Joseph Glanvill [9] (1636-1680) and Thomas Burnet of the *and* Charterhouse (1635?-1715). Glanvill, in his *Vanity of Dogmatizing* (1661), *Thomas* which he recast once as *Scepsis Scientifica* (1665) and again as a part of his *Burnet* *Essays on Several Important Subjects in Philosophy and Religion* (1676), had influence in developing the doctrine of skepticism (or the open mind) as a method in thinking. The changes in style in the forms of this work, furthermore, indicate neatly the nature of the influences (the Royal Society and moral honesty among other things) that were modernizing English prose style. His *Plus Ultra* (1668) shows his belief in progress, and his *Essay concerning Preaching* (1678) had potency in reducing pulpit oratory to a sensible plainness and clarity. In structural form Glanvill's work is not a part of the essay tradition; his attitude towards style, however, may have helped prepare the way for the ease and informality of the essay. Burnet's *Telluris Theoria Sacra* (2 volumes, 1681-9), the first volume of which was made English as *A Sacred Theory of the Earth* (1684), is similarly a treatise, not an essay; but it is glowingly written, and with the Boyle lectures of men like John Ray (1627-1705) and William Derham (1657-1735) is an important influence in leading poets and essayists to describe and praise the works of the visible creation.

These men represent the religious tradition behind the essay. Politics was hardly less favored as a subject for incisive prose. Somewhat like Temple in policy and temper and yet very different from him, was Sir George Savile,[10] who became the Marquis of Halifax and one of the chief counselors

[9] Ferris Greenslet, *Joseph Glanvill* (1900); Moody E. Prior, "Joseph Glanvill, Witchcraft, and Seventeenth-Century Science," *MP*, xxx (1932). 167-193; Hartwig Habicht, *Joseph Glanvill* (Zurich, 1936).

[10] Sir George Savile (1633-1695), created successively Viscount (1668), Earl (1679) and Marquis of Halifax (1682), was in his time a courtier of unsurpassed intellectual power and sharpness of wit. He served on many diplomatic missions and held many high offices. His caustic tongue made him enemies at court, but that fact did not silence him. He was a most able critic of the Cabal ministers, but when restored to the royal council in 1679 he tempered his wit in the King's presence and became a notable favorite. His reputation for moderate policies dates from the hysteria over the Popish Plot (1678). The defeat of the Exclusion Bill in 1680 was largely due to Halifax, who spoke sixteen times in the debate, answering Shaftesbury. At the end of 1680 he briefly withdrew from the battle; for while he had blocked the Monmouth faction, he had no enthusiasm for the succession of the Catholic Duke of York (James II). Within six months, however, he was back at court, where the rising influence of the Duke of York and his succession to the throne in 1685 reduced Halifax's influence, and caused him to turn hopefully towards William of Orange. In 1688 Halifax was a leading peer in the effort to secure the crown jointly to William and Mary. He was much attacked by extremists in policy, and, as his health failed, withdrew from public office, especially during his last

*Politics
and the
Essay*

of state after 1672. By temperament he was a mediator, an apostle of compromise; and when Sir Roger L'Estrange's periodical *The Observator* (December 3 and 4, 1684) attacked such moderation in a discourse on *The Character and Humour of a Trimmer,* Halifax wrote in reply his celebrated *Character of a Trimmer,* which circulated for some time in manuscript copies and was printed in 1688. It embodies with dignity and insight the essential spirit of the revolution of 1688. Shrewdly he says:

> This innocent word *Trimmer* signifieth no more than this, That if Men are together in a Boat, and one part of the Company would weigh it down on one side, another would make it lean as much to the contrary; it happeneth there is a third Opinion of those, who conceive it would do as well, if the Boat went even, without endangering the Passengers; now 'tis hard to imagin by what Figure in Language, or by what Rule in Sense this cometh to be a fault, and it is much more a wonder it should be thought a Heresy.

In this spirit Halifax promoted moderate ideas as to the necessity of law in the functioning of constitution, prince, and parliament. He was a firm Protestant and a reasonable opponent of the papists. He was an ardent nationalist; he adored, with unusually elevated rhetoric, "the Goddess Truth," and in a good-natured and witty conclusion expressed the opinion that from climate to laws England is by nature in all respects a Trimmer.

Shortly after the death of Charles II Halifax wrote his *Character of King Charles II.* This is less a pamphlet than is the *Trimmer,* and it is rather a series of essays on various aspects of the late monarch's personality—his religion, his dissimulation, his amours, his conduct to his ministers, his wit, his talents, and his disposition. It is a portrait etched with acid of deceptive strength, yet tempered finally with subservient kindliness. The writing here is more aphoristic, the style more terse and clipped; the weightiness of the work, however, as in the *Trimmer,* lies in its large yet acrid worldly wisdom. On the King's talent of "finding out other Men's weak sides" and neglecting his own faults, Halifax comments:

> Men love to see themselves in the false Looking-glass of other Mens Failings. It maketh a Man think well of himself at the time, and by sending his Thoughts abroad to get Food for Laughing, they are less at leisure to see Faults at home. Men choose rather to make War in another Country, than to keep all well at home.

Such moral commonplaces are perfect essay material. Halifax's other public pamphlets include two concerning the readiness of dissenters to club with

three years. — *Miscellanies* (1700, 1704, 1717); *The Life and Letters of . . . Halifax, with a new Edition of his Works,* ed. H. C. Foxcroft (2v, 1898); *Complete Works,* ed. Walter Raleigh (Oxford, 1912); *A Letter to a Dissenter . . . By T. W.* (1687, 6 eds.); *The Character of a Trimmer. By the Honorable Sir W. C.* (1688); *The Anatomy of an Equivalent* (1688); *The Lady's New-Year's-Gift* (1688); ed. Bonamy Dobrée (1927); *Maxims Found amongst the Papers of the Great Almanzor* (1693); *A Character of King Charles the Second* (1750); ed. Peter Davies (1927); *Savile Correspondence* (Camden Society, 1858). — H. C. Foxcroft, *Sir George Savile, Marquis of Halifax* (2v, 1898); G. P. Gooch, *Political Thought from Bacon to Halifax* (1914); A. W. Reed, "George Savile, Marquis of Halifax," in F. J. C. Hearnshaw, *The Social and Political Ideas . . . of the Augustan Age* (1928).

the Catholics in the matter of toleration, and his *Maxims of State,* which illustrates his skill in turning out *pensées.*

Not excepting even the *Trimmer* his most popular work was the series of essays written for his daughter Elizabeth (who later became the mother of the famous Earl of Chesterfield) and published under title of *The New-Year's-Gift: or, Advice to a Daughter* (1688). Written seriously and affectionately, these advices on such topics as religion, a husband, housekeeping and family, behavior, friendships, censoriousness, vanity, pride, and diversions, introduced the young lady to a rather melancholy social system in which women must study to protect their reputations and to manage patiently and tactfully "in case a *Drunken Husband* should fall to your share." These essays contain a great deal of long-refrigerated common sense, and were highly valued for a century or more by well-meaning parents. They reached at least a fifteenth edition by 1765. Halifax in a letter to Charles Cotton concerning Cotton's popular translation (1685) of Montaigne's *Essays* called the essays "the Book in the World that I am the best entertain'd with"; but in Halifax's own writing there is little of the discursiveness or of the geniality of Montaigne; he sticks to the point, illuminates his thinking with frequent brief similes but almost never by anecdote. His strength, as Dryden pointed out in *Absalom and Achitophel,* lay in "piercing wit and pregnant thought." Of these he is master. Apart from his *New-Year's-Gift* he is a pamphleteer rather than an essayist.

Lighter in tone and effect, though still didactic in avowed purpose, is the type of essay that influenced Halifax, the "character." [11] This sort of writing had become well established early in the century by the work of such authors as Bishop Hall, Sir Thomas Overbury, and John Earle,[12] and it continued to be popular and fundamentally unchanged throughout the century. Upon the prose character the Restoration period patterned satirical portraits in verse as a popular extension of the type. Ralph Johnson in his *Scholar's Guide* defined the prose character as "a witty and facetious description of the nature and qualities of some person, or sort of people." In method it was analytical and abstractionist rather than concrete, dramatic, or vivid. It presented the traits essential to define a type or a quality, but did not strive to make the type live. In such variations from the norm as Richard Head's wheedling *Shopkeeper* there is attention to external objectivity; and in such other deviations as Halifax's *Charles II* or Richard

Marginal notes: Advice to a Daughter — *The Theophrastan Character*

---

[11] On the "character" one may well consult: Gwendolen Murphy, *A Bibliography of English Character-Books* (The Bibliographical Society, Oxford, 1925); Henry Morley, *Character Writings of the Seventeenth Century* (1891); E. C. Baldwin, "The Relation of the English 'Character' to its Greek Prototype," *PMLA,* xviii (1903). 412-423; G. S. Gordon, "Theophrastus and his Imitators," in *English Literature and the Classics* (Oxford, 1912); Chester N. Greenough, "The 'Character' as a Source of Information for the Historian," in *Massachusetts Hist. Soc. Proc.,* LIV (1922). 224-235; reprinted in *Collected Studies* (Cambridge, Mass., 1940), pp. 123-153; Gwendolen Murphy, *A Cabinet of Characters* (Oxford, 1925); E. N. S. Thompson, "Character Books and Familiar Letters," in *The Seventeenth-Century English Essay* (Iowa City, Ia., 1926); the late Chester N. Greenough's *Bibliography of the Theophrastan Character in English,* ed. J. Milton French (Cambridge, Mass., 1947).

[12] Concerning the early, formative period of the "Character" Professor Benjamin Boyce has in press an extensive study (Cambridge, Mass.).

Flecknoe's *Worthy Nobleman* (William, Duke of Newcastle), not types but individuals are represented, and this is usually the procedure in characters in satirical verse. Religious and political characters usually become controversial in tone and purpose, but the normal prose character remained in spite of variations a witty and facetious analysis of a type, a class, or an abstract moral quality.

Flecknoe and Butler   Its best practitioners in the Restoration period were Dryden's zany Richard Flecknoe and Samuel Butler, famous as the author of *Hudibras*. Flecknoe,[13] whose work is by no means so contemptible as Dryden reported, relies on wit for success in such pieces (from his total of 119 characters) as those about *A School-Boy, A Talkative Lady,* or *An Immitable Widdow*. A Catholic priest, he is habitually caustic when writing of religious sects and is severe also on the little hypocrisies that he detects among his own co-religionists. His passion for rewriting his characters is unusual: they appeared, many of them, in at least three different forms. Flecknoe recognized that "Wit ... is no solid food of life, but an excellent sawce or seasoning" to wisdom. As compared with the learned and subtle Butler [14] his wisdom is commonplace. Butler's scope and satiric edge are hardly paralleled among the writers of characters. Possibly because he was aware of his incautious savageness on political and religious topics, Butler never published his characters, which were first printed in 1759. In politics he gives us accounts of *A Modern Politician, A Republican, A Leader of a Faction,* that are so virulent as to imply perhaps a personal animus behind them. Both in these and in his diverse sketches of religious eccentricity—*An Hypocritical Nonconformist, A Fifth-Monarchy-Man, A Ranter, A Latitudinarian,* etc., he shows the biases one might expect from the author of *Hudibras*. On literary or antiquarian types he is also mordant: his accounts of *A Small Poet, An Imitater,* or *A Modern Critic* are important evidences of common literary predilections. The style is bluntly rough, terse, and spiced with what in an earlier age might have been called ale-house metaphors.

A Degenerate Noble: or, One that is proud of his Birth, Is like a Turnep, there is nothing good of him, but that which is under-ground, or Rhubarb a contemptible Shrub, that springs from a noble Root.

13 Of the life of Richard Flecknoe (1620?-1678?) little is known. He was very likely not Irish, as Dryden led people to believe. He was a Roman secular priest, and he traveled perhaps as widely as his *Relation of Ten Years' Travels* asserted; that is, from England to Constantinople and the Greek islands; to the Cape Verde islands, Teneriffe, Funchal, and Brazil. He achieved posthumous notoriety when in 1682 Dryden entitled his attack on Shadwell *MacFlecknoe;* before this event his reputation had not been altogether contemptible. — Apart from five plays his chief works were *Miscellania* (1653); *A Relation of Ten Years' Travels* (1654?); *The Diarium, or Journal, in Burlesque Rhime* (1656); *Enigmatical Characters* (1658; rev. 1665); *Heroick Portraits* (1660); *A Farrago of Several Pieces* (1666); *The Life of Tomaso the Wanderer* (1667); ed. George Thorn-Drury (1925); *Epigrams* (1669, 1670, 1671, 1673, each ed. with additions). — Anton Lohr, *Richard Flecknoe, Eine Literarhistorische Untersuchung* (Leipzig, 1905); Paul H. Doney, *The Life and Works of Richard Flecknoe* (unpublished Harvard diss., 1928).
14 On Samuel Butler's career and poems see above, ch. IV, n. 2.

A Republican ... is so much a Fool, that, like the Dog in the Fable, he loses his real Liberty, to enjoy the Shadow of it.

A Leader of a Faction ... is like a Figure in Arithmetic, the more Ciphers he stands before, the more his Value amounts to.

In pungency and satirical force Butler's characters are unsurpassed.

The character, as Halifax's *Trimmer* shows, tended at times to become a controversial pamphlet; and the pamphlet itself, as well as the essay, was closely bound up with journalism.[15] As early as 1621 Burton's *Anatomy* had dolefully proclaimed that "If any read nowadays, it is a playbook or a pamphlet of news," and pamphlets that either reported events or (more frequently) expressed fierce opinions about events were common throughout the century. Early newspapers were too small to devote much space to editorial comment; and before 1695 when the Licensing Act finally lapsed, such comment was limited; after 1695 it was made at the peril of the author. The most meager news-sheets, however, tended to be violently partisan.[16] Just as the *Mercurius Britannicus* (No. 1: August 29, 1643) was founded as a counter to the royalist *Mercurius Aulicus* (January, 1643), so after 1695 George Ridpath's *Flying-Post* (1695-1731) was bitterly Whig while Abel Roper's *Post-Boy* (1695-1736) was a Tory organ. More closely related to intellectual and literary interests, and hence to essay writing, were journals which, instead of featuring news, disseminated opinion or information on popular subjects. Of these Sir Roger L'Estrange's *Observator* [17] (1681-87) devised a question and answer method of controversial exposition, which, however, speedily became a dialogue between the Observator and an op-

The Rise of Journalism

---

[15] Among many books that deal in part with early journalism may be noted the following: as bibliographies, "J. B. Williams" [i.e., J. G. Muddiman], *The Times Tercentenary Handlist of English and Welsh Newspapers, Magazines, and Reviews* (1920) [arranged chronologically]; Ronald S. Crane and Fred B. Kaye, *A Census of British Newspapers and Periodicals, 1620-1800* (Chapel Hill, N. C., 1927) [arranged alphabetically]; and *CBEL*, II. 688-739; as histories, H. R. Fox Bourne, *English Newspapers* (2v, 1887); Stanley Morison, *The English Newspaper* (Cambridge, 1932); and Laurence Hanson, *Government and the Press, 1695-1763* (Oxford, 1936).

[16] The official government organ for the dissemination of news during this whole period was founded in 1665 at Oxford, and was called for 23 numbers *The Oxford Gazette;* in February 1666 it was transferred to London and became *The London Gazette.* It appeared twice a week normally, and has had a continuous existence since its founding. Its early specialty was foreign news, and the Gazetteer (its author) was attached to the office of the Secretary of State.

[17] Sir Roger L'Estrange (1616-1704) came of a loyalist family, and throughout a stormy career he was loyalist and Tory. After the Restoration he was appointed surveyor of printing presses and licenser of the press. In the ensuing struggle for freedom of the press he was powerfully active for government control and for censorship. He was knighted by James II in 1685, and, more or less by ministerial command, was returned M.P. for Winchester. The Whig triumphs in the Revolution of 1688 spelled ruin for Sir Roger, whom the Whigs regarded as a most notorious enemy to all liberty in England. He was thereafter imprisoned three separate times, and his writing after 1688 was practically all pot-boiling translation. He was earlier connected with two or three newspapers apart from his *Observator,* and he was the author of something like three score of political pamphlets. One of the earliest of these was a retort to John Milton called *No Blinde Guides* (1660). His most popular translations, often reprinted, were: *The Visions of Quevedo* (1667), *Five Love Letters from a Nun to a Cavalier* (1678), Seneca's *Morals* (1678), Tully's *Offices* (1680), *Twenty Select Colloquies out of Erasmus* (1680), *The Fables of Aesop*, et al. (1692), Terence's *Comedies* (1694), and *The Works of Flavius Josephus* (1702). For complete details with a bibliography, see George Kitchin, *Sir Roger L'Estrange* (1913).

posing straw-man—a Whig, or a Courantier, or a Trimmer. Less political
and more intellectual was *The Athenian Gazette: or Casuistical Mercury*
(1691-97), a project of the eccentric bookseller John Dunton,[18] whose staff
for his periodical included Richard Sault, John Norris, Samuel Wesley
(father of the founder of Methodism), and others. These men composed an
"Athenian Society" and undertook to answer in the *Mercury* all questions
on all topics. Most commonly questions related to matrimony or love, to
theology or to ethical problems, to popular science or pseudo-science. Occasionally literary criticism had its day, as when the question appeared
(January 16, 1692) "Whether Milton and Waller were not the best English
poets? and which the better of the two?" Answers to a dozen or more
questions in the space that a *Spectator* paper would fill (a folio half-sheet
printed in two columns) produced paragraphs rather than essays; but the
tendency towards essay writing is obvious. *The Athenian Mercury* was very
popular in literary circles, and its editorial "Society" was praised in verses
written by Nahum Tate (the poet laureate), Peter Motteux, Defoe, and
Swift.

"Learned"   None of the periodicals so far named made a habit of reviewing con-
Journals   temporary belles-lettres. There had been in France and the Low Countries
various periodicals that reviewed learned works, chiefly in the fields of
theology, archaeology, or classical literature, and these began to be imitated
in England. The Huguenot Jean de la Crose tried it in his *History of Learning* (1691-4) and his *Memoirs for the Ingenious* (1693), and at the end of the
century was begun the more durable *History of the Works of the Learned*
(1699-1712). There were several such "learned" journals. Apart from them
stands the work of the Frenchman Peter Motteux (1663-1718) in a periodical
that has obvious pioneering aspects in the field of belles-lettres, *The Gentleman's Journal* (1692-94). This is a periodical of miscellaneous contents.
more like a modern magazine than any other periodical for years to come.
It contained news, short stories, fables, poems, songs (with music), many
essays, and comments on contemporary publications in the field of belles-
lettres. Once or twice a whole number was the product of Motteux's sole
pen, but generally contributors were numerous. Among them are named
Congreve, Prior, Sedley, Tate, Tom Brown, Durfey, Southerne, Dennis,
Crowne, Gildon, Oldmixon, and Tutchin. Motteux was that rare thing
for his day, a kindly, commending critic; but either personal instability or
lack of support made three volumes the extent of his *Journal's* life. Motteux
is also known as the author of plays and operas and as the translator of
Rabelais and Cervantes.[19]

---

[18] Dunton left an amusing life of himself, *The Life and Errors of John Dunton, late Citizen
of London* (1705); ed. John Nichols (1818). In *Collected Studies* (Cambridge, Mass., 1940) of
C. N. Greenough there are two essays on "John Dunton's ·*Letters from New England*" and
Dunton's borrowings in his writing. See also Harrison R. Steeves, "The Athenian Virtuosi and
the Athenian Society," *MLR*, VII (1912). 358-371.
[19] Robert N. Cunningham has done a biographical and critical study called *Peter Anthony
Motteux* (Oxford, 1933), and also "A Bibliography of the Writings of Peter Anthony Motteux,"
Proc. of the Oxford Bibl. Soc., III (1933). 317-337.

A more specialized periodical which had influence on later essay writing *Ned Ward* was Ned Ward's *London Spy* (1698-1700).[20] This was less an imitation of the popular *Turkish Spy* (1687, 1694) than it was a product of Ward's natural love for describing the low life of his day. In 18 monthly numbers of sixteen folio pages each the "Spy" and a friend visit such tourist spots as the tombs of Westminster Abbey, the law courts in Westminster Hall, St. James's Park, the zoo in the Tower as well as low-lived taverns, bagnios, and prisons of the city. For some years Ward himself kept a public-house in Moorfields, and it was in such locales that his genius was most at home. His method is narrative interspersed with songs, characters, and other devices for variety. The language is frequently so much the slang of its day as to be somewhat difficult 250 years after the fact; but his diction normally is pungent and apt as are his vigorous but vulgar similes. The material often is shamelessly nasty and usually vividly detailed. In style the matter seems subjected to a definitely fluid and fluttering mind; and so the sentences float wittily onward in rather formless or casual fashion. As social documents the narratives are invaluable. The same comment may serve for Ward's satirical voyage pamphlets. His *Trip to Jamaica* (1698) gives a vivid picture of a transatlantic voyage in his day, and a most uncomplimentary account of the island itself. The chief pleasures of the voyage were lucrative backgammon and harmony made "in Lyricking over some *Antiquated Sonnets* and for varieties sake now and then a *Psalm*." In Jamaica he had difficulty with tropical dishes:

They make a rare *Soop* they call *Pepper-Pot;* its an excellent Breakfast for a *Salamander,* or a good preparative for a *Mountebanks Agent,* who Eats Fire one day, that he may get better Victuals the next. Three Spoonfuls so Inflam'd my Mouth, that had I devour'd a Peck of *Horse-Radish,* and Drank after it a Gallon of *Brandy* and *Gunpowder,* (*Dives* like) I could not have been more importunate for a Drop of Water to cool my Tongue.

His *Trip to New England* (1699) begins with the assertion that "Bishops, Bailiffs, and Bastards, were the three Terrible Persecutions which chiefly drove our unhappy Brethren to seek their Fortunes in our Forreign Colonies." Naturally he is caustic about the Boston blue laws—especially those against kissing; but he finds "one very wholesome Law"—that of punishing a scold by making her stand for a fixed period at her own door, gagged!

---

[20] Edward ("Ned") Ward (1667-1731), definitely a journalistic genius, wrote numerous pieces in Hudibrastic verse and much humorous prose. After his visits to America he settled in London and kept a tavern, to which men of High Church political sympathies were particularly welcomed. For the anti-Whig tendencies of his *Hudibras Redivivus* in 1705 he was condemned twice to stand in the pillory. He offended Alexander Pope in *The Poetical Entertainer* (1712-13), was put in *The Dunciad,* and retaliated in *Durgen* (1729) and *Apollo's Maggot in his Cups* (1729). His fame rested on *The London Spy.* — A list of his works may be found in *CBEL,* II, 596-599. *The London Spy* has been reprinted for the Casanova Society (1924) and has been edited by Arthur L. Hayward [1927]. *Five Travel Scripts Commonly Attributed to Edward Ward* have been reproduced by the Facsimile Text Society (1933) with a bibliographical note by Howard W. Troyer. Professor Troyer is the author of an excellent biographical and bibliographical study, *Ned Ward of Grubstreet* (Cambridge, Mass., 1946). See also Claude E. Jones, "A Short-title Checklist of Works Attributed to Edward Ward," *N&Q,* CXC (1946). 135-139.

Ward also seems to have had a hand in two related periodicals called *The Weekly Comedy as it is dayly acted at most Coffee Houses* (1699) and *The Humours of a Coffee-House, a Comedy* (1707-8), which are among the notable predecessors of *The Tatler*. Much of Ward's prose shows interests parallel but inferior to those of Richard Steele's work. His many verses— chiefly Hudibrastic—seem usually to lack the edged life of his prose.

Tom Brown   A somewhat similar writer, though one of more varied gifts, was Tom Brown,[21] whose prose illustrates most of the types popular in the period. His most remunerative work was probably translation; for through the years he was concerned, as collaborator at least, in translations of Mme D'Aulnoy, Saint-Évremond, LeClerc, Fontenelle, Scarron, Cicero, and Lucian. Early in his career he entered the lists against Dryden with three witty, satirical pamphlets in dialogue form: *The Reasons of Mr. Bays Changing his Religion* (1688), *The Late Converts Exposed* (1690), *The Reasons of Mr. Joseph Hains the Player's Conversion & Reconversion* (1690). These placed Brown at once high among the true blue Protestant wits approved by King William's court, and presently, after some more dialogues, some political poems, and a group of letters from the dead to the living, he attempted at the moment of the popularity of Dunton's *Athenian Mercury* a rival periodical, *The London Mercury* (32 numbers, 1692), which much annoyed Dunton. About the same time he made at least a small contribution to his friend Motteux's *Gentleman's Journal,* and had great success with his translation of Mme D'Aulnoy's letters, which he called *Memoirs of the Court of Spain* (1692). In 1700 his *Amusements Serious and Comical* were obviously in the tradition of *The London Spy,* though Brown, while by no means completely decent, is less crude than Ward. His *Laconics: or, New Maxims of State and Conversation* (1701) remind one of Halifax's *Maxims;* but these *New Maxims* deviate from aphoristic *pensées* in that they frequently illustrate a central point by facetious anecdote. From the Lucianic device of dialogues between famous dead celebrities Brown and some friends evolved, with an eye on recent French models, a considerable series of *Letters from the Dead to the Living* (1702-3; 1707). Neither so witty nor so intellectual as their greater predecessors, these letters are entertainingly scurrilous and topical. The deceased correspondents, writing from the lower regions, are less concerned with "the present state of the

---

[21] Thomas Brown (1663-1704), was born in Newport (Salop.), and was educated in the Grammar School there and in Christ Church, Oxford (1678-84), from which he was graduated B.A. in 1684. Probably while at Christ Church he composed out of disrespect to the famous Dean, Dr. Fell, his one "surviving" poem—an imitation of Martial, I. 32:

I do not love you Dr. *Fell,*
But why I cannot tell;
But this I know full well,
I do not love you, Dr. *Fell.*

For at least two or three years Brown taught school near London, and by 1688 he was established in the metropolis as a Grub-street Tory pamphleteer, which function was to occupy the rest of his grimy life. He was to suffer arrests for his scurrilities, and was to know debt as the driving force behind his pen. Much of his prose falls into letter form, dialogue, or allegorical fable. He campaigned against the "Pindarick way of preaching"—against an ornate or metaphorical pulpit style. An excellent account of Brown is given in Benjamin Boyce's *Tom Brown of Facetious Memory* (Cambridge, Mass., 1939), which includes a list of his works.

Plutonian kingdom" than they are with scandalous revelations which now they are able to make concerning the living. The device is made personal, topical, journalistic, and blithely shameless. In this journalistic tendency Brown had been somewhat anticipated by the *Dialogues of the Dead Relating to the Present Controversy concerning the Epistles of Phalaris* (1699) by William King of Christ Church—though King avoided the nastiness that Brown evidently loved. Apart from all this variety of journalistic prose Brown produced much negligible verse. It is dutiful to recall that *The Adventures of Lindamira* (1702) is perhaps the first real epistolary novel in English, and though possibly not altogether Brown's work,[22] is a work creditable to his eager pioneering spirit.

Most of the writers here surveyed tended to cultivate wit, ease, and plain- *Prose Style* ness—ideals that may suit a leisurely or a workaday world. The styles used range from the poised and measured elegance of Sir William Temple to the pert and nasty pungency of Ward and Brown. Among the scientists the ideals of exactness and functional plainness were cultivated with a persuasiveness that influenced literary circles also; but exactness outside of scientific circles was less sought than an elegant and conversational ease. The style of Dryden's *Essay of Dramatic Poesie* illustrates this ease at its best. In this dialogue gentlemen and noblemen converse on dignified topics; in the dialogues and letters of Brown we may still be listening to gentlemen, but we hear them only in their tavern hours talking about tavern subjects. In the sermons of Archbishop Tillotson (whose style many, following Dryden's lead, strangely overpraised) and in the work of the philosopher Locke ideals of plainness were coupled with distinguished ability to marshal materials in orderly and effective fashion. By practically all of these writers the richness of imagery and the stately, somewhat cumbrous sentence structure of the early century had been discarded. They achieved familiarity and naturalness, but tended to lose individuality and subtlety. At worst their ease is that of negligent vulgarity; commonly it is that of casual and amiable informality. They lack finish and elegance in their commonplace "middle" style, to which presently Joseph Addison will add distinction by means of polish.

[22] The title-page reads: *The Adventures of Lindamira, a Lady of Quality. Written with her own Hand to her Friend in the Country; in Four Parts. Revised and Corrected by T. Brown.* These words have led careful students to doubt Brown's entire authorship, but a natural interpretation would be that the statements represent a typical attempt to authenticate the letters for an age that loved only "true stories." Internal evidence may cast doubt on Brown's authorship; but if one recalls that years later Richardson pretended in print to be only "the publisher" of Clarissa's letters, and that officially Rousseau was "editeur" of his *Nouvelle Héloïse*, the evidence of Brown's title-page against his authorship is weak.

BOOK III

The Restoration and Eighteenth Century (1660-1789)

✧

PART II

Classicism and Journalism

Guide to reference marks

Throughout the text of this book, a point . ● set beside a page number indicates that references to new critical material will be found under an identical paragraph/page number (set in **boldface**) in the BIBLIOGRAPHICAL SUPPLEMENT.

In the Index, a number preceded by an **S** indicates a paragraph/page number in the BIBLIOGRAPHICAL SUPPLEMENT.

I

Eighteenth-Century Quality

Few centuries have with more facility been reduced to a formula than the Labels for the Century eighteenth;[1] and yet it has been questioned whether the century began "spiritually" with the days of John Locke and the glorious revolution of 1688 or whether it began with the accession of Queen Anne in 1702: it may also be questioned whether the century properly ended with the dawn of the French Revolution in 1789 or with the publication of the *Lyrical Ballads* in 1798. One can seldom date with exactitude the important turnings of history; but certainly to divide the Restoration period competely from the eighteenth century by stressing the numerical accident of 1700 is quite without logic. Few centuries, to be sure, have demonstrated more unity of

[1] In addition to the works cited in ch. 1 on the Restoration period, many of which are valuable also for later periods, the following titles are more specifically applicable to the first half of the eighteenth century. — For general or somewhat specialized histories of the literature of the time see Thomas S. Perry, *English Literature in the Eighteenth Century* (1883); Sir Edmund Gosse, *A History of Eighteenth Century Literature* (1889); Austin Dobson, *Eighteenth Century Vignettes* (Three Series, 1892-96: Dobson also published other volumes of delightful and valuable essays); John Dennis, *The Age of Pope* (1894); William Minto, *The Literature of the Georgian Era* (Edinburgh, 1894); Oliver Elton, *The Augustan Ages* (Edinburgh, 1899); David H. Stevens, *Party Politics and English Journalism, 1702-42* (Chicago, 1916); Oliver Elton, *A Survey of English Literature 1730-1780* (2v, 1928); Ray W. Frantz, *The English Traveller and the Movement of Ideas, 1660-1732* (Lincoln, Neb., 1934); F. C. Green, *Minuet: A Critical Survey of French and English Literary Ideas in the Eighteenth Century* (1935); Hoxie N. Fairchild, *Religious Trends in English Poetry, 1700-1780* (2v, 1939-42); Marjorie Plant, *The English Book Trade* (1939); Francis Gallaway, *Rule, Reason, and Revolt in English Classicism* (1940). — For political history see William E. H. Lecky, *A History of England in the Eighteenth Century* (8v, 1878-90; 7v, 1916-17); I. S. Leadam, *The History of England from the Accession of Anne to the Death of George II (1702-60)* (1909, 1921); *The Cambridge Modern History* (Vol. vi, by various authors, Cambridge, 1909); Charles Bechdolt Realey, *The Early Opposition to Sir Robert Walpole, 1720-27* (Lawrence, Kan., 1931); Keith G. Feiling, *A History of the Tory Party, 1640-1714* (Oxford, 1924); Keith G. Feiling, *The Second Tory Party (1714-1832)* (1938); George M. Trevelyan, *England under Queen Anne* (3v, 1930-34); Laurence Hanson, *Government and the Press, 1695-1763* (Oxford, 1936); William T. Laprade, *Public Opinion and Politics in Eighteenth Century England to the Fall of Walpole* (1936); Winston Spencer Churchill, *Marlborough, his Life and Times* (4v, 1933-38); Basil Williams, *The Whig Supremacy, 1714-1760* (Oxford, 1939); Basil Williams, *Carteret and Newcastle* (Cambridge, 1943); and William T. Morgan, *A Bibliography of British History, 1700-1715* (5v, Bloomington, Ind., 1935-42). — For ecclesiastical history see Charles J. Abbey, *The English Church and its Bishops, 1700-1800* (2v, 1887); John H. Overton and Frederic Relton, *The English Church, 1714-1800* (1906); N. Sykes, *Church and State in England in the Eighteenth Century* (1930). — For the intellectual background of the period see Sir Leslie Stephen, *History of English Thought in the Eighteenth Century* (2v, 1876); Carson S. Duncan, *The New Science and English Literature in the Classical Period* (Menasha, Wis., 1913); Fossey J. C. Hearnshaw (ed.), *The Social and Political Ideas of Some English Thinkers of the Augustan Age* (by various authors, 1928); Arthur O. Lovejoy, "The Parallel of Deism and Classicism," *MP*, xxix (1932). 281-299; Preserved Smith, *A History of Modern Culture*, Vol. ii (1934); Arthur O. Lovejoy, *The Great Chain of Being* (Cambridge, Mass., 1936); Richard F. Jones, *Ancients and Moderns: A Study of the Background of the Battle of the Books* (St. Louis, 1936); Basil Willey, *The Eighteenth Century Background* (1940). — For social life see Thomas Wright, *England under the House of Hanover* (2v, 1848); Thomas Wright, *Carica-*

character than, superficially considered, the eighteenth seems to have possessed. To the facile-minded it is composed merely of neo-classicism and a romantic revolt against that constricting tradition. The more careful historian, forgetting verbal labels, sees in it a unique fusion of ingenuity with traditionalism, of decorum with realism, of Stoic coolness with sentimental effusion, of simplicity with rococo ornamentation, and of aristocratic pomp with the manner of a "free" and hireling press. It preserves the Restoration love of rational simplification in life, thought, and art; it endorses the Restoration confidence in common sense as contrasted with logic-chopping; it trusts empirical thinking rather than the "high priori" road to metaphysical truth; and it sustains Restoration skepticism so far as the application of finite reason to problems of the infinite is concerned. The ideals of the later seventeenth century continue into the eighteenth.

Benevolism: 1. Collier   To anyone obsessed with the notion that all Restoration gentlemen were rakes at heart and libertines in conduct this last statement may be surprising; for the gentlemen of the early eighteenth century (Isaac Bickerstaff, for example, in his *Tatler*) looked upon their Restoration predecessors with self-respecting horror. Yet the Dorimants and Mirabels of comedy were less typical of their time than were the noble Clarendon, the industrious and life-loving Pepys, or the public-spirited Evelyn. Not all courtiers were rakes, nor did all the Puritans drop dead upon the coronation of Charles II. During the seventeenth century, as we have seen, there was a shift from the epic and Roman conception of "heroic virtue" as indispensable to the true gentleman, from ideals of composure, of *nil admirari,* and of Stoic restraint, to the ideal of the gentleman as a benevolent and Christian citizen of the world.[2] By 1700, certainly, the favored concept of the gentleman made him

---

ture History of the Georges [1868]; John Ashton, *Social Life in the Reign of Queen Anne* (2v, 1882; 1925); Henry B. Wheatley, *London Past and Present* (3v, 1891); H. D. Traill and J. S. Mann, *Social England* (6v, 1894-7; esp. Vol. IV [1663-1714] and Vol. V [1714-1815]); Sir Walter Besant, *London in the Eighteenth Century* (1903); William E. Mead, *The Grand Tour in the Eighteenth Century* (Boston, 1914); Myra Reynolds, *The Learned Lady in England, 1650-1760* (Boston, 1920); Edwin Beresford Chancellor, *The Eighteenth Century in London* (1920); Mary Dorothy George, *English Social Life in the Eighteenth Century* (1923) and *London Life in the XVIIIth Century* (1926); Dorothy Marshall, *The English Poor in the Eighteenth Century* (1926); A. S. Turberville, *English Men and Manners in the Eighteenth Century* (Oxford, 1926); R. B. Mowat, *England in the Eighteenth Century* (1932); Robert J. Allen, *Clubs of Augustan London* (Cambridge, Mass., 1933); John E. Mason, *Gentlefolk in the Making: Studies in the History of English Courtesy Literature from 1531 to 1774* (Philadelphia, 1934); Rosamond Bayne-Powell *English Country Life in the Eighteenth Century* (1935); Rosamond Bayne-Powell, *Eighteenth-Century London Life* (1937). — On the fine arts in this period see Sir Reginald Blomfield, *The Formal Garden in England* (1892); Sir Reginald Blomfield, *A History of Renaissance Architecture in England, 1500-1800* (2v, 1897); C. H. Collins Baker, *Lely and the Stuart Portrait Painters* (2v, 1913); Col. Maurice S. Grant, *Old Landscape Painters, Sixteenth to Nineteenth Centuries* (2v, 1925); William T. Whitley, *Artists and their Friends in England, 1700-1799* (2v, 1928); Albert R. Powys, *The English House* (1929); C. H. Collins Baker and Montague R. James, *British Painting* (1933); C. Reginald Grundy, *English Art in the Eighteenth Century* (1928); Beverley Sprague Allen, *Tides in English Taste, 1619-1800* (2v, Cambridge, Mass., 1937); Robert J. Allen, *Life in Eighteenth Century England* (Illustrative Set Number Four, The Boston Museum of Fine Arts, Boston, Mass., 1941).

[2] See the admirable studies of W. L. Ustick, "Changing Ideals of Aristocratic Character and Conduct in Seventeenth-Century England," *MP*, XXX (1932). 147-166; R. S. Crane, "Suggestions toward a Genealogy of the 'Man of Feeling,'" *ELH*, I (1934). 205-230; and W. E.

disinterestedly compassionate and moral, and useful rather than merely ornamental. In 1694 Jeremy Collier in a dialogue (*Of General Kindness*) between a benevolist and a disciple of Hobbes argues comprehensively in favor of "universal benevolence." He says:

My first Argument then shall be drawn from Community of Nature. We are all cast in the same *Mould,* allied in our Passions, and in our Faculties: We have the same Desires to satisfy, and generally the same Pleasure in satisfying of them. All Mankind is as it were one great *Being,* divided into several Parts; every Part having the same Properties and Affections with another. Now as we can't chuse but desire Accommodations for our own Support and Pleasure; so if we leave Nature to her Original Bias, if we hearken to the undepraved Suggestions of our Minds, we shall wish the same Conveniences to others.[3]

Along with Collier we find curiously different proponents of benevolism or "good nature." Among these the most influential was the third Earl of Shaftesbury[4] whose *Characteristicks* (1711) was widely read, much approved, and much attacked. Like the theodicies of his day Shaftesbury's work expounded the perfection of the universe, and particularly the naturalness of virtue in man. He believed it

2. Shaftesbury

impossible to conceive that a rational creature coming first to be tried by rational objects, and receiving into his mind the images or representations of justice, generosity, gratitude, or other virtue, should have no liking of these or dislike of their contraries. . . . Sense of right and wrong therefore being as natural to us as natural affection itself, and being a first principle in our constitution and make, there is no speculative opinion, persuasion, or belief, which is capable immediately or directly to exclude or destroy it.

His lordship thus concluded man to be endowed with a "Moral Sentiment" that instinctively instructed one in matters of right and wrong. The development of this faint non-rational monitor is the chief duty of man; and to this elegant peer perfect virtue is the result of an acquired perfect taste in morals. The relaxed and discursive suavity of Shaftesbury's style won

---

Houghton, "The English Virtuoso in the Seventeenth Century," *JHI*, III (1942). 51-73; 190-219.

[3] *Essays upon Several Moral Subjects* (5ed., 1703), pp. 151-152. It is worth noting that here universal benevolence (sometimes regarded as a "romantic" notion) is based on the idea of the uniformity of mankind, commonly thought a "classical" concept. The classical-romantic dichotomy here, as frequently, is not merely useless but confusing.

[4] Anthony Ashley Cooper (1671-1713), third Earl of Shaftesbury, was the grandson of the first Earl, Dryden's Achitophel. The third Earl's education was supervised by his grandfather's protégé, John Locke, whose philosophy the third Earl disliked. He studied at Winchester and traveled on the Continent. For three years (1695-8) he sat in the House of Commons, and succeeded to the title in 1699. Bad health compelled him to withdraw from public life, and ultimately (1711) to retire to Italy. He died at Naples in 1713. — *Characteristicks of Men, Manners, Opinions, Times* (3v, 1711); ed. John M. Robertson (2v, 1900); *Life, Unpublished Letters, and Philosophical Regimen,* ed. Benj. Rand (1900); *Second Characters,* ed. Benj. Rand (Cambridge, 1914). — Thomas Fowler, *Shaftesbury* (1881); Cecil A. Moore, "Shaftesbury and the Ethical Poets in England, 1700-1760," *PMLA,* XXXI (1916). 264-325; W. E. Alderman, "Shaftesbury and the Doctrine of Moral Sense in the Eighteenth Century," *PMLA,* XLVI (1931). 1087-1094; and "Shaftesbury and the Doctrine of Optimism," *Trans. Wisconsin Acad.,* XXVIII (1933). 297-305.

him friends and annoyed his enemies. In attacking the idealism of his lordship, Bernard Mandeville used in his *Fable of the Bees* (1714) a blunt, pungent, and earthy idiom.

3. Steele   Shaftesbury as a deist preached the natural beauty of virtue and benevolence. Richard Steele in his first work, *The Christian Hero* (1701), showed the superiority of Christian benevolence over Stoic arrogance of virtue. He formulates an answer to his own inquiry, "Why is it that the Heathen struts, and the Christian sneaks in our Imagination?" His conclusion, announced in his subtitle, is "No principles but those of religion [are] sufficient to make a Great Man." "Thus," he remarks, "are we fram'd for mutual Kindness, good Will and Service, and therefore our Blessed Saviour has been pleased to give us ... the Command of Loving one another." He thinks "the two great Springs of Human Actions are Fame and Conscience" (self-approbation?), and observes that Christianity, unlike Stoicism, does not require "an utter Extirpation, but the Direction only of our Passions." Under the Christian dispensation the passions are serviceable: love of fame stimulates us to great actions and conscience directs our acts to be useful to God and Man—all with the hope (and hope is a passion) of ultimate reward in heaven. Many another dogmatist in benevolence might be cited; but clearly Collier the non-juror, Shaftesbury the deist, and Steele the latitudinarian Captain of the Tower Guard approach the problem differently, yet all with strong emphasis on the emotional rather than the rational aspects of consciousness.

Practical   These are not matters merely speculative in the early days of the century.
Benevolence Both piety and morality were encouraged through practical, organized effort. Two important religious organizations, the Society for the Propagation of Christian Knowledge, founded in 1699, and the Society for the Propagation of the Gospel in Foreign Parts were in a flourishing state; equally significant at the time was the Society for the Reformation of Manners, founded shortly after the revolution of 1688 and patronized by Archbishop Tenison and other important clergymen as well as by the King and Queen. The reformation of manners in these hands was clearly on a neo-puritan basis, and the Society specialized, through a complex and far-flung organization, in punishing those guilty of lewdness, swearing, and profanation of the Lord's Day. It published pamphlets and books calculated to promote piety, and was behind attempts to purify the theatre as well as literature itself. One suspects, however, that whereas the sublime trait of benevolence was most commonly predicated of the upper classes, the need of reforming manners was viewed in relation to the lower ranks.[5]

If feeling, benevolism, or sentiment is so operative in the thought and good works of this era, what becomes of the notion that it was essentially

---

[5] See *An Account of the Societies for the Reformation of Manners* (1699); White Kennett, *A Complete History of England*, III (1706). 642-645; and John Strype, *Stowe's Survey of London* (1720), Book V, ch. III. A most important aspect of the social history of the century is the frequent founding of benevolent, charitable societies or institutions. See the careers of Thomas Coram, General James E. Oglethorpe, Henry Fielding, Sir John Fielding, Jonas Hanway, John Howard—and many others.

an Age of Reason? Man still, it must be avowed, finds himself described *Reason and*
as *animal rationale:* it is still reason that differentiates him from the brutes.[6] *Common*
Reason, furthermore, is uniform in all men who are uncorrupted by bad *Sense*
education, false religion, or faulty social institutions; for "we are all cast
in the same mould." Uniformity encourages individualism in that, being
the rational equal of his fellowmen, the individual may trust his own powers
—the light of reason should shine undiffracted within him. On the other
hand, in case of doubt, there is appeal to the common sense *(consensus
gentium)* of all men similarly endowed; one's ideas to be sound must accord
with such common sense. To prefer one's "private" sense to common sense
is irrational enthusiasm. To think in universal rather than parochial terms
is an obvious duty; hence our rationalist may be a citizen of the world, a
cosmopolitan. To prefer the Golden Age, untarnished by rational complexity
or errors, over the corrupted present is also obvious good sense; hence the
illuminated rationalist is frequently a primitivist, or at least regards the
history of man since the patriarchal ages as a tragic record of rational defeat.
Pierre Bayle in his *Dictionary* enjoyed repeating a sixteenth-century remark
to the effect that the title of Orosius's history, *De miseria humana,* "was a
very proper title, which well becomes history in general."

To these dogmas concerning reason, and to such corollaries as deism and
neo-classicism, the uniformity of Nature led men. But the rationalism of
the century has an inductive, a scientific and even journalistic, aspect that
demands attention. In the period when Spinoza was exemplifying beautiful syllogistic argument, a great distrust of logic had developed. Divine
truth, men said, should of its nature be clear and should need no intricate
exegesis. This attitude is seen in one of the more extreme panegyrics to
reason in the period, the fourth voyage of *Gulliver's Travels.* Here the
Houyhnhnms represent "perfection of nature" (i.e., of reason), and, we
are told,

their grand Maxim is, to cultivate *Reason,* and to be wholly governed by it.
Neither is *Reason* among them a Point problematical as with us, where Men
can argue with Plausibility on both Sides of a Question; but strikes you with
immediate Conviction; as it needs must do where it is not mingled, obscured, or
discoloured by Passion and Interest.

Obviously it is only a step from such a conception of reason to something
very like common sense. Swift, though he praises reason, prefers common
sense to intricate reasonings, and like the benevolists really exalts the non-
reasoning aspects of the mind over logic. Ingenious and novel *imaginings*
the author of *Gulliver,* like many others of his day, would be loath to decry;
in his suspicion of ingenious and novel *reasonings* or opinions he is typical
of his time.

The fact is that Reason, Nature, Truth, are ultimate norms not easily *"Nature"*
capable of definition, especially if one begins and ends with the dogma of *as Norm*

---

[6] The rationalism of the time has been well analyzed and related to literary tradition by
A. O. Lovejoy, "The Parallel of Deism and Classicism," *MP,* XXIX (1932). 281-299.

uniformity. A disputatious, and hence ungenteel, love of logic had little affinity with these undefined ultimates. Men agreed with Aristotle that art was to imitate Nature; and obviously such imitation was not to be photographic or realistic, but was to attend to essential meanings or principles. When the young Cicero applied to the Delphic Oracle for counsel in his ambition to become a great orator, he heard the portentous injunction: "Follow Nature!" These two words were doubtless the categorical imperative of the neo-classical period. "Nature" was the complex system or set of principles divinely ordained and manifested in the Creation. To this system man should conform; of this system the moralist and the poet were the interpreters; by this system the critical intelligence could evaluate either life or letters. So Pope enthusiastically voiced the view of his day when he affirmed that

> Unerring nature, still divinely bright,
> One clear, unchanged, and universal light,
> Life, force, and beauty, must to all impart,
> At once the source, and end, and test of art.

George Berkeley

To such views led the widely diffused principles of uniformity and universality, the sense of allegiance to the whole system. Such untechnical thinking on the part of literary men was balanced by more elaborate works of technical philosophers. John Locke had stimulated "practical" ideas about government and society, but he had also promoted speculations in the field of the theory of knowledge—as to *how* we know and *what* we know. This type of theorizing was continued by the greatest thinker of the first third of the century, George Berkeley [7] (1685-1753), who in his *Treatise concerning the Principles of Human Knowledge* (1710) expounded a theory of immaterialism based on the proposition *esse est percipi*: to be is to be perceived. Material objects do not exist except in our minds, or if they do we can know them only in our minds. Such limitation of our knowledge, which Berkeley defended adroitly in his *Three Dialogues between Hylas and Philonous* (1713), inadvertently opened the way to David Hume's cogent skepticism. In 1713 and later Berkeley, who was a man of great personal charm and who commanded an English style few philosophers, if any, have surpassed, was on friendly terms with the leading literary men of London. Swift introduced him everywhere; he was Pope's friend; he wrote several essays for Steele's *Guardian,* and achieved a just and considerable reputation as a writer. In 1728 he went to America with the project of founding a college for the education of both the Indians and the colonists. The project was not realized, but while living at Newport, Rhode Island, he wrote his popular dialogues, *Alciphron: or, The Minute Philosopher*

[7] Berkeley's *Works* have been edited by Alexander C. Fraser (4v, Oxford, 1871; rev., 1901) and by George Sampson (3v, 1897-8). — Joseph M. Hone and Mario M. Rossi, *Bishop Berkeley: His Life, Writings and Philosophy* (1931); John Wild, *George Berkeley: A Study of his Life and Philosophy* (Cambridge, Mass., 1936); T. E. Jessop, *A Bibliography of George Berkeley* (Oxford, 1934).

(1732). In America he also acquired a great faith in the medicinal uses of tar-water, which became for him almost a panacea. Historically, Berkeley is known for his doctrines of philosophical immaterialism: in his own day he was most favorably known for his *Alciphron* and for his *Siris: A Chain of Philosophical Reflections and Inquiries concerning the Virtues of Tar-Water* (1744). Men of his day could be both extremely theoretical and extremely practical in their thinking.

Although he was a good servant of his Church, and rose to be a bishop, *Bishop* Berkeley's writings were less ecclesiastical or ·spiritual than the writings of *Butler and* two other men. The first was Bishop Joseph Butler (1692-1752). No man *William* of the moment was comparable to Berkeley in speculative skill, but Butler *Law* acquired permanent fame as author of one of the most impressive attempts in English to construct a rationalist demonstration of the existence of the deity.[8] This attempt, his masterly *Analogy of Religion, Natural and Revealed, to the Constitution and Course of Nature* (1736), undermined most of the argumentative positions taken by the deists of the period and either terminated the controversies they had for a generation maintained or at least caused a considerable shift of ground. Faith less dependent than Butler's on man's philosophizings was alive at this time, but not common. Its great exemplar was William Law (1686-1761), who in his *Serious Call to a Devout and Holy Life* (1728) produced a work of permanent and compelling power, expressive of fervent spirituality and consecration in the highest degree.[9] In the early thirties John and Charles Wesley were briefly Law's disciples, and later at King's Cliffe, Northamptonshire, his home, the aunt of the historian Gibbon and a wealthy friend of hers were devoted followers of his systematic spirituality. In London he had been sought after by John Byrom (1692-1763), eccentric poet and religious writer. Law had no large following.

Unlike Butler, Law engaged in controversies: he took part in the Bangor- *The Criti-* ian controversy (1717) by attacking Bishop Hoadly; he answered Mande- *cism of* ville's *Fable of the Bees,* and his opinion of the theatre of the time was *Experience:* more condemnatory than that of his fellow non-juror, Jeremy Collier. Law *Reform and* was a mystic, but he was also a practical reformer—and many men in his *Satire* day assumed this latter rôle. The empirical method led men to accumulate, abstract, and generalize the experience of the day; and this led them to be critical of experience, for their task was to relate the truth of the moment to the whole system of things, to evaluate the detail as a part of "unerring

---

[8] Apart from the *Analogy* Butler's reputation rests upon his *Fifteen Sermons Preached at the Chapel of the Rolls Court* (1726). Butler's *Works* are edited by John H. Bernard (2v, 1900). The *Analogy* has been often edited and is available in the Everyman's Library (ed. Ronald Bayne) and in the Oxford World's Classics (ed. William E. Gladstone). See Frederick D. Maurice, *The Conscience* (1872); W. M. Egglestone, *Stanhope Memorials of Bishop Butler* (1878); Ernest C. Mossner, *Bishop Butler and the Age of Reason* (1936); William J. Norton, *Bishop Butler, Moralist and Divine* (New Brunswick, N. J., 1940).

[9] Law's *Works* (9v, 1753-76); ed. G. B. Morgan (Brockenhurst, 1892-3, privately printed); *A Serious Call* is edited by John H. Overton (1898) and C. Bigg (1899). — John H. Overton, *William Law, Nonjuror and Mystic* (1881); G. Moreton, *Memorials of the Birthplace and Residence of Law at King's Cliffe* (Guildford, 1895).

Nature." Otherwise "the truth of today" remained unstable and perhaps trivial. Increasingly, through distrust of present achievement, the century looked before and after, and became either primitivist or perfectionist. The critical attitude towards the diversity of present experience borrowed warrant from the classical traditions of satire, chiefly from Horace, but also from Juvenal, Martial, and Persius, and gave the early eighteenth century its most typical literature, a literature that castigated the follies of fashionable life (particularly feminine foibles), the corruptions of political and commercial affairs, the vulgar taste of the numerous *nouveaux riches,* and even the petty jealousies of literary men towards rivals.

Peace and Controversy   The age has been praised for its love of peace, and, considering the fact that between the accession of William and Mary (1688) and the Peace of Utrecht (1713) England had been at war for all but four of twenty-five years, one can understand a frequent outcry for peace. But it is mere Whiggery to assume that the Revolution of 1688 had solved all problems in church and state, and had secured peace—whether political or spiritual. The Church was beset by lassitude within and by Catholics, sectaries, and deists from without. One has only to recall the lot of non-jurors, or to compare the fictitious Big-Endians and Little-Endians in *Gulliver* with the actual if grotesque indecorums of the Bangorian controversy, to see that the Church was hardly at peace. In politics things were no better. "One half the Nation," Voltaire remarked, "is always at Variance with the other half. I have met People who assur'd me that the Duke of *Marlborough* was a Coward, and that Mr. *Pope* was a Fool." [10] Even the succession to the throne was threatened at least slightly by the death of Queen Anne (1714), by the Atterbury plot of 1723, and by the Jacobite invasion of 1745. The burdensome national debt resulting from the long wars drove England to lotteries and to experimentation in stock companies, many of which were formed at this time, frequently on the pattern of the long-established East India Company. Of these imitations the South Sea Company was the most notable. Incorporated in 1711, and possibly a project from the mind of the ingenious Daniel Defoe, this company was accorded an extensive trade monopoly in return for taking over a sizable part of the national debt. The Company at times rivaled in influence even the Bank of England (incorporated in 1694); but the highly inflated value of its stock caused in 1720 England's first great panic in the stock market. Of the immediate effects of this panic, Dr. Arbuthnot wittily remarked that "the Government and South Sea Company have only locked up the money of the people upon conviction of their lunacy, as is usual in the case of lunatics, and intend to restore them as much as is fit for such people, as they see them return more and more to their senses." Of the long-term chastening effects of the bursting of this bubble there is much evidence, which includes even a revulsion from the mercantilist worship of Commerce to the physiocratic idea that wealth comes basically from the soil.

[10] In his *Letters concerning the English Nation* (1733) as translated by John Lockman (ed. Charles Whibley, 1926), p. 162.

If a widespread preoccupation with one's chances in lotteries and in the *Utilitarian* stocks did not make for peaceful relaxation, it may perhaps account in part *Values in* for the insistence on utilitarian values. Literature, with its unparalleled *the Arts* development of journalism and with its preoccupation with daily life and how best to lead it, had obviously "useful" ideals to accord with its Roman traditions. In the other fine arts a similar attention to pragmatic needs was apparent. Although Sir Christopher Wren's masterpiece was St. Paul's Cathedral (built 1675-1710), the great achievement in the architecture of his day was not in public buildings but in the transformation of domestic architecture from the frequently gloomy Tudor Gothic to the lighter, more spacious and definitely more comfortable "Queen Anne" mansion of Italian origin. Under the patronage of Pope's friend the third Earl of Burlington (1695-1753) various architects developed a style for small houses that was severely neo-Palladian and chastely elegant: they saved England, largely, from the excesses of the Continental rococo.[11] Such residences demanded landscaping, and the shift from the rigidly formal gardens, produced by Dutch designers brought over by William III, to a more "natural" and "picturesque" system was early urged by Addison and Pope, as well as by Pope's influential professional friends Charles Bridgman and William Kent, and by "Capability" Brown. Proper settings for stately homes were effectively devised by such men. Interiors in some sense were improved—at least lightened—by the substitution of paint or of the increasingly fashionable and artistic wallpapers for dark oak paneling or tapestry hangings. Domestic furniture of the day was assuming new patterns of elegance and delicacy as oak gave way to the mahogany of Central America; the great designers, however—Chippendale, Hepplewhite, Sheraton, and the Adam brothers— belong to the middle and later part of the century. New paintings for the walls were of less distinction than they had been in the days of Van Dyck, since the visiting Continental artists were less eminent. Sir Godfrey Kneller was perhaps the best of these. Of native English painters William Hogarth (1697-1764) was easily the greatest. The authentic, journalistic realism of his numerous conversation pieces, designed frankly to correct the manners of the time, was so finely detailed that its lack of elegance proved no barrier to popularity. Since Hogarth began as an engraver, his paintings were commonly popularized by engraving. In general the best work of this kind at this time was done by imported French artists; but the English practitioners of the mezzotint method were producing by the beginning of the century brilliant and delicately shaded portraits. John Smith (1652?- 1742) was perhaps the most eminent early artist in this method, which was to become famous as *la manière anglaise*. Smith's mezzotint (1703) of Lely's portrait of Wycherley is a well-known specimen.

[11] Fiske Kimball, "The Creation of the Rococo," *Jour. Warburg and Courtauld Institutes,* IV (1941). 119-123; "Burlington Architectus," *Jour. Royal Institute of British Architects,* October 15, 1927, pp. 675-693 [cf. George Sherburn, " 'Timon's Villa' and Cannons," *Hunting- ton Library Bull.,* No. 8 (1935). 132n]; "Les influences anglaises dans la formation du style Louis XVI," *Gazette des Beaux-Arts,* V (1931). 29-44; 231-2⁵⁵; and *The Creation of the Rococo* (Philadelphia, 1943).

Opera   In the early century, music, which had long been among the most favored
of English arts, was hardly regarded as a "useful" art; for the time was
torn with arguments concerning the "absurdities" of Italian opera. With
the passing of the great English musical tradition of the sixteenth and
seventeenth centuries, the arrival (1710) of George Frederick Handel [12]
(1685-1759) in London gave impetus to the fashionable amusement of
opera, and for half a century English music was Handel and opera. The
overelaborate scenic effects and the supposed absurdity of dialogue sung
in an unintelligible foreign language caused the *Tatler* and *Spectator,* among
others, to attack opera as completely non-intellectual and hence contemptible.
John Dennis (doubtless intended in *Tatler* No. 4 as the "great critic" who
"fell into fits in the gallery, at feeling, not only time and place, but language
and nations confused in the most incorrigible manner"), like Mme Dacier
in France, regarded opera as coöperating perfectly with evil manners to
corrupt the taste of the time. To many a critic or supporter of the drama,
opera was as sinister in the early eighteenth century as the cinema has
seemed in the twentieth. The English were still great music-lovers, but as
the century advanced their music was with growing frequency produced for
them by imported composers and performers.

Formalism   Italian opera, like the other arts of the period, was marked by extreme
in Art   formalism—even more extreme than in the dramas of the century. Popularity
of arts so rigidly controlled by tradition naturally has led critics to label
the period "artificial." The term, of course, is always equivocal and relative.
Clearly the period frequently regarded technical ingenuity as highly as it did
substance. The very formality of the Roman, Italian, or French traditions
imposed ingenuity as the *sine qua non* of novelty, and novelty is insisted
on by all traditionalist critics. (Dulness, as Pope was to say in so many
ingenious ways, is the worst of aesthetic crimes.) Artificiality and frivolity
can easily be asserted of a century, the arts of which were dominated by
a regard almost exclusively directed to the upper classes and to luxurious
amusement. But one must remember that behind this superficial gaiety
England was in the eighteenth century building a far-flung empire by
means of a reputation for commercial honesty that was world-wide except
in England itself—where one thought every man had his price. It was
an age of crudely robust aspects, in which a Richard Savage, a James Annesley, an Elizabeth Canning could look Defoe's personages—Moll Flanders
or Colonel Jacque—in the eye and remind them that real life is stranger
than fiction. One must remember this fact when faced with the facile
generalizations that stress the peace and nobility of these second-generation
Augustans and neglect the more or less honest rough and tumble of their
daily life. Along with their devotion to the Roman tradition they developed
a sentimental cast of thought and at the same time a libelous journalism
that should not be forgotten.

12 He was born, of course, Georg Friedrich Händel in Halle (Saxony) and received much
of his musical training in Italy.

II

The Critical Temper and Doctrine, 1700-1750

The unpeaceful nature of the early eighteenth century can be seen *The Dis-*
nowhere more clearly than in literary criticism. Much of this sort of writing *repute of*
was not of permanent eminence, but it does illuminate both the mood and *Criticism*
the intellectual quality of the period.[1] The critical function and temperament were freely disparaged on a variety of grounds. One of these was the
quarrel over the relative merits of ancient and modern writers—a quarrel
long current in both France and England. In the preface to his edition
of Sir Charles Sedley's *Miscellaneous Works* (1702) Captain William Ayloffe
bursts out:

Parnassus is in Arms against it self, and the Daughters of *Helicon* as mutinous,
as the execrable Sons of the Earth. The Factious Ensigns are every where display'd, and the Various Wits rank'd in formidable Batallions. If a Man sets up
for a Poet he is immediately attacqu'd by a Satyrical Party; Destruction is the
Word; and, as for Quarter, they give none; these are the blood-thirsty Hussars
of *Parnassus,* cut out for the ruine of others, tho' rarely with any great Honour to
themselves.

Politics also muddied the springs of criticism. In 1705 Ned Ward in his
Hudibras Redivivus, No. 1, gave writers advice from the gutter:

> For he that writes in such an Age,
> When Parties do for Pow'r engage,
> Ought to chuse one Side for the Right,
> And then, with all his Wit and Spite,
> Blacken and vex the Opposite.

[1] Important further aid in the study of the criticism of this period will be found in the
following: P. Hamelius, *Die Kritik in der englischen Literatur des 17. und 18. Jahrhunderts*
(Leipzig, 1897); George Saintsbury, *A History of Criticism and Literary Taste in Europe* (3v,
Edinburgh, 1900-4); Louis Charlanne, *L'Influence française en Angleterre au XVIIᵉ siècle*
(Paris, 1906); G. M. Miller, *The Historical Point of View in English Literary Criticism from 1570-*
1770 (Heidelberg, 1913); *Critical Essays of the Eighteenth Century 1700-1725,* ed. Willard H.
Durham, [introduction] (New Haven, 1915); Caroline M. Goad, *Horace in the English Litera-*
ture of the Eighteenth Century (New Haven, 1918); John W. Draper, "Aristotelian Mimesis in
Eighteenth-Century England," *PMLA,* xxxvi (1921). 372-400; Raymond D. Havens, *The In-*
fluence of Milton on English Poetry (Cambridge, Mass., 1922); A. F. B. Clark, *Boileau and*
the French Classical Critics in England, 1660-1830 (Paris, 1925); Marvin T. Herrick, *The*
Poetics of Aristotle in England (New Haven, 1930); John W. Draper, *Eighteenth Century*
English Aesthetics: A Bibliography (Heidelberg, 1931); Samuel H. Monk, *The Sublime: A*
Study of Critical Theories in XVIII-Century England. (1935); Beverley S. Allen, *Tides in*
English Taste, 1619-1800 (Cambridge, Mass., 1937); Ronald S. Crane, "Neo-classical Criticism,"
in *Dictionary of World Literature,* ed. Joseph T. Shipley (1943), pp. 193-203.

> Scurrility's a useful Trick,
> Approv'd by the most Politic;
> Fling Dirt enough, and some will Stick.

As for the manners and morals of criticism—on that subject Jonathan Swift was superlatively opprobrious. In his *Battle of the Books* he describes Criticism as

a malignant Deity ... extended in her Den, upon the Spoils of numberless Volumes half devoured. At her right Hand sat *Ignorance,* her Father and Husband, blind with Age; at her left, *Pride* her Mother, dressing her up in the Scraps of Paper herself had torn. There, was *Opinion* her Sister, light of Foot, hoodwinkt, and headstrong, yet giddy and perpetually turning. About her play'd her Children, *Noise* and *Impudence, Dullness* and *Vanity, Positiveness, Pedantry,* and *Ill-Manners.* The Goddess herself had Claws like a Cat: Her Head, and Ears, and Voice, resembled those of an *Ass.* ...

In his "Digression concerning Criticks" in *A Tale of a Tub* Swift is equally caustic, and more personal:

Every *True Critick* is a Hero born, descending in a direct Line from a Celestial Stem, by *Momus* and *Hybris,* who begat *Zoilus,* who begat *Tigellius,* who begat *Etcætera* the Elder, who begat *B—tly,* and *Rym—r,* and *W—tton,* and *Perrault,* and *Dennis,* who begat *Etcætera* the Younger.

Abuse of the critical function was often blamed on antiquarian specialization such as that of Bentley, Rymer, Tom Hearne, and Lewis Theobald. Verbal criticism, as textual emendation was called, was abused as pedantry. Even before Swift wrote, Dennis, for example, had a reputation as an ill-natured critic. He at one extreme was frequently castigated for subservience to rules, and at the other extreme blows fell upon sprightly authors who defended irregularities by remarking pertly, "Shakespear writ without rules."

John Dennis

Most notable among the so-called "rules" critics of the period was doubtless John Dennis,[2] who, like Dryden, struggled intermittently to reconcile divergent critical traditions, and who, like Rymer, ultimately tended to rely on rules and common sense. Dennis began in the last decade of the seventeenth century as a poet, dramatist, pamphleteer, and critic. In the last capacity

[2] John Dennis (1657-1734), born in London, educated at Harrow and Cambridge (M.A., 1683) made the grand tour in 1688, and upon his return became a frequenter of Will's and other London coffee-houses and a valued, if at times eccentric, member of the literary circle whose center was John Dryden. "Before 1706," Mr. Hooker tells us, "he had produced six plays, seven critical treatises, four long poems, at least three political treatises, a collection of letters together with a translation of Voiture, a translation of part of Tacitus, and various shorter items of a miscellaneous nature." His later years were marred by poverty, ill health, and controversy; but his pen kept busy. Apart from his unfortunate attacks on Pope and other literary men his later works dealt with attacks on Tories, with the theatre, or with religion. His publication of *Letters upon Several Occasions* (1696) and *Original Letters, Familiar, Moral and Critical* (2v, 1721) marks a departure that Pope and many another literary man were to follow. His plays and poems are at this distance negligible. His *Critical Works* have been admirably edited by Edward N. Hooker (2v, Baltimore, 1939-43) with a long introduction in Vol. II; and his life is well treated by H. G. Paul, *John Dennis* (1911). See also Fred Tupper, "Notes on the Life of John Dennis," *ELH,* v (1938). 211-217; and Hoxie N. Fairchild, *Religious Trends in English Poetry,* I (1939). 183-189, *et passim.*

he achieved a considerable reputation. His critical writing appeared in about a dozen longer pieces as well as in shorter prefaces, dedications, and letters. His views derived, on the one hand, from the traditions of Aristotle, Horace, Boileau, Bossu (whose treatise on the epic was standard), Rapin (who was the favorite commentator on Aristotle), St. Évremond, and Dryden. On the other hand, he owed much to his strong admiration for Shakespeare and Longinus and to his worship of John Milton. He is the first admirer of Milton to put himself extensively in print. Dennis thus combines a rationalist tradition with an unbounded love of sublimity and enthusiastic passion. He was ridiculed often for his love of such words as "furious" and "tremendous."

Like Dryden his difficulty in reconciling his diversities was augmented *Dennis on* by accidental circumstance. Himself an unsuccessful playwright, he believed *the Drama* wholeheartedly in the stage as an instrument in reforming manners, and defended the theatre as an institution even though vehement in condemning its increasing decadence in his time. He replied to Collier's attack caustically in his *Usefulness of the Stage* (1698) and again in *The Person of Quality's Answer to Mr. Collier's . . . Disswasive from the Play-house* (1704). He replied to William Law's *Absolute Unlawfulness of the Stage-Entertainment* (1726) in his *Stage Defended* (1726). In *An Essay on the Operas* he had in 1706 attacked Italian opera, which he regarded as both aesthetically and morally corrupting. He ably defended Etherege's *Sir Fopling Flutter* in 1722, and more than once attacked plays and playwrights (notably Richard Steele) of the rising sentimental school.

His more important early critical treatises were his *Impartial Critick His Major* (1693), a reply to Rymer's *Short View of Tragedy; The Advancement and Treatises Reformation of Modern Poetry* (1701), which states his central critical positions, and the similar *Grounds of Criticism in Poetry* (1704). His attack on Rymer, concerned with the attempt to force a chorus on modern tragedy, states a position of relativity with regard to the rules that would have been of great importance if Dennis had firmly adhered to it. He here holds that devices, such as a chorus, "adapted to the Religion and Temper" of the Greeks, may not be at all effective in a nation of different religion, climate, and customs. In general, however, Dennis firmly supports the "ancient" rules as the established guides to good writing, though they must be intelligently used. He praises Milton for rising above the rules in *Paradise Lost,* and blames Addison for slavish and ineffectual following of them in *Cato.* His handling of the last act of Addison's tragedy has much of the prosaic common-sense method that Rymer used on *Othello.* Later in his unpublished attack on Welsted, *The Causes of the Decay and Defects of Dramatick Poetry,* he depends on the rules unquestioningly, and in his *Essay on the Genius and Writings of Shakespear* (1712) he regrets that Shakespeare, "one of the greatest Genius's that the World e'er saw for the Tragick Stage," could not have "join'd to so happy a Genius Learning and the Poetical Art." Poetical Art means the rules! It is, however, the general rule of decorum and regularity rather than the more mechanical rules of the unities that Dennis cherishes.

ion and More interesting to post-romantic students is Dennis's theory of the *husiasm* relation of religion and passion to poetry. Historically, Dennis here has great importance in showing that sound neo-classicism held no brief for poetic frigidity. To Dennis, as well as to Milton and other neo-classicists, passion is a chief element in poetry; but no other critic of the time has so explicitly expounded this view. Poetry must please in order to instruct: there is no pleasure without passion; there is no religion without passion. Passions are in Dennis's system of two kinds: ordinary, which arise from known, objective causes, and enthusiastic, which arise from unknown causes, in contemplation. The chief enthusiastic passions are admiration and terror; horror, joy, sadness, and desire are also mentioned. In his love of passionate sublimity he clearly owes much to both Longinus and Milton. Enthusiasm, condemned by Dennis and all other churchmen when it means non-rational religion, is praised as a divinely given element in poetic pleasure. This view, stated by Dennis in his *Advancement and Reformation of Poetry* and in *The Grounds of Criticism in Poetry,* was to be popularized, as we shall see, in Shaftesbury's *Moralists.* Divinely given enthusiasm or passion joins poetry and religion, and Dennis's notion of "advancement and reformation" depends upon his belief that the ancients, where they have excelled the moderns, have relied upon their religion for material; but since the moderns have a true religion, they may, if they will infuse their poetry with divine spirit, as Milton has done, easily surpass the ancients. This sort of reasoning frequently misleads Dennis. Of all the defenders of passion that criticism has produced surely he is the most devoted to categories and to "logic."

His Con- One wonders how far Dennis's precepts conditioned his perceptions. He *ditioned* has a glowing admiration for Milton and a great, if qualified, admiration *Perceptions* for Shakespeare. He is capable of feeling "a delightful Horrour, a terrible Joy" over Alpine scenery that made him lyrical; and he felt strongly impressed by that "incomparable Statue of *Laocoon,* which," he says, "I saw at *Rome,* in the Gardens of *Belvidere,* and which is so astonishing, that it does not appear to be the Work of Art, but the miserable Creature himself, like *Niobe,* benumm'd and petrify'd with Grief and Horror." Perception could move him: precept by contrast frequently made him a victim. His least happy *idée fixe* was the depravity of the taste of his day. The corollary was that if a new piece of writing was popular, it was bad, and duty required him to attack it. So in his later days he attacked many of Pope's works as well as *The Tatler, The Spectator, Cato,* and *The Conscious Lovers.* Criticism, as we have seen, had in general a bad reputation, and as early as 1696 in his *Remarks* on Blackmore's *Prince Arthur,* Dennis found it advisable to protest against the charge of ill nature. After 1705, when he began to "retire from the world," and particularly after 1711, when he became embroiled with Pope and Steele, his fame for ill nature increased. But there was an honest directness and vigor about Dennis's thought and insight into poetic problems that continued to command respect. His rages were obvious and amazing; his calmer thought was commonly of obvious value. The frequent disparagement that he and Pope bestowed on each other in their writings is one of the more disgraceful episodes of the period, but in spite of what they printed it is probable that each respected the other's abilities. In fact, Pope advertised in 1730 that he would take any victim out of his *Dunciad* if the man would present a certificate of his being a wit or a poet "from any *three of his companions* in the Dunciad, or from Mr. *Dennis singly,* who is esteemed equal to any three of the number." Not a high compliment perhaps; for Pope knew Dennis's habitual scorn for most of his contemporaries; but still it represents an official opinion. If Dennis's views on passion had been more widely heeded, later Augustan poetry would certainly have been more declamatory: conceivably it might have been more truly moving.

Contrasting with Dennis in many ways and yet often agreeing with *Shaftesbury* him stood the famous philosopher, the third Earl of Shaftesbury.[8] His lord- *as Critic* ship was perhaps hardly a critic at all. He theorizes about the art of poetry interestingly, but his applied criticisms are hardly reputable. He had less taste than Dennis for "our old dramatic poet" Shakespeare, but allowing for the dramatist's "natural rudeness, his unpolished style, and antiquated phrase and wit, his want of method and coherence, and his deficiency in almost all the graces and ornaments...yet by the justness of his moral, the aptness of many of his descriptions, and the plain and natural turn of several of his characters, he pleases the audience, and often gains their ear without a single bribe from Luxury or Vice." *Hamlet* is called "that piece of his which appears to have most affected English hearts," and is praised as being "almost one continued moral." In general, the English muse is regarded by his lordship as not yet out of swaddling clothes. Many of his judgments—those on Dryden and Sir Christopher Wren's new St. Paul's notably—must have been colored by personal prejudice. He believes in ridicule as a test of truth, but no words are too harsh to express his de-testation of the ridicule found in Swift's *Tale of a Tub.* On the other hand, he praises the Duke of Buckinghamshire's *Essay on Poetry* (after all—*a duke!*), admires French tragedy and its rules, and so naturally thinks well of Rymer as a critic.

His theories spring from his belief that harmony with Nature leads to that *On Taste* *summum bonum,* serenity; that the three major aspects of Nature, the Good, the Beautiful, and the True, are at bottom one. A difficulty in his philosophizings was to reconcile *(a)* the idea that this is a divinely created and ordered, a perfect, world, and *(b)* the idea that man should strive to improve his world. Shaftesbury, then, stresses man's *natural appetite* for these ultimates of Goodness, Beauty, and Truth, which drives man towards

---

[8] On Shaftesbury's philosophy and life see above, Part II, ch. 1, n. 4. On his criticism see two papers by Alfred O. Aldridge, "Lord Shaftesbury's Literary Theories," *PQ,* XXIV (1945). 46-64, and "Shaftesbury and the Test of Truth," *PMLA,* LX (1945). 129-156.

an ideal quasi-Platonic goal. He endows man with a "moral sentiment," a natural faculty or internal sense which enables one to distinguish deformity from beauty and vice from virtue. This faculty is at times called *taste*. The seeds of taste exist naturally in man's mind; but they must be cultivated: taste is by no means subjective or even easy to attain. In the *Advice to an Author* he exclaims, " 'Tis not by wantonness and humour that I shall attain my end and arrive at the enjoyment I propose. The art itself is severe, the rules rigid." And again, in his *Miscellanies* (III, ii): "A legitimate and just taste can neither be begotten, made, conceived, or produced without the antecedent labour and pains of criticism."

Thus he resents the facility of the young coffee-house wit who alleges "that we Englishmen are not tied up to such rigid rules as those of the ancient Grecian or modern French critics." In his opinion "there is nothing more certain than that a real genius and thorough artist in whatever kind can never, without the greatest unwillingness and shame...be prevailed with to prostitute his art or science by performing contrary to its known rules." It is then natural that he condemns tragicomedy, and in general follows Continental traditions of art and opinions of the English genius.

On the Imagination He is aware of the difference between imaginative delusion and imaginative illusion, and endorses the latter highly.

We may...presume to infer from the coolest of all studies, even from criticism itself... "that there is a power in numbers, harmony, proportion, and beauty of every kind, which naturally captivates the heart, and raises the imagination to an opinion or conceit of something majestic and divine." ...Without this imagination or conceit the world would be but a dull circumstance, and life a sorry pastime. Scarce could we be said to live.

But the trained imagination abominates the particular image. It could easily make every subject "appear unlike anything extant in the world besides. But this effect the good poet and painter seek industriously to prevent. They hate minuteness, and are afraid of singularity."

On Enthusiasm In the first treatise in his *Characteristicks*, "A Letter concerning Enthusiasm," Shaftesbury had attacked religious enthusiasm (that is, irrationality), and had stated the notion "that provided we treat religion with good manners, we can never use too much good-humor, or examine it with too much freedom and familiarity." From this and other dangerous positions he evolved the notion that ridicule is admirable as a test of truth—a view that may have stimulated writers to use ridicule in satire. His attitude towards enthusiasm, however, cannot be taken from a reading of this first treatise alone, though even here he asserted that enthusiasm sits "gracefully with an ancient," and again that "No poet...can do anything great in his own way without the imagination or supposition of a divine presence, which may raise him to some degree of this passion [enthusiasm] we are speaking of." [4] The fifth treatise in his *Characteristicks*, "The Moralists, a Philosophical

---

[4] On the "rationalist" or scientific attitude towards enthusiasm see George Williamson's excellent article on "The Restoration Revolt against Enthusiasm," *SP*, XXX (1933). 571-603.

Rhapsody," was largely devoted to an exposition of the approved or "sweet" enthusiasm. Shaftesbury called this treatise his "principal performance." In it Theocles, a lover of nature and romantic solitude, converts Philocles by showing him the transcendent beauty of the landscape at dawn. The scene reaches its climax in the famous apostrophe to Nature ("Moralists," III, i), after which Philocles concludes,

"The transports of poets, the sublime of orators, the rapture of musicians, the high strains of the virtuosi—all mere enthusiasm! Even learning itself, the love of arts and curiosities, the spirit of travelers and adventurers, gallantry, war, heroism—all, all enthusiasm!" 'Tis enough; I am content to be this new enthusiast in a way unknown to me before....For is there a fair and plausible enthusiasm, a reasonable ecstasy and transport allowed to other subjects, such as architecture, painting, music; and shall it be exploded here?

Such passages in Shaftesbury certainly helped to turn poets to a new enthusiasm for nature—to be seen later in James Thomson, Joseph Warton, William Whitehead (his *Enthusiast*), and many another.[5] Enthusiasm as related to religion was still deplorable, but as applied to the arts it was more than desirable. It is his moral philosophy and such incidental passages scattered through his other writings that made Shaftesbury an influence in shaping literary ideals. In his third treatise, "Advice to an Author," he devoted a section (II, ii) to a defense of criticism. His consistent *politesse,* dignity, and serenity all served as examples to turbulent commoner critics.

Less ostentatiously noble than his lordship but equally devoted to high moral ideals for criticism and poetry was Richard Steele's collaborator in *The Spectator,* Joseph Addison.[6] More widely and more intelligently read than his lordship, Addison seems (though by no means a critic greatly daring) far more modern than either Dennis or Shaftesbury. After several years at Oxford and a residence of four years on the Continent, including a scholarly tour of classic Italy, Addison could still live with the coffee-house wits as a *bon vivant*—he drank copiously and soberly—and as a scholar who was no pedant. He seemed to Pope in days of hostility—

Addison as Critic

born to write, converse, and live with ease.

Thus to him as to Shaftesbury the critic was at best the ideal fine gentleman. In *Spectator* No. 291, where he lays down qualifications for the true critic, he remarks contemptuously, "A few general rules extracted out of the French authors, with a certain cant of words, has sometimes set up an illiterate heavy writer for a most judicious and formidable critic." Addison doubtless believed in the rules; but he more than once disparaged them casually, and he commonly found other things to talk about. With him perception outweighed precept in importance. The true critic essentially

On the Character and Training of a Critic

---

[5] See two notable articles by Cecil A. Moore: "Shaftesbury and the Ethical Poets in England, 1700-1760," *PMLA,* XXXI (1916). 264-325, and "The Return to Nature in English Poetry of the Eighteenth Century," *SP,* XIV (1917). 243-291.

[6] On Addison's career and writings apart from criticism see Part II, ch. v.

was the man of taste, and a fine taste seemed "the utmost perfection of an accomplished man." To test one's taste he advised in *Spectator* No. 409 three procedures: (1) see if the generally approved classics afford delight; (2) see if the individual quality of different authors is felt; and (3) see if disparate statements of the same thought by a great author and an ordinary writer produce different effects. Psychological response rather than correspondence with precedent was stressed. Taste depended on training, which included reading the best authors, conversation with men of politeness, familiarity with the best critics ancient and modern, a love of simplicity rather than of artificial ingenuity, and development of one's imagination.

On Genius   Possibly Addison's eleven *Spectator* papers on the Pleasures of the Imagination (Nos. 411-21) are his most original contributions to the theory of criticism.[7] A rival for this honor would be *Spectator* No. 160, which gives account of two types of geniuses—the natural, "who by the mere strength of natural parts, and without any assistance of art or learning" have delighted readers, geniuses like Shakespeare and Pindar; and, secondly, the trained geniuses, "that have formed themselves by rules, and submitted the greatness of their natural talents to the corrections and restraints of art"—men like Plato, Aristotle, Virgil, Tully, and Milton. This dual concept of genius had enormous influence; but it is perhaps less important than Addison's papers on imagination.

On the   Dennis, Shaftesbury, and Addison differed notably in their accounts of
Imagination the imagination. To Dennis its function was to vivify, to present absent objects to the mind as if present. Images of "absent terrible objects" move one violently, and for him constitute the source of enthusiasm in poetry. Like Hobbes and Locke, Dennis stresses the importance of judgment as a control over the imagination. To Shaftesbury imagination is primarily the force that elevates the mind, not to passion, but to the lofty serenity that his admiration for Plato led him to love. Addison is less philosophic and more scientific. He is the empiricist who, somewhat after the manner of Hobbes and Locke, wishes to examine into the workings of the imagination and its effects on the mind. These last are pleasurable, and he finds (in No. 412) that such pleasures coming from outward objects arise from "what is great, uncommon, or beautiful."[8] The general effect of these pleasures is refining: "A man of polite imagination is let into a great many pleasures, that the vulgar are not capable of receiving." A more specialized effect is felt by the imaginative writer:

---

[7] In recent times there has been controversy over these essays. W. B. Worsfold's *Principles of Criticism* (1897), chs. III-V, exaggerated and mistook their importance; others have denied them any importance. Beyond doubt they meant much to the eighteenth century. See C. D. Thorpe, "Addison's Theory of Imagination as 'Perceptive Response'," *Papers of the Michigan Academy*, XXI (1936). 509-530. On Addison's predecessors in this field see Donald F. Bond, "The Neo-Classical Psychology of the Imagination," *ELH*, IV (1937). 245-264. Also D. F. Bond's "'Distrust' of Imagination in English Neo-Classicism," *PQ*, XIV (1935). 54-69.

[8] By this statement he encouraged a host of succeeding theorists to analyze sublimity, beauty, the picturesque, and other types of imaginative stimuli. Francis Hutcheson (1694-1746) in his *Inquiry into the Original of our Ideas of Beauty and Virtue* (1725) and in his *Essay on ... the Passions* (1728) was an early disciple. See Clarence D. Thorpe, "Addison and Hutcheson on the Imagination," *ELH*, II (1935). 215-234.

It would be in vain to enquire, whether the Power of imagining Things strongly proceeds from any greater Perfection in the Soul, or from any nicer Texture in the Brain of one Man than of another. But this is certain, that a noble Writer should be born with this Faculty in its full Strength and Vigour, so as to be able to receive lively Ideas from outward Objects, to retain them long, and to range them together, upon occasion, in such Figures and Representations as are most likely to hit the Fancy of the Reader. A Poet should take as much Pains in forming his Imagination, as a Philosopher in cultivating his Understanding. He must gain a due Relish of the Works of Nature, and be throughly conversant in the various Scenery of a Country Life.

Such forming of the poet's mind results in the forming of pleasing images in his poetry, in that final "Embellishment to good Sense" that "makes one Man's Compositions more agreeable than another's." Judgment, Addison thinks, must operate along with imagination (No. 416); but he talks much less of the necessity of control than had the critics of Dryden's day—including Dennis. Addison also is less worried by the possibility of the imagination's overwhelming the understanding. He is less concerned with the confusion between illusion in practical matters (which is delusion) and that in poetical matters, where illusion, provided it is an embellishment to *good sense,* cannot be dangerous.

By nature Addison loved the simple and the direct rather than the complex *On Classical* and the fanciful, but he had commendation for all these qualities. His *Simplicity* mind shows a delicate balance between an easy-going common sense that could in *Spectator* No. 40 condemn poetic justice as unnatural and a somewhat rigid rationalism that in the same essay could also condemn tragicomedy as unnatural. Although he follows the French classical critics in his method of praising the ballad of *Chevy Chase* (*Spectator* No. 70), his love of sensible simplicity is here admirably expressed:

I know nothing which more shews the essential and inherent Perfection of Simplicity of Thought, above that which I call the Gothick Manner in Writing, than this, that the first pleases all Kinds of Palates, and the latter only such as have formed to themselves a wrong artificial Taste upon little fanciful Authors and Writers of Epigram.

Trivial ornament, often called "Gothick" at this time, he opposed to the universality of simplicity.

If he was bold in this admiration of ballads,[9] he was also outspoken in his admiration of the complex art of John Milton. After Dennis he is one *On Milton* of the very first to praise Milton extensively. In method, the eighteen papers in his series on *Paradise Lost* (*Spectator,* No. 267, and thereafter on Saturdays until No. 369) are most revealing. The first four are, in his phrase, done "according to Aristotle's method." That is, they deal with the topics treated in the *Poetics* in connection with the epic. Here the rules become principles

---

[9] See S. B. Hustvedt, *Ballad Criticism . . . during the Eighteenth Century* (1916), pp. 65-78; E. B. Reed, "Two Notes on Addison" [one on ballads], *MP,* VI (1908). 186-189; and E. K. Broadus, "Addison's Influence on the Development of Interest in Folk-Poetry in the Eighteenth Century," *MP,* VIII (1910). 123-134.

of criticism, and the critic's observations are conventional. In No. 291 he
in a sense defines the function of criticism so as to defend the next paper
(No. 297) on the imperfections of the poem. Thereafter (Nos. 303 to 369)
he devotes one paper to the beauties of each of the twelve books. Evidently
it is twelve times as important to point out beauties as it is to find faults.
It is possible that in these papers, which quote Milton with exquisite taste
but comment somewhat perfunctorily upon the quotations made, Addison
more or less founds a school of "beauties" criticism; for throughout the
ensuing century almost every important author has his merits displayed
in a volume (sometimes two), the title of which begins "The Beauties
of ——." In any case Addison exhibits the sensitiveness that results from
genteel training of imagination reinforced by good sense. Occasionally—for
instance in his praise of *Chevy Chase* or in his opinion that Caliban, as a
product of sheer imagination, is a greater effect of genius than Hotspur
or Julius Caesar—Addison surprises one by his independent insight.[10]
Usually, however, as in his dispraise of Italian opera as non-intellectual, he
spoke for better or worse the wisdom of his time. The fact that he spoke
it unassumingly and elegantly and in the highly popular *Spectator* gave
it enormous vogue and influence.

Pope as Critic   In similar fashion poetic eminence gave vogue to the critical writing of
Alexander Pope.[11] His almost juvenile *Essay on Criticism* was, to be sure,
published before he was eminent, and it speedily became a bible for neo-
classicists. The rest of Pope's output in criticism, except for *The Dunciad*
and for fairly brief passages in other poems, was in prose. Most notable are
the prefaces to his *Iliad* (1715), to his edition of Shakespeare (1725), and
to his collected *Works* (1717). His general position as a critic has been too
frequently deduced only from his early writing, such as the *Essay on Criticism,* a poem published before he was twenty-three and perhaps written
before he was twenty-one. His *Discourse on Pastoral Poetry* was apparently
written before 1709, though published in 1717. In these works Pope is
the elegant amateur and the complete traditionalist. In the preface to his
Works (1717) he affectedly remarks that poetry and criticism are "only the
affair of idle men who write in their closets, and of idle men who read there";
and with equal self-depreciation he remarks as a traditionalist, "All that
is left us is to recommend our productions by the imitation of the Ancients."
But no one should imagine those were his permanent views. At the end
of the noble account of the evolution of Society in Epistle III of the *Essay
on Man,* at the point where tyranny and superstition have enslaved man,
appears the poet as reformer:

> 'Twas then the studious head or gen'rous mind,
> Follow'r of God, or friend of human-kind,

[10] Both Addison and Steele make admirable comments on Shakespeare. See J. H. Neumann,
"Shakespearean Criticism in *The Tatler* and *The Spectator,*" PMLA, xxxix (1924). 612-623.
[11] On Pope's criticism see Austin Warren, *Alexander Pope as Critic and Humanist* (Princeton,
1929), and John E. Butt, *Pope's Taste in Shakespeare* (a paper read before the Shakespeare
Association, 1936). On Pope's poetry see Part II, ch. VIII.

Poet or patriot, rose but to restore
The faith and moral Nature gave before. . . .

To Pope as, later, to Johnson evidently the poet might be "the interpreter
of nature and the legislator of mankind."

His theory of poetry and criticism is usually, however, deduced from the *An Essay on*
Essay on Criticism. This poem has as its general office the same function *Criticism*
Shaftesbury performed in Part II, Section ii, of his "Advice to an Author";
namely, the rehabilitation of the critic in good nature and good manners.
Only the first 200 lines of the poem concern the theory of the art of letters;
the rest deals with the manners appropriate to a polite critic. In the first
section Pope starts with the view that as poets must by natural endowment
have genius, so critics must have taste; that most men "have the seeds of
judgment in their mind," and that this natural taste must be developed
by a study of Nature (that is, of the moral system of the universe together
with its manifestations) and a study of the ancients and of ancient rules. One
may, he suggests, rise above the rules, but that way danger lies. The rules
have authority, not because they are ancient or Aristotelian, but because
they are "nature methodised"—are based in reason. Pope, like Addison,
Hobbes, and Locke, stands in the empirical tradition: the rules are simply
the procedure of ancient authors codified. In all this there is nothing new,
and Pope intended there should be nothing new: he was stating only the
accepted wisdom of his day. But the brilliance of the statement kept his
precepts in vogue long after their early vitality had evaporated. It was this
vogue fully as much as any essential falseness of doctrine that later enraged
romantic critics—De Quincey, for example.

Pope in his satirical writing is rationalist in temper, and even has much
of the common-sensical attitude towards the handling of material. In his
Bathos (*The Art of Sinking in Poetry*) (1728) he ridicules the affected
diction of many contemporaries, and in *The Dunciad,* a poem devoted to
good common sense as well as to virulent personal satire, he attacks pre-
tentiousness in scholarship, criticism, and editing. In various critical passages
found in his letters he writes in a similar tone. His attack, in one letter, on
the poetry of Crashaw foreshadows remotely that of Johnson on the metaphysical poets.

In the prefaces to the *Iliad* and to his edition of Shakespeare Pope is *Pope on*
somewhat more incisive. He glories in Homer's "invention," and while he *Homer and*
analyzes the poem according to Aristotle's method, he uses the theme of *Shakespeare*
invention to unify the analysis. He gives a striking comparison of Homer
and Virgil, from which dates the unexpected eighteenth-century preference
of Homer, the poet of nature, to Virgil, the poet of art. In his account of
Homer's imperfections he adopts the typical idea of his day that progress
has improved manners. His successors argued long over the question of
the purity or the corruptness of manners in Homer's pristine time. Pope's
account of his own attempts to preserve in English Homer's fire and sim-

plicity shows insight into problems that were perhaps beyond him to solve. The preface to Shakespeare is less notable. Pope neatly tries to throw the blame for imperfections on Shakespeare's first publishers, who were, he thought, ignorant actors. His appreciation of Shakespeare's characters and of his power over the passions is admirable. His bold opinion that "To judge . . . of Shakespear by Aristotle's rules, is like trying a man by laws of one country, who acted under those of another" is creditable and on the whole typical of the time: but it was an opinion that neither the time nor Mr. Pope could consistently cling to.

His Notes on Homer   Pope's method is very like Addison's in applied criticism. This can best be seen in the notes to the *Iliad* and *Odyssey,* which were widely studied during the whole century. Some notes are almost little essays in themselves. The character of Axylus, "a friend to mankind," inserted as a note to *Iliad* VI, 16, is a striking portrait of "the good man" as drawn after Homer. More literary in content are notes to such lines as VI, 595, on the domestic scene between Hector and his infant son. Here, typically, Pope uses the analogy of poetry with painting; he concludes with the important comment that *"Longinus* indeed blames an author's insisting too much on trivial Circumstances," but Pope holds "There is a vast difference betwixt a *small* Circumstance and a *trivial* one, and the smallest become important if they are well chosen, and not confused." More conventional seems the note to Book XI, line 669, on "low" words in poetry—with the influential passage from Boileau quoted. Pope's method in all these notes, however antiquarian some may be, is to exhibit the beauties of the poetry. This purpose he asserts at the beginning of the notes to both the *Iliad* and the *Odyssey*. He goes further in defining his purpose by being depreciatory of commentators who are always giving us exclamations instead of criticisms. This is the fault of his French predecessor, Mme Dacier: she often gives only "general Praises and Exclamations instead of Reasons." Criticism to Pope is a reasoned discourse about art: in his mature criticism he seldom indulges in stale or unintelligent thinking, though he does not escape the prejudices that were traditional in his day.

Lesser Critics: Textual Criticism   The numerous lesser critics of the period resemble in many ways these four critics just considered. Their vehicles were pamphlets, prefaces, and, increasingly, the periodical essay. There was also a weighty amount of textual criticism done in editions of ancient or modern authors. Shakespeare found in the period 1709-47 five different editors, of whom Pope and Lewis Theobald (1688-1744) are most often recalled. Theobald in his periodical *The Censor* (1715-17) published some brief essays about Shakespeare; and his later remarks on Pope's negligent editing won for him the distinction of being Prince of Dulness in *The Dunciad*. None of Shakespeare's editors before Edmond Malone equaled in editorial care or scholarship the work of Richard Bentley (1662-1742) on Horace (1711), though Bentley lost much of his reputation in 1732 by his tinkerings with the text of *Paradise Lost*. The most scrupulous editing in the period was the work of Thomas

Hearne (1678-1735), the greatest medievalist of the century,[12] and the scholarly edition of Thuanus (7 volumes, folio, 1733) produced by Samuel Buckley (1673-1741) with the aid of the Jacobite historian Thomas Carte (1686-1754) and the wealthy and learned physician Dr. Richard Mead (1673-1754). In comparison with the volumes of these competent editors, the textual work of purely literary men, like Pope and (later) Bishop Percy, is inferior. The relatively amateurish editing of Shakespeare, however, together with the increase of dramatic criticism in the periodical essays augmented the popularity of that great dramatist. By 1737 Pope could write of him as "the divine, the matchless, what you will"; and a torment of "rules" critics was the unblinkable fact that "Shakespear writ without rules."

In the less technical sorts of criticism the minor men followed the methods *Gildon* of the greater critics. Charles Gildon [13] (1665-1724), an admirer of Dryden, *and Others* Congreve, and Dennis, was avowedly a "modern," but a modern who was obsessed by the practices of the ancients—and by rules. Lewis Theobald in his edition of Shakespeare curiously remarked that Gildon was "one attached to Rymer by a similar way of thinking and studies." He certainly was a "rules" critic, but in his early *Miscellaneous Letters and Essays* (1694) he was strong on the side of Shakespeare and opposed to Rymer. His last critical work of note was *The Laws of Poetry ... Explain'd and Illustrated* (1721) in commentaries on the critical poems of three noble lords—Buckinghamshire, Roscommon, and Lansdowne: like much of Gildon's hack work it was obviously a bid for patronage in days when he was both poor and blind. In his *Complete Art of Poetry* (1718) and elsewhere he showed an admiration for Shakespeare but no really stimulating thought. The *Art of Poetry* was for a time kept in memory by a couplet in *The Spleen* by Matthew Green, who asserts of his Muse that she

> Draws from the spring she finds within;
> Nor vainly buys what Gildon sells,
> Poetic buckets for dry wells.

Such buckets, however, had a market; for one Edward Bysshe had brought out *The Art of English Poetry* in 1702, which ran to ten editions by 1739. More interesting than these men was Leonard Welsted (1688-1747), who in addition to poems of some slight repute brought out a translation of Longinus in 1712 with "Remarks" added "on the English Poets" (chiefly Shakespeare and Milton); and in 1724 his prefatory "Dissertation concerning the Perfection of the English Language, the State of Poetry, etc." appeared in a volume of his *Epistles, Odes, etc.* These two essays illustrate the average

---

[12] When Hearne's library was to be sold the *London Daily Post* (February 21, 1736) printed an epigram that exhibits the gift of the time for such witticism as well as Hearne's high reputation as a scholar:
> "Pox on't, quoth Time, to Thomas Hearne,
> Whatever I forget, you learn!"

[13] On Gildon's career see Paul Dottin, "An Essay on Gildon's Life," in Gildon's *Robinson Crusoe Examin'd and Criticis'd* (1923).

taste of the time rather than independent thinking. A work of like interest is *The Arts of Logick and Rhetorick* (1728) which John Oldmixon (1673-1742) based upon *La Manière de Bien Penser* (1687) of Father Dominique Bouhours, a highly valued French critic and essayist. Oldmixon, like most of these minor critics, had found himself placed among Pope's dunces, and this book contains personal retorts of stale virulence. Among the few critics to defend Pope in print was Joseph Spence (1699-1768), who won affection by *An Essay on Pope's Odyssey: in which Some Particular Beauties and Blemishes ... are Consider'd* (1726-7). The display of his beauties led Pope to forgive the blemishes, which Spence pointed out chiefly as faults in over-decorative style. Spence's collections of important literary *ana,* mostly about Pope, were published long after his death as *Anecdotes* (1820). His largest work was a tall folio called *Polymetis* (1747), which was a popular classical handbook for the later century.

Critical Agreements and Dis-agreements   Criticism in the early eighteenth century had a small core of generally accepted doctrine, including beliefs in the moral function of poetry, the value of the ancients as guides or models, the necessity of probability in one's poetic fictions, and the necessity of art to correct nature and to give to form a desirable directness and clarity. There was, however, no agreement on such matters as tragicomedy and poetic justice, and the three unities were in general respected but not carefully observed.[14] There were differences of opinion on the matter of rime vs. blank verse, and, more significant, about the function—but not the importance—of the imagination. Simplicity, sublimity, elegance, and ease were differently, if highly, valued. Even where there was basic agreement, there was likely to be difference in emphasis. The rules of Nature must be observed; the rules of France might be slighted, at the cost of elegance, for the sake of vigor, variety, and richness. As Pope himself put it:

> The rules a nation, born to serve, obeys;
> And Boileau still in right of Horace sways.
> But we, brave Britons, foreign laws despised,
> And kept unconquered, and uncivilized.

But, as he continued in his *Essay on Criticism,* some among "the sounder few" had labored to restore "wit's fundamental laws," and laws were essential. There was, finally, a faint awareness that while the Greco-Roman tradition was dominant, China and Peru and all sorts of other sources of law were waiting to be heard from.

[14] Clarence C. Green's *Neo-Classic Theory of Tragedy in England during the Eighteenth Century* (Cambridge, Mass., 1934) gives a good account of divergences of opinion over dramatic rules.

III

Defoe and Journalism

The art of pamphleteering throve mightily in the seventeenth and eight- *Pamphlets* eenth centuries. Essentially it had little in common with the classical dignity *and News-* and magnificence that characterized nobler forms of writing: it was perhaps *papers* the reverse side of the tapestry. In the eighteenth century the pamphlet supplemented the newspaper; arguments, that is, that were too long for the single folio sheets or half-sheets that then constituted newspapers, dilated in independent publications of moderate size. The newspaper itself took on life after 1695 when the Licensing Act lapsed.[1] Not that the lapsing of this act made journalism a safe profession: it long remained an anonymous and furtive employment. Immediately in 1695 the Tories founded an "organ," *The Post-Boy* (1695-1735), edited at first by Abel Roper; and the Whigs countered with their *Flying-Post* (1695-1731), long presided over by George Ridpath. *The Post-Man* (1695-1730) was also Whig in bias. Few newspapers of the day lived as long as these; journals were born to argue over a crisis, and they ceased when new topics came into play. The first successful daily, *The Daily Courant* (1702-35), published by Samuel Buckley, was during its early and prosperous existence a commercial sheet of Whig tendencies that grew violent later.

Certain periodicals specialized in comment on news or in essay material *Comments* rather than in printing news itself. L'Estrange's *Observator* and Dunton's *on Current* *Athenian Gazette* [2] had ceased publication before 1700, but their formerly *Affairs* popular methods of dialogue or question and answer still occasionally found able if vituperative imitators. In 1702 John Tutchin (d. 1707), whose poem *The Foreigners* had provoked Defoe's *True-Born Englishman*, founded a Whig *Observator* (1702-12), borrowing the title from Sir Roger L'Estrange's earlier success. This, in turn, inspired the non-juring Tory,

---

[1] The best bibliographies concerning the history of English periodical publications—essays, reviews, newspapers—are those made by H. G. Pollard for the *Cambridge Bibliography of English Literature* (Cambridge, 1940), II. 656-739. The section dealing with "The Periodical Essay" (pp. 660-668) is by Walter Graham. For newspapers see II. 688-739. Useful among histories of journalism for this period are the following: H. R. Fox Bourne, *English Newspapers* (2v, 1887); Edwin B. Chancellor, *The Annals of Fleet Street* (1912); David H. Stevens, *Party Politics and English Journalism, 1702-1742* (Chicago, 1916); Walter Graham, *English Literary Periodicals* (1930); Stanley Morison, *The English Newspaper* (Cambridge, 1932); David Nichol Smith, "The Newspaper," *Johnson's England*, ed. A. S. Turberville (Oxford, 1933), II. 331-367 (dealing in part with this period); James R. Sutherland, "The Circulation of Newspapers and Literary Periodicals, 1700-1730," *Library*, XV (1934). 110-124; Laurence Hanson, *Government and the Press* (Oxford, 1936). The *Census of British Newspapers and Periodicals, 1620-1800* made by Ronald S. Crane, F. B. Kaye, and M. E. Prior (Chapel Hill, 1927) is useful both as a bibliography and as a finding-list for American holdings.

[2] See above, Part I, ch. IX, n. 18.

Charles Leslie, to start *The Rehearsal* (1704-9), which attacked Tutchin's *Observator*, Defoe's *Review*, and other Whig utterances.

litics and By 1709 London had at least eighteen separate papers, issuing in all about *journalism* fifty numbers a week;[3] and the power of the newspaper as a political influence was becoming such that in 1712 the Tory ministry evolved a clever scheme of a stamp tax of a halfpenny per issue on each paper, and the added cost to the buyer crushed Whig journals: Tory papers perhaps were secretly subsidized. Any setback to "Grub-street," as the press was now called, was temporary. Upon the death of Queen Anne the Tories went out of power, and then new Whig journals appeared. Every crisis brought out new papers: Addison and Steele argued on opposite sides of the Peerage Bill in 1719 in their serial pamphlets *The Plebeian* (Steele) and *The Old Whig* (Addison). In the same year John Trenchard (1662-1723) founded, with the able aid of Thomas Gordon (d. 1750), *The London Journal*, in which they published a notable series of essays, collected in 1724 into four volumes called *Cato's Letters*. These argued for punishment of South Sea directors after their "bubble" burst, and for various other good Whig causes. Gordon became one of Sir Robert Walpole's writers, and, apart from politics, published in 1728-31 a valued translation of Tacitus. During Walpole's term of office (1721-42) as prime minister the press became more violent than it had been, but no more soundly intellectual.[4] Attacks on his ministry were led by a coalition of "Patriots," who under the guidance of Viscount Boling-broke sponsored *The Craftsman* (1726-47). Walpole's most annoying organ was *The Daily Gazetteer* (1735-48), which absorbed three government papers, and was said to be delivered gratis throughout the land in support of the minister. Walpole habitually employed untalented but obedient hacks for his journals, men who could be bought and controlled. Throughout the first half of the century, however, almost all writers from Defoe to the Earl of Chesterfield dabbled overtly or secretly in journalism. Henry Fielding, for example, was intermittently concerned with at least four or five newspapers. Like most of the abler literary personalities of the early forties, he wrote against Walpole.

News Many newspapers featured the leading article or essay, and when space *Pamphlets* did not permit long accounts, or when the proprietor of the journal did not wish to risk suppression, a pamphlet was the normal result. In form the pamphlet was most diverse: it might be narrative—realistic or allegorical— it might be argumentative, it might be dialogue, and it was very likely to be cast in the form of a letter. It might be a "feature story," as was Defoe's brilliant *True Relation of the Apparition of one Mrs. Veal*[5] (1706); it

---

[3] See Stanley Morison, *op. cit.*, p. 84.

[4] On the literary opposition to Walpole see Charles B. Realey, *The Early Opposition to Sir Robert Walpole, 1720-1727* (Lawrence, Kan., and Philadelphia, 1931); William T. Laprade, *Public Opinion and Politics . . . to the Fall of Walpole* (1936); and Keith G. Feiling, *The Second Tory Party, 1714-1832* (1938), as well as the works already cited, especially Hanson.

[5] On this clear case of actual journalistic reporting see Sir Charles H. Firth, "Defoe's *True Relation of the Apparition of Mrs. Veal*," *RES*, VII (1931). 1-6; and Dorothy Gardiner's "What Canterbury knew of Mrs. Veal and her Friends," *RES*, VII (1931). 188-197.

might be a practical joke as were the numerous Bickerstaff-Partridge pamphlets of 1708-9, which prophesied the death of the Tory almanac-maker Partridge, and after the fatal evening jeered at him for not admitting his decease.[6] It loved ingenuity, and rose to allegorical excellence in the masterpiece of Dr. John Arbuthnot [7] (1667-1735), now known as *The History of John Bull* (1712), in which the whole futility of the War of the Spanish Succession was displayed from the point of view of an English Tory under guise of a lawsuit between Lord Strutt (Spain) and Lewis Baboon (Louis XIV of France) and John Bull (England). "John Bull" as symbolizing England is Arbuthnot's invention. Pamphleteers loved irony, and achieved their most incisive and dangerous appeal through this device. Defoe suffered in the pillory for his ironic *Shortest Way with the Dissenters* (1702); Swift has been castigated for his ironic pre-Malthusian *Modest Proposal for Preventing the Children of Poor People from being a Burther to Their Parents* (1729); and Fielding's burlesque biography of *Jonathan Wild* (1743) used irony to cover a shrewd attack on party politics if not on Walpole himself. Pamphleteering might be dangerous if directed against the ministry (such attacks were frequently ruled seditious) or in favor of the Pretender—such writing was high treason. In 1719 an unfortunate eighteen-year-old printer, John Matthews, was hanged, drawn, and quartered for aiding the publication of a Jacobitical pamphlet called *Vox Populi, Vox Dei*. Such grim facts darkened the careers of even the masters of this type of writing, and darkened few careers more than they did that of Daniel Defoe.

No writer of the whole century had a life more full of strange surprising adventures than did Defoe [8] (1660-1731). Son of a dissenting tallow-chandler of London named James Foe (Daniel added the genteel "De" when over forty years of age), he rebelled with Monmouth in 1685 and escaped without punishment. Already well married (1684), he for some years prospered by trading in hosiery, though various lawsuits indicate that his reputation for honesty was sadly tarnished even before 1692, when war ruined his export trade and caused his failure for the sum of £17,000. One way or another

Daniel Defoe

---

[6] William A. Eddy, "Tom Brown and Partridge the Astrologer," *MP*, xxviii (1930). 163-168.

[7] Arbuthnot, a royal physician and popular wit, with his close friends Swift, Pope, Gay, and Parnell, constituted the Scriblerus Club, and was largely concerned in the "Memoirs of Martinus Scriblerus," published by Pope in 1741. His *Life and Works*, ed. George A. Aitken (Oxford, 1892) is the only modern edition of his writings. An excellent study of his mind and genius is found in Lester M. Beattie's *John Arbuthnot Mathematician and Satirist* (Cambridge, Mass., 1935). Herman Teerink's edition of *John Bull* (Amsterdam, 1925) has textual usefulness: his ascription of the work to Swift lacks proof.

[8] There is no complete edition of Defoe's works, which run to over 400 titles. The titles are best listed in *CBEL*, ii. 495-514. Collected editions—chiefly of the novels—have been made; see *Romances and Narratives*, ed. George A. Aitken (16v, 1895) and *Works*, ed. Gustavus H. Maynadier (16v, 1903-4), and *Novels and Selected Writings* (14v, Oxford, 1927-8). For biographies see William Lee, *Life and Recently Discovered Writings, 1719-29* (3v, 1869); Thomas Wright, *Life* (1894; rev. ed., 1931); William P. Trent, *Daniel Defoe: How to Know Him* (Indianapolis, 1916); Paul Dottin, *Daniel De Foe et ses romans* (3v, Paris, 1924), cheapened in an English translation of Vol. 1 (1929); James R. Sutherland, *Defoe* (1937: the best one-volume life); John R. Moore, *Defoe in the Pillory and Other Studies* (Bloomington, Ind., 1939). For criticism see Arthur W. Secord, *Studies in the Narrative Method of Defoe* (Urbana, Ill., 1924).

much of this indebtedness was later paid off; but for the rest of his career Defoe had in his heart the strong dread of the law and the fear of a debtor's prison. He learned the trick of quiet disappearance, and practised it often when legal danger threatened—and more than once it threatened because of his career as a writer, which he undertook when his chosen function of "true-born merchant" was closed to him. Practically all of his writing was done after he was thirty-five, and the first of his famous stories, *Robinson Crusoe,* was the work of his sixtieth year.

Defoe's Personal Character   His personal character as seen in his writings is worth considering.[9] As seen in real life it was none too favorably regarded by his critics. In the bitter days of 1713 when his *Mercator* was supporting Tory ideas of trade, that firm Whig Joseph Addison, in his *Tryal of Count Tariff,* spoke of Defoe as "a false, shuffling, prevaricating rascal ... unqualified to give his testimony in a Court of Justice." This from one who at times tactfully hinted faults and hesitated dislikes, is unduly severe; one must at least allow that when Defoe's own fortunes were not at stake, he had frequently a disinterested and highly intelligent attitude towards the public welfare. Like Robinson Crusoe and all his fictitious heroes, he was suspiciously shrewd and excessively ingenious; he was as a partisan or a businessman slippery and changeable: one could not tell which side he was on or even which side he thought he was writing on—such was his gift of irony. But in his more disinterested moments his ingenuity is amusingly canny. His first real book, for example, called *An Essay upon Projects* (1697), is significantly public spirited. Some of his projects, here presented, with regard to reforms in legal procedure are doubtless the result of his own sad experiences; but his desire to see the highways of England improved (by means of humanely directed slave labor!), his plan for an asylum for idiots and, at the other extreme, for an academy to correct and stabilize the English language, and, above all, his projected "academy for women," which shows his confidence in the capabilities of women along with suspicions of their discretion—all these projects display the desire of his time to improve practical conditions of life. Such desires never left Defoe, and they operate in very diverse fields. In 1724-7, for example, appeared one of his most popular and useful works, *A Tour thro' the Whole Island of Great Britain* (three volumes),[10] which was important for fifty years as a guidebook and even longer as a document in the economic history of England. It is by a tradesman, and is about trade for the most part; but when he reaches Windsor Castle, he remarks, "I must leave talking of Trade, River, Navigation, Meal, and Malt, and describe the most beautiful, and most pleasantly situated Castle, and Royal Palace, in the whole Isle of Britain." And when he describes the paintings in St. George's Hall and tells us, "I had some Pretensions to Judgment of pictures," the reader may recall that in 1720 he had

---

[9] On this difficult subject see Hans H. Andersen, "The Paradox of Trade and Morality in Defoe," *MP,* xxxix (1941). 23-46, and John R. Moore, "The Character of Daniel Defoe," *RES,* xiv (1938). 68-71.

[10] Edited by George D. H. Cole (2v, 1927, and also for Everyman's Library).

published a translation of Du Fresnoy's *Compleat Art of Painting*. He was furthermore well informed in the history of modern Europe, and his geographical knowledge was far from contemptible. His intellect was eager, retentive, far-ranging, shrewd, and ingenious: what he lacked was a just and tenacious adherence to honest dealing in practical matters.

Any career as political writer was dangerous; and Defoe, as a dissenter, a writer for hire, and an ironist, seems usually to have been in danger. He began as a satirical political poet; and by the time (1703) when he first collected his works, he had produced several poems of this kind. His most effective and popular verse was doubtless the *True-Born Englishman* (1701), which defended William III against the prejudices of such subjects as disliked the King's Dutch origin or Dutch advisers. He begins briskly— *Defoe's Adventurous Career*

> Where-ever God erects a House of Prayer,
> The Devil always builds a Chapel there:
> And 'twill be found upon Examination,
> The latter has the largest Congregation.

And he concludes in a rugged fashion natural to a bourgeois—

> Fame of Families is all a Cheat,
> *'Tis Personal Virtue only makes us Great.*

In 1706 he published an almost epic satirical attack (in twelve books) on divine right, called *Jure Divino*. But prose was his trade—even when he used metre and rime; and his crucial writings were prose pamphlets. As a dissenter he early engaged, somewhat equivocally at times, in the arguments over "occasional conformity," by which practice of occasionally taking the Anglican communion—a practice which Defoe called "playing-Bopeep with God Almighty"—dissenters might qualify for public office. In his *Enquiry into the Occasional Conformity of Dissenters* (1698) he remarks of such fellow dissenters as thus conformed, "These are Patriots indeed, that will damn their Souls to save their Countrey." In 1701, according to his own boast, "guarded with about sixteen gentlemen of quality," he entered the House of Commons and presented Mr. Speaker with *Legion's Memorial to the House of Commons*. The foolhardiness of this act at such a moment can be guessed if one reads the threatening end of the pamphlet, which told Mr. Speaker that "Englishmen are no more to be slaves to Parliaments than to a King. Our name is LEGION, and we are many." The pamphlet succeeded in its aims; but the next year its author had no such luck. His *Shortest Way with the Dissenters* (1702) he had conceived as a playful ironic attack on the extreme High Church people who believed that "if the Gallows instead of the Counter, and the Gallies instead of the Fines, were the Reward of going to a Conventicle, to preach or hear, there wou'd not be so many Sufferers." Defoe's irony here backfired: both dissenters and churchmen were offended, and the government ordered his arrest. After successfully hiding for over four months, he was taken, tried, and condemned to pay a heavy fine and to stand in the pillory three times. A sentence of such severity was a thunderbolt: in Defoe's time more than one sinner died from the effects of missiles hurled at pilloried heads. But our hero's ingenuity was equal to the occasion: his friends were rallied about him; he composed a *Hymn to the Pillory,* which sold well during his exposure; and when he came down "from his Wooden Punishment" the crowd treated him, so a Tory journalist complained, "as if he had been a Cicero that had made an excellent oration in it." [11] After this uncomfortable triumph Defoe was returned to Newgate for an indeterminate sentence, totally unable to pay the large fine that had been imposed along with the pillory. His tile works at Tilbury were gone; he was now irretrievably bankrupt a second time, with no prospect of release from prison. Late in 1703, however, his fine was suddenly paid by the Crown, and Defoe, bound over to good behavior, was released. Good behavior apparently meant becoming the man Friday of Robert Harley, a rising politician soon (1704) to be Secretary of State and later (1710-14) to be a Tory prime minister.[12]

Defoe's Review   During the first decade of the century Defoe's important achievements were to aid, by journalism or by pamphlet or by confidential personal work, the Union with Scotland (1707) and to further the Whig cause and English trade in his extensive journal, *A Review of the Affairs of France* (1704-13).[13] It will be remembered that during these years England and France were at war. Defoe's *Review* was actually a political or economic serial pamphlet that appeared, during most of its run, in four quarto pages three times a week. So far as is known, Defoe wrote its nine volumes singlehanded—an almost unparalleled feat in the journalism of the day, all the more surprising because of the time Defoe was out of London—even as far away as Scotland, where he was serving as confidential agent of the government. The *Review* has not much in common with the lighter periodical essay of the type of *The Tatler;* but Defoe and others have thought that his moralizings and the amusing sections captioned as "Advice from the Scandalous Club" were among the formative influences of *The Tatler.* When Harley and the Tories came into power in 1710 the influence of the Whig *Review* declined, and presently in its place Defoe was writing for the Tories a new trade journal called *Mercator, or Commerce Retriev'd* (1713-14).

Other Newspaper Connections   After 1715 he was connected with various papers, among which *Mercurius Politicus* (1716-20), *The Daily Post* (1719-25), Applebee's *Weekly Journal* (1720-26), and Dormer's *News-Letter* (1716-18) mark, with one exception, his principal periods and places of journalistic employment. The exception is significant. In 1717 he was as a reputed Tory secretly placed by the Whig

[11] Theodore F. M. Newton, "William Pittis and Queen Anne Journalism," *MP,* xxxiii (1935-6). 169-186; 279-302. The quotation is from p. 181.
[12] David H. Stevens, "Defoe and the Earl of Oxford," *Party Politics and English Journalism* (Chicago, 1916), pp. 47-60.
[13] Recently the *Review* has been made available for study in a beautiful facsimile edition made by the Facsimile Text Society—with an excellent introduction by Arthur W. Secord. The *Review* shows Defoe's ability as a social and economic thinker at his best. See A. E. Levett, "Daniel Defoe," *The Social and Political Ideas . . . of the Augustan Age,* ed. F. J. C. Hearnshaw (1928), and John R. Moore, "Daniel Defoe and Modern Economic Theory," *Indiana Univ. Studies,* xxi (1934). 1-28.

ministry on the staff of the Tory-Jacobite *Weekly Journal; or, Saturday's Post*, published by Nathaniel Mist. It was his task to moderate the fury of this journalistic storm-center, and until 1724 he had some success in the attempt: in all such government jobs he was likely to be acting a part—and not too sincerely. More than once he was writing for both Whig and Tory journals at the same time. Just after *Robinson Crusoe* (1719), he began work on Applebee's *Journal*, writing stories about Jack Sheppard and other criminals, which led him into the genre of criminal biography.

Most of Defoe's longer works were in part related to his journalism or to his love of "projects." That he wrote his longer stories at all was probably due to the unexpectedly great success of *Robinson Crusoe,*[14] the first part of which was a fictional grafting upon the story of Alexander Selkirk, who had lived alone on Juan Fernandez from 1704-9, and whose return to England in 1711 had caused the publication of many narratives of his history. Defoe's masterpiece was acclaimed at once, and when four editions were called for within four months, he followed it with a second volume of *Farther Adventures of Robinson Crusoe*, which was not worthy of the first. In 1720 a moralizing treatise was added as a third volume; it was entitled *Serious Reflections...of Robinson Crusoe*. Only the first *Strange Surprising Adventures of Robinson Crusoe* won fame, and its popularity was and remains enormous.[15] "There is not an old Woman," wrote Gildon, enviously attacking, "that can go to the Price of it, but buys...and leaves it as a Legacy, with the *Pilgrim's Progress*, the *Practice of Piety*, and *God's Revenge against Murther*, to her Posterity." It was, however, to be more than a middle-class masterpiece: though sprawling in structure and careless in detail, it expressed the eighteenth-century epic theme of the power of the average man to preserve life and to organize an economy in the face of the most unpromising environment. A modern novelist would focus on the horrors of isolation, the loneliness of Crusoe's island; for Defoe these things hardly existed: his mind, as always, was on the God-given power of sinful man to win through—and on the human ingenuity that embellishes the effort.

His Longer Works: Robinson Crusoe

This success led rapidly to other long narratives, produced with a speed almost unaccountable if we consider that in addition to books he was turning out newspaper leaders and pamphlets in quantity. Within twelve weeks in the summer of 1720 he published his historical romance *The Memoirs of a Cavalier*, his *Captain Singleton*, which was another voyage story with pirates featured, and his *Serious Reflections* of Crusoe. During the year 1722 his longer books included *Moll Flanders, Due Preparations for the Plague, Religious Courtship, A Journal of the Plague Year*, and his *Colonel Jacque. Roxana* appeared in 1724, *Capt. George Carleton* in 1728, and in

His Facility in Writing

---

[14] Henry C. Hutchins, *Robinson Crusoe and its Printing, 1719-31* (1925), gives a thorough account of the early editions.

[15] The story even created in Germany a literary type known as *Robinsonaden*. See H. Ullrich, *Robinson und Robinsonaden* (Weimar, 1898), and the learned work of Philip B. Gove, *The Imaginary Voyage in Prose Fiction* (1941), pp. 122-154.

1729 *Robert Drury's Journal,* a work about Madagascar that seems at least in part Defoe's. His *Compleat English Gentleman,* incomplete at his death, was published in 1890. Not all of these works are certainly the exclusive creations of Defoe; but on the other hand it is probable that other books unidentified, especially translations, were made by him.

The Vivid-ness of His Plague Year   Obviously his pen was indefatigable; equally obvious is the fact that his art was chiefly nature: he wrote rapidly, revised seldom,[16] and succeeded through a natural gift for ingenious episode and specific detail. Some of the details in his *Journal of the Plague Year* are so living and horrible as to seem the plausible memories of an eye-witness rather than the work of an author who was only five years old when in 1665 the plague ravaged London.[17] The bellman walking by night in front of the dead-cart, ringing his bell and calling "Bring out your dead!" appalls the memory. The "agony and excess of sorrow" of the pitiful stranger "muffled up in a brown cloak" and come to the great pit to see the body of some one dear to him buried is communicated to us with the full horror of the scene. For sheer grimness this book is Defoe's masterpiece; but all his stories are full of what he calls "speaking sights."

His Charac-terizations   His gifts in characterization can easily be underrated. The spiritually gaunt and awesome figure of Moll Flanders, victim of society and of the Devil, born in Newgate of bad blood that could come to no good, and the more gracious figure of Colonel Jacque—born with genteel blood in him, fortunately—form two of the best contrasting genre pictures of the century. Crusoe and Friday, Singleton and his Quaker William are as authentic as they are casual in portrayal. More than one of these characters illustrates some editorial point. William dramatizes Defoe's prejudice against Quakers [18] —together with his admiration for their shrewdness; Moll Flanders illus-trates the techniques of thieves and adventuresses; Colonel Jacque illustrates the inequity of Spanish trade barriers. Defoe always admires the merchant, and his heroes are always adding up their financial profits, frequently for Defoe's delight rather than for the reader's pleasure.

Lack of Structure   He lacks well-knit structure; several of his stories show a break near the middle which might suggest that Defoe has for the moment run out of adventures, and presently must open a new vein. When Crusoe has estab-lished his economy, there is a pause; then the footprint is seen, Friday is introduced, and we can observe education impressing the blank sheet which is the mind of the man of Nature. *Captain Singleton* is half devoted to a trip across central Africa and half devoted to pirate adventures. *The Memoirs of a Cavalier* divides interest between Continental wars of the seventeenth century and the Cavalier's services to King Charles I in the English Civil

[16] William T. Hastings, in "Errors and Inconsistencies in Defoe's *Robinson Crusoe," MLN,* XXVII (1912). 161-166, points out amusing bits of carelessness.
[17] Watson Nicholson's *Historical Sources of Defoe's Journal of the Plague Year* (Boston, 1919) is valuable as a study of Defoe's factual sources: the book fails in the author's purpose to depreciate Defoe's imaginative gifts.
[18] Ezra K. Maxfield, "Daniel Defoe and the Quakers," *PMLA,* XLVII (1932). 179-190.

Wars. *Moll Flanders,* in many ways his most naturally constructed work, deals first with her amorous adventures and in middle age her adventures as a thief. *Moll* comes closer to standard technique in novel writing in that a nucleus of a social group is reunited at the end of the story. Normally only the central character continues throughout the whole story. Defoe seldom uses chapter divisions, and thus lacks an easy mechanical aid in emphasizing dramatic moments as well as preparation for and punctuation of minor climaxes.

In pattern, his narratives are fictional autobiographies always pretending to be "true" stories, and so cleverly authenticated with fictional detail that it is at times difficult to believe that they have no basis in actuality. *The Memoirs of a Cavalier* has been the object of several attempts—all fruitless —to identify the hero with an actual cavalier. *Moll Flanders* ends with the gratuitous note, "Written in the year 1683"; but the date is obviously impossible. In general Defoe's sense of the passing of time in a story is vague and poor. Crusoe's adventures and Moll Flanders' love affairs drift on through an excessive number of years. Lacking neat arts of construction, Defoe excelled in rich variety of superbly devised episode. An adventure to Defoe was not so much a hairbreadth escape as it was an exercise of human ingenuity or a piece of surprising and delightful good luck. The bit about the small Jacque's hiding his money in the hollow tree is a perfect synthesis of Defoe elements: Jacque's vanishing sense of wrong-doing, his fear of being done out of his stolen prize, his sense of his own incompetence, his grief at his supposed loss when the money falls down inside the tree, and, above all, the final "revolution and discovery" that terminates this little financial tragicomedy, are all essential Defoe. By turns he is to be seen counting his profits, or listening to the voice of a very circuitous and personal Devil, or considering the moral or social implications of his episodes.

"Truth" in His Fiction

The relation of Defoe's longer narratives to the tradition of the English novel has been debated.[19] He has been regarded as following the picaresque type of fiction, and if the word *picaresque* is loosely used—as it certainly is by critics—one understands what is meant. But actually Defoe wrote rogue biography rather than the true picaresque. The eighteenth century was to conceive the picaresque in the light of René LeSage's masterpiece, *Gil Blas* (1715-35). There the tradition as formulated required biographical pattern, episodic structure with the protagonist living by his wits and passing from one social stratum to another or from one professional class to another, the object of the change being diversified social exposé or satire. This tradition is common in eighteenth-century novels, and is seen in Sarah Fielding's *David Simple* (1744-53), Francis Coventry's *Pompey the Little* (1751), Charles Johnstone's *Chrysal* (1760-65), Smollett's *Adventures of an Atom* (1769), and many other minor masterpieces; but with this

The Picaresque Tradition

[19] It is shrewdly argued in Arthur W. Secord, *Studies in the Narrative Method of Defoe* (Urbana, Ill., 1924).

tradition, so far as conscious social exposé is concerned, Defoe has little in common. His traditions are clearly those of biography, voyage literature, and the moral treatise—of which last he himself produced various examples.[20] It is from the manual of piety that Defoe acquired his moralizing tone— which is hortatory rather than satirical. With the types of novel destined to be popular later in the century Defoe has less in common than one might think; but, on the other hand, with the spontaneous, unsophisticated methods of narration, far more fundamental than the temporary fashions that shaped the novel ten years or more after his death, Defoe has a great deal in common. He lacks power over domestic emotions, and these were to be the stock in trade of the sentimentalists; but his gifts are more basically sound than theirs, and his influence will endure as long as theirs. He is perhaps more realistic than many of them are; but he never seems to worry about conscientious fabrication of real life: he is, like the truly natural storyteller, content to create elaborate illusions of reality, and makes no attempt to build up a complete and authentic picture of Life for us. His stimulus— monetary returns apart—is that of his century: appetite for reflection upon the duty of man to man in a social world. The moral treatise thus becomes the positive pole in his fictional creations; adventure becomes the negative pole.

Preacher and Commentator   From first to last we may call him the preacher or editorial commentator. Crusoe is disobedient to his parents and to the God who had appropriately placed him in the scale of being; as a consequence of sin in leaving his proper station he is thereafter to feel frequently that he was "the most miserable wretch that ever was born." In *Moll Flanders* Defoe glides easily and briefly into editorial comments on the advantages of a foundling asylum, and *A Journal of the Plague Year,* written when a recurrence of the plague was feared in London, takes time to argue the inhumanity of so vital a matter as quarantine. His voyage stories like to expose the unfair trading practices of low foreigners, who—to make matters worse in his extreme Protestant mind—are Catholics as well as foreigners. His historical romances at times reflect the ideas of the Good Old Cause of the sixteen-forties. His geographical and historical detail is the product of much journalistic reading, and it is this reading, together with his shrewd observation of contemporary life, that gave both the rich variety and the vivid detail of his narratives. The vitality and fecundity of genius shown by Defoe after he was sixty years old remain as astonishing as are the earlier wily arts of the ablest journalist and pamphleteer of his time.

[20] His *Family Instructor* (1715) was frequently reprinted and so was his *Religious Courtship* (1722).

IV

Jonathan Swift

In some ways Jonathan Swift's career [1] parallels that of Daniel Defoe.[2] Both were considerably occupied in the dangerous career of political writer, and both were energetic supporters of Robert Harley, Earl of Oxford. The contrast between the two has been symbolized by the supposition that *Swift and* Swift was received by the front door whereas Defoe waited on the back *Defoe: a* stairs. Defoe was, to be sure, a tradesman, and Swift came of somewhat *Contrast* more genteel stock; but the real difference in the men lies in the fact that Defoe was a dissenter and had a middle-class practical education. Swift was a churchman, and *speciali gratia* a university graduate. An independent neo-classicist, Swift had and knew how to use brilliantly a "good classical training." Defoe was hardly conscious of the classics as patterns for writing. Both men were endowed with a strong common sense; both viewed mankind with curiosity—and suspicion. Defoe possessed a wide factual knowledge of the political, social, and economic conditions of England, whereas Swift was content to condemn "conditions"—rashly at times—because he found them abysmally divorced from his ideals. He viewed conditions with

[1] The *Works* of Swift, collectively published by George Faulkner in 1735 (4v, Dublin), *et seq.*, have been edited as follows: by John Hawkesworth (12v,.1755; 20v, 1764-79), Thomas Sheridan (17v, 1784), Sir Walter Scott (19v, Edinburgh, 1814, 1824), Temple Scott (Bohn Library, 12v, 1897-1908), and Herbert Davis (1939 ff., in progress). The *Poems* have been superbly edited by Harold Williams (3v, Oxford, 1937) and the *Correspondence* by F. Elrington Ball (6v, 1910-14). See also *Vanessa and her Correspondence with Jonathan Swift*, ed. Alexander M. Freeman (1921); and *The Letters of Swift to Charles Ford*, ed. David Nichol Smith (1935); *A Tale of a Tub* (1704, 1710); ed. A. C. Guthkelch and David Nichol Smith (Oxford, 1920); *Gulliver's Travels* (1726, 1735 [in *Works*]); ed. G. Ravenscroft Dennis (Bohn Library *Works*, Vol. VIII, 1899); Harold Williams (1926); Arthur E. Case (1938); Herbert Davis and Harold Williams (Oxford, 1941). — Among the many biographies may be mentioned those of John, fifth Earl of Orrery (*Remarks*, 1752); John Hawkesworth (1755); Deane Swift (1755); Samuel Johnson (*Lives of the Poets*, 1781); Thomas Sheridan (1784); John Forster (1875); Sir Henry Craik (1882; 2v, 1894); John Churton Collins (1893); Carl Van Doren (1930); Bertram Newman (1937); and Robert W. Jackson (1939). — The best commentaries are William A. Eddy, *A Critical Study of Gulliver's Travels* (Princeton, 1923); Sybil Goulding, *Swift en France* (Paris, 1924); Emile Pons, *Swift: Les années de jeunesse et le Conte du Tonneau* (Strasbourg, 1925); F. Elrington Ball, *Swift's Verse* (1928); Herbert Davis, "Swift's View of Poetry," *Studies in English* (Toronto, 1931); Harold Williams, *Dean Swift's Library* (1932); Marjorie Nicolson, *The Microscope and English Imagination* (Northampton, Mass., 1935); Richard F. Jones, *Ancients and Moderns: A Study of the Background of the Battle of the Books* (St. Louis, 1936); Ricardo Quintana, *The Mind and Art of Jonathan Swift* (1936). — Bibliographies of Swift have been published by W. Spencer Jackson in Vol. XII of the Bohn Library (Temple Scott) ed. of Swift's *Prose Works* (1908), by Dr. H. Teerink (Hague, 1937), by Harold Williams in *CBEL*, II. 581-596, and by Louis A. Landa and James E. Tobin, *Jonathan Swift, A List of Critical Studies Published from 1895 to 1945* (1945). More specialized aids are cited below in footnotes.

[2] See John F. Ross, *Swift and Defoe: a Study in Relationship* (Berkeley and Los Angeles, 1941); ably reviewed by Louis A. Landa in *PQ*, XXI (1942). 221-223.

contempt, and hence has been called a cynic; but if a cynic is one who denies the existence of humane values, the term cannot be applied to him; for his excellent sense of values is implicit in all that he wrote. He wrote contemptuously and vexatiously, if you like, yet always for the good of mankind. Curiously enough, like Defoe, when he was sure a public measure was right—and, when sure, he was likely to be very sure—he was sometimes unscrupulous in his means of supporting that measure. The personal reputations of Defoe and Pope have suffered because critics have known them only partially. Swift, more than any man of his day, has suffered from deliberate romanticizing of his career. It is true that he, more than most geniuses, fancied himself in the rôle of merit unrewarded; it is true that he writes frequently in an emotionally intense manner: his external frigidity indicates ardor within; but it is also true that he writes with exquisite playfulness. The romantics exaggerated the blackness of his grumblings and intensities, and forgot his gifts for sheer fun.

Aspects of Swift's Career — Intellectually his career has ecclesiastical, political, social, and even philosophical aspects: chronologically it has four or five phases that must be surveyed if we are to understand him. He was born (1667) of English parents living in Ireland; and there he was educated. He was graduated from Trinity College, Dublin, with some difficulty because of his refusal to study logic, and he left Ireland for England at the time of the Revolution (1688). This first phase of his career, in which his rôle had been that of dependent poor relation, had unfortunately built up in the young man an inordinate and overbearing pride.

Swift at Moor Park — His second rôle was that of secretary to Sir William Temple, then living in retirement chiefly at Moor Park, Surrey. While Swift languished here, his former schoolmate and friend, William Congreve, was winning fame in London. Eyeing, therefore, the metropolis, Swift was discontented at Moor Park. There were compensations—some perhaps unappreciated. He there met distinguished guests—among them King William himself; and he learned from Temple much about politics [3] and absorbed Temple's disbelief in the idea of progress, his belief in cycles of change whereby civilization graced now China, now Peru, now Greece and Rome. Clearly he must have enjoyed his duty of supervising the education of the eight-year-old child, Esther Johnson, who perhaps was Sir William's natural daughter. Swift later developed an appetite for improving the minds of ladies whom he knew: Stella (as he later called Esther Johnson, after she had gone to live in Ireland) was his first and his only "perfect" pupil. In her, mind predominated, as he thought it should, over emotion.

His Early Odes — During his periods of service at Moor Park, ending with Sir William's death in 1699, Swift read and thought much, and wrote. His writing rather strangely began with a group of Pindaric odes, of which he published only one. This *Ode to the Athenian Society,* printed in *The Athenian Gazette*

---

[3] Robert J. Allen, "Swift's Earliest Political Tract and Sir William Temple's Essays," *Harvard Studies & Notes in Phil. & Lit.,* xix (1937). 3-12.

(1692), is like the odes which he did not publish, turgid, lofty, and obscure: not at all like Swift! If Dryden ever made the alleged remark, "Cousin Swift, you will never be a poet," it may well have been made as a critique on this ode. His unpublished epistles to Congreve and to Sir William are similarly involved and artificial: being in couplets they have no duty to rise to Cowleyan ecstasy. Never again was Swift to try lofty flights except to burlesque them. He evidently decided that thereafter any verse of his must be natural in a realistic, functionalist sense: his poetry was to be as "unpoetical" as possible, without ornament or high emotional glow.

At Moor Park also he wrote (1696-8) his first and very important prose, *A Tale of a Tub* and *The Battle of the Books,* which he published in 1704. Infinitely superior to his odes, these pieces are, nevertheless, akin to the *Early Prose* method of those early poems in their effervescence, in the way his fancy *Masterpiece* coruscates around the ideas it wishes to express or to discredit: there is no urge to forward-moving, direct structure here in his thought. These works had their origin in the so-called quarrel between the ancients and the moderns, which Temple's essay *Of Ancient and Modern Learning* (1690) had fanned into flame. William Wotton, a Cambridge don, in his *Reflections upon Ancient and Modern Learning* (1694), patiently explained to Temple and the world the real advances of modern science, and attacked Temple's ignorance as shown in his remarks about the antiquity of Aesop and the *Epistles* of Phalaris. In 1693 the Christ Church wits of Oxford set on young Charles Boyle, later Earl of Orrery, to edit the *Epistles* of Phalaris and thus exhibit their true quality—without repeating Temple's errors. The edition (1695) attacked Richard Bentley, then royal librarian at St. James's, for alleged discourtesy. Bentley, ever a fighter, had aided Wotton with a "Dissertation" appended to his *Reflections* in 1697, and retorted also in a second *Dissertation.* Swift, doubtless perceiving the impossibility of a crushing answer, began his part in the struggle, which was to pour out his already copious supply of contempt upon the whole silly controversy, and, more broadly, upon the conceited complacency of modern scholarship, criticism, and poetry. His vehicle in the simpler *Battle of the Books* (out of respect to Bentley the battle took place in the royal library) is the prose mock-heroic, and here Swift exhibits at its best the love of classical epic techniques that marked his period. The mock epic simile in which Bentley and Wotton are spitted on a single spear and the episode of the spider and the bee, with the fine moral by Aesop, constitute perfection in neo-classical writing. *A Tale of a Tub* is of wider scope and less unified structure. In the narrative sections about the three brothers, Peter (the Roman Church), Martin (the Lutheran or Anglican Church), and Jack (the English dissenters or extreme Protestants), he burlesques church history and dogma in a rash and, so others felt, sacrilegious fashion.[4] In the Digressions of the *Tale* he satirizes modern learning, criticism, and the general self-sufficiency of "moderns."

---

[4] On Swift's attitude towards religion, learning, and pedantry see David Nichol Smith, "Jonathan Swift, Some Observations." *Trans. Royal Soc. of Lit.,* XIV (1935). 29-48.

Here also, as in the section on "The Mechanical Operation of the Spirit," there are philosophical implications as to the methods of knowledge that have significance in the period. Practically no political issues are raised in this book.

In 1694, ambitious of a more independent career than Moor Park promised, Swift had returned to Ireland and become an ordained Anglican priest.[5] During a dull year in an Irish parish he found time to fall in love with a Belfast heiress, who regarded her ill health and his meager income as barriers to the marriage which in 1696 he much desired. Disappointed, he returned to Moor Park, and when, after Temple's death, he was back in Ireland as chaplain to the Earl of Berkeley and the heiress tried to reopen negotiations for a match, he concluded the affair with chilly regrets that neither his fortune nor her health had greatly improved. His reputation in the first decade of the new century doubtless depended on *A Tale of a Tub,* which was a sensation if not altogether a success, and on his position as editor of Temple's *Letters* and *Memoirs.* In the Berkeley household he produced certain literary witticisms that are typical of his playfulness—the best of these in verse is the burlesque *Petition of Frances Harris,* the maidservant who lost her purse and so her parson too. In prose his solemn banter of Lady Berkeley's fondness for the Hon. Robert Boyle's pious *Meditations* produced a delightful trifle, his *Meditation upon a Broomstick,* with its pontifical conclusion, "Surely Man is a Broomstick." Grave buffoonery was already his forte.

His London Years   From 1708 to 1714 Swift was chiefly in London, and these years, especially those after 1710, represent his period of triumph and disillusionment in public affairs. Some of his innocent playfulness persists in the early works of this period. *The Predictions for the Year 1708 ... by Isaac Bickerstaff, Esq.,* for example, and its succeeding pamphlets, in which the pseudonymous author (Bickerstaff) [6] of the later *Tatler* is created, are a real contribution to the literature of laughter, and the poetic rendering, new style, of Ovid's *Baucis and Philemon* shows Swift's gift of visual myth-making. In *Baucis and Philemon,* however, there is a savage undertone in the poet's attitude towards the village "Pack of churlish Boors," who may be thought to represent average mankind.

But by 1708 Swift had more serious work to do—though always he would do it with a mixture of savagery and mirth. His duty in London was to serve as a sort of representative of his Archbishop in attempting to regain for the Irish church certain tithes, which Queen Anne had remitted to English parishes but not to those in Ireland. He is consequently involved

[5] On the much disputed problems concerning Swift's religion see C. Looten, *La Pensée religieuse de Swift et ses antinomies* (Lille and Paris, 1935); Hans Reimers, *Jonathan Swift: Gedanken und Schriften über Religion und Kirche* (Hamburg, 1935); see also F. M. Darnall, "Swift's Religion," *JEGP,* xxx (1931). 379-382; and especially Louis A. Landa, "Swift, the Mysteries, and Deism," *Studies in English, University of Texas* (Austin, 1945; dated 1944). pp. 239-256.
[6] W. A. Eddy, "Tom Brown and Partridge the Astrologer," *MP,* xxviii (1930). 163-168, illuminates this procedure.

in ecclesiastical politics, and these concerned the Bill for Occasional Con- *Ecclesiasti-* formity. As early as Section xi of *A Tale of a Tub* Swift had disapproved *cal Politics* of the occasional conformity [7] of the Lord Mayor of 1697, as Defoe had done in his *Enquiry into the Occasional Conformity of Dissenters;* and now Swift in his *Letter ... concerning the Sacramental Test* (1709) opposed repeal of the Test, even for Ireland. The Letter is supposedly by a member of the Irish Parliament, who assures his English cousins: "If your little finger be sore, and you think a poultice made of our vitals will give it any ease, speak the word and it shall be done." The argument and tone of the *Letter,* typical of Swift's method of inflaming rather than convincing, estranged him from the government of Godolphin and Sunderland, whose price for the desired tithes was repeal of the Test in Ireland. Consequently when in 1710 these Whigs went out of office and Swift's personal friend Robert Harley, a moderate Tory, became Lord Treasurer, it was easy for Swift to shift allegiance in party alignments that meant little at the time. In ecclesiastical issues he made no change: his brilliantly ironical *Argument to prove that the Abolishing of Christianity in England, may ... be Attended with some Inconveniences* (1711) continues his bitter attack upon those who would abolish the Test. It is one of his best ironical pieces.

For nearly four years (1710-14) he supported Robert Harley and Henry *His Services* St. John, each ennobled presently, the former as Earl of Oxford and the *to Robert* latter as Viscount Bolingbroke. Support of these moderate Tories cost *Harley* him the friendship of Addison and Steele, and doubtless of many others. The new ministry had started a paper called *The Examiner* (August 3, 1710 to July 26, 1714). It had not gone too well, but when Swift briefly took charge in October, 1710 (Nos. 14-46), it became a powerful aid to the ministry. Among its writers were Dr. William King (1663-1712), Mrs. Mary Manley, the novelist, and others—notably William Oldisworth (1680-1734), who was editor after the first volume, which ended in July, 1711. Before *The Examiner* Swift had had experience in writing for Steele's *Tatler* and later for his friend Harrison's continuation of *The Tatler.* Both in *The Examiner* and in his pamphlets Swift's function was to aid the ministry by discrediting the war party, especially the great general, John Churchill, Duke of Marlborough, and to persuade the public that the war was being prolonged because there was money in it for such men as the general, and James Brydges as paymaster and Robert Walpole as Secretary at War. The first step was to urge the selfishness of England's allies, to persuade readers that this had become a Continental, not an English fight. In his great pamphlet, *The Conduct of the Allies* (1711) and in its pendant *Some Remarks on the Barrier Treaty* (1712) Swift did these things effectively and perhaps

---

[7] The Corporation Act of 1661 and the Test Act of 1672 had required all officers of the Crown to take oaths of allegiance and to receive the sacrament of the Lord's Supper in the established church. These acts excluded Catholics from public office, but dissenters frequently did not scruple to take the Anglican communion occasionally, and thus qualify for office. Extreme high-churchmen were eager to promote bills forbidding this Occasional Conformity. To abolish "the Test," Swift says with supreme hyperbole, would be to abolish Christianity; but he is not sure that prohibiting Occasional Conformity is expedient.

sincerely: in politics it was easy for him to believe as he chose to believe. Among several other pamphlets in this process his *Public Spirit of the Whigs* (1714) was dangerously successful. It was a blistering reply to Steele's *Crisis* (1713), and it led the House of Lords to vote Swift's piece "a false, malicious, and factious libel" and to offer a reward of £300 for the discovery of the author. The Lord Treasurer reassured the author privately with a gift of £100, and when the new Parliament met, Steele, because of *The Crisis* and other impudent behavior, was expelled from the House of Commons. For all these trying and dangerous labors Swift naturally hoped for public rewards. More than once when opportunities for ecclesiastical preferment seemed promising he jogged the memory of the Lord Treasurer, and so did his friends. In April, 1713, he was finally made Dean of St. Patrick's Cathedral, Dublin—a place that paid better than some English bishoprics, but still it was in a sense exile, and he was not a bishop! Although he spoke often of the ingratitude of ministers, Swift continued to esteem and to correspond with both Harley and St. John. These two ministers had not well coöperated, and their ministry was a failure before the Queen died in August, 1714. The Tory party then totally disintegrated. Wittily perverting the posy from Virgil, famous as the motto of the East India Company, Dr. Arbuthnot, physician to her late Majesty, wrote, "Fuimus Tories." The *ingens gloria* of Swift was also eclipsed.

Non-political Writing   A gentleman's pen is by no means so tireless as a hack writer's; hence during his period of party politics Swift produced no works of imaginative importance. He had written admirable *Tatlers,* and deserves credit for formulating some methods of that periodical. He had written only one pamphlet with his name signed to it. Early in 1712 he had addressed to Lord Oxford *A Proposal for Correcting, Improving and Ascertaining the English Tongue,* in which he advocated the establishment of an English Academy, but without success: "precision and perspicuity," as the Earl of Chesterfield was later to remark, "not being in general the favourite objects of ministers." Swift at various times in his career exhibits an amateur interest in purity and decorum of language. In his *Proposal* he praises notably the simplicity, beauty, and strength of the King James version of the Bible and the "true sublime eloquence" of the English liturgy. His wish to reform speech and style appears again most favorably in his *Letter to a Young Clergyman* (1721), where he defines a true style as "Proper words in proper places." His insistence on elegance in conversation is seen also in his essays on education and in his masterly satire on trite diction in his *Complete Collection of Genteel and Ingenious Conversation,* published in 1738 but probably written some years earlier.

To posterity the most attractive of Swift's writings during his political activities in London is probably the volume that contains his letters to *The Journal to Stella*   Esther Johnson and her duenna Rebecca Dingley. These were first published in 1766-8, and since 1784 have been printed under the title of *Journal to Stella*—though the name Stella was apparently not used by Swift for Esther

Johnson at that period (1710-13) or in the correspondence. The letters give a most vivid picture of daily life in London and a behind-the-scenes account of the politics of the day, detailed if not altogether unprejudiced. But because of the title, *Journal to Stella,* interest has fallen upon the display and the nature of the affection Swift so obviously felt for these ladies, particularly for Stella. His somewhat crudely jocose attitude towards the duenna "Bec" is not without affection or respect; but for her he would not indulge, as he does for Stella, in the baby-talk language that sprinkles the correspondence. Some of Swift's acquaintance believed that in 1716 he was secretly married to Stella: such gossip was common about other men of Swift's day, and the evidence in his case, in some ways plausible, is not perfectly convincing in view of the unaccountable fact that Swift and Stella never lived under the same roof or met in private.[8] The *Journal,* however, is a most delightful document, and shows Swift at his playful best, whether in giving accounts of his drunken servant Patrick, who liked to read Congreve's plays, or in apostrophizing an unanswered letter from Stella:

And now let us come and see what this saucy dear letter of MD says. Come out, letter, come out from between the sheets; here it is underneath, and it won't come out. Come out again, I say; so there. Here it is. What says Presto [Swift] to me, pray? says it. Come, and let me answer for you to your ladies. Hold up your head then, like a good letter. There.

After his retirement to Dublin in 1714 Swift spent several doleful years. *The Irish Patriot* Always an insatiate and witty grumbler, he uses expressions in letters to his English friends that can be much discounted and yet still convey deep depression. "You are to understand," he writes to Pope, "that I live in the corner of a vast unfurnished house...and when I do not dine abroad, or make an entertainment, which last is very rare, I eat a mutton-pie, and drink half a pint of wine. My amusements are defending my small dominions against the archbishop, and endeavouring to reduce my rebellious choir. *Perditur haec inter misero lux.*" For a time he wrote little; but after a few years he began, either out of sense of the injustices that Ireland suffered or out of his desire to vex the English ministry, to write pamphlets like the *Letter to a Young Clergyman,* which was designed to improve the Irish priesthood, or like his vexatious *Proposal for the Universal Use of Irish Manufacture* (1720), which urged a complete boycott of English imports.

[8] In view of this last fact the relevance of the marriage ceremony to any understanding of Swift's work is hard to see. Yet much ink has been shed on this subject. In his *Jonathan Swift* (1893) J. Churton Collins argued against the ceremony. In the Temple Scott edition of Swift's *Works,* XII (1908). 83-106, the Rev. J. H. Bernard summarized the evidence and believed in the marriage. In *PMLA,* XLII (1927). 157-161, Marguerite Hearsey presented "New Light on the Evidence for Swift's Marriage," and the whole controversy is summarized by Maxwell B. Gold, *Swift's Marriage to Stella* (Cambridge, Mass., 1937). Mr. Gold is convinced that there was a marriage ceremony, that Swift offered to announce the marriage publicly, and that his (alleged) impotence precluded consummation. For this somewhat curious position Mr. Gold has less new evidence of importance than he imagines; and without further new evidence the marriage ceremony can neither be proved nor disproved. R. K. Root has admirably reviewed Gold's book in *PQ,* XVII (1938). 205-206. A general view of "Swift and Marriage" is given by George Hand in *Essays and Studies by Members of the Department of English of the University of California,* XIV (1943). 73-92.

His position among the Irish was completely changed by the appearance
of a series of pamphlets published in 1724, and commonly known as *Drapier's
Letters*. Like all pamphleteers Swift liked to write in an assumed character,
and here he signed his letters "M. B. Drapier." He was taking occasion
again to inflame passions rather than to calm the minds of such people
as believed that a patent granted to one William Wood to coin halfpence
for Irish use was a "vile job" designed to cheat impoverished Irish subjects
by false or debased coinage. Wood's halfpence were, as the Master of the
Mint—Sir Isaac Newton himself!—certified, a sound coinage; but throughout most of 1724 Dublin was in a tumult, and Swift was fanning the flames.
In October, after his fourth letter had breathed defiance and urged a boycott
of the coinage, a reward of £300 was offered for discovering the author:
the printer was already in confinement. The authorship was no secret, but
proof of authorship was not to be bought. With fervor Irish mouths were
quoting I Sam. 14: 45: "Shall *Jonathan* die, who hath wrought this great
salvation in Israel? God forbid: as the Lord liveth, there shall not one hair
of his head fall to the ground; for he hath wrought with God this day."
It was one of Swift's greatest triumphs, and Pope's lines upon the affair were,
Swift thought, "the greatest honor I shall ever receive from posterity."
Pope wrote:

> Let Ireland tell, how Wit upheld her cause,
> Her Trade supported, and supply'd her Laws;
> And leave on SWIFT this grateful verse ingrav'd,
> The Rights a Court attack'd, a Poet sav'd.

After 1724 Swift was not merely the "Hibernian Patriot"; he was the best
loved man in Dublin, far more of a personage than he could ever be anywhere in England. In 1726 when he landed in Dublin after a sojourn of
over four months in England, upon his arrival all the church bells were
rung and bonfires blazed at night. A hostile English newspaper commented,
"There's scarce a Street in Town without a Representation of him for a
Sign." On his birthday (November 30) thereafter Dublin celebrated fre-
·quently with peals of bells, bonfires, and illuminations; and on July 1, 1740,
in celebration of the fiftieth anniversary of King William's victory at the
Boyne, the Dean, in turn, gratified the populace with "the largest bonfire`
ever seen" in Dublin. Building bonfires of one sort or another had long
been his sport.

Gulliver's   Before he undertook the rôle of Drapier, Swift had already completed much
Travels   of his masterpiece, *Travels into Several Remote Nations of the World*,[9]

[9] For editions of *Gulliver* see n. 1 of this chapter. For commentaries, not in editions, see
Henry M. Dargan, "The Nature of Allegory as Used by Swift," *SP*, XIII (1916). 159-179;
Sir Charles H. Firth, "The Political Significance of *Gulliver's Travels*," *Proc. of the British
Academy*, IX (1920), reprinted in Firth's *Essays Historical and Literary* (Oxford, 1938);
Lucius L. Hubbard, *Contributions toward a Bibliography of Gulliver's Travels* (Chicago, 1922);
William A. Eddy, *A Critical Study of Gulliver's Travels* (Princeton, 1923); Marjorie Nicolson
and Nora M. Mohler, "The Scientific Background of Swift's 'Voyage to Laputa'," *Annals of
Science*, II (1937). 299-334, and by the same authors, "Swift's Flying Island in the 'Voyage to
Laputa'," *Annals of Science*, II (1937). 405-430; R. W. Frantz, "Gulliver's 'Cousin Sympson',"

which was printed in London in 1726. Though some parts may have been devised in the days of the Scriblerus Club (*c.* 1713-14), most of it was certainly written in the years 1721-5. Of all Swift's writings it best shows the merits of his mind and his gifts of expression. The voyages to Lilliput and to Brobdingnag illustrate the increasing tendency of the day to see truth in relative terms: as Gulliver is to the Lilliputians, so are the Brobdingnagians to him. Under the microscope truths assume different shapes. These first two voyages focus attention on the corruptions of court life; but Lilliput had had a noble past (chapter VI) before sophistication and chicanery had corrupted "original institutions," and the Brobdingnagians are for the most part large of mind as well as of body. Both of these nations, pictured with richly ingenious and delightful surface detail, have lessons for Gulliver, and throughout these two voyages Swift's playfulness is dazzling. The next voyage to be written was the fourth, to Houyhnhnmland, where animal man, the Yahoo, is contrasted with the "perfection of nature" seen in the Houyhnhnms—who are figured as horses. Again Swift gives childlike play to surface ingenuity in his depiction of the human habits of these "horses"—their weaving of mats, threading of needles, etc. Gulliver is not quite identified with the loathsome Yahoos, but his kinship is as unquestionable as is his admiration for Houyhnhnm virtues. Although this voyage is Swift's most misanthropic writing, yet he makes Gulliver profit in truthfulness, cleanliness, and devotion to the life of reason, from his association with these ideal people. His unsociability upon his return to human society is doubtless misanthropic: it illustrates Swift's fundamental horror of the gulf between the actual and the ideal. The fourth voyage, with the third, which was the last to be written, deals with corruptions of theoretical reason, while the first two voyages had dealt with matters of practical reason. Gulliver's Houyhnhnm master "dreaded lest the corruption of 'reason' might be worse than brutality itself," and in the third voyage Gulliver met men whose thirst for theory and for novelty in technical method—whether in the writing of books, in the manufacture of sunbeams, or the making of clothes—made them to him more dreadful than brutes. Technical knowledge had been disparaged in the first two voyages in brief passages where the educational methods of the nations visited were described. In this third voyage technical knowledge is extensively derided: he regards its ingenuity as misplaced, its passion for novelty as unnatural, and its preoccupations in general as unfitting man for society. And the chief function of reason, according to eighteenth-century views, was to fit man for a happy life among his fellows. As a whole *Gulliver's Travels* has the multiple intentions of a masterpiece: it can be read by children for its narrative and descriptive charm; it can be read by learned historians as an allegory of the political life of Swift's time; it can be read as a burlesque

HLQ, I (1938). 329-334; John R. Moore, "The Geography of *Gulliver's Travels*," *JEGP*, XL (1941). 214-228; Merrel D. Clubb, "The Criticism of Gulliver's 'Voyage to the Houyhnhnms,' 1726-1914," *Stanford Stud. in Lang. and Lit.* (1941), pp. 203-232; Arthur E. Case, *Four Essays on Gulliver's Travels* (Princeton, 1945).

of voyage literature; it can be read (at least it has been read) as a master-piece of misanthropy; it is perhaps best read as the ingenious reflections of a thoughtful man on the abuses of human reason. It fascinates the reader by the seemingly unaffected directness and simplicity of its manner or by the subtlety of its reflections on man and his corrupt behavior at court, at home, or in his study. It is important to realize that it could be written only by one who had the highest ideals for human achievement and who despaired of the achieving.

Later Occasional Pieces

After his exploits as Drapier Swift wrote less and less, and what he wrote tended to be *jeux d'esprit* merely. One of his best poems, *Cadenus and Vanessa,* which had been written in 1712 or 1713 to cure Esther Van-homrigh of a passion for Swift, appeared in 1726, three years after the lady's death. On one level it is a piece of autobiography; on a higher level it is again Swift's program for the improvement of the feminine mind. It was in this latter fashion that contemporaries took it, without looking for scandal. It thus finds a less imaginative equivalent in his prose *Letter to a very Young Lady on her Marriage.* In more savage tone appeared in 1729 his *Modest Proposal for Preventing the Children of Poor People from Being a Burthen to their Parents or Country.* By this proposal that the starving Irish should sell their own infants as food and thus make a modest, inoffensive livelihood, Swift is again charging the British Parliament with gross injustice to Ireland,[10] and is, at least in method, mimicking the "political arithmeticians" who held that people are "a most precious *commodity*," as one of them said. The Laputanlike "systems" of such projectors as con-tinually sent the ministry wild projects for raising money must have irked Swift, who, with his Brobdingnagians, derided the mystery of politics and preferred a modicum of moral common sense. Thus he rises to an ironic climax when he exclaims, "Let no man talk to me of other expedients," such as—and he enumerates several devices agreeable to justice and good sense that might serve rulers actuated by morality and benevolence. Unlike Burke at the other end of the century, he does not *seem* to rail at the rising influence of "sophisters, economists, and calculators" who were thought to subvert political honor. Swift assumes the quiet tone of a humble projector, who, weary of visionary schemes, has fortunately fallen upon this proposal, "which as it is wholly new, so it hath something solid and real, of no expense and little trouble, full in our power, and whereby we can incur no danger in *disobliging* ENGLAND." And, like a good scientist, he is willing to consider any other project "equally innocent, cheap, easy, and effectual." Irony can go no further than in this pamphlet.

The publication of many of Swift's small things was left to his friend Pope, who in four volumes of *Miscellanies* (1727-32) grouped together pieces by members of the Scriblerus Club. Swift here made a dominant showing. In 1735, as we now know, he coöperated with his Dublin publisher in

---

[10] See Louis A. Landa's two articles: "*A Modest Proposal* and Populousness," *MP,* XL (1942). 161-170; "Swift's Economic Views and Mercantilism," *ELH,* X (1943). 310-335.

bringing out his *Works,* and almost his last literary labors must have been the revision of his letters to Pope, which Pope had sent him, already printed in a volume, with an anonymous letter suggesting publication. All of Swift's major works were published with some background of mystification, and he evidently understood and abetted Pope's schemes. The letters appeared in the early summer of 1741: Pope in London published the text he had prepared; Faulkner in Dublin used the text Swift had revised for him. Pope protested hypocritically at the "tricks" of publishers; the Dean, so far as we know, said nothing.[11]

Swift had from his early years suffered from labyrinthine vertigo; before *His Mental* he was sixty he was very deaf; and in his seventy-fifth year (March, 1742) *Decay* guardians were appointed, since his mind—said in the application for the appointment of guardians to have been failing for eighteen months—was then much decayed. He had long been socially difficult, what with his quick temper, his pride, and his love of practical jokes; and his relatives tended to stress his violence of mood. He himself had long complained of loss of memory, and such complaints increased, justifiably, in the last years. It is doubtfully accurate, however, to say that Swift went mad. Old age, aggravated by vertigo and deafness, caused the decay of his faculties. Violence there doubtless was: there had always been a tendency to violence in Swift, and with the restraining power of reason weakened, childish indulgence of wrath developed. It is said that when his mind was quite gone, his servants used to take money for allowing people to come in and stare at him. He died thus "a driveler and a show" in 1745.

In the case of more than one great writer a single phrase seems to sum *Indignation* up the characteristic quality of the man. Thus *saeva indignatio* has been *and a Sense* the fixed label for Swift's dominant mood. Such a summation is dangerous, *of Values* since, for example, it excludes totally the quality of effervescent playfulness that is almost equally important; but a mordant indignation certainly explains much of Swift. His lack of peace within himself was due to many things, but certainly was in large part due to the abysmal gulf between his ideals for human nature and human nature as he found it. He called himself a misanthrope, and it is clear that for human nature as found in the mass he had unlimited contempt. But he had also a high and clear sense of values, and this caused his contempt to tear his heart with an anxiety to improve humanity. His passion for improving women is obvious: not merely little Stella, the heiress Varina, and the passionate Vanessa were subjected to his instruction: the Countess of Burlington, Lady Betty Germain, Lady Acheson, and even the ineffable Letitia Pilkington, were all his pupils. He might occasionally make them cry, but they all loved and respected their "teacher." (One must never forget that most people found Swift a very companionable person.) He was constantly trying to improve the government, the English language, the Irish clergy, Trinity College Dublin,

[11] Maynard Mack, "The First Printing of the Letters of Pope and Swift," *Library,* XIX (1939). 465-485; and Capt. Vinton A. Dearing, "New Light on the First Printing of the Letters of Pope and Swift," *Library,* XXIV (1943). 74-80.

and all the world besides, for he wrote chiefly for the mankind that he despised. A man so devoted to human uplift is a strange sort of misanthrope —one who despairs and believes at once.

Reason and Dogmatism   To Swift "reason" was the good word. His most significant comments on reason are to be found in the Digression IX "On Madness" in *A Tale of a Tub*, in *The Mechanical Operation of the Spirit*, published with the *Tale*, and in the last two voyages of *Gulliver*. In his discourse "On Madness" he applies a highly skeptical analysis to the act of intellectual conviction, to the problem of just what happens in the mind when we are "convinced." To him it seems not to be a rational process but rather a matter of two minds vibrating in unison, or some such thing. The proselytizer or the conqueror, who wishes to make men agree with *him,* is mad. So are the enthusiasts who imagine they have private revelations or inspirations about spiritual truths. He holds that the more a man "shapes his understanding by the pattern of human learning, the less he is inclined to form parties after his particular notions." Swift is a conservative, believing in common sense, not in private notions, but in the uniformity of nature. One should accept things as they are, to be happy; one should (ironically) "content his ideas with the films and images that fly off upon his senses from the superficies of things.... This is the sublime and refined point of felicity, called, the possession of being well deceived; the serene peaceful state, of being a fool among knaves." In less ironical vein another might have said: "Be content with what the physical senses offer, and know that The Whole is designed and governed by the All-wise Creator." That was the road many of his generation took; but Swift was no optimist. He assented to orthodox Anglican doctrine dogmatically; he tolerated no argument about such matters: they were settled. But he was at the same time temperamentally despondent and even skeptical: only dogmatism could keep the peace. He came to attach almost a transcendent meaning to reason, but what he really valued was the concept of the "light of reason" as opposed to any logical argumentative faculty. Hence Swift is an anti-rationalist and almost an enthusiast when he praises reason in its perfection. He is normally a common-sense rationalist, and despises strange new doctrines: his contempt for the Laputan thirst for novelty in practical matters is paralleled by his hatred of new theories in religion, statecraft, or in society. "Common sense suffices," might almost have been his remark. In the Digression on Madness he exclaims: "But when a man's fancy gets astride on his reason, when imagination is at cuffs with the senses, and common understanding, as well as common sense, is kicked out of doors; the first proselyte he makes, is himself, and when that is once compassed, the difficulty is not so great in bringing over others; a strong delusion always operating from without as vigorously as from within." That sentence contains by implication Swift's basic theory of writing: it is useless to argue with Men; the thing to do is to warm and dazzle them with a bonfire.

Swift's art, then, is as significant as his intellectual content. But it is not so much the structural or architectural design of his greater works that *Method and* is impressive. The alternating narrative (*dulce*) and digression (*utile*) of *Substance* *A Tale of a Tub* have been rhapsodically praised, though that method seems to be a novelty that Swift himself should have seen as confusing and ineffectual. Likewise the multiplication of preliminaries to the *Tale*, though each is in itself a gem, is excessive. In *Gulliver* he has more control, and shapes his materials more easily than he did in the *Tale*. But there is still a curious duality, which makes easy contrasts in relative values, but is essentially, and quite satisfactorily, episodic. Like the other writers of his day Swift achieves highest excellence in the invention of detail. In his gift for allegory and for myth-making he certainly surpasses all others of his time. Here he is supreme, ranging from the spider and the bee to Lilliput and Brobdingnag. One may note also such typical small bits as the incisively casual ending of his *Seasonable Advice* [as Drapier] *to the Grand Jury*, which might be forced into indicting him:

Once upon a time the *Wolves* desired a League with the *Sheep*, upon this Condition; that the Cause of strife might be taken away, which was the Shepherds and *Mastiffs;* this being granted, the *Wolves* without all Fear made Havock of the Sheep.

This ability to strike out analogies that are simple-appearing but serpentlike in implication marks one of Swift's great merits—perhaps his greatest. He is constantly praised for his precision, plainness, and purity of language. (Purity is here used in its rhetorical sense: his passion for arousing disgust by the frank use of foul words and images is of course one of his abnormalities.) He knows how to make words do what he wants them to do as well as any man who ever wrote English; but sometimes he is not clear as to just what he wants to do, and allows himself a virtuosity of witty effervescence that delights or wounds by turns: it consistently dazzles. Sensitive minds find a lack of shading in his images, which do come forth with tense explicitness usually, with every phrase in perfect individual focus. He represents at its best the eighteenth-century ambition to combine clarity and strength of style. He and Defoe together represent two different approaches to problems of life, the aristocratic classicist and the middleclass economist. The writings of both, though aiming to reform, call attention to the numerous abuses of the *ancien régime,* and so become an important part of the movement of illumination that led to the abolition of this regime that they merely wished to reform.

V

Addison, Steele, and the Periodical Essay

The Nature of the Periodical Essay

The periodical essay, "invented" towards the very end of the seventeenth century, reached its acme of achievement early in the eighteenth in the work of Richard Steele (1672-1729) and Joseph Addison (1672-1719). It maintained a great popularity throughout the century, and disappeared about 1800.[1] Rigorous definition of this peculiarly eighteenth-century type of publication is not very helpful. The "dialogue" papers, such as Sir Roger L'Estrange's *Observator* (1681-7), *The Athenian Gazette* (1690-97), Tutchin's *Observator* (1705-6), and Charles Leslie's *Rehearsal* (1704-9), as well as others of the same type, used material similar to that embodied in the periodical essay, but, because of their mechanical dialogue form, never achieved essay structure. "Learned" periodicals were more technical and bookish in substance than essays should be, and hence most of the work of Jean de la Crose in his various periodicals or of such writers as Richard Willis in his *Occasional Paper* (1697-8) fell into the class of book-reviewing. Popular monthly reviews we shall find established in the second half of the eighteenth century; and the magazine, as they knew it—a storehouse for fugitive reprints from weekly newspapers,—has been regarded as beginning in 1731 with *The Gentleman's Magazine*. The periodical essay has been aptly described as dealing with morals and manners, but it might in fact deal with anything that pleased its author. It covered usually not more than the two sides (in two columns) of a folio half-sheet: normally it was shorter than that. It might be published independently of other material, as was *The Spectator*, except for advertising; or it might be the leading article in a newspaper.

Formative Influences

The shaping influences of this essay were journalistic rather than the traditions of Montaigne, Bacon, or Cowley. There is a considerable influence of the seventeenth-century "character";[2] and such pictures of daily life as

[1] For a bibliography of the periodical essay see Ronald S. Crane and F. B. Kaye, *A Census of British Newspapers and Periodicals, 1620-1800* (Chapel Hill, 1927) or Walter Graham in *CBEL*, II. 660-668. For histories and criticism see Nathan Drake, *Essays ... Illustrative of the Tatler, Spectator, and Guardian* (3v, 1805); John Nichols, *Literary Anecdotes of the Eighteenth Century* (9v, 1812-15. Index in Vol. VII); H. R. Fox Bourne, *English Newspapers* (2v, 1887); Lawrence Lewis, *The Advertisements of the Spectator* (1909); Hugh Walker, *The English Essay and Essayists* (1915); George S. Marr, *The Periodical Essayists of the Eighteenth Century* (1924); Walter Graham, *English Literary Periodicals* (1930); James R. Sutherland, "The Circulation of Newspapers and Literary Periodicals, 1700-1730," *Library*, xv (1934). 110-124.
[2] Walter Graham, "Some Predecessors of the *Tatler*," *JEGP*, xxiv (1925). 548-554; and "Defoe's *Review* and Steele's *Tatler*—the Question of Influence," *JEGP*, xxxiii (1934). 250-254; Edward C. Baldwin, "The Relation of the Seventeenth-Century Character to the Periodical Essay," *PMLA*, xix (1904). 75-114.

those in Ned Ward's *London Spy* (1698-1700)—supposedly descended from
G. P. Marana's *Turkish Spy* (which was not a periodical)—clearly had
influence also. The periodical or pamphlet cast in the form of a letter, like
Willis's *Occasional Paper* or the anonymous *Miscellaneous Letters* (1694-6),
helped to popularize the use of the letter as an essay device. The periodical
essay usually had a dual aim: to amuse and to improve. It was through
deft management of the second of these, while not neglecting the first,
that Steele and Addison achieved their great success. The editorial devices
that they adopted—the single editor, aided by relatives or friends, or the
club of editors—had existed before them. The Observator was the best
known type of editorial personality of earlier times, and *The Weekly Comedy*
(12 numbers, 1699) and *The Humours of a Coffee-House* (1707-8), both
probably by Ned Ward, who had the assistance of William Oldisworth in
the second, showed how use could be made of a club or of a group of persons
that parallels noticeably the club of *The Spectator*. Editorial personalities
were not very carefully delineated at best. The Tatler, Isaac Bickerstaff,
frequently forgets his age of sixty-four and his profession as astrologer. The
Spectator is supposed to be a very taciturn man; but he gossips with all
the garrulity of his tattling predecessor. Serial publication fully as much
as collaboration is probably responsible for the inconsistencies of age and
behavior seen in the portraiture of both the Spectator and his friend Sir
Roger de Coverley.

One must conclude that the superiority of *The Tatler* and *The Spectator*[8]
over all other such periodicals—even those done separately by Steele and
Addison—is in part due to the happy combination of these two authors.
In literary reputation Addison[4] far surpasses Steele, but in his prose he is
never at his best except when working beside Steele.[5] Steele may have done
his most agreeable writing in the periodical essay, but as a pamphleteer
he was more stirring than Addison, and as a playwright he had more
influence than Addison—though he never produced a tragedy. The two

*The Early
Careers of
Addison
and Steele*

[8] The first collected edition of *The Tatler* was in four volumes, 1710-11. There were at
least 25 editions reprinted before 1800. It has been edited notably by John Nichols (6v, 1786),
Robert Bisset (4v, 1797), Alex. Chalmers (4v, 1803), George A. Aitken (4v, 1898-9). The
first collected edition of *The Spectator* was the small octavo (8v, 1712-15). It has been edited
by John Nichols (8v, 1789), Robert Bisset (8v, 1793-4), Alex. Chalmers, (8v, 1806), G.
Gregory Smith (8v, 1897-8; 1907 in Everyman's Library), George A. Aitken (8v, 1898).
[4] Addison's collected *Works* (with or without the periodical essays) have been edited by
Thomas Tickell (4v, 1721; 3v, 1726); Richard Hurd (6v, 1811); George W. Greene (6v,
1856); A. C. Guthkelch (2v, 1914). His *Letters* have been edited as a part of the *Works*
by Hurd, and separately by Walter Graham (Oxford, 1941). There is no first-rate life of
Addison, but lives have been written by Samuel Johnson (*Lives of the Poets*, ed. G. B. Hill,
Oxford, 1905, II. 79-158); Lucy Aiken (2v, 1843); William J. Courthope (1884). Bonamy
Dobrée in his *Essays in Biography* (Oxford, 1925) gives an interesting but somewhat prejudicial account of Addison.
[5] Steele's *Dramatic Works* were collected in 1723, 1734, etc. They have been edited by
George A. Aitken (1894, 1903). French translations of his political pamphlets were collected
as *Œuvres diverses sur les affaires de la Grande Bretagne traduit de l'Anglois* (Amsterdam,
1715). His miscellaneous prose is well edited by Rae Blanchard as *Tracts and Pamphlets*
(Baltimore, 1944). Steele's *Correspondence* is edited by John Nichols (1787, 1809) and by
Rae Blanchard (Oxford, 1941). The best biographies are those by Austin Dobson (1886),
George A. Aitken (2v, 1889), and Willard Connely (1934). That by Aitken contains an excellent bibliography, as does the *CBEL*.

men had been schoolmates in the Charterhouse, and had been at Oxford together, though not in the same college. From the University their paths seemed to diverge: Steele went into the army, became a captain of the Tower Guard, definitely a "city captain's" job, and there wrote his first book, *The Christian Hero* (1701), a pamphlet in commendation of King William III and of Christian as opposed to Stoic morals.[6] After producing three "reformed" comedies, and contributing verses to a monthly miscellany called *The Muses Mercury* (1707), he went into politics, and became the writer of the official *Gazette,* a periodical which he wrote from 1707 to 1710 "without ever erring against the rule observed by all Ministries, to keep that paper very innocent and very insipid." *The Tatler,* which he began April 12, 1709, and which appeared three times a week, until he suddenly dropped it with No. 271 (January 2, 1711), gave some release from this enforced tameness as Gazetteer.

Addison's
Early
Works When Steele left Merton College, Oxford (1694), without a degree, to enlist in the Duke of Ormonde's regiment of horse guards, his friend Addison, already an M.A., stayed on in various capacities, attaining in 1698 a fellowship in Magdalen College, which, though most of the time out of residence, he held until 1711. At Oxford he won some reputation for his verses, especially for those in Latin, which are still regarded as among the most correctly elegant to come from an English pen.[7] Among these his *Pygmaio-geranomachia* (1698) ("The Battle of the Pigmies and the Cranes") has been especially praised as inaugurating the typical eighteenth-century mock-heroic tradition and as demonstrating better than other poems by Addison his imaginative deftness. Deciding to make diplomacy his career, he spent the years 1699-1703 in a leisurely grand tour that enabled him to acquire the necessary languages and acquaintance with the courts of France, Italy, Germany, and Holland. During the years after his return he published certain classical translations; a poetical *Letter from Italy* to his patron Charles Montagu, Earl of Halifax; and, his great success, *The Campaign* (1705), a patriotic celebration of the Duke of Marlborough's victories. This poem was his best liked work before *The Spectator,* and in some sense it made his reputation. Most of his English poems, except his hymns, *Milton's Stile Imitated in a Translation out of ...the Third Aeneid* (1704), and his *Song for St. Cecilia's Day* (1694), are in the heroic couplet. His opera *Rosamond* (1707) pleased the Marlboroughs, who now owned Fair Rosamond's manor of Woodstock, but to the general public it seemed dismal. *The Campaign,* more successful as a party pamphlet perhaps than as a poem, procured its author's advancement to be Under-Secretary of State (1706-8). In 1709 his brother died in India, and shortly thereafter Addison is evidently, in contrast to Steele, a comparatively rich man. His career had none of the

---

[6] Ed. Rae Blanchard, with an Introduction (Oxford, 1932).
[7] Leicester Bradner, "The Composition and Publication of Addison's Latin Poems," *MP,* xxxv (1938). 359-367.

happy-go-lucky character of Steele's, and his position among men of letters and among statesmen was assured.

When Steele began *The Tatler*, Addison was in Ireland as Secretary to *Steele and* the Lord Lieutenant of that realm. To Steele, consequently, belongs all the *The Tatler* credit for the initiation of *The Tatler*, though he had some help from Swift, with whom he was then on terms of intimacy. The first four numbers were distributed gratis; thereafter it sold for a penny. It consisted of a folio half-sheet, and it was published on the days the London post went to the country, Tuesdays, Thursdays, and Saturdays. In the dedication to the first collected volume Steele wrote: "The general purpose of this paper, is to expose the false arts of life, to pull off the disguises of cunning, vanity, and affectation, and to recommend a general simplicity in our dress, our discourse, and our behavior." But with this attention to the *utile* Steele wisely heeded the appetite for the *dulce,* for amusement. Diversity was the great need, and so at the start he divided each paper into contrasting sections that derived from various sources, chiefly coffee-houses, in which he had (so he jokingly said) agents. "All accounts of gallantry, pleasure, and entertainment" were to come from the fashionable White's Chocolate-house—near St. James's Palace. Swift got his letters at White's, which became increasingly notorious for its gaming for high stakes. Poetry was to be reported from Will's Coffee-house, already made famous by Dryden, Wycherley, Congreve, and others, and the meeting place of Addison and his little coterie until they moved to Button's—founded apparently for their use. "Learning" was reported from the Grecian, near the Inns of Court, and "foreign and domestic news" came from St. James's Coffee-house, again near the palace. All other subjects, he concludes, "shall be dated from my own apartment." In No. 18 Steele remarked that his "chief scenes of action" were "coffee-houses, play-houses, and my own apartment"; that, consequently, he should find a public "as long as there are men or women, or politicians, or lovers, or poets, or nymphs, or swains, or cits, or courtiers in being." The days of publication show that he aimed to reach the country as well as "the cits"; this account of his audience again shows his breadth of intended appeal. For the first forty numbers his motto was Juvenal's *Quicquid agunt homines . . . nostri farrago libelli,* and his other favorite was the Horatian *Celebrare domestica facta.* As time went on and his success was quite assured, the number of sections in a given issue began to decline, until seldom more than two sections appeared, and "From my Own Apartment" became by all odds the favorite source of writing.[8] The precedent of division, however, enabled Steele, even in *The Spectator,* when time pressed and he was lazy, to slap together three letters that correspondents had sent in (and which he usually seems to have revised or rewritten), and call the three letters an essay.[9]

[8] Chester N. Greenough, "The Development of the Tatler," *PMLA,* xxxi (1916). 633-663.
[9] In 1725 Charles Lillie, the perfumer, to whose shop Tatler-Spectator correspondence had been addressed, was allowed to publish two volumes entitled *Original and Genuine Letters Sent to the Tatler and Spectator.* These volumes show the quantity and diversity of letters sent in. A few here printed had been used actually in the periodicals, but in a revised form.

Two
tyists
npared

Out of the 271 numbers of *The Tatler* Steele wrote 188, and Addison only 42; together they did 36 others.[10] Steele's prose never attained the elegant ease and correctness of Addison's, and yet it is probable that his tendency to warm to a subject and to write intimately and personally, as the reader's friend, contributed much to the success of the paper. Addison's best essays here are the result of his slightly chilly insight into the typical mental attitudes of his day. His portraiture of Ned Softly (No. 163), the pest who insisted on reading his verses aloud to the frequenters of Will's, exhibits a mastery of good-natured satire; and his Tom Folio (No. 158) is highly typical of the day in its laughter at pedantry. Much used by later writers was his depiction of the Political Upholsterer (Nos. 155, 160, etc.), an ignorant reader of news comically eager to know what the Czar of Muscovy was about but unregardful of the doings of his own family. His device in narrating the adventures of a shilling (No. 249) was also much imitated. These are papers of ingenious insight. Steele had the more pedestrian sections to do—the news, the theatre, and all that. But Steele had an interest in family affairs and a kindly way of writing about "the fair sex"[11] that won him friends and readers. Bickerstaff writes about his nephews (Nos. 30, 207), about the relations of parents and children (Nos. 235, 263),[12] and about the death of his father (No. 181)—surely Steele's own memories here—in an autobiographical intimacy exceedingly rare in that or any day. In view of the frequent essays on love and marriage, and also in view of the attitude of the Restoration period towards matrimony, it is interesting to read the comments of John Gay in his *Present State of Wit* (1711),[13] and see that he regards the Steele type of paper as giving *The Tatler* its peculiar appeal. He is enthusiastic in his praise, and remarks:

It would have been a jest some time since, for a man to have asserted that any thing witty could be said in praise of a married state; or that devotion and virtue were any way necessary to the character of a fine gentleman. ... [Bickerstaff's] writings have set all our wits and men of letters upon a new way of thinking, of which they had little or no notion before; and though we cannot yet say that any of them have come up to the beauties of the original, I think we may venture to affirm, that every one of them writes and thinks much more justly than they did some time since.

"It is no small thing," wrote Taine, "to make morality fashionable";[14] and Steele and Addison between them did more to rehabilitate English

---

[10] These are the figures of Nathan Drake, *Essays...Illustrative of the Tatler, Spectator, and Guardian*, III (1805). 376. The figures are very likely not too exact.

[11] Rae Blanchard, "Richard Steele and the Status of Women," *SP*, XXVI (1929). 325-355; also Joachim Heinrich, *Die Frauenfrage bei Steele und Addison* (Leipzig, 1930).

[12] No. 189, one of the best of these family papers, shows Steele's technique of using material from real life: here from the Molesworth family. See Robert J. Allen, "Steele and the Molesworth Family," *RES*, XII (1936). 449-454.

[13] Gay's remarkably good-natured pamphlet is reprinted in Edward Arber's *English Garner*, VI, (1883). 503-512, and from there in John Churton Collins, *An English Garner: Critical Essays and Fragments* [n.d.], pp. 201-210.

[14] Hippolyte A. Taine, *History of English Literature* (trans. by H. Van Laun, 1871), II. 103.

manners after the Restoration excesses than any other two men—not excepting the clergy.

The Spectator is of course by far the best of all periodical essays.[15] It also **The**
was a folio half-sheet, but unlike *The Tatler* it appeared daily—a severe **Spectator**
strain on the versatility and industry of its authors. It began two months
after Steele had suddenly abandoned *The Tatler,* and it ran from March
1, 1711 to December 6, 1712 (555 numbers) as a collaborative project. It
was then discontinued; but in June 1714 Addison, without Steele's aid, revived it, and saw it through another volume, somewhat more staid than
earlier volumes had been. Steele probably had wished to attend to other
matters—politics in particular. The paper had by no means abated in popularity, so far as one can observe. When, on August 1, 1712, Bolingbroke's
halfpenny tax was levied and many newspapers immediately disappeared,
The Spectator had doubled its price to twopence, and gone bravely on its
way. But soon thereafter the members of the Spectator's Club began to
die or to get married and go to live in the country. Clearly Steele foresaw
an end to *The Spectator,* and he did not wish piratical successors to plagi-
arize the personalities Addison and he had created.

In *The Spectator* Addison did by all odds his best writing—writing so
polished and easy that it makes his other works seem cold and formal.
Here he wrote rather more papers than Steele did,[16] and almost fifty were
contributed by such men as Eustace Budgell (1686-1737), John Hughes
(1677-1720), Alexander Pope, and others. At the time Steele was commonly
regarded as "Mr. Spectator," and he doubtless had the editorial responsibility.
The first essay, by Addison, gave a sketch of Mr. Spectator's character, and
in the second Steele introduced the famous Club. Of its members the
Templar (student of law), the Clergyman, and Captain Sentry (reporting
on military affairs) showed again the desire for diversity in point of view;
but neither they nor the slightly more useful Will Honeycomb ("the man
about town") and Sir Andrew Freeport (the merchant) are prominent
in many papers. Sir Roger de Coverley, however, appeared in many of the
most delightful essays. At first he was designed to be the survival of a
Restoration rake, but by an inconsistent transformation he became the Tory
country squire, aged and lovable, but politically incompetent.[17] As an

---

[15] The collected sets were in eight volumes. Addison's revival ran from No. 556 to 635
(June 18, 1714 to December 20, 1714). A ninth volume, by William Bond, Nos. 636-695
(January 3, 1715 to August 3, 1715), had of course no real relationship to its distinguished
predecessors. Bond was a writer "of very little genius" who later assisted Aaron Hill in his
Plain Dealer (1724-5). Bond died in 1735.

[16] N. Drake, *Essays . . . Illustrative of the Tatler,* etc. (1805), III. 377-379, reports that Addison wrote 274 complete papers; Steele 240; Budgell 37; John Hughes 11, etc. Fifty-three are left
anonymous. It is difficult to be exact in this matter. Addison began signing his essays with
one of the four letters *C, L, I, O*; Steele thereupon began using *R* and *T.* Budgell used *X,*
and *Z* stands for Hughes or some unknown person. In the original sheets these isolated letters
were at times badly placed, and they were sometimes omitted or changed in the collected
editions. The first collected edition changed or dropped 18 of these signatures from the
original sheets, and later changes have been made. Almost no two editions seem to agree in
their uses of these letters.

[17] Émile Legouis, "Les deux Sir Roger de Coverley," *Revue Germanique,* II (1906). 453-471.

outmoded figure he was once or twice contrasted with the Whiggish Sir Andrew Freeport in a manner prophetic of the social and economic revolution that was to occur in England at the end of the century.

Moral rpose

The purpose of the papers, well announced in No. 10, was "to enliven morality with wit, and to temper wit with morality." Addison continued: "It was said of Socrates, that he brought philosophy down from Heaven to inhabit among men; and I shall be ambitious to have it said of me, that I have brought philosophy out of closets, and libraries, schools, and colleges, to dwell in clubs and assemblies, at tea-tables and in coffee-houses." The success of the essays depended precisely on the ability of the two authors to do just this—to popularize moralizing. Steele, more than any man of equal literary ability in his day, reacted against the immorality of the Restoration. His dramatic criticism in both *The Tatler* and *The Spectator* is filled with this animus. His attacks on Etherege in Nos. 51 and 65 of *The Spectator* are significant of the changed taste. Steele is quite conscious of his bias, and comments on it in a letter supposedly from a gentleman aged "between fifty and sixty" who had enjoyed the best company in "the joyous reign of Charles the Second." He writes to Steele in No. 158:

> I have observed through the whole Course of your Rhapsodies, (as you once very well called them) you are very industrious to overthrow all that many your Superiors who have gone before you have made their Rule of writing....It is monstrous to set up for a Man of Wit, and yet deny that Honour in a Woman is anything else but Peevishness, that Inclination is the best Rule of Life, or Virtue and Vice any thing else but Health and Disease. We had no more to do but to put a Lady in good Humour, and all we could wish followed of Course. Then again, your *Tully,* and your Discourses of another Life, are the very Bane of Mirth and good Humour. Prithee don't value thy self on thy Reason at that exorbitant rate, and the Dignity of humane Nature; take my Word for it, a Setting-dog has as good Reason as any Man in *England....* I shall sum it up all in this one Remark, In short, Sir, you do not write like a Gentleman.

Mr. Spectator might have replied (had reply been necessary) that the character of the gentleman, *si quid mea carmina possunt,* was being reformed.

Its Social Criticism

Social comment in the essays was, then, diverse both in matter and in tone. Many papers laughed at the follies and foibles of the ladies: the periodical was a tea-table companion. Problems regarding love and marriage appear continually. Wifely extravagances are chided (328); giggling damsels in church are reproved (158); the feminine violence in party politics is gently ridiculed in the famous paper about party patches (81). There is much puffing of favorite plays or actors, much ridicule of Italian opera as nonrational pleasure; there are amusing skits on the fashionable puppet-show (then in its Golden Age in England) and on the more robust inelegant athletic combats of Hockley-in-the-Hole. There are sobering narratives such as Steele's famous retelling of the tale of Inkle and Yarico (11),[18] Addison's

---

[18] Lawrence M. Price, *Inkle and Yarico Album* (Berkeley, 1937).

Vision of Mirza (159), the account of the career of that typically prosperous "cit," Sir John Anvil (299), or of the weaver's unhappy wife who lost her benefit in the lottery (242). From these the material ranges to philosophical or moral disquisitions on benevolence (Nos. 27, 169, 177, 181, etc.) or on courage (350), on tranquillity (196), or even on immortality (111); to dissertations upon instincts in brutes (Nos. 120, 121, 128), to exhortations against "the two great errors into which a mistaken devotion may betray us"—enthusiasm and superstition; or, finally, to the popular doctrines about self-love, expounded by Henry Grove in No. 588. Steele's essay for Good Friday, 1712 (No. 356), well illustrates the suiting of material to occasion, certainly a part of the journalistic art here required.

Many of the best papers rely for interest on descriptions of everyday *Its Pictures* life. In No. 454 Mr. Spec. rises at 4 A.M. at Richmond and takes boat for *of Daily* London and Covent Garden Market. Similarly Sir Roger's visits to West- *Life* minster Abbey (329) and to Vauxhall (383) are vivid reflections of London, as, on another level, is Tom Trusty's story of his life as a servant (96). Probably the best descriptive papers, however, are those dealing with country life. Budgell's account of a country wake (161), Addison's pictures of Sir Roger at the assizes (122), of the fashions of the Western Circuit (129), and Steele on the pains and pleasures of married life in the country (254) are all good documentary records of their day. For real charm the sketches of life in Coverley Hall, with Will Wimble (a younger son), Moll White the witch, the family portraits, Mr. Spectator philosophizing amongst the poultry, and Sir Roger at church—these are among the best the essays offer in this kind.

Almost any subject might be treated in these essays. We have seen how excellent Addison was in criticism, and on the drama Steele certainly was both wise and influential: as bookish men they might be expected to write *Its Avoid-* about books. One topic that might be expected, however, they firmly banned. *ance of* "I never espoused any Party with Violence, and am resolved to observe *Politics* an exact Neutrality between the Whigs and Tories, unless I shall be forced to declare myself by the Hostilities of either Side." This stand in No. 1 is reiterated in No. 262 and elsewhere. Probably what was intended was a promise to avoid attacks on ministers of state as well as to avoid the extreme party spirit then prevalent. The Tories were in power; Addison and Steele were out of office, and *The Spectator* papers were a sort of holiday exercise: it was a pleasure to avoid acrimony—and perhaps to feel superior to it all. Later in his satirical portrait of Addison, Pope, as will be remembered, applied to him, in partial compliment, the name of Cicero's non-partisan friend, Atticus. Addison was born "to converse with ease," [19] and not to write political pamphlets. The non-partisan promise in *The Spectator* by and large was kept. There were, to be sure, moments when

---

[19] To Joseph Spence (*Anecdotes*, 1820, p. 50) Pope remarked that with intimates Addison "had something more charming in his conversation than I ever knew in any other man: but with any mixture of strangers, and sometimes only with one, he seemed to preserve his dignity much."

they came close to the line—when they printed the suppressed preface to the Bishop of St. Asaph's *Four Sermons* (384), a procedure which as a party stroke contravened all their nobly protested principles, and when they praised Prince Eugene (340) and the Duke of Marlborough (139 and in the dedication to Volume IV of the collected editions). But consistently their attitude was cool and dignified: they were never rabid partisans in *The Spectator.*

Its Interest in Trade

Addison at least was so filled with a healthy interest in trade that his Whig instincts could not be suppressed there. They were not, however, argumentatively presented. Probably no one—least of all Addison himself —realized the possible party bias of his ideas. He was one among the nation of traders that was bestirring itself in this century. Like Defoe, he praises the merchant frequently and highly. The merchant is the true internationalist: he brings the culture of all the world to the Thames, and makes mankind one. In the Royal Exchange (and Mr. Spectator was on 'Change far more often than most readers realize) Addison is nobly moved: "I am a Dane, Swede, or Frenchman at different times, or rather fancy my self like the old Philosopher, who upon being asked what Country-man he was, replied, That he was a Citizen of the World.... As I am a great Lover of Mankind, my Heart naturally overflows with Pleasure at the sight of a prosperous and happy Multitude, insomuch that at many publick Solemnities I cannot forbear expressing my Joy with Tears that have stolen down my Cheeks." Addison's sound mercantilism does not normally give way to emotion so extremely, but in his day many an English heart was being warmed by prosperity.

Its Vogue and Influence

If one wishes to know what the eighteenth-century Londoner and his environment looked like, the best source of information is the paintings and engravings of William Hogarth; if one wishes to know what the eighteenth-century Londoner thought about, one can do no better than to read *The Spectator:* it both conditioned and freshened the minds of its readers, and it was read throughout the century. The collected editions sold far better than did the original sheets. The influence of these essays is not due to any great mental power of their authors. It is due rather to their natural journalistic sympathy with their environment and the people in it; it is due above all to charm of style. It is well known how Benjamin Franklin in far-off Boston as a boy taught himself to write by imitating *The Spectator* and how Hugh Blair in 1760 and for more than a score of years thereafter, in reading his Lecture XIX [20] and there giving "directions concerning the proper method of attaining a good style in general," approved a process with regard to imitating *The Spectator* that was substantially the one Franklin, and doubtless many another, had followed. Addison's style was the model for simplicity, plainness, and elegance during more than a century. Its best praise and shrewdest criticism came perhaps from Dr. Johnson at the very end of his *Life* of Addison:

[20] Hugh Blair, *Lectures on Rhetoric and Belles Lettres* (2v, 1783).

His prose is the model of the middle style; on grave subjects not formal, on light occasions not groveling; pure without scrupulosity, and exact without apparent elaboration; always equable, and always easy, without glowing words or pointed sentences. Addison never deviates from his track to snatch a grace; he seeks no ambitious ornaments, and tries no hazardous innovations. His page is always luminous, but never blazes in unexpected splendour.

It was apparently his principal endeavour to avoid all harshness and severity of diction; he is therefore sometimes verbose in his transitions and connections, and sometimes descends too much to the language of conversation: yet if his language had been less idiomatical it might have lost somewhat of its genuine Anglicism. What he attempted, he performed; he is never feeble, and he did not wish to be energetick; he is never rapid, and he never stagnates. His sentences have neither studied amplitude, nor affected brevity; his periods, though not diligently rounded, are voluble and easy. Whoever wishes to attain an English style, familiar but not coarse, and elegant but not ostentatious, must give his days and nights to the volumes of Addison.

Both *The Tatler* and *The Spectator* had immediate imitators. In *Tatler* **Imitators** No. 229 Addison mentioned *Tit for Tatt* (5 numbers, 1710), *The Whisperer* (1709), and *The Female Tatler* as rivals or critics. The last of these ran to 115 numbers (July, 1709-March, 1710), and hence it may be thought abler than the others. There were also *The North Tatler, The Tory Tatler,* etc. When Steele suddenly stopped *The Tatler* it was continued by at least three would-be successors. One of these, William Harrison, whom Swift aided, continued his essays through one volume (52 numbers) rather wearily. Of the continuations of *The Spectator* by Addison and, *longo intervallo*, by William Bond, mention has already been made. The best successor was Steele's own *Guardian,* which ran daily for 175 numbers in 1713 (March 12 to October 1) under the editorship of "Mr. Nestor Ironside," whose relations in the Lizard family aided him.·

If *The Spectator* had not existed, *The Guardian* might outrank all period- **The** icals of this kind; but it is shaded by its predecessor, and the fact that **Guardian** Addison—busy with his tragedy, *Cato*—had no part in the early numbers certainly diminished its interest. In No. 98 Addison considers the imitators who have tried the "diurnal" essay and justly finds them deficient. Some *Guardians* concern the lion's mouth erected for a post-box at Button's Coffee-house and are triflingly amusing; another series concerns the absence of a "tucker" from the latest fashions in ladies' dress—a change that left their bosoms less covered than heretofore. "Let him 'fair sex' it to the world's end," might have been the reaction of Steele's now estranged friend Swift, whom Steele had attacked rashly in *Guardian* No. 53. There was a great deal of politics and of piety in *The Guardian* and relatively less light and effective satire. There was little literary criticism of first interest. A series of papers on the pastoral (Nos. 22, 23, 28, 30, and 32), probably by Thomas Tickell,[21] had praised the pastorals of Ambrose Philips, and

---

[21] Richard Eustace Tickell, *Thomas Tickell* (1931), p. 26; and John E. Butt in *Bodleian Quar. Rec.,* v (1928). 299.

led Pope, whose jealousy was aroused because of lack of mention of his own pastorals, to submit anonymously an attack on Philips in No. 40. Such procedure caused difficulties among the staff contributors. Pope wrote at least eight papers for Steele, of which No. 78 ("A Receit to Make an Epick Poem") and No. 173 ("On Gardens") are notable. In general *The Guardian* has the diversity of its great predecessors, but not their distinction.

*Addison
nd Steele
n Politics*

The Guardian found its writers in a bitter season of politics. The Tory peace of Utrecht was signed in April, 1713, and all poets, Whig and Tory alike, burst into early songs thereupon. The Pretender, the Whigs were certain, would be brought in if the Tories and the Catholics could do it. New peers, it was rumored, were to be created to support a Tory majority, and Steele protested in a pamphlet *Letter to Sir M[iles] W[arton] Concerning Occasional Peers* (March 5, 1713). In April Addison's *Cato* had a great welcome as a political document from both Whigs and Tories; but more typical of the moment was his partisan pamphlet *The Tryal of Count Tariff.* Religion got sadly mixed with politics. A Tory parson at Putney preached a sermon *Whigs no Christians,* and Whig retorts were as numerous as they were Christian. *The Guardian* itself was often attacked for its politics, especially by the Tory *Post Boy,* probably because at the moment Steele was the most vigorous of Whig writers. Defoe was working for Harley and the Tories. Parliament was dissolved, but both Steele and Addison were reëlected—Steele with some difficulty. In the late summer he began his attacks on the ministry for not compelling the French to destroy the harbor at Dunkirk, as the late treaty required, and on this subject he wrote often, most effectively perhaps in *The Importance of Dunkirk Consider'd* (September, 1713). He dropped *The Guardian,* and within the week began the more partisan *Englishman* (57 numbers: October 6, 1713 to February 15, 1714). In his fiery pamphlet *The Crisis* (January, 1714) he turned to attack the Tories on the prejudicial grounds that they were at heart Catholics and Jacobites, and during the months to follow he and his fellow Whig writers repeated these unjust charges. A solid Tory vote speedily expelled him from the House of Commons, but that did not quiet his pen. He continued to harp upon Dunkirk, religion, and the succession, and in *Mr. Steele's Apology for Himself and his Writings* (October, 1714) made an able defense of his career. There was scant application of reason to politics while the succession was in doubt. The Hanoverian Prince George was not popular: he was a German. The Jacobite Pretender ("James III") was unpopular: he was a Catholic. Religion settled the matter, and when the Queen died (August 1, 1714), the Protestant succession was readily secured, and in spite of the Jacobite invasion of the North in 1715, George I was King of England.[22]

The remaining periodicals published by Steele and Addison are of slight

---

[22] The new King's mother, Sophia, Electress of Hanover, was granddaughter of King James I of England. The Electress Sophia had longed to be Queen; but she died, aged 83, less than two months before Queen Anne. Soon after King George the First's arrival in England Steele was made governor of Drury Lane Theatre and in April, 1715, he was knighted.

literary influence. Steele's *Lover* (40 numbers: February 25 to May 27, 1714) was an attempt to recapture the playful attention of the fair sex; Addison's *Freeholder* (55 numbers: December 23, 1715 to June 29, 1716) *Their Later* was a combination of polite small talk with politics and trade. Steele's lesser *Periodicals* efforts, *The Reader* (1714), *Town Talk* (1715-16), *The Tea Table* (1715-16), and *Chit Chat* (1716) were all short lived. In 1719 he and Addison found themselves, with only temporary acrimony, on opposite sides in the debate concerning the proposal of the Whig ministers to limit the size of the peerage. Steele in *The Plebeian* (4 numbers, March and April, 1719) opposed his party chiefs, and lost standing in consequence. Addison, more conservative, supported the limitation, like the reliable party man that he was, in his *Old Whig* (2 numbers, March and April, 1719). Addison died within two months after this final effort.[23] Steele's stand cost him his place as governor of Drury Lane Theatre, and turned his writing into theatrical channels for most of the rest of his career. His projected "fishpool"—a vessel to bring fish alive from the sea by means of allowing salt water to flow through the ship's bottom—was a characteristic and ineffective attempt to get rich through inventive ingenuity.[24]

The more successful minor writers of periodical essays must be men- *Lesser* tioned briefly. During the first half-century notable political-literary period- *Essayists* icals were John Trenchard's and Thomas Gordon's *Independent Whig* (1720-21) and their *Cato's Letters,* collected from *The London Journal*[25] (1720-23); *Pasquin* (1722-4) by George Duckett, Nicholas Amhurst, and Steele; *The Craftsman* (1726-47); and *Common Sense* (1737-43), a paper in opposition to Walpole, managed by Charles Molloy for the Earl of Chesterfield, George Lyttelton, and others. Henry Fielding combined literature and politics in his *Champion* (written with James Ralph, 1739-44), in *The True Patriot* (1745-6), *The Jacobite's Journal* (1747-8), and *The Covent-Garden Journal* (1752).[26] This last periodical conducted a "paper war" with Sir John Hill's *Inspector,* a newspaper essay that ran to 152 numbers (1751-3). More definitely literary and moralistic was *The Lay Monk* (40 numbers, 1713-14) by Sir Richard Blackmore and John Hughes; Ambrose Philips's *Freethinker* (350 numbers, 1718-21) was one of the ablest in this kind; Eustace Budgell, Addison's eccentric cousin, conducted *The Bee* (118 numbers, 1733-5); and Aaron Hill's *Plain Dealer* (117 numbers, 1724-5) and his *Prompter* (173 numbers, 1734-6) are interesting for their attention to the theatre. Eliza Haywood, the novelist, wrote for more than one periodical: her slight success is best seen in *The Female Spectator*

---

[23] Steele was distressed that Addison made Thomas Tickell his literary executor. When Tickell published Addison's *Works* (4v, 1721) Addison's unsuccessful and unacknowledged play *The Drummer* (1716) was omitted. Because of Steele's protest in the dedication (to Congreve) which he prefixed to an edition of the play (1722), Tickell included it in the smaller trade edition of Addison's *Miscellaneous Works* (3v, 1726).

[24] In November, 1718, Steele published *An Account of the Fish-pool* in the hope of attracting investors.

[25] Charles B. Realey, *The London Journal and its Authors, 1720-1723* (Lawrence, Kansas, 1935; *Bull. Univ. of Kansas,* xxxvi).

[26] Ed. Gerard E. Jensen, with introduction (2v, New Haven, 1915).

(24 numbers, 1744-6). There were two interesting "literary" newspapers of the time that featured leading essays: *The Universal Spectator* (907 numbers, 1728-46), written by Defoe's son-in-law, Henry Baker, with help from James Ralph, and *The Grub-street Journal* (418 numbers, 1730-37), written by the non-juror, Richard Russel, and the Cambridge botanist, John Martyn.[27] Clinging for a while to Alexander Pope's coat-tails, this paper threw mud at his enemies—and sometimes at his friends. Their most independent policy was to oppose deism and support Jeremy Collier's attacks on the theatre. This last aim involved Russel unpleasantly with Henry Fielding. By the middle of the century periodical essays might deal with any subject in any.tone; and their subjects and tones might vary from day to day: they were personal organs unless guided by party politics; and as personal organs, their interest depended on the compelling power of the author's personality and style. None of them approached with any consistency the excellence of those produced by Steele and Addison.

[27] James T. Hillhouse, *The Grub-street Journal* (Durham, N. C., 1928) gives an excellent account of this journal. Professor Hillhouse is one of many who think that Pope was actually—as Russel wished them to think—the manager or editor of the *Journal*.

VI

The Drama, 1700-1740

Although the eighteenth century is not a brilliant period in English drama, the first half of it saw two developments of historical importance in the theatre. The one was a change in the quality of the managers of the playhouses, and the other was the moral reform (accompanied by increasing sentimentality) in comedy.[1]

In the days of Charles II the licensed theatres were managed by courtiers, friends of the King. In the early eighteenth century the management passed for the most part into the hands of professional theatrical people, usually actors. The normal number of major theatres in London during the first half of the century was two—Drury Lane and Lincoln's Inn Fields, or after 1732 Covent Garden; while a third house in the Haymarket, designed by Sir John Vanbrugh,[2] was acoustically suited only for opera. Of the lesser theatres the so-called Little Theatre in the Haymarket is of peculiar interest as showing the farces of the mad Samuel Johnson of Cheshire, of Henry Fielding, and later of Foote. The change in the social and, perhaps, intellectual class of managers in these theatres brought a different type of author to write for the stage. Restoration comedies were likely to be written by gentlemen and about people who imagined themselves to be gentlemen and ladies. The comedy of the eighteenth century was written by authors who would stoop to allow mere actors to revise and reshape their work;

Theatres and Playwrights

[1] For large collections of eighteenth-century plays see *Bell's British Theatre, Consisting of the Most Esteemed English Plays* (21v, 1776-81; 36v, 1791-1802); *The British Theatre; or, a Collection of Plays*, ed. Eliz. Inchbald (25v, 1809; 20v, 1824); *A Collection of Farces and other Afterpieces Selected by Mrs. Inchbald* (7v, 1809, 1815). — For smaller anthologies one may mention David H. Stevens, *Types of English Drama, 1660 to 1780* (Boston, 1923); Dougald MacMillan and Howard M. Jones, *Plays of the Restoration and Eighteenth Century* (1931); and George H. Nettleton and Arthur E. Case, *British Dramatists from Dryden to Sheridan* (Boston, 1939). — For general histories of the drama of the period the following are useful: Colley Cibber, *An Apology for the Life of . . . Written by Himself* (1740); ed. Robert W. Lowe (2v, 1889); David E. Baker, *The Companion to the Playhouse* (2v, 1764; reworked and enlarged by Isaac Reed and Stephen Jones under the title of *Biographia Dramatica*, 3v, 1812); John Genest, *Some Account of the English Stage from 1660 to 1830* (10v, Bath, 1832); Percy Fitzgerald, *A New History of the English Stage* (2v, 1882); Ashley H. Thorndike, *Tragedy* (Boston, 1908), and *English Comedy* (1929); George H. Nettleton, *English Drama . . . 1642-1780* (1914); George C. D. Odell, *Shakespeare from Betterton to Irving* (2v, 1920); Joseph W. Krutch, *Comedy and Conscience after the Restoration* (1924); Allardyce Nicoll, *A History of Early Eighteenth Century Drama* (Cambridge, 1925) [very valuable for its play lists with dates of performances]; Hazelton Spencer, *Shakespeare Improved* (Cambridge, Mass., 1927); Frederick W. Bateson, *English Comic Drama, 1700-1750* (Oxford, 1929); Charles H. Gray, *Theatrical Criticism in London to 1795* (1931); Clarence C. Green, *The Neo-Classic Theory of Tragedy in England during the Eighteenth Century* (Cambridge, Mass., 1934).

[2] Robert J. Allen, "The Kit-Cat Club and the Theatre," *RES*, VII (1931). 56-61. The building of this house makes an interesting story.

and that meant that frequently it was by men and women writing for money and taking an attitude towards human nature and genteel manners not unlike that found among the citizens who had been the objects of satire in Restoration comedy. Playwrights like Susanna Centlivre and Henry Fielding complained loudly of the difficulty of pleasing the whims of un-educated managers; and the audiences, frequently disorderly if not actually riotous, were also difficult.[3] The net result was a period of confused and mediocre writing, which did not entirely cease when in 1747 Garrick took over the management of Drury Lane.

New Tendencies in Plays
The plays were marked by an increased avoidance of both bawdiness and wit, though neither was usually quite absent from a successful play. There was, as we shall see, a considerable accession of sentimentality. The stage at times became a part of the political battleground of the period. *The Beggar's Opera* (1728) stimulated the development of a type of musical show that was part farce and part political propaganda. Henry Fielding wrote political farces of such brilliance and virulence that Parliament passed in 1737 the Licensing Act, by which all plays had to be read and approved by deputy licensers appointed by the Lord Chamberlain before they could be performed on the stage. Unless made topical, farcical, or sentimental, comedy could hardly hold the stage—so little salt of true wit did new plays have. As a result there arose a variety of dramatic "entertainments" inci-dental to the legitimate types of plays, the chief of which was the com-pletely non-literary pantomime.[4]

The witty comedy of manners fared badly. Not that Jeremy Collier drove either immorality or profaneness completely from the stage: the very plays that he condemned, in fact, still held the boards moderately well. Play-wrights continued also to rework Elizabethan plays or French plays; but the really new thing was the "reformed" or "genteel" or "sentimental" comedy. Based partly upon the honest habit of audiences in all ages to glow emotionally over happy or distressful domestic scenes and partly upon the benevolist view of human nature that Hobbes had provoked in the clergy, in the Cambridge Platonists, and in deists of the type of Lord Shaftesbury, the sentimental view of man was so common that inevitably it appeared on the stage.[5] The passion to reform, to set the human heart in harmony with those principles of virtue that are Nature, produced moral plays as readily as it did moral periodical essays.

[3] Julian L. Ross, "Dramatist versus Audience in the Early Eighteenth Century," *PQ*, XII (1933). 73-81.
[4] See three articles by Emmett L. Avery: "Dancing and Pantomime on the English Stage, 1700-1737," *SP*, XXXI (1934). 417-452; "Vaudeville on the London Stage, 1700-1737," *Research Studies of the State College of Washington*, V (1937). 65-77; and "The Defense and Criticism of Pantomimic Entertainments in the Early Eighteenth Century," *ELH*, V (1938). 127-145. See also Charles R. Baskervill, "Playlists and Afterpieces of the Mid-Eighteenth Century," *MP*, XXIII (1926). 445-464.
[5] See Ronald S. Crane, "Suggestions toward a Genealogy of the 'Man of Feeling'," *ELH* I (1934). 205-230. For special histories of sentimental comedy see Arthur Eloesser, *Das bürgerliche Drama. . . . im 18. und 19. Jahrhundert* (Berlin, 1898); Osborn Waterhouse, "The Development of English Sentimental Comedy in the Eighteenth Century," *Anglia*, XXX (1907). 137-172; 269-305; and Ernest Bernbaum, *The Drama of Sensibility* (Boston, 1915).

It is no longer possible to say that sentimental comedy began with Cibber's *Love's Last Shift* (1696); [6] but since Cibber was the most influential theatrical personage during much of the half-century, it will be convenient to treat him as our first nexus of dramatic sentimentalism. Son of a Danish sculptor whose career had been English, Colley Cibber (1671-1757) achieved notable success as an actor and as a comic playwright; he was also from about 1710 to 1733 the dominant force in the management of Drury Lane.[7] It is important to remember that Cibber's characteristic rôles throughout his career were those of fops, and that in his first play, *Love's Last Shift*, he created a somewhat new type of fop for himself in his Sir Novelty Fashion, a rôle perfected in Vanbrugh's continuation of Cibber's plot, *The Relapse* (1696), where Sir Novelty was ennobled as Baron Foppington. Cibber's fops were not merely overdressed effeminates; rather they were ostentatiously simple-minded or vapid. He acted these rôles so well that in the eyes of his public he *was* the vapidity that he counterfeited. Thus it was easy for his critics (whom Pope led) to regard him as a dunce. From school days, Cibber tells us, "A giddy negligence always possess'd me." In large part, however, this may have been pose; for Cibber was a shrewd and even courageous manager of Drury Lane. His intriguing personality conditioned his contemporary reputation as manager, actor, playwright, and heir apparent to the throne of Dulness in Pope's *Dunciad*.

During almost fifty years' work as playwright he produced over a score of plays, afterpieces, or ballad operas, most of which were well received. But a giddy negligence certainly possessed him when it came to the apt use of words, and he failed in several attempts to write tragedy. As a writer of comedy he realized that he was no wit, and he depended on story and situation rather than on well-written dialogue. His favorite early trick of situation was to reform an erring male suddenly—almost accidentally—in the last act. So Loveless in *Love's Last Shift* is restored to conjugal fidelity when his forsaken wife masquerades as a prostitute to win him back. Again in *The Careless Husband* (1704) a wife, through a casual act of kindness, shames the heart of a moderately shameless husband. At these

Colley
Cibber

---

[6] DeWitt C. Croissant, "Early Sentimental Comedy," *Parrott Presentation Volume* (Princeton, 1935), pp. 47-71; Kathleen M. Lynch, "Thomas D'Urfey's Contribution to Sentimental Comedy," *PQ*, IX (1930). 249-259.

[7] The small events of Cibber's life are too complex for brief recording. His distinguished theatrical career was eclipsed by the subsequent phase as poet laureate (1730 ff.). His odes for the New Year and for the King's birthday justly occasioned much ridicule. Pope had disliked him from about 1717, and after 1730 Fielding continually ridiculed him. In 1743 Pope made Cibber the hero of his revised *Dunciad*. That Cibber had an ambitious genius may be seen from his autobiography (his *Apology*—by all odds his most valued work) and also from his boldness in publishing a quarto volume of nearly 300 pages called *The Character and Conduct of Cicero Considered* (1747) and a poetical *Rhapsody upon the Marvellous: Arising from the First Odes of Horace and Pindar* (1751). His *Letter from Mr. Cibber to Mr. Pope* (1742) had a considerable success in its jocular attack on the poet. — Only his *Plays* have been collected (2v, 1721; 4v, 1760; 5v, 1777). By writing his own life in his *Apology* (1740) Cibber made it difficult for modern biographers. Richard H. Barker's *Mr. Cibber of Drury Lane* (1939) may be recommended, as, for commentary on his plays, may be DeWitt C. Croissant's *Studies in the Work of Colley Cibber* (Lawrence, Kan., 1912). On Fielding's criticism of Cibber see Houghton W. Taylor, "Fielding upon Cibber," *MP*, XXIX (1931). 73-90.

facile redemptions the audience shed honest tears, and the historians have since hailed Cibber as a reformer of comedy. Shamelessness for four acts he counterbalanced by an artificial and sudden triumph of virtue in the last. Cibber was no moral reformer: he realized that a new tone would please, and he hit upon the one most likely to please. His cleverness as a playwright lay in devising situations and stage business and in the rapid movement of his plots. .Typical in these matters are two notable successes, *Love Makes a Man* (1700) and *She Wou'd and She Wou'd Not* (1702). Like most practical playwrights he did not disdain topical aids to success: his *Non-Juror* (1717) is a clumsy secondhand adaptation of Molière's *Tartuffe* to the anti-Catholic fervor of the time [8] (heated by the Bangorian controversy just then), and his *Refusal* (1721) attempted to capitalize on the furor over the South Sea Bubble. His service to patriotism and the Whigs in *The Non-Juror* was rewarded in 1730 when he was made poet laureate. His best play was probably *The Careless Husband,* of which in 1764 David Erskine Baker could write extravagantly:

This comedy contains, perhaps, the most elegant dialogue, and the most perfect knowledge of the manners of persons in real high life, extant in any dramatic piece that has yet appeared in any language whatever.

Though the play was extremely popular, these judgments were most absurd. Cibber's writing was at times effective but never subtle. His early critics, John Dennis, Pope, and Fielding, for example, thought Cibber a most egregious murderer of the King's English. While the absurdities of his plays were obvious, the sprightliness, variety, and individuality of his work, aided by his ability to create effective rôles for leading members of the Drury Lane company, made many, if not most, of his comedies consistently "good theatre."

Cibber's friend Richard Steele was a different sort.[9] "At the Restoration," Dennis said scornfully, "the Theaters were in the Hands of Gentlemen." *Sir Richard* In some moods he did not allow this quality (except by birth) to Steele, *Steele* who nevertheless was the chief instrument in the attempt to get the theatre back into genteel hands. At the beginning of 1715, already a licensed partner in Drury Lane, Steele petitioned (successfully) the King for a life-patent to the theatre, urging "That the use of the Theatre has for many years last past been much perverted to the great Scandal of Religion and Good Government." From 1715 to 1719 Steele apparently was in close contact with other licensees; but after the presentation of *The Conscious Lovers* (1722) there is little evidence of his active participation in anything except the profits from the theatre. During the first years of his connection with Drury Lane he probably exercised a strong informal influence, but this is difficult to define or to establish except through his essays.

[8] See three articles by Dudley H. Miles: "The Original of *The Non-Juror*," *PMLA*, xxx (1915). 195-214; "The Political Satire of *The Non-Juror*," *MP*, xiii (1915). 281-304; "A Forgotten Hit: *The Non-Juror*," *SP*, xvi (1919). 67-77.

[9] On Steele's career see Part ii, ch. v. Even on his plays the best factual commentary is in George A. Aitken's *Life of Richard Steele* (2v, 1889).

His plays are definitely on the side of gentility and bourgeois respectability. Three came out early in the century, before he was engrossed in politics. *The Funeral: or Grief a-la-Mode* (1701) was a comedy of manners and intrigue in which Lord Brumpton feigns death in order to test the affection of his wife as well as that of his son, whom the villainous and actually bigamous wife has persuaded him to disinherit. The hypocrisy of the "widow's" grief and the moral prating of the vulturous undertaker afford some comedy here, as do two pairs of lovers—the one coyly hesitant, the other somewhat more boisterously active. Both of the young gentlemen are officers in the army (like Steele), and both are far more reputable and more human than their immediate predecessors in comedy. Steele boasted of the innocence of the play in his preface. This success encouraged performance of *The Lying Lover* (1703), a play of much the same sort, but too serious in tone for its time. It was, as Steele himself confessed, "dam'd for its piety." His object in the play was, he said, to promote "Simplicity of Mind, Good-nature, Friendship, and Honour" and "to attempt a Comedy, which might be no improper Entertainment in a Christian Commonwealth." Steele here took occasion to demonstrate, as throughout his career he liked to do, the evils of dueling. None of these objectives, obviously, was generative of true comedy. He had better luck with his next, *The Tender Husband* (1705), which is again in the sentimental moralizing mood, but has a better story, one dealing, as we are told in conclusion, with "A Son too much confin'd—too free a Wife." The "free" wife, Mrs. Clerimont, is scared into virtue by a device worthy of Cibber: her husband disguises his mistress Fainlove as a man, who is to be compromisingly discovered with Mrs. Clerimont, who in turn is unaware of the trick. Young Clerimont has the more rational design of marrying an heiress, and since he has been "a great Traveller in Fairy-land," and knows "Oroondates, Cassandra, Astraea, and Clelia" as "intimate Acquaintance," he easily impresses the romance-reading city heiress, Biddy Tipkin, and saves her from a hateful marriage to a country lumpkin named Gubbin—who ultimately marries Fainlove. This seems a more normal play for the time, with an artificial intrigue, with scenes in the Park rather than in Newgate, as in *The Lying Lover*. But it is still a play stressing serious and domestic rather than frivolous and elegant problems.

For years thereafter Steele in his periodical essays preached the gospel of reformed gentility, of the true gentleman as compared with Etherege's Dorimant. Finally in 1722 he brought out his best play, which he once intended to call "The Fine Gentleman," but actually called *The Conscious Lovers*. The contrast with the Restoration is here complete—as it was not in *The Tender Husband*. The characters are frankly middle-class; the lovers are not in doubt about each other's affection, though no word of affection has passed between them: their love is "conscious," i.e., mutually understood. The character of young Bevil is thoroughly upright and worthy; his sense of filial duty (derived in part from Terence's *Andria*) is extreme

The Conscious Lovers

for anything except a sentimental comedy, and his attitude towards Indiana is so excessively idealized as to be unrealistic but still commendable. The treatment of marriage as properly an affair of love rather than of marriage settlements is typically sentimental, and still another mark of the type is the reiterated prejudice against dueling. The piece is not only, however, a storehouse of sentimental clichés, but also a play of well-knit structure. The dénouement—the discovery that Indiana is Sealand's daughter—is certainly conventional; but it is here handled with a sure and restrained touch. The neatness of plotting and the naturalness of expression make the play the best sentimental comedy before Hugh Kelly's *False Delicacy* (1768). But in its moral intention it is in no wise truly comic. Fielding ironically made worthy Parson Adams characterize the superiority of its morals: " 'Aye, there is nothing but heathenism to be learned from plays,' replied he, 'I never heard of any plays fit for a Christian to read, but *Cato* and the *Conscious Lovers;* and, I must own, in the latter there are some things almost solemn enough for a sermon.' " John Dennis, again, summed up clearly Steele's divergence from the classical theory of comedy as curative of men's follies through ridicule. In comedy ideal patterns of conduct tend to be implicit, not explicit, as in Steele. So Dennis tells us:

> How little do they know of the Nature of true Comedy, who believe that its proper Business is to set us Patterns for Imitation: For all such Patterns are serious Things, and Laughter is the Life, and the very Soul of Comedy. 'Tis its proper Business to expose Persons to our View, whose Views we may shun, and whose Follies we may despise; and by shewing us what is done upon the Comick Stage, to shew us what ought never to be done upon the Stage of the World.

Other "Reformed" Comedies

Dennis's theories were sound, but the difficulty in an increasingly prudish and genteel age was to find respectable and interesting follies of any variety to dramatize. After *The Conscious Lovers* many a play was written with the polite intention, as the Rev. James Miller remarked in the Dedication to his comedy *The Man of Taste* (1735), "to entertain the Town, without giving Offence, either to Virtue, Decency, or Good Manners." In general these plays are comedies of manners or of intrigue with sentimental elements added. Such had been the character of the plays of Thomas Baker, Charles Burnaby, Charles Johnson, and even of Addison's neglected comedy *The Drummer* (1716); it was to be the nature of the plays of James Miller and Robert Dodsley, the latter of whom as an ex-footman naturally and effectively featured somewhat proletarian emotions. Perhaps the best of the more sentimental mid-century plays was *The Foundling* (1748) by Fielding's friend Edward Moore [10] (1712-1757), whose masterpiece, however, was his bourgeois tragedy, *The Gamester* (1753).

Susanna Centlivre

Among comic writers depending less on these sentimental motivations of action one must consider Mrs. Susanna Centlivre and Henry Fielding. After a picturesque early life Mrs. Centlivre turned to the exasperating

[10] John H. Caskey, *The Life and Works of Edward Moore* (New Haven, 1927). Moore's collected *Poems, Fables, and Plays* were published in 1756.

career of playwright.[11] She wrote fourteen comedies, two tragedies, and three farces, and of the comedies at least four achieved and deserved great success, not so much for their literary quality as for their brisk movement of intrigue and easy flow of incident. Her fourth comedy, *The Gamester* (1705), builds in the fourth act to a thrilling scene in which the gaming lover first sweeps the boards, and then loses all to his lady (disguised as a man), including, finally, her own picture set in diamonds. His cure from gaming—and his marriage to the lady—result. In *The Busie Body* (1709) there is even livelier intrigue, and the rôle of Marplot was long a favorite with many comic actors. *The Wonder: A Woman Keeps a Secret* (1714), a similar triumph of theatrical instinct and sound plot construction, kept the stage for well over a century, and in Don Felix furnished Garrick with one of his best rôles. More wit and perhaps even hardness of style is seen in her last great success, *A Bold Stroke for a Wife* (1718). Here and in her other late plays Mrs. Centlivre has been thought to imitate Congreve; but marriage is her theme, and in these plays as in sentimental comedies (unlike the Restoration plays), there is little or no aversion to matrimony or coyness in confessing a passion.

Henry Fielding's abilities as playwright are so greatly overshadowed by his fame as novelist that they have hardly been properly recognized.[12] Although he was not at his best in comedy, he at least illustrates the difficulty of writing comedy of manners in his day. He has been thought too imitative of Congreve and Wycherley; actually the trouble was that comedy of manners was a constricted genre, and that the life had gone out of it. Other difficulties arose from his ideas that "the highest life is much the dullest," and that London high society was incorrigibly shameless. He saw

Fielding's Comedies

[11] Mrs. Centlivre's *Works* have been collected (3v, 1760-61; 3v, 1872). There is no good biography. See John W. Bowyer, "Susanna Freeman Centlivre," *MLN*, XLIII (1928). 78-80; James R. Sutherland, "The Progress of Error: The Biographers of Mrs. Centlivre," *RES*, XVIII (1942). 167-182. For critical commentary see R. Seibt, "Die Komödien der Mrs. Centlivre," *Anglia*, XXXII (1909). 434-480; XXXIII (1910). 77-119; and also Ezra K. Maxfield, "The Quakers in English Stage Plays Before 1800," *PMLA*, XLV (1930). 256-273. Paul B. Anderson, in his "Innocence and Artifice: or, Mrs. Centlivre and *The Female Tatler*," *PQ*, XVI (1937). 358-375, gives some reasons for thinking Mrs. Centlivre a writer of *The Female Tatler*. The real contribution of his article, however, is to show the hard life of the female author. Walter Graham in his "Thomas Baker, Mrs. Manley, and *The Female Tatler*," *MP*, XXXIV (1937). 267-272, leads one to doubt the validity of Professor Anderson's tests for authorship.

[12] On Henry Fielding see Part II, ch. x. His dramatic career lasted from 1728 to 1737, though three of his plays were first performed later than 1737. His plays have been collectively published in his *Works* since 1762. The most complete collection of them appears in the *Works* as edited by William E. Henley (16v, 1903). [The plays are in Vols. VIII-XII.] James T. Hillhouse has admirably edited *The Tragedy of Tragedies* (New Haven, 1918). For the history of Fielding's theatrical career see Wilbur L. Cross, *The History of Henry Fielding* (3v, New Haven, 1918)—to be supplemented by later studies such as Emmett L. Avery's article, "Fielding's Last Season with the Haymarket Theatre," *MP*, XXXVI (1939). 283-292. See also Helen S. Hughes, "Fielding's Indebtedness to James Ralph" [for stimulus to burlesque the amusements of the town], *MP*, XX (1922). 19-34; Charles W. Nichols, "Social Satire in Fielding's *Pasquin* and *The Historical Register*," *PQ*, III (1924). 309-317, and "Fielding's Satire on Pantomime," *PMLA*, XLVI (1931). 1107-1112; G-E. Parfitt, *L'Influence française dans les œuvres de Fielding et dans le théâtre* (Paris, 1928); Charles B. Woods, "Notes on Three of Fielding's Plays" [*The Letter-Writers*, *The Modern Husband*, *Eurydice Hiss'd*], *PMLA*, LII (1937). 359-373; Winfield H. Rogers, "Fielding's Early Aesthetic and Technique," *SP*, XL (1943). 529-551.

nothing comic about it. His first play, *Love in Several Masques* (1728), staged before he was twenty-one, could not equal *The Beggar's Opera,* with which it tried to compete, but it was a lively, light comedy. *The Temple Beau* (1730) shows more firmness of character-drawing, but, except for touches of realism in his handling of the life of law students, it is not of vivid interest. In *The Modern Husband* (1732) and *The Universal Gallant* (1735) Fielding presented his frank condemnation of London high life— later to be elaborated in Tom Jones's Lady Bellaston and in the noble lords and colonels in *Amelia.* "The decency of polite life" was not here preserved, and the audience was not amused. On the other hand, in a completely unlocalized play like his *Miser* (1733), which is the best English version of Molière's *L'Avare,* he maintained both decency and lightness of touch. Of his five-act comedies this adaptation alone kept the stage with a long and distinguished history.

His Predecessors in Farce   But comedy was not Fielding's true *métier*: he was really at home in his farces, which have hardly been surpassed in English. He had some notable predecessors, but only John Gay [13] in his *Beggar's Opera* (1728) compares with Fielding. Gay's sense of absurdity in dramatic situations or verbal idioms was early well displayed in his afterpiece *The What D'Ye Call It* (1715), which burlesqued *Cato* and other toplofty plays. The excessive dependence on the absurd limited Gay's success in some plays. In *Achilles* (1733), for example, the Greek slacker-hero appeared among the spinning maidens wearing women's clothes *over his armor.* In his great success, *The Beggar's Opera,* which had an unparalleled run, he burlesqued Italian opera, satirized aristocratic marriage customs, and brought on the stage a symbolic representation of the famous fight Walpole had had with his brother-in-law and fellow minister, Lord Townshend, a representation which coupled farce with political satire. The biting irony and not too bitter cynicism of Gay's lines and his exquisitely turned lyrics gave him preëminence in the tradition that he more or less began. Another predecessor of Fielding's wrote a quite unintentional burlesque of the heroic plays of the day. This was the mad Samuel Johnson of Cheshire—not the Doctor—who in 1729 got produced in the Little Theatre in the Haymarket his very "poetic" drama *Hurlothrumbo: or, the Super-Natural,* which was downright insanity with hardly a lucid interval, but which in its mad imagery and diction is as good a burlesque of dramatic fustian as was ever penned.

Fielding's farces made much use of these ingredients just indicated: po-

---

[13] On John Gay see Part II, ch. VIII. His plays have been collectively printed as *Plays* (1760; 2v, 1923), and in his *Works* (4v, Dublin, 1770, 1772, 1773). His *Poetical Works,* ed. G. C. Faber (Oxford, 1926) contains the major plays and fragments of the others. *The Beggar's Opera* has been edited by Oswald Doughty (1923) and Frederick W. Bateson (1934). For comment on his dramatic work see Lewis Melville, *Life and Letters of John Gay* (1921); A. E. H. Swaen, "The Airs and Tunes of John Gay's *Beggar's Opera*," *Anglia,* XLIII (1919), 152-190; William E. Schultz, *Gay's Beggar's Opera: Its Content, History, Influence* (New Haven, 1923); Frank Kidson, *The Beggar's Opera: Its Predecessors and Successors* (1922); George Sherburn, "The Fortunes and Misfortunes of *Three Hours after Marriage*," *MP,* XXIV (1926). 91-109; Edmond M. Gagey, *Ballad Opera* (1937); William H. Irving, *John Gay* (Durham, N. C., 1940); Bertrand H. Bronson, "The Beggar's Opera," *Studies in the Comic* (*Univ. of California Pub. in English,* 1941), pp. 197-231.

litical satire, satire on the absurd manners of "high" people, satire on the irrational amusements of the town, and satire on the irrationally inflated diction of supposedly rational dramas. His farces varied in length according *Fielding's* to their function as brief afterpieces or as half of an evening's entertainment. *Farces* He apparently liked the idea of the "double feature," an equal division of the evening between two pieces. The afterpiece is represented by his *Mock Doctor* (1732), based on Molière; by *Tumble-Down Dick* (1736), a screaming vulgarization of the Phaeton story; and by *Eurydice* (1737), a burlesque that involved giving the lady of Orpheus the psychology of a prudish "fine lady." In his longer farces we find him successful in reviewing episodically the topical follies of his day. *The Author's Farce* (1730) burlesqued the amusements of the town; and *Pasquin* (1736) and *The Historical Register for 1736* (1737) continued this theme, adding savage attacks on the political corruption of the day. These last two plays largely provoked the Licensing Act of 1737[14] that shut Fielding off the stage. These two, it may be noted, were of the "Rehearsal" pattern, in which Fielding excelled. His *Welsh Opera* (1731) was a ballad opera burlesquing the royal family, and *Don Quixote in England* (1733) had attacked corruption in elections: such satire was permitted, but the Walpole ministry was dangerous to satirists. *The Letter-Writers* (1731) and *The Lottery* (1732) were topical skits—as indeed all his farces are. With slight annotation they come to life, and display all the incongruous disparity that marked society during the reign of Sir Robert Walpole.

The *Tragedy of Tragedies; or, the Life and Death of Tom Thumb the Great* (1730), as his best farce was called in its last form, stands somewhat apart. It is a literary burlesque surpassing even Buckingham's *Rehearsal* by its incisive exposé of rhetorical absurdity in the heroic tragedy of the seventeenth and eighteenth centuries. It is, of course, also a satire on courtly "greatness," but its chief merit lies in the skill with which he parodies or quotes verbal absurdity; no one has ever doubted Fielding's sense of excellence or bathos in diction. This farce, he pretended, was a newly discovered Elizabethan play of great influence, a device which enabled him to display the "influence" in footnotes showing parallels, which he was burlesquing. *Tom Thumb*, as well as one or two others of Fielding's farces, broke all records of the time for long runs. Their topical nature, however, made all except *Tom Thumb* relatively short lived; while they lived, they enjoyed all the triumphs of boisterous journalism dramatized.

Contemporary with Fielding's plays in the thirties and stimulated by much the same influences, were the theatrical pieces produced by Henry Carey (1687?-1743). After two farces, one of which, *The Contrivances* *Henry* (1715), he remade in 1729 into a ballad opera, Carey as dramatist—he *Carey* was also a nondramatic poet of ability—concentrated on operas and burlesques. His productions *Amelia* and *Teraminta* (both 1732) were

---

[14] For other influences as well, see P. J. Crean, "The Stage Licensing Act of 1737," *MP*, xxxv (1938). 239-255.

English operas after the Italian manner, and were only moderately success-ful as poetic operas. But his burlesque tragedy *Chrononhotonthologos* (1734), "Being the Most Tragical Tragedy, that ever was Tragediz'd," fared better as a Fielding-like criticism of the amusements of the town. It was staged at the Little Theatre in the Haymarket, and its frank criticism of the theatre of its day may have caused Drury Lane to decline his next ballad farce, *The Honest Yorkshire-Man* (1735), which, however, proved a great success. So did his next piece, a burlesque opera, *The Dragon of Wantley* (1737), with a story as grotesque as Gay's *Acis and Galatea,* taken from a ballad that told how Moor of Moor Hall slew a terrible dragon and thus won Margery for his bride. The inevitable sequel pictured Margery as a shrew. The title *Margery: or, A Worse Plague than the Dragon* (1738) indicates the tone. Carey was a clever lyrist, and his inventions caught the mood of his decade ably.

The Weak-ness of Tragedy   Turning now from low farce to lofty tragedy we find ourselves in a period, as Dr. Johnson admirably put it, when

> crush'd by Rules, and weaken'd as refin'd,
> For Years the Pow'r of Tragedy declin'd;
> From Bard, to Bard, the frigid Caution crept,
> Till Declamation roar'd, while Passion slept.
> Yet still did Virtue deign the Stage to tread,
> Philosophy remain'd, though Nature fled.

It is not true that there was no passion in the tragedies of the time; but the passion was falsified by sentimentality or weakened by flat details of middle-class life. There was a considerable amount of domestic pathos, but the tones of noble Roman declamation were more artificially valued. Limited in literary ability, tragic writers took refuge in gloomy stage settings such as Congreve used in *The Mourning Bride*—settings which, it will be re-membered, evoked the high admiration of Dr. Johnson. Rowe was more melodramatic than Congreve, and he set the last act of his *Fair Penitent* in

A Room hung with Black; on one Side, Lothario's Body on a Bier; on the other, a Table, with a Scull and other Bones, a Book and a Lamp on it. Calista is discovered on a Couch, in Black; her Hair hanging loose and disordered. After soft Music, she rises and comes forward.

Daggers, bones, tolling bells, and corpse-laden biers were easy supports for deficient imaginative power and stylistic frigidity.

Nicholas Rowe   Of the tragic writers Nicholas Rowe [15] (1674-1718) was probably the

[15] Rowe was a native of Bedfordshire, the son of a barrister. In 1688 he entered West-minster School, but soon left, entered the Middle Temple, was called to the bar, but abandoned the law for literature. As a writer of tragedies he came to know all the literary men of his day, especially Addison and Pope. In 1709 he published an edition of Shakespeare's *Works* (6v; 9v, 1714), and became in a sense the first editor of the plays. In 1715 he succeeded Nahum Tate as poet laureate, and as an ardent Whig received other small rewards. — His plays have been collected in various editions (2v, 1720; in *Works,* 3v, 1728; 2v, 1736). For commentary see Edmund K. Broadus, *The Laureateship* (Oxford, 1921); Alfred Jackson, "Rowe's Historical Tragedies," *Anglia,* LIV (1930). 307-330; James R. Sutherland, *Three Plays* [and introduction] (1929).

ablest: his plays at least were most often acted.[16] Practically all of his seven tragedies were successes, and he was obviously less "crush'd by rules" than others of his day, since he harked back to various English traditions. His first tragedy, *The Ambitious Stepmother* (1700), is a play of palace intrigue with echoes of Restoration heroic plays; but the rants have been cut in favor of pathos in Otway's manner, which is what Rowe admired. *Tamerlane* (1701), his most frequently performed play, was a part of the chorus of commendation of King William III, in which we have seen Defoe, Swift, and Steele also joining in this same year. Tamerlane stands for King William and Bajazet for his base opposite, Louis XIV. The play showed what could be done with political tragedy; for it was regularly acted throughout most of the century on King William's birthday (November 4) and frequently also on November 5, the anniversary of his landing in England in 1688. *The Fair Penitent* (1703) had a more genuine popularity: the "gay Lothario" and the "fair Calista" became patterns for later characterizations, such as Richardson's Lovelace in *Clarissa* and Fielding's Miss Matthews in *Amelia*. The play, though perhaps melodrama rather than true tragedy, must nevertheless have been thrilling theatre. For diversity Rowe then turned to classical and heroic rant in his *Ulysses* (1705) and to the days of Hengist in medieval Kent for his pathetic *Royal Convert* (1707)—which was not one of his most popular plays. *Jane Shore* (1714), which, so Rowe fondly imagined and even stated on the title-page, was "written in imitation of Shakespear's style," was another success of pathos and feminine distress. Shakespeare apart, Rowe here created a magnificent rôle for an emotional actress. His last play, *Lady Jane Grey* (1715), again focused attention on the distress of a lady. This tradition of "she-tragedies," as they were called, derived from Otway and perhaps Racine. Clearly Rowe ranged widely for materials; he observed the rules loosely; he concentrated his powers on depicting distress. The woes depicted are more likely, even in the historical plays, to arise from domestic rather than from national situations. Thus he works in the same vein as the sentimental playwrights who were producing lachrymose comedies.

Many of the tragedies of the time were less in the English tradition than in the Franco-Roman. One such play, Addison's *Cato*, was perhaps the most esteemed tragedy of the half-century, and one of the most frequently performed. *Cato* by any other author than Addison,[17] however, might have been less regarded. It is the product of a formally correct rather than a nobly sympathetic mind, and it owed its first popularity (as did

Addison's Cato

---

[16] In *Research Studies, State College of Washington*, IX (1941), 115-116, Professor Emmett L. Avery has a note on "The Popularity of *The Mourning Bride*," in which he lists the number of performances given to the most frequently acted tragedies during the period 1702-76. They are in part as follows:

Otway, *The Orphan*	314		Otway, *Venice Preserved*	269	
Rowe, *Tamerlane*	282		Rowe, *The Fair Penitent*	261	
Rowe, *Jane Shore*	279		Addison, *Cato*	226	
Southerne, *Oroonoko*	272		Congreve, *The Mourning Bride*	205.	

[17] On Addison see Part II, ch. v.

Rowe's *Tamerlane*) to a political situation. Written for the most part ten years before it was performed, it was staged in 1713, pretty surely as a political document. The Whigs identified Cato with the Duke of Marlborough; the Tories identified Marlborough with Caesar, the would-be dictator. Each party presented Barton Booth (who made his reputation as Cato) with a purse of fifty guineas, and both parties were loud in their applause of the play. Addison, of course, protested his innocence of any political intention. After Rowe's warm scenes the love dialogue in *Cato*—there is not much of it—is positively frigid; but the play is full of noble Roman sentiments that were cherished by patriots for a century or more. Americans will remember Nathan Hale when they hear Cato saying:

> What pity is it
> That we can die but once to serve our country!

Somewhat more aptly English and rational is Cato's noble injunction:

> Remember, O my friends, the laws, the rights,
> The gen'rous plan of power delivered down,
> From age to age, by your renowned forefathers,
> (So dearly bought, the price of so much blood)
> O let it never perish in your hands!
> But piously transmit it to your children.
> Do thou, great Liberty, inspire our souls,
> And make our lives in thy possession happy,
> Or our deaths glorious in thy just defense. (III, v)

Such eloquence, one hopes, is not merely a sublimation of anti-Jacobitical emotions.

Cato is the zenith in English neo-classical tragedy. Before Addison, Dennis had also used the patriotism resulting from victories over the French to *Other* create interest in his *Appius and Virginia* (1709), which was not a success, *Tragedies* though it was less criticized than his later reworking of *Coriolanus* as *The Invader of his Country* (1719).[18] *Cato's* chief rival was its immediate predecessor, Ambrose Philips's adaptation from Racine's *Andromaque* (1667), called *The Distrest Mother* (1712). The wits of Button's coffee-house formed more or less a claque for this play, which, however, deserved the aid. Other classical stories were handled by many authors, of whom the most eminent (but not for tragedy) was James Thomson,[19] author of *The Seasons* and of five not very notable tragedies. As Dr. Johnson said so often, classical stories were becoming trite and stale in the hands of second-rate writers.

Oriental Other sources of story for tragedy were chiefly two: Oriental tales and *and English* English history, frequently medieval. The best Oriental tragedies were at-*Plots* tractive in part for their deistic tendency to contrast Mohammedan virtue with Christian, with the preference going frequently to the former; for

---

[18] On Dennis see Part II, ch. II. The best discussion of his plays and the pamphlets they provoked will be found in his *Critical Works* as edited with introduction by Edward N. Hooker, Vol. II (Baltimore, 1943).

[19] On James Thomson (1700-1748) see Part II, ch. IX.

virtue like all else of value was universal. Among these Oriental plays were *Busiris* (1719) and *The Revenge* (1721), both by Edward Young,[20] author later of the *Night Thoughts;* John Hughes's *Siege of Damascus* (1720), and Aaron Hill's[21] adaptations from Voltaire, the tragedies *Zara* (1735) and *Merope* (1749). Hill also sought variety, as Rowe had done, by going to English history for tragic story, as one sees in his *Elfrid* (1710), which he reworked in 1731 as *Athelwold.* The egregious novelist and journalist, Mrs. Mary Manley, used history for the story of her tragedy *Lucius, the First Christian King of Britain* (1717), and Ambrose Philips also tried his hand at English historical material in his tragedies *The Briton* (1722) and *Humfrey, Duke of Gloucester* (1723). Of all these attempts Philips's were the best written, but neither his nor the others met success comparable to that of Rowe. Such plays, however, show a tendency to depart from classical material to a "medieval revival" that undermines classicism in matter but not in manner: the new material is still poured into the same traditional Franco-Roman forms.

All these tragic writers were conscious of the rules; but usually they departed in some respects from strict observance of dictated procedure. Naturally in adapting Racine, Philips tried, as Steele in his prologue for *The Distrest Mother* says, to observe the rules duly. "Our author," Steele says, *Tragedy and the Rules*

> Not only rules of time and place preserves,
> But strives to keep his characters intire,
> With French correctness, and with British fire.

The spirit of such "brave Britons" who studied "wit's fundamental laws" as set down by the French, normally infused a certain independence into the traditionalism that dominated tragedy more than any other genre. To modern readers, and even to Dr. Johnson, these tragic poets seemed "crush'd by rules"; but foreign eyes saw the matter quite differently. The master of the Italian comedians in Paris, Luigi Riccoboni, an authority on all the theatres of Europe, in his *Historical and Critical Account of the Theatres in Europe* (1741) gives his reactions to English tragedy, formed in 1727, when he visited England. The English theatre is highly praised. He writes as follows:

> Reason alone sketched out the first Rules of the Theatre in the *Grecian* Tragedies: *Aristotle* established an Art, and made the Laws for us; the *Latins*

20 On Young see Part II, ch. IX.
21 Aaron Hill (1685-1750) was educated at Barnstaple with John Gay, and later at Westminster. When young he traveled much, and in 1710 and thereafter he was intermittently concerned with writing for the stage or managing theatrical or operatic companies. In addition to seven tragedies he produced a very successful farce, *The Walking Statue* (1710). He wrote much about the theatre in his periodicals *The Plain Dealer* (1724-5) and *The Prompter* (1734-6). His *Collection of Letters between Mr. Aaron Hill, Mr. Pope, and Others* (1751) have theatrical interest also. Hill and Pope were alternately friends and enemies, and kept the public informed (at least Hill did) of their attitudes. — Hill's *Works* (4v, 1753), published for the benefit of his family, include letters, plays, poems, and some prose. There is a good biography by Dorothy Brewster (1913). Some of his plays are treated by Harold L. Bruce, *Voltaire on the English Stage* (Berkeley, Calif., 1918).

adopted them, and Moderns have confirmed them by the Heaps of Poems, by the so great Number of Dramas, which the *Italians,* and, still more, the *French* have already, and yet continue to supply us incessantly with. One therefore can't step aside from these Rules without incurring the Censure of the whole World. Otherwise nothing can be objected to the *English* Poets, but their having received a particular Maxim, which differs from those of other Countries, and which does not want its Defenders to support it. In such a general Agreement of Opinions authorized by Good-Sense, I am persuaded that the Men of Learning in *England* are sensible of the Irregularity of their Stage, and that (like the *Spaniards*) they are the first who take Notice of it. Were it permitted to depart from these Rules, which Reason itself hath dictated, the *English* Theatre would be able to balance in Reputation both the Ancient and the Modern. The Excellence of the English excels all the Beauties which the other Theatres in *Europe* can shew us; and if some time or other the *English* Poets would submit themselves to the three Unities of the Theatre, and not expose Blood and Murder before the Eyes of the Audience, they would at least partake of that Glory which the other more perfect modern Theatres enjoy.

Present-day students of these tragedies are likely to feel that more than a respect for rule was needed to vivify and make natural the materials that went into these plays, whether classical, Oriental, or medieval English.

Lillo's Innovation

Truly fresh substance, however, is seen in the two successful tragedies of George Lillo [22] (1693-1739), author of at least five. In the first of these, *The London Merchant: or, The History of George Barnwell* (1731), Lillo flung a challenge in the face of neo-classical tragedy. His hero was an apprentice, who, corrupted by the siren Millwood (the only really authentic characterization in the play), murdered his wealthy benefactor. This plot discards all theory as to "greatness" in a tragic hero: the story comes from an Elizabethan ballad, and deals with middle-class people only. And it is written in plain prose, though the ends of scenes may be tagged with couplets. It is the stark honesty of the grim bare presentation of a type story, together with the freshness of the theme, that gave the play its initial success. So sound a neo-classicist as Alexander Pope attended and approved the first performance. Lillo evidently knew he had not invented a genre but was simply reviving an Elizabethan tradition; for he made a version of *Arden of Feversham* (performed 27 May 1736), and he definitely associated George Barnwell with the Elizabethan, not the Georgian, period. In spite of the reputation of his play for moral power (until the middle of the nineteenth century it was regarded as an "improving" holiday amusement

---

[22] Concerning Lillo's life little is known. See Drew B. Pallette, "Notes for a Biography of George Lillo," *PQ,* xix (1940). 261-267. His *Works* were collectively published after his death, in 1740, and were republished with a life by Thomas Davies (2v, 1775, 1810). The best account of Lillo and his plays is found in Sir Adolphus W. Ward's edition [with introduction] of *The London Merchant* and *Fatal Curiosity* (Boston, 1906). On Lillo's influence see Jacob Minor, *Die Schicksalsdrama* (1884); H. W. Singer, *Das Bürgerliche Trauerspiel in England* (1891); A. Kunze, *Lillos Einfluss auf die Englische und die Deutsche Literatur* (Magdeburg, 1911); William P. Harbeson, *The Elizabethan Influence on the Tragedy of the Late Eighteenth and the Early Nineteenth Centuries* (Lancaster, Pa., 1921); Fred O. Nolte, *Early Middle Class Drama, 1696-1774* (Lancaster, Pa., 1935); T. Vincent Benn, "Notes sur la fortune du *George Barnwell* de Lillo en France," *RLC,* vi (1926). 682-687.

for apprentices), Lillo stimulated practically no disciples in England. In France and Germany, however, the play caused the production of Lessing's *Miss Sara Sampson* (1755), the initial example of *bürgerliches Trauerspiel*, and in France Diderot's *Le Fils Naturel* (1757) had a deliberate intention of revolutionizing French tragedy. When these Continental influences reacted on England at the beginning of the nineteenth century, the result was melodrama rather than new tragedies. In 1736 Henry Fielding, a close friend of Lillo's, brought out Lillo's second success, *Fatal Curiosity,* as half of the evening's bill in the Little Theatre in the Haymarket—the other half being a Fielding farce (*Tumble-Down Dick*). *Fatal Curiosity,* in honestly plain blank verse, was a short tragedy in three acts—again a family tragedy. Its length fitted it for Fielding's purpose of half an evening's entertainment, but made it less useful for ordinary performance. It had less vogue in England than in Germany, where it stimulated the writing of tragedies of fate. Thus Lillo became more important as an influence than for absolute achievement. He illustrates well, however, the feeling of a need for novelty in dramatic method and the turning from aristocratic to middle-class material. It was, for the most part, unorthodox people like Fielding and Lillo who, writing somewhat eccentrically, kept alive true theatrical instincts in the face of a crushing traditionalism, more powerful in the drama than elsewhere in literature.

VII

Traditions in Early Eighteenth-Century Poetry

The Concept of Genres

Poets and critics in the early eighteenth century thought of poetry as consisting of various specialized traditions called *genres*.[1] The classical traditionalist did not sit down to write a poem; he attempted a certain kind of poem—an epic, a great ode, a satire, an elegy, an epistle, a song, or a pastoral. And he had precedent for the general procedure that each tradition or genre entailed and even for various minutiae within the general pattern; he had in addition a storehouse of apt phrases that had accumulated in the previous masterpieces of the genre chosen, and these phrases were to be treated at will as heirloom jewels to be reset and effectively used again and again. With these definitely constricting influences of tradition it was the fate of the eighteenth century to struggle. The poets whom we are now to consider believed in liberty, but in liberty within the law—and they stressed law. But they were not slaves to one tradition, and in addition to the classical genres they built for themselves various non-classical traditions, such as the burlesque (which they thought had classical warrant and which usually depended on a classical generic pattern), narratives in the manner of fabliaux, ballads, biblical narratives, hymns, descriptive topographical poems, and many others. Even in this period the classical genre was not the sole possible precedent.

Decay of the Genres

In fact, the classical genres had seen their best days before 1700. Milton had achieved greatness in the epic, but Sir Richard Blackmore in his repeated attempts showed piety, patriotism, and the desire to achieve greatness—but never true epic quality itself.[2] The Miltonic influence led to a lamentable number of biblical epics of no distinction. *The Life of Our Blessed Lord* (1693) by the elder Samuel Wesley (1662-1735) and Aaron Hill's Pindaric *Gideon* (1749) may serve as examples. The most discussed epic of the half-century was doubtless Richard Glover's *Leonidas* (1737), which enjoyed approval or disparagement according to one's attitude towards the ministry of Sir Robert Walpole; for *Leonidas* was

---

[1] In addition to the general histories of the period it is helpful to consult on poetry William J. Courthope, *A History of English Poetry*, Vol. v (1905); and, as always, Samuel Johnson's *Lives of the English Poets* (1779-81); ed. George Birkbeck Hill (3v, Oxford, 1905); William J. Courthope, *Life in Poetry and Law in Taste* (1901); Raymond D. Havens, *The Influence of Milton on English Poetry* (Cambridge, Mass., 1922); and Hoxie N. Fairchild, *Religious Trends in English Poetry, 1700-1780* (2v, 1939-42).

[2] On the epic see René Le Bossu, *Traité du poème épique* (1675; in English 1695, 1719); Alexander Pope, "A General View of the Epic Poem ... extracted from Bossu," in Pope's *Odyssey* (1725); Elizabeth Nitchie, *Vergil and the English Poets* (1919); Hugh T. Swedenberg, Jr., *The Theory of the Epic in England, 1650-1800* (Berkeley, Calif., 1944).

written in support of that oppositional "patriotism" that Dr. Johnson came to regard as "the last refuge of a scoundrel." The reputation of *Leonidas,* however, was such that its original nine books in blank verse were in 1770 enlarged to twelve, and the poem was translated into French and German.[8] Epics were essential to poetic respectability, but they were relatively few in number and feeble in merit. Odes, on the other hand, were numerous but undistinguished.[4] From the time of Congreve's *Ode to the Queen* (1706), with its important Discourse in protest against the "irregular" odes of Cowley, poets knew the duty of Pindaric regularity, but preferred the laxness of Cowley's form. This laxness led only to mediocrity, and while practically every poet from 1700 to 1750 attempted a Cowleyan ode, even Pope himself failed in his *Ode for Music*—though it may be noted that Pope, like many such ode writers, was attempting only a libretto. In the forties Collins, Warton, and Gray showed how odes might be written well. In satire during the first quarter of the century success depended on more than adherence to the Horatian or Juvenalian tradition:[5] Samuel Wesley (1662-1735) in 1700 produced a satirical epistle *On Poetry* and his friend Blackmore in the same year published his *Satyr against Wit;* but pious railing alone availed little. Sir Samuel Garth found a way more pleasing to the time in his satirical mock-epic, *The Dispensary* (1699), which in its day made exciting reading, but is so topical that it is now unreadable. Its wealth of satire on individual physicians and apothecaries of the time followed the tradition of personal satire that Dryden and Boileau had sponsored, and that Pope was to follow. The first Horatian satires to achieve real success were the seven that Edward Young published in 1725-8 as *Love of Fame, the Universal Passion.* Practically all of Pope's satires postdated these of Young, which were highly praised. Among the numberless imitators of Horace Pope alone in this period won permanent reputation. The same limited success could be pointed out for other classical genres. The pastoral, attempted with credit by Ambrose Philips and Pope,[6] was

[8] Richard Glover (1712-1785), one of the relatively few poets frankly and profitably engaged in trade, published in 1739 *London; or, The Progress of Commerce,* in blank verse, and also a very popular ballad, *Admiral Hosier's Ghost,* on naval events in 1726. He wrote three tragedies, *Boadicea* (1753), *Medea* (1761), and *Jason* (1799). After his death the publication of a second long epic, *Athenaid* (1787), aroused no interest. He was an amateur Greek scholar, and his *Medea,* in form a Greek tragedy, was a part of the "Greek revival" in the mid-century. See J. G. Schaaf, *Richard Glover, Leben und Werke* (Leipzig, 1900).

[4] On the ode see George N. Shuster, *The English Ode from Milton to Keats* (1940); also Oswald Doughty, *English Lyric in the Age of Reason* (1922).

[5] On satire see C. W. Previté-Orton, *Political Satire in English Poetry* (Cambridge, 1910); Caroline M. Goad, *Horace in the English Literature of the Eighteenth Century* (New Haven, 1918); Hugh Walker, *English Satire and Satirists* (1925); David Worcester, *The Art of Satire* (Cambridge, Mass., 1940); Mary Claire Randolph, " 'Hide and Seek' Satires of the Restoration and XVIII-Century," *N&Q,* CLXXXIII (1942). 213-216; and "The Structural Design of the Formal Verse Satire," *PQ,* XXI (1942). 368-384.

[6] On the pastoral see Fontenelle, *Poésies pastorales, avec un discours sur la nature de l'eclogue* (1688, translated into English, 1695); *The Guardian,* Nos. 22, 23, 28, 30, 32 [by Thomas Tickell], and No. 40 [by Pope] (all in April, 1713); Harold E. Mantz, "Non-Dramatic Pastoral in Europe in the Eighteenth Century," *PMLA,* XXXI (1916). 421-447; Richard F. Jones, "Eclogue Types in English Poetry of the Eighteenth Century," *JEGP,* XXIV (1925). 33-60; Marion K. Bragg, *The Formal Eclogue in Eighteenth-Century England* (Orono,

better done either in John Gay's burlesques of the genre or in the type of descriptive writing that is either topographical, in the manner of Sir John Denham's *Cooper's Hill,* or philosophical, in the manner of Thomson's *Seasons.* Early in the century there developed in the pastoral, as in the epic, a burlesque tradition of "town eclogue" which Swift, Gay, and Lady Mary Wortley Montagu tried successfully. Burlesques, it may be remarked, may serve as playful expressions of affection for a genre: they do not necessarily imply contempt for it.[7]

Modified Patterns in Poetry

But the constricting rigidity of the classical genres easily drove poets to experiment with other patterns of writing. Some poets could dominate a tradition; most preferred to follow tradition loosely or to follow new or blurred patterns. They were encouraged in departures from the classical by their great admiration for earlier English poets. Shakespeare, whom a wit from Button's coffee-house could call "perhaps the greatest Genius the World ever saw in the Dramatick way" in a newspaper article of 1722, and whom according to Pope in 1737 every playhouse bill styled "the divine," had a general influence, which became specific at times in the drama.[8] Spenser, still called "our arch-poet," was imitated, though feebly, by several poets,[9] among them, Samuel Croxall (d. 1752) and Thomas Purney [10] (*c.* 1717) the riming chaplain in ordinary to Newgate Prison, and more reputably by Prior and James Thomson. John Hughes edited Spenser (1715) with interesting critical essays. Lesser poets claimed disciples also. Ned Ward and the other numerous followers of *Hudibras* were naturally not regardful of classical tradition. Defoe, whose rough-hewn couplets in his early satires constitute some of the most respectable if least attractive verse of the first decade of the century, could simply write an argument in verse as a more effectual and dignified vehicle than prose, and could write with little or no attention to what classical satirists had done. Narrative poets liked to versify Bible stories—frequently in the Cowleyan form of the ode, which was thought appropriate to the enthusiastic Oriental style—or to invent fables in the manner of Aesop, or fabliaux in the manner of Chaucer, or simply in the manner of one retelling a practical joke. Swift's *Baucis and Philemon* has a relationship to Ovid, but it has an equally close relationship to English village life. Hardly a volume of miscellanies appeared in the years 1700-1750 that did not contain jocose narratives of rural life.

Me., 1926); J. E. Congleton, "Theories of Pastoral Poetry in England, 1684-1717," *SP,* XLI (1944). 544-575. On the Georgic see Marie L. Lilly, *The Georgic* (Baltimore, 1919); Dwight L. Durling, *Georgic Tradition in English Poetry* (1935).

7 On burlesque see Albert H. West, *L'Influence française dans la poésie burlesque en Angleterre entre 1660 et 1700* (Paris, 1931); Richmond P. Bond, *English Burlesque Poetry, 1700-1750* (Cambridge, Mass., 1932).

8 We need a thorough study of Shakespeare's reputation for the years 1700-1750. See George C. D. Odell, *Shakespeare from Betterton to Irving* (2v, 1920); Hazelton Spencer, *Shakespeare Improved* (Cambridge, Mass., 1927); James R. Sutherland, "Shakespeare's Imitators in the Eighteenth Century," *MLR,* XXVIII (1933). 21-36.

9 See Herbert E. Cory, *The Critics of Spenser* (Berkeley, Calif., 1911); and Harko G. de Maar, *A History of Modern English Romanticism,* I (1924).

10 Thomas Purney's *Works,* ed. H. O. White (Oxford, 1933). Also H. O. White, "Thomas Purney, a Forgotten Poet and Critic," *E&S,* XV (1929). 67-97.

Reflective or discursive poetry, fairly independent of Horace, had been stimulated by Dryden as well as by the philosophic tendencies of the time. Bernard Mandeville's *Grumbling Hive* (1705) was destined to have fame when made a part of *The Fable of the Bees:* such a poem carries more weight of thought than an Aesopian fable. Blackmore's *Nature of Man* (1711), his *Creation* (1712), and *Redemption* (1722) are all works that regard very little classical forms while faithfully versifying rationalist doctrines about the duties of man and about the superiority of religious to philosophical solutions of moral problems as then seen. Without denying revelation Blackmore in *Creation* tries to support religion on the grounds of natural reason. Similar poems appear throughout the century: the most read were Pope's *Essay on Man* and Young's *Night Thoughts.* Less known was Aaron Hill's Pindaric *Creation* (1720) with its long preface in praise of the "terrible simplicity" and "magnificent plainness" of Hebrew poetry.

Various patterns more or less new were used also for descriptive poems.[11] *Descriptive reflective Patterns* Parks and estates were described, partly because of their beauties and partly because praise might open the door to patronage. Denham's *Cooper's Hill* and Waller's *Poem on St. James's Park* (1661) were forerunners of much of this writing; the one glorifying picturesque "prospects" from a hill-top and the other praising the beauties of the gardener's art. All these descriptive types are likely to be as much interested in moral reflections as in description; but the description aided readability. Addison's disciple Thomas Tickell (1685-1740) in 1707 brought out a poem on *Oxford* and later one describing *Kensington Garden;* Pope's *Windsor Forest,* with reflections about civic glory and the pleasures of peace, succeeded so well that two years later his friend Sir Samuel Garth[12] printed his *Claremont* (1715) in praise of the beautiful villa of the Earl of Clare. Dozens of such poems appeared, the best of which were by John Dyer. Thomson's *Seasons* belong rather outside this topographical tradition since they are, as we shall see, less focused on description and more philosophical in intention.

The tendency to grandiose ideals led poets who might have written what we now call lyrics to express their emotions in Pindarics rather than in less swollen lyric forms. There are, however, two commendable developments *Songs and Ballads* in the shorter forms that call for mention: the development of hymn writing, and the awakening of literary interest in ballads. What we now call lyrics they called songs, and the tradition of the cavalier lyrists persisted in song, with no access of merit except when the singer took on a witty or satiric tone. That there was a strong tradition of song in the century, leading straight to Robert Burns, will be seen if one recalls the fact that in 1688 *Lillibulero* "sang James II off his throne," that *Rule Britannia* was first

---

11 Robert A. Aubin, *Topographical Poetry in XVIII-Century England* (1936).

12 Sir Samuel Garth (1661-1719), born a Yorkshireman, educated at Cambridge and Leyden, became a well-known London physician and wit in the nineties. He was also known as a religious freethinker. An ardent Whig, he was knighted in 1714 and appointed a royal physician. *The Dispensary* is said to have achieved ten editions by 1741. His other poems are chiefly political in stimulus, but a notable achievement was the translation of Ovid's *Metamorphoses* (1717) "by several hands," which he supervised and in part translated.

sung in 1740, and that succeeding generations have delighted in Henry Carey's *Sally in our Alley,* Gay's *'Twas When the Seas Were Roaring* (not to mention the ever-delightful songs of his *Beggar's Opera*), and Fielding's *Roast Beef of Old England.*

Songs and ballads were hardly differentiated in this period, which nevertheless saw the emergence of an interest in balladry that was to become important later.[13] The ballad was a song of narrative nature. Swift's two saints found the cottage walls of Baucis and Philemon plastered with broadside ballads, and aesthetic judgments of such poems are usually biased by their social humility. The dean of ballad writers was Tom D'Urfey, who published many songbooks before his death in 1723, but few poets failed to write ballads, and none lived without knowing well ballads that as yet had hardly got into reputable print in spite of a long traditional existence. Addison's praise of *Chevy Chase* we have seen; and though greeted jocosely, it doubtless promoted genteel interest in ballads. Prior based his *Henry and Emma* upon *The Nut-brown Maid;* Thomas Tickell produced a tragic love ballad in his *Colin and Lucy,* which had enduring popularity; in 1719 appeared Lady Wardlaw's *Hardyknute,* long supposed to be a genuine piece of antiquity and admired as such by all the ballad scholars of the century; in the same year Thomas Hearne in the preface to his edition of William of Newburgh's *Historia* quoted from the *"Cantilena celebratissima ... volgo vocata* Chevy-chase"; and in 1723 David Mallet brought out his imitation ballad *William and Margaret,* which was at once popular. Collections of ballads began to appear. In 1723-5 were published three volumes called *A Collection of Old Ballads,* the first collection of such materials. Though the collection was too miscellaneous to accord with later tastes in ballads, it did pioneer work, and had at least the success of a third edition (1727). On slight evidence the editor has been thought to have been Ambrose Philips, who certainly had a connection with a songbook called *The Hive* (1724; fourth edition, 1732-3). This, however, contained little ballad material.[14]

llan
Ramsay

The work of Allan Ramsay (1686-1758) [15] in editing from the Bannatyne

[13] Sigurd B. Hustvedt, *Ballad Criticism ... during the Eighteenth Century* (Cambridge, Mass., 1916).

[14] Mary G. Segar in *LTLS,* Dec. 6 and 13, 1923 and also March 3, 1932, gives the slight evidence for Philips's editing. Lillian de la Torre Bueno, "Was Ambrose Philips a Ballad Editor?" *Anglia,* LIX (1935). 252-270, argues against Philips's connection with the work. *The Monthly Chronicle,* I (1728). 239, lists the third edition of *The Hive,* "To which is prefix'd a Criticism on Song-Writing. By Mr. Philips." *The Daily Journal,* May 5, 1735, in advertising the fourth edition, ascribes the prefatory essay to "A. Philips." Has the *Collection of Old Ballads* become confused with *The Hive?*

[15] Ramsay, born in Lanarkshire, passed most of his life in Edinburgh, where he was socially an important literary figure early in the century. He kept a bookshop, and about 1725 there started one of the first circulating libraries in Great Britain. The Scottish songs and poems that he printed from the MS collection (1568) of George Bannatyne were not traditional poems, but Ramsay's public was not discriminating in such matters. Their appetites had been stimulated by the *Choice Collection of Comic and Serious Scots Poems* (1706-11 and several reprints) published by James Watson (d. 1722). Ramsay himself was a popular song writer (*The Lass o' Patie's Mill, Lochaber no More,* etc.), and he delighted in the pastoral also. His most popular success was his pastoral drama *The Gentle Shepherd* (Edinburgh, 1725).

MS *Christ's Kirk on the Green* (1718) and a volume of *Scots Songs* (1718, 1720), and in his miscellanies *The Ever-Green* and *The Tea-Table Miscellany* (both 1724) was also important, if only for his known influence on Robert Burns. Ramsay did not hesitate to modernize or "improve" texts of the ballads he printed, but he included an increasing number of traditional folk ballads as new editions of *The Tea-Table* were called for. The popularity of the work is seen in the numerous editions that appeared throughout the century. Ramsay had no definite concept of true balladry. He regards *Hero and Leander* as a ballad, and evidently values ballads for their "merry images of low character." The tradition of the ballad, in any case, was purely native and throve alongside of more sophisticated genres.

The English hymn is a similar phenomenon. While the great honors in hymnology are given to the Wesleys, who are treated later in this volume, the early eighteenth century produced at least one great writer of hymns. Isaac Watts (1674-1748), one of the most scholarly and talented writers among the dissenters of the time,[16] wrote spiritual manuals, a much-used *Logic* (1725), and various theological works. More permanently important were his volume of *Hymns* (1707) and his *Psalms of David* (1719)—a total of several hundreds of songs designed for dissenting congregations. Of these about a dozen are among the finest of English hymns. The poetic art of the day excelled in expressing public rather than private emotion, and its sense of the metrical line fitted the quaint necessity of Watts's school of worship—the giving out the hymn line by line for singing. Thus Watts's magnificent "Our God, our help in ages past" has the dignity of established tradition coupled with the fervor of dissenting piety. Watts's diction and imagery are by no means always so august as in this hymn or so easy as in his well-known "Jesus shall reign where'er the sun" and "When I survey the wondrous cross." Among other writers of hymns must be named the saintly non-juring bishop Thomas Ken (1637-1711) whose morning and evening hymns, ending with the doxology, "Praise God from Whom all blessings flow," have remained in widespread use. Bishop Ken during his residence at Longleat exercised a spiritual influence on Mrs. Elizabeth Singer

English Hymns

After 1730, though he continued to write, he ceased publishing. His son Allan (1713-84) was a celebrated painter. — *Poems* (1720 ff.); *Poetical Works*, ed. Charles Mackay (2v, 1866-8); *Burns, Ramsay, and the Earlier Poets of Scotland*, ed. Allan Cunningham and Charles Mackay (2v, 1878). — Leigh Hunt, *A Jar of Honey from Mt. Hybla* (1848), ch. VIII; Daniel T. Holmes, *Lectures on Scottish Literature* (1904); John W. Mackail, "Allan Ramsay and the Romantic Revival," *E&S*, x (1924). 137-144; Burns Martin, *Allan Ramsay, a Study of his Life and Works* (Cambridge, Mass., 1931). — *Bibliography of Allan Ramsay* (Glasgow Bibliographical Society, 1931).

[16] Watts's father kept a boarding school at Southampton, and saw that his son had a good education in dissenting schools. Intellectually very able, young Watts became the preacher of a London congregation; but, his health breaking, he passed the last thirty-six years of his life quietly in the house of friends at Theobalds, or at Stoke Newington. — His collected works are edited by D. Jennings and P. Doddridge (6v, 1753), G. Burder (6v, 1810-11; 9v, Leeds, 1812-13). See Thomas Milner, *The Life and Times, and Correspondence of I. Watts* (1834); Edwin Paxton Hood, *Isaac Watts, His Life and Writings* (1875); Thomas Wright, *Isaac Watts and Contemporary Hymn-Writers* (1914); Wilbur M. Stone, *The Divine and Moral Songs of Isaac Watts: An Essay thereon and a Tentative List of Editions* (1918); Vivian de Sola Pinto, "Isaac Watts and the Adventurous Muse," *E&S*, xx (1935). 86-107; Arthur P. Davis, *Isaac Watts, His Life and Works* [1943].

Rowe—also a hymn-writer. Joseph Addison also should be here named for two small poems which he published in the *Spectator*. The first, found in No. 453, is the well-known stanzas beginning "When all thy mercies, O my God"; and the second, published a fortnight later in No. 465, is the "Ode" as he called it, the first stanza of which is so typical of the physico-theological view of the universe popular at the time:

> The spacious firmament on high,
> With all the blue etherial sky,
> And spangled heav'ns, a shining frame,
> Their great Original proclaim:
> Th' unwearied Sun, from day to day,
> Does his Creator's power display,
> And publishes to every land
> The work of an Almighty hand.

Watts as Critic and Secular Poet   Like Addison, Watts had literary interests outside of hymn-writing. His critical ideas were fresh and independent. Like Dennis he believed that modern poetry can be elevated only by avoiding profaneness and cultivating a fervor of faith. Like Dennis he believed in Longinus and the sublime; but his idea of sublimity was less rhetorical than that of Dennis and most writers of the century. Like the French critic Rapin he preferred incessant study of the true eloquence of the biblical prophets to the daily and nightly reading of the *exemplaria Graeca* recommended by Horace. Concerning his handling of the couplet he says:

In the poems of heroic measure, I have attempted in rhyme the same variety of cadence, comma, and period, which blank verse glories in as its peculiar elegance and ornament. It degrades the excellency of the best versification when the lines run on by couplets, twenty together, just in the same pace, and with the same pauses. It spoils the noblest pleasure of the sound: the reader is tired with the tedious uniformity, or charmed to sleep with the unmanly softness of the numbers, and the perpetual chime of even cadences.

It is a pity such sense on the technique of the couplet, published in 1706, could not have prevented more often the faults thus early proscribed. Watts's independence is further seen when he passes to the subject of blank verse, which he highly approved. His translation of Casimir's *Dacian Battle* into blank verse has a dignity and strength worthy of Dr. Johnson's praise. The Doctor liked its imagination, and possibly he could the more easily praise this poem because the blank verse was avowedly not Miltonic. In his preface Watts says:

In the essays without rhyme, I have not set up Milton for a perfect pattern; though he shall be for ever honoured as our deliverer from the bondage. His works contain admirable and unequalled instances of bright and beautiful diction, as well as majesty and sereneness of thought ... yet all that vast reverence ... cannot persuade me to be charmed with every page of it. The length of his periods, and sometimes of his parentheses, runs me out of breath: some of his numbers seem too harsh and uneasy. I could never believe, that roughness and obscurity added anything to the true grandeur of a poem; nor will I ever affect archaisms, exoticisms, and a quaint uncouthness of speech, in order to become perfectly Miltonian. It is my opinion, that blank verse may be written with all due elevation of thought in a modern style.

Again one wishes that James Thomson, for example, might have profited by this lesson—which Dr. Johnson, the purist, would certainly approve, though regretting Watts's too frequent avoidance of rime. Johnson regrets also that some of Watts's odes were "deformed by the Pindaric folly then prevailing." In some of these Pindarics Watts talks of his muse in a manner anticipatory of Collins. In three poems—*Two Happy Rivals (Devotion and the Muse), Free Philosophy,* and *The Adventurous Muse*—he shows this attitude:

> I hate these shackles of the mind
>   Forged by the haughty wise;
> Souls were not born to be confin'd,
>   And led, like Samson, blind and bound. . . .

Such a passage of antinomianism may bring us to a last trait in Watts's genius—his childlikeness. His volume of *Divine Songs Attempted in Easy Language for the Use of Children* (1715) is an early volume of children's verses, many of them hymns and all of them very moral. The tradition of English-speaking dissent, at least, absorbed, almost as folklore, his stanzas beginning "Let dogs delight to bark and bite," "Birds in their little nests agree," and "How doth the little busy bee." For at least two centuries, also, his *Cradle Hymn* ("Hush, my dear, lie still and slumber") was the lullaby most familiar in many a humble home. In several respects his verses for children anticipate no less a person than William Blake. Watts's contrasts—*Against Quarrelling and Fighting* and *Love between Brothers and Sisters,* his busy bee and his sluggard—show something of Blake's tone, purpose, and symbolic imagery. So does the following passage, among others, which comes from *Innocent Play:*

> Abroad in the meadows to see the young lambs
> Run sporting about by the side of their dams,
>   With fleeces so clean and so white;
> Or a nest of young doves in a large open cage,
> When they play all in love, without anger or rage,
>   How much may we learn from the sight.

Watts does interestingly what Blake was later to do superlatively.[17]

It becomes clear that patterns of poetry varied considerably in the early eighteenth century, and the work of Watts shows that the variation was not altogether due to different attitudes towards classical genres but in many cases was due rather to bias in the individual poet or to his accidental

---

[17] V. de S. Pinto, "Isaac Watts and William Blake," *RES,* xx (1944). 214-223.

status in society. It may be well to examine the work of certain authors who illustrate personal influences in their writing. The slight fame of Anne Finch, Countess of Winchilsea,[18] as poet derives in part from the passing mention that Wordsworth gave her in his "Essay Supplementary to the Preface" (1815). He thought her *Nocturnal Reverie* and Pope's *Windsor Forest* the only poems between *Paradise Lost* and *The Seasons* that contained "a single new image of external nature." Those who have echoed Wordsworth's rash praise have probably imitated him in forgetting the stilted and conventional opening lines of this admirably descriptive poem. In her own day Lady Winchilsea had modest and deserved repute; on her contemporaries the effect of a countess poetizing paralleled the later effect on Dr. Johnson of a woman preaching. Ardelia (as her ladyship called herself in print) did it surprisingly well. Her work is characteristic of the late seventeenth century, in which most of it was written. She published in two or three miscellanies and in a volume called *Miscellany Poems on Several Occasions, Written by a Lady* (1713). She wrote two plays (not intended for the stage); several fables from La Fontaine, among which *The Atheist and the Acorn* is admirable; various Pindarics of a tame sort; satires; religious poems, and several songs. In *Fanscomb Barn* she imitates Milton in a plain blank verse, used, perhaps in burlesque, to present the antics of vagrants frequenting the barn. Burns's *Jolly Beggars* was in spirit more than a century distant from this only moderately amusing attempt. In her *Petition for an Absolute Retreat* there is none of the enthusiasm of Shaftesbury's praise of solitude and nature; we have rather the celebration of the classic theme of the golden mean, much in the fashion of the popular *Choice* by John Pomfret (1667-1702), which in 1700 and 1701 had gone through several editions, won instant fame, and was long regarded as perhaps the most read of English poems.[19] Her simple honesty of description is seen at its best in such poems as *The Nightingale, To the Eccho,* and *A Nocturnal Reverie.* In contrast with the female dramatists and novelists of the time the Countess and her very religious friend Elizabeth Singer Rowe (1674-1737) illustrate the improvement of the times in decorum and virtue.[20] Mrs. Rowe (whose husband's uncle was the schoolmaster of Isaac Watts) wrote numerous pastorals, hymns, "devout soliloquies," Pindarics,

The
Countess of
Winchilsea

Elizabeth
Singer
Rowe

[18] Anne Kingsmill Finch (1661-1720), of an ancient Hampshire family, served as Maid of Honor to Mary of Modena (queen of James II) in 1683, with Catherine Sedley and with Anne Killigrew, to whom Dryden addressed his famous ode. In 1684 Anne Kingsmill married Heneage Finch and withdrew from court. Mr. Finch was in the service of James II, and after 1689 he and Anne lived at Eastwell Park (Kent) with the fourth Earl of Winchilsea, to whose title the non-juring Heneage succeeded in 1712. Most of her ladyship's poems were probably written before 1712, and many of them she left in MS unpublished. — *Poems,* ed. Myra Reynolds (Chicago, 1903) [introduction]; John M. Murry, "Anne Finch, Countess of Winchilsea," *New Adelphi,* I (1927). 145-153; Helen S. Hughes, "Lady Winchilsea and her Friends," *London Mercury,* XIX (1929). 624-635; Reuben A. Brower, "Lady Winchilsea and the Poetic Tradition of the Seventeenth Century," *SP,* XLII (1945). 61-80.
[19] E. E. Kellett, "Pomfret's 'Choice,'" *Reconsiderations* (Cambridge, 1928), pp. 163-181.
[20] Helen Sard Hughes, *The Gentle Hertford, Her Life and Letters* (1940), presents an illuminating account of the social background of Mrs. Rowe. The "gentle Hertford" is, of course, Frances Thynne (1699-1754) for years a patroness of letters when she was Countess of Hertford and, more briefly, Duchess of Somerset.

and paraphrases of Scripture stories; but her literary merits were somewhat inferior to her piety. Dr. Johnson was sure that Isaac Watts and Mrs. Rowe were "applauded by angels and numbered with the just." Beautiful as well as pious, it was the lot of this young woman to have two poets as diverse as Watts and rakish Matt Prior in love with her:[21] at thirty-five she married tuberculous young Mr. Rowe, aged twenty-two.

Lady Winchilsea and her applauded friend may be balanced as personal exhibits in poetry by two men of Oxford, Christ Church wits, who achieved fame with less of gravity in it. John Philips (1676-1709) and Edmund Smith (1672-1710) were more than typically brilliant students and more than usually lax with regard to college regulations. Smith had written Latin Alcaics on the death of Dr. Pocock (1691), which Dr. Johnson found not "equalled among modern writers"; yet Smith, called "Captain Rag" and "the handsome sloven," after several years of exasperating conduct in the University, was expelled. "At Oxford, as we all know," remarks Dr. Johnson, "much will be forgiven to literary merit"; and Smith's youthful promise had been brilliant.[22] When Swift's anonymous *Tale of a Tub* appeared in 1704, Atterbury thought Smith and Philips were the authors of it. At Christ Church Philips also was "eminent among the eminent."[23] Though a less witty tavern-companion than Smith, he was still convivial, and the opening lines of his first poem, *The Splendid Shilling* (1701), indicate the carefree nature of his Oxford existence:

"Rag" Smith and John Philips

> Happy the Man, who void of Cares and Strife,
> In Silken, or in Leathern Purse retains
> A *Splendid Shilling:* He nor hears with Pain
> New Oysters cry'd, nor sighs for chearful Ale;
> But with his Friends, when nightly Mists arise,
> To *Juniper's, Magpie,* or *Town-Hall* repairs:
> Where, mindful of the Nymph, whose wanton Eye
> Transfix'd his Soul, and kindled Amorous Flames,
> *Chloe,* or *Phillis;* he each Circling Glass
> Wisheth her Health, and Joy, and equal Love.
> Mean while he smoaks, and laughs at merry Tale,
> Or *Pun* ambiguous, or *Conundrum* quaint.

All Philips's English poems are in blank verse, and on relatively prosaic subjects all make either serious or jocose use of Milton's lofty manner. For facetious effect the device soon wears thin, and the author's one serious use of it in praise of Marlborough, *Blenheim* (1705), was rough in rhythm and

---

[21] H. B. Wright, "Matthew Prior and Elizabeth Singer," *PQ*, XXIV (1945). 71-82, prints very interesting letters from Prior to Miss Singer, and concludes that the friendship was literary rather than amorous.

[22] Smith's *Works* were edited by Oldisworth in 1714 and were reprinted in 1719 and 1729. — Johnson's *Lives of the Poets* (Oxford, 1905), II. 1-23. Elizabeth M. Geffen's two biographical articles support Johnson's account. See *N&Q*, June 6, 1936, pp. 398-401 and *RES*, XIV (1938). 72-78. Smith's best work was his tragedy, *Phaedra and Hippolitus* (1707), based on Racine's *Phèdre*.

[23] John Philips, *Poems,* ed. M. G. Lloyd Thomas (1927) [introduction].

disparate in imagery and diction. *Cyder* (1708), one of the happiest frivolous imitations of the *Georgics,* was his most approved work. After Philips's death, Edmund Smith wrote in heroic couplets an epistolary elegy in his memory, which consists in part of a defense of blank verse for "lower themes." Philips's genius was essentially realistic, and his use of Miltonic verse in such case becomes an interesting and not too fortunate accident. There is some slight reason for thinking that blank verse had influential supporters at Christ Church. In view of the complete devotion of these two university wits to classical patterns one may surely assume that Philips's desire to free himself from the bondage of "Gothic rhyme" was due to the lack of rime in classical poetry.

Poets of the "Little Senate"

Ambrose Philips [24] (1674-1749), not a relative of John Philips, belongs with Thomas Tickell [25] (1685-1740), Leonard Welsted [26] (1688-1747), and others in the little senate that was attentive at Button's coffee-house to Joseph Addison. In his own day Ambrose acquired some fame both for his *Pastorals,* which exceeded Pope's in popularity and showed a discipleship of Spenser, and also for his infantile trochaics addressed to children. "To Miss Margaret Pulteney" he wrote on April 27, 1727:

> Dimply damsel, sweetly smiling,
> All caressing, none beguiling,
> Bud of beauty, fairly blowing,
> Every charm to nature owing,
> This and that new thing admiring,
> Much of this and that enquiring. . . .

And so forth. It was these or similar verses that led the wits to describe the style as "namby-pamby," which became a derogatory nickname for "Amby" Philips. A certain personal pomposity that ill accorded with this infantile style doubtless aggravated the mirth; for Philips was not without ability. His translations of Pindar are undistinguished, but his stanzas from Sappho ("Bless'd as the immortal gods is he") have sure and lovely rhythms and apt diction. His *Winter Piece,* sent from Copenhagen in 1709, is an attempt at descriptive writing, which, however, fails really to bring before us either a definite picture or the moods of winter.

Ten years older than most of the poets we have been considering, and far abler, was Matthew Prior [27] (1664-1721), who was, however, their con-

[24] Ambrose Philips, born in Shropshire and educated at St. John's College, Cambridge (1693-6), spent the decade 1696-1706 as a fellow of St. John's, visited Denmark, became a member of the Addison circle, and was in 1713 involved in a literary quarrel with Pope over his *Pastorals.* With the accession of George I, he was made justice of the peace for Westminster, was given the commissionership of the lottery (1714), became a member of the Irish Parliament (1727) and Registrar of the prerogative court (1734). His *Poems* are edited by Mary G. Segar (1937) [introduction].

[25] John E. Butt, "Notes for a Bibliography of Thomas Tickell," *Bodleian Quar. Rec.,* v (1928). 299-302; R. Eustace Tickell, *Thomas Tickell and the Eighteenth Century Poets* (1931).

[26] Welsted's *Works* were edited by John Nichols (1787) with a memoir.

[27] For Prior's collected works see *Poems on Several Occasions* (1707, 1709, 1718, etc.); *Miscellaneous Works* (2v, 1740); *Writings,* ed. A. R. Waller (2v, 1905-7). — Francis Bickley, *Life of Matthew Prior* (1914); L. G. Wickham Legg, *Matthew Prior* (1921); Oswald Doughty,

temporary and superior in repute. Like many poets Prior came of a good *Matthew* family much reduced in circumstances. As a boy he worked in his uncle's *Prior: His* tavern in Charing Cross and attended Westminster School. His skill at *Education* Latin verses was discovered by the poetic Earl of Dorset, who became his patron and ultimately sent him to Cambridge. The influence of the witty Dorset and his friends Sir Charles Sedley and Fleetwood Shepherd on the budding poet was ineradicable. He became perhaps the ideal neo-classicist, writing with both lightness and a noble urbanity, with elegant ease and a deft and imaginative use of classical mythology unequaled in the century. He avoided the pedantry involved in minute attention to classical patterns, yet he captured the mood and felicity of both Horace and Anacreon. His favorite English poet was Edmund Spenser, at whose feet in Westminster Abbey he was at his own desire buried.

> I'll follow Horace with impetuous Heat,
> And cloath the Verse in Spenser's Native Style,

he says in an ode on *The Glorious Success of Her Majesty's Arms* (1706), written in a modified Spenserian stanza.

From boyhood Prior wrote verses, and at Cambridge he acquired a local reputation, which became national when he and his friend Charles Montagu (later Earl of Halifax) burlesqued Dryden's *Hind and the Panther* in their *Story of the Country-Mouse and the City-Mouse* (1687). Poetry was Prior's *Autobio-* acknowledged vocation, but he was ambitious to advance his fortunes, and *graphical* his friends aided his start in the world of politics and particularly of diplo- *Elements* macy. Poetry became during the many busy years that followed either a *in His* relaxation or a device for flattering patrons into attention or a vehicle for *Poetry* serious philosophizing. Much of his verse, like his early epistles to Fleetwood Shepherd, is definitely and intimately autobiographical, so intimately that at times the personal references are not too illuminating. His career as diplomat in Holland or France was crowned by his acting as plenipotentiary in negotiating the peace of Utrecht (1713), known derisively as "Matt's peace." As a result the Whigs, when again in power, kept him in confined arrest for over a year (1715-16). He had been a protégé of Robert Harley—as Defoe, Swift, and Pope were also. Harley (in 1711 created Earl of Oxford) remained Prior's good friend in the last years, after both were released from their Whiggish imprisonments, and he provided the poet with a country residence, Down Hall, about one visit to which Prior wrote some of his most amusing "cantering anapestics." Harley assisted Prior also in arrangements for the magnificent subscription edition of his *Poems* (1718), which is said to have netted the author something like four thousand guineas. It was a moment when society was being kind to

---

"The Poet of the 'Familiar Style' " *English Studies,* vii (1925). 5-10; W. Knox Chandler, "Prior's *Poems,* 1718: a Duplicate Printing," *MP,* xxxii (1935). 383-390; Charles K. Eves, *Matthew Prior, Poet and Diplomatist* (1939). Professor H. Bunker Wright and Henry C. Montgomery have recently illuminated a little-known aspect of Prior's career—his collection of paintings—in their article on "The Art Collection of a Virtuoso in Eighteenth-Century England," *Art Bulletin,* xxvii (1945). 195-204.

poets: Pope was getting a modest fortune for his *Iliad;* Addison was retiring as Secretary of State with a generous pension; even Dick Steele had his sinecures.

Types of His Poetry
Prior's volume was called *Poems on Several Occasions,* and the best pieces here collected were personal, if not autobiographical. Three types of poem, however, lie outside this personal field: his verse narratives, his Anacreontics, and his philosophical poems. The narratives—*The Ladle, Paulo Purganti,* and *Hans Carvel,* are deftly handled, and are the best of a type popular at the time but not too creditable to it. They parallel the century's love of practical jokes, preferably crude ones. The Anacreontics are elegantly frivolous and excel in the lightness of touch that characterizes Prior's work to a rare degree. *Cupid Turned Stroller* is a good example. The philosophical poems, which he thought his important works in verse, are now hardly readable except as intellectual documents for the time. The first poem in all his collections was the college Pindaric On Exodus *iii:14. I Am that I Am,* which avows the limitations of human reason in what might be skeptical fashion except for a bow to Faith in the last lines. *Solomon on the Vanity of the World,* published in 1718 but written earlier, is a dignified soliloquy in three books of despondent heroic couplets, in which Prior expresses the Christian pessimism common to his century and to his race. Neither knowledge, pleasure, nor power avails in the face of human vanity of reason and effort. "The Pleasures of Life do not compensate the Miseries."

> Alas! We grasp at Clouds and beat the Air,
> Vexing that Spirit We intend to clear.
> Can Thought beyond the Bounds of Matter climb?
> Or who shall tell Me, what is Space or Time?
> In vain We lift up our presumptuous Eyes
> To what our Maker to their Ken denies:
> The Searcher follows fast; the Object faster flies.
> The little which imperfectly We find,
> Seduces only the bewilder'd Mind
> To fruitless Search of Something yet behind.

Prior, having an unusually fine library, was widely read, and this poem, the product of his great reading and reflection, he regarded as his masterpiece. While under arrest in 1716, he wrote—hastily and carelessly, so he said—*Alma: or, the Progress of the Mind,* which manifests again his skeptical tendency by ridiculing all systems of philosophy. It is supposedly a dialogue between Prior and his friend Richard Shelton, and its burlesque is neatly cast in the tetrameter couplet, in which Prior wrote both frequently and excellently.

His Playfulness
These poems illuminate their age and Prior's mind; but they are relatively impersonal; Prior is more pleasing when he is easily and elegantly familiar and facetious or when sentimentally melancholy. Love and poetry were his favorite relaxations, and he mingled the two in the eighteenth-century

manner that employed a touch of acid cynicism, a touch of affectionate playfulness, and a great deal of implicit physical desire. In his tradition, as in Restoration comedy, love was a game in which one's emotions should not become too much involved. Contrary to the decorum of the time Prior's loves were seldom bestowed upon ladies but rather upon barmaids of wit and willingness.[28] *The Secretary* (1696) gives the tone for a week-end relaxation from his diplomatic activities at the Hague:

> While with labour assid'ous due pleasure I mix,
> And in one day atone for the bus'ness of six,
> In a little Dutch-chaise on a Saturday night,
> On my left hand my Horace, a Nymph on my right.
> No Memoire to compose, and no Post-Boy to move,
> That on Sunday may hinder the softness of love;
> For her, neither visits, nor parties of tea,
> Nor the long-winded cant of a dull refugée.
> This night and the next shall be her's, shall be mine,
> To good or ill fortune the third we resign:
> Thus scorning the world, and superior to fate,
> I drive on my car in processional state.

His various poems to Cloe are happy descendants of Horace, and might well as graphic portrayal have been "painted" by Watteau, Fragonard, or Boucher. Their bouquet is unique in eighteenth-century England. The acidulated seriousness of the quatrain *The Lady who offers her Looking-Glass to Venus* (an episode in his "pastoral war" with Cloe) is quintessential Prior:

> Venus, take my Votive Glass:
> Since I am not what I was;
> What from this Day I shall be,
> Venus, let Me never see.

Thus love and beauty are reduced to ingenious tragicomical wit.

Prior's mock seriousness enables him to do admirably what Ambrose Philips did intolerably: write verses to and about children. *To a Child of Quality Five Years Old (The Author Suppos'd Forty)* is sheer wit, but his grown-up tone in his brief *Letter to the Honourable Lady Miss Margaret Cavendish-Holles-Harley* is equally deft and more substantial. In *Cupid Turned Stroller* we see again his ability to grasp and sophisticate a small child's point of view. For the debutante age we have his account in *The Female Phaeton* of how Lady Catherine Hyde ("Kitty"), who later became perhaps the most beautiful woman of her age and, as Duchess of Queensberry, patroness to John Gay, persuaded the Countess her mother (as Phaeton had persuaded Apollo his father) to lend her the family car:

His Poems to Children

---

[28] On two such that appear in his poems see H. B. Wright, "Matthew Prior: A Supplement to his Biography," *Northwestern University Summaries of Doctoral Dissertations*, v (1937). 34-38; and by the same author, "Matthew Prior's Cloe and Lisetta," *MP*, xxxvi (1938). 9-23.

Fondness prevail'd, Mamma gave way;
Kitty, at heart's desire,
Obtained the chariot for a day,
And set the world on fire.

In these last two poems the poet shows what genius can do with classical mythology in days when such tricks were hackneyed.

Prior's wit from early manhood was cut by a constitutional melancholy, the result perhaps of early dissipations and disappointments. In all his reflective poems this tone crops out, and phrases like "this cheat of life" are common. His sense of history as tragedy, expressed in the lines *Written in the Beginning of Mezeray's History of France,* is but the public aspect of "the cheat of life," and his *Epitaph* for Saunt'ring Jack and Idle Joan expresses the same feeling for private life. Such melancholy is the moving element in his masterly epitaph for *Jinny the Just*—published only in 1907 —and is seen also in the words of the landlady in *Down-Hall:*

Why Things since I saw you, most strangely have vary'd,
And the Hostler is Hang'd, and the Widow is Marry'd.

And Prue left a Child for the Parish to Nurse;
And Sisley went off with a Gentleman's Purse;
And as to my Sister so mild and so dear,
She has lain in the Church-yard full many a Year.

Well, Peace to her Ashes; what signifies Grief:
She Roasted red-*Veal,* and she Powder'd lean-*Beef:*
Full nicely she knew to Cook up a fine Dish;
For tough was her *Pullets,* and tender her *Fish.*

This tone of realistic and melancholy frivolity is pervasive in Prior: it may be the mark of a superficial nature, but his frivolities are universally moving. The lesson of life possibly may be, as he says at the start of *Solomon* "That We pursue false Joy, and suffer real Woe"; but it seems rather to be that since real woe is our lot, all transitory joys are to be cherished. He was essentially Epicurean.

His Artistic Conscience

Much of Prior's conscience was aesthetic: elegance and finish and neat ingenuity were the things that mattered most to him in art and life, and he had the gift of finding these traits where others could and can see chiefly vulgarity; but however Hogarthian his landladies and barmaids were in real life, in his poems they are refined into figures by Boucher. Not content with refining such dross into gold, he further worked the gold into exquisite filigree marked by delicacy and sure firmness of form. His rhythms and metres are tactfully chosen and lightly manipulated. In his preface to *Solomon* he expresses a feeling, more common in his age than one is likely to think, that the heroic couplet is far from a perfect vehicle. Donne and his contemporaries had so blurred it with enjambement that it "was found too dissolute and wild, and came very often near Prose." As "corrected" by Davenant, Waller, and Dryden, "It is too Confined":

It cuts off the Sense at the end of every first Line, which must always rhime to the next following; and consequently produces too frequent an Identity in the Sound, and brings every Couplet to the Point of an Epigram. It is indeed too broken and weak, to convey the Sentiments and represent the Images proper for Epic. And as it tires the Writer while he composes, it must do the same to the Reader while he repeats; especially in a Poem of any considerable length.

Prior was at his best in the tetrameter couplet, which certainly avoids the sedateness and heaviness of the longer line.

Having seen how these various poets differ in their bias of literary or *Metrical* personal tradition, we may profitably summarize their more technical biases *Tendencies* in metrics. Obviously the romantic notion that they could excel in only one metre—that of Dryden and Pope—is untenable. It is true that the numerous imitators of Milton's blank verse, being otherwise realists in attitude towards poetry, were unhappy in their attempts to marry his exotic idiom to everyday detail; but their attempts show that they valued blank verse. Not all blank verse, as we have seen, is Miltonic in pattern. Various quaint habits contrived to undermine the repute of the measure: Dr. Fell preached at Christ Church, Oxford, *in blank verse,* and in 1712 John Ozell (d. 1743), a hack translator, brought out a version of the *Iliad* in blank verse, but printed as prose. The fact that such men confused unrimed verse with prose does not mean that all men did: there are plenty of witnesses to the contrary. Even Pope with patience heard Bishop Atterbury frequently condemn rime, and promised, evidently without seriousness, "to allow it unfit for long works ... as soon as Homer is translated." It was post-Miltonic performance fully as much as prejudice that limited the repute of blank verse.

Apart from the heroic couplet and blank verse the favorite metres were chiefly two. The tetrameter couplet, as practised by Swift and Prior, is handled with admirable individuality: the use of feminine rimes is not too frequent, and Prior, unlike Swift, avoids both the cleverness and the grotesqueness of Hudibrastic rime. There is more tendency to stop the lines than in *L'Allegro* and *Il Penseroso,* and variety is secured rather by change of tone and by varying light stresses. After the heroic couplet that with four stresses is the best metre of the period. The Pindaric, in Cowley's manner, is frequently used, but almost invariably is flawed by an elaborate tumidity or a prosaic bathos or—which is worse—by both together jostling each other in the same passage; but somehow the metre maintained popularity. The thirst for regularity crept in upon the Pindaric, and Congreve's prefatory Discourse to his *Ode to the Queen* marks a terminal point in the definition of this form. Like octosyllabics and Pindarics the measures used in songs were less varied and more regular than formerly; but it would be easy to exaggerate the regularity here. Trisyllabic measures in song decrease, although Prior in *Down Hall* and *Jinny the Just* had used anapestics with rollicking charm. That this rhythm could be used in song is seen in the popular lines addressed to Mrs. Howard (Countess of Suffolk), supposedly by the Earl of Peterborow (1658-1735):

> I said to my heart, between sleeping and waking,
> "Thou wild thing! that always art leaping or aching,
> What Black, Brown, or Fair, in what clime, in what nation,
> By turns has not taught thee a pit-a-pat-ation?"

Such "society verse" had its obvious usefulness, but short poems and irregular metres, though they existed, were not highly valued. The stage was set for Pope and regularity.

VIII

Pope and His Group

The masters whom Pope followed most consistently in his career were Horace and Boileau. His *Pastorals* were, to be sure, of Virgilian derivation, but if he wrote a little "Ode to Solitude," it was perfect Horace; his *Essay on Criticism* was formed after both Horace and Boileau, and his satires and epistles show the same discipleship.[1] Nevertheless, Pope owed much to native English writers: he is "discovered" at three different periods of his career reading the *Faerie Queene;* investigation has brought to light as many echoes of Miltonic phrases in his work as any other poet of the century can show;[2] his versification was a development from the techniques of Dryden. In him, without animosity, diverse traditions meet. To both Pope and his school true poetry was universal, and on such principle one should admire both Horace and Spenser, both Boileau and his greater contemporary, John Milton. The antagonisms later premised between classic and romantic were non-existent in his day: one was both—though doubtless Horace and Boileau were the dominant influences.

Pope's Masters in Poetry

Although Pope was frequently annoyed—to put it mildly—by criticisms of his own work, he was tolerant of various traditions in poetry. This fact is evident if we consider the sort of poetry written by some of his closest friends, whom it may be well to consider briefly before passing to Pope's own writing. These friends may be divided into several groups: his early friends included William Walsh, Wycherley, Garth, Granville, Southerne, and Congreve; his next close friends and associates were Rowe, Swift, Gay, Arbuthnot, and Parnell, and his assistants on the *Odyssey,* Fenton and Broome. Here also may come Lady Mary Wortley Montagu, who about the time of *The Dunciad* became Pope's bitter enemy. His friends who were in part disciples—his imitators speedily were innumerable—would include Aaron Hill (1685-1750), Samuel Wesley the younger (1691-1739), Joseph Spence (1699-1768), Robert Dodsley (1703-1764), David Mallet (1705?-1765), George, Lord Lyttelton (1709-1773), and the Rev. Walter Harte (1709-1774). His champion in later years and literary executor, William Warburton (1698-1779), though not among the poets, deserves mention as an example of how Pope's prestige could be imparted posthumously to a

His Friends

---

[1] W. H. Williams, "Pope and Horace," *Temple Bar,* cxv (1898). 87 ff.; James W. Tupper, "Pope's Imitations of Horace," *PMLA,* xv (1900). 181-215; A. F. B. Clark, *Boileau and the French Classical Critics in England* (Paris, 1925); Émile Audra, *L'Influence française dans l'œuvre de Pope* (Paris, 1931). For further works about Pope see below, note 12.

[2] Raymond D. Havens, *The Influence of Milton on English Poetry* (Cambridge, Mass., 1922), pp. 573-583.

brash and inferior personage. His other friends included the most interesting men of his day—George Berkeley (1685-1753) the philosopher; the architectural Earl of Burlington (1695-1753), who with Pope and others fought to preserve classicism from the rococo; William Kent (1684-1748), who as painter, architect, and landscape gardener worked out new ideas—perhaps Pope's —in landscaping; Charles Jervas [3] (1675?-1739), who taught Pope painting and in whose London house Pope frequently stayed; Sir Godfrey Kneller (1646-1723), and the two Jonathan Richardsons, who were later to be his chief painting friends. With musicians he was less intimate perhaps, but he evidently had some acquaintance and friendly relations with both Buononcini and Handel. The friendly Countesses of Burlington and Peterborow were both musical. The list might be expanded indefinitely. When Pope wrote, "Envy must own, I live among the great," it is to be feared that he was not thinking of the famous persons just enumerated but rather of the various and numerous noble lords and ministers of state with whom he was on intimate terms. He numbered dukes among his friends, though not among his closest friends; and duchesses and countesses were his humble servants. At the other end of his scale, writers like Mrs. Catharine Cockburn and Defoe's son-in-law Henry Baker apparently pined in vain for his acquaintance. He was much sought after socially, a fact that gives the lie to the sentimental notion that a keen satirist must be fundamentally an ill-natured man. Such an idea was the product of a romantic sentimental period, and not of the late seventeenth-century tradition in which Pope was reared.

William Walsh

His early friends were men older than himself and not of the rising sentimental group. The literary work of Wycherley, Southerne, Congreve, Garth, and Rowe, has been at least briefly treated elsewhere in this volume. William Walsh, more notable as a courtier than as a poet, had in his own day excessive reputation. Dryden had called him "the best critic of our nation"—meaning doubtless of our coffee-house society. His poems consist of pastorals, elegies, songs, and love lyrics, all of which express tender conventional images in smooth verse.[4] His personal charm and magnificence— he was tall and, as Dennis tells us, "loved to be well dressed"—dazzled the young Pope, and his chief title to fame is the fact that in some measure he formed Pope's genius. To Spence Pope said:

> About fifteen, I got acquainted with Mr. Walsh. He used to encourage me much, and used to tell me, that there was one way left of excelling: for though we had several great poets, we never had any one great poet that was correct; and he desired me to make that my study and aim.

In 1707 the youthful poet journeyed to Worcestershire and spent several weeks there with Walsh. Some of his early poems were submitted to Walsh

---

[3] Jervas has claim to literary reputation through his admirable translation of *Don Quixote*, published in 1742 after his death.

[4] Walsh's *Works in Prose and Verse* were published by Pope's enemy Edmund Curll in 1736. His poems are in Samuel Johnson's collection (Vol. XII); in R. Anderson (Vol. VI), and in Alex. Chalmers (Vol. VIII). For his biography see *DNB*.

for correction, and it is probable that under his influence the *Essay on Criticism* was conceived. To Walsh's memory, in effect, the poem is in its conclusion dedicated, and there can be no doubt that his influence on Pope was considerable.

Another elderly wit and man of the world who was Pope's early friend was George Granville, Baron Lansdowne (1666-1735). The poetical son of Waller, Granville as a young man wrote songs to a cruel north-country beauty whom he called Myra. In the didactic couplet tradition his chief performance was his *Essay on Unnatural Flights in Poetry,* which was among the forerunners of Pope's *Essay on Criticism.* He wrote four plays, some of which enjoyed a considerable success in their seasons.[5] In the Tory régime of 1710-14 he was Secretary at War, was created a peer in 1712, was sent to the Tower in 1714, and in 1720 began nine years of discreetly self-imposed exile as a debtor and a Jacobite. To Granville, Pope had addressed his *Windsor Forest,* and in a later poem, published within a month after Lord Lansdowne's death, Pope admirably summed up his lordship's character in the phrase, "Granville the polite." The early commendation of distinguished elderly courtiers like Wycherley, Walsh, and Granville, left Pope somewhat unprepared for the distinctly smaller enthusiasm that writers of his own age felt for his youthful poems, and led to a certain, perhaps natural, irritation.

"Granville the Polite"

In 1713, if not before, Swift, Gay, Parnell, and Pope were occasionally meeting with Dr. Arbuthnot in his apartments in St. James's Palace as members of what has been called "The Scriblerus Club."[6] The Club was informally under the patronage of the Prime Minister (the Earl of Oxford); but it was not political in purpose. Arbuthnot,[7] a court physician, an amateur in music, an expert card-player, and a supreme wit, was probably the center of this group, who were inventing "The Memoirs of Martinus Scriblerus" as a burlesque on the various sorts of pedantry rampant in their day. The *Memoirs* were ultimately published by Pope in 1741 long after the deaths of all the group except Pope and Swift. The satiric impulse of the Club, however, bore minor fruit much earlier. The wit of Arbuthnot had been shown in his *John Bull* and his *Art of Political Lying* (1712). His verses, of which his philosophical poem *Know Yourself* (1734) was the most ambitious example, were never notable except for small bits of epigrammatic wit. Of Swift's poetry, already mentioned, hardly more need be said, except that unlike Pope he seldom uses the heroic couplet and is normally a realist with small traces of the noble Roman in his verse. Thomas Parnell (1679-1718), a protégé of Swift's from Ireland, was less interested in satire than his fellow Scriblerians; but he doubtless enjoyed the conviviality of their

The Scriblerus Club

---

[5] Granville's *Poems upon Several Occasions* (1712) went through at least four editions during his lifetime. Elizabeth Handasyde, *Granville the Polite* (Oxford, 1933), stresses properly his public career but gives a full account of his writings.
[6] On the Scriblerus Club and its productions see Robert J. Allen, *The Clubs of Augustan London* (Cambridge, Mass., 1933), pp. 260-283, and George Sherburn, *The Early Career of Alexander Pope* (Oxford, 1934), pp. 69-82.
[7] On Arbuthnot see Part II, ch. III, n. 7, and on Swift Part II, ch. IV.

meetings.[8] He published little in his lifetime, and that little chiefly in miscellanies. Much of the summer of 1714 he spent at Binfield with Pope, and for a time aided in the preparation of notes for Pope's *Iliad* and of a prefatory discourse on "The Life, Writings, and Learning of Homer." He was an admirer of Milton, and his best poems, like Pope's, are full of Miltonic echoes. His *Hermit* is a retelling of an ancient story designed to illustrate the ease with which the limited human mind mistakes the ways of Providence. *A Night-Piece on Death* is an obvious forerunner of the "graveyard" school: Goldsmith rashly preferred it to Gray's *Churchyard*. Among his other pieces *A Fairy Tale* and the *Hymn to Contentment* are admirable. His less distinguished work consists of numerous "divine poems" based on Bible stories: these are in the heroic couplet. Some of his better poems use the tetrameter in the manner of *Il Penseroso,* and his Arthurian *Fairy Tale* is in somewhat too regular *rime couée.* Parnell should have had a more productive career, but he was naturally idle, and sorrow over the death of his wife drove him to intemperance and away from poetry.

John Gay   Like Parnell, John Gay [9] (1685-1732) worked closely with Pope but independently. Contemporaries at times gave Pope partial credit for some of Gay's successes; but the twentieth century has more justly recognized Gay as a genius in his own right, whose reputation suffered unduly in being shadowed by Pope's supposed aid. Gay's first printed piece apparently was *Wine* (1708), an imitation of Milton and of the latest poetic hit, Philips's *Cyder.* Gay evidently had read *Paradise Lost* with keen attention to mannerisms of style, and it is interesting to see him copying Milton's stateliness rather than attempting the elegant informality that Philips coupled with the great master's idiom. Gay never again seems to have tried nondramatic blank verse, and one suspects that *Wine* was an opportunist attempt to score in the vein in which, four months previously, the Oxonian Philips had won success. It must have been a hasty piece of work, and Gay did not include it in his *Poems* (1720).

Wine was a burlesque, and this type of writing was to be Gay's favored province. Four of Ambrose Philips's *Pastorals* had been printed in 1708, and all six were printed at the beginning of Tonson's *Poetical Miscellanies* (1709). Pope's *Pastorals,* which had perhaps been in Tonson's hands since

---

[8] Parnell's *Poems on Several Occasions* (1722) were published by Pope, and his enlarged *Works in Verse and Prose* (1755) include hitherto unpublished pieces. *Poems,* ed. George A. Aitken (1894); *Minor Poets of the Eighteenth Century* (Everyman's Library, 1930). Parnell's life has been written by Oliver Goldsmith (1770; in Goldsmith's *Works,* ed. J. W. M. Gibbs, IV (1885). 155-178), and by Samuel Johnson, *Lives of the Poets,* ed. Hill, II (1905). 49-56.

[9] Gay's formal education took place in the Grammar School of Barnstaple (Devon), his native town, where the schoolmaster (Robert Luck) was a poet and where Aaron Hill and William Fortescue (later Master of the Rolls and lifelong friend of Gay and of Pope) were schoolmates. Of a moderately well-to-do family Gay became at about the age of seventeen apprentice to a London silk mercer. This apprenticeship he quit in 1706, and presently seems to have started a career as writer with the aid of Aaron Hill. In 1713 he served as secretary to the Duchess of Monmouth, widow of the rebel son of King Charles II. Thereafter he was usually in minor public employments, and was the protégé of the Earl of Burlington, William Pulteney (later Earl of Bath), and the Duke and Duchess of Queensberry. — For his bibliography see Part II, ch. VI, n. 13. His *Poems,* first collected in 1720, are edited by John Underhill (2v, 1893), Francis Bickley (1923), and G. C. Faber (Oxford, 1926).

1706, and had been highly praised when in manuscript by Pope's elderly admirers, were first printed at the end of this miscellany. Philips's poems seem to have been preferred to Pope's by the writers of periodicals, and such preference came to annoy Pope. It was partly a matter of Whig prejudice against him among the wits at Button's coffee-house. In 1713, in *Guardian* No. 40, he provoked a pastoral war by ironically praising Philips highly— for his faults, which were made evident! In this war Gay was Pope's chief ally. Philips, following Spenser distantly, had endeavored to strike out a pastoral manner both English and "different": Pope had composed in the French-Roman tradition relying, with warrant, on his melodic lines for whatever distinction he might have. Gay, and in 1717 Thomas Purney, really struck out new lines in rural poetry, not so much through the burlesque of pastoral artificiality as through particularity in rural details. Pope, and even Gay himself, pretended at times that Gay had no knowledge of the country; but in his *Rural Sports*—where he addresses Pope as "You, who the sweets of rural life have known" and paints himself as one who never "brightened plough-shares in paternal land"—and especially in his *Shepherd's Week* (written in part to discredit Philips),[10] Gay gave readers more of country sights, sounds, and folklore than any poet of the half-century if we except Thomson—and even Thomson did not use folklore as did Gay. The details are never sentimentalized, and for that reason are neglected by romantic critics who love sentimental rustic details. The influence of this pastoral war and of Gay's poems in it would be hard to trace. Clearly there existed along- side the neo-classical "elegant" rural tradition a jocose rural type of poem; and of this type such poems as these by Gay and later Shenstone's *School- mistress* (1737-42) are important.

In most of his poems in the pentameter couplet Gay preserved an Trivia informal if not a burlesque tone. *Trivia; or, The Art of Walking the Streets of London* (1716) is the most admired of the longer "town eclogues" or burlesque Georgics such as Swift, Lady Mary Wortley Montagu, and others were popularizing. In this imitation of Virgil's *Georgics,* Gay, like many realists, stressed the gutter to the neglect of more pleasant prospects; but for the foot passenger his warnings were vivid and sage. Like Hogarth he paints the grotesque reality of London life for purposes of not too serious instruc- tion. *Trivia* shows his most mature and careful use of the couplet, and while many passages are quite in accord with Pope's rhythms, many are not. Witness the enjambement of the following somewhat Swiftian passage:

> The man had sure a palate cover'd o'er
> With brass or steel, that on the rocky shore
> First broke the oozy oyster's pearly coat,
> And risqu'd the living morsel down his throat.
> What will not lux'ry taste? Earth, sea, and air
> Are daily ransack'd for the bill of fare.

[10] Hoyt Trowbridge, "Pope, Gay, and *The Shepherd's Week,*" MLQ, v (1944). 79-88.

In his later epistles—the one to the Earl of Burlington (*A Journey to Exeter*) or the one to Pulteney from Paris—Gay is less studied than in *Trivia*, and allows metrical substitutions that Pope would have balked at.

Gay's Love of Burlesque

Informality and burlesque permeated most of Gay's work. In his *Letter to a Lady* (1714), really to the Princess of Wales newly arrived from Germany, he practically burlesqued the congratulatory epistle, and his libretto for *Acis and Galatea* (set by Handel) was a delightfully spirited burlesque of one of Ovid's *Metamorphoses*. He carried the spirit of burlesque, or at least of satire, even into his songs, which are among his finest achievements. Apart from *Black-ey'd Susan*, which is in the true spirit of balladry, his best songs are in his plays. In *Acis and Galatea* occur the robust lines:

> O ruddier than the cherry,
> O sweeter than the berry—

which owe much of their fame doubtless to Handel's setting. In *The Beggar's Opera* we have his most finished lyrics—and there is no really good reason for thinking that he did not write every one of them himself. Peachum's opening song is the key to the whole vein of political satire in the play:

> Through all the employments of life
> Each neighbour abuses his brother;
> Whore and Rogue they call Husband and Wife:
> All professions be-rogue one another.
> The Priest calls the Lawyer a cheat,
> The Lawyer be-knaves the Divine;
> And the Statesman, because he's so great,
> Thinks his trade as honest as mine.

Such political lyrics satirize cuttingly and cynically the modes of the court, and in this dangerous kind Gay set an example for Fielding and many another lyrical critic of the Walpole régime. Gay's range is seen in his love songs, which vary from "The Turtle thus with plaintive crying" to the amusing duet between mother and daughter, "O Polly, you might have toy'd and kist," and the famous masculine protest of Macheath, "How happy could I be with either." Similarly the drinking songs range from the boisterous chorus of highwaymen, "Fill every glass," to Lucy's more seductive, "Come, sweet lass."

In the twentieth century *The Beggar's Opera* has surpassed all Gay's other writing in popularity, but in his own century, and even into the nineteenth, his *Fables* (1727-38) had rivaling vogue.[11] The first fifty of these, addressed to the small but royal Duke of Cumberland, made, with its engrav- ·ings, a charming book, though the wisdom inculcated was far from being weakly sentimental or childlike. Sixteen additional fables were published in 1738, six years after Gay's death, and this second group is frankly addressed to adults, as indeed the first might well have been. Story element

---

[11] The *CBEL* tells us that there were more than sixty editions of the *Fables* before 1800.

is neglected in all these fables in favor of a worldly wisdom that is often bitterly caustic. *The Hare and Many Friends* has thus been interpreted as an autobiographical reproach to Gay's friends, but there is no reason for such an interpretation. The *Fables* prepare one somewhat for the epitaph which Gay composed for himself and which somewhat strangely stares at the tourist in Westminster Abbey from Gay's tomb:

> Life is a jest; and all things show it.
> I thought so once; but now I know it.

So spoke the spirit of the age through a genius that was essentially good-natured and very highly talented.

We come finally to the greatest poet of this group—and of the century— Alexander Pope.[12] Born of Catholic parents six months before the glorious and Protestant Revolution of 1688 and dying in 1744 when the last attempt at a Catholic and Jacobite invasion was imminent, he proudly suffered throughout his life minor disabilities for a religion regarded as almost treasonable; and he perhaps unconsciously fostered instincts of furtiveness that adherence to a proscribed cult entailed. He was debarred from a university training, but from tutors at home in Windsor Forest or from friends he acquired and indulged a great appetite for reading and at least superficial learning. From childhood he composed verses, and while Pope was still seventeen, Jacob Tonson, the leading publisher of poetry at the time, a publisher who owned—or thought he owned—the copyrights in Shakespeare

Alexander Pope: His Early Life

12 Pope's life, except for literary quarrels, was uneventful. Shortly after his birth in London, the family left the City, and most of the years between 1700 and 1716 were passed at Binfield in Windsor Forest. After perhaps two years' residence at Chiswick he and his mother moved to Twickenham, his home for the rest of his life. His career as writer is easily divided into three periods: 1709-17 (early works), 1715-26 (translating and editing), 1728-44 (satires and epistles). — His *Works*, collected in several editions in his lifetime, were edited by his literary executor and friend, William Warburton (9v, 1751—often reprinted in the eighteenth century); by Joseph Warton (9v, 1797, 1803, 1822); by William Lisle Bowles (10v, 1806; 8v, 1812); by William Roscoe (10v, 1824; 8v, 1847); by Whitwell Elwin and William J. Courthope (10v, 1871-89). The Twickenham Edition (ed. John Butt, Geoffrey Tillotson, James R. Sutherland, and others, 1939—) is in progress: three volumes of six have appeared; *The Prose Works*, Vol. I, ed. Norman Ault (Oxford, 1936). — *The Iliad of Homer Translated* (6v, 1715-20); ed. Gilbert Wakefield (5v, 1806; 3v, 1817); *The Odyssey of Homer* (5v, 1725-6); ed. Gilbert Wakefield (4v, 1806; 2v, 1817); *The Works of Shakespear* edited (i.e., the plays only, 6v, 1725; 8v, 1728; 10v, 1728; 9v, 1731, 1735; 8v, 1734-6, etc.). — Thomas J. Wise, *A Pope Library* (1931); Reginald H. Griffith, *Alexander Pope: A Bibliography* (2v, Austin, Texas, 1922-7); James E. Tobin, *Alexander Pope: A List of Critical Studies from 1895-1944* (1945). — Edwin Abbott, *A Concordance to Pope* (1875). There are biographies by Samuel Johnson, *Lives of the English Poets*, ed. G. B. Hill, III. 82-276; Robert Carruthers (1853; improved ed., 1857); Sir Leslie Stephen (1880); William J. Courthope (1889, Vol. v of the *Works*); "George Paston" [Miss E. M. Symonds], *Mr. Pope* (2v, 1909); George Sherburn, *Early Career* (Oxford, 1934). For criticism see Joseph Spence, *An Essay on Pope's Odyssey* (1726-7); Jean Pierre de Crousaz, *Examen de l'Essai ... sur l'Homme* (Lausanne, 1737; Paris, 1748, 1766), Crousaz, *Commentaire sur ... l'Essai sur l'Homme* (Paris, 1738); Joseph Warton, *Essay on the Genius and Writings of Pope* (2v, 1756, 1782; 1806); Joseph Spence, *Anecdotes*, ed. Samuel W. Singer (1820); Matthew Arnold, *On Translating Homer* (1861); Charles W. Dilke, *Papers of a Critic* (2v, 1875); Émile Montégut, *Heures de lecture d'un critique* (1891); William E. Mead, *The Versification of Pope* (Leipzig, 1889); James T. Hillhouse, *The Grub-street Journal* (Durham, N. C., 1928); Austin Warren, *Pope as Critic and Humanist* (Princeton, 1929); Edith Sitwell, *Alexander Pope* (1930); Willard H. Durham, "Pope as Poet," *Essays in Criticism, Second Series* (University of California, 1934), pp. 93-110; Geoffrey Tillotson, *On the Poetry of Pope* (Oxford, 1938); Robert K. Root, *The Poetical Career of Alexander Pope* (Princeton, 1938).

and Milton, solicited the privilege of publishing Pope's *Pastorals* for him.
By 1709, when these poems appeared, the young poet had been introduced
to the London coffee-house circles by his elderly sponsors, and was launched
on a career at twenty-one. His *Essay on Criticism* [13] (1711) gained him a
considerable fame, as did *Messiah,* first published by Steele in *The Spectator*
for May 14, 1712, where the unnamed author was called "a great genius."
When in 1713 he announced a subscription for a translation of the *Iliad,*
his friends were enthusiastic, and his acquaintances were inclined to lift
eyebrows over the idea that a young man without academic training should
try to translate the greatest of all poets. The moment was tense and violently
partisan so far as politics and religion were concerned; Pope furthermore
had estranged the wits at Button's (good Whigs!) by his war with Philips
and by his friendship with the "turncoat" Swift. While he was translating
the *Iliad* (1713-20), Pope was frequently attacked in print, chiefly for his
religion and for his alleged incompetence in Greek. The attacks were the
more annoying because the *Iliad* was most cordially received practically
everywhere except at Button's. Two days after Pope's first volume of Homer
appeared, Thomas Tickell published a translation of *Iliad* I, said privately
to have been done with the aid of Addison. The attempt, if it was one, to
show how superior a translation an Oxonian poet could produce, was a
failure—but it did not fail to irritate Pope. It was in part the attacks on his
work during the nine long years of translation (for when the *Iliad* was
completed, he presently went on with the *Odyssey*) that changed Pope into
a satirist.

Pope's
Poems
(1717)
    In 1717 he collected his *Poems* in a volume that marks the end of his early
experimental period. Associated with the *Pastorals* in this volume was
Windsor Forest, a poem devoted to praise of the retired life and of the peace
of Utrecht. It is not in intention a descriptive poem [14] so much as a meditation on court life, retirement, peace, prosperity, and other topics. There were
descriptive details, but they in no way surpass the best passages of his
Pastorals, with which also his *Messiah* (an imitation of Virgil's fourth
Eclogue) is usually associated. Less important were certain poems collected
from various miscellanies: his first epistle in verse (1712) addressed *To a*
Young Lady with the Works of Voiture, several versions of Ovid and other
ancients, two modernizations from Chaucer, and various small pieces. *The*
Temple of Fame had been published separately in 1715, and his *Epistle to*
Charles Jervas, significant as showing Pope's interest in his other art of
painting, had been prefixed to Dryden's translation of Du Fresnoy in 1716.

Two Poems
of Pathos
    Two poems first printed in this volume have unusual interest as being
studies in highly emotional expression: the *Verses to the Memory of an*
Unfortunate Lady and *Eloisa to Abelard.* The *Unfortunate Lady* is confused
and somewhat theatrical—possibly it is emulous of the manner of his friend

[13] On this poem see Part II, ch. II, n. II.
[14] On the arguable matter of Pope's descriptive powers see the incisive remarks of Ann
Winslow, "Re-evaluation of Pope's Treatment of Nature," *Univ. of Wyoming Pub.,* IV (1938).
21-43.

Rowe.[15] The confusion is curiously evident in Dr. Johnson's violent common-sensical comment on the poem, which he summarizes in favor of the harsh uncle and characterizes the whole as "the amorous fury of a raving girl." But since the girl has committed suicide, clearly it is not *her* raving, though it at times might seem to be. *Eloisa to Abelard,* based on John Hughes's translation of the famous love letters, is a greater work. Like the *Unfortunate Lady* it is a tragic monologue, but the "raving" of Eloisa has a definite and powerful story behind it, which makes the tragedy moving. As eloquent Roman pathos the poem is not surpassed in English. It is also tensely dramatic—witness Eloisa's sense of sacrilege as she takes her vows as nun with her thoughts and eyes all on Abelard:

> As with cold lips I kiss'd the sacred veil,
> The shrines all trembled, and the lamps grew pale:
> Heav'n scarce believ'd the conquest it survey'd,
> And Saints with wonder heard the vows I made.
> Yet then, to those dread altars as I drew,
> Not on the Cross my eyes were fix'd, but you....

The poem is a fusion of medieval and Ovidian material. In the volume we have evidence of Pope's love of Chaucer, and about this time he was doing verses for the Rev. Aaron Thompson's translation of Geoffrey of Monmouth (1718), which in turn probably stimulated the project of an epic in blank verse on the story of Brutus, supposed founder of the British empire.[16] This project was never completed. The casting of *Brutus* into the form of a classical epic and *Eloisa* into the form of Ovid's *Heroides* shows the spirit of Pope's work: there is no feeling on his part that traditions should be kept "pure"; romantic medieval material is recast in preferred classical forms.

But even *Eloisa* is of less interest than the gem of the 1717 volume— **The Rape of the Lock** *The Rape of the Lock.*[17] Published in a brief form in 1712 the poem was enlarged in 1714 most advantageously by adding the "machines"—sylphs, gnomes, etc.—and other important details. Thus executed, the poem was at once recognized as a masterpiece; it remains for many Pope's most delightful poem, and for all, the best mock-heroic poem in the language. It may then be read as a burlesque of classical epic devices—the proposition, the invocation, the epic speeches, the episodes of games or of the descent to the lower regions are all delightfully depreciated here without being vulgarized—and vulgarization was usual in these mock-heroics. Pope's elegance as compared with the realism of Swift or even of Gay is characteristic. *The Rape* may also be read as a poem on an occasion, as designed to reconcile Arabella Fermor (Belinda) and her family with the family of Lord Petre, he being

---

15 Geoffrey Tillotson, "Lady Mary Wortley Montagu and Pope's ... *Unfortunate Lady,*" *RES,* XII (1936). 401-412.

16 Pope's prose summary of his projected *Brutus* was printed in Owen Ruffhead's *Life of Pope* (8vo, 1769), pp. 410-424. See also Friedrich Brie, "Popes *Brutus,*" *Anglia,* LXIII (1939). 144-185.

17 The best commentary on this poem is that of Geoffrey Tillotson in Pope's *Poems* Twickenham ed. (1940), Vol. II.

the baron who in real life had cut the lock. As such the poem is enormously clever in making Belinda charming (though her bereaved screams were excessive in a decorous age) and in making the lock ultimately immortal and, meanwhile, trivial. As "society verse" it takes superlative rank, and is comparable with Sheridan's later *School for Scandal* as a completely satisfying depiction, in laughing satire, of the frivolities of a polite age. Considered as a work of imagination the poem is perhaps Pope's highest achievement. It has been urged that Ariel is borrowed from *The Tempest* and that the sylphs and gnomes come from the Rosicrucian *Comte de Gabalis* by Montfaucon de Villars. But both Ariel and the sylphs are handled with originality. The sylphs in particular are purified of the dross of sex that Rosicrucians imputed to them. The best imaginative achievement in the poem lies in the element of burlesque. "Burlesque," Addison had said in *Spectator* No. 249, "is ... of two kinds, the first represents mean persons in the accoutrements of heroes; the other describes great persons acting and speaking, like the basest among the people." Pope's talent is exercised both in diminution and in aggrandizement: Agamemnon's scepter dwindles to become Belinda's bodkin; Clarissa swells and talks like a Homeric sage. Finely turned are the passages where Belinda's dressing-table becomes an altar, Belinda's mirrored image becomes the goddess, and her maid "the inferior priestess." More ingeniously sustained is the heroic battle of ombre in Canto III, but skilful ingenuity is present in every exquisite page of the work.

Pope's Homer For a decade or more Pope was engrossed in translating the *Iliad* and the *Odyssey*, and editing Shakespeare's plays. From translation in Pope's day one could acquire both fame and fortune; from editing less could be expected. Pope's gains from Homer have been variously estimated: all one can do is to guess at them, but he may have got as much as £9000, which seems to be an unparalleled return for such labors. In spite of Pope's obvious deficiencies in academic training and in spite of many attacks by envious minor authors, the translation was well received, and it deserved to be. Unfortunately the synchronized publication of his first volume of the *Iliad* (June 6, 1715) and Tickell's translation of Book I (June 8, 1715) caused a sharp breach in his relations with Addison,[18] to whom Pope forthwith addressed the satirical portrait (published about six years later), which in its final form was to appear in the *Epistle to Dr. Arbuthnot* (1735) as the portrait of "Atticus." Pope's performance in the *Odyssey* brought less fame and more obloquy because while he announced himself as "undertaking" the translation, that ambiguous word concealed the fact that his friends Elijah Fenton[19] (1683-1730) and William Broome (1689-1745) were to translate half the poem. Pope was unjustly accused of underpaying his assistants: what they chiefly complained of was that concealment of their

[18] Arthur E. Case, "Pope, Addison, and the Atticus Lines," *MP*, XXXIII (1935). 187-193; Norman Ault, "Pope and Addison," *RES*, XVII (1941). 428-451.

[19] For Fenton's poems see the collections of Samuel Johnson, Robert Anderson, and Alexander Chalmers. His letters to and from Pope and Broome are in Pope's *Correspondence*, ed. Sherburn (Oxford, 1956).—W. W. Lloyd, *Elijah Fenton* (1894); Earl Harlan, *Elijah Fenton* (Philadelphia, 1937).

part in the matter robbed them of just fame. It is probable that, as Broome said, Pope revised every page of their work to give integrity of style to the whole.

Pope's success with Homer, though thus qualified, was great. He made the father of all poetry live for those of his day who were not scholars, and though he wrote for his day, his translation still remains about the most lively and readable of poetic translations. Less encrusted with magnificent imagination than Chapman's version, it has more, and more varied, narrative movement; not so simple or plain as Cowper's version, it has more nervous power and is less relaxed. It is naturally not a very faithful translation, if by that adjective one means *literal*. Pope follows the ideals in translation stated by his French contemporary Houdar de la Motte, who in his *Iliade* (1714) tried to make Homer write like an eighteenth-century poet. So Pope omits or multiplies lines as he pleases in order to make Homer more vivid for readers of 1715. The diction of his translation has been criticized perhaps severely, but there is ground for criticism. He is timid about everyday words that might seem "low." In his day English was regarded as both an inferior and a "failing" language. Pope himself had written, "And such as Chaucer is, shall Dryden be," and the line was quite in keeping with the ideas of his day. The Greek of Homer was regarded as changelessly and supremely poetic, and the consequent problem was to bridge the linguistic abyss between the two tongues. Pope was much influenced by the success of Milton in giving to English an epic dignity, but the influence did not operate happily. It resulted frequently in an inflated phrasing stiffened with Latinity that was neither felicitous nor Miltonic. Even in other poems Pope was capable—for the sake of rime—of using heavy Latin derivatives: his "lab'ring oxen . . . from the field *retreat.*" Another false taste of his day was for terse epigram or moral commonplace as well as for elegant periphrasis. "Glitt'ring forfex" is admirable as witty periphrasis for Lord Petre's scissors; but there is obvious affectation in "finny prey" for fish and "fleecy care" for sheep. It is unjust to represent Pope as inventing any of these mannerisms, but his Homer, remarkable in general for its eloquent dignity and its nervous speed, did at times propagate such heresies. In spite of these faults his translation is far more readable than some critics would have one believe.

His edition of Shakespeare was again a qualified success.[20] Like the *Iliad* and the *Odyssey* the bulky quarto volumes of these plays were published by subscription—for the benefit in this case of Jacob Tonson the bookseller, not for Pope's benefit. Pope was paid only moderately for this enterprise; but he was given paid helpers—Gay, Fenton, and possibly others. The edition was at first unpopular because expensive. Cheaper reprints in smaller format (of which there were at least four in Pope's lifetime) were better

His Edition of Shakespeare

---

[20] On the history of this edition see Thomas R. Lounsbury, *The First Editors of Shakespeare* (London, 1906) or *The Text of Shakespeare* (New York, 1908). The two titles are for a single work. Also David Nichol Smith, *Shakespeare in the Eighteenth Century* (Oxford, 1928); Ronald B. McKerrow, *The Treatment of Shakespeare's Text by his Earlier Editors, 1709-1768* (British Academy Lecture, 1933).

liked. Pope's preface indicated an understanding of the nature of an editor's textual duty and an appreciation of the excellences of Shakespeare's genius and style, though the great bard's defects were allowed to loom large. Pope indicated the "best" passages in the plays, in a somewhat casual fashion,[21] by placing inverted commas in the margins opposite choice bits. In making his text he had a fairly good collection of early folios and quartos to work from, but the tediousness of the labor was too much for him. His chief improvements in the text lie in his restoring "prose" passages to their original blank-verse form, in the addition of passages from the quartos hitherto omitted in folio reprints, and in his occasionally happy textual emendations. In days when clarity of style was a cult and when textual emendation à la Richard Bentley was a mania, it was inevitable that Shakespeare's complex language should be tinkered with inexpertly; but while Pope's ignorance of the meanings of words in Elizabethan English (for which dictionaries were quite inadequate) led him to grotesque definitions, it also probably restrained him from lavish emendation. It was his failure to do an all-out job on the text that Lewis Theobald [22] (1688-1744) reproached Pope for in his two-hundred page review of Pope's work on *Hamlet*, published in 1726 as *Shakespeare Restored: or, a Specimen of the Many Errors, as well Committed, as Unamended, by Mr. Pope*. Theobald had read much more Elizabethan English than had Pope, and many of his criticisms were just; almost an equal number, however, were either wrong or petty. When in 1734 Theobald published his own edition of Shakespeare (dated 1733) it was a considerable advance upon Pope's, but it was not then generally so regarded—perhaps because meanwhile, as a reward for *Shakespeare Restored*, Pope had made Theobald the "hero" of his *Dunciad*.

In Pope's later career, chiefly that of satirist, three important works or groups of works appear: *The Dunciad*, the "Moral Essays" (including the *Essay on Man*), and his imitations of Horace and similar epistles or satires. For many critics *The Dunciad* is the climax of Pope's achievement. There are, however, certainly two and possibly three *Dunciads*. The first,[23] composed in part under the influence of Swift, appeared in three books (1728) as a counterblast to all critics of Pope's works, to all bad poets, to publishers,[24] and to all professors of pedantry such as Theobald, who is now the hero, and thus expresses his ardent devotion to the Goddess, Dulness:

The Dunciad

> For thee I dim these eyes, and stuff this head,
> With all such reading as was never read;
> For thee supplying, in the worst of days,
> Notes to dull books, and prologues to dull plays;

---

[21] John E. Butt, *Pope's Taste in Shakespeare* (Shakespeare Assoc., 1936); James R. Sutherland, " 'The Dull Duty of an Editor,' " *RES*, XXI (1945). 202-215.

[22] Richard F. Jones, *Lewis Theobald* (1919).

[23] R. H. Griffith, "The *Dunciad* of 1728," *MP*, XIII (1915). 1-18; cf. *Colophon*, III (1938). 569-586.

[24] The most poisonous of the publishers of the day was Edmund Curll (1675-1747). See Ralph Straus, *The Unspeakable Curll* (1927). The first modern copyright law was passed in 1709, and the ensuing years of confusion and of piracies agonized marketable authors.

> For thee explain a thing till all men doubt it,
> And write about it, Goddess, and about it;
> So spins the silkworm small its slender store,
> And labours, 'till it clouds itself all o'er.

In 1729 Pope reissued this version with changes and elaborate burlesque apparatus as *The Dunciad Variorum*.[25] The poem was still a satire on pedantry: *dunce* is derived from Duns Scotus. But the modern meaning of *dunce* opened the way for a shift in emphasis, when in 1742, probably at the suggestion of William Warburton (like Theobald an editor), the poem was in part recast to make Colley Cibber the hero and vapidity the essential quality of dulness. A fourth book, published as *The New Dunciad* (1742) advertised the coming change, and *The Dunciad in Four Books* appeared [26] late in 1743. The very conclusion of the fourth Book rises to something like nobility in expressing scorn of cheap, dull art, and this Book as a whole is one of Pope's most richly imaginative and wise pieces. The merit of the poem as a whole lies in its generalized satirical insight expressed in barbed couplets; the personal spites of the author may be set down as defects for the most part. Even these personal stimuli, however, can be generalized. Whether Pope succeeded, however, in emancipating himself from personal spite and in generalizing his dislikes has been doubted. Theory and practice do not always accord. Certainly there is more of personal animus in *The Dunciad* than in any other great English satire; but there is also a universal lesson for humanists which textual critics and professors of literary pedantry would do well to keep always in mind.

By 1730, if not earlier, Pope was at work on his "ethic epistles," which he projected in several parts. Two parts were actually written: the "Moral Essays" and the *Essay on Man*. The first of the "Moral Essays" to appear (1731) is now number four. It was addressed to the Earl of Burlington, an architect and an important patron of architecture. It was called "Of Taste," "Of False Taste," and finally "Of the Use of Riches." It was Pope's first publication after *The Dunciad,* and it turned his satirical shafts away from Grub-street scribblers towards the palatial and tasteless lavishness of *nouveaux riches,* whose new mansions lay heavy on the earth. The dunces waiting their chance, insisted, without much ground, that the satire was largely directed through "Timon" against the Duke of Chandos, who had subscribed generously to Pope's *Iliad*.[27] Thus from his alleged treatment of Addison and the Duke, Pope's enemies built up the legend of his constitutional ingratitude. The real importance of the poem is its aid in promoting plainer tastes in architecture and more natural and picturesque methods of landscaping one's garden and park. Among the other "Moral Essays" the

The "Moral Essays"

[25] James R. Sutherland, "The *Dunciad* of 1729," *MLR*, xxxi (1936). 347-353. See also the introductory essay by Robert K. Root to his facsimile edition of *The Dunciad Variorum* (Princeton, 1929).

[26] Its appearance was probably delayed by litigation over the copyright, which Pope had sold in 1729. See Howard P. Vincent, "Some *Dunciad* Litigation," *PQ*, xviii (1939). 285-289.

[27] George Sherburn, " 'Timon's Villa' and Cannons," *Huntington Library Bull.*, No. 8 (1935). 131-152.

third, to Lord Bathurst, attacks avarice and allied vices. It ends with the brilliant story of the career of Balaam the India merchant, a shrewd piece of apparently impersonal satire. The essay addressed "To a Lady" (Pope's lifelong friend, Martha Blount) "Of the Characters of Women" is an elaborate compliment to Miss Blount, who amidst the *varium et mutabile* of her sex is said to be *semper eadem*. The famous character of Atossa, probably originating in that of Katherine, Duchess of Buckinghamshire, was added to the poem only after the Duchess's death and just before Pope died. The first of these "Moral Essays," addressed to Lord Cobham, "Of the Knowledge and Characters of Men," is Pope's best statement of the favorite theme of his day, the fallible limitations of human reason. Brilliantly written, it is in doctrine closely related to the *Essay on Man*.

An Essay on Man: Its History and Doctrine

This "philosophical poem," which along with the *Essay on Criticism* became an integral part of the eighteenth-century intellectual tradition, was published in four epistles during twelve months of 1733-4. Pope's ingenuity was again active. Realizing that his dunces would attack whatever he printed as his, he planned to publish this poem anonymously and at the same time to publish other poems over his own name, so that his authorship of the *Essay* might be unsuspected and the unknown "new" author of the *Essay* be praised. The scheme worked, and the poem, soon acknowledged by Pope, attained even international fame. Presently a Swiss professor of logic named Crousaz attacked the poem as heterodox and Leibnitzian. Although William Warburton came forward as Pope's defender, lovers of orthodoxy began to waver in their admiration, and by 1781 Dr. Johnson,[28] who earlier had defended the poem, attacked its doctrines strongly. It was admired by many, however, including Immanuel Kant, and has frequently been a favorite literary document with scientists and philosophers, though not a favorite piece of philosophizing with Anglican literary critics. No idea in the poem is new or peculiar to Pope or to Lord Bolingbroke, who had encouraged and greatly influenced Pope in writing the *Essay*. The first epistle discusses the relation of man to God, and presents an exposition of the idea of the universe as a "great chain of being," a rising continuous scale, ideally perfect in its completeness, its order, and its unity.[29] As corollary to this notion of divine design permeating the whole universe, Pope concludes, "Whatever is, is right." In so concluding he does not deny the existence of evil, but asserts that ultimately evil works God's will. He essayed the impossible task of reconciling these views with the doctrine of free will and the obligation to moral effort. The second epistle discusses man's psychological nature, and

[28] See Allen T. Hazen and E. L. McAdam, Jr. in the *Yale Univ. Library Gazette*, x (1936). 45-51; and Georges A. Bonnard, "Note on the English Translations of Crousaz' Two Books on Pope's *Essay on Man*," *Recueil de Travaux* (Université de Lausanne, VII (1937). 175-184. Hazen and McAdam established finally the fact that Dr. Johnson translated Crousaz's *Commentary* in 1739. The footnotes of Johnson show less hostility to Pope than does Johnson's *Life* (1781). See also A. W. Evans, *Warburton and the Warburtonians* (1932) for Warburton's entrance into the controversy.

[29] The classic treatment of this idea so fundamental in the thought of the early eighteenth century is Professor Arthur O. Lovejoy's *Great Chain of Being* (Cambridge, Mass., 1936).

while stressing the dichotomy of passion and reason, tries to reconcile the two. The third presents a sentimental picture of man's social coöperativeness and an account of the evolution of society from a primitive state to its present decadent condition. Some months after these three Pope published the fourth epistle, "Of Happiness." One may justly question whether Pope or many of his orthodox readers realized the essential, but not quite inevitable, deistic bias of these epistles: Pope was trying to build a rational or empirical system of ethics independent of metaphysics or religion, but without denying the latter. No one has ever been competent to achieve this feat, and Pope was far from competent.

The poem is a crucial instance of the problematical relation of reason and prose to poetry. In his preface on "The Design" Pope recognizes this aesthetic and intellectual problem, and shows that he realized somewhat the *The* deficiencies of his work. Certain matters, he said, needed more detail; but *Aesthetic* detail would be tedious: other parts should have been more "poetical," but *Problem of* that could not be gained "without sacrificing perspicuity to ornament." In *Reasoning in Poetry* other words, Pope believed in the poetry of statement; and it is obvious that in such poems as Tennyson's *In Memoriam* or in T. S. Eliot's intellectual poems, meaning is poetical but is sacrificed for sense images, which, if not ornament, surely bear some occasional relationship to ornament or to periphrasis. It was inevitable and just that the mutual incoherence of Pope's various paragraphs should be exposed; it is also just to recognize that many paragraphs taken as such are crisp and brilliant meditations on ideas that writers of many ages have treated—whether in prose or verse—somewhat fumblingly. If one believes in the possibility of intellectual poetry, the *Essay on Man* is a masterpiece—not as the "system" Pope thought it, but rather as a cluster of sparkling passages that make an obviously incoherent whole. If one holds the strange doctrine of Matthew Arnold that Pope was essentially a prose writer, one is still bound to reckon with tangible and brilliant merits in expression. And as far back as Aristotle it was thought doubtfully wise to try to trace precisely the boundaries that separate poetry from prose.

As early as 1729 Pope told Fenton "that for the future he intended to write *His Imita-* nothing but epistles in Horace's manner." Such he considered the epistles *tions of* that form the "Moral Essays" and the *Essay on Man*. The modern reader *Horace* is likely to apply the remark rather to Pope's "imitations" (translation plus modernization) of Horace. Of these in the thirties he did almost a dozen, and with them may be associated two adaptations from the satires of John Donne and the two other poems that became the "Prologue" and the "Epilogue" to these satires. His satires are basically directed against the follies of polite society, against corruption in politics, and against false values in art, particularly the art of poetry. All three of these join at times, as in his *Epistle to Augustus* (Horace, Epistle ii, i). His political position was complex. One of his closest friends was Bolingbroke, and yet while close to this leader of the Opposition, Pope was on dining terms with Sir Robert

Walpole. It is corruption rather than corrupt leaders that he attacks,[30] and in the *Epilogue to the Satires* (originally called *One Thousand Seven Hundred and Thirty-eight*), where he excoriates the follies of the year, he depicts (lines 141-170) eloquently the "triumph" of corruption.

His Defense of Satire

In more than one poem, evidently aware of the increasing aversion of sentimentalism to satire, Pope defends his cruel art. This is done in his "Prologue," in the "Epilogue," and in the *Imitation of the First Satire of the Second Book of Horace* (1733), which he addresses to his eminent friend in the law, William Fortescue. His best defense is his *Epistle to Dr. Arbuthnot,* ultimately called by Warburton the "Prologue" to the Satires. The poet here vividly pictures himself as pestered by applications from Grub-street authors, and justifies his defensive aggressive treatment of them by a rose-colored summary of his early career of forbearance. Here he introduces the justly famous character of Atticus (Addison), the jealous genius who, having arrived, complacently encouraged critics to keep others from like success. Presently Pope passes to a harshly caustic portrait of "Sporus," a name here applied to John, Lord Hervey, towards whom Pope felt an intense hostility of unknown cause. In 1733 and possibly earlier Hervey and Lady Mary Wortley Montagu had attacked Pope viciously: here the poet retorts, though Lady Mary gets off, as usual, with brief but scathing scorn. All that friendship was now over. Pope ends the poem with an account of his parents, since his "obscure birth" had been sneered at in Hervey's attack, and the account is composed of sincerity and pose mixed. All Pope's critics admit he was a good son, but regret, some of them, that he was aware of the fact. The poem is among Pope's most spirited and finished works, one in which much of the time mere pique transforms itself into valid universal meanings.

Publication of His Letters

These poems of self-defense, which strive to place the poet in a good light as a moral crusader, agree in aim with Pope's publication of his private correspondence, publication which went on over a period of years (1735-42). It was not "correct" to publish one's private letters, and for this reason, at least in part, Pope resorted to chicanery to make it appear that the publications were unauthorized and piratical. He at times falsified the texts of letters, but the falsification is one of general pose usually rather than of specific fact. His great rival for epistolary fame in his half-century is Lady Mary Wortley Montagu (1689-1762), whose letters published after her death [31] deal with her travels and life as ambassador's wife in Turkey, her insatiable appetite for gossip about the irregularities of polite society in Eng-

Lady Mary Wortley Montagu's Letters

---

[30] Lady Mary Wortley Montagu in her little known periodical, *The Nonsense of Common Sense* (eight numbers, 1737-8), written in answer to the *Common Sense* of Chesterfield, Lyttelton, *et al.*, ardently supports Walpole and at the same time attacks corruption as nobly as did the Opposition.

[31] These letters, published under strange circumstances, in four volumes, 1763-7, are to be found in Lady Mary's *Works*, ed. James Dallaway (5v, 1803); Lord Wharncliffe (3v, 1837; 2v, 1861). — Charles W. Dilke, *Papers of a Critic*, I (1875). 343-359; "George Paston" [Miss E. M. Symonds], *Lady Mary Wortley Montagu and her Times* (1907); Lewis Melville, *Life and Letters* [1925]; Helen S. Hughes. "A Letter from Lady Mary to Mr. Wortley Montagu," *RES*, IV (1928). 327-330.

land, and her residence after 1739 on the Continent. More than Pope she shows an objective interest in the world about her; more than his letters hers are valuable as a record of the life of her time. It is to be feared, however, that she is an irresponsible if sprightly gossip: one hates to believe English society was as bad as she in her letters and Lord Hervey in his *Memoirs* paint it. Pope hardly paints society at all in his letters, which are (i.e., the ones he published) largely a personal record of mental life. In his own day Pope's letters were accepted as a sincere record; in the nineteenth century there was an excessive reaction against the supposed trickery involved in the processes of publication and "cooking" the texts. To modern readers Pope's letters are usually somewhat dull and moralistic, but for his own century his deft and elegant phrase encouraged a development of the art of letter-writing that is one of the significant aspects of the century. To Pope and to *The Spectator,* which published many personal letters, should go much of the credit for this development.

As an artist Pope is remarkable for clean-cut, incisive phrasing: his verbal *Pope's* marksmanship is unparalleled. In his early poems and in the Homer he *Methods* erred from the paths of simple plainness, but after *The Dunciad* of 1728 *as Artist* he is normally elegant and conversational in tone; a studied ease is his great achievement. In versification, if not in rime, he is one of the great masters, although he worked within self-imposed limits that would have been intolerable to another of equal ability. He learned metrics from Dryden, but he excluded Dryden's somewhat obvious devices for variety—the Alexandrine and the triplet—and depended normally on subtle variations of rhythms within the closed couplet, further hampered by a common tendency to balance and antithesis. Professor Saintsbury—and not he alone—is content to illustrate Pope's metrics from the opening lines of Canto II of *The Rape of the Lock* as showing the "rocking-horse" movement of Pope's monotonously antithetical lines. The passage (lines 1-18) is really typical only in that Pope is indulging in a *tour de force* which amounts almost to a burlesque of the antithetical half-lines that he loved with conscious excess. Even in this passage there is more variety in emphasis and in placing of the caesura than Saintsbury admits. It is true, furthermore, that the "closed" quality of Pope's couplets has been exaggerated. Couplets are curiously detachable even when lacking grammatical independence. Take the most quoted couplets:

> Slave to no sect, who takes no private road,
> But looks through Nature up to Nature's God.

Or

> Damn with faint praise, assent with civil leer,
> And without sneering, teach the rest to sneer.

Grammatically these couplets must be joined to context: they are not completely self-contained in spite of end-pauses. The second couplet, it may be noted, is part of a perfect periodic sentence which includes the whole Atticus portrait and runs on for practically twenty-two lines. The *Essay on Man* is full of couplets that are linked in groups of two or three with varying pauses at the ends of lines, or in the middle. For example,

> Of Systems possible, if 'tis confest
> That Wisdom infinite must form the best,
> Where all must full or not coherent be,
> And all that rises, rise in due degree;
> Then, in the Scale of reas'ning life, 'tis plain,
> There must be, somewhere, such a rank as Man:
> And all the question (wrangle e'er so long)
> Is only this, if God has placed him wrong?

Such a passage is far more characteristic of Pope's graceful rhythms than the opening lines of Canto II of *The Rape.* Pope's manner fascinated his inferiors for almost fifty years. As Cowper put it in 1782 in *Table Talk:*

> Then Pope, as harmony itself exact,
> In verse well disciplin'd, complete, compact,
> Gave virtue and morality a grace,
> That, quite eclipsing pleasure's painted face,
> Levied a tax of wonder and applause,
> Ev'n on the fools that trampled on their laws.
> But he (his musical finesse was such,
> So nice his ear, so delicate his touch)
> Made poetry a mere mechanic art;
> And ev'ry warbler has his tune by heart.

The mechanics of Pope's art were so subtle that mere "warblers" missed them: even Cowper, delightful as he is, lacks Pope's sparkle and dignity. There was more to the art than mere mechanics, but the mechanics were so exacting and constricting that one wonders how William Walsh could ever have advised them. Those who fail, however, to hear the delicately varied rhythms in Pope are akin to music "critics" who hear nothing but mechanic skill in Mozart. In the larger traditionalism of Pope's generic patterns as well as in the preoccupation with public emotion eloquently expressed Pope is the acme of "correct" neo-classical excellence. He is, perhaps permanently, our great example in English of "the poet of reason," of intellectuality in the poetic art. It is, of course, clear, as Joseph Warton pointed out in 1756, that Pope practised only the lesser genres of poetry, but it is perhaps also clear (as Warton says) that "in that species of Poetry wherein Pope excelled, he is superior to all mankind"—in other words, the greatest of didactic and satirical poets.

IX
New Voices in Poetry

In his *Theory of Moral Sentiments* (1759) Adam Smith, not yet a famous economist, expressed the following opinions as to the state of English poetry:

In our own language, Mr. Pope and Dr. Swift have each of them introduced a manner different from what was practised before, into all works that are written in Rhyme, the one in long verses, the other in short. The quaintness of Butler has given place to the plainness of Swift. The rambling freedom of Dryden and the correct but often tedious and prosaic languor of Addison are no longer the objects of imitation, but all long verses are now written after the manner of the nervous precision of Mr. Pope.

There is much truth in these statements, but they are not, as this chapter *Were Swift* will show, altogether true. They rather express a common feeling as to the *and Pope* obsessive influence that Swift and Pope exerted. During the second quarter *Dominant?* of the century, however, at a time when Swift and Pope were in their prime, new tendencies in poetry began to appear. These tendencies were hardly rebellious against the dominance of Swift and Pope, but they do evade the influence of those poets and of their tradition as it stemmed from Dryden and others. The developments include an increasing awareness of landscape as material for poetry, coupled, curiously enough, with an increased use of philosophical reflections in poetry. More noticeable than heretofore and parallel to the Dryden-Pope school is a Miltonic tradition, manifest metrically in the use both of blank verse and of the tetrameter couplet of *L'Allegro* and *Il Penseroso*. The idiom of Milton also is increasingly cultivated.

When in 1731 Edward Cave (1691-1754) founded the most interesting magazine of the century, *The Gentleman's Magazine,* he assumed as editor the pseudonym of Sylvanus Urban.[1] The very name suggests the bifurcation in poetic subject matter that was taking place: description of woods and meadows of rural England might now be interspersed with reflections on the manners and morals of urban society. Among several assistants presently working for the *Magazine* Cave had Dr. Johnson, who regarded the full tide of human existence as flowing at Charing Cross, and among his poetical advisers he had Moses Browne (1704-1787), who in 1729 had published *Town and* vividly descriptive *Piscatory Eclogues* that featured successfully rural scenery *Country* and folk superstition. Though there are obviously the two tendencies, it is *Poets* not possible to divide poets thus easily into town and country bards; for

---

[1] Dr. Johnson wrote for *The Gentleman's Magazine* (February, 1754) a life of Cave. As revised in 1781 it appears in his *Works,* vi (Oxford, 1825). 428-435.

some descriptive poets lived in town, and some moral-reflective poets inhabited the country. Nor is it possible to regard descriptive poets as *ipso facto* "romantic." [2] A favorite model, loosely followed, is Virgil, both in his *Eclogues* and in his *Georgics*. The latter type divides into poems that describe objective processes—Dyer's *Fleece* is an example—and poems that are speculative, in the manner of the dozens of imitations of the *Essay on Man*. Descriptive poetry is habitually blended with moralizing, and accounts of descriptive poetry, such as the *Critical Essays on Some of the Poems of Several English Poets* (1785) by John Scott of Amwell, included Denham and Pope as well as Thomson, Dyer, and others. One must not lightly call blank verse a sign of romanticism: the escape from Gothic rime had a classical as well as a libertarian bias. The entire lack of cleavage involved between "neo-classical" and "new" tendencies at this time can be seen in the explanatory note printed in 1737 at the end of a blank-verse poem (anonymous) called *Albania: a Poem Address'd to the Genius of Scotland:*

The above Poem (*Albania*) was wrote by a Scots Clergyman some Years ago, who is since dead. The fine Spirit of Poetry which it breathes, its Classic Air, but above all the noble Enthusiasm he discovers for his Country, cannot fail to make it agreeable to such as have a Taste for that Simplicity of Nature, and that beautiful Diversification of Epithets, which constitute the principal *Excellencies of Antiquity*.

Among the more urban poets of the time we may here mention such minor writers as James Ralph [3] (1705?-1762), better known for his prose and for having been a friend of Benjamin Franklin and of Henry Fielding, than for his blank-verse descriptive poems, *The Tempest* (1727), *Night* (1728), and *Zeuma, or the Love of Liberty* (1729)—this last an American poem—or his unhappy attack on Pope, *Sawney, an Heroic Poem occasioned by the Dunciad* (1728), which won for Ralph a dubious immortality among the dunces. More friendly to Pope among poets of the urban type were Richard Savage, David Mallet, and George, Lord Lyttelton.[4] Lyttelton's second poem was *An Epistle to Mr. Pope* (1730), and one of his four eclogues on *The Progress of Love* (1732) was dedicated to Pope. His most discussed poem, the *Monody* (1747), on his wife's death, was in somewhat monotonous Pindaric form. Lyttelton, again, is better known for his prose and for his political influence with Frederick, Prince of Wales (whose secretary he was). Isaac Hawkins Browne (1706-1760) produced early poems of interest and a *magnum opus* in Latin hexameters *De Animi Immortalitate* (1754). In 1736, after preliminary circulation and piratical publication, he brought out his *Pipe of Tobacco*,[5] a masterly set of imitations of contempo-

---

[2] A. O. Lovejoy, "On the Discrimination of Romanticisms," *PMLA*, XXXIX (1924). 229-253; Raymond D. Havens, "Romantic Aspects of the Age of Pope," *PMLA*, XXVII (1912). 297-324.

[3] On Ralph see *CBEL*, II. 443. Also Helen S. Hughes, "Fielding's Indebtedness to James Ralph," *MP*, XX (1922). 19-34.

[4] On Lyttelton see Part III, ch. IV, n. 2.

[5] Browne's *Pipe of Tobacco* is edited by H. F. B. Brett-Smith (Oxford, 1923).

rary poets and a masterpiece of light verse at the same time. It continues the tradition of elegant informality, of which Prior is the best exemplar.

These urban poets are surpassed in interest by the "sylvan" poets, at least by the ones devoted to description. These men, though some of them passed their "career" years in or near London, were animated by a real love of "external nature" and by memories at least of a pleasant past amid rural surroundings.[6] The most important of them, James Thomson, came from Scotland; John Dyer came from Wales, and a group of west-country poets including Lyttelton, Shenstone, Somerville, and Jago, also made their reputations during this period, though their careers lasted on to a point where they properly become "mid-century" poets. Memories and pleasures of rural life were supported in many cases by literary or artistic precedent: Dyer, being a painter as well as a poet, was influenced by the landscapes painted by Poussin, Salvator Rosa, and Claude Lorrain.[7] The literary influences came largely from the pastoral tradition, from the *Georgics,* from the topographical school of Denham involving descriptions of prospects or estates, or from the modest and ingratiating pattern of *L'Allegro* and *Il Penseroso.*

James Thomson [8] (1700-1748) was much influenced by these literary tradi- *Thomson's* tions, which reinforced a true love of natural scenery, acquired from the *Career* Scottish lowlands where he was born and from which he was sent to Edinburgh for university training—supposedly for the ministry. Hesitant for some reason to continue his theological studies, he traveled to London by boat in 1725, where, still undecided as to a future career, he became tutor to the small son of a Scottish family. He had in David Mallet and others good friends who encouraged his bent to poetry, which he had manifested as early as 1720 by then publishing three poems in the *Edinburgh Miscellany.* One of these, *Of a Country Life* (in couplets), was prophetic of *The Seasons.* Mallet and Thomson exchanged manuscripts and criticized each other's verses during these years when Thomson was writing *The Seasons* and Mallet his *Excursion* (1728). They remained lifelong friends. *The Seasons* (1726-30) established Thomson's fame, and secured for him a place as traveling tutor to young Charles Talbot, son of the future Lord Chancellor. After their return from the Continental tour Thomson was made Secretary

---

[6] On "the return to nature" see Myra Reynolds, *The Treatment of Nature in English Poetry between Pope and Wordsworth* (2d ed., Chicago, 1909); Cecil A. Moore, "The Return to Nature in English Poetry of the Eighteenth Century," *SP,* XIV (1917). 243-291; Christopher Hussey, *The Picturesque* (1927); C. E. de Haas, *Nature and the Country in English Poetry of the First Half of the Eighteenth Century* (Amsterdam, 1928); G. G. Williams, "The Beginnings of Nature Poetry in the Eighteenth Century," *SP,* XXVII (1930). 583-608; Cecil V. Deane, *Aspects of Eighteenth Century Nature Poetry* (Oxford, 1935).
[7] Elizabeth W. Manwaring, *Italian Landscape in Eighteenth Century England* (1925), esp. pp. 98-102.
[8] Thomson's *Works,* ed. George, Baron Lyttelton (4v, 1750 ff.); Sir Harris Nicholas (2v, 1830); Peter Cunningham (2v, 1860 ff.); Duncan C. Tovey (2v, 1897); *Poetical Works,* ed. Charles Cowden Clarke (Edinburgh, 1868); J. Logie Robertson (Oxford, 1908); *The Seasons* (1730, 1738, 1744, 1746); critical ed. by Otto Zippel (Berlin, 1908); John Beresford (1927). — Léon Morel, *James Thomson, sa vie et ses œuvres* (Paris, 1895); George C. Macaulay, *James Thomson* (1907); Alan D. McKillop, *The Background of Thomson's Seasons* (Minneapolis, 1942).

of Briefs in the Court of Chancery (1733-7) with a stipend of £300 a year. When the Lord Chancellor died, Thomson, who by now had become allied with the opposition poets, lost his place; but his good friend Lyttelton persuaded the Prince of Wales to give the poet a pension of £100. On this and the income from his poems and plays he lived quietly in Kew Lane, Richmond, after 1736. Here was his "Castle of Indolence," where in good-natured and almost phlegmatic mood he passed a life very different from that of such contemporaries as his neighbor (and friend) Pope at Twickenham or the even busier Fielding in London.

The
Seasons

The Seasons is both descriptive and philosophical in nature. Moral reflection was indispensable, but description was what gave novelty and charm. Even landscape painters of the time always placed somewhere in their canvases human figures: Aristotle had announced that men in action were the proper subjects of poetry. Mere description, with no attention to manners, was juvenile. In 1756, writing about Pope, Joseph Warton remarked "that description of the external beauties of nature, is usually the first effort of a young genius, before he hath studied manners and passions." Warton may here be laboring under the prejudice of Pope's opinion that youth was the time

> When pure description held the place of sense;

but the opinion lasts on, and Gibbon, for example, in his *Essai sur l'Étude de la Littérature* (1761) thought "the external beauties of nature" were not advantageous if used as substance rather than ornament.

By enlarging *The Seasons* in successive revisions Thomson made them increasingly episodic.[9] *Winter* first appeared, in 1726, as a poem of 405 lines; it went through several editions with augmentation: in the first collected edition of *The Seasons* (1730) it included 787 lines and in its final revised edition (1746) had 1069 lines. Similarly *Summer*, which in the first edition had 1146 lines, grew to 1805; *Spring* (1728) and *Autumn*, which, with the important *Hymn to the Seasons*, appeared first in the collected edition of 1730, each added about 100 lines. The evolution of the final text is complicated, but the essential structure, of which Thomson was perhaps more careful than most authors of his day who produced works of similar length, remained fairly fixed. *Autumn* and *Winter* are organized on a loose narrative pattern, following the progress of the season in time. *Summer* presents a typical day, with passages devoted to dawn, forenoon, noon, and so on through sunset to contemplation of the nightly stars and Serene Philosophy. *Spring*, finally, presents the effects of the season on the rising scale of being: "on inanimate matter, on vegetables, on brute animals, and last on Man; concluding with a dissuasive from the wild and irregular passion of Love, opposed to that of a pure and happy kind." There is, obviously, in all four poems an expository as well as a descriptive purpose, and these devices of organization are hardly more than strings upon which to hang episodes or

[9] Otto Zippel, *Entstehungs- und Entwicklungsgeschichte von Thomsons "Winter"* (Berlin, 1907), and Thomson's *Poetical Works*, ed. J. Logie Robertson (Oxford, 1908), pp. iii-viii.

individual landscapes. Even the episodes may be organized for expository purposes: in *Winter* the reflections on poverty (lines 322-388), appended to the brief death of the husbandman frozen in the snow, arouse sentiments of sympathy just as in the same poem the famous passage on the robin (lines 245-256) dramatizes the sympathy that should exist between man and the lower animate creation.

Thomson has doubtless favorite ideas that he wishes to express; but in his choice of materials for description it is hard to find favorite scenes. Forest, river, sky, sea, plains, mountains, meadows, valleys, flowers, and animals, are all presented with an equal eye in varying aspects: the mass of detail is most inclusive. It has been urged that his repeated use of the epithet "horrid" for mountains expresses a conventional dislike rather than a romantic love of the rougher aspects of landscape.[10] But the truth seems to be that he felt sympathy for titanic as well as for intimate details. He ranges from "the repercussive roar" of thunder to a thoroughly sentimental treatment of the domestic animals:[11] "rapturous terror" and "generous purpose" are both characteristic of his moods. Familiarity was no pedantic requisite: he gives us the wolves of the Alps and Apennines and the sand storms of the desert along with the British countryside. In general his descriptive passages are marked by motion and change and are not composed pictures of landscapes. There is a keen love of varying light and shade, of changing mood and shifting color. His colors are treated definitely in a kaleidoscopic fashion, as one sees in his apostrophe to the sun in *Summer:*

Descriptive Details

> At thee the ruby lights its deepening glow,
> And with a waving radiance inward flames.
> From thee the sapphire, solid ether, takes
> Its hue cerulean; and, of evening tinct,
> The purple-streaming amethyst is thine.
> With thy own smile the yellow topaz burns;
> Nor deeper verdure dyes the robe of Spring,
> When first she gives it to the southern gale,
> Than the green emerald shows.

Such lines are typical also of the large vague effects that he loves. He is seldom minutely particular, but he is capable both of massing specific detail and of a realistic observation unusual, and practically unknown, in his time:

> not a breath
> Is heard to quiver through the closing woods,
> Or rustling turn the many-twinkling leaves
> Of aspen tall.

[10] P. K. Das, "James Thomson's Appreciation of Mountain Scenery," *ESt,* LXIV (1929). 65-70. On the general topic of attitudes towards mountain scenery see Claire-Eliane Engel, *La Littérature alpestre en France et en Angleterre au XVIIIme et au XIXme siècle* (Chambéry, 1930), and Professor R. S. Crane's comment in *PQ,* XI (1932). 175-177.

[11] Dix Harwood, *Love for Animals and How It Developed in Great Britain* (1928).

Coupled with his love of motion is an exuberance in the presentation of his details that is highly significant: in Thomson it is the plenitude rather than the order of nature that arouses enthusiasm—though both principles are felt. His picture of man in the primitive state of the Golden Age "replete with bliss" as well as the benevolent aspect of nature itself is full of this mood:

> Clear shone the skies, cooled with eternal gales,
> And balmy spirit all. The youthful sun
> Shot his best rays, and still the gracious clouds
> Dropped fatness down; as o'er the swelling mead
> The herds and flocks commixing played secure.
> This when, emergent from the gloomy wood,
> The glaring lion saw, his horrid heart
> Was meekened, and he joined his sullen joy.
> For music held the whole in perfect peace:
> Soft sighed the flute; the tender voice was heard,
> Warbling the varied heart; the woodlands round
> Applied their quire; and winds and waters flowed
> In consonance. Such were those prime of days.

Thomson and Physico-Theology

Many passages like this, better in feeling than in poetic expression, suggest reflective processes going on behind the descriptions. Thomson observes and loves details in external nature; he does not much depend on the nostalgic love of scenes once dear in childhood, such as Goldsmith later was to feel for "Sweet Auburn," and he has less of the mere sense of the picturesque in nature than had Dyer and perhaps others of his day. Fundamentally his love of nature is in a large sense philosophic. There is, to be sure, a religious aspect in it, seen in the appended *Hymn to the Seasons* and in various passages such as *Summer,* lines 185-191, in which he echoes the Psalmist's theme, "All Thy works praise Thee!" This idea, much used by deistical believers in natural religion, may perhaps be called the basic warrant for the mass of descriptive detail Thomson lovingly presents. There is, however, an added attitude, derived from the physico-theologists like John Ray and William Derham, the scientific theologians like Sir Isaac Newton, and such widely read works as Shaftesbury's *Moralists.* It is difficult to disentangle the various strands of influence here involved: [12] Shaftesbury contributes the vague enthusiasm for contemplation of nature; the more scientific writers support a rational reflection upon the divine *teachings* of nature. Nature is a book to be reverentially studied:

---

[12] On Thomson's intellectual background see chiefly McKillop, *op. cit.,* and also Cecil A. Moore, "Shaftesbury and the Ethical Poets in England, 1700-1760," *PMLA,* XXXI (1916). 264-325; Raymond D. Havens, "Primitivism and the Idea of Progress in Thomson," *SP,* XXIX (1932). 41-52; and several articles on the influence of Newton on Thomson by Herbert Drennon as follows: *PMLA,* XLIX (1934). 71-80; *SP,* XXXI (1934). 453-471; *PQ,* XIV (1935). 70-82; *ESt,* LXX (1936). 358-372. On the philosophic aspects of Newton's work see Hélène Metzger, *Attraction universelle et religion naturelle chez quelques commentateurs anglais de Newton* (Paris, 1938), and Marjorie H. Nicolson, *Newton Demands the Muse* (Princeton, 1946).

> To me be Nature's volume broad displayed;
> And to peruse its all-instructing page,
> Or, haply catching inspiration thence,
> Some easy passage, raptured, to translate,
> My sole delight.

Thomson has the curiosity of a scientist. The passage quoted about the sun and its gem-like diffractions is not merely a passage delighting in color: it has behind it notions as to the origin of precious stones. Many times Thomson insists that the study of nature frees us from the credulous superstition of the ignorant. He appended his *Hymn to the Seasons* as an important justification and explanation of the rational purpose that he fuses with enthusiastic delight in nature. It is this latter that now captures romantic critics: in his own day the philosophy was probably of equal importance.

Thomson's favorite ideas occur in poems other than *The Seasons*. While writing these four poems he had published some smaller pieces, two of which are notable. His *Hymn on Solitude*,[13] published in James Ralph's *Miscellaneous Poems by Several Hands* (1729), is an evening piece contemplating nature somewhat more sedately than Theocles had done at dawn in *The Moralists*. Thomson here uses a simpler and more pleasing idiom than in *The Seasons*. So likewise in the other poem, *To the Memory of Sir Isaac Newton* (1727), the elegiac tone softens the blank verse, and enables the poet to pay dignified and worthy praise to the great scientist, to whom his mind owed so much stimulus. *[marginal note: Hymn on Solitude]*

It is, however, in *Liberty*, published in five parts in 1735-6, that Thomson most explicitly expresses ideas concerning society and government that had been incidental in *The Seasons*. The poem to Newton had been dedicated, apparently without due response, to Sir Robert Walpole, and though in sympathies a Whig, Thomson passed to the group of "Patriots" who under the guidance of Lyttelton were attacking the Walpole ministry. Thomson was an ardent nationalist and a sentimental benevolist: his political ideas followed somewhat the line of his Patriot group and somewhat that of his own contradictory personality. By nature indolent, he throughout his career praises industry perhaps more often than any poet has done. In *Autumn* there are several passages that enunciate the principle that *[marginal note: Politics and Industry]*

> All is the gift of industry—whate'er
> Exalts, embellishes, and renders life
> Delightful.

And in the second part of his *Castle of Indolence* the Knight of Art and Industry is the rescuing hero. *Liberty* is in a sense a "progress piece," in which Thomson traces the development of civil liberty from Greece and Rome to Britain—and into the future prospects. His philosophy of history, like that of many of his contemporaries, involved a worship of primitive

---

[13] Abbott C. Martin, "The Love of Solitude in Eighteenth Century Poetry," *So. Atl. Quar.* XXIX (1930). 48-59.

times and a belief, not so contradictory as it at first sight appears, in progress. The pristine days were the best man had known, but man could not retrace his steps: his best hope, then, was to "relume the ancient light" (as Pope phrased it) in some millennial day far ahead. With a divine origin behind him man could only work towards a heavenly city of the future. So Thomson repeatedly, in the best Whig fashion, condemns luxury, praises the simple virtues and the force of the arts, and, looking before and after, at times laments the decadence of man in the Walpole era and at times is optimistic concerning men, industry, and trade. Of course victims of an undue thirst for gold are, as he had shown in *Summer*, enemies of human progress:

> Ill-fated race! the softening arts of peace,
> Whate'er the humanizing muses teach,
> The godlike wisdom of the tempered breast,
> Progressive truth, the patient force of thought,
> Investigation calm whose silent powers
> Command the world, the light that leads to Heaven,
> Kind equal rule, the government of laws,
> And all-protecting freedom which alone
> Sustains the name and dignity of man—
> These are not theirs.

Here and in many other passages speaks the spirit of Illumination. Thomson, like his patron Lord Talbot, was alive to the humanitarian movements of his day. As solicitor-general Lord Talbot had acted (1729) for the crown in the prosecution of Bambridge, the inhuman warden of Fleet prison, and thereafter Thomson more than once expressed enthusiasm for prison reform, and for the work of General Oglethorpe both in that respect and in regard to the colony of Georgia. Among other humane projects he praised, in the last, prophetic part of *Liberty*, the not yet realized project of Thomas Coram for a foundling hospital—

> The dome resounding sweet with infant joy,
> From famine saved, or cruel-handed shame.

The Castle of Indolence   After *The Seasons* Thomson wrote over a period of fifteen years five tragedies, which were staged with only moderate success. His final work of distinction was his *Castle of Indolence*, published a few weeks before his death in 1748. Somewhat deficient in action (it tells merely how the wizard Indolence enticed pilgrims into his castle, and how the Knight of Art and Industry liberated them), the poem is one of the best imitations of Spenserian melody and descriptive techniques in the language,[14] and is by all odds metrically the most harmonious of Thomson's poems. It is rich in portraiture, and has fewer passages devoted to the prosaic topics treated in *Liberty*. The description of the castle and its environs at the opening of the poem is both admirable Spenser and admirable "atmosphere":

[14] Herbert E. Cory, "Spenser, Thomson, and Romanticism," *PMLA*, xxvi (1911). 51-91.

> A pleasing land of drowsyhed it was:
> Of dreams that wave before the half-shut eye;
> And of gay castles in the clouds that pass,
> For ever flushing round a summer sky:
> There eke the soft delights, that witchingly
> Instil a wanton sweetness through the breast,
> And the calm pleasures always hovered nigh;
> But whate'er smacked of noyance, or unrest,
> Was far far off expelled from this delicious nest.

The life of the enchanted idle pilgrims is like a dream—

> As when a shepherd of the Hebrid Isles,
> Placed far amid the melancholy main,
> (Whether it be lone fancy him beguiles,
> Or that aerial beings sometimes deign
> To stand embodied to our senses plain)
> Sees on the naked hill, or valley low,
> The whilst in ocean Phoebus dips his wain,
> A vast assembly moving to and fro;
> Then all at once in air dissolves the wondrous show.

From this bit of supernaturalism the poet has some difficulty recalling himself without breaking the mood: he describes some of the rooms of the castle and with stanza lvi turns to sketching the characters of some of the idlers. These stanzas—very likely among the earliest to be written—sketch actual friends of the poet, and stanza lxviii (by a friend, except for the first line) portrays Thomson himself:

> A bard here dwelt, more fat than bard beseems. . . .

Obviously here we have left the abode of Indolence for some House of Good Fun, and the spell of "drowsyhed" is gone. Though lacking in substance, the poem is in many ways the author's most poetical effort.

The individuality and merit of Thomson's work can be easily grasped if one considers the moment at which *The Seasons* appeared. Their chief rivals in immediate vogue were the seven satires by Edward Young, called *Love of Fame,* and Pope's *Dunciad.* It was a moment when poets, animated by a desire to ennoble the poetic art, were "stooping to truth" and moralizing their songs; but while both Young and especially Pope were dealing with petty particularities, Thomson was dealing with more general and fundamentally moral subjects. If Pope was in part led to write satirical epistles because of the success of *Love of Fame,* it is conceivable that in writing his *Essay on Man,* which he began during the first vogue of *The Seasons,* he was influenced by Thomson. At least the two men are expressing very similar sets of ideas—the one in rather harsh and unmelodious "rhyme-unfetter'd verse," the other in smooth and polished couplets. But Thomson anticipated Pope in expressing the benevolism of Shaftesbury in verse, and he avoided some of Pope's difficulties by being vaguely optimistic and

The Novelty and Merit of The Seasons

forbearing to attack head-on, so to speak, the problem of evil and of man's moral responsibility. Neither in blank verse nor in the Spenserian stanza was Thomson a pioneer, but his success helped to popularize these metres and to subvert the couplet. As description his work is vastly superior to *The Excursion* of his more ambitious and sensational friend Mallet. Thomson's excellence clearly lay in his sensitiveness to sense impressions and his confident use of such impressions: his blank verse is not smoothly rhythmed, and his diction is, like that of Young, greatly inferior to Pope's. Pope could never have passed a cacophonous line like

> Who nobly durst, in rhyme-unfetter'd verse;

and he would surely have pilloried (if *Liberty* had been written in time) the bathos of such another as

> And ventilated states renew their bloom.

Other oppressive artifices are his self-conscious compound epithets, which no page is without, and his love of polysyllabic monstrosities like *irriguous, contiguous, convolutions,* etc. Not Thomson's gifts of expression but rather his natural poetic sensitiveness that emerges in spite of the heavy-going style makes him a memorable part of the movement to reform poetry as the drama and prose style were being "reformed." In his preface to the second edition of *Winter* Thomson voices this objective:

That there are frequent and notorious abuses of Poetry is as true as that the best things are most liable to that misfortune.... To insist no further on this head, let poetry once more be restored to her ancient truth and purity; let her be inspired from heaven, and in return her incense ascend thither; let her exchange her low, venal, trifling, subjects for such as are fair, useful and magnificent; and let her execute these so as at once to please, instruct, surprise, and astonish ... and poets [shall] yet become the delight and wonder of mankind.

In certain aspects such ideals and Thomson's application of them to his work tend towards the romantic; they more clearly tend towards the quality that Matthew Arnold aptly called "high seriousness." [15]

John Dyer   In 1726, possibly before *Winter,* appeared the one important poem by John Dyer [16] (1699-1757), *Grongar Hill.* During the year the poem was

[15] Thomson's extensive Continental influence is with justice regarded as "romantic." See K. Gjerset, *Der Einfluss von James Thomsons Jahreszeiten auf die deutsche Literatur des achtzehnten Jahrhunderts* (Heidelberg, 1898); B. G. Halberstadt, *De Nederlandsche Vertalingen en Navolgingen van Thomson's Seasons* (Leipzig, 1923); and Margaret M. Cameron, *L'Influence des Saisons de Thomson sur la poésie descriptive en France, 1759-1810* (Paris, 1927).

[16] John Dyer was born in Wales and passed much of his life there. He attended Westminster School briefly, studied law, and (after his father's death) painting—this last with Jonathan Richardson. He tried painting and farming in Wales, and eventually became a clergyman. The circumstances of publication of *Grongar Hill* are obscure. It is conceivable that the *New Miscellany: Being ... Pieces from Bath, Tunbridge ... in the Year 1725 ... Written chiefly by Persons of Quality* appeared in 1725, and so represents first publication. The miscellany of David Lewis, possibly Dyer's former master at Westminster, called *Miscellaneous Poems by Several Hands,* was published in June, 1726, and Savage's *Miscellaneous Poems and Translations* was being reviewed in September. Savage's volume contained the Pindaric form of the poem and also *The Country Walk* and other small poems by or about Dyer. Dyer's

printed in at least three different miscellanies, with differing texts. In the last of the three the poem is cast in Pindaric form; but since this version is far less attractive than the tetrameter couplets of other texts, it has been assumed to be a first form of the poem: it was not the first form printed. The immediate influence of Dyer's poem is perhaps comparable to that of *The Seasons*. In a companion piece, *The Country Walk*, Dyer was less happy; for the mood of *L'Allegro* (which it affected) had less appeal at the moment than that of *Il Penseroso*, and it is in the tradition of evening contemplation that Dyer cast *Grongar Hill*. His interest in landscape was that of both painter and poet: he gives us more of settled scene than does Thomson in *Winter*, even though his confusion of background and foreground is open to criticism. He notes picturesque detail, such as "streaks of meadow" in the distance, or ancient ruined towers, but his reactions are likely to be those of common sense: ruins at a distance are picturesque, but close by they are fearful; for "there the pois'nous adder breeds." His distant purple hills tipt with golden sunset, his wide valleys in the manner of Claude, his deep shade at the river's bank, give us the ingredients of a typical painting of his day. The mood is contemplative and even melancholy. He at times surpasses his elegiac rivals with such graceful, if chilly, comment as:

> A little rule, a little sway,
> A sun beam in a winter's day,
> Is all the proud and mighty have
> Between the cradle and the grave.

His poems are most sincere, and can be astonishingly honest. In *The Country Walk*—published when our urban poets were afraid of "low" details— Dyer uses the language of the kitchen and the stable fearlessly in his depiction of an old man at work in his small garden:

> Here he puffs upon his spade,
> And digs up cabbage in the shade;
> His tatter'd rags are sable brown,
> His beard and hair are hoary grown.

Such lines are almost prophetic of the vogue of such rural scenes as Gainsborough was to popularize later in the century. They were almost unknown in 1726. The prosaic honesty of these lines serves to indicate the difficulty Dyer had in his longer poems. *The Ruins of Rome* (1740) is both too uneven poetically (it has its moments!) and too discursive to achieve great

---

friends in London included Jonathan Richardson, Aaron Hill, Richard Savage, Martha Fowke, and Benjamin Victor—all of whom are at least mentioned in Savage's Miscellany.—Dyer's *Poems* (1761, 1765, 1770); ed. Robert A. Willmott (1855); Edward Thomas (1903); Hugh I'A. Fausset (Everyman's Library, 1930); *Grongar Hill*, ed. Richard C. Boys (Baltimore, 1941) [Introduction].—William Gilpin, *Observations on the River Wye Relative chiefly to Picturesque Beauty* (1782); John Scott of Amwell, *Critical Essays on Some of the Poems of Several English Poets* (1785); Helen S. Hughes, "John Dyer and the Countess of Hertford," *MP*, xxvii (1930). 311-320; Edward Parker, "John Dyer" [biographical data], *LTLS*, July 22, 1939, p. 437.

pute, and *The Fleece* (1757) deals somewhat too bluntly with the details of sheep-raising and of the wool trade even for devoted Virgilians. It has again some good landscapes. It is landscapes, in the first place, and then the use of picturesque ruins and other devices for gentle melancholy that characterize the "newer" elements in Dyer's work. Moral reflections are a less novel staple.

dactic
,oems

Apart from Thomson and Dyer the poets of the second quarter of the century limited themselves closely to the moralizing tradition, which of course both these poets encouraged. There were many didactic poems, among which the concrete "process" poem, remotely or closely in the manner of the *Georgics,* aroused interest long before *The Fleece*. The best of these was *The Chace* (1735) by William Somervile [17] (1675-1742), a blank-verse poem that celebrates in honest detail the joys of the hunt, the breeding and training of hounds, and the attendant outdoor pleasures of a country squire. Earlier Somervile had published fables and verse tales of rural life, and later he published *Hobbinol, or the Rural Games* (1740) and *Field Sports* (hawking) in the year of his death; but *The Chace* alone pleased greatly. All three of his sporting poems are in blank verse of a quality undeserving Dr. Johnson's prejudiced description as "crippled prose." In *The Chace* his diction is less artificial and conventional than in the other two poems. Dr. Johnson's verdict ("he writes very well for a gentleman") suggests the probable nature of Somervile's early vogue.

Somervile's objective didacticism is less characteristic of the period than the more philosophical efforts that appeared after the *Essay on Man*. Among these, *Universal Beauty* (1735) by Henry Brooke (1703?-1783) and *The Pleasures of Imagination* (1774) by Dr. Mark Akenside [18] (1721-1770) have especial literary interest. Brooke,[19] known for his plays and better still for his novel *The Fool of Quality* (1765-70), in *Universal Beauty* shows typical influence of Shaftesbury on aesthetic minds in his harmonizing of beauty, nature, and truth. It was the plenitude and diversity of the scale of being that aroused his devout enthusiasm and (to be frank) at times upset the clarity of his couplets. Dr. Akenside's early important poem blended the influence of Shaftesbury with that of Addison and others, and was influential in preaching the importance of imagination to both poet and reader. A youthful poem, it was revised, or rather rewritten, in maturer years, which led Akenside to retrench the lushness of his earlier style. Dr. Johnson, who respected but disliked Akenside, thought that in some respects the poet was "perhaps superior to any other writer of blank verse." Pope had encouraged Dodsley to pay well for the poem, and it is obvious that neither Pope nor the poets of this chapter shared Dr. Johnson's opinion that blank verse was "in description exuberant, in argument loquacious, and in narration tiresome."

17 On Somervile see Johnson's *Lives of the Poets* (ed. G. B. Hill), III. 1-66; also Raymond D. Havens, "William Somervile's Earliest Poem," *MLN*, XLI (1926). 80-86.

18 On Akenside see Part III, ch. IV, n. 12.

19 On Brooke see Part III, ch. V, n. 11.

Far more famous in their day, but hardly more readable now than Brooke   *Young's*
and Akenside, the *Night Thoughts* of Edward Young [20] (1683-1765) are   Night
with *The Seasons* and Cowper's *Task* the most important blank-verse poems   Thoughts
of the century. Young "arrived" slowly. Five years older than Pope, his
fame postdated Pope's *Iliad* by a decade. His satires, *The Universal Passion*
(1725-8), were his first great success, and that success determined him to
take holy orders and become a royal chaplain. The *Night Thoughts* (1742-
5) was his masterpiece, but his prose *Centaur not Fabulous* (1754) notably
strengthened the common condemnation of the follies of high society,
and his *Conjectures on Original Composition* (1759) have been thought
(mistakenly) to mark a revolution in criticism. Young's achievement was
in seizing his moments and thus making rather common ideas strike his
readers as important novelties. In this respect *Night Thoughts* "on life,
death, and immortality," among other things, won European fame for a
century.

The work was essentially an exercise in Christian apologetics,[21] but its
appeal lay in its concentration on death, on its macabre detail. It is a
poetical *memento mori,* and an argument for the truths of Christianity as
guides to paradise. Young's intellectual intent was to stress apologetics;
his readers loved his thrilling mortuary images—

> The knell, the shroud, the mattock, and the grave;
> The deep damp vault, the darkness, and the worm.

Such sensationalism was ably reinforced by an autobiographical back-   *The Ele-*
ground, in part fictitious, that made many passages seem expressions of   *ment of*
poignant personal grief. Death had aimed his darts freely and successfully   *Auto-*
at the sixty-year-old poet's closest and dearest. He had in 1731 married the   *biography*
Lady Elizabeth Lee (granddaughter of Charles II), and she had died in
January, 1740. Young's grief over this loss may have been poignant, but
within four months he was paying his aging addresses to another lady of
fifty winters and some fortune—discreetly! [22] Lady Elizabeth's daughter,
called Narcissa in the poem, had died in 1736, and Narcissa's husband

[20] Young, the son of the rector of Upham near Winchester, studied at Winchester, at New
College, Corpus Christi, and All Souls. He became a well-known but not intimate member
of London literary circles by 1713. After 1730 he was rector of Welwyn (Herts), where he
led a life of dignified retirement, interspersed with trips to Bath, Tunbridge Wells, etc.—
Complete Works, ed. J. Doran (2v, 1854); *Poetical Works* (2v, 1741; 4v, 1757, etc.); ed. J.
Mitford [Aldine ed.] (2v, 1830); *Dramatic Works* (1778); *Conjectures on Original Compo-
sition* (1759); ed. M. W. Steinke (Philadelphia, 1917); Edith J. Morley (Manchester, 1918);
"One Hundred and Fifty Original Letters between Dr. Edward Young and Mr. Samuel
Richardson," *Monthly Magazine,* Dec. 1813-Aug. 1818. — George Eliot, "Worldliness and
Other-worldliness: The Poet Young," reprinted from *Westminster Review* for January, 1857,
in *Essays and Leaves from a Notebook* (1884); W. Thomas, *Le Poète Edward Young* (Paris,
1901); Henry C. Shelley, *The Life and Letters of Edward Young* (1914); Alan D. McKillop,
"Richardson, Young, and the *Conjectures,*" *MP,* xxii (1925). 391-404. H. H. Clark, "The
Romanticism of Edward Young," *Trans. Wisconsin Acad.,* xxiv (1929). 1-45.

[21] See the excellent article of Isabel St. J. Bliss, "Young's Night Thoughts in Relation to
Contemporary Christian Apologetics," *PMLA,* xlix (1934). 37-70.

[22] H. T. Swedenberg, Jr., "Letters of Edward Young to Mrs. Judith Reynolds," *HLQ,* ii
(1938). 89-100. (The death of Lady Elizabeth Young is announced in *The Daily Post,* January 30, 1740, as having taken place "yesterday.")

(Philander in the poem) had died in August, 1740. There had been other losses, but of these three Young, with a certain amount of poetic license, made his "Complaint" to Death in the first of his *Night Thoughts:*

> Insatiate Archer! could not one suffice?
> Thy shaft flew *thrice,* and *thrice* my peace was slain;
> And thrice, ere thrice yon moon had fill'd her horn.

Romantic subjectivity does not require factual accuracy, and these three, as one can see upon careful reading, turn out to be chiefly "cases" that evoke specialized reflections on death: Narcissa died young and beautiful and in her "bridal hour"; Philander, the good man, died suddenly; of Lady Elizabeth the poet tells us she

> Not early, like Narcissa, left the scene,
> Nor sudden, like Philander. What avail?

Of Narcissa's furtive midnight burial in France, where Protestants were not normally buried in consecrated ground (though in England Catholics were buried even in Anglican churches), the poet (III. 150-88) gave so lurid an account as to provoke shedding of ink in international literary recrimination. (In England, it may be noted, throughout Young's lifetime burials were customarily at night.)

Their Moral Aim   It is this element of personal narrative with its great wealth of somewhat melodramatic woe that gave these poems vogue. The moral reflections on the duty of Being Prepared were all aimed at a possibly fictitious "silken son of pleasure" called Lorenzo—one whose "fond heart dances while the siren sings." To the reflections on sudden death, on the triumphant death of the virtuous, the pitiful deaths of the young and beautiful, the case of the ill-living Lorenzo adds an ominous note about the death of the infidel. And thus after many winged reflections through three "Nights," we have in the fourth "The Christian Triumph." These four poems, almost Christian *Georgics,* were then "collected" (1743), and ran through six editions in six months. In December, 1743, the poet resumed his profitable task with a fifth "Night," "The Relapse," and the series ran to nine "Nights" by January, 1746. The later group confined itself more closely to theological argument, and hardly achieved the popularity of the earlier parts.

Intellectually Young is conventional. His neo-puritan antipathy for the silks and sirens of wealthy sinners and for what he calls "art, brainless art," has led to a hasty association of him with evangelical or even Wesleyan tendencies. He holds, rather, a normal latitudinarian position. He touches but lightly on the doctrine of the entire corruption of man, and rather stresses the seeds of natural virtue or even the nobility of man. He emphasizes neither the doctrine of grace nor the importance of a conscious act of conversion. He does stress the necessity of strong faith built upon a foundation of sound reason. Night IV comes nearest to evangelicalism, but even it accords with latitudinarian ideas. Young's eloquence in all these argumentative parts of the *Night Thoughts* was doubtless impressive; for a century after his poems appeared virtuous young Christians were instructed to "think much on death," and the *Night Thoughts* were a useful stimulant in that good work.

It is, then, the pious gloom and the seemingly personal feeling of these *Graveyard* poems that gave them their European vogue. The melancholy tradition *Poetry* in England was of long standing.[23] In *Tatler* No. 89 Steele had remarked that "That calm and elegant satisfaction which the vulgar call Melancholy, is the true and proper Delight of Men of Knowledge and Virtue." Many poets from the time of *Il Penseroso* had agreed, and the wealth of funeral elegies in the eighteenth century forms an impressive background for *Night Thoughts*.[24] Young's own early poem, *The Last Day* (1713), and Parnell's *Night Piece on Death* (1722) anticipate *Night Thoughts;* and *The Grave* by Robert Blair (1699-1746)[25] achieved fame in 1743 along with Young's masterpiece. It is also notable that Thomas Gray began work on his *Elegy Written in a Country Churchyard* during the time when *Night Thoughts* was being completed. In prose the tradition of pious melancholy is interminable: in the eighteenth century two very popular works of the sort were Mrs. Elizabeth Rowe's *Friendship in Death* (1728) and James Hervey's *Meditations and Contemplations* (1746), the first part of which was called "Meditations among the Tombs."

Young's poetic art is most uneven. His diction and his rhythms can be flatly prosaic. Witness his enumeration of themes that puzzle him:

> The importance of contemplating the tomb;
> Why men decline it; suicide's foul birth;
> The various kinds of grief; the faults of age;
> And Death's dread character. (v, 295-298)

He, like Thomson, is victimized by heavy phrases such as the "feculence *Young's* of falsehood," and he is also unfortunate in his metaphors: *Diction and Eloquence*

> Lean not on earth; 'twill pierce thee to the heart.

Or

> Fired is the Muse? and let the Muse be fired.

He warns that the delights of the flesh pall; that the roué gets no pleasure even from memory:

[23] On this tradition see Raymond D. Havens, "Literature of Melancholy," *MLN*, XXIV (1909). 226-227; Harry H. Clark, "A Study of Melancholy in Edward Young," *MLN* XXXIX (1924). 129-136, 193-202; Amy L. Reed, *The Background of Gray's Elegy: a Study in the Taste for Melancholy Poetry, 1700-1751* (1924); P. Van Tieghem, "La Poésie de la nuit et des tombeaux," *Le Préromantisme*, série 2 (Paris, 1930); also Oswald Doughty, "The English Malady of the Eighteenth Century," *RES*, II (1926). 257-269.

[24] John W. Draper, *The Funeral Elegy and the Rise of English Romanticism* (1929).

[25] Robert Blair was born in Edinburgh and was educated there and in Holland. Having prepared for the ministry he in 1731 received the living of Athelstaneford, East Lothian, and there spent the remainder of his life, as minister and student of poetry and botany.—*Poetical Works of Beattie, Blair, and Falconer*, ed. G. Gilfillan (Edinburgh, 1854).—W. A. Drake, "A Note on Robert Blair." *Freeman*, VIII (1924). 516-518.

> On cold-served repetitions he subsists,
> And in the tasteless present chews the past;
> Disgusted chews, and scarce can swallow down.

And again he warns Lorenzo:

> A languid, leaden iteration reigns,
> And ever must, o'er those whose joys are joys
> Of sight, smell, taste.

He has the gift of his century for sententiousness, and many a "familiar quotation" comes from his pen:

> Procrastination is the thief of time.

> Who does the best his circumstance allows,
> Does well, acts nobly; angels could no more.

> How blessings brighten as they take their flight.

> Death loves a shining mark, a signal blow.

In sustained passages Young is best when indulging a clerical bent for stately, if emotional, eloquence. A good example is the prayer (lines 36-54) with which *Night Thoughts* begins. His style lacks all the unassuming tenderness that Dyer had: it is formal and somewhat overbearing. To explain the European vogue of *Night Thoughts* one must recall the thirst for melancholy as well as the growing love of personal emotion.[26] The poems blended "what oft was thought" with what the circumstances of the moment led the poet personally to feel. Then too, Young had a real gift in sensationalism: he was frequently absurd here, but he evidently captured the taste of the time perfectly. His artifices, after all, were no more obvious and self-conscious than those of Macpherson's Ossian, which also pleased all Europe.

New Tones and Tendencies   International reputations in poetry are perhaps unaccountable, but one of the important aspects of the history of European civilization is the fact that during the eighteenth century southern Europe awoke to the artistic existence of the northern countries. At the beginning of the century almost all of the Elizabethans were unknown in the Latin countries. Boileau pretended to a total ignorance of English poetry and even of the name of his contemporary, John Dryden. During the first half of the century this ignorance of English poetry ceased. Milton and Pope led the way, and Thomson and Young were not far behind in vogue. Romanticism, and more than romanticism, came out of England to change the course of European poetry. Roman eloquence, notable in all four of these poets, was soon to lose its prestige in favor of a more personal expression of subjective emotion; the tradition of ancient models for poetry—desiccated through petty rules—gave way to new tones and modified patterns in writing. The transformation did not take place rapidly; it came about rather slowly and unob-

[26] J. L. Kind, *Edward Young in Germany* (1906); Fernand Baldensperger, "Young et ses *Nuits* en France," *Études d'histoire littéraire* (Paris, 1907), pp. 55-109.

trusively. Without the noble Roman tone and the use of generic classical patterns familiar throughout Europe English poets would not have had a Continental hearing. But the patterns and the tones were being modified. The models, for example, first substituted for the Virgilian pastoral tradition, as we have seen in this chapter, were in no way hostile to Virgilian ideals: all they did was gently to push the *Eclogues* and the *Georgics* more to the background as models, and to attempt, at times awkwardly and unskilfully, to forsake the pattern of the ancient poems while still preserving their spirit of true poetry. By the middle of the century these new tendencies were no more than tendencies, tentatives reaching out without conscious program—other than the desire to make poetry more noble by making it more philosophical—and without conscious rebellion against the tyranny of tradition that had operated so long.

The Mid-Century Novel

By the middle of the century (1740-54) three great novelists had permanently modified the art of English fiction: [1] of these Richardson dilated the short story or "novel," as it was called before his day, by means of psychological or sentimental detail; Fielding added structure, style, and a realistic attitude towards life; and Smollett excelled in the invention and crisp presentation of unforgettably vivid burlesque episode. Through these men fiction acquired a sense of pattern or structure, richness of varied detail, and gravity as well as comedy. All three were critics of manners. Fielding was both an artist and a critic of his art, which he analyzed in brilliant essays or prefaces and which he dignified by associating it with the noblest of narrative forms, the epic. As psychologists the three vary considerably, but each has his excellences. Their purposes were avowedly moral; they taught men to know themselves and their proper "spheres" and appropriate manners.

This last aspect of their work differs somewhat from that of their immediate predecessors. Defoe, to be sure, made great pretensions to moral instruction; but his real interest, like that of any inspired story-teller, was in the ingenious thrills of his rogues. Life stimulated the telling of such adventure stories, and Defoe's tales were hardly more "strange and surprising" than the adventures of Count Grammont in high society,[2] of James Annesley,[3] heir perhaps to an Irish earldom but "trepanned" into America by a wicked uncle, or of Elizabeth Canning,[4] servant girl in the city of London. Life—or appetite for "innocent" libel—also stimulated

---

[1] For bibliographies of the prose fiction of this period see *CBEL*, II. 488-553. The fullest history is that of Ernest A. Baker, *The History of the English Novel*, Vols. III and IV (1930). Good short histories are Sir Walter Raleigh, *The English Novel* (1894); Wilbur L. Cross, *The Development of the English Novel* (1899); George Saintsbury, *The English Novel* (1913); Robert M. Lovett and Helen S. Hughes, *The History of the Novel in England* (Boston, 1932); and Edward Wagenknecht, *Cavalcade of the English Novel* (1943).

[2] Anthony Hamilton, *Memoirs of the Life of Count de Grammont* (in French, 1713; trans. by Abel Boyer, 1714); ed. Sir Walter Scott, Bohn Library (1846); ed. Gordon Goodwin (1908); ed. Peter Quennell (1931). See also Ruth Clark, *Anthony Hamilton* (1921).

[3] *The Case of James Annesley* (1743); Andrew Lang, *The Annesley Case* (1912). The story is used by Sir Walter Scott in *Guy Mannering* (1815), by Charles Reade in *The Wandering Heir* (1872), and by Robert Louis Stevenson in *Kidnapped* (1886). Annesley was made hero of an anonymous contemporary novel, featuring sentimental distress, called *Memoirs of an Unfortunate Nobleman Return'd from a Thirteen Years Slavery in America* (2v, 1743).

[4] Of the scores of pamphlets concerning the disappearance of Elizabeth Canning in 1753 one may cite Henry Fielding's *Clear State of the Case of Elizabeth Canning* (1753) in his *Works*, ed. Wm. E. Henley, XIII (1903). 221-255. For modern accounts see Arthur Machen, *The Canning Wonder* (1926); Barrett R. Wellington, *The Mystery of Elizabeth Canning* (1940), and Lillian de la Torre Bueno, *"Elizabeth is Missing"* (1945).

the production of gossip tales called "scandal chronicles." Mrs. Mary Delariviere Manley (1663-1724) was the early leader in this genre. Her masterpiece, *Secret Memoirs and Manners of Several Persons of Quality . . . from the New Atalantis* (1709-10), was a daring satire on great personages of her day—the names concealed transparently under pseudonyms, which are sometimes explained at the end in a "key." [5] Mrs. Eliza Haywood (1693?-1756), who had begun her long career as a playwright and novelist (i.e., short-story writer), inherited Mrs. Manley's love of scandal in her *Memoirs of Utopia* (2 volumes, 1725), in which she indulged in slurs on Lord Bolingbroke, Mrs. Howard (the royal mistress), and Martha Blount, a procedure which, since these were all friends of Pope, won Mrs. Haywood a mean rôle in *The Dunciad*.[6] She later learned much from her betters, and such novels as her *Fortunate Foundlings* (1744), which was based remotely on scandals in the family of the Duke of Rutland but was also a good historical novel in Defoe's manner with sentiment added, *Life's Progress through the Passions* (1748), and especially her *Betsy Thoughtless* (1751) and her *Jemmy and Jenny Jessamy* (1753), are interesting pieces of work, verging towards excessive pathos and melodrama. She had a long and voluminous career.

What Defoe and the writers of short "novels" lacked was emotional appeal. This element was perhaps acquired from France. Both Mrs. Manley and Mrs. Haywood used French sources at times, and the tradition of *grands sentiments*, which Ménage found in the romances of his friend Mlle Scudéry, was in French fiction well established.[7] During the decade after Defoe's death the best fictional reading the English had came from France and from the pens of the comic writer Marivaux and the sentimental Prévost. The first part of Marivaux's *Vie de Marianne*, which was in English by 1736, is thought by some to have influenced Richardson's *Pamela*,[8] and there is no doubt that Fielding knew Marivaux's *Paysan Parvenu*, translated in part in 1735. Prévost's masterpiece, *Manon Lescaut*, had little vogue in eighteenth-century England; but it as well as his other two important novels—*Cleveland, the Natural Son of Cromwell* and *The Dean of Coleraine*—was translated into English before 1743. Prévost's periodical *Pour et Contre* (1733-40) was an important vehicle in conveying a knowledge of current English literature to France. His novels must have stimulated the sentimental love of pathos already known in the drama, and he in turn was to be the translator of Richardson into French.

Emotional Appeal of French Fiction

[5] Paul B. Anderson, "Delarivière Manley's Prose Fiction," *PQ*, XIII (1934). 168-188.
[6] George F. Whicher, *The Life and Romances of Mrs. Eliza Haywood* (1915).
[7] Edith Birkhead, "Sentiment and Sensibility in the Eighteenth-Century Novel," *E&S*, XI (1925). 92-116; Paul Van Tieghem, "Le Roman sentimental en Europe de Richardson à Rousseau," *RLC*, XX (1940). 129-151.
[8] See Helen S. Hughes, "Translations of the *Vie de Marianne* and their Relation to Contemporary English Fiction," *MP*, XV (1917). 491-512; Ronald S. Crane, "Richardson, Warburton, and French Fiction," *MLR*, XVII (1922). 17-23; George R. Havens, *L'Abbé Prévost and English Literature* (Princeton, 1921); J. R. Foster, "The Abbé Prévost and the English Novel," *PMLA*, XLII (1927). 443-464. Prévost's first novel, *Memoires et aventures d'un homme de qualité qui s'est retiré du monde* (7v, 1728-31), contains episodes that take place in England. These have been translated and published with an interesting introduction by Mysie E. I. Robertson, *The Adventures of a Man of Quality* (1930).

Richardson
and the
Distresses
of Love

French fiction at any rate makes a plausible bridge to carry one from the relatively unemotional, ingenious adventures of Defoe's characters to the intense distress to which the central persons in Samuel Richardson's novels are subjected. If Richardson [9] (1689-1761) were a lone phenomenon, one might credit the access of emotion to his own personal bent, which obviously accounts for much. He had been an industrious apprentice and had risen to be one of the most reputable and prosperous printers in London. Long before that, however, as a boy in Derbyshire, he had been the confidential adviser for damsels despondently in love. He had written their love letters for them, had in the process acquired a curiosity about the feminine emotional life, and had developed an imagination that delighted in projecting in extreme detail fantasies concerned with the distresses of love. One suspects that he must have read stories of the sort; for his own love life seems to have been steady and (with all respect to his prudently chosen and dutiful wives, each of whom bore him six children) unimaginative. His loving care in building up fantasies with complex emotional situations is his chief asset as a novelist. He had also defects: "Surely, Sir, Richardson is very tedious," protested a friend to Dr. Johnson, and the Doctor in his famous reply conceded, "Why, Sir, if you were to read Richardson for the story, your impatience would be so much fretted that you would hang yourself. But you must read him for the sentiment." Besides tediousness (which implies a deficiency in sense of style), Richardson also suffered from a total lack of humor, a naïve and snobbish veneration of rank and respectability, and an undue devotion to the principle of poetic justice. These are almost insuperable limitations, but his minute imaginative construction of his central situations was so careful and so detailed that if read in small portions any one of his novels in his own day was bound to be impressive. The general love of elegance in literature as well as his own neo-puritanism kept him from handling his sex situations with blunt realism or crudity; but his prolix fondling of episodes was even more indecent than vulgarity would have been.

He specialized in the portrayal of divided minds, and the materials got him always into a dilemma from which he was not clever enough to escape

---

[9] Richardson's *Works* have been edited by Edward Mangin (19v, 1811); by Sir Leslie Stephen (12v, 1883-4); his *Novels* are found edited by Austin Dobson and Wm. L. Phelps (18v, 1901-3), by Ethel M. M. McKenna (20v, 1902); Blackwell ed. (19v, Oxford, 1930). — *Letters Written to and for Particular Friends, Directing the Requisite Style and Forms . . . in Writing Familiar Letters* (1741); ed. Brian W. Downs (1928), as *Familiar Letters . . .* [this is Richardson's manual of letter-writing]. *The Paths of Virtue Delineated* (1756), a condensation in 250 pages of Richardson's three novels, "adapted to the capacities of youth," who thus early found the originals far too long. *The Correspondence of Samuel Richardson,* ed. Anna L. Barbauld (6v, 1804); *The Letters of Dr. George Cheyne to Samuel Richardson* (Columbia, Mo., 1943). A highly useful volume is Wm. M. Sale, *Samuel Richardson: A Bibliographical Record* (New Haven, 1936). Also Clara L. Thomson, *Samuel Richardson* (1900); Aleyn L. Reade, "Samuel Richardson and his Family Circle," *N&Q*, Sept. 2, 1022 to June 30, 1923; Brian W. Downs, *Richardson* (1928); Paul Dottin, *Samuel Richardson, imprimeur de Londres* (Paris, 1931); Alan D. McKillop, *Samuel Richardson, Printer and Novelist* (Chapel Hill, 1936); and the same author's "Samuel Richardson's Advice to an Apprentice," *JEGP*, XLII (1943). 40-54.

without fundamental imaginative self-contradiction. He saw the central *His Por-* problem of each story very simply—perhaps too simply. In 1739 while *trayal of* working on a manual of letter-writing that two booksellers had asked him *Indecisive* to do, Richardson took time off to write his first novel, *Pamela, or Virtue* *Minds* *Rewarded*. The problem posed in a series of letters was one of decorum: how was the fifteen-year-old servant girl Pamela to resist the improper advances of her mistress' son now that her mistress was dead, and what would be the reward of decorous resistance? The novel, published in two volumes in 1740, was an enormous success; a continuation came out a year later, and here the problem in simplest terms was, how would Pamela, now virtuously wedded to her young master, succeed socially in "high life"? Presently (1744-8) Richardson was at work on a second novel, *Clarissa* (1747-8), and again the central problem was clearly conceived: can Clarissa, a paragon of virtue and decorum, violated by an earl's nephew (Lovelace) who believes no woman truly chaste, be rewarded for her virtue on earth or must she look to a better world for justice? Any indecision here exists not in Clarissa's mind but in that of Lovelace—and of the reader! In his third and last novel, *Sir Charles Grandison* (1753-4), Richardson's hero, the fine gentleman, must decide which of two young ladies would make the appropriate wife. In all three cases there is a problem of indecision, a divided mind: should Pamela quit her master's house or stay to complete embroidering his waistcoat and to finish other assigned tasks? Is Lovelace merely a brutal investigator of chastity or does he truly love Clarissa? Can she marry Lovelace and thus become an "honest woman" or should she droop and die like a broken flower? Which of two ladies did Sir Charles prefer with all his heart and with all his mind, the Lady Clementina della Porretta (an Italian Catholic) or Harriet Byron, a nice English girl?

The central problems may be simple in all senses of that word, but the *Problems* difficulties arise in the process of vivid and realistic dilation. We suspect *of Detail* the disinterestedness of Pamela's virtue when we see her disinclination to leave Squire B——'s house after her complete awareness of extremities to be expected if she remains. She is to be sure very young; but she is also very clear-eyed, is said to be intelligent and capable. Her attempts to escape from the Lincolnshire estate are inept. Unsympathetic readers (Fielding, for example) regarded Pamela as a shrewd schemer, determined all along to marry her master. The possibility of such calculation is suggested by Richardson himself in various remarks. Early in the continuation it occurs to Pamela (now a lady), and to Richardson, that her letters to her parents narrating vividly the various attempts on her honor are being shown to all the neighboring gentlemen, who may form strange ideas from her love of explicit detail. Lady Davers reassures her by saying that

except one had known these things, one could not have judged of the merit of your resistance, and how shocking those attempts were to your virtue, for that life itself was endangered by them: nor, let me tell you, could I, in particular, have so well justified him for marrying you (I mean with respect to his own

proud and haughty temper of mind), if there had been room to think he could have had you upon easier terms.

There is inevitably a danger of compromise between sentimental ideals and selfish "terms" in all Richardson's fully expanded plots.

This is least true, of course, of his masterpiece, *Clarissa*. Here we have more direction in narrative movement, less wavering. The story is easily likened to a five-act tragedy with a rising and falling action, a crisis in the rape of Clarissa, and a dual tragic catastrophe. There is a considerable use of dramatic mannerism in writing. Sentences take the form of stage directions such as "(Enter Dorcas in a hurry)"; parenthetical adverbs often indicate the precise tone of a speaker's voice, and at times epistolary form is so far forgotten that the author gives us dialogue presented as in a play. More important, however, is the fact that in *Clarissa* Richardson's imagination functions substantially without self-contradiction: the details here "click," and if the novel is read slowly and reflectively, as it must be if read at all, its effect is even today overwhelming. Few novels in any language have the wealth of organic detail, the focus on a rather simple train of events, and the emotional power of *Clarissa*.

His Heroines   The dilemmas of Richardson's novels are usually psychological, and the modern reader must consider the vastly changed status of women and maintain a historical attitude in part. But even to Fielding Pamela and possibly also Clarissa (though *Clarissa* he praised highly in print) seemed as heroines too passive and helpless. Sophia Western is in almost as great distress as Clarissa; but one has perfect confidence in Sophia's abilities to evade danger. Clarissa is so perfect a creature that in spite of Richardson's exceedingly deft exposition of the situation in the Harlowe family at the start of the novel, one is a little surprised to find her writing to Miss Howe most caustic criticisms of her brother and sister. One is not surprised, of course, at her refusal to compromise her ideals with the "respectable" mores of high society in the falling action; but one is here, more than elsewhere, bored by the prolongation of distress. With Lovelace the dilemma was reversed: Richardson's respect for rank and his ready belief in the combinations of vice and merit that were to be expected in the heirs to earldoms, led him to make Lovelace too charming for the good of his lady readers, and he had to blacken the portrait.[10] Lovelace must attract Clarissa, but she must recognize and shun (shall we say?) his cloven hoof. Unlike Clarissa, Lovelace does not suffer from the need of self-exposition imposed on epistolary heroines. Pamela, Clarissa, and Harriet Byron all have to make clear their more than modest merit, and they record in some detail at times their triumphs and the various pretty compliments paid them. This dilemma, heightened by the need of frank criticism of her family by Clarissa and the need of something very like moral blind-

---

[10] H. G. Ward in his "Richardson's Character of Lovelace," *MLR*, VII (1912), 494-498, suggests that Lovelace is drawn after the "gay Lothario" of Nicholas Rowe's *Fair Penitent*. Miss Matthews in Fielding's *Amelia* more than once associates herself with Lothario's Calista.

ness on the part of Pamela, is perhaps inevitable in the epistolary method of story-telling.

Through focus on a single situation such as might heretofore have been treated in a short novel, Richardson created the "dilated novel," and his *His In-* performance was revolutionary so far as material and structure went. His *fluence* success led to a great vogue of epistolary novels, though he himself used the letter form loosely.[11] The early letters of *Pamela* are reasonably brief; letters XVII-XXXI become longer, and are followed by an interruption not in epistolary form. Thereafter, in Lincolnshire, Pamela's "letters" become a very detailed journal. Even in *Clarissa* and *Grandison* the letters frequently turn into journal form, and at no time in his novels did Richardson imagine that he was writing model letters. That function was performed in his manual of *Familiar Letters* (1741). For the rest Richardson's great influence was due to his focus on sensational love problems, his use of the highest and purest ideals in morals, his adoption of the moral clichés popularized by benevolists and sentimental dramatists, and his unquestioning faith that

> What nothing earthly gives, or can destroy,
> The soul's calm sunshine, and the heart-felt joy,
> Is virtue's prize.

It very likely did not occur to him, as it did to his Yankee contemporary, Benjamin Franklin, that "to be proud of one's virtue is like poisoning one's self with the antidote."

Franklin's view did appeal to Henry Fielding [12] (1707-1754), whose social outlook might well have been complementary to Richardson's, but seems in many respects antithetical. Great-grandson of an earl, son of a general, *Fielding's* educated at Eton and (briefly) at the University of Leyden, Henry Fielding *Moral and* was a gentleman more experienced both in society and in books than was *Social Bias*

11 Helen S. Hughes, "English Epistolary Fiction before *Pamela*," *Manly Anniversary Studies* (Chicago, 1923), pp. 156-169; Godfrey F. Singer, *The Epistolary Novel* (Philadelphia, 1933); F. G. Black, "The Technique of Letter Fiction from 1740 to 1800," *Harvard Studies and Notes*, XV (1933). 291-312; Paul Dottin, "Samuel Richardson et le roman épistolaire," *Revue Anglo-américaine*, XIII (1936). 481-499; Katherine Hornbeak, "Richardson's *Familiar Letters* and the Domestic Conduct Books," *Smith College Stud. in Mod. Lang.*, XIX, ii (1938). 1-50; and see also Miss Hornbeak's "Complete Letter-Writer in English, 1568-1800," *ibid.*, XV (1934). 1-150; Frank G. Black, *The Epistolary Novel in the Late Eighteenth Century* (Eugene, Oregon, 1940).

12 On Fielding's career as dramatist see Part II, ch. VI. Fielding's *Works* are edited as follows: by Arthur Murphy (4v, 1762, etc.); Sir Leslie Stephen (10v, 1882); George Saintsbury (12v, omitting much, 1893); Sir Edmund Gosse (12v, novels only, 1898-9); Wm. E. Henley, *et al.* (16v, 1903); Basil Blackwell ed. of novels (10v, Oxford, 1926). The novels have been often reprinted separately; *Joseph Andrews* is notably edited by J. Paul de Castro (1929). Parts of *The Covent-Garden Journal* are edited by Gerard E. Jensen (2v, New Haven, 1915). — G. M. Godden, *Henry Fielding* (1910); Wilbur L. Cross, *The History of Henry Fielding* [with a bibliography] (3v, New Haven, 1918); Aurélien Digeon, *Les Romans de Fielding* (Paris, 1923; in English, 1925); Hiran K. Banerji, *Henry Fielding* (Oxford, 1929); Ethel M. Thornbury, *Henry Fielding's Theory of the Comic Prose Epic* [reprints the sale catalogue of Fielding's library] (Madison, Wis., 1931); Maria Joesten, *Die Philosophie Fieldings* (Leipzig, 1932); Benjamin M. Jones, *Henry Fielding: Novelist and Magistrate* (1933); Annelise Studt, "Fieldings Charakterromane," *Britannica*, XIII (1936). 101-118; Richard Haage, "Charakterzeichnung und Komposition in Fieldings *Tom Jones* in ihrer Beziehung zum Drama," *Britannica*, XIII (1936). 119-170; Howard P. Vincent, "The Childhood of Henry Fielding," *RES*, XVI (1940). 438-444.

Richardson. Yet Fielding was definitely *déclassé*. He was poor, and he had a rugged contempt for the social and political corruption of his day. To Richardson high society was either "calm sunshine" or titillating vice: Fielding's comment in *Tom Jones*, xiv, i, was that "the highest life is much the dullest, and affords very little humor or entertainment." Nor would Fielding think of virtue as merely a state of being. He regards virtue (*Tom Jones*, xv, i) as "a certain relative quality, which is always busying itself without-doors, and seems as much interested in pursuing the good of others as its own." Poverty and contempt are as likely to be the reward of virtue as is felicity; and if he agrees with Mrs. Heartfree, whose burlesque adventures in *Jonathan Wild* end with her surest conviction "that Providence will sooner or later procure the felicity of the virtuous and innocent," he agrees with the reservation that one may not surely expect just rewards in this life.

Shamela and Joseph Andrews

Richardson's extravagant pride in Pamela's virtue as well as his critics' extravagant praise of the morality of the novel evidently annoyed Henry Fielding, and made him in his first burlesque of the novel, *Shamela* (1741), take the attitude that this type of virtue was a sham. The highly indecent boisterousness seen in this burlesque became more refined and truly comic in a second attempt, *The History of the Adventures of Joseph Andrews, and of His Friend Mr. Abram Adams Written in Imitation of the Manner of Cervantes* (1742). Here Pamela's newly invented brother Joseph refuses the overtures of Squire Booby's sister-in-law, and, promptly dismissed from her service, takes the road to Somersetshire where lives the damsel of his heart, Fanny. On the way he meets the parish parson, the quixotic Adams, and their adventures occupy the middle half of the novel. In Book iv they reach Lady Booby's country house, where in a burst of delicious snobbery Pamela arrives to plead with Joseph to marry Lady Booby and thus elevate the station of the Andrews family additionally. This last book shows a doubtless excessive influence of stagecraft on Fielding's art. The farcical revolutions and discoveries come thick and fast. The real art, however, lies not in the puppet-like manipulation of the persons but in their psychology. Parson Adams is the first of Fielding's portraits of "the good man," and easily the best. Heartfree in *Jonathan Wild* lacks Adams's brains, as indeed does Tom Jones's foster father Allworthy. Dr. Harrison in *Amelia* has learning but he has no witty fecundity of argument or happiness in self-contradiction such as Adams shows. Parson Adams is guileless as an apostle; his naïve virtue busies itself without-doors as well as within; it seeks the good of others always—and occasionally the means of defraying his own expenses of travel. The element of paradoxical discussion that he introduces into the novel gives the book its true character, and we forget the Boobys gladly. The novel is full of high spirits, rough horse-play, and a healthy sense of the comedy of life.

The burlesque *Life of Mr. Jonathan Wild the Great*, published in Fielding's *Miscellanies* (1743), continues, in reverse, the intellectual attitudes of

Parson Adams.[13] The central formula here is the ironical contrast between Jonathan
Wild "goodness" and "greatness." [14] Wild the criminal, hanged in 1725, had become the symbol of political knavery, and Fielding capitalizes on the tradition. In *Joseph Andrews* he had followed (except for the burlesque of Richardson) the quixotic pattern of master and man meeting adventure on the road. In *Jonathan Wild* the pattern is that of biography with a feminine burlesque of voyage adventures added for Mrs. Heartfree. The intention is chiefly moral. The good man, Heartfree, virtuously free from suspicion of others, is easily victimized. The "great man," whether conqueror or prime minister, or thief, is thoroughly selfish—"a bold heart, a thundering voice, and a steady countenance" make up his transcendent nature. "Mankind," Fielding tells us prophetically, "are first properly to be considered under two grand divisions, those that use their own hands, and those who employ the hands of others" (I, xiv). The great thief, like a prime minister, works through a cabinet or gang. In spite of much evidence to the contrary Fielding avows that he is not here attacking a particular prime minister (Walpole was just out of office). "Roguery, not a rogue," is his game. Rich in irony, this book is primarily a moral apologue with wounding cuts at political and economic abuses. The persons tend, under these aims, to become mere intellectual formulae.

For both *Joseph Andrews* and *Jonathan Wild* Fielding had written very Tom Jones important prefatory statements about his artistic and moral intentions.[15] He was first to make his ideas effective in his masterpiece, *The History of Tom Jones, a Foundling* (1749). In his preface to *Joseph Andrews* Fielding had talked both of structure and of characterization, and had used the notable phrase "the comic epic poem in prose." The epic was the only narrative form to have been much the object of critical formulation: it had a central plot idea; it moved steadily towards a desired terminal objective; it used episodes, but the episode contributed to the general narrative pattern. In *Tom Jones* application of these doctrines produced one of the best-plotted novels in English. Obviously Fielding had learned much from the drama as well as from the epic tradition, and he had learned much also from life. Foundlings in the decade after the Hospital in Bloomsbury was opened were a popular social problem, and Tom as a foundling had to discover his birth—which must be such as to make him worthy of his lovely Sophia Western. The pattern followed is biography, with unusual stress placed upon the boyhood of Tom. The word *history,* found in the title, suggests an avoidance of the lofty, the marvelous, and the fantastic, and the adherence to "the plain and simple workings of honest nature" as seen in real life. The focus of incident resembles somewhat that of *Joseph Andrews.* The first third takes place at the house of Squire Allworthy in Somersetshire; the middle section deals with adventures on the

---

13 William R. Irwin, *The Making of "Jonathan Wild"* (1941).
14 F. McD. C. Turner, *The Element of Irony in English Literature* (Cambridge, 1926).
15 Richmond C. Beatty, "Criticism in Fielding's Narratives and his Estimate of Critics," *PMLA* XLIX (1934). 1087-1100.

roads to London; and the last third takes place in that city. At the exact middle of the narrative in Books ix and x we reach a comic (if not farcical) plateau of dramatic episode in the inn at Upton-on-Severn. But the high jinks of these books are all neatly woven into the organic structure of the whole in a fashion not attempted in the complications of the farcical elements in the last book of *Joseph Andrews*.

Inter-weaving Detail and Episode

It is the skilful interweaving of small detail or episode that best characterizes the economy of Fielding's art in this story. Every appearance of Attorney Dowling, for example, signals information to the reader clearly but not too obviously. The bank note appropriated by Black George becomes gradually a significant device in complicating and unraveling the plot. And most of the episodes illustrate some favorite idea of the author's. Human characters are mixed, good and bad, he thinks, and the world is most obtuse in perceiving true merit. Thus at first Blifil is preferred to Tom. Though a member of a military family, Henry Fielding did not like soldiers as a class; though a resident of London, he had little respect for the high society of that city. Consequently Ensign Northerton and Lady Bellaston will be unsavory types. Tom must, so his foster father Allworthy tells him, acquire prudence and religion, and when Tom leaves what has been home he matures rapidly: he lectures the hard-hearted Quaker at Hambrook, and the Man of the Hill near Upton, and young Nightingale in London. He becomes a sound Christian apologist on the subject of misanthropy. In or near London he meets, among others, an honest highwayman, Mrs. Miller, and Mr. Fitzpatrick, who in his hour of deepest disfavor become indispensable witnesses to the real goodness of his nature. A wealth of highly diversified episode is fitted together by the hand of a master craftsman into a perfectly organized whole. Practically everything except the introductory essays to the eighteen books is organic; and since these essays are as brilliantly written as any essays in this essay-writing century, only harassed undergraduates wish them away.

Human Nature and Psychological. Clichés

Here as in all his novels Fielding devises his persons from observation or from psychological clichés. Virtue is easily deceived, he thinks; and thus Squire Allworthy (whom he designs, so he says, in compliment to his patrons Ralph Allen and George, Lord Lyttelton as prototypes) becomes a mere formula, not a live person. Allworthy's opposite, Squire Western, is the classic Tory country squire of the century, so truly and roughly is he drawn. Lady Bellaston is the hardened female commonly seen on the Drury Lane stage; her opposite, Molly Seagrim, smells of Somerset loam. The balance between characters taken from life and those taken from Fielding's intellectual preconceptions dips probably in favor of the latter source. In the principal pair of opposites, Tom and Blifil, Fielding seems to be playing with the problem of fate or predestination, which fascinated him. These two lads have the same mother, similar fathers (though Tom's is superior), the same environment and education. Yet one is fated to be a sneak and a villain and the other, though young, rash, full of impulse, is full also of benevolence and what Fielding calls "good nature." In the prologue to Part v of *The Cry* his sister Sarah well expresses a common view of psychological determinism:

Altho' it might be absurd to assert that any man is entirely bad, or completely good; yet there is surely no absurdity in declaring, that every individual possessed of rationality is absolutely in the path to goodness, or in the road to corruption. . . . There appears to be but two grand master passions or movers in the human mind, namely, Love and Pride. . . . Thus a man may be more or less proud; but if Pride be his characteristic, he cannot be a good man. So a man may be more or less attracted by love, and rouzed to benevolent actions; but whilst he preserves Love as the characteristic of his mind, he cannot be a bad man.

According to some such theory of master passions, Tom and Blifil move apart. Another contrasting pair are Thwackum and Square, the former a typical polemical divine stressing total depravity and redeeming grace, whereas the latter, a Stoic deist, cants of "the natural beauty of virtue," "the unalterable rule of right, and the eternal fitness of things"—and both have long since discarded benevolence and "all natural goodness of heart." Fielding prefers Square over Thwackum, but Square's final on-stage appearance in Molly Seagrim's attic chamber is a quaint comment on the "eternal fitness of things." The intellectual by-play in *Tom Jones* is far more a matter of careful intention than the casual reader imagines.

Certainly in Fielding's last novel intellectual and social intentions are obvious. *Tom Jones* and *Joseph Andrews* had appealed because written generally in high spirits and with nimble wit. But when Fielding wrote of London life, as in his comedies of manners and in the last part of *Tom Jones,* his picture was grim and his tone lacking in spirit and comedy. And so *Amelia* (1751), awaited with great expectation, was a disappointment. In some ways it is Fielding's most pretentious and yet his least finished work.[16] He had been appointed justice of the peace for Middlesex in 1749 and his daily duties in court thereafter left him little time for careful writing. He defended the novel warmly in his *Covent-Garden Journal,* remarking in No. 8 (January 28, 1752):

The Epic Quality of Amelia

I go farther, and avow, that of all my Offspring she [*Amelia*] is my favourite Child. I can truly say that I bestowed a more than ordinary Pains in her Education; in which I will venture to affirm, I followed the Rules of all those who are acknowledged to have writ best on the Subject; and if her Conduct be fairly examined, she will be found to deviate very little from the strictest Observation of all those Rules; neither Homer nor Virgil pursued them with greater Care than myself, and the candid and learned Reader will see that the latter was the noble model, which I made use of on this Occasion.

Thus designedly the epic action of *Amelia* really begins *in medias res* with the modern Dido (Miss Matthews) listening to Captain Booth's military adventures and seducing him in the "cave" of Newgate prison. It is an

---

[16] George Sherburn, "Fielding's *Amelia:* an Interpretation," *ELH*, iii (1936). 1-14.

unheroic beginning, but this is an epic *in prose,* with the "proposition" articulated in the first sentence: "The various accidents which befel a very worthy couple after their uniting in the state of matrimony will be the subject of the following history." This prosaic announcement is a product of Fielding's theory of realism. In his autobiographical *Voyage to Lisbon* (1754) he says:

> I must confess I should have honoured and loved Homer more had he written a true history of his own times in humble prose, than those noble poems that have so justly collected the praise of all ages; for though I read these with more admiration and astonishment, I still read Herodotus, Thucydides and Xenophon, with more amusement and more satisfaction.

Its Social and Moral Themes
The events of this prose epic, "accidents" that befell a very worthy couple, are shaped largely from two sources of motivation. As in an epic, there is a national theme: the hardness of a social system that keeps Booth from getting back his commission. There is also a personal theme; and for the wrath of Achilles and the piety of Æneas we have Booth's lack of courage to battle against the social system and make a living for his family and for his courageous wife, Amelia. After Parson Adams, Booth is easily Fielding's best educated protagonist; he has an excellent army record, and his chief faults before the story begins are his desire to appear as a gentleman rather than a mere farmer and his lack of courage for the struggle of life: he is a fatalist of sorts—as Fielding makes evident in a crucial passage from Claudian which he did not translate for his readers. At the end of the story Amelia unexpectedly inherits a fortune, Booth suddenly "gets religion," and a happy ending is enforced. Between the events in Newgate and his final happiness the episodes are largely such as should have pleased Richardson's admirers—a series of attempts to seduce Amelia, who, however, is a courageous mother and a faithful wife. Yet the scenes of extreme poverty, the lack of luck that attends all Booth's actions, and other things such as his somewhat American willingness to do a part of the housework make the story unattractive, and certainly the general hardness of life for the underprivileged offers no catharsis. Booth's personal failing is remedied at the end by a reading of Dr. Barrow's sermons and a sort of conversion; but the public problem of the story—the lack of patronage for merit—is, naturally, unsolved. Noble lords will get commissions for their footmen pimps, but for a demobilized officer of distinguished record in the service they will do nothing. The reader must exclaim with Amelia:

> "Good Heavens! . . . what are our great men made of? are they in reality a distinct species from the rest of mankind? are they born without hearts?"
> "One would, indeed, sometimes," cries Booth, "be inclined to think so. In truth, they have no perfect idea of those common distresses of mankind which are far removed from their own sphere. Compassion, if thoroughly examined, will, I believe, appear to be the fellow-feeling only of men of the same rank and degree of life for one another, on account of the evils to which they themselves are liable. Our sensations are, I am afraid, very cold towards those who are at a

great distance from us, and whose calamities can consequently never reach us. . . . Where ambition, avarice, pride, or any other passion [than benevolence], governs the man and keeps his benevolence down, the miseries of all other men affect him no more than they would a stock or a stone. And thus the man and his statue have often the same degree of feeling or compassion." (x, ix)

Here Fielding touches one of the social sores in a period that was by turns vaguely benevolist and brutally hard. Similar comments can be found in other novels—notably Smollett's—as well as in Johnson's *Life of Richard Savage* and his celebrated letter to the Earl of Chesterfield. Fielding does not organize *Amelia* either for mere entertainment or for any revolutionary action: he simply presents grim truths in uncolored prose.

Fielding and Richardson gave form and pattern to the novel. Fielding added dignity to the art of fiction by imitating the epic and by cultivating serious criticism of manners. Tobias Smollett (1721-1771) was to excel in vivid human detail rather than by structure.[17] Like Richardson and Fielding he was a critic of manners; but being a "lousy Scot" and a surgeon to boot he lacked entrée to high society and wrote always as an external observer and critic. A born storyteller, he paid little attention to premeditated effects; his narrative and descriptive gifts were sufficient to keep readers keenly interested and amused. He expressed his conception of what a novel should be in his preface to *Ferdinand Count Fathom*: *Smollett's Achievement*

A novel is a large diffused picture, comprehending the characters of life, disposed in different groups, and exhibited in various attitudes, for the purposes of an uniform plan, and general occurrence, to which every individual figure is subservient. But this plan cannot be executed with propriety, probability, or success, without a principal personage to attract the attention, unite the incidents, unwind the clue of the labyrinth, and at last close the scene, by virtue of his own importance.

[17] Smollett's *Miscellaneous Works* (6v, Edinburgh, 1790, 1796; 12v, 1824); ed. Thomas Roscoe (1841, etc.); *Works*, ed. John Moore (8v, 1797; 1870, etc.); ed. Wm. E. Henley and T. Seccombe (12v, 1899-1901); ed. George Saintsbury (12v, 1895, etc.); ed. Gustavus H. Maynadier (12v, 1902). *Novels* (11v, Oxford, 1925-6). *Letters*, ed. Edward S. Noyes (Cambridge, Mass., 1926). Apart from fiction Smollett's most popular work was *The Complete History of England* (4v, 1757-8; 11v, 1758-60). *Continuation of the History of England* (5v, 1760-5). Among Smollett's translations were *Gil Blas* (4v, 1749), *Don Quixote* (2v, 1755), *The Works of M. de Voltaire* (Smollett and others: 36v, 1761-9), *Adventures of Telemachus* (2v, 1776). He edited *The Critical Review* in its early years, 1756-63, and *The British Magazine*, 1760-67, *The Briton*, 1762-3, and contributed to other periodicals. The luckless tragedy that he brought up to London in 1739 was called *The Regicide* (1749). On it see *Roderick Random*, chs. 61-63.— Scholarly treatment of Smollett is moderately recent: Howard S. Buck, *A Study in Smollett, Chiefly "Peregrine Pickle"* (New Haven, 1925); H. S. Buck, *Smollett as Poet* (New Haven, 1927); Lewis M. Knapp, "Smollett's Early Years in London," *JEGP*, XXXI (1932). 220-227; George M. Kahrl, "The Influence of Shakespeare on Smollett," *Essays in Dramatic Literature: the Parrott Presentation Volume* (Princeton, 1935); Eugène Joliat, *Smollett et la France* (Paris, 1935); Lewis M. Knapp, "The Publication of Smollett's 'Complete History' and 'Continuation,' " *Library*, XVI (1935). 295-308; L. F. Powell, "William Huggins and Tobias Smollett" [Letters, 1756-61], *MP*, XXXIV (1936). 179-192; James R. Foster, "Smollett's Pamphleteering Foe Shebbeare," *PMLA*, LVII (1942). 1053-1100; Claude E. Jones, *Smollett Studies* (Berkeley and Los Angeles, 1942); Louis L. Martz, *The Later Career of Tobias Smollett* (New Haven, 1942); Henry W. Meikle, "New Smollett Letters," *LTLS*, July 24 and 31, 1943, pp. 360, 372; George M. Kahrl, *Tobias Smollett, Traveler-Novelist* (Chicago, 1945).

Practically all of his stories thus fall into the picaresque tradition of rambling episode, though he sometimes neglects the picaresque function of exposing the vices and follies of various social classes or professions. Sometimes for the social class he substitutes racial distinctions such as the Welsh or Irish or Scotch. This trick of racial characterization was very popular by the end of the century. For inventiveness and diversity of episode, vivid particularity of detail to the point of caricature, and energy of style Smollett is hardly excelled. He is to the eighteenth-century novel what Hogarth is to painting—a savage realist with an eye for eccentric character, which he discovers in all classes.

Roderick Random

His first novel, *Roderick Random* (1748), antedated *Tom Jones* by about a year and was, so Smollett wrongly thought, a source from which Fielding plagiarized. The novel was in part autobiographical. Like Smollett, Roderick after some training in surgery came from Scotland to London, where, after suffering from poverty, he, like Smollett, secured a place as surgeon's mate on a man-of-war and sailed away to the West Indies to take part in the unfortunate expedition against Carthagena (1740-1). Roderick's journey up to London in company with the ineffable Strap and the ghastly pictures of life aboard the *Thunder* and the *Lizard* in the West Indies are outstanding episodes, the life aboard a man-of-war being a complete novelty in English fiction.[18] He returned from these naval exploits; and after a brief episode in Sussex where he fell in love with Narcissa, military adventures on the Continent, including the battle of Dettingen, enabled Smollett to express caustic opinions of French fighters. Supported by Strap's money "Rory" next went on a hunt for a rich wife at Bath (scene of a failure on Smollett's part as surgeon). In London's Marshalsea prison Roderick listened to Melopoyn's (Smollett's) account of a luckless tragedy. Here Smollett anticipated the attack on patrons that Fielding and Dr. Johnson were soon to make. Finally—and how fortunately!—Rory discovered a long lost, wealthy father, married Narcissa, repurchased the family estate in Scotland, and showed his scorn for those relatives who had at the beginning of the story scorned him. The exile had returned triumphant.

Clearly such a tale must depend upon vividness for its appeal. In his preface Smollett tells us that he "attempted to represent modest merit struggling with every difficulty to which a friendless orphan is exposed"; but Roderick finds friends at need, and he evokes no more sympathy than does a Defoe protagonist. He, like Smollett, is fighting for a place in the sun, and he is ingenious and not too scrupulous in battling for the rights of "modest merit." Thinking Roderick's chief misfortune was his being a

Peregrine Pickle

Scot, Smollett created for his second novel, *Peregrine Pickle* (1751), an English hero, who might well have been Roderick's twin. The supporting cast, however, is much improved. Commodore Hawser Trunnion, whose country

[18] Charles N. Robinson and John Leyland, *The British Tar in Fact and Fiction* (1909); Lewis M. Knapp, "The Naval Scenes in *Roderick Random*," *PMLA*, XLIX (1934). 593-598; Louis L. Martz, "Smollett and the Expedition to Carthagena," *PMLA*, LVI (1941). 428-446.

house observes the routine of a battleship, is Smollett's most sympathetic creation, but as an eccentric he is almost equaled by the man-hunting spinster Grizzle Pickle and by the misanthropic Cadwallader Crabtree. The art of caricature is here seen at its best, and burlesque episodes abound, such as, for example, the famous dinner in the manner of the ancients (chapter 44). The novel was made less readable by the insertion, doubtless at the financial instance of Lady Vane, the author, of the long interrupting section (chapter 81) called "Memoirs of a Lady of Quality." This chapter—of one hundred and fifty pages—has no connection with the rest of the story, and lacks the spice that one expects from the apologies for their lives not infrequently written about this time by ladies charged with frailty.

In his later novels Smollett was inclined to experiment. *The Adventures of Ferdinand Count Fathom* (1753) recounted the heinous deeds of a Continental villain and through appeal to the "impulses of fear" professed to hope to terrify into virtue those hesitating "on the brink of iniquity." Much of this book is mere melodrama; at times it anticipates the so-called "novel of terror." In 1760-1 he brought out *The Adventures of Sir Launcelot Greaves,* a curious attempt to adapt *Don Quixote* to the eighteenth century by creating a benevolist reformer so disinterested as to seem (and be) a madman. The *Adventures of an Atom* (1769), which pretended to be about Japan, is a coarse and virulent satire on important political issues and persons in the troubled early years of George III. In method it owed something to Charles Johnstone's *Chrysal, or the Adventures of a Guinea* (1760-5). *[margin: Count Fathom]*

Smollett's best experiment was his last novel—and his masterpiece—*The Expedition of Humphry Clinker,* which appeared in 1771 shortly before Smollett's death. Stimulated by his prejudice against Bath and all watering places and by the poetical epistles of the witty and popular *New Bath Guide* (1766) by Christopher Anstey, Smollett designed this expedition, which started from Brambleton Hall (Wales) and journeyed through Gloucester, Bath, London, Harrowgate, Scarborough, Berwick, Edinburgh, Cameron (the Smollett "seat"), Glasgow, Carlisle, Manchester, and again home. The novelist's virtuosity in devising variety of happenings ranges from practical jokes of a dubious sort to attendance at a Methodist meeting where our footman hero is the preacher. In this book Smollett discards the method of travel narrative used in his early novels and suddenly shows himself a great master of the epistolary method. Each correspondent has a highly individual style and characterizes (or caricatures) himself with facility. Matthew Bramble is the *pater familias,* and externally, as his name indicates, he is what the world thought Tobias Smollett—thoroughly irascible; but his true self is what Smollett thought his to be—easily moved to benevolent action. Squire Bramble is making this journey in part to distract the mind of his young niece, Lydia Melford, who has fallen in love supposedly with a strolling player. Tabitha Bramble, Matt's sister, is an *[margin: Humphry Clinker]* aging spinster in violent search for a husband, whom she finds in the priceless veteran of Indian warfare, Lismahago.[19] At Marlborough Downs, needing a new postilion, they add Humphry Clinker to the party—and Humphry turns out to be the natural son of Matt, and the devoted admirer of Winifred Jenkins, Tabitha's maid, supreme among illiterate servants. With at least three major plots to unravel and several minor episodic suspenses the book is easily Smollett's richest picture of English and Scottish life, and his most entertaining narrative. He always had viewed life as a traveler, and here his critical and descriptive powers find natural scope and blend with a somewhat less tough-minded attitude towards mankind than his earlier work had shown.

Smollett's Place in Fiction   Like Fielding Smollett wrote a great deal apart from his prose fiction. He turned out political pamphlets and periodical essays; he edited two magazines,[20] and was a voluminous translator. Almost to the twentieth century he was regarded as a rather "low" author, and no one of his novels is without vulgarity. He was from the start, however, a novelist's novelist, and many writers of prose fiction are obviously in his debt. Sterne's Uncle Toby derives in part from Hawser Trunnion, and his *Sentimental Journey* is in part a counterblast to Smollett's *Travels through France and Italy* (1766). Fanny Burney will be presently his disciple in the method of caricature, and Walter Scott, Dickens, and many another have since lifted good devices from his pages. His contribution to fiction is a fusion of ingenuity with humorous and highly particularized caricature, just as Fielding and Richardson contributed dignity, structure, and emotional psychology. *Clarissa, Tom Jones,* and *Humphry Clinker* remain among the greatest masterpieces of English fiction. In the eighteenth century only Sterne's work is comparable to these three novels. The work of Richardson and Fielding was complete by 1754, when Fielding died. Smollett had by that year established his fame, but his career was longer and outlasted that of Sterne who began significant publication in 1759.

[19] Smollett probably discovered a prototype for Lismahago in Captain Robert Stobo; see George M. Kahrl's article in the *Virginia Mag. of Hist. and Biog.,* XLIX (1941). 141-151, 254-268.

[20] See, for Smollett's work on periodicals, Part III, ch. VII.

BOOK III

The Restoration and Eighteenth Century (1660-1789)

✁

PART III
The Disintegration of Classicism

Guide to reference marks
Throughout the text of this book, a point • set beside a page number indicates that references to new critical material will be found under an identical paragraph/page number (set in **boldface**) in the BIBLIOGRAPHICAL SUPPLEMENT.

In the Index, a number preceded by an **S** indicates a paragraph/page number in the BIBLIOGRAPHICAL SUPPLEMENT.

I

Accentuated Tendencies

To define precisely the change that came over the second half of the *The Vogue* eighteenth century is difficult.[1] It is not quite enough to say that the Age *of Senti-* of Reason gave way to an Age of Sentiment. Undoubtedly there was an *ment* access of sentimentality after the vogues of Richardson and Rousseau were established; but sentiment had existed before their day, and the phrase "Age of Reason" was used by Tom Paine to describe the period of the French Revolution. Nevertheless, one chief mark of the change was not merely an increase in sentimentality but also a modification of attitude towards sentiment. While Richard Steele in his *Christian Hero*—and other authors of his day as well—had perceived rather the utility of sentiment, authors later in the century indulged in the delicate enjoyment of their own emotional thrills. Where Addison and others had praised the rationality of simplicity, Burns will display the picturesqueness of the quality. The ablest men of the second half of the century still were proponents of

[1] Most of the many references given in Part II, ch. I are useful also for the latter half of the century. Certain additions, however, may be made: Thomas Seccombe, *The Age of Johnson* (1899); William L. Phelps, *The Beginnings of the English Romantic Movement* (1893); Henry A. Beers, *A History of Romanticism in the Eighteenth Century* (1899); John H. Millar, *The Mid-Eighteenth Century* (1902); John Bailey, *Dr. Johnson and his Circle* (1913); Arthur S. Collins, *Authorship in the Days of Johnson, Being a Study of the Relationship between Author, Patron, Publisher, and Public, 1726-1780* (1927); David Nichol Smith, *Shakespeare in the Eighteenth Century* (Oxford, 1928); Robert W. Babcock, *The Genesis of Shakespeare Idolatry, 1766-1799* (Chapel Hill, 1931); Francis Gallaway, *Reason, Rule, and Revolt in English Classicism* (1940); Walter J. Bate, *From Classic to Romantic: Premises of Taste in Eighteenth-Century England* (1946). — For the political history add William Hunt, *The Political History of England*, Vol. x: *From the Accession of George III to the Close of Pitt's First Administration* (1905); Basil Williams, *William Pitt, Earl of Chatham* (2v, 1913); Lewis B. Namier, *The Structure of Politics at the Accession of George III* (2v, 1929); L. B. Namier, *England in the Age of the American Revolution* (1930); Philip W. Wilson, *William Pitt the Younger* (1933); R. B. Mowat, *The Age of Reason—the Continent of Europe in the Eighteenth Century* (1934); Sir Charles Petrie, *The Four Georges* (1935); L. B. Namier, *In the Margin of History* [collected essays] (1939).—For the intellectual and social background add Trueman Wood, *Industrial England in the Eighteenth Century* (1911); Louis W. Moffit, *England on the Eve of the Industrial Revolution* (1925); Ephraim Lipson, *Economic History of England* (1931), Vols. II and III; *Johnson's England*, ed. A. S. Turberville (2v, 1933); J. H. Whiteley, *Wesley's England: A Study of ... Social and Cultural Conditions* (1938); H. N. Fieldhouse, "Bolingbroke and the Idea of Non-Party Government," *History*, XXIII (1938). 41-56; Charles Reith, *The Police Idea: Its History and Evolution* (Oxford, 1938); Wilmarth S. Lewis, *Three Tours through London in the Years 1748, 1776, 1797* (Colver Lectures at Brown University: New Haven, 1941); Maurice J. Quinlan, *Victorian Prelude: a History of English Manners, 1700-1830* (1941).—On the household arts see A. T. Bolton, *The Architecture of Robert and James Adam* (1922); Oliver Brackett, *Thomas Chippendale: A Study of his Life, Work, and Influence* (1924); Percy Macquoid and R. Edwards, *The Dictionary of English Furniture* (3v, 1924-7); Sir Kenneth Clark, *The Gothic Revival* (1928); Sacheverell Sitwell, *Narrative Pictures* (1937); G. C. Williamson, *English Conversation Pictures* (1931); Chauncey B. Tinker, *Painter and Poet* (Cambridge, Mass., 1938).

⌐ and common sense; but they were also (Dr. Johnson or Burke, for ⌐mple) likely to be men of strong emotional natures. It is significant ⌐at Hume's philosophical writing was practically done by 1750; thereafter he was to be the historian and essayist. Hume's highly logical thinking, one may say, served but to subvert the classical integrity of man's reason, and throughout the century there had been a strong anti-rational prejudice against "mere" logic. The change is at once felt if we place the leading poets of the Queen Anne group—Pope and Swift—in comparison with *fin de siècle* poets such as Cowper and Burns. It is a change obviously that does not imply an access of intellectual power but does imply increased delight in subjective emotional states. The later century tends to glorify the individual's sensations whether merely thrilling or (as they seemed at times) revelatory of new, vague truths.

The Able Conserva- tives Lovers of romanticism have liked to picture this last half-century as a slow awakening to a better artistic life, an awakening from constrictive tradition. There is truth in the picture, but not the whole truth. The ablest writers and thinkers of the period were still traditionalists—Johnson, Reynolds, Gibbon, and Burke. The awakening was not altogether an advance except in the field of graphic art. In the field of music, the most purely emotional of the arts, there was something like an eclipse in the second half of the century as compared with the periods of Purcell and Handel. Waging war was almost an inveterate pursuit of the whole century, but the second half of the century produced no general comparable to Marlborough and no prime minister equal to Walpole (though the younger William Pitt was more picturesque). If the latter half-century produced no poet comparable to Pope, it did perhaps produce a larger number of writers of high importance, and it did move forward to the period of the highest regard for the dignity and transcendent nobility of the individual soul and its potentialities. Even Dr. Johnson believed in progress, and his contemporaries in general glorified the idea.

Religion and Politics There were obvious repercussions in religion and politics. In the second third of the century the evangelical movement of Methodism became notable; by the end of the century it had softened and civilized the spirit of the lower classes, and was rapidly elevating many to a rank in the middle class that was to be so commended during the nineteenth century. This development, with its emphasis on emotional "conversion" to a Christian faith and its reassertion of the importance of the individual soul, was moving in the main channel of tendencies of the time. Such tendencies in politics were not to be viewed with equanimity by conservatives. The law of subordination, Dr. Johnson feared, was being relaxed—dangerously. While enterprising Englishmen were building a British empire across various seas, the politicians in Parliament (now regarded as "the finest club of gentlemen in Europe") were wittily or eloquently confusing themselves and the electorate over the rights of electors (notably the electors of Middlesex) and the rights of the crown as opposed to the rights of Parliament.

It was a period of argumentative vituperation and chicanery among partisans, and a field-day for not too scrupulous trouble-makers like John Wilkes and "Junius." In such a period Edmund Burke seems to resemble a colossus of integrity. The loss of thirteen American colonies was an episode in this period of confused and selfish politics.

The humanitarianism of the time led to increased feeling of social responsibility for the underprivileged. Such feeling had stimulated the work of Henry Fielding as justice of the peace for Middlesex and as author of the *Enquiry into the Late Increase of Robbers* (1751). Henry's work was continued with distinction by his blind brother, Sir John, and later by John Howard (1726?-1790), whose *State of the Prisons* (1777 ff.) is a landmark in the literature of reform, and by William Wilberforce (1759-1833), who added to an interest in prison reform a great zeal in the cause of anti-slavery. The career of Jonas Hanway (1712-1786) also is a typical record of labors for the Foundling Hospital, the Magdalen House, the Marine Society, and other similar institutions. *Humanitarian* was not a word to be found in Johnson's *Dictionary*, but the trait was coming more and more into existence.[2] That it was coupled with the sentimental ideas of "universal benevolence" can be seen by the international nature of John Howard's work, and, concretely, by the epitaph placed on his remote Russian grave:

Humanitarianism

> WHOEVER THOU ART, THOU STANDEST AT
>
> THE TOMB OF THY FRIEND.

Prosperity as well as a strongly utilitarian bias led to the development of such arts as made for dignified and beautiful living conditions. Architecture throve under the guidance of Sir William Chambers (1726-1796) and, among others, James (d. 1794) and Robert Adam (1728-1792). In London Sir William's final achievement was Somerset House—which since his day has been much enlarged. Along the Thames also the Adam brothers similarly showed their finest work in the pretentious façade of their Adelphi buildings (1768-71). These were classical buildings—Sir William being more correctly traditionalist than the brothers, who displeased Horace Walpole by their "warehouses laced down the front." They had a touch of rococo, but not much of it. Walpole, of course, at Strawberry Hill, was promoting the vogue of Gothic, and between 1757 and 1762 Sir William Chambers was adorning Kew Gardens for the dowager Princess of Wales with the *chinoiseries* that, with Gothic, became the fantastic but modishly popular extremes of taste. Possibly when all is said, the great architectural achievement of the half-century is to be seen at Bath, where a most brilliant experiment in community architecture took place in the rebuilding of

The Useful and Fine Arts

[2] Wilmarth S. Lewis and R. M. Williams, *Private Charity in England, 1747-1757* (New Haven, 1938); Frank J. Klingberg, "The Evolution of the Humanitarian Spirit in Eighteenth-Century England," *Pennsylvania Magazine of Hist. and Biog.*, LXVI (1942). 260-278; Frank J. Klingberg, *The Anti-Slavery Movement in England* (New Haven, 1926); Wylie Sypher, *Guinea's Captive Kings: British Anti-Slavery Literature of the XVIIIth Century* (Chapel Hill, 1942); John H. Hutchins, *Jonas Hanway, 1712-1786* (1940).

the city, chiefly on designs by John Wood (1705?-1754) and his son of the same name. Through their efforts Bath became the most stately city in England and an admirable example of the classical tradition. At a slightly later date the Adam brothers were designing beautifully and building solidly new streets, squares, public buildings, and palatial residences for the Scottish capital, Edinburgh.

Interiors of buildings were fully as lovely as exteriors. Excessive rococo ornamentation was less common in England than on the Continent, and the less ornate English interiors of the time had a cheerful repose and a spacious dignity hardly excelled. The walls of these houses were hung with the work of the greatest painters England has yet produced. In 1768 Benjamin West, a native of Pennsylvania and an historical painter who enjoyed the patronage of George III, founded, with the aid of the King and of three fellow artists, the Royal Academy of Arts, of which Sir Joshua Reynolds became the first president. These were the great days of Reynolds (1723-1792) and Gainsborough (1727-1788), who surpassed such earlier masters as Joseph Highmore, Richard Wilson, Allan Ramsay the younger, Paul Sandby, and the Cozenses, and were ably supported in a glorious second rank by such men as Romney, Beechey, Zoffany, Raeburn, Hoppner, Opie, Morland, and others. Painting was perhaps the most highly developed of the fine arts in this period, but love of beautiful interiors also stimulated the production of finely designed furniture, and an English school of cabinet-makers throve, equal almost to the painters as artists. The relative heaviness of the designs of William Kent now gave way to the lightness that the greatest of these designers, Thomas Chippendale (1718-1779), was enabled to give to mahogany—which now displaced walnut as a favorite wood. Chippendale's styles included much from earlier English traditions, much from contemporary French, and much from Chinese and even Gothic patterns. His rococo tendency was corrected in favor of a less fanciful type of classicism in the elegant designs of Robert Adam, George Hepplewhite, and Thomas Sheraton. The essential quality that marked the work of all these men and the interiors that they adorned was elegance.

In literature there was perhaps no truly comparable achievement; but literature, being more important than household arts and being more accessible for general study, has naturally been basic in all descriptions of the period. If one focuses attention merely on literature, one has to conclude that the second half of the century is still the victim of the first. Authors may now more readily disparage the rules, may seek to strike out new paths for the imagination; but they are still inhibited by excessive attention to decorum, by a fear of not being correct, of being the object of satire because of a lack of common sense. One feared to have too much epic quality in one's elegy: Gray's use of the pentameter in his *Churchyard* was suspected of this fault. One had to watch one's manners: Evelina is merely a projection of music-master Burney's daughter, who through decorum rose to be a friend and critic even of royalty. One wished to be thought exquisitely normal in action, to avoid above all being fantastic. One took refuge in *domestica facta,* in realistic matters of daily life, and rested there with little overt rebellion against the classical tradition. One simply thought about other things and gently disregarded the classical pastoral, the Punic War, classical mythology, and much else that seemed merely the stale clap-trap of schoolmasters and schoolboys.[3]

So-called classical tendencies varied in value and in the amount of approbation they received throughout the century. *Sub specie aeternitatis* their theory might be excellent; in the closets where poets wrote they received a decreasing amount of attention. Subversive and disintegrating tendencies were seldom openly or clearly opposed to classicism, but at bottom they were hostile. Three of these tendencies may be briefly described.[4] First, there was the much-vaunted English love of liberty. The French might accept Boileau in right of Horace as an absolute literary monarch: the English still kept "unconquered and uncivilised." For ancient authority the English had largely substituted the more abstract sanction of truth, reason, or nature; the ancients were now simply the best guides. As the Enlightenment advanced, there was a marked tendency to insist on the impossibility of absolute standards, to believe in progress, change, novelty—in a word, in relative if not subjective standards of excellence.

Secondly, doubts arose as to whether truth—poetic truth at least—*was* "one clear, unchanged, and universal light," and the belief in uniformity and universality gave way to a love of diversity that led to revolutions. Truth was less often conceived as quite external to the poet; it was seen filtered through the varying lights and shades of the poet's mood. Before the Restoration a poet's personality had had relatively little to do with understanding his art. The ancients normally had glorified art rather than artists. But Milton, Dryden, and Pope were all men of commanding personalities apart

Classicism Subverted:

1. By English Love of Liberty

2. By Subjective Attitudes towards Truth; by Moods

[3] Dr. Johnson, of course, was hardly gentle in his disregard of these matters. See Joseph E. Brown, *The Critical Opinions of Samuel Johnson* (Princeton, 1926), pp. 154-160. On the frigidity of the use of mythology by the poets of the time see Douglas Bush, *Mythology and the Romantic Tradition in English Poetry* (Cambridge, Mass., 1937).

[4] The paragraphs immediately following describe tendencies that without much meaning might be called "the beginnings of romanticism." Some years back the academic discussion of eighteenth-century literature eddied about the "romanticism" of the second half of the century. To the present writer it seems that such discussion has tended to describe the eighteenth century as seen distorted through the spectacles of the nineteenth. Furthermore, the term *romantic,* as Professor Lovejoy has clearly shown ("On the Discrimination of Romanticisms," *PMLA,* xxxix [1924]. 229-253), has been used in divergent and even self-contradictory senses. In so far as the term is a comprehensive label covering the general quality of the literature of the early nineteenth century, it has a limited but not very descriptive usefulness for that century. When it is used so loosely as to be a synonym of "imaginative" or to be merely a blanket term of approbation, it ceases to be historically or critically illuminating. Hence the term is here used infrequently and, it is hoped, cautiously. Other writers on the subject may be consulted as follows: J. G. Robertson, *Studies in the Genesis of Romantic Theory in the Eighteenth Century* (Cambridge, 1923); Harko G. de Maar, *A History of Modern English Romanticism,* Vol. 1: *Elizabethan and Modern Romanticism in the Eighteenth Century* (1924); Paul Van Tieghem, *Le Préromantisme* (2v, Paris, 1924, 1930); Paul Kaufman, "Defining Romanticism: A Survey and a Program," *MLN,* xl (1925). 1-12; Fernand Baldensperger, " 'Romantique,' ses analogues et ses équivalents: tableau synoptique de 1650 à 1810," *Harvard Studies and Notes in Philology and Literature,* xix (1937). 13-105; Arthur O. Lovejoy, "The Meaning of Romanticism for the Historian of Ideas," *JHI,* ii (1941). 257-278.

from their gifts as writers; and it was natural that in a journalistic period when literature and politics were so near allied, personalities should come increasingly to influence reputation. Speedily writers developed the self-conscious sensitive mind: the cult of genius accentuated the tendency. The sensitive mind is likely to be a restless mind, and that mood characterizes authors of this period. Even Dr. Johnson's mind must be classified as restless. Serenity, however desirable, was at best a dream, at worst a delusion.

The moods of these sentimental self-tormentors most commonly operative can be roughly classified. There was the benevolist filter. This had been used even in the late seventeenth century as producing serenity: clearly it might do that. It might also be the mood of an eager and generous soul wishing to pour itself out for the improvement of the human lot, or even for the sole pleasure of outpouring. Benevolism had made for stable equilibrium; it will now begin to work for instability. One of Pope's phrases most often quoted in the fifty years after his death and quoted significantly as applying to the whole consciousness of the sensitive man is "tremblingly alive all o'er." Another mood is that of melancholy. This was not new, but it was greatly (even tediously) accentuated in the later century. To Continental observers hypochondria was notoriously *The English Malady* before 1733 when Dr. George Cheyne published his book of that title. Night, death, and the graveyard became favorite topics in poetry; and the English acquired an international reputation for suicide. ("These are the dark November days," said Voltaire, "when the English hang themselves!") A third mood much affected was that of sublimity. Founded fully as much on the rhetorical precepts of Longinus (whose thesis was that sublimity could, if one followed his precepts, be attained by conscious effort) as on the superlative achievement of John Milton,[5] the cult of the sublime subverts common-sense rationalism, and hence points in part away from so-called classical tendencies. In so far as it opened new channels for noble Roman rhetoric it is hardly so "romantic" as many have thought. Thomas Gray did some lofty and thrilling things in this mood, but more truly serviceable were those who by applying some of the enthusiasm of this mood to subjects less titanic and noisy than *The Descent of Odin* or *The Progress of Poesy* became poets of humble life, and with their mildly warming glow of imagination anticipated Wordsworth himself. The cult of Longinus stimulated perhaps this quiet antithesis to itself that is more truly characteristic of a period devoted to simplicity[6] than was the somewhat rococo sublime. Collins and Cowper illustrate this quiet and at times pedestrian mood. Increasingly poets are creatures of mood rather than the eloquent announcers of general truths.

Thirdly, we may note the tendency away from Horatian or French classicism in the less frequent and inexact attention on the part of the abler

---

[5] Arthur Barker, " '. . . And on his Crest Sat Horror': Eighteenth-Century Interpretations of Milton's Sublimity and his Satan," *Univ. of Toronto Quar.*, xi (1942). 421-436. For a more extensive treatment see Samuel H. Monk, *The Sublime: A Study of Critical Theories in XVIII-Century England* (1935).

[6] Chauncey B. Tinker, *Nature's Simple Plan* (Princeton, 1922).

poets to the imitation of established generic models. A poet like Goldsmith, *3. By Neg-* conservative in many of his sympathies, could sit down to write poems like *lect of* *The Traveller* and *The Deserted Village* without asking himself whether *Horace and* he was writing a Georgic, an elegy, or a pastoral. Such emancipation is quiet *the Genres* but fundamental. More learned poets, still dependent upon patterns to follow, passed from the Roman genres to other models. There was a revival of interest in Greek, which in the mid-century encouraged William Mason to attempt two plays, or, as he called them, dramatic poems "Written on the Model of the Ancient Greek Tragedy." Adaptations of both his *Elfrida* and his *Caractacus* were performed at Covent Garden long years after those poems had been printed; but both were monuments of piety to a Greek form rather than attempts at a popular success in the theatre. More than one poet of the mid-century wrote monostrophic odes of the type used in Greek tragedy.[7] Still others, like Gray in *The Descent of Odin* and in *The Fatal Sisters,* attempted to recapture the tone of primitive lyricism; Macpherson is obviously in this tradition. There was also a naturally increasing tendency to use English models, which nationalist critics approved. It is not easy to see why Spenser and particularly Milton should be thought more "romantic" than Ovid, for example; but the imitation of English models, if still imitation and still not too clearly romantic, at least broadened the field of poetic method and subject matter. Milton, known as a political revolutionary, was frequently called by critics "the assertor of English liberty" in that he freed poetry from "the bondage of rime." Of course Milton himself adopted blank verse as approximating classical metrical forms; but again, reasons apart, the cultivation of nondramatic blank verse in the early eighteenth century had certainly increased the number of standard metrical forms from which a poet *de longue haleine* might choose.

In all these additions to poetic matter or manner was apparent an increas- *Love of* ing love of novelty. The conservative opinion about this was stated by Henry *Novelty* Felton in his *Dissertation on Reading the Classics* (1713): " 'Tis easier to strike out a new Course of Thought, than to equal old Originals, and there-fore it is more Honour to surpass, than to invent anew." This was, however, distinctly a minority view. A mere newspaper critic in *The Daily Gazetteer* (September 25, 1741) states the opposite position: "I would be content to inculcate a Desire of Excelling, rather by striking out new Paths, than by treading very circumspectly in the old ones. I have shewn, that it is natural for our Contemporaries to be pleased with anything that is tolerable if it be new, rather than a better Thing if it be evidently an Imitation."

That new paths were being more and more frequently trod is seen if we *English vs.* look at some specimens of new subject matter. It may be noted that here *Classical* Horace himself seems to countenance undermining classical imitation. On *Story* one page he could advocate using known fables (*ex noto fictum carmen sequar*) and on another could urge forsaking Greek paths (*vestigia Græca*)

---

[7] Bernard H. Stern, *The Rise of Romantic Hellenism in English Literature, 1732-1786* (Menasha, Wis., 1940).

and using native material (*domestica facta*). This patronage of English or everyday materials was in a way forced on writers. Classical story might be excellent; but after a dozen costive poets have moaned over Hero and Leander, other writers, if wise, are likely to choose another fable for their poem. Take Orpheus, or whatever classical story you will, and the condition will be similar: the tragedies of Thomson and dozens of forgotten narrative poems all attest the fact that classical story was an exhausted vein for the moment at least. It is an attractive hypothesis that a story tradition appeals when first well known, as the classics did in the Renaissance, or when again sporadically recovered, as in the nineteenth century. In any case, by 1756, Joseph Warton was simply expressing a general desire when he said: "It is to be wished, that our writers would more frequently search for subjects, in the annals of England, which afford many striking and pathetic events, proper for the stage. We have been too long attached to Grecian and Roman stories. In truth, the DOMESTICA FACTA, are more interesting, as well as more useful...." Dr. Johnson, though the author of the pseudo-oriental *Rasselas,* expressed the same idea earlier than Warton, and more frequently. Nicholas Rowe, Aaron Hill, and John Home illustrate the tendency to use the "annals of England" popularly in tragedy. Thomas Leland's *Longsword* (1762) marks the same purpose in fiction. George Lillo and his friend Henry Fielding are among the numerous authors who use "daily life" in the drama, the novel, the essay-story, or in poetry.

Medieval-ism

If a genuine thirst for novelty cannot be quenched by classical story, it is not likely to be satisfied for long by stories of one's own day. There was a turning from the "annals of England" as well as from Greece and Rome, a turning that took two lines of escape, one temporal, the other geographic. The first was a return to the Middle Ages. This sort of "revival" is always going on. Milton meditated the Arthurian legend as a subject; Dryden retold several medieval tales; Blackmore wrote Arthurian epics, and Pope added greatly to the fame of one medieval love story by his poem *Eloisa to Abelard.* He might have done more had he written his projected epic about Brutus, the founder of the British nation. This interest in medieval story was intensified by the middle of the century. Frequently it extended, as in the case of Richard Hurd, to hardly more than the chivalry of Spenser's *Faerie Queene;* at times, as in the case of Gray, it included Scandinavian lore.[8] There was also an increased interest in Welsh and Irish stories,[9] and Macpherson achieved an extravagant success in his Ossian. At times, of course, medievalism became mere clap-trap, as in Walpole's influential *Castle of Otranto.*

Oriental Exoticism

The other escapist path led to remote lands. Under the stimulus of *The Arabian Nights,* first translated into occidental languages in the first two decades of the century, and of Jesuit "relations" as well as of the literature

[8] Frank E. Farley, *Scandinavian Influences in the English Romantic Movement* (Boston, 1903).
[9] Edward D. Snyder, *The Celtic Revival in English Literature, 1760-1800* (Cambridge, Mass., 1923); Russell K. Alspach, *Irish Poetry from the English Invasion to 1798* (1943).

of travel and trade, there were definite idealizations of Chinese, Persian, Arabian, and other Oriental peoples. These again were not new, nor were they ever vividly realistic. "Local color" and particularity were not yet. In the Oriental tale we get usually a medium for philosophizing. This is most marked in *Rasselas*. The love of oriental luxury and magnificence is seldom so stressed as in Beckford's *Vathek* (1786).

Another sort of incidental material that came much into use was outdoor scenery.[10] After the example of James Thomson writers used landscape increasingly because of a deistical preoccupation with the design of the universe or of a more orthodox belief in the benevolence of the Deity as seen in His works. The use of landscape backgrounds in novels was encouraged by Rousseau's *Julie* (1761). Landscapes turn up somewhat unexpectedly in such novels as Thomas Amory's *John Buncle* (1756-66) and Richard Graves's satirical story *The Spiritual Quixote* (1773). By the time of Ann Radcliffe the use of landscape illustrates what Ruskin was to stigmatize as "the pathetic fallacy." Cowper and possibly some others felt at least a medicinal, if not a spiritual, influence from nature; but Wordsworth had yet to formulate and vivify such concepts in poetry. *Description of Landscape*

Preoccupation with landscape, like other novelties in subject matter here mentioned, was induced from books as well as from life. It was an easily acquired focus of attention. The unstable equipoise of the sensitive mind— Cowper's, for example—sought tranquillity outside itself in nature, and it had not far to seek, for in the eighteenth century one could walk from central London into the country, and apart from London there were few large towns.[11] To the end of the century England was still a nation of villagers and husbandmen. Even the woolen industry was for the most part rural rather than urban: the factory system was largely the invention of the early nineteenth century, though the increase in coal mining and the mechanical inventions of Arkwright and Watt had fully prepared the way during the last third of the century for the institution of large factories. At the moment, however, industrial matters had little place in literature. In spite of Blake's prompt perception (1804) of the evil of "dark Satanic mills," even he recognized that largely England was still a "green and pleasant land." For the most part poets were to be and to remain preoccupied with greenness and pleasantness. *Approaching Economic Changes*

The subject matter of literature in the later eighteenth century thus added new and varied materials, and at the same time writers became in manner

---

[10] Alfred Biese, *The Development of the Feeling for Nature in the Middle Ages and Modern Times* (1905).

[11] According to the census of 1801 London was a city of about 900,000 inhabitants. The changes in size of certain English cities were due to their positions as ports: Bristol had a population of 64,000; Liverpool had displaced Chester as a northwest port, and had grown rapidly to 78,000; Plymouth had 43,000. Of the mushroom manufacturing towns Manchester-Salford had 84,000, Birmingham 74,000, and Leeds 53,000. Of the older towns of importance Norwich, possibly in 1660 the second city of England, was now eighth with 37,000 inhabitants. Other towns that had populations of between thirty and forty thousand were Bath, Portsmouth-Portsea, Sheffield, and Hull. Twenty-five towns had populations of between ten and twenty-five thousand.

and form less dependent on classical genres. Above all, the tone became more elegant and soft. One has only to contrast Swift and Burke (both of whom knew how to inflame) or Pope and Cowper or Addison's *Cato* and Home's *Douglas* to see the effects of increasing sentiment or fervor. There is no great increase in intellectual power; there is perhaps (Blake apart) none in imaginative power; but there is an increased effort for emotional appeal. This is objectively visible if we compare the method of Hogarth with that of the popular illustrator of books Thomas Stothard (1755-1834). Stothard embodies the spirit of his time in that his every line is graceful and elegant. He lacks the harsh robustness of Hogarth—is, in fact, somewhat anemic if placed beside that great graphic satirist; but his appeal is more facile and more agreeable. So perhaps is the appeal of the latter half of the eighteenth century as compared with the earlier half.

II

Opinions of Critics

As the eighteenth century moved on, there were changes of emphasis and tone with regard to many critical positions. There was no small amount of confused statement, in large part due to failure of the critic to make clear whether he was talking about (*a*) the nature of literature itself, (*b*) the psychological experience of enjoying literature, (*c*) the processes involved in the creation of literature, or (*d*) the intellectual process of evaluating literary achievement. The conscious changes in doctrine were less trenchant than they seem at first sight. *Rules* and *imitation* continued a tendency to become "indecent" words; but the art of literature remained representational (mimetic) in the minds of practically all writers except Blake, and the battle between controlled and spontaneous art continued—with much of the shouting done by the believers in spontaneity.

In the case of imitation there were changes in doctrine which are not easily analyzed without false simplification or systematization. Pope in the preface to his *Works* (1717) had modestly justified his youthful efforts by the statement, "All that is left us is to recommend our productions by the imitation of the Ancients." This statement should be compared with the more intelligent remarks on imitation in the first Observation[1] affixed to Book 1 of his translation of the *Iliad*—and with other such passages. Failing such comparisons, critics have placed Pope too easily among the supporters of servile rather than emulous imitation. That he was so placed was in part due to his official editor, pugnacious William Warburton, who expounded Pope *ex cathedra,* and was by accident or through controversies hostile to views expressed by others, such as Akenside, Spence, and Joseph Warton.

To an edition of Horace's *Epistle to Augustus* Warburton's friend Richard Hurd in 1751 added a *Dissertation on Poetical Imitation,* which attempted to defend something more or less like Pope's true position. "Every wondrous *original,* which ages have gazed at, as the offspring of creative fancy" is, so Hurd asserts, the result of "mimetic arts"—"is itself but a *copy,* a transcript from some brighter page of this vast volume of the universe." Whatever originality we can achieve must lie in our *manner* of imitation or representation. Homer in "rosy-fingered" conveys the "precise idea," and

---

[1] "Observations," p. 5 (of the first edition): "Imitation does not hinder Invention: We may observe the Rules of Nature, and write in the Spirit of those who have best hit upon them, without taking the same Track, beginning in the same Manner, and following the Main of their Story almost step by step; as most of the modern Writers of Epic Poetry have done."

so shows original genius. "General appearances," or the "objects of imitation," are a common stock; it is the effect of the poet's mind operating on these objects that will show his originality. There are obviously servile imitators, whom Hurd is ready to "resign to the shame and censure which have so justly followed them in all ages." "Successful imitation" is another matter. The two types of imitators suggest the journalistic formula of lofty "Parnassians" and vile "Grubeans" so much used in the pages of the *Grub-street Journal* twenty years before Hurd wrote.

Hurd's friends at Cambridge—including Thomas Gray and William Mason—were evidently interested, and at Mason's request Hurd wrote another dissertation, *On the Marks of Imitation* (1757). This is somewhat less theoretical, but in it from various favorite passages by many poets Hurd defends parallel expressions of ideas or sentiments.

Hurd's views were by no means accepted by all his contemporaries, though clearly they were not unusual. Dr. Johnson, at about the same time, in *Rambler* No. 143, condemned plagiarism but allowed imitative echoing of the "successful" sort. The blunt dictum of *Rasselas,* chapter x, that "no man was ever great by imitation," represents another aspect of the case, which the Doctor possibly would not always support. Boswell much later speaks of Hurd's commentaries as of the "Warburtonian School," and that label would not indicate popularity. To Joseph Warton the notes of Pope's first editor are not always pleasing, but he speaks pleasantly of "the ingenious Mr. Hurd," and in his oftenest quoted piece of criticism, his *Essay on Pope* (1756), he seldom, if ever, disparages any but ineffective imitation. In the *Adventurer* No. 63 (June 12, 1753) he commended several passages in which Pope had improved hints from others, and in this paper Warton speaks of poetry as "an art whose essence is imitation." [2] In the same passage he praises originality as a superlative and inevitably rare achievement. Edward Gibbon in his *Journal* for 1762 rigorously interprets Hurd's argument as an attempt to make anything but imitation impossible. Hurd, he says, "endeavours to prove, by a very elaborate deduction, that both the ideas, and the methods, employed by the ancients, were not only *natural ones,* but the *sole natural ones;* so that if succeeding poets, endued with judgment, looked abroad into nature, they not only *might,* but *must* meet with them; while men of irregular fancies could avoid *them only* by avoiding truth and probability." Hurd's position Gibbon regards as extreme.

Young's Conjectures   It was, so Warton said, Pope's remark in his preface of 1717 that led Dr. Young, author of *Night Thoughts,* to write in his old age a pamphlet called *Conjectures on Original Composition in a Letter to the Author of "Sir Charles Grandison"* (1759). Boswell records that Johnson, to whom the *Conjectures* were read before publication, "was surprized to find Young receive as

---

[2] His brother Thomas, in the preface to his *Five Pastoral Eclogues* (1745), says, "The learned reader will observe, that the author has endeavour'd to imitate the simplicity of the ancients in these pieces, as thinking it not only more particularly adapted to pastoral, but the true ornament of all kinds of poetry in general." Ancient simplicity and "romantic" simplicity are frequently indistinguishable.

novelties, what he thought very common maxims"; but in spite of this expert opinion, historians in general have regarded Young as here advanced in his views. In many respects he agrees perfectly with Warton. While "imitation must be the lot (and often an honourable lot it is) of most writers," it is one's first duty and highest possible achievement to be "original." If all the literati could have read Young's *Conjectures,* perhaps he might have achieved the banishment, not of the representational concept of literature but of the notion of imitation as copying other masterpieces. In the *Conjectures* originality is not, as sometimes elsewhere, confused with novelty. Originality to Young consists in going back to the originals of things, in not going to "copies" made by others. Unlike Pope's Maro, he finds that Homer and Nature are *not* the same, though both must be very highly regarded; and the discovery, if not precisely new, is one that in his day had to be made again and again. His other significant doctrine is his insistence on the importance of the mind of the writer. *Know thyself; reverence thyself:* these are his two remedial principles. Genius comes before learning; "the divinely-inspired enthusiast" before "the well-accomplished scholar." In spite of his high metaphorical style, Young's effectiveness lay in his enthusiastic tone rather than in much of his content. The Warburtonians did not like the pamphlet, which seems to have aroused little immediate interest in England. Its influence in Germany, where it had some vogue, has been variously estimated. Young's essential position on imitation had been more quietly stated by Burke two years earlier when he remarked that poets had been "confined in so narrow a circle" because "they have been rather imitators of one another than of nature."

The best example of the continuance of conservative ideas on imitation *Reynolds'* may be seen in the fifteen *Discourses* of Sir Joshua Reynolds, delivered Discourses before the Royal Academy during the years 1769 to 1790. These lectures, in spite of William Blake's contempt for them, are a distinguished statement of the case for traditionalism and mimesis in the art of painting. They apply equally well to literature. Reynolds does not too much stress rules, but thinks some attention to them is essential. "The rules by which men of extraordinary parts . . . work, are either such as they discover by their own peculiar observations, or of such a nice texture as not easily to admit being expressed in words"; but, even unexpressed, "they are still seen and felt in the mind of the artist." Artists must begin by imitating other artists, but their goal is the representation of ideal beauty in the "great style." Again and again he insists, "This idea of the perfect state of nature, which the artist calls the ideal beauty, is the great leading principle by which works of genius are conducted." What Dr. Johnson says bluntly ("Nothing can please many, and please long, but just representations of general nature") Reynolds says with elegant dignity and with noble and subtle reasoning that makes him the most impressive defender of mimesis and of tradition in his century.

Thus the question of imitation was kept alive; though Sir Joshua's reiteration of his views may indicate that he felt restatement necessary because of

Poetry and
Painting

apparent lack of receptiveness on the part of the young artists of his day. The prestige of imitation had of course been undermined by more than one writer on the graphic arts, in which the inferiority of merely representing or "copying" nature was peculiarly apparent. In 1719 the Abbé Du Bos had brought out a work ultimately translated by Thomas Nugent as *Critical Reflections on Poetry, Painting, and Music* (3 volumes, 1748). Even before the translation appeared similar discourses on the allied arts were fashionable. After 1750 they were numerous. Among the most influential early works doubtless Joseph Spence's *Polymetis* (1747) should stand first. These genteel dialogues developing a parallel between Roman poetry and ancient sculpture were ushered into the world after long preparation with a list of subscribers worthy of Pope himself. In some sense this work supplanted Andrew Tooke's *Pantheon* (1698), which Swift had forced upon Lady Acheson in an endeavor to improve her taste. *Polymetis* doubtless was of aid in the Greek revival of the later century and prepared a public for the beautiful sculpture of John Flaxman. To some extent these parallels between the arts undermined false notions of mimesis and encouraged sound redefinitions of aesthetic principles in the belles lettres.

As the century progressed, talk about imitation decreased. It was agreed that imitations of masterpieces were generally inferior to direct imitations of nature, called "originals."

Originality
and Genius

Talk about "genius" and "imagination" certainly increased: these were the good words. *Genius* had by the mid-century supplanted *wit* as the creative force in an author's mind. Following a remark from *Spectator* No. 253, the Abbé Yart in his critical sketch of Pope's career observes, in fashion typical of the time, that "wit consists in adorning well-known thoughts, but genius is creative." [3] More commonly genius is associated with *original* (almost a synonym of *creative*),[4] and this fact indicates a tendency to abandon the well-worn stories of Greece and Rome. Dr. Johnson himself was an ardent proponent of *domestica facta,* and disparaged the use of classical stories and even of classical allusions. The Trojans, he asserted apropos of Pope's projected *Brutus,* "were a race upon whom imagination has been exhausted and attention wearied." One remembers also his lack of interest in Catiline and the Punic Wars. This appetite for new material hardly agrees with Hurd's idea that originality can consist only in manner, and it indicates Johnson's sympathy with the popular search for new materials. Joseph Warton was on record to the same effect. The desire of novelty drove authors to escape from classical material by turning to realism or by going to exotic subject matter—Peruvian, American, Indian, Scandinavian, Mohammedan, or Chinese. Bishop Lowth's Latin lectures *De Sacra Poesi Hebraeorum* (1753), which went through several editions and were finally (1793) translated into English, certainly stimulated the already keen taste for the so-called *style oriental.* In the work of a writer lacking genius these exotic

[3] *Idée de la poësie angloise,* III (1753). 18n.
[4] Paul Kaufman, "Heralds of Original Genius," in *Essays in Memory of Barrett Wendell* (Cambridge, Mass., 1926), pp. 191-222.

materials would be classed as somewhat grotesque novelties; the "original genius" alone can effectively "explore unbeaten tracks ... invent new designs, and perfect the productions of Art."

Such at least was the opinion of one of the clearest and most methodical *Duff on* of the many writers about genius, William Duff (1732-1815). When this *Genius* pious Scot published his *Essay on Original Genius* (1767), so much had been written on the subject that he made no pretense of novelty in many of his views and hence may serve as a convenient summarizer. The most important ingredient of genius was generally thought to be imagination; but Duff, with apology, adds other elements that temper and exalt each other. The effect, Duff tells us, of "a plastic and comprehensive imagination, an acute intellect, and an exquisite sensibility and refinement of taste" in union, "will be very extraordinary." He always glorified imagination, but still judgment is once or twice mentioned as a sensible guide to the glowing and impulsive faculty. Wit and Humor are "nearly allied to true Genius," but are the offspring of "a rambling and sportive Fancy," while Genius "proceeds from the copious effusions of a plastic Imagination." Swift was a wit rather than a genius of any "exalted kind"; Ossian was obviously no wit. This dichotomy of interest, especially since Duff, suggests that "men of genius, conscious of possessing superior talents, are not very ambitious of acquiring the reputation which arises from Wit." Such ideas become the highway from the *riant* art of the classical age to the mansions of high seriousness. But Duff can still see that "Genius derives vivacity from Wit, and Wit derives justness and extent of comprehension from Genius." In view of attempts at philosophical poetry in his day it is interesting to find him asserting that while "Original Philosophic Genius is that which is distinguished by regularity, clearness, and accuracy, ... Original Genius in poetry is that whose essential properties are a noble irregularity, vehemence, and enthusiasm." We later learn that to Duff the normal manifestation of irregularity is "a mixture of great beauties and blemishes," and that Shakespeare illustrates the quality. The path of Genius, "as the course of a comet, is blazing, though irregular; and its errors and excellencies are equally inimitable." The cult of correctness is losing its charm.

So also is the Renaissance idea that a poetic genius should be learned. One *Genius and* may depend on the force of nature as sufficient aid, and may believe in *Learning* geniuses quite untaught. Joseph Spence and some Wiltshire friends had stimulated these ideas when in 1730 they sent up to court "the thresher poet," Stephen Duck. Spence's account of Magliabecchi and even his insistence on Alexander Pope's rôle as automath also indicate his obsession with the force of nature as effective inspirer. Young enthusiastically proclaims: "Many a Genius, probably, there has been, which could neither write, nor read." This would have appalled Rymer or even the dunce who asserted bluntly that Pope had not that sufficient learning necessary to make a true poet. Shakespeare again was the chief exhibit among unlearned geniuses;

but after Stephen Duck had achieved royal patronage the number of them became legion.

Imagination   The force of nature manifested itself in geniuses through imagination. This commonplace of the seventeenth century was enthusiastically reiterated by critics throughout the Augustan period. The poets of the eighteenth century seem particularly fond of stressing the creative in this connection.[5] Joseph Warton, who as a critic affected the word, used it most notably in his dedication to his *Essay on Pope* when he announced that "it is a creative and glowing IMAGINATION, *acer spiritus ac vis*, and that alone" that can entitle a writer to the name of poet.[6] There is no serious objection on the part of his contemporaries to this view, nor is there any serious analysis of the creative imagination as seen in operation. The tone and frequency of such remarks is more novel and significant than is their content. We still find in Duff's *Essay* and elsewhere insistence on the old alliance of imagination and judgment. In one passage Duff makes imagination subordinate to judgment. Unregulated imagination, he thinks, may "throw glaring colours on objects that possess no intrinsic excellence," and thus "mislead the mind." More than once this element of *glare* is mentioned by critics with disfavor.

Sympathetic   Duff's generation made perhaps its chief contribution to an understand-
Imagination ing of the imagination by adapting principles concerning the association of ideas and by a notion of intuitive, sentimental, or "sympathetic" imagination.[7] From 1749, when David Hartley's *Observations on Man* appeared, down to Archibald Alison's *Essays on Taste* (1790) and of course even to Coleridge's day, critics made increasing use of association of ideas in explaining imaginative appeal. Duff specifies also a duality of function in the imagination that harks back perhaps to the days of Hobbes: the faculty had both powers of association and powers of creation. Wit and humor are, as in the days of Hobbes, associational; but poetic genius now is creative. These views are interesting further because Duff tends, in anticipation of Wordsworth and Coleridge, to name the associative power, *fancy*.[8]

Taste and   From early in the century views of the imagination were tied up with
Judgment another favorite topic: *taste*. Addison and others had stressed the power of imagination to refine taste, to make one in some sort the *honnête homme;* and the later century, equally devoted to refined elegance, wrote interminably on the subject. It was largely accident if concepts of taste undermined neo-classical uniformity. That was not the intention. The situation was that, having like sensible men first abandoned the authority of Aristotle and the ancients for the authority of those indefinable absolutes, Truth (*Rien n'est*

---

[5] Logan Pearsall Smith, "Four Words: Romantic, Originality, Creative, Genius," *S.P.E. Tract* No. XVII (1924), pp. 21-22.
[6] See Hoyt Trowbridge, "Joseph Warton on the Imagination," *MP*, XXXV (1937). 73-87 (esp. pp. 82-84).
[7] Walter J. Bate, "The Sympathetic Imagination in Eighteenth-Century English Criticism," *ELH*, XII (1945). 144-164.
[8] John Bullitt and Walter J. Bate, "The Distinctions between Fancy and Imagination in Eighteenth-Century English Criticism," *MLN*, LX (1945). 8-15.

beau que le vrai), Nature (the source, end, and test of art), and Reason (which "wants not Horace to support it"), they were next compelled, as good empiricists, to limit their regard to the authority of experience, which was "taste." Nature methodized gave rules; experience methodized gave taste. In the realm of judicial criticism the one was to replace the other: taste was to be a faculty of judgment.

More readily, however, from the Addisonian point of approach, taste became a faculty of enjoyment. Taste may be innate in part, but training is likely to be stressed as an aid. Through refinement of imagination, one associates the "right" ideas—not the vulgar. Dr. John Armstrong in his poem *Taste* [9] (1753) is still echoing Pope's outcry against the crude false taste of the *nouveaux riches*. Enjoyment of the best depends on delicate sensibility. It is not, except for critical judgments, necessary to transmute sensibility into a standard. In his important essay *Of the Standard of Taste* (1757) Hume in stating a point of view different from his own makes a distinction between sentiment and judgment that really is not alien to his own way of thinking: *Taste and Enjoyment*

Hume on Taste

All sentiment is right; because sentiment has a reference to nothing beyond itself, and is always real, wherever a man is conscious of it. But all determinations of the understanding are not right; because they have a reference to something beyond themselves, to wit, real matter of fact; and are not always conformable to that standard. Among a thousand different opinions . . . there is one, and but one, that is just and true; and the only difficulty is to fix and ascertain it.

Taste as a faculty of enjoyment, then, is quite subjective and unpredictable so far as particular enjoyments go. In another essay, *Of the Delicacy of Taste and Passion,* Hume praises this sensibility as desirably refined and as tempering our interest in the cruder passions of real life. He gives us the cool, well-bred point of view of the eighteenth-century Francophile.

But even if the *enjoyment* of literature can be left, within genteel limits, to individualism, taste as a faculty of *judgment* is in theory quite another thing. Hume summarizes an opinion somewhat divergent from his own as saying that "Beauty is no quality in things themselves: It exists merely in the mind which contemplates them; and each mind perceives a different beauty." For enjoyment this may do, but for the further purpose of evaluation we must search for what Hume calls "a *Standard of Taste;* a rule, by which the various sentiments of men may be reconciled; at least, a decision, afforded, confirming one sentiment and condemning another." Hume himself asserts: "Though it be certain, that beauty and deformity . . . are not qualities in objects, but belong entirely to the sentiment; . . . it must be allowed, that there are certain qualities in objects, which are fitted by nature to produce those particular feelings." It is on this correspondence between cause in the object and effect in the sentiment that Hume bases his belief

[9] *Taste* is probably the most readable of this medicinal poet's writings. For an account of his amazingly varied friendships with many literary folk see the excellent article by Lewis M. Knapp, "Dr. John Armstrong, Littérateur . . . ," *PMLA,* LIX (1944). 1019-1058.

..andard of taste. In similar fashion Alexander Gerard in his more
..sive *Essay on Taste* (1759) by implication differentiates the tasteful
..ader from the critic: [10] "A critic must not only *feel*, but possess that
accuracy of discernment, which enables a person to *reflect* upon his feelings
with distinctness, and to explain them to others." In 1759 Burke prefixed to
his *Sublime and Beautiful* an introduction in which he also insists that the
recording faculty is essential as an ingredient in taste. In general, so far as
"taste" critics focused attention on nameless graces, on the *je ne sais quoi*,
they headed towards a subjective anarchy in criticism; but with regard to
other "graces" their normal aim was to replace outworn sanctions by a
criterion empirically established. In his important dissertation *Of the
Standard of Taste*, Hume, as a conservative disciple of French taste, was
impelled towards the belief that a uniform standard of excellence exists;
but, as a skeptic, he could not feel that such a standard could easily be determined. "Every voice," he says, "is united in applauding elegance, propriety,
simplicity, spirit in writing; and in blaming fustian, affectation, coldness,
and a false brilliancy: But when critics come to particulars, this seeming
unanimity vanishes; and it is found, that they had affixed a very different
meaning to their expressions." The quotation perhaps exaggerates the skeptical nature of Hume's conclusion. He goes on to show how the standard
of taste is to be determined, and is able to conclude thus: "But in reality the
difficulty of finding, even in particulars, the standard of taste, is not so great
as it is represented. Though in speculation, we may readily avow a certain
criterion in science and deny it in sentiment, the matter is found in practice
to be much more hard to ascertain in the former case than in the latter."
He holds that even "amidst all the variety and caprices of taste, there are
certain general principles of approbation or blame," but the difficulty is that
"though the principles of taste be universal, and, nearly, if not entirely the
same in all men; yet few are qualified to give judgment on any work of
art, or establish their own sentiment as the standard of beauty." The critic,
he sees, may lack delicacy, or such sureness as comes from practice, or the
skill that compares works justly, or the necessary freedom from bias. The
fundamental difficulty lies in "the different humours of particular men" or
in "the particular manners and opinions of our age and country."

The Galli-
cism of
Hume's
Taste

Of this last limitation, it may be remarked parenthetically, Hume himself
is a sweet example. His Francophile manners, for instance, amusingly lead
him to adopt the current reservations as to Homer's heroes: "The sage
Ulysses in the Greek poet seems to delight in lies and fictions.... But his
more scrupulous son, in the French epic writer,[11] exposes himself to the
most imminent perils, rather than depart from the most exact line of truth
and veracity." Of the death of old Memnon in Rowe's *Ambitious Stepmother* it is easy for him to say, "The English theatre abounds too much
with such shocking images." His encouragement of his friend and cousin,

10 The Select Society of Edinburgh had awarded Gerard's *Essay* a prize. Hume had been
one of the judges, and he helped see the *Essay* through the press.
11 The reference is to Fénelon's *Avantures de Télémaque fils d'Ulysse* (1699).

John Home, the author of *Douglas,* is sufficient evidence of his loyalty to old Scotia's grandeur. Significantly in a letter he urged Home: "For God's sake, read Shakespeare, but get Racine and Sophocles by heart. It is reserved for you, and you alone, to redeem our stage from the reproach of barbarism." Such an adviser could readily see the French objections to Shakespeare.

This elegant, clear-eyed critic was not the man to break a butterfly on the wheel; but more than one of his contemporaries was. In analyzing taste they could not be content with Hume's admired universals—"elegance, propriety, simplicity, spirit"—as telling adequately what qualities please the imagination. In largest terms these qualities were to them the beautiful, the sublime, and, sometimes, the picturesque.[12] The first two of these were incessantly subjected to analysis in this period. The greatest English painter of the midcentury, William Hogarth (1697-1764), gave an influential and typical account of the first in his *Analysis of Beauty* (1753), where appeal is said to arise from the following: fitness of the parts in a design, variety, uniformity, regularity or symmetry (but these can only subserve fitness or design), simplicity, intricacy, and magnitude (the cause of admiration and awe). Burke in his *Sublime and Beautiful* did not admit fitness, proportion, or perfection as sources of beauty, but named different elements in his more psychological analysis into such component parts as smallness, smoothness, variation from straight lines, delicacy, and color. Alexander Gerard, making beauty one of several principles of taste (which are, according to him, novelty, grandeur, beauty, imitation, harmony, ridicule, and virtue), analyzes it into figure (uniformity, variety, proportion), utility (fitness to design), and color.

Analysis of Beauty

And so, with variations, these qualities were again and again regurgitated. In 1761 Dodsley reprinted Spence's *Crito* (1752), in which beauty falls under the four heads of color, form, expression, and grace. Spence regarded virtue as the chief beauty, and it may be said in passing that most of these men, however much they expatiate on the beautiful, were at heart moralists. Lord Kames in his *Elements of Criticism* (1762) based beauty and ugliness on the emotions of pleasure and pain, after the fashion of Hume and many others; and Kames reverted to earlier theorists for the idea that beauty belongs to objects of sight and is either intrinsic or relative to other objects. The constituent parts of intrinsic beauty he found to be utility, color, figure (which depends on regularity, uniformity, proportion, order, simplicity), motion, and simplicity. He stressed most, perhaps, figure and simplicity.

---

[12] Since the "picturesque," the seeing of landscape itself or the use of it in terms of the graphic arts, is not early formalized in theory, it is not further treated here. While picturesqueness dominated the literary use of landscape for two-thirds of a century, it was theorized late chiefly by William Gilpin and Sir Uvedale Price. Its early manifestations grew out of schools of landscape painting or gardening or out of accidental personal interests uniting the graphic arts and literature in such individuals, for example, as John Dyer, Jonathan Richardson, William Mason, William Shenstone, Philip de Loutherbourg, etc. The idea of picturesqueness influenced profoundly the description of landscape, but it did not receive the repeated analysis bestowed on the beautiful and the sublime. See Elizabeth W. Manwaring, *Italian Landscape in Eighteenth Century England* (1925), Christopher Hussey, *The Picturesque* (1927), Chauncey B. Tinker, *Painter and Poet* (Cambridge, Mass., 1938).

In 1790 Archibald Alison in his *Essays on the Nature and Principles of Taste* adopted a newer method of approach, the association of ideas, upon which rather than perception he based aesthetic pleasure.

Analysis of the Sublime: Burke

Contemplation of the *disiecta membra* of beauty was not enough: the sublime must also be anatomized. Before the mid-century there were glimmerings of this attempt, and possibly the two most significant relationships stressed are the relation of the sublime to novelty or astonishment, which harks back to a baroque theory of art, and its relation to the pathetic. Writers such as John Baillie [13] (for whom chiefly vastness but also novelty and uniformity stimulate the sublime mood) and Bishop Lowth [14] (who commends agitation, amplification, and passion, as sublime) groped towards analysis; but Edmund Burke first arrived at detailed and avowed sources of the mood. In his early work, *A Philosophical Enquiry into the Origin of Our Ideas of the Sublime and Beautiful* (1757), he based the sublime emotions on terror, and on the astonishment and amazement that accompany terror. These subsidiary states of mind recall not merely Longinus but the appeal that even the early seventeenth century found in baroque art. The qualities stimulating these sublime emotions are listed as obscurity ("It is one thing to make an idea clear, and another to make it affecting to the imagination"), power, privation (i.e., vacuity, darkness, solitude, and silence), vastness, infinity (including succession, uniformity, and magnitude), difficulty (i.e., objects or effects that are the result of "immense force"), magnificence (profusion plus, sometimes, a desirable disorder), light, color, loud sounds, as well as other sensory and emotional affects. This is clearly a confusingly inclusive list, which provoked both hostility and discipleship. Burke used physiological as well as psychological data, and found the theory of the association of ideas somewhat useful. In his opinion that the strongest sublime emotion is one of distress, he came dangerously near to wedding sublimity and sentimentalism. Unsatisfactory as Burke's thought may appear, his point of view is purely scientific and disinterested. He was simply describing mental reactions to certain types of stimulation; he had no purpose either to heighten enjoyment or to guide judgment. Yet in his purely descriptive function he had no idea that he was at work on a subjective chaos. In the introduction "On Taste" he said: "If taste has no fixed principles, if the imagination is not affected according to some invariable and certain laws, our labour is likely to be employed to very little purpose; as it must be judged an useless, if not an absurd undertaking, to lay down rules for caprice and to set up for a legislator of whims and fancies." Principles, standards, even rules, are not yet intentionally replaced by "individualism," but the appeal of subject matter is rapidly being redefined in very new terms.

Burke was followed by dozens of writers and analysts. Gerard in his *Essay on Taste* relates the sublime to quantity or amplitude, to simplicity,

---

[13] *An Essay on the Sublime* (1747).
[14] Robert Lowth (1710-1787), *De Sacra Poesi Hebraeorum Praelectiones* (1753).

to vastness, etc., but not to terror. Lord Kames in his *Elements of Criticism* *Others on* devoted a conventional chapter to "Grandeur and Sublimity." Priestley's *the Sublime* ideas combined views of Gerard and Hartley. Blair objected, in lectures delivered in 1759 and later, to founding the sublime solely on terror or on vastness; he preferred "mighty force or power." It is unnecessary to list further suggestions. The critics here mentioned show that by no psychological technique available could satisfactory principles or rules for a faculty of judgment be deduced. Unintentionally what these analysts had accomplished was a shift from the relatively unified sanctions of Reason, Truth, and Nature to dozens of new and diverse qualities that appealed to imagination. While hunting through experience for a uniform standard, they introduced the Trojan horse, diversity.

They hardly accomplished more in the direction of a standard than to *Permanence* stress such criteria as permanence and universality of appeal, but these had *and* already been derived at least in part from the anti-rationalist concept of *Historical* common sense (*consensus gentium*). The criterion of permanence of appeal *Criticism* had an interesting development in the historical criticism which was practiced much in the later century. It centers, perhaps accidentally, on the study of such authors as Homer, Shakespeare, and Spenser. There was in editing masterpieces a strong scholarly tradition, paralleled by a more genteel amateurish tradition. From Richard Bentley and Tom Hearne to Richard Porson and Edmond Malone there were fine scholars who were good editors. Though this sound scholarship aided the editors of Shakespeare, most of them from Rowe to Blair were ready, as Bishop Percy was with his ballads, to falsify without warning as well as to modernize the original texts with which they dealt. But after the work of Pope and Theobald it was obviously necessary to study an author's vocabulary in the light of his own generation. Elizabethan puns and humor were explained as the result of the dramatist's necessary appeal to the groundlings. Similarly, as we have seen in Hume's remark on Odysseus's disregard of honesty, there were things to be explained about Homer's heroes. These, among other matters, were discussed in such works as Thomas Blackwell's *Enquiry into the Life and Writings of Homer* (1735) and Robert Wood's *Essay on the Original Genius and Writings of Homer* (1769). One remark by Wood explains his point of view: "I must confess I am a little surprized ... that those who have affected to discover so perfect a system of morals and politics in Homer, should have bestowed so little consideration upon the character of the times for which this instruction was calculated." And Wood suggests that the age of Homer differed from that of Madam Dacier "as we do ... from our Gothic ancestors in the days of Chivalry and Romance." Relative conditions as formative of genius were becoming important for the critic's thorough understanding of a masterpiece, not merely of its morals but of its entire nature as well. This type of study is best illustrated by Thomas Warton's *Observations on the Faerie Queene* (1754, 1762). To aid the critic of Spenser, Warton says, "I have considered the customs and genius of his age; I have searched his contemporary writers, and examined the books on which the peculiarities of his style, taste and composition, are confessedly founded." Beside this passage may be placed his repeated belief that in criticizing our "elder poets ... not only a competent knowledge of all antient classical learning is requisite, but also an acquaintance with those books, which, though now forgotten and lost, were yet in repute about the time in which each author respectively wrote, and which it is most likely he had read." In such remarks we see the scholarly critical conscience growing; the first law of sound criticism is to be complete understanding. Thomas Warton was not a systematic historian, but his pioneer *History of English Poetry* (3 volumes, 1774-81) is full of a rich store of learning and of admiration for the Middle Ages.[15] His enthusiasm was shared by Richard Hurd, who, in glorifying "Gothic Chivalry," found, as did others of his day, its best embodiment in *The Faerie Queene*. Hurd's *Letters on Chivalry and Romance* (1762) show the same revulsion from the pedestrian life of his own day that Horace Walpole was expressing in his *Castle of Otranto*. Hurd sees that common-sense *vraisemblance* has "perfectly dissolved ... the magic of the old Romances," and he concludes with his well-known lament for the loss of "fine fabling."

The Drift of Opinion   This "romantic" observation comes from a critic who, it must be remembered, was an ardent defender of imitation. Such apparent confusion must be expected in most so-called "liberal" critics of the time. It is customary to read Joseph Warton's dedication to his *Essay on Pope* and having read no further pronounce him a revolutionary. But Warton always regarded Pope as among the half-dozen first poets of England: his dedication simply calls attention to the fact that Pope, while the greatest of poets in the genres he attempted, did not attempt the highest genres. It should be remembered also that Warton appended to the first volume of Virgil's *Works in Latin and English* (1753) "Reflections on Didactic Poetry," which, even if colored by the idea that "Men love to be moved, much better than to be instructed," is lacking neither in sympathy for this type of poetry nor in the magisterial tone sometimes associated with rules of criticism. It is, then, possible to exaggerate the conscious "romanticism" of such men as Young, Hurd, and the Wartons. It is wise to remember that the best brains of the mid-century— Hume, Gibbon, Reynolds, and Dr. Johnson—were in many respects the most fervent "classicists" of the whole century. The drift was away from authority, tradition, and formalism, to diversity, to originality, and to admiration of a "creative and glowing IMAGINATION, *acer spiritus ac vis.*" This drift, fortunately or unfortunately, was not entirely conscious: it was inconsistently maintained, and the opposition to parts of the tendency were stated with shrewdness and above all with magisterial emphasis.

---

[15] René Wellek, *The Rise of English Literary History* (Chapel Hill, 1941), gives a comprehensive view of the beginnings of historical criticism and of Warton's place in the development. On Hurd one may compare the divergent emphasis of two articles: Audley L. Smith, "Richard Hurd's *Letters on Chivalry and Romance*," ELH, VI (1939). 58-81; and Hoyt Trowbridge, "Bishop Hurd: a Reinterpretation," PMLA, LVIII (1943). 450-465. On another aspect of historical criticism see Donald Foerster, "Mid-Eighteenth Century Scotch Criticism of Homer," SP, XL (1943). 425-446.

III

Dr. Johnson

Samuel Johnson (1709-1784), who at the age of fifty-five became Doctor *Samuel*
of Laws, and was thereafter known as "Doctor," was doubtless the most *Johnson*
magisterial among the conservatives of the later eighteenth century.[1] His
very great achievement was two-fold: that of writer and that of conversationalist. One might add a third function: being the subject of the greatest
biography ever written, that by James Boswell. Largely through Boswell's
picturesque efforts Johnson still lives, and through his own gifts in conversation as well as through Boswell's gifts in retailing small anecdotes, he lives
chiefly as a psychological eccentric—which he certainly was. In thinking of
him, however, as representative of his period and in some sense of his race,
we must not forget to conceive of him as a man of typical *mind*.

A native of Lichfield, son of a provincial bookseller, he contracted

[1] *The Works of Samuel Johnson,* ed. Sir John Hawkins and others (15v, 1787-9); Arthur
Murphy (12v, 1792); Oxford English Classics (11v, 1825).—*Poems,* ed. David Nichol Smith
and Edward L. McAdam (Oxford, 1941); *The Rambler,* ed. Alex. Chalmers, British Essayists,
Vols. XIX-XXII (1802); *Rasselas,* ed. Oliver F. Emerson (1895); Robert W. Chapman (1927);
The Idler, ed. Alex. Chalmers, British Essayists, Vols. XXXIII, XXXIV (1802); *A Journey to
the Western Islands of Scotland,* ed., with Boswell's *Tour,* Robert W. Chapman (1924); *The
Lives of the Poets,* ed. Mrs. Alexander Napier and John W. Hales (3v, 1890); Arthur Waugh
(6v, 1896); George Birkbeck Hill (3v, Oxford, 1905); *Johnsonian Miscellanies* (includes
Prayers and Meditations), ed. George Birkbeck Hill (2v, Oxford, 1897); *Prefaces & Dedications,*
ed. Allen T. Hazen (New Haven, 1937); *Letters,* ed. Hester Lynch [Thrale] Piozzi (2v, 1788);
George Birkbeck Hill (2v, Oxford, 1892, 1897); *The Queeney Letters* [from Johnson and Mrs.
Thrale to Hester Maria Thrale], ed. the Marquis of Lansdowne (1934). Dr. R. W. Chapman
is preparing a new edition of all Johnson's letters. The best bibliography of Johnson is that
by William P. Courtney and David Nichol Smith (1925). "A Supplement to Courtney" by
R. W. Chapman and A. T. Hazen appeared in *Proc....Oxford Bibl. Soc.,* v (1938). 117-166
— James Boswell, *Life of Samuel Johnson* (2v, 1791); ed. Edmond Malone (4v, 1799, 1804, etc);
John W. Croker (5v, 1831); George Birkbeck Hill (6v, 1887, rev. by L. F. Powell, 6v, 1934 —
in progress), and many other eds. Other biographical works about Johnson include those by
Hester Lynch Piozzi (*Anecdotes,* 1786; in Hill's *Johnsonian Miscellanies,* 1897; ed. S. C.
Roberts, Cambridge, 1925), Sir John Hawkins (1787), Arthur Murphy (1792), John W.
Croker (*Johnsoniana,* 1836), Alexander M. Broadley (*Dr. Johnson and Mrs. Thrale,* 1910),
Aleyn L. Reade (*Johnsonian Gleanings,* 10 Parts, 1909-46), Mildred C. Struble (*A Johnson
Handbook,* 1933), Sydney C. Roberts (*Dr. Johnson,* 1935), James L. Clifford (*Hester Lynch
Piozzi,* Oxford, 1941); Joseph W. Krutch (*Samuel Johnson,* 1944). — Of general interpretative
value are the following: Thomas B. (Lord) Macaulay, "Samuel Johnson" (*Edinburgh Review,*
Sept., 1831; ed. David Nichol Smith, Edinburgh, 1900; Chester N. Greenough, 1912); Thomas
Carlyle, "Samuel Johnson" (*Fraser's Magazine,* May, 1832; reprinted separately, 1853); Sir
Walter Raleigh, *Six Essays on Johnson* (1910); Chauncey B. Tinker, *Dr. Johnson and Fanny
Burney, Being the Johnsonian Passages from the Works of Mme d'Arblay* (1912); Percy H.
Houston, *Dr. Johnson: A Study in Eighteenth-Century Humanism* (Cambridge, Mass., 1923);
Joseph Epes Brown, *The Critical Opinions of Samuel Johnson* (Princeton, 1926); David Nichol
Smith, Robert W. Chapman, and L. F. Powell, *Johnson and Boswell Revised by Themselves
and Others* (three essays, Oxford, 1928); Hugh Kingsmill (ed.), *Johnson without Boswell:
A Contemporary Portrait* (1940); Bertrand H. Bronson, *Johnson and Boswell* (Berkeley, Calif.,
1944); Sydney C. Roberts, *Samuel Johnson* (British Academy Lecture, 1944).

His Educa-tion scrofula in infancy from his nurse, and thereby his eyesight was impaired. Nevertheless he grew up a lad of unusual physical strength and robustness as well as an omnivorous reader. In spite of poverty he was sent briefly, it seems (1728-9), to Pembroke College, Oxford, in which "nest of singing birds" he distinguished himself for his pride as well as for his learning. Of these poverty-stricken days, when tutors and students both loved him and thought him "a gay and frolicksome fellow," he said: "Sir, I was mad and violent. It was bitterness which they mistook for frolick. I was miserably poor, and thought to fight my way by my literature and my wit; so I disregarded all authority." Poverty drove him back to Lichfield without a degree, and for six years he was a schoolmaster or bookseller and, as always, a rapid and desultory reader. In 1731 he first became a published author when his Oxford friends printed without his consent his Latin version of Pope's *Messiah,* and in 1735 a friendly bookseller employed him to translate a book on Abyssinia. In this same year he married a widow twice his age, to whom beyond her death (1752) he remained touchingly devoted. By 1737 he had written a tragedy, *Irene,* and he thereupon hopefully abandoned schoolteaching and trudged up to London with one of his pupils named David Garrick. Thereafter Johnson was to be a Londoner.

Early Years in London In the metropolis he made curious, amusing, and useful friends. Richard Savage, whose *Life* Johnson wrote in 1744, initiated him into the seamy life of the hack writer, and Edward Cave, proprietor of *The Gentleman's Magazine,* gave him employment of various sorts, notably (1738-43) in helping prepare the semi-allegorical and almost illegal accounts of the "Senate of Lilliput," which gave the public some notion of the speeches made in the Houses of Parliament. For another bookseller, Thomas Osborne, he used his erudition in preparing a catalogue of the famous Harleian Library (5 volumes, 1743-5), and wrote proposals and a Preface for *The Harleian Miscellany* (1744). He was making himself useful and respected both for his learning and for his poetry.

His Poetry It was, after all, poetry that had brought Johnson to London. *Irene* was not acted until 1749 when Garrick, then famous and in power at Drury Lane, produced it.[2] In it Johnson had transformed a savage story into a fable carrying fine moral implications expressed in formal but noble eloquence that aroused respect but evoked no tears. He long believed in the play, and it is pathetic to find him years later leaving a room where it was being read aloud to friends. When asked why he left, he replied, "Sir, I thought it had been better." Johnson's reputation as a poet had been made on other pieces.[3] *London,* an imitation of Juvenal's third satire, was published in 1738 on the same day as Pope's *Epilogue* to his satires. Though the work of a new poet it was thought to compare favorably with Pope's mature eloquence. Both Pope and Johnson attacked the corruption of the times in typical fashion.

[2] David Nichol Smith, *Samuel Johnson's "Irene"* (Oxford, 1929); reprinted in part from *E&S,* xiv (1928). 35-53.
[3] T. S. Eliot, Introduction to *London and The Vanity of Human Wishes* (1930); R. W. Chapman, "Dr. Johnson and Poetry," *Sat. Rev. of Lit.* (Aug. 17, 1929), pp. 49-51.

Johnson's picture of the town in this poem is, however, not comparable to that given in his *Life of Savage,* which is the best account of Grub-street existence that we have. In 1747, at Garrick's request, he wrote a prologue for the opening of the season at Drury Lane, which was remarkable for its pungent and imaginative statements by way of dramatic criticism. In sixty-two lines he sketched incisively the development of English drama with particularly neat lines devoted to neo-classical tragedy. In 1749 another important poem, *The Vanity of Human Wishes,* appeared. Pessimism such as it expresses permeates Johnson's whole life. The vanity of literary or scholarly fame is colored by personal feeling in the couplet:

> There mark what ills the scholar's life assail,
> Toil, envy, want, the patron, and the jail.

Five years earlier Savage had died in a debtor's jail, and Johnson's collaborator on *The Harleian Miscellany,* William Oldys, was from 1751 to 1753 in Fleet prison for debt. The word *patron* was substituted for *attic* after Johnson's failure to get patronage from Lord Chesterfield. The magnificent and marmoreal gloom of the couplets about Charles XII remind one of later conquerors:

> He left the name, at which the world grew pale,
> To point a moral, or adorn a tale.

He could command this stately eloquence, but tenderness of strong personal emotion left him inarticulate. Even his quiet lines *On the Death of Dr. Robert Levet,* who had for many years been a member of Johnson's household, lack intimacy.

He was essentially a prose man, as he himself realized, and he won high reputation as a scholar and a prose moralist. As a scholar he had shown ability first in his work on the Harleian Library. His major reputation in his own time was perhaps gained from his *Dictionary of the English Language* (1755), for which in 1747 he had addressed a *Plan* to the third Earl of Chesterfield. Failing to get response in the way of patronage until the work was completed, Johnson wrote in 1755 the famous (and impertinent) letter to Chesterfield denouncing patrons in general. The *Dictionary* had been composed with the aid of a half-dozen amanuenses (chiefly Scottish), employed to transcribe the illustrative quotations that were a feature.[4] Johnson had a naturally defining mind, and his definitions of words were usually excellent—though now chiefly remembered are the jocose or erratic examples cited by Boswell and others. These were at times merely playful,

His Wo
as a Sch

---

[4] Sir James A. H. Murray, *The Evolution of English Lexicography* (Romanes Lecture, 1900); Percy W. Long, "English Dictionaries before Webster," *Bibl. Soc. of America, Papers,* IV (1910). 25-43; Stanley Rypins, "Johnson's Dictionary Reviewed by his Contemporaries," *PQ,* IV (1925). 281-286; Allen W. Read, "The Contemporary Quotations in Johnson's Dictionary," *ELH,* II (1935). 246-251; Philip B. Gove, "Notes on Serialization and Competitive Publishing: Johnson's and Bailey's Dictionaries, 1755," *Oxford Bibl. Soc.,* V (1940). 305-322; De Witt T. Starnes and Gertrude E. Noyes, *The English Dictionary from Cawdrey to Johnson, 1604-1755* (Chapel Hill, 1946).

and at times they aired Johnson's cherished prejudices. A *lexicographer* was "a harmless drudge, that busies himself in tracing the original, and detailing the signification of words." *Network* was "anything reticulated or decussated, at equal distances, with interstices between the intersections." He kept up the feud with the Scots in defining *oats*—"A grain, which in England is generally given to horses, but in Scotland supports the people." *Whig,* tersely, is "the name of a faction." And after 1762, when through his Scottish prime minister, Lord Bute, King George III bestowed a pension on Johnson, the joke was on the Doctor because of his definition of *pension*—"An allowance made to any one without an equivalent. In England it is generally understood to mean pay given to a state hireling for treason to his country." In revising the work later Dr. Johnson did not meddle with these *jeux d'esprit.* The preface to the *Dictionary,* while not the best of his notable series of prefaces, is rich in sound sense, in general observation, and in the stylistic mannerisms already demonstrated in *The Rambler* and elsewhere. His plea for mercy from critics is memorable for all such works:

> In this work, when it shall be found that much is omitted, let it not be forgotten that much likewise is performed; and though no book was ever spared out of tenderness to the author, and the world is little solicitous to know whence proceeded the faults of that which it condemns; yet it may gratify curiosity to inform it, that the *English Dictionary* was written with little assistance of the learned, and without any patronage of the great; not in the soft obscurities of retirement, or under the shelter of academick bowers, but amidst inconvenience and distraction, in sickness and sorrow; and it may repress the triumph of malignant criticism to observe, that if our language is not here fully displayed, I have only failed in an attempt which no human powers have hitherto completed.

The work, naturally, was faulty: the derivations, for example, because of the backwardness of studies in English etymology were not too creditable; but the undertaking as a whole was both highly useful and nobly monumental in scope and effect. As Carlyle remarked in his *Heroes, Hero-Worship,* etc., "Had Johnson left nothing but his *Dictionary,* one might have traced there a great intellect, a genuine man."

Shake-
speare's
Plays

Even before he published his *Plan* for the *Dictionary* Johnson had formed a hope of editing Shakespeare's plays. In 1745 he had shown critical insight appropriate to such a task in his *Miscellaneous Observations on the Tragedy of Macbeth;* and, again, after the *Dictionary* was off his hands, he published *Proposals* (1756) for an edition of Shakespeare.[5] Subscriptions were received, but Johnson was scandalously dilatory in performing the task. Friends tried to urge industry, and foes, like Charles Churchill in his *Ghost* (1762), added perhaps more effective jeers:

[5] Sir Walter Raleigh, *Johnson on Shakespeare* (selections edited with a preface, 1908); David Nichol Smith, *Eighteenth Century Essays on Shakespeare* (Glasgow, 1903) and *Shakespeare in the Eighteenth Century* (1928); Karl Young, "Samuel Johnson on Shakespeare: One Aspect" [i.e., source study], *Univ. of Wisconsin Studies,* XVIII (1923). 147-227; Robert W. Babcock, *The Genesis of Shakespeare Idolatry, 1766-1799* (Chapel Hill, 1931).

He for *Subscribers* baits his hook,
And takes their cash—but where's the Book?

In 1765 the volumes finally appeared, and, while attacked in part as coming
from a pensioner, they were well received and greatly stimulated scholarship
concerning Shakespeare. Johnson's contribution was less textual than it was
interpretative and historical. He, first, pointed out many sources for the
plays, and his notes on individual passages were usually sound and illuminating, and frequently provocative of comment by others. The preface was one
of the best pieces of prose Johnson ever wrote—manly, incisive, and sensitively phrased.

Its doctrine was sensible rather than new. Neither Johnson nor Garrick   *The Preface*
nor their half-century "discovered" Shakespeare or made his reputation.   *to Shake-*
That was long since assured. Nor was Johnson's defense of Shakespeare's   *speare*
failure to follow the "rules" wholly revolutionary: Addison and Pope (with
all Pope's respect for both Rymer and for rules) and many others had already
indicated similar positions. But Johnson's statements concerning the nature
of Shakespeare's genius and work are more complete and more explicit
than those of his predecessors, and they are in general admirable. Three
points may be noted: (1) Johnson appeals to the imaginative basis of literature in attacking the unities: "The objection arising from the impossibility
of passing the first hour at Alexandria, and the next at Rome, supposes, that
when the play opens, the spectator really imagines himself at Alexandria,
and believes that his walk to the theatre has been a voyage to Egypt, and
that he lives in the days of Anthony and Cleopatra. Surely he that imagines
this may imagine more." And the Doctor goes on to give an exposition of
imaginative truth that should cause critics that talk of the "distrust of the
imagination" to read him again. (2) His conception of "general" nature is
here well expressed. Johnson may be deficient in a liking for the fantastic
or the particular. Shakespeare he likes because "Shakespeare always makes
nature predominate over accident." To Johnson nature is essential humanity,
not accidental or minute detail. On the other hand extreme attention to
decorum of character leads to trivialities that are "the petty cavils of petty
minds." "Just representations of general nature" require the elimination of
irrelevant detail. The poet does not, as he remarks in the famous passage
in *Rasselas* (chapter x), present *all* details or even irrelevant details such as
the "streaks of the tulip," but rather "such prominent and striking features,
as recall the original to every mind." The chosen detail must induce imaginative recall, but the detail may be small since "There is nothing, Sir, too little
for so little a creature as man." The sort of imaginative recall demanded by
art (in Johnson's opinion) is that which serves to lead one to general truth.[6]
(3) Dr. Johnson is in regard to Shakespeare, as with regard to all literature,
moralistic in his approach. Shakespeare is, he believes, a great moral teacher;
but only by accident, not by effort. In general it may be confessed Johnson
had an extensive conception of Shakespeare's defects—he is always a judicial

6 Arthur Friedman and W. K. Wimsatt, Jr., in *PQ*, xxi (1942). 211-213; xxii (1943). 71-76.

critic, and must find fault—but he had a noble and manly sense of the excellences as well.

Johnson as Essayist

Apart from these works of scholarship Johnson had made a great reputation as a moral essayist before either the *Dictionary* or the edition of Shakespeare appeared.[7] "He who thinks reasonably must think morally," was with him a fundamental principle, and with him all art as well as philosophy was a guide to life. In 1748 he contributed to Dodsley's *Preceptor* an allegory called *The Vision of Theodore, the Hermit of Teneriffe,* which Johnson once said was "the best thing he ever wrote." It couples allegory with moral precept, and has interest as an early expression of Johnson's fear of habit as deadening the sincerity of religious devotion. It was inevitable that presently Johnson should try his hand at a periodical essay; and his *Rambler* (208 numbers, 1750-52) is, after *The Tatler* and *The Spectator,* the most respected effort in this form, and it did much to make his early reputation.[8] In the years 1758-60 he contributed to a newspaper, *The Universal Chronicle,* a series of nearly a hundred essays called *The Idler,* which were fully as amusing as but less meaningful than *The Rambler* had been. He contributed also essays in *The Adventurer* (1753-4), and wrote book-reviews and articles for various magazines at this period.

As a Moralist: Rasselas

The best piece of moral writing by Johnson is found in his *History of Rasselas, Prince of Abissinia.* This was an Oriental apologue related to the sort of thing he had occasionally done in *The Rambler* but nearer to his heart and more significant. It was rapidly written in January, 1759, and hastily published in April to defray the funeral expenses of his mother. It is his most appealing presentation of his ideas on the vanity of human wishes, on the impossibility of complete happiness in the imperfect human lot. Animals can eat, sleep, and be content; man who is both animal and immortal is torn by desires that this world cannot satisfy; for him a "stagnant mind" is brutal, a restless mind inevitable—and unhappy. It is interesting to see Johnson, who hated deism, here writing a book that is almost as despondent as the freethinker Voltaire's *Candide,* which was published probably in February, 1759, but did not reach England until after *Rasselas* appeared. Voltaire is content to scoff at the optimism of Leibniz and Pope, which (he mistakenly believes) denies the existence of evil. Johnson is not so much concerned in *Rasselas* with "the system of things," or with universal harmony, as he is with the imperfect ability of man to adjust himself to practical life. The two works are only superficially parallel. As a devout, though despondent, Christian Johnson might have saved the case for cheerfulness by introducing the popular orthodox idea of rewards and punishments in a future state; but this he refrains from doing. The "fable" is highly episodic; but the episodes are admirably pointed and are used to expose the vanity of many ideas current in his day apart from rationalistic optimism: he pays his respects to pastoral life, to the hermit's solitary flight from

[7] O. F. Christie, *Johnson the Essayist* (1924).
[8] On *The Rambler* see below. ch. VII.

temptation, to monastic life, to Stoic pride, to the life according to nature, and to many another recipe for happiness. His "Orientalism" like that of most Oriental tales is purely a device for effacing any bias of locality and reducing life to a sort of biblical universality.[9] The action is seldom vivid, though there are many moments that might have been dramatic. The escape from the Happy Valley is unexciting, and the ultimate return from the region of Cairo to Abyssinia—where, as Imlac had foretold, they would find themselves unknown and unregarded—is left equivocal as between the futility of their search for happiness and the aimlessness of a nondescript wandering existence. The author's reflections whether implicit or explicit are the important matter. He is sincerely and profoundly realistic about happiness, and here more than in his other prose he suffuses his reflections with emotional power.

After getting his pension in 1762 Johnson tended to write less than before. Two major works, however, appeared after that date. His *Journey to the Western Islands* (1775) is an account of a long-projected tour with Boswell, finally made in 1773 when Johnson was sixty-four years old. The journey was not merely primitive; it was at times positively dangerous. In a letter to Mrs. Thrale Johnson wrote: *Journey to the Western Islands*

> You remember the Doge of Genoa, who being asked what struck him most at the French court, answered, 'Myself.' I cannot think many things here more likely to affect the fancy than to see Johnson ending his sixty-fourth year in the wilderness of the Hebrides.

His book is shaded by Boswell's *Tour of the Hebrides* (1785), which excels precisely because Boswell can feature the picturesqueness of Johnson as well as of the Hebrides. He can show us Johnson sleeping in barns with no bed except hay or Johnson dragging his feet all day astride an undersized pony guided only by a halter—and longing "to be back in a land of saddles and bridles." Johnson, however, shows an interesting eye for detail and, as one would expect, rises to nobility in his moral reflections. His historical reverence for Iona leads him to express the moral stimulus of all history:

> Whatever withdraws us from the power of our senses; whatever makes the past, the distant, or the future predominate over the present, advances us in the dignity of thinking beings. Far from me and from my friends, be such frigid philosophy as may conduct us indifferent and unmoved over any ground which has been dignified by wisdom, bravery, or virtue. That man is little to be envied, whose patriotism would not gain force upon the plain of *Marathon,* or whose piety would not grow warmer among the ruins of *Iona!*

The net result of the journey was to confirm Johnson in his opinion that Macpherson's Ossian was a fraud and that primitive life and institutions were loathsome. He had experienced "simplicity" and found it "a native of the rocks." He made some attempt to control his anti-Scottish prejudices,

[9] Geoffrey Tillotson, *"Rasselas and the Persian Tales," Essays in Criticism and Research.* (1942), pp. 111-116.

but witticism would break through, and his caustic passages probably helped the sale of the book and temporarily increased its vogue.

Lives of the English Poets

His last work, the series of prefatory *Lives of the English Poets* (1779-81), has survived as easily his best. Begun in his sixty-eighth year and completed in his seventy-second, these fifty-two lives in their vigor and keenness would have been a major achievement for any author, young or old. The book-sellers who employed Johnson decided that the series should begin with Cowley; Johnson suggested a few modifications of their list of authors, but in general followed their choice. Many of the briefer lives are obviously perfunctory, but Johnson was devoted to both poetry and "the biographical part of literature"—which, as he told Boswell, "is what I love most"; and his *Lives* are in general written *con amore*.[10] He had had earlier experience in writing lives for *The Gentleman's Magazine,* and his *Life of Savage* was a small masterpiece. In literature Johnson valued "what comes near to our-selves, what we can turn to use," and he found that in biography. He had a sense of both the uniformity and the diversity of mankind, and advocated the presentation of minute biographical facts. The enforced brevity of his own *Lives,* however, precluded the use of much minute detail. The *Lives* excel not so much for their intimacy as for their solid judgment and their terse, finished phrasing. They abound also in authoritative enunciations of general wisdom, such as (concerning education), "We are perpetually moral-ists, but we are geometricians only by chance."

Johnson regarded as most important the authors of the Restoration and the Queen Anne periods—Dryden, Pope, Swift, and Addison. These men gave scope to his moralistic approach to literature, and their works were based on the principles of "general nature" that he valued. He is illuminating in his understanding both of these men as men and of their works—though by no means blind to some of their limitations. But to many poets he was less sympathetic.[11] To Cowley and especially to Milton among his earlier poets, he was unfair, though he himself preferred his *Life of Cowley* to all the rest "on account of the dissertation it contains on the Metaphysical Poets." This dissertation is indeed a brilliant and justly famous passage, still the classic verdict on the metaphysicals. Among the later poets he was not altogether kind in his estimates of certain contemporaries, notably Gray, Lyttelton, Shenstone, and even Collins, though for Collins he had a strong personal affection. His worst case of critical blindness is Milton, for whom he had a dislike grounded on religious and political issues which carried over to the poet's language and versification. Yet it must be remembered that the *Life of Milton* is full of mixed praise and blame, and that the compliments are so noble that Milton might well have retorted, as a man of less merit did, to Johnson's two-edged praise and blame, "Nay, Sir, Alexander the Great, marching in triumph into Babylon, could not have desired to have had more said to him." It would be difficult to determine

[10] Bergen Evans, "Dr. Johnson's Theory of Biography," *RES,* x (1934). 301-310.
[11] Meyer H. Abrams, "Unconscious Expectations in the Reading of Poetry," *ELH,* ix (1942). 235-245.

whether the greatest excellence of these *Lives* lies in Johnson's fine understanding of human nature manifested as poetical genius or in his vigorous and sensible criticism of individual poems. His comprehension of the mixed characters of men like Savage, Swift, Pope, and Addison shows masterful insight, kindliness, and tolerance; his views of the poetry surveyed are normally judicious and beautifully articulated. The romantics found easy grounds for discounting Johnson's taste, but at this distance it seems inevitable that any man's taste may be invigorated by spending his days and nights on *The Lives of the English Poets.*

Even before he secured leisure through his pension, Johnson was well *The Club* advanced in reputation from his other career, that of conversationalist. He met Boswell in 1763, and thereafter we naturally have more records of his talk. In 1764 the Club was founded, and Johnson there had the best conversation in the kingdom. Sir Joshua Reynolds first proposed the Club, and the original members included Reynolds, Johnson, Burke, Goldsmith, and· lesser friends in their circle. "They met," Boswell tells us, "at the Turk's Head in Gerrard-street, Soho, one evening in every week at seven, and generally continued their conversation till a pretty late hour." Other than charter members, in Johnson's day, were Bishop Percy, Garrick, Joseph and Thomas Warton, Fox, Gibbon, and Adam Smith. In 1773 Boswell himself was elected. One sees at a glance that Johnson enjoyed the company of the most interesting men of his time. He was in a sense driven to club life and eating abroad because of conditions at home. His wife had died in 1752, and he gradually surrounded himself with a strange assortment of dependents whom he received in charity but who behaved at times without that quality. Apparently at home he could be sure of neither good-natured conversation nor well-prepared food: hence in the years before the wealthy Thrales rescued him (1765), club life was important.

Conversation was Johnson's greatest pleasure, and it was also a necessary *Conversa-* anodyne. All his adult life he suffered from melancholia, at times to the *tion and its* very point of insanity. Increasingly he hated to be alone; talk was medicinal *Functions* to his mind. It was also a positive delight and an art conscientiously and joyously cultivated. With his temperament conversation was bound to be mercurial. Like the sluggish bear, whose external traits he seemed to have, he required prodding into activity; and the resulting talk might at times be "mad and violent" and at times hilarious and triumphant. "Well," he said to Boswell on one classic occasion, "we had good talk." "Yes, Sir," came the reply, "you tossed and gored several persons." Such was often the drama of his talk, but what he said made sense, and it was said with deliberate impressiveness, with wit, and with definitive finality. The idiom of his phrasing was picturesque and perfectly individual. According to Malone, he was "as correct and elegant in his common conversation as in his writings." He complimented his hearers by talking above them, and they only listened the more attentively. In general, he "laid it down as a fixed rule to do his best on every occasion and in every company; to impart whatever he knew in the most forcible language he could put it in." There was little doubt of his force: as Goldsmith complained, "When his pistol misses fire, he knocks you down with the butt-end of it." He was essentially kind but not sensitively polite. In view of the Boswellian record it is surprising that Malone could say, "I have been often in his company, and never *once* heard him say a severe thing to anyone; and many others can attest the same." One must assume that these friends meant that he never used undeserved severity.

Boswell concludes his *Life of Johnson* with the opinion that in conversation Johnson was essentially a virtuoso, who in a group delighted in showing his dexterity even to the extent of making sophistry acceptable. But talking more privately, or on topics concerning which he had settled convictions, he was genuinely and constantly sincere. He admitted that he often "talked for victory," and Boswell's recordings of Johnson's voice are so perfect that readers of Boswell are easily led to regard Johnson's conversation as a "performance" and to forget that the talk had a mind behind it. To do this is to be unfair to the intellectual quality of the Doctor, though it is true that he talked and at times wrote rashly and that his mental processes were not always logically consistent. Boswell expresses this mental self-contradiction admirably:

His mind resembled the vast amphitheatre, the Colisæum at Rome. In the centre stood his judgement, which, like a mighty gladiator, combated those apprehensions that, like the wild beasts of the *Arena,* were all around in cells, ready to be let out upon him. After a conflict, he drove them back into their dens; but not killing them, they were still assailing him. To my question, whether we might not fortify our minds for the approach of death, he answered, in a passion, 'No, Sir, let it alone. It matters not how a man dies, but how he lives. The act of dying is not of importance, it lasts so short a time.' He added, (with an earnest look,) 'A man knows it must be so, and submits. It will do him no good to whine.'

This is a picture of a mind with judgment and emotions perpetually in unstable equilibrium, a mind capable of gladiatorial combat or of furious refusal to fight.

Johnson on Religion

Johnson's best topics—whether in conversation or in print—were religion, politics, and literature. In matters of religion his mind worked with intense feeling.[12] "Religion appears, in every state of life," he thinks, "to be the basis of happiness, and the operating power which makes every good institution valid and efficacious." In his *Vision of Theodore* and in *Idler* No. 41 he insists again that religion is the only source of whatever happiness we have. Yet his written *Prayers* and Boswell's record indicate that his own religion lacked joyfulness. He approved Hugh Blair's sermon on Devotion, but objected to Blair's "rash" assertion that "he who does not feel joy in religion is far from the kingdom of heaven." Johnson's fear of the Deity

[12] William H. Hutton, "The Religion of Dr. Johnson," *Burford Papers* (1905), pp. 277-281; Stuart G. Brown, "Dr. Johnson and the Religious Problem," *English Studies,* xx (1938). 1-17, 67; W. T. Cairns, *The Religion of Dr. Johnson and Other Studies* (1946).

outweighed his love. Much of his religious longing was "the pursuit of perfect peace," which seemed to him "the great, the necessary, the inevitable, business of human life." This passion for a divine equilibrium is frustrated by the necessity of hope, which destroys poise. "Where there is no hope, there can be no endeavour"; and endeavor is the essence of moral and religious life. Johnson believed in the necessity of regularity in both public and private devotions, and suffered greatly over his negligences or even his tardinesses in worship.

The second half of the eighteenth century was a period wearied by the theological acrimony of the preceding century and deficient in creative theology of its own. Johnson recognized and condemned its "prevailing spirit" as one of "skepticism and captiousness, of suspicion and distrust, a contempt of all authority, and a presumptuous confidence in private judgment; a dislike of all established forms, merely because they are established, and of old paths, because they are old." He himself held that "the Bible tells us in plain and authoritative terms, that there is a way to life and a way to death." Essentials were clear and not to be questioned; he had no tolerance for "private judgment" in essentials. In theory he had little tolerance for any heterodoxy. His primitive conclusion was, "Every man has a right to utter what he thinks truth, and every other man has a right to knock him down for it. Martyrdom is the test." But in practice he could be more civilized, and could, in trying days, speak with moderation of either Catholics or Methodists. He much enjoyed the conversation of his overbusy friend and fellow high-churchman, John Wesley. The two had in common a spiritual intensity that showed itself most diversely. Johnson was possibly too conscious that his own sin was idleness. Perhaps (in view of his chronic fear of death) the most touching of his prayers is the "Ejaculation Imploring Diligence": "O God, make me to remember that *the night cometh when no man can work.*"

Religion, to repeat, is "the operating power which makes every good institution valid and efficacious." Johnson has no use for primitive society, Stoic poise, or (above all) for a cloistered retreat from temptation. Man's place is in society, and in a society based on Christian submission to the fundamental principle of subordination. "Order," he held, "cannot be had but by subordination." He also scorned equality as a political principle. "There may be community," he remarks through Imlac, "of material possessions, but there can never be community of love or of esteem. It must happen that one will please more than another." Unscrupulous demagogues talked of "natural equality, the absurdity of 'many made for one,' the original compact, the foundation of authority, and the majesty of the people," and Johnson regretted their ascendency. He felt that the chain of subordination was being relaxed, but solaced himself with the notion as to the English lower classes "that their insolence in peace is bravery in war." Of the cant of his day about liberty he was contemptuous. "All boys," he said, "love liberty, till experience convinces them they are not so fit to govern themselves as they

Johnson on Subordination

.gined. We are all agreed as to our own liberty; we would have as much ɔf it as we can get; but we are not agreed as to the liberty of others." Similar opinions are found throughout Johnson's writings.

In practical politics he was again conservative. He was reared as a Tory and a Jacobite; but by the time of George III he had concluded that long establishment of the Hanoverian family justified their claim to the throne. In his early London years he had written mildly against Walpole in his *Marmor Norfolciense* (1739), for example; but his chief political attitudes developed later, and concerned colonial possessions and the constitutional crisis in Parliament. Johnson was a violent anti-imperialist. In his *Observations of the State of Affairs in 1756* he condemns war with the French over boundaries in America on the ground that neither the French nor the English have any just title since both were robbers of the Indians. This basic injustice to the aborigines will, he thinks, make America "a perpetual ground of contest." In his *Political State of Great Britain* he disparages the motives of colonists, men either disaffected or bankrupt, who, loving adventure and enterprise, settled in "Canada, a cold, uncomfortable, uninviting region, from which nothing but furs and fish were to be had, and where the new inhabitants could only pass a laborious and necessitous life, in perpetual regret of the deliciousness and plenty of their native country." In his later outbursts about colonies he showed a prudential legalistic attitude rather than any economic awareness of the advantage of imperial outposts. He castigated the "howling violence of patriotick rage" over the Falkland Islands, which had "exasperated to such madness, that, for a barren rock under a stormy sky, we might have now been fighting and dying, had not our competitors been wiser than ourselves." For the most part he was sure the Islands would be but "a station for contraband traders, a nursery of fraud, and a receptacle of theft." In view of such opinions it is not surprising that when thirteen American colonies proved "disloyal" he poured forth scorn on the passion of the hypocritical "slave-drivers" for liberty. He had some awareness of the constitutional inconsistencies of the colonists but little comprehension of their economic grievances. He did not "take to" his fellow club-member, Adam Smith, and like Burke might on occasion couple economists with "sophisters."

At home he attacked vehemently rabble-rousers like John Wilkes. His *False Alarm* (1770) defended Parliament for refusing to seat Wilkes on the ground that a man convicted of "sedition and impiety" should not serve as "one of the guardians and counsellors of the church and state." In *The Patriot* (1774), written to aid his friend Thrale get elected to Parliament, he delivers his best blows at "false" patriotism and defends admirably the toleration of Catholicism in Quebec—six years before the Gordon Riots. In his earlier pamphlet on Falkland's Islands (1771) he had paid his respects to the ablest of the rabble-rousers, the mysterious Junius. It is perhaps Junius's "blaze of impudence" that appealed to Johnson, who condemned his morals but not his faculties:

It is not by his liveliness of imagery, his pungency of periods, or his fertility of allusion, that he detains the cits of London, and the boors of Middlesex. Of style and sentiment they take no cognizance. They admire him, for virtues like their own, for contempt of order, and violence of outrage; for rage of defamation, and audacity of falsehood. The supporters of the bill of rights feel no niceties of composition, nor dexterities of sophistry; their faculties are better proportioned to the bawl of Bellas, or barbarity of Beckford; but they are told, that Junius is on their side, and they are, therefore, sure that Junius is infallible. Those who know not whither he would lead them, resolve to follow him; and those who cannot find his meaning, hope he means rebellion.

There is more than alliterative pomposity in this passage. Johnson could not stem the rising tide of democracy, and that he wished to do so was doubtless due to his keen perception of the imperfections of democratic procedure as of 1771. He turned shuddering from such corruptions to fly, like Goldsmith, from lesser tyrants to the impartial protective authority of the throne. He was blindly conservative, and in politics he had an unfortunate knack of starting from sound principles and ending in conclusions quite mistaken.

This knack betrayed him in the field where he was most at home—literary *Johnson as* criticism. His blindness and prejudice in respect to Milton, his neglect of the *a Literary* Elizabethans [13] (except Shakespeare), and his dislike of contemporaries have *Critic* cost him reputation as a critic. He is often outrageously wrong but seldom corruptingly wrong: his errors are gross, open, and palpable. His strength lies in his directness and clarity of insight, in his defined and articulate thinking, in his typically eighteenth-century insistence that life is the best commentary on art. "Books," he quotes Bacon as saying, "can never teach the use of books." And he adds: "The student must learn to reduce his speculations to practice, and accommodate his knowledge to the purposes of life." The function of criticism was "to form a just estimate" of a work. The critic-judge must understand the case before him and the principles, rules, or laws applicable to it. Principles or rules are essential but relative: they are "the instruments of mental vision, which may indeed assist our faculties when properly used, but produce confusion and obscurity by unskilful application." Principles were an aid to perception, but no substitute for it. More than once he speaks of "the cant of those who judge by principles rather than perception." The real enemies of just criticism, however, were in his opinion not the rules so much as "the anarchy of ignorance, the caprices of fancy, and the tyranny of prescription." One can recognize in these enumerated faults the errors of Johnson himself as well as of all critics.

His conception of the nature and function of poetry is of his age. Its end *His Con-* is "to instruct by pleasing." It is the work of genius, and genius is "that *ception of* power which constitutes a poet; that quality without which judgment is *Poetry* cold and knowledge is inert; that energy which collects, combines, amplifies, and animates." Genius includes invention, imagination, and judgment, and Johnson while affirming that "no man ever yet became great by imitation"

---

[13] Dr. Johnson read them at least! See Walter B. C. Watkins, *Johnson and English Poetry before 1660* (Princeton, 1936).

of his predecessors merely, believes that genius must be trained by study. In *Adventurer* No. 85 he eloquently denounces a recent statement of an author who had "been able to learn nothing from the writings of his predecessors." "The highest praise of genius is original invention," he says elsewhere; but he makes imagination merely a recombining, not a creative, faculty. It is not reasonable, however, to cite such *loci* as chapter XLIII of *Rasselas* on "The Dangerous Prevalence of Imagination" (frequently only this title is cited) as showing that Johnson distrusted poetical imagination. In practical or philosophical matters it is to be distrusted when it prevails over reason and becomes insanity or practical delusion—as in the chapter cited.[14] To Johnson imagination in poetry is a vivifying and delightful faculty: it objectifies truth, recombines experience, "and produces novelty only by varied combinations." Finally, we should recall the noble passage in *Rasselas,* chapter x, where it is said that the poet "must write as the interpreter of nature, and the legislator of mankind, and consider himself as presiding over the thoughts and manners of future generations; as a being superiour to time and place." Johnson has no truck with such notions as the unhappy bit of insincerity expressed by the youthful Alexander Pope in his first preface about "poetry and criticism being by no means the universal concern of the world, but only the affair of idle men who write in their closets, and of idle men who read there." After religion and morality poetry was to Johnson the most important thing in the world. It was, in fact, the attendant and indispensable servant of both religion and morality. It is consequently not strange that he should show prejudice towards the writing of the anti-episcopal republican, John Milton, or against the metaphysicals whose calculated playfulness of wit failed, in his opinion, to achieve either the pathetic or the sublime. His prejudices were strong; but his values— sense, morality, power, novelty, and durability—are manly, sound, and usually judiciously applied.

On Poetic Diction   Johnson is especially competent and interesting as a critic of diction. He is a purist, and that fact makes him condemn the artificial re-creation of Latinate idiom that Milton used in *Paradise Lost*. Dryden forced language to the very "brink of meaning" and loved to "hover over the abyss of unideal vacancy." In diction Pope is preferred to Dryden. With regard to Gray's diction probably prejudice again operated, though one may well recall that Wordsworth as well as Johnson objected to Gray's artificiality or inexactness. Johnson had a real if clouded interest in poetic diction, and might have made history if he could have paused in his preoccupation with morality long enough to have thought through his theories as to the language proper for poetry.

[14] Irving Babbitt's "Dr. Johnson and Imagination," *Southwest Rev.*, XIII (1927). 25-35, should be read only as preliminary to F. B. Kaye's trenchant comment on it in *PQ*, VII (1928). 178; Raymond D. Havens, "Johnson's Distrust of the Imagination," *ELH*, x (1943). 243-255; Stuart G. Brown, "Dr. Johnson, Poetry, and Imagination," *Neophilologus*, XXIII (1938). 203-207; W. B. C. Watkins, "Dangerous Prevalence of the Imagination," *Perilous Balance* (Princeton, 1939), pp. 71-98.

His own prose style is perhaps the greatest of his achievements.[15] It con- *His Prose*
stantly and aptly expresses the essential directness of his mind. A typical bit *Style*
of his idiom is his characterization of Otway's bottle companions: "Their
fondness was without benevolence, and their familiarity without friendship."
This has significant balance, conscious structure and rhythm; it has pithiness
(the phrasal components of his sentences are normally brief); and it has
exquisite precision in its choice of abstract nouns. It also has an illusion of
Latinity. By habit he writes in abstract terms, and such terms tend to seem
Latin even when they are not. His fondness for polysyllables produced the
heaviness of style that has unjustly been called Johnsonese. The same tendency is visible in Congreve's plays, in Thomson's blank verse, and in Walter
Scott's novels, in all of which it is less appropriate than in Johnson's more
abstract disquisitions. His choice of words is at least correct, and both his
example and his *Dictionary* begot correctness in others. Arrangement of
clauses consciously in parallel or balanced patterns is also typical of his prose.
He almost never uses parenthetical clauses, but builds short members into
complex but easily grasped sentences. An unusual proportion of his sentences
are periodic in structure: he forms subjects from infinitives or "that" clauses,
which are then elaborated and finally concluded by a brief, forceful predicate.
Objective "that" clauses are piled up. His lives of Roscommon and Pitt each
have a sentence ending with a series of five such clauses, and the concluding
sentence of the life of Cowley has six. A more famous example of balanced
elaboration comes in the well-known letter to Chesterfield:.

> The notice which you have been pleased to take of my labors
>   had it been early,   had been kind;
> but it has been delayed
>   till I am indifferent,   and cannot enjoy it;
>   till I am solitary,   and cannot impart it;
>   till I am known,   and do not want it.

Johnson's position in the history of eighteenth-century prose is individual
and influential. Among the stylists of his day Hume, Gibbon, Burke, and
Johnson himself are eminent for care, vigor, and elegance of expression. All
four are notable practitioners of the grand or formal style. They mark a
general revulsion against the easy, fluent, unobtrusive style which Addison
had made perfect, and which his followers had made commonplace. To that
style Johnson pays high tribute in his *Life of Addison,* and of William
Whitehead's opposite style he expresses the immortal opinion that "grand
nonsense is insupportable." Yet his own manner is definitely of the formal
or noble sort. It varies with the subject, but it is always dignified and never,
for long at least, colloquial. He was doubtless consciously avoiding the errors

---

[15] W. V. Reynolds, "Johnson's Opinions on Prose Style," *RES,* IX (1933). 433-446, and
"The Reception of Johnson's Prose Style," *RES,* XI (1935). 145-162; William K. Wimsatt,
Jr., *The Prose Style of Samuel Johnson* (New Haven, 1941); Morley J. Mays, "Johnson and
Blair on Addison's Prose Style," *SP,* XXXIX (1942). 638-649.

of his predecessors; his clauses are of Attic brevity: his arrangement of clauses might be Ciceronian, but he economizes on connective words—omitting conjunctions with increasing frequency as he grows older—and he substitutes for the Ciceronian suavity a vigorous directness. His sentences have a more apparent structural unity than those of his seventeenth-century masters. In severity of design they are true Palladian; they lack any Corinthian or baroque ornateness. With the other great stylists of his day Johnson signalizes a moment of architectural formality and correctness that had been preceded by the easy journalistic prose of the early periodical essayists or by the rather facile Ciceronianism of Shaftesbury or Bolingbroke. It was followed in the early nineteenth century by the intimate and charming but highly careless prose of the romantic essayists. No writer in the eighteenth century achieved a style at once so nobly dignified and so individual as Samuel Johnson.

IV

Mid-Century Poets

The taste of readers of poetry in the mid-century is revealed by Dodsley's *Dodsley's*
Collection of Poems, by Several Hands, which first appeared in three duodec- Collection
imo volumes in 1748. Robert Dodsley,[1] the footman poet, who by the middle
of the century had become a fashionable bookseller and the leading publisher
of English poetry, was so successful with this *Collection* that by 1758 it had
grown to six volumes, and between 1748 and 1782 it was reprinted eleven
times. It was in these volumes largely that people of the day read their "contemporary" poetry. The authors included Dodsley's friends, especially those
for whom he was publisher, and other poets who were pleased to be
included. One or two, like Robert Nugent (1702-88) and George, Lord
Lyttelton, were there perhaps less as poets than as men of fashion and of
influence in the world of letters.[2] Shenstone and Akenside got generous
recognition because they were Dodsley authors; Collins, Gray, and others
were doubtless there because they were eminent in public esteem. Poets such
as Beattie or Chatterton, considered in this chapter along with these Dodsley
protégés, emerged just too late to be included in the *Collection.*[3]

---

[1] Robert Dodsley (1703-1764), though more important as an editor and publisher than as
a writer, began his career as a footman who turned poet just as Stephen Duck, the thresher
poet, was acquiring fame. Of Dodsley's early poems *The Muse in Livery* (1732) and *An
Epistle to Mr. Pope* (1734) won favorable attention. In the years 1735-58 he wrote a half-
dozen theatrical pieces, of which *The Toy-Shop* (1735) and *The King and the Miller of
Mansfield* (1737) were the most esteemed. In 1735 Pope set him up as a bookseller and publisher, and he published for Pope, Young, Laurence Sterne, and many others. In addition to
his *Collection of Poems* he published *A Select Collection of Old Plays* (12v, 1744), perhaps
his greatest service to literature, since the *Collection* served to keep in mind the lesser
Elizabethans. With the aid of Edmund Burke he began to publish in 1759 his *Annual Register.*
Some of his pieces were collected as *Trifles* (1745; 2v, 1777). See also Alex. Chalmers, *British
Poets* (1810), Vol. xv.—Ralph Straus, *Robert Dodsley* (1910); William P. Courtney, *Dodsley's
Collection of Poetry, Its Contents and Contributors* (1910), is superseded by R. W. Chapman,
"Dodsley's *Collection of Poems,"* *Oxford Bibl. Soc.,* iii, iii (1933). 269-316.

[2] George Lyttelton (1709-1773), however, was fully represented in the *Collection* by no
less than thirty-three poems—all of his significant verse. His early epistles and songs seem
now perfectly conventional. His *Monody* (1747) written in memory of his first wife was one
of the most discussed irregular odes of the mid-century. Lyttelton, for a time secretary to the
Prince of Wales, was an essayist as well as a poet. He turns up in literary circles as the friend
of Pope, Thomson, and Fielding, the object of attack by Smollett, and in other connections.
He is, as Gray called him in a letter to Horace Walpole reviewing Dodsley's *Collection,* "a
gentle elegiac person"—as were too many writers of verse in his day. See Sydney C. Roberts,
An Eighteenth-Century Gentleman (Cambridge, 1930); Ananda V. Rao, *A Minor Augustan*
(Calcutta, 1934); and Rose M. Davis, *The Good Lord Lyttelton* (Bethlehem, Pa., 1939).

[3] For further accounts of the poetry here treated see William Minto, *The Literature of the
Georgian Era* (1895), ch. vii; John H. Millar, *The Mid-Eighteenth Century* (1902), ch. v;
William J. Courthope, *A History of English Poetry,* Vol. v (1905), esp. ch. xii; *CHEL,* Vol. x,
ch. vi, vii, and x; Thomas Seccombe, *The Age of Johnson* (1899), ch. x; Oliver Elton, *A Survey
of English Literature, 1730-1780* (2v, 1928), ch. xiii, xiv, xv. Inferior texts of these poets can

More illuminating historically if one is not obsessed with the idea that poetry was steadily tending towards romanticism, the *Collection* reveals no marked sense of cleavage with the past. After all, Dodsley owed his start in life both as poet and as publisher to Pope's kindness, and he was hence likely to admire Pope's work. He was not permitted to include much of it in his *Collection,* but the influence of Pope is pervasive. There are Mason's *Musaeus* and a half-dozen other poems chiefly concerned with Pope, and still others mention him with high respect. From the early century are re-printed poems by William King (1663-1712), Abel Evans, Dr. Arbuthnot, Lord Bolingbroke, William Harrison, and Thomas Tickell. With these appear the leading poets of the mid-century: Akenside, Collins, William Whitehead (the laureate), the Wartons, Shenstone, Mason, and Gray. There is nothing from Edward Young. Thomson is represented by three short poems, among which is his admirable *Hymn on Solitude.* The Thomson influence, however, is apparent neither in extended description of landscape nor in the use of his type of blank verse.

Its Typical Subject Matter The tone and subject matter are seldom novel: there is much moralizing, if not so much satire; there are epistles, though these tend to be less formal than those of Horace and Pope; there are sedate elegies, but not much compelling grief; there is little landscape, but much "rural elegance"; there are poems of humble life, which tend to be realistic and jocose rather than idyllic. The many songs are likely to be neatly turned and witty—almost as witty as the numerous epigrams. Most of the poems could in 1750 easily be classed according to one or another tradition then well recognized. Possibly Roman-French devices decline in favor of native English or classic Greek forms. There is much prettiness, sweetness, and softness; there is relatively little robustness save in the attempts after sublimity and in the moralizing couplet poems (Dr. Johnson's three most important poems are here) and in the poems of rural life that remotely resemble the fabliau. Still we find chiefly "poems on occasions," and the occasions are public and the poetic manner is usually rhetorically effective rather than intimate or private.

Its Metrical Habits In general the metres used are what we should expect. Of the poems that run to over twenty pages in length, eleven are in the heroic couplet; four in the Spenserian stanza, and two in blank verse, at least in part. Most of the blank-verse poems are short and tend to a simpler, less sublime idiom than that of *The Seasons* or *Paradise Lost.* The rimed poems, especially those in tetrameter couplets, abound in phrasal echoes of Milton's shorter poems. There are dozens of odes, which range from the Horatian to the Cowleyan, to the "true" Pindaric, and to poems in non-classical stanza forms. The Cowleyan odes here are likely to be called "irregular." The other most popular metres are the tetrameter couplet (used for fables and for light as well as pensive effects), the various standard quatrains, and six-line stanzas of varying structure.

be found in *The Works of the British Poets,* ed. Robert Anderson (13v, 1792-5) and in *The Works of the English Poets from Chaucer to Cowper,* ed. Alexander Chalmers (21v, 1810). These collections in other notes for this chapter will be cited as Anderson or Chalmers.

By the middle of the century, then, if one may judge from Dodsley's *Collection*, the divergence from traditional metres and materials is not marked. What is notable is that one or two real geniuses appear in Dodsley, who have either new subjects to treat or new voices with which to speak. High among these would surely be William Collins (1721-1759) and Thomas Gray. Collins,[4] naturally, does not occupy many pages, for his total poetic output was a scant score of poems; but he is represented here by five poems somewhat strangely chosen. His *Epistle Addresst to Sir Thomas Hanmer* is his longest poem included, and it, in spite of its common neglect by romantic critics, is a striking poem to come from a university undergraduate. It is not typical Collins, however. His other poems used by Dodsley are the elegiac *Ode to a Lady on the Death of Colonel Ross*, the small but perfect *Ode Written in the Beginning of the Year 1746*, the *Ode to Evening*, and the early *Song from Shakespeare's Cymbeline*. Probably all of Collins's poems were available to Dodsley, and it is perhaps significant that he neglected to use the more complex odes. The two longer poems used had an obvious topical appeal through their connections with Hanmer and Colonel Ross. The three shorter poems are certainly among Collins's best so far as delicacy of feeling, clarity, and structure are concerned. The first of these qualities Collins evinces in all his poems; the other two he less often achieves.

William Collins

His first published poem appeared in 1739 when he was still a boy in Winchester College, and his last written ode, *On the Popular Superstitions of the Highlands of Scotland*, was at least sketched in 1749. A career of a decade, terminating before Collins was thirty years old, and productive of only about a score of poems, cannot be expected to show much development, or great range and diversity. We can now see more easily than could Dodsley or Dr. Johnson the quality of Collins's art, because his methods embody a type of romanticism with which poetry since 1800 has been more or less familiar. Although it is untrue that Collins was in his own century neglected, it is probable that he was not completely and sympathetically understood.

The Brevity of His Career

Among his immediately popular poems were his youthful *Persian Eclogues*, which had, as he himself saw, a merely conventional prettiness and grace under the thinnest of "Persian" veneers. His later poems frequently offer what seems like a quite new poetic idiom. The aphoristic didacticism, the chiseled phrases of Dryden and Pope are absent—though more than once his phrases are based on those of Dryden or Pope. His style

His Mannerisms

4 Collins's *Poems* are found in Anderson, Vol. IX and in Chalmers, Vol. XIII. The best modern eds. are those by Walter C. Bronson (Boston, 1898), Christopher Stone (1907, rev. 1917, rev. 1937), and Edmund Blunden (1929). Bibliographies are available in Bronson's edition and in Iolo A. Williams's *Seven XVIIIth Century Bibliographies* (1924). See Samuel Johnson, *Lives of the English Poets* (1781); ed. George Birkbeck Hill (Oxford, 1905), III. 334-342; John W. Mackail, "Collins and the English Lyric," *Trans. Royal Soc. of Lit.* (1921), reprinted in *Studies of English Poets* (1926), pp. 135-156; John Middleton Murry, "William Collins," *Countries of the Mind* (1922), pp. 81-99; H. O. White, "The Letters of William Collins," *RES*, III (1927). 12-21; Alan D. McKillop, "The Romanticism of William Collins," *SP*, xx (1923). 1-16; Heathcote W. Garrod, *Collins* (1928); Edward G. Ainsworth, *Poor Collins* (Ithaca, N. Y., 1937); Arthur S. P. Woodhouse, "Collins and the Creative Imagination: A Study in the Critical Background of his Odes," *Studies in English by Members of University College, Toronto* (Toronto, 1931), pp. 59-130.

is exclamatory rather than reflective; it is full of emotional apostrophe: "Oh thou" or its equivalent can be found in almost every poem, and more than once. Next, one notes that, in his longer odes, freed from couplet-control, his sentences drift on until they become so involved or so lost among parentheses that doubtless even the poet himself could hardly untangle them. Smaller mannerisms are his love of personifications (which, were they not so frequently statuesque evocations in highly particular poses, would be strictly neo-classical) and his perpetuation of the seventeenth-century habit of suffixing the letter *y* to adjectives ("the folding-star's *paly* circlet," for example). More important and equally clear is it that Collins had the true poetic gift of myth-making, of bodying forth his impressions in phrases fused with delicate and individual imagination. This is done in fragmentary flashes, possibly because he lacked the gift of sustained imaginative constructions and possibly because he chose to work with sudden strokes. To line 82 of his *Ode to Liberty* he appends a footnote recounting a traditional mermaid story about the Isle of Man. Many a poet of his inclinations would have made a whole poem out of this story: Collins makes one line—and a line quite unintelligible without the footnote. It is this condensed, at times incoherent, imaginative fusion that sets Collins apart from the placid poets of his day.

The Poetical Character

Poetry to him—as he tells us in his *Ode on the Poetical Character*—is essentially imaginative; it is divine in origin, wild and impassioned in method and insight; and its approved exemplars are Shakespeare, Spenser, and, most of all, Milton. He disparages gently "Waller's myrtle shades," and obviously he is not of the Dryden-Pope tradition. The form affected in most of his poems is the ode, both in simple Horatian stanza and in the strict Pindaric or the monostrophic form. In spite of superficial appearances of irregularity Collins's odes are metrically well controlled except in *The Passions* and in the irregular (and unfinished) *Ode on the Popular Superstitions of the Highlands*.[5] In a sense he belongs to the line of ode-writers who, after Congreve, reacted against the irregularities popularized by Cowley. His unrimed *Ode to Evening* is not free verse but is a skilful classical imitation in metres used by Horace and Milton. All told, his appeal is to our love of dim, dreamlike effects; and if he does not warm us with poignant humanity, he delights by his ornate and curious fantasy.

Christopher Smart

The poetic idiom of Collins is fantastic but not really mad. That of Christopher Smart [6] (1722-1771), does at best actually approach the insane. Domi-

---

[5] Arthur S. P. Woodhouse, "Collins and Martin Martin," *LTLS*, Dec. 20, 1928 (concerns the sources of this Ode).

[6] *Poems* (omitting much, 2v, Reading, 1791); also in Anderson, Vol. XI and Chalmers, Vol. XVI. *A Song to David* (1763) has been edited by John R. Tutin (1898), Richard A. Streatfield (1901), Edmund Blunden (1924); Oxford facsimile reprint (1926); *Rejoice in the Lamb*, ed. William Force Stead (1939).—George J. Gray, *A Bibliography of the Writings of Smart*, in *Trans. Bibl. Soc.*, VI (1903); reprinted separately (1903).—Sir Edmund Gosse, "Smart's Poems," *Gossip in a Library* (1891), pp. 183-199; K. A. McKenzie, *Christopher Smart, sa vie et ses œuvres* (Paris, 1925); C. D. Abbott, "Christopher Smart's Madness," *PMLA*, XLV (1930). 1014-1022; F. T. Wood, "Christopher Smart," *ESt*, LXXI (1936). 191-213; Edward G. Ainsworth and Charles E. Noyes, *Christopher Smart, A Biographical and Critical Study* (Columbia, Mo., 1943).

ciled as student and fellow in Pembroke Hall, Cambridge, in the years 1740-49 (before Thomas Gray moved across from Peterhouse), this wildly convivial genius, who was about the most delightful alehouse companion in Cambridge, seemed to Gray in 1747 to be headed for a debtor's prison or for Bedlam. In the fashion of needy authors, he migrated to London; and although his early fame rested upon his pious blank-verse Seatonian Prize poems, his meager income in London was that of a periodical essayist, pamphleteer, wit, and satirist.

After years of avoiding the debtor's jail and after having been privately confined for a year as mentally unbalanced, Smart achieved the madhouse in 1757. His mania was largely religious: he was obsessed by the command to "pray without ceasing," and upon impulse would kneel in the traffic of busy streets. Probably he was liberated a few weeks before the publication in 1763 of his masterpiece, *A Song to David*. Although without contemporary favor, the poem has enjoyed belated repute since Browning's *Parleyings with Certain People* (1887) appeared. More than some admirers admit, the poem relates to eighteenth-century traditionalism, with obvious debts to *Paradise Lost, The Seasons,* the *Essay on Man,* the Boyle lectures, and Smart's own earlier blank-verse poems. Regard for the vast scale of being directs David's choice of themes and man's adoration. Despite its rambling structure, small groups of stanzas within it are beautifully and deftly interrelated. Verbal play—the shifting position, for example, of the repeated phrase *for adoration*—is quite in keeping with the eighteenth-century love of ingenious effects. But in sustained lyric intensity, in bold transitions from the homely to the sublime, in exotic imagery, and in its piercing, mystical piety, it is unique in the century. Although Smart's madness may not have been such as to prevent his writing the *Song* while confined, there is no evidence that it was written during his confinement for madness. But his *Rejoice in the Lamb, a Song from Bedlam* (Smart's own title was *Jubilate Agno*) was so composed. It lacks the form of the *Song to David,* but it is a rich document in imaginative madness, and may even be regarded as in some sense prophetic of Blake. The tradition of literary madness from the *Hurlothrumbo* (1729) of Samuel Johnson of Cheshire through Collins, Smart, and Cowper, to William Blake, is both amazing and alluring. In this tradition and in any tradition of religious lyricism, *A Song to David* is a glowing achievement. It appeared too late for use by Dodsley.

The Wartons

More typical of the normal lyric mood of the mid-century was the work of Collins's friend Joseph Warton. Collins and Warton had talked of publishing their odes in a joint volume, but eventually (December, 1746) they published separately, and two years later some of their poems were found together in Dodsley's *Collection*. The Wartons, three of them, have been given perhaps an exaggerated rôle in the development of a romantic tradition. Thomas the father (*c.* 1688-1745), who was Professor of Poetry at Oxford in the years 1718-28, showed at least a slight primitivistic tendency in choosing to write *An American* [Indian] *Love-Ode* and *A Runic Ode*.

These, with other poems,[7] were edited by his elder son, Joseph, in 1748. In general the volume is Horatian and biblical in tone, with phrasal echoes also from the greater English poets; on the whole, it is a typical and not a very distinguished collection of early eighteenth-century verses. Warton's sons, Joseph and Thomas, are somewhat more clearly romantic at times, but they are far from being complete romanticists.

Joseph Warton   Joseph Warton (1722-1800) is a sort of focus of transitional tendencies.[8] We have already seen certain ambivalences in his criticism, and it may be again recalled that his reputed hostility to Pope was a source of grief to him. He always admired Pope, and in his old age edited Pope's *Works* (1797). In his own poems, however, Warton avoided didactic materials, and cultivated idyllic moods. Both he and his brother Thomas preferred rural to urban subjects. The preface to Thomas's *Five Pastoral Eclogues* (1745) shows this preference diffidently, and it is stressed in Joseph's *Enthusiast* (1744). In this last poem, however, the most primitivistic passages (lines 79 ff., 87 ff., 104 ff., and 119 ff.)[9] are quite in the Roman tradition, being based, as the first edition points out in footnotes not commonly reprinted, on Lucretius, Tibullus, and Horace. *The Enthusiast* combines other "romantic" traits with its borrowed primitivism,[10] such as the praise of idyllic simplicity, the preference of nature to art, the delight in objective natural beauty, the innocence of America, aesthetic irregularity, and sentimental melancholy in the vein of *Il Penseroso*. Its blank verse is quieter than that of Thomson and the followers of *Paradise Lost*. Quietness, placidity, are qualities that mark pleasingly most of Joseph's poems. His *Ode to Evening* as compared with that of Collins is relaxed, and is without imaginative perplexity.

Thomas Warton the Younger   The younger Thomas Warton (1728-1790), similarly, cultivates the relaxed mood of *Il Penseroso* in his *Pleasures of Melancholy* (1747).[11] But in more than one poem he preserves the neo-classical love of gayer, lighter verse; for example, in his *Panegyric on Oxford Ale*, which Dodsley placed in his *Collection*. In their odes as well as in their other poems the Wartons seek new materials, but they lack high imaginative gifts and intellectual strength; for the most part they fail to rise above the timid but graceful conventions

---

[7] *Poems on Several Occasions* (1748; reprinted by Facsimile Text Society, 1930).—D. H. Bishop, "The Father of the Wartons," *So. Atl. Quar.*, XVI (1917). 357-368; E. E. Willoughby, "The Chronology of the Poems of Thomas Warton, the Elder," *JEGP*, XXX (1931). 87-89; Leo Kirchbaum, "The Imitations of Thomas Warton the Elder," *PQ*, XXII (1943). 119-124; XXIV (1945), 89-90.

[8] In Chalmers, Vol. XVIII; for selections see also *The Three Wartons: a Choice of their Verse*, ed. Eric Partridge (1927).—John Wooll, *Biographical Memoirs* (1806); Hoyt Trowbridge, "Joseph Warton on the Imagination," *MP*, XXXV (1937). 73-87.

[9] In most later texts the passages in question begin with lines 87, 97, 115, 135.

[10] A. O. Lovejoy, in *PMLA*, XXXIX (1924). 237-245, discusses incidentally the "romanticism" of *The Enthusiast*. See also Audley L. Smith, "The Primitivism of Joseph Warton," *MLN*, XLII (1927). 501-504.

[11] In Chalmers, Vol. XVIII. See also Eric Partridge, *The Three Wartons* (1927).—Clarissa Rinaker, *Thomas Warton, a Biographical and Critical Study* (Urbana, 1916); Raymond D. Havens, "Thomas Warton and the Eighteenth-Century Dilemma," *SP*, XXV (1928). 36-50; René Wellek, *The Rise of English Literary History* (Chapel Hill, 1941), esp. ch. VI, "Thomas Warton."

of their day. Thomas, to be sure, was one of the few writers of sonnets in his century, and he is to be remembered as a medievalist notable in his day and as the first historian of English poetry.

The last two volumes (1758) of Dodsley's *Collection* begin with fifty or *Akens*
more pages of poems by William Shenstone and Dr. Mark Akenside,[12] respectively. Both had been Dodsley authors for years. Akenside (1721-1770) is represented in the *Collection* by typically dignified odes and "Inscriptions," full of naiads, dryads, nymphs, classical allusions, and frequent exhibitions of what Dr. Johnson termed "an unnecessary and outrageous zeal for what he called and thought liberty." These poems now have lost most of their charm. Some of the mythology is used gracefully:

> Tonight retired the queen of Heaven
> With young Endymion stays;

but most of it is perfunctory. Years before, Dodsley had printed Akenside's *Pleasures of Imagination* (1744), and for Dodsley during 1746-7 Akenside had supervised, and written for, a not uninteresting periodical called *The Museum*.

William Shenstone (1714-1763), represented in Dodsley's *Collection* by *Shenstone* no less than forty-seven poems,[13] is chiefly known for his Spenserian imitation, *The Schoolmistress*, for his *Pastoral Ballad*, and for the concluding quatrain of his lines *Written at an Inn at Henley*:

> Whoe'er has travell'd life's dull round
> Where'er his stages may have been,
> May sigh to think he still has found
> The warmest welcome at an inn.

His prose essays contain interesting observations on literature, and his sprightly letters, addressed to a wide circle of literary friends, are still entertaining. His *ferme ornée*, Leasowes, was a miniature show place competing for attention with its magnificent neighbor, Hagley Park, residence of Lord Lyttelton, and, in spite of its somewhat cluttered prettiness, deserving a place alongside of Gothic Strawberry Hill in the newer modes of gardening already in vogue. Dr. Johnson's unkind remark that "the pleasure of Shen-

---

12 *Poetical Works* in Anderson, Vol. IX; in Chalmers, Vol. XIV; also ed. Alexander Dyce, Aldine ed. (1835, 1894); R. A. Willmott (1855).—Johnson's *Lives* (ed. George Birkbeck Hill, Oxford, 1905), III. 411-420; Iolo A. Williams, *Seven . . . Bibliographies* (1924), pp. 75-97; George R. Potter, "Mark Akenside, Prophet of Evolution," *MP*, XXIV (1926). 55-64; Howard S. Buck, "Smollett and Dr. Akenside," *JEGP*, XXXI (1932). 10-26; Alfred O. Aldridge, "The Eclecticism of Mark Akenside's "The Pleasures of Imagination'," *JHI*, V (1944). 292-314; Charles T. Houpt, *Mark Akenside: A Biographical and Critical Study* (Philadelphia, 1944).

13 *Works* (2v, 1764; 3v, 1769); ed. George Gilfillan (Edinburgh, 1854); in Anderson, Vol. IX, and Chalmers, Vol. XIII; *Letters*, ed. Marjorie Williams (Oxford, 1939); and by Duncan Mallam (Minneapolis, 1939).—Iolo A. Williams, *Seven . . . Bibliographies* (1924), pp. 41-71.—Richard Graves, *Recollections of . . . the late William Shenstone, Esq.* (1788) and *Columella* (1779), a novel about Shenstone's life; Samuel Johnson, *Lives* (ed. George Birkbeck Hill), III. 348-359; Marjorie Williams, *William Shenstone, a Chapter in Eighteenth-Century Taste* (Birmingham, 1935); Helen S. Hughes, "Shenstone and the Countess of Hertford," *PMLA*, XLVI (1931). 1113-1127; A. R. Humphreys, *William Shenstone* (Cambridge, 1937).

...s all in his eye" implies a more serious deficiency of mind behind
...e. Shenstone's poems, like those of other minor bards of his day, are
...ther the sport than the business" of a mind, and serve to prophesy that
romantic poetry is to be sensuous rather than intellectual. An admirer and
acquaintance of James Thomson, Shenstone continued the tradition of descriptive poetry, loving above all, as he said, "odd picturesque description." He
was averse to Thomson's Miltonic grandeur, to the "present pomp and
haughtiness of style instead of sentiment"; and he consciously cultivated
an artificially simple and pretty style. Like many a sentimentalist he was
emotionally timid, and excused his *Schoolmistress* to the critical by means
of its jocose and burlesque details. He felt a need repeatedly to "spruce up"
the "trivial" poem, and so he recast it more than once. Similarly he defended
the genuineness of feeling in his *Elegies* by insisting that they were about
his own farm and his own sheep! He belonged to the conscious admirers
(so numerous in his day) of simplicity, rural elegance, picturesqueness,
informality, melancholy, and ornate prettiness. His liking for ballads led
him not merely to compose poems in that form (the best of which is doubtless *Jemmy Dawson*) but also to aid his friend Thomas Percy in the preparation of the *Reliques of Ancient English Poetry* (1765). He used a diversity
of metres pleasingly; his early success, *The Judgment of Hercules* (1741),
was in the heroic couplet, but that was a metre which in general he avoided.
The pentameter quatrains of his too numerous elegies reflect the popularity
of James Hammond's *Love Elegies* (1743) and perhaps also of Gray's
Churchyard.[14] For the grand style, the lofty, conscious art, Shenstone had
little affection. "The public," so he writes to a friend, "has seen all that art
can do, and they want the more striking effects of wild, original, enthusiastic
genius."

Thomas Gray

With the last part of this opinion Shenstone's greatest mid-century contemporary, Thomas Gray, would have agreed; but Gray was also and above
all a poet of art.[15] Among the most learned of English poets, he was widely

[14] J. Fisher, "James Hammond and the Quatrain of Gray's *Elegy*," *MP*, xxxii (1935). 301-
310, and "Shenstone, Gray, and the 'Moral Elegy'," *MP*, xxxiv (1937). 273-294.

[15] Thomas Gray (1716-71), son of a London exchange broker, entered Eton in 1725, where
he formed a friendly "quadrumvirate" with Horace Walpole, Richard West, and Thomas
Ashton. In 1734 he went on to Peterhouse, Cambridge, but left in 1738 without a degree. In
1739 he accompanied Horace Walpole on a tour of France and Italy, and as a result of a
quarrel returned to England alone in 1741. The next year he was back at Cambridge studying
law; and most of the rest of his career is associated with that place. In 1745 his friendship with
Walpole was renewed, and Walpole ultimately printed some of Gray's pieces on his Strawberry
Hill press. As a result of a practical joke by undergraduates Gray left Peterhouse (1756) and
moved to Pembroke College. During the years 1759-61 he settled in London in order to read
in the newly opened British Museum. In 1768 he was appointed Professor of Modern History
at Cambridge. He visited the Scottish Highlands in 1765, and in 1769 made a tour of the
English lakes, which he described in his journal kept for Dr. Wharton. In 1771 he was contemplating a journey to Switzerland to visit his young friend Charles Victor de Bonstetten,
but death prevented the journey.—Clark S. Northup, *A Bibliography of Thomas Gray* (New
Haven, 1917).—Gray's *Poems* have been edited by William Mason (York, 1775, etc.); Gilbert
Wakefield (1786); John Mitford (1814). His *Works* have been edited by John Mitford (2v,
1816; 4v, 1835-7); Sir Edmund Gosse (4v, 1884); William Lyon Phelps (Selections, Boston,
1894); Duncan C. Tovey (Cambridge, 1898); A. L. Poole and Leonard Whibley (Oxford,
1937). His *Correspondence* has been rather badly edited, but the best edition is easily that
of Paget Toynbee and Leonard Whibley (3v, Oxford, 1935).—Samuel Johnson, *Lives* (ed.

and intelligently read in the Romans, in the Greek lyrists and tragedians, in his great English predecessors, and, significantly, in such versions of Old Norse and Welsh poems as were available in his day. He typifies the transitional poet who loved tradition yet courted novelty. He excelled his contemporaries in meticulous workmanship and in ability to use new materials—medieval Welsh or Scandinavian—with dramatic imaginative power. He sought sublime moods, *sensations fortes,* and elevated even primitive materials to noble Roman or heroic levels.

Various explanations have been offered of the quantitative limitation of *Gray's* Gray's output. Perhaps he felt that devotion of all of his leisure to mere *Limitation* versifying would annul his position of genteel amateur. Gray, furthermore, could savor his refined sensations without the urge to share them with strangers. His delight in Alpine scenery led to no Coleridgean *Hymn before Sunrise;* and his pleasure in the English Lake region would not have made him a Wordsworth, had he lived longer. He did not "pour himself out": he was perceptive and receptive rather than publicly articulate. Although his letters to his intimates are easy and informal, his public appearances in print are dignified, stately, "official." He was certainly learned; that he was intellectually very creative is doubtful in view of his small prose output and of his appetite for "eternal new romances of Marivaux and Crebillon." Whether at Cambridge, Stoke Poges, or the newly opened (1759) British Museum reading-room, he was absorbed and stimulated by books. Unlike Walpole or Fielding, and unlike any typical poet of his day, he was shy. While hardly more melancholy than other lovers of *Il Penseroso,* he was a true hypochondriac, and both his character and his poetry were affected somberly by sorrows—such as, for example, the death of his closest friend, Richard West. Lastly, he was a fastidious exquisite. He perceived and delighted in beauty; over the exacting expression of beauty in poetry he labored as few English poets have done. His *Churchyard*—not really a long or complex poem—occupied his creative hours during perhaps six years. Of his projected but unwritten history of English poetry Walpole wrote, "If he rides Pegasus at his usual foot-pace, [he] will finish the first page two years hence."

Slow, stately, and impersonal as Gray's genius was, some of his earlier *His* poems are nevertheless derived chiefly from his personal experience of life; *"Occa-* they are, like those of so many "bards" of his day, actually "poems on several *sional"* occasions." A distant prospect of Eton College, where ten years before he *Poetry*

George Birkbeck Hill, Oxford, 1905), III. 421-442; Charles V. de Bonstetten, *Souvenirs* (Paris, 1832); Matthew Arnold, "Thomas Gray," *Essays in Criticism* (Second Series, 1888); Duncan C. Tovey, *Gray and His Friends* (Cambridge, 1890); Charles Eliot Norton, *Gray as a Naturalist* (Boston, 1903); Amy L. Reed, *The Background of Gray's Elegy* (1924); Roger Martin, *Essai sur Thomas Gray* (Paris, 1934); Robert W. Ketton-Cremer, *Thomas Gray* (1935); La Rue Van Hook, "New Light on the Classical Scholarship of Thomas Gray," *AJP*, LVII (1936). 1-9; William Powell Jones, *Thomas Gray, Scholar* (Cambridge, Mass., 1937); Herbert W. Starr, *Gray as a Literary Critic* (Philadelphia, 1941); M. H. Griffin, "Thomas Gray, Classical Augustan," *Classical Jour.,* XXXVI (1941). 473-482; Geoffrey Tillotson, "Gray the Scholar-Poet," *Essays in Criticism and Research* (Cambridge, 1942), pp. 124-126.

had been a schoolboy, led in 1742 to the composition of an ode on the subject that involved obviously heartfelt reflections on the hidden future sorrows awaiting the happy youngsters seen at play. Here, as in his *Ode on the Spring,* the diction is ornately Augustan, as indeed Wordsworth found it also in the *Sonnet on the Death of Richard West.* The *Ode on the Death of a Favourite Cat* (belonging to Horace Walpole) is a neat and laughing *jeu d'esprit* that Gray could approve. Another such, *The Long Story* (1753), was less pointed and finished; and it Gray excluded from the 1768 edition of his poems. Cowper knew this tune better; there was little of the *riant* in the genius of Gray.

His Elegy
    The greatest of Gray's poems—possibly the greatest of his century—is his *Elegy Written in a Country Churchyard.* Though perhaps motivated in part by sorrow over the death of West, the poem is not "particular": it is an Elegy for Man, or at least for all "average" and obscure men. Both in its attempt to work thus in universal terms and in its unrivaled purity, propriety, and harmony of diction the poem is a great realization of the ideals of its day: in its placid melancholy and its rustic setting it is perhaps slightly romantic. In its treatment of the common man it is heroic and even majestic; it has not the tone of Wordsworth. The poem is compact of what Tennyson called "divine truisms," and these are universally, if decorously, affecting. Among poems embodying the noble ideal of

> What oft was thought but ne'er so well expressed,

this *Elegy* must always rank high. Persons with an aversion to reflective commonplaces in poetry may, as T. S. Eliot has done, question the subtlety of the *Churchyard;* but critics who admit *both* clarity and subtlety as merits will be content with the noble and finished transparency of this poem. Its achievement is, of its very nature, the opposite of facile: *"divine* truisms" are not so easily come by!

Inspiration from Books
    After 1751 Gray derived poetic stimulus from his reading of books rather than from life itself. After the *Elegy* came his two regular Pindaric odes, *The Bard* and *The Progress of Poesy.* Although his contemporaries appreciated the clarity and reflective moralizing of the *Elegy,* they found the energetic and rhapsodical quality of these odes difficult. The imagery of *The Progress of Poesy* dazzled more readers than Dr. Johnson; [16] the frequent classical allusions in Milton's vein recalled to them the schoolroom rather than the glory and grandeur of Greece or Rome; and the management of persons in *The Bard* required a sort of study familiar to Browning's readers but unfamiliar in 1757. Yet neither ode is so obscure as it at first seemed; both have unusual energy and imaginative shimmer. The medieval fable in *The Bard* has dramatic power hardly equaled between Milton and Byron. These odes approach the sublime as do few others in this age that adored Milton and Longinus. Though their rhythms at first sound dithyrambic, they are rigidly correct within the true Pindaric form. Gray published in his

16 W. P. Jones, "The Contemporary Reception of Gray's Odes," *MP,* XXVIII (1930). 61-82.

lifetime no poems in the heroic couplet, though he had used it in a few brief translations and had begun in it his didactic *Education and Government*. Yet his achievement in other metres and his critical interest in them give him high importance in the history of English metrics. His range from the somewhat cold pomp of the heroic quatrains in his *Elegy* to the energetic outburst of his Pindarics and his later primitive chants is unparalleled in his century.

As historian and antiquary, Gray had long been interested in early verse forms and medieval poetic materials. Paul Henri Mallet's *Introduction à l'Histoire de Dannemarc* (1755) drew him to Norse antiquities and poetry; Bartholin's *De Causis Contemptae . . . Mortis* (Copenhagen, 1689) offered two Norse poems which Gray translated as *The Fatal Sisters* and *The Descent of Odin;* and Evans's *Some Specimens of the Poetry of the Ancient Welsh Bards* (1764), viewed in manuscript by Gray in 1760, furnished materials for *The Triumphs of Owen* and *The Death of Hoel*. Gray and others significantly turned, as Gibbon did not, from the Graeco-Roman tradition to Northern antiquities, from classically correct elegies and Pindarics to the primitive minstrelsy of the North.[17] In 1768, when Gray for the last time carefully edited his poems, he also became Professor of Modern History at Cambridge; and it is remarkable that learning and poetry marry so perfectly in the wild "runic" chants of these last products of his muse. *His Scandinavian and Celtic Poems*

Gray, however, was not the first to exploit heroic Celtic story.[18] He was a distinguished, if independent, admirer of Macpherson's Ossian, and Ossian importantly reinforced Sir William Temple's view that all nations, not merely Greece and Rome, had their artistic distinction. "Imagination," as Gray wrote after reading Ossian, "dwelt many hundred years agoe in all her pomp on the cold and barren mountains of Scotland. . . . she reigns in all nascent societies of Men, where the necessities of life force every one to think & act for himself." The cult of imagination, the belief in cycles of culture outside the Graeco-Roman tradition, the belief in primitive nature (seen in "nascent societies of Men") as more potent than formalized art— all these influences and more had been long preparing the way for James Macpherson (1736-1796) and his supposed versions of Ossianic poems.[19] The aesthetic rightness of the moment is seen if we remember how unpopular *Macpherson's Ossian*

---

[17] George L. Kittredge, "Gray's Knowledge of Old Norse," *Selections from Gray*, ed. William L. Phelps (Boston, 1894), pp. xli-l.

[18] Edward D. Snyder, "Thomas Gray's Interest in Celtic," *MP*, XI (1914). 559-579.

[19] *The Works of Ossian*, ed. William Sharp (Edinburgh, 1896); *Ossian. Faksimile-Neudruck der Erstausgabe von 1762/63 mit Begleitband: die Varianten*, ed. Otto L. Jiriczek (3v, Heidelberg, 1940); *Fragments of Ancient Poetry* (1760); ed. Otto L. Jiriczek (Heidelberg, 1915); *Fingal. An Ancient Epic Poem* (1762); *Temora. An Ancient Epic Poem* (1763).—G. F. Black, "Macpherson's Ossian and the Ossianic Controversy: A Contribution towards a Bibliography," *Bull. New York Public Library*, XXX (1926). 424-439; 508-524.—Hugh Blair, *A Critical Dissertation on the Poems of Ossian* (1763); Thomas B. Saunders, *The Life and Letters of James Macpherson* (1894); John S. Smart, *James Macpherson* (1905); Paul Van Tieghem, *Ossian et l'Ossianisme dans la littérature européenne au XVIIIᵉ siècle* (Groningen, 1920) and "Ossian et l'Ossianisme au XVIIIᵉ siècle," *Le Préromantisme* (Paris, 1924), II. 197-284; Edward D. Snyder, *The Celtic Revival in English Literature* (Cambridge, Mass., 1923), ch. IV.

Scots were in London in the days of Lord Bute, John Wilkes, Charles Churchill, and the arch-enemy, Dr. Johnson, and if we remember how Scottish poets had recently failed to "take" in London. For unpretentious homely geniuses such as Allan Ramsay (1686-1758) and Robert Fergusson (1750-1774) one need not expect a fashionable vogue; but John Home, author of *Douglas,* had not overwhelmed London, as he had Edinburgh, in his rôle of "the Scottish Shakespeare," and William Wilkie (1721-1772), author of *The Epigoniad* (1757), had been even less welcomed as a "Scottish Homer." But Macpherson fared better—fared beyond all expectation, so that his success became even embarrassing.

As early as 1749, when John Home, not yet a Shakespeare, was returning to Scotland, Collins in his unpublished *Ode on the Popular Superstitions of the Highlands* had urged him to sustain the "rural faith," "the themes of simple, sure effect," and to collect legendary materials in the Highlands both from the "well-taught hind" and from the more credulous shepherd.

> Old Runic bards shall seem to rise around,
> With uncouth lyres, in many-colour'd vest,
> Their matted hair with boughs fantastic crown'd. . . .

Ten years later Home met James Macpherson and found in him the man who should answer the wishes not merely of Collins but of all well-disposed antiquaries, nationalists, and primitivists. Under encouragement of Home, Hugh Blair, and other patriotic Scots, Macpherson in 1760 published in Edinburgh a small volume of *Fragments of Ancient Poetry Collected in the Highlands of Scotland.* An instant success, it lighted a poetic fire that for a half-century was to rage throughout all Europe. The widespread appetite for primitive poetry found its fullest gratification in Ossian.

Insistent Scottish supporters forced Macpherson to collect and "translate" other Gaelic poems. Ignorant of Gaelic and perhaps confused as to the relation of his fragments to each other and to their romantic cycles, Macpherson was reluctant; but, fired with the enthusiasm of his backers, he continued his work. Challenged by Dr. Johnson and others to authenticate the antiquity of his fragments, he could produce no ancient manuscripts, and lacked, in the discussion of oral transmission, any scholarly understanding which might have aided him. The controversy over the genuineness of his poems became bitter, but it did not, at least for some years, greatly affect their popular vogue.

The Melancholy of Ossian The materials which he had gathered from the mouths of not too well-taught hinds bore, in general, relationships to the Fenian cycle of Celtic romance. Macpherson adapted or even invented his episodes, as any eighteenth-century "translator" might have done. The Ossianic poems were in one respect peculiarly fitted to his needs. They were retrospective in method. Macpherson found in the dark backward and abysm of time, Ossian: Ossian, in turn, sang mournfully of glories that had vanished before his day. The effect of remoteness was doubled, and the tender melancholy implicit in all reminiscence added a touch of sentiment, without which in 1760 there was little chance of success. The method and style of this poetic prose may be called Macpherson's own in spite of the fact that it is largely biblical in coloring and owes much to Homer, Milton, Pope's *Iliad,* and even to bits of more recent authors. A happy invention, it answered to the full the eighteenth-century concept of primitive objectivity, naturalness, and sublimity. Designed to show that, ages long ago, Ossian on the cold and barren mountains of Scotland had equaled, if not surpassed, Homer on Scamanderside, it actually achieved almost the full synthesis of romantic primitivism.

Thomas Percy (1729-1811) was more of an antiquarian than was Macpherson, and certainly more of a scholar; but he also was hardly more than an amateur in the work of "old runic bards," and his chief success was to be less their editor than their popularizer.[20] Aware of the public's avidity for the exotic, he sponsored the translation of a Chinese novel, *Hau Kiou Choaan,* and wrote two other volumes concerning China; stimulated by Macpherson's success, he brought out *Five Pieces of Runic Poetry* (1763) from the Icelandic and *Northern Antiquities* from the French of Mallet. As late as 1775 he was preparing a volume of *Ancient Songs ... Translated from the Spanish.*[21] His greatest work, the enhancing of popular regard for early English ballads, began about 1758, when he had secured from his friend Humphrey Pitt of Shifnal a folio manuscript volume of old ballads. With the encouragement of Shenstone, Thomas Warton, and others, Percy assembled enough ballads to make three volumes called *Reliques of Ancient English Poetry* (1765). As an editor of ballads Percy had had more than one predecessor in the earlier eighteenth century; but since the sixties had witnessed an increase in the appetite for "ancient poetry," he had more success and influence than his predecessors. The volumes stimulated an extensive rehabilitation of the repute of English balladry. Percy does not belong to the tradition of good editing in his century—that of Tom Hearne and Edmond Malone—but to that of the popularizers and improvers of texts, the tradition of Pope among others. He selected his materials capriciously, frankly mixing old ballads, such as *Chevy Chase, Edom o' Gordon,* and *Sir Patrick Spens* with political songs of the seventeenth century, and

Thomas Percy

[20] There is no collected edition of Percy's writings; his *Reliques* is edited by Henry B. Wheatley (3v, 1886) and by M. M. Arnold Schröer [a critical edition] (2v, Berlin, 1889-93). For a bibliography see L. F. Powell, "Percy's *Reliques,*" *Library,* IX (1928). 113-137.—Alice C. C. Gaussen, *Percy, Prelate and Poet* (1908); Hans Hecht, "Kleine Studien zu Graves, Shenstone und Percy," *Anglia,* LVIII (1934). 103-112, 131-154; Clarissa Rinaker, "Percy as a Sonneteer," *MLN,* XXXV (1920). 56-58; Leah Dennis, "The Text of the Percy-Warton Letters," *PMLA,* XLVI (1931). 1166-1201 and "Percy's Essay 'On the Ancient Metrical Romances'," *PMLA,* XLIX (1934). 81-97; Vincent H. Ogburn, "Thomas Percy's Unfinished Collection, *Ancient English and Scottish Poems,*" *ELH,* III (1936). 183-189; "Further Notes on Thomas Percy" [biographical], *PMLA,* LI (1936). 449-458; and "A Forgotten Chapter in the Life of Bishop Thomas Percy," *RES,* XII (1936). 202-208; Irving L. Churchill, "William Shenstone's Share in the Preparation of Percy's *Reliques,*" *PMLA,* LI (1936). 960-974; Walter J. Bate, "Percy's Use of his Folio Manuscript," *JEGP,* XLIII (1944). 337-348; *The Percy Letters,* general editors, David Nichol Smith and Cleanth Brooks: *Correspondence of Percy & Edmond Malone,* ed. Arthur Tillotson (Louisiana State Univ., 1944); *Correspondence of Percy & Richard Farmer* (Louisiana State Univ., 1946). Other vols. will follow.

[21] First published with a preface by David Nichol Smith (Oxford, 1932).

with ballads by his contemporaries, and by himself. He used certain interesting devices of "salesmanship," such as the transference of *Chevy Chase* at the very last moment from Volume III to the beginning of the first volume, where this song about a Percy followed a dedication to the Countess of Northumberland, "in her own right Baroness Percy," etc. Thus the son of the Bridgnorth grocer capitalized on the accident of his own name, and began his rise to the spiritual lordship of Dromore.[22]

Beattie's Minstrel

To his *Reliques* he added essays historical and critical on various aspects of English verse, essays which interested and encouraged Thomas Warton in his *History of English Poetry* and one of which, on ancient minstrels, stimulated James Beattie [23] (1735-1803) to one of the longest and certainly one of the best poems of the century in the Spenserian stanza, *The Minstrel* (1771-4). Here we find a sketch of the training of Edwin (Beattie himself), a modern "minstrel." In the first Book the simplicities of rural life and the beauties of landscape seem educational:

> Lo! where the stripling, wrapt in wonder, roves
> Beneath the precipice o'erhung with pine;
> And sees, on high, amidst th' encircling groves,
> From cliff to cliff the foaming torrents shine:
> While waters, woods, and winds, in concert join,
> And Echo swells the chorus to the skies.

The "mighty masters of the lay" also instruct the youth, and in Book II philosophy and history aid in the task apparently still essential of curbing "Imagination's lawless rage." The poem in some passages seems a graceful but not compelling predecessor of Wordsworth's *Prelude*. Beattie's *Essays* are of more interest than his poems apart from *The Minstrel;* for the latter tend to be conventional odes, elegies, and translations.

Thomas Chatterton

The cults of genius and of medieval minstrelsy, so enthusiastically fostered by these poets in the sixties, meet in the tragic career of Thomas Chatterton (1752-1770), "the marvellous boy" who began publishing poems before he was twelve, and ended with suicide before he was eighteen.[24] To the succeeding great romantics Chatterton became the myth or symbol of "heaven-born

[22] Leah Dennis, "Thomas Percy: Antiquarian vs. Man of Taste," *PMLA*, LVII (1942). 140-154.

[23] Beattie's poems are found in Chalmers, Vol. XVIII, and in the Aldine edition, ed. A. Dyce (1831, etc.).—Sir William Forbes, *An Account of the Life and Writings of James Beattie, Including Many of his Original Letters* (2v, Edinburgh, 1806); Margaret Forbes, *Beattie and his Friends* (1904); E. A. Aldrich, "James Beattie's *Minstrel:* Its Sources and Influence," *Harvard Summaries of Theses* (Cambridge, Mass., 1931), pp. 117-119.

[24] *Works*, ed. Thomas Tyrwhitt [*The Rowley Poems*] (1777); Robert Southey and J. Cottle (3v, 1803); Walter W. Skeat (2v, 1871); Henry D. Roberts (2v, 1906); Maurice E. Hare, *The Rowley Poems* (Oxford, 1911).—Francis A. Hyett and W. Bazeley, *Chattertoniana* [bibliography] (Gloucester, 1914).—Helene Richter, *Thomas Chatterton* (Vienna and Leipzig, 1900); Eduard H. W. Meyerstein, *A Life of Thomas Chatterton* (1930); Esther P. Ellinger, *Thomas Chatterton, the Marvellous Boy* (Philadelphia, 1930); L. F. Powell, "Thomas Tyrwhitt and the Rowley Poems," *RES*, VII (1931). 314-326; A. Watkin-Jones, "Bishop Percy, Thomas Warton and Chatterton's Rowley Poems (1773-1790)," *PMLA*, L (1935). 769-784; Eduard H. W. Meyerstein, "Chatterton: his Significance To-day," *Essays by Divers Hands (Transactions of the Royal Society of Literature)*, XVI (1937). 61-91; Wylie Sypher, "Chatterton's *African Eclogues* and the Deluge," *PMLA*, LIV (1939), 246-260.

Genius" suffering from "want and the bleak freezings of neglect." Dull as Bristol schoolboy and attorney's apprentice, he brightened in his favorite haunt, the church of St. Mary Redcliffe. Among the muniments of this church, of which his family were almost hereditary sextons, he learned according to myth to read black letter before he knew Roman type, and to adore illuminated parchments. His "medievalism," since it began before he was twelve, may well have been spontaneous rather than owing to the *ersatz* of Ossian or *The Castle of Otranto;* but it flowed in somewhat similar channels. Endowed with a gift for lyric, satire, and literary mimicry, Chatterton composed work supposedly by poets of Chaucer's day and later, chief among them a feigned Bristol monk, Thomas Rowley. Chatterton's counterfeiting of spelling and diction has been disparaged; yet the style was archaic enough to delight many contemporary readers, though Gray, Mason, Walpole, and others—made wary by Macpherson's work—remained unconvinced and unsympathetic. Such counterfeiting wore out its success easily, and Chatterton, denied both bread and fame, in bitter pride and despondency drank arsenic and died.

The real quality of Chatterton's gifts is difficult to dissociate from his tragic career. Actually his stimulus was Elizabethan and Spenserian rather than Chaucerian or fifteenth-century. This is especially true of his best poem, *An Excelente Balade of Charitie.* Here we have colorful Renaissance imagery and the stateliness of rime royal modified by a Spenserian Alexandrine. Always Chatterton showed a pretty gift in his figurative and decorative language and in the warm tunefulness of his lines. More than Macpherson, Percy, or Gray, he could emancipate himself from the mannerisms of his own century, and escape to the imaginary world of fifteenth-century Bristol, his own created city of refuge. It is, after all, this frustrated escape rather than the achievement of poems actually written that became important to his romantic idolaters. They praised his gifts rather than his poems; he was regarded by them as first among "the inheritors of unfulfilled renown." The transition from Chatterton to Coleridge, Shelley, or Keats is in many ways a short step.

Another able poet, whose career like Chatterton's postdated Dodsley's *Collection,* was Charles Churchill (1731-1764), a dissipated clergyman, who during the last four years of his life acquired notoriety and fame as a satirist.[25] His first important poem, *The Rosciad* (1761), attacked theatrical personalities with a verve that made the poem, in the opinions of some later critics, the outstanding success in personal satire between Pope's *Dunciad* and Byron's *English Bards and Scotch Reviewers.* It was soon supported by an attack on Smollett in Churchill's *Apology to the Critical Reviewers*

Charles Churchill

25 Churchill's *Poems* were collected in 1763 and thereafter; they are found in Anderson, Vol. x, and Chalmers, Vol. xiv, and are edited by James Laver (2v, 1933). For biographies (there is no first-rate life of Churchill) and special articles on Churchill see CBEL, ii. 340-342, especially the biographical articles there listed as by Joseph M. Beatty. See also George Nobbe, *The North Briton, a Study in Political Propaganda* (1939), and Wallace C. Brown, "Charles Churchill: A Revaluation," *SP*, xl (1943). 405-424.

(1761) in the form of an epistle to his close friend Robert Lloyd [26] (1733-
1764). This attack in turn led to an alliance with the author of *The North-
Briton,* John Wilkes, that shaped much of Churchill's later poetry. *The
Prophecy of Famine* (1763) continued Wilkes's outcry against the Scotch;
the *Epistle to Hogarth* (1763) was a bitter revenge on the aging artist for
his caricature of Wilkes drawn in the courtroom; *The Duellist* (1764) was
a defense of Wilkes's rôle in his duel with Samuel Martin; and *The Candidate* (1764) renewed onslaughts on Wilkes's hypocritical enemy, the fourth
Earl of Sandwich. *The Times* (1764) was an unsavory depiction of the vices
of the day with emphasis at times on vices to which Churchill himself was
perhaps not a stranger. Less satirical was his rambling *Gotham* (1764),
which expounded ideas of political and social freedom and gave way to
humanitarian reflections that pleased his former schoolmate, William
Cowper. That Churchill had a remarkable gift for satirical portraiture is
attested by his laughter at Dr. Johnson (Pomposo) in *The Ghost* (1762-3)
and his more virulent satire on Wilkes's enemies, Warburton and Lord
Sandwich, in *The Duellist.* As favorite metres he used both the four- and
the five-stressed couplets, and was happier in his use of the latter. For some
reason—possibly because he hated Pope's editor, Warburton—he disliked
Pope, and cultivated the vigorous flow of Dryden, which more suited his
genius. In *Gotham* he remarks

> Nothing of Books, and little known of men,
> When the mad fit comes on, I seize the pen,
> Rough as they run, the rapid thoughts set down,
> Rough as they run, discharge them on the Town.
> Hence rude, unfinish'd brats, before their time,
> Are born into this idle world of rime....

In substance and manner the passage is typical, though the poet's gross
energy and power are better seen in his acrid and mordant personalities. But
satire's preoccupation with the "Sons of Sin" (Churchill's phrase), when
stressed by such a sinner, was naturally suspect. That vein had been worked
out; [27] and Churchill remains a journalist, a savage and incisive editorial
commentator or propagandist who happened to write best—and it was very
well—in eloquent couplets. His art looks backward to a rhetorical school,
whereas Chatterton and others, looking farther back, were renewing aged
and unfamiliar poetic strains.

[26] On Robert Lloyd see *CBEL,* II. 370, and Austin Dobson's essay on Lloyd in *At Prior
Park and Other Papers* (1912); also I. R. Halsband, "The Poet of *The North Briton,*" *PQ,*
XVII (1938). 389-395.

[27] Worked out, but not abandoned! Witness the frequently lively and witty attacks on Pitt
and his partisans by members of the Esto Perpetua Club in their burlesque epic, *The Rolliad,*
with also the *Criticisms on The Rolliad* that furthered the burlesque in 1784 and for a decade
thereafter. The multitudinous lampoons that, during the last quarter of the century, poured
from the pen of John Wolcot (1738-1819), or "Peter Pindar," as he called himself, show also
that energy still endured in satire though deftness and elegance had ceased to be notable
traits

V

The Novel After 1760

Excessive articulation of the rules of poetry, constricting one to the traditions of Homer, Aristotle, and Horace, might stimulate subversion of such rules, but since tradition in the English novel was brief and relatively unformulated, no similar revolution in taste is here to be expected. The very popularity of a new form, of course, tended to withdraw attention from the classical traditions. In the novel, changes in form or emphasis will relate to changes in attitude towards the phenomenon *man* and his daily life and not to remote literary precedent.[1]

The function of the novel remained the study of man and his manners and morals. The most notable developments are those due to emphasis on the emotions or sentiments of men—and of women!—rather than on their rational endowments. But just as the light of reason was regarded as uniform in all right-minded men, so were the sentiments of the heart. Rousseau's Julie reproaches her lover for his preoccupation with "those peculiarities of manners and decorum, which ten years hence will no longer exist" and for his neglect of "the unalterable springs of the human heart, the constant and secret workings of the passions." It is these last which, under the influence of Richardson and Rousseau, engrossed novelists increasingly, though study of manners was by no means excluded. Manners were found interesting among humble folk as well as among aristocrats, in *domestica facta* as well as in foreign society.[2] The problem of how far the particular (the *trivial*, novelists and critics termed it frequently) might augment or diminish universality was seldom faced by writers. They seem, however, conscious that changeable manners and values that were only relative possessed the appeal of novelty and diversity. Strange Rousseauistic moral ideas crept into novels. Julie avowed, "My virtue is unblemished, and my love has left behind no remorse. I glory in my past life." But such a view was foreign to English sense of decorum; no English heroine of comparable behavior thus regarded her eccentricities. If highly particular psychological reactions were to be depicted, they must normally be kept in some way "universal." So Sterne managed

Manners, Morals, and Sentiments

[1] For additional details on the novel of this period consult Ernest A. Baker, *The History of the English Novel*, Vols. IV (1930) and V (1934); J. M. S. Tompkins, *The Popular Novel in England, 1770-1800* (1932); Charlotte E. Morgan, *The Rise of the Novel of Manners* (1911); Robert M. Lovett and Helen S. Hughes, *The History of the Novel in England* (Boston, 1932). For further bibliography see *CBEL*, II. 488-490, 521-553.

[2] See Houghton W. Taylor, *The Idea of Locality in English Criticism of Fiction, 1750-1830* (Chicago, 1936), and his "Modern Fiction and the Doctrine of Uniformity," *PQ*, XIX (1940). 225-236; and again by the same author, " 'Particular Character': An Early Phase of a Literary Evolution," *PMLA*, LX (1945). 161-174.

...iis Shandean sentiments; so Fanny Burney shaped her notorious and specialized "character-mongering."

In practice there were also other modifications. The neat, suspensive struc-

irtuosity
in Structure ture formulated by Fielding and Richardson, through its very excellence perhaps, led virtuosos like Sterne and his imitator Mackenzie (in *The Man of Feeling*) to play tricks with structure. Normally, of course, matrimony remained the terminal point in plots, but frequently writers discard plot and affect the loose patterns in vogue in Defoe's time. Setting became definitely more important: medieval or Oriental or other remote backgrounds indicated a superficial interest in the exotic and, more significantly, a disgust with trivial daily life as matter for fiction. The introduction of landscape backgrounds that were peacefully idyllic or wildly sublime or mysterious was a development important for the future though at first used—by Ann Radcliffe, for example—somewhat artificially. This "poetic" tendency illustrates a natural desire on the part of the undervalued art of storytelling to elevate its status, a desire seen also in the habit of inserting poems in the text to give a "literary" tone or in the use of a style at times excessively dignified or polysyllabic. These last habits, for better or worse, carried over into the next century, and are all to be seen in the work of Sir Walter Scott among others.

The incurably sentimental tone of most novels of this period is in part due to feminine influence. Women were the novel-reading public, and there were a surprising number of women novelists.[3] Among these were Mrs.

Feminine
Influences Charlotte Lennox (1720-1804), the American, whose work was approved by Dr. Johnson; Mrs. Sarah Scott (1723-1795), author of one very successful book, *Millenium Hall* (1762); Mrs. Frances Sheridan (1724-1766), the dramatist's mother, whose *Miss Sidney Bidulph* (1761-7) and *History of Nourjahad* (1767) went through several editions; Mrs. Frances Brooke (1724-1789), author of *Lady Julia Mandeville* (1763), and a further train of other ladies somewhat too seriously sentimental for long popularity. These would include Mrs. Elizabeth Griffith, Clara Reeve, Charlotte Smith, and the romantic Mrs. Elizabeth Inchbald. So many women tried their hands at elegant tales of feminine distress that in Smollett's *Humphry Clinker* (1771) Tim Cropdale's failure is excused because novel-writing "is now engrossed by female authors, who publish merely for the propagation of virtue, with so much ease, and spirit, and delicacy, and knowledge of the human heart, and all in the serene tranquillity of high life, that the reader is not only enchanted by their genius, but reformed by their morality." Tobias Smollett, horse of another color, thus paid his ironic respects to the gray mare of the

Sterne's
Sense of
Comedy moment.

The basic attitude of the most eminent novelist of the period, Laurence Sterne,[4] was by nature not very different from Smollett's with regard to this

[3] R. B. Johnson, *The Women Novelists* (1918); also Miriam R. Small, *Charlotte Ramsay Lennox* (New Haven, 1935); Walter M. Crittenden, *The Life and Writings of Mrs. Sarah Scott* (Philadelphia, 1932); William McKee, *Elizabeth Inchbald, Novelist* (Washington, D. C., 1935); Florence M. A. Hilbish, *Charlotte Smith, Poet and Novelist* (Philadelphia, 1941).
[4] Laurence Sterne (1713-1768) was born in Ireland, son of an English army officer and

facile ease, spirit, and "knowledge of the heart," affected by his contemporaries. At the beginning of his brief literary career, at least, he saw all these matters as materials for comedy, if not for grotesque farce. In his first, unsuccessful attempt (May, 1759) to sell Volume I of *Tristram Shandy* to Dodsley, he described the work as "taking in, not only, the Weak part of the Sciences, in which the true point of Ridicule lies—but every Thing else, which I find Laugh-at-able in my way." He thought, so he wrote Garrick, that a "Cervantic comedy" might be drawn from Volumes III and IV. The first volumes were certified by Cambridge friends as the "best & truest & most genuine original & new Humour, ridicule, satire, good sense, good nonsense ever put forth." But even before sending the manuscript to Dodsley, Sterne had learned by reading parts of the story to his convivial and tolerant friends at Stillington Hall[5] that much of it was too gross. Even after revision the work, when published, was widely condemned as too indelicate for a clerical pen. In later volumes he in part curbed his salacious bent, and wrote, with or without his tongue in his cheek, something more apparently sentimental. But the "serene tranquillity of high life" at Shandy Hall has little in common with that of Rousseau's Eloisa at Clarens—or with the scenes depicted by Sterne's female contemporaries: the Shandy brothers led a life that was essentially tranquil—and essentially comical.

Sterne's significant output was limited to two pieces of fiction, seven small volumes of *Sermons* (1760-69), and his correspondence, which includes the *Letters from Yorick to Eliza* (1773). To modern readers he is the author of *The Life and Opinions of Tristram Shandy* (1759-67) and its by-product

Tristram Shandy

---

an Irish mother. His early years were spent moving about with the regiment; during the years 1723 to about 1731 he was in school in Yorkshire. Receiving the B.A. in Jesus College, Cambridge, in 1737, he took orders the same year, and in 1738 obtained the vicarage of Sutton-in-the-Forest, near York. He later received other livings, and resided chiefly in or near York itself. His great-grandfather had been Archbishop of York, and an uncle was archdeacon in the diocese during Sterne's career. A chapter quarrel indirectly led to Sterne's first imaginative writing, *A Political Romance* (1759), later called *The History of a Good Warm Watch Coat*. In 1760, upon the publication of the first of *Tristram Shandy*, he was lionized by London society. Ill health—he had long been consumptive—made advisable a visit to France in 1762; but here despite his health he plunged into fashionable society. Again in 1765 London fêted him, and again recuperation required a seven-months' tour of France and Italy. While in London in 1768 to superintend publication of the *Sentimental Journey*, he died. He had married Eliza Lumley in 1741; but the match was completely incompatible. During his last hectic winter in London Sterne indulged in a passionate but Platonic intrigue with Mrs. Eliza Draper, the young wife of a Bombay official in the East India Company. Sterne's letters to this Eliza, written after she sailed for Bombay, became his *Journal to Eliza*.—Of his works the edition by Wilbur L. Cross (12v, 1904) and that from the Shakespeare Head Press (7v, Oxford, 1926-7) are standard. His *Letters* (3v, 1775) are best edited by Lewis P. Curtis (Oxford, 1935). The standard life is by Wilbur L. Cross (2v, 1925); other lives by Percy Fitzgerald (2v, 1864) and H. D. Traill (1882) are of some value. For Sterne's Continental vogue see Harvey W. Hewett-Thayer, *Sterne in Germany* (1905); Francis B. Barton, *L'Influence de Sterne en France* (Paris, 1911); Gertrude Hallamore, *Das Bild Laurence Sternes in Deutschland von der Aufklärung bis zur Romantik* (Berlin, 1936); and F. Louise W. M. Buisman-de Savornin Lohman, *Laurence Sterne en de Nederlandse schrijvers van c. 1780-c. 1840* (Wageningen, 1939). See also Lewis P. Curtis, *The Politicks of Laurence Sterne* (Oxford, 1929).

[5] This was the seat of John Hall-Stevenson, the original of Eugenius in *Tristram Shandy*, and author, among other things, of *Crazy Tales* (1762).

A Sentimental Journey through France and Italy (1768), and these works are a most highly individual achievement. It was Sterne's intention to bring out *Tristram Shandy* in annual installments during the rest of his life.[6] This his health did not permit; but the method of the story is in part dictated by the plan for interminable serial publication. As in comic-strip drawings in present-day newspapers, it was essential here to husband one's material, to work with minutiae—in short, to get nowhere. The structural results are apparent. Sterne used small scenes—snapshots one might call them—and cultivated variety and surprise to the utter neglect of continuity or progress. The art of digression was never so continually or successfully cultivated.

Digressions [Sterne tells us], incontestably, are the sunshine;—they are the life, the soul of reading;—take them out of this book for instance,—you might as well take the book along with them;—one cold eternal winter would reign in every page of it; restore them to the writer;—he steps forth like a bridegroom,— bids All hail; brings in variety, and forbids the appetite to fail.

After the close organization of *Tom Jones* and the tragic rise and fall of complication in *Clarissa,* such apparent chaos would be intolerable except in the hands of a great genius.

s Time
cheme
    The chaos is more apparent than actual. There was both a method and a (concealed) plan. On the original title-page Sterne announced in a Greek tag from Epictetus that not deeds but the teachings of deeds are what concern men. So his pages are devoted to adumbrations of trivial occurrences, and his overtones are both rich and amusing, if not logically arranged. Furthermore, although he conceals the fact, he does have a complete chronological conception of the events he is presenting, and he does live up to his title, *The Life and Opinions of Tristram Shandy,* more fully than a casual reader realizes. Since the nine published volumes are only a beginning, Tristram's elders naturally occupy the center stage, but in the sequel Tristram would have come to that position himself. As matters stand, we know the dates of Uncle Toby's and Trim's active military careers and the years of the campaigns on the bowling-green at Shandy Hall. We know that the maneuvers relating to the Widow Wadman fall chiefly in the years 1713-14; that Tristram was born on November 5, 1718; that after attending Jesus College, Cambridge, he made the grand tour—and that, like a good comic-strip artist, Sterne planned to send with him most of the male dramatis personae of the book: how many volumes that might have made! We know that in 1741 Tristram attended Mr. Noddy's son as governor in Denmark; that in 1748 Parson Yorick died; and that Tristram supposedly began his latest volume on or about August 12, 1766.[7]

But chronology or "plot" was not the principle on which *Tristram Shandy* was built. Not deeds but the implications of deeds engrossed Sterne: it is

---

[6] The facts concerning the composition and history of the novel are admirably summarized in the edition prepared for the Odyssey Press (1940) by James A. Work.

[7] Theodore Baird, "The Time-Scheme of *Tristram Shandy* and a Source," *PMLA*, LI (1936), 803-820.

the emotional aura of these things and especially their comic aspects that he was dramatizing. He was much influenced by John Locke's theory as to the irrational nature of the association of ideas; Tristram calls Locke's *Essay* "a history-book ... of what passes in a man's own mind"; and since association is thought an accidental or whimsical process, it easily lends itself to a comedy of intellectual incoherence. Hence the casual, digressive motion of the work; hence the tragicomic interruption in the first chapter and other *non-sequiturs* in many other chapters. When Dr. Slop avers, "It would astonish you to know what improvements we have made of late years in all branches of obstetrical knowledge," Uncle Toby wistfully replies, "I wish you had seen what prodigious armies we had in Flanders." At Lyons when the commissary of the post politely asks, "And who are you?" Tristram *en philosophe* replies, "Don't puzzle me!" When at the visitation dinner the learned Kysarcius—his very name a monument to Locke's theory—triumphantly summarizes the weighty proofs that led all ecclesiastical authorities to agree that the Duchess of Suffolk was not of kin to her own child, Uncle Toby, with human eagerness, cries out, "And what said the Duchess of Suffolk to it?" This interplay of pedantry and natural humanity is one of Sterne's favorite sports: it has both comic and sentimental aspects.

Comedy from the Association of Ideas

Comedy also arises from fundamental idiosyncrasy of character. Corporal Trim learned his catechism in a military fashion, so to speak; and so he must deliver it. Uncle Toby, who devoted his waking hours to war games, was nevertheless the most pacific of mortals with "scarce a heart to retaliate upon a fly." At the start of the painful story of LeFevre, he sighed, "I wish, Trim, I was asleep." With preparations befitting a foreign embassy, he waited upon the Widow Wadman to tell her he was in love; but at that moment taking up the Bible and happening upon the siege of Jericho, he forgot completely the rest of his intended discourse. Uncle Toby's "hobby-horse" (war) furnished Sterne with the best possible burlesque of the popular eighteenth-century doctrine of the "ruling passion."

Comedy from the Ruling Passion

Sterne's forte is in the sensitive perception of the comedy that goes on in our minds; there are less attractive aspects of his fooling. One tolerates his use of blank pages, black pages, and marbled pages, his placing his preface in the middle of the book, his dots, dashes, and index hands, and other tricks that Joseph Addison would have classed as "false wit." It is less easy to tolerate his recurrent grossness. Quite possibly the comedy of the human mind depends much upon the grotesquely indecent associations found even in the purest minds. In general, however, Sterne's grossness is not subtly psychological; it derives from the sort of stimulus that moves the urchin to scrawl with chalk upon a sidewalk—the desire to be bold and shocking, to evoke a snigger. His prurience is, however, by intention and in effect comic rather than corrupting.

Sterne's Indecency

Adverse criticism resulted, and there was less indecency later. If one compares Volume VII of *Tristram* (1765), the record of Tristram's tour of

France, with Yorick's travels as recounted in *A Sentimental Journey through France and Italy* (1768) one appreciates readily this increasing refinement. The grotesque tricks of *Tristram*—its first illustrator was appropriately William Hogarth himself [8]—are replaced by something approaching elegance; the comedy of mental processes becomes more sweetly tender. The use of *sentimental* in the title puzzled English as well as Continental readers. Sterne himself perhaps conveyed its meanings when he wrote to a friend: "I told you my design in it was to teach us to love the world and our fellow creatures better than we do—so it runs most upon those gentler passions and affections." Similarly in the work itself he says, " 'Tis a quiet journey of the heart in pursuit of NATURE, and those affections which arise out of her." Yorick was not the philosophical traveler like Goldsmith, nor the "proud traveler" like Dr. Samuel Sharp, whose *Letters from Italy* (1766) won him Sterne's notice as "Mundungus," nor yet the jaundiced traveler such as Smollett ("Smelfungus"), whose *Travels through France and Italy* were anathema to Sterne. Yorick savored the situation of the moment—usually as trivial as fiction could produce—with sweet emotion, the result in part of Sterne's consumptive hyperesthesia. Long a very sick man, he was throughout the composition of his last work face to face with death.

Of Sterne's *Sermons* it may be said that their publication brought him money; of his letters that they show him carrying on his inveterate clowning, delicate or indelicate by turns, off stage as well as on. Those addressed to Mrs. Eliza Draper and published as his *Journal to Eliza* in a synthetic text enjoyed much popularity in an age that overvalued emotional facility. His epistolary style has charm of the same sort as that seen in his public works, but not of the same degree; for before publishing his stories Sterne revised, recast, and filed his phrases in order to perfect the apparently spontaneous effervescence that is his glory. He writes the language of conversation with a finished and economic sureness and an attention to overtones that are with him unique.

As he had no important and close predecessors—though there is the intriguing *Life and Memoirs of Mr. Ephraim Tristram Bates, Commonly Called Corporal Bates* [9] (1756)—he had likewise no worthy followers. Most novelists of his time, to be sure, featured emotions of obvious stimulus, ranging from domestic tenderness and the sorrows of abandoned beauty, such as those of Sterne's Maria of Moulines, to more self-conscious public emotions, such as love of liberty, symbolized by Sterne's caged starling. But other sentimentalists had neither his ingenious facility nor his light sureness of touch. Sentimental clichés are of course found everywhere in the novels and plays of the time. Goldsmith's *Vicar*, commonly regarded as a sentimental achievement, contains no comedy worthy of Sterne, and seems more or less earnest in dramatizing a virtuous fortitude in the face of distress

---

[8] Thomas Cary Duncan Eaves, *Graphic Illustration of the Principal English Novels of the Eighteenth Century* (unpub. Harvard diss., 1944), pp. 211-261.
[9] Helen S. Hughes, "A Precursor of *Tristram Shandy*," *JEGP*, xvii (1918). 227-251.

rather than any abandonment to mere tenderness. Closest to Sterne, perhaps, but far behind him, is "the Northern Addison," Henry Mackenzie,[10] whose *Man of Feeling* (1771) imitates *Tristram* in a pretended structural incompleteness, a reminiscent pathos, and a certain quality of dreamlike fantasy. Mackenzie's hero, Harley, faced with the hard facts of existence, exhibits a sentimental incompetence, which, though common in literature at this time, is not characteristic of the Shandys nor altogether of Goldsmith's Vicar—though Dr. Primrose can be inept on occasion. Harley seems rather akin to Rousseau's St. Preux and Goethe's Werther (1774). In general *The Man of Feeling* is crammed with sentimental motifs, such as the loneliness of the delicate soul (not the delicate female soul!), unhappy love, the hardness of life for a private soldier and for the victims of the enclosure movement or of business trickery; it is also filled with the customary glorification of benevolence.

Henry Mackenzie

Mackenzie's companion-piece to his first novel is the more luridly melodramatic *Man of the World* (1773). The villainous protagonist is significantly named Sindall, and he is a cruder descendant of Richardson's villains; the heroine, naturally of mysterious birth, is the perfection of innocence in extremes of distress; and the hero, true to type, is a "friend of humanity." Both *The Man of Feeling* and *The Man of the World* are set down in an extremely stilted and inflexible style. The love scenes are as formal in diction as they are in human conduct.

More effectively theatrical is Mackenzie's third novel, *Julia de Roubigné* (1777), obviously a Puritan's reworking of the basic story of Rousseau's *Julie*. Mlle de Roubigné is preserved chaste, is separated from her true love, Savillon, is married through family pressure to the Count de Montaubon, who upon Savillon's return from Martinique imitates not Wolmar but Othello and in groundless jealousy brings tragedy upon Julia and himself. Little is new or subtle in this, but the motives are well sustained, and the story—granted its author and tradition—is not too baldly narrated. Sir Walter Scott reports that in this novel Mackenzie tried to avoid using the devices of melodramatic villainy. In his substitution of complications resulting from misunderstanding or bad timing of actions he is in accord with the better practice of his day, as Fanny Burney was shortly to show. He gives us bits of romantic scenery as background—following Rousseau here—and motivates the whole upon the principle that "memoirs of sentiment and suffering, may be found in every condition," not merely among the great.

One of the richest fictional storehouses of sentimental clichés is by another contemporary of Sterne's, the Irishman Henry Brooke.[11] His *Fool of Quality*

---

[10] Henry Mackenzie (1745-1831) was born, was educated, and lived most of his life in Edinburgh, where he was from the time of David Hume to that of Sir Walter Scott a notable leader in the political, legal, literary, and social activities of the northern capital. He produced three novels and four plays—the four are of no great distinction—and won reputation by his essays contributed to *The Mirror* (1779-80) and to *The Lounger* (1785-87). His life has been written by Harold W. Thompson in *A Scottish Man of Feeling* (Oxford, 1931).

[11] Henry Brooke (c. 1703-1783), was the son of an Irish Protestant clergyman. After studying in Trinity College, Dublin, he went to London to study law in 1724, but turned rather

Brooke's
Fool of
Quality

as a narrative is complex and confused; it includes in a seventeenth-century manner transverse episodes and biographies, and it pauses for set discussions of economic, political, religious, and educational problems. Except possibly for Sarah Fielding's *Governess* (1749) it is the first important English educational novel, and it follows the English sentimental tradition as well as that of Rousseau in his *Émile* (1762) and other works. It presents, as Charles Kingsley remarked, "the education of an ideal nobleman by an ideal merchant prince"; and it teaches that "all virtues, even justice itself, are merely different forms of benevolence." From this book nonconformists as well as churchmen learned (in Kingsley's ardent phrase) "more which is pure, sacred, and eternal, than from any which has been published since Spenser's *Faerie Queene.*" In so extreme a benevolist there is bound to be not a little naïveté. His hero, young Harry Moreland, destined to become Earl of Moreland and to marry a Princess of Morocco, from childhood showers guineas—seldom less—on all the needy, so thoroughly is he imbued with "generosity." Cosmopolitanism readily extends to marriage with a blond African princess who has a twin brother "of sable hue." The power of sympathy agitates the merchant-prince when seated in a side-box at the Paris opera next to "one of the loveliest young fellows I ever beheld"—who turns out to be a future brother-in-law. "The truth is," our author remarks, "that people live incomparably more by impulse and inclination than by reason and precept." "Even the wild Indians" feel "the sweet compunctions and emotions of the human heart." It is such opinions that make the *Fool of Quality* an interesting "document," and not its superfluity of episode, of thrilling heroism, of astonishing coincidence, or revolutions, discoveries, and deferred, heart-melting reunions. Its teachings commended the work even to so austere a mind as that of John Wesley, who in 1781 issued a condensed edition of it.

The strong set of the time was doubtless towards all these "sweet compunctions" and benevolences; but there were many readers and some writers who protested that while nature might be nature "wherever placed," it was

Walpole's
Reaction to
Novels

more effective in drama and novel if highly placed, if aristocratic. Horace Walpole [12] was one. It is easy to isolate excessively so-called "Gothic" or "terror" fiction from the sentimental tendencies of the time. Walpole in his second preface to his *Castle of Otranto* (1765) states that his story was "an attempt to blend the two kinds of romance, the ancient and the modern."

---

to letters, became acquainted with Pope, Lyttelton, and others, and in opposition to George II became a zealous adherent of Frederick, Prince of Wales. His tragedy *Gustavus Vasa* was forbidden to be acted because of political bias. In 1740 he returned to Ireland, where he lived the life of a country gentleman noted for his benevolence and generosity.—His works have been collected as *A Collection of Plays and Poems* (4v, 1778) and as *Poetical Works* (4v, Dublin, 1792). These include, in part, *Universal Beauty, A Poem* (1735); *Gustavus Vasa* (1739); *The Farmer's Six Letters to the Protestants of Ireland* (Dublin, 1745); *The Secret History and Memoirs of the Barracks of Ireland* (1745); *The Case of the Roman Catholics of Ireland* (Dublin, 1760); *The Fool of Quality; or the History of Henry Earl of Moreland* (5v, 1764-70; 2v [condensed by John Wesley], 1781); ed. Charles Kingsley (2v, 1859); ed. Ernest A. Baker (1906); *Juliet Grenville; or, The History of the Human Heart* (3v, 1774).
[12] For Walpole's career and his other writings see below, ch. VIII, n. 23.

By this he seems to mean an attempt to revive in briefer compass the marvelous or supernatural elements of seventeenth-century French romance, on which he had been reared, and to avoid any too "strict adherence to common life." Of Richardson and Fielding he had no great opinion. He stopped at the fourth volume of *Sir Charles Grandison*: "I was so tired of sets of people getting together, and saying, 'Pray, Miss, with whom are you in love?'" His own work would be more brief, more exotic, less bourgeois.

But his persons in *Otranto* are still the children of his own day rather than of the Middle Ages. Manfred, the blood-stained usurper, is Sindall in a costume rôle; Hippolita is a tearful, subservient wife of 1765; Conrad, the sickly heir, might be Harry Moreland's elder brother; Mathilda is the idyllic heroine hopelessly in love; Isabella is persecuted eighteenth-century innocence; and Theodore, the mysterious heir—"a lovely young prince, with large black eyes, a smooth white forehead, and manly curling locks like jet." This exquisite personage must, like Tom Jones, establish his birth and thus win estate and love. The ground bass of this performance, then, is familiar; it is the descant that is fantastically "Gothic," supernatural, and full (so the author hoped) of terror. With the supernatural causes of terror, however— his giant swords and helmets, his bleeding statues and walking portraits— Walpole was not too effective; with natural causes he was happier. His use of gloomy cloisters, strange sounds, and breathless flights—with the fragile Isabella panting out in the very nick, "Oh transport! here is the trap-door"— these were new and alluring; these chiefly his followers imitated. A less effective but much copied device is the attempt to get comic relief through excessive and ill-timed loquacity of servants, who here and in later tales are drawn after Dogberry, Verges, and Juliet's Nurse, but so feebly that they fail almost totally in comic power.

His significant Gothicism derives from medieval architecture, the theatrical gloom and mystery of which had been more slightly exploited in a scene in Congreve's *Mourning Bride* and in Pope's *Eloisa*. By rebuilding his house, Strawberry Hill, in Gothic style Walpole stimulated others to regard that style more favorably, but in literature his uses of Gothic background are less new or picturesque than sensational.[13] He knew something about medieval life, doubtless, but he embodied little knowledge in his story. A Gothic castle with subterranean passages, gloomy stairways, long corridors, and remotely slamming heavy doors—plus supernatural happenings—rescued one from "common life" and furnished thrills. Walpole's chief contribution to fiction is his reliance on exotic stage-sets; his primary aim was to avoid vulgar triviality. For novel-writers this medieval escape was never antiquarian, seriously historical, or learned; it simply provided a no-man's-land where startling, thrilling, sensational happenings might be frequent. In this vein Walpole was imitated by Clara Reeve, Ann Radcliffe, and many others.

Otranto a "Costume" Piece

Its Medievalism

13 Wilmarth S. Lewis, *The Genesis of Strawberry Hill* (Metropolitan Museum Studies, v [1934]) and W. H. Smith, *Architecture in English Fiction* (New Haven, 1934). The best life of Walpole is that by Robert W. Ketton-Cremer (1940).

tle of Otranto was crammed with absurdities not manipulated with
cal finesse; but the story was highly regarded, and its influence was
rmous.[14]

Another similar escape was to the Oriental.[15] Early in the century translations and pseudo-translations of Arabic, Persian, Turkish, and Chinese tales
flooded England, and thereafter the Oriental story or the essay with Oriental
background had great vogue. Usually these Oriental stories are short and
imbued with a moral-philosophical aim or with criticism of manners. At
times they are fantastic and horrible and relate thus to the novel of terror;
at times again they are merely sentimental with an exotic background used
to make displays of emotion plausible. Of such attempts in this vein as those
of John Hawkesworth (*Almoran and Hamet,* 1761), Mrs. Sheridan (*Nourjahad,* 1767) Charles Johnstone (*Arsaces,* 1774), and Robert Bage (*The Fair
Syrian,* 1787) little need be said; the tradition produced in this period only
two indubitable and yet very different masterpieces—Johnson's *Rasselas,*
which excels, as we have seen, not in its veneer of orientalism, but in its
dignity and wisdom of life, and William Beckford's *Vathek,* which excels
in its varied, theatrical fantasy.

Beckford's
Vathek

Beckford,[16] born to great wealth, social eminence, and idle amateurism,
expressed himself exotically. The enormous structure of his rebuilt palace,
Fonthill Abbey, represented an extreme of Gothicism, and the gloom of its
great hall has been said to have inspired his dreams of the Hall of Eblis in
Vathek. His later architectural creation, Lansdown Tower, near Bath, was
exotic if not Gothic. In literature his one notable achievement is *Vathek, an
Arabian Tale* (1786). This was written first in French, of which Beckford
had a fairly competent command, and was translated into English for him
by the Reverend Samuel Henley, who, contrary to Beckford's injunctions,
published his English version before the French had appeared. Beckford,
long afterwards, told his first biographer:

I wrote Vathek when I was twenty-two years old. I wrote it at one sitting, and
in French. It cost me three days and two nights of hard labour. I never took my
clothes off the whole time. This severe application made me very ill.

[14] This influence is studied in *Le Roman terrifiant* (Paris, 1920, 1923) by Alice M. Killen.
[15] Martha P. Conant, *The Oriental Tale in England in the Eighteenth Century* (1908).
[16] William Beckford (1760-1844), son of a Lord Mayor of London and heir to great
wealth, was born at Fonthill-Gifford, Wiltshire, was privately educated, traveled extensively,
and after 1784, despite frequent trips to the Continent, was, except for the years 1795-1805, a
Member of Parliament until 1820. Before that date he had long secluded himself at Fonthill.
He twice rebuilt the house on an increasingly grand scale, and added a tower 300 feet high,
which, when it soon fell, he replaced with another. Extravagance and neglect of business
matters forced him in 1822 to sell Fonthill, and he retired to Bath, where he died.—Guy
Chapman and John Hodgkin, *A Bibliography of William Beckford* (1930).—*Vathek* (trans-
lated into English by Samuel Henley as *An Arabian Tale,* 1786; in French, Lausanne, 1787;
Paris, 1787; ed. [English text] Richard Garnett, 1893, 1900; ed. [French text] Guy Chapman,
2v, 1929); *Modern Novel Writing* (2v, 1796); *Italy, with Sketches of Spain and Portugal*
(2v, 1834); *The Episodes of Vathek* (translated into English by Sir F. T. Marzials, ed.
"Lewis Melville" [L. S. Benjamin], 1912; the French text is in Chapman's *Vathek,* 2v, 1929);
The Travel-Diaries, ed. Guy Chapman (2v, 1928); *The Vision, Liber Veritatis,* ed. Guy Chapman (1930).—Cyrus Redding, *Memoirs* (1859); "Lewis Melville," *Life and Letters of Beckford*
(1910); John W. Oliver, *Life of Beckford* (1932); Guy Chapman, *Beckford* (1937).

Conceivably but not too probably this is true concerning a first draught of the story: Beckford's letters show him at work on the tale for a period of several weeks early in 1782, and it undoubtedly received from him all the care of which he was capable. On the three *Episodes* (first in English in 1912) designed for ultimate insertion towards the end of *Vathek* he worked intermittently over a longer period. They are far less inspired than *Vathek* itself. The story of how that sensual and sadistic young caliph sold his soul to the devil is a somewhat cynical, witty contribution to the literary satanism of a generation that also produced Goethe's *Faust* and the adolescent horrors of Lewis's *Monk*. Its prose has a brittle brilliance and is slyly ironical; in the final scene where the hearts of the newly damned are suddenly set aflame with infernal fire it achieves a superb theatrical quality that has been more than once mistaken for a sudden moral qualm on the part of the author. Beckford's Orientalism derived largely from the *Arabian Nights* and its train of imitations; he antedates the scholarly interest in the Orient fostered notably by Sir William Jones (1746-94), but by some happy accident of natural sympathy for his material his *Vathek* is the most successfully imaginative piece of exotic fiction in his century.

All these Gothic and Oriental tales form a small current in the stream of English fiction. Preoccupation with "common life" and with manners, in spite of Walpole, dominated novel-writing, and a fairly large number of the novels of manners escaped the drug of sentimentalism, and preserved, if not a high sense of human comedy, at least a satiric attitude. Both Mrs. Haywood in her *Betsy Thoughtless* (1751) and Sarah Fielding in her *Countess of Dellwyn* (1759) maintain a generally critical attitude towards female difficulties and dangers. True comedy is found at its best in this field in the work of Fanny Burney; but social satire abounds elsewhere. The curious thing about many of these satirical novels is their lack of technical progress. They hark back to the picaresque pattern—particularly to that of *The Golden Ass* of Apuleius, encouraged perhaps by Le Sage, by *The Sopha* (1742) of Crébillon *fils,* and by much of Smollett. Instead of a human adventurer they, like Apuleius, frequently substitute some unhuman piece of "currency"; Smollett used an atom; Francis Coventry in *Pompey the Little* (1751) used a lap-dog; an anonymous author (1760) produced *The Life and Adventures of a Cat;* and in *Chrysal* (1760-65) Charles Johnstone used a guinea. All these devices enabled authors to pass in satiric review various classes and professions in corrupt society. A persisting theme was the insensibility of the patron to humble merit, but in these tales the hard-hearted man of wealth is not treated with true sentimental horror. *Chrysal* was perhaps the most notable, or even notorious, of this type, with its glimpses of corruption in high places, its scandals about the Medmenham "monks," and its relations to the career of John Wilkes.

Other rambling satirical novels persisted in attempts at the pattern of *Don Quixote*. Among these were Smollett's *Sir Launcelot Greaves* (1760-61), Mrs. Lennox's *Female Quixote* (1752), in satire of the novel-reading girl,

Contemporary Manners Still Preferred

Novels of Episodic Pattern

and, more interesting, Richard Graves's *Spiritual Quixote* (1773), in which Whitefield and Methodist preachers are satirized in the adventures of Sir Geoffrey Wildgoose. This novel is also notable for its charming and frequent uses of English landscape backgrounds. Graves has a pretty gift of ridicule; he is neither too savage nor too absurd. There were also numberless novels of the loose biographical pattern, such as Thomas Amory's *John Buncle* (1756-66) or the fictional lives turned out by Edward Kimber.[17]

Fanny Burney

Fanny Burney [18] in her social attitude belongs to the courtesy-book tradition. She was no careless workman, and, aware of the traditions of her great predecessors, fashioned her neat plots with matrimony as a terminus, and formed her perfect characters on Richardsonian ideals, her eccentrics in the mode of Smollett. Perhaps instinctive and extreme decorum was naturally strong in her; in any case circumstances developed such instincts. Her father was a music master—a distinguished one, to be sure, and famous in his own right as author of a notable *History of Music* (1776-89)—but still a music master, and hence on the very edge of polite society. Socially the Burneys watched their steps and particularly Miss Fanny, who, like her heroines conscious of an insecure position, sought something more assured. She was a sensible, sensitive, decorous maiden with a very just feeling for social values—and a resulting tincture of snobbishness. Her sense of the socially ridiculous was acute and comprehensive. After all, her contemporaries were trying to live up to their setting—to their grand houses and magnificent gardens, to their furniture by Chippendale, Heppelwhite, Sheraton, or Adam, to their portraits by Reynolds, Gainsborough, or Romney, to their ruffles and laces, which required delicate gestures. No English generation before her day had been called upon to grace an environment so exquisite. Miss Burney saw, valued, and shared the attempt—and laughed at its incongruities.

Evelina

Evelina (1778), her first and most regarded novel, appeared at an auspicious moment when little or no coolly decorous and elegant fiction—in contrast to sentimental ardors—was being produced. It appeared anonymously, most of her family pretending at least ignorance of her authorship.

[17] F. G. Black, "Edward Kimber: Anonymous Novelist," *Harvard Studies & Notes in Phil. & Lit.*, XVII (1935). 27-42.

[18] Miss Burney (1752-1840) was the daughter of Dr. Charles Burney (1726-1814), organist and historian of music. Among Dr. Burney's early friends of influence was Fulke Greville (proud but second son of the fifth Lord Brooke), whose wife, Walpole's "pretty Fanny Macartney," was Fanny Burney's godmother. Another friend of Dr. Burney's, Samuel Crisp, became the "adopted father" (called "Daddy Crisp") of the Burney girls. He was Fanny's closest confidant and doubtless a prototype of Evelina's Mr. Villars. With the success of *Evelina* Miss Burney, aged 26, became the admired friend of Dr. Johnson and all his circle, particularly of Mrs. Thrale, who introduced her widely in society. (See James L. Clifford's *Hester Lynch Piozzi,* 1940). During the years 1786-91 Fanny was second keeper of the robes to Queen Charlotte. In 1793 she married a refugee from France, General d'Arblay, and during the decade 1802-1812 they lived in France. After their return to England, and especially after his death in 1818, Mme d'Arblay lived out her long old age in quiet retirement.— Apart from her novels she wrote *Memoirs of Dr. Burney* (3v, 1832), *The Diary and Letters of Madame d'Arblay* (7v, 1842-46), and *The Early Diary of Frances Burney* (2v, 1889). Biographical studies have been written by Austin Dobson (1903), by Constance Hill (*Juniper Hall,* 1904; *The House in St. Martin's Street,* 1907; *Fanny Burney at the Court of Queen Charlotte,* 1912), by R. B. Johnson (1926), and by Christopher Lloyd (1936).

It was an instant and enormous success among the best people. All the world from Dr. Johnson, Sir Joshua Reynolds, and Edmund Burke to Mrs. Delany and the Duchess of Portland were most complimentary—as one can see from Miss Burney's *Diary* where their favorable comments are carefully recorded. In *Evelina* as elsewhere Miss Burney wisely limited herself to a field that she understood, and she published only after a long apprenticeship. The story is in most senses an antithesis to *Tom Jones*. Evelina, with a stigma on her birth, must be owned by her father and show herself socially worthy of her paragon of masculine decorum, Lord Orville. The plot device most commonly used is summed up in the French term *contretemps:* unseasonable coincidence complicates many a simple circumstance. A vulgar grandmother intrudes most unhappily; people hear and misinterpret half-heard remarks or catch glimpses of seemingly equivocal but actually innocent situations. The inexperience of Evelina constantly gets her into small difficulties from more than one of which the impeccable Orville somewhat frigidly rescues her. The reader is ultimately almost as much surprised as Evelina herself to find that his lordship is in love with her.

Among her vulgar characters Miss Burney is happiest. Mr. Smith, the "gentleman *manqué*," was a great favorite, and the Branghtons, Evelina's crude kinfolk, were a great cause of mirth. Here the author's sense of ridicule and insight into degrees and kinds of "low" behavior serve her well. She is unhappy in her practical-joking sea-captain, Mirvan, and is not altogether sure in her handling of the "French" grandmother, Mme Duval, but for the rest her gallery of eccentrics is full, varied, and convincing. As her *Diary*— perhaps her greatest work after all—shows, she almost transcribes more than one eccentric from real life. Certainly she forgets "universality" in the face of an original character.

Evelina is effectively cast in epistolary form; only *Humphry Clinker* uses letters to better effect. But in her second novel, *Cecilia* (1782), which deals **Cecilia** with similar material, she discarded letters, and wrote in ten "books" subdivided into chapters of greatly varying lengths. The reason very possibly is that after *Evelina* she was urged to write a comedy. Significantly, she shrank from the stage as unsuitable for a lady; but in her second novel she wished perhaps to show that she could build up highly dramatic scenes of some length, and this could not be done well in letters. Even in *Evelina* she is as much interested in dramatic situation as she is in the sort of emotional analysis that made the letter a good form for Richardson and others.

Cecilia Beverley's difficulty is that her fortune has been left her on condition that she marry a man who will take her name. By *contretemps* she falls in love with young Delvile, who ardently returns her affection; but his family is proud of its antiquity, and he alone can perpetuate its name; hence their love is frustrated through four volumes and unspeakable agonies. Then a secret marriage takes place, but again misunderstandings, baseless jealousies, separate them until Cecilia runs mad at night in the streets of London and is only recovered by Delvile through a shopkeeper's notice inserted in an early "agony column" of *The Daily Advertiser*. *Cecilia* has less of grotesquely comic vulgarity than *Evelina,* but the heroine has a galaxy of three guardians each in his way unbelievable, and there is a mad moralist, Albany, who appears at the oddest moments to utter diatribes against the follies of fashionable life. The story is more melodramatic than *Evelina,* more sentimental, less comic, but equally thrilling.

With *Cecilia* Miss Burney's career as novelist really stopped. *Camilla* (1796) and *The Wanderer, or Female Difficulties* (1814) were tediously lacking in narrative interest, and were in fact courtesy books rather than stories. Her years at court in the service of the Queen had increased her regard for formality; and the horrors of the French Revolution doubtless heightened her belief in the best people. She was proud of having made the novel a valued and respectable vehicle for social instruction, and this pride with an increasing sense of the dignity of her function expressed itself in a cumbrous style that has been blamed on her personal admiration for Dr. Johnson. If a similar style were not to be found in other novelists who strove to be literary, the explanation might be satisfactory. But as the letter to her father prefixed to *The Wanderer* shows, she had come to regard the novel as by no means trivial in nature though of "frivolous exterior." Her late attempt to dignify this exterior was unfortunate; her early success in writing letters in a natural style and in portraying social correctness and social eccentricities, in creating a type of novel that, through manipulation of accidental misunderstanding or unseasonable coincidence, delineated "female difficulties" thrillingly, is undoubted. This fictional genre she passed on to her great superior, Jane Austen; and it is notable that a moral passage in the last chapter of *Cecilia* gave not merely the theme but even the title to *Pride and Prejudice.*

*Miss
Burney's
Later
Novels*

VI

The Drama, 1740-1785

The year 1740 saw the publication of Colley Cibber's *Apology,* which included an account of the drama from 1660 to the time in the thirties when the old Drury Lane company of actors finally disappeared.[1] In 1741 emerged the greatest theatrical genius of the century, David Garrick, whose success in *Richard III* at the unlicensed theatre in Goodman's Fields made him instantly the idol of theatre-goers. With him emerged a more natural method of acting; but increased dependence on histrionic skill did not tend to promote literary quality in the drama. With such performers as Macklin, Quin, Barry, J. P. Kemble, Kitty Clive, Peg Woffington, and, lastly, the tragedy queen, Sarah Siddons, who after 1782 dominated performances at Drury Lane, it was not necessary to have great playwrights, and almost none appeared. Three or four theatres at most easily accommodated patrons. Drury Lane, under the distinguished management of Garrick[2] (till 1776), of Sheridan (till 1788), and thereafter of J. P. Kemble, Mrs. Siddons' brother, was the "first" theatre normally. Covent Garden was in general less distinguished, but George Colman the Elder while in charge there (1767-77)

Personalities of the Theatre

[1] For the drama of this period histories with varying amounts of detail are as follows: David E. Baker, Isaac Reed, and Stephen Jones, *Biographia Dramatica* (3v, 1812); John Genest, *Some Account of the English Stage* (10v, Bath, 1832); Percy H. Fitzgerald, *A New History of the English Stage* (2v, 1882); George H. Nettleton, *English Drama of the Restoration and Eighteenth Century (1642-1780)* (1914); Ernest Bernbaum, *The Drama of Sensibility* (Boston, 1915); Alwin Thaler, *Shakspere to Sheridan* (Cambridge, Mass., 1922); Allardyce Nicoll, *A History of Late Eighteenth Century Drama, 1750-1800* (Cambridge, 1927). For two volumes of invaluable theatrical records of this period see Dougald MacMillan, *Drury Lane Calendar, 1747-1776* (Oxford, 1938) and, by the same scholar, *Catalogue of the Larpent Plays in the Huntington Library* (San Marino, Calif., 1939).

[2] David Garrick (1717-1779) was born at Hereford and educated in Lichfield and in Samuel Johnson's "academy" at Edial. In March, 1737, he came up to London with Johnson. Presently he and his brother started a wine business, but this proving unsuccessful David, already interested in dramatic writing, tried acting. His speedy success enabled him in 1747 to purchase a part of the patent for Drury Lane, and his career as manager began. He did much to revive the popularity of Shakespeare, and he wrote himself numerous pieces—many of them afterpieces or farces and others light comedies that furnished good rôles for himself and his company. Their literary merit was, on the whole, inconsiderable. After 1766 he ceased to act much, but continued as manager. In 1769 he organized the Shakespeare Jubilee at Stratford, and in 1773 he was elected to Johnson's Club. In 1776 he took leave of the stage by playing once again a complete round of his favorite characters.—*Dramatic Works* (3v, 1798); *Poetical Works* (2v, 1785); *Private Correspondence,* ed. James Boaden (2v, 1831-2); *Some Unpublished Correspondence,* ed. George P. Baker (Boston, 1907); *Pineapples of Finest Flavor* [letters], ed. David M. Little (Cambridge, Mass., 1930).—Thomas Davies, *Memoirs of Garrick* (2v, 1780; rev. S. Jones, 2v, 1808); Arthur Murphy, *Life of Garrick* (2v, 1801); Sir Joshua Reynolds, *Johnson and Garrick* (1816); ed. R. B. Johnson (1927); Percy H. Fitzgerald, *Life of Garrick* (2v, 1868; rev., 1899); Florence Parsons, *Garrick and his Circle* (1906); Dougald MacMillan, "David Garrick as Critic," *SP,* xxxi (1934). 69-83; Elizabeth P. Stein, *David Garrick, Dramatist* (1938).

staged both of Goldsmith's comedies, which had been refused by Garrick, and thus gave the house distinction. In the sixties, the supreme mimic of the period, Samuel Foote, got control of the Little Theatre in the Haymarket, famous earlier for Fielding's robust farces, and there in midday performances indulged his gifts for impersonations, farces, musical shows, and other entertainments. Whereas Drury Lane and, to a less degree, Covent Garden, stuck to the stereotyped sort of comedy and tragedy, the Little Theatre in the Haymarket was "experimental" (if one wishes to be polite)— or scurrilous. Foote's impersonations made him many enemies. Dr. Johnson, when asked how he escaped exhibition, replied of Foote: "Sir, fear restrained him; he knew I would have broken his bones." But Foote in spite of the libelous quality of his satire preserved a vital if unorthodox theatrical tradition.

Stagecraft

Except with new or very popular plays theatres normally offered as an evening's entertainment a major piece, either tragedy or comedy, and an afterpiece [3] of contrasting character. Between the acts frequently appeared singers, dancers, acrobats, or strong men—to keep the audience quiet. Afterpieces and even the major piece might frequently be musical comedies, such as Bickerstaffe's *Love in a Village* (1762) or Sheridan's *Duenna* (1775). In stagecraft the period shows some advance in lighting methods, and, after the coming of the Alsatian De Loutherbourg to Drury Lane in 1771, a considerable advance in the realism of scene painting.[4] The costumes usually made little pretense to historicity. Any lesser lady of the stage was proud to act "in a *cast* gown of some person of quality." Fashion rather than history was attended to. In 1764 *Richard III* was performed "in the Habits of the Times," and in 1773 *Macbeth* was staged in Scottish costumes: "modern dress," however, was the normal thing. Exotic performances or spectacles got special treatment. In 1785 John O'Keeffe and De Loutherbourg staged at Covent Garden a pantomime called *Omai, or a Trip round the World,* a landmark in the stagecraft of local color.[5] Omai, a noble savage from the South Seas, had visited England (1774-6) as a result of Captain Cook's second voyage to the South Seas, and had been a notable social success. With him had been brought back drawings of local costumes, weapons, and utensils, all of which were later used to give this pantomime a great pretense of local authenticity. It was at once a symbol of the cult of the noble savage, of British empire-building, and of the apparent intellectual bankruptcy of the London theatre. Outward realism already was a frequent substitute for sound psychology and good plotting in these days of pantomimes.

The more legitimate plays of the period were less novel than *Omai*. They were usually of obvious derivation and story. During the period of Garrick's

[3] C. R. Baskervill, "Play-lists and Afterpieces of the Mid-Eighteenth Century," *MP*, XXIII (1926). 445-464.

[4] W. J. Lawrence, "The Pioneers of Modern English Stage Mounting: De Loutherbourg," *The Magazine of Art* (March, 1895). Also Russell Thomas, "Contemporary Taste in the Stage Decorations of London Theaters, 1770-1800," *MP*, XLII (1944). 65-78.

[5] William Huse, "A Noble Savage on the Stage," *MP*, XXXIII (1936). 303-316; Thomas B. Clark, *Omai* (San Francisco, 1940).

dominance the tragedies and romantic comedies of Shakespeare[6] and other *Dr...*
Elizabethans were frequently revived or, even more frequently, reworked. *Fare*
Restoration comedies had to be made moral: Garrick himself made Wycher- *Time*
ley's country wife a decent woman in his own *Country Girl* (1766), and
there were numerous similar moral improvements. Translations of French
plays—those of Destouches, Voltaire, Diderot, and many others—were a
chief source throughout the period, and after 1786 German plays were
adapted with success, with the work of Kotzebue having enormous vogue
in the last decade of the century. The narrow vein of stereotyped comedy of
manners was nearing exhaustion, and neo-classical tragedy practically had
reached that point. The result was that not merely sentimental comedy but
also pantomimes, musical comedies, and burlettas, throve—and these last are
almost never drama in any literary sense.

The tragedies of this period lacked both novelty and freshness. As in the *Tragedies*
first fifty years of the century, there were attempts to use native historical
stories for tragic plots, but this was usually done without great success. To
be sure, Henry Brooke's use of the worn story of *The Earl of Essex* (1750)
had still some individuality. Hall Hartson's *Countess of Salisbury* (1767)
was a sentimental yet successful adaptation of the novel *Longsword*
(1762) written by Hartson's tutor, Dr. Thomas Leland; Thomas Francklin
reworked a play by J.-F. de la Harpe called *The Earl of Warwick* (1766);
William Woodfall, the journalist and actor, reworked Richard Savage's *Sir
Thomas Overbury* with success in 1777, and Hannah More's pseudo-historical *Percy* was well received at the end of the same year. Some of Shakespeare's historical plays were very popular, but no new tragedies on English
stories held the boards really well.

More successful were a few plays based upon a more modern interpretation of *domestica facta* that encouraged the writing of "domestic" or bourgeois tragedy. Edward Moore's prose *Gamester*[7] (1753) was a proper successor to *George Barnwell*. The hero, Beverley, confirmed in the vice of
gaming, loses his whole fortune through the machinations of a melodramatic
villain-friend (who remotely recalls Iago and Jonathan Wild), is accused of
murder, and poisons himself just before learning that he has succeeded to
the wealth of his uncle. The tears of the virtuous Mrs. Beverley doubtless
seemed both affecting and "natural." Similarly in the very successful
Douglas (1756), the masterpiece of "the Scottish Shakespeare," John Home[8]
(1722-1808), Lady Randolph's ever fresh grief for an infant son lost twenty
years ago, and now recovered only for a tragic fate, marks the play as
devoted to "simple nature." Its emotional power kept it on the stage for a
century or more in spite of obvious defects. Richard Cumberland's prose
tragedy, *The Mysterious Husband* (1783), with a plot based on secret marriages, was somewhat less lurid than Walpole's unacted *Mysterious Mother*

---

[6] On the adaptations of Shakespeare see George C. D. Odell, *Shakespeare from Betterton
to Irving* (2v, 1920), and Hazelton Spencer, *Shakespeare Improved* (Cambridge, Mass., 1927).
[7] John H. Caskey, *The Life and Works of Edward Moore* (New Haven, 1927).
[8] Alice E. Gipson, *John Home* (Caldwell, Idaho, 1917).

out not powerful enough to strengthen the domestic tradition in ...y, which was doing better in France and Germany than in its native .gland. Remotely lofty plots were still in demand; and if stories from English history were used with increasing frequency, Orientals, Peruvians, royal slaves, and noble Romans still made highly acceptable tragic heroes. The continued influence of Voltaire, from whom, for example, Arthur Murphy's *Orphan of China* (1759) derived, may account in part for the Oriental vogue. Pretentious poets, like William Whitehead, might still use classical stories, but the swing was away from that cult. William Mason, to be sure, used Greek tragedy as a model for his British stories of *Elfrida* and *Caractacus,* thus combining two traditions. But tragedy lacked the freshness necessary to hold its own against the increasing popularity of sentimental comedy.

Not that all comedy was sentimental. Comedy of manners was frequently attempted with success, and the loosely wrought comedy (or farce) that was topical and personal in its satire continued to find a home in the theatre where Henry Fielding had domesticated it, the Little Haymarket. The *Samuel* libelous work of Samuel Foote[9] (1720-1777) in the third quarter of the *Foote* century illustrates this at its most sensational limit. His plays are frequently devised to give the author-actor opportunity to show his gifts of impersonation, not merely in his noonday skits *The Diversions of the Morning* (1747), *An Auction of Pictures* (1748), and *Taste* (1752)—which are all practically identical except for their titles—but in his "scandal-chronicle" comedies as well. In *The Minor* (1760) he indulges in the popular sport of satirizing George Whitefield the Methodist; in *The Patron* (1764) he depicts Bubb Dodington (1691-1762), and in *The Maid of Bath* (1771) he derides the pre-Sheridan suitors of Miss Elizabeth Linley, the beautiful singer soon to be Mrs. Sheridan. These are but specimens. All of Foote's pieces are loosely constructed and, through their personalities, cheaply effective—grand vehicles for his talents in mimicry. The vitality of his performances can be judged in part by the influence they had on Garrick and even on Sheridan's play, *The Critic.*

It is usual to classify the comedies of this period, on the one hand, as old-fashioned witty plays that aimed to provoke laughter and amusement, *Laughing* and, on the other hand, as sentimental plays that avowed morality as their *and* object and at least secured tears as a response. Actually all comedies of the *Weeping* time have rid themselves of Restoration looseness of morals: the real diver-*Comedies* gence is between laughter and sentiment. Managers—Garrick and Colman, for example—were officially in favor of mirth; but their commercial instincts

9 Foote spent three years (1737-40) in Worcester College, Oxford, and thereafter had a career in London as young man about town. Having dissipated his fortune, he became an actor and was a great success because of his astonishing gifts of mimicry. In 1766 he obtained from the Duke of York the patent for a theatre in Westminster as compensation for a practical joke that had cost him his leg. He built the new Haymarket Theatre the following year, and continued to hold it until 1777, when he sold it to Colman.—*Works* (4v, 1786); ed. John Badcock (3v, 1830).—Percy H. Fitzgerald, *Samuel Foote: A Biography* (1910); Mary M. Belden, *The Dramatic Work of Samuel Foote* (New Haven, 1929).

made them very tolerant of "the luxury of tears." Playwrights found it somewhat easier to produce sentimental plays, which depended more on mystery and plot, than to turn out plays rich in sparkling wit, incisive and novel perception of faulty manners, and pointed situations. Even the best Restoration comedies lacked story and neat plot construction: in days of less witty genius when taste was returning to the story-drama of Shakespeare's age, a sentimental plot was both a refuge and an asset.

There were, however, many plays that relied on *vis comica*. Among these *Arthur* may be ranged those of Arthur Murphy [10] (1727-1805), who between 1756 *Murphy* and 1777 produced over a dozen farces or comedies. Tired of life as a bank clerk Murphy set up as journalist-essayist in 1752, and two years later began appearances as an actor. His brief career as such contributed something to his first play, a farce called *The Apprentice* (1756). His best afterpiece, *The Citizen* (1761), and a rewritten farce, *Three Weeks after Marriage* (1776), bring to the old sport of baiting citizens a new edge due to Murphy's own brief sojourn in a banking house. Drugget, in *Three Weeks,* one of Murphy's best characters, is the parvenu citizen of taste, a belated expert in topiary work, who wishes to cut two fine yews to represent Gog and Magog, because, as he says, "I won't have anything in my garden that looks like what it is." His best five-act comedies are *The Way to Keep Him* (1760) and *Know Your Own Mind* (1777). In this last-named play Murphy presents three well-contrasted ladies—Miss Neville, who arouses our pity for poor relations of charm; Lady Jane and Lady Bell, the shy and witty pair of sisters. Lady Bell speaks out to her shy sister: "You may let 'concealment feed on your damask cheek.' My damask cheek, I hope, was made for other purposes." Even these best of Murphy's comedies owe much to French sources; they are true comedies of manners, but are somewhat deficient in lightness, ease, and elegance of dialogue. Though at his real best in comedy, Murphy produced a half-dozen successful tragedies. The earliest was his *Orphan of China* (1759), adapted from Voltaire, and his best were *The Grecian Daughter* (1772) and *Alzuma* (1773), which blends classical and Peruvian elements. Habitually in most of his plays Murphy took his inspiration from books, but he usually adapted his borrowings effectively to the taste of the moment.

In native ability George Colman the Elder [11] (1732-1794) surpassed

---

[10] Murphy was born in Ireland and educated at the English College in St. Omer (France). He returned to England and Ireland for commercial employment, became interested in both the theatre and the law, entered Lincoln's Inn (1757), and although devoting most of his time to dramatic writing, continued to practise law until his retirement from the bar in 1788. He was Commissioner of Bankrupts, and at the end of his life had an annual pension of £200.—*Works* (7v, 1786). His periodical essays include *The Gray's Inn Journal* (52 nos., 1753-4; reprinted 2v [104 nos.], 1756); *The Test* (with Henry Fox and others, 35 nos., 1756-7); *The Auditor* (43 nos., 1762-3).—Jesse Foot, *Life of Arthur Murphy* (1811); John Homer Caskey, "Arthur Murphy and the War on Sentimental Comedy," *JEGP*, xxx (1931). 563-577; Howard H. Dunbar, *The Dramatic Career of Arthur Murphy* (1946; *MLA Revolving Fund Ser.*, xiv); John P. Emery, *Arthur Murphy, an Eminent English Dramatist of the Eighteenth Century* (Philadelphia, 1946).

[11] Colman the Elder was born in Florence, where his father was British envoy. He was educated at Westminster, Christ Church, Oxford, and in Lincoln's Inn. During the middle fifties, with other friends of Westminster days—notably Bonnell Thornton, Robert Lloyd, and William Cowper—he formed a "Nonsense Club." He became intimate with Garrick (1758),

Murphy, but the early promise of Colman's career was not fulfilled. After a half-dozen years (1760-66) of producing comedies and farces of vivid reality and vigor, managerial duties, or some other cause, brought about a decline in the quality of his plays. Although he wrote a variety of pieces during the years 1760 to 1786, many of these are so obviously derivative that he hardly deserves the credit for them. One of his most significant adaptations was Beaumont and Fletcher's *Philaster* (1763), which remained popular for years. In 1777 his *Spanish Barber* was based on *Le Barbier de Séville,* the famous new comedy by Beaumarchais; and his last play, *Tit for Tat* (1786), was based on a recent Dublin success, which in turn derived from Marivaux. Colman's first work, *Polly Honeycombe* (1760), was a gay afterpiece satirizing the novel-reading girl and warning that soon, if not already, it would be more reprehensible to read novels than plays. Polly, like her descendant, Lydia Languish (and also, vaguely, Lydia Melford in *Humphry Clinker*), frequents the circulating library—"that evergreen tree of diabolical knowledge." [12] In 1761 in *The Jealous Wife* Colman contrived a somewhat novel plot in the distresses of Harriot Russet, whose initial situation reminds one of Sophia Western in London: Harriot escapes from the advances of Lord Trinket in her aunt's house, and finds shelter with the Oaklys; Mrs. Oakly is the jealous wife, but all turns out happily when her husband reduces her jealousy to ridicule, and then Harriot and young Charles Oakly, true lovers, are made happy. *The Jealous Wife* was one of the most popular and most truly comic plays of the century. Its equal in character interest and skilful construction was the play in which Colman had the considerable aid of David Garrick, *The Clandestine Marriage* (1766). Here Lord Ogleby has brought his nephew, Sir John Melvil, to arrange a marriage with the elder daughter of the newly rich Sterlings. Both nephew and uncle, however, successively are smitten with the younger daughter, Fanny, who is already secretly married to her father's clerk, Lovewell. Much of the comedy depends on the matriarchal Mrs. Heidelberg, on the superannuated foppishness of Lord Ogleby, and on satire of the *nouveau riche* taste in gardening and other foibles of the day. The serious complications come to a thrilling climax, and when the clerk Lovewell announces that he is "the happiest of men," the faithful maid Betty sobs, "I could cry my eyes out to hear his magnimity." It has been suspected that the audience shared in this benevolent sobbing. The seriousness of the suspense in the Fanny-Lovewell action brings to the play the mixture of comic and sentimental elements that is the normal characteristic of the drama at this time.

---

devoted himself increasingly to dramatic writing, and upon the death of his uncle, William Pulteney, Earl of Bath (1764), he abandoned the law. For the years 1767-77 he was manager of the Covent Garden theatre and during 1777-89 of the Haymarket theatre. He became insane shortly before his death.—*Dramatic Works* (4v, 1777).—George Colman the Younger, *Random Records of my Life* (2v, 1830); Richard B. Peake, *Memoirs of the Colman Family* (2v, 1841); Joseph M. Beatty, "Garrick, Colman and *The Clandestine Marriage*," *MLN*, xxxvi (1921). 129-141; Eugene R. Page, *George Colman the Elder* (1935); Howard P. Vincent, "Christopher George Colman, 'Lunatick'," *RES*, xviii (1942). 38-48.

[12] Austin Dobson, " 'Polly Honeycombe'," in *Eighteenth Century Vignettes, Third Series* (1896), pp. 83-103.

Chief among the sentimental playwrights were Hugh Kelly (1739-1777) *Hugh* and Richard Cumberland (1732-1811). Kelly's career was brief and very *Kelly* successful.[13] A needy Irishman, for the first years of his residence in London, 1760-67, he relied on contributions to periodicals and work on newspapers for a living. Garrick took him into protection, and he won fame by his first comedy, *False Delicacy* (1768), which was staged in successful rivalry with Goldsmith's first play, *The Good Natur'd Man*. *False Delicacy* was acted over twenty times the first season, and within the year ten thousand printed copies of it were sold. The plot employs a triple intrigue, giving rise to much complexity of situation. Lady Betty, a young widow, too delicate for the impropriety of a second marriage, will not have Lord Winworth, whom secretly she loves. He consequently turns to her protégée, Miss Marchmont— who, though in love with Sidney, is under obligations to Lady Betty, who *seems* to wish Miss Marchmont to make Lord Winworth happy. Meanwhile Miss Rivers, in love with Sir Harry, must have the delicacy to obey her father and marry Sidney. The false delicacy of these three ladies is cured by the two anti-sentimental characters, Mrs. Harley and Cecil, who furnish the comedy in the play. As a result of his new fame it was alleged that Kelly received a pension from the unpopular minister Lord North, and when his second comedy, *A Word to the Wise* (1770), was brought on, it was at once damned by political cabal. After a negligible tragedy, *Clementina* (1771), *The School for Wives* (1773), the least sentimental of Kelly's plays, was successfully produced. It, like *False Delicacy,* ends in three weddings after misunderstood situations. In 1774 Kelly produced his last play, was called to the bar, and gave up literature—both the theatre and newspaper work. The play, *The Romance of an Hour,* is a two-act afterpiece, in which Zelida, a *petite Hindoue,* "a character of perfect simplicity," finally marries the man she loves rather than the Colonel to whom her father had bequeathed her. The comedy comes largely from a near-admiral whose manners and lan-guage, as his wife judiciously remarks, are those of the forecastle. In concern over the distress of Zelida this would-be wit hopes that the arrival of the Colonel "will prevent the worms of her sorrow from eating into the planks of her constitution."

Richard Cumberland [14] had a longer, more distinguished, and more

---

[13] *The Works of Hugh Kelly, to which is Prefixed his Life* (1778).—Mark Schorer, "Hugh Kelly: His Place in the Sentimental School," *PQ,* XII (1933). 389-401.

[14] Richard Cumberland, son of the Master of Trinity College, Cambridge, and-grandson of a more famous Master of the College (Richard Bentley), was born in the Master's Lodge, February 19, 1732. He was educated in Bury St. Edmunds, Westminster, and Trinity College, Cambridge. His brilliant record as a student helped him to both academic and civic employ-ments. His work was concerned with the Board of Trade and with various American colonies. He was briefly (1780-1) Ambassador to Spain, from which mission he returned distressed in health and in finances. His last years were spent in Tunbridge Wells, where he devoted most of his time to varied literary work. He died in 1811, the acquaintance of Byron, Tom Moore, and Scott.—Five from his forty plays (never collected in one edition) are found in Vol. XVIII of Mrs. Inchbald's *British Theatre* (1808). He also published translations, poetry, religious tracts, essays, conducted *The London Review* (2v, 1809), wrote two novels, *Henry* (1795) and *John de Lancaster* (3v, 1809), and published his own *Memoirs* (2v, 1806-7). Stanley T. Williams has written the standard biography, *Richard Cumberland* (New Haven, 1917), and has published additional articles in *MLN* during 1920 and 1921.

*Richard
Cumber-
land*

quarrelsome career than did Kelly. His eye for good materials was both covetous and furtive, and although he borrowed plots or situations freely, he was from the beginning of his career sensitive to accusations of such thefts. Thus he was easily identified as the original of Sir Fretful Plagiary in Sheridan's *Critic*. He first achieved success in his comedy *The Brothers* (1769), and while he produced a half-dozen tragedies and a few musical comedies, his real success lay in sentiment. *The Brothers* is typical of its day in its complicated plot, its deep-dyed villain contrasting with a completely virtuous younger brother, its use of a secret marriage, of a quarrelsome married couple, and its enveloping gloom of distress. His best comedy, *The West Indian* (1771), introduces an element notable in several of his plays, the defense of character types formerly treated as ridiculous. In his *Memoirs* he explains his object: "I introduced the characters of persons who had been usually exhibited on the stage as the butts for ridicule and abuse, and endeavoured to present them in such lights as might tend to reconcile the world to them, and them to the world." In *The West Indian* these puffed characters are the Irishman O'Flaherty, who is made genteelly winsome, and Belcour, the West Indian, a child of nature in Rousseau's pattern. Belcour is certainly one of the most attractive heroes of sentimentality. The same method of characterization is used in other plays: in *The Fashionable Lover* (1772) he combats the prejudice against Scots by creating the virtuous steward, Colin Macleod; and in *The Jew* (1794) he created Sheva to combat anti-Semitism. Allied with this element of purpose Cumberland had an obvious tendency to melodrama. *The Wheel of Fortune* (1795), his most appealing play of this sort, was long enormously successful. Its central character, Penruddock, is an interesting summation of much in the whole period. He is the Man of the Hill in *Tom Jones* and a dozen other places: the unsocial hermit, here devoted to the thought of revenge for long past wrongs, but (since this is a moment for facile moral reform) here to be converted to ultimate benevolence. The character of mixed good and evil, with good bound to win through ultimately, made Penruddock one of the best emotional rôles of the day. The moving performance of J. P. Kemble, who created the rôle, doubtless gave the play much of its power. Cumberland's last comedy, *The Widow's Only Son*, was staged in 1810. His death in the following year and burial in the Poet's Corner in the Abbey ended one of the longest careers known for an English dramatist.

*Opposition
to Senti-
mental
Comedy*

Throughout his fifty years as playwright there had been notable objection to the sort of play called comedy by Cumberland and his admirers. Garrick himself passed jokes about the advisability of putting a steeple on the playhouse now that it was a temple of virtue, and sneered gently at "these our moral and religious days." Avowedly it was a warfare between two schools, one stressing the desire to promote morality and the other a desire to promote mirth and entertainment. But the contrast thus stated is surely too strong. If Hugh Kelly and Cumberland made obvious concessions to mirth, so Goldsmith and Sheridan, the two great writers supposed hostile to "weeping comedies," made concessions to morality. All plays, one may rashly say, were now moral; but some preached more explicitly than others. In general, also, the morality of the sentimentalists was excessively facile: from Cibber's *Love's Last Shift* (1696) to Cumberland's *First Love* (1795) the erring are shamed into virtue with surprising—and unconvincing—ease. The situation, suggesting at times a not too sincere didacticism, is simply explained by the fact that audiences were readier to pay for tears than for laughter.

The subservience of the managers to their own commercial interests was what first moved Goldsmith to animosity,[15] and his attack on the managers in the chapter "Of the Stage" in his *Enquiry into the Present State of Polite Learning in Europe* (1759) was not forgiven by Garrick. He declined both Goldsmith's plays for Drury Lane, and in 1768 injured the success of *The Good Natur'd Man* by producing in competition with it Hugh Kelly's new comedy, *False Delicacy*. Shortly before submitting *She Stoops to Conquer* to public censure, Goldsmith published in *The Westminster Magazine*[16] his essay *A Comparison between Laughing and Sentimental Comedy*. He bluntly queries "whether the exhibition of human distress is likely to afford the mind more entertainment than that of human absurdity?" He asserts that "the distresses of the mean by no means affect us so strongly as the calamities of the great." "While we melt for Belisarius, we scarcely give halfpence to the beggar." Goldsmith thinks that the success of so-called sentimental comedies, "in which the virtues of private life are exhibited, rather than the vices exposed, and the distresses rather than the faults of mankind make our interest in the piece," may be due to novelty or to "their flattering every man in his favorite foible." But he thinks such plays deficient in *vis comica,* and thinks audiences likely by being "too fastidious" to banish humor from the stage.

Goldsmith's Views

In his *Good Natur'd Man* Goldsmith had not been too fastidious; he had instead offensively put fine sentiments about generosity into the mouth of a low bailiff—and of that scene the exquisite auditors forced the excision. But as a partial concession to such possible critics he had combined in his hero, Young Honeywood (as he had in Beau Tibbs and the Man in Black in his essays), both sentiment and criticism of sentiment. Young Honeywood, to his uncle's disgust, "loves all the world"; and such "love" is undiscriminating. "His good-nature arises rather from his fears of offending the importunate, than his desire of making the deserving happy." Thus Goldsmith preaches, here as elsewhere, a *prudent* benevolism. Honeywood, like Fielding's good men, is unsuspicious and easily deceived: the play is the history of his education, and in the process Miss Richland aids more actively than most eighteenth-century heroines could have done. The subplot resembles that of Bevil Junior and Indiana in *The Conscious Lovers:* it is, if anything, less carefully constructed than Steele's story. Croaker—an obviously "humorous" character of the late Elizabethan type—is used to subvert sentimentality:

Goldsmith's Plays

---

[15] For treatment of Goldsmith's nondramatic works see below, ch. VII.
[16] For January, 1773; also in his *Works* (ed. J. W. M. Gibbs), I. 398-402.

"Ah! my dear friend," he croaks, "it is a perfect satisfaction to be miserable with you." The play got little recognition from its early audiences, since in spite of its easy dialogue the whole lacks focus and structure, and even the comic effect its author sought.

She Stoops to Conquer (1773), on the other hand, was an immediate success, and has always remained one of the half-dozen most popular comedies in English. From the start it was recognized as almost farce; but even in days when it was ill-bred to laugh loudly, this play made Horace Walpole and the other exquisites "laugh very much." All English audiences since 1773 have joined in the laughter, and in spite of defects in structure, plausibility, and characterization, its appeal has hardly waned. Enjoyment here is not much heightened by analysis. One sees the improbability of the continued misapprehension that the Hardcastle mansion is a country inn; one can accept the comic bashfulness of Young Marlow, but not his inability to distinguish a barmaid from a young lady; one is pleased with Tony Lumpkin's ability to display his Latinity in his song on The Three Pigeons in Act I, but surprised to find him practically illiterate in Act IV (he is of course stupid or shrewd as the individual situation demands); and one finds Mrs. Hardcastle's kneeling to her own husband in her own garden and fancying herself forty miles away on Crackskull Common face to face with a highwayman—one finds this a strain on the bedazzled imagination. These defects would kill any other comedy, and yet they count as nothing in this jolliest of all plays. Whatever its absurdities, the action seems to move naturally and among natural homely people—not the artificially sensitive persons found in sentimental comedy nor the hard, brittle wits of high comedy. The characters are all easily individualized—drawn again in the "humorous" Jonsonian fashion—and they are all individuals new to the drama of their day. The historic excellence of the work lies not in the fact that it is apparently anti-sentimental or that it is obviously attempting a revival of the comedy of manners. It is *sui generis,* not sentimental and not overtly anti-sentimental. It has been likened to the work of Farquhar, but it is better written and is morally innocent. Like much of Goldsmith's work, it is casually rather than carefully organized; and it is not too surely prophetic of more dramatic masterpieces from Goldsmith. He died a twelvemonth after its success. The play has succeeded perfectly in being what its author hoped it would be—one of the most entertaining plays in English.

Sheridan   Richard Brinsley Sheridan,[17] ordinarily regarded as Goldsmith's aid and

[17] Sheridan (1751-1816) was the grandson of Swift's friend, Dr. Thomas Sheridan. His father was an actor, who, when Richard was not yet twenty, left London for Bath, where he taught elocution. Richard's mother, Frances Sheridan (1724-66), was the author of two novels and of three plays. Some translations, popular verses, and an unaccepable farce were the products of her son's early years. In 1772 the beautiful singer, Elizabeth Linley, persecuted by undesired suitors, persuaded young Richard to escort her to a refuge in a religious house in France. In France they were allegedly married, the ceremony being repeated in England a year later. Meanwhile Sheridan fought two duels with a less fortunate suitor, and was "rusticated" at Waltham Abbey by his father. In the late summer of 1774 he wrote *The Rivals,* and for the next five years his chief activities were theatrical. In 1776 he became part owner and manager of the Drury Lane theatre, and in 1777 he was elected a member of

successor in the attempt to restore comedy to its own province of mirth, had almost as brief a career as Goldsmith. In the years 1775-79 he produced five plays and two afterpieces. One of these was a very successful comic opera, *The Duenna* (1775), which beat all records for full-length plays with seventy-five performances in its first season. Its long popularity was due to ingenious plotting and to its music rather than to any notable brilliance or wit in the lines. Another play, *A Trip to Scarborough* (1777), is a competent sterilized version of Vanbrugh's *Relapse*. The sex of the bawd Coupler is changed; Loveless and Berinthia overstep the bounds of decorum but not of morality, and the ingenious double plot is preserved effectively. Sheridan's last play, *Pizarro* (1799), adapted from the popular Kotzebue, adds nothing to his fame.

There remain, then, three original comedies, and since the last of these, *The Critic* (1779), is least important, it may be first disposed of. In method it is a "rehearsal" in the tradition instituted by the Duke of Buckingham in 1671, brought to its cleverest development by Fielding's *Tom Thumb* (1730), and used by various playwrights, among them Garrick in his *Peep behind the Curtain* (1767). It is highly significant, as Mr. Rhodes has shown, that the methods of Sheridan involve caricature rather than parody, of which last there is little in *The Critic*. The verbal dexterity of Buckingham and Fielding is discarded for impersonation and mimicry: the result is perhaps more theatrical but less literary. By the same token it tends to be more perishable because of its topical nature. Sir Fretful Plagiary is Richard Cumberland, but since here the burlesque is good satire, it transcends the personality of one man, and becomes a lasting symbol of the vanity and irritability of bards born without thick skins; and yet it remains Cumberland. Lesser burlesques are traceable, but less tangibly. The play is also a "war" play: Spain had declared war on England three or four months before *The Critic* with its rehearsal of a new tragedy called "The Spanish Armada" was presented. Thus the immediate success of the piece was topical in part; the ultimate value lies in the theatrical wisdom shown in the implicit and explicit observations made on the nature of tragedy and in the element of robust good fun that dominates every scene. Sheridan was already looking forward in 1779 to a political career, and this farcical treatment of tragedy and of public affairs came as an appropriate transition.

Sheridan's great service to English drama lies in his two high comedies.

The Critic

---

the Club on motion of Dr. Johnson himself. He was in Parliament from 1780 to 1812, and politics withdrew his attention from the theatre. His gifts as orator equaled those as playwright. With Burke he was very active in the impeachment of Warren Hastings, and his speeches were as much enjoyed as Burke's were admired. He was long the confidential adviser of the Prince Regent, who remained his generous friend to the time of Sheridan's death. Personally Sheridan was a brilliant wit of charm and fascination. Although his later years were financially perplexed, he lived gaily, drank to excess, and was an artful and scheming gallant "among fine ladies." Wit and charm made these faults venial in the Regency period. —Much myth has arisen among the facts of Sheridan's life. The best biography perhaps is *Harlequin Sheridan* by R. Crompton Rhodes (1933). Other lives, among many, are those by Walter Sichel (2v, 1909) and W. A. Darlington (1933). For the standard text see *The Plays and Poems of Sheridan*, ed. R. C. Rhodes (3v, Oxford, 1928).

The Rivals   *The Rivals* [18] and *The School for Scandal* are amazing for their period and excellent for any period. They represent a return to the ideals of witty, elegant comedy, purged of its Restoration impurities, but a return that preserves an amusing consciousness of contemporary sentimental absurdities. *The Rivals* was soundly damned at its first performance on January 17, 1775. While in rehearsal the play had been puffed as "the *ne plus ultra* of comedy," and this boast for a new playwright not yet twenty-four years old may have antagonized other literati. The title, with the knowledge that the scene was Bath, may have suggested that the squabbles over the fair Elizabeth Linley, "The Maid of Bath," were to be served up again, and that idea might stimulate to opposition Sheridan's rivals in love. But the performance was inadequate, and the play faulty. Shuter as Sir Anthony Absolute made little pretense of having learned his lines, and Lee as Sir Lucius O'Trigger was ineptly cast. The rôle of Sir Lucius, furthermore, was regarded as insulting to the Irish gentry. Coming after Cumberland's gracious O'Flaherty in *The West Indian* the rôle of Sir Lucius, as first written, naturally grated on Irish sensibilities. All told, the performance had too much buffoonery and it lasted an hour longer than usual. The only parts generally liked were the sentimental scenes between Julia and Faulkland. And so the play was withdrawn that its faults might be corrected. The rôle of Sir Lucius was largely rewritten, and the dialogue much improved. Clinch replaced Lee as actor of the rôle; Shuter learned his lines; the whole was shortened, and Sheridan's personal enemies remained quiet: the net result was that the second performance (eleven days after the first) was greeted with agreeable convulsions of laughter, and the play was repeated twelve times or more that season. It became from that moment a permanent part of English dramatic repertoire.

The intrigue of *The Rivals* is not too original, but it is skilfully conducted, and the humors of Mrs. Malaprop, Sir Anthony, Bob Acres, and indeed the whole cast are triumphs of theatrical genius. Even borrowed bits—the novel-reading girl, the coward forced into a duel, the rebellious son bent on marrying to please himself and not his father and yet making love unwittingly to the very girl his father wants him to wed—all such bits, though not new, are treated so vividly that Sheridan makes them easily his own. Even more surely did he appropriate to himself the device now called "malapropism," which had been popular since the days of Mistress Quickly, and had renewed its popularity many times in the eighteenth century. Every admirer has his favorites among Mrs. Malaprop's "nice derangement of epitaphs," but her projected schooling for girls may serve as an example:

I would send her, at nine years old, to a boarding-school, in order to learn a little ingenuity and artifice.—Then, Sir, she should have a supercilious knowledge in accounts;—and as she grew up, I would have her instructed in geometry, that she might know something ôf the contagious countries;—but above all, Sir Anthony, she should be mistress of orthodoxy, that she might not mis-spell, and mis-pro-

[18] *The Rivals* has been admirably edited by Richard L. Purdy (Oxford, 1935).

nounce words so shamefully as girls usually do; and likewise that she might reprehend the true meaning of what she is saying.—This, Sir Anthony, is what I would have a woman know;—and I don't think there is a superstitious article in it.

Auditors in the theatre catch but fragments of this word-play, but from its profusion enough is grasped to make its uproarious effect unfailing. In lightness, crispness, and elegance of point the dialogue of the play is unsurpassed, unless by Congreve, who in wit is Sheridan's only real competitor.

Two years later (1777) the only rival to the fame of *The Rivals* was staged: *The School for Scandal*. This was carefully prepared; Sheridan was now the author-manager, and could cast his own players. In the opinion of Horace Walpole, "there were more parts performed admirably...than I almost ever saw in any play." The dialogue this time was set down with such exquisite Congreve-like precision that it enforced excellence of delivery. James Boaden thought the comedy "better *spoken,* in all its parts, than any play that I have witnessed upon the stage." Unlike *The Rivals,* then, it sailed to success with poise, dignity—and with a dazzling glitter of wit. It has indeed been urged that even the stupid characters are here made witty, that there is a surfeit of wit. The assumption seems to be that characters—particularly servants—ought to use "the language of real life," which is a strange idea if applied to eighteenth-century servants at least. Audiences seldom balk at too much wit; only critics do that.

Much in the play is partly familiar; but here it strikes us always with the pleasure of novelty: the quarrelsome couple, here the old husband and the young wife from the country; the two brothers, one impulsive and feckless like Tom Jones, the other mouthing fine sentiments like Blifil, and plotting mischief; the "scandal-club" of Lady Sneerwell—and more besides are all familiar; yet here are felt to be endowed with new life. Apart from the dialogue, the pride of the play is doubtless the perfect manipulation of the intrigue leading inevitably to the thrilling resolution in the famous screen scene. More than marital worries are here resolved: at this crucial moment Sheridan pays his cutting respects to the sentimentalists. In this play he makes no concessions to Julias and Faulklands. He presents Charles Surface, the true man of feeling who gaily eschews fine sentiments, and Joseph, the hypocritical man of feeling, who conceals malice under falsely moral or noble sentiments. Thus, early in the screen scene, Joseph has reproached Charles for having given Sir Peter cause to suspect Lady Teazle: "I'm sorry to find, Charles, you have lately given that worthy man grounds for great uneasiness"; and before the screen goes down Sir Peter has urged Charles to be like Joseph: "He is a man of sentiment.—Well, there is nothing in the world so noble as a man of sentiment!" After the screen is down, Charles makes (for Sheridan) his retort about sentiments:

Egad, you seem all to have been diverting yourselves here at hide and seek, and I don't see who is out of the secret.—Shall I beg your ladyship to inform me? Not a word!—Brother, will you be pleased to explain this matter? What! is

The School for Scandal

Morality dumb too?—Sir Peter, though I found you in the dark, perhaps you are not so now! All mute! ... so I'll leave you to yourselves—[*Going*] Brother, I'm sorry to find you have given that worthy man grounds for so much uneasiness.—Sir Peter! there's nothing in the world so noble as a man of sentiment!

If Sheridan's object was to discredit sentimentalism, this retort should have accomplished it; but sentimentalism is only an ingredient in the rich sauce of his satire. He gives us the quintessence of a scandal-loving society, its brilliantly lacquered veneer, its less lovely basic substance. He can be serious, but is not too serious; he keeps to the comic aspects of the foibles of the day, and enlivens the whole with incessant sparkling wit.

Later Sentimental Plays   It is very wrong to assume that Goldsmith and Sheridan gave notable pause to sentimentalism. It went marching on, specializing at the end of the century in either melodrama as in the early plays of George Colman the Younger [19] (1762-1836) or in the drama of humanitarian purpose as in the plays of such revolutionists as Thomas Holcroft [20] (1745-1809) and Mrs. Elizabeth Inchbald [21] (1753-1821) or of Thomas Morton (1764?-1838), author of *Speed the Plough* (1800) and *The Slave* (1816). In *Such Things Are* (1787) Mrs. Inchbald portrayed the great prison-reformer, John Howard, under the name of Haswell, who in a Sumatra prison converses with a noble savage, Zedan. The Indian has stolen Haswell's pocketbook, hoping to buy his freedom. As Haswell repasses with the Keeper, there ensues the following conversation—sufficiently indicative of the persistence of sentiment:

Keeper. [*To Zedan.*] What makes you here?—still moping by yourself, and lamenting for your family? [*To Haswell.*] That man, the most ferocious I ever met with, laments, sometimes even with tears, the separation from his wife and children.

Hasw. [*Going to him.*] I am sorry for you, friend: [Zedan *looks sullen and morose.*] I pity you.... Poor man! bear your sorrows nobly.—And, as we are alone, no miserable eye to grudge the favour—[*Looking round.*] take this trifle —[*Gives Money.*] it will, at least, make your meals better for a few short weeks, till Heaven may please to favour you with a less sharp remembrance of the happiness you have lost.—Farewell.

[Zedan *catches hold of him, and taking the Pocket-book from his Belt, puts it into* Haswell's *Hand.*]

Hasw. What's this?

Zedan. I meant it should gain me my liberty—but I will not vex you.

Hasw. How came you by it?

Zedan. Stole it—and wou'd have stabb'd you, had you been alone—but I am glad I did not—Oh, I am glad I did not!

Hasw. You like me then?

Zedan. [*Shakes his Head, and holds his Heart.*] 'Tis something that I never

[19] Colman the Younger's *Dramatic Works* were edited, with a Life, by J. W. Lake (4v, Paris, 1827). Colman wrote an autobiography covering his life to about 1790, which he published (2v) in 1830 as *Random Records*. See also Richard B. Peake, *Memoirs of the Colman Family* (2v, 1841).

[20] On Thomas Holcroft see Elbridge Colby, "A Bibliography of Thomas Holcroft," *Bull. New York Public Library* (1922), and articles by Mr. Colby as listed in *CBEL*, II. 470.

[21] James Boaden, *Memoirs of Mrs. Inchbald* (2v, 1833).

felt before—it makes me like not only you, but all the world besides.—The love of my family was confined to them alone—but this sensation makes me love even my enemies.

Hasw. O, nature! grateful! mild! gentle! and forgiving!—worst of tyrants they, who, by hard usage, drive you from men's breasts.

It may gratify the reader to know that at the end of the play Zedan is given his freedom.

VII

The Periodicals and Oliver Goldsmith

In the thirties when Johnson and Smollett came up to London armed with their tragedies, the most likely openings for needy authors were in the fields of periodical literature. The same situation held in the late fifties when Goldsmith reached London. Literature, in fact, was increasingly "periodical." The lowest and most completely anonymous employments of this sort were offered by newspapers, which sooner or later got involved dangerously in politics. The most ambitious efforts in the field were put forth in following the path marked out by the *Tatler* and *Spectator,* in the periodical essay.[1] The golden mean of effort between these two extremes was solicited by the newly developing magazines and reviews. It may help if we survey developments in these fields as a background for the career of the most attractive essayist of the time, Oliver Goldsmith.

The history of the periodical essay in the later part of the century is one of decline and of absorption into newspapers as a "feature." Such an opinion is unfair to the serial which more than any one other work made the reputation of Dr. Johnson—*The Rambler* (1750-52), a periodical doubtless second only to *The Spectator* and possibly to *The Tatler.* But *The Rambler* ran only for 208 numbers as compared with *The Spectator's* 555, and it appeared only twice a week instead of six times. After two years of "the anxious employment of a periodical writer," Johnson was delighted to quit. It is true that his essays were considerably longer than those of Addison and Steele, and that fact augmented their difficulty by making it more necessary to have significant content. The earlier essayists wrote playfully, like statesmen out of office, on a vacation: Johnson and many of the later essayists were more serious.[2] Bluntly, the contrast is between entertaining journalism and the ingenious display of mind. Such a contest is likely to be weighted in favor of entertainment as opposed to intellect.

Johnson displayed high intellectual quality, but he and his generation lacked lightness and informality. The "principal design" of *The Rambler* was "to inculcate wisdom or piety." Possibly, as Johnson said in his conclud-

The Rambler

---

[1] Information concerning the development of the essay must largely be sought in the biographies of the various essayists. In addition to the more general works cited on the periodical essay in Part II, ch. v, the following are useful for the period after 1750: Arthur S. Collins, *Authorship in the Days of Johnson* (1927); David Nichol Smith, "The Newspaper," *Johnson's England,* ed. Arthur S. Turberville (2v, Oxford, 1933), II. 331-367; Benj. C. Nangle, *The Monthly Review (1749-89): Indexes of Contributors and Articles* (Oxford, 1934); Laurence Hanson, *Government and the Press, 1695-1763* (Oxford, 1936); George Nobbe, *The North Briton: A Study in Political Propaganda* (1939).

[2] O. F. Christie, *Johnson the Essayist* (1924).

ing paper, he produced some essays "of which the highest excellence is harmless merriment," but gaiety of tone is not here really obtrusive. He had little assistance, and that little came also from persons of sobriety: Elizabeth Carter, Catherine Talbot, Hester Mulso (later Mrs. Chapone), each wrote one or two, and Samuel Richardson, the novelist, wrote No. 97, which is said to have outsold all other numbers. Significantly, Richardson suggests that more attention be paid in *The Rambler* to ridicule of "fashionable follies" in the manner of *The Spectator*. Johnson recognized this lack of lightness and variety, and at the end feared that "the severity of dictatorial instruction has been too seldom relieved, and that he [the reader] is driven by the sternness of The Rambler's philosophy to more cheerful and airy companions"; but if the author "can be numbered among the writers who have given ardor to virtue and confidence to truth," he will rest content. He has some amusing papers: No. 16, about the woes of eminence in authorship, is facetious in tone, and so is the project analogous to Fielding's "universal register" in No. 105. He gives us also allegories, Oriental tales, and sketches—not too vivid—of London life. It is the critical essays that have most permanent interest: No. 4 on modern romance, No. 60 on biography, No. 93 on prejudice in criticism; No. 125 on tragedy and comedy, No. 152 on letter-writing, and Nos. 156 and 158, in which he attacks the rules—all these and others demonstrate Johnson's ability. These, standing out above the Johnsonian average, are among the best brief critical essays of the century; they are models of thoughtfulness. Later Johnson wrote at least twenty-five essays [3] for *The Adventurer* (1752-54) of his friend John Hawkesworth (1715?-1773), Swift's editor and a notable figure in the periodical literature of the day.

Other writers of periodical essays that appeared independent of news or other condiments fared less well in general than Johnson. *The World* (209 nos., 1753-56), conducted by Edward Moore, the dramatist, would seem to have been the most popular series, and if we can believe its claims its circulation at times reached 2500. *The Rambler,* which averaged less than 500, was, however, far more highly regarded in reprinted editions. *The World* probably at first had a considerable snob appeal as well as undoubted merit; for its contributors included Lord Chesterfield, Horace Walpole, Richard Owen Cambridge, Soame Jenyns, and others of note.[4] If Johnson could find

Other Periodical Essays

---

[3] L. F. Powell, "Johnson's Part in *The Adventurer*," RES, III (1927). 420-429.

[4] The blue-stocking ladies called the last three of these gentlemen "the old wits"; and the group represents a stately tradition soon to be discarded for something less formal. Cambridge (1717-1802) led an amiable, pious, and complacent life, passed chiefly at Twickenham Meadows on the banks of the Thames. He was an amateur poet and essayist, but achieved distinction chiefly through elegant and kindly hospitality. His *Works* were collected into a quarto volume with a life by his son George in 1803, and his career has recently been well depicted by Richard D. Altick in *Richard Owen Cambridge: Belated Augustan* (Philadelphia, 1941).—Soame Jenyns (1704-1787) did not, like Cambridge, shun public employment, and he made more pretense to intellectuality than most of his group. He was not, however, capable of profound reasoning, and his *Free Enquiry into the Nature and Origin of Evil* (1757) was the object of a famous review by Dr. Johnson that is somewhat surprising for its extremely caustic tone. Jenyns's *View of the Internal Evidence of the Christian Religion* (1776) was much read and was at the time overvalued by the orthodox.

a Hawkesworth and these aristocratic personages find a Moore who would shoulder responsibility for a periodical, the tradition was still possible; but such editors were rare. Lesser successes were achieved by Fielding in his various essay newspapers and by Arthur Murphy in his *Gray's-Inn Journal* (1753-4) where one may find some excellent criticism, especially on the drama. The Nonsense Club (Bonnell Thornton, George Colman, Robert Lloyd, William Cowper, *et al.*) in their *Connoisseur* (1754-6) met with less success than one would have expected. In Edinburgh, where many of the most distinguished thinkers and writers lived, the novelist Henry Mackenzie won distinction as chief author of *The Mirror* (1779-80) and *The Lounger* (1785-87).

Newspapers   The truth is that long before the time of *The Grub-street Journal* (1730-37) and *The Universal Spectator* (1728-46) newspapers had begun to absorb essay writers and use them as authors of leading articles, frequently of a literary character. Such "leaders" need not have merit sufficient to stand alone, and need not always appear regularly. The drudgery was therefore less than in "the anxious employment" of the independent essayist, who constantly faced a deadline. After 1750 many essay series, literary in character, appeared in newspapers. Sir John Hill's *Inspector* (1751-3) was printed in *The Daily Advertiser;* the *Idler* essays, to the number of 104, all but twelve of which were by Johnson, graced the front page of John Payne's *Universal Chronicle* for two years (1758-60); and Goldsmith's "Chinese Letters" were read first in *The Public Ledger.* Hardly any newspaper of considerable duration failed to have an essayist among its contributors some of the time, and though such writers naturally tended to be topical or political or religious, they were often literary.

It may perhaps here be remarked that while in the second half of the century newspapers continued to be usually very short-lived, stability was definitely emerging. No newspaper, except the official *Gazette,* had weathered the whole period 1700-50; but at least two tri-weekly evening papers founded before 1750 continued beyond the end of the century. These were *The London Evening Post* (1727-1806) and *The General Evening Post* (1733-1813). *The Daily Advertiser* (1730-98) had the longest life of any daily. Of the papers founded in the second half of the century *The London Chronicle* (1757-1823), for which Dr. Johnson wrote the first leader, had notable literary interests. "It was," so Boswell tells us, "constantly read by Johnson himself; and it is but just to observe, that it has all along been distinguished for good sense, accuracy, moderation, and delicacy." John Newbery's new daily, *The Public Ledger* (1760-) during its first twenty months of existence, featured Goldsmith's "Chinese Letters," as indicated above, and *The Chronicle* at much the same time (1760-62) carried a series called "The Schemer." At almost the same moment (1761) Bonnell Thornton and George Colman started *The St. James's Chronicle,* in which Colman published essays called "The Genius." Of greater commercial and political weight in the nineteenth century were *The Morning Chronicle* (1769-1862),

The Morning Post (1772-1937), and finally *The Times* (1788), which survives to the present day. The battle for "freedom of the press" was largely won in the eighteenth century, but in times of stress the journalist was still precariously placed. It will be recalled that in 1719 John Matthews was hanged, drawn, and quartered, for a technically treasonable piece of journalism; John Wilkes's troubles over his *North Briton* No. 45 (1763) were notorious,[5] and in the last decade of the century James Perry was repeatedly prosecuted for sarcasms in his *Morning Chronicle*. But Perry in general defended himself with ease and success. There had been great progress in this important matter.

If the newspapers continually featured poems, stories, and essays, that was in part due to competition arising from the development of magazines and reviews in the period. In the history of magazines the landmark doubtless was the founding in 1731 of *The Gentleman's Magazine*[6] by Edward Cave (1691-1754), its publisher. This magazine appeared monthly until 1907, and was at its inception a pioneer influence. Its contents were most miscellaneous, including a section devoted to poetry, another to news summaries for the month—births, deaths, marriages, preferments, lists of books published during the month—and a third section, the magazine's real specialty, abridgments or quotation of interesting essays printed in the newspapers. In the introduction to the first volume Cave announced his aim as "to give Monthly a View of all the Pieces of Wit, Humour, or Intelligence, daily offer'd to the Publick in the News-Papers, (which of late are so multiply'd, as to render it impossible, unless a Man makes it a Business, to consult them all)." Naturally he was accused of plagiarism, but the "plagiarism" proving profitable was speedily and often imitated by rivals. Of these *The London Magazine* (1732-85) was a powerful and closely imitative competitor. In it Boswell published his "Hypochondriack" essays (1777-83). *The Scots Magazine* (1739-1817), which carried the "digest" idea to Edinburgh, had a long run; as did also *The Universal Magazine* (1747-1814). By the middle of the century two obvious developments took place. *The Magazine of Magazines* (1750-51) instituted the further plagiaristic synthesis of all monthly periodicals; and, secondly, by this time original material formed a notable part of the matter of each number of the well-established magazines. Original poetry from the start was included by Cave, and by 1735 letters from readers were frequently printed. Johnson was an early contributor of verse in the *Gentleman's*, and early was concerned in writing up the debates in Parliament for Cave. He also contributed ten biographies of distinguished persons, most of them recently deceased. Other prominent contributors were (Sir) John Hill, Christopher Smart, John Hawkesworth, Sir John Hawkins, and John

The
Gentleman's
Magazine

---

5 See George Nobbe's book on *The North Briton* (1939).
6 John Nichols, "An Account of the Rise and Progress of *The Gentleman's Magazine*," in *A General Index to The Gentleman's Magazine* [*from 1731 to 1818*] (4v, 1789-1821), Vol. III (1821). Also Carl Lennart Carlson, *The First Magazine: A History of The Gentleman's Magazine, with an Account of Dr. Johnson's Editorial Activity and of the Notice Given America in the Magazine* (Providence, R. I., 1938; *Brown University Studies*, Vol. IV). Review article by Donald F. Bond, *MP*, xxxviii (1940). 85-100.

.combe. After Cave's death successive editors included David Henry ..ave's brother-in-law), Francis Newbery, and the eminent antiquarian, ,ohn Nichols (1745-1826). The magazine eventually depended less and less on abridgments from the newspapers, and came to be a miscellany with considerable emphasis on science, religion, and politics as well as on literature.

*ed
ines
Along with the imitations came specialization. Perhaps to relieve pressure for the publication of religious material, the resourceful John Newbery founded in 1760 *The Christian's Magazine,* apparently the first to be devoted to popular religious topics. *The Arminian Magazine* (1778-97) was the organ of the Wesleyan Methodists. Various short-lived periodicals were devoted to theatrical matters. *The Town and Country Magazine* (1769-96) specialized in literary and aristocratic entertainment. In literature its most famous contributor was the boy Thomas Chatterton. Since the days of Richard Steele the fair sex had been reading periodicals, and now there were magazines for ladies. It is amusing that no less a person than Goldsmith himself, under the pen-name of the "Honourable Mrs. Caroline Stanhope," [7] edited for a while *The Lady's Magazine; Or, Polite Companion for the Fair Sex* (1759-63), and there were several other magazines for this clientele. So also lawyers, builders, farmers, musicians, and other particular groups all had their own magazines.

The
Annual
Register
Hardly a magazine in the usual sense but still an important example of a specialized periodical is *The Annual Register,* founded in 1758 with Dodsley as publisher and the youthful Edmund Burke as first author. The annual volume thus published contained a retrospective account of the year, even including reviews of a few chosen books. Somewhat imitative in concept of earlier registers, such as John Meres's *Historical Register* for the years 1714-1738, it transcended its predecessors by being more inclusive and more literary. Burke was "during the space of one-and-thirty years, the principal conductor" of this undertaking, of which he made an enormous success. [8]

The
Monthly
Review
Soon after the eager market for magazines was evident, reviews also entered the popular field. Throughout the first half of the century there had been reviews devoted to learned publications, especially in the field of theology and of classical literature. For contemporary belles-lettres reviewing had been casual and rare. Compliments to fellow authors appear not infrequently in *The Spectator* and in other periodical essays; but usually reviewing in the early period would be found in unfriendly pamphlets. A periodical devoted to reviewing relatively untechnical books was instituted by Ralph Griffiths in his *Monthly Review* (1749-1845). At first, under the influence perhaps of the magazine plan of abridgments, the accounts of books tended to be summaries, with a minimum of critical comment. This is not the worst possible fault since reviewers can hardly summarize without reading. In fact, one of the merits of Griffiths' review articles is that

[7] Ronald S. Crane, *New Essays by Oliver Goldsmith* (Chicago, 1927), pp. xxxii, n. 2 and 89, n. 1.
[8] An admirable account of Burke and the *Register* may be found in Thomas W. Copeland's "Burke and Dodsley's *Annual Register*," PMLA, LIV (1939). 223-245.

they focus attention on the nature of the work rather than on the nature of the anonymous critic's response. That emphasis would come in the reviews later in the century and in the early nineteenth century. Griffiths' bias was that of a nonconformist, and several of his assistants were dissenting clergymen. It was this anti-ecclesiastical tendency that made Johnson give so unfavorable an account of the undertaking to the King. Griffiths, in spite of Goldsmith's opinion, apparently paid well, was the sole responsible chief, and secured, when possible, genuine experts to write for him.[9] These he protected normally by a complete anonymity. His classical reviewers, as we know, were Porson, Parr, and Fanny Burney's brother Charles—three of the best classical scholars of the day. For drama he had Arthur Murphy[10] and George Colman the elder; for belles-lettres, Goldsmith (very briefly!), John Langhorne, John Hawkesworth, John Wolcot ("Peter Pindar"), and others. Science, theology, Oriental studies, and other fields were similarly well covered. In the spring of 1757 Goldsmith was resident in Griffiths' house as an important and adequately paid assistant on the *Monthly*. The arrangement proved unsatisfactory at the end of six months, though Goldsmith contributed four reviews to the *Monthly* for December 1758 before quarreling with Griffiths the following month. When Goldsmith's *Enquiry* (1759) appeared, it was reviewed by a new writer for the *Monthly*, William Kenrick (1725?-1779), a man whose libelous asperities foreshadowed—and surpassed—the savagery of early nineteenth-century reviewers. Griffiths' chief assistant at the start was the cultivated dissenter William Rose; at the very end of the century the revolutionary William Taylor of Norwich was beginning in the *Monthly* a career as critic with an enthusiasm for things Continental, especially German. According to the exaggerated compliments of the day Taylor stimulated Walter Scott to be a poet and Hazlitt to be a critic.

The cultural superiority of the *Monthly* did not escape challenge. Dr. *Other* Johnson edited and wrote much of *The Literary Magazine: or Universal Reviews Review* (1756-8); his contributions constitute some of his best writing, especially on political subjects. Church and Tory interests joined in support of the real rival of the subversive *Monthly*, which was *The Critical Review* (1756-1817). This was edited at first by Tobias Smollett with the aid of three or four others of doubtful identity. There was no admitted chief as in the case of Griffiths. Joseph Robertson (1726-1802) informs us that he contributed to *The Critical Review* more than 2600 articles between the years 1764 and 1785. William Guthrie (1708-1770) and Percival Stockdale (1736-1811) were successively important staff members in the years after Smollett left the *Critical*. Less able than the *Monthly*, the *Critical* had nevertheless notable

9 Aubrey Hawkins, "Some Writers on *The Monthly Review*," RES, VII (1931). 168-181; also Benj. C. Nangle, *The Monthly Review* (1749-89): *Indexes of Contributors and Articles* (Oxford, 1934).
    10 In 1757-8 Murphy may have been contributing to a section in *The London Chronicle* called "The Theatre." See J. P. Emery, "Murphy's Criticisms in *The London Chronicle*," *PMLA*, LIV (1939). 1099-1104.

contributors. Johnson wrote at least three good articles, and Goldsmith in 1759 and 1760 wrote over fifteen reviews. Presently the rows between the rival reviews were aired in the satirical *Battle of the Reviews* (1760); and Charles Churchill (1731-1764), in his *Apology Addressed to the Critical Reviewers* (1761) and in others of his satires, ridiculed Smollett and his collaborators. Smollett's health forced him to withdraw from the *Critical* in 1763, and Kenrick at the end of 1765 left writing for the *Monthly*. In 1775 in his own periodical, *The London Review of English and Foreign Literature,* Kenrick continued decrying and even libeling Johnson, Goldsmith, and most of the geniuses of the age. Among other notable reviews of the period were Gilbert Stuart's *English Review* (1783-95), published by John Murray, and Thomas Christie's *Analytical Review* (1788-99), which attracted the revolutionary literati. Other leading conservative reviews included *The British Critic* (1793-1826), edited by William Beloe and Robert Nares, and *The Anti-Jacobin Review and Magazine* (1798-1821), edited by "John Gifford" (i.e., James R. Green) and Robert Bisset. Among all such periodicals Griffiths' *Monthly* continued the leader until in 1802 *The Edinburgh Review* was founded.

Periodicals such as these here presented formed the background for the career of the foremost of hackwriters, Oliver Goldsmith.[11] Bibliographies of his work indicate that in the years 1757 to 1762 Goldsmith contributed to at least ten periodicals of differing kinds. The serial miscellany that he himself wrote, *The Bee* (1759), ran to only eight weekly numbers, but these early years of magazine writing in general served him well. He made many friends, and in 1764, when his first signed work, *The Traveller,* was published, he was already one of the original members of Dr. Johnson's Club. The magazines and reviews, however, were not sufficiently lucrative, and

[11] Oliver Goldsmith (1730?-1774) was born in Ireland, where he received most of his education. From Trinity College, Dublin, he received the degree of B.A. in 1749. He studied medicine in Edinburgh, 1752-3, but took no degree there. He continued his medical studies at the University of Leyden, and traveled on the Continent through France, Switzerland, and Italy. After his return to London in 1756 he attempted for two strenuous years to establish himself as a physician in Southwark and to augment his meager earnings by writing reviews for the magazines. In 1759 he published his first book, *An Enquiry into the Present State of Polite Learning in Europe,* and by this time was launched on a busy career as writer. By steady use of his facile pen he eventually made a good income, but he was apparently improvident, and died leaving debts amounting to about £2000. On these debts Dr. Johnson made the proud comment: "Was ever poet so trusted before?"—Goldsmith's *Works* (4v, 1801); ed. Sir James Prior (4v, 1837); J. W. M. Gibbs (5v, 1884-6); *Plays,* ed. Austin Dobson (1893, 1901); *Complete Poetical Works,* ed. Austin Dobson (1906); *New Essays by Oliver Goldsmith,* ed. Ronald S. Crane (Chicago, 1927); *The Collected Letters of Oliver Goldsmith,* ed. Katharine C. Balderston (Cambridge, 1928).—Iolo A. Williams, "Oliver Goldsmith," *Seven XVIIIth Century Bibliographies* (1924), pp. 117-177; Temple Scott, *Oliver Goldsmith Bibliographically and Biographically Considered* (1928); R. S. Crane, "Oliver Goldsmith," in *CBEL,* II. 636-650 (the most complete list of writings by and about Goldsmith).—Thomas Percy, "The Life of Dr. Oliver Goldsmith," in *The Miscellaneous Works of Oliver Goldsmith,* Vol. I (1801); see Katharine C. Balderston, *The History and Sources of Percy's Memoir of Goldsmith* (Cambridge, 1926); Sir James Prior, *The Life of Oliver Goldsmith* (2v, 1837; still the most authoritative life); John Forster, *The Life and Adventures of Oliver Goldsmith* (1848), with notes as *The Life and Times of Oliver Goldsmith* (2v, 1854); Austin Dobson, *Life of Oliver Goldsmith* (1888); Arthur L. Sells, *Les Sources françaises de Goldsmith* (Paris, 1924). For many special studies of the canon and sources of Goldsmith see *CBEL.*

once his reputation was established Goldsmith took to translation and compilation as a means of further income. Among the many works in which he was concerned at least as reviser may be listed an abridgment of Plutarch's *Lives* in five volumes (1762), a *History of England* (1764) in two volumes, another in four volumes (1771), *The Roman History* in two volumes (1769), *The Beauties of English Poesy* in two volumes (1767), *The Grecian History* in two volumes (1774) and, most extensive and perhaps most interesting of all his compilations, *An History of the Earth and Animated Nature* (1774) in eight volumes.[12] During the fifteen years that elapsed between his first original book, his *Enquiry into the Present State of Polite Learning in Europe* (1759), and his death, Goldsmith must have either written, revised, translated, compiled, or supervised over two score volumes. No one will accept Horace Walpole's verdict that "Goldsmith was an idiot, with once or twice a fit of parts"; but it is evident that he was a professional maker of books, who affords high delight from a relative few of his writings.

As an essayist he achieved his earliest and perhaps his greatest success.[13] *Goldsmith as an Essayist* In his own days his essays could be read in the original periodicals or in three collections, to the sum of which later additions have been made. These collections were *The Bee* (not a reprint), *The Citizen of the World* (1762), collected from *The Public Ledger*, in which they had appeared serially as "Letters" (1760-61); and the *Essays by Mr. Goldsmith*, assembled from the magazines and newspapers into a volume in 1765.

Before these volumes appeared Goldsmith's *Enquiry* had helped readers *The Enquiry* to understand certain typical positions of its author. The book, to be sure, lacks the charm of the essays partly because, as Davies said, "the Doctor loved to dwell upon grievances." It is one of the long series of complaints made by writers that their art is both unappreciated and unrewarded. The mid-eighteenth century was vocal in its complaints of this sort. From another point of view the volume might seem to be a prose "progress of poesy"; for "polite learning" is here belles-lettres. Goldsmith's survey of the cultural state of the countries of Europe anticipated his *Traveller,* and is typically facile and moralistic. Everywhere he finds decay of the arts, and, since he thus seems an "ancient" rather than a "modern," one might think him a pessimist negating the popular belief in progress. Actually he believes in a theory of cyclic change with new achievement compensating for the obvious decay of parts. Almost a *philosophe* in his devotion to finite causes of the human state, he blames the decline of the arts on faulty education (he is typically for the elegant, the humane, and opposes the technical and pedan-

---

12 James H. Pitman, *Goldsmith's Animated Nature* (New Haven, 1924); Winifred Lynskey, "The Scientific Sources of Goldsmith's *Animated Nature,*" SP, XL (1943). 33-57.
13 The publication of Professor Ronald S. Crane's *New Essays by Goldsmith* (Chicago, 1927) has greatly stimulated a mass of research concerning the sources and the canon of Goldsmith's essays. This work has been done by A. J. Barnouw, H. J. Smith, A. L. Sells (pioneers in the field), and by R. W. Seitz, J. H. Warner, and Arthur Friedman. The extensive record of these researches may be found in the excellent bibliography of Goldsmith in CBEL, II. 636-650. The results of the work make it apparent that Goldsmith was capable of frequent, interesting plagiarisms. Professors Crane and Friedman are preparing an edition of Goldsmith's works.

tic), on lack of patronage by the aristocrats, and, perhaps most surprisingly, on the literary critics, who discourage genius and malign all innovation. These positions, like many of Goldsmith's, are easily taken and not thoroughly considered. The author himself was making an income as a critic; and such remarks as "The author who draws his quill merely to take a purse, no more deserves success than he who presents a pistol," somewhat naturally provoked sneers from his former employers on *The Monthly Review*.

His essays were less querulous and more varied in tone. *The Bee*, a periodical miscellany in octavo format, which appeared on eight Saturdays in October and November, 1759, contains some of his best small poems as well as an amusing diversity of prose—dramatic criticisms, moral tales, serious or fanciful discourses. Among the last perhaps the most famous is the *Resverie* ("The Fame Machine"), in which he compliments *The Rambler* highly. Goldsmith excels in human details. In *The Bee* and in his other groups of essays we find interesting ideas expressed and we meet such amusing personages as the Strolling Player, who reminds us of Goldsmith himself as well as of George Primrose in the later *Vicar;* the Private Sentinel, that colossal monument to human distress and fortitude; and, above all, the immortal Beau Tibbs, surely one of the most delightful brief characterizations of the century. The Strolling Player and the Private Sentinel remind one at least vaguely of Addison's Political Upholsterer in *Tatler* Nos. 155, 160, and 178. The methods of Addison and Goldsmith can be studied illuminatingly in these essays. The earlier writer is more definitely pointed and more brilliant in his satirical concept; the Upholsterer was a clearer comment on an age recently exposed to newspapers and their wild daily rumors. Goldsmith, on the other hand, is contentedly preoccupied with vivid and rich human detail; he creates his persons not merely as mouthpieces or as gorgeous eccentrics: strange as they are, he really likes them as people.

He does, of course, at times use persons as topics or as mouthpieces. Mistress Quickly in the *Reverie at the Boar's Head Tavern*, certainly one of Goldsmith's happiest efforts, is vivaciously human, but she is obviously borrowed from Shakespeare for the purpose of avowing that it is futile to mourn over the degeneracy of the age, since "every age is the same." There is neither progress nor regress: there is compensated change always. Similarly, the figure of *Asem the Man Hater* merely is a personal center for a fantasy of various favorite ideas. Asem is taught the necessity of having the life of pure reason stimulated by emotion. He is taught the complementary lesson of the necessity of controlling one's rash benevolence by prudence. He illustrates the theory of cyclic change embodied in an individual life. Almost alone among the eighteenth-century descendants of Timon, Asem is cured of his misanthropy—by means of regenerated social emotions. At the end of the tale he is starting on a new cycle dominated again by benevolence; but the new round is to be an improvement; for his benevolence now is to be not rash, like Timon's, but prudent.

His Methods as Essayist

The Citizen of the World [14] is perhaps Goldsmith's best sustained work.
It is certainly the best example in English of the essay device so popular at
the time in France, which made the essayist a foreign traveler (preferably
Oriental; for philosophy came from the East) who wrote letters to his home
country describing and criticizing the strange customs of the lands through
which he passed. The device, initiated in the late seventeenth century by
G. P. Marana's *L'Espion Turc* and perfected in Montesquieu's *Lettres
Persanes* (1721), throve in France where the critics of established institutions
sheltered themselves behind the pretense of being foreigners. From Montesquieu's imitator, the Marquis d'Argens, author of a series of *Lettres
Chinoises* (1739), Goldsmith drew much inspiration and even many small
plagiarized passages.[15] Long before D'Argens such writers as Le Comte and
Du Halde had started a Chinese tradition that was invaluable to both
D'Argens and Goldsmith. As this tradition developed, the Chinese were
made into a race of philosophers, embodiments of simple reason and common sense; people who lived in a patriarchal society or under an absolute
but perfectly benevolent emperor. They honored men of letters above
conquerors and military heroes, and were in religion rationally devout,
tolerant—and altogether void of bigotry and "superstition." In a word, the
Chinese traveler embodied the pure light of reason, and his mind played
effectively over the customs of England and of Christendom in an impartial
and at times devastating fashion. To him nothing established had an
absolute validity: in the Orient, as these essayists all loved to remark, polygamy was perfectly respectable; in Christendom the marriage customs were
frequently shocking. All things were relative. The *philosophe* had quite
emancipated himself from the ecclesiastical interpretation of the universe.
The excellence of all customs was to be estimated according to human and
common-sense standards. If Goldsmith's "Chinese Letters" are less brilliantly
trenchant than the best of his French models, it is in part due to the fact that
England was, by definition almost, the land of liberty, and the English,
unlike the French, did not have "God and the king to pull down"—to
borrow Walpole's phrase. Goldsmith is more playful, more relaxed, more
superficial, more of the literary man, less of the revolutionary.

Thus these Chinese letters are most useful in giving a picture of Goldsmith's mind and the temper of his time. From the very beginning of his
career he had loved to set the qualities of one country over against the quali-

[14] *The Citizen of the World*, ed. Austin Dobson (1891); Hamilton J. Smith, *Oliver Gold-
Smith's "The Citizen of the World"* (New Haven, 1926); also Martha P. Conant, *The Oriental
Tale in England in the Eighteenth Century* (1908).
[15] Ronald S. Crane and Hamilton J. Smith, "A French Influence on Goldsmith's *Citizen of
the World*," *MP*, xix (1921). 83-92. A noteworthy English link between Montesquieu and
Goldsmith was the *Letters from a Persian in England* published in 1735 by George (later
Baron) Lyttelton. This youthful and undistinguished piece of writing Lyttelton revised for a
fifth edition (1744). It contains interesting political and social criticisms, and had obvious but
not very important influence on Goldsmith. Lyttelton tried his hand at another popular type
of essay in 1760 when he brought out his *Dialogues of the Dead*. Mrs. Elizabeth Montagu
of Blue-Stocking fame contributed three dialogues to this volume. On Lyttelton's *Letters from
a Persian* see Samuel C. Chew, "An English Precursor of Rousseau," *MLN*, xxxii (1917).
321-337.

ties of another. He is a patriot, but a patriot who is sure each nation has its individual and superlative merit—as well as a contrasting defect. Upon this concept his poem *The Traveller* is based. The philosophic mind, he thinks, will attempt to absorb the diverse goods of all nations. It was, then, appropriate to call the "Chinese Letters," when they were reprinted, by a title that haunted Goldsmith, *The Citizen of the World*. This phrase, picturesque and cogent from the ancient moment when Dionysius put it into the mouth of Plato, had a particular appeal to the illuminati, who abhorred the parochial. Goldsmith had used the phrase in his essay on *National Prejudices* (1760), in his *Memoirs of M. de Voltaire* (1761), and in the twentieth and the twenty-third of his series of Chinese letters. The title is philosophical rather than political in implication; for Goldsmith, like many another proponent of cosmopolitanism in his day, believed that one should be aware and tolerant of the curious opinions and customs of strange nations, but he did not deny the duty of a local allegiance; he rather insisted that local allegiance be subordinated to allegiance to the Whole.

In these "Chinese Letters" as well as elsewhere Goldsmith is also typical of his day in his praise of simplicity. Here Nature's "simple plan" (Letter III) is the catchword. To be sure, he is at times equivocal. Where wealth accumulates, men decay; but where there is no wealth, there are no arts, no graces of civilization; and these last are what the century really valued. Plain living and rigid intellectualism might easily become to Goldsmith a meager, bleak existence. He certainly tends to idealize something like an opulent patriarchal society, but even in his picture of "Sweet Auburn" or of the Vicar's family of Wakefield, he forgets his dictum that "every age is the same," and shares the predilection of his time for the simple, though not for the truly primitive.

Goldsmith excelled in other types of writing as well as in the essay, and the mental processes seen in these essays carry over into his plays,[16] his one novel, and even into his poems. He illustrates the economic methods of the less shrewd authors of his day in his magazine work, and he also illustrates

The Vicar   the curious equivocal emancipation of mind typical of many men in his day. His attitude towards sentimentalism and towards "trade" are cases in point, and can be studied in *The Vicar of Wakefield*.[17] The plot of the *Vicar* is not complex: clouds gather more and more blackly over the poor Primroses; finally when their complete misery seems assured, the sun shines out, all woes vanish, and we leave the family living happily ever afterwards. Goldsmith loved to portray simplicity, but his love of idyllic simplicity was curiously modified by economic considerations. After the South Sea Bubble a conservative reaction towards a trust in the land as the source of wealth and well-being prepared the way for the idealized farmer-philosopher. Consequently, when *The Vicar of Wakefield* finally appeared in 1766 (it was at

---

16 On Goldsmith's plays see Part III, ch. VI, n. 15.
17 Among the very many editions of the *Vicar* may be mentioned for their introductions and notes those by Austin Dobson (1883) and by Oswald Doughty (1928).

least partly written four years earlier), its public was prepared for a "hero" who united in himself "the three greatest characters upon earth:...a priest, an husbandman, and the father of a family." There is, obviously, a connection here with sentimentalism, but the sentimental bearings of the *Vicar* are difficult to grasp justly.[18] Here as elsewhere—especially in the "Distresses of a Private Sentinel" (*Citizen of the World*, cxix)—Goldsmith lavishly uses "distress" as material; but his attitude towards distress demands acute attention. The distresses of the Sentinel are so gross as to be absurd: they are far from moving tears, and at the end of the essay one can see the logical conclusion: "Thus saying, he limped off, leaving my friend and me *in admiration of his intrepidity and content;* nor could we avoid acknowledging that an habitual acquaintance with misery is the truest school of fortitude and philosophy." We are not invited to weep; we are asked to admire intrepidity. Similarly we are told in the *Vicar* that "after a certain degree of pain, every new breach that death opens in the constitution, nature kindly covers with insensibility." Submission, intrepidity, fortitude, these are the lessons Goldsmith wishes us to learn from the distresses of the virtuous. The tone of the novel is emotional and benevolist, but it must be noted that the good vicar himself is habitually caustic as to the absurdities of his socially ambitious females. The popularity of the book was and is doubtless due not to its overt moral purpose but to the author's attitude towards his material. Like his vicar, he seems "by nature an admirer of happy human faces"— preferably faces distinctly self-conscious in their happiness. One thinks of Greuze and the *Accordée de Village*. Both author and painter are self-conscious; their sentimentalism is intended to serve a moral or even divine purpose—not, however, quite too deep for tears.

Dr. Johnson's opinion of the *Vicar* was expressed to Fanny Burney: "It is very faulty; there is nothing of real life in it, and very little of nature. It is a mere fanciful performance." This verdict is surprisingly severe, but not altogether unjust. The faults of the *Vicar,* like those of *She Stoops to Conquer,* are palpable, and yet for most people these works make still very pleasant reading. The charm is in part due to the imaginative glow that Goldsmith so effortlessly casts over the action of the *Vicar* (after all *Daphnis and Chloe* has its absurd side!), and to his flexible and easy style.

Much praise has been given to his style, which is indeed attractive. It lacks the coldness of the aristocratic manner, and it escapes the tendency of his generation to follow Johnson into excessive heaviness of diction and balanced formality of sentence structure. The unfriendly review [19] of his *Enquiry* in *The Monthly Review* shows that Goldsmith's former colleagues were aware of his criteria of style—his avoidance of "the quaintness of antithesis, the prettiness of points, and the rotundity of studied periods"; and yet they professed to feel a "remarkable faultiness" in expression. Probably even for them Goldsmith was hardly bookish enough to be a "fine writer." *Goldsmith's Prose Style*

---

[18] W. F. Gallaway, "The Sentimentalism of Goldsmith," *PMLA,* xlviii (1933). 1167-1181.
[19] *Monthly Review,* xxi (1759). 381-389. The reviewer was William Kenrick.

It is precisely for this lack of formality and for his graceful and sensitive ease, fluency, and vividness that we value his style.

His Poems   At his death Goldsmith was commended usually for his poems; obituaries mentioned *The Traveller* and *The Deserted Village* rather more frequently than any of his prose works. Apart from these two masterpieces, and perhaps *Retaliation,* which is remembered for biographical rather than aesthetic reasons, his verse is interesting but unimportant. In these two poems he succeeds signally in the couplet tradition, in which most of his contemporaries were commonplace. *The Traveller* contains glowing statements of his cosmopolitanism, of his patriotic Toryism, and of his favorite notion of compensation; *The Deserted Village* presents the economic difficulties of rural life, the dangers of luxury and "trade's unfeeling train." [20] These two are eighteenth-century masterpieces of the poetry of statement: in them current ideas and attitudes are caught and are suffused sufficiently with genuine feeling to make them stir our imaginations to this day. They are the work of a gifted author, happy in not too much education but richly endowed with human insight. Aesthetically he was a traditionalist; mentally he was of the Enlightenment; he was too hard-headed to be a thorough sentimentalist, and too sympathetic to be an outright satirist. In spite of the pot-boiling nature of most of his books, his complex personal endowments with his especial gifts of flexible expression enabled him in several of his works to achieve fame as one of the most readable writers of his century.

[20] On the general background of *The Deserted Village* see Julia Patton, *The English Village: A Literary Study, 1750-1850* (1919). For a literary antecedent by Goldsmith in prose see Ronald S. Crane, *New Essays by Oliver Goldsmith* (Chicago, 1927), pp. 116-124 and the introduction. See also Howard J. Bell, Jr., "*The Deserted Village* and Goldsmith's Social Doctrines," *PMLA,* LIX (1944). 747-772.

VIII

Biography and Letter-Writing

To a century devoted to the proper study of mankind biography was a natural medium.[1] To a century devoted to communication in the coffee-house and by means of rambles through the countryside to gracious Georgian country seats, letter-writing was a natural means of conversing with absent friends. In many periods biographies and letters are merely invaluable sources for historical study, but in the eighteenth century they frequently serve for a delight as well. The didacticism of the age led to an insistence on the significant, the morally useful; a sense of realism, furthermore, encouraged scrupulous attachment to truth and to a love of picturesque detail; and an insatiable human curiosity encouraged a love of trivial anecdotes, which added an element of drama to the universality and uniformity that characterized most views of human nature at the time. Thus grew up a belief that the lives even of "average" men might furnish materials for virile, witty, and perhaps even noble personal writing.

In biography the century had a long way to go before it reached Johnson and Boswell, the greatest practitioners of the art. It developed away from the distant formality advised by Addison in *Freeholder* No. 35 and towards the judicious realism advised by Johnson. Addison had correctly condemned the Grub-street authors who added a new terror to death by rushing to "Curll's chaste press" with garbled and jumbled "lives." Although these works are now usually negligible, often valuable are such brief lives as are found in the biographical dictionaries of the time. A thirst for information about celebrities is marked in the *Life of Francis Bacon* (1740) by David Mallet, the "beggarly Scotchman" who later published Bolingbroke's *Works* (1754), and in such pedestrian compilations as John Jortin's *Erasmus* (2v, 1758-60) and Ferdinando Warner's *Sir Thomas More* (1758). New techniques gradually mingled with established methods. The noble Roman style of Conyers Middleton's *Life of Cicero* (1741), at which Fielding sneered but which Fanny Burney and others thought "manly and elegant," was less significant than Middleton's effective use of Cicero's letters as jewels set in

The Development of Biography

---

[1] The following general sources on biography may well be consulted: Anna R. Burr, *The Autobiography* (1909); Waldo H. Dunn, *English Biography* (1916); Mark Longaker, *English Biography in the Eighteenth Century* (Philadelphia, 1931); John C. Major, *The Role of Personal Memoirs in English Biography and Novel* (Philadelphia, 1935); Donald A. Stauffer, *The Art of Biography in Eighteenth Century England* (2v, Princeton, 1941). Stauffer's second volume contains an "Alphabetical Index of English Biographies and Autobiographies, 1700-1800."

,graphical narrative. This method was developed by William Mason [2] _4-1797) in the "Memoirs" he prefixed to his edition of his friend Thomas ray's *Poems* (1775). Mason used many letters and thus stimulated the tradition of combining "life and letters" which was later common, and was followed by Boswell. Unfortunately for Mason's ultimate reputation he garbled inexcusably the texts of the letters used.

*nce's
Anecdotes*

Joseph Spence (1699-1768) in some respects anticipated the techniques of Boswell. His type of favorite subject differed from Boswell's in that he had a predilection for natural, self-taught geniuses such as Stephen Duck, "the thresher poet," and Thomas Blacklock, a blind Scottish poet: of both these men he wrote lives. More popular was his account of the Italian Magliabecchi in his *Parallel in the Manner of Plutarch* (1758). As a definitely limited predecessor of Boswell in method, Spence attached himself after 1726 to Alexander Pope and collected supposedly verbatim records of Pope's conversation and that of other eminent persons as well. Unlike Boswell, Spence was himself too timid to make any real use of these collected materials, but Pope's editor, Warburton, and Dr. Johnson were allowed to use some of them. They were published as *Anecdotes* (1820) long after Spence's death at a time when the influence of Boswell had increased the value of such intimate matter.

*Boswell's
Career*

James Boswell [3] (1740-1795), when first he met Dr. Johnson in 1763, was known in his native Edinburgh as a convivial and witty member of Scottish literary circles, as the friend of Lord Elibank, Lord Kames, of Robertson, Hume, and Blair among others. He was the author of certain anonymous poems and pamphlets, and was eager for literary fame. His correspondence with the Hon. Andrew Erskine, upon publication in 1763, was hailed as a

---

[2] John W. Draper, *William Mason* (1924); on Mason's handling of Gray's letters see *Correspondence of Thomas Gray,* ed. Paget Toynbee and Leonard Whibley (3v, Oxford, 1935), I, pp. xiii-xvi.

[3] James Boswell was the eldest son of Alexander Boswell, who on being raised to the bench took the title of Lord Auchinleck (pronounced *Affléck*) from the family estate in Ayrshire. Boswell studied law in Edinburgh and Glasgow, with little enthusiasm, and on a visit to London in 1763 met Johnson. After a Continental tour (December 1763-February 1766), he lived chiefly in Scotland, marrying his cousin there in 1769. Usually he visited London in the spring of the year, and saw much of Johnson at such times. After the death of his father in 1782, Boswell, having succeeded to the family estate, became politically ambitious, with no great success. At the end of 1788 he removed to London and devoted himself to seeing the *Life of Johnson* through the press. His remaining years were marked by a continual decline in health and spirits. — Apart from his *Life of Johnson* (for which see Part III, ch. III), his principal works are *Dorando, A Spanish Tale* (1767); *The Essence of the Douglas Cause* (1767); *An Account of Corsica* (1768); ed. Sydney C. Roberts (Cambridge, 1923); *The Journal of a Tour to the Hebrides* (1785), ed. George Birkbeck Hill (1887), Robert W. Chapman (1924), and from the original MS by Frederick A. Pottle and Charles H. Bennett (1936); *Letters,* ed. Chauncey B. Tinker (2v, 1924); *The Hypochondriack* (70 nos., 1777-83, reprinted from *The London Magazine*), ed. Margery Bailey (2v, Stanford University, 1928); *Private Papers of James Boswell from Malahide Castle,* ed. Geoffrey Scott and Frederick A. Pottle (18v, 1928-34, privately printed). — Frederick A. Pottle, *The Literary Career of James Boswell, Esq., being the Bibliographical Materials for a Life of Boswell* (Oxford, 1929); F. A. Pottle, *The Private Papers of James Boswell from Malahide Castle: A Catalogue* (1931); Claude C. Abbott, *A Catalogue of Papers Relating to Boswell ... found at Fettercairn House* (Oxford, 1936). — Charles Rogers, "Memoir" prefixed to *Boswelliana* (1874); Percy H. Fitzgerald, *Life of Boswell* (2v, 1891); Chauncey B. Tinker, *Young Boswell* (Boston, 1922); John L. Smith-Dampier, *Who's Who in Boswell* (1935); L. F. Powell, "Boswell's Original Journal of his Tour to the Hebrides and the Printed Version," *E&S,* XXIII (1938). 58-69.

work of "true genius"; his pamphlets about the Douglas Cause, including the allegorical *Dorando* (1767), attracted attention on the Continent as well as in England; and his writings in favor of the brave Corsicans—the result of a visit to the "enslaved" island in 1765—gave him European fame. His *Account of Corsica* (1768) is still a most readable book. Besides General Paoli, the Corsican patriot and apostle of freedom, Boswell had met in his travels Voltaire, Rousseau, and other celebrities. He returned to England in 1766 escorting thither the mistress of Rousseau, who at that time was making his unfortunate sojourn in England. By this time Boswell had probably decided to write a "great" life of his friend Johnson; but his duties as a Scottish advocate and his interest in politics make it wrong to suppose Johnson the sole center of Boswell's existence. Apart from his *Life of Johnson* Boswell had a very considerable career as writer, and as a writer of travels he was far more interesting than was Johnson. As an essayist he was inferior, but his *Hypochondriack* indicated some ability in a form of writing to which he made contributions at times jocose and at times sedate or even melancholy.

But if not the center of Boswell's existence, Johnson was certainly Boswell's best subject. Boswell excelled in insight into human nature and in ability to dramatize a situation. For such purposes Johnson was God's plenty, and when relatively rare occasions offered through the years, Boswell watched and listened and collected materials for the great work. His methods in collecting have been differently described. Rarely he perhaps made notes on the spot as conversation ran its fascinating course. Usually he recorded the day's gleanings in his journal from memory, and in the process he sometimes fell into arrears of over a fortnight.[4] He questioned Johnson himself; he pestered Johnson's friends; he visited Lichfield; and, after the Doctor's death, was indefatigable in collecting letters and anecdotes, and in verifying details not earlier settled. His memory was prodigious and accurate. He would not have thought of himself as a trained scholar, but actually his devotion to truth of detail and his ideals of thoroughness would do credit to many such. These qualities evidently, and fortunately, won the respect and aid of the ablest research scholar of the day, Edmond Malone—a man whose illuminating work on such figures as Dryden and Shakespeare still demands veneration. Boswell knew material; Malone knew a competent workman, and so gave up any desire he had to write Johnson's life and by his discreet and judicious aid helped to settle Boswell's final draught of the greatest of biographies.

Boswell was not merely a conscientious preserver of detail; he was also an inspired shaping artist. He knew, and transmits, the sound of his subject's voice to a degree unparalleled in other biographers. From the Malahide Papers we now learn that frequently Johnson's talk is more characteristically

Boswell's Method with Johnson

---

[4] Geoffrey Scott, *The Making of the Life of Johnson*, Vol. VI of *The Private Papers of James Boswell from Malahide Castle* (1929). See also Frederick A. Pottle and Charles H. Bennett, "Boswell and Mrs. Piozzi," *MP*, XXXIX (1942). 421-430.

Johnsonian in the final form Boswell gave it than it was in the first form—that in which very likely it fell from Johnson's lips. Not merely remarks but scenes doubtless undergo this artistic reshaping to give them character. At least many scenes, such as the first meeting of Boswell with Johnson and the famous dinner with Wilkes in 1776, come to mind as masterpieces of theatrical manipulation, in which every detail has been given priceless organic value. It is only to a casual reader that Boswell at first sight seems a biographical annalist swamped with magnificent detail.

His Ideal of Complete Portrayal   Completeness of portrayal was certainly Boswell's aim—and his accomplishment. For this he labored, prodding the sluggish mind of Johnson that appeared to him like a great mill needing grist; and prodding also at times the sluggish body. In his sixty-fourth year the Doctor was persuaded to visit Scotland and its Western Islands. It would have been a difficult journey for a younger man, but from all points of view the adventure was a great success. Both men wrote accounts of the journey, and, some richly Johnsonian passages apart, Boswell's *Tour,* published ten years after Johnson's *Journey* and a year after Johnson's death, is easily superior. Here his narrative flows more smoothly and is perhaps more steadily entertaining even than in the *Life of Johnson.* The work was less weighty, less rich: completeness did not oppress here as a duty—after all, the journey was a holiday.

Problems of Particularity   By his contemporaries Boswell was castigated for his fondness for petty personal detail, for exhibiting flaws and foibles as well as virtues. It was in this actually that he excelled his master, Johnson, who understood through his intellect while Boswell used also his senses and intuitions. Not that Johnson was averse to particularity. When Boswell sought his counsel, the Doctor remarked, "There is nothing, Sir, too little for so little a creature as man." Johnson excelled in a sense of human values; Boswell triumphs by means of his sense of vital particular detail that gives significant lifelike quality. Truth and particularity for him went hand in hand "in the Flemish picture which I give of my friend." "By how small a speck," he exclaims, "does the *Painter* give life to an Eye!" His friend Sir Joshua Reynolds was not so tolerant of these Flemish methods in painting, but Boswell was on the side of the future, and the remark of Hazlitt—"I did not then, nor do I now believe, with Sir Joshua, that the perfection of art consists in giving general appearances without individual details, but in giving general appearances with individual details"—was a remark that Johnson and Boswell would have endorsed for biography. It was a crucial part of Boswell's magic to give significance and vitality to the apparently trivial; it is this trait, together with his notable accuracy and unparalleled completeness of portraiture, that made him, in one of the few Macaulay phrases still quotable about Boswell, "the Shakespeare of biographers."

Autobiographies   In theory at least autobiography was preferable to biography. "Those relations are therefore commonly of most value," announced Johnson in *Idler* No. 84, "in which the writer tells his own story"; and both Johnson and John Wesley continually urged their friends to keep journals. The diversity of the autobiographies of the time is astonishing. Cibber's *Apology* (1740) stimulated others to autobiographical self-defense. A revision of the alleged autobiography of Bampfylde-Moore Carew became *An Apology for the Life of Bampfylde-Moore Carew ... commonly known throughout the West of England by the Title of King of the Beggars* (1749); but this is perhaps rogue fiction rather than autobiography.[5] Cibber's youngest daughter brought out *A Narrative of the Life of Mrs. Charlotte Charke* (1755), which in robust and varied episode surpasses fiction, and gives, incidentally, one of the most authentic accounts of strolling players of the time. The theatre stimulated more egoists than Cibber to paint themselves as well as their trade: Benjamin Victor's *History of the Theatres of London and Dublin* (1761-71) and Tate Wilkinson's *Memoirs of His Own Life* (1790) are important in their material but not in their literary quality. This lack of art is also notable in the stories written by more or less lovely ladies who, having been indiscreet, desired to publish and justify their indiscretions. Among these Letitia Pilkington's *Memoirs* (1748) with its sidelights on Dean Swift, Con. Phillips's *Apology* (1748-9), and above all, Lady Vane's memoirs, inserted in *Peregrine Pickle* (1751), are significant of the marital infelicities of the day.

More significant and varied are the numberless specialized autobiographies that give accounts of voyages—round the world as in the cases of Anson and *Narratives* Cook—or simply to the Continent as in the work of Henry Fielding, Tobias *of Voyages* Smollett, James Boswell, Dr. Charles Burney, William Beckford, and Arthur Young.[6] Throughout the century voyage narratives had formed an important part of the popular reading matter and had had an enormous influence on literature—witness *Robinson Crusoe* as well as *Roderick Random*. Large "Collections" of voyages had been frequently reprinted, and the enterprising publisher John Newbery (1713-1767) brought out in the second half of the century one of the largest in *The World Displayed; or, a Curious Collection of Voyages and Travels*.[7] Voyages had influence at various levels: we have seen how they affected such authors as Smollett and Sterne; it is also clear that such books as Arthur Young's *Travels in France* (1792) had notable implications for the political economy ·of his revolutionary times. Still another sort of possible influence is seen in such a work as the *Authentick Narrative* (1764) by Cowper's evangelical friend, the Rev. John Newton, who had pictured himself vividly as a brand plucked from the burning, and as a sailor sinful and repentant he foreshadowed a type transcendently treated by Coleridge in *The Ancient Mariner*.

Of the less adventurous autobiographies written in this half century the

---

[5] The *Apology* is edited by C. H. Wilkinson (Oxford, 1931) under the more usual title, *The King of the Beggars*.
[6] It is doubtless invidious to mention these few and omit many others. For extensive classified lists of voyages one should consult the admirable bibliography prepared by R. W. Frantz for *CBEL*, II. 739-757.
[7] 20v, 1759-61; 1774-8; 1790.

Edward
Gibbon

subtlest and smoothest was that of the historian Edward Gibbon,[8] who was so fascinated by the problem of self-portrayal that he left six draughts of his own life, which his friend Lord Sheffield blended for publication in Gibbon's *Miscellaneous Works* (1796). The reserved honesty of the portrayal and the crystal hardness and clarity of the style make this work a masterpiece. Unlike most autobiographers Gibbon is no obvious eccentric. "My name may hereafter be placed among the thousand articles of a Biographia Britannica," he writes; "and I must be conscious that no one is so well qualified as myself to describe the series of my thoughts and actions." Of his native endowments he says bluntly, "Wit I have none"; but his gift of phrasing and of incisive arrangement of details furnishes a very fair imitation. Unforgettable is his comment on his second tutor at Oxford, who "well remembered that he had a salary to receive, and only forgot that he had a duty to perform." The termination of his romance—by parental edict—with the lady who later was to be the mother of Mme de Staël is equally characteristic: "I sighed as a lover, I obeyed as a son." Elegant and cool irony is surely an acceptable ingredient of wit. A more obvious limitation is confessed when he says, "My temper is not very susceptible of enthusiasm"; and yet no one has conveyed more justly the genuine thrill a true neo-classicist felt upon first visiting the *fons et origo*, the eternal city of Rome. Nor have historians ever recorded with truer emotion the moments of conception or termination of an enormous piece of work. "It was at Rome, on the 15th of October 1764, as I sat musing amidst the ruins of the Capitol, while the barefooted fryars were singing vespers [what sacrilege!] in the Temple of Jupiter, that the idea of writing the decline and fall of the city first started to my mind." The emotions of deliverance from the task, twenty-three years later, on the night of June 27, 1787, are equally fine. Certainly the dramatic impact of Rome on Gibbon represents one of the supreme moments in neo-classicism. But the autobiography of Gibbon is a part of an essentially rhetorical tradition: it is done in the forum rather than in the closet; it is personal without being extremely intimate; it has all the reserve and composure of a public performance.

Less designed for the public were the diaries and private letters of the time: these were the raw materials for biography, and according to traditions well established were not to be published until revised and purged of intimate details in which only gossips might have a natural interest. Probably none of these diaries or correspondences was first published without excision or adaptation. It is natural that the *Memoirs of the Reign of George the Second*, actually an autobiography of John, Lord Hervey (1696-1743) for the years 1727-37, should have been kept from publication for a century, since his frankness and brilliant wit, which at times is almost brutal in its hardness, especially in his reflections on his good friends of the royal family, would have been offensive at an earlier period. Of other journals the very

Lord
Hervey's
Memoirs

---

[8] For bibliographical references for Gibbon see below, ch. IX, n. 6. All six versions of the autobiography are printed in *The Autobiographies of Edward Gibbon*, ed. John Murray (1896).

bulk as well as their uneven interest has hindered complete publication. No one in the age is a Samuel Pepys.

For about fifty-five years John Wesley (1703-1791), the founder of Method- *John* ism, kept a journal which, while its entries are fragmentary and brief for *Wesley* the general reader, has for historians enormous social and religious importance.[9] In 1729, while a fellow of Lincoln College, Oxford, Wesley joined with his brother Charles and a group of like-minded young men in systematic ("methodic") devotions and undertook preaching to prisoners and doing religious work among undergraduates. In spite of opposition the work of the group prospered. Wesley's *Journal* begins in 1735 with his embarkation for Georgia on an unsuccessful two-year mission. After his return in 1738 he began his lifelong, stupendous activity in preaching and organizing religious societies. For fifty years or more he traveled on an average of 4500 miles a year, preaching almost every day three times (the first at five A.M.), writing letters about his work, and doing a mammoth job of organization. He throve on persecution, and met riots and mobs with indomitable composure. Gradually he won his way. Soldiers, respecting his courage, came to listen and, if need be, defend. Colliers venerated him, and the upper classes were in the end usually respectful. He was miraculously active to the age of eighty-five, and continued preaching, on occasion held up in the pulpit by assistants, almost up to his death at the age of eighty-seven.

He represents a curious combination of emotional, intellectual, and practical tendencies. He regarded fervent spirituality as of more importance than theological dogma, which he neglected. While remaining to the end a loyal high-churchman, he stressed a belief in the necessity of conversion, in particular Providence, and in good works. He was a scholarly gentleman, an astonishing reader of ancient and modern literature, and in his travels keenly observant of architecture, parks, gardens, and works of art. Oxford was always his norm of beauty. Returning there at the age of eighty-two he notes: "I once more surveyed many of the gardens and delightful walks. What is wanting but the love of God to make this place an earthly paradise?" But from this paradise he was self-exiled to a life arduous beyond belief, devoted to illiterate and brutalized colliers, felons, tradesmen, and, when they would listen, "the better sort of people." Whether one believes in modern wise that Wesley "set back the clock" of progress by preventing a proletarian revolution in England comparable to that in France,[10] or whether one regards him as a man who labored, not entirely in vain, to realize the Kingdom of Heaven on this earth and among humble folk, one

[9] Wesley's *Works* (32v, Bristol, 1771-4; 11th ed., 15v, 1856-62); *Journal* (4v, 1827); ed. Nehemiah Curnock (8v, 1909-16); *Letters*, ed. John Telford (8v, 1931). — Richard Green, *Bibliography of the Works of John and Charles Wesley* (1896). — Biographies are numerous: John Whitehead (2v, 1791-93), Robert Southey (2v, 1820), Luke Tyerman (3v, 1870-71), John H. Overton (1891), Caleb T. Winchester (1906), William H. Hutton (1927). Brief discussions of the *Journal*, with extracts and with other examples of this type of writing, may be found in the volumes by Arthur, Baron Ponsonby, *English Diaries* (1923), *More English Diaries* (1927), and *Scottish and Irish Diaries* (1927).
[10] Wellman J. Warner, *The Wesleyan Movement in the Industrial Revolution* (1930).

must recognize and admire the magnificent personal achievement recorded in his *Journals*.

Thraliana   Less important but more amusing than Wesley's writing are the diaries of two ladies, who are in part coadjutors of Boswell in preserving Dr. Johnson's life and the manners of his day. These are the *Thraliana* of Mrs. Hester Lynch Thrale, later Mrs. Piozzi, and the diaries of Fanny Burney, later Mme d'Arblay. Only recently has *Thraliana* been published in its entirety, so that its total effect has been until now unappreciated. It is more than a source for anecdotes about Johnson; it is a partly unconscious piece of realistic self-portraiture of high value. Mrs. Thrale [11] kept other journals and wrote hundreds of letters, not for the most part published. *Thraliana* begins in 1776, and its last entry dates 1809. It is not a mere diary; it is a "repository" of anecdotes, jests, poems by herself or others, as well as a record of her life and emotions. "Strange Farrago as it is," she writes, "of Sense, Nonsense, publick, private Follies—but chiefly my own— & *I* the little Hero &c. Well! but who should be the Hero of an *Ana?*" So she rambles on, fluttering from records that concern all members of the Johnson circle to inferior verses of her own composing and to jests that savor at times almost of the bawdy house. She sets down voluminously and interestingly, perhaps not too scrupulously, the "small talk" of a gossiping age. Her taste is as far from being impeccable as her conduct was from being stately: she gives an unvarnished portrait of herself and astonishing glimpses into the society of her day. The total effect is one of liveliness and surprising charm: we see her defects, but see also the gaiety and unstable warmth that led Johnson in his more generous moments to call her "the first of women."

Fanny   Mrs. Thrale's protégée and friend, Fanny Burney,[12] is of course prac-
Burney's tically always impeccable. Her diaries, covering most of her long life after
Diaries   she was sixteen, show a discretion in her recordings that Mrs. Thrale never

[11] Mrs. Thrale (1741-1821) was born Hester Lynch Salusbury, in a distinguished but impoverished Welsh family. She was educated at home by her mother and by Dr. Arthur Collier (1707-77), who also taught Sarah Fielding, Henry's learned sister. In the fifties Miss Salusbury began to keep diaries, of which some thirty odd, covering much of her later life, have been at least in part preserved. In 1763 she was married to the wealthy brewer, Henry Thrale, and thereafter lived for many years either in Southwark or in Streatham. She became the mother of many children, only four of whom (daughters) survived to maturity. In 1765 Johnson was first entertained by the Thrales, who thereafter for about fifteen years afforded him a sort of second home. After Mr. Thrale's death (1781) Johnson and Mrs. Thrale saw less of each other, and when the wealthy widow married Gabriel Piozzi (1784), she was temporarily estranged from Johnson, her family, and from many friends. After 1795 she lived chiefly in Wales or at Bath. — With more facility than distinction she wrote several books for publication. Her *Anecdotes of the Late Samuel Johnson* (1786), ed. in *Johnsonian Miscellanies* by G. B. Hill (Oxford, 1897) and separately by Sydney C. Roberts, (Cambridge, 1925), is her most valued book. She also edited (badly) Johnson's *Letters* (2v, 1788). Apart from *Thraliana*, ed. Katharine C. Balderston (2v, Oxford, 1942), other diaries or journals have been published: *Observations and Reflections Made in the Course of a Journey through France, Italy, and Germany* (2v, 1789); her Welsh journal of 1774 in *Dr. Johnson and Mrs. Thrale* by A. M. Broadley (1910); her *French Journals*, ed. Moses Tyson and Henry Guppy (Manchester, 1932); her *Autobiography, Letters, and Literary Remains*, ed. Abraham Hayward (2v, 1861), and Percival Merritt, *Piozzi Marginalia* (Cambridge, Mass., 1925). The standard biography is that by James L. Clifford, *Hester Lynch Piozzi* (Oxford, 1941).

[12] For bibliographical references regarding Miss Burney see Part III, ch. v, n. 18.

coveted. To be sure, Mme d'Arblay in her old age erased and expunged, and left us texts both improved and imperfect; but doubtless even the indiscretions excised would not if extant undermine the natural dignity and poise of "little Burney." She is far less occupied with herself than with the pageant of life about her, and since her part of the pageant included the most important figures of a long and thrilling period, her record is priceless. Her attitude towards others was reserved, sophisticated, even critical. Possibly a sense of social limitation—after all her father, known through Europe later as a musicologist, started life as a mere music master—led her to be amusedly critical of the manners and minds of others. She was herself a "junior" blue-stocking, but she could see the comedy of their self-important prosy remarks. A gem from the lips of Mrs. Vesey is perfect Burney:

"Did you know Mr. Wallace, Mr. Cambridge?" [Mrs. Vesey asks.]
"No, ma'am."
"It's a very disagreeable thing, I think," said she, "when one has just made acquaintance with anybody, and likes them, to have them die."
This speech set me grinning so irresistibly, that I was forced to begin filliping off the crumbs of the macaroon cake from my muff, for an excuse for looking down.

She records long conversations naturally; her characterizations are incisive and revealing. Obviously more prudish than Mrs. Thrale, her prudery is never annoying; she perceives that she herself also has comical aspects. If she records all the compliments that she ever heard of as paid to her *Evelina,* she must be pardoned as being in general the most self-effacing of diarists. She is by habit the demure but shrewd spectator, whether reporting by letter to her sisters or to Daddy Crisp or recording the opinions of the literati gathered by the Thrales at Streatham or the horrors of the ogress Mrs. Schwellenberg, her *bête noire* at Court during the period when she served as second Mistress of the Robes to Queen Charlotte, or later the troubles of the French *émigrés,* one of whom, General d'Arblay, she married when she was forty-one. Her *Early Diaries* (1768-77) are the more easy and sprightly, more full of "worldly dross"; as she grew older, her natural sedateness developed at times into something remotely resembling a heavy self-consciousness; but her materials are everywhere interesting and her methods pleasantly dramatic.

Letter-writing was more commonly approved than the writing of diaries *Blue-* or journals, which at least one early adviser of Miss Burney regarded as *stocking* "the most dangerous employment young persons can have." One was taught *Letters* to write letters; and, in fact, many pages of Miss Burney's diaries were really transcripts of her long journal-like letters. She, her sisters, and all the sobering company of her intellectual friends were notable correspondents. The "Blue-stocking Club," an unorganized circle of ladies who loved literary or intellectual conversation ("Babels" these gatherings seemed to Horace Walpole), was at its prime in the early sixties.[18] Some of these ladies

18 Chauncey B. Tinker, *The Salon and English Letters* (1915).

published essays, frequently in epistolary form, or poems; Hannah More even wrote plays. Mrs. Elizabeth Montagu, "Queen of the Blues," achieved her loudest fame as writer by her exasperating defense of Shakespeare against Voltaire in her *Essay on the Writings and Genius of Shakespeare* (1769). But it is by recording vivid impressions of men, manners, and books in private letters that these ladies and their friends, Mrs. Mary Delany (1700-1788), Mrs. Elizabeth Vesey, called "The Sylph" (1715?-1791), Elizabeth Carter (1717-1806), and Hester Mulso Chapone (1727-1801), have achieved their permanent modicum of repute.[14]

The Queen of the Blues   Mrs. Montagu [15] (1720-1800), though she wrote letters by the thousand, probably will always be best remembered as a charming hostess. In her luxurious houses in Hill Street and in Portman Square, she gathered London literary society about her and acquired fame as a patroness of the arts, without perhaps too much strain on her purse-strings, considering the fact that she was about the wealthiest woman in England. She was allowed to add three dialogues to the *Dialogues of the Dead* (1760) by Lord Lyttelton, always a close friend, who was defended by her and her feminine myrmidons when Johnson's *Lives of the Poets* seemed not sufficiently aware of his lordship's merits. In this case as well as in that of her patronage of James Beattie, she exaggerated her own literary influence: doubtless she had influence, but her real place is rather in social than in literary history.

Chesterfield's Letters   Among the more specialized letter-writers of the period must be placed one of the leading statesmen of the reigns of the first two Georges, the fourth Earl of Chesterfield (1694-1773). The general correspondence of this noble lord,[16] so famous for being, and for not being, a patron of letters, must

---

[14] *Autobiography and Correspondence of Mary Granville, Mrs. Delany,* ed. Lady Llanover (6v, 1861-62); *A Series of Letters between Mrs. Elizabeth Carter and Miss Catherine Talbot . . . To which are added Letters from Mrs. Carter to Mrs. Vesey,* ed. Montagu Pennington (4v, 1809); *Letters from Mrs. Elizabeth Carter to Mrs. Montagu,* ed. Montagu Pennington (3v, 1817); Hester Chapone, *Letters on the Improvement of the Mind, Addressed to a Young Lady* (2v, 1773); *The Works of Mrs. Chapone* (2v, Dublin, 1786; 4v, 1807); *Posthumous Works of Mrs. Chapone* (2v, 1807); *Letters of Elizabeth Montagu,* ed. Matthew Montagu (4v, 1809-13); other volumes are edited by John Doran (1873), Emily J. Climenson (2v, 1906), R. Blunt (2v, 1923), and Maud Wyndham (2v, 1924).

[15] René Huchon, *Mrs. Montagu* (1907).

[16] Philip Dormer Stanhope, fourth Earl of Chesterfield, may be said to have inherited his interest in courtliness, since his mother was the Lady Elizabeth Savile for whom the Marquis of Halifax had written his *Advice to a Daughter* (1688). Largely privately educated, the future fourth Earl at twenty traveled on the Continent, and speedily was embarked on one of the more distinguished diplomatic and administrative careers of the century. After serving as Ambassador to the Hague (1728-32) he returned to England, accompanied by his mistress; their son, Philip, on whose education the Earl was to spend unusual effort, was born two months later (May, 1732). His lordship was long in public employment, but becoming deaf and ill he continued an interest in politics only for the sake of his son, who died in 1768. Thereafter his lordship concentrated on the education of his godson and presumptive heir to his title, who also was named Philip. The arts of life, particularly literature, had always interested the fourth Earl. In youth a friend of Pope, Arbuthnot, Gay, and others, he later cultivated Voltaire, Rousseau, and Montesquieu. His interest in writers was normally so generous that his neglect of Samuel Johnson was probably not intentional and certainly was not characteristic. — His *Letters to his Son* were published (1774) immediately after his death by his son's widow, and they have often been republished. *Miscellaneous Works,* ed. Dr. Matthew Maty and John O. Justamond (2v, 1777; 4v, 1779); *Letters* (2v, 1774); ed. Lord Mahon (5v, 1845-53); John Bradshaw (3v, 1892); Bonamy Dobrée (6v, 1932). The *Letters to his Godson* were first edited by the Earl of Carnarvon (1890). — Sidney L. Gulick, *A*

have been dominantly political; but his fame will probably always rest on the series of courtesy-book letters addressed to his illegitimate son, Philip. A similar series, addressed to his godson (1761-73) and first published in 1890, serves to reinforce the doctrines of the earlier series. Chesterfield in many ways was a belated Ciceronian in life as in epistolary style. His counsels to his son are based on the noblest "Roman" principles; but the object is policy. According to his contemporary, the Philadelphia printer, Dr. Franklin, honesty was the best policy; according to Chesterfield, manners were the best policy. To his bookish, shy, and awkward son, he preaches in his letters the art of pleasing—always for a purpose: he wished his son to have a distinguished political or diplomatic career. Young Philip had excellent training for this end, but he lacked grace, social charm, and even the inclination to win by diplomacy. His father has been castigated as worldly and insincere; he seems merely to be at times cynical about public intelligence. At least he realized that a compromise between ideals and conduct is inevitable in public life. That he was himself an honest and amiable diplomat and an affectionate parent is indubitable. His knowledge of men was wide and shrewd: "Whatever poets may write, or fools believe, of rural innocence and truth, and of the perfidy of Courts, this is most un-doubtedly true—that shepherds and ministers are both men; their nature and passions the same, the modes of them only different." Such worldly wisdom is deftly stated; but the primitivists and sentimentalists of 1774 regarded such opinions as insensitive and artificial, and probably even fellow peers felt that Chesterfield worked too hard at being noble. He certainly lacked warmth of style but not sound perception of social values. His Augustan spirit is seen when he applies Horace's precepts for the poet to a wider field: "To avoid extremes, to observe propriety, to consult one's own strength, and to be consistent from beginning to end, are precepts as useful for the man as for the poet." The ideal of noble diplomacy has hardly found a sounder proponent in English.

In violent contrast to the special province of Chesterfield is that of Gilbert White [17] (1720-1793), who in his thirties retired from a useful career as an Oxford don to his native and ancestral Hampshire village, Selborne, there to pursue his real career as natural historian. His letters (1767-87) to his fellow observers of nature, Thomas Pennant and Daines Barrington, which were first published in 1789 under the title *The Natural History of Selborne*,

Gilbert White

Chesterfield Bibliography to 1800 (Chicago, 1935; *Papers of the Bibl. Soc. of America*, Vol. xxix). — Samuel Shellabarger, *Lord Chesterfield* (1935); Sidney L. Gulick, "The Publication of Chesterfield's Letters to his Son," *PMLA*, LI (1936). 165-177; Willard Connely, *The True Chesterfield* (1939); Virgil B. Heltzel, "Chesterfield and the Anti-Laughter Tradition," *MP*, xxvi (1928). 73-90.
[17] Gilbert White's *Writings* (incomplete), ed. H. J. Massingham (2v, 1938); *The Natural History and Antiquities of Selborne* (1789; 2v, 1802, with "A Naturalist's Calendar"), ed. Edward T. Bennett, et al. (1837); Sir Wm. Jardine (Edinburgh, 1829); Frank Buckland (2v, 1876); John Burroughs (2v, 1895); Grant Allen (1900); L. C. Miall and W. Warde Fowler (1901); World's Classics (Oxford, 1902); B. C. A. Windle (Everyman's Library, 1906). — *Life and Letters of Gilbert White*, ed. Rashleigh Holt-White (2v, 1901); *Journals*, ed. Walter Johnson (1931). — Edward A. Martin, *A Bibliography of Gilbert White* (1934); Walter Johnson, *Gilbert White: Pioneer, Poet, and Stylist* (1928).

embody a world of curious fact about the weather, the soil, the animals, and the birds of the secluded and beautiful region in which he lived. At first sight the letters take us quite out of the world of men; nature is their subject, and while the villagers appear briefly, White never deviates into "world topics" of the day. A young neighbor, "a young gentleman in the service of the East-India Company," is mentioned, not as an empire-builder, but as one who "has brought home a dog and a bitch of the Chinese breed." White's observations, especially of birds, are said to have notable value to science. His literary charm depends largely on his obvious but unconscious and restrained affection for what he sees, and on his interest in the instincts and almost human behavior of birds and animals. On the instinctive anger of fangless, unborn vipers torn from the belly of their dam, just dead, he comments: "To a thinking mind nothing is more wonderful than that early instinct which impresses young animals with the notion of the situation of their natural weapons, and of using them properly in their own defense, even before those weapons subsist or are formed." Of unwieldy, disproportioned, newly hatched swifts he says: "We could not but wonder when we reflected that these shiftless beings in a little more than a fortnight would be able to dash through the air almost with the inconceivable swiftness of a meteor; and perhaps, in their emigration must traverse vast continents and oceans as distant as the equator. So soon does nature advance small birds to their ἡλικία, or state of perfection; while the progressive growth of men and large quadrupeds is slow and tedious!" Accurate and diverse curiosity and an unceasing wonder at the mysteries of creation, together with a "thinking mind," have in these letters created that rarity, a scientific literary masterpiece.

But most letter-writers are not so specialized as Lord Chesterfield or Gilbert White. Most of them are content, without plan, to make their letters merely friendly communications. This is especially true of literati, among whom for the moment we may place the great actor and less great playwright, David Garrick (1717-1779). Although preoccupied in his letters with the details of his career as actor and manager, Garrick writes from the time he is sixteen amiable, natural, sprightly letters that at times rise to wit and brilliance.[18] He approaches the task of letter-writing normally with a special point of view, if not a new histrionic individuality, for each important effort. He is sincere, but shows the emotional flexibility of a great actor, even though, as he says, he writes "upon the gallop." His letters gain interest in part from the fact that his correspondents included not only theatrical celebrities and members of the Johnson circle (Burke is his closest friend here), but also other leaders of the social and political life of the day. His chief interest, however, in spite of his wide acquaintance is to students of theatrical history.

Among the poets more than one is distinguished for epistolary charm: perhaps the three most commonly praised are William Shenstone, Thomas

---

[18] On Garrick see Part III, ch. VI, n. 2.

Gray, and William Cowper. Of these Shenstone [19] is in all respects the least, *Poets as* but he is by no means contemptible. From the ornamented rusticity of *Letter-* Leasowes he wrote interestingly on literary topics to the publisher Robert *Writers:* Dodsley, to Bishop Percy, to Richard Graves, author of *The Spiritual* *Shenstone* *Quixote,* to the Edge Hill poet Richard Jago, and to William Somervile, author of *The Chace.* To his neighbor fifteen miles away, Lady Luxborough (half-sister of Lord Bolingbroke), he confided his emotional state and his gardening projects. Apart from gardening, his "rural allusions" in his letters, as in his poems, suffer from self-consciousness. His epistolary style is easily overpraised: his sentences straggle and sprawl—inelegantly at times but almost always interestingly and naturally.

Thomas Gray is in all respects a greater epistolary artist.[20] Gray, in fact, *Thomas* seems more natural and easy in his letter-writing than elsewhere. Here the *Gray* true warmth and fineness of his personality are evident. Frequently erudite, a trait unavoidable in "the most learned man in Europe," he was even more frequently colloquial, witty, and genuinely affectionate. There is none of the stiffness that his normal reserve in company would lead one to expect. The mere fact that he called his friend the Rev. William Mason "Scroddles" alone speaks volumes of his gift for affectionate informalities. Mason, Nicholls, and the young Swiss Bonstetten all won Gray's affections as young men. Such major correspondents as Horace Walpole and Richard West had been boyhood friends at Eton. At Cambridge Dr. Thomas Wharton, Fellow of Pembroke College from 1739 to 1747, became Gray's closest friend, and to him in 1769 Gray sent as an account of his tour of the Lake Region a series of letters that of itself would establish the poet's epistolary fame.[21]

Apart from the unconscious revelation of himself, Gray's letters have at least three notable topics: antiquities, literature, and the beauties of land-scape. The letters are a chief clue to his great learning, and they also con-stitute him, in well-chosen excerpts, a notable critic of poetry and prose fiction. Most interesting, because unusual, is his ability to convey his delight in the wilder aspects of nature. It is absurd to imagine that Gray was the first Englishman really to feel the titanic beauty of the Alps or the quieter loveliness of the English lakes; but he is perhaps the first to express this beauty in words of distinction. Thomas Amory, for example, in his fantastic *John Buncle* (Volume I, 1756) had made the attempt, and he shows that Westmorland already had a reputation for wild natural beauty. He also shows that a taste for the sublime may exist without gifts of expressing the sublime. Throughout his life Gray's mind recorded delicate impressions of

[19] On Shenstone see Part III, ch. IV, n. 13.
[20] In addition to the references on Gray given in Part III, ch. IV, n. 15, see Geoffrey Tillotson, "On Gray's Letters," in *Essays in Criticism and Research* (Cambridge, 1942), pp. 117-123.
[21] Dr. Wharton had planned to accompany Gray, but asthma prevented. Consequently Gray kept for his friend a detailed journal of the tour in pocket note-books, from which letters were extracted and sent to Wharton. See Gray's *Correspondence,* ed. Paget Toynbee and Leonard Whibley (Oxford, 1935), III. 1074 ff.; esp. the footnote on pp. 1074-5. Gray's interest in nature at times approached the purely scientific. See, for example, Charles Eliot Norton's *The Poet Gray as a Naturalist* (Boston, 1903), which publishes some of his learned marginalia.

beautiful landscapes, and, unlike others, he had a special gift for conveying his impressions through words. His letters record a rich experience of books, men, and nature, and the record is warmly intimate yet restrained; informal yet, of its epoch, dignified.

William Cowper

William Cowper,[22] in spite of his intermittent periods of mental derangement, led a more serene and winsome existence than did busy intellectuals like Gray or Shenstone; and this quiet life of virtue and piety is beautifully mirrored in his letters. For over forty years he sent his friends charming accounts of his life—his country walks, his adventures with "Puss" and his other hares and pets, his religious agonies, his reading, and his own labors as a poet, together with observations on the life of the parish in which he happened to be living. As Johnson represents the literary life in town, so Cowper symbolizes the refined aspects of village life of the late century. In his letters, he writes with an ease, limpidity, naturalness, and elegance that is hardly found elsewhere in letters. It is perhaps true that one remembers Cowper for a relatively small number of superlatively excellent letters—those in which ease is spiced by his exquisite humor rather than made painful by his religious depression; but the average quality of his prose is high and the total effect of self-portrayal is most attractive. Doubtless he is the most lovable of letter-writers.

Horace Walpole

In the opinion of his editor Thomas Wright, Cowper "is universally acknowledged to be the greatest of English letter-writers." Such assertion will provoke opposition from the many admirers of Gray or, more evidently, of Horace Walpole [23] (1717-1797), though they will probably admit that in many ways Cowper had a quiet integrity and personal charm that Walpole lacks. But Walpole has everything else: brilliance, wit, humor, knowledge of society, politics, literature, architecture, painting, and an ability always to be—at some slight cost of conscious effort—extremely entertaining. Among the thousands of his letters there are relatively few that are not enlivening. He was personally "spirits of hartshorne" to his intimates. At first sight Walpole seems merely a superficial, elegant amateur, to whom no high human experience came. From another point of view, however, all experi-

---

[22] On Cowper see references given below, ch. x. To these may be added articles by Kenneth Povey: "The Text of Cowper's Letters," *MLR*, XXII (1927). 22-27; "Notes for a Bibliography of Cowper's Letters," *RES*, VII (1931). 182-187; VIII (1932). 316-319; x (1934). 76-78; XII (1936). 333-335.

[23] *The Works of Horatio Walpole*, ed. Mary Berry *et al.* (9v, 1798-1825). Apart from his letters his major contribution to the history of his own time is made in his *Memoirs of the Last Ten Years of . . . George the Second*, ed. Lord Holland (2v, 1822) and in his *Memoirs of the Reign of George the Third*, ed. Sir D. Le Marchant (4v, 1845). His *Correspondence* has been often edited since 1820 when four volumes appeared. The best editions are by Peter Cunningham (9v, 1857), Mrs. Paget Toynbee (16v, Oxford, 1903-5; Supplements by Paget Toynbee, 3v, Oxford, 1918-25; 2v, Oxford, 1915). These, however, are to be supplanted by the magnificent Yale Edition now in progress, edited by Wilmarth S. Lewis. This began in 1937, and to date 12 volumes have appeared. The completed edition may run to over fifty volumes. — Austin Dobson, *Horace Walpole, a Memoir* (1890, 1927); Paul Yvon, *La Vie d'un dilettante: Horace Walpole* (Paris, 1924); Leonard Whibley, "The Foreign Tour of Gray and Walpole," *Blackwood's Magazine*, CCXXVII (1930). 813-827; Warren H. Smith, *Architecture in English Fiction* (New Haven, 1934); Robert W. Ketton-Cremer, *Horace Walpole, a Biography* (1940); Isabel W. U. Chase, *Horace Walpole, Gardenist* (1943).

ence came his way, and found in him an attentive and amused observer and recorder. His most famous remark was, "The world is a comedy to those who think, a tragedy to those who feel." He chose to be a comic artist.

Born the youngest son of the great prime minister, Horace was in his ninth year sent to Eton, where he formed ardent boyish friendships with Thomas Ashton and two other boys—Richard West (1716-1742) and Thomas Gray. This "Quadruple Alliance" lasted for some years. Another Eton group was called "The Triumvirate": it included George Montagu, *His Early* later Walpole's correspondent to whom social gossip was confided, and *Years* Charles Lyttelton, brother of the "good" Lord Lyttelton and later Bishop of Carlisle. The years (1727-34) at Eton meant much to Walpole—far more than the succeeding years at Cambridge (1735-9), though there he continued his friendship with Ashton and Gray. Both Gray and Walpole were intended for the law, but neither fancied that fate, and both welcomed the opportunity of making the grand tour together. Before they got to Calais differences in temperament between the volatile and theatrical Walpole and the shy, proud Gray manifested themselves; but together they delighted in Paris, the Alps, Florence, and Rome, and perhaps had no more psychological rubs than befall the average fellow travelers. At Florence they met and enjoyed the hospitality of Horace Mann, destined, in spite of the fact that Walpole never saw him after this tour, to receive the most voluminous and valued of Walpole's correspondences. In the spring of 1741 the two travelers parted company for some unknown and probably unimportant reason: the coolness was not removed until late in 1745. This tour through France and Italy was most influential in the development of Walpole's social and artistic tastes.

During the period 1741-68 Walpole was a member of Parliament, and though he seldom spoke in the House, he was active and even influential in discreet and respectable wire-pulling. The most trying moment in his career came at its beginning when his father in 1742 was forced to resign by means so treacherous, Horace felt, as to be eternally unforgivable. Other tense moments came at crises in the career of his cousin, the Hon. Henry Seymour Conway, who as member of Parliament and even as Secretary of State deferred—but not always—to Walpole's advice. In 1747 Walpole acquired in Twickenham a small house, presently rechristened Strawberry Hill, and set about a career first as gardener and by 1750 as architect.

To the surprise of some of his friends he decided to do the house in *Strawberry* Gothic style. There was nothing really revolutionary in the decision. Gothic *Hill* was never totally "out"; antiquarians had almost consistently praised it, and clergymen and others sporadically throughout the first half of the century had been pointing the windows of their cottages and at the same time adding "Chinese" porches to their doorways. For music and dining *al fresco* one of the most fashionable places of resort after 1732 was Vauxhall Gardens, and here Gothic design had been freely used. The distaste for this style came normally from those who loved simplicity and plainness. The chapel of

Henry VII in the Abbey had seemed to John Evelyn "lace ... cut-work, and crinkle crankle." The ingenuity of baroque ornamentation and the artifice of decorative Gothic were regarded, however, as akin rather than as hostile. In 1717 that true Palladian architect, Colin Campbell, had charged that post-Palladian "Italians can now no more relish the antique simplicity, but are entirely employed in capricious ornaments, which must at last end in the Gothick." The vexed problem of ornamentation in art rather than any love or even understanding of pure Gothic forms is at the bottom of most eighteenth-century controversy over architectural styles. Since practically all architectural revivals are easily dated fifty years after the fact, it need surprise no one that Walpole's somewhat rococo Gothic was, to say the least, impure. He had no intention of making his house a perfect period piece devoid of modern convenience: being naturally an exotic, somewhat disillusioned with the life of his own day, he sought a remote style that would gratify his antiquarian tastes and also give play to the multiplicity of decorative effects that were his delight. By 1753 the first stage of his gothicizing was accomplished, but at intervals for twenty years he greatly enlarged the house, adding a cloister, towers, and several spacious rooms and other architectural features. If he did not originate the Gothic revival either in architecture or in literature, he certainly gave aristocratic sanction and popular vogue to both. Curious visitors became so frequent that tickets were issued and rules of visit established. Walpole's house aroused more interest in his own day than did any of his other activities.

The Strawberry Hill Press

Near his house Walpole's experimental nature led him to set up a private printing press, and the press stimulated him to authorship. Here he published his friend Gray's two great odes (the first productions of the press; brought out in 1757), as well as other works not by himself.[24] Of his own writings he did not publish all at Strawberry Hill. Naturally the anonymously produced *Castle of Otranto* (1765) did not come from his own press, but his *Fugitive Pieces in Verse and Prose* (1758) and his tragedy, *The Mysterious Mother* (1768), did. Although this last work, dealing with a morbid story of incest, was unfitted for stage production, it is his most powerfully written imaginative work.

Even in his original writing Walpole was the amateur medievalist, and the most regarded works of the Strawberry Hill press that came from his pen were genteelly historical. His *Catalogue of the Royal and Noble Authors of England* (2 volumes, 1758) was an amusing compilation of literary and antiquarian gossip, and his *Historic Doubts on Richard III* (1768), which was not printed at Strawberry Hill, was an interesting if unsoundly argued attempt to clear Richard from his alleged murders and other misdeeds. It was in part, as Mr. Ketton-Cremer says aptly, a work of "disdainful amateurishness." Of far different merit and far more typical of Walpole's

---

[24] Allen T. Hazen and J. P. Kirby, *A Bibliography of the Strawberry Hill Press, with a Record of the Prices at which Copies have been Sold* (New Haven, 1942). This excellent work supersedes all other secondary sources of information about Walpole's press.

natural interests was his production, on the Strawberry Hill press, of his *Anecdotes of Painting in England* (4 volumes, 1762-71). This work, based on the valuable note-books of the famous engraver George Vertue (1684-1756), which Walpole had purchased from Vertue's widow, made Walpole a pioneer in the history of English painting; and when in the twentieth century a society was founded for the promotion of the historical study of English art, it was appropriately named the Walpole Society.

As the son of a notable prime minister Walpole had naturally an interest *Walpole's* in the political history of his own day. Before he bought Strawberry Hill *Memoirs* he had begun to envisage himself as a historian of his own time; and in this difficult rôle he produced his *Memoirs,* covering much of the latter half of his century. These show his limitations (a capricious hatred of his father's enemies being one), and yet show also his keen observation and wide knowledge of the political alignments of his day, a knowledge invaluable for its frequent illumination of the tortuous political quarrels and friendships so perplexing to later historians.

Possibly, as has been suggested, Walpole came to regard his voluminous correspondences not merely as the raw materials for memoirs but as themselves the best memoirs he could bequeath to posterity. If so, he thought wisely. He was an artist in miniature work; for the large canvas of formal history he lacked the indispensable quality of settled industry and the ability to make coherent and large interpretations. In letters he becomes legitimately *His Letters* the vivid and intelligent reporter of the specific scene. At present scholars *as Memoirs* believe that Walpole selected his correspondents as worthy recipients of specialized materials: to Horace Mann in distant Florence was consigned the matter of politics; to George Montagu went society gossip, and to William Cole talk of antiquities. One can perhaps exaggerate this conscious and somewhat pedantic specialization in correspondences, but clearly to some degree it existed. It enabled Walpole to leave a diversified record of the life of his time, and his concentration on the specialized aspect of the moment helped to make each letter an individual and artistic achievement.

Historically the letters have the value of a thousand examples of that modern work the "documentary film"; artistically the letters are superior to any graphic portrayal of their time. He gives us "shots" of everyone—the beautiful Countess of Coventry, the chivalrous highwayman, M'Lean, the notorious Fanny Murray, clapping the despised gift of a twenty-pound note between two pieces of bread and eating it!—they are all there. We have pictures of the trials and executions of the Jacobite lords, of the funeral of George II, of a score of other historic—and possibly grotesque—moments. He recaptures for nostalgic minds a whole social era in a sentence: "Old Cibber plays tonight, and all the world will be there." His art, formed on the model of Madame de Sévigné's, is at its best in focused episode or anecdote. At times he certainly has the modern journalistic defect of overconfidence in the authenticity of his information; yet he was not intentionally the irresponsible gossip, and he doubtless was the best informed gossip of his century. His deftness and lightness—tinged at times with cynicism—together with a keen sense of humor make him supreme among the wits of a decreasingly witty period. His personality, his artifice, have been decried; but from one point of view his personality is negligible: it is the wealth of his material that counts. From another point of view, however, the catholicity of his perceptions *is* his personality. Life for him was a "dome of many-colored glass" and from it he caught a myriad of brilliant diffractions. Of the serious religious or intellectual life of his time he is, like a good popular journalist, almost totally unaware: in *comédie humaine* he would rank near the top in any period. He is the most voluminous and, by all odds, the most entertaining practitioner of the art of letter-writing in the period that is clearly the golden age of that art.

IX

Intellectual Prose

In David Hume, Edward Gibbon, and Edmund Burke are seen tendencies *Reason* that indicate significant, if diversely individual, developments in style and *Subverted* in modes of thinking. Their very diversity suggests intellectual disintegration in the period, but all three seem alike in that they mark a transition from the mechanistic a priori thinking of many early Augustans towards a new organic concept of man and of human institutions. The first two of our trio were skeptics; Burke was a man of faith, but he too tended to rely on a psychological pragmatism or opportunism rather than on abstract theory— a position that subverted trust in reason. "Reason," as a matter of fact, was claimed as on the side of the French Revolution: Burke was not. We must ask, then, how do these three men illuminate the movements of their day?

Hume's[1] preëminence is supremely that of a philosopher; but he was *David* also an historian and an essayist of worth. His philosophy was embodied *Hume* in early works that won recognition too slowly to suit their ambitious author.

[1] David Hume (1711-1776) was born in Edinburgh, and was educated there in the University. He spent the years 1734-7 in France, where he wrote his first *Treatise*. After publishing it in London, he returned to Scotland, but failing to secure a professorial appointment, he became (1745-6) a nobleman's tutor, and presently he was with General Sinclair at Lorient and later in Vienna and Turin. In 1749 he returned to Scotland, where he wrote (1751) his *Dialogues concerning Natural Religion* (1779). Because of clerical opposition he failed (1752) of appointment as successor to Adam Smith in the chair of logic at Glasgow. From 1752 to 1757 he was Keeper of the Advocates' Library, and became a leader in the distinguished intellectual society of Edinburgh. After serving (1763-66) as secretary of the British Embassy in Paris, where he was a great social success, he returned to England, escorting the philosopher Rousseau to an English refuge. A famous quarrel between the two resulted. In 1767 Hume was Conway's under-secretary of state; but most of the rest of his life was spent among his Scottish friends, who included Hugh Blair, John Home, Adam Ferguson, Lord Kames, William Robertson, and Adam Smith. In his autobiography, dated April 18, 1776, he expects "a speedy dissolution." The calm cheerfulness of his demise four months later greatly annoyed the orthodox. His character was both upright and amiable; his life attempted a demonstration of a proposition very dear to the free-thinkers of his century: that virtue could exist independent of religion. — Rudolf Metz, "Bibliographie der Hume-Literatur," in *Literarische Berichte aus dem Gebiete der Philosophie*, XV-XVI (1928). 39-50; Thomas E. Jessop, *A Bibliography of David Hume*, etc. (1938). — Hume's writings have been collected as *Essays and Treatises* (4v, 1753-6; 1758, 1760, etc.); as *Philosophical Works* (4v, 1826, etc.); as *A Treatise of Human Nature*, ed. Thomas H. Green and T. H. Grose (2v, 1874) and *Essays Moral, Political, and Literary*, ed. Thomas H. Green and T. H. Grose (2v, 1875). His histories have been published as follows: *History of Great Britain*, Vol. I [Reigns of James I and Charles I] (Edinburgh, 1754); Vol. II [The Commonwealth, Charles II, and James II] (1757); *History of England under the House of Tudor* (2v, 1759); *History of England from the Invasion of Julius Caesar to the Revolution of 1688* (8v, 1763; and many eds. thereafter; after 1793 with continuations by Smollett to 1760 and by others later for later periods). — *The Life of David Hume, Esq., written by Himself* (1777; and in most eds. of the *Essays* thereafter); *The Letters of David Hume*, ed. John Y. T. Greig (2v, Oxford, 1932). The standard biography is that of John H. Burton, *Life and Correspondence of David Hume* (2v, 1846); Ernest C. Mossner gives an illuminating account of Hume's personal relations with contemporaries in *The For-*

The core of his thinking was precociously formed, and was expressed in a *Treatise of Human Nature,* completed when he was twenty-five and published anonymously in 1739. "It fell *dead-born from the press"* was the author's pained comment. In his final edition of his *Essays* (1777) he included an Advertisement requesting that only pieces published later than the *Treatise,* a "juvenile work," be "regarded as containing his philosophical sentiments and principles." His later work in philosophy, however, is by and large a restatement and development, in more polished and strategic form, of positions taken in the *Treatise.* The most inclusive single reworking was his *Enquiry concerning Human Understanding* (1748), the second edition of which was the first volume to bear the author's name. In his *Four Dissertations* (1757) that on the passions frankly uses material drawn verbatim from the *Treatise,* and these ideas had already been fundamental to the work that was his favorite, his *Enquiry concerning the Principles of Morals* (1751). It was chiefly in posthumous works, particularly the smoothly written *Dialogues concerning Natural Religion* (1779), that Hume trenchantly extended his skepticism (always outspoken in other directions) to the field of religion.

Hume's Skepticism   Beyond doubt Hume was the most thoroughgoing and strategically logical skeptic to come out of Great Britain. Carrying the empiricism of Locke and Berkeley to its extreme conclusion, Hume held that nothing can be known by the mind but its own "impressions" (sensations) and "ideas" (faint copies of impressions). He is opposed to all a priori thinking and to most metaphysical concepts. He builds inductively from psychological data; but his service is less the erection of a new system than it is the destruction of doctrines to him either irrelevant or baseless. He combats such arguments from "design" as the physico-theologists had indulged in; and in his *Dialogues concerning Natural Religion* he ridicules current speculation about the divine attributes. His logical legerdemain is everywhere dazzling, and perhaps nowhere more so than in the sections of his *Human Understanding* which analyze the concept of Causation. Naturally he will have no traffic with supernaturalism in religion; and if he does admit—somewhat strangely—an idea of "necessary connection" or even at rare moments "an eternal inherent principle of order" that ranges and rules our "impressions," he rigorously opposes any analogy between this principle and intelligence whether human or divine. He clears the way, in metaphysics, for the positivism of the nineteenth century. In ethics he as clearly prepares for utilitarianism. He proves to his own satisfaction that while the passions cause actions, reason is neither a guide nor a controlling force in the face of passion. Ethical choice he bases altogether on utility, on a *sentiment* that declares a preference of pleasure to pain. Reason and the earlier concepts of

gotten Hume (1943). On the trouble with Rousseau see Albert Schinz, *État présent des travaux sur J.-J. Rousseau* (New York, 1941) and H. Roddier in *RLC,* xviii (1938). 452-477.— Charles W. Hendel, *Studies in the Philosophy of David Hume* (Princeton, 1925); André Leroy, *La critique et la religion chez David Hume* (Paris, 1930); John Laird, *Hume's Philosophy of Human Nature* (1932); Norman K. Smith, *The Philosophy of David Hume* (1941).

conscience are modified in nature and in power. Belief itself in Hume's eyes is a *sentiment,* "which depends not on will, nor can be commanded at pleasure." If there ever was an age of reason in Matthew Arnold's sense of the phrase, surely Hume with skilful logic was its treacherous, subversive high priest. In his thinking "eternal verities" disappear, and his probable answer to the question as to what kept his world from being merely a chaos of sensation would be "the principles of the association of ideas." "Common sense" was the answer later urged by some of his Scottish compatriots and critics.

Hume's early works, as we have said, were less cordially received than his thirst for fame desired. This was due less to an immediate realization that, if he was right, all the theologians and a priori rationalists were hopelessly wrong, than it was to the fact that he wrote in a cool, quiet fashion when the reasoners of the moment (like William Warburton and his school) were excitingly abusive or paradoxically or ironically entertaining. Hume's *Philosophical Essays concerning Human Understanding* was, he said, eclipsed by Conyers Middleton's *Free Enquiry into the Miraculous Powers,* an unintentionally subversive work of the same year. Possibly the excitement over Bolingbroke's posthumous *Works* (1754) held back readers from Hume; but he was gradually coming into his own, and presently was to be spoken of as "the fashionable Hume." Eventually he acquired a comfortable income through the very large sale of his books.

Vogue of the "fashionable" sort he doubtless sought, but he wisely sought *Hume's* it through literary efforts in the form of essays. In 1741-2 Hume brought out *Essays* two volumes of essays, which he had accumulated with the unrealized intention of using them in a weekly periodical; some were social and moral— remotely patterned after *The Spectator;* others were political, somewhat in the manner of *The Craftsman.* One of these latter was an uncomplimentary "Character of Sir Robert Walpole"—discreetly published just after the great statesman's fall. Of the two types the political essays, especially those on economic subjects,[2] have been at times highly regarded, though their cool moderation would hardly have fired readers used to *The Craftsman* or *The Daily Gazetteer.* Hume was practising to gain an elegant style fit for *salons;* but he lacked the lightness, the playfulness, and the wit, as well as the feeling for details of human interest that are required of the journalist-essayist. Almost ten years before *The Rambler* he was demonstrating the unfitness of the clear, abstract thinker for the task so well performed by Steele and Addison. The net result of the experience gained through these twenty-seven essays was that Hume effectively cast his *Human Understanding* in brief essay-like sections. The most readable of his *Essays* are those on literary topics or his sketches ("characters") of the Epicurean, the Stoic, the Platonist, and the Skeptic. The style usually is unadorned, but where it departs from the simplicity and refinement that he normally sought and achieved, it departs

---

[2] Hume's influence on Adam Smith is perhaps exaggerated by James Bonar, *Philosophy and Political Economy* (1893), pp. 105-129.

in the tradition of classical oratory or history. His most finished writing is found in the *Dialogues concerning Natural Religion,* which was suppressed until after his death.

Strangely enough this gifted thinker was to achieve his greatest popular success in the field of history, where his endowments were less remarkable than in philosophy. An appointment (1752) as Keeper of the Advocates' Library (now the National Library of Scotland) put at his disposal what *His* History seemed large resources for writing in the neglected field of history, and thus encouraged him to realize long-cherished ambitions to shine as an historian of Great Britain. His first volume, dealing with the early seventeenth century, which was to him "the most curious, interesting, and instructive part of our history," was not well received. Hume as a Scot was naturally pro-Stuart;[3] but he had thought himself open-minded and impartial. Reactions to his work were disappointing. "I was assailed," he writes, "by one cry of reproach, disapprobation, and even detestation; English, Scotch, and Irish, Whig and Tory, churchman and sectary, free-thinker and religionist, patriot and courtier, united in their rage against the man, who had presumed to shed a generous tear for the fate of Charles I and the Earl of Strafford." This extreme picture is hardly congruent with his further complaint that only forty-five copies of the work were sold during a year. The second volume, with Charles I out of the way and the glorious Revolution of 1688 as terminal point, was less offensive, and "helped buoy up its unfortunate brother" (Volume 1). The next installment, on "The House of Tudor," was criticized; but when the whole was completed in 1762, and became in the following year the *History of England from the Invasion of Julius Caesar to the Revolution of 1688* in eight volumes, Hume had achieved the first satisfactory history of England to be written. Its defects are now obvious: it is not very soundly based in careful study or research; the Middle Ages are ignorantly defamed and in later fields there is bias. The organizing purpose—Hume's desire to illustrate the dangers of violent faction to a state—had more appeal in his time than in later days. But the work supplied a great lack, and it was readable. Its fame outlived that of Hume's contemporary rivals, Robertson[4] and Smollett, and was for over a century the most read history of England. In 1828 Macaulay[5] admitted that Hume was "the ablest and most popular" of English historians, and a more recent historian, the

---

[3] E. C. Mossner defends Hume's position in "Was Hume a Tory Historian?" *JHI,* II (1941). 225-236, and in "An Apology for David Hume, Historian," *PMLA,* LVI (1941). 657-690, gives a more general account of Hume as historian, and gives a good bibliography of other accounts of Hume's work as historian. These papers are shrewdly reviewed by William Davidson, *PQ,* XXI (1942). 206-209.

[4] William Robertson (1721-1793), a Scottish Presbyterian minister, was a charter member (1754) of the "Select Society," a club of fifteen eminent Scots, including David Hume, Adam Ferguson, Monboddo, Kames, and Adam Smith. His fame was established by his *History of Scotland during the Reigns of Queen Mary and of King James VI* (2v, 1759), and was sustained by his *Charles V* (3v, 1769), and his *History of America* (2v, 1777). Both in style and in scholarship his work is comparable with Hume's, but his subjects were less popular in appeal. For Smollett see above, Part II, ch. x, n. 17.

[5] In a review article on Neele's *Romance of History* in the *Edinburgh Rev.,* XLVII (1828). 331-367.

Right Honorable Winston Churchill, has called the work his "boyhood's manual."

In 1752 Viscount Bolingbroke brought out his much read *Letters on the Study of History*. These in England and—much more significantly—the work of Montesquieu and Voltaire in France and Vico in Italy were modifying the concept of history. Hume would have agreed with the fundamental precept of Bolingbroke, borrowed from the ancients, that "history is philosophy teaching by examples." For although he did not write history like a philosopher, Hume's purpose was fundamentally didactic. Unlike the French illuminati, who stressed the criminal wrongs of the past, Hume was a pioneer giving an account of a great nation that had recently emerged as a power and a cultural force in Europe.

Curiously enough the historian Gibbon [6] is somewhat more philosophical than the historian Hume, and even more typical of the aristocrats of his age. *Gibbon's* Like Hume and Voltaire, Gibbon was anticlerical; his mind had "emerged *Decline* from superstition to skepticism." Like Voltaire he inclined to the tragedy *and Fall* rather than the comedy of man's past. He was less keen than Voltaire on finding ideas behind actions, but was far more interested in causal sequences than was Hume. Above all, he was in coolness of temperament and in his veneration for the civilization of ancient Rome the perfect neo-classicist. The fascination that the pageantry of imperial Rome had for Gibbon stimulated him to spend more than twenty years of his life in the research for and composition of his great masterpiece, *The Decline and Fall of the Roman Empire*. In his *Autobiography* he remarked:

My temper is not very susceptible of enthusiasm, and the enthusiasm which I do not feel I have ever scorned to affect. But, at the distance of twenty-five years, I can neither forget nor express the strong emotions which agitated my mind as I first approached and entered the *eternal city*. After a sleepless night, I trod, with a lofty step, the ruins of the Forum; each memorable spot where Romulus *stood,* or Tully spoke, or Caesar fell, was at once present to my eye; and several days of intoxication were lost or enjoyed before I could descend to a cool and minute investigation.

[6] Edward Gibbon (1737-1794) was born in Putney, near London, of a well-to-do family. His youth was sickly, and his early education irregular. After fourteen months at Magdalen College, Oxford (1752-53), he became a convert to Catholicism and was dismissed. His father thereupon placed him under the care of a Calvinist minister in Lausanne, and Gibbon soon abandoned the Roman faith—and all faith. Lausanne became a second home to him, and French a second language. In 1757 he returned to England, where he served two years as captain in the Hampshire Militia (1760-62), and then devoted himself to historical studies and writing. In 1764 he visited Rome, and there conceived the project of writing the history of the decline and fall of the city. In 1774 he was admitted to Dr. Johnson's "Club," and became a Member of Parliament. He served on the Board of Trade and Plantations 1779-82, but retired from politics when the coalition government of 1783 was formed. Thereafter he lived at Lausanne; but in 1793 he paid a visit to his friend Lord Sheffield in England, became ill, and died there. — Jane E. Norton, *A Bibliography of the Works of Edward Gibbon* (Oxford, 1940). — *Miscellaneous Works*, ed. the first Earl of Sheffield (5v, 1814). — J. B. Black, *The Art of History* (1926); Vernon P. Helming, "Edward Gibbon and Georges Deyverdun," *PMLA*, XLVII (1932). 1028-1049; Shelby T. McCloy, *Gibbon's Antagonism to Christianity* (1933); Edmund Blunden, *Edward Gibbon and his Age* (1935); Robert B. Mowat, *Gibbon* (1936); David M. Low, *Edward Gibbon* (1937); I. W. J. Machin, "Gibbon's Debt to Contemporary Scholarship," *RES*, xv (1939). 84-88.

Years of this cool and minute research followed; for Gibbon far surpassed the historians of his time in devotion to careful study: Rome merited such consecration of effort. If he found history brick and left it nobly marble, the change doubtless was due to inspiration from that ancient civilization the decay of which was his tragic theme. He was among the last and among the best of the true Augustans.

Its Scope   Through the years of his labor the scope of Gibbon's project steadily enlarged itself. His first idea was to write "the decline and fall of the city" of Rome. He early expanded this to include the fall of the Western Empire, a field covered in the first three volumes of the published work (1776-81). Then after a year of hesitation and of political confusion (1783), he began work looking towards a history of the fall of the Eastern Empire, which he completed at Lausanne, June 27, 1787. After all those years the great work was done, and a "sober melancholy," as if at losing "an old and agreeable companion," was Gibbon's natural mood. Seldom has so extensive and prolonged a piece of study been so thoroughly a labor of love.

The effect on his readers is that of dignified and magnificent pageantry. The narrative unfolds in smooth, living details—not details that are full of vague overtones: they are sharply defined and register in the mind without much imaginative repercussion. Imaginative impressiveness comes less from individual pictorial passages than from the tremendous and complete marshaling of great masses of material. Gibbon's aim is to *portray* fully and accurately; he makes the somewhat austere remark that "Diligence and accuracy are the only merits which an historical writer may ascribe to himself." To a surprising extent even after 150 years the accuracy of much of his wealth of fact is not impugned. Nowadays a scholarly historian might evaluate sources more carefully, and nowadays more sources are available; but if one recognizes on Gibbon's part a failure to understand Byzantine civilization or the play of economic forces, if one sees and regrets a too frequent bias through anticlericalism or other limitations of Gibbon's mind and day, one still finds an amazing amount of sound fact and shrewd interpretation.

History and Causation   Authenticity and the ability to unfold a stupendous panorama clearly and smoothly have been granted Gibbon, but there have been regrets that he lacked "philosophy." This is in part a Victorian indictment of all eighteenth-century skeptics; and it must be admitted that they lack metaphysics. But Gibbon is precisely the first great English historian to stress causation as a philosophic basis for the writing of history. He does not use the causes of decline and fall as devices for organization, but he does pause at times in his narrative for formal discussions of this or that cause. At other times a cause is briefly, almost slyly, adverted to in the course of narrative or description. Only in his last chapter does he summarize methodically.

After a diligent inquiry, I can discern four principal causes of the ruin of Rome, which continued to operate in a period of more than a thousand years. I. The injuries of time and nature. II. The hostile attacks of the barbarians and Christians. III. The use and abuse of the materials. And, IV. The domestic quarrels of the Romans.

These causes of the ruin of the city of Rome suggest the causes of imperial ruin—which obviously would be more complex. It is notable that while all these causes are informally and briefly introduced into Montesquieu's work translated in 1734 as *Reflections on the Causes of the Grandeur and Declension of the Romans,* the extensive development and application of them is Gibbon's own. One of his editors (J. B. Bury) has stressed Gibbon's remark about cause III: "In the preceding volumes of this History, I have described the triumph of barbarism and religion." To isolate this remark as indicating total cause is debatable justice. In his summary Gibbon carefully subordinates the subversive rôle of Christianity; but his anti-Christian remarks occur *Gibbon and* slyly, frequently, and pervasively; and they constitute evidence that prej- *Christianity* udices the rôle of religion as villainous. Byron expressed a widespread awareness that Gibbon was

> Sapping a solemn creed with solemn sneer.

To evaluate the relative importance in Gibbon's mind of the manifold causes of decline would be difficult, because this summary for the city of Rome is the nearest to a complete summary that we get. Causes normally are expressed recurringly, like *leitmotivs* or themes in a symphony. Such a method in historical discourse is obviously diplomatic if one is subverting religion; and while the method in the hands of a journeyman might be dangerous to logic and clarity, in the hands of a masterworkman it is adroit. He has made "diligent inquiry," and a diligent reader will find plenty of causes emerging effectively. To present a unique cause would falsify.

The art of Gibbon is nowhere more noticeable than in his manner of expression. This is marked by a clear flow of narrative expressed in diction of unvarying nobility. Like a true neo-classicist he shuns "low" everyday words: a physically small man himself, he compensates with a pompous *Gibbon's* style of rhythmic sonority, definitely "noble Roman." It is obvious that he *Art* frequently writes as he does merely for the sake of the sound. Conscious effort here succeeds: the sound is always musical, and the pomp has true majesty. His phrasing is not especially decorative. One has to forgive excessive melodramatic heightening such as the murder of Probus (chapter XII) or the theatrical apparition of the King of the Goths:

A victorious leader, who united the daring spirit of a Barbarian with the art and discipline of a Roman general, was at the head of an hundred thousand fighting men; and Italy pronounced, with terror and respect, the formidable name of Alaric.

In general the style, vivid in description and fluid in narration, enlarges and elevates the mind of the reader in spite of a chill formality. Its idiosyncrasy is doubtless irony—seen at its most devastating in the offensive chapters (xv and xvi) that terminated his first volume and with covert sacrilege pictured the rise of Christianity. Of the early saints he could write, four years before the Gordon riots:

It is a very ancient reproach, suggested by the ignorance or the malice of infidelity, that the Christians allured into their party the most atrocious criminals, who, as soon as they were touched by a sense of remorse, were easily persuaded to wash away, in the water of baptism, the guilt of their past conduct, for which the temples of the gods refused to grant them any expiation. . . . The friends of Christianity may acknowledge without a blush that many of the most eminent saints had been before their baptism the most abandoned sinners. Those persons who in the world had followed, though in an imperfect manner, the dictates of benevolence and propriety, derived such a calm satisfaction from the opinion of their own rectitude, as rendered them much less susceptible of the sudden emotions of shame, of grief, and of terror, which have given birth to so many wonderful conversions.

It is this suave, almost unctuous, irony that gives the Gibbon tone quality. His external mannerisms are typical of the day: there is much antithesis, though it is more sinuous and varied than Dr. Johnson's type, much aphorism, and much beautiful design in his finely chiseled sentences. A common mannerism here is the "Attic" [7] tendency to economize on subordinate clauses, to omit connectives, and to make logical relations implicit yet plain simply by arrangement of detail. Of Bernard of Clairvaux he remarks:

A philosophic age has abolished, with too liberal and indiscriminate disdain, the honours of these spiritual heroes. The meanest amongst them are distinguished by some energies of the mind; they were at least superior to their votaries and disciples; and in the race of superstition they attained the prize for which such numbers contended.

Clearly, in artistic conscience, as well as in lucid order and conscious elevation, Gibbon is among the foremost neo-classic stylists. He owed much to Livy and Tacitus; he owed more to his own personality and to the age in which he lived, to the elegant, cool and spacious drawing-room environment, in which he existed. With successful artifice he fused congruous elements into a manner that was highly individual. The small details of the work are as clearly executed as the design of the whole is architecturally unified. Gibbon gave distinction to historical writing by his style just as he gave meaning to historical thinking through his focus on the organizing idea of "decline and fall." Rome was the world's greatest art object in institutional civilization; Gibbon believed in progress, and the lesson of Rome was that man's progress

has been irregular and various, infinitely slow in the beginning, and increasing by degrees with redoubled velocity; ages of laborious ascent have been followed by a moment of rapid downfall. . . . The splendid days of Augustus and Trajan were eclipsed by a cloud of ignorance; and the Barbarians subverted the laws and palaces of Rome.

---

[7] See M. W. Croll, " 'Attic Prose' in the Seventeenth Century," *SP*, xviii (1921). 79-128.

In passing from Gibbon to Burke,[8] we pass from history to actuality. In *Edmund* the Restoration period it was possible to believe that even at that moment *Burke* England was renewing the splendid days of Augustus. By Burke's day—and before—the consciousness was growing that what had happened to Roman liberty could also happen to the English. To Gibbon, obviously, Rome was remote, and was an awful warning. Burke was not especially interested in history;[9] he was devoted to the processes of administering government rather than to tracing its origins. He was both a political philosopher and a practical politician; and as such he fell upon relatively evil days—days of constitutional crisis, of selfish intrigue, of covertly shifting personal allegiances, and even of corruption. His mind was too good for its tasks: he was set to "cut blocks with a razor." The blocks were too hard for him, but although he was normally in the minority in the House of Commons, he exercised through his intellectual quality, his evident integrity, and his fervid logic, a far-reaching influence.

The method of his thinking combined practical empiricism with a neo- *A Practical* classical veneration for established precedent and for Law that was com- *Statesman* patible with a faith in metaphysical absolutes. As an empiricist he appealed to "the wisdom of our ancestors" as if to established authority. He abhorred

8 Edmund Burke (1729-1797) was the son of an Irish Protestant attorney. He was educated in Trinity College, Dublin, and in 1750 entered the Middle Temple. He now, with introductions by William Burke (always his closest friend), became a typical literary Templar, frequenting coffee-houses and the society of writers. His marriage in 1757 made publication a financial necessity, and his important connection with the *Annual Register* resulted. He was in 1763 an original member of the Club, and in 1765 he became secretary to the prime minister, the Marquis of Rockingham, and entered Parliament. He was a leader among the Rockingham Whigs, and when in 1782 the coalition ministry fell and Rockingham became again, briefly, prime minister, Burke was Paymaster of the Forces—his highest office. After 1783 he was in the opposition, and in 1794 he retired from Parliament. — *Works*, ed. F. Laurence and W. King (8v [quarto], 1792-1827; 16v [octavo], 1803-27; 12v, Boston, 1897; 8v, 1901-6). The best editing of Burke is that of Edward J. Payne, *Select Works* (3v, Oxford, 1874-8). The six volumes in the World's Classics (1906-7) are useful and moderately priced. — *A Vindication of Natural Society* (1756); *A Philosophical Enquiry into the Origin of our Ideas of the Sublime and Beautiful* (1757 and [with the *Discourse on Taste* added] 1759); *An Account of the European Settlements in America* (with William Burke, 2v, 1757); *Thoughts on the Cause of the Present Discontents* (1770); *Speech on American Taxation* (1774); *Speech on Conciliation with the Colonies* (1775); *A Letter to the Sheriffs of Bristol* (1777); *Two Letters on Ireland* (1778); *Speech on Oeconomical Reformation* (1780); *Speeches at the Bristol Election* (1780); *Speech on Mr. Fox's East India Bill* (1784); *Speech on the Nabob of Arcot's Debts* (1785); *Articles against Warren Hastings* (1786); *Reflections on the Revolution in France* (1790); ed. Edward J. Payne (1875); ed. Walter A. Phillips (1875); *A Letter to a Member of the National Assembly* (1791); *An Appeal from the New to the Old Whigs* (1791); *A Letter to Sir Hercules Langrishe on the Subject of the Roman Catholics of Ireland* (1792); *A Letter to a Noble Lord* (1796); *Two Letters on the Proposals for Peace with the Regicide Directory of France* (1796; Third Letter, 1797; Fourth Letter, 1812); *Correspondence*, ed. Earl Fitzwilliam and Sir R. Bourke (4v, 1844); *Correspondence with William Windham*, ed. J. P. Gilson (Roxburghe Club, 1910). — Robert Bisset, *The Life of Burke* (1798; 2v, 1800); Sir James Prior, *Memoir of Burke* (1824, 5th ed., 1854); Thomas Macknight, *History of the Life and Times of Burke* (3v, 1858-60); John (Viscount) Morley, *Edmund Burke* (1867, 1893); John MacCunn, *The Political Philosophy of Burke* (1913); A. P. I. Samuels, *The Early Life, Correspondence, and Writings of Burke* (1923); Dixon Wecter, "The Missing Years in Edmund Burke's Biography," *PMLA*, LIII (1938). 1102-1125; D. Wecter, "Edmund Burke and his Kinsmen," *Univ. of Colorado Studies* (Boulder, Colo., February, 1939) ["A Study of the statesman's financial integrity and private relationships"]; Thomas W. Copeland, "Burke and Dodsley's *Annual Register*," *PMLA*, LIV (1939). 223-245; Donald C. Bryant, *Edmund Burke and his Literary Friends* (St. Louis, 1939).

9 For mention of Burke's interest in literary criticism see Part III, ch. II.

the doctrinaire notions of Rousseau and others concerning the natural rights of man: man, he thought, had only such rights as continuous precedent gave him in a civil state. The appeal to experience was attended by a reverence for continuity, for institutions developed through agelong trial; and this sense of the value of continuity became a fundamental part of Burke's method of thought. As a practical politician he was insistent on the necessity for lawmakers to understand the state of mind of the governed. In such matters he was a social psychologist, and in a sense an idealistic opportunist. "The temper of the people amongst whom he presides ought," he urged, "to be the first study of a statesman." This is the crux of the matter in his doctrine of conciliation with the American colonies. A governor must choose between practical wisdom and unsound theory. Sound theories, so Burke thinks, will fit the facts.

A strong common-sense dislike of unproved theory was on the whole convenient in the confused and tortuous years of Burke's career. But common sense was not all: study was essential, and no member of Parliament gave more time to study of the great problems of the day than did Burke. Among *His Fields* the political problems upon which he brought his powers to bear, one may *of Activity:* isolate five. First would come the constitutional crisis precipitated when *1. Domestic* King George III attempted to choose ministers responsible to himself rather *Issues* than to Parliament. This imbroglio was a part of the loose construction of constitutional rights that led the Commons to deny John Wilkes a seat in Parliament in spite of his repeated elections to that House.[10] Burke's respect for legal procedure is the high ground here on which he attacks both the King and "the King's Men" in his *Thoughts on the Present Discontents,* one of his early major efforts. His enemies retorted with the specious charge that Burke was the concealed author of the *Letters of Junius,*[11] which were *2. America* appearing in the *Public Advertiser* (1769-72). Secondly, Burke dealt with the more unified problem of the American colonies. Here his gospel is expediency. Not the natural rights but the natural grievances of the colonists were what he wished to satisfy. He had studied American conditions thoroughly, and was convinced that the practical course was conciliation. Ultimately he hoped for a system that might preserve both English superiority and colonial liberty. In favor of the cause of the Americans Burke composed two great speeches—that on *American Taxation* (1774) and that on *Conciliation with America* (1775). For his resolution in favor of conciliation his speech won only 58 votes, but it has generally been regarded as one of the great examples of classical eloquence in English. Burke continued

[10] The story of Wilkes and his rôle in the fight for a free press has been interestingly told by George Nobbe, *The North Briton* (1939).
[11] Junius himself chose 69 letters from the series for a collected edition in 1772. Before 1812 at least 70 reprintings of this collection had been issued. The identity of Junius has never been determined. Over 40 people have been accused of writing the letters. The most generally favored "victim" is Sir Philip Francis. Junius evidently had access to highly confidential official information, which he used against the ministers who alone should have had the information. The unsolved authorship is one of the most fascinating mysteries of the century. See *CBEL,* II. 630-632.

his support of the colonies even after they took up arms, in his *Speech on the Address to the King* (1777) and his *Letter to the Sheriffs of Bristol* (1777), as well as in the House of Commons. Thirdly, Burke faced crises in matters of trade. The unjust restrictions upon Irish trade concerned him **3. Irish** in 1779 and later, and naturally the problems of his native country were **Trade** always close to his heart. In 1780 he presented an elaborate bill for Economic Reform, and on February 11 made one of his most brilliant speeches on the subject. His proposals at that time were rejected. Presently he was advocating, without immediate success, humane regulation of the Negro slave trade, and was supporting justice for Roman Catholics in the face of the rabid intolerance that led in June 1780 to the anti-Catholic Gordon riots. In the autumn these various activities cost him the support of his Bristol constituency, which he quitted with triumphant dignity: "The charges against me are ... that I have pushed the principles of general justice and benevolence too far." Bristol trade would not be augmented by these activities as it would have been by prevention of war with the colonies! Burke was of course promptly chosen by another borough.

The fourth great field that exercised Burke's genius was India. Of this **4. India** domain like that of America Burke was a profound student, and from 1783 through much of the rest of his career in Parliament it engrossed his attention. At the end of 1783 he eloquently supported Fox's bill to reform Indian administration, a bill that so annoyed the King that he dismissed his ministers who had supported the rejected bill, and chose William Pitt the younger, aged twenty-four, to be his prime minister. Early in 1785 Burke countered a royal desire to keep Indian issues quiescent by one of his most eloquent speeches, that on the Nabob of Arcot's debts (February 28, 1785). To the present day this speech is still full of dynamite for statesmen concerned with the exploitation of "backward" peoples. Burke had long been critical of the administration of the Governor-General of India, Warren Hastings, and in January 1786 he with others began to draw up charges. Fox and R. B. Sheridan (the dramatist) were Burke's coadjutors, and the trial was a series of field-days for orators. Sheridan's most glowing attack was his speech on the Begum charge (February 7, 1787). For four days, February 15-19, 1788, Burke spoke on an average of three hours daily, and in 1794 (for the trial was interminable—with evidence far off in Asia) he spoke in summing up for nine days in succession. On April 23, 1795, the lords voted a verdict of acquittal. The scenes in Westminster Hall had been theatrical beyond belief. Seats were in great demand—£50 being "cheerfully" given for one; beautiful ladies fainted; and the histrionic Sheridan himself at the end of one speech collapsed into the arms of Burke with the words, "My Lords, I have done!" Burke's motives were certainly those of integrity: he wished justice and sound administrative procedure. He had here a relatively popular cause at first, but favor veered to Hastings, and Burke lost the verdict—as so often happened in his career.

Before the Hastings trial was over, Burke had become involved in his fifth and last great public effort, opposition to the French Revolution. No one in England was more astounded and horrified than Burke by the Fall of the Bastille and the subsequent irregular proceedings. He had a high admiration for the brilliant and intellectual aristocrats whom he had met in Paris, and he was totally ignorant of the grievances of France as a whole. Sound administration and dutiful obedience to such administration were the highest public duties, and he had no doubts as to the abilities of French rulers. Furthermore, *continuity* in institutional life was in his eyes the great test of merit: it was to him almost a religion. He loved civil liberty, and the revolution seemed to him to have substituted the capricious tyranny of a riotous mob for the settled government, which, to his way of thinking, should have been amended, not destroyed. During and after the summer of 1789 Burke privately in conversation and in his letters expressed hostility to the Revolution. Early in 1790 he broke off his friendship with Sheridan, who in Parliament endorsed the new freedom and found Burke's animosity to it inconsistent with his earlier American sympathies. Later Burke renounced friendship with Fox also on the same disagreement in views. The behavior of the revolutionaries became an obsession, and in November 1790 he published a formal and eloquent explanation of his attitude, *Reflections on the Revolution in France.*

Cast in the form of a letter (volume-long!) to a French gentleman who sought his views, it took occasion for offense from the fact that the well-known dissenter, Dr. Richard Price [12] (1723-1791), had just preached a sermon before the Revolution Society (founded to commemorate the English Revolution of 1688) in which he felicitated the French on their achieving liberty. Burke was enraged that the glorious and orderly change of 1688 should be connected with the mob riots of the French. "I flatter myself," he writes, "that I love a manly, moral, regulated liberty as well as any gentleman of that society." But before he congratulates a mob on its "liberty," he feels one must ask, What are you going to do with your liberty? That question he felt sure the followers of doctrinaires like Voltaire and Rousseau, believers in natural rights, could not answer wisely. Among the most picturesque and emotional passages in the book are those that narrate the violation of Versailles on October 6, 1789, or describe the young Queen, Marie Antoinette, as he had seen her long ago "glittering like the morning star." His sincere grief is summed up in the sentences: "But the age of chivalry is gone. That of sophisters, economists, and calculators has succeeded; and the glory of Europe is extinguished forever." Burke's *Reflections* in its magnificence of rhetoric surpassed all other attacks on the Revolution; and in argumentative force also, in spite of his obvious ignorance of conditions in France and in spite of its emotional bias in favor of the grace and elegance of the *ancien régime,* the work compares favorably with other attacks. The chief reply was

---

[12] This "apostle of liberty" was invited in 1778 by the American Congress "to consider him as a Citizen of the United States," and if possible to remove to America, where his services as a financial expert were badly needed. He of course did not accept the invitation. See Roland Thomas, *Richard Price* (Oxford, 1924).

Tom Paine's *Rights of Man*,[13] which defended the bases of the Revolution, asserted that every civil right is derived from a natural right, and reproached Burke's love of monarchical pageantry: "He pities the plumage and forgets the dying bird." Possibly the most cogent answer was Arthur Young's *Travels in France* (1792), in which is revealed the actual condition of France, which was unknown to Burke. Among all the thinkers and writers of Europe Burke was immediately preëminent as champion of the old order. He continued his attacks, notably in his *Letter to a Member of the National Assembly* (1791), in his *Appeal from the New to the Old Whigs* (1791), and in his *Letters on a Regicide Peace* (1796). Of this last prophetic vision of woes to come he remarked, "It may have the weakness, but it has the sincerity of a dying declaration." He died a year later (July 9, 1797).

Burke's fame is that of a thinker and of a superb rhetorician. As a thinker *Burke as a* his doctrines were practical but idealistic common sense. Bolingbroke's *Thinker* friend Pope had achieved a popular witticism in his *pensée:* "Party is the madness of Many for the gain of a Few." Party was faction. This favorite idea of *The Craftsman,* embodied in Bolingbroke's *Dissertation upon Parties* (1735), angered Burke. One of his functions was to popularize somewhat a better concept:

Party is a body of men united for promoting by their joint endeavours the national interest upon some particular principle in which they are all agreed.

He was firmly insistent that a party in power must govern with an unselfish regard for the welfare of the nation. In a period of confused personal alliances in politics and of loose concepts as to the constitutionality of measures, Burke's influence here was most salutary. Again it may be repeated that he was a practical psychologist. As applied to America this method is exhibited in his remark, "The question with me is, not whether you have a right to render your people miserable; but whether it is not your interest to make them happy." The value that he set upon continuity as a test of efficiency need not be further stressed. Mr. Brailsford has given a brief summary of the doctrines of William Godwin which were in a sense the intellectual background of the English romantics in their revolutionary mood. The summary may well serve to indicate most of the things at the turn of the century that Burke abhorred:

perfectibility, non-resistance, anarchism, communism, the power of reason and the superiority of persuasion over force, universal benevolence, and the ascription of moral evil to the desolating influence of "positive institution." [14]

Two or three of these, with different connotations, Burke might favor, but the attitudes of the two men towards institutions and government were antithetical. All Burke's doctrines were recognized as those of a man highly respected for his integrity. This respect came from his disinterested, modest

[13] Hastily but vigorously written and published (1791-2) in two parts within four months after Burke's *Reflections* appeared.

[14] H. N. Brailsford, *Shelley, Godwin, and their Circle* [1913], p. 219.

action and also from the lofty plane upon which his mind and his rhetoric habitually moved.

Burke as a Rhetorician   During a career of over forty years as writer Burke's command of all the arts of persuasion steadily increased. In 1794, disheartened and despondent, embittered against his former satellites, Sheridan and Fox, for their sympathy with revolution, Burke withdrew from Parliament after nearly thirty years of distinguished services. A year later these were recognized by royal grants of pensions, and the reward caused repercussions even in the House of Lords, where the radical Duke of Bedford, whose enormous family fortunes were due to royal favor dating from the sixteenth century, attacked the grants—and Burke. Burke replied in what is perhaps the masterpiece of decorative classical rhetoric in English—his *Letter to a Noble Lord* (1796). Reply to his grace was easy, almost superfluous; and Burke indulges in arguments of the moment and for the man. The wealthiest of dukes was an improper person to object to royal rewards; an improper person to object to Burke's attacks on levellers and revolutionaries. The rhetoric used is typical. In one of the finest passages Burke weaves together the ideas that the British Constitution is both a citadel and a temple, the symbol of Law, Order, and Security for wealthy dukes and all British subjects. *As long as* it endures, the "dykes of the low, fat Bedford level will have nothing to fear from all the pickaxes of all the levellers of France." Like a symphonic composer Burke allows his central theme on this subject—*continuity*—to announce itself repeatedly in parallel clauses beginning *as long as;* and he concludes in a burst of extra-rational rhetoric:

as long as these endure, so long the Duke of Bedford is safe: and we are all safe together—the high from the blights of envy and the spoliations of rapacity; the low from the iron hand of oppression and the insolent spurn of contempt. Amen! and so be it: and so it will be,

> Dum domus Aeneae Capitoli immobile saxum
> Accolet; imperiumque pater Romanus habebit.

It is typical of Burke's mind that, sure of itself, its point well made, it should, so to speak, overflow in a purely emotional climax. He borrows the majestic lines from the ninth *Aeneid,* where Virgil prophesies that the fame of two young heroes, Nisus and Euryalus, shall endure

> Long as th' imperial capitol shall stand,
> Or Rome's majestic lord the conquer'd world command!

and transfers the permanence of heroic fame to the duration of British rights of property. As pure poetry the borrowing is effective; but it is a beautiful dilation of mood rather than a triumph of logic. The echo from Virgil may serve to remind us that Burke's art came from the ancients, and that with the figured and fervent mood of his last works eighteenth-century prose goes out in a blaze of noble artifice. One may say justly of Edmund Burke's mind that it too was both a citadel and a temple.

X
Cowper and Burns

By 1780 the mid-century poets were mostly gone, and a new generation was arising. In it among the most distinguished were William Cowper, Robert Burns, William Blake, George Crabbe, and Samuel Rogers.[1] Cowper and Burns alike mark a tendency to use subjective, autobiographical material and to write of rural domesticity: they were among the latest flowerings in the eighteenth century of the cult of simplicity. Since it chances that Cowper's dates (1731-1800) are exactly a century later than John Dryden's, it is interesting to compare these last voices in the neo-classic choir (if indeed they belong there) with the tones of Dryden and Pope, the partial founders of the tradition. Obviously the century elapsed has grown tender; Burns and Cowper both write satires, but these are relatively good-humored— perhaps too good-humored. Cowper's satire in particular lacks hardness, flash, and cutting edge. Burns, like Dryden and Pope, has sympathetic, generalized observations to make about man, but like Blake and Cowper he is most aroused concerning underprivileged men. Burns and Blake have faith in progress and in the ability of man to achieve his own destiny. Cowper, like Dryden and Pope, has a sense of man's limitations; but Cowper would have man rely on God's help, on a divine plan, whereas Pope had fitted man into a philosophic chain of being, in which duty urges him to be a competent link or a submerged atom. There is, however, little in the observations of these later poets about man that would revolt Dryden or Pope, and both Cowper and Burns echo the *Essay on Man* with some sympathy—though Cowper could tolerate no attempt (such as Pope's fundamentally seemed) to build up a moral philosophy independent of religion. The earlier poets had featured impersonal material, "what oft was thought"; Cowper and Burns stress what *they* have thought and felt, though they value impersonal aphoristic wisdom. The later poets tend to talk to themselves or to a small audience; they lack—Cowper always and Burns usually— the loud, noble eloquence of the earlier poets. The tendency is increasingly subjective and lyrical; it expresses not so eagerly an acquired wisdom of life as it does a personal experience of life. The later poets are less intellectual than Dryden and Pope, more intimately emotional. Cowper and Burns are transitional poets.

The important part of Cowper's[2] career as poet was relatively brief. His

---

[1] Blake, Crabbe, and Rogers are here regarded as members of a later generation of poets.
[2] William Cowper (1731-1800) came of distinguished ancestors. Since his mother, a descendant of the Elizabethan John Donne, died before Cowper was six, he was then sent to

Cowper's Career

first extant poem, *On the Heel of 'a Shoe,* was written in 1748, and in the years following he addressed poems to his cousin Theodora, and wrote essays and witticisms in the period (1754) of the Nonsense Club. But poetry as a professional recreation—its major function to Cowper—began to occupy him after he had lived in rural Olney for some years. His first independent volume was his *Poems* (1782), which included various lyrics but chiefly his eight moral essays—discursive, reflective poems in the heroic couplet. These rapidly written, carefully revised essays in verse reflect the activities of Cowper's mind. Quite suddenly in the winter of 1780-81 he had begun to amuse himself by putting on paper *The Progress of Error* and *Truth* (together over 1200 lines, composed in December and January), and speedily thereafter *Table Talk* and *Expostulation* were completed. *Hope, Charity, Conversation,* and *Retirement* were products of the summer of 1781, the period of the poet's first friendship with Lady Austen. These poems are all reflective rather than descriptive. *Table Talk* has interesting comments on the poetry of the century; *Conversation, Retirement,* and *The Progress of Error* attack the follies of high life; *Expostulation* condemns anti-Semite prejudice; and the others represent the religious thinking of the poet. They are all medleys of reflective passages, with very serious and very obvious moral purpose. The volume, unpretentious and pious, met in general with a favorable reception.

Under the stimulus of success and of new-found encouragement from Lady Austen, Cowper continued to write. In 1782 he composed his noble patriotic lyric *On the Loss of the Royal George* as well his humorous master-

a boarding school, where he was persecuted by one of the older boys. Later (*c.* 1741-48) he was happier at Westminster School, where his friends included Robert Lloyd, Charles Churchill, George Colman the Elder, Bonnell Thornton, and Warren Hastings. His favorite master here, Vincent Bourne, was perhaps the best Latin poet of the century in England. Later, in the Middle Temple, Cowper studied law, and was called to the bar in 1754. He had fallen in love with his cousin Theodora ("Delia" in his poems), whom, in 1756, presumably because already he had suffered one lapse from sanity, he was forbidden to marry or to see. In 1763, overwhelmed by an approaching examination for a clerkship in the House of Lords, he went mad a second time, and attempted suicide. After a long convalescence, he settled for two years at Huntingdon as a lodger in the house of the Rev. Morley Unwin. Upon Mr. Unwin's death (1767) Mrs. Unwin ("My Mary"), her daughter, and Cowper moved to Olney, where they lived for almost twenty years, then removing to Weston Lodge, a mile outside the town. At Olney the vicar was, until 1780, the Rev. John Newton (1725-1807), who became one of Cowper's closest friends and upon removal to London a frequent correspondent. In 1773 another period of madness resulted from a terrible dream, "before recollection of which all consolation vanishes," and thereafter he suffered intermittently from melancholia, most seriously in 1787 and 1794. At East Dereham, Norfolk, where they spent their last years, Mrs. Unwin died in 1796, and Cowper less than four years later. — *Works,* ed. John Newton (10v, 1817); ed. with a "Life" by Robert Southey (15v, 1835-7; 8v, Bohn Library, 1853-5); ed. Thomas S. Grimshawe (8v, 1835, 1836), with the Life and Letters by William Hayley and an Essay on Cowper by John W. Cunningham; *Poems* (2v, 1782-5; 3v, 1815); ed. John Bruce (Aldine ed., 3v, 1865); ed. Sir Humphrey S. Milford (1905 ff.); ed. Hugh L'A. Fausset (Everyman's Library, 1931); *Letters,* with a Life by William Hayley (4v, Chichester, 1809); ed. Thomas Wright (4v, 1904); *Unpublished and Uncollected Letters,* ed. Thomas Wright (1925). — There are biographies by William Hayley (3v, Chichester, 1803-4); Goldwin Smith (1880); Thomas Wright (1892; rev. 1921); Hugh I'A. Fausset, *William Cowper* (1928); Lord David Cecil, *The Stricken Deer; or, The Life of William Cowper* (1929); Gilbert Thomas, *William Cowper and the Eighteenth Century* (1935). See also Robert E. Spiller, "William Cowper: A New Biographical Source: Rev. J. Johnson's Holograph Memorandum Book, 1795-1800," *PMLA,* XLII (1927). 946-962; cf. Hoxie N. Fairchild, *PMLA,* XLIII (1928). 571-572.

piece, *John Gilpin's Ride*. The first of these, strangely enough, was published only after Cowper's death; but *John Gilpin,* sent to a newspaper in November 1782, was instantly a popular success. Humor was becoming rare and precious in poetry. In July, 1783, Lady Austen urged Cowper to attempt blank verse, and upon his protest that he had no subject, she replied, "Oh, you can never be in want of a subject; you can write upon any—write upon that sofa!" Accepting the assignment, Cowper was able somewhat over a year later to send the result, called *The Task,* to the printer. It was over 5000 lines in length. In composing this poem Cowper strengthened his animus against the couplet and Pope, and thus was persuaded to set about (1784-91) rescuing Homer from the clutches of rime and artificial elevation. Homer, he thought, was more remarkable than any book except the Bible "for that species of the sublime that owes its very existence to simplicity." If his translation fails in competition with Pope, the failure is not due to lack of simplicity but rather to inability to capture the vigor of the ancient epics.

For thirty-five years William Cowper lived as retired a village life as one *Cowper's* could imagine, but he took an intelligent, if mild, interest meanwhile in the *Interest in* outside world, and the issues of the day form a noticeable part of the more *Public* impersonal subject matter of his verses. A typical passage is the opening of *Affairs* Book IV ("The Winter Evening") of *The Task.* The post rides into the village bringing news of all the world—received with tolerant interest:

> have our troops awak'd?
> Or do they still, as if with opium drugg'd,
> Snore to the murmurs of th' Atlantic wave?
> Is India free? and does she wear her plum'd
> And jewell'd turban with a smile of peace,
> Or do we grind her still? The grand debate,
> The popular harangue, the tart reply,
> The logic, and the wisdom, and the wit,
> And the loud laugh—I long to know them all;
> I burn to set th' imprison'd wranglers free,
> And give them voice and utt'rance once again.
>   Now stir the fire, and close the shutters fast,
> Let fall the curtains, wheel the sofa round,
> And, while the bubbling and loud-hissing urn
> Throws up a steamy column, and the cups,
> That cheer but not inebriate, wait on each,
> So let us welcome peaceful ev'ning in.   (ll. 25-41)

Here is quiet and gentle curiosity—no burst of eloquence. Such is Cowper's usual reaction to outside stimuli, whether the subject is India, America, prison reform, slavery, or the French Revolution. On many of these topics he is very intelligent; but unlike Dryden, Swift, or Pope, he is rarely an eager crusader for a cause. He does appear such in his lines *On the Loss of the Royal George;* in his castigation of war as the sport of kings in Book V of *The Task;* and in such passages as his defense (*Hope,* ll. 554-593) of the eminent Methodist, George Whitefield (1714-1770), who had in his lifetime been grossly slandered.

His Religion   Cowper's ardent, evangelical Calvinism led to expressions of despair, of hope, and of firm doctrinal assertion typical of his day. Biographers have found in religion the key and cause of Cowper's melancholia. The most terrifying moment of his life came on January 24, 1773, when in a "fatal dream" a word, apparently of divine condemnation, seemed to enjoin eternal and complete despair. "Nature," he wrote to Newton years later, "revives again, but a soul once slain lives no more." At other times, however, there were glimpses "of heavenly light by the way" or whispers saying "Still there is Mercy." Critics ought to remember constantly that if religion was an undoubted cause of despair to Cowper, it was also a great source of comfort. Doctrinally he was true to type. Much of his didactic verse about religion is anti-deistic and anti-philosophical. In *Charity* come the lines—

> That man, in nature's richest mantle clad,
> And grac'd with all philosophy can add,
> Though fair without, and luminous within,
> Is still the progeny and heir of sin.
> Thus taught, down falls the plumage of his pride;
> He feels his need of an unerring guide....

Pride is, as he shows in *Truth,* the most insidious foe of the Gospel. Being no deist, he substitutes for man's philosophizings

> Heav'n's easy, artless, unincumber'd, plan!

and his Calvinism rejects as "outrageous wrong" the idea of

> Ten thousand sages lost in endless woe,
> For ignorance of what they could not know.

In many passages he stresses the sole efficacy of grace, and doctrinal points turn up at times even in his hymns.

It is one of the contradictions of history that the eighteenth century, known as an age of doubt and skepticism, is also the great age of English *His Hymns* hymnody, and Cowper is notable as a writer of great hymns.[3] Earlier in the century hymns such as those by Isaac Watts tended to be "congregational" in point of view, but the best known hymns of Charles Wesley and of his brother John are more personal, intimate, and evangelical. Cowper's "Oh! for a closer walk with God" is comparable, and superior, to Wesley's

---

[3] Cowper contributed 67 hymns to John Newton's *Olney Hymns* (1779). Newton included 281 of his own, among the most popular of which is "Glorious things of thee are spoken." Charles Wesley was doubtless the greatest of the hymn-writers of the time, and the Wesleyan love of music did much to promote congregational singing. Among Charles Wesley's famous hymns are the well-known "O for a thousand tongues to sing," "Hark! the herald angels sing," "Arise, my soul, arise," "Love divine, all loves excelling," and "Jesus, Lover of my soul." John Wesley's notable contributions are translations of German hymns. Among other well-known hymns of this period may be mentioned Augustus Toplady's "Rock of Ages," and Edward Perronet's "All hail the power of Jesus' name." See John Julian, *A Dictionary of Hymnology* (1892; rev. ed., 1921).

popular "Jesus, Lover of my soul"; and the tone of "Sometimes a light surprises" reminds one—as some other of his hymns do not—that

> True piety is cheerful as the day.

The frequent fault of hymn-writers is their incongruous mixture of secular metaphor with biblical symbolism. Cowper is not an outrageous offender here except in "There is a fountain filled with blood." Cheerful or not, his religious poems, while doctrinally sound, are sufficiently emotional to avoid the heaviness of theological argument. The language is always that of unaffected and sincere devotion.

Religion and current public issues as treated in Cowper's verse have less *Nature as* appeal than do his descriptions of nature. Unlike his predecessors Cowper *an Escape* describes and reflects about landscape details, but rather seldom philosophizes about the abstraction "Nature." In a few such passages as *The Task*, Book VI, lines 198-261, to be sure, he urges that there can be no Law of Nature apart from God's law:

> The Lord of all, himself through all diffus'd,
> Sustains, and is the life of all that lives.
> Nature is but a name for an effect,
> Whose cause is God.

But it is not the theological aspect of the creation that preoccupies and consoles Cowper: it is rather the extra-theological innocence of Nature; for Nature is free from the primal curse, depravity; and a consciousness of this happy fact encourages Cowper in his escape from the moral to the natural world. From another point of view Cowper's love of rural life resembles the common-sense attitude of the Sabine farmer, Horace, or of people who, like Henry Fielding, did not love "the town." In any case, the gambols of Cowper's hares or the antics of his many other pets as well as the spring zephyr or the slow-winding Ouse were innocence itself. The inanimate world was to Cowper a plaything, a "bauble," as he loved to call it, to distract his mind from manic gloom. The moral world was full of terrors; the amoral, full of innocent delights that

> Exhilarate the spirit, and restore
> The tone of languid Nature.

And so, in his most famous aphorism, he could say,

> God made the country, and man made the town.

The "Not-me" is then a broad and tranquilizing stream that flows peacefully through his consciousness. It is panorama, motion, normally—not the static picturesque. Nature dreads

> An instant's pause, and lives but while she moves....

> Oceans, rivers, lakes, and streams,
> All feel the fresh'ning impulse, and are cleans'd
> By restless undulation: ev'n the oak
> Thrives by the rude concussion of the storm.

His Taste in Land- scape   Being thoroughly individual, Cowper avoids the common predispositions of his day. He recognizes that the creation is "an effect whose cause is God," but he does not play with the rationalist tradition that places "the Book of Nature" beside the Bible. Nor does he affect the dramatic or thrilling arrangement of detail that constituted the Italian picturesque. Even less does he, loving tranquillity, gratify any romantic appetite for the "delightful horrors" of the artificial sublime promoted by Burke and others. He loves tame nature and everyday phenomena—*domestica facta*. After his visit in 1792 to Hayley at Eartham, he wrote to Newton:

> The cultivated appearance of Weston suits my frame of mind far better than wild hills that aspire to be mountains, covered with vast unfrequented woods, and here and there affording a peep between their summits at the distant ocean. Within doors all was hospitality and kindness, but the scenery *would* have its effect; and though delightful in the extreme to those who had spirits to bear it, was too gloomy for me.

Cowper's evocation of the sights and sounds of the "tame" Olney region was delicate, precise, and full of placid glamour. Neither he nor his neo- classic predecessors normally cultivated *sensations fortes,* and in romantic days to come this fact was held a limitation by lovers of intense effects. Certainly a violent and "outrageous thirst for stimulation" was no source of Cowper's art. The homely household occupations, images such as the danc- ing light on his shaded pathway, sounds such as that of small streams

> chiming as they fall
> Upon loose pebbles—

these were the simple natural facts of experience that moved him delicately. There is no great admixture of strangeness in his beauty and no intense neurotic passion for nature: simply a genuine, normal, and constant attach- ment. If there had never been a Wordsworth, Cowper would be more highly and justly regarded.

The Task   In its day *The Task* seemed a masterpiece: it satisfied the taste (soon to vanish) for long poems. It preserved the discursive rambling structure that the eighteenth century liked in such poems, but it added to reflection what Cowper's "moral essays" lacked—description of nature. The poet in Book I soon left the assigned topic ("The Sofa"), and started describing a morning walk to Weston. Delightful bits of typical English landscape are simply and naturally presented:

> hedge-row beauties numberless, square tow'r,
> Tall spire, from which the sound of cheerful bells
> Just undulates upon the list'ning ear,
> Groves, heaths, and smoking villages, remote. . . .

In Book II he relapses into moral reflection—on Sicilian earthquakes, on "our own late miscarriages" ("England, with all thy faults, I love thee still"), on the necessity of discipline in education, and on various other topics. In Book III comes the famous passage

> I was a stricken deer, that left the herd
> Long since; with many an arrow deep infixt
> My panting side was charg'd . . .

and here he celebrates "domestic happiness" and gardening as giving "blest seclusion from a jarring world." The last three books, written in winter, describe the tranquillity of home in "The Winter Evening" (IV), and walks at morning (V) and at noon (VI). In these books again description is pleasingly blended with reflection.

The art of the poem seems transparent. Cowper in general avoids the "poetic diction" long stereotyped for objective detail. Usually simple and precisely plain, he employs a characteristic idiom, which at best prophesies Wordsworth and at second best tries to recapture the tones of Thomson. But unlike Thomson and Young, Cowper has a nice word sense, and the polysyllables which he evidently loves could not be better chosen had Johnson himself culled them. One suspects that at times Cowper fell into polysyllables but out of slight poetic embarrassment; for example, in his dutiful account of the gardener's dunghill in *The Task* (III, 463-475). *Yardley Oak* illustrates his most effective use of such diction.

In the blank verse of *The Task* and of *Yardley Oak* Cowper achieves *His Blank* more individuality than in the couplet. He may have believed that he as *Verse* well as "every warbler" had Pope's tune by heart, but actually his couplets, as compared with those of Dryden and Pope, are languid and lack both edge and, above all, vigorous variety. In blank verse he is a pioneer in the humble vein in which Wordsworth (perhaps alone) achieves distinction. Cowper's lines are relaxed and are rhythmically much less constricted in blank verse than in the couplet. He had not learned Pope's art of building two or three couplets, each technically closed, into a unified easy period; but in blank verse, though too many lines are still end-stopped, he works with more ease and grace.

From the brevity of Cowper's creative period in the early eighties one *His Merits* must not expect much in the way of artistic development. Furthermore, *and Defects* another cause impeding development was the poet's essential amateurishness. His reflections may rise out of deep conviction, but his poems as such are casual. He can "write upon the sofa" or on any topic assigned. He is in love with "baubles"; and apart from religion most topics are to him equally significant. He keys his flights so low that he frequently achieves mere prose.

> Who loves a garden loves a green-house too,

he chants; and he seems frequently thus in love with platitude or bathos. His very gift of raising, not always but usually, obvious everyday life into the realm of the poetic is the quality that makes him in many ways the most typical poet of his century. Fidelity to truth is a fundamental neo-classic ideal seen in Cowper as admirably as anywhere except perhaps in Gray's *Churchyard*. He achieves the Horatian *simplex munditiis,* but lacks the Horatian finish, felicity, and pleasing acidity. At times he is delicately and placidly lyrical. His painter's eye is excellent, and his ear is one of the nicest.

> The poplars are fell'd, farewell to the shade
> And the whispering sound of the cool colonnade

is an excellent beginning. It is, however, with the vice of moralizing, immediately watered down to insipidity. Most pathetically personal is the tragic final lyric, *The Castaway.* Although one of Cowper's less typical pieces, this poem through autobiographical intensity has to this day an appeal that his more placid verses lack. He is, like his favorite beverage, at best cheering, never inebriating. After the French Revolution there was a demand rather for poetical *aqua vitae.*

Robert Burns: A Natural Genius   Robert Burns,[4] like Cowper, is largely a poet of domestic emotion; but whereas Cowper loved environment for its own sake, Burns loved it for the human relationships implied in it. *The Cotter's Saturday Night* is an obvious illustration. Burns also found his local background a grim stimulus towards an escape to a larger life, a life which he rebelliously believed the just destiny of all men in a state of freedom. A great difference between the two poets lies in the fact that while Cowper came of a distinguished family of notable ability and of rich cultural opportunity, Burns was a "sport" in a family of humble uprightness and poverty-stricken integrity, but without a spark of genius except in Robert. Burns was an untaught genius, or, to use his epithet applied to Fergusson, "Heaven-taught." As such he was the realiza-

[4] Robert Burns (1759-1796) was born at Alloway in Ayrshire, a county in which most of his life was passed. His father William Burnes (as he spelled it) was a tenant farmer in a region where rentals were so high as to make certain the poverty of the tenant. At Mount Oliphant (1765-77), Lochlie (1777-84), and at Mossgiel, it was the same story of heart-eating labor, and poverty its reward. In 1781 Burns spent some months in Irvine learning to dress flax, but that work proving unattractive, he returned to the farm. Upon the death of their father (1784), Robert and his younger brothers moved the family to Mossgiel in Mauchline parish. Before this time Robert had commenced writing verses and making love. His sexual activities were promiscuous as well as fruitful. Jean Armour of Mauchline, whom he married in 1788, if not earlier, bore him twins in 1786 and again in 1788. Mary Campbell ("Highland Mary") apparently died in childbirth in 1786. There were several others also. In 1786 appeared his first book, *Poems, Chiefly in the Scottish Dialect,* printed at neighboring Kilmarnock. This brought local fame, and during the following winter Burns was in Edinburgh, where he conducted himself with dignity even though in more intellectual or aristocratic society than he had hitherto seen. Two reprintings of his poems, with some additions, were made in Edinburgh in 1787, and a second winter there was devoted in part to adjusting financial returns, which were considerable. The volume was also brought out in London, and within two years piracies appeared in Dublin, Belfast, Philadelphia, and New York. Burns now decided, after brief vacation tours in the summer of 1787, to return to the farm, and presently to marry Jean Armour. They settled at Ellisland, near Dumfries, and after a last unsatisfactory attempt to make a rented farm pay, removed in 1791 to Dumfries itself, where Burns got a place as an officer in the excise. In spite of gossip to the contrary, and in spite of ill health, it is certain that the last five years of Burns's life were those of a valued and respected citizen, of a well-known poet, who up to the last was busy in his attempt to aid George Thomson in his projected *Select Scottish Airs,* designed to glorify Scots song-writing. — The most scholarly *Life of Robert Burns* is that by Franklyn B. Snyder (1932); those by Hans Hecht (trans. by Jane Lymburn, 1936) and by John De Lancey Ferguson (*Pride and Passion,* 1939)

tion of an eighteenth-century dream that went back even further than *Spectator* No. 160. At the beginning of Alexander Pope's career a hostile critic could assure him: "You have not that sufficient learning necessary to make a poet." The idea of learning as essential to a poet perished in the eighteenth century. Stephen Duck, the thresher poet, Ann Yearsley, the milkmaid, and Thomas Chatterton all aspired to the rôle of natural genius— and to the grief of possible sponsors seemed deficient in quality. Robert Burns consciously attempted the part, and succeeded beyond all rivals. His outcry against such college wits as "think to climb Parnassus / By dint o' Greek" would have annoyed Pope's critic:

> Gie me ae spark o' Nature's fire,
> That's a' the learning I desire;
> Then, tho' I drudge thro' dub an' mire
>   At pleugh or cart,
> My Muse, tho' hamely in attire,
>   May touch the heart.

Burns was by no means so untaught as this would seem to say, but the stanza constitutes at least a declaration of poetical independence of learning. It is, on the other hand, implicitly a reaffirmation of the favorite dogma of the century, "Nature is nature wherever placed." The ability of "the force of Nature" to arrive at heights, if unimpeded, or even to arrive in spite of impediment, had been a cherished notion throughout the period of Illumination, and Burns was a complete demonstration of the idea. Later, it may be noted, natural genius will be regarded as "spontaneous" rather than untaught; but Burns was proud of his careful revision of his poems: they came from the heart rather than the head, but they are no "profuse strains of unpremeditated art." His career, however, as well as the idea of spontaneity, encouraged the romantic heresy that a true genius could bloom into a finished poet overnight.

An untaught genius naturally had to be proletarian—a thresher, a milkmaid, a farmer. Burns's pride in his humble origin is no self-conscious literary pose, as we shall see, but fitted into a tradition glorifying the farmer that went back to the days (1728) when Lord Bolingbroke had rakes, hoes, and other farm implements painted on the walls of the entrance hall of his house, named, in mock modesty, Dawley Farm. Bolingbroke, of course, had his eye on the rôle of Cincinnatus. The tradition was promoted by the later physiocrats, and echoed, for example, in the "Advertisement" in Goldsmith's *Vicar,* where Dr. Primrose is said to unite in himself "the three greatest characters upon earth"—the priest, the farmer, and the father of a family.

are also excellent. Most lives are quite unreliable. The most authentic text of the poems is found in *Robert Burns, The Poems,* ed. Charles S. Dougall (1927). The one-volume Cambridge Edition (Boston, 1897), a condensation of the four-volume edition by William E. Henley and T. F. Henderson (1896-7), is useful except for the untrustworthy introduction. Professor Ferguson has well edited *Selected Poems of Robert Burns* (1926) and has published the only reliable edition of the *Letters* (2v, Oxford, 1931).

The world was ready for a genius like Burns, who should be a farmer, a family man, and a great poet.

Hard Labor and Books　　The farming was inevitable; his father and grandfather before him had struggled to wrest a livelihood from the farms of Ayrshire, and the poet followed the family tradition. It was a hard life, and was—both for the boy at Mount Oliphant, overworking and thus undermining his health, and later for the married man with children—a losing fight. Almost from the start there were three worlds closing and opening on the poet bewilderingly. The first was the back-breaking world of hard work. Farm life to Burns was never sincerely idyllic. The second was the world of books; for his father and many another Ayrshire man were "reading people," and the poet early and always loved books. He cherished a schoolbook, Arthur Masson's *Collection of Prose and Verse,* which gave him his first knowledge of bits of Shakespeare, Dryden, Addison, and others. Later he knew well the work of Milton, Pope, Thomson, Gray, Shenstone, Beattie, and Goldsmith; and his bias to sentiment is seen in his love for Sterne's and Mackenzie's novels. Even more important was his affection for his Scottish predecessors, Allan Ramsay and Robert Fergusson, and his long passion for Scots songbooks encouraged his great lyric gift. In various other unrelated fields he read widely—in theology, philosophy, and even in agriculture. From this reading in prose as well as from the controversies between the "Auld Lichts" and the "New Lichts" current throughout Scottish life in his day and violent in the more rustic parishes, Burns very likely acquired his anti-Calvinistic belief in the natural goodness of man—a belief that did much to develop a sense of the injustice of the poor farmer's lot and to make him what he speedily became—a social rebel.

Love vs. Law　　This attitude was stimulated not merely by philosophy and by exhaustion from "the thresher's weary flingin-tree," but also through influence of the third world that opened so maddeningly upon the high-strung youth, when, as his Muse in *The Vision* says—

> youthful Love, warm-blushing, strong,
> Keen-shivering, shot thy nerves along.
>
> ·　　　·　　　·　　　·　　　·
>
> I saw thy pulse's maddening play,
> Wild-send thee Pleasure's devious way,
> Misled by Fancy's meteor-ray,
> 　　　　By passion driven;
> But yet the light that led astray
> 　　　　Was light from Heaven.

The young poet, rebelliously guilty, disclaims moral responsibility in these last lines; but his whole psychology belies such fatalism: his loves were consciously sinful, and he rationalizes excuses by blaming Heaven or by such brilliant satire on the faults of others as is found in *The Holy Fair*— to which Fair he represented himself as going accompanied by the "hizzie" Fun, to keep an eye on Superstition and Hypocrisy. He concludes:

There's some are fou o' love divine;
There's some are fou o' brandy;
An' monie jobs that day begin
May end in houghmagandie
Some ither day.

The poet eagerly makes us feel the comedy of the sinful hypocrites; open sin
seems thus the less reprehensible. His amours have obvious if inadequate
excuse in the drabness of the life to which he seemed unjustly condemned.

There's nought but care on ev'ry han',
In every hour that passes, O:
What signifies the life o' man,
An' 'twere nae for the lasses, O.

Burns thus begins his career with an apologetic and allegedly heaven- *Burns's*
authorized defiance of convention, due in part to the rigorous morality *Politics*
his father had attempted to instill, in part to his conscious rationalizing of his
own errors, in part to his growing class-consciousness; and ultimately to his
political heterodoxy. This last was somewhat notorious after 1788 when he
became an exciseman in the employ of His Majesty the King. By this time
class-consciousness was reinforced by a rational love of freedom, a sympathy
first with the American colonies and later with the French revolutionaries—
and, natural to a Scot, a not too serious notion that Charles III or his
daughter "the bonie lass of Albanie" would fill the throne of England with
more grace than a mad Hanoverian. His Jacobitism is negligible, but his
anger at political or social injustice is true, eloquent, and pervasive. It may
be seen in *The Twa Dogs, A Dream, Is there for Honest Poverty,* and in
the romantic anarchy of the last chorus of *The Jolly Beggars.*

From the worlds of work, love, and books, there was, then, this other
opening that he had found: the world of poetry. Probably in 1781 occurred
the episode recorded in his letter to his friend Richard Brown, December
30, 1787:

Do you recollect a Sunday we spent in Eglinton Woods? you told me, on my
repeating some verses to you, that you wondered I could resist the temptation of
sending verses of such merit to a magazine: 'twas actually this that gave me an
idea of my own pieces which encouraged me to endeavour at the character of
a Poet.

His first volume assured his fame and indicated fully the nature of that *A Poet of*
fame. He, like Cowper, was to be a poet of rural, daily life. He aimed *Rural Life*
humbly "at the character of a Poet," and his notion of that character was
thoroughly that of his time:

. . . manners-painting strains,
The loves, the ways of simple swains—

these were to be his subjects, and one might add to them the portrayal of
the hypocrisies of the townsfolk of Ayrshire and, occasionally, the injustices

of the larger world of statecraft. But chiefly he focused on men and their interrelations—their loves, their revels, their labors, and their sorrows. Landscape is incidental. As in *The Holy Fair,* he frequently commences with a bit of description; he uses imagery with brief poignant effect, but almost unawares—

> The wan moon sets behind the white wave,
> And Time is setting with me, O.

If he writes of animals or flowers, they are companions—the farmer's mare Maggie, the child's pet sheep Mailie, or the Mouse, or the Mountain Daisy—to all of whom (*which* would be improper!) he ascribes human traits, a human lot.[5] The focus is on Man still, and from many of his poems— the less glowing ones perhaps—one could deduce parts which, if grouped, would show that Burns, still of his century, conceived his work, his "manners-painting strains," as an essay on man. The final injunction in *The Vision* is,

> Preserve the dignity of Man
> With soul erect;
> And trust the Universal Plan
> Will all protect.

His subject matter, then, is what we might expect: love songs, drinking songs, humorous satires on the religious hypocrites of the Mauchline region, glowing eloquence on the theme of the rights of man, and the pervading incidental use of bits of rural life that becomes only slightly artificial even when self-consciously idyllic as in *The Cotter's Saturday Night.* He is never far from the soil, and never fails in a human sympathy for whatever subject he treats.

His Use of Folk Superstitions
Even when he makes use of the folk superstitions of the Ayr region he shows these same qualities of homeliness and humanity. For sophisticates like Matthew G. Lewis or (at a proper interval) Wolfgang von Goethe, Satanism was a taste largely acquired from books. But Burns, or rather his neighbors, believed firmly that a personal devil, who lived "in yon lowin heugh," might be met casually and frightfully in many "lanely glens"; and it was well established, they were certain, that he and his witches haunted the ruined Alloway Kirk, less than a mile away from the house where the poet was born. Burns himself evidently took his devils with several grains of humor, as one can see in his Halloween poems or in his account of the peripatetic mores of "Auld Hornie" in the *Address to the Deil:*

> Whyles, ranging like a roarin lion,
> For prey, a' holes an' corners tryin;
> Whyles, on the strong-wing'd tempest flyin,
> Tirlin the kirks;
> Whyles, in the human bosom pryin,
> Unseen thou lurks.

[5] On the treatment of animals in literature see the interesting book by Dix Howard, *Love for Animals and How it Developed in Great Britain* (1928).

Auld Hornie himself seems to share the poet's high spirits, and possibly in the prank of "tirlin the kirks" his sense of humor also. Any poet deserves acclaim whose imagination can evoke witches in the road that runs past his own house, and that is substantially what Burns did in his narrative master-piece of *Tam o' Shanter,* a triumph of creative imagination through its vividness, its vigor, and its combination of local color with the supernatural. He makes us hear Nannie and her infernal crew come galloping from the kirk to the river in full cry after poor Tam. The reader is left wide-eyed and breathless—and at the same time, highly amused. It is one of the best fusions of diverse grotesque elements to be found in the century.

In his handling of all his created persons, from "the deil" to Tam Glen, *His Adaptation of Genres* Burns's method is flexible, rich, and supremely sure. One is always confident that Burns will not fumble, no matter in what varied genre he chooses to write. In view of his exquisite humor his frequent use of the elegy is surprising. His admiration for Shenstone was doubtless excessive, and this, with his own tendency to melancholy, led him to write such pieces as *Man was Made to Mourn, To a Mouse,* and other despondent pieces. He is, however, especially delightful in mock-elegies such as those for Poor Mailie and Tam Samson. His satire also is cut by humor, though *Holy Willie's Prayer* (which was published posthumously) is savagely caustic. *The Holy Fair* is perhaps his most typical assault in satire on the hypocrisy that so offended him. His epistles are notably independent in form and conversational in tone: he knew Pope's work in this sort, but his own is perfectly independent of the Horatian tradition, though his *Epistle to J. Lapraik* is in some sense an *ars poetica.* The eighteenth century had been fond of humorous verse—"the Muse in a good humor"—but Burns stood on the threshold of the era of high seriousness, and while he may not have been the last British humorous poet, no poet since his day has surpassed him in rich and varied gaiety.

His lyrics are also diverse in mood and method. His songs of wooing *His Songs* range from the tender in *Mary Morison* to archness in *Tam Glen,* to a jocose treatment of bashfulness in *Duncan Gray,* and to uproarious delight in the story of *Last May a Braw Wooer.* There are happy songs of married life, such as *Contented wi' Little* and the salvaged treasure of *John Anderson my Jo,* among others. Absence, though not his common theme, is sweetly treated in *Of a' the Airts,* and the elegiac tone of *Banks o' Doon* and *Highland Mary* expresses beautifully the tragedy of lost love. *Tam o' Shanter* alone would prove that Burns had superlative gifts in poetic narrative, but in his songs he seldom relies on story for substance. In *Auld Rob Morris, Open the Door,* and *Tam Glen,* however, story is exquisitely implied. The lover at parting perhaps protests too much in *Ae Fond Kiss,* but in the fervidly hyperbolic *Red, Red Rose* we surely have authentic passion if ever words conveyed it. His more "public" songs, such as the reworked *Auld Lang Syne, Is there for Honest Poverty,* and above all the battle song of *Scots Wha Hae* are in their respective modes supremely eloquent.

It was a principal function of Burns to add dignity and life to the folk-song of his people. He was almost a learned expert as well as a poetic genius in this field, and to such collections as James Johnson's *Musical Museum* (1787-1803) and George Thomson's *Select Scottish Airs* (1793-1841) he gave much of the labors of his last years. Unfortunately the settings of *Select Scottish Airs* by Haydn and Beethoven, among others, transformed the folk-song into the art-song; and the nineteenth-century poets, lacking Burns's sure sense of recurring rhythms, turned from the song to the "art lyric" that was quite independent of song. After Burns, Tom Moore and Mrs. Hemans represent the tradition of song: Shelley, Keats, and Tennyson the art lyric.

Universality and Ayrshire Life   Burns's high and individual achievement depended largely on his intense and tender insight into social relations. In these his scope was wide: they might be as private as love or as public as monarchy; but at his best Burns drew from the social problems keenly felt in the laborious farm life that was his lot. His literary ambitions were two-fold: he hoped to be a poet like Thomson, Gray, or Shenstone (*The Vision*), but he distrusted his abilities; he hoped more confidently to be a local poet following a Scottish muse and singing the scenes from which "old Scotia's grandeur springs." The two ambitions get mixed. To be a universal poet, he thought, required the ability to strike out aphoristic reflections; but this art had perished, and in such lines as

Anticipation forward points the view,

Burns showed that he could not recapture it. No more could Byron, of whom Goethe remarked, "The minute he reflects, he is childish." It is not that Burns could not write well in English; his letters would do credit to any writer of English, and show conclusively that it was as natural for him to write English as it was to speak Scots. But to Burns poetry was rhythm and sound as well as meaning; and the sound of his native Scots gave him courage, and gave his writing life, vigor, and savor. He got his more un-usual stanza forms from Ramsay's *Ever Green* (1724) or from songbooks; his superbly firm and fine sense of musical rhythm was presumably native with him. He was always excessively modest, and after a pleasant winter in Edinburgh society, including duchesses, he was content to retire to the misty moors of Ayrshire and do his duty by Jean Armour. His "ain countree" gave him courage to be himself and integrity to win, in spite of his moral flaws, the respect of the best people with whom he came in contact. His personality was vibrant and glowing, and it had life-giving power to bestow on the essentially and frankly autobiographical and local material that con-stitutes his best poetry. On a more serene level Cowper's achievement was similar. The stage was well set for the autobiographical Wordsworth.

BOOK IV
The Nineteenth Century
and After (1789-1939)

～⊙๏～

Guide to reference marks
Throughout the text of this book, a point . • set beside a page number indicates that references to new critical material will be found under an identical
paragraph/page number (set in **boldface**) in the BIBLIOGRAPHICAL SUP-
PLEMENT.
In the Index, a number preceded by an S indicates a paragraph/page number in the BIBLIOGRAPHICAL SUPPLEMENT.

to the French National Assembly on the triumph of liberty over arbitrary power. This message roused Edmund Burke to the composition of his *Reflections on the Revolution in France* (1790). The anti-revolutionary opinions so widely disseminated in this pamphlet did not go unchallenged.[2] Mary Wollstonecraft [3] (1759-1797) attacked Burke for his reliance upon the past and his contempt of the poor; but though charged with generous feeling her *Vindication of the Rights of Men* (1790) was too hastily written and too emotional to be very effective. Nor was the *Vindiciae Gallicae* (1791) of James Mackintosh [4] (1765-1832) widely influential, for it was too refined in its Whig liberalism. But the demagogic style in which Thomas Paine [5] (1737-1809) wrote *The Rights of Man* (1791) made it at once a textbook of popular radicalism. Anyone, even if unable to follow close reasoning, could comprehend his ringing assertions that "man has no property in man" and that "there is a morning of reason rising upon the world." The violence of Paine's attack upon the British monarchy was, however, prejudicial to his own cause, and he harmed it further by the crass anti-Christianity of *The Age of Reason* (1794). In contrast to this fanaticism is the cool argument in *Letters to the Right Honourable Edmund Burke* (1791) by Joseph

[2] With Burke's opponents may be associated Arthur Young (1741-1820), whose defense of the French Revolution was none the less telling for being indirect. He was already an expert observer of agricultural and social conditions and had published three *Tours* (1768-1770) through different parts of England and a *Tour in Ireland* (1780) when in 1787 he made the famous tour of which he gave an account in *Travels in France* (1792); ed. M. Bentham-Edwards (1924). By exposing the rottenness of economic conditions under the *ancien régime* this work demonstrated the inevitability of the Revolution.

[3] After early experience as a teacher (see her *Thoughts on the Education of Daughters*, 1787), Mary Wollstonecraft became literary adviser to Joseph Johnson, a publisher. Her *Original Stories* (1791) were illustrated by Blake; ed. E. V. Lucas (1906). *A Vindication of the Rights of Women* (1792) argues for equality of education for both sexes and state control of co-education. In Paris in 1792-1793 she formed an attachment with Gilbert Imlay, her principles forbidding her to marry. Their daughter, Fanny, has a part in Shelley's story. On discovering Imlay's infidelity, Mary attempted to drown herself in the Thames but was rescued. Imlay deserted her and she returned to work in Johnson's shop, where in 1796 she met William Godwin. The union between these two was regularized by marriage in 1797 in order to safeguard the legal rights of a coming child. This was a daughter, Mary, who became Shelley's second wife. At her birth Mrs. Godwin died. — *Posthumous Works*, ed. William Godwin (4v, 1798), of which the *Love Letters to Gilbert Imlay*, ed. Roger Ingpen (1908), were originally part. See William Godwin, *Memoirs of the Author of a Vindication of the Rights of Women* (1798); ed. W. C. Durant (1927) and J. M. Murry (1930); G. R. S. Taylor, *Mary Wollstonecraft* (1911); H. R. James, *Mary Wollstonecraft* (1932); G. R. Preedy, *This Shining Woman* (1937).

[4] In later years, shocked by the excesses of the revolutionists, Mackintosh came to agree entirely with Burke. But he continued to advocate parliamentary reform. His fragmentary *History of the Revolution in England* (posthumous, 1834) points forward to Macaulay. — R. J. Mackintosh, *The Life of Sir James Mackintosh* (1836).

[5] In early life Paine was an exciseman. A meeting with Benjamin Franklin in London led him to go to America in 1774. In January, 1776 he published *Common Sense*, arguing for the separation of the colonies from Britain and their union in a republic. During the American Revolution he was an energetic pamphleteer. Returning to England, he issued *Prospects on the Rubicon* (1787), pleading for friendship with France. *The Rights of Man* led to his indictment for high treason, but he escaped to France. *The Age of Reason* (1794) mingles lofty morality with rough ridicule. He returned to America in 1802 and died in New York in 1809. — *Writings*, ed. M. D. Conway (4v, 1894-1896); *Representative Selections*, ed. H. H. Clark (1944). See M. D. Conway, *The Life of Thomas Paine* (1892); M. A. Best, *Thomas Paine, Prophet and Martyr of Democracy* (1927); Hesketh Pearson, *Tom Paine, Friend of Mankind* (1937); Frank Smith, *Thomas Paine, Liberator* (1938); W. E. Woodward, *Tom Paine: America's Godfather* (1946).

Priestley [6] (1733-1804). That this first clear enunciation of the doctrine of perfectibility came from a chemist was significant, for the scientific advances of the later eighteenth century stimulated ideas of progress and social evolution. John Thelwall [7] (1764-1834) expounded his social radicalism in a miscellany of prose and verse entitled *The Peripatetic* (1793), but his direct answers to Burke were in speeches delivered in 1795 and in two pamphlets of 1796.

William Godwin [8] (1756-1836) began to write *Political Justice* in 1791, though it was not published till 1793. It is at once a criticism of existing society, a system of social ethics, and a series of prophecies for the future. Godwin shared with other radicals an optimism founded upon their confidence in the power of the human reason. Ignoring the obvious lessons which might have been drawn from the past of the very society that he criticized, he held that truth must prevail because the arguments supporting it are in the nature of the case stronger than those supporting error. Truth needs no sanction but itself. Vice is an error of judgment. Adopting the sensationalistic interpretation of Locke's theory of knowledge, Godwin believed that judgments, falsified by passion and ignorance, could be rectified by education.[9] Though, like the physical world, the mind of man is subject to necessity (the invariable sequence of cause and effect) and though the basic motive of morality is the desire for pleasure and the avoidance of pain, education can make the individual adapt his own interests to the common good. This "enlightened self-interest," which in the moral sphere cor-

Godwin and Radicalism

---

[6] The discoverer of oxygen was a voluminous writer on natural science, metaphysics, theology, sociology, and other topics. His idea of perfectibility influenced the Marquis de Condorcet, whose *Esquisse d'un tableau historique du progrès de l'esprit humain* (1794) is one of the documents of revolutionary optimism. Priestley emigrated to America (1794) and settled in Pennsylvania, where he died.

[7] Thelwall's ideas influenced Coleridge and Wordsworth; there are definite parallels between *The Peripatetic* and *The Excursion.* — Charles Cestre, *John Thelwall* (1906).

[8] Godwin began his career as a Calvinist minister but soon adopted the principles of the "Enlightenment." He wrote much, but nothing of importance, before *Political Justice* (1793). This was followed by *Caleb Williams*, on which and on his other novels see below, ch. VIII. After the death of his first wife he married a Mrs. Clairmont, one of whose children by a former marriage was Jane ("Claire") Clairmont. In later life Godwin was in constant pecuniary difficulties, wrote many ephemeral literary and historical works, and carried on a small publishing business. — *Political Justice*, ed. and abridged by R. A. Preston (1906); C. K. Paul, *William Godwin, his Friends and Contemporaries* (2v, 1876); Raymond Gourg, *William Godwin* (Paris, 1908); H. N. Brailsford, *Shelley, Godwin and their Circle* (1913); F. K. Brown, *The Life of William Godwin* (1926); George Woodcock, *William Godwin* (1946); Sir Leslie Stephen, *English Thought in the Eighteenth Century* (ed. 1902), II. 264-281; Basil Willey, *The Eighteenth Century Background* (1940), pp. 217-239.

[9] The basic document of romantic theories of education is *De l'esprit* (1758) by Claude Adrien Helvétius. The author follows Condillac's interpretation of Locke's epistemology. The mind is at birth a *tabula rasa*; ideas come solely through sensation, the mind adding nothing but merely arranging the data of sense. Hence the supreme importance of an education which will provide the right sensations. The destructive side of Helvétius's thought is his attack upon conservatism and tradition, kings, priests, and hereditary rights. A more superficial book (which had, however, a great influence) is the Baron d'Holbach's *Système de la nature* (1770). Here the mechanistic theory of the universe coupled with the materialistic monism logically deducible from the sensationalistic interpretation of Locke results in absolute atheism. Reason is the only guide. In lieu of threats of supernatural vengeance as a sanction a right education becomes an assurance of morality. See further Daniel Mornet, *French Thought in the Eighteenth Century*, trans. L. M. Levin (1929).

responds to the "will of the majority" in the political, points forward t𝗍 the Utilitarians; Jeremy Bentham had, indeed, already adumbrated it in his *Fragment on Government* (1776). Only create the right environment for a proper education, Godwin urged, and limitless development in the right direction is possible. In a well ordered society reason, not law, will maintain the social equilibrium. Men will require no political control and government will be reduced to a minimum or will altogether disappear. (It is difficult to distinguish between Godwin's theory of government and pure anarchy.) The institution of private property will not be destroyed, but men will be too reasonable to claim more than their just shares. Marriage, a form of tyranny, will disappear. The penal code and other social conventions will be reformed. This utopian vision is not a "return to nature" in accordance with the usual English interpretation of Rousseau's doctrines,[10] for Godwin advocates not innocent ignorance but virtuous wisdom. When Southey and Coleridge, influenced by *Political Justice,* devised their "pantisocratic" society, they were doubtful of the possibility of reforming their own minds, already warped by wrong education, but planned for the next generation an environment from which opportunities for evil would be shut out and only right sensations impressed upon the mind. These poets and Wordsworth moved away from Godwinian ideas; and Godwin moved away, as it were, from himself. In place of the cool, analytical theory of *Political Justice* his later books substitute a sentimental naturalism.

Though English radicalism was in close touch with Paris, English societies were not planned upon French models. "The Friends of the People" (1791) was moderate in its program of parliamentary reform, though Fox and the New Whigs, who for all their sympathy with France were not "levelers," stood aloof from it. "The London Corresponding Society" (1792), which had branches all over the country, planned to unite the common people for the purpose of making their wishes felt. But by 1792 the increasing violence of the French Revolution strengthened reaction in England. Already in 1791 a "Church and King" mob in Birmingham had burned Priestley's home and laboratory, but this riot had expressed hostility to Dissent rather than to advanced political opinion. Societies appeared dedicated to "the protection of Liberty and Property against republicans and levelers." Men who had formerly sympathized with France began to waver in their optimism. Pamphlets celebrating the blessedness of the English Constitution found ready readers. Loyal addresses flooded the government; newspapers were subsidized; informers wormed their way into radical meetings; and a heresy-hunt began.

ar with
ance
When the reactionary powers of the Continent made their first attack upon France (1792), Pitt had refused to join them; but the French Convention's invitation to a general revolution of all peoples and its indiscriminate defiance of all sovereigns, coupled with the attack upon the Nether-

---

[10] The English notion of Rousseau's teaching derived primarily from the ideas in his two early *Discours* which were modified and qualified in the writings of his maturity.

lands, brought England into the war early in 1793. Pitt's object was to prevent the annexation of the Low Countries and to meet the cost of hostilities by seizing French colonies in the West Indies. After the expulsion of her army in 1794 England's military rôle on the Continent was almost negligible till the beginning of the Peninsular War in 1808. Her successes in the West Indies were purchased at a high cost in lives and money and contributed little to her ultimate victory. Her practical control of the sea after the Battle of the Nile (1798) was complete after Trafalgar (1805). But meanwhile Napoleon remained invincible on land. The Treaty of Amiens (1802) as much as recognized the oceans as England's sphere, Europe as Napoleon's. But England interpreted the treaty as setting a limit to French conquests, while Napoleon proceeded with his annexations. Consequently Amiens turned out to be but an uneasy truce. Pitt's methods of financing the war by indirect taxation (the income tax was not introduced till 1798) bore heavily upon that part of the population which could least afford to pay, and rising prices and food scarcity increased suffering and discontent. The strange remoteness from the war on the part of many members of the cultivated and wealthy classes was due in part to the fact that they were so little affected by taxation, in part to the fact that the navy was manned by means of the press-gang and there was no call for service in the army save for the short time of threatened invasion in 1805, and in part to the disaffection of the Whigs who, though alienated from France, were half-hearted in support of the war and remained aloof, enjoying a life of wealth and ease.

The outbreak of war in 1793 led to the so-called "Anti-Jacobin Terror" *Anti-* of 1794. Daniel Isaac Eaton, the publisher of the newspaper *Hog's Wash* *Jacobinism* (its name an ironical allusion to Burke's scornful phrase, "the swinish multitude"), was tried but acquitted; but in Scotland cruel sentences were imposed upon the victims of the public panic. In the autumn Horne Tooke, John Thelwall, and other radicals were brought to trial for high treason. Their advocate, Thomas Erskine, exposed the falsity of the evidence against them. Several were acquitted and the rest released without trial. Whereupon the volatile populace, which had been strongly anti-Jacobin, celebrated this triumph of freedom of speech and assembly over governmental tyranny. This outcome encouraged the societies, which had been lying low, to become active again for reform. The government countered in 1795 with acts more rigorously defining treason and prohibiting public gatherings without special authorization. To the word *Convention* events in France had attached a sinister meaning; it was feared that assemblies would attempt to overawe or even supersede Parliament. Seething unrest in Ireland, a mutiny in the fleet, and great suffering among the poor were further causes for alarm. The ministry at length suspended habeas corpus. Pitt's motives in putting into force these repressive measures have been much disputed. There seems to be little doubt that he genuinely feared sedition; but he appears to have stimulated panic as a means to rouse the country to support the war.

Freedom of the press, resting upon the Common Law, was never completely suppressed, though actions for libel and sedition were frequent. The two ablest newspapers, *The Morning Chronicle* and *The Morning Post* (for which Coleridge wrote), were bitter opponents of the ministry. Pitt, on the other hand, had the support of the two cleverest caricaturists of the day, James Gillray and Thomas Rowlandson; and in 1797-1798 George Canning, George Ellis, and J. H. Frere championed the government and defended the system of taxation in their brilliant newspaper, *The Anti-Jacobin*. The chief purpose of their satire was to contrast abstract republican philanthropy with the actual cruelties of the Jacobins. This satire was at once strengthened and lightened with parodies of those English poets who expressed sympathy with radical ideas. The contributors had also an eye for other absurdities of modern thought and fashion.[11]

With the spread of opinion hostile to France the situation eased at the turn of the century, but with the renewal of the war in 1803 fears of subversive activities were again rife. It was in this year that William Blake was brought to trial on the charge of sedition. It was difficult to advance the cause of any reform, no matter how obviously salutary it might be. The argument with which conservatives met the advocates of change was that English society, which had rejected reform, had survived, while French

[11] See *Parodies and Other Burlesque Pieces by George Canning, George Ellis and John Hookham Frere with the whole Poetry of the Anti-Jacobin*, ed. Henry Morley (1890). The most effective part of this weekly paper was the verse. In it appeared *The Needy Knife-Grinder*, by Canning and Frere, a parody on Southey; *The Loves of the Triangles*, a parody of Erasmus Darwin's *Loves of the Plants*; *The Progress of Man*, a parody of Richard Payne Knight's *Progress of Civil Society*; and similar pieces. Canning was the chief author of *The New Morality* which vigorously satirizes Coleridge, Southey, Paine, Priestley, and other radicals; renders Burke's ideas into verse; and closes with a lofty exhortation to Britain to be true to her noblest traditions. — George Canning (1770-1827), a young protégé of Pitt, became a great statesman. See Dorothy Marshall, *The Rise of George Canning* (1938), pp. 175-188. George Ellis (1753-1815) contributed to the *Probationary Odes for the Laureateship* (1784 and following years; collected, 1791). He is remembered also for his antiquarian studies of which the most distinguished result is his *Specimens of Early English Metrical Romances* (1805). John Hookham Frere (1769-1846) pointed the way towards Byron's *Don Juan* (see below, ch. XI) and occupied the leisure of a diplomatic career with his translation of Aristophanes (1839). See Gabrielle Festing, *J. H. Frere and his Friends* (1899); Albert Eichler, *J. H. Frere, sein Leben und seine Werke* (Vienna, 1905). — The editor of *The Anti-Jacobin* was William Gifford (1756-1826). Gifford was schooled in boyhood in hard experience but through the kindness of a philanthropist obtained an Oxford education. His stern nature found congenial stuff in the satires of Juvenal and Persius; and the latter was his model for *The Baviad* (1791) in which with a weight of learning and invective he crushed the poor butterflies who fluttered round Robert Merry, the chief "Della Cruscan" poetaster. The feeble verses of this coterie of sentimentalists had appeared in the *World* newspaper and were gathered into a volume. Gifford followed up his first attack with *The Mæviad* (1795), this time dividing his attention between his former victims and the absurdities of the contemporary stage. The harsh energy and assumption of righteous indignation in these satires are due as much to Gifford's Latin model as to any personal feeling. See J. M. Longaker, *The Della Cruscans and William Gifford* (Philadelphia, 1924). In 1809 Gifford became editor of *The Quarterly Review* where his notices of new literature were often written in the current "slashing" style. He edited Ben Jonson (1816) and John Ford (1827). See R. B. Clark, *William Gifford, Tory Satirist, Critic, and Editor* (1930). — Apart from the *Anti-Jacobin* group was Thomas James Mathias (1754-1835) whose *Pursuits of Literature* appeared in three installments, 1794-1797. In form, dialogues modeled on Pope, these satires derive in thought from Burke. Mathias denounced and ridiculed everything contaminated with revolutionary ideas. He smelt a rat in every corner and many of his corners were small and dark. Most of his victims are forgotten today. See further C. W. Previté-Orton, *Political Satire in English Poetry* (Cambridge, 1910), pp. 154-164; W. J. Courthope, *A History of English Poetry*, VI (1910), ch. VI.

society, which had welcomed it, had collapsed; and that changes were entering wedges proposed by dangerous persons who planned to "go further." The one great accomplishment of these years, the abolition of the slave trade, belongs to the interim of Tory governments when Fox headed the Ministry-of-All-the-Talents. Samuel Romilly [12] carried on his agitation for the reform of the cruel and illogical penal code under a cloud of anti-Jacobin prejudice. Sir Francis Burdett,[13] to whom Shelley dedicated *The Wandering Jew* (1810), was a leader in the attacks upon the government. Among the many victims of the policy of repression were John and Leigh Hunt, who were prosecuted in 1811 for exposing the cruelty of flogging in the army. On the same charge William Cobbett was fined and imprisoned. The trial of Daniel Isaac Eaton in 1812, on the charge of reprinting Paine's *Age of Reason,* was the occasion of Shelley's *Letter to Lord Ellenborough.* The Luddite riots of 1811 led to the Frame-Breaking Bill (1812) which made it a capital offense to destroy manufacturing machinery. Against this bill Byron delivered his maiden speech in the House of Lords. Under its terms various unfortunate victims of technological unemployment were executed in the presence of sullen crowds cowed by the military. The state of the public's nerves is shown by the fact that when in 1812 there was a strike among the Scottish weavers a panic spread over Britain. Scott wrote to Southey: "The country is mined beneath our feet." [14]

II

The restrictions upon popular liberty were war measures, but they were *Reactions* not withdrawn after Waterloo and for years the movement for reform was *and Social* impeded because it was associated with sedition.[15] The retention of office by *Unrest* Tory governments till 1830 was at first due to the prestige of victory, but more largely to the divisions among the Whigs, who by failing to agree among themselves on a plan of parliamentary reform deprived themselves of their one chance of gaining popularity. For the misery and unrest of 1815-1817 several causes are apparent. The growth of population came partly from Irish immigration but chiefly through the decline in the infantile death-rate. Consequent upon this growth was the overcrowding in the new cities of the Midlands with all the horrors of slums and cellar-dwellings. Discharged soldiery swelled the ranks of those thrown out of work by the

[12] *Memoirs of Sir Samuel Romilly written by Himself* (3v, 1840).
[13] M. W. Patterson, *Sir Francis Burdett and His Times* (2v, 1931).
[14] Sir Walter Scott, *Letters,* ed. Sir H. J. C. Grierson, III. 125.
[15] The classical survey of English society in 1815 is Elie Halévy, *Histoire du peuple anglais au dix-neuvième siècle,* I (3 ed., 1923); Vols. II and III (1923) bring the story down to 1841. See also E. L. Woodward, *The Age of Reform, 1815-1870* (Oxford, 1938); J. H. Clapham, *Economic History of Modern Britain,* I (1930); F. O. Darvall, *Popular Disturbances and Public Order in Regency England* (1934). There is a wealth of illustrations in E. B. Chancellor, *Life in Regency and Early Victorian Times* (1927). Of Rudolph Ackermann's *The Microcosm of London* (3v, 1808-1811) with its color-plates by A. C. Pugin and Thomas Rowlandson there is a reprint (3v, 1904). This is an unrivaled evocation of the outward appearance of Regency London. See also M. J. Quinlan, *Victorian Prelude: a History of English Manners, 1700-1830* (1941).

new machinery. Hand-looms gave place to power-looms slowly—more slowly in the woolen industry than the cotton, but fast enough to cause distress. The decline in trade and fall in prices coincided with the repeal of the income tax with the consequent burden of indirect taxation upon the poor. The fall in the price of corn brought about the enactment of the Corn Laws with their "sliding scale" which afforded protection to the farmers and the landed interests at the expense of the laboring and mercantile classes. In 1816 there was destruction of machinery, agitation among the colliers, and the circulation of petitions to Parliament, and in December a great meeting at Spa Fields, organized by "Orator" Hunt,[16] was accompanied with rioting. The ministers, alarmed, suspended habeas corpus and had an act passed making seditious meetings unlawful. With a temporary revival of trade, panic subsided; but a new depression began in 1819. In August a huge crowd, estimated at 50-60,000, gathered in St. Peter's Field at Manchester to hear an address by Hunt. The crowd was orderly, but the authorities lost their heads, and when soldiers dispersed the gathering, eleven persons were killed and about four hundred wounded. This "Peterloo Massacre," which prompted Shelley to write *The Masque of Anarchy*, roused indignation even in the upper classes. The Six Acts regulating agitation, assembly, and arrest followed. Immediately afterwards came the "Cato Street Conspiracy," so called because in that street were arrested some fanatics who were plotting to blow up the cabinet. The ill repute of the Prince Regent had its share in inflaming popular feeling, as did the indifference and isolation of the Whigs with their leisured, luxurious, cultivated, and often profligate life. When divorce proceedings were brought against Queen Caroline (1820), and when at her husband's coronation (1820) she claimed the right to be crowned, popular opinion rallied round her as a symbolic victim of oppression. In the popular mind Viscount Castlereagh was associated with the policy of repression because he was the leader of the House of Commons. Actually his own interests and great achievements were in the domain of foreign affairs, in bringing back peace to Europe.[17] But his was a Tory mentality and he supported harsh measures. Hence the almost symbolic position that he occupies in the poetry of Byron and Shelley. His suicide in 1822 marked the close of the worst years of reaction.

Cobbett The fear of the "mob," grounded upon shocked observation of the French Terror, was enhanced by the violence of radical pamphleteering. The most influential of the agitators was William Cobbett [18] (1766-1835), whose early

[16] Henry Hunt (1793-1835) was a disciple of Horne Tooke. In 1810 he was a fellow-prisoner with William Cobbett. In prison, to which he was sentenced after "Peterloo," he wrote his *Memoirs* (1820). He was elected to Parliament in 1830.

[17] C. K. Webster, *The Foreign Policy of Castlereagh, 1815-1822* (1934).

[18] After experience as a soldier (1784-1791) and six months in France (1792) Cobbett lived in America (1792-1800), where as "Peter Porcupine" he was a satiric pamphleteer and publisher, intensely pro-British, anti-French, and anti-Republican. He was prosecuted and fined for libel. After his return to England he veered gradually from support of the Tories towards radicalism. His imprisonment for exposing the cruelties of flogging in the army followed in 1809. On his release he became so much involved in debt that in 1817 he fled to the United States. On his return home he stood repeatedly for Parliament, was elected, 1830,

anti-Jacobinism gave way to an ardor for reform after his return from America in 1800. He began publication of *The Political Register* in 1802. In its pages and in other writings vivid observation, loud-voiced denunciation, and conviction-compelling sincerity attracted wide attention. In many journeys through the length and breadth of England, recorded in *Rural Rides* (1830), he made himself the master of the "condition of England question." Though fined and imprisoned, weighed down with debts, and compelled to exile himself for a time in the United States, he lived to become a member of the first reformed Parliament. With him in the history of the struggle for a free press may be associated two publishers. William Hone [19] (1780-1842) was tried in 1817 on the charge of sedition and blasphemy for publishing parodies on the Creed, the Litany, and the Catechism. He was acquitted. But in 1818 Richard Carlile [20] (1790-1843) was fined and imprisoned for reprinting Hone's parodies and Paine's works.

Meanwhile the tide of reform was slowly coming in. The act of 1819 limiting the hours of child labor in the cotton mills to eleven, pitiable though the concession was, was important in that it recognized the principle of parliamentary interference. Another favorable sign after 1815 was the headway made by the movement for working class education. The "Mechanics' Institutes" and similar organizations were philanthropic responses to the argument that leisure for the poor was a social evil because they had no opportunity for harmless recreation. The experiments which Robert Owen (1771-1858) had been conducting since 1800 at his mills in New Lanark near Glasgow set an example not only in the educational field but in the whole field of social amelioration. Owen's conviction that human character depended upon a right environment was the basis of the principles set forth in his *New View of Society* of which the first part appeared in 1813. His attempts to reconcile the conflict between hand labor and machinery, to organize labor, to manage a business upon a profit-sharing basis, and to establish model communities, with (at a later date) his labor exchange system and socialistic propaganda, were important influences upon the social legislation of the Victorian period and upon the social economics of John Ruskin.

In the years between Waterloo and the Reform Bill the doctrines which

The Advance of Reform

Bentham

re-elected, 1834. — Based on his *Life and Adventures of Peter Porcupine* (1798) and on autobiographical memoranda is *The Progress of a Plough-boy to a Seat in Parliament*, ed. William Reitzel (1933). See also Lewis Melville [pseudonym for L. S. Benjamin], *Life and Letters of William Cobbett* (2v, 1913); *Letters to Edward Thornton*, ed. G. D. H. Cole (1937); G. D. H. Cole, *The Life of William Cobbett* (1924); Marjorie Bowen, *Peter Porcupine, a Study of William Cobbett* (1936); M. C. Clark, *Peter Porcupine in America: the Career of William Cobbett, 1792-1800* (Philadephia, 1939); George Saintsbury, "William Cobbett," *Collected Essays and Papers* (1923), I. 268-301.

[19] F. W. Hackwood, *William Hone, His Life and Times* (1912); Augustus de Morgan, "Hone's Famous Trials," *A Budget of Paradoxes* (Chicago, 1916), I. 180-187; W. H. Wickwar, *The Struggle for the Freedom of the Press, 1819-1832* (1928).

[20] Theophila Carlile Campbell, *The Battle of the Press as told in the Story of the Life of Richard Carlile* (1899).

Jeremy Bentham [21] (1748-1832) had begun to promulgate at a much earlier date began to bear practical fruit. His theory of the pursuit of happiness is open to much question; but at a time when the social conscience was awakening, the doctrine of the "greatest happiness of the greatest number" was a criterion of practical service. It made for reforms in the direction of peace and public order. Bentham's chief concern was not with private morals but with the betterment of society. He was no revolutionary but trusted in parliamentary procedure, advocating governmental supervision but not governmental control. His was a logical rather than a historical method. For the heritage of the past he had an entire contempt unless a reason for survival could be found in a satisfactory answer to his persistent question: "What is its use?" The test of usefulness was of utmost value in the revision and codification of the law. He was especially active in the reform of criminal law; but less directly his doctrines bore upon the problem of a fairer and wider suffrage. Through his disciples, James Mill [22] (1773-1836) and John Stuart Mill [23] (1806-1873), who put much of his memoranda into final shape, he became the father of the Utilitarian school of philosophy.

*he Re-
orm Bill*
Against this background of reform the Tories held office during the eighteen-twenties. The death of Castlereagh opened the era of George Canning's dominance (1822-1827). Canning represented a liberal Toryism which was opposed to the high Toryism of Wellington and Eldon. This division and the separation of the Whigs into three groups had the advantage that different sides of public opinion were reflected in Parliament. The prosperity of the early twenties was a support to public order and good feeling. After Canning's death, power came into the hands of the more reactionary Tories; but so great was the pressure of public opinion that they repealed the Test and Corporation Act (1828) and emancipated the Roman Catholics (1829). The pressure for parliamentary reform was led by Francis Place (1771-1854) whose tailor-shop was the rallying-ground of moderate radicalism. Place was active in gathering petitions presented to Parliament by his collaborator, Joseph Hume. The French Revolution of July, 1830 was a further incentive. There was an outbreak of strikes, violent agitation, and arrests. The Whigs' concession to the demand for a more just representation was due to their realization of the strength of popular opinion. There is no need here to repeat the familiar story of the confusion between party lines, the swift

---

[21] Bentham possessed private means which enabled him to pursue his interests. He studied law but was more concerned with the reform of legal abuses than with establishing a practice. His *Fragment on Government* (1776), published anonymously, was a criticism of the English Constitution and manifested both his indifference to historical considerations and his test of utility. In 1789 appeared his *Principles of Morals and Legislation*. He worked for the abolition of the system of transportation for crime, and the establishment of prisons on lines invented by himself. In 1823 he founded *The Westminster Review* as the organ of philosophic radicalism.

[22] The elder Mill collaborated with Bentham and wrote voluminously on history (*The History of India*, 1818), economics (*Elements of Political Economy*, 1821), psychology (*Analysis of the Human Mind*, 1829), and public affairs. As an economist he was a follower of David Ricardo; as a psychologist he developed associationism. In his political writings he advocated a wide extension of the franchise. He was one of the founders of the University of London (1825).

[23] On the younger Mill see below, ch. xxi.

alternations of governments, the threats uttered by the reformers, and the prophecies of disaster made by the reactionaries. In the end fifty-six boroughs were disfranchised and the membership of thirty others was reduced. Representation was given to many new centers of population. The franchise was limited to householders, copyholders, leaseholders, and freeholders. The day of manhood suffrage was still far off and the laboring classes remained in large part without direct representation. The Reform Bill of 1832 shifted the center of political power to the middle classes.

II

Romanticism

The French Revolution, the Napoleonic Wars, and the progress of domestic reform enlarged the boundaries and enriched the content of English romanticism,[1] but these social and political events did not initiate the movement. For its origins search must be made deep into the past, perhaps into the very nature of the human spirit. Upon that quest we cannot embark here. The word *romans* meant originally a vernacular descended from the Latin; then the literature written in the vernacular; and then the prevailing kind of that literature. The adjective *romantic* (with variants) first appeared in English in the mid-seventeenth century as a word to describe the fabulous, the extravagant, the fictitious, and the unreal. From this disrepute it was rescued during the following hundred years by being used to describe pleasing scenes and situations of the sort appearing in "romantic" fiction and poetry.[2] Gradually the term *Romanticism* came to be applied to the resurgence of instinct and emotion which the prevalent rationalism of the eighteenth century never wholly suppressed. More or less timid and tentative manifestations of this revolt against "common sense" have been recognized in the previous section of this History. The choice of the word *Romanticism* was perhaps unfortunate, because it begs the question whether there is any such single cultural phenomenon in Europe; but it is too firmly fixed to be discarded. The confusion prevalent in recent discussions of the matter may be clarified in a measure if we remember that it springs from the use of the same term for different tendencies. Romantic phenomena vary in different countries, and even within the same country no two writers are necessarily romantic in the same way or to the same degree, nor is a writer necessarily romantic in all his work or throughout his life. The term some-

[1] H. N. Fairchild, *The Romantic Quest* (1931), to which this chapter is especially indebted; H. N. Fairchild, Elizabeth Nitchie, and others, "Romanticism: a Symposium," *PMLA*, LV (1940). 1-60; Paul Elmer More, *The Drift of Romanticism* (1913); Irving Babbitt, *Rousseau and Romanticism* (1919); Lascelles Abercrombie, *Romanticism* (1926); F. L. Lucas, *The Decline and Fall of the Romantic Ideal* (1936); B. I. Evans, *Tradition and Romanticism* (1940); Jacques Barzun, *Romanticism and the Modern Ego* (1944); Ernest Bernbaum, *Guide through the Romantic Movement* (1930), especially pp. 438-459; Sir H. J. C. Grierson, "Classical and Romantic," in *The Background of English Literature* (1925); W. P. Ker, "Romantic Fallacies," in *The Art of Poetry* (1921); Alfred North Whitehead, "The Romantic Reaction," in *Science and the Modern World* (1925); C. H. Herford, "Romanticism in the Modern World," *E&S*, VIII (1922). 109-134; A. O. Lovejoy, "On the Discrimination of Romanticisms," *PMLA*, XXXIX (1924). 229-253. — Annual bibliographies on the Romantic Movement have been published in *ELH* (1937-49), *PQ* (1950-64), and *ELN* (1965-   ) .

[2] Logan P. Smith, *Four Words, S. P. E. Tract*, No. XVII (1924), pp. 3-17.

times implies a theory, a formulated code, a "school"; but in England romanticism was informal and almost wholly unattached to any doctrinaire program. Though often used of writers in rebellion against classical rules of composition, romanticism is not merely a matter of technique. It is true that many of these writers were deficient in critical control of their material, but the technical excellencies usually praised as classical may be found in association with elements of romanticism. As a recognition of the need to discriminate among many tendencies, it has been proposed that the plural *romanticisms* be employed; but other scholars, rejecting this counsel of despair, pursue the quest for some underlying principle or common denominator binding together the various phenomena of this movement of thought and emotion.

The romanticist is "amorous of the far." He seeks to escape from familiar experience and from the limitations of "that shadow-show called reality" which is presented to him by his intelligence. He delights in the marvelous and abnormal. To be sure, loving realistic detail and associating the remote with the familiar, he is often "true to the kindred points of heaven and home." But he is urged on by an instinct to escape from actuality, and in this escape he may range from the most trivial literary fantasy to the most exalted mysticism. His effort is to live constantly in the world of the imagination above and beyond the sensuous, phenomenal world. For him the creations of the imagination are "forms more real than living man." He practises willingly that "suspension of disbelief" which "constitutes poetic faith." In its most uncompromising form this dominance of the intuitive and the irrational over sense experience becomes mysticism—"the life which professes direct intuition of the pure truth of being, wholly independent of the faculties by which it takes hold of the illusory contaminations of this present world." [3] Wordsworth described this experience as "that serene and blessed mood" in which, "the burden of the mystery" being lightened, he "sees into the life of things." Blake, who seems to have lived almost continuously in this visionary ecstasy, affirmed that the "vegetable universe" of phenomena is but a shadow of that real world which is the Imagination. To the romanticist not the thing perceived is important but the thing imagined. But it is difficult to sustain for long this vision of the archetypal reality. The attempt to find some correspondence between actuality and desire results in joy when for fleeting moments the vision is approximated, but in despondency or despair when the realization comes that such reconciliations are impossible. Thus, Byron's Lucifer tempts Cain to revolt by forcing upon him an awareness of "the inadequacy of his state to his conceptions." [4] A sense of this contrast is expressed by Shelley in those poems in which there is a sudden fall from ecstasy into disillusionment. The same sense adds a new poignancy to the melancholy strain inherited by the romantic poets

"Amorous of the Far"

[3] L. Abercrombie, *Romanticism*, p. 107.
[4] Byron, *Letters and Journals*, ed. Prothero, v. 470.

from their predecessors.[5] If the vision embraces the concept of perfection in this present life ("perfectibilitarianism"), the poet, becoming aware of the unattainability of this ideal here and now, tends to escape from actuality into "the innermost stronghold of his own spirit." There is a "withdrawal from outer experience in order to concentrate upon inner experience."[6] A reliance upon the life within carries with it the belief that in that life there is liberty to realize some perfection inherent in the nature of man. There is a trust in the validity of natural impulses, in "the holiness of the heart's affections."[7] At its boldest (as in Blake) the self-sufficient imagination is utterly confident. "The classical writer," it has been said,[8] "feels himself to be a member of an organized society; the romantic is in rebellion against external law. He asserts the rights of his individuality *contra mundum.*"

Extremes of Sensibility   With this confidence in intuition goes an expanding imaginative sensibility which in extreme instances may take exotic and disquieting forms, as in the Byronic concepts of the daemonic male and the *femme fatale*. Emphasizing the abnormal element, some scholars have singled out the morbidly erotic and deranged as distinguishing marks of romanticism, interpreting this as evidence of the part played by the less conscious impulses of the mind and noting that a larger number of English writers of the period approached the borders of insanity or went beyond, than can be accounted for on the ground of mere coincidence. That several were attracted to the theme of incest is sometimes thought to be significant.[9] Yet when all is said, there is little exploitation of perversity in English literature between 1789 and 1832 and, on the higher literary levels, little of the grotesque and bizarre. In line with this reticence is the almost unanimous refusal of the English romanticists to attract attention in vulgar fashion by outlandish pose. William Beckford, who exhibits the romantic mood in an unqualified form, says of the incestuous loves of the brother and sister in one of his tales, that there had entered into them "the ardent elixir of a too exquisite sensibility and the poison of an insatiable desire."[10] This is a memorable formula for the extremes of the romantic attitude; but to select, with Paul Elmer More,[11] as "the essential type and image of the romantic life and literature" Beckford's vision of the damned moving ever round the throne of Eblis with hands upon flaming hearts, is to generalize extravagantly, for the English genius, with its instinct to compromise, seldom pursued the primrose path the entire way to the everlasting bonfire. Is not the hunger

[5] See E. M. Sickels, *The Gloomy Egoist: Moods and Themes of Melancholy from Gray to Keats* (1932); Oswald Doughty, "The English Malady of the Eighteenth Century," *RES*, II (1926). 257-269.

[6] L. Abercrombie, *op. cit.,* p. 51.

[7] Keats, *Letters,* ed. M. B. Forman (1931), I. 72.

[8] J. Middleton Murry, *The Problem of Style* (1922), p. 146.

[9] On the abnormal extremes of the romantic temperament see Mario Praz, *The Romantic Agony* (1933), and for an argument based upon psychoanalytic theories of the Ego, Super-Ego, and "Reality Principle" see F. L. Lucas, *op. cit.,* chs. I and II.

[10] Beckford, "The Story of Zulkaïs," *The Episodes of Vathek,* trans. by Sir F. T. Marzials (ed. 1922), p. 197.

[11] P. E. More, *op. cit.,* p. 36, referring to the final episode in *Vathek.*

for illusion balanced in the English mind by the steadying influence of common sense? Only seldom are the poet's flights of fancy taken with metaphysical seriousness; rarely is he lost in "an O *Altitudo*." The romanticist's attempts to find a rational justification for the pleasures of the imagination were misleading; but modern opponents of romanticism fall into the opposite error when they repudiate these pleasures because they belong to the realm of desire and dream.

In the romantic mood there has been detected the influence of the Oriental mind which had flowed into the West through the channels of Neo-Platonic speculation. Whereas the classical mind of Greece had sought for the Divine in the qualities of order, restraint, and proportion, the East associated the Divine with the vast and vague. In Gnosticism and other ancient heresies there are elements of what many centuries later came to be called romanticism—the identification of the intellect with desire; the dominance of emotion over reason; the assertion of the Ego above the claims of society.[12] As the eighteenth century moved on, the instinctive side of personality asserted itself ever more strongly and in more individuals. The check provided by tradition, morality, and religion upon human potentialities was relaxed. Rousseau's doctrine that man, by nature good but corrupted by bad laws and customs, should be freed from these and left to the guidance of his own personality, was an impelling force.[13] The Calvinistic conviction of predestination to salvation modulated into "a sense of goodness and freedom" in the individual "which must somehow find corroboration in the nature of the universe"; and even Hume's self-destructive psychology, discrediting the very rationalism by which it worked, "gave encouragement to those who desired to believe in the truth of the unaccountable and the uncriticized."[14] This anti-intellectualism is expressed by Wordsworth when he denounces "that false secondary power by which we multiply distinctions"[15] and by Blake when he pictures Urizen at his sad and evil task of breaking up the primal unity into rational categories.[16] Again, when Keats declares that "Philosophy will clip an angel's wings,"[17] we are reminded of one of Blake's emblems where purblind Reason is clipping the wings of Love.[18]

Anti-intellectualism

This anti-intellectualism was no sudden manifestation of a spirit of revolt; it had been swelling in volume for many years. In the thought of the predecessors of the great romantic poets there had been a tendency to view learning with suspicion as allied to vice and to commend ignorance as concomitant with virtue. The idealization of the "noble savage," the peasant, and the child had come about in greater or less degree long before Coleridge

[12] P. E. More, *op. cit.*, pp. 21-31.
[13] The influence of Rousseau upon romanticism was stressed by Irving Babbitt, *op. cit.* and by T. E. Hulme in "Romanticism and Classicism," *Speculations*, ed. Herbert Read (1924), pp. 113-140, especially p. 116.
[14] H. N. Fairchild, in his contribution to the symposium, *PMLA*, LV. 21.
[15] *The Prelude*, II. 216-217.
[16] *The First Book of Urizen*.
[17] *Lamia*, II. 234.
[18] "Aged Ignorance," *The Gates of Paradise*, Emblem XI; *Writings*, Nonesuch Edition, III. 344.

and Southey conceived their plan to emigrate to America, and Wordsworth chose his dalesmen as fit characters for poetry, and Blake sang his *Songs of Innocence*. The confidence in the intuitive wisdom of childhood runs parallel with the exaltation of the primitive life of rustics and savages; and both are aspects of the romantic "escape" from actuality. This primitivistic tendency was one of the powerful impulses upon the revolutionary movement in France; and conversely, the same tendency received a powerful new impulse from the democratic forces let loose by the French Revolution. But obviously, sympathy with the Revolution cannot be considered an infallible "touchstone" of English romanticism since many of its elements had appeared before 1789.[19]

The attraction of the remote from social sophistication—the simple, the rustic, the democratic—found various forms of expression. It is a "return to nature." It is behind the cult of mountains and desert islands and the virgin lands of the New World, unstained by the slow contagion of civilization. This primitivism explains the taste for the "reliques" of ancient poetry; it is behind the romantic conception of genius and of poetry as a gift of nature, not an acquired art. With such currents of thought and feeling flowing, it *The* was natural that the Middle Ages were regarded with a fresh sympathy, *Middle* though not, be it said, with accurate understanding. It is true that there were *Ages* those who, like Shelley, seeking to reshape the present in accordance with desire, did not revert to the past but pursued their ideal into a utopian future. But to others the Middle Ages offered a spiritual home, remote and vague and mysterious. The typical romanticist does not "reconstruct" the past from the substantial evidence provided by research, but fashions it anew, not as it was but as it ought to have been. The more the writer insists upon the historical accuracy of his reconstruction the less romantic is he. Under the stimulus of the Napoleonic Wars this love of the past tended to become nationalistic, with a special emphasis upon antiquarian and regionalist elements in English history. But this nationalism is an accidental characteristic of some phases of romanticism rather than a component part of the movement as a whole. The tremendous public events of the time brought out the patriotism of the older generation of romantic poets, but the younger generation remained cosmopolitan in outlook.

The remote in place offered an appeal similar to that of the remote in time, and in innumerable cases the two attractions are combined. From castles in "the wind-grieved Apennines" the romantic imagination passed *The Super-* easily to those haunted castles whose magic casements opened upon the *natural* perilous seas of fairyland. The archetypal romantic poet "lures his fancy to its utmost scope." In the company of Coleridge we visit the enchanted palace of Kubla Khan, the vampire-haunted castle of Christabel, the demon-

---

[19] The direct influence of the French revolutionary philosophers upon the English romantic poets was formerly somewhat overestimated; but through Godwin and other radicals the new ideas were assimilated into English poetry. See Edward Dowden, *The French Revolution and English Literature* (1897); A. E. Hancock, *The French Revolution and the English Poets* (1899); Charles Cestre, *La révolution française et les poètes anglais* (Paris, 1906).

infested seas of the Ancient Mariner. With Keats we stand in the church-portal on Saint Mark's Eve or attend the wedding-banquet of Lycius and the lamia in the palace at Corinth. Upon the lower levels of romanticism the revolt from intellectualism and "common sense" produced mere spectre-ballads and "Gothicism," but upon the higher levels we have the true "Renaissance of Wonder" of Watts-Dunton's famous definition.[20]

The typical romanticist is a dreamer, though no single writer conforms wholly, consistently, and uninterruptedly to the type. In dreams a great significance attaches to symbolism. A wealth of symbols enriches romantic literature.[21] There is a persistent resort to suggestiveness in language, to overtones of meaning, and to the dreamy associations that attach to words.

[20] "The Renascence of Wonder in English Poetry," originally the introduction to *Chambers' Cyclopaedia of English Literature* (1903), Vol. III; reprinted with additional material in *Poetry and the Renascence of Wonder*, ed. Thomas Hake (1916).

[21] The interpretation of romantic symbolism is carried to extremes of complexity in G. Wilson Knight, *The Starlit Dome* (1941).

III

William Blake

I

The first clear voice of romanticism was that of William Blake [1] (1757-1827). It was almost unheeded. There were times when the failure of his fellow-men to respond to his message moved him to indignant protest; but beneath his anger there was always an abiding happiness, for this neglect was but an incident in the warfare which his imagination waged with spiritual enemies. That the few men who recognized his genius did not comprehend his ideas and that the world passed him by was of little moment to one who knew that his works were the delight of the archangels. [2] The *Descriptive Catalogue* of his pictures closes with these noble and prophetic words:

If a man is master of his profession, he cannot be ignorant that he is so; and if he is not employed by those who pretend to encourage art, he will employ himself, and laugh in secret at the pretences of the ignorant, while he has every night ... a reward for the labours of the day such as the world cannot give, and patience and time await to give him all that the world can give. [3]

He was content with his "great task" which was "to open the immortal Eyes of Man inwards into the Worlds of Thought." [4]

[1] *The Writings of William Blake*, Nonesuch Edition, ed. Geoffrey Keynes (3v, 1925); *Prose and Poetry*, Nonesuch Edition (1932), complete but without textual apparatus; *Works*, ed. E. J. Ellis and W. B. Yeats (3v, 1893); *Prophetic Books*, ed. D. J. Sloss and J. P. R. Wallis (2v, 1926). — Geoffrey Keynes, *Bibliography* (1921); Mona Wilson, *Life of William Blake* (1927); Thomas Wright, *Life of William Blake* (2v, 1929); Alexander Gilchrist, *Pictor Ignotus: The Life of William Blake* (1863), ed. Ruthven Todd (Everyman's Library, 1942); Helene Richter, *William Blake* (Strassburg, 1906); Pierre Berger, *Mysticisme et Poésie: William Blake* (Paris, 1907; trans. D. H. Conner, 1914); A. C. Swinburne, *William Blake* (1868); Arthur Symons, *William Blake* (1907); E. J. Ellis, *The Real Blake* (1907); Basil de Selincourt, *William Blake* (1909); S. Foster Damon, *William Blake, his Philosophy and Symbols* (1922); H. L. Bruce, *William Blake in this World* (1926); Osbert Burdett, *William Blake* (EML Series, 1926); J. Middleton Murry, *William Blake* (1933); J. Bronowski, *William Blake: A Man without a Mask* (1943); M. Plowman, *Introduction to the Study of Blake* (1927); Denis Saurat, *Blake and Milton* (1920; reissued 1935); Helen C. White, *The Mysticism of William Blake* (1927); M. O. Percival, *William Blake's Circle of Destiny* (1938); Emily S. Hamblen, *On the Minor Prophecies of William Blake* (1930); Laurence Binyon, *The Engraved Designs of William Blake* (1926); Darrell Figgis, *The Paintings of William Blake* (1925); J. B. Wicksteed, *Blake's Vision of the Book of Job* (1910). Mark Schorer, *William Blake: The Politics of Vision* (1946) appeared when this chapter was in type. It presents an "anti-mystical" interpretation of Blake and relates him closely to movements of political and social thought.
[2] See the letters to Thomas Butts, January 10, 1802, and July 6, 1803; *Writings*, II. 199 and 246.
[3] *Writings*, III. 120.
[4] *Jerusalem*, I; *Writings*, III. 169.

There are three periods in Blake's life. The first extends from his birth (November 28, 1757) to his marriage in 1782 and the publication of *Poetical Sketches* in 1783. Within the second period (1783-1803) we note especially the years 1793-1800 when he lived in Lambeth and the years 1800-1803 when he lived at Felpham on the Sussex coast. During the last period (1803-1827) he lived in London. The first is the time of his apprenticeship in poetry and the arts of design; the second, of his fully coherent powers as a poet and of his earliest mature designs; the third, of increasing extravagance in poetry followed by twenty years of almost unbroken silence, and of full power as an artist, increasing till the year of his death. Throughout it is possible to trace, sometimes clearly, sometimes obscurely, the development of his ideas. There are contradictions of detail which cannot be resolved, incoherences which no amount of exegesis has made clear; but fundamentally there are no inconsistencies; what seem to be such are alterations of emphasis.

From childhood, when he saw a tree full of angels, and his youth, when *The* in Westminster Abbey he had visions of ancient kings, to his old age, when *Visionary* he drew "spiritual portraits" of the mighty dead, he consorted with beings from the world of the imagination, rising ever higher into mystical illusion. Unlike the Christian mystics his apprehension was not of Divinity in its nameless essence but of a cloud of heavenly witnesses that compassed him about. The record of his visions is in his poems and designs. They are not drug-inspired hallucinations or literary fancies. In his youth, the stream of mystical thought in England which, flowing apart from the main current of ideas, had never wholly evaporated, was swollen by the writings of Emmanuel Swedenborg. Reading him, Blake was impelled to elaborate what he conceived to be true in the doctrines of the Church of the New Jerusalem and to refute what was false. He studied Behmenism, Rosicrucianism, and other esoteric ideas which came from Neo-Platonism, Gnosticism, and other well-springs of profound, if often confused, speculation. This reading confirmed him in his confidence in the validity of his own experiences. Into the problem of the causes of mystical phenomena we cannot enter here. Suffice it to say that they are manifested in Blake. There is that sense of the inadequacy of this world to satisfy the aspirations of the soul which in the mystic inspires, in a sort of transport, a realization here and now of the perfections of Eternity. There is the feeling of exultation and power, the sense of illumination, the confidence that the rapt soul is in the possession of absolute Truth. Mysticism not seldom challenges orthodoxy, for it claims an immediate apprehension of Truth from God unaided by any Church to which has been committed the duty of revelation. Blake belongs among those mystics who repudiate allegiance to the Church.

While Blake was an apprentice to Basire the engraver and afterwards while seeking his livelihood from the booksellers, he wrote his first poems.

Poetical Sketches

Well-intentioned people whom he met at the home of Mrs. Henry Mathew [5] assisted him financially in the publication of *Poetical Sketches* [6] (1783). Among these some pieces of cadenced Ossianic prose are ominous of the turgid style of the "Prophetic Books." *Fair Elenor* is an exercise in the Gothic mode but of an impassioned intensity beyond the capabilities of any Gothicizer. *To the Evening Star* and the four poems on the seasons are suggestive of Collins but with exquisite faltering rhythms which sound an individual note. *King Edward the Third* is an imitation of Elizabethan tragedy crude and boyish enough but with passages of fine energy. There are echoes of Jacobean song, such as *My Silks and Fine Array*, so unexpected in the period of classical decline as to be fresh creations. In the *Mad Song* there is a boldness of metrical innovation for which nothing in contemporary poetry prepares the reader. Everywhere a freshness of utterance springs from the poet's own genius. Joy, laughter, love, and harmony are the prevailing notes. The Muses, who, forsaking poetry, had fled from England, were ready to return. A new star had risen, but there were few to watch its rising.

Innocence and Experience

The qualities of spontaneity and simplicity undeformed by sentimentality are more fully apparent in *Songs of Innocence* (1789). This lovely little volume enriched the resources of English prosody.[7] Blake learned from the ballads and perhaps from Chatterton the principle of "substitution" or "equivalents" and carried it beyond the limits of his models, anticipating effects of *Christabel*. There are shifting patterns, quiet modulations from one key into another, or sudden changes in metrical schemes. Accents fall upon light syllables more boldly than in Augustan poetry. Pauses in breathing take the place of missing syllables. The laughter and glee which ring and tinkle through these lyrics are indicative of Blake's personal happiness, but they also symbolize the joy in that primal unity of which the child, type of unfallen mortality, is still aware, doomed though he be to the "shades of the prison-house." As that shadow is the obverse of the light, so are the later *Songs of Experience* (1794) implicit in those of *Innocence*. For that Blake was already apprehending both sides of his thought, the negative as well as the positive, is shown by the rapidity with which *The Marriage of Heaven and Hell* [8] (1790) followed the songs of childhood.

Without qualification or reserve and with an almost terrifying downrightness this strange work denies the validity of the moral law. The god of

[5] Blake was introduced into this circle by John Flaxman, the sculptor. For his own relief and not for publication he composed *An Island in the Moon*, an amusing but incoherent and in parts very coarse satire upon the habitués of Mrs. Mathew's salon. It contains drafts of some of the *Songs of Innocence*. From one passage we learn that Blake had already devised his method of "illuminated printing."

[6] See M. R. Lowery, *Windows of the Morning* (New Haven, 1940), a critical study of *Poetical Sketches*.

[7] See George Saintsbury, *A History of English Prosody* (1910), III. 8-29.

[8] This was issued by the method of "illuminated printing" (the text as well as the illustrations engraved, and each copy colored by hand). With this method Blake had already experimented in the two tiny booklets, *There is No Natural Religion* and *All Religions are One* (both about 1789), in *Songs of Innocence*, and in *Tiriel* and *Thel*, the earliest of the "Prophetic Books."

Sinai is a jealous and evil god. Satan is the type of energy, desire, and will. Action is good; slave-morality is sin. Joy is its own justification. The anti-nomianism, expressed with splendor and audacity in the famous *Proverbs of Hell*, is intertwined but not completely fused with Blake's positive doc-trine of the One-ness of the Human and the Divine. "Those who envy or calumniate great men hate God; for there is no other God."

In the bookshop of Joseph Johnson, Blake met Paine, Priestley, Godwin, *The Early* and Mary Wollstonecraft. He was soon alienated by their rationalism; but *Prophetic* meanwhile expositions of the new revolutionary ideas confirmed him in his *Books* own rebelliousness. In 1791 Johnson published *The French Revolution, a Prophecy*. The metrical form of this poem is the unrimed "fourteener," loosely handled but not entirely undisciplined. Blake viewed events in France as an opening episode in the cosmic warfare which would lead ultimately to the overthrow of morality and law and the triumph of instinct and freedom. From France in the throes of revolution he then turned to the triumph of revolution across the Atlantic, and in *Visions of the Daugh-ters of Albion* and *America, a Prophecy* (both 1793) he interpreted the War of Independence symbolically. The action takes place on two planes, the natural and the supra-mundane; Washington and his colleagues consort with the strange spirits of Blake's imagination. There is some incoherence, but the general drift is clear. Orc, symbol of vital passion and desire, exults in his victory over Urizen (Reason). He tramples to dust the stony law of the commandments and scatters religion as a torn book, proclaiming that

> everything that lives is holy, life delights in life;
> Because the soul of sweet delight can never be defil'd.[9]

In *The First Book of Urizen* (1794) the metrical form is further broken down, the incoherence more pronounced, and the action more tumultuous. Violent, shapeless beings weep and shriek and roar and bellow through the abyss. Urizen finds not joy but anguish in his nefarious task of dividing and measuring time and space, breaking the primal unity into categories, setting up the reign of law, and snaring the five senses in the net of religion. *Urizen* was followed by *Europe* (1794) and *The Song and Book of Los* and its sequel *The Book of Ahania* (both 1795). In these three some of the symbolic characters and their actions have defied the ingenuity of all the commentators.

The "Lambeth Period" was at first fairly prosperous. Blake received numerous commissions to engrave the designs of other artists, and also gave drawing-lessons to a few pupils. His fecundity of invention was shown in no less than 537 designs for Young's *Night Thoughts* (1797). But in 1798 commissions fell off and he plunged into the composition of the longer "Prophetic Books." To this time belongs *The Four Zoas* (also called *Vala*) which he never engraved. This obscure chaos of dross and treasure later

9 *America; Writings*, I. 265.

served as a reservoir of incidents and ideas drawn upon for the *Milton* and *Jerusalem*.

At Felpham

When penury threatened in 1799, Blake found in Thomas Butts a generous friend.[10] Through Flaxman he also met William Hayley [11] who invited him to live on his estate at Felpham. The next three years saw the tragicomedy of the relations of a great genius with a kindly but overbearing patron who had no conception of the quality of the man whom he sheltered. At first all went well; Felpham was a paradise. But as Blake found himself obliged not only to furnish designs for Hayley's books but to listen to his verses, while his own work was blandly discouraged or ignored, happiness turned to uneasiness and then into resentment. Gradually there was a spiritual restoration. He busied himself with the designs for Milton's poems and the Bible. Hayley's loyalty during the quarrel with the drunken soldier Schofield satisfied Blake that he was a friend; and when they parted in the autumn of 1803 it was upon amicable terms.

Once more in London, Blake was at first cheerfully active. He began the *Milton*, on which he worked till about 1808, and the *Jerusalem*, which occupied him intermittently till 1820. Between 1804 and 1809 there was much painting and engraving. In the ill treatment which he received from R. H. Cromek, print-seller and publisher,[12] he saw an incident in his warfare with the powers of darkness. In 1809 he issued the *Prospectus* interpreting his engraving of the Canterbury Pilgrims, and the greatest of his prose works, the *Descriptive Catalogue* for the exhibition of his paintings which he now held and which was almost completely ignored. This and other writings of the time are eloquent of his sense of neglect but also of his entire self-confidence. After the failure of the exhibition he passed into almost

"I am hid"

complete obscurity. "I am hid," he wrote.[13] Till 1818 there are no extant letters. Hayley and even Butts disappear. Journeyman-work as an engraver supported him and his wife, and there was much painting in water-color, but save for work on *Jerusalem* there was little poetry. The view, however, that his increasing mystical tendency destroyed in him the power to write is scarcely tenable, for in 1818 he showed undiminished energy in *The Everlasting Gospel* and in the final version of *The Gates of Paradise*. New friends now appeared: John Linnel, an artist; John Varley, painter and astrologer; Henry Crabb Robinson, the diarist, who left invaluable impressions of Blake; and a group of young artists who gathered round the aging genius.[14]

[10] Butts was for years a steady purchaser of Blake's works. See Blake's *Letters to Thomas Butts*, facsimiles of the manuscripts, introduction by Geoffrey Keynes (1926).

[11] William Hayley (1745-1820), friend and biographer of Cowper, was a well-to-do amateur of letters, critic, poetaster (*The Triumphs of Temper* (1781) and other works), connoisseur, and something of an arbiter of taste.

[12] Cromek commissioned Blake to make the designs for Blair's *Grave* (1808) but engaged another artist to engrave the plates. He saw Blake's design for the Canterbury Pilgrims, pirated the idea, and commissioned Thomas Stothard to make a rival engraving. Blake's lampoons on Cromek were committed to a note-book and not intended for publication.

[13] An annotation to Sir Joshua Reynolds' *Discourses; Writings*, III. 5.

[14] The gentle pastoralism of Blake's designs for Thornton's edition of Virgil's *Eclogues* influenced these disciples, especially Samuel Palmer. See Laurence Binyon, *The Followers of William Blake* (1926). Palmer was a connecting link between Blake and the Pre-Raphaelites.

To the last years of intense activity in the graphic arts belong the woodcuts for Thornton's *Virgil,* the "spectral" portraits, the illustrations to the *Divine Comedy,* and the *Job.* Gradually, but in serenity and spiritual joy, Blake's health failed, and he died on August 12, 1827. The site of his grave in Bunhill Fields is unknown. Frederick Tatham, a friend of orthodox mind, destroyed the plates of his engravings and burned or dispersed his manuscripts.

II

In the eighteenth century Gothic art was what English genius, too long *Blake's* fettered with conventions, needed and was groping after. Blake found it in *Symbolism* boyhood and it did his genius harm. His mind was undisciplined; it lacked the balance, scope, and tolerance which a classical training might have provided. Disgust with classical art (known to him only in plaster replicas of late Greco-Roman statues) closed his imagination to a whole series of traditional forms. The medieval tombs at Westminster confirmed an instinctive taste for the enormous and distorted; and from amorphous things he sought to shape his symbols. The mystic movement of his mind required metaphor; he saw not likenesses but identities. Upon an age not accustomed to think in symbols he tried to impose those of his own devising or drawn from esoteric sources. The task would have been difficult had he tried to force upon rationalists the traditional symbolism of Christianity or such august pagan symbols as Fortuna or Chronos. As it was, from the first his purpose was hopeless of success. His imagination was "in rebellion, not only against the limits of reality, but against the only means by which he could make vision visible to others." [15] He possessed his own associations but could communicate only a fraction of them, leaving scattered clues but no key to unlock all doors. He held that "that which is not too explicit is fittest for instruction, because it rouses the faculties to act." [16] But the faculties, overdriven, may lapse into lethargy. He defined "the most sublime poetry" as "Allegory addressed to the Intellectual powers while it is altogether hidden from the Corporeal Understanding." [17] But he relied too confidently upon powers not as extraordinary as his own and lacking his private key to the great secrets. "He forgets," it has been said,[18] "that he is talking to men on the earth in some language which he learnt in heavenly places." His symbolism embraces all time and space; vague, tremendous forms with uncouth and hideous names; contemporary events and people; personages of the past; continents, oceans, and points of the compass; provincial towns; districts of London; incidents in his own life. Many of the actors in his mighty drama remain mere names; from others a meaning may be wrested by care-

[15] Arthur Symons, *William Blake,* p. 217.
[16] *Writings,* II. 175.
[17] *Ibid.,* II. 246.
[18] Arthur Symons, *William Blake,* p. 84. On the distinction between single vision, twofold, three-fold, and even four-fold vision in Blake see J. W. Beach, *The Concept of Nature in Nineteenth Century Poetry* (1936), pp. 112-113.

...ion of reference with reference. Whether the result is worth the ef-
... a question which the interpreters, dazzled by the light they have
...osed, are perhaps not best qualified to judge.

Upon the "wide, wallowing waves" of shifting and partially contradictory detail the main themes float apprehensibly. Blake continued to love all the forms of nature so long as they are understood to be but the phenomenal expression of the Divine Reality, and he never ceased to draw imagery from the natural world. But since "Mental Things are alone Real," there is in the later "Prophetic Books" scorn and even hatred of the symbol. Hence his disapproval of the poetry of Wordsworth who, he thought, loved the mere phenomenon and forgot the Reality of which it was but the sign. Poetry founded upon reason (Pope and Dryden); realistic art (as represented by the Venetians, Rubens, and Reynolds); rationalism (as represented by Voltaire and Rousseau); and science or "Single Vision" (of which Bacon, Newton, and Locke are the usual symbols)—all these come within the compass of Blake's indignation as agents of Urizen.

The Cosmic Warfare

The mythology of the "Prophetic Books" is a perversion of Milton's theodicy, reënforced from Job, the apocalyptic books of the Bible, and such texts as Eph. 6:12, from Boehme and Swedenborg, notions of the Neo-Platonic Trinity perhaps derived from the English Platonist Thomas Taylor, and from fragments of a long tradition of occultism. In this mythology Blake recounts the pre-mundane and supra-mundane origins of his beliefs. They are based upon his instinctive dualism; yet he was not a Manichee, for as boldly as the author of Isa. 45:7, he would have asserted that the Lord is responsible for both light and darkness, good and evil. "Without Contraries is no progression," he said; and "To be an Error and to be Cast out, is a part of God's design." [19] The recurrent theme is the War in Heaven, but the battlefield is on two planes: the cosmic and within the mind of man. Blake envisages the destiny of the universe but also (like Dante) the cycle through which the individual soul moves. The process is from Unity through Diversity to the restoration of Unity. Urizen (the Reason), rebelling against the Eternals, is cast out and fashions the world of Time and Space, subject to Law. He is the Creator (Blake often identifies him with Jehovah). He symbolizes discipline, rule, order, limitation, abstinence, asceticism, science, analysis, self, separation from the Unity which is God—who is the Imagination. The force and variety with which this concept is suggested account for the seeming ubiquity of evil and disharmony in Blake's visions. But against Urizen and his cohorts are arrayed the mighty opposites, symbols of Spiritual Freedom (Orc), Poetry (Los), Love (Enitharmon), Passion (Luvah), and other champions. The strategy is confused, but there is an ever-present sense of the mightiness of the issues at stake. The antinomianism is paramount, though only in *The Everlasting Gospel* (which is not a "Prophetic Book") and in short poems is it expressed with

---

[19] *The Marriage of Heaven and Hell; Writings,* I. 182; *A Vision of the Last Judgment; Writings,* III. 156.

no shadow of symbolism upon its clarity. But though the gratification of desire is freedom and freedom is the only good, and though the attacks upon continence, obedience, modesty, restraint, and discipline are thoroughgoing, yet there is a standard of conduct, a sanction: not an obligation imposed by church or state, but Love, symbolized in the Christ, the Saviour, and identified with the Imagination, Poetry, Art. (Blake seems not to have recognized that while the Kingdom of Love requires no Law, the absence of Law does not necessarily lead to the Kingdom of Love.) Every act of the sympathetic Imagination is a triumph over Urizen and a step in the conquest of Jerusalem. Thus the soul mounts the *Scala Perfectionis,* "the ever-varying spiral ascents to the heavens of heavens."[20] "Perfect Love casteth out fear." "Love is the fulfilling of the Law."

Blake is representative of the new age in the congenital enthusiasm of his *Blake's* temperament, his exquisite apprehension of beauty, his passion for freedom, *After-Fame* the largeness of his vision, the fascination which the supernatural exerted upon him, his faith in the imagination, his anti-intellectualism, his lyric thought. But, as he said, "Genius is always above the age"; and though not completely ignored he remained almost isolated in his time. Genuine interest in his poetry and (apart from a narrow circle) in his designs dates from the middle of the nineteenth century. His ideas were then found to be in harmony with new ethical and spiritual tendencies. His defiance of traditional morality was congenial to bold spirits. His view of Christ's message as one of joy was a protest against the Carlylean doctrine of renunciation and sorrow. His insistence upon what came to be called "fullness of life" was agreeable to the generation influenced by Swinburne and Pater. His non-orthodox mysticism appealed strongly to Rossetti,[21] and, later, to Yeats. His conviction that the Human and the Divine were One resembled that "Religion of Humanity" brought into England by the disciples of Auguste Comte. It is not insignificant that interest in him synchronized with the first real appreciation of Shelley and with the "discovery" of Walt Whitman by young Englishmen. In our own day Blake's realization of the force of the subconscious and his efforts to break down moral inhibitions have attracted new attention to him, with the consequence that in the spiritual chaos of the decades intervening between two wars there was a tendency to view him as a philosopher whose message the world must heed.[22] Even those who question this exalted status or deny it to him altogether acknowledge the perennial fascination which he exercises as poet and artist and man.

[20] *Europe; Writings,* I. 299.
[21] On the spiritual affinities of these two poets see Kerrison Preston, *Blake and Rossetti* (1944).
[22] Denis Saurat, *Blake and Modern Thought* (1929) and various studies of the last two decades listed in our bibliography; but not Osbert Burdett's biography, which supplies a valuable corrective.

IV

William Wordsworth [1]

Wordsworth's claim to preëminence among modern English poets has often been made to rest upon qualities not strictly poetical. He has been loved and revered as a far-seeing statesman, a penetrating moralist, a great critic, a philosopher, a guide and counselor to multitudes of readers. But by success in none of these rôles is a poet rightly judged. He was also a great, albeit not always dependable, artist. In recent criticism this has not always been remembered. He has been made the subject and sometimes the prey of the psychologist and the historian of ideas. The disclosure in 1916 of his French love affair provided "psychoanalytical" biographers with an explanation of his revolutionary enthusiasm, subsequent despondency, so-called "apostasy," and loss of poetic power. This explanation has not survived calm scrutiny, and today the obsession with Annette Vallon is disappearing. More important was the appearance in 1926 of the original version of *The Prelude,* a poem which had hitherto been known only as altered into conformity with the poet's later beliefs.

The Prelude—the autobiographical account of "the growth of a poet's mind"—is the primary subject of Wordsworthian studies. To satisfy himself of his capacity to write the philosophical poem on Man, Nature, and Society which he contemplated, Wordsworth felt the need to probe into his memories of the past, tracing the development of his powers. His record

[1] *Poetical Works*, ed. William Knight (11v, 1882-1886; 8v, 1896); *Poems*, ed. N. C. Smith (3v, 1908); *Poems*, ed. E. de Selincourt, I-III (1940-6), in progress, with full *apparatus criticus*; *Representative Poems*, ed. Arthur Beatty (1937); *The Prelude*, ed. E. de Selincourt (1926), texts of 1805-1806 and 1850; *Prose Works*, ed. W. Knight (2v, 1896); *Guide to the Lakes*, ed. E. de Selincourt (1906); *Letters of William and Dorothy Wordsworth*, ed. E. de Selincourt (6v, 1935-1939); *Literary Criticism*, ed. N. C. Smith (1905). — G. M. Harper, *William Wordsworth: His Life, Works, and Influence* (2v, 1916; revised, 1929); C. H. Herford, *Wordsworth* (1930); Herbert Read, *Wordsworth* (1930); H. I'A. Fausset, *The Lost Leader* (1933); Emile Legouis, *La Jeunesse de Wordsworth* (Paris, 1896), English trans., *The Early Life of William Wordsworth* (1897); G. W. Meyer, *Wordsworth's Formative Years* (Ann Arbor, 1943); critical studies: Walter Raleigh, *Wordsworth* (1909); Arthur Beatty, *William Wordsworth: His Doctrine and Art in their Historical Relations* (Madison, 1922); H. W. Garrod, *Wordsworth* (Oxford, 1927); Marian Mean, *Four Studies in Wordsworth* (1928); M. M. Rader, *Presiding Ideas in Wordsworth's Poetry* (1931); *Wordsworth and Coleridge: Studies*, ed. E. L. Griggs (Princeton, 1939); S. F. Gingerich, *Essays in the Romantic Poets* (1924); pp. 91-191; R. D. Havens, *The Mind of a Poet: a Study of Wordsworth's Thought with Particular Reference to "The Prelude"* (Baltimore, 1941); Basil Willey, *The Eighteenth Century Background* (1940), ch. XII; J. W. Beach, *The Concept of Nature*, chs. IV-VI; Eric Robertson, *Wordsworth and the English Lake Country* (1911); Lane Cooper, *Concordance* (1911). — *The Poetry of Dorothy Wordsworth*, ed. Hyman Eigerman (1940); *The Journals of Dorothy Wordsworth*, ed. E. de Selincourt (2v, 1941); C. M. MacLean, *Dorothy Wordsworth: the Early Years* (1932); E. de Selincourt, *Dorothy Wordsworth, a Biography* (1933). — *Letters of Dora Wordsworth*, ed. H. P. Vincent (1944).

must be used with circumspection. Though he realized the danger of confounding "present feelings" with those of long ago and knew that his memory transfigured even though it did not distort actuality, yet he claimed for the mind the position of "lord and master" over fact.[2] When "the consecration and the poet's dream" were added, incidents took on a deeper meaning in retrospect than they had possessed when they occurred. Not only in *The Prelude* but (with some notable exceptions in which the effect of spontaneity strikes the reader with overwhelming force) generally throughout his poetry he wrote from a point of view in after-time. Hence there is much pathos in Wordsworth, but little or no command of tragedy. He is the least dramatic of great poets. Few men and women in his pages stand out with individualized clarity. In human portraiture as in his landscapes he does not scrutinize minutely but selects the traits that appeal to him; and even these he views from a distance, as it were. He has been called a great narrative poet; but he is not, for he does not so much tell a story as dwell upon the impression of an event or character upon himself. This self-centeredness, to which Hazlitt and Keats called attention, might be repellent (as, indeed, it is to some readers) were it not that he is a figure so majestical that an understanding of his development, achievement, and decline sheds light upon his entire epoch. To resolve the ambiguities in the record is the task of the scholarship which traces Wordsworth's course from his neoclassical apprenticeship to his dominant position in romanticism, from his advocacy of revolution to his support of the established order, from his trust in the "visionary gleam" to his meek acceptance of divine grace.

The life of William Wordsworth (1770-1850) presents no such clear-cut *The Three* pattern as does Blake's. His own scheme of the Three Ages or stages in the *Ages* mental history of every individual—Childhood, the age of sensation; Youth, the age of simple ideas and emotions; Manhood, the age of complex ideas and emotions—is too much generalized to serve as an outline. What is discernible from a distance is the central, lofty plateau of the *decennium mirabile* (1797-1807). The way to this height moves from his childhood in the Lake Country, through his career as an undergraduate at Cambridge (1787-1790) and the years of *Sturm und Drang* (1791-1795), to the years of recovered serenity and assured purpose (1796-1797). At mid-point in the great decade Wordsworth married and settled at Grasmere (1802) and in the immortal *Ode* bade farewell to the visions of youth and welcomed the consolations of the "philosophic mind." The rate and gradient of ascent are not identical for Wordsworth as an artist and as a thinker. As a stylist he rose slowly and awkwardly from the low level of contemporary verse till the sudden upward movement to the heights of 1797. His progress in thought was steadier from point to point. In the descent after 1807 the reverse of this process took place. In his thinking the decline into orthodoxy was precipitate, while for another ten years in poetic power he remained al-

---

[2] Bennett Weaver, "Wordsworth's *Prelude*: the Poetic Function of Memory," *SP*, xxxiv (1937). 552-563; and "Wordsworth: Forms and Images," *SP*, xxxv (1938). 433-445.

ms

impaired. Yet poems comparable to the best work of the great decade
more and more sparsely interspersed among what Wordsworth himself
d (ominously) "valuable chains of thought." After 1817 the poetic
cline was rapid, but till about 1835 he remained, as it were, incalculable;
that is, though the reader must prepare for the worst, he can never be certain
that he may not meet with poems equal almost to the best. Such, in brief, was
the progress and regress which must now be traced more carefully.

In his earliest noteworthy poem, *The Vale of Esthwaite*[3] (1787), of interest only for some direct transcriptions of Westmorland scenery, Wordsworth mixed Gothicism and sentiment in the current mode. A little later
he began *An Evening Walk,* which is chiefly the work of his Cambridge
years. For it he borrowed material from various prose descriptions of the
Lake Country[4] and also from the bucolic poets who were in fashion in
France.[5] In style he adhered to the artificial idiom and vocabulary of the
period and in subject conformed to the conventions of regional poetry.[6]
No uninformed reader could deduce from it that already, while it was being
written, Wordsworth in the summer of 1788 had become "a dedicated
spirit," unconscious though he then was of the "vows" made for him;[7]
and that in the summer of 1790 during a walking-tour on the Continent he
had been brought into contact with revolutionary events. Of his impressions
of this tour he left two major records. That written later—part of the sixth
book of *The Prelude*—is more trustworthy than the earlier *Descriptive
Sketches,* a conventional travel poem, composed in 1792, into which he
introduced sentiments which he had not felt two years before. The conception of the Swiss as the ideal society of freemen is founded not upon his own
observations but upon his reading of Ramond de Carbonnières[8] whose eloquent prose Wordsworth paraphrases closely in several places. In style
Descriptive Sketches belongs to the school which he was afterwards to repudiate; and its mingling of history, landscape, and moral reflections is
characteristic of the not very attractive genre of which it is a favorable
specimen.

On leaving Cambridge early in 1791[9] Wordsworth passed four months
in London and then went for a second time to France. Here he lived till
the fall of 1792, pausing but briefly in Paris and remaining for long periods

[3] Long thought to be lost. See Ernest de Selincourt, *The Early Wordsworth* (1936).

[4] Especially William Gilpin, *Observations on the Mountains and Lakes of Cumberland and
and Westmorland* (1786).

[5] Rosset, *L'Agriculture* (1774 and 1782), Roucher, *Les Mois* (1779), Delille, *Les Jardins*
(1780), and other poems.

[6] R. A. Aubin, *Topographical Poetry in the Eighteenth Century* (1936), pp. 217-219;
Christopher Hussey, *The Picturesque* (1927), ch. IV: "Picturesque Travel."

[7] *The Prelude,* IV, 309-338. (All references to *The Prelude* are to the line-numbering in
the text of 1850).

[8] To a lesser extent Wordsworth was also indebted to William Coxe, *Sketches of Swisserland*
(1779), of which Ramond's book is a translation "augmentée des observations faites par le
traducteur" (1781). See C. E. Engel, *La littérature alpestre en France et en Angleterre aux
xviii° et xix° siècles* (Chambéry, 1930), Part II, ch. V, and Part III, ch. II.

[9] On Wordsworth's environment at the University see D. A. Winstanley, *Unreformed
Cambridge, a Study of Certain Aspects of the University in the Eighteenth Century* (1935).

at Orleans and Blois. The magnificent chateaux of the region stirred him *France* to imaginative sympathy with the aristocratic life of the past, but friendship *and* with Michel Beaupuy, an officer in the revolutionary army, brought him to *Annette* the popular side.[10] Of the love of Wordsworth for Annette Vallon little need *Vallon* be said.[11] To them a daughter, Caroline, was born in December, 1792. Want of funds forced Wordsworth to return to England. His uncles, however, refused to supply him with money or to help in any way to regularize the liaison. War intervened and he was shut off from France,[12] though he remained in occasional communication with Annette. The view that in later years he was plagued with remorse which he sublimated by writing poems about forsaken women and unmarried mothers has little to commend it.[13]

But anxiety for Annette and Caroline deepened Wordsworth's despond- *Godwinism* ency when, once more in London, he watched the Revolution degenerate into the Reign of Terror. England's entry into the war against France shocked him as a betrayal of the cause of liberty, and to it he ascribed the opportunity afforded the extremists in Paris to seize the reins of power. Under the influence of the radicals who frequented Joseph Johnson's book-shop [14] he continued work on *Guilt and Sorrow*,[15] a poem begun in 1791. In using the Spenserian stanza instead of the couplet and in striving for simplicity of language and syntax, Wordsworth evinced dissatisfaction with the neo-classical tradition. The intertwined stories of a soldier's destitute widow and of a discharged soldier who is driven by penury to crime expose the miseries of war, the injustices of the penal code, and the wrongs inflicted by the privileged upon the defenseless poor. This indictment of society is Godwinian. To the same period (1793) belongs the *Letter to the Bishop of Llandaff*,[16] which is really a reply to Burke. Bishop Richard Watson, defending the established social order, had expounded in a sermon the wisdom and justice of God in creating rich and poor. In his noble pamphlet Wordsworth admitted that to put power into the hands of the people before they were ready to wield it wisely might be, as the Terror showed, only a change in the forms of tyranny. But he defended the republican principle, blaming upon iniquitous institutions that "terrific reservoir of guilt and ignorance" [17]

10 On the character and opinions of Michel-Armand Beaupuy see *The Prelude*, IX. 288-552. On Wordsworth and the French Revolution see, in addition to authorities already cited, Sir H. J. C. Grierson, *Milton and Wordsworth* (1937), ch. VII.

11 See, in addition to all the biographies published since Professor Harper's disclosure of the story in 1916, Émile Legouis, *William Wordsworth and Annette Vallon* (1922) and *Wordsworth in a New Light* (1923).

12 There is some evidence that he returned to France in the autumn of 1793. If he did so, he ran a great risk and there is no evidence that he saw Annette. See G. M. Harper, "Did Wordsworth Defy the Guillotine?", *The Quarterly Review*, CCXLVIII (1927). 254-264, and letters in *LTLS*, May 1 and 29 and June 12, 1930.

13 These poems are *The Ruined Cottage* (afterwards imbedded in *The Excursion*, I. 871-916), *The Thorn*, and *Ruth*.

14 Johnson published *An Evening Walk* and *Descriptive Sketches* (both 1793).

15 This poem was repeatedly revised. The present ending with the soldier's acceptance of his death as an expiation probably takes the place of an original condemnation of capital punishment. See O. J. Campbell and Paul Mueschke, "Wordsworth's *Guilt and Sorrow*," *MP*, XXIII (1926). 293-306; and R. D. Havens' comments, *RES*, III (1927). 71-73.

16 First published in *Prose Works*, ed, Grosart, I. 3-23.

17 *The Prelude*, X. 476-480.

which must burst and flood the land before a new order, based upon political justice, could be secured. The comments upon hereditary privileges, the laws for the protection of property, the penal code, and the miseries of war expressed the sentiments of the English radicals. It is unknown whether this letter was sent to Watson. It was not published. To have advertised an open alliance with the extremists might have cut short a career as a poet before it was well begun.

Forced by his radical convictions to suppress his patriotic instincts and to condone the Terror, Wordsworth was in an unhappy state of mind. He attempted a satire on Pitt and English society but soon abandoned it. Gradually he was tempted into the region of abstract Godwinian speculation; but reliance upon syllogistic reasoning brought him to the point where he "yielded up moral questions in despair." [18] The distrust of logic is not, however, to be understood as a repudiation of "Reason in her highest mood"; there is the same distinction which Kant had drawn and Coleridge was to draw between the "higher" reason and the understanding.[19] From the slough of despond into which he fell in 1793 Wordsworth extricated himself with painful slowness. It is impossible to trace here the course of his spiritual convalescence. The transition came in the autumn of 1795 when, having settled at Racedown with his sister Dorothy,[20] he turned from France and Godwin to a political philosophy more in harmony with Burke, and to the loveliness of the natural world. Dorothy's companionship and a legacy which relieved his financial anxieties played their parts in this recovery. Thwarted political enthusiasm was turned into imaginative channels; and in 1796-1797 he wrote the tragedy of *The Borderers*.[21] This laborious effort in the "German" fashion is of slight moment as drama but of much as a milestone on Wordsworth's progress. The story of the villain Oswald who, after committing a crime, banishes remorse by condemning all human feeling as weakness and thus becomes a malignant moral skeptic is intended to demonstrate that though the attempt to live by the light of reason may be a noble aspiration, yet to discard affections and "prejudices" leaves not reason but the passions supreme. The play is, moreover, not merely a negation of Godwinism but an affirmation of the reconciliation of man and nature.[22]

"Despondency Corrected"

The poet had met Coleridge in 1795, and by the summer of 1797, when the Wordsworths moved to Alfoxden, near Nether Stowey where Coleridge lived, the friendship had ripened into intimacy. Coleridge's influence gradually "turned Wordsworth's work from fragmentary descrip-

---

[18] *The Prelude*, XI. 305.

[19] J. W. Beach, "Reason and Nature in Wordsworth," *JHI*, I (1940). 335-351.

[20] Bergen Evans and Hester Pinney, "Racedown and the Wordsworths," *RES*, VIII (1932). 1-18.

[21] Not published till 1842. No early draft exists to show how much it was revised. A preface, long believed to be lost, has been recovered; see E. de Selincourt, *Oxford Lectures on Poetry* (1934), pp. 157-179.

[22] O. J. Campbell and Paul Mueschke, "*The Borderers* as a Document in the History of Wordsworth's Aesthetic Development," *MP*, XXIII (1925-1926). 465-482.

tions of impressions and emotions into the expression of a comprehensive *The Influ-*
philosophy." [23] Whether through this guidance or from independent *ence of*
reading. Wordsworth had now absorbed the associationist philosophy of *Hartley*
David Hartley's *Observations on Man* [24] (1749). This type of empiricism, which denies the existence of innate ideas, teaches that all sense
impressions originate in external things. Through the power of association the simple ideas deriving from sensation combine into larger and
more highly organized units. Hence the character of a man's higher
ideas is determined by the character of his sensations; the "sense" is the
guardian of the heart and soul of the moral being.[25] Each faculty of the
mind is produced by a transformation of the faculty next below it in rank;
and at the summit is the moral sense. The three-fold hierarchy of sensations,
simple ideas, and complex ideas Wordsworth found to correspond to the
Three Ages or stages in mental development. When he wrote of those
sensations which pass from the "blood" into the "heart" (or feelings) and
thence into the mind he was expounding Hartley's psychology.[26] But according to Hartley, the mind has no control over the physical or mechanical
necessity by which it acts; he allows it the power of classifying ideas into
categories of pleasure and pain, but nothing else. In Wordsworth's view, on the
other hand, though experience may be merely passive and in that case the
theory is necessitarian, this is not always the case; the influence of natural
objects may depend in part upon us; we are then not merely passive recipients but "half create" that which we perceive.[27] This belief may become
a claim for the superior validity of imaginative experience over the data
communicated by sense. In other words, Wordsworth imposed upon associationism a Platonic principle of mystical insight—"another gift of aspect
more sublime." [28]

During the year at Alfoxden Wordsworth and Coleridge, in revolt from *Lyrical*
the contorted and artificial phrasing of contemporary verse, evolved the *Ballads*

---

[23] See the excellent review of Wordsworth's state of mind when he met Coleridge and of the
immediate influence of each poet upon the other in Lawrence Hanson, *The Life of Coleridge:
the Early Years* (1939), pp. 163-202. The opinion that each poet was incomplete without
the other is well stated in F. W. Bateson, "Wordsworth and Coleridge," in *From Anne to
Victoria*, ed. Bonamy Dobrée (1937), pp. 546-559.
[24] Wordsworth's debt to Hartley was first fully demonstrated in Arthur Beatty, *William
Wordsworth: His Doctrine and Art* (1922). Beatty summarizes his argument in the introduction to his edition of *Representative Poems*. An important corrective to this view is Melvin
Rader, "The Transcendentalism of William Wordsworth," *MP*, xxvi (1928-1929). 169-190.
See also J. D. Rea, "Coleridge's Intimations of Immortality from Proclus," *MP*, xxvi (1928-
1929). 201-213. Both articles emphasize the anti-associationist elements in Wordsworth's
thought. Other influences than Hartley are brought out in N. P. Stallknecht, "Wordsworth and
Philosophy," *PMLA*, xl (1925). 346-361. For the "neo-humanistic" attack upon Wordsworth's
naturalism see Barry Cerf, "Wordsworth's Gospel of Nature," *PMLA* xxxvii (1922). 615-638,
to which J. W. Beach offers an "Expostulation and Reply," *ibid.*, xl (1925). 346-361. See
also O. J. Campbell and Paul Mueschke, "Wordsworth's Aesthetic Development, 1796-1802,"
Essays and Studies in English and Comparative Literature (Ann Arbor, 1933), pp. 1-57.
[25] *Lines Composed a Few Miles above Tintern Abbey*, lines 108-111.
[26] *Ibid.*, lines 28-29.
[27] Coleridge goes further: "We receive but what we give" (*Dejection: an Ode*, line 47).
[28] *Tintern Abbey*, lines 36-37. Compare Lascelles Abercrombie (*Romanticism*, p. 63): "The
power of the unknown can only reside within. The senses can but deal with what they know."

theory (towards which Coleridge had long been moving and which had connections with associationism) that poetry should be written in "a selection from the real language of men in a state of vivid sensation"; [29] and in accordance with this theory and with Hartley's psychology they composed many of the poems on rustic and humble life collected in *Lyrical Ballads* (1798). The as yet unnamed *Prelude* was conceived to justify or, more happily, remove the misgivings which Wordsworth felt as to his strength for a yet greater task, *The Recluse, or Views on Man, Nature, and Society.* Of this the autobiographical poem was at first planned as a part; but it grew to independent proportions.[30] After a long interruption there was continuous work in 1804 and it was completed in 1805. As originally planned *The Prelude* had only five books and culminated in the "consecration" episode of 1788. But Wordsworth realized the need to carry the story through the two sojourns on the Continent, the Revolution, life in London, despondency, and release; and he added nine books more. In so doing he enriched *The Prelude* but impoverished *The Recluse* where much of this material might have been used to good advantage.

In broad outline the pattern of *The Prelude* is suggested in the *Lines Composed a Few Miles above Tintern Abbey,* the incomparably beautiful result of a walking-tour in June, 1798. This was inserted at the very end of *Lyrical Ballads with a few other Poems* [31] which Joseph Cottle of Bristol published in September. With this off their hands, the Wordsworths and Coleridge set sail for Germany. Having separated from their companion, Wordsworth and Dorothy passed a somewhat dull and lonely winter at Goslar.[32] To this period belong various narrative pieces afterwards incorporated in *The Prelude,* and the cycle of five poems commemorative of "Lucy." There has been much speculation as to her identity. Coleridge's idea that the poems reflect Wordsworth's love for Dorothy must certainly be rejected. Efforts to discover an English girl whom he had loved and lost have been fruitless. The view that "Lucy" is purely ideal and imaginary must overcome the not insuperable objection that seldom, if ever, elsewhere does Wordsworth display such objective power. It has been shown that the region of "the springs of Dove" was a commonplace in ballad topography and that the name "Lucy" was conventional in elegies. The exquisite little cycle may therefore be regarded as the poet's evocation in an uncongenial foreign city of an ideal that is simple, humble, rustic, and English.

Returning to England in the spring of 1799, the Wordsworths after some

The "Lucy" Poems

---

[29] See Mrs. M. L. Greenbie, *Wordsworth's Theory of Poetic Diction* (1917).

[30] Garrod's opinion that *The Prelude* was begun at Racedown in 1797 is contested by D. H. Bishop, who holds that the beginning was at Grasmere in 1799. See D. H. Bishop, "Wordsworth's 'Hermitage,' Racedown or Grasmere?", *SP,* XXXII (1935). 483-507, and "The Origin of *The Prelude* and the Composition of Books I and II," *SP,* XXXVIII (1941). 494-520.

[31] Facsimile ed. (Oxford, 1926).

[32] That the influence of German literature and culture upon Wordsworth, at this time and earlier and later, was comparatively slight is shown by M. J. Herzberg, "William Wordsworth and German Literature," *PMLA,* XL (1925). 302-345.

wandering settled at Dove Cottage on the outskirts of Grasmere.[33] In the Grasmere
summer Wordsworth and Coleridge were engaged upon the enlarged second
edition of *Lyrical Ballads* (1800) which included, besides *Michael,* the finest
of the "pastorals," the preface which grew out of Wordsworth's realization
that it was necessary to educate his readers by explanation as well as examples of his work. Here, in a central paragraph, is a concentrated statement
of his convictions and intentions: to draw material for poetry from humble
and rustic life because on that social level the "essential passions" are "less
under restraint"; to set forth the chosen incidents in a selection from the
language really used by men; to throw over them "a certain colouring of
the imagination"; and to trace in them "the primary laws of our nature."

Save for work on *The Prelude* and on the fragment of *The Recluse* which
(apart from the magnificent Proem) was not published till 1888, the year
1801 was comparatively barren. The state of Coleridge's health caused increasing anxiety; and Wordsworth was conducting his courtship of Mary
Hutchinson. But 1802 was an eventful year. *The Leech-Gatherer,* renamed
Resolution and Independence, of which the germ is recognizable in Dorothy's Journal in September, 1800, was composed, and the *Ode on Intimations* 1802
of Immortality was begun. The Peace of Amiens provided the opportunity
for a final settlement with Annette Vallon; and in July Wordsworth and
Dorothy met her at Calais. Association with his old love and with their
child Caroline heightened by contrast the poet's devotion to his own country,
and this was rendered the more ardent by his increasing distrust of Napoleon's ambitions. The mood had found voice before his departure from
England; it reached a climax at Calais; and was still strong upon him for
a while after his return. Impassioned protests against Napoleon's suppression of liberty in nations and individuals mingle with exhortations to England to be worthy of her past glory and of the "exultations, agonies, love,
and man's unconquerable mind" which are her great allies. Yet there is a
clear-sighted recognition of England's spiritual weakness. "O Grief"—not
"O Joy"—he exclaims, "O Grief, that earth's best hopes rest all in thee!"
These *Sonnets Dedicated to National Independence and Liberty* are a spontaneous overflow of patriotic feeling without parallel in English literature
since Milton.[34]

Wordsworth married Mary Hutchinson on October 4, 1802, and on that Farewell to
day Coleridge published *Dejection: an Ode,* which has an obvious affinity Childhood
to the *Ode on Intimations of Immortality.* In the latter poem the preëxistence
theme, which Wordsworth probab'y derived from Coleridge and which is
scarcely more than mythological machinery, has the unfortunate effect of
falsifying the poet's characteristic view of Nature and degrading her into
the rôle of a foster-mother who weans the child from recollection of the
heavenly mansions whence he came. More fundamental is the theme of the

---

[33] When Dove Cottage became too small for Wordsworth's family, he moved twice and
finally, in 1813, settled at Rydal Mount.
[34] Amid these patriotic utterances the only sonnet bearing directly upon Wordsworth's
personal affairs is that addressed to his daughter, beginning "It is a beauteous evening."

Three Ages which relates the *Ode* to the *Tintern Abbey* lines and to *The Prelude*; and it is with certain passages in *The Prelude* in mind that it is to be interpreted. In intimacy with the natural world Wordsworth had found the corrective to despondency; the beauty of natural objects had made "sorrow and despair from ruin and from change" seem but "an idle dream."[35] These experiences of contact and response had been peculiarly vivid in childhood. His effort now was to recapture in recollection those "spots of time"[36] so that he could draw "invigorating thought from former years."[37] The consciousness that this power of immediate apprehension was passing from him he expressed with poignant foreboding:

> The soul,
> Remembering how she felt, but what she felt
> Remembering not, retains an obscure sense
> Of possible sublimity;[38]

and again:

> I see by glimpses now; when age comes on
> May scarcely see at all.[39]

In the light of these passages the *Ode* is seen to be a farewell to the past and an impassioned celebration of the vitality of childhood.[40] The assertion that for the lost gift of apprehension the years have brought "abundant recompense" in the consolations of the philosophic mind does not carry complete conviction.[41]

On a tour of Scotland in 1803, whence he returned with the exquisite *Highland Reaper* and other *Memorials,* Wordsworth met Sir Walter Scott, whose influence is apparent in the *Song at the Feast of Brougham Castle* (1807) and other poems. The loss at sea of his beloved brother John Wordsworth (1805) is the "deep distress" which, in the *Elegiac Stanzas on a Picture of Peele Castle,* has "humanized" the poet's soul, making him aware of the stormy reality of life which contrasts with the poetic dreams of youth. With this brother (and perhaps Beaupuy and Lord Nelson) in mind he wrote *The Character of the Happy Warrior,* and in the same mood the *Ode to Duty.* The three poems are closely related. In the *Ode to Duty* the romantic conviction of the inherent goodness of man has declined into a belief that though there are some *schöne Seelen* whom Nature "saves from wrong," most men must depend for guidance upon the sense of Duty, "stern daughter of the voice of God." The *Happy Warrior* affords a specific illustration of this doctrine.

These pieces, with the political sonnets, the *Memorials of a Tour in Scot-*

[35] *The Excursion,* I. 949-952.
[36] *The Prelude,* XII. 208.
[37] *Ibid.,* I. 621.
[38] *Ibid.,* II. 315-318.
[39] *Ibid.,* XII. 281-282.
[40] A. C. Babenroth, *English Childhood: Wordsworth's Treatment of Childhood in the Light of English Poetry from Prior to Crabbe* (1922).
[41] On the structure and prosody of the *Ode* see Oliver Elton, *Survey of English Literature, 1780-1830* (1920), II. 78.

land, and much else, were published in *Poems in Two Volumes* (1807). The collection marks the culmination of Wordsworth's work and the end of the great decade. His reading of the finished *Prelude* to Coleridge at this time thus takes on a symbolic significance: his youth is rounded out. A friendship of several years' standing with Sir George Beaumont, a wealthy patron of the arts, now furthered the drift towards conservatism, and in Coleridge's absence Wordsworth was also drawn closer to Southey, with the same consequences. The course of Napoleon's tyrannical progress through Europe had forced upon the poet a re-orientation of his political and social ideas. The change is marked in the prose tract on *The Convention of Cintra* [42] (1809) in which, while indicating with Miltonic eloquence England's place and duty in the comity of nations, Wordsworth enunciated an anti-democratic doctrine of leadership which foreshadows the "hero-worship" of Carlyle.[43] A respect for tradition which owes much to Burke, a growing affection for the past as enshrined in English institutions, awakened his sense of the political value of the ecclesiastical Establishment and a reverence for the means whereby Christianity has given formal expression to religious concepts. Trust in the inner "gleam" yielded to the acceptance of divine grace through the mediation of the Church. These changes brought to a close Wordsworth's early turbulent spiritual life. His "anticlimax" was at hand.[44] To what degree this decline—for despite special pleading [45] the fact of the decline is undeniable—was due to psychological disturbances resulting from the French love affair and its long aftermath, or to the alienation from Coleridge, or to the acceptance of conservatism, or to an awareness that the themes for poetry to which he had committed himself were exhausted, or merely to a weakening in inspiration not without parallels in the case of other poets approaching middle life, or to all these causes combined, is a debated question which does not admit of a solution acceptable to everyone.

The Decline

The great task of the succeeding years was *The Excursion* (1814), the central portion of the never finished *Recluse.* The first two books, which were written in 1797, are fastened to what follows rather than fused with it. There is not only a shift in topography but a change in mood; the spirit of social protest and of oneness with the cause of the poor and outcast, expressed at the beginning, disappears, and in the later books Wordsworth seems to look with complacency upon their sufferings, content with the promise of a heavenly recompense for earthly trials. Such was the view of Bishop Watson whom the poet had formerly refuted so passionately. *The Excursion* exhibits a dichotomy not only in structure but in themes; there is a cleavage but awkwardly bridged between those portions which deal

The Excursion

---

[42] Ed. A. V. Dicey (1915). See A. V. Dicey, *The Statesmanship of Wordsworth* (1917), a study reflecting the crisis amid which it was written but still of value.

[43] See B. H. Lehman, *Carlyle's Theory of the Hero* (Durham, N. C., 1928), pp. 138-144.

[44] See W. L. Sperry, *Wordsworth's Anti-Climax* (Cambridge, Mass., 1935).

[45] See Edith Batho, *The Later Wordsworth* (1933); Mary E. Burton, *The One Wordsworth* (Chapel Hill, 1942).

with high metaphysicalities and those which recount rather flatly the simple annals of the poor. As in the narrative, so in the style there is a jarring contrast between the homeliness of these stories and the Miltonic sublimity of the speculative passages. Wordsworth was probably insensitive to this disharmony. He heard "humanity in fields and groves pipe solitary anguish" and for this misery he offered counsel and consolation. But the transitions from the one mood to the other, from the chronicler of humble life to the rapt affirmer of immortal glory, are too abrupt. The need for modulation is not satisfied. The general pietistic tone of the poem contrasts strangely with the magnificent Proem or *Prospectus* in which the poet with mystic confidence passes Jehovah and his angels "unalarmed" and ascends to

> breathe in worlds
> To which the heaven of heavens is but a veil.

The four principal characters are but so many aspects or facets of Wordsworth himself: the Poet, who is for the most part a silent listener; the Wanderer, to whom are assigned most of the arguments supporting Christian optimism; the Pastor, who tells the stories of the departed dalesmen; and the Solitary, a disillusioned rationalist who is what Wordsworth, but for the grace of God, might have been, and whose function is to state objections to religious faith in order that they may be refuted by his companions. In the colloquies among these four Wordsworth resumes the argument advanced by Pope in the *Essay on Man*. In the vast Chain of Being man has his appointed place. The defectiveness of his faculties is appropriate to his position in the scale.[46] The principle of universal harmony, an optimistic necessitarianism, supports the argument that "what may seem ill from a restricted point of view is seen to be good by reference to the design and intention of the whole." [47] The "final causes of natural things"—that is to say, the ends which God has in mind—must be kept in view. Wordsworth widens the scope of Pope's argument, resting it not only upon experience but upon faith. He proves nothing except that he is himself convinced.[48] To apply to *The Excursion* the touchstones of great poetry recommended by Wordsworth himself is a profitable exercise of the critical intelligence. In the preface to the collected edition of his poems (1815) he listed the "powers requisite for the production of poetry." These are: Observation and Description; Sensibility; Reflection; Imagination and Fancy; Invention; and Judgment. The list is as illuminating for what is omitted as for what it contains; but if these criteria, such as they are, are applied to *The Excursion* it becomes apparent that some of these requisite powers are absent and others disproportionately relied upon.

Wordsworth followed the *Song at the Feast of Brougham Castle* (1807) with *The White Doe of Rylstone* (1815). Though these poems show some affinity to Scott's metrical romances, the resemblances to typical antiquarian

[46] See A. O. Lovejoy, "Optimism and Romanticism," *PMLA*, XLII (1927). 921-945.
[47] J. W. Beach, *The Concept of Nature*, p. 176.
[48] G. M. Harper, *William Wordsworth* (1916), II. 224.

poems are only superficial. Wordsworth was not interested in re-creating the past or in the action of his tales. *Brougham Castle* celebrates the advantages of a life in communion with nature; *The White Doe* exposes the futility of the life of action and recommends a wise passiveness as the cure for sorrow.[49] A new departure, foreshadowed by passages in earlier poems and supported by sympathetic allusions in *The Excursion* to the value of pagan myths as symbols of the religious imagination,[50] was made in *Laodamia* (1814) and *Dion* (1816).[51] The Virgilian tone of wistful beauty and austere melancholy in the former poem is profoundly authentic and deeply moving. In the advocacy of rational self-discipline some readers may detect a rebuke to the poet's own passionate youth. The alteration in his conception of Laodamia's fate in the other world—a "weak pity" for her in the original version giving place in the later to righteous condemnation and retribution—is indicative of the change coming over Wordsworth's temperament and outlook. In these poems Wordsworth re-created mythological poetry and established a tradition which his successors from Keats to Bridges were to follow.

The Preface of 1815 contains the memorable distinction (pointing back *Expanding* to discussions with Coleridge many years earlier and forward to the *Bio-* *Fame* *graphia Literaria*) between the Imagination, which is serious and penetrating and detects moral associations, and the Fancy, which is frivolous and arbitrary. *Peter Bell,* a poem of 1797 long withheld from publication, appeared in 1819 and provoked much ridicule. But the poet had now triumphed over earlier neglect. The expansion of his fame after 1814-1815 is shown by Leigh Hunt's estimate of him not only as the greatest of living poets but as the founder and leader of a school of naturalistic poetry which succeeded the artificial poetry of the preceding era. Among the disciples of this new school Hunt numbered not only himself but Keats; and, indeed, the influence of Wordsworth in general and of *The Excursion* in particular was strong upon Keats. It is obvious also in Shelley's poetry and for a time in Byron's. On his visits to London the reverence with which the members of Hunt's circle regarded Wordsworth as a poet was strongly tinged with dislike because of his egotism.[52] In the wider world his fame was growing as teacher and moralist; the "healing power" of his poetry was exerting a benignant influence.

The didactic and austere sonnets, *The River Duddon* (1820), derive little from regional legend, for there was little to be found, and owe to Coleridge's projected but never written poem, *The Brook,* the idea of tracing a stream from its mountain source to the sea. The metaphor of the stream

[49] C. B. Bradford, "Wordsworth's *White Doe of Rylstone* and Related Poems," *MP*, xxxvi (1938). 59-70.
[50] *The Excursion*, iv. 718-762; 847-887; vi. 538-547.
[51] Douglas Bush, *Mythology and the Romantic Tradition in English Poetry* (Cambridge, Mass., 1937), pp. 56-70. (Hereinafter referred to as Bush).
[52] Wordsworth saw a good deal of the painter Benjamin Robert Haydon (1786-1846) in these years and addressed three sonnets to him. The impressions of the poet in Haydon's *Autobiography and Journals* are vivid and valuable.

The Last Phase

was employed to bind together the *Ecclesiastical Sonnets* [53] (1822), Wordsworth's homage to tradition and the Established Church. Gleams of the old splendor appear fitfully in both these series. Meanwhile, *Memorials of a Tour on the Continent* (1820) were laborious and solemn records and impressions of a journey through France and Italy.[54] Much time in later years was expended upon the revision of *The Prelude* and upon the preparation of successive editions of the collected works. *Yarrow Revisited* (1835) and *Poems, Chiefly of Early and Late Years* (1842) were the last new publications. During the last two decades Wordsworth's continued interest in public affairs took generally the form of a dread of change. He professed an interest in Chartism; but he opposed parliamentary reform, holding that the extension of the suffrage would put power into the hands of men who would proceed quickly to violence. He opposed the emancipation of Catholics, the secret ballot, and even the abolition of capital punishment for various minor offenses. His sister's tragic lapse into premature senility and a daughter's death were devastating blows under which his fortitude bowed. Always austere and repressed, he now drooped sadly.[55] There are many extant records of the gloom of Rydal Mount in these last years. He died on April 23, 1850, and was buried in Grasmere Churchyard.

[53] Ed. A. B. Potts (1922).

[54] A later tour (1837) which Wordsworth made in the company of Henry Crabb Robinson, the diarist, was not productive of any poetry. Robinson (1777-1867) was a friend of the entire Wordsworth-Coleridge circle and of many other celebrities of the age. In his voluminous diaries he has left invaluable records and impressions of innumerable people. See Edith J. Morley, *The Life and Times of Henry Crabb Robinson* (1935); *Correspondence with the Wordsworth Family*, ed. E. J. Morley (2v, 1927); *Henry Crabb Robinson on Books and their Writers*, ed. E. J. Morley (2v, 1938).

[55] On the death of Southey in 1843 Wordsworth accepted the post of poet laureate but on condition that he should not be expected to produce "official" poems. The only such poem published under his name was actually written by his son-in-law. — For the last phase of his life see Frederika Beatty, *William Wordsworth of Rydal Mount: an Account of the Poet and his Friends in the Last Decade* (1939).

V

Samuel Taylor Coleridge

The verdict passed upon Coleridge [1] that his legacy to posterity consists of "a handful of golden poems" and "a will-o'-the-wisp light to bemused thinkers" [2] is one-half disputable, but it points the contrast between the radiant months of 1797-1798 (with their afterglow in 1802) when most of the "golden poems" were written and the long years before and after when Coleridge followed the light, often flickering and uncertain, of philosophy. From his youth up he was both poet and philosopher; the "inspired Charity-boy" of Lamb's famous reminiscence [3] was "metaphysician" as well as "bard"; and though lovers of poetry may regret that the fertile gardens of Xanadu were abandoned for "the holy jungle of metaphysics," it must be remembered that Coleridge conceived as part of his life work the fructification of receptive minds. Not only through his writings but through his talk [4] he impressed his ideas upon such contemporaries as Wordsworth, Hazlitt, and De Quincey and upon younger men of promise, including even John Stuart Mill and the recalcitrant Carlyle. How fruitful was the impregnation is obvious in many fields of inquiry: in the theory and practice of literary criticism, the theory of the state, psychology, the interpretation of German

Metaphy-sician and Bard

---

[1] There is no definitive edition. *Complete Works*, ed. W. G. T. Shedd (7v, 1858); *Complete Poetical Works*, ed. E. H. Coleridge (2v, Oxford, 1912); *Biographia Literaria*, ed. John Shawcross (2v, Oxford, 1907); *Literary Remains*, ed. H. N. Coleridge (4v, 1836-1839); *Anima Poetae*, from the unpublished Note-books, ed. E. H. Coleridge (1895); *Specimens of the Table-Talk*, ed. H. N. Coleridge (2v, 1835); *Shakespearean Criticism*, ed. T. M. Raysor (2v, 1930); *Miscellaneous Criticism*, ed. T. M. Raysor (1936); *Literary Criticism*, ed. J. W. Mackail (1931), a selection; *Select Poems*, ed. A. J. George (Boston, 1905); *Select Poetry and Prose*, ed. Stephen Potter (1933); *Coleridge on Logic and Learning*, ed. A. D. Snyder (New Haven, 1929); *Treatise on Method*, ed. A. D. Snyder (1934); *Letters*, ed. E. H. Coleridge (2v, 1895); *Unpublished Letters*, ed. E. L. Griggs (2v, New Haven, 1933). — T. J. Wise, *Bibliography* (1913) and *Coleridgiana* (1919); V. W. Kennedy, *Bibliography* (Baltimore, 1935); Lawrence Hanson, *The Life of S. T. Coleridge: the Early Years* (1939); Sir Edmund Chambers, *Samuel Taylor Coleridge* (1938); J. Dykes Campbell, *Samuel Taylor Coleridge, a Narrative of the Events of his Life* (1894); H. I'A. Fausset, *Coleridge* (1926); John Charpentier, *Coleridge, the Sublime Somnambulist*, trans. by M. V. Nugent (1929); J. H. Muirhead, *Coleridge as Philosopher* (1930); A. D. Snyder, *The Critical Principle of the Reconciliation of Opposites as employed by Coleridge* (Ann Arbor, 1918); R. W. White, *The Political Thought of S. T. Coleridge* (1938); C. R. Sanders, *Coleridge and the Broad Church Movement* (Durham, N. C., 1942); *Coleridge: Studies by Several Hands*, ed. Edmund Blunden and E. L. Griggs (1934); *Wordsworth and Coleridge: Studies*, ed. E. L. Griggs (Princeton, 1939); S. F. Gingerich, *Essays in the Romantic Poets* (1924), pp. 17-87; L. W. Willoughby, "Coleridge as a Philologist," *MLR*, xxxi (1936). 176-201; Walter Graham, "Contemporary Critics of Coleridge the Poet," *PMLA*, xxxviii (1923). 278-289.

[2] Sir Edmund Chambers, *Coleridge*, p. 331.

[3] *Essays of Elia: Christ's Hospital Five-and-Thirty Years Ago.*

[4] R. W. Armour and R. F. Howes, *Coleridge the Talker. A Series of Contemporary Descriptions and Comments* (Ithaca, N. Y., 1939). The introduction discusses Coleridge's technique as a conversationalist.

romantic philosophy, the reconciliation of Trinitarian Christianity with Neo-Platonic thought, and other speculative problems. The immense and intense, albeit undisciplined, mental activity which lay behind both the written and the spoken word has been too much obscured by the record of irresponsibility in practical affairs, of grandiose plans unrealized, of promises broken and pledges unredeemed. The friends who, yielding to the fascination of his personality, gave him financial assistance which he was all too willing to accept seem not to have considered their investment wholly unprofitable. This fact must be set against Southey's harsh strictures, Lamb's mockery of the good intentions of the "archangel somewhat damaged," the anxieties and disappointments of the Wordsworths, and Coleridge's oft-repeated self-reproaches.

Samuel Taylor Coleridge (1772-1834), the precocious and dreamy youngest son of a Devonshire clergyman, had acquired many of his lifelong traits of character by the age of ten when he entered Christ's Hospital school. Already he was willing to cadge for small sums of money; already he was planning for himself careers beyond his powers of realization. The faculty of winning friends and the need for affection and the ability to evoke it were conspicuous. At school began the friendship with Charles Lamb, lifelong and but once momentarily clouded over. Already a "library cormorant" (as he later called himself), he was in the process of substantiating his later assertion that he had read almost everything and was "deep in all out of the way books." He discovered the Neo-Platonists [5] and unfolded to admiring auditors "the mysteries of Iamblicus." His earliest sonnets, feeble in sentiment, and diction, and structure, were his response to the influence of William Lisle Bowles,[6] in whose insipidities he discerned a sincere nature poetry uncontaminated by fashionable artifice. From the shackles of the contemporary mode Coleridge, however, was not himself free. His addiction to "turgid ode and tumid stanza," [7] clogged with pompous rhetoric and frigid personification, is evident in the *Destruction of the Bastille* (1789), in which he expressed radical political sentiment, and in the *Monody on the Death of Chatterton* which was later (1794) completely rewritten.

Coleridge entered Cambridge in January, 1791, with a reputation for astonishing erudition; but almost at once his career there became so erratic as to disappoint his friends. There is some evidence of fast living. There were indiscretions when he aired opinions which were republican in politics

---

[5] It is possible, though not proved, that Coleridge knew at this time the translations of Plotinus and Proclus by Thomas Taylor "the Platonist" (1758-1835). He read Taylor's works later, but was already able to read the Neo-Platonists in the original Greek. On Taylor, who also influenced Wordsworth, Blake, and Shelley, see F. B. Evans, "Thomas Taylor, Platonist," *PMLA*, LV (1940), 1060-1079, and authorities there cited.

[6] The Rev. W. L. Bowles (1762-1850) published in 1789 *Fourteen Sonnets* notable for simplicity of diction, purity of form, and sensitiveness of observation, though they lacked sturdiness of thought. His later, longer poems—*The Spirit of Discovery* (1804), *The Grave of the Last Saxon* (1822), and others—are forgotten. *Poetical Works*, ed. George Gilfillan (2v, 1855); Garland Greever, *A Wiltshire Parson and his Friends: the Correspondence of W. L. Bowles* (1926). For his controversy with Byron over the merits of Pope's poetry see ch. XI., note 33, below. — Coleridge was also influenced by Charlotte Smith's *Elegiac Sonnets* (1784).

[7] Byron, *English Bards and Scotch Reviewers*, line 256.

and Unitarian in theology. Debts piled up; from study he was distracted by his love for Mary Evans (whom he had met while still at school); and in December, 1793, he suddenly left the university. The serio-comic episode of his enlistment in the dragoons followed. From this predicament he was rescued by his family and reinstated in Cambridge. In the summer of 1794 came, at Oxford, the first meeting with Robert Southey. The two young *Meeting* men, both infected with radical doctrine, were soon deep in plans to emi- *with* grate to America and establish there a "pantisocratic" community free from *Southey* prejudice and tradition and based upon "the generalization of individual property." Coleridge's immoderate enthusiasm is reflected in certain sonnets on Pantisocracy and in *The Fall of Robespierre* (1794), a worthless drama composed in collaboration with Southey. The same impulsiveness took a tragic turn when, because matrimony was an essential factor in the American scheme, he affianced himself at Bristol to Sarah Fricker, the sister of the young woman to whom Southey was betrothed. When it was "too late" he learned that his love for another woman, Mary Evans, was reciprocated.[8] The reaction from high hopes which bore little relation to reality was expressed in one of the earliest and not least poignant of those many passages of self-depreciation which are not to be judged insincere merely because Coleridge evidently derived a perverse satisfaction from inditing them:

> To me hath Heaven with bounteous hand assign'd
> Energic Reason and a shaping mind,
> The daring ken of Truth, the Patriot's part,
> And Pity's sigh, that breathes the gentle heart—
> Sloth-jaundic'd all! [9]

A long though irregular connection with the newspapers began with the publication in *The Morning Chronicle* (December, 1795—January, 1796) of a dozen *Sonnets on Eminent Characters*—Pitt, Priestley, Godwin, Bowles, and others. Seeking employment, Coleridge went to London, where he lingered long, associating with Lamb and reluctant to face his responsibilities in the west of England. In July Southey practically compelled his return. The two poets lectured at Bristol—Southey on history, Coleridge on politics and religion [10]—as a means of raising money for their passage to America; but Coleridge's untrustworthiness now led to an estrangement which was not bridged over till after Southey's return from Portugal and then without a renewal of confident intimacy. Coleridge had married Miss *Marriage* Fricker in October, 1795; and shortly afterwards he toured England, lecturing and canvassing for subscriptions to a proposed journal of public affairs. Of this journal, *The Watchman*, ten issues appeared in the spring of 1796. By the impartiality of his attacks on both Godwin and Pitt Coleridge managed to alienate both radical and conservative readers. A weak will was

---

[8] *On a Discovery Made Too Late; Poetical Works*, ed. E. H. Coleridge, I. 72.
[9] *Lines on a Friend who Died of a Frenzy Fever;* lines 39-43; *Poetical Works*, I. 72.
[10] Three of Coleridge's lectures were published as tiny pamphlets: *A Moral and Political Lecture; Conciones ad populum;* and *The Plot Discovered* (all Bristol, 1795).

unequal to the drudgery involved in the undertaking; there was too much dependence for "copy" upon parliamentary reports; subscriptions fell off; and soon *The Watchman* "ceased to cry the state of the political atmosphere." At this juncture a few guineas came to hand from Joseph Cottle, who not only published but paid for Coleridge's *Poems on Various Occasions* (1796). In this volume he had intended to include *The Destiny of Nations*, which he had permitted Southey to use as part of *Joan of Arc* and which he now reclaimed and expanded; but submitting to Lamb's advice he suppressed it and it was not published till 1817 in its entirety. The most ambitious piece in the volume of 1796 is *Religious Musings* upon which Coleridge had been at work since Cambridge days. In it the French Revolution is idealized; Priestley's Unitarianism is praised; there are signs of adherence to Hartley's psychology and its implications; and a vague current of mysticism marks the drift away from Godwinian rationalism. One or two small poems, such as the *Song of the Pixies,* show a timid venturing into the realms of the glamorous where Coleridge was soon to be at home. The *Poems* were not ill received and a second edition was called for.[11]

In desultory search for congenial employment Coleridge went about the country, preaching in Unitarian chapels.[12] On one of these journeys he received word of the birth of his eldest son, Hartley, and composed a sonnet in which the Platonic idea of preëxistence points forward to Wordsworth's *Ode.* In the autumn he was in correspondence with John Thelwall, the radical;[13] and to the same period belongs his first admission that he was addicted to opium.[14] A desire to live in the country and the fantastic conviction that he could earn a livelihood by farming led him, notwithstanding the warnings of his sensible friend Thomas Poole,[15] to move into a cottage at Nether Stowey among the Quantock hills. The year 1796 closed with an *Ode to the Departing Year* in which a belief that "Divine Providence regulates into one vast harmony all the events of time, however calamitous some of them may appear to mortals,"[16] struggles for expression through the conventional poetic diction.

The spring of 1797 was occupied with a tragedy undertaken on an invitation from Sheridan, the manager of Drury Lane. This was *Osorio.* The plot was adapted from part of Schiller's novel *Der Geisterseher* which was

---

[11] To the second edition (1797) were added poems by Charles Lamb and Charles Lloyd.

[12] At this time Hazlitt first met Coleridge, as he records in *My First Acquaintance with Poets.*

[13] See the famous letter to Thelwall (November, 1796) containing the self-portrait ("indolence capable of energies"); *Letters,* ed. E. H. Coleridge, I. 178-181. Thelwall visited Coleridge at Nether Stowey.

[14] *Letters,* I. 173 and 240. Opium had, however, been prescribed much earlier to alleviate the rheumatic pains from which Coleridge suffered from childhood.

[15] See the letter to Poole of mid-December, 1796; *Letters,* I. 187-193. — In later years Poole was a tower of strength to Mrs. Coleridge. See *Minnow among Tritons; Mrs. S. T. Coleridge's Letters to Thomas Poole, 1799-1834,* ed. Stephen Potter (1934). See also Mrs. Henry Sandford, *Thomas Poole and his Friends* (2v, 1888). — Another loyal and generous supporter of Coleridge at a later date was Thomas Wedgwood, one of the famous family of manufacturers of pottery.

[16] Coleridge's Argument prefixed to the *Ode; Poetical Works,* ed. E. H. Coleridge, I. 160.

soon to contribute something to *The Ancient Mariner*. The play caters to some extent to the "Gothic" taste with an incongruous but not uncharacteristic mingling of a politico-philosophic strain. On the ground of the obscurity of the later acts it was, after long delay, rejected. Many years later (1813) Coleridge revised it and as *Remorse* it reached the stage.

The first meeting with Wordsworth at an undetermined date late in 1795 had developed by the summer of 1797 into close friendship. Coleridge visited the Wordsworths at Racedown in June [17] and persuaded them to move to Alfoxden. The Wordsworthian influence is apparent in *This Lime-tree Bower My Prison* both in its stylistic freedom from Augustan idiom and in the heightened sensitiveness to the minutiae of the natural world. Parallels between Coleridge's poetry of the succeeding year and the contemporary entries in Dorothy's Journal show that not to her brother only (as he testified) but to Coleridge also the "exquisite sister" gave eyes and ears. During the wonderful half-year between November, 1797, and May, 1798, *The Rime of the Ancient Mariner*, the First Part of *Christabel*, and the fragment of *Kubla Khan* were composed; a projected tale, *The Wanderings of Cain*, was outlined; the theory of poetic diction was discussed; and a decision was reached as to the respective shares of the two poets in a volume to be published jointly. Wordsworth was to give "the charm of novelty to things of every day," while Coleridge's province was to be "persons and characters supernatural, or at least romantic," but with an attachment to them of "a human interest and a semblance of truth sufficient to procure for these shadows of imagination that willing suspension of disbelief for the moment, which constitutes poetic faith." [18]

For a study in "the ways of the imagination" as exemplified in the history of the composition of *The Ancient Mariner* there is abundant material in the records of Coleridge's "cormorant" reading.[19] For years a chaotic medley of ideas and images had sunk into "the deep well" of his "unconscious cerebration." An adept in recondite lore of many kinds, he had been accustomed to follow from book to book chance references to anything that attracted his all-devouring attention. In the literature of travel—from Herodotus and Strabo through Hakluyt and Purchas to Bartram and Bruce —he had found multitudes of facts and fictions about the sea in storm and calm, about tropic heat and austral cold, about phosphorescent and auroral phenomena, about strange creatures of the deep. For his never realized project of six *Hymns* to the Sun, the Moon, and the Four Elements he had been accumulating ideas of the most varied kinds, from Neo-Platonic speculations on tutelary spirits to the latest researches reported in the scientific publications of the day. At Bristol he had consorted with seafaring men. He had read of ships guided by the dead. From Schiller

The
Ancient
Mariner

---

[17] See the enthusiastic impressions of Wordsworth ("I feel myself a little man by his side"), *Letters*, I. 221.

[18] Coleridge, *Biographia Literaria*, beginning of ch. XIV.

[19] See J. L. Lowes, *The Road to Xanadu: A Study in the Ways of the Imagination* (1927), one of the most fascinating of all products of literary research.

and other sources his imagination had been fired by the legend of the Wandering Jew and, as we have seen, he was meditating a story upon the doom of Cain. Deep in the unconscious these and numberless other images became associated together. Wordsworth's suggestion (which he derived from an incident in George Shelvocke's *Voyage*) of the theme of retribution for the crime of slaying a bird beloved by an elemental spirit [20] acted upon all these images as a drop of chemical upon a solution held in suspense. The poem was precipitated; or rather, more accurately and changing the metaphor, the ideas, richly encrusted with associated imagery, rose to the surface of thought, there to be subjected to the conscious working of "the shaping spirit of imagination." The choice of the ballad-measure, the discussions with Wordsworth on the reform of poetic diction, and a white-hot imaginative apprehension of his subject combined to rid Coleridge of the old trammels of the Augustan style.[21] The resultant poem is the most enchanting of all evocations of the romantic spirit of wonder, winning by means of the clarity of its general design, the realism of detail, and the unanalyzable amalgam of the natural and the marvelous an unreluctant "suspension of disbelief" from every reader.

Christabel   The First Part of *Christabel* was begun after, and finished before, *The Ancient Mariner*. In the Second Part, not composed till 1800, the imaginative tension is somewhat relaxed; and despite Coleridge's assurances that he had the entire design in mind, the poem was never completed. Coleridge thought that he had invented the metre—the line consisting of four stressed and a varying number of unstressed syllables; but it is really a revival of an old form. In its tantalizing state the story has invited much speculation as to his intentions.[22] Fragments of his reading of Percy's *Reliques*, Lewis's *The Monk*, and Mrs. Radcliffe's romances went into the poem. It seems that classical ideas of the lamia and medieval ideas of the vampire, conflated in the person of Geraldine, were to be crossed with the theme of vicarious suffering as expiation for a wrong. After Coleridge settled in the Lake Country he introduced into Part II something of the traditions and landscape of Westmorland. The fire-lore which shone more luridly in the first

[20] To the summer of 1797 (and therefore several months earlier than the conception of *The Ancient Mariner* in November of that year) belongs *The Raven* (*Poetical Works*, I. 169-171), a little poem which Coleridge dismissed as "doggerel" and which is strangely unnoticed by the biographers and commentators, but which is significant because of its freedom from metrical and rhetorical conventions, its faint anticipation of the "magical" quality of Coleridge's masterpieces, and its theme—the vengeance wreaked upon a ship and its company for a wrong done to a bird.

[21] The archaisms of the version of 1798 were much reduced in number in the version of 1800 and there was less of macabre grotesquerie. The beautiful marginal glosses, though perhaps composed at an early date, did not accompany the poem till the version of 1817.

[22] Lowes did not include *Christabel* in *The Road to Xanadu* because he could not discover "the mysterious tracks from which it rose." A. H. Nethercot, *The Road to Tryermaine* (1939), has assembled much interesting erudition and comes nearest to a solution. See also B. R. McElderry, "Coleridge's Plan for Completing *Christabel*," *SP*, XXXIII (1936). 437-455; D. R. Tuttle, "*Christabel* Sources in Percy's *Reliques* and the Gothic Romance," *PMLA*, LIII (1938). 445-474.

version of *The Ancient Mariner* than in the revised form burns mysteriously in *Christabel.*[23]

In *Kubla Khan* (composed, if we accept Coleridge's statement,[24] in an opium-induced dream) the images which had been deposited in the unconscious from Coleridge's reading about subterranean rivers, pleasure-palaces, and other esoteric scenes and marvelous phenomena surged up and were expressed immediately in words without the exercise of conscious art. On waking he began to write the poem but was interrupted by an intrusive stranger, and afterwards neither the words nor the vision could be recaptured; and Coleridge, who persuaded himself that he would one day finish *Christabel,* made no effort to complete this other fragment of haunted and haunting beauty.

Kubla Khan

Below the level of these three "golden poems" but very memorable nevertheless are other pieces of 1798: *Fire, Famine, and Slaughter,* an excoriating attack upon William Pitt; *Frost at Midnight,* close in sentiment and beauty to Wordsworth's *Tintern Abbey* lines; *The Nightingale,* with its lovely picture of the father stilling his infant's sobs by showing him the moon; *The Three Graves,* an attempt, such as Wordsworth made in *Peter Bell,* to suggest mystery and horror without recourse to the supernatural; and *France: an Ode,* a magnificent plea to Freedom for forgiveness because the poet had mistakenly identified her with revolutionary France. Over these and other things we must pass without further comment. Coleridge's greatest work as a poet was now all but done; and the long remainder of his life must here be surveyed with utmost brevity.

Before his departure for Germany (September, 1798) Coleridge had been busy with his versions of Schiller's *Piccolomini* and *The Death of Wallenstein,*[25] a task brought to completion after his return in 1799. From Germany he carried home quantities of books and the determination to devote himself to philosophy. He was now employed by *The Morning Post,* and some of his articles on public affairs attracted such wide attention that Daniel Stuart, the editor, offered him an editorial position at a handsome salary. Coleridge, however, would not commit himself to a partisan policy— or to fixed obligations. In 1800 he settled at Greta Hall on the outskirts of

---

[23] What sight met Christabel's gaze when Geraldine laid bare her bosom? Did she have eyes in her breasts? Compare the well-known story of Shelley's hallucination at Geneva in 1816, and the epithet "bosom-eyed" in *The Witch of Atlas,* XI. 8. Or did flames, forked-tipt like a serpent's tongue, jut from her breasts? A tradition says that this was the conception may have been handed down in the Pre-Raphaelite circle and is recorded in Watts-Dunton's *Aylwin.* Or was her heart enveloped in flames, like the hearts of the damned in Beckford's *Vathek?* "Bosom-eyed" monsters occur in the travel books Coleridge had read. Whether he had read *Vathek* has never been proved but seems certain.

[24] As does Lowes, *The Road to Xanadu,* Book IV. But see Elisabeth Schneider, "The 'Dream' of *Kubla Khan,*" *PMLA,* LX (1945). 784-801.

[25] P. Machule, "Coleridge's Wallensteinübersetzung," *ESt,* XXXI (1902). 182-239. Some of Coleridge's supposed mistranslations have been shown to be due to the fact that he worked from Schiller's manuscripts, which differed from the later published versions. — On the wider subject of Coleridge's relations with German thought and culture see J. L. Haney, *The German Influence on Coleridge* (Philadelphia, 1902); F. W. Stokoe, *German Influence in the English Romantic Period* (1926), pp. 89-143; A. C. Dunstan, "The German Influence on Coleridge," *MLR,* XVII (1922). 272-281, and XVIII (1923). 183-201.

Opium

Keswick, and prepared with Wordsworth the second edition of *Lyrical Ballads*. The opium habit had now taken firm hold upon him. Love for his wife, which had never been deep-rooted, faded and died.[26] Increasing anxiety for him found repeated expression in Dorothy Wordsworth's Journal; and at this time Wordsworth drew his portrait in the *Stanzas Written in a Copy of Thomson's "Castle of Indolence."* In October, 1802, he published his last great poem, the poignant *Dejection: an Ode* in which he lamented the loss of the faculty of response from within to the beauty of the natural world and of that "shaping spirit of Imagination" which nature had given him at his birth.[27] Desire to escape from Greta Hall and to seek health in a warmer climate led to his acceptance of a secretarial appointment at Malta, and he was absent from England for more than a year. On his return the alienation from Mrs. Coleridge drifted into a separation [28] which was none the less final because never put upon a legal basis. Henceforth he lived mostly in London. He wrote for *The Courier*; he began in 1808 the first of various courses of lectures on Shakespeare and other poets and on metaphysical topics. During nine months of 1809-1810 he issued *The Friend*, a journal of philosophical, political, and literary opinion, irregular in its dates of appearance, and often dull in its contents, though enlivened with *Satyrane's Letters*, written from Germany in 1798-1799 and afterwards included in the *Biographia Literaria*. The estrangement from Wordsworth in 1810, brought about by Basil Montague's indiscreet report of Wordsworth's confidential warning against Coleridge's habits, increased his despondency. There was, however, a constant though at first unsuccessful struggle against opium. The lectures on Shakespeare in 1812 were attended by the world of fashion and were brilliantly successful. Coleridge, who owed a good deal to Lessing

Lectures

and other German critics, emphasized the philosophic aspect of Shakespeare, reading more into the subject than the text always warranted and neglecting the outer form for the sake of what he held to be the inner reality. The dramas were for him a spiritual as well as an aesthetic experience.[29] In 1813-1814 he delivered four courses of lectures, mostly on literary subjects, at Bristol. Through Lord Byron's persuasion and mediation *Remorse* (the revised *Osorio*) was produced at Drury Lane (1813). A second drama, *Zapolya* (1816), was rejected. Coleridge's dark pathway was still illuminated with visionary projects. In 1814 these took the form of a great treatise on *Christianity, the One True Philosophy*. This design came to nothing—or very little; but it marks his severance from Unitarianism

[26] The tone of Coleridge's letters to his wife is generally kindly; but for cruel candor see *Unpublished Letters*, ed. E. L. Griggs, I. 218-222.

[27] *Dejection* is closely associated with Coleridge's unhappy love for Sara Hutchinson, to which allusion is made in various poems between 1801 and 1810. See T. M. Raysor, "Coleridge and 'Asra,'" *SP*, xxvi (1929). 305-324. The original version of the ode is printed and discussed by E. de Selincourt, "Coleridge's *Dejection: an Ode*," *E&S*, xxii (1937). 7-25.

[28] After their daughter Sara's marriage there was a partial reconciliation and from about 1822 till the end Coleridge and his wife occasionally met in London.

[29] Augustus Ralli, *History of Shakespearean Criticism* (1932), I. 126-143. For Coleridge's relation to earlier English criticism of Shakespeare see R. W. Babcock, *The Genesis of Shakespeare Idolatry* (1931).

and acceptance of a Neo-Platonic form of Christianity. That it was intended to be "illustrated by fragments of Autobiography" shows that he was now contemplating another work. In 1816 he put himself under the care and into the household of James Gillman, a physician at Highgate.[30] His determination was to submit to an anti-narcotic regimen "not only firm but severe." In this year *Christabel* and *Kubla Khan* (both by now famous in literary circles from recitations and manuscript copies) were published, together with *The Pains of Sleep* (written in 1803) which conveyed a picture contrasting with the glories of Xanadu. Many more poems were assembled in *Sibylline Leaves* (1817).

The *Biographia Literaria,* which had gone through numerous vicissitudes, at length appeared in 1817. Despite digressions, the first volume was fairly coherent, but in the second the plan broke down and it was expanded to the proportions of the first only by a reprint of *Satyrane,* an acrimonious critique of Maturin's *Bertram,* and a rambling concluding chapter. The most important chapters are those on the Wordsworthian theory of poetic style and those formulating a theory, based upon the Kantian distinction between the *Vernunft* and the *Verstand* (with heavy obligations to Schelling), distinguishing between the Fancy, which is merely "a mode of Memory emancipated from the order of time and space" and which, like Memory, receives its material from the laws of association, and the Imagination, which transcends sensational material and brings the mind into direct connection with the ultimate and supersensuous reality.[31] The *Biographia* was harshly reviewed by Hazlitt;[32] and *Blackwood's*[33] was so outrageously personal in its attack upon Coleridge's private life that he thought of bringing suit for libel.

Biographia Literaria

In later years Coleridge renewed intercourse with Southey, was more closely in touch with Wordsworth, revived for a short time the publication of *The Friend,* delivered a last series of lectures in 1819, published a miscellany of philosophy, piety, and literary criticism entitled *Aids to Reflection* (1825), struggled manfully and on the whole successfully with the old enemy, opium, was almost crushed with the disgrace of his son Hartley's expulsion from Oxford, and gathered round him disciples of the younger generation, including Edward Irving, John Sterling, Frederick D. Maurice, and other religious-minded liberals, who absorbed his discourses at Highgate. In 1827-1828 there was a St. Martin's-Summer revival of the poetic instinct and he wrote *The Garden of Boccaccio* and *Love, Hope and Patience.* The moving *Epitaph* for his own grave was composed in failing health in November, 1833. He died on July 25, 1834, and was buried in

Last Years

---

[30] L. E. Watson, *Coleridge at Highgate* (1925); A. W. Gillman, *The Gillmans of Highgate* (1895).

[31] I. A. Richards, *Coleridge on Imagination* (1935). For criticism of Richards' views see F. L. Lucas, *The Decline and Fall of the Romantic Ideal* (1936), ch. IV.

[32] In the *Edinburgh Review,* August, 1817; *Collected Works,* ed. A. R. Waller and Arnold Glover, x. 135-158.

[33] October, 1817; reprinted in *Notorious Literary Attacks,* ed. Albert Mordell (1926), pp. 20-62. The authorship has been ascribed to John Wilson, but this is doubtful.

Highgate cemetery. Southey pursued his memory, in private letters, with shocking rancor. Lamb mourned for him during the short remainder of his life. Wordsworth pronounced him "the most wonderful" man he had ever known and referred in magnificent lines to the marvelous intellectual power of

> The rapt One, of the godlike forehead,
> The heaven-eyed creature.[34]

The attempt of Coleridge's literary executors to piece together the much talked-of philosophical and religious *magnum opus* failed; but his nephew, Henry Nelson Coleridge (who married the poet's daughter, Sara [35]), gathered together the *Literary Remains* and published the fascinating record of his "Table-Talk."

[34] *Extempore Effusion on the Death of James Hogg.*
[35] See E. L. Griggs, *Coleridge Fille. A Biography of Sara Coleridge* (1940). Sara Coleridge edited many of her father's writings.

VI
Robert Southey, Walter Savage Landor, and Other Poets

I

The reputation of Robert Southey [1] (1774-1843) has suffered from his *Southey* association with men of far greater genius than was his, from the mass and unevenness of his work, from his undertaking tasks in poetry beyond his powers, and from the circumstance that he is often judged simply as a poet rather than as a professional man of letters. His own self-confidence betrayed him. He was convinced that he was planting acorns which would grow into great oaks in whose shade posterity would find recreation. The trust in posterity has proved fallacious. His epics are unread and—with the doubtful exception of *Roderick*—unreadable; the historical works on Brazil and on the Peninsular War and his editions of various books [2] have been superseded; *The Doctor* may, at most, be dipped into here and there; most of the shorter poems have turned out to be ephemeral; and Southey's reputation as a poet is kept alive by a few things, such as *The Inchcape Rock, The Battle of Blenheim,* and *My Days among the Dead are Passed*; as a writer of prose by *The Life of Nelson* and perhaps *The Life of Wesley*; [3] and as a man by his connection with Wordsworth and Coleridge, his change in political opinions, and his quarrel with Lord Byron.

Yet because of his personal relationships, the early date at which he was active in revolutionary and romantic literature, the significant changes in opinion which are illustrated by his conspicuous example, and his range and choice of themes in prose and poetry he remains an important historical figure. His early life and later years are clearly divided from one another in 1803, when he settled at Keswick. Before that time he had been expelled from school; gained little from life at Oxford; been inspired by the French

---

[1] *Poetical Works* (10v, 1837-1838); *Poems*, ed. M. H. FitzGerald (Oxford, 1909), containing the longer poems except *Joan of Arc*, and a selection from the minor poems; *Select Prose*, ed. Jacob Zeitlin (1916). There is no collected edition of the prose works. *Life and Correspondence*, ed. C. C. Southey (6v, 1849-1850); *Correspondence with Caroline Bowles*, ed. Edward Dowden (Dublin, 1881); *Letters*, ed. M. H. FitzGerald (Oxford, 1912), a selection. — Edward Dowden, *Southey* (EML Series, 1874); Jack Simmons, *Southey* (1945); William Haller, *The Early Life of Robert Southey* (1917); George Saintsbury, "Southey," *Collected Essays and Papers* (1923), I. 239-268.

[2] *Amadis of Gaul*, the *Chronicle of the Cid*, Chatterton's *Poems*, *Specimens* of the English poets, and so forth.

[3] *The Life of Nelson*, ed. H. B. Butler (1911); *The Life of Wesley*, ed. M. H. FitzGerald (1925).

Revolution to compose an epic on *Joan of Arc*[4] (1793; published 1796) and *Wat Tyler*, a two-act drama which remained long in manuscript; met Coleridge, with whom he evolved the "pantisocratic" scheme and wrote *The Fall of Robespierre* (1794); collaborated with Robert Lovell on a volume of *Poems* (1795); traveled with an uncle in Portugal and Spain;[5] published *Minor Poems* (1797-1799); studied law half-heartedly; visited Portugal for a second time; and completed there *Thalaba the Destroyer* (1801). The radicalism of his youth had been put behind him by the time that he established himself at Keswick for the long remainder of his busy life. He accumulated a vast library and vaster stores of erudition. To the "Poet's Corner" of *The Morning Post* and to other newspapers and periodicals he contributed countless ephemeralities. *Metrical Tales* appeared in 1805. An ambitiously planned history of Portugal never materialized in entirety, but the *History of Brazil* (1810-1819) is part of it. After the initiation of *The Quarterly Review* (1809) he was for many years a regular and voluminous contributor. Meanwhile he had the epic poems long in hand. *Madoc* appeared in 1805, *The Curse of Kehama* in 1810, *Roderick the Last of the Goths* in 1814, and *A Tale of Paraguay* (of less than epic proportions) in 1825. The little masterpiece of pellucid prose, *The Life of Nelson*, belongs to 1813. In that year, on the death of Henry James Pye,[6] Southey was made poet laureate.[7] Southey's "official" poems, of which *Carmen Triumphale* for the year 1814 is the most inflated and *A Vision of Judgment* (1821) the best remembered (because of Byron's parody), are among his least happy efforts. There is space to note here only two of his miscellaneous prose works. In *Sir Thomas More, or Colloquies on the Progress and Prospects of Society* (1829), the form of which owes something to Landor's *Imaginary Conversations*, he showed his distrust in democracy and lasting desire for social betterment by urging a return from modern competition to coöperative feudalism and by stressing the helpful interdependence of medieval society. This reverence for tradition is a heritage from Burke; but William Cobbett had been writing along similar lines and Carlyle and Ruskin were soon to do so. *The Doctor*[8] (1834-1847) is an *omnium gatherum* of lore and learning, anecdote and fantasy, serious thought lightly expressed and facetiousness laboriously hammered out, all of the most various kinds. To read it entire

---

[4] The Christian "machinery" of the original version was discarded in the revision of 1798 and Joan became a "child of Nature," guided, like Wordsworth's Lucy, by her benign influence. Joan is of course the champion of liberty. In his preface to the final edition (1837) Southey confessed that when writing the poem he "was ignorant enough of history and of human nature to believe that a happier order of things had commenced with the independence of the United States, and would be accelerated by the French Revolution."

[5] Southey, *Letters written during a Short Residence in Spain and Portugal* (1797).

[6] H. J. Pye (1745-1813), author of *Alfred*, an epic (1801) and many other volumes of worthless verse; poet laureate, 1790-1813.

[7] The new Tory laureate was embarrassed when in 1814 Richard Carlile, the radical publisher, having obtained possession of the manuscript, piratically published *Wat Tyler*, a drama of Southey's long-since-vanished revolutionary youth. The process of Southey's change in political opinion is analogous to that of Wordsworth but less complex.

[8] Seven volumes, the last two posthumous. *Selections from The Doctor, Etc.*, ed. R. B. Johnson (n.d.).

is beyond most modern capacities; to dip into it is to discover matter both informative and entertaining. In later life Southey's career was clouded with losses and sorrows, a son dying in 1816 and a favorite daughter in 1826. His wife, who had gone insane, died in 1837. Two years later he married Caroline Bowles, whose claims to remembrance for her own literary works are of the slightest. Not long afterwards his mind began to fail, and after a period of pathetic incompetence he died in 1843.

Southey's failures or at best partial successes as a poet ought not to obscure *The Epics* the fact that he was early in many fields of romance and in some led the way followed by greater poets. In *Thalaba the Destroyer* and in *The Curse of Kehama* he penetrated into Arabia and the further East; [9] in *Madoc* into Wales and America; in *Roderick* into Spain. In the Oriental epics immense learning at second-hand, displayed in elaborate explanatory notes, is no acceptable substitute for actual experience and imaginative grasp. There are arresting episodes in both poems, such as the description of the "Hand of Glory" in *Thalaba* [10] and the pageant-like opening of *Kehama,* but they are not enough to give life to the whole. Southey's choice of metre in *Thalaba* was ill-advised.[11] The rimeless lines of varying length, contracting and expanding according to no discernible principle of either sense or form, seem but so much prose chopped up indiscriminately; the reader is constantly looking for a pattern that is not there. Southey may have been uneasy, for he introduced rimes into *Kehama*; but the objection still stands, for they are inserted so irregularly that while holding out the promise of design they fail to fulfill it. Even so, Southey was in this matter a precursor, for where he failed later poets, managing more subtly the cadences which distinguish free verse from prose, have succeeded. These undisciplined forms encouraged a volubility which was not checked when, in *Madoc,* Southey reverted to blank verse. Here, following the lead of Gray and other poets of the earliest romantic generation, Southey tells a story of barbarous Celtic violence, crossing it with traditions of the "Aztecas" of America, the land to which Madoc emigrates.[12] It is refreshing to turn from this to the clear-cut tale of Count Julian's betrayal of Spain to the Moors in revenge for the seduction of his daughter by King Roderick—an appropriate theme when Wellesley's campaigns were turning the thoughts of Englishmen to the Iberian peninsula.[13] The opening of the story with Roderick's penitence is perhaps due to Scott's treatment of the legend, and Southey owed some-

[9] See A. Waechter, *Ueber Robert Southeys Orientalische Epen* (Halle, 1890).
[10] Book v, stanza xxvii. Compare Scott, *The Antiquary,* ch. xvii.
[11] In his preface Southey acknowledged his indebtedness to Francis Sayers of Norwich who in his *Poems* (1792) had used irregular rimeless verse. Sayers in turn derived the form from William Collins who, however, had used it in the ode *To Evening* with far more delicacy and within manageable limits.
[12] This is based on the tradition (found in Hakluyt and Drayton) of Madoc's discovery of America three centuries before Columbus. — Coleridge, Pantisocracy, and Spain all have their places in *Madoc.* See H. G. Wright, "Three Aspects of Southey," *RES,* ix (1933). 37-46.
[13] Compare Scott, *The Vision of Don Roderick* (1811) and Byron, *Childe Harold* (1812), I. xxxv. For the kernel of history in the legend see *The Cambridge Medieval History,* ii. 48 and 265.

thing to Landor's *Count Julian*.[14] The initial situation is an arresting one and stimulates interest in the earlier episodes to which the poem folds back. Southey realized the tragic power of the grim tale; unfortunately his blank verse is a slow-moving and creaking vehicle.

The Shorter Poems

From the inexhaustible resources of his learning Southey drew the materials for those of his shorter poems into which he instilled most life. He employed the ballad-measure at a date which may have been earlier than that at which Coleridge was writing in the same form; the question of priority is not important because Coleridge is incomparably more skilful than Southey. Southey's crude and jaunty anapaests owe, admittedly, something to M. G. Lewis, to whose *Tales of Wonder* he contributed. He is at his best in ballads where the supernatural is treated lightly, with touches of humor, or where the horrible is crossed with the grotesque. The finest examples in these kinds are his rendering of the legend of Bishop Hatto and the still well-known *Old Woman of Berkeley*. Something like irony is substituted for humor in *The Well of St. Keyne* and *The Inchcape Rock*, where the supernatural is muted though still present. In *Blenheim* the weird and wondrous notes are not sounded. Southey's handling of even such short pieces is seldom certain; but even the less good are of historical interest because Southey helped to liberate romantic prosody from eighteenth-century restrictions. In both matter and form his exploitations of the macabre point the way towards Hood, Praed, and *The Ingoldsby Legends*. While his acorns mouldered in the ground, these small seeds took root.

II

Landor

The traditional concept of Walter Savage Landor [15] (1775-1864) as an austere and lonely figure is founded upon the self-portraits which he liked to draw; actually there is as little of truth in it as in the notoriously irascible poet's proud assertion that he strove with none for none was worth his strife. From boyhood when he won the friendship of the great scholar Samuel Parr to old age when he was protected by Browning and received Swinburne's homage, he enjoyed the admiration of many famous men, not excluding Byron, whose satiric thrust at "that deep-mouthed Bœotian Savage Landor" [16] is not wholly unlaudatory, and Dickens, whose caricature of him as Boythorn in *Bleak House* is, in intention at any rate, good-natured. Landor's wide circle of friends embraced many people who were not authors, and in particular various gracious women to whom he offered the tribute

---

[14] See E. Schwichtenberg, *Southeys Roderick und Landors Count Julian* (Königsberg, 1906).

[15] *Complete Works*, ed. T. E. Welby and Stephen Wheeler (16v, 1927-1936), not absolutely "complete"; *Poetical Works*, ed. S. Wheeler (3v, 1937). — T. J. Wise and S. Wheeler, *Bibliography* (1919); John Forster, *Walter Savage Landor* (1869); Sidney Colvin, *Landor* (EML Series, 1881); Helene Richter, "Walter Savage Landor," *Anglia*, L (1926). 123-152, 317-344; LI (1927). 1-30; H. C. Minchin, *Last Days, Letters and Conversations of Walter Savage Landor* (1934); Malcolm Elwin, *Savage Landor* (1941); George Saintsbury, "Landor," *Essays and Papers*, II. 110-131; Bush, pp. 229-245.

[16] *Don Juan*, XI. lix.

of his courtly verses. He was not isolated from the world (even during the years in Italy) save toward the end and then through his own fault. Nor are his writings, either poetry or prose, so much apart from the currents of the age as is sometimes said. His Jacobinism in the days when he joined the Spanish revolutionaries and hoped to live to see King George III hanged between the two archbishops was one bond of sympathy with Southey, though unlike him Landor remained loyal to his republican convictions. The Orientalism which is one strand in the fabric of his works links him to Southey, Byron, and Moore. In his evocations of the past he worked, with all the obvious dissimilarities, along lines parallel with Scott. The chastity of phrase and style in his poetry shows a connection with those minor poets in whom the tastes and traditions of the eighteenth century lived on into the nineteenth. The elaborations of his prose remind the reader, notwith-standing the differences in the harmonies, that De Quincey (one of Landor's earliest admirers) was a contemporary who likewise pulled out all the organ-stops of the language. The "marmoreal" quality of his best verse is suggestive of Keats's latest style and may have had an influence upon it. A passionate love of Italy Landor shared with Byron and Shelley, and, like them, he, an aristocratic republican, dedicated his powers to the service of the cause of Italian unity and independence. Again like these and other poets of the period, he experimented in the dramatic form. The Grecian *Idylls* point the way toward Tennyson's classical pieces; some of the dialogues approximate to forms which Browning later employed. At all these and yet other points he touches one or another of the romantics. Why, then, does he seem so solitary a figure? One reason may be found in the quarrels which marred his middle life, and the violent scandal of 1857 which forced him to leave England and left a memory of lonely exile. Another reason is that his long life embraced three literary generations, so that it is difficult to classify him with any. A third is that because he is of equal note as poet and as writer of prose it is difficult to fit him into either category.

The juvenile phase during which Landor was an imitator of older poets was quickly passed through. The tumidity of the odes in the *Poems* of 1795 is not a characteristic of his mature work. He never ceased to fancy himself as a satirist; but though almost always missing the mark, he fails in an indi-vidual way not attributable to imitation of his predecessors. Profound know-ledge of Latin led him into his own path. In Clara Reeve's *Progress of* Gebir *Romance* [17] he discovered a story which, with free adaptations and embel-lishments from other sources, he fashioned into *Gebir* (1798). This he began in Latin verse, and after the publication of the English form he returned to the Latin and completed *Gebirus* (1803). The tale of ancient Egypt in-volves enchantments, a descent into hell, and the death of the hero in a horrifying manner. The Latinate syntax, the heavily charged style, and the

---

[17] The dialogue form of this book may have suggested to Landor the form of the *Imaginary Conversations* (see a letter by M. F. Ashley-Montague in *LTLS*, January 27, 1940). But there were older and better precedents for him to follow.

allusive indirectness of the narrative make *Gebir* a burden to read entire, consecutively. Few pieces of comparable length gain more from selection; and the selections are usually such brief passages as the famous lines on the sea-shell. The men and women of the story, for all the violence of the issues in which they are engaged, are not dynamic. They are, in Arthur Symons' apt metaphor,[18] figures in low relief—figures, one may add, upon a stele, for about them there is a death-like stillness.

Poems by the Author of Gebir[19] (1802) contains, along with much of interest only as anticipations of greater things to come, one short piece, *Regeneration,* in which the passion for Greek antiquity and the passion for liberty are blended as they were later to be in Byron's poetry, but with a stylistic control that is not Byronic. In succeeding years Landor, who possessed independent means, lived much in Italy, engaged in litigation and personal quarrels, and wrote a quantity of Latin verse which he later trans-lated into English. In 1812 appeared his tragedy of *Count Julian* on the story of Don Roderick. The indirectness of Landor's approach, the intricacy of style, and the assumption that the reader can supply from his own knowl-edge what it is the dramatist's business to impart spoil this play beyond redemption even by the occasional passages of noble eloquence.

Imaginary Conversa-tions

The first series of *Imaginary Conversations* (1824) was followed by others to the number of five by 1829, and more were published at later dates, the latest (save those published posthumously) in 1848. With them may be considered *The Citation and Examination of William Shakespeare* (1834) and *The Pentameron* (1837), while on the periphery of this immense mass of prose is *Pericles and Aspasia* (1836). In time the *Conversations* range from remote antiquity to Landor's own day.[20] The characters are nearly always historical. The author never intrudes himself save when he is an interlocutor; but though he is not present we have seldom any sense of impartiality, for the arguments are so managed as to reveal and support Landor's opinions. Frequently Landor draws out the thread of his verbosity finer than the staple of his argument; the style is nobler than is appropriate to the thinness of the idea; an obvious thought is swathed in metaphor; and the restrained feeling contrasts with the magniloquence with which the very restraint is expressed. Landor can be intolerably dull, as in the colloquies on statecraft and public policy; and the elephantine humor of some of his attacks upon ecclesiasticism is equally tedious. But in the best of the *Conversations* there are passion and vitality and a genuine realization of a dramatic situation, as when Achilles confronts Helen or Henry VIII Anne Boleyn. His learn-ing and intuition harmonize when he imagines great men giving expression

---

[18] *The Romantic Movement in English Poetry* (1909), p. 179.

[19] On the poems up to 1802 see William Bradley, *The Early Poems of Landor: A Study of his Development and Debt to Milton* (1914).

[20] Their geographical distribution may be summarized by noting the arrangement adopted in Welby's edition (numerals indicate the number of conversations in each category): Greek (18), Roman (12), Italian (29), English (35), Scottish (2), Irish (5), American (3), Spanish (5), French (17), German (7), Russian (7), Oriental (8), various (4). See H. M. Flasdieck, "Landor und seine *Imaginary Conversations,*" *ESt,* LVIII (1924). 390-431.

to his own serenely epicurean outlook upon life.[21] Between these philosophic dialogues and those on purely literary subjects there is no well-defined boundary. Those concerned with problems of criticism and taste are often delightful, for Landor, though whimsical and unreliable, is a stimulating guide through the world of books. Generally he introduces but two speakers, the interest being thus concentrated upon the clash of two personalities or upon their perfect accord; but in a few cases he brings on three or even four people. There are practically no "stage-directions," the *mise-en-scène* being indicated with deft touches in the dialogue or left to the reader's knowledge of the situation.

The *Pentameron* may be regarded as one of the *Conversations* extended through five days of uninterrupted leisure during which Petrarch and Boccaccio discuss life and letters with special reference to the character, thought, themes, and poetic style of Dante. But though the interlocutors are the fourteenth-century humanists, the thoughts are Landor's, for neither Petrarch nor Boccaccio can be imagined as holding such opinions of Dante as they are made to express; the disparagement is Landor's, not theirs. The homely incidents, intended to provide "relief," are not quite in keeping, though the humor is above Landor's average level. Variety of a more welcome kind is supplied in the beautiful narratives of dreams.

Landor dared even more greatly than usual when he undertook to show the youthful Shakespeare on trial before Sir Thomas Lucy for deer-stealing. The high spirits of the *Citation* make it a pleasant volume to dip into, but it is difficult to sustain attention throughout its length. Had Landor curbed his prolixity and refrained from long digressions which blur the wit and retard the action, he might have produced an almost convincing portrait of the young genius who is at once so clever, so impudent, and so eloquent. But just when we are about to believe that this is how the charming deer-stealer would have spoken, his voice falls silent and for long whiles we hear Landor speaking.

The most ambitious of all Landor's works is *Pericles and Aspasia,* not a series of conversations (though much dialogue is recorded) but of imaginary letters exchanged between Aspasia and her friend Cleone, with occasional letters from others of the Periclean circle. Into this picture of the Golden Age of Athens Landor unfortunately permitted allusions by indirection to modern England to intrude, and he committed the fundamental mistake of making Aspasia the mouthpiece for his own opinions. These concern a variety of subjects—war, politics, the drama, and (very interestingly) the Homeric question. But the disputations are so cloudy as to obscure the lovely evocations of ancient Greece. The dramatic effect of the first short, swift letters is not sustained in the sequel, save in occasional pas-

Pericles and Aspasia

---

[21] See especially the colloquy between Scaliger and Montaigne. A comparison between this and Water Pater's portrait of Montaigne in *Gaston de Latour* brings out interesting likenesses and dissimilarities between Landor and Pater. Pater's *Imaginary Portraits* owe something to Landor; and note also the "Conversation Not Imaginary" (which is a version of one of Lucian's dialogues) in *Marius the Epicurean* (ch. xxiv).

sages such as the narrative of the plague. The book would have been better
had it been one-third as long; as it is, the anthologist must do for Landor
what he would not do for himself.

Turning now to Landor's poetry, we may dismiss the Neapolitan trilogy [22]
with a few words. Despite warm pleadings in their behalf,[23] to peruse them
is an ordeal for which the occasional passages of stately eloquence in these
most shut-in of all closet dramas afford but little compensation. Landor did
not know how to conduct a dramatic action. The reader is bewildered with
the intricacies of the historical situation, which is rendered only the darker
by the rare flashes of familiar episode, as when Boccaccio and Fiammetta
cross the stage. Even the figure of the evil monk Rupert—straight out of
Gothic romances but tinged with the deeper dye of Landor's anti-ecclesiastical prejudices—looms dimly through the haze of policy and words. Save
momentarily and then for but a few lines, the characters all talk alike—
pure Landor.

The Shorter Poems

Of the short poems—some of them of but relative brevity by Landorian
standards, for they range in length from one line (literally) to four or five
hundred—a few, such as *Rose Aylmer* and *Past Ruined Ilion Helen Lives*
(that incomparable expression of the poet's pride and confidence in his art)
have won universal admiration.[24] In these pieces of marmoreal loveliness
Landor seems to remember that upon a monument there is room for but
a short inscription. Yet there is none of the dryness of epigraphy. The heat
of passion is there, though it is so firmly constricted that it cannot burst
into flame. For the reader weary of the more exuberant romantics there is
refreshment in this proud reticence. In elegy and courtly compliment there
are never those false notes that occasionally mar Landor's prose. The
Hellenics (1847) are more difficult to judge. The best—such as *The Death of
Artemidora*—are very beautiful; but their studied quiet is suggestive of the
calm of a Street of Tombs. Nowhere is the "arrestedness" of which Landor's
critics have often written more apparent. These men and women, youths
and maidens of ancient Hellas move slowly or not at all. The sacrificial
victim approaches the altar but is not slain; the lover for all his boldness
does not achieve the embrace. Though the landscape is sun-drenched, the
prevailing atmosphere is of a sad serenity. Landor is master of a firmly-
wrought blank verse oftener eloquent than poetic, but he is as restricted
in metrical forms as in his style. In all his poetry he uses familiar traditional
metres and seems never to have been tempted to experiments in prosody.

To know and love the best of Landor there is needed a sense of dedication
to a heavy task. Much that is tedious and otiose must be passed through in
order to discover what is perfect in its kind. He who endures—not neces-

---

[22] *Andrea of Hungary* and *Giovanna of Naples* (both together, 1839); *Fra Rupert* (1840).
[23] Notably by Oliver Elton, *Survey . . . 1780-1830*, II. 22-24.
[24] Other poems in this group are *Dirce; Mother, I Cannot Mind my Wheel; Soon, O Ianthe;
From You, Ianthe, Little Troubles Pass; I Strove with None;* and *Death Stands Above Me,
Whispering Low.*

sarily to the end—may find himself in the select company of those who have delighted to pay him homage.[25]

III

Remoter than Landor from the main tendencies of the age was George *Crabbe* Crabbe [26] (1754-1832), who might have been considered in the previous section of this *History* but for the fact that the works in which his genius found full expression appeared at so late a date as to bring them into chronological relationship with the great romantic poets. Crabbe's earliest poems attracted no attention, despite his plea to the reviewers in *The Candidate* (1780); but a letter with samples of his verses won the consideration of Edmund Burke and through his influence Crabbe obtained ordination and the curacy of his native village of Aldeburgh on the Suffolk coast. Later, an accumulation of livings assured him a competency. *The Village* (1783) displayed his maturing powers. In succeeding years he wrote much and destroyed much, but with negligible exceptions published nothing till the *Poems* of 1807 in which *The Parish Register* is the principal item. Then followed *The Borough* (1810), *Tales in Verse* (1812), and *Tales of the Hall* (1819). He won a wide following and became a well-known figure in London society though his home in later life was in Wiltshire.

Admirer of Pope and arch anti-romantic though he was, Crabbe has this *Anti-ro-* in common with Wordsworth, that he brought within the horizon of poetry *manticism* the characters and social condition of poor and humble people. But while Wordsworth sought to throw "a certain colouring of imagination" over "incidents and situations" in ordinary life, Crabbe worked with absolute realism in the sphere of the lowly and the ignoble. When he portrayed loftier social circles it was generally to darken by contrast the humiliation to which privileged persons subject interlopers from the nether world. The exaggerations in his picture were due to his unflinching determination not to soften or mitigate the sordid and the squalid elements in these lowly lives. In the poetry of his master he found justification for this realism, noting *Realism* that "Pope himself had no small portion of this actuality of relation, this nudity of description, and poetry without an atmosphere." [27] In his reaction

[25] Landor's brother, Robert Eyres Landor (1781-1869), has been brought back into notice by Eric Partridge who has edited *Selections* from his poetry and prose (1927). He gains from judicious anthologizing. The beauties of his plays—*The Count Arezzi* (1824), *The Earl of Brecon, Faith's Fraud,* and *The Ferryman* (all 1841)—must otherwise be sought in a mass of gnarled, crude 'matter. Their obscurities make the effort scarcely worth while. Two pieces of elaborate prose show the attraction of ultra-romantic subjects to an austere scholar. *The Fawn of Sertorius* (1846), an attempt at historical romance based upon Plutarch, introduces a supernatural being who is the guide and companion of a Roman general. *The Fountain of Arethusa* (1848) brings together ·two modern explorers and the ancient ghosts whom they meet in a subterranean cavern in Derbyshire. After the opening lively narrative there is an over-plus of dialogue.

[26] *Works* (8v, 1834); *Works,* ed. A. W. Ward (3v, Cambridge, 1906). — George Crabbe (son), *The Life of the Rev. George Crabbe* (1834); René Huchon, *George Crabbe and his Times,* trans. Frederick Clarke (1907); J. H. Evans, *The Poems of George Crabbe: a Literary and Historical Study* (1933); George Saintsbury, "Crabbe," *Essays and Papers,* I. 1-25; V. H Lang, "George Crabbe and the Eighteenth Century," *ELH,* v (1938). 305-333.

[27] Preface to *Tales: Works,* ed. Ward, II. 10.

from contemporary romanticism he was hostile rather to the novel of sentiment and wild adventure than to romantic poetry, for when he became
fixed in his style and outlook the great romantic poets had not appeared. He
expressed his contempt for Gothic inventions, those "shadows of a shade"
upon which as a boy he had wasted his "sixpences and tears." [28] The particularity of his realistic detail is shot through with satiric comments, though
these are not directed against recognizable individuals.

> Man's Vice and Crime I combat as I can,
> But to his God and conscience leave the Man.[29]

Nature he delineated not for her own sake but as an accessory to man, the
somber background for the tragedy of poor outcasts. Fogs and storms and,
oftener, autumnal mists and decay (as in *The Patron* [30]) are suggestive of
the hard human lot and are symbols of the death of men's hopes. A recurring note of disappointment and disillusion sounds sometimes with mere
mournful iteration but more rarely with moving power, as in the story of
the condemned felon's dream of pardon.[31] He despised the old pastoral vein
of rustic verse and the idealization of village life. There is pathos, humor,
and resignation in some of his characters; but he is pitiless to the wicked.
No sudden "conversion" ever brings one of his tales to a forced "happy
ending." There is a grim monotony in his manner, and his themes, as
Hazlitt remarked, "turn, one and all, on the same sort of teasing, helpless,
unimaginative distress." [32] Enmeshed in the particular, he rarely, if ever,
rises to a universal view of life. Stressing the consequences rather than the
causes of folly or sin, he shows himself, like Hogarth, as much a penologist
as a psychologist. Even in his more lightly ironic stories there is a sardonic
tone; and a note of morbidness was sounded when in later life he became
addicted to opium. The effect of the drug is evident in some of his poems.[33]

In structural capacity he was weak. *The Village* is but loosely held together, and the letter form adopted for various sections of *The Borough* is
inappropriate. In the preface to the *Tales* he discussed the possibility of connecting them "by some associating circumstance" in the manner of Chaucer
and Boccaccio but concluded that he could not avail himself "of the benefit
of such artificial mode of affinity." [34] For *Tales of the Hall* he did, however,
invent a simple "frame," contrived from the reunion of two long separated
brothers. Most of his poetry is written in rimed couplets; it is perhaps significant that for the two pieces in which the influence of opium is most
apparent he chose stanzaic forms. In his fidelity to harsh actuality he was

---

[28] *The Borough*, xx. 11-32; *Works*, I. 470. Compare the satiric description (*ibid.*, xx. 59-77)
of the decayed chateau through which the wind and the heroine "sweep."
[29] *The Borough*, xxiv. 450-451; *Works*, I. 524.
[30] Lines 426-433; *Works*, II. 78-79.
[31] *The Borough*, xxiii. 226-332; *Works*, I. 509-511.
[32] *The Spirit of the Age; Collected Works*, ed. Waller and Glover, IV. 352.
[33] Especially in *Sir Eustace Grey* (*Works*, I. 238-251) and *The World of Dreams* (*Works*,
III. 403-413). See Meyer Abrams, *The Milk of Paradise* (Cambridge, Mass., 1934), pp. 13-21.
[34] *Works*, II. 7.

sometimes positively unfair to life, for his eye and mind rejected those mitigating circumstances that seldom fail to soften even the unhappiest fate. Gifford was justified in protesting against Crabbe's "contempt for the *bienséances* of life, and rage for its realities." [35] This "rage" explains his most conspicuous weakness: an inability to select. Every detail must be set down, not only what adds to the effect of a scene but what the reader may claim the right to take for granted. A lack of sensitiveness to language, which is sometimes definitely vulgar, is admitted even by Crabbe's warmest admirers; and there are few passages in his verse that would lose much if recast in prose. Among his admirers have been Scott and Byron; his influence is apparent in the later realistic novel; and there are still a few to praise his "hard, human pulse, . . . his plain excellence and stubborn skill." [36]

Samuel Rogers [37] (1763-1855) is of interest not for his ineffectual poems *Rogers* but because he is a typical figure in a period when taste vacillated between the old classicism and the new romanticism. His wealth enabled him to write with no thought of pleasing the public. Commencing with an *Ode to Superstition* (1786), adorned with historical allusions and formal personifications, he passed on to *The Pleasures of Memory* (1792), in which Archibald Alison's theory of the association of ideas [38] is paraphrased in polished couplets and illustrated with refined instances of the awakening of the imagination by the crowding associations of certain objects and places. In the *Epistle to a Friend* (1798) he celebrated the joys of the art-collector. For years thereafter Rogers wrote no more verses. *The Voyage of Columbus* (1812) shows an advance, or rather a change, in his poetic course; he was no longer dwelling in the sanctuary of classicism but ventured timidly forth. The abrupt and fragmentary manner of the narrative, the attempts at suggestion rather than direct representation, the adventurous theme of storms and mutiny, and the unintentionally absurd supernaturalism of the conspiracy of the gods of America to turn Columbus back, all show Rogers attempting to adapt his "Muse" to romantic tastes. In his next poem, *Jacqueline* (1813), he withdrew to the tame subject of a country maiden whose run-away match is forgiven by her father. He returned in *Human Life* (1819) to the sedately reflective manner best suited to his slender talent. *Italy* (1822), his best-known poem, is a collection of fifty-two sections of impressions and anecdotes of which five are in prose and the remainder might as well have been, though they are in blank verse. Here, with divagations, Rogers followed in the footsteps of Childe Harold from Switzerland to Venice, to Florence, and to Rome. The impressions are often sensitively set down and the tales well told, but only once, in the touching tribute to

[35] *The Quarterly Review*, IV (1810). 281-312 (a notice of *The Borough*).
[36] Edwin Arlington Robinson, "George Crabbe," *Collected Poems* (1922), p. 93.
[37] *Poetical Works* (1875). — *Table-Talk*, ed. Alexander Dyce (1856); G. H. Powell, *Reminiscences and Table-Talk of Samuel Rogers* (1903); P. W. Clayden, *The Early Life of Samuel Rogers* (1887) and *Rogers and his Contemporaries* (1889); R. E. Roberts, *Samuel Rogers and his Circle* (1910).
[38] Based on Hartley's psychology and set forth in *Essays on the Nature and Principles of Taste* (1790).

Byron's memory,[39] does the writing approximate to poetry. Thereafter, through the long remainder of his life, though he refurbished his verses, Rogers wrote little that was new; but he employed two artists—J. M. W. Turner and Thomas Stothard—to do what he could not do for himself: insure the survival of his poems in the memory of posterity. In their editions of *Italy* (1830) and the miscellaneous *Poems* (1834) the matchless delicacy of the vignettes reveals the technique of line-engraving at its best. Rogers was a sort of arbiter of taste in London society. He knew everybody; and to be invited to one of his famous breakfasts was an accolade. The sharpness of his wit contrasted with the gentleness of his verse. He lived long enough to be offered the laureateship on the death of Wordsworth; declining the post, he gave his voice for Tennyson.

Campbell   Another transitional figure was Thomas Campbell [40] (1777-1844), a Scot long resident in London. Campbell withstood the pressure of romanticism and yet was restive under classical restraint. *The Pleasures of Hope* (1799) reveals a temperament which was essentially lyrical struggling to free itself from didactic form. During travels on the Continent in 1800 he composed some of his finest martial lyrics. The outbreak of war between England and Denmark was celebrated in *The Battle of the Baltic,* a poem whose fervent splendor was not justified by an exploit of which England has long since ceased to be proud. Newspaper work, lecturing, and the editorship of *The New Monthly Magazine* supported him in London. Of several narrative poems [41] *Gertrude of Wyoming* (1809) alone retains any interest, and that not much. It stands between Beattie's *The Minstrel* and Byron's *Childe Harold* in its employment of the Spenserian stanza. The exotic American setting is a bid for popular approval; but the story of a massacre of settlers by the Indians is told with an inappropriate fastidiousness. The fire which is missing from the long poems blazes in some of the short pieces. *Ye Mariners of England* still stirs the blood; and in *Hohenlinden* Campbell expressed with memorable power the tragedy and heroism and futility of battle.[42] *The Soldier's Dream* is on a somewhat lower level, as is the once so popular ballad of *Lord Ullin's Daughter.* Two great Scottish themes, the Jacobite rising of 1745 and the gift of second-sight, are combined in *Lochiel's Warning.* These and other short things are more spontaneous (or seemingly so) than the long narratives, which Campbell polished till all the vital ruggedness appropriate to his subjects was smoothed away.

A more brilliant and popular figure in the literary circle of the Whigs was

---

[39] *Italy* (ed. 1830), pp. 97-99.
[40] *Complete Poetical Works,* ed. J. L. Robertson (Oxford, 1908); *Life and Letters,* ed. William Beattie (3v, 1849); J. C. Hadden, *Thomas Campbell* (Edinburgh, 1899).
[41] *Theodric: a Domestic Tale* (1824) and *The Pilgrims of Glencoe* (1842) have faded from remembrance. — Campbell wrote several biographies, of which the most ambitious, *Frederick the Great and his Times* (1842-1843), has been for long lost to sight in the shadow of Carlyle.
[42] See George Saintsbury, "English War-Songs—Campbell," *Essays and Papers,* I. 330-355. To Campbell, as to Byron, was sometimes attributed the most enduringly popular of poems inspired by Napoleonic events, *The Burial of Sir John Moore* (1816), by a young Irishman, Charles Wolfe (1791-1823), who wrote nothing else of consequence.

Thomas Moore [43] (1779-1852) in whose early work there are vestiges of *Moore* classicism while the later is entirely romantic. Moore, who was born in Dublin, came to London in 1798. A version of the *Odes of Anacreon* (1800) was followed by *The Poetical Works of the Late Thomas Little, Esq.* (1802) the insipid amatory improprieties of which gained for Moore, whose authorship was soon known, a notoriety among the prurient. In 1803-1804 he occupied an official post in Bermuda, but having left it in charge of a deputy he traveled in the United States and Canada and then returned to England. *Epistles, Odes and other Poems* (1806) contains impressions of these wanderings. He attempted formal satire in Pope's manner, but not very successfully. Installments of *Irish Melodies* began to appear in 1807 "with symphonies and accompaniments" by Sir John Stevenson and some airs composed by Moore himself. The instant success was furthered among the privileged by Moore who himself sang sweetly in fashionable drawing-rooms. The series of *Melodies* continued intermittently till 1834. Among them were sheaves of *Sacred Songs* and *National Songs*. Moore's satiric talent found an informal outlet in the political squibs and gay lampoons which, beginning in the columns of *The Morning Chronicle,* he published in seven volumes between 1812 and 1835. Of these *The Fudge Family in Paris* (1818) and *Fables for the Holy Alliance* (1823) are representative. *Lalla Rookh* was begun in 1812 and published in 1817. The deputy in Bermuda embezzled funds for which Moore was legally responsible, and between 1818 and 1822 he had to live on the Continent beyond the bailiff's reach. In Venice he associated with Byron who had been his close friend since 1812; but he was more at home in Paris. His last considerable poem was *The Loves of the Angels* (1823). Of much miscellaneous prose work his biography of Byron (1830) is the most noteworthy. In his last years senile dementia overclouded the wit and charm which for long had dazzled society.

To read Moore's poems is to feel, in his own simile, like one who treads "some banquet-hall deserted" with garlands dead and lights extinguished. His works are old-fashioned without being venerable. There are few things more pathetic than faded frivolousness and outmoded sentiment. Only a few of the "melodies"—*Believe Me, if All Those Endearing Young Charms; The Young May Moon is Beaming; Oft in the Stilly Night*—are kept in remembrance, and some of them as much for the sake of the airs as for the words. He is memorable as the first of a long line of singers of Ireland's woes; but he sang them with a sentiment too facile and superficial to be comparable to the poignant laments of the bards of Young Ireland of later date. His light-hearted nature found a proper medium for his easy Muse in the political and social lampoons which were seldom cruel (even against

[43] *Poetical Works* (9v, 1840-1842); a tenth volume, added later, contains a reprint of *The Epicurean* (1827), a philosophical romance of third-century Egypt, Moore's only attempt at prose fiction. *Memoirs, Journal and Correspondence of Thomas Moore,* ed. Lord John Russell (8v, 1853-1856); *Poetical Works,* ed. A. D. Godley (Oxford, 1910). — Stephen Gwynn, *Thomas Moore* (EML Series, 1904); W. F. Trench, *Tom Moore* (Dublin, 1934); H. M. Jones, *The Harp that Once—A Chronicle of the Life of Thomas Moore* (1937); L. A. G. Strong, *The Minstrel Boy: a Portrait of Tom Moore* (1937).

the Prince Regent) and never mean. But with the fading from memory of the occasions and persons that prompted them these things have lost their interest; scholarly commentary sits heavily upon thistledown. In *Lalla Rookh,* which was an instant success all over Europe and was translated, imitated, and turned into an opera, he rode on the crest of the wave of Orientalism which had been long gathering. The poem can still please those who enjoy large expanses of prettiness, and there is wit in it for those who have the patience to search; but there is no strength beneath the surface coloring. *The Loves of the Angels,* taken in part from the Moslem legend of Haruth and Maruth,[44] challenged comparison with Byron's *Heaven and Earth,* which appeared at exactly the same time. It tells of three "sons of God" who fell in love with "the daughters of men" with consequent punishments fitting their greater or lesser degrees of rebelliousness. As originally written, the poem derived from Gen. 6: 1-4 rather than from the *Koran,* and there was an outcry against the juxtaposition of religion and eroticism. Moore promptly "turned his angels into Turks"—that is, into Moslem angels. The episode is characteristic of a poet whose artistic conscience did not much trouble him.

V

Hunt

The last poet to be considered in this chapter brings us even closer than does Moore to the younger generation of the great romantic poets. Leigh Hunt[45] (1784-1859) inherited from his father the eccentricity and improvidence which caused him endless difficulties and humiliations, and from his mother the charm and gentle courage which won him hosts of loyal friends. His first collection of poems, candidly entitled *Juvenilia* (1801), has signs of discipleship to Thomson and Collins but with a reversion in prosody from the "closed" couplet of Pope to the freer manner of Dryden. The importance of Hunt's lasting liking for run-on lines is that it influenced Keats's early poetry. While still a youth Hunt began his career as a journalist and handy-man-of-letters, contributing to periodicals conducted by his elder brother, John. In 1808 John Hunt began to issue on Sundays *The Examiner* which quickly became a formidable opponent of the Tory government.[46] For it Leigh Hunt did the literary and theatrical criticism.[47] In 1811 the

[44] Richard Laurence's translation (1823) of the Ethiopic version of *The Book of Enoch,* manuscripts of which James Bruce had discovered in Abyssinia in 1771, probably called Byron's and Moore's attention to the theme. Analogous subjects were popular among the romantic poets. James Montgomery wrote *A World before the Flood* (1813) as did Reginald Heber (*Poetical Works* (1853), pp. 93-105); George Croly wrote *The Angel of the World* (1820). Lamartine, Vigny, and Hugo wrote similar poems under Byron's influence.

[45] *Poetical Works,* ed. H. S. Milford (Oxford, 1923); *Essays and Poems,* ed. R. B. Johnson (2v, 1891); *Selections in Prose and Verse,* ed. J. H. Lobban (1909); *Prefaces,* ed. R. B. Johnson (1930); *Correspondence,* ed. Thornton Hunt (2v, 1862). — Edmund Blunden, *Leigh Hunt* (1930); Edmund Blunden, *Leigh Hunt's "Examiner" Examined* (1928); Louis Landré, *Leigh Hunt. Contribution à l'histoire du romantisme anglais* (2v, Paris, 1935-1936); Barnette Miller, *Leigh Hunt's Relations with Byron, Shelley, and Keats* (1910).

[46] Michael Roberts, "Leigh Hunt's Place in the Reform Movement, 1808-1810," *RES,* xi (1935). 58-65.

[47] He had already been theatrical critic of *The News* in 1805-1807. See the selection of his *Dramatic Essays,* ed. William Archer and R. W. Lowe (1894). Hunt, says Archer, was "the

Hunts were prosecuted for exposing the barbarities of army discipline; and in 1812 the brothers were fined and imprisoned for denouncing the Prince Regent as a rake and a liar. Meanwhile Hunt had published *The Feast of the Poets* (1811), a satire in which the chief poets of the age appear. In later editions the text and commentary were expanded and altered to suit Hunt's changing tastes.

Hunt was in prison from early in 1813 till February, 1815. He obtained permission to have his wife and children live with him, to carry on his literary work, and to receive visits from friends old and new (the latter attracted by his martyrdom). While incarcerated he published *The Descent of Liberty: a Mask* (1814) in celebration of the downfall of Napoleon, which caused Hazlitt to brand him as an apostate. After his release he lived in the "Vale of Health" in suburban Hampstead, where he was soon associating with two young admirers, Shelley and Keats. A change came over him after his emergence from prison. He held loyally to his political opinions, but he tended to withdraw into the world of books, trusting to his followers the furtherance of the cause for which he had suffered. Benevolent himself, he became increasingly dependent upon the benevolence of friends, not to the advantage of his credit in business affairs.

The Story of Rimini (1816) was Hunt's most ambitious bid for fame as a serious poet. The "free and idiomatic use of language" and the run-on couplets which are characteristics of this poem were of value in promoting a less austere vocabulary and metrical flexibility; but Hunt's taste was insufficiently secure to manage these liberties without adopting a jaunty and familiar style, as of a novelette, disastrously ill-suited to the tragic Dantesque matter of his narrative.[48] The effect of his slipshod vulgarity upon Keats's early style was soon realized by the younger and immeasurably greater poet, with the result that Keats gradually freed himself from Hunt's influence. The taint of low breeding gave some warrant for Lockhart's notorious attack upon the "Cockney School of Poetry" in *Blackwood's Magazine*[49] (October, 1817), though it did not excuse its brutality.

Hunt's Prosody

---

first writer of any note who made it his business to see and report upon all the principal theatrical events of the day." Hunt denounces the venality and incompetence of most contemporary theatrical criticism.

[48] Hunt's critical writings and conversation did much to direct the attention of Keats and other young poets to Italian literature. For interest in Italy during the preceding generation see R. Marshall, *Italy in English Literature, 1755-1815* (1934), and for Hunt's interest in Dante see Paget J. Toynbee, *Dante in English Literature from Chaucer to Cary* (2v, 1909), II. 116-164. The first published English version of the *Divine Comedy* was made by Henry Boyd: the *Inferno* (1785); the entire *Comedy* (1802), but this was not so much a translation as an expanded paraphrase. See Toynbee, I. 410-419. Boyd's version was superseded by the famous translation by the Rev. Henry Francis Cary (1772-1844). Of this the *Inferno* appeared in 1805-1806 and the entire poem in 1814 with the title: *The Vision: or Hell, Purgatory, and Paradise, of Dante Alighieri*. The work was almost unnoticed till 1818 when a recommendation of it by Coleridge in one of his lectures called attention to it. See Toynbee, I. 455-502. Cary numbered many men of letters among his friends and was on terms of intimacy with Charles Lamb. See R. W. King, *The Translator of Dante: The Life, Work, and Friendships of Henry Francis Cary* (1925).

[49] Reprinted in *Notorious Literary Attacks*, ed. Albert Mordell (1926), pp. 11-19.

Foliage (1818) contains, along with some admirable translations, one poem of lasting interest. This is *The Nymphs,* the foster-sister, as it were, of *Endymion.* It throws light upon the aesthetic milieu in which Keats's poem was written. The two narratives in *Hero and Leander; and Bacchus and Ariadne* (1819) show that Hunt had not learned that great subjects were beyond his capability as a poet. *The Indicator* (1819-1821), a literary weekly, contained some of Hunt's pleasantest essays, things trivial in themselves but written with the easy discursiveness of the born journalist. In 1822 Byron and Shelley invited him to join them in the project of a new quarterly to be called *The Liberal.* This ill-fated scheme brought Hunt and his family

At Pisa to Italy shortly before Shelley was drowned. Four issues of *The Liberal* appeared, but Byron lost heart in the undertaking and Hunt's situation in Italy became forlorn. In Florence he consorted with Landor and Hazlitt. The latter's portrait of Hunt in *The Spirit of the Age,* while candid in revealing his faults both as a writer and a man, was in the main so generous in advertising his virtues and accomplishments that it did much to cheer the now wayworn author.

Later Years Hunt returned to England in 1825. Obliged by necessity, he consented to publish his reminiscences of Byron at this time when there was a great demand for Byroniana. In these articles, which, with additional matter, were made into *Lord Byron and Some of his Contemporaries* (1828), Hunt, without any fundamental falsification of the truth, unwisely avenged himself for humiliations to which Byron had subjected him. The book occasioned an acrimonious quarrel with Thomas Moore.[50] Between 1830 and 1832 Hunt conducted *The Tatler,* issued in rivalry to the newly founded *Spectator.* For the loss of old friends there was partial compensation in the gain of new, among them Browning, Dickens, and Carlyle. Carlyle has left a vivid pen-sketch of Hunt and his family, concluding: "A most interesting, pitiable, lovable man, to be used kindly but with discretion."[51] Dickens' caricature of him as Harold Skimpole in *Bleak House* (1852) was not in intention unkind, but it wounded by the thoughtless implication that the dishonesty belonging to the fictitious person was a characteristic of the real prototype. In his later years a vast quantity of miscellaneous matter poured from Hunt's pen. *A Legend of Florence* (1840), a play neither better nor worse than the usual run of poetic drama, had a *succès d'estime* in his circle. In 1850 he published the most delightful of his books, the *Autobiography;*[52] and in the same year, when mentioned for the laureateship, generously supported the claims of Tennyson.

As a poet Hunt is remembered for *Abou ben Adhem,* which passes from anthology to anthology; for a few bits of graceful trivia such as *Jenny Kissed Me* (the kiss was Mrs. Carlyle's compliment to him; the verses, his to her); for the forceful indictment of militarism in *Captain Sword and Captain*

[50] Moore attacked Hunt in an unpleasant satiric fable, *The Living Dog and the Dead Lion.*
[51] J. A. Froude, *Thomas Carlyle: The First Forty Years* (ed. 1910), II. 354-355.
[52] Ed. Roger Ingpen (1903); World's Classics ed. (1928).

Pen; and for his serious but fortunately temporary misguidance of Keats. The issues upon which he wrote were often fine, but his spirit was seldom finely touched to them. For the sake of spontaneity he sacrificed art; for the sake of liveliness he sacrificed dignity. Grave themes generally betrayed him into falsities of taste; light themes into sentimentality and triviality. The taint of vulgarity is on most of his verse. It is less apparent in his prose because, making less effort, he stumbled less often. Most of his essays and miscellaneous prose writings have proved ephemeral; they were good journalism in their day but are of little moment in ours. He could handle acceptably, and occasionally adorn, any subject that occurred to his quick and facile fancy.

VII

Reviews and·Magazines: 1802-1830; The Essayists

I

The old distinction between the "review" and the "magazine" was still in force at the beginning of the nineteenth century. The function of the former was to survey politics, literature, science, and art; the latter, as its name implied, was a storehouse of literary and antiquarian learning with an infusion of more fanciful prose and verse. *The Gentleman's Magazine,* the greatest of its kind, continued uninterruptedly till mid-Victorian times and with vicissitudes almost to our own day. It was without party affiliations and existed solely to instruct and entertain. The organs of political and religious opinions which after 1802 had to struggle against fresh, vigorous rivals had once numbered great men of letters among their occasional contributors, but in general they were written by slovenly and ill-paid hacks who as literary critics made scarcely a pretense to independence, being cowed by their editors. These in turn were dependent upon the booksellers whose wares they advertised; consequently they did not dare to criticize adversely. Criticism was not only venal but quite non-selective. Whether valuable or worthless, books that were advertised were noticed.

The
Edinburgh
Review

Such, in brief, was the situation when in 1802 a new stage in the history of English periodicals began. Three young men then living in Edinburgh—Francis Jeffrey, an advocate; Henry Brougham, a barrister; and Sydney Smith, an Anglican clergyman—found themselves at one in conservative literary tastes and liberal political outlook. Alarmed by the strength of entrenched Toryism, they determined to found a review which should support the Whigs in the advocacy of reform. With Constable of Edinburgh and Longman and Rees of London as publishers and with Jeffrey as editor, they launched *The Edinburgh Review and Critical Journal* in October, 1802. In politics and literature alike the *Edinburgh* spoke as one having authority and not as the scribblers. It aimed not only to reflect but to mold political opinion in the Whig interest. But unlike the old partisan· organs, it was written by men of vigorous minds and independent judgment. Its repute was enhanced by the policy of anonymity. The voice was not that of an individual, however eminent, but of a group, a party, one-half England. The strong personality of the editor imposed a unity of tone, but the contributors wrote from conviction, not of necessity. Pay at rates hitherto unheard of commanded the services of the most distinguished talent, and though there was grumbling at editorial changes and condensations, these writers felt themselves protected by anonymity and very few severed their profitable and congenial connection. Among these few was Sir Walter Scott who, when the Whiggery of the *Edinburgh* became too disturbingly pronounced, transferred his allegiance to the *Quarterly*. But the genial independence of spirit which characterized the group is evinced by the lasting personal friendship between Scott and Jeffrey. The vigor and authoritativeness of its style, its indubitable independence, and the policy of selecting for comment only publications which possessed some value made the *Edinburgh* an instantaneous success. Its circulation rose steadily to a maximum of about 14,000 in 1818, a figure which, however, does not represent the public it reached, for copies passed from hand to hand and there was a constant demand for reprints in bound volumes.

Of the *Edinburgh* triumvirate the chief was the editor, Francis Jeffrey [1] *Jeffrey* (1773-1850), who held his post till 1829. The tone he set was exasperating to many, yet warranted to attract attention and to impose opinion upon countless readers who desired guidance. He applied to criticism a versatile, legalistic, and dogmatic mind. He was the last considerable English critic who held to the high a priori road, bringing imaginative literature to the bar of established forms and conventions. Yet the classical tradition to which he was loyal struggled with a reluctant admiration for the new romanticism. Late in life he admitted that his early judgments of the Lake Poets were at fault, and there is wistfulness in his famous retrospective farewell to the "rich melodies" of Keats and Shelley, the "splendid strains" of Moore, and the "blazing star" of Byron.[2] The fascination which romance exercised upon this precise, sharp dogmatist is evident in his love of the lesser Elizabethan dramatists. Jeffrey was not a great critic, but he was honest, independent, and influential, and by making his *Review* a medium for critics more profound and sensitive than himself he raised the general level of the profession. His miscellaneous articles, ranging over law, politics, biography, history, travel, and other subjects, have proved ephemeral.

His colleague Henry Brougham [3] (1778-1868), afterwards Lord Chancellor, stands on the extreme periphery of literary history. Brougham's courageous *Brougham* endeavors in the cause of political, social, and educational reform, his gifts as statesman and orator, his defects of character, and his quarrels and controversies are subjects that concern the biographer and political historian. So close was his connection with the *Edinburgh* and so large his services to it that in later years, when Macvey Napier was editor, he attempted to

---

[1] Afterwards (1834) Lord Jeffrey. — *Contributions to the Edinburgh Review* (4v, 1844); *Selections*, ed. L. E. Gates, (1894); *Literary Criticism*, ed. D. Nichol Smith (1910). — H. T. Cockburn, *Life of Lord Jeffrey* (1852); George Saintsbury, "Jeffrey," *Essays and Papers*, I. 79-105.

[2] *The Edinburgh Review*, L (1829). 47.

[3] *Works* (11v, Edinburgh, 1872-1873); *Life and Times of Lord Brougham Written by Himself* (3v, 1871-1872). — G. T. Garratt, *Lord Brougham* (1935); A. M. Gilbert, *The Work of Lord Brougham for Education in England* (Chambersburg, Pa., 1922); Arthur Aspinall, *Lord Brougham and the Whig Party* (Manchester, 1927).

dictate its policies and regarded it almost as his personal organ. This attitude involved him in many disputes, notoriously with his hated rival, Macaulay. Of the vast number of his contributions to the *Review* not one is read today.

Sydney Smith [4] (1771-1845) is one of those figures about whom it is easy to say much and difficult to say little. His famous wit is more easily discoverable in letters and anecdotes than recoverable from his formal writings, partly because it is there imbedded in the context and partly because it has faded with the issues that inspired it. This wit too frequently swelled to mere high spirits which sound coarsely rollicking to our ears; but some of his sayings and even some of his practical jokes are classics in their kind, and beneath his jesting were ardent sincerity and immense vigor dedicated to many good causes. He was the mainstay of the *Edinburgh* in its championship of a variety of reforms, from the emancipation of Catholics to changes in the game laws, from the elevation of female education to the abolition of mantraps. His powers as a satirist and advocate of reform are seen at their best in the *Letters on the Subject of the Catholics* (1808), generally known from the pseudonym on the title-page as *The Plymley Letters*.

Of the contributors whom Jeffrey gathered round him by far the greatest was Sir Walter Scott. By 1806 Scott had written ten articles for the *Edinburgh,* but in that year he withdrew his support and began negotiations with John Murray for the establishment of a new review which should challenge the dominance of the Whigs and supply a counterpoise to "the disgusting and deleterious doctrines with which the most popular of these periodicals disgraces its pages." [5] Scott was offered but declined the editorship of *The Quarterly Review,* and it went to the learned but acidulous and unimaginative William Gifford [6] who impressed his own dull aridity upon the initial number (February, 1809). From this unpromising beginning there was a recovery, but though the *Quarterly* soon rivaled the *Edinburgh* in circulation and authority it was never so uniformly brilliant in style. Scott wrote frequently for it, and Southey so voluminously that Gifford regarded him as "the sheet anchor of the *Review.*"

The pontifical ponderousness of the *Quarterly* suggested the desirability of a more nimble weapon against the Whigs. This need was apparent to William Blackwood [7] of Edinburgh who desired also to promote the fortunes of his publishing house at the expense of Constable, his competitor. In 1817 *Blackwood's Edinburgh Magazine* got off to a discouraging start

---

[4] *Works* (4v, 1839-1840); *Selections,* ed. Ernest Rhys (1892). — Lady Holland, *Memoir of the Rev. Sydney Smith* (2v, 1855); G. W. E. Russell, *Sydney Smith,* (EML Series, 1905); André Chevrillon, *Sydney Smith et la renaissance des idées libérales en Angleterre au xix* siècle (Paris, 1894); George Saintsbury, "Sydney Smith," *Essays and Papers,* I. 53-78.

[5] Scott to Gifford, October 25, 1808; *Letters,* ed. Grierson, II. 105.

[6] On Gifford see ch. I, n. 11, above. — A regular contributor to the *Quarterly* was Macaulay's enemy, John Wilson Croker (1780-1857), a bigoted Tory politician and atrabiliar pedant, best remembered for his edition of Boswell's *Johnson.* Croker wrote the review of Keats's *Endymion* (1818) for which the *Quarterly* has suffered merited obloquy. — The *Croker Papers,* ed. L. J. Jennings (2v, 1884); M. F. Brightfield, *John Wilson Croker* (Berkeley, 1940). See also in general Walter Graham, *Tory Criticism in the Quarterly Review, 1809-1853* (1921).

[7] M. O. Oliphant, *Annals of a Publishing House: William Blackwood* (3v, 1897).

but quickly recovered itself when the proprietor procured the services of three clever writers, John Gibson Lockhart and James Hogg (who as poets and novelists are considered later in the present work) and John Wilson [8] (1785-1854), poet, scholar, and forceful personality. A *succès de scandale* engineered by these three set the new magazine on its feet. *The Chaldee MS*, a biblical parody, subjected to ridicule the entire entourage of *The Edinburgh Review* and many other respectable personages in the northern metropolis. The point of this satire is now blunted, and it is difficult to understand why even at the time it roused much interest south of the Border; but the fact is that it took all Britain by storm. The actions for libel which resulted served merely as more advertisements for *Blackwood's*. This success fixed the tone of flippant and cruel satire which was characteristic of the magazine for many years, though after the duel which resulted in the death of John Scott, Lockhart became more seemly and the manners of the group gradually improved. In 1819 Blackwood added to his ranks the wayward Irishman, William Maginn [9] (1793-1842), scholar, wit, and improvisor of burlesques. From him may have come the suggestion for the *Noctes Ambrosianae* which began in 1822 and became a popular feature of the magazine. The chief author of these papers was, however, John Wilson. Taking its name from a public-house where the friends met together, the *Noctes* is a record of real or imaginary conversations on life and letters, enthusiastic, romantic, satirical, derisive, and rowdy by turns. In it Hogg appears *in propria persona;* Wilson in the pseudonymous guise of "Christopher North"; Maginn as "O'Doherty"; and other characters, some fictitious, others real, appear from time to time, the real people not always with their own consent. The raciness and realism of the dialogues have given them something of enduring vitality and they are still enjoyable. In this department as in all the editorial contributions a Tory flavoring was maintained; but *Blackwood's* also offered entertainment unattached to political party. It published verse and fiction.[10]

   To the success of *Blackwood's* was due a new venture, the brilliant and

---

[8] Wilson's poem *The Isle of Palms* (1812) is quietly lovely and Wordsworthian; *The City of the Plague* (1816) is a succession of dramatic episodes based upon Defoe's *Journal of the Plague Year*. His fiction is of little moment. In 1820, notwithstanding his slender qualifications and the rival candidacy of Sir William Hamilton, the Tory majority of the town council elected Wilson to the chair of moral philosophy in the University of Edinburgh. As a professor he influenced generations of students who admired the man and were indifferent to his lack of philosophic profundity. — *Works*, ed. J. F. Ferrier (12v, 1855-1858); *Essays, Critical and Imaginative* (4v, 1856); *Noctes Ambrosianae*, ed. R. S. Mackenzie (5v, 1854), containing only the *Noctes* written by Wilson, about half the total number; *Recreations of Christopher North* (2v, 1887); *Poetical Works* (Edinburgh, 1896). — Mary Gordon, *Christopher North, a Memoir of John Wilson* (2v, Edinburgh, 1862); George Saintsbury, "Wilson," *Essays and Papers*, I. 184-209.

[9] *Miscellaneous Writings* (5v, 1855-1857). — The best biography of Maginn, relieving him of the serious charges brought against him by an enemy and recently revived by Michael Sadleir, is in M. M. H. Thrall, *Rebellious Fraser's* (1934), pp. 161-244. In later life Maginn's convivial habits degenerated into confirmed drunkenness, but he deserves to be remembered for himself as well as for Lockhart's lines on "bright, broken Maginn."

[10] The popularity of this fiction is attested by three series of *Tales from Blackwood* (12v, 1858-1861; 12v, 1878-1880; 6v, 1889). Many are still readable, notably *The Iron Shroud* which may have suggested to Poe *The Pit and the Pendulum*.

The
London
Magazine

short-lived (1820-1829) *London Magazine.* Its editor, John Scott [11] (1783-1821), gathered round him a notable variety of talents, including Lamb, Hazlitt, and De Quincey. In so far as it concerned itself with politics the *London* was liberal, and its literary sympathies were with the romantic school. Its most serious rival, save *Blackwood's,* was Colburn's *New Monthly Magazine,* which was for long popular under the successive editorships of Campbell, Bulwer, Hook, and Hood. Though faintly Whig in tint, it tried to eschew politics altogether. *The Westminster Review,* a publication of graver import, was founded in 1824 as the organ of the "Philosophic Radicals" led by Bentham and the Mills.[12] It offered trenchant criticism of Whigs and Tories alike. While the great reviews pursued their equable courses the magazines which aimed to entertain came to depend more and more upon serialized fiction and thus provided one of the two media (the other being publication in the form of monthly parts) for the Victorian

Fraser's

novelists who were appearing upon the scene. *Fraser's Magazine,*[13] long-lived and very influential, managed to combine amusement with the serious advocacy of many reforms. Its proprietor engaged the services of William Maginn as editor. Under his pen-name of "Oliver Yorke" he is known to all readers of *Sartor Resartus;* but those who remember Carlyle's satire do not always appreciate the liberalism of the editorial mind which gave hospitality to a work of literature so new and strange as *Sartor.* With the appearance of *Fraser's* in 1830 the modern era of periodical publications may be considered to begin.[14]

II

Lamb

Charles Lamb [15] (1775-1834) was born in the heart of the great city which throughout his life was his home and his delight. Though he had happy

[11] Scott had been editor of *The Champion* and had attracted attention with his brilliant impressions of Paris in 1814 and 1815 which Thackeray commended long afterwards as "famous good reading" (*The Newcomes,* ch. xxii). Among his admirers were Wordsworth and Byron. In *The London Magazine* (May, 1820) Scott attacked the Blackwood group for their satiric scurrilities. Lockhart challenged him to a duel. The quarrel was settled in so bungling a fashion that Lockhart's friend C. H. Christie imputed cowardice to Scott. Whereupon Scott challenged Christie. In the duel Scott was mortally wounded and died in a few days (February, 1821).

[12] G. L. Nesbitt, *Benthamite Reviewing: Twelve Years of the Westminster Review, 1824-1836* (1934).

[13] Among the contributors to *Fraser's* in its early days were Carlyle, Thackeray, Crofton Croker (the Irish folklorist), Hook, Galt, Lockhart, and Francis Mahony ("Father Prout"), the charming ex-Jesuit and author of *The Shandon Bells.* See M. M. H. Thrall, *Rebellious Fraser's* (1934). On its lighter side *Fraser's* was a precursor of *Punch* (founded in 1841) for which many of its staff wrote in later years.

[14] Of special studies of Victorian periodicals the most important are W. B. Thomas, *The Story of the Spectator* (1928), E. M. Everett, *The Party of Humanity: The Fortnightly Review and its Contributors, 1865-1874* (1939), L. A. Marchand, *The Athenaeum: a Mirror of Victorian Culture* (1941), and M. M. Bevington, *The Saturday Review, 1855-1868* (1941). See also E. E. Kellett, "The Press," in *Early Victorian England,* ed. G. M. Young (1934), ii. 3-97, and references there given to histories of *The Times, Punch,* and so forth.

[15] *Life and Works,* ed. Alfred Ainger (12v, 1899-1900); *Works,* ed. E. V. Lucas (7v, 1903); *Works in Prose and Verse,* ed. Thomas Hutchinson (2v, Oxford, 1909); *Works,* ed. William Macdonald (12v, 1903); *Letters,* ed. E. V. Lucas (3v, 1935); *Twenty Essays of Elia,* ed. Daniel Varney (1932); *Essays and Letters,* ed. J. M. French (1937), a selection. — J. C. Thomas,

recollections of the rural holidays of his childhood, spent vacations in various parts of England, and became the friend of the great poets who made a cult of nature, he was as urban as Doctor Johnson. He told Wordsworth that he did not care if he never saw a mountain, and on a visit to Keswick he affirmed that he would not exchange Fleet Street for Skiddaw. In this indifference to nature he stands apart from all his friends.

At Christ's Hospital,[16] where he was educated, he formed a lifelong friendship with Coleridge, and through Coleridge he later met Wordsworth, whom he never ceased to regard as the greatest of living poets. On leaving school he was employed for a short time in South Sea House [17] and then, in 1792, entered upon his long career of secure routine as a clerk in East India House. Wisely he chose to depend upon this post for his livelihood and not upon his talent as a writer. Four sonnets by him appeared without his name among Coleridge's *Poems* of 1796; other pieces, this time ascribed to him, were added in the edition of 1797. He helped a friend, James White, with the ingenious skit which claimed to be *Original Letters, etc., of Sir John Falstaff* [18] (1796). There was insanity in Lamb's family, though he was himself touched with it but once, at the age of twenty. But in 1796 came the dreadful blow when his sister Mary (1764-1847) in sudden mania killed their mother. Unwilling to have Mary permanently put away, Lamb made himself for the remainder of his life responsible for her. Much of the time she was normal and shared in his literary tastes and pursuits; but at intervals, on the appearance of premonitory symptoms, she had to be consigned to an asylum. This is the melancholy background of Lamb's character and humor—and intemperance.

Through Coleridge Lamb met Charles Lloyd,[19] a Quaker with a thin poetic talent, in collaboration with whom he published a volume baldly entitled *Blank Verse* (1798). This contained his best-known poem, *Old Familiar Faces,* which in its gentle pathos and nostalgia for the past is characteristic of the author, though he was but twenty-three years old. To the same year belongs *The Tale of Rosamund Gray,* part fiction, part reminiscence, not very coherent, but delicate in its humor, descriptions, and characterizations. *John Woodvil* (1802) is a clumsily constructed and almost

Bibliography (1908); E. V. Lucas, *Life of Charles Lamb* (2v, 1905); F. V. Morley, *Lamb before Elia* (1932); Edmund Blunden, *Charles Lamb and his Contemporaries* (1933); A. C. Ward, *The Frolic and the Gentle: a Centenary Study of Charles Lamb* (1934); J. May Lewis, *Charles Lamb* (1934); Orlo Williams, *Charles Lamb* (1934); E. C. Johnson, *Lamb Always Elia* (1935); E. C. Ross, *The Ordeal of Bridget Elia: a Chronicle of the Lambs* (Norman, Okl., 1940); Katharine Anthony, *The Lambs* (1945); M. H. Law, *The English Familiar Essay in the Early Nineteenth Century* (Philadelphia, 1934).

16 Edmund Blunden, "Elia and Christ's Hospital," *E&S,* XXII (1937). 37-60.

17 To save the feelings of his elder brother John, who spent his life as a clerk there, Lamb wrote under a pseudonym when he published *Recollections of the South-Sea House,* the first of the *Essays of Elia* (*The London Magazine,* August, 1820). The name Elia was that of an Italian clerk who had been employed in South Sea House.

18 Ed. C. E. Merrill (1924). — The skit was prompted by W. H. Ireland's "Shakespearean" fabrication, *Vortigern,* which had been produced in this same year, 1796.

19 Charles Lloyd (1775-1839), author of *Edmund Oliver* (1798), a novel containing a satiric portrait of Coleridge, and of several volumes of poems for the most part feebly Wordsworthian in tone. He translated the tragedies of Vittorio Alfieri (1815).

plotless drama, but lively in movement and noble in sentiment. Its period is the Restoration and its protagonist an old parliamentarian; but in atmosphere and style it is a precursor of the "Elizabethan Revival" which Lamb, as critic and anthologist, presently did much to initiate. Between 1802 and 1804 he wrote for various newspapers and through association with ill-conditioned hacks was confirmed in his taste for alcohol. But these men were not his intimates. At his famous "Wednesday evenings," of which Hazlitt has left a vivid description, men of talent or genius forgathered and they became a notable feature of literary London.

Lamb's farce, *Mr. H——* (1806), though no worse than the general run of its kind, met with failure upon the stage. Its buffoonery—good enough for a passing jest but thin and stupid when stretched to an evening's entertainment—is a reminder of the need to distinguish between Lamb's humor, which is subtly perceptive of the incongruities of life, and his jocosity, which is a matter of puns and horseplay not always in the best of taste. His humor was known to the privileged few long before it delighted readers. His earliest public efforts to be funny were often laborious and sometimes grim, and to the end he was not always sure of himself but liable, when writing against the grain of melancholy, to strike a forced and false note. A strange streak of the sardonic, which is often overlooked in accounts of "the frolic and the gentle" Lamb, appears in some anecdotes of his behavior and in some passages in his letters.

'ales from
hake-
peare

Though his name appeared alone on the title-page of *Tales from Shakespeare* (1807), actually he wrote only the six tragedies and his sister the fourteen comedies. The histories, the Roman plays, and two of the comedies were omitted. The skill with which Shakespeare's language is retained in simplified form and so carefully dovetailed into the narrative that the joints are almost invisible is matched by the exquisite tact with which the essentials of the stories are preserved yet adapted to an immature intelligence and moral sense.[20] The style, without being pastiche, is so perfectly in keeping as to suggest that these are the original tales, here recovered, whence Shakespeare derived his plots. Though addressed to children, this charming book reached an adult audience at the moment when romantic "bardolatry" was raising Shakespeare to his modern position of supreme national poet.[21] A companion book entirely by Charles, *The Adventures of Ulysses* (1808), though written with spirited directness, suffers from too close a dependence upon Chapman's *Odyssey*. In 1808 came also the *Specimens of the English Dramatic Poets who Lived about the Time of Shakespeare,* one of the finest of all anthologies. Save for an inadequate appreciation of Marlowe's genius Lamb's taste is faultless. The great scenes of Heywood, Webster, Dekker, Fletcher, Middleton, and Ford were here restored to remembrance, and

---

[20] The problem which *Othello* presented Lamb solved beautifully by treating passionate love in the guise of a supreme affection which comes within the compass of a child's understanding. See Oliver Elton, *Survey . . . 1780-1830* (1920), II. 341-342.

[21] On the earlier stages of this movement see R. W. Babcock, *The Genesis of Shakespeare Idolatry* (Chapel Hill, 1931).

the passages chosen were illuminated with brief comments which contain some of the best-known *obiter dicta* in English criticism.

Mrs. Leicester's School (1809) contains ten tales of childhood (three by Charles and seven by Mary), supposedly related by the "young ladies" of the school and set down by their teacher. In these slight, tender, delicate things memories are interwoven with fiction. Close to them is another joint work, *Poems for Children* (1809), mainly by Mary, simple little bits of moralizing but with a humor and pathos which raise them above the level of the apologues which it was then the educational mode to inflict upon the young. This was the last book the Lambs published together.

The letters of the following decade, addressed to Wordsworth, Coleridge, George Dyer, and other friends, are filled with critical comment upon contemporary poetry and older literature and are among the most precious of Lamb's writings. For the public he wrote comparatively little. In Leigh Hunt's *Reflector* were published (1811) the penetrating but somewhat labored studies of Hogarth and of Shakespeare's tragedies.[22] *Recollections of Christ's Hospital* (in *The Gentleman's Magazine*, 1813) gave promise of *Elia*, still several years off. The *Confessions of a Drunkard* (in *The Philanthropist*, 1813) was, though exaggerated, founded upon personal experience and not without serious intent. Lamb impishly reprinted it in *The London Magazine* in 1822 as a sort of pendant to De Quincey's *Confessions of an English Opium-Eater*.

To *The London Magazine* Lamb contributed between 1820 and 1825 the essays signed "Elia." A first collection of these was made in 1823;[23] and *The Last Essays of Elia* (gathered from various magazines) appeared in 1833. Their descent is from the "familiar" essay of the eighteenth century, but in color and warmth they are romantic and there are closer affinities to seventeenth-century prose. Lamb had long since imitated with extraordinary fidelity the manner and mood of Robert Burton;[24] and in the essays the wide-ranging curiosity and delight in strange learning recall Burton. Some of the deliberate archaisms of style are traceable to the same source and others to Sir Thomas Browne, and in phrase and cadence and in the solemn, elaborate treatment of small things there are suggestions of Browne. The sixteen *Popular Fallacies* of the *Last Essays* were obviously imitated from the *Vulgar Errors*. Temple, Taylor, Fuller, and the "Character-Writers" were also laid under contribution. Lamb's retentive memory betrayed him at times into something like plagiarism; but what he took he made his own. He was master of a simple, direct manner when it was appropriate to his subject; but with De Quincey he was responsible for restoring to English style the elaborate harmonies of pre-Augustan prose. Like all the romantics he is self-revelatory, but there is nothing in him of the

"Elia"

22 See Augustus Ralli, *A History of Shakespearean Criticism* (1932), I. 143-145.
23 *Elia, Essays which have Appeared under that Signature in The London Magazine.*
24 The *Fragments of Burton*, first published with *John Woodvil* (1802), were not really intended to deceive and are therefore not, properly speaking, fabrications. They include an astonishing imitation of Burtonian melancholy in the poem *Hypochondriacus.*

"egotistical-sublime." Experience had made him too clear-sighted to take any individual, least of all himself, too seriously. The admissions of his own weaknesses, follies, and prejudices are so many humorous warnings to his readers. In middle age Lamb found his most characteristic subject in the *recherche du temps perdu.* Past time is viewed through glowing mists of memory which distort the actual without entirely falsifying it. The point where fact shades into fancy is so indefinite that he is not trustworthy and does not pretend to be, for he was a pseudonymous essayist, not a sworn witness before a jury of biographers. The affection for children is rooted in memories of his own childhood, and odd characters and situations, recollected from his own youth, are the material for many of the essays. The prevailing mood is pathos, but Lamb is a humorist and when on the verge of sentimentality can almost always check himself with laughter, and recognizing the nearness of laughter to tears, he accomplished many of his most individual effects through this proximity. The contrast and convergence of the two moods were for him the stuff of human life.

Humor and Pathos

Ill health led to his resignation from East India House in 1825. *The Superannuated Man* is a memorial of his freedom and a complaint that he now had too much time on his hands. He severed his connection with *The London Magazine,* but continued to contribute to other periodicals. *The Wife's Trial* (1827) is a comedy in blank verse founded upon Crabbe's tale, *The Confidant.* His sister's periods of insanity and his own intemperance were increasing strains upon his health. In 1830 his poems were gathered together in *Album Verses.* Some of these occasional pieces are quaint and charming; there are lovely echoes of the seventeenth-century poets; and one sonnet, *The Gypsy's Mansion,* rises far above the modest level of "album" poetry. The *Last Essays* appeared in 1833, and in the following year "the frolic and the gentle" Lamb "vanished from his humble hearth." Mary, whose remarkable personality has been too much obscured by her brother's, survived him thirteen years.

Lamb seldom permitted his profounder views of life to appear above the humorous, pathetic, and ironical surface of his writings. In religion he sympathized with the Unitarians; in politics (in so far as he had any political opinions) he was a radical with many reservations. He never pretended to frame a consistent philosophy, nor did he aim to teach or to lead; but, loving his fellow-men, he asked, if for anything, for their affection. This he won in abundance from countless friends and from generations of readers who love him not only for his writings but even more for himself.

III

Hazlitt

In this matter of friendship and affection the contrast which William Hazlitt [25] presents is extraordinary. "Call me Ishmael!" he might have ex-

[25] *Complete Works,* ed. P. P. Howe (21v, 1930-1933); *Collected Works,* ed. A. R. Waller and Arnold Glover (12v, 1902-1904; Index, 1906), does not include the *Life of Napoleon* nor the pieces first assembled in *New Writings,* ed. P. P. Howe (2v, 1925 and 1927); *Essays by*

claimed. His temperament drove him into the very dissidence of dissent, sometimes into a minority of one. He was the target of scurrilous attacks and gave as good as he got. He was often contemptuous, sometimes malignant. He quarreled with all his friends save Lamb—and nearly quarreled with him. He bore misfortune not with the quiet fortitude of Lamb but morbidly, angrily, acrimoniously. His enemies gloated over his solitude and misery. Yet he was not miserable. He nursed his wrath to keep it warm and possessed a proud self-confidence in adversity. He railed against people and institutions but not against life. His story is unhappy in the telling; but on his death-bed he declared that he had had a happy life. He made his own way, was never seduced from honest conviction by considerations of worldly interest, and was no man's hireling. For all his egotism, he was passionately devoted to the rights and liberties of mankind. This devotion to freedom is the thread which binds together all his work. It explains his seemingly perverse idolatry of Napoleon, for in the downfall of this foe of the old hereditary despotisms he recognized the triumph not of liberalism but of reaction. Hazlitt's prejudices sometimes blinded him to merit. His jealousy of rank probably colored his estimate of Shelley, and instinctive hostility to a lord worked against his sympathy with Byron's liberalism. But more often his political opinions were not allowed to warp his judgment and taste as a literary critic. He detested Burke's politics but lavished praise upon him as a writer. He regarded Wordsworth as a turn-coat but also as the greatest poet of the age. He would kneel, he said, to the author of the Waverley Novels, but he would not shake hands with the Tory Sir Walter Scott.

William Hazlitt (1778-1830), the son of a nonconformist minister, passed his youth in Shropshire.[26] Characteristically, his earliest piece of writing was a letter (1791) to a Shrewsbury newspaper defending Joseph Priestley and remonstrating against the outrage done him by the Birmingham mob. With almost no regular education, he read and meditated and walked about the country. In 1798 he met Coleridge, who invited him to Nether Stowey where he met Wordsworth. These new friends shaped his course toward literature, but his ambition was to become a painter. The Peace of Amiens in 1802 afforded an opportunity to visit Paris, where he copied Titians in the Louvre and was enraptured with the works of art which

William Hazlitt, ed. P. V. D. Shelly (1924); Selected Essays, ed. Geoffrey Keynes (1930); Hazlitt on English Literature, ed. Jacob Zeitlin (1913). — Geoffrey Keynes, Bibliography (1931); P. P. Howe, The Life of William Hazlitt (1922); Augustine Birrell, William Hazlitt (EML Series, 1902); C. M. Maclean, Born under Saturn: A Biography of William Hazlitt (1944); M. H. Law, The English Familiar Essay in the Early Nineteenth Century (Philadelphia, 1934); W. P. Ker, "William Hazlitt," Collected Essays (1925), I. 242-257; George Saintsbury, "Hazlitt," Essays and Papers, I. 106-133; Virginia Woolf, "William Hazlitt," The Second Common Reader (1932), pp. 186-199; H. W. Garrod, "The Place of Hazlitt in English Criticism," The Profession of Poetry and other Lectures (Oxford, 1929), pp. 93-109; S. P. Chase, "Hazlitt as a Critic of Art," PMLA, XXXIX (1924). 179-202; P. L. Carver, "Hazlitt's Contributions to the Edinburgh Review," RES, IV (1928). 385-393.

26 He was with his family for three years in America, but was too young to absorb any memories save of the beauty of the New England country.

were the trophies of Napoleon's victories. After his return home he struggled to master his chosen profession, but though there is evidence of talent in his portrait of Lamb, in the end he abandoned the attempt. It bore fruit, however, in his writings upon art and in his friendships with Flaxman, Haydon, and Northcote.[27] Meanwhile, intercourse with Coleridge had turned his mind toward philosophy, and in 1805 he published *An Essay on the Principles of Human Action*. This has been judged amateurish, but the basic pluralism which he expounded is the key to his sporadic pronouncements upon aesthetics and prepares the reader for his catholic sympathies as a critic of art and literature.

Hazlitt's marriage (1808) to Sarah Stoddart, a friend of the Lambs, forced him to seek a livelihood as a journalist and lecturer. For years after 1813 he wrote theatrical criticisms, which were collected in *A View of the English Stage* (1818). His enthusiasm was not for the scholarship or antiquarianism of the theatre, but for the actual plays, new or revived, for the actors, for the audience, and for his own responses. To the subject of his first considerable book, the *Memoir of Thomas Holcroft* (1816), he was drawn not only by Holcroft's political radicalism but by his talent as a dramatist. Hazlitt's knowledge of the practical problems of the stage helped *Lectures* to vitalize the lectures on the *Characters of Shakespeare's Plays* (1817) in which, ignoring historical and philological research, he shared with his readers an enjoyment of Shakespeare's profound and varied panorama of human life.[28] Many short papers on miscellaneous topics, somewhat in the manner of the old "familiar" essay, were published in *The Examiner* and collected in *The Round Table* (1817). There are good things here, such as the characterization of Rousseau and the papers on Milton, but Hazlitt's expansive genius needed ampler room. This he had in the three books that followed: *Lectures on the English Poets* (1818); *Lectures on the English Comic Writers* (1819), which reached beyond the announced subject to include Montaigne, *Don Quixote,* and *Gil Blas;* and *Lectures on the Dramatic Literature of the Age of Elizabeth* (1820), which with broader sweep carried on the work begun by Lamb. *Table-Talk* (1821-1822) ranges over literature and life and contains such examples of Hazlitt's finest writing as the essays *On Going a Journey* and *On the Fear of Death*. The *Epistle to William Gifford, Esq.* (1819) is strong but distasteful. Gifford was a disagreeable person who deserved a dressing-down, but Hazlitt almost overreached himself as he poured out the vials of his spleen and hatred upon the Tory editor who had treated him so insolently.[29]

When he was at the top of his powers, Hazlitt became involved in the

---

[27] Hazlitt's *Conversations of James Northcote* (*The New Monthly Magazine,* 1826; ed. Edmund Gosse, 1894) made much trouble for the artist and his friends because of the record of pungent personalities.

[28] See Augustus Ralli, *A History of Shakespearean Criticism* (1932), I. 145-157; H. T. Baker, "Hazlitt as a Shakespearean Critic," *PMLA,* XLVII (1932). 191-199; G. Schnöckelborg, *A. W. Schlegels Einfluss auf William Hazlitt als Shakespeare-Kritiker* (Emsdetten, 1931).

[29] Gifford's outrageous notice of *The Round Table* (*The Quarterly Review,* April, 1817) is reprinted in *Notorious Literary Attacks,* ed. Albert Mordell (1926), pp. 1-10.

sordid and unhappy love affair which led him to divorce his wife and which
he recorded in *Liber Amoris* (1823). Sarah Walker, the girl with whom he Liber
was madly enamoured, was the daughter of his landlord. A knowledge of Amoris
her duplicity did not check the course of Hazlitt's erotomania. The frankness and power of self-analysis with which this "expense of spirit in a waste
of shame" is narrated is a reminder that Hazlitt idolized Rousseau and
that it is with the *Confessions* that this book must be compared. When he
had cleansed his bosom of this perilous stuff, he entered into a second marriage (1824) and with his new wife set out upon a Continental tour. With a
mixture of enthusiasm for art and scenery and a Smollett-like repugnance
for foreigners he contributed his impressions to *The Morning Chronicle*
and collected them in *Notes on a Journey through France and Italy* (1826).
His finest books belong to these years: *The Spirit of the Age* (1825), in
which fair-mindedness in criticism of his contemporaries is but occasionally
betrayed by his prejudices, and *The Plain Speaker; or Opinions on Books,
Men, and Things* (1826), which ranges more widely and on the whole
more serenely. In 1827 the second marriage terminated. The last years of
his life were mostly wasted upon a *Life of Napoleon* (1828-1830), intended
as a rejoinder and corrective to Scott's biography.

Hazlitt's enemies sneered at his want of education and at the narrow
limits of his reading. He admitted the truth of both charges. In youth his
reading had been random and undisciplined; in later life he came actually
to dislike reading and depended largely upon memories. Like Lamb, he
relied upon the impressions of former years. Passionate retrospection is *Retrospec-*
a prevalent note in his essays. His early admiration for Raphael, Titian, *tion*
Poussin, and Claude provided him with the touchstones in his criticism of
art. His emphasis upon the literary content of painting anticipated the
typical Victorian approach to art, and in his rapturous descriptions of
masterpieces as well as in his insistence upon the moral and intellectual aspects
of the arts he was a precursor of Ruskin. All this is very old-fashioned
today, but Hazlitt's enthusiasm is still infectious. The incidental utterances
on aesthetics can be reduced to coherence only with the aid of the aestheti-
cians, to whom we must leave this task.[30]

In the love of painting, literature, and natural scenery the discords of *"Depth of*
Hazlitt's nature were resolved into harmony. His function as a critic was, *Taste"*
he said, "to feel what is good and give reasons for the faith that is in me."
That faith was grounded upon his own convictions. He would not repeat
what other critics had written, but would "give words and intelligible symbols
to that which was never imagined or expressed before." He wished to
share his enjoyment with the many, not to keep it to himself or reserve it
for a privileged coterie. His criticism depended not upon his breadth of
knowledge but upon what Keats called his "depth of taste." How seldom
he went astray is nowhere better shown than in *The Spirit of the Age* in
which the estimates of his contemporaries more often than not indicate the

30 Elisabeth Schneider, *The Aesthetics of William Hazlitt* (Philadelphia, 1933).

direction which the judgment of posterity was to take. This holds generally for his appraisals of older literature as well.

There is a lack of serenity and composure in Hazlitt's writings, and those who seek these qualities had best turn to Lamb. There is also a want of unity. An idea starts each essay off; there is a rush of associations; and when the torrent subsides an end but not a conclusion is reached. The method of comparison is constantly employed, with one great painter or writer balanced against another or a greater enhanced by contrast with a less. In the antitheses

Style

and terse clarity of his style he is a link between the eighteenth century and Macaulay, with the lucidity and often the moderation of the one and the force and conciseness of the other. Yet as a stylist he commands a wider range. *My First Acquaintance with Poets* is as lyrically reminiscent as anything of Lamb's; *On the Feeling of Immortality in Youth* is imposingly ornate without dependence upon archaisms; *On Going to a Fight,* a theme which invited the use of slang, is loyal to pure English, yet none the less virile for its purity; the *Farewell to Essay-Writing* is charged with romantic emotionality. Whatever the style or subject, it is Hazlitt's own. Like his favorite Montaigne, he could assure the reader that his was *un livre de bonne foi.*

IV

De Quincey

The vagrant and patternless life of Thomas De Quincey [31] (1785-1859) is not easily summarized. When once he began to write for a living, he wrote unceasingly and on an immense variety of subjects; but almost all his works came out in periodicals where they were left till during his last decade he issued the first collected edition of his writings; and books—the to-be-expected milestones along an author's path—are in his case but three in number: *The Confessions of an English Opium-Eater* (1822); *Klosterheim* (1832), a tedious novel of the Thirty Years' War; and the negligible *Logic of Political Economy* (1844). De Quincey came of a well-to-do family and inherited a patrimony which might have launched him smoothly upon life; but being impractical in worldly affairs he soon squandered his little fortune and fell into the hands of the money-lenders. To learning he had taken with the aptitude of a genius whose native home was the intellectual sphere, and at fifteen he could converse fluently in Greek. But he ran away from school, wandered in Wales, and in 1802-1803 found himself, homeless and penniless, in London. There he was sheltered by a girl of the streets, that Ann who soon disappeared from his ken but never from his dreams.

[31] *Collected Writings,* ed. David Masson (14v, 1889-1890); *Uncollected Writings,* ed. James Hogg (2v, 1890); *Posthumous Works,* ed. A. H. Japp (2v, 1891); *Selected Writings,* ed. P. Van D. Stern (1939); *Confessions of an English Opium Eater* [the text of 1822] *with Notes of De Quincey's Conversations with* [Richard] *Woodhouse,* ed. Richard Garnett (1885); *Literary Criticism,* ed. H. Darbishire (1909); *A Diary of Thomas De Quincey for 1803,* ed. H. A. Eaton (1927). — J. A. Green, *Bibliography* (1908); H. A. Eaton, *Thomas De Quincey, a Biography* (1936); E. Sackville-West, *Thomas De Quincey: his Life and Work* (1936); J. C. Metcalf, *De Quincey, a Portrait* (1940); Sigmund Proctor, *Thomas De Quincey's Theory of Literature* (Ann Arbor, 1943).

In 1804 he first had recourse to opium for the relief of toothache. The habit *Opium* grew fast upon him and he was presently consuming enormous quantities of the drug. For years he wrestled with the vice, sometimes victorious, sometimes backsliding, never wholly acquiescent in its tyranny. Meanwhile he had come to terms with his guardians and was able to pass five years (1803-1808) at Oxford. But he left the university without a degree. Alert to novel excellence in literature, he was one of the first men to recognize Wordsworth's genius. He became his friend, advised him on the composition of the tract on Cintra, and saw it through the press. Notwithstanding differences due to his tactlessness and Wordsworth's self-esteem, this friendship endured till 1834 when the publication of De Quincey's too candid reminiscences of life at Grasmere caused a permanent separation. With Lamb and Coleridge he was also on terms of intimacy. From 1809 till 1820 he lived at Grasmere. There, in 1816, he married Margaret Simpson, the "dear M" of the *Confessions* and the most patient of wives. For a time he was editor of *The Westmorland Gazette*. In 1819 he made a connection with *Blackwood's,* and in the following year took up his abode in London and was introduced by Lamb to the proprietors of *The London Magazine.*

At this point De Quincey's literary life really began. In the *London* (September and October, 1821) appeared *The Confessions of an English Opium-Eater,* which attracted wide attention and made him famous, for though published anonymously the authorship was soon an open secret. Late in life (1856) De Quincey enlarged it greatly. There are precious things in the expanded version, but one needs to know also the first brief, direct narrative before it was confused with divagations. After 1825 De Quincey lived in Edinburgh, Glasgow, and other parts of Scotland, moving from lodging-house to lodging-house, industrious but desultory, contributing to *Blackwood's,* consorting (as the *Noctes Ambrosianae* record) with Wilson and others of "Maga's" staff, never precisely a popular author but one for whose writings there was a market in various periodicals. Had he possessed worldly wisdom, the days of pecuniary stress would have been over; as it was, though most of the time he kept himself and his large family out of misery, he lived in an almost constant state of impecuniosity.

De Quincey's fame depends upon a small fraction of the mass of his *Miscel-* writings. His vast learning and all-embracing curiosity enabled him to *laneous* turn to his own purposes (and not always with the acknowledgements of *Writings* indebtedness that are customary) whatever came to hand. Like the young Carlyle, he stimulated, while he helped to supply, the demand for translations from the German romanticists. He interpreted Kant, though he evinced no interest in later developments of German idealism. Among critical articles on German literature is the curiously ill-balanced estimate of Goethe in which *Faust* is dismissed in a single sentence. To some extent he drew from German scholarship the materials for his historical papers. Of these *The Spanish Military Nun,* in which a groundwork of fact is richly embroidered with fancy, is the most interesting. The chief monument of his classical erudition is the series of biographies of *The Caesars* in which he generally restrained his tendency to discursiveness. A lifelong student of political economy, he defended the theories of Ricardo against Malthus. He wrote constantly on English literature, interweaving biography and criticism. Of the vivid and pungent impressions and reminiscences of his contemporaries [32] it must suffice to say that the candor with which they were written wounded, though to wound was far from the intention of De Quincey's childlike unworldliness. His literary criticism, with the exception of *On the Knocking on the Gate in Macbeth,* survives in fragments, often illuminating and penetrating but seldom of impressive length, sometimes incoherent, and occasionally, as in the remarks on Keats, quite perverse.

All this was far enough above the level of periodical ephemeralities to justify its being assembled into more than one collected edition, but much of it was not sufficiently far above that level to keep it in remembrance. Employing De Quincey's own familiar categories, one may dismiss most of this miscellaneous popularized and stylized erudition as belonging to that "Literature of Knowledge" which sooner or later is always superseded. In some places—in *The Revolt of the Tartars,* for example, and in passages of noble eloquence in *The Caesars*—the creative artist was at work and the erudition was so strongly impregnated with imagination as to rise into the higher category of the "Literature of Power." There the aim is not to instruct but to move. This level is attained more often in De Quincey's narratives and descriptions than in his critical and expository writings. His gift for portraiture enabled him to vitalize figures even of the far past. The nearer his own day the more vivid the portrait; and the most striking likenesses are of men who came within the compass of his own experience—Wordsworth, Coleridge, and Lamb.

Of himself his experience was intensest, and consequently he was most able to move when he wrote about himself. He is in the company of self-revelatory romanticists. There is much to be said for the view that undue attention has been paid to De Quincey as a "damaged soul." [33] Had he not been a genius opium would not have made him one, for though the drug may destroy or perhaps stimulate talent it cannot originate. It is not always borne in mind that the *Confessions* were not a despairing farewell but a confident introduction to his literary career. Nearly forty years of industry followed the book which fastened upon him forever the soubriquet of "the Opium-Eater." Like Lamb, he shaped his recollections, unreliable in detail but true in substance, into the form of art. The splendor of his dream-narratives makes it difficult to estimate the importance of his dream-life in relation to other experiences. The later autobiographical reminiscences which developed from the *Confessions* must be known if the balance is to be redressed. Yet De Quincey will always be remembered chiefly for his ad-

Self-revelation [marginal note]

[32] A convenient collection is: *Reminiscences of the English Lake Poets* (Everyman's Library, 1911).

[33] On the effects of opium upon De Quincey see Jeannette Marks, *Genius and Disaster* (1925); M. H. Abrams, *The Milk of Paradise* (Cambridge, Mass., 1934).

ventures in the world of dreams. He was not content merely to relate them, *The World* but aimed to show the stuff of actuality—the encounter with Ann; the visit *of Dreams* of the Malay at Grasmere; the first news of Waterloo; the reading of Livy; the night-journey in the stage-coach—upon which his dreams were based. Providing some of the material for modern students of abnormal psychology and anticipating some of their conclusions, he recorded the enormous distortions of time and space; the sense that stupendous issues are involved in the situations in which the dreamer finds himself; the monstrous animals; the persistent crowds and tumults; the claustrophobia. Some of these hallucinations haunted his waking intelligence; the obsession of crowds explains his furtiveness. Yet though shy and solitary and never precisely convivial, De Quincey was no misanthrope but courtly and urbane in any company.

Discursiveness, a major flaw in romantic literature, is De Quincey's besetting fault as a writer. He cannot resist the temptation to divagate. The flood-gates of erudition are always ready to burst open; and then he is swept far off his course into inlets and swamps of learning and argument. But this want of control must be distinguished from the deliberate art with which he prepares, with leisurely and, as it seems, wandering garrulity, for *Style* the great effects of ·his prose. The organ-stops are pulled out one by one till the music swells and rolls in amplitude, as in the great evocation of "just, subtile, and mighty Opium," or in the *Dream-Fugue* following the *Vision of Sudden Death,* or the concluding address to the Bishop of Beauvais in the *Joan of Arc,* or the three-fold description of "Our Ladies of Sorrow." In general he reserved his most elaborate style for the record of meditations and of dreams; but in somewhat less ornate form such passages occur in unexpected places, even in the biographical sketches and literary criticism. The technical means by which he accomplished his mighty effects have been often analyzed [34]—the cadenced antitheses, the balanced phrases and clauses, the cycles and epicycles of verbal elaboration. He brought his imaginings to the furthest borderland of language, where the "prose poem" impinges upon the province of music.[35] Tastes in style, which during the era of Ruskinian prose carried De Quincey to the top of his reputation, have turned against the ornate periods of which he was the greatest master since the seventeenth century; but there are signs that the winds of opinion are again shifting in his favor. It is unlikely that any fluctuation will restore nine-tenths of his writings to remembrance; but there may be a new appreciation of the remaining tenth.

[34] Excellently, though briefly, by Oliver Elton, *Survey . . . 1780-1830* (1920), II. 327-331. Comparisons with Landor are frequent in studies of De Quincey's style.
[35] De Quincey was conscious of this proximity. In the foreword to *The Vision of Sudden Death* he explains that "the ultimate object was the Dream-Fugue, as an attempt to wrestle with the utmost efforts of music in dealing with a colossal form of impassioned horror."

VIII
Gothic Romance and the Novel of Doctrine

I

The antithesis suggested in the title of this chapter is, as a matter of fact, somewhat blurred, for not only was English fiction [1] during the last decade of the eighteenth century and the first decade of the nineteenth developing along other lines besides the Gothic romance and the doctrinaire novel but such categories as have been set up are ill-defined and the characteristics of one kind are often found in another. Writers whose aim is to entertain and astound often aim also to edify; and conversely, writers whose intention is starkly doctrinal often employ the technique of the romancers. Between extreme specimens of one group and another there may be nothing in common; but in general the classes tend to shade off into one another. Looked at from a distance, fiction at this time seems to be at once sentimental, doctrinal, historical, and Gothic.

Between 1790, when William Lane, the busiest caterer to the popular taste, named his publishing house "The Minerva Press," [2] and 1814, when *Waverley* appeared, so great was the flood of extravagant fiction that even today it has not all been canalized into bibliographies. The tributaries to this stream were sensational Jacobean drama, seventeenth-century romance, translations and adaptations of Prévost and the *frénétique* fiction and drama of Baculard d'Arnaud, and some native English novels. The horrors of Smollett's *Ferdinand Count Fathom* and the naïve supernaturalism of Walpole's *Castle of Otranto* had been portents; and now a current already flowing was swollen by a torrent from Germany. One result of the romantic interest in North European culture was an attention to German literature which had hitherto been practically non-existent in England. It began with translations from Klopstock and Gessner. William Taylor of Norwich [3] (1765-1836) was in Germany as early as 1781. Throughout his life he exerted

The German Influence

---

[1] E. A. Baker, *The History of the English Novel*, v (1934), chs. VIII and IX (hereinafter referred to as Baker); Montague Summers, *The Gothic Quest* (1939) and *A Gothic Bibliography* (1941); Edith Birkhead, *The Tale of Terror* (1921); Eino Railo, *The Haunted Castle* (1927); Mario Praz, *The Romantic Agony* (1933), ch. II, on the hero-villain; J. M. S. Tompkins, *The Popular Novel in England, 1770-1800* (1932), chs. V-VIII; A. S. Collins, *The Profession of Letters . . . 1780-1832* (1929), on the relation of authors to their publishers; R. E. Prothero (Lord Ernle), *The Light Reading of Our Ancestors* (1927); Amy Cruse, *The Englishman and his Books in the Early Nineteenth Century* (1930). The most recent general survey is Edward Wagenknecht, *Cavalcade of the English Novel* (1943), with excellent bibliographies.

[2] Dorothy Blakey, *The Minerva Press, 1790-1820* (1939), with bibliography.

[3] J. A. Robberds, *Memoir of William Taylor of Norwich* (2v, 1843).

an influence which reached from Scott to Carlyle, writing hundreds of articles on German subjects. His activities culminated in the *Historic Survey of German Poetry* (1828-1830). In 1792-1793 Matthew Gregory Lewis made a long sojourn at Weimar. Schiller's drama *Die Räuber* was translated in 1792 and attracted the enthusiastic attention of Coleridge and Scott. The following years saw many translations from the German. Typical of these is Christiane Naubert's *Herman of Unna* (1794), which contains the elements of mystery, terror, and suspense presently exploited by the English Gothicizers, and Earl Grosse's *Horrid Mysteries* (1796), which has been kept in remembrance by Jane Austen's satire.

Less extravagant, indigenous ingredients were combined with the German infusion to form Gothic romance. A distinction is to be drawn between "Terror Gothic" and "Historical Gothic." [4] The earliest English experiments in the historical novel have already received notice. Following in the steps of the pioneers came Sophia Lee (1750-1824) who did gross violence to history in *The Recess* (1785), the story of two daughters of Mary Queen of Scots by a clandestine marriage with the Duke of Norfolk. Miss Lee contributed two stories to *Canterbury Tales* (1797-1805), mainly by her sister Harriet Lee [5] (1757-1851). Jane Porter (1776-1850) adapted history to her purposes in *Thaddeus of Warsaw* (1803) and *The Scottish Chiefs* (1810), though she did not mistreat Clio so miserably as her predecessors had done. But the gain in accuracy has carried with it no gain in lasting vitality. Miss Porter's early readers found her thrilling, but her laborious adaptations of chronicle material are today as lifeless as anything in outmoded fiction.

Charlotte Smith [6] (1749-1806) is in the line of descent from Fanny Burney, but the lineage has been modified by an infiltration of romance. From her first novel, *Emmeline, the Orphan of the Castle* (1788) to *The Old Manor House* (1793), her best-known book, there is increasing attention to the scenic background. In the latter story the dilapidated mansion, deep woods, moonlight, and moaning wind are designed to harmonize with the tale. Mrs. Smith's characters are generally those of domestic fiction, but the situations in which she places them are often romantic in the extreme. She makes use of mysterious occurrences, secret passageways, and such typically Gothic themes as that of the long-lost, rightful heir. In her imagination the dissolute seducer of Richardson has taken on a Gothic gloom, and her sentimental lovers have read *The Sorrows of Werther*. Along with much senti-

---

[4] See Gerard Buck, *Die Vorgeschichte des historischen Romans in der modernen englischen Literatur* (1931); George Saintsbury, "The Historical Novel, I: The Days of Ignorance," *Essays and Papers*, III. 1-20; Montague Summers, *The Gothic Quest*, ch. IV. — On a contemporary parodist of these early historical novels see J. M. S. Tompkins, "James White, Esq., a Forgotten Humourist," *RES*, III (1927). 146-156. — Ill-informed efforts to recreate the medieval scene in literature synchronized with the growing interest in Gothic architecture. See W. H. Smith, *Architecture in English Fiction* (New Haven, 1934); Kenneth Clark, *The Gothic Revival* (1928), ch. IV: "Romanticism and Archaeology."

[5] One of Harriet Lee's tales, *Kruitzner,* is of genuine power and gave Byron the plot of his tragedy, *Werner.*

[6] F. M. A. Hilbish, *Charlotte Smith, Poet and Novelist* (1941).

ment there is some satire, and occasionally she touches upon contemporary problems. *Desmond* (1792) shows her sympathy with the French Revolution, and *The Young Philosopher* (1798), the story of an idealist who is disillusioned with Europe and seeks refuge in America, reveals the influence of Rousseau. Here Mrs. Smith is close to the doctrinaire novelists; but in general she is closer to Ann Radcliffe.[7]

Ann Radcliffe

Mrs. Radcliffe [8] (1764-1823), a quiet lady who never had an adventure in her life, is the arch-Gothicizer of them all. After an unpromising first attempt, she produced in *A Sicilian Romance* (1790) a full-blooded horror-story of a wicked husband, imprisoned wife, and guileless daughter. Though indebted to French romancers for certain incidents,[9] she is here already mistress of her peculiar art. *The Romance of the Forest* (1791), in part derivative, relies for its effect upon the gloom of forests and Gothic ruins where villains absolute in wickedness wreak their rage upon good people who are flawlessly refined. The influence of Rousseau is apparent in Mrs. Radcliffe's descriptions of nature, and there is something of the atmosphere of the paintings of Salvator Rosa. This story was followed by Mrs. Radcliffe's masterpiece, *The Mysteries of Udolpho* (1794), in which her technique of terror by suggestion—often through strange sounds—is fully displayed. A basic rationalism forbade her to do more than touch the marvelous. The compromise adopted is never quite satisfactory, for her mysteries are often held so long in suspense that the rational explanations, when they come, fail to satisfy a curiosity which is no longer alert. It was beyond her ability, and aside from her purpose, to people her stage with convincing human beings; the dialogue put into the mouths of her characters is of a stiltedness that must be sampled to be imagined. But there is no denying the effectiveness of her tenebrous landscapes and atmosphere.

The portrait of the criminal monk, Schedoni, in her next book, *The Italian* (1797), owes something to Lewis's portrait of Ambrosio in *The Monk*; but Lewis was but repaying a debt, for Montoni in *The Mysteries of Udolpho* had given him suggestions for Ambrosio. The anti-sacerdotalism of both Mrs. Radcliffe and Lewis had deep roots in Protestant prejudice and roots of more recent growth in the attacks on the Jesuits in many Continental countries. Schedoni, with his mysterious origin, his somber mien, his pallor, his arresting eyes, the aura round him of unspeakable guilt, and the horror touched with pity which he inspires, is the type-figure of the romantic *homme fatal,* the precursor of Byron's Lara and Manfred. He dominates the story as he dominates the lovers who are caught in the toils of the Inquisition. In certain episodes a sense of spiritual wicked-

---

[7] The romances of S. E. Brydges, the antiquarian, are modeled upon Mrs. Smith's. See M. K. Woodworth, *Sir Samuel Egerton Brydges* (Oxford, 1936).

[8] See, in addition to the general authorities, A. M. Killen, *Le Roman terrifiant ou roman noir de Walpole à Ann Radcliffe* (1924); C. F. McIntyre, *Ann Radcliffe in Relation to her Time* (1920); A. A. S. Wietens, *Mrs. Radcliffe: her Relation towards Romanticism* (1926); E. Margraf, *Der Einfluss der deutschen Litteratur auf der englischen Schauerroman* (1901); Jakob Brauchli, *Die englische Schauerroman* (1928).

[9] J. R. Foster, "The Abbé Prévost and the English Novel," *PMLA*, XLII (1927). 443-464.

ness is conveyed which may still appall the sympathetic reader, keyed to the right pitch of emotion. The contrasting scenes of Neapolitan loveliness and the dark recesses of the great abbey are managed admirably. But the modern reader finds it difficult to stomach the melodrama, crudities of drawing, and incredible complexities of iniquity.

Gaston de Blondeville, Mrs. Radcliffe's last novel (written in 1802), is an unsuccessful compromise between Gothicism and history. Hitherto she had rejected the responsibilities assumed by the novelists who claimed to recreate an authentic past; in this story she tried to be conscientious and succeeded merely in being tedious. Moreover, she succumbed at last to the lure of the unexplained supernatural and introduced a genuine ghost. Whether because of this intrusion or because she was sensitive to Miss Austen's satire, Mrs. Radcliffe did not publish this novel and it appeared posthumously (1826).

No rationalistic scruples inhibited Matthew Gregory Lewis (1775-1818). "*Monk*" His reading of Tieck, Spiess, Musäus, and other prolific spawners of the *Lewis* macabre filled his head with fantasies of the grotesque, the horrible, and the criminal. But in his notorious romance, *The Monk* [10](1797), a nightmare of fiendish wickedness, ghastly supernaturalism and sadistic sensuality, there is almost indubitably something else than mere literary sensationalism; it gives evidence of a psychopathic condition perhaps inherent in the extremes of the romantic temperament.[11] The crude purposes to which Lewis adapted the great themes of Faust and Ahasuerus suggest deliberate parody; but he was intensely serious, though capable only of such coarse, broad strokes in characterization and setting as make his scenes of lust and torture and rotting corpses repellent beyond description. They are even more revolting in the original version which, in fear of legal action, Lewis afterwards modified. *The Monk* still has its admirers,[12] but to most critics it is of interest only because it combines various literary traditions in a monument of romantic extravagance. Lewis won the regard of great men; Scott and Southey were contributors to his anthologies, Byron and Shelley his friends in Switzerland. On the stage his *Castle Spectre* (1798) and later pieces were successful. His death at sea on a return voyage from Jamaica, where he possessed property, is said to have been in circumstances worthy of his own spectral imagination.[13]

---

[10] Ed. E. A. Baker (1907); (3v, 1913).

[11] Or (to regard the matter with less gravity), *The Monk* may be considered the dream of an "oversexed" adolescent, for Lewis was only twenty when he wrote it.

[12] With Montague Summers' immoderate praise (*The Gothic Quest*, pp. 212-223) contrast the just estimate in Baker, v. 207-211. See also Eino Railo, *The Haunted Castle*, chs. II and IV.

[13] Many romances were written in imitation of *The Monk*. Edmund Montague's *The Demon of Sicily* (1807) is a specimen of extreme extravagance. Charlotte Dacre's *Zofloya, or the Moor* (1806; ed. M. Summers, 1927) is of interest for its influence on Shelley. H. J. Sarratt's *Koenigsmark the Robber, or the Terror of Bohemia* (1801) is an adaptation from the German of R. E. Raspe. Raspe put this story into the mouth of Baron Münchhausen. There is thus a connection with the famous popular saga which, beginning with Raspe's *Baron Munchausen's Narrative of his Marvellous Travels and Campaigns in Russia* (1785), received in later recensions facetious and extravagant accretions. Raspe lived in England and wrote in English. *Munchausen* is therefore entitled to be regarded as an English classic.

Mrs.
Shelley

Mary Wollstonecraft Shelley [14] (1797-1851) wrote *Frankenstein* (1817), the only novel of terror that is still famous. Gothic horrors, sentimental humanitarianism, and the current pseudo-scientific theory of vitalism or the "vital spark" are combined in the story of the man-made monster. Among Mrs. Shelley's other novels *The Last Man* (1826), on the destruction of human society by a pestilence, and *Lodore* (1835), based on the privations which the Shelleys had suffered in 1814, are of some interest for their "fictionized" portraits of Byron and Shelley.[15]

Maturin

Charles Robert Maturin [16] (1780-1824) showed himself in his first romance, *The Fatal Revenge* (1807), as a disciple of Mrs. Radcliffe; but in *The Wild Irish Boy* (1808) and *The Milesian Chief* (1812) he gave voice to Irish nationalistic feeling. His tragedy, *Bertram* (1816), won at Drury Lane a success which was deserved, for despite the accumulation of Gothic accouterments its action is swift and its emotion genuine. Then came *Melmoth the Wanderer* [17] (1820), Maturin's masterpiece and the greatest novel of the school of terror. Its structure is complicated and obscure, but there is inventive ingenuity in each of the six episodes into which it is divided. The theme of the Wandering Jew, or more broadly, of the never-ending life, which haunted the imagination of the period,[18] is impressively developed. The idea of combining the stories of Ahasuerus and Faust might have resulted in a pretentious failure, a mere variant upon *The Monk;* but *Melmoth* is not imitative, is not a failure; and it has strongly impressed various great writers.[19]

In the sub-literary depths of romanticism there were hundreds of stories in imitation of Mrs. Radcliffe, Lewis, and the horror-mongers of the Continent. Here iniquity rioted in ruined castles and dim oratories and crypts and dungeons, where monstrous villains oppressed the innocent, and ghosts walked, and demons lured their victims to destruction. But into these noisome fastnesses we need not descend.

[14] Mrs. Julian Marshall, *The Life and Letters of Mary Wollstonecraft Shelley* (2v, 1889); *Letters of Mary W. Shelley*, ed. Frederick L. Jones (2v, Norman, Okla, 1944); R. Glynn Grylls, *Mary Shelley, a Biography* (1938).

[15] W. E. Peck, "The Biographical Element in the Novels of Mary Wollstonecraft Shelley," *PMLA*, XXXVI (1923). 196-219.

[16] Nielo Idman, *Charles Robert Maturin: His Life and Works* (1923); William Scholten, *Charles Robert Maturin, the Terror Novelist* (Amsterdam, 1933).

[17] Ed. anonymously (3v, 1892), with memoir and bibliography.

[18] Lewis attached the story of the Wandering Jew loosely to the main plot of *The Monk*. The theme is used by Wordsworth, Coleridge, Godwin, and Shelley. It reappears in Thomas Medwin's poem, *Ahasuerus the Wanderer* (1823) and in George Croly's flamboyant romance, *Salathiel the Immortal* (1827). See Werner Zirus, *Der ewige Jude in der Dichtung vornehmlich in der englischen und deutschen* (Leipzig, 1928); A. M. Killen, "L'Évolution de la légende du Juif errant," *RLC*, v (1925). 5-36; Eino Railo, *op. cit.*, ch. v.

[19] Balzac's *Melmoth réconcilié* is a sort of sequel. Maturin influenced Hugo's *Han d'Islande*. Vigny, Baudelaire, and Villiers de l'Isle Adam were among the admirers of the book, as were Rossetti and Poe. Oscar Wilde after his disgrace took the pen-name of "Sebastian Melmoth" (the saint pierced with arrows associated with the doomed wanderer).

II

Fiction in the late eighteenth century became a convenient medium for *The Novel* promulgating the new social theories which were entering England from *of Doctrine* France.[20] Rousseau's *Emile* (1762) was soon known in England, and one of its chief themes—education not by coercion but by persuasion and guidance —is found in Henry Brooke's *The Fool of Quality* (1765-1770) and is the basis of *Sandford and Merton* (1783) by Thomas Day (1748-1789). Sandford is reared close to nature with the result that he is healthy, kindly, and sensible, while Merton, having had the conventional education of a gentle- man, is a headstrong weakling. Elizabeth Inchbald [21] (1753-1821) used the *Mrs.* subject twice. *A Simple Story* (written in 1777 though not published till *Inchbald* 1791) presents the contrast between a mother who has been educated in the old fashion and a daugher who has benefited from the new ideas. What might seem unpromising material for fiction is vitalized by Mrs. Inchbald's art, which, though serene, is capable of scenes of passion and tragedy. A masculine variant of the theme is presented in her second novel, *Nature and Art* (1796). Henry, one of the protagonists, who has been brought up on "Zocotora Island," brings to English society the simplicity and candor of a child of nature, while William, the cousin who has been educated in England, is a rake and a hypocrite. Henry befriends the woman whom William has seduced and abandoned. Later, in a memorable scene, William, now a judge, sentences this unfortunate woman to death.

This novel shows the influence of Robert Bage (1728-1801), whose earlier *Bage* satiric stories must be passed over,[22] but whose last novel, *Hermsprong, or Man as He is Not* (1796), is, notwithstanding its conventionally happy end- ing, a significant indictment of society. The hero, having been reared among the Redskins, is a candid *homme sauvage* who criticizes sophisticated so- ciety in a manner which recalls the "Foreign Visitor" of Montesquieu, Lyttelton, and Goldsmith. Bage makes telling points in his exposure of the abuses perpetrated by rank and wealth. But the frankness of the hero is often both coarse and dull. Bage had little talent for characterization, and his good people and bad are scarcely more than personifications of the virtues and vices.[23]

In William Godwin's *Caleb Williams, or Things as They Are* [24] (1794) *Godwin* the antithesis is not between nature and conventionality but between the power possessed by the privileged and the helplessness of the lowly. This novel is intended to illustrate by a particular case the general indictment

[20] Allene Gregory, *The French Revolution and the English Novel* (1915).
[21] William McKee, *Elizabeth Inchbald* (Washington, 1935).
[22] See J. M. S. Tompkins, *The Popular Novel*, pp. 194-196, for an appreciation of Bage's earlier novels as in some measure anticipating Peacock and even Thackeray.
[23] With *Hermsprong* may be associated Thomas Holcroft's *Anna St. Ives* (1792) in which the revolutionary program of "perfectibility" is put into the form of fiction. The idealistic hero confounds the machinations of the aristocratic villain and in the end converts him to a better view of life.
[24] Ed. E. A. Baker (1903). — On Godwin see above, ch. I.

of society which Godwin had drawn up in *Political Justice*. But far from being merely a polemic, *Caleb Williams* is an absorbingly interesting story of suspense and fear, connected with the tales of terror and even anticipating in some measure the design and technique of detective fiction. Caleb, a youthful servant, has become possessed of the secret that his master, Falkland, has committed a murder; but the social prestige of Falkland enables him to retain the mastery and pursue his victim implacably. Godwin's quite definitely Gothic *St. Leon* (1799), a pseudo-historical tale of the sixteenth century, deals clumsily with the themes of the "eternal wanderer" and the philosopher's stone. His later novels are heavy and lifeless, the narratives being burdened with philosophic disquisitions. Into *Fleetwood* (1805) he introduced his subversive opinions about marriage, but it is more important as showing that Godwin, like some of his disciples, abandoned his early opinions. He is here no longer the rationalist and necessitarian but has come under the influence of romantic anti-intellectualism and nature-worship.

Maria Edgeworth   The doctrinaire novel shades off into the novel of manners.[25] The novels and tales of Maria Edgeworth [26] (1767-1849) are in the line from Miss Burney but with ingredients from Day and other writers who used fiction as an instrument for reform. She points forward to both Jane Austen and Sir Walter Scott. Her social philosophy separates her from them and connects her with the reforming group; but her pictures of society have much of the shrewdness, though little of the subtlety, of Jane Austen, and her "regional" settings in Ireland suggested to Scott the possibilities of a Scottish background for fiction. From her father, Richard L. Edgeworth, she obtained not only many of her ideas on education and society but—with unfortunate consequences to her art—aid in the composition of many of her books. *The Parents' Assistant,* a series of moral tales which between 1796 and 1800 grew from one volume to six, was designed as a supplement to Mr. Edgeworth's treatise on *Practical Education* (1798). The titles of these little stories—*Forgive and Forget; Waste Not, Want Not;* and the like—indicate their quality and purpose. For a century they remained part of the nursery regimen. From these humble and utilitarian beginnings Miss Edgeworth graduated to the composition of novels of full length for readers of mature years. Yet the didacticism of her stories for children reappears in her writings for adults and would be the ruin of them were it not that, for all her faults and theories, she knew how to tell a tale, to paint scenery with minute yet interesting accuracy, and to represent the clash of characters in their social relations. Viewed as a historical novel *Castle Rackrent* (1800)

---

[25] Amelia Opie (1769-1853), a member of Godwin's circle, wrote fiction—*Father and Daughter* (1801), *Tales of Real Life* (1813), and many other books—in which the purpose to instruct is often present but almost always subordinated to sentiment. Mrs. Opie's plots are often intricate and in some of them use is made of mystery and villainy.

[26] *Novels and Tales* (18v, 1832-1833); *Novels* (12v, 1893); *Castle Rackrent* and *The Absentee*, ed. Brander Matthews, in Everyman's Library. — E. A. Edgeworth, *A Memoir of Maria Edgeworth* (3v, 1867), privately printed and very rare; A. J. C. Hare, *The Life and Letters of Maria Edgeworth* (2v, 1894); Emily Lawless, *Maria Edgeworth* (EML Series, 1904); Friedrich Michael, *Die irischen Romane von Maria Edgeworth* (Königsburg, 1918); Theodore Goodman, *Maria Edgeworth, Novelist of Reason* (1936); Baker, VI, chs. I and II.

is more accurate and vivacious than any such work of fiction before Scott. On the technical side it is a milestone in the development of the novel. The fortunes of a family through several generations are seen from the point of view of a character in the book who tells the story. This is a structural innovation of great consequence. Being almost without any tincture of her social theories, *Castle Rackrent* remains Miss Edgeworth's most attractive book. The novelettes in the first series of *Tales of Fashionable Life* (1810) require no comment, but in the second series (1812) the principal item is *The Absentee,* a long short story or short novel which many good judges reckon her masterpiece. Here London society and the life of the Irish gentry are wittily contrasted, and the scenes of low life in Ireland are contrived with much animation. There is still great vitality in the book, marred though it is by didacticism and by a conventional scale of social values. In Miss Edgeworth's later books—*Patronage* (1814), *Ormond* (1817), and others that must be passed over—the leading figures seem patterned according to a formula; only from the minor people does human nature extrude. When her sense of humor is not clogged with theory Miss Edgeworth can delineate her men and women with a minuteness of observation and a shrewdness of understanding not unworthy of Jane Austen; but she has not Miss Austen's aloofness and objectivity and finesse.

IX

Jane Austen

The happiest and most productive years in the life of Jane Austen [1] (1775-1817) were passed in two small towns of Hampshire. She was the seventh of the eight children of the rector of Steventon. In the Austen family there existed a sympathetic affection based upon an identity of tastes and an outlook upon life illuminated by lightly ironic detachment. Jane's juvenilia— *Love and Freindship* and the little pieces collected in *Volume the First*— are mostly burlesques and parodies written for the amusement of the family. She moved in this intimate circle throughout her uneventful life. However, her experience of provincial society gradually broadened, and she had visited Bath before, on her father's retirement, the Austens settled there in 1801. By that time she had written, besides a number of minor things, first versions of three of her novels. In the uncongenial atmosphere of Bath she accomplished little; nor were the three years (1806-1809) in Southampton, where, after her father's death, she lived with her mother, more fruitful. Not until she breathed again the congenial air of the provincial town of Chawton did the creative instinct reassert itself. There she was very active till, shortly before her death, she moved to Winchester.

Line of Development

Apart from *Lady Susan,* a false start from which she quickly withdrew herself, Miss Austen began as a satirist of the current sentimental mode— that romantic view of life which trusts to the dictates of the heart.[2] *Northanger Abbey* treats this theme superficially, and *Sense and Sensibility* analyzes with greater profundity the contrast between a woman who submits herself to the guidance of common sense and one who follows impulse. The theme of *Pride and Prejudice* is announced in its original title—*First*

---

[1] *Novels,* ed. R. W. Chapman (5v, Oxford, 1923), the definitive edition of the six novels. The juvenilia and fragments are all accessible in modern editions: *Love and Freindship* (1922; 1929); *Lady Susan* (1925); *Sanditon* (1925); *Plan of a Novel* (1926); *The Watsons* (1927); *Volume the First* (1933). *Letters,* ed. R. W. Chapman (1932).—R. W. Chapman, *Bibliography* (1929); J. E. Austen-Leigh, *A Memoir of Jane Austen* (1870), ed. R. W. Chapman (1926); Leonie Villard, *Jane Austen: sa vie et son œuvre* (Paris, 1915), trans. by Veronica Lucas as *Jane Austen: a French Appreciation* (1924); C. Linklater Thomson, *Jane Austen, a Survey* (1929); R. Brimley Johnson, *Jane Austen: Her Life, her Work, her Family, and her Critics* (1930); John Bailey, *Introductions to Jane Austen* (1931); David Rhydderch, *Jane Austen, Her Life and Art* (1932); Guy Rawlence, *Jane Austen* (1934); Lord David Cecil, *Jane Austen* (1935); Mary Lascelles, *Jane Austen and her Art* (1939); Elizabeth Jenkins, *Jane Austen, a Biography* (1939); A. C. Bradley, "Jane Austen," *E&S,* II (1911). 7-36; Baker, VI, chs. III-V. — Miss Austen was four years younger than Sir Walter Scott, but her first published novel appeared three years before, and she died three years after, the publication of *Waverley* and is therefore considered here before Scott.

[2] See J. M. S. Tompkins, *"Elinor and Marianne:* a Note on Jane Austen," *RES,* XVI (1940). 33-43.

Impressions, which are not to be trusted but must be corrected by experience and afterthought. In the last three novels there is no longer a preoccupation with sentimentalism. *Mansfield Park* presents the antithesis between wordliness and unworldliness. *Emma,* her most thoughtful comedy, is a study in the self-deceptions of vanity. *Persuasion,* more definitely a love story than its predecessors, develops the contrast between true love and prudential calculations. From the appended table,[3] in which the somewhat complex facts of the dates of composition, the revisions, the changes in title, and the publication of the novels are summarized, it will be seen that they fall into two groups, separated by a sterile decade. These "silent years" are accounted for by Miss Austen's discouragement; for the original version of *Northanger Abbey* a publisher had given her a pittance, but he had not issued it; and *First Impressions* had been rejected, unread. But it is a mistake to differentiate too sharply between the earlier and the later novels, for the three in the first group were subjected to revision during the years when she was engaged upon the three in the second. All that can be safely said is that the element of burlesque gradually disappeared; that in the later books there is an increasing gravity, an occasional frostiness of tone, and perhaps a suspicion of heaviness of handling; and that at the close she permitted herself a guarded display of emotion which the readers of her first books could not have expected of her.

The Austen family were, as Jane said, "great Novel-readers and not *Tastes and* ashamed of being so."[4] This reading embraced not only the classics of *Interests* eighteenth-century fiction and Fanny Burney and Maria Edgeworth; the Austens read and enjoyed, though they laughed at, Mrs. Radcliffe and other purveyors of terror and sentimentalism. From most of her predecessors Jane learned one or another of the secrets of her craft, what to do and what to avoid; but she learned more from her own practice. Her tastes, grounded upon Richardson, the essayists, Cowper, and her "dear Doctor Johnson,"[5]

---

[3] *c.* 1790-1793: *Love and Freindship; Volume the First.*
  Before 1796: *Elinor and Marianne* (not extant); recast, 1797-1799, as *Sense and Sensibility;* further revision, 1809-1810; published 1811.
  1792-1796(?): *Lady Susan;* survives in a fair copy of *c.* 1805 or later; first published in Austen-Leigh, *Memoir,* second ed., 1871.
  1796-1797: *First Impressions* (not extant); rewritten, *c.* 1812, as *Pride and Prejudice;* published 1813.
  1797-1798: *Susan* (not extant); recast and much expanded as *Northanger Abbey,* 1805; posthumously published 1818.
  1803: *The Watsons* (a fragment); first published in Austen-Leigh, *Memoir,* 1871.
  1811-1813: *Mansfield Park;* published 1814.
  1814-1815: *Emma;* published towards the end of 1815 or more probably early in 1816.
  1815-1816: *Persuasion;* published posthumously 1818.
  1817: *Sanditon* (a fragment to which this title was given by the Austen family); first published from the manuscript in 1925.

[4] Jane Austen to her sister Cassandra, December 18, 1798. On Miss Austen's reading see Mona Wilson, *Jane Austen and Some of her Contemporaries* (1938), pp. 1-42.

[5] Resemblances to Johnson have been noted: her distrust in any indulgence in emotion; her penetrative honesty in observing human nature. That Johnson's influence was not uniformly fortunate is evident from those rare passages in the novels where, essaying a full and heightened style, Miss Austen gives an impression of strain.

were so much of the eighteenth century that her mind has been called "femininely Augustan." [6] She lived when the tide of romanticism was at the flood, yet was never borne upon it or even sprinkled with its foam. Not only did she not frequent literary society; she had not a single literary correspondent during her entire life. Scott's poetry entertained her—but she mocked at it. *Waverley* she admired—but reluctantly. To Wordsworth, Coleridge, and Byron she was completely indifferent. Romanticism gave her an opportunity to ridicule Mrs. Radcliffe; it affected her in no other way. There is nothing surprising in the absence of a large historical perspective and wide social view from her novels; fiction was not expected to deal with such matters. But the fact remains that even in her letters Miss Austen exhibits practically no interest in social problems and public events. The Napoleonic Wars swept past and left little trace upon her books. This lack of concern reflects the state of mind of county society. The "lower orders," portentously upsurging across the Channel, appear seldom and casually in the novels and only in their proper position as subservient to gentle folk. She never wrote the annals of the poor; she was not interested in the simple or the primitive. Collective humanity never puts in its appearance in her stories; there is no mob or any scene of public disturbance. Her people are unaffected by the drift of contemporary thought; they have no concern with abstract ideas; no anxiety about destiny disturbs them; and if death must come it will come at some indeterminate date beyond the *finis* of their story.

Weaknesses of character are the stuff from which these novels are fashioned; but there is little of positive evil. Miss Austen's sole experiment in the delineation of a thoroughly bad woman is *Lady Susan*. This story of an adventuress who schemes to sell her daughter to a rake while entrapping for herself the daughter's young lover is an advance upon Miss Austen's early burlesques of circulating-library fiction in that her intention seems to be to draw a credible bad woman in contrast to the incredible ones of popular fiction. But that it was huddled up to an abrupt conclusion [7] is a sign of her distaste for such a theme. She thought that "guilt and misery" were "odious subjects," [8] and from them she escaped quickly on the rare occasions when she had to deal with them at all. There are no adventures, properly so called, in the novels; and only in *Persuasion* is there a physical accident, external to character, which alters the course of events. In the work of few other novelists does coincidence play so small a part. She was much concerned with the effects of emotion upon human beings; but the emotion itself is almost always indicated by implication. All her plots revolve upon love; but only once (in the case of Mr. Knightley) do we hear a lover declare himself. There is no lack of knowledge of passion or of interest in it; but there is an instinctive reticence. She can be sympathetic even while seeing the ironical and satiric implications in character and situation. She

---

[6] F. E. Pierce, *Currents and Eddies in the English Romantic Generation* (1918), p. 310.
[7] It is not a fragment, as some writers (e.g., CHEL, xii. 259) call it.
[8] *Mansfield Park*, ch. xli.

is, as one of her successors has remarked, "a mistress of much deeper emotion than appears upon the surface. She stimulates us to supply what is not there." [9] In the story of the woes of Marianne, told though it is with no blindness to absurdities, "the burning human heart" was, as George Moore maintained,[10] revealed for the first time in English fiction.

She pictured a limited part of the English scene. "Three or four Families in a Country Village is," she said, "the very thing to work upon." Her small world is that of the provincial gentry. But her oft-quoted metaphor of the "small square two inches of ivory" is too modest a self-estimate. She leaves out many aspects of experience, but what she pictures is grounded upon so comprehensive a knowledge of human nature as to universalize it; her men and women, true of their own period, are true also of all time. Wisely she stayed "within the range of her imaginative inspiration"; [11] that range was of almost the same circumference as her own personal experience. It has often been remarked that she never describes a scene in which no woman is present. She knew nothing about finance, and the prestige and power of money play little part in her stories. When her niece, writing a novel, sought counsel of her, Miss Austen wrote: "Let the Portmans [characters in the novel] go to Ireland, but as you know nothing of the Manners there, you had better not go with them." The niece should "stick to Bath" where she would be "quite at home." [12] The familiar incident of Miss Austen's correspondence with the domestic chaplain to the Prince of Wales cannot be omitted here, for it shows that even a message from royalty could not distract her from her path. The chaplain suggested that in her next novel she might delineate the character of a clergyman; and Jane, sensing that the hints which he supplied were based upon his own experience, mischievously replied that she might be equal to "the comic parts of the characters" but "not the good, the enthusiastic, the literary." Her correspondent then, with amusing insensitiveness, suggested that "any historical romance illustrative of the history of the august House of Cobourg, would just now be very interesting." But Jane was not to be enticed; she must, she felt, "go on in [her] own way." [13]

That way led her through the world of men and women in their personal relationships. She regarded them with the shrewdness and acumen of the satirist but without losing sight of moral values. There is no distortion in her perspective. She shows us the tangle resulting from conflicting personalities; we hear the jangle of incongruous temperaments. Her province is not that of somber delinquency but of venial error. The faults in her characters are mostly due to bad training or want of training in youth. In older people these are often beyond repair; but in young, especially the young lovers,

Jane Austen's "World"

[9] Virginia Woolf, *The Common Reader* (1925), p. 174.
[10] *Avowals* (1919), pp. 43-44.
[11] Lord David Cecil, *Jane Austen*, p. 8.
[12] *Letters*, p. 395.
[13] *Ibid.*, pp. 429-430, 443, 445, 451. This correspondence inspired Miss Austen to write the *Plan of a Novel* in which she burlesques those faults and falsities in fiction which she was most careful to avoid.

they are purged and done away through tribulations which are none the less poignant for being generally mere misunderstandings. Each book is thus a history of self-education and self-correction. Miss Austen proffers no counsels of perfection, for her practical idealism is content with the implied lesson that a sound education, a marriage based upon congenial dispositions as well as passion, and social decorum give the best promise of happiness in life.

Characteri-
zation   But to make "the dreary intercourse of daily life" significant a novelist must be able to create living characters. This ability Jane Austen possessed in a measure never excelled among writers of fiction. We have been made to know her people so well that when a crisis arrives they act as we expect them to act; their behavior never astonishes us.[14] Miss Austen knew them so well that she would narrate to her family incidents in their lives which do not occur in the books. *Tout comprendre c'est tout pardonner* is not a proverb to be applied unreservedly to her; she does not always forgive. But those whom she forgives she often loves. There may be truth in the tradition that it was because she "fell in love with" Catherine Morland that she expanded what was probably a mere skit upon Gothic romance into *Northanger Abbey*.[15] The element of burlesque which was probably conspicuous in the original form of *Sense and Sensibility* disappeared in the revision, and for all the sharp, satiric thrusts there is affection for the emotional Marianne. Elizabeth in *Pride and Prejudice* Miss Austen loved unreservedly, declaring her to be "as delightful a creature as ever appeared in print."[16] Emma, on the other hand, she described as "a heroine whom no one but myself will like much,"[17] thus doing less than justice to her art and to her readers, for with all Emma's faults we are attracted to the self-deceived woman who is the profoundest of Miss Austen's characterizations. In *Persuasion,* where the satire is directed almost entirely against Bath society, there is nothing but sympathy for the long-parted lovers who are at length united. An unwonted self-revelatory tone, new to this most impersonal of artists, has made many readers suspect that in this book Jane Austen for once unlocked her heart.

The plots are so firmly integrated that it is impossible to isolate even the subsidiary characters (as is so easily done in Dickens). Each is part of a

[14] It must be admitted, however, that in some moments of strain they do not talk as we should expect. See on this point Herbert Read, *English Prose Style* (1928), pp. 119-120.

[15] Montague Summers projected an edition of the seven "horrid" novels which Miss Andrews recommended to Isabella Thorpe, but only two—*Horrid Mysteries* and *The Necromancer of the Black Forest*—appeared. See also Michael Sadleir, *The Northanger Novels: a Footnote to Jane Austen* (1927). — Before the final revision of *Northanger Abbey* in 1816 two books had appeared which may have convinced Miss Austen that the two decades intervening since she wrote her satire had not rendered it obsolete. One of these books is Sarah Green's *Romance Readers and Romance Writers* (1810), in which the heroine's head is turned by too much reading of extravagant fiction. The other is Eaton Stannard Barrett's *The Heroine* (1813; ed. Walter Raleigh, 1909), in which the satiric parody, though amusing in spots, is carried to such cruel lengths that Cherubina's plights, intended to expose her to ridicule, actually make her pitiable. On Barrett see further Edith Birkhead, *The Tale of Terror* (1921), pp. 133-137.

[16] *Letters,* p. 297.

[17] J. E. Austen-Leigh, *Memoir,* ed. R. W. Chapman, p. 157.

closely woven fabric. All are what a modern novelist has described as "three-dimensional" or "round" figures, as contrasted with "two-dimensional" or "flat" characters in which a single quality or factor is portrayed.[18] In other words, there are no throw-backs, as in Scott or Dickens, to the old-fashioned "humors." Miss Austen's men and women are seen from a thousand facets. In depicting them she very rarely introduces herself, as Fielding had done and Meredith was to do; still less does she plead with and cajole her readers as some novelists do. Direct record of dialogue and action, not interpolated comment, conveys her impressions and opinions. At times, however, the task of interpreting people and events is shared between the anonymous, impersonal, omniscient narrator and certain of her dramatis personae. Thus, we accept Elizabeth Bennett's point of view as on the whole a reflection of the author's; and in general the tangle in which the characters are enmeshed is observed from a single angle.[19]

There are qualities of Miss Austen's style—the delicate precision, the nice *Style* balance, the seeming simplicity which often masks subtlety, the lucidity and vitality and ironic wit—which remind many readers of Congreve's comedies.[20] Certainly in the neat rhythms of her dialogue the resemblance to stage-comedy is apparent; it is particularly close when she verges upon the farcical, as in the scene of Mr. Collins' proposal of marriage to Elizabeth. It has been remarked that the three-volume form in which the novels were first published brings out an analogy which is obscured in modern one-volume editions, for as in a three-act comedy there is a crescendo, a crisis, and a dénouement.[21] *Pride and Prejudice,* the most dramatic of them all, has even been analyzed into five acts.[22] Miss Austen's preference for the dramatic method involved a severe economy in the use of description; or, putting it the other way round, perhaps her slight interest in the external appearance of people or the details of places led her to adopt the dramatic method. This technique reaches perfection in *Pride and Prejudice.* In the last three books there is more description with more color and sensitiveness; but there is a corresponding loss in animation and a new sobriety of tone. *Mansfield Park* is the least dramatic of the series, and though the half dozen strands of the story are interwoven with wonderful skill, something was sacrificed along with unity of plot. In *Emma* there was a recovery of concentration, and here we have for our delight Miss Austen's greatest comic creations, Mr. Woodhouse and Miss Bates, a superbly natural pair who would be recognizably at home if we saw them on the boards. The resemblance to drama is much less marked in *Persuasion.* Here Miss Austen seems to be feeling her way towards a new technique. What seems a new

---

18 E. M. Forster, *Aspects of the Novel* (1927), pp. 112-113.
19 Perhaps Miss Austen abandoned the novel-in-letters because in that form the point of view necessarily shifts from writer to writer.
20 Congreve, however, she never mentions and may not have read.
21 C. L. Thomson, *Jane Austen,* p. 233.
22 Baker, VI, 84-87. Only *Pride and Prejudice* begins with a dialogue; the other openings are quietly expository.

departure in *Sanditon* may have been due to a desire to work with fresh materials, perhaps to a belief that the original vein was running thin. But this fragment had not advanced far enough at the time of her death to warrant guesses as to the direction in which it and its author's genius might have developed.[23]

Through almost all her life Jane Austen might have said, with Blake, "I am hid." Few of her books reached a second edition in her lifetime. Only towards the end were there signs of coming recognition.[24] Yet it was long retarded. The collected edition of 1833 supplied the market till 1882. From about 1890 biographies and appreciative estimates began to multiply, and the twentieth century has atoned for the neglect of most of the nineteenth. There have been many studies of her mind and art, her style and technique. There is not a fragment of her writings that has not been edited with loving care. Scholars have scrutinized and interpreted every detail of her picture of English society. Those who have made her the object of a cult have not alienated from her the wider circle of readers. The fact that she wrote comparatively little and that that little is almost always of the highest quality has resulted in the unique distinction which her reputation now enjoys, that she is the only author of her period whose works can be read, and are read, today with delight in their entirety.

[23] For some speculations on this problem see Virginia Woolf, *The Common Reader,* pp. 203-206.

[24] Especially Sir Walter Scott's article on the novels in *The Quarterly Review,* October, 1815; reprinted in *Famous Reviews,* ed. R. B. Johnson (1914).

X

Sir Walter Scott

I

The genial manliness of Scott's character, his fame first as a poet and then as a novelist, the crash of his fortunes, and the heroism with which in broken health he assumed responsibility for a vast debt form a tale which has become part of the British heritage. Possessing a pattern as clear-cut as any story of his own invention, it reveals the fatal flaw in character which brings about a catastrophe, but also the strength without which there is no true tragedy.

Born into an honorable but not lofty position in a society where the *Youth* feudal tradition was still strong, Walter Scott [1] (1771-1832) cherished the ambition to become a landed aristocrat. The Scottish past, legendary and historical, whether of families or clans or regions or the entire country, fascinated him. An incurable lameness, without making him a recluse, led him to devote much time as a boy to reading. He learned Latin, French, and Italian, and later more than a smattering of German. An encyclopedic knowledge of European history was stored in his phenomenal memory. Fairy tales, Oriental fables, romances of chivalry, balladry, and folklore fed his imagination. A brief experience in the dragoons started a lifelong interest in soldiering; and the study of the law, while providing him with a profession, accounts for the legal technicalities in some of his novels and for the effectiveness of his trial scenes. His young days were not devoted wholly to libraries, for loving a life of action he rode about Scotland, drinking and gossiping with humble folk, collecting from their lips quantities

[1] *The Waverley Novels*, Abbotsford Edition (12v, 1842-1847); Border Edition, ed. Andrew Lang (48v, 1892-1894); Oxford Edition (25v, 1912); *Poetical Works* (12v, Edinburgh, 1820), with Scott's notes; Globe Edition, ed. F. T. Palgrave (1866 and reprints); Oxford Edition, ed. J. L. Robertson (1904); *Miscellaneous Prose Works* (30v, 1834-1871); *Letters*, ed. Sir H. J. C. Grierson (12v, 1932-1937); *Private Letter-Books*, ed. Wilfred Partington (1930); *Journal, 1825-1832*, ed. David Douglas (2v, 1890); *Journal, 1825-1832*, ed. J. G. Tait (3v, 1939-1947).— Greville Worthington, *Bibliography* (1930); William Ruff, *Bibliography of the Poetical Works, Transactions of the Edinburgh Bibliographical Society*, I, Part II (1937); J. C. Corson, *A Bibliography of Sir Walter Scott* (1943); J. G. Lockhart, *Memoirs of the Life of Sir Walter Scott* (7v, Edinburgh, 1837-1838); Sir H. J. C. Grierson, *Sir Walter Scott, Bart.* (1938), supplementing and correcting Lockhart. See also Sir H. J. C. Grierson, *Lang, Lockhart, and Biography* (1934); Stephen Gwynn, *Life of Sir Walter Scott* (1930); John Buchan, *Sir Walter Scott* (1932); Archibald Stalker, *The Intimate Life of Sir Walter Scott* (1921); Donald Carswell, *Scott and his Circle* (1930); Wolfgang Keller, *Walter Scott* (Münster, 1933); Lord David Cecil, *Sir Walter Scott* (1933); *Sir Walter Scott To-Day*, ed. Sir H. J. C. Grierson (1932), essays by various authors; W. H. Hudson, *Sir Walter Scott* (1901); C. A. Young, *The Waverley Novels, an Appreciation* (Glasgow, 1907); Margaret Bail, *Sir Walter Scott as a Critic of Literature* (1907); C. F. Fiske, *Epic Suggestion in the Imagery of the Waverley Novels* (New

of traditional ballads, and enlarging his knowledge of peasant types and manners, architectural antiquities, places already famous in song and story, and other places to which he would one day impart a like renown.

Ballads   Enthusiasm for balladry was heightened by his study of German;[2] and he "commenced poet" with a free version entitled *William and Helen* (1796), of *Lenore*, G. A. Bürger's ballad on the theme of the spectre bridegroom.[3] In 1797 he married Charlotte Carpenter.[4] He had already experienced the passion and pain of an unsuccessful love affair,[5] and he put no such ardor into his marriage, these emotions coming, as he said, but once in a lifetime. His activities as a folklorist brought Scott into touch with "Monk" Lewis, who included some of his pieces in *Tales of Wonder* (1801). Among his collaborators Scott had John Leyden, an erudite Scottish peasant, and James Hogg, the eccentric shepherd-poet. He benefited also from the counsel of Joseph Ritson.[6] The example of earlier anthologies encouraged him to prepare with Leyden the *Minstrelsy of the Scottish Border* (1802-1803) in which, along with authentic ballads, more or less retouched, were original pieces by Scott or Leyden to take the places of lost ballads. Scott admitted that he added and emended freely, and, though in this matter not perfectly lucid, he did not attempt to palm off his own compositions as genuine antiques. That the learned Ritson approved of his work should have put the question of his essential honesty beyond dispute; it has, nevertheless, been disputed.[7] An edition of the metrical romance of *Sir Tristrem*, retouched and expanded, followed in 1804.

The Lay of the Last Minstrel   Then came *The Lay of the Last Minstrel* (1805), which put Scott in the forefront of living poets. There was an eager public for the Gothic stuff from which its confused plot was fashioned. The "frame" in which the tale is set —an aged minstrel reciting the *Lay*—was a happy device, linking the poem to the genuine heritage of old narrative verse and helping to justify the

Haven, 1940); O. F. Emerson, "The Early Literary Life of Sir Walter Scott," *JEGP*, xxiii (1924). 28-62, 241-269, 389-417; W. P. Ker, "Scott," *Collected Essays* (1920), i. 161-179; Baker, vi, chs. vi-ix; Edwin Muir, "Sir Walter Scott," in *From Anne to Victoria*, ed. Bonamy Dobrée (1937), pp. 528-545; P. N. Landis, "The Waverley Novels, or A Hundred Years After," *PMLA*, lii (1937). 461-473.

[2] See F. W. Stokoe, *German Influence in the English Romantic Period* (Cambridge, 1926), ch. iv and appendices i-iii. — In 1799 Scott published a version of Goethe's *Götz von Berlichingen*. Another drama influenced by German Gothicism is *The House of Aspen* which Scott wrote in 1799 but did not publish till 1820.

[3] A better version of *Lenore*, by William Taylor of Norwich, also appeared in 1796; and three other renderings were published in the same year.

[4] The mystery of Miss Carpenter's origin and family has been cleared up, so far as seems possible, by Grierson, *Sir Walter Scott*, ch. iii.

[5] See Grierson, *op. cit.*, pp. 28-32.

[6] See B. H. Bronson, *Joseph Ritson, Scholar-at-Arms* (2v, Berkeley, 1939). On the work of Ritson and other antiquaries and anthologists see also F. E. Pierce, *Currents and Eddies in the English Romantic Generation* (1918), ch. iii.

[7] See the *Minstrelsy*, ed. T. F. Henderson (1892). The case against Scott is presented in F. Elliot, *Trustworthiness of the Border Ballads* (Edinburgh, 1906) and *Further Essays on the Border Ballads* (Edinburgh, 1910). For the defense see Andrew Lang, *Sir Walter Scott and the Border Minstrelsy* (1910). See also Oliver Elton, *Survey* ... *1780-1830* (1920), ii. 303-304.

extravagant flights of fancy. The metre was modeled upon the ballads with some intermixture from *Christabel,* which Scott had heard recited. The carelessnesses of style, looseness of structure, and crudeness in characterization—defects easily discernible now—were not stumbling-blocks to the first readers of a poem whose vital energy carried everything before it. Scott did not at once follow up this success. While writing his next poem he was busy professionally and socially and engaged in the finest of his scholarly undertakings, the edition of Dryden (1808), and in negotiations which initiated *The Quarterly Review.* In 1808 appeared *Marmion,* a poem less varied   Marmion in prosody than the *Lay* and more clear-cut in conception, a tale of private adventure set against the background of public events which culminated in the defeat of James IV at Flodden Field. Marmion, the lordly scoundrel, troubles our psychological scruples; but to such heroes the taste of the day was accustomed. The introductions to the several cantos, verse epistles to various friends, are not quite in keeping with the context; but their tributes to Nelson, Pitt, and Fox harmonized with the martial spirit of the narrative and roused patriotic feeling at a time when every Briton needed to have a stout heart.

In *The Lady of the Lake* (1810), which was inspired by Scott's enthusiasm   *Later* for the wild country of Loch Katrine, the plot, though better managed than   *Poems* the plots of the earlier poems, is subordinate to the descriptive passages, to such episodes as the stag-hunt and the gathering of the clans, and to the beautiful songs, *Rest, Warrior, Rest* and the plangent *Coronach. The Vision of Don Roderick* (1811), which preceded Southey's and Landor's versions of the legendary crime of the last of the Goths, is a *pièce d'occasion.* To its lack of interest may be in part attributed the blame for the falling off in Scott's popularity which he later ascribed wholly to the emergence of Byron. The sales of *Rokeby* (1813) were alarmingly small. Scott had no intimate knowledge of the Yorkshire setting and consequently the "thunderous, cumulative topography" [8] which is a feature of the Scottish poems is diminished. The heroine is the first of various tenderly reminiscential portraits of Scott's first love. Of more significance is the figure of Bertram, in whom we observe the characteristics of the Byronic hero-type—the somber personage compounded of crime, remorse, and magnanimity—in all its features, antedating *Lara* by a year. [9] The period is that of the Cavaliers and Roundheads; in choice and treatment of materials the poem points the way towards the historical novels. We may glance beyond Scott's shift to prose fiction to notice the remaining poems. *The Bridal of Triermain* (1813) is the first experiment by a nineteenth-century poet with the "Matter of Arthur." In it Scott virtually tells as an Arthurian story the tale of the Sleeping Beauty, thus crossing different strains of folklore with the easy

---

[8] John Buchan, *Sir Walter Scott,* p. 113.
[9] The concept, deriving in long descent from Milton's Satan and immediately from heroes of Gothic romance, shows that "Byronism" was already prevalent when Byron availed himself of it. See Byron, *Childe Harold and other Romantic Poems,* ed. S. C. Chew (1936), pp. xxv-xxvi.

license of the medieval romancers.[10] *The Lord of the Isles* (1815), on the wanderings of Robert Bruce, adheres more closely to history than the earlier poems and is redeemed from dullness only by the fine narrative of Bannockburn. In *Harold the Dauntless* (1817) Scott made the mistake of not taking his own wild theme quite seriously and introduced an element of burlesque which consorts ill with a fierce northern saga.

*Poetic
Style*

Scott's prosody, a compound of interwoven rimes in the ballad measure, of octosyllabics, and of cataracts of rime which continue sometimes for five or six lines, is at its best well adapted to the matter of the narratives, but combined with his inexhaustible memories and affluent imagination it produced stories and descriptions that are almost always too long. His finest vein is that of rapid and tumultuous action, when we hear

> sounds of insult, shame and wrong,
> And trumpets blown for wars.

In the analysis both of private motive and of those considerations of state which result in great events he is feeble, often abandoning such problems to the reader's surmise. He could manage mysteries fairly well (as that of the disguised De Wilton in *Marmion*), but he did not know the value of reticence. Overtones of meaning, the substitution of suggestion for statement, were beyond his powers. Only in the lyric did he curb his redundancy and often achieve a condensed poignancy. The most memorable passage in the *Lay* is the version of the *Dies Irae*. More stirringly than in any passage of narrative is the martial spirit conveyed to the reader in the *Pibroch of Donald Dhu* and in *Macgregor's Gathering;* and in *Proud Maisie* (the song in *The Heart of Midlothian*) romantic pathos is quintessentialized as it is in none of the long poems or novels.

II

Abbotsford

In 1812 Scott purchased a farm on the Tweed and began not only to build Abbotsford but to acquire more and more land. Thus, through the disastrous realization of the dreams of childhood, the foundation was laid for a pyramid of debts. Involved financial obligations culminated in his ruin.[11] The first omens of the disaster which his arrangements with James Ballantyne and Archibald Constable were to bring upon him appeared as early as 1813 and emphasized the need to check the decline in popularity with efforts along new lines. Long since he had tried his hand at fiction, beginning novels on Thomas the Rhymer and on the Civil Wars.[12] In

[10] See Howard Maynadier, *The Arthur of the English Poets* (1907), pp. 336-340. In this same year (1813) Scott's friend Reginald Heber (1783-1826), the famous hymn-writer, was at work upon his *Morte d'Arthur*, which remained a fragment. See Maynadier, pp. 340-342.

[11] Grierson, *Sir Walter Scott*, is largely concerned with the problem of disentangling the complicated evidence and apportioning blame for the crash. Scott's folly and indiscretion, into which his social ambitions drove him, are now seen to have been more blameworthy than Lockhart admitted or Scott himself seems to have realized.

[12] In an appendix to the General Preface to the collected edition of 1829 Scott outlined the plot and printed a fragment of the romance of Thomas the Rhymer.

1805 he had begun *Waverley*, only to lay it aside, discouraged perhaps by the failure of *Queenhoo Hall* (1808), a historical romance by Joseph Strutt which, after the author's death, Scott completed and prepared for the press. The discarded manuscript was now taken up again, and in 1814 *Waverley, Waverley or 'Tis Sixty Years Since* was published anonymously. Scott thought it beneath his dignity as an official of the law to attach his name to a novel; it might also cheapen his reputation as a poet and hinder him from producing tales as rapidly as, with his teeming memory and imagination, he was planning to do. Later, when *Waverley* and its successors were enormously popular, he enjoyed the mystification as to the authorship, though it cannot be denied that it involved him in falsehoods.[13]

In his youth Scott had had from elderly people first-hand reminiscences of the "Forty-five." These he used to make *Waverley* in part a "novel of manners" of the comparatively recent past. But in it history, romance, scenery, folklore, and humor are blended as they had never been before in prose fiction. The different materials are not very well fused; the plot is conventional and the hero not only feebly characterized but representative of a more refined state of society than is quite credible at the epoch and in the environment. But the success of the book was instantaneous and Scott set himself to hold the market he had won.[14] *Guy Mannering* (1815) was written in six weeks, a feat as amazing physically as intellectually. This is a picture of society rather than a historical novel. The period is recent; the setting a remote part of Scotland. The well-worn plot of the missing heir is intricate and incoherent but may be disregarded, for the story's charm lies in the vivid episodes, the brilliant drawing of the subsidiary figures, and the cheerful gusto of the telling. In *The Antiquary* (1816)[15] Scott repeated the plot of the missing heir, contriving it very clumsily and setting it in a period of which he had youthful memories. *Tales of My Landlord* (1816) contains two works, the crudely Gothic *Black Dwarf*[16] in which Scott descended to the level from which he had been rescuing romance, and the splendid *Old Mortality*, a story centering in the rising of the Covenanters in 1685. In *Rob Roy* (1818) Scott's design was, as he noted in the introduction, to contrast the "cultivated mode of life" in southern Scotland with the "wild and lawless adventures" still to be met with in the Highlands. Rob Roy is but a secondary figure in the book, overshadowed by Di Vernon;

[13] From the first the authorship was apparent to good judges (Miss Austen, for example). In 1822 J. L. Adolphus, in *Letters to Richard Heber containing Critical Remarks on the Series of Novels beginning with Waverley*, arguing from the resemblances between the novels and Scott's poems, put the matter beyond all doubt—though by then few had any doubts. In the introduction to *Chronicles of the Canongate*, First Series (1825), Scott avowed himself as "the sole and unaided author of these Novels of Waverley," a fact by that time universally known.

[14] The fecundity of Scott's first few years as a novelist has suggested the theory (for which there is no real evidence) that he had in hand drafts of at least six of the books which he poured out in rapid succession. See Una Pope-Hennessey's letter in *LTLS*, April 28, 1932.

[15] Impressions of a visit to the Continent in 1815 were recorded in *The Field of Waterloo*, a poem, and in *Paul's Letters to his Kinsfolk*, journalistic impressions of the state of Europe. Both were published in 1816.

[16] See C. O. Parsons, "The Original of the Black Dwarf," *SP*, XL (1943). 567-575.

the most winning of Scott's heroines. The second series of *Tales of My Landlord* was taken up wholly with *The Heart of Midlothian* (1818), the finest of all the Waverley Novels. In it Scott made amends to the memory of the Covenanters to whom, in *Old Mortality,* he had shown himself, if not unjust, at any rate less than sympathetic. Jeanie Deans represents the covenanting spirit among the peasantry at its noblest. Between 1817 and 1819 Scott was often ill with gall-stones. The disease was at its worst when he wrote the third series of the *Tales* (1819). *The Legend of Montrose,* on

The Bride of Lammermoor

the campaign against Argyle, is a slight thing; but *The Bride of Lammermoor* is very different not only from its companion tale but from all the other books. It was dictated during such agonies that when he read it afterwards Scott remembered not a scene or word. *The Bride* has been well described as "that masterpiece of Gothic fiction which so many had been trying to write and never succeeding." [17] It is a reversion to such stories of doom as the ballads tell, with disasters foretold by soothsayers and sped with curses dark; the violent death of bride and bridegroom; and the extinction of an ancient house.[18] Unlike Scott's other heroes, Ravenswood is the center of his story; but his tragedy is external to his character and is brought upon him by malignant fate. The comic scenes of the faithful retainer are wearisomely prolonged and so farcical as to defeat their purpose of darkening the tragedy by contrast. But the powerful portents uttered by the witch-woman have been likened, not unjustifiably, to the prophecies in *Macbeth.*

Ivanhoe

A recovery of health which, however, left Scott with but half his former physical strength, was signaled by a new departure. *Ivanhoe* (1820) [19] is his first incursion into the Middle Ages. In this romance of adventure, history is accommodated to the exigencies of the plot. In pattern *Ivanhoe* is more firmly knit than are most of the Waverley Novels; and though it was long since relegated to the category of "books for boys" (a position which it now holds very precariously), it contains episodes which, once read (and perhaps never read again), are never forgotten and characters which remain unfadingly vivid. In this year, 1820, Scott wrote far too much. The protracted and confused story of *The Monastery,* with its supernatural absurdities and lack of understanding of "monkish" ideals, gives evidence of hasty writing. Its sequel, *The Abbot,* is much better. For all the violence done to fact, this tale of Mary Queen of Scots combines history and romance in a setting of memorable charm. Scott was now advised by Constable to write a story to be called *The Armada*; but in wisely rejecting the title he relieved himself of the responsibility which would have been his had he put into the forefront of his book the quarrel with Spain. Instead, he chose as his center the apocryphal legend of the death of Amy Robsart and as his setting

[17] Baker, VI (1935). 168. — Consciously or unconsciously Scott took the main situation of *The Bride* from C. R. Maturin's *The Milesian Chief* (1812).

[18] See C. O. Parsons, "The Dalrymple Legend in *The Bride of Lammermoor,*" RES, XIX (1943). 51-58.

[19] In this year, 1820, a baronetcy was bestowed upon Scott.

a romantic spot which he had visited; and the result was *Kenilworth* (1821). *The Pirate* (1822), founded on impressions of the northern islands received in 1814 and on his interest in the Norse sagas, is second-rate work partially redeemed by fine descriptions of coast and storm. *The Fortunes of Nigel* (1822) shows us London in the reign of James I; there is very little history and consequently little violence is done to it. The evocation of the streets and crowds and iniquities of London is masterly; the opportunity to set Scottish eccentrics against a contrasting background is well exploited; and the character of the King is Scott's most careful historical portrait. Working under deplorable pressure, Scott produced a third novel in this same year: *Peveril of the Peak*. The characters and locality were unfamiliar to him; he did not grasp the complex horrors of the so-called Popish Plot; and the dull story is drawn out to intolerable length. Here we have the first evidence of Scott's decline.

Again there was recovery in *Quentin Durward* (1823), Scott's first foray into French history, based on the *Chronicles* of Philippe de Commines and dealing with the quarrel between Louis XI and Charles the Bold. It falls into the same category with *Ivanhoe,* and judgments passed upon that romance apply equally well to this. In *St. Ronan's Well* (1824) an experiment was made with a story of contemporary life, but the combination of light social satire with a tragic theme was an unhappy one and the book must be judged a failure. On a much higher plane is *Redgauntlet* (1824), the last novel of first rank. Here, reverting to a subject near to his heart, Scott showed the tragic though futile nobility of Jacobitism. The private story (such as it is) is combined with the unfounded tradition of the Young Pretender's secret visit to London. There is more of personal recollection than in any of the other books, much law which derives from the writer's experiences, and memories of his first love affair. The famous inset, *Wandering Willie's Tale,* gives to the book a peculiar prestige. This masterpiece of supernaturalism attains its effect in part by the skilful juxtaposition of the matter-of-fact and the weird and in part by the sense it conveys of mounting terror as the unhurried narrative with which it opens gives way to horror. The climax of the grisly revel is tremendous. *Tales of the Crusaders* (1825) is made up of *The Betrothed* and *The Talisman,* the former an almost negligible piece of Gothicism (though the appearance of Vanda in the haunted chamber is memorable), the latter a lively adventure-story with robust characters and brightly colored Syrian landscape.

Then, when in 1825 England plunged into an economic depression, the *Debts* crash came, and Scott found himself burdened with debt, permitted to retain some of his possessions only through the indulgence of creditors to whom he bound himself by hard conditions, and doomed to seven years of unremitting toil from which he was released only by death. In this year he began to keep the *Journal* which is one of the most moving of autobiographic documents. Turning to one of the first historical themes to attract his attention, the English Civil Wars, he had begun *Woodstock* (1826) amid anxieties but before the wrecking of his fortunes. The unusual care with which it is composed is a sign, perhaps, of his sense of responsibility to his creditors. In the first series of *Chronicles of the Canongate* (1827) he placed in an attractive frame several novelettes, of which some are inconsiderable Gothic fantasies of ghost-lore and divination while two, *The Highland Widow* and *The Two Drovers,* are little tragedies of condensed power. A second series of the *Chronicles* (1828) has as its main offering *The Fair Maid of Perth,* which interweaves a love story with a picture of the conflict between nobles and townsfolk in the Scottish Middle Ages. The psychological insight shown in the delineation of the cowardly young chief of the clan Quhele is noteworthy. Three series (1828, 1829, and 1831) of *Tales of a Grandfather* are not fiction but simplifications of Scottish and French history addressed to youthful intelligences. In *Anne of Geierstein* (1829) he returned to Franco-Burgundian history in the fifteenth century. Here the flame gives light for the last time. In *Count Robert of Paris,* a story of eleventh-century Byzantium taken largely from Gibbon, it flickers fitfully; and in *Castle Dangerous* it goes out in smoke. These last two romances appeared together as the fourth series of *Tales of My Landlord* (1832). Heart and brain had been overdriven; and with "the retinue of the world's good wishes" Scott sought health in Italy. But it was too late. He was brought back to Abbotsford to die (September 21, 1832).[20]

III

The
Marvelous

    Scott defined romance as "a fictitious narrative in prose or verse, the interest of which turns upon marvelous and uncommon incidents," and the novel as "a fictitious narrative, differing from the romance, because the events are accommodated to the ordinary train of human events, and the modern state of society."[21] Classified accordingly, almost all his fictitious narratives are romances rather than novels. By combining direct observation and imaginative apprehension he blended elements of wonder from old romance with elements of real life into a new synthesis of historical prose romance.[22] With an inveterate taste for "bogles and brownies and

[20] From the above chronological survey the dramas and the miscellaneous prose works have been omitted. Such interest as the former still possess lies in their reflection of contemporary tastes. *The Doom of Devorgoil* (published 1826 but written long before) is a "melo-drama" (in the contemporary sense) with serio-comic goblins, songs, and music. *Halidon Hill* (1822) is a clearly drawn sketch from history, full of movement. *Auchindrane* is a domestic tragedy. Scott's major work as an editor, besides the Dryden (1808), is the Swift (1814), a less congenial task. He also edited several collections of letters, memoirs, and state papers. *The Border Antiquities of England and Scotland* (1817) have to do with the scenery and architecture of the region. *Letters on Demonology and Witchcraft* (1830), though a somewhat chaotic compilation, was written *con amore* and retains its interest.

[21] *Essay on Romance,* published in the Supplement to the *Encyclopædia Britannica* (1824); reprinted in *Miscellaneous Prose Works* (1827).

[22] Max Korn, "Sir Walter Scott und die Geschichte," *Anglia,* LXI (1937). 416-441. G. E. Smock, *Sir Walter Scott's Theory of the Novel,* a Cornell University dissertation, 1934, is not yet published.

lang-nebbit things frae the neist world," Scott never entirely freed himself from dependence upon the marvelous.[23] This varies in tone and atmosphere from the crudest supernaturalism [24] to such a moving evocation of awe and dread as the apparition of old Alice to Ravenswood. The many failures in this kind are partly due to Scott's failure to take the supernatural seriously. The White Lady of Avenel (a grotesque sister of Fouqué's Undine), which even Lockhart admitted to be a "blot" upon *The Monastery*,[25] is a shocking mixture of farce and fantasy. Elspeth the witch in *The Antiquary* and Norna of the Fitful Head in *The Pirate* are the merest pieces of theatrical clap-trap. That he had overdone this sort of thing Scott implied in the introduction to *The Fortunes of Nigel* where he promised to make no use of "dreams, or presages, or obscure allusions to future events," "not so much as the poor tick of a solitary death-watch in the wainscot."

The farther back in time the stories are placed the larger the element of romance and the smaller the attention paid to "the ordinary train of human events." Those whose period is the eighteenth century are, for all their romantic qualities, also novels of manners, and are sometimes so advertised on title-page or in introduction. Since types and manners change slowly in Scotland, the same may be said of *Old Mortality* and *The Heart of Midlothian*. But in the fifteenth and sixteenth centuries Scott was less at home, and when we have retreated to the Middle Ages we are in a dream-world where Scott cheerfully admits that he "may have confused the manners of two or three centuries." [26] A distinction must be made between anachronisms due to insufficient knowledge or sympathy and the deliberate distortions of history designed to heighten the interest of the story. He could on occasion master a historic situation supremely well, as the Covenanters in *Old Mortality* and the Porteous Riots in *The Heart of Midlothian* bear witness. He knew as well as his critics that in *Kenilworth* events are condensed and telescoped, that Dudley's marriage to Amy Robsart was not a secret and that her death had occurred long before the period of the story; but when he made Shakespeare a figure renowned at court at a date when he was really a child he allowed himself too great a liberty. There are times when his failure to grasp a situation bewilders and exasperates his readers. The desperate confusion in *The Monastery* is a case in point; and there, too, we note his incompetence when he deals with a subject with which he has no sympathy. The monastic ideal and consequently the tragedy of its degeneracy were beyond his range. The aesthetic question is whether his offenses against Clio are of a nature to shock the sensibilities not only of a

The Treatment of History

---

[23] C. O. Colman has published many studies of Scott's use of folklore and the supernatural. See especially N&Q, CLXXXIV (1943). 95-97; 358-363; CLXXXV (1943). 4-9; 92-100;CLXXXVIII (1945). 2-8; 30-33; 76-77; 98-101.

[24] Such as the apparition of the Bodach Glas in *Waverley* or the wraith which appears on the battlefield in *A Legend of Montrose*.

[25] Lockhart, *Life of Scott*, ch. L. Lockhart argued that Scott erred in dwelling too long upon the phantom: "The phantom with whom we have leisure to become familiar is sure to fail." The assertion is debatable; and even a very little of the White Lady would have been too much.

[26] Introduction to *Ivanhoe*.

professional historian, like Freeman,[27] but of the usually indulgent general reader. Of profounder moment are Scott's "moral anachronisms," when he ascribes to men and women of past ages the thoughts, tastes, and emotions of his own day. In this respect he followed, probably unconsciously, the example of the rationalistic historians of the preceding age who accepted the principle of immutable natural laws which included human behavior, making the motives of men subject to the same influences in all times and places. In general he showed wisdom in relegating great historical figures to the middle distance or the background. When they are thrust forward to the footlights they are sometimes rather stagey. This is certainly true of his Mary Queen of Scots, though she is made a queenly and romantic personality. But the failure to face the problem of her guilt or innocence in the murder of Darnley makes his portrait psychologically valueless; and the inconclusive end of *The Abbot* at Langside leaves her tragedy but half told. Only once in *Kenilworth* does Queen Elizabeth rise to the height of her reputation; and Louis XI in *Quentin Durward* is a portrait verging upon caricature, unforgettable though the grotesque bigot may be. Scott's most convincing regal figure is James I in *The Fortunes of Nigel,* an eccentric pedant with a strain of vulgarity crossed with kingly dignity.

Characteri-
zation

Scott's supreme feat was to make the past alive again. His best work was done within the world he knew: the past of Scotland within about a hundred years, that, is within the memory of people he had known in his youth. It has been said that he looked on a man "as an antiquarian looks on a house." [28] He had an eye for every portion of the structure, recognizing that this characteristic was due to this inherited trait and that to that circumstance of environment. He envisaged a man as being colored by the social conditions into which he is born and of which he is heir. With the anxieties and aspirations of men and women considered as individuals he concerned himself scarcely at all; their private lives are of interest only as they are part of history. Working within these limitations he could not give a "three-dimensional" quality to his heroes and heroines; but at his best he imparted a tragic dignity to large situations: revenge, remorse, or the struggle of rival loyalties. His greatest creations usually have but a small part in the conventional plot of the story or are altogether independent of it. They belong to regions which he knew and loved. Not the ineffectual hero but Fergus MacIvor and the Baron of Bradwardine give vitality to *Waverley.* The "wax-work" protagonists of *Guy Mannering* are easily forgotten, but we remember the crowds of peasants and especially Meg Merrilies. Jonathan Oldbuck in *The Antiquary* elbows the nominal hero out of the way and shares his claim to attention only with the vagabond Edie Ochiltree. Bailie Nicol Jarvie and the lying braggart Andrew Fairservice, with their humorous vernacular,[29] are the life of *Rob Roy.* Even in *The*

[27] See the strictures on *Ivanhoe* in E. A. Freeman, *The Norman Conquest,* v, Note W.
[28] Lord David Cecil, *Sir Walter Scott,* p. 7.
[29] The dialect is generally of Scott's own district. Sometimes it is "broad"; or he may make a concession to southern readers by coloring standard English with local idioms and

Heart of Midlothian, where the principal characters count for more than in the general run of the novels, the most vivid figures are the criminals. Just as he made of the Scots dialect an instrument for the expression of a wide range of emotion, so Scott is always excellent when he is portraying social outcasts, treating them often humorously, but as often horrifyingly. He is, in fact, a much more convincing artist when he deals with the humorous, the eccentric, the squalid, even with the downright villainous, than when he delineates the morally irreproachable.

In a few cases Scott took pains with the structure of an entire story; but *Great* generally we remember the novels for separate episodes rather than for any *Scenes* total artistic effect. Innumerable scenes are greater than the stories that contain them. Sometimes these are scenes of hair-breadth escapes, as when Queen Mary escapes from Loch Leven or when Charles I appears as a fugitive. Of like kind is the scene in *Old Mortality*—one of the supreme things in the novels—when Claverhouse saves Morton from the fanatics who are attending his midnight doom. The confrontation of mighty opposites is a challenge to all Scott's powers. Scenes of action are more congenial to him than are interludes of calm. He and his public were overfond of weird and horrible episodes; but when his imagination was excited to its depths, as in the scene of the corpse-winding in *The Bride of Lammermoor,* he rose far above the level of contemporary Gothicism. The total effect was generally marred because Scott seldom conceived a unified design. He displayed a brilliant but disorderly pageant, imposing upon this vital confusion a semblance of order by means of the artificial plot. Some of the novels are too long in getting started; he seems to be letting his pen drive on while deciding what to write about. Others continue after the real story is wound up; the long anticlimax of *The Heart of Midlothian* was stitched on because the book had to be extended to the contracted length. The conventional reversal of fortune at the close of some stories is a concession to his public, Scott being one who, living to please, had to please to live.[30] An anxiety not to alienate readers resulted in the hopeless marring of *St. Ronan's Well* where last-minute changes in the plot blurred the whole point of the intrigue.[31]

Of any profound philosophic conception of life there is no trace in Scott. *Tastes and* He would have been bewildered had he guessed it would be sought for. *Sympathie* There is no speculation in his eyes. His sympathies were aristocratic, almost feudal; he enjoyed the position of the bountiful laird surrounded by loyal retainers; and he delighted to pay homage to his liege lord—even though that liege was George IV. This loyalty to the House of Hanover did not

---

words. Scott knew no Gaelic, and Celtic scholars have criticized his attempts to render Gaelic idiom. In the medieval romances the problem of the style of the dialogue was met by not making it so obsolete as to be incomprehensible nor so modern as to jar upon the sensibilities of the trained reader; but it was not very well solved, for the antique effects are often of the sort known as "Wardour Street English."

30 "No one shall find me rowing against the stream—I write for general amusement' (Introductory Epistle to *The Fortunes of Nigel*).

31 See Baker, VI. 194-195.

clash with the purely sentimental "Charlie-over-the-Waterism" which Borrow was later to laugh at. His sympathies were with the Cavaliers—which is why he was somewhat less than just to the Roundheads; but in dealing with history he generally avoided controversial issues, preferring to accept the current popular judgment. Love, though the major theme of his plots, is not the major theme of his books. They have to do with warfare and adventures, wild, curious and improbable, dangers by flood and field. Such subjects consorted with his taste for chivalry and "gramarye," ancient architecture, armor, heraldry, old sports and pastimes, and folk-legends. His robust interest in art and antiques was not discriminating, as the miscellaneous assortment of objects assembled at Abbotsford testified. He had little love of music save when a melody called to mind the words of songs.

During the last decade of his life a legion of now forgotten imitators trailed after him. His immediate contemporaries among Scottish novelists worked mostly along other lines.[32] Later came Ainsworth, Bulwer-Lytton, and G. P. R. James; then Reade and Kingsley; and much later Stevenson. The French romanticists—Vigny, Dumas, Hugo, and even (though with a difference) Mérimée—were his followers in the field of the historical novel.[33] Without Scott, Manzoni's *I Promessi Sposi* is inconceivable. In Germany a school of novelists regarded him as their master, and G. M. Ebers applied his methods to stories of ancient Egypt. In England and America his reputation is probably somewhat higher today than it was a generation ago; but from the ardor of some vocal admirers one must not infer an increase in the number of his readers.[34]

[32] See ch. xvi, below.

[33] Louis Maigron, *Le roman historique à l'époque romantique: essai sur l'influence de Walter Scott* (Paris, 1898).

[34] For a survey of the fluctuations in the prestige of the novels see J. T. Hillhouse, *The Waverley Novels and their Critics* (Minneapolis, 1936).

XI

Lord Byron

I

It is a commonplace of criticism to distinguish between the poetry which Byron composed before his final departure from England in 1816 and the poetry of his later years. The break in continuity was not complete. He vacillated between rationalism and romantic illusionism, between respect for convention and defiant revolt, between loyalty to the old classicism and adherence to the new fashions in poetry. There are satiric elements in his romantic poems; and, conversely, there are romantic passages in his satires.[1]

George Gordon Byron[2] (1788-1824), who at the age of ten became Lord Byron of Newstead, inherited from both sides of his ancestry an emotional

---

[1] Helene Richter, "Byron, Klassizismus und Romantik," *Anglia,* XLVIII (1924). 209-257. Miss Richter makes much of this dichotomy in her *Lord Byron: Persönlichkeit und Werk* (Halle, 1929).

[2] *Works: Poetry,* ed. E. H. Coleridge; *Letters and Journals,* ed. R. E. Prothero (13v, 1898-1904); *Poetical Works,* ed. P. E. More (1905); *Correspondence,* ed. John Murray (2v, 1922); *Don Juan and other Satirical Poems,* ed. L. I. Bredvold (1935); *Childe Harold's Pilgrimage and other Romantic Poems,* ed. S. C. Chew (1936). — T. J. Wise, *Bibliography* (2v, 1932-1933); Ethel C. Mayne, *Byron* (2v, 1912; revised, 1924); John Drinkwater, *The Pilgrim of Eternity: Byron—A Conflict* (1925); André Maurois, *Byron* (2v, Paris, 1930); Harold Nicolson, *Byron: The Last Journey, 1823-1824* (1924); Peter Quennell, *Byron: The Years of Fame* (1935) and *Byron in Italy* (1941); Ethel C. Mayne, *The Life of Lady Byron* (1929). On the Byron "Problem" see also Ralph Milbanke, Earl of Lovelace, *Astarte: A Fragment of Truth concerning . . . Lord Byron* (privately printed, 1905; ed. Mary, Countess of Lovelace, 1921); John Murray, E. H. Pember, and R. E. Prothero, *Lord Byron and his Detractors* (privately printed, 1906); Richard Edgcombe, *Byron: The Last Phase* (1909); Sir John Fox, *The Byron Mystery* (1924). Monographs on special topics: Charles du Bos, *Byron et le besoin de la fatalité* (Paris, 1929; English trans., by E. C. Mayne, 1932); W. J. Calvert, *Byron: Romantic Paradox* (Chapel Hill, 1935); S. C. Chew, *The Dramas of Lord Byron* (Göttingen, 1915); C. M. Fuess, *Lord Byron as a Satirist in Verse* (1912); C. T. Goode, *Byron as Critic* (Weimar, 1923); Dora N. Raymond, *The Political Career of Lord Byron* (1924). On Byron's reputation and influence: S. C. Chew, *Byron in England: His Fame and After-Fame* (1924); W. E. Leonard, *Byron and Byronism in America* (1905); Edmond Estève, *Byron et le romantisme français* (Paris, 1907); G. Muoni, *La Fama del Byron e il Byronismo in Italia* (Milan, 1903); Max Simhart, *Lord Byrons Einfluss auf die italienische Literatur* (Munich, 1909); Antonio Porta, *Byronismo Italiano* (Milan, 1923); W. Ochsenbein, "Die Aufnahme Lord Byrons in Deutschland," *Untersuchungen zur neueren Sprach- und Literaturgeschichte,* VI (Berne, 1905); Cedric Hentschell, *The Byronic Teuton* (1939); P. H. Churchman, "The Beginnings of Byronism in Spain," *Revue hispanique,* XXIII (1910). 333-410. Important critical estimates are: P. E. More, "The Wholesome Revival of Byron," *Atlantic Monthly,* LXXXII (1898). 801-809; W. P. Trent, "The Byron Revival," *Forum,* XXVI (1898). 242-256; George Rebec, "Byron and Morals," *International Journal of Ethics,* XIV (1903). 39-54; J. F. A. Pyre "Byron in our Day," *Atlantic Monthly,* XCIX (1907). 542-552; S. F. Gingerich, *Essays in the Romantic Poets* (1924), pp. 243-276; H. W. Garrod, *Byron: 1824-1924* (1924), a lecture; Lord Ernle (R. E. Prothero), "The Poetry of Byron," *Quarterly Rev.* CCXLI (1924). 229-263; H. M. Jones, "The Byron Centenary," *Yale Rev.* XIII (1924). 730-745; Bertrand Russell, "Byron and the Modern World," *JHI,* I (1940). 24-37. — Parts of this chapter are taken, by permission of the Odyssey Press, from the writer's introduction to the volume of selections mentioned above.

instability bordering upon madness.[3] His father, having had by a first marriage a daughter, Augusta, had married Catherine Gordon of Gight; and having depleted her small dowry, he decamped to France where he died when his only son was three years old. Congenital lameness, narrow circumstances in his childhood at Aberdeen,[4] and alternating indulgence and abuse from his mother fixed in the boy a subconscious sense of inferiority which found expression in pride, scorn, and contemptuousness. Of several precocious love affairs, one, with a cousin, Mary Chaworth, he later made famous to all the world. At Harrow he won some distinction for oratory; and at Cambridge (1805-1808), where dissipation distracted him from study, he made friends with John Cam Hobhouse[5] and with the mysterious "Thyrza" whose death in 1812 he mourned in a cycle of elegies. In 1806 his *Fugitive Pieces* appeared privately, only to be suppressed because of the impropriety of one poem. After a second false start, *Poems on Various Occasions* (1807), Byron sought a wider audience and published *Hours of Idleness* (1807). These poems, reprinted in the main from the two previous volumes, are imitative and pretentious, facile and rhetorical, commendable only for the sincere love of Highland scenery expressed in some of them. Henry Brougham's slashing criticism in *The Edinburgh Review*[6] goaded Byron to the discovery of his powers as a satirist. He kept his anger under control, proceeded slowly, and did not publish *English Bards and Scotch Reviewers* till 1809. It attracted some attention. That its author was young and injudicious was evident; but that he could polish an epigram and hit hard was undeniable.

Shortly after this, Byron, having attained his majority and taken his seat in the House of Lords, set out with Hobhouse for the Levant. They traveled by way of Portugal and Spain, sailed to Malta and thence to Albania, and at length came to Athens.[7] There Byron celebrated the charms of Teresa Macri in *Maid of Athens,* the best known of his songs. At Smyrna he completed the first two cantos of *Childe Harold's Pilgrimage.*[8] Of a sojourn at Constantinople (May to July, 1810) we know little, for the travel poem was not carried on to this point and later gossip is mostly baseless. Hobhouse then returned home; but Byron lingered for a second stay in Athens and did not reach England till July, 1811. He brought with him the manuscripts of several poems.

[3] Of various studies of Byron's mental health-history the latest is J. H. Cassity, "Psychopathological Glimpses of Lord Byron," *Psychoanalytic Review,* XII (1925). 397-413. See also Hermann Conrad, "Byrons Vorfahren und Kindheit," *Anglia,* LI (1927). 164-173, 372-383.

[4] The early Scottish influence upon Byron is stressed in J. D. Symon, *Byron in Perspective* (1925), and in T. S. Eliot, "Byron," in *From Anne to Victoria,* ed. Bonamy Dobrée (1937), pp. 601-619.

[5] J. C. Hobhouse (1786-1869), created Lord Broughton, entered Parliament, championed reform, and was a member of Grey's, Melbourne's, and Russell's cabinets. His *Recollections of a Long Life* (2v, 1909) contains much information on Byron.

[6] January, 1808; reprinted in *Letters and Journals,* ed. Prothero, I, 344-349.

[7] Harold Spender, *Byron and Greece* (1924); Karl Brunner, "Griechenland in Byrons Dichtung," *Anglia,* LX (1936). 203-210.

[8] Hobhouse's *A Journey through Albania and other Provinces of Turkey* (1813) supplements Byron's second canto.

A friend, R. C. Dallas, was disappointed in *Hints from Horace,* a laborious sequel to *English Bards.* *The Curse of Minerva,* attacking Lord Elgin for the vandalism committed upon the Parthenon, was set aside because possibly actionable.[9] Dallas·then read the verse narrative of Byron's travels and recognizing it to be a work of genius, persuaded the poet to consent to its publication by John Murray. Subjected to revision while passing through the press, it received the stamp of Byron's moody loneliness, intensified by the death of his mother and of two dear friends, in the months following his return to England. But he now met two influential men of letters, Rogers and Moore, and by them was introduced to the brilliant Whig society which centered in Holland House.[10] His beauty, youth, and ancient name, the romantic journey which he had accomplished, reports of his genius, and rumors of his wickedness were more than sufficient to offset his self-conscious gaucherie; and the years of his notoriety began. The morning when he "awoke and found himself famous" was March 10, 1812, when *Childe Harold's Pilgrimage* appeared. The way for it had been prepared by the people who molded literary taste; there was nothing disconcertingly novel in a narrative and reflective poem in the Spenserian stanza; the poet's rank and reputation stimulated curiosity; the Iberian setting of the first canto was of topical interest; the Levantine setting of the second appealed to the taste for Oriental travel books;[11] and the *leitmotif* of disillusioned skepticism was attractively romantic and melancholy. The crudities of these cantos are now all too obvious; but they may be still enjoyed by anyone who is stimulated by contact with a young mind of exceptional energy. *Childe Harold*

Byron's cynicism appraised popular applause correctly, but he made the most of it while it lasted. More sought after than seeking, he passed from one love affair to another, sensual or sentimental. The most conspicuous was the liaison with Lady Caroline Lamb; the most serious was the incestuous relationship with his half-sister, Augusta Leigh. Happiness fled before him who sought to find it in pleasure. Gloom and satiety were none the less sincere for being theatrically displayed. In the midst of amatory and social triumphs he turned out the three Oriental Tales—*The Giaour, The Bride of Abydos* (both 1813), and *The Corsair* (1814), rhetorical narratives of mysterious adventure and sentimental love which are today readable only for their occasional passages of genuine poetry. In *Lara* (1814) Byron turned from the East and employed the Gothic mode for the delineation of the "Byronic" hero. The type is descended from the Miltonic Satan and the criminal heroes of Mrs. Radcliffe; but the lowering doom is *The Oriental Tales*

[9] Privately printed (1812) and pirated in mangled form, but not included in Byron's works till after his death. The famous opening lines describing sunset on the Acropolis were transferred to *The Corsair,* Canto III.

[10] See the Countess of Airlie, *In Whig Society, 1775-1818* (1921); Lord David Cecil, *The Young Melbourne* (1939), pp. 47-80; Marjorie Villiers, *The Grand Whiggery* (1939), pp. 236-303.

[11] The best account of these is in Wallace C. Brown's as yet unpublished study, *The Gorgeous East in Fee.*

darkened by Byron's sense of predestination, and "the fire which preys on lonely bosoms" is kindled by personal guilt and remorse. The portrait of Lara has been regarded as a masterpiece of self-revelation, but the "self" revealed is to some degree a deliberate fabrication.[12]

Marriage and Separation

Through 1814 Byron was looking about for a wife to mend his fortunes and, perchance, his ways. His choice fell upon Anna Isabella Milbanke, who, having wisely rejected him, yielded when he addressed her a second time; and they were married on January 2, 1815. The unhappy story of the marital year does not need retelling. *Parisina* and *The Siege of Corinth* are the chief poems of this period. Byron was often drunken, saturnine, and taciturn, brutal and unfaithful to his wife. Their only child, Augusta Ada,[13] was born in December; and in January, 1816, Lady Byron left her husband.[14] Negotiations followed, but in the end Byron consented to a separation. He found revenge in two poems which piratical publishers circulated as *Poems on his Domestic Circumstances*. One was a sentimental farewell to his wife, the other a lampoon upon her female companion—both in the worst of taste. A few friends rallied round him; the romantic Jane Clairmont[15] ("Claire") offered herself as his mistress. The storm of social ostracism raged too high and in April he left England forever.

Switzer- land

By way of Waterloo[16] and the Rhine Byron journeyed to Geneva, where he rejoined Jane Clairmont, who was living with Shelley and Mary Godwin. Association with Shelley enlarged the humanitarian sentiment to which Byron had already given expression;[17] and from Shelley came also an understanding of Wordsworth which did not last but which helped to inspire the nature feeling of the third canto of *Childe Harold* and the style of *Churchill's Grave*. Shelley and "Monk" Lewis (who joined the company at Geneva) introduced Byron to Goethe's *Faust*, with profound effect upon his imagination.[18] To the early summer belong *The Dream*, a cruel in-

[12] Compare Charles du Bos, *Byron et le besoin de la fatalité* (Paris, 1929), pp. 70-78, with T. S. Eliot's comment thereon in *From Anne to Victoria*, p. 614.

[13] Afterwards Countess of Lovelace, mother of the author of *Astarte* and mother-in-law of the poet-traveler Wilfrid Scawen Blunt.

[14] It seems clear that Lady Byron knew of the relationship which had existed between Byron and Mrs. Leigh; but having received the latter's assurances that it had been broken off before Byron's marriage, she extended her forgiveness and protection to her sister-in-law. The incest was, therefore, not the cause of the separation. So long as Lady Byron suspected (with good reason, as modern alienists hold) that her husband was insane, she was determined to remain with him; but when a physician assured her that Byron was mentally responsible for the outrages committed against her, she decided, on her father's advice, to demand a separation. Byron made a great show of "going into court" rather than submit; but when his bluff was called he capitulated.

[15] A. C. Gordon, *Allegra: the Story of Byron and Miss Clairmont* (1926).

[16] The narrative of Waterloo in *Childe Harold*, III, is followed by the most elaborate of Byron's estimates of Napoleon's character. See Gerhard Eggert, "Lord Byron und Napoleon," *Palæstra*, CLXXXVI (Leipzig, 1933).

[17] In February, 1812, Byron had spoken in the House of Lords in defense of the Nottingham frame-breakers, and in April, 1812, on behalf of the repeal of Catholic disabilities. In June, 1813, he presented a petition from an advocate of parliamentary reform who had been mishandled by the military. For a letter refusing to present a petition for the amelioration of the conditions in which debtors were detained see *The Nation* (N. Y.), CVI (1918). 473-474.

[18] See J. G. Robertson, *Goethe and Byron* (1925; *Publications of the English Goethe Society*, n.s., II); F. W. Stokoe, *German Influence in the English Romantic Period* (1926), ch. VII.

discretion against his wife and Mary Chaworth, and the *Epistle to Augusta,* in which, employing *ottava rima* for the first time, he displayed his "bleeding heart." The intense and fiery *Prometheus,* one of Byron's grandest utterances, is of a Shelleyan nobility of thought. The two poets made a voyage round Lake Leman which is recorded in *Childe Harold,* III, and in Shelley's letters and bore fruit also in *The Prisoner of Chillon.* After parting from Shelley Byron visited the Bernese Oberland. The Jungfrau and the Valley of Lauterbrunnen provided the setting for *Manfred,* a wildly Gothic drama in which Promethean and Faustian elements are combined with extravagances taken from Beckford's *Vathek,* Chateaubriand's *René,* the legend of the Wandering Jew, and remorseful memories of Augusta Leigh. In October Byron crossed the Simplon into Italy and after a stay in Milan arrived in *Italy* Venice in November.

In the licentiousness of the next few months, recorded in the most brilliant and boisterous of his letters, there was a defiance of the English "code" which betokened something like desperation. After the Carnival of 1817, when he wrote the exquisite lyric, *So we'll go no more a-roving,* Byron settled into a more regular way of life; and all the while he had not wasted himself entirely upon the society of gondoliers and their wenches but had studied Italian, read the poets, visited the galleries, and frequented the salons. Among his few English visitors was Hobhouse, with whom he went southward in April. Ferrara suggested to him *The Lament of Tasso.* By way of Florence and Umbria he came to Rome, where he completed *Manfred* and in Hobhouse's expert company surveyed the antiquities.[19] The summer was passed near Padua with Byron engaged upon the fourth canto of *Childe Harold,* that splendid panorama of human destiny inspired by Italian history. Renewed association with Shelley at this time is recorded for us in Shelley's *Julian and Maddalo.* Before the end of the year Byron had finished *Childe Harold,* and in the poetry of Luigi Pulci had found a new and very different inspiration.

II

Byron seems never to have read William Tennant's *Anster Fair*[20] (1812), *The Mock-*
the poem which introduced the Italian mock-heroic style into modern *heroic*
English literature. In 1816 he had read—or looked into—Giovanni Battista
Casti's *Gli Animali Parlanti* (1794-1802), a late survival of the style;[21]
but he did not know *The Court and Parliament of Beasts* (1816), the version
of Casti by William Stewart Rose.[22] He may have known one or two poems

[19] See Hobhouse's *Historical Illustrations of the Fourth Canto of Childe Harold* (1818).

[20] For a specimen of *Anster Fair* see Ward's *English Poets* (1892), IV, 304-308.

[21] Casti's poem is a satiric improvisation in which the conflict between the *ancien régime* and the new republicanism is transferred to the antediluvian animal world. The subject appealed to Byron's political sympathies.

[22] W. S. Rose (1775-1843) was living in Venice during Byron's sojourn there. See his letter in *ottava rima* to Byron, *Letters and Journals,* ed. Prothero, IV. 212-214. Rose translated Ariosto's *Orlando Furioso* (1823 and 1831). — Byron may have read the samples of the *Morgante Maggiore* translated by J. H. Merivale (1806-1807) and the same scholar's rendering of the

of this sort in the Venetian dialect; but the real incentive came from John Hookham Frere's mock-heroic poem entitled *Prospectus and Specimen of an intended National Work, by William and Robert Whistlecraft ... intended to comprise the most interesting particulars relating to King Arthur and his Round Table* [23] (1817). "Whistlecraft" opened Byron's eyes to the wide possibilities inherent in this kind of satire, taught him to base it upon a famous legend, and led him straight to Pulci, the "sire of the half-serious rhyme."[24] In the *Morgante Maggiore* [25] Pulci, inheriting an older Italian tradition of burlesquing the legend of Charlemagne, narrated the romantic, amorous, comic, and heroic exploits of the Paladins. Running through his vast poem is a vein of moral, political, social, and philosophical comment, generally bantering in tone but capable on occasion of profound seriousness. The connection of Pulci with Byron is direct, but a long rambling tradition must also be reckoned with which leads through Rabelais and Cervantes, Tassoni's *La Secchia Rapita,* Butler's *Hudibras,* and Boileau's *Le Lutrin,* to Pope's *Rape of the Lock* and other mock-heroic poems of the English Augustan age.

In the autumn of 1817 Byron first experimented in the Pulcesque vein. *Beppo,* a Venetian tale of Carnival-time, is frivolous and facetious and just sufficiently naughty to startle the prudes. By a multitude of digressions this

Don Juan

trifle is expanded to ninety-nine stanzas. It gives a foretaste of *Don Juan.* In September, 1818, Byron wrote to Moore that he had begun a new poem "meant to be a little quietly facetious upon everything" but perhaps "too free for these very modest days." [26] This is his first allusion to his masterpiece.[27] Whence came his knowledge of the legend of Don Juan Tenorio? [28] What is the relationship between the legend and his poem? Why did he choose this subject? Almost certainly he did not know at first-hand Tirso de Molina's *El Burlador de Sevilla* (1630) or later Spanish versions of the story. Molière's tragicomedy he may have read, and he may have attended per-

---

final episode, *Orlando in Roncesvalles* (1814). For Byron's own version of the first canto of Pulci (1820) see *Poetry,* ed. Coleridge, IV. 279-309. — On the broader movement of which these translations and imitations were part see R. W. King, "Italian Influence on English, Scholarship and Literature during the Romantic Revival," *MLR,* xx (1925). 48-63, 295-304; xxi (1926). 24-33.

[23] Expanded as *The Monks and the Giants* (1818); ed. R. D. Waller (Manchester, 1926). On Frere see also above, ch. I, n. 11.

[24] *Don Juan,* IV, vi.

[25] The *Morgante* was published in 1480; the enlarged version (hence *Maggiore*) in 1482. — Byron's debt to Pulci has never been fully explored. The Satan of *The Vision of Judgment* owes something to the courtly demon Astarotte. The flight through space in *Cain* may owe a hint to Astarotte's transportation of Rinaldo from Egypt to Roncesvalles; but from Lucian to Shelley there are many magical flights in poetry and legend. Astarotte, who insists that he is a fallen angel, not a mere tricksy imp, may have given Byron a suggestion for *Heaven and Earth.* And there are other parallels.

[26] *Letters and Journals,* IV. 260.

[27] See E. F. Boyd, *Byron's Don Juan: A Critical Study* (New Brunswick, 1945); P. G. Trueblood, *The Flowering of Byron's Genius: Studies in Byron's Don Juan* (Stanford University, 1945).

[28] George Gendarme de Bévotte, *La Légende de Don Juan. Son évolution dans la littérature des origines au romantisme* (Paris, 1906); Hans Heckel, *Das Don Juan-Problem in der neueren Dichtung* (Stuttgart, 1915).

formances of Goldoni's comedy and of Mozart's opera. He had seen at Covent Garden the pantomime in which Grimaldi, the famous clown, took the part of Scaramouch. There is little in common between the titanic figure of the Spanish tradition and the adventurous young rake of Byron's poem; but the problem of how youthful innocence could develop into a personage so formidable as the legendary Don Juan was perhaps at the back of Byron's mind. It may be that with recollections that he had been attacked as a "Don Juan" and a "Sardanapalus" he undertook to portray analytically these types of licentiousness, Sardanapalus with grave sympathy, Juan with sardonic humor. Between September, 1818, and March, 1823, Byron wrote sixteen cantos. The first five were published anonymously by John Murray (1819 and 1821); the later cantos, declined by Murray, were published by John Hunt (1823 and 1824). The political radicalism, blasphemy, and immorality of the first installment occasioned a great outcry; but Byron stood his ground.[29]

Into *Don Juan* Byron put his abundant knowledge of the world and what wisdom he had garnered from experience. It is a brilliant picture of life in many lands, furnished with a running commentary, satirical, sardonic, or serious, upon men, women, and affairs. It exhibits Byron's admirable gift of friendship; his sensual view of women; his clear-sighted superiority to the conventions of society and the fads of the moment; his political convictions; his memories of romantic wanderings in the Levant; his titanic questionings of the cosmos; his poetic sense of the grandeur of nature and the contrasting pettiness of man. All life is here in its various phases of love and joy, suffering and hate and fear. The poem is a satire on social usage, sham and cant and humbug, pride of place, the ostentation and vanity of glory, the wickedness and needlessness of war, the hypocrisies of conventional morality. A great variety of human beings crowd its pages, friends and enemies[30] of Byron's, acquaintances, and strangers whom he had passed by. It is a poem of many moods. There is more of romance and of "the mannerly obscene" in the early cantos, of public affairs in the middle, and of social satire in the closing episodes, where Byron's attitude towards England is strangely tolerant, as that of a man of the world rather than of a romantic outcast. The changes in mood are reflected in the constant surprises in the rimes;[31] and the *ottava rima* lends itself to many tones. It is admirably adapted to satirical purposes, for a situation can be set forth in the sestet and the required epigrammatic verdict rendered in the couplet. But though the serio-comic is the most characteristic mood, the evil of the world is not sensed the less sharply because the corrective supplied is that of ridicule. Sometimes the Comic Muse withdraws and the poem is flooded with ro-

[29] S. C. Chew, *Byron in England*, ch. IV: "The Reception of Don Juan." Imitators were at once in the field with "forged *Don Juans*," and when at Byron's death the poem was left a fragment there were many attempts to carry it on. See *ibid.*, ch. v: "The Continuations of *Don Juan*." A fragment of the genuine Canto XVII was first published in 1904.

[30] Byron suppressed his ferocious dedication to Southey when it was decided to publish the poem anonymously; and it first appeared after Byron's death.

[31] E. Eckhardt, "Lord Byrons komische Reime," *ESt*, LXX (1935-1936). 198-208.

mantic sunshine or clouded over with philosophic speculation. *Don Juan,* a wonderful memorial to a society that has "gone glimmering through the dreams of things that were," is yet true to the enduring facts of human nature. Almost it deserves the title which some admirers have bestowed upon it—"the epic of modern life." There are signs that our own disillusioned generation has returned to it with a fresh understanding of its significance.

Ravenna

The five years during which Byron had *Don Juan* in hand were filled with other activities. In April, 1819, he met at Venice the Countess Teresa Guiccioli, who fell passionately in love with him. As her *cavaliere servente* he lived near her in Ravenna from December, 1819, till October, 1821. Through her brother, Count Pietro Gamba, Byron came into touch with the conspiratorial organization called the Carbonari which was working for the liberation of Italy. Political liberalism, already voiced in *Childe Harold,* found expression in *The Prophecy of Dante* (1819), in the later cantos of *Don Juan,* and in the two Venetian plays, *Marino Faliero* (1820)

The Tragedies

and *The Two Foscari* (1821). The story of the Doge Faliero who joined the rebels against the state of which he was titular head and whose private animus against his own social order became merged in, and subordinate to, the larger issue of freedom against tyranny, inspired Byron to some of his noblest utterances. Unfortunately, in protest against the contemporary degenerate stage (with which he later sought to come to terms in his tragedy, *Werner* [32]) and in line with his advocacy of "regularity" and classical restraint,[33] Byron took as his model the tragedies of Alfieri and composed his drama in accordance with the pseudo-classical "rules," with the consequence that the action begins at so late a point in the story that the cumulative effect of the Doge's resentment is lost.[34] The dramatization of the story of the Doge Foscari who was in duty compelled to pass sentence upon his own son is less impressive. *Sardanapalus* (1821), the most strictly regular of Byron's tragedies, is also the most poetic and personal. In the character of the last Assyrian monarch Byron discerned his own features—his sensuality and love of ease, his detestation of tyranny and wars of conquest, his skepticism and championship of free inquiry, his intellectual probity, his ability to shake off lassitude and act in a righteous cause.

Cain

To the Ravenna period belong the two biblical "mysteries," *Cain* and *Heaven and Earth* (both 1821). They are challenges to submissive orthodoxy and assertions of man's right to exercise the reason implanted in him. *Cain*

[32] Byron began *Werner* in 1815 and returned to it in 1821-1822. So lacking in the typical Byronic qualities that it has even been suspected that he did not write it, it had, nevertheless, more success upon the stage than any other of his plays. See T. H. V. Motter, "Byron's *Werner* Re-estimated," *Essays in Dramatic Literature,* ed. Hardin Craig (Princeton, 1935), pp. 243-275. See also D. V. Erdman, "Byron's Stage Fright: the History of his Ambition and Fear of Writing for the Stage," *ELH,* VI (1939). 218-243.

[33] In 1821 Byron defended Pope against the strictures in W. L. Bowles's *Invariable Principles of Poetry* (1819). See J. J. Van Rennes, *Bowles, Byron, and the Pope Controversy* (1927); *Letters and Journals,* ed. Prothero, v. 522-592.

[34] Swinburne's tragedy *Marino Faliero* (1885) was partly inspired by his sensitiveness to the defects of style and structure in Byron's. For a comparison of the two plays see S. C. Chew, *Swinburne* (1929), pp. 215-219.

owes little to the narrative in Genesis and nothing to the medieval plays on the theme. Lucifer (as Byron was careful to note) resembles the Satan of *Paradise Lost;* he stands in somewhat the same relation to Cain as does Goethe's Mephistopheles to Faust. From Pierre Bayle's *Dictionary* Byron derived various ideas, especially the Manichaean doctrine of the Two Principles, which he seems not to have fully understood. The Promethean motif, already noted in *Manfred,* reappears, for Cain is not a mere egoistic rebel but "a symbol and a sign to Mortals of their fate and force." [35] His intellect "recoils from its encumbering clay"; [36] and· Lucifer brings him into the state of mind which leads to the catastrophe by showing him "infinite things and his own abasement," so that "the rage and fur• against the inadequacy of his state to his conceptions" discharges itself "rather against Life, and the author of Life, than the mere living." [37] In thus interpreting his theme, the poet illuminated the very core of Byronism. Like his own Lucifer, he was one of those

> Souls who dare look the Omnipotent tyrant in
> His everlasting face, and tell him that
> His evil is not good.[38]

Reason's challenge to Omnipotence he resumed in *Heaven and Earth.*[39] This "mystery" on the subject of the loves of the sons of God for the daughters of men breaks off abruptly at the coming of the flood, probably because Byron was put to it to devise a sequel.[40]

Byron's political liberalism and his challenge to orthodoxy were behind the quarrel with Robert Southey which culminated in *The Vision of Judgment* (1821), the tremendous parody of the laureate's elegy on George III.[41] Into this little masterpiece Byron put all his "tempest-anger, tempest-mirth," his contempt for the man whom he considered a Tory renegade, his scorn of sycophancy and compromise, his hatred of reactionary despotism. With the exception of the concluding cantos of *Don Juan* this was his last great work.[42]

When the police forced the Gamba family to leave the States of the *Pisa* Church, Byron moved to Pisa. His old connection with John Murray was

---

[35] Byron, *Prometheus,* lines 45-46.
[36] Byron, *The Prophecy of Dante,* IV. 21-22.
[37] *Letters and Journals,* v. 470. Compare *Cain,* I. i. 174-178.
[38] *Cain,* I. i. 138-140. For the outcry occasioned by *Cain* and Byron's disingenuous attempt to set up an analogy with *Paradise Lost* see S. C. Chew, *Byron in England,* ch. VI: "The Reception of *Cain.*"
[39] This was rejected by Murray and published in the second number of *The Liberal* (January, 1823). On the resemblances to James Montgomery's *The World before the Flood* (1812), George Croly's *The Angel of the World* (1820), Thomas Dale's *Irad and Adah, a Tale of the Flood* (1821), and Thomas Moore's *The Loves of the Angels* (1822) see S. C. Chew, *The Dramas of Lord Byron* (Göttingen, 1915), pp. 137-140.
[40] Another fragment, written at Pisa in 1822, is *The Deformed Transformed,* a variation on the Faust theme.
[41] On the origins and development of the quarrel with Southey see *Letters and Journals,* VI. 377-399.
[42] *The Island* (1823), on the story of the mutiny of the *Bounty,* is a reversion to romantic primitivism.

severed on account of the publisher's reluctance to be associated with poems denounced for their impiety, obscenity, and seditiousness. At Shelley's invitation Leigh Hunt arrived at Pisa and the publication of a new quarterly, *The Liberal,* was initiated. Another member of the Pisan circle was Edward John Trelawny.[43] Shelley's death in July, 1822, led to the break-up of the group, and Byron rejoined the Countess Guiccioli at Genoa. He was bored, depressed, resentful of his entanglement with Hunt, aware of a falling off in his reputation in England, perhaps conscious of a decline in poetic power. In this mood he undertook the expedition to Greece. A revolt against the Ottoman overlordship had broken out in 1821 and from the Morea had spread into Attica and Albania. A wave of Philhellenism swept through Western Europe, and a group of Greek nationalists who arrived in London early in 1823 to plead for intervention succeeded in establishing a "Greek Committee" of which Trelawny was a member. Through him and other friends Byron became associated with this organization, and after months of negotiations he sailed from Genoa with Trelawny, Pietro Gamba, and

The Last Journey

other followers, in July, 1823. He went with little hope of success, believing himself to be on "a fool's errand," but liking the cause and determined to "stick to it." A long delay followed while Byron, in Cephalonia, reached a decision as to the Greek leader to whom he would throw the weight of his prestige and resources, for though there had been military victories there was political confusion among the rival native leaders. He wisely chose Prince Mavrocordatos, the ablest of them, and arrived at his headquarters at Missolonghi early in January, 1824. What followed is known to all the world: the disputes composed genially by Byron; the squalor, and unceasing rain, and hardships bravely borne; the poem written on his thirty-sixth birthday in which he looked forward to a soldier's death; the fever which struck him down; and the end, on April 19, 1824. When the news reached England a month later, animosities were almost universally forgotten and to most men it seemed as though the sun had vanished from the heaven of poetry.[44] His body was brought home and buried in the family church at Hucknall Torkard, near Newstead.

It is difficult to pass judgment upon a poet so *divers et ondoyant* as Lord Byron. His imperfections as an artist are exaggerations of faults common to all the romanticists, and it is unnecessary to amplify his own self-condemnation: "No one has done more through negligence to corrupt the language." His impact upon the reader comes from the mass and weight of

Romance and Satire

his entire work. Today his reputation as a satirist is far higher than as a writer of romantic poems; but his letters and all his poetry, save the negligible juvenilia, must be read if you would know him; and he must be known as a romanticist, representative of his own age, as well as a satirist, belated representative of the Augustans. In one mood he would have sym-

[43] On Trelawny see below, ch. xvi.
[44] See S. C. Chew, *Byron in England,* ch. xi: "The Death of Byron." For the decline in Byron's reputation, the revival of interest in the eighteen-sixties (due largely to the growth of liberal feeling), and later phases of his "after-fame" see *ibid.,* subsequent chapters.

pathized with George Meredith's ridicule of the ultra-romanticism of *Manfred*; but his readiness to turn quizzically upon his own extravagances must not be taken as a token that his tempestuous and introspective moods were insincere. He calculated the value of theatrical posturing to hold attention, but the pose was natural to him. The sense of sin in the Byronic hero comes from his own accusing conscience, and the sense of doom was part of his Calvinistic heritage. He played to perfection the rôle of *l'homme fatal* (with which some of his precursors had experimented) because it was in character. Yet to his despondency and melancholy he could apply the corrective of his cynicism and wit and reasonableness. His opinions on religion are difficult to apprehend because of his instability and two-sidedness.[45] From the Calvinism of his childhood he worked gradually through negation to a vague deism with attendant doubts about immortality illogically at variance with a strong, abiding predestinarianism. Apart from a brief period of derivative transcendentalism in 1816, he found in the natural world not God but an escape from mankind. His poetic imagery [46] is drawn *Imagery* generally from the great natural forces and phenomena, winds and sun and clouds, mountains and the sea. But though he affects to withdraw from his fellows, Byron is to a far greater degree than the other romanticists the poet of humankind. He conveys with tremendous power the majesty and desolation of history, the vanity of pomp and pride, the transitoriness of fame. And he is the poet of contemporary society, keen to discern the false and the corrupt, courageous in denunciation, yet with pity for the young and innocent and with signs of a broader tolerance towards the end.[47] Among the signs of his greatness are his refusal to placate or compromise, his honesty in facing fact, the resolution with which he kept his eyes open to evil in himself as in other men, and the steady decline in affectation and increase in sincerity of purpose as his poetry matured. As a man he will continue to present to posterity a problem which does not admit of a universally acceptable solution. As a poet he mirrored brilliantly and without distortion an absorbingly interesting world.

[45] Manfred Eimer, *Byron und der Kosmos* (Heidelberg, 1912; *Anglistische Forschungen,* XXXIV); E. M. Marjarum, *Byron as Skeptic and Believer* (Princeton, 1938).

[46] See G. Wilson Knight, *The Burning Oracle* (1939), ch. VI: "The Two Eternities: an Essay on Byron," where extravagant claims are made for the metaphysical significance of Byron's imagery.

[47] See G. R. Elliott, "Byron and the Comic Spirit," *PMLA*, XXXIX (1924). 897-909.

XII

Percy Bysshe Shelley

I

Consistency of purpose runs through Shelley's career.[1] In boyish letters the ideas of his maturity pulsate with embryonic life. The continuity is obscured by the contrast between the fanaticism of his undisciplined youth and the growing tolerance and moderated hopes of his last years. But the change was in strategy, not in aim. Realizing that premature direct action by reformers would defeat their ends, he came to rely upon poetry as one of the "instruments with which high spirits call the future from its cradle." [2] By gradual modulation rather than abrupt change the radical pamphleteer developed into the greatest of radical poets. The time when one phase

[1] *Complete Works,* Julian Edition, ed. Roger Ingpen and W. E. Peck (10v, 1926-1930); *Poems,* ed. C. D. Locock (2v, 1911); *Selected Poems, Essays, and Letters,* ed. Ellsworth Barnard (1944); *Narrative Poems,* ed. C. H. Herford (1927); *Letters,* ed. Roger Ingpen (2v, 1909); *Shelley's Lost Letters to Harriet,* ed. Leslie Hotson (1930); *Note-Books,* ed. H. B. Forman (3v, privately printed, St. Louis, 1911); *Verse and Prose from the Manuscripts,* ed. Sir J. C. E. Shelley-Rolls and Roger Ingpen (1934); *Letters of Mary W. Shelley,* ed. F. L. Jones (2v, Norman, Okla., 1944). — Bibliography in T. J. Wise, *A Shelley Library* (privately printed, 1924). Newman I. White, *Shelley* (2v, 1940), the definitive biography, and *Portrait of Shelley* (1945); Edmund Blunden, *Shelley: A Life Story* (1946); Edward Dowden, *The Life of Percy Bysshe Shelley* (2v, 1886); W. E. Peck, *Shelley: His Life and Work* (2v, 1927); Olwen W. Campbell, *Shelley and the Unromantics* (1924); Roger Ingpen, *Shelley in England* (2v, 1917); Helen Rossetti Angeli, *Shelley and His Friends in Italy* (1911); T. J. Hogg, *After Shelley: Letters to Jane Williams,* ed. Sylva Norman (1934); Thomas Medwin, *Life of Shelley,* ed. H. B. Forman (1913); *The Life of Percy Bysshe Shelley as Comprised in the Life of Shelley by T. J. Hogg, the Recollections of Shelley and Byron by E. J. Trelawny, and Memoirs of Shelley by T. L. Peacock,* introduction by Humbert Wolfe (2v, 1933); Jane, Lady Shelley, *Shelley and Mary* (4v, privately printed, 1882); R. M. Smith and others, *The Shelley Legend* (1945), on which see strictures by N. I. White, *SP,* XLIII (1946). 522-544; F. L. Jones, *PMLA,* LXI (1946). 848-890; K. N. Cameron, *JEGP,* XLV (1946). 369-379. — Critical studies: Francis Thompson, *Shelley* (1909), a famous rhapsody; Edward Dowden, Richard Garnett, and W. M. Rossetti, *Letters about Shelley* (1917), informal consultations among three Shelleyans; A. T. Strong, *Three Studies in Shelley* (1921); Floyd Stovall, *Desire and Restraint in Shelley* (Durham, N. C., 1931); Bennett Weaver, *Toward the Understanding of Shelley* (Minneapolis, 1932); B. P. Kurtz, *The Pursuit of Death* (1933); C. H. Grabo, *The Magic Plant: the Growth of Shelley's Thought* (Chapel Hill, 1936); Ellsworth Barnard, *Shelley's Religion* (Minneapolis, 1936); O. W. Firkins, *Power and Elusiveness in Shelley* (Minneapolis, 1937); A. P. Cappon, *The Scope of Shelley's Philosophic Thinking* (Chicago, 1938); Lillian Winstanley, "Platonism in Shelley," *E&S,* IV (1913). 72-100; Gingerich, *Essays in the Romantic Poets* (1924), pp. 195-239; M. A. Bald, "Shelley's Mental Progress," *E&S,* XIII (1928). 112-137; Herbert Read, *In Defence of Shelley and Other Essays* (1936), pp. 1-86; George Cowling, *Shelley and Other Essays* (Melbourne, 1936), pp. 13-108; Bush, ch. IV; Edmund Blunden, *Shelley and Keats as They Struck Their Contemporaries* (1925); N I. White, *The Unextinguished Hearth: Shelley and His Contemporary Critics* (Durham, N. C., 1938); F. C. Mason, *A Study in Shelley Criticism, 1818-1860* (Mercersburg, Pa., 1937); Henri Peyre, *Shelley et la France* (Cairo, Egypt, 1935); M. L. G. de Courten, *Shelley e l'Italia* (Milan, 1923); Solomon Liptzin, *Shelley in Germany* (1924) — F. S. Ellis, *Concordance* (1892).

[2] Shelley, *Epipsychidion,* lines 520-521.

yielded to the other cannot be determined precisely; the years 1812-1818 saw the transition.

In outline and in many romantic, distressing, or grotesque particulars the life of Percy Bysshe Shelley (1792-1822) is a familiar story. But it is hard to keep the details in mind; they involve the dreary complexities of pecuniary entanglements and the record of constant changes of abode. The fact that at times Shelley was perilously close to madness chastens amusement when we contemplate his impulsive eccentricities of conduct, his swift revulsions from affinities, his humorless resolution in translating theory into practice, the compromises into which he was forced, the contrast between his visions and reality, the contrast between his genius and the milieu whence he sprang.

His family possessed Whig convictions and recently acquired wealth. From *Boyhood* his father, Timothy Shelley, he appears to have inherited no trait of character save the stubbornness with which he held to his opinions. The life of the imagination led with the little sisters whom he charmed with weird and marvelous tales was enriched by the reading of Gothic romances, whence he derived a hatred of tyrants and a desire to emulate the rescuers of damsels in distress. His first love affair, with a cousin, Harriet Grove,[3] was conducted with an ardor as much philosophical as sentimental, for he intended that she should be the first convert to his doctrines. Her betrothal to a man whom Shelley considered "a clod of earth" was the first great disappointment in his life. At Eton this sensitive boy suffered from bullies and from the system of fagging, and his sympathy with the oppressed was deepened. He pursued his hobby of scientific experimentation, with startling immediate results and with a strong ultimate effect upon his imagination. He wrote and even had published a romance, *Zastrozzi* (1810), which was followed by another, *St. Irvyne* (1811).[4] The portrayal in them of despotic iniquity and oppressed virtue is characteristic, but they are the veriest Gothic rubbish, of no promise whatsoever. Equally worthless is *Original Poetry by Victor and Cazire*[5] (1810), written in part by Shelley's sister, Elizabeth. In *The Wandering Jew*[6] appears the figure of Ahasuerus, who was to loom large in *Queen Mab* and *Hellas*.

Shelley entered Oxford in 1810 and soon became intimate with Thomas *Oxford* Jefferson Hogg (1792-1862). The youths absorbed together the ideas of the Neo-Platonists, the French philosophers of the preceding age, the English political radicals, and contemporary writers on natural science. Shelley's childish, unthinking acceptance of orthodox religion had changed to a militant rationalism, and with rhetorical rancor he was dedicating himself to a Voltairian warfare against Christianity. In *Posthumous Fragments of*

---

[3] See *The Journal of Harriet Grove for the Years 1809-1810*, ed. Roger Ingpen (privately printed, 1932). N. I. White incorporates in his biography the portions significant for the study of Shelley.

[4] A. M. D. Hughes, "Shelley's *Zastrozzi* and *St. Irvyne*," MLR, VII (1912). 54-63.

[5] Ed. Richard Garnett (1898).

[6] Shelley's cousin, Thomas Medwin, collaborated with him on this poem. See Manfred Eimer, "Zu Shelley's Dichtung *The Wandering Jew*," *Anglia*, XXXVIII (1914). 433-476.

Margaret Nicholson [7] (1811) poems attacking despotism are mingled with others exploiting Gothic horrors or expressing personal melancholy. In · February, 1811, appeared *The Necessity of Atheism*. This is a less blatant performance than those who know it only by its challenging title infer. It is really a brief, precise bit of dialectic culminating in the signature: "Thro' deficiency of proof, an Atheist." Shelley's expulsion from the university followed promptly, not on the ground of his authorship of the pamphlet but for contumacy in refusing to answer questions. Hogg was equally obdurate and shared his friend's fate.

Timothy Shelley mismanaged the situation in a tragicomic fashion; and his son, leading a lonely life in London, was soon in a serious plight. An interest in Elizabeth Hitchener, a Sussex schoolteacher was now developing into the attachment of two kindred souls. More ominous for the future was Shelley's concern for his sisters' beautiful young friend, Harriet Westbrook, who was unhappy at school. For Shelley schools were synonymous with oppression. When Harriet threw herself upon his protection, like a knight of romance he was impelled to rescue her. An elopement followed, and their marriage in Edinburgh in August, 1811. Shelley subscribed to Godwin's anti-matrimonial theories, but (like his future father-in-law) disregarded them in practice, holding that till society was educated free love worked too great a hardship upon a woman. Leaving his wife at York under the protection of Hogg, he set out to negotiate a financial settlement with his father (which came to nothing); and in his absence Hogg treacherously attempted to seduce Harriet. When he learned of this, Shelley reasoned with Hogg and forgave him, but perfect congeniality was not for a long while, if ever, restored.

Harriet West-brook

The next sojourn was at Keswick. Here Shelley saw a good deal of Southey, whose poetry he admired. But repeated contacts convinced him that the elder poet was a turn-coat and time-server.[8] A letter to William Godwin established a relationship long before Shelley met him face to face.[9] Ill health at Keswick (as often afterwards) was concurrent with mental anxiety; and at this time occurred the first grave case of the hallucinations which Shelley experienced thereafter from time to time. With Harriet's elder sister, Eliza, the Shelleys set out for Ireland in February, 1812. The Irish cause was to be the starting-point of a movement to emancipate the human spirit. In Dublin Shelley issued an *Address to the Irish People* and *Proposals for an Association*. The spectacle of three young dreamers distributing tracts on street-corners has obscured the fact that the proposals were moderate in tone and scope. Shelley was aware of the perils of secret societies and mob violence, and while expressing confidence

Ireland

---

[7] The point of the hoaxing title is that twenty-five years earlier Margaret Nicholson had attempted to assassinate George III.

[8] See K. N. Cameron, "Shelley vs. Southey: New Light on an Old Quarrel," *PMLA*, LVII (1942). 489-512.

[9] See Paul Elsner, *Shelleys Abhängigkeit von William Godwins "Political Justice"* (Berlin, 1906).

that the Catholics would soon be emancipated and the Union repealed, cautioned the Irish against over-optimism; misery and crime would not disappear with the accomplishment of their immediate program. His written words were supplemented by an address to a meeting in Dublin. But the sight of the abject poverty depressed him and initial confidence gave way to discouragement. "I make myself," he wrote to Godwin, "the cause of an effect which will take place ages after I have mouldered in the dust." [10]

They were in England again in April. Shelley occupied himself with radical propaganda in Devonshire and Wales. He read Sir James Henry Lawrence's utopian romance, *The Empire of the Nairs,* whose ideas entered into *Queen Mab* and later poems.[11] The prosecution of Daniel Eaton prompted a *Letter to Lord Ellenborough* (distributed privately) in which Shelley attacked Christianity and defended the right of free speech. In Wales he threw himself, Faust-like, into a project for the reclamation of waste land. Miss Hitchener was now a member of his household; but the belief that she was the "sister of his soul" did not long survive close association, and they parted with bitter feeling on both sides. A short stay in London, where he at last met Godwin, was followed by another sojourn in Wales, a second visit to Ireland, and a return to London.

Queen Mab appeared in the summer of 1813.[12] Parts of it are in the irregular rimeless verse of Southey's *Thalaba;* the rest, in blank verse, is clear and forceful radical oratory without shade or subtlety. The vision unfolded to Ianthe by the Spirit was suggested by Volney's *Les Ruines des Empires;* the harshly anti-Christian rationalism comes from Volney, Voltaire, Holbach, Paine, and Godwin. Ahasuerus, the type of sufferer from vengeful power, denounces God, the cruel tyrant who is the depraved creation of the human mind. Kings and priests are the instruments of tyranny. Other subversive doctrines are introduced. In revised form, as *The Dæmon of the World,* the least "dangerous" parts of *Queen Mab* reappeared in the *Alastor* volume (1816); but the complete poem, though subjected to repeated prosecutions, made its way in pirated editions and became a *vade mecum* among the radicals.[13]

After the birth of their daughter Ianthe, the alienation from Harriet which had begun long before kept pace with his growing attachment to Godwin's daughter Mary. Affairs moved to a crisis in June, 1814, when he eloped with Mary and in company with Jane Clairmont set off upon a fantastic

Queen Mab

Mary Godwin

[10] March 18, 1812; *Works,* Julian Edition, VIII. 302.
[11] Walter Graham, "Shelley and the *Empire of the Nairs,"* PMLA, XL (1925). 881-891. On the sources of certain details in *Queen Mab* see Carlos Baker, "Spenser, the Eighteenth Century, and Shelley's *Queen Mab,"* MLQ, II (1941). 81-98. See also in general D. J. MacDonald, *The Radicalism of Shelley and its Sources* (Washington, D. C., 1912).
[12] To the same period belong two pamphlets: *A Vindication of Natural Diet,* advocating vegetarianism (a subject which intrudes incongruously into *Queen Mab*), and *A Refutation of Deism,* in which Shelley employs a method of controversy vaguely anticipating the ironical attack upon revealed religion in Samuel Butler's *The Fair Haven.*
[13] N. I. White, "Shelley and the Active Radicals of the Early Nineteenth Century," *So. Atl. Quar.,* XXIX (1930). 248-261.

journey to Switzerland. The restless trio soon returned to England. In London late in 1814 Shelley sank to the nadir of his fortunes, hounded by bailiffs, cast off by Godwin, and in constant controversy with the forsaken Harriet. All that must be said here of the tragedy of Shelley and his first wife is that though his actions were in accord with his avowed principles and were supported by an unshakable consciousness of rectitude, a "conviction of sin" such as a Christian would have confessed would not have made him a less noble man. Intercourse with Hogg and the friendship of Thomas Love Peacock were props to his mind in these dark days. Financial burdens were lightened on the death of his grandfather; but his impractical generosity in dealings with Godwin and in alleviating the poverty of others kept him till the end of his life under the shadow of debt.

Alastor

Shelley's depression and sense of isolation found expression in *Alastor, or the Spirit of Solitude* (1816). For the plain rhetoric of *Queen Mab* there is here substituted a delicate, elusive symbolism, employed to give to mental experiences the guise of persons, events, and the forms of nature. The Poet is the devotee of the Ideal; his journey, the quest thereof; his death, his failure to find it in the actual world.[14] That Shelley had in mind the greatness and decline of Wordsworth is likely;[15] but on its deeper levels *Alastor* is indubitably autobiographical.

Switzer-land

The summer of 1816 was passed in Switzerland. The climate benefited Shelley's health, and association with Byron was a stimulus to both poets.[16] At this time the *Hymn to Intellectual Beauty*—to that unseen Power which consecrates all human thoughts and forms—marked a further stage in Shelley's progress from Godwinian necessitarianism towards Platonic idealism. Later in the summer Shelley visited Chamounix, where in an inn-album he subscribed himself ᾽άθεος. This audacity, reported in England with scandalous gossip about the Geneva household,[17] blackened a reputation already dark. When "Monk" Lewis joined the group, Shelley's interest was excited in Goethe and he translated some scenes from *Faust*.[18]

The Death of Harriet

The return to London in September was followed by a series of disasters. The suicide of Mary's half-sister, Fanny Imlay, though for it Shelley was not responsible, was none the less a shock. Harriet's suicide in November and the consequent embittering of the quarrel with the Westbrook family led to the long-drawn-out suit in Chancery which deprived the poet of the

---

[14] B. P. Kurtz, *The Pursuit of Death*, p. 89. See also H. L. Hoffman, *An Odyssey of the Soul, Shelley's Alastor* (1933); R. D. Havens, "Shelley's *Alastor*," PMLA, XLV (1930). 1098-1115.

[15] Paul Mueschke and E. L. Griggs, "Wordsworth as the Prototype of the Poet in Shelley's *Alastor*," PMLA, XLIX (1934). 229-245.

[16] Manfred Eimer, *Die persönlichen Beziehungen zwischen Byron und den Shelleys* (Heidelberg, 1910); I. C. Clarke, *Shelley and Byron, a Tragic Friendship* (1934). — Byron's physician, J. W. Polidori, was a member of the group. See his *Diary, 1816*, ed. W. M. Rossetti (1911).

[17] That there was a love-affair between Shelley and Jane Clairmont is argued by J. H. Smith, "Shelley and Claire Clairmont," PMLA, LIV (1939). 758-814. This theory is controverted by F. L. Jones, "Mary Shelley and Claire Clairmont," So. Atl. Quar., XLII (1943). 406-412. See also R. Glynn Grylls, *Claire Clairmont* (1939).

[18] On Shelley's German studies and translations from Goethe see F. W. Stokoe, *German Influence in the English Romantic Period* (1926), ch. VI and appendix IV.

custody of his two children by Harriet, Ianthe and the infant Charles. Marriage to Mary, who had borne him a son, William, and was again with child, followed quickly upon Harriet's death. Shelley's burdens increased when in February, 1817, Jane Clairmont gave birth to Byron's daughter, Allegra. Till the death of this child in 1822 he had constantly to act as mediator between the mother and Lord Byron.

Much of 1817 was spent at Marlow, near Windsor. Here the friendship and encouragement of Horace Smith [19] and Leigh Hunt [20] were of utmost value, and Shelley gradually recovered his spirits and creative energy. *Laon and Cythna,* which in slightly revised form became *The Revolt of Islam,* was now written.[21] The copious monotony and confused detail of the action of *The Revolt of Islam* repel all but the most sympathetic readers; but there are passages of lofty beauty and others of macabre horror. The story reflects the hopes and disappointments of the French Revolution; but it is intended to show—and here Shelley's optimism is in impressive contrast to Wordsworth's despondent revulsion from early confidence—that the Revolution had failed not in consequence of the ideas whence it arose but because of the violence and vengeance with which it was prosecuted. The contrast between the tolerance of this poem and the fanaticism of *Queen Mab* is a measure of the distance Shelley's thought had moved during four years. In the end the lovers die; but they are sustained by the hope that their love will endure and by a "mystical faith that annihilates the differences between fact and dream." [22]

Two shorter poems of the same period are *Prince Athanase,* which draws from Plato's *Convivium* the comparison between the Uranian and Pandemian Love, and *Rosalind and Helen,* which contrasts true love, unlegalized, with marriage unsanctified because without true love.[23]

In quest of a salubrious climate the Shelleys, with their son, William, an infant daughter, Clara, Jane Clairmont (who now called herself Claire), and Allegra, left England in March, 1818. Shelley was about to reach his full stature as a poet.

II

At Pisa the Shelleys began a friendship with John and Maria Gisborne; and then, pursuing negotiations relative to Allegra, Shelley met Byron at

---

19 Horace Smith (1779-1849) was co-author with his brother James Smith (1775-1839) of *Rejected Addresses* (1812), a series of clever, good-natured parodies of contemporary poets pretending to be submitted in competition for the prize offered for an address to be recited at the opening of the new Drury Lane theatre. The brothers also wrote together *Horace in London* (1813). In later life Horace Smith was the author of many historical novels. His *Gaieties and Gravities* (3v, 1826) contains the still remembered *Address to the Mummy in Belzoni's Exhibition.*

20 R. B. Johnson, *Shelley-Leigh Hunt. How Friendship Made History* (1928).

21 See F. L. Jones, "The Revision of *Laon and Cythna,*" *JEGP,* XXXII (1933). 366-372.

22 B. P. Kurtz, *The Pursuit of Death,* p. 121. The close of *The Revolt of Islam* contains important evidence for the development of Shelley's ideas on immortality, on which see Kurtz, pp. 122-135. On the indebtedness to Volney's *Les Ruines* see K. N. Cameron, "A Major Source of *The Revolt of Islam,*" *PMLA,* LVI (1941). 175-206.

23 R. D. Havens, "Rosalind and Helen," *JEGP,* XXX (1931). 218-222.

Venice

Venice. There Mary joined him, bringing with her the ailing baby Clara, whose death followed in a short time. Mary seems to have held Shelley responsible for this distressing loss, because he had urged her to come to Venice. A spiritual alienation and physical revulsion from her husband which she evinced may be the explanation of the long, latter portion of Shelley's *Julian and Maddalo*. The opening of this poem, a philosophical conversation-piece between Julian (Shelley) and Maddalo (Byron), is but loosely connected with what follows. It has been generally believed that the Madman's desperate story shadows forth the tragedy of Shelley and Harriet, but there are better reasons for associating it with the change in Shelley's and Mary's relations.[24] A despondency less close to insanity but scarcely less profound is expressed in the *Lines Written among the Euganean Hills*, a poem beautifully constructed around the hours of the day, evoking the loveliness of Italian landscape, and containing a magnificent tribute to Byron.

That Shelley carried his melancholy with him to the South in the winter of 1818-1819 is evident from the *Lines Written in Dejection, near Naples;*[25] but in the spring when he went to Rome there was a renewal of confidence and even a measure of happiness, as may be seen in the letters of this time to T. L. Peacock. In that "divinest climate" he resumed work upon *Pro-metheus Unbound*, which had been begun in the previous autumn, and completed the drama as originally conceived. Act IV, the cosmic choral hymn celebrating the victory of Prometheus, was written later. The prosodic triumphs of this massive yet iridescent drama range from the gentle songs of the comforting spirits, through the rhapsodic *aria*, "Life of Life," to the mighty orchestration of the fourth act. It was once the fashion to interpret Shelley's meaning in terms of formal allegory,[26] but this method is now generally discarded in favor of explications of his erudite symbolism.[27] Of this the reader must be apprised if he would wrest the meaning from *Prometheus*. Even if some of the supposed resemblances to Platonic thought and contemporary scientific theory are discounted as unconscious reminiscences, sufficient remain to indicate that Shelley aimed at a synthesis of his youthful radicalism, his mature Platonism, Christian ethics, and modern science. The fourth act, for example, certainly cannot be understood without recourse to theories of electric phenomena, vitalism, and "animal

*Prome-
theus
Unbound*

---

[24] N. I. White, *Shelley*, II. 38-56. In the light of Professor White's discussion the theory cf R. D. Havens, "Julian and Maddalo," *SP*, XXVII (1930). 648-653, that the Madman is drawn from Tasso must be modified though not necessarily abandoned.

[25] Light has been thrown by N. I. White, *Shelley*, II. 71-83, on the mystery of Shelley's "Neopolitan ward." According to the register of births at Naples a daughter, Elena, was born to Shelley and Mary. That this parentage was impossible at the time is certain. A review of all the possibilities supports the hypothesis that Shelley falsely affirmed the parentage of an adopted child; but Professor White's theory has not been accepted by all Shelley scholars.

[26] One form of allegorical interpretation is represented by W. M. Rossetti's lectures of 1886-1887 (*Shelley Society Papers*, I); another by V. D. Scudder in her edition of *Prometheus Unbound* (1892). For objections to these and other interpretations see N. I. White, "*Prometheus Unbound*, or Every Man His Own Allegorist," *PMLA*, XL (1925). 172-184. See also K. N. Cameron, "The Political Symbolism of *Prometheus Unbound*," *PMLA*, LVIII (1943). 728-753.

[27] C. H. Grabo, *A Newton among Poets* (Chapel Hill, 1930) and *Prometheus Unbound: an Interpretation* (Chapel Hill, 1935).

magnetism." In *Queen Mab* the Spirit of Nature had symbolized Necessity, that is, the uninterrupted sequence of cause and effect in the intellectual and material world. But Shelley saw that by observing cause and consequence we can modify conduct and opinion through persuasion and exhortation. To do this is the poet's function, and in this sense, as he afterwards proclaimed, "poets are the unacknowledged legislators of the world." Instead of attacking institutions Shelley came to realize that evil is in man's own mind. If the will did not enchain us to evil, "we might be otherwise." [28] The titan's "unbinding" comes about through the birth of pity, the disappearance of the desire for vengeance, and repentance for evil done. The conquest of Jupiter takes place within the mind of Prometheus. Thus the overthrow of the despotic God who is the creature of man's own imagination is brought about, and the mind is united with Ideal Love. Shelley's concept of the Utopia which follows upon this union has been derided as both Godwinian and sentimental; but it needs to be observed that in the closing words of the drama there is warning as well as triumph; the Golden Age, though won, may be lost again; in the great cycle of renewal and decline the struggle may have to be resumed.

Shelley employed his symbolism to convey suggestions of ideas almost *Symbols* beyond the reach of language. We may pause to note a few examples. [29] By a strange distortion, images ordinarily associated with evil are often made images of good in Shelley's poetry. Thus, the serpent generally represents the good principle. [30] Meteors, which are maleficent in popular superstition, are sometimes beneficent in his imagination, though at others the word *meteor,* in the sense of marsh-light or will-o'-the-wisp, is used with an evil connotation. Metaphors of poison—the poisoned cup or chalice, or poisoned springs, or the air, or the dew—occur often; and in general an obsession with the sinister [31] is the obverse of Shelley's idealism and reflects his passionate consciousness of evil in the world. His boyish Gothic fancies and later hallucinations contributed to the charnel-house imaginings and strange associations of loveliness with terror and decay which, sometimes in swift metaphor, sometimes in elaborated symbol, darken his poems and reach a climax of horror in the ghastly garden described in *The Sensitive Plant.* A favorite symbol of evil is that of the scorpion which (as in the old emblem-books) stings itself to death; for evil is in its nature self-destroying. A symbol may have more than one meaning, even contradictory meanings. Thus, the oft-recurring image of the veil may mean hypocrisy, which hides injustice and selfishness; but "the painted veil which men call life" separates the ideal from the errors of the phenomenal world. The moon is another favorite image, sometimes employed with a Keatsian connotation, or as an

[28] Shelley, *Julian and Maddalo,* lines 170-172.
[29] A. T. Strong, "Shelley's Symbolism," *Three Studies in Shelley,* pp. 67-106.
[30] For this Shelley had the warrant of the Serpent in the Wilderness, the snake associated with Aesculapius, the serpent as the emblem of wisdom and eternity, and so forth. In *The Revolt of Islam,* I, sts. XXVI-XXXIII, the serpent struggles with the eagle. The eagle as an emblem of evil was suggested by the eagle of despotic Rome.
[31] A. T. Strong, "The Sinister in Shelley," *Three Studies in Shelley,* pp. 107-147.

emblem of mutability, or with suggestions of thaumaturgic power. In *Alastor,* in Asia's song in *Prometheus,* and elsewhere we note the image of the boat, which either bears the soul or *is* the soul, and floats beyond death into the regions of the ideal. Sometimes the boat is associated with caverns, and it may be steered by a fair woman, who is Intellectual Beauty. Even in such apparently airy fantasies as *The Cloud* Shelley's poetic imagery is generally the outer covering of profound meaning.

The Cenci   *The Cenci,*[32] which was written in Leghorn in the autumn of 1819, was intended for the theatre, but though it contains a few scenes of dramatic power and of an intensity almost Websterian, it has never proved to be suited to the stage. The conflict presented between good and evil bears an obvious resemblance to *Prometheus;* Beatrice is, however, not a titanic figure but rather a representative victim of an evil society and religion. Before this tragedy was written another calamity had fallen upon Shelley and Mary—the death of their little son William. Mary was plunged into bitter despair from which she rallied slowly. In Florence Shelley received news of the "Peterloo Massacre" and was moved to compose the *Masque of Anarchy* in forceful, downright terms comprehensible to working-men.[33] An unfinished and for long unpublished prose work, the *Philosophic View of Reform*[34] (1819), confirms our impression that though extreme in the poetic statement of his ideals, Shelley was moderate in his practical program. He wrote of the widening gap between wealth and poverty created by the class of fund-holders (the "tax-eaters" of Cobbett's fulminations) who live on the interest on the public debt. He believed that this debt could be abolished by the confiscation of capital. A truly representative Parliament would provide a solution. Yet he believed that England was not yet prepared for universal suffrage, and he advocated armed insurrection only as a last resort if parliamentary action failed. Late in 1819 he wrote *Peter Bell the Third,* a satiric narrative of Wordsworth's apostasy; and he wrote also the

Ode to the   incomparable *Ode to the West Wind* in which, gathering together a wealth West Wind   of symbolism already adumbrated in earlier poems, he employed not only his powers of metrical orchestration at their mightiest but also a structural art that is by no means invariably characteristic of his poetry. The adaptation of *terza rima* to a stanzaic form is no less wonderful than is the development of the symbols of wave and leaf and cloud.

Pisa   The last years of his life,[35] from the beginning of 1820, were spent in Pisa and its neighborhood. Serenity and kindliness are in the *Letter to Maria Gisborne,* in which Leigh Hunt's familiar style is used without a trace of Hunt's vulgarity; there is piercing pathos in *To a Skylark;* and there is airy loveliness in *The Witch of Atlas,* in which the theme of Intellectual

[32] See E. S. Bates, *A Study of Shelley's Drama The Cenci* (1908); *The Cenci,* ed. G. E. Woodberry (Boston, 1909); *The Stage Version of Shelley's Cenci,* ed. A. C. Hicks and R. M. Clarke (1945).

[33] This was intended for *The Examiner* but remained unpublished till 1832.

[34] Ed. T. W. Rolleston (1920).

[35] Shelley's and Mary's youngest child, Percy Florence Shelley, was born in Florence, November, 1819.

Beauty is treated with a fantastic grace hiding from all but the initiated the recondite sources of its lore.[36] How ample was Shelley's range is shown by contrasting this poem with his *Swell-Foot the Tyrant,* a satiric drama on the divorce proceedings brought against Queen Caroline. Here Shelley combined Aristophanic motifs with others suggested by contemporary caricatures and lampoons.[37] But the satire is too learned to be effective.

In the person of Emilia Viviani,[38] a lovely Italian girl "imprisoned," as *Episychi-* he fancied, in a convent-school, Shelley found for the last time in mortal *dion* form "the likeness of what is perhaps eternal," and to *la figlia della sua mente, l'amorosa idea* he addressed the impassioned rhapsody *Epipsychidion* (1821). In this poem the symbols of the sun and the moon recognizably mean Emilia and Mary respectively; other symbols are used, as Shelley hints, rather to conceal than to reveal. The invitation to Emilia to fly with him to a far-off island is not quite in keeping with the exalted Platonism of the earlier part of the poem and was perhaps an afterthought. *The Defence of Poetry* (called forth by T. L. Peacock's *Four Ages of Poetry*) is an eloquent affirmation of the supreme social and moral value of the poet.[39] On hearing of Keats's death in February, 1821, Shelley was moved to write *Adonais,* second only to *Lycidas* among English elegies. The classical conven- *Adonais* tions of the opening stanzas are not managed quite convincingly; the self-pity in the likening of one of the mourners to a stricken deer shows that Shelley's thoughts were as much upon his own wrongs as Keats's; the curse launched against the reviewers strikes a false note; but towards its close *Adonais* rises into a sublime hymn to the eternal Principle of Beauty. Sympathy with the Greek revolutionists now bore fruit in *Hellas,* a topical drama curiously aloof from contemporary events and redeemed from mediocrity only by the splendid choruses. *The Triumph of Life,*[40] the last, unfinished poem, bears the marks of the study of Dante and especially of Petrarch's *Trionfi.* It is too fragmentary to permit speculation as to Shelley's intentions. The concept of the victims of Life is desolating in its despondency.

Byron, Trelawny, and other friends gathered round him. His last days were happy in association with Edward and Jane Williams to whom he had been introduced by Tom Medwin. To Jane he addressed a few beautiful short poems. Edward Williams shared with Shelley a love of sailing. In the summer of 1822 the Shelleys lived near Lerici on the Gulf of Spezia. Early in July he and Williams sailed to Leghorn to greet the arrival of Leigh Hunt from England. On the return voyage Shelley and Williams

[36] C. H. Grabo, *The Meaning of "The Witch of Atlas"* (Chapel Hill, 1935); E. E. Kellett, *Suggestions* (1923), pp. 109-136.
[37] N. I. White, "Shelley's *Swell-Foot the Tyrant* in Relation to Contemporary Political Satires," *PMLA,* xxxvi (1921). 332-346.
[38] E. V. Della Robbia, *Vita di una Donna* (Florence, 1936), a biography of Emilia Viviani.
[39] *Peacock's Four Ages of Poetry; Shelley's Defence of Poetry; Browning's Essay on Shelley,* ed. H. F. B. Brett-Smith (1923). The relation of Shelley's essay to Sidney's *Apologie for Poetry* is generally recognized; for the indebtedness to the discourse on poetry in Johnson's *Rasselas* see K. N. Cameron, "A New Source for Shelley's *A Defence of Poetry,*" *SP,* xxxviii (1941). 629-644.
[40] F. M. Stawell, "Shelley's Triumph of Life," *E&S,* v (1914). 104-131.

Death

were caught in a squall, and drowned on July 8, 1822. Some days later the bodies were washed ashore, and in the presence of Byron and Trelawny were committed to the flames. Shelley's ashes were buried in the new Protestant Cemetery in Rome. The pathetic group which had been held together by the magic of his personality dispersed.

Mary Shelley returned to England to keep alive her husband's memory in the face of the opposition of his father, who desired that he be forgotten. Under the threat of withdrawing financial support from his little grandson, Percy Florence Shelley, Timothy Shelley was able to impose the condition that there should be no biography of the poet. Mary was able to circumvent this prohibition in a measure by the publication of the *Posthumous Poems* (1824) and the *Works* (1839). Leigh Hunt and other admirers worked for the expansion of his fame. *Queen Mab* continued to make its way among the radicals, but till the publication of the Galignani edition in 1829 Shelley's other poems were difficult to procure. In that year there took place a famous debate between a group of Cambridge undergraduates (of whom Arthur Henry Hallam was one) and a group of Oxford undergraduates. Cambridge defended the merits of Shelley against the Oxford upholders of Byron. Byron's cause triumphed; but the significant fact is that the question was considered a matter for debate. The young poets had no doubts. Beddoes was Shelley's disciple; Browning hailed him as the "Sun-treader."

XIII

John Keats

Thought and Sensation

Keats,[1] like Théophile Gautier, was "a man for whom the physical world exists." His genius was objective and concrete, moving not so readily in the world of abstract thought as in the world of imaginative realization.[2] Yet critics who regard him as the lover and creator of sensuous beauty are opposed by those who contend that he is a great philosophic poet.[3] The truth probably lies between these two extremes. Efforts to synthesize his ideas do not carry conviction, for later views of life would, had he lived longer, probably have been as much subject to change as had been those of earlier date. All that can be discerned clearly is the drift from romantic egocentricity towards objectivity. The problem of his development is one of the most fascinating of literary studies because of the wealth of evidence both in his poems and letters and in the records accumulated by his friends.[4]

[1] *Poetical Works and Other Writings,* Hampstead Edition, ed. M. Buxton Forman (8v, 1938), based on ed. H. Buxton Forman (5v, 1900) with additional material; *Poems,* ed. Ernest de Selincourt (1926), with admirable commentary; *Poetical Works,* ed. H. W. Garrod (1939), with full collation of texts; *Complete Poems and Selected Letters,* ed. C. DeW. Thorpe (1935); *Letters,* ed. M. B. Forman (2v, 1931). — Sir Sidney Colvin, *John Keats: His Life and Poetry, His Friends, Critics and After-Fame* (1917; revised, 1925); Amy Lowell, *John Keats* (2v, 1925); R. M. Milnes (Lord Houghton), *Life, Letters, and Literary Remains of John Keats* (2v, 1848; Everyman's Library, 1927); C. L. Finney, *The Evolution of Keats's Poetry* (2v, Cambridge, Mass., 1936), to which the present chapter is much indebted; Lucien Wolff, *John Keats, sa vie et son œuvre* (Paris, 1910); Albert Erlande, *Life of John Keats,* trans. by Marion Robinson (1929); H. I'A. Fausset, *Keats, a Study in Development* (1922); Dorothy Hewlett, *Adonais: A Life of John Keats* (Indianapolis, 1938); B. C. Williams, *Forever Young* (1943); E. V. Weller, *Autobiography of John Keats, Compiled from his Letters and Essays* (Palo Alto, Cal., 1933); Edmund Blunden, *Shelley and Keats as They Struck Their Contemporaries* (1925); Edmund Blunden, *Keats's Publisher: A Memoir of John Taylor (1781-1864)* (1936). — Among studies primarily critical, not biographical, are: C. DeW. Thorpe, *The Mind of John Keats* (1926); H. W. Garrod, *Keats* (1926); J. Middleton Murry, *Keats and Shakespeare: A Study of Keats's Poetic Life* (1925); J. M. Murry, *Studies in Keats* (1930; enlarged, 1939); W. J. Bate, *Negative Capability: the Intuitive Approach to Keats* (Cambridge, Mass., 1939) and *The Stylistic Development of Keats* (1945); A. W. Crawford, *The Genius of Keats* (1932); *John Keats Memorial Volume,* ed. G. C. Williamson (1921); Robert Bridges, "A Critical Introduction to Keats," *Collected Essays* (1929), IV, originally the introduction to Keats's *Poems* in the Muses' Library (1895); A. C. Bradley, "The Letters of Keats," *Oxford Lectures on Poetry* (1909), pp. 209-244; Bush, ch. III. — D. L. Baldwin and others, *Concordance* (Washington, D. C., 1917).

[2] This antithesis is stated in unqualified form by J. M. Murry, *Keats and Shakespeare,* p. 7.

[3] For these opposing views see Royall Snow, "Heresy concerning Keats," *PMLA,* XLIII (1928), 1142-1149, and M. E. Shipman, "Orthodoxy concerning Keats," *ibid.,* XLIV (1929), 929-934. The first effort to interpret Keats as a philosophic and not merely a sensuous poet was F. M. Owen, *John Keats* (1880). Today this view is represented in its extreme form by J. Middleton Murry. For the interpretation of Keats as a sensuous poet see H. N. Fairchild, *The Romantic Quest,* ch. XXII.

[4] Hunt, Clarke, Haydon, Dilke, Mathew, Reynolds, Severn, and other friends left their testimony. The two men to whom posterity is most indebted are Richard Woodhouse, who made manuscript collections of Keatsiana which have been used by many scholars, and Charles Armitage Brown, whose *Life of John Keats,* ed. D. H. Bodurtha and W. B. Pope, remained

The swiftness of his progress is almost without parallel in the history of the arts. There were retardations and perturbations, returning eddies which swept him upstream to points which he had left behind; but always his exalted conception of poetry made him dissatisfied with each stage as it was reached and determined to press on further. What his goal might have been we cannot say. He expressed the hope to live to write "a few great plays"; but there is little evidence to support the opinion that his true bent was towards the drama. On better grounds it may be held that with longer life he would have written more, and greater, narrative poetry, in which human characters portrayed with psychological insight would have moved before a background of romantic beauty.[5] But this is mere speculation. What we know is that in the three or four crucial years (1816-1819) there was a struggle between what Keats thought of as the Wordsworthian conception of the poet's function and what he thought of as the Shakespearean, a struggle, that is, between the opposing ideals of a reasoned humanitarianism and an objective dispassionateness of suspended judgment.

Born in London in the milieu of an humble trade but of people self-respecting and fairly well-to-do, John Keats (1795-1821) at an early age lost his father; then his mother; and then the grandmother who after his parents' death had given him a home. The terms of a trust deprived him of the share in a modest estate which would have relieved him of anxieties and perhaps prolonged his life. At school at Enfield (1803-1811) he made friends with Charles Cowden Clarke, the son of the headmaster. There are records of Keats's vivacious personality, pugnacity, sense of humor, and love of sport, but not of any special interest in literature till at the age of fifteen Clarke helped to awaken in him a love of mythology and travel-lore. In 1811 his guardian apprenticed him to an apothecary-surgeon at Edmonton.[6] His reading of *The Faerie Queene* resulted in 1813 in the first poem that is still extant, an *Imitation of Spenser* of little value. The influence which the poems of Mary Tighe had upon him has been exaggerated.[7] That Keats knew and admired Mrs. Tighe's *Psyche* (1805) is indubitable; but most of the parallels noted between her poetry and his are due to their common use of conventional and sentimental diction. Nothing is unimportant in tracing the development of such a genius; but the student must turn to larger treatises for the details of Keats's juvenilia. Among them is an *Ode to Apollo* in the manner of Gray, and sonnets addressed to the memory of

venilia

in manuscript till 1937. For the squabbles over rival claims to be Keats's first biographer see the introduction to this biography. See also *Some Letters and Miscellanies of Charles Brown*, ed. M. B. Forman (1937).

[5] This was A. C. Bradley's opinion. See *Oxford Lectures on Poetry* (1909), p. 239. For the unusual view that Keats would not have accomplished greater things had he lived see G. R. Elliott, "The Real Tragedy of Keats," *PMLA*, xxxvi (1921). 315-331.

[6] Sir W. Hale-White, *Keats as a Medical Student* (1925) and *Keats as Doctor and Patient* (1938).

[7] *Keats and Mary Tighe: The Poems of Mary Tighe with Parallel Passages from the Works of John Keats*, ed. E. V. Weller (1928). — A stronger and longer lasting influence was that of C. M. Wieland's romantic poem, *Oberon*, which Keats knew in William Sotheby's translation (1798). See W. W. Beyer, *Keats and the Dæmon King* (1947).

Chatterton, to Byron, and to Leigh Hunt (lately released from prison). The influence of Byron was ephemeral; that of Chatterton subtly pervasive; Hunt's for a time paramount.

In October, 1815, Keats became a medical student in the London hospitals. A verse epistle to a friend, G. F. Mathew, is in a genre descending from Drayton. For the run-on couplets with many double rimes and accented light syllables there was Elizabethan precedent as well as Hunt's example; but the displeasing colloquialisms are due to Hunt's vulgarization of the Wordsworthian principle of simplicity of diction. With the desire to emulate *The Story of Rimini* Keats began a romantic narrative, but this *Specimen of an Induction to a Poem* got no further than the title indicates, for the story refused to "come." Of *Calidore*, an offshoot from *The Faerie Queene,* only the opening episode was written. The jauntiness of the narrative shows that Hunt, not Spenser, was Keats's model. The luscious vocabulary includes some of Hunt's favorite words, notably those soft adjectives ending in *y* which for so long were blemishes on Keats's style. In the *Epistle to My Brother George,* written in August, 1816, Keats debated the choice between surgery and poetry as a profession; by September, as we learn from the *Epistle to Charles Cowden Clarke,* the die had been cast. Then suddenly, as though to put the seal upon an irrevocable decision, in October he wrote the sonnet *On First Looking into Chapman's Homer,*[8] drawing a magnificent simile from Robertson's narrative of Balboa's first sight of the Pacific Ocean and another from Bonnycastle's narrative of Herschel's discovery of Uranus. We feel that to the excitement of the exploration of the earth, the heavens, and the golden realms of poetry Keats was adding the ardor of the exploration of his own poetic powers. This impression connects the Chapman sonnet with *Sleep and Poetry,* upon which he was engaged in the autumn, after he and Hunt had become friends. This poem, which contains the famous description of Hunt's study at Hampstead, is the fullest expression of Keats's discipleship. Hunt's teaching is recognizable in the survey of the three schools of English poetry: the "Italian," which was dominant from Chaucer to Milton; the "French," in which a foppish and barbaric "crew" obeyed the rules dictated by Boileau; and the new, "natural" school of which Wordsworth is the master and to which Hunt and, by implication, Keats himself belong. A contrast is drawn between the poetry of natural loveliness which is presided over by "Flora and old Pan" and the poetry which reveals "the agonies, the strife of human hearts." The need to choose between the two kinds remained the burning problem in Keats's thought.[9] In a companion poem without title, beginning "I stood

Influence of Hunt

"The Realms of Gold"

[8] C. L. Finney, *The Evolution of Keats's Poetry,* I. 121-128; G. W. Landrum, "More concerning Chapman's Homer and Keats," *PMLA,* XLII (1927). 986-1009; B. I. Evans, "Keats's Approach to the Chapman Sonnet," *E&S,* XVI (1931). 26-52.

[9] Though Keats kept political questions almost entirely out of his poetry (unless, as some have thought, *Hyperion* reflects the French Revolution), his letters reveal liberal opinions which by no means merely echo Hunt. He sympathized with Cobbett, with the prosecuted radical publishers, and with the victims of the "Peterloo Massacre." He was opposed to the Holy Alliance and to the restored, reactionary Continental dynasties. See H. G. Wright, "Keats and Politics," *E&S,* XVIII (1933). 7-23.

tip-toe upon a little hill," Keats described the stimulus to the poetic faculty afforded by natural beauty and developed the Wordsworthian doctrine that the poets of ancient Greece were inspired by that beauty to create myths. This piece is, then, a sort of proem to *Endymion*.

Intimacy with Hunt reached a climax on the day when the two poets crowned each other with laurel. Of the effusiveness and affectation of this "intercoronation" episode Keats was soon ashamed, as he confessed in an *Ode* in which he asked forgiveness of Apollo. He had now met Benjamin Robert Haydon, the painter and art-critic, lately victorious in his battle for recognition of the Phidian workmanship and supreme aesthetic value of the Elgin marbles.[10] Haydon's efforts to emancipate the young poet from discipleship to Hunt bore first fruit in the sonnet *On Seeing the Elgin Marbles*. The first period in Keats's career was rounded out in March, 1817, when his first volume, entitled simply *Poems*,[11] was published. The few reviews, though slight, were not altogether unfavorable. Keats had progressed far enough to accept the admonition to eschew affectation and shun bad models.

Endymion,[12] which marks a transitional phase in Keats's development,
Endymion was written between April and October, 1817. A close study of Shakespeare's diction, style, and imagery began early in this year.[13] The study of Milton and of Dante (in Cary's translation) was encouraged by a new friend, Benjamin Bailey, a theological student, who also turned the poet's thoughts towards humanitarianism. The incubus of Hunt's bad taste could not be shaken off easily; colloquialisms, vulgarisms, and a soft lusciousness of style and sentiment mar *Endymion,* particularly in the amorous passages; but on the other hand there are exquisite felicities, single lines of terse grandeur, and (memorably in the "Song of Sorrow") a prodigal wealth of imagery drawn from poetry, mythology, and the fine arts. The too abundant use of run-on couplets, imitated not so much from Hunt as from Drayton, William Browne, and other poets of the English Renaissance, gives a slipshod effect that is due not to carelessness but to faulty taste. The reviewers who noted that the rimes often seem to dictate the sense rather than the sense the rimes made a valid criticism. Keats took the story of the love of Endymion and Diana from Drayton's *The Man in the Moon* and perhaps from the same poet's *Endimion and Phoebe*. Some suggestions seem to have come from Lyly's court-satire, *Endimion,* and others from allusions to the myth in other Renaissance poets. Lemprière's *Classical Dictionary* and other books of reference were at hand. The interwoven episodes of Venus and Adonis, Glaucus and Scylla, and Alpheus and

[10] S. A. Larrabee, *English Bards and Grecian Marbles* (1943), ch. IX.
[11] *Poems of 1817*, Noel Douglas Replica (1927).
[12] Published 1818. Type-facsimile, ed. H. C. Notcutt (1927). See Leonard Brown, "The Genesis, Growth, and Meaning of *Endymion*," *SP*, XXX (1933). 618 653.
[13] See C. F. E. Spurgeon, *Keats's Shakespeare, a Descriptive Study Based on New Material* (1928).

Arethusa came from like sources. Drayton had used the moon as a symbol of Ideal Beauty; but Keats's central idea, the Platonic theme of the quest of a unity transcending the flux of the phenomenal world, came in the main from Spenser's *Four Hymns,* with suggestions from Shelley's *Alastor.*[14] The thread of this theme, though never broken, is often lost to sight in the luxuriant decorative detail. Endymion passes through four stages of experience, to each of which one of the four books of the poem is devoted. On his progress towards the attainment of "fellowship with Essence" he experiences the beauty of Nature; of Art (and more especially of Poetry); of Friendship; and of Love. The Renaissance concept of friendship as the love of man for man Keats converted, under the influence of Wordsworth, into philanthropy or universal humanitarianism. Unlike the Platonists of the Renaissance, he placed love higher than friendship; but, as he afterwards recognized, he failed to mark the distinction between the Uranian and Pandemian Aphrodite and fused and confused spiritual and physical love. Keats was dissatisfied with *Endymion* and even before its completion he had passed beyond it into another stage. This being the case, it might have been wiser, and certainly would have served his prospects better, had he left the poem unpublished. For the manners of the malignant reviewers there is neither excuse nor forgiveness; but the magnanimity with which Keats faced ridicule was due in part to his recognition that in some of their strictures there was justice.

Frequent personal contact with Wordsworth disillusioned Keats, because of the elder poet's complacency, egotism, and didacticism; and as a consequence there was during the winter of 1817-1818 a drift away from humanitarianism. The counterbalance was an ever-deepening appreciation of the impartiality and impersonality of Shakespeare. This antithesis may have been sharpened for Keats by Hazlitt's comment upon the "intense intellectual egotism" of Wordsworth and his observation that Shakespeare enters so completely into his various characters as "scarcely to have an individual existence of his own."[15] It may have been with this distinction between objective and subjective genius in his memory that Keats evolved his famous doctrine of "Negative Capability."[16] By this not very happily *"Negative* chosen term he meant, he said, "when a man is capable of being in un- *Capability"* certainties, mysteries, doubts, without any irritable reaching after fact and reason." As examples by contrariety he chose Wordsworth, who imparted a direct philosophical view of life, and Coleridge, who was "incapable of remaining content with half-knowledge." The poetic ideal after which Keats was here reaching is that of imaginative insight and suspended judgment, "a selfless sympathy" not only with other human beings but

14 Keats's indebtedness to Shelley, in *Endymion* and elsewhere, is demonstrated (and exaggerated) in L. J. Thompson, *More Magic Dethroned* (1925). The desire to retain his "unfettered scope" kept Keats from responding to Shelley's advances in 1817; and in 1820 he was too ill to respond.
15 Hazlitt, "On Mr. Wordsworth's *Excursion"* and "On Posthumous Fame," *The Round Table; Works,* ed. Waller and Glover, I. 113 and 23.
16 Keats, *Letters,* I. 77 (December 28, 1817).

with all life. Of himself he said that he could enter into a sparrow's personality and "pick about the gravel."

While seeing *Endymion* through the press, Keats planned with John Hamilton Reynolds [17] a series of narrative poems based upon stories from the *Decameron*. Since this project was an outgrowth from Hunt's recommendations of Italian literature as affording subjects for poetry, it is not surprising to note in *Isabella, or The Pot of Basil* [18] a reversion to the cloying diction of Hunt. Yet there is an increased firmness of style, and the handling of *ottava rima* is masterly. The digressions, such as the invocation of Boccaccio and the complaint to Melancholy, are in imitation of old conventions. The touches of the macabre anticipate a taste of the eighteen-twenties.

Shortly after the publication of *Endymion* (April, 1818) Keats was separated from his brother George, who with his bride set sail for America. The illness of his second brother, Tom, who was now stricken with tuberculosis, proved to be a severe test of the ideal of suspended judgment, and we find Keats expressing his longing for a fixed philosophy based upon reason.[19] It may be, however, that students of Keats have taken these fluctuations of opinion too seriously, for Keats's nature was of a chameleon-like sensitiveness to his surroundings. How strong the influence of Wordsworth was upon him still is shown in the famous letter in which he likened

The Chambers of Life" life to "a mansion of many apartments." [20] Of these, two only were as yet open to him: "the infant or thoughtless chamber" and "the chamber of Maiden-Thought." In the latter "we see nothing but pleasant wonders, and think of delaying there for ever with delight." At his present point of growth he was conscious of passing thence, of being "in a mist," unable to balance good and evil but aware of the "burden of the mystery." Keats expressly drew the analogy to Wordsworth's case (as recorded in *Tintern Abbey*) and believed that the elder poet had explored those further chambers, those "dark passages" which were as yet closed to himself.

A strong vein of humanitarianism continued to manifest itself in Keats's letters during the walking-tour with Charles Armitage Brown in the summer of 1818. The friends visited the Lowlands of Scotland, the Lake District, and, for a fleeting moment, Ireland. By overtaxing his physical powers this tour hastened Keats's decline. The vicious attacks on *Endymion* in the *Quarterly* and *Blackwood's* were accepted with the nobly philosophic re-

[17] On Reynolds see below, ch. xiv.
[18] For his material Keats went not directly to Boccaccio but to an English version first published in 1620. See H. G. Wright, "Keats's *Isabella*," *LTLS*, April 17, 1943, p. 192.
[19] *Letters*, I. 132. This was in March, 1818. Three months earlier Keats had expressed the oft-quoted aspiration "O for a Life of Sensations rather than of Thoughts!" (*ibid.*, I. 73). Professor Finney (*op. cit.*, I. 301) argues that Keats has here in mind Wordsworthian or Hazlittian empiricism. "The sensations which a man receives from natural objects, he [Keats] believed, produce strong passions or emotions in him and induce a state of ecstasy in which his imagination, stimulated by his passions, apprehends or intuits truth in the form of being." The context of the letter hardly supports the weight of this interpretation. Contrast H. N. Fairchild's matter-of-fact interpretation of Keats's use of "sensation" (*The Romantic Quest*, p. 414).
[20] *Letters*, I, 156.

mark: "I was never afraid of failure, for I would sooner fail than not be among the greatest." [21] But later these hostile reviews undermined his confidence, as he came to realize that by warning the public away from him they had deprived him of the hope of winning a livelihood from poetry.

In the late summer of 1818 Keats began work on *Hyperion*.[22] The theory that *The Fall of Hyperion*, the "dream" version commonly regarded as an attempt to recast the original poem, is really a preliminary draft [23] has met with no acceptance; but the alternative view which accepts the traditional chronological order probably over-simplifies the problem. The view which, though it rests upon internal evidence, best meets the case is that Keats began *Hyperion* under the influence of Wordsworth, composing the introductory colloquy with Moneta in which the goddess upbraids him for having been "a dreaming thing, a fever of thyself" and declares that none can usurp the heights of poetic power save those "to whom the miseries of the world are misery." [24] In revulsion from this humanitarian sentiment he may have set aside this introduction and made a new beginning with the objective and Miltonic version of which he had completed two books and begun a third by the spring of 1819. The sensuousness, subjectivism, and exuberant beauty of the fragmentary third book reflect the heightening of Keats's personal emotion consequent upon his meeting with Fanny Brawne, with whom he had fallen passionately in love.[25] This ardent feeling, which for a time conquered the despondency caused by his brother's death in December, 1818, burns brightly in the theme of *Hyperion*. From allusions in Renaissance poetry and from works of reference Keats took the story of the fall of the Titans and triumph of the Olympians. The celestial warfare is reminiscent of *Paradise Lost,* of which there are many echoes in the diction; and such stylistic features as repetition, inversion, elliptical construction, and elaborate simile come from close study of Milton.[26] The landscape and imagery owe something to Keats's recent impressions of rugged mountain scenery; and the marmoreal quality of certain passages (notably the opening scene) are suggestive of his contemplation of Greek sculpture. To all this he gave a modern coloring. Whether or not the history of the French Revolution was in the back of his mind as he wrote, his theme is progressive evolution. Up the Scale of Being evolution must move, towards the ideal. Each generation of the gods is supplanted by another more beautiful, for "the first in beauty should be first in might."

The change in tone in Book III is a modulation from *Hyperion* to the

Hyperion

---

[21] *Ibid.,* I. 243.
[22] Facsimile of Keats's autograph manuscript of *Hyperion*, ed. E. de Selincourt (1905).
[23] Amy Lowell, *The Life of John Keats*, II. 339-348.
[24] *The Fall of Hyperion*, I. 148-149; 168-169. — The theory here outlined is that of C. L. Finney, *The Evolution of Keats's Poetry*, II, ch. v.
[25] Whether or not Fanny Brawne appreciated the greatness of her lover's genius is a hotly disputed problem. Over against the notorious letter in which she expressed the wish that his memory might be permitted to die must be set the evidence in the *Letters of Fanny Brawne to Fanny Keats*, ed. Fred Edgecumbe (1936).
[26] On Keats's indebtedness to Milton see in general R. D. Havens, *The Influence of Milton on English Poetry* (1922), ch. x.

poem which occupied Keats early in 1819. In *The Eve of St. Agnes* youthful, romantic love is set against a background of family feud, coarse carousing, storm, and bitter cold. Memories of *Romeo and Juliet* and *Cymbeline* and of the Gothic romances [27] are here combined with quaint superstitions and folk-rites about which Keats had read in Ben Jonson, Burton, and Brand's *Popular Antiquities*. Keats's creative art was at its happiest and most spontaneous in this poem. The diction is of a flawless purity. Though the Spenserian stanza is employed and the sensuous imagery and lavish adornment of the narrative are suggestive of Spenser, there is nothing that is merely imitative. The reliance upon elaborate and vivid presentation rather than upon suggestion differentiates the quality of Keats's romanticism from Coleridge's.

But alarming symptoms of tuberculosis were developing, among which are to be numbered the torments of jealousy expressed in the first ode *To Fanny*. It is likely, as Rossetti suggested long ago, that there is a connection of thought and mood between this ode and the fragmentary *Eve of St. Mark*.[28] According to the old belief, those who watch in the porch of the parish church on this eve will see shadowy forms pass into the portal. The forms that do not pass out again are of those who are doomed to die within the succeeding year. Is it Fanny who watches by the church-door? Is Keats the lover who passes in, not to reappear? In April, 1819, he wrote *Bright Star* (miscalled his "Last Sonnet"), and shortly afterwards the agonizing second ode *To —— [Fanny]* and *La Belle Dame Sans Merci*, that miraculously weird evocation of the *femme fatale* which exalts to the highest imaginative plane the fatal thraldom in which Keats found himself.

He was now discontented with the sonnet form which he had used with such mastery, and while expressing his dissatisfaction in the irregular sonnet, "If by dull rhymes our English must be chain'd," he experimented with three new patterns which proved to be unsuccessful. Keats's music tends to move in stanza lengths. His "continuous verse" is either diffusive or else falls into such well defined paragraphs as the opening movement of *Hyperion*, which is precisely the length of a sonnet. The theory is acceptable that these experiments in new sonnet forms led directly to the series of odes

composed in the late spring and early summer of 1819.[29] The scanty external evidence as to their order of composition may be supplemented by study of the links of thought between the odes and the growth and decline of mastery of the form. The *Ode to Psyche* was probably written first. It is more in the tradition of the pseudo-Pindaric than are the other odes; a

---

[27] M. H. Shackford, "*The Eve of St. Agnes* and *The Mysteries of Udolpho*," PMLA, xxxvi (1921). 104-118.

[28] In an undated letter (August, 1820 ?) to Fanny Brawne (*Letters*, ii. 548) Keats refers to a poem which he has in mind but which his health does not permit him to write. Rossetti believed that the reference was to the unfinished *Eve of St. Mark*. The overlapping of ideas between this poem and *The Cap and Bells* may also be significant. See C. L. Finney, *The Evolution of Keats's Poetry*, ii. 566-567; and, more specifically on this poem, W. E. Houghton, "The Meaning of Keats's *Eve of St. Mark*," ELH, xiii (1946). 64-78.

[29] This theory was first advanced by H. W. Garrod, *Keats* (1926).

formal pattern has not yet been established. The Wordsworthian theme that the poet is the myth-maker provides a link, not present in the other odes, between the *Psyche* and Keats's earlier thought. The *Ode to a Nightingale,* in which the happy world of natural loveliness is contrasted with the human world of pain, is flawless in design and expression and almost perfect in the development of its theme.[30] It seems likely that it preceded the *Ode on a Grecian Urn* where another contrast is developed, that of the permanence of art with the fleetingness of human passion. For all its beauty this ode is not quite flawless,[31] and the oft-quoted conclusion is open to the charge of ambiguity.[32] The *Ode to Indolence* is on a lower level of achievement, and both in subject and treatment reflects the poet's spiritual apathy after a period of intense creation. A study of the sources in literature, art, and personal experience of Keats's imagery in the odes, of their varying stanzaic patterns or approximations to pattern, and of the beautiful, tenuous links among them (as of the night-moth, the Grecian vase, Lethe, and drowsiness) is one of the most rewarding of literary investigations.

By midsummer of 1819 Keats's health was failing and he was living under the pressure of dire poverty. While staying in Winchester he and his friend Charles Brown collaborated upon a tragedy with the hope that they might dispose of it to the theatre and that Edmund Kean would assume the title-rôle. This drama, *Otho the Great,* is on a historical theme of the tenth century and involves the rivalry of two brothers and a conflict between father and son. The tradition is that Brown supplied the characters and action, scene by scene, and that Keats wrote the dialogue from this outline; but it is probable that Keats shared the responsibility for the general plan and concept. The question is of no great importance, for though there are a few passages of fine poetry in the play,[33] as a whole it must be adjudged a failure.

Another attempt to win attention with something in a popular vein is **Lamia** of much more consequence. This is *Lamia,* composed in the late summer. The story of the serpent-woman who fell in love with a youth of Corinth and was detected and exorcised by Apollonius, the philosopher, Keats drew from Burton's *Anatomy of Melancholy.* Dryden's verse was the model for the firmly wrought couplets with well-spaced triplets and alexandrines in which it is composed; and the astringent style of the latter part of the poem is also suggestive of Dryden. The contrast between the romantic beauty and mystery of Part I and the intrusive cynicism in Part II is, indeed, remarkable. It is probably explicable on biographical grounds. A little earlier Keats had written what he described as the "flint-worded" letters to Fanny Brawne—hysterical, passionate outcries of agony in the face of consuming

---

[30] "Almost perfect"—the description of the nightingale's song as a "plaintive anthem" in the final stanza contradicts, and jars ever so slightly upon, the earlier indications of its happiness and ecstasy. What had been purely objective becomes subjective.

[31] The flaw is in stanza v; the ugly repetition of sound in "O Attic shape! Fair attitude!"

[32] The best discussion of "Beauty is Truth, Truth Beauty" is in J. M. Murry, *Studies in Keats* (ed. 1930), pp. 71-92.

[33] For example, Ludolph's speech at IV, ii. 18.

love and jealousy, encroaching disease, and the ever-more-certain threat of death with work unfinished and ambitions unrealized. In these letters he affirmed his dedication to poetry and resolve to reject the distractions of love.[34] About the same time he wrote in a mood of desperate cynicism three stanzas expanding the narrative of the meeting of the lovers in *The Eve of St. Agnes.* These were ruinously out of keeping with the rest of the poem, and Keats afterwards wisely let himself be persuaded to suppress them. But they help to account for the satiric element in *Lamia.* Is there autobiographical symbolism in the story of Lycius and the serpent-woman?[35] Is "the tender-personed lamia"—who is beautiful, mysterious, and *not* malign—the Poetic Imagination? Is her lover, Lycius, the poet Keats? Does the feast at Corinth symbolize the publication of his poems? Are the guests the reading-public? If this interpretation holds, then Apollonius symbolizes the reviewers who destroyed the Imagination and—tragic prescience on Keats's part!—brought about the poet's death.[36]

What remains to tell is a story of decline. The ode *To Autumn,* for all its gorgeous sensuousness, shows no intellectual advance. *The Fall of Hyperion* is (if the view here adopted be generally accepted) an attempt to dovetail the original Wordsworthian opening into the second, Miltonic fragment, with other revisions under the influence of Dante's *Purgatorio.* There was a passionate revulsion of feeling expressed in a letter to Fanny Brawne on October 10, 1819, and in the moving but languorous sonnet *The Day is Gone.* An effort to write a chronicle play, *King Stephen,* was beyond Keats's strength, and the opening scenes remain a fragment of high but uncertain promise. *The Cap and Bells,* patterned upon Ariosto and *Don Juan* and combining fairy-lore and topical allusion in a satire on the Prince Regent with side-glances at Lord Byron, was tragically alien from Keats's genius and was set aside. At the close of the manuscript of this fantasy are found the beautiful and terrible lines beginning "This living hand," without title but undoubtedly addressed to Fanny Brawne.

During 1820, which he called his "posthumous year," Keats wrote no poetry. In February came the first hemorrhage from the lungs. He was watched over by Brown, then by the Hunts, and then by Mrs. Brawne and Fanny. In the spring he prepared his last volume for the press, and in July was published *Lamia, Isabella, The Eve of St. Agnes, and Other Poems,*[37] the greatest single volume of English poetry of the nineteenth century. In September, with his faithful friend Joseph Severn, he sailed for Italy in search of health. The quest was hopeless. He died in Rome on February 23, 1821, and was buried in the old Protestant Cemetery, close to the pyramid of Caius Cestius which serves as a beacon for pilgrims to his grave.

Death

---

[34] *Letters,* II. 400-403 (August 17, 1819).
[35] C. L. Finney, *The Evolution of Keats's Poetry,* II. 696-702.
[36] This interpretation accounts for the denunciation of "cold Philosophy" and meets Robert Bridges's objection, *Collected Essays* (1929), IV. 127, that the poem should not have ended with the death of Lycius.
[37] *Poems of 1820,* Noel Douglas Replicas (1927).

The evidence of Shelley's letters supplements the impression from *Adonais* that Shelley was not aware of the greatness of Keats's accomplishment. The elegy is a chivalrous protest against Keats's detractors; but together with Byron's pitying scorn of one who had let himself "be snuffed out by an article" it helped to keep alive the false tradition that Keats was a weakling. The loyal friends who preserved Keats's letters and assembled a vast quantity of records of his life provided for posterity the means to refute this conception. But even the temporary prevalence of this opinion and the association of his name with the "Cockney School" did not long retard his fame and influence. That influence is visible in the poetry of Darley and Hood, Tennyson and the youthful Browning. After 1848, the year when R. M. Milnes's biography of the poet with his letters and literary remains appeared, the poetry of Keats became the greatest single influence upon the poetry and painting of the Victorian generation.[38] Emphasis upon the value of Keats's thought is a phenomenon of the criticism of our own day.

[38] See G. H. Ford, *Keats and the Victorians. A Study of his Influence and Rise to Fame* (New Haven, 1944).

XIV

Thomas Hood, Thomas Lovell Beddoes, and Other Poets

In the eighteen-twenties a number of poets appeared of whom some died early and some, discouraged, subsided into silence, while others continued to write for many years. There was abundant talent in most of them and two possessed powers beyond their actual achievement; but none was a poet of anywhere near the first order. They do not divide the Romantic Period, narrowly so called, from the Victorian, but illustrate the continuity of the romantic tradition. They are not a very homogeneous group, but several among them are near allied and there are loose links among the rest.

Of these points of connection the most conspicuous is the taste for the extravagant, the weird, and the horrible which they acquired from Gothic romance. The popular art of the period catered to the same liking for the *The* "horrid." The grotesque and the macabre are dominant motifs in the designs *Grotesque* of Thomas Rowlandson and George Cruikshank.[1] Pater's doctrine, that *and the* in romantic art strangeness is allied to beauty and that if the strangeness *Macabre* is exaggerated the beauty tends to disappear and we have the grotesque, is of dubious validity as a generalization; but it is applicable here. Only a poet of austere soul can invest the terrors of the charnel-house with an aura of beauty. The Italian Leopardi had done so; but few of these English poets possess, even momentarily, the austerity of a Leopardi. Generally they do not take their horrors quite seriously. Like their French *confrères* they seek to provoke a "new shudder"; but they smile or even chuckle when their readers are horrified. Some of their poems are weirdly romantic and others wittily satirical, and the one kind shades off into the other. An expert technique with surprising effects of rimes, curious stanzaic forms, and startling juxtapositions of images is employed for either purpose. Yet beneath the surface of grim or merry wit there is, in almost every case, an underlying sadness. Sometimes this contracts to a point of personal introspection where all that is expressed is a sense of the aimlessness and futility of life; but at other times it broadens from the characteristic romantic sympathy with the unfortunate into a bold and not uninfluential poetry of social protest dealing with substantial wrongs.

---

[1] Noteworthy is the reappearance of the "Dance of Death" theme in art. Rowlandson's *English Dance of Death* (1816) and Dagley's *Death's Doings* (1826) are examples. The material in Francis Douce's *Dissertation on the Dance of Death* (1833) had been collected much earlier.

I

The entire gamut, from romantic loveliness, through weirdness and horror, *Hood* and wit and humor, to satiric protest and the championship of the oppressed, is sounded in the poetry of Thomas Hood [2] (1799-1845). It is not apparent that the quality and range of his writings were conditioned by the circumstances of his career, for though amid disappointments, poverty, drudgery, and sickness he was, as he said, "a lively Hood for his livelihood," it is improbable that health and affluence would have altered his congenital disposition. His humor was that of his time and milieu. He was a friend of Charles Lamb, the master of the art of punning, and a contemporary of Theodore Hook, the master of the craft of "high jinks." The use of verbal play for serious poetic effects has the warrant of long lineage, and in Hood's day not all the good puns had been perpetrated. Nevertheless, this part of Hood's work in verse and prose—work it often was rather than play—is now sadly faded.

But the sparkle which has vanished from these things still plays upon the seas of old romance which Hood viewed from the magic casements thrown open for him by Keats. He was the earliest and closest disciple of that master.[3] His *Hero and Leander* is "Elizabethan" in a sense but with a difference; and the difference is due to Keats. *The Two Swans,* though a poem in the Spenserian tradition, is closer to *Isabella* than to *The Faerie Queene*; and its heavy, sultry imagery and slow-moving cadences anticipate effects with which Tennyson, likewise taught by Keats, was soon to be experimenting. *The Plea of the Midsummer Fairies* (1827), Hood's most extended effort in the romantic line, can still charm those who have the abundant time needed for its perusal, provided they are not offended by the passages of light quaintness and grotesquerie which do not quite harmonize with the context. The influence of Keats, evident in these longer things, is still more apparent in various short pieces; in *Ruth* and *Autumn,* especially, one is brought up abruptly with the consciousness of having heard the same thing before. But the echoes are so beautiful that Hood may claim them for his own.

An undertone of horror is audible in some of these poems. Horror is clangorous in *The Dream of Eugene Aram*. Though in metrical effects and turns of phrase it owes much to *The Ancient Mariner,* this narrative resembles the popular broadside ballads of the seventeenth century, even in such particulars as the edifying emphasis upon the murderer's remorse and the crude woodcuts with which the original edition was adorned. Quieter, more subtle, and more allusive are *The Elm-Tree* and *The Haunted House*

---

[2] *Works* (11v, n.d. [1882?]); *Poetical Works,* ed. Walter Jerrold (1906). — Mrs. F. F. Broderip (Hood's daughter), *Memorials of Thomas Hood* (2v, 1860); Walter Jerrold, *Thomas Hood: His Life and Times* (1907); Emil Oswald, *Thomas Hood und die Soziale Tendenzdichtung seiner Zeit* (Vienna, 1904); George Saintsbury, "Thomas Hood," *Essays and Papers,* II. 132-150.

[3] Shelley's influence is visible in a few pieces, notably *Lycus the Centaur.*

in which Hood gains his effects by means of indirection and understatement. Through other horror-pieces we are led into the region of the humorous-grotesque, where Hood is in line of descent from Southey and in proximity to *The Ingoldsby Legends*.[4] On occasion he can use his peculiar technique for serious purposes; and this he does in *Miss Kilmansegg and her Precious Leg*. The froth of fun has long since evaporated from this extravaganza, but a precipitate of serious intent remains—the intent to satirize the tragic absurdity of man's pursuit of gold.

Hood's touch is in general too light and his nature too kindly to admit him to the company of formidable satirists; but he first attracted attention by the *Odes and Addresses to Great People* (1825) in which he collaborated with some other writers. His manner here is suggestive of a better-bred "Peter Pindar"; and the ingenious rimes owe something to *Don Juan*. Topical poetry of this kind does not last well; but the humorous sympathy of the address to Mrs. Fry (the worker among the prisoners of Newgate) is still attractive, and there is sharp and effective indignation in the *Ode to Rae Wilson, Esquire*, in which Hood castigates a hypocrite. The indignation which is buoyed up with humor in some pieces is entirely serious in others of later date. The aims of the social reformers who worked to remedy conditions among the poor during the "Hungry Forties" were expressed by Hood in such poems as *The Lay of the Labourer, The Workhouse Clock*, and—on a higher level of workmanship and celebrity—*The Bridge of Sighs* and *The Song of the Shirt*. Distilling into a few stanzas the awareness of social wrongs which Dickens scattered through many volumes, Hood proved himself to be as influential as Dickens in aiding the reformers who were driving through Parliament the factory, mining, and sanitation acts. A problem which the modern sociologist faces in a different though not less sympathetic spirit is faced by Hood in *The Bridge of Sighs* with a pathos redeemed from mawkishness by its sincerity. The over-ingenious rimes are sustained upon the emotion of the poem, with its picture of the black-flowing river, the dark arch, and the unfortunate victim of man's inhumanity to woman. There is less beauty but more energy in the companion-piece on the misery of the sweat-shop worker. This *Song of the Shirt* rang through England as did Mrs. Browning's *Cry of the Children*. Its publication in *Punch* was the foundation of the popularity of that hitherto not very successful periodical. Appropriately and at his own request there was inscribed upon Hood's tombstone: "He Sang *The Song of the Shirt*."

---

[4] Richard Harris Barham (1788-1845), who used the pen-name "Thomas Ingoldsby," began to publish legends in prose and verse, whimsical and grotesque but stuffed with sound antiquarianism, in 1837. A First Series of these pieces was collected as *The Ingoldsby Legends* (1840); Second and Third Series (1847). The complete edition (1870; Oxford, 1926) contains a memoir of the author by his son, R. H. D. Barham. "Ingoldsby" descends from Southey's grotesques, is immediately contemporary with "Bon Gaultier" (see ch. xiv, n. 29, below), and points forward to some of the *Bab Ballads* of W. S. Gilbert (see ch. xxxviii). — More completely fantastical than Barham's inventions (some critics now say surrealist) are *The Book of Nonsense* (1848) and its successors by Edward Lear (1812-1888). In Lear's "limericks" and other pieces there are elements which give promise of the work of "Lewis Carroll" (see below, ch. xxi).

Near Hood may be grouped several lesser men. Ebenezer Elliott [5] (1781- *Ebenezer* 1849) is best remembered as a poet of social protest. A Yorkshire laborer *Elliott* who rose to be an iron-manufacturer in Sheffield, he knew well the hardships of the lives of industrial workers and rustics. He was closest to poetry when closest to the soil. In the very early poem *A Vernal Walk* (1801) he obviously chose Thomson for his guide. But when after many years he returned to verse his masters were Campbell and Byron, who had taught him a fierce rhetoric. In *The Ranter* (1827) and *Corn-Law Rhymes* (1828) he exposed the horrors of factories and slums and the injustice to workingmen of the law against the importation of foreign cereals. In such fiery poems as *Child, Is Thy Father Dead?* and *Day, like our Souls, is fiercely Dark,* commonplace but easily comprehended words are set to commonplace but memorable cadences. The "Corn-Law Rhymer" helped to mold sentiment which led two decades later to repeal. He was an excellent propagandist and occasionally a true poet, albeit more often inflated than inspired. The tales in *The Village Patriarch* (1829) in which he depicts with stern clarity the lives of humble folk show him to be a disciple of Crabbe.

On the other side of Hood are two poets who have little in common with *J. H.* Elliott's reforming spirit but much with Hood's facile romanticism and *Reynolds* satiric wit. John Hamilton Reynolds [6] (1794-1852) is remembered as the friend of Keats, but his poems show the influence of almost all the greater poets of the time. *The Eden of the Imagination* (1814) is an introspective analysis of his own emotional and imaginative development. *Safie* (1814) is an Oriental tale in the manner of Byron. The Elizabethan influence is obvious in some fairy poems which foreshadow Hood and Darley; the "Cockney" influence is apparent in the imperfections of his style. Reynolds is nearest to Keats in *The Garden of Florence* (1821) which is a story from the *Decameron* (and hence is like *Isabella*) in couplets on Dryden's model (and hence is like *Lamia*). The romantic vein presently ran out, and most of Reynolds' energy went thereafter into the practice of law and what remained for literature into satire. His *Peter Bell* [7] is a parody not of Wordsworth's poem in particular but of the general spirit and manner of the *Lyrical Ballads.* It is fairly amusing, but pert rather than really clever.

Romance and satiric wit are allied in the verses of Winthrop Mackworth *Praed ·* Praed [8] (1802-1839) with the added factor of an intimate knowledge of well-bred English society. Praed's narratives of King Arthur owe something, metrically, to Coleridge and more, for their manner, to Scott, while from Frere he seems to have taken the hint to season his romantic tales with a dash of topical satire. Abandoning romance, Praed came to specialize in the

---

[5] *Poems* (2v, 1876). — January Searle, *Memoirs of Ebenezer Elliott* (1852).
[6] *Prose and Poetry* (selections), ed. G. L. Marsh (1928).
[7] This preceded Shelley's satire, which is why Shelley called his poem *Peter Bell the Third.* See G. L. Marsh, "The *Peter Bell* Parodies of 1819," *MP*, XL (1943). 267-274.
[8] *Select Poems,* ed. W. M. Praed, with introduction by A. D. Godley (1909). — Derek Hudson, *A Poet in Parliament: The Life of William Mackworth Praed* (1939); Mathilde Kraupa, *W. M. Praed, sein Leben und seine Werke* (Vienna, 1910); George Saintsbury, "Praed," *Essays and Papers,* II. 31-52.

grotesque. Of his poems in this kind *The Red Fisherman* is the best and best known; its grim humor and facility anticipate Barham's characteristic effects. On a smaller scale Praed used the technique of surprising rimes and ingenious stanzaic schemes in a large amount of *vers de société*, touched with light malice but essentially kindly. Some of these things, such as *The Belle of the Ball* and *The Letter of Advice*, still possess a winning freshness and grace. Related to them but more serious in purpose and untouched with sentiment are his political pieces. These squibs and skits, which he wrote from experience, for he sat in Parliament and supported the movement for reform,[9] have lost most of their interest with the fading from memory of the persons and events which prompted them; but the best, such as *Stanzas on Seeing the Speaker Asleep*, retain some residue of their pungency. Praed's manner was often too light for the seriousness of his subjects, and his good-nature generally restrained him from penetrating to his victim's quick; but in a few poems, notably the *Counsels of a Father to his Son*, the stiletto reached vital parts.

II

Beddoes   The most memorable figure of these transitional years is Thomas Lovell Beddoes [10] (1803-1849). Just before his death he wrote: "I ought to have been—among other things—a good poet." The fact is, he was a "good" poet and "ought to have been" a great one. The failure to realize his potentialities is attributable to various causes—to distracted aims, for he was a physician and anatomist and, in later years in Germany and Switzerland, something of a political agitator; to discouragement, for *The Improvisatore* (1821) and *The Bride's Tragedy* (1822), which he published while an Oxford undergraduate, met with no success; to isolation, for he got out of touch with English literary society and came to feel that his native English was being supplanted by his acquired German; and to a profound melancholy and lethargic eccentricity which made him skeptical of the value of effort. After the two volumes just named he published no more. His most famous work, *Death's Jest-Book*, was begun about 1825 and for a quarter of a century he tinkered with it, revising, deleting, and expanding. He

---

[9] Yet not without misgivings; see Praed's *The New Order of Things* (1830). In his last years he was shifting towards the Tories.

[10] A selection from the mass of Beddoes' writings was published posthumously in 1851 by a devoted friend, Thomas Kelsall. *Death's Jest-Book*, as it then appeared, was a patchwork of several different versions left in manuscript. Beddoes' manuscripts were bequeathed by Kelsall to Robert Browning, who intended to "do something" with them but procrastinated. After his death the box of papers passed to Browning's son, and after *his* death it was reported as lost beyond recovery. Years later it became known that the elder Browning had permitted J. Dykes Campbell to make copies of the entire contents of the box; and from these transcripts it has been possible to publish at long last a definitive edition of the poetry and prose. This is *Works*, ed. H. W. Donner (1935), superseding all earlier editions. Supplementing this is *The Browning Box, or the Life and Work of T. L. Beddoes as reflected in Letters by his Friends and Admirers*, ed. H. W. Donner (1935). — H. W. Donner, *Thomas Lovell Beddoes: The Making of a Poet* (1935); R. H. Snow, *Thomas Lovell Beddoes, Eccentric and Poet* (1928); Lytton Strachey, "The Last Elizabethan," *Books and Characters* (1922), pp. 235-265.

wrote the massive fragments in dramatic form, *Torrismond* and *The Second Brother;* began but made little headway with a strange visionary romance, in mixed verse and prose; and composed a quantity of lyrics and lyrical fragments, some of ethereal loveliness and others harsh and grotesquely humorous. Friends in England received occasional letters and verse epistles in which he commented with engaging and often caustic candor upon the stage and theatrical criticism, upon the state of literature in England and Germany, and upon his own shortcomings as a poet. The more self-revealing of these letters suggest that his eccentricity was at times close to madness. At Zurich, in circumstances of eerie lugubriousness he committed suicide.

In youth Beddoes was one of the earliest admirers of Shelley. It is easy to detect Shelley's influence upon him, but it is equally easy to over-emphasize it. The dozen perfect lyrics—*Dream-Pedlary, If Thou Wilt Ease Thine Heart*, and the rest—are worthy of Shelley, but the rarified atmosphere in which the music sounds, the Debussy-like delicacy of the fingering, the pure, thin tone—these are Beddoes' own peculiar qualities. Equally individual are the repulsively grotesque ditty, *Lord Alcohol,* and the uncanny song of which the refrain is "In the ghosts' moonshine." Beddoes' fondness for sinister and spectral imagery probably owes something to Shelley; but both poets were influenced by tales of terror and Jacobean tragedies.

Beddoes was, indeed, at the very center of the Elizabethan revival. It is not a matter of imitation of the gnomic Webster, the dour Tourneur, the acrid Marston; rather it is a spiritual kinship or, more accurately, an identity of imaginative processes. To this Jacobeanism were added ingredients from German romanticism. That Beddoes had read Tieck we know; and something of tender sentiment (like that in *Undine*) and of ghostly and diabolic horror (like that in *Sintram*) probably came from De la Motte Fouqué. Ballads of the "Spectre Bridegroom" type stirred his imagination. How often must he have contemplated old German paintings and engravings in which the figure of Death appears among the living! [11] Through his anatomical studies in textbooks and the laboratory he became familiar with, and hence, as he said, contemptuous of, the horrors of mortality. To this exotic and sinister amalgam was added an awareness of new scientific speculation and experiment in dim regions of physiology and psychology. First among English poets he used as material for poetry the discoveries of the paleontologists. "The mighty thought of an old world," where amid the fern wildernesses titanic reptilian forms glistened, troubled his somber fantasy.[12] There are passages in his poetry which suggest that he believed in the evolution of species.[13]

[11] Particularly the numerous engravings of Death and the Maiden, and Death and the Lovers. The analogy to *Death's Jest-Book* is startling in the case of Hans Sebald Beham's exquisite little engraving of Death and the Woman (1541). Here the skeleton wears a fool's cap and carries a fool's bauble.

[12] Beddoes, *Song by Thanatos; Works*, ed. Donner, p. 142.

[13] G. R. Potter, "Did Beddoes Believe in the Evolution of Species?" *MP*, XXI (1923). 89-100.

Death's
Jest-Book

The two fragmentary dramas are not carried far enough to permit us to guess their intended course. The plot of *Death's Jest-Book* in summary reads like a parody of Jacobean tragedies of revenge: a duke who commits a murder; an avenger who disguises himself as a court-jester; the victim who rises from the tomb and at the close conducts his murderer into the world of the dead. Beddoes' imagery is powerful, condensed, aphoristic, disturbing. Earth is "this grave-paved star"; ivy, a "creeping darkness"; Time is a cataract falling into Eternity over ruined worlds. Death lurks always very near. So close are tombs together that those of latest date lie just beneath the surface of life in "the garrets of Death's town." "Death is old and half worn out; are there no chinks in it?" a character asks; and the reply takes the form of the numerous dead who rise, not furtive and wraith-like but social and substantial, and hobnob with the living, warning, counseling, mocking them; who chat and sing and dance, as they do in Holbein or Rowlandson; but who can be tender as well as terrible. In Beddoes' drama there is much of madness and more of sin; but horror is not the soul of the plot. There is a weird glee not only in some of the interspersed lyrics but in the antic prose; there is subtlety of thought and fancy; and over all there is cast a veil of shimmering loveliness. Beddoes did not possess the strength of character and structural skill to carry to completion a greatly conceived design. To ask of him significance of plot or profundity of psychology is to ask for what he cannot give. He is memorable for scattered lines and passages, cadences of haunting beauty, and images of arresting grandeur.

III

Of the other poets who belong to the Elizabethan revival those who won any considerable success in the theatre are noticed in the next chapter. The rest may be considered here. Of these the least in merit but personally closest to Beddoes was Bryan Waller Procter [14] (1787-1874), who wrote under the pen-name of "Barry Cornwall." He is a link between Shelley's generation [15] and the Victorians, for he was a friend of Browning and a recipient of Swinburne's homage. Procter began with *Dramatic Scenes* (1819), limpid little pieces, one of which is on the story in the *Decameron* which Tennyson afterwards dramatized in *The Falcon*. A tragedy, *Mirandola* (1821), was a success at Covent Garden rather because of its striking theme—the marriage of a father to his son's betrothed—than for any distinction of style or technique. It is obviously patterned upon Massinger, but in it the wine of the old drama is diluted to a feeble draught. Procter's contemporary fame rested upon his *English Songs* (1832)—of the sea and of love and of the jolly life. Some of them are faintly Shelleyan, others obviously Tom-Moorish.

"Barry
Cornwall"

[14] *Poetical Works* (3v, 1822). There is no modern edition. — Franz Becker, *B. W. Procter* (Vienna, 1911).
[15] He and Beddoes helped to bear the cost of printing Shelley's *Posthumous Poems*.

Charles Jeremiah Wells [16] (1800-1879), another link between the genera- *Wells* tions, was in youth a friend of Keats and in old age a protégé of the Pre-Raphaelites. His *Stories after Nature* (1822), from the *Decameron,* are one more instance of the influence of Boccaccio at this time. The sprawling and grandiloquent dramatic poem, *Joseph and His Brethren* (1824), is in its prosody and more than life-size characterizations sufficiently like Marlowe's plays to resemble more nearly the plays of Marlowe's imitators. Wells could catch the large utterance of the early gods; but he could not catch the attention of the public. *Joseph* passed promptly into oblivion and its author, being possessed of a competence, to an aimless existence in France. Both were rediscovered half a century later by Rossetti and Swinburne, who persuaded the old man to permit the republication of his play. For a while *Joseph* was a touchstone of taste in Rossetti's circle. Today it is sinking into a second obscurity which it does not altogether deserve, for in it there are passages of torrential poetry, a richly laden Oriental atmosphere, and keen glimpses into human character. But it is better to dip into than to read entire; the monotony of its rhetorical splendor soon becomes a burden on the spirit.[17]

More versatile and persevering than Wells was the Irishman George *Darley* Darley [18] (1795-1846). His first volume, *The Errors of Ecstasie* [19] (1822), was neglected and is negligible save as a precursor of the "spasmodic" poetry of the mid-century. But the dramatic criticism and prose tales [20] which he contributed to *The London Magazine* attracted attention. One of his tales, *Lillian of the Vale,* he reshaped into *Sylvia, or the May Queen* (1827), a resuscitation of the fairy-lore of Shakespeare, Drayton, and Fletcher. The Lilliputian warfare of fairies and fiends over Sylvia is pleasant, but this delicate fretwork in a complicated pattern is marred by incongruous clownish jocosity. The play is scarcely more than a vehicle for some lovely songs. Darley could sing an individual melody.[21] From light Fletcherian grace he passed on to a graver style. *Nepenthe* (1836) is incoherent in its rush of words, but the tragedies, *Thomas à Becket* (1840) and *Ethelstan* (1841), have something of the sober dignity of Massinger.

Grave, high-minded, labored, and slow-moving are the "closet" dramas of

---

[16] *Joseph and His Brethren,* introduction by A. C. Swinburne (1876; World's Classics, 1908); *Stories after Nature,* ed. W. J. Linton (1891).

[17] Another "Elizabethan" of even slenderer renown is Thomas Wade (1805-1875). His drama on the Griselda-theme, *Woman's Love, or the Triumph of Patience* (1828), was a success at Covent Garden, but *The Jew of Arragon* (1830), reminiscent of Marlowe, failed. Before and after these plays Wade published volumes of lyrics and sonnets, the former Shelleyan in manner, the latter curiously Shakespearean.

[18] *Complete Poetical Works,* ed. Ramsay Colles (The Muses' Library, n.d.) — C. C. Abbott, *The Life and Letters of George Darley, Poet and Critic* (1928).

[19] This contains a strange dialogue between a Mystic and the Moon in which the Moon argues for the Golden Mean between metaphysical speculation and sensuous enjoyment.

[20] Gathered into *The Labours of Idleness* (1826). These are mainly sketches in the manner of Washington Irving.

[21] He could also recapture the tune of cavalier lyric, as he did in *It is not Beauty I Demand* which F. T. Palgrave mistook for genuine seventeenth-century work. From another of Darley's songs George Meredith seems to have taken the stanza of *Love in the Valley.*

Taylor

Sir Henry Taylor [22] (1800-1886). *Philip Van Artevelde* [23] (1834) is not a stage-play but a historical romance cast in dramatic form. Its theme is the contrast between the *vita contemplativa* and the *vita activa*. For his people's sake Artevelde dedicates himself to soul-destroying service, moving from the life of thought to that of political power, and from power to personal ambition. There is noble poetry in this work and it was for long admired by thoughtful readers. Taylor's other plays—*Isaac Comnenus* (1827), *Edwin the Fair* (1842)—are of less interest. Richard Henry Horne [24] (1803-1884) is remembered for *Orion* (1843), a poem which he called an epic but which is rather a symbolic romance, a work of overwrought and clouded imagination, not without passages of splendor. Much of Horne's intense activity went into poetic drama. *Cosmo de' Medici* (1837) is another example of the attraction of Italian themes. *The Death of Marlowe* [25] (1837) is violent and vivid. The social and literary studies in Horne's *New Spirit of the Age* [26] (1844) are written with forceful conviction and are interesting for their indications of changing taste.

Horne

Scotch Poets

Allan Cunningham [27] (1784-1842), a Scot, tried his hand at sensational drama in *Sir Marmaduke Maxwell* (1822) and other plays, but he is remembered today for the sea-chantey *A Wet Sheet and a Flowing Sea,* and for a few other lyrics. With him may be grouped two older minor poets of Scotland, Hector MacNeill (1746-1818), whose serious verse is forgotten but whose whimsical humor touched with sentiment (as in *Saw Ye My Wee Thing?*) possesses a lasting charm, and Carolina, Lady Nairne (1766-1845), whose *Land o' the Leal* was often mistakenly ascribed to Burns. Through these and other writers [28] the tradition of Scottish humor, sentiment, and loyalty to the Jacobite cause was passed down to William Edmonstoune Aytoun (1813-1865), in whose *Lays of the Scottish Cavaliers* (1848) Jacobitism received almost its last poetic expression.[29]

[22] *Works* (5v, 1883); *Autobiography* (2v, 1885); *Correspondence,* ed. Edward Dowden (1888).

[23] The preface to *Artevelde,* a defense of Wordsworth and an attack upon Byronism, arguing that reason should dominate imagination in poetry and reflection should dominate emotion, is a document of importance in the history of taste.

[24] Or Richard Hengist Horne, as he called himself. Horne had an early life of adventure in America and in Australia. In England he was a civil commissioner engaged on the problem of child labor, and in that capacity inspired Elizabeth Barrett to write *The Cry of the Children.* His correspondence with her (1839-1846) was published in 1877. She was one of his collaborators in *The New Spirit of the Age.* Horne's works range from *Judas Iscariot,* a miracle play, to *The South Sea Sisters,* a masque. He also wrote novels, travel narratives, biographies, and books for children. — E. J. Shumaker, *Bibliography* (Granville, Ohio, 1943) and a forthcoming biography.

[25] Reprinted in Marlowe's *Works,* ed. A. H. Bullen (1885), III, Appendix.

[26] In the World's Classics, introduction by Walter Jerrold (1907).

[27] Cunningham, who began life as a mason, was for many years manager of the studio of F. L. Chantrey, the sculptor. Of his prose work the *Lives of Eminent British Painters, Sculptors, and Architects* (1829-1833) is entertaining and still worth consulting. He edited Burns and *Songs of Scotland* and palmed off as genuine antiques some dialect ballads of his own composition.

[28] For example, Mrs. Anne Grant (1755-1838), the author of *O Where, Tell Me, Where Has My Highland Laddie Gone?*

[29] *Poems* (1921). Aytoun, though of a younger generation, may be noticed here. The *Lays* include the moving *Execution of Montrose* and the plangent, martial *Burial March of Dundee.* An appendix in which Aytoun crosses swords valiantly with Lord Macaulay is note-

IV

Enduring popularity for other than strictly literary reasons is assured to *The Hym-* some of the writings of the hymnodists. There is necessarily a rhetorical *nodists* rather than strictly poetical quality in the impassioned, up-surging, eminently singable, and movingly devout hymns of Reginald Heber [30] (1783-1826). *From Greenland's Icy Mountains, The Son of God Goes Forth to War*, and *Holy, Holy, Holy* are in the great tradition of dignified Anglicanism inherited from the eighteenth century. They are of slightly earlier date than most of the work mentioned in this chapter. A note of more personal devotion is heard in the equally popular hymns of James Montgomery [31] (1771-1854), such as *For Ever with the Lord* and *Hail to the Lord's Annointed*. Montgomery's reforming spirit expressed itself also in secular verse, a little in the manner of Cowper, as in his poems of protest against the employment of tiny boys as chimney-sweeps. His longer poems are forgotten. Comment upon John Keble's *The Christian Year* (1827) belongs to our account of the Oxford Movement,[32] but here it may be noted that some stanzas of the *Evening Hymn* in that collection form one of the best loved of all hymns, *Sun of my Soul, Thou Saviour Dear*. Through Heber, Montgomery, and Keble the tradition of devotional song descended from Watts, Toplady, and Cowper to the greatest of Victorian hymnodists, John Mason Neale.[33]

Connected with the Oxford Movement by personal ties was the Hispano- *Blanco* Irish poet Blanco White (1775-1841), whose reputation rests upon one great *White* sonnet, *On Night* (1829), praised by Coleridge and expressing the devout but uncertain speculations of an inquiring spirit.

The sonnet was the favorite medium of expression used by Hartley *Hartley* Coleridge [34] (1796-1849). He wrote in other forms: the idyll, the meditative *Coleridge* lyric, even the heroic couplet (in which he praised various English poets of former times); but he found his true voice—humble, penitent, and devout— within the sonnet's narrow limits. He seldom rises above a level of quiet

---

worthy. In *Firmilian . . . a Spasmodic Tragedy* (1854) Aytoun parodied and satirized tellingly Alexander Smith and Sidney Dobell at the moment when Tennyson, in *Maud*, was under the influence of these poets. See below, ch. xxvi, n. 12. The rollicking and robust fun at *Ta Fhairson* is still enjoyable. This is one of the *Ballads by Bon Gaultier* which Aytoun wrote with Theodore Martin. They were collected in 1845.

[30] *Poetical Works* (1841).

[31] *Poetical Works* (4v, 1850). — John Holland and James Everett, *Memoirs of the Life and Writings of James Montgomery* (2v, 1854).

[32] See below, ch. xviii.

[33] J. M. Neale (1818-1866) belongs to the next generation but it is appropriate to notice him in this connection. He wrote fiction, theological works, and books for young people, but is best remembered for his hymns. *Art Thou Weary?* is exceptionally beautiful and *Christian, Dost Thou See Them?* exceptionally vigorous; but the best known are *Jerusalem the Golden* and its three companion excerpts from his translation of *The Rhythm of Bernard of Morlaix on the Celestial City* (1859). According to *DNB* one-eighth of the entire contents of the original edition of *Hymns Ancient and Modern* was by Neale, original or translated. — See Eleanor A. Towle, *John Mason Neale, D. D., a Memoir* (1906).

[34] *Poems*, with a Memoir by Derwent Coleridge (2v, 1851); *Poems*, ed. Ramsay Colles (2v, 1908); *New Poems*, ed. E. L. Griggs (1942); *Letters*, ed. G. E. and E. L. Griggs (1936). — E. L. Griggs, *Hartley Coleridge. His Life and Work* (1929); Herbert Hartman, *Hartley Coleridge: Poet's Son and Poet* (1931).

competence, but on rare occasions he can be magnificent, as in the self-revelatory *Let Me Not Deem that I Was Made in Vain* and in the profoundly religious *Multum Dilexit*. His prose criticism, ranging from the early Tudors to the eighteenth century, is not unworthy of the great tradition in which he was reared. The story of the bright promise of his youth and the tragic failure of his young manhood is today better known than his poetry or criticism.

Clare   Another pathetic figure is that of John Clare [35] (1793-1864), the Northamptonshire peasant-poet, who, because of the affinity of his nature poetry to that of William H. Davies and Edward Thomas, has of late been overpraised for his sensitive descriptions of the small sights and sounds of the natural world. After an obscure youth as a ploughboy in such circumstances as the romanticists, with their confidence in the virtues of primitive man, loved to contemplate as the natural nursery of genius, Clare won sudden fame with his *Poems Descriptive of Rural Life* (1820). Other volumes—*The Village Minstrel* (1821) and *The Rural Muse* (1834)—were less well received. Clare was as "uneducated" (in Southey's phrase) [36] as Robert Bloomfield,[37] but he had in him more of the genuine poetic quality, a quality like that of the brook which in "the leafy month of June" hums "a quiet tune" to itself. As the observer of nature he descends from Thomson, Cowper, and Wordsworth; as the special poet of a particular corner of England he points forward to later regionalists. But he was ill content with the sequestered way of life of which he sang; Melancholy marked him for her own; and in later life he passed into the twilight of lunacy. The verses which he wrote in an asylum have a childlike charm for those who ignore the circumstances in which they were written and a painful interest for those who remember them. His *Last Lines* are in a different key from that characteristic of him; and their poignancy is somewhat rhetorical.

Mrs.   Women writers, very active in the field of popular fiction, produced little
Hemans   poetry at this time. Two only are of any consequence. The lofty intentions, moral purity, and generous nature of Felicia Dorothea Hemans [38] (1793-1835) attracted the large contemporary audience who praised her innumerable and exuberant poems, lyrical, narrative, dramatic, and meditative. Only once or twice, however, as in *England's Dead*, did she discipline her redundance into noble form. It has been the misfortune of this "holy spirit" (as Wordsworth called her, mourning her death) to be chiefly remembered —and then with a disdainful smile—for *Casabianca*. Even more popular

[35] *Poems*, ed. Arthur Symons (1908); *Poems*, ed. J. W. Tibble (2v, 1935); *Poems chiefly from Manuscript*, ed. Edmund Blunden and Alan Porter (1920); *Sketches in the Life of John Clare Written by Himself*, ed. Edmund Blunden (1931). — J. W. and Anne Tibble, *John Clare, a Life* (1932); M. Chaning-Pearce, "John Clare," *Hibbert Journal*, xxxix (1941). 291-298.
[36] See Southey's *Lives and Works of the Uneducated Poets*, ed. J. S. Childers (1925). This was originally the introduction to *Attempts in Verse, by John Jones, an Old Servant* (1831).
[37] The career of Robert Bloomfield (1766-1823) overlaps that of Clare, for Bloomfield's *Mayday with the Muses* appeared so late as 1823.
[38] *Poetical Works* (1914).

was Letitia Elizabeth Landon, "L.E.L.," [39] (1802-1838). Her life—gay in *"L.E.L."* its promise, tragic in its ending—has an abiding interest not found in her poetry. She supplied her public with sentiment and prettiness in the manner of the "annuals" to which she was a contributor.[40]

[39] D. E. Enfield, *L. E. L., a Mystery of the Thirties* (1928); M. M. H. Thrall, *Rebellious Fraser's* (1934), ch. IX.

[40] From the above survey many minor poets have necessarily been excluded. There is room here to mention three more. Bernard Barton (1789-1849), the Quaker poet, is better remembered as the friend and correspondent of Charles Lamb and Edward FitzGerald than as the author of feeble and ineffectual verse. Robert Pollok (1798-1827) achieved among the devout a high reputation which now seems almost inexplicable, with his pretentious apocalyptic poem in blank verse, *The Course of Time* (1827). See David Pollok, *The Life of Robert Pollok* (1843). The same public found edification and consolation in *The Omnipresence of Deity* (1828) and *Satan* (1830) by Robert Montgomery—or Gomery (1807-1855), who is now remembered as the subject of an excoriating review (1830) by Macaulay.

XV
The Drama in Decline[1]

Of the nine theatres in regular use in London at the beginning of the nineteenth century the two principal houses were soon destroyed by fire, Covent Garden in 1808 and Drury Lane in 1809. They were rebuilt. Most of the others underwent drastic alterations. The enormous growth of the city during the next four decades created a demand for places of amuse-

ment which was met by the construction of new theatres in and around London. These were more receptive to innovations than the two great houses. Forbidden to offer "legitimate" drama,[2] their managers were ingenious in providing substitutes—melodramas, burlettas, extravaganzas, farces, operettas, and other sorts of entertainment that were within the law. Machinery was elaborate; ghosts and demons rose through traps of various device; goblins and fairies floated on wires through the air. Some theatres, notably Sadler's Wells (because of its proximity to the New River), made a specialty of water-spectacles with practicable ships; the Olympic Pavilion was licensed for pantomime and equestrian acts; other houses catered to the taste for performing animals—not only dogs and horses but sometimes larger and wilder beasts. Under a thin veneer of drama these variety entertainments were often little more, and no better, than circuses.

Certain technical innovations wrought great changes. The apron, which had formerly jutted far out into the pit, continued to shrink; and as the actors retreated behind the proscenium arch, the "picture-frame" stage assumed almost its modern form. The removal of the old proscenium doors and stage-boxes widened the gap between actors and spectators. The introduction of illumination by gas afforded opportunities for effects hitherto undreamed of. Scenery was elaborate, and talented decorators and skillful machinists were employed; but because of the great cost of mounting, large numbers of sets were kept in stock, and scenes made for one play often did service in another, with a resulting incongruity which amused discriminating

---

[1] *Representative British Dramas, Victorian and Modern,* ed. M. J. Moses (1937), with introductions and bibliographies; Allardyce Nicoll, *A History of Late Eighteenth Century Drama, 1750-1800* (1927) and *A History of Early Nineteenth Century Drama, 1800-1850* (2v, 1930); John Genest, *Some Account of the English Stage* (10v, Bath, 1832); E. B. Watson, *Sheridan to Robertson: A Study of the Nineteenth-Century London Stage* (Cambridge, Mass., 1926); N. W. Sawyer, *The Comedy of Manners from Sheridan to Maugham* (Philadelphia, 1931); U. C. Nag, "The English Theatre of the Romantic Revival," *Nineteenth Century and After,* CIV (1928). 384-398; A. E. DuBois, "Shakespeare and Nineteenth-Century Drama," *ELH,* 1 (1934). 163-196.

[2] This prohibition was lifted from the Haymarket during the two summer months when Drury Lane and Covent Garden were closed. The Licensing Act was repealed in 1843.

patrons. Antiquarian research and the vogue of the historical novel encouraged a relative accuracy of costume and setting in plays on subjects from times past; and in such plays a reliance upon pageantry enabled Covent Garden and Drury Lane to compete with those minor theatres that were noted for spectacular performances. The immense size of the two licensed houses made for a robust style of acting, loudly rhetorical and dependent upon large, conventional gestures, and dictated the choice of grandiose and spectacular pieces, since quiet, austere drama was unsuited to these vast spaces.

Under the pressure of Evangelical opinion most sober and godly people *The* avoided the theatres. Patronage came from rough and disreputable elements: *Audience* the well-to-do fast set occupying the boxes; their footmen crowding the galleries; and the bullies and prostitutes disgracing the side-boxes and the lobbies. The turbulence of audiences is suggested by the obsequious requests for order found in many prologues. In the face of this unruliness the aristocracy deserted the theatres almost altogether and frequented the opera instead. Yet long before the Victorian era the decorousness of moral tone and respect for the proprieties of language in the plays offered often amounted to prudishness. The Lord Chamberlain's censorship was vigilant in condemning anything indecent or tending to bring religion into disrespect or seeming to countenance sedition. Allusions hostile to government were forbidden; but contemporary events might be dramatized provided they appealed to the emotion of patriotism.

Some of the minor theatres were run at a profit, but the two patent houses were constantly in financial difficulties. The salaries of leading actors rose steadily during the first half of the century; the pay-rolls were very large, since separate stock companies were maintained for tragedy, comedy, opera, and pantomime and were on salary even when idle; the scenery and machinery cost a great deal. The management never solved the dilemma that if they raised prices the mob raised riots [3] and if they lowered them expenses could not be met. They resorted to versions of French plays for which they paid next to nothing; since copyright was insecure there was much piracy; and the native playwrights received starvation wages. Notwithstanding these and other economies the history of Covent Garden and Drury Lane is a succession of bankruptcies and consequent changes in management.

The Romantic Period was an age of great actors. Yet the genius and *The* prestige of Kemble, Kean, and Macready were partly responsible for the *Actors* drama's decline, for the star sacrificed the other actors to his own glory, brought his own part too prominently into the limelight, and made a proper coördination of effects difficult or impossible. Old texts were often mangled to bring the principal rôle into still greater prominence. When

---

[3] The most notorious disturbance occurred in 1809 when Kemble reopened Covent Garden at advanced rates and the "O. P. riots" lasted nearly seventy nights till the old prices were restored, save for the boxes.

playwrights wrote with particular stars in view, the setting of the luminaries was apt to carry the plays into oblivion. A further consequence of the star-system was the small demand for new plays. The star's desire was to challenge comparison with his predecessors in famous rôles. A like situation obtains in opera today. In comedy and farce the talents of a remarkable line of actors (Liston, Munden, Johnstone, and others) popularized contemptible pieces which, less well acted, would have been hissed off the stage.

In general the plays produced had the least pretensions to literary merit, while those deserving the respect of people of refined taste were as a rule shut out from the theatres. Actable plays came almost entirely from ready writers with little or no artistic conscience, working for a pittance and subservient to imperious managers and stars. Yet from Gifford's *Maeviad* to Byron's prefaces to his plays there was a succession of pleas for the reform of the stage; and all the distinguished poets tried their hands at drama. Not one of them succeeded perfectly and most of them failed altogether. The dramas written by the great romanticists have therefore been noticed in connection with their other work. They never grasped the basic principle that "those who live to please must please to live." They did not cater to the public taste. Their subjects were mostly remote from contemporary interests and their style was derivative. Mistakenly, they laid their stress upon poetry at the expense of action. Naturally exuberant (not to say long-winded), they made no attempt to master the condensation and restraint required for effective drama. The self-centeredness of most of them was ill-suited to the playwright's art. It may also be that they shrank from the rude ordeal of facing the disapproval of ill-mannered audiences.

The French Revolution made no break in the continuity of English drama. Some writers, notably Thomas Holcroft, injected cautious hints of radical opinions into their plays, and others, notably Mrs. Inchbald, used their plays as vehicles for social criticism. But in general the stage was not alive to the great political issues of the age. Types of drama inherited from the previous era underwent slow change or disappeared.[4] In the last years *The* of the century, coinciding with the vogue of German romance, there was a *German* phenomenal demand for German plays. The democratic sentiments in the *Vogue* plays of the Austrian dramatist August von Kotzebue were in harmony with current sentiment, and his technical cleverness (as in *The Stranger*) went well in the theatre. Sheridan's *Pizarro* (1799) is a feeble version of Kotzebue's *Die Spanier in Peru*; and there were translations of other plays of his. Gothic romance influenced the melodramas which were in vogue before a name for them was imported from France.[5] These were spectacular

---

[4] The few belated examples of neo-classical tragedy are of no account. George Lillo's plays failed to establish domestic tragedy as a popular genre. Parallel with the beginnings of the historical novel came plays on subjects from English history but none are of consequence. Cumberland invaded the historical field once with *The Days of Yore* (1796), a drama laid in Anglo-Saxon times.

[5] The first English play to be announced as a "melo-drama" was Holcroft's *Tale of Mystery* (Covent Garden, 1802), a free version of *Coeline, ou l'enfant du mystère* by Guilbert de Pixérécourt, the chief French writer of *melodrame*. The incidental music which the etymology of the word *melodrama* implies gradually ceased to be an essential feature of the genre.

productions, gloomy and mysterious, sometimes introducing the supernatural, infused strongly with sentimental morality, and ending in accordance with "poetic justice." Typical and among the most successful of
this kind are *The Castle Spectre* (1798) by "Monk" Lewis and *The Iron
Chest* (1796) by George Colman the Younger.

Sentimental comedy continued to be popular. The veteran Richard
Cumberland (1732-1811) was active in this and in other kinds of drama.
The Wheel of Fortune (1795), one of his best plays, provided John Kemble
with the famous part of the misanthropist who cannot forget his wrongs
but learns to forgive. In the social comedies of Mrs. Elizabeth Inchbald [6]
(1753-1821)—*I'll Tell You What* (1785) and later plays—the sentimentalism
is lightened by wit and technical expertness which make her a not altogether
unworthy successor of Goldsmith and Sheridan. Sentimentalism is but one
ingredient in the plays of Thomas Holcroft [7] (1745-1809), the most considerable dramatist at the turn of the century. Holcroft owed his outstand- *Holcroft*
ing success to the practical knowledge of the theatre which he acquired
as a prompter in Dublin and member of a strolling company. In Paris
shortly before the Revolution he attended performances of Beaumarchais'
Le Mariage de Figaro [8] and absorbed the new political and social ideas.
These he expressed in guardedly general terms in his famous sensational
and sentimental drama, *The Road to Ruin* (1792), in which are shown the
inevitable disasters attendant upon gambling. Holcroft's mastery of stage
technique is demonstrated by the fact that at so late a date as 1873 a revival
of this play ran for more than a hundred nights. Other playwrights at this
time were Frederick Reynolds, author of *The Dramatist* (1793), and Thomas
Morton, author of *Speed the Plough* (1800).

Between 1800 and 1830 there was a long series of adaptations and imitations of Guilbert de Pixérécourt, followed from about 1825 till the mid-
century by versions of Eugène Scribe. From native sources came numerous
adaptations of novels, particularly those of Scott and at a later date of
Cooper, Bulwer, Ainsworth, Egan, and Dickens. Burlettas (comic pieces
with accompanying music) were sometimes founded upon Shakespeare's
plays; and how confidently the theatres could count upon familiarity with
Shakespeare is shown by the number of travesties. Farces and extravaganzas, flimsy in plot, loose in construction, and dependent upon humorous
types such as the "stage Irishman," were poured out by the hundreds down
to the mid-century. Among writers of these things may be mentioned
Edward Fitzball [9] (1792-1873), J. R. Planché (1796-1880), and Douglas
Jerrold [10] (1803-1857). In *Black-eyed Susan* (1829) Jerrold turned his early

[6] S. R. Littlewood, *Elizabeth Inchbald and her Circle* (1921), and see above, ch. VIII.

[7] V. R. Stallbaumer, "Thomas Holcroft: a Satirist in the Stream of Sentimentalism," *ELH*,
III (1936). 31-62.

[8] Holcroft's version of this was produced as *The Follies of the Day* (Drury Lane, 1784).

[9] Fitzball was successful in many genres. He specialized in nautical dramas such as *The
Floating Beacon* (1824), which ran for 140 nights, and *The Pilot* (1825), which ran for two
hundred. Among his many melodramas is *Jonathan Bradford, or the Murder at the Roadside
Inn* (1833). He also wrote opera librettos.

[10] On Jerrold's nondramatic work see ch. XVI, below.

nautical experiences to good account and won an enormous and long-lived success. Dion Boucicault [11] (1822-1890) belongs in the main to the post-Robertson period, but his first success, *London Assurance* (1841), held out, in its attempt at realism of dialogue and situation, accompanied by a more naturalistic style of acting, some promise of better things to come.

Midway between the successful plays of little or no literary value and the closet dramas by the great romanticists which were either not aimed at the theatres or else missed their mark are certain tragedies and tragi-comedies written with more literary taste than the former and more knowledge of stagecraft than the latter. In this category belong the plays of

Joanna Baillie

Joanna Baillie [12] (1762-1851), who, having been vastly overrated by Sir Walter Scott, has been somewhat underrated ever since. Her *Plays on the Passions* appeared in four series between 1798 and 1836.[13] She believed that of late the stage, in concentrating upon grand vicissitudes of fortune and startling dramatic situations, had neglected its true mission, and she would recall it to "the boundless variety of nature" by portraying in each of her plays a single ruling passion. Reducing action to a minimum and concentrating upon the exposition of motive by means of dialogue, she foreshadowed Byron's tragedies (as he recognized) and even Browning's. Her aim was a high one; but the faulty psychology inherent in her theory is ineradicable, and Hazlitt hit the mark when he said that she was "a Unitarian in poetry. With her passions are, like the French Republic, one and indivisible; they are not so in nature, or in Shakespeare." [14]

Poetic Tragedy

The triumphs of the great tragedians—the Kembles, Kean, and Miss O'Neil—encouraged in the years after 1810 the writing of poetic tragedies. Coleridge's *Remorse* was produced at Drury Lane in 1813. The large borrowings from Shakespeare in his second play, *Zapolya,* which the Drury Lane committee rejected, show how heavily the dead hand of Elizabethanism lay upon the talent of the time. Of the five tragedies by Henry Hart Milman (1791-1868) the best is *Fazio* (Covent Garden, 1816), an Italianate-Elizabethan drama of jealousy and crime. Milman's interest in biblical studies is reflected in three other plays; and his last is on the story of Anne Boleyn (1826). Richard L. Sheil [15] (1791-1851) wrote half a dozen plays, of which *The Apostate* (1817) and *Evadne* [16] (1819) are the best. James Sheridan Knowles [17] (1784-1862) had the advantage of practical experience as an actor before he won his first success with *Leo* (1810). *Virginius* (1820) provided Macready with one of his most famous parts. Other plays by Knowles are *William Tell* (1825) and *The Hunchback* (1832), which re-

[11] Townsend Walsh, *The Career of Dion Boucicault* (1915).

[12] *Dramatic and Poetical Works* (1851).—M. S. Carhart, *The Life and Work of Joanna Baillie* (New Haven, 1923).

[13] See the discourse prefixed to *Plays on the Passions,* Series I. Favorable specimens of her plays are *De Montfort* (hate) and *Ethwald* (ambition).

[14] Hazlitt, *Lectures on the English Poets; Works,* ed. Waller and Glover, V. 147.

[15] W. T. M'Cullagh, *Memoirs of Richard Lalor Sheil* (2v, 1855).

[16] *Evadne* is an amalgam of motifs from James Shirley's *The Traitor* and Massinger and Field's *The Fatal Dowry.*

[17] L. H. Meeks, *Sheridan Knowles and the Theatre of his Time* (Bloomington, Ind., 1933).

mained for a long time in the theatrical repertory. Among several plays by Mary Russell Mitford [18] (1787-1855) may be mentioned *Foscari* (1826), which challenged comparison with Byron, and *Rienzi* (1828), which had a considerable run. On a higher level are two tragedies on classical themes by Sir Thomas Noon Talfourd (1795-1854). In *Ion* (1836) and in *The Athenian Captive* (1838) there is grave dignity; but these and Talfourd's other plays did not long maintain themselves upon the stage. Brilliant and eminently actable was Edward Bulwer's [19] *Richelieu* (1839), which kept its place in the repertory down to the time of Irving. His comedy, *The Lady of Lyons* (1838), with its romantic plot won immediate and prolonged popularity. In *Money* (1840) Bulwer dealt seriously with contemporary questions and showed himself definitely a precursor not only of Robertson but of later dramatists. Most of the plays of John Westland Marston (1819-1890) are merely derivative, but in *The Patrician's Daughter* (1841) he accomplished the noteworthy feat of adapting the Elizabethan form to a modern subject.

Glancing back over the poetic drama of the first half of the century, we observe that the closer the dramatists adhered to Elizabethan models in subject, style, and technique, the further were they from the modern stage. At one end of the line are such poets as Beddoes and Wells who wrote only to be read; at the other end are Bulwer and Marston, who almost freed themselves from traditionalism. Beddoes in one of his letters passes judgment upon himself and his fellow-poets:

These reanimations are vampire-cold. Such ghosts as Marlowe, Webster &c are better dramatists, better poets, I dare say, than any contemporary of ours—but they are ghosts—the worm is in their pages. . . . With the greatest reverence for all the antiquities of the drama, I still think that we had better beget than revive—attempt to give the literature of this age an idiosyncrasy and spirit of its own and only raise a ghost to gaze on, not to live with—just now the drama is a haunted ruin.[20]

---

[18] Miss Mitford is better remembered for *Our Village* (1819), sketches of rural life, character, and scenery, suggestive of Crabbe in their wealth of homely "Dutch" detail, but genial and without Crabbe's censoriousness.

[19] On Bulwer's novels and other nondramatic work see below, ch. xxv.

[20] *Works*. ed. H. W. Donner, p. 595. The letter is of January, 1825.

XVI

The Novel Between Scott and Dickens

The *terminus a quo* of this chapter is 1814, the year of *Waverley*, but there is no precise *terminus ad quem*, for much of the fiction to be considered here appeared later than 1837, the year of *Pickwick Papers*.[1] Bulwer and Disraeli are not included, because though they began to publish before Dickens and exhibit certain characteristics of this period of transition, their activities extended over so many years and their books are so intimate a part of the Victorian scene that to treat of them at this point would be an anachronism. Peacock will be taken up first and in isolation, for his idiosyncrasies are marked, and he cannot be forced into a category. Among the other novelists of this time certain groups and lines of development are discernible. Hope, Morier, Trelawny, and Marryat have this in common, that they all draw upon their own experiences in distant lands. The historical material in Hope's and Marryat's fiction relates them to the novelists who followed the path blazed by Scott. Sir Walter's Scottish followers and successors include two men—Lockhart and Hogg—who, though active in other fields of literature besides fiction, are most conveniently disposed of here; and among the Scottish writers are two other novelists—John Galt and Susan Ferrier—who depart widely from the pattern laid down by Scott. From them we shall pass to the English writers of historical fiction, with the reminder that a part of Bulwer's work might be studied in this connection but for the reasons already given. The Irish novelists are also deeply indebted to Scott, whether they deal with the historic past of their country or apply something of his technique to their treatment of the contemporary state of Irish politics and society. But there was in them a vein of broad humor and low farce like that in the English novelists of sporting life. This group of Englishmen and the artists whose designs in color or black-and-white accompanied their "letter-press" portrayed "life in London" in a manner foretelling the advent of "Boz." In summary fashion we have thus set up a series of sign-posts along the way which we are now to travel.

---

[1] Only the specialists, and not all of them, have read all the novels of all the novelists of this period of transition. The present chapter is largely indebted to Baker, VII, chs. I-IV, and to George Saintsbury, *The English Novel* (1913), chs. VI-VII. The subject is well treated in Oliver Elton, *Survey of English Literature, 1830-1880* (1920), II, ch. XX, though Professor Elton admits that some of his facts and opinions are taken from the writings of the specialists.

I

After trying his hand at poetry and after years of indecision, Thomas *Peacock* Love Peacock[2] (1785-1866) found a comfortable berth as an official of the East India Company. The friendship of this classically-minded and sophisticated man with Shelley may have awakened in him his critical and satiric talent, for though he is not precisely an anti-romantic (as sometimes rated) and though his poems are in the current mode,[3] he was alert to the excesses and vagaries of the romantic pose. Yet two of his little novels— *Maid Marian* (1822) and *The Misfortunes of Elphin* [4] (1829)—are steeped in fantasy and in them the satire is almost mute. He is more famous for, and his peculiar flavor may be more pungently tasted in, his five other tales: *Headlong Hall* (1815), *Melincourt* (1817), *Nightmare Abbey* (1818), *Crochet Castle* (1831), and *Gryll Grange* (1860). In each of these the setting is romantic; the plot is so simple as to be almost non-existent; and the characters and their conversations are all-important. In a slightly ambiguous tribute Shelley said that Peacock's "fine wit makes such a wound, the knife is lost in it." [5] This wit is directed against fanatics and bigots, the frenetic enemies of classical serenity and the pretentious purveyors of panaceas for the ills of humanity, "perfectibilitarians, deteriorationists, statusquo-ites, phrenologists, transcendentalists, political economists, theorists in all sciences, projectors in all arts, morbid visionaries, romantic enthusiasts," and any and every sort of humbug. Peacock's method is to bring a company of such eccentrics together and let them talk. Their conversation is their undoing. Many great figures are recognizable among them: Wordsworth, Coleridge, and Southey; Byron and Shelley. The twist given to their sentiments and opinions is seldom so violent as to be mere caricature, but rather, just sufficient to make them ridiculous. The portraits of Wordsworth and Coleridge are unkind; but the song which Mr. Cypress (Byron) sings [6] is better than parody—it is triple-distilled Byronism; and Shelley was not offended by the portraits of himself. Peacock does not direct the "silvery arrows of the Comic Spirit" only against individuals; he shoots Folly wherever it flies, mocking at theories of political economy, at the newspapers, at the Gothic revival in architecture, at the movement for popular education, at reform—but also

[2] *Works,* Halliford Edition, ed. H. F. B. Brett-Smith and C. E. Jones (10v, 1924-1934), with a biography in Vol. 1; *Novels,* ed. R. B. Johnson (2v, n.d.). — Carl Van Doren, *The Life of Thomas Love Peacock* (1911); J. B. Priestley, *Thomas Love Peacock* (EML Series, 1927); Jean-Jacques Mayoux, *Un Épicurien anglais: T. L. Peacock* (Paris, 1932); George Saintsbury, "Peacock," *Essays and Papers,* II. 82-109.

[3] *Poems,* ed. R. B. Johnson (n.d.). Peacock's chief poems are *Palmyra* (1806), *The Genius of the Thames* (1810), and *Rhododaphne* (1818). *The Four Ages of Poetry* (1820) is his only important prose work outside the novel. In this paradoxical piece of whimsicality Peacock argued that poetry moves through the iron or "bardic" ages to the golden ages (represented by Homer and Shakespeare), thence to the silver ages (Virgil and the period of Dryden and Pope), and ultimately to the brazen age (his own). The essay is memorable chiefly for having called forth Shelley's *Defence of Poetry.*

[4] On the setting of *Elphin* see Herbert Wright, "The Associations of T. L. Peacock with Wales," *E&S,* XII (1926). 24-46.

[5] For Shelley's tribute to Peacock see the *Letter to Maria Gisborne,* lines 232-247.

[6] "There is a fever of the spirit," in *Nightmare Abbey,* ch. XI.

at the Tory enemies of reform. In his last book there is more urbanity, and the wit has been diluted by old age. Yet Peacock remained a singularly homogeneous writer, an epicurean humanist impatient of pretense. Something of his temper was transmitted to his son-in-law, George Meredith, and his books admirably illustrate Meredith's doctrine of "thoughtful laughter" and saving common sense.[7] Of recent years there have been signs of Peacock's influence upon contemporary novelists who portray groups of argumentative intellectuals and who use the novel-form as a vehicle for criticism and satire.[8]

II

A parallel to the historical novel was fiction dealing not with past times but with remote parts of the world. The eighteenth-century roots of Oriental exoticism were kept alive during the Romantic period by the Byronic vogue, the popularity of travel literature, and interest in the Greek

Hope

War of Independence. Thomas Hope (*c.* 1770-1831), a wealthy art collector and connoisseur who had traveled extensively in the Near East, was the author of *Anastasius, or Memoirs of a Greek* [9] (1819). This is a cross between historical and picaresque romance. Hope's failure to correlate the incidents in his tale betrays his dependence upon the note-books of his own travels, and the amount of attention paid to authentic but obscure history does not make for liveliness. The hero, a puzzling compound of profligacy and sentiment, generosity and greed, becomes involved in the Russo-Turkish war which Byron, who admired *Anastasius,* afterwards introduced into *Don Juan.*[10] There are exciting episodes and vigorous descriptions in Hope's book, but the interest is not well sustained.

Morier

Far more entertaining are two books by James Morier (1780-1849): *Hajji Baba of Ispahan* (1824) and its sequel, *Hajji Baba in London* [11] (1828). Morier, an explorer, linguist, and diplomat, made two wide journeys through the Near and Middle East.[12] Among the Persians he had close friends. He knew intimately the court etiquette, the domestic life, the bazaars, the religious beliefs, and the manners of Persia. With sympathetic understanding but with an eye for absurdities he turned this knowledge to the purposes of fiction in the two delightful books which carry on the tradition of the pseudo-Oriental *conte.* When he brings his exotic hero to London he happily combines the old literary convention of the "Foreign Visitor" with his own

[7] Meredith, however, never mentions Peacock in the *Essay on Comedy.*
[8] For example, in the novels of Aldous Huxley and, in lighter vein, in J. B. Priestley's *Adam in Moonshine.*
[9] There is no biography of Thomas Hope and no modern edition of *Anastasius.* Scott praised it along with Morier's *Hajji Baba* in the introduction to *The Talisman* (ed. 1832).
[10] See Anton Pfeiffer, *Thomas Hope's "Anastasius" und Lord Byron's "Don Juan"* (Munich, 1913).
[11] *Hajji Baba of Ispahan,* with an introduction by E. G. Browne (Blue Jade Library, n.d.); with an introduction by C. W. Stewart (World's Classics, 1923); *Hajji Baba in London* (World's Classics, 1925).
[12] Morier's *Journey through Persia* (1816) and *Second Journey* (1818) are as brightly informative as his novels.

experiences as an English official attached to the retinue of a Persian envoy to England. In later novels Morier failed to repeat the success of *Hajji Baba*.

The life of Edward John Trelawny [13] (1793-1881) bridges the long in- *Trelawny* terval between Byron and Swinburne. His *Adventures of a Younger Son* (1831) resembles Hope's and Morier's stories in its exotic scenes and its foundation in personal experience. How much there is of autobiography in it is a disputed problem. That the author was a pretty ruffianly buc- caneer is certain, and the "primitive" hatred of civilization expressed in the book is in keeping with the man; but the adventurous and amorous exploits and even the brutality are probably greatly exaggerated. It is safest to describe it as an autobiography heightened in color, with some incidents invented and many others "arranged."

Captain Frederick Marryat [14] (1792-1848) worked autobiography into *Marryat* fiction, but he was also in a sense a historical novelist, for he drew largely upon his experiences in the Mediterranean and the West Indies where he served as a naval officer from 1806 till the close of the Napoleonic Wars. He crosses history with other strains, following Smollett as a chronicler of adventures at sea, with touches of his master's Gothicism. Though he yields occasionally to the lure of the supernatural, as in *The Phantom Ship* (1839), on the theme of the Flying Dutchman, his proper vein is more realistic and there is more of comedy than of terror. Marryat draws blackguards admir- ably; he can be both coarse and gruesome; but he possessed a genuine feel- ing for the hardships and heroisms of the sailor's lot, and he used his talent effectively for the reform of naval administration and discipline. The best remembered of his books are *Midshipman Easy* (1836), a mixture of ad- venture, humor, and naval history, and *Masterman Ready* (1841), which has points of resemblance to *Robinson Crusoe*. Having descended the scale of literary values till they became "standard juveniles," these books held that place till the close of the nineteenth century when they were ousted by Stevenson's stories of adventure.

III

Of the Scottish novelists two might have been considered elsewhere in this *Lockhart* history because of the miscellaneous character of their writings. The learned, arrogant, and fastidious John Gibson Lockhart [15] (1794-1854) is known to everybody as the biographer of his father-in-law. After his early career on

[13] *The Adventures of a Younger Son*, with an introduction by Ethel C. Mayne (World's Classics, 1925); *Letters*, ed. H. B. Forman (1910); *Recollections of the Last Days of Byron and Shelley* (1858). — H. J. Massingham, *The Friend of Shelley. A Memoir of Edward John Trelawny* (1930); Margaret Armstrong, *Trelawny: a Man's Life* (1940).

[14] *Novels*, ed. R. B. Johnson (26v, 1929-1930). — Florence Marryat, *The Life and Letters of Captain Marryat* (2v, 1872); Christopher Lloyd, *Captain Marryat and the Old Navy* (1939); Michael Sadleir, "Captain Marryat, a Portrait," *London Mercury*, x (1924). 495-510.

[15] Andrew Lang, *The Life and Letters of John Gibson Lockhart* (1897); Gilbert Macbeth, *John Gibson Lockhart, a Critical Study* (Urbana, 1935); George Saintsbury, "Lockhart," *Essays and Papers*, ii. 1-30; Donald Carswell, *Scott and his Circle* (1930), pp. 216-270. For the many short contributions on Lockhart and his circle by A. L. Strout see the annual bibliographies in *PMLA*.

the staff, of *Blackwood's,* where his malicious satire and cruel reviews earned for him the sobriquet of "the Scorpion," he was for long editor of *The Quarterly Review* and an influence in criticism and scholarship.[16] His original verse and translations are nearly forgotten.[17] The deft characterizations of Edinburgh types in *Peter's Letters to his Kinfolk* (1819) exhibited some of the talents of a novelist; but his *Valerius* (1821), in which he tried to use Scott's technique in a romance of ancient Rome, is a·failure. The short novel *Adam Blair* (1822), the story of a Calvinistic minister who is guilty of adultery, is memorable for its anticipation of the theme of Hawthorne's *Scarlet Letter.*[18] *Matthew Wald* (1824), a powerful study of mental and moral degradation, owes something to William Godwin's fiction and resembles Hogg's *Justified Sinner* which appeared in the same year.

Hogg   James Hogg, "the Ettrick Shepherd" [19] (1770-1835), had published much verse before he made his name with *The Queen's Wake* (1813), a collection of narrative poems supposedly sung before Mary Stuart by rival poets in whom are recognizably mirrored Hogg himself and his contemporaries. The charming "frame," the ballad of *The Witch of Fife,* and the lovely other-worldliness of *Kilmeny* compensate for the poor quality of the other pieces. In *The Poetic Mirror*[20] (1816) Hogg imitated and parodied the "Living Bards of Britain," but succeeded in revealing his own vanity more clearly than his victims' shortcomings. Hogg is better in the lyric than in poems of ambitious length; his *Skylark* and *When the Kye Comes Hame* live in the anthologies. His efforts to rival Scott in the field of historical fiction need not be mentioned; but *The Private Memoirs and Confessions of a Justified Sinner* [21] (1824) is still not only readable but read. It is at once a satire on the unco guid, a powerful example of the macabre fiction with which the *Blackwood's* group supplied their public, and a strange re-creation of the Faust story in an Edinburgh setting in a period not long after that of *Old Mortality.* The fact that it has more coherence than most of Hogg's writings led George Saintsbury to suspect that Lockhart had a hand in it; [22] but Saintsbury's arguments have not carried conviction.

Galt   John Galt [23] (1779-1839), a man widely experienced in business and travel, success and failure, was scarcely at all influenced by Scott and much by Smollett. *The Ayrshire Legatee* (1820) is a satiric sketch in letter-form

---

[16] As a critic Lockhart wrote much on modern foreign literatures and paid special attention to Spanish culture and antiquities.

[17] Some of Lockhart's original verse is serious and sentimental, but his best piece is *The Mad Banker of Amsterdam* (1818-1819) , a serio-comic poem in *ottava rima,* following Tennant and Frere and immediately contemporary with Byron's *Beppo.*

[18] See Henry James's comparison of the two in his *Hawthorne* (EML Series), pp. 114-117.

[19] Edith C. Batho, *The Ettrick Shepherd* (1927); Donald Carswell, *Scott and his Circle* (1930), pp. 171-215; A. L. Strout, "The *Noctes Ambrosianae* and James Hogg," *RES,* XIII (1937). 46-63; 177-189; A. L. Strout, *The Life and Letters of James Hogg* (Vol. I, Lubbock, Texas, 1947).

[20] Ed. T. Earle Welby (1929).

[21] Ed. T. Earle Welby (1924).

[22] George Saintsbury, "Hogg," *Essays and Papers,* I. 49-51.

[23] *Works,* ed. D. S. Medrum and William Roughhead (10v, Edinburgh, 1936). — J. W. Aberdein, *John Galt* (1936); F. H. Lyell, *A Study of the Novels of John Galt* (Princeton, 1942).

closely modeled upon *Humphry Clinker*. *Annals of the Parish* (1821) displays powerfully though coarsely drawn types of the new industrialists; *The Provost* (1822) is the story of a self-made man in the period of the industrial revolution; and *The Entail* (1823) covers the fortunes of a family through three generations. These are all of value to the social historian and are precursors of an important kind of Victorian fiction. Later Galt wrote too much and sometimes condescended to Gothic supernaturalism which was uncongenial to his broad comedy and hard realism. His biography of Byron (1830) is the shrewdest of all early portraits of the poet; and his *Autobiography* (1833) is also noteworthy. Another descendant from Smollett was Michael Scott (1789-1835) whose *Tom Cringle's Log* (1833) and *The Cruise of the Midge* (1834), based on personal experiences in the West Indies, contain nautical adventures, sensational incidents, and grotesque characterizations in the manner of *Roderick Random*. Susan Edmonstone Ferrier [24] (1782-1854) is in the line from Fanny Burney on a much lower level than Jane Austen. The best of her three novels is *Marriage* (1818) in which the union of an English girl and a Highlander brings out the contrast between two modes of life. *The Inheritance* (1824) is on the old theme of the changeling who turns out to be the rightful heir. Miss Ferrier's good-natured satire tends toward caricature. The identifiable pen-portraits of real people in her books were a factor in their success.

In the generation after Scott two English writers shared with Bulwer the field of historical fiction. G. P. R. James [25] (1801-1860), who began under Sir Walter's auspices and was finished by Thackeray's satire,[26] was a prolific writer in this kind. Among his subjects are Cardinal Richelieu, Henry of Navarre, and Monmouth's rebellion. Till the middle of the century he was enormously popular, a rival of both Dickens and Thackeray. He remains an interesting figure but his books are no longer read. In style he is pompous and frigid; he has no humor or talent for characterization; his conventional characters are involved in webs of intrigue every strand of which James painstakingly disentangles, leaving no smallest knot for the reader's intelligence to untie. The works of William Harrison Ainsworth [27] (1805-1882) are of more lasting interest. Beginning with old-fashioned Gothic stories, he turned out a long series of pseudo-historical romances of which *The Tower of London* (1840), *Old Saint Paul's* (1841), *Windsor Castle* (1843), and *The Lancashire Witches* (1849) are the best. On a ground of solid

Michael Scott

Susan Ferrier

G. P. R. James

Ainsworth

[24] *Novels*, ed. R. B. Johnson (6v, 1894); *Memoirs and Correspondence*, ed. J. A. Doyle (1898).

[25] S. M. Ellis, *The Solitary Horseman: G. P. R. James* (1927). Many of James's stories open with a solitary horseman crossing a dark and desolate landscape; hence the title of this biography. On James, Lever, and Marryat see Lionel Stevenson, "The Novelist as Fortune-Hunter," *Virginia Quar. Rev.*, XIII (1937). 376-390. — On the historical novel after Scott there is material in H. Butterfield, *The Historical Novel* (1924) and A. T. Sheppard, *The Art and Practice of Historical Fiction* (1930).

[26] The tricks of James's manner are caught in *Barbazure*, the cleverest of Thackeray's *Novels by Eminent Hands*.

[27] S. M. Ellis, *William Harrison Ainsworth and his Friends* (2v, 1911); Harold Locke, *Bibliographical Catalogue of . . . Ainsworth* (1925).

antiquarianism Ainsworth applied "local color" thickly, touching it off with sentiment, rhetoric, and horror. The horrific has proved to be his most memorable note; and with the help of Cruikshank's illustrations there are episodes in *The Tower of London* which may still provoke a shudder.

IV

Irish Novelists

Only the most important of the Irish novelists can be brought within our survey.[28] They followed not the lead of Miss Edgeworth but that of Scott, finding in the struggles of Ireland with England and of Catholic Ireland with the Protestant North, and in the relationship of landlord with tenant, materials which could be treated in a fashion analogous to that which Scott used in his stories of border warfare. After the Act of Union (1798) fiction was employed in Ireland as an instrument of political agitation. The "stage Irishman" of the English tradition appears in some novels, but in general there was an honest effort to picture the land, the people, and the problems realistically. As a part of the regional atmosphere much of this fiction introduces Celtic superstitions of fairies, leprechauns, and similar sprites.[29] Social themes are generally treated in a bitterly controversial and polemical spirit. The brothers Banim—Michael (1796-1874) and John (1798-1842)— proposed to "insinuate through fiction the causes of discontent" and to show how discontent leads to crime. Often they point the contrast between the lives of the gentry and the lives of the peasants. But they wasted their talents upon melodrama and ghastly criminality. The three series of their *Tales by the O'Hara Family* (1825-1829) have to do with outlawry, the cruel suppression of sedition, and Celtic superstitions. John Banim's *The Boyne Water* (1826) challenges Scott directly. In this story of William III's suppression of the Irish supporters of James II there is so much careful history that much of the narrative is not fictitious at all. The most powerful of the Irish writers was William Carleton[30] (1794-1869). His many stories of peasant life are too long drawn out and have in them a superfluity of coarse humor, rollicking, and buffoonery. But he had a gift for lively dialogue, intimate knowledge of Irish folk-beliefs, and an awareness of the various causes and expressions of discontent—the miseries of famine and typhus, the cruelties of eviction, the callousness of absentee landlords, the

Michael and John Banim

Carleton

---

[28] H. S. Krans, *Irish Life in Irish Fiction* (1903); Father S. J. Brown, *Ireland in Fiction* (1916); and for the further background Fritz Mezger, *Der Ire in der englischen Literatur bis zum Angang des 19. Jahrhunderts* (Leipzig, 1929). — Three lesser Irish novelists may be mentioned. Sydney, Lady Morgan (1775-1859) won her greatest success with *The Wild Irish Girl* (1806). William Hamilton Maxwell (1792-1850), parson and sportsman, wrote many sketches and untidy tales of a kind better represented by the work of Lever. Gerald Griffin (1803-1840), poet, dramatist, and folklorist, as well as novelist, dealt with the lives of fishermen and smugglers, with feuds, and with the clash of peasantry and gentlefolk. From his novel, *The Collegians* (1828), Dion Boucicault made his famous melodrama, *The Colleen Bawn*. On these and other Irish novelists see Baker, VII (1936), ch. I.

[29] This element brings Irish fiction close to the records of the folklorists, and consequently at this point may be mentioned Thomas Crofton Croker (1798-1834) whose *Fairy Legends of the South of Ireland* (1825) was the precursor of a large literature on such subjects.

[30] *Stories of Irish Life* (new ed., 1936). — D. J. Donoghue, *The Life of William Carleton* (2v, 1896); Rose Shaw, *Carleton's Country* (1930).

secret societies, the "Peep o' Day Boys," and the ruffians bred by social distress. Samuel Lover (1797-1868), who, like his friend Tom Moore, wrote *Lover* songs and sang them sweetly, is a more trivial figure than Carleton. *Handy Andy* (1842) and his other books are in the main farcical and burlesque, depending too much upon high jinks and broad jokes to retain lasting esteem. Charles Lever [31] (1806-1872) had a more varied talent. Belonging *Lever* to the gentry and of half-English blood, he looked at the peasantry from outside and from above. He began with *The Confessions of Harry Lorrequer* [32] (1839) and other farragoes of military and sporting life, wenching and drinking, in the tradition of the old jest-books and the picaresque; but in *Charles O'Malley, the Irish Dragoon* (1841), along with realistic or farcical pictures of high and low society in Ireland, there is a good deal of history, for the hero goes through the Peninsular and Waterloo campaigns. In later books Lever became more serious, facing the problems of poverty, the decline of great estates, and the misery of the peasants.

The noisy farce of Lover and Lever and their scenes of sporting life connect them with a contemporary group in England. Pierce Egan (1772-1849) *Egan* is now remembered chiefly for the color-plates which illustrate his *Life in London* (1821-1828), vivid evocations of the rough vitality of the Regency and reign of George IV. With buffoonery in the manner of the jest-books and coney-catching pamphlets of an earlier age he mixed scandalous gossip and libelous caricatures of actual people of the day. He held up the well-to-do, flashy sporting set to the mingled admiration, envy, and emulation of the masses. Theodore Hook [33] (1788-1841) lies on the borderland between *Hook* literature and journalism. His scandalous newspaper, *John Bull*, was conducted with much vigor and an entire lack of principle. His novels mixed practical jocosity with libelous gossip and were dangerous at the time but are unreadable today save by historians who discover in their coarse realism a presage of Dickens without Dickens' humanity. Robert S. Surtees [34] (1803- *Surtees* 1864) has retained a specialized renown as the annalist of the hunting field which he depicted in *Handley Cross* (1843), *Mr. Sponge's Sporting Tour* (1853), and many other books. But Surtees' view is broader than that of his fox-hunters; he chronicled all sorts of amusements, not always without satiric intent. Samuel Warren (1807-1877) contributed to *Blackwood's* a *Warren* series of powerful short stories which he gathered together as *Passages from the Diary of a Late Physician* (1838). The ghoulish horrors of these pieces are in "Maga's" tradition but they are combined with realistic pictures of degraded life. Warren's *Ten Thousand a Year* (1841) is rough satire, farcical

[31] *Novels* (37v, 1897-1899). — W. J. Fitzpatrick, *The Life of Charles Lever* (1884); Edmund Downey, *Charles Lever: His Life in his Letters* (2v, 1906); Lionel Stevenson, *Dr. Quicksilver: the Life of Charles Lever* (1939).
[32] Reprinted in the Nelson Classics (1937).
[33] M. F. Brightfield, *Theodore Hook and his Novels* (Cambridge, Mass., 1928).
[34] E. D. Cummings, *Robert Smith Surtees, Creator of Jorrocks* (1924); A. Steel, *Jorrocks' England* (1932); Frederick Watson, *The Life of R. S. Surtees* (1933) and *R. S. Surtees, a Critical Study* (1933). One of the most typical of Surtees' books, *Hillingdon Hall*, has been reprinted with an introduction by Siegfried Sassoon (1931). — On the novel of hunting and sporting life see Harvey Darton, *From Surtees to Sassoon* (1931).

humor, and squalid melodrama, a portrayal of dishonesty, greed, and imposture. It was one of the most popular novels of the period, and for those who can stomach its crude pathos, too obvious moralizing, and other extravagances it is readable for the sake of its swiftly moving plot. Lastly, the tradition that Douglas Jerrold [35] (1803-1857) was a great humorist is still alive, though most of his jokes are forgotten. His *Mrs. Caudle's Curtain Lectures* (1846) helped to establish the popularity of *Punch*.[36]

Jerrold

[35] *Works*, with an introductory memoir by Jerrold's son (4v, n.d.).

[36] Two women-novelists wrote on fashionable life: Mrs. Catherine Gore (1799-1861) and Mrs. Frances Trollope (1780-1863). On the latter see below, ch. xxiv, n. 8. On the "fashionable novel" of the period see M. W. Rosa, *The Silver Fork School* (1936).

XVII
The Background: 1832-1868
The Progress of Reform

The precisian may limit the Victorian period to the years between the Queen's accession in 1837 and her death in 1901, but a new era really began with the passage of the Reform Bill in 1832 and closed at the end of the Boer War in 1902. The seven decades between these two dates are often divided into three phases of national life, what is called the "Mid-Victorian" period being considered as embracing the years 1855 to 1879 from the ascendency of Palmerston to the great economic depression. For our purposes, however, it is more convenient to recognize but two divisions—"Early" and "Late"—of almost exactly equal length. According to this scheme the Early Victorian period extends from the Reform Bill of 1832, which coincides with the death of Scott, the definite emergence of Carlyle, and the publication of Tennyson's first significant volume, to the formation of Gladstone's first administration in 1868, the year which saw the climax of Browning's career with the appearance of *The Ring and the Book* and of Morris's with *The Earthly Paradise*. Of the thirty-six years to be surveyed in this chapter the first fourteen were filled with unrest, alarm, and misery, and they contrast with the growing prosperity and general good feeling of the succeeding twenty-two years when England, having committed herself to industrialism and free trade, became for a time "the workshop of the world."[1]

Of purely political history little more than a reminder is needed here. The rearrangement of the old Whig and Tory groups which resulted in the modern Liberal and Conservative parties is of small significance for the student of literature. Party intrigues provided material for such writers of

[1] E. L. Woodward, *The Age of Reform 1815-1870* (1938); G. M. Trevelyan, *History of England* (1926), Book VI, ch. II, and *English Social History* (1942), ch. XVII; Gilbert Slater, *The Making of Modern England* (rev. ed., 1915), chs. VII-XVII; Elie Halévy, *Histoire du peuple anglais au dix-neuvième siècle* (1923; English trans., 1924-1927) had reached the year 1841 before the author's death; H. W. C. Davis, *The Age of Grey and Peel* (1929); F. E. Gillespie, *Labor and Politics in England, 1850-1867* (1927); S. Maccoby, *English Radicalism 1832-1852* (1935); M. Hovell, *The Chartist Movement* (1918); J. L. and B. Hammond, *The Age of the Chartists* (1930); G. D. H. Cole, *Chartist Portraits* (1941); R. J. Conklin, *Thomas Cooper the Chartist* (1935); C. R. Fay, *Life and Labor in the Nineteenth Century* (1920) and *The Corn Laws and Social England* (1932). An elaborate survey of many phases of the life and activities and tastes of the period, by a corps of experts, is *Early Victorian England*, ed. G. M. Young (2v, 1934). The final chapter, by the editor, is reprinted, expanded to cover the entire period to 1901, in *Victorian England: Portrait of an Age* (1936). A. L. Hayward, *The Days of Dickens: a Glance at Some Aspects of Victorian Life in London* (1926) is in popular vein but informative and supplied with an abundance of illustrations.

memoirs as Creevey [2] and Greville [3] and for a kind of fiction revived by Disraeli and carried on by Trollope—the political novel. But Carlyle, Ruskin, and other writers who were concerned with the pressing social problems of the time viewed with scornful impatience the parliamentary see-saw of "Ins" and "Outs." Postponing to the next two chapters the subject of the religious revival and the repercussions of evolutionary speculation, we shall here summarize the history of the progress of reform. The awakened social conscience is, it is safe to say, the predominant theme in Early Victorian literature. But first we must have in mind the most important changes in administrations.

Whigs vs. *Conservatives*
The Whigs under Melbourne kept office till 1841 when they were succeeded by Sir Robert Peel's Conservative ministry. Peel, who in the "manifesto" to his constituents at Tamworth (1834) had accepted parliamentary reform as a *fait accompli,* had amalgamated the *disjecta membra* of the old Tory party with certain of the Whig oligarchs into the new Conservative party. His conversion to the principle of free trade, of which the sweeping reduction in tariffs in 1842 was a sign, was completed with the repeal of the Corn Laws in 1846. This act, with which the history of "modern" England is sometimes considered to begin, split the Conservatives into protectionists and Peelites. The former group found a nominal leader in the Earl of Derby [4] but their real new leader was Benjamin Disraeli. The cynical opportunism which was part of Disraeli's character as a politician was evinced when within a short time of his denunciation of Peel as a betrayer of party principles he admitted that the issue of protection was "dead and damned." The Peelites, of whom Gladstone was the greatest, presently coöperated with the Whigs and ultimately formed the core of the modern Liberal party. Peel's downfall and the division in the ranks of the Conservatives led to the administration (1846-1852) of the arch-Whig, Lord John Russell,[5] which, after a brief interim under Derby, was succeeded by Aberdeen's coalition of Whigs and Peelites. The inefficient conduct of the Crimean War (1854-1855) forced Aberdeen's resignation and the Palmerstonian era began, to continue, with the short interruption of Derby's second ministry, till Palmerston's death in 1865. Russell then became prime minister again and brought in a bill for the further extension of the franchise. The defection of some of his Whig supporters ("the Adullamites") led to the rejection of this measure and Russell resigned. Derby's third administration was formed,

---

[2] Thomas Creevey (1768-1838) belongs in the main to an earlier period, but many of his most vivid impressions are of the eighteen-thirties. See *The Creevey Papers: a Selection from the Correspondence and Diaries of the late Thomas Creevey,* ed. Sir Herbert Maxwell (2v, 1903).

[3] Charles Cavendish Fulke Greville (1794-1865) belonged to the world of high society, fashion, and sport. As secretary of the Privy Council he had unrivaled opportunities for many years to possess himself of information and gossip. His diaries, parts of them in short-hand, cover the years 1815-1860. — *The Greville Memoirs,* ed. Lytton Strachey and Roger Fulford (8v, 1938). *The Greville Diary, Including Passages Hitherto Withheld from Publication,* ed. P. W. Wilson (2v, 1927), is a selection only.

[4] As a scholarly poet Derby is remembered for his translation of the *Iliad* (1864).

[5] Lord John Russell (1792-1878), afterwards first Earl Russell, wrote, besides stories and essays which are now forgotten, a biography of Charles James Fox (1859-1866).

and Disraeli, as leader of the House of Commons, introduced a suffrage act in some respects more far-reaching than that which had just been defeated. Thus the Conservatives "dished the Whigs" with the Reform Bill of 1867 which Disraeli in a famous phrase called "the leap in the dark" and which Carlyle called "shooting Niagara." After Derby's resignation in 1868 Disraeli was prime minister for a few months, but in the general election of that year the Conservatives were driven from office—largely by the votes of the very classes whom they had just enfranchised—and Gladstone's first ministry, the high tide of English Liberalism, began.

With this brief outline in mind, we may now turn back to the eighteen-thirties to consider the progress of social reform. For want of firm leadership and a sound financial policy the large Whig majority under Melbourne gradually disintegrated. It bought the unreliable support of the Irish members of Parliament (led by Daniel O'Connell) with palliative measures which did not meet the chronic distress in Ireland. Consequently the dismal round of concession and coercion continued in the government of that country. The most important immediate legislative accomplishment of the reformed Parliament was the emancipation of slaves in British dominions. This triumph (1833) of the long struggle of the abolitionists (about which something more will be said in the next chapter) was not won without *Abolition* recalcitrance on the part of the slave-owners, especially in Jamaica, notwith- *of* standing the fact that they were compensated for their losses. The dis- *Slavery* turbance in Jamaica coincided with turbulence in Canada where the clash between the English and French races and between the dominant families and the new settlers reached the proportions almost of an insurrection. The pacific settlement of the Canadian disputes embodied in Lord Durham's famous Report (1838) became the basis of the new system of English colonial administration and of the relations between the dominions and the mother country.

The impetus of reform had other progressive results. The admission of Quakers to Parliament, with the substitution of an affirmation for the oath, was a notable advance in toleration. Steps towards the abolition of various cruel forms of sport were signs of increasing refinement and compassion. The first effective act regulating child labor in factories was passed in 1833. *Child* From the beginning of the century there had been measures to protect *Labor* orphan apprentices from merciless exploitation, but these had been easily evaded because the responsibility for inspection and enforcement had been left to the local justices of the peace. After several years of agitation in Lancashire and the West Riding of Yorkshire, a Royal Commission was appointed in 1833 which took testimony from the victims of industrial oppression and made recommendations embodied in the Factory Act of that year. This act, which applied to all the textile industries but only to them, limited the hours and kinds of child labor and provided for inspectors to enforce its provisions. Its passage was largely due to the efforts of Lord

Ashley (afterwards Earl of Shaftesbury), one of the most energetic and enlightened philanthropists of the age.

Under pressure of the Benthamite radicals in and out of Parliament the government faced the problem of pauperism. The old method of out-door relief with parochial responsibility for the indigent was often corrupt and almost always inefficient in administration. The reckoning of the amount of relief on the basis of the number of children, legitimate or illegitimate, put a premium upon improvident marriages and even upon immorality. The general tendency was to pass responsibility from parish to parish. The *The New* Poor-Law-Amendment Act of 1834 abolished out-door relief and parochial *Poor Law* responsibility. The system of workhouses which already obtained in London was applied to the whole country, contiguous parishes being amalgamated into a "union" and central control over the entire system of unions being vested in three commissioners. In lieu of the compulsory, unpaid services of citizens in the different localities, full-time salaried civil servants were employed in each workhouse. The ignorance, incapacity, and heartlessness of many of these employees moved Dickens and other writers to bitter satire; but the new policy was a change in the right direction. More broadly, the policy underlying the New Poor Law was not to help the deserving unfortunate who might be in temporary difficulties owing to illness or unemployment but to give food and shelter in the workhouses only to the absolutely destitute who would be driven to apply for it only when they had exhausted all possible means of self-support. Life in the workhouse was deliberately standardized below the meanest obtainable at the lowest wage of the independent laborer. Not until the Lancashire cotton famine during the American Civil War did it come to be realized that another criterion than mere destitution must guide relief work among the deserving poor. The failure to search out, and attempt to deal with, the causes of indigence was the fundamental fault with the legislation of 1834. Honest workmen in distress were not carried over bad times but left to shift for themselves till it was too late for anything but the workhouse. A stigma attached to poverty as such, irrespective of its causes, because of the acceptance by the governing class of the Malthusian doctrine attributing social misery to the tendency of population to increase faster than the means of subsistence. The "lower orders" were themselves to blame for breeding too abundantly. The new law, though an advance upon the old methods of dealing with pauperism, was enforced with a grim Benthamite rigidity and impersonality which caused needless suffering and humiliation. The later policy of segregating children from adults, the healthy from the diseased, and the innocent from the morally corrupt greatly improved conditions among these unfortunates. The picture in *Oliver Twist* (1838) is of the typical workhouse in the years before experience and protests introduced ameliorating modifications in the administration of the law. Hatred of the workhouse, a threat constantly hanging over the head of the laboring man, was one cause of the social unrest of the time.

The Chartist Movement sprang from "the social degradation produced by the unregulated growth of industry and by the subordination of human to commercial interests." [6] Unrestricted private enterprise, which found theoretical justification in the doctrine of laissez faire advanced by David Ricardo and the political economists of the so-called "Manchester School," made for intolerable relations between labor and capital. Until Peel reintroduced the income-tax in 1842 as a compensation for the loss of revenue from tariffs, indirect taxation bore down heavily upon the working classes. Laborers without reserve funds for hard times lived from hand to mouth at the mercy of the fluctuations in trade. The rapidly increasing population which was concentrated in London, Liverpool, Glasgow, and the new manufacturing *Social* towns of the Midlands [7] lived in circumstances of physical and moral wretch- *Conditions* edness. The "rookeries" of London and Westminster were pestiferous dens of iniquity, and a large fraction of the populations of Liverpool, Manchester, and other towns lived in crowded cellars. The lack of sanitation of even the most rudimentary kinds was scandalous—the water-supply costly, inadequate, and often contaminated; proper means for the disposal of sewage and refuse non-existent; noisome graveyards in immediate proximity to the living. The pictures of the London slums in *Oliver Twist* and of the cemetery in *Bleak House* are not the romantic exaggerations of a Gothic imagination but transcripts from actuality that can be verified. The demand for new houses was met by jerry-builders, under no control of government and guided by no city-planning, who ran up cheap and flimsy dwellings which soon fell into disrepair and became new slums. The efforts of social workers to improve sanitation were impeded by the "vested interests" of undertakers, the private water companies, the "dustmen" such as figure in *Our Mutual Friend,* and other vultures who preyed upon the public. The visitations of cholera, a pestilence closely associated with filth, in 1831, 1848, and 1853-54, at length taught the necessity of remedial action to secure pure and abundant water, proper drainage, and the closing of the old graveyards. The activities of Edwin Chadwick [8] in this field of social reform are worthy of honorable remembrance. In the next generation there were many to heed Disraeli's counsel: *Sanitas sanitatum, omnia sanitas!*

Between 1832 and 1836 a greater confidence, born of good harvests, brisk *Chartism* trade, railway building,[9] and higher wages, led to increased activity in the trade-unions. In 1836 the "London Workingmen's Association" determined to embark upon a campaign of political propaganda and drew up a

---

[6] Gilbert Slater, *The Making of Modern England* (ed. 1915), p. 214.

[7] Manchester and Birmingham were without representation till 1832 and were not incorporated till 1838. The Municipal Reform Act (1835) established a uniform system of town government throughout England. It did not, however, include London, which had its own system.

[8] Charles Kingsley drew Chadwick's portrait as Tom Thurnall in *Two Years Ago* (1857).

[9] The railway boom of 1835-1836 collapsed in 1837. There was a revival of construction in 1840 which led on to the "railway mania" of 1845. Acts of Parliament regulated the new companies. These enormous enterprises withdrew capital from other businesses but created a huge demand for labor and before long were a great source of new wealth. Armies of "navvies" (construction gangs) were familiar sights in Early Victorian times both along the rights of way and in the city terminals.

"Charter" which embodied and enlarged upon the demands in the petition of 1819. Of the six "points" in the Chartists' program, four—manhood suffrage, the removal of property qualifications for membership in the House of Commons, the payment of members, and the secret ballot—have long since become part of English law; while the two others—annual Parliaments and equal electoral districts—remain to this day unrealized. Though this program was on the face of it political, the basic purpose of the Chartists was the redress of social grievances which could, they held, be accomplished only when workingmen had representation in Parliament. There were two conflicting elements in Chartism—the men who relied upon moral suasion and those who advocated the use of threats and force. For want of possessing votes with which alone pressure could be brought upon their governors, and also for want of wise leadership, a unified purpose, and funds with which to propagandize, the movement fizzled out. A national convention of workingmen held in London to present a petition and overawe Parliament failed; the moderate men withdrew timidly, and the physical force party was easily dispersed by the authorities. This failure had much to do with Carlyle's increasing conviction that in democracy there lay no hope for radical reform. Yet Carlyle recognized in Chartism a symptom of a diseased society.[10] During the "Hungry Forties" it hung over England like a threatening cloud, while in the minds of the prosperous classes two fears were ever present—terror of pestilence and terror of a rising of the "mob." Tennyson discerned this omen of conflict between the laboring and governing classes:

> Slowly comes a hungry people, as a lion creeping nigher
> Glares at one that nods and winks behind a slowly-dying fire.[11]

The revival of Chartism in 1846-1848, when a "monster petition" of nearly two million signatures was presented to Parliament, was the last flicker of what had once threatened to become a conflagration.

The Anti-Corn Law League

Meanwhile, in contrast to the ill-managed fanaticism of this movement, had been the efficient and well-directed purposefulness of the Anti-Corn-Law League. The League had the advantages of ample funds and of guidance by Richard Cobden.[12] The repeal of the Corn Laws was only part of their larger program of freedom of trade. Even after 1832 the landed interests controlled four-fifths of the votes in the House of Commons while the industrial and commercial classes controlled but one-fifth; but the ability and influence of the latter group was out of all proportion to its numerical membership. The free traders had the further advantage that they adhered to the classical doctrine of Adam Smith and had the support of the Manchester economists. Commerce and industry opposed the tariff on cereals on grounds of self-interest because cheap bread would mean

---

[10] See especially Carlyle's *Chartism* (1839).
[11] *Locksley Hall* (published 1842 but probably written some years earlier), lines 135-136.
[12] John Morley, *The Life of Richard Cobden* (2v, 1881).

lower wages and an English market for foreign food-stuffs would enable foreign countries to pay for English manufactured goods. But these employers, among whom were multitudes whom Ruskin would have described as "thoroughly honest merchants" and who possessed stout nonconformist consciences, were actuated by other considerations, disinterested and patriotic. They were convinced that peace and friendliness among nations would be secured by freedom of trade. The League was supported not only by the mercantile class and urban labor but by many landless rural workers who were without security. It was opposed by the landed interests, both gentry and freehold farmers. An indirect result of the clash between the protectionists and the advocates of free trade was the further advance of social reform, for when the industrialists upbraided the land-owners for the low wages paid rural labor the land-owners countered with reproaches against the conditions of labor in factories and mines.[13]

As early as 1842 Peel reduced the tariff on a large number of articles. The *Repeal* failure of the potato crop and the consequent famine in Ireland in 1845 *of the* convinced him of the necessity of repeal. In 1846 an act provided that the *Corn Laws* "sliding scale" of duties on cereals should be reduced gradually till after three years a uniform duty of one shilling a bushel was to be reached. The dire consequences of repeal predicted by the protectionists did not eventuate —at least immediately. Trade expansion and higher wages, which came in part from the new markets for English manufactured goods in food-selling countries, and in part were the result of the discovery of gold in California and Australia, enabled the working classes to eat more bread, so that foreign cereals supplemented the home-grown crops and did not drive them off the market. But in the long run the revolutionary change in British fiscal policy ruined the native agriculture, especially after the building of railways in the United States opened the vast granary of the Middle West. England, predominantly industrial, found herself dependent upon supplies of food from abroad. The complacent confidence and ostentatious prosperity of the "Mid-Victorian" period show how blind the newly powerful English middle class was to the future. The European nationalistic conflicts of 1856-1870 retarded the industrial development of the Continent, and with her favorable position in advance of her neighbors England did not see that she could remain "the workshop of the world" only so long as other nations did not industrialize themselves in imitation of her. For the time prosperity brought an era of good feeling, making it possible to widen the franchise

[13] In briefest summary here are some of the most important steps in advance. In 1842 an act prohibited the employment of women and children in underground places, and this was followed in 1847-1850 by more measures of protection. In 1862 it was required that ventilation and safety devices be installed in mines. Imprisonment for debt was abolished in 1843. In 1848 came the first Public Health Act. The first society for the suppression of the liquor traffic was organized in 1853. The great Education Act of 1870 belongs to the next period, but it had tentative forerunners. These and many other measures, such as the "Baths and Wash-Houses Act," the "Housing of the Working Classes Act," and the "Free Libraries Act" were expressions of the social conscience which had been roused by philanthropists, enlightened officials, the sociological novelists, and clergymen who preached "the social implications of the Gospel."

in 1867 with but few of those forebodings of disaster which had preceded the earlier Reform Bill.

A few words only need be added on foreign affairs. Between 1832 and 1848 England, preoccupied with domestic problems, kept herself pretty much aloof from the Continent; but as one result of increasing prosperity and confidence and also of the rising tide of liberal sentiment, this attitude changed in the mid-century. Four decades of peace and the rise of a generation which remembered nothing of the horrors of the Napoleonic Wars account for the blitheness with which England plunged into the needless

The Crimean War

conflict with Russia in the Crimea (1854-1855). The unthinking emotionality of the time is reflected in Tennyson's *Maud* (1855) and in the writings of the "Spasmodic" poets. Tennyson went so far as to preach a doctrine, as incomprehensible as it is atrocious, of the purifying influence of war. It is difficult to see why he expected a struggle by a professional army in a remote Russian province to remedy social abuses at home. The course of the conflict brought England to her senses. Mismanagement in strategy, sanitation, and the organization of supply taught valuable lessons. Though the necessary reforms in army administration had to wait for the coming of Cardwell in Gladstone's ministry, the inefficiency of government was brought to light, since war is an activity which even the most extreme supporter of laissez faire cannot leave to private enterprise. The work of Florence Nightingale in the hospitals of Scutari raised permanently the public estimation of the capacity of women for professional work. The alliance with France helped to ward off a long-threatening war with that country.

England gave nothing but ineffectual moral support and sympathy—and even that only from private individuals and not officially from her government—to the Continental revolutionists of 1848. But during the Palmerston era (1855-1865) English diplomacy was exerted with such skill by playing off France and Austria against each other that without active intervention an important part was taken in the later course of the Italian Risorgimento which led to the liberation and unification of Italy. This sympathy with the aspirations of peoples struggling for national independence was eloquently expressed by Mrs. Browning, Meredith, and Swinburne. But this period of interference in Continental affairs was brought to a close with England's failure when, after threatening military intervention, she found herself unable to make good her threat to stop Prussia's raid upon Denmark in 1864. She stood meekly aside when Prussia defeated Austria in 1866 and France in 1870. Over Germany the clouds were darkening, but in England there were few to discern what the future held in store.

XVIII
The Religious Revival
and Its Expression in Literature

I

The influx of revolutionary ideas from France had the negative result *The Evan-* of strengthening the Evangelical party in the Church of England and *gelical* gradually rousing the High Church party from its long somnolence.[1] The *Party* Evangelicals were descendants of those followers of John Wesley who did not pass with the Methodists into schism but aimed to regenerate the Establishment from within. By the close of the eighteenth century they had mostly fused with the old Low Church party, whose rationalistic tendencies declined and pietism increased under the impact of Jacobinism. The Evangelicals rejected the doctrine of the Apostolic Succession, regarded the sacraments as mere "forms," and emphasized the "Protestant" position of the Church. For them personal conversion to Christ was the center of religion. Their creed rested upon the infallibility and inerrancy of the Bible as the very Word of God. Its three chief articles were the total depravity of man, the substitutionary atonement of Christ, and justification by faith. But a concern for the reform of manners had the consequence among many Evangelicals of a softening of the Calvinistic elements in their theology, so that both faith and works were recognized as essential to salvation. Their reliance upon the emotional element in religion—their "enthusiasm"—was distrusted by moderate men, but their hold upon the masses of the people was firm. By the time we reach the Victorian era Evangelical morality affected not only the great majority of middle-class people but most of the great leaders as well, whatever their doctrinal beliefs.

At the beginning of the nineteenth century the Evangelicals were an organized party within the Establishment, with a clerical center at Cam-

[1] F. W. Warre Cornish, *History of the English Church in the Nineteenth Century* (1910); H. O. Wakeman, *History of the Church of England* (6ed., 1899), chs. xix and xx; V. F. Storr, *The Development of English Theology in the Nineteenth Century* (1913) and *Freedom and Tradition: a Study of Liberal Evangelicalism* (1940); R. W. Church, *The Oxford Movement* (1891); S. L. Ollard, *A Short History of the Oxford Movement* (1915); P. M. P. Thureau-Dangin, *The English Catholic Revival in the Nineteenth Century*, trans. by Wilfred Wilberforce (2v, 1915); W. J. Warner, *The Wesleyan Movement in the Industrial Revolution* (1930); A. W. Benn, *History of English Rationalism in the Nineteenth Century* (2v, 1906); H. N. Fairchild, "Romanticism and the Religious Revival in England," *JHI*, ii (1941). 330-338; and the relevant chapters in general histories of the period. There is much material in biographies and memoirs. See also W. E. Gladstone, *Correspondence on Church and Religion*, ed. D. C. Lathbury (2v, 1910), and Lord Acton, *Letters to Mary Gladstone*, ed. Herbert Paul (1904).

bridge and another center, made up mainly of laymen, at Clapham near London—the so-called "Clapham Sect." Several of this group were members of Parliament, and through their connections with the country gentry they were able to bring pressure upon the politicians and to win the adherence of men of education, wealth, and social prestige. A leader of the community at Clapham was William Wilberforce [2] (1759-1833), the author of *A Practical View of the Prevailing Religious System of Professed Christians in the Higher and Middle Classes in this Country Contrasted with Real Christianity* (1797), which is a foundation-stone of the Religious Revival of the following half-century. Wilberforce denounced the silence of the Anglican pulpit on points of doctrine and its inculcation of mere morality. Looking upon the self-assertion of the individual (a cardinal tenet of revolutionary thought) as an offence against the Divine Unity, he was convinced of the corruption of human nature and the need for redemption through Christ. His teaching foreshadows the Tractarian Movement, for Newman, who was reared in the Evangelical milieu, did not so much alter this theology as enrich it with elements rescued from the past. The *Practical View* sets forth a rigid code of behavior in which may be detected germs of Victorian sabbatarianism. Along with Thomas Clarkson, Wilberforce conducted the campaign for the abolition of the slave trade.[3] In other fields of endeavor [4] he was close to Hannah More.

Wilberforce

Hannah More [5] (1745-1833), who in youth had moved in the circles of Johnson and Garrick and later won some reputation as a dramatist,[6] turned her vivacious common sense to the services of practical piety. Her *Estimate of the Religion of the Fashionable World* (1790) anticipates in lighter vein the conclusions of Wilberforce's *Practical View*. She assailed Jacobinism, and in a long series of ethical tracts, including the enormously popular *Coelebs in Search of a Wife* (1809), which is in the form of fiction, exposed the corrupting influences of Regency "high life." Her enthusiasm brought against her the charge of "Methodism," and she was subjected to clerical abuse; but she did not waver in her philanthropic work. Her favorite field was among the children of the poor, especially in the mining districts.

Hannah More

There were no such shining lights of energy and devotion in the old High Church party. The characteristic feature of this group was a feeble loyalty to the historic claims of the Church, to the Prayer Book, and to the sacraments. Amid social distractions their conduct of the services of the Church

The High Church Party

---

[2] R. I. and Samuel Wilberforce, *The Life of William Wilberforce* (5v, 1838).

[3] The Society for the Abolition of the Slave Trade was founded in 1787. See E. L. Griggs, *Thomas Clarkson, the Friend of Slaves* (1936) and for the background of the movement Wylie Sypher, *Guinea's Captive Kings: British Anti-Slavery Literature in the Eighteenth Century* (Chapel Hill, 1942). — *The Christian Observer*, the organ of the abolitionists, was edited by Zachary Macaulay, father of the historian.

[4] Wilberforce was an advocate of educational reform, a champion of the cause of the poor curates against the greed of the higher clergy, and one of the founders of the London Missionary Society (1795) and of the British and Foreign Bible Society (1804).

[5] Charlotte M. Yonge, *Hannah More* (1888); "Marion Harland" (pseudonym), *Hannah More* (1900).

[6] *Percy*, a tragedy (Covent Garden, 1779); *Sacred Dramas* (1782).

had degenerated into a lifeless routine. During the Whig supremacy of the Walpole era they had commanded little influence, but with the Tory dominance of the Revolutionary and Napoleonic period their authority increased. The ecclesiastical constitution of England harmonized with the political, in that power was in the control of the landed proprietors. The episcopal bench presented a solid phalanx of Tories. Church emoluments were controlled and enjoyed by aristocratic families. As in the civil administration so in the ecclesiastical, a profitable appointment was regarded as a sinecure, its duties being deputized to an underling. During the wars other careers were open to talents; but after 1815 the younger sons of great families crowded into the Church. With no sense of vocation or dedication, they regarded the ministry as they did any other profession in which they might make their way.[7] The evils of pluralities and of non-residence were scandalous. While a small privileged group of clerics were very wealthy,[8] the hard-working curates without influence lived—or starved—on pittances. The shift of populations from old centers to the new industrial towns left many of the cathedrals over-staffed and largely empty of worshipers, while in the new communities there were too few churches. Though some beneficed divines feared for their own emoluments should the ecclesiastical revenue be reapportioned to meet this need, the more disinterested clergy contemplated with alarm the free field left to the proselytizers of dissent; and defenders of political stability and the established order recognized the danger of leaving the "masses" exposed to Jacobin propaganda (as indeed they were). These considerations led to the organization of the Church Building Society (1818) and the passage of an act granting a million pounds for new churches in populous districts.[9]

Neither the Evangelicals nor the High Church party paid much heed to theological studies. There was no examination in theology for candidates for holy orders at the universities, though at Cambridge the beginnings of reform in this matter date from 1809. Only the vaguest notion existed of the biblical scholarship of Germany, where, following the earliest disintegrating analysis of the Pentateuch, the theory of a lost proto-gospel had already been advanced. The standard textbook of ethics was William Paley's *Principles of Moral and Political Philosophy* (1785) which formulated the teaching of Christ in purely utilitarian terms. The same author's *View of the Evidences of Christianity* (1794) is a notorious specimen of Low Church rationalizing. In his *Natural Theology* (1802) Paley elaborated in the light of scientific observations the argument from design which had long been prevalent, instancing the adjustments of organ to function and of organism to environment as proofs of the existence and providence of

Paley

[7] What seems to be cynicism in Jane Austen on the choice of the ministry as a profession (*Sense and Sensibility*, ch. XIX; *Pride and Prejudice*, ch. XVI) merely reflects the ordinary contemporary state of mind.
[8] For examples of the abuse of the ecclesiastical revenues see E. L. Woodward, *The Age of Reform*, pp. 489-492.
[9] On the so-called "commissioners' churches" see Kenneth Clark, *The Gothic Revival* (1928), pp. 116-119.

God. The effort of lecturers at the universities was to minimize the miraculous and sacramental elements in Christianity, while moralizing and rationalizing the contents of the Creeds.

The Broad Church Group

As yet the Broad Church group, which was more scholarly than the other two and better informed of the new criticism that was fermenting in Germany, had scarcely emerged as a separate party. Later it was to provide the leaders of the attack upon the Tractarians. Conspicuous in this group were Richard Whately [10] (1787-1863), the logician, and Thomas Arnold [11] (1795-1842), the historian. To both men the mystical element in Tractarian thought and the emotional element in Evangelicalism were alike incomprehensible. Both tended to reduce the content of Christianity to the absolute minimum of belief in the divinity of Christ; all else was, they held, a matter not of faith but of "order." To the historic claims of the Church they were indifferent. Arnold's point of view was Erastian, that is, he desired to subordinate the ecclesiastical to the secular power.

II

Ecclesiastical Reform

Three measures of reform roused the opposition of the Establishment. In 1828 the Tory ministry under Wellington, under compulsion of the Whigs, repealed the Test and Corporation Act. For many years annual acts of indemnity had rendered this oppressive law inoperative, but now dissenters were placed on a basis of legal equality with members of the Church of England. The opponents of this just and salutary reform argued that the House of Commons as the representative assembly of the Church of England could not manage ecclesiastical affairs if it were opened to nonconformists. The logical reply was disestablishment; but though this would have made the Church of England autonomous it was a remedy which most of the clergy rejected because it would entail the sacrifice of revenue and prestige. The final triumph in 1829 of the long struggle for Catholic Emancipation in Ireland was a second blow to the Establishment. Partisans, blind to the inherent justice of this act, argued that it had been forced upon England under duress. This was to a degree true, for Emancipation was intended to pacify Irish discontent which under O'Connell's leadership had threatened open war. When the Reform Parliament met in 1833 a bill was introduced for the suppression of ten Anglican bishoprics in Ireland. The measure was reasonable and just, for the number of such sees was out

[10] Whately is still remembered for his *Historic Doubts relative to Napoleon Bonaparte* (1819), a brilliant parody of the skeptical methods of critics of the Gospel history. His *Christian Evidences* (1837) was influential, widely used, and translated into many tongues. He became Archbishop of Dublin. See his *Life and Correspondence,* edited by his daughter (1864).

[11] Arnold was headmaster of Rugby (1827-1841) and professor of modern history at Oxford (1841-1842). His chief works, besides volumes of sermons, are his edition of Thucydides and his *History of Rome* (3v, 1838-1843). The influence of his character and thought upon younger men, notably his own son, Matthew Arnold, was profound. See A. P. Stanley, *The Life and Correspondence of Thomas Arnold* (1844), and for modern estimates the clever but distorted portrait in Lytton Strachey, *Eminent Victorians* (1918), pp. 205-242, and the sympathetic and just characterization in Lionel Trilling, *Matthew Arnold* (1939), pp. 39-76.

of all proportion to the non-Catholic population. But Lord Grey's frankly Erastian purpose—and Erastianism was anathema to the High Church party—was to reapportion the diocesan revenues so that they might be used in place of certain hated taxes which it was determined to abolish. In the minds of a number of devout clergymen, consulting together in the common-room of Oriel College at Oxford, the affair of the Irish bishoprics brought matters to a crisis. The "crisis," save in so far as the Irish Church Bill was an assault upon ecclesiastical property and inferentially upon the principle of Establishment, was a figment of their cloistered imagination. But it initiated the Tractarian Movement at Oxford.[12]

The initiator of the Movement was John Keble [13] (1792-1866) who had *Keble* lately returned to Oxford from a curacy in Gloucestershire. In 1827 he had published anonymously *The Christian Year*, a cycle of devotional poems which combine simple piety with a mildly Wordsworthian love of nature. In these pieces the Anglican prerogative is assumed and the emotionalism of the Evangelicals is raised to a higher and drier level. Today their senti- mental piety seems to be charged with the religiosity they were designed to combat. Keble's reputation as a poet and scholar led to his appointment as professor of poetry at Oxford in 1831. His part in the Movement will appear presently. His later life was passed in a parish near Winchester, whence his sanctity shed its influence upon a younger generation. A second member of the group was Richard Hurrell Froude (1803-1836), a brother *R. H.* of the historian. The impression of great ability made upon his friends is *Froude* scarcely substantiated by his posthumous *Remains* (1836). He was the con- necting link between Keble and John Henry Newman [14] (1801-1890). Friendship with Keble and Froude led Newman away from the Calvinistic *Newman* Evangelicanism in which he had been brought up. In 1828 he was appointed vicar of St. Mary's in Oxford, whose pulpit he was to make famous.[15] Dur- ing a sojourn for his health in Italy in 1832 he was impressed with what he termed "the polytheistic, degrading, and idolatrous Roman Catholic religion." On his voyage home he wrote *The Pillar of the Cloud*, better known as the hymn *Lead, Kindly Light*. The fourth leader of the Move- ment (which, however, he did not join actively till 1835) was Edward Bouverie Pusey [16] (1800-1882). Pusey had studied Oriental languages and *Pusey*

[12] On the environment of the Movement and of the later, liberal reaction see W. S. Knickerbocker, *Creative Oxford: Its Influence on Victorian Literature* (1925).

[13] *The Christian Year, Lyra Innocentium, and other Poems. Together with* [Keble's] *Sermon on "National Apostasy"* (1914); *Lectures on Poetry*, translated by E. K. Francis (2v, 1912). The lectures were delivered in Latin and so published (1844). — Sir John Taylor Coleridge, *A Memoir of John Keble* (1869).

[14] *The Life and Correspondence of John Henry Newman*, ed. Anne Mozley (1892); Wilfrid Ward, *The Life of John Henry Cardinal Newman* (2v, 1912); William Barry, *Newman* (1904); C. F. Harrold, *John Henry Newman* (1945); J. J. Reilly, *Newman as a Man of Letters* (1925); T. B. Kittredge, *The Influence of Newman on the Oxford Movement* (Berkeley, 1914).

[15] *Parochial and Plain Sermons*, ed. W. J. Copeland (8v, 1868), originally published in various volumes between 1834 and 1843.

[16] H. P. Liddon, J. C. Johnston, and R. J. Wilson, *The Life of Edward B. Pusey* (5v, 1893-1899). — The popular name "Puseyism" came to be attached to the Movement because the first of the *Tracts for the Times* (No. xviii) not published anonymously was from his pen.

theology at Göttingen, was in advance of most English scholars in mastery of the new biblical criticism, and was professor of Hebrew at Oxford. Like Keble, he never wavered in his allegiance to the Church of England, and after the Movement at Oxford had disintegrated he was for many years a leader of the Anglo-Catholics.

At the opening of the Oxford Assize in July, 1833, Keble preached a sermon on "National Apostasy" in which he attacked the Whig government as traitors to the Church. The passionate intolerance of this utterance created a sensation which reverberated beyond the university, and Newman and his associates, looking beyond the ephemeral political "crisis" and desiring to awaken the Church of England to a consciousness of her Catholicity, at once planned to enlarge upon Keble's appeal. The result was the

Tracts for the Times

initiation of the *Tracts for the Times* [17] (as they came later to be called). The early Tracts were generally brief notes on doctrinal, historical, liturgical, and disciplinary subjects. Later, especially when Pusey's heavy hand contributed to them, they became less personal and direct in appeal and more elaborate treatises upon theological tradition and documents. [18] From the start they were Catholic in teaching, but there was no defiant severance from the Protestant party in the Church of England till the publication of Tracts xxxviii and xli in the summer of 1834, in which Newman expounded the doctrine of the *Via Media*. Concurrently with the series were the beautiful and persuasive sermons at St. Mary's in which Newman exploited the charm of his eloquence and personality. Opposition was soon vocal and the charge of "Romanizing" was raised. In 1836 the publication of Froude's posthumous writings seemed to confirm these accusations; and in the same year the appointment of R. D. Hampden to a professorship of divinity was bitterly but unsuccessfully opposed by the Tractarians on the ground of his Arianism. Prejudice was enhanced by Newman's lectures on *The Prophetical Office of the Church, Viewed Relatively to Romanism and Popular Protestantism* [19] (1837), in which, developing further the doctrine

The "Via Media"

of the *Via Media,* he claimed for the Church of England a position midway between absolute submission to infallible authority and entire freedom of private judgment, a firm middle ground traceable unbroken back to apostolic times, free alike from the errors which had accumulated in the Church of Rome and those which owed their inception to the Reformation. In later life Newman repudiated this as a "paper theory" irreducible to practice, where, as he said, he could find no sure footing between Roman Catholicism and agnosticism. The term *Via Media* was widely misapprehended, suggesting as it did not the Golden Mean but a compromise for the sake of gaining adherents.

[17] *The Oxford Movement. Being a Selection from the Tracts for the Times,* ed. W. G. Hutchinson (1906), eighteen *Tracts,* including Nos. xxxviii and xc.

[18] As a supplement to the later Tracts, designed to make original sources available to readers who knew no Greek or Latin, Pusey, Newman, and Keble began in 1838 *The Library of the Fathers,* which, extending to forty-five volumes, was not completed till 1885.

[19] Reprinted in *The Via Media of the Anglican Church* (1877), where it occupies the whole of Vol. I.

In the next years several Tracts that were markedly Catholic in tone [20] led to the climax of the Movement. Newman argued that the two signs of Catholicity were world-wide extension and the preservation of the primitive faith intact; on the score of universality Rome could support her claim; but in view of certain of her dogmas how could she pretend to hold unaltered the Faith once for all delivered? Much later, Newman found in his "doctrine of development" the answer to this question; but in 1838 it seemed to him an irrefutable argument against the Roman position. Early in 1841 Newman issued Tract xc. He undertook to demonstrate that the Thirty-Nine Arti- *Tract XC* cles of Religion in *The Book of Common Prayer,* popularly regarded as a stronghold of Protestantism, were, though hostile to Rome, not hostile to Catholic principles; that they condemned not uses but abuses; and that they were susceptible of Catholic interpretations which would remove from the path of his disciples the stumbling-block of obligatory subscription.[21] To accomplish this it was necessary in some cases to resort to a non-natural meaning in order to wring a reluctant Catholicity from Protestant doctrines. This laid Newman open to the charge of sophistry, a charge from which he is not entirely relieved by the fact that, whether or not the Anglican divines who framed the Articles in 1563 were deliberately ambiguous,[22] long experience has shown that they can be conscientiously signed by men who hold different opinions. Tract xc occasioned a great scandal; many men who had till now favored the Movement withdrew their support; the Bishop of Oxford requested Newman to discontinue the series; and the *Tracts for the Times* came to an end.

To recount briefly the story of Newman's alienation from the Church of England is to over-simplify what he has told with incomparably subtle self-analysis.[23] Studying certain heresies of the early Church, he was struck by the fact that though possessing valid orders they were separated from the Church of Rome. Consequently valid orders, which he believed that the Anglican communion possessed, did not constitute a proof of Catholicity. The proud words of St. Augustine—*Securus judicat orbis terrarum* [24]—rang in his ears as a death knell of his loyalty to Anglicanism. Then the arrangement between England and Prussia whereby each government should alternately appoint a bishop of Jerusalem seemed to Newman an official recognition of the practical identity of Lutheranism and Anglicanism. This was a repudiation of all he stood for. He retired into lay communion, yet still hesitated upon the brink, for certain "errors" of the Roman Church

[20] Especially *On Reserve in Religious Teaching,* by Isaac Williams, Newman's curate, and *On the Catholicity of the English Church,* by Newman himself.

[21] The line of argument was not original; it had been followed by Laudian controversialists.

[22] F. D. Maitland held that the charge of deliberate ambiguity could not fairly be brought against the sixteenth-century divines. Maitland's chapter, "The Anglican Settlement," *Cambridge Modern History,* II. 550-598, should be read in connection with Tract xc.

[23] *Apologia pro Vita Sua,* Parts v and vi.

[24] "The slightest reflection would have told [Newman] that the Catholic Church of St. Augustine's time was but a small fraction of the earth's population, and was controlled by a small minority of its own members" (A. W. Benn, *English Rationalism,* I. 17-18).

The Doctrine of Development

seemed to him insurmountable. But in his "doctrine of development" he found a satisfying solution.[25] He did not argue, as is sometimes said, that new religious truths gradually develop but that men slowly grasp the complete implications of the Truth "once for all delivered to the saints." He was, in fact, opposed to the liberal Protestant conception of religion as developmental or evolutionary. His doctrine is more truly analogous to the "preformationism" of the naturalist Charles Bonnet. "The original world-plan was like a photographic roll which had been exposed but not developed. The pictures were already there potentially, so pour on the 'developer' of time and circumstance and they will come out."[26] This theory enabled Newman to accept Roman dogmas which, as he now came to hold, were implicit but not explicit in primitive Christianity. Thus his sole remaining doubt was swept away, and in October, 1845, he was received into the Roman Catholic Church.

For a long while Newman lived in loneliness, isolated from old friends and not altogether trusted by new. In 1848 he received permission to found a house of the Oratorians at Birmingham, which was his home thereafter. In 1851 he helped to organize the Catholic University of Dublin of which he was appointed Rector.[27] The Achilli trial[28] (1851-1853) helped to re-establish his prestige and public confidence in his integrity. But he was still living under a cloud when in 1864 Charles Kingsley accused him slanderously of having informed the world that "truth for its own sake" need not be, and on the whole ought not to be, "a virtue with the Roman clergy."[29]

Apologia pro Vita Sua

Newman's publication of the inconclusive exchange of letters which followed inspired Kingsley's boisterous and unconvincing attempt at a refutation, *What, then, does Dr. Newman Mean?* in reply to which Newman wrote the *Apologia pro Vita Sua*[30] (1864).

Newman's style was normally suave and urbane,[31] but at Oxford, by his own admission, he had delighted in logical fence and in the use of irony

[25] *An Essay on the Development of Christian Doctrine* (1845). — For the part played by the impetuous logician W. G. Ward, a follower of Newman who led his chief Romeward, see Ward's *Ideal of a Christian Church* (1844) and Wilfrid Ward, *William George Ward and the Oxford Movement* (1889).

[26] Woodbridge Riley, *From Myth to Reason* (1926), p. 260. — There is some irony in the fact that Newman opposed the promulgation of the dogmas of the Immaculate Conception (1854) and of Papal Infallibility (1869).

[27] The discourses which Newman delivered at Dublin, collected in *The Idea of a University* (new edition, 1903), combat the opinion that theology is not a science and therefore has no part in the curriculum and discuss the relation of theology to physical science and literature. Newman declares that science and faith inhabit separate spheres. In his novel *Callista* there is a witch who symbolizes physical science and her son is modern liberalism.

[28] On this notorious case see Wilfrid Ward, *Life of John Henry Cardinal Newman*, I, ch. x.

[29] This statement appeared in a review of J. A. Froude's *History of England* in *Macmillan's Magazine*, January, 1864.

[30] The reissue of 1865 with the passages on Kingsley omitted bore the title *History of My Religious Opinions*. The original title was afterwards restored. The edition by Wilfrid Ward (1913) contains the texts of 1864 and 1865 with the pamphlets which led up to the *Apologia* and other supplementary material.

[31] As seen not only in his sermons but in his attempts at fiction: *Loss and Gain: the Story of a Convert* (1848) and *Callista: a Sketch of the Third Century* (1856). The former contains some sharply polemical passages, but in general the suavity in these two books is a little soft and there is a strained emotionalism.

to disconcert opponents, and years of controversy had sharpened a weapon of formidable temper. But when once by means of the finest irony he had disposed of his blustering antagonist, he resumed his accustomed urbanity. His purpose in the *Apologia* was not to proselytize but to justify himself. He knew that to remove prejudice he must exhibit himself as he really was; as in the pulpit so here he relied upon his personality. *Cor ad cor loquitur.* He employed persuasion rather than syllogistic reasoning. The emotional stress under which this spiritual autobiography was composed did not distract his attention from the subtlest influences upon his long and at times almost imperceptible progress towards Rome. At the risk of wearying his readers every particle of the truth must be revealed. Candor, quiet humor, psychological insight, understatement, sudden, piercing irony—these are the qualities of a style which represents the classical tradition of confidence and repose as contrasted with the stormy romanticism of Carlyle and Ruskin. Yet at the heart of the *Apologia,* as in his most characteristic sermons, there is a sense of the mystery of existence which allies him with the romanticists.[32] Newman shows himself, as in the sermons, to be a great though quiet rhetorician; but rhetoric is never employed for its own sake. The irony is not merely destructive but has a positive argumentative value. Even those who were not convinced of the validity of his opinions were convinced of his sincerity. His reputation was henceforth secure.

With the subsidence of turmoil Newman turned to the composition of poetry of which he had written little since about 1836.[33] Warned by a physician of his precarious state of health and under a vivid apprehension of approaching death, he wrote *The Dream of Gerontius* [34] (1866), a semi-dramatic poem in which the Soul passes from the body, is borne by the Guardian Angel through the abyss, and having come to the Judgment Seat, is carried thence to Purgatory. The death bed with which the poem opens, the passing of the Soul into silence and solitude, the consciousness of the angelic presence, and the colloquy between the Soul and the Angel are rendered with a solemn dignity which makes the *Dream* one of the most moving of religious poems.

(margin note: The Dream of Gerontius)

The last decades of Newman's life were of ever-widening recognition.[35] In 1879 he was created a cardinal, with special permission (rarely granted to non-diocesans) not to reside in Rome. He died in Birmingham in 1890. On his tomb are the words: *Ex umbris et imaginibus in veritatem.*

---

[32] The sense of mystery is never of mystic intensity. P. E. More (*The Drift of Romanticism,* p. 65) remarks that Newman was unable to understand the position of the pure mystic, dependent as he was upon revelation through the Church.

[33] Newman contributed more than a hundred poems to *The British Magazine.* These, with contributions by Keble, Froude, and others, were gathered together in *Lyra Apostolica* (1836), ed. H. S. Holland and H. C. Beeching (1899). Of Newman's short pieces only a few are of great merit: *The Pillar of the Cloud, Refrigerium,* and *A Voice from Afar.*

[34] Ed. M. F. Egan (1919). Sir Edward Elgar's oratorio (1900) has maintained the fame of Newman's poem. It is likely that Newman, who was a musician and who loved every association with St. Philip Neri, had the oratorio form in mind.

[35] The last of Newman's major works is *The Grammar of Assent* (1870), an examination of the grounds of religious belief.

III

Broadly speaking, the Oxford Movement was part of the Romantic Revival. Newman himself recognized the influence of Sir Walter Scott in turning men's minds back to the Middle Ages and thus making them sympathetically receptive to Catholic dogma. The revival of Gothic architecture antedated the Tractarians and was independent of them, but Pugin was a romantic medievalist whose theory and practice were in harmony with their teaching; and as the clergy came to lay more emphasis upon proper ritualistic observance they were able to correct the technical errors of the earlier Gothicizers.[36] The Tractarians' insistence upon the principle of authority resembles the conservative reaction of the early nineteenth century from the intellectual emancipation of eighteenth-century radicalism. Their pessimistic view of this present world was a like reaction from the unlimited confidence of the perfectibilitarians. Their rejection of Reason as a guide is characteristic of romanticism; Truth for them as for the transcendentalists is above Logic. The use in Newman's sermons and in Tractarian poetry of symbols drawn from the natural world to suggest the supernatural is thoroughly romantic.

Apart from Newman's writings few of the polemical and exegetical works produced by the Tractarians are remembered today. Newman's poetry, Keble's *Christian Year,* and the hymns of John Mason Neale,[37] with three or four by Isaac Williams and F. W. Faber, make up their contribution to English poetry, though their beliefs strongly influenced Christina Rossetti, a poet of genius. More broadly, the Movement colored Tennyson's conception of the religious life of the Middle Ages and helped to shape the mood of the early poetry and painting of the Pre-Raphaelites. Of the many religious novels emanating from Tractarianism or combatting it scarcely any are readable today, though the stories of Charlotte M. Yonge once enjoyed a great vogue.[38] Less definitely it contributed something to the writings of Joseph Henry Shorthouse; and the ritualistic or ceremonial expression of High Anglicanism appealed strongly to Walter Pater. Mingled with other streams of thought and emotion the influence of Anglo-Catholicism is discernible in many other places and has been perpetuated to the present time.[39]

To Evangelicalism the Tractarians contributed little save a more reverent regard for the visible Church as the Body of Christ and a new feeling for

---

[36] On the architectural work of A. W. N. Pugin see Kenneth Clark, *The Gothic Revival,* ch. VII, and on the influence of ecclesiology upon architecture, *ibid.,* ch. VIII.

[37] On Neale see above, ch. XIV, n. 33.

[38] On Anglo-Catholic novels, Evangelical attacks on the Tractarians in the guise of fiction, and so forth see J. E. Baker, *The Novel and the Oxford Movement* (Princeton, 1932). See also Amy Cruse, *The Victorians and their Reading* (1935), chs. II and III.

[39] The student who is neither a theologian nor a liturgist may obtain an idea of the questions still at issue from A. H. T. Clarke, "The Passing of the Oxford Movement," *The Nineteenth Century and After,* LXXI (1912). 133-147, 341-346; and the rejoinder by E. G. Selwyn, "The Future of the Oxford Movement," *ibid.,* 532-546. See also H. L. Stewart, *A Century of Anglo-Catholicism* (1929). The vitality of these issues is further shown by the preoccupation with them in the writings of T. S. Eliot.

the dignity of worship. In both respects the Evangelicalism of the mid-century was different from what it had been fifty years earlier, and the difference was due to the Oxford men.

Yet there is a measure of truth in Mrs. Browning's remark that the *Tracts* **Liberal** were not "for" but "against" the times. The direction in which the winds **Theology** of doctrine were blowing is shown by the growth of the Broad Church party. This group was profoundly affected by romantic philosophy, especially as interpreted by Coleridge, and was well informed on the new discoveries of science and biblical scholarship. In the eighteen-fifties the influence of F. C. Bauer and the "Tübingen School" of biblical studies began to make itself seriously felt in England. Their recognition of a primitive Judaistic form of Christianity; the distinction which they drew between the teaching of Jesus and that of Paul; and especially their arguments against the traditional authorship of the Fourth Gospel (which they regarded as an allegorical work of the second century)—these and similar opinions permeated the thought of the Broad Churchmen. This influence is well illustrated by the career of Carlyle's friend, John Sterling; [40] but it is more significant in that it was a chief force in alienating men from the Oxford Movement. Two men are of special note because each was a brother of a leading Tractarian. Francis W. Newman [41] (1805-1897) has suffered in **F. W.** reputation from Arnold's incisive criticism of his translation of Homer; but **Newman** his spiritual history makes him a representative of the spirit of the age. The course of his renunciation of supernatural Christianity, while retaining a vague belief in a vague Divinity, is set forth in his autobiography, *Phases of Faith* (1850). James Anthony Froude (1818-1904) chose the form of semi- **J. A.** autobiographical fiction—*Shadows of the Clouds* (1847); *The Nemesis of* **Froude** *Faith* (1849)—in which to trace the stages of the disintegration of his beliefs. He had been a Tractarian and had taken orders; his final revulsion from what he regarded as the superstitions of the Anglo-Catholic revival was experienced while translating one of the Tractarian series of *The Lives of the Saints*. The reaction from childish legends diverted Froude's attention to the English Reformation, with consequences for historiography which will engage our attention in a later chapter. [42] Other latitudinarians who were conspicuous figures in the Victorian scene were F. D. Maurice [43] and H. L. Mansel. [44]

[40] See Anne K. Tuell, *John Sterling, a Representative Victorian* (1941); A. W. Benn, *English Rationalism*, I. 385-390.

[41] The account of F. W. Newman in Lionel Trilling, *Matthew Arnold* (1939), pp. 168-178, is witty but biased. His importance is stressed by Benn, *op. cit.*, II. 17-36.

[42] See below, ch. XXI.

[43] Frederick Denison Maurice (1805-1872) commanded a great personal following because of his piety and social-service work. He exerted a strong influence upon Charles Kingsley in the field of Christian Socialism.

[44] Henry L. Mansel (1820-1871), professor of philosophy at Oxford and afterwards Dean of St. Paul's, was a follower of Sir William Hamilton. His most famous work is *The Limits of Religious Thought* (1858) in which Christian apologetic is based upon agnosticism. God, in His essence, and "absolute morality" are alike beyond the reach of human knowledge. Therefore, Mansel argues, since knowledge is only relative, theological doctrines based upon human conceptions of good and evil may be accepted. Mansel was a notable stylist, combining

Timidity and a reluctance to challenge accepted beliefs kept some scholars silent and others but semi-articulate, but notwithstanding bitter hostility the "higher criticism" continued to gather force. In 1860 a group of seven writers, among whom were Benjamin Jowett, afterwards Master of Balliol, and Frederick Temple, afterwards Archbishop of Canterbury, spoke out in a manifesto entitled *Essays and Reviews*. The counsel communicated to Christians in this eloquent and courageous book was that the new discoveries in natural science and biblical scholarship should be accepted as not threatening but reinvigorating faith. One writer went so far as to commend Darwin's *Origin of Species* as "a masterly book" which would revolutionize opinion "in favor of the grand principle of the self-evolving powers of Nature." The volume made a great stir. Frederick Harrison, the Positivist, and Arthur P. Stanley, afterwards Dean of Westminster, were among its defenders; but Pusey attacked it with acrimony and circulated a declaration of belief in biblical infallibility to which no less than eleven thousand clerical signatures were obtained. The seven authors were prosecuted and condemned in the ecclesiastical court. Two years later controversy broke out afresh, when Bishop J. W. Colenso,[45] who by arithmetical methods had demonstrated "the unhistorical character of very considerable portions of the Mosaic narrative," was tried for heresy. Colenso's reputation has suffered from Matthew Arnold's supercilious ridicule. Other phases of the warfare between orthodox Christianity and science will be touched on in the next chapter.

---

effects obviously derived from the seventeenth-century divines with others echoing Newman. See George Saintsbury, *A History of English Prose Rhythm* (1912), pp. 416-420.

[45] *A Critical Examination of the Pentateuch and the Book of Joshua* (1862). See Benn, *op. cit.*, II. 135-145.

XIX

The Theory of Evolution and Its Repercussions

The concept of the Scale of Being or Ladder of Life, widely disseminated *"The Scale* in the eighteenth century,[1] influenced the speculations of evolutionists, *of Being"* though in itself it was creationist rather than evolutionary.[2] What was envisaged was not a series of events in chronological order but a sequence of hierarchies extending upwards through the stages of organized life to its culmination in man. The metaphysical implications of this concept were worked out by Schelling and other German thinkers and attracted the attention of Coleridge.[3] Buffon, Diderot, and Kant had conjectured that species have not remained unalterable through all time but that "higher" forms have been derived by natural means from "lower" forms. But for definite statements of the idea of the mutability of species we must turn to the poet-naturalist Erasmus Darwin[4] (1731-1802). The faults of Dr. Darwin's *Erasmus* poetic style are of no moment in this connection; his fame as a pioneer in *Darwin* scientific speculation is secure. His theories are set forth in the medico-

[1] A. O. Lovejoy, *The Great Chain of Being* (1936); J. W. Beach, *The Concept of Nature,* pp. 172-176. Famous allusions to the concept are in Pope, *Essay on Man,* I. 233-240; Akenside, *The Pleasures of Imagination,* first version, II. 323-350; and Thomson, *The Seasons, Summer,* lines 333-337.

[2] The present writer does not claim to speak with authority in this chapter nor to have controlled more than a fraction of the enormous literature of the subject. Works which he has found of special value are: H. F. Osborn, *From the Greeks to Darwin* (2ed., 1898), which, however, needs correction at many points; J. W. Judd, *The Coming of Evolution* (1912); S. C. Schmucker, *The Meaning of Evolution* (1916), a popular account; A. F. Shull, *Evolution* (1936), especially ch. XI; L. T. More, *The Dogma of Evolution* (1925), an impressive corrective to overconfidence; Douglas Dewar, *Difficulties of the Evolution Theory* (1931); A. M. Davies, *Evolution and its Modern Critics* (1937), in part a reply to Dewar; Julian Huxley, *Evolution: The Modern Synthesis* (1942); J. A. Thomson, *Darwinism and Human Life* (1910; 1946). See also L. J. Henkin, *Darwinism in the English Novel, 1860-1910* (1940).

[3] As Professor Beach has pointed out, Coleridge's phraseology is so ambiguous that when he writes of the efforts of "lower natures" to ascend (*Aids to Reflection; Complete Works* (ed. 1868-1871), I. 181), he might seem to be enunciating evolutionary doctrine did we not know that elsewhere he repudiated the hypothesis, branding as "absurd" the notion "of man's having progressed from an ourang-outang state—so contrary to all history, to all religion, nay, to all possibility" (*Letters,* ed. E. H. Coleridge, II. 648). — Lord Monboddo (1714-1799), in *The Origin and Progress of Language* (1773), classified man and the ourang-outang as species of the *genus Homo.* But Monboddo was a creationist; he made no suggestion of transmutation, but merely drew the line below, not above, the highest apes; and the line demarking species from species remained impassable. Thomas Love Peacock's satire in *Melincourt* (1817) keeps Monboddo in remembrance.

[4] Hesketh Pearson, *Doctor Darwin* (1930). On Darwin's *The Loves of the Plants* (1789) and *The Botanic Garden* (1791) see W. J. Courthope, *History of English poetry,* VI (1910). 33-40. See also Ernst Krause, *Erasmus Darwin und seine Stellung in der Geschichte der Descendenz-theorie* (Leipzig, 1887; translated by W. S. Dallas, 1889); and monographs by Leopold Brandl on *The Temple of Nature* and *The Botanic Garden* (Vienna, 1902 and 1909). On Darwin the poet see J. V. Logan, *The Poetry and Aesthetics of Erasmus Darwin* (Princeton, 1937).

philosophical work, *Zoönomia* (1794-1796), and in the posthumously published poem, *The Temple of Nature* (1803). From Greek and later theorists he derived his belief in the spontaneous origin of life in minute forms in the ocean. Thence came fishes, and from fishes amphibians, and finally terrestrial animals. Discerning the significance of accidental variations which are of value to the organism acquiring them, he believed that transformations were produced by the exertions of the organisms themselves, in response to pleasures and pains. These acquired forms and propensities are transmitted to posterity—a clear anticipation of the doctrine of Lamarck. Darwin described what later came to be called "the struggle for existence" but saw in it merely a check upon overcrowding, thus missing the connection between this struggle and the principle of the survival of the fittest.

Lamarck   Whether the Chevalier de Lamarck (1744-1829) knew Darwin's writings is not demonstrable but appears probable. The fame of Lamarck's work, based upon wide knowledge of botany and zoology and upon precise powers of description, obscured the speculations of his predecessor. Altered wants (*besoins*) through changes in environment lead, Lamarck holds, to altered habits, and hence to the formation of new organs and the modification or disappearance of those already existing. Organs do not give rise to habits, but habits give rise to organs. Living beings have not been created for a certain mode of life; it is the mode of life which has created the beings. Within the organism there is a "will" to adapt itself. This is the theory of appetency or of variation "definitely directed" from within. The desire for any action on the part of an animal leads to efforts to accomplish that desire; environment furnishes the stimuli for these adaptive changes; and the resultant organ and its functions can be transmitted to future generations. The crux of the conflict between the Lamarckians and the Darwinians is in this theory, for Charles Darwin held that variation is indefinite and in all directions and that with change in environment a *chance* variation may prove advantageous to the organism and is then continuously and increasingly selected. The question at issue is crisply summarized in the title of one of Samuel Butler's books: *Luck or Cunning?*

Cuvier and Catastrophism   Lamarck, who was ridiculed for the extravagances of his illustrative examples (as in his discussion of the way in which the snake lost its legs), was further discredited by the opposition of the great naturalist, George Cuvier [5] (1769-1832). Cuvier, a Catholic and creationist, opposed transmutationism. Yet his creationism, which was supposed to harmonize the evi-

---

[5] Cuvier adumbrated his theory in various earlier works before he presented it in its most extravagant form in the third edition of his *Discours sur les révolutions sur la surface du globe* (1825).Though the *Discours* was not translated into English until 1829, his views were accessible in English in his *Essay on the Theory of the Earth*, translated by Robert Kerr (1813) and stirred the imagination of Byron, who combined catastrophism with the "poetical fiction" of the pre-Adamites which he took from Beckford's *Vathek*. See *Cain*, II. ii. 130-147; *Don Juan*, IX. xxxvii-xxxviii; *Heaven and Earth*, I. iii. 40-46; and *Letters and Journals*, ed. R. E. Prothero, v. 368. — On catastrophism see further Charles Singer, *The Story of Living Things* (1931), pp. 231-232, and Erik Nordenskiöld, *The History of Biology* (1928), pp. 338-339.

dence of science with the narrative in Genesis, differed widely from the old orthodoxy. He inherited and enlarged upon the "Theory of Catastrophes" or doctrine of discontinuity, that is, of cataclysmic changes in the earth's history necessitating supernatural intervention. On the evidence of the stratification of the rocks and of the abrupt extinction of organisms as evinced by fossils it was argued that the earth had undergone a series of convulsive changes alternating with periods of calm. Cuvier himself held that after each catastrophe "such few beings as escaped have spread and propagated their kind"; but as popularized by some of his followers the theory took the extreme form that in each cataclysm all life had been destroyed and a new series of creations by God had followed. The view that at different moments in the past God interfered with natural processes, repairing the damage which He was, it would seem, unwilling or power-less to prevent, is the ignoble doctrine of "special creation" which for many years satisfied the orthodox. The advance of evolutionary theory is partly due to the quest for a tenable alternative hypothesis.

Materials for the refutation of catastrophism had been patiently assembled by the English geologists, James Hutton, John Playfair, and William Smith,[6] and the *coup de grâce* was delivered by Sir Charles Lyell (1797-1875), whose monumental *Principles of Geology* (1830) overthrew the doctrine of dis-continuity and, inferentially, of special creation. Moreover, by showing that natural causation is competent to account for the inorganic portion of our globe, Lyell raised the question why it should not also account for the living part. Thus, his uniformitarianism prepared the way for Charles Darwin; and it is significant that one of the works which Darwin studied during the voyage of the *Beagle* was Lyell's *Geology*. Lyell did not seek to explain the origin of life, but he demonstrated that geological history is one of gradual development and that the evidence of fossils supports the belief that living organisms, since their first appearance on earth, have continued to exist thereon.[7] Lyell was not a transmutationist; but his chronological sequence from lower to higher forms tended, like the hierarchic sequence of the Scale of Being, to over-emphasize progress and the idea of betterment. The Victorian evolutionists who adhered to the idealistic notion of a steady and inevitable progress towards a state of perfection were as much influ-enced by Lyell as by the philosophic perfectibilitarians.

Lyell and Uniformi-tarianism

During the three decades intervening between *The Principles of Geology* and *The Origin of Species* a number of convergent lines of argument were

---

[6] James Hutton, *Theory of the Earth* (1785; expanded, 1795); John Playfair, *Illustrations of the Huttonian Theory of the Earth* (1802); William Smith, *Order of the Strata and their embedded Organic Remains, in the Neighborhood of Bath* (1799) and *A Geological Map of England and Wales* (1815).

[7] It is now generally held that Lyell overstated his case. The modern view is that at the close of each geological era there were large redistributions of land and water which caused changes of climate with which multitudes of species were unable to cope. Some geologists now calculate that in the intense cold of the Permian period with which the Palaeozoic era closed twenty-nine out of every thirty species perished. Lyell did not make sufficient allowance for the effect of these perturbations. Moreover, he did not recognize the importance of degenera-tion, that is, of reversion to earlier modes of life.

*The Evo-
lutionary
Hypothesis*

assembled in support of the evolutionary hypothesis.[8] The general presumption of science was against "supernatural" explanations of phenomena. If astronomical and geological phenomena are shown to be the result of the operation of natural "laws,"[9] why not biological? Are we to believe that organisms fossilized in strata which have come about through natural means are themselves the result of special acts of creation? Cuvier had argued, with reservations which destroyed the validity of his contention, that no fossil species had analogues among living species. The proof to the contrary was emphasized by Chambers in 1844 and this argument from the persistence of types was a telling blow to the special creationists. The argument from homologies in vertebrates had been recognized by eighteenth-century naturalists and much new evidence along this line had been gathered by the comparative anatomists. The theory of recapitulation in stages of embryo life was pressed for as much as it was worth—or more. The existence of vestigial organs was taken as evidence of ancestral forms of independent species. The argument from the variability of existing species was advanced; but one of the most telling arguments of the anti-evolutionists (afterwards candidly recognized by Darwin) was the lack of evidence of variations so wide as to produce varieties sterile *inter se*. Such sterility is a mark of distinct species. Finally, there was the argument from the sequence of types in paleontology. The abrupt extinction of multitudes of species as we pass from one geological stratum to the next was an argument for catastrophism and special creationism. In fossils there was very little evidence of continuity. The negative argument of course does not hold, for the chances of fossilization are small and the opportunities for destruction immense. The evolutionists searched for "missing links" with the result that in later years several convincing "form-series" were discovered.[10]

Despite the force of these arguments the opinion of the majority of scientists remained creationist. Some may have believed in evolution *in petto* but they were either ambiguous in statement or else kept silent. The difficulties confronting the pious geologist who sought to reconcile the chronology deduced from the biblical narrative with the testimony of the rocks are illustrated in the writings of William Buckland (1784-1856): *Reliquiae Diluvianae* (1823) and *Geology and Mineralogy* (1836), the latter one of the famous *Bridgewater Treatises* which were designed to exhibit "the power, wisdom, and goodness of God, as manifested in the creation." When a human skeleton was discovered in strata containing the bones of "antediluvian" animals, Buckland would not accept the evidence before his eyes but argued that the skeleton was of recent date and had by accident in-

Buckland

[8] The summary which follows is condensed from A. O. Lovejoy, "The Argument for Organic Evolution before *The Origin of Species," Popular Science Monthly,* LXXV (1909). 499-514, 537-549.
[9] The Nebular Hypothesis of Laplace was widely accepted at this time. The dynamic difficulties which disposed of it in its original form were not demonstrated till 1859.
[10] The example most familiar to every visitor to our museums of natural history is that of the *Equidae.* Huxley made much of the ancestry of the horse in his address to the Geological Society in 1870.

truded into the lower level of stratification. This resort to sophistry by a scientist of repute is significant of the spiritual unease of the time. A more curious case is that of the naturalist Philip Henry Gosse, the author of *P. H.* *Omphalos: an Attempt to Untie the Geological Knot* (1857). This book's *Gosse* quaint title is taken from the problem, which had vexed Sir Thomas Browne, as to whether painters err who depict Adam and Eve with navels. Just as God—so runs Gosse's argument—actualized his *idea* of Adam and Eve when they had reached maturity but included in their forms characters from earlier stages of growth through which they had passed only in His mind, so the earth was created at the moment when, though its earlier phases had had only an ideal existence, it had reached that stage in the mind of God which is recorded in the geological evidence. "We might still speak of the inconceivably long duration of the processes in question," Gosse concedes, "provided we understand *ideal* instead of actual time—that the duration was projected in the mind of God and not really existent." [11] Gosse, who hoped to satisfy alike the believers in revelation and in scientific induction, was mortified when, far from ingratiating himself with either party, he was upbraided for picturing God as a manufacturer of false evidence. [12]

While the professional scientists temporized and the pious retreated to *Chambers* one or another untenable position, some of the poets evinced an awareness of the startling new speculations, [13] and a brilliant amateur of science spoke out boldly. In 1844 Robert Chambers (1802-1871) published anonymously *Vestiges of the Natural History of Creation*. The outcries which greeted this book are indicative of the general state of mind. [14] Though some scien-

---

[11] *Omphalos*, p. 369.

[12] For the entire episode see Edmund Gosse, *Father and Son* (1907), ch. v.

[13] Lionel Stevenson, *Darwin among the Poets* (Chicago, 1932); J. W. Beach, *The Concept of Nature*, chs. xv and xvi. — As an undergraduate at Cambridge Tennyson discerned in the Nebular Hypothesis the implications for geology and biology and advanced the theory that "the development of the human body might possibly be traced from the radiated, vermicular, molluscous, and vertebrate organisms" (*Alfred Lord Tennyson: a Memoir by his Son*, I. 44). *In Memoriam* (1850) has as its groundwork the idea of the steady upward progress of organized life; and in the memorable section cxviii the poet sketches the hypothesis that the earth began "in tracks of fluent heat," implies that man rose from "brutish forms," and expresses the belief that man is "the herald of a higher race." Yet in no poem is there a clear indication that Tennyson believed in transmutation and he certainly did not account for the presence of mind in man as due to natural evolution—as Meredith did later. In later life he held, cautiously, that "evolution in a modified form was partially true" (*Memoir*, II. 167). See W. R. Rutland, "Tennyson and the Theory of Evolution," *E&S*, xxvi (1941). 7-29. On the evolutionary passages in Browning's *Paracelsus* and *Cleon* and on his tentative admission, in *Prince Hohenstiel-Schwangau* (1871), of the theory of the genesis of the human being from lower forms, see J. W. Beach, *op. cit.*, pp. 437-447. The new ending which in 1869 Arnold supplied to *In Utrumque Paratus* (1849 or earlier) presents the view that man has grown out of the "stuff" of inorganic matter. Arnold later deleted this stanza and reverted to the original ending. See C. B. Tinker and H. F. Lowry, *The Poetry of Matthew Arnold: A Commentary* (1940), p. 55. On Beddoes and evolution see above, ch. xiv.

[14] Among various attempted refutations of Chambers—e.g., S. R. Bosanquet, *Vestiges . . . the Arguments Examined and Exposed* (1845) and T. M. Mason, *Creation by the Immediate Agency of God, as opposed to Creation by Natural Law* (1845)—the most popular and influential was Hugh Miller's *Footprints of the Creator* (1849). Here much is made of the negative evidence from the discontinuity of organisms between geological periods. Hugh Miller (1802-1856) was an enormously popular and thoroughly devout writer on geology, to which subject he had been drawn from work as a stone-mason. His careful and abundant observations won the respect of Agassiz and other scientists; the charm of his descriptions won the public. His chief books, besides the *Footprints*, are *The Old Red Sandstone* (1841) and *The*

tists were scornful of the *Vestiges* and made much of its errors of detail, Chambers had grasped firmly and stated clearly nearly all the arguments which, after 1859, were adopted by Huxley, one of his severest critics. Darwin and Spencer were more tolerant of the small mistakes for which the force of the general argument afforded ample compensation. Chambers denied that he intended to advance a system "independent or exclusive of Deity." Natural laws are "only the instruments in working out and realizing" "the original Divine conception of all the forms of being." The impulse imparted by God advances all forms of life, from lower to higher and from simpler to more complex. The consequent gap at the bottom of the scale is, Chambers seems to think, filled by continuous spontaneous generation. To the objection that the idea of man's descent from lower animals is degrading Chambers replies that this impression may be due simply to human prejudice and that in any case "it is our part to admire and to submit." [15]

Spencer   The *Vestiges* influenced the early thought of Herbert Spencer (1820-1903), who by 1850 had realized that in the absence of any third reasonable hypothesis it was necessary to choose between that of a series of special acts of creation and that of the production of species through the gradual modification of simpler forms.[16] In *The Development Hypothesis* (1852) he opposed the theory of special creation, though he offered no explanation of how development has come about. In *Progress: Its Law and Cause* (1857) he stressed the influence of changes in climate and environment upon life and argued for the development of the heterogeneous from the homogeneous. These books, like the *Vestiges,* are precursors of Darwin's *Origin of Species,* though Spencer's vast attempt to synthesize all knowledge by means of the evolutionary concept did not begin until 1862.[17]

Charles   Charles Darwin [18] (1809-1882), the grandson of Erasmus Darwin, had
Darwin   an early training in biology and geology which led to his appointment as Naturalist on the scientific expedition of the *Beagle* round South America (1831-1836). His observation of the near resemblance, but not identity, between animals of neighboring latitudes and between existing species and fossils of recent date illuminated the theories of Lamarck as discussed in Lyell's *Geology,* which Darwin studied on the voyage. After his return to England, while publishing the scientific results of the expedition,[19] he

Testimony of the Rocks (posthumous, 1857). — Chambers replied to his critics and amplified, clarified, and corrected his book in *Explanations: a Sequel to "Vestiges of the Natural History of Creation"* (1845). On the reception of *Vestiges* see Amy Cruse, *The Victorians and Their Reading,* pp. 84-90. See also Disraeli's witty satire on "The Revelations of Chaos" (i.e., the *Vestiges*) in *Tancred* (1847), Book II, ch. VIII.

[15] *Vestiges* (ed. New York, 1845), pp. 177-178.

[16] See D. Duncan, *Life and Letters of Herbert Spencer* (1908), II. 317.

[17] See below, ch. XXI.

[18] Francis Darwin, *The Life and Letters of Charles Darwin* (3v, 1887); Geoffrey West, *Charles Darwin, the Fragmentary Man* (1937).

[19] The first edition of Darwin's Diary of the voyage forms Vol. III of the official *Voyages of H. M.'s Ships Adventure and Beagle,* ed. Robert Fitzroy (1839). It was issued separately later in the same year. The definitive edition is *Charles Darwin's Diary of the Voyage of H. M. S. "Beagle,"* ed. Nora Barlow (Cambridge, 1934). The zoology and botany of the expedition were published by Darwin and assistants (8v, 1840-1846).

began an intensive study of artificial selection by breeders of domestic animals. (It needs to be remembered that much of his material was not scientifically controlled, having been derived at second-hand from pigeon-fanciers, stud-breeders, and kennel-men.) By selective breeding the fancier can produce the fan-tail or the pouter. How can nature apply such methods? That was Darwin's problem. In 1838 he read Malthus' *Essay on the Principle of Population* in which it was argued that since the food supply increases by arithmetical progression while the population increases by geometrical progression, starvation must ensue unless the population is kept down by war, vice, disease, and misery. Upon this ground of the struggle for existence Darwin erected the hypothesis that variations (however originating), if favorable to the struggle, would become emphasized; if unfavorable would lead to the extinction of the individual or type retaining them.[20] Darwin's later claim that he worked in strict accord with the Baconian method of induction is not admissible, for he had arrived at his hypothesis long before all his evidence was assembled. His method was really that of inverse deduction. Though he was as careful to note evidence against his theory as for it, there must have been some bias in favor of the hypothesis. His hesitations and modifications show that he was not absolutely satisfied. By 1844 he had advanced far enough to compose a preliminary summary. Another summary followed, and then in 1858 came the dramatic communication from Alfred Russell Wallace [21] (1823-1913) sug- *Wallace* gesting almost the same hypothesis (with minor technical differences). By a strange coincidence Wallace's hypothesis, like Darwin's, had been suggested to him by a reading of Malthus. He was also influenced by Chambers. Darwin had already confided his theory to Lyell and other friends; there was therefore no possibility of any charge of non-independence. The two men displayed the finest reciprocal magnanimity, and Wallace's essay and Darwin's summary were published together in *The Journal of the Linnean Society,* in June, 1858.

In 1859 appeared the epoch-making volume *On the Origin of Species by* On the *Means of Natural Selection, or the Preservation of Favoured Races in the* Origin of *Struggle for Life.* The arguments supporting the fact of evolution were Species already, as we have seen, assembled; what was lacking was a convincing explanation of the means whereby it was brought about.[22] Darwin denied the Lamarckian principle that there is a "necessary progression" or "prin-

[20] In 1813 W. C. Wells had advanced the theory that species originated by means of natural selection; and in 1831 Patrick Matthew arrived independently at the same opinion. But of their writings Darwin knew nothing till after the publication of his book. He then acknowledged their priority in handsome terms—terms beyond their claims since their views were based on little evidence or research.

[21] Author of *Darwinism: an Exposition of the Theory of Natural Selection* (1889); *Man's Place in the Universe* (1903); *My Life: a Record of Events and Opinions* (1905); and other works. — James Marchant, *Alfred Russell Wallace: Letters and Reminiscences* (1916).

[22] Darwin's case would have been stronger had he known of the experiments conducted by Mendel at this very time. Mendel's report on his researches was not delivered till 1865, but there is no reason why Darwin should not have known of them while they were in progress. Yet even in later editions of the *Origin of Species* no reference to them was introduced.

ciple of improvement" within organisms. His search had been for something natural to supplant the breeder as a selective agent. This he found in the usefulness or harmfulness of the qualities of the organisms themselves. How the original minute variations which are subsequently developed occur he did not attempt to explain, but took them for granted. His emphasis upon "natural selection" was due in part to his inheritance from Paley of the idea that all characters in an organism are useful; actually it is often difficult to find a utilitarian explanation of the differences which mark distinct species. He did not sufficiently perceive that "natural selection" is generally a destructive agency, acting not on the "fit" but on the unfit or less fit. He and his first disciples did not realize how small is the fraction of extinct forms of life ancestral to existing forms; how incomplete is the evidence; how dependent upon chance the investigator is to fill the gaps.[23] The vastness of geological time and the multitude of steps in the process of evolution have become more apparent to his successors than these factors were to him. In later years he somewhat modified his views, and in his final position he recognized a three-fold causation—natural selection, the inheritance of the effects of use and disuse, and the direct action of the environment. Sexual selection, upon which at first he set considerable store, he later minimized. He was silent with regard to the problem of the origin of life, and in 1859 he had little to say about the ancestry of man save by inference in the famous promise that his theory would throw light upon "the origin of man and his history."

The great book did not immediately excite opposition. That the first small edition was exhausted on the day of publication was probably due to the interest of theologians and scientists who were already aware of evolutionary speculation. Many older scientists were reluctant to accept Darwin's conclusions. Agassiz remained a stubborn creationist; Lyell hesitated and temporized; Richard Owen never accepted the Darwinian explanation, though he recognized a progressive or ascending course of evolution. But younger men rallied to Darwin's side. With some reservations [24] Huxley accepted the theory, and, since his master was by temperament ill-suited to controversy, constituted himself, as he said, Darwin's "bull-dog." Quickly mounting clerical hostility reached its climax at the meeting of the British Association at Oxford in 1860 when Huxley made his famous, crushing rejoinder to the sarcastic remarks of Bishop Samuel Wilberforce.[25] But the Broad Church party, expressing itself in *Essays and Reviews,* was, as we

---

[23] On the extreme imperfection of the paleontological record see A. M. Davies, *Evolution and its Modern Critics,* pp. 105-106.

[24] Huxley's reservations were partly due to his previous acceptance of Cuvier's doctrine of four *embranchements,* corresponding to archetypal "ideas" in the mind of the Creator. Within each of these four groups are variations which are, however, subordinate to conformity in essentials to the archetype. — Huxley never accepted Darwin's theory of pangenesis, put forward in *The Variations of Animals and Plants under Domestication* (1868). This is the theory that every separate unit or cell of an organism reproduces itself by contributing its share to the germ or bud of the future offspring.

[25] The several versions of this famous story are identical in essentials. See Leonard Huxley, *Life and Letters of Thomas Henry Huxley,* I. 196-203.

have seen, willing to face the implications of new truths. In succeeding years the storm rumbled on. Huxley's *Man's Place in Nature* (1863), in which the theory was explicitly applied to "the human animal" (an expression which was now, significantly, becoming current), occasioned a new outcry. But when Darwin published *The Descent of Man* [26] (1871), though Pusey and Gladstone attacked it, there was no general excitement. The public was becoming accustomed to the new ideas, and the Church was retreating to new lines of defense. When Darwin died in 1882 he was buried in Westminster Abbey.

In contrast to Darwin, Thomas Henry Huxley [27] (1825-1895) possessed gifts of style which could popularize science by lucid and readily intelligible presentation, as in the renowned lecture *On a Piece of Chalk*. His discoveries as a scientist lie beyond the horizon of the historian of literature. He did useful work in advancing the cause of popular education, though, as Arnold argued, he laid too much emphasis upon the value of the natural sciences as a discipline at the expense of the older humane curriculum. Unlike Darwin, he was not content with the task of merely assembling facts and drawing inferences from them but regarded this as the preliminary spadework for philosophy. Beyond Darwin's range but characteristic of Huxley is, for example, the profound suggestion, with its social implications, that the organism can adapt itself to environment not by modifying itself but by altering the environment. Endowed as he was with a self-assurance that invited controversy, he attacked orthodox theology harshly,[28] even while evincing sympathy with ethical aspects of Christian doctrine. Though his championship of freedom of thought, unfettered by tradition, dogma, or prejudice, is memorable and honorable, it cannot be held, in the light of the

T. H. Huxley

[26] Here Wallace parted company with Darwin, arguing that natural selection could have endowed a savage with a brain only a little superior to that of the ape. To which the thorough-going Darwinian replies that the great difference between ape and man is easier to account for than would be the sudden substitution of a new law for one which operates everywhere else through nature. — In these years the public became aware of the quest for types intermediate between man and the anthropoid apes, and the term "missing link" was on everybody's lips. The fossil evidence was still extremely scanty, consisting of but two anthropoids and two skulls of *Homo neanderthalensis.*

[27] *Collected Essays* (9v, 1893). — Leonard Huxley, *Life and Letters of Thomas Henry Huxley* (2v, 1900); P. C. Mitchell, *Thomas Henry Huxley* (1900); Clarence Ayres, *Huxley* (1932). — Huxley's famous Edinburgh address, *The Physical Basis of Life* (1868), is included in *Lay Sermons* (1870). His little volume on *Hume* (1879), in the *EML Series*, is important for the background of Huxley's "agnosticism" (a word of his invention). The Romanes lecture *Ethics and Evolution* (1893) is based upon his dualistic belief that the cosmic process has no sort of relation to moral ends, man's moral nature being a striving against the stream.

[28] See the controversy with Gladstone on the reliability of the narrative of the creation in Genesis, in the *Nineteenth Century,* November and December, 1885, January and February, 1886; and the satiric attack on Gladstone in "The Keepers of the Herd of Swine," *ibid.,* December, 1890 (reprinted in *Collected Essays,* v). Controversial papers by Huxley, Gladstone, and others are gathered together in *The Order of Creation: The Conflict between Genesis and Geology* (n.d., 1890 ?). In 1888-1889 a lively discussion went on between Huxley and the Rev. Henry Wace, Principal of King's College, London, in the pages of the *Nineteenth Century.* In this Mrs. Humphry Ward and W. G. Magee (the Bishop of Peterborough) took part; and W. H. Mallock intervened in the *Fortnightly Review.* These important papers are assembled in *Christianity and Agnosticism: a Controversy* (1889).

evidence, that his claim to be regarded as the uncompromising disciple of Truth is invulnerable.[29]

Any discussion of the present state of evolutionary theory, requiring as it would a mastery of genetics, embryology, and other disciplines, is beyond our province and the writer's competence; but a few remarks may be offered by way of postscript to this chapter. In contrast to those Victorians who thought that they discerned "one increasing purpose" running through the cosmic process, the modern evolutionist is likely to hold to the view that this apparent purpose is but a product of blind forces. The old common conception that evolution implies "an intrinsic tendency in everything to become something higher"[30] cannot survive the evidence that, while there are dominant types which have acquired a greater and greater independence of environment, there are, equally, other dominant types which have been forced by their very control over environment into lines of specialization from which there is no escape. Moreover, the misconception, when the argument was by an insecure analogy transferred from the biological to the social sphere, has resulted in bitter disappointment. The doctrine of the survival of the fittest had dangerous points of connection with the doctrine of the dominant race, implicit in Carlyle's teaching. Popular thought seized upon natural selection to the exclusion of other factors which Darwin had taken into account. "As applied to human society," says Professor Whitehead, "this theory is a challenge to the whole humanitarian movement.... Instead of dwelling on the brotherhood of man, we are now directed to procure the extermination of the unfit."[31]

[29] See the devastating exposure of Huxley's claim in L. T. More, *The Dogma of Evolution*, pp. 256-267.
[30] F. H. Collins, *An Epitome of the Synthetic Philosophy of Herbert Spencer* (1889), p. 351.
[31] A. N. Whitehead, *Adventures of Ideas* (1933), pp. 44-45.

XX
Thomas Carlyle

I

Born at Ecclefechan in the Scottish Lowlands, Thomas Carlyle [1] (1795- *Youth and*
1881) was the eldest child of pious and intelligent peasants. From the Annan *Education*
Grammar School he proceeded to the University of Edinburgh, where, while
making fair progress in the classics, he showed an aptitude for mathematics.
In 1814 he began to teach at Annan, and two years later transferred to a
school at Kirkcaldy, where he became intimate with Edward Irving, a
somewhat older man of brilliant promise, and fell in love with Margaret
Gordon, the original of Blumine in *Sartor Resartus*.[2] Hating teaching, he
abandoned it at the end of 1818 and returned to Edinburgh. Already he had
read widely. Mme de Staël's *De l'Allemagne* had opened to him the treasures
of German thought and fixed his romantic conception of German literature.
Gibbon, Hume, and Voltaire were leading him into the paths of history.
His study of Newtonian physics and eighteenth-century rationalism had
undermined his inherited Calvinistic creed. Religious doubts, the mech-

[1] *Works*, Centenary Edition, ed. H. D. Traill (30v, 1897-1901); *Reminiscences*, ed. J. A.
Froude (1881), ed. C. E. Norton (2v, 1887); *Two Notebooks*, ed. Norton (1898); *Early Letters*,
ed. Norton (1887); *Letters, 1826-1836* (2v, 1888); *Correspondence between Goethe and Carlyle*,
ed. Norton (1887); *Correspondence of Carlyle and Emerson*, ed. Norton (1886); *Letters to
his Youngest Sister*, ed. C. T. Copeland (1899); *New Letters*, ed. Alexander Carlyle (2v, 1904);
Early Letters of Jane Welsh Carlyle, with some of Thomas Carlyle (1889); *Love Letters of
Thomas Carlyle and Jane Welsh*, ed. A. Carlyle (2v, 1909); *Letters to John Stuart Mill, John
Sterling, and Robert Browning*, ed. A. Carlyle (1923); *Briefwechsel mit Varnhagen von Ense*,
ed. R. Preuss (Berlin, 1892); *Last Words of Thomas Carlyle* (1892); *Letters and Memorials
of Jane Welsh Carlyle, Prepared for Publication by Thomas Carlyle*, ed. J. A. Froude (3v, 1883);
New Letters and Memorials of Jane Welsh Carlyle, Annotated by Thomas Carlyle, ed. A.
Carlyle (2v, 1903); *Jane Welsh Carlyle: Letters to Her Family, 1839-1863*, ed. Leonard Huxley
(1924). — I. W. Dyer, *Bibliography* (Portland, Maine, 1928). — James Anthony Froude,
Thomas Carlyle: History of the First Forty Years of his Life (2v, 1882) and *Thomas Carlyle:
History of his Life in London* (2v, 1884). On the "Froude Controversy" see David Masson,
Carlyle Personally and in his Writings (1885); D. A. Wilson, *Froude and Carlyle* (1898) and
The Truth about Carlyle (1913); J. A. Froude, *My Relations with Carlyle* (posthumous, 1903);
J. Crichton-Browne, *Froude and Carlyle* (1903); J. Crichton-Browne and Alexander Carlyle,
The Nemesis of Froude (1903). The case is reviewed and a verdict rendered generally
favorable to Froude in Waldo Dunn, *Froude and Carlyle* (1930). — D. A. Wilson, *Life of
Carlyle* (6v, each with individual title; Vol. vi finished by D. W. MacArthur, 1923-1934);
R. S. Craig, *The Making of Carlyle* (1908); Louis Cazamian, *Carlyle* (Paris, 1913), English
translation by E. K. Brown (1932); Bliss Perry, *Carlyle: How to Know Him* (Indianapolis,
1915); Emery Neff, *Carlyle* (1932); Norwood Young, *Carlyle: His Rise and Fall* (n.d.,
1936 ?); W. S. Johnson, *Thomas Carlyle: a Study of his Literary Apprenticeship, 1814-1831*
(New Haven, 1911); Osbert Burdett, *The Two Carlyles* (1931); Elizabeth Drew, *Jane Welsh
and Jane Carlyle* (1928).
[2] R. C. Archibald, *Carlyle's First Love: Margaret Gordon, Lady Bannerman* (1910). —
Blumine has also been identified, less plausibly, with a Miss Kirkpatrick whom Carlyle knew
in 1824.

anistic materialism which was the current philosophy, the selfish individualism which passed for ethics, disappointment in love, poverty, and an ailing stomach (for already he was afflicted with the dyspepsia which was to be a lifelong complaint) combined with a consciousness of the possession of powers which had as yet found no outlet and produced misery. He was in the clutches of "the Everlasting No," the Spirit that denies.

To me the Universe was all void of Life, of Purpose, of Volition, even of Hostility: it was one huge, dead, immeasurable Steam-engine, rolling on, in its dead indifference, to grind me limb from limb. O, the vast gloomy, solitary Golgotha and Mill of Death!

But he met the devil of despair and defied him, asserting: "I am not thine, but Free, and forever hate thee!" Thus, having repudiated the evidence that no moral order sustains the world, he accepted "the Everlasting Yea," faith in the Divine Fatherhood and adherence to the gospel of self-renunciation and duty.[3]

ne
illie
elsh
To this stage Carlyle had progressed by 1821 when he fell in love with Jane Baillie Welsh, a girl of brilliant intellect and charm, his superior in social status. She recognized his genius and force of character, and her admiration soon deepened into love. He had obtained commissions to write some articles for *The Edinburgh Encyclopaedia*[4] and to translate Legendre's *Geometry*; and in 1822 he got the tutorship of the two sons of wealthy people named Buller, in whose company he saw something of the world of fashion —and despised it. Studies in German literature provided him with literary material and shaped his philosophy.[5] His biography of Schiller appeared in *The London Magazine*[6] (1823-1824), and in 1824 he published a translation of the first part of Goethe's *Wilhelm Meister*. The book trade was flourishing; there was a special demand for works on German culture; and encouraged by the situation and by Goethe's commendation, Carlyle committed himself to a life of letters.

Visiting London in 1824, he met Coleridge and was probably more impressed with him than he permitted to appear when years later he composed his famous pen-portrait of the sage of Highgate.[7] Other men of letters seemed to him of small account; both at the time and in old age he expressed contemptuous pity for Lamb, De Quincey, and Campbell. In a fortnight's visit to Paris he saw much that remained vividly in memory. In 1825, despite misgivings on both sides, he and Jane Welsh became engaged.

---

[3] *Sartor Resartus*, Book II, chs. VII-IX. — On this "conversion" and related aspects of Carlyle's life and ideas see C. F. Harrold. "The Mystical Element in Carlyle," *MP*, XXIX (1932). 459-475.

[4] These articles were first collected in *Montaigne and other Essays*, ed. S. R. Crockett (1897).

[5] C. F. Harrold, *Carlyle and German Thought* (New Haven, 1934); C. E. Vaughan, "Carlyle and his German Masters," *E&S*, I (1910). 168-196; Margaret Storrs, *The Relation of Carlyle to Kant and Fichte* (Bryn Mawr, 1929); Susanna Howe, *Wilhelm Meister and his English Kinsmen* (1930); J. A. S. Barrett, "Carlyle's Debt to Goethe," *Hibbert Journal*, XXX (1931). 61-75; F. Kuchler, "Carlyle und Schiller," *Anglia*, XXVI (1903). 1-93, 393-446.

[6] In book form, enlarged, 1825.

[7] *The Life of John Sterling* (1851), Book I, ch. VIII.

Carlyle's plan for living at Craigenputtock, her ancestral farm near Dumfries, she rejected, for she dreaded its rude isolation; and having decided upon a house on the outskirts of Edinburgh, they were married in October, *Marriage* 1826. Meanwhile, the financial crash of 1825 had caused the bottom to drop out of the book market and Carlyle's situation was precarious. He was at work upon a philosophic novel, *Wotton Reinfred*,[8] but this was abandoned, for the creative imagination which was soon to mold the facts of history to Carlyle's purposes was impeded by the necessity to invent incident, just as his genius, master of a thousand effects in prose, was fettered when he tried to write in verse.

A meeting with Francis Jeffrey was happily fruitful, for the editor of *The* *First* *Edinburgh Review* was in search of fresh talent and recognized Carlyle's *Essays* promise. He commissioned him to write an article on Jean Paul Richter (1827), the first of the *Miscellaneous and Critical Essays.*[9] This was followed by a more important essay, *The Present State of German Literature.* An attempt to meet Scott came to nothing, for Scott, in the midst of distracting anxieties, did not reply to a letter from Carlyle. This discourtesy, as he thought it, colored Carlyle's later estimate of Sir Walter.[10] Contact with John Wilson was not congenial, though Carlyle attended a session of the Ambrosian Nights. He translated and published four volumes of *German Romances*[11] (1827); but the market was glutted with such things and the work did not sell. At this juncture the launching of *The Foreign Review* provided him with a new medium, and before this periodical stopped in 1830 he had written for it eight essays, including *Goethe's Helena, Goethe, Voltaire,* and the second *Richter.* In the *Edinburgh* appeared the *Burns* (1828) and *Signs of the Times* (1829), the first of the articles on contemporary social problems. Most of these essays were written at Craigenputtock, whither, for economy's sake, the Carlyles had gone in 1828. Loneliness was a hardship to Mrs. Carlyle, who loved society; but the domestic jars of this period, though they existed, are exaggerated in Froude's biography. New commissions were not forthcoming and financial anxieties increased. Jeffrey, who had been forbearance itself, found Carlyle's radicalism increasingly out of harmony with the opinions of the *Edinburgh*; and after his retirement from the editorship his successor, Macvey Napier, employed his irascible contributor but seldom and then upon non-controversial literary topics.

In 1830 Carlyle began a history of German literature (which survives, however, only in fragments sold to periodicals), formed a friendship with John Stuart Mill which opened to him the pages of *The Westminster Re-*

---

[8] First published in *Last Words of Thomas Carlyle* (1892). *Wotton Reinfred* underlies the biographical portion of *Sartor Resartus.*
[9] This general title was first used by Carlyle in the collected edition of 1839.
[10] H. J. C. Grierson, "Scott and Carlyle," *E&S*, XIII (1928). 88-111.
[11] In selecting these romances Carlyle sought the advice of Henry Crabb Robinson. To placate the popular taste he translated folk-tales by Musäus and Tieck, a fantasy by Hoffmann, and Fouqué's *Aslauga's Knight;* but he went on to Richter (very difficult to translate and hitherto accessible in English only in fragments) and to the second part of *Wilhelm Meister.*

view, and established contact with the newly founded *Fraser's Magazine*. In October he noted in his diary: "Written a strange piece 'On Clothes.' Know not what will come of it." What came of it was *Sartor Resartus*, for when the "strange piece" was rejected by London editors, Carlyle, instead of setting it aside, enlarged it into a book. This was rejected by Murray and Longman and at length appeared serially in *Fraser's* (1833-1834). Meanwhile the magnificent essay, *Characteristics*, designed to prepare the public for the vagaries of style and strangeness of thought in *Sartor*, came out in the *Edinburgh* (1831). Goethe's death in 1832 was the occasion for the solemnly elegiac *Death of Goethe* and the *Goethe's Works*. In the latter, as in the *Johnson* (also 1832), Carlyle's concern is not for the "work" but for the author's personality as revealed in the work. Carlyle's drift towards revolutionary France as the theme of a book, already apparent in the *Voltaire*, became more marked in the *Diderot* (1833). He was confirmed in his choice of subject when Mill, abandoning a similar design, turned over his materials to him. He had formed his conviction that history is a revelation of the "Divine Idea" and had determined the manner in which his should be composed. A first experiment in the "poetico-historical" kind was the article on Count Cagliostro (1833), the "arch-quack" whose career, as Carlyle viewed it, was symptomatic of the rottenness of the *ancien régime*. A companion-piece, *The Diamond Necklace*, did not reach publication till 1837.

In 1834 the Carlyles moved to London and settled permanently in Cheyne Row, Chelsea. For the next three years he published nothing save an obituary article on Irving. The labor upon his history was increased when the manuscript of the first volume, entrusted to Mill, was accidently destroyed by fire. At length financial need forced him to raise money by an article on Mirabeau (1837). *The Diamond Necklace* was also published. By the time when the great work was completed Carlyle was in distress for want of funds, and friends arranged for a series of lectures on German Literature, a subject on which he could discourse with little or no fresh preparation.[12] Immediately afterwards *The French Revolution: A History* was published,[13] and Carlyle's position in the top rank of living writers was secure.

II

For a while he rested, lying fallow. The only noteworthy essay of 1838 is the *Sir Walter Scott*, which distressed the admirers of the critic and his subject alike. A course of lectures on the history of literature was carefully prepared and enthusiastically received.[14] A third series, on the revolutions

[12] No report of this course is extant.

[13] Ed. C. R. L. Fletcher (3v, 1902); ed. J. Holland Rose (2v, 1909).

[14] Leigh Hunt reported this course in somewhat disputatious vein in *The Examiner*. The reporter for *The Times*, almost certainly Thackeray, was very eulogistic. T. C. Anstey, an admirer of Carlyle, took stenographic notes which he afterwards amplified from a "lecture-book" borrowed from Mrs. Carlyle. This amalgam was eventually published as *Lectures on the History of Literature*, ed. J. R. Greene (1892).

of modern Europe, was given in 1839; [15] and in 1840 a fourth and final series, the famous lectures *On Heroes, Hero-Worship, and the Heroic in History*.[16] A misunderstanding broke off work on an essay on Cromwell which Mill had suggested for the *Westminster*; but the labor was not wasted as this was the start of his second great historical work. Carlyle was now reaching an ever widening audience. Through Emerson came an invitation to visit America, which was declined. In 1839 the sales of the collected edition of the miscellaneous essays, of the first English edition of *Sartor*, of the second edition of *The French Revolution*, and of *Chartism* [17] brought in sufficient funds to enable Carlyle to devote himself to research. His original intention to write the history of the Puritan revolution was narrowed to a collection of Cromwell's letters and speeches with interspersed narrative, character-portraits, and comment. This rehabilitation of the Puritan "hero" was his principal work during the next four years. In 1843 he turned aside to write *Past and Present*,[18] a remarkable exercise of the historical imagina- **Past and** tion in which twelfth-century leadership in the person of Abbot Samson [19] **Present** is contrasted with the chaos of modern individualism. An article (1844) on Dr. Francia, the dictator of Paraguay, was the first alarming indication of the extreme to which he was later to push his doctrine of leadership. *Oliver Cromwell's Letters and Speeches. With Elucidations* appeared in 1845.[20] **Cromwell**

For several years Carlyle remained comparatively idle, much sought after in society. In his gruff fashion he enjoyed this lionizing; but it was a sad time for Mrs. Carlyle, who was jealous of the attentions lavished on her husband by the wealthy Lady Harriet Baring (later Lady Ashburton). Froude made too much of the resultant partial estrangement, but some later biographers have made too little. The neglect of his wife was the chief cause of Carlyle's poignant remorse after her death.

Impressions of Ireland, gained hurriedly in 1846, brought home to him vividly the Irish troubles of 1847-1848. He talked about writing a book on the subject, but the intention was never fulfilled. Watching Continental **Anti-** events during the Year of Revolutions, he predicted that the French Re- **democratic** public could not endure, and though ties of friendship bound him to Maz- **Views** zini he was convinced that that leader's triumph in Rome was but temporary. The failure of the European revolutionists and the second Chartist fiasco in London confirmed him in his negation of the democratic principle. His

---

[15] Very few notes on this course survive; Hunt's reports were meager and irregular.

[16] Published, with emendations and additions, in 1841.

[17] Lockhart had regretfully rejected *Chartism* as too extreme in its opinions for *The Quarterly Review*, and it was consequently published as a book.

[18] Ed. Oliphant Smeaton (1902).

[19] To the subject Carlyle was attracted by Jocelin of Brakelond's *Chronicle* of the reforms of Abbot Samson in the monastery of St. Edmundsbury, which had just been published by the Camden Society (1840).

[20] Ed. Mrs. S. C. Lomas (3v, 1904). — Among additions to the second edition of the *Cromwell* (1846) were the so-called "Squire forgeries" whose acceptance by Carlyle as authentic had occasioned ironic comment upon the ease with which the arch-foe of sham was taken in by documents obviously spurious. See C. H. Firth's introduction to *Cromwell*, ed. Lomas, I. xlii-xiv; and the less judicious consideration of the subject in Norwood Young, *Carlyle: His Rise and Fall*, pp. 214-224.

first violently anti-democratic pamphlet was *The Nigger Question* (1849), to which Mill replied vigorously, thus terminating a friendship which had hitherto stood the strain of opposed opinions.[21] During 1850 the vituperative and declamatory *Latter-Day Pamphlets* were issued in eight monthly parts. The extreme violence with which Carlyle's views on modern society were here displayed roused the opposition of every supporter of laissez faire, alienated the doubtful, and bewildered many of Carlyle's disciples; and in consequence his reputation suffered an abrupt decline. To recover serenity and to pay personal homage to a dead friend he wrote the quietly beautiful *Life of John Sterling* (1851).

Frederick the Great

He considered and rejected the career of the Cid as the subject of a book. The mists of distance and the incrustations of legend round the Spanish hero would have presented great difficulties; yet the theme might have been a happier choice than that actually selected—the career of Frederick the Great.[22] He plunged into thirteen years of research, not without ceaseless lamentations on the stupidity of "Dryasdust" and the hardness of his own lot. The toil was interrupted by two visits to Germany (1852 and 1858) to survey Frederick's battlefields.[23] The moral problem whether the evidence really supported his interpretation of Frederick's character troubled him; but he suppressed these scruples and persevered. The huge work appeared in three installments, the last in 1865.[24] Now at the summit of his fame, Carlyle was elected rector of the University of Edinburgh and was received

Death of Mrs. Carlyle

with great acclaim when he delivered his inaugural address in April, 1866. Immediately afterwards came the news of his wife's sudden death; and he passed into his grief-stricken and desolate old age.

He arranged and annotated the *Letters and Memorials* of his wife.[25] In 1867 he published *Shooting Niagara: and After?* in protest against the second Reform Bill. His championship of Governor Eyre, brought to trial for the cruelty with which he had suppressed an uprising of the Negroes in Jamaica, is another indication of the extreme to which the doctrine of leadership had now advanced. In 1871, in a letter to the *Times*, he defended Prussia's annexation of Alsace-Lorraine and contrasted "noble, patient, deep, pious, and solid Germany" with "vapouring, vainglorious, gesticulating, quarrelsome, restless, and over-sensitive France."[26] Once more, in 1876, he intervened in public affairs, warning his countrymen of the danger that

---

[21] Emery Neff, *Carlyle and Mill, Mystic and Utilitarian* (1924).

[22] On earlier and contemporary English interest in this subject see Hans Marcus, *Friedrich der Grosse in der englischen Literatur* (Leipzig, 1930).

[23] See Carlyle's diary, *Journey to Germany: Autumn 1858*, ed. R. A. E. Brooks (New Haven, 1940).

[24] Abridgment by E. Sanderson (1909); *The Battles of Frederick the Great, abstracted from Carlyle's Biography*, ed. C. Ransome (1892).

[25] Carlyle turned these papers over to Froude with the injunction that they be not published without editorial excisions. In 1883 Froude published them with no deletions, and when the storm of controversy burst round him pleaded that Carlyle had rescinded verbally his previous directions.

[26] The *Times* refuted editorially Carlyle's arguments and rejected his conclusions. — As much for his services in 1871 as for his tribute to Prussia in *Frederick the Great* Bismarck bestowed on Carlyle the Order of Merit.

Disraeli might involve them on the side of Turkey against Russia in the Eastern Crisis.[27] In so doing he was consistent, for in 1854, despising Napoleon III and favoring the Russian method of despotic rule, he had opposed the Crimean War.

After losing the use of his right hand he resorted to dictation, but the only *Last* results were the two essays, *Norse Kings* and *Portraits of John Knox* (both *Years* 1875). In his increasing feebleness devoted disciples—Froude, Ruskin, Huxley, Tyndall, and others—ministered to him, harkening to the prophecies of woe to fall upon a world which, heedless of his warnings, was moving towards catastrophe. The death of his brother John (1878) severed almost the last link with the far past. He lingered three years longer, dying in February, 1881. Burial was offered in Westminster Abbey, but by his directions his body was committed to the ground at Ecclefechan.

III

In temperament, manner, and intensity of conviction Carlyle was more closely akin to the Hebrew prophets than to any counselor of the people of his own day. His concern was to rescue society from materialism, greed, irresponsibility, uncontrolled competition, and industrial chaos. The value of history, in his estimate, lay in the lessons of the past which are applicable to the present; and he believed that a right interpretation of the contemporary situation would throw a beam of light into the darkness of the future. Thus he combined the functions of the historian, social reformer, and *Transcen-* prophet; and he based them upon a transcendental metaphysic. Dissatisfied, *dentalism* like his fellow romanticists, with the science of Newton, the epistemology of Locke, the skepticism of Hume, and the ethics of the Utilitarians, he turned to his own intuitions, finding sustenance for them in German romantic philosophy. From his superficial knowledge of Kant he derived the distinction between the Reason and the Understanding and the concept of the ideality of Space and Time. His debt to Fichte was far greater—to Fichte's popular expositions of his philosophy rather than to his earlier, more technical writings. Fichte taught Carlyle to respect the outward world and scientific law as revelations of Divine power and idea. From him, rather than from a mere phrase in Hume, came the doctrine of heroes and hero-worship. Fichte's teaching that in the struggle between the Self and the Non-Self each individual must by means of justice, love, and sympathetic understanding spiritualize the world of matter was translated into the practical terms of aiding the work of scientific progress and social amelioration. These ideas came to Carlyle largely through the imaginative interpretations of Novalis and especially Goethe. In Goethe to a greater degree than in any other modern man Carlyle discerned the inward experiences which gave meaning

---

[27] This second letter to the *Times* prompted Swinburne's eloquent and bitter attack on Carlyle and the pro-Russian party: *Notes of an English Republican on the Muscovite Crusade* (1876).

to life. He recognized Goethe's tolerance (though he himself rarely imitated it) and the submission to the inevitable upon which that tolerance was founded. He imagined that Goethe taught a philosophy of self-renunciation. Actually Goethe's ideal was to subordinate the "lower" elements in human nature in order to gain a harmonious development of the whole, a line of thought to which Carlyle gave a puritanically ascetic twist which owes more to Geneva than to Weimar.

Sartor Resartus [28] is the most eloquent and elaborate statement of Carlyle's transcendental philosophy. There was nothing that was novel in its essence, for the illusioned romanticists should have accustomed readers to the ideas set forth in the "Clothes Philosophy"—that Language is the clothing of Thought, the Body the vestment of the Soul, the entire Universe the "living Garment of God" woven upon the roaring loom of Time. Moreover, Carlyle had prepared the way for Sartor in earlier writings in which he adumbrated his concepts of "the greatness of great men" and of the Divine Idea underlying the world of phenomena. But the fantastic style in which these ideas were conveyed—the Germanic locutions, the vast range of allusions, the bold colloquialisms, the rhetorical flights, the proximity of the ridiculous and the sublime, and the heterogeneous mixture of autobiography, romance, satire, ethics, metaphysics, and humor—bewildered the English public.

"Hero-Worship"

Elements from many sources had sunk into Carlyle's memory to come forth fused by his fiery imagination into the doctrine of "hero-worship." [29] The Hebraic concept of the divinely appointed Messiah, the Platonic concept of the philosopher-king, and the Plutarchian concept of the law-giver were combined with eighteenth-century speculations upon genius and with the romanticists' idea of the "great man." [30] In Fichte Carlyle thought he discovered a philosophic support for the idea. Liberty is the reign of law; compulsion must be applied to rebellious individuals for whom is secured thereby their only true freedom, which is found in the fostering, not thwarting, of the general will. Within each soul burns, more brightly or more dimly, an awareness of the Divine Idea of the World. The hero is distinguished from the common throng by his possession of this consciousness to an extraordinary degree. His shape is Protean; he may be a man of action or of thought—god, prophet, priest, poet, king, man of letters (or other manifestation, for Carlyle's categories in Heroes and Hero-Worship are limited only by the number of his lectures). The leader's shape is conditioned by the exigencies of the time in which he appears. There are ages in which

[28] Ed. Archibald MacMechan (Boston, 1896); ed. P. C. Parr (1913).
[29] B. H. Lehman, Carlyle's Theory of the Hero: Its Sources, Development, History, and Influence on Carlyle's Work (Durham, N. C., 1928). — On Heroes and Hero-Worship, ed. A. MacMechan (Boston, 1901); ed. P. C. Parr (1910).
[30] Wordsworth turns often to the idea of the leader. See, for instance, The Prelude, xiv, 112: "Such minds are truly from the Deity," and the sonnet "Great men have been among us." Coleridge's view of the statesman as a "Coadjutor with God" is set forth in The Friend, The Statesman's Manual, and elsewhere. Shelley shows the Liberator failing in The Revolt of Islam but triumphant in Prometheus Unbound. Compare also Keats's sonnet "Great spirits now on earth are sojourning." Lehman detects something of the idea even in the Byronic rebel; but this is doubtful.

no hero comes forth; but when he does so he responds to the needs of his time. He has the right and the duty to compel mankind, representing the *Staatslehre* in which is the compulsive power ordained by God. Carlyle was not unmindful of the problem, noted by Mill in his review of *The French Revolution,* of the means by which the hero is to be discovered. Burke had held that men instinctively subordinate themselves to declared authority; but Carlyle found an answer to Mill's question in the Goethean doctrine of "reverence," the faculty natural to men of recognizing and becoming obedient to the heaven-sent leader. With Emerson's later effort, in *Representative Men,* to reconcile the idea of leadership with the democratic principle of free choice Carlyle had no sympathy. His anti-democratic social radicalism was a reversion to the feudal concept of obedience to the lord who in return vouchsafes protection to his followers. How ominous an anticipation it was of the modern *Führerprinzip* is obvious.[31]

The development of this doctrine may be traced through Carlyle's literary *Criticism* essays.[32] He conceived the critic's function to be the interpretation of the poet's revelation of the Divine Idea.[33] The poet—and within this term Carlyle includes the historian, the man of letters, the philosopher—puts this revelation into a form apprehensible by the senses. More than this, the poet is himself, as is every man to a greater or less degree, a revelation. Thus Carlyle shifts the emphasis from the work of art to the man who made the work. From the first his approach was biographical. "What manner of man was this?" is his question. The *Burns* (1828) attempts to answer it rather than to solve any problem in literary history. The *Johnson* (1832), written during the agitation for reform, takes Boswell's *Life* as a text for a sermon on hero-worship and an excuse for a tract for the times. *Goethe's Works* (1832) tells us little about the "works" and rhapsodizes on Goethe. In the *Scott* (1838) Carlyle touched lightly upon the novels and passed upon the man a judgment which scandalized contemporaries but is now seen to be almost uncannily shrewd. The same increasing emphasis upon biography is seen in the essays on French subjects as we pass from the *Voltaire* through the *Diderot* to the *Mirabeau*. These, like *Cagliostro* and *The Diamond Necklace,* prepare the way for *The French Revolution.*

Eighteenth-century rationalism, in line with the Cartesian principle of *History* immutable natural laws, held that history must reveal the uniformity and regularity of recurring phenomena. As a historian [34] Carlyle opposed this rationalistic historiography, finding for this opposition support in various elements of romantic thought and practice. Burke had regarded history as a reservoir of the accumulated wisdom of the past. Coleridge affirmed that the philosopher must reinterpret to each generation the Idea underlying

[31] Sir H. J. C. Grierson, *Carlyle and Hitler* (1930).
[32] F. W. Roe, *Thomas Carlyle as a Critic of Literature* (1910).
[33] K. E. Gilbert and Helmut Kuhn, *A History of Esthetics* (1939), pp. 407-409.
[34] Louise M. Young, *Thomas Carlyle and the Art of History* (Philadelphia, 1939), to which the discussion which follows is much indebted. See also G. P. Gooch, *History and Historians in the Nineteenth Century* (1913), pp. 323-332; René Wellek, "Carlyle and the Philosophy of History," *PQ,* XXIII (1944). 55-76.

human institutions. Scott supplied an example of the blend of a wide observation of the manners of the present with an imaginative apprehension of the life of the past. Herder and other German romanticists, rejecting the notion of universally valid "laws," showed Carlyle how the destiny of every nation is conditioned by its "Folk-Spirit" and taught him the importance of the irrational and individualistic elements in history. Schiller helped to form his concept of the historian as the artist who selects those facts which are related to the present constitution of society and molds them into form.

The Divine Idea is revealed in man, in institutions, and in universal history. History is the indubitable proof of a purposeful Deity shaping the destiny of man. The loftiest visible emblem of the Idea is poetry; and of poetry history is the highest order. Thus religion, poetry, and history are fused.[35] Carlyle repudiates the theory of the contractual basis of society. Institutional and social origins lie deep in the primal chaos, the unconscious having been informed with the law of order and righteousness. Carlyle adheres to the evolutionary concept of a slow, upward-moving spiral, as opposed to the Platonic concept of recurring historic cycles; but he is more interested in the process of progress than in its goal. There is a periodicity or rhythm; successive ages are critical or creative, characterized by faith or skepticism. From the mutability which is a primary quality of the social organism comes Carlyle's concentration upon periods of revolution in which the process of change is speeded up. Not that he considered revolution the inevitable mode of change; on the contrary, he held that institutions and states grow more steadily when they grow calmly. Upheavals are the penalty for stagnant disobedience to the laws of normal development. Revolution to be justified must spring from the profound instinctual level of a people's consciousness. The mandate to revolt against outworn institutions is communicated to society through the hero. Carlyle's interest in what he called "the Revolution Prodigy" accounts for the limitations which he imposed upon his treatment of the French Revolution, his concern being neither for causes nor for aftermath but for the phenomenon in itself. In similar fashion he concentrated upon Cromwell as the embodiment of the Puritan Revolution, which collapsed after the leader's death. The achievements of Frederick were revolutionary because in his age Prussia emerged from the dominance of decadent France and the anachronistic Holy Roman Empire.

Carlyle's perennial interest was in Man, in the motives which underlie human behavior. History, in his famous phrase, "is the essence of innumerable biographies"; and through it we may hope to gain "some acquaintance with our fellow creatures, though dead and vanished." [36] The artist's effort is to identify himself with his subject, to "blow his living breath between dead lips," to abolish by his own life the death in things. Carlyle therefore

---

[35] Hill Shine, *Carlyle's Fusion of Poetry, History and Religion by 1834* (Chapel Hill, 1938) and *Carlyle and the Saint-Simonians: The Concept of Historical Periodicity* (Baltimore, 1941)

[36] *On History* (1830); *Works*, Centenary Edition, xxvii. 86. See Godfrey Davies, "Biography and History," *MLQ*, i (1940). 79-94.

distinguishes between the archivist—the "simple husbandman" who labors mechanically and for whom, as "Dryasdust" or "Smelfungus," he expressed an unwarranted contempt—and the artist-historian who has the right to exercise judgment in his choice of emphasis and whose duty it is to select and condense, since under the pressure of contractions and epitomes untruths and trivialities disappear.[37] "The two pinions on which History soars," he wrote, "are stern Accuracy in inquiring, bold Imagination in expounding and filling-up."[38] His method (which entailed greater risks of error than 'Dryasdust" was ready to run) was to depend not upon notes but on the upsurging stores of memory. His plastic imagination molded into artistic form the visual and the concrete, presenting with unequaled vividness the appearances of people, their clothes and complexions and mannerisms, and the sounds of individual voices and of the uproar of the mob or the hurlyburly of battle. When engaged upon the last volume of *The French Revolution* he wrote to his wife:

It all stands pretty fair in my head, nor do I mean to investigate much more about it, but to splash down what I know in large masses of colours, that it may look like a smoke-and-flame conflagration in the distance, which it is.[39]

Critics have done him wrong who have taken this to mean that he had not "investigated" thoroughly. To the materials assembled by laborious research he applied his power of revivifying the past, of probing into motive, and of sociological analysis.

The unanswerable charge against Carlyle is that he made history serve the ends of his transcendental philosophy. The spectral effects of his great dioramas are achieved with superb literary art; but as history they are not trustworthy. For the validity of the doctrine that history is a revelation of the Divine Idea he can offer his vehemently affirmed convictions but not an atom of proof. Was he not a victim of romantic illusionism? And even as an artist his technique is uncertain and fumbling. The story of Abbot Samson in *Past and Present* is told not only forcefully but with exquisite clarity; but in the sequel the presentation of the contemporary situation as a chaos is as much due to Carlyle's confused vision as to the confusions of modern life. He abandoned the plan to tell the story of the Puritan Revolution because he could not mold it into shape. The *Frederick*, with its dull reversion to the far past and its alternately narrowing and expanding perspectives, is badly designed, admirable in scattered passages of narrative and analysis, unreadable as a whole.[40] As a work of art *The French Revolution*,

[37] *On History Again* (1833); *Works*, XXVIII. 172.
[38] *Count Cagliostro* (1833); *Works*, XXVIII. 259-260. Carlyle attributes the aphorism to his imaginary friend "Sauerteig" and admits that in the particular case of Cagliostro he is committing himself in the main to the "pinion" of Imagination.
[39] J. A. Froude, *Thomas Carlyle: Life in London*, I. 65.
[40] The charges of inaccuracy brought against the magnificent narratives of Frederick's battles (see, e.g., Norwood Young, *Carlyle: His Rise and Fall*, p. 291) have been convincingly disproved by R. A. E. Brooks in his edition of Carlyle's *Journey to Germany*, appendices I-XII. More serious is the evidence that Carlyle was deliberately reticent when, as his investigations progressed, he realized that his original conception of Frederick's character was a mistaken one.

The
French
Revolution

with its beautiful trifold structure—the destruction of the old; the purging by terror; the beginnings of the new—stands alone among his historical writings. To echo a judgment which has been delivered of Gibbon's *History* —it has been superseded but has not been surpassed. He studied the Revolution as a sociological phenomenon and thus earned the disapproval of the "scientific" historians who were more intent to note his errors and omissions than to comprehend his intentions. The lack of any thorough treatment of constitutional and economic problems, of events in the provinces, and of foreign relations and wars is due to the concentration upon his chosen aspect. The episodic treatment came naturally from Carlyle's epic imagination, but it is also due to the limitations of the source-material at his command.[41] There are no more preconceptions than in other narratives of the Revolution written before the criterion of dispassionate objectivity was established by historians of a later school. In this respect Carlyle's book, with its emphasis upon retributive justice, is no more biased than Michelet's interpretation of the Revolution as the "birth-throes" of democracy, or Guizot's prejudice in favor of the English form of government, or the socialism of Louis Blanc, or the narrow constitutionalism of Thiers, or the anti-French position of Sybel and Treitschke.

Carlyle's reputation as a historian did not pass unchallenged in his own day and suffered a decline after his death. The influence of Henry Thomas Buckle's *History of Civilization* (1857) was adverse, for Buckle reduced the process of history to laws based upon man's physical environment. The historical materialism of Karl Marx, with its emphasis upon economic forces, was opposed to Carlyle's transcendentalism. The critical methodology of the "scientific" school, represented by William Stubbs, E. A. Freeman, and J. R. Green, relied upon archivistic research with a corresponding distrust of the recreative imagination.

The lessons of history Carlyle sought to apply to the problems of his own day. He taught, and would fain have believed, that the world was God's; but beneath his loudly proclaimed trust there were gloomy doubts. The *Ewige Nein* was never completely exorcised. While blind to the signs of progress in his own day, he was ruthless in his exposure of the shortcomings of modern society—the widening gap between rich and poor; the callous indifference of the "ruling classes"; the failure of the promises held out by the advocates of parliamentary reform; the bewildered gropings of the Demos. But he offered no counsel of value for the reconstruction of a democratic society. He had no trust in collective humanity or in the organic unity

---

[41] Of about 1700 paragraphs in *The French Revolution* about 1200 are narrative and descriptive, the rest Carlyle's reflections. An examination of Carlyle's sources (some 83) confirms his general soundness and good faith. Concrete detail is sometimes exaggerated and there are a very few violations of chronological order. See C. F. Harrold, "Carlyle's General Method in *The French Revolution*," *PMLA*, XLIII (1928). 1150-1169. The great French authority, Aulard, has testified that Carlyle used nearly everything available at the time he wrote, and, moreover, used it with discriminating judgment. Contrast the extremely unfavorable verdict passed upon Carlyle by Lord Acton, *Letters to Mary Gladstone*, ed. Herbert Paul (1904), pp. 170-171, and *Lectures on the French Revolution* (1910), pp. 358-359.

of the race. The one popular right, he held, is to be well governed. He is nearer to Gobineau, with his theory of the dominant race, than to Marx, with his theory of the class-conflict; and nearest to Nietzsche, with his division of humanity into Supermen and Helots. His views he expounded with somber vehemence and in later life with violent extravagance. To their exposition he brought all the resources of his genius as a writer: pathos and gloom; humor, ridicule, and sarcasm; an intense earnestness; and a style completely individualized.[42] After Carlyle's death George Meredith wrote of him:

He was the greatest of the Britons of his time—and after the British fashion of not coming near perfection; Titanic, not Olympian; a heaver of rocks, not a shaper.[43]

[42] The range of Carlyle's style is best displayed in *Sartor.* Verbal coinages, elaborate metaphors, apostrophes; rhetorical questions, compounds of various kinds, and the use of nicknames are among its chief characteristics. The style seems to owe something to Richter but more came from Carlyle's native Annandale than from any literary model. It is constantly suggestive of spoken—or shouted—words; and there is testimony that Carlyle talked almost as he wrote.

[43] George Meredith, *Letters,* ii. 333.

XXI
Philosophy, History, and Miscellaneous Prose

I

It is difficult to determine the boundary beyond which the historian of literature need not, or may not, pass into the various fields of specialized and technical writing. The choice, which to some extent must be arbitrary, should be based in part upon a writer's greatness of stature but chiefly upon the qualities of style and breadth of popular appeal which entitle him to a place in the history of literature as well as of thought. When marginal cases are discarded,[1] there remain among English philosophers Mill and Spencer.

Mill   John Stuart Mill [2] (1806-1873), the last great figure in the history of British empiricism, was like most English thinkers no recluse but rather a man active in the world of affairs—editor of *The Westminister Review,* an official at India House, a worker for practical reform, and in his later years a member of Parliament. The remorselessly rigorous education to which, in accordance with Benthamite principles, he was subjected by his father would have turned into a hopeless prig the boy who at the age of fifteen had formed a little society of "Utilitarians" had not his character contained hidden elements of greatness. At the age of twenty he passed through a "spiritual crisis" from which he emerged with an awareness of reaches of experience beyond the comprehension of the strict Benthamites. Though, like all members of the philosophical sect in which he was reared, he would continue to "calculate," henceforth the influence of poetry and the fine arts was to enter into Mill's calculations. The poetry of Wordsworth and the speculations of Coleridge helped to shape his new ideas. The struggle in his mind was between the old "enlightenment" and the new "romanticism," or, as he displayed it antithetically in two great essays published

---

[1] Among the philosophers more or less reluctantly set aside are Sir William Hamilton, James Mill, Alexander Bain, James Martineau, and J. F. Ferrier.

[2] *Autobiography* (1873), ed. J. J. Coss (1924); ed. H. J. Laski (1944); *Principles of Political Economy,* ed. W. J. Ashley (1909); *On Liberty; Representative Government; On the Subjection of Women,* ed. M. C. Fawcett (World's Classics, 1912); *Letters,* ed H. S. R. Elliot (2v, 1910). — W. L. Courtney, *Life of John Stuart Mill* (1889); Leslie Stephen, *The English Utilitarians* (3v, 1900), III; H. K. Garnier, *John Stuart Mill and the Philosophy of Mediation* (1919); Emery Neff, *Carlyle and Mill* (1924); C. L. Street, *Individualism and Individuality in the Philosophy of John Stuart Mill* (Philadelphia, 1926); A. W. Levi, *A Study in the Social Philosophy of John Stuart Mill* (Chicago, 1940); James Seth, *English Philosophers and Schools of Philosophy* (1912), pp. 246-278; Rudolf Metz, *A Hundred Years of British Philosophy* (1938), pp. 62-74; J. S. Schapiro, "John Stuart Mill, Pioneer of Democratic Liberalism in England," *JHI,* IV (1943). 127-160.

in *The Westminster Review,* between Bentham (1838) and Coleridge (1840). The opposition was essentially this, that "Coleridge's doctrine is ontological, conservative, religious, concrete, historical, and poetic, while Bentham's is experimental, innovative, infidel, abstract, matter-of-fact, and essentially prosaic." [3] Mill made the attempt to master the premises and combine the methods of these two thinkers. Later there was a reaction in the direction of Bentham; but Mill's ethics, as set forth in *Utilitarianism* (1863), differed from the system which he had learned from his father and his father's master, in that by distinguishing between the qualities of various pleasures he introduced a criterion above that of ethical hedonism. Mill's *System of Logic* (1843) followed Whately in reviving interest in a subject which had been long neglected in England. Denying intuitive knowledge, he studied the inductive process, dealt with the problem of causation, and theorized on the formation of scientific concepts and the conduct of exact inquiry by means of induction, ratiocination, and verification. But the *Logic,* like the *Principles of Political Economy* (1848), in which he followed Adam Smith and simplified David Ricardo, scarcely belongs, by any stretching of the terms of definition, to literature. Long used as standard textbooks, both these works have now been superseded.

Mill's lasting fame rests, so far as the general reader is concerned, upon the three long essays or short books, *On Liberty* (1859), *Considerations on Representative Government* (1861), and *On the Subjection of Women* (1869). The ringing assertions that "genius can only breathe freely in an atmosphere of freedom," that to silence the expression of opinion is to rob the human race, that "the despotism of custom is everywhere the standing hindrance of human advancement," and that "society has now fairly got the better of individuality; and the danger which threatens human nature is not the excess but the deficiency of personal impulses and preferences" serve to show why *On Liberty* is regarded as one of the finest expressions of nineteenth-century liberalism. Like Herbert Spencer, Mill insisted that "the individual is not accountable to society for his actions, in so far as these concern the interests of no person but himself." He deplored the world's loss in promising intellects combined with timid characters who refrain from following out a train of thought for fear lest "it land them into something considered irreligious or immoral." In *Representative Government* he demonstrated the superiority of free institutions to even the best of despotisms, discussed the provision of checks upon the power of government, and argued for a system of proportional representation. In his third treatise he showed that the principles of liberty and representation were as applicable to women as to men, and he provided what was one of the greatest impelling forces of the movement for the political emancipation of women.

The posthumous publication of *Three Essays on Religion* (1874) came as a surprise to those who had regarded Mill as a "saint of rationalism." In them he went beyond his basis in empiricism to a discussion of transcen-

[3] Thus condensed by Metz, *op. cit.,* p. 65.

dental problems. They show how much there was latent in him which did not find a place in his inherited system. In harmony with the moral and religious experience of mankind he found the idea of a morally perfect God whose power is not infinite and who, needing the active coöperation of man in the struggle against the negative world-principle, leads the cosmic process upward.[4]

II

Spencer

Today the dust lies thick upon the work and reputation of Herbert Spencer.[5] The *Synthetic Philosophy* was so exact an expression of Victorian liberalism that with the passing of the age which produced it, it, too, has become discredited. The pioneering originality of a great mind has been obscured by the fact that many of the theories which were fructifying in their originality sixty or seventy years ago have been absorbed into the general body of ideas, while many of the other theories which were poured forth so lavishly have been falsified by events. Science in an age of specialization was from the first suspicious of one who took all knowledge as his province and who had the super-Baconian energy not only to envisage a new Organon but to design and construct it in almost all its parts. The trend towards socialism and state-control was hostile to the fundamental Spencerian argument for the free development of the individual, and the mounting armaments of the age into which the philosopher unhappily lived seemed a mockery of his devotion to the cause of peace. Spencer himself recognized the eternal "flux"—devolution following evolution and evolution devolution—but it is unlikely that with another turn of the cosmic wheel his ideas will reappear.

In youth as throughout his life Herbert Spencer (1820-1903) was not amenable to intellectual discipline save in so far as it was self-imposed. There were as great gaps in his education as in what he afterwards claimed to be his philosophic synthesis. Intellectually, as in his celibate life, he was very largely independent. This tended to make him arrogant and censorious, but it provided him with the immense self-confidence and the will to persevere which in spite of poverty and ill health enabled him, through thirty-six years (1860-1896) of arduous work, to carry to completion his vast design, a synthesis of all knowledge under the universal law of evolution.

[4] Rudolf Metz, *A Hundred Years of British Philosophy*, p. 74.

[5] Herbert Spencer, *Autobiography* (2v, 1904); David Duncan, *Life and Letters of Herbert Spencer* (1908); William Henry Hudson, *Introduction to the Philosophy of Herbert Spencer* (1894) and *Herbert Spencer* (1908); J. Arthur Thomson, *Herbert Spencer* (1906); Hugh Elliot, *Herbert Spencer* (1917); J. Rumney, *Herbert Spencer's Sociology* (1934); James Seth, *English Philosophers and Schools of Philosophy* (1912), pp. 284-297; Rudolf Metz, *A Hundred Years of British Philosophy* (1938), pp. 98-110. For the opposition in this country to Spencer's competitive individualism see Richard Hofstadter, *Social Darwinism in American Thought, 1860-1915* (Philadelphia, 1944). — The range of Spencer's interests is well illustrated for the ordinary reader in his miscellany entitled *Facts and Comments* (1902), in which he treats of law and justice, imperialism, militarism, slavery, education, gymnastics, music, sanitation, and much else.

In the essay on *Progress, its Law and Cause* (1857) Spencer offered an exposition of the universality of the evolutionary process, founded upon his study of the nebular hypothesis and of the Lamarckian theory of the inheritance of acquired characters. In the next year he chanced in his reading upon the observation that organisms tend to develop from homogeneity to heterogeneity, and wrote to his father that his "ideas on various matters have suddenly crystallized into a complete whole." [6] That "whole," that basic law, he afterwards condensed into his famous definition of evolution as "an integration of matter and concomitant dissipation of motion, during which the matter passes from an indefinite incoherent homogeneity to a definite coherent heterogeneity and during which the retained motion undergoes a parallel transformation." In 1859 Darwin provided him with another explanation of the phenomenon of organic evolution, and without entirely discarding the theory of the inheritance of acquired characters Spencer at once absorbed natural selection into his system. His life work was now laid out for him. In *First Principles* (1862) he adumbrated his plan to present a genetic history of the universe in terms of matter, motion, and force. From the first his object was fundamentally ethical, to provide "a basis for a right rule of life, individual and social." [7] The bibliography of the successive installments of the *Synthetic Philosophy* is too complicated to be presented here, for there were overlappings, revisions, enlargements, and confusing changes of titles; but broadly speaking the chronology is as follows: *The Principles of Biology* (1864-1867), *The Principles of Psychology* (1855-1872), *The Principles of Sociology* (1876-1896), and *The Principles of Ethics* (1879-1893). Of the subsidiary works may be mentioned *Education* (1861), of which the argument runs counter to the modern claim to equal education for all but which strongly influenced modern theory and practice; *The Man versus the State* (1884), the most thoroughgoing exposition of Spencer's individualism; the suppressed volume on *The Nature and Reality of Religion* (1885); and the posthumously published *Autobiography* (1904).

The Synthetic Philosophy

The synthesis was incomplete from the very start, for Spencer never included save by implication and in the early essay on the nebular hypothesis, the realm of inorganic matter, and by not considering "the step preceding the evolution of living forms" failed to force into his scheme the all-important problem of the origin of life. There is another unbridged gap between his *Biology* and *Psychology,* that is, between matter and mind. The phenomena of social life no less than of organic nature were shown to conform to law, for as in organisms so in society (the "super-organic") there is a tendency to the increased specialization of interdependent elements. In Spencer's *Sociology* state-control is reduced to the minimum needed for the coöperative life (protection against external enemies and the maintenance of internal order), and individual liberty is expanded to the maximum possible in the state. Competition is the condition of progress. He would

The Individual and Society

[6] *Autobiography,* ii. 19.
[7] *Ibid,* ii. 314.

turn over to private competing companies not only such affairs as the postal service but sanitation and the measures necessary for public health. Spencer's ethics were an outgrowth from utilitarianism. The end of conduct is the complete life. Holding that morality becomes instinctive (an "acquired character"), he foresaw the day when there would be an "approximately complete balance" between the desires of the individual and the needs of society. When this adjustment is effected, all sense of compulsion will disappear, and with it the need to exercise a moral choice.

Notwithstanding the immense and imposing accumulation of facts, Spencer's process of reasoning is essentially deductive, not inductive. He admitted that his mind was "ready to receive" material which could be taken into his system, while "ideas and sentiments of alien kinds, or unorganizable kinds" were either rejected "or soon dropped away." [8] A Spencerian theory has been likened to a magnet; as it is passed over particles of different metals, the iron facts cling to it; the rest are left behind.

Spencer attempted a reconciliation of science and religion in the common meeting-ground of reverent contemplation of the Unknowable and Absolute First Cause which he found to be behind both religious beliefs and scientific observation and experiment. But in this cold abstraction the religious-minded found no substitute for faith in a Divine Father; and science refused to be turned from its task of enlarging the boundaries of the known to pay homage to what was beyond the reach of knowledge.

Spencer's style is dry, technical, cumbrous, and pedantic, but it is always precise, sometimes fervent, and on occasion of a lofty dignity. A panoramic view of the *Synthetic Philosophy* inspires admiration for the patient ingenuity which fitted the interdependent parts into the vast, definite, and coherent heterogeneity.

III

Historians   With the exception of Carlyle (to whom some would deny the title altogether), no historian of high rank as a figure in English literature appeared between the death of Gibbon and the advent of Macaulay. [9] The authority of many works has declined because their writers did not submit themselves to the discipline of the new science of the analysis of evidence which, initiated in Germany, made its way slowly in England. Moreover, such works as William Mitford's *History of Greece* (1784-1810) and Sir Archibald Alison's *History of Europe* (1833-1842) were colored by their authors' intense anti-Jacobin prejudices. Connop Thirlwall's *History of Greece* (1835-1847) is, however, dispassionate in its massive intellectual power, and George Grote's *History of Greece* (1846-1856) is still a recognized authority. The Roman histories of Thomas Arnold and Charles Merivale have been quite

---

[8] *Autobiography,* I. 242.

[9] On writers in the fields of European and English history see G. P. Gooch, *History and Historians in the Nineteenth Century* (1913), pp. 282-294, and in the field of ancient history, *ibid.*, pp. 308-322. See also T. P. Peardon, *The Transition in English Historical Writing, 1760-1830* (1933); E. L. Woodward, *British Historians* (1943).

superseded. The works of Henry Hart Milman (1791-1868) have a special claim upon our attention because of their connection with liberal theology and biblical criticism. His *History of the Jews* (1829) was denounced by the High Church party for its semi-rationalistic outlook. In the *History of Christianity* (1840) Milman adopted the theory of "accommodation" which holds that a belief in miracles has suited certain stages of religious progress and that this belief, though not the miracles themselves, is the work of God— an uncomfortable, not to say blasphemous, compromise. The liberal reaction had set in by the time his *History of Latin Christianity* appeared (1855).

Sharon Turner's *History of the Anglo-Saxons* (1799-1805), a pioneer effort to reconstruct a culture and civilization, supplied a demand for information about the national past in which the literary antiquarians were rousing interest. Henry Hallam (1777-1859), on the other hand, lacked the sympathetic imagination to re-create a past epoch, and in his *Europe in the Middle Ages* (1818) he was not so much a narrator as a moralist, drawing from the past lessons applicable to his own age. His *Constitutional History of England* (1827) broke with the tradition of Tory history, inherited from Hume, and thus led directly to Macaulay. The *Introduction to the Literature of Europe in the Fifteenth, Sixteenth, and Seventeenth Centuries* (1838-1839) surveys a vast number of books and hazards many broad generalizations of varying degrees of validity. Among Hallam's works it retains perhaps most interest for the general reader.

IV

The precocious childhood of Thomas Babington Macaulay [10] (1800-1859)   *Macaulay* was passed among the Evangelicals of Clapham. After a brilliant career at Cambridge he published his first essays in *Knight's Quarterly Review* (1823-1824). The first of his contributions to *The Edinburgh Review* was the essay on Milton (1825) which owed its success in part to qualities of style but also to the author's prestige in Whig society where his powers as a conversationalist were already famous. In 1829 he was elected to Parliament. His five speeches in advocacy of the Reform Bill were an invaluable aid to Lord Grey's government. Between 1834 and 1838 he was in India as a member of the Supreme Council. His labors there resulted in educational reforms which lasted almost to our own day. On his return to England Macaulay was a member of Melbourne's ministry. In 1847 he lost his seat in Parliament, retired from public life, and devoted himself entirely

[10] *Works,* ed. Lady Trevelyan (8v, 1866); *Critical and Historical Essays,* ed. F. C. Montague (3v, 1903); *Miscellaneous Writings,* ed. T. F. Ellis (2v, 1860); *History of England,* ed. Sir Charles Firth (6v, 1913-1915). — Sir G. O. Trevelyan, *Life and Letters of Lord Macaulay* (2v, 1876); Arthur Bryant, *Macaulay* (1932); R. C. Beatty, *Lord Macaulay, Victorian Liberal* (Norman, Oklahoma, 1938); Sir Charles Firth, *A Commentary on Macaulay's History of England* (1938); G. P. Gooch, *op. cit.,* ch. xv; John Morley, "Macaulay," *Critical Miscellanies* (1908), I. 253-291. — Macaulay was raised to the peerage as Baron Macaulay of Rothley in 1857.

The
Essays

to the *History of England,* which appeared in three installments (1848, 1855, and 1861), the last unfinished and posthumous.

In later years Macaulay was ashamed of the superficial glitter of the *Milton;* but the essay exhibits many of the characteristics of his mature style.[11] The opinions expressed may be unreliable, but they are set forth with perfect clarity in pure English. The marked intellectual arrogance probably came from associations in boyhood with the high-minded but opinionated men of Clapham. The rough give-and-take of parliamentary debate presently increased the brutality of his style. Inexcusably severe is the attack on Southey (1830) who had argued in the *Colloquies* that all was not well with plutocratic England. The Whig essayist rages at the suggestion that the doctrine of a "stake in the country" was open to question and that the prosperity of the moneyed classes was perhaps not essential to the well-being of the "lower orders." Still worse is Macaulay's onslaught (1830) on the pathetic poetaster Robert Montgomery, where he seems to delight in invective for its own sake. A quarrel with the Tory John Wilson Croker culminated in a savage attack upon Croker's edition of Boswell's *Johnson* (1831), in which Macaulay outdid the current vituperative manner of the reviewers. The party animus is here so flagrant that Macaulay's intellectual integrity may well be questioned.[12] For the quarrel with Henry Brougham there was even less excuse, for Brougham had been his father's friend, was of Macaulay's own party, and had helped to give the young man his first step up the political ladder. That Macaulay could, however, estimate justly the achievement of a great man is evident from the article on Clive (1841), and that when his prejudices were not excited he could be both courteous and respectful is shown by the review of Ranke's *History of the Popes* (1841), where, for once, he seems almost humble in the presence of a historian greater than himself. The essay on Warren Hastings (1841) established the celebrity of his subject but is one of the least accurate of Macaulay's historical portraits. That on Frederick the Great (1842), though inaccurate and incomplete, is more penetrating than usual. The essays on men of letters are generally unreliable; Macaulay was himself dissatisfied with most of them. The *Dryden* (1828) is a study of the status of a man of letters in an uncongenial age when science was the center of interest. In the *Byron* (1830) there is not much more than shallow shrewdness. The portraits of Johnson and Boswell are notoriously flagrant caricatures. The *Walpole* (1834) is distorted by the writer's lack of sympathy with his subject's tastes and temperament. The *Lord Bacon* (1837) exposes Macaulay's incompetence to write on philosophical subjects. The account therein of Platonic doctrine is of a superficiality to shame Macaulay's own proverbial "school-boy"; and Bacon's achievement in inductive science is magnified beyond all reason, as is, antithetically, his moral turpitude. Only in the

---

[11] That it owed a good deal in ideas and style to Hazlitt is shown by P. L. Carver, "The Sources of Macaulay's *Essay on Milton,*" *RES,* vi (1930). 49-62.
[12] R. C. Beatty, *Lord Macaulay,* p. 143.

Addison (1843) have we a thoroughly trustworthy piece of literary criticism. The *Lays of Ancient Rome* (1842) are vigorous narratives from Livy, lacking shade and subtlety of diction and cadence but written with a forthright clarity which made them immediately popular. *Horatius* is still recitable; the other *Lays* are now neglected. They are the work of a historian interested in the problem of the transmission of traditions. Reversing the process whereby Livy composed his narrative, Macaulay attempted to reconstruct something like the lost ballad sources which the Roman historian had used.[13]

Lays of Ancient Rome

In the essay entitled *History* (1828) Macaulay set forth the ideal which he was himself to follow. "By judicious selection, rejection, and arrangement" the perfect historian, he says, "gives to truth those attractions which have been usurped by fiction." Macaulay would, then, redeem for history the provinces too frequently abandoned to the novelist: those small and vivid incidents and circumstances which restore life to the past; the rich cultural and social background without which the great figures of history have no perspective; the vast and variegated assortment of facts which earlier historians in England had rejected as beneath the dignity of their calling. He had ample precedent for employing history to maintain or refute opinions currently debated. The choice of his subject was determined by his devotion to the principles upon which the compromise of 1689 was founded; and this choice was confirmed when Sir James Mackintosh's fragmentary and posthumous *History of the Revolution in England in 1688* appeared (1834). Macaulay's criticism of his immediate predecessors was that they "miserably neglected the art of narrative." His own *History* is at its best when a great episode distracts him momentarily from his prejudices and he is content to be a literary artist working in a field not far removed from that of the historical novelist. In the narrative of Jeffrey's "Bloody Assizes" and of the last interview of the condemned Monmouth with King James the novelists were challenged and beaten on their own ground. In sweep and grasp nothing comparable to the great third chapter, surveying England in 1685, had appeared since Gibbon's prologuizing panorama of Rome in the age of the Antonines. There is, of course, perpetual overvehemence; and, in contrast to Gibbon, Macaulay never realized the value of condensation. His points are made, not by packing them into single sharp sentences, but by expanding them into paragraphs. The prolixity of parts of the narrative cannot be denied; but they are forgotten in the excited and impetuous flow at dramatic moments. The parade of historical parallels is occasionally tiresome; but by parallels of another sort—modern analogies—interest is sustained and the reader is made to understand the importance of the past for a comprehension of the present.

The History of England

Macaulay collected his material with astonishing energy and rapidity. He

[13] On a level higher than Macaulay elsewhere reached in verse is the *Epitaph on a Jacobite* (strange and moving theme for the arch-Whig to choose!) which has a deserved place in several anthologies.

went about England visiting the scenes which he intended to describe; he read (though he did not always inwardly digest) innumerable pamphlets and manuscript sources; and having accumulated these impressions in his miraculous memory he composed a draft with great swiftness, afterwards expending much toil upon the process of revision. The opinion of Brougham that Macaulay was never in search of truth but aimed only to produce "an effect of glitter and paint" is in harshness worthy of Macaulay himself, but it is not without warrant. The dazzling style is without shade; neither the whites (generally the Whigs) nor the blacks (generally the Tories) admit of any adulteration of gray. There is not even an appearance of impartiality. For the reliability of evidence he cared less than for its usefulness for the purposes of his argument.[14] "He marches," says John Morley, "through the intricacies of fact with a blaze of certainty." Yet recognition is due to the intellectual power which wrests the evidence to the support of a thesis. Those aspects of his subject which did not enlist his interest or did not lend themselves to his thesis he tended to neglect; there is, for example, little about England's relations with her colonies and with the Continental powers; the *History* is as insular as Macaulay himself.[15] The basic opinions maintained throughout are that all the blessings of England have flowed from the settlement of 1689 and that the present era in England is the most prosperous and enlightened age in the history of mankind. The gospel of material wealth is promulgated in a tone of infallibility. The moral complacency is extreme.[16]

V

Froude

When James Anthony Froude [17] (1818-1894) had broken with the Tractarians,[18] he turned to historical research. From the mid-century, date the earliest of the essays, published in the *Westminster Review, Fraser's Magazine,* and elsewhere, which were later gathered into the four series of *Short Studies on Great Subjects* (1867-1883). Among these papers that on *The Oxford Counter-Reformation* presents most interestingly the Protestant obverse of the Catholic picture drawn in Newman's *Apologia.* With it may

Short
Studies

[14] Various parts of the *History* provoked refutations. Of these the most penetrating is a series of papers, dealing chiefly with Macaulay's estimate of Marlborough, contributed by John Paget to *Blackwood's* in 1859. These have been reprinted with an introduction by Winston S. Churchill as *The New Examen* (1934).

[15] Macaulay admitted as much: "The book is quite insular in spirit. There is nothing cosmopolitan about it" (Trevelyan, *Life,* II. 390).

[16] A word must be added on Macaulay's private Journals. Trevelyan made some use of them and Professor Beatty much more, but as a whole they are still unpublished. Scholars who have read the manuscripts at Cambridge have brought away a disquieting impression of the self-portrait they contain. The censoriousness which Macaulay inherited from the Clapham group became even more extreme in his later life. An attitude of hatred and contempt towards nearly all contemporaries who were not in precise accord with his opinions was uniformly maintained. Disparagement was his almost unvarying position not only towards open foes but towards many who considered themselves his friends. The consciousness of his own rectitude was unfaltering.

[17] Herbert Paul, *Life of Froude* (1905); Algernon Cecil, *Six Oxford Thinkers* (1909), pp. 156-213; G. P. Gooch, *op. cit.,* pp. 332-339. On the Froude-Carlyle controversy see above, ch. xx, n. 1.

[18] See above, ch. xviii.

be associated the coldly analytical review of Newman's *Grammar of Assent.*
England's Forgotten Worthies is a spirited tribute to those Elizabethan adventurers whose exploits are brought into the forefront of Froude's *History.*
The sketches of travel reveal an interest in colonial problems and point
forward to Froude's *Oceana, or England and her Colonies* (1886) which
was an influence upon the growing imperialistic sentiment of the time. *The
Scientific Method applied to History* is in part an exposition of Froude's
opinion that history is an art, not a science; it contains the startling pronouncement that "the most perfect English history which exists is to be
found, in my opinion, in the historical plays of Shakespeare." [19] The remark
casts a flood of light upon Froude's own methods and standard of accuracy,
and it reveals the gulf fixed between him and his opponents. The biography
of Carlyle (1882-1884) and the controversy which sprang from it have
already been touched on. The biographical studies of Caesar and Luther
and some other minor works have not proved to be of lasting value.

In revulsion from Anglo-Catholicism Froude, as we have seen, was at- The
tracted to the subject of the Protestant Reformation in England, which History of
preserved English liberties from the temporal ascendency of the Papacy. England
This dominant theme accounts for the modification of Froude's original
plan, which was to narrate the history of the reign of Elizabeth. But on the
one hand he worked back to the reign of Henry VIII and on the other he
brought his story to a close with the artistic and historical climax of the
Battle of the Armada. The first installment of his *History of England,* which
at once rivaled Macaulay's *History* in popularity, appeared in 1856; the last
in 1870. In the choice both of theme and emphasis Froude was influenced
and encouraged by his master, Carlyle, though his pure English style is
quite uncontaminated with "Carlylese." Froude made much use of documentary material hitherto unexplored, but with gross carelessness, much
misinterpretation of evidence, and a complete inability to maintain a judicial impartiality. The anti-Catholic bias which pervades the whole work is
as notorious in the bitter blackening of the character of Mary Stuart as in
the "white-washing" of Henry VIII. The celebration of the triumph of
Protestantism perhaps necessitated a glorification of the instrument which
made that triumph possible; but the special pleading in the matter of the
King's marriages, the denial that he was a despot, the misinterpretation of
the position and power of Parliament, the defense of the execution of More
and Fisher, the condoning of atrocities provided they were committed on
the Protestant side, and the eagerness to let ends justify the most revolting
means, all are characteristics of the *History* which have led modern historians to declare bluntly that Froude's work must be done over again.
Even those who recognize his splendid pictorial gift (as in the famous opening chapter which is comparable to the analogous panoramas in Gibbon
and Macaulay) and equally admirable gift of narrative (as in the death-
scene of Henry VIII or Mary's flight from Scotland or the scene at Fother-

[19] *Short Studies on Great Subjects* (ed. 1910), II. 471.

ingay) repudiate Froude's authority as a historian. Freeman's attacks were of such unmeasured violence as to do as much harm to himself as to Froude; but the more calmly pronounced strictures of Stubbs are in substance as condemnatory; and a representative modern opinion is that "Froude closes the age of the amateurs, whose brilliant writings belong as much to literature as to history."[20] The worship of force, which Froude learned from Carlyle, is displayed most repulsively in the narrative of Elizabethan rule in Ireland; and this part of the subject is carried in a later work, *The English in Ireland* (1872-1874), down to the Act of Union. Froude's argument that a policy of conciliation was useless was his unhappy contribution to contemporary discussions of the Irish problem; and the opinion expressed that the right of a small people to self-government depends upon their power to defend themselves was, like Carlyle's doctrines, ominous of the appalling disasters which were later to fall upon the little nations.

Like Carlyle, Froude emphasized the influence of great men—a Henry VIII or a Burleigh—in shaping the course of history. Opposed to this view and probably a reaction from the exaggerations of Carlyle was the doctrine of impersonal laws determining the progress of mankind which was set forth by Henry Thomas Buckle (1821-1862) in his unfinished *History of Civilization in England* (1857-1861). The less speculative inquiries of W. E. H. Lecky (1838-1903)[21] furthered the growth of toleration. Of the so-called "Oxford School" of historians[22] only John Richard Green (1837-1883) won the attention of a large public. Into his *Short History of the English People* (1874) he introduced the cultural and scientific aspects of the nation's life and thus satisfied readers who wished for something else than constitutional, military, and diplomatic history. The prestige of William Stubbs (1825-1901) on account of his impartiality and intellectual grasp has proved lasting among professional historians, but his *Constitutional History of England* (1873-1878) and many monographs scarcely belong to literature. Unlike Stubbs, Edward Augustus Freeman (1823-1892) refused to divorce the chronicle of fact from a moral judgment of the fact. His studies in Ottoman history (1877) helped to stimulate anti-Turkish opinion during the Near East Crisis. His best-known work is the *History of the Norman Conquest* (1867-1879). To his influence is in part attributable the concept, popular at the end of the century, of the superiority of the Anglo-Saxons to the "lesser breeds." At Cambridge the massive erudition of J. E. E. D. Acton, Baron Acton (1834-1902) failed to bear fruit in books of great scope. He never wrote the "History of Liberty" which he planned as his life-work.[23] The royalist and parliamentary causes in seventeenth-century

The Oxford School

Other Historians

[20] G. P. Gooch, *op. cit.*, p. 339.
[21] *A History of the Rise and Influence of Rationalism in Europe* (1865); *A History of European Morals from Augustus to Charlemagne* (1869).
[22] G. P. Gooch, *op. cit.*, ch. xviii.
[23] Three volumes of Acton's historical studies were issued posthumously, ed. J. N. Figgis and R. V. Laurence (1907-1910). See F. A. Gasquet, *Lord Acton and his Circle* (1906).

England were interpreted with equal insight and impartiality by Samuel R. Gardiner (1829-1902); his *History* has yet to be superseded.[24] Justin McCarthy (1830-1912) wrote in more popular vein a *History of the Four Georges and of William IV* (1884-1901). Goldwin Smith (1828-1910), vigorous and voluminous controversialist, colored his interpretation of history with his anti-imperialist opinions; in *The Empire* (1863) he urged that the colonies should separate from England. Sir John R. Seeley (1834-1895), on the other hand, sensed the inevitable process of empire-building and in *The Expansion of England* (1883) and other writings was influential in impressing upon his countrymen the idea of "the White Man's Burden." [25]

Walter Bagehot [26] (1826-1877), a writer whom it is difficult to classify, was *Bagehot* a man of business, publicist, economist, historian, and literary critic. In *The English Constitution* (1867) he argued against the separation of the legislative and executive functions and commended their practical fusion through the cabinet in the English system. *Physics and Politics* (1869), one of the first attempts to apply to the study of politics the methods of psychology, developed the implications of Darwinism by describing the evolution of communities of men. Among Bagehot's *Literary Studies* (collected in 1879 but written much earlier) may be mentioned that on Wordsworth, Tennyson, and Browning as examples of pure, ornate, and grotesque art, and that on Shakespeare with its illuminating discussion of "experiencing nature" and its effort to discover the personality of the man behind the poet and dramatist.

VI

In the mid-nineteenth century a series of narratives of travel in the Near *Travel* and Middle East points forward to the great books by Doughty and Colonel Lawrence. Alexander William Kinglake (1809-1891) followed in *Eothen* [27] (1844) the English tradition of treating "Oriental encounters" in the spirit of comedy. The little book still retains its fresh charm. On an ampler scale but without Kinglake's touch of genius Eliot Warburton (1810-1852) wrote *The Crescent and the Cross* (1844). Robert Curzon (1810-1873) told of the quest of ancient manuscripts in his *Monasteries of the Levant* [28] (1849), and Sir Austen Henry Layard (1817-1894) reported vividly upon some of the most notable archaeological achievements of the age in *Discoveries at Nineveh* (1851) and later books. The life of Sir Richard Francis Burton [29]

---

[24] *History of England, 1603-1642* (1863-1882); *The Great Civil War* (1886-1891); *Commonwealth and Protectorate* (1895-1901).

[25] Seeley's early work, *Ecce Homo* (published anonymously, 1866), a study of the life of Christ, occasioned wide discussion.

[26] William Irvine, *Walter Bagehot* (1939).

[27] Ed. David G. Hogarth and V. H. Collins (1906); also in Everyman's Library.

[28] Ed. David G. Hogarth (1916).

[29] N. M. Penzer, *Bibliography* (1923); Thomas Wright, *The Life of Sir Richard Francis Burton* (2v, 1906); Fairfax Downey, *Sir Richard Burton: Arabian Nights Adventurer* (1931); Seton Dearden, *The Arabian Knight: a Study of Sir Richard Burton* (1936); H. J. Schonfield, *Richard Burton, Explorer* (1936); Sir Arnold Wilson, *Richard Burton* (1937). — For the student, though not for the general reader, Burton's translation of *The Thousand Nights and a Night* (1885-1888) superseded the expurgated and condensed version which Edward William

(1821-1890) belongs to the history of heroism rather than of literature. *A Pilgrimage to Al-Medinah and Meccah* [30] (1855) is the record of his most famous achievement; but the style is both random and braggart, the color laid on too thick, and the sardonic humor overdone. These strictures hold for Burton's other narratives of exploration.[31] Other explorers in Hither Asia and Africa who gave accounts of their accomplishments were W. G. Palgrave (1826-1888), David Livingston (1813-1893), Sir Henry Morton Stanley (1841-1904), and John Hanning Speke (1827-1864), the discoverer of the sources of the Nile.

Borrow   George Borrow [32] (1803-1881) was a wanderer over Europe, and his best books are the records of his wanderings. The amount of fiction that he mixed with autobiography cannot be estimated precisely. His versatility as a linguist was extraordinary, though his pretentions as a philologist rest on slender foundations. The strident anti-popery to which he gave voice was genuine, but the piety which won him his job as an agent of the Bible Society in Russia and Spain was of a dubious sort. His associations with rough characters lost nothing in the telling, but he did know gypsy life intimately. Humor, sentiment, graphic observation, satire, erudition, and romance mingle in the books of this eccentric individualist. The basic ingredient is a love of the open road and "the wind on the heath." *The Bible in Spain* (1843), *Lavengro* (1851), *The Romany Rye* (1857), and *Wild Wales* (1862) are episodic, inchoate, and inconsequential; but these strange, untidy, racy books still appeal not only to "the Borrovians" but to all lovers of the picaresque.

VII

"Lewis   From such exotic lands as Russia and Arabia we may pass to the authentic
Carroll"   wonderlands down the rabbit-hole and behind the mirror. The transition is sufficiently logical to satisfy "Lewis Carroll" [33] (Charles L. Dodgson, 1832-1898), the author of *Alice in Wonderland* (1865) and *Through the Looking-Glass* (1871). Written by an eccentric Oxford don to amuse his little girl-friends, these two world-famous books have proved to be enduringly delightful and are the best of all memorials of the Victorian love of nonsense. In them are elements of satire and parody which connect them with a long tradition, but they are shot through with a quaintly distorted

Lane (1801-1876) had published in 1838-1840. Burton's version has been praised by Arabists for its fidelity to the tone and idiom of the original, but it lacks the literary quality of John Payne's translation.

[30] Ed. Isabel, Lady Burton and S. Lane Poole (2v, 1906).

[31] Among which the best are *First Footsteps in East Africa* (1856), *Unexplored Syria* (1872) *The Land of Midian* (1879), and the books on Brazil (1869) and Paraguay (1870).

[32] *Works*, ed. Clement K. Shorter (16v, 1923-1924). — W. I. Knapp, *Life, Writings and Correspondence of George Borrow* (2v, 1899); R. A. J. Walling, *George Borrow, the Man and his Work* (1909); C. K. Shorter, *George Borrow and his Circle* (1913); R. T. Hopkins, *George Borrow, Lord of the Open Road* (1922); S. M. Elam, *George Borrow* (1929).

[33] S. H. Williams, *Bibliography* (1924; rev. ed., 1931); S. D. Collingwood, *Life and Letters of Lewis Carroll* (1898); *Selection from Letters of Lewis Carroll to his Child-Friends*, ed. E. M. Hatch (1933); Langford Reed, *Life of Lewis Carroll* (1932); Walter de la Mare, *Lewis Carroll* (1932); F. B. Lennon, *Victoria through the Looking-Glass* (1945).

logic (for their author was a professional mathematician and logician) which is inimitable and unique. It is a misfortune that of late years Dodgson and his charming books have been somewhat besmirched by the prying hands of the psychologists. "Lewis Carroll's" other writings (apart from professional papers) include *The Hunting of the Snark* (1876), a fantastical narrative poem, and the much less successful *Sylvie and Bruno* (1889-1893). Sir John Tenniel's illustrations to the *Alice* books share the fame of the text.

XXII
John Ruskin

Before 1860 Ruskin [1] was primarily an aesthetician and historian of art; afterwards he was primarily a social economist and reformer. But there was no interruption of continuity; the course of evolution from his first dominant interest to his second was consistent.

It is now known that John Ruskin (1819-1900) was a mental invalid; the attacks of insanity in his old age were the culmination of manic disturbances which manifested themselves, with periods of remission and exacerbation, from early life. The evidence for this is overwhelming.[2] What concerns us is the effect upon his work—the arrogance, dogmatism, capriciousness, self-contradictions, petulance, discursiveness, and alternations from depression to elation, from furious activity to gloomy indolence. His greatness is undeniable; but the thin partitions which divide great wits from madness were in his case distressingly insecure.

The education given him by fond and wealthy parents was neither normal nor wise. An only child, he had no companions of his own age, little regular instruction, and strict religious discipline. His tastes were indulged and it was assumed that he was a genius. He accompanied his father on his travels, and *The Iteriad,* a memorial of a visit to the Lake Country in 1830,[3] is one

[1] *Works*, Library Edition, ed. E. T. Cook and Alexander Wedderburn (39v, 1903-1912); Vols. xxxvi-xxxvii contain a selection from Ruskin's vast correspondence but many letters are still unprinted or scattered through various publications; Vol. xxxviii contains a bibliography exhaustive down to 1910. — E. T. Cook, *The Life of John Ruskin* (2v, 1911); R. H. Wilenski, *John Ruskin: an Introduction to further Study of his Life and Work* (1933); Alice Meynell, *John Ruskin* (1900); Frederick Harrison, *John Ruskin* (EML Series, 1902); A. C. Benson, *John Ruskin, a Study in Personality* (1911); Amabel Williams-Ellis, *The Exquisite Tragedy: an Intimate Life of John Ruskin* (1929). Older books still useful are E. T. Cook, *Studies in Ruskin* (1891); Charles Waldstein, *The Work of John Ruskin: its Influence on Modern Thought* (1894); J. A. Hobson, *John Ruskin, Social Reformer* (1898); J. Bardoux, *Le mouvement idéaliste et social dans la littérature anglaise au XIXe siècle: John Ruskin* (Paris, 1900). On Ruskin's aesthetic see Robert de la Sizeranne, *Ruskin et la religion de la beauté* (Paris, 1909); H. A. Ladd, *The Victorian Morality of Art: an Analysis of Ruskin's Esthetic* (1932); Bernard Bosanquet, *History of Aesthetics* (ed. 1934), pp. 447-454; Katharine E. Gilbert and Helmut Kuhn, *History of Esthetics* (1939), pp. 412-422; K. E. Gilbert, "Ruskin's Relation to Aristotle," *Philosophic Rev.*, xlix (1940). 52-62. See also F. W. Roe, *The Social Philosophy of Carlyle and Ruskin* (1921); E. B. Hagstotz, *Educational Theories of John Ruskin* (Lincoln, Neb., 1942). Various estimates are collected in *Ruskin the Prophet and other Centenary Studies*, by John Masefield, Laurence Binyon, and other writers, ed. J. H. Whitehouse (1920).

[2] R. H. Wilenski, *John Ruskin*, pp. 27-181, and the "synoptic tables," pp. 15-24.

[3] *On Skiddaw and Derwent Water*, a poem written at the age of nine, was Ruskin's first published piece; *The Spiritual Times*, February, 1830 (*Works*, II. 265-266). Other poems appeared in *Friendship's Offering* in 1835 and 1836. At Oxford, after two unsuccessful attempts, Ruskin won the Newdigate Prize with *Salsette and Elephanta* (1839). Ruskin's father privately printed *Poems. By J. R.* (1850). In this were collected almost all the poems already in print with a few others published for the first time. The poems are gathered together in *Works*, II.

of many poems composed and illustrated by the young prodigy. In 1832
Samuel Rogers' *Italy* with Turner's vignettes opened to him two worlds at *J.M.W.*
once; in 1833 he first saw Chamounix and in 1835 Venice, his "two homes *Turner*
on earth." Three articles which appeared in 1834 [4] manifest the interest in
natural science which was one of the bases of his art criticism. In 1836 the
impudent strictures of *Blackwood's* upon Turner's recent paintings moved
Ruskin to write a reply [5] which he afterwards described as a "first chapter"
of *Modern Painters*; but the germs of his principles are more clearly discernible in the articles on *The Poetry of Architecture* [6] (1837-1838). Illness cut
short his career at Oxford, and after a period of desultory activity he was in
Italy in 1840-1841. New attacks on Turner provoked him to another defense
(1842); and then, in 1843, appeared the book whose long original title accurately indicated its contents: *Modern Painters: Their Superiority in the* Modern
Art of Landscape Painting to all the Ancient Masters proved by Examples Painters
*of the True, the Beautiful, and the Intellectual, from the Works of Modern
Artists, especially those of J. M. W. Turner. By a Graduate of Oxford.* [7] The
notion that Turner was "unknown" till Ruskin came to his rescue is, of
course, baseless. He was famous, but his later manner was not intelligently
appreciated. Ruskin held him up to admiration at the expense of Claude
and Salvator Rosa who for a century had been in English estimation touchstones of artistic achievement. An Evangelical zeal, both moral and religious,
permeates the book and biases the critic's judgment. Art being, as he held,
"a noble and expressive language," it follows that "the greatest picture is
that which conveys to the mind of the spectator the greatest number of the
greatest ideas." [8] What, then, are the ideas conveyed by art? In answer
Ruskin formulated the five categories of Power, Imitation, Truth, Beauty,
and Relation. Thus, he, the least systematic of writers, involved himself
from the outset in a show of system. Actually his attention was concentrated,
as was proper in a treatise on aesthetic, upon the idea of Beauty; but his
definitions were so broad that his discursive mind could range as widely as
it would.

From sojourns abroad (1844-1845) he returned with impressions of Venetian and Florentine art which provided the material—displayed in descriptive
passages of gorgeous coloring and elaborate cadence, yet with minute
fidelity in verbal renderings of paintings and natural scenery—for a second
volume (1846). Because of the Protestant bigotry of its outlook Ruskin came
later to dislike this book; but it is one of his most significant. Religion is
the basis of the aesthetic which he expounds. The "theoretic faculty" is

[4] In *Loudon's Magazine of Natural History*, on the causes of the color of the water of the
Rhine, on the perforation of a leaden pipe, and on the strata of Mont Blanc—remarkable
topics for discussion by a boy of fifteen. See *Works*, I. 190-196.
[5] This, though submitted to Turner at the time, was first published in *Works*, III. 635-640.
[6] In *The Architectural Magazine*. The full title almost constitutes a program of Ruskin's
art criticism: *Introduction to the Poetry of Architecture; or, the Architecture of the Nations
of Europe considered in its Association with Natural Scenery and National Character*. The
papers were signed "Kataphusin" (i.e., "According to Nature"). Reprinted in *Works*, I. 5-188.
[7] The authorship, soon known in Ruskin's circle, was first publicly acknowledged in 1849.
[8] *Modern Painters*, I. i. 2; *Works*, III. 92.

The
"Theoretic
Faculty"

opposed to the merely aesthetic, that is, the moral perception of beauty is contrasted with the sensuous. The mind must confront Beauty with reverent contemplation (*theoria*) because through Beauty the attributes of God are revealed. It is plain how close this is to Carlyle's teaching that the visible universe is "the living Garment of God." With faulty logic Ruskin went on to develop his theme that "all Art being the formative action of a Spirit, the character of the Deed must necessarily depend upon that of the Doer, and according to that character the Deed is bad or good." [9] In other words, no "bad" man can be a great imaginative painter. Hence the first essentials for good art are true faith, sound morality, right education, and proper social conditions. This thought was to lead through the two treatises on architecture to Ruskin's social economics. The latter part of *Modern Painters, II,* is devoted to the three forms of the imagination: the associative, the penetrative, and the contemplative.

Work on *Modern Painters* was interrupted for a decade during which a vast growth in knowledge, necessitating some modification of his views, was accompanied by an illusory conviction of rightness upon every matter upon which he elected to speak. In 1848 Ruskin married [10] and passed his honeymoon in Normandy studying the cathedrals. Something of the excitement of French politics went into *The Seven Lamps of Architecture* (1849) in which the object was to show "that certain right states of temper and moral feeling were the magic powers by which all good architecture had been produced." [11] The line of thought which led him from the Venetian School of painting to the most communal of the arts was his realization of the historic importance of architecture as the record of the life of a people. Since, as he held, great art depends upon nobleness of life, it is the visible sign of a nation's virtue, and debased art is a sign of national decadence. Where it ministers only to luxury and pride it contributes to that decadence and itself degenerates. In this way of looking at architecture there was nothing new. A. W. N. Pugin and his fellow Gothicizers had already "tried to gauge the merit of a building by the virtue of its builders." [12] But Ruskin's eloquence forced a hearing where Pugin was unheeded. The "lamps" burning before God's altar are Sacrifice, Truth, Power, Beauty, Life, Memory, and Obedience. Discussions of such technical problems as the proportions of color, light, and shade and the use of honest materials are interrupted by passages of impassioned exhortation. The book offended architects because an amateur had intruded into their professional preserve with attacks upon the tastelessness and ignorance of contemporary design, the deceptions prac-

The
Seven
Lamps

---

[9] *Ibid.*

[10] The marriage to Euphemia Chalmers Gray ended in an annulment in 1854. For the circumstances see the letters in "Ruskin and the Women," ed. Peter Quennell, *Atl. Mo.,* CLXXIX (1947), Feb., pp. 37-45.

[11] *The Crown of Wild Olive,* II; *Works,* XVIII. 443.

[12] Kenneth Clark, *The Gothic Revival* (1928), p. 253. Pugin's delightful and ingenious *Contrasts; or a Parallel between the Architecture of the Fifteenth and Nineteenth Centuries* (1836) is essential to an understanding of the aesthetic "atmosphere" in which Ruskin's taste and theory developed.

tised in materials and workmanship, and the gross errors of the self-styled "restorers" of ancient buildings. But the resonant voice raised in the "Age of the Ugly" was gradually heeded, and to this noble book, with its bold attack upon conventions, its background of social concern, its plea for a dignified and truly representative national style, its practical lessons, and its moral fervor, is largely due the regeneration of English taste.

Living in Venice, Ruskin now dedicated himself to the "hard, dry, mechanical toil" of assembling material for *The Stones of Venice* (1851-1853), a particular exemplification of the general principles of *The Seven Lamps*. Of all his major works this is the most orderly in design, the three volumes being devoted to the periods, respectively, of origins and growth, of full flowering in the Byzantine and Gothic buildings of the city, and of decline in morals, life, and art. He found it difficult to adjust history to his theory because of the paradox that Venetian art reached its apogee amidst Renaissance pride and worldliness when the religious faith of the Republic had declined. The heights of his flamboyant, romantic prose (into which the rhythms of blank verse persistently force themselves) are attained in the description of St. Mark's; [13] and the central chapter on "The Nature of Gothic," [14] which became the bible of the new aesthetic school, contains the quintessence of his teaching. Since all art is for the glory of God, the concept is of more significance than the execution—or, as Browning was putting it at just this time, "a man's reach should exceed his grasp." Moreover, since a man is not a mere tool and true workmanship is imaginative creation, every workman must design for himself and not be a mere copyist.

The Stones of Venice

So complex are the wheels within wheels of Ruskin's mobile energy that it is difficult to compress into short space an indication of his activities during the eighteen-fifties. In 1851 he championed the Pre-Raphaelites, in whose paintings he detected, as he thought, some of the results of his own teaching.[15] Turner's death involved him in the long toil of cataloguing the paintings and drawings bequeathed to the nation.[16] In 1853 he lectured publicly for the first time; thereafter such appearances were frequent and this mode of communication enhanced his tendency to dogmatize. In 1854 he was one of the founders of the Working Men's College, where he gave drawing lessons and lectured. For his pupils he wrote the very popular

Many Activities

[13] *The Stones of Venice*, II, ch. IV, section 14; *Works*, x. 82-83. See George Saintsbury, *A History of English Prose Rhythm* (1912), pp. 395-396.

[14] *The Stones of Venice*, II. ch. VI, sections 1-78; *Works*, x. 180-245. These sections deal with the "mental expression" of Gothic architecture; the remainder of the chapter is concerned with technical problems of "material form."

[15] Two letters on the Pre-Raphaelites appeared in the *Times* in 1851; two more in 1854; all four were reprinted in *Arrows of the Chace* (1880); *Works*, xII. 317-335. A longer defense is *Pre-Raphaelitism* (1851); *Works*, xII. 337-393. Ruskin's association with Rossetti as patron and self-appointed mentor is one of the most interesting episodes in his life. In the end Rossetti could no longer tolerate Ruskin's arrogance and the friendship was ruptured.

[16] On the dispute in Chancery about Turner's will, Ruskin's renunciation of the executorship, and his subsequent work on the bequest see E. T. Cook, *The Life of John Ruskin*, I. 411-417. Ruskin issued various letters, notes, and catalogues dealing with the collection. All this material on Turner is gathered together in *Works*, xIII.

Elements of Drawing (1857) and the more technical *Elements of Perspective* (1859), both admirable pieces of exposition. The courageous address on *The Political Economy of Art*,[17] delivered at Manchester in 1857, expounds the relationship between employers and workmen and between government and industry; it is the bridge between Ruskin's earlier and later career. Annually, in his self-assigned rôle of arbiter of taste, he issued his *Academy Notes* (1855-1859). The third and fourth volumes of *Modern Painters* appeared in 1856 and the final volume in 1860.

The best-known chapters in Volume III are those on the "Grand Style" and on the "Pathetic Fallacy"; but the most coherent and characteristic are those contrasting classical, medieval, and modern landscape. From the formalism of Renaissance architecture studied in *The Stones of Venice* Ruskin had turned with enthusiasm and evident relief to the study of natural beauty. A moving epilogue, for which the reader is quite unprepared, is on the Crimean War. Volume IV was planned to be an analysis of the beauty of mountains, trees, and clouds; but love of the Alps won the mastery and the book became "a hymn to the mountains." It is the most clearly designed of all the five. The first seven chapters deal quite strictly with Turner's technique in mountain landscape; the next four, written with intense imaginative power controlling a mass of scientific detail, analyze the materials of the mountains and give an account of the geological changes from which they have resulted. Chapters XIV-XVIII are laboriously technical discussions of the resultant forms. Then, in chapters XIX and XX—"The Mountain Gloom" and "The Mountain Glory"—comes the response to the question: "What actual effect upon the human race has been produced by the generosity, or the instruction of the hills?" The splendid rhetoric of Ruskin's reply does not conceal a stubborn disregard of fact. Without thought of the great painters of the Low Countries he asserts that the fountain-heads of art are in the mountains, and argues from the lack of any great poet in Antwerp and Amsterdam without asking himself whether Switzerland has produced any such. The volume closes with the peroration recounting three scriptural mountain scenes: the death of Aaron, the death of Moses, and the Transfiguration. Volume V, in portions of which the incoherence is pronounced, is chiefly notable for the elaborate contrasts of the attitudes towards death displayed by various artists. This survey leads up to "The Two Boyhoods," one of Ruskin's most famous chapters, in which he points the contrast in the upbringing of Giorgione and Turner by rhapsodizing on Venice and then grimly describing modern London.

Social Economy

Unto This Last, the "truest, rightest, most serviceable" of all his books (as Ruskin afterwards described it), appeared in *The Cornhill Magazine* in 1860. This series of papers on political economy was to be longer, but Thackeray, the editor, alarmed by the hostility of reviewers and defections among his subscribers, brought the work to an abrupt close. The same fate

---

[17] Renamed, when republished in expanded form in 1880, *"A Joy For Ever"; (and its Price in the Market); Works,* XVI. 3-169.

overtook four *Essays on Political Economy* [18] published in *Fraser's* in 1862-1863. In letters to the newspapers, gathered together in *Time and Tide* (1867), Ruskin defended and elaborated his opinions. For them he did not claim originality, for he was one of a group who, following Owen and Carlyle, revolted against the classical school of mercantile economics which postulated "economic man" without the social and moral elements in human nature and by deductive reasoning arrived at absolute "laws" that were vitiated by application to concrete cases into which the social and moral elements always entered. Without denying men opportunities for self-development Ruskin urged that government should regulate and limit freedom of competition. From the analogies of the household, the professions, and the army Ruskin argued that in commerce and industry unselfish treatment of employees would give employers the best return. His appeal to the honor of manufacturers is reminiscent of Carlyle's hope for a "Working Aristocracy." The vigor of the protests against these views (which today seem old-fashioned in their mildness) is a measure of the strength of individualism, social irresponsibility, and belief in unrestricted competition in the mid-century. For long ridiculed or ignored, *Unto This Last* gradually made its way and was a telling influence upon the labor movement of the last decades of the century. *Time and Tide* contains scattered suggestions for an ideal commonwealth which passed into the program of William Morris and later Socialists.[19] Ruskin's more technical theories—his definition of wealth; his view that there is no profit in exchange; his conviction that all interest is usury—must be left to the economic historians. What concerns us is the burning sense of wrong and the militant social conscience which he evinced.

The years 1861-1863 were unhappy. Ruskin's religious views were unsettled and his incursion into the economic field had displeased his father. More alarming was the growth of a morbid attachment to the child Rose La Touche in whom his thoughts were henceforth centered and whom he later desired to marry. The story of this obsession, as of his over-emotional friendships with other girls of tender age, is a painful one. All this was a premonition of his later mental collapse. The death of Ruskin's father in 1864 may have caused a subconscious relief; at any rate a new period of intense activity began in that year. He could not find repose. The dogmatism and irritability increased and sought release in frequent lecturing, his audiences ranging from boarding-school girls to the Institute of British Architects. *The Cestus of Aglaia* (1865-1866), a series of papers on the laws of art, exhibits an eccentric discursiveness. To 1865 belongs the most widely popular of all his books: *Sesame and Lilies,* that is, in Ruskin's symbolism, the

---

[18] Reissued as *Munera Pulveris* (1872).

[19] Ruskin argued that the form of government is of no consequence; its efficiency in promoting social welfare is all-important. It must regulate marriage and provide compulsory schools. Occupations will be adapted to the tastes and talents of the workmen. The so-called "law" of supply and demand will prevail no longer, having been rooted in injustice. The rate of wages will depend not upon the supply of labor but upon the quality of the work. The working day will be eight hours. Menial tasks will be imposed upon a slave-caste, drawn perhaps from the criminal element. The suffrage will be limited by intelligence.

magic of right reading which opens the treasuries of human thought, and the purity which is the scepter with which women rule. Today the book seems as tritely Victorian as *The Princess*; but once upon a time it pointed towards the future when girls would have an education equal to that for boys, and there would be free public libraries, and better sanitation. Included in the volume was the beautiful and somber lecture on *The Mystery of Life and its Arts* which Ruskin later suppressed temporarily because of the evidence in it of religious unrest. It leads on to the eloquent discourses in *The Crown of Wild Olive* (1866), Ruskin's closest approximation to the agnosticism of the period.

The amazing versatility which came from the urge to be always active and the inability to concentrate upon one occupation is seen in the lectures on Greek mythology published as *The Queen of the Air* (1869); the consultations with Miss Octavia Hill, the social worker, on housing schemes for the poor; the visits to Switzerland and Italy; the botanizing and geologizing; the grandiose design to curb the Alpine torrents and conserve the waterfall; and yet other expressions of extreme mobility of interests. When in 1869 Ruskin was appointed Slade Professor of Fine Arts at Oxford, he undertook his new duties with feverish enthusiasm, publishing six volumes of lectures, writing guides for art-lovers, teaching drawing, trying to turn his doctrines to practical account, giving generously to museums of art, and exerting his influence upon younger men. Between 1871 and 1878 he was also much occupied with St. George's Guild and with *Fors Clavigera*. The Guild was a coöperative agricultural and manufacturing organization which he endowed with a tithe of his fortune. Essentially it was an attempt to revert to an irrevocable past, to establish a sort of neo-feudalism in industry. In plan it was in some respects practical, in others hopelessly utopian. Profits were to be shared; but there were no profits to share. The fortunes of the Guild were entangled with Ruskin's conviction that all interest upon capital is usury. The communistic basis led to disagreements and disappointments. The long series of letters addressed to the "Workmen of England" which Ruskin cryptically entitled *Fors Clavigera* [20] express many of his interests; but those critics who consider *Fors* the finest of Ruskin's works are misled by the richness of the medley. The style, in its relative simplicity, is far removed from the gorgeous periods of *Modern Painters*; but it is so flexible that Ruskin can bend it to any purpose. Inconsistent and pugnacious, sometimes blatantly boastful, often bitterly satiric, and always garrulous, these letters range over countless topics. Ruskin was, as it were, thinking on paper, following the train of thought wherever it led him. Often the drift is hard to follow and the rambling discontinuity painfully pronounced. But the mind is not everywhere unstable, and of its nobility there can be no question. The serenest portions are the "readings" in history, mythology, and literature. Other papers are on social economics, education, and the creed and

St. George's Guild

Fors Clavigera

---

[20] Nos. 1-87 appeared regularly in monthly installments, 1871-1878; Nos. 88-96 at irregular intervals, 1880-1884. The title is based upon Horace, *Odes*, I, 35.

rule of life of the Guild. Throughout the series runs a kind of diary of the author's activities, and in the occasional reminiscences of his early years are the germs of *Praeterita*.

Obsessions multiplied [21] and the relationship with Rose La Touche became more distressing till her death in 1875. In 1876-1877 Ruskin was in Venice, occupied with *St. Mark's Rest*, a history of the city. After his return home came the first complete breakdown, and he had to resign his professorship.[22] The story of the onslaught upon J. M. Whistler and the suit for libel which went against Ruskin is amusing only to those who are not aware of his malady.[23] In 1880 he recovered sufficiently to write the brilliant but erratic essays entitled *Fiction, Fair and Foul*. On a visit to France he began *The Bible of Amiens* (published 1885). In the lectures on *The Art of England* (1883) and *The Pleasures of England* (1884) insight flashes from tenebrous mists of eccentricity. The evidence of mental aberration is even more apparent in *The Storm-Cloud of the Nineteenth Century* (1884). *Mental* Repeated attacks of delirium now led to his permanent retirement to Brant- *Breakdown* wood, the home on Lake Coniston which he had purchased in 1871. There, in periods of temporary recovery between 1885 and 1889, he wrote *Praeterita*, the touching and delightful memories of his youth. The last decade—when by a tragic irony his prestige and influence were at their height—was, save for rare lucid intervals, a living death in which periods of violent excitement alternated with periods of gloomy silence. When he died in 1900 the age against whose cruel individualism and social apathy he had waged valiant warfare was passing and a new age which he had attempted to direct towards the light was at hand. At his funeral a wreath sent by one of his disciples bore the inscription: "There was a man sent from God whose name was John."

[21] The obsession with roses is of obvious origin. The obsession with young girls was expressed in his extravagant admiration for Kate Greenaway's pictures and even in his interpretation of Carpaccio's St. Ursula. The obsession with fireflies and lights against darkness has a direct bearing upon his violent criticism of Whistler's painting of fireworks in Cremorne Gardens.

[22] 1878; resumed for a short time in 1882.

[23] See J. M. Whistler, *Whistler v. Ruskin* (1878); reprinted in *The Gentle Art of Making Enemies* (ed. 1912), pp. 1-34. See also E. R. and J. Pennell, *The Life of James McNeill Whistler* (5ed, 1911), ch. xix.

XXIII
Charles Dickens,
Wilkie Collins, and Charles Reade

I

Some recent writers on Dickens blame him unfairly for faults that he had in common with his age and social class. But without accepting all the conclusions of the psychoanalysts one may recognize that certain defects in his character help to explain the shortcomings in his achievement. There is evidence in his novels and his life that a troubled childhood left its mark upon the man and his work. The sense of power and the self-assertion, combined with an incapacity for self-criticism, were perhaps compensations for the frustrations of his early years.

Early Years

Charles Dickens [1] (1812-1870) came of a family of the lower middle-class which regarded itself as genteel, yet tended to decline in the scale of consequence. Though born on the South coast, he was so young when brought by his parents to the outskirts of London that it is to the Kentish background of *Great Expectations* we must look for his earliest memories. His father, an ineffectual person destined to be caricatured as Mr. Micawber, went up and down in the world; and it was during one of his periods of degradation in a debtor's prison that Charles, then nine years old, was apprenticed in a blacking warehouse, a humiliating experience to the sensitive boy. After two years, better family fortunes enabled him to continue schooling; but his real education came from his reading and from wanderings in

[1] *Works*, Gadshill Edition, with introductions by Andrew Lang and B. W. Matz (36v, 1897-1908); Nonesuch Edition (23v, 1937-1938), with the largest collection of Dickens' letters. — John Forster, *The Life of Charles Dickens* (3v, 1872-1874), ed. B. W. Matz (2v, 1911), ed. J. W. T. Ley (1928), abridged by George Gissing (1898); G. K. Chesterton, *Charles Dickens* (1906) and *Appreciations and Criticisms of the Works of Charles Dickens* (1911); George Gissing, *Dickens, a Critical Study* (1898); A. W. Ward, *Charles Dickens* (EML Series, 1902); A. C. Swinburne, *Charles Dickens* (1913); J. W. T. Ley, *The Dickens Circle* (1918); Edward Wagenknecht, *The Man, Charles Dickens* (1929); A. S. G. Canning, *Dickens and Thackeray* (1911); Bernard Darwin, *Dickens* (1933); Stephen Leacock, *Charles Dickens: His Life and Work* (1933); Thomas Wright, *The Life of Charles Dickens* (1935); T. A. Jackson, *Dickens: The Progress of a Radical* (1938); Gladys Storey, *Dickens and His Daughter* (1939); Humphry House, *The Dickens World* (1941); Una Pope-Hennessy, *Charles Dickens* (1945); W. C. Phillips, *Dickens, Reade and Collins, Sensation Novelists* (1919); Pearl S. Buck, "My Debt to Dickens," *English Review*, LXII (1936). 408-412; E. R. Davis, "Dickens and the Evolution of Caricature," *PMLA*, LV (1940). 231-240; Lord David Cecil, "Dickens," *Early Victorian Novelists* (1935), pp. 37-74; Sir Arthur Quiller-Couch, *Charles Dickens and Other Victorians* (1925), pp. 3-99; George Santayana, "Dickens," *Soliloquies in England* (1924), pp. 58-73; Edmund Wilson, "Dickens: The Two Scrooges," *The Wound and the Bow* (1941), pp. 1-104. — *The Dickensian* (1905—in progress), the publication of the Dickens Fellowship, contains stores of information. — At this point a general reference may be made to Cornelius Weygandt, *A Century of the English Novel* (1925).

London and beside the Thames estuary. In 1827 he was articled to a solicitor, meanwhile mastering shorthand and attending sessions of the courts. He became parliamentary reporter for a small newspaper and then for *The Morning Chronicle*. By 1833, when the first of his sketches of London life appeared, he had had his share of hardships and humiliations, but also of small triumphs; he knew the metropolis and its infinite variety of human types; and he possessed abounding energy and self-assurance. Henceforth the story of his life is, for us, in the main the story of his books; but before turning to them let us glance ahead along his course. The success of his first volume enabled Dickens to marry Catherine Hogarth in 1836, though it was to her sister Mary that he was romantically attached. Mary is idealized in more than one of the novels, while poor Mrs. Dickens, who bore her husband many children, became the butt of the crude jocosity at the expense of over-fecund females that crops up persistently in the novels. The marriage ended in a separation in 1856. Dickens pressed the advantage of immediate success for all that it was worth—perhaps for more, for in the not very long run the burden of commitments was greater than even his tremendous *An* vitality could sustain. The widening of literacy was opening a vast market *Exhausting* to enterprising publishers who, to meet the new demand, purveyed fiction *Burden* in cheap form in monthly parts or serially in magazines. The need to swell a novel to proportions that could be spread over a year or eighteen months explains the unconscionable padding characteristic of this fiction; and the need to hold interest from month to month forced the novelist to close each installment with an unsolved mystery or on a note of interrogation. These requirements of his trade left their stigmata upon Dickens' art; and they kept his imagination upon a strain, for often he foresaw no more than his readers what was to happen next. More than once he began a fresh novel before he had completed its predecessor. Then there were his burdens as editor of *Bentley's Miscellany* (1837-1839), of *Household Words* (1850-1859), and later of *All the Year Round*. His many friendships brought a delightful but wearying round of social distractions of which we have the record in his letters and in Forster's *Life*. Responsibility for a large establishment and family often involved him in debt and necessitated the constant pursuit of profits. Amateur and semi-professional theatricals were emotionally exhausting, and towards the end there were the yet more exacting public "readings" from his books. Small wonder that he died, worn out, at the age of fifty-eight.[2]

Dickens' impressions of the world around him began to appear in periodi- Sketches cals in 1833, and in 1836 were gathered together as *Sketches by Boz, Illustra-* by Boz *tive of Every-Day Life, and Every-Day People,* with plates by George

[2] Hugh Kingsmill, *The Sentimental Journey* (1935), applies the methods of psychoanalysis in a cynical and exaggerated fashion to the interpretation of Dickens' character and writings. Bernard Darwin (*Dickens*, p. 114) and Baker (vii. 306) protest against Thomas Wright's disclosure of Dickens' relations with the actress Ellen Lawless Ternan, insisting that the "proof" advanced is mere hearsay. But Kingsmill and Edmund Wilson, among other recent writers, accept the story as true.

Cruikshank. A second series followed in 1837 and a complete edition in 1839. These evocations and episodes of London life, which contain the germs of much that is characteristic of his later work, spring partly from the ancient tradition of "character-writing," partly from Leigh Hunt's impressionistic essays and Washington Irving's *Sketch-Book* (1819), but in the main from the author's own talent as a keen observer of the superficialities of the human comedy. The success of the *Sketches* brought an invitation to contribute the "letter-press" to a series of jocular prints to be designed by Robert Seymour portraying the adventures of a club of amateur sportsmen. Thus, in *The Posthumous Papers of the Pickwick Club* (1836-1837), Dickens came to rival and immediately outstrip Hook, Egan, and Surtees in the field of episodical, anecdotal, facetious fiction concentrating upon sporting life.[3] Obligated to make his cockney clubmen merely ridiculous, Dickens got off to something of a false start. Seymour's suicide might have brought the plan to disaster, but in H. K. Browne ("Phiz") an ideal collaborator was found, and Dickens, no longer the minor partner, took the reins into his own hands. The character of Mr. Pickwick developed quickly from a mere figure of fun into something more attractive and substantial, and after Sam Weller appeared, these two—simple, kindly idealism supported by homely common sense—became as inseparable as Don Quixote and Sancho Panza. A note of richer humor was struck in the characterization of the elder Weller. Gradually a panoramic view of English life unfolded. The element of farce was never entirely abandoned, but there were hints of tragic implications, an awareness of injustice, an admiration of moral courage. The scenes in the Fleet prison point forward to Dickens' later advocacy of penal reforms. What seemed to be inexhaustible material encouraged the author to depend upon improvisation. *Pickwick* is loosely put together with the formlessness of life itself. The scene shifts from the London streets to rural leisure, from the world of sport to the tumult of an election, from the public-house to the prison and the law-courts. A romantic love affair, humorously treated, leads on to the thrilling narrative of a wild pursuit with coach-and-horses through the night. Ladies and gentlemen, politicians, lawyers and journalists, jailers and jail-birds, humbugs, eccentrics, snobs and charlatans, with a mixture of undifferentiated humanity, jostle one another in these crowded pages. *Pickwick,* the first fruit of Dickens' genius, remains in the opinion of many readers the most delightful of all his books.

From this humorous extravaganza Dickens turned in *Oliver Twist* (1837-

_____

[3] The picaresque element owes much to Smollett. In the character of Mr. Pickwick there are close resemblances to the comic protagonist of William Combe's *Dr. Syntax* (1812, 1820, and 1821). See William Dibelius, "Zu den *Pickwick Papers,*" *Anglia,* xxxv (1912). 101-110. — William Combe (1741-1823) had already written many ephemeralities before *The Tour of Dr. Syntax in Search of the Picturesque* made him famous when it appeared serially in 1809-1811. The subsequent *Tours* are *in Search of Consolation* and *in Search of a Wife.* They owed their popularity as much to Thomas Rowlandson's coarsely vigorous illustrations as to Combe's pseudo-Hudibrastic verse, which is not much above the level of doggerel. *The English Dance of Death* and *The Dance of Life* are also more memorable for Rowlandson's designs than for Combe's "letter-press."

ickwick
apers

1838) to the novel of crime and terror, following where Bulwer and Ains- Oliver
worth had led the way but refusing to idealize criminals as they had done. Twist
Some of the effects are modernizations and urbanizations of Gothic devices
and others are borrowed from the melodrama of the popular stage. Some
characters are drawn with humorous realism, but for the most part humor
is dimmed by gloomy memories of the author's own neglected childhood,
and sensational scenes are shrouded in an atmosphere genuinely eerie and
sinister. The few pleasant people heighten by contrast the brutality of Bill
Sykes and Fagin the Jew, which is very little relieved by the squalidly
pathetic figure of Nancy. That Dickens shared with his contemporaries
the conviction that the novel should be an instrument of social reform is
evident in *Oliver Twist*.

At this time disquieting rumors were current about the mismanagement Nicholas
of certain private schools in Yorkshire. The outcome of a journey to investi- Nickleby
gate the conditions said to prevail in these institutions was the picture in
Nicholas Nickleby (1838-1839) of Mr. Squeers and his academy, a caricature so much exaggerated as to spoil its effect as an indictment though not
as a series of coarsely humorous episodes. The plot of this novel is more
complex than in the earlier books. To sustain the interest of his subscribers
Dickens provided a series of climaxes, but between them are long level
stretches where the interest sometimes flags. Attention is often distracted
from the nominally principal figures to the subordinate. Nicholas himself
is colorless in comparison with his mother, Mr. Squeers and his daughter,
Mr. and Mrs. Mantalini, and Crummles. The Cheeryble brothers are among
the earliest of those "good" characters for whom Dickens bespoke more
affection than the modern reader is inclined to give them.

Master Humphrey's Clock was designed as a "frame" in which are set The Old
The Old Curiosity Shop and *Barnaby Rudge* (1840-1841). The clumsy Curiosity
"clock" matter was afterwards discarded and the two main stories issued Shop
independently. In *The Old Curiosity Shop* Dickens pulled out the *vox
humana* and *tremolo* stops upon his organ. In *Oliver Twist* indignation
had held pathos in restraint, but in the story of Little Nell no curb was put
upon emotion. A more cynical age than his is inclined to question the
sincerity of Dickens' pathos; but the fact that it is overwrought and that
Dickens, knowing that his readers enjoyed a "good cry," made it his practice
to wring the last possible tear from a situation does not prove that his
sentiments were feigned. He was as much moved as were his readers; he
and they were alike inheritors of the romantic conception of childhood
surviving into an industrial civilization which tolerated the employment of
little children in mines and workshops. Not all the Victorians were blind
to this contrast between their ideal and the actuality; that is one reason
why they wept. Little Nell and her Grandfather move through a crowd of
secondary figures, among them Dick Swiveller and the Marchioness and
Mrs. Jarley and that monstrous but effective embodiment of evil, the dwarf

Quilp. The earlier horror-romancers had devised nothing so memorably gruesome as Quilp's death in the slimy waters.

Barnaby Rudge

Scott's exalted example made it incumbent upon every ambitious novelist to try his hand at historical fiction, and this Dickens essayed in *Barnaby Rudge*. How closely he followed Scott appears from a comparison of his scenes of the Gordon riots with the Porteous riots in *The Heart of Midlothian*. The narrative of the outrages committed by the London mob is thrilling, but it would have gained in power from more restraint in style. In the episodes of ordinary life there is little attempt to differentiate the eighteenth-century scene from that of Dickens' own day. The absurd misrepresentation of the character of Lord Chesterfield in the figure of Sir John Chester shows that Dickens possessed nothing of Scott's ability to breathe life into people of the real past. With all this more or less authentic history a love story and an intrigue of crime and mystery are interwoven. A faded charm still lingers about Dolly Varden; and her lover is a not unattractive lad. But the mystery of the crime no longer rouses interest, for Dickens was both inept and stingy in providing clues. The poor simpleton Barnaby is a painful rather than pathetic figure; and Dennis the hangman is drawn in Ainsworth's Gothic style. On the whole this experiment in historical fiction was an aberration from Dickens' appropriate path.

Martin Chuzzlewit

After a visit to the United States [4] Dickens published *American Notes* (1842), by no means altogether hostile but a foretaste of what followed in *Martin Chuzzlewit* (1843-1844). The picture here painted of American vulgarity, boastfulness, and dishonesty wounded and offended Dickens' admirers over here, and the long, dreary episode is in inartistic contrast to the English scenes. The latter are rich in fantastic creations—Mr. Pecksniff, the quintessence of hypocrisy; Mrs. Gamp and Betsy Prig and that immortal shadow, Mrs. Harris; Todgers, sprung from the heart of cockney London; Tom Pinch, the most appealing of Dickens' pathetic figures; and Jonas Chuzzlewit, perhaps the most terrible of his villains.

Dombey and Son

The small sales of this novel indicated a decline in popularity, and Dickens, apparently realizing that his original vein was exhausted, struck out on new lines. Absence from familiar scenes while he lived on the Continent may explain his choice as the setting of *Dombey and Son* (1847-1848) of a higher social stratum than he had hitherto done more than glance at. But a sympathy with the aristocracy, new to him, is visible in the portrait of Cousin Feenix, who, though drawn humorously, behaves in a crisis as a gentleman should. Unusual care was devoted to the style and construction of this book. Yet the shift of interest after Little Paul's death to his sister might have been better prepared for and is accomplished not without some break in continuity. Mr. Carker is a vestige of theatrical melodrama, but his last journey and terrible death are narrated with great power. The serious

---

[4] W. G. Wilkins, *Charles Dickens in America* (1911). — *A Christmas Carol* (1843) is the first of the *Christmas Books*, short stories of a fantastic or fairy-tale kind which included, among other things, *The Chimes* (1845), *The Cricket on the Hearth* (1846), and *The Haunted Man* (1848).

story is lightened by the humorous characters, Major Bagstock (who is tiresome), Susan Nipper, and the delightful Captain Cuttle, who belongs to the tribe of Smollett's sea-faring folk. In general tone and atmosphere *Dombey and Son* is closer to actuality than Dickens had come hitherto; but this may be due as much to a decline in vitality as to deliberation.

Dickens' preference for *David Copperfield* (1849-1850) among all his David books has been shared by the great majority of his readers. The early, more Copper-closely autobiographical chapters contain the most vivid and moving pages field in all the novels; when purely fictitious incidents take the place of elaborated memories the later portions show some falling off. The comparative vagueness in the character of David himself, by some critics considered a weakness, is really part of the story's charm. David's are the eyes through which the other characters are seen; and what an array they are!—the Murdstones and Aunt Betsie Trotwood; the Peggottys; the Micawbers; Dora and her family; Uriah Heep. Mr. Dick is the least offensive of the simpletons and crazy folk whom Dickens, following an old tradition, turned to purposes of comedy. Mr. Micawber is perhaps the best of all his comic creations. There are both melodrama and false sentiment in the story of Steerforth's seduction of Little Em'ly; but in general this novel stays within the bounds of probability and truth to life.

When Dickens founded *Household Words* in 1850, he enlisted as contributors a group of younger authors, chief among them Wilkie Collins. The influence of this master of the technique of fiction dependent upon sensation, mystery, and intrigue is apparent in the more firmly knit plot of *Bleak House* (1853), where the story of the endless Chancery suit is in- Bleak geniously intertwined with that of Lady Dedlock's sin and retribution. An House immense number of characters are wonderfully differentiated. The satire on the law's delays was of practical value in exposing the need of reforms. Never before or after did Dickens picture more vividly the London streets, the quiet of the precincts of the law-courts, the horror of the city graveyards, the gruesome and degraded atmosphere of old houses tainted with old crimes. Death broods over the somber story. The pathos of the end of poor Joe, the crossing-sweeper, still moves the sensitive reader; and there is real spiritual terror in the narrative of the death of Mr. Tulkinghorn.

The shift of interest in *Hard Times* (1854) was strangely sudden. The Hard intention to use fiction for purposes of social protest, already apparent in the Times earlier books, now became the principal motive of an entire novel. The story, appropriately dedicated to Carlyle, was based on Dickens' own observations of industrial conditions in Manchester. The bitter sincerity of Dickens' social indignation, which before now had led him to sacrifice artistic refinement and reticence in order to bring home the wrongs of society to the consciences of his readers, lessens the value of this book as a work of art. His passion makes him unfair, for though employers like Bounderby may have existed they did not represent their entire class, nor was the almost saintly patience of Dickens' workingman and working-girl typical of theirs.[5] Dickens was within his rights in using the novel as a medium for agitation, and while he had no other solution of the problem of industrial relations than an emphasis upon benevolence, as an artist he was justified in declining to discuss practical remedies.

Little Dorrit (1857) shows a serious falling off in power. The stagy scenes in the Clennam residence are so many remnants of Gothic romance. The dreary business of the "Circumlocution Office" is topical satire on bureaucratic inefficiency. In the foreign episodes Dickens went far beyond the range within which he was master. The scenes in the Marshalsea are somberly autobiographic, and the distressing delineation of Flora Finching almost justifies the conclusions drawn from it by the psychoanalytical critics. On the whole, *Little Dorrit* is, of all Dickens' books, that which has worn least well.

A Tale of Two Cities (1859), inspired by Carlyle's *French Revolution* and planned with an intricate artifice suggestive of Wilkie Collins, is a second effort in the field of historical fiction. About it there is a pretentious grandiosity, as though Dickens had set himself to a task on lines to which his admirers were unaccustomed. There is too much of mystery and melodrama; but the opening scene in the stagecoach, the pictures of the bloodthirsty women of the Parisian proletariat, and the death of Sydney Carton have secured places in the memory of three generations of readers.

After the comparative failure of the three preceding books Dickens made a recovery in *Great Expectations* (1861), where loose capaciousness gives place to clear-cut condensation in plot, and the usual slipshod style is brought into order and beauty. The famous opening in the dismal Kentish lowlands is an evocation of Dickens' early memories. Pip, the hero, is less of a lay-figure than Copperfield had been, not only an observer of other people but an actor in his own drama who is not the less alive for being far from faultless. There is much stirring adventure, but it seldom goes beyond the bounds of plausibility, though Miss Havisham and her strange household are one more reminiscence of Gothic grotesquerie. The convict and Joe Gargery and Mrs. Joe are among Dickens' less extravagant creations, neither the grimness of the one nor the humors of the other two being overdone. Of Estella's rôle there are two opinions, some holding that Dickens should have retained his original conception of her as the evil principle in Pip's life, while others welcome the sacrifice of that conception for the sake of the romantically happy ending. This vivid, simply contrived and compellingly interesting story was the last expression of Dickens' full power.

The decline in *Our Mutual Friend* (1865) is obvious to most readers. The plot, with its absurdity of the supposed dead man who slinks through the story in disguise, is a tissue of crossed motives scarce worth the unraveling. The character of Riah, the pious old Jew, is too obviously an atonement for

---

[5] Ruskin (*Unto This Last*, I, 10; *Works*, XVII. 31) commended *Hard Times* but thought that its usefulness was diminished by the error of making Bounderby "a dramatic monster" and Stephen Blackpool "a dramatic perfection."

the prejudices revealed in the early portrait of the malignant Fagin. The satire on snobbery and social ambitions is even more heavy-handed than it had been in *Little Dorrit*. The mingling of comedy and pathos in the character of the doll-dressmaker is laborious, as are the futile humor-studies of the Golden Dustman and Silas Wegg. The book is partially redeemed by the powerful, though overwrought, delineation of Headstone's tragic passion for Lizzie Hexam and by the magnificent opening scene on the Thames and other episodes along the water-front.

The scale upon which Dickens lived kept him burdened with debt. He worked the gold mine of public readings and in 1867 made a second tour of the United States. Avoiding the strain of original composition, he underwent the severer strain of these readings into which he threw himself with all the force of his emotional temperament. He returned home exhausted, but heedless of advice continued his public appearances till 1870. In that year he began the publication of *The Mystery of Edwin Drood,* which was inter- The rupted, with the mystery unsolved, by his death. Many attempts have been Mystery made to construct the probable ending. No solution is satisfactory, though of Edwin the most nearly convincing relates the plot to Dickens' interest in the secret Drood society of Thugs in India.[6]

II

Adapting with many reservations Dryden's characterization of Shake- *"A Com-* speare, one may say of Dickens that he was of all the Victorian novelists *prehensive* the man of most comprehensive soul. He saw life, as no earlier novelist had *Soul"* seen it, from the point of view of the poor of a great city. Possessed of a buoyant temperament, it is the more remarkable that he was not deceived by the blatant assurances of industrialism, but sought to mitigate its evils. He worked for practical reforms without advocating any change in the system of society because he believed that when institutions and their administration were remedied the fundamental goodness of human nature would make the reform of individuals an easy matter. Nearly all his bad characters are capable of conversion, and many are converted. Through most of his life he addressed his appeals for reform to the middle classes, and though towards the end there are signs that he was turning from hope in them to hope in the aristocracy, his pictures of the upper classes are almost always prejudiced and exaggerated, generally inaccurate, seldom kindly. His basic belief in the primary benevolent impulses of man—affection, charity, gaiety, fun, kindliness, spontaneity—brought within the compass of his sympathy any man or woman in whom he discerned the working of these impulses.

But he had not a Shakespearean understanding of evil. His unconverted *Characters*

[6] For a list of solutions of the problem of *Edwin Drood* see Thomas Wright, *The Life of Charles Dickens,* Appendix IV, to which add Howard Duffield, "John Jasper—Strangler," *The Bookman,* LXX (1930). 581-588.

"bad" people are saved from absolute condemnation only if, like Silas Wegg or Mrs. Gamp, they can be delineated grotesquely. The characters therefore tend to fall into two classes, almost as sharply differentiated as are the Virtues and Vices of the old moralities. But Dickens was not a creator of types; his figures are seldom truly representative of humanity at large. When he draws from observation of real people, as in his portraits of Landor and Leigh Hunt, the result is caricature. He is at his best when, peopling a world of his own devising with creatures of his own imagination, he fashions individuals who are beyond caricature because they are not distorted reflections of someone else but are themselves. No one has ever encountered a Mrs. Gamp or a Silas Wegg; but they are alive in their own right. To object that Dickens exaggerates is to question the very basis of his art. "It would be as sensible," says an excellent critic, "to criticize a gargoyle on the ground that it is an exaggerated representation of the human face" as to criticize Pecksniff because he is an exaggerated representation of a hypocrite.[7] This creative imagination is exercised upon literally hundreds of characters, each unlike all the rest, so that individual traits distinguish one charlatan from another, one shabby old woman from another, one villain from another, even one good man or "hero" from another. This intense individualization is accomplished by emphasizing the innumerable external qualities which are present in different combinations and permutations in every man and woman, marking the distinction of each from other. Dickens is far less alert to the underlying traits in which all human beings share and share alike. The colonel's lady and Judy O'Grady may be sisters under the skin, but since Dickens does not look beneath the surface he is not struck by the family resemblance. His is essentially a grotesque art, the art of the caricaturist, even when the result is not, properly speaking, caricature. But though to secure an effect a weakness is overemphasized, there is unerring insight in detecting the weakness. He sees the outward man rather than the inward motive; there is little effort to trace the development of character; and when once the idiosyncrasy or "humor" is established, the person either remains what he is to the end of the story or else undergoes a violent and unconvincing change at the close for the sake of the plot. A disconcerting feature of Dickens' work is the juxtaposition of the fantastic and the real. Creatures who live only in his imagination, though there with unexampled vitality, jostle with people drawn from actuality. Similarly, melodramatic incident protrudes with startling suddenness from a context which is real. Limelight and daylight play upon the scene at the same time.[8] Like Scott and unlike Jane Austen, Dickens focuses the interest upon characters and episodes irrelevant to the main story. The structural center is seldom the center of interest. For long stretches of narrative the principal plot—often a tangle of intrigue so elaborate that the reader follows it with difficulty or is quite indifferent to it—

Plot and Setting

[7] Lord David Cecil, *Early Victorian Novelists*, p. 44.
[8] *Ibid.*, p. 39.

is neglected, while the vital, though nominally subordinate, figures live and move before us. For plots Dickens relied with cheerful brazenness upon the shoddy and paltry devices of romance—the disguised lover, the long-lost heir, mistaken identity, the supposed dead who turn up in the nick of time, and other such tricks of the trade. But though Dickens' craftmanship and taste are alike defective, reflecting as they do the vulgarity and false sentiment of his age and class, the setting of these plots is almost always admirable. From the Gothic romancers he inherited a love of the fantastic in places, houses, objects, and names. He rendered marvelously the sights and sounds and smells of London—the fog, the drizzle, the slime, the dust, the crowded streets, picturing with equal authenticity the river, the water-side, the City, the law-courts, the West End, the suburbs. At further removes he was equally successful only when equally at home, as in the scenes beyond London in *David Copperfield* and *Great Expectations*. When he ranged beyond his own intimate experience, as in the Italy of *Little Dorrit* or the America of *Martin Chuzzlewit,* he was not at ease.

III

Wilkie Collins [9] (1824-1889) served under Dickens on the staff of *House- *hold Words* and, later, *All the Year Round*. Dickens' shift from novels of humorous character to novels of sensational intrigue was partly due to Collins' precepts and example. But there are differences. Whereas Dickens conceived his characters and then invented a plot to set them in motion, Collins invented his plot and then fitted characters into it. Far more than Dickens, Collins depended upon the technique of the popular sensational theatre; how closely is shown by the ease with which he adapted several of his novels to the stage. His tales contain almost invariably three ingredients: an intricate plot; humor in not very good imitation of Dickens; and a love-story. He often tells his story through the mouths of different characters, sacrificing continuity for the sake of startling effects. His three best books are *The Woman in White* (1860), the story of a crime based upon the resemblance of two women of whom one turns out to be the illegitimate sister of the other; *Armadale* (1866), where an ingenious plot is unfolded in an atmosphere of sinister eerieness; and *The Moonstone* (1868), on the theme (which Collins passed on to many imitators) of a jewel stolen from an Indian idol and retrieved by Brahmin conspirators. Collins was a master of climax and suspense, but the men and women in his tales are scarcely

Wilkie Collins

---

[9] S. M. Ellis, *Wilkie Collins, Le Fanu and Others* (1931); Baker, VIII. 191-201. — Other sensation novelists of the mid-century were Joseph Sheridan Le Fanu (1814-1873), an Irishman with a mastery of the occult, the uncanny, and the ominous; Mary Elizabeth Braddon (1837-1914), whose *Lady Audley's Secret* (1862) won for her a devoted public, though her realistic and historical novels are now forgotten; Mrs. Henry Wood (1814-1887), whose *East Lynne* (1861) is still remembered and who depended less upon sensationalism than realism; and Marie Louise de la Ramée, "Ouida" (1840-1908), whose love of the gorgeous and stupendous endeared her to a public blind to her meretriciousness. *Under Two Flags* (1867) is her best-known book. See Yvonne ffrench, *Ouida, a Study in Ostentation* (1938).

:harles
eade

characterized at all, being but pawns upon his chessboard of intrigue. He
was in some ways an ancestor of modern writers of detective fiction.

Charles Reade [10] (1814-1884) was not so close to Dickens. Before turning
to fiction he had been a successful dramatist, and his novels, with their
crudity and violence and large dependence upon dialogue and dramatic
presentation, have an affinity to the stage. *Peg Woffington* (1853), the first
of them, was made over from his comedy, *Masks and Faces.* Like Dickens
he used the novel to expose abuses and advocate reforms. *It's Never Too
Late to Mend* (1856) has to do with the management of prisons and the
mistreatment of criminals; *Hard Cash* (1863) with the scandals of private
lunatic asylums. In *Put Yourself in His Place* (1870) Reade attacked the
trade-unions. His other books are not to the same degree novels with a
purpose. Several, of which the powerful but too vehement *Griffith Gaunt*
(1866) is the best, are studies in character. Like Emile Zola, whose *L'As-
sommoir* he dramatized as *Drink* (1879), Reade accumulated and classified
in huge ledgers and notebooks immense amounts of material for his studies
of the human situation, drawing it from personal observation, newspapers,
reports of commissions of inquiry, and other sources. Generally his imagination was stifled rather than vitalized by all this information. He followed
the same method in the composition of *The Cloister and the Hearth* (1861),
putting into that great and still widely read historical novel material from
Erasmus, Froissart, Luther, the chronicles, the old jest-books and beggar-
books, and quantities of miscellaneous erudition. The remoteness of the
scene and period imparted geniality to a style made coarse and brutal by
sincere but too vociferous indignation in the propaganda novels. The resultant picture of Europe at the dawn of the Renaissance—its every level
of life from palace and monastery to tavern and highroad; its every type of
character from bishop and burgomaster to beggar and freebooter—is at
once spacious and dignified and beautiful and wonderfully informed with
life. *The Cloister and the Hearth* was an entire departure, and a welcome
one, from Reade's predictable line of development. Its interest and value
have proved lasting; and Reade is likely to be remembered as *homo unius
libri.*

10 C. L. Reade and Compton Reade, *Charles Reade, a Memoir* (2v, 1887); Malcolm Elwin,
Charles Reade, a Biography (1931); Léonie Rives, *Charles Reade: sa vie, ses romans* (Toulouse,
1940); A. C. Swinburne, "Charles Reade," *Miscellanies* (1886), pp. 271-302; Baker, VIII. 202-
213; A. M. Turner, *The Making of the Cloister and the Hearth* (1938). Important articles on
Reade by E. G. Sutcliffe are in *SP*, XXVII (1930). 64-109; 654-688; *ibid.*, XXXVIII (1941). 521-
542; *PMLA*, XLVI (1931). 1260-1279; *ibid.*, XLVII (1932). 834-863.

XXIV

Thackeray and Trollope

I

Thackeray's injunction to his daughters, "Mind, no biography!" was prompted not by fear of discreditable disclosures but by distrust of cant and insincerity. In default of an "official" *Life*, scholars have ransacked his writings for autobiographical allusions. Something has been detected and more has been surmised; there are few untouched transcripts from actuality but many portraits of real people "worked up" into imaginative creations. This search for "originals" has, however, been carried too far.

William Makepeace Thackeray [1] (1811-1863) was born in Calcutta of a *Early* family of Anglo-Indian officials. After his father's death his mother sent *Years* him as a child back to England. School-days at Charterhouse were not a happy time, though memory softened asperities and what he had once called "Slaughter House" became the kindly "Grey Friars" where Colonel Newcome died a pensioner. In 1829 he entered Trinity College, Cambridge, where he and Edward FitzGerald became intimate friends. Between them there was a spiritual kinship; each found in his own breast an echo of the words *Vanitas Vanitatum, omnia Vanitas!* Leaving Cambridge without a degree and with but a smattering of classical education, Thackeray traveled in Germany, visited Paris, and returning to London entered the Middle Temple. From the study of law he derived little save memories afterwards used in *Pendennis*. The loss of a small legacy in speculation and gaming was also turned later to good account in fiction. Like Clive Newcome, he had a talent for caricature and hoped to be an artist. This, in the severest technical sense, he never was; but only a very crotchety aesthetician can fail to enjoy his illustrations to many of his own writings. The date of his first contact with *Fraser's Magazine* is uncertain; few contributions from his pen have been identified with certainty of an earlier date than 1835, when he

[1] *Works*, Centenary Biographical Edition, introductions by Anne, Lady Ritchie (26v, 1910-1926); Oxford Edition, introductions by George Saintsbury (17v, 1908); *Letters and Private Papers*, ed. G. N. Ray (4v, Cambridge, Mass., 1945-1946); *Letters to an American Family* (1904); other letters by Thackeray are in *Letters of Anne Thackeray Ritchie*, ed. Hester Ritchie (1924). — Lewis Melville, *The Life of William Makepeace Thackeray* (2v, 1899), which contains a bibliography (II, 133-376); Charles Whibley, *Thackeray* (1903); G. K. Chesterton, *Thackeray* (1909); A. J. Romilly, *Thackeray Studies* (1912); Raymond Las Vergnas, *Thackeray: l'homme, le penseur, le romancier* (Paris, 1932); Malcolm Elwin, *Thackeray, a Personality* (1932); H. N. Wethered, *On the Art of Thackeray* (1938); J. W. Dodds, *Thackeray: a Critical Portrait* (1941); J. C. Bailey, "Thackeray and the English Novel," *The Continuity of Letters* (1923), pp. 193-217; Lord David Cecil, *Early Victorian Novelists* (1935), ch. III; Baker, VII, ch. VII; J. W. Dodds, "Thackeray as a Satirist before *Vanity Fair*," *MLQ*, II (1941). 163-178; Lionel Stevenson, *The Showman of Vanity Fair* (1947).

figures in Maclise's drawing of the "Fraserians." [2] He began as a trenchant critic and an imitator of Maginn's burlesques. In 1836 he married. His wife's insanity, after a few years of marriage, is the tragedy of Thackeray's life. Round his two daughters his affections clung, and in his later years he made a home for them. Solaces of different kinds were provided by the friendship with Mrs. Brookfield and by an ever increasing habit of "dining out."

Early Writings

The miscellaneous writings that appeared before his great year, 1847-1848, are not to be enumerated exhaustively here. The majority were published in *Fraser's,* but after 1841 Thackeray was on the staff of *Punch* [3] and connected also with other publications. After his home was broken up he lived in London clubs or at Brighton or Paris, or wandered from place to place. *The Paris Sketch Book* (1840) is a miscellany of small, uncomfortable episodes of travel, ephemeral and not very well considered chat on French politics and history, and comment on the art, literature, and theatres of contemporary Paris. Rather incongruous intrusions are two stories in the grotesque vein, *The Painter's Bargain* and *The Devil's Wager*. *The Irish Sketch Book* (1843) has an abundance of anecdote and local color but evinces little sympathetic understanding of Ireland and its problems; it was as a disillusioned tourist that Thackeray remembered the discomforts of journeys more vividly than the sights he went to see. In 1845 he undertook the tour of the Levant recounted in *Notes of a Journey from Cornhill to Grand Cairo* (1846) where the excellent writing does not conceal the fact that when contemplating the wonders of antiquity he was as much of a Philistine as Mark Twain.

Yellow-plush

Meanwhile he had been progressing towards the novel. *The Memoirs of Mr. C. J. Yellowplush* and *The Diary of C. Jeames de la Pluche* (1837-1838) have to do with a footman who makes a fortune by gambling in railway shares. Fashionable life is viewed from the servants' hall, and the satiric thrusts at what Mr. Yellowplush calls—or rather spells—"fashnabble novvles" are directed at Bulwer. The ingenuities of Jeames's phonetic spelling are still amusing, though this device has been staled by imitators. Bulwer and Ainsworth, as novelists of crime, are assailed in *Catherine* (1839-1840), the detestable story of a woman who murdered her husband and was burned at Tyburn, founded upon an actual case of 1726. Thackeray's intention was to deflate the pretensions of the criminal-as-hero; but as in other early work in lighter vein his footing is unsteady. To the novel of crime he returned with more assurance in *Barry Lyndon* (1844), recounting with ironic detachment a rascal's actual exploits. *Jonathan Wild* was his model, but Thackeray could not, or at any rate did not, sustain his irony throughout and obscured his effect by endowing Lyndon with genuinely attractive qualities. In the *Novels by Eminent Hands,* originally called *Punch's Prize*

---

[2] On Thackeray's connection with, and contributions to, *Fraser's* see M. M. H. Thrall, *Rebellious Fraser's* (1934), pp. 55-80, 295-298. See also H. S. Gulliver, *Thackeray's Literary Apprenticeship* (1924).

[3] M. H. Spielmann, *The Hitherto Unidentified Contributions of W. M. Thackeray to "Punch." With a ... Bibliography from 1843 to 1848* (1900).

Novelists (1847), Thackeray parodied more directly his favorite victim, Bulwer, along with Disraeli, G. P. R. James, and other popular writers of fiction. During these years some very amusing things, along with others that have not worn so well, appeared in *Punch* and annuals and "Christmas Books." The fantastic romance, *A Legend of the Rhine,* is still attractive; *Mrs. Perkins's Ball* is a lively succession of social caricatures; *Rebecca and Rowena* is good sense and sound criticism as well as enjoyable parody; and *The Rose and the Ring* (published so late as 1855) is Thackeray's masterpiece in this minor kind, unforgettable for its illustrations, its rimed page-headings, its speeches in inflated verse embedded in the prose, its sense and nonsense, parody and romance.

Reverting to an earlier date, we remark that in its opening chapters *A Shabby-Genteel Story* (1840) gives promise of the serious realism lightened with ironical comedy of which Thackeray was afterwards a master. But at this time he was distracted and distressed by his wife's breakdown, and after some fumbling he fell into mere burlesque where the note is pathetically forced. Much later Thackeray attached to this story *The Adventures of Philip,* but the sequence of events is not made clear. A new tenderness and delicacy of treatment, probably not unconnected with the author's personal sadness, is apparent in *The History of Samuel Titmarsh and the* Titmarsh *Great Hoggarty Diamond* (1841), the story of the morally innocent but foolishly gullible employee in a swindling company who is involved in the crash in its affairs and goes to prison. There is a recovery of spirits and a significant change in spirit in *The Snobs of England. By One of Themselves* (*Punch,* 1846-1847), better known by its later title, *The Book of Snobs.* Thackeray had formerly known the word *snob* as Cambridge slang, but he now used it with serious intent. Snobbery is "toad-eating," "climbing," and vulgar humbug. In his definition the snob is one who, seeking to emulate his social superiors, "meanly admires mean things."

Up to this time Thackeray's writings, for all their variety and brilliance, Vanity had not been commensurate with his powers. The failure to establish him- Fair self on an equality with Dickens and above other contemporary novelists had weighed upon his spirits. But when *Vanity Fair* appeared in twenty serial numbers in 1847-1848, it was not long in making its way to the summit of contemporary fiction. In setting the events back a generation and thus not criticizing his own period too directly Thackeray perhaps displayed a little timidity; but essentially this is a novel of contemporary life. He had often mocked at sensational romances and historical novels. Now he picked up the thread of the novel of manners where Jane Austen had let it fall, and wove his pattern upon a vastly larger loom than hers. He employs no romantic machinery, no intrigue to be unraveled, no secrets to be disclosed. Apart from the episode of Waterloo (where the battle reverberates in the distance), he is concerned with the commonplaces in the life of people who, as he says, have "no reverence except for prosperity, and no eye for anything beyond success," "a set of people living without God in the world."

His anxiety lest he be taken in by such men and women is responsible for the tendency to associate cleverness with evil and goodness with foolishness, and this was the basis for the charge that he was cynical. Conventional categories of human types were disregarded in favor of an individualization so complete that we know the characters better than we know our friends. The very fact that a few inconsistencies can be detected is evidence of the fullness of our knowledge. To this day the debate continues as to whether Becky Sharp killed Joseph Sedley. Thackeray, when asked, said that he did not know; and when readers give reasons for this verdict or that, they are transferring the problem from the domain of fiction to actuality. This is the very triumph of art. A triumph of another kind is the portrayal of Becky in all her wicked worldliness yet with revealing touches that explain her attractiveness.

Pendennis   *Pendennis* (1849-1850) has had its enthusiastic admirers but is little read today. In its scenes in town and country and university there is the plotlessness of life itself, and, as in life, there are stretches of tedium. The surface is broad, but the deeps are seldom plumbed. Thackeray drew upon his own experiences of school and university and the world of journalism; but Pen, though a "portrait of the artist as a young man," is so with variations which make him no mere copy from memory. Major Pendennis has been thought in some respects a portrait of the novelist in his maturity. Rather he is what Thackeray might have been but for the grace of his genius.

Henry   The hero of *Henry Esmond* (1852) is another self-portrait, such a man as
Esmond   Thackeray might have been had he lived a century and a half earlier. The grave detachment and serene melancholy in Esmond's bearing are suggestive of the novelist, as is the awareness of all-pervading futility and vanity. The political, social, and cultural background of the reign of Queen Anne is painted with a masterly confidence grounded upon long familiarity and lately refreshed by the lectures on *The English Humorists of the Eighteenth Century* which Thackeray had delivered in 1851.[4] Breathing, as it were, the very atmosphere of Augustan England, Thackeray attempted to write *Esmond* in the style of the period. The archaism is an appropriate artifice, but the pastiche is far from convincing. The supreme creation is the character of Beatrix in her fascinating and imperious beauty, her calculating worldliness, and her tragedy. Thackeray was justified in his daring when he portrayed her in her old age in *The Virginians,* for the Baroness de Bernstein is the person whom Beatrix was fated to become.

With the lectures on the *Humorists* as his wares to sell, Thackeray, who needed money, visited the United States in 1852-1853, and with another series on *The Four Georges* made a second tour in 1855-1856.[5] Whether because he was forewarned by Dickens' experiences or because he was more disillusioned and therefore more tolerant, he had on the whole a happy

---

[4] The word *humorist* is used not in the loose modern sense but with the old meaning of one who displays the *humors* of mankind.
[5] J. G. Wilson, *Thackeray in the United States* (2v, 1904).

time on both visits. He was willing, as Dickens had not been, to see the greatness of the country and recognize that the promise of the future atoned for the shortcomings of the present. His American connections were pleasant and the tours profitable. Impressions of the second tour were worked·into *The Virginians* (1857-1859), a rambling novel with characters connected by ties of blood with those in *Esmond* but in a period two generations later. It suffers, as does Dickens' *Chuzzlewit*, from the shifting of scenes between England and America. Between his first transatlantic journey and the second came *The Newcomes* (1853-1855), in the opinion of many readers his most beautiful book. But such readers are swayed by memories of the closing pages and by the character of Ethel Newcome, Thackeray's warmest tribute to the noble qualities of womanhood; and they forget the bitter insistence upon the follies and infirmities and depravities of life. For all the beauty of his nature Colonel Newcome is both fond and foolish; and the portraits of Barnes Newcome, the meanly successful worldly man, and of Clive's mother-in-law, "the Old Campaigner," are terrible in their uncompromising clarity.

In 1859 Thackeray accepted the editorship of the newly founded *Cornhill Magazine*. The duties irked him and he soon resigned; but the last two novels and the fragment of a third appeared in its pages. In *Lovel the Widower* (1860) comic power is wasted upon dull and disagreeable people. *The Adventures of Philip* (1861-1862) has its defenders but betrays to most people flagging invention. There was promise of recovery in *Denis Duval* (posthumous, 1864), a historical romance of the late eighteenth century, but Thackeray's death left this unfinished. It has roused no controversy like that which has raged round *Edwin Drood* because the plan of what was to follow is known. The little that was written has a vigor and expansive charm making the loss the more regrettable.[6]

The Virginians

The Newcomes

Last Novels

II

Did Thackeray spend so much time parodying and satirizing romantic sentiment because he recognized and distrusted sentimentality in himself and subjected himself to his own satiric scrutiny? *The Book of Snobs,* it will be recalled, was written "by one of themselves." He possessed a terrible power to detect and expose men's self-deceptions, shams, pretenses, and unworthy aspirations. Disillusionment was dominant in his temperament from early life, and the tragedy which shattered his home fixed the mood upon him. He can show anger and indignation, but his usual manner is urbane. He was, as has often been remarked, a spectator of the battle of life, not a com-

Point of View

---

[6] Thackeray's poetry has been overshadowed by the novels. He belongs in the company of Victorian writers of light verse touched with sentiment. As in his early prose burlesques, so in his early verse-parodies his footing is not quite certain and the effects aimed at are not always hit—at any rate from our modern angle of vision. But the best of his *vers de société* are of a finesse beyond the reach of his master, Maginn, and comparable to those of Praed. *The Willow Tree* is a unique thing, a double parody; the first part takes off romance with such delicacy that, as in some things by Peacock, almost one is persuaded of the seriousness of the poet's intentions; and then a second part broadly, but with equal cunning, burlesques the first. *The Ballad of Bouillabaisse* combines sad and tender memories of the past with the gourmet's enjoyment of the immediate present; and the incongruous combination is made

batant therein. For this detachment he has incurred the charge of cynicism, because the Victorians expected of their novelists that they would crusade for good causes, and Thackeray, unlike Dickens, was no crusader. Comparisons with Dickens have always been as inevitable as those of Tennyson with Browning; and most of them are inept. But two points of contrast are as important as they are obvious. One is that whereas we are interested in the creatures of Dickens' imagination because they are unlike anyone we have ever known, our interest in Thackeray's is due to their resemblance to people within the experience of most of us. The other is that while Dickens depended for his best effects upon externalities of setting, in Thackeray a moral atmosphere is created.

Thackeray suffered, and complained of suffering, from the prudish inhibitions of his time. Many modern critics have held against him that he ignored or at most hinted at "the sins of the flesh"; but had he defied convention he would not have gained an audience. In the tendency to divide his characters into good and bad he reflects an age which was uncompromising on moral issues; yet here he struggles against convention, insinuating mitigating circumstances into "wicked" natures and showing how often "good" people are weak and foolish.

Technique   The technical and structural defects of the novels are obvious—the habit, inherited from Fielding, of stepping down to the footlights and discoursing in his own person; the occasional inconsistencies and lapses of memory; the garrulity and repetitiousness for which he now pays dearly in the loss of readers; the slack and patternless structure. But in his hands the novel advanced in several ways, upon only two of which there is space here to remark. In *Vanity Fair* events are seen not from the point of view of any one character, and there is no one with whom the reader is expected especially to sympathize. Yet the reader does not survey the scene precisely from the author's angle of vision. A double emotion is imparted: that of the actors in the events and that of the author who records them. There is alternately a withdrawal for the sake of a wider view and an approximation for the sake of minute scrutiny. In all the novels the reader is made aware of the flight of time, of renewal and decay, of the generations trodden down by their successors. This effect of time's remorseless flow, associated with such later novelists as Bennett and Galsworthy, Thackeray first introduced into English fiction.

III

Anthony Trollope [7] (1815-1882) came naturally by the novelist's trade

touching and beautiful. The half-humorous, half-pathetic is the kind in which Thackeray worked most successfully, but some of his extravaganzas are still amusing and once at least, in *The Chronicle of the Drum*, he was wholly serious with success. The translations from Béranger are worth mentioning, for as a poet Thackeray exhibits some affinity with the French song-writer and satirist.

[7] There is no definitive edition of Trollope's writings. The Shakespeare Head Edition was designed to fill this want, but since the publication of the *Autobiography* and the *Barchester Novels*, ed. Michael Sadleir (14v, 1929) has proceeded no further. Of some novels there are

(the term is used advisedly), for his mother was a prolific writer.[8] After a *Anthony* boyhood which, as he admits in his candid *Autobiography,* had been un- *Trollope* promising, he obtained a position in the Post Office administration which, with a brief but memorable interim, kept him busy in Ireland from 1841 to 1859. A ramble among the ruins of an Irish mansion gave him the idea for his first novel (1847) which, with its immediate successor, is in the tradition of Carleton and Lever. These books are no longer esteemed even by Trollope's devotees. When he held temporarily an inspectorship in the west of England, the cathedral close of Salisbury opened his imagination to the little world of clerical society. The result was *The Warden* (1855), followed by *Barchester Towers* (1857) and *Doctor Thorne* (1858). *Framley* *The* *Parsonage* appeared in *Cornhill* (1859-1860) and, as Thackeray generously *Barchester* acknowledged, was responsible for the immediate success of the new maga- *Novels* zine. *The Small House at Allington* (1864) followed, and the series of *Barchester Novels* was closed with *The Last Chronicle of Barset* (1867). Trollope's attention was not limited to the region he knew so intimately; *Can You Forgive Her?* (1864), *The Claverings* (1865), *The Belton Estate* (1866), and other books show a wider outlook. Moreover, he visited many countries and recorded his observations in travel books. In 1867 he resigned from the Post Office and in 1868 stood unsuccessfully as a Liberal candidate for Parliament. The disappointment of defeat could not have been great, for he had neither an aptitude for a public career nor stoutly held political convictions. His candidacy merely shows that as a novelist his interest was veering to the political scene. Among the novels on public life are *Phineas* *Other* *Finn* (1869) and *The Prime Minister* (1876).[9] With the systematic industry *Novels* of which he has given an account in the *Autobiography* he turned out novel after novel almost faster than admirers could devour them. The specialists have classified them,[10] and only the specialists have read them all. In addition to the Barchester series and the political novels, there are novels of "manners, convention, and the social dilemma"; half a dozen social satires; four Irish and two Australian novels; four historical and romantic novels; six "psychological analyses and stories of single incident"; four collections of short stories; and (in a class by itself) *The Fixed Period* (1882), one of those glimpses into futurity of which the late nineteenth century produced

---

many reprints, in Everyman's Library, the World's Classics, and elsewhere. *The Warden,* ed. R. M. Gay (1935) is of special value. — Michael Sadleir, *Bibliography* (1928) and *Anthony Trollope, a Commentary* (1927; rev. ed., 1945); T. H. S. Escott, *Anthony Trollope, his Works, Associates, and Literary Originals* (1913); S. van B. Nichols, *The Significance of Anthony Trollope* (1925); Hugh Walpole, *Anthony Trollope* (EML Series, 1928); L. P. and R. P. Stebbins, *The Trollopes: the Chronicle of a Writing Family* (1945); J. H. Wildman, *Anthony Trollope's England* (Providence, 1940); Baker, VIII, ch. IV; George Saintsbury, "Trollope Revisited," *Essays and Papers* (1923), II. 312-343. See also *The Trollopian* (1945-   ).

[8] Mrs. Frances Trollope (1780-1863), author of the *Domestic Manners of the Americans* (1832), which gave great offense in the United States; *The Vicar of Wrexall* (1837), an anti-clerical novel; and forty-odd other books. The recent vogue of Anthony Trollope has resulted in some overestimates of her worth as a novelist. See Michael Sadleir, *Anthony Trollope,* pp. 29-97. — Anthony's elder brother, Thomas Adolphus Trollope (1810-1892), lived long in Italy and wrote popular history, miscellaneous fiction, and stories of Italian society.

[9] M. E. Speare, *The Political Novel* (1924), ch. VII.

[10] Michael Sadleir, *Anthony Trollope,* pp. 415-419.

many examples. It is a very unconvincing forecast of life in 1980; Trollope was no visionary. All told, these categories embrace some fifty titles.

When it is remembered that he was forty when *The Warden* appeared and over fifty when the Barchester series was closed, it is not surprising that many of the later books are of little value and the best of them uneven in quality. The general line of his development was from the familiar to the exceptional and abnormal. There were early raids into strange countries but he did not attempt to occupy them till he was too old to become ac-climated. "His great, his inestimable merit," said Henry James, "was a complete appreciation of the usual" [11]—an opinion which George Moore repeated in a less bland fashion when he said that Trollope "carried commonplace further than anyone dreamed it could be carried." [12] In the parsonage or bishop's palace or cathedral stall or close he observed the immemorial round of English custom. It chanced that he selected for his freshest scrutiny "scenes of clerical life," but that other representatives of the "governing classes" served his purposes almost as well is shown by the glimpses of the political world that appear in his pictures of the ecclesiastical and by the ease with which he turned from the latter to the former. His clergymen are Englishmen first and divines only a long way after. Such a book as Mrs. Humphry Ward's *Robert Elsmere* was beyond his intellectual range and beside his artistic purpose. With the problems of faith and doubt, religious meditation, and the theological issues that were dividing the churches he evinces no concern, just as in the political novels he is not interested (as was Disraeli) in the great questions of the day but in the party game. The little world of a diocese is a stage broad enough for him. Whole classes of society that live in the sociological fiction of the period never appear in his pages. In his microcosm the lesser faults and foibles of human nature are displayed—the heart-burnings of social aspirants; the distinctions of caste and class; the gossip and scandal, jealousy and arrogance of petty people. Serious moral obliquity is rarely his theme, save in *The Eustace Diamonds* (1873) and in *The Way We Live Now* (1875). The latter, openly but unsuccessfully challenging comparison with *Vanity Fair*, is one long piece of satiric invective against modern life, surprising as coming from a writer usually so genial and tolerant. Because his intention is generally to "sport with human follies, not with crimes," Trollope's natural manner suggests indulgent amusement. When derisive or censorious he generally fails, for his laughter, unlike Meredith's, is not "corrective." He did not use the novel as a vehicle for a "philosophy of life" which he did not claim to possess.

Henry James observed that of the two kinds of literary taste, "the taste for the emotion of surprise and the taste for the emotion of recognition," Trollope gratified the latter.[13] Here he resembled his master, Thackeray.

"The Usual"

---

11 Henry James, *Partial Portraits* (ed. 1919), p. 100.
12 George Moore, *Avowals* (1919), p. 89.
13 *Partial Portraits*, p. 133.

Excluding from his best work the exceptional and minimizing the improbable, he was truthworthy in his reading of life. He knew men and women not in those isolated examples of moral grandeur which make us proud of our human nature nor in those of turpitude which horrify and shame, but on the average level where contemplation makes us tolerant and a little humble. His method as an artist was to begin with a group of such characters and *Method* having set them in relation to one another, to depend upon the logic of circumstances for the "plot" which was bound to result from the clash of opposing egotisms. Knowing intimately the people of his imaginary world, very rarely could he bring himself to violate the probabilities of motive and action for the sake of the "story." A technical device, used rarely but always with startling effectiveness, is his sudden intrusion in his own person (though he has no part in the story) to record an encounter with this character or that. The reappearance of people in novel after novel, sometimes in principal, sometimes subordinate capacities, enhances this sense of intimacy. All this coming and going produces an impression of an actual world like that of the *Comédie Humaine*. A realism less sincere would have been hopelessly deformed by Trollope's adherence to the old convention of bestowing upon his characters such fantastic names as Mr. Quiverful, Mr. Stickatit, or Dr. Fillgrave. This was all very well so long as people so encumbered remained in the background behind Archdeacon Grantly or Mrs. Proudie; but when in later novels men with names suggestive of *Pilgrim's Progress* are promoted (as is Mr. Quiverful) to a principal rôle the blemish is serious and the reader does not without effort suspend disbelief. Faith is put to a severer test by Trollope's unnecessary and persistent habit of reminding us that the story he tells is, after all, only make-believe.[14] In the long run his meticulousness in detail, his insistence upon explanation, his inability to let suggestion do the work of statement, his too faithful record of tedious conversation, his prolixity, his undistinguished style (a heavy-footed amble for which George Moore found the wittily apt epithet "Trollopy")—all this will tell against his reputation.

Trollope's posthumous revelation of his calculated, scheduled, daily stint *Post-* was responsible for the conception of him as a mere industrious journeyman- *humous* of-letters. Obviously, without methodical habits he could not have accom- *Vogue* plished his immense amount of work. Obviously, had he written less he would probably have written better. In the period between the World Wars his reputation rose to new heights. This revival of interest was initiated by the recommendations of a few authoritative critics who, however, would not have been heeded had not Trollope appealed to a disillusioned and anxious generation, skeptical of the heroic virtues and amused by a candid and psychologically convincing picture of average humanity.

[14] James, who remarks upon this habit, calls it "suicidal" (*ibid.*, p. 116).

XXV
Other Novelists of the Mid-Century

To complete a survey of Victorian fiction before the appearance of Meredith and Hardy we must revert to the eighteen-twenties when Bulwer and Disraeli published their first novels.

I

Edward Bulwer

The life of Edward Lytton Bulwer [1] (1803-1873) as politician and "dandy" cannot be recounted here, and there is space to touch on only the most significant of his novels.[2] The earliest of these are tainted with Gothic and Godwinian insincerities. The first that is memorable is *Pelham* (1828), a picture of fashionable society whose satiric intent was not apprehended by Carlyle.[3] With *Paul Clifford* (1830) Bulwer started the vogue of romances of crime and social injustice, and continued this vein in *Eugene Aram* (1833), inventing a motive for the murder, with which motive the reader is asked to sympathize. In a series of historical novels he followed Scott with much careful and self-conscious documentation. *The Last Days of Pompeii* (1834) presents the contrast of pagan brutality, sensuality, and superstition with the simplicity and piety of primitive Christianity. *Rienzi* (1835), on the medieval Roman "tribune," *Leila* (1838), on the Conquest of Granada, *The Last of the Barons* (1843), on the Wars of the Roses, and *Harold* (1848), on the Norman Conquest, followed. All display the same qualities of careful, scholarly preparation, smoothness of construction, over-facility of style, and a bookishness which makes for an effect of low vitality. Romance and history are conjoined in them, and though in places the romance is heavily laid on, for long stretches it is quite subordinated to history. Questions of relative merit apart, a point of contrast with Scott is that Bulwer built his stories round some great personage of authentic history,

Historical Novels

---

[1] On inheriting Knebworth Bulwer took the additional surname of Lytton; he was knighted; and in 1866 was created Baron Lytton. — *Novels*, New Knebworth Edition (29v, 1895-1898). — The Earl of Lytton, *The Life of Edward Bulwer, First Lord Lytton* (2v, 1913); Michael Sadleir, *Bulwer, a Panorama: I: Edward and Rosina* (1931). When the projected "panorama" was abandoned, Mr. Sadleir renamed this book *Bulwer and his Wife* (1933). Material for the intended second part went, with a shift of emphasis, into *The Strange Life of Lady Blessington* (1935). See also E. B. Burgum, *The Literary Career of Edward Bulwer, Lord Lytton* (1924).

[2] On Bulwer's plays see above, ch. xv. On his pretentious poem *King Arthur* (1848), of interest only as a precursor of Tennyson's *Idylls of the King*, see Howard Maynadier, *The Arthur of the English Poets* (1907), pp. 351-352. His other poems are forgotten. Still of some value as a document is *England and the English* (1833), a shrewd and lively survey of contemporary society and culture, with an emphasis upon snobbery and class-consciousness.

[3] *Sartor Resartus*, Book iii. ch. x.

whereas Scott relegated illustrious figures to the middle distance or the background, reserving the foreground for characters of his own creation.

Bulwer did not limit himself to historical fiction. *Zanoni* (1842) is a fantastic romance of terror, supernaturalism, and occultism. The protagonist is granted immortality on the condition that he never yield to the dictates of human sympathy; but after five thousand years he sacrifices himself during the French Revolution, for the sake of the woman he loves. Bulwer returned more than once to supernatural themes, and in *A Strange Story* (1862) he almost succeeded in creating a masterpiece of weird terror. What he called "Varieties of English Life" (though there is not much variety) he depicted in a succession of realistic stories of which the best are *The Caxtons* (1849) and *My Novel* (1853). *The Coming Race* (1871) is a utopian fantasy of a lost subterranean people. In *Kenelm Chillingly* (1873) Bulwer's sociological speculations came down—or up—to earth. The wealthy hero is a "muscular Christian" who lives in the slums and works as a laborer. *Other Novels*

Bulwer was a writer whose restless and versatile talent took color from some fashions and helped to shape others. An opportunist alike in his parliamentary and literary career, and driven on by need of money, he wrote too much and too fast in too many genres of literature. It is only as a novelist that he is remembered—and even as such he is in peril of oblivion.

The crowded life of Benjamin Disraeli [4] (1804-1881) belongs to political rather than literary history, and a survey of his novels may be undertaken with little reference to his career. In *Vivian Grey* (1826) the young author's limited experiences and unlimited aspirations are attached to a story of political intrigue enlivened with witty dialogue in the manner of Peacock. Dialogue is the main ingredient in the Lucianic fantasies, *The Voyage of Popanilla* (1828) and *Ixion in Heaven* (1833). *The Young Duke* (1831) is so much encumbered with ephemeral politics as to be today unreadable. *Contarini Fleming* (1832) is chiefly interesting for what is obviously a self-portrait set against the background of the Levant where Disraeli had traveled in 1828-1831. The political theme is abandoned in *Henrietta Temple* (1836) in favor of a love story. The hero is loved by two women, to one of whom he is betrothed while with the other he is infatuated. Disraeli was always unable to render passion convincingly; the effort to remedy this defect merely heightened the affectations of his style. *Venetia* (1837) has been kept in remembrance because two of the characters share between them, with a curious redistribution, the traits and circumstances of Byron and Shelley, about whom Disraeli, through his father [5] and John Murray, *Benjamin Disraeli*

---

[4] *Novels and Tales*, Bradenham Edition, introduction by Philip Guedalla (12v, 1926-1927). — W. F. Monypenny and G. E. Buckle, *The Life of Benjamin Disraeli, Earl of Beaconsfield* (6v, 1910-1920) in which the following parts are important for Disraeli as a writer: I, chs. VI, X, XV; II, chs. VII, IX; III, ch. II; V, chs. IV and Appendix; VI, ch. XV. See also M. E. Speare, *The Political Novel* (1924), chs. II-VI; F. T. Russell, *Satire in the Victorian Novel* (1920).

[5] Isaac Disraeli (1766-1848), author of *The Curiosities of Literature* (five series, 1791-1834), *The Calamities of Authors* (1812-1813), *The Quarrels of Authors* (1814), and other works.

possessed somewhat more information than was then known to the public.

When Disraeli became a member of the parliamentary group of "Tory Democrats" known as "Young England," he promulgated their theories and program in a trilogy of novels dealing, respectively, with the political, social, and religious problems of the day. *Coningsby* (1844) pictures the English governing classes. The slender plot unfolds the development of the political ideas of the hero, a young aristocrat with a sense of social responsibility. Contrasted with him is his grandfather, a man of immense wealth and immovable conservatism. Disraeli's fondness for the pseudo-occult finds an outlet in the theatrical character of the Jew, Sidonia, through whom the wisdom of the East is brought to bear upon the problems of the West. "Comic relief" is provided by the figures of the political agents; there is a variety of swiftly moving scenes; and a great deal of discussion reminiscent of Peacock but without Peacock's brilliant brevity. *Sybil* (1845) has for its theme the "Two Nations," that is, the rich and the poor of England. Disraeli had supported the Chartists' petition to Parliament, had visited Manchester, and had studied the reports of Shaftesbury's committee on mines and factories. There is consequently real feeling springing from first-hand observation in his portrayal of industrial squalor and agricultural misery, the cruelty to children, and the brutalization of the poor. The contrast between the two divisions of society is epitomized in the splendor of Mobray Castle and the wretchedness of the town of Mobray near by. Disraeli's indictment of Whigs and Tories alike is that for all their public protestations they are indifferent to social wrongs. The hero, a "Tory Democrat," who falls in love with the daughter of one of the Chartists, argues that the people are too weak to right these wrongs themselves; hope lies in the awakening of the aristocracy to a sense of their responsibilities as hereditary leaders. There is thus a close connection between *Sybil* and Carlyle's *Chartism* and *Past and Present,* though Carlyle, without faith in the degenerate aristocracy, sought to arouse the new "Captains of Industry," and though Disraeli was without Carlyle's moral fervor. *Tancred* (1847) centers attention upon religious issues and contains some of Disraeli's strongest satire and absurdest occultism. The wisdom of the East is again summoned to the aid of occidental bewilderment; but the consequence is merely more bewilderment; there is no revelation of saving truth, and though the hero's journey to Jerusalem provides the occasion for some fine descriptions of landscape, the dabbling in supernaturalism is but so much clap-trap and the famous "Great Asian Mystery" remains unexplained and inexplicable.

Not till the close of his first ministry did Disraeli again occupy himself with fiction. The central figure in *Lothair* (1870) is a young man of wealth and title who is in quest of the true path. A number of recent conspicuous conversions to Roman Catholicism suggested the admirable narrative of Catholic intrigue and the recognizably real people engaged therein. The rival claims of Canterbury and Rome are argued in Peacockian style. The theme of the three women who influence the hero is a fanciful variation

"The Two Nations"

upon the part played by female friendships in the author's own career. Lothair goes to Italy during the Risorgimento and is wounded at the battle of Mentana. But here Disraeli touches only the fringes of a great subject and his treatment of Italian politics and aspirations cannot bear comparison with Meredith's in *Vittoria*. Before the end we have once more the appeal to the wisdom of the East, for Disraeli, though a Christian, was in mind and temperament an Oriental Semite; the ancient East, for romantic Englishmen a way of escape, was his racial and spiritual home. *Endymion* (1880), written after Disraeli's second and final retirement from the premiership, proved not so intimately autobiographical as the public had hoped, but is a backward glance over the author's triumphant career. Again there is the romantic fantasy of the influence of feminine friendships upon the hero; but more interesting are the vivid pictures of Whig and Tory politics, of the Tractarian Movement, the railway mania and collapse, and many other events and affairs, all set against the opulent background of high society.

This taste for opulence is the conspicuous weakness of Disraeli as a novelist *Character-* of social reform. As in Bulwer so in Disraeli, a genuine sympathy with the *istics* poor and outcast is vitiated by a delight in luxury and display and a fondness for "great" people. Another and more fundamental weakness is the want of a creative imagination. Disraeli is not a Protean artist, able to assume many shapes. He can manage skilfully not only events but characters and thoughts so long as they are within the range of his own experiences, hopes, and dreams; but when he attempts to create a character with whom he has nothing in common, his power fails and he can draw only conventional figures or caricatures. The flamboyance of his style, the inconclusiveness of his arguments, and the ephemerality of many of his themes are severe handicaps upon his books. They are no longer widely read, but it is likely that the lasting fascination of Disraeli's personality and career will keep them long in remembrance.

II

Charles Kingsley[6] (1819-1875), clergyman, naturalist, sportsman, and *Charles* something of a poet,[7] employed fiction for purposes of propaganda more *Kingsley* effectively than Bulwer and Disraeli because his sympathies were more sincerely engaged than theirs in the task of social reform. He began to write

[6] *Life and Works* (19v, 1901-1903), Vols. I-IV being a reprint of *Charles Kingsley. His Letters and Memories of his Life*, ed. by his wife (1877). — S. E. Baldwin, *Charles Kingsley* (Ithaca, 1934); M. F. Thorp, *Charles Kingsley* (Princeton, 1937); L. Cazamian, *Le Roman social en Angleterre* (Paris, 1903), pp. 436-531; L. Cazamian, *Kingsley: le socialisme chretien* (Paris, 1904); Ella Juhnke, "Charles Kingsley als sozialreformatorischer Schriftsteller," *Anglia*, n.f., xxxvii (1925). 32-79; M. W. Hanavalt, "Charles Kingsley and Science," *SP*, xxxiv (1937). 589-611; Baker, viii. 166-176; Karl Brunner, "Charles Kingsley als christlich-sozialer Dichter," *Anglia*, xlvi (1922). 289-322; xlvii (1923). 1-33.

[7] *Andromeda* (1858), in hexameters, is Kingsley's most ambitious poem; *The Sands of Dee* his best known. *The Saint's Tragedy* (1848), a closet-drama on St. Elizabeth of Hungary, is in blank verse with passages in prose. — Kingsley published lectures on history and science, sermons, and social and theological tracts. *The Water-Babies* (1863) has slipped from the high place it formerly occupied among children's books.

novels under the inspiration of the eloquent theorizing of Carlyle and the practical Christian Socialism of F. D. Maurice. Along with faint echoes of Carlyle's style there are repetitions, rather than mere echoes, of his doctrines of work and duty, leadership and silent strength. Kingsley's books express the stirring social conscience of the mid-century, and it is not without significance that his first novel appeared in 1848, the Year of Revolutions. This was *Yeast,* followed by *Alton Locke* (1850). The title of the former is symbolic of the ferment of new ideas. Both are as much sociological tracts as works of fiction, with little plot and a great deal of discussion (in which there are reminiscences of Disraeli's *Sybil*). In *Alton Locke* an old Chartist, after the failure of the movement, renounces force as an instrument of reform in favor of moral suasion; and in both books there is offered in place of discredited Chartism that Christian philanthropy which is a form of benevolent individualism. Trade-unionism is attacked, but the horrors of insanitation and slum-dwellings are exposed and there is an ardent advocacy of free schools, country life, and hygiene.

Kingsley dared greatly and did not quite succeed when he used the historical novel for the purpose indicated in the title *Hypatia: New Foes with an Old Face* (1853). Accepting the principle that human nature does not change, he transplanted modern moral and intellectual types to ancient Alexandria, implying parallels between nineteenth-century controversies and the old antagonisms of Jews, Christians, heretics, and pagans. The analogies are forced, but they may be disregarded while we watch the turbulence of the cosmopolitan city which is depicted with considerable brilliance and archaeological accuracy. *Westward Ho!* (1855) was written with the intention to brace English nerves in wartime by means of a recital of the Elizabethan adventurers' heroic deeds. But to fasten upon these grand old sea-rovers a code of morals characteristic of mid-Victorian England was a gross anachronism, and the Protestant bias is as extreme as Froude's. The high spirits and martial fervor of the tale made it enormously popular, and the genuinely tragic close is still moving.

From antiquity and the Elizabethan age Kingsley returned to his own time in *Two Years Ago* (1857), the title pointing back to the year of the Crimean War. Here Kingsley preached the gospel of strength and self-sacrifice and the ennobling virtues of war. More appealing to us is the narrative of bravery shown amid the ravages of the cholera. The transformation which various characters undergo under the stress of war is not explained psychologically but merely stated sentimentally. The same compound of manly virtues which Kingsley celebrated in earlier books appears for the last time in *Hereward the Wake* (1866) where, turning back to a heroic age, Kingsley captures at least suggestions of the tragic grandeur of the Norse sagas, the self-reliance and dauntless courage of brutal and passionate primitive heroes.

The declamatory verve with which Kingsley expressed an admiration for strength and courage combined with his genuine high-mindedness to win him an enormous following in his own generation. The Victorians found satisfaction in seeing young men exchange ledgers for swords. We have become more doubtful of the benefit, and our doubts overshadow Kingsley's reputation today.[8]

III

As the wife of a Unitarian minister in Manchester, Elizabeth Cleghorn Gaskell [9] (1810-1865) worked among the poor, knew at first-hand the misery of the industrial areas, and was in the midst of the Chartist agitation. As the champion of the mill-hands she first appeared as a novelist with *Mary Barton, a Tale of Manchester Life* (1848). The melodramatic plot is of no consequence in a book which, exposing the callousness of employers to the sufferings of the operatives, is memorable as a specific, if perhaps not entirely impartial, illustration of the social wrongs against which Carlyle was fulminating in more general terms. *Ruth* (1853) is for its date a bold, if over-emotional, plea for a "single standard" of sexual morality; it points forward to *Tess of the d'Urbervilles*. When invited by Dickens to contribute to *Household Words*, Mrs. Gaskell turned from these sociological problems to the memories of her own childhood in Cheshire. *Cranford* (1853) is not precisely a novel, but rather a series of sketches of simple, often humble, provincial people. There is little satire but an abundance of quiet humor and sympathy (reminiscent of Goldsmith) in the narration of the little incidents that make up their lives. Mrs. Gaskell worked the same vein but with less simplicity and success in later books. In *North and South* (1855) she reverted to the serious theme of the struggle between capital and labor. As the title promises, there is presented a contrast between the old agricultural gentry of the South of England who with their wealth have inherited a feudal sense of responsibility, and the new moneyed industrialists of the North. Mrs. Gaskell's endeavor to be fair is seen in her portrayal of a philanthropic manufacturer. Types of importance for understanding the period are the clergyman who relinquishes his living because he cannot still

Elizabeth Gaskell

---

[8] Henry Kingsley (1830-1876) possessed a subtler and at the same time less effective mind than his brother Charles. With no great gift for narrative he displays considerable psychological insight. Having lived in the Antipodes, he made use of his experiences in *Geoffrey Hamlyn* (1859). *Ravenshoe* (1862; World's Classics, 1925) is his best book, hopelessly confused in narrative but with some fine episodes and appealing characters which are drawn from the author's benevolent view of human nature. — See S. M. Ellis, *Henry Kingsley: Towards a Vindication* (1931). — Charles Kingsley's insistent preaching of the gospel of health and the out-of-doors connects his books with the enormously popular *Tom Brown's School Days* (1856) by Thomas Hughes (1823-1897) which spread the doctrines of "Muscular Christianity" and pictured young men with, as was said, "the souls of saints and the bodies of vikings." Another novelist who glorified the saga-spirit was G. A. Lawrence (1827-1876), the author of *Guy Livingston* (1857) and other tales depicting heroes of magnificent courage and physique. This "physical force" school of fiction was of practical benefit in promoting interest in games and athletics.

[9] *Works*, Knutsford Edition, introduction by A. W. Ward (8v, 1906); *Letters of Mrs. Gaskell and C. E. Norton*, ed. Jane Whitehill (1932). — A. S. Whitfield, *Mrs. Gaskell: Her Life and Work* (1929); G. De W. Sanders, *Elizabeth Gaskell* (New Haven, 1929), with bibliography by C. S. Northup; Elizabeth Haldane, *Mrs. Gaskell and her Friends* (1930).

his spiritual doubts and the trade-unionist official who combines social radicalism with militant atheism. This book has obvious connections with Dickens' *Hard Times* and Charlotte Brontë's *Shirley*. Mrs. Gaskell's last novel, *Wives and Daughters* [10] (1866), delineates two daughters of contrasting temperaments, who are further contrasted with their foolish mother, Mrs. Gibson. The mother is a memorable creation because though humorously drawn she is kept within the bounds of truth. The satire on snobbishness, though more gentle in manner than Thackeray's, is none the less penetrating.

Mrs. Gaskell has points of connection with George Eliot as a woman who turned fiction to the purposes of morality, though she carried the burden of her mission more lightly than George Eliot did hers. As a shrewd observer of the provincial scene she is allied to Trollope and as a novelist of social reform to Charles Kingsley. There are echoes of Charlotte Brontë in her books, and as a compensation for the lack of the passion which her friend possessed abundantly, she shows a humorous aloofness which is wanting in the novels of that greater woman of genius. Mrs. Gaskell's *Life of Charlotte Brontë* (1857) is a masterpiece of biography.[11]

IV

he
rontës The three Brontë sisters [12] have been overlaid with so much biography, criticism, and conjecture that in reading about them there is danger lest their own books be left unread. Theory and surmise, taking their start from the indubitably autobiographic. character of parts of Charlotte's novels, have

[10] Posthumous; completed all but a few pages at the time of Mrs. Gaskell's death.

[11] Other women novelists who were interested in social reform used fiction for moral and uplifting purposes. Harriet Martineau (1802-1876), the daughter of James Martineau the philosopher and Unitarian divine, besides writing copiously on public affairs, travel, history, Positivism, and economics, resorted to fiction in her *Illustrations of Political Economy* (1831) and *Illustrations of Taxation* (1834). Frankly didactic, these tales were immediately popular and very influential. She also published two novels less directly tendentious. See Theodora Bosanquet, *Harriet Martineau* (1927). — Dinah Maria Mulock, Mrs. Craik (1826-1887), was the author of *John Halifax, Gentleman* (1856), one of the most famous of Victorian "best-sellers." In it the hero rises from poverty to wealth without sacrificing his integrity. Mrs. Craik's other novels are forgotten. — Charlotte Mary Yonge (1823-1901) commanded a wide audience. *The Heir of Redclyffe* (1853), another "best-seller," develops with characteristic earnestness the theme of wrong and expiation. *The Daisy Chain* (1856) shows Miss Yonge's intimate connection with High Anglicanism. *The Dove in the Eagle's Nest* (1866) is the best example of her historical novels; she ranged widely through history and took great liberties with it. Among her stories for children *The Little Duke* (1854) is still attractive. She also specialized in chronicles of family life. — The two Jane Austen-like novels of Emily Eden (1797-1869), *The Semi-attached Couple* and *The Semi-detached House* (both 1860), were rescued from oblivion by reprints in 1928 when their light irony made a special sophisticated appeal.

[12] *The Shakespeare Head Brontë*, ed. T. J. Wise and J. A. Symington (20v, 1931-1940), contains, besides the novels, poems and juvenilia, the correspondence, some unpublished material, and a biography; *Life and Works of Charlotte Brontë and her Sisters*, Haworth Edition, with introductions to the novels by Mrs. Humphry Ward and to Mrs. Gaskell's *Life* (see below) by C. K. Shorter (7v, 1899; many reprints); Emily Brontë, *Complete Poems*, ed. C. W. Hatfield (1941); Charlotte Brontë, *The Twelve Adventurers*, ed. C. W. Hatfield (1925) and *The Spell: an Extravaganza*, ed. G. E. MacLean (1931); *Brontë Poems: Selections*, ed. A. C. Benson (1915). — Laura L. Hinkley, *Charlotte and Emily: The Brontës* (1945); Mrs. E. C. Gaskell, *The Life of Charlotte Brontë* (2v, 1857), ed. May Sinclair (1908); C. K.

played fantastic tricks with probability. *Wuthering Heights* has been assigned in part to their brother, Branwell, or, taken wholly from Emily, has been attributed to Charlotte.[13] The origins of their genius have been traced to such diverse stimuli as their Celtic ancestry [14] or their unfortunate wastrel of a brother [15] or their reading of Methodist magazines.[16] The novels have been interpreted as *romans à clef* (which to some extent they are), and there is scarcely a character or scene that has not been identified with actuality.[17] The postponed publication and slow release of materials kept from psychologists information that might have modified their conclusions.[18]

The Rev. Patrick Brontë [19] was an Irishman; his wife came from Cornwall. To this pair were born six children: two elder daughters, then Charlotte (1816-1855), Patrick Branwell (1817-1848), Emily Jane (1818-1848), and Anne (1820-1849). Shortly after Anne's birth the family came to Haworth parsonage in Yorkshire, and there in 1821 the mother died. Mr. Brontë invited his sister-in-law, Elizabeth Branwell, to live with him and share the responsibility for the rearing of his children. In 1824 all the girls

Shorter, *The Brontës and their Circle* (1896) and *The Brontës: Life and Letters* (2v, 1908); Ernest Dimnet, *Les Soeurs Brontë* (Paris, 1910), translated by Louise M. Sill (1927); May Sinclair, *The Three Brontës* (1914) Mrs. E. H. Chadwick, *In the Footsteps of the Brontës* (1914); J. C. Wright, *The Story of the Brontës* (1925); Romer Wilson [Mrs. F. R. M. O'Brien], *All Alone: The Life and Private History of Emily Jane Brontë* (1928); K. A. R. Sugden, *A Short History of the Brontës* (1928); Emile and Georges Romieu, *La Vie des soeurs Brontë* (Paris, 1930), English translation, *Three Virgins of Haworth* (1931); E. M. Delafield, *The Brontës* (1935); E. F. Benson, *Charlotte Brontë*, (1932); I. C. Willis, *The Brontës* (1933); W. B. White, *The Miracle of Haworth: a Brontë Study* (1937); F. E. Ratchford, *The Brontës' Web of Childhood* (1941), of first importance; *The Transactions of the Brontë Society* (Bradford, 1895—in progress); Baker, VIII. chs. I and II; J. C. Smith, "Emily Brontë," *E&S*, V (1914). 132-152; Janet Spens, "Charlotte Brontë" *E&S*, XIV (1929). 54-70.
13 Some critics believe that Branwell wrote the first two chapters. He claimed to be joint-author, but his word is not to be trusted. Emily may have talked over her plans with him, but at the time the book was written he was too far gone in drink to have contributed much to it. For the theory of Charlotte's authorship see J. M. Dembley, *The Key to the Brontë Works* (1911); I. C. Willis, *The Authorship of Wuthering Heights* (1936).
14 C. O'Bryne, *The Gaelic Source of the Brontë Genius* (1933). See also William Wright, *The Brontës in Ireland* (1894) and A. M. MacKay's reply, *The Brontës: Fact and Fiction* (1897), which also reviews other Brontë "myths."
15 E. E. Kinsley, *Pattern for Genius: a Story of Branwell Brontë and his Three Sisters* (1939). See also F. A. Leyland, *The Brontë Family with Special Reference to Patrick Branwell Brontë* (2v, 1886).
16 Mrs. G. E. Harrison, *Methodist Good Companions* (1935), ch. v: "Reactions in Haworth Parsonage." It is here shown that these magazines, with their accounts of revivalist meetings, fanaticism, hysteria, and preternatural manifestations, had some influence upon the sisters. For their effect upon Emily see Baker, VIII. 72. note 1.
17 *Sources of Charlotte Brontë's Novels, Persons and Places; Publications of the Brontë Society*, VIII, Part IV (1935). Isabel Clarke, *Haworth Parsonage* (1927), introduces into her narrative a conjectured love affair between Emily and her father's curate Weightman for which there is not a shred of evidence. On the basis of an incorrectly deciphered manuscript annotation Emily has been given a lover who never existed; see Virginia Moore, *The Life and Eager Death of Emily Brontë* (1936), and C. W. Hatfield's letter in *LTLS*, August 29, 1936, showing that Miss Moore misread Charlotte Brontë's annotation "Love's Farewell" as "Louis Parensell" and thus created the lover. On the basis of Emily's occult experiences she has also been given a kind of demon-lover in whom (if one understands the theory) the features of Lord Byron are faintly discernible. There are of course Byronic and "Satanic" elements in Emily's thought. See Helen Brown, "The Influence of Byron on Emily Brontë," *MLR*, XXXIV (1939). 374-381.
18 Rosamond Langbridge, *Charlotte Brontë: a Psychological Study* (1929); Lucile Dooley, "Psycho-Analysis of Charlotte Brontë as a Type of the Woman of Genius," *American Journal of Psychology*, XXXI (1920). 221-273.
19 On Patrick Brontë's earlier career see W. W. Yates, *The Father of the Brontës: His Life and Work at Dewsbury and Hartshead* (1897).

but Anne were put into a school for clergymen's daughters, where the two eldest died—of under-nourishment and harsh discipline, as Charlotte thought,[20] but more likely of tuberculosis. Charlotte and Emily were brought back to Haworth, where, though their father guided them in unmethodical study, they were left largely to their own devices, to play among the graves in the churchyard, roam over the moors, and build a world of their own imagining. At this time they began those strange, famous little books, gener-ally written in microscopic hands, wherein Charlotte, with some bungling help from Branwell, recorded the adventurous, passionate lives of the people of "Angria," [21] while Emily composed the *Gondal Chronicle* [22] on the wars and intrigues of Royalists and Republicans in a mysterious kingdom of the North.[23] In Charlotte's childish and adolescent fantasies have been discovered anticipations, in characters and situations, of her mature work. Emily continued to make the *Gondal Chronicle* a receptacle for her poems and was working on it as late as 1845; but the prose cycle was destroyed. When her poems were published the links with Gondal were as far as possible obliterated.

In 1831 Charlotte was sent to a boarding-school where she made friends with Mary Taylor and Ellen Nussey to whom in later years many of her most interesting letters were addressed. Once more at Haworth, she helped in the education of her younger sisters, and four years later returned to the same school, this time as a governess, while Emily and then Anne were pupils for a short time. After filling two other posts as governess, she planned with Emily to open a school of their own; and to gain proficiency in French and other polite accomplishments the two sisters went to Brussels, with funds provided by their aunt, and became pupils in the Pensionnat Héger. Eight months of 1842 were passed there till they were called home by the death of their aunt. For Charlotte there was a second, longer sojourn in Brussels in 1843-1844, this time as a teacher in the same establishment. Her loneliness and despondency and what most biographers have interpreted as her passion for Constantin Heger enter into *Villette*. When she rejoined Emily at Haworth, the sisters advertised for pupils—but none came. In the following years they watched with sorrow and shame the moral degradation of their brother whose talents were wasted long before he went to a drunk-ard's grave in 1848. In 1845 Charlotte made the accidental discovery of Emily's poems in manuscript; Anne had also been writing verse; and

---

[20] Mrs. Gaskell made it clear that the Clergy Daughters School at Cowan Bridge, of which the Rev. W. C. Wilson was the principal, is the "Lowood" of *Jane Eyre*. See Henry Shepheard, *A Vindication of the Clergy Daughters School and the Rev. W. Carus Wilson from the Re-marks in the Life of Charlotte Brontë* (1857).

[21] F. E. Ratchford, "Charlotte Brontë's Angrian Cycle of Stories," *PMLA*, XLII (1928). 494-501.

[22] Emily Brontë, *Gondal Poems*, ed. Helen Brown and Joan Mott (1938); M. H. Dodds, "Gondaliand," *MLR*, XVIII (1923). 9-21, and "A Second Visit to Gondaliand," *ibid.*, XXI (1926). 373-379; F. E. Ratchford, *Two Poems by Emily Brontë: with the Gondal Background of her Poems and Novel* (Austin, 1934).

[23] Anne, though in Emily's confidence, never entered so deeply into these imaginary countries as did her elder sisters.

Charlotte herself had composed many poems. The result of this discovery was *Poems by Currer, Ellis and Acton Bell* (1846); it attracted no attention whatsoever. All three were now busy writing novels. *The Professor,* Charlotte's first novel, a determined effort to escape from the romantic dream-world of Angria into actuality, went the round of the publishers; but Smith, Elder and Company, in rejecting it, intimated that they would be glad to consider another story of "more varied interest." *Jane Eyre* was submitted immediately and on its publication (1847) achieved a sensational success.[24] Another publisher brought out together Emily's *Wuthering Heights* and Anne's *Agnes Grey*, and taking advantage of the popularity of *Jane Eyre,* accepted Anne's *The Tenant of Wildfell Hall* (1848), letting a rumor get about that the pseudonyms Currer and Acton Bell concealed the same individual. To prove the contrary Charlotte and Anne visited London and showed themselves to the former's publisher. They had not long been home when Branwell died; and in December Emily died. An attempt to arrest the course of Anne's disease by seeking a change of air proved unavailing, and she died at Scarborough in May, 1849. Charlotte was left alone, to continue her writing and care for her father, now going blind.

Shirley, begun in confidence, was resumed in distress; the transition occurs in the chapter entitled "The Valley of the Shadow of Death." In sorrowful loneliness Charlotte could not bring herself to adhere to what was apparently her original intention, to bring the story to a tragic ending, and wrenching probabilities, she closed it in happiness. It was published in the autumn of 1849. The years of social lionizing followed when in London and elsewhere she met Thackeray, Matthew Arnold, Mrs. Gaskell, Harriet Martineau, and other famous people. *Villette* appeared in 1853. Having already rejected three suitors, Charlotte married her father's curate, the Rev. Arthur Bell Nichols, who long outlived her. Less than a year afterwards she died in March, 1855. *The Professor,* her first novel, was published posthumously in 1857, and *Emma,* a short fragment, in 1860.

The pathos and nobility of the story of the Brontës must be read between the lines of the above brief summary of these lives which were almost as circumscribed as Haworth churchyard, almost as illimitable as the sky above the Yorkshire moorland.

V

Charlotte Brontë's four novels have generally been regarded as variations upon her own story of frustrated passion. While her great predecessor, Jane Austen (to whom she never did justice), had looked deep into the human heart, she had been reticent about what she saw there and had kept her own heart veiled from public view. Charlotte Brontë, in her subjectivism, her dwelling in the world of the inner life, her reliance upon her own experi-

Charlotte Brontë

---

[24] Upon the chorus of acclaim broke belatedly the hostile voice of Elizabeth Rigby (afterwards Lady Eastlake) in the *Quarterly Review,* December, 1848; reprinted in *Notorious Literary Attacks,* ed. Albert Mordell (1926), pp. 101-121. On the reception of *Jane Eyre* see further Amy Cruse, *The Victorians and their Reading* (1935), pp. 263-265.

ences, was an innovator in bringing English fiction into the domain of the writer's own emotional consciousness. The demonstration of the close parallels between the novels and the Angrian stories, while it reduces the element of autobiography, does not altogether invalidate the traditional view that directly or indirectly she wrote of her love for Héger, the accomplished Belgian scholar, married to another, who was her friend and mentor. *The Professor,* her first tedious and clumsy effort, thinly disguises autobiography by a curious inversion of the principal rôles, Crimsworth, the professor, being Charlotte. There is much reliance upon actuality, all the chief characters being identifiable. The provinciality of tone, the stylistic uncertainties, the artificiality of the dialogue (defects that Charlotte never rid herself of, though she was overcoming them at the time of her death) are at their worst in this story, which is now unreadable save for the light it casts upon the

Jane
Eyre

author and her later works. The sudden change that is seen in *Jane Eyre* is most plausibly accounted for by a liberation from inhibitions effected by the power and passion of her sister's *Wuthering Heights* and a consequent reversion to the romantic wonderland of Angria. Yet the faults are still evident—the unsophistication which would provoke a smile were it not pathetic; the prim and stilted dialogue when she tries to imitate the chit-chat of society folk of whom she knew next to nothing; the unmodulated alterations of style from homely colloquialism to the most turgid rhetoric; the distressing attempts at humor and the heavy satire; the blunders in depicting social conventions; the inability to be tolerant or nonchalant; and all the rest of the familiar indictment. Though the love of Jane Eyre for Rochester, the married man, parallels the love of Charlotte for Héger, Rochester is not a portrait from actuality but an ideal of strong and ruthless masculinity painted by a woman who knew very little of men but had for years dreamed of the supermen of Angria. The setting of the central episodes recalls the *mise-en-scène* of the Gothic romances, and none of the Gothicizers invented an incident more sensational than that of the mad wife kept in the husband's house.[25] Melodrama is the stuff of the plot, but though it held readers to breathless attention and can still hold them, such greatness as *Jane Eyre* possesses lies not in the story but in the fiery imagination and poetic passion with which characters and situations are realized. Anxious dread of the developing situation with Branwell at Haworth threw a shadow over the narrative; but apart from this, the wildness, the sense of tremendous issues involved in humble scenes, and the illimitable passions of people outwardly insignificant, the atmosphere of sinister gloom, the suggestions of the occult and mysterious, all qualities that we associate rather with poetry than with fiction and that remove the book utterly from the field of the novel of man-

---

[25] Despite the anticipations discovered by Miss Ratchford in the Angrian cycle, there remain resemblances so close as to indicate unconscious borrowing from J. S. Le Fanu's *A Chapter in the History of a Tyrone Family* (1839), reprinted in *The Watcher and other Weird Stories* (1894). The story is summarized in *CHEL*, XIII. 460-463. — The qualities in *Jane Eyre* that "date" may be indicated by the fact that Ainsworth was inclined to attribute the authorship to G. P. R. James.

ners, are of the essence of the Brontë genius. Romance, which in its pro-founder sense had till now shunned prose fiction, took to itself this new domain.[26] With an emotional tension hitherto unknown in the novel and foreshadowing the work of George Meredith, Charlotte Brontë portrayed the ecstasies of love, as in the unforgettable scene when Rochester meets Jane in the garden while the nightingales sing. The human story is set against a background so intimately realized that nature seems to have her part in it; the constantly recurring "pathetic fallacy" seems not fallacious because it is so intense.

For *Shirley* Charlotte chose a setting foreign to her own experience, the *Shirley* industrial troubles between mill-owners and operatives in Yorkshire ir 1807-1812.[27] Nevertheless, the unrequited love of Caroline for Robert Moore has been thought to be another reflection of the Brussels episode. The book contains what are probably portraits from real life, chief among them the splendid, clear-sighted Shirley, drawn, not with entire convincingness, from Emily. The somewhat wearisome discussions of the rights of women are reflections of contemporary opinion. The distrust of beauty and honest joy, the censoriousness, the sternness of moral commendation or condemnation which makes the clashing characters almost symbols of the warfare between sin and virtue, come from a nature that was grand and formidable but neither easy-going nor lightly tolerant. The harshness of judgment becomes positively repellent in the savage, rasping satire on the curates, who labor under the disadvantage of belonging to the only class of men whom Char-lotte had had the opportunity to observe with coldly analytical disapproval.

Villette is usually described as a reversion to direct autobiography. The *Villette* transcription from real life, with a multitude of betraying details, was considered so close that protests were later forthcoming from Brussels. The portrait of Lucy Snowe in her love-sick longing reflects, according to the traditional view, Charlotte's hopeless passion; and Paul Emanuel, with his insight and power to dominate, is Héger. Yet there is more of Angria in *Villette* than in any of the other novels, and before committing ourselves to the autobiographical theory we must weigh in the balance the parallels from Charlotte's dream-world of a date before she had visited Brussels. The plot relies upon gross improbabilities and various incredible coincidences, yet the story holds the reader's attention for its own sake, and to those who accept it as autobiography its stark self-revelation is almost painful.

VI

To turn from Charlotte's novels [28] to *Wuthering Heights* is to turn from *Emily* schools and parsonages, governesses and curates, to the wild moorlands and *Brontë*

[26] See Baker, viii. 11-25.
[27] In a newspaper file she "read up" conscientiously the Luddite riots; but there had been industrial troubles in Angria!
[28] And Anne's. No injustice is done to Anne Brontë's reputation by limiting remarks upon her novels to a footnote, for only her connection with her sisters has kept them in remem-

the free air of heaven, and from faulty works redolent of genius to the masterpiece of a greater genius. Emily's life, so far as we know, was almost without outer event. From the age of seven till sixteen she was never away from Haworth, and in the last seven years of her brief life only once and then for but a few days. Little is to be gathered of her personality, though much of her opinions, from Charlotte's portrait of her as Shirley. The virginal passion, the strength of soul, the maintenance of complete integrity of thought and expression are revealed in her one novel—call it rather her prose-poem—and in the best of her poems. Perpetually conscious of two planes of life, she manifested that conjunction of transcendentalism and descendentalism which marks the Romantic Movement in its deepest implications. Like Wordsworth, she was "true to the kindred points of heaven and home." Yet she was not so near to Wordsworth as to Blake, of whom she probably never so much as heard. Like Blake, she was "beyond Good and Evil," repudiating restraint and law, relying upon freedom and passion and the unfettered imagination. Blake had said that "no bird soars too high if it soars with its own wings"; and Emily rose to the empyrean upon her own strength. That to put it this way is not mere rhetoric will be acknowledged by anyone who has read such poems as *The Prisoner, Remembrance, The Old Stoic, The Visionary,* and *No Coward Soul is Mine.*[29] What is fragmentary and only partially expressed in the poems is fused into a consistent whole in *Wuthering Heights.*[30] There is no evidence that she was deeply read in the literature of mysticism, but there is equally no doubt that she was a mystic.[31] Unlike Blake, however, who was constantly "under the direction of messengers from heaven," it seems from the testimony of her poems that Emily had attained the mystical experience in its entirety only in early youth, possibly only once. Later it returned fitfully and more dimly. The memory of that early union with the Divine is the "rapturous pain," the "divinest anguish," of which she sings in one of her grandest poems; no human lover has lain for "fifteen wild Decembers" "cold in the earth" (*Remembrance*). In another poem she exclaims:

ystic

---

brance. *Agnes Grey,* a plain, honest, dull narrative, without satire, passion, or romantic illusion, possesses autobiographic value for its picture of the trials of a governess in an unamiable family. *The Tenant of Wildfell Hall* goes beyond the range of Anne's experience into fast society which she knew only from reading fiction. Arthur Huntingdon has been thought to be a portrait of the degraded Branwell but the differences between the imaginary figure and the real are greater than the resemblances. See W. T. Hale, *Anne Brontë: Her Life and Writings* (Bloomington, Indiana, 1929).

[29] Generally but inaccurately known (from Charlotte's statement) as *Last Lines*; but probably written about three years before Emily's death.

[30] K. W. Maurer, "The Poetry of Emily Brontë," *Anglia,* LXI (1937). 443-448.

[31] See J. C. Smith, "Emily Brontë: a Reconsideration," *E&S,* v (1914). 132-152; Charles Morgan, "Emily Brontë," in *The Great Victorians,* ed. H. J. and Hugh Massingham (1932), pp. 63-79; C. F. E. Spurgeon, *Mysticism in English Literature* (1913), pp. 80-84. Charlotte Brontë refers to Shirley's (i.e., Emily's) visions and trances and "genii-life." On the ground that the poems are part of the lost Gondal cycle in prose and are therefore dramatic and not self-revelatory, Miss Ratchford denies that Emily was a mystic. But it is not obvious why poems put into the mouths or minds of imaginary characters should not have been inspired by personal experience.

Speak, God of visions, plead for me,
And tell me why I have chosen thee!

This "God of visions" is the "strange Power" for whose return she looks
at twilight and whose might she trusts as she bids him trust her constancy
(*The Visionary*).[32] In *The Prisoner* the crude Gondalian Gothicism is
merely the frame for the central description of the ecstatic vision. As in the
case of Blake, so in her case there is neither room nor need to discuss here
the explanations of the mystical phenomena. All that requires insistence is
that in her case as in his there can be no question of the sincerity of the
passionate conviction of their authenticity.

Wuthering Heights must be read in the light of this fact. To seek in this   Wuthering
wonderful book a successor to the Gothic romances to which, superficially,   Heights
it owes something, is to misapprehend it quite. It is of an altogether different kind. The attempts to connect it with the lost Gondal stories do not
carry us very far. Though firmly based upon the moorlands, with peasant
characters as realistic as Hardy's, it is not to be judged by standards of
realism and probability. *Wuthering Heights* is not merely an allegory of
the intersecting relationship between the earthly and the divine plane of
being but a vision of their interpenetration.[33] The cosmic vision is of two
contending principles, the one dynamic, the other passive. Both principles
are good. But dynamism, diverted from its proper course, becomes a power
of destruction; and this is the tragedy of Heathcliff. Like will to like;
Heathcliff and Catherine Earnshaw are affinities. When Catherine marries
Edgar Linton storm and calm are mismated and disaster follows. In the
second generation the union of the dynamic characters is renewed upon
the spiritual plane and the passive characters find happiness on earth. The
pattern is much more complex than can be indicated briefly here, and the
best interpreters have shown that it accounts triumphantly for the construction of the story, which, on grounds applicable to any ordinary novel, has
been criticized as awkward and uncouth. When the book opens, the first
Catherine is already dead; her pale ghost flutters at the window, imploring
admission to Wuthering Heights. To plunge, as Emily did, not merely into
the midst of the action but into the very conclusion of the whole matter
(for Heathcliff is near his death) was to challenge the laws of narrative.
But Emily knew that it was impossible to lead the reader by degrees into
the occult realm of her story; the fortress of incredulity must be taken at
once and by storm. From this beginning at the end, the tale folds back, first
in the narration by Nelly Deans, afterwards in part by Lockwood, the in-
truder from the outside world to whom are allotted the immortal concluding words of the story.

---

[32] The last eight lines of this poem were added by Charlotte to the Gondalian opening twelve
lines; but the present writer finds it impossible to believe they are not by Emily. Charlotte
probably transcribed them from another copy.
[33] The construction as well as the thought of the book Lord David Cecil discusses admirably
in *Early Victorian Novelists* (1935), ch. v. See also "C. P. S.," *The Structure of Wuthering
Heights* (1926).

Much might be—much has been—said of the intensity and solidity of Emily's imagination, of her strong apprehension of character, situation, and underlying theme. Too much cannot be said in praise of the style of the book, at once subtle and colloquial, imparting new vitality to conventional idiom, as exhilarating as the moorland winds, evoking the beauty of the world, capable of candid ferocities. Its rhythms, piercingly sad or exultantly joyous, invigorate even those readers who have no sympathy with occultism and mysticism. When Catherine tells of her vision the voice is Emily's own:

> I see a repose which neither earth nor hell can break, and I feel an assurance of the endless and shadowless hereafter, ... where life is boundless in its duration, and love in its sympathy, and joy in its fullness.

VII

George Eliot

Not without effort is the mind adjusted to a new point of view as one turns from a novel which has proved to be of enduring vitality to the writings of George Eliot.[34] No other Victorian novelist of major rank is so little read today. The effort to lift fiction to a higher plane than that upon which her predecessors and contemporaries were satisfied to work, though it brought her immense temporary prestige, has ultimately been responsible for this decline. Whereas Dickens, Kingsley, and Mrs. Gaskell, when they used the novel as an instrument for social agitation, did not forget to mix pleasure with edification, in George Eliot's hands the novel was not primarily for entertainment but for the serious discussion of moral issues. If these issues are no longer felt to be vital, as the Victorians felt them, and if the solutions proposed now seem unsatisfactory, the *raison d'être* of the stories which are but vehicles for these ideas is enfeebled, if, indeed, it does not vanish altogether. Moreover, George Eliot's own uneasiness as to the honesty of invention in fiction was from the beginning a hazard in the way of lasting success. "Have I any time," she asked herself, "to spend on things that never existed?" [35] Such a question, which would never disturb a born novelist, might have given her pause. To teach was, she held, the paramount purpose in authorship. What, then, did she aim to teach? "My artistic bent," she told her publisher, "is directed not at all to the presentation of eminently

[34] *Works*, Warwickshire Edition (25v, 1908); *George Eliot's Life as Related in her Letters and Journals*, ed. J. W. Cross (2v, 1885); *George Eliot's Family Life and Letters*, ed. Arthur Paterson (1938); *Letters*, ed. R. B. Johnson (1926); G. S. Haight, *George Eliot and John Chapman* (1940), contains hitherto unpublished correspondence. — Leslie Stephen, *George Eliot* (EML Series, 1902); E. S. Haldane, *George Eliot and her Times* (1927); J. Lewis May, *George Eliot; a Study* (1930); E. and G. Romieu, *La Vie de George Eliot* (Paris, 1930), trans. by B. W. Downes (1932); A. T. Kitchel, *George Lewes and George Eliot: a Review of Records* (1933); P. Bourl'honne, *George Eliot: Essai de biographie intellectuelle et morale, 1819-1854* (Paris, 1933); Blanche C. Williams, *George Eliot: a Biography* (1936); M. C. Wade, "George Eliot's Philosophy of Sin," *English Journal*, XIV (1925). 269-277; J. J. Bassett, "The Purpose in George Eliot's Art," *Anglia*, LIV (1930). 338-350; Helene Richter, "Die Frauenfrage bei George Eliot," *Anglia*, XXVII (1903-1904). 333-380; Lord David Cecil, *Early Victorian Novelists*, pp. 291-336; Baker, VIII, ch. VI.
[35] *Letters and Journals*, I. 38.

irreproachable characters, but to the presentation of mixed human beings in such a way as to call forth tolerant judgment, pity, and sympathy." She exhibits men and women in relation to an ideal based on certain principles of truth and goodness. She inculcates the importance of being earnest; but the virtues so earnestly striven after—industry, self-restraint, conscientiousness—are very drab; "school-teachers' virtues," they have been unkindly called.[36]

Mary Anne (or Marian) Evans (1819-1880), who after 1857 was known to the world as George Eliot, began to write fiction when on the verge of middle age. Behind her were memories of girlhood in Warwickshire and of the spiritual conflict of the severance from her father's religion. Under the influence of friends in Coventry, Charles Bray and Charles Hennell, she had been drawn to the "advanced" biblical and theological scholarship of Germany, and this led to her translation (1846) of D. F. Strauss's *Leben Jesu*. Her father, whom she had distressed by her skepticism, died in 1849. After a sojourn on the Continent Marian Evans was brought into touch with a group of rationalists in London of whom the chief figure was John Chapman. Chapman, who was engaged in resuscitating *The Westminster Review*, took her on as assistant editor, a post which she occupied from 1851 to 1854. In the set in which she moved there were men of brilliant gifts and others of decidedly "bohemian" standards of morality. Herbert Spencer became a close friend, and through him she met George Henry Lewes.[37] Lewes was separated from his wife but could not obtain a divorce. In 1854 Miss Evans took the defiant step of entering into an irregular union with him which lasted till his death in 1878. The moral conflict of this situation is part of her background as a novelist. In all but the law they regarded each other as man and wife and were accepted as such by their friends. For a time they lived in Germany, occupied with philosophical and psychological studies.

In 1857 George Eliot (the pseudonym which she now assumed) published in *Blackwood's* her first works of fiction—*Amos Barton, Mr. Gilfil's Love-Story*, and *Janet's Repentance*, three short stories which were gathered together in the same year as *Scenes of Clerical Life. Adam Bede*, the first full-length novel, followed quickly (1857), and then *The Mill on the Floss* and *Silas Marner* (both 1860). A visit to Florence roused her interest in the Italian Renaissance and after laborious studies and with elaborate documentation she produced *Romola* (1863). From this not completely successful excursion to the realm of the historical novel she returned to modern England in *Felix Holt, the Radical* (1866) and *Middlemarch* (1871-1872), the longest and most crowded of her books. The last work, *Daniel Deronda* (1876), is an illustration of her moral philosophy in which the characters

---

[36] Lord David Cecil, *Early Victorian Novelists*, p. 327.

[37] G. H. Lewes (1817-1878) was the author of many works on philosophy, natural science, and literary history, including a *Life of Goethe* (1855). He was instrumental in introducing knowledge of Comte's Positivism into England. On the foundation of *The Fortnightly Review* he was its first editor (1865-1867).

The Novels

are but so many examples of the theory she expounds. After Lewes's death she married J. W. Cross (1880). She died in the same year.

Memories of Warwickshire furnish the background of the novels of modern England, though not all are actually laid in that county. George Eliot's world is that of town folk and peasantry. Her concern is for absolutely commonplace people, and this concern is without a trace of patronage. The quiet humor is often of the sort we associate with Thomas Hardy. It is limited in range by her avoidance of any trace of unkindness and her stern discrimination between subjects that may be treated humorously and those that may not. Mrs. Poyser, in *Adam Bede,* is a humorous character in the mode of Dickens; more representative of George Eliot's own peculiar quality are some of the lesser figures in *Silas Marner.* But no matter how attractive a subsidiary character may be, she never lets him run away with her imagination. In the ability to concentrate attention upon the chief figures in her story she differs markedly from most of her predecessors in the novel. These principal persons are very unlike the conventional run of heroes and heroines, for she discarded the standardized formula of plot-construction in which the tale is built round an attractive young pair who are to be married in the last chapter. Along with this conventional couple the old convention of the "happy ending" sometimes goes into the discard. Wrenching probability, she did close *Adam Bede* with the marriage of Adam and Dinah; [38] but *The Mill on the Floss* ends distressfully; and all the others more or less somberly. In *Middlemarch* there is no central figure at all, interest being divided among several groups of people whose fates are entangled with much ingenuity though not without some bewilderment to the reader. In this book some fifty characters are not only drawn but analyzed. Nowhere else is George Eliot's peculiar power of describing how character develops more fully exhibited. An entire world, albeit a little world, which she knew intimately is here depicted, on a scale and with a thoroughness unexampled elsewhere in Victorian fiction. When, however, she attempted in *Romola* to portray in similar detail the crowded and tempestuous scene of the Italian Renaissance she passed beyond her range. She endows the men and women of fifteenth-century Italy with the moral sense and standard of her own age and milieu. They are transplanted Victorians. Leslie Stephen says roundly that Romola and Tito Melema did not really live in old Florence. "They were only masquerading there, and getting the necessary properties from the history-shops at which such things are provided for the diligent student." [39] The labor with which George Eliot "got up" her history resembles that with which she amassed from her memories and wide reading the material for the novels of modern England. This thoroughness of preparation has naturally suggested comparisons with the method of Flaubert, and George Eliot has frequently been described as the first English writer of the *roman expérimental.* But the resemblances

[38] J. S. Diekhoff, "The Happy Ending of *Adam Bede,*" ELH, III (1936). 221-227.
[39] Leslie Stephen, *George Eliot,* p. 136.

to Flaubert are not so obvious as the dissimilarities, and in particular her humane feeling for her men and women, commonplace as they almost always are and often both unattractive and futile, contrasts with the French novelist's feelings of lofty and bitter contempt as displayed in *Madame Bovary* and *L'Education sentimentale.*

Aware though she was of the influence of environment upon character, *The* George Eliot never showed environment determining character. In each *Moral* novel there is a moral clash, generally involving the need for a woman to *Basis* choose between two men or a man between two women. She maintained firmly her belief in the freedom of the will. The moral choice is everything. "Our deeds," she says in *Adam Bede,* "determine us as much as we determine our deeds." With stern, sad firmness, with a massive implacability that is at once impressive and depressing, she insisted upon the importance and irrevocability of actions. Moral degeneration follows acts committed from selfish motives; moral regeneration is accomplished by acts of love unregardful of self. Consequently, we have on the one hand such selfish characters as Tito or Hetty or Arthur Donnithorne, and on the other such grand figures as Romola or Dinah Morris or Daniel Deronda. But George Eliot's moral theories often interfere with the spontaneity of her imagination. More than once what she exhibits as the working of immutable moral law—"the wages of sin"—turns out to be the working of crass "poetic justice," a mere literary device which is something quite different. In homely phrase, the punishment does not invariably fit the crime. Nor is she content to let the reader draw for himself the required lesson from the narrative but must constantly intersperse philosophic remarks to serve her didactic purpose.[40]

Close to George Eliot in one department of her work was the popular *Mrs.* and enormously prolific novelist Margaret Oliphant (1828-1897). The re- *Oliphant* semblance is particularly marked when, as in *Salem Chapel* (1863), she pictures the world of dissent. The accuracy of her delineation of Scottish life has been commended by no less an authority than Sir James Barrie. Mrs. Oliphant also wrote stories of the occult, among which *A Beleaguered City* (1880) is memorable. Her miscellaneous writings include biographies and historical studies.

---

[40] It was not for want of industry and determination that George Eliot did not succeed in becoming a poet. There is too much sententiousness and too little spontaneity in her verse. Her best-known poem is a sort of Positivist hymn, beginning "O may I join that choir invisible." There is genuine charm in *How Lisa Loved the King* (1869) on a story in the *Decameron* which suggested to Swinburne his *Complaint of Lisa. The Legend of Jubal* (1869; published 1874) tells the old story of the return of the aged inventor of the art of music to his old home, to find that he is himself forgotten but also to find consolation in the honor in which his art is held. George Eliot's most ambitious poem, *The Spanish Gypsy* (1868), is an amalgam of narrative, dramatic scenes, lyrics, and choral commentary. The theme is the conflict of the rival loyalties of love and race. This piece, to which she devoted only too much labor and learning, has sunk out of sight under its own weight.

XXVI

Alfred Tennyson

Alfred Tennyson [1] (1809-1892) came of a family of scholarly tastes and some literary accomplishments. His father, a clergyman at Somersby in Lincolnshire, could turn "a copy of verses," and two of his brothers, Frederick and Charles,[2] possessed in slight measure the poetic gift. Alfred passed quickly through an imitative phase of discipleship to Thomson in descriptive poetry and to Scott in narrative. A clever little play, *The Devil and the Lady* (published posthumously), exhibits boyish fun, a taste for the grotesque, and the beginnings of a tendency to speculate upon the mystery of existence. A collective venture of the three brothers was in deference to Frederick's modesty entitled *Poems by Two Brothers* (1827). A rather winning self-conscious pride in wide-ranging erudition both classical and modern, an attraction to Oriental themes, and a prevalent Byronism are the chief characteristics of a volume which contains little

Poems
by Two
Brothers

[1] *Life and Works* (12v, 1898-1899), includes the *Memoir* (see below); *Works*, ed. Hallam Lord Tennyson (6v, 1908); *Poetic and Dramatic Works*, ed. W. J. Rolfe (1898); *The Devil and the Lady*, ed. Charles Tennyson (1931); *Unpublished Early Poems*, ed. Charles Tennyson (1931); *Tennyson and William Kirby: Unpublished Correspondence*, ed. L. A. Pierce (1929); *Selections*, ed. W. C. and M. P. DeVane (1940); *Representative Poems*, ed. S. C. Chew (1941); *A Selection*, introduction by W. H. Auden (1944). — T. J. Wise, *Bibliography* (1908), to be used with caution because it includes the forgeries exposed by John Carter and Graham Pollard in *An Enquiry into the Nature of Certain Nineteenth Century Pamphlets* (1934); T. G. Ehrsam, R. H. Deily, and R. M. Smith, "Tennyson," *Bibliographies of Twelve Victorian Authors* (1936), pp. 299-362 (hereinafter referred to as Ehrsam, *Bibliographies*); Hallam Lord Tennyson, *Alfred Lord Tennyson, a Memoir* (2v, 1897) and *Tennyson and his Friends* (1911); Andrew Lang, *Tennyson* (1901); R. M. Alden, *Tennyson: How to Know Him* (1917); A. C. Benson, *Tennyson* (1907); H. I'A. Fausset, *Tennyson: a Modern Portrait* (1923); Sir A. C. Lyall, *Tennyson* (EML Series, 1902); Harold Nicolson, *Tennyson: Aspects of his Life, Character and Poetry* (1923); T. R. Lounsbury, *The Life and Times of Tennyson* (1915), an account of the critical reception of Tennyson's earlier work; Morton Luce, *A Handbook to the Works of Alfred Lord Tennyson* (1906); J. F. A. Pyre, *The Formation of Tennyson's Style* (Madison, 1921); W. P. Mustard, *Classical Echoes in Tennyson* (1904); A. E. Baker, *Concordance* (1914) and *A Tennyson Dictionary* (1916); Sir T. Herbert Warren, *The Centenary of Tennyson* (1909), a lecture; A. C. Bradley, *The Reaction against Tennyson, English Association Pamphlets*, No. 39 (1917); Alfred Noyes, "Tennyson and Some Recent Critics," *Some Aspects of Modern Poetry* (1924), pp. 133-176; Lascelles Abercrombie, "Tennyson," *Revaluations: Studies in Biography* (1931), pp. 60-76; G. N. G. Orsini, *La Poesia di Alfred Tennyson* (Bari, 1928); Cornelius Weygandt, *The Time of Tennyson* (1936). — Passages in this chapter are taken, by permission of the Odyssey Press, from the writer's introduction to *Representative Poems*. — In 1884 Tennyson was raised to the peerage as Baron Tennyson of Aldworth.

[2] Frederick Tennyson (1807-1898) published four volumes of verse, of which *Days and Hours* (1854) is the best. Charles Tennyson-Turner (1808-1879) published his *Sonnets* in 1830 and added to them in successive editions till the final *Collected Sonnets, Old and New* (posthumous, 1880), with an appreciative essay by James Spedding. There is a quality of wildness in Frederick's poetry, as in his strange personal life, that is characteristic of the Tennysons. The Wordsworthian influence is strong in Charles. Examples of their work are included in *Representative Poems*, ed. S. C. Chew, Appendix III.

promise of what was soon to come. When Tennyson went to Cambridge and made friends with several brilliant young men—Arthur Henry Hallam,[3] Edward FitzGerald, James Spedding, and Richard Monckton Milnes (afterwards Lord Houghton)—the Byronic influence waned and he was soon aware of the two rising stars of English poetry, Shelley and Keats, posthumously renowned. The effect of Shelley upon him was intermittent and slight; but that of Keats was profound, as is seen in the luxuriant texture and rich coloring of some of the *Poems, Chiefly Lyrical* (1830), such as *Recollections of the Arabian Nights* and *Mariana,* which are connecting links between Keats and the Pre-Raphaelites. The imaginary portraits of fair women in this collection of 1830 show that Tennyson was not unaffected by the vogue of prettiness exemplified in the immediately contemporary gift-books and annuals. Tennyson never quite rid himself of the feminine ideal they are intended to suggest. There is real passion, bolder and less characteristic, in the *Ballad of Oriana.* Other poems sound a morbid note and in yet others the young poet luxuriates in stately melancholy. Experiments in novel metrical combinations, though the fingering was as yet uncertain, gave promise of a fresh music in English poetry. *[margin: Poems, Chiefly Lyrical]*

Without denying that the expansion of Tennyson's emotional and intellectual horizon and his mastery of style and technique were slow processes covering many years, one may recognize the next two years as the most remarkable period of growth. This was a happy time of close association with Hallam. The two young men went to Spain together with the quixotic intent to aid the insurgents; and Tennyson returned with memories of Pyrenean landscape which he worked into his poetry. Hallam, betrothed to the poet's sister, was a regular visitor at Somersby where Tennyson lived with his widowed mother, devoting himself to the cultivation of his art. The imagery and accessories of *A Dream of Fair Women* show the affinity to Keats. *The Hesperides,* which Tennyson afterwards suppressed, reveals that wildness in his nature which was too often subdued to Victorian sobriety. In *Œnone* a moral purpose is infused into old myth; the colors are radiant, but the Judgment of Paris is told from the point of view of the forsaken wife and the speech of Pallas is the central incident. In this poem, as in *The Lotos-Eaters,* Tennyson was feeling his way towards the dramatic monologue. *Œnone* is, however, an idyll in which a story is related, not a monologue in which the situation is implied; and *The Lotos-Eaters,* after the introductory narrative in Spenserian stanzas, is a choric song which the sailors chant in unison. The conflict between Wisdom and Beauty, the theme of *The Palace of Art,* suggests a deliberate effort at self-discipline as though the poet were rejecting the aestheticism to which he had been devoting his gift. At Cambridge he had thought of writing a poem or drama on the Arthurian legend upon which he would impose an allegorical inter-

---

[3] Contemporary testimony is unanimous as to the brilliant promise of A. H. Hallam (1811-1833), son of the historian. *Remains in Verse and Prose* (1834); *Writings,* ed. T. H. V. Motter (1943).

pretation (Arthur representing "Religious Faith" and the Round Table "Religious Institutions") with the intent to enrich its meaning for the modern world. But of this purpose there is no sign in *The Lady of Shalott* or in *Sir Launcelot and Queen Guinevere*. The pieces named in this paragraph form the principal contents of *Poems* published at the close of 1832.

Death of A. H. Hallam

So far, life had been full of happy promise; but in the autumn of 1833 came the crushing blow of Hallam's sudden death. This loss combined with symptoms of failing eyesight and the contemptuous reception accorded his poems by hostile critics [4] to weigh him ·down. *The Two Voices* (originally entitled *Thoughts on Suicide*) discloses his state of mind in the dark days when *In Memoriam* was begun. Tennyson became betrothed to Emily Sellwood, but the uncertainty of his prospects put marriage out of the question for a long while. The next years were passed mainly at Somersby till 1837 when the family were turned out of the rectory.[5]

Little verse was written till about two years after Hallam's death. In lyric elegy the poet recalled "the tender grace of a day that is dead"; but in the magnificent dramatic monologue *Ulysses* he looked to the future, albeit without the "old strength." The determination to follow knowledge wherever it may lead is characteristic of the period which was becoming aware of the perilous seas of scientific speculation. Thus Tennyson poured the new wine of modern thought into the old wine-skins of mythology. *Tithonus,*[6] though lacking the immediacy of application obvious in *Ulysses,* is perhaps an even finer poem. The art with which the shimmering lights and cool airs of the Palace of the Dawn are suggested by words and cadences is as wonderful as are the full-voiced vowels of the companion piece, suggesting the ocean beating upon a rocky coast; and as in *Ulysses* the ancient theme is brought home to the modern reader by means of the emphasis upon knowledge and unyieldingness, so the situation in *Tithonus,* beyond all human experience, is yet humanized by the speaker's longing to share the common lot of mortality. During an entire decade Tennyson published nothing [7] save *O that 'twere possible,* out of which *Maud* afterwards developed, and *St. Agnes' Eve,* the first of his evocations of the asceticism of the Middle Ages. Both poems belong to 1837. In the following five years he was active in the revision of old work and the composition of new. In 1842 he emerged from the long twilight with *Poems in Two Volumes.* To contrast the earlier and later versions of famous poems is to learn much about the development and refinement of his art. Thus, in *Œnone* the central episode of Pallas was expanded and the landscape background redrawn in closer

Poems, 1842

---

[4] See E. F. Shannon, Jr., "Tennyson and the Reviewers, 1830-1842," *PMLA,* LVIII (1943). 181-194. The most notorious of these attacks was in the *Quarterly Review,* XLIX (1833). 81-96. This, long attributed to Lockhart, was written by J. W. Croker.

[5] There were several changes of residence before Tennyson settled at Farringford in the Isle of Wight in 1853. Subsequently he built himself another home, Aldworth, in Surrey.

[6] *Tithonus,* though not published till 1860, belongs to about the same date as *Ulysses.* On Tennyson's treatment of classical themes see Bush, ch. VI; W. P. Mustard, *Classical Echoes in Tennyson* (1904).

[7] *The Lover's Tale* was printed in 1833 but immediately suppressed and not published till 1879.

resemblance to the Troad; and in *The Lotos-Eaters* the Lucretian picture
of the careless gods was added and the conclusion altered into its final
superb form. In these and other cases, though there may be some sacrifice
of beauty of detail, the new version, whether in the precision of the rendering
of mental states or in the delicacy of the visualization of outward objects,
is better than the old.

The new poems which made up the second volume of the collection of
1842 show a large expansion of interests and sympathies. Besides *Ulysses,*
another dramatic monologue is *St. Simeon Stylites,* a study in religious
psychopathology which impinges upon Browning's province. The "Matter
of Arthur" is represented by *Sir Galahad,* which is off the road leading to
epical narrative, and the *Morte d'Arthur,* which points forward to the *Idylls
of the King.* Tennyson sets the narrative of Arthur's last battle within a
"frame" of modern life. A young poet (recognizably a self-portrait) reads
to his friends the fragment of an epic. The inference is plain that Tennyson
had already in mind a poem of epical proportions. The homely realism of
this "frame" has something in common with the poems of "domestic" life
which bulk large in this collection. *Dora* and *The Gardener's Daughter* still
possess a quiet prettiness, and their lovely passages descriptive of "haunts
of ancient peace" show Tennyson's kinship to the English school of landscape painters. But there is little vitality in the men and women who people
this tranquil world, and no conceivable retrogression of taste is likely to
reverse the modern repudiation of Tennysonian sentiment. The Queen of
the May has suffered the fate of Little Nell. Fashioned out of more substantial
stuff is *Locksley Hall,* the first of Tennyson's poems of social protest and
very moving to those of his contemporaries who were active in reform. The
"rowdy or bullying element" in Tennyson's poetry which William Morris
found distasteful [8] is audible here. Was he as angry as he appeared to be?
At heart he was content with his time, on the side of the Church in religion
and of the middle classes in economics, less boastful than Macaulay but
none the less complacent in his assurance that the "Anglo-Norman race" is
"the noblest breed of men." To many readers the rhetorical denunciations
of the pursuit of gain do not ring true. The assumption that a poet must
be "a leader of thought" led him too often to the choice of subjects unsuited
to his temperament and artistry.

The Princess (1847), while a disappointment to the judicious, suited the
general taste because of its mild liberalism and "gentlemanly" support of the
cause of female education. The theme of this versified novelette is one which
might have been handled entertainingly as an intellectual comedy; but wit
was not among Tennyson's gifts. There are amusing episodic passages, but
the reasoning was inconclusive at the time and is negligible today. Only
the two lyrics in blank verse (*Tears, Idle Tears* and *Come down, O Maid*)
and the intercalary songs are of perennial loveliness.[9]

[8] J. W. Mackail, *The Life of William Morris* (Pocket Edition, 1912), I. 47-48.
[9] The six songs were added in the third edition (1850).

In
Memoriam

Tennyson's structural skill was not sufficiently robust to build a poem of more than medium length. *In Memoriam* [10] (1850) is no exception to this statement. Periods of intermittent composition extended over seventeen years, and the task of welding the disparate parts into something approximating a unified whole was accomplished in the later eighteen-forties. Many sections were then written to clarify the connections of thought and progress of emotion. The links are often weak, but the use of the same stanzaic form throughout imposes an outward semblance of unity.[11] Such inner harmony as *In Memoriam* possesses comes from the drift of spiritual experience rather than from the too laborious artistic effort. The tradition of the English elegy is followed, in that the note of mourning modulates into a hymn of faith; as in *Lycidas* and *Adonais,* the turning point is discernible, but the looser structure involves a recurrence of earlier moods, so that the pattern is less precise. For this reason, among others, the poem is poignantly convincing as an expression of personal loss, the alternate subsidence and upwelling of grief, and the outcome in renewed happiness. Seeking to impose upon the original simple "elegies" a vague hint of allegorical intent, Tennyson spoke of *In Memoriam* as "a Way of the Soul." The value of the poem, however, is not in this philosophic afterthought but in its lyrical and meditative record of changing moods. There is the gradual healing of grief with the continuance and widening of a love so spiritualized that it can exist without the presence of the beloved.

In some sections Tennyson sought to reconcile traditional faith with the new ideas of evolutionary science; but in others faith and reason are opposed. From both the poetical and psychological points of view this dichotomy is part of the lasting attractiveness of *In Memoriam.* The concessions to the scientific spirit have been derided as feeble attempts to rescue something from the wreck of creeds; they express a characteristic Victorian state of mind. The contrasting mood comes and goes, as do all mystical experiences, with the breath of the spirit; it is revealed in passages of profound feeling and haunting beauty, especially in the incomparable ninety-fifth section, perhaps Tennyson's supreme utterance. These passages are founded upon certain trance-like experiences in which the poet seemed to be, like St. Paul, caught up into a region beyond earth. They are equally beyond the region of argument in which much of the poem moves. The course of speculation passes through doubt to an affirmation of belief in personal immortality. The future life is contemplated as a continuation of the evolutionary process ever nearer and nearer to God.

In Memoriam was received with approbation by leaders of the most diverse schools of thought. The imagery drawn from recent discoveries in astronomy and geology attracted the attention of the scientists, who also marked the poem's underlying evolutionary assumptions. The liberals wel-

---

[10] A. C. Bradley, *A Commentary on Tennyson's "In Memoriam"* (1901).
[11] Tennyson thought he had invented the tetrameter quatrain with inner rimes (*abba*); but it had been used by Lord Herbert of Cherbury and other poets.

comed its attempted compromise between science and religion. The orthodox recognized the effort to save faith from the grip of conquering
materialism. Modern readers, brushing aside these old claims upon their
attention, are still won by its sustained beauty, its deep feeling, its wealth
of imagery, now tender and intimate, now gorgeous and elaborate, and its
revelation of the poet's personality. It is easier today to sympathize with
Tennyson's wistful yearning after certainty than with arrogant dogmatism.
The fused tremulousness of doubt and faith makes the poem the more
moving.

In 1850, the year of his marriage, Tennyson succeeded Wordsworth as *Poet*
poet laureate. The seriousness with which he undertook the duties of an *Laureate*
office which had hitherto been little more than a sinecure is shown by the
dignity of the "poems on affairs of state" produced in his official capacity,
such as the gravely eloquent *Ode on the Death of the Duke of Wellington*
(1852), the *Welcome* to Princess Alexandra (1863), and various poems for
special occasions and elegies on public men. But his position gradually
committed him to an increasingly complacent acceptance of English institutions and virtues.

There is, however, no complacency in *Maud* (1853), which reflects the *Maud*
irresolution and uncertainty to which Arnold and Clough were giving expression at the same time, and which voices this mood in the manner of
the poets of the "Spasmodic School," then in the midst of their brief vogue.[12]
That Tennyson was influenced by these poets is evident from the discontinuity of the thought and the extravagances of the style.[13] *Maud* is a
"monodrama," that is, an extension of the form of the dramatic monologue
through a succession of episodes wherein the story is unfolded in soliloquies.
Those who identified the speaker with the poet were to this degree correct,
that the moody side of Tennyson's nature is mirrored in the character of
the hero. The plot, with its poor but proud lover pitted against the heroine's
wealthy family and his haughty rival, and leading to death and madness, is
quite commonplace. The self-revelations of a speaker of abnormal mentality
owe something to the scenes of madness in prose fiction. The hysterical tone,

---

12 The "Spasmodic" poets were Sydney Dobell (1824-1874) and Alexander Smith (1830-
1867). Dobell wrote *The Roman* (1850), *Balder* (1854), *England in Time of War* (1856),
and other poems. See his *Poetical Works* (2v, 1875); *Life and Letters* (2v, 1878). His finest
piece is the weird ballad, *Keith of Ravelston*. The dominant note in his verse is the struggle
of free men against autocracy. His style is over-excited, often to the point of incoherence; and
from passages of power he lapses into banality. Some of his poems on the Crimean War
were written in collaboration with Alexander Smith, author of *A Life-Drama and other
Poems* (1855), *City Poems* (1857), and the charming volume of essays, *Dreamthorp* (1863).
The best estimate of the poetry of Dobell and Smith is in Hugh Walker, *The Literature of the
Victorian Era* (1910), pp. 513-526. They were satirized in W. E. Aytoun's parody, *Firmilian:
a Spasmodic Tragedy* (1854). Walker writes: "What Aytoun condemned in them was the
confusion and inequality and extravagance of their work, its passion piled on passion, its
thought disjointed from thought, the rant and fustian of the style, the lavishly sprinkled and
overwrought metaphors."

13 Walker, *op. cit.*, p. 514, says that *Maud* "is just a very fine example of many of the
faults and of more than all the merits" of the "School." Aytoun reviewed *Maud* savagely as
"an ill-conceived and worse-expressed screed of bombast," in *Blackwood's Magazine*, September, 1855; reprinted in *Notorious Literary Attacks*, ed. Albert Mordell (1926), pp. 138-161.

dubiously appropriate, to a madman, is close to fustian when used to denounce the evils of modern society; and the advocacy of war as a remedy for these ills is both unreasonable and shocking. *Maud* presents the paradox of worthlessness as a story, as a psychopathological study, and as a contribution to social criticism, and yet of enduring readability beyond most of Tennyson's poetry. The form has kept the matter alive; the prosody is a triumph of the adaptation of various metres to varying moods.

Idylls
of the
King

Tennyson now devoted himself to his long-meditated great task. The Tractarian Movement, the historical novel, the Gothic revival in architecture, and the writings of Pugin and Ruskin had all served to intensify interest in the Middle Ages, and the Arthurian theme was in the air of the mid-century. Bulwer had published his epic, *King Arthur* (1848); Arnold, his *Tristram and Iseult* (1853); the young painters of Rossetti's circle had chosen subjects from the legend for their murals at Oxford (1857); Morris had published *The Defence of Guenevere* (1858); and Tennyson's friend Robert Stephen Hawker was writing *The Quest of the Sangraal* (not published till 1864). Tennyson's *Idylls of the King* appeared in 1859.[14] These original four *Idylls* display a symmetry that is lacking in the completed twelve parts of the poem. Almost, if not quite, devoid of allegorical implication, they are studies in contrasted types of womanhood, "the True and the False." Judged as metrical tales, they are not very different from the domestic "Idyls" on modern subjects. Though there is little of the authentic medieval flavor, it is but fair to insist that Tennyson, in subjecting the legends to modern treatment, was following the same procedure successfully used in his renderings of classical myths. Disregarding for the moment his other poems, we may look ahead to consider the *Idylls* as a whole. *The Holy Grail and other Poems* (1869) contained, beside the title poem and two other idylls, an expanded version of the old *Morte d'Arthur* with a new title, *The Passing of Arthur*. *The Last Tournament* and *Gareth and Lynette* were published together in 1872. In that year the *Enid* of 1859 was split into two idylls, *The Marriage of Geraint* and *Geraint and Enid*. *Balin and Balan,* though written about 1870, was not published till 1885, when it rounded out the cycle to twelve.

The Coming of Arthur, the opening idyll, shows the imperfect success with which Tennyson wrestled with the difficulty of making clear the various motives intended to bind together a series of narratives composed dispersedly over many years. He never welded into a jointless whole the medieval, supernatural stories, their modern application, and the allegorical significance he attached to them. The difficulty is not that there is too much allegory but that there is too little and that little too vague. Tennyson expects his readers to rise to the allegorical plane, but he does not hold them there

---

[14] Two "trial issues," privately printed, preceded the published volume. These are, *Enid and Nimuë; or, the True and the False* (1856) and *The True and the False: Four Idylls of the King* (1857). — See in general M. W. MacCallum, *Tennyson's Idylls of the King and Arthurian Story from the Sixteenth Century* (Glasgow, 1904); Howard Maynadier, *The Arthur of the English Poets* (1907), ch. XXII.

securely. Arthur, who is "Faith," is constantly becoming Arthur the deceived husband. In the former capacity he acts in character; in the latter he is both self-righteous and ungentlemanly. Trouble of another sort was encountered when, as in the cases of the legends of Tristram and Balin, Tennyson, in order to fit them into the allegorical conception of the corruption of society, was forced to degrade noble material. Only when allegory was practically in abeyance, as in the tales of Enid and Lynette, or when, as in *The Holy Grail,* the theme was precisely congenial to the poet's purpose, is the result satisfactory. In the tales of the two "true" women the narrative flows as gently as the limpid brooks which Tennyson loved; and the story of the quest of the Grail is shrouded in mystery through which the lights shine as they do through the mist when Guinevere sees Arthur for the last time.

While the *Idylls* were expanding, Tennyson produced some of the most characteristic poems of his middle period. *Enoch Arden* (1864) was one of the most popular of all his poems, but with the exception of the "inset" of gorgeous tropical description it is flat and commonplace. *The Northern Farmer, Old Style,* and its companion piece, *New Style,* are vigorous monologues in Lincolnshire dialect, contrasting the type of tenant farmer, who was disappearing with the new freeholders. *Lucretius* (1868), the longest of the poems on classical subjects, is both eloquent and erudite, and so unwontedly bold in its treatment of an erotic subject as to make critics suspect that, consciously or unconsciously, Tennyson was challenging comparison with Swinburne.

About 1870 a reaction began to set in against Tennyson's position of un- *Reaction* questioned supremacy among the poets of the period. It was expressed *Against* privately by George Meredith [15] and publicly by Swinburne in *Under the* *Tennyson* *Microscope* [16] (1872), where there is a savage onslaught on Tennyson's treatment of the Arthurian story. There were other signs that the laureate's reputation was under a cloud. He had to compete with Browning, who had won belated popular recognition with *The Ring and the Book*; with Swinburne, whose *Poems and Ballads* had taken the world by storm; with Morris, whose *Earthly Paradise* had just appeared; and with Rossetti, whose *Poems* of 1870 brought the "new poetry" to a climax. The progress of his fame was, moreover, impeded by the imitators who trailed behind him.[17] Within

[15] Meredith, *Letters* (1912), I. 197.
[16] *Under the Microscope* (ed. 1872), pp. 36-45; *Works,* Bonchurch Edition (1925-1927), XVI. 377-444.
[17] Echoes of Tennyson's style are audible in much late Victorian poetry, particularly in the work of writers not susceptible to the influence of Rossetti and Swinburne. The Earl of Lytton (1831-1891), diplomat and Viceroy of India, published a dozen volumes of verse under the pen-name of "Owen Meredith." Of these the best remembered are *Tannhäuser* (1861), which is of some slight Wagnerian interest because of its date, and *Lucile* (1860), a novel in verse, both romantic and witty. Lytton's poetry is fluent and facile, lax and slovenly. Tennyson was but one of many poets whom he imitated, sometimes so closely that the charge of plagiarism can in some cases be sustained. See *Personal and Literary Letters of Robert First Earl of Lytton,* ed. Lady Betty Balfour (2v, 1906); A. B. Harlan, *Owen Meredith* (1945). — Sir Edwin Arnold (1832-1904), who passed much of his life in the East, is remembered for *The Light of Asia* (1879), a poem on the life and teaching of the Buddha. Half a dozen other volumes of poetry deal in the main with Oriental themes. In subject Arnold's work has little in common with Tennyson's, but his blank verse is closely imitative. See his *Poetical*

*The
Dramas*

a shadow of comparative indifference he remained for a decade. These years were devoted in the main to the three tragedies—*Queen Mary* (1875), *Harold* (1877), and *Becket* (1879)—in which he sought to dramatize the story of "the Making of England." Unremitting toil was expended upon these earnest, bulky, and stagnant things, but Tennyson had neither the practical experience of the theatre nor the gift of delineating characters and making them interact upon one another without which plays cannot live. These tragedies and four other plays—*The Falcon* (1879), *The Cup* (1881), *The Promise of May* (1892) and *The Foresters* (1892)—have shared the fate of almost all the poetic dramas of the nineteenth century. Several of them reached the boards, but only *Becket* had a successful run and that only after it had been much revised by Sir Henry Irving.

After this unprofitable decade Tennyson returned to the kinds of poetry of which he was a master. The abandonment of the historical drama may have brought a relief which accounts for the recovery of genius in his seventieth year. There was also a noticeable withdrawal from the position of *vates* or counselor to his countrymen which he had assumed in middle life. Save in a few pieces such as the ranting, ineffectual *Locksley Hall, Sixty Years After,* he was content in this final period to resume once more the manner and matter native to his genius as a poet of solemn, introspective, and melancholy moods, of romantic atmosphere and lovely landscape, and as an elegist and the contemplator of the mysteries of life and death. In 1878 appeared the spirited ballad of *The Revenge. Ballads and other Poems* (1880) ushered in the final decade of his glory in which his reputation in England and America eclipsed all competitors. This volume was followed by four other collections of miscellaneous lyrical, narrative, and meditative verse: *Tiresias and other Poems* (1885), *Locksley Hall, Sixty Years After, Etc.* (1886), *Demeter and other Poems* (1889), and *The Death of Œnone, Akbar's Dream, and other Poems* (posthumous, 1892). That the old laureate possessed a wonderful reserve of power is proved by the admirable *Rizpah,* the address *To Virgil,* the symbolic narrative, *The Voyage,* the allegorical autobiography, *Merlin and the Gleam,* and the last poems on

*The
Last
Decade*

Works (8v, 1888). — Sir Lewis Morris (1833-1907), after publishing *Songs of Two Worlds* (1871), established a fame that has proved ephemeral with *The Epic of Hades* (1876-1877), a series of monologues by characters in Greek mythology whom the poet meets in the other world. *A Vision of Saints* (1890), on Christian themes, is similar in design. In these and numerous other volumes Morris wrote smoothly and cheerfully in the style Tennyson had made popular. — Alfred Austin (1835-1913), whom Lord Salisbury rewarded with the laureateship for services rendered to Tory journalism, was Byronic rather than Tennysonian, so far as he was anything. His two score volumes of worse than mediocre verse include satires, dramas, lyrics, the pretentious narrative poem, *The Human Tragedy* (1862; revised 1876) and *England's Darling* (1896), a play on Alfred the Great. *The Poetry of the Period* (1870) is a piece of impudently cocksure criticism of some interest for its connection with Browning. *The Garden that I Love* (1894) is a pleasant piece of prose, once quite popular. Austin's *Autobiography* (2v, 1911) is a curious revelation of overweening self-esteem.— On an even lower level than Austin was an older poetaster, Martin Tupper (1810-1889), whose enormous popularity in the mid-century is a phenomenon in the history of taste. His innumerable poems and ballads on public affairs, emigration, the Crimean War, and so forth are patriotic in feeling and shot through with complacent Whiggery. His once-famous and still proverbially bad *Proverbial Philosophy* (four series, 1838-1867) expresses in unrimed verse a facile and pretentious but doubtless sincere morality.

classical themes (though these incorporate some work of early years).[18] In meditative pieces Tennyson sought again and again to epitomize his thoughts on life. Many poems are in memory of departed friends. The purely lyrical note is seldom sounded, perhaps most clearly in *The Silent Voices,* for *Crossing the Bar* does not belong in the category of song. He was engaged upon his latest poems till shortly before his death (October 4, 1892).[19]

Tennyson's posthumous reputation passed through a period of more *After-* violent denigration than that suffered by any of his great contemporaries. *fame* Of this there had been anticipations in the strictures passed upon the *Idylls of the King* by Meredith and Swinburne. It reached its most forceful expression in *Tennyson as a Thinker* (1893) by Henry S. Salt, the rationalist, and survived to color critical pronouncements of the nineteen-twenties. The gravamen of adverse criticism has been concerned with the disproportion between the manner and the matter of Tennyson's poetry. Subjects either outmoded or essentially insignificant are made to bear too heavy a weight of ornament, and this ornamentation is designed in accordance with a formula of imagery and cadence which, once devised, is repeated again and again. The elaborate surface covers a paucity of ideas; and such thought as exists is timid, complacent, conventional when critical of society, and fundamentally conservative. His wide-mindedness made him aware of contemporary issues and tendencies, but he was a follower, a popularizer, not an originator. His poetry is therefore of little consequence as a "criticism of life." Such was the indictment. The wind of extreme disfavor, which has carried his dramas, his "domestic" pieces, and his poetry of social protest into something like oblivion, has now passed by; and recent criticism has readjusted the balance which sank too far against him. The meditative poems, often touched with the majestic Virgilian melancholy; the poems on classical subjects and a few other dramatic monologues, such as the magnificent *Rizpah;* some of the shorter narrative pieces and some episodes in the *Idylls of the King;* the poems of moods and places far withdrawn; the all too few lyrics; *Maud,* not for its subject but for its mastery and range of prosody; and *In Memoriam,* in which faith and doubt contend for the possession of a soul—these parts of Tennyson's work belong in the enduring heritage of English poetry.

[18] In *Tiresias* it is easy to discriminate between the early work (the prophet on the mountain; the vision of Pallas; the forecast of the prophet's death) and the later.
[19] For a list of a score of elegies inspired by Tennyson's death, mostly by writers of note, see *Representative Poems,* ed. S. C. Chew, pp. lv-lvi. By far the finest of these is Sir William Watson's *Lachrymae Musarum,* published in the *Illustrated London News,* October 15, 1892; *Poems* (2v, 1905), I. 3-8.

XXVII
The Brownings

I

Part of the heritage of Robert Browning [1] (1812-1889) from his well-to-do parents was a love of books, pictures, and music. Their home was near Dulwich, and the gallery there was one of the boy's favorite haunts. His father shared with his son a passion for old tales of intrigue and violence, and the two followed together the latest crime-stories in the newspapers. In the light of Browning's subsequent predeliction for criminal types and morally warped characters this early shaping influence upon his imagination requires emphasis. For the austere atmosphere of worship in the religion of Evangelical dissent in which his mother instructed him he retained a reverence which long afterwards he expressed in his poetry. Of his childhood there are the usual stories of precocity; his father was proud of his juvenile verses. After the age of fourteen he had no regular education, but in the library at home he read widely and acquired the taste for out-of-the-way books which was to furnish him with his vast but undisciplined erudition. "Ossian" and Byron were his first masters, but in 1826 he met with the poems of Shelley and became an avowed disciple of the "Sun-treader." [2] Attendance at the theatres roused his ambition to be a "maker of plays";

---

[1] *Works*, Centenary Edition, ed. Sir F. G. Kenyon (10v, 1912); *New Poems*, ed. Kenyon (1914); *Works*, ed. H. E. Scudder (1895); *Works*, ed. C. Porter and H. A. Clarke (12v, 1910). No edition is absolutely complete. *Shorter Poems*, ed. W. C. DeVane (1934). *Letters of Robert Browning and Elizabeth Barrett Barrett, 1845-1846* (2v, 1899); *Robert Browning and Alfred Domett*, ed. Kenyon (1906), a collection of letters; *Letters of Robert Browning to Miss Isa Blagden*, ed. A. J. Armstrong (1923); *Letters of Robert Browning, Collected by T. J. Wise*, ed. T. L. Hood (1933); *Robert Browning and Julia Wedgwood. A Broken Friendship as Revealed by Their Letters*, ed. Richard Curle (1937); *Letters of Elizabeth Barrett Browning*, ed. Kenyon (2v, 1897); E. B. Browning, *Letters to her Sister, 1846-1859*, ed. Leonard Huxley (1929). — T. J. Wise, *Bibliography* (1897); H. W. Griffin and H. C. Minchin, *Life of Robert Browning* (1910; rev. ed. 1938); W. C. DeVane, *A Browning Handbook* (1935), an invaluable reference-guide; Mrs. Sutherland Orr, *Life and Letters of Robert Browning* (1891), ed. Kenyon (1908); G. K. Chesterton, *Robert Browning* (EML Series, 1903); C. H. Herford, *Robert Browning* (1905); Pierre Berger, *Robert Browning* (Paris, 1912); L. Whiting, *The Brownings: Their Life and Art* (1917); Osbert Burdett, *The Brownings* (1929); H. L. Hovelaque, *La Jeunesse de Robert Browning* (Paris, 1932); J. P. McCormick, *As a Flame Springs* (1940); Mrs. Sutherland Orr, *Handbook to the Works of Robert Browning* (1886), still important because authorized by Browning; W. L. Phelps, *Browning: How to Know Him* (1931); F. G. R. Duckworth, *Browning: Background and Conflict* (1931); Edward Berdoe, *The Browning Cyclopaedia* (1897); L. N. Broughton and B. F. Stelter, *Concordance* (2v, 1924-1925); George Santayana, "The Poetry of Barbarism," *Interpretations of Poetry and Religion* (1900), pp. 166-216, relates Browning to Walt Whitman and is hostile to both. — Baylor University, Waco, Texas, has been made an important center of Browning studies under the direction of A. J. Armstrong, who has published there various monographs and brochures.

[2] F. A. Pottle, *Shelley and Browning, a Myth and Some Facts* (Chicago, 1923).

but first he conceived the idea of writing a poem, an opera, and a novel, each to appear under a different pseudonym. Nothing more is heard of the opera and novel, but the poem was *Pauline* which came out anonymously Pauline in 1833.[3] The heroine of this has no function save to listen to the confidences of the young poet (an Alastor-like creation) who lays bare his soul. Scattered lines and passages give promise of a greatness which *Pauline,* in its incoherent entirety, does not display. A copy of it with manuscript comments by John Stuart Mill got back to Browning. Some of Mill's remarks were beside the point, but his reproof of the writer's self-centeredness and morbidness was salutary. Browning shifted his point of view with swift determination and henceforth regarded *Pauline* as a false start which he preferred to have forgotten.

In 1834 he made a journey to St. Petersburg in company with a Russian consul. Not till late in life did he make poetic use of impressions gathered there. On his return home he applied for a post in a mission to Persia but failed of appointment. His interest in the wiles and casuistry of diplomatic dealings may have been fed by the Russian experience; and the Persian dream may have been transmuted long afterwards into *Ferishtah's Fancies.* But travel and plans for a career did not turn him from his vocation. He had written as wonderful a poem as ever came from a youth of genius: *Paracelsus*[4] (1835). It had little success with the public, but recognition Paracelsus by Wordsworth, Landor, and other men of influence started Browning on the road to the renown which he might have reached soon had he courted readers instead of alienating them. Macready asked him to write a tragedy[5] and the poet's response was *Strafford* (1837) which ran feebly for five performances.[6] He had now for long been wrestling with the subject of his next poem, and to acquire a first-hand knowledge of its setting and atmosphere he went to Italy in 1838. He brought back not only the impressions immediately needed but a love of the country that was lifelong. *Sordello* Sordello (1840) did almost irreparable harm to his reputation, for it became promptly a byword for wilful and impenetrable obscurity in subject, treatment, and style. To this day, even after a century of interpretation, its difficulties remain well-nigh insuperable and, for most people, not worth the trouble of surmounting. The tangled political situation in medieval Italy with which it deals had called for clarity of treatment, and the young poet, blindly confident that matters plain to him would be plain to his readers, had not responded. During seven years of composition there had been successive

[3] *Pauline,* ed. N. H. Wallis (1931).
[4] On the reception of *Paracelsus* see T. R. Lounsbury, *The Early Literary Career of Robert Browning* (1911), pp. 29-44. This book carries the story of the reception of Browning's work by the reviewers down to 1846.
[5] *Diaries of William Charles Macready,* ed. William Toynbee (2v, 1912), contains much information on the relations between the actor and the poet.
[6] Browning helped John Forster with the biography of Strafford contributed to Lardner's *Cyclopaedia* (1836); but F. J. Furnivall exaggerated when he reprinted this as *Robert Browning's Prose Life of Strafford* (Browning Society, 1892). — On Browning's misinterpretations of history in the play but essential truth of characterization see S. R. Gardiner's preface to *Strafford,* ed. E. H. Hicksey (1884).

stages of incubation, involving radical alterations in the theme, and vestiges of earlier concepts remain in the later strata.[7] When Sordellists expound the theme ultimately chosen, the candid reader is inclined to repeat Lowell's judgment: "It was a fine poem before the author wrote it."

Bells and Pomegranates

Between 1841 and 1846 Browning published eight little pamphlets entitled *Bells and Pomegranates*.[8] The first of these was *Pippa Passes* which, had not *Sordello* frightened readers away, might have been at once what it ultimately became, one of Browning's most popular poems. Five of the *Bells* contained six dramas. *A Blot on the 'Scutcheon* [9] was the cause of a bitter quarrel with Macready. After writing *A Soul's Tragedy* Browning abandoned his long effort to write for the stage. He had found in the dramatic monologue the medium ideally suited to his genius. Of poems in this form *Dramatic Lyrics* contained, among other things, *My Last Duchess* and *Soliloquy in a Spanish Cloister*. The perfection of these famous pieces is of a narrower order than that of some of the more elaborate monologues of later date. *Dramatic Romances and Lyrics* included, with much else on a somewhat lower level, the lastingly popular *How They Brought the Good News from Ghent to Aix, The Flight of the Duchess,* the first nine sections of *Saul,* and that masterpiece of psychological and historical insight, *The Tomb at St. Praxed's*.[10] Here, too, was *The Lost Leader,* the attack on Wordsworth (which Browning afterwards regretted), written under the impetus of the sympathy with liberalism which had permeated *Strafford* and *King Victor and King Charles*.

Meanwhile Browning had visited Italy for a second time in 1844. In that year Elizabeth Barrett published her *Poems* in one of which Browning read a commendation of himself. He and the poetess already had friends in common, and now he addressed her a letter of admiration which led at once to friendship and soon (impetuously on his part and timidly on hers) to love. The earliest of her *Sonnets from the Portuguese* date from this time. Browning's virile confidence triumphed over paternal despotism [11] and Elizabeth's ill-health, and on September 12, 1846, the lovers eloped. Mr. Barrett never forgave his daughter.

Marriage and Italy

They went to Italy, and after a short stay at Pisa settled in Florence at Casa Guidi which was their home from 1847 till Mrs. Browning's death in 1861. For years their financial situation was precarious till a munificent

---

[7] W. C. DeVane, "Sordello's Story Retold," *SP,* xxvii (1930). 1-24.

[8] 1: *Pippa Passes* (1841); 11: *King Victor and King Charles* (1842); 111: *Dramatic Lyrics* (1842); iv: *The Return of the Druses* (1843); v: *A Blot on the 'Scutcheon* (1843); vi: *Colombe's Birthday* (1844); vii: *Dramatic Romances and Lyrics* (1845); viii: *Luria* and *A Soul's Tragedy* (1846).

[9] The plot—a melodramatic quarrel between two noble houses in the eighteenth century—is of Browning's invention, but it has points of resemblance to *Romeo and Juliet,* just as in *Luria,* on a quarrel between Florence and Pisa in the fifteenth century, there are similarities to *Othello.* For a general discussion see G. R. Elliot, "Shakespeare's Significance for Browning," *Anglia,* xxxii (1909). 90-162.

[10] Renamed in 1849 *The Bishop Orders His Tomb at St. Praxed's Church.*

[11] For the view of Mr. Barrett's feelings for his daughter spread abroad in Rudolf Besier's successful play *The Barretts of Wimpole Street* (1931) there is no valid evidence whatsoever.

bequest from John Kenyon in 1856 put them beyond anxiety. In 1849 their son was born. Mrs. Browning, impressionable and emotional, was no sooner established in Italy than she became an enthusiastic partisan of the Italian patriots struggling for freedom. Browning, though he shared her sympathies, remained cool and more detached. To her Italy meant mainly contemporary politics; to him, painting, music, history, landscape, and the complex temperament of a fascinating people. He observed disapprovingly the elaborate ritual of Catholic worship, contrasted it with the simple piety of English dissent, and from his reading of Strauss's *Leben Jesu* [12] drew out the further contrast between faith and rationalism. Such was the trifold subject of *Christmas-Eve and Easter-Day* (1850). A critique of Shelley, attached to a collection of Shelley letters that turned out to be forgeries (1852), is Browning's only work in prose and is important for an understanding of his conception of poetry. The Brownings visited London in 1855. *Men and Women*, a collection of fifty poems, was now published. The enthusiasm of Rossetti and his circle furthered the immediate sales of the new work, but these soon dropped off and though reviews were generally favorable few readers seem to have discerned the surpassing excellence of many of these poems. Among the few, however, were some of the foremost men of the time. Carlyle had long been Browning's admirer; Landor ranked him with Chaucer; Ruskin praised him in *Modern Painters*, IV. *Men and Women*

At the time of their return to Florence in 1856 a shadow of difference had come between husband and wife, for Mrs. Browning had been taken in by D. D. Home, the American medium, while Browning was completely skeptical about spiritualistic phenomena. *Mr. Sludge, "the Medium,"* in which he satirized Home, was not published till after Mrs. Browning's death. In 1860 Browning discovered on a Florentine bookstall an "Old Yellow Book" containing a collection of records of a murder trial at Rome and the execution of the murderer in 1698. Only gradually did the poet come to realize that this was material precisely, almost providentially, suited to his interest in psychology, in casuistry, in the criminal mind, and in Italian social history, and to the technique of the dramatic monologue. Meanwhile his wife's health was declining; she was overwrought when Italian hopes languished after the Peace of Villafranca; and she died in 1861. Life in Florence was henceforth impossible for Browning; he left the city, never to return; and with his son made his home in London with occasional sojourns in France.[13] *Dramatis Personae* (1864) shows a shift of interest from Italian to English themes and an alert attention to such vital issues of the day as the Darwinian hypothesis (*Caliban upon Setebos*) and the "higher criticism" (*A Death in the Desert*). An increased ruggedness of manner and a *The "Old Yellow Book"* *Death of Mrs. Browning*

---

[12] K. Goritz, "Robert Browning's *Christmas-Eve and Easter-Day* und *Das Leben Jesu* von D. F. Strauss," *Archiv*, CXLVII (1924). 197-211; W. O. Raymond, "Browning and Higher Criticism," *PMLA*, XLIV (1929). 590-621.

[13] On his return to London Browning began the correspondence with Isa Blagden which is a chief source of information for the next decade. The letters in Armstrong's edition (1923) are supplemented by others in the Wise collection, ed. T. L. Hood (1933).

The Ring and the Book

greater emphasis upon the grotesque presage the work of his last two decades. The next years were devoted to *The Ring and the Book,* which was published in four installments, 1868-1869. This masterpiece was received with almost universal acclaim; in popular estimation Browning was henceforth second only to Tennyson among living poets and by many he was accorded the first place.

In 1871 came the affair of his proposal of marriage to Lady Ashburton, which was made with such tactless, albeit touching, loyalty to the memory of his wife that the lady had no choice but to refuse his hand. Browning bitterly regretted not that he had been rejected but that he had made the offer. Covert allusions to the unhappy incident occur in later poems. *Balaustion's Adventure* (1871) is his first extended incursion into the field of classical mythology which he was now for some years to cultivate diligently.[14] The choice of the theme of Alcestis is a tribute to his dead wife. Bewilderingly unlike this offshoot from Euripides is the intricate and crabbed *Prince Hohenstiel-Schwangau* (1871). The speaker of this long monologue is, as was clear to all readers, Napoleon III. The inception of the poem and possibly parts of it date from 1859; it was resumed after the fall of the French Empire. The harshness of style and fine-drawn psychologizing, with the many no longer easily comprehensible allusions to contemporary affairs, make it one of the least readable of Browning's poems.

Fifine at the Fair

To 1872 belongs *Fifine at the Fair.* This involved but to some tastes fascinating study in erotic psychology is connected only by the names of the husband and wife with the legend of Don Juan and Elvire; but it has an immediate contemporary reference in that it is a commentary by indirection upon the Rossetti-Buchanan quarrel and is inferentially a partial condemnation of Rossetti's poetry.[15] Even while strengthening the admiration of devotees who now clustered round the poet, the two volumes just named alienated many readers; for they justified the old charge of harsh obscurity which had been less vocal during his middle years. The fascination which crime and the mentality of criminals had for Browning now led him into the dark thickets of *Red Cotton Night-Cap Country* (1873). The uncouth title [16] is as repellent as the sordid narrative. It concerns an actual con-

[14] The short and beautiful *Artemis Prologuizes* is of earlier date. — On the relation of Browning's Alcestis to other modern versions of the myth see E. M. Butler, "Alkestis in Modern Dress," *Jour. of the Warburg Institute,* I (1937-1938). 46-60. On Browning's poems on classical subjects see Bush, pp. 358-385; T. L. Hood, "Browning's Ancient Classical Sources," *Harvard Studies in Classical Philology,* xxxiii (1922). 79-180. On the relation of *Cleon* (a study of dying paganism as *A Death in the Desert* is of dawning Christianity) to Arnold's *Empedocles on Etna* see A. W. Crawford, "Browning's *Cleon*," *JEGP,* xxvi (1927). 485-490.

[15] On the autobiographical element in *Fifine* (Browning's proposal of marriage to Lady Ashburton) see W. O. Raymond, "Browning's Dark Mood," *SP,* xxxi (1934). 578-599. On the relation of the poem to Rossetti's *Jenny* see W. C. DeVane, "The Harlot and the Thoughtful Young Man," *SP,* xxix (1932). 463-484. Rossetti detected the allusions to himself in *Fifine* and broke off his long friendship with Browning.

[16] Not to vindicate but to explain the title it may be noted that a friend of Browning's called the Calvados country of Normandy "White Cotton Night-Cap Country" with reference to the head-dresses worn by women there. Browning changed the color to "red" in allusion to the bloody tragedy narrated in his poem.

temporary French trial involving a contested will and a suspected suicide. Another psychological study of villainy is *The Inn-Album* (1875) founded upon the case of a card-sharper in *The Greville Memoirs,* with material inserted from the case of the Tichborne Claimant, which had just been engaging public attention. To 1875 belongs also *Aristophanes' Apology,* a sequel to *Balaustion's Adventure* and a defense at once of Euripides against current detraction and of Browning's own poetic faith and practice.[17]

In tone different from all Browning's other books is the curious volume *Of Pacchiarotto and How He Worked in Distemper* (1876). Alfred Austin, a journalist and poetaster, had criticized Browning in impudent fashion in *The Poetry of the Period* (1870) and for years had been sniping at him in the newspapers. Browning now turned on him savagely but not very effectively, for his invective is overloaded with erudition and the grotesque rimes employed as a weapon of satire are not handled with the requisite light Byronic touch. That Austin had held up Byron as a model for contemporary poets to copy accounts for Browning's mockery of *Childe Harold,* which, beginning in *Fifine,* had been continued in *The Inn-Album* and reappeared in *Pacchiarotto.*[18] Two other poems in the same volume are of personal interest: *House* is apparently an indirect reproof of Rossetti, a remonstrance against the intimate revelations of *The House of Life; St. Martin's Summer,* in which the ghost of an old love intervenes in a belated love affair, is obviously an atonement to the memory of his wife for the proposal of marriage made to Lady Ashburton.

Browning's version of *The Agamemnon of Aeschylus* (1877) is the most unattractive of all his books. He seems deliberately to have reproduced as closely as possible, and with clumsy literalness, the harshness and obscurity of the Greek, doing this as a vindication of his beloved Euripides from those who exalted Aeschylus at the expense of the younger dramatist. Thus to load the dice against the author to whose text he devoted so much toil was a curiously perverse occupation.

In 1877 a newly founded periodical, *The Nineteenth Century,* attracted wide attention by publishing under the general title *A Modern Symposium* a series of articles by a distinguished group of intellectuals, Sir James Stephen, W. G. Ward, Frederick Harrison, and others. Among the problems discussed were the influence of morality upon religious beliefs and "The Soul and Future Life." [19] Browning followed these essays with eager attention, and *La Saisiaz* (1878), a poem inspired by the death of a friend, is in

---

[17] F. M. Tisdel, "Browning's *Aristophanes' Apology,*" *University of Missouri Studies,* II (1927). 1-46; Donald Smalley, "A Parleying with Aristophanes," *PMLA,* LV (1940). 823-838.

[18] See *Letters of Robert Browning,* ed. T. L. Hood, pp. 358-363; W. L. Phelps, "Robert Browning and Alfred Austin," *Yale Review,* n.s. VII (1918). 580-591; and on Browning's earlier and later opinions of Byron, S. C. Chew, *Byron in England* (1924), p. 237 and pp. 285-287.

[19] This was the title of an article by Frederick Harrison, *The Nineteenth Century,* I (1877). 623-636 and 832-842. To it Lord Selborne and others replied, and Harrison was permitted the last word, *ibid.,* pp. 497-536. To these articles Browning alludes by title in *La Saisiaz.*

La
Saisiaz

a way an intervention in the debate. The uncharacteristic gloom of this poem culminates in an emphatic and disturbing asseveration:

> I must say—or choke in silence—"Howsoever came my fate,
> Sorrow did and joy did nowise—life well weighed—preponderate." [20]

This solemn statement is not always taken into account by those who speak of the "facile optimism" of Browning. *La Saisiaz* shows that he did not easily come by his assurance of God's Love. *The Two Poets of Croisic* in the same volume is, however, in lighter mood; and in the first series of

Later
Poems

Dramatic Idyls (1878) there are a vigor of narrative, a freshness, and an interest that, despite the verbosity and the mannerisms, are fairly well sustained. This group of stories is the most readable of the later books. *Dramatic Idyls, Second Series* (1880) shows a sudden and pathetic loss of spontaneity: the fantastic rimes are but so much misapplied ingenuity; the grotesquerie is wearisome; the tales are obscure and dull, fit exercise only for the minds of the Browning Society, which began its activities in the following year. *Jocoseria* (1883) is, as the title promises, a miscellany in light vein; the most interesting of its contents are the renderings of rabbinical legends, and of these the best is *Solomon and Balkis*.[21] *Ixion,* almost the last fruit of Browning's love of Greek myth, interprets the familiar story in a novel fashion; by softening Ixion's guilt Browning is able to fulminate against tyrannical omnipotence in a manner reminiscent of Shelley. *Ferishtah's Fancies* (1884) is a group of little tales that are with one exception of Browning's own invention. There is a thin veneer of Eastern coloring, but the Persian sage is transparently the poet himself. *Parleyings with Certain People of Importance in Their Day* (1887) is a stumbling-block in the path of even the most devoted admirers of the poet. These pieces are desperately crabbed, obscure, verbose, and dull; nowhere else is the subtlety more intricate and tedious. It has been shown that the seven men with whom the "parleyings" are carried on were not chosen at random but represent the seven major interests in Browning's life: philosophy, history, poetry, painting, politics, Greek, and music.[22] Lacking this autobiographical key, reviewers of the day were bewildered; and it may be questioned whether, possessing it, many modern readers find pleasure in unlocking the mystery.

In the summer of 1889, turning over the pages of the newly published *Letters* of Edward FitzGerald, Browning came across a passage in which FitzGerald wrote: "Mrs. Browning's death is rather a relief to me, I must say: no more Aurora Leighs, thank God!" This was addressed to a private correspondent and should not have been published; at worst the writer is to be blamed only for tasteless facetiousness. But, agitated and furious,

---

[20] *La Saisiaz,* lines 332-333. Compare the bitter doubts expressed in the *Epilogue* to *Ferishtah's Fancies.*

[21] Solomon confesses to his royal visitor that his vanity is stronger than his wisdom. W. C. DeVane, *A Browning Handbook,* p. 416, compares FitzGerald's version of Jami's *Sálamán and Absál* where the king confesses that his basic emotion is avarice, not love of wisdom.

[22] W. C. DeVane, *Browning's Parleyings: the Autobiography of a Mind* (New Haven, 1927).

Browning wrote the vituperative sonnet *To Edward FitzGerald who Thanked God My Wife was Dead.*[23] The painful episode is of biographical importance because it shows the passionate tenderness of the poet's memories and because the shock probably hastened his end. In the autumn he visited his beloved Asolo and then became a guest in his son's home in Venice, where he died on December 12, 1889. On the morning of that day he found *Death* pleasure in the telegraphed word of the favorable reception of his last volume, *Asolando: Fancies and Facts.* This is a sheaf of love lyrics, versified anecdotes, and philosophical pronouncements. It closes with the *Epilogue* in which Browning described himself as

> One who never turned his back but marched breast forward,
>> Never doubted clouds would break,
> Never dreamed, though right were worsted, wrong would triumph,
> Held we fall to rise, are baffled to fight better,
>> Sleep to wake.

II

Life meant "intensely" to Browning, and meant "good." His confidence in *Love* the final triumph of the right was based upon a belief in the Divine Love which he found manifested through power in nature and through intellect in mind. The antithesis which he intended to make plain in *Paracelsus* is not only between one who would know and one who would love, but between two conceptions of love. The dying Paracelsus realizes that love is not a passion for human perfection but a divine condescension to human frailty.[24] The alterations in the theme of *Sordello* show successive stages in the young Browning's thought. Directly from Dante he had taken the conception of his hero as a poet whose high visions had failed. This had shifted to the theme of martial glory versus human love; and in the final concept Sordello becomes the champion of the poor against the powerful. The poem thus expresses the same humanitarianism which in *Strafford, King Victor and King Charles,* and *Colombe's Birthday* is a championship of popular rights. The disillusioned tone of *A Soul's Tragedy* is an indication that Browning became dissatisfied with political liberalism. In *Christmas-Eve and Easter-* *Faith* *Day* he searched for a secure ground for modern faith and found it neither in nature nor intelligence but in love. How did he arrive at this principle? Quite empirically; love underlay the facts of life as he experienced them; love in the human heart was for him the best evidence of God's providential Love. In the face of intellectual incertitude he asserted with forcible iteration the ultimate validity of his own emotions and intuitions. Critics contemptuous of Browning's sentimental optimism—both those who are complete

---

[23] On second thoughts Browning attempted to recall the lines, but it was too late; they were published in *The Athenaeum,* July 13, 1889. In the next issue W. A. Wright, the editor of FitzGerald's *Letters,* apologized for the oversight in printing the offensive passage.

[24] W. O. Raymond, "Browning's Conception of Love as represented in *Paracelsus,*" *Papers of the Michigan Academy of Science, Arts and Letters,* IV (1924). 443-463.

skeptics and those who rely on dogma—have pointed out that such assevera-
tions are not argument. But the tenuousness of the analogy between human
love which could be tested by experience and the Divine Love which could
only be inferred therefrom was plain to Browning himself. In general he
was convinced of the superiority of the intuitive faculties over the intellectual in giving man a knowledge of God. But there were moments when
he was not convinced; there was the heart-rending moment when he questioned whether the parallel between human love and the Divine was not
a deceit—

> Only, at heart's utmost joy and triumph, terror
> Sudden turns the blood to ice: a chill wind disencharms
> All the late enchantment: What if all be error—
> If the halo irised round my head were, Love, thine arms? [25]

Doubt

What, indeed! Fortunately for his robust confidence, for the boisterous joy
in life which has discredited him with many readers of a later day, the
question does not often arise. When it does, Browning seeks assurance in
an illogical and paradoxical attainment of faith through doubt; St. Michael
stands the more secure just because he feels the serpent writhe beneath his
feet.[26] Doubt is a spiritual Purgatorio and cleanses the soul; the error is to
turn it into a guiding principle instead of regarding it as a stage through
which to pass.

Evil

But if there is an overruling providential Love, what of evil in the
world? Browning is constantly preoccupied with the problem. Evil and
falsehood have no real existence in themselves but are manifestations by
contrariety of love and truth. Care and pain are pledges of the divine regard.
Strength comes from an obstructed road; assurance would breed torpor, but
difficulty increases power. The thought is in line with German idealism
which taught that the imagination creates evil in order that by combatting
it the moral will may be strengthened. Hence "the paradox that comforts
while it mocks," the doctrine of the spiritual value of failure. This doctrine,
which the poet's contemporaries found of inestimable worth, our generation
has contemptuously rejected, perhaps because our failures have been in-
calculably disastrous and our values have gone awry. Aspiration, the poet
taught, should exceed man's grasp; achievement is not evidence of greatness
but of an easy objective. Ruskin counseled his readers "not to set the meaner
thing, in its narrower accomplishment, above the nobler thing, in its mighty
progress." [27] Browning shared the Victorian belief in progress; Time, he
declared,

> means amelioration, tardily enough displayed,
> Yet a mainly onward moving, never wholly retrograde.[28]

---

[25] *Epilogue* to *Ferishtah's Fancies.*
[26] *Bishop Blougram's Apology.*
[27] *The Stones of Venice,* II, ch. VI.
[28] *La Saisiaz.*

But the mighty progress of the nobler thing is beyond the possibility of *Immor-*
fulfillment in this life. Thus failure is used as an argument for belief in *tality*
immortality; the disappointments of this world are so great that in another
there must be reparation. Virtue and happiness will ultimately be brought
into harmony with one another through the agency of God. No shadow of
proof is offered for this assertion.[29] That most people seem to be made
less rather than more fitted for the things of the spirit by their experience
of the world does not trouble Browning overmuch. In the case of most of
his villains he seeks to show that they have become wicked through the
perversion of good; and though Guido Franceschini's very element seems,
like Iago's, to be wickedness, yet Browning leaves it an open question
whether Guido's last cry to Pompilia was not a recognition of the truth and
consequently a sign of salvation; and even if the cry was of despair his soul
went not to hell but to the "sad sequestered place" where God remakes it.

If for the sake of the artist we ignore Browning's pontifical didacticism, *Characters*
we see that his acceptance of the world as he finds it makes him the great
creator of character that he is. Sense as well as spirit has its value; human
life, full and vigorous, of the past and the present,[30] but always grounded
upon reality, is his theme. He is like Shakespeare in the absolute centering
of his interest in humanity, and Shakespearean in his understanding of the
weak, the erring, and the self-deceived. His theatre is the human spirit, his
great subject the soul's development. The regular dramas are failures because
the interest in the plot is sacrificed to inquiry into motive. What men aspire
to be and are not is a proper subject for discussion; but the stage demands *The*
action. Consequently he found his medium in the dramatic monologue, *Dramatic*
where the subject's case could be presented from the inside. The "Old Yel- *Monologue*
low Book" [31] provided him with a perfect theme since the recorded testi-

[29] In an early satire which he did not publish Swinburne, while echoing Arnold's *Empedocles,*
mocks at Browning:

> Thus runs our wise men's song:
> Being dark it must be light;
> And most things are so wrong
> That all things must be right;
> God must mean well, he works so ill by all men's laws.

[30] Browning's antiquarian enthusiasms which made him so lavish with historical detail
obscure the fact that though he used subjects from the past as frequently as from the present
his emphasis is upon those aspects of human nature which do not change. His concern, between
1870 and 1882, with subjects from classical antiquity was probably a revulsion from stories of
sordid crime. But a notable characteristic of the classical pieces is the realistic treatment of
persons and setting. In *Gerard de Lairesse* (*Parleyings*) he insists, as Mrs. Browning had done
in *Aurora Leigh*, upon the need to choose modern subjects. Poets must not "push back reality,
repeople earth with vanished shapes." It is thought that he had Morris's *The Earthly Paradise*
in mind as an example of what the poet should *not* do.

[31] The literature of *The Ring and the Book* is extensive. See especially A. K. Cook, *Commentary upon Browning's The Ring and the Book* (1920), indispensable; C. W. Hodell, *The
Old Yellow Book with Translation, Essay and Notes* (Washington, 1908), a photo-reproduction
of the original now at Oxford; the translation is reprinted in Everyman's Library (1911); J. M.
Gest, *The Old Yellow Book* (1925), which corrects Hodell's translation at important points
and shows that Browning altered the characters in the story more profoundly than had hitherto
been thought; W. O. Raymond, "New Light on the Genesis of *The Ring and the Book*,"
MLN, XLIII (1928). 357-368 and cf. *ibid.*, 445-450; Sir Frederick Treves, *The Country of
the Ring and the Book* (1913); F. T. Russell, *One Word More on Browning* (1927), which
argues that Browning deliberately misrepresented Pompilia and Caponsacchi. That in drawing

mony of the murder trial suggested that the character of the several speakers would alter their presentation of the facts and their presentation of the facts would shed light upon the character of the speakers. The conclusion we are to draw, however, is not that truth is relative but that somewhere in the maze of casuistry and deceit it can be found and is absolute.

The number and variety of the men and women whom he created make for the illusion that Browning possessed a wide range of ideas; but the fact is that he illustrated by innumerable case-histories a small recurring group of themes. He seeks to understand people of the most varied sorts; and because the "good" people present fewer problems he is fascinated by the "bad." His poems of most lasting appeal are psychological stories. The intricacies of motive are disentangled and light is thrown upon the self-deceiver even as he seeks to justify himself. Browning's rich though amateurish scholarship attracted him to subjects from authentic history. His assertion that in *The Ring and the Book* he made no alteration in fact is not supported by the documents; but essentially he aimed at a psychological interpretation of actual fact. The subtlety of this interpretation, necessitating, as he thought (often mistakenly), expansive treatment, makes his poems almost always too long. Moreover, though he wrote very little "nature poetry," he set an elaborate background for his spiritual dramas. His antiquarian enthusiasm spares no detail of architecture and ornament; his quick-darting mind can resist no temptation to digress. This wealth of interests finds appropriate expression in the labyrinthine Gothicism of his verse, the range of effects in his blank verse, the almost unrivaled variety of his stanzaic

Style forms. The illusion of breadth is enhanced by the confused energy of his style, the reposelessness, the persistent allusiveness, and the quality that an unsympathetic critic has described as "garrulous pedantry" and "lumpy and gritty erudition." [32] On occasion the exuberant vitality offended or even scandalized contemporary admirers, as in the notorious case of *The Statue and the Bust* where, censuring the lovers who had not the courage to fulfill their destiny, he seemed to advocate adultery. To many modern readers his dynamism is an offense. [33] Yet he will certainly outlive the detraction from which his fame has suffered since about 1910. Much of his work is dead—but of what poet of vast productivity cannot this be said? At every stage in his career he wrote too much and at too great length and too often sank the poet in the teacher. But the residue is large and very vital and very grand;

Pompilia the poet had in mind his own wife and that Caponsacchi's rescue of her is reminiscent of the Brownings' elopement has long been suspected. The idealization of Pompilia as a tribute to Mrs. Browning in the manner of Dante's idealization of Beatrice is studied by J. E. Shaw, "The 'Donna Angelicata' in *The Ring and the Book*," *PMLA*, xli (1926). 55-81.
[32] Bush, p. 373.
[33] F. R. G. Duckworth, *Browning, Background and Conflict* (1932), contains a survey of Browning's reputation in the eighteen-fifties, in the decade following his death, and in the nineteen-twenties. See also D. C. Somervell, "The Reputation of Robert Browning," *E&S*, xv (1929). 122-138.

and there are few good judges who will reject the opinion that *The Ring and the Book* is the greatest English poem of the Victorian Period.[34]

III

When Robert Browning had not yet emerged from the shadow of *Sordello* and his wife was the most highly esteemed poetess of England, there were few to foresee the day when an estimate of her achievement would properly be a short appendage to an extended account of his; but the authoress of the *Sonnets from the Portuguese* realized what would be the comparative opinions of posterity.

Mrs. Browning

The story of Elizabeth Barrett Browning [35] (1806-1861) is familiar to thousands of people who never read her poems.[36] She began to write under the influence of Byron (*The Seraphim*, 1838) and passed thence to the company of the "Spasmodic" poets (*A Drama of Exile*, 1845). She was too emotional and overstrained to receive either influence without disaster. Of the generosity of her enthusiasms—for Greek literature (she translated the *Prometheus* twice); for social reform (*The Cry of the Children*, 1843); for the lower classes and the rights of women (*Aurora Leigh*, 1857); for the cause of Italian freedom (*Casa Guidi Windows*, 1851; *Poems before Congress*, 1860); and for other noble causes—there can be no question; but much of what she had to say might have been better said in prose, and more succinctly. Her intensity of feeling was rarely controlled by the discipline of form. The verse is too fluent and too facile, and the fact that the many false rimes and approximations to rime were introduced in accordance with a theory that she herself expounded is an explanation of their presence rather than an excuse for it. She depended upon large and loose effects, and rarely sought or found the perfect cadence or the inevitable word. The poems of social protest connect her with the movement for reform; the poems dealing with the Risorgimento contain vivid descriptions of the Florentine scene during the eventful year 1848, and though (as she later realized) she backed the wrong horse when she praised Napoleon III, these pieces form a not unworthy link between Byron and Shelley before her and Swinburne and Meredith after. But only in the sonnets addressed to her husband did she fashion her feeling into the form of art. It would seem that her profounder emotions were the more controlled, for in the *Sonnets from the Portuguese* (1850) there is little of the "confused impetuosity" [37] of *Aurora Leigh*. Though written over a period of several years, the sonnets form a homo-

[34] The "modern" view of the poem discounts the religious and ethical aspects and finds interest in the "novel" element—the complications, the suspense, the entanglements of motive, the conflicts of testimony, the bustle and excitement; while objecting to the arguments, casuistries, doubts, and aspirations. See V. S. Pritchett in *The New Statesman*, xx (1940). 66.
[35] On Elizabeth Barrett's forebears in Jamaica and on her "health-history" see Jeannette Marks, *The Family of the Barrett* (1938).
[36] Familiar from Rudolf Besier's play mentioned above and from Virginia Woolf's *Flush, a Biography* (1933).
[37] The phrase is Virginia Woolf's, who has said all that can be said, and more than most critics would say, for *Aurora Leigh*. See *The Second Common Reader* (1932), pp. 218-231.

geneous sequence. In tone they are almost uniform; occasional attempts at lightness of touch are not very successful, but on other occasions (as in the magnificent twenty-second sonnet) she rises to a height she nowhere else attains. There was abundant fire in Mrs. Browning's spirit, but generally it burned with more smoke and heat than light. In some of the *Sonnets* it is pure flame.

XXVIII

Matthew Arnold and Arthur Hugh Clough; Edward FitzGerald and James Thomson ("B.V.")

I

The story of Clough's spiritual conflict is important for an understanding *Clough* of Arnold and therefore we begin this chapter with the less famous of the two Oxford poets. The early promise of Arthur Hugh Clough [1] (1819-1861) failed of fulfillment because of indecisiveness. At Rugby the influence of Dr. Arnold induced in him an excessive introspectiveness, and at Oxford the Tractarians drew him one way and the liberal theologians another with the consequence that he wandered between two worlds, a perplexed spirit, hesitating almost to the point of paralysis, yet maintaining a receptive openmindedness. He was one of those who retained for the word *skepticism,* which for many contemporaries had become the polite term for the rejection *Skepticism* of religious beliefs, its proper meaning of suspension of judgment. Clough's skepticism was due to the destructive conclusions of the new biblical criticism. Not without poignant misgivings did he relinquish his faith in orthodox Christianity, and he continued to recognize that to submit to reason was as blind a course as to adhere to dogma. *The New Sinai,* a satiric poem, expresses his distrust in science. Several poems reveal the effect of the "higher criticism" upon his hypersensibility. When (in *The Shadow*) men repeat the arguments for the Resurrection, the ghost of Jesus knows no such arguments. In *Easter-Day* the evidence for the Resurrection is rejected; but the poem goes on to a second part in which it is affirmed that in an ideal sense Christ has indeed risen.[2] Clough tries to accept the Carlylean counsel to "do the duty that lies nearest thee." Only—by what criterion can duty be recognized? That question gives him pause. He said of Carlyle that "he led us out into the wilderness and left us there."

The poet soon passed into the wilderness of the world. He recanted his *Principal* subscription to the Thirty-nine Articles and resigned his Oriel fellowship. *Poems*

[1] *Poetical Works,* ed. Charles Whibley (1913); *The Emerson-Clough Letters,* ed. H. F. Lowry and R. L. Rusk (Cleveland, 1934). — Ehrsam, *Bibliographies,* pp. 67-75; Goldy Levy, *Arthur Hugh Clough* (1938); Laura Lutonsky, *Arthur Hugh Clough* (Vienna, 1912); J. I. Osborne, *Arthur Hugh Clough* (1920); Stopford A. Brooke, *A Study of Clough, Arnold, Rossetti and Morris* (1908), pp. 26-48; H. W. Garrod, *Poetry and the Criticism of Life* (1931), pp. 109-127.

[2] A. W. Benn, *English Rationalism,* II. 48, emphasizes the significance of these two poems. Other short pieces recording Clough's spiritual struggles are *Qui Laborat Orat, Blank Misgivings, A Song of Autumn, Qua Cursum Ventus, Sic Itur,* and *Parting.* The most popular of his poems, *Say Not the Struggle Nought Availeth,* is not quite typical.

In the next years (1848-1850) he wrote his three principal poems. *The Bothie of Tober-na-Vuolich*, a novelette in hexameters [3] with amusing Scarron-like echoes and burlesques of Virgilian effects, tells of the love of a radical young Oxonian for a Highland girl who rejects him on the ground of the differences in their stations in life. But when he suggests that they emigrate to New Zealand she accepts him.[4] The grace and charm of the love scenes, the clever argumentation, and the zestful cheerfulness of the poem reflect Clough's temporary buoyancy after his escape from entanglements at Oxford. A second story in hexameters, *Amours de Voyage*, was written in Rome in 1849 during the short-lived Republic. In mood, if not in incident, it is autobiographical. The desire for action with doubts as to its efficacy is thoroughly characteristic. The overintellectualized art student who is the hero is representative of "feeble and restless youth born to inglorious days." His languid love affair with an English girl ends in separation. The emotional situations are subtly analyzed; the episodes are entertainingly developed; and the background of great events is sketched with a vividness due to the poet's own presence upon the scene whereof he wrote. The despondent and wayward ending of the *Amours* points forward to *Dipsychus*, which Clough began and left unfinished at Venice in 1850. This has been called "a little Victorian *Faust*." The debt to Goethe and Byron is obvious, and Clough had also in mind a poem then widely read though unreadable today, the *Festus* of Philip James Bailey.[5] The Spirit with whom Dipsychus holds converse is not "a fallen and hateful fiend" but his own worldly common sense. In the end he submits to the standards of the world, with a consequent coarsening of his moral fiber and with regret for forsaken ideals.

In his last years Clough wrote little. The voice of doubt and despondency was not suited to the contentment he at length won. He made a happy marriage, found work in the Education Office, and assisted Florence Nightingale in her philanthropic activities. He and Arnold, close friends at Oxford and for several years thereafter, drifted apart, estranged by Arnold's impatience with Clough's indecisiveness. In failing health he went to live in

---

[3] In 1847 Longfellow, in *Evangeline*, had revived the English hexameter. For Arnold's defense of its use see *On Translating Homer*, pp. 210-216.

[4] Emigration was in the air of the mid-century. Tennyson thought of going to Australia; Thomas Woolner, the sculptor, went there. Samuel Butler farmed sheep in New Zealand. Compare the concluding pages of *David Copperfield* and Ford Madox Brown's popular picture "The Last of England."

[5] Philip James Bailey (1816-1902) published *Festus* in 1839 and enlarged it in subsequent editions to some forty thousand lines. In scope the poem is cosmic; in style occasionally noble, more often inflated and absurd; in form it is semi-dramatic, a succession of fifty-two scenes in which Festus, Lucifer, and other characters engage in colloquies. Bailey does not fear to challenge comparison with Milton, Byron, and Goethe; he comes off the worse from these encounters. Two English versions of Goethe's *Faust*, Part I, were current (Hayward's, 1832; Anster's, 1835); but Bailey, though he did not know much German, borrows also from Part II, which was not translated till much later. See G. A. Black, "Bailey's Debt to Goethe's *Faust*," *MLR*, xxviii (1933). 166-175. The contemporary popularity of *Festus* was due to its theme of universal salvation. See Emil Goldschmidt, "Der Gedankengehalt von Baileys *Festus*," *ESt*, lxvii (1932). 228-237. For an estimate with favorable specimens of its style see Hugh Walker, *The Literature of the Victorian Era* (1910), pp. 346-349.

Florence and died·there in 1861. Not till three years later did Arnold write *Thyrsis* in which the greater poet, not without hints of his own superior moral strength which led him to share in the intellectual warfare of the age, sang of his dead friend's choice of an easier road. Thyrsis could not wait the passing of the storm that raged. "It irk'd him to be here; he could not rest."

II

In his essay on George Sand, Arnold outlined unconsciously the pattern *Arnold* of his own development, the "grand elements" which he distinguished in the mind of the French novelist being discernible in his own. Each inherited from the French Revolution "the cry of agony and revolt" and "the aspiration towards a purged and renewed human society," and each possessed a trust in nature as "a vast power of healing and delight for all." [6] The cry of revolt sounds in the poetry of Arnold's earlier life; the aspiration towards a new society in the prose writings of his later years.

Matthew Arnold [7] (1822-1888), the son of Arnold of Rugby, passed much of his boyhood in the Lake Country, and the beauty of Westmorland, "where mountains make majestical man's lowliest fate," [8] impressed upon him forever a sense of the healing power of nature. The heritage from Dr. Arnold was of utmost importance in shaping the son's ideas on religion and society—religion conceived not in terms of dogma and ritual but of an organization to be remolded on nationally comprehensive lines for social and ethical betterment; society conceived in terms of the state strong enough to exert authority over warring factions and classes. In his historical studies Dr. Arnold had emphasized the need to understand the development of institutions; and the obligation to adjust the mind to social and political change became part of the son's message to his countrymen. Of the many

---

[6] Matthew Arnold, "George Sand," *Mixed Essays* (ed. 1904), p. 241.

[7] There is no complete edition. *Works* (15v, 1903-4); *Poems* (3v, 1889; often reprinted); *Poems (1840-1867)*, introduction by Sir A. T. Quiller-Couch (1930); *Arnold: Prose and Poetry*, ed. Sir E. K. Chambers (1939); *Culture and Anarchy*, ed. J. Dover Wilson (1932); *Thoughts on Education Chosen from the Writings of Matthew Arnold*, ed. Leonard Huxley (1912); *Note-Books* (1902); *Essays in Criticism, Third Series*, ed. E. J. O'Brien (Boston, 1910), hitherto uncollected essays; *Letters, 1848-1888*, ed. G. W. E. Russell (2v, 1895); *Unpublished Letters*, ed. Arnold Whitridge (New Haven, 1923); *Letters to Arthur Hugh Clough*, ed. H. F. Lowry (1932). — T. B. Smart, *Bibliography* (1892); Ehrsam, *Bibliographies*, pp. 14-45. George Saintsbury, *Matthew Arnold* (1899); Herbert W. Paul, *Matthew Arnold* (EML Series, 1902); Stuart Sherman, *Matthew Arnold: How to Know Him* (Indianapolis, 1917); Hugh Kingsmill, *Matthew Arnold* (1928); Lionel Trilling, *Matthew Arnold* (1939); C. B. Tinker and H. F. Lowry, *The Poetry of Matthew Arnold, a Commentary* (1940); J. B. Orrick, *Matthew Arnold and Goethe* (1928); Otto Elias, *Matthew Arnolds Politische Grundanschauung* (Leipzig, 1931); Iris E. Sells, *Matthew Arnold and France: The Poet* (1935); F. L. Wickelgren, "Arnold's Literary Relations with France," *MLR*, xxxiii (1938). 200-214; L. Bonnerot, "La Jeunesse de Matthew Arnold," *Revue Anglo-Américaine*, vii (1930). 520-537; John Drinkwater, "Some Letters from Matthew Arnold to Robert Browning," *Cornhill Mag.*, n.s. lv (1923). 654-664; W. S. Knickerbocker, "Matthew Arnold at Oxford," *Sewanee Rev.*, xxxv (1927). 399-418; C. B. Tinker, "Arnold's Poetic Plans," *Yale Rev.*, n.s. xxii (1933). 782-793; Margaret Woods, "Matthew Arnold," *E&S*, xv (1929). 7-19; T. Sturge Moore, "Matthew Arnold" *E&S*, xxiv (1938). 7-27; H. W. Garrod, *Poetry and the Criticism of Life* (1931), pp. 3-84.

[8] Sir William Watson, *In Laleham Churchyard* (an elegy on Arnold).

men whom the elder Arnold prepared for life none bore his impress more deeply than his son.

The prize-poems *Alaric at Rome* (1840) and *Cromwell* (1843) are more or less derivative, but the austerity and restraint are characteristic of Arnold's mature poetry. Yet the young man who entered Balliol in 1841 was distinguished rather for a protectively ironical manner than for "high seriousness." Something of this manner he retained throughout life and his persiflage was at times offensive to his opponents. At Oxford he appeared gay and self-assured, but the restless play of his mind as he sought in the welter of modern thought for a criterion of conduct is reflected in the letters to Clough.

"Marguerite"

In Switzerland in 1848 Arnold fell in love with a French girl, the "Marguerite" of the cycle of poems from which some biographers have tried to reconstruct the course of the fascination, the passion, and the parting.[9] All that can safely be conjectured is that, distrusting impulse and aware of unbridgeable differences of "race" and breeding, Arnold rejected the dictates of his heart and reluctantly withdrew. The poems written in retrospect show that the experience left its scar; but in 1851 he married an English woman. Appointed to an inspectorship of schools, he threw himself into the arduous work of a post which he did not relinquish till near the close of his life. The reports written for the Education Department [10] are, with the possible exception of *A French Eton* (1864), of no moment as literature, but they have their place among the records of educational reform.

Poetry

Almost all Arnold's poetry was written during his young manhood. The few pieces of later date are for the most part resuscitations of earlier moods. The poems are generally variations upon the themes of youthful anguish and aspirations. When Arnold described them as recording a "main movement of mind" of his generation he did not mean that they reflected the confident, expanding world of Whig commercialism but that they expressed the thoughts of the intellectuals who, disturbed by new, subversive ideas, found themselves adrift from old moorings upon a wide, uncharted sea. This poetry is contained in five slender collections: *The Strayed Reveller and other Poems. By A.* (1849); *Empedocles on Etna and other Poems. By A.* (1852); *Poems* (two volumes, 1853), where Arnold's name first appeared upon a title-page; *Poems, Second Series* (1855); and *New Poems* (1867). There was a good deal of suppression, reprinting, and rearrangement from volume to volume; [11] *Empedocles* disappeared till, at Browning's solicita-

---

[9] The "Marguerite Cycle" is contained in two groups of poems, *Switzerland* and *Faded Leaves*; it is possible, however, that one or two in the latter group may have been addressed to Frances Lucy Wightman, whom Arnold married. For a highly dubious psychoanalytical interpretation see Hugh Kingsmill, *Matthew Arnold* (1928). A more sympathetic, not to say sentimental, view is set forth in I. E. Sells, *Matthew Arnold and France* (1935), chs. VIII and IX. See also Tinker and Lowry, *Commentary*, pp. 153-157.

[10] *Reports on Elementary Schools, 1852-1882*, ed. Sir Francis Sanford (1889); new edition with additional material and an introduction by F. S. Marvin (1908).

[11] For details see Tinker and Lowry, *Commentary, passim*.

tion, it was republished in the *New Poems* of 1867. Save for that belated volume and the drama *Merope* (1858), most of Arnold's verse had been written by 1855. To the volume of 1853 he attached a preface in which he deprecated "timeliness" as a requisite in poetry, urged the importance of the choice of subject, and counseled poets not to waste their art upon random verbal felicities but, mindful of "total effect," to strive for a unified and consistent impression.

The half-dozen poems of considerable length support the opinion that *The* Arnold's genius was not quite equal to the task of such sustained efforts in *Longer* poetry and was at ease only within narrow compass. *Tristram and Iseult Poems* (1852), the first modern version of the legend,[12] betrays in its imperfectly coördinated metrical experiments the characteristics of the transition period between Tennyson and the Pre-Raphaelites. The prominence accorded to the Second Iseult—Tristram's wife—is perhaps not without personal significance, as is the brooding regret for the brevity of passionate youth. *Empedocles on Etna,* though semi-dramatic in form,· is meditative in tone. The reminiscences of *Paracelsus* pleased Browning but may account for Arnold's dissatisfaction with the poem. The theme is the contrast of the life of the reason, in the character of Empedocles, with that of the imagination, in the character of Callicles. The long discourse in which Empedocles recommends compromise and submission to the limitations of life concludes with the philosopher's suicide because he cannot bring himself to follow his own counsel—an end which Arnold intended to be moving but which, despite the grave sonority of the verse, is faintly ridiculous.[13] *Sohrab and Rustum* (1853) displays an effort towards complete "objectivity"; the choice of a story from Firdawsí's *Shah Nameh*[14] is an illustration of Arnold's contention that poetry should be remote from contemporary issues; but the theme of the son slain by the mightier father is susceptible of a personal interpretation.[15] In *The Church of Brou* (1853) the simple, Scott-like opening narrative and the quiet Wordsworthian description in the second part enhance by contrast the superb concluding section in which the poet imagines the awakening of the lovers from their tomb.[16] Is it fanciful to discern a personal application in this dream of reunion? *Merope* (1858), a drama classical in

[12] Howard Maynadier, *The Arthur of the English Poets* (1907), pp. 382-389. — The tentative beginnings of Richard Wagner's *Tristan und Isolde* date from 1852, but the opera was composed in the main between 1857 and 1859. It is probable that Wagner knew, and took some hints from, Arnold's version.

[13] George Meredith laughed at it, as he did at *Manfred* and *Hernani*. See his impish but wise little poem, *Empedocles; Poetical Works,* ed. G. M. Trevelyan (1912), pp. 411-412.

[14] Arnold took his story not directly from Firdawsí but from Sainte-Beuve's review of Jules Mohl's translation of the *Shah Nameh*. He borrowed details of Oriental atmosphere and color from Sir John Malcolm's *History of Persia* and Sir Alexander Burnes's *Travels into Bokhara*. See Tinker and Lowry, *Commentary,* pp. 75-85.

[15] Lionel Trilling, *Matthew Arnold*, pp. 134-135.

[16] For the indebtedness of this final section to Edgar Quinet's essay on the Church of Brou in his *Mélanges* (1839) see Charles Cestre, "*The Church of Brou* de Matthew Arnold," *Revue Germanique*, IV (1908). 526-538; I. E. Sells, *Matthew Arnold and France*, pp. 202-207. The topographical errors in the poem were soon commented on and were the cause of Arnold's dissatisfaction with it. See Tinker and Lowry, *Commentary*, pp. 38-41.

form, is on a subject [17] hardly worthy of the austere dignity of the style and is so flat a failure that we may pass it by. Arnold's laborious effort to be impersonal and remote from modernity was wasted; *Merope* has no particle of life in it.

The cornerstone of Arnold's meditative and elegiac verse is doubt. This comes as much from the *Zeitgeist* as from his own temperament. Though he could not as yet share the confidence of the rationalists, the tradition of skepticism reasserted itself in a mind uninfluenced by transcendentalism. He is consistent in his denial of revelation, but a feeling for the grandeur of the Christian tradition and for the influence of the historic Jesus (he was never much concerned with Strauss's "Christ-mythus") acts as a check upon his agnosticism. He shares the tendency of the mid-century to subordinate faith to conduct. "Has man no second life? Pitch this one high!" [18] The categorical imperative is accepted with a realization of the formidable responsibility it places upon the individual. How is the standard to be maintained? Arnold's answer is: through self-trust. Meditations upon the self-contained soul provide one of the most persistent motives in his poetry.[19] Goethe is the type and exemplar of this ideal. The need for self-sufficiency strengthens, at the same time that it is intensified by, the sense of estrangement from one's fellows. Images of the castaway, of wreckage, and of the sea which isolates man from man recur frequently. The calm, confident unity of the Middle Ages is gone forever; the French Revolution was a great watershed of history dividing the present from the past. The poet and his generation wander between a dead world and a world "powerless to be born." In this bewildering turmoil the need is for a fixed ideal; and those great figures whom Arnold holds up to admiration—Sophocles, Shakespeare, Wellington, his own father—possessed a "vision of the general law," chose a "path to a clear-purposed goal," and "saw life steadily." [20] So long as Arnold was primarily a poet, he yearned to set his feet upon the secure path; his verse records the quest and the disappointment.

There can be but partial substitutes for lost faith in supernatural religion. What are these substitutes? Mere "natural" life is not an ultimate resource and guide; Arnold rejects that illusion of the romanticists.

[17] A son, returning home in disguise, barely escapes being murdered by his mother. The situation is uncomfortably close to that in George Lillo's *Fatal Curiosity*.

[18] *The Better Part, Poems* (ed. 1889), I. 260. Compare Rossetti's early sonnets, *The Choice*, in *The House of Life*, lxxi-lxxiii. Similar sentiments, nobly expressed, are in the Preface to Ruskin's *Crown of Wild Olive* and in a famous letter by Huxley on the death of his son (Leonard Huxley, *Life and Letters of Thomas Henry Huxley*, I. 237).

[19] See, for examples, the close of *Mycerinus*; the salutation to Emily Brontë as "the spirit which dared trust its own thoughts" (*Haworth Churchyard*); the lament that we modern men "never once possess our soul" (*A Southern Night*); the poet's desire to withdraw from the world "till I possess my soul again" (*Stanzas from the Grande Chartreuse*).

[20] *To a Friend; Shakespeare; To the Duke of Wellington; Rugby Chapel*. The famous line "Who saw life steadily and saw it whole" is often misunderstood. Arnold does not make for Sophocles the extravagant claim that he saw the whole of life. What came within the range of his vision he saw integrally.

> Know, man hath all which Nature hath, and more,
> And in that *more* lie all his hopes of good. . . .
> Man must begin, know this, where Nature ends.[21]

Nor is there ever a suggestion of a sensual anodyne; Omar's solace is to Arnold nothing else than abhorrent "lubricity." To follow the counsel of the Spirit in Clough's *Dipsychus* and feign an outward conformity is a solution which Arnold spurns. May one, then, fly from the fevered conflict of modern civilization? The temptation to do so is well-nigh overwhelming. Arnold feels an affinity to souls who have fled from life,[22] finding in Nature, "calm soul of all things,"[23] the promise of spiritual restoration. But he inherited too impelling a consciousness of moral responsibility to rest content in such a solution. Is action, then, the remedy? Is the Carlylean Gospel of Work the outlet from the Everlasting No? In the practical sphere, despite intellectual doubts, Arnold resolutely followed this counsel; but it did not satisfy him as a poet. What remains? A Stoic resignation. Man, *in utrumque paratus,* **Stoicism** must "waive all claim to bliss and try to bear,"[24] recognizing that the secret of life is "not joy but peace."[25] But this attitude of serene acquiescence, characteristic of Arnold at his noblest, he does not always maintain. In the poem which the modern reader (not without cause) has taken to his heart **Despair** as he has no other of Arnold's there is a despair as desolating as James Thomson's:

> The world, which seems
> To lie before us like a land of dreams,
> So various, so beautiful, so new,
> Hath really neither joy, nor love, nor light,
> Nor certitude, nor peace, nor help for pain;
> And we are here as on a darkling plain
> Swept with confused alarms of struggle and flight,
> Where ignorant armies clash by night.[26]

Arnold's finest poems are reveries, profoundly personal and introspective. In verse he rarely assumes the function of the teacher and guide. He feels the need for a new social order but is powerless to suggest the way. This critical and melancholy ineffectuality reveals his spiritual kinship to Clough. In harmony with this prevailing mood is the chill aloofness of his treatment of subjects which have given other poets the opportunity for passionate expression. Marguerite is a fading memory; the lovers in the Church of Brou

[21] *In Harmony with Nature.* In Arnold's use the word *Nature* means the "world of things" as opposed to the moral world of man. This is in contradistinction to the use to designate "the natural order" which includes both worlds, material and moral. See J. W. Beach, *The Concept of Nature,* pp. 397-405.

[22] For example, Senancour, Amiel, Wordsworth (as Arnold interpreted him), the Scholar-Gipsy.

[23] *Lines written in Kensington Gardens.*

[24] *The Scholar-Gipsy.*

[25] *Resignation.*

[26] *Dover Beach.* See Tinker and Lowry, *Commentary,* pp. 172-178.

lie in their tombs; even the story of Tristram focuses sympathy not upon the lovers but upon the widow and her children.This austere control of emotion has its counterpart in Arnold's technique. Save for his experiments in cadenced rimeless verse, he was content to write in a few traditional metres and stanzaic forms. His imagery is remarkable for a few oft-recurring figures drawn from his love of flowers and streams and mountains. In contrast to the Venetian richness of Tennyson's color-sense, his poetry is in *grisaille*; the impression it imparts is of grays and cold moonlight.

III

*he
riticism
: Life*

The spiritual void of modern life had been the theme of Arnold's poetry. In prose his effort was to give shape to his "aspiration towards a purged and renewed human society." On his election (1857) to the professorship of poetry at Oxford he chose for his inaugural theme *The Modern Element in Literature*.[27] He lectured in English, not Latin as his predecessors had done, and thus underscored his conviction that literary studies must be pursued not in aesthetic isolation but in intimate relation with the largest issues of social life. Later he delivered two formal series of lectures. In those *On Translating Homer* (1861-1862), with a discriminating insight which has won the praise of so exacting a scholar as A. E. Housman, he discussed the Homeric poems with the object of analyzing the constituent elements of the "grand style," showing to what extent and with what shortcomings each English translator has succeeded in rendering the qualities of the original. The problem has the widest social significance, for the "grand style" is an expression of the nobility of the human spirit and Arnold felt that the conditions of contemporary life had diminished the stature of that spirit.[28] The lectures *On the Study of Celtic Literature* (1867) are in part vitiated by Arnold's acceptance of the prevalent theory of "race" which enabled him with a confidence hardly justified by the disputable evidence to isolate those elements in the English temper that spring, respectively, from Celtic, Saxon, and Norman ancestors. Once more the emphasis is upon the social importance of literary studies.

*ssays in
riticism*

Meanwhile the first series of *Essays in Criticism* had appeared (1865). This famous volume represents a reaction from romanticism and from earlier, insular standards of English literary criticism. By the term *criticism* Arnold intends something much broader than literary scholarship. It embraces all branches of knowledge with the object of making "the best" prevail. The critic, drawing upon all the resources of cosmopolitan culture,

---

[27] Published in *Macmillan's Magazine*, February, 1869; never reprinted by Arnold; first gathered into his works in *Essays by Matthew Arnold* (Oxford, 1914), pp. 454-472. — Arnold's pamphlet *England and the Italian Question* (1859) is an early example of his cosmopolitan outlook. Rising above the immediate issues of Napoleon III's campaign and the policy of Lord Derby's ministry, Arnold relates the problem to the larger one of the need for the English aristocracy to adapt itself to democratic change.

[28] Lionel Trilling, *Matthew Arnold*, p. 174; T. S. Omond, "Arnold and Homer," *E&S*, III (1912). 71-91.

seeks to supply what is lacking in the English character and thus to remedy the defects in English society. The endeavor is towards an integration of the individual and the social order. Arnold dwells upon the virtue born of the submission of individual genius to general law. Taking as his illustration the great tradition cherished by the French Academy, he urges the need to impregnate the English genius with that flexibility of intelligence and "regard for the whole" which are the marks of the classic spirit. In the English poetry of the romantic era there had been a lack of what T. S. Eliot was later to call "the objective correlative"; too much energy had been expended to too little purpose. On the same grounds Arnold deprecates Carlyle's exaltation of the German romanticists and turns to Heine, the intellectual liberator. The intense, preoccupied individualism of the English poets finds its parallel on a lower level among those people who believe that the greatness of England depends upon her material prosperity and who are indifferent to the things of the spirit. These people are the "Philistines," enemies of the "Children of Light." They are characterized by their concern for their own interests at the expense of society as a whole. Criticism rises above this "practical view of things" to a universality of outlook grounded upon disinterestedness. The emphasis laid upon poetry in these discussions comes from Arnold's conviction that since the great problem of modern life is the disunity which has been brought about by the decline of faith, poetry must assume the function of a religion to bind life afresh into a whole. For the poet sees life steadily and in its entirety. In this sense "Poetry is a Criticism of Life."

These lines of thought were extended and their practical application clarified in *Culture and Anarchy* (1869). Robust people (Walt Whitman among them) derided the term *culture* for its supposed connotation of snobbish, academic fastidiousness. For this misunderstanding Arnold's own self-deprecation was in part to blame. Actually the term embraces the complete realization of the potentialities of the human spirit under the guidance of reason. The argument (obviously directed against Mill's essay *On Liberty,* though Arnold does not refer to it directly) is for an authority strong enough to discipline the individual's claim to liberty of action. The English tradition of unrestrained individualism encourages that "dissidence of dissent" which is characteristic of the Protestant mind and which, if unchecked, inevitably breeds anarchy. It must be combatted by the disinterested objectivity which regards society as a whole. To the three classes of society—aristocracy, the middle class, and the lower classes—which are opposed in interests to one another Arnold attaches the famous nicknames of Barbarians, Philistines, and Populace; but to bestow such names is not argument. He makes great play with "the God-given right of every Englishman to do as he likes" and with light irony exposes the pettiness of the self-styled "practical" men, who, blind to universal issues, expend their energies upon the passage of an act permitting a widower to marry his sister-in-law. (This satiric method of argument was continued in *Friendship's Garland,* 1871). But the irritating

[margin: Culture and Anarchy]

*Hellenism
and
Hebraism*

flippancy does not conceal the serious intent. Necessary to the argument is the antithesis between Hellenism and Hebraism, the illuminated mind which sees things as they are and the moral conscience which is obsessed with thoughts of sin. Admitting that "Conduct is three-fourths of Life," Arnold contends that Puritanism has expanded it yet further, thus affording another illustration of that regard for the parts which is inimical to the well-being of the whole. But Culture opens the mind to the possibilities of perfection. "Not a having and a resting but a growing and a becoming, is the character of perfection as culture conceives it." In this respect "it coincides with religion." The individual self must become part of the "best self," the "national right reason" upon which the State must be founded. "Individual perfection is impossible so long as the rest of mankind are not perfected along with us." It was of this doctrine of a disciplined community whose members rise above self-interest that H. G. Wells was thinking when in the midst of a great crisis he affirmed roundly in *Mr. Britling Sees It Through* (1916) that "the trouble with England is that she did not listen to Arnold."

*Biblical
and
Theological
Essays*

The space devoted in *Essays in Criticism* to religious problems (especially in the two papers on the Guérins) was indicative of the direction in which Arnold's thought was soon to move. With *St. Paul and Protestantism* (1870) he entered upon a decade dedicated largely to biblical and theological controversy. With his favorite technique of antithesis he contrasted the spirit of contentiousness which informs Protestantism with the "sweet reasonableness" of St. Paul. But he refashioned St. Paul in his own image and wrested his meaning to his own purposes. In his quest for a concept of God that would satisfy the rationalist and scientist he resorted to a method of interpretation entirely without warrant in the text of the Epistles. Thus, while wounding the orthodox, his attempt to effect a compromise alienated the secularists. His rash amateurishness shocked biblical scholars who had devoted their lives to the textual and historical problems which he handled so lightly. The shakiness of his reasoning, as when he defined religion as "morality touched with emotion," exposed him to a devastating onslaught by F. H. Bradley, the great logician.[29] Furthermore, serious-minded people were offended by his levity of manner in dealing with sacred things.[30] In *Literature and Dogma* (1873) the attempted demonstration that the ancient Hebraic concept of God was identical with the idea of Righteousness led on to his own definitions of God as "a stream of tendency," "a something not ourselves that makes for righteousness." Once more he laid himself bare

---

[29] Lionel Trilling, *Matthew Arnold*, pp. 357-359 and index. — Francis Herbert Bradley (1846-1924), who lived to become the most influential English philosopher of his time, first revealed his critical power in *Ethical Studies* (1876). His *Principles of Logic* (1883) broke with, and advanced beyond, the accepted empirical logic of the time. *Appearance and Reality* (1893) is his most famous book and is the representative exposition of Bradley's idealism. *Essays on Truth and Reality* (1914) appeared when his influence was waning. Almost alone among modern British philosophers Bradley had at his command a prose style of a grace and beauty that won him readers beyond the boundaries of the schools.

[30] Arnold defended his levity; see *Letters*, ed. Russell, II. 120.

to the logician's scourge. *God and the Bible* (1875) is a defense of his position and an interpretation of details in the two earlier books. Later he became conscious of a revulsion of public feeling from the hard and narrow rationalism of the past two decades and expressed a belief that he might end his days "in the tail of a return current of popular religion, both ritual and dogmatic." [31]

Gradually Arnold forsook religious controversy. He wrote on the Irish question and in an eloquent estimate of George Sand returned to literary criticism.[32] In 1883 he retired from professional work and visited the United States, where he lectured on *Democracy,* on *Literature and Science* (here crossing swords with Huxley), and on *Emerson.*[33] His latest manner, in the essays on Wordsworth, Byron, Shelley, and Keats in *Essays in Criticism, Second Series* (1888), is more intimate and winning than that of former books; the levity and the superciliousness have almost disappeared. The mixture of biography and critical comment in these essays approximates to the method and style of Sainte-Beuve.[34] The purity and refinement of Arnold's prose (traits which he generously attributed to the influence of Newman), the qualities of grace and repose and calm clarity are here exhibited at their most persuasive. On occasion he is master of a restrained eloquence with no false or forced note. The fastidiousness which was displeasing when he dealt with social problems, suggesting as it did that he was more offended with the hideousness of poverty and crime than moved to deep moral indignation, was a useful instrument for the analysis of literary values. Yet Arnold's values have not been universally accepted. The interpretation of Wordsworth is curiously one-sided. The generous estimate of Byron is colored by mid-century liberalism. The opinion of Shelley's "ineffectuality" has been hotly contested. The concept of Keats is warped and limited. But for their suggestiveness, their sureness of touch, their display of wide horizons of culture, their cosmopolitan outlook, these final essays remain the part of Arnold's prose writings which posterity has valued most highly.

Arnold died suddenly in 1888. Sir William Watson's *In Laleham Churchyard* is not a mere conventional elegiac tribute but an analysis of the strength and grace and lucidity of Arnold's genius, of that element of the "worldling" that mingled with "the bard and sage," that shunning of "the common touch" which was his weakness, and that preservation of "the fortress of his 'stablished soul" which was his strength.[35]

(margin: Last Essays)

[31] Arnold to Grant Duff, August 22, 1879, *Letters,* ed. Russell, II. 187.

[32] *Mixed Essays* (1879); *Irish Essays* (1882).

[33] *Discourses in America* (1885).

[34] Arnold wrote the article on Sainte-Beuve in *Encyclopaedia Britannica,* ninth edition. His obituary notice of Sainte-Beuve (*Academy,* November 13, 1869) is reprinted in *Essays by Matthew Arnold* (Oxford, 1914), pp. 482-487. See Paul Furrer, *Die Einfluss Sainte-Beuve auf die Kritik Matthew Arnolds* (Zurich, 1920).

[35] Sir William Watson, *Poems* (2v, 1905), I. 27-30.

IV

tzGerald   Of all poems written during the Victorian period that which is best known today came from the pen of a scholarly recluse whose other writings never reached many readers. The intellectual powers of Edward FitzGerald [36] (1809-1881) were highly prized by contemporaries at Cambridge. But temperament and a small competence led him into a pleasant rural life where an uncongenial marriage, followed by a separation, scarcely ruffled the surface of his placid existence. *Dolce far niente.* Actually, FitzGerald found it sweet to do not precisely nothing but only what he wished to do. This was to read, visit London for the sake of music and the theatre, acquire a knowledge of exotic tongues, and correspond with his friends. His letters are among the most charming in English literature. They lack the wide social horizon of Walpole's, the homely humor and pathos of Cowper's, the tempestuous wit of Byron's; but their intimacy and whimsicality picture for us a personality of singular charm. As the century moved towards its self-confident middle years, FitzGerald, like the recluse he was, found himself out of sympathy with the new tendencies. Yet his thought and feeling were in the very vortex of one of the principal currents of the age. So passed a harmlessly selfish, gently hedonistic life. He set down his meditations in a prose dialogue, *Euphranor* (1851), whose delicacy of style befits the insignificance of its contents. He made paraphrases from the Greek and Spanish.[37] He cultivated his garden.

he   And then the study of Persian led him, after two preliminary experiments
báiyát   in translation,[38] to Omar Khayyám. In the *Rubáiyát* or quatrains of the twelfth-century poet he found the revelation of a kindred heart. He rendered into English the quintessence of their thought and emotion. Persian scholars who have compared the version with the original tell us that much has been omitted but little added; that quatrains separated in the alphabetical sequence of the Persian have been brought together for the sake of coherence; that what is loose and lax has been tightened and what is coarse has been refined away.[39] The metrical pattern lent itself admirably to English adapta-

[36] *Poetical and Prose Writings*, ed. George Bentham (7v, 1902); *Letters and Literary Remains*, ed. W. A. Wright (7v, 1902-1903). The four versions of *The Rubáiyát of Omar Khayyám* (1859, 1868, 1872, 1879) were reprinted together with the original prefaces and notes in 1890; the first and fourth versions, with variants from the other two, are in the Golden Treasury Series (1899). Facsimile of ed. 1859 (1939). — Ehrsam, *Bibliographies*, pp. 78-90; John Glyde, *Life of Edward FitzGerald* (1900); A. C. Benson, *Edward FitzGerald* (EML Series, 1905); Thomas Wright, *The Life of Edward FitzGerald* (2v, 1904); N. C. Hannay, *A FitzGerald Friendship* (1932), with hitherto unpublished letters to W. B. Donne; A. M. Terhune, *The Life of Edward FitzGerald* (1947), with many hitherto unpublished letters.

[37] The best of these is *Such Stuff as Dreams Are Made Of*, from Calderón's *La Vida es Sueño* (*Six Dramas of Calderón*, 1853).

[38] The *Sálamán and Absál* of Jamí and *The Bird Parliament* (or *The Language of Birds*) of Attar. On FitzGerald's version of Jamí see E. G. Browne, *Literary History of Persia*, III (1928). 523-526. Browne does not mention the version of Attar.

[39] E. H. Allen, *Edward FitzGerald's Rubáiyyát of 'Omar Khayyám with their Original Persian Sources* (1898). The statistical results of Allen's investigation are interesting: 49 of the quatrains are from 49 originals; 44 are condensations of more than one original quatrain,

tion. FitzGerald wisely discarded the scheme with four like rimes and retained the alternative design in which the rimeless third line has the effect of a thought hovering or fluttering before finding repose, an effect either of lyrical delicacy or of witty sharpness. Other poets have since used the form,[40] but in the history of English prosody it remains the "FitzGerald stanza."

The *Rubáiyát* (1859) attracted no attention till Rossetti came across it and introduced it to his friends. Very soon the little book "caught on." On the whole it is proper that the fourth version should be the definitive text; yet there is an occasional Oriental boldness of imagery in the version of 1859 which we see sacrificed with regret.[41]

Two modes of thought and feeling are intertwined in the poem. One is *Hedonism* the desire to snatch the utmost of pleasurable sensation from the irretrievable passing moment, for (as Pater was soon to be warning the young Oxonians who were among the first readers of the *Rubáiyát*) "we have an interval and then our place knows us no more." The nightingale and the harkening poet alike vanish from the garden, and the moon looks down upon other pleasure-lovers who will vanish in their turn. It is as obvious as are all the eternally repeated forms of human experience; but it is expressed with a freshness and beauty comparable to Ecclesiastes and with the same burden: "Rejoice, O young man, in thy youth," for "there is no work, nor device, nor knowledge, nor wisdom in the grave, whither thou goest." Time's wingéd chariot hovers near, and audible is the noise of greedy Acheron.

But with this desire to enjoy while it is day the fleeting loveliness of the light mingle more somber thoughts of the Power that has created beauty and in man a capacity to appreciate beauty but has cursed him with transience and holds him responsible for the actions of a nature not determined by himself. But should the pots blame the potter for fashioning this one ugly and that one fragile? Wherefore not, if the potter attaches to the pots blame for ugliness or fragility not of their choosing? Is justice conceivable in the scheme of things?[42] Had the thought of the *Rubáiyát* been expressed in the terms of modern occidental philosophy it would have won adherents

---

2 are found in only one text of Omar; 2 reflect the spirit of the whole but are not direct translations; 4 are from other Persian poets; 3 (which appeared in the first and second versions but were afterwards suppressed) are not attributable to any Persian poet. — In Persian poetry a quatrain is invariably a complete and isolated unit; there is no such thing as a poem composed of a number of quatrains. The units are assembled in mere alphabetical order according to the rime-word.

[40] Swinburne used the form with ingenious variations. In *Laus Veneris* each pair of quatrains is linked together by riming the third lines. In the elegy on Gautier the FitzGerald stanza is crossed with *terza rima* to produce a new form, *quarta rima*.

[41] See, for example, the very opening. In the fourth version the Sun "strikes the Sultan's Turret with a Shaft of Light," but in the first "the Hunter of the East" has caught "the Sultan's Turret in a Noose of Light."

[42] FitzGerald wrote but, anxious lest he give offense (and probably conscious that anger was out of keeping with the prevailing calm of the poem), suppressed this quatrain:
Nay, but for terror of His wrathful face,
I swear I will not call Injustice Grace;
Not one good fellow of the tavern but
Would kick so poor a coward from the place.

but not devotees and lovers. Not in the garb of harsh, repellent materialism, but voluptuous, genial, courteous, ceremonious, and sadly smiling, cloaked in gorgeous and elaborate imagery, came forward into the Victorian world the figure of the astronomer-poet of Persia.[43] He spoke with the authority of age-long experience and with the wisdom of the East. *Ex oriente lux!* "But if thy light be darkness, how great is that darkness!" In words and cadences of haunting loveliness a desolating message was communicated to numberless hearts. The *Rubáiyát* helped to shape the melancholy hedonism and moral incertitude of late nineteenth-century England.

V

James Thomson ("B.V.")

In social standing and way of life the translator of Omar and the author of *The City of Dreadful Night* were worlds apart; but money might have made of Thomson another such hedonistic recluse as FitzGerald, and poverty might have driven FitzGerald to drink and despair as it did Thomson. The depths of their natures were much alike, though FitzGerald kept them hid and Thomson exposed them bleakly to the world.

The most formidable and uncompromising use of the speculations of the mechanistic materialists for the purposes of poetry is in *The City of Dreadful Night* by James Thomson [44] (1834-1882). It is difficult to imagine "this poetical offense of dark monotonousness" (in Meredith's phrase) being written at any other time or by any other poet. By heredity, poverty, ill fortune, bad habits, and intense conviction Thomson was prepared for his gloomy task. From personal experience he drew his material, and he had "the largeness of utterance" (as George Eliot said of him) and the sense of form to shape his nightmare into a work of art. His father was a drunken sailor; his mother a woman of sensitiveness and refinement; both died when he was a child, leaving to him the heritage of an addiction to alcohol and a love of poetry. With little regular education, the orphan boy read widely. The initials "B. V." over which he published much of his verse memorialize two of his early passions, "B" standing for "Bysshe" (that is, Shelley) and "V" for "Vanolis" (an anagram of Novalis, the German romanticist). From 1854 till 1862 he was a schoolmaster to soldiers' children at an army-post in Ireland. There he fell in love with the daughter of the regimental ser-

---

The denunciation is as audacious as that of the speaker in Thomson's dark City who would not, even were he rewarded with God's power and glory, assume His "ignominious guilt." Compare also the famous middle chorus in Swinburne's *Atalanta in Calydon*. On the "cosmic irony" or "ironic reproach" which FitzGerald added to Omar and which is heard also in Thomson's poem see David Worcester's suggestive study, *The Art of Satire* (1940), pp. 132-135.

[43] A. C. Benson, *Edward FitzGerald*, p. 97.

[44] *Poetical Works* (2v, 1895); *The City of Dreadful Night and Other Poems*, ed. Bertram Dobell (1910); ed. G. H. Gerould (1927); ed. Edmund Blunden (1932). — H. S. Salt, *James Thomson* (1889); Josefine Weissel, *James Thomson der Jüngere, sein Leben und seine Werke* (Vienna, 1906); Bertram Dobell, *James Thomson* (1910); J. E. Meeker, *The Life and Poetry of James Thomson* (1917); B. I. Evans, *English Poetry in the Later Nineteenth Century* (1933), ch. IX.

geant. She died; and without sentimentality it may be said that from the shadow of her loss his soul was never henceforth lifted.

Thomson was dismissed from his post on an unspecified charge (perhaps *Early* drunkenness) and through friendship with Charles Bradlaugh, the atheistic *Poems* radical, obtained work on *The National Reformer*. From 1862 till 1874 he contributed to the secularist press. He had already written some verse, including a long poem, *The Doom of a City* (1857). The descriptive passages foreshadow some of the imagery in Thomson's masterpiece, and there is an evident trend towards pessimism, but the basic contrast is more striking than the superficial resemblance, for in this early poem there is still a recognition of Divine Providence.

Sunday at Hampstead (1863) and *Sunday up the River* (1865), transcripts of cockney life, show inherent capacities for humor and realism which in happier circumstances the poet might have developed further. *The Naked Goddess* (1866) has a Shelleyan element of vague allegory combined, not very successfully, with satiric passages. *Weddah and Om-el-Bonain* (1868) shows a romantic yearning for beauty which, when we remember Thomson's circumstances, is pathetic. But it is not by these poems that he is remembered.

The line of development from *The Doom of a City* brings us to *A Festival of Life* (1859), describing a dance where the masquers are startled by the appearance ever and anon of two hooded strangers who conduct away now one and now another of the guests. The resemblance to Poe's *Masque of the Red Death* is apparent, and the two aspects of Death, as a gracious deliverer and a malignant demon, suggest that Thomson knew Alfred Rethel's engravings of "Death the Avenger" and "Death the Friend." To the same year belongs *Mater Tenebrarum*, a poem of agonizing sensibility which is suggestive of De Quincey. In *Our Ladies of Death* (1861) the threefold concept of Death as Beatitude, Annihilation, and Oblivion is reminiscent of De Quincey's *Levana and Our Ladies of Sorrow*. Then came the prose phantasmagoria, *A Lady of Sorrow* (1862). Sorrow appears to the poet in three guises: first as an Angel in the form of the lost Beloved; then as a Siren, symbolizing the effort to forget the past in sensuality; lastly as a constantly attending Shadow. There are striking anticipations of the imagery of *The City of Dreadful Night*; indeed, the value of this feverish little piece is that it enables us to watch Thomson's conceptions taking their final form.

The City of Dreadful Night [45] appeared in *The National Reformer*, *The City* March-May, 1874. The keynote of the poem is the motto from Leopardi: *of Dread-* "In thee, O Death, our naked nature finds repose; not joyful, but safe from *ful Night* the old sadness." Prologuizing, the poet asks why he should write, and answers that to express his woe in words imparts a sense of power and passion.[46] The structure of the poem, hard, obvious, and unsubtle, is massively impressive in its clarity. In alternate sections there are descriptions of

[45] See L. A. Cotten, "Leopardi and *The City of Dreadful Night*," *SP*, XLII (1945). 675-689.
[46] Compare Tennyson's *Lucretius*, lines 223-225: "Shutting reasons up in rhythm . . . To make a truth less harsh."

the City and a series of episodes recounting the death-in-life therein. The general sections are in a seven-line stanza riming *ababccb,* with double endings in the fifth and sixth lines whose effect of weighty, mournful iteration suits the mood.[47] The episodic sections are in a variety of stanzaic forms, with one in blank verse. The topography of the City—the river, the embankment, the tenebrous streets, the enormous cathedral, the suburbs rising to the North—is drawn from London. Only three or four of the most memorable episodes can be noticed here. In the famous "As I came through the desert" (the desert of life) the traveler is the poet as he now is, while the figure seen mourning by the dead is the poet as he had been in the far past when the loss of his beloved was fresh upon him. This motif is repeated in the central scene in the vision of the young man who kneels beside a bier in the *chapelle ardente.* In the tremendous dialogue between a demonist and a determinist, the poet is to be identified not with the former, who in hysterical fashion seeks to fix the blame for circumstance upon some malevolent divinity, but with the latter, who with grim-eyed resolution expounds the same mechanistic materialism that is later the subject of the sermon to which the brotherhood of sorrow listen in the cathedral. The poem rises at its close almost to sublimity in the description of the great statue of Melancholia (drawn in every particular from Dürer's engraving) which broods over the City as the emblem of despair.

The impact of the poem upon a sensitive reader is so soul-shaking that there is danger lest it be appraised too highly. Guidance to a sounder judgment may be had from Arnold's remark (in his Preface of 1853) that there is one kind of situation unsuitable for poetry because it cannot give that joy which great art imparts, namely, a situation "in which a continuous state of mental distress is prolonged, unrelieved by incident, hope, or resistance, in which there is everything to be endured, nothing to be done."

During his last decade Thomson made some notable translations from Leopardi and wrote some not very distinguished critical papers. Friends were loyal to him and he won the attention of influential people.[48] By 1880 he had gained sufficient fame to warrant the publication of two volumes of poetry.[49] But it was too late. Sleeplessness, whose horrors are described in the impressive poem *Insomnia,* was added to his afflictions, and his drunkenness increased to dipsomania. He died in distressing circumstances in 1882, leaving a few friends to cherish his reputation till the coming of a later generation which has sensed his genius and his tragedy.

[47] The rime-scheme, but without the double-endings in the fifth and sixth lines, had been employed in *Our Ladies of Death.* Thomson is said to have taken the stanza from Browning's *The Guardian Angel;* but it is also the stanza of Vigny's *La Maison du Berger* where there are striking anticipations of Thomson's thought and manner.
[48] Notably George Meredith. See Meredith's *Letters* (1912), II. 302, 307, 413, and 437 for some illuminating comments upon Thomson and his work. The blind poet P. B. Marston and the poetical bookseller Bertram Dobell were close friends of his last years.
[49] *The City of Dreadful Night and other Poems* and *Vane's Story, Weddah and Om-el-Bonain and other Poems* (both 1880). *Essays and Phantasies* (1881) is a collection of prose. *A Voice from the Nile and other Poems* appeared posthumously (1884).

XXIX
Rossetti and His Circle

I

Dante Gabriel Rossetti [1] (1828-1882) was the son of Gabrielle Rossetti, a political exile from Italy, poet, opera librettist, and student of Dante.[2] The future poet-painter passed his youth in the Italian colony in London, but his father was a constitutional royalist and saw little of Mazzini and the other exiled republicans.[3] A characteristic indifference to politics dates probably from Rossetti's boyhood. His education was irregular and mostly at home. He and his brother and two sisters [4] were brought up under "the shadow of Dante," who remained one of the great influences upon his imagination.[5] To the later poets of Italy he was never much attracted, nor did he ever visit the land of his ancestors. He was a child of precocious promise, writing a drama at the age of four, imitating in early drawings the style of contemporary German illustrators, and, when he was twelve, composing a ballad, *Sir Hugh the Heron,* in the manner of Scott. A few

[1] *Works,* ed. W. M. Rossetti (4v, 1911); *Poems,* ed. W. M. Rossetti (2v, 1904), valuable for the illustrations; *Poems,* ed. P. F. Baum (1937), including also a selection from the prose; *Family Letters,* ed. W. M. Rossetti (2v, 1895); *Letters to William Allingham,* ed. G. B. Hill (1897); *Letters to F. S. Ellis,* ed. Oswald Doughty (1928); *Three Rossettis: Unpublished Letters,* ed. J. C. Troxell (Cambridge, Mass., 1937); *Letters to Fanny Cornforth,* ed. P. F. Baum (Baltimore, 1940). — Ehrsam, *Bibliographies,* pp. 201-225; W. M. Rossetti (ed.), *Ruskin, Rossetti, Preraphaelitism* (1899) and *Preraphaelite Diaries* (1900); A. C. Benson, *Rossetti* (EML Series, 1904); Henri Dupré, *Un Italien d'Angleterre, le poète-peintre Dante Gabriel Rossetti* (Paris, 1921); Frances Winwar, *Poor Splendid Wings: the Rossettis and their Circle* (1933); William Gaunt, *The Pre-Raphaelite Tragedy* (1942); Evelyn Waugh, *Rossetti: His Life and Works* (1928); R. L. Mégroz, *Dante Gabriel Rossetti: Painter-Poet of Heaven in Earth* (1929); R. D. Waller, *The Rossetti Family, 1824-1854* (Manchester, 1932). There is much information in memoirs and biographies; see especially, G. Burne-Jones, *Memorials of Edward Burne-Jones* (2v, 1912); W. Holman Hunt, *Pre-Raphaelitism and the Pre-Raphaelite Brotherhood* (2v, 1905); J. W. Mackail, *The Life of William Morris* (2v, 1899); William Bell Scott, *Autobiographical Notes,* ed. William Minto (2v, 1892). The superb caricatures in Max Beerbohm, *Rossetti and his Circle* (1922) are valuable as criticism and literary history.

[2] Gabriele Rossetti's autobiography in Italian verse was translated by W. M. Rossetti. His theory, based upon a symbolic interpretation of *The Divine Comedy,* that Dante was a precursor of the Reformation is expounded in *Disquisitions on the Antipapal Spirit which produced the Reformation: its Secret Influence on the Literature of Europe,* translated by Caroline Ward (1834). See E. R. P. Vincent, *Gabriele Rossetti in England* (1936).

[3] For the Italian exiles, their British connections, and their influence on English literature see H. W. Rudman, *Italian Nationalism and English Letters: Figures of the Risorgimento and Victorian Men of Letters* (1940).

[4] William Michael Rossetti (1829-1919) became the prosy but indispensable chronicler of the Pre-Raphaelite movement and of his family. Maria Francesca Rossetti (1827-1876) wrote, among other things, *The Shadow of Dante,* a commentary. On Christina Rossetti see further on in this chapter.

[5] B. J. Morse, "Rossetti and Dante Alighieri," *ESt,* LXVIII (1933-1934). 227-248; R. D. Waller, "The Blessed Damozel," *MLR,* XXVI (1931). 129-141, on the debt to Dante and to the *dolce stil nuovo.*

years later he made versions of Bürger's *Lenore* and of portions of the *Nibelungenlied*. His interests were always divided evenly between poetry and painting,[6] and while he studied at the Royal Academy and afterwards as a pupil of Ford Madox Brown,[7] he began a translation of the *Vita Nuova*. The poetry of Keats [8] and Browning, the tales and poems of Edgar A. Poe, and the Gothic romances were among the formative influences; and after he made the lucky purchase of a manuscript volume of unpublished poems by Blake, that poet, then practically unknown, also influenced him.[9] During 1847-1848 he composed the first versions of *The Blessed Damozel, The Portrait,* and other poems which, circulating in manuscript, established his reputation in a privileged circle as a new force in poetry long before he became known to the public. In 1848 he and six friends [10] formed the Pre-Raphaelite Brotherhood.

The   The "P.R.B." aimed to reclaim for the artist the freedom in manner
"P.R.B." and choice of subject which he was supposed to have exercised befoie Raphael's example and prestige became dominant. The movement was also a protest against the influence of Sir Joshua Reynolds and the tradition of the "grand style." These young men would paint what they saw, not what the artists of the past who were held up to them as models had seen. They rejected various established principles of technique. Their special preoccupation was with problems of light. They altered the conventional proportions and distribution of light which academic theorists had legislated from the practice of Rembrandt. They discarded the use of bitumen as a groundwork, and instead of building up their lights from shade they built up their shades from light. They were thus feeling their way along the same line as that of the young Impressionists of France. But unlike the French group, so great was their devotion to religious, medieval, and romantic themes that their art was often subservient to literature. Moreover, while the French school, reacting against the newly invented art of photography, moved away from representation, the "P.R.B.", influenced by photography, became entangled in minute representationalism. Their meticulous attention to detail often involved the sacrifice of central emphasis; and when they first exhibited in 1849 this fidelity to fact was thought to be unworthy of religious art and Millais was even accused of blasphemy. In 1850 Rossetti and some
The   of his colleagues initiated a little periodical, *The Germ,* as a medium for
Germ the promulgation of their doctrines and a vehicle for their poems; but it died after four numbers. In later years the movement disintegrated, some of the brethren compromising with the general taste, and Rossetti going his

---

[6] Eva Tietz, "Das Malerische in Rossettis Dichtung," *Anglia,* LI (1927). 278-306.

[7] F. M. Brown (1821-1893), associated with the "P. R. B." but not a member, later became a member of Morris's firm of decorators. A few poems which he wrote to accompany his paintings show Rossetti's influence.

[8] Hill Shine, "The Influence of Keats upon Rossetti," *ESt,* LXI (1926-1927). 183-210.

[9] Preston Kerrison, *Blake and Rossetti* (1944); B. J. Morse, "D. G. Rossetti and William Blake," *ESt,* LXVI (1931-1932). 364-372.

[10] This Pléiade was composed of Rossetti, W. Holman Hunt, John Millais, Thomas Woolner the sculptor, Walter Deverell who died young, James Collinson, and W. M. Rossetti.

own way. Analogies drawn between one art and another are seldom secure, and in the case of the Pre-Raphaelites they are tenuous and difficult to discern. There is a certain naïveté, not without some affectation, in their early poems and paintings; in both arts there is painstaking representationalism; in both there is religiosity rather than deep religious feeling; in both a love of romantic subject-matter; and the use of color words in their poems corresponds to the brilliant coloring of their canvases. But in the poems of Rossetti's maturity there is little to remind one of the theories of the Brotherhood.

In 1857 Rossetti collaborated with Morris and Burne-Jones upon the now vanished murals of the Oxford Union and at this time he met Swinburne. The impact of Rossetti's powerful personality is apparent in the early poetry of Morris and Swinburne. To 1857 belongs the famous volume of Tennyson's poems illustrated by the brethren. Many of Rossetti's finest paintings date from 1850 to 1860 before the morbid mannerisms of his later style had mastered him. To these years belongs also the friendship with Ruskin to which, as to the subsequent estrangement, reference has been made in an earlier chapter. In 1860 Rossetti married Elizabeth Siddal, one of his models.[11] Fragile in beauty and in health, she was loved by Rossetti after his fashion, though he was unfaithful to her. She pined and, in peculiarly distressing circumstances, died in 1862. As a token of penitence he placed the manuscripts of his poems in her coffin.

In 1861 he had published *The Early Italian Poets,*[12] a series of translations. Rallying after a while from the despondency into which he sank after his wife's death, he set up house in Cheyne Walk. In the luxuriant paintings of the following years may be traced chronologically the growth of mannerism and obsession. Symptoms of eye-strain led him to renew his activities as a poet in 1868, and in 1869, acting upon the counsel of friends, he consented to the opening of his wife's grave that his manuscripts might be retrieved. The way for the reception of his *Poems* (1870) had been for so long prepared by volumes from other members of his circle that the degree to which he was the master and impelling force of the new movement was not so apparent to the public of the day as it is now. Nevertheless the book was well received till in the following year Robert Buchanan perpetrated his cruel and foolish attack, *The Fleshly School of Poetry.*[13] Without considering the personal issues involved in the celebrated quarrel that followed,[14] we may note that the effect upon Rossetti was to increase his gloom and isolation. The last decade is the story of chloral and its conse- *Poems, 1870*

[11] Violet Hunt, *The Wife of Rossetti* (1932).

[12] Revised as *Dante and his Circle* (1874).

[13] Reprinted in *Notorious Literary Attacks,* ed. Albert Mordell (1926), pp. 185-213. — Robert Buchanan (1841-1901), a Scot, published *London Poems* (1866) and many later volumes, including plays and novels. That he had genuine power is shown by *Judas Iscariot* and a few other things, but his talent was dissipated over too many fields and his nature was corroded by jealousy of his betters. — See A. S. Walker, *Robert Buchanan, the Poet of Modern Revolt* (1901).

[14] For a succinct account of the quarrel, in which Swinburne became involved, see S. C. Chew. *Swinburne* (1929), pp. 242-243.

quences. A friend, ignorant of the dangers of the newly discovered drug, had recommended it as a cure for insomnia. An attempt at suicide by an overdose was barely averted in 1872. A mental disorder took the form of suspicion of hidden enemies and the conviction that his friends were treacherous. Morris did what he could for Rossetti, bearing the discomfort of his presence at Kelmscott House. Despite the ravages of disease, there were periods of intellectual vigor in both the arts. The paintings of this last phase show mannerisms pathologically exaggerated, but there are still power and splendor in them. In poetry Rossetti wrote *The White Ship* and *The King's Tragedy* in 1880 and so late as 1881 published the volume of *Ballads and Sonnets*. Two new young friends, Hall Caine and William Sharp,[15] were much with him towards the end. He died in 1882.

Rossetti's personality dominated all who knew him; and upon posterity he makes the impression of a genius greater than anything that he accomplished. Whatever the judgment of his accomplishments as a painter, there can be no question of the integrity and consistency of his work as a poet. He became grasping in his negotiations with clients and often the merely salable was his aim in the atelier; but no such commercialism mars his poetry. At times an overelaboration of detail obscures the central effect. The thronging images, balanced between decoration and symbol, blur the concept. Yet, generally speaking, the luxuriance is but the covering of a fundamental austerity and a sense is imparted of intellectual control over the exuberant sensuousness. So careful were successive recensions that earlier and later versions of many of the poems might well serve as illustrations of a treatise upon the poetic process. Thus, *The House of Life,*[16] which is the connecting link between his early and late poetry, was not a coherent sequence when parts of it, intermingled with lyrics, were published in 1870; but in subsequent years, while expanding it greatly, he molded it into form. Rossetti seems never to have improvised, but brooded long over his poems. Through intellectual contemplation he disciplined sensuous feeling. Everywhere there is a syntactical tightness, and there is little unnecessary dilation of figures of speech. This discipline he had in mind when he insisted upon the "fundamental brain-work" requisite for the production of poetry. Consequently, almost alone among poets of the nineteenth century, he does not require of the critic that the work of high excellence be separated from the mediocre. He wrote comparatively little and his poems are almost all on a singularly even level of accomplishment.

Italian and "Gothic" strands are interwoven in the rich fabric of his verse. The influence of Dante was, though limited, profound. The exacting task of the translations from the poets of the *dolce stil nuovo* helped to give

"Funda-mental Brain-work"

---

[15] Caine's *Recollections of D. G. Rossetti* (1882) is still of some value; Sharp's *D. G. Rossetti: a Record and a Study* (1882) was a hasty supply for the market and is of no importance.

[16] *The House of Life,* ed. P. F. Baum (Cambridge, Mass., 1928); R. C. Wallerstein, "Personal Experience in Rossetti's *House of Life*," *PMLA,* xlii (1927). 492-504.

his own style firmness, though it probably confirmed him in certain technical mannerisms (such as the employment of imperfect rimes and of rimes upon unaccented syllables) which he later exaggerated into defects. But apart from a conception of love—half personified, half spiritualized, never wholly apprehended—he took less from Dante and his contemporaries than from the somber superstitions of the North.[17] From boyhood, when he read *Melmoth the Wanderer* and translated *Lenore,* Rossetti was fascinated by the weird, the occult, the supernatural, the unknown. He read Hoffmann and Chamisso and other German exploiters of terror and wonder. The theme of the Doppelgänger troubled his imagination as it had Shelley's. The visionary instinct also found sustenance in medieval dream-literature and in the ritual and symbols of the faith of his forefathers.

In tracing Rossetti's development it must be kept in mind that the dates of his two volumes of original poetry are misleading both because many pieces in them were written long before publication and because he subjected them to repeated revisions. A few memorable poems are not characteristic. *Jenny,* with its pathos and delicate irony, stands as much apart from the rest of his verse as does *Found* from his other pictures. *A Last Confession* is Browningesque pastiche. Such poems as *On the Sunrise of 1848* and the tribute to Wellington are quite uncharacteristic. Along his true path he moved from the realistic Pre-Raphaelitism of some of the early poems ever deeper into the world of dreams. The conflict of the realistic and the visionary is wonderfully resolved in *The Blessed Damozel* in which elements from the atelier combine with motives inspired by Dante. *The Burden of Nineveh* and *Dante at Verona* are sustained midway between the outer and the inner world. In both these poems the corridors of time past are seen in strange perspective. Rossetti never wrote purely descriptive poetry, but for the purpose of simile natural imagery is beautifully employed. In *The House of Life* nature is representative of every mood, changing as the mood changes. In many poems the human situation has its harmonizing background—the wind in *Sister Helen*; the thunder and dull rain-drops in *The Portrait.* Rossetti penetrates far into the twilit recesses of life: forests with dim waters where silence and shadow reign, fit abodes of a spirit oppressed with "sick fervor" and vain longing. In such places he is aware of mystery: there ghosts walk and the phantom double. His imagination broods upon ancient magical lore: the beryl-stone and the waxen image; and upon non-human beings or women with thaumaturgic powers: Lilith or Sister Helen. The extant prose fragments (most of them synopses of poems never written) are variations upon themes that are somberly ominous. The dream-world was for him no mere piece of poetic decoration derived from old literary traditions; in his mind the barriers between the conscious and the subconscious were thin. From some of the sonnets in *The House of Life* it is difficult or impossible to wrest a logical meaning; but it is not to be

The World of Dreams

---

[17] L. A. Willoughby, *Dante Gabriel Rossetti and German Literature* (1912).

inferred that this is due to confusion of thought; the obscure inapprehensibility is deliberately contrived to convey a sense of the stress of an unresolved emotional conflict. It is the more impressive because he retained command of another and simpler style, rich in recondite archaisms and steeped in eerie atmosphere but more direct and objective than are the introspective poems. To this style belong such early pieces as *The Staff and Scrip* (1851-1852) and *Sister Helen* (of which the first version dates from 1851-1854); such poems of his middle years as *Eden Bower* and *Troy Town;* and the two narrative pieces, *The White Ship* and *The King's Tragedy,* which were written in intervals of comparative calm shortly before the end. From first to last the impression of concentrated thought and constricted energy dominates the effects of sensuousness.

II

Christina Rossetti

Not the leader of the Pre-Raphaelites but his almost cloistered sister, Christina Georgina Rossetti [18] (1830-1894), first attracted attention to the new movement in poetry. Her *Goblin Market* (1862) offered something very different from the conventional Tennysonian diffuseness and sentimentality, something strange and fantastic and resolute. She presents points of resemblance and contrast to her brother. They are alike in the intensity and concentration of their work; but he is generally elaborate and ornate while she is simple and spontaneous. The sensuality of his nature is opposed to the asceticism of hers. Both were drawn to Catholicism, but he by its aesthetic charm and she by its devotional appeal. Yet it was the unbelieving brother who often hovered on the verge of mystical experience from which the devout sister was shut off. She longed for the visionary ecstasy but was too honest and humble to lay claim to what she did not possess. Within the Anglican communion she found her spiritual home; but though her opinions are those of the Tractarians and though there are similarities between her poetry and Keble's,[19] a closer affinity is with the devotional poetry of Herbert and Vaughan. She found contentment in the family circle and in friendships with people of talent or genius; but she refused to marry James Collinson, the man she loved, because of differences on matters of faith. This renunciation is the subject of the sonnet-sequence *Monna Innominata,* the shorter sequence *By Way of Remembrance,* and various individual poems. Apart from this her life is the record of her books.[20] In the devo-

[18] *Poetical Works,* ed. W. M. Rossetti (1904). — Ehrsam, *Bibliographies,* pp. 189-199; Dorothy M. Stuart, *Christina Rossetti* (EML Series, 1930); Fredegond Shove, *Christina Rossetti: a Study* (1931); Eleanor W. Thomas, *Christina Georgina Rossetti* (1931); M. A. Sandars, *The Life of Christina Rossetti* (n.d.).

[19] The poems in *Some Feasts and Fasts,* a section of her work written at long intervals between 1853 and 1893, follow the Church Calendar in the manner of Keble's *The Christian Year.*

[20] She published seven poems in *The Germ* (1850). Her volumes of poetry are: *Goblin Market* (1862); *The Prince's Progress* (1866); *Sing-Song* (1872); *A Pageant, and other Poems* (1881); *Verses* (1893); and *New Poems* (posthumous, 1896).

tional works in prose,[21] which contain a good deal of verse subsequently assembled with her other poetry, she places much emphasis upon the symbols lying, or supposed to lie, beneath the literal surface of the Bible.

Like all her family, she enjoyed the eerie fantasies of German romanticism. In several poems [22] she played variations upon the theme of the spectre bride or bridegroom, imparting to it a Christian interpretation. *Goblin Market*,[23] for all its lightly tripping measures, is not gay or trivial but sinister, for the creatures of the other world are malignant, not frolicsome, sprites. For those who could "catch the clues" there is a warning against the spiritual wickedness with which the soul must wrestle. When, expanding the lyric dirge *Too late for Love, too late for Joy*, she turned the tale of the Sleeping Beauty into the romantic narrative of *The Prince's Quest*, it is as much a parable as a fairy tale, for the lover who lets himself be tempted by the pleasures of the way arrives too late and finds the bride dead who had long awaited him. Who will may disregard the symbolism; but it is there. Other, shorter poems are simple allegories of the Way of the Soul—the Choice of the Paths, the distractions of the World, the frustrations of Love, the journey of Life towards Death. Of such pieces the most impressive is *Up-Hill*. But Christina Rossetti has lighter moments, and when the allegory is ignored some of these pieces are almost as childlike as the nursery rimes which she gathered in *Sing-Song*. The lilt and jingle of these tiny ditties show the lightness of her fingering and her command of rime. Something of their simplicity reappears in her lovely carols, of which an example is *In the Bleak Mid-Winter*.[24] In another direction the nursery rimes point towards the pageant of *The Months*. All these things modulate by almost imperceptible shades and almost inaudible overtones into her austere religious verse. Many of the latter bear the general title *Songs for Strangers and Pilgrims*. She moved through this life conscious of its transitoriness and desirous of a better country. This desire is expressed perfectly in *Marvel of Marvels* and *Passing away, saith the World*. Both these are built upon monorime. The danger of this metrical form is that it may seem a mere *tour de force*; but from this Christina Rossetti escapes through the energy and intensity of her desire. Of a quieter beauty is the little poem for Whitsunday, "We know not the voice of that River," in which is quintessentialized that mood of longing which does not attain to the immediacy of the mystic vision.

(margin notes: Goblin Market; Religious Poetry)

[21] *Seek and Find* (1879); *Called to be Saints* (1881); *Letter and Spirit* (1883); *Time Flies* (1885), which is semi-autobiographic; and *The Face of the Deep* (1892), a commentary on the Apocalypse. All were published by the S. P. C. K.

[22] *The Hour and the Ghost; The Poor Ghost; The Ghost's Petition.*

[23] B. I. Evans, "The Sources of Christina Rossetti's *Goblin Market*," MLR, xxviii (1933). 156-165.

[24] Widely popular today in the beautiful setting by Gustav Holst.

III

A number of lesser poets moved in Rossetti's circle. Among them were William Bell Scott [25] (1812-1892), the painter, and Thomas Woolner [26] (1825-1892), the sculptor. Many of Rossetti's best letters are addressed to the Anglo-Irish poet William Allingham [27] (1824-1889). Another Anglo-Irish poet in the same group was Arthur O'Shaughnessy [28] (1844-1881). The misfortunes of the blind poet Philip Bourke Marston [29] (1850-1887) evoked tender responses from the Pre-Raphaelites. John Payne [30] (1842-1916), who won renown as a translator, was a more independent figure moving in the same circle. William Sharp [31] (1855-1905) regarded Rossetti as his master and shows his influence in the poetry published under his own name; but his fame was due to the verse and prose published under the pseudonym "Fiona Macleod" which are in the most exaggerated manner of the writers of the "Celtic Twilight" school. At a further remove from Rossetti but influenced by his work in translation were the writers of *vers de société*, a genre fashionable in the eighteen-seventies.[32] Impeccably moral itself, this light verse preluded the "Decadence" by its emphasis upon form. The early poems of Andrew Lang [33] (1844-1912) stem directly from Rossetti's versions

[25] Scott's long poems, *Hades* (1838) and *The Year of the World* (1846) are pseudo-Shelleyan in style and thought and were written before he felt Rossetti's influence. *Poems* (1854) and later volumes show his new orientation.

[26] Woolner published four volumes of verse. His once popular *My Beautiful Lady*, a soft and silly thing which reads almost like a parody of the Pre-Raphaelite manner, he later expanded (1863) under the influence of Patmore's *The Angel in the House*.

[27] Between 1850 and 1887 Allingham published a dozen volumes of verse. See also his *Diary*, ed. H. Allingham and D. Radford (1907). Allingham's place in the Irish Literary Revival is as a poet who sensed the *genius loci* rather than as a nationalist. He had a pleasant fancy for witches and leprechauns and an ear for light lyric. He exercised a considerable influence upon the young Yeats.

[28] *Poems*, ed. W. A. Percy (1923). O'Shaughnessy's first book, *An Epic of Women* (1870), is in an ironic manner afterwards abandoned. *Music and Moonlight* (1874) is more characteristic. *The Fountain of Tears* and *We Are the Music Makers* are his best-known poems.

[29] Marston's four volumes of verse were collected together in 1892. His poems are shot through with Pre-Raphaelite imagery and mannerisms, but in their mood of resignation mingled with revolt there is an individual note.

[30] *Poetical Works* (2v, 1902). There are Pre-Raphaelite elements in such pieces as *The Rhyme of Redemption* and evidence of indebtedness to Swinburne elsewhere. The marsh-lights which play over *Lautrec* are the product of the decomposition of romanticism. Payne translated Villon, Boccaccio, Omar, Hafiz, Heine, and *The Thousand Nights and a Night*. — See Thomas Wright, *The Life of John Payne* (1919); C. R. H. Williams, *John Payne* (Paris, 1926).

[31] *Earth's Voices* (1884); *Romantic Ballads* (1888). Among the "Fiona Macleod" volumes *From the Hills of Dream* (1897) is the best. The problem of Sharp's "dual personality" concerns the psychologist rather than the literary historian. See *The Writings of "Fiona Macleod,"* ed. Elizabeth A. Sharp (7v, 1909-1910); E. A. Sharp, *William Sharp (Fiona Macleod), a Memoir* (1910); P. E. More, "Fiona Macleod," *The Drift of Romanticism* (1913), pp. 119-143.

[32] The vogue began with *Lyra Elegantiarum* (1867), edited by Frederick Locker-Lampson (1821-1895) who was in the line of descent from Prior through Praed. Elegance, sparkle, light irony, and perfect finish are the effects aimed at in this genre.

[33] *Ballads and Lyrics of Old France* (1872); *Ballads in Blue China* (1880-1881). Lang's *Helen of Troy* (1882), a narrative poem reminiscent in manner of William Morris, is related to his Homeric studies and to his translations, done in collaboration, of the *Odyssey* (1879) and the *Iliad* (1883). A sonnet on the *Odyssey* is his best-known poem. — *Poetical Works* (2v, 1923). On Lang's prose work see below, ch. XLII.

of Villon. Austin Dobson [34] (1840-1921) and Edmund Gosse [35] (1849-1928) were accomplished practitioners of these dainty forms, and the parodies and witty verses of Charles Stuart Calverley [36] (1831-1884) and James Kenneth Stephen [37] (1859-1892) display something of the same manner.

[34] *Vignettes in Rhyme* (1873); *Proverbs in Porcelain* (1877); *Old-World Idylls* (1883); *Complete Poetical Works* (1923). Dobson shaped his fragile material exquisitely and in his hands the rondeau and the triolet attained their trivial perfection. His besetting fault was sentimentality. On his prose see ch. XLII, below.

[35] *On Viol and Flute* (1873). See also Gosse's "Plea for Certain Exotic Forms of Verse," *Cornhill Mag.*, XXXVI (1877). 53-71, which makes apparent the indebtedness of this school to the French poet Théodore de Banville. *Firdausi in Exile* (1885) is Gosse's most substantial poem. *Collected Poems* (1911). On Gosse's prose see ch. XLII, below.

[36] *Fly Leaves* (1872); *Complete Works* (1901). See also P. L. Babington, *Browning and Calverley* (1925), where *The Cock and the Bull* is reprinted with the relevant passages from *The Ring and the Book*; and R. B. Ince, *Calverley and Some Cambridge Wits* (1929).

[37] *Lapsus Calami* (1891).

XXX
William Morris

I

The career of William Morris [1] (1834-1896) falls into two well-defined periods: till 1877 he was primarily concerned with poetry and the fine arts; thereafter with the ills and problems of modern society.

The Middle Ages A boyish love of everything medieval led him to the study of architecture, armor, heraldry, romance, and Chaucer. At Oxford he was attracted to Anglo-Catholicism, and he and his closest friend, Edward Burne-Jones (1833-1898), planned to take orders and establish a monastery. Ruskin was their master; the famous chapter on "The Nature of Gothic" their inspiration.[2] His teaching and the activities of the "Christian Socialists" directed their attention to actual conditions in England. Meanwhile, drawing and architectural design were the first outlets for their creative enthusiasm. By 1855 Morris was composing poems and prose romances; and some of these things were printed in 1856 in *The Oxford and Cambridge Magazine*. From the manner of his early verse Morris afterwards made a wide departure; but the tales in prose foreshadow in their languorous rendering of action that is often violent the style of his latest romances.

The strong personality of Rossetti, whom these two young men now met, confirmed the decision to devote themselves to art, and they began to put into practice the aesthetic doctrines which Ruskin preached. In London in 1857 they set up house in Red Lion Square in what they called their "Palace of Art." The same year saw the decoration of the Oxford Union. Morris's share in this joint enterprise was an episode from the legend of Tristram *The Defence of Guenevere* and Iseult. *The Defence of Guenevere and other Poems* (1858) was the first public indication that a new movement in poetry was under way. Morris had in mind a cycle of Arthurian stories, in style and treatment unlike

---

[1] *Collected Works,* introductions by May Morris (24v, 1910-1915), supplemented by May Morris, *William Morris: Artist, Writer, Socialist* (2v, 1936), which contains hitherto unpublished material, an index to the *Works,* and an essay by George Bernard Shaw; *Prose and Poetry, 1856-1870* (1913). — Ehrsam, *Bibliographies,* pp. 161-187; J. W. Mackail, *The Life of William Morris* (2v, 1899), Pocket Edition (2v, 1912); Elizabeth L. Cary, *William Morris: Poet, Craftsman, Socialist* (1902); A. Clutton-Brock, *William Morris: His Work and Influence* (1914); John Drinkwater, *William Morris* (1912); Alfred Noyes, *William Morris* (EML Series, 1908); Holbrook Jackson, *William Morris* (1908; revised edition, 1926); B. I. Evans, *William Morris and His Poetry* (1925); *Some Appreciations of William Morris,* ed. G. E. Roebuck (Walthamstow, 1934), essays by Lascelles Abercrombie, J. W. Mackail, G. B. Shaw, and others; L. W. Eshleman, *A Victorian Rebel* (1940); Oliver Elton, *Poetic Romance after 1850* (1914); J. Middleton Murry, *Heroes of Thought* (1938), ch. xxvii; Karl Litzenberg, "William Morris and the Reviews: A Study in the Fame of the Poet," *RES,* xii (1936). 413-428.
[2] They were also influenced by Henry Kenelm Digby's *The Broad Stone of Honour* (1829).

Tennyson's *Morte d'Arthur* though owing something to *The Lady of Shalott,* in intensity of phrase stimulated by *Maud,* and in technique reminiscent of Browning's dramatic monologues. The mystic coloring of *The Chapel in Lyoness* is foreign to Morris's temperament and probably due to Rossetti's influence. The obscurity of some pieces comes not from profundity of thought but from an as yet incomplete mastery of expression; yet the roughness of rhythms is not to be ascribed to an inadequate prosodic technique but to a deliberate avoidance of the patterns of mid-Victorian metrics as long since fixed by Tennyson. The niceties of character are seldom delineated, but there is a genuine realization of tragic moments. How astonishing is the abrupt opening of the *Guenevere,* without scene-setting or explanation, the poet driving impetuously into the central situation! The Middle Ages are conceived not in the guise of Victorian sentiment, but as rough, hard, and barbarous. Thus, these early Arthurian pieces point forward to Morris's interpretations of the heroic sagas of Iceland. *Sir Galahad* marks his revulsion from his youthful ascetic ideal. The "gramarye" of *Rapunzel* points back to Coleridge rather than forward along the course he was to take. *Sir Peter Harpdon's End* is a tragic incident from Froissart dramatized with conspicuous, though not precisely dramatic, power. In one respect Morris never fulfilled the poetic promise of this first book. Save in brief infrequent passages, the later poetry does not possesss the force, the passion, the concentrated energy of these poems of his early manhood. Perhaps it was because, as he became active in many affairs, he came to look upon poetry as a recreation and relaxation. Certainly the poetic fiber was relaxed.

In 1859 Morris married the beautiful Jane Burden. The failure to find satisfactory furniture for their home in Kent led to the establishment in 1861 of the firm of "Morris, Marshall, Faulkner and Co., Fine Art Workmen in Painting, Carving, Furniture, and the Metals." [3] For some time Morris had little opportunity to write, but by 1865, when he returned to London to live, his business was prospering along several lines, he was freed from the necessity of immediate supervision, and time was released for literary work. He planned a cycle of poems on the Fall of Troy, but of these only two parts were written.[4] Plans for *The Earthly Paradise* were now taking shape, but one of the stories intended for it outgrew the space provided and was published separately. This was *The Life and Death of Jason* [5] (1867). His intention was to tell the old story as a troubadour would have told it, with sources freely adapted, with no striving for archaeological accuracy, with, indeed, a flavor that was deliberately medieval rather than classical. The

Jason

[3] See the Prospectus in J. W. Mackail, *The Life of William Morris,* Pocket Edition, I. 154-156. Among the craftsmen employed by Morris was William F. De Morgan (1839-1917) who in old age came before the public, like an apparition from another world, as the writer of sprawling, long-winded novels: *Alice-for-Short* (1907), *Somehow Good* (1908), and others with more faults and fewer merits. In them De Morgan combined elements from Dickens and Trollope. Their great vogue proved to be temporary.

[4] *Scenes from the Fall of Troy; Collected Works,* XXIV. 3-51. See Bush, pp. 298-303.

[5] Ed. E. Maxwell (1914). Morris drew his material from Ovid, Apollodorus, and Apollonius of Rhodes, with details from Lemprière. See Bush, pp. 303-313.

pictorial style, the subdued coloring, and the modulation from episode to episode without any abrupt discontinuity have been likened to the effects of tapestry, and the comparison is apt, for Morris loved old tapestries. The exquisite interspersed lyrics make scarcely a ripple on the surface of a narrative which flows with leisurely amplitude, its strength consisting not in isolated passages but in the cumulative impression till in the final book the pace quickens with the vengeful meditations of the abandoned Medea. No longer, as in the early poems, is there any obscurity or hesitation; but with the gain in clarity and confidence there is loss in intensity. Morris's besetting fault of over-fluency becomes apparent and the passion, though genuine, is watered down with words. There is no conscious intention to pour the new wine of modern thought into the old wine-skins of myth, but the recurrent motives of the beauty and brevity of life, the inevitability of death, and the dark uncertainty of any future existence color the poem's elemental pathos with modern skepticism.

The Earthly Paradise

Morris now hastened through the composition of the forty-two thousand lines of *The Earthly Paradise*. It was published in four volumes in two installments (1868 and 1870).[6] The tales are set in an ingenious "frame": to escape a visitation of the Black Death a company of Germanic, Norse, and Celtic folk of the Middle Ages sail westward and come to an island inhabited by descendants of the ancient Greeks who, cut off from the world, have kept their traditions and culture unalloyed. This artifice affords an opportunity for contrasts which Morris, who was no subtle psychologist, did not fully realize. The story-tellers, Greek and medieval, are old men, wistfully looking back to their lost youth. The situation enabled the poet to juxtapose tales in which the clear beauty of classic myth contrasts with the somber fantasies of barbaric ages and climes.[7] There are twenty-four stories, two for each month of the year, linked by lovely descriptive interludes. As the calendar moves round, the temper of the stories changes, becoming stronger and darker, and at the end the tone is sinister. Thus, the full effect can be gained only by continuous and consecutive reading—but this is a heavy task. The interludes are personal utterances, glimpses into the poet's mind, for though Morris disapproved of introspective poetry he did not altogether avoid it. They repeat with variations the keynote of the Prologue in which he declares that he, "the idle singer of an empty day," has no power to sing of heaven or hell or to make death durable. This characterization of himself as "idle" and his day as "empty" has been thought an affectation, but it is not; by an idle song he intended one which

---

[6] A plan to issue the poem in folio with five hundred illustrations by Burne-Jones was abandoned for want of trained wood-engravers.

[7] E. C. Kuster, *Mittelalter und Antike bei William Morris* (Berlin, 1928). The twelve stories of classical antiquity are from Homer, Herodotus, Apollodorus, Ovid, and other obvious sources. Some of the eleven western medieval tales come from the *Gesta Romanorum*, the *Legenda Aurea*, William of Malmesbury, and Mandeville. *The Hill of Venus* is from Tieck's *Erzählen*. *The Lovers of Gudrun*, from the *Laxdaela Saga*, is the first heir (other than translations) of Morris's Icelandic studies. *The Man who Never Laughed Again*, the only Oriental tale, is from the *Arabian Nights*. For stories which Morris discarded see *Collected Works*, XXIV. 87-316.

would afford distraction from everyday cares; and he was ever conscious of a spiritual emptiness. The general design—the outer "frame," the linking "months," and the balanced pairs of stories—is beautifully symmetrical. The deepening of tone, partly a matter of conscious art, is due also to the change from the romantic to the epic manner as Morris became more influenced by Norse myths. Through the whole there runs a note of doubt and despondency, a mild skepticism in harmony with the poet's ingenuous pity for humanity. There is an elemental vigor, a sense of the glory of youth and power and possessions and love; but these things that make life worth while are envisioned in the memories of aged men. The narrative, even though the action be swift and strong, is generally slow-moving; the diffuseness of the poem stands between us and it. There is little attempt to individualize the characters, either the tale-tellers or the actors in the tales. Once more we are reminded of figures on tapestries.[8]

In 1871 came the removal to Kelmscott on the upper Thames and the first visit to Iceland; in 1872 the "morality play" *Love is Enough*. The tenuous connection of this semi-dramatic poem with the old moralities is just sufficient to alienate it from most modern sympathies. There is too much comment and didacticism at the expense of action; and the metre used for the central theme (an adaptation of the old alliterative verse) encouraged diffuseness. Yet the poem is of singular loveliness. The intricate structure involves five concentric "layers" of the action. On the periphery are two peasants, sweethearts, who comment upon the morality and upon the Emperor and Empress, who, somewhat removed from ordinary humanity, watch the performance given in celebration of their wedding-day. Then, there is the figure of Love, who, bearing emblems which change from episode to episode, acts as the Expositor. The play shows the quest of Pharamond for Azalais. At the center of the design, and its essence, is the Music. All these motives are interwoven in a kind of poetic counterpoint and at the climax they combine in full harmony. The Music, Morris's most wonderful achievement in prosody, modulates on each of its soundings from mood to mood till it reaches a triumphant tone in the famous "Love is enough: ho ye who seek saving." This "morality" is not so remote from modern issues as it seems; indeed in one passage it looks forward to the social revolution: Love proclaims that he will be the leader at Armageddon.

In the next years Morris's activities were multifarious. He visited Italy and was disappointed. He went to Iceland for a second time. To his earlier translations from the Icelandic he added *Three Northern Love Stories* (1875). He translated the *Aeneid* (1876), not very satisfactorily. A disagreement with his partners forced him to reconstruct his business. Yet he had time to write his greatest narrative poem, *Sigurd the Volsung*[9] (1876),

Love is Enough

Sigurd the Volsung

---

[8] See Bush, pp. 313-327, on Morris' medievalizing treatment of classical myth in *The Earthly Paradise*.

[9] The story is from the *Volsunga Saga* which Morris had already translated (1870) in collaboration with Eiríkr Magnússon, his teacher of Icelandic. See D. M. Hoare, *The Works of Morris and Yeats in relation to Early Saga Literature* (1937).

a strong and massive evocation of the passion and heroism of the North. In it he reveals his deepest thoughts upon human destiny. There is a lowering sense of doom; the Norns are heavy and hard and determine man's fate regardless of his efforts. There may be truth in the suggestion that the stimulus of the rugged North helped to turn Morris's thoughts towards Socialism. How acute was his discontent with modern civilization is apparent from various passages in *Sigurd*. At all events the following year is a turning point in his life.

II

The part Morris now played in two undertakings enlarged his sense of social responsibility. He organized the Society for the Protection of Ancient Buildings; and during the crisis of 1877-1878 he was an active member of the Eastern Question Association which supported Gladstone in his pro-Russian attacks upon Disraeli's pro-Turkish policy. These activities brought Morris into contact with the leading radicals.

ocialism   His Socialism [10] was founded upon the teaching of Ruskin, but that teaching was tested by his practical and experienced intelligence. Everywhere he saw round him vulgarity, debased Gothic, machine-made ornament, ugliness, and squalor. His disgust was enhanced by his experiences in trying to procure first-rate material from which to manufacture his furniture, wall-papers, fabrics, and other articles. He raised the condition of life of his own workmen and later shared profits with them; but he could not, without action, contribute to any general amelioration of the conditions in which laborers lived. His knowledge of the Middle Ages confirmed Ruskin's doctrine that only in a society in which the need to work was not divorced from happiness would it be possible to produce a truly popular art of sound design and craftsmanship. He repudiated, however, Ruskin's neo-feudalism with its acceptance of social inequality; and though he was strongly affected by the medieval institution of the craft-guilds, he advocated no archaistic "return to the Middle Ages." Abandoning hope in the propertied classes as agents of reform, he came to believe not only that the advent of revolution would be speedy but that it was desirable. Only after a catharsis could the classless society be established. He studied *Capital,* and while admitting that he did not understand Marx's theory of surplus value he was deeply impressed with the historical parts of the book, drawn as they were in large measure from social and economic conditions in England. The lethargy and caution of the Liberal government in the enactment of social legislation and their coercive policy towards Ireland were factors in Morris's decision to join the Socialist Party. In 1881 H. M. Hyndman had founded the Demo-

---

[10] A. A. Helmholtz-Phelan, *The Social Philosophy of William Morris* (Durham, N. C., 1927); Granville Hicks, *Figures of Transition* (1939), ch. II (to which the present account is especially indebted); M. R. Grennan, *William Morris, Medievalist and Revolutionary* (1945); William Sinclair, "Socialism according to William Morris," *The Fortnightly Review*, n.s., LXXXVIII (1910). 722-735; J. B. Glasier, *William Morris and the Early Days of the Socialist Movement* (1921), of value as the narrative of a fellow-worker with Morris.

cratic Federation, the first modern English Socialist body. This Morris joined in 1883, but, distrusting Hyndman, he left it in 1884 to found the Socialist League. Early in 1885 he brought out the first number of *The Commonweal,* a periodical designed to spread the doctrine of the League.

Morris's views are simplifications of Marxian doctrine for popular consumption. They are familiar to everyone today, but because they are basic to an understanding of Morris they must be summarized. There are two classes of society, the wealth-possessing and the wealth-producing, the former controlling the instruments for making wealth—lands, machinery, capital; the latter using these instruments only by permission of, and for the benefit of, the former. Capital lives on the efforts of labor; labor strives to better itself at the expense of capital. The aim in work is to obtain a profit. The workers must sell their labor on terms imposed by the capitalists. Hence comes the competition among workers for a share in wages and among employers for a division of profits. The result is the hideous squalor in the lives of the proletariat. Morris's positive program was equally simple in its essentials. All means of production are to be held in common for all by the state. The motive of production and distribution is to be a decent livelihood for all, not the profit of the few. Duty to the commonweal is to be substituted for obedience to any system of private ethics. Education shall fit the tastes and talents of each individual. Hard, distasteful, but necessary work shall be apportioned equably among all the able-bodied. In his own labor the workman will find joy. Morris believed that under Socialism art, now the possession of the few and unknown to, and unenjoyed by, the many, would flourish.

These propositions and corollaries he enunciated in *The Commonweal* and from the lecture-platform. They are implicit in *The Day is Coming* and *All for the Cause* and other pieces in *Poems by the Way* (1891). At Oxford, at a meeting presided over by Ruskin, he announced them boldly, causing a considerable furore. So late as 1893 he wrote with E. Belford Bax *Socialism, its Growth and Outcome.* Bax was probably chiefly responsible for the theoretical portions of this treatise, but Morris certainly subscribed to them and he illuminated the whole with his imagination and his minute knowledge of the Middle Ages. Long before this, in 1885, he had been arrested for joining in a demonstration. However, after witnessing the riots in Trafalgar Square on "Bloody Sunday" in November, 1887, he deplored mere scuffling with the police and argued that education must precede any revolutionary action that could hope to succeed. Consequently he came to believe that the way advocated by Sidney Webb and the other Fabians was the only right way; but feeling that his talents were not adapted to the Fabian organization he retired after 1889 into "passive Socialism," keeping the communistic cause alive in the group gathered round him at Kelmscott.

The essays and lectures on Socialism which bulk so large in the *Collected Works* are not "literature" in the narrow sense of the word. They were part of a program of action: to instruct, controvert, convert, encourage, and agitate. But two books which supplement this propaganda are parts of Morris's literary work of lasting beauty and value. *The Dream of John Ball* (1888) is not a treatise but an imaginative romance, not a connected system of sociology but a reverie. The narrator returns in a dream to fourteenth-century England and finds himself in the midst of the Peasants' Revolt. He hears a fiery speech by John Ball and afterwards talks long and earnestly with the peasant leader. He tells him all the woes which must come to pass before the fulfillment of Ball's ideal; yet the preacher dies for that ideal. Awaking, the narrator hears the factory whistles of modern industrialism calling the people to work. There is thus a projection from the fourteenth century into the nineteenth. The lesson is that change, even with advancement, means new problems. The ideal will not be quickly or easily attained.

Unlike Marx and Engels, who discouraged the planning of Utopias and declined to predict the form which the classless society would take, Morris gave free play to his imagination. Stimulated by Edward Bellamy's *Looking Backward* (1887) but disagreeing radically with it, he wrote *News from Nowhere* (1890). Bellamy predicted that when capitalism had become all-embracing it would be taken over by the state without the necessity of any violence. Morris held that monopoly would never become co-terminal with society but that there would be disintegrations and rearrangements, accompanied by competition and wars, till the revolution destroyed the entire system. Bellamy held out the promise of a reduction of labor to a minimum; Morris the promise of a reduction of the pains of labor. In *News from Nowhere* we have again a dreamer, who this time finds himself in the classless future. Surroundings are beautiful and healthy; the profit motive has vanished and men are happy in their work. The sanction of morality rests upon active endeavor for the common good. Details of this Utopia which are discussed at tedious length we must pass over, to note the burning emotion with which the book is brought to a close and which has made it a classic in the literature of Socialism.

Refusing to postpone activities in the arts till the cause had triumphed, Morris did not limit himself to revolutionary propaganda in his later years. He helped to organize the Guild of Arts and Crafts whose first exhibition was held in 1888. He began to issue books from the Kelmscott Press in 1891. The Kelmscott *Chaucer* (1894) was the crown of his lifework in the arts. He composed a series of prose stories based upon medieval themes.[11] As in *The Earthly Paradise* there had been a movement from romance to epic, so in this sequence there is a withdrawal from epic to romance. We move from a tale of the Roman conflict with the heroic North to a tale laid in a soft and lovely fairyland. In these romances Morris had no motive save to entertain; he aimed to provide solace as the reward of work well done. Yet there are connections with his writings on Socialism, for the dream-

[11] *The House of the Wolfings* (1889); *The Roots of the Mountains* (1890); *The Story of the Glittering Plain* (1891); *The Wood beyond the World* (1894); *The Water of the Wondrous Isles* (1897); and *The Sundering Flood* (1897), the last two posthumous.

world or fairyland of these books has much in common with the world of the future which he envisaged. A seemingly simple style only half conceals the artifice. In *The Wolfings* there is much archaism of idiom and vocabulary; [12] this is gradually reduced in subsequent tales to the point where it is but a beautifully appropriate coloring.

When Morris died in 1896 Swinburne sang his praises as the "warrior and dreamer" who strove to redeem the world "by sword and by song." [13] In a better ordered society Morris would not have concerned himself with the problems which even the ideal commonwealth will have to face. Like all good workmen he would have dedicated himself to the work for which his talents suited him. He would have remained in his shops and library. But faced with society as it is and being what he was, and therefore unable to "escape" with the archaistic dreamers into the past, he was compelled to practical effort. He could not remain within the shelter of art. With Ruskin he might have written:

For my own part I will put up with this state of things, passively, not an hour longer. . . . I simply cannot paint, nor read, . . . nor do anything else that I like . . . because of the misery that I know of, and see signs of, where I know it not, which no imagination can interpret too bitterly.[14]

Narrative Gift

Poetry was for Morris what he intended it to be for his readers—a recreation and a delight. It was at once a picture and a tale. He did not see things in generalizations or symbols or abstractions but as concrete pictures, dream-like, tapestry-like, but clearly realized. As the world was to Shakespeare a drama, so to Morris it was a tale. He wrote lovely lyrics but primarily he was a narrative poet. Without Chaucer's genius for characterization, he lacked also Chaucer's humor. He was not a subtle artist (though not so naïve as he wished his readers to think) and he depended upon broad effects, not upon the inevitable and ultimate phrase. He did not load every rift of his subject with ore but spread the gold-leaf over as large a surface as possible.

Melancholy

For all his almost miraculous accomplishments in so many arts,[15] for all his enthusiasm and renown, there is a vein of sadness in his poetry, wistful, never plangent, but the more poignant because restrained. Why this undercurrent of melancholy? He could not avoid his age and environment. The

---

[12] The paraphrase of *Beowulf* which Morris made with A. J. Wyatt (1895) is so archaic as to be disconcerting to the reader who knows no Old English.

[13] Swinburne, *A Channel Passage and Other Poems* (1904), *Dedication* to the memory of Morris and Burne-Jones.

[14] Ruskin, *Fors Clavigera*, I (1871); *Works*, XXVII. 13.

[15] Morris's firm began with ecclesiastical work, wall-papers, and furniture. After 1875 he was sole proprietor and manager and in that year began to print and weave fabrics. In 1877 tapestry-weaving commenced and in 1879 carpets and rugs. In 1881 larger and better equipped works were opened at Merton Abbey. Morris never supplied a large part of the general market, but gradually his example was followed by other firms with consequent improvements in design. In particular he undermined the Victorian confidence in machine-made ornament. In addition to these arts and crafts and his typography Morris illuminated manuscripts, bound books, carved in wood and stone, made architectural designs, and worked in metal, jewelry, and stamped leather. He was an expert cook. He said he avoided music because he was afraid that if he devoted himself to it he would be distracted from his other work.

heavy and weary weight of an unintelligible world pressed upon him. At times he must have felt acutely the odds against any individual at war with capitalistic society. But there was something deeper yet. Like all Cyrenaics, he was possessed with a heart-stabbing sense of the brevity of life and the swift approach of death. He insisted on the duty of each individual to labor for the happiness of the community, but he knew that each moment of that temporal happiness is lost as soon as it is gained. He who filled each day to the full longed for that immortality in which he could not believe. The central fires of his spirit shine in *The Story of the Glittering Plain* where he pictures the "Acre of the Undying," the Norse Elysium, where youth is renewed forever and men live without the fear of death.

XXXI
Algernon Charles Swinburne

I

At the moment when, in 1879, Swinburne was entering upon a new life *"Thalas-* in which he was to become gradually reconciled to colorless respectability he *sius"* looked back with wistful detachment to his experiences in past years and composed the allegorized autobiography, *Thalassius*. He was the child of the Sun (Reason and Art and Song) and the Sea (Liberty). A foster-father (Landor or, rather, Landor's writings) reared this child, teaching him to love truth and hate tyranny. Love, first, and then Lust, led Thalassius astray into disillusionment, satiety, and skepticism; and escaping thence he reverted to his first ideals. The poem is as significant for its reticences as for its candor. In particular, there is no direct allusion to the influence of Mazzini and the Italian Risorgimento upon the poet's thought. The renunciation of sensuality must be regarded as an aspiration rather than an accomplished fact.

Although born in London, Algernon Charles Swinburne [1] (1837-1909) was of North-Country blood with a tradition of rebelliousness as part of his heritage. At Eton his frail physique and peculiarities of temperament isolated him from other boys. He arrived at Oxford with a budding reputation as a poet, tastes formed from reading "Dodsley's grand old plays," sub- *Oxford* versive opinions that derived from Landor, Shelley, and Hugo, and the manuscripts of his first experiments in tragedies of lust and violence modeled on those of the Jacobeans. At Balliol he became intimate with John Nichol, a dour and forceful Scot, who strengthened him in his dangerous views. In politics the two young men were republican and in religion nihilistic. Nichol was an ardent disciple of Mazzini and under this influence Swinburne composed a perfervid *Ode* to the exiled Italian patriot.[2] His mind was a receptacle for those mid-century streams of tendency which we

---

[1] *Complete Works*, Bonchurch Edition, ed. Sir Edmund Gosse and T. J. Wise (20v, 1925-1927). This, despite its title, is not complete. Among other things omitted are letters in Thomas Hake and Arthur Compton-Rickett, *Letters of Swinburne. With Some Personal Recollections* (1918) and in Coulson Kernahan, *Swinburne as I Knew Him* (1919). — T. J. Wise, *Bibliography*, (2v, 1919-1920), rev. ed. in Bonchurch Edition, xx; Ehrsam, *Bibliographies*, pp. 263-297; Sir Edmund Gosse, *The Life of Swinburne* (1917), rev. ed. in Bonchurch Edition, xix; Georges Lafourcade, *La Jeunesse de Swinburne, 1837-1867* (2v, 1928) and *Swinburne: a Literary Biography* (1932); Edward Thomas, *Swinburne* (1912); John Drinkwater, *Swinburne: an Estimate* (1913); W. B. D. Henderson, *Swinburne and Landor* (1918); T. E. Welby, *A Study of Swinburne* (1926); Harold Nicolson, *Swinburne* (EML Series, 1926); S. C. Chew, *Swinburne* (1929); Paul de Reul, *L'œuvre de Swinburne* (Brussels, 1922); W. R. Rutland, *Swinburne, a Nineteenth Century Hellene* (1931); C. K. Hyder, *Swinburne's Literary Career and Fame* (Durham, N. C., 1933); Ludwig Richter, *Swinburnes Verhältnis zu Frankreich und Italien* (Leipzig, 1911).

[2] The fullest study of the influence of Mazzini on Swinburne is in H. W. Rudman, *Italian Nationalism and English Letters* (1940).

have already observed elsewhere. He was, as Tennyson said later, "a reed through which all things blow into music." A sense of dedication to the cause of liberty was counterbalanced by a conviction that art was of value for its own sake, and a confidence in progress by an underlying feeling of disillusionment and despair. From republican politics and Jacobean pastiche he was diverted in 1857 when he met Rossetti and Morris. Under the influence of the one he composed poems of aesthetic religiosity, and of the other a never finished narrative poem on Tristram and Iseult.[3] Indiscretions in behavior alarmed the authorities (among whom was Benjamin Jowett who recognized his pupil's genius), and to escape being expelled Swinburne withdrew from the university.

The "demoniac youth" (as Ruskin called him) published together two little plays in 1860: *The Queen-Mother* and *Rosamond*. The latter has an attractive Pre-Raphaelite, thin freshness. The former, a more substantial work, shows a variety of influences, among them that of Beddoes. Its darkly passionate theme, set against the background of the Massacre of St. Bartholomew, makes it, as it were, an antechamber to the later trilogy on Mary Queen of Scots. The failure to attract attention by these two dramas may account for a waste of time during the next two years, which are notable only for a visit to Italy in 1861. To 1862 belongs *Laus Veneris* on the theme of Tannhäuser; and in that year disappointment in his only serious love affair inspired one of the greatest of his poems, *The Triumph of Time.* Swinburne contributed several articles to *The Spectator,* among them a review of Baudelaire's *Les Fleurs du Mal* and a defense of Meredith's *Modern Love*; but presently R. H. Hutton, the editor, severed relations with him. In 1863 he visited Paris and met Manet and Whistler. That summer he

**Atalanta
in
Calydon**

began the composition of *Atalanta in Calydon*. On a second visit to Italy[4] (1864) occurred the famous meeting with Landor when England's "youngest singer" offered to her oldest the dedication of his Greek tragedy. *Atalanta* appeared in 1865, winning the applause of the critics but attracting no wide attention; and later in the same year came *Chastelard,* for the moment an independent play but destined to be the first part of a dramatic trilogy. It is written with a passionate *brio* suggestive of the libretto of some Italian opera. Through these years Swinburne had been writing the lyrical and meditative poems, narratives, and dramatic monologues which in the sum-

**Poems
and
Ballads**

mer of 1866 burst upon the world as the first series of *Poems and Ballads*. The resultant scandal, when the reviewers, led by John Morley,[5] pursued the poet as the laureate of libidinousness and the apostle of despair, is one

---

[3] The first canto appeared in *Undergraduate Papers* (December, 1857); five more were privately printed by T. J. Wise (1918); the six (all written of an intended ten) are assembled in *Complete Works,* I.

[4] *Notes on Designs of the Old Masters at Florence,* written at this time, is an essay which anticipates the method and manner of Pater's art criticism. Pater acknowledged his indebtedness to Swinburne.

[5] Morley's anonymous onslaught in the *Saturday Review,* August 4, 1866, is reprinted in *Notorious Literary Attacks,* ed. Albert Mordell (1926), pp. 171-184. W. M. Rossetti defended Swinburne, with qualifications, in *Swinburne's Poems and Ballads: a Criticism* (1866).

of the most familiar episodes in the history of English taste and morals. Swinburne stood his ground and struck back in the eloquent though overwrought *Notes on Poems and Reviews* in which he proclaimed the doctrine of "Art for Art's Sake," interpreted certain of the poems, and derided the idyllic domesticity of Tennyson and Coventry Patmore.

During the later eighteen-sixties Swinburne's genius was in full flower. *Ave atque Vale* (1867), the tribute to Baudelaire, stands at the summit of his elegiac poems and near the summit of English elegiac poetry. In its grave, elaborate beauty it suggests a closer affinity between Swinburne and the author of *Les Fleurs du Mal* than actually existed. *William Blake* (1868), the first considerable work in prose, is historically important because it blazed a trail through the jungle of the Prophetic Books. Before the close of the decade he had composed the rapturous *Prelude* to *Tristram of Lyonesse*. Before coming into intimate contact with Mazzini he had written that cataract of fervent lyricism, *A Song of Italy* (1867). It was not personal friendship with Mazzini that turned Swinburne's genius from eroticism *"Songs* and nihilism to the service of the republican cause, for the old political en- *of the* thusiasm of Oxford days, though for long subordinated to other passions, *Republic"* had never vanished. This enthusiasm now surged into the forefront of his poetic consciousness. The English tradition of love of Italy and championship of her aspirations which descended to Swinburne from Byron, Shelley, Landor, and the Brownings reached its climax in *A Song of Italy.* In *Songs before Sunrise* (1871), though some of the poems are immediately topical, the rapture is transcendentalized. In so far as these poems are on historical subjects the situation which most of them reflect is that of 1848 rather than of 1870. The sun which Swinburne hailed did not rise; Italy was suffused not with the flush of dawn but with the drab twilight of the Sabaudean monarchy. The failure of Mazzini's hopes—which were also Swinburne's— accounts for the poet's rapid withdrawal from the field of political poetry. There was no formal recantation; he sang no palinode; but the disillusionment influenced his gradual change in political opinions and long before the end he had entered the company of "lost leaders."

Much—too much—research was undertaken in preparation for *Bothwell* (1874), the huge second part of the Scots trilogy. Save in a few passages that are dramatic in their intensity, the monotony of sustained eloquence obscures the genuine grasp of character and motive. In 1875 Swinburne collected a number of critical articles in *Essays and Studies.* At this point *Critical* we may turn aside and look ahead to consider briefly Swinburne's work in *Studies* criticism. His exuberance, verbosity, inflated style, and tendency to exaggerated statements conceal the general soundness of his judgment and taste. Violent in controversy and not suffering pedants gladly, he was an unsafe guide when he assumed a hostile position; but if the rhetoric be overlooked and the exaggerations reduced to a normal scale of values, there is matter of permanent worth in his appreciations. The study of Blake was, as we have noted, a trail-blazer. The *Study of Shakespeare* (1880), in some respects the greatest of his prose works, is fundamentally sound, for all its verbiage, and in places brilliantly illuminating. In the *George Chapman* (1875), the *Study of Ben Jonson* (1889), *The Age of Shakespeare* (1908), and many briefer appraisals of the old dramatists (including a sequence of sonnets in their honor) he carried on the work of Charles Lamb. The *Study of Victor Hugo* (1886) is a set-piece of laudation like Swinburne's various poetic tributes to his French master; as criticism it is almost negligible. The most weighty collection of critical papers is the *Miscellanies* (1886). Of the literary polemics the most powerful and sustained is *Under the Microscope* (1872), occasioned by Robert Buchanan's diatribe, *The Fleshly School of Poetry*. Of the essays on English poets the earlier article on Byron is genuinely appreciative and nobly eloquent, the later a notorious and prejudiced attack. The accompanying estimate of Wordsworth is half-hearted and one-sided.[6] That on Keats is quite inadequate; and Swinburne never gave the world a full appreciation of his master, Shelley. The essay on Rossetti is a review of the *Poems* of 1870, occasional in manner and biased by friendship. Other critical and controversial papers must be passed over here; nor is there room for comment upon Swinburne's letters, which contain much excellent informal criticism of his own and others' work. His highest merit as a critic may be indicated by his own words: "I can enjoy and applaud all good work.... I have never been able to see what should attract men to the profession of criticism but the noble pleasure of praising."[7]

We return to Swinburne's poetry. *Erechtheus* (1876) is a second tragedy on the Greek model, lofty in sentiment, learned in structure, diffuse in diction, and Mazzinean rather than truly classical in thought. Most of the contents of *Poems and Ballads, Second Series* (1878) were composed years before they were collected here. Unless this matter of dates be kept in mind, the solemn splendor of *Ave atque Vale* and the challenging paganism of *The Last Oracle* may give a false impression of Swinburne's development. The "perfume of old passion" envelops some of these poems, but the prevailing mood is elegiac, the poet seems to be withdrawn into the world of books, and in *A Vision of Spring in Winter* he bids farewell to his lost youth. It must not, however, be inferred from the serenity of this beautiful volume, that Swinburne's life was serene. The fact is that alcoholism was now rapidly undermining his health, and by 1879 his life was despaired of. At this juncture his legal adviser (not, as yet, an intimate friend), Walter Theodore Watts,[8] took charge of the situation, removed Swinburne from

Watts-Dunton and Putney

[6] The article "Wordsworth and Byron" (*Nineteenth Century,* April and May, 1884; reprinted in *Miscellanies,* 1886) was a reply to Matthew Arnold's exalted estimate of these two poets in his essay on Byron (1881). In the resultant controversy W. E. Henley, W. H. White ("Mark Rutherford"), Alfred Austin, and Andrew Lang took part. See S. C. Chew, *Byron in England* (1924), pp. 305-312; H. J. C. Grierson, *Lord Byron: Arnold and Swinburne* (1921).
[7] *Notes on Poems and Reviews* (1866), p. 22.
[8] Thomas Hake and Arthur Compton-Rickett, *The Life and Letters of Theodore Watts-Dunton* (2v, 1916); James Douglas, *Theodore Watts-Dunton: Poet, Novelist, Critic* (n.d.). — Watts (1832-1914), who took the additional surname Dunton late in life, was an East Anglian who came to London to practise law; was brought through his professional services into contact with Rossetti and his circle; and became the closest friend of Swinburne and the confidential

his London lodgings, and nursed him back to health at his home in Putney. The famous tragicomedy of life at "The Pines" had begun.

There was an immediate recovery of energy and productiveness. *Songs of the Springtides* and *Studies in Song* both appeared in 1880. Swinburne resumed and pushed to completion the dramatic trilogy which closed with *Mary Stuart* (1881), and *Tristram of Lyonesse* (1882). Much later *Tristram* was followed by a second Arthurian poem, *The Tale of Balen* (1896). With waning power and ever-increasing reliance upon self-imitations, a succession of volumes of miscellaneous poetry marked the passage of the years: *A Century of Roundels* (1883); *Poems and Ballads, Third Series* (1889), to which a misleading impression of freshness was imparted by the inclusion of a group of ballads in northern dialect written long since at Oxford; *Astrophel* (1894), largely literary and elegiac in themes; and *A Channel Passage* (1904), a most heterogeneous collection. During these years Swinburne was encouraged by Watts to expend much effort upon poetry of nature description to which his gifts were not suited. There are, however, gorgeous passages in *By the North Sea* and *A Swimmer's Dream*; and in *The Garden of Cymodoce* and *A Nympholept* suggestions of experiences of almost mystical intensity. Watts also undertook to mold Swinburne's political opinions with the consequence that the poet composed a number of rash anti-Gladstonian tirades against Home Rule. A nobler patriotism informs *Athens: an Ode,* where the parallel is drawn between Greece and England; the less formal ode on *The Armada*; and *The Commonweal,* Swinburne's contribution to the celebration of Victoria's Golden Jubilee (1887). In yet other poems there is a wistful groping after belief in personal immortality, which comes strangely from the once vociferous nihilist.

A continuing interest in the drama was evinced in *Marino Faliero* (1885), the last expression of Swinburne's Mazzinean ideals; *Locrine* (1887), the reworking of an Elizabethan theme interesting for its metrical experiments; *The Sisters* (1892), a tragedy of modern life barely redeemed from failure by passages of autobiographic interest; *Rosamund, Queen of the Lombards* (1899), on the ghastly, barbaric story of the queen forced by her husband to drink from her father's skull; and *The Duke of Gandia* (1908), a brief dramatic episode which is almost all that took form from an early plan to

The Tragedies

---

counselor of Rossetti. See H. W. Wright, "Unpublished Letters from Theodore Watts-Dunton to Swinburne," *RES,* x (1934). 129-155 (on Swinburne's tangled financial affairs in 1872 and showing Watts already in his capacity as a literary adviser). Watts nourished literary ambitions beyond his talents but had a considerable critical faculty and a flair for personalia which he exercised for many years in *The Athenaeum.* Some of his essays are reprinted in *Old Familiar Faces* (1916). *Poetry and the Renaissance of Wonder* (1916) consists of a reprint of the article on "Poetry" in *The Encyclopaedia Britannica,* ninth edition, and the introduction to the third volume of *Chambers' Cyclopaedia of English Literature* (1904). *Aylwin* (1898), a romance, was a momentary sensation because of the recognizable portraits of Rossetti and other celebrities it contained. Its gypsy-lore connects it with George Borrow. But the romanticism is thin and it is no longer readable. Watts-Dunton's poetry was collected in *The Coming of Love* (1897). There is some personal interest in a few pieces, and an intimate knowledge of gypsy life supplies an individual note; but on the whole his verse is of little moment. The problem of his influence on Swinburne has been much debated; for the present writer's view see S. C. Chew, *Swinburne,* pp. 273-278.

write a tragedy on the Borgias.[9] Swinburne's tragedies are to be numbered among the closet dramas which were mostly still-born of romanticism. The unpublished juvenile imitations of the Jacobeans are mere curiosities. *Chastelard* is informed with beauty and passion, but in the two later parts of the Scots trilogy Swinburne became bogged in a morass of complex historical intrigue. That he weighed carefully the conflicting evidence may be seen from his article on Mary Stuart in *The Encyclopaedia Britannica*; but the conscientiousness of the historian was no substitute for the technique of the dramatist which he did not possess. The characterization of Knox is admirable and the scene of Darnley's murder really well handled; but the general impression that remains after reading the trilogy is of mere torrential eloquence. *Marino Faliero* is of interest for the improvements in design and dramatic technique and the more convincing interpretations of motive as compared with Byron's play on the same subject. The later tragedies have little to commend them.

The long seclusion at Putney, while transforming the apostle of liberty into an opponent of Home Rule, an imperialist, and a champion of England against the Boers, changed also the disquieting phenomenon of the eighteen-sixties into a respectable little old man of letters; the "crimson mackaw among owls" (of Gosse's metaphor) had himself, through the agency of time and Watts, become owlish. To regret the transformation is an affectation. But for Watts, Swinburne would have died in 1879; and, besides, the Putney period provides the antithesis which is essential to the Swinburne legend. In 1904 the first collected edition of his poems and tragedies was published, prefaced by a remarkable survey and estimate of his achievement.[10] Swinburne died in April, 1909; and by his express direction the burial service was not read over his grave at Bonchurch on the Isle of Wight.

II

Style

The Word is omnipotent in Swinburne's poetry; language breaks through all structural barriers. The stanzaic patterns (of which he invented a large number while adapting to new effects many that were traditional) are invariably impeccable and often marvels of complex ingenuity. But in a larger sense his poems are often formless. When once the verbal music has begun there is no logical reason why it should ever cease; the only end is the end of exhaustion. The fact can easily be put to experimental test, that almost any stanza or scattered groups of stanzas may be omitted without loss of any, save a quantitative, effect. No developing sequence of emotions and ideas is interrupted by such excisions. The music—whether the bright,

---

[9] See also the fragmentary, posthumous prose "chronicle," *Lucretia Borgia*, ed. Randolph Hughes (1943).

[10] Unaccountably omitted from the Bonchurch Edition of Swinburne's *Works*. — About 1900 Swinburne wrote but did not publish a vigorous and vitriolic reply to those who accused him of having abandoned the political opinions and literary tastes of his earlier life. See C. K. Hyder, "Swinburne: *Changes of Aspect* and *Short Notes*," *PMLA*, LVIII (1943). 223-244.

swift melody of the Spring Chorus in *Atalanta,* or the convolutions of *Dolores,* or the muted notes of *The Garden of Proserpine,* or the sultry monotone of *Laus Veneris,* or the plangent passion of *The Triumph of Time,* or the elaborate harmonies of *Ave atque Vale,* or the trumpet-call of *Mater Triumphalis,* or the full orchestration of the *Prelude* to *Tristram* and *The Last Oracle,* or such dexterous counterpointing as *At a Month's End*— sings itself in the memory; but it is immaterial which stanzas are got by heart. No other poet of equal rank has implanted fewer individual lines of verse in the general memory. The too luxuriant alliteration is mere ara- besque, not (as in Gerard Hopkins) a series of hammer-blows to rivet an image upon the mind. The flower-soft spilth of fluent verbiage leaves behind it but a thin precipitate of imagery. The virtuoso plays innumerable varia- tions upon a few themes—the sea and the sun, flowers and foam and blood. A concordance to Swinburne's poetry (did one exist) would reveal the meagerness of his vocabulary and the constant repetition of a few character- istic epithets in new stanzaic patterns. His color sense was weak; there is no such variety and gradation of tone as is observed in Keats's and Tenny- son's poetry; and to a degree greater even than Shelley Swinburne depended upon effects of light.

This is not to reaffirm the old charge that Swinburne "lacked thought," *Fatalism* that he was, as Browning said, "a fuzz of words." On the contrary, till his *and* retirement to Putney he was sensitively responsive to contemporary ideas. *Satiety* In *Atalanta in Calydon* the pseudo-Hellenism [11] made for a sense of detach- ment from modern issues; but the bitter fatalism of the tragedy—the es- sential nobility of helpless man in the presence of malignant fate—was a direct challenge to the religious ideas of Victorian England. The philosophy of despair enunciated in the second Chorus and culminating in the tre- mendous indictment of "the supreme evil, God," relates *Atalanta* to the *Rubáiyát* and *The City of Dreadful Night.* The shimmering beauty of the verse, the metrical artifices, the far-off idealized landscape, and the seeming remoteness of the theme obscured to many contemporaries the implications of the play; but they are clear to us. The Chorus beginning "We have seen thee, O Love, thou art fair" associates love with pain and bitterness and death and connects *Atalanta* with *Chastelard.* In that drama Mary Stuart is the *femme fatale* of the romantic imagination and her lover is the victim of a *belle dame sans merci.* Thus *Chastelard* points forward to those pieces in *Poems and Ballads* which electrified the English imagination—*Laus Veneris, Dolores, Anactoria, Faustine,* and the rest. To our taste these may seem a little tawdry and obvious both in sentiments and rhythms; but to Swinburne's contemporaries, accustomed to the ideal of domestic love set before them by Tennyson, they were "a wind of liberation," at once destroy- ing and invigorating. The positive motif of *Poems and Ballads* was hedon- istic, anticipating the doctrine which Pater was presently to impose upon

---

[11] For opposing views of *Atalanta* and of *Erechtheus* see W. R. Rutland, *Swinburne, a Nineteenth Century Hellene* (1931), and Bush, ch. x.

the "aesthetic" generation. The negative note was that of satiety, disillusion, and despair. Thus was the range of poetry extended beyond the limitations erected by the poet laureate. It is not surprising that young men and women, chanting this new music that seemed to them miraculous, hailed Swinburne as a portent.

Liberty may relax into license; and license brings satiety; satiety leads to perversity; and perversity breeds despondency and despair. Bitter is the fruit of these flowers of evil. Love is associated with Death, as cause with consequence. The sequence closes with somber probings into the ultimate mystery; and upon that dark quest Swinburne, in *Ave atque Vale,* led his readers far into "that low land" where the "sun is silent." To this theme he returned in later poems, in a mood of elegiac wistfulness (as in *A Vision of Spring in Winter*), or of passionate regret for the "perfume" of lost days (as in *At a Month's End*), or of almost exultant recognition of Time's power over all things (as in *A Forsaken Garden*). The retrospective mood dominated his poetry from a period of life when normal persons are still living in the full tide of the present.

But liberty need not degenerate into license; it may be a stern and exacting discipline. As such it is celebrated in many of Swinburne's noblest poems. He was not, as he is sometimes described, the prophet merely of a federated republic of Europe or a "Parliament of Man." He proclaimed himself the herald and "trumpet" of Mater Triumphalis, Hertha, the Life-Force working not only in each individual but in the social order. Society cannot progress save through the exertion of conscience and reason; and it is this action, thus working, that Swinburne contemplated when, in *A Song of Italy* and in the more visionary and less topical of the *Songs before Sunrise,* he hailed the Republic which is to be. For that ideal the individual must be glad to die. This sacrifice is the theme of *Super Flumina Babylonis, The Pilgrims,* and *Teresias.* It is implicit in *Erechtheus,* which is more nearly related to Mazzinean doctrine than to Greek thought. In the thick darkness of the cosmos which seemed to envelop him when Mazzini's dream vanished, Swinburne found no star to guide him "save his own soul." This thought, which enters his poetry in the *Prelude* to *Songs before Sunrise,* is the motive of many poems of his middle years and the burden of *The Altar of Righteousness,* his final testament to the world. The thought is positivist and secularist. A confidence in man's ability to conquer evil leads the poet to the conclusion of his *Hymn of Man:* "Glory to Man in the highest, for Man is the master of things!" [12] That such an assertion would be ridiculous were it not pathetic is obvious to us who have lived amid the disasters of the twentieth century. But it reflected the confidence of a time which John Morley described as "an epoch of hearts uplifted with hope, and brains

The "Life-Force"

---

[12] The *Hymn of Man* was composed for recitation at the anti-Catholic Council which met at Naples in 1869 during the sitting of the Oecumenical Council in Rome. This meeting adjourned, however, before the poem was completed. See Lafourcade, *Swinburne, a Literary Biography,* pp. 172-175.

made active with sober and manly reason for the common good." [18] Moreover, Swinburne does not say that this mastery over "things" is yet attained; it is to be realized when the sun has risen, and before that glad confident morning there must be toil and sacrifice. Hard tasks are imposed upon the individual for the benefit of the race.

[18] Lord Morley, *Recollections* (1917), II. 365.

XXXII

The Background: The Victorian Decline (1868-1901) and the Aftermath (1901-1939)

The Late Victorian Period,[1] three decades of waning confidence, commercial and industrial rivalries, imperial expansion, and increasing political, economic, social, and spiritual anxieties, extends from the beginning of Gladstone's first administration in 1868 to the death of Queen Victoria in 1901 and the close of the Boer War in 1902. In literary history it extends from the beginning of the Aesthetic Revival with Pater's first essays (1867-1868) to the death of Ruskin in 1900 and of Spencer in 1903. The activities of many of the writers already surveyed continued, but with few exceptions they are more characteristic of an earlier era. Thus, Herbert Spencer's huge project unfolded, but its inception dates from the mid-century; Ruskin had still to publish many volumes, but his work of most value had been done by 1868; Morris's career as a Socialist was yet to come, but his best poetry had been written; and though Rossetti and Swinburne overlap the dividing line (the latter by many years), Rossetti is obviously a mid-century figure and Swinburne's later poetry is in the main derivative from his earlier. On the other hand, though Meredith published his first noteworthy book as early as 1859, he seems to belong beyond the watershed; and Hardy's first published novel dates from 1871.

The High-tide of Liberalism The extension of the franchise (1867) brought the Liberals into power on a tide of confidence in 1868. Among the writers who gave expression to the rationalistic liberalism and radicalism characteristic of the time were Frederic Harrison[2] (1831-1923) and Sir Leslie Stephen[3] (1832-1904). On

---

[1] R. C. K. Ensor, *England, 1870-1914* (1936); G. M. Trevelyan, *British History in the Nineteenth Century* (1922) and *English Social History* (1942), chap. xviii; Elie Halévy, *Histoire du peuple anglais: Epilogue I: 1895-1905* (1926); G. P. Gooch, *History of Modern Europe, 1878-1919* (1923); J. H. Clapham, *Economic History of Great Britain*, II (1933), for the period before 1886; R. E. Prothero (Lord Ernle), *English Farming, Past and Present* (1927); Sidney and Beatrice Webb, *The History of Trade Unionism* (rev. ed., 1920); and the biographies of Disraeli, Gladstone, Parnell, Salisbury, Chamberlain, and other leaders.

[2] A leader of the Positivists and active in political reform, working-class legislation, and jurisprudence. Harrison's writings, often trenchantly controversial, represent but a fraction of his accomplishment. *The Choice of Books* (1886), the studies assembled in *Early Victorian Literature* (1896), and the life of Ruskin (1902)—an act of homage by a disciple to his master—are on a level of serenity above the battles in which he engaged in public life. See also his *Collected Essays* (4v, 1907-1908) and *Selected Essays* (1925).

[3] Stephen applied the principles of rationalism to the interpretation of the history of ideas. The world of the "Enlightenment" was his intellectual home; and *English Thought in the Eighteenth Century* (1876-1881) his most massive work. His other principal book is *The English Utilitarians* (1900). Relatively lighter fare is to be had in *Hours in a Library* (1892). *An Agnostic's Apology* (1893) is characteristic not only of Stephen (who had renounced holy

taking office Gladstone put through three great measures of reform: the Irish Church Disestablishment Act; the first Irish Land Act (a half-way measure but a step toward the solution of the problem of landlords, tenants, and eviction for non-payment of rent)'; and the Education Act, which established primary education upon a national basis, practically abolished illiteracy, and disciplined the hitherto uncared-for hordes of slum children. Army reform and the beginnings of naval expansion were signs that England read correctly the omens drawn from the victory of Prussia over France in 1870-1871. The effect of German predominance on the Continent was to dampen in England the cosmopolitan liberal spirit. A wave of pessimism and materialism, spreading across the Channel from defeated France, swept many men of letters into an aesthetic isolation from practical life and was one cause of the "Art for Art's Sake" movement. But there were other writers who remained in close touch with political and social events and were strongly affected by the Irish Question, imperial expansion, and the economic decline. In retrospect the growing German peril, while the struggle for colonies, raw materials, and markets developed, is seen as the most significant current of the time. Sir George Chesney's sensational pamphlet, *The Battle of Dorking* (1871), brought home a realization of the German threat and the possibility of invasion, but the alarm it created soon subsided. The traditional enmity with France loomed larger in the contemporary consciousness because of the intense rivalry with England in Africa.

The election of 1874 showed that the Liberal impetus of the past six years had spent its force; Gladstone's ministry had become, in Disraeli's famous phrase, "a row of extinct volcanoes." A new personality now came to the fore. By 1870 Ireland had recovered from the prostration which followed the great famine, and the movement for the repeal of the Act of Union was again under way. The Home Rule party, an outgrowth from the older Fenian Movement, emerged in 1874, and in the following year Charles Stewart Parnell began his obstructionist tactics in the House of Commons. The Irish Land League, a strong influence upon the Irish Literary Revival, was formed in 1879. Ireland was now governed by coercion, and the problem of a settlement of the Irish Question was a legacy from the Conservatives to Gladstone in 1880.

Parnell and Home Rule

During his second administration (1874-1880) Disraeli was anxious to demonstrate the connection between Conservatism and social reform. New sanitary measures were initiated, but before much could be accomplished the economic depression of 1876-1881 set in and the problem of the unemployed came to the fore. Disraeli's interest centered in foreign affairs and the expansion of the British Empire. The day was long past when he had described the colonies as "millstones" around England's neck. After the

---

orders) but of his time. Much of his energy was expended upon the *DNB* of which he was the first chief editor. In all his writings there is much light but little warmth. See his *Collected Essays* (10v, 1907); F. W. Maitland, *Life and Letters of Sir Leslie Stephen* (1906); Desmond MacCarthy, *Leslie Stephen* (1937). Stephen was the brother of Sir James Fitzjames Stephen the philosopher, and the father of Virginia Woolf the novelist.

Mutiny the government of India had been transferred from the old East India Company to the Crown; and in 1876, following the purchase of the shares in the Suez Canal (1875) which made England more conscious of her destiny in the East, Victoria was proclaimed Empress of India. The Near East Crisis of 1875-1878, temporarily composed at the Congress of Berlin (1878), was provoked in part by dread of Russian expansion, in part by generous indignation against the Ottoman treatment of subject Christian populations in the Balkans. This indignation was fanned by Gladstone in the most eloquent of Victorian political pamphlets, *The Bulgarian Horrors and the Question of the East* (1876). In South Africa Zulu barbarities were suppressed and the Transvaal was annexed for the first time (1877). On the Northwest frontier of India the Afghan War led to Lord Roberts' triumph at Kandahar (1879).

How far-flung were England's powers and responsibilities was made manifest by these and other events. But in reaction from Tory "jingoism" the Liberals were reinstated in 1880. The chief successes of Gladstone's second ministry were the new Land Act for Ireland (1881), which gave greater security of tenure and an assurance of equitable rent; and the extension of the franchise to miners and agricultural laborers. The long-predicted decline in agriculture now moved downward precipitously, hastened by the importation of frozen meat and the increased consumption of American wheat. The position of England as "the workshop of the world" was imperiled in the Continental countries, which were becoming industrialized and were erecting tariff walls against English goods. The early eighteen-eighties saw the rise of Socialism and of the new Birmingham radicalism of which Joseph Chamberlain was spokesman. Attacks upon irresponsible wealth divorced from association with the land helped to stimulate class hatred. The famous "unauthorized program" of Chamberlain and Dilke was one expression of radical sentiment.

Economic Depression

The problem of the relations of the English and the Cape Dutch was another legacy from Disraeli to Gladstone, who after the defeat at Majuba decided to cut England's losses and recognize the independence of the Transvaal. This proved to be but a temporary palliative, for the grievances of the "Uitlanders" remained to plague England in the closing years of the century. Turkish misrule of Egypt and the mismanagement of the Khedive's finances led to the British occupation of that country in 1882, with the suppression of Arabi's revolt. A premature effort to conquer the Sudan resulted in the death of General Gordon at Khartoum (1885), a blow from which Gladstone's prestige never entirely recovered. Only after England's predominant position in Egypt had been established by Cromer was she able to extend her power permanently in the South (1898). The immediate consequence of the disaster of 1885 was the defeat of Gladstone at the polls. Lord Salisbury's first Conservative government proved to be of short duration and little consequence, for the Home Rule Party under Parnell held the balance of power between the two English parties. Gladstone came to

Egypt

an agreement with Parnell with the result that Salisbury was defeated and Gladstone's third ministry was formed. Conspicuous among his lieutenants were two prominent men of letters, John Morley [4] (1838-1923) and James Bryce [5] (1838-1922). The First Home Rule Bill, embracing Protestant Ulster in its scope, was introduced (1886). In the general election consequent upon the defeat of this measure in Parliament the Conservatives with the Liberal Unionists who had seceded from the Gladstonian Liberals obtained a majority over the latter party and the Irish Home Rulers combined. The new ministry resorted to the strictest coercion in governing Ireland, with Arthur James Balfour [6] (1848-1930) as Irish Secretary. The attempt to discredit Parnell by means of the forged letters published in *The Times* roused intense feelings which made a rational settlement impossible; and in 1890 the O'Shea divorce case in which Parnell was cited as co-respondent shattered the leader's prestige with the tragic consequence that the solution of the Irish Question was postponed for a generation.

The First Home Rule Bill

Meanwhile, during Salisbury's second ministry (1886-1892), there was social unrest but also social progress. The theories of Henry George set forth in *Progress and Poverty* (1877) were of widening influence. *Fabian Essays* (1889) by Sidney Webb and other advanced thinkers was followed by William Booth's powerful exposure of the social question, *In Darkest England and the Way Out* (1890). Robert Blatchford's *Merrie England* (1894) was another stimulus to practical action. Statistical research exposed conditions in the slums of London and other great cities; great strides were made in municipal reform; and volunteer "settlements" such as Toynbee Hall sprang up in various localities. Symptomatic of the changed balance of

Social Progress

---

[4] Afterwards Viscount Morley. His career as a statesman, which does not concern us here, overshadows his claim to notice as a writer. He had already acquired a reputation for aggressive radicalism and agnosticism and for his forceful literary criticism when he became editor of *The Fortnightly Review* in 1867. (See E. M. Everett, *The Party of Humanity*, Chapel Hill, 1939). In 1878 he initiated as editor the EML series of biographies. His own writings have largely but not exclusively to do with the "Enlightenment" and the Utilitarians. Of both these movements he was the Late Victorian heir and representative. His Stoicism and uncompromising moral integrity, wide intellectuality, and weight of style made him one of the great forces of the dying Liberalism of the late century. His literary judgments, expressed with a restrained eloquence, moral fervor, and on occasion grave irony, are often founded upon values not strictly literary. His principal books are *Voltaire* (1872); *Rousseau* (1873); *Diderot* (1878); *Burke* (1879); *Walpole* (1889); *Studies in Literature* (1890); *The Life of W. E. Gladstone* (1903); *Literary Essays* (1906); *Recollections* (1917). The last, a noble *apologia* not so much for himself as for Victorian Liberalism, will perhaps be remembered longest. — *Works* (15v, 1921). F. W. Hirst, *Early Life and Letters of John Morley* (2v, 1927); G. M. Harper, *Lord Morley and Other Essays* (1920); J. D. MacCallum, *Lord Morley's Criticism of English Poetry and Prose* (Princeton, 1921); F. M. Knickerbocker, *Free Minds: John Morley and His Friends* (1943); Warren Staebler, *The Liberal Mind of John Morley* (1943); Algernon Cecil, *Six Oxford Thinkers* (1909), pp. 252-301.

[5] Afterwards Viscount Bryce. He made an early reputation with the brilliant historical sketch, *The Holy Roman Empire* (1864). *The American Commonwealth* (1888), a study of institutions in the United States, is a classic in its field. From wide experiences of travel he made several books, notably *Transcaucasia and Ararat* (1877). — H. A. L. Fisher, *James Bryce* (2v, 1927).

[6] Afterwards prime minister and Earl of Balfour. The claim of Balfour to be taken quite seriously as a philosopher was hindered by a reputation for dilettantism and flippancy, but his *Defence of Philosophic Doubt* (1879), *Foundations of Belief* (1895), and later studies in theism reveal a critical mind of considerable power, though Balfour contributed little to the philosophic currents of his time.

political power was the popular press, led by Harmsworth's *Daily Mail,* which reached an enormous semi-educated public and exerted a dangerous influence. In foreign affairs Salisbury's second ministry is memorable for the policy of "splendid isolation" which kept England without an ally while the Continental powers were forming the rival groups of the Triple Alliance (Germany, Austro-Hungary, and Italy.) and the Dual Alliance (France and Russia). Till the close of the century English policy was on the whole Germanophile, a deterioration in relations not setting in till the Kaiser embarked upon his program of naval expansion. French relations remained precarious because of disputes over spheres of influence in Africa. The Fashoda incident of 1898 was the culmination of a series of misunderstandings and brought the two countries to the verge of war. Not for several years thereafter did the growing danger of Germany lead to a reorientation of policy resulting in the Entente Cordiale. But this is to look ahead.

The Second Home Rule Bill   By 1892 the Unionists [7] had fulfilled their mandate and in the general election Gladstone was returned to office, though not to power because he was dependent for a majority upon the support of the Irish members. By this association he was committed to a Second Home Rule Bill, which met defeat in the House of Lords. On Gladstone's resignation in 1894 the Earl of Rosebery [8] (1847-1929) became prime minister. The Liberal interlude of 1892-1895 is notable for the formation of the Independent Labor Party under Keir Hardie and for the development of imperialistic thought, expressed in the political world by Chamberlain, in South Africa by Cecil Rhodes, and in the world of letters by Rudyard Kipling. In the election of 1895 the Unionists swept the country but were forced to share power with the radical Chamberlain who had allied himself with the Unionists on the Irish issue. Chamberlain, though never prime minister, was as potent as Salisbury and more potent than A. J. Balfour, who succeeded Salisbury in 1902. He chose the cabinet post of Colonial Secretary which had hitherto been held in small estimation. In so choosing he rode the crest of the wave

Imperialism   of Imperialism. This reached its climax of grandiose display at the Queen's Diamond Jubilee of 1897; and though Kipling sounded an impressive warning in the *Recessional,* the country drifted confidently towards war in South Africa. The steps towards war were, briefly, these: the intensification of the

The Boer War   hostility between the old Boer farmers of the Transvaal and the new British diamond-miners and gold-miners; the increasing power of Rhodes's Chartered Company; the settlement of Rhodesia; the haste to push northward in order to check German expansion east and west which threatened to block the British dream of an empire extending from the Cape to Cairo; the impatience of Rhodes with the Boer President, Paul Kruger, which

---

[7] The coalition of Conservatives and anti-Home-Rule Liberals and radicals called themselves Unionists because the maintenance of the Act of Union of Ireland and Great Britain was their basic principle.

[8] In literature as in political life Rosebery failed to fulfill his early promise, but his brief monographs on Pitt (1891) and Peel (1899) and the more famous *Napoleon, the Last Phase* (1900) are historical miniatures revealing a gift for characterization.

culminated in Dr. Jameson's Raid (1895); and the decision of Chamberlain and Sir Alfred Milner to settle the question at issue by war. English men of letters were as sharply divided as statesmen as to the justification of the conflict which began in 1899. Public confidence was rudely shaken by the stupidity of English strategy, bad organization, and underestimation of the Boers' powers of resistance. Victoria's reign ended (1901) during the final, terrible phase of the Boers' guerilla warfare and Kitchener's concentration camps. The treaty of peace (1902) led on to the wise and magnanimous pacification accomplished by Sir Henry Campbell-Bannerman after the Liberal triumph of 1905.

It is customary today to look back upon the reign of Edward VII (1901- *The* 1910) as a period of opulent ease and blind complacency. For this notion *Reign of* there is no foundation in the facts. At no time in English history has the *Edward* strife of parties been more bitter. The differences between Balfour and *VII* Chamberlain over fiscal policy led to the Unionist defeat and the return of the Liberals to office, but the outstanding features of the election of 1905 were the appearance of Labor as a separate party in the house of commons and the power exercised by John Redmond, the Irish leader. A contentious Unionist minority, a series of industrial strikes, and the militant activities of the advocates of woman suffrage embittered public life. During the pre-war years of the reign of George V these and other disturbing movements were intensified, but they were already apparent in his father's reign. Europe moved through a series of crises—over German claims in Morocco in 1905 and 1911; over Austria's annexation of Bosnia in 1908; and a chain of events links the first of these to the outbreak of the Italo-Turkish war in Tripoli (1911) and the two Balkan wars (1912-1913) which were preludes to the catastrophe of 1914. Germany's intransigence in the matter of the limitation of naval armaments led to the Entente Cordiale with France (1904) and the later understanding with Russia which produced the Triple Entente as a counterpoise to the Triple Alliance. For England's military preparedness—such as it was—the chief credit attaches to the War Secretary, Lord Haldane.[9] The increased naval appropriations forced upon England were the main cause of Lloyd George's sensational budget of 1909, which in turn caused the bitter quarrel between the two houses of Parliament. After two general elections the Lords' veto-power was abolished by the Parliament Act of 1911. The Liberal government under Asquith (who had succeeded Campbell-Bannerman as prime minister in 1908) attempted a new solution of the Irish Question, but racial and religious antagonisms were even stronger than they had been in 1886 and the plan to include Ulster in a scheme satisfactory to the Roman Catholic majority of Irishmen met with an opposition which under the leadership of Sir Edward Carson had almost

[9] Richard B. Haldane (1856-1928), later Viscount Haldane, brought from Germany, his "spiritual home" (his own famous phrase which temporarily ruined his career in 1914), the knowledge of Schopenhauer whose *World as Will and Idea* he translated (1883-1886). Haldane's weightiest philosophic writings—*The Reign of Relativity* (1921) and *The Philosophy of Humanism* (1922)—belong to his closing years.

reached the point of open rebellion in the summer of 1914. These were some of the principal factors making for a pervasive sense of social disintegration which, though more fully expressed in the post-war years, was already a "note" in modern literature before the outbreak of the Great War.

Beyond August, 1914, it is unnecessary to carry this sketch of the political and social background. Any indication of the underlying and immediate causes of the war would take us beyond our space and beside our purpose. It is impossible to generalize as to the mood in which the English people entered the conflict. There were those who, like Rupert Brooke, welcomed it as a relief from domestic controversy and the feeling of personal frustration. Others felt the pity and tragedy of the breakdown of western civilization, and to this feeling John Masefield gave expression in his poem *August, 1914.* Yet others, looking beyond the dark present, discerned a brighter future, as did H. G. Wells in his pamphlet, *The War that Will End War,* and in other utopian visions. The contrast between the hope of a better world and the actuality of the Peace of Versailles; between the politicians' promise of "a land fit for heroes to live in" and the actuality of unemployment, distressed areas, strikes, the long-drawn agony of the struggle in Ireland before the establishment of the Free State, the rise of the Continental dictatorships, the economic depression, and the waning prestige of the League of Nations—these and other contrasts between the vision of desire and the desolating reality confirmed in many thoughtful minds the sense that old moorings had been cast off, that humanity was adrift upon a chartless sea, that inherited criteria of conduct no longer possessed authority, and that all values had been discredited. True, there were still some voices bidding men hope, but the prevailing mood was one of futility and frustration. During the Long Armistice those able to interpret the signs of the times were uttering warnings of a worse disaster to follow in a world where, as Yeats said,

Between Two Wars

> The best lack all conviction, while the worst
> Are full of passionate intensity.

XXXIII

George Meredith

I

George Meredith [1] (1828-1909) declared that he would "most horribly haunt" anyone who should write his biography. After his death it became known that there were facts about his origin he wished to conceal. They are trivial, but their concealment is significant. Did he hope to dictate the estimate of himself to be held by posterity? Were we to see in him something of proud, elaborate, Olympian indifference, with much of the clearsightedness, touched with light malignancy, of the Comic Spirit? Admit a suspicion of "the taint of personality" and he is seen, not seated overhead with this Spirit, but himself the target of its volleys of silvery laughter. The poet who described the distempered devil of Self was caught in the snares of that "scaly Dragon-fowl." His proud declaration that "station is nought, nor footways laurel-strewn" consorts ill with evident restiveness under by no means total popular indifference to his work.

But though he did not take the world into his confidence, there was no *Birth and* self-deception. Evan Harrington, who was ashamed of his low birth and *Breeding* "would be a gentleman," is a piercing satire upon Meredith's own mortification because of his socially inferior connections. Of Welsh and Irish descent, he was the son and grandson of naval outfitters at Portsmouth. His mother died when he was a child; he was estranged from his father; and two impressionable years (1842-1844) were spent at a Moravian school at Neuwied on the Rhine. Here a wise and gentle education encouraged a tolerant and cosmopolitan outlook upon life. Here also he acquired a love

[1] *Works*, Memorial Edition (29v, 1909-1912); *Poetical Works*; ed. G. M. Trevelyan (1912); *Letters*, ed. W. M. Meredith (2v, 1912); *Letters to Edward Clodd and C. K. Shorter*, ed. T. J. Wise (privately printed, 1913); *Letters to Alice Meynell* (1923). — M. B. Forman, *Bibliography*, (1922) and *Meredithiana* (1924); S. M. Ellis, *George Meredith: his Life and Friends in Relation to his Work* (1919); J. B. Priestley, *George Meredith* (EML Series, 1926); René Galland, *George Meredith: les cinquante premières années* (Paris, 1923); M. S. Gretton, *The Writings and Life of George Meredith* (1926); R. E. Sencourt, *The Life of George Meredith* (1929); J. H. E. Crees, *George Meredith: A Study of his Works and Personality* (1918); E. J. Bailey, *The Novels of George Meredith* (1907); James Moffatt, *George Meredith: A Primer to the Novels* (1909); J. W. Beach, *The Comic Spirit in George Meredith* (1911); Constantin Photiades, *George Meredith: sa vie, son imagination, son art, sa doctrine* (Paris, 1910; trans. by A. Price, 1913); H. B. Forman, *George Meredith: Some Early Appreciations* (1909); J. A. Hammerton, *George Meredith in Anecdote and Criticism* (1909); G. M. Trevelyan, *The Poetry and Philosophy of George Meredith* (1907); Robert Peel, *The Creed of a Victorian Pagan* (Cambridge, Mass., 1931); M. E. Mackay, *Meredith et la France* (Paris, 1937); J. W. Beach, *The Concept of Nature*, ch. xviii; Baker, viii (1937). chs. vii-ix; O. J. Campbell, "Some Influences of Meredith's Philosophy upon his Fiction," *Univ. of Wisconsin Stud. in Lang. and Lit.*, ii (1919). 323-339; C. D. Locock, "Notes on the Technique of Meredith's Poetry," *ESt*, xlvi (1912-1913). 86-97.

for the extravagances of German romanticism. Features of his style that suggest Carlyle are in part imitations of Jean Paul Richter. Meredith had not long returned to England when the generous liberalism of 1848, sweeping from a Continent in revolt, helped to mold his political opinions. He now met Thomas Love Peacock and fell in love with his daughter, a widow nine years his elder. After their marriage (1849) they lived with or near Peacock, whose influence was strong upon him.[2] Peacock had drawn cranks and eccentrics; he had attacked sentimentality and egoism; he had affirmed the intellectual equality of women; he believed in the corrective power of laughter. There is no sign of this influence in Meredith's first book, *Poems* (1851), which contained the first version of *Love in the Valley* and won Tennyson's commendation; but the Peacockian strain of fantasy, mockery, and grace is present in *The Shaving of Shagpat* (1855), an oriental extravaganza hovering on the brink of allegory, in which are the germs of Meredith's later advocacy of the active life in accord with nature. Different ingredients are mixed in *Farina: a Legend of Cologne* (1857): romantic supernaturalism purposely reduced to absurdity, sentimentality half-serious and half-mocking, and bits of picaresque that give promise of *Harry Richmond*. Meredith was still experimenting.

Meanwhile his marriage had proved disastrous and in 1858 his wife left him, going to the Continent with a lover. She died in 1861. Something of his own experience went into the tragic-ironic narrative poem, *Modern Love* (1862), and it influenced the choice of unsuccessful marriage as the subject of several of the novels. A run-away wife and the problem of a father left to educate his son form the autobiographical background of *The Ordeal of Richard Feverel* (1859). Though not his greatest book, this is one of the most memorable, for its freshness and the plenitude of joy and pity. Already the defects of Meredith's qualities are apparent: the tendency towards too elaborate characterization; the overplus of shadowy minor figures; the aphorisms which flash too frequently, though as yet they are not dark with excessive light. The greatness of the book does not lie in the entire conception, which is incoherent, but in certain scenes—the idyllic raptures of first love; the news of his son's marriage brought to Sir Austin Feverel; the "Enchantress" chapter (though this is overwrought); the parting of Richard and Lucy; and Richard's walk in the forest after hearing of his son's birth. Whether the final catastrophe of Lucy's death is properly prepared for or whether Meredith forces the issue has always been disputed. The basic irony is in the antithesis between romance and reality; and the satire is expended upon a system of education through which human nature insists upon breaking. There are reminiscences of Sterne, Dickens, and Bulwer; but the novel breaks new ground. Beneath the brilliant satire and lyrical romanticism there is an idea that is fundamental to all Meredith's thought: Richard should have worked to-

Richard
Feverel

[2] A. H. Able, *George Meredith and Thomas Love Peacock: A Study in Literary Influences* (Philadelphia, 1933).

wards brain and spirit through the blood; but this natural development was thwarted; and when one part of the Meredithian Triad is sundered from the rest, disaster follows.

Evan Harrington [3] (1860) showed no advance. It concerns the conflict of Evan's love for Rose Jocelyn with his duty to pay his dead father's debts and maintain the business which he had inherited and of which he was ashamed. In the end he is ashamed of his shame. The theme is not rich enough for a long novel and it is expanded by the story of Evan's three beautiful sisters who storm society by making advantageous marriages. In this study of snobbery there is thus a conflict of different social strata. The portraits from real life are of Meredith himself and his three aunts. The book wounded his father, as well it might, for the "great Mel," the dead tailor, is drawn from family reminiscences of Meredith's grandfather. `Evan Harrington`

Modern Love and Poems of the English Roadside appeared in 1862. The title poem, though founded upon Meredith's own marital unhappiness, presents a more complex situation than that of his own experience.[4] In intensity and beauty of phrase, variety of styles to suit the different situations, incisiveness of psychological analysis, dramatic power, and grasp of character it stands alone among Meredith's poems. Among other things in this volume, *Juggling Jerry* and *The Old Chartist* are monologues somewhat reminiscent of Browning's manner, and the *Ode to the Spirit of Earth in Autumn* [5] is the first of Meredith's important nature poems written under the influence of the evolutionary concept. `Modern Love`

In 1864 Meredith married again. The union was a happy one.[6] In the same year he published *Sandra Belloni* (originally called *Emilia in England*). In the character of Wilfrid Pole he offered his most elaborate analysis of sentimentalism, and in the characters of Pole's sisters, of social affectation. Opposed to Wilfrid is the exquisite figure of Sandra, as yet an immature girl but already adumbrating that "ideal of the heroical feminine type" to which she would approximate in the sequel. The course of Pole's degeneration as the sentimental egoist is traced downward to the point where his story would later be resumed. But before that sequel appeared, Meredith turned aside to a rural theme and in *Rhoda Fleming* (1865) challenged comparison with George Eliot. Dahlia Fleming, a girl of the yeoman class, has been seduced by Edward Blancove, the squire's son. His nefarious design to marry her off to a bribed ruffian and the reappearance of the latter's wife `Sandra Belloni` `Rhoda Fleming`

[3] In 1860 Meredith became literary adviser to the firm of Chapman and Hall. He rejected Mrs. Henry Wood's *East Lynne* (1861), which became a best-seller, Butler's *Erewhon*, which became famous, and early work of G. B. Shaw. On the other hand, he gave encouragement to Hardy and Gissing. See B. W. Matz, "George Meredith as Publisher's Reader," *Fortnightly Review*, n.s., LXXXVI (1909). 282-298.

[4] The story is told in fifty sixteen-line sonnet-like stanzas. Having a definite plot, involving four characters, it resembles the Victorian sonnet-sequences, such as Mrs. Browning's and Rossetti's, less than it does William Ellery Leonard's *Two Lives*.

[5] This is a reworking of *South-West Wind in the Woodland* (1851).

[6] Meredith's sorrow and quest of consolation at the time of his wife's death (1885) are recorded in *A Faith on Trial*, the *Hymn to Colour*, and other poems included in *A Reading of Earth* (1888).

at the moment to prevent this iniquity are of the stuff of melodrama, as is Edward's sudden change of heart. The story centers in the efforts of the strong-minded sister, Rhoda, to right her sister's name. Dahlia, far from belonging to the Victorian type of "fallen" woman, develops, as do all Meredith's women, under adversity. Rustic characters providing a lighter vein are well drawn but without that affectionate intimacy of understanding which George Eliot and Hardy display and with a not altogether agreeable "superior" tolerance. This novel is strangely off the line of Meredith's predictable development.

Vittoria

Sandra's story is continued in *Vittoria* (1866), Meredith's only historical novel. It deals with the outbreak of 1848 in Milan against the Austrians and the Italian defeat at Novara.[7] Political and military events are, however, impressionisticly related or hinted at, and though there are recognizable historical portraits (memorably of "the Chief," who, though not named, is Mazzini), and though the scene is crowded with soldiers, politicians, and conspirators, the heroine is the central figure and her growth in dignity and personality from the promise of her girlhood is the central theme. There are superb episodes, such as the meeting of the plotters on the mountain behind Stresa, the performance at La Scala when Vittoria sings the patriotic song which initiates the revolt, and the duel in the mountain pass; but much of the story is obscurely told by indirection. Wilfrid Pole reappears among the minor figures, but his sentimentalism is of small consequence amid great events. Meredith's concept of the Risorgimento was strongly influenced by Swinburne, contact with whom affected not only his political ideas but his naturalistic philosophy.

Harry Richmond

In *The Adventures of Harry Richmond* (1871) Meredith mingled realism and fantasy in the strangest fashion, bringing together characters taken directly from English life and others that are the creation of his poetic humor. Though told from the point of view of the son, Harry, this is really the story of the father, the magnificent and, in the end, disgraced charlatan, Richmond Roy. The general tone is of comic and romantic extravagance, but there is tragedy in Harry's gradual disillusionment. To the boy his father had been all that was wonderful; the shock is the greater as he is revealed in his true character. The revelation culminates in the famous scene of Squire Beltham's denunciation of the rogue. The women in the story are among the most attractive in all the Meredithian gallery of radiant female portraits. The exuberance of Meredith's fancy made the story far too long, but the vitality never flags. He seems, for once, to have written solely for the pleasure of creating and without thought of imparting any doctrine.

Beauchamp's Career

Beauchamp's Career (1875) is a love story combined with politics. The love story is more intelligible than are the affairs of state, for the distinctions among grades and shades of political opinion are tenuous and are obscured

---

[7] Meredith was special correspondent of *The Morning Post* during the Austro-Italian War of 1866. — Between 1860 and 1866 he had been on the staff of *The Ipswich Journal* and later wrote leaders for the *Post*. He seems to have quieted his own conscience, but the spectacle of a leading radical writing in the Conservative interest has troubled many of his admirers.

by the artifices of a style more epigrammatic and tortuous than in any earlier book. The hero was drawn from one of Meredith's friends, and the program of state control, universal suffrage, limitation of private wealth, and provision for future generations is that of the radicals of the period. Beauchamp's mentor, the philosophical Dr. Shrapnel, though the mouthpiece for Meredith's own views, seems to be drawn in part from Carlyle. Less even than in the case of Lucy Feverel is the reader prepared for the death with which the story ends. Beauchamp's drowning in saving a boy demonstrates the tragic irony of the accidental.

In 1877 came the lecture on *The Idea of Comedy and the Uses of the Comic Spirit*.[8] After a brilliant survey of writers of comedy, Meredith contrasts comedy with irony, farce, and satire, and develops themes already touched on in the novels: that comedy is the sword of common sense, the corrective of vanity, egoism, and sentimentality, and that under the aegis of the Comic Spirit women attain equality—and more than equality—with men. But comedy is not mere castigating; it is "the sacred chain of man to man," binding together the members of an intelligent, forward-looking society.[9] A most complex example of the corrective power of thoughtful laughter is supplied in *The Egoist*[10] (1879). In this story of the mortification of the jilted lover, Sir Willoughby Patterne, Meredith pushed the analytical method to such an extreme that the narrative takes far longer than the events narrated. It is overlaid with digressions and confused with a crowd of supernumerary people. The tendency becomes marked to make characters the vehicles of the novelist's doctrines; and persons in fiction do not easily stay alive when such a burden is imposed upon them. The brilliant manner has become a brilliant mannerism. The reader is blinded with the blaze and sputter of aphoristic pyrotechnics. Subtlety of thought is refined to the point of extinction, elliptical expression has become mercilessly obscure, spontaneousness is no longer the quality of the dialogue, and matters essentially trivial are anatomized microscopically. Humiliation at his failure to win wide popular recognition was at the bottom of the stubborn exaggeration of the defects of Meredith's style and mode of narrative.

Having read the story of the love affair of Ferdinand Lassalle and Helene von Dönniges and of the death of the famous Jewish Socialist in a duel with the man who became Helene's husband,[11] Meredith wrote in impassioned haste *The Tragic Comedians* (1880) which is of little interest today save as an experiment in a hybrid literary form that came into vogue forty years later—the "fictionized" biography. *Poems and Lyrics of the Joy of Earth* (1883), Meredith's finest volume of verse, contains the enlarged version of

The Comic Spirit

The Egoist

8 Ed. Lane Cooper (1918).
9 See G. F. Reynolds's study of the *Ode to the Comic Spirit* in "Two Notes on the Poetry of George Meredith," *Univ. of Colorado Stud.*, xv (1925). 1-12.
10 To 1879 belongs also the finest of Meredith's three short stories, the tragic *Tale of Chloe*, an episode of Bath society in the eighteenth century.
11 Meredith took his material from Helene von Dönniges' *Meine Beziehungen zu Ferdinand Lassalle* (Breslau, 1879).

Love in the Valley; The Day of the Daughter of Hades, the most notable of his renderings of classical myth; [12] and the two most important statements of his philosophy of naturalism: *The Woods of Westermain* and *Earth and Man.*

Diana of the Cross-ways

The popular success of *Diana of the Crossways* (1885) was due in part to the influence of such admirers as Stevenson and Henley upon the general taste and in part to the faint aroma of scandal which emanated from the book. It was founded on the career of Sheridan's granddaughter, Mrs. Caroline Norton, against whom the false charge had been brought that she had given to Delane of *The Times* confidential news of Peel's conversion to free trade.[13] Meredith afterwards added a cryptic foreword to the effect that the accusation was unfounded and that the story was to be "read as fiction." The real difficulty is that he fails to make Diana's action plausible; nothing in her character leads us to expect her to be guilty of such disloyalty—or stupidity. In a few episodes (notably Dacier's denunciation of Diana for her betrayal of the secret of state) Meredith surpassed himself in brilliance; but the old vice of narrative by indirection is more pronounced than ever, the epigrams are of too studied a polish, and the metaphors at once too laborious and too quick-darting.

Two volumes of verse now intervened before fiction was resumed. *Ballads and Poems of Tragic Life* (1887) contains much that is harsh and clangorous in style and desperately obscure in subject. *A Reading of Earth* (1888) is more varied in manner and substance, from the simple melodiousness of the *Dirge in Woods* to the condensed thought of the *Hymn to Colour* and the repellent turgidity of the *Ode to the Comic Spirit.* Admirers of Meredith who fancied that in *Diana* they had caught up with him were deceived, for he escaped from them into yet more tangled jungles of language. *One of*

Later Novels

Our Conquerors (1891) is the most ruthless of all his assaults upon the loyalty of readers. Syntax, diction, and allusion are alike obscure; there are constant irrelevancies; and the narrative is carried on in so indirect a fashion that the situation is often lost to sight. This is the greater pity because the story of the tragic Nataly and her illegitimate daughter is a moving one, and there is wonderful delicacy in the analysis of the young girl's feelings when the secret of her parents' irregular relations becomes known to her. *Lord Ormont and his Aminta* (1894) presents another matrimonial entanglement in a more lucid and vivacious style; but the fantastic plot overtaxes credulity. *The Amazing Marriage* (1895) is a better story, albeit tortuously told. Moved by sudden impulse, the hero, a sort of Byronic type, proposes marriage to the heroine, a simple child of nature. He regrets his impulse, but is forced into marriage by the girl's uncle. He leaves his wife, only to realize her worth when it is too late. But Meredith's vein was now

---

[12] On Meredith's classical poems see Bush, pp. 385-395.

[13] Lord Aberdeen, not Mrs. Norton, was the guilty party. — Mrs. Norton, having been sued by her husband for her earnings from writing, published *English Laws for Women in the Nineteenth Century* (1853), a pamphlet which led eventually to the passing of the Married Women's Property Act. Her part in this needed reform certainly attracted Meredith's sympathy.

running thin, and the story is supplemented with persistent disquisition.[14]

Of the four *Odes in Contribution to the Song of French History* (1898) *France* the finest, *France: 1870*, had been published at the time of the Prussian victory. The others—*The French Revolution, Napoleon,* and *Alsace-Lorraine* —belong to the eighteen-nineties. The connecting theme is the faithfulness and unfaithfulness of France to her true lover, Liberty, "the young Angelical." To this union France has aspired constantly and has been as constantly distracted from her path. During the earlier stages of the Revolution she was clasped in this lover's embrace; her first disloyalty was during the Terror. Victory over external foes raised in her the lust for glory. She abandoned her heavenly lover and turned to Napoleon, the demoniac chief, "earth's chosen, crowned, unchallengeable upstart." The Emperor's triumphs and ultimate overthrow are narrated in verse which reverberates as with cannon-shot. Then, amidst the gross materialism of the Bourbon reaction, Napoleon's legend shapes itself

> like some rare treasure-galleon,
> Hull down, with masts against the Western hues.

France: 1870 has for its theme retributive justice, a vindication of the moral order. The mother of pride and luxury is overthrown; but being also the mother of reason, France must herself justify the blow. She who under Napoleon had sown in blood must reap in blood. The Napoleonic conquests are the cause of her present shame. The final ode, *Alsace-Lorraine,* traces the regeneration of France after 1870. In harsh and puzzling metaphors the course of French history during the next three decades is traced, with the legitimist conspiracies, the sporadic revival of Napoleonism, and the gradual decline of the spirit of *revanche.* In the light of subsequent history Meredith's belief that France was abandoning her claim to the lost provinces is now seen to have been tragically impercipient.[15]

Meredith's last volume of poems, *A Reading of Life* (1901), broke no fresh ground. In his last two decades he was the recipient of many honors, succeeding Tennyson as President of the Society of British Authors and made one of the original members of the Order of Merit. He died in 1909, and was buried near his home at Box Hill in Surrey. On his grave is the inscription, from the song in *Vittoria:*

> Life is but a little holding, lent
> To do a mighty labour.

II

It is likely that Meredith's poems, though temporarily somewhat discredited, will prove to be of more lasting value than his novels. Truths

[14] After Meredith's death the fragment of another novel, *Celt and Saxon*, was published (1910). The date of its composition is unknown. It appears to be fairly early work overlaid with later highly mannered revision. It is a conversation-piece breaking off with no indication of the course events were to take. — *The Sentimentalists* is Meredith's only attempt at drama.

[15] In another poem, *England before the Storm*, Meredith showed himself as tragically perⲥipient; he pictured an ill-prepared England confronting the peril of invasion by Germany.

applicable to all humanity shine in his prose and reënforce the teaching of the poems; but there is a limitation of time and nationality and social stratum that already "dates" this fiction; too much of the nineteenth century, of Victorian England, and of the manners and motives of a self-styled "upper

Mere-dith's "World" class." Meredith's satire was salutary and is still invigorating; but already the point of many of his shafts is blunted. He is concerned with artificial people —the landed aristocracy, the ruling classes. When he descends to the "lower levels" the tendency to caricature, inherited from Dickens, becomes pronounced. In *Rhoda Fleming,* notwithstanding a deep feeling for social injustice, he depicted a world whose intimate history remained closed to him Though some parts of Meredith's political and social gospel are in advance of the position we have yet reached, the general trend has been along other lines than he predicted and his radicalism will not necessarily keep him in remem-

Women brance. His championship of women represents a great advance from the conventional adoration combined with secret patronage which Tennyson offered them; he protested against this "charity of chivalry." The novels of his last phase helped to shape opinion in favor of women who, suffering from the injustice of the marriage laws, had no redress. He looked forward to the time when the minds of women, nourished by "light," would no longer need to flatter "a tyrant's pride," but with equal economic opportunities based upon equal educational advantages would meet men as equals in a marriage of true minds. But the reformer of yesterday enunciates the commonplace of today. Meredith realized this when he said that another generation reaps that which we speak in protest.[16]

Evolution The great and memorable theme of all Meredith's writings, in verse and prose, is the frank and joyous acceptance of the idea of evolution, of life as a process of becoming. The troubled generation that preceded him had faced this idea with anxiety and alarm. Although Tennyson, superficially considered, had seemed to meet the scientists half-way, he was at bottom suspicious and hostile towards the new order. But Meredith hymns gladly that "Philosophy of Change" which teaches that progress is the law of all being.

> Sameness locks no scurfy pond
> Here for Custom crazy-fond:
> Change is on the wing to bud
> Rose in brain from rose in blood.[17]

Men have "come out of brutishness," "not forfeiting the beast with which they are crossed" but moving upward towards the "stature of the Gods." [18] As the race has emerged from savagery and is passing through supernaturalism (which is grounded in egoism) to a faith in the natural order, so the individual, avoiding alike the ascetic rocks and the sensual whirlpool, must

---

[16] *The Empty Purse.* — For a brilliant "modern" estimate of Meredith's novels, on the whole adverse, see Virginia Woolf, *The Second Common Reader* (1932), pp. 245-256.
[17] *The Woods of Westermain.*
[18] *Hymn to Colour.*

achieve a harmony of blood, brain, and spirit, the Triad in whose union *"The* true felicity is attained. Meredith's use of the word *spirit,* to which old *Triad"* religious meanings that he discards are traditionally attached, presents some difficulty; but it appears to be the equivalent of the social sense, the sense of society and the moral order, rising above egoism. Men must cease to question Whence? and Whither? and must learn from nature to live in their offspring. A true marriage—"the senses running their live sap, and the minds companioned, and the spirits made one by the whole-natured conjunction"—is "more than happiness"; it is "the speeding of us ... to the creation of certain nobler races, now very dimly discerned." [19] In *The World's Advance* this progress is likened to a reeling spiral with many backslidings yet upward moving. The soul is "wind-beaten but ascending." Struggle is of the essence of life, and in the course of that struggle consciousness and a moral sense have been evolved. Meredith does not feel, as does Hardy, "the intolerable antilogy" of this birth of consciousness and morality in men and women who are the creatures of impercipience. He is an empiricist; he cannot explain the "Why" of evolution but rejoices in the fact, loving nature "too well to ask." He counsels submission to "those firm laws which we name gods," that unalterable reign of law evidenced in the steadfast course of the stars at the sight of which Lucifer sank back reproved.[20] This confidence in the moral order sustained his faith in severest trials.[21] Throughout his life he faced the prospect of personal dissolution with serenity. The "Daughter of Hades" was content with her day of life in the sunlight. The stars are not "frosty lamps illumining dead space," mere cogs in the great machine which grinds out good and ill indifferently, but spirits, sisters of the earth, fellow-workers that still sojourning still move onward in silent joy. Here and there these ideas are touched with a transcendentalism inherited from the romantic generation, but in the main there is a firm refusal of illusion, and what seems to be of religious and even mystical intent is due to the use of traditional figurative language without the traditional connotations. Man must not appeal with "wailful prayers" from nature to the Invisible, nor search mystically for "symbol-clues" in the facts of life. Life for those who hold the freedom of the Woods of Westermain is "a little holding, lent to do a mighty labor." Accepting this privilege and responsibility, man craves no further goal than to live in his offspring and bequeath the young generation no broken house; [22] and when his hour arrives he can fall without shuddering "into the breast that gives the rose."

[19] *Diana of the Crossways.*
[20] *Lucifer in Starlight.*
[21] *A Faith on Trial.*
[22] *The Empty Purse.* — See James Moffat, *"The Empty Purse,* a Meredithian Study for the Times," *Hibbert Journal,* XIV (1916). 612-626.

XXXIV
Thomas Hardy

I

The ideas and emotions which Hardy cautiously termed his "tentative metaphysic" took shape so gradually that no point in his career can be indicated where the fatalism of his youth gave way to the determinism of his old age. There are anticipations of his final convictions in his earliest writings and vestiges of early speculation in his latest. Nor does the publication of his first volume of poems in 1898 mark a clear division, since Hardy wrote poetry in his youth, turned to prose only when he could not find an audience for his verse, never renounced his intention to be a poet during the quarter of a century of novel-writing, and, abandoning fiction, reverted to poetry at last. It is impossible, therefore, to divide his career into "periods," and perhaps the question had best be left where he left it in the contrasting titles of the two volumes of his memoirs—titles (as their muted despondency makes evident) indubitably suggested by himself: "The Early Life" and "The Later Years."

The Past   Born in a small hamlet close to the wild stretch of upland in Dorsetshire which he called Egdon Heath, Thomas Hardy [1] (1840-1928) came of old

[1] *Works*, Wessex Edition (22v, 1912-1922); *Works*, Mellstock Edition (37v, 1921-1922); *Collected Poems* (1919); *The Dynasts*, one-vol. ed. (1919); *Poems*, Golden Treasury Series (1920); *Selected Poems*, ed. G. M. Young (1940). Hardy never reprinted his occasional essays and letters to the press, but there is a convenient, albeit unauthorized, collection, *Life and Art*, ed. Ernest Brennecke (1925). — A. P. Webb, *Bibliography* (1916); R. L. Purdy, *Thomas Hardy: Catalogue of Memorial Exhibition* (New Haven, 1928); Professor Purdy has in preparation a definitive *Bibliography* of Hardy's writings; C. J. Weber, *The First Hundred Years of Thomas Hardy, 1840-1940: a Centenary Bibliography of Hardiana* (Waterville, Me., 1942); Ehrsam, *Bibliographies*, pp. 91-125; Florence Emily Hardy, *The Early Life of Thomas Hardy, 1840-1891* (1928) and *The Later Years of Thomas Hardy, 1892-1928* (1930), of which Mrs. Hardy was rather the compiler than author, for to a large extent the writing, as well as the work of assembling material from letters, diaries, note-books, etc., was Hardy's own; Lionel Johnson, *The Art of Thomas Hardy* (1894; ed. with a chapter on the poetry by J. E. Barton, 1923); F. A. Hedgcock, *Thomas Hardy: Penseur et artiste* (Paris, 1910); Lascelles Abercrombie, *Thomas Hardy: A Critical Study* (1912); S. C. Chew, *Thomas Hardy: Poet and Novelist* (1921; rev. ed., 1928), from which are drawn some parts of the present chapter; J. W. Beach, *The Technique of Thomas Hardy* (1922); Ernest Brennecke, *Thomas Hardy's Universe* (1924); H. B. Grimsditch, *Character and Environment in the Novels of Thomas Hardy* (1925); Pierre d'Exideuil, *Le Couple humain dans l'œuvre de Thomas Hardy* (Paris, 1928; translated by F. W. Crosse, 1929); H. M. Tomlinson, *Thomas Hardy* (privately printed, 1929); Federico Olivero, *An Introduction to Thomas Hardy* (Turin, 1930); Arthur McDowall, *Thomas Hardy* (1931); Louise de Ridder-Barzin, *Le Pessimisme de Thomas Hardy* (Paris, 1932); A. P. Elliott, *Fatalism in the Works of Thomas Hardy* (Philadelphia, 1935); H. C. Duffin, *Thomas Hardy: A Study of the Wessex Novels, the Poems, and The Dynasts* (Manchester, 1937); W. R. Rutland, *Thomas Hardy: A Study of his Writings and their Background* (1938); C. J. Weber, *Hardy of Wessex: His Life and Literary Career* (1940) and *Hardy in America* (1946); for Professor Weber's smaller, but valuable, contributions to Hardy-

yeoman stock. From childhood the impressions of the past—Celtic, Roman, Saxon, medieval, Georgian—were strong upon him. Vestiges of primitive ideas and superstitions, folkways and folklore, thrust themselves through the more superficial modern and sophisticated strata of his writings.[2] Though under the impact of scientific speculation he discarded old beliefs, he was always attentive to the uncanny and preternatural. Peasant song and dance and old church music never ceased to fascinate him. His father's trade of master-builder helped to dictate the choice of architecture as a profession, and at the time when the movement for church-restoration was in full swing he was articled to a local practitioner. Later he pursued this vocation in London; but his natural bent was towards literature. He was at the center of intellectual ferment during the critical eighteen-sixties; and reading Spencer's *First Principles* he meditated upon the unknown First Cause and upon the incalculable element of "Casualty" in human destinies. At this *Early* time he wrote a good deal of verse. Many of these pieces were afterwards *Poems* destroyed, but some remain and others are probably imbedded or reworked in poems of much later date. The freaks and pranks of the purblind "Doomsters" who mismanage man's life are the themes of some poems, and in a few there are hints of the contrast between the "unweening" First Cause and the human consciousness which by some unaccountable cosmic irony has evolved from that Cause. Chance is sometimes personified as a malignant deity who deliberately "sports" with human misery. For this angry fatalism Hardy found support in Swinburne's upbraiding of "the gods"; and in fact Swinburne was a strong influence upon him. Sensitive to the intellectual and emotional atmosphere of the time, he thus shaped his thoughts towards that "twilight view of life" which Meredith was later to deprecate. This despondency was lightened by his rustic humor and at other times darkened with resentment against the social distinctions of which he was more conscious in London than in his native Dorset. Something of the spiritual conflict of these early years is certainly recorded in the narrative of Angel Clare's renunciation of the Christian ministry in *Tess,* and something of the social conflict in Jude Fawley's thwarted aspirations in *Jude the Obscure.*[3]

But there was probably little of metaphysical speculation though much *The First* social radicalism in Hardy's first novel, *The Poor Man and the Lady* (1867- *Novel* 1868), which mingled scenes of rural life with satire directed against the metropolitan "upper classes." This book was rejected by three publishers. Portions of it were incorporated in later novels; one section survives as the novelette, *An Indiscretion in the Life of an Heiress* (1878); the remainder

study, too numerous to list here, see the annual bibliographies in *PMLA*; Edmund Blunden, *Thomas Hardy* (EML Series, 1942); Lord David Cecil, *Hardy, the Novelist* (1943). Of many books on the Hardy country the best is Herman Lea, *Thomas Hardy's Wessex* (1913). The *Southern Rev.,* VI (Summer, 1940), is a "Thomas Hardy Centennial Issue" devoted to articles on Hardy by W. H. Auden, Allen Tate, Bonamy Dobrée, and others. Baker, IX (1938), chs. I and II; D. H. Lawrence, "A Study of Thomas Hardy," in *Phoenix: The Posthumous Papers of D. H. Lawrence* (1936), pp. 398–516.

[2] Ruth A. Firor, *Folkways in Thomas Hardy* (Philadelphia, 1931).

[3] In old age Hardy denied the existence of any autobiographical substratum in his novels; it is there nonetheless, though not to be interpreted too literally.

was ultimately destroyed. But it is possible to reconstruct the original with some plausibility.[4] Both John Morley and George Meredith, who were then publishers' readers, recognized the promise of the book; and Meredith advised Hardy to try again, this time avoiding social satire and contriving an intricate plot. The result was *Desperate Remedies* (1871), a highly improbable tale of mystery and murder which in its sensational incidents and complex concatenation of circumstances reveals the influence of Wilkie Collins. *Under the Greenwood Tree* (1872) is a slight tale of rural courtship and feminine wiles mingled with episodes of rich rustic humor. *A Pair of Blue Eyes* (1873) combines sensational intrigue and incredible coincidences in the swiftly moving narrative of a romantic tragedy. The yokels in the humorous or gruesome episodes are drawn with a more intimate art than are their social superiors in the main plot. The success of this romance brought an invitation from Leslie Stephen to contribute to *Cornhill*, where in 1874 appeared Hardy's first masterpiece, *Far from the Madding Crowd*.[5] Its anonymity provoked widespread speculation as to its authorship; its success was enormous; and Hardy, now securely launched upon his career, was able to marry. His bride was Emma Lavinia Gifford to whom he had become betrothed four years earlier when engaged upon church-restoration work in Cornwall. After a honeymoon in France and Belgium, the Hardys lived either in London or in one or another southern town till 1885, when they settled at Max Gate on the outskirts of Dorchester, Hardy's home for the long remainder of his life.

Popular Success

Resenting the attribution of *Far from the Madding Crowd* to George Eliot, which he interpreted as a charge of imitation, Hardy essayed in his next book, *The Hand of Ethelberta* (1876), something wholly different and achieved only a negligible piece of frivolity. But this was followed by the book which in its balance and control is his greatest work of fiction, *The Return of the Native* (1878). It was rejected by Leslie Stephen on the ground that a tale of tragic passion would displease *Cornhill's* clientèle and was accepted by *Belgravia* only when Hardy had consented to bring the secondary plot of Venn and Thomasin to the "happy ending" which was *de rigueur* in current fiction.[6] *The Trumpet-Major* (1880), the most genial of the Wessex Novels, was the first considerable sign of Hardy's interest in Napoleonic traditions. Criticism of *A Laodicean* (1881) is disarmed by the fact that, having been contracted for, it was composed during convalescence from a severe illness. It is quite worthless. *Two on a Tower* (1882), though fragile in theme and almost dream-like in tone, is memorable for its projection of human passion against the background of starry distances. Hardy's

---

[4] See *An Indiscretion in the Life of an Heiress*, ed. C. J. Weber (Baltimore, 1935).

[5] Here Hardy first revived the ancient name of Wessex for the southern and southwestern counties and fixed imaginary names to many identifiable actual places. In later editions of the first three novels he revised the nomenclature to conform to this scheme. See *Far from the Madding Crowd*, ed. C. J. Weber (1937).

[6] On the alterations in the various novels to conform to the requirements of editors see Mary E. Chase, *Thomas Hardy from Serial to Novel* (Minneapolis, 1927). Professor Weber also has made valuable contributions to the history of Hardy's texts.

outspokenness in this book on the subject of the sexual relation did not conform to contemporary standards of literary propriety and "rumblings of British prudery" were audible. Apart from the pretty novelette, *The Romantic Adventures of a Milkmaid* (1883), nothing more was published for four years. The resultant reserve of energy was expended upon *The Mayor of Casterbridge* (1886). Here the interest is not divided among four or five main characters as in the earlier books but is concentrated upon the figure of Michael Henchard; and though external circumstance and crass coincidence continue to play their part, there is a new emphasis upon faults in Henchard's character which the directing Force of the universe uses to bring him to destruction. The book is firmly constructed and austere in tone almost to brutality. What it lacks as compared with the earlier novels is charm and sweetness and poetry. Two of these qualities and something of bitter-sweet as well are abundantly present in *The Woodlanders* (1887), the tenderest of Hardy's stories, thrilling in its narrative power and memorable both for the nobility of its two central figures and for its exquisitely observed scenes and customs of the woodland folk.

A first set of short stories, assembled as *Wessex Tales* (1888), was followed by *A Group of Noble Dames* (1891), *Life's Little Ironies* (1894), and *A Changed Man and Other Stories* (1913). Disregarding chronology for a moment, we may notice these together. Hardy was not a great short-story-teller, though he wrote a few fine short stories. *The Three Strangers, The Withered Arm, The Distracted Preacher, On the Western Circuit, For Conscience' Sake*, and *A Tragedy of Two Ambitions* are little masterpieces, exhibiting a wide range of power—ironic, humorous, grim, sardonic, or eerie. But too frequently Hardy's tales are either trivial or extravagant local anecdotes cast in literary form or else give the impression of being sketches or drafts for full-length novels. The tone of many is bitter or sinister, though they do not afford scope for much explicit comment upon the human quandary.

Short Stories

Hardy needed a larger canvas for an exposition of the view of life he now held. The first notes for *Jude the Obscure* were jotted down in 1887 and the composition of *Tess* was begun not much later. For these books he attempted to prepare the public by two articles in the nature of manifestoes: *The Profitable Reading of Fiction* (1888) and *Candor in English Fiction* (1890).[7] In these he asked for the novelist the right to treat controversial topics with the same sincerity as is permitted in private intercourse, to discuss candidly the sexual relation, the problems of religious belief, and the position of man in the universe. Notwithstanding this urgent argument, he was forced, for the sake of his livelihood, to bowdlerize and dismember *Tess of the d'Urbervilles* when he published it serially in 1891;[8] and this, the most famous of his novels, was bitterly denounced when its integrity was restored in the book form. The two-fold polemic—against social prejudice and against

Tess

---

[7] Reprinted in *Life and Art*, pp. 56-74; 75-84.
[8] C. J. Weber, "On the Dismemberment of *Tess*," *Sat. Rev. of Lit.*, XI (1934). 308-309.

of the Immortals"—roused a storm of protest. *The Well-
*,[9] a semi-allegorical Platonic fantasy, shows a temporary ex-
 the profound emotional effort called forth by *Tess*; nor did
ely recover his artistic control in the last novel, *Jude the Obscure*
powerful but overwrought story of "the derision and disaster that
 the wake of the strongest passion known to humanity." That a
 such formidable candor could achieve publication shows that Vic-
 prudery was waning; that it caused a great scandal shows that that
ery was not extinct. The experience "cured" Hardy, as he wrote after-
rds, of any desire to write more novels. As a matter of fact, he had had
is say in a medium which, for all his mastery, was never entirely congenial
to him and was ready to turn again to poetry, the native country of his mind.

Wessex Poems (1898) and *Poems of the Past and the Present* (1902)
preceded the epic-drama, *The Dynasts* (1903-1906-1908), the stupendous result of his life-long interest in the Napoleonic Wars, and, more than this, an
exposition upon the amplest scale of his mechanistic determinism. Subsequent collections of short poems were *Time's Laughing-Stocks* (1909),
Satires of Circumstance (1914), *Moments of Vision* (1917), *Late Lyrics and
Earlier* (1922), *Human Shows* (1925), and *Winter Words* (posthumous,
1928). *The Queen of Cornwall* (1923), a short drama on the legend of Iseult,
is an attempt, more ingenious than convincing, to harmonize the two conflicting versions of the story. In his later years Hardy also occupied himself
with the memoirs which appeared after his death as a biography professedly
by his widow. When his first wife died in 1912, his thoughts turned to their
romance of long ago and he wrote a series of poignant little elegies. Differences of temperament and opinion had come between the pair, but there
had never been an entire estrangement.[10] In a second marriage (1914), to
Florence Emily Dugdale, he found congeniality and happiness. During the
last two decades his fame widened enormously. He bore his honors with
deprecating modesty, yet was curiously sensitive to the few voices of dissent.[11] He died in January, 1928, and his ashes were placed in Westminster
Abbey among England's poets.[12]

[9] Not published in book form till 1897.

[10] Distorted rumors of scandalous estrangement form the basis of Somerset Maugham's
roman à clef, Cakes and Ale. For a clear and candid statement of the matter see C. J. Weber,
Hardy of Wessex (1940), ch. xv.

[11] The present writer knew of the anxiety at Max Gate when report came of George
Moore's intention to attack Hardy. Moore's violent but not altogether unwarranted onslaught,
prompted by jealousy, was published in *Conversations in Ebury Street* (1924), ch. vi. Moore
attached to Hardy the blame for some of the extravagant expressions of praise on the part of
Hardy's admirers—which was scarcely fair. J. Middleton Murry replied to Moore in a hysterically
abusive brochure, *Wrap Me Up in My Aubusson Carpet* (1925). A campaign of denigration
against Hardy of another sort made way under the leadership of T. S. Eliot. The most arrogant statement of this critic's disapproval is in *After Strange Gods* (1934), pp. 59-62. Mr.
Eliot has criticized Hardy with the acerbity of a spiritual pride which, the Christian may hold,
gives greater offense to God than Hardy's irremediable impercipience.

[12] Hardy had expressed the wish to be buried in Stinsford churchyard, near Max Gate. The
universal opinion that burial must be in the Abbey resulted in a compromise: the heart was
cut out and buried at Stinsford; the ashes after cremation were taken to the Abbey. The
almost pagan primitiveness of this proceeding was not out of keeping with the man.

II

As a regionalist Hardy had forerunners of a kind in Maria Edgeworth *Region-* and other Irish novelists and in John Galt and other Scots; but those writers *alism* had not confined themselves to a small, well-defined area and were national-istic rather than regionalist. In a modest way the claim to be Hardy's predecessor belongs to the Dorset poet, William Barnes.[13] But though, like Barnes, he was steeped in the traditions of his countryside, Hardy was not primarily "folkloristic." His yokels do not form a class entirely apart from the other characters in the Wessex Novels, but by almost imperceptible gradations, through persons of middle rank, are connected with the char-acters who are higher in the social scale. From the latter the rustics are distinguishable by their use of dialect and by the serenity with which they hold their place in the world. Hardy laid no stress upon their poverty and insisted that their misery had been much overestimated.[14] They have dis-covered the secret of happiness, which, as is said in *The Woodlanders,* lies in limiting one's aspirations. Many are shrewd, some witty, nearly all un-consciously humorous. They are at once a part of the Wessex background and a sort of chorus commenting upon the actions in which their superiors are engaged. Apart from the villains, who are almost always sophisticated intruders from the outside world, the leading characters are of Wessex blood. When, as in some of the minor novels, Hardy ventured beyond Wessex he was beyond his range. On his chosen, restricted stage as high drama could be enacted as in parts of the world seemingly more significant, for, like Wordsworth, he believed that in rustic life "the essential passions of the heart find a better soil" and are "less under restraint" than in urban society. The closer man lives to nature in humility and ignorance the likelier *Nature* he is to be happy, for knowledge is sorrow. But nature[15] is full of cruelty, and Hardy stresses those aspects of the natural world that are hostile to man. Yet with faulty logic he is on the side of natural impulse (as in *Tess* or *Jude*) in opposition to social law, convention, and restrictions. Nature is not a setting for his stories but an integral part of them. Man is a plaything in the grip of vast forces. The dominant theme is the ineffectual struggle of the individual against the obscure power which moves the universe. Since love accentuates individuality, it is in love that the conflict of humanity with destiny is at its most intense. In such earlier masterpieces as *The Return of the Native* and *The Mayor of Casterbridge* the blows of fate are to some

[13] William Barnes (1801-1886), clergyman, poet, and local antiquary, author of three series of *Poems of Rural Life in the Dorset Dialect* (1854, 1859, 1862; collected ed., 1879). These are little eclogues, love poems, nature pieces, bits of folklore and superstition, and the like. See his *Select Poems,* chosen by Thomas Hardy (1908). — Another ''regionalist" poet was Thomas Edward Brown (1830-1897) who wrote narrative and lyrical verse, some in standard English, much in the Manx dialect. *Collected Poems,* ed. W. E. Henley (1901); *Letters,* ed. S. T. Irwin (2v, 1900).

[14] See Hardy's article on "The Dorsetshire Labourer," *Longman's Mag.,* July, 1879, and his letter "On the Use of Dialect," *Spectator,* October 15, 1881. Both are reprinted in *Life and Art,* pp. 20-47; 114-115.

[15] See J. W. Beach, *The Concept of Nature,* pp. 503-521.

extent consequent upon weaknesses of character, so that one may speak of "blame" and "retribution"; but in *Tess* and *Jude* culpability is of no consequence because blind destiny strikes the innocent and the guilty with stupid impartiality. Hardy came to view man and nature as fellow-sufferers from the cosmic imbecility. His myth-making imagination gave "a kind of rationality to the hoary old superstitions of hostile or capricious powers which he cherished and half-believed." [16] But he was really a scientific determinist, and by "Fate" or "Chance" or "Casualty" meant human life as determined by all antecedent circumstances in a chain of causality.[17] Groping for a name for this concept, he abandoned such terms as "Nature," "Hap," or "God" and finally—whether or not after reading Schopenhauer [18]—chose to call the unintelligent and unconscious urge or impulse in things the Immanent Will. But this term is nothing more than a "metaphysical convenience" to express the unity and pattern of existing things.[19] Critics have deplored the sacrifice of tragic grandeur which this concept requires, for since human protagonists are reduced to automata so that even in their struggles against destiny they are merely pulled to and fro by the "halyards" of the Will, there is no room for that internal conflict which is the essence of tragedy. Hardy would have agreed; the root of his indictment against life was "the intolerable antilogy of making figments feel." "The emotions," he remarked, "have no place in a world of defect, and it is a cruel injustice that they should have developed in it." [20] Yet in the inexplicable evolution of human consciousness from the Unconscious and of intelligence from the Unknowing lay Hardy's strange, dim hope that "in some day unguessed of us" the Will may "lift its blinding incubus" and, becoming informed by consciousness, "fashion all things fair." [21]

In personal relations Hardy was jovial, but his temperament was fundamentally saturnine and he found this "twilight view of life" congenial to him. A rich fund of sympathy with suffering often made him angry and indignant and (again with a want of logic) he indicted Circumstance and the miseries of man's own contriving alike. He was not a sociological novelist, but he was happy to recognize that reforms often begin in sentiment and sentiment sometimes begins in a novel.[22] As a professional man of letters it was

"The Immanent Will" (margin note)

[16] Baker, ix. 81.

[17] J. W. Beach, *op. cit.*, p. 511.

[18] Agnes Steinbach, *Thomas Hardy und Schopenhauer* (Leipzig, 1925), pp. 434-474; H. Garwood, *Thomas Hardy: An Illustration of the Philosophy of Schopenhauer* (Philadelphia, 1912).

[19] J. W. Beach, *op. cit.*, p. 518.

[20] Florence E. Hardy, *The Early Life of Thomas Hardy*, p. 192.

[21] *The Blow*; and the ·final Chorus of the Pities in *The Dynasts*. Professor Beach repudiates this "mitigating concession" as not a serious element in Hardy's philosophy; but the idea, that just as man has attained consciousness through some evolutionary process so conceivably may the Immanent Will, recurs constantly in Hardy's poetry. In the practical, unspeculative sphere Hardy described himself as a meliorist, and in a poem addressed to "the Unknown God" he hymned the praise of the Divinity because he saw here and there "old wrongs dying as of self-slaughter." But he said to the present writer and to others that had he written *The Dynasts* after the Treaty of Versailles he could not have closed it upon a note of hope.

[22] Final preface to *Tess*. Compare George Moore's satisfaction when *Esther Waters* was efficacious in suggesting practical philanthropies.

his business to entertain, and only gradually, when he had made his way, did he come to use fiction openly for polemic. But what finally became explicit had always been implicit. In "loading the dice" against his characters and in relying to an extravagant degree upon coincidence he was at once following the sensational fashion in fiction and hinting at his indictment of life. It has been held that in the end—that is, in *Jude*—the bitterness of his indignation overreached itself; but even those who do not feel the spiritual terror of that book see that the element of realism is subordinated to something like allegory—the old allegory of the Choice of the Two Paths. The suicide of Jude's son, whether or not suggested by Hartman's *Philosophy of the Unconscious,* is an omen of humanity's escape from life; the Will-Not-to-Live is to triumph ultimately over the Life-Urge.

With his architect's training in design Hardy found satisfaction in the symmetry of his plots. Today, when mere plot is at a discount in fiction, the almost diagrammatic regularity of his plans is severely criticized. "Slices of life" do not fall into such symmetrical segments. The even tenor of life attracted neither his interest nor that of the readers for whose suffrages he first bid. But he held, when inventing sensational incident, that "the uncommonness must be in the events, not in the characters." Of the melodramatic quality of many of his "events" it is unnecessary to speak; some are merely preposterous. His characters fall into a few recurrent types which reveal his prepossessions in favor of honest worth and his prejudices against sophistication. A master of narrative, he was less successful in dialogue, where, save in the peasant scenes, there is almost always more than a touch of the artificial and declamatory. In the decades when the doctrine of impersonality in art was gaining ground he continued to avail himself of the privilege of the Victorian novelist to intrude his own opinions into his stories. Whatever the value as propaganda for the reform of sentiment and convention, the savage satire with which he attacked the Church, the universities, marriage, and various social prejudices marred his last two novels as works of art.[23]

Structure of the Novels

---

[23] The influence of the Wessex Novels is apparent to a greater or less degree in the writings of various regionalists; and others, though perhaps not directly affected by Hardy's example, show affinities to him.

Richard D. Blackmore (1825-1900) won a single great success with *Lorna Doone* (1869), a historical novel in the line of descent from Scott but with elements of mystery and melodrama imitated from Wilkie Collins. It is permeated with a love and knowledge of Exmoor. In later novels, now forgotten, Blackmore imitated Hardy. See Q. G. Burris, *R. D. Blackmore, His Life and Novels* (Urbana, 1930).

Sabine Baring-Gould (1834-1924) exploited the antiquities and folklore of Devon and Cornwall in stories ranging from antiquity to the very recent past.

William Black (1841-1898) specialized in the regionalism of the Highlands and the Hebrides with elaborate landscapes and seascapes and with the traditional contrast between remote simplicities and modern sophistication.

Samuel R. Crockett (1860-1914) told tales of his native Galloway with so lavish a use of dialect that a glossary was compiled for his readers. See M. M. Harper, *Crockett and Grey Galloway: The Novelist and his Works* (1907).

Closer in mood though not in form to Hardy is Richard Jefferies (1848-1887), the author of *The Story of My Heart* (1883) and of novels and fantasies many of which are set in Wiltshire. There is a passionate "paganism" in his celebration of love, and his philosophic determinism is characteristic of his time. See *Selections,* ed. H. Williamson (1937); *Jefferies'*

III

Short
Poems

Besides *The Dynasts* Hardy wrote about nine hundred short poems.[24] No other considerable poet exhibits a like contrast between a single work of ample scope and a multitude of little things; but the sheer bulk of the miscellaneous poetry is a counterbalance to the epic-drama and an essential supplement to it. A good deal of this minor verse must go into the discard. Such idiosyncrasies of style as violent inversions of word-order, uncouth neologisms, the wrenching of words from their familiar meanings, the revival of half-intelligible archaisms, and the drastic clipping of words to force them into a metrical pattern, though by such means as these he sometimes achieved his best effects, impose a strain upon the reader which is not tolerable when his theme is trivial or cynical or would-be humorous. On the other hand, a great deal remains. Returning to poetry when his position was assured, he was under obligations to no school (though he betrays stylistic affinities to Browning and was himself conscious of an indebtedness to Donne) and could experiment as he liked. Some of his innovations are analogous to those of Hopkins and Doughty, but in the main his poetry stands apart from that of his time. There is an avoidance of the decoration and embroidery of decadent romantic verse. The trained storyteller is seen in the vigorous ballads (such as *A Tramp-Woman's Tragedy,* which was his own favorite among his poems), the ironic "satires of circumstance," and the little incidents told with sardonic humor. His poems, he said, were "explorations of reality." There is a ruthless insight, a precision that needs no over-emphasis, a lovely quietness, and an ability to achieve his purposes without resort to merely verbal imagery. A gruesome humor in many pieces was not, he insisted to friends, to be taken too seriously; some of his many graveyard poems show a sort of cheerful ghoulishness; but others are cynical, sardonic, melancholy, tender, eerie, or wonderfully spectral. In many poems he exposed the disenchantments and incompatabilities of love; but he was convinced that in the marriage of true minds men and women find the best that life has to offer. The most beautiful of his short poems was ad-

---

England: *Nature Essays,* ed. S. J. Looker (1937); Edward Thomas, *Richard Jefferies* (1909); C. J. Masseck, *Richard Jefferies* (Paris, 1913).

Eden Phillpotts (1862-1960) was Hardy's closest disciple, though the influence is less marked in his late books. The setting of his best novels, of which *The River* (1902) is a good example, is generally in the western country beyond Wessex. The congenital wisdom of Phillpotts' yokels is precisely in the manner of the master. Phillpotts has also written plays, several volumes of poems, and a number of mere "thrillers."

The novels of Mary Webb (1885-1927) have wider affiliations, but her emphasis upon her native region (the Welsh marches) owes much to Hardy. Her literary ancestry is, however, complex. Characteristic books are *The House in Dormer Forest* (1920) and *Precious Bane* (1924). *Novels,* Sarn Edition (7v, 1942); *A Mary Webb Anthology,* ed. H. B. L. Webb (1940); Thomas Moult, *Mary Webb: Her Life and Work* (1932).

[24] On Hardy's verse technique see E. C. Hickson, *The Versification of Thomas Hardy* (Philadelphia, 1931); G. R. Elliott, "Spectral Etching in the Poetry of Thomas Hardy," *PMLA,* XLIII (1928). 1185-1195; and several of the articles in "Hardy Centennial Issue" of the *Southern Review.* See also Amiya Chakravarty, *The Dynasts and the Post-War Age in Poetry* (1938).

dressed to the woman who became his second wife. He has the ability to cast an unfamiliar light upon familiar things, to contrast the fugitive and the permanent, and (in Tennyson's words) to give "a sense of the abiding in the transient." Occasionally but less characteristically he was master of the grand style, as in the lines written in Gibbon's garden or in the sonnet *At a Lunar Eclipse*. There is no room to say more, though much more might be said, save to indicate his range by naming a few poems in addition to those to which attention has been directed already. These are: *Heiress and Architect, The Impercipient, The Oxen, The Darkling Thrush, Let Me Enjoy, The Blow, Jubilate, A Singer Asleep, Quid hic agis?, The Clock-Winder,* and *Afterwards.* The list might be greatly extended; but every reader can make his own anthology. Today, after a shorter period of denigration than usually follows the death of a famous writer, critics are again studying in minutest detail his technique and style, and the opinion prevalent in the nineteen-twenties is once more expressed that even if Hardy was not a great poet he wrote great poetry.

Concerning *The Dynasts* opinion has not yet crystallized. The general tendency is to assert that a partial failure is redeemed by the greatness of the conception. As the appropriateness of the poetic style to the structure and theme becomes more apparent it is likely that this half-heartedness will give way to less qualified admiration. Upon a scale of cosmic proportions Hardy undertook to exhibit the Immanent Will, which "like a knitter drowsed" weaves "with absent heed," entangling in its web human automata. It was not Hardy's purpose to contribute anything new to the analysis of Napoleon's character or that of any other figure in the tragedy of the "Clash of Peoples." The conduct of the action upon two planes—Europe and the Over-World where dwell "the great intelligences . . . which range above our mortal state" —is an extraordinary feat of the creative imagination. In the group of overseeing spirits the poet succeeded in rendering in dramatic form abstractions of human emotion and experience. Parts of the material assembled with the conscientiousness of a historian proved intractable to verse; but almost invariably the poetry rises to greatness upon great occasions. Some of the choruses are of tragic grandeur and others are beautiful and tender or bluff and hearty or of sinister humor. The "stage-directions" in prose are of a wonderful imaginative clarity, whether the scene is viewed near at hand or is a vast panorama spread before spirit-eyes from celestial heights. With such palpitating excitement yet historical accuracy are the battles dramatized that these scenes have been likened to those in Tolstoy's *War and Peace.* The rustic episodes are beyond compare with anything of the kind save those in Shakespeare and in some of Hardy's own romances. The glimpse of the mad King George III is as convincing in its pathos as is that of the rakish Prince Regent in its satiric realism. The death of Nelson; the burial of Sir John Moore; the deserters skulking in a Spanish cellar; the retreat from Moscow; the return from Elba; and the entire Waterloo campaign—

The Dynasts

these are a few of the high points in a drama which sometimes sinks, as does life itself, to lower levels, but rises majestically upon fit occasion. To read it is to have implanted in the memory forever the august and tragic spectacle of humanity entangled in the web of "the all-urging Will, raptly magnipotent."

XXXV
Aestheticism and "Decadence"

I

The origins of the Aesthetic Movement [1] are found in various streams of speculation. At Oxford in the eighteen-sixties the Hegelian evaluation of the various kinds of human experience was expounded by Thomas Hill Green (1836-1882) and was of primary importance for the determination of Walter Pater's point of view.[2] At just this time Swinburne, following Gautier and Baudelaire, was controverting the Utilitarian criticism which demanded of art a moral emphasis and declaring that art should serve no religious, moral, or social end, nor any end save itself. Rossetti, while avoiding precept and controversy, was a strong and disturbing example of the artist dedicated wholly to his art. By seeking to make the social order comely, Ruskin, even while insisting upon moral values in art, prepared the way for Pater's doctrine of the comeliness of the individual life as a criterion of right conduct. Behind these and other expressions of dissatisfaction with the dominant Utilitarian creed was the pessimism of the mid-century which was a further stimulus towards hedonism. After the French defeat of 1870 the withdrawal of French artists and men of letters from the political and social arena into aesthetic isolation was a gesture imitated in England.

For want of an authoritative biography it is difficult to determine the *Pater* degree to which early influences of family and environment shaped the temperament of Walter Horatio Pater [3] (1839-1894), the somewhat reluctant leader of the Aesthetic Movement. *The Child in the House* is indubitably an evocation of his own early years; but here, as in his accounts of the boyhood of Marius, Gaston, and Emerald Uthwart, it is impossible to draw a precise line between the imaginary and the autobiographical. Throughout his books there are obscure personal allusions. Florian Deleal, the child who

[1] A. J. Farmer, *Le Mouvement esthétique et "décadent" en Angleterre, 1873-1900* (Paris, 1931); Louise Rosenblatt, *L'Idée de l'art pour l'art dans la littérature anglaise pendant la periode victorienne* (Paris, 1931); William Gaunt, *The Aesthetic Adventure* (1944); Albert Cassagne, *La Théorie de l'art pour l'art en France* (Paris, 1906).

[2] B. Fehr, "Walter Pater und Hegel," *ESt*, L (1916). 300-308.

[3] *Works*, Library Edition (10v, 1910); *Selected Essays*, ed. H. G. Rawlinson (1927). — Thomas Wright, *The Life of Walter Pater* (2v, 1907); A. C. Benson, *Walter Pater* (EML Series, 1906); Edward Thomas, *Walter Pater, a Critical Study* (1913); A. J. Farmer, *Walter Pater as a Critic of English Literature* (Grenoble, 1931); H. H. Young, *The Writings of Walter Pater, a Reflection of British Philosophical Opinion from 1860 to 1890* (Bryn Mawr, 1933); J. G. Eaker, *Walter Pater, a Study in Methods and Effects* (Iowa City, 1933); R. C. Child, *The Aesthetic of Walter Pater* (1940); Algernon Cecil, "Walter Pater," *Six Oxford Thinkers* (1909), pp. 214-251.

possessed "a positive genius for tranquility,"[4] suggests the actual man who at Oxford passed a life of almost quietistic seclusion and who emerged but rarely, and then shyly, into London society. Save for a few visits to the Continent Pater's career was almost eventless. At Oxford he assembled round him a small company of disciples, meanwhile publishing in periodicals a series of essays of which most, with some new material, were collected as *Studies in the History of the Renaissance*[5] (1873). Other essays in philosophy, literature, and the fine arts followed, with a little group of highly characteristic "portraits," some purely fictitious, others with some historical foundation. Much of this miscellaneous work was assembled in *Imaginary Portraits* (1887), *Appreciations* (1889), and *Plato and Platonism* (1893), while much else was first gathered together or first published in posthumous volumes.[6] Though, like his own Marius, "essentially but a spectator" even in "his most enthusiastic participation" in the ways of the restricted world in which he moved,[7] Pater came to feel a responsibility towards those of the younger generation who, following his leadership, evinced a misunderstanding of his teaching; and after the appearance of W. H. Mallock's *The New Republic* (1877), in which his doctrines were cruelly caricatured,[8] he undertook an elaborate *apologia* which resulted in his masterpiece, *Marius the Epicurean* (1885). A second effort along similar lines, *Gaston de Latour*, was abandoned after five chapters had been published in 1888. Pater was at work upon an essay on Pascal when he died suddenly at the height of his powers and prestige.

In an age of doctrinal controversies often productive of bitter personalities Pater held himself aloof from quarrels; and equally he had no share in the humanitarian movement of the time. Even though his mature thought found a place for compassion, it is not on record that this sympathy was ever expressed in any positive, remedial social action. He virtually never sounded any other note than that of appreciation, keeping silent on his antipathies. Of two dominant traits of temperament which helped to shape his thought, one was his extraordinary keenness of sensitivity: of Florian he wrote that he "seemed to experience a passionateness in his relation to fair outward objects," and of Gaston, that he tended towards "a new religion, or at least a new worship, maintaining and visibly setting forth a single overpowering apprehension."[9] With this hypersensuousness was

---

[4] See *The Child in the House*, in *Miscellaneous Studies*.

[5] Renamed *The Renaissance. Studies in Art and Poetry*.

[6] *Miscellaneous Studies* and *Greek Studies* (both 1895); *Gaston de Latour* (1896); *Essays from "The Guardian"* (1896); *Sketches and Reviews* (1919).

[7] *Marius the Epicurean*, I. 46.

[8] William H. Mallock (1849-1923) voiced in a succession of volumes his hostility to the tendencies of his time, his opposition to advancing democracy and Socialism receiving final expression in *Memories of Life and Literature* (1920). But he never repeated the success of *The New Republic*. In this pseudo-Peacockian satire most of the characters, identifiable as Ruskin, Tyndall, and other eminent Victorians, are drawn sympathetically. Not so "Mr. Rose," i.e., Pater, in whose portrait there is deliberate malice. In contemporary keys "Mr. Rose" is identified with Rossetti, an error showing how little Pater was known to the general public, which associated Rossetti with the movement of "Art for Art's Sake."

[9] *The Child in the House*, *Miscellaneous Studies*, p. 186; *Gaston de Latour*, p. 70.

combined a poignant awareness of the brevity of life which directed his *Cyrenai-*
thought towards Cyrenaicism, that philosophy which has "no basis of un- *cism*
verified hypothesis" and relies upon the security of the present moment
"set between two hypothetical eternities."[10] To fill each passing moment
with intense experience, "to maintain this ecstasy," is success in life. Yet
this passionate apprehension of beauty and the sense of its fleetingness do
not bring happiness. Not only in Pater's early writings but in the works of
his maturity there is a troubling unwholesomeness. The famous "meditation" upon the Mona Lisa, the exquisite penultimate paragraph of *The
Poetry of Michelangelo,* the narrative of Flavian's death in *Marius,* the
appearance of Denys from the tomb, and the gruesome episode of the
extraction of the bullet from the dead heart of Emerald Uthwart are examples of this morbidity, this unhealthy curiosity. The attraction exerted by
mysterious iniquity is expressed with greatest power in *Apollo in Picardy,*
one of the "portraits" of latest date (1893). The fascination which the theme
of the pagan gods who have "grown diabolic among ages that would not
accept [them] as divine" exercised upon Pater is one expression of this recurrent mood.[11] This aspect of his work is premonitory of the coming
"Decadence." But it must not be overemphasized, for there was a development in Pater's thought. In *Diaphanéité,* his earliest extant essay (1864),
and even so late as *Marius* the counsel is that life should be lived in the spirit
of art; but almost from the first there was the realization that though
pursued for its own sake, art does contribute to the ethical nature of man;
and towards the end there was an increasing emphasis upon the beauty of
order and upon the need to discipline the soul. At times there is an ambiguity, a suggestion of transcendental possibilities, an open-minded recognition of the *grand peut-être.*

When Pater began to write, Ruskin's exaltation of the Middle Ages and
denigration of the Renaissance had given the latter period the attraction of
a fresh subject.[12] In approach and in critical theory Pater was quite un-
Ruskinian. He is nearer to Arnold in his fastidiousness, though without

[10] *Marius the Epicurean,* I. 149; *Conclusion* to *The Renaissance.*

[11] See J. S. Harrison, "Pater, Heine, and the Old Gods of Greece," *PMLA,* xxxix (1924).
655-686.

[12] This field of research was intensively cultivated by John Addington Symonds (1840-
1893). *The Renaissance in Italy* (7v, 1875-1886) is desultory in design, flamboyant in style,
and not altogether trustworthy; but a fine descriptive talent displays the rich coloring, violent
movement, and strong personalities of the Renaissance. Symonds also wrote *Sketches in Italy
and Greece* (1874), *Studies of the Greek Poets* (1873 and 1876), biographies of Michelangelo,
Sidney, and Shelley, and critical studies of Dante, Whitman, and Shakespeare's predecessors
in the English drama. *In the Key of Blue* (1893) is a significant volume of essays. The qualities
conspicuous in his critical and historical work—the scholarship, the love of art and the classics,
the sensitiveness to the genius of places, the febrile response to the loveliness of Italian and
Alpine scenery—are present also in Symonds' verse: *Many Moods* (1878); *New and Old*
(1880). Occasionally he gives expression to the mood of late-century dejection and suggests
the quandary into which mechanistic materialism has led thoughtful men. — With Pater may
also be associated Violet Paget (1856-1935), whose pen-name was "Vernon Lee." Among
her studies in art, literature, and aesthetics are *Euphorion* (2v, 1884) and *Genius Loci* (1899).
Ariadne in Mantua (1903) is a delicately graceful "dramatic romance." Her novels are of
little moment, but later books, such as *Gospels of Anarchy* (1908) and *Vital Lies* (1912), show
that she kept abreast of the age, refusing to be a mere belated voice of aestheticism.

Arnold's superciliousness.[13] But he accepted as the function of criticism the duty to "see the object as it really is"; and his modification of this rule introduced by the question "What is it to *me*?" has been misunderstood by those who have disregarded the context in the preface to *The Renaissance*. Nevertheless it cannot be convincingly denied that his subjective impressionism led to a confusion between the critical and creative processes which involved him in falsifications of history and contributed to the distortion of his theory in Oscar Wilde's *The Critic as Artist*.[14] At times this subjectivity reduces criticism to Anatole France's oft-quoted definition: "the adventures of a sensitive soul among masterpieces." (But though there are resemblances between Pater and France, the English writer is less profoundly sensual and has austere depths beneath his suave and polished surface.) [15] In some of the studies in *The Renaissance,* notably that on Leonardo da Vinci, the method is that of the *Imaginary Portraits,* and this method betrayed Pater into misinterpretations of evidence even in the *Plato and Platonism,* a work of his latest years.[16]

But from the beginning he advocated, though he did not always follow, another conception of the aesthetic function—to discover and analyze each particular manifestation of beauty, the "active principle" of the mind of each individual artist. This quest of the "formula" (which he may have learned from Baudelaire's criticism) led him, for example, to construct his essays on Leonardo and Sir Thomas Browne around the word "curiosity," the study of Wordsworth on the importance of contemplation in the conduct of life, the essay on Lamb on his subject's dainty epicureanism, and so forth. Of the suggestiveness of the method there can be no question, but every resultant portrait is to some degree distorted and "imaginary," and when we note that in each case the quality selected for emphasis is one possessed by Pater himself, we find it difficult to refute the charge that his subjects are projections of his own personality.

Marius the Epicurean and the unfinished *Gaston de Latour* are projections of Pater's inner life into other epochs, transitional as was his own. The former book, a body of doctrine rather than a novel,[17] was undertaken to clarify, or rather to modify, the "dangerously" misleading Cyrenaicism of the *Conclusion* to *The Renaissance.*[18] Though it is admitted that "the

---

[13] Contrasts rather than resemblances are brought out in T. S. Eliot, "Arnold and Pater," *Selected Essays* (1932), pp. 346-357.

[14] The meditation on the Mona Lisa, which carries to its zenith the romantic cult of the *femme fatale,* Wilde described as "criticism of the highest kind. It treats the work of art simply as a starting point for a new creation." The beholder "lends the beautiful thing its myriad meanings." See E. J. Bock, *Walter Paters Einfluss auf Oscar Wilde* (Bonn, 1913).

[15] See Irving Babbitt, *Masters of Modern French Criticism* (1912), p. 322.

[16] A special kind of unwarranted manipulation of literary material is exposed in S. C. Chew, "Pater's Quotations," *Nation* (N. Y.), xcix (1914). 404-405.

[17] Ed. Sir J. C. Squire (2v, 1929); Joseph Sagmaster (1935). For what can be said of *Marius* as fiction, as of Pater's related minor works, see Baker, ix (1938). 209-213. See also Louise Rosenblatt, "*Marius l'Epicurien* de Walter Pater et ses points de départ français," *RLC,* xv (1935). 97-106.

[18] The *Conclusion* was suppressed in the second edition, to reappear, with the addition of one quiet but all-important concessive clause, in the third edition, where there is a footnote directing the reader's attention to *Marius.*

burden of positive moral obligation" rested lightly upon Marius, Pater fashioned of "the New Cyrenaicism" a philosophy not of pleasure but of "fullness of life" which embraced, or might embrace, disinterested activity, kindness, compassion, and self-sacrifice. Passing from his ancestral religion through stages of Epicureanism and Stoicism, Marius is brought to the threshold of Christianity and in the end meets a death approximating to martyrdom. But the picture drawn of the Church in the age of the Antonines is as false to history as is Pater's delineation of Sparta in *Plato and Platonism*. In *The Renaissance* he had implied a valuation of all religions for their beauty, strangeness, and passion, and in *Marius* a lively sympathy with ecclesiastical tradition and a delight in the aesthetic charm of ritual are all that are offered as a substitute for faith. There is a report that towards the end of his life Pater was contemplating the resumption of a youthful intention to take holy orders. It is as well for his reputation that he did not do so, for he remained always a fastidious pragmatist.[19] It is not surprising that in the minds of young men who sought in *Marius* not fiction but a rule of life the evolution of Marius towards Christianity went unnoticed while the cult of Beauty gained new adherents. Nor is it without significance that Pater, dissatisfied, abandoned work on *Gaston* in which he had made a further effort to reconcile "the exigence of his sensibility with the needs of his conscience."[20]

Notwithstanding the subtlety and austerity of his thought, the impression *Style* will not down that in Pater's writings the manner is more important than the matter. In the infinitely patient discrimination of his own impressions, the elaborate artistry displayed in the precise expression of every shade of idea and sentiment with a constant introduction of hair-splitting qualifications seems often to be undertaken as much for the sake of the musical cadence of the sentences as for the ideas expounded in them. To most readers the verbal virtuoso appears more memorable than the humanist. In the judgment of the greatest of his disciples (and the adjective is employed relatively, for Pater influenced no mind of absolutely first rank), he was "all-powerful in written word, impotent in life."[21]

II

Not the greatest but certainly the most famous of the followers of Walter *Oscar* Pater was Oscar Wilde [22] (1856-1900). The story of his rise to the dizzy *Wilde*

[19] Compare James Huneker, *The Pathos of Distance* (1913), p. 280: "In the Aristippean flux and reflux of his ideas we discern a strong family likeness to the theories of William James and Henri Bergson, a pragmatism poetically transfigured."

[20] A. J. Farmer, *Le mouvement esthétique*, p. 64.

[21] George Moore, *Avowals* (1919), p. 215.

[22] *Works* (14v, 1908); *Complete Works* (4v, Paris, 1936); *Selected Works*, ed. Richard Aldington (1946). — Frances Winwar, *Oscar Wilde and the Yellow 'Nineties* (1940), with bibliography; Lord Alfred Douglas, *My Friendship with Oscar Wilde* (1932), an *apologia*, notwithstanding the same writer's *Without Apology* (1938); Frank Harris, *Oscar Wilde: His Life and Confessions* (2v, 1918), to be used with caution; R. H. Sherard, *Life of Oscar Wilde* (1906; 1928) and *The Real Oscar Wilde* (1917), by a loyal friend; W. W. Kenilworth,

summit of fame and of his catastrophic fall will be remembered when oblivion, the penalty for their fundamental insincerity, overtakes most of his writings. To the historian he is already the symbol of a period.

Inheriting artistic tastes from his clever mother, Wilde came to Oxford in 1874. There he attended Ruskin's lectures and, while differing radically on the question of the function of art in society, he caught from the master a sympathy with the poor and outcast that helps explain his views on Socialism. But a stronger influence was that of Pater whose favorite disciple he became. Adopting a pose of extravagant aestheticism, he dressed exotically, paraded his love of "blue china" and other objects of virtu, and discoursed upon the complete indifference of art to morality or to anything save itself. Having won the Newdigate prize with *Ravenna* (1878), a negligible piece of Swinburnian pastiche, he left Oxford in 1878, traveled in Greece, and by 1881 had achieved in London sufficient celebrity to give point to Gilbert and Sullivan's *Patience* and to a long series of satiric thrusts by Du Maurier in *Punch*. Only popular curiosity about Wilde can account for the success of *Poems* (1881) which went through five editions within the year. The poems are imitations of Rossetti and Swinburne discordantly juxtaposed to borrowings from Milton, Wordsworth, Tennyson, and Arnold. The sympathy expressed at once with radicalism and Catholicism is specious, and the adaptation of so many styles and moods to the purposes of artifice reveals at once Wilde's facility and his want of truth. From the first he was a literary opportunist.[23]

A lecture-tour of the United States [24] (1882) during which Wilde carried the gospel of aestheticism to the Philistines was followed by several comparatively barren years of less eccentricity but probably not less depravity. He edited *The Woman's World,* published essays, including *The Decay of Lying* and *The Critic as Artist* which elaborated his theory of the complete indifference of art to subject-matter, and then, somewhat unexpectedly, *The Happy Prince and Other Tales* (1888), a collection of graceful fairy stories with wittily satiric allusions to contemporary topics and (in some of them) an expression of his humanitarian sentiments and sympathy with the sufferings of the poor. It is in the light of this latter motive that must be read the more pretentious essay, *The Soul of Man under Socialism* (1891), in which are ideas borrowed from Morris and G. B. Shaw and which indicates that Wilde's way of life was in part at least due to dissatisfaction with the contemporary state of society. *Lord Arthur Savile's Crime and Other Stories,*

A Study of Oscar Wilde (1912); Arthur Ransome, *Oscar Wilde, a Critical Study* (1912); O. T. Hopkins, *Oscar Wilde, a Study of the Man and His Work* (1916); Arthur Symons, *A Study of Oscar Wilde* (1930); G. J. Renier, *Oscar Wilde* (1933); Vincent O'Sullivan, *Aspects of Wilde* (1936); Boris Brasol, *Oscar Wilde, the Man, Artist, and Martyr* (1938); Hesketh Pearson, *Oscar Wilde, His Life and Wit* (1946). — On the background of the period see Holbrook Jackson, *The Eighteen Nineties* (1913); Richard Le Gallienne, *The Romantic Nineties* (1925); Thomas Beer, *The Mauve Decade* (1926); Joseph and E. R. Pennell, *The Life of James McNeill Whistler* (1908); Sir William Rothenstein, *Men and Memories* (2v, 1931-1932); W. B. Yeats, *The Trembling of the Veil* (1916).

[23] See further B. I. Evans, *English Poetry in the Later Nineteenth Century* (1933), ch. xiv.
[24] Lloyd Lewis and H. J. Smith, *Oscar Wilde Discovers America* (1936).

Intentions (a collection of essays chiefly memorable for the further develop-ment of the implications underlying his theory of the uselessness of art), and *The Duchess of Padua,* a tragedy in verse, all followed in 1891; and in the same year came *The Picture of Dorian Gray,* a novel which is the most typical product of the "Decadence." The "unwholesome" overtones audible in this book and in the earlier *Portrait of Mr. W. H.* (a theory of Shake-speare's Sonnets couched in the form of fiction) increased Wilde's notoriety.

A series of successful comedies now carried Wilde to the zenith of his *Plays* career. *Lady Windermere's Fan* (produced 1892; published 1893), *A Woman of No Importance* (1893; 1894), and *The Ideal Husband* (1895; 1899) have much in common with one another. The presence of a "problem" shows that Wilde, always the opportunist, was conscious of the influence of Ibsen, probably through the medium of Pinero's plays; but the substance is thin and out of accord with the coruscating epigrams and paradoxes. In 1893 a license was refused ·for the performance of *Salomé.* It was written in French [25] and was produced in Paris by Sarah Bernhardt in 1894. To that year belongs *The Sphinx,* a revery upon the lusts of ancient times closing upon the note of renunciation and acceptance of religion which is sug-gestive of Joris-Karl Huysmans and very typical of the eighteen-nineties.[26] In 1895 came Wilde's masterpiece of comedy, *The Importance of Being Earnest,* in which, for once, he achieved a perfect combination of theme and style in airily insolent and witty paradox.

This play and *The Ideal Husband* were both running at London theatres when Wilde's world crashed round him. The Marquis of Queensberry (the father of Lord Alfred Douglas) accused him of homosexual practices. Wilde brought suit for libel; lost it; was at once arrested and put on trial; and having been convicted was sentenced to two years' imprisonment. Before his release in 1897 he had written *De Profundis,*[27] an *apologia* that is an expres-sion of self-pity and wounded pride rather than of contrition. Even in the depths of mortification he found satisfaction in his pose. *The Ballad of Reading Gaol* (1898), written, as Wilde's letters show, under the impulse of intense emotion, is moving in its expression of sympathy with outcasts from society; but the rhetorical exaggeration and the inappropriate echoes from other poets smack of artifice, and the basic theme, that "all men kill the thing they love," is an absurd generalization from Wilde's personal ex-perience. Two years followed of squalid life in exile upon the Continent from which he was relieved by death in Paris in 1900. Upon his grave Jacob Epstein's gigantic sphinx presses down.

[25] The English version was made by Lord Alfred Douglas (1870-1945). Douglas's original verse of later years has had its admirers. His best work is in the sonnet form. *Complete Poems* (1928). See W. Sorley Brown, *Lord Alfred Douglas: The Man and the Poet* (1918); Patrick Braybrook, *Lord Alfred Douglas: His Life and Work* (1931).

[26] Even the stanzaic form betrays the insincerity and artifice of this poem. The interior rimes were commended for their ingenuity; but the stanza is simply that of *In Memoriam* printed as two long lines instead of four short lines. — Another poem of this period is *The Harlot's House,* a rhetorical but not unimpressive allegory of the degeneration of love.

[27] Published posthumously, with excisions, in 1905; complete text, 1949.

Wilde struck in various directions, but not at random, against contemporary standards of taste and morality, and more fundamentally at contemporary society.[28] In his social criticism he was probably as sincere as it was in his nature to be; but one feels that he desired a free society rather for the sake of the freedom it would give him than for the general good. His "Socialism," like his aestheticism, was a rationalization of his own sensual impulses. The real Wilde, so far as he is discoverable at all, is to be found not in *De Profundis* but in *The Picture of Dorian Gray*. The analysis of the search for rare sensations clarifies the logical consequences of the acceptance of Pater's doctrines without the moralistic concessions which Pater had suggested; and in so far as the novel is an apologue of divided personality it is prophetic of the ruin into which its author was soon to fall.

III

The
Yellow
Book

Though the most conspicuous figure of the "mauve decade," Wilde was not the leader of the group of writers and artists who formed the "Rhymers' Club," published jointly slim volumes of verse, and in 1894 were associated together in John Lane's quarterly, *The Yellow Book*.[29] The real leader of the "Decadence" was the artist Aubrey Beardsley [30] (1872-1898) whose drawings of exquisite, sinuous line and startling contrasts of light and shade quintessentialize in their morbidity and perversity the audacities of the movement. As art-editor of *The Yellow Book* Beardsley coöperated with Henry Harland (1861-1905), the literary editor, afterwards author of *The Cardinal's Snuff-Box* (1900) and other short novels notable for a dainty wit that does not conceal their lack of substance. John Lane, the publisher, anxious not to offend, included among his contributors Henry James, Richard Garnett, Edmund Gosse, and other writers, and Leighton and other artists; and the respectable tone given by them to the quarterly was intended to offset the impression made by the more troubling minority. Even so, the tone set by Beardsley's drawings was dominant and after several numbers had appeared during 1894-1895, William Watson, according to the well-known story, issued an ultimatum to Lane that either Beardsley's work must be suppressed or else he, Watson, would sever his connection with the periodical. As a consequence Beardsley left *The Yellow Book* (which with dwindling brilliance continued for another two years) and launched

The
Savoy

The Savoy (1896) with Arthur Symons as editor. Among its contributors

[28] See Granville Hicks, *Figures of Transition* (1939), ch. VI.
[29] One of the contributors to *The Yellow Book* was Frederick William Rolfe (1860-1913) who called himself "Baron Corvo." An isolated figure, shabby and sinister, Rolfe was utterly *fin de siècle*. "Caviare to the general" best describes his work, but, as D. H. Lawrence said, "if caviare, at any rate it came from the belly of a live fish." Six *Stories Toto Told Me* (1898), published in *The Yellow Book*, were expanded as *In His Own Image* (1900; ed. Shane Leslie, 1925). *Chronicles of the House of Borgia* (1901) is a learned, highly colored, and extravagant history. Rolfe is best remembered for *Hadrian the Seventh* (1904), a romance heavily charged with autobiography, and a "compensation" for the writer's failures and disrepute. *Don Tarquinio* (1905) and later books are of less interest. — See A. J. A. Symons, *The Quest for Corvo* (1934).
[30] H. Macfall, *Aubrey Beardsley, the Man and his Work* (1928).

were G. B. Shaw, Max Beerbohm, W. B. Yeats, Ernest Dowson, and the artists Charles Conder and William Rothenstein. *The Savoy* was decidedly more "advanced" than its predecessor, in fact so far ahead or to one side of the public taste that after running for a year it failed for lack of support. Wilde's downfall had discredited aestheticism; and with England rapidly approaching a crisis in her old quarrel with the Boers the strident voices of the imperialists drowned out the delicate music of decadent literature.

The exquisite grace and urbane artificiality of decadent prose at its best is seen in the essays of Max Beerbohm [31] (1872-1956). More characteristic, however, is the work in verse and prose of Arthur Symons [32] (1865-1945). *Arthur* In his poetry there is a remoteness from contemporary society that expresses *Symons* the point of view of the entire group of "Decadents." The substitution of suggestion for statement; the effects of "correspondences" of words and music and color; the dim sadness and misty unwholesomeness; the profound sensuality; and the reliance upon symbols—these are characteristics which Symons shares with his French masters, Verlaine and Mallarmé. His critical study, *The Symbolist Movement in Literature* (1899), though inadequate from the historian's point of view, is of historical importance as a sort of belated manifesto. Richard Le Gallienne (1866-1947), though ranging more widely and vigorously than most of the writers considered in this chapter, displays *fin de siècle* traits in much of his work. The two series of *Prose Fancies* (1894-1896) are typical of the time and the man. The many essays and impressionistic sketches cannot be enumerated here. The novels, which do not fall into any simple category, are, like Le Gallienne's verse, mostly forgotten, though *The Quest of the Golden Girl* (1896) still has the interest of a period-piece.

Many writers on the periphery of the "Decadence" will be considered *Ernest* later. We may conclude this chapter with the typical figure of Ernest Dow- *Dowson* son [33] (1867-1900). His febrile, sordid and lonely, pathetic and tragically short life was in strictest harmony with *fin de siècle* aestheticism. Influences from Swinburne, Verlaine, Catullus, and Propertius are intertwined in his poetry with others from the Catholic liturgy and hymnology. An exquisite technician within a narrow range, he sang of chaste and tender love, of un-controlled passion resulting in remorse, of renunciation of the world, and of the fleetingness of mortality. His prose is of little moment and his play,

[31] *Works* (1896); *More* (1889); *And Even Now* (1920); and other volumes of essays; and in fiction: *The Happy Hypocrite* (1897) and *Zuleika Dobson* (1911). Sir Max Beerbohm was the most brilliant caricaturist of his time. The student of literature must know his two volumes, *The Poet's Corner* (1904) and *Rossetti and His Circle* (1922).

[32] *London Nights* (1895); *Images of Good and Evil* (1899); *Poems* (2v, 1902), a severely sifted collected edition; and later volumes. In prose, besides impressionistic studies of men and places, Symons wrote more elaborately on Blake, Hardy, Rossetti, Swinburne, and the Elizabethan dramatists. — See his autobiographical *Confessions* (1930) and T. E. Welby, *Arthur Symons, a Critical Study* (1925).

[33] Contributions to *The Book of the Rhymers' Club* (1892) and their *Second Book* (1894); *Verses* (1896); *Decorations* (1899); *Poetical Works*, ed. Desmond Flower (1934); *Stories*, ed. Mark Longaker (Philadelphia, 1947). The most extended study is Mark Longaker, *Ernest Dowson* (Philadelphia, 1944).

The Pierrot of the Minute (1897), a slight thing; but the best poems in *Verses* (1896)—such poems as *Nuns of the Perpetual Adoration, Amor Umbratilis,* and the famous *Non sum qualis eram bonae sub regno Cynarae* —possess a quality of permanence because of their sincerity of passion and their individuality of style that sets them apart from the ephemeral sensualities and sadnesses of the other "Decadents."

XXXVI

The Novel: Naturalism and Romance

I

To include Samuel Butler among the novelists is perhaps to suggest a *Samuel* false emphasis, since this man of versatile talents wrote but one novel; but *Butler* *The Way of All Flesh* is substantial enough to validate the claim, and the element of fiction is considerable in three of his other books.

Samuel Butler [1] (1835-1902) was the son of a clergyman and grandson of Bishop Samuel Butler whose biography he wrote (1902). In boyhood he suffered from the extremes to which parental control was then generally carried, and in *The Way of All Flesh* he later took vengeance upon his father.[2] The gradual process of escape from the strict educational discipline and sanctimonious priggishness imposed upon him is narrated ironically but with scarcely any embroidery upon the facts. Butler was destined for the ministry, but after graduation from Cambridge religious doubts led to the abandonment of an intention that had been his family's rather than his own. In 1859 he emigrated to New Zealand [3] where he accumulated a small fortune through sheep-farming. Here began the friendship with C. P. Pauli which was to cost him much money and more pain, for, by an arch-irony, Butler, the ironist, was hoodwinked by this handsome, fascinating man who sponged shamelessly upon his benefactor. The relationship is central to an understanding of Butler's character. He could satirize his father and family, his enemies and some of his friends; but the wound made by Pauli's unfaithfulness was too deep to be cauterized by satire.

An interest roused by *The Origin of Species* was expressed in articles con-

---

[1] *Works,* Shrewsbury Edition, ed. H. F. Jones and A. T. Bartholomew (20v, 1923-1926); *Erewhon,* ed. Aldous Huxley (1934); *The Way of All Flesh,* ed. G. B. Shaw (World's Classics, 1936). — A. J. Hoppé, *Bibliography* (1925); H. Festing Jones, *Samuel Butler, a Memoir* (2v, 1919); Gilbert Cannan, *Samuel Butler, a Critical Study* (1915); J. F. Harris, *Samuel Butler, the Man and His Work* (1916); C. E. M. Joad, *Samuel Butler* (1924); Mrs. R. S. Garnett, *Samuel Butler and His Family Relations* (1929); C. G. Stillman, *Samuel Butler: A Mid-Victorian Modern* (1932); J. B. Fort, *Samuel Butler. Etude d'un caractère et d'une intelligence* (Bordeaux, 1924) and *Samuel Butler. Etude d'un style* (Bordeaux, 1925); R. F. Rattray, *Samuel Butler, a Chronicle and an Introduction* (1935); Malcolm Muggeridge, *The Earnest Atheist: A Study of Samuel Butler* (1936); Madeleine L. Cazamian, *Le Roman et les idées en Angleterre,* I (Strassburg, 1923), ch. III; Baker, x. 244-270.

[2] The letters from Theobald Pontifex to Ernest are almost exact transcripts from the letters of Canon Butler to his son.

[3] Butler's letters home were put together by his father as *A Year in Canterbury Settlement* (1863). — See Donald Cowie, "Samuel Butler in New Zealand," *London Mercury,* xxxv (1937). 480-488.

tributed to a New Zealand newspaper.[4] Here began Butler's speculations upon evolution. After his return to England in 1864 he devoted himself to painting, exhibiting regularly at the Royal Academy between 1868 and 1876.[5] At art school he met Eliza M. A. Savage, a clever spinster of homely appearance and tart disposition with whom he corresponded for many years.[6] Quantities of her witty observations he borrowed for his own books. Art did not distract him from the problems of religion and science. In *The Evidence for the Resurrection of Jesus Christ* (privately printed, 1865) he subjected the Gospel narratives to an ironical analysis. This pamphlet was afterwards incorporated in *The Fair Haven* (1873) with the pretense that it had been written by a certain John Pickard Owen, lately deceased, whose biography, purporting to be written by a surviving brother, serves as an introduction. In this ruthlessly clever skit the irony is maintained with such quiet skill that more than one Evangelical reviewer was misled into commending *The Fair Haven* as a serious defense of Christian doctrine.

Erewhon

Meanwhile Butler had published *Erewhon, or Over the Range* (1872), his only book to win fame among his contemporaries. Mr. Higgs, the hero (if he may be so called), traverses the mountains of New Zealand and finds himself in a hitherto undiscovered country among strange people. Butler's imaginary commonwealth is not an ideal state, though some of its characteristics—gracious living, prosperity, physical health—reflect Butler's ideal. But in other respects—the worship of the goddess Ydgrun ("Mrs. Grundy," i.e., respectability) and the institution of the Musical Banks (conventional religion based upon pharisaic smugness)—the story is a satiric and ironic mirror of English society, resembling parts of *Gulliver's Travels* but described with a cool amusement in which there is nothing of Swift's *saeva indignatio*. Fallacies are exposed by means of ingenious paradox, and with infinite cleverness cogent reasoning is conducted from designedly unsound premises. The theory that machines are extensions of human organs is a parody of popular Darwinism but not without tragic implications for the future of mankind. Butler's modernity is also evinced in his doctrines of the rectifiability of moral error and the criminality of disease as an offense against the race.

On a visit to Canada in 1875 Butler composed a little masterpiece in verse, *A Psalm of Montreal*, in which the contrast between the virile beauty of the neglected Discobolus and the repulsive drabness of the taxidermist symbolizes the contrast between pagan grace and nineteenth-century respectability.

Evolution

During the following decade much of his energy went into the exposition of his biological theories in a series of volumes: *Life and Habit* (1877), *Evolution, Old and New* (1879), *Unconscious Memory* (1880), and *Luck or*

---

[4] *The Press*, Christchurch. *Darwin among the Machines* was afterwards incorporated in *Erewhon. Darwin on the Origin of Species, a Philosophical Dialogue* (1862) was reprinted at Christchurch in 1912.

[5] Butler's best-known painting, "Mr. Heatherley's Holiday," is now in the National Gallery of British Art. His "Family Prayers" recalls the atmosphere of Ernest Pontifex's boyhood.

[6] *Letters between Samuel Butler and Miss E. M. A. Savage* (1935).

Cunning? (1887).[7] Butler was at first not unsympathetic with Darwin and had been in personal touch with him in 1872. It is needless to retell the story of their quarrel.[8] Apart from the personal disagreement involved, Butler deceived himself in believing that the professional scientists had organized "a conspiracy of silence" against him. Patient experimenters are justified in ignoring the guesswork of a brilliant amateur. It helped Butler's fame immensely that the progress of research brought evolutionary doctrine in some particulars into harmony with his theories; but the same position would have been reached had he never lived. As an amateur he accepted the data collected by the professionals; but questioning their lines of reasoning and their conclusions, he repudiated the purposelessness inherent in Darwin's theory, and in place of "small fortuitous variations" he argued for purposive evolution. Without altogether eliminating the part played by "luck" in the evolutionary process, he held that needs, intelligence, and memory are implied in any acceptable theory. There is a deliberate intention in the individual cell which so acts upon its chance environment as best to serve its own ends. Butler thus restored, with a difference, the teleological argument of the pre-Darwinian evolutionists. Moreover, he found evidence of an unconscious racial memory in which serviceable habits are stored up. This memory asserts itself through the "identity" of parents and offspring. From this he deduced the doctrine of "vicarious immortality" which is the subject of the sermon in *Erewhon Revisited* and of the sonnet *Not on Sad Stygian Shore,* and also the doctrine of "the omnipresence of mind and intelligence throughout the universe to which no name can be so fittingly applied as God."[9]

The shaping influence of inherited habits is illustrated in the long account of Ernest Pontifex's ancestors which opens *The Way of All Flesh* so unpromisingly. This largely autobiographical novel was written between 1873 and 1885.[10] Butler himself appears in two characters, the hero and the hero's counselor and friend. He put into the book his parents, Pauli, Miss Savage, and other people he had known. Irony is employed for a serious and legitimate purpose, and though the candor is unreticent and unrelenting there is a sincere effort to avoid exaggeration. Realism is made a vehicle for a philosophy of wordly wisdom, the advocacy of a *via media* that is not golden but commonplace, with a recognition of the world's frauds and fallacies and with a confidence reposing upon sound physical health, the practice of the "comely virtues," and the possession of a sufficient income. The satiric picture of family life in mid-Victorian England is so vivid that the story

The Way of All Flesh

---

[7] See also parts of *God the Known and God the Unknown,* a series of articles in *The Examiner* (1879); in book form posthumously (1909). Many of the memoranda posthumously published in *The Note-Books* (1912) have to do with the subject of evolution.

[8] The conclusion reached by impartial inquiry is that Butler, not having been informed of the accident whereby Darwin cut out of the proofs of the preface to Krause's volume on evolution his acknowledgement of the use of Butler's *Life and Habit,* was justified in believing that a slight was intended. Much bad feeling might have been avoided if Darwin had followed his family's advice to offer an explanation instead of Huxley's, that Butler be ignored.

[9] H. Festing Jones, *Samuel Butler,* II. 41.

[10] Published posthumously, 1903.

is a document as well as an indictment. With all its wit and wisdom *The Way of All Flesh* is a sad and bitter book. Satire was the cloak with which Butler covered a brooding, suspicious, and disappointed nature.

Italy; Handel; Homer

Yet he had his compensations, chief among them Italy and the music of Handel. The fruit of many visits to the land he loved are the two travel books, *Alps and Sanctuaries* (1881) and *Ex-Voto* (1888), in which he recounted his wanderings in Piedmont and his appreciation of the votive chapels on the Sacro Monte at Varallo. The composition of an oratorio, *Ulysses,* in imitation of Handel, turned his thoughts to Homeric problems. After a visit to Asia Minor he evolved the theory that the *Iliad* was written by a Greek of the Troad secretly in sympathy with the Trojans. But he was convinced that the *Odyssey* had been written at Trapani in Sicily and by a woman. Upon *The Authoress of the Odyssey* (1897) he wasted elaborate pains. Butler's reputation as an ironist led many to take this for a hoax, but he was as serious as he was perverse, and the annoyance of the bigwigs of scholarship was merely a by-product of his work.[11] An equal amount of energy was expended upon *Shakespeare's Sonnets Reconsidered* (1899) in exposition of a theory that has not even the merit of being original. In his later years he spent much time arranging and docketing his correspondence and other papers against the day when a biography might be called for.

Erewhon Revisited (1901) is as closely related to *The Fair Haven* as to the original *Erewhon,* for, occupying his mind with the problem of the origins of religious beliefs, Butler hit upon the notion that the escape of Mr. Higgs had been interpreted by the Erewhonians as a miracle, had taken on legendary accretions, and had given rise to "Sunchildism," a new religion. The story, written with much spontaneity, is the most artistic of Butler's creations; there is pathos and gentleness in it as well as wit and humor; but these qualities do not conceal the fierceness of the caricature of revealed religion. George Bernard Shaw, who had a hand in its publication, did much to enhance Butler's posthumous fame, declaring that he was, in his own special department of satire, the greatest English author of the second half of the nineteenth century.

II

William Hale White

If the semi-autobiographical novels of William Hale White (1831-1913), who wrote under the pen-name of "Mark Rutherford," [12] are kept in remembrance, it will be rather as documents in the history of certain phases of Victorian thought than as works of imaginative literature. A few short

---

[11] B. Farrington, *Samuel Butler and the Odyssey* (1939). — Butler published translations of the *Iliad* (1898) and the *Odyssey* (1900), rendering the Greek into what he called "Tottenham Court Road English." See also his pleasant lecture, *The Humor of Homer* (1892).
[12] The three series of "Mark Rutherford's" *Pages from a Journal* (1900; 1910; 1915) are important supplements to his novels. — Sir W. R. Nicoll, *Introduction to the Novels of Mark Rutherford* (1924); H. W. Massingham, "Memorial Introduction" to *The Autobiography of Mark Rutherford* (ed. 1923); A. E. Taylor, "The Novels of Mark Rutherford," *E&S,* v (1914). 51-74; Baker, IX (1938). 97-115.

stories apart, White showed in his loosely woven, inconsequential books little evidence of structural capacity. He pictures with sympathy rather than disgust the nonconformist world of small shopkeepers and laborers who live in the borderland between indigence and ignoble decency. His special province is that of the religious-minded fundamentalists who are shaken in their faith by the new ideas of science and the new criticism of the Bible. Much of White's own experience went into *The Autobiography of Mark Rutherford* (1881) and *Mark Rutherford's Deliverance* (1885), the former dealing with his emancipation from Calvinism, the latter with the nether world of London. *The Revolution in Tanner's Lane* (1887), set in the period of industrial unrest following Waterloo, tells of the emancipation of a mind brought up in nonconformity and obtaining glimpses in the poetry of Wordsworth and Byron of a larger world of thought and emotion. Characteristic of White as of his time is the close association of religious doubt with sociological discussion and social reform. He had little humor but commanded a quiet kind of satire.

Immediately contemporary with White's narratives of the doubts and deliverance of Rutherford is *The Story of an African Farm* (1883) by Olive Schreiner [13] (1855-1920). Because of its passionate intensity and also because of the relationship of the two principal characters by affinity of temperament this story reminded its first readers of *Wuthering Heights*; but though the descriptions of the African veldt are not altogether unworthy of comparison with Emily Brontë's descriptions of the Yorkshire moors, the story does not really bear comparison with that masterpiece. The clumsy narrative concerns the efforts of certain sensitive souls to find a philosophy of life after abandoning the religion of childhood. The characterization of the heroine is one of the earliest expressions of the "new" femininism which was to gain ground during the last years of the century. *Olive Schreiner*

The conflict of faith and doubt is the motive running through the novels of Mrs. Humphry Ward (1851-1920). *Robert Elsmere* (1888), which made a great stir and troubled Mr. Gladstone, is the story of a clergyman in whom skepticism triumphs over faith with a consequent estrangement from his wife. Mrs. Ward, who was a niece of Matthew Arnold, reflected in her books the controversial issues of her youth long after the world had passed them by. Consequently her later novels seemed to be "dated" even at the time of their appearance. Today they are chiefly interesting for their recognizable portraits of actual people. *Mrs. Humphry Ward*

An unceasing attention to religious problems connects these writers with Joseph Henry Shorthouse [14] (1834-1903), though in his case the problem is that of reconciling mystical insight with orthodoxy and Roman Catholicism *Short- house*

[13] S. C. Cronwright, *The Life of Olive Schreiner* (1924).
[14] *Life, Letters and Literary Remains*, ed. Sarah Shorthouse (2v, 1905); M. Polak, *The Historical, Philosophical and Religious Aspects of John Inglesant* (1934); P. E. More, "Shorthouse," *Shelburne Essays*, III (1905). 213-243; W. K. Fleming, "Some Truths about *John Inglesant*," *Quarterly Rev.*, CCXLV (1925). 130-148. — Shorthouse's five other novels are nearly negligible, but *The Countess Eve* is notable for its spiritual feeling and delicate morbidity.

with Anglicanism. In *John Inglesant* (1880) Shorthouse transferred the questions at issue in the Tractarian Movement to an appropriate seventeenth-century setting. The hero, a mystic misled for a time into worldliness, is a courtier of Charles I, comes under the influence of Little Gidding, is present at a Papal consistory, and is in Naples during a visitation of the plague. His private story, which involves an avenging quest of his brother's murderer, is interwoven with public affairs in a panorama of European life which remains impressive even after Shorthouse's inaccuracies have been exposed. With infinite pains Shorthouse put together in a sort of mosaic countless passages from seventeenth-century books, but though no acknowledgment is made, the result is not plagiarism but something highly original. When Pater's *Marius the Epicurean* appeared readers were quick to notice an unlike likeness between the two books.

III

Gissing   George Gissing [15] (1857-1903) is the most significant figure in the period of transition from the Victorian to the modern novel. Tastes and scholarship fitted him for an academic career; but while a student at Manchester an infatuation with a girl of the streets whom he desired to "rescue" involved him in thefts for which he served a short prison term. Thus his hopes were ruined. On his release he attempted a new start in life in the United States, where he underwent the great hardships afterwards turned to the account of fiction in *New Grub Street*. He sold to the Chicago *Tribune* a few short stories [16] (1877). On his return to England he quixotically married the woman who had been the occasion of his misfortunes. The union was a wretched failure, endured in direst poverty and ending in a separation. Kept from starvation by tutoring and clerical jobs, he wrote a first novel which did not find a publisher and has disappeared. A small legacy carried him over the writing of *Workers in the Dawn* [17] (1880), which was published at his own expense. Though commercially a failure, it attracted the attention of Frederick Harrison, who gave Gissing employment as tutor to his sons and proved a valuable friend. For the next twenty years Gissing published on the average one novel a year, and though he was subjected

[15] There is no collected edition of Gissing's works; some of the novels are out of print. *Letters of George Gissing to Members of his Family*, ed. A. and E. Gissing (1927) is indispensable for want of anything better, but passages in the letters are suppressed with no indication of lacunae and towards the end of the book allusions to "Mrs. Gissing" are deliberately misleading. Other correspondence has been privately printed. *Selections, Autobiographical and Imaginative*, introduction by Virginia Woolf (1929). — A definitive biography is needed. Morley Roberts, *The Private Life of Henry Maitland* (1912), a biography thinly disguised as fiction, must serve till superseded, but it is a disservice to Gissing's memory by one of his oldest friends. Frank Swinnerton, *George Gissing, a Critical Study* (1912); see R. C. McKay, *George Gissing and his Critic Frank Swinnerton* (Philadelphia, 1933); May Yates, *George Gissing, an Appreciation* (Manchester, 1923); Anton Weber, *George Gissing und die Soziale Frage* (Leipzig, 1932); S. V. Gapp, *George Gissing, Classicist* (Philadelphia, 1936); Baker, IX, ch. IV.

[16] Eleven stories are reprinted in *Sins of the Fathers and Other Tales*, ed. Vincent Starrett (Chicago, 1924) and *Brownie*, ed. G. E. Hastings, Vincent Starrett, and T. O. Mabbott (1931).

[17] Ed. Robert Shafer (1935), with introduction and bibliography.

to incessant drudgery, never becoming a popular author and often reduced to despair, he won the esteem of so discriminating a judge as Henry James [18] and the friendship of various men of letters, notably H. G. Wells.[19] After the death of his first wife he repeated the mistake of his youth by making a second ill-fated marriage. With the years of abject poverty behind him, he was able, by practising severest economies, to gratify his scholarly longing to see the lands of classical antiquity, visiting Greece once and Italy three times. From his wanderings in Calabria in 1897 he drew the material for a travel book, *By the Ionian Sea* [20] (1901). Unable to obtain a divorce from his second wife, Gissing in his last years found solace in an irregular union with a French woman of refined tastes with whom he lived in the Pyrenees. The quiet pessimism of his final phase is expressed in *The Private Papers of Henry Ryecroft* (1903), a beautifully composed series of *pensées* which has often, but mistakenly, been taken as autobiographical. Into this book he put many of his ripest, but not all his deepest, thoughts on human experience. Before his death he brought almost to completion *Veranilda*,[21] a historical novel on the struggle of the dying Roman Empire with the Goths. With this he had been occupied for many years, and upon it he lavished an erudition comparable in richness though not in imaginative intensity to that of Flaubert's *Salammbô*. Apart from his novels the tale of his books is rounded out with two inconsiderable collections of short stories [22] and a monograph on Dickens (1898) which illuminates not only the subject but the mind of the critic.[23] Dickens was Gissing's first master and remained a paramount influence upon him.

In Gissing's novels the continuity of English fiction is preserved yet at the same time deflected from its former course by the attraction of French and Russian writers and by the doctrine of *l'art pour l'art*. In his studies of environment he follows Dickens, but he probes deeper and does not gloss over with humor and sentiment the appalling conditions of the life of the poor. Nor does he often offer human kindliness as a compensation or remedy for this state of affairs. It is sometimes said that he cherished the ambition to write an English *Comédie Humaine;* but he lacked Balzac's energy and wide-ranging curiosity and variety of social experience. There is a closer analogy to Zola, the Goncourts, and the French naturalistic movement in general.[24] But Gissing, though his "saturation" in his subject won the commendation of Henry James, did not rely upon "scientific" documentation, and, unlike Zola, he was not involved by his concern with the

Naturalism

[18] Henry James, *Notes on Novelists* (1914), pp. 437-443.
[19] H. G. Wells, *Experiment in Autobiography* (1934), pp. 481-493.
[20] New ed., with introduction by Virginia Woolf (1933).
[21] Posthumous, 1904, with preface by Frederick Harrison.
[22] *Human Odds and Ends* (1898); *The House of Cobwebs* (posthumous, 1906), with a "Survey" of Gissing's work by Thomas Seccombe.
[23] Supplementing this formal study is a series of prefaces written for the never completed Rochester Edition of Dickens' works and gathered together as *Critical Studies of the Works of Charles Dickens*, ed. Temple Scott (1924).
[24] See W. C. Frierson, *L'Influence du naturalisme français sur les romanciers anglais de 1885 à 1900* (Paris, 1925), especially pp. 205-218.

problem of environment in the related problem of heredity. Save perhaps in *Demos* (1886), where he demonstrates the failure of Socialism, and in *Born in Exile* (1892), in which he narrates the efforts of a young man to rise above his own social class, there is little in these novels to remind one of Zola's characteristic stress upon a central theme or thesis. Moreover, though there is a conscientious effort to be "objective," Gissing does not succeed in being impersonal; his own tastes, prejudices, and opinions persistently intrude. Nevertheless the emphasis upon the brutalized poor, upon pestiferous crowds, and upon squalid amorousness is suggestive of Zola, albeit a Zola restrained by English reticences. The connection with Flaubert is more remote, though there are resemblances between *Madame Bovary* and *The Whirlpool* (1897). The Russians Gissing knew in French or German translations; there is something of Turgenev in his outlook, but, save in *Isabel Clarendon* (1886), where the imitation may have been deliberate, little of Dostoëvsky in his art.[25] Basically he remained in the native tradition. Till his later books Gissing was committed to the old "three-decker" Victorian novel, with its elaborate and often melodramatic plot, its crowd of supernumerary characters, its different groups of people, its tendency to argue about them instead of making them self-revealing, and its tidy ending. In his studies in abnormal temperaments he was in advance of his time, but he subjected them to the caprice of old-fashioned intrigue. Yet in his experiments with a purely dramatic method and his attempts, albeit never completely successful, to stand, as an artist, outside his work, he points the way towards a more modern technique.

Studies in Environment and Psychology

The two categories into which these novels (apart from *Veranilda*) fall are suggested by the contrasted aims of the two authors who are principal characters in *New Grub Street* (1891). Biffen's object was to secure "absolute realism in the sphere of the ignobly decent," while Reardon was "a psychological realist for the more cultivated." The keynote of many of the studies in environment is the ignobility of poverty. In some, notably *The Nether World* (1889), the lowest classes of slum life are portrayed with intense realism and from personal experience—but experience, as it were, from the outside, for Gissing, even in the worst days of his youth, was never a part of the life he was compelled to lead and viewed it with a horror and loathing which left no room for any comprehension of the mitigating circumstances of habit and insensitivity that perhaps dull the miseries of the very poor. In other novels he rises to a slightly higher social stratum of suburban or provincial life, but a life still under the burden of a poverty perhaps all the more intolerable because not so degraded. *New Grub Street,* the finest of the novels dealing with the lower middle class, makes use of Gissing's own bitterly familiar acquaintance with the life of writers who, having once aspired to literary renown, have sunk to the ranks of literary hacks. Of the many authors packed into this book one dies of starvation and another commits suicide. Apart from the novels of environment are the

[25] Helen Muchnic, *Dostoëvsky's English Reputation* (Northampton, Mass., 1939).

studies in psychological analysis. Of these the most elaborate is *Thyrza* (1887) in which the character of the heroine, torn between her low-born fiancé and her high-born lover, is portrayed with elaborate, loving, and sentimental care. Here it may be remarked that in almost all his books Gissing's grim realism is softened by the charm and tenderness with which at least one woman in each story is idealized. In *A Life's Morning* (1888), where he evidently imitated *Richard Feverel*, and in *The Crown of Life* (1899) the influence of Meredith is apparent; but Gissing was not fortified with that master's comic spirit and poetry and confidence in life.

Longing for the "retired leisure" of which *Ryecroft* is the dream and compelled to drudge without rest and without hope yet with an artistic conscience that permitted no compromise with the popular taste of the day, Gissing viewed life with humorless disgust. He had no trust in the processes of democracy. He was skeptical of the promises held out by the Socialists. No other writer of the period foresaw more clearly the catastrophe towards which the world was heading and no other prophesied so forcefully and repeatedly the coming of "a time of vast conflicts which will pale into insignificance the thousand wars of old." [26]

Several lesser novelists have points of connection with Gissing. Sir Walter Besant (1836-1901) used fiction in advocacy of social reforms. *All Sorts and Conditions of Men* (1882) portrays life in the East End of London, and later novels expose the miseries of urban labor. In fiction of another sort Besant, who was an authority on the antiquities of London, re-created the life of the metropolis in the eighteenth century. Resembling Gissing in that they wrote novels about the lives of the lowly are Richard Whiteing (1840-1928), author of *No. 5 John Street* (1889), and Arthur Morrison (1863-1945), author of *Tales of Mean Streets* (1894) and *A Child of the Jago* (1896). Israel Zangwill (1864-1926) pictured humble Jewish life in *Children of the Ghetto* (1892) and later stories and plays. Closer to Maupassant in technique but related to Gissing by virtue of his unflinching realism was Leonard Merrick (1864-1938), author of *Conrad in Quest of His Youth* (1903) and other novels much admired by his fellow-craftsmen. [27] The debt to Gissing both in subjects and technique is apparent in the work of several younger novelists whose achievement will be noticed in a later chapter.

IV

The career of George Moore [28] (1852-1933) seems to be as sinuous and *George* unaccountable as his personality, but for all its diversity it is unified by *Moore*

---

[26] *The Private Papers of Henry Ryecroft,* "Winter," xviii.

[27] See the introductory tributes by H. G. Wells, Maurice Hewlett, and other writers in Merrick's *Works* (12v, 1918-1919).

[28] *Works,* Carra Edition (21v, 1922-1924); Ebury Edition (20v, 1936-1938). There is no complete edition of Moore's works, and so long as his testamentary directions are in force there may not be. He suppressed some of his books altogether and ruled others out of the "canon" without prohibiting their publication. *Letters,* introduction by John Eglinton (1942). — I. A. Williams, *Bibliography* (1921), needing revision and amplification: Joseph Hone, *The Life of*

unfailing signs of his dedication to art. After ,an undisciplined boyhood at
Moore Hall in Ireland, where he learned more from stablemen and book-
makers than at school, he went to Paris to study painting, consort with
artists and men of letters, and live the *vie de Bohème*. His nature was, he
said, as receptive to impressions as a sheet of wax. In the milieu of Médan
he assimilated the doctrines of the *roman expérimental*—naturalism and
"scientific" impersonality in fiction. But he also absorbed much from Balzac
and Flaubert, and in French translation he read Turgenev. Agrarian troubles
in Ireland reduced his income and forced him to return to London in 1880.
A volume of verses, *Flowers of Passion,* had appeared in 1878 and was followed by *Pagan Poems* in 1881. These bits of Baudelairian pastiche are precursors of the "decadent" poetry of the eighteen-nineties.

Moore's first phase as a novelist (1883-1894) began with an adherence to
strict Zolaesque naturalism and moved towards a freer and sincerer realism
upon which the greatest influence was Balzac's. *A Modern Lover* [29] (1883),
written with a challenging candor that provoked protests, closely resembles
Maupassant's *Bel-Ami* but preceded that story by two years. *A Mummer's
Wife* (1884) is naturalistic in its painstakingly detailed portrayal of the life
of a squalid troupe of actors. The emphasis upon the forces of heredity and
environment derives from Zola, but the narrative of Kate Ede's degradation
through drink is suggestive of Flaubert and there is a striking likeness to
the work Gissing was doing at just this time. The outcry against *A Mummer's Wife* and the prosecution of the publisher of translations of Zola's
novels for which Moore was partly responsible occasioned his forceful
pamphlet, *Literature at Nurse* (1885), an attack upon the circulating libraries which by means of financial pressure imposed strait-laced moral
standards upon English literature. From the drab seriousness of Kate's story
Moore turned, in *A Drama in Muslin* (1886), to a frivolous picture of well-
to-do Irish society. Here the new naturalism is strangely crossed with a
manner reminiscent of Jane Austen. That Moore had been studying
Huysmans is shown by the close parallels in *A Mere Accident* (1887) to *A
Rebours*; a more poetic quality now informed a style that had hitherto
been as commonplace as the subject-matter. The *Confessions of a Young
Man* (1888), which attracted the somewhat condescending attention of
Walter Pater who doubtless recognized in it the evidence of his influence,[30]
reveals Moore as definitely a precursor along lines that were to lead to the
"Decadence." Noteworthy are the sensuality and fastidiousness, the attacks
on materialism and Philistinism, and the modish and probably insincere

George Moore (1936); John Freeman, *A Portrait of George Moore in a Study of his Work*
(1922); Charles Morgan, *Epitaph on George Moore* (1935); A. J. Farmer, *Le Mouvement
esthetique et "décadent" en Angleterre* (Paris, 1931), Part I, ch. III; W. C. Frierson, *L'Influence
du naturalisme français sur les romanciers anglais* (Paris, 1925), pp. 83-120; Baker, IX, ch. V.
For a personal impression of Moore and his opinions by the present writer see *Readings from
the American Mercury,* ed. G. C. Knight (1926), pp. 61-81.
    [29] Rewritten as *Lewis Seymour and Some Women* (1917) and ultimately ruled out of the
"canon."
    [30] R. P. Sechler, *George Moore, a Disciple of Walter Pater* (Philadelphia, 1931).

expressions of admiration for the Roman liturgy and for the literature of the late Roman Empire. With the *Confessions* may be grouped *Impressions and Opinions* (1891) and *Modern Painting* (1893), the latter influential in spreading knowledge of the French Impressionists. Passing over a couple of novels and a play, we reach the fine book with which Moore's first phase closed.

This is *Esther Waters* (1894). That the influence of Zola was now no longer paramount is evident from the fact that the cardinal tenet of "scientific" naturalism—the crushing power of heredity and environment over the individual—is disregarded in this history of a girl who struggles against adversity and social prejudice and in the end triumphs. The novel has something in common with *Germinie Lacerteux*, but whereas the lowly heroine of the Goncourts is merely pathetic, Esther possesses courage and strength of character. The resemblance to Hardy's *Tess* is the more striking because of the nearness in dates of publication of the two books; but in Moore's realism there is nothing of Hardy's coloring of romance and no indictment of malignant Fate. The story, which is told with an artistic impersonality so complete that the author's genuine feeling must be read between the lines, is of the seduction of a young girl; her valiant and successful efforts to rear her son to sturdy manhood; and her life with her husband, the racetrack bookmaker and public-house keeper. The style is serious, honest, humane, and restrained. There are no digressions into the facetious, the grotesque, or the romantic. The Victorian principle of alternation, with the interest shifting from one group of characters to another, is discarded in favor of a restricted point of view, so that every chapter is mainly about Esther.[31] This technique Moore learned from Flaubert, Turgenev, and Henry James. *Esther Waters*

The next seven years form a somewhat unfruitful intermediate phase. *Celibates*[32] (1895) is a group of short stories of more or less abnormal and neurotic people. *Evelyn Innes* (1898) and *Sister Teresa* (1901) are really one novel in two parts. Again the point of view is restricted, attention being concentrated upon the aesthetic, emotional, and intellectual life of the heroine. In the analysis of the conflicting claims of the world and of religion the influence of Huysmans has been detected; but there is more of difference than of resemblance. Ultimately Moore came to condemn these books as insincere and ruled them out of the "canon." Whether faked or not, they are undeniably dull and "dated," memorable, if at all, for the appreciations of Wagner's music.

The shock of the Boer War and especially the cruelty of Kitchener's concentration camps alienated Moore from English life and in 1901 he returned to Ireland. During the ten years of his "Irish" phase he associated with Yeats, Synge, Lady Gregory, Edward Martyn, A. E., and other writers who were active in the Irish Literary Renaissance. For a time he was an *Ireland*

---

[31] J. W. Beach, *The Twentieth Century Novel* (1932), pp. 135-138.
[32] Revised as *In Single Strictness* (1922) and again as *Celibate Lives* (1927).

enthusiastic supporter of the Abbey Theatre and as enthusiastic an amateur of folk-tales. The story of these years he afterwards told with infinite zest and unscrupulousness in *Hail and Farewell,* manipulating the characters of actual people for the purposes of something that is close to fiction. He had brought to Ireland the ripe experience of a novelist who had at last found himself—or one of his many selves. Trained to observe the human scene and to analyze the human heart, he was able to store up a multitude of impressions to which he gave literary form. *Memoirs of my Dead Life* (1906) looks backward to former times and is largely devoted to amatory episodes which lose nothing in the telling. *The Untilled Field* (1903) is a collection of stories of Irish life, intended for translation into Irish [33] and deeply marked with the impress of Turgenev. The racy idiom may well, as Moore claimed, have influenced Synge's dialogue style. In general the tales are straightforward, but in some there is a suggestive, latent symbolism which shows how sensitive Moore was to contemporary currents in literary theory and practice. Symbolism is again apparent beneath the surface of *The Lake* (1905), in purity of English and clarity of design one of the most beautiful of Moore's books. This story of the escape of a young priest from the "prison-house of Catholicism" is an outgrowth from the earlier analysis of the spiritual misgivings of Evelyn Innes; but its searching into the roots of religious belief indicates the direction in which Moore's thoughts were moving. He described this novel as "an uninterrupted flow of narrative." The author's ideas are never permitted to intrude; and with an art reminiscent of Henry James the action is witnessed entirely from the point of view of Father Gogarty.

In 1911 Moore returned to England. His relations with the Irish writers, his enthusiasm, and his disillusionment form the principal subject of the autobiographical trilogy, *Hail and Farewell* (1911, 1912, 1914) in which wit, malice, perversity, impishness, and insinuation are inextricably intertwined, and fact and fancy so cleverly fused that it is difficult to determine just where truth yields place to something very like mendacity. His former associates (most of whom, not unnaturally, never forgave him) are caricatured in a manner which Moore himself likened to that of Max Beerbohm. There is a keen sense of the comedy of enthusiasm, and even more remarkable is the self-revelation—call it rather self-creation. The zestful and challenging critical ideas point forward to *Avowals* (1919) and *Conversations in Ebury Street* (1924).

The
Brook
Kerith

Concurrently with the autobiography Moore began work on *The Brook Kerith* (1916), the germ of which is in *The Apostle* (1911), a drama on the character of Saint Paul. Adopting the rationalistic theory that Jesus did not die on the cross but was taken down by Joseph and secretly nursed back to health, Moore led the story to a tremendous climax when the fanatical missionary Paul comes face to face with the man whose resurrection and divinity he had proclaimed. Moore's prejudices are visible only in his portrayal of the apostles as stupid men; and his unseemly desire to

---

[33] The versions in Irish appeared (1902) before the English originals.

shock for the sake of shocking is suppressed save in the lubricity of one comic episode. The narrative is conducted without the irony which Anatole France would have employed and with no such complacent delight in exposing a fraudulent fable as Butler exhibited in *The Fair Haven*. The Syrian landscape is beautifully delineated from actual observation, for Moore, who could sacrifice himself for his art if for nothing else, made a toilsome journey to Palestine for the purpose. Serene or lively pastoral incidents fill the background without distracting attention from the theme. The narrative flows smoothly on with no interruption for comment or philosophic digression. The influence of Landor and Pater is apparent and was proudly acknowledged by the author; but he is more humane than Landor and more cosmopolitan than Pater. Everywhere there is the effect, as it were, of the speaking voice.

This method of "oral narrative," deriving from Irish folk-tale and polished by Moore's practice of dictating to a secretary, reached perfection in *Heloïse and Abelard* (1921) in which he re-created the twelfth century as an exotic dream world despite his display of antiquarian detail and philosophic background. A multitude of clerics and scholars, trouvères and gleemen, lords and ladies, monks and nuns move to and fro through perilous woods or flowery fields or beside pleasant rivers or through the streets of Paris and Blois. The landscape often suggests some mural by Puvis de Chavannes, and there are exquisite little genre scenes in the manner of Pater's *Imaginary Portraits*. With perfect judgment Moore brings the story to a close when the lovers, separated forever, are about to begin to write the famous *Letters*. All the pulsing life of the time is seen through the eyes of Heloïse to whom Moore devotes his most sympathetic knowledge of the depths and wanderings of the human heart. The sinuous prose, seemingly artless but the result of numberless revisions, has been likened to that of Morris's romances; but Moore is less luxuriant than Morris and more restrained. The resemblance is closer to Pater.

The same style, suggestive as ever of the human voice, is heard again in *Ulrick and Soracha* (1926), a tale of medieval Ireland; in *A Story-Teller's Holiday* (1928), a group of Irish stories; and in *Aphrodite in Aulis* (1930), where the manner has become almost a parody of itself. In its intimacy this style is perfectly appropriate to the two volumes of literary dialogues. Various books of earlier date were heavily revised to bring them into conformity with this latest manner. At the time of his death Moore was working upon *A Communication to My Friends*, telling once again the oft-told, much-loved story of his life and opinions.

To peruse in sequence all Moore's books is to receive the impression of an extreme mobility and sensitivity of mind. He led the way along naturalistic and "decadent" lines only to turn from them to new sources of inspiration in Ireland, classical and biblical antiquity, and the Middle Ages. In his earlier work he aimed at a critical interpretation of life (implicit rather than explicit, because his objective method did not permit the intrusion of per-

Heloïse and Abelard

Characteristics

sonal opinion save in the avowedly autobiographical books). With as little dependence as possible upon imagination and with a contempt for the old intrigues of outmoded fiction he presented contemporary people confronted with actual problems. His naturalism was informed with bold candor and clarity of purpose. The psychological insight laboriously attained he afterwards applied to his resuscitations of the life of former ages, for, as he often insisted, human nature has not changed. Often he wasted time and talent upon trivial literary gossip and the satisfaction of that jealousy of distinguished contemporaries which was the worst defect in his character. Often he seemed to be playing upon the mere surface of men and things. He could be insincere and factitious, but he could also be tender and grave and deeply moved and moving. He had at his command a variety of styles, from the robust, straightforward English of *Esther Waters* and the impassioned, poetic prose of *The Lake* to the witty malice of *Hail and Farewell* and the slippered ease of *Avowals.* The famous final manner, with its trailing sentences in which coördinate clauses so rarely make way for the subordinate, has a unique beauty at its best, but it is often languid and it can be tedious. Moore set an example to all artists of absolute devotion to his art. A consciousness of widening experience and increasing expertness and a sense of the contrast between conception and execution led to his unremitting rearrangements and rewritings of his books, and to the peremptory rejection of many of them. His achievement, it has been said, was a series of experiments; and dissatisfaction with anything that fell short of his ideal in style and design was a characteristic of his genius.

V

The tradition of the personal charm of Robert Louis Stevenson [34] (1850-1894) still colors most estimates of his work. It is difficult to deal dispassionately with a man whose life was a ceaseless and gallant search for health. The quest took him from his native Scotland to Switzerland, to southern Europe, to the Far West, to Saranac, and ultimately to the South Seas. He was sustained by the zest of adventure, and from every part of the world that he visited he derived material for his essays. The charm of personality permeates his radiant letters, mingling with impressions of people, places, and books. It is significant that he was an essayist and writer of short stories before he attempted the novel form, and to the end he was more successful in briefer than in more expanded fiction. The record of his

[34] *Works,* Pentland Edition, ed. Edmund Gosse (20v, 1906-1907); Vailima Edition, ed. Lloyd Osbourne and F. Van de G. Stevenson (26v, 1922-1923); *Letters,* ed. Sidney Colvin (2v, 1899). — W. F. Prideaux, *Bibliography* (rev. ed., 1917); Ehrsam, *Bibliographies,* pp. 227-261; Graham Balfour, *The Life of Robert Louis Stevenson* (2v, 1901; new ed., 1912); John A. Steuart, *Robert Louis Stevenson, a Critical Biography* (2v, 1924); L. C. Cornford, *R. L. Stevenson* (1899); Frank Swinnerton, *R. L. Stevenson, a Critical Study* (1914); R. O. Masson, *The Life of Robert Louis Stevenson* (1923); Lloyd Osbourne, *An Intimate Portrait of R. L. S.* (1924); G. S. Hellman, *The True Stevenson: a Study in Clarification* (1925); D. N. Dalglish, *Presbyterian Pirate: a Portrait of Stevenson* (1937); Janet A. Smith, *Robert Louis Stevenson* (1937); Baker, IX. 296-327.

early wanderings on the Continent is in *An. Inland Voyage* (1878), about a trip by canoe in Belgium and France, and in *Travels with a Donkey in the Cevennes* (1879). In both there is evident the incipient romancer alert to discern and exploit the picturesque in incident and locale. A first visit to the United States (1879), whither he was drawn by love of the woman whom he married in California, is memorable for his experience of life in a rough mining-camp. Many years later he recalled this pioneer life in *The Silverado Squatters* (1893). On his return to Europe tuberculosis drove him to Davos Plaz. There he composed some of his essays which, with others of earlier date, form *Virginibus Puerisque* (1881), an intimate and self-revelatory book. More critical in tone but still informal and personal is the set of papers entitled *Familiar Studies of Men and Books* (1882). Though he had not yet attracted wide attention, he had published various short stories which were now assembled in *New Arabian Nights* (1882), a collection memorable for the little masterpiece of sinister scene-painting, *The Pavilion on the Links*. Fame and fortune arrived with the publication of *Treasure Island* (1883), a swashbuckling tale of the quest for Captain Kidd's hidden loot, the rivalry of two parties on the search, and the triumph of the hero. This was intended for young readers who, reading it for its adventurous story, were doubtless indifferent to the care with which it was stylized and psychologized.

Encouraged by this success, Stevenson brought out *A Child's Garden of Verses* (1885), followed by *Underwoods* (1887), a second volume of poems, addressed for the most part to readers of maturity. In these years Stevenson collaborated with William Ernest Henley upon a few plays, but both men were without experience in the theatre and they did not achieve success. *Prince Otto* (1885) is a story of ultra-romantic kind, redeemed from being no more than an anticipation of *The Prisoner of Zenda* type of tale by the delicacy of Stevenson's psychological analysis. *Kidnapped* (1886), another tale of adventure, is primarily for a juvenile audience; its sequel, *Catriona*, did not appear till 1893. *Dr. Jekyll and Mr. Hyde* (1886), immediately and lastingly Stevenson's most famous story, is a moral apologue of divided personality. A collection of short stories, *The Merry Men* (1887), included the very powerful tales, *Markheim* and *Thrawn Janet*. While all this work was in progress Stevenson was ceaselessly and unsuccessfully in search of health. During 1887-1888 he lived at Lake Saranac where he wrote *The Master of Ballantrae* (1889) and many essays. His last wanderings were in the Antipodes. From 1890 till his death he lived in Samoa where his feverish energy involved him actively in native politics. He collaborated with his stepson, Lloyd Osbourne, on *The Wrong Box* (1889), *The Wrecker* (1892), and *The Ebb-Tide* (1894). The fragment that remains of *Weir of Hermiston* [35] shows that in the months before his death Stevenson had attained a power

---

[35] Published posthumously, 1896. The central motive is the old one of the father, a judge, who condemns his son to death; but the fragment breaks off before the two great scenes which we know Stevenson had planned—the trial and the subsequent rescue of the hero from prison. — Another fragment, *St. Ives* (1897), was completed by Sir Arthur Quiller-Couch ("Q").

of character analysis and a strength of style beyond the promise of any of his earlier books. His grave, "under the wide and starry sky," is on the summit of a mountain overlooking the Pacific.

*Art and
Morality* Stevenson's work was conditioned on the one side by his theological and ethical heritage and on the other by his literary environment. While, like many of his contemporaries, repudiating the opinion that art has a direct ethical function, he confessed that morality was always his "veiled mistress." It is characteristic of a spirit which along some lines was ready to compromise that he concealed his agnosticism.[36] Yet the Calvinism from which he could not wholly escape forced the intrusion of moral issues into his fiction. The essay form, where the discussion of such issues is appropriate, he practised throughout his life with grace and vigor. It colors not only the short moral apologues but some of the longer works of fiction. He was inclined to blame the restrictions imposed by British reticence for turning him from the novel of real life to romance. It is sometimes said that he would not risk the loss of public approbation by a resolute adoption of the principles of naturalism. But his mastery of horror, his suggestions of supernaturalism, and his pleasure in the ingenuity of his own inventions support the suspicion that, for all his obsession with moral issues and all his awareness of the direction in which the novel was moving, he was a romancer not through compulsion but free choice. He sought to give psychological depth to the characters of romance. This is apparent even in *Treasure Island*. Scott's influence is at its most effective in *Weir of Hermiston*, but in the character of the father-judge Stevenson surpasses all but the greatest of Scott's portraits. Again Scott's influence is discernible in *The Master of Ballantrae* but combined with fantastic and somber motives from other sources and even with overtones that suggest Meredith. The Meredithian influence is even more apparent in *Prince Otto*. Stevenson is often suspected

Style of attitudinizing in style as in personal pose. There is some foundation for both accusations, yet neither is entirely just. What he imitated he made his own, whether it was the elaborate, periodic sentence of Sir Thomas Browne or De Quincey, or the confidential familiarity of Lamb, or the subtle character-analysis of Meredith. He was strongly affected by current discussions of *l'art pour l'art*. He insisted upon skill in handling material, both in the largest structural sense and also in finesse of detail, rather than upon the value of ideas. The extreme labor and sedulous attention to the great masters with which he cultivated his style often resulted in a manner disproportionate in elaborateness to the matter of his books. It is significant that his influence was effective not upon the psychological novelists or the naturalists or the experimenters in new forms of fiction but upon a group of writers of romance.

[36] Stevenson's first biographers did his memory a disservice by concealing the fact of his agnosticism. Moreover, the history of his various youthful amatory indiscretions did not become known till long after his death. He was entitled to his own reticences, but the something other than candor of the early biographers has in some recent estimates been transferred to Stevenson himself.

In some of his "regional" stories Stevenson invaded the province of the *The* so-called "Kailyard School." Sir James Barrie's novels have connections with *"Kailyard* this group. The typical "Kailyarder" was John Watson (1850-1907) who *School"* under the pen-name of "Ian Maclaren" wrote *Beside the Bonnie Briar Bush* (1894) and *The Days of Auld Lang Syne* (1895). Their wide contemporary popularity has not proved lasting and today the sentiment seems forced and the regionalism factitious. Stronger, and truer to actualities, is *The House with the Green Shutters* (1901) by George Douglas Brown ("George Douglas," 1869-1902) which was intended in part as a corrective of false notions of Scottish life. S. R. Crockett, who has already been noticed as a regionalist, was a "Kailyarder."

Sir Henry Rider Haggard (1856-1925) had an immense following for *Romance* his ultra-romantic stories, *King Solomon's Mines* (1885), *She* (1887), and *Allan Quatermain* (1887). Less extravagant were the semi-historical romances of Stanley J. Weyman (1855-1928), of which *A Gentleman of France* (1893) is the best. Here belong the adventure stories of Sir Arthur Quiller-Couch, "Q" (1863-1944), of which *The Splendid Spur* (1889) and *The Ship of Stars* (1899) are among the best. Many of these tales have a Cornish background. "Q" was a genial professor, prolific critic, and the most influential anthologist of our day. Sir Arthur Conan Doyle (1859-1930) wrote *The White Company* (1891), *Rodney Stone* (1896), and other romances, some of them based on history, but it is as the creator of the most famous character in all English fiction that he is known to everybody. Sherlock Holmes [37] made his first appearance in *A Study in Scarlet* (1887). Presently millions of readers were watching him applying his "methods" in *The Adventures of Sherlock Holmes* (1892), *The Hound of the Baskervilles* (1902), and other books. The dashing tales of Sir Anthony Hope Hawkins [38] ("Anthony Hope," 1863-1933), *The Prisoner of Zenda* (1894) and *Rupert of Hentzau* (1898), contrast strangely with the witty social sophistication of his *Dolly Dialogues* (1894). Of all the romancers Neil Munro (1864-1930) was nearest to Stevenson. His *John Splendid* (1898) owes much to Scott, but the analysis of character and motive is in Stevenson's manner. The resounding success of these and other purveyors of romance proves that decadent aestheticism and stern naturalism were by no means the only currents in literature at the end of the century.

Maurice Hewlett [39] (1861-1923) offered in his early books an unusual

---

[37] H. W. Bell, *Sherlock Holmes and Dr. Watson* (1932); Vincent Starrett, *The Private Life of Sherlock Holmes* (1933), with bibliography. For the development of the detective story from the days of Poe and of Dickens' Inspector Buckett, through Wilkie Collins and Emile Gaboriau, to Doyle and beyond see H. D. Thomson, *Masters of Mystery: A Study of the Detective Story* (1931); Howard Haycraft, *Murder for Pleasure: The Life and Times of the Detective Story* (1942); F. W. Chandler, *The Literature of Roguery* (2v, 1907), ii, ch. xiii; and the introductions to *The Great Detective Stories*, ed. W. H. Wright (1927); *Crime and Detection*, ed. E. M. Wrong (World's Classics, 1926); and *Great Short Stories of Detection, Mystery, and Horror*, ed. Dorothy L. Sayers (1928).

[38] Sir Charles Mallet, *Anthony Hope and His Books* (1936).

[39] *Letters*, ed. Laurence Binyon (1926). Milton Bronner, *Maurice Hewlett* (1910); A. B. Sutherland, *Maurice Hewlett: Historical Romancer* (Philadelphia, 1938); H. W. Graham, "Maurice Hewlett," *Fortnightly Rev.* lxxiv (1925). 47-63.

combination of romance, erudition, artifice, and modernism. *The Forest Lovers* (1898) is a medieval tale avowedly modeled on Malory but too softly voluptuous to remind many readers of its prototype. *Little Novels of Italy* (1899) have some resemblance to Pater's *Imaginary Portraits*. *Richard Yea-and-Nay* (1900) and *The Queen's Quair* (1904) in which something of Meredith's manner and technique are applied to the elucidation of the characters, respectively, of Richard Coeur de Lion and Mary Queen of Scots, are the most substantial re-creations of history in the form of fiction produced in the period. Stylistic artificialities and a naturalistic philosophy alike reminiscent of Meredith are combined in *Halfway House* (1908), *Open Country* (1909), and *Rest Harrow* (1910), the trilogy on John Senhouse, lover of flowers and enemy of marriage.[40]

VI

ipling

Rudyard Kipling[41] (1865-1936) was born in India, where his father, the accomplished John Lockwood Kipling, had been appointed to a chair of sculpture in the University of Bombay. A multitude of impressions of the East were already stored in memory when at the age of six the child was sent to England. There he led at first a lonely and unhappy life with relatives. These experiences he afterwards turned to literary use in *Baa-baa, Black Sheep* and in the opening chapters of *The Light that Failed*. Presently he was put into the school for the sons of army and navy men of which he afterwards drew a picture in *Stalky and Co.*, a boisterous and rowdy tale of the pranks and adventures of boys who fancied themselves outlaws.[42] But the young Kipling did other things besides cut up. Verses which he sent home to his family in India his proud father had privately printed as *Schoolboy Lyrics* (1881). Here, among much that is, naturally enough, merely imitative, there is one piece, *Ave Imperatrix,* that strikes for the first time the authentic Kipling note of service to the British Empire.

[40] Hewlett's *Song of the Plough* (1916), an "epic" (or rather a series of episodes) of the life of Hodge (the typical English agricultural laborer) from the Norman Conquest to modern times, evinces sincere feeling and intimate knowledge (for Hewlett, though urbane in literary tastes, lived close to the soil), but it fails as a poem for want of profundity, freshness of imagery, and any novelty of technique.

[41] *Writings in Prose and Verse* (36v, 1898-1937); Burwash Edition (28v, 1941); and many other collected editions; *A Choice of Kipling's Verse*, introduction by T. S. Eliot (1941). — There is as yet no definitive "Life and Letters." Mrs. F. V. Livingston, *Bibliography* (1927); Ehrsam, *Bibliographies,* pp. 127-160; Edward Shanks, *Rudyard Kipling, a Study in Literature and Political Ideas* (1940), an excellent corrective to the denigrations of recent criticism; Hilton Brown, *Rudyard Kipling* (1945); Sir George MacMunn, *Rudyard Kipling, Craftsman* (1938); Cyril Falls, *Rudyard Kipling, a Critical Study* (1915); W. M. Hart, *Kipling, the Story-Writer* (Berkeley, 1918); A. M. Weygandt, *Kipling's Reading and its Influence upon his Poetry* (1939); R. A. Durand, *A Handbook to the Poetry of Rudyard Kipling* (1914); W. A. Young, *A Dictionary of the Characters and Scenes of the Stories and Poems of Rudyard Kipling, 1886-1911* (1911); André Chevrillon, *Three Studies in English Literature* (1923), I: "Rudyard Kipling's Poetry"; Baker, x (1939), ch. III; Edmund Wilson, "The Kipling that Nobody Read," in *The Wound and the Bow* (1941), pp. 105-181.

[42] G. C. Beresford, the original of M'Turk, gives a picture of these boys' doings and of the school somewhat at variance with Kipling's. See his *Schooldays with Kipling* (1936). See also General L. C. Dunsterville's *Stalky's Reminiscences* (1928) and Kipling's own memoirs, *Something about Myself* (posthumous, 1937).

Returning to India at the age of seventeen, Kipling became sub-editor of *India*
the Lahore *Gazette,* thus serving an apprenticeship in journalism which
taught him to observe sharply, judge quickly, and report tersely. To the
paper he contributed with precocious virtuosity the verses and tales that
were collected, respectively, in *Departmental Ditties* (1886) and *Plain Tales
from the Hills* (1888). The latter were followed by others of the same kind,
among them *Soldiers Three* and *The Phantom 'Rickshaw,* in separate,
pamphlet form for reading on railway journeys. The last-named story shows
the attraction which the occult had for Kipling, and others are colored by
somewhat cruel humor and a love of the gruesome. In many of these
juvenilia Kipling displayed a cynicism, crude jocularity, coarse flippancy,
and brutality that were expressed with a slick assurance of style that merited
and won the epithet "brassy." Style and pattern owed something to Bret
Harte and perhaps to Maupassant, but the themes were Kipling's own—
the comic or tragic scandals of Anglo-Indian society, the hardships and
courage of common soldiers, the patient efficiency of the Civil Servants,
and the misery and mystery of the teeming native life. The reappearances
of various characters (especially the famous "soldiers three," Mulvaney,
Ortheris, and Learoyd) helped to bind this heterogeneous mass of verse and
fiction into a whole which, as it grew enormously in later years, remained
coherent in manner and atmosphere.

A shipment of the *Ditties* and *Plain Tales* to England revealed Anglo-
Indian life to stay-at-homes with the consequence that Kipling's fame preceded his own return. A leisurely journey home took him through China
and Japan and across the United States. To the Allahabad *Pioneer* he sent
back impressions which were later collected in *From Sea to Sea* (1899), a
volume now obscured by the fame of his other work but which is not
negligible journalism because in it may be found his characteristically
forcible criticism of inefficiency, his distrust of democracy, his belief in
authority, and his advocacy of war as a necessary instrument of good government.

The vigor, snap, vividness, self-assurance, and even the vulgarity of the
early tales won Kipling an immediate audience and on his arrival in England he found himself *persona grata* with publishers. Stories published in
Macmillan's Magazine were collected in *Life's Handicap* (1891). *The Light
that Failed* [43] (1891), Kipling's first attempt at full-length fiction, cannot
be judged an entire success, though the character of Maizie Duncan is finely
drawn. W. E. Henley published in *The National Observer* the poems which, *Barrack-*
when collected as *Barrack-Room Ballads* (1892), enormously widened Kip- *Room*
ling's fame. Many a pithy phrase and many a resonant line were soon on *Ballads*
everybody's lips. With suggestions from Burns for the use of dialect and

[43] As an example of publishers' exigencies (compare the case of Hardy's *Tess*) it may be
noted that in the magazine version this novel ended "happily." In book form Kipling reverted
to the original tragic ending. — *The Maulakha* (1891), a novel written in collaboration with
Wolcott Balestier, an American whose sister Kipling married in 1892, must be judged a
failure.

with a gift for mating Swinburnian measures to the style of music-hall lyric he had evolved a poetry all his own. In other pieces there are reminiscences of Browning's manner which read almost like parody but are not. Greatly daring, he had seen the possibilities for music, pathos, and humor in the speech of the cockney, a dialect hitherto despised as low and sub-literary. If some of the results were vulgar, brash, and blatant, in others he created things of beauty such as *The Road to Mandalay.* Association with Henley fortified Kipling's imperialism [44] and encouraged the didacticism which grew upon him with the years.

Many Inventions (1893)—far too many, indeed, to be recorded by title here—is another collection of stories, among them such little masterpieces as *His Private Honor* and *Love o' Women.* The famous but overpraised *Man Who Was* gives expression to the jingoism which Kipling both echoed from the crowd and further stimulated. Even more noteworthy is *In the Rukh,* in the same volume, for here Mowgli, though grown-up, makes his first appearance.[45] Kipling saw that in this human companion of the beasts there was the making of a myth, and altering his conception just sufficiently, he wrote, at the top of his inspiration, *The Jungle Book* (1894) and *The Second Jungle Book* (1895). These are beast-fables, not of the old kind which attributed human qualities to animals but of a new which attempted to see into the very depths of animal natures (granting the convention of endowing them with speech). With a like sympathetic selflessness Kipling in other stories laid bare the "souls" of ships and locomotives and other inanimate things. He was now at the height of a fame that was maintained, if not enlarged, by the poems in *The Seven Seas* (1896); by *Captains Courageous* (1897), a novel-length yarn of the redemption of a spoilt child of the rich who, falling overboard from a liner, learns courage and self-sacrifice among the fishermen of Newfoundland; and by *The Day's Work* (1898), another batch of stories.

In July, 1897, the English-speaking world was electrified by the publication of the *Recessional.* This, as Kipling afterwards said, was written to "avert the evil eye" directed against England because of the *hubris* of the Diamond Jubilee. The rôle of counselor of the people sat well upon him, and in 1899 he spoke again, in *The White Man's Burden,* this time on the duties of the imperial races towards "the lesser breeds." During the South African War he voiced no vindictiveness against the Boers but only an anxiety for the welfare of Tommy Atkins and an insistence that lessons for the future be drawn from the inefficient management of the campaign. In the midst of the war appeared *Kim* (1901), a picaresque yarn on the largest scale, evoking life in India. The inaccuracies in the interpretation of native character are redeemed by wisdom, geniality, and humor. Notwithstanding his brutal

----

[44] On the origins and development of the "imperial theme" in English literature see Friedrich Brie, *Imperialistische Strömungen in der englischen Literatur* (Freiburg, 1928).

[45] For this greatest creation of his imagination Kipling probably owed something to remarks upon legends and rumors of children suckled by wolves in his father's undeservedly neglected book, *Man and Beast in India* (1891).

common sense the mysterious East always fascinated Kipling; he could not share its visions but he could suggest their infinitude.[46] In the charming *Just-So Stories* (1902) his humor, often an uncertain quality, is at its best.

With the close of the Boer War the mood of England to which Kipling had given such vigorous expression changed. Though his popularity with the masses did not wane, he was, not altogether fairly, identified with the blatant, jingoistic imperialism of the preceding decade, and his reputation began to decline. A mellower Kipling drew for his countrymen the lesson from the late struggle that if civilization was to be guarded, order, authority, and discipline must be enforced. In these years he was living in Sussex, where the consciousness of an age-long civilization [47] inspired *Puck of Pook's Hill* (1906) and its sequel, *Rewards and Fairies* (1910). These stories are grounded upon England's past and illustrate the continuity of tradition. On the outbreak of the Great War he bade his countrymen in stern and measured rhetoric protect the ramparts of civilization against the barbarians at the gate. In a sense he had foreseen what was coming, though in former years he had held, as was natural from the point of view of an Anglo-Indian, that the arch-foe was not Germany but Russia. Against the "Hun" he wrote with a fierce hatred that contrasts with his earlier attitude towards the Boers. They were the betrayers of Western Civilization, disloyal to "the Law." [48] He lived long enough to be vigilant against the renewal of the German menace. Within our limits it is impossible to record all his later publications. He had little that was new to say in verse, and the last two series of prose stories, though written with the old mastery of technique, contain little that is fresh in substance.

It being impossible to divorce the two departments of Kipling's achieve- *Poetry* ment, something further must be said here of his poetry. As a virtuoso in verse he had more than one style at his command. The swagger and swash-buckling are often detestable, but he could give expression alike to Tommy Atkins' hopes for loot and to his weariness when upon the march. The cockney dialect is sometimes used for mere music-hall vulgarities but again for lovely verbal music. Of a different order are the surging rhythms of *The Last Chantey* and *The Long Trail*. Alone among poets his ear caught the cadences of clanking machinery and pulsating ships. There is a solemn rhetoric in the prophetic tones of counsel and warning to England, though in some pieces the gnomic style is so terse that the meaning is with difficulty interpreted. No other writer was capable of uttering such a *sursum corda* in time of national peril. There was always something of the journalist in the absorbed attention he gave to public affairs. As the unofficial laureate of his people he could express their feelings on great occasions of state, as in *The Dead King,* where the impressiveness lies in the very contrast be-

---

[46] See A. Rumson, *Kipling's India* (1915).
[47] See R. T. Hopkins, *Kipling's Sussex* (1921).
[48] Realizing that England had not learned the lessons of the Boer War, Kipling was forced in 1914-1918 to bring renewed charges of inefficiency against those responsible for operations, especially in the Mesopotamian campaign.

tween the poet's estimate of Edward VII and the actuality. More rarely he was master of a subtler music, as in the beautiful *Epitaph*, "Call me not false, beloved."

"The Law"

Implicit in all his writings, explicit in the *Jungle Books*, and first emphasized in *The Day's Work* is the central theme of obedience to "the Law"— the law whereby civilized society is so ordered that every man can obtain from life the fruits thereof within the limits of his obligations to his fellowmen. Kipling was not an "authoritarian" in the modern "totalitarian" sense. Men are not the servants of the state, but trained experts are the servants of the community. Tools to the hands of those who can use them! His criticism of democracy [49] was that ill-informed people choose representatives who legislate upon subjects about which they know nothing. With such he contrasts the efficiency of the specially trained, whether the Roman soldier guarding the Wall, or the Sussex farmhand inheriting an age-long technique, or the Civil Servant organizing famine-relief in India, or the proconsul directing the restoration of order in the chaotic Sudan. The praise of machinery, the delight in engineering technicalities displayed in the story *The Bridge-Builders,* in *M'Andrew's Hymn,* and in a hundred other places, is due to Kipling's admiration of the coördination of functions of which the machine is not only a symbol but the perfect example. He seems to have had no foresight of the perils to a civilization that had become "the Machine Age."

[49] This criticism deeply wounded many of Kipling's American admirers. Kipling lived for several years in Vermont, having married an American. His attitude towards the United States, in the worst tradition of British superciliousness, is partly to be explained by a bitter quarrel with his brother-in-law. See F. F. Van de Water, *Rudyard Kipling's Vermont Feud* (1937).

XXXVII
The Irish Literary Renaissance

The Irish political leaders who, abandoning their efforts to effect reforms within the British Parliament, gradually roused the national enthusiasm which prepared the way for Home Rule have a stronger claim than the regionalists in Irish fiction to be regarded as the precursors of the Irish Literary Renaissance.[1] From about 1830 Trinity College, Dublin, became a center of political and literary activity, and in 1833 *The Dublin University Magazine* was founded. Among its contributors was James Clarence Mangan [2] *Mangan* (1803-1849) who because of his personal history has been called "a sort of Irish Poe." Besides such self-revelatory poems as *The Nameless One,* Mangan wrote verse paraphrases of Gaelic songs from prose translations supplied (for he knew no Gaelic) by his friends. Among these is the fervently patriotic address to Ireland, *My Dark Rosaleen.* Mangan contributed also to *The Nation,* of which the founders (1842) were Charles Gavan Duffy [3] (1816-1903) and Thomas O. Davis [4] (1814-1845). These men and their collaborators, impatient of the cautious policy of Daniel O'Connell, seceded from his following to form the group known as "Young Ireland." It had little immediate *"Young* practical effect and after 1848 seemed to dwindle away. But part of the *Ireland"* program was to stimulate patriotism by rousing interest and pride in the national past, and of that past legend, lore, and literature were the chief glories. Thus it came about that (with no separation from the men active in contemporary politics) antiquarians, philologists, and historians advanced to the foreground of the Irish picture. Sir Samuel Ferguson [5] (1810-1886), who, unlike Mangan, was a Gaelic scholar, was the first to make known to *Ferguson* Englishmen and to Irishmen lacking knowledge of their ancestral language, *and* in anything like their original form and fullness the cycle of epic legends *O'Grady* of the deeds of Cuchulain and the loves of Deirdre. With no claim to rank

[1] E. A. Boyd, *Ireland's Literary Renaissance* (1916); N. J. O'Conor, *Changing Ireland: Literary Background of the Irish Free State, 1889-1922* (1924); David Morton, *The Renaissance of Irish Poetry* (1929); Cornelius Weygandt, *Irish Plays and Playwrights* (1913) and *The Time of Yeats* (1937); A. E. Malone, *The Irish Drama* (1929); Una Ellis-Fermor, *The Irish Dramatic Movement* (1939). There is much material in the more or less autobiographical writings of the leading figures in the movement. See especially W. B. Yeats, *Autobiographies* (1926) and "The Irish Dramatic Movement," in *Plays and Controversies* (1923); Lady Gregory, *Our Irish Theatre* (1914); George Moore, *Hail and Farewell* (1911-1914); Lady Gregory, *Diaries* (1946).
[2] *Poems* (Dublin, 1903). — D. J. O'Donoghue, *The Life of James Clarence Mangan* (1897).
[3] Sir C. G. Duffy, *My Life in Two Hemispheres* (1898). Duffy's *Ballad Poetry of Ireland* (1843) is noteworthy.
[4] *Poems* (1846); *Selections* (1915). — Sir. C. G. Duffy, *The Life of Thomas Davis* (1890).
[5] Lady Ferguson, *The Life of Sir Samuel Ferguson* (2v, 1896).

as an original poet Ferguson performed as an antiquarian, through his *Lays of the Western Gael* (1865), *Congal* [6] (1872), and *Deirdre* (1880), an inestimable service to Ireland in restoring to the general consciousness these monuments of the heroic past. Work equally necessary as a preliminary to a cultural renaissance was done by Standish James O'Grady (1846-1915) in his *History of Ireland: Heroic Period* [7] (1878-1880). In surging, eloquent prose O'Grady vitalized the ancient stories of the Gael. The original materials for work of this kind were now being made available by archaeological and philological societies. During the ascendency of Parnell, Irish energies were mostly diverted from literature to politics; but after the recuperation from the shock of his downfall the claims of Irish culture were reasserted. In 1892 there was organized at Dublin the Irish Literary Society, of which the first president was George Sigerson (1839-1925), a productive scholar. Of the Gaelic League (1893) the first president was Douglas Hyde (1860-   ) who has lived to become President of the Irish Free State. Hyde was influential as a folklorist, editor, translator, and writer of original poetry in Gaelic. His *Literary History of Ireland* (1899) did much to advance the claims of Irish letters to be judged independently of English literature.

Meanwhile there had appeared an anthology of *Poems and Ballads of Young Ireland* (1888). Among the poets here represented was John Todhunter (1839-1916) who, after several earlier volumes of verse, had turned his attention to the bardic legends in *The Banshee and Other Poems* (1888). Despite the sincerity of his sympathies Todhunter belonged among the expatriated Anglo-Irish writers of London.[8] Another poet in the anthology was Katharine Tynan, afterwards Mrs. Hinkson [9] (1861-1931). She had been influenced in her early work by the Pre-Raphaelites, and her devotional poetry connects her with the group of Roman Catholic poets.[10] But this association links her poetry also to the tradition of the Irish religious lyric. Gaelic themes are dominant in her *Shamrocks* (1887) and *Ballads and Lyrics* (1891), and much later she published *Irish Poems* (1913). Her talent was sweet but fragile and her popularity has now declined.

Yeats   The editor of this anthology was William Butler Yeats [11] (1865-1939),

[6] Founded on the bardic romance, *The Battle of Moyra*.

[7] O'Grady later attached to the *History* an essay on *Early Bardic Literature* (1879). His more conventional *History of Ireland* (1881) remains a fragment. Of his historical romances the best are *Red Hugh's Captivity* (1889) and *The Flight of the Eagle* (1897). *The Bog of Stars* (1893) is a collection of short stories.

[8] An Anglo-Irish poet of the previous generation was Aubrey de Vere (1814-1902). His mild Wordsworthian verse covers many subjects, classical, medieval, hagiological, political, and religious. *Inisfail* (1862) and various other poems are Irish in subject; but in general he was apart from the Movement. — For two other Anglo-Irish poets, Allingham and O'Shaughnessy, see above, ch. xxix, notes 27 and 28.

[9] *Collected Poems* (1930).

[10] See below, ch. xxxix.

[11] *Collected Works* (8v, 1908); *Collected Poems* (1933; expanded edition, 1950); *Collected Plays* (1935); *New Poems* (1938); *Letters on Poetry to Dorothy Wellesley* (1940). — A. J. A. Symons; *Bibliography* (1924); Joseph Hone, *W. B. Yeats* (1943), the authorized biography; Forrest Reid, *William Butler Yeats, a Critical Study* (1915); C. L. Wrenn, *William Butler Yeats, a Literary Study* (1920); J. H. Pollock, *William Butler Yeats* (Dublin, 1935);

then at the outset of his career. Sprung from Irish Protestantism and the son of an Irish painter, Yeats was born in Dublin, but his childhood was passed in London save for vacations in the west of Ireland. Some early attempts at poetic drama were in the nature of a false start. The first poem that matters was *The Wanderings of Oisin* [12] (1889), the volume with which the Irish Literary Revival attained complete self-consciousness. No intrusion of modern political ideas sullies the other-worldly atmosphere, but the Gaelic theme of the pagan who relates to St. Patrick his adventures in fairyland is overlaid with stylistic ornament reminiscent of Spenser, Shelley, and William Morris,[13] and the design of the poem owes something to *Endymion*. Though in succeeding years Yeats was a member of the coterie of poets and aesthetes in London, he was already in quest of a fresh tradition and an individual style. There is little that is derivative from English sources in the poetic plays, *The Countess Cathleen* (1892) and *The Land of Heart's Desire* (1894), or in the lyrics and ballad-pieces that accompanied the former. The delicate light rimes (frequently "off-rimes" and assonances), the insubstantial rhythms, and the vague outlines are characteristics of Yeats's first manner. The aesthetic theory of the separation of art from life, which Yeats was later to repudiate, is implicit; and the exploitation of the strange and the intense and of spiritual weariness ("the soul with all its maladies") is characteristic of the time and milieu rather than of the poet himself. His *Poems* were collected in 1895, but for several years he was chiefly occupied with prose. The contrast between the simple fairy-lore of *The Celtic Twilight* (1893) and the difficult occultism of *The Secret Rose* (1897) is a measure of his advance during these years. The studies which *Symbolism* had resulted in his edition of Blake's *Works* (1893) strengthened his interest in symbols, and at a later date a meeting with Mallarmé and association with Arthur Symons confirmed his acceptance of the doctrines of the Symbolists. The influence of the French school and of Maeterlinck is apparent in *The Wind among the Reeds* (1899), a new collection of verse. Some of the early symbols, particularly those drawn from the natural world, are simple enough; the moon stands for weariness (as often in Shelley),

---

J. P. O'Donnell, *Sailing to Byzantium, a Study in the Development of the later Style and Symbolism of W. B. Yeats* (Cambridge, Mass., 1939); Louis MacNeice, *The Poetry of W. B. Yeats* (1941); V. K. N. Menon, *The Development of William Butler Yeats* (1942); Edmund Wilson, *Axel's Castle* (1931), ch. II; David Daiches, *Poetry and the Modern World* (1940), chs. VII-VIII; *The Southern Review*, VII (Winter, 1941-1942), "William Butler Yeats Memorial Issue," essays by T. S. Eliot, J. C. Ransom, and other poets and critics; *Scattering Branches,* ed. Stephen Gwynn (1940), memorial articles by Maud Gonne MacBride, Lennox Robinson, and others.

[12] On turning to Ireland Yeats was influenced by Sigerson's *Poets and Poetry of Munster* (1860) and later by Hyde's *Love Songs of Connacht* (1893) where the syntax is partly Gaelic and the vocabulary partly Elizabethan. Yeats, who did not know Gaelic, occasionally used the Anglo-Irish of the peasantry, but most of his poetry is written in standard English, refreshed from new sources in imagery rather than vocabulary. Space is lacking here to record the heavy revisions and significant modifications to which Yeats afterwards subjected much of his early work. — Yeats's indebtedness to the eighteenth-century Irish poet Michael Comys and to other sources acknowledged and unacknowledged is demonstrated by R. K. Alspach, "Some Sources of Yeats's *The Wanderings of Oisin*," PMLA, LVIII (1943). 849-866.

[13] Morris said to Yeats: "You write my sort of poetry" (Yeats, *Autobiographies,* p. 181).

water for the fleetingness of beauty, and the rose, over and over again, for the principle of Eternal Beauty. The life of ecstatic reverie, hidden from the world, is suggested by the image of the veil. But in Irish mythology Yeats had found a treasury of symbols hitherto unused in English poetry. The clues to these are not always readily accessible and the precise significance of some figures is often difficult to apprehend. Fairyland itself—the country of the Sidhe, the Irish fairy-folk—is itself a symbol of the imagination. Over against the world of the imagination is set the naturalistic, scientific world, sometimes symbolized by Yeats in hostile allusions to Huxley or Tyndall.

Yet gradually there was a drift towards actuality. The influence of Ibsen's problem plays has been discerned. And notwithstanding Yeats's aloofness, there was the influence of Irish politics. He could not escape from his environment—the less so because he was in love with the fiery Nationalist, Maud Gonne. In 1899 he and Lady Gregory founded the Irish National Theatre Society which was presently housed in the Abbey Theatre in Dublin.[14] Isabella Augusta, Lady Gregory (1859-1932) was a forceful influence upon the entire Irish movement. Of her many translations *Gods and Fighting Men* (1904) is typical. Her explorations of folklore and legend are recorded in various volumes. But her principal work was in the drama. She collaborated with Yeats in *The Unicorn from the Stars* (1908) and other plays. Of her own comedies some are in one act, others full-length. Not all are of much literary value, but they display an insight into peasant character and are full of humor. *The Rising of the Moon* and *The Workhouse Ward* are perhaps her best, showing as they do her deft craftsmanship and economy of means. Her tours of the United States with the Abbey company in 1911-1913 are memorable for her difficulties and triumphs. In Dublin the company maintained their enthusiasm despite discouragements and they persisted in the face of violent and occasionally riotous opposition provoked by their supposed "blasphemy" in some cases and their supposedly discreditable portrayal of Irish character in others.

Yeats's energetic activity during the formative, combative period of the Abbey Theatre had a profound effect upon him as a poet, but the theatre was not a perfectly appropriate medium for his imagination. Notwithstanding his practical experience, he did not always grasp either its opportunities or its limitations. Of sturdier texture than the dramatic fairy fantasies of his youth are the *Plays for an Irish Theatre* (1904), and of these the finest is *Cathleen ni Houlihan* (performed 1902) in which beneath the dramatiza-

Lady Gregory

---

14 With Yeats and Lady Gregory was associated Edward Martyn (1859-1923), author of *The Heather Field* (1899) and *The Tale of a Town* (1902), the latter adapted by George Moore as *The Bending of the Bough*. The maliciously witty portrait of Martyn in Moore's *Hail and Farewell* requires a corrective. See Denis Gwynn, *Edward Martyn and the Irish Literary Revival* (1930). — Yeats and Lady Gregory had the good fortune to secure the services of the talented actors, Frank and William Fay. See W. G. Fay and Catherine Carswell, *The Fays of the Abbey Theatre* (1935). See also in addition to authorities already cited, Dawson Byrne, *The Story of Ireland's National Theatre* (1929); Camillo Pellizzi, *English Drama: the Last Great Phase*, trans. by Rowan Williams (1935), ch. VI; Lennox Robinson (ed.), *The Irish Theatre* (1939). lectures by Robinson, T. C. Murray, and others.

tion of a story of 1798 there is discernible a symbolic nationalism. In other plays subjects are taken from the heroic sagas, as in the tragic *Deirdre* (1907). At a later date Yeats was occupied with obscure and difficult abstractions in which he made use of dancers, musicians, and masked actors. These pieces, for which he derived suggestions from the Nōh plays of Japan, were collected as *Four Plays for Dancers* (1921).

For a time during his middle years Yeats seemed to be less dependent upon symbolism. *In the Seven Woods* (1904) and *The Green Helmet* (1910), the latter a reworking in ballad metre of an earlier play in prose, are hard and dry in manner. Yet concurrently with his substitution of lively, homely detail for the dreamy vagueness of background in his renderings of Irish myths, his studies were becoming increasingly esoteric. The symbolism which he evolved is extremely difficult. It is true that he sometimes drew upon traditional and hence easily intelligible sources (such as Plato), but he inquired also into astrology, theosophy, the phenomena of clairvoyance, oriental speculation, and various "hermetic" writings. At the time when he was engaged upon *Reveries over Childhood and Youth* (1915) and *The Trembling of the Veil* (1922)—afterwards printed together as *Autobiographies* [15] (1926)—he came to use events in his own life as symbols for his poetry that are often "private" and obscure to the verge of incommunicability. Increasingly he had to rely upon prose comments appended to the poems. In later work there are often multiple connotations which are not successfully communicable. A few (such as the cat-headed figures) are utterly uncouth. Yeats was profoundly interested in, and disturbed by, reports of mystic experiences; but though he would have liked to be, he never was a genuine mystic. The theory of the "Earth Memory" which he held in common with his friend A. E. (who, however, held it with sincere conviction) is in Yeats little other than a literary device; and in all the ingenuity and complexity of the theory elaborated in *A Vision* (privately printed, 1926), with its exposition of the phases of human experience symbolized by the Hunchback, the Saint, and the Fool, and with its great show of secret *gnosis,* in this pseudo-mystic erudition, one detects something of sham. Did not Yeats himself admit that it might be no more than metaphors for poetry, "a painted scene"? There was a core of rationalism in Yeats's nature. Nevertheless, though at bottom he remained unconvinced, these speculations provided for him the wonderful contrasts conveyed in his verse between the pagan world and the Catholic, between the natural and the supernatural, between the transient and the abiding. The sense of the conflict between soul and sense, between Being and Becoming, is suggested with greatest depth and splendor in *Sailing to Byzantium,* one of the finest of his later poems.

Later Poems

[15] In various collections of essays Yeats expounded his views on poetry, symbolism, the theatre, and other subjects. The principal volumes are *Ideas of Good and Evil* (1903); *Discoveries* (1907); *The Cutting of an Agate* (1912); and *Per Amica Silentia Lunae* (1918). Yeats's reception of the Nobel Prize for Literature in 1923 inspired the tribute, *The Bounty of Sweden* (1925). See also *Dramatis Personae* (1936).

A reaction from what he considered the weak sentiment of his earlier poetry was sometimes pushed to the extreme of sheer brutality. It took the form of substituting for the old suggestiveness the precise, hard-hitting word. He was dissatisfied because formerly he had separated his imagination from life; yet he was dissatisfied with life itself—"this pragmatical pig of a world." This is expressed with terrible and prophetic force in various poems, notably *The Second Coming* where some readers have detected a prediction of the world catastrophe which came about in the year of his death. Yeats seemed to abandon the effort to give, through his art, order to a chaotic world. From *The Tower* (1928) onward, humor, sarcasm, scorn, audacity, and a most unexpected sensuality mark his final phase. He resisted and resented the on-coming of old age. In his latest poems there is at once a passionate regret for the passing of the passionate experiences of youth and at the same time an indignant remoteness from the world. The gyre, the spiral, and the winding stair are constantly recurring symbols of the cyclic philosophy which he had evolved from reading and from life.

"A. E."   The mysticism which in Yeats is no more than the expression of a poetic mood is accepted, experienced, and revealed as profoundest truth by A. E., George W. Russell [16] (1867-1935), artist, poet, philosopher, journalist, economic theorist, and practical worker for agricultural reform in Ireland. The immense services which A. E. rendered to Ireland do not all belong to a history of literature; a considerable portion of his prose was ephemeral in subject. The insight and foresight which he applied to public affairs are also found in those poems in which he urges upon his fellow-countrymen a new outlook: "the first-born of the coming race" rather than "the last splendors of the Gael." But in most of his poems and in the beautiful fragment of autobiography entitled *The Candle of Vision* (1918) he is concerned with the varying manifestations of the one and eternal Truth of which intimations had come to him through his mystic experiences. There is a special devotion to evening, night, and dawn, when the soul is at furthest remove from the care and turmoil of the day. A quietism of Oriental intensity is combined with a devotion to the Earth, the Earth Memory, and the divinity of Earth. These ideas were expressed in *Homeward: Songs by the Way* (1894), in *The Earth Breath and other Poems* (1897), and in several volumes of later verse. There is necessarily a certain monotony of subject-matter but it is more than atoned for by the exquisite beauty with which A. E. plays his gentle and profound variations upon the theme of vision. How intensely, nevertheless, this visionary felt the charm of the world of phenomena is revealed in *The Symbol Seduces,* one of his loveliest poems.

Yeats made one of his most memorable contributions to the Irish Theatre

---

[16] *Collected Poems* (1913); the volumes of later date have not yet been collected; *The Living Torch,* ed. Monk Gibbon (1937), a selection from A. E.'s writings in *The Irish Statesman,* of which he was editor. — John Eglinton (pseudonym for W. K. Magee), *A Memoir of A. E.* (1937).

when he persuaded John Millington Synge [17] (1871-1909) to return from **Synge**
Paris in 1898 to his native land. Synge brought back with him a tinge of
Maeterlinck's nature mysticism and an acquaintance with Pierre Loti's
stories and studies of the Breton peasantry; but he owed little to these
Continental influences. In the Aran Islands [18] he absorbed the rich dialect
of a people quite uncontaminated with modern sophistication. Observing
the precepts and practice of Lady Gregory and Douglas Hyde, which were
strengthened by his own sense of style, he elevated and purified the peasant
idiom till it became the singularly vigorous and poetic medium of his plays.
Synge kept apart from Irish politics, and he indulged neither in didacticism
nor in metaphysical implications. He was concerned with the motivating
ideas and emotions of small groups of isolated men and women. (In his
hands even the traditional grandiosity of the Deirdre story is simplified).
He was aware of the savagery in human nature and he loved wildness in
nature and in men. Occasionally, especially in farcical situations, his plays
are brutal. He depicted a hard, coarse life and the unrestrained feelings,
alike in joy and sorrow, of simple people, close to earth. The background
of mist and mountain is essential to the effect of *The Shadow of the Glen,*
and the ocean, though never personified in the dialogue, seems to be one
of the dramatis personae in *Riders to the Sea.* There was an elemental quality
in his imagination which gave something of universality to the comedy and
tragedy of humble folk.

Setting aside a negligible farce, a few undistinguished poems and translations, and his accounts of the Aran Islanders and the people of West Kerry,
we are concerned with five plays, all work of his last decade. *The Shadow
of the Glen* (1903), a one-act piece about a miser who by pretending to
be dead entraps his wife (a theme as old as the story of the Widow of
Ephesus), is no more than a sketch, too abrupt in its brevity and puzzlingly
poised between farce and melancholy. Far finer (partly because the subject lent itself to condensation in a single act) is *Riders to the Sea* (1904), **Riders**
on the struggles of the fisher-folk with the element which is at once their **to the**
livelihood and their doom. In swift cumulativeness of effect and in piercing **Sea**
sweetness and direct incisiveness of speech Synge never surpassed this little
play. *The Well of the Saints* (1905), a full-length play, is set in a vague
period of the past; very wonderful is the effect throughout of strange remoteness from modernity. The theme, which is suggestive of old French
fabliaux, is bitter, melancholy, and sardonic. A man and woman, beggars
old and blind, have their sight restored with consequences other than had
been hoped for. Synge's instinct for theatrical effectiveness is at its best in

---

[17] *Complete Works* (1935) and other collected editions. — Maurice Bourgeois, *John Millington Synge and the Irish Theatre* (1913); P. P. Howe, *John Millington Synge, a Critical Study*
(1912); Daniel Corkery, *Synge and Anglo-Irish Literature* (1931); A. D. Estill, *The Sources
of Synge* (Philadelphia, 1939); John Masefield, *J. M. Synge. A Few Personal Recollections
with Biographical Notes.* (1921).

[18] For Synge's informal impressions of the peasantry of the west of Ireland see *The Aran
Islands* (Dublin, 1907), with drawings by Jack B. Yeats. Supplementary to this are the prose
sketches, *In Wicklow, In West Kerry,* and *In the Congested Districts.*

the postponed entry of the Saint who accomplishes the miracle. The uses to which Martin Doul puts his recovered sight gave offense in Dublin as a supposed reflection upon the national character. But the affront to Irish sensibilities on both religious and nationalistic grounds was more serious when Synge's most famous play, *The Playboy of the Western World* (1907), was produced. The protests and disturbances it occasioned in Dublin and later in the United States are part of Irish literary history. It was suggested by an actual case of parricide, but by substituting for the crime Christy Mahon's mistaken notion that he had killed his father, Synge, while retaining tragic overtones, turned the subject into vigorous, brilliant, and extravagant comedy—a comedy too exceptional in its subject, however, to claim the place among masterpieces which some admirers have assigned it. At the time of his death Synge was at work upon *Deirdre of the Sorrows* (posthumous, 1910), on the legendary theme of Beauty doomed to early death. In its bleak and tragic intensity of style *Deirdre*, unfinished though it is, is Synge's greatest work.

Padraic Colum

The intentions and the earlier accomplishments of the Irish playwrights had been poetic and folkloristic; but the study of actual peasant types, the adoption of the living idiom, the proximity of social and political agitation, and the impact of the English problem play opened the door to realism. The pioneering examples of realistic drama are the plays of Padraic Colum (1881-   ): *Broken Soil* (1903), later rewritten as *The Fiddler's House; The Land* (1905); and *Thomas Muskerry* (1910). A finer and more experienced craftsman was Lennox Robinson (1886-1958), director, actor, and producer, whose plays have been among the mainstays of the Abbey Theatre in recent years. In them there is scarcely a trace of the old folklore and in mood and technique they are not far apart from the work of Galsworthy and Granville-Barker. *The Whiteheaded Boy* (1916) is one of Robinson's liveliest comedies. He sometimes drew his subjects from recent Irish history, most notably in *The Lost Leader* (1918), which is founded on the popular report that Parnell had not died but was still alive under an assumed name. In his later plays Robinson tended to touch comedy with sentiment. There is room here but to name other contemporary realistic dramatists who have portrayed the changing conditions of Irish life—T. C. Murray, J. B. MacCarthy, George Shiels, and Brinsley MacNamara.

Lennox Robinson

Sean O'Casey

Towering above these writers was Sean O'Casey (1884-1965), who in three masterpieces dramatized the tragic events in which he took part. Born among the poor of Dublin, he passed his youth in humble labor, and in 1916 participated in the Easter Rebellion.[19] His first play, *The Shadow of a Gunman,* was produced at the Abbey Theatre in 1923. It is on the struggle between the Sinn Feiners and the English soldiery in 1920; the violence of

[19] See O'Casey's prose narrative of the Rebellion, *The Story of the Irish Citizen Army* (1919). — The three volumes of O'Casey's as yet unfinished autobiography—*I Knock at the Door* (1939), *Pictures in the Hallway* (1942), and *Drums under the Windows* (1946)—possess vivid intensity and brutal power.

conflict in the streets of Dublin forms effectively the background for scenes in the life of poor people in a tenement. In *Juno and the Paycock* (1924) the civil war of 1922 between the new-born Free State and the bitter-end Republicans is the setting of the story of a poor family's expectation of an inheritance and their subsequent disappointment. Bitter comedy and stark tragedy clash in violent contrast with no softening by means of such glamorous poetic style as Synge would have introduced. *The Plough and the Stars* (1926), on the Easter Rebellion, reaches in the final act a climax of horror in which national and private tragedy intermingle. In *The Silver Tassie* (1928) O'Casey turned to the larger subject of the Great War, making use of an "expressionistic" technique to bring a theme so huge within the boundaries of the theatre. The rejection of this play by the Abbey Theatre occasioned a notorious exchange of letters between O'Casey and Yeats in which the former had the better of the argument. *Within the Gates* (1933) deals, with an even freer technique, with the subject of the unemployed; the scene is Hyde Park. It shows how deeply O'Casey was moved by the plight of the poor. His torrential and often virulent power of language; the moral integrity which refuses to devise for the sake of aesthetic satisfaction a technical unity of fundamentally discordant elements; and the ability to show the impact of mighty events upon humble people, thus universalizing the tragedy of the life of the poor—these gifts mark him as one of the greatest writers of the Irish Literary Renaissance.[20]

[20] The writings of James Stephens (1882-1950) are almost entirely apart from the Irish theatre. In fiction and poetry he has delineated peasant life and made use of Irish folklore and supernaturalism. His charm and fantasy are at times contaminated with the merely whimsical. *The Crock of Gold* (1912) and *The Demi-Gods* (1914) are his best-known books. Several volumes of his verse were collected in 1926, and he wrote much in later years.—The talent of Daniel Corkery (1878-   ) is of a kind less popular but more distinguished and of probably more lasting quality. Dramatist, scholar, and author of one novel, Corkery is best known for the short stories collected in *A Munster Twilight* (1917), *The Hounds of Banba* (1920), and *Earth out of Earth* (1939). In them there are tragedy and pathos, an effect of remoteness, and often a strange poetic quality.

XXXVIII
Modern Drama

I

In the mid-nineteenth century, well before the "renovation" of the theatre associated with the names of T. W. Robertson and Sir Squire and Lady Bancroft, there was a vital and developing stagecraft, albeit unaccompanied by any literary drama worthy of the name.[1] Since evasions of the old monopolies had been permitted, or at any rate winked at, the repeal of the Licensing Act (1843) caused little or no immediately perceptible change, though in the long run the effect was wholesome. The minor theatres were already coming into prominence. Reforms for which Robertson has often been given credit were, it is now recognized, under way before he appeared. Apart from technical innovations in the structure of the theatres and the mounting of plays, there was evidence of progress in various kinds of drama. In melodrama the development was from vulgar staginess to a considerable degree of dignity and fidelity to reality, and in naturalistic burlesque, as performed by Mme Vestris and Charles Mathews, a piquant contrast between the extravagances of sentiment and situation and the quietness of acting and deportment. Before 1865 a decidedly realistic kind of acting had appeared in the London theatres. What was lacking was a playwright to provide dramas giving scope to the actors of the new school.

Boucicault Neither Dion Boucicault [2] (1820?-1890) nor Tom Taylor [3] (1817-1880) could satisfy this requirement. Boucicault, whose first successes were in the
Tom eighteen-forties, fixed the type of Victorian melodrama, adapted plots from
Taylor Dumas *fils* and other foreign writers, and in *The Colleen Bawn* (1860) and later plays exploited Irish subjects. Taylor's talent was facile and prolific. In *Our American Cousin* (1858) the "character-part" of Lord Dundreary points the way towards individualization as opposed to reliance upon con-

[1] For antecedents of the modern period see E. B. Watson, *Sheridan to Robertson* (1926) and Ernest Reynolds, *Early Victorian Drama: 1830-1870* (1936). William Archer, *The Theatrical World* (5v, 1894-1898), contemporary surveys of the crucial years 1893-1897; F. W. Chandler, *Aspects of Modern Drama* (1914); P. P. Howe, *Dramatic Portraits* (1913); Graham Sutton, *Some Contemporary Dramatists* (1924); Frank Vernon, *The Twentieth Century Theatre* (1924); J. W. Cunliffe, *Modern English Playwrights* (1927); Ramsden Balmforth, *The Problem-Play and its Influence on Modern Thought and Life* (1928); B. H. Clark, *A Study of the Modern Drama* (1928); W. P. Eaton, *The Drama in English* (1930); T. H. Dickinson, *The Contemporary Drama in England* (1931); Camillo Pellizzi, *Il Teatro Inglese* (Milan, 1934), trans. by Rowan Williams as *English Drama: The Last Great Phase* (1935); Allardyce Nicoll, *A History of Late Nineteenth Century Drama, 1850-1900* (2v, Cambridge, 1946).
[2] See above, ch. xv.
[3] Journalist, wit, critic, and editor (1874-1880) of *Punch.* — See Winton Tolles, *Tom Taylor and the Victorian Drama* (1940).

ventional stage types. *The Fool's Revenge* (1859), adapted from Hugo, is the best of Taylor's pseudo-historical plays, and *The Ticket-of-Leave Man* (1863) is the best of his melodramas.

The effort of Thomas William Robertson [4] (1829-1871) was towards *Robertson* naturalism in dialogue, feeling, and situation and the creation of the atmosphere of modern life with no artificialities of plot or violence of passion. In Marie Wilton (afterwards Lady Bancroft) he found an actress-manager in sympathy with his views, and in her small, intimate theatre a place where he could put into practice his ideal of restrained acting and contemporaneousness of effect. When *Society* was produced (1865) some critics sneered at the new "cup-and-saucer" comedy, but London flocked to see it. Robertson followed this success with *Ours* (1866), *Caste* (1867), and three other plays. To us his technique seems elementary, his dialogue flat or stilted, his fidelity to actuality questionable; and the literary value of his plays is of the slightest. But in the history of modern drama he has a secure place as a pioneer.

Sir William S. Gilbert [5] (1836-1911) wrote many farces and pantomimes *Gilbert* and in several comedies combined something of Robertson's technique with *and* a cynicism that was all his own. There are motives in his "fairy comedies" *Sullivan* as well as in his *Bab Ballads* (1867-1869) that reappear in the "Savoy Operas" [6] (1875-1889) which he wrote for Sir Arthur Sullivan's music. These operettas are unique among librettos in that they are enjoyable even apart from the music. Lyric charm and lightly parodied romantic themes are joined to a cynicism that is often quietly ruthless and to mordant satire upon contemporary fads and humbugs. The formula requires a humorous topsy-turviness of situation and reasoning; and over all there is a dainty, shimmering grace.

II

The French ideal of the *pièce bien faite*—exposition; situation; "great scene"; disentanglement—lived on till the close of the century, but in the eighteen-eighties the tide of Ibsenism began to flow.[7] The "discoverer" of *Ibsenism*

[4] *Principal Dramatic Works* (2v, 1889); *Caste* and *Society*, ed. T. E. Pemberton (1905). — T. E. Pemberton, *Life and Writings of T. W. Robertson* (1893); Sir Squire and Lady Bancroft, *Recollections of Sixty Years* (1909); Sir Arthur W. Pinero, "The Theatre of the 'Seventies," in *The Eighteen-Seventies*, ed. H. Granville-Barker (1929), pp. 135-163.

[5] *The Savoy Operas* (1926); *The Bab Ballads* [and] *Songs of a Savoyard* (1919). — Isaac Goldberg, *Sir William S. Gilbert: a Study in Modern Satire* (1913) and *The Story of Gilbert and Sullivan* (1929); Hesketh Pearson, *Gilbert and Sullivan: A Biography* (1935); G. K. Chesterton, "Gilbert and Sullivan," in *The Eighteen-Eighties*, ed. Walter de la Mare (1930), pp. 136-158.

[6] *Trial by Jury* (1875); *H. M. S. Pinafore* (1878); *The Pirates of Penzance* (1880); *Patience* (1881); *Iolanthe* (1882); *The Mikado* (1885); *Ruddigore* (1887); *The Yeoman of the Guard* (1888); *The Gondoliers* (1889). Gilbert and Sullivan quarreled in 1889. After their reconciliation they collaborated again but without their former success.

[7] Miriam A. Franc, *Ibsen in England* (1919); Elizabeth Robins, *Ibsen and the Actress* (*Hogarth Essays*, Series II, xv, 1928); Harley Granville-Barker, "The Coming of Ibsen," in *The Eighteen-Eighties* (1930), pp. 159-196; Halvdan Koht, *The Life of Ibsen* (English translation, 1931), II. 114-115 and 266-270; and the table of dates, based on Koht, in Una Ellis-Fermor, *The Irish Dramatic Movement* (1939), Appendix 3.

the Norwegian dramatist had been Edmund Gosse, who since 1871 had written several critiques bringing him to notice [8] and in 1876 had translated *Emperor and Galilean*. In 1880 William Archer's [9] translation of *Pillars of Society* appeared, and in 1884 Henry Arthur Jones collaborated on a bowdlerized perversion of *A Doll's House*. With the production in 1889 of Archer's faithful rendering of that play the storm began to rise, Clement Scott, the dramatic critic, being the leader of the opposition, and Sir Henry Irving, the foremost actor of the period, setting his face against the "new" drama. When in 1891 the Lord Chamberlain refused to license *Ghosts,* the controversy became acute. To this year belongs G. Bernard Shaw's *The Quintessence of Ibsenism,* the expansion of a lecture of the previous year. The organization of the Independent Theatre in London (1891), following the lead of the Théâtre Libre in Paris (1887), provided an outlet for serious realistic drama. With Elizabeth Robins' production of *Hedda Gabler* in 1892 the status of Ibsen began to be accepted and controversy gradually subsided. That the English theatre preferred the social plays of Ibsen's middle period to his earlier poetic plays and continued to prefer them to his later symbolic dramas was not the fault of the pioneer Ibsenites but due rather to the prominence of the contemporary "problem novel" and to current sociological speculation. The "bleak Norwegian" furnished weighty support to English criticism of middle-class society. Fearlessly confronting subjects hitherto proscribed, he was as fearless in driving forward from ominous situations to their logical conclusions. His emphasis upon heredity and the marital relation brought sexual problems into startling prominence, and the tendency towards pessimism was pronounced. Ibsen's English disciples imitated for the most part no more than his external audacities without penetrating to the revolutionary foundations; but at least they advanced the cause of the theatre's claim to deal seriously and purposefully with "the whole of life."

Jones   Yet the two most successful playwrights of the period were anti-Ibsenite or at most pseudo-Ibsenite. Henry Arthur Jones [10] (1851-1929), having scored a great hit with *The Silver King* (1882), a melodrama which won Matthew Arnold's commendation, did prudish violence, as we have noted, to *A Doll's House* in *Breaking a Butterfly* (1884). At that time he knew, as he afterwards said, "nothing of Ibsen, but a great deal of Robertson." Thereafter he moved away from the old allegiance without ever unreservedly accepting the new. He had nothing of Ibsen's ability to universalize the characters and situations of a particular time and place, but he had some-

---

[8] Gosse's principal papers on Ibsen (1873 and 1889) are reprinted in *Northern Studies* (1890), pp. 38-104.
[9] 1856-1924. — See Charles Archer, *William Archer: Life, Work and Friendships* (1931).
[10] Of Jones's hundred plays a good many were never published. *Representative Plays of Henry Arthur Jones,* ed. Clayton Hamilton (4v, 1926). Of Jones's writings on the drama the most important are collected in *The Renascence of the English Drama* (1895) and *Foundations of a National Theatre* (1912). — See Doris Arthur Jones [Mrs. Thorne], *Life and Letters of Henry Arthur Jones* (1930); R. A. Cordell, *Henry Arthur Jones and the Modern Drama* (1932); Marjorie Northend, "Henry Arthur Jones and the Development of Modern English Drama," *RES,* XVIII (1942). 448-463. — The dates given are of stage production.

thing of the master's polemic fervor in his effort to reclaim for the drama the lost provinces of religion and morality. He was influenced by the ideas of Ruskin and Morris, but with a social conscience never greatly troubled he did not enlist in the cause of any thorough-going rebellion against "things as they are," for he remained involved in the prejudices of the age and, like Tennyson, criticized a social system with which he was at heart content. Writing and lecturing ceaselessly on the dramatist's function and opportunity in society, on the play-reading public, in advocacy of a subsidized National Theatre, and on similar topics, he constituted himself a propagandist for the stage, insisting that the art of the drama was not merely a matter of cleverly devised situations and effective "curtains" but the portrayal of life as a whole. But he never really freed himself from the demands of the commercial theatre. To write with one eye on the actor-manager and the other on the box-office is not to write at liberty. The fact is that Jones's position as a critic was always in advance of that which he assumed as a playwright. How narrowly he was content to circumscribe the freedom he professed is shown by the contrast between the claims advanced in the preface to *Saints and Sinners* (1884) and the timid sentimentality of the play itself. *Michael and His Lost Angel* (1896), the story of an erring Anglican clergyman, concludes with a scene of false theatricality. (Jones turned in other plays to the provincial nonconformist world from which he sprang, hating it but bearing the scars of cast-off chains.) In this play, as in others, the satiric exposure of social corruption is but incidental to this basic sentimentality. The theme of marital infidelity in *The Case of Rebellious Susan* (1894) and the problem of divorce as adumbrated in *The Liars* (1897)—the latter a technically admirable example of the "well-made play" against which Shaw fulminated—are handled in a manner that now seems old-fashioned. Jones continued to exploit social problems in *Mrs. Dane's Defense* (1900), but in *Dolly Reforming Herself* (1908) there is genuine high comedy and a mellow art instead of the old hard vehemence. From about 1897, coincident with Kipling and the Boer War, an "imperialistic" note had sounded in some of his plays. This grew in volume and fervor after 1914, and it was over differences of opinion regarding England's policy in war and peace that Jones quarreled bitterly with Shaw and H. G. Wells.[11]

Sir Arthur Wing Pinero [12] (1855-1934) learned his craftsmanship in the *Pinero* school of Scribe and Sardou and never discarded completely the conventions of the *pièce bien faite* with its over-ingenious plotting, its "great scene," its conversational exposition, and its use of "asides." From 1877 he put out a succession of comedies and farces, light in substance and noteworthy only for the expertness with which comic entanglements are devised and resolved.

[11] See especially Jones's *My Dear Wells* (1921), ch. xix. Cf. Archibald Henderson, *Bernard Shaw, Playboy and Prophet* (1932), pp. 648-655.
[12] *Social Plays*, ed. Clayton Hamilton (4v, 1917-1922). — Hamilton Fyfe, *Sir Arthur Wing Pinero's Plays and Players* (1930); W. Stocker, "Pinero's Dramen," *Anglia*, xxxv (1912). 1-79. The account of Pinero in P. P. Howe, *Dramatic Portraits*, is exquisitely cruel. Pinero's *Stevenson the Dramatist* (*Publications of the Dramatic Museum of Columbia University*, 1914) is illuminating on his own ideals and limitations. — The dates given are of stage production.

Overtones of melancholy and hints of serious purpose gradually became audible. For *The Profligate* (1889) he wrote alternative dénouements—a suicide or a technically happy ending; the theatre-folk chose the latter but Pinero published the play with the tragic close. *The Second Mrs. Tanqueray* (1893), the tragedy of a "woman with a past," must be judged not only in relation to Ibsen (at the height of whose notoriety it was produced) but to several immediately contemporary novels such as *Tess, Esther Waters,* and Grant Allen's *The Woman Who Did.* Pinero's skill is displayed in the admirable exposition and in the tense critical scenes; but the tragic conclusion is melodramatic, and Shaw's indictment of the play—that the tragedy does not develop from character but from an exceptional and improbable chain of events—is justified. From a situation which would have provided Ibsen with crushing accusations against society Pinero extracted good "theatre." In subsequent plays he continued to exploit "delicate"—or, as Shaw wittily called them, "Pinerotic"—subjects. *The Gay Lord Quex* (1899) is notable for its wit, its ingenious stage-setting, and its deft adjustment of the audience's sympathies whereby the "villain" becomes the "hero." Pinero's technique in tragedy can be best studied in *Iris* (1901), old-fashioned though it now is. *Mid-Channel* (1909), Pinero's most powerful play, is a study in neurasthenia leading to a wrecked marriage. Pinero continued to write till about 1930; but his post-war plays are, like Jones's, of little consequence.

Whatever the shortcomings of their plays as literature, Jones and Pinero are significant transitional figures in the revival of the theatre, for they set examples of formal excellence. As expert craftsmen they claim more attention than the bare mention usually vouchsafed them in histories of English literature.

III

Shaw

George Bernard Shaw [13] (1856-1950), Irish in birth but of Yorkshire blood, commanded for his campaign of ideas the position of vantage of a man without a country. After his childhood in Dublin, his youth was a period of poverty and struggle in London. He became attached to the Socialist movement and a member of the Fabian Society (1884) for which he wrote the *Manifesto.* Later he collaborated with Sidney and Beatrice Webb on the *Fabian Essays* (1889). With a natural forensic gift he developed into an alert and hard-hitting debater and public speaker. Meanwhile, between 1879 and 1883, he had written five novels. *Cashel Byron's Profession* (1882;

[13] *Collected Works* (30v, 1930-1931); *Complete Plays* (1931); *Prefaces* (1934). — G. H. Wells, *Bibliography* (1925-1929); C. L. and V. M. Broad, *Dictionary to the Plays and Novels of Bernard Shaw, with a Bibliography* (1929); Archibald Henderson, *George Bernard Shaw: His Life and Work* (1911) and *Bernard Shaw, Playboy and Prophet* (1932); *Table Talk of G. B. S. Conversations . . . between Bernard Shaw and His Biographer* [Henderson] (1925); H. L. Mencken, *G. B. Shaw: His Plays* (1905); G. K. Chesterton, *George Bernard Shaw* (1909); Charles Cestre, *Bernard Shaw et son œuvre* (Paris, 1912); P. P. Howe, *Bernard Shaw: A Critical Study* (1915); E. C. Wagenknecht, *A Guide to Bernard Shaw* (1929); R. F. Rattray, *Bernard Shaw: A Chronicle and an Introduction* (1934); Sen Gupta, *The Art of Bernard Shaw* (1936); T. A. Knowlton, *The Economic Theory of George Bernard Shaw* (1936); H. C. Duffin, *The Quintessence of Bernard Shaw* (1939); Hesketh Pearson, *G. B. S.: A Full-Length Portrait* (1942).

published 1885-1886), the best of them, was later dramatized as *The Admirable Bashville* (1901). *Love among the Artists* (1881; published 1886) is concerned largely with music. Wagner had been one of the shaping influences on Shaw's youth; and it was as a musical critic for *The Star* (1889) and art critic for *The World* (1890-1894) that he first attracted attention.[14] The keen and forthright dramatic criticisms in *The Saturday Review* (1895-1898) made the initials "G. B. S." famous.[15]

Long before that time this immensely energetic journalist, critic, publicist, and reformer had found in the drama the congenial medium for the dissemination of his ideas. In 1885 he and William Archer had attempted to collaborate on a play. It did not come off; but in 1892, with Ibsen as an incentive rather than a model, Shaw drastically altered the play into *Widowers' Houses*, which was produced by the Independent Theatre group. This grotesque and ironical exposure of slum landlordism and municipal graft is crude enough, but the rapid interchange of ideas gives life to the characters. *The Philanderer* (1893), which did not achieve production, is a disagreeable piece no longer vitalized by its ephemeral topicalities on the Ibsenites, the vivisectionists, and the "new women." *Mrs. Warren's Profession* (1894) ran afoul of a censorship which could not stomach a serious treatment of the "social evil." In it Shaw broadens an attack upon the problem of the prostitute and the procuress into an apologue of the iniquities of industrialism. By this time Shaw had probably derived suggestions from the sparkling dialogue and impudent paradoxes of Wilde's comedies,[16] but independently of Wilde he possessed from the first a sense of style which distinguishes his dialogue from the usual commonplaces of Jones and Pinero. The gay and witty comedy *Arms and the Man* (1894), which under the patronage of Emily Horniman (later the financial "backer" of the Irish Players) had a limited success with an intellectual coterie but failed to win the larger public, satirizes romantic notions of military glory and false ideals of heroism.

If people would not attend performances of his plays, perhaps he could persuade them to read them. *Plays Pleasant and Unpleasant* (1898) collect in the latter category Shaw's first three pieces and in the former *Arms and the Man, Candida, The Man of Destiny,* and *You Never Can Tell.* In *Candida* the contrast is developed between the large, unpractical vision of a poet and the narrow but boldly benevolent opinions of a Christian Socialist clergyman. Candida, the parson's wife, is the most charming of Shaw's heroines (he designed the rôle for Ellen Terry [17]) and in no other play till

Plays Pleasant and Unpleasant

[14] Reprinted as *London Music in 1888-9* (1937) and *Music in London, 1890-1894* (1932). Shaw's most important contribution to musical criticism, *The Perfect Wagnerite* (1898), expounds the revolutionary thought in *The Ring of the Nibelungs* with a characteristic neglect of the emotional content.
[15] Assembled as *Our Theatres in the Nineties; Collected Works,* xxiii-xxv.
[16] See above, ch. xxxv.
[17] What has been called the struggle of Shaw and Irving for the possession of the soul of Ellen Terry (too complex a story to be related here) typifies the conflict between the modern and the traditional-classic view of the function of the stage. See *Ellen Terry and Bernard Shaw: A Correspondence* (1931).

Saint Joan did this dramatist who is so nearly pure intelligence approach so closely to an understanding of emotion. *The Man of Destiny* carries on the attack upon the falsity of martial glory by contrasting the historic Bonaparte with the Napoleon of legend. *You Never Can Tell* is an irresponsible farce-comedy almost wholly devoid of social theses save what may be read into the contrast between the kindly wisdom and lowly social status of William the Waiter. He is one of the most memorable creations of the English Comic Muse.

Of *Three Plays for Puritans* (1901) *The Devil's Disciple* is a melodrama of the American Revolution, *Captain Brassbound's Conversion* a comedy, and *Caesar and Cleopatra* the delineation of a supremely famous man who, true to his own nature, does not need the pedestal of legend for the recognition of his genius. The amusing anachronistic topical allusions are part of Shaw's method of bringing history home to the modern spectator. But after the admirable opening episode of Caesar's first encounter with Cleopatra, action and characterization are blurred by too much sheer talk. *Man and Superman* (1903) presages the philosophy to be elaborated later; but lacking Act III (the Dream of Hell), which is almost always omitted on the stage, this is a disconcerting comedy of a woman's pursuit and capture of a reluctant male. Marriage is "a man-trap baited with ... delusive idealizations." What is implied in the comedy is made explicit in John Tanner's dream of Don Juan Tenorio and still more so in the Preface to the play. Woman is the agent of the "Life-Force" which directs her more strongly than it does man towards procreation, the supreme end of the species. With suggestions of Bergson's doctrine of creative evolution (the *élan vital*) and hints from Schopenhauer, Nietzsche, and Samuel Butler are combined "advanced" views on eugenics and selective breeding. Shaw the philosopher dominates Shaw the dramatist.

Man and Superman [margin]

Till 1904 Shaw had had but a limited theatrical success and had been almost wholly dependent upon provincial audiences and the coterie acclaim of the semi-private Stage Society, but now came fame and financial success. Harley Granville-Barker and J. E. Vedrenne began their brilliant management of the Court Theatre where by 1907 there were several hundred productions of nearly a dozen of Shaw's plays. At the summit of renown, he was also at the top of his form. *John Bull's Other Island,* a wise and witty comedy on Irish character and politics, was rejected by the Abbey Theatre for which it was written, produced in London, and published with *Major Barbara* (1907). In power of thought and brilliance of style Shaw never surpassed the latter play, and when the prestige of some of his later dramas has declined it may come to be considered his masterpiece. In the munitions business he found a peculiarly hateful example of the evils of industrialism and in Undershaft, the war-profiteer, an illustration of man's following of self-interest disguised as duty. The Salvation Army provides the other side of the picture and affords an occasion for the development of the theme,

Major Barbara [margin]

taken directly from Samuel Butler, that "poverty is the worst of crimes" and the lack of money the root of all evil.

There was now some evidence of decline in power. *The Shewing-up of Blanco Posnet* (1909), refused a license but acted in Dublin beyond the Lord Chamberlain's jurisdiction, evinces some understanding of crude religiosity but is not worth the pother about it in Shaw's preface. *Misalliance* (1910) is scarcely more than a specific illustration of the matters discussed in the appended "Treatise on Parents and Children." *Getting Married* (1908), is really not a play at all but a dialogue, much of it tedious. *The Doctor's Dilemma* (1911), written, according to the report, to meet Archer's challenge that Shaw had never attempted a death scene, does not meet it successfully. The incidental attacks upon the medical profession as an organization preying upon the public spill over into a huge preface. *Fanny's First Play* (1911), which on the stage scored one of Shaw's greatest hits, uses the old device of the play-within-the-play and reminiscences of *The Rehearsal* and *The Critic* to satirize the dramatic critics. *Androcles and the Lion* (1913) afforded much mirth to those who were not shocked by the mingling of buffoonery with the serious presentation of different types of Christian faith. The play is not wanting in passages of solemn beauty, and the lion is really funny. *The Dark Lady of the Sonnets* (1910) is amusing, if unconvincing, as a comedy of the court of Queen Elizabeth, and more serious as an argument for a National Theatre. In reply to Frank Harris's accusation that Shaw had pilfered the "Mary Fitton" theory of Shakespeare's *Sonnets* from him, Shaw in his preface gave an account of Thomas Tyler, the originator of that theory. *Pygmalion* (1913) is a satire on snobbery and a contribution of no great value to educational theory. That the normalization of Judy O'Grady's use of the aspirates will make her the equal of the Colonel's lady does not carry us very far.

Shaw's expression of opinions during the War of 1914-1918 cost him temporarily his popularity. Actually he directed his attack not against England's participation in the war but against the official justification of her entrance into the conflict. But as his arguments were nearly identical with those in German propaganda he was accused, not without reason, of giving aid and comfort to the enemy. Certainly his levity of tone was ill-timed and seemed heartless. Shaw's far-sighted proposals for the peace may have had some influence upon Woodrow Wilson. The "playlets of the war" (as he called a few dramatic sketches) are negligible topicalities. *Heartbreak House* (1917), attacking the ruling classes held responsible for the crash of civilization, is an inartistic amalgam of discussion and farce, making use of parable and symbol and anticipating the mood of disillusioned futility which was to prevail in the literature of the nineteen-twenties. The cycle of five plays entitled *Back to Methuselah* (1921), beginning with the Garden of Eden and peering into the future "as far as thought can reach," develops with unrestrained garrulity the theme of creative evolution. Death is a mere device of natural selection and if prolongation of life is ever found necessary for the preservation of the race it will be prolonged. "The power that produced Man when the monkey was not up to the mark, can produce a higher creature than Man if Man does not come up to the mark." Yet the pallid and sexless "vortices of thought" towards which humanity is held to be evolving seem singularly dispiriting. Shaw's anti-Neo-Darwinism and his arguments for a restatement of religious mythology in modern terms are more convincingly presented in his preface (a hundred pages of his finest prose) than in the plays themselves. *Saint Joan* (1923) was a great success in the theatre, partly because the circumstance of the former self-proclaimed atheist offering his homage to a heroine of religion seemed piquant. But the characterization of Joan of Arc is regarded as a purely intellectual problem; the emotional content of religion, though not ignored, is misunderstood. The great trial-scene gave Shaw an opportunity to dramatize a clash of opposites wherein Joan's enemies are permitted to have the better of the arguments. This satisfies logic at the expense of intuition; but a "vortex of pure thought" cannot be expected to comprehend the character of a saint. Shaw's plays after *Saint Joan,* such as *The Apple Cart* (1930) and *Geneva* (1939) were either topicalities or "tomfooleries" (his own term) and may be passed over without comment.

Saint Joan

"In all my plays," Shaw remarked to his authorized biographer, "my economic studies have played as important a part as a knowledge of anatomy does in the works of Michael Angelo." These studies led to his rejection of the Marxian theory of value, while practical experience with workingmen and revolutionists led to a denial of the existence of the "class-conflict." Revolutionists, he found, were generally intelligent, and therefore dissatisfied, members of the bourgeoisie, at war with their own class, while self-interest attached the proletariat to the capitalistic system which exploited it. From revolutionary Marxism Shaw passed to the conviction that public ownership would come gradually. Not till late in his career did he bring together his ideas on society in *The Intelligent Woman's Guide to Capitalism and Socialism* (1928), but from the beginning his effort was, as he said, "to force the public to reconsider its morals," especially current morality as to economic and sexual relations. To this end (and not merely for self-advertisement) he used every resource of a nature that was never loath to clown, to shock, and to parade, but also to fight hard and generously against cruelty and hypocrisy. The ardor of his convictions made for the volubility and repetitiousness which are his greatest weaknesses as a writer and for the persistent confusion of art and ethics which turned so many of his plays into pieces of propaganda. There is little or nothing that is original in his thought. His gift was for the vigorous enunciation and brilliant illustration of the ideas of other men. His satire ranged over the church, the law, penology, medicine ("organized" medicine and the vivisectionists), science (especially Neo-Darwinism which he opposed as cruel, mindless, and futile), and numberless other subjects. A distrust of emotional values led

The Drama of Ideas

to his derision of romantic notions of love; love he regarded as a biological mechanism for the propagation of the race. War he exposed as futile folly, but he argued that at the present stage of evolution man is naturally destructive though he invents such excuses as justice and patriotism. This is a particular example of Shaw's exposure of the contrast between the public profession of ideals of conduct and society and the secret evasion of those ideals. Men search for high-sounding excuses for following the path of desire. What is wrong with civilization? is his ever-recurring question. Consequently his basic concern was not with individual characterization but with problems in character and conduct of universal import, with the further consequence that in the later plays there is a tendency towards the symbolic which accounts for the resemblance that has been found between his plays and the Jonsonian Comedy of Humors. There are no real villains in the plays, or rather, Society as it exists is the villain, for, as Shaw asserted, "until Society is reformed, no man can reform himself except in the most insignificant small ways." His aim was not to tell a story but to convey ideas. In this there is the danger to Shaw's future reputation that these ideas will be absorbed into, or rejected by, the general consciousness. Putting it more hopefully, not the ideas but the entertaining way in which they are illuminated will keep the comedies in remembrance. In some plays he does not entirely discard the *raisonneur* or disinterested *tertium quid* of whom Jones and Pinero made so much use; but more frequently, seeking a perpetual display of contrary arguments, Shaw permits the characters, who are sometimes mere burlesques, to illustrate and comment upon the author's theses. Often they are no more than his mouthpieces. "Debated drama," Shaw called this kind of play; that is, the discussion of the mental and spiritual states and changes in the characters of men and women who are involved in a situation rather than an action.[18]

IV

The dramatist most closely associated with Shaw was Harley Granville-Barker (1877-1946). Early experience as an actor and producer contributed to his success as a playwright. At the Court Theatre he created several of Shaw's most famous rôles. In the years shortly before the First World War he was responsible for Shakespearean productions which are famous in stage history for their beauty and intelligence. With Gordon Craig he was an innovator in methods of mounting and illumination. His three important

Granville-Barker

[18] St. John Hankin (1860-1909) was another contributor to the "drama of ideas," but in a sense other than that in which the phrase is applied to Shaw. The dramatist's business, Hankin said, is to "represent life, not argue about it." The life he represents affords the spectator the satisfaction of recognition rather than of surprise. Instead of making his plays vehicles of ideas, as did Shaw, he used a clear-cut idea, apt for comedy and touched with cynicism, as the central motive in each. Hankin avoided cheap theatrical effects, sudden "curtains," and the like. A feeling for style makes his plays more readable today than are most of the period. *The Cassilis Engagement* (1905) is probably his best play, and *The Last of the De Mullins* (1908) his most serious. — *Plays*, introduction by John Drinkwater (2v, 1923).

plays all belong to the first decade of the century. These varied experiences as actor, manager, producer, playwright, translator, adapter and experimenter lie behind the brilliant Shakespearean and other dramatic criticism of his later years, in which the emphasis is upon the practical problems of the theatre.[19]

The Marrying of Ann Leete (1901), Granville-Barker's first significant play, deals with the problem of *mésalliances* into which the heroine and her brother are driven by the "Life-Force." Ideas suggestive of Shaw and George Meredith[20] are combined with elements of fantasy and symbolism faintly resembling Barrie's work. *Prunella* (1904) is a light and charming thing written in collaboration with Laurence Housman. *The Voysey Inheritance* (1905) presents the conflict between the older generation, represented by an energetic, dishonest father, and the younger, represented by the sensitive son who must face a heritage of debt and dishonor. The conflicting counsel given him by his sister and his betrothed provides a clash of opposites, and at the close the situation is left in dramatic suspense. *Waste* (1907), which the censor refused to license, is a somber "domestic" tragedy of a young politician who when his mistress dies as the result of an operation to escape child-bearing is left without the son he longed for and the woman he loved and, faced with a scandal ruinous to his career, kills himself. *The Madras House* (1910) is another study of the conflicting generations and reflects also the "feminist" agitation of the pre-war years. *The Secret Life* (1923) reflects the moral and spiritual desolation of the post-war world, mooting questions to which no answer is forthcoming. Characteristic of this small body of work of high distinction are an extreme precision in dialogue, an intimate sympathy with the characters he has created, a most effective employment of understatement, an ability to make details contribute to the mood of an entire play, and a sensitiveness to the subtle relationships existing between small things and great.

Houghton   The theatre at Manchester supported by Miss Horniman afforded an outlet for several dramatists of whom William Stanley Houghton (1881-1913) was the most distinguished. A direct, frank realism in which there is nothing of the doctrinaire is characteristic of his best play, *Hindle Wakes* (1912). This is an austere and genuinely modern treatment of the problem of the "double standard." Fanny passes a holiday at the seaside with Alan; facing a scandal the parents try to force marriage upon them. The weak Alan is brought to the point of proposing marriage, but it is Fanny who refuses; she does not love him and declines to let a passing affair enmesh her for life. The play ends without any attempt to solve the underlying problem.

It seems likely that John Galsworthy[21] will be longer remembered for

[19] *Prefaces to Shakespeare* (4v, 1927-1945); *On Dramatic Method* (1931); *Associating with Shakespeare* (1932); and other works.

[20] Compare Granville-Barker's discussion of *The Sentimentalists* in "Tennyson, Swinburne, and Meredith—and the Theatre," in *The Eighteen-Seventies* (1929), pp. 187-193.

[21] For the novels and for general bibliographical references see ch. XL, below. Galsworthy's plays are collected in seven series (1909-1930). See also his *Representative Plays*, ed. G. P. Baker (1924). The correspondence with Edward Garnett in H. V. Marrot, *The Life and Letters*

one work of fiction than for his plays. He had already published several *Galsworthy* novels and begun *The Forsyte Saga* when his first play, *The Silver Box,* was produced by Granville-Barker (1906). Standing as always within the confines of the privileged class, Galsworthy here indicts society for its contrasting treatment of two men, the one rich the other poor, who are guilty of the same crime. *Strife* (1909) presents the conflict of extremes as represented by capital and labor, the lock-out, and the strike. In the end and after much misery, both parties repudiate their recalcitrant leaders and accept a compromise ready at hand from the beginning of the dispute. The fact that *Justice* (1910) led to reforms in prison-administration is more to Galsworthy's credit as a humanitarian than as a dramatist. Falder, the protagonist, is neither innocent nor an incorrigible criminal; but when after the theatrically effective trial scene and the harrowing episode of the solitary confinement Falder, now a ticket-of-leave man, forges references in order to find employment, is again arrested, and in the act of escape meets his death, no solution of the problem of the ex-prisoner has been offered; the dramatist has merely put before us an extreme case. *The Pigeon* (1913) contrasts the treatment of social outcasts by a charitable sentimentalist with the treatment accorded by three types of social workers. *The Skin-Game* (1920) presents yet another contrast, this time between the "county families" and the newly rich. In *Loyalties* (1922) sympathy is extended to a vulgar young Jew from whom a "gentleman" has stolen money to buy off his former mistress. Facing discovery, the thief shoots himself. *Old English* (1924), which in mood is nearest of the plays to *The Forsyte Saga,* studies the vanishing type of ruggedly individualistic man of affairs. From this rapid survey a dozen lesser plays, no longer acted or read, have been omitted. The charge brought against Galsworthy at the beginning of his career that he was cold and "inhuman" in his impartiality yielded later to the criticism that he was sentimental, that his sympathy was not untouched with aristocratic patronage of the unfortunate, and that his pity often sinks into the lachrymose. He applied an anxious seriousness, unalleviated by wit or humor, as much to the effective theatrical arrangement of his material as to his exposure of defects in modern society. The desire to be fair to both sides carries in later plays the consequence not only of over-symmetry of design but also of seeming to refuse to take a firm stand. His lucid and all too facile compassion was expended rather upon social groups than upon individuals, and his hostility, like Shaw's, was to institutions rather than to men and women. He is the perpetual pleader of those extenuating circumstances which society must often brush aside if it is to protect itself. The criticism that while demonstrating the need for reform he was not a reformer is true of the plays but not of the man, as his correspondence with Winston Churchill and other public officials shows. His hope was in social evolution, not revolution; but in his desire to be just to the under-dog he did less than justice to society itself.

---

of John Galsworthy (1936) is illuminating for his intentions and techniques. See also his essay, *Some Platitudes concerning the Drama,* in *The Inn of Tranquility* (1912), pp. 189-202.

Maugham   William Somerset Maugham [22] (1874-   ) is destined to be remembered rather for his novels (or one of them) than for his numerous plays. Like Galsworthy, he was already a writer of fiction when the Stage Society produced his first play, *A Man of Honor,* in 1903. This tragedy of mismating gave promise of profounder things, but Maugham chose to expend his polished technique for many years upon already well-worn themes. The literary grace of such an essentially trivial play as *The Land of Promise* (1909) marks its descent from Oscar Wilde and its cynicism is suggestive of Restoration comedy. The same manner survives in some of his post-war plays, *The Constant Wife* (1926), for example. More substantial and on the highest level of his craftsmanship is *The Circle* (1921). Often he satirized the self-assured pose of the "Bright Young Things" of the post-war generation, and his somewhat supercilious sophistication sometimes anticipates the tone of Noel Coward. But in his final phase as a dramatist Maugham, writing not "what the public wants" but what he wished to write, rose to a high level of sincerity and power. *The Breadwinner* (1930), deft in craftsmanship and sardonic in humor, is suggestive of Maugham's novel, *The Moon and Sixpence. For Services Rendered* (1932) is a grim commentary upon the politicians' promise of "a land fit for heroes to live in." In the last act of *Sheppey* (1933) the action shifts most impressively from the realistic to the symbolic plane, with the introduction of the old morality motive of the Coming of Death. Maugham had for long followed the melodramatic or farcical path of least resistance, but from it he turned to express his cynical contempt for the world in which he has been forced to live.

Barrie   While some of the novels of Galsworthy and Maugham are more likely to survive than their plays, the converse is true of Sir James Matthew Barrie [23] (1860-1937). Like them he was practised in other literary forms before he turned to the drama. In his early writings he sketched with humor and pathos the life of Kirriemuir: *Auld Licht Idylls* (1888) and *A Window in Thrums* (1889) are Scottish regionalism of the "Kailyard School." The sketches in *My Lady Nicotine* (1890) are somewhat broader in scope. *The Little Minister* (1891), humorous and unabashedly sentimental, won success as a novel and far more success when it was dramatized (1897). The humorous types in *The Professor's Love Story* (1894) are steeped in cloying sentiment. But that there was a hard core beneath Barrie's surface softness was shown in the two novels, *Sentimental Tommy* (1896) and its sequel *Tommy and Grizel* (1900). The costume-play *Quality Street* (1902) treats with genuinely moving tenderness the old theme of lovers meeting after

[22] *Collected Plays* (6v, 1931-1934). For the novels and for bibliographical references see below, ch. XL.
[23] *Works,* Kirriemuir Edition (10v, 1922), Peter Pan Edition (18v, 1929-1941); *Plays,* Uniform Edition (10v, 1918-1938); *Plays,* Definitive Edition, ed. A. E. Wilson (1942); *Letters,* ed. Viola Meynell (1942). — Herbert Garland, *Bibliography* (1928); Denis Mackail, *Barrie* (1941); J. A. Hammerton, *Barrie: The Story of a Genius* (1929); H. M. Walbrook, *J. M. Barrie and the Theatre* (1922); J. A. Roy, *J. M. Barrie* (1937); W. A. Darlington, *J. M. Barrie* (1938). — Barrie's plays were generally printed several years after their appearance on the stage; the dates here given are those of production.

long separation. *The Admirable Crichton* (1902) is sturdier stuff. With The perfect mastery of his art Barrie presents the imperturbable, sagacious butler Admirable who when the fashionable people by whom he is employed are wrecked on Crichton a desert island assumes the leadership for which his nature fits him. He becomes arrogant and plans to marry his master's daughter. But the party is rescued and with the return to Mayfair he returns to his menial rank. The sound social criticism in all this came appropriately from a countryman of Burns, but it is kept implicit and does not clash with the comedy of the situation. *Peter Pan* (1904) developed from the somewhat shadowy elfin-child in the volume of fantasies called *The Little White Bird* (1902). The boy who, dwelling in the "Never-Never Land," refused to grow up and carried Wendy and his companions to the fairy world, to the pirate ship, and to his home in the tree tops, has assumed the proportions of a myth in the imagination of modern England. Certainly the merging of reality and dream is accomplished with most delicate art; but, whatever may be the case with juvenile readers and spectators, to most adult minds there is something a little distasteful in the combination of humor and adventure with sentimentality. Passing over a number of not very substantial pieces, we come to Barrie's masterpiece, *Dear Brutus* (1917). Here once more, Dear reality fades into dream and dream into reality. In the magic wood just Brutus outside old Lob's house each character in a mixed company of guests has his or her "second chance" at life. The awakening in the third act, which in other hands might have been grim or tragic, is kept perfectly within the region of comedy, and the moral—that "the fault, dear Brutus, is not in our stars, but in ourselves"—is as clear as it is unobtrusive. Barrie's short war-plays are of no lasting interest. In *Mary Rose* (1920) a dramatized ghost-story is touched with symbolism. *Shall We Join the Ladies?* (1921) is a murder play beginning with a startling interest that is scarcely sustained. *The Boy David* (1936) depended upon Barrie's renown for such success as it achieved.

There is altogether too much *larmoyante* sensibility and pathos in Barrie's writings, especially when he expends his sympathy upon women and children, but there is also mockery, slyness, and, for all his apparent want of robustness, a disillusioned, quietly ironical view of life, not without hints of cruelty. He skirts round tragedy only by constantly availing himself of the by-path of fantasy. His plays are consequently nearer to the poetic drama than to the drama of social reform.

That poetic tragedy might be reinstated in the theatre was the promise *Phillips* held out by the brief, brilliant success of Stephen Phillips (1868-1915) during the first years of this century.[24] But this flash in the pan was quickly extinguished. *Paolo and Francesca* (1899; acted 1902), his first and best play, has an operatic kind of theatricality which imposed itself upon audiences for a while. Thereafter there was a decline through the lyricism of *Herod*

[24] Phillips first attracted attention with his nondramatic poem *Christ in Hades* (1896). The contemporary evaluation of Phillips is shown by the space allotted to him in F. W. Chandler, *Aspects of Modern Drama* (1914), pp. 382-394.

(1901) and the episodic pageantry of *Ulysses* (1904) to later plays that need not be listed. The large, unsubtle rhetoric of these plays, easily mouthed and easily comprehended, with their dependence upon panoramic spectacle, exotic costumes, and theatrical emotionality, provided the public with refreshment from the staple fare of the problem play.

Bottomley   Gordon Bottomley [25] (1874-1948) applied the large utterance of his nondramatic poetry to his strenuous and closely-knit plays in which there is a brutal force and directness that is not mere theatricality nor pseudo-Jacobean pastiche but springs from something primitive in the poet's own nature. After three one-act pieces he wrote *The Riding to Lithend* (1909), *King Lear's Wife* (1915), and his two finest dramas, *Gruach* and *Britain's Daughter* (both 1921). It remains to be seen whether posterity will make to these strong, sincere, and highly individual creations reparation for the neglect from which they have suffered.

Dunsany   Edward J. M. D. Plunkett, Lord Dunsany [26] (1878-1957) was an Irishman and was briefly associated with the Abbey Theatre; but instead of availing himself of Celtic legends for his stories and plays he invented a mythology of his own. Of the volumes in which Dunsany shaped his fantasies into narrative form the best are *Time and the Gods* (1906), *The Book of Wonder* (1912), *Tales of Wonder* (1916), and the exquisite little masterpiece, *The Charwoman's Shadow* (1926). In other books of more recent date he drew upon his own experiences of war and far travel. In the within narrow limits and not without repetition he achieved effects of sometimes a little suggestive of Blake. A more clearly discernible influence is that of Maeterlinck. The symbolism underlying his stormy gods and helpless mortals is apprehensible, if at all, only with difficulty; yet working within narrow limits and not without repetition he has achieved effects of weird, romantic beauty. *The Gods of the Mountain* (1914) and *A Night at an Inn* (1917) are among his best plays.

Masefield   As poet laureate John Masefield requires consideration in a later chapter.[27] In his first play, *The Tragedy of Nan* (1909), which was produced at Manchester, the influence of Synge is apparent. But a manner natural to the west of Ireland is less appropriate to the west of England. A grim story, culminating in a moment of sheer horror, is played out against the background of the Severn river and its mighty tides. A dignified prose style is employed to better purpose in *The Tragedy of Pompey the Great* (1910). *Good Friday* (1915) pointed forward to *A King's Daughter* (1923) —the story of Jezebel, *The Trial of Jesus* (1925), *The Coming of Christ* (1928), and *Easter* (1928). *Tristan and Isolt* (1927) and *End and Beginning* (1933), on Mary Queen of Scots, are, like the plays on biblical themes, noble if not entirely successful experiments in interweaving verse and prose,

---

[25] Bottomley's first five plays were collected in 1920; the later plays have not yet appeared in a collected edition. For his nondramatic poetry see below, ch. XLI.

[26] *Five Plays* (1914); *Plays of Gods and Men* (1917); *Seven Modern Comedies* (1928); and other dramas. — See E. H. Bierstadt, *Dunsany the Dramatist* (1917).

[27] See ch. XLI, below.

dialogue and choruses. The quest for freedom from modern conventionalities of form and diction led Masefield back to something like the medieval mystery plays.

Experience as an actor and as author of several now forgotten plays was *Drink-* behind John Drinkwater [28] (1882-1937) when *Abraham Lincoln* (1918) *water* made him famous. The great theme of the captain slain at the moment of the safe arrival of the victor ship evoked an immediate response at a time when the forward-looking, with malice towards none and charity to all, were seeking to bind up the wounds of a broken world. The play, though of late unjustly denigrated, is memorable not only for nobility of sentiment and dignity of versification but for the occasional deliberate manipulations of history which raise mere fact to the level of the artistic sense of fact. Later plays, *Mary Stuart* (1921), *Oliver Cromwell* (1921), and *Robert E. Lee* (1923), though equally competent, did not equally engage public attention.

[28] *Collected Plays* (2v, 1925). On Drinkwater's nondramatic poetry see ch. XLI, below. He wrote also critical studies of Morris and Swinburne and biographies of Byron, Charles James Fox, and Pepys.

XXXIX

Other Late-Victorian Poets[1]

I

Patmore

Coventry Patmore[2] (1823-1896) inherited from an eccentric father[3] a marked individuality of temperament, but his strength of purpose was his own. His *Poems* (1844), of which the best reappeared with new pieces in *Tamerton Church Tower* (1853), introduced him to the Pre-Raphaelite circle, and he contributed to *The Germ*. To the Pre-Raphaelites and Browning his wife's beauty was an inspiration, as it was to himself. Wedded love is the theme of *The Angel in the House* (1854) with its sequels, *The Espousals* (1856) and *Faithful Forever* (1860), as it is of *The Victories of Love* (1863).[4] In 1862 Mrs. Patmore died. In 1864 Patmore became a Roman Catholic and married again. The *Odes* (1868) are in a new, elaborate, irregular style which is fully developed in *The Unknown Eros* (1877). In later life there was little poetry, but Patmore wrote a treatise on English metrics, some rather eccentric literary criticism, and several essays in mystical speculation, among them the lost *Sponsa Dei* the manuscript of which he destroyed at the behest of his spiritual advisers.

The Two Styles

Patmore believed that the poet possesses a supersensual knowledge which he imparts by means of symbols and parables drawn from sensible things.[5] This is the unifying principle binding together his earlier and later work. There was no real breach of continuity when, about 1862, his first manner, simple and sentimental to the point of insipidity, modulated into his second style, heightened, ornate, and occasionally sublime. The figure of him drawn

[1] Brief estimates of certain lesser poets of the late nineteenth century have been introduced, as seemed appropriate, in earlier chapters. The rest, now to be passed in review, are so grouped that points of contact of either a common faith or a common skepticism are emphasized. This chapter is limited, with two exceptions, to writers who had obtained recognition or had at any rate done their best work by the beginning of the present century. The exceptions are Hopkins, who was unknown to the general public till long after his death, and Doughty, who though self-dedicated to poetry from his early years, published his first poem of consequence in 1906.

[2] *Poems* (4v, 1879); *Selected Poems*, ed. Derek Patmore (1931). Patmore's prose works include: *Principle in Art* (1889); *Religio Poetae* (1893); *The Rod, the Root, and the Flower* (1895). — Basil Champneys, *Memoirs and Correspondence of Coventry Patmore* (2v, 1900); Edmund Gosse, *Coventry Patmore* (1905); Osbert Burdett, *The Idea of Coventry Patmore* (1921); Frederick Page, *Patmore: A Study in Poetry* (1933). See also G. N. Shuster, *The Catholic Spirit in Modern English Literature* (1922).

[3] Peter George Patmore, a friend of Hazlitt and author of *My Friends and Acquaintances* (1854), the indiscretions in which occasioned much scandal.

[4] In the final version of *The Angel in the House* the three installments were amalgamated into two books. *The Victories of Love*, though a sequel, is an independent poem, telling with more "plot" the story of another wedded pair.

[5] *Religio Poetae* (ed. 1898), p. 3.

by Francis Thompson is of one who held in one hand "a cup of milk and honey" and in the other "a lightning-bolt." [6] In *The Angel in the House* the husband tells of the courtship and marital happiness over which the Angel (spiritual love) keeps watch and ward. The art of sinking in poetry has seldom been exemplified more candidly than in the smooth-flowing quatrains of these "idyls of the dining-room and the deanery." [7] But if the poem sinks it can also rise, as it does in the "preludes" and other passages *The* Odes of symbolic interpretation. Needing a grander style for his symbolism, Patmore resorted to the irregular ode, made up of longer and shorter lines with rimes falling capriciously, which had its precursors in Cowley and Crashaw and in the *Canzoniere* of Petrarch. Verbal and metrical splendor support themes so simple as to seem inappropriate to the style; yet in this very contrast are found Patmore's finest effects, for from the lowliest experiences of domestic life (as in *The Toys*) he drew analogies of eternal significance. The prevailing symbols are parental and marital love. For the analogy of the sexual relationship to the relationship of God and the soul Patmore had the sanction of traditional interpretations of The Song of Songs and the ecstasies of the love-mystics. This symbolism was developed in *The Unknown Eros* and was, it seems, carried from resemblance to identification in the destroyed *Sponsa Dei*. In the nature of married love Patmore found a clue to the problems of life. Man, the rational soul, is wedded to woman, the sensitive soul. Only in marriage can humanity's natural goodness and nobility find their scope. Thus an ideal—both a philosophy and a creed—is founded upon commonplace experience. With this love, death is associated in Petrarchan or Pre-Raphaelite fashion, as in the memorials to his wife (*The Azalea, Departure,* and *A Farewell*) which are among Patmore's finest odes.

Francis Thompson [8] (1859-1907), weak in will but strong in faith, pre- *Thompson* served his spiritual integrity in circumstances of poverty and degradation. The Roman Catholic college into which he was put could do little for the slovenly and shiftless boy. Drifting to London (1885), he plumbed the depths, selling matches on the street. Forlorn and faint, he outwatched the inquisitive stars, and in the extremity of illness was given shelter by a girl of the streets who shared with him her "scant pittance," asked no reward, and was afterwards sought for in vain. [9] The resemblance of this episode to the story of Ann in De Quincey's *Confessions* is no reason for questioning

[6] Francis Thompson, *Ode for the Diamond Jubilee*; *Works*, II. 139.
[7] Swinburne, *Notes on Poems and Reviews* (1866), p. 22. Swinburne's cruel but amusing parody, *The Person of the House*, written in 1859, was published in *The Heptalogia* (1880).
[8] *Works* (3v, 1913); *Poems*, ed. T. L. Connolly (1941); *Selected Poems*, ed. Wilfrid Meynell (1912). — Everard Meynell, *The Life of Francis Thompson* (1913); R. L. Mégroz, *Francis Thompson: The Poet of Earth in Heaven* (1927); T. H. Wright, *Francis Thompson and His Poetry* (1927); Agnès de la Gorce, *Francis Thompson et les poètes catholiques d'Angleterre* (Paris, 1932); Federico Olivero, *Francis Thompson* (Turin, 1938); Katherine Tynan, "Francis Thompson," *Fortnightly Rev.*, n.s. LXXXVII (1910). 349-360; Cornelius Weygandt, *Tuesdays at Ten* (Philadelphia, 1928). ch. XI; F. B. Tolles, "The Praetorian Cohorts: a Study of the Language of Francis Thompson's Poetry," *English Studies* (Amsterdam), XXII (1940). 49-64.
[9] *A Child's Kiss*, from *Sister Songs*.

its authenticity. Poems submitted to *Merry England,* a magazine edited by Wilfrid Meynell, were accepted, and in its pages appeared *The Hound of Heaven* in 1891 and other pieces earlier or later. Thompson's worst days were now over. He was taken up by the genial circle of the Meynells, and in 1893 a volume of *Poems* appeared. That here was a new poet of power and promise was evident, though conservative critics could not comprehend this new idiom with its elaborate rhythms, exotic vocabulary, and startling and strained imagery. *Sister Songs* (1895) and *New Poems* (1897) followed; but in his last years Thompson declined into journalism, producing little that was not ephemeral save the rhapsodic essay on Shelley. Consumption and laudanum hastened his end. Among poems published posthumously the greatest is *The Kingdom of God.*

· For all its individuality the poetry of Thompson is steeped in tradition. His immediate master was Patmore—the later Patmore of the *Odes.* The use of archaic and exotic words is reminiscent of Rossetti and the rhapsodic passages sometimes echo Shelley. But the searcher after influences must look further back, for Thompson was one of the first to reintroduce a strain of "metaphysical" conceit into English poetry. That he had pondered upon Donne is evident, but Crashaw's amorous mysticism had a more profound effect upon him. Dantesque elements are also present, and the sonorous Latinisms are often drawn from the liturgy. Hypersensitive, withdrawn, a recluse by temperament and (in later years) by addiction to opium, Thompson is one of the most introspective of poets. He fashioned his poetry from his memories, weaknesses, gratitudes, spiritual fears, even from his art itself. The "objective" poems have often a false and heavy pomp, but only let him write of himself and there is nothing of the meretricious in his splendor. When commissioned to write an elegy on Cardinal Manning he does not "perturbate the paradisal state" of the dead by needless praise but takes the "holy soul" apart "to press a private business"—has the poet's devotion to his art been to the detriment of his immortal soul? This catechizing of a released spirit might, had it been managed less subtly, have been absurd; in Thompson's hands it is profoundly moving. So with *The Hound of Heaven.* The conception of Christ, the Lover, pursuing the Soul, the Beloved, was one to appeal to a baroque Spanish mystic; but there were modern Englishmen who, forgetting the ancient symbols of Lamb and Fish and Pelican and Phoenix, were shocked by the symbol of the Hound. The poem is charged with extravagant imagery. The Soul flees down the labyrinthine ways of the mind. The casements of the heart are blown to with the gust of the divine approach. God chars the wood before he can limn with it. Other poems contain metaphors of like bold magnificence: Time "shoots his barbed minutes"; Death flushes "the cumbered gutters of humanity." The Body is a house at whose "clay-shuttered doors" the pinions of the angels beat. Thompson's imagery is often merely thick and clotted. His vocabulary of almost unequaled gorgeousness is often turgid. He falls into far-fetched

The
Hound
of
Heaven

conceit when inspiration fails. But he rises to majestic heights when impassioned fervor fuses thought and style.

The poetry of Alice Meynell [10] (1847-1922), though spread through nine volumes from *Preludes* (1875) to *Last Poems* (1923), is small in quantity. Her spiritual reticence, her inhibitions, and her exacting standards of craftsmanship limited her output; nor did she have a great deal to say. Her faculty, when she looked out upon the world, was for the exquisite rendering of little things, and when she looked inward, for the analysis of her own religious and emotional experiences. Whether this still, small voice will continue to be heard is doubtful, but her two best-known poems, the *Letter from a Girl to Her Own Old Age* and the sonnet *Renouncement*, should remain in the anthologies.[11] *Alice Meynell*

Lionel Pigot Johnson [12] (1867-1902), who became a Roman Catholic by conversion in early life, was a contributor to the *Book of the Rhymers' Club* and in touch with the Irish Literary Renaissance. Apart from his fine study, *The Art of Thomas Hardy* (1894), and the literary essays collected posthumously in *Post Liminium* (1911), his writings are found in *Poems* (1895) and *Ireland and Other Poems* (1897). He shared with Thompson a cloistered medievalism of outlook, but there is nothing of Thompson's grandiloquence in his spare and chiseled verse. He derived inspiration from his classical scholarship, and, as became a son of Oxford, he attached himself to "lost causes and impossible loyalties," as in his finest poem, *By the Statue of King Charles at Charing Cross*. Drink undermined his delicate health; but the motive of contrition which in some writers seems a "decadent" pose was in his case indubitably sincere. The faith that gave him assurance despite the bleak tragedy of his life is expressed with stern grandeur in *The Dark Angel*. *Lionel Johnson*

With all the foregoing may be associated two men of the older generation who were not Roman Catholics but in whose verse the religious element predominates. Roden B. W. Noel [13] (1834-1894) expresses the reaction from pessimistic realism to religious faith. *A Little Child's Monument* (1881) is a series of elegies illuminated with Christian hope. From experiences of oriental travel he derived the subjects of various poems. Others show his sympathy with the workers for social betterment, and yet others his prescience of the disaster towards which militarism was driving the world. Frederick W. H. Myers [14] (1843-1901) is best remembered for his long dra- *Roden Noel* *Myers*

[10] *Poems*, Complete Edition (1940); *Selected Poems* (1930); *Selected Essays* (1926). — Viola Meynell, *Alice Meynell* (1929); A. K. Tuell, *Mrs. Meynell and her Literary Generation* (1925).

[11] Mrs. Meynell wrote a good deal of literary criticism, distinguished for its subtlety and note of calm authority, but not without its limitations (seen, for example, in her attack on Gibbon).

[12] *Poetical Works*, introduction by Ezra Pound (1915); *Selections* (1908); *A New Selection*, ed. H. V. Marrot (1927); *Reviews and Critical Papers* (1921). — Cornelius Weygandt, *Tuesdays at Ten* (Philadelphia, 1928), ch. III.

[13] *Behind the Veil* (1863); *Songs of the Heights and Deeps* (1885); and many other volumes of verse; *Poems*, introduction by Robert Buchanan (1890); *Collected Poems* (1902).

[14] *Collected Poems*, ed. E. Myers (1921); *Saint Paul*, ed. E. J. Watson (1916); *Wordsworth* (EML Series, 1880); *Science and a Future Life* (1893); and other books.

matic monologue *Saint Paul* (1867), fervent in feeling for the character of the militant apostle and composed in a clarion-like metre which Swinburne borrowed for *Mater Triumphalis*. Myers' literary criticism is Arnoldian in substance and in manner too close an imitation of Pater.

II

Dixon

The oldest member of the group of which Robert Bridges was the center was Richard Watson Dixon [15] (1833-1900). He was a friend of William Morris, and in *The Wizard's Funeral* and other early poems are a sense of "wonder" and love of the supernatural characteristic of the circle he frequented. His first volume, *Christ's Company* (1861), carries to excess the Pre-Raphaelite quaintness and search for curious words and rimes. The poems on Wellington and Marlborough which gave the title to *Historical Odes and Other Poems* (1864) reflect Dixon's scholarly interests. *Mano* (1883) is a long poem in harsh *terza rima* on an obscure tenth-century theme. In later years he accomplished some of his best work, dealing often with the thoughts and moods provoked by consciousness of advancing age. His range is narrow and his monotonous somberness, though not without moments of real greatness, expresses a religious faith without religious joy. In practically all his work there is a technical roughness and uncouthness, especially in the matter of faulty rimes. His friendship with Father Hopkins resulted in a noteworthy correspondence and the friendship with Bridges bore fruit in the volume of selections from his poems by which Bridges made him better known. Another poet who owed such reputation as he won to

Dolben

Bridges' influence is Digby Mackworth Dolben [16] (1848-1867) in whom a religious ardor which, had he lived, might have carried him, like Hopkins, to Rome, is blended with a love of pagan beauty. Dolben is best when he is

Mary Coleridge

simplest, as in the tender little poem *Homo Factus Est*. Mary Elizabeth Coleridge [17] (1861-1907), the friend of Dixon and Bridges, occasionally suggests Christina Rossetti, but there are also signs in her work of the influence of Blake and the "metaphysical" poets, and there are reminiscences of a greater Coleridge in the fantasy of such pieces as *The Witch* and *Wilderspin*. In general her poems record the varying moods of a steadfast religious experience.

Hopkins

Unknown to the public but in close touch with Patmore, Dixon, and Bridges, Gerard Manley Hopkins [18] (1844-1889) wrote the poems which

[15] *Poems, a Selection,* with memoir by Robert Bridges (1909). Dixon was a Canon of Carlisle Cathedral and author of a voluminous *History of the Church of England* (1870-1902).
[16] *Poems,* ed. Robert Bridges (1911).
[17] *Poems,* ed. Sir Henry Newbolt (1908); *Gathered Leaves,* with a memoir by Edith Sichel (1910).
[18] *Poems,* ed. Robert Bridges (1918); revised and enlarged with introduction by Charles Williams (1931); *Correspondence with Richard Watson Dixon* (1935); *Letters to Robert Bridges* (1935); *Further Letters* (1938), all ed. C. C. Abbott; *Note-Books and Papers,* ed. Humphry House (1937).—G. F. Lahey, *Gerard Manley Hopkins* (1930); E. E. Phare, *The Poetry of Gerard Manley Hopkins: A Survey and a Commentary* (1933); John Pick, *Gerard Manley Hopkins: Priest and Poet* (1942); W. H. Gardner, *Gerard Manley Hopkins* (1944);

were published posthumously in 1918. As a student at Oxford he was interested in stylistic and prosodic theory, though what little survives of his early verse shows no radical departure from tradition. He destroyed nearly all his manuscripts when, in 1868, he became a Jesuit. His career as teacher and preacher does not concern us. Hopkins' superiors in the Society encouraged him to resume the writing of poetry, and when he did so (1875) it was with a change of manner for which his speculations had prepared him but for which little in the previous course of English poetry prepares the reader who comes for the first time upon *The Wreck of the Deutschland*. The drowning of some nuns in a disaster at sea moved the devout priest to this passionate, ejaculatory mingling of prayer and amazement. Bridges likened the poem to a great dragon coiled at the entrance to the cavern which is Hopkins' poetry. To this day, despite the panegyrics and the interpretations, the dragon remains frightening to many would-be explorers of the cave.[19] Hopkins' letters, note-books, and other papers contain unorganized critical and theoretical discussion and *dicta* which illuminate his practice and aims. Yet obscurities remain, partly because he trusted to the insecure analogies of musical terminology, partly because he used technical terms of his own devising to describe metrical and stylistic phenomena which were innovations only in the extremes to which he carried them, thus persuading himself (and many of his admirers) that he had invented something when he was really calling an old thing by a new name. His "sprung rhythm" is a principle which poets have had ready at hand since Anglo-Saxon times—the employment of a fixed number of stressed syllables and a varying number of unstressed in each line. What he called "counterpoint" is much the same as resolved stress or what Saintsbury called "equivalence"—the occasional substitution of a different foot for the foot that is the norm of the metrical pattern. The stylistic quality which he tried to secure in his own poetry he called "inscape." This term has provoked much discussion of pattern, texture, and what not, but essentially a poem possesses "inscape" when the design is perfectly adapted to the theme; it is "the suiting of the unique experience to a unique form." Hopkins outran Browning in his search of far-fetched rimes (for example, "boon he on"—"Communion"); but whereas Browning aimed generally at the grotesque, Hopkins, even in his worst offences, was intensely serious. Moreover, he revived from the seventeenth century the ugly device of the "run-over" rime.[20] For the use of alliteration he had vener-

---

Eleanor Ruggles, *Gerard Manley Hopkins* (1944); B. I. Evans, *English Poetry in the Late Nineteenth Century* (1933), pp. 210-218; F. R. Leavis, *New Bearings in English Poetry* (1938), pp. 159-193; David Daiches, *Poetry and the Modern World* (1940), pp. 24-34; J. G. Southworth, *Sowing the Spring: Studies in British Poets from Hopkins to MacNeice* (1940), pp. 15-32; Herbert Read, *In Defence of Shelley and other Essays* (1936), pp. 111-144; four articles in the *Kenyon Rev.* (Summer, 1944), occasioned by the Hopkins centenary.

[19] See W. H. Gardner, "The Wreck of the Deutschland," *E&S*, xxi (1936). 124-152, an elaborate study illustrating the lengths to which Hopkins' devotees have gone; useful also, perhaps, as a counterbalance to the present writer's distaste for Hopkins.

[20] Thus in *The Windhover*, one of the poems most extravagantly admired, Hopkins uses a "run-over" rime at the end of the first line, so that the first syllable of "kingdom" rimes with "wing" in line four.

able precedent and many of his best effects of detonating impetuousness are gained by this device. He tried to eliminate every colorless, passive, merely connective word (especially the relative pronouns) so that only the poetic vocables should remain—every substantive a picture, every verb a deed. This "passionate condensation" is, at best, a sort of poetical shorthand, at worst, an intolerably licentious violation of every law of syntax. That his ardor, which instead of finding an outlet in luxuriant verbosity sought an extreme condensation, could impart new life and color to over-worn words is not to be denied; but generally condensation was purchased at too high a cost. The stylistic rebelliousness may have come from his isolation as a Jesuit, and the delight in oddness and incoherence may have been a reaction from ascetic discipline and an ordered philosophy. The sympathetic student recognizes that Hopkins' "altogether unusual problem of personal adjustment sought expression in an altogether unusual style." That he wrestled in spiritual anguish the moving sonnets, *No worse, there is none* and *Thou art indeed just, Lord,* make manifest. His eager apprehension of natural loveliness, as in *Inversnaid* and *The Starlight Night* and *The Windhover,* is one expression of his worship. Probing, as in *The Loss of the Eurydice,* into the mystery of God's ways, he possessed "a passionate sense of the terror of the nearness of God." Spiritual grief, not spiritual joy, is his theme. But even when the mystery was darkest he rejected the "carrion comfort," despair. Not Hopkins' religion, however, but his poetic style attracted the admiration of the post-war generation. This poetry, completely independent of the Victorian tradition, has appealed to those who fail to recognize that imagery is a good servant but a bad master; who are in quest of "something craggy to break the mind upon"; and who do not distinguish between the thought that is obscure because it is difficult and the thought that is difficult because it is obscurely expressed. Interesting experiment has been mistaken for accomplishment.

Robert
Bridges

Robert Bridges [21] (1844-1930) emerged slowly into prominence. While a practising physician he wrote verse, and in 1882 he abandoned medicine to dedicate himself wholly to his art. Between 1873 and 1896 came eight little pamphlets of verse, afterwards brought together in the *Shorter Poems. The Growth of Love* (1876), a sonnet-sequence later much expanded, expresses the resolve to remain faithful to the poet's calling even though it goes against the scientific tendencies of the age. Love gives new values to life and new spurs to the searcher after beauty. *Prometheus the Firegiver* (1883) is composed in austere blank verse with choric interludes. Bridges called it "a Mask in the Greek Manner." He seems to have hesitated between a mere

[21] *Poetical Works* (6v, 1898-1905); *Poetical Works* (1912), excluding the eight dramas; *Collected Essays, Papers, etc.* (10v, 1927-1936). — There is as yet no full biography. G. L. McKay, *Bibliography* (1933); Sir T. Herbert Warren, *Robert Bridges, Poet Laureate* (1913); L. P. Smith, *Robert Bridges,* S. P. E. Tract, xxxv (1931); F. E. Brett Young, *Robert Bridges: A Critical Study* (1914); G. S. Gordon, *Robert Bridges* (1932); Albert Guérard, Jr., *Robert Bridges: A Study of Traditionalism* (1941); Edward Thompson, *Robert Bridges* (1944); B. I. Evans, *English Poetry in the Late Nineteenth Century* (1933), pp. 219-243; Ernest de Selincourt, "Robert Bridges," *Oxford Lectures on Poetry* (1934), pp. 233-256.

"reconstruction" of the lost first part of the Aeschylean trilogy and a fresh, individual interpretation of the myth, and as a consequence the piece is neither the one nor the other; nor is it a true masque. *Eros and Psyche* (1885), which appeared in the same year with Pater's *Marius* with its beautiful prose version of Apuleius' tale, implicitly challenged comparison with the version in *The Earthly Paradise*, for Bridges was antagonistic to Morris's loose and facile manner of story-telling. It was perhaps to suggest this challenge that Bridges divided his poem into the twelve months of the year (as *The Earthly Paradise* is planned), going Morris one better by assigning to each month as many stanzas as it contains days. Beneath these surface artifices Bridges' interpretation of the myth (so far as he suggests any) connects it with Keats's ode *To Psyche*. Beauty allied to love permits man to "gather an enchantment" from life which would otherwise pass unregarded. While these longer poems were being written, Bridges' lyrical, meditative, and elegiac faculty was developing from the first blossoms to the fairest fruit. How soon he attained the simplicity that is the very refinement of art is shown by *Long are the Hours the Sun is above,* a perfect poem and of *The* very early date. The delicate cadences of the lyrics sometimes echo the *Shorter* Elizabethan song-writers, and those of richer texture Edmund Spenser; but *Poems* though traditional they are not merely imitative. The more elaborate nature-pieces, such as *London Snow,* come later, as do the grander harmonies of *Whither, O Splendid Ship,* the elegy *On a Dead Child,* and the great *Elegy on a Lady.* These and countless other "shorter poems" convey that sense of the wide variety of experiences and intellectual interests to be found in the world which at the end of Bridges' life was to make *The Testament of Beauty* so rich a store of wisdom and erudition. But Bridges was no mere "intellectual.'" He knows that beauty fades and he is capable on rare occasions of a poignant expression of grief, but "the best of his art is gay" and he is the votary of that beauty which liberates the human spirit from the tyranny of circumstance and of that deep but untumultuous love which the gods approve.

Between 1885 and 1905 Bridges wasted much labor upon poetic dramas. *The* The uncongenial subject of *Nero* (two parts, 1885 and 1894) did not permit *Dramas* him to grasp firmly his own purpose. *The Return of Ulysses* (1890) might have been handled acceptably in episodic narrative but it proved recalcitrant to the dramatic form. To imitate Terence displayed Bridges' scholarship but not any gift for comedy. The adaptations from Calderon took him into a world of "cloak-and-sword" intrigue where he was not at home. *Demeter* (1905) is a lovely but slight thing.

Close study of the principles of English metrics led to the treatise on *Milton's Prosody* (1893; final revision, 1921) and later to the unattractive experiments in quantitative metres. Gradually Bridges worked out the form which in *New Verses* (1921) he called "Neo-Miltonic syllabics" and in *The Testament of Beauty* "loose alexandrines" based on "the secure bedrock of Milton's prosody." In the explorations of metrical law and the experiments in new rhythms Bridges followed the lead of Father Hopkins but with less waywardness and a more disciplined taste. Hopkins' example is behind his use of "counterpoint" and internal rime. The final manner is fully displayed in *The Testament of Beauty* (1929). Bridges had made no effort to secure a large audience. Forty years earlier he had had the recognition of such authoritative critics as Dowden and Lang, but his emergence had proceeded so slowly that when, in 1913, he had been appointed poet laureate he was still generally unknown. The subsequent absorption in prosodic experimentation did not broaden his reputation. Consequently he was as much surprised as gratified when *The Testament of Beauty*,[22] appearing on his eighty-fifth birthday, became a popular success. Circumstances extraneous to the poem's intrinsic merit account for this—the great age of the poet and his dignity, and the phenomenon, not to have been expected in the cynical nineteen-twenties, of a poem exalted in theme, of ample scope, containing the wisdom and learning of a long life, and representative of the great tradition of English poetry. The genitive case of the title is both objective and subjective. This is the poet's testament concerning Beauty but it is also Beauty's testimony, her "witness." The theme is that which runs through all Bridges' poetry, that in the life of man

The Testament of Beauty

> Beauty is the prime motiv of all his excellence,
> his aim and peaceful purpose.

"Self" and "Breed" (by which Bridges intends the instinct of propagation which by slow degrees rises into the most exalted love) draw man up the "ladder of joy" to his "peace with God." There is an elaborate attempt to fuse this Platonic concept with modern evolutionary thought. The poem is, indeed, overburdened with scientific theory. In speculations upon the future course of society Bridges opposes Socialism and champions "individual worth." He put into his *Testament* anything and everything that came within his wide intellectual horizon, from the dawn of the inventive faculty to the airplane and the radio, from the excavations at Ur and Kish to "far Pasadena's roseland." At first the poem was rated too highly and there has since been time for second thoughts. Difficulties of phrase, idiom, and allusion which immediately inspired commentaries are not to be held against it; and objections to the superficial eccentricities of "reformed" spelling and elocutionary punctuation may be set aside. Of the nobility of certain parts (especially the opening and the close) there can be no question. Yet doubts remain. Obviously here was the material out of which a great poem might have been molded, but to many critics it is equally obvious that a truly great poem has not been molded out of this material. Bridges' fame rests more securely upon his lyrical poetry.

[22] N. C. Smith, *Notes on The Testament of Beauty* (1931); H. W. Garrod, "The Testament of Beauty," *Poetry and the Criticism of Life* (1931), pp. 129-147; Ernest de Selincourt, "The Testament of Beauty," *Oxford Lectures on Poetry* (1934), pp. 233-256.

III

By a hard irony the fame of Charles Montagu Doughty [23] (1843-1926) *Doughty*
rests upon "the secure bedrock" of the *Travels in Arabia Deserta* while his
poetry remains almost unknown. Yet the Arabian adventure (1876-1878)
and the following decade employed in writing the narrative of it were but
interludes in a life dedicated to the cultivation of "the Muse of Britain."
There was a massive, primitive simplicity about Doughty's character which
perhaps explains the early choice of geological and philological studies; and
these studies in turn help to explain the qualities of his poetry. The heavy
beat of the accents, the abundant alliteration, the clashing epithets, and the
harsh yet majestic march of the rhythm have their far-descended historical
justification. Self-taught and self-secure, he was the disciple of Chaucer,
Langland, and Spenser; and passionately patriotic, he would redeem his
native tongue from modern feebleness and vulgarity. Having completed his
prose masterpiece in 1888, he spent a decade and a half in writing *The
Dawn in Britain* (1906), an epic in six volumes.[24] Space is lacking here to
discuss the word-lore that filled, and the verbal experimentation that issued
from, his vigorous but undisciplined mind. The epic [25] moves ponderously
through the vast period of British history from the taking of Rome by
Brennus to the revolt of Bonduca. There is a vague underlying allegorical
intent suggesting the conflict between the forces of darkness and light in
the contrast between the woad-stained pagans and the meek Christian
missionaries who come to Britain. Defective in the large matters of composition and exasperatingly humorless, the poem contains passages of stately
narrative, gentle pastoral episodes, and an abounding spiritual joy. But
there are few readers to be found willing to overcome the difficulties of the
way for the sake of the occasional rewards. *Adam Cast Forth* (1908) is as
rugged as the stony desert through which our First Parents wandered, but
it is shorter and simpler than the epic and not without a grave gentleness.
It is the best introduction to Doughty's poetry; few readers will go further.
The Cliffs (1909) and *The Clouds* (1912) were intended to arouse England
to an awareness of the imminent peril of war with Germany. In them
Doughty's wisdom attained to "something like prophetic strain," for there
are few stranger episodes in literary history than the fulfillment of his vision,
not merely of the actualities of submarine and aerial warfare but in his
clairvoyant sense of the spirit of a people threatened with the horrors of
invasion. Both poems contain interludes, not very well integrated with the

[23] D. G. Hogarth, *The Life of Charles M. Doughty* (1928); Barker Fairley, *Charles M. Doughty: A Critical Study* (1927); Anne Treneer, *Charles M. Doughty: A Study of his Prose and Verse* (1935), with bibliography; Walt Taylor, *Doughty's English,* S. P. E. Tract, LI (1939); Barker Fairley, "The Modern Consciousness in English Literature," *E&S,* IX (1923). 127-144. Some sentences in the present discussion are taken from S. C. Chew, "The Poetry of Charles Montagu Doughty," *No. Amer. Rev.,* CCII (1925-1926). 287-298. — On the *Arabia Deserta* see ch. XLII, below.
[24] Centenary Edition in one volume (1943), with introduction by Ruth C. Robbins.
[25] See Friedrich Brie, "Charles Doughty und sein Epos *The Dawn in Britain,*" *Anglia,* LXIV (1940). 256-295.

context, in which, by night while the human actors sleep, gnomes and dapper elves disport themselves and play their part in the protection of Britain. *The Titans* (1916) is an obscure allegory of man's gradual conquest of the forces of nature. In Arabia, when the Bedouin inquired of him "Who art thou?" Doughty's answer had been: "God's wanderer, who, not looking back to his worldly interest, betakes himself to the contemplative life's pilgrimage." *Mansoul, or the Riddle of the World* (1920) is the record, under the medieval convention of the poet's dream, of the life-long effort to discover

> What were indeed right paths of a man's feet,
> That lacking light wont stumble in World's murk?

The poet (who is not clearly differentiated from his companion Minimus) is guided by Mansoul into the world of the dead where he confronts the prophets and sages with this persistent question. At the close the words "that abide, a perfume in our hearts" are those of Jesus: "Fear ye not, little flock; God is Love." Doughty's poetry has its advocates, few but ardent; but it must be said that had he deliberately set out to do so, he could not have erected between himself and all but the most intrepid reader more effective barriers than those of his archaistic vocabulary, dialect words, eccentricities of syntax and style, harsh and monotonous prosody, and massive and uncouth mythology. Those who force their way into his fastness will discover flowers of poetry growing amid the rocks.

IV

The poets now to be considered all express the pessimism and skepticism of the period, though the expression ranges from a serene "paganism" to an iron-shod despair.

John B. Leicester Warren, Lord de Tabley [26] (1835-1895) obtained belated recognition when at the end of his life he gathered the best work of many volumes into *Poems Dramatic and Lyrical* (1893 and 1895). In the sad dignity of his bearing he typifies a late Victorianism untouched by the "Decadence." Of all the lesser poets of the period he missed greatness by the narrowest margin. Those who would know him at his lofty best must read his *Napoleon the Great* and the three odes: *To Astarte, To Aphrodite,* and *Sire of the Rising Day.*

For Wilfrid Scawen Blunt [27] (1840-1922) poetry was a by-product of a life of travel and political agitation. Of the poems written for purposes of propaganda we need notice only *Satan Absolved* (1899), a *Faust*-like "Mystery" satirizing imperialistic expansion and the current cant of "the White Man's

[26] *Collected Poems* (1903); *Select Poems*, ed. John Drinkwater (1924). — Robert Bridges, "Lord de Tabley's Poems," *Collected Essays, Papers, etc.*, VII (1931).

[27] *Poetical Works* (2v, 1914); *Poems*, ed. Floyd Dell (1923). The six volumes of Blunt's memoirs or "Secret History" deal with public affairs in England, Ireland, Egypt, and India, together with much matter of social and literary interest. They are a mine of not absolutely trustworthy material on the period. — Edith Finch, *Wilfrid Scawen Blunt* (1938); Sister Mary Joan Reinehr, *The Writings of W. S. Blunt* (Milwaukee, 1940).

*ord de
*abley

3lunt

Burden." But Blunt is remembered as a "love poet." Sincerity of passion and self-revelation is the characteristic of *The Love-Sonnets of Proteus*[28] (1881). "Sad child of doubt and passionate desires," he describes himself. The happy moments of triumphant love are set against a background of dark fatalism, and the course of passion is traced to satiety and estrangement. There are resemblances to Meredith's *Modern Love,* but the moods are more fluctuating and the art is less well sustained. The sonnet's laws are infringed by irregular rime-schemes and by the extension of members of the sequence, when the thought refuses to be compressed, to eighteen or twenty lines. *Proteus* is less memorable as a whole than for such splendid individual sonnets as *Lost Opportunity* and *Sibylline Books.* A second sequence, *Esther* (1882), is a narrative of the fascination exerted upon a young man by a beautiful woman, older and more experienced than he.

Eugene Lee-Hamilton[29] (1845-1907) has been undeservedly neglected. His first noteworthy volume is *Imaginary Sonnets* (1891), each a tiny dramatic monologue on themes from the German and Italian Renaissance. His fragile art attained maturity in *Sonnets of the Wingless Hours* (1894), written during years of illness. In some of these a puckish fancy plays, but others are macabre and most are burdened with the pessimism of the epoch. The beautiful sonnet-sequence *Mimma Bella* (1909), in memory of his little daughter, expresses "the burden of the mystery" with a despair that is restrained by perfect artistry.

Lee-Hamilton

The poetry of Sir William Watson[30] (1858-1935) is often dismissed as "derivative," but it is at any rate in a great tradition going back through Arnold to Wordsworth and Landor. In it there is a revulsion from Swinburne's flamboyance to austerity. In *Wordsworth's Grave* (1890), in *Lachrymae Musarum,* an elegy on Tennyson (1892), and in poems on Burns, Shelley, and Arnold, Watson used verse for laudatory estimates of fellow poets. Notable is his mastery of *rime couée* (the "Burns stanza") in *A Child's Hair* and elsewhere. There is sometimes passion held in severe control (as in *The Glimpse* and *Lux Perdita*); but generally, as he asserts in his *Apologia,* his art is dedicated to other emotions than that of love. The splendid, fervent *Ode in May* is on the highest level of his achievement. In *The Hope of the World* and *The Dream of Man* the agnosticism and the evolutionary meliorism show the influence of Herbert Spencer. Watson's courageous opposition to the Boer War placed him beside Blunt and against Kipling and Henley.[31] He could command the trenchant phrase, but this faculty easily degenerates into rhetoric. The poetic gift, though genuine, was soon exhausted and the long remainder of his life was pathetically ineffectual.

Watson

[28] Expanded from *Songs and Sonnets by Proteus* (1875) with the omission of the songs, and further expanded after 1881.
[29] There is no collected edition or biography. See the brief biographical preface by his widow in *Mimma Bella* (1909).
[30] *Poems,* with an introduction by J. A. Spender (2v, 1904); *Poems: 1878-1935* (1936). No biography has yet appeared.
[31] *For England: Poems written during Estrangement* (1903).

Henley   William Ernest Henley [32] (1849-1903) wrote verse in various modes and moods. His best-known poem exhibits him as braggartly superior to the blows of fortune; but to keep in mind that he was a cripple is to forgive— perhaps to admire—this posturing. In the poems on his own illness entitled *In Hospital* he experimented in unrimed, irregularly cadenced forms and in harshly realistic subject-matter; and in *London Voluntaries* (1893) he sketched the streets and squares of his city. Henley, who was in close touch with Kipling, sounded the imperialistic note in *England, My England, The Song of the Sword,* and *For England's Sake* (1900). He was skilled in the use of the "old French forms," but employed them for other purposes than Dobson's or Gosse's, often producing new effects by crossing these artifices with intense realism. Like Kipling, he sometimes had recourse to slang and "low" dialect. Rarely, he commanded a more delicate style, as in the elegy on his child and in *Some Twilit Garden Grey with Dew.* With him may

Newbolt   be grouped Sir Henry Newbolt [33] (1862-1937) to whom came temporary fame when he expressed the inarticulate feelings of a people deeply moved by the approach of the Boer War. The titles of his two principal volumes of verse—*Admirals All* (1897) and *The Island Race* (1898)—suggest his dominant themes and his limitations. "The strength and splendor of England's war" is a recurring motive.

Davidson   Imperialism is one note in the poetry of John Davidson [34] (1857-1909) who came to London from a Scotch Calvinistic milieu "where savage faith works woe." In his *Ballad in Blank Verse of the Making of a Poet* he tells how he revolted from this upbringing and adopted a militant atheism. After several false starts the real Davidson began to emerge in *Smith, a Tragic Farce* (1888), with its hints of autobiography, its description of society as "the mud wherein we stand up to the eyes," and its counsel: "Obey your nature, not authority." *Scaramouch in Naxos* (1888) is an extravaganza on the theme of "the gods in exile." *In a Music-Hall* (1891) and *Fleet Street Eclogues* (1893; second series, 1896) turn urban modernity to the uses of poetry somewhat as Henley was doing. Then followed Davidson's best work, in *Ballads and Songs* (1894), *New Ballads* (1897), and *The Last Ballad and Other Poems* (1899). One of the first Englishmen to be influenced by Nietzsche, Davidson gave a new turn to romantic subjects by introducing vigorous modern ideas of self-expression and the fulfillment of desire. Thus, in *A New Ballad of Tannhäuser* the knight is not contrite but exultant when he returns to Venus, and in *The Ballad of a Nun* the Blessed Virgin takes

---

[32] *Poems* (1912); *Works* (7v, 1908; 5v, 1921). — L. C. Cornford, *William Ernest Henley* (1913); Kennedy Williamson, *William Ernest Henley, a Memoir* (1930); J. H. Buckley, *William Ernest Henley* (Princeton, 1945). — On Henley's criticism see ch. XLII, below.

[33] *Collected Poems* (1910). — Newbolt wrote several historical works, popular and patriotic. *Modred* (1895) is a rather conventional Arthurian tragedy.

[34] There is no collected edition or full-length biography. *Selected Poems* (1905). — Davidson wrote novels, including the satiric *Earl Lavender* (1895); essays, notably those in *A Random Itinerary* (1894); and literary criticism. — H. Fineman, *John Davidson: A Study of the Relation of his Ideas to his Poetry* (Philadelphia, 1916); Gertrud von Petzold, *John Davidson und sein geistiges Werden unter dem Einfluss Nietzsches* (Leipzig, 1928); B. I. Evans, *English Poetry in the Later Nineteenth Century* (1933), ch. XIII.

the place of Sister Beatrice in the convent because she sympathizes with her desire to escape and experience life to the full.[35] There is a like exaltation of egoism in the tremendously forceful *Ballad of Hell*. But this note, over-driven, modulated into morbidly subjective poems, fiercely indignant against the hardships of life, in which Davidson wrote of his own disappointments and distresses. In some poems he fused the current imperialism with the philosophic concept of the superman. When he turned again to the dramatic form the most notable results were *Self's the Man* (1901) and the unfinished trilogy *God and Mammon* (1907-1908). Lack of wide recognition and con-stant poverty preyed upon him; the morbidity and bitter satire of his later work gradually approached the borders of the psychopathic; and there were hints of contemplated suicide. A confused and violent "Satanic" philosophy sought to identify the Self with the God which is Energy. This is the theme dominating the series of strange, ill-organized, repellent *Testa-ments: Of a Vivisector* (1901), *Of a Man Forbid* (1901), *Of an Empire-Builder* (1902), *Of a Prime Minister* (1904), and *Of John Davidson* (1908). In these there are passages of power and passion, such as the vision of hell in *The Empire-Builder*; but as a whole they are unrewarding. There is much that is crude and something that is vulgar in Davidson's verse, but in the best work of his middle years, there are also energy and vitality, and, occasionally a true lyric gift. In *The Man Forbid* a materialist banished by the orthodox finds comfort in the springtime on the sea-bordered hills. Davidson disappeared near Penzance in March, 1909; months later his body was found in the sea. There was no proof of suicide, but it is believed that he threw himself from the cliffs.

The enigmatic personality of Alfred Edward Housman [36] (1859-1936) *Housman* contrasts so strangely with the crystal clarity of his poetry that critical inquiry has been directed less towards *A Shropshire Lad* (1896) than towards its author. How explain that "continuous excitement" in the spring of 1895 under which, as he told long afterwards, most of the poems were written? How did it come about that what is evidently his own pessimism was pro-jected into the figure of the "lad"? Is this pessimism to be traced to a lasting melancholy caused by the early death of an adored mother? Or is it to be ascribed to disappointment and wounded pride when he failed in "Greats" at Oxford? Was there a tragic love affair of which the secret has been kept? Or (remembering that the poems have far more to do with "lads" than "lassies") was there some friendship whose rupture left a lasting wound? To what degree did thwarted ambition and a consciousness of intellectual

---

[35] The thirteenth-century story (an *exemplum* of the boundless range of divine forgiveness to the penitent however late) had been retold by Adelaide Proctor in *A Legend of Provence*. There are other modern English versions. Compare also Maeterlinck's *Sœur Beatrice* and Humperdinck's opera.

[36] *Collected Poems* (1940). — T. G. Ehrsam, *Bibliography* (1941); R. W. Stallman, "An-notated Bibliography," *PMLA*, LX (1945). 463-502; A. S. F. Gow, *A. E. Housman: A Sketch together with a List of his Writings* (1936); Laurence Housman, *My Brother, A. E. Housman: Personal Recollections* (1938); Percy Withers, *A Buried Life: Personal Recollections of A. E. Housman* (1940); *A. E. Housman* (1937), recollections by A. W. Pollard, R. W. Chambers, and others.

superiority mold his temperament? Does the explanation lie in Housman's consciousness that accepted standards were crumbling, that with the disappearance of old values reliance must be placed in stoic pride and personal integrity? Or was his despair due not to experience of life but to a preconception of life's futility? There may be some truth in an affirmative answer to each of these questions. It is obvious that Housman's nature, like Hardy's, was one that became "vocal to tragedy," that saw the frustrations of life more clearly than its satisfactions, though his bitter pity has in it little of Hardy's all-embracing compassion. With laconic brevity, forceful directness, and exquisite simplicity a dark fatalism was expressed. Carouse and make love, lad, and enjoy youth and the loveliness of the spring while you can, for death comes quickly—and it may come violently or shamefully. This grim counsel was set to the music of familiar metres, with cadences from ballads and well-loved hymns and with echoes, never too recondite, from Latin poetry. After 1895 the impulse to write verse subsided as suddenly as it had swelled, to reappear fitfully thereafter. Housman was determined to leave a lasting monument in English verse, and his standards of excellence were as rigorous in original composition as in his professional classical studies, where, as the arrogant prefaces to his edition of Manilius show, he was always willing to wound and never afraid to strike. The *Last Poems* (1922) and the posthumous *More Poems* (1936) contain, along with other things of less excellence, some as perfect in their kind as anything in *A Shropshire Lad*. This poetry, so narrow in range of thought and emotion and so slender in quantity, bids fair to survive current efforts at detraction. It may be read in the light of the sardonic and deliberately disillusioning lecture on *The Name and Nature of Poetry* (1933) which is Housman's only prose work apart from his classical papers.[37]

[37] The exquisitely refined style of William Johnson Cory (1823-1889), author of *Ionica* (1858, and later, expanded editions), was certainly an influence upon Housman. Cory aimed at the effects of the Greek Anthology. *Mimnermus in Church*, a beautifully restrained expression of "pagan" agnosticism, and *Heraclitus*, a version of a Greek epigram, are his best known poems. He expressed a pensive wistfulness very different from the "horror and scorn and hate and fear and indignation" of the *Shropshire Lad*.

XL
The Modern Novel[1]

I

The task of making an estimate of the achievement of Henry James [2] (1843-1916) proportionate in scale to its significance may be renounced on *James* the ground that though he became an Englishman shortly before his death his writings belong to the history of American Literature. But because he was, by temperament and taste, long residence, and passionate devotion to the country of his adoption, an Englishman, and also because his work occupies "a pivotal position in the development of the twentieth-century novel," [3] he must be included within this survey.

James came of the well-to-do, erudite, and highly individualistic family of which he wrote long afterwards in *A Small Boy and Others* (1913) and *Notes of a Son and Brother* (1914). Visits to England, France, and Italy roused in his "famished" American soul a yearning to become part of an old culture, richer in tradition and associations than his native land could provide. While engaged upon his first reviews, travel sketches, and attempts in fiction, he alternated wanderings abroad with sojourns in the United States. He did not quickly reach a decision, but the desire to regain the lost heritage of the past led him in 1880 to settle permanently in England. He never married, took no part in public affairs, and never evinced any genuine

[1] Percy Lubbock, *The Craft of Fiction* (1921); E. M. Forster, *Aspects of the Novel* (1928); Edwin Muir, *The Structure of the Novel* (1928); C. H. Grabo, *The Technique of the Novel* (1928); J. W. Beach, *The Twentieth Century Novel: Studies in Technique* (1932), henceforth referred to as Beach; David Daiches, *The Novel and the Modern World* (1939); W. C. Frierson, *The English Novel in Transition, 1885-1940* (Norman, Okla., 1942); Philip Henderson, *The Novel Today* (1936); Abel Chavelley, *Le Roman anglais de notre temps* (1921); Agnes C. Hansen, *Twentieth Century Forces in European Fiction* (1934); Herbert Muller, *Modern Fiction: A Study in Values* (1937); Helen E. Haines, *What's in a Novel* (1942); Elbert Lenrow, *Reader's Guide to Prose Fiction* (1940).

[2] *Novels and Tales*, New York Edition (26v, 1907-1917). James excluded some novels and many short stories from the canon of his collected works. Some of the omitted items are accessible in recent reprints. *Short Stories*, ed. Clifton Fadiman (1945). The Prefaces are assembled in *The Art of the Novel: Critical Prefaces*, ed. R. P. Blackmur (1934). James's theories may also be studied in *Notes on Novelists* (1914) and *Notes and Reviews* (1921). There is no definitive biography but much material for one may be found in James's *Letters*, ed. Percy Lubbock (2v, 1920). — F. M. Hueffer, *Henry James, a Critical Study* (1913); Rebecca West, *Henry James* (1916); J. W. Beach, *The Method of Henry James* (1918); Van Wyck Brooks, *The Pilgrimage of Henry James* (1925); H. L. Hughes, *Theory and Practice in Henry James* (1926); Pelham Edgar, *Henry James, Man and Author* (1927); Theodora Bosanquet, *Henry James at Work* (1927); Morris Roberts, *Henry James's Criticism* (1929); C. P. Kelley, *The Early Development of Henry James* (1930); Leon Edel, *The Prefaces of Henry James* (Paris, 1931); C. H. Grattan, *The Three Jameses, a Family of Minds: Henry James, Sr., William James, Henry James* (1932); F. O. Matthiessen, *Henry James: The Major Phase* (1944).

[3] Beach, p. 186.

understanding of the economic and social changes that were shaking the foundations of his world. Even of that world of international society whose centers were London, Paris, and Rome (with New York and Boston hull-down upon the horizon) he remained a spectator. From the beginning his department of fiction was a restricted section of the novel of manners—the manners of wealthy, leisurely, sophisticated people, steeped in tradition, trained in a code, so subtle in their reactions one to another that they appear to belong not in the rough work-a-day world but in a world of James's imagining, where motives are more complex and the discrimination of values more microscopic than in what we call reality. In James's absorbed attention to the ultimate refinements of sensibility and of moral and social scruple, in his reliance upon exquisite taste, tact, and fineness of perception, and in his increasingly tortuous and abstruse exploration of mental states there is a resemblance to Pater's critical theories and practice. For James, as for Pater, life was a fine art.

The International Scene

The typical character in such outstanding novels of James's first phase as *Roderick Hudson* (1875) and *The American* (1877) is the American abroad, and the typical theme is the clash between transatlantic Puritanism and European tolerance.[4] The comic aspects of situations developing from these antagonistic traditions James very rarely explored; he was more interested in serious social contrasts. During his first years in Europe he was a fasci-nated observer of Mayfair and the Quartier St. Germain, the world of privilege and prestige. There was a gradual diminution of emphasis upon the theme of the expatriated American, and by the time we reach *The Portrait of a Lady* (1881), the masterpiece of this first period, the fact that Isabel Archer is an American is an almost immaterial consideration in her story.

The First Phase

As the original glamour faded, there crept in a note of disillusion which is characteristic of James's middle years. In *The Princess Casamassima* (1886) he showed himself dimly and disturbingly aware of restlessness beyond the boundaries of his world. It is significant that in *The Tragic Muse* (1890) he quite obviously champions the cause of the artist against aristocratic society. This change in tone is accounted for by his somewhat bewildered resentment of the fact that he had failed to win any popular success.[5] For some years after 1890 he neglected fiction, other than the short story, in favor of the drama, but though two of his plays were performed there was no genuine success. These experiments, however, were not unprofitable since they helped him to solve problems of craftsmanship in fiction: the approximation to the dramatic form; the selection of those aspects of experience to be presented; the complete separation of the author from his work.

The Second Phase

The gradual assumption of a stoical indifference to popular neglect led

[4] The few novels, such as *Washington Square* (1881), in which the scene is laid in America did not call for the exercise of James's full powers because he never "saturated" himself in material which he regarded as thin.

[5] Save in the early, unimportant novel, *Daisy Miller* (1877), which was widely read and provoked much discussion because its heroine was declared to be "a libel on young American womanhood."

James to the determination to write only to please himself and his limited *The* clientèle. This state of mind is characteristic of his third period. There was *Third* increasingly a limitation of the field of vision with a correspondingly en- *Phase* riched saturation in the social and psychological situation and an intense preoccupation with the problems of selection, approach, arrangement, and emphasis. Broad and comparatively superficial evocations of the social scene were abjured in favor of an intimate concentration upon situations composed out of innumerable touches of finesse in a kind of literary *pointillisme*. There were vibrations of sensibility almost beyond the human auditory range. To many readers the subjects of the later books seem to be crushed by the weight of the technique. *The Spoils of Poynton* (1897) is, in comparison with James's former novels, restricted in scope, but what is lost in range is gained in profundity and insight. *What Maisie Knew* (1897) is a display of technical virtuosity, the lives of corrupt worldlings being seen exclusively through the eyes of an innocent little girl. *The Awkward Age* (1899) is an attempt to apply the dramatist's technique to fiction, the action being conducted almost entirely in dialogue.[6] These comparatively slight books lead to the massive novels of James's last years. In *The Wings of the Dove* (1902) the faint suggestions of an underlying symbolism reveal James's sensitiveness to at least one contemporary tendency; and there is also an obscure obsession with evil which had already betrayed itself in earlier books and is most manifest in the famous short story, *The Turn of the Screw*. That problems of moral obliquity fascinated James is evident, but there is little to be said for the theory that this fascination was due to a "guilt-complex" arising from his failure, as a young man, to take part, as his brothers had done, in the War between the States. Rather it was a special product of his interest in any and every variety of mental experience. The same explanation holds for his stories of the occult, whether of the supernatural, as in the story just named, or the supernormal, as in *The Altar of the Dead*. He worked this ground only in short stories, though in *The Sense of the Past* (posthumous, 1917) the uncanny experiences of the young American who tries to live into the past approximate the occult in their effect upon the reader. In his last books James reverted to his old interest in international social relations. *The Ambassadors* (1903), in which an American is brought into contact with French traditions of the richest texture, is a delight to those for whom the enjoyment of a novel consists in observing and analyzing technical skill, for the chief protagonist is at once the "reflector" of the situation and the leading actor therein. In the international complication here set forth with what most readers deem wearisome elaboration, American Philistinism comes off the worse from the encounter. But in *The Golden Bowl* (1905), which many devotees of James consider the crown of his life's work, the most mellow and exquisitely sensitive of his books, that same Philistinism, in its finer guise of Puritanism, is vindicated in its struggle with moral turpitude.

---

[6] The approximation to the form of drama is carried even further in *The Outcry* (1911).

The change from the Victorian to the modern novel has been accounted for as due to the weakening of traditional values, with the consequence that the novelist, no longer able to rely upon truth as viewed in terms of the conventions and assumptions of a stable civilization, came to depend more and more upon his own individual experiences.[7] To all outward seeming James was confident in the stability and enduring value of his world. Yet we remark in him, as in his successors, that "the personal sense of truth replaces the formulas of a civilization."[8] He set the example of attempting to make the mind of the artist "a clear glass through which objective truth can pass undisturbed,"[9] but since the choice of persons and things to be represented depends upon the artist's personal estimate of their value, this quest of entire objectivity, in James as, again, in his successors, ends in complete subjectivity. He is present in every page of every book from which he sought so assiduously to eliminate himself. In the prefaces to the New York Edition of his collected works[10] and, less directly, in various studies of other novelists, James expounded the principles of the art of fiction. These principles have been as influential as his practice upon such successors as Conrad, Galsworthy, Katherine Mansfield, Virginia Woolf, and Dorothy Richardson. The reader is required to focus his attention not upon the mere "fable" but, increasingly, upon the manner of presentation, the point of

The Point of View

view—which is not the simplest and clearest but deliberately the most arduous, the richest in overtones of meaning. To an extent differing in different books James employed the dramatic method—the projection of the mind of a character without comment or explanation. The effort is to have the author, as a separate individuality, cease to exist, and to impart to the reader the illusion of being present at the moment of the action. For the old formal, descriptive introductions of the persons in a story James substituted a gradual unfolding of characters by means of a multitude of fine touches. This was intended to impart that "solidity of specification" upon which he set supreme value. The data, once selected, must be composed, arranged, and set in the appropriate lights. In the effort to hide behind his work he made much use of persons in whose minds actions, characters, and situations are mirrored. He remarked upon his preference "for dealing with [his] subject-matter ... through the opportunity and the sensibility of some more or less detached, some not strictly involved, though thoroughly intelligent, witness or reporter." Occasionally he preferred the fitting together of parts of a tale known fragmentarily to various witnesses—a mode of narration which he passed on to Conrad. But is there an honest reader who can affirm that in absorbed attention to James's creations he forgets James himself? Though ever so artfully hidden, is not the puppeteer pulling the strings? Does not

---

[7] This is the central thesis of David Daiches' book, *The Novel and the Modern World* (henceforth, in this chapter, referred to as Daiches). Professor Daiches does not include James within his survey.

[8] Daiches, p. 78.

[9] *Ibid.*, p. 72, and compare Katherine Mansfield's *Journals, passim.*

[10] Gathered together as *The Art of the Novel*, ed. R. P. Blackmur (1934).

James seem always to be demanding of his reader not that he listen to what is being told but that he observe with unflagging attention how it is being told? And does not this demand divert attention from the work of art to the artist? An affirmative answer to these questions does not cast doubt upon the significance of James's experiments in craftsmanship. He turned the course of the novel into new directions (though some of these directions, as is beginning to be apparent, were blind alleys). He might have applied his method to material of a different kind, but his technical dexterity was ideally suited to the subject-matter of his choice. The lessons in craftsmanship, taught and exemplified, remain fruitful. But with the disappearance of his "world" the books in which the theories were given practical application are likely to become, save in the estimation of a small and diminishing band of devotees, mere documents in the history of a phase of European sensibility almost as remote from today's actualities as is the *Carte du Tendre.*

II

The unique position of Joseph Conrad [11] in English literary history is due   *Conrad* not only to the fact that he wrote in a language not native to him but to his isolation from the main movement of the novel. In some respects his work resembles that of Henry James and in other more superficial respects the work of Kipling and Stevenson. But he made no contribution either to the novel of manners or to sociological fiction, and even in the few stories having a European setting the subjects are remote from typical western experience.

Jozef Teodor Konrad Nałęcz Korzeniowski (1857-1924)—the name afterwards so nobly simplified—came by inheritance to his chivalrous and romantic temperament and outlook upon life. Resenting the undifferentiated designation as a Slav, he insisted upon his Polish blood. As a Pole his cultural connections were with the West. From childhood he knew French and to the end of his life would resort to it when at a moment's loss for an English word. But his father was a student of English literature, and in translation the boy read Shakespeare and Dickens. In his veins ran the blood of martyrs for freedom, and it is not too fanciful to suppose that the

---

[11] *Collected Works*, Memorial Edition (21v, 1925); there are several other collected editions. *Letters, 1895-1924* [to Edward Garnett] (1928); *Letters to a Friend* [Richard Curle] (1928); *Lettres françaises*, ed. G. Jean-Aubry (Paris, 1929); *Letters to Marguerite Poradowska*, translated from the French, ed. J. A. Gee and P. J. Sturn (1940); parts of Conrad's correspondence are still unpublished. — T. J. Wise, *Bibliography* (1921); G. T. Keating, *A Conrad Memorial Library* (1929); G. Jean-Aubry, *Joseph Conrad: Life and Letters* (2v, 1927); Gustav Morf, *The Polish Heritage of Joseph Conrad* (1930); Richard Curle, *Joseph Conrad, the History of His Books* (n.d.) and *The Last Twelve Years of Joseph Conrad* (1928); Jessie Conrad, *Joseph Conrad and His Circle* (1935); W. W. Bancroft, *Joseph Conrad, His Philosophy of Life* (Boston, 1933); R. L. Mégroz, *Joseph Conrad's Mind and Method* (1931); Edward Crankshaw, *Joseph Conrad: Some Aspects of the Art of the Novel* (1936); Raymond Las Vergnas, *Joseph Conrad* (Paris, 1938); J. D. Gordan, *Joseph Conrad, the Making of a Novelist* (1940); M. C. Bradbrook, *Joseph Conrad, England's Polish Genius* (1941); J. H. Retinger, *Conrad and His Contemporaries* (1943); F. M. Stawell, "Conrad," *E&S*, VI (1920). 88-111; W. L. Cross, *Four Contemporary Novelists* (1930), ch. II; Baker, x (1939), chs. I and II; Beach, pp. 337-365 and *passim*.

Poland

sense of man's conflict with terrific powers, which was afterwards heightened by Conrad's experiences at sea, derived ultimately from the Polish dread and hatred of Russia. In this scion of a land-locked race rose strangely the desire to follow a sailor's life. In overingenious detail the theory has been developed that throughout Conrad's books there is evidence of an obsession, a "guilt-complex," originating in his abandonment of Poland. Certainly the cases are very numerous of disloyalty, infidelity, sullied honor, and hidden shame, as also of retribution or the restoration of self-respect through self-immolation.

Not without opposition from his family was the lad able to fulfill his desire. In 1874 he made his way to Marseilles, where he was involved in gun-running adventures for the Spanish Carlists and in the conspiratorial and emotional experiences afterwards recalled in *The Arrow of Gold*. He soon joined the English merchant service and was at sea for the next twenty years, rising gradually from a common sailor to mate and master. He learned English (though he always spoke it with an accent), and so strong a hold did the idiom, the cadences, and the rich vocabulary of the language have upon him that, as he afterwards said, when he began to write he did not adopt English but it adopted him. To beguile the hours of calm weather all sailors spin yarns; and it was in part from "tales of hearsay" in fo'c'sle

Hearsay

and master's cabin that Conrad shaped his technique as a novelist. His themes were drawn from people he had known or heard of, places he had visited or coasted past, and the storms and calms of the ocean. He had tried his hand at one or two short things before he began, while still at sea, to write the story of a Dutchman whose moral nature had been degraded through long years among aliens in the tropics. From the first, Conrad's imagination exercised itself not in the invention of incident and character but in the shaping and interpretation of reality. The circumstances in which this first novel was written are a principal subject of *A Personal Record,* his autobiographical recollections. *Almayer's Folly* was published in 1895, at a time when the first successes of Kipling, a long series of travel books, and the British consciousness of world-wide responsibilities had stimulated interest in distant parts of the world and in people and things remote from occidental experience. It is noteworthy that W. H. Hudson's and Cunninghame Graham's books, on the borderland of fiction and travel literature, began to appear about the same time. The personality of Almayer remains shadowy notwithstanding the patient probing into character and motive, and the style is lush and over-written, but there was promise in the gorgeous descriptions of the tropical environment and in the portrayal of the natives of the Malay peninsula. Into a second novel, *An Outcast of the Islands* (1896), Conrad brought many of the characters of his first book, reverting, however, to an earlier period of this Dutch-Malayan history.

In both these novels there is a leisurely and elaborate scrutiny of the consequences of the impact of events upon character. In other books—short stories or narratives that are expansions of the short-story technique—

Conrad's aim was to give the effect of immediate contact with events. The change from the one to the other method and style is apparent in *The Nig-* *Experience* *ger of the "Narcissus"* (1897) where in place of events observed or surmised Conrad offers something from his own experience. This same firm foundation underlies his greatest short pieces, *Youth* (1902), *Heart of Darkness* (1902), and *Typhoon* (1903). These do not have the amplitude, movement, and pattern of novels, each being the elaboration of a single episode. As *Youth* was, by Conrad's own admission, "a feat of memory," so in *Heart of Darkness* he carried the situation only a little beyond his own experience of a journey to the Congo in order, as he said, to add to it "a sinister resonance." We are to note that Conrad leaves unexplained the remorse which weighs upon the dying Kurtz and, further, that there is a symbolic darkness in Kurtz's own heart. Conrad admitted the presence of overtones of symbolism in many of his books. In *Youth* Marlow first makes his appearance. This narrator (who in the very long run became tiresome and pretended to an oracular wisdom and psychological insight not convincingly in the character of a ship's officer) obviously found his original among yarn-spinning seamen. Marlow was a means of bringing stories close to the reader by avoiding the old convention of the omniscient author. He pieced them together from scraps of hearsay and observation. This, subtilized almost beyond recognition, was the way in which Conrad had heard sailors tell their tales. It was also a device to maintain the artist's attitude of aloofness, as though the irony and compassion expressed were not Conrad's but Marlow's. The objection is that the effect of corroborative testimony which Conrad sought is often marred by complexities. The reader does not always suspend his disbelief in Marlow's phenomenal memory for the *ipsissima verba* of lengthy dialogues and for the subtle minutiae of appearance, gesture, and changing countenance.

Upon a notorious actual case of a pilgrim-ship which was abandoned by *Lord* her officers in a supposedly sinking condition but which nevertheless got *Jim* to port [12] Conrad based *Lord Jim* (1900). It is a story of betrayal of trust, shame, and the redemption of character and the regaining of self-respect. Lord Jim becomes the trusted counselor of the natives and dies in the performance of a deed of chivalrous generosity. In none of the earlier stories had Conrad made use of so complex a method of indirect narration.[13] But this pattern is simple in comparison with the intricacies of *Nostromo* (1904). The South American people and environment Conrad had to divine from very little experience of his own. The confusing and overopulent story of revolution and the theft of a cargo of silver is told from various points of view and by the most obscure indirection. It cost Conrad agonizing efforts

[12] See the discussion of the incident of the *Jeddah* (which took place in 1880) in J. D. Gordan, *Joseph Conrad: The Making of a Novelist*, pp. 60-63, and the nearly contemporary allusion to this scandal in Wilfrid Scawen Blunt, *The Future of Islam* (1882), p. 30.

[13] Conrad wrote *The Inheritors* (1901) and *Romance* (1902) in collaboration with Ford Madox Hueffer (Ford) (1873-1939). Of Ford's many novels four on the First World War, *Some Do Not* and its sequels (1924-1928), are the most noteworthy; but his fiction has failed to take a lasting place. His critical studies in art and literature are intensely personal.

in the composition and it imposes a heavy burden upon the reader. Perhaps it was an association of ideas which led Conrad from a story of revolution in South America to narratives of European revolutionists. *The Secret Agent* (1907) is founded upon the fact that a Russian *agent provocateur* had attempted in 1894 to blow up the Greenwich Observatory as a means of rousing British indignation against the Nihilists. Conrad's Russophobia is apparent in the sinister atmosphere of the underworld of terrorists. A circle of international conspirators in Geneva forms the setting of *Under Western Eyes* (1911), the most Slavic of his books. Razumov, the conspirator turned informer, is one of the most memorable of Conrad's creations. Much in his motives is left unexplained, for, piecing together fragments of impression and rumor, Conrad gains his effects in part by his professed inability to understand his characters completely.

Later Novels   He now returned to stories of the sea. *Chance* (1913) is a not altogether successful blend of a love story with a tale of sordid wickedness, drifting or sinking towards the close into mere melodrama. The irony of haphazard works not only in the chances that keep the lovers apart but in the chance that unites them at the end. Marlow tells the story. He had had a part in the events, but much of his knowledge consists of deductions from what he had been told by another actor in them. *Victory* (1915), grounded upon personal acquaintance with Heyst and Mr. Jones (the latter the most repulsive of all Conrad's villains), is in tone much like *Chance;* and to an even greater degree the mingling of sensationalism, hideous crime, and idealized love is unconvincing. *The Shadow-Line* (1919) conveys strange hints of the occult. The reader is left to 'guess whether the spirit of the wicked dead captain is responsible for the criminal substitution of salt for quinine with the consequence that the sailors are fever-stricken. This touch of supernaturalism is quite uncharacteristic of Conrad, for whom there were mysteries enough in nature without exploring beyond the boundaries of the natural world. The Carlist adventures of his youth which he had related succinctly in *The Mirror of the Sea* (1906) are reworked elaborately in *The Arrow of Gold* (1919), in which obscure rumors are pieced together into a story of which the reader may make as much as he can. *The Rescue* (1920) is too long, intolerably repetitious, and dull. *The Rover* (1923) is Napoleonic in theme, and *Suspense* (posthumous, 1925), long meditated, obviously planned on a large scale, and left unfinished when Conrad died,[14] has as its basis the return of Napoleon from Elba. These last half-dozen novels, appearing in the years when Conrad's long delayed but at length immense reputation was at its height, were over-praised by contemporary critics. His fame rests more securely upon his earlier work.[15]

---

14 There has been a good deal of discussion of Conrad's probable design in *Suspense*. For the present writer's suggested solution see *Sat. Rev. of Lit.,* II (November 14, 1925).

15 Five collections of short stories are to be noted: *Tales of Unrest* (1898), of which some are of lyrical intensity and others labored; *A Set of Six* (1908), a Napoleonic, nautical, and terroristic miscellany; *'Twixt Land and Sea* (1912), memorable for the romantic story of Freya and for *The Secret Sharer*, a little masterpiece; *Within the Tides* (1915), of less note; and *Tales of Hearsay* (posthumous, 1925), another miscellany covering the years from 1884

Life, Conrad was wont to say, is a spectacle of terror and pity, yet also of *Conrad's* beauty. His reason is baffled by the mystery of a world whose beauty holds *World* him in thrall. His most characteristic situation shows the conflict of the primitive and the civilized. Europeans who in their own environment might have led normal lives are set in alien circumstances which bring to the surface the best or the worst qualities in human nature. Puny and courageous man struggles with natural forces but also with forces within his own nature. Conrad's interest is not in the typical human being but in the exceptional, whether in moral heroism or moral degradation. Cautious mediocrity provokes his contempt. In his ability to draw inferences from minute externalities of appearance, gesture, and behavior he is like Henry James. He described James as "the historian of fine consciences," and he was such a historian himself. Cases of puzzling mental pathology, studies in hopeless degeneration, fascinated him, but though he sometimes contemplated them with sardonic detachment he was pitiful, not cruel. In particular he sought to trace the weakening of character through environment. Action is of secondary importance, despite the violence of many crucial episodes. Those critics are mistaken who hold that his "psychology" is merely one ingredient of his atmosphere. Rather the sensitive subtleties of atmosphere are part of the psychology. His gorgeous word-painting, especially in the earlier books before he pruned his luxuriance, won him more readers than did his probings into the human heart. He conveyed the spell·of eastern islands lying "clothed in their dark garments of leaves, in a great hush of silver and azure, where the sea without murmur meets the sky in a ring of magic stillness." But all this was only the setting for the tragedy of man. The loneliness of an alien environment is often the symbol of the soul's loneliness.

III

A meeting with John Galsworthy on shipboard was the chance that gave *Gals-* Conrad the first step up the ladder to fame as a writer; but though the *worthy* two men became close friends there is an utter dissimilarity in their novels both in form and subject-matter. John Galsworthy [16] (1867-1933) viewed English society from within the pale of the well-bred and well-to-do upper bourgeoisie. He possessed little real understanding of the great world beyond and beneath his class, and though, as in his plays, he expressed a sense of "injustice" and a troubled compassion, he was unaware of the full extent of the social disintegration going on around him. Late-Victorian and post-

---

to post-war England. *The Mirror of the Sea* (1906) supplements both the autobiographical *Personal Record* and the novels and tales.

[16] *Novels, Tales and Plays*, Devon Edition (22v, 1926-1929); Manaton Edition (30v, 1922-1933); *Autobiographical Letters* [to Frank Harris] (1933); *Letters* [to Edward Garnett] (1934). — H. V. Marrot, *Bibliography* (1928) and *The Life and Letters of John Galsworthy* (1936); Joseph Conrad, *John Galsworthy, an Appreciation* (1922); L. M. Schalit, *John Galsworthy, a Survey* (1929); Edouard Guyot, *John Galsworthy* (Paris, 1933); Natalie Croman, *John Galsworthy, a Study in Continuity and Contrast* (1933); Hermon Ould, *John Galsworthy* (1934); Baker, x (1939). 319-344; Beach, ch. xxi; Daiches, ch. iii. — On Galsworthy's plays see ch. xxxviii, above.

Victorian life is criticized in his novels by exposing not the miseries of the poor but the complacency of the propertied class, acquisitive and possessive. Galsworthy neither offers any profound diagnosis of social ills nor suggests any drastic remedy. His characteristic combination of gentility, fastidiousness, and pity often degenerates into sentimentality. There is always something ineffectual about his indignation, a lack of emotional force, though there is no reason for questioning his sincerity. His later books betray a wistful fondness for the very society which he began by satirizing.

His first four novels, published between 1897 and 1901 under the pseudonym "John Sinjohn," must be disregarded here. *The Man of Property* (1906) was not conceived as the first part of a trilogy; it is a well-made and well-rounded novel, complete in itself. From this first chronicle of the Forsyte family Galsworthy turned to other subjects. In *Fraternity* (1909) he looked from the world of property into the world of poverty which he did not understand. *The Dark Flower* (1913) recounts with genuine but soft and overwrought emotion a man's three love affairs, in the spring, summer, and autumn of his life. Other novels of these middle years are *The Patrician* (1911), *The Freelands* (1915), and *Saint's Progress* (1919).[17] Galsworthy then resumed the Forsyte series. From the opulent Victorianism of *The Man of Property*, *In Chancery* (1920) brings us to the period of the Boer War and *To Let* (1921) to the years immediately following the Armistice of 1918. With the addition of short connecting links these three books were brought together as *The Forsyte Saga* (1922). The chronicle was carried into the age of the "bright young people" of the nineteen-twenties in *The White Monkey* (1924), *The Silver Spoon* (1926), and *Swan Song* (1928) which together form a second trilogy, *A Modern Comedy* (1929). Even then Galsworthy was not done with his Forsytes; further episodes appeared between 1931 and 1933 and were assembled as *End of the Chapter* (posthumous, 1934). The half-dozen later installments of this huge "novel in sequence" carry the story into the post-war world of which Galsworthy, a disapproving and bewildered spectator, knew little. They are scarcely more than bi-annual journalistic records, thrown into the form of fiction, and they are on a much lower level than the original trilogy.

The
Forsyte
Saga

Galsworthy's fame rests upon *The Forsyte Saga* and even there somewhat precariously. The *Saga* is not a *Comédie Humaine,* broad-based as society itself; nor does it concentrate narrowly upon a few individuals. Galsworthy "expatiates free" over an entire class whose types are represented by the different members of a large family. The Forsytes belong to what seems a stable and secure stratum of society whose roots are money. Soames Forsyte is "the man of property" whose claims extend even to a reluctant wife. Irene's first effort towards emancipation ends with the accidental death of the artist who loves her. In the second part of the trilogy the ill-mated pair are divorced and each marries again. The third part centers in the love that

---

[17] Fifty short stories, an ample selection from five original collections, were gathered together in *Caravan* (1925).

springs up between the children of these second marriages, Soames's daughter and Irene's son. Throughout, Irene stands outside the circle of the Forsytes and is seen only through the eyes of members of the family—a device of technique to which Galsworthy himself called attention. To her, as to Old Jolyon Forsyte and to various inanimate objects, Galsworthy attaches a symbolic value, but this value is lessened by the persistent sentimentality. Galsworthy's greatest accomplishment from the point of view of the craftsman in fiction is the presentation of the flow of time. This sense of the tragic passage of the years is concentrated in the character of Soames Forsyte, Galsworthy's greatest creation. Beginning by detesting him, the novelist gradually grows fond and understanding of Soames as he survives, almost the last vestige of Victorian stability, into the restless, rootless postwar world. On the whole, however, the *Saga* offers little of interest to the student of technique. The perpetual shifting of the point of view is distracting and is in keeping with the clear but shallow delineation of character. Since the world which Galsworthy knew widely and intimately, though scarcely with psychological profundity, has disappeared, the question arises in his case, as in the case of Henry James, whether the reflection in the mirror of Galsworthy's art possesses sufficient vitality of its own to endure now that the thing mirrored is gone.

Arnold Bennett [18] (1867-1931), Galsworthy's exact contemporary, came *Bennett* from one of the "Five Towns" of Staffordshire, the district known as "the Potteries." Many of his books, including his two masterpieces, are set wholly or in part in this grimy and unlovely locality, and his affectionate knowledge of it made him one of the foremost of the regionalists. After a start in journalism he began to write fiction in 1898 and evinced serious promise in *Anna of the Five Towns* (1902). *The Old Wives' Tale* (1908) put him in the forefront of contemporary novelists. *Clayhanger* (1910) is the first part of a trilogy which would have been his greatest work had not the sequels, *Hilda Lessways* (1911) and *These Twain* (1915), showed a decline in power which was still more evident in subsequent books. There was some recovery in *Riceyman Steps* (1923), though Bennett here seems· overwhelmed in detailed documentation of his own accumulation; and the immense expenditure of effort upon *Imperial Palace* (1930) turned out to be not worth while. Much of Bennett's work was ephemeral, and even of the large portion that has not lost its vitality we must here pass over a good deal: shorter novels, farcical tales, "thrillers," plays, criticism, impressions of art and travel, popular counsel, and autobiographical notes, including *Things That Have Interested Me* (three series, 1906-1925) and the posthumous *Journals*.

Bennett's candor on the subject of his financial success has obscured to

[18] There is no collected uniform edition of Bennett's works. In addition to the novels, plays, and miscellaneous more or less journalistic productions the posthumous *Journals* (3v, 1932-1933) and the *Letters to his Nephew* (1936) are illuminating. — There is as yet no definitive biography. Dorothy C. Bennett, *Arnold Bennett* (1935); Rebecca West, *Arnold Bennett* (1931); Geoffrey West, *The Problem of Arnold Bennett* (1932); J. B. Simons, *Arnold Bennett and His Novels* (1936); Georges Lafourcade, *Arnold Bennett* (1939); Baker, x (1939). 288-319; Beach, pp. 238-245.

some critics the fact that though he made much money by his art he was first and foremost an artist. He was fascinated by vast enterprises and by the processes of wealth and luxury, as symbolized, for example, in the complex organization of a modern hotel. But there was no sycophancy in the attention he paid to such large affairs. It was part of his intense interest in life itself, an interest lavished even more abundantly upon the poor and humble. His province is not the "nether world" of Gissing's most despairing books but the urban lower-middle class which he depicted not with fastidious distaste but with affectionate sympathy. Unlike the naturalists who preceded him, he was not in quest of ugliness for the sake of "documented" art or for less valid reasons—in fact, not in quest of ugliness at all. In unlikely places he perceived a homely beauty or at any rate the beauty of homeliness. He is concerned with small lives, but in narrowly circumscribed environment the souls of his people are not small. He conveyed the excitement and significance of commonplace experiences in the unromantic, normal give-and-take of family life. A rich knowledge of his characters is imparted not through ever deeper probing and analysis but by enabling the reader to live with them, as it were, through the long lapse of time. There is pathos rather than tragedy in his books. No other novelist has narrated with such intensity and precision the circumstances of non-violent, natural death; and few have rendered more impressively than Bennett, in the history of Constance and Sophia, the sense of the relentless passage of the years. But Bennett's was a nature which became vocal to comedy rather than to tragedy. He was no crusader, no reformer; and if a teacher, the lesson he taught was "how to get the best out of life." An expert craftsman, he was content in general with the older forms of the novel and made no innovation of consequence. From the point of view of technique, both *The Old Wives' Tale* and the *Clayhanger* trilogy repay study for the alternation of sections in which the lives of the chief characters are concurrently narrated with other sections in which they are told separately, either because the characters have not yet met (as with Clayhanger and Hilda Lessways) or because they have drifted apart (as with Constance and Sophia in *The Old Wives' Tale*).

Wells   Herbert George Wells [19] (1866-1946), journalist, propagandist, and reformer, used fiction as a vehicle for his criticism of existing society and for his utopian visions of the future. His early training in biology (which he studied under Huxley) accounts for his confidence that scientific progress will bring about the social millennium, his basic error in underestimating the force of irrational impulses in man, and his persistent denigration of the arts.

[19] *Works,* Atlantic Edition (28v, 1925-1927); the books since· 1927 have not yet been collected together. — F. A. Chappell, *Bibliography* (1924); Van Wyck Brooks, *The World of H. G. Wells* (1915); Edouard Guyot, *H. G. Wells* (1920); J. S. Price, *The World in the Wellsian Era* (1923); Sidney Dark, *Outline of Wells* (1924); Geoffrey West, *The Works of H. G. Wells: A Bibliography, Dictionary and Subject-Index* (1926) and *H. G. Wells, a Sketch for a Portrait* (1930); F. H. Doughty, *H. G. Wells, Educationist* (1926); George Connes, *Etude sur la pensée de Wells* (Paris, 1926) and *A Dictionary of the Characters and Scenes in the Novels, Romances and Short Stories of H. G. Wells* (1926).

To the opinion that artistic considerations were always secondary with him certain exceptions must, however, be made. The early "scientific" fantasies such as *The Time Machine* (1895), *The Stolen Bacillus* (1895), *The Island of Dr. Moreau* (1896), and *The Invisible Man* (1897) are beautifully written with a clarity of design and economy of means that put them on an altogether higher level than that of their prototypes in Jules Verne. Criticism of society is delicately handled in *The Wonderful Visit* (1895)—the visit of an angel to the earth. In *The War of the Worlds* (1898) an invasion of the Martians is made wonderfully convincing by means of touches of minute realism. Wells was least the reformer and most nearly the artist in fiction of sustained length in such comedies of middle-class life as *Love and Mr. Lewisham* (1900), *Kipps* (1905), and *The History of Mr. Polly* (1910). *When the Sleeper Wakes* (1899) began the series of utopian novels that was carried on in *In the Days of the Comet* (1906), *The Dream* (1924), *The Autocracy of Mr. Parham* (1930), and other books. In *Ann Veronica* (1909) the balance is sustained between form and substance, plot and thesis. This was the first of various books—among them *Joan and Peter* (1918) and *Christina Alberta's Father* (1925)—having as their theme sexual disharmony and advocating utopian schemes for the relationship of the sexes which it is often difficult to distinguish from libertinage. In the earlier books, even those that were most argumentative, Wells displayed a rich inventive faculty and, when depicting commonplace people, kindly humor and pathos. But he did not possess the born novelist's interest in individual human beings; he was more concerned with ideas. The tendency to overweigh the thesis at the expense of the story is apparent in *Tono-Bungay* (1909), amusing as it is in its exposure of crafty business practices barely within the law; and even more so in *The New Machiavelli* (1911) which deals with the world of politics. *Mr. Britling Sees It Through* (1916) is a piece of war-propaganda which was very effective in its day. *The Undying Fire* (1919) proclaimed Wells's "discovery" of a finite God who in his struggle with evil needs the aid of man. In some of these books and in others not named it is at times difficult to discern the point where the novel form gives place to the sociological treatise. In *The World of William Clissold* (1926) the protagonist's experiences, amatory and otherwise, are thinly imagined and the narrative is constantly being interrupted by massive blocks of discussion of one or another of Wells's many interests. From such a novel, so-called, as this it is but a step to treatises from which the needless element of story has been eliminated, such as *The Work, Wealth, and Happiness of Mankind* (1931) and *The Shape of Things to Come* (1933). Since from the past, if from anywhere, man must draw lessons for the future, it was to be expected that Wells, whom no task could daunt, should tell the story of mankind. Discarding nationalistic history in favor of a world-view and interpreting that story in terms of evolutionary speculation, he wrote *The Outline of History* (1920), a more remarkable achievement than most professional historians have been willing to admit.

The Novel of Ideas

From the above brief survey many volumes have perforce been omitted. The task of selection from Wells's eighty-odd books has indeed already been accomplished in large measure by the lapse of time, for in much of his writing there is too little of artistic value to give enduring life to subject-matter that was of transitory interest. Wells moved with the times, leaving quantities of his books and pamphlets behind him and behind the times. Repetitiveness, long-windedness, and an inability to distinguish between the trivial and the significant impose an insuperable barrier between his work as a whole and any reader too young to have read his Wells in installments from year to year—almost, like his newspaper, from day to day. His novels offer little of interest to students of craftsmanship, for far from introducing innovations in the art of fiction, they generally exhibit a reversion to Victorian formlessness. In his use of fiction to convey ideas he followed the Victorian sociological novelists, while carrying further than they had done the custom of making plot and characterization mere pegs upon which to hang disquisitions on every sort of topic. For the future historian of the political, economic, social, moral, and religious unrest and aspirations of the first forty years of our century his books provide a mountain of evidence of varying degrees of value and reliability, to be sifted, assorted, and condensed. The number and variety of his Utopias have often been derided; but actually they testify to the alertness and fecundity of an imagination ready to discard an old, and embrace a new, idea in accord with social change. The buoyant optimism of this writer who held that we fall to rise and are baffled to fight better was a tonic through years of skepticism, lassitude, and despair.

IV

Joyce

James Joyce [20] (1882-1941) is reported to have declared that to understand him the reader must devote his life to the study of his books. The readjustment of values that is sure to come will spare future lovers of literature this self-immolation, and meanwhile the commentators supply short cuts. Already it is apparent that startling innovations in technique are not in themselves evidence of artistic success, and even among Joyce's admirers there are those who admit that one of his two massive books is but partially successful and the other a failure. Joyce's contemporary renown was in part due to factors extraneous to literary excellence. These are so notorious as to call for no comment here. Of his mastery of language—indeed, his tyranny over it—there can be no question, nor of the beauty, profundity, strength, and significance of parts of his achievement. But the separation of the author from any considerable body of readers, already apparent in his early books,

---

[20] Herbert Gorman, *James Joyce* (1940), the authorized biography, complete to within a year of the subject's death; Frank Budgen, *James Joyce and the Making of Ulysses* (1934); Stuart Gilbert, *James Joyce's Ulysses, a Study* (1931); Harry Levin, *James Joyce, a Critical Introduction* (1941); Edouard Dujardin, *Le Monologue intérieur, son apparition, ses origines, sa place dans l'œuvre de James Joyce* (Paris, 1931); R. M. Kain, *Fabulous Voyager* (1947); Edmund Wilson, *Axel's Castle* (1931), ch. VI; Beach, ch. XXXII; Daiches, chs. VI-IX.

became a chasm only to be bridged by the erudite in *Ulysses* and a great gulf of incommunicability in *Finnegans Wake*.

A Dubliner educated by the Jesuits for the priesthood, Joyce rebelled against the inhibiting forces of family, church, and native country. Despite the encouragement given him by Yeats, he stood completely apart from the Irish Literary Revival. Yet in a sense he could no more escape from the Ireland of his youth than from his education. Few readers possess the inti- *Dublin* mate knowledge of Irish history and politics and of Dublin life and topography requisite for a thorough understanding of his local and topical allusions. The main fact about his life—his self-imposed Continental exile from 1904 till his death—is also the main fact about his art: he was absolutely aloof from the society which with his phenomenal memory he depicted in such detail. Using for defense, as he said, the weapons of "silence, exile, and cunning," he lived at first in Paris and later in Trieste, Rome, and Zurich, supporting himself as a bank-clerk and as a teacher in the Berlitz schools, while with single-minded determination he pursued his path. His poetry is over-valued by the enthusiasts. *Chamber Music* (1907) attracted almost no attention, and Joyce returned only once to verse (apart from *jeux d'esprit*) when he published *Pomes Penyeach* (1927). *Dubliners* (1914), a collection of short stories including one, *The Dead,* that is a little masterpiece, showed him to be not only a keen observer of the squalid life of his native city but also an exquisite artist in language and in the delicate patterning of apparently casual accumulations of seemingly unrelated detail. *A Portrait of the Artist as a Young Man* (1916), of which the posthumously published *Stephen Hero* (1944) is all that remains of a first draft, is autobiographical; Stephen Dedalus, who purges himself of racial and religious inhibitions, is obviously Joyce himself. The book is, further, a necessary prologue to the *Ulysses* greater work which followed. *Ulysses* (1922), published in Paris, was suppressed in England and the United States. The blasphemy and obscenity which gained it immediate notoriety insured its success as a commercial venture but were of little moment to those who recognized the book's significance as an ambitious experiment in creative literature along new lines. The correspondence between the experiences of Leopold Bloom on a single day in Dublin and the adventures of Ulysses is not, as some critics have declared, a mere scholarly jest or *tour de force* but is fundamental to the design. Joyce held that Ulysses, far more than Hamlet or Faust, was the "complete" or representative man—son, husband, father; wise, courageous, shrewd; subject to many trials. Each episode in *Ulysses* has its parallel in the *Odyssey*, as when Dedalus finds himself between the Scylla of Aristotelian realism and the Charybdis of Platonic mysticism. For the detection of many of these parallels the reader needs the guidance of the commentators. The episodes are, moreover, associated each with an hour of the day and an organ of the body, and each may be connected with one of the arts and may have its peculiar color and symbol and "technique." There are innumerable reticulations and decussations of recurrent motives, many of them so tenuous as to be discernible only after the closest scrutiny. Not every reader finds the effort always rewarding. Joyce had an astonishing command of the resources of the English language, and when conventional vocabulary and syntax failed to meet his requirements he had recourse to neologisms, truncated and telescoped words, and a sort of counterpoint derived from his knowledge of music. In one chapter the development of the embryo from conception to birth is symbolized by a chronological succession of English prose styles imitated with dazzling virtuosity. The technical expertness often overreaches itself, for though there are passages of lucid beauty more often there is an orgiastic tumult of vocables. Joyce plumbed the depths of the subconscious to draw thence half-formed thoughts and unspeakable desires. These are interlaced with description, narrative, and dialogue. The *monologue intérieur* is carried beyond the limit of candor and length in the famous reverie of Molly Bloom with which *Ulysses* concludes. Though the end is a magnificent glorification of the "life-urge," the prevailing tone of the book is of a desolating irony; and though there is abundant humor it is a mistake to describe it as Rabelaisian, unless we apply to Joyce Coleridge's characterization of Swift as an *anima rabelaisiana habitans in sicco*. The book succeeds best where it communicates most, as when we follow Bloom's thoughts in the cemetery or when Dedalus develops his theory of *Hamlet* in the library. When it fails, the failure is in communication; contact between author and reader can be established, if at all, only through the mediation of the commentators.

This fundamental objection to *Ulysses* applies *a fortiori* to *Finnegans Wake* [21] (1939). From Giambattista Vico's theory of the three phases of civilizations Joyce here built up a vast phantasmagoria of the stream of time. The thoughts and activities are those of the world of dreams. Though Joyce never makes clear how the mind of the Dublin public-house keeper, H. C. Earwicker, became charged with such a wealth of knowledge and associations, this extraordinary phenomenon is evidently suggested by Jung's theory of the "collective consciousness." The distortions and convolutions of language transcend the extreme limits of intelligibility. Single sentences are brilliant, ingenious, amusing, or profound.[22] The extraordinary linguistic acrobatics may hold the reader's attention for a while. But before long, light dies before Joyce's "uncreating word" "and universal Darkness buries All." Joyce has retired so far within himself as to be beyond reach.

The modern cultural phenomenon of the artist who, amid the disruption of society, withdraws into the stronghold of his own personality is illustrated

[21] The clearest exposition is Edmund Wilson, "The Dream of H. C. Earwicker," in *The Wound and the Bow* (1941), pp. 243-271. But the light provided by Mr. Wilson is quickly extinguished in the phantasmagoric darkness of the text. — See also J. Campbell and H. M. Robinson, *A Skeleton Key to Finnegans Wake* (1946).

[22] Here is a relatively simple example (cited by Mr. Wilson): "Nobirdy aviar soar anywing to eagle it" which is a *Jabberwocky* distortion of: "Nobody ever saw anything to equal it."

in another way in the case of David Herbert Lawrence [23] (1885-1930). Liter- *D. H.* ary criticism cannot disengage itself from the record of the neuroses, fixa- *Lawrence* tions, and complexes, originating in his social and psychological maladjustment, which is found in the autobiographical stratum of his books and in the frequently conflicting testimony of his friends and biographers. Lawrence, the son of a Nottinghamshire miner, was encouraged by the forceful mother to whom he was excessively attached, to get himself some education and become a schoolteacher. Brooding resentment of his social inferiority found expression in suspiciousness, and compensation in arrogance. For the obsession with sex which tormented him throughout his career there was perhaps a physiological or psychic explanation. His earliest poems, published by F. M. Ford in *The English Review* in 1908, show that already he aimed to interpret all life in terms of his own personal experience. Two novels—*The White Peacock* (1911), which is faintly Hardy-esque, and *The Trespassers* (1912), the romanticized record of a trivial love affair —preceded *Sons and Lovers* (1913), which remains his greatest book. The story is composed out of the "passionate experience" of the conflict between Lawrence's mother and the woman to whom he was attached (the "Miriam" of the novel and the "E. T." of actuality). At this time, when psychoanalysis was directing attention to the Unconscious but apparently before he had read Freud, Lawrence began in this book his probings into the "underground roots," "the dark founts of creative life." It needs to be noted, however, that despite his sexual obsession, he never accepted Freud's theory as to the predominance of the sexual instinct but subordinated it to the "male passion of collective purpose." In *The Rainbow* (1915) he explored the problem of successful mating in the cases of three pairs of lovers. This book brought him into conflict with the police. Its suppression enraged and humiliated him, for not only was he sincere in the assertion of his high moral purpose but he knew that the prosecution was actuated in part by his anti-militaristic opinions and the fact that he had married a German woman. Henceforth he ate his heart out in bitterness. *Women in Love,*

[23] There is no collected edition. In addition to the books mentioned in the text the following may be noted. *Love Poems* (1913); *Amores* (1916); *Birds, Beasts and Flowers* (1923) and other volumes of verse were collected in 1928, after which five other volumes appeared, including *Last Poems*, ed. Richard Aldington (1932). Much of Lawrence's most beautiful writing is in the travel books, *Twilight in Italy* (1916), *Sea and Sardinia* (1921), and *Mornings in Mexico* (1927). *Fantasia of the Unconscious* (1922) is important for its criticism of Freud. *Studies in Classic American Literature* (1923) contains some first-rate criticism mixed with eccentricities. *Letters*, ed. Aldous Huxley (1932), are of more value for Lawrence's life than the biographies. *Apocalypse* (1932) is a posthumous "revelation" of his view of life. *Phoenix*, ed. E. D. McDonald (1936), contains the posthumous papers. — E. D. McDonald, *Bibliography* (1925), with *Supplement* (1931); J. Middleton Murry, *Son of Woman: The Story of D. H. Lawrence* (1931) and *Reminiscences of D. H. Lawrence* (1933); Stephen Potter, *D. H. Lawrence* (1930); Catherine Carswell, *The Savage Pilgrimage, a Narrative of D. H. Lawrence* (1932); Ada Lawrence and G. S. Gelder, *Young Lorenzo, the Early Life of D. H. Lawrence* (1931); Dorothy Brett, *Lawrence and Brett: A Friendship* (1933); Horace Gregory, *Pilgrim of the Apocalypse, a Critical Study of D. H. Lawrence* (1933); Frieda Lawrence, *Not I but the Wind* (1934); E. T. ["Miriam"], *D. H. Lawrence, a Personal Record* (1935); Paul de Reul, *L'Œuvre de D. H. Lawrence* (1938); Knud Merrill, *A Poet and Two Painters: A Memoir of D. H. Lawrence* (1938); Hugh Kingsmill, *D. H. Lawrence* (1938); W. Y. Tindall, *D. H. Lawrence and Susan His Cow* (1939); Baker, x (1939), ch. VIII; Beach, ch. XXX.

a sequel to *The Rainbow,* did not find a publisher till 1921. Meanwhile, in 1919, Lawrence had left England, and for the remainder of his life he was a wanderer, impelled by his sense of the post-war chaos to try to construct a social group round himself but taking with him wherever he went his resentments and his fears. In Italy he wrote *The Lost Girl* (1920), in which he compromised with, or rather concealed, his convictions in order to re-establish a besmirched reputation. *Aaron's Rod* (1922), partly Italian in setting, contains hints of his sympathy with the incipient Fascist movement. Lawrence then lived for a time in Australia. There he wrote *Kangaroo* (1923), an interminable discussion-novel in which the advocacy of the principle of "leadership" is downright and there are violent and obscure expatiations upon a darkly "mystical" concept of God. *The Boy in the Bush* (1924) is a work of collaboration. There followed the sojourn in Taos, New Mexico, of which members of Lawrence's coterie have given contradictory accounts. In Mexico he wrote *The Plumed Serpent* (1926), an occult and macabre, exotic and hysterical book, which contains the fullest and most fantastic expression of his awareness of "old life-modes," his sense of modern man's heritage from primitive ancestors. It is, however, impossible to take quite seriously the narrative of the upsurging of the old soul of Mexico through the crust of Spanish civilization and its triumph in a new Fascist order which would revive the brutal horrors of the old Mexican religion. Yet there is here something premonitory of the Nazi cult of the old Germanic pantheon. Lawrence's defiant repudiation of modern society now goaded him to write the notorious novel, *Lady Chatterley's Lover* (1929). The bitter indictment of the hypocrisies of civilization shows Lawrence at his strongest; the calculated improprieties are forcibly-feeble and the phallic obsession which led alike to the book's suppression and its surreptitious success is of a naked shamelessness which would be ridiculous were it not a painful symptom of exacerbated nerves. *The Virgin and the Gipsy* (1930) repeats the theme of the woman of higher social rank who finds emotional satisfaction in the embraces of a man of brutish primitiveness. Lawrence published many short stories. The requirements of magazine publication kept a rein upon his tendency to divagate and his urge to shock, and many of these tales have a raciness and even a humor that the full-length novels do not display. Over these things, as over his poems and travel books, we must pass without comment. The last journey was to the French Riviera where he died of tuberculosis.

The testimony of those who knew Lawrence confirms the impression made by his books of a powerful, ruthlessly dominating personality. He was a genius, albeit an ill-directed genius. He attempted to harmonize the intellectual and emotional forces in human nature, yet in exasperated revolt against intellectualism he overvalued the significance of the primitive and instinctive. "The body is the soul," he said, without ever making clear what he intended by this paradox. Again, he was wont to declare that the flesh is wiser than the intellect—an assertion which students of his own case may be inclined to call in question. He was primarily concerned not with individual characterization or even with broad human types but with the "life-urge" common to all humanity and pulsing throughout the cosmos. With this all-pervading force he sought obscurely to identify himself. In the exposition of his erotic psychology he could descend to vulgar self-exhibitionism, but he could also ascend to the heights of vision. He carried extraordinarily far the analysis of the complexities of modern emotional reactions and responses. The strained metaphors, the violences and incoherencies are due to the effort to achieve an idiom suitable for the exploration of the Unconscious. The chaos of Freudian depths is illuminated by flashes from whirling thunderheads of words. Lawrence's mastery of style is best displayed not in the expositions of his cloudy "mysticism" but in his descriptions of desert and mountain landscape.

Like Lawrence, Aldous Huxley [24] (1894-1963) repudiated contemporary society, in terms, however, not of fury and hatred but of cynical disgust.[25] Earth seemed to him a sterile promontory and the air a foul and pestilent congregation of vapors. This grandson of a great Victorian scientist found the old belief in scientific progress a vain deceit. Life, standardized and mechanized, has been bereft of joy. Endeavor, disinterested or otherwise, leads to frustration. Sensual satisfactions turn to dust and ashes. There is a nostalgic envy of the happy few who hold sincerely to the ancient ways of faith, but religion is mostly a pretense. That aesthetic values are still vital Huxley's essays on the arts prove, but in his novels art, too, is sterile. A Swiftian obsession with stench and filth comes from an indignant realization that romance is an illusion. This bitterly jesting Pilate's pursuit of truth carried him, in his attempt to isolate himself from a society which appalled him, into a sort of pseudo-Hindu quietism. Huxley, as he acknowledged in drawing his own portrait in the character of Philip Quarles in *Point Counter Point,* was not "a congenital novelist" but a thinker using fiction as the vehicle for his ideas. His are "discussion-novels" in which the plot is negligible or non-existent and the action consists in the clash of contrary opinions.[26] As in Peacock's books, the setting is chosen merely

Aldous Huxley

24 See Daiches, ch. xi; Beach, ch. xxxvi. There is no satisfactory full-length criticism of Huxley's work. — Much of Huxley's best writing is in his essays and travel books. Among the former are *Essays New and Old* (1926), *Proper Studies* (1927), and *Holy Face* (1929); and among the latter *Along the Road* (1925), *Jesting Pilate* (1926), and *Beyond the Mexique Bay* (1934). Earlier biographical studies led the way to *Grey Eminence* (1941), a biography of Richelieu's counselor Father Joseph. Into this Huxley introduces his own despairing repudiation of the active life and his advocacy of withdrawal into a *vita negativa.*

25 The cynical, urbane wit of Hector H. Munro ("Saki," 1870-1916) was anticipatory of a dominant mood of the nineteen-twenties. He satirized society from the point of view of aristocratic Toryism in short stories (collected posthumously from half a dozen volumes in 1930). His deft competence has in the long run failed to conceal his shallowness.

26 A significant discussion-novel of slightly earlier date than Huxley's is *South Wind* (1916) by Norman Douglas (1868-1952). The boldness of Douglas's assault upon conventional moral standards is indicative of that disintegration of values of which the period affords so many other signs. Equally indicative is his inability to supply any positive convictions (other than a delight in scholarship and exotic landscape) to take the place of those he ruthlessly discards. Douglas recorded life in southern Italy in *Old Calabria* (1931) and a series of books on Capri (collected in 1930). He also wrote essays, literary criticism, and technical monographs. See H. M. Tomlinson. *Norman Douglas* (1931).

to account for the presence together of a group of intellectual eccentrics, each representative of a point of view. The character of each person is implied in the ideas of which he is the mouthpiece. Huxley's early novels— *Crome Yellow* (1921), *Antic Hay* (1923), and *Those Barren Leaves* (1925), and the short stories in *Limbo* (1920), *Two or Three Graces* (1926), and other volumes have something of Peacock's concise wit; but in the later books, though he retains his method, there is a ponderous elaboration of ideas. *Point Counter Point* (1928) is his best balanced and most representative book. *Brave New World* (1932) is a utopian nightmare of the futility of scientific "progress." If the cynical skepticism of *Eyeless in Gaza* (1936) and the contemptuous satire directed in *After Many a Summer* (1939) against the waste land of materialism and sensuality are fair pictures of the *vita activa,* small wonder that Huxley sought to withdraw into the *vita contemplativa.* The burden of topicality bodes ill for the lasting popularity of these novels, but they will remain valuable as records of a prevailing mood in the dark transition period between the two wars.

Both Lawrence and Huxley are off the path trodden by the experimenters in technique. On that path, parallel with rather than stemming from Joyce, are several women-novelists. Between 1915 and 1938 Dorothy M. Richardson [27] issued *Pilgrimage* in a dozen installments, each with its individual title. When she began this novel Marcel Proust was engaged on his task of reconstructing experience from within the mind of a single individual. Miss Richardson was not influenced by him but was, as it were, aware of his proximity. Henry James had already often depended upon the eye of a single observer of the human conflict. But while James had permitted himself to interpret and explain, Miss Richardson, seeking to identify herself completely with her heroine, does not intrude *in propria persona.* There is never a lapse from the technique of the stream of consciousness—the succession of fleeting images of the external world mingled with thoughts and half-thoughts and shadows of thought attached to the immediate present or moving back and forth in memory. There is the variety, but also the insignificance, of ordinary experience, and the effect is of garrulous, meandering, and objectless fluidity. It is a pity that Miriam, the heroine, is so dull and commonplace a person. Men who doubt whether the record of so much that is tedious and trivial is worth while must leave to women the decision as to whether this study in feminine psychology rings true. *Pilgrimage* has not been widely read, but as an experimenter Miss Richardson has influenced other novelists. One who helped to gain her a hearing was May Sinclair (1879-1946). After winning a success with *The Divine Fire* (1904), a novel traditional in form, Miss Sinclair turned to Freudianism and the stream of consciousness in *Mary Olivier* (1919) and other books. Her touch is lighter than Miss Richardson's and she does not discard the element of plot or detach her subjects wholly from the external world.

Dorothy M. Richardson

May Sinclair

[27] *Pilgrimage* (4v, 1938), with a foreword by the author. — J. C. Powys, *Dorothy M. Richardson* (1931); Beach, ch. xxxi. Professor Beach relates Miss Richardson's work to the poetry of the Imagists.

Virginia Woolf [28] (1882-1941) owed a good deal to the example of *Ulysses* *Virginia* and *Pilgrimage,* but she was without Joyce's amplitude and creative vitality *Woolf* and her range of experimentation, though wider, was on a smaller scale than Miss Richardson's. A first novel, *The Voyage Out* (1915), is fairly conventional in pattern, and the impressive climax is too long in preparation. The short stories or sketches in *Monday and Tuesday* (1921) show her feeling her way towards one of her methods—the method of impressionism. *Jacob's Room* (1922) is not concerned with Jacob's view of the world but with the world's view of Jacob, the hero's portrait being built up from the hinted testimony of friends and strangers. In *Mrs. Dalloway* (1925) the limit of time to a single day and of place to a single city is suggestive of *Ulysses.* The stream of consciousness technique is employed, with this difference that we pass from mind to mind through transitional impressions of environment. When within a personality the movement is back and forth through time, and during the meticulously indicated pauses in time the movement is from one personality to another. The aim is to convey a sense of immediacy, but the effect upon some readers is of a refined remoteness from actuality, a pale, stylized intellectuality. A setting far withdrawn from the busy stir of life is best suited to Mrs. Woolf's method, and for this reason *To the Lighthouse* (1927) is the most successful of her novels. The interrelated problems of time and personality are turned to fantastic account in *Orlando* (1929) which, despite its brilliant evocation of periods of the past, is an unconvincing *tour de force. The Waves* (1931), with its incredibly elaborate soliloquies, *The Years* (1933), and *Between the Acts* (1941) are further experiments in pattern and method. The attempt is to rarify life to its quintessence and then enrich that refined distillation with all the resources of elaborately intellectual metaphor. There was an ever-increasing remoteness till at length Mrs. Woolf of her own volition withdrew from life. She had once compared life to "a luminous halo, a semi-transparent envelope surrounding us" and she had conceived it to be the novelist's task to impart to the reader a sense of this "unknown and uncircumscribed spirit." But is not this luminous halo a mist that slips between Mrs. Woolf's fingers as she attempts to apprehend it? [29]

[28] Daughter of Sir Leslie Stephen; married Leonard Woolf (1880-   ), sociologist and journalist. In addition to books mentioned in the text Mrs. Woolf's work includes the critical essays in *The Common Reader* (two series, 1925 and 1932) and in *The Death of the Moth* (1942), and *Flush* (1933), the story of the Brownings from the point of view of Mrs. Browning's pet dog. — E. M. Forster, *Virginia Woolf* (1942); David Daiches, *Virginia Woolf* (1942); Joan Bennett, *Virginia Woolf* (1945); Beach, pp. 428-432, 490-493; Daiches, ch. x.

[29] If promise and not performance were the historian's criterion, Katherine Mansfield (pseudonym for Kathleen Beauchamp) (1888-1923) would be a major figure. She wrote no full-length novel. *In a German Pension* (1911), *Bliss* (1920), and *The Garden Party* contain short stories in the impressionistic manner of Chekhov. Plot counts for very little. Delicate observation is recorded with exquisite precision of phrase and the subtlest choice of detail. The tensity of emotion and clarity of insight into character are remarkable. On her art and intentions see her *Journal* (1927) and *Letters* (2v, 1928), both edited by her husband, J. Middleton Murry. See also R. E. Mantz and J. M. Murry, *The Life of Katherine Mansfield* (1933).

V

E. F.
Benson
Several novelists of distinguished talent stand apart from the experimenters in technique who have attracted most critical attention. As these writers do not fall into obvious categories it is best to consider them in chronological order. Edward Frederick Benson (1867-1940) created a sensation with his first novel, *Dodo* (1893), which was followed by many other lightly satirical novels of different strata of society. Among them the "Lucia"

Montague
books and *Paying Guests* (1929) may be mentioned. Benson also wrote stories of the supernatural. Charles Edward Montague (1867-1928), a first-rate journalist, was a novelist rather by taking thought than by native endowment. From his experiences in the First World War he drew the material for *Disenchantment* (1922) and *Rough Justice* (1926), the latter containing an unforgettable account of a soldier's cowardice. In these books there is little of the bitter revulsion from warfare which was a dominant note of many "war novels." Some of these, written by poets, receive notice in the next chapter. Montague's *Right Off the Map* (1927) is a disillusioned liberal's satiric fantasy of international relations. His literary criticism is of

Tomlinson
value, especially *A Writer's Notes on His Trade* (1930). Henry Major Tomlinson (1873-1958), journalist, critic, and author of books of travel of which *The Sea and the Jungle* (1912) is the best known, won a place among novelists with his *Galleon's Reach* (1927), a romance of the Far East which calls Conrad to mind, and *All Our Yesterdays* (1930), a story notable for its indictment of the civilization which culminated in catastrophe. An admirable stylist, Tomlinson was as individualistic in his choice of imagery as in his love of obscure, exotic, far-off places. Often he blended fiction with personal experience, especially in the world of docks and ships; *London*

Beresford
River (1921) and similar books are filled with the *genius loci*. The social disintegration which Gissing had predicted is mirrored in the novels of John Davys Beresford (1873-1947). His realism and gift for psychological analysis have fullest scope in the *Jacob Stahl* trilogy (1911-1915). A second novel in sequence is made up of *The Old People* (1931), *The Middle Generation* (1932), and *The Young People* (1933). Beresford also wrote novels and short stories in lighter vein. There is said to be much autobiography in his fiction.

Maugham
William Somerset Maugham [30] (1874-1965) began his career as a conscious or unconscious disciple of Gissing. *Liza of Lambeth* (1897) and other early books offered a promise that was impressively fulfilled in the powerful, partly autobiographical novel, *Of Human Bondage* (1915), which in the opinion of many good judges remains his best book. *The Moon and Sixpence* (1919) is based upon the career of the painter Gauguin, and *Cakes and Ale* (1930) upon gossip about Hardy's private life. Other novels, earlier

---

[30] C. S. McIver, *William Somerset Maugham, a Study of Technique and Literary Sources* (Philadelphia, 1936); R. H. Ward, *William Somerset Maugham* (1937); R. A. Cordell, *W. Somerset Maugham* (1937). On Maugham's plays see above, ch. xxxviii.

and later in date, must be passed over without mention. Half a dozen volumes of short stories are reprinted in *Altogether* (1934). In parts of his work the influence of Maupassant is paramount and there is often a strain of exoticism. A favorite setting is the tropics, as in the famous short story, *Rain*. In general Maugham's tales exhibit technical expertness rather than depth of feeling; in fact, the restraint imposed upon his own emotions sometimes gives the effect of callousness. He likewise wrote volumes of impressions, opinions, and recollections of art, letters, peoples, and countries. *The Summing Up* (1938) contains illuminating accounts of his intentions and ideals in fiction and the drama.

The most widely read novel of Edward Morgan Forster [31] (1879-   ) is *A Passage to India* (1924); its fame is in part due to considerations adventitious to its high merits in style, pattern, characterization, and atmosphere. Of his four other novels, all of earlier date, *A Room with a View* (1908), which is set in part in Italy, and *Howards End* (1910), which is on an ampler scale, may be mentioned. Veins of quietism and symbolism run through Forster's books with a constantly recurring contrast between the inner and the outer life. A peculiar characteristic is the sudden interruption of delicate psychological analysis with episodes of melodramatic violence. A debt to Henry James is apparent, but also, curiously crossed with it, a debt to Gissing. Resemblances to the novels of D. H. Lawrence have often been remarked upon, and it is indeed likely that Forster influenced Lawrence. The subtlety but also the limitations of his opinions on the art of fiction are shown in his *Aspects of the Novel* (1927). His essays and a few short stories afford small compensation for the abrupt and as yet unexplained cessation of novel-writing in early middle life.

Forster

Of younger writers only a few can be singled out for mention. Compton Mackenzie (1883-   ) never fulfilled the promise of his first success, *Sinister Street* (1913-1914), though he wrote a vast number of other novels. The book just named is memorable for its descriptions of life at Oxford and its narrative of a conversion to Roman Catholicism. Ralph Hale Mottram (1883-   ) is the author of *The Spanish Farm Trilogy* (1924-1926) which is of lasting value for its rendering of the spiritual atmosphere of Europe at the close of the First World War. Frank Swinnerton (1884-   ), a disciple of Gissing, has dealt in the main with lower middle-class urban society. *Nocturne* (1917), *Young Felix* (1923), *The Georgian House* (1932), and a dozen other novels have generally to do with the seamy side of city life, viewed, however, with more of Arnold Bennett's cheerfulness than of Gissing's gloom. Swinnerton's candid and amusing impressions, *The Georgian Literary Scene* (1934), may be recommended to students of the period. The contemporary popularity of the novels of Sir Hugh Walpole (1884-1941) does not seem likely to endure. Out of his experiences of war in Russia came *The Dark Forest* (1916) and *The Secret City* (1919) in

Compton Mackenzie

Mottram

Swinner-ton

Hugh Walpole

[31] Rose Macaulay, *The Writings of E. M. Forster* (1938); Lionel Trilling, *E. M. Forster* (1943).

which are strains of "mysticism" obviously foreign to his temperament. Equally foreign, though deftly accomplished, are the stories of mystery and horror,[32] *Portrait of a Man with Red Hair* (1925) and *Above the Dark Circus* (1931). Walpole was more sincere in tales of ecclesiastical society suggestive of Trollope and in romances that owe something to Scott. His most ambitious, not to say pretentious, efforts went into the "Herries" series: *Rogue Herries* (1930), *Judith Paris* (1931), *The Fortress* (1932), and *Vanessa* (1933). He was a master of smoothly flowing narrative, but he carried to great lengths analyses of character which give the effect of being somewhat beyond his intellectual capacity. Much more likely to be permanently remembered though for the time being neglected by critics who are obsessed with problems of technique are the best novels of Francis Brett Young (1884-1954). Among these some readers give their suffrage to *Cold Harbour* (1924), others to *Portrait of Clare* (1927). The grim terror of the one contrasts with the graciousness of the other. Young always ranged widely in settings, themes, and moods. Many of his stories take place in the border-country between England and Wales; others in ports; others at sea or in countries oversea. A devotion to beauty expressed in his early novels and in his study of Robert Bridges (1914) later yielded place to attacks upon "progress," sometimes angry or complaining, sometimes lightly satirical. The prediction may be ventured that when the reappraisal of this accomplished stylist and incisive commentator upon society is made—it is long overdue—Young will be accorded a high rank among the novelists of his generation.

F. B.
Young

    With two women we close this chronological survey. Rose Macaulay (who seems to have kept secret the date of her birth) portrayed the generation between the wars with an acidulous wit and an alert intellectualism which cover but do not conceal her profound pessimism. Among her many novels, *Potterism* (1920), a satire on middle-class values, *Dangerous Ages* (1921), analysing the motives and standards of the modern "career-woman," and *Told by an Idiot* (1923) are still the best. Others books are in the field of the historical novel, or are exotic in setting, or are merely topical. She also wrote literary criticism and verse. The most impressive work of Rebecca West (1892-   ) has been done outside fiction, though she rates as a considerable novelist by virtue especially of *The Judge* (1922). Her hard, clear intelligence, of the sort which men like to call "masculine," has been largely directed to the elucidation of political and social problems;

Rose
Macaulay

Rebecca
West

---

[32] For really excellent tales of mystery and the supernatural we must turn to three older writers. The best ghost-stories of the period were written by the great scholar Montague Rhodes James (1862-1936); he published three series of them (1904, 1911, 1919). William W. Jacobs (1863-1943) specialized in the humors and human oddities of London dock-land in short stories collected in three "omnibus" volumes (1931-1934); but his most powerful work has been done in tales on the borderland of the supernatural, as in the truly horrifying story, *The Monkey's Paw*. Algernon Blackwood (1869-1951) explored the same borderland and beyond, achieving effects of genuine spiritual terror in *The Empty House* (1906), *The Listener* (1907), and other stories of the occult and the supernatural of which the best are collected in *The Willows and Other Queer Tales* (1932).

and in her comments upon events and personalities she is by turns bantering, satiric, serious, and impassioned. *Black Lamb and Gray Falcon* (1942), an account of a visit to Jugoslavia, with divagations anthropological, cultural, literary, philosophical, and emotional, is her most massive work and is likely to be long remembered.

XLI
Poetry in the Twentieth Century

Tradition and Innovation

In essaying a sketch of the progress of English poetry from the beginning of the present century to the outbreak of the Second World War, the historian must select from among the almost innumerable poets of the period.[1] A catalogue of names would be unprofitable, and a mere chronological survey would bring together writers who have nothing but birth-years in common with one another. This chapter begins with poets in whom the Victorian tradition was still alive, and proceeds through the era of experimentation that became apparent about 1910 to the innovators who captured critical attention during the period between the two wars. The rough classifications "traditionalists" and "experimenters" are employed without prejudice. The poet who works within the frame of a great tradition is entitled to consideration provided he has something to say. On the other hand, it is possible to overestimate the significance of innovations.

There was no abrupt break in the continuity of English poetry during, or immediately after, the war of 1914-1918. The war did not initiate change, though it probably hastened it. Actually, one of the most remarkable of the innovators, Father Hopkins, had died as long ago as 1889, though the delay in publishing his *Poems* (1918) postponed the impact of his experiments in style, syntax, prosody, and imagery. Of other poets already noticed in this history several who lived far down into this century endeavored, each in his own way, to liberate poetry from late-Victorian debasement, reinvigorating the idiom and enlarging and refreshing the vocabulary. The great variety of readers, receptive, as usual, to the familiar rather than to the strange, supported the traditionalists, while the innovators only gradually roused interest. Even so, that interest has been generally limited to circles of "intellectuals." A remarkable phenomenon in English literary history between 1918 and 1939 is the alienation of poets who have been competent masters of their art from the large public consciousness.

[1] H. P. Collins, *Modern Poetry* (1925); E. L. Davison, *Some Modern Poets* (1928); Charles Williams, *Poetry at Present* (1930); R. L. Mégroz, *Modern English Poetry, 1882-1932* (1933); Geoffrey Bullough, *The Trend of Modern Poetry* (1934); Cornelius Weygandt, *The Time of Yeats* (1937); F. R. Leavis, *New Bearings in English Poetry* (1938); Cleanth Brooks, *Modern Poetry and the Tradition* (1939); H. W. Wells, *New Poets from Old: A Study in Literary Genetics* (1940); David Daiches, *Poetry and the Modern World* (1940); J. G. Southworth, *Sowing the Spring: Studies in British Poets from Hopkins to MacNeice* (1940); H. V. Routh, *English Literature and Ideas in the Twentieth Century* (1945).

I

The typical traditionalist of the period was Alfred Noyes [2] (1880-1958) whose poetry was never touched by the theories and experiments of his *Noyes* contemporaries. His fluently melodious *Poems* (1904), in which were echoes of Tennyson, Swinburne, Kipling, and the old ballads, won him a large audience and some of his pieces found their way promptly into the repertories for school recitations. This is no reason for despising them provided they are good of their kind; and *The Barrel-Organ* and *The Highwayman* are good of their kind. But there was something factitious about Noyes's Orientalism in *The Flower of Old Japan* (1903), his "gramerye" in *The Forest of Wild Thyme* (1905), his medievalism in the drama *Robin Hood* (1911), and his Elizabethanism in the epic poem *Drake* (1906-1908) and in *Tales of the Mermaid Tavern* (1913). The trilogy of *The Torch-Bearers* (1922-1930), a poem of epical proportions on man's achievements in invention and discovery, exhibits Noyes beyond his depth though not beyond an audience that liked poetry to be instructive. Another poet carrying on the late romantic mood and idiom was Herbert Trench [3] (1865-1923) who *Trench* was attracted to classical and Celtic themes, retained the Victorian love of Italy, and even in his war poems, such as the *Requiem of Archangels for the World,* relied upon a derivative style. Richard Middleton [4] (1889-1911), *Middleton* whose death by his own hand seems a pathetically belated *fin de siècle* gesture, carried into the pre-war years a pseudo-Swinburnian floridness of style and a passionately "pagan" outlook upon life not unlike the early work of Rupert Brooke. The longevity of established modes is further illustrated in the poetry of Humbert Wolfe (1885-1940). He, too, depended *Wolfe* upon a Swinburnian facility and intricacy of rhythm and rime. In *Kensington Gardens* (1924), *The Unknown Goddess* (1925), and other volumes this virtuoso accomplished a semblance of freshness by the skill with which he played variations upon old themes. There is an elaborate patterning in his formerly much-praised *Requiem* (1927) on the "Losers" and "Winners" of the world. That he was not wholly out of accord with the temper of post-war England is shown by *Lampoons* (1925) and *News of the Devil* (1926), and it is a pity that he did not exercise more freely his gift for satire.

Robert Laurence Binyon [5] (1869-1943) made no radical break with tra- *Binyon* ditional forms, but he experimented in elaborate stanzas and played individualized variations upon inherited melodies. His poetry bears the impress of a cosmopolitan culture. The narratives and dramas are less likely to be remembered than some of his lyrical and elegiac poetry. Representative volumes are *London Visions* (1896), *Porphyrion* (1898), *Odes* (1901), *The*

---

[2] *Collected Poems* (2v, 1928) and later volumes; also various volumes of prose, chiefly critical.

[3] *Collected Poems* (3v, 1924); *Selected Poems,* ed. H. Williams (1924).

[4] Middleton published only in periodicals; his verse was collected posthumously in *Poems and Songs,* two series (1912 and 1913).

[5] *Collected Poems* (2v, 1931); *Selected Poems* (1922). The best study of Binyon's poetry is in J. G. Southworth, *Sowing the Spring,* pp. 46-63.

Secret (1920), and *The Sirens* (1924). Binyon always evinced an aware-ness of contemporary sentiment, even when, as often, he did not share it. *For the Fallen*, the best-known of his war poems collected in *The Four Years* (1919), though it went to the heart of England as did few poems of the time, is not really typical of Binyon's response to the world calamity. The note usually struck is that war must be accepted as a temporary deflec-tion from the main current of life. In an age of discouragement he offered the bracing doctrine of regeneration through contact with the common life of man. In a restrained style he advocated "excess"—but an excess of kind-ness, mercy, and courage. The heart, he declared, should "overbrim."

De la Mare

The poetry of Walter de la Mare [6] (1873-1956) shows how a strong individuality, intensity of feeling, and an exquisite sense of style may revitalize old romantic themes without recourse to any novelty of technique. De la Mare was accused of being an "escapist" from real life—but what is called "reality" was never his home; and it has been said that his poetry can be appreciated by the half-awake intelligence—but that is precisely the mental state he required for its reception. The familiar touched with mystery has been a note often sounded since the onset of romanticism; in De la Mare, from his earliest work to *Alone* (1927) and *The Fleeting* (1933), it was dominant. While cautioning himself against the instinct to "lure his fantasy to its utmost scope," he was always "amorous of the far" and his conscience indicted his mind less "for idle days than of which he wrote in *Songs for Children* (1902) and *Peacock-Pie* (1913); are close to one another, children are at home in those parts of his world of which he writes in *Songs for Children* (1902) and *Peacock-Pie* (1913); but other parts, where ghosts and demons walk beneath a waning moon, are morbid, terrible, and dreadful. *The Listeners* (1912), one of his most famous poems, cannot be read without a shudder; and there is a sense of awe imparted by the Ozymandias-like poem, *The Image*, De la Mare could be genial, as in *Jenny Wren* or *Titmouse*; but generally he suggests the instability of the world, and there is an underlying pessimism as he gropes his way through the cosmic mystery. Sometimes the theme is so vague that the reader is left in doubt as to the poet's intentions—a state of mind which it was his intention to induce. Of De la Mare's prose stories *Henry Brocken* (1904) is a literary fantasy that does not quite succeed, and *Memoirs of a Midget* (1921), apart from the implicit symbolism, is morbid to excess. His delight in curious lore is shown in *Desert Islands and Robinson Crusoe* (1930) and he threw more light upon his strange and fascinating mind in *Pleasures and Speculations* (1940).

T. Sturge Moore

Thomas Sturge Moore [7] (1870-1944), engraver, art critic, and aesthetician, was one of the first modern poets to attempt to reform poetic diction. This independence in style is a curious feature of the work of one who was

---

[6] *Collected Poems* (1942); *Poems for Children* (1930). — R. L. Mégroz, *Walter de la Mare, a Biographical and Critical Study* (1924); Forrest Reid, *Walter de la Mare, a Critical Study* (1929).

[7] *Poems*, collected edition (4v, 1931-1933); *Selected Poems* (1934).

peculiarly faithful to classical and mythological themes, as in *Danaë* (1903), and later poems on Pan, Theseus and Medea, the Centaurs, and the Amazons. Of his dramas *Aphrodite against Artemis* (1901) and *Tragic Mothers* (1920) are the most impressive; but the dramatic form seems not really congenial to him. His thought is often recalcitrant to expression, as in the obscurely powerful *Judas* (1923). There is an austerity and rugged grandeur about Sturge Moore's best work that is suggestive of Doughty, though the stylistic eccentricities are less extreme. He expounded his aesthetic in various prose works, notably *Life and Art* (1910) and *Armour for Aphrodite* (1929).

Gordon Bottomley [8] (1874-1948) likewise sought to redeem the language *Bottomley* of poetry from sweetness and sentimentality. How far he had to go before he mastered his mature style is shown by the lavish sensuousness of his early *Poems at White Nights* (1899). The contrast is extreme in the two series of *Chambers of Imagery* (1907 and 1912), *A Vision of Giorgione* (1910), and *Poems of Thirty Years* (1925). Here, as in the dramatic poems mentioned in an earlier chapter, there is a strength of utterance suggestive of, and perhaps imitated from, the Jacobean dramatists. There is a closely knit texture of thought and rhythm and an exploitation of themes of weirdness and horror with a violence that sometimes stuns and sometimes merely deafens the reader. Like other contemporary poets Bottomley often wrote on rural subjects, and these pieces are occasionally meditations upon those "nameless men" of the far past who fashioned what are now prehistoric antiquities. Bottomley led a secluded life, but that he was not unaware of contemporary stirrings in the social order is evident from various poems, notably *To Iron-Founders and Others.* Somewhat resembling Bottomley's is the poetry of Lascelles Abercrombie [9] (1881-1938), but though *Abercrom-* often gnarled and contorted, its stern thoughtfulness is without Bottomley's *bie* violence. Abercrombie did not attempt to sever himself completely from the Victorian tradition; there are, in fact, many signs of Browning's influence upon him. But he offers yet another example of the effort to rescue style from the languor of the "Decadents." He made frequent use of the dialogue form; and *Emblems of Love* (1912), "designed in several discourses," connect closely with his verse-plays. Of the latter *The Sale of Saint Thomas* (published in part in 1911 but not entire till 1930) is the most memorable. Remarkable, too, is *The End of the World*—one of *Four Short Plays* (1922)—where there is comedy as well as grimness in the portrayal of the superstition-ridden yokels. Abercrombie, however, was seldom attracted to comic situations. He was a master of horror and dread, though he sometimes descended to the lurid and condescended to the supernatural. His reputation was academic rather than popular, and his hold upon the intellectuals was strengthened by his work in criticism and aesthetics. *An Essay towards a Theory of Art* (1922), *The Idea of Great Poetry* (1925), *Romanticism* (1926), and *Principles of Literary Criticism* (1932) are weighty professorial pronouncements.

[8] On Bottomley's plays see ch. xxxviii, above.
[9] *Poems,* Oxford Edition (1930).

Gibson

Wilfred Wilson Gibson [10] (1878-1962) passed a long apprenticeship to Tennysonian sweetness and Swinburnian passion before discovering his proper subjects in the lives of poor and humble folk—fishermen, track-walkers, charwomen, industrial workers, a drover lost in the snow, a miner lost underground. These people are often of his native Northumberland, and occasionally he employed dialect. To this extent he was a regionalist, and he was obviously close to the naturalists in prose fiction. In reading his poetry George Crabbe comes to mind, though the resemblance has been denied on the ground that whereas Crabbe is diffuse Gibson's best effects are of an energetic condensation. In his use of the dramatic monologue he is suggestive of Browning. His most powerful poems are in *Daily Bread* (1910), a series of dramatized incidents; *Fires* (1912); *Thoroughfares* (1914); and *Livelihood* (1917), a series of what he called "dramatic reveries" or interior monologues. From narratives such as *The Blind Rower* and dialogues such as *The Operation* he moved on to the plays, *Krindlesyke* (1922) and *Kestrel Edge and Other Plays* (1928). Here, however, he over-extended himself, for he was most effective in incidents lending themselves to restricted treatment. Like various contemporaries, he enlarged the boundaries of poetry by bringing within its purview modern industrial life. His grim realism informs the controlled, ironic bitterness of poems on the war. Gibson was no innovator in technique; his diction is quite commonplace and his versification frequently crude; but these are qualities in keeping with his themes.

Masefield

The rough, stark life of the poor was the subject of the poem that made John Masefield [11] (1878-   ) famous. He had had his own experiences of hardship. Before he came of age there had been three years at sea in the merchant service and two more years of earning a living at odd jobs in and around New York. On his return to England he published *Salt-Water Ballads* (1902). That most of these derive from Kipling, with sailors' chanteys substituted for barrack-room ditties, is plain enough, but in *Sea-Fever* and a few other pieces there is a fresh note. In the proem to this collection Masefield "consecrated" himself to themes of the lowly, the burdened, and the forlorn. Then came *The Everlasting Mercy* (1911), being the confessions of a drunken poacher who is converted to gentleness. The tough subject, set forth in tough language, stood out against the idyllic background of the nature poetry that was the mode of the moment, and the poem made a sensation. Less violent than *The Everlasting Mercy* is *The Widow in the Bye Street* (1912) about a mother who loses her reason after her son is hanged for murder. *The Daffodil Fields* (1913) is another piece of stern realism. The comment of the sociological critics that Masefield is moved not by indignation against the condition of outcasts but by a sense of its picturesqueness is unfair to a poet who is manifestly burdened with the pitiful-

[10] *Collected Poems, 1905-1925* (1926); *Sixty-three Poems* (1926); and later volumes.
[11] *Collected Poems* (1932); *Selected Poems* (1938); and later volumes. — C. H. Simmons, *Bibliography* (1930); W. H. Hamilton, *John Masefield, a Critical Study* (1922); Cecil Biggane, *John Masefield, a Study* (1924); Gilbert Thomas, *John Masefield* (1933). — On Masefield's plays see ch. xxxviii, above.

ness of life, but it is to this extent justified, that the devotee of Beauty, as Masefield declares himself, can face ugliness only by showing how it can be transmuted into the beautiful. Later narrative pieces are less depressing in tone. *Dauber* (1913) contains Masefield's memories of the sea in calm and storm. *Reynard the Fox* (1919) has a prologue describing in a manner intended to resemble Chaucer's the characters who assemble at a meet. The story of the hunt which follows is not important enough to bear the weight of this introduction. *Right Royal* (1920) is about horse-racing; *Enslaved* is a bit of melodramatic orientalism; and *The Wanderer of Liverpool* (1930) is a medley of verse and prose. Only in this last is there a suggestion of some symbolic intent below the surface of the narrative. The crudities and violences (though often deliberate), the lack of insight into character, the colors too thickly laid on, and all the noise and glare of these pieces have deafened and blinded many readers who have consequently missed the quieter tones and subtler shades of Masefield's lyrical and meditative poetry, in *Lollingdon Downs* (1917) and elsewhere. His appointment as poet laureate in 1930 did not meet with the approval of the intellectuals, but it was a deserved recognition of the only poet of the period who had won a nation-wide audience; and to a traditional office it was proper to appoint a traditionalist. Masefield's plays have been considered in an earlier chapter, and space is lacking to do more than mention by title the best of his novels, *Sard Harker* (1924) and *Bird of Dawning* (1933), and the best of his criticism, *Shakespeare* (1911), *Ruskin* (1920), and *Chaucer* (1931). Two other works are in a special category as narratives of tragic heroism: *Gallipoli* (1916) and *The Nine Days' Wonder* (1941), the latter on the evacuation of Dunkirk.

William Henry Davies [12] (1871-1940), peddler, mendicant, and "super- *Davies* tramp," knew what it was to be poor. After rough experiences in the United States he became a poet at the age of thirty-four, and presently a picturesque and patronized figure in London society. Among a score of volumes of poems *Songs of Joy* (1911) and *Raptures* (1918) may be named because their titles convey his peculiar quality. He could be odd or grim, but he had found the secret of happiness in a fresh contact with the natural world of fields and woodlands, flowers, birds, and small four-footed creatures. He jogged merrily along the footpath way of life, a sort of modern improvisatore whose facility often betrayed him into doggerel but whose joy was like Blake's and whose content was like Dekker's. The resemblances were not coincidental, for Davies was steeped in English lyric poetry. His apparent artlessness was in harmony with the more self-conscious simplicities of other poets of the pre-war years, and he became one of them. Like him, but with less fecundity, Ralph Hodgson (1871-1962) sang of his delight in creatures *Hodgson* and the creation. *The Bull* is the best of many poems about animals written at just this time because it does not assimilate animal and human nature

---

[12] *Collected Poems* (1929) and later volumes, including *Poems* (1934). — Thomas Moult, *William H. Davies* (1931).

but recognizes the barriers between. *A Song of Honour* is rapturous in a manner a little too like Christopher Smart's *Song to David*. These poems are both of 1913; in later years Hodgson failed to fulfill their promise. Edward Thomas [13] (1878-1917) is as close to nature as Davies or Hodgson but in a different way. His early essays show an affinity to Richard Jefferies and his attempts at fiction to Hardy. Towards the end of his life he turned to poetry, adopting the pen-name of "Edward Eastaway." He was killed in the battle of Arras. *Poems* (1917) and *Last Poems* (1918) show in their delicately precise observation the influence of contemporary theory and experiment and in their predominantly rural themes the prevailing mood of pre-war poetry; but the peculiar angle of his approach individualizes his subjects in a way that is more easily felt than described. Thomas's literary scholarship was a bond between him and three other poets. John Freeman [14] (1880-1929), an accomplished critic, published about ten volumes of verse between 1909 and 1926, the high point of his reputation being reached in *Poems New and Old* (1920). Sound in craftsmanship and sincere in thought, he was not very original in either. John Drinkwater [15] (1882-1937) profited by his reputation as a dramatist, critic, and biographer to gain a hearing for his nondramatic verse, the bulk of which is much larger than his present fame. Occasionally he tried to be stark and strong in the manner of his friends Gibson and Abercrombie, but generally his poetry is nearer to that of Edward Thomas in its quietness and love of nature. Sir John C. Squire [16] (1884-1958) managed to save from his life as a journalist time enough for a dozen volumes of polished but not very significant serious verse. *Steps to Parnassus* (1913) and *Tricks of the Trade* (1917) are of more lasting interest, for they show, as only good parody can show, the response of a conservative taste to innovation.

James Elroy Flecker [17] (1884-1915), who passed the fruitful years of his life in the Near East, was not so remote from his contemporaries as this geographical factor might indicate, for many of them were "amorous of the far," whether it were Babylon or Cotopaxi. In *The Golden Journey to Samarkand* (1913) and in the formerly overpraised poetic drama *Hassan* (posthumous, 1922) Flecker's object was to evoke the splendor and color of the Orient in a style stript of romantic excess and a mood purged of romantic subjectivity. His masters were the French Parnassians with their

Thomas (margin)
Freeman (margin)
Drink-water (margin)
Squire (margin)
Flecker (margin)

[13] Robert Eckert, *Edward Thomas* (1937).
[14] *Collected Poems* (1928); *Last Poems*, ed. Sir J. C. Squire (1930). Freeman's critical studies include *A Portrait of George Moore* (1922) and *Herman Melville* (1926).
[15] *Collected Poems* (1923); *Summer Harvest: Poems, 1924-1933* (1933). — On Drinkwater's plays see ch. xxxviii, above.
[16] *Poems*, collected edition (1926); *Collected Parodies* (1921). Squire's critical articles, written under the pen-name of "Solomon Eagle," are collected in *Books in General*, three series (1918, 1920, 1921). His play, *Berkeley Square* (1928), written in collaboration with J. L. Balderston, was a success on stage and screen. Squire's monthly journal, *The London Mercury* (1919-1934), patronized new writers provided they were not too radical, but its cautious modernity disguised basic conservatism.
[17] *Collected Poems* (1923); *Collected Prose* (1920); *Letters* (1926); *Letters from Abroad* (1930). — Douglas Goldring, *James Elroy Flecker, an Appreciation* (1922); Geraldine E. Hodgson, *The Life of James Elroy Flecker* (1925).

doctrines of cool objectivity and the statuesque. Today Flecker is a faded figure, yet of interest for his attempt to escape from Victorianism.

II

The half-decade before the First World War was enlivened with new movements in poetry and the other arts. The famous "Futurist" Manifesto issued by the Italian Filippo Tomaso Marinetti dates from 1909; Cubism was a sensation in New York in 1911; Richard Strauss was at the top of his fame; and the Russian Ballet was the rage. That the yeast was working in the post-Victorian dough is evident in much of the poetry we have passed in review; and some of the younger poets were attempting to design new bottles for their new wine. That the period-adjective "Georgian" became current within a year or two of the accession (1910) of George V is an indication of the self-consciousness of the time. *Georgian Poetry,* an anthology edited by Edward Marsh, appeared in 1912; sequels with the same title in 1915, 1917, 1919, and 1922. De la Mare, Davies, and Gibson were represented in the first four of these compilations; other poets appeared less often; a few soon drifted away; and fresh talent was recruited for the later volumes. A few contributors, notably Chesterton on the extreme "right" and D. H. Lawrence on the extreme "left," were strangely out of place in this company. With such a variety of tastes, talents, and points of view, the limits of the group of "Georgian" poets were ill-defined and it is difficult to generalize. In so far as these poets shared a common program, it was an unexcited protest against the meretricious passion of the "Decadents" and against the stylistic flaccidity and lassitude of late-nineteenth-century verse. There was a revulsion from urban life into a sentimentalized rusticity. The prevailing mood was of quiet decorum. The "Georgians" did not extend the boundaries of poetry, and it is obvious today that theirs was not a revolution but a retreat. These generalizations do not apply to some of the contributors to Marsh's anthologies, but they are true of the movement as a whole. One of the poets repeatedly represented in these volumes was Harold Munro [18] (1879-1932). Munro's own verse is of less importance than his management of the "Poetry Bookshop" where poets forgathered to read and discuss their writings, and whence were issued the short-lived *Poetry Review* (1912) and later *The Chapbook* (1919-1921). These were but two of various "little magazines" whose aim was to stimulate interest in poetry and the other arts. Another outlet for new poets was the periodical *Rhythm* (1911-1912), edited by J. Middleton Murry and Katherine Mansfield. Binyon, Gibson, and Davies were among the poets who appeared in its pages. *New Numbers* (1914) was edited, and largely written, by Gibson, Abercrombie, Drinkwater, and Rupert Brooke. Much more radical than any of these publications was *Wheels* of which six annual issues appeared between 1916 and 1921. The moving spirits of *Wheels* were Edith Sitwell and her two brothers,

Georgian Poetry

Harold Munro

Wheels

[18] *Collected Poems* (1933), with memoir by F. S. Flint and introduction by T. S. Eliot.

Sacheverell and Osbert. Their object was to rouse public interest by deliberate eccentricity and aggressive self-advertisement; and in tone and technique their poetry was premonitory of tendencies of the nineteen-twenties. For this reason "the Sitwells" can best be considered when we reach the post-war years.

Imagism Contemporaneous with these magazines and annuals were certain publications in the United States. This it is necessary to note because the Imagist movement of the same years was not limited to English poets but was Anglo-American.[19] As in the case of the "Georgians," the boundaries of the Imagist group were vague, for some writers seceded, others joined up, some were always on the periphery, and in later years most of them found the form with which they had experimented too constricted for their purposes. In the end they went their several ways. Within the limits of the form nothing was accomplished commensurate with the amount of discussion of theories and intentions. In its use of *vers libre* with cadences governed by breath-pauses instead of regular metres following the beat of the metronome, Imagism owed something to Whitman and Henley and much to the French Symbolists; it was also much influenced by tiny poetic forms from Japan. But (though there was some confusion on this point) Imagism was not a matter of prosody; an Imagist poem might have been written in regular metres or even in rime. It aimed at a "hard and dry" clarity and precision in the rendering of natural objects and of ideas, and it was opposed to exuberance, sentiment, and cloudily romantic lushness. The "tree of language" was, as Osbert Sitwell put it, to be pruned of its "dead fruit." The anti-

Hulme romantic opinions of Thomas Ernest Hulme[20] (1883-1917) provided a theoretical basis for Imagism, and the scanty sheaf of what now seem to be his quite insignificant poems exemplified the practice. Five of these (thirty-three lines in all) were first published in 1912 by the American poet Ezra Pound. In the same year some early Imagist poetry was published in America. In 1914 Pound issued *Des Imagistes: An Anthology;* and after he had withdrawn from the movement another American poet, Amy Lowell, brought out three more Imagist anthologies (1915, 1916, 1917). Among the

Flint English members of the group was Frank Stewart Flint[21] (1885-1960) whose one significant volume is *Cadences* (1915). After 1920 Flint aban-

Aldington doned poetry in favor of work as a translator. Richard Aldington[22] (1892-1962) and his wife, the American poet "H. D." (Hilda Doolittle), were the most expert of the Imagists. The exquisite purity, clarity, and restraint of some of "H. D.'s" poems inspired by Greek subjects show Imagism at its finest. Aldington's *Images* (1915), *Images of War* (1919), and *Images of Desire* (1919) are the fruits of his search for new cadences in *vers libre* with precise attention to the exclusion of every word that does not contribute to the presentation of the subject. Later on, Aldington loosened his ties with

[19] Glenn Hughes, *Imagism and the Imagists* (1931).
[20] Michael Roberts, *T. E. Hulme* (1938). Appendix 1 contains Hulme's eight poems.
[21] *In the Net of Stars* (1909); *Cadences* (1915); *Otherworld, Cadences* (1920).
[22] *Collected Poems* (1928); *Poems* (1934).

Imagist theory, developed a talent for satire, and made odd but effective use of colloquialisms in verse. Turning to prose, he wrote short stories and novels. One of the latter, *Death of a Hero* (1929), is a bitter indictment of war. The Imagists did not hold together long; but while the movement lasted it helped to cleanse and discipline poetic diction and cadence, and its indirect influence both on later poets such as T. S. Eliot and upon the impressionistic technique of the stream of consciousness novelists was considerable.

III

The First World War produced little poetry of a high order of excellence. Such poems as *The Spires of Oxford* by Winifred Letts and *In Flanders Fields* by John McCrae were of poignant significance at the time because the poets were experiencing that of which they wrote and their readers that of which they read. After August, 1914, every living poet was to a greater or less extent a "war poet." There were, however, a few young men who formed a more or less homogeneous group; and of these Rupert Brooke [23] (1887- 1915) remains in the general memory as the typical poet of the war, because of his radiant personality and his Byronic death in one of "the isles of Greece." The five war sonnets called *1914* are the best known of all poetic utterances inspired by the conflict. In the nineteen-twenties the reaction following Brooke's tremendous posthumous renown took the form of sneering at the mood in which he had welcomed the coming of war. Had he lived, it is likely that he would have had his own second thoughts on that subject. In fact, in some of his pre-war pieces there is an incipient cynicism which might have developed into something congenial to the mood of post-war disillusionment. Other early poems, such as the still charming *Grantchester,* show the characteristically "Georgian" love of "haunts of ancient peace." Probably a much greater poet was lost when Wilfred Owen [24] (1893-1918) was killed in battle a week before the Armistice. In his poetry Owen moved rapidly from indignant renderings of the horrors of battle (as in *The Disabled* and *Dulce et Decorum*) to elegiac meditations upon the tragedy of youth sacrificed. In the preface to a projected volume which he did not live to publish he wrote: "My subject is War and the Pity of War. The Poetry is in the Pity." His *Anthem for Doomed Youth* and *Strange Meeting* are of lasting value not merely as records of a dominant mood of 1918 but as poetry. Owen's experiments in imagery, half-rime, and consonance suggest that, had he lived, he would have been a leader of the innovators of the nineteen-twenties. Another young poet slain in battle was Francis Led-

The "W< Poets"

Brooke

Owen

[23] *Collected Poems* (1915); *Complete Poems* (1932); *Letters from America* (1916), with a preface by Henry James. Brooke's *John Webster and the Elizabethan Drama* (1916), an undergraduate essay, is of interest as anticipating the taste for Jacobean drama evinced by poets after the war. — E. H. Marsh, *Rupert Brooke, a Memoir* (1918); Walter de la Mare, *Rupert Brooke and the Intellectual Imagination* (1919); Maurice Browne, *Recollections of Rupert Brooke* (1927).

[24] *Poems,* ed. with "notices of his life and work" by Edmund Blunden (1931).

Ledwidge widge [25] (1891-1917). This Irish peasant was torn from the fairies and folklore of which he had written, and he visualized the war as a bad dream against the reality of the rustic Ireland of happier days. In the war poems of

Blunden Edmund Blunden [26] (1896-   ) there is pity, not anger or disgust; the futile strife is contrasted with memories of times of peace. Blunden carried into the war something of the pastoral mood of the "Georgians" and he carried over something of this mood into his poetry of the post-war years. Contrasting with Blunden's quiet pity are the horror and hate and scorn of

Sassoon Siegfried Sassoon [27] (1886-   ). Sassoon's early poems, from about 1906, are acrid satires and parodies that stand out against the decorous "Edwardian" background. In the war his was one of the earliest and most influential expressions of satiric revulsion from the elation of Rupert Brooke. From his own experiences he wrote the brief and bitter poems in *The Old Huntsman* (1917) and *Counter-Attack* (1918) against profiteers and place-hunting politicians and the obscene fiction of military "glory." It is easy to deplore the crude violence of such pieces as *The General* or *Suicide in the Trenches,* but it is also heartless, for Sassoon wrote these aggressive poems with his heart's blood. After the war he continued to publish verse, often under assumed names, generally satiric. His two autobiographies in the guise of semi-fiction, *Memoirs of a Fox-Hunting Man* (1928) and *Memoirs of an Infantry Officer* (1930), the one picturing the old country life of hunting, racing, and cricket, the other a grim narrative of war, present the contrast between what was gone forever and what had taken its place.[28]

Graves His friend Robert Graves [29] (1895-   ) opposed British policy and leadership with equal aggressiveness but less art. After the war Graves satirized and parodied most of his poetic contemporaries in somewhat indiscriminate fashion, and in a dozen volumes published his own abstruse and increasingly "metaphysical" verse. His autobiography, *Good-bye to All That* (1929), which was suppressed in its original form, had a success of notoriety. Two novels re-creating the Rome of the Emperor Claudius were much esteemed in 1934, and later novels are set in seventeenth-century England and prehistoric Greece.

IV

Poetry Between the Two Wars During the period between the two wars the significance of a poet could not be measured on the scale of popularity. It is a question whether poetry became esoteric because the public had abandoned it or whether the public abandoned it because it had become esoteric. Conscious of the political and social chaos caused by the war and its aftermath and of the moral chaos

---

[25] *Complete Poems* (1926). — Another casualty of the war was Charles Hamilton Sorley (1895-1915). His posthumously published *Marlborough and Other Poems* (1916) and *Letters* (1919) give evidence of his bright promise.
[26] *Poems, 1914-1930* (1930); *Undertones of War* (1928). Blunden has done notable work as a critic and biographer especially attached to the Romantic Period.
[27] *War Poems* (1919); *Selected Poems* (1925).
[28] See also *The Weald of Youth* (1942).
[29] *Poems, 1914-1926* (1927) and later volumes.

consequent upon the widespread acceptance of Freudian psychology; repudiating this chaotic world yet reflecting in his work the chaos which disgusted him, the post-war poet claimed to be the voice of "a generation for whom the dissolution of value had in itself a positive value." [30] By the larger public the voice was unheeded, not because there was not sympathy with the point of view but because contemporary novelists such as Aldous Huxley mirrored the scene of moral desolation more clearly. The poet came to feel that he was living in a world hostile to the artist, and realizing that he was no longer popular he had "no incentive to gild his poetry with the stuff of entertainment." [31] "Communication" was enfeebled and often completely interrupted. Poetry became obscure, experimental, irregular, antagonistic to didacticism, indifferent to any social value, the private language of small coteries, with much dependence upon verbal subtleties and patterns of association so complex, unstable, and fleeting as sometimes to become presently incomprehensible to the writers themselves. For some of the critics the interpretation of poetry became a sort of game; one of them has acknowledged the "thrill" experienced in "decoding" modernistic verse. The need was to fashion a new technique in diction and prosody to meet the requirements of the new subject-matter of a changing world. How much of the effort was the exploration of blind alleys and how much the blazing of a highway into the future of English poetry only time can tell. We are still too close to the brilliant and bewildering phenomena to judge dispassionately. Critical pronouncements were, however, clear. An arrogant assumption of authority in matters of taste was a characteristic of the period; personal predilections were mistaken for dogma. From judgments enunciated *ex cathedra* there could be, it was implied, no appeal. The poets and critics of poetry encouraged the widespread skepticism with regard to inherited ideals and established reputations. The great names and achievements in literature were subjected to a fresh valuation. Milton was dethroned in favor of Donne, in whose poetry was found a satisfying and imitable fusion of sensibility and intellectuality. The romantic poets were excommunicated and Dryden and Pope canonized. Into limbo went all the Victorian poets save Hopkins—who was not really Victorian. These "moderns" went in quest of strange gods—John Skelton and Thomas Middleton; Laudian divines; baroque and rococo artists. There was a great display of abstruse learning—in Sanskrit or Provençal or Japanese or what not, ostentation overreaching itself in the Sitwells' poems, and the *Cantos* of the American Ezra Pound, and the notes to T. S. Eliot's *The Waste Land*. The capriciousness of taste during these unstable years was astonishing. Thus, T. S. Eliot placed a vulgar little ditty in one of Dryden's plays on a par with the final chorus in Shelley's *Hellas,* and pronouncing *Hamlet* "a failure as a work of art" declared that *Coriolanus* was Shakespeare's greatest play. Another arbiter of taste said that Father Hopkins' *The Windhover* was the

---

[30] T. S. Eliot, writing of Marcel Proust, in *The Criterion*, IV (1926). 752-753.
[31] C. Day Lewis, *Revolution in Writing* (1934), p. 34.

greatest of all English poems. Such absurdities had no effect upon sound literary scholarship, but scholarship must notice them because they are symptomatic of the time. Adrift from old moorings, there were sensitive spirits who sought safe anchorages in some strong principle of authority. In this quest of "a help and stay secure" there was something touching; and equally touching at this distance of time seems the cynical repudiation of all standards, which was another expression of the *Zeitgeist.*

Satire

Satiric poetry, dormant since Byron's time, expressed the prevailing sense of the fatuousness and futility of post-war life. We have already glanced at the satiric elements in the later poetry of Aldington, Sassoon, and Wolfe. But scorn and anger whose roots were very deep generally wasted itself upon the agreeable task of breaking butterflies. Roy Campbell (1902-   ), who had exhibited an exuberance of imagery in *The Flaming Terrapin* (1924) and other volumes of verse, chastised in *The Georgiad* (1931) the pre-war poets and the social basis of their point of view, while Osbert Sitwell, in *The Jolly Old Squire* (1922), expended a lot of ammunition upon *The London Mercury,* its editor, and its group of poets. Little of this satiric verse is likely to survive, but that it was produced is of interest to the historian because it helps to explain the early poetry of T. S. Eliot and the writings and attitudes of the Sitwells.

Roy Campbell

The Sitwells

The Sitwell trio—Edith (1887-1964), Sir Osbert (1892-   ), and Sacheverell (1897-   )—have their different individual qualities, Edith being the most caustic, Osbert the most robust, and Sacheverell the most learned; but they have worked harmoniously and may be considered together.[32] Reared in an aristocratic tradition of wealth, leisure, and culture, they have delighted to bait the reviewers and *épater la bourgeoisie* with a showy clowning and self-exhibitionism that disguise a fundamental seriousness and sadness. From the Philistinism they abhor they have sought an escape into the past. Their eclecticism is wide-ranging, but their favorite period has been that of the baroque and the rococo. Their poetry draws imagery and allusion from the refined artificiality of the *commedia dell' arte,* the opera, and the ballet; from Claude and Poussin; from periwigs and lacquers and chinoiserie and all the pleasing extravagances of Augustanism. Allusions remote in origin from one another are patterned into strange mosaics; but all this museum bric-à-brac is assimilated into modern idioms and themes, and Edith's verse in particular was influenced by the new rhythms of contemporary music. With her brother Osbert she published *Twentieth Century Harlequinade and Other Poems* (1916), and afterwards, singly, *Façade* (1922), *Elegy on Dead Fashion* (1926), *Five Variations on a Theme* (1933), and other and later volumes. Beneath the glitter and artificiality of her verse there is the pathos of the fleetingness of youth and a haunting fear of old age and death. Osbert Sitwell's poetry is generally satiric. He is less learnedly allusive than

---

[32] Edith Sitwell, *Collected Poems* (1930) and later volumes; Osbert Sitwell, *Collected Satires and Poems* (1931). There is no collected edition of Sacheverell Sitwell's poems. See Sir Osbert Sitwell, *Left Hand, Right Hand!* (1944) for the family background. This autobiography is continued in *The Scarlet Tree* (1946), and three later volumes.

she, and, unlike her, he does not hold the modern world at arm's length, for he wants to hit it hard. More notable than his poetry is his novel, *Miracle on Sinai* (1933), a *roman à clef*. Sacheverell Sitwell's most memorable poem is the as yet unfinished *Doctor Donne and Gargantua* (1921-1930), which, beginning with the statement of a moral problem, modulates into a pastoral ballet. The best introduction to the poetry of this remarkable trio is their critical work in literature and the fine arts. Edith's biography of Alexander Pope (1930) is, notwithstanding its extravagance, a valuable corrective to Victorian denigration of that master. Her three anthologies—Augustan, Romantic, and Victorian—entitled *The Pleasures of Poetry* (1930-1932) illuminate her tastes. *The English Eccentrics* (1933) is a witty piece of literary and antiquarian research. Osbert Sitwell's *Discursions on Travel, Art, and Life* (1925) and *Winters of Content* (1932) have opened the eyes of many tourists to the charms and glories of South Italian baroque art. Sacheverell Sitwell's prose is more voluminous and even more learned. Besides lesser travel books, there are the three influential studies of the baroque—Southern (1924), German (1927), and Spanish (1931); the study of medieval life, art, and thought entitled *The Gothick North* (1929); and the intricately erudite phantasmagoria, *Splendours and Miseries* (1943). A reading of their prose confirms the impression made by their poetry, that their delight in a sophisticated culture, their fastidious eclecticism, and their frivolousness are grounded upon despair of the modern world. The curtain of their persiflage muffles this note but does not render it inaudible.

The most famous and influential poet of the post-war period was *T. S.* Thomas Stearns Eliot[33] (1888-1965), who, born in America, embraced *Eliot* English citizenship in 1927. The story of his progress from disdainful desperation to spiritual peace within the Anglican fold can be traced with such precision in his poetry that almost it appears to have been patterned beforehand. There may seem to be nothing in common between the creator of Prufrock, Burbank, Bleistein, and Sweeney and the theologian who was a mainstay of the Malvern Conference, but it is possible to follow each step along this pilgrim road. The journey starts with the poems collected in *Prufrock and Other Observations* (1917), *Ara Vos Prec* (1919), and *Poems* (1920). In many of these the barrenness of the present is contrasted with the fruitfulness of the past. There is an apparent casualness in weaving together banal modern allusions and literary references which widen the vista and embrace tradition. With a boldness that at once attracted attention, imagery was drawn from things hitherto regarded as "unpoetic"—coffee-spoons, and trouser-cuffs, and an etherized patient; but recourse was also had to allusive quotations that demanded for their comprehension a certain amount of specialized scholarship. In style the modern and the traditional were fused into a new synthesis: on the one hand, there is an indebtedness

[33] *Collected Poems, 1909-1935* (1936) and later volumes; *Selected Essays* (1932); *Essays Ancient and Modern* (1936). — H. R. Williamson, *The Poetry of T. S. Eliot* (1932); F. O. Matthiessen, *The Achievement of T. S. Eliot* (1935); G. W. Foster, "The Archetypal Imagery of T. S. Eliot," *PMLA*, LX (1945). 567-585.

to Ezra Pound and the Imagists and to certain French poets, particularly Tristan Corbière and Jules Laforgue; and on the other, there is the use of simple, inherited verse forms, especially the quatrain, and blank verse modeled upon that of Webster and Middleton. The contemporary is set in the frame of a long tradition, for Eliot's is the head upon which all the ends of the world are come, and his eyelids are a little weary. In a bare, dry, satiric tone he makes his statements without qualification, expressing with seeming flippancy his contempt for vulgarity. Modern types are characterized, or rather caricatured, in such poems as the *Portrait of a Lady;* and the vulgarity of *l'homme sensuel moyen* is exposed in the poems on Prufrock, Sweeney, and the tourists in Venice. Eliot's early success was not the reward of his occasional profundities but of his witty and blasé unmasking of shallowness. His essential qualities of austerity and precision in the use of words, of novelty in rhythms and cadences, and of intensity of observation were present in these first poems. But already there was an attempt to generalize about life on the basis of a narrow, academic, almost cloistered existence.

The
Waste
Land

    The poem *Gerontion*—"thoughts of a dry brain in a dry season"—is the connecting link between the early poems and *The Waste Land* (1922). This most famous of modern poems is not merely, as is sometimes said, a picture of the spiritual and moral vacuity of the post-war period. It had, indeed, its contemporary significance, but as always in Eliot's writings, the contemporary is bound to the past in a thousand ways. The present fades into the past and the past into the present. The remote is near. The "Waste Land" is the fallen nature of humanity. The rôle of the prophet Tiresias as the focus of the present and the past is central to an understanding of the poem. Alternately the horizon expands and contracts in a phantasmagoria resembling some of the effects accomplished by James Joyce. Everyone knows that the poem is based upon Jessie L. Weston's *From Ritual to Romance,* a monograph relating the Grail legend to the fertility cults of Tammuz and Adonis. There is consequently much sexual symbolism. Other images are taken from *The Golden Bough.* But this anthropological lumber is incompletely assimilated, and chips and splinters strew the footnotes. With all this are interwoven allusions to Dante, Buddhism, the Jacobean dramatists, and much else. Cleopatra and Dido, Tristan and Isolde, Queen Elizabeth and Leicester, Spenser, Goldsmith, Saint Augustine, and the Buddha —these and other figures loom dimly through the chaos. The figure of the Vegetation God is dominant, ranging in his Protean manifestations from the Crucified Jesus to the Hanged Man of the Tarot cards. Eliot realized that "communication" with the reader was incomplete and he attached notes which leave most matters unexplained. *The Waste Land* is not an artistic entity since even the attempt to grasp its meaning leads us to something outside itself. It has been held that this is not merely a poem of despair of the present but of hope and promise for the future, since at the close the thunder speaks, foretelling the coming of the life-giving rain. But no rain falls. The same mood is continued in *The Hollow Men* (1925), a picture of the "inert resignation" of those who breathe the small, dry air of modern spiritual emptiness. The change came in *Ash-Wednesday* (1930) of which the theme is the search for peace found in humble and quiet submission to God's Will. This is a poem not of Easter joy but of the beginning of the penitential season. The mystic vision is not attained, but there is the record of the steps along the mystic way. Depending upon a great tradition of Dantesque and liturgical imagery, *Ash-Wednesday* is comparatively easy to understand and loses nothing for being comprehensible. "Intellect," as Eliot says of Donne, "is at the tip of the senses"; and the most beautiful part of the poem is found in the sensuous loveliness of the evocation of the New England coast. But the impression that remains is of an intellectual effort to find faith rather than of a spiritual conviction surging from within. *(margin: Ash-Wednesday)*

The poems of the following decade show for the most part an increasing hardness and thinness of manner, with rhythms often scarcely distinguishable from prose. *Sweeney Agonistes* (1932) marks a reversion to the early mood of satiric revulsion from modern vulgarity. In *The Rock* (1934) the words only are Eliot's, the scenario of this ecclesiastical pageant having been supplied by someone else. It contains interesting experiments in rhythms and the characteristic juxtaposition of the exalted and the commonplace. *Murder in the Cathedral* (1935), a drama on Thomas à Becket, has as much significance for the dogmatist and moralist as for the student of drama. The sequence collectively entitled *Four Quartets,* beginning with *Burnt Norton* (written in 1935 though not published till 1939) and continuing through *East Coker* (1940) and *The Dry Salvages* (1941) to its culmination in *Little Gidding* (1942), brings together the intricacies of modern technique and imagery and the simplicities of traditional lyric measures. In the austere asceticism and confident dogmatism of these poems there is an impressive restatement of Christian belief in terms of contemporary poetic idiom and contemporary speculations about time.

Space is lacking for a full estimate of Eliot's work as a critic. The six volumes from *The Sacred Wood* (1920) to *Elizabethan Essays* (1934) contain the richest collection of critical pronouncements our age has to show. To be sure, they contain eccentricities of judgment sufficient to illustrate a primer of modern critical heresy. Often mistaking personal predilections for principles of universal validity, Eliot, by the pontifical self-assurance of his manner, imposed his tastes and opinions upon his following. But no other modern critic has so thoroughly ploughed the old fields of literature, bringing forth new fruit by forcing even his opponents to subject inherited values to new scrutiny. *Homage to John Dryden* (1924) and *For Lancelot Andrewes* (1928) exhibit characteristic lines of thought and feeling. *Dante* (1929) is Eliot's profoundest piece of criticism and *After Strange Gods* (1931) his most arrogant. Occasional essays of recent date have often been on theological subjects. *(margin: Eliot's Criticism)*

The poets born in the present century are still young and in full productivity and some of them, one assumes, still immature. Their point of view *(margin: Younger Poets)* was conditioned not by the immediate aftermath of the First World War, for at that time they were still schoolboys, but by the problems of unemployment and the distressed areas, by ideological discussion, communist and anti-communist, by the economic depression, and by the encroaching menace of Fascism. In their early verse they made so much use of cryptic symbolism comprehensible only to the initiated that, when published, these poems, as one of the group expressed it, were "private faces in public places." But the extremes of esotericism of the years 1925-1935 provoked a reaction, and these younger poets have of late retreated from snobbish and sophisticated exclusiveness and have attempted, by employing an idiom more widely intelligible, to come to terms with a larger body of readers than the coteries could supply. Running the gamut from wrath to pity, they have attacked the privileged classes and denounced social conditions calling for radical change, and they have intermingled these politico-sociological motives with sympathetic analyses of abnormal sexual psychology. In style they have ranged from spluttering incoherence to forceful clarity. The most conspicuous of these poets is Wystan Hugh Auden (1907-   ) who first challenged attention with *The Orators* (1932), a loud and confused piece of rhetoric from which the reader was expected to gather that nought was well with England. Much of Auden's work has been done in collaboration with other writers. His finest verse is in *The Ascent of F. 6* and in *Look, Stranger* (both 1936). In *Letters from Iceland* (1936) and *The Double Man* (1941) he has simplified his technique, not, however, without a descent to levels close to ephemeral journalism. Of finer quality is *For the Time Being* (1944) which contains some remarkable prose. His *Selected Poems* (1940) show the range of his modes, moods, and themes. Stephen Spender (1909-   ) is subtler, more pitiful, and less violent than Auden (with whom he is closely associated in the public consciousness). The titles of his volumes—*Forward from Liberalism* (1937), *Poems for Spain* (1939), and *Ruins and Visions* (1941)—suggest the history of recent tragic years. Other poets of this group are Cecil Day Lewis (1904-   ) and Louis MacNeice (1907-1963). Apart from them stands F. J. Ronald Bottrall (1906-   ) whose *Festivals of Fire* (1934) and *The Turning Path* (1939) may one day win him more renown than has yet come to him.[34]

Auden

[34] From this summary final paragraph many names have necessarily been omitted. Here may be added Hugh MacDiarmid, the Scots communist (*Selected Poems,* 1940), and Dylan Thomas, (1914-1953), *Collected Poems* (1952).

XLII
Anthropology; Travel; History; Criticism

I

Two writers of the closing years of the nineteenth century helped to lib- *Carpenter* eralize thought and in particular to extricate the study of problems of sex from prurient obscurantism. Edward Carpenter [1] (1844-1929), who was active in Socialist agitation, proclaimed his vision of a pure and primitivistic democratic society, expressing emotionally in his poems *Towards Democracy* (1883-1902) and *Chants for Labour* (1888) the ideals for which he argued in *Civilization: Its Cause and Cure* (1889) and other prose works. *Love's Coming of Age* (1896) and other books gave him a special reputation, but his thought ranged widely over literature, aesthetics, sociology, ethics, and religion. Carpenter was much influenced by Walt Whitman (whom he visited twice) and by Thoreau and Tolstoy; and a journey to India left the impress of Oriental mysticism upon his thought. The charm of his personality is revealed in his autobiography, *My Days and Dreams* (1916). The emotional exuberance of his style alienates many even of those readers who are in entire accord with his objectives, but the influence of his nobly ardent nature will not quickly disappear. Another courageous pioneer was Havelock Ellis [2] (1859-1939) whose *Studies in the Psychology* *Ellis* *of Sex* (1897-1928) brought him an un-sought-for notoriety. For long these monographs could be procured only surreptitiously in England, and by the time they became easily accessible Ellis's researches had been absorbed into those of his successors. Ellis explored in many other directions, being a literary critic, traveler, essayist, philosophic exponent of the art of living, and counselor-at-large to the English people. *The New Spirit* (1890) is still of value for the appreciations of Whitman, Ibsen, and Tolstoy. *The Soul of Spain* (1908) reveals a remarkable insight into the spirit of a people alien from most Englishmen. *The Dance of Life* (1923), advocating grace, pattern, and rhythm in the conduct of life, contains much of Ellis's ripest wisdom, and a like sagacious serenity informs the three series of his *Impressions and Comments* (1914, 1921, and 1924).

[1] Edward Lewis, *Edward Carpenter: An Exposition and an Appreciation* (1915); A. H. M. Sime, *Edward Carpenter: His Ideas and Ideals* (1916); G. Lowes Dickinson, Havelock Ellis, and others, *Edward Carpenter: In Appreciation* (1931).
[2] Isaac Goldberg, *Havelock Ellis, a Biographical and Critical Survey* (1926); Houston Peterson, *Havelock Ellis, Philosopher of Love* (1928), with bibliography; Bertrand Russell, H. L. Mencken, and others, *Havelock Ellis: In Appreciation* (1929).

Tylor

The assault upon Victorian reticence was prosecuted vigorously upon the battleground of religious beliefs, where inquiry extended beyond biblical criticism into the wider problems of the origins of religion and the different levels of belief and ritual. Sir Edward B. Tylor (1832-1917) helped to re-shape ideas and to awaken the modern interest in prehistory. *Primitive Culture* (1871), the most influential of his works, deals with the beginnings and early stages of development of mythology, philosophy, religion, art, and culture. A more impassioned but less scientific book is *The Martyrdom*

Winwood Reade

of Man [3] (1872) by Winwood Reade (1838-1875), a survey of human history divided and recomposed under the heads of War, Religion, Liberty, and Intellect. Reade's indignant agnosticism is expressed with a "fine gloom"

William Robertson Smith

for which he was commended by H. G. Wells.[4] William Robertson Smith (1846-1894), the chief editor of the ninth edition of *The Encyclopaedia Britannica* (to which he contributed articles of great pith and moment on biblical subjects), was one of the last victims of the Victorian heresy-hunters, being deprived of his professorship at Aberdeen. His chief works are *The Prophets of Israel* (1882) and *The Religion of the Semites* (1889), the latter an outstanding example of the methods and results of comparative criticism.

Frazer

Smith was the revered master of Sir James George Frazer [5] (1854-1941), classical scholar, translator of Pausanias (1898), anthropologist, historian of various forms of religious beliefs, and author of *The Golden Bough* (1896; third edition, greatly expanded, 1912), from which have branched out sub-sidiary studies of totemism, the worship of the dead, the religion of nature, Old Testament folklore, and related problems. *The Golden Bough* did more than any other single book to reorient men's minds towards fundamental questions of custom and belief. Many of Frazer's theories are now dis-credited; the evidence upon which he drew is of varying degrees of reli-ability; the pseudo-scientific "laws" which he detected at work beneath savage custom emphasize the logical at the expense of the emotional element in the savage mind; and since Frazer's day the methods of anthropology have changed. But however much it has been discredited as science, *The Golden Bough* endures as literature, an immense and fascinating repository of curious and far-fetched lore, arranged according to a vast design, and set forth in a prose style of pellucid grace touched with an irony suggestive of Anatole France. Of anthropologists of a younger generation there is room

Sir G. Elliot Smith

to mention only Sir G. Elliot Smith (1871-1937), who was the center of con-troversy as the leader of the "diffusionist" school of prehistorians. *The Ancient Egyptians and the Origins of Civilization* (1923) argued the thesis that civilization originated in the Valley of the Nile and spread thence to

---

[3] New edition, in the Travellers' Library, with an introduction by J. M. Robertson (1927).
[4] See the preface to *The Outline of History*, where Wells acknowledges his indebtedness to Reade. — Reade's *African Sketch-Book* (1873) is a vivid narrative of exploration.
[5] R. A. Downie, *James George Frazer: A Portrait of a Scholar* (1940). For a more extended estimate by the present writer than is here possible see "Nemi and the Golden Bough," *No. Amer. Rev.*, ccxxviii (1923). 814-824. — Andrew Lang, an expert in controversy, was among the first to show how insecure was Frazer's "high-piled castle of hypotheses." See Lang's *Magic and Religion* (1901), which is largely concerned with *The Golden Bough*.

the uttermost parts of the planet. This theory, much discussed without evoking much credence, is opposed to that of Tylor and Frazer who did not derive all cultural elements from any single source but accounted for resemblances on the ground that at any given stage of social development the human mind reacts to similar circumstances in similar ways.

II

The anthropologists who, like Frazer, were not themselves field-workers *Travel* depended largely upon the reports of travelers. To the literature of travel there have been notable additions since the mid-nineteenth century. The temptation must be resisted to review the narratives of exploration in the Arctic and Antarctic, in Central Asia and Tibet, in the Australian desert, and in many other perilous and remote portions of the globe. The modern *Mountain* sport of mountaineering has produced a literature of its own. Of this, *Hours eering of Exercise in the Alps* (1871) by the scientist John Tyndall (1820-1893), *Peaks, Passes and Glaciers* (1859-62), and Sir Leslie Stephen's *The Playground of Europe* (1871) are popular examples.[6] Sir Martin Conway (1856-1937) went farther afield, writing narratives of adventure in the Himalayas and the Andes. The recent attempts upon the summits of Mt. Everest and other Himalayan peaks have been recorded in narratives distinguished for nobility of spirit. The Far East was productive of no great travel book. That strange exotic, Lafcadio Hearn (1850-1904), who became a citizen of Japan *Lafcadio* and married a native, made his adopted country the subject of *Glimpses of Hearn Unfamiliar Japan* (1894) and other impressionistic volumes.

From experiences in the Near and Middle East have been shaped those travel books that have best claims upon our attention, for since the days of Burton, Palgrave, and Warburton,[7] Englishmen have been irresistibly attracted to the rock-strewn wilderness of Arabia and have given us a series of narratives unequaled elsewhere in the literature of man's wanderings "on sands and shores and desert wildernesses." Edwin Henry Palmer (1840-1882), a distinguished Arabist, wrote *The Desert of the Exodus* (1871), which was *Palmer* long afterwards Colonel Lawrence's authority for the topography of Sinai. Its vivid accuracy is lightened with a humor that now seems old-fashioned. *Lady* Lady Anne Blunt (1837-1917) accompanied her husband, Wilfrid Scawen *Anne* Blunt, on journeys recorded in her *Bedouin Tribes of the Euphrates* (1879) *Blunt* and *Pilgrimage to Nejd* (1881). Topographically to one side of the explorers of Arabia stands Edward G. Browne (1862-1925), the historian of Persian *Browne* literature. His exquisitely written book, *A Year among the Persians* [8] (1893), is touched with the mystery and mysticism of Babism. *Persian Pictures*

[6] *The Englishman in the Alps*, ed. Arnold Lunn (1927), is an excellent anthology.
[7] See ch. XXI, above. — There is excellent literary criticism in D. G. Hogarth, *The Penetration of Arabia* (1904).
[8] New edition, with a memoir by Sir E. Denison Ross (1926). — Without the charm of Browne's book but a work of broader scope distinguished for its authoritativeness is *Persia and the Persian Question* (1892) by George Nathaniel Curzon, Marquis Curzon (1859-1925).

Gertrude Bell

Hogarth

Other Arabists

Doughty

(1894) by Gertrude Bell [9] (1868-1926) is a slighter work than Browne's, but her account of Syria, *The Desert and the Sown* (1907), is a classic in its field. During the First World War she was associated with David G. Hogarth (1862-1927) in the Arab Bureau in Cairo. Hogarth's reminiscences of archaeological experiences, *A Wandering Scholar in the Levant* (1896) and *Accidents of an Antiquary's Life* [10] (1910), won, and still hold, admiration. Of Arabists still living mention must be made of Eldon Rutter, whose *Holy Cities of Arabia* (1928) received Colonel Lawrence's praise; Bertram Thomas, whose superb feat in crossing the Rub'-al-Khāli is narrated in *Arabia Felix* (1932); and St. John Philby, an English Moslem, whose later accomplishment of the same arduous journey is the subject of *The Empty Quarter* (1933).[11] The books in which Miss Freya Stark has recorded her explorations and adventures in Arabia are of even more recent date. These were all men and women of high courage and renown; there remain to be noted two men of genius associated with Arabia.

The famous adventure of Charles Montagu Doughty [12] was, as has been noted in an earlier chapter, but an interlude in a life dedicated to poetry. After his return from Arabia Doughty devoted a decade to the composition of *Travels in Arabia Deserta* [13] (1888) which won the admiration of William Morris, Wilfrid Blunt, and other good judges but remained unknown to the general public for many years and at length, partly through the support of Colonel Lawrence, received acclaim as a masterpiece of English prose and a work of first magnitude in the history of travel. It is a surpassingly sincere, sure, and sensitive record of Arabian life both among the Bedouin and in the oasis towns. But it is more than that. With dim suggestions of allegorical intent, it shows the solitary man upon some exalted spiritual journey, groping for light through "the moral desolation of the world." Doughty was drawn to the barren peninsula (1876-1878) by his philological, geological, and antiquarian studies and his feeling for the primitive and the near to earth. Throughout his wanderings and afterwards while composing his masterpiece he remained true to his vocation as a poet. The prime consideration was that his language should be "right English of the best period." The *Arabia Deserta* is a supreme experiment in style, the result of an effort to refresh and invigorate the mother tongue, redeeming it from modern venality and flaccidity by a return in idiom and vocabulary to the larger utterance of an earlier and nobler time. The archaisms, neologisms, and absolute constructions; the effects of the spoken word; the use of Arabic terms and turns of phrase; and the other elements of Doughty's

[9] *The Letters of Gertrude Bell,* ed. Lady Bell (2v, 1927). — Ronald Bodley and Lorna Hearst, *Gertrude Bell* (1940), an inadequate biographical sketch which must serve for the present for want of anything better.

[10] The best parts of both these books have been combined to form *The Wandering Scholar* (1925).

[11] Both Thomas and Philby have written other books on Arabia.

[12] For Doughty's poetry see ch. xxxix, above, where will also be found a bibliography.

[13] New edition, with introduction by T. E. Lawrence (2v, 1921); *Wanderings in Arabia* (1908), an abridgment made by Edward Garnett; *Passages from the Arabia Deserta,* selected by Edward Garnett (1931).

style are matters for special study. It must be granted that he "writ no language" and that mastery of the great book is not won without toil; but this extraordinary archaistic revival in style is magnificently in keeping with Doughty's noble simplicity of personality and with the primitive society in which he lived through two memorable years.

Among the younger English Arabists for whom the *Arabia Deserta* was the bible of their profession was Thomas Edward Lawrence [14] (1888-1935). Lawrence went to Syria to pursue studies in military architecture of which the fruit was a monograph, *Crusader Castles,* published posthumously (1936). On the outbreak of war in 1914 he was attached to the Arab Bureau in Cairo where Hogarth was his chief and Gertrude Bell a colleague. There followed the celebrated mission which resulted in the rising of the Arab tribes against their Ottoman overlords. In conjunction with Allenby's advance through Palestine, Lawrence directed the desert campaign which terminated in the Turkish defeat and the occupation of Damascus. Lawrence, though always (as is not always remembered) subordinate to Allenby, proved himself a master of the strategy of open warfare. For a time he was a prisoner in the hands of the Turks and endured shameful experiences that left a sense of defilement upon him. Moreover, he found that he had been made the medium for conveying to the Arabs promises which were incompatible with English commitments to the French. It was therefore in a mood of disillusionment and mortification that he pleaded unavailingly the cause of Pan-Arabism at Versailles. Afterwards he assisted Winston Churchill in securing a reasonably equitable settlement in the Near East. But he had lost faith, and, changing his name first to "Ross" and then to "Shaw", he sought seclusion from the world, ultimately finding in the R. A. F. a sort of modern equivalent to medieval monastic life. Yet he never escaped from his enormous celebrity, nor can it be said that he really desired to do so. The manuscript of the first draft of his narrative of the Arab revolt was lost and never recovered. In its second version, *Seven Pillars of Wisdom* was privately printed in 1922 and in definitive form in a limited, costly edition in 1926.[15] For anything like a final judgment of this book the needed perspective is as yet lacking, and criticism is of many minds. Lawrence's romantic and baffling personality, in which, if there was not (as is sometimes held) something of the charlatan, there was certainly much of the showman, but to whose extraordinary greatness there is ample testimony, stands between us and his book. The extent and significance of his contribution to Allenby's

T. E. Lawrence

[14] *Secret Despatches from Arabia* (1938); *Oriental Assembly* (1938); *Men in Print* (1940); *Letters,* ed. David Garnett (1939); *Letters to his Biographers Liddell Hart and Robert Graves* (2v, 1938); *Letters to H. S. Ede* (1942). — Liddell Hart, *Colonel Lawrence: The Man behind the Legend* (1934); Robert Graves, *Lawrence and the Arabian Adventure* (1928); *T. E. Lawrence by his Friends,* ed. A. W. Lawrence (1937). For more extended estimates by the present writer than are here possible see *New York Herald Tribune Books,* April 8, 1934; July 4, 1937; January 8, 1939.
[15] Lawrence would not permit the publication of an ordinary edition in his lifetime; consequently *Seven Pillars of Wisdom* was first published in regular fashion in 1935. *Revolt in the Desert* (1927), a so-called abridgment, is really a hasty affair of scissors-and-paste, published to defray the costs of the limited edition of the complete work.

plan of campaign, his mastery of strategy, his gullibility as a diplomat—
these are not problems for the literary critic, but for the moment they con-
fuse critical judgment. Certainly, in clarity of execution *Seven Pillars of
Wisdom* does not match the desert campaign. Though overlong and over-
written, it is yet so incomplete that to be fully understood the narrative
must be supplemented from other sources. Its levities seem mistimed, its
touches of malice misplaced. Parts are greater than the whole; and these
parts include the analysis of the character of the Semite, the story of the
approach to Arabia, the assembling of the tribes, the destruction of the
Meccan railway, the battle in the narrow defile, and the final scenes in
Damascus. There are magnificent descriptions of desert landscape and
vigorous characterizations of Arab personalities. At times (as in the *Arabia
Deserta*) there are hints that the story is moving upon two planes—
Lawrence journeyed upon a spiritual as well as a military road to Damascus.
The monotony and incoherence of parts of the narrative suggest the chaotic
monotony of war. In later years, when new perils lowered over England,
there were those who hoped that Colonel Lawrence would emerge from
his seclusion to become a leader of his people. It was not to be. He was
killed when thrown from his motor-cycle while riding at reckless speed.[16]

Cunning-
hame
Graham

Life among the Moslems formed only part of the far-flung adventures of Robert B. Cunninghame Graham [17] (1852-1936)—"Don Roberto,"
"Hidalgo," "Modern Conquistador," as he was called. He never won in
the United States the fame that was his due, perhaps because he included
all Americans within his stormy, aristocratic scorn of comfort-loving, lethargic
Philistinism. Nor has he yet achieved the legendary reputation of a Burton
or a Lawrence, though with both he may be compared. Scottish but of partly
Spanish descent, bold, generous, emancipated, and vehement, Cunninghame
Graham had adventures and opinions and learning and prejudices enough
to fill many volumes—and he did, in fact, fill three dozen. In youth he was
a gaucho in the Argentine, a farmer in Mexico, and a soldier in Uruguay.
Like his friend W. H. Hudson, he loved the wild men, wild animals, and
wild vegetation of the pampas. Many of his reminiscences and semi-fictitious
sketches and most of his historical and biographical works have a South
American setting. But, unlike Hudson's, no years of his life were sedentary.
His finest book, *Mogreb-el-Acksa* (1898), tells of his journey in the disguise
of a Turkish physician beyond the Atlas mountains where he was arrested
and held captive. Another time he joined the Meccan *haj*. At home he
threw himself into the Labor movement and sat for a while in Parliament.
"Don Roberto" had as rich and full a life as ever falls to the lot of man; it
offers alluring material to the biographer. That material will be quarried

---

[16] Lawrence made a prose translation of the *Odyssey* (1932; reissued in paperback ed., Oxford,
1956). A long and candid account of life in the Royal Air Force, entitled *The Mint*, finally
appeared in 1955.
[17] There is no collected edition. *Thirty Tales and Sketches*, ed. Edward Garnett (1929) and
Rodeo: a Collection of Tales and Sketches, ed. A. F. Tschiffely (1936) offer characteristic
examples of Cunninghame Graham's work. — See H. F. West, *A Modern Conquistador:
Robert Bontine Cunninghame Graham: His Life and Works* (1932).

from his books, but probably they will themselves never be widely read. In theme they are often too remote from ordinary English interests, and they are too allusive, caustic, and ironical. Writing was one of Graham's ample, magnificent gestures. He waved the pen as he did the sword and made as few concessions to his reader as to an opponent in a quarrel. The pride that ruled his years was not so becoming in his books as in his noble and picturesque personality. Life was to him more than letters; he lacked the patience which is part of genius in the arts.

William Henry Hudson [18] (1841-1922) is sometimes numbered among *Hudson* writers of fiction, but this is to suggest a false emphasis, for he was a novelist only sporadically and inexpertly. His own preference would have been for a place among adventurers who tell of wild and lawless lands. Of English stock but American parentage, he was born in the Argentine and remained in South America till 1874 when he went to live in England. "My life ended when I left the pampas," he said; rather, it became a *recherche du temps perdu.* Hudson hated the drab, urban civilization in which, matched with an uncongenial wife, he was fated to live in poverty; and though he loved the intimate English countryside and instilled a quiet charm into such books as *Birds in London* (1898), *Afoot in England* (1909), and *A Hind in Richmond Park* (1922), his dreams were of the solitary grandeur of the Patagonian desert, the Argentine plains silent under the stars, the impetuous, fantastic gauchos, and the turbulent, revolutionary life of South America in the days of his youth. *The Purple Land* [19] (1885), a tale of revolution in Uruguay, is of little moment as fiction, but the rich incidental descriptive passages are exquisite evocations of memories of long ago. *Green Mansions* (1904), the only other "novel" that counts, is set in the tropical jungles of Venezuela where Hudson had never been, so that this romantic creation is an ideal contemplated in compensation for the ugly realities of Bayswater. The character of Rima in this story is intended to suggest natural beauty as opposed to nature's cruelties. But the transcendental and human elements in the tale are not well harmonized. *El Ombú* (1912) is a collection of sketches, rather than of short stories, of the gauchos, full of violence and anguish, poverty and cruelty. In all these the mode of tale-telling is quite artless, dependent upon Hudson's own experiences or upon hearsay. His material was not unlike Conrad's, but though he was that master's admiring friend, he was without Conrad's subtleties in "arranging" the data stored in memory. But how astonishing was the memory of this "traveller in little things"! Gilbert White's *Selborne* was one of his favorite books; he resembles White in his patient observation and faithfulness in description of minute objects. But his approach to nature was not "scientific"; in his books there are a latent symbolism (especially when he wrote of birds—

---

[18] *Collected Works* (24v, 1922-1923); *Letters to Edward Garnett* (1925). — G. F. Wilson, *Bibliography* (1922); Morley Roberts, *W. H. Hudson: A Portrait* (1924); R. H. Charles, "The Writings of W. H. Hudson," *E&S,* xx (1935). 135-151; Baker, x (1939). 86-94.

[19] Originally entitled *The Purple Land that England Lost*—that is, by her failure to seize and colonize Uruguay in the early nineteenth century.

Rima chirps like a bird) and a pantheistic fervor that put him in the line of Thoreau and the other transcendentalists. The passionate love of wild nature, animate and inanimate, and the intensity of his fellow-feeling with animals show his affinity to D. H. Lawrence, as does his hatred of the urban middle-class. In old age he wrote *Far Away and Long Ago* (1918), the history of his early life, recalling in it the animistic sense which he possessed in youth and which, he held, is at the root of all nature-worship. Rejecting Darwin's explanation of the evolutionary process, he responded to the Lamarckian theory because it made room for intelligence and desire.

III

The Cambridge Histories

Much of the historical research accomplished in an era of minute specialization is beyond the horizon of the historian of literature. The most imposing monuments of recent English historical scholarship are the three series, *The Cambridge Ancient History* (12 volumes, 1923-1939), *The Cambridge Medieval History* (8 volumes, 1911-1936), and *The Cambridge Modern History* (12 volumes, 1902-1910).[20] Lord Acton, laying down the plan of the *Modern History,* had defined as his object a work which should be "not a rope of sand but a continuous development, ... not a burden on the memory but an illumination of the soul." [21] This aspiration and ideal cannot be accepted as a summary of accomplishment except with more reservations than can be considered here. Professor Toynbee, drawing an analogy from the industrialist's search for raw materials, exploitation of sources, and division of labor, has described the *Cambridge Histories* as "monuments of the laboriousness, the factual knowledge, the mechanical skill, and the organizing power of our society." [22] The analogy is acceptable with qualifications, but it fails in appreciation of the highly individualized excellence of many of the contributions to the Cambridge volumes. In the *Ancient History,* more particularly, there are chapters worthy of the finest tradition of English historiography.

"The Hammonds"

The specialized work of two pairs of scholars must be mentioned for its bearing upon the growth of Socialism and consequently upon a main movement in modern creative literature. John L. Hammond (1872-1949) and his wife Lucy B. Hammond (1873-) investigated the social conditions of the working-classes during the Industrial Revolution. Their three volumes covering the period from 1760 to 1832 on *The Village Labourer* (1911), *The Town Labourer* (1917), and *The Skilled Labourer* (1919), with the two sequels, *The Rise of Modern Industry* (1925) and *The Age of the Chartists* (1930), are outstanding examples of contemporary economic history. Sidney

"The Webbs"

Webb (1859-1947) and his wife Beatrice Potter Webb (1858-1943), later Lord and Lady Passfield, collected evidence and disseminated humane ideas

[20] Specialists of many nations were among the contributors, but the great majority were English historians.
[21] Lord Acton, *Lectures on Modern History* (1907), p. 317.
[22] Arnold J. Toynbee, *A Study of History,* I (1934). 4.

in their *History of Trade Unionism* (1894), *Industrial Democracy* (1897), *Problems of Modern Industry* (1898), and later books. As one of the original Fabians, Webb was closely associated with George Bernard Shaw. The writings of "the Webbs" can scarcely be judged as literature, but every creative writer who has touched on the field of sociology has, directly or indirectly, been influenced by them.

For all its devotion to the task of assembling and organizing masses of fact, the period has not lacked historians capable of brilliant synthesis and popular exposition. John B. Bury (1861-1927) made a special reputation as *Bury* an authority on the Byzantine Empire, but he may be longer remembered for a by-product of his original research, his indispensable edition of Gibbon (1896-1900). As Acton's successor at Cambridge, it was appropriate that Bury should write a *History of Freedom of Thought* (1913), albeit on a scale too small for the greatness of the theme and with a liberal-minded hopefulness that has been refuted by subsequent events. Bury's successor at Cambridge was George Macaulay Trevelyan (1876-1962), great-nephew of *Trevelyan* Lord Macaulay and most widely known for his brilliantly presented brief *History of England* (1926). On an ampler scale and in a style that has won him deserved popularity Trevelyan wrote two historical trilogies, one on Garibaldi's part in the Risorgimento—*Garibaldi's Defence of the Roman Republic* (1907), *Garibaldi and the Thousand* (1909), and *Garibaldi and the Making of Italy* (1911); the other on the reign of Queen Anne—*Blenheim* (1930), *Ramelies and the Union with Scotland* (1932), and *The Peace and the Protestant Succession* (1934). With the latter trilogy may be associated the chief historical work of Winston Spencer Churchill (1874-1965), *Marlborough: His Life and Times* (4v, 1933-1938), which presents the *Churchill* writer's ancestor against the background of the age of which he was the greatest figure. Churchill had already displayed his narrative talent in volumes on the Boer War and on Kitchener's conquest of the Sudan; in these history is mingled with personal reminiscence. Vaster conflicts, *quorum magna pars fuit,* form the subject of Churchill's *The World Crisis* (4v, 1923-1929), with its supplementary volume on the Eastern Front entitled *The Unknown War* (1931). In this massive work, part history, part *apologia,* there surges and thunders the grand rhetoric which since the retreat from Dunkirk has become familiar to all the world. Churchill's war-speeches have been collected in several volumes. Upon his mastery of the tradition of parliamentary oratory it is needless to comment.

The Oxford tradition of historiography was ably maintained by Herbert *Fisher* A. L. Fisher (1865-1940). His *Napoleon* (1913) is a little masterpiece of condensation. In his *History of Europe* (1935) he evinced remarkable powers of organization and clarification. Oxford-trained is the most interesting historian of our time, Arnold Joseph Toynbee (1889-   ). Only a provisional opinion can be offered of his *Study of History* (6v, 1934-1939) *Toynbee* for it is still unfinished. Moved by "the deep impulse to attempt to envisage and comprehend the whole of life" and taking all historical knowledge (and much else) as his province, Toynbee has undertaken to define the political, social, economic, and cultural characteristics whereby a civilization or "great society" can be distinguished; to isolate for examination such portions of each society as the "dominant minority" and the "internal" and "external" proletariat; to formulate such general principles as those of "apparentation and affiliation," "challenge and response," and "withdrawal and return"; and, in a word, to discover the "laws" governing the rise, florescence, and decline of civilizations. The general course of the argument is overlaid with much erudite detail, not all of it obviously pertinent. Till the remaining portions of the *Study* appear, judgment cannot be passed upon the validity of this vast interpretation of human experience; but it is already evident that in scale, organization, and profundity of both thought and feeling this is a work of major importance. Its great theme has a solemn significance for our time. By a tragic coincidence, the point in the discussion reached at the outbreak of the Second World War was the problem of the breakdown and disintegration of civilizations.

IV

Lang   From these professional historians we turn to men of letters who combined the writing of history with activity in other departments of literature. Andrew Lang [23] (1844-1912) with immense industry touched and adorned many subjects. The eclecticism of his interests led to a dissipation of his talents with the consequence that he accomplished absolutely first-rate work in no one field. *Myth, Ritual and Religion* (1887), his best-known book, connects him with Tylor and other inquirers into the origins of religious beliefs. The popular series of vari-colored *Fairy Books* were by-products of his investigations into folklore. To problems of occult phenomena, forgeries, and other debatable subjects he applied a shrewdly analytical and argumentative intelligence. He was most stimulating, though not always most reliable, when discussing such matters as the significance of totemism, or ballad origins, or the Homeric problem, or the authenticity of the Casket Letters, or what you will. Of Lang's historical works the best is *The History of Scotland* (1890-1897). Among his minor books may be mentioned the witty and attractive *Letters to Dead Authors* (1886)—some of which are in verse.

Belloc   Joseph Hilaire Pierre Belloc [24] (1870-1953), while all too productive in many departments of literature, was primarily a historian. Born in Paris and of French blood with a dash of Irish, Belloc was Roman Catholic by birth and conviction and Continental in his outlook upon English history and institutions. He began as a humorist—often a savage humorist—with *The Bad Child's Book of Beasts* (1896), a volume that had several sequels. In

[23] R. L. Green, *Andrew Lang: A Critical Biography* (1946), with bibliography. On Lang's poetry see ch. XXIX, n. 33, above.
[24] C. C. Mandell and Edward Shanks, *Hilaire Belloc, the Man and his Works* (1916), needs to be supplemented by a survey of Belloc's later writings.

verse he was an effective satirist, though not always a fair one. His small amount of serious poetry is deft and delicate, and there is reticent good taste in his poems on religious subjects. Of a score of collections of essays, often trivial though generally amusing, it is unnecessary to give the titles here. Particularly noteworthy among many impressions of travel are *The Path to Rome* (1902) and *The Old Road* (1904). Belloc was an expert in combining with history something of the qualities of an informal guide-book, as in *The River of London* (1912) and *The Stane Street* (1913). He wrote several novels, but it is evident that he did not take them quite seriously, nor is the historian of literature obligated to do so. Of numerous historico-biographical monographs his *Wolsey* (1930), *Cranmer* (1931), and *Cromwell* (1934) are representative. As a historian he was con-troversial, partisan, and tendentious, most trustworthy, though not always most effective, when his sectarian prejudices were least engaged. His *History of England* (1925-1931) is so strongly Roman Catholic in bias as to be illuminating rather of his mind than of his subject. Its inaccuracies have been severely criticized. A controversy with H. G. Wells which began with Belloc's *Companion to Mr. Wells' "Outline of History"* (1926) is worth mentioning. *The Servile State* (1912), Belloc's most influential book, is an attack at once upon capitalistic industrialism and upon the socialistic Utopias of the opponents of capitalism.

Gilbert Keith Chesterton [25] (1874-1936), who was not a historian though he took large liberties with history, may be introduced at this point as Belloc's co-religionist, ally, and sharer in his opinions and prejudices. His innumerable books are known *in toto* today only to those old enough to have read them as they appeared. His *Browning* (1903) and *Dickens* (1903) reveal him as an acutely analytical, if often wayward, critic. These two ex-uberant writers were congenial to his temperament. Sometimes he resorted to fiction of a fantastic sort to convey his ideas, as in *The Napoleon of Not-ting Hill* (1904), *The Man Who Was Thursday* (1908), *The Flying Inn* (1914), and the series of detective-stories (with a strong distillation of re-ligiosity) which began with *The Innocence of Father Brown* (1911). *The Ballad of the White Horse* and *Lepanto* (both 1911) have a fine swash-buckling rhetoric, but Chesterton was not a poet as Belloc, within narrow limits, was. Like his partner, Chesterton tried to lead men away from capi-talism towards a kind of neo-medievalism of craft guilds. Both men fash-ioned out of their dreams and fantasies a medieval England that had never existed—a "Merrie England" of hearty faith and brotherhood.[26] Chesterton

Chesterton

---

[25] Patrick Braybrooke, *Gilbert Keith Chesterton* (1922); G. W. Bullett, *The Innocence of G. K. Chesterton* (1923); G. N. Shuster, *The Catholic Spirit in Modern English Literature* (1922).

[26] The most formidable opponent of Belloc and Chesterton in exposing the inaccuracies in their conception of the Middle Ages was George Gordon Coulton (1858-1947). His case, based on wide knowledge of first-hand evidence, is not demolished by Belloc's wittily insolent satire beginning:

> Remote and ineffectual don
> Who dares attack my Chesterton.

did not enter the Church of Rome till 1922, but the direction in which he was moving was obvious as early as 1909 when he published *Orthodoxy*. Of the miscellaneous controversial works of his later years, apologetical and polemic, *The Everlasting Man* (1925) is representative. Chesterton was primarily a journalist and consequently wasted much talent on ephemeral subjects. His best work was accomplished before his mannerisms became fixed upon him. The perpetual effort to be clever was often misdirected into mere silliness, and the reliance upon the see-saw of antithesis and the whimsicalities of paradox became tiresome. Yet he forced readers to think, though they often thought the worse of Chesterton. It would be unsafe to predict confidently of any of his books that they will be long remembered. Yet this pillar of conservatism and reaction was in his day a significant figure of protest against the current winds of doctrine and streams of tendency.

Strachey   Blown by those winds and floating on those streams was Giles Lytton Strachey (1880-1932), the most brilliant representative in the field of historico-biographical studies of the cynical skepticism towards established reputations which we have noted as characteristic of the nineteen-twenties. Having attracted some attention with his *Landmarks of French Literature* (1912), a little book that remains the best balanced of his works, Strachey turned in the last and most disillusioned year of the First World War to the agreeable task of "de-pedestalizing" popular idols. Discarding reverence and reticence, he relied upon ironic wit, urbanity, and ultra-sophistication. "Psychography," as it was called, would discover by a facile use of what was believed to be the Freudian method the hidden weakness and lay bare the "damaged soul." By means of the disillusioning anecdote and caricaturing detail Strachey aimed to strip the great of their false trappings and expose the hollowness of their pretentions. He did not realize that greatness is not dependent upon externalities. The four subjects of *Eminent Victorians* (1918), dissimilar in other respects, possessed in common religious convictions and moral fervor. Strachey and his readers had no understanding of religious experience and no sympathy with moral fervor. By emphasizing Dr. Arnold's pompousness, Florence Nightingale's bustling activity, General Gordon's addiction to brandy (a malicious calumny), and Cardinal Manning's worldly ambitions he would "deflate" these eminent reputations. When, however, in *Queen Victoria* (1921), he attempted to apply the formula again, he had enough of fairness to capitulate to the evidence of genuine greatness, and having come to scoff he remained to praise. *Elizabeth and Essex* (1928) displays a minimum of research and a maximum of manner. He had always used something of the method of the novelist, with the telling episode, the

---

Coulton dared attack, and attacked successfully, other partisan, sectarian historians. He was the guiding spirit of a Cambridge school of medievalists who have not permitted romantic idealizations to hide from them "the spotted actuality." Coulton's *Chaucer and his England* (1909) is an admirable introduction to the subject. The *Five Centuries of Religion* (3v, 1923-1926, in progress) is his most massive work. *A Medieval Panorama* (1938), an excellent synthesis, is the ripest fruit of a fine scholarship. — See his *Four Score Years* (1944), an autobiography memorable for the account in the last two chapters of one of the fiercest controversies in which he was engaged.

avoidance of the tedious even where it is relevant, and an unwarranted employment of the "interior monologue"; and in this last book he approximated to the hybrid type of "fictionized biography" for whose florescence in the nineteen-twenties his example was in part responsible. With Strachey it is natural to group Philip Guedalla (1889-1944), though this is unfair to *Guedalla* a historian whose solid research and serious intent are hidden from the eyes of most readers by the too unremitting brilliance of his style. *The Second Empire* (1922), *Palmerston* (1926), and *Wellington* (1931) are Guedalla's finest books.[27]

V

A number of miscellaneous writers—scholars, journalists, publicists, and *Nevinson* essayists—cannot be forced into a category. Henry W. Nevinson (1856-1941), for long on the staff of *The Manchester Guardian,* was a war-correspondent in many parts of the world between 1897 and 1918. His outspoken *Essays in Freedom and Rebellion* (1921) are still of value for the light they cast upon Liberal sentiment and policy in the first post-war years. *In the Dark Backward* (1934) is on the borderland of the essay, travel book, history, and fiction. Goldsworthy Lowes Dickinson [28] (1862-1932), historian, sociologist, *G. Lowes* internationalist, and "Good European," was representative of much that is *Dickinson* finest in the Liberal tradition. *The Greek View of Life* (1896) established his reputation. His impartial and lucid intelligence enabled him to assume other points of view than his own, as in the anonymous *Letters from a Chinese Official* (1903) which certain people accepted as genuinely Oriental, and in *A Modern Symposium* (1905). Other important books are *Religion, a Criticism and a Forecast* (1905) and *War: Its Nature, Cause and Cure* (1923). The Platonic dialogue was a form ideally adapted to the purposes of this admirably fructifying mind, and Dickinson's last book was appropriately *Plato and His Dialogues* (1931). Gilbert Murray (1866-1957), classical *Gilbert* scholar, philosopher, and publicist, is famous for his verse-translations from *Murray* Euripides and Aeschylus. These have been criticized as too unliteral paraphrases, but they have the great merit of being fine poetry and alive in their own right. Among Murray's classical studies are *The Rise of the Greek Epic* (1907) and *Euripides and His Age* (1913). In later years Murray devoted much of his energy to supporting the League of Nations and to the furtherance of international coöperation. *The Problem of Foreign Policy* (1921) advances ideas and suggestions of which the fault is that they are too good for an evil world. Both in his life and writings Murray was representative of the best hopes that struggled to keep alive during the Long Armistice. Maurice Baring (1874-1945), a widely traveled connoisseur of the art of *Baring* living, was a poet whose verse leaves an impression of graceful talent rather than of any creative urge. His best work was in prose. Novels, such as *Cat's*

---

[27] On Strachey and Guedalla see Mark Longaker, *Contemporary Biography* (Philadelphia, 1934), chs. II and VI.

[28] E. M. Forster, *Goldsworthy Lowes Dickinson* (1934).

Cradle (1925) and *Tinker's Leave* (1927), are easy to read and easy to forget. His *Dead Letters* (1910) and *Unreliable History* (1934) show a gift for burlesque and not too unkindly satire. As a critic Baring wrote with special authority on Russian life and literature. *The Puppet Show of Memory* (1922) tells the story of his life. Percy Lubbock (1879-1965), friend and disciple of Henry James, wrote several biographies, something like an autobiography in *Earlham* (1922), something approximating to fiction in *Roman Pictures* (1923), and an extremely subtle study, *The Craft of Fiction* (1921). The most notable art critics of the period have been the poet Laurence Binyon (1869-1943), Roger Fry (1866-1934), and Clive Bell (1881-1964). Binyon spoke with special authority on the art of the Far East. Fry was influential as an interpreter of contemporary French painters. Bell, in addition to his criticisms of modern painting, wrote an excellent study of Proust (1928) and in *Civilization* (1928) ventured into the arena of social problems. Arthur Christopher Benson (1862-1925) wrote verse and fiction of little consequence and won the esteem of a wide, gentle public with *The House of Quiet* (1904) and other volumes of semi-autobiographic meditations which were "comforting," mildly pietistic, and not too profound; but his most sensitive writing is in his studies of Tennyson, Ruskin, FitzGerald, Rossetti, and Pater. Edward Verrall Lucas (1868-1938), disciple, biographer (1908), and editor of Charles Lamb, was a voluminous essayist, critic, novelist, gentle satirist, and "wanderer" in famous cities. For many years he was on the staff of *Punch.* Another essayist, less widely ranging than Lucas, was Robert Lynd (1879-1949), who combined experiences of travel and a love of books and animals in pleasing and witty fashion.

VI

Of the great company of literary critics of the late Victorian period and after, only the most prominent can be mentioned here. To obviate invidiousness, they are considered in chronological order. Stopford Augustus Brooke (1832-1916), an influential nonconformist divine, was the author of a widely used manual of English Literature and of many popular studies of the poets. His most distinctive interest is displayed in *English Literature from the Beginning to the Norman Conquest* (1898). Richard Garnett (1835-1906) was engaged in history, biography, and criticism. With Edmund Gosse he collaborated on the well-known *Illustrated Record* of English Literature (1903-1904). Garnett's poems are now lost to sight, but still attractive is *The Twilight of the Gods* [29] (1888; enlarged edition, 1903), a series of learned, witty, and sardonic tales and apologues. Henry Austin Dobson [30] (1840-1921) took the eighteenth century as his province, writing biographies of Hogarth, Horace Walpole, Goldsmith, and Fanny Burney, and many

[29] New edition, with introduction by T. E. Lawrence (1926).
[30] See Cornelius Weygandt, *Tuesdays at Ten* (Philadelphia, 1928), ch. XIII: "Austin Dobson, Augustan." — On Dobson's poetry see ch. XXIX, n. 34, above.

critical papers. The grace and lightness of his verse are characteristics also of his prose, but there is more substance in the prose. William John Courthope (1842-1917), assuming the task which Thomas Gray had projected and Thomas Warton had left unfinished, wrote a *History of English Poetry* (6v, 1895-1910), ample in design and philosophical in temper but in usefulness marred by a too strict adherence to the thesis that there is a close connection between literary fashions, tastes, and values and contemporary social and political opinions and conditions. Edward Dowden [31] (1843- *Dowden* 1913) made a great reputation with his *Shakespeare: His Mind and Art* (1873), the most influential "subjective" treatment of the subject till the appearance of Bradley's work. Dowden was the most famous of the critics who professed an ability to discern in the plays evidence of Shakespeare's own intellectual, moral, and spiritual experiences. For a *Life of Shelley* (1886) the family documents were made available to Dowden, but the biography was too partisan and too emotional in tone to remain definitive. Miscellaneous critical essays show this scholar to greater advantage than these two ambitious works. Andrew Cecil Bradley (1845-1933) brought to a climax in his *Shakespearean Tragedy* (1904) the Coleridgian tradition of *A. C.* philosophic and subjective criticism. In the Shakespearean world, it is safe *Bradley* to say, his was the dominant voice for thirty years, and it is still harkened to. His *Oxford Lectures on Poetry* (1909) are partly on Shakespeare, partly on the Romantic and Victorian poets. George Edward Bateman Saints- *Saintsbury* bury [32] (1845-1933) was an omnivorous, genial, zestful, and indefatigable critic and historian of literature. Of his vast and varied work there is room to note only the *Short History of French Literature* (1882), the *Short History of English Literature* (1898), the *History of Criticism* (1900-1904), the *History of English Prosody* (1906-1910), the *History of English Prose Rhythm* (1912), and the *History of the French Novel* (1917-1919). The *Collected Essays and Papers* (4v, 1923) contain the best of his innumerable lesser studies. The tonic quality of Saintsbury's criticism is found in his undeviating loyalty to values that were strictly literary and strictly his own. Neither his clear-sightedness nor occasional wrong-headedness was borrowed from other men. His style—informal, circumlocutory, and allusive, with parenthetical qualifications and concessions—was often the despair of the precisian, but it reflected the man. Sir Edmund Gosse [33] (1849-1928) ranged *Gosse* through English literature, was influential in introducing modern Scandinavian culture to English readers, and has claims to be regarded as the initiator of the modern vogue of John Donne, whose *Life and Letters* (1899) is his most substantial work. Gosse was an adept in the *causerie* and literary portrait, deft, sly, and often lightly malicious, hinting faults and hesitating dislikes. His reticences and innuendoes are abundant in his biography of Swinburne (1917). His scholarship, though wide, was often inaccurate. In *Father and*

[31] *Letters of Edward Dowden,* ed. E. D. and H. M. Dowden (1914).
[32] A. B. Webster, *George Saintsbury* (Edinburgh, 1934).
[33] *Collected Essays* (12v, 1912-1927). — Evan Charteris, *The Life and Letters of Sir Edmund Gosse* (1931). On Gosse's poetry see ch. XXIX, n. 35, above.

Son (1907), a document in the history of the mid-nineteenth century con-flict between the older and younger generations, there are subtleties and profundities to which Gosse's other writings afford no parallel and which support the opinion (for which there is other evidence) that he was aided in its composition by George Moore. William Ernest Henley [34] (1849-1903), poet, critic, and reviewer, was editor of *The National Observer,* which boasted of a brilliant company of contributors, and of *The New Review,* where Conrad and Wells got their start. With T. F. Henderson, Henley edited the works of Burns, his special contribution being the forceful and candid estimate of the poet's genius and achievement. As a critic Henley was often truculent, especially when attacking the "Aesthetes" and the Socialists, and his strength was lessened rather than enhanced by an affecta-tion of bravado; but he had the hard-hitting courage of convictions that were not notably original. Augustine Birrell [35] (1850-1933) wrote biographies of Marvell and Hazlitt, but is better known for the essays on life and letters in *Obiter Dicta* (1884, 1887, and 1924) and in *Res Judicatae* (1896). Birrell was a master of the essay form, graceful, easy, and sincere, with a wit that never condescended to facetiousness. The literary studies of William Paton Ker [36] (1855-1923) covered English literature from the Middle Ages to the nineteenth century and reached into foreign fields. His *Epic and Romance* (1896) has a weight impressively in contrast to its slight mass. Sir Walter Raleigh [37] (1861-1922) possessed a style happily compounded of grace and vigor. He first won attention with a compact monograph on *The English Novel* (1894), continued with studies of Milton (1900) and Wordsworth (1909), and proved worthy of the responsibility and honor when he was chosen to supply the long-missing volume on Shakespeare (1907) for the *English Men of Letters Series.* For condensed suggestiveness, regard for basic principles, and conscientious avoidance of personal eccentricities in theory and judgment this small book remains without a rival among intro-ductions to Shakespeare. An admirable essay on *The English Voyagers* appended to a reprint of Hakluyt (1905) shows that Raleigh yearned for a life of action, and at the close of his life he was engaged upon a *History of the Royal Air Force.* Charles Whibley (1862-1930) has claims on our gratitude as editor of the series of *Tudor Translations.* His *Literary Por-traits* (1904) and *Literary Studies* (1919), though marred by the intrusion of his Tory prejudices, display a wide culture and a distinguished style. This paragraph would have to be greatly extended if it were to include critics and historians in the fields of foreign literatures.

(margin notes: Ienley, rrell, er, aleigh, hibley)

---

[34] *Works* (5v, 1921); *Views and Reviews* (1890). On Henley's poetry, and for bibliography, see ch. XXXIX, and n. 32, above.
[35] *Collected Essays and Addresses* (3v, 1922). Birrell was in public life and was Secretary of State for Ireland in Asquith's cabinet.
[36] *Collected Essays,* ed. Charles Whibley (2v, 1925).
[37] *Letters,* ed. Lady Raleigh (2v, 1928).

Here, with homage offered to the memory of this last group of writers, representative of the much larger company who have devoted their learning and insight to the history and interpretation of English literature, and with the wish that "what we have written may be read by their light," we bring this history to a close. New names and new talents appear each year, and of these some will doubtless claim places of honor in chapters that cannot yet be written. As the historian of English literature turns his face from the past to look into the future, he feels that he is standing upon a shore

> where a confident sea
> Is ever breaking, never spent.

BIBLIOGRAPHICAL
SUPPLEMENT

Boldface numbers refer to pages in text

BOOK I: THE MIDDLE AGES
Part I. The Old English Period (to 1100)

I. Folk, State, and Speech

3 At this writing the latest book-length survey of the Old English period is S. B. Greenfield's *Critical History of Old English Literature* (1965), with generous bibliographical footnotes. See also his bibliography of Old English in D. M. Zenser, *Guide to English Literature* . . . (1961). W. Bonser's *Anglo-Saxon and Celtic Bibliography 450-1087* (Oxford, 1957) excludes "all material dealing with literature and linguistics as such" (viii). A second ed. of Stenton's *Anglo-Saxon England* came out in 1947. See also P. H. Blair, *An Introduction to Anglo-Saxon England* (Cambridge, 1956); D. Whitelock, *The Beginnings of English Society* (1952); N. R. Ker, *Catalogue of MSS Containing Anglo-Saxon* (Oxford, 1957); P. Clemoes (ed.), *The Anglo-Saxons* (1959); and K. Sisam, *Studies in the History of Old English Literature* (Oxford, 1953). K. Jackson's *Language and History in Early Britain* (Cambridge, Mass., 1953) deals chiefly with Celtic matters, as do, in part, C. Fox and B. Dickins (eds.), *The Early Cultures of Northwest Europe* (1950). On the Sutton Hoo archeological finds see C. Green, *Sutton Hoo* (1963) and the writings listed by F. P. Magoun and J. B. Bessinger in *Speculum,* xxix (1954). 116-124 and xxxiii (1958). 515-522 respectively.

4 See also J. Godfrey, *The Church in Anglo-Saxon England* (Cambridge, 1962).

5 A short Old English grammar, with special attention to syntax, is that of R. Quirk and C. L. Wrenn (1955; 2ed, 1958). A longer one, for more advanced students, is that of A. Campbell (Oxford, 1959).

11 A fuller sketch of Old English times is that of K. Malone, *Emory University Quar.,* v (1949). 129-148.

II. Anglo-Latin Writings

12 M. L. W. Laistner's *Thought and Letters in Western Europe A.D. 500-900* (2ed., 1957) throws light on Anglo-Latin writers and their sources of information.

13 On Aldhelm see also E. R. Curtius, *Europäische Literatur und Lateinisches Mittelalter* (Bern, 1958), pp. 53-54, 454-455.

15 Two MSS of Bede's *Historia* . . . are now available in the series *Early*

English MSS in Facsimile: the Leningrad MS, ed. O. Arngart, and the Moore MS, ed. P. H. Blair (Copenhagen, 1952 and 1959). On Bede see also Curtius, *op. cit.,* pp. 54-55. Bede's *Opera de Temporibus* have been edited by C. W. Jones (Cambridge, Mass., 1943). For Bede studies in recent years see W. F. Bolton, "A Bede Bibliography," *Traditio,* xviii (1962). 436-445.

16 Bede's metrical life of Cuthbert has been edited by W. Jaager (Leipzig, 1935); his prose life, with the anonymous life, by B. Colgrave (Cambridge, 1940). The Whitby life of Pope Gregory has been translated by C. W. Jones, *Saints' Lives and Chronicles in Early England* (Ithaca, N.Y. 1947), pp. 95-121.

18 Eadmer's life of Anselm is now to be had in a separate edition by R. W. Southern (1963); see also Southern's *St Anselm and His Biographer* (1963). The following recent editions are noteworthy: F. Barlow, *Vita Ædwardi Regis* (1962) and A. Campbell, *Chronicon Æthelweardi* (1962).

III. The Old Tradition: Poetic Form

20 For the Germanic background see also J. de Vries, *Die geistige Welt der Germanen,* (2ed., Hall/Saale, 1945). On speakings, see also H. M. Chadwick, *The Heroic Age* (Cambridge, 1912), of which *The Growth of Literature* is an expansion. The studies of Mr and Mrs Chadwick were carried further by Milman Parry in his papers on Homer (see *Harvard Stud. in Classical Phil.,* xli. 73-147 and xliii. 1-50 and *Trans. Amer. Phil. Assoc.,* lxiv. 179-197) and by Parry's disciple A. B. Lord in *The Singer of Tales* (Cambridge, Mass., 1960), a work which, like the Chadwicks' book (ii. 299-456) and Parry's papers, leans heavily on Yugoslavic speakings. Parry's method in isolating the set phrases ("formulas") of Homeric diction has been applied to Old English poetry by F. P. Magoun and others, with results still in the stage of learned debate. See Magoun's paper in *Speculum,* xxviii (1953). 446-467 and R. Quirk's critique in *Early English and Norse Studies presented to Hugh Smith in Honour of his sixtieth Birthday* (1963), pp. 150-171. The Chadwicks summed things up as follows (iii. 753): "The diction of heroic narrative poetry tends everywhere to abound in static epithets, descriptive circumlocutions, kennings, repetitions and recurrent formulae." This statement of the case will doubtless be generally accepted. And Cædmon, the earliest English poet known to us by name, was an illiterate singer as Bede tells the tale. But it need not follow that all or even many of the Old English poems committed to writing were composed by such singers. Cædmon's was a special case: his songs were written down (from dictation) because thought to be divinely inspired, but speakings as a rule did not win written record. Indeed, why should they? The clerical poets made free use, naturally enough, of the conventional poetic diction familiar to them from childhood. In so doing they were following in the steps of Cædmon, who had turned the native English way of versifying into a tool for God's service; see p. 60. But their compositions, made to be read aloud, were writings, not speakings.

On the runes see R. W. V. Elliott, *Runes: An Introduction* (Manchester, 1959); K. Schneider, *Die germanischen Runennamen* (Meisenheim, 1956); and R. Derolez, *Runica Manuscripta* (Bruges, 1954).

21 The Franks Casket is better dated in the sixth century. See K. Schneider in *Festschrift für Walther Fischer* (Heidelberg, 1959), pp. 4-20.

23 A more recent metrical study is that of A. J. Bliss, *The Metre of Beowulf* (Oxford, 1958); reviewed by W. P. Lehmann in *JEGP*, LIX (1960). 137-142, by G. Storms in *ES*, XLVI (1965). 418-422.

29 See H. Marquart, *Die altenglischen Kenningar* (Halle/Saale, 1938); reviewed in *JEGP*, XXXVIII (1939). 282-285 and *MLN*, LV (1940). 73-74.

30 On the supposed Old English poetic *koiné* see F. Klaeber, *Beowulf* (3ed, Boston, 1936). lxxxviii and K. Malone in *Revue belge de Philologie et d'Histoire*, XLII (1964). 155-156.

IV. The Old Tradition: Popular Poetry

32 A second ed. of K. Malone's *Widsith* is now in print (Copenhagen, 1962).

34 On the Runic Poem see K. Schneider, *Die germanischen Runennamen* (Meisenheim, 1956), *passim*.

35 Note also F. E. Harmer, *Anglo-Saxon Writs* (Manchester, 1952).

38 Grendon has been superseded by G. Storms, *Anglo-Saxon Magic* (The Hague, 1948). See also K. Schneider, *Festschrift . . . Spira* (Heidelberg, 1961), pp. 38-56.

41 K. Schneider takes *eorþan modor* (rightly, no doubt) for a compound word; see his *Runennamen* 605 top. One may compare the *fæmnanþegn* of *Beowulf* 2059.

43 On words of wisdom in *Beowulf* see K. Malone, *Humaniora, Essays honoring Archer Taylor* (Locust Valley, N.Y., 1960), pp. 180-194.

V. The Old Tradition: Courtly Poetry

45 A second ed. of K. Malone's *Widsith* has come out in the series *Anglistica* (XIII, Copenhagen, 1962). See also his papers in *Festschrift für L. L. Hammerich* (Copenhagen, 1962), pp. 161-167 and *Speculum*, XXXIX (1964). 35-44.

48 K. Malone's *Deor* is now in its fourth edition (1966). See also H. Hallmundsson, *American-Scandinavian Rev.*, L (1962). 267-271; M. W. Bloomfield, *PMLA*, LXXIX (1964). 534-541; and N. E. Eliason, *SP*, LXII (1965). 495-509.

50 From *Beowulf* 1125-1128 one gathers that the *wealaf* after swearing allegiance to Finn are released by him and take ship for Denmark, all but Hengest, whom Finn holds (as hostage?); see K. Malone, *Festschrift für Walther Fischer* (Heidelberg, 1959), pp. 1-3.

57 On *Maldon* see now *CL*, XIV (1962). 23-35 (by J. B. Bessinger) and 53-70 (by R. W. V. Elliott).

VI. Religious Poetry: Cædmon and his School

60 See C. L. Wrenn, *The Poetry of Cædmon* (1947) and the reviews in *MLR*, XLIII (1948). 250-252 and *MA*, XVII (1948). 56-57. On Bede's account of Cædmon see F. P. Magoun, *Speculum*, XXX (1955). 49-63 and K. Malone, *MLN*, LXXVI (1961). 193-195.

61 A later edition of the Old English *Exodus* is that of E. B. Irving (New Haven, 1953), reviewed by E. V. K. Dobbie in *JEGP*, LIII (1954). 229-231; by S. Potter in *MA*, xxv (1956). 30-33; and by C. L. Wrenn in *RES*, VI (1955). 184-189.

62 B. F. Huppé in his *Doctrine and Poetry: Augustine's Influence on Old English Poetry* (Albany, N.Y., 1959) includes a close study of *Genesis A*. On *Genesis* and *Exodus* see further *Anglia*, LXX (1952). 285-294; LXXV (1957). 1-34; LXXVII (1959). 1-11; and LXXX (1962). 363-378.

67 The latest editions of *Judith* are those of B. J. Timmer (1952) and E. V. K. Dobbie, in Krapp-Dobbie IV.

68 A tenth-century dating of *Judith* is now usual: see Timmer, ed., pp. 6-11, Dobbie, ed., p. lxiv, and H. M. Flasdieck, *Anglia*, LXIX (1950). 270. The poem as it has come down to us is in the West Saxon dialect, with some admixture of Anglian forms. These were formerly explained as relics of an Anglian original but are otherwise accounted for (not very convincingly) by F. Tupper and his followers; see *JEGP*, XI (1912). 82-89. The theory of a poetic *koiné* is likewise dubious; see F. Klaeber, *Beowulf* (3ed.), p. lxxxviii.

VII. Religious Poetry: Cynewulf and his School

70 On Cynewulf's poetry see also Marguerite-Marie Dubois, *Les Éléments Latins dans la Poésie Religieuse de Cynewulf* (Paris, 1943) and Claes Schaar, *Critical Studies in the Cynewulf Group* (Lund, 1949), with K. Malone's review of the latter in *Anglia*, LXX (1952). 444-450. Later editions: R. Woolf, *Juliana* (1955) and P. O. E. Gradon, *Cynewulf's Elene* (1958). *The Fates of the Apostles* follows *Andreas* in the Vercelli Book and the two poems are usually edited together, though they are otherwise unconnected.

74 On the runic passages of Cynewulf's poems see also R. W. V. Elliott's paper in *ES*, XXXIV (1953). 49-57 and K. Schneider, *Die germanischen Runennamen* (Meisenheim, 1956), pp. 548-557.

75 A recent ed. of *Andreas* and *Fates of the Apostles* is that of K. R. Brooks, reviewed by R. Willard in *MP*, LXII (1963). 45-51 and K. Malone, *Revue belge de Philologie et d'Histoire*, XLII (1964). 154-160. An important article by Hans Schabram, "*Andreas* und *Beowulf*," *Nachrichten der Giessener Hochschulgesellschaft*, XXXIV (1965). 201-218, attacks vigorously the view that the *Andreas* poet used *Beowulf*. For Felix's life of Guthlac see now the definitive ed. by B. Colgrave (Cambridge, 1956).

76 A recent ed. of *Phoenix* is that of N. F. Blake (Manchester, 1964); see also his paper in *Anglia*, LXXX (1962). 50-62.

VIII. Religious Poetry: Poems on Various Themes

78 The Dickins-Ross *Rood* is now in its fourth edition (1963).

79 The Advent poem has now been edited by J. J. Campbell with the title *The Advent Lyrics of the Exeter Book* (Princeton, 1959).

81 *Doomsday A* is to be dated early in the eleventh century according to Max

Förster, *Anglia*, LXXIII (1955). 7. F. Mossé, *Études Germaniques*, III (1948). 157-165, argues that *Doomsday C* had an Old Saxon original.

83 For the passages in *Solomon and Saturn* (first poem) that incorporate runes see K. Schneider, *op. cit.*, pp. 558-569. On *Gifts of Men* see J. E. Cross, *Neophilologus*, XLVI (1962). 66-70. *Falseness of Men* is called *Homiletic Fragment I* in Krapp-Dobbie II. 59 and *Admonition* is called *Homiletic Fragment II* in Krapp-Dobbie III. 224. For *Seafarer* see now the ed. of I. L. Gordon (1960). For editions of *Wanderer* and *Riming Poem* see Krapp-Dobbie III. 134-137 and 166-169. On *Wanderer* and *Seafarer* see also the following: D. Whitelock in the Chadwick Memorial Studies, *Early Cultures of N.W. Europe* (1950), pp. 259-272; R. M. Lumiansky, *Neophilologus*, XXXIV (1950). 104-112; S. B. Greenfield, *JEGP*, L (1951). 451-465; E. G. Stanley, *Anglia*, LXXIII (1955). 413-466; G. V. Smithers, *MA*, XXVI (1957). 137-153 and XXVIII (1959). 1-22; W. Erzgräber, *Festschrift . . . Spira* (1961), pp. 57-85; and A. A. Prins, *Neophilologus*, XLVIII (1964). 237-251.

85 It is now fashionable to date *Riming Poem, Wanderer,* and *Seafarer* late or latish and to doubt their Anglian origin; see esp. Mrs. Gordon's ed. *Seafarer*. But E. Ekwall, *Philologica: the Malone Anniversary Studies* (1949), p. 28, and H. M. Flasdieck, *Anglia*, LXIX (1950). 167-171, keep the older view and strengthen it with new evidence; see also G. V. Smithers, *English and Germanic Stud.*, IV (1951-1952). 84-85, who favors a latish date but a "Northern" origin for *Wanderer*. The Benedictine Office is now available in an edition by J. Ure; see Chapter X (Literary Prose) below. For the *Paris Psalter* see now B. Colgrave's edition in *Early English MSS in Facsimile*, VIII (Copenhagen, 1958).

IX. Secular Poetry

88 On the date of the *Durham Poem* see *JEGP*, LXI (1962). 591-594. *Ruin* is included in R. F. Leslie (ed.), *Three Old English Elegies* (Manchester, 1961). On the riddles, see the following: for text and notes, Krapp-Dobbie III; for text and translation, the *EETS* ed. of the Exeter Book; for the Leiden Riddle, R. W. Zandvoort, *English and Germanic Stud.*, III (1949-1950). 42-56; for other riddles, *Neophilologus*, XXX (1946). 126-127, XXXI (1947). 145-158; *PMLA*, LXI (1946). 620-623, 910-915, LXII (1947). 1-8, LXIII (1948). 3-6, LXIV (1949). 884-888; *MLN*, LXII (1947). 558-559, LXV (1950). 93-100; *Philologica: the Malone Anniversary Studies* (1949), pp. 1-19; *MA*, XXI (1952). 36-37; *SP*, XLIX (1952). 553-565; *ES*, XXXV (1954). 259-262; *RES*, IX (1958). 241-252; and *MS*, XX (1958). 93-97.

90 On *Eadwacer* and *Wife's Lament* as Old English representatives of the widespread *Frauenlied* genre see K. Malone, *CL*, XIV (1962). 106-117. *Wife's Lament* is included in R. F. Leslie (ed.), *Three Old English Elegies* (Manchester, 1961).

91 *Lover's* or *Husband's Message* is included in Leslie's book mentioned above. A. C. Bouman, *Patterns in Old English . . . Literature* (Leiden, 1962), tries to reconstruct a story pattern which, he thinks, underlies *Wife's Lament* and *Lover's* or *Husband's Message* but his pattern is not convincing, depending as it does on a reading in the latter poem which R. E. Kaske has shown to be highly unlikely; see *MA*, XXXIII (1964). 204-206. See also K. Malone, *ES*, XLVI (1965). 492-493. On the runes in *Lover's Message* see K. Schneider, *Die germanischen Runennamen* (Meisenheim, 1956), pp. 570-574.

92 A second ed. of Zupitza's *Beowulf* with new facsimile photographs and an introductory note (v-xvii) by Norman Davis is now available in the *EETS* series, No. 245 (1959). See also *Early English MSS in Facsimile*, I (1951) and XII (1963), both edited by K. Malone. Heyne-Schücking's *Beowulf* (ed. E. von Schaubert) is in its eighteenth edition (1963), and Chambers' *Beowulf, An Introduction* is in its third (1959), with a supplement by C. L. Wrenn, whose own *Beowulf* edition (1953) was issued in revised and enlarged form in 1958. A good prose translation is that of J. R. Clark Hall, as revised and annotated by C. L. Wrenn, with a Preface on words and meters by J. R. R. Tolkien (1940). Critical studies of *Beowulf* are too many to be listed here, but the following cannot go without mention: D. Whitelock, *The Audience of Beowulf* (Oxford, 1951); K. Sisam, *The Structure of Beowulf* (Oxford, 1965); and A. G. Brodeur, *The Art of Beowulf* (Berkeley, 1959), reviewed by J. C. Pope in *Speculum*, XXXVII (1962). 411-417, by Ad. Bonjour in *ES*, XLIII (1962). 501-504, and by K. Malone in *MLN*, LXXV (1960). 347-353. See also Bonjour's *Twelve 'Beowulf' Papers 1940-1960* . . . (Geneva, 1962), Charles Donahue, "Beowulf and Christian Tradition," *Traditio*, XXI (1965). 55-116, and L. E. Nicholson (ed.), *An Anthology of Beowulf Criticism* (South Bend, Indiana, 1963), the last but not the least item of the list.

93 On the date of *Beowulf* see also G. Bond, *SP*, XL (1943). 481-493 and H. M. Flasdieck, *Anglia*, LXIX (1950). 135-171; Flasdieck concludes that "the date of the original MS of *Beowulf* cannot be later than c. 725 and, more probably, is between 675 and 700" (p. 171). But D. Whitelock, *op. cit.*, contends that the poem may have been composed as late as the latter half of the eighth century.

X. Literary Prose

96 On English prose before Alfred note R. J. Menner's dictum: "Prose must have been cultivated in the Anglian kingdoms before the time of Alfred, . . ." (*Philologica: the Malone Anniversary Studies*, p. 56). In the paper from which this dictum is taken Menner shows that the Blickling homilies were of Anglian origin (they have come down to us in a tenth-century Saxonized version) but he does not venture to date their composition. Flasdieck however sees no difficulty in setting this date "as early as the beginning of the 8th c." (*Anglia*, LXIX. 168).

97 Authoritative translations of the *Old English Annals* are those of G. N. Garmonsway, in Everyman's Library, No. 624 (1953) and of S. I. Tucker, edited by D. Whitelock with D. C. Douglas (1961). The editor's Introduction to the latter translation is the latest if not the last word on the origins and history of the versions. Miss Whitelock also gives us the most recent study of the Old English Bede, in *Proc. Brit. Acad.* XLVIII (1963 for 1962). 57-90. The Bodleian MS Hatton 20, with Alfred's translation of Gregory's *Regula Pastoralis*, has been published in the series *Early English MSS in Facsimile*, VI (Copenhagen, 1956), ed. N. R. Ker, and in the same series (III, 1953) we have the Tollemache Orosius (BM MS Add. 47967), ed. A. Campbell. This translation has been compared with the Latin text by S. Potter, *Anglia*, LXXI (1953). 385-437 and by J. Bately, *Classica et Mediaevalia*, XVII (1961). 69-105; the latter, who studied a large number of codices and established many variant readings hitherto unknown to Alfredian

scholarship, has shown that Alfred departed from his Latin text much less often than had previously been thought. On Alfred's *Blostman* see S. Potter in *Philologica: the Malone Anniversary Studies* (Baltimore, 1949), pp. 25-30. On the West Saxon prose translation of Psalms 1-50 see now J. I'a Bromwich, *The Early Cultures of Northwest Europe* (Cambridge, 1950), pp. 289-303; he tells us that "King Alfred has just as good a claim to the translation of the prose portion of the Paris Psalter as he has to the Cura Pastoralis and the Boethius" (103).

101 Ælfric's *De temporibus anni* (in English despite its title) is to be had in H. Henel's ed. of 1942; see C. L. Wrenn's review in *RES*, xx (1944). 232-234. On Ælfric's rhythmic alliterative prose see esp. O. Funke, *Anglia*, lxxx (1962). 9-36 and *ES*, xliii (1962). 311-318. Marguerite-Marie Dubois's *Ælfric, Sermonnaire, Docteur et Grammairien* (Paris, 1943) is a full-scale study.

103 In recent years much work has been done on Wulfstan. See esp. D. Whitelock (ed.), *Sermo Lupi ad Anglos*, 3ed. (1963), with bibliography, which brings Wulfstan scholarship and criticism up to date in the form best suited to the student. Special mention, besides, must be made of the following: A. McIntosh, "Wulfstan's Prose," *Proc. Brit. Acad.*, xxxv (1949). 109-142; K. Jost, *Wulfstan studien* (Bern, 1950); K. Jost (ed.), *Die 'Institutes of Polity, Civil and Ecclesiastical'* (Bern, 1959); D. Bethurum, *The Homilies of Wulfstan* (Oxford, 1957); J. Ure, *The Benedictine Office* . . . (Edinburgh, 1957); and P. Clemoes, "The Old English Benedictine Office . . ." in *Anglia*, lxxviii (1960). 265-283. The *Blickling Homilies* MS (now owned by W. H. Scheide of Princeton, N.J.) is now to be had in facsimile: *Early English MSS in Facsimile*, x (Copenhagen, 1960), ed. R. Willard. On the dialect in which the homilies were composed see above (suppl. to p. 96).

104 A saint's life of some importance recently edited (though not for the first time) is that of St. Chad (Amsterdam, 1953), ed. R. Vleeskruyer; see A. Campbell's review in *MA*, xxiv (1955). 52-56. Of interest, too, is the first article of the Nowell codex, a fragment of a life of St. Christopher, ed. S. Rypins (1924; *EETS*, 161), pp. 68-76; see K. Sisam, *Studies in the History of Old English Literature* (Oxford, 1953), pp. 65-72 and K. Malone (ed.), *The Nowell Codex* (Copenhagen, 1963), pp. 114-115, 119. *Bald's Leech Book*, on which Cockayne drew for the second volume of his *Leechdoms* . . . , is now available in the series *Early English MSS in Facsimile*, v (Copenhagen, 1955), ed. C. E. Wright. The Old English *Apollonius* has been edited by J. Raith (Munich, 1956) and by P. Goolden (Oxford, 1958).

Part II. The Middle English Period (1100-1500)

I. General Characteristics of the Period

109 A new edition of Wells' *Manual* is in preparation under the general editorship of J. Burke Severs. There are new editions of Renwick and Orton (1952) and Loomis's *Reading List* (1948). To the Brown-Robbins *Index* there is now a Supplement by Rossell H. Robbins and John Cutler (Lexington, Ky.,

1965) as well as William Ringler, "A Bibliography and First-Line Index of English Verse Printed through 1500: A Supplement to Brown and Robbins' *Index of Middle English Verse*," *Papers of the Bibl. Soc. of America*, XLIX (1955). 153-180. The texts and editions cited in the *Middle English Dictionary* offer a very useful list, available separately: *A Bibliography of Middle English Texts*, by Margaret S. Ogden, Charles E. Palmer, and Richard L. McKelvey (Ann Arbor, 1956). The *Annual Bibliography of English Language and Literature*, published by the Modern Humanities Research Assoc., and the Annual Bibliography compiled by Paul A. Brown and numerous collaborators for *PMLA*, which since the issue for 1956 has been international in scope, are indispensable for all periods of English literature; the student will find convenient the surveys in *The Year's Work in English Studies*, issued annually since 1919 by the English Assoc., and *The Year's Work in Modern Language Studies*, since 1931, published by the M.H.R.A. The first issue of Rossell H. Robbins, "Middle English Research in Progress," appeared in *Neuphil. Mitteilungen*, LXV (1964). 360-366, with continuations appearing annually.

110 More recent general surveys of Middle English literature, at least in part, include H. S. Bennett, *Chaucer and the Fifteenth Century* (1947) and E. K. Chambers, *English Literature at the Close of the Fifteenth Century* (1946), both in the *Oxford History of English Literature;* George Kane, *Middle English Literature: A Critical Study of the Romances, the Religious Lyrics, 'Piers Plowman'* (1951); Margaret Schlauch, *English Medieval Literature and Its Social Foundations* (Warzawa, 1956); John Speirs, *Medieval English Poetry: The Non-Chaucerian Tradition* (1957); *The Pelican Guide to English Literature*, ed. Boris Ford: Vol. 1: *The Age of Chaucer* (1954, rev. 1963). The collected essays of Dorothy Everett, *Essays on Middle English Literature*, ed. Patricia Kean (Oxford, 1955), and of Laura Hibbard Loomis, *Adventures in the Middle Ages* (1962), gather together conveniently articles previously scattered. *Middle English Survey*, ed. Edward Vasta (Notre Dame, Ind., 1965) is an anthology of critical and interpretive articles.—For the Old French background Paul Zumthor, *Histoire littéraire de la France médiévale* (Paris, 1954), and Jessie Crosland, *Medieval French Literature* (Oxford, 1956), the latter often perceptive in its critical appraisals, may be consulted. R. Bossuat, *Manuel bibliographique de la littérature française du moyen âge* (Melun, 1951; two supplements, Paris, 1955, 1961) is indispensable in spite of many small inaccuracies. Ernst R. Curtius, *European Literature in the Latin Middle Ages*, trans. W. R. Trask (1953; German text, 1948), is broad in range and stimulating. W. T. H. Jackson, *The Literature of the Middle Ages* (1960), will help the student to see English literature in its European context.—The historical background has been enriched by several additional volumes in the *Oxford History of England:* Austin L. Poole, *From Domesday Book to Magna Carta, 1087-1216* (2ed, 1955), F. M. Powicke, *The Thirteenth Century, 1216-1307* (2ed, 1962), May McKisack, *The Fourteenth Century, 1307-1399* (1959), and E. F. Jacob, *The Fifteenth Century, 1399-1485* (1961). A revised and rewritten edition of *Medieval England* is ed. by A. L. Poole (2v, Oxford, 1958). Two excellent shorter treatments are Doris M. Stenton, *English Society in the Early Middle Ages, 1066-1307* (2ed, 1952), and A. R. Myers, *England in the Late Middle Ages, 1307-1536* (1952), both Pelican Books. *The Shorter Cambridge Medieval History*, ed. Philip Grierson (2v, 1952) is an abridgment of the

larger work. Indispensable for the background of much religious literature are Dom David Knowles, *The Monastic Order in England* (2ed, Cambridge, 1963), and *The Religious Orders in England* (3v, Cambridge, 1948-59).

II. The Survival of the Native Tradition

118   The items of R. M. Wilson in note 6 have been incorporated in *The Lost Literature of Medieval England* (1952). Cecilia Sisam, "The Scribal Tradition of the *Lambeth Homilies*," *RES*, n.s. II (1951). 105-113, is a valuable study leading to important general conclusions.

123   Betty Hill, "The 'Luue Ron' and Thomas de Hales," *MLR*, LIX (1964). 321-330, supplies important new data. Thomas of Hales wrote also in Latin and French. For an Anglo-Norman sermon by him see M. Dominica Legge, *Anglo-Norman Literature and Its Background* (Oxford, 1963). Of great interest for the Katherine Group is the *Facsimile of MS Bodley 34: St. Katherine, St. Margaret, St. Juliana, Hali Meiðhad, Sawles Warde*, ed. N. R. Ker (1960; EETS, 247).

125   The edition of the *St. Juliana* by Miss d'Ardenne mentioned in note 20 has been reprinted (1961; EETS, 248).

126   Additional evidence for Herefordshire is offered by Cecily Clark, "*Sawles Warde* and Herefordshire," *N&Q*, CXCIX (1954). 140.

III. The Ancrene Riwle

127   The intention of the *EETS* mentioned in note 1 is steadily being carried out. The following MSS have been printed: Cotton MS Nero A. XIV, ed. Mabel Day (1952; *EETS*, 225); Gonville and Caius College MS 234/120, ed. R. M. Wilson, 1954; *EETS*, 229); BM MS Royal 8 C.i., ed. Albert C. Baugh (1965; *EETS*, 232); Corpus Christi College, Cambridge MS 402 (*Ancrene Wisse*), ed. J. R. R. Tolkien (1962; *EETS*, 249); Cotton MS Titus D. XVIII, ed. Frances M. Mack (1963; *EETS*, 252); the second French version, from Trin. Coll., Cambridge MS R. 14. 7, etc., ed. W. H. Trethewey (1958; *EETS*, 240). See also W. H. Trethewey, "The Seven Deadly Sins and the Devil's Court in the Trinity College Cambridge French Text of the *Ancrene Riwle*," *PMLA*, LXV (1950). 1233-1246; John H. Fisher, "The French Versions of the *Ancrene Riwle*," *Middle Ages—Reformation—Volkskunde: Festschrift for John G. Kunstmann* (Chapel Hill, 1959; *Univ. of No. Carolina Stud. in the Germanic Lang. and Lit.*, No. 26), pp. 65-74; *The Ancrene Riwle: The Corpus MS. Ancrene Wisse*, trans. M. B. Salu (1955; *Orchard Books*); E. J. Dobson, "The Affiliations of the Manuscripts of *Ancrene Wisse*," *English and Medieval Studies Presented to J. R. R. Tolkien* (1962), pp. 128-163; Charlotte D'Evelyn, "Notes on Some Interrelations between the Latin and English Texts of the *Ancrene Riwle*," *PMLA*, LXIV (1949). 1164-1179.

128   That English was the original language of the *Ancrene Riwle* has become clear from Miss D'Evelyn's article just mentioned and especially from Hans Käsmann, "Zur Frage der ursprünglichen Fassung der *Ancrene Riwle*,"

Anglia, LXXV (1957). 134-156. *The Tretyse of Loue,* ed. John H. Fisher (1951; *EETS,* 223), derives in part from the *Ancrene Riwle.* See also John H. Fisher, "Continental Associations for the *Ancrene Riwle,*" *PMLA,* LXIV (1949). 1180-1189.

133 C. H. Talbot, "Some Notes on the Dating of the *Ancrene Riwle,*" *Neophilologus,* XL (1956). 38-50, offers important evidence for dating the work in the latter half of the twelfth century, possibly the closing years of the century. Peter Hackett, "The Anchoresses' Guide," *The Month,* n.s. XXIII (1960). 227-240, is a sensible survey.

134 *þe Wohunge of Ure Lauerd,* ed. W. Meredith Thompson (1958; *EETS,* 241).

IV. Anglo-Norman Literature

135 The best treatment of Anglo-Norman literature is now M. Dominica Legge, *Anglo-Norman Literature and its Background* (Oxford, 1963), to which may be added her earlier book, *Anglo-Norman in the Cloisters: The Influence of the Orders upon Anglo-Norman Literature* (Edinburgh, 1950; *Edinburgh Univ. Pub.: Lang. & Lit.,* No. 2). The *Dictionnaire des lettres françaises publié sous la direction du Cardinal Georges Grente. Le Moyen Age,* préparé par R. Bossuat, *et al.* (Paris, 1964), contains articles (of unequal value) on all the works mentioned in the present chapter. Much the best review of the current status of Anglo-Norman scholarship is K. V. Sinclair, "Anglo-Norman Studies: The Last Twenty Years," *Australian Jour. of French Stud.,* II (1965). 113-155, 225-278. Ruth J. Dean, "A Fair Field Needing Folk: Anglo-Norman," *PMLA,* LXIX (1954). 965-978, is useful.

136 On Eleanor of Aquitaine see E. R. Labande, "Pour une image véridique d'Aliénor d'Aquitaine," *Bull. Soc. des Antiquaires de l'Ouest,* 4th Ser., II (1953). 175-234; Rita Lejeune, "Rôle littéraire d'Aléanor d'Aquitaine et de sa famille," *Cultura Neolatina,* XLV (1954). 5-57, both being supplementary to the basic account in Alfred Richard, *Histoire des comtes de Poitou, 778-1204* (Paris, 1903), II. 54-457. The major part of W. F. Schirmer and U. Broich, *Studien zum literarischen Patronat im England des 12. Jahrhunderts* (Köln, 1962), is the discussion (by Broich) of Henry II as a literary patron. Florence McCulloch, *Medieval Latin and French Bestiaries* (Chapel Hill, 1960; *Univ. of No. Carolina Stud. in the Romance Lang. and Lit.,* No. 33), may be read in connection with the *Bestiaire* of Philippe de Thaün.

137 The Latin and Anglo-Norman lives of St. Edmund by Matthew Paris are discussed by C. H. Lawrence in *St. Edmund of Abingdon: A Study in Hagiography and History* (Oxford, 1960). Alexander Bell, "Notes on Two Anglo-Norman Saints' Lives," *PQ,* XXXV (1956). 48-59, discusses a *St. Osith* in the Welbeck Abbey MS and *La Passiun de Seint Edmund* in a Caius MS. *The Life of St. Catherine* by Clemence of Barking is edited by William Macbain (Oxford, 1964; *Anglo-Norman Text Soc.,* No. 18).

138 Alexander Bell (ed.), *L'Estoire des Engleis* by Geffrei Gaimar (Oxford, 1960; *Anglo-Norman Text Soc.,* Nos. 14-15) on which Ronald N. Walpole, "A

New Edition of Geffrei Gaimar's *L'Estoire des Engleis*," *PQ*, XLI (1962). 373-385, is a critique.

139 Iain MacDonald, "The Chronicle of Jordan Fantosme: Manuscripts, Author, and Versification," *Studies in Medieval French Presented to Alfred Ewert* (Oxford, 1961), pp. 242-258. The *Chronicle* of the Dominican friar Nicholas Trevet (*c*. 1335) has not yet been edited. See, however, Ruth J. Dean, "The Manuscripts of Nicholas Trevet's Anglo-Norman *Chronicles*," *Medievalia et Humanistica*, XIV (1962). 95-105. Also pertinent here are Isabel S. T. Aspin (ed.), *Anglo-Norman Political Songs* (Oxford, 1953; *Anglo-Norman Text Soc.*, No. 11) and Carl Selmer (ed.), *Navigatio Sancti Brendani Abbatis from Early Latin MSS* (Notre Dame, 1959). R. L. G. Ritchie, "The Date of the *Voyage of St. Brendan*," *MA*, XIX (1950). 64-66, suggests that it was dedicated to Queen Maud and dates it before May 1, 1118, possibly *c*. 1106.

140 Sister Amelia Klenke has edited *Three Saints' Lives by Nicholas Bozon* (St. Bonaventure, N.Y., 1947; *Franciscan Inst. Pub., Hist. Ser.*, No. 1) and *Seven More Poems by Nicholas Bozon* (St. Bonaventure, N.Y., 1951; same ser., No. 2), the attribution of some of the latter being open to question. In "Nicholas Bozon," *MLN*, LXIX (1954). 256-260, she continues to argue that Bozon belonged to the diocese of York rather than Lincoln. New data on Peter of Peckham are given by M. Dominica Legge in "*La Lumiere as Lais*—a Postscript," *MLR*, XLVI (1951). 191-195, and *Anglo-Norman in the Cloisters*, pp. 63-68. For a summary of and selections (modernized) from the *Lumiere* see Charles V. Langlois, *La Vie en France au moyen âge* (4v, Paris, 1924-28), IV. 66-119. William of Wadington's authorship of the *Manuel des Péchés*, long considered doubtful, is now generally given up. The text is being edited for the Anglo-Norman Text Society by E. J. Arnould. See also Charlton Laird, "Character and Growth of the *Manuel des Pechiez*," *Traditio*, IV (1946). 253-306. Though not mentioned in the text, worth noting is Henry of Lancaster's *Livre de Seyntz Medicines* (1352), ed. E. J. Arnould (Oxford, 1940; *Anglo-Norman Text Soc.*, No. 2). Cf. also the editor's study, *Étude sur le Livre des saintes medecines du duc Henri de Lancastre* (Paris, 1948), and R. W. Ackerman, "The Traditional Background of Lancaster's *Livre*," *L'Esprit Créateur*, II (1962). 114-118.

141 On Robert de Boron see Mary E. Giffin, "A Reading of Robert de Boron," *PMLA*, LXXX (1965). 499-507. *The Romance of Horn by Thomas*, ed. Mildred K. Pope and T. B. W. Reid (2v, Oxford, 1955-64; *Anglo-Norman Text Soc.*, Nos. 9-10, 12-13). Brian Foster, "The *Roman de toute chevalerie*: Its date and author," *French Studies*, IX (1955). 154-158, assigns the romance to shortly after 1150. E. A. Francis, "The Background of 'Fulk FitzWarin,'" *Studies in Medieval French Presented to Alfred Ewert* (Oxford, 1961), pp. 322-327, may be mentioned.

V. Early Latin Writers

144 On John of Salisbury see Hans Liebeschütz, *Medieval Humanism in the Life and Writings of John of Salisbury* (1950; *Stud. of the Warburg Inst.*, 17), Georg Misch, *Studien zur Geschichte der Autobiographie*, V: *Johann von Salisbury und das Problem des mittelalterlichen Humanismus* (Göttingen, 1960;

Nachrichten der Akad. der Wissenschaften in Göttingen, 1960, No. 6), and *The Metalogicon of John of Salisbury, a Twelfth-Century Defense of the Verbal and Logical Arts of the Trivium*, trans. Daniel D. McGarry (Berkeley, 1955).

145 André Boutemy, *Gautier Map, conteur anglais* (Brussels, 1945).

146 H. G. Richardson, "Gervase of Tilbury," *History*, XLVI (1961). 102-114, is a good appraisal. For Giraldus Cambrensis should be noted *The First Version of the Topography of Ireland*, trans. John J. O'Meara (Dundalk, 1951), and Thomas Jones, *Gerald the Welshman's 'Itinerary through Wales' and 'Description of Wales': An Appreciation and Analysis* (Aberystwyth, 1950; also in *The National Library of Wales Jour.*, VI).

147 *The Historia Novella* by William of Malmesbury and the *Gesta Stephani* have both been edited by K. R. Potter (1955) for *Nelson's Medieval Classics*.

148 Richard Vaughan, *Matthew Paris* (Cambridge, 1958; *Cambridge Stud. in Medieval Life and Thought*, n.s., vol. 6) is excellent.

149 Geoffrey B. Riddehough, "A Forgotten Poet: Joseph of Exeter," *JEGP*, XLVI (1947). 254-259, and "Joseph of Exeter: The Cambridge Manuscript," *Speculum*, XXIV (1949). 389-396, should be noted. New translations of some Goliardic poems have been published by the translator, George F. Whicher, *The Goliardic Poets: Medieval Latin Songs and Satires* (n.p., 1949). On Serlo of Wilton see Albert C. Friend, "The Proverbs of Serlo of Wilton," *MS*, XVI (1954). 179-218, and *Serlon de Wilton: Poèmes latins, texte critique* . . . ed. Jan Öberg (Stockholm, 1965; *Acta Universitatis: Studia Latina*, XIV). The best treatment of Nigel Wireker (properly Nigel de Longchamps) is the introduction to A. Boutemy, *Nigellus de Longchamp, dit Wireker*, vol. 1 (Paris, 1959). The *Speculum Stultorum* has been edited by by J. H. Mozley and R. R. Raymo (Berkeley, 1960; *Calif. Stud. in English*) and there is now an excellent translation, *The Book of Daun Burnel the Ass*, trans. Graydon W. Regenos (Austin, Texas, 1959).

150 Theodore Silverstein, "Daniel of Morley, English Cosmogonist and Student," *MS*, X (1948). 179-196. E. Westacott, *Roger Bacon in Life and Legend* (1953), Theodore Crowley, *Roger Bacon: The Problem of the Soul in his Philosophical Writings* (Dublin, 1950), Stewart C. Easton, *Roger Bacon and His Search for a Universal Science: A Reconsideration of the Life and Work of Roger Bacon in the Light of His Own Stated Purposes* (Oxford, 1952), and Erich Heck, *Roger Bacon: Ein mittelalterlicher Versuch einer historischen und systematischen Religionswissenschaft* (Bonn, 1957, offset typescript) contribute, each by its own approach, to our understanding of Bacon. On Ailred of Rievaulx see Amédée Hallier, *Un éducateur monastique: Aelred de Rievaulx* (Paris, 1959); *The Life of Ailred of Rievaulx by Walter Daniel*, trans. F. M. Powicke (1950); and Carleton M. Sage, "The Manuscripts of St. Aelred," *Cath. Hist. Rev.*, XXXIV (1949). 437-445. We should now add to note 19 Sir Maurice Powicke, "Robert Grosseteste, Bishop of Lincoln," *Bull. John Rylands Library*, XXXV (1953). 482-507, and D. A. Callus (ed.), *Robert Grosseteste, Scholar and Bishop: Essays in Commemoration of the Seventh Century of His Death* (Oxford, 1955). Alfred C. Friend, "Master Odo of Cheriton," *Speculum*, XXIII (1948). 641-658, includes new biographical material and a consideration of the dates of his works. N. Denholm Young, "Richard de Bury (1287-1345)," *Trans. Royal Hist. Soc.*, 4th Ser., XX (1937), reprinted in his *Collected Papers on Mediaeval Subjects* (Oxford,

1946), pp. 1-25, makes significant additions to our knowledge, especially to the important articles of J. DeGhellinck, "Un évêque bibliophile au XIVᵉ siècle: Richard Aungerville de Bury (1345)," *Revue d'histoire ecclésiastique*, xviii (1922). 271-312, 482-508; xix (1923). 157-200. New evidence on the date of Bromyard's *Summa Predicantium* (earlier fourteenth century) is given in W. A. Pantin, *The English Church in the Fourteenth Century*, p. 147.

VI. Wit and Wisdom

153 The work of Arngart has been completed by a second volume (Lund, 1955), containing the texts.

154 Most important is N. R. Ker's *The Owl and the Nightingale, reproduced in facsimile from the surviving manuscripts, Jesus Coll. Oxford 29 and B. M. Cotton Caligula A. IX* (1963; EETS, 251). The Cotton MS has been edited by Eric G. Stanley (1960; *Nelson's Medieval and Renaissance Library*). There is a verse translation of the poem by Graydon Eggers (Durham, N.C., 1955). The following items deserve mention: Bertil Sundby, *The Dialect and Provenance of the Middle English Poem 'The Owl and the Nightingale': A Linguistic Study* (Lund, 1950; *Lund Stud. in English*, xviii), Robert M. Lumiansky, "Concerning *The Owl and the Nightingale*," PQ, xxxii (1953). 411-417, and A. C. Cawley, "Astrology in *The Owl and the Nightingale*," MLR, xlvi (1951). 161-174, the last discussing an astrological allusion possibly bearing on the date of the poem.

VII. For Their Soul's Need

158 J. E. Turville-Petre, "Studies on the *Ormulum* MS," *JEGP*, xlvi (1947). 1-27, R. W. Burchfield, "*Ormulum*: Words Copied by Jan Van Vliet from Parts Now Lost," *English and Medieval Studies Presented to J. R. R. Tolkien* (1962), pp. 94-111, and E. S. Olszewska, "Alliterative Phrases in the *Ormulum*: Some Norse Parallels," *ibid.*, pp. 112-127, are all useful.

162 Nita Scudder Baugh, *A Worcestershire Miscellany, Compiled by John Northwood, c. 1400, ed. from B. M. MS. Add. 37,787* (Philadelphia, 1956), prints the text of the *Body and Soul* and explains the hitherto puzzling disarrangement of the stanzas in this manuscript. Special aspects of the poem are discussed in Robert W. Ackerman, "*The Debate of the Body and the Soul* and Parochial Christianity," *Speculum*, xxxvii (1962). 541-565, and Sister M. Ursula Vogel, *Some Aspects of the Horse and Rider Analogy in* The Debate between the Body and the Soul (Washington, D.C., 1948).

VIII. The Arthurian Legend to Layamon

165 The work of Bruce, while still valuable, must now yield to *Arthurian Literature in the Middle Ages: A Collaborative History*, ed. Roger S. Loomis (Oxford, 1959). See also R. S. Loomis, *Arthurian Tradition and Chrétien de Troyes* (1949) and *The Development of Arthurian Romance* (1963); Jean Marx,

La légende arthurienne et le Graal (Paris, 1952) and *Nouvelles recherches sur la littérature arthurienne* (Paris, 1965). The annual bibliography in *MLQ,* begun by J. J. Parry and continued by Paul A. Brown was discontinued in 1963; the best current guide to Arthurian scholarship is the annual *Bulletin bibliographique de la Société Internationale Arthurienne* (Paris, in prog.). To note 2 should be added *The Continuations of the Old French* Perceval *of Chrétien de Troyes: The First Continuation,* ed. William Roach (3v in 4 to date, Philadelphia, 1949-55).

167   The *Mabinogion* should now be read in the scholarly translation of Gwyn and Thomas Jones (1950). On the historicity of Arthur and the beginnings see Thomas Jones, "The Early Evolution of the Legend of Arthur," *Nottingham Mediaeval Stud.,* VIII (1964). 4-21; John J. Parry, "The Historical Arthur," *JEGP,* LVIII (1959). 365-379, which makes some useful points; William A. Nitze, "Arthurian Names: *Arthur,*" *PMLA,* LXIV (1949). 585-596, 1235.

169   A *Variant Version* of the *Historia Regum Britanniae* was edited by Jacob Hammer (Cambridge, Mass., 1951). On the date of this version see Robert A. Caldwell, "Wace's *Roman de Brut* and the *Variant Version* of Geoffrey of Monmouth's *Historia Regum Britanniae,*" *Speculum,* XXXI (1956). 675-682. For a full discussion of Geoffrey of Monmouth see J. S. P. Tatlock, *The Legendary History of Britain: Geoffrey of Monmouth's Historia Regum Britanniae and Its Early Vernacular Version* (Berkeley, 1950).

170   On Wace see Michel de Roüard, "A propos des sources du *Roman de Rou,*" *Recueil de Travaux offert à M. Clovis Brunel* (2v, Paris, 1955), I. 178-182, Urban T. Holmes, Jr., "Norman Literature and Wace," in *Medieval Secular Literature: Four Essays,* ed. William Matthews (Berkeley, 1965), and Elspeth Yeo, "Wace's *Roman de Brut:* A Newly Discovered Fragment," *Manuscripta,* VIII (1964). 101-104. A new edition of Layamon's *Brut,* ed. G. L. Brook and R. F. Leslie, Vol. I [to line 8020] (1963; *EETS,* 250). See also W. J. Keith, "Laȝamon's *Brut:* The Literary Differences between between the Two Texts," *MA,* XXIX (1960). 161-172, and Herbert Pilch, *Laȝamons 'Brut': Eine literarische Studie* (Heidelberg, 1960; *Anglistische Forsch.,* 91).

IX. The Romance: I

173   The following items concern the Middle English romances generally: Karl Brunner, "Middle English Metrical Romances and Their Audience," *Studies in Medieval Literature,* ed. MacEdward Leach (Philadelphia, 1961), pp. 219-227 (inferences drawn from the character of the MSS) and "Die Überlieferungen der mittelenglischen Versromanzen," *Anglia,* LXXVI (1958). 64-73 (interesting statistics on the dates and the number of the MSS); Dieter Mehl, "Die kürzeren mittelenglischen 'Romanzen' und die Gattungsfrage," *Deutsche Vierteljahrsschrift für Litteraturwissenschaft und Geistesgeschichte,* XXXVIII (1964). 513-533; Albert C. Baugh, "The Authorship of the Middle English Romances," *Annual Bull. of the Modern Humanities Research Assoc.,* No. 22 (1950). 13-28 and "Improvisation in the Middle English Romance," *Proc. Amer. Philos. Soc.,* CIII (1959). 418-454; Gerald Bordman, *Motif-Index of the English Metrical Romances* (Helsinki, 1963; *FF Com.,* vol. 79, no. 190).

175   D. M. Hill, "An Interpretation of *King Horn*," *Anglia*, LXXV (1957). 157-172, finds symbolism in the poem; Charles W. Dunn, "Havelok and Anlaf Cuaran," *Franciplegius: Medieval and Linguistic Studies in Honor of Francis Peabody Magoun, Jr.* (1965), pp. 244-249.

181   On the legend of Alexander see George Cary, *The Medieval Alexander* (Cambridge, 1956).

X. The Romance: II

189   The English Arthurian romances in alliterative verse are discussed by J. L. N. O'Loughlin in *Arthurian Literature in the Middle Ages*, ed. Roger S. Loomis (Oxford, 1959), pp. 520-527, the others by Robert W. Ackerman, *ibid.*, pp. 480-519. Ackerman has also published a most useful *Index of the Arthurian Names in Middle English* (Stanford, 1952; Stanford Univ. Pub., Univ. Ser., Lang. and Lit., x). On the short poem known as *Arthur* see J. Finlayson, "The Source of *Arthur*, an Early Fifteenth-Century Verse Chronicle," *N&Q*, CCV (1960). 46-47, who finds that the principal source is Wace.

190   *Ywain and Gawain* has been edited by A. B. Friedman and N. T. Harrington (1964; *EETS*, 254). *Sir Gawain and the Carl of Carlisle* has been twice edited: by Robert W. Ackerman (Ann Arbor, 1947; *Univ. of Michigan Contrib. in Mod. Phil.*, No. 8) and by Auvo Kurvinen (Helsinki, 1951; *Annales Academiae Scientiarum Fennicae*, Ser. B, vol. 71, pt. 2). M. Mills, "A Mediaeval Reviser at Work," *MA*, XXXII (1963). 11-23, concerns *Libeaus Desconus*.

191   William Matthews, *The Tragedy of Arthur: A Study of the Alliterative 'Morte Arthure'* (Berkeley, 1960); Angus McIntosh, "The Textual Transmission of the Alliterative *Morte Arthure*," *English and Medieval Studies Presented to J. R. R. Tolkien* (1962), pp. 231-240. William A. Nitze, *Perceval and the Holy Grail* (Berkeley, 1949; *Univ. of Calif. Pub. in Mod. Phil.*, vol. 28, no. 5).

192   Thomas C. Rumble, "The Middle English *Sir Tristrem:* Toward A Reappraisal," *Compar. Lit.*, XI (1959). 221-228.

193   Mabel VanDuzee, *A Medieval Romance of Friendship—Eger and Grime* (1963) is a study of the romance.

194   Charles W. Dunn, *The Foundling and the Werwolf: A Literary-Historical Study of 'Guillaume de Palerne'* (Toronto, 1960). L. F. Casson, *The Romance of Sir Degrevant: A Parallel-Text Edition* (1949; *EETS*, 221).

195   Robert J. Geist, "Notes on *The King of Tars*," *JEGP*, XLVII (1948). 173-178, studies the relationship of the MSS and the dialect. Thomas C. Rumble, *The Breton Lays in Middle English* (Detroit, 1965), is a welcome edition of the principal texts. G. V. Smithers, "Story-Patterns in Some Breton Lays," *MA*, XXII (1953). 61-92, is concerned especially with English examples.

196   William C. Stokoe, Jr., "The Double Problem of *Sir Degaré*," *PMLA*, LXX (1955). 518-534, corrects the views set forth by Faust and in the still earlier study of Clark H. Slover, *Sire Degarre: A Study of a Mediaeval Hack Writer's Methods* (Austin, Texas, 1931; *Univ. of Texas Stud. in English*, No. 11). Mention should be made of the edition of *Sir Degare* by Gustav Schliech (Heidelberg, 1929; *Englische Textbibliothek*, xix), based on all the MSS. A. J. Bliss (ed.), *Sir Launfal* (1960; *Nelson's Medieval and Renaissance Library*) contains also *Sir Landevale* and Marie's *Lanval* in the Appendix. See also M. Mills, "The Composition and Style of the 'Southern' *Octavian, Sir Launfal* and *Libeaus Desconus*," *MA*, xxxi (1962). 88-109. On *Sir Orfeo* see the edition of A. J. Bliss (Oxford, 1954); J. Burke Severs, "The Antecedents of *Sir Orfeo*," *Studies in Medieval Literature*, ed. MacEdward Leach (Philadelphia, 1961), pp. 187-207; D. M. Hill, "The Structure of *Sir Orfeo*," *MS*, xxiii (1961). 136-153; Dorena Allen, "Orpheus and Orfeo: The Dead and the *Taken*," *MA*, xxxiii (1964). 102-111, an interesting theory that the romance represents the classical story as understood by a Celt and represents it in the light of Celtic popular beliefs; B. Mitchell, "The Faery World of *Sir Orfeo*," *Neophilologus*, xlviii (1964). 155-159.

198 Beverly Boyd (ed.), *The Middle English Miracles of the Virgin* (San Marino, Calif., 1964; *Huntington Library Pub.*). See also R. W. Southern, "The English Origins of the 'Miracles of the Virgin,'" *Medieval and Renais. Stud.*, iv (1958). 176-216, and Harold F. Folland, "Our Lady and Her Miracles," *Western Humanities Rev.*, iii (1949). 285-302. Two additional studies of the fabliau should now be consulted: Per Nykrog, *Les Fabliaux: Étude d'histoire littéraire et de stylistique médiévale* (Copenhagen, 1957), and Jean Rychner, *Contributions à l'étude des fabliaux: Variantes, remaniements, dégradations* (2v, Geneva, 1960).

XI. The Omnibus of Religion

200 A number of the works treated in this chapter are considered in W. A. Pantin, *The English Church in the Fourteenth Century* (Cambridge, 1955), chap. x: Religious and Moral Treatises in the Vernacular. See also Morton W. Bloomfield, *The Seven Deadly Sins: An Introduction to the History of a Religious Concept* (East Lansing, 1952).

202 On John Peckham and his Constitutions see Decima L. Douie, *Archbishop Pecham* (Oxford, 1952).

204 D. W. Robertson, Jr., "The Cultural Tradition of *Handlyng Synne*," *Speculum*, xxii (1947). 162-185.

206 Philip Buehler, "The *Cursor Mundi* and Herman's *Bible*—Some Additional Parallels," *SP*, lxi (1964). 485-499; Henning Larsen, "Origo Crucis," in *If by Your Art* (Hunt Festschrift, 1948), pp. 27-33; Paul E. Beichner, "The *Cursor Mundi* and Petrus Riga," *Speculum*, xxiv (1949). 239-250; J. J. Lamberts, "The Noah Story in Cursor Mundi (vv. 1625-1916)," *MS*, xxiv (1962), 217-232, is an attempt at a critical edition of this portion. An edition of *The South English Legendary* has been published by Charlotte D'Evelyn and Anna J. Mill (3v, 1956-9; *EETS*, 235, 236, 241). See also Beverly Boyd, "New Light on *The South English Legendary*," *Texas Stud. in English*, xxxvii (1958). 187-194, and Theodor Wolpers, *Die englische Heiligenlegende des Mittelalters: Eine Formgeschichte des Legendenerzählens von der spätantiken lateinischen Tradition bis zur Mitte des 16. Jahrhunderts* (Tübingen, 1964; *Anglia Beireihe*, 10). After a lapse of many years the edition of an early fifteenth-century Biblical paraphrase is being completed and deserves mention: *A Middle English Metrical Paraphrase of the Old*

Testament, ed. H. Kalen and U. Ohlander (Vols. I-IV, Göteborg, 1922-63; the last three volumes are in *Gothenburg Stud. in English*). See also Urban Ohlander, "Old French Parallels to a Middle English Metrical Paraphrase of the Old Testament," *Gothenburg Stud. in English*, XIV (1962). 203-224.

XII. The Lyric

208 The following discussions and editions may be noted: Arthur K. Moore, *The Secular Lyric in Middle English* (Lexington, Ky., 1951); Rossell H. Robbins (ed.), *Secular Lyrics of the XIVth and XVth Centuries* (2ed, Oxford, 1955); the same editor's *Historical Poems of the XIVth and XVth Centuries* (1959); Henry A. Person (ed.), *Cambridge Middle English Lyrics* (2ed, Seattle, 1962), seventy lyrics from MSS in Cambridge college libraries; R. T. Davies (ed.), *Medieval English Lyrics: A Critical Anthology* (1963); Nita Scudder Baugh (ed.), *A Worcestershire Miscellany Compiled by John Northwood, c. 1400, from B. M. Add. MS 37,787* (Philadelphia, 1956), a collection of religious pieces, mostly lyrical. See also Rossell H. Robbins, "Middle English Lyrics: Handlist of New Texts," *Anglia*, LXXXIII (1965). 35-47.

209 On the sources of the vernacular lyric see Peter Dronke, *Medieval Latin and the Rise of European Love-Lyric* (Cambridge, 1965).

211 For the student who wishes to explore further the convention of Courtly Love, the starting point is the treatise *De Amore* of Andreas Capellanus (*c.* 1185), ed. E. Trojel (Copenhagen, 1892), English translation by John J. Parry, *The Art of Courtly Love* (1941). See also Alexander J. Denomy. *The Heresy of Courtly Love* (1947), D. W. Robertson, Jr., "The Subject of the *De Amore* of Andreas Capellanus," *MP*, L (1953). 145-161, and Don K. Frank, "The Corporeal, the Derogatory and the Stress on Equality in Andreas' *De Amore*," *Medievalia et Humanistica*, XVI (1964). 30-38. Courtly love, as implied in the text, is illicit, the devotion of the lover to a married woman, exemplified by the relations of Lancelot and Guinevere.

213 Most welcome is the *Facsimile of British Museum MS. Harley 2253*, with intro. by N. R. Ker (1965; *EETS*, 255). Also to be noted are G. D. Brook (ed.), *The Harley Lyrics: The Middle English Lyrics of MS. Harley 2253* (Manchester, 1948) and the important article of Theo. Stemmler, "Zur Datierung des MS. Harley 2253," *Anglia*, LXXX (1962). 111-118, which draws some of its best evidence from an unpublished M.A. thesis by J. A. Gibson (Univ. of London). Political and other allusions require a date about 1340. The Leominster origin rests on dubious evidence (see Ker).

215 Bukofzer's contention has been seriously challenged by B. Schofield, "The Provenance and Date of *Sumer is Icumen in*," *Music Rev.*, IX (1948). 81-86. For the religious lyric see Stephen Manning, *Wisdom and Number: Toward a Critical Appraisal of the Middle English Religious Lyric* (Lincoln, Neb., 1962); Sister M. Aquinas Chester, "The Latin Hymn and the Middle English Lyric," *Papers of the Michigan Acad.*, XL (1954). 271-283; Ruth E. Messenger, *The Medieval Latin Hymn* (Washington, D.C., 1953); Theodor Wolpers, *Geschichte der englischen Marienlyrik im Mittelalter*," *Anglia*, LXIX (1950). 3-88.

221 On the carol: Richard L. Greene (ed.), *A Selection of English Carols* (Oxford, 1962); Rossell H. Robbins (ed.), *Early English Christmas Carols* (1961); "The Middle English Carol Corpus: Some Additions," *MLN*, LXXIV (1959). 198-208, and "Friar Herbert and the Carol," *Anglia*, LXXV (1957). 194-198; J. Copley, "The 15th Century Carol and Christmas," *N&Q*, CXCIX (1954). 242-243, and "John Audelay's Carols and Music," *ES*, XXXIX (1958). 207-212; and Richard L. Greene, "The Meaning of the Corpus Christi Carol," *MA*, XXIX (1960). 10-21.

XIII. Richard Rolle and Other Mystics

225 Hilda Graef, *The Light and the Rainbow* (1959) traces the history of mysticism from Old Testament times to the late Middle Ages. Shorter surveys are Gerard Sitwell, *Medieval Spiritual Writers* (1961) and Ray C. Petry, *Late Medieval Mysticism* (Philadelphia, 1957).

226 For English mysticism see David Knowles, *The English Mystical Tradition* (1961), Conrad Pepler, *The English Religious Heritage* (1958), Richard M. Wilson, "Three Middle English Mystics [Rolle, Julian of Norwich, Margery Kemp]," *E&S*, n.s. IX (1956). 87-112, and Eric Colledge, *The Medieval Mystics of England* (1962), the last a book of selections with short introductions.

227 An important Rolle text is now available for the first time, the *Melos Amoris*, ed. E. J. F. Arnould (Oxford, 1957). The editor's "Richard Rolle of Hampole," *The Month*, n.s. XXIII (1960). 13-25, is an excellent brief account.

228 The text of the *Incendium Amoris* is available in two editions: *The Incendium Amoris of Richard Rolle*, ed. Margaret Deanesly (Manchester, 1915; *Pub. of the Univ. of Manchester, Hist. Ser.*, No. XXVI) and Dom N. Noetinger, *Le Feu de l'Amour, le Modèle de la Vie Parfaite, le Pater, par Richard Rolle de Hampole* (Tours, 1928). The *De Emendatione Vitae* should be consulted in the edition of Leopold Denis, *Du Péché à l'amour divin ou l'Amendement du Pécheur* (Paris, 1926). See also Margery M. Morgan, "Versions of the Meditations on the Passion Ascribed to Richard Rolle," *MA*, XXII (1953). 93-103.

229 Two additional translations of *The Cloud of Unknowing* have appeared, one by Ira Progoff (1959), the other by Clifton Wolters (1961; *Penguin Books*). *Deonise Hid Diuinite and Other Treatises on Contemplative Prayer Related to 'The Cloud of Unknowing'*, ed. Phyllis Hodgson (1955; *EETS*, 231). Miss Hodgson in "Walter Hilton and *The Cloud of Unknowing*: A Problem of Authorship Reconsidered," *MLR*, L (1955). 395-406, concludes that the *Cloud* is not by Hilton. There are two additional translations of Hilton's principal work: *The Scale of Perfection*, trans. Gerard Sitwell (1953; *Orchard Books*), and *The Ladder of Perfection*, trans. Leo Sherley-Price (1957; *Penguin Books*). Cf. S. S. Hussey, "The Text of *The Scale of Perfection*, Book II," *Neuphil. Mitt.*, LXV (1964). 75-92. Attributed to Hilton is *The Goad of Love: An Unpublished Translation of the Stimulus Amoris formerly attributed to St. Bonaventura*, ed. Clare Kirchberger (1952).

230 For Julian of Norwich the following items should be noted: *The Revelations of Divine Love*, trans. James Walsh (1961; *Orchard Books*); *A Shewing* of God's Love: The Shorter Version of Sixteen Revelations, ed. Sister Anna M. Reynolds (modernized) (1958); P. Franklin Chambers, Juliana of Norwich: An Introductory Appreciation and an Interpretative Anthology (1955); Paul Molinari, Julian of Norwich: The Teaching of a 14th Century English Mystic (1958); Anna M. Reynolds, "Julian of Norwich," The Month, xxiv (1960). 133-144. Katharine Cholmley, Margery Kempe: Genius and Mystic (1947) may be added to the references in note 15.

XIV. The Alliterative Revival

233 On the Pearl poet the following should be noted: Henry L. Savage, The Gawain Poet: Studies in His Personality and Background (Chapel Hill, 1956); The Complete Works of the Gawain-Poet, in a Modern Version with a Critical Introduction, by John Gardner (Chicago, 1965); Coolidge O. Chapman, An Index of Names in Pearl, Purity, Patience, and Gawain (Ithaca, N.Y., 1951; Cornell Stud. in English, xxxviii). There is an edition of Pearl by E. V. Gordon (Oxford, 1953) and an edition with translation and interpretation by Sister M. Vincent Hillmann (Convent Station, N.J., 1961). Among many attempts at explanation and interpretation may be mentioned: Milton R. Stern, "An Approach to The Pearl," JEPG, liv (1955). 684-692; John Conley, "Pearl and a Lost Tradition," ibid., 332-347; Marie P. Hamilton, "The Meaning of the Middle English Pearl," PMLA, lxx (1955). 805-824; Stanton D. Hoffman, "The Pearl: Notes for an Interpretation," MP, lviii (1960). 73-80; F. E. Richardson, "The Pearl: A Poem and Its Audience," Neophilologus, xlvi (1962). 308-316; H. Pilch, "Das mittelenglische Perlengedicht," Neuphil. Mitt., lxv (1964). 427-446; Robert W. Ackerman, "The Pearl-Maiden and the Penny," Romance Phil., xvii (1964). 615-623; C. Carson, "Aspects of Elegy in the Middle English Pearl," SP, lxii (1965). 17-27; A. R. Heiseman, "The Plot of Pearl," PMLA, lxxx (1965). 164-171; P. M. Kean, "Numerical Composition in Pearl," N&Q, ccx (1965). 49-51, the last considering the problem of the extra stanza.

235 John W. Clark, "Observations on Certain Differences in Vocabulary between Cleanness and Sir Gawain and the Green Knight," PQ, xxviii (1949). 261-273. Charles Moorman, "The Role of Narrator in Patience," MP, lxi (1963). 90-95.

236 Much has been written in recent years about the "meaning" of Sir Gawain and the Green Knight, finding a particular allegory or symbolism by emphasizing one or another feature of the poem. Only a limited number of articles can be listed here: John Speirs, "Sir Gawain and the Green Knight," Scrutiny, xvi (1949). 274-300; D. E. Baughan, "The Role of Morgan le Fay . . . ," ELH, xvii (1950). 241-251; G. J. Englehardt, "The Predicament of Gawain," MLQ, xvi (1955). 218-225; Alan M. Markman, "The Meaning of Sir Gawain and the Green Knight," PMLA, lxxii (1957). 574-586; Laura H. Loomis's general survey in Arthurian Literature in the Middle Ages, ed. R. S. Loomis (Oxford, 1959), pp. 528-540; S. R. T. O. D'Ardenne, " 'The Green Count' and Sir Gawain and the Green Knight," RES, n.s. x (1959). 113-126, the Green Count being Amadeus VI, Count of Savoy (1334-83); Hans Schnyder, Sir Gawain and the Green Knight: An Essay in Interpretation (Bern, 1961), exemplifying the exegetical approach, to which M. Mills, "Christian Significance and Romance Tradition in *Sir Gawain and the Green Knight*," *MLR*, LX (1965) 483-493 is a useful caveat; Morton W. Bloomfield, "Sir Gawain and the Green Knight: An Appraisal," *PMLA*, LXXVI (1961). 7-19; Larry D. Benson, "The Source of the Beheading Episode in *Sir Gawain and the Green Knight*," *MP*, LIX (1961). 1-12; Marie Borroff, *Sir Gawain and the Green Knight: A Stylistic and Metrical Study* (New Haven, 1962; *Yale Stud. in English*, 152); G. V. Smithers, "What *Sir Gawain and the Green Knight* is about," *MA*, XXXII (1963). 171-189, with which may be read John Burrow, "The Two Confession Scenes in *Sir Gawain and the Green Knight*," *MP*, LVII (1959). 73-79; R. H. Bowers, "*Gawain and the Green Knight* as Entertainment," *MLQ*, XXIV (1963). 333-341; R. G. Cook, "The Play-Element in *Sir Gawain and the Green Knight*," *Tulane Stud. in English*, XIII (1963). 5-31; Mother Angela Carson, "The Green Chapel: Its Meaning and Its Function," *SP*, LX (1963). 598-605; David F. Hills, "Gawain's Fault in Sir Gawain and the Green Knight," *RES*, n.s. XIV (1963). 124-131; Stephen Manning, "A Psychological Interpretation of *Sir Gawain and the Green Knight*," *Criticism*, VI (1964). 165-177; Theodore Silverstein, "The Art of *Sir Gawain and the Green Knight*," *UTQ*, XXXIII (1964). 258-278; Larry D. Benson, *Art and Tradition in Sir Gawain and the Green Knight* (New Brunswick, N. J., 1965); T. McAlindon, "Magic, Fate, and Providence in Medieval Narrative and *Sir Gawain and the Green Knight*," *RES*, n.s. XVI (1965). 121-139, which relates the poem to the tradition of Christian hero and magical opposition. See also Larry D. Benson, "The Authorship of St. Erkenwald," *JEGP*, LXIV (1965). 393-405.

XV. Piers Plowman and Other Alliterative Poems

240 On the literature of social protest in general see John D. Peter, *Complaint and Satire in Early English Literature* (Oxford, 1956) and Rossell H. Robbins, "Middle English Poems of Protest," *Anglia*, LXXVIII (1960). 193-203. To note 1 should also be added T. W. Ross, "On the Evil Times of Edward II: A New Version from MS. Bodley 48," *Anglia*, LXXV (1957). 173-193. Jerry D. James, "The Undercutting of Conventions in *Wynnere and Wastoure*," *MLQ*, XXV (1964). 243-258, sees irony and humor as important stylistic features of the poem.

241 There is a new edition of *The Parlement of the Three Ages* by M. Y. Offord (1959; *EETS*, 246). Since note 7 was originally written two new editions of the A-text of *Piers Plowman* have appeared: *Piers the Plowman: A Critical Edition of the A-Version*, ed. Thomas A. Knott and David C. Fowler (Baltimore, 1952), and *Piers Plowman. Vol. 1: The A-version: Will's Visions of Piers Plowman and Do-Well. An edition in the form of Trinity College, Cambridge, MS. R. 3. 14 corrected from other manuscripts with variant readings*, by G. Kane (1960). The translation by Henry W. Wells has been reissued (1959) and a new translation by J. F. Goodridge has been published (1959; *Penguin Books*).

246 J. R. Hulbert, "*Piers the Plowman* after Forty Years," *MP*, XLV (1948). 215-225, challenges R. W. Chambers' arguments for unity of authorship. Other discussions of the three versions include: A. G. Mitchell and G. H. Russell, "The Three Texts of *Piers the Plowman*," *JEGP*, LII (1953). 445-456; B. F. Huppé, "The Authorship of the A and B Texts of *Piers Plowman*," *Speculum*, XXII (1947).

578-620; David C. Fowler, *Piers the Plowman: Literary Relations of the A and B Texts* (Seattle, 1961; *Univ. of Wash. Pub. in Lang. and Lit.*, 16); Gordon H. Gerould, "The Structural Integrity of Piers Plowman B," *SP*, XLV (1948). 60-75; T. P. Dunning, "The Structure of the B-Text of *Piers Plowman*," *RES*, n.s. VII (1956). 225-237; E. Talbot Donaldson, *Piers Plowman: The C-Text and its Poet* (New Haven, 1959; *Yale Stud. in English*, 113); and the same author's "Langland on the Incarnation," *ibid.*, n.s. XVI (1965). 349-363; Willi Erzgräber, *William Langlands 'Piers Plowman' (Eine Interpretation des C-Textes)* (Heidelberg, 1957; *Frankfurter Arbeiten aus dem Gebiete der Anglistik u. der Amerika-Studien*, 3); G. Kane, *Piers Plowman: The Evidence for Authorship* (1965).

247 Critical and interpretive studies: D. W. Robertson and Bernard F. Huppé, *Piers Plowman and Scriptural Tradition* (Princeton, 1951; *Princeton Stud. in English*, 31); S. S. Hussey, "Langland, Hilton, and the Three Lives," *RES*, n.s. VII (1956). 132-150; Robert W. Frank, Jr., *'Piers Plowman' and the Scheme of Salvation: An Interpretation of 'Dowel, Dobet, and Dobest'* (New Haven, 1957; *Yale Stud. in English*, 136); John Lawler, *Piers Plowman: An Essay in Criticism* (1962); Elizabeth Salter, *Piers Plowman: An Introduction* (Cambridge, Mass., 1962); Morton W. Bloomfield, *Piers Plowman as a Fourteenth-Century Apocalypse* (New Brunswick, N. J., 1962) and for a briefer statement an article with the same title in the *Centennial Review of Arts and Sciences* (Michigan State Univ.), V (1961). 281-295; Nevill Coghill, "God's Wenches and the Light That Spoke (Some notes on Langland's kind of poetry)," *English and Medieval Studies Presented to J. R. R. Tolkien* (1962), pp. 200-217; Hans Bruneder, *Personifikation und Symbol in William Langlands* Piers Plowman (Vienna, 1963); P. M. Kean, "Love, Law, and *Lewte* in *Piers Plowman*," *RES*, n.s. XV (1964). 241-261; Marshall Walker, "Piers Plowman's Pardon: A Note," *English Studies in Africa*, VIII (1965). 64-70. Because of an important allusion in the poem, mention may be made of *The Sermons of Thomas Brinton, Bishop of Rochester (1373-1389)*, ed. Sister M. Aquinas Devlin (2v, 1954; *Camden Soc.*, Third Ser., LXXXV-LXXXVI), and William J. Brandt, "Remarks on Bishop Thomas Brinton's Authorship of the Sermons in MS. Harley 3760," *MS*, XXI (1959). 291-296, the last a reply to a review in *Speculum*, XXX (1955). 267-271. Brinton, of course, is also known as Brunton.

248 Arthur B. Ferguson, "The Problem of Counsel in *Mum and the Sothsegger*," *SRen*, II (1955). 67-83.

XVI. Chaucer: I

249 The standard edition of Chaucer's works by F. N. Robinson appeared in a revised edition in 1957. *Chaucer's Major Poetry*, ed. Albert C. Baugh (1963) also offers a critical text of nearly all the poetry with extensive annotation. Dudley D. Griffith's *Bibliography of Chaucer, 1908-1953* (Seattle, 1955) supersedes his compilation of 1928. Albert C. Baugh's "Fifty Years of Chaucer Scholarship," *Speculum*, XXVI (1951). 659-672, may permit more recent work to be seen in perspective.

A number of overall treatments of the poet are to be noted, although they vary in character and value: Nevill Coghill, *The Poet Chaucer* (1949); J. S. P. Tatlock, *The Mind and Art of Chaucer* (Syracuse, 1950); Kemp Malone, *Chapters on Chaucer* (Baltimore, 1951); Gordon H. Gerould, *Chaucerian Essays* (Princeton, 1952); G. K. Chesterton, *Chaucer* (1956); Mary Giffin, *Studies on Chaucer and His Audience* (Quebec, 1956); Paull F. Baum, *Chaucer: A Critical Appreciation* (Durham, N. C., 1957); D. S. Brewer, *Chaucer* (2ed, 1960) and *Chaucer in His Time* (1963); Bertrand H. Bronson, *In Search of Chaucer* (Toronto, 1960); Marchette Chute, *Geoffrey Chaucer of England* (2ed, 1962); Edwin J. Howard, *Geoffrey Chaucer* (1964). Collections of reprinted articles and essays have been edited by Edward Wagenknecht (1959) and by Richard J. Schoeck and Jerome Taylor (2v, Notre Dame, 1960-1), both collections in inexpensive paperback form.

As this is being written a new edition of the *Chaucer Life Records*, ed. M. M. Crow and C. C. Olson, is announced as about to appear by the Oxford University Press. P. Godeile, "Chaucer en Espagne?", *Recueil de Travaux offert à M. Clovis Brunel* (2v, Paris, 1955), II. 9-13, calls attention to a document long in print but previously overlooked, indicating that Chaucer was in Spain in February, 1366, on an official mission. P. R. Watts, "The Strange Case of Geoffrey Chaucer and Cecilia Chaumpaigne," *Law Quar. Rev.*, LXIII (1947). 491-515, views the episode as a modern lawyer sees it, but cf. T. F. T. Plucknet, *ibid.*, LXIV, 33-36. Valuable background on life in Chaucer's day is provided in Edith Rickert, *Chaucer's World*, ed. C. C. Olson and M. M. Crow (1948), and, mainly in pictures, Roger S. Loomis, *A Mirror of Chaucer's World* (Princeton, 1965). There is a revised edition of Walter C. Curry, *Chaucer and the Medieval Sciences* (1960). An important article casting doubt on Chaucer's acquaintance at first hand with rhetorical treatises, as claimed by Manly in a widely accepted article, is James J. Murphy, "A New Look at Chaucer and the Rhetoricians," *RES*, n.s. xv (1964). 1-20, in connection with which may be noted the same author's "The Arts of Discourse, 1050-1400," *MS*, XXIII (1961). 194-205, and "The Medieval Arts of Discourse: An Introductory Bibliography," *Speech Monographs*, XXIX (1962). 71-78.

The interpretation of medieval poetry by methods familiar in early scriptural exegesis, with its emphasis on allegory and symbolism, is a subject on which scholars strongly disagree. Its current vogue and attendant reaction spring from two books: D. W. Robertson, Jr., *A Preface to Chaucer: Studies in Medieval Perspective* (Princeton, 1963) and D. W. Robertson, Jr. and Bernard F. Huppé, *Piers Plowman and Scriptural Tradition*, mentioned under the preceding chapter, together with earlier articles by the same authors. Among discussions of the method may be mentioned "Patristic Exegesis in the Criticism of Medieval Literature," *English Inst. Selected Papers, 1958-1959* (1960), a symposium participated in by E. T. Donaldson (The Opposition), R. E. Kaske (The Defense), and Charles Donahue (Summation); Morton W. Bloomfield, "Symbolism in Medieval Literature," *MP*, LVI (1958). 73-81; and R. E. Kaske, "Chaucer and Medieval Allegory," *ELH*, XXX (1963). 175-192, Francis L. Utley, "Robertsonianism Redivivus," *Romance Phil.*, XIX (1965). 250-260, the last two review articles on Robertson's book.

251 On Thomas Chaucer's daughter, presumably the poet's granddaughter, see Marjorie Anderson, "Alice Chaucer and her Husbands," *PMLA*, LX (1945). 24-47. On Chaucer's French affiliations see Charles Muscatine, *Chaucer and the French Tradition: A Study in Style and Meaning* (Berkeley, 1957) and Haldeen

Braddy, *Chaucer and the French Poet Graunson* (Baton Rouge, 1947). A new text of the *Roman de la Rose* is being published by Felix Lecoy (vol. 1, Paris, 1965; *CFMA*, 92).

252-6   On the influence of Dante and Boccaccio see Howard Schless, "Chaucer and Dante," *English Inst. Selected Papers, 1958-1959* (1960), pp. 134-171, and Robert A. Pratt, "Chaucer's Use of the *Teseida*," *PMLA*, XLII (1947). 598-621. On the period of Chaucer's work discussed in the present chapter see Wolfgang Clemen, *Chaucer's Early Poetry*, trans. C. A. M. Sym (1964), a translation of *Chaucers frühe Dichtung* (Göttingen, 1963), itself a reworking of the author's earlier *Der junge Chaucer* (1938); Bernard F. Huppé and D. W. Robertson, Jr., *Fruyt and Chaf: Studies in Chaucer's Allegories* (Princeton, 1963), on *The Book of the Duchess* and *The Hous of Fame;* Georgia R. Crampton, "Transitions and Meaning in *The Book of the Duchess*," *JEGP*, LXII (1963). 486-500; *The Parlement of Foulys*, ed. D. S. Brewer (1960); J. A. W. Bennett, *The Parlement of Foules: An Interpretation* (Oxford, 1957); Charles O. McDonald, "An Interpretation of Chaucer's *Parlement of Foules*," *Speculum*, XXX (1955). 444-457; Sanford B. Meech, *Design in Chaucer's 'Troilus'* (Syracuse, N. Y., 1959); Robert A. Pratt, "Chaucer and *Le Roman de Troyle et de Criseida*," *SP*, LIII (1956). 509-539; John J. O'Connor, "The Astronomical Dating of Chaucer's *Troilus*," *JEGP*, LV (1956). 556-562. A second astronomical treatise which there is good reason to believe is by Chaucer has been discovered: *The Equatorie of the Planetis*, ed. from Peterhouse MS. 75. 1, by Derek J. Price (Cambridge, 1955).

XVII. Chaucer: II

258   A. C. Cawley (ed.), *Canterbury Tales* (1958; Everyman's Library, 307) reprints Robinson's text. The following books and articles deserve mention: Muriel Bowden, *A Commentary on the General Prologue to the Canterbury Tales* (1948); Robert M. Lumiansky, *Of Sundry Folk: The Dramatic Principle in the Canterbury Tales* (Austin, Texas, 1955); William W. Lawrence, *Chaucer and the Canterbury Tales* (1950); T. W. Craik, *The Comic Tales of Chaucer* (1964); Ralph Baldwin, *The Unity of the Canterbury Tales* (Copenhagen, 1955; *Anglistica*, v); Harold F. Brooks, *Chaucer's Pilgrims: The Artistic Order of the Portraits in the Prologue* (1962); C. Owen (ed.), *Discussions of the Canterbury Tales* (Boston, 1961); Robert A. Pratt, "The Order of the *Canterbury Tales*," *PMLA*, LXVI (1951). 1141-1167; Donald C. Baker, "The Bradshaw Order of *The Canterbury Tales*: A Dissent," *Neuphil. Mitt.*, LXIII (1962). 245-261; Bernard F. Huppé, *A Reading of the Canterbury Tales* (1964); Paul G. Ruggiers, *The Art of the Canterbury Tales* (Madison, 1965). It is impossible to list the many articles, critical and interpretive, of the individual tales and their tellers; for these the reader is referred to the annual bibliographies mentioned under chap. 1. Because of the interest in and importance of the Wife of Bath mention may be made of Robert A. Pratt, "The Development of the Wife of Bath," *Studies in Medieval Literature*, ed. MacEdward Leach (Philadelphia, 1961), pp. 45-79, and "Jankyn's Book of Wikked Wyves: Medieval Matrimonial Propaganda in the Universities," *Annuale Mediaevale*, III (1962). 5-27.

XVIII. Other Contemporaries of Chaucer

264 John H. Fisher, *John Gower: Moral Philosopher and Friend of Chaucer* (1964) is the first full length treatment of the poet. The same author has published "A Calendar of Documents Relating to the Life of John Gower the Poet," *JEGP*, LVIII (1959). 1-23. Other discussions include Gardiner Stillwell, "John Gower and the Last Years of Edward III," *SP*, XLV (1948). 454-471; Dorothea Siegmund-Schultze, "John Gower und seine Zeit," *Zs. für Anglistik u. Amerikanistik*, III (1955). 5-71; J. B. Dwyer, "Gower's *Mirour* and Its French Sources: A Reexamination of Evidence," *SP*, XLVIII (1951). 482-505; Lewis Thorpe, "A Source for the *Confessio Amantis*," *MLR*, XLIII (1948). 175-181.

267 Josephine W. Bennett, *The Rediscovery of Sir John Mandeville* (1954; *MLA Monograph Ser.*, XIX) must be given precedence over the references in note 11. Mrs. Bennett vigorously attacks the testimony of Jean d'Outremeuse, produces many additional John Mandevilles in England, including the region of St. Albans, and believes that some one of them was the probable author. She argues (less convincingly) for 1356 as the date of composition. Malcolm Letts, *Sir John Mandeville: The Man and His Book* (1949), retains more of the older views. Letts has also edited the French text (2v, 1953; *Hakluyt Soc.*). An abridged English version is edited by M. C. Seymour, *The Bodley Version of Mandeville's Travels . . . with Parallel Extracts from the Latin Text* (1963; *EETS*, 253) and has discussed "The Origin of the Egerton Version of *Mandeville's Travels*," *MA*, XXX (1961). 159-169. J. D. Thomas, "The Date of *Mandeville's Travels*," *MLN*, LXXII (1957). 165-169, dates the English translation between 1367 and 1370.

268 David C. Fowler throws "New Light on John of Trevisa," *Traditio*, XVIII (1962). 289-317. Two items on Usk deserve mention: Claes Schaar, *Notes on Thomas Usk's 'Testament of Love'* (Lund, 1950; *Acta Univ. Lundensis*, N. F. avd. 1, Bd. 46, pp. 1-46) and S. K. Heninger, Jr., "The Margarite-Pearl Allegory in Thomas Usk's *Testament of Love*," *Speculum*, XXXII (1957). 92-98.

270 There have been important developments in Wyclif studies, especially the Wyclifite Bible. To be noted are Joseph H. Dahmus, *The Prosecution of John Wyclyf* (New Haven, 1952); Kenneth B. McFarlane, *John Wycliffe and the Beginnings of English Nonconformity* (1952); Edward A. Block, *John Wyclif, Radical Dissenter* (San Diego, Calif., 1962; *San Diego State Coll., Humanities Monograph Ser.*, Vol. 1, No. 1); J. A. Robson, *Wyclif and the Oxford Schools: The Relation of the 'Summa de Ente' to Scholastic Debates at Oxford in the Later Fourteenth Century* (Cambridge, 1961; *Cambridge Stud. in Medieval Life and Thought*, n.s. VIII); Margaret W. Ransom, "The Chronology of Wyclif's English Sermons," *Research Stud. of the State College of Washington*, XVI (1948). 67-114. The most important contribution to our knowledge of the Wyclif Bible since the present chapter was written is Sven L. Fristedt, *The Wycliffe Bible*, Part I: *The Principal Problems connected with Forshall and Madden's Edition* (Stockholm, 1953; *Stockholm Stud. in English*, IV). Whether we accept his views as to Wyclif's more direct participation in the work of translation and revision, Fristedt's book must be the starting point for any future work in both text and authorship. See also the same author's "The Authorship of the Lollard

Bible: Summary and Amplification of the Wyclyffe Bible, Part I," *Studier i Modern Språkvetenskap* (Uppsala), xix (1956). 28-41, a necessary supplement to his book. Bodl. MS. 959, though not the original copy of the translator, as Forshall and Madden thought, is (the part from Genesis to Baruch 3:20) still the earliest and most important MS of the Early Version. This is being edited by Conrad Lindberg (3v, Stockholm, 1959-63; the last two volumes are in *Stockholm Stud. in English*, viii, x). See also Sven L. Fristedt, "The Dating of the Earliest Manuscript of the Wycliffite Bible," *Studier i Modern Språkvetenskap*, n.s. 1 (1956-9). 79-85. Mention may also be made of Henry Hargraves, "An Intermediate Version of the Wycliffite Old Testament," *Studia Neophil.*, xxviii (1956). 130-147, and David C. Fowler, "John Trevisa and the English Bible," *MP*, lviii (1960). 81-98, which claims a part for Trevisa in the work of translation.

XIX. The Beginnings of the Drama

273   Carl J. Stratman, *Bibliography of Medieval Drama* (Berkeley, 1954) is a convenient tool. Hardin Craig, *English Religious Drama of the Middle Ages* (Oxford, 1955) is a valuable contribution. Arnold Williams, *The Drama of Medieval England* (East Lansing, 1961) is a briefer treatment. O. B. Hardison, Jr., *Christian Rite and Christian Drama in the Middle Ages: Essays in the Origin and Early History of Modern Drama* (Baltimore, 1965), questions some of the traditional views. Useful for comparison with English developments is Grace Frank, *The Medieval French Drama* (Oxford, 1954).

276   *Le Mystère d'Adam* (*Ordo representacionis Ade*) has been edited by Paul Aebischer (Geneva, 1963).

277   The first volume of Glynne Wickham, *Early English Stages, 1300 to 1660* (1959) treats the period here discussed. On the English cycles in general see Eleanor Prosser, *Drama and Religion in the English Mystery Plays: A Re-evaluation* (Stanford, 1961; *Stanford Stud. in Lang. and Lit.*, xxiii) and Jerome Taylor, "The Dramatic Structure of the Middle English Corpus Christi, or Cycle Plays," in *Literature and Society*, ed. Bernice Slate (Lincoln, Neb., 1964), pp. 175-186.

279   A modernized version of the *York Plays* has been prepared by John S. Purvis (1957). See also J. W. Robinson, "The Art of the York Realist," *MP*, lx (1963). 241-251.

280   The translation of *The Wakefield Mystery Plays* by Martial Rose (1961) has a useful introduction. Other discussions of the Towneley cycle include: Arnold Williams, *The Characterization of Pilate in the Towneley Plays* (East Lansing, 1950); Martin Stevens, "The Composition of the Towneley *Talents* Play: A Linguistic Examination," *JEGP*, lviii (1959). 423-433; A. C. Cawley (ed.), *The Wakefield Pageants in the Towneley Cycle* (Manchester, 1958); John E. Bernbrock, "Notes on the Towneley Cycle *Slaying of Abel*," *JEGP*, lxii (1963). 317-322; Howard H. Schless, "The Comic Element in the Wakefield Noah," *Studies in Medieval Literature*, ed. MacEdward Leach (Philadelphia, 1961), pp. 229-243; Francis J. Thompson, "Unity in *The Second Shepherds' Play*," *MLN*, lxiv (1949). 302-306.

281   F. M. Salter, *Mediaeval Drama in Chester* (Toronto, 1955).

283 Arnold Williams, "The English Moral Play before 1500," *Annuale Mediaevale*, IV (1963). 5-22.

285 Jacob Bennett, "The *Castle of Perseverance:* Redactions, Place, and Date," *MS*, XXIV (1962). 141-152; Richard Southern, *The Medieval Theatre in the Round: A Study of the Staging of 'The Castle of Perseverance' and Related Matters* (1957); John J. Molloy, *A Theological Interpretation of the Moral Play, Wisdom, Who Is Christ* (Washington, D. C., 1952); Sister Mary P. Coogan, *An Interpretation of the Moral Play 'Mankind'* (Washington, D. C., 1947); Donald C. Baker, "The Date of *Mankind*," *PQ*, XLII (1963). 90-91, suggests 1464-69 on numismatic evidence.

286 Everyman has been edited by A. C. Cawley (Manchester, 1961). See also Henry de Vocht, *Everyman: A Comparative Study of Texts and Sources* (Louvain, 1947; *Materials for the Study of the Old English Drama*, n.s. xx); J. Van Mierlo, *De prioriteit van Elckerlyck tegenover Everyman gebandhaafd* (Antwerp, 1948; *Kon. VI. Acad. voor Taal en Letterkunde*, Reeks III, Nr. 27); R. W. Zandvoort, "Everyman—Elckerlijc," *Études Anglaises*, XI (1953). 1-15; Lawrence V. Ryan, "Doctrine and Dramatic Structure in *Everyman*," *Speculum*, XXXII (1957). 722-735.

XX. Ebb Tide

288 H. S. Bennett's *Chaucer and the Fifteenth Century* has been mentioned under Chap. I.

289 Elizabeth Zeeman, "Nicholas Love—a Fifteenth-Century Translator," *RES*, n.s. VI (1955) is a good treatment.

293 Ethel Seaton, *Sir Richard Roos, c. 1410-1482, Lancastrian Poet* (1961) identifies the poet (not the Richard Ros previously accepted), traces his family and his own career in detail, and claims on highly questionable grounds his authorship of a large corpus of English verse. There is an edition of *The Floure and the Leafe* and *The Assembly of Ladies* by D. A. Pearsall (1962). See also this editor's "*The Assembly of Ladies* and *Generydes*," *RES*, n.s. XII (1961). 229-237. The Scottish Chaucerians are discussed in A. M. Kinghorn, "The Mediaeval Makars," *Texas Stud. in Lit. and Lang.*, I (1959). 73-88, Kurt Wittig, *The Scottish Tradition in Literature* (Edinburgh, 1958), and James Kinsley (ed.), *Scottish Poetry: A Critical Survey* (1955), pp. 1-32 (by the editor).

294 There has been considerable interest in Henryson: Marshall W. Stearns, *Robert Henryson* (1949); Charles Elliott (ed.), *Robert Henryson: Poems Selected* . . . (Oxford, 1963; *Clarendon Medieval and Tudor Ser.*); Mary Rowlands, "The Fables of Robert Henryson," *Dalhousie Rev.*, XXXIX (1960). 491-502; Denton Fox, "Henryson's *Fables*," *ELH*, XXIX (1962). 337-356; David K. Crowne, "A Date for the Composition of Henryson's *Fables*," *JEGP*, LXI (1962). 583-590, suggesting a date not long after 1485 or 1486; Richard Bauman, "The Folktale and Oral Tradition in the Fables of Robert Henryson," *Fabula*, VI (1963). 108-124. On *The Testament of Cresseid* see excellent essay by E. M. W. Tillyard in *Five Poems, 1470-1870* (1948); A. C. Spearing, "*The Testament of Cresseid* and the 'High Concise Style'," *Speculum*, XXXVII (1962). 208-225; Douglas Duncan,

"Henryson's *Testament of Cresseid*," *EIC*, XI (1961). 128-135; Sydney Harth, "Henryson Reinterpreted," *ibid.*, 471-480 (a reply to the preceding item); Charles Elliott, "Two Notes on Henryson's *Testament of Cresseid*," *JEGP*, LIV (1955). 241-254. Charles d'Orléans' authorship of the English renderings of his poems has been denied. See Daniel Poirion, "Création poétique et composition romanesque dans les premiers poèmes de Charles d'Orléans," *Revue des sciences humaines*, n.s. fasc. 90 (1958). 185-211, and Sergio Cigada, *L'Opera poetica di Charles d'Orléans* (Milan, 1960). But see the vigorous rebuttal of John Fox, "Charles d'Orléans, poète anglais," *Romania*, LXXXVI (1965). 433-462. See also Harold Watson, "Charles d'Orléans: 1394-1465," *RR*, LVI (1965). 3-11.

295 W. F. Schirmer, *John Lydgate: A Study in the Culture of the XVth Century* (1961) is a translation by Ann E. Keep of the German original (Tübingen, 1952). Alain Renoir, "John Lydgate, Poet of the Transition," *English Miscellany*, XI (1960). 9-19, is a suggestive article, and see his *John Lydgate, Poet of Transition* (Cambridge, Mass., 1966).

296 See Alain Renoir, "The Immediate Source of Lydgate's *Siege of Thebes*," *Studia Neophil.*, XXXIII (1961). 86-95 and James M. Clark, "The Dance of Death in Medieval Literature: Some Recent Theories of Its Origin," *MLR*, XLV (1950). 336-345. The Pynson edition (1511) of *The Gouernaunce of Kynges and Prynces* is edited in facsimile by D. T. Starnes (Gainesville, Fla., 1957; *SF&R*).

297 There is an essay on Hoccleve in H. S. Bennett, *Six Medieval Men and Women* (Cambridge, 1955). The same author notes in "Thomas Hoccleve's Death," *LTLS*, Dec. 25, 1953, p. 833, that Hoccleve's corrody in the priory of Southwick was given to another on Aug. 18, 1437, which would normally imply his death, but so early a date would leave unexplained the *Balade to my gracious Lord of York* which has generally been dated *c.* 1448. See also H. C. Schulz, "Thomas Hoccleve, Scribe," *Speculum*, XII (1937). 71-81, which should have been mentioned in the original edition of this book, and Beverly Boyd, "Hoccleve's Miracle of the Virgin," *Univ. of Texas Stud. in English*, XXXV (1956). 116-122.

298 A. I. Doyle, "More Light on John Shirley," *MA*, XXX (1961). 93-101, offers new biographical matter including Shirley's will.

XXI. Looking Forward

300 Robert W. Ackerman, "Henry Lovelich's *Merlin*," *PMLA*, LXVII (1952). 473-484.

302 J. A. Mulders (ed.), *'The Cordyal' by Anthony Woodville, Earl Rivers* (Nijmegen, 1962). K. B. McFarlane, "William Worcester: A Preliminary Survey," *Studies Presented to Sir Hilary Jenkinson* (1957), pp. 196-221; Thomas D. Kendrick, "John Rous and William of Worcester," in his *British Antiquity* (1950), pp. 18-33.

303 *Paston Letters*, selected and ed. by Norman Davis (Oxford, 1958); Norman Davis, *The Language of the Pastons* (1955; *Sir Israel Gollancz Memorial Lecture*). There is a new edition (1957) of the book by R. Weiss mentioned in note 33.

304 Everett H. Emerson, "Reginald Pecock: Christian Rationalist," *Speculum*, xxxi (1956). 235-242.

305 The discovery and publication of the Winchester MS has greatly stimulated the study of Malory. The text of Vinaver's edition without the commentary is available in one volume (Oxford, 1954). Essays by several hands make up two collective volumes: *Essays on Malory*, ed. J. A. W. Bennett (Oxford, 1963), and *Malory's Originality: A Critical Study of Le Morte Darthur*, ed. (and partly written by) Robert M. Lumiansky (Baltimore, 1964). One essay in the former volume and all in the latter oppose Vinaver's contention that the *Morte Darthur* is really eight separate tales rather than a unified work. The controversy has also been carried on in articles in the learned journals. For these the student must be referred to the annual bibliographies mentioned in this Supplement under p. 109. Of general interest is Arthur B. Ferguson, *The Indian Summer of English Chivalry: Studies in the Decline and Transformation of Chivalric Idealism* (Durham, N.C., 1960).

308 Two excellent collections of ballads are now available in Evelyn K. Wells, *The Ballad Tree: British and American Ballads, Their Folklore, Verse, and Music, together with Sixty Traditional Ballads and Their Tunes* (1950) and MacEdward Leach, *The Ballad Book* (1951). Of first importance is Bertrand H. Bronson, *The Traditional Tunes of the Child Ballads, with their Texts* (3v, Princeton, 1959-65, in prog.). Two other books should be mentioned: Tristram P. Coffin, *The British Traditional Ballad in North America* (Philadelphia, 1951; Pub. Amer. Folklore Soc., Bibl. Ser., 11) and MacEdward Leach and Tristram P. Coffin (eds.), *The Critics and the Ballad* (Carbondale, Ill., 1961), selected essays.

BOOK II. THE RENAISSANCE
Part I. The Early Tudors (1485-1558)
I. Links with the Past

315 See C. F. Bühler, *William Caxton and his Critics: a Critical Reappraisal of Caxton's Contribution to the Enrichment of the English Language* (Syracuse, N.Y., 1960).

316 Polydore Vergil's *Anglica historia* has been ed. and tr. by Denis Hay (1960; *Camden Soc.*). See also D. Hay, *Polydore Vergil, Renaissance Historian and Man of Letters* (Oxford, 1952).

317 *The Chronicles of Jean Froissart in Lord Berners' Translation* has been ed. by Gillian & William Anderson (Carbondale, Ill., 1963).—A reprint of W. M. Mackenzie's ed. of Dunbar's poems, with a little revision, has appeared (1960) as well as a new ed. by James Kinsley (Oxford, 1958). *The Chepman and Millar Prints*, ed. William Beattie (1950; *Edinburgh Bibl. Soc.*) includes facsimiles of early printings of several poems by Dunbar. Denton Fox, "The Chronology of William Dunbar," *PQ*, xxxiv (1960). 413-425 assigns him the dates c. 1456-c. 1513. See also J. W. Baxter, *William Dunbar* (Edinburgh, 1952); Edwin Morgan, "Dunbar and the Language of Poetry," *EIC*, ii (1952). 136-157; Isabel Hyde, "Primary Sources and Associations of Dunbar's Aureate Imagery," *MLR*, li (1956). 481-492; John Leyerle, "The two Voices of William Dunbar," *UTQ*, xxxi (1962). 316-338. On *The Golden Targe* see D. Fox, *ELH*, xxvi (1959). 311-334.—Dunbar and the other Scottish poets are discussed in John Speirs, *The Scots Literary Tradition* (1940, rev. 1962); Kurt Wittig, *The Scottish Tradition in Literature* (Edinburgh, 1958); and (more briefly) *Scottish Poetry: a Critical Survey*, ed. James Kinsley (1955).

319 Vols. ii-iv (the text) of *Virgil's Aeneid Translated into Scottish Verse by Gavin Douglas*, ed. D. F. C. Coldwell (1957-1960; *STS*, 3rd ser., 25, 27, 28) have been issued. Coldwell's *Selections from Gavin Douglas* (Oxford, 1964) are nearly all drawn from the *Aeneid*. See also L. B. Hall, "An Aspect of the Renaissance in Gavin Douglas' *Eneados*," *SRen*, vii (1960). 184-192; Bruce Dearing, "Gavin Douglas' *Eneados*: a Reinterpretation," *PMLA*, lxvii (1952). 845-862; Hans Käsmann, "Gavin Douglas' *Aeneis*-Übersetzung," *Festschrift für Walter Hübner*, ed. Dieter Riesner & Helmut Gneuss (Berlin, 1964), pp. 164-176.— Priscilla Preston, *MA*, xviii (1959). 31-47 and F. H. Ridley, *Speculum*, xxxii (1959). 402-412 both question Douglas' authorship of *King Heart*.

324 There is an ed. of *Squyer Meldrum* by James Kinsley (1959).

II. The New Learning

326   On the sixteenth-century acceptation of the phrase "new learning" see A. G. Chester, "The New Learning: a Semantic Note," *SRen*, II (1955). 139-147. —A revised ed. of Weiss's *Humanism in England during the Fifteenth Century* has been published (Oxford, 1957; *MA Monographs*, IV). See also Fritz Caspari, *Humanism and the Social Order in Tudor England* (Chicago, 1954).

327   On Linacre see Roberto Weiss, "Un allievo inglese del Poliziano" in *Il Poliziano e i suoi tempi: atti del IV convegno internazionale di studi sul Rinascimento* (Firenze, 1957), pp. 231-236; W. D. Sharpe, "Thomas Linacre, 1460-1524: an English Physician Scholar of the Renaissance," *Bull. Hist. of Medicine*, XXXIV (1960). 233-256; C. D. O'Malley, *English Medical Humanists, Thomas Linacre and John Caius* (Lawrence, Kans., 1965; *Logan Clendenning Lectures on the History & Philosophy of Medicine*, 12th ser.).—On Colet see E. F. Rice, Jr., "John Colet and the Annihilation of the Natural," *Harvard Theological Rev.*, XLV (1952). 141-163; P. A. Duhamel, "The Oxford Lectures of John Colet: an Essay in Defining the English Renaissance," *JHI*, XIV (1953). 493-510; E. W. Hunt, *Dean Colet and his Theology* (1956); Leland Miles, *John Colet and the Platonic Tradition* (La Salle, Ill., 1961; *Fishers with Platonic Nets*, I); Sears Jayne, *John Colet and Marsilio Ficino* (1963).

328   *A Shorte Introduction of Grammar by William Lily* has been ed. by V. J. Flynn (1945; *SF&R*). See also C. G. Allen, "The Sources of Lily's Latin Grammar," *Library*, 5th ser., IX (1954). 85-100.

329   On Elyot see S. E. Lehmberg, *Sir Thomas Elyot: Tudor Humanist* (Austin, Tex., 1960); J. M. Major, *Sir Thomas Elyot and Renaissance Humanism* (Lincoln, Nebr., 1964).

331   On Elyot's translations see James Wortham, "Elyot and the Translation of Prose," *HLQ*, XI (1948). 219-240.

332   For some biographical notes on Baldwin see Arthur Freeman, *N&Q*, CCVI (1961). 300-301.

333   On Ascham see L. V. Ryan, *Roger Ascham* (Stanford, 1963). On his *Report* see W. F. Staton, Jr., "Roger Ascham's Theory of History Writing," *SP*, LVI (1959). 125-137.

334   On Leland see T. S. Dorsch, "Two English Antiquaries: John Leland and John Stow," *E&S*, n.s. XII (1959). 18-35; James Hutton, "John Leland's *Laudatio pacis*," *SP*, LVIII (1961). 616-626.

335   On Camden see Maurice Powicke, "William Camden," *English Stud.* (*E&S*, n.s.), I (1948). 67-84; Stuart Piggott, "William Camden and the *Britannia*," *Proc. Brit. Acad.*, XXXVII (1951). 199-217; F. J. Levy, "The Making of Camden's *Britannia*," *Bibl. d'Humanisme et Renaissance*, XXVI (1964). 70-97.

III. The New World

337   Two editions of the works of Sir Thomas More are currently under way. Of the facsimile of the 1557 *Works* ed. Frank Sullivan, three fascicles have so far appeared (Los Angeles, 1957-1964). Of the Yale edition of the complete works two volumes have been published: *The History of King Richard III*, ed. R. S. Sylvester (New Haven, 1963), and *Utopia*, ed. E. L. Surtz and J. H. Hexter (1965). In the concurrent series of modernized texts *Selected Letters*, ed. E. F. Rogers (1961) and *Utopia*, ed. E. L. Surtz (1964) have appeared. R. W. Gibson has published a bibliography (unhappily inaccurate): *St. Thomas More: a Preliminary Bibliography of his Works and of Moreana to the Year 1750* (New Haven, 1961); see also Frank and M. P. Sullivan, *Moreana: Materials for the Study of St. Thomas More* (2v, Los Angeles, 1964, in progress).—See also Germain Marc'hadour, *L'Univers de Thomas More: chronologie critique de More, Erasme, et leur époque (1477-1536)* (Paris, 1963); R. P. Adams, *The Better Part of Valor: More, Erasmus, Colet, and Vives on Humanism, War, and Peace* (Seattle, 1962); Pearl Hogrefe, *The Sir Thomas More Circle: a Program of Ideas and their Impact on Secular Drama* (Urbana, Ill., 1959); R. J. Schoeck, "Sir Thomas More, Humanist and Lawyer," *UTQ*, xxiv (1964). 1-14.—On the interpretation of *Utopia*, see Russell Ames, *Citizen Thomas More and his "Utopia"* (Princeton, 1949); J. H. Hexter, *More's Utopia: the Biography of an Idea* (Princeton, 1952), and "The Loom of Language and the Fabric of Imperatives: the Case of *Il principe* and *Utopia*," *American Hist. Rev.*, LXIX (1964). 945-968; E. L. Surtz, *The Praise of Pleasure: Philosophy, Education, and Communism in More's Utopia* (Cambridge, Mass., 1957), and *The Praise of Wisdom: a Commentary on the Religious and Moral Problems and Backgrounds of St. Thomas More's Utopia* (Chicago, 1957; *Jesuit Stud.*); P. R. Allen, "*Utopia* and European Humanism: the Function of the Prefatory Letters and Verses," *SRen*, x (1963). 91-107; R. C. Elliott, "The Shape of Utopia," *ELH*, xxx (1963). 317-334; A. R. Heiserman, "Satire in the *Utopia*," *PMLA*, LXXVIII (1963). 163-174.

338 Cavendish's life of Cardinal Wolsey has been ed. by R. S. Sylvester (1959; *EETS*, 243), by Roger Lockyer (1962; *Folio Soc.*), and by R. S. Sylvester and D. P. Harding in *Two Early Tudor Lives: The Life and Death of Cardinal Wolsey, by George Cavendish; The Life of Sir Thomas More, by William Roper* (New Haven, 1962). See also Sergio Rossi, "George Cavendish e il tema della fortuna," *English Miscellany*, ix (1958). 51-76; R. S. Sylvester, "Cavendish's *Life of Wolsey*: the Artistry of a Tudor Biographer," *SP*, LVII (1960). 44-71.—Roper's life of More has also been ed. by J. M. Cline (1950).—Starkey's *Dialogue* has been ed. by K. M. Burton (1948).

339 On early Tudor poetry see H. A. Mason, *Humanism and Poetry in the Early Tudor Period* (1959); John Stevens, *Music and Poetry in the Early Tudor Court* (1961).

340 *The Collected Poems of Sir Thomas Wyatt*, ed. Kenneth Muir (1949; *Muses' Library*) is now the standard edition. Muir's *Unpublished Poems by Sir Thomas Wyatt and his Circle* (Liverpool, 1961; *English Reprint Ser.*, no. 18) makes some additions to the canon. *The Arundel Harington Manuscript of Tudor Poetry*, ed. Ruth Hughey (Columbus, O., 1960) gives the text of a contemporary collection of poems by Wyatt and others. Some studies are Sergio Baldi, *La poesia di Sir Thomas Wyatt, il primo petrarchista inglese* (Firenze, 1953); Otto Hietsch, *Die Petrarcaübersetzungen Sir Thomas Wyatts* (Wien, 1960; *Wiener Beiträge*, 67); K. Muir, *The Life and Letters of Sir Thomas Wyatt* (Liverpool, 1963; *Liverpool English Texts and Stud.*, 12); Patricia Thomson, *Sir Thomas Wyatt and his Background* (Stanford, Calif., 1964); Winifred Maynard, "The Lyrics of Wyatt: Poems or Songs?" *RES*, n.s. XVI (1965). 1-13, 245-257.

342 Wyatt's versification is still a matter of dispute: see Hallett Smith, "The Art of Sir Thomas Wyatt," *HLQ*, IX (1946). 323-355; D. W. Harding, "The Rhythmical Intention in Wyatt's Poetry," *Scrutiny*, XIV (1947). 90-102; Alan Swallow, "The Pentameter Line in Skelton and Wyatt," *MP*, XLVIII (1950). 1-11; R. O. Evans, "Some Aspects of Wyatt's Metrical Technique," *JEGP*, LIII (1954). 197-213; Elias Schwartz, "The Meter of some Poems of Wyatt," *SP*, LX (1963). 155-165.—Surrey's poems have been ed. by Emrys Jones (Oxford, 1954) and his translation of the *Aeneid* by F. H. Ridley (Berkeley, 1963; *Univ. of California Pub., English Stud.*, 26).

IV. Satire

346 *John Skelton: a Selection from his Poems* has been ed. by V. de Sola Pinto (1950). Skelton's translation of the *Bibliotheca historiae* of Diodorus Siculus has been ed. by F. M. Salter & H. L. R. Edwards (2v, 1956-1957; *EETS*, 233, 239). There are new biographies by H. L. R. Edwards (*Skelton: the Life and Times of an Early Tudor Poet*, 1949) and Maurice Pollet (*John Skelton (c. 1460-1529)*, Paris, 1962; *Études anglaises*, 9). For discussions of his work see E. M. Forster, *Two Cheers for Democracy* (1951), pp. 145-161; R. S. Kinsman, "Skelton's 'Uppon a Deedmans Hed': New Light on the Origin of the Skeltonic," *SP*, L (1953). 101-109; John Holloway, "Skelton," *Proc. Brit. Acad.*, XLIV (1958). 83-102, reprinted in *The Charted Mirror* (1960); Robert Graves, "The Dedicated Poet," *Encounter*, XVII: vi (1961). 11-18, reprinted in *Oxford Addresses on Poetry* (1962), pp. 1-26; A. R. Heiserman, *Skelton and Satire* (Chicago, 1961); S. E. Fish, *John Skelton's Poetry* (New Haven, 1965).

347 See J. S. Larson, "What is *The Bowge of Court?*" *JEGP*, LXI (1962). 288-295.

349 See R. S. Kinsman, "The Voices of Dissonance: Pattern in Skelton's *Colyn Cloute*," *HLQ*, XXVI (1963). 291-313.

351 On Barclay see Selma Guttman, "Alexander Barclay: a Product of his Age," *Papers of the Michigan Acad.*, XXXV (1949). 317-328.

352 On *Cock Lorell's Boat* see P. R. Baumgartner, "From Medieval Fool to Renaissance Rogue: *Cocke Lorelles Bote* and the Literary Tradition," *Annuale Mediaevale*, IV (1963). 57-91.

353 A reprint of *Merie Tales of the Mad Men of Gotam*, ed. S. J. Kahrl, has been published by the Renaissance English Text Soc. (Evanston, Ill., 1965).

354 *John Heywood's Works and Miscellaneous Short Poems* have been ed. by B. A. Milligan (Urbana, Ill., 1956; *Illinois Stud. in Lang. and Lit.*, 41); this includes the 1562 ed. of the *Proverbs*.

357 The 1546 ed. of the *Dialogue of Proverbs* has been ed. by R. E. Habenicht (Berkeley, 1963; *Univ. of California Pub., English Stud.*, 25).

V. The Interlude

358 Recent studies of the drama before 1576 are A. P. Rossiter, *English Drama from Early Times to the Elizabethans: its Background, Origins, and Developments* (1950); T. W. Craik, *The Tudor Interlude: Stage, Costume, and Acting* (Leicester, 1958); Bernard Spivack, *Shakespeare and the Allegory of Evil: the History of a Metaphor in Relation to his Major Villains* (1958); D. M. Bevington, *From Mankind to Marlowe: Growth of Structure in the Popular Drama of Tudor England* (Cambridge, Mass., 1962).—On *Fulgens and Lucres* see E. M. Waith, "*Controversia* in the English Drama: Medwall and Massinger," *PMLA*, LXVIII (1953). 286-303.

359 On Redford see Arthur Brown, *MLR*, XLIII (1948). 508-510, XLIV (1949) 229-232, *PQ*, XXVIII (1949). 430-442.

360 *The Marriage of Wit and Science* has been ed. by Arthur Brown (1961; *Malone Soc.*).

361 On Heywood see S. A. & D. R. Tannenbaum, *John Heywood: a Concise Bibliography* (1947); Ian Maxwell, *French Farce and John Heywood* (Melbourne, 1946); William Elton, "John Heywood's 'Johan Johan'," *LTLS*, 24 February 1950, p. 128; T. W. Craik, "The True Source of John Heywood's 'Johan Johan'," *MLR*, XLV (1950). 289-295.—The Malone Soc. reprint of *Gentleness and Nobility*, ed. A. C. Partridge & F. P. Wilson (1950), is the only complete and accurate text of the play.

362 On *Magnificence* see W. O. Harris, "Wolsey and Skelton's *Magnyfycence*: a Re-valuation," *SP*, LVII (1960). 99-122.—On Bale see Honor McCusker, *John Bale, Dramatist and Antiquary* (Bryn Mawr, Penna., 1942); E. S. Miller, "The Roman Rite in Bale's *King John*," *PMLA*, LXIV (1949). 802-822.

363 *Ane Satyre of the Three Estates* has been ed. by James Kinsley (1954).

365 Woodes's *Conflict of Conscience* has been ed. by Herbert Davis & F. P. Wilson (1952; *Malone Soc.*).—On *Cambises* see W. A. Armstrong, "The Authorship and Political Meaning of *Cambises*," *ES*, XXXVI (1955). 280-299.

366 *A Knack to Know a Knave* has been ed. by G. R. Proudfoot (1964; *Malone Soc.*).

VI. Religious Prose

367 On Tyndale see W. E. Campbell, *Erasmus, Tyndale and More* (1949), E. G. Rupp, *Six Makers of English Religion 1500-1700* (1958).

368 On Coverdale see J. F. Mozley, *Miles Coverdale and his Bibles* (1954).

369 On the influence of the King James Bible see C. S. Lewis, *The Literary Impact of the Authorized Version* (1950).

370 On Cranmer see F. E. Hutchinson, *Cranmer and the English Reformation* (1951); G. W. Bromiley, *Thomas Cranmer: Archbishop and Martyr* (1956), *Thomas Cranmer, Theologian* (1956); Theodore Maynard, *The Life* *of Thomas Cranmer* (1956); Jasper Ridley, *Thomas Cranmer* (Oxford, 1962).

372 On the sermon see J. W. Blench, *Preaching in England in the Late Fifteenth and Sixteenth Centuries* (Oxford, 1964) and the references cited.— On Latimer see H. S. Darby, *Hugh Latimer* (1953); A. G. Chester, *Hugh Latimer, Apostle to the English* (Philadelphia, 1954).

374 On Foxe see William Haller, *Foxe's Book of Martyrs and the Elect Nation* (1963; American ed., *The Elect Nation: the Meaning and Relevance of Foxe's "Book of Martyrs,"* 1964).

375 On Becon see D. S. Bailey, *Thomas Becon and the Reformation of the Church in England* (Edinburgh, 1952).—On Puritan propaganda see D. J. McGinn, *The Admonition Controversy* (New Brunswick, N.J., 1949); *Cartwrightiana*, ed. Albert Peel & L. H. Carlson (1951; *Royal Hist. Soc.*).

378 On Hooker see F. J. Shirley, *Hooker and Contemporary Political Ideas* (1949); Peter Munz, *The Place of Hooker in the History of Thought* (1952); A. S. P. Woodhouse, "Religion and some Foundations of English Democracy," *Philosophical Rev.*, LXI (1952). 503-531; A. S. McGrade, "The Coherence of Hooker's Polity: the Books on Power," *JHI*, XXIV (1963). 163-182.

Part II. The Reign of Elizabeth (1558-1603)

I. The Elizabethan Lyric

383 Some comprehensive works of literary history are V. de Sola Pinto, *The English Renaissance 1510-1688* (1938; *Introductions to English Literature*, II; rev. ed., 1950); Hallett Smith, *Elizabethan Poetry, a Study in Conventions, Meaning, and Expression* (Cambridge, Mass., 1952); M. C. Bradbrook, *Shakespeare and Elizabethan Poetry* (1952); C. S. Lewis, *English Literature in the Sixteenth Century, excluding Drama* (Oxford, 1954; *Oxford Hist. of English Literature*, III); Maurice Evans, *English Poetry in the Sixteenth Century* (1955); *The Age of Shakespeare*, ed. Boris Ford (Harmondsworth, 1955; *A Guide to English Literature*, 2; rev. 1961); Helen Morris, *Elizabethan Literature* (1958). —See also Dámaso Alonso, "Poesia correlativa inglesa en los siglos XVI y XVII," *Filologia Moderna*, I: 2 (1961). 1-47; H. S. Bennett, *English Books and Readers 1558 to 1603, being a Study in the History of the Book Trade in the Reign of Elizabeth* I (Cambridge, 1965).—Catherine Ing, *Elizabethan Lyrics: a Study in the Development of English Metres and their Relation to Poetic Effect* (1951) and John Thompson, *The Founding of English Metre* (1961) treat versification.—On literary patronage see Eleanor Rosenberg, *Leicester, Patron of Letters* (1953).

384 The surviving fragments of *The Court of Venus* have been ed. by R. A. Fraser (Durham, N.C., 1955); he has also published the pious parody of it by John Hall, *The Court of Vertue* (1961).

385 On Breton see S. A. & D. R. Tannenbaum, *Nicholas Breton, a Concise*

Bibliography (1947); *Poems by Nicholas Breton* (*not Hitherto Reprinted*), ed. Jean Robertson (Liverpool, 1952).

386 On *Love's Martyr* see T. P. Harrison, "*Love's Martyr*, by Robert Chester: a New Interpretation," *Texas Stud. in English*, xxx (1951). 66-85. On *The Phoenix and Turtle*, Shakespeare's contribution to *Love's Martyr*, see J. V. Cunningham, " 'Essence' and the *Phoenix and Turtle*," *ELH*, xix (1952). 265-276; Heinrich Straumann, *Phönix und Taube* (Zürich, 1953); A. Alvarez, "How to Read a Poem (iii): Shakespeare's 'The Phoenix and the Turtle'," *Mandrake*, ii (1955), 395-408, reprinted in *Interpretations*, ed. John Wain (1955), pp. 1-16; Daniel Seltzer, " 'Their Tragic Scene': *The Phoenix and Turtle* and Shakespeare's Love Tragedies," *SQ*, xii (1961). 91-101; W. T. Matchett, *The Phoenix and the Turtle: Shakespeare's Poem and Chester's Loues Martyr* (The Hague, 1965; *Stud. in English Lit.*, 1).

387 C. T. Wright, "Anthony Mundy and the Bodenham Miscellanies," *PQ*, xl (1961). 449-461 assigns the editorship of *Belvedere* to Munday.

389 On the song books see Bruce Pattison, *Music and Poetry in the English Renaissance* (1948); Floris Delattre & Camille Chemin, *Les Chansons élisabéthaines* (Paris, 1948; *Bibl. des langues modernes*, 2); Alfredo Obertello, *Madrigali italiani in Inghilterra* (Milano, 1949); Joseph Kerman, "Elizabethan Anthologies of Italian Madrigals," *Jour. of the Amer. Musicological Soc.*, iv (1951). 122-138; W. L. Woodfill, *Music in English Society from Elizabeth to Charles I* (Princeton, 1953); John Stevens, *Music and Poetry in the Early Tudor Court* (1961); John Hollander, *The Untuning of the Sky: Ideas of Music in English Poetry 1500-1700* (Princeton, 1961); G. L. Finney, *Musical Backgrounds for English Literature 1580-1650* (New Brunswick, N.J., 1962).

391 *Selected Poems of Barnaby Googe* have been ed. by Alan Stephens (Denver, 1961). *The Zodiacke of Life* has been ed. by Rosemond Tuve (1947; *SF&R*). See P. E. Parnell, "Barnabe Googe: a Puritan in Arcadia," *JEGP*, lx (1961). 272-281.

393 Charles & Ruth Prouty, "George Gascoigne, *The Noble Arte of Venerie*, and Queen Elizabeth at Kenilworth," *J. Q. Adams Memorial Studies*, ed. J. G. McManaway *et al.* (Washington, 1948), pp. 639-664 assemble the evidence which shows Gascoigne to be the translator.

396 *An Humble Supplication to her Majestie* has been ed. by R. C. Bald (Cambridge, 1953). There is a biography of Southwell by Christopher Devlin, *The Life of Robert Southwell, Poet and Martyr* (1956). L. L. Martz, *The Poetry of Meditation* (New Haven, 1954) pictures Southwell as a forerunner of the religious poets of the seventeenth century. Toshihiko Kawasaki, "From Southwell to Donne," *Stud. in English Lit.*, xxxix (1963). 11-31 finds as many differences as likenesses between them. H. C. White, "Southwell: Metaphysical and Baroque," *MP*, lxi (1964). 159-168 describes Southwell as a pioneer of the baroque.

II. Verse Narrative

398 Recent studies of narrative poetry are L. R. Zocca, *Elizabethan Narrative Poetry* (New Brunswick, N.J., 1950); E. M. W. Tillyard, *The English*

Epic and its Background (1954).—On *A Mirror for Magistrates* see Alwin Thaler, "Literary Criticism in *A Mirror for Magistrates," JEGP,* XLIX (1950). 1-13; E. M. W. Tillyard, *"A Mirror for Magistrates* Revisited," *Elizabethan and Jacobean Studies Presented to F. P. Wilson* (Oxford, 1959), pp. 1-16, reprinted in *Essays Literary and Educational* (1962).

400 On Churchyard see C. A. Rahter, "Some Notes on the Career and Personality of Thomas Churchyard," *N&Q,* ccv (1960). 211-215.

401 On *Albion's England* see Robert Birley, *Sunk without Trace: some Forgotten Masterpieces Reconsidered* (1962).

402 Daniel's *Civil Wars* has been ed. by Laurence Michel (1958); see the corrections in *MLR,* LIV (1959). 587-588, *SQ,* x (1959). 442-443. For studies of Daniel's works see May McKisack, "Daniel as Historian," *RES,* XXIII (1947). 226-243; M. H. Shackford, "Daniel's Poetical 'Epistles'," *SP,* XLV (1948). 180-195; C. C. Seronsy, "Well-languaged Daniel: a Reconsideration," *MLR,* LII (1957). 481-497, "Daniel's *Complaint of Rosamond:* Origins and Influence of an Elizabethan Poem," *Lock Haven Bull.* ser. 1, II (1960). 39-57; William Blissett, "Samuel Daniel's Sense of the Past," *ES,* XXXVIII (1957). 49-63; Joan Rees, *Samuel Daniel* (Liverpool, 1964).

403 A corrected ed. of Drayton's *Works,* ed. Hebel, Mrs. Tillotson, and Newdigate, has been published (5v, 1961). *The Poems of Michael Drayton,* ed. John Buxton (2v, 1953; *Muses' Libr.*), is a selection. See Joan Grundy, "'Brave translunary things'," *MLR,* LIX (1964). 501-510; P. G. Buchloh, *Michael Drayton: Barde und Historiker, Politiker und Prophet* (Neumünster, 1964; *Kieler Beiträge zur Anglistik und Amerikanistik,* I).

405 On the influence of Boccaccio in general see H. G. Wright, *Boccaccio in England from Chaucer to Tennyson* (1957).—A new revised ed. of Bush's *Mythology and the Renaissance Tradition* has been published (1963).

406 *Elizabethan Minor Epics,* ed. E. S. Donno (1963) reprints 13 Ovidian poems.—Fraunce's *Arcadian Rhetorike* has been ed. by Ethel Seaton (Oxford, 1950; *Luttrell Soc.,* 9).—W. F. Staton, Jr., "The Influence of Thomas Watson on Elizabethan Ovidian Poetry," *SRen,* VI (1959). 243-250, imputes to Watson's Latin *Amyntas* (1585) and its translation into English by Abraham Fraunce, *The Lamentation of Amyntas for the Death of Phillis* (1587), the stimulation of the vogue of Ovidian poetry.

407 On Barnfield see Harry Morris, *Richard Barnfield, Colin's Child* (Tallahassee, Fla., 1963; *Florida State Univ. Stud.,* 38).

409 *The Poems of John Marston* have been ed. by Arnold Davenport (Liverpool, 1961). They have been studied by John Peter, *Complaint and Satire in Early English Literature* (1956) and Alvin Kernan, *The Cankered Muse: Satire of the English Renaissance* (New Haven, 1959; *Yale Stud. in English,* 142).

410 E. M. W. Tillyard has reprinted *Orchestra* (1945) and also discussed it in *Five Poems* (1948). Robert Krueger, "Sir John Davies: *Orchestra* Complete, *Epigrams,* Unpublished Poems," *RES,* n.s. XIII (1962). 17-29, 113-124, describes a manuscript with the conclusion of *Orchestra,* wanting in all the printed eds. See also G. A. Wilkes, "The Poetry of Sir John Davies," *HLQ,* XXV (1962). 283-298.

III. Prose Narrative: I. Lyly and his Predecessors

412 *A Hundred Merry Tales and other English Jestbooks of the Fifteenth and Sixteenth Centuries,* ed. P. M. Zall (Lincoln, Nebr., 1963) reprints five jestbooks of which three are not in Hazlitt's collection. See also Fernando Ferrara, *Jests e merry tales: aspetti della narrativa popolaresca inglese del sedicesimo secolo* (Roma, 1960; *Nuovi saggi, 27*).

413 On prose fiction see C. C. Mish, *English Prose Fiction 1600-1640* (Charlottesville, Va., 1952; *Bibl. Soc. of the Univ. of Virginia*); Sterg O'Dell, *A Chronological List of Prose Fiction in English Printed in England and other Countries* (Cambridge, Mass., 1954); G. B. Parks, "Before *Euphues,*" *J. Q. Adams Memorial Studies,* ed. J. G. McManaway et al. (Washington, 1948), pp. 475-493; Margaret Schlauch, *Antecedents of the English Novel 1400-1600 (from Chaucer to Deloney)* (Warsaw, 1963).

414 F. S. Hook has ed. *The French Bandello, a Selection: the Original Text of Four of Belleforest's* Histoires tragiques *Translated by Geoffrey Fenton and William Painter Anno 1567* (Columbia, Mo., 1948; *Univ. of Missouri Stud.,* XXII: 1).

415 On Pettie see Ludwig Borinski, "The Origin of the Euphuistic Novel and its Significance for Shakespeare," *Studies in Honor of T. W. Baldwin,* ed. D. C. Allen (Urbana, Ill., 1958), pp. 38-52.

416 One copy of *Philotimus* is dated 1582 and the book was probably printed at the end of that year; see Ralph Maud, "The Date of Brian Melbancke's *Philotimus,*" *Library,* 5th ser., XI (1956). 118-120.—*The Adventures of Master F. J.* is reprinted in *Elizabethan Fiction,* ed. Robert Ashley & E. M. Moseley (1953), along with *Euphues, the Anatomy of Wit, The Unfortunate Traveler,* and *Jack of Newbury.* See also R. P. Adams, "Gascoigne's *Master F. J.* as Original Fiction," *PMLA,* LXXIII (1958). 315-326.

417 *Euphues, the Anatomy of Wit* is reprinted in *The Descent of Euphues: Three Elizabethan Romance Stories,* ed. James Winny (Cambridge, 1957), along with *Pandosto* and *Piers Plainness,* as well as in the collection mentioned above. See also J. A. Barish, "The Prose Style of John Lyly," *ELH,* XXIII (1956). 14-35; G. K. Hunter, *John Lyly: the Humanist as Courtier* (1962).

IV. Prose Narrative: II. Greene and his Followers

421 On Greene see Fernando Ferrara, *L'opera narrativa di Robert Greene* (Venezia, 1957). On *Mamillia,* Jaroslav Hornát, "*Mamillia:* Robert Greene's Controversy with *Euphues,*" *Philologica Pragensia,* V (1963). 210-218.

423 *Ciceronis amor* and *A Quip for an Upstart Courtier* have been ed. by E. H. Miller (1954; *SF&R*).

425 *The Third Part of Cony-catching* is reprinted in *Three Elizabethan Pamphlets,* ed. G. R. Hibbard (1952), along with *Pierce Penniless* and *The Wonderful Year.*

426 On the possibility that *A Quip for an Upstart Courtier* was written in collaboration with Nashe see D. J. McGinn, "A Quip from Tom Nashe," *Studies in the English Renaissance Drama in Memory of K. J. Holzknecht*, ed. J. W. Bennett *et al.* (1959), pp. 171-188.

429 Riche's *Farewell to Military Profession* has been ed. by T. M. Cranfill (Austin, Tex., 1954); *Faultes Faults and Nothing else but Faults* by M. H. Wolf (Gainesville, Fla., 1965; *SF&R*). See further T. M. Cranfill & D. H. Bruce, *Barnaby Rich, a Short Biography* (Austin, Tex., 1953); P. A. Jorgensen, "Barnaby Rich: Soldierly Suitor and Honest Critic of Women," *SQ*, VII (1956). 183-188; J. L. Lievsay, "A Word about Barnaby Rich," *JEGP*, LV (1956). 381-392; Fernando Ferrara, "Barnabe Riche, difensore del soldato inglese e autore di *A Larum for London*," *English Miscellany*, VIII (1957). 21-54.—Munday's *Zelauto* has been ed. by Jack Stillinger (Carbondale, Ill., 1963).

430 On Lodge see P. M. Ryan, Jr., *Thomas Lodge, Gentleman* (Hamden, Conn., 1958).

431 On *The Unfortunate Traveler* see A. K. Croston, "The Use of Imagery in Nashe's *The Unfortunate Traveller*," *RES*, XXIV (1948). 90-101; A. M. C. Latham, "Satire on Literary Themes and Modes in Nashe's 'Unfortunate Traveller'," *English Stud. (E&S,* n.s.), I (1948). 85-100.—*The Novels of Thomas Deloney* have been ed. by M. E. Lawlis (1961). See also M. E. Hablützel, *Die Bildwelt Thomas Deloneys* (Bern, 1946; *Schweizer anglistische Arbeiten,* 16); Torsten Dahl, *An Inquiry into Aspects of the Language of Thomas Deloney* (Aarhus, 1951; *Acta Jutlandica,* XXIII, *Humanistick Serie,* 36); E. D. Mackerness, "Deloney and the Virtuous Proletariat," *Cambridge Jour.,* V (1951). 34-50; M. E. Lawlis, *Apology for the Middle Class: the Dramatic Novels of Thomas Deloney* (Bloomington, Ind., 1961; *Indiana Univ. Pub., Humanistic Ser.,* 46).

432 That Munday was not born till 1560 is now reasonably clear: see I. A. Shapiro, "Mundy's Birthdate," *N&Q,* CCI (1956). 2-3; Leslie Hotson, "Anthony Mundy's Birth-date," *N&Q,* CCIV (1959). 2-4; see also Mark Eccles, "Anthony Munday," *Studies in the English Renaissance Drama in Memory of K. J. Holzknecht,* ed. J.W. Bennett *et al.* (1959), pp. 95-105. On his works see Mary Patchell, *The Palmerin Romances in Elizabethan Prose Fiction* (1947; *Columbia Univ. Stud. in English and Comparative Literature,* 166); C. T. Wright, "Young Anthony Mundy Again," *SP,* LVI (1959). 150-168.

V. Miscellaneous Prose

434 Yong's translation of the third part of Montemayor is in *Diana enamorada (1564) together with the English Translation (1598),* ed. R. L. & M. B. Grismer (Minneapolis, 1959).—*Orlando Furioso: John Harington's Translation* has been ed. by Graham Hough (1962) and selections from it by R. B. Gottfried (Bloomington Ind., 1963). K. M. Lea, "Harington's Folly,"*Elizabethan and Jacobean Studies presented to F. P. Wilson* (Oxford, 1954), pp. 43-53 is a study of the text.—E. B. Knowles, "Thomas Shelton, Translator of *Don Quixote*," *SRen,* V (1958). 160-175 and J. George, "Thomas Shelton, Translator, in 1612-14," *Bull of Hispanic Stud.,* XXXV (1958). 157-164 provide new biographical data.—On translations from the Spanish in general see D. B. J. Randall, *The Golden Tapestry: a Critical Survey of Non-chivalric Spanish Fiction in English Translation* (*1543-1657*) (Durham, N.C., 1963).—On linguistic problems see R. F. Jones, *The Triumph of the English Language: a Survey of Opinion concerning the Vernacular from the Introduction of Printing to the Restoration* (Stanford, Calif., 1953).

435 *Wilson's Arte of Rhetorique, 1553* has been ed. by R. H. Bowers (1962; *SF&R*). See also A. J. Schmidt, "Thomas Wilson, Tudor Scholar-statesman," *HLQ*, xx (1957). 205-218; R. H. Wagner, "Thomas Wilson's *Arte of Rhetorique*," *Speech Monographs*, xxvii (1960). 1-32.

436 On literary theory see J. W. H. Atkins, *English Literary Criticism: the Renascence* (1947; 2ed., 1951); Rosemond Tuve, *Elizabethan and Metaphysical Imagery* (Chicago, 1947); O. B. Hardison, Jr., *The Enduring Monument, a Study of the Idea of Praise in Renaissance Literary Theory and Practice* (Chapel Hill, N.C., 1962).—On Stanyhurst see J. L. Rosier, "Richard Stanyhurst and Sixteenth-century Lexical Usage," *Studia Neophil.*, xxxiii (1961). 115-127.—On quantitative versification see G. L. Hendrickson, "Elizabethan Quantitative Hexameters," *PQ*, xxviii (1949). 237-260.

437 Richard Wills, *De re poetica, Translated and Edited from the Edition of 1573* by A. D. S. Fowler (Oxford, 1958; *Luttrell Reprints*, no. 17) antedates most other Elizabethan treatises.

438 On the Nashe-Harvey quarrel see W. Schrickx, *Shakespeare's Early Contemporaries: the Background of the Harvey-Nashe Polemic and* Love's Labour's Lost (Antwerp, 1956); David Perkins, "Issues and Motivations in the Nashe-Harvey Quarrel," *PQ*, xxxix (1960). 224-233.—On the canceled passages in *A Quip* see I. A. Shapiro, "The First Edition of Greene's *Quip for an Upstart Courtier*," *Stud. in Bibliography*, xiv (1961). 212-218.—McKerrow's ed. of *The Works of Thomas Nashe* has been reprinted with corrections and supplementary notes by F. P. Wilson (5v, Oxford, 1958). See also G. R. Hibbard, *Thomas Nashe, a Critical Introduction* (1962).

440 Harington's *New Discourse of a Stale Subject, called the Metamorphosis of Ajax* has been ed. by E. S. Donno (1962).

443 On Stubbes see T. P. Pearson, "The Composition and Development of Phillip Stubbes's 'Anatomie of Abuses'," *MLR*, lvi (1961). 321-334.

445 On Prynne see W. M. Lamont, *Marginal Prynne, 1600-1669* (1963; *Toronto Stud. in Political Hist.*, 3).

VI. Elizabethan Comedy

446 Greg's *Bibliography* is now complete in 4 vols. (1939-1959). A revised ed. of Harbage's *Annals*, ed. Samuel Schoenbaum (1964) is available.—Alternatives to J. C. Adams's reconstruction of the Globe playhouse are expounded by C. W. Hodges, *The Globe Restored* (1953), A. M. Nagler, *Shakespeare's Stage* (New Haven, 1955), and Richard Hosley, "The Discovery-space in Shakespeare's Globe," *ShS*, xii (1959). 35-46, "The Origins of the Shakespearian Playhouse," *SQ*, xv:ii (1964). 29-39. Leslie Hotson, *Shakespeare's Wooden O* (1959) argues that Elizabethan plays were performed in the round. See also Glynne Wickham,

Early English Stages 1300 to 1660 (2v, 1959, 1963, in progress); J. W. Saunders, "Staging at the Globe," *SQ*, xi (1960). 401-425. Richard Southern, *Changeable Scenery: its Origin and Development in the British Theatre* (1952) begins just before the closing of the theaters in 1642.—On the question whether Elizabethan acting was formal or realistic see Bertram Joseph, *Elizabethan Acting* (1951, *Oxford English Monographs, 2*; 2ed., 1964), *Acting Shakespeare* (1960); Marvin Rosenberg, "Elizabethan Actors: Men or Marionettes?" *PMLA*, lxix (1954). 915-927; R. A. Foakes, "The Player's Passion," *E&S*, n.s. vii (1954). 62-77. On the social status of the actor see M. C. Bradbrook, *The Rise of the Common Player* (1962).—Some studies of broad scope are M. T. Herrick, *Comic Theory in the Sixteenth Century* (Urbana, Ill., 1950; *Illinois Stud. in Lang. and Lit.*, 34); Madeleine Doran, *Endeavors of Art: a Study of Form in Elizabethan Drama* (Madison, 1954); M. C. Bradbrook, *The Growth and Structure of English Comedy* (1955); J. V. Curry, *Deception in Elizabethan Comedy* (Chicago, 1955); Irving Ribner, *The English History Play in the Age of Shakespeare* (Princeton, 1957; 2ed., 1965); W. W. Main, "Dramaturgical Norms in the Elizabethan Repertory," *SP*, liv (1957). 128-148.—Recent anthologies of plays include *Four English Tragedies of the Sixteenth and Seventeenth Centuries*, ed. J. M. Morrell (1953); *Three Elizabethan Plays*, ed. James Winny (1959); *Six Elizabethan Plays*, ed. R. C. Bald (Boston, 1963); *Elizabethan History Plays*, ed. W. A. Armstrong (1965; *World's Classics*). Three series of play texts are currently in progress: the Revels Plays (Methuen), the Regents' Renaissance Drama Series (Univ. of Nebraska Press), the New Mermaid Dramatists (Benn).

447 *Henslowe's Diary* has been ed. by R. A. Foakes & R. T. Rickert (Cambridge, 1961).—On the private playhouses see W. A. Armstrong, *The Elizabethan Private Theatres: Facts and Problems* (1958; *Soc. for Theatre Research*). Irwin Smith, *Shakespeare's Blackfriars Playhouse, Its History and Design* (1964) attempts a detailed reconstruction.

448 On *Jack Juggler* see R. Marienstras, "*Jack Juggler:* aspects de la conscience individuelle dans une farce du 16ᵉ siècle," *Études anglaises*, xvi (1963). 321-332. —On *Ralph Roister Doister* see A. W. Plumstead, "Satirical Parody in *Roister Doister:* a Reinterpretation," *SP*, lx (1963). 141-154.

450 D. M. Bevington, "*Misogonus* and Laurentius Bariωna," *ELN*, ii (1964). 9-10 confirms the identification of the author as Lawrence Johnson.

451 *Damon and Pythias* has been ed. by Arthur Brown & F. P. Wilson (1957; *Malone Soc.*). See also W. A. Armstrong, "*Damon and Pythias* and Renaissance Theories of Tragedy," *ES*, xxxix (1958). 200-207.—J. I. Cope, "'The Best for Comedy': Richard Edwards' Canon," *Texas Stud. in Lit. and Lang.*, ii (1961). 501-519 attributes *Common Conditions* and *Sir Clyomon and Clamydes* to Edwards.

452 On Lyly's plays see B. F. Huppé, "Allegory of Love in Lyly's Court Comedies," *ELH*, xiv (1947). 93-113; R. Y. Turner, "Some Dialogues of Love in Lyly's Comedies," *ELH*, xxix (1962). 276-288.

455 Two volumes of a new ed. of Peele's works have been published: *The Life and Minor Works*, ed. D. H. Horne (New Haven, 1952); *Edward I*, ed. F. S. Hook, *The Battle of Alcazar*, ed. John Yoklavich (1961). On *The Old Wive's Tale* see Herbert Goldstone, "Interplay in Peele's *The Old Wives' Tale*,"

Boston Univ. Stud. in English, IV (1960). 202-213; M. C. Bradbrook, "Peele's *Old Wives' Tale:* a Play of Enchantment," *ES,* XLII (1962). 323-330.

457 *Friar Bacon and Friar Bungay* has been ed. by Benvenuto Cellini, with *John of Bordeaux* (Firenze, 1953) and by Daniel Seltzer (Lincoln, Nebr., 1963). On Greene see Norman Sanders, "The Comedy of Greene and Shakespeare," *Early Shakespeare,* ed. J. R. Brown & B. Harris (1962; *Stratford-upon-Avon Stud.,* 3); Kenneth Muir, "Robert Greene as Dramatist," *Essays on Shakespeare and the Elizabethan Drama in Honor of Hardin Craig* (Columbia, Mo., 1962), pp. 45-54.

458 *The Downfall of Robert Earl of Huntingdon* has been ed. by J. C. Meagher (1964; *Malone Soc.*).—On Porter see A. C. Partridge, *Orthography in Shakespeare and Elizabethan Drama* (1964).

VII. Elizabethan Tragedy

460 Recent studies are Wolfgang Clemen, *Die Tragödie vor Shakespeare* (Heidelberg, 1955; *Schriftenreihe der deutschen Shakespeare-Gesellschaft,* 5).— C. S. Lewis, *The Discarded Image* (Cambridge, 1964) is another account of the Elizabethan world picture.—On Seneca see *Les Tragédies de Sénèque et le théâtre de la Renaissance,* ed. Jean Jacquot & Marcel Oddon (Paris, 1964; *Centre National de la Recherche Scientifique*). R. G. Palmer, *Seneca's De remediis fortuitorum and the Elizabethans* (Chicago, 1953) attributes more influence to Seneca's ethical writings than to his plays.

461 On *Gorboduc* see Jacobus Swart, *Thomas Sackville* (Groningen, 1949); Paul Bacquet, "Structure et valeur dramatique de *Gorboduc,*" *Filološki Pregled,* I-II (1964), pp. 247-259.

463 An enlarged ed. of F. S. Boas's *Works of Kyd* has been published (Oxford, 1955). The most recent eds. of *The Spanish Tragedy* are those of P. W. Edwards (1959) and B. L. Joseph (1964). The Malone Soc. has reprinted the earliest surviving ed. (1592), without the additions, ed. W. W. Greg & D. N. Smith (1949). Félix Carrère, *Le Théâtre de Thomas Kyd* (Toulouse, 1951) is a comprehensive study giving disproportionate attention to Kyd's supposititious works. See also Kurt Wittig, "Gedanken zu Kyd's *Spanish Tragedy,*" *Strena Anglica: Otto Ritter zum 80. Geburtstag* (Halle, 1956), pp. 133-177; J. D. Ratliff, "Hieronimo Explains Himself," *SP,* LIV (1957). 112-118; W. H. Wiatt, "The Dramatic Function of the Alexander-Viluppo Episode in *The Spanish Tragedy,*" *N&Q,* CCIII (1958). 327-329; C. K. Cannon, "The Relation of the Additions to *The Spanish Tragedy* to the Original Play," *SEL,* II (1962). 229-239; S. F. Johnson, "*The Spanish Tragedy,* or Babylon Revisited," *Essays on Shakespeare and Elizabethan Drama in Honor of Hardin Craig,* ed. R. Hosley (Columbia, Mo., 1962), pp. 23-36.

466 *The Tragedy of Philotas* has been ed. by Laurence Michel (New Haven, 1949). G. A. Wilkes, "Daniel's *Philotas* and the Essex Case: a Reconsideration," *MLQ,* XXIII (1962). 233-242 deprecates finding the story of the earl in the play.

468 *Thomas of Woodstock* has been ed. by A. P. Rossiter (1946).—For the latest discussion of the problems of *Sir Thomas More* see Harold Jenkins, *Malone*

Soc. Collections, vi (1961). 179-192.—*Jack Straw* has been ed. by Kenneth Muir & F. P. Wilson (1947; *Malone Soc.*).

469 *Arden of Feversham* has been ed. by Hugh Macdonald (1947; *Malone Soc.*).

470 *The Tragedy of Hoffman* has been ed. by Harold Jenkins (1951; *Malone Soc.*).—K. G. Cross, "The Authorship of *Lust's Dominion*," *SP*, lv (1958). 39-61 would join Marston to Dekker.

VIII. Sidney and the Sonneteers

472 *The Poems of Sir Philip Sidney*, ed. W. A. Ringler, Jr. (Oxford, 1962) is now standard. J. C. A. Rathmell has ed. *The Psalms of Sir Philip Sidney and the Countess of Pembroke* (1963). Some recent studies are Michel Poirier, *Sir Philip Sidney, le chevalier poète élizabéthain* (Lille, 1948; *Travaux et mémoires de l'Univ. de Lille*, n.s., *Droit et lettres*, 26); John Buxton, *Sir Philip Sidney and the English Renaissance* (1954; 2ed., 1964); R. L. Montgomery, Jr., *Symmetry and Sense: the Poetry of Sir Philip Sidney* (Austin, Tex., 1961); David Kalstone, *Sidney's Poetry: Contexts and Interpretations* (Cambridge, Mass., 1965). John Thompson, *The Founding of English Metre* (1961) finds Sidney's achievement to be crucial.

474 On the *Arcadia* see J. F. Danby, *Poets on Fortune's Hill* (1952; 2nd impression, *Elizabethan and Jacobean Poets*, 1964); W. R. Davis & R. A. Lanham, *Sidney's Arcadia* (1965; *Yale Stud. in English*, 158).

477 *The Defense of Poesy* has been ed. by W. H. Clemen (Heidelberg, 1950) and by Geoffrey Shepherd (1965). See further John P. McIntyre, "Sidney's 'Golden World'," *CL*, xiv (1962). 356-365.

479 On *Astrophel and Stella* see Jack Stillinger, "The Biographical Problem of *Astrophel and Stella*," *JEGP*, lix (1960). 617-639; A. R. Howe, "*Astrophel and Stella*: 'Why and How'," *SP*, lxi (1964). 150-169; R. B. Young, "English Petrarke: a Study of Sidney's *Astrophel and Stella*," *Three Studies in the Renaissance* (New Haven, 1958; *Yale Stud. in English*, 138).

480 On the sonnet see J. W. Lever, *The Elizabethan Love Sonnet* (1956); Claes Schaar, *On the Motif of Death in Sixteenth Century Sonnet Poetry* (Lund, 1960; *Scripta minora Regiae Societatis Humaniorum Litterarum Lundensis 1959-1960*, iii).—*The Hecatompathia or Passionate Century of Love (1582)*, by *Thomas Watson* has been ed. by S. K. Heninger, Jr. (Gainesville, Fla., 1964; *SF&R*). See also C. G. Cecioni, "Appunti per una biografia di Thomas Watson," *Siculorum Gymnasium*, xvi (1963). 101-131, "Introduzione all' Ἑκατομπαθία di Thomas Watson," *Ibid.*, xvii (1964). 8-22.—On *Delia* see Diethild Bludau, "Sonettstruktur bei Samuel Daniel," *Shakespeare-Jahrbuch*, xciv (1958). 63-89. —*The Poems of Henry Constable* have been ed. by Joan Grundy (1960; *Liverpool English Texts and Stud.*). See also George Wickes, "Henry Constable, Poet and Courtier (1562-1613)," *Biographical Stud. 1534-1829*, ii (1954). 272-300.

481 *The English Works of Giles Fletcher, the Elder* have been ed. by L. E. Berry (Madison, 1964). Berry has also published a bibliography in the *Trans. Cambridge Bibl. Soc.*, iii: iii (1961). 200-215.

482   The sonnets are of course included in the facsimile of the earliest printings of *Shakespeare's Poems* (New Haven, 1964). An old-spelling text of the
sonnets has been published by Martin Seymour-Smith (1963), an elaborately
annotated text by W. G. Ingram & Theodore Redpath (1964), and a text with
prose paraphrases by A. L. Rowse (1964). A. Nejgebauer, *ShS,* xv (1962). 10-18
surveys twentieth-century studies of the sonnets. On the date see Leslie Hotson,
Shakespeare's Sonnets Dated and Other Essays (1949); T. W. Baldwin, *On the
Literary Genetics of Shakespeare's Poems and Sonnets* (Urbana, Ill., 1950); Claes
Schaar, *Elizabethan Sonnet Themes and the Dating of Shakespeare's Sonnets*
(1962; *Lund Stud. in English,* 32): all of them would date the sonnets, or some
of them, earlier, sometimes much earlier, than is usual. New candidates for the
distinction of being the rival poet and the fair youth are proposed by Robert
Gittings, *Shakespeare's Rival* (1960) and Leslie Hotson, *Mr W. H.* (1964). Some
recent studies are Edward Hubler, *The Sense of Shakespeare's Sonnets* (1952;
Princeton Stud. in English, 33); G. K. Hunter, "The Dramatic Technique of
Shakespeare's Sonnets," *EIC,* III (1953). 152-164; G. W. Knight, *The Mutual
Flame: an Interpretation of Shakespeare's Sonnets* (1954); Claes Schaar, *An
Elizabethan Sonnet Problem: Shakespeare's Sonnets, Daniel's Delia, and their
Literary Background* (1960; *Lund Stud. in English,* 28); J. B. Leishman, *Themes
and Variations in Shakespeare's Sonnets* (1961); Joan Grundy, "Shakespeare's
Sonnets and the Elizabethan Sonneteers," *ShS,* xv (1962). 41-49; Hilton Landry,
Interpretations in Shakespeare's Sonnets (Berkeley, 1963; *Perspectives in Criti-
cism,* 14); J. D. Wilson, *An Introduction to the Sonnets of Shakespeare for the
Use of Historians and Others* (Cambridge, 1964).

IX. Edmund Spenser

483   The Variorum ed. of Spenser is now complete in 9 vols. (Baltimore, 1932-
1949), besides an index by C. G. Osgood (Baltimore, 1957). W. F. McNeir &
Foster Pruvost, *Annotated Bibliography of Edmund Spenser, 1937-1960* (Pitts-
burgh, 1962) continue the bibliographies of Carpenter and Miss Atkinson. R. M.
Smith, "Spenser's Scholarly Script and 'Right Writing'," *Studies in Honor of
T. W. Baldwin,* ed. D. C. Allen (Urbana, Ill., 1958), pp. 66-111 lists the known
documents in Spenser's hand and studies his orthography. *That Soveraine Light:
Essays in Honor of Spenser,* ed. D. C. Allen & W. R. Mueller (Baltimore, 1952)
and *Spenser's Critics: Changing Currents in Literary Taste,* ed. W. R. Mueller
(Syracuse, N.Y., 1959) are anthologies of criticism. Some recent general studies
are W. B. C. Watkins, *Shakespeare and Spenser* (Princeton, 1950); C. R. Sonn,
"Spenser's Imagery," *ELH,* xxvi (1959). 156-170; Veselin Kostić, "Spenser and
the Bembian Linguistic Theory," *English Miscellany,* x (1959). 43-60; *Form and
Convention in the Poetry of Edmund Spenser: Selected Papers from the English
Institute,* ed. William Nelson (1961); William Nelson, *The Poetry of Edmund
Spenser, a Study* (1963). Alastair Fowler, *Spenser and the Numbers of Time*
(1964) is a numerological study.

484   An ed. of *The Shepherds' Calendar* by A. M. Crinò (Firenze, 1951) has
been published. See also P. E. McLane, *Spenser's* Shepheardes Calender, *a Study*

in Elizabethan Allegory (South Bend, Ind., 1962); S. K. Heninger, Jr., "The Implications of Form for *The Shepheardes Calender*," *SRen*, IX (1962). 309-321.

485 See V. K. Whitaker, *The Religious Basis of Spenser's Thought* (Palo Alto, Calif., 1950; *Stanford Univ. Pub.: Lang. and Lit.*, VII: 3).

486 On Spenser's early poems see A. W. Satterthwaite, *Spenser, Ronsard, and DuBellay: a Renaissance Comparison* (Princeton, 1960).

488 On *Colin Clout* see Sam Meyer, "Spenser's *Colin Clout:* the Poem and the Book," *Papers of the Bibl. Soc. of America*, LVI (1962). 397-413.

489 On Spenser's sonnets see Diethild Bludau, "Humanismus und Allegorie in Spensers Sonetten," *Anglia*, LXXIV (1956). 292-332; L. L. Martz, "The *Amoretti:* 'most goodly temperature'," *Form and Convention in the Poetry of Edmund Spenser*, ed. William Nelson (1961), pp. 146-168, 180.

491 On the *Epithalamion* see A. K. Hieatt, *Short Time's Endless Monument: the Symbolism of the Numbers in Edmund Spenser's "Epithalamion"* (1961); T. M. Greene, "Spenser and the Epithalamic Convention," *CL*, IX (1957). 215-228.

492 See Robert Ellrodt, *Neoplatonism in the Poetry of Spenser* (Geneva, 1960; *Travaux d'humanisme et Renaissance*, XXXV).

X. The Faerie Queene: The Spenserians

496 On *The Faerie Queene* see A. S. P. Woodhouse, "Nature and Grace in *The Faerie Queene*," *ELH*, XVI (1949). 194-228; W. J. B. Owen, "The Structure of *The Faerie Queene*," *PMLA*, LXVIII (1953). 1079-1100; John Arthos, *On the Poetry of Spenser and the Form of Romances* (1956); H. P. Guth, "Unity and Multiplicity in Spenser's *Faerie Queene*," *Anglia*, LXXIV (1956). 1-15; M. Pauline Parker, *The Allegory of* The Faerie Queene (Oxford, 1960); J. B. Dallett, "Ideas of Sight in *The Faerie Queene*," *ELH*, XXVII (1960). 87-121; A. C. Hamilton, *The Structure of Allegory in* The Faerie Queene (Oxford, 1961); Northrop Frye, "The Structure of Imagery in *The Faerie Queene*," *UTQ*, XXX (1961). 108-127, reprinted in *Fables of Identity* (1962); Millar MacLure, "Nature and Art in *The Faerie Queene*," *ELH*, XXVIII (1961). 1-20, "Spenser's Allegories," *UTQ*, XXXII (1962). 83-92; Graham Hough, *A Preface to* The Faerie Queene (1962); J. F. Kermode, "Spenser and the Allegorists," *Proc. Brit. Acad.*, XLVIII (1962). 261-279; Kathleen Williams, "Romance Tradition in *The Faerie Queene*," *Research Stud. of Washington State Univ.* XXXII (1964). 147-160. The following treat particular books of *The Faerie Queene*: Harry Berger, Jr., *The Allegorical Temper: Vision and Reality in Book II of Spenser's "Faerie Queene"* (New Haven, 1957); T. P. Roche, Jr., *The Kindly Flame: a Study of the Third and Fourth Books of Spenser's* Faerie Queene (Princeton, 1964); E. W. Tayler, *Nature and Art in Renaissance Literature* [book VI] (1964).

502 *Tasso's* Jerusalem Delivered: *the Edward Fairfax Translation* has been ed. by Roberto Weiss (1962). See also C. G. Bell, "Fairfax's Tasso," *CL*, VI (1954). 26-52.

503 On Drayton's odes and others see Carol Maddison, *Apollo and the Nine: a History of the Ode* (1960).

504 On Phineas Fletcher see R. G. Baldwin, "Phineas Fletcher: his Modern Readers and his Renaissance Ideas," *PQ*, XL (1961). 462-475.

506 On Henry More see R. L. Colie, *Light and Enlightenment: a Study of the Cambridge Platonists and the Dutch Arminians* (1957); Aharon Lichtenstein, *Henry More: the Rational Theology of a Cambridge Platonist* (Cambridge, Mass., 1962).

XI. Christopher Marlowe

508 Eds. of Marlowe's plays have been published by Leo Kirschbaum (1962) and Irving Ribner (1964). For critical studies see Nicola D'Agostino, *Marlowe* (Roma, 1950); Michel Poirier, *Christopher Marlowe* (1951); Harry Levin, *The Overreacher: a Study of Christopher Marlowe* (Cambridge, Mass., 1952); F. P. Wilson, *Marlowe and the Early Shakespeare* (Oxford, 1953); Denis Marion, *Christopher Marlowe, dramaturge* (Paris, 1955); Douglas Cole, *Suffering and Evil in the Plays of Christopher Marlowe* (Princeton, 1962); J. B. Steane, *Marlowe: a Critical Study* (Cambridge, 1964); A. L. Rowse, *Christopher Marlowe* (1964); Jocelyn Powell, "Marlowe's Spectacle," *Tulane Drama Rev.*, VIII: iv (1964). 195-210.

514 On *Hero and Leander* see R. A. Fraser, "The Art of *Hero and Leander*," *JEGP*, LVII (1958). 743-754; Clifford Leech, "Marlowe's Humor," *Essays on Shakespeare and the Elizabethan Drama in Honor of Hardin Craig*, ed. R. Hosley (Columbia, Mo., 1962), pp. 69-81.

515 A later date for *Dido* is advocated by T. M. Pearce, "Evidence for Dating Marlowe's *Tragedy of Dido*," *Studies in the English Renaissance Drama in Memory of K. J. Holzknecht*, ed. J. W. Bennett *et al.* (1959), pp. 231-247.

516 On *Tamburlaine* see G. I. Duthie, "The Dramatic Structure of Marlowe's *Tamburlaine the Great*, Parts I and II," *English Stud. (E&S*, n.s.), I (1948). 101-126; Katherine Lever, "The Image of Man in *Tamburlaine*, Part I," *PQ*, XXV (1956). 421-427; Donald Peet, "The Rhetoric of *Tamburlaine*," *ELH*, XXVI (1959). 137-155; E. M. Waith, *The Herculean Hero in Marlowe, Chapman, Shakespeare and Dryden* (1962), cf. Rolf Soellner, "The Madness of Hercules and the Elizabethans," *CL*, X (1958). 309-324; Robert Kimbrough, "*Tamburlaine*: a Speaking Picture in a Tragic Glass," *Renaissance Drama*, VII (1964). 20-34; Clifford Leech, "The Structure of *Tamburlaine*," *Tulane Drama Rev.*, VIII: iv (1964). 32-46.

517 *Marlowe's* Doctor Faustus *1604-1616, Parallel Texts*, ed. W. W. Greg (Oxford, 1950) exhaustively compares the several texts of the play. Greg has also published a critical text in modern spelling (Oxford, 1950); a still more recent ed. is that of J. D. Jump (1962). The latest discussion of the date of the play, C. A. Zimansky, "Marlowe's *Faustus*: the Date again," *PQ*, XLI (1962). 181-187, favors an early date; it refers to previous speculations. On the interpretation of the play see Nicholas Brooke, "The Moral of Doctor Faustus," *Cambridge Jour.*, VII (1952). 662-687; Robert Ornstein, "The Comic Synthesis in *Doctor Faustus*," *ELH*, XXII (1955). 165-172; R. M. Frye, "Marlowe's *Doctor Faustus*: the Repudiation of Humanity," *So. Atl. Quar.*, LV (1956). 322-328; J. T. McCullen, "Dr.

Faustus and Renaissance Learning," *MLR*, LI (1956). 6-16; J. P. Brockbank, *Marlowe: Dr. Faustus* (1962; *Stud. in English Lit.*, 6); Joseph Westlund, "The Orthodox Christian Framework of Marlowe's *Faustus*," *SEL*, III (1963). 191-205; C. L. Barber, "The Form of Faustus' Fortunes Good or Bad," *Tulane Drama Rev.*, VIII: iv (1964). 92-119; D. J. Palmer, "Magic and Poetry in *Doctor Faustus*," *Critical Quar.*, VI (1964). 56-67; Arieh Sachs, "The Religious Despair of Doctor Faustus," *JEGP*, LXIII (1964). 625-647.—There is a new ed. of *The Jew of Malta* by R. W. Van Fossen (1964). See also Antonio D'Andrea, "Studies on Machiavelli and his Reputation in the Sixteenth Century: Marlowe's Prologue to 'The Jew of Malta'," *Medieval and Renais. Stud.*, V (1961). 214-248; Alfred Harbage, "Innocent Barabas," *Tulane Drama Rev.*, VIII: iv (1964). 47-58.

518 On *Edward II* see Robert Fricker, "The Dramatic Structure of *Edward II*," *ES*, XXXIV (1953). 204-217; Clifford Leech, "Marlowe's *Edward II*: Power and Suffering," *Critical Quar.*, I (1959). 181-196.

XII. Shakespeare to 1603

519 Recent bibliographies are G. R. Smith, *A Classified Shakespeare Bibliography, 1936-1958* (University Park, Penna., 1963); Ronald Berman, *A Reader's Guide to Shakespeare's Plays: a Discursive Bibliography* (1965). Useful reference books are K. J. Holzknecht, *The Backgrounds of Shakespeare's Plays* (1950); F. E. Halliday, *A Shakespeare Companion 1550-1950* (1952; 2ed, 1964). Some new biographies are M. M. Reese, *Shakespeare: his World and his Work* (1953); G. E. Bentley, *Shakespeare: a Biographical Handbook* (New Haven, 1961); A. L. Rowse, *William Shakespeare, a Biography* (1963).—Some comprehensive studies are Alfred Harbage, *As They Liked It: an Essay on Shakespeare and Morality* (1947); Henri Fluchère, *Shakespeare: dramaturge élisabéthain* (Toulouse, 1948; English tr., 1953); Arthur Sewell, *Character and Society in Shakespeare* (Oxford, 1951); Max Lüthi, *Shakespeares Dramen* (Berlin, 1957); L. C. Knights, *Some Shakespearean Themes* (1959); A. P. Rossiter, *Angel with Horns and Other Shakespeare Lectures* (1961); Peter Alexander, *Shakespeare* (1964); John Wain, *The Living World of Shakespeare* (1964). F. E. Halliday, *Shakespeare and his Critics* (1949; 2ed, 1958) is an anthology of criticism.—On Shakespeare's technique see T. W. Baldwin, *Shakespeare's Five-act Structure* (Urbana, Ill., 1947); H. T. Price, *Construction in Shakespeare* (1951; *Univ. of Michigan Contrib. in Mod. Phil.*, VII); Arthur Gerstner-Hirzel, *The Economy of Action and Word in Shakespeare's Plays* (Bern, 1957; *Cooper Monographs*); H. L. Snuggs, *Shakespeare and Five Acts* (1960); Wolfgang Clemen, *Shakespeare's Soliloquies* (Cambridge, 1964); Nevill Coghill, *Shakespeare's Professional Skills* (Cambridge, 1964).—On his language see E. A. Armstrong, *Shakespeare's Imagination: a Study of the Psychology of Association and Inspiration* (1946; new ed., Lincoln, Nebr., 1963); Sister Miriam Joseph, *Shakespeare's Use of the Arts of Language* (1947); Wolfgang Clemen, *The Development of Shakespeare's Imagery* (1951, a tr., revised, of *Shakespeares Bilder*, Bonn, 1936); Milton Crane, *Shakespeare's Prose* (Chicago, 1951); Helge Kökeritz, *Shakespeare's Pronunciation* (New Haven, 1953); M. M. Mahood, *Shakespeare's Wordplay* (1957); B. I. Evans, *The Language of Shakespeare's Plays* (2ed, 1959); H. M. Hulme, *Explorations* in *Shakespeare's Language* (1962).—On the sources of the plays see E. C. Pettet, *Shakespeare and the Romance Tradition* (1949); F. P. Wilson, "Shakespeare's Reading," *ShS*, III (1950). 14-21; M. C. Bradbrook, *Shakespeare and Elizabethan Poetry* (1951); J. A. K. Thomson, *Shakespeare and the Classics* (1952); V. K. Whitaker, *Shakespeare's Use of Learning* (San Marino, Calif., 1953); Geoffrey Bullough, *Narrative and Dramatic Sources of Shakespeare* (5v, 1957-1964, in progress); Kenneth Muir, *Shakespeare's Sources: 1, Comedies and Tragedies* (1957); R. M. Frye, *Shakespeare and Christian Doctrine* (Princeton, 1963).

520 See Bernard Beckerman, *Shakespeare at the Globe 1599-1609* (1962).

521 Of the Shakespeare Association's facsimiles of the quartos, ed. W. W. Greg & Charlton Hinman, so far 14 vols. have appeared (1939-1964). The facsimile of the first folio ed. Helge Kökeritz & C. T. Prouty (New Haven, 1954) is less satisfactory than those which preceded it. The New Variorum ed. now includes 23 plays (besides the poems and the sonnets) and a supplement to *1 Henry IV*, ed. G. B. Evans (1956). The New Shakespeare, ed. A. T. Quiller-Couch, J. D. Wilson, and others, is now virtually complete (37v, 1921-1962). In the Arden series 25 vols. have been issued in revised form (1951-1965). New eds. of the complete works in a single volume are those of Peter Alexander (1951) and C. J. Sisson (1953).—On the text and its transmission see Alice Walker, *Textual Problems of the First Folio:* Richard III, King Lear, Troilus and Cressida, 2 Henry IV, Hamlet, Othello (Cambridge, 1953; *Shakespeare Problems Ser.*, VII); W. W. Greg, *The Shakespeare First Folio: its Bibliographical and Textual History* (Oxford, 1955); Leo Kirschbaum, *Shakespeare and the Stationers* (Columbus, O., 1955); Fredson Bowers, *On Editing Shakespeare and the Elizabethan Dramatists* (Philadelphia, 1955), *Textual and Literary Criticism* (Cambridge, 1959); Charlton Hinman, *The Printing and Proof-reading of the First Folio of Shakespeare* (2v, Oxford, 1963); E. A. J. Honigmann, *The Stability of Shakespeare's Text* (1965); J. M. Nosworthy, *Shakespeare's Occasional Plays, their Origin and Transmission* (1965).

523 On the poems see F. T. Prince's ed. (1960; *Arden Shakespeare*); J. W. Lever, "The Poems," *ShS*, xv (1962), 18-30, a review of criticism; R. P. Miller "The Myth of Mars's Hot Minion in *Venus and Adonis*," *ELH*, xxvi (1959). 470-481; A. C. Hamilton, " 'Venus and Adonis'," *SEL*, I: i (1961). 1-15; H. R. Walley, "*The Rape of Lucrece* and Shakespearean Tragedy," *PMLA*, LXXVI (1961). 480-487.

524 On the history plays see Raymond Chapman, "The Wheel of Fortune in Shakespeare's Historical Plays," *RES*, I (1950). 1-7; Harold Jenkins, "Shakespeare's History Plays: 1900-1951," *ShS*, vi (1953). 1-15; M. M. Reese, *The Cease of Majesty: a Study of Shakespeare's History Plays* (1961); S. C. Sen Gupta, *Shakespeare's Historical Plays* (Oxford, 1964).—The opinion that Shakespeare is the sole author of *1 Henry VI* is maintained by Leo Kirschbaum, "The Authorship of *1 Henry VI*," *PMLA*, LXVII (1952). 809-822, by A. S. Cairncross in the Arden ed. of the play (1962), and by C. G. Harlow, "A Source for Nashe's *Terrors of the Night*, and the Authorship of *1 Henry VI*," *SEL*, v (1965). 31-48, 269-281; J. D. Wilson in the New Cambridge ed. (1952) disagrees. In *"The Contention" and Shakespeare's "2 Henry VI," a Comparative Study* (New Haven, 1954) C. T. Prouty argues that *The Contention* is an older play which

Shakespeare revised as 2 *Henry VI;* J. G. McManaway, *"The Contention* and *2 Henry VI,"* Studies in English Language and Literature Presented to Karl Brunner (1957; *Wiener Beiträge,* LXV), pp. 143-154 reaffirms the derivative nature of the text of *The Contention.* Marco Mincoff, *"3 Henry VI* and *The True Tragedy," ES,* XLII (1961). 273-288 concludes that the latter is also a reported text. See J. P. Brockbank, "The Frame of Disorder—*Henry VI," Early Shakespeare,* ed. J. R. Brown & B. Harris (1961; *Stratford-upon-Avon Stud.,* 3) and R. Y. Turner, "Characterization in Shakespeare's Early History Plays," *ELH,* XXXI (1964). 241-258 for studies of these plays.—On *King John* see Adrien Bonjour, "The Road to Swinstead Abbey: a Study of the Sense and Structure of *King John," ELH,* XVIII)1951). 253-274.—On *Richard III* see J. K. Walton, *The Copy for the Folio Text of* Richard III (1955; *Auckland Univ. Coll. Monograph Ser.,* 1); Wolfgang Clemen, *Kommentar zu Shakespeare's* Richard III (Göttingen, 1957).—On *Richard II* see L. F. Dean, *"Richard II:* the State and the Image of the Theatre," *PMLA,* LXVII (1952). 211-218.—On *Henry IV* see Leslie Hotson, "Ancient Pistol," *Yale Rev.,* XXXVIII (1948). 51-66, reprinted in *Shakespeare's Sonnets Dated* (1949), pp. 57-75; William Empson, "Falstaff and Mr. Dover Wilson," *Kenyon Rev.,* XV (1953). 213-262.—On the comedies see J. R. Brown, "The Interpretation of Shakespeare's Comedies: 1900-1953," *ShS,* VIII (1955). 1-13; D. L. Stevenson, *The Love Game Comedy* (1946; *Columbia Univ. Stud. in English and Compar. Lit.,* 164); S. C. Sen Gupta, *Shakespearian Comedy* (Calcutta, 1951); J. R. Brown, *Shakespeare and his Comedies* (1957); C. L. Barber, *Shakespeare's Festive Comedy* (Princeton, 1959); Bertrand Evans, *Shakespeare's Comedies* (Oxford, 1960); J. D. Wilson, *Shakespeare's Happy Comedies* (1962); Northrop Frye, *A Natural Perspective: the Development of Shakespearean Comedy and Romance* (1965).

525 On *Love's Labour's Lost* see Bobbyann Roesen, *"Love's Labour's Lost," SQ,* IV (1953). 411-426; Cyrus Hoy, *"Love's Labour's Lost* and the Nature of Comedy," *SQ,* XIII (1962). 31-40.—On *The Two Gentlemen of Verona* see J. F. Danby, "Shakespeare Criticism and *The Two Gentlemen of Verona," Critical Quar.,* II (1960). 309-321.—On *The Comedy of Errors* see H. F. Brooks, "Themes and Structure in *The Comedy of Errors," Early Shakespeare,* ed. J. R. Brown & B. Harris (1961; *Stratford-upon-Avon Stud.,* 3), pp. 55-71; T. W. Baldwin, *On the Compositional Genetics of* The Comedy of Errors (Urbana, Ill., 1965).—That Shakespeare was the sole author of *The Taming of the Shrew* seems now to be generally agreed: see Karl Wentersdorf, "The Authenticity of *The Taming of the Shrew," SQ,* V (1954). 311-332. On the relation of the play to *The Taming of a Shrew* opinion is still vexed. The idea that *A Shrew* is the main source of *The Shrew* has largely been abandoned except by J. W. Shroeder, *"The Taming of a Shrew* and *The Taming of the Shrew:* a Case Reopened," *JEGP,* LVII (1958). 424-443. Opinion is divided between the supposition that both *A Shrew* and *The Shrew* are derived from a lost play and that *A Shrew* is a bad quarto of *The Shrew:* see Richard Hosley, "Sources and Analogues of *The Taming of the Shrew," HLQ,* XXVII (1964). 289-308, who chooses the latter alternative. Some recent studies are M. C. Bradbrook, "Dramatic Role as Social Image: a Study of *The Taming of the Shrew," Shakespeare-Jahrbuch,* XCIV (1958). 132-150; Richard Hosley, "Was there a 'Dramatic Epilogue' to *The Taming of the Shrew?" SEL,* I: ii (1961). 17-34; C. C. Seronsy, " 'Supposes' as

the Unifying Theme in *The Taming of the Shrew,*" *SQ,* xiv (1963). 15-30.—
On *The Merry Wives* see William Green, *Shakespeare's* Merry Wives of Windsor
(1962).—On *Much Ado about Nothing* see C. T. Prouty, *The Sources of Much
Ado about Nothing* (New Haven, 1951); T. W. Craik, "Much Ado about
Nothing," *Scrutiny,* xiv (1953). 297-316; Francis Fergusson, *"The Comedy of
Errors* and *Much Ado about Nothing,"* *Sewanee Rev.,* lxii (1954). 24-37, reprinted in *The Human Image in Dramatic Literature* (1957), pp. 144-157.—
On *As You Like It* see Harold Jenkins, *"As You Like It,"* *ShS,* viii (1955).
40-51.—On *Twelfth Night* see Leslie Hotson, *The First Night of* Twelfth Night
(1954); L. G. Salingar, "The Design of *Twelfth Night,"* *SQ,* ix (1958). 117-
139; Harold Jenkins, "Shakespeare's *Twelfth Night,"* *Rice Inst. Pamphlet,* xlv
(1959). 19-42.

526 On the tragedies see L. L. Schücking, *Shakespeare und der Tragödi-
enstil seiner Zeit* (Bern, 1947); H. B. Charlton, *Shakespearian Tragedy* (Cam-
bridge, 1948); J. V. Cunningham, *Woe or Wonder: the Emotional Effect of
Shakespearean Tragedy* (Denver, 1951); Robert Speaight, *Nature in Shake-
spearean Tragedy* (1955); Brents Stirling, *Unity in Shakespearean Tragedy: the
Interplay of Theme and Character* (1956); F. M. Dickey, *Not Wisely but too
Well: Shakespeare's Love Tragedies* (San Marino, Calif., 1957); H. S. Wilson,
On the Design of Shakespearian Tragedy (1957; *Univ. of Toronto Dept. of
English Stud. and Texts,* 5); R. F. Hill, "Shakespeare's Early Tragic Mode,"
SQ, ix (1958). 455-469; John Lawlor, *The Tragic Sense in Shakespeare* (1960);
William Rosen, *Shakespeare and the Craft of Tragedy* (Cambridge, Mass., 1960);
John Holloway, *The Story of the Night: Studies in Shakespeare's Major Trag-
edies* (1961); C. J. Sisson, *Shakespeare's Tragic Justice* (1962).—The question
of Shakespeare's authorship of all of *Titus Andronicus,* especially Act I, is still
open; the latest word is R. F. Hill, "The Composition of *Titus Andronicus,"*
ShS, x (1957). 60-70. Some studies are R. M. Sargent, "The Source of *Titus
Andronicus,"* *SP,* xlvi (1949). 167-183; E. M. Waith, "The Metamorphosis of
Violence in *Titus Andronicus,"* *ShS,* x (1957). 39-49; Horst Oppel, *Titus Andronicus: Studien zur dramengeschichtlichen Stellung von Shakespeares früher
Tragödie* (Heidelberg, 1961; *Schriftenreihe der deutschen Shakespeare-Gesell-
schaft,* n.F., 9).—On *Romeo and Juliet* see Herbert McArthur, "Romeo's Lo-
quacious Friend," *SQ,* x (1959). 35-44; Harry Levin, "Form and Formality in
Romeo and Juliet," *SQ,* xi (1960). 3-11.

527 On the Roman plays see J. C. Maxwell, "Shakespeare's Roman Plays:
1900-1956," *ShS,* x (1957). 1-11; T. J. B. Spencer, "Shakespeare and the Elizabethan Romans," *ShS,* x (1957). 27-38; J. L. Barroll, "Shakespeare and Roman
History," *MLR,* liii (1958). 327-343; Maurice Charney, *Shakespeare's Roman
Plays: the Function of Imagery in the Drama* (Cambridge, Mass., 1961).—On
Julius Caesar see Adrien Bonjour, *The Structure of* Julius Caesar (Liverpool,
1958).—On *Hamlet* see P. S. Conklin, *A History of Hamlet Criticism, 1601-1821*
(1947); *Readings on the Character of Hamlet, 1661-1947,* ed. C. C. H. William-
son (1951); Clifford Leech, "Studies in *Hamlet:* 1901-1955," *ShS,* ix (1956).
1-15; Stanley Wells, "A Reader's Guide to 'Hamlet'," *Hamlet,* ed. J. R. Brown
& B. Harris (1963; *Stratford-upon-Avon Stud.,* 5), pp. 200-207; Harold Jenkins,
"'Hamlet' then till now," *ShS,* xviii (1965). 34-45; Salvador de Madariaga, *On
Hamlet* (1948, rev. 1964); Roy Walker, *The Time is out of Joint: a Study of*

Hamlet (1949); Francis Fergusson, "Hamlet and the Analogy of Action," *Hudson Rev.*, II (1949). 165-210, reprinted in *The Idea of a Theater* (Princeton, 1949), pp. 98-142; Richard Flatter, *Hamlet's Father* (1949); G. R. Elliott, *Scourge and Minister, a Study of Hamlet as Tragedy of Revengefulness and Justice* (Durham, N.C., 1951); Maynard Mack, "The World of Hamlet," *Yale Rev.*, XLI (1952). 502-523; Peter Alexander, *Hamlet, Father and Son* (1955); Rebecca West, *The Court and the Castle* (New Haven, 1957); H. D. F. Kitto, *Form and Meaning in Drama* (1959); Harry Levin, *The Question of Hamlet* (1959); L. C. Knights, *An Approach to "Hamlet"* (1960); Weston Babcock, *Hamlet: a Tragedy of Errors* (1961); E. A. J. Honigmann, "The Politics in *Hamlet* and 'the World of the Play,'" *Hamlet*, ed. J. R. Brown & B. Harris (1963; *Stratford-upon-Avon Stud.*, 5), pp. 129-147.

Part III. The Early Stuarts and the Commonwealth (1603-1660)

I. Shakespeare under James

533 On the dark comedies see E. M. W. Tillyard, *Shakespeare's Problem Plays* (Toronto, 1949); Ernest Schanzer, *Shakespeare's Problem Plays* (1963).— On *Troilus and Cressida* see R. K. Presson, *Shakespeare's* Troilus and Cressida *and the Legends of Troy* (Madison, 1953); Kenneth Muir, "*Troilus and Cressida*," *ShS*, VIII (1955). 28-39; M. C. Bradbrook, "What Shakespeare did to Chaucer's *Troilus and Criseyde*," *SQ*, IX (1958). 311-319.

534 On *All's Well that Ends Well* see W. N. King, "Shakespeare's Mingled Yarn," *MLQ*, XXI (1960). 33-44; S. Nagarajan, "The Structure of *All's Well that Ends Well*," *EIC*, X (1960). 24-31.—On *Measure for Measure* see Clifford Leech, "The 'Meaning' of *Measure for Measure*," *ShS*, III (1950). 66-73; Mary Lascelles, *Shakespeare's "Measure for Measure"* (1953); D. L. Stevenson, "Design and Structure in *Measure for Measure*," *ELH*, XXIII (1956). 256-278; Robert Ornstein, "The Human Comedy: *Measure for Measure*," *Univ. of Kansas City Rev.*, XXIV (1957). 15-22.

535 On *Othello* see Harley Granville-Barker, *Othello* (1946; *Prefaces to Shakespeare*, 4th ser.); G. G. Sedgewick, *Of Irony, especially in Drama* (Toronto, 1948); Richard Flatter, *The Moor of Venice* (1950); Helen Gardner, "The Noble Moor," *Proc. Brit. Acad.* XLI (1955). 189-205; R. B. Heilman, *Magic in the Web: Action and Language in* Othello (Lexington, Ky., 1956); Marvin Rosenberg, *The Masks of Othello: the Search for the Identity of Othello, Iago, and Desdemona by Three Centuries of Actors and Critics* (Berkeley, 1961).

536 On *Lear* see Edwin Muir, *The Politics of "King Lear"* (Glasgow, 1948); R. B. Heilman, *This Great Stage: Image and Structure in King Lear* (Baton Rouge, La., 1948), cf. W. R. Keast, "Imagery and Meaning in the Interpretation of *King Lear*," *MP*, XLVII (1949). 45-64; J. F. Danby, *Shakespeare's Doctrine of Nature: a Study of King Lear* (1949); J. M. Lothian, King Lear, *a Tragic Reading of Life* (Toronto, 1949); Salvatore Rosati, *Il giro della rota* (Firenze,

1958); Barbara Everett, "The New *King Lear*," *Critical Quar.*, II (1960). 325-339; Maynard Mack, "The Jacobean Shakespeare," *Jacobean Theatre*, ed. J. R. Brown & B. Harris (1960; *Stratford-upon-Avon Stud.*, 1); R. A. Fraser, *Shakespeare's Poetics in relation to* King Lear (1962).

537 On *Macbeth* see Roy Walker, *The Time is Free: a Study of* Macbeth (1949); H. N. Paul, *The Royal Play of Macbeth* (1950); R. M. Frye, "*Macbeth* and the Powers of Darkness," *Emory Univ. Quar.*, VIII (1952). 164-174; Francis Fergusson, "*Macbeth* as the Imitation of an Action," *English Inst. Essays 1951*, pp. 30-43, reprinted in *The Human Image in Dramatic Literature* (1957), pp. 115-125; G. R. Elliott, *Dramatic Providence in* Macbeth: *a Study of Shakespeare's Tragic Theme of Humanity and Grace* (Princeton, 1958); H. L. Rogers, "*Double Profit*" in Macbeth (Melbourne, 1964).—On *Antony and Cleopatra* see J. F. Danby, "The Shakespearean Dialectic: an Aspect of 'Antony and Cleopatra'," *Scrutiny*, XVI (1949). 196-213, reprinted in *Poets on Fortune's Hill* (1952).

538 On *Coriolanus* see Harley Granville-Barker, *Coriolanus* (1948; *Prefaces to Shakespeare*, 5th ser.).

539 On *Timon of Athens* see J. C. Maxwell, " 'Timon of Athens'," *Scrutiny*, XV (1948). 195-208; Andor Gomme, "*Timon of Athens*," *EIC*, IX (1959). 107-125; E. A. J. Honigmann, "*Timon of Athens*," *SQ*, XII (1961). 3-20.—On the last plays see J. F. Danby, *Poets on Fortune's Hill: Studies in Sidney, Shakespeare, and Beaumont and Fletcher* (1952; 2nd impression, *Elizabethan and Jacobean Poets*, 1964); D. A. Traversi, *Shakespeare: the Last Phase* (1954); D. R. Marsh, *The Recurring Miracle: a Study of* Cymbeline *and the Last Plays* (Durban, 1962).—On *Pericles* see John Arthos, "*Pericles, Prince of Tyre*," *SQ*, IV (1953). 257-270.

540 On *The Winter's Tale* see S. L. Bethell, The Winter's Tale: *a Study* (1947); Adrien Bonjour, "The Final Scene of *The Winter's Tale*," *ES*, XXXIII (1952). 193-208; Northrop Frye, "Recognition in *The Winter's Tale*," *Essays on Shakespeare and Elizabethan Drama in Honor of Hardin Craig*, ed. R. Hosley (Columbia, Mo., 1962), pp. 235-246, reprinted in *Fables of Identity* (1963), pp. 107-118.—On *The Tempest* see Bonamy Dobree, "The Tempest," *E&S*, n.s. V (1952). 13-25; Bernard Knox, " 'The Tempest' and the Ancient Comic Tradition," *English Stage Comedy*, ed. W. K. Wimsatt, Jr. (1954; *English Inst. Essays*), pp. 52-73.—On Shakespeare's share in *The Two Noble Kinsmen* see Kenneth Muir, *Shakespeare as Collaborator* (1960).—Shakespeare's share in *Henry VIII* is still an open question or at least is still debated: the latest proponent of the idea that he is the sole author is R. A. Foakes in the Arden ed. of the play (1957); of the view that it is by Shakespeare and Fletcher, A. C. Partridge, *Orthography in Shakespeare and Elizabethan Drama* (1964), pp. 141-163.

II. Jacobean Drama: I. Dramatists of the Old School

541 Bentley's *Jacobean and Caroline Stage* is now complete except for the last two volumes (5v, Oxford, 1941-1956). Some comprehensive studies are F. S. Boas, *An Introduction to Stuart Drama* (Oxford, 1946); Robert Ornstein, *The Moral Vision of Jacobean Tragedy* (Madison, 1960); Irving Ribner, *Jacobean*

Tragedy: the Quest for Moral Order (1962). Recent anthologies include *Five Stuart Tragedies,* ed. A. K. McIlwraith (1953; *World's Classics*); *Early Seventeenth Century Drama,* ed. R. G. Lawrence (1963, Everyman's Library); *The Anchor Anthology of Jacobean Drama,* vol. 1, ed. R. C. Harrier (1963).—*The Dramatic Works of Thomas Dekker* have been ed. by Fredson Bowers (4v, Cambridge, 1953-1961). See also M. T. Jones-Davies, *Un Peintre de la vie londonienne: Thomas Dekker* (*circa 1572-1632*) (2v, Paris, 1958; *Coll. des études anglaises,* 6).

543 On Heywood see Michel Grivelet, *Thomas Heywood et le drame domestique élizabéthain* (Paris, 1957). *The Fair Maid of the Exchange* has been ed. by P. H. Davison & Arthur Brown (1963; *Malone Soc.*).

544 Ernest Schanzer, "Heywood's *Ages* and Shakespeare," *RES,* xi (1960). 18-28 suggests 1611 as the date.

545 *The Captives* has been ed. by Arthur Brown (1953; *Malone Soc.*).

546 *Dick of Devonshire* has been ed. by J. G. & M. R. McManaway (1955; *Malone Soc.*).

547 There is an ed. of *A Woman Killed with Kindness* by R. W. Van Fossen (1961). See also P. M. Spacks, "Honor and Perception in *A Woman Killed with Kindness,*" *MLQ,* xx (1959). 321-332; David Cook, "*A Woman Killed with Kindness:* an Unshakespearian Tragedy," *ES,* xlv (1964). 353-372. —On *The English Traveller* see Michel Grivelet, "The Simplicity of Thomas Heywood," *ShS,* xiv (1961). 56-65; Norman Rabkin, "Dramatic Deception in Heywood's *The English Traveller,*" *SEL,* 1: ii (1961). 1-16.—On Webster see Lord David Cecil, *Poets and Story-tellers* (1948); Ian Jack, "The Case of Webster," *Scrutiny,* xvi (1949). 38-43; Clifford Leech, *John Webster, a Critical Study* (1951); Gabriele Baldini, *John Webster e il linguaggio della tragedia* (Roma, 1953); Travis Bogard, *The Tragic Satire of John Webster* (Berkeley, 1955); H. T. Price, "The Function of Imagery in Webster," *PMLA,* lxx (1955). 717-739; Mina Irgat, "Disease Imagery in the Plays of John Webster," *Studies by Members of the Istanbul Univ. English Dept.,* ii (1955). 1-26; Inga-Stina Ekeblad, "The 'Impure Art' of John Webster," *RES,* ix (1958). 253-267; Johanna Glier, *Struktur und Gestaltungsprinzipien in den Dramen John Websters* (München, 1957); R. W. Dent, *John Webster's Borrowing* (Berkeley, 1960); M. R. Ridley, *Second Thoughts* (1965), pp. 74-132.

548 *The White Devil* has been ed. by J. R. Brown (1960). See also Gunnar Boklund, *The Sources of* The White Devil (1957; *Uppsala English Inst. English Stud.,* 17); B. J. Layman, "The Equilibrium of Opposites in *The White Devil:* a Reinterpretation," *PMLA,* lxxiv (1959). 336-347.

549 *The Duchess of Malfi* has been ed. by J. R. Brown (1964) and E. M. Brennan (1964). See also F. W. Wadsworth, "Webster's *Duchess of Malfi* in the Light of some Contemporary Ideas on Marriage and Remarriage," *PQ,* xxxv (1956). 394-407; C. G. Thayer, "The Ambiguity of Bosola," *SP,* liv (1957). 162-171; Clifford Leech, *Webster: The Duchess of Malfi* (1963; *Stud. in English Lit.,* 8).

551 On *A Cure for a Cuckold* see Inga-Stina Ekeblad, "Webster's Constructional Rhythm," *ELH,* xxiv (1957). 165-176.

III. Jacobean Drama: II. The Satiric Group

552 *The Three Parnassus Plays* have been ed. by J. B. Leishman (1949).
554 On Chapman's continuation of *Hero and Leander* see D. J. Gordon, "Chapman's 'Hero and Leander'," *English Miscellany*, v (1954). 41-94.
556 On *The Widow's Tears* see S. Schoenbaum, "*The Widow's Tears* and the Other Chapman," *HLQ*, XXIII (1960). 321-338.—On Chapman's tragedies see Edwin Muir, " 'Royal Man': Notes on the Tragedy of George Chapman," *Essays on Literature and Society* (1949); J. W. Wieler, *George Chapman: the Effect of Stoicism upon his Tragedies* (1949); Jean Jacquot, *George Chapman (1559-1634), sa vie, sa poésie, son théâtre, sa pensée* (Lyon, 1951; *Annales de l'Univ. de Lyon, troisième série*, 19); Ennis Rees, *The Tragedies of George Chapman* (Cambridge, Mass., 1954); Marcello Pagnini, *Forme e motivi nella poesia e nelle tragedie di George Chapman* (Firenze, 1959); Allardyce Nicoll, "The Dramatic Portrait of George Chapman," *PQ*, XLI (1962). 215-228.—*Bussy d'Ambois* has been ed. by N. S. Brooke (1964) and R. J. Lordi (Lincoln, Nebr., 1964). See also W. G. McCollom, "The Tragic Hero and Chapman's *Bussy d'Ambois*," *UTQ*, XVIII (1949). 227-233.

558 On *Caesar and Pompey* see Elias Schwartz, "A Neglected Play by Chapman," *SP*, LVIII (1961). 140-159.

559 The Herford-Simpson ed. of Jonson is now complete (11v, Oxford, 1925-1952). Recent studies of the plays are H. W. Baum, *The Satiric and the Didactic in Ben Jonson's Comedy* (Chapel Hill, N.C., 1947); H. L. Snuggs, "The Comic Humours: a New Interpretation," *PMLA*, LXII (1947). 114-119; F. L. Townsend, *Apologie for Bartholomew Fayre: the Art of Jonson's Comedies* (1947; *M.L.A. Revolving Fund Ser.*, xv); A. H. Sackton, *Rhetoric as Dramatic Language in Ben Jonson* (1948); E. V. Pennanen, *Chapters on the Language in Ben Jonson's Dramatic Works* (1951; *Annales Universitatis Turkuensis*, ser. B, XXXIX); A. C. Partridge, *Studies in the Syntax of Ben Jonson's Plays* (Cambridge, 1953), *The Accidence of Ben Jonson's Plays, Masques and Entertainments with an Appendix of Comparable Uses in Shakespeare* (Cambridge, 1953); J. J. Enck, *Jonson and the Comic Truth* (Madison, 1957); S. Musgrove, *Shakespeare and Jonson* (1957; *Auckland Univ. Coll. Bull.*, 51); E. B. Partridge, *The Broken Compass: a Study of the Major Comedies of Ben Jonson* (1958); J. A. Barish, *Ben Jonson and the Language of Prose Comedy* (Cambridge, Mass., 1960); C. G. Thayer, *Ben Jonson: Studies in the Plays* (Norman, Okla., 1963); R. E. Knoll, *Ben Jonson's Plays: an Introduction* (Lincoln, Nebr., 1964).—The conclusions of G. E. Bentley in *Shakespeare and Jonson* are disputed by David Frost, "Shakespeare in the Seventeenth Century," *SQ*, XVI (1965). 81-89.

561 On the war of the theaters see Alfred Harbage, *Shakespeare and the Rival Traditions* (1952).—*Sejanus* has been ed. by J. A. Barish (New Haven, 1965). On Jonson's tragedies see Ralph Nash, "Jonson's Tragic Poems," *SP*, LV (1958). 164-186.

562 *Volpone* has been ed. by A. B. Kernan (New Haven, 1962) and by J. B. Bamborough (1964). See also J. A. Barish, "The Double Plot in *Volpone*," *MP*,

LI (1953). 83-92; S. L. Goldberg, "Folly into Crime: the Catastrophe of *Volpone*," *MLQ*, xx (1959). 233-242.

563 *Bartholomew Fair* has been ed. by E. A. Horsman (1960), E. M. Waith (New Haven, 1963), E. B. Partridge (Lincoln, Nebr., 1964), Maurice Hussey (1964).—On Marston see Samuel Schoenbaum, "The Precarious Balance of John Marston," *PMLA*, LXVII (1952). 1069-1078; Gustav Cross, "Some Notes on the Vocabulary of John Marston," *N&Q*, CXCIX (1954). 425-426; continued in volumes CC-CCVIII; A. J. Axelrad, *Un Malcontent élizabéthain: John Marston (1576-1634)* (Paris, 1955); Anthony Caputi, *John Marston, Satirist* (Ithaca, N.Y., 1962).

564 Both *Antonio and Mellida* and *Antonio's Revenge* have been ed. by G. K. Hunter (Lincoln, Nebr., 1965); *The Malcontent* by M. L. Wine (Lincoln, Nebr., 1964); *The Fawn* by G. A. Smith (Lincoln, Nebr., 1965).

565 *The Dutch Courtesan* has been ed. by M. L. Wine (Lincoln, Nebr., 1965).—Skepticism about Tourneur's authorship of *The Revenger's Tragedy* persists: the latest discussion is P. B. Murray, "The Authorship of *The Revenger's Tragedy*," *Papers of the Bibl. Soc. of Amer.*, LVI (1962). 195-218. Some studies of Tourneur are Samuel Schoenbaum, "*The Revenger's Tragedy*: Jacobean Dance of Death," *MLQ*, xv (1954). 201-207; John Peter, "*The Revenger's Tragedy* Reconsidered," *EIC*, VI (1956). 131-143, 482-486; P. B. Murray, *A Study of Cyril Tourneur* (Philadelphia, 1964). *The Atheist's Tragedy* has been ed. by Irving Ribner (1964).

566 On Middleton see Samuel Schoenbaum, *Middleton's Tragedies, a Critical Study* (1955; *Columbia Univ. Stud.*, 168), "Middleton's Tragicomedies," *MP*, LIV (1956). 7-19; R. H. Barker, *Thomas Middleton* (1957); Mark Eccles, "'Thomas Middleton a Poett'," *SP*, LIV (1957). 516-536.—*A Mad World, my Masters* has been ed. by Standish Henning (Lincoln, Nebr., 1965).

567 *The Changeling* has been ed. by N. W. Bawcutt (1958), Patricia Thomson (1964), and M. W. Black (Philadelphia, 1965). See K. J. Holzknecht, "The Dramatic Structure of *The Changeling*," *Renaissance Papers*, ed. A. H. Gilbert (Columbia, S.C., 1954), pp. 77-87; Christopher Ricks, "The Moral and Poetical Structure of *The Changeling*," *EIC*, x (1960). 290-306.—On *Women Beware Women* see Christopher Ricks, "Word-play in *Women Beware Women*," *RES*, XII (1961). 238-250.

570 Some recent studies of the masque are E. W. Talbert, "The Interpretation of Jonson's Courtly Spectacles," *PMLA*, LXI (1946). 454-473; A. H. Gilbert, *Symbolic Persons in the Masques of Ben Jonson* (Durham, N.C., 1948); Otto Gombosi, "Some Musical Aspects of the English Court Masque," *Jour. of the American Musicological Soc.*, I: iii (1948). 3-19; D. J. Gordon, "Poet and Architect: the Intellectual Setting of the Quarrel between Ben Jonson and Inigo Jones," *Jour. Warburg and Courtauld Inst.*, XII (1949). 152-178; Dolora Cunningham, "The Jonsonian Masque as a Literary Form," *ELH*, XXII (1955). 108-124; W. T. Furniss, "Ben Jonson's Masques," *Three Studies in the Renaissance* (1958; *Yale Stud. in English*, 138), pp. 89-179; J. C. Meagher, "The Dance and the Masques of Ben Jonson," *Jour. Warburg and Courtauld Inst.*, XXV (1962). 258-277; Stephen Orgel, *The Jonsonian Masque* (Cambridge, Mass., 1965). A. J. Sabol has published two collections of musical scores: *Songs and Dances for the*

Stuart Masque (Providence, 1959), *A Score for "Lovers Made Men," a Masque by Ben Jonson* (Princeton, 1963). W. W. Greg has ed. Jonson's *Masque of Gipsies* (1952) and R. C. Bald, Middleton's *Honourable Entertainments,* a series of civic shows (1953; *Malone Soc.*).

IV. Jacobean Drama: III. The Romantic Playwrights

571 *Law Tricks* has been ed. by John Crow (1950; *Malone Soc.*).

573 On Beaumont and Fletcher see J. F. Danby, *Poets on Fortune's Hill: Studies in Sidney, Shakespeare, Beaumont and Fletcher* (1952; 2d impression, *Elizabethan and Jacobean Poets,* 1964); E. M. Waith, *The Pattern of Tragicomedy in Beaumont and Fletcher* (1952; *Yale Stud. in English,* 120); W. W. Appleton, *Beaumont and Fletcher* (1956); Cyrus Hoy, "The Shares of Fletcher and his Collaborators in the Beaumont and Fletcher Canon," *Stud. in Bibliography,* VIII (1956). 129-146, IX (1957). 143-162, XI (1958). 85-106, XII (1959). 91-116, XIII (1960). 77-108, XIV (1961). 45-68, XV (1962). 71-90; Philip Edwards, "The Danger not the Death: the Art of John Fletcher," *Jacobean Theatre* (1960; *Stratford-upon-Avon Stud.,* 1), pp. 159-177; Clifford Leech, *The John Fletcher Plays* (1962).—*A King and no King* has been ed. by R. K. Turner, Jr. (Lincoln, Nebr., 1963).

574 On *The Faithful Shepherdess* see Nicoletta Neri, *Il Pastor fido in Inghilterra con il testo della traduzione di Sir Richard Fanshawe* (1963; *Univ. di Torino Pub. della Facoltà di Magistero,* 21).

575 See further M. T. Herrick, *Tragicomedy, its Origin and Development in Italy, France, and England* (1955; *Illinois Stud. in Lang. and Lit.,* 39).— Manuscript copies of *The Humorous Lieutenant* (called *Demetrius and Enanthe*) and of *Bonduca* exist and have been published by the Malone Soc., ed. M. M. Cook & F. P. Wilson (1951) and by W. W. Greg (1951) respectively.

V. Caroline Drama, 1625-1642

578 On Massinger see T. A. Dunn, *Philip Massinger, the Man and the Playwright* (1957). L. G. Clubb discusses "*The Virgin Martyr* and the *Tragedia Sacra*," *Renaissance Drama,* VII (1964). 103-126.

579 *A New Way to Pay Old Debts* has been ed. by M. St. C. Byrne (1949) and by T. W. Craik (1964).

580 *The City Madam* has been ed. by Cyrus Hoy (1964) and by T. W. Craik (1964).—On Ford see Robert Davril, *Le Drame de John Ford* (Paris, 1954; *Bibl. des langues modernes,* 5); H. J. Oliver, *The Problem of John Ford* (Melbourne, 1955); Clifford Leech, *John Ford and the Drama of his Time* (1957).

581 On *Love's Sacrifice* see Peter Ure, "Cult and Initiates in Ford's *Love's Sacrifice*," *MLQ,* XI (1951). 298-306.

582 *The Broken Heart* has been ed. by Brian Morris (1965). Alfred Harbage, "The Mystery of *Perkin Warbeck,*" *Studies in Renaissance Drama in*

Memory of K. J. Holzknecht, ed. J. W. Bennett *et al.* (1959), pp. 125-141 suggests Dekker as part-author.

583 *The Plays of Nathan Field* have been ed. by William Peery (Austin, Tex., 1950).—On Brome see R. J. Kaufman, *Richard Brome, Cavalier Playwright* (1962).

585 On Shirley see Richard Gerber, *James Shirley, Dramatiker der Dekadenz* (Bern, 1952; *Schweizer anglistische Arbeiten,* xxx).

586 *The Cardinal* has been ed. by C. R. Forker (Bloomington, Ind., 1964; *Indiana Univ. Pub., Humanities Ser.,* 56); *The Traitor* by J. S. Carter (Lincoln, Nebr., 1965).

587 *Six Caroline Plays,* ed. A. S. Knowland (1962; *World's Classics*) reprints *The Lady of Pleasure* and *The Wedding,* along with Brome's *Mad Couple Well Matched* and *The Antipodes,* Davenant's *Wits,* and Killigrew's *Parson's Wedding.*

588 *The Lady Mother by Henry Glapthorne* has been ed. by Arthur Brown (1959; *Malone Soc.*).

VI. Seventeenth-century Prose: I. Bacon and the Prose of Utility

590 More recent anthologies of seventeenth-century prose are *Seventeenth-century Prose 1620-1700,* ed. Peter Ure (1956); *Seventeenth-century English Prose,* ed. M. A. Shaaber (1957).—A revised ed. of Bush's *English Literature in the Earlier Seventeenth Century* has been published (Oxford, 1962). See also C. V. Wedgwood, *Seventeenth Century English Literature* (Oxford, 1950); *From Donne to Marvell,* ed. Boris Ford (1956; *A Guide to English Literature,* 3; rev. ed., 1962).—M. W. Croll's papers on prose style have now been collected under the title *Style, Rhetoric and Rhythm,* ed. J. M. Patrick *et al.* (Princeton, 1966). See also D. C. Allen, "Style and Certitude," *ELH,* xv (1948). 167-175; George Williamson, *The Senecan Amble, a Study in Prose from Bacon to Collier* (Chicago, 1951); F. P. Wilson, *Seventeenth-century Prose* (Berkeley, 1960).

591 On Chamberlain see Wallace Notestein, *Four Worthies* (1957).— James Craigie has ed. *The Basilicon Doron of King James VI* (2v, 1944-1950; *STS*) and *The Poems of James VI of Scotland* (2v, 1955-1958; *STS*). D. H. Willson, *King James VI and I* (1956) and W. L. McElwee, *The Wisest Fool in Christendom: the Reign of King James I and VI* (1958) are recent biographies.

593 Selections from Holland's translation of Pliny have been ed. by Paul Turner (1962) and by J. Newsome (Oxford, 1964).—*Ben Jonson's Timber or Discoveries* has been ed. by R. S. Walker (Syracuse, N.Y., 1953). See also C. J. Sisson, "Ben Jonson of Gresham College," *LTLS,* 21 Sept. 1951, p. 604.—V. B. Heltzel has ed. *The Complete Gentlemen* [in part], *The Truth of our Times, and The Art of Living in London by Henry Peacham* (Ithaca, N.Y., 1962).

594 Cornwallis' *Discourses upon Seneca the Tragedian (1601)* has been ed. by R. H. Bowers (Gainesville, Fla., 1952; *SF&R*), as also *Essaies or rather Imperfect Offers (1607) by Robert Johnson* (Gainesville, Fla., 1955; *SF&R*).— R. W.

Gibson has published *Francis Bacon: a Bibliography of his Works and of Baconiana to the Year 1750* (Oxford, 1950), with a supplement (Oxford, 1959). Some studies of Bacon are F. H. Anderson, *The Philosophy of Francis Bacon* (Chicago, 1948); Benjamin Farrington, *Francis Bacon, Philosopher of Industrial Science* (1949); J. W. Crowther, *Francis Bacon, the First Statesman of Science* (1960); C. D. Bowen, *Francis Bacon: the Temper of a Man* (1963); L. C. Eiseley, *Francis Bacon and the Modern Dilemma* (1962); Anne Righter, "Francis Bacon," *The English Mind: Studies . . . Presented to Basil Willey*, ed. H. S. Davies & G. Watson (Cambridge, 1964), pp. 7-29.

595 On Bacon's ideas about literature see T. H. Jameson, *Francis Bacon: Criticism and the Modern World* (1954); J. L. Harrison, "Bacon's View of Rhetoric, Poetry, and the Imagination," *HLQ*, xx (1957). 107-125.

596 *The Political Writings of James Harrington* have been ed. by Charles Blitzer (1955). See also C. B. Macpherson, "Harrington's 'Opportunity State,'" *Past & Present*, xvii (1960). 45-70; Charles Blitzer, *An Immortal Commonwealth: the Political Thought of James Harrington* (1960; *Yale Stud. in Political Science*, 2).—On *The Anatomy of Melancholy* see W. R. Mueller, *The Anatomy of Robert Burton's England* (Berkeley, 1952; *Univ. of California Pub., English Stud.*, 2); Lawrence Babb, *Sanity in Bedlam: a Study of Robert Burton's* Anatomy of Melancholy (East Lansing, Mich., 1959).

598 On Fuller see William Addison, *Worthy Dr. Fuller* (1951); S. C. Roberts, *Thomas Fuller, a Seventeenth-century Worthy* (Manchester, 1953).

599 J. O. Wood has ed. *Thoughts and Contemplations by Thomas Fuller* (1964).

600 A selection from *The Worthies of England* has been ed. by John Freeman (1952).—On Baxter see Roger Thomas, *The Baxter Treatises: a Catalogue of the Richard Baxter Papers (other than the Letters) in Dr. Williams's Library* (1957); Hugh Martin, *Puritanism and Richard Baxter* (1954); R. B. Schlatter, *Richard Baxter and Puritan Politics* (New Brunswick, N.J., 1957).

VII. Seventeenth-century Prose: II. Character Books. Autobiography. Walton

602 On the character see C. N. Greenough & J. M. French, *A Bibliography of the Theophrastan Character in England with several Portrait Characters* (Cambridge, Mass., 1947; *Harvard Stud. in Compar. Lit.*, xviii); Benjamin Boyce, *The Theophrastan Character in England to 1642* (Cambridge, Mass., 1947), *The Polemic Character 1640-1661* (Lincoln, Nebr., 1955).—*Heaven upon Earth and Characters of Vertues and Vices by Joseph Hall* have been ed. by Rudolf Kirk (1948; *Rutgers Stud. in English,* 6); *The Collected Poems of Joseph Hall* by Arnold Davenport (1949; *Liverpool English Texts and Stud.*). See also T. F. Kinloch, *The Life and Works of Joseph Hall, 1574-1656* (1951). Hall's Senecan style is discussed by P. A. Smith, "Bishop Hall, 'our English Seneca,'" *PMLA*, lxiii (1948). 1191-1204; Audrey Chew, "Joseph Hall and neo-Stoicism," *PMLA*, lxv (1950). 1130-1145; Harold Fisch, "The Limits of Hall's Senecanism,"

Proc. Leeds Philos. Soc., VI (1950). 453-463.—On Overbury see William McElwee, *The Murder of Sir Thomas Overbury* (1952).

605 S. B. Ewing describes a hitherto unnoticed manuscript of Greville's life in *MLR*, XLIX (1954). 424-427.

606 On Greville see H. N. Maclean, "Fulke Greville on War," *HLQ*, XXI (1958). 95-109; G. A. Wilkes, "The Sequence of the Writings of Fulke Greville, Lord Brooke," *SP*, LVI (1959). 489-503; Ivor Morris, "The Tragic Vision of Fulke Greville," *ShS*, XIV (1961). 66-75.

607 On Lord Herbert see M. M. Rossi, *La vita, le opere, i tempi di Edoardo Herbert di Cherbury* (3v, Firenze, 1947); Margaret Bottrall, *Every Man a Phoenix: Studies in Seventeenth-century Autobiography* (1958), which also treats Browne and Baxter.

608 On Digby see R. T. Petersson, *Sir Kenelm Digby, the Ornament of England 1603-1665* (Cambridge, Mass., 1956); Vittorio Gabrieli, *Sir Kenelm Digby: un inglese italianato nell'èta della controriforma* (Roma, 1957; *Storia e Letteratura*, LXIV).

609 On *Eikon Basilike* see F. F. Madan, *A New Bibliography of the Eikon Basilike of King Charles I with a Note on the Authorship* (1950; *Oxford Bibl. Soc. Pub.*, n.s. III).

610 On Walton's *Lives* see Donald Novarr, *The Making of Walton's Lives* (1958; *Cornell Stud. in English*, 41); I. A. Shapiro, "Walton and the Occasion of Donne's *Devotions*," *RES*, IX (1958). 18-22.

611 A recently-discovered sixteenth-century book on angling, *The Arte of Angling* (1577) has been ed. by G. E. Bentley (Princeton, 1956), discussed in relation to Walton by M. S. Goldman in *Studies in Honor of T. W. Baldwin*, ed. D. C. Allen (Urbana, Ill., 1958), pp. 185-204, and attributed to the Rev. William Samuel by T. P. Harrison, *N&Q*, CCV (1960). 373-376.

VIII. Seventeenth-century Prose: III. The Baroque Glory

613 On the baroque see Mario Praz, "Il barocco in Inghilterra," *Manierismo, barocco, rococo: concetti e termini* (Roma, 1962; *Problemi attuali di scienza e di cultura*, 52), tr. as "Baroque in England," *MP*, LXI (1964). 169-179.—*The Sermons of John Donne*, ed. E. M. Simpson & G. R. Potter (10v, Berkeley, 1953-1962) is now standard. See also E. M. Simpson, "The Biographical Value of Donne's Sermons," *RES*, II (1951). 339-357; R. L. Hickey, "Donne's Art of Preaching," *Tennessee Stud. in the Humanities*, I (1956). 65-74; D. B. Quinn, "Donne's Christian Eloquence," *ELH*, XXVII (1960). 276-297, "John Donne's Principles of Biblical Exegesis," *JEGP*, LXI (1962). 313-329; W. R. Mueller, *John Donne, Preacher* (Princeton, 1962); Joan Webber, *Contrary Music: the Prose Style of John Donne* (Madison, 1963).

615 On Lancelot Andrewes see M. F. Reidy, *Bishop Lancelot Andrewes, Jacobean Court Preacher: a Study in Early Seventeenth-century Religious Thought* (Chicago, 1955; *Jesuit Stud.*); P. A. Welsby, *Lancelot Andrewes, 1555-1626* (1958); Joan Webber, "Celebration of Word and World in Lancelot

Andrewes' Style," *JEGP*, LXIV (1965). 255-269.—A revised ed. of Keynes's *Works of Sir Thomas Browne* has been published (4v, 1964). *Religio Medici and Other Works*, ed. L. C. Martin (1964) contains all of Browne's works except *Pseudodoxia epidemica*. For recent biographical and critical studies see J. S. Finch, *Sir Thomas Browne: a Doctor's Life of Science and Faith* (1950); Austin Warren, "The Style of Sir Thomas Browne," *Kenyon Rev.*, XIII (1951). 674-687; J.-J. Denonain, *La Personnalité de Sir Thomas Browne* (Paris, 1958; *Pub. de la Faculté des lettres et sciences humaines d'Alger*); M. F. Moloney, "Metre and *Cursus* in Sir Thomas Browne's Prose," *JEGP*, LVIII (1959). 60-67; William Whallon, "Hebraic Synonymy in Sir Thomas Browne," *ELH*, XXXVIII (1961). 335-352; F. L. Huntley, *Sir Thomas Browne: a Biographical and Critical Study* (Ann Arbor, 1962); Joan Bennett, *Sir Thomas Browne: a Man of Achievement in Literature* (Cambridge, 1962); N. J. Endicott, "Some Aspects of Self-revelation and Self-portraiture in *Religio Medici*," *Essays in English Literature . . . Presented to A. S. P. Woodhouse* (Toronto, 1964), pp. 85-102.— J.-J. Denonain has published three eds. of *Religio Medici*: one which sets forth the variants in the surviving manuscripts as well as the printed eds. (Cambridge, 1953), one with biographical notes (Cambridge, 1955), and one which reproduces the text of the manuscript which, in the editor's opinion, is closest to Browne's first draft (Paris, 1958; *Faculté des lettres de l'Univ. d'Alger Pub.*, sér. 2, no. 36). Other eds. have been published by Vittoria Sanna (2v, 1958; *Annali della Facoltà di lettere, filosofia e magistero dell'Univ. di Cagliari*, XXVI: i-ii) and James Winny (Cambridge, 1963).

618 *Urne Buriall and The Garden of Cyrus* have been ed. by John Carter (Cambridge, 1958).

619 On Jeremy Taylor see C. J. Stranks, *The Life and Writings of Jeremy Taylor* (1952); Thomas Wood, *English Casuistical Divinity during the Seventeenth Century, with Special Reference to Jeremy Taylor* (1952); J. R. King, "Certain Aspects of Jeremy Taylor's Prose Style," *ES*, XXXVII (1956). 197-210; H. T. Hughes, *The Piety of Jeremy Taylor* (1960).

621 V. M. Hirst defends "The Authenticity of James Howell's Familiar Letters," *MLR*, LIV (1959). 558-561.

623 On Coryate see Michael Strachan, *The Life and Adventures of Thomas Coryate* (1962).—Lithgow's originality is impugned by Pierre Grandchamp, "Le Prétendu voyage de William Lithgow dans les états de Barbarie (1615-1616)," *Revue Africaine*, XCI (1948). 213-234.—On exploration and discovery see A. L. Rowse, *The Expansion of Elizabethan England* (1955), *The Elizabethans and America* (1959).

IX. Seventeenth-century Poetry: I. The Olympians

624 Some studies of seventeenth-century poetry are Ruth Wallerstein, *Studies in Seventeenth-century Poetics* (Madison, 1950); M. H. Nicolson, *The Breaking of the Circle: Studies in the Effect of the "New Science" upon Seventeenth Century Poetry* (Evanston, Ill., 1950; 2ed, 1960); Patrick Cruttwell, *The Shakespearean Moment and its Place in the Poetry of the Seventeenth Century*

(1954); M.-S. Røstvig, *The Happy Man: Studies in the Metamorphoses of a Classical Ideal 1600-1700* (1954; *Oslo Stud. in English*, 2; 2ed, 1962); Arno Esch, *Englische religiöse Lyrik des 17. Jahrhunderts: Studien zu Donne, Herbert, Crashaw, Vaughan* (Tübingen, 1955); Geoffrey Walton, *Metaphysical to Augustan: Studies in Tone and Sensibility in the Seventeenth Century* (1955); Siegfried Korninger, *Die Naturauffassung in der englischen Dichtung des 17. Jahrhunderts* (1956; *Wiener Beiträge zur englischen Philologie*, 64); Josephine Miles, *Renaissance, Eighteenth-century, and Modern Language in English Poetry* (Berkeley, 1960).—A revised ed. of Miss Latham's *Poems of Sir Walter Raleigh* has been published (1951). She has also made an anthology of *Selected Poetry and Prose* (1965). Walter Oakeshott, *The Queen and the Poet* (1960) proposes a few additions to the canon. Of the many biographies of Raleigh, Philip Edwards, *Sir Walter Raleigh* (1953) pays more attention to his writings than most. On his life see A. M. C. Latham, "A Birth Date [1554] for Sir Walter Raleigh," *Études anglaises*, IX (1956). 243-245; A. L. Rowse, *Sir Walter Raleigh and the Throckmortons* (1962); A. M. Crinò, *Sir Walter Raleigh nella letteratura e nella storia* (Verona, 1963; *Atti dell'Accademia di Agricoltura, Scienze e Lettere*, serie VI, XIII). On his thought see E. A. Strathmann, *Sir Walter Raleigh: a Study in Elizabethan Skepticism* (1951). On his poems, Peter Ure, "The Poetry of Sir Walter Raleigh," *REL* I: iii (1960). 19-29; Donald Davie, "A Reading of 'The Ocean's Love to Cynthia'," *Elizabethan Poetry*, ed. J. R. Brown & B. Harris (1960; *Stratford-upon-Avon Stud.*, 2), pp. 71-89.

626 *Chapman's Homer: the Iliad, the Odyssey and the Lesser Homerica* has been ed. by Allardyce Nicoll (2v, 1956; *Bollingen Ser.*, XLI). See also H. C. Fay, "Poetry, Pedantry, and Life in Chapman's *Iliads*," *RES*, IV (1953). 13-25; G. deF. Lord, *Homeric Renaissance: the Odyssey of George Chapman* (1956; *Yale Stud. in English*, 131).

627 Jonson's poems have been ed. by G. B. Johnston (1954; *Muses' Libr.*) and W. B. Hunter, Jr. (1963). See also Wesley Trimpi, *Ben Jonson's Poems: a Study of the Plain Style* (Stanford, Calif., 1962); Hugh Maclean, "Ben Jonson's Poems: Notes on the Ordered Society," *Essays in English Literature . . . Presented to A. S. P. Woodhouse* (Toronto, 1964), pp. 43-68.

631 A 3d ed. of Keynes's bibliography of Donne has been published (Cambridge, 1958). The most comprehensive study of Donne is J. B. Leishman, *The Monarch of Wit: an Analytical and Comparative Study of John Donne* (1951; 4ed, 1962). See also Leonard Unger, *Donne's Poetry and Modern Criticism* (Chicago, 1950); A. J. Smith, "Sources of Difficulty and of Value in the Poetry of John Donne," *Littérature moderne*, VII (1957). 182-190; Arnold Stein, *John Donne's Lyrics: the Eloquence of Action* (Minneapolis, 1962). On the dating see Robert Ellrodt, "Chronologie des poèmes de Donne," *Études anglaises*, XIII (1960). 452-463. On Donne's satires see N. C. J. Andreasen, "Theme and Structure in Donne's *Satyres*," *SEL*, III (1963). 59-75. For recent biographical studies see R. C. Bald, *Donne and the Drurys* (Cambridge, 1959); B. D. Whitlock, "The Heredity and Childhood of John Donne," *N&Q*, CCIV (1959). 257-262, 348-353, "The Family of John Donne," *N&Q*, CCV (1960). 380-386, "Donne's University Years," *ES*, XLIII (1962). 1-20.

632 Some further studies of Donne and kindred poets are L. E. Berry,

A Bibliography of Studies in Metaphysical Poetry, 1939-1960 (Madison, 1964); Itrat-Husain, *The Mystical Element in the Metaphysical Poetry of the Seventeenth Century* (Edinburgh, 1948); L. L. Martz, *The Poetry of Meditation: a Study in English Religious Literature of the Seventeenth Century* (1954; Yale Stud. in English, 125); J.-J. Denonain, *Thèmes et formes de la poésie "métaphysique"* (Alger, 1956); Robert Ellrodt, *L'Inspiration personnelle et l'esprit du temps chez les poètes métaphysiques anglais* (3v, Paris, 1960); Joan Bennett, *Five Metaphysical Poets: Donne, Herbert, Vaughan, Crashaw, Marvell* (Cambridge, 1964), a revision of *Four Metaphysical Poets* (1934).

633 Annotated eds. of the *Songs and Sonnets* have been published by Theodore Redpath (1956) and (with the elegies) by Helen Gardner (Oxford, 1965). See also A. J. Smith, *John Donne: the Songs and Sonnets* (1964; *Stud. in English Lit.,* 17). Perhaps the two most debated poems are "The Canonization" and "The Ecstasy." On the former, the latest word is J. A. Clair, "Donne's 'The Canonization'," *PMLA* LXXX (1965). 300-302; on the latter, John Carey, "Notes on two of Donne's *Songs and Sonets,*" *RES,* n.s. XVI (1965). 51-53, which refers to earlier discussions.

634 An ed. of the *Anniversaries* by Frank Manley has been published (Baltimore, 1963). L. L. Martz, "Donne in Meditation: the Anniversaries," *ELH,* XIV (1947). 247-273 ascribes the structure of the anniversaries to the influence of the Ignatian method of meditation, and in *The Poetry of Meditation* (cited above) he extends this influence to metaphysical poetry in general, virtually equating metaphysical poetry and the poetry of meditation. This thesis has elicited some support and some skepticism. Examples of the support are J. M. Wallace, "Thomas Traherne and the Structure of Meditation," *ELH,* XXV (1958). 79-89 and T. F. Van Laan, "John Donne's *Devotions* and the Jesuit Spiritual Exercises," *SP,* LX (1963). 191-202; of the skepticism—besides reviews such as that by Helen Gardner in *RES,* n.s. VIII (1957). 194-200—Stanley Archer, "Meditation and the Structure of Donne's 'Holy Sonnets'," *ELH,* XXVIII (1961). 137-147 and George Williamson, "The Design of Donne's *Anniversaries,*" *MP,* LX (1963). 183-191, reprinted in *Milton & Others* (1965), pp. 150-164.

635 *John Donne: the Divine Poems* have been ed. by Helen Gardner (Oxford, 1952).

X. Seventeenth-century Poetry: II. The Moral Tradition

637 Some recent anthologies are *Seventeenth-century Verse and Prose,* ed. H. C. White, R. C. Wallerstein, & Ricardo Quintana (2v, 1951); *The Metaphysical Poets,* ed. Helen Gardner (1957); *Seventeenth-century English Poetry,* ed. R. C. Bald (1959); *Wayside Poems of the Seventeenth Century,* ed. Edmund Blunden & Bernard Mellor (1963); *The Meditative Poem, an Anthology of Seventeenth-century Verse,* ed. L. L. Martz (1964).

638 The 1605 ed. of Du Bartas, with an introduction by F. C. Haber, has been reprinted (Gainesville, Fla., 1965; SF&R). See also John Arthos, *The Language of Natural Description in Eighteenth-century Poetry* (1949; *Univ. of Michigan Pub., Lang. and Lit.,* 24); V. L. Simonsen, "Joshuah Sylvester's

English Translation of Du Bartas' *La première semaine,*" *Orbis Litterarum,* VIII (1950). 259-285.

639 On Sandys see F. T. Bowers & R. B. Davis, "George Sandys: a Bibliographical Catalogue of Printed Editions in England to 1700," *Bull. N. Y. Public Library,* LIV (1950). 159-181, 223-244, 280-286; R. B. Davis, *George Sandys, Poet-adventurer: a Study in Anglo-American Culture in the Seventeenth Century* (1955).—On Wither's enormous output after 1625 see Allen Pritchard, "George Wither: the Poet as Prophet," *SP,* LIX (1962). 211-230.

641 John Horden has compiled *Francis Quarles (1592-1644): a Bibliography of his Works to the Year 1800* (1948; *Oxford Bibl. Soc.,* n.s. 11) and also ed. *Hosanna and Threnodes* (1960; *Liverpool English Reprints Ser.,* 15).

642 Praz's *Studies in Seventeenth-century Imagery* has been supplemented by a second volume, a bibliography of the emblem books (1947). See further Rosemary Freeman, *English Emblem Books* (1948).—On John Taylor see Wallace Notestein, *Four Worthies* (1956).—*The Latin Poetry of George Herbert* has been ed. and tr. by Mark McCloskey & P. R. Murphy (Athens, O., 1965). Some recent studies of Herbert are Rosemond Tuve, *A Reading of George Herbert* (Chicago, 1952), "George Herbert and *Caritas,*" *Jour. Warburg and Courtauld Inst.,* XXII (1959). 303-331; J. H. Summers, *George Herbert, his Religion and his Art* (1954); Marchette Chute, *Two Gentle Men: the Lives of George Herbert and Robert Herrick* (1959); R. L. Montgomery, Jr., "The Province of Allegory in George Herbert's Verse," *Texas Stud. in Lit. and Lang.,* 1 (1960). 457-472; M. E. Rickey, "Herbert's Technical Development," *JEGP,* LXII (1963). 745-760. In *The Poetry of Meditation* (New Haven, 1954) L. L. Martz imputes a unified design to the order of the poems of *The Temple;* so does J. D. Walker, "The Architectonics of George Herbert's *The Temple,*" *ELH,* XXIX (1962). 289-305, only a different design; George Watson, "The Fabric of Herbert's *Temple,*" *Jour. Warburg and Courtauld Inst.,* XXVI (1963). 354-358 finds the temple a significant symbol but the order of the poems casual.

646 A new ed. of Crashaw's *Poems,* ed. L. C. Martin, has been published (Oxford, 1957). See further Mario Praz, *The Flaming Heart: Essays on Crashaw, Machiavelli, and other Studies in the Relations between Italian and English Literature* (1958), pp. 204-263, tr. from *Secentismo e Marinismo in Inghilterra* (Firenze, 1925); Laura Petoello, "A Current Misconception concerning the Influence of Marino's Poetry on Crashaw's," *MLR,* LII (1957). 321-328; M. E. Rickey, *Rhyme and Meaning in Richard Crashaw* (Lexington, Ky., 1961); G. W. Williams, *Image and Symbol in the Sacred Poetry of Richard Crashaw* (Columbia, S.C., 1963).

648 E. L. Marilla has compiled *A Comprehensive Bibliography of Henry Vaughan* (1948; *Univ. of Alabama Stud.,* 3). A new ed. of *The Works of Henry Vaughan,* ed. L. C. Martin, has been published (Oxford, 1957), besides *The Secular Poems of Henry Vaughan,* ed. E. L. Marilla (1958; *English Inst. of the Univ. of Uppsala Essays & Stud.,* 21) and *The Complete Poetry of Henry Vaughan,* ed. F. R. Fogle (1964). See further F. E. Hutchinson, *Henry Vaughan: a Life and Interpretation* (Oxford, 1947); Ross Garner, *Henry Vaughan: Experience and the Tradition* (Chicago, 1959), *The Unprofitable Servant in Henry Vaughan* (1963; *Univ. of Nebraska Stud.,* 3); E. C. Pettet, *Of Paradise and*

Light: a Study of Vaughan's Silex Scintillans (Cambridge, 1960); R. A. Durr, *On the Mystical Poetry of Henry Vaughan* (Cambridge, Mass., 1962); L. L. Martz, *The Paradise Within: Studies in Vaughan, Traherne, and Milton* (New Haven, 1964).

649 H. M. Margoliouth has ed. *Thomas Traherne: Centuries, Poems, and Thanksgivings* (2v, Oxford, 1958). The *Centuries* have been ed. by John Hayward (1951) and John Farrar (1960). See further M. E. Willy, *Life was their Cry* (1950); C. A. Owen, "The Authorship of 'Meditations on the Six Days of Creation' and the 'Meditations and Devotions on the Life of Christ'," *MLR*, LVI (1961). 1-12; K. W. Salter, *Thomas Traherne, Mystic and Poet* (1964); J. M. Osborn, "A New Traherne Manuscript," *LTLS*, Oct. 8, 1964, p. 928.

XI. Seventeenth-century Poetry:
III. The Academic and Courtly Tradition

651 *The Poems of Richard Corbett* have been ed. by J. A. W. Bennett & H. R. Trevor-Roper (Oxford, 1955).—*The Poems of Henry King* have been ed. by Margaret Crum (Oxford, 1965). See further R. F. Gleckner, "Henry King: a Poet of his Age," *Trans. Wisconsin Acad.*, LXV (1956). 149-167; Ronald Berman, *Henry King and the Seventeenth Century* (1964).—"Sir John Beaumont's *Crowne of Thornes*, a Report" by Ruth Wallerstein is in *JEGP*, LIII (1954). 410-434.

652 Stanley's *Poems and Translations* have been ed. by G. M. Crump (Oxford, 1962). See also Margaret Flower, "Thomas Stanley (1625-1678): a Bibliography of his Writings in Prose and Verse (1649-1743)," *Trans. Cambridge Bibl. Soc.*, I (1950). 139-172; J. M. Osborn, "Thomas Stanley's Lost 'Register of Friends'," *Yale Univ. Library Gazette*, XXXII (1958). 122-147.—*The Poems and Translations of Sir Edward Sherburne* have been ed. by J. F. Van Beeck (Assen, 1961).—Two of John Hall's prose works have been reprinted: *An Humble Motion to the Parliament of England concerning the Advancement of Learning*, ed. A. K. Croston (Liverpool, 1953), and *Paradoxes (1650)*, ed. D. C. Allen (Gainesville, Fla., 1956; *SF&R*).—On Benlowes see Harold Jenkins, *Edward Benlowes (1602-1676): Biography of a Minor Poet* (1952).—On Chamberlayne see A. E. Parsons, "A Forgotten Poet: William Chamberlayne and 'Pharonnida'," *MLR*, XLV (1950). 296-311.—Chalkhill is identified by P. J. Croft, *LTLS*, June 27, 1958, p. 365, Aug. 15, 1958, p. 459.—Beedome's *Poems Divine and Humane* have been ed. by Marcello Pagnini (Pisa, 1954; *Studi e Testi*, 8).

653 On Drummond see F. R. Fogle, *A Critical Study of William Drummond of Hawthornden* (1952).

654 *A Cypress Grove* is a revised version of *A Midnight's Trance* (1619); the latter has been reprinted by its discoverer, Robert Ellrodt (1951; *Luttrell Soc. Reprints*, 10).

655 *The English and Latin Poems of Sir Robert Aytoun* have been ed. by C. B. Gullans (1963; *STS*).—On Randolph see S. A. & D. R. Tannenbaum, *Thomas Randolph, a Concise Bibliography* (1947).

656 *The Plays and Poems of William Cartwright* have been ed. by G. B. Evans (Madison, 1951).

657 *The Poems of Thomas Carew with his Masque* Coelum Britannicum have been ed. by Rhodes Dunlap (Oxford, 1949). See further R. A. Blanshard, "Thomas Carew and the Cavalier Poets," *Trans. Wisconsin Acad.*, XLIII (1954). 97-106, "Thomas Carew's Master Figures," *Boston Univ. Stud. in English*, III (1957). 214-227; E. I. Selig, *The Flourishing Wreath: a Study of Thomas Carew's Poetry* (New Haven, 1958).

658 *Sir John Suckling's Poems and Letters from Manuscript* have been ed. by Herbert Berry (1960; *Univ. of Western Ontario Stud. in the Humanities*, 1). See further L. A. Beaurline, "The Canon of Sir John Suckling's Poems," *SP*, LVII (1960). 492-518, "New Poems by Sir John Suckling," *Ibid.*, LIX (1962). 651-657, "An Editorial Experiment: Suckling's *A Sessions of the Poets*," *Stud. in Bibliography*, XVI (1963). 43-60.

659 On Cleveland see J. L. Kimmey, "John Cleveland and the Satiric Couplet in the Restoration," *PQ*, XXXVII (1958). 410-423; Eleanor Withington, "The Canon of John Cleveland's Poetry," *Bull. N. Y. Public Library*, LXVII (1963). 307-327, 377-394; D. H. Woodward, "Notes on the Canon of John Cleveland's Poetry," *Ibid.*, LXVIII (1964). 517-524.

660 On Lovelace see D. C. Allen, "An Explication of Lovelace's 'The Grasse-hopper'," *MLQ*, XVIII (1957). 35-43.

661 On Montrose see C. V. Wedgwood, "The Poems of Montrose," *E&S*, n.s. XIII (1960). 49-64.—Complete eds. of Herrick's poems have been published by L. C. Martin (Oxford, 1956) and J. M. Patrick (1963). See further S. A. & D. R. Tannenbaum, *Robert Herrick, a Concise Bibliography* (1949); S. Musgrove, *The Universe of Robert Herrick* (Auckland, N.Z., 1950); T. R. Whitaker, "Herrick and the Fruits of the Garden," *ELH*, XXII (1955). 16-33; M. K. Starkman, "*Noble Numbers* and the Poetry of Devotion," *Reason and the Imagination: Studies in the History of Ideas, 1600-1800*, ed. J. A. Mazzeo (1962), pp. 1-27; M. L. Reed, "Herrick among the Maypoles: Dean Prior and the *Hesperides*," *SEL*, V (1965). 133-150; D. H. Woodward, "Herrick's Oberon Poems," *JEGP*, LXIV (1965). 270-284.

XII. Seventeenth-century Poetry:
IV. Links with the Restoration

665 *The Poems of William Habington* have been ed. by Kenneth Allott (1948; *Liverpool English Texts and Stud.*).—On Cowley see J. C. Ghosh, "Abraham Cowley (1618-1677)," *Sewanee Rev.*, LXI (1953). 433-447; Ulrich Suerbaum, *Die Lyrik der Korrespondenzen: Cowleys Bildkunst und die Tradition der englischen Renaissance-dichtung* (Bochum, 1958; *Beiträge zur englischen Philologie*, 40); R. B. Hinman, *Abraham Cowley's World of Order* (Cambridge, Mass., 1960).

668 A 2nd ed. of Margoliouth's *Poems & Letters of Andrew Marvell* has appeared (2v, Oxford, 1952). Selections from Marvell's work have been published by Dennis Davison (1952) and an edition of the poems by Hugh Macdonald (1952; *Muses' Libr.*). Some critical studies are C. E. Bain, "The Latin

Poetry of Andrew Marvell," *PQ*, xxxviii (1959). 436-499; A. Alvarez, "Marvell and the Poetry of Judgment," *Hudson Rev.*, xiii (1960). 417-428; J. B. Leishman, "Some Themes and Variations in the Poetry of Andrew Marvell," *Proc. Brit. Acad.*, xlvii (1961). 223-241; Dennis Davison, *The Poetry of Andrew Marvell* (1964; *Stud. in English Lit.*, 18); L. W. Hyman, *Andrew Marvell* (1964); Pierre Legouis, *Andrew Marvell, Poet, Puritan, Patriot* (Oxford, 1964); E. W. Tayler, *Nature and Art in Renaissance Literature* (1964); H. E. Toliver, *Marvell's Ironic Vision* (New Haven, 1965). All of Marvell's principal poems have been enthusiastically interpreted of late, but "The Garden," "The Nymph Complaining for the Death of her Faun," and the "Horatian Ode" have perhaps provoked the widest divergences of opinion. On the first, the latest word is M.-S. Røstvig, "Andrew Marvell's 'The Garden': a Hermetic Poem," *ES*, xl (1959). 65-76; on the second, Ruth Nevo, "Marvell's 'Songs of Innocence and Experience'," *SEL*, v (1965). 1-21; on the third, J. S. Coolidge, "Marvell and Horace," *MP*, lxiii (1965). 111-120. Each refers to earlier discussions.

670 On Waller see A. W. Allison, *Toward an Augustan Poetic: Edmund Waller's "Reform" of English Poetry* (Lexington, Ky., 1962).

671 On Davenant see J. P. Feil, "Davenant Exonerated," *MLR*, lviii (1963). 335-342.—On *Cooper's Hill* see Rufus Putney, "The View from Cooper's Hill," *Univ. of Colorado Stud. in Lang. and Lit.* vi (1957). 13-22; E. R. Wasserman, *The Subtler Language* (Baltimore, 1959), pp. 45-88.

XIII. Milton, "The Last Elizabethan"

673 Some recent eds. of Milton are *John Milton's Complete Poetical Works Reproduced in Photographic Facsimile*, ed. H. F. Fletcher (4v, Urbana, Ill., 1943-1948); *Poems of Mr. John Milton: the 1645 Edition with Essays in Analysis*, ed. Cleanth Brooks & J. E. Hardy (1951); *The Poetical Works of John Milton*, ed. Helen Darbishire (2v, Oxford, 1952-1955); *The Poems of John Milton*, ed. J. H. Hanford (2v, 1953); *Milton's Poems*, ed. B. A. Wright (1956; Everyman's Library); *John Milton: Complete Poems and Major Prose*, ed. M. Y. Hughes (1957); *The Complete English Poetry of John Milton*, ed. J. T. Shawcross (1963); *The Complete Poetical Works of John Milton*, ed. Douglas Bush (Boston, 1965).—New reference books include Calvin Huckabay, *John Milton: a Bibliographical Supplement, 1929-1957* (Pittsburgh, 1960); E. S. Le Comte, *A Milton Dictionary* (1961).—Among recent biographical studies are J. M. French, *The Life Records of John Milton* (5v, New Brunswick, N. J., 1949-58); Piero Rebora, "Milton a Firenze," *Il sei-settecento* (Firenze, 1956; *Pubb. della Libera Cattedra di Storia della Civiltà Fiorentina*), pp. 249-270. On Milton's early education see D. L. Clark, *Milton at St. Paul's School* (1948). H. F. Fletcher, *The Intellectual Development of John Milton* (2v, Urbana, Ill., 1956, 1961, in progress) exhaustively surveys the furniture of his mind. On particular interests see Kester Svendsen, *Milton and Science* (Cambridge, Mass., 1956); W. C. Curry, *Milton's Ontology, Cosmology, and Physics* (Lexington, Ky., 1957).—Recent general discussions of Milton and his works are J. H. Hanford, *John Milton, Englishman* (1949); Kenneth Muir, *John Milton* (1955; 2ed, 1960); A. S. P. Woodhouse, *Milton the Poet* (Toronto, 1955); W. B. C.

Watkins, *An Anatomy of Milton's Verse* (Baton Rouge, La., 1955); David Daiches, *Milton* (1957); M. H. Nicolson, *John Milton: a Reader's Guide to his Poetry* (1963); Douglas Bush, *John Milton: a Sketch of his Life and Writings* (1964). James Thorpe has ed. an anthology of *Milton Criticism* (1950). T. S. Eliot, who gave the cue for the detraction of Milton, has since at least partly recanted; see his lecture in *Proc. Brit. Acad.*, xxxiii (1947). 61-79. His disciple F. R. Leavis, however, remains adamant; see "Mr. Eliot and Milton," *Sewanee Rev.*, lvii (1949). 7-30. The attack is maintained in A. J. A. Waldock *Paradise Lost and its Critics* (Cambridge, 1947) and John Peter, *A Critique of Paradise Lost* (1960). B. A. Wright, *Milton's "Paradise Lost"* (1962) is a comprehensive brief for the defense. See also R. M. Adams, *Ikon: John Milton and the Modern Critics* (Ithaca, N. Y., 1955); Bernard Bergonzi, "Criticism and the Milton Controversy," *The Living Milton,* ed. Frank Kermode (1960), pp. 162-180.—On Milton's style and language see T. H. Banks, *Milton's Imagery* (1950); E. S. Le Comte, *Yet once more: Verbal and Psychological Pattern in Milton* (1954); F. T. Prince, *The Italian Element in Milton's Verse* (Oxford, 1954); E. M. Clark, "Milton's English Poetical Vocabulary," *SP*, liii (1956). 220-238; Helen Darbishire, "Milton's Poetic Language," *E&S*, n.s. x (1957). 31-52; C. L. Wrenn, "The Language of Milton," *Studies in English Language and Literature Presented to Karl Brunner* (1957; *Wiener Beiträge*, lxv), pp. 252-267; J. B. Broadbent, "Milton's Rhetoric," *MP*, lvi (1959). 224-242; Albert Cook, "Milton's Abstract Music," *UTQ*, xxix (1960). 370-385; Christopher Ricks, *Milton's Grand Style* (Oxford, 1963); R. D. Emma, *Milton's Grammar* (The Hague, 1964; *Stud. in English Lit.*, ii).

674 On Milton and the poets of his time see E. M. W. Tillyard, *The Metaphysicals and Milton* (1956).—On the Nativity ode see Rosemond Tuve, *Images and Themes in Five Poems by Milton* (Cambridge, Mass., 1957), which also discusses *L'Allegro, Il Penseroso, Lycidas,* and *Comus.*

675 On the twin poems see J. B. Leishman, "*L'Allegro* and *Il Penseroso* in their Relation to Seventeenth-century Poetry," *E&S*, n.s. iv (1951). 1-36.

677 On *Comus* see J. C. Maxwell, "The Pseudo-problem of Comus," *Cambridge Jour.*, i (1948). 376-380; D. C. Allen, "Milton's *Comus* as a Failure in Artistic Compromise," *ELH*, xvi (1949). 104-119; R. M. Adams, "Reading *Comus,*" *MP*, li (1953). 13-32, reprinted in *Ikon: John Milton and the Modern Critics* (Ithaca, N. Y., 1955); E. F. Haun, "An Inquiry into the Genre of *Comus,*" *Essays in Honor of W. C. Curry* (Nashville, Tenn., 1955; *Vanderbilt Stud. in the Humanities,* ii), pp. 221-239; A. E. Dyson, "The Interpretation of *Comus,*" *E&S*, n.s. viii (1955). 89-114; John Arthos, "Milton, Ficino, and the *Charmides,*" *SRen*, vi (1959). 261-274; Sears Jayne, "The Subject of Milton's Ludlow *Mask,*" *PMLA,* lxxiv (1959). 533-543.

678 On *Lycidas* see Wayne Shumaker, "Flowerets and Sounding Seas: a Study in the Affective Structure of *Lycidas,*" *PMLA,* lxvi (1951). 485-494; R. L. Brett, *Reason and Imagination* (1960); M. H. Abrams, "Five Ways of Reading *Lycidas,*" *Varieties of Literary Experience,* ed. Stanley Burnshaw (1962), pp. 1-29. *Milton's "Lycidas": the Tradition and the Poem,* ed. C. A. Patrides (1961) is an anthology of criticism of the poem.

679 On Milton's sonnets see Macon Cheek, "Of two Sonnets of Milton,"

Renaissance Papers (Columbia, S.C., 1956), pp. 82-91; Fitzroy Pyle, "Milton's First Sonnet on his Blindness," *RES*, n.s. IX (1958). 376-387; Taylor Stoehr, "Syntax and Poetic Form in Milton's Sonnets," *ES*, XLV (1964). 289-301. On the controversy over which wife Milton refers to in the 23d sonnet see Thomas Wheeler, *SP*, LVIII (1961). 510-515, who mentions earlier discussions.

XIV. Milton's Latin Poems and Prose Works

682 On Charles Diodati see D. C. Dorian, *The English Diodatis: a History of Charles Diodati's Family and of his Friendship with Milton* (New Brunswick, N.J., 1950).

685 *The Complete Prose Works of John Milton*, ed. D. M. Wolfe *et al.* is in progress (3v, New Haven, 1953-1963). For more or less comprehensive studies see L. A. Sasek, "Milton's Patriotic Epic," *HLQ*, XV (1956). 1-14; B. K. Lewalski, "Milton: Political Beliefs and Polemical Methods, 1659-1660," *PMLA*, LXXIV (1959). 191-202; Ernest Sirluck, "Milton's Political Thought: the First Cycle," *MP*, LXI (1964). 209-224.

686 *An Apology against a Pamphlet* has been ed. by M. C. Jochums (Urbana, Ill., 1950; *Illinois Stud. in Lang. and Lit.*, XXXV: 1-2).—On the divorce pamphlets see William Haller, " 'Hail Wedded Love'," *ELH*, XIII (1946). 79-97.—*Areopagitica* has been ed. by Olivier Lutaud (Paris, 1956).—On the *History of Britain* see Constance Nicholas, *An Introduction and Notes to Milton's* History of Britain (Urbana, Ill., 1957; *Illinois Stud. in Lang. and Lit.*, 44).—On the *Christian Doctrine* see H. F. Robins, *If this be Heresy: a Study of Milton and Origen* (Urbana, Ill., 1963; *Illinois Stud. in Lang. and Lit.*, 51).

687 *Pace* William Empson, *Milton's God* (1961), Milton's alleged complicity in the publication of "the king's prayer" is disposed of by F. F. Madan, *A New Bibliography of the Eikon Basilike of King Charles I* (1950; *Oxford Bibl. Soc. Pub.*, n.s. III) and M. Y. Hughes, "New Evidence on the Charge that Milton Forged the Pamela Prayer in the *Eikon Basilike*," *RES*, n.s. III (1952). 130-140.

XV. Milton in the Restoration

689 On *Paradise Lost* see Helen Gardner, "Milton's Satan and the Theme of Damnation in Elizabethan Tragedy," *English Stud.* (*E&S*, n.s.), I (1948). 46-66; A. E. Barker, "Structural Pattern in *Paradise Lost*," *PQ*, XXVIII (1949). 16-30; Watson Kirkconnell, *The Celestial Cycle: the Theme of* Paradise Lost *in World Literature, with Translations of the Major Analogues* (Toronto, 1952); E. L. Marilla, *The Central Problem of* Paradise Lost: *the Fall of Man* (Uppsala, 1953; *Essays & Stud. in English Lang. and Lit.*, XV); Arnold Stein, *Answerable Style: Essays on* Paradise Lost (Minneapolis, 1953); I. G. MacCaffrey, Paradise Lost *as "Myth"* (Cambridge, Mass., 1959); J. B. Broadbent, *Some Graver Subject: an Essay on* Paradise Lost (1960); R. M. Frye, *God, Man, and Satan* (Princeton, 1960); J. I. Cope, *The Metaphoric Structure of* Paradise Lost (Baltimore, 1962); D. P. Harding, *The Club of Hercules: Studies in the*

Classical Background of Paradise Lost (Urbana, Ill., 1962; *Illinois Stud. in Lang. and Lit.,* 50); J. H. Summers, *The Muse's Method: an Introduction to "Paradise Lost"* (Cambridge, Mass., 1962); A. D. Ferry, *Milton's Epic Voice: the Narrator in* Paradise Lost (Cambridge, Mass., 1963).

691 On Milton's geographical surveys see R. R. Cawley, *Milton and the Literature of Travel* (1951; *Princeton Stud. in English,* 32).

693 On *Paradise Regained* see E. M. Pope, *Paradise Regained: the Tradition and the Poem* (Baltimore, 1947); Frank Kermode, "Milton's Hero," *RES,* n.s. IV (1953). 317-330; A. S. P. Woodhouse, "Theme and Pattern in *Paradise Regained,*" *UTQ,* XXV (1956). 167-182; Northrop Frye, "The Typology of *Paradise Regained,*" *MP,* LIII (1956). 227-238; Arnold Stein, *Heroic Knowledge: an Interpretation of* Paradise Regained *and* Samson Agonistes (Minneapolis, 1957); B. K. Lewalski, "Theme and Structure in *Paradise Regained,*" *SP,* LVII (1960). 186-220.

695 A separate ed. of *Samson Agonistes* has been published by F. T. Prince (1957). See further F. M. Krouse, *Milton's Samson and the Christian Tradition* (Princeton, 1949); A. S. P. Woodhouse, "Tragic Effect in *Samson Agonistes,*" *UTQ,* XXVIII (1959). 203-222; Watson Kirkconnell, *That Invincible Samson: the Theme of* Samson Agonistes *in World Literature with Translations of the Major Analogues* (Toronto, 1964); A. E. Barker, "Structural and Doctrinal Pattern in Milton's Later Poems," *Essays in English Literature . . . Presented to A. S. P. Woodhouse* (Toronto, 1964), pp. 169-194.—For the opinion that *Samson* was written long before it was published see W. R. Parker, "The Date of *Samson Agonistes,*" *PQ,* XXVIII (1949). 145-166; A. H. Gilbert, "Is *Samson Agonistes* Unfinished?" *Ibid.,* pp. 93-106; J. T. Shawcross, "The Chronology of Milton's Major Poems," *PMLA,* LXXVI (1961). 345-358. It is rejected by Ants Oras, "Milton's Blank Verse and the Chronology of his Major Poems," *SAMLA Studies in Milton,* ed. J. M. Patrick (Gainesville, Fla., 1953), pp. 128-197, and Ernest Sirluck, "Milton's Idle Right Hand," appendix, *JEGP,* LX (1961). 773-781.

BOOK III. THE RESTORATION AND EIGHTEENTH CENTURY (1660-1789)

The following abbreviations are used for various *Festschriften:*

Carré Festschrift. Connaissance de l'Étranger: Mélanges offerts à la mémoire de Jean-Marie Carré (Paris, 1964).

Jones Festschrift. The Seventeenth Century: Studies in the History of English Thought and Literature from Bacon to Pope, by Richard Foster Jones and Others writing in his Honour (Stanford, Calif., 1951).

McKillop Festschrift. Restoration and Eighteenth-Century Literature: Essays in Honor of Alan Dugald McKillop. Ed. Carroll Camden (Chicago, 1963).

Nicolson Festschrift. Reason and the Imagination: Studies in the History of Ideas, 1600-1800. Ed. J. A. Mazzeo (1962).

Pottle Festschrift. From Sensibility to Romanticism: Essays presented to Frederick A. Pottle. Ed. Frederick W. Hilles and Harold Bloom (1965).

Powell Festschrift. Johnson, Boswell and their Circle: Essays presented to Lawrence Fitzroy Powell in Honour of his Eighty-fourth Birthday (Oxford, 1965).

Sherburn Festschrift. Pope and His Contemporaries: Essays presented to George Sherburn. Ed. James L. Clifford and Louis A. Landa (Oxford, 1949).

Tinker Festschrift. The Age of Johnson: Essays presented to Chauncey Brewster Tinker (New Haven, 1949).

Willey Festschrift. The English Mind: Studies in the English Moralists presented to Basil Willey. Ed. Hugh Sykes Davies and George Watson (Cambridge, 1964).

Woodhouse Festschrift. Essays in English Literature from the Renaissance to the Victorian Age presented to A. S. P. Woodhouse, 1964. Ed. Millar MacLure and F. W. Watt (Toronto, 1964).

Part I: The Rise of Classicism

I. The Spirit of the Restoration

699 Additional general studies: Alan D. McKillop, *English Literature from Dryden to Burns* (1948); Louis I. Bredvold, "The Literature of the Restoration and Eighteenth Century," in *A History of English Literature,* ed. Hardin Craig (1950), pp. 343-459; Stanley J. Kunitz and Howard Haycraft, *British Authors before 1800: a Biographical Dictionary* (1952). Gilbert Highet's *The Classical Tradition: Greek and Roman Influence on Western Literature* (1949) has special relevance for this period, both as a survey and a bibliography. An important side of Restoration publishing is treated by Roy M. Wiles, *Serial Publication in England before 1750* (Cambridge, 1957). In addition to the MHRA *Annual Bibliography, The Year's Work in English Studies* (1921—) contains chapters surveying the scholarship of the Restoration and eighteenth century, and the *Annual Bibliography* in the Spring issue of *PMLA* provides (from 1956) a comprehensive coverage of scholarship. A supplementary Vol. v of *CBEL*, ed. by George Watson, was published in 1957 (for errors see the review by Gwin J. Kolb in *MP*, LVI (1959). 197-203). Of major importance for the Restoration period is Donald Wing's *Short-Title Catalogue, 1641-1700* (for supplements and additions see Donald F. Bond, *A Reference Guide to English Studies* (Chicago, 1962), pp. 82-83). Annual surveys of scholarship in this period also appear in *SEL*: the first, by Donald J. Greene, "Recent Studies in the Restoration and Eighteenth Century," *SEL*, 1 (1961). 115-41 (continued by other scholars). Beljame's classic work appeared in English translation by E. O. Lorimer in 1948 (New York, 1953), with introduction and notes by Bonamy Dobrée. For the influence of the King see James Sutherland, "The Impact of Charles II on Restoration Literature," *McKillop Festschrift* (Chicago, 1963), pp. 251-63.

700   G. N. Clark (Sir George Clark), *The Later Stuarts, 1660-1714*, has appeared in a revised ed. (Oxford, 1955).

For the influence of science see also Francis Christensen, "John Wilkins and the Royal Society's Reform of Prose Style," *MLQ*, VII (1946). 179-187, 279-290; Marie Boas, *Robert Boyle and Seventeenth-Century Chemistry* (Cambridge, 1958); R. F. Jones, "The Rhetoric of Science in England of the Mid-Seventeenth Century," *McKillop Festschrift* (Chicago, 1963), pp. 5-24.

Sprat's *History of the Royal Society* has been edited by Jackson I. Cope and Harold W. Jones (St. Louis, 1958); see the important review of this by R. S. Crane in *PQ*, XXXIX (1960). 357-359. Newton's *Correspondence* is being edited by H. W. Turnbull (Cambridge, 1959—), of which three volumes (to 1694) have appeared. Andrew Motte's (1729) translation of Newton's *Mathematical Principles of Natural Philosophy and his "System of the World,"* rev. and ed. by Florian Cajori (2v, Berkeley, 1962). For early expositors of Newton see E. W. Strong, "Newtonian Explications of Natural Philosophy," *JHI*, XVIII (1957). 49-83. A useful survey is provided by I. Bernard Cohen, "Newton in the Light of Recent Scholarship," *Isis*, LI (1960). 489-514.

R. F. Jones's *Ancients and Moderns*, (rev. ed., St. Louis, 1961).

701   Ernest L. Tuveson, *Millenium and Utopia: A Study in the Background of the Idea of Progress* (Berkeley, 1949).

702   George Williamson, *The Senecan Amble: A Study in Prose Form from Bacon to Collier* (1951).

703   G. R. Cragg, *From Puritanism to the Age of Reason: A Study of Changes in Religious Thought within the Church of England, 1660-1700* (Cambridge, 1950). On the Quakers: Catherine Owen Pearce, *William Penn: A Biography* (Philadelphia, 1957); *The Journal of George Fox*, rev. ed. by John L. Nickalls (Cambridge, 1952); Jackson I. Cope, "Seventeenth-Century Quaker Style," *PMLA*, LXII (1956). 725-754.

The importance of John Tillotson (1630-1694), Archbishop of Canterbury 1691-1694,—both in the religious thought of the time and in his influence upon prose style—has been underlined in a number of recent studies: Louis G. Locke, *Tillotson: A Study in Seventeenth-Century Literature* (Copenhagen, 1954); Norman Sykes, "The Sermons of Archbishop Tillotson," *Theology*, LVIII (1955). 297-302; David D. Brown, "The Text of John Tillotson's Sermons," *Library*, XIII (1958). 18-36, and "John Tillotson's Revisions and Dryden's 'Talent for English Prose,'" *RES*, n.s. XII (1961). 24-39; Irène Simon, "Tillotson's Barrow," *ES*, XLV (1964). 194-211, 273-288.

704 D. G. James, *The Life of Reason: Hobbes, Locke, Bolingbroke* (1949). Alfred O. Aldridge, "Polygamy and Deism," *JEGP*, XLVIII (1949). 343-360.

705 Filmer's *Patriarcha and Other Political Works*, ed. Peter Laslett (Oxford, 1949).

706 *Locke's Travels in France, 1675-79, as related in his Journals, Correspondence and Other Papers*, ed. John Lough (Cambridge, 1953); *Essays on the Law of Nature*, ed. W. von Leyden (Oxford, 1954); *A Letter concerning Toleration: Latin and English Texts* rev. and ed. by Mario Montuouri (The Hague, 1963). On Locke see also Gabriel Bonno, *Les Relations intellectuelles de Locke avec la France* (Berkeley, 1955); John Hampton, "Les Traductions françaises de Locke au XVIIIᵉ siècle," *RLC*, XXIX (1955). 240-251; Maurice Cranston, *John Locke: A Biography* (1957); Theodore Redpath, "John Locke and the Rhetoric of the Second Treatise," *Willey Festschrift* (Cambridge, 1964), pp. 55-78.

708 David Green, *Grinling Gibbons: His Work as Carver and Statuary, 1648-1721* (1964).

II. Literary Criticism of the Restoration

710 R. S. Crane's "Neo-Classical Criticism" is reprinted ("English Neo-classical Criticism: An Outline Sketch") in *Critics and Criticism* (Chicago, 1952), pp. 372-388. Cf. also his article, "On Writing the History of English Criticism, 1650-1800," *UTQ*, XXII (1953). 376-391, apropos of the book by J. W. H. Atkins, *English Literary Criticism: 17th and 18th Centuries* (1951). Other books dealing with particular aspects: Marjorie H. Nicolson, *The Breaking of the Circle: Studies in the Effect of the "New Science" upon Seventeenth Century Poetry* (Evanston, 1950; rev. ed., New York, 1960), and Alexander W. Allison, *Toward an Augustan Poetic: Edmund Waller's "Reform" of English Poetry* (Lexington, Ky., 1962). The most comprehensive work on the subject is Alexandre Maurocordato, *La Critique classique en Angleterre de la Restauration à la mort de Joseph Addison: Essai de définition* (Paris, 1964). Some of the French critical essays are collected in *The Continental Model: Selected French Critical Essays of the Seventeenth Century, in English Translation*, ed. Scott Elledge and Donald Schier (Minneapolis, 1960). Other important items: Harold F. Brooks, "The 'Imitation' in English Poetry, especially in Formal Satire, before the Age of Pope," *RES*, XXV (1949). 124-140; H. V. S. Ogden, "The Principles of Variety and Contrast in Seventeenth Century Aesthetics, and Milton's Poetry," *JHI*, X (1949). 159-182; Louis I. Bredvold, "The Rise of English Classicism: Study in Methodology,"

CL, II (1950). 253-268; George Williamson, *The Proper Wit of Poetry* (1961); K. G. Hamilton, *The Two Harmonies: Poetry and Prose in the Seventeenth Century* (1963).

714 Hugh Macdonald and Mary Hargreaves, *Thomas Hobbes: A Bibliography* (1952). George Watson, "Hobbes and the Metaphysical Conceit," *JHI*, XVI (1955). 558-562 (comment by T. M. Gang, *Ibid.*, XVII (1956), 418-421); Samuel I. Mintz, *The Hunting of Leviathan: Seventeenth-Century Reactions to the Materialism and Moral Philosophy of Thomas Hobbes* (Cambridge, 1962); J. W. N. Watkins, *Hobbes's System of Ideas* (1965).

716 Dryden's critical essays have been edited by George Watson (*Of Dramatic Poesy and Other Critical Essays*) in Everyman's Library (2v, 1962) with excellent notes. On this early masterpiece see Frank L. Huntley, *On Dryden's "Essay of Dramatic Poesy"* (Ann Arbor, 1951) and Dean T. Mace, "Dryden's Dialogue on Drama," *Jour. Warburg and Courtauld Inst.*, XXV (1962). 87-112; and for Dryden's revisions in this essay Irène Simon in *RES*, n.s. XIV (1963). 132-141, and Janet M. Bately, *Ibid.*, XV (1964). 268-282. Also on Dryden's criticism: Max Nänny, *John Drydens rhetorische Poetik* (Bern, 1959); Barbara M. H. Strang, "Dryden's Innovations in Critical Vocabulary," *Durham Univ. Jour.*, LI (1959). 114-123; John M. Aden, *The Critical Opinions of John Dryden, A Dictionary* (Nashville, 1963); Niall Rudd, "Dryden on Horace and Juvenal," *UTQ*, XXXII (1963). 155-169. For the "Heads of an Answer to Rymer" see George Watson, "Dryden's First Answer to Rymer," *RES*, n.s. XIV (1963). 17-23.

719 *The Critical Works of Thomas Rymer*, ed. Curt A. Zimansky (New Haven, 1956).

721 Wesley's *Epistle to a Friend concerning Poetry*, with an Introduction by Edward N. Hooker (1947; *ARS*, No. 5).

III. The Poetry of Dryden

723 Dryden's *Poetical Works*, ed. Noyes (rev. and enlarged ed., Boston, 1950); *Dryden: Poetry, Prose and Plays*, ed. Douglas Grant (1952). The first volume of the new California edition of Dryden, ed. E. N. Hooker, H. T. Swedenberg, and others, is devoted to *Poems, 1649-1680* (1956). *The Poems of John Dryden*, ed. James Kinsley (4v, Oxford, 1958). *The Prologues and Epilogues of John Dryden: A Critical Edition*, ed. William B. Gardner (1951).

For bibliography: Samuel H. Monk, *John Dryden: A List of Critical Studies published from 1895 to 1950* (Minneapolis, 1950); cf. review by W. R. Keast in *MP*, XLVIII (1951). 205-210. Single volume studies include: David Nichol Smith, *John Dryden* (Clark Lectures, 1948/9) (Cambridge, 1950); Kenneth Young, *John Dryden: A Critical Biography* (1954); Charles E. Ward, *The Life of John Dryden* (Chapel Hill, 1961); and George R. Wasserman, *John Dryden* (1965). Cf. Pierre Legouis, "Ouvrages récents sur Dryden," *Études anglaises*, XVII (1964). 148-158. On the poetry: Guy Montgomery, *Concordance to the Poetical Works of John Dryden* (Berkeley, 1957); Arthur W. Hoffman, *John Dryden's Imagery* (Gainesville, Fla., 1962); Earl Miner, "Some Characteristics of Dryden's Use of Metaphor," *SEL*, II (1962). 309-320; Reuben A. Brower, "Dryden and the 'Invention' of Pope," *McKillop Festschrift* (Chicago, 1963), pp. 211-233; Alan Roper, *Dryden's Poetic Kingdoms* (1965).

724   Bruce A. Rosenberg, *"Annus mirabilis* Distilled," *PMLA*, LXXIX (1964). 254-258.

725   John Harrington Smith, "Some Sources of Dryden's Toryism, 1682-84," *HLQ*, XX (1957). 233-243; Bernard N. Schilling, *Dryden and the Conservative Myth: A Reading of "Absalom and Achitophel"* (New Haven, 1961) (rev. by Samuel H. Monk in *MP*, LXI (1964). 246-252).

727   On *Mac Flecknoe:* G. Blakemore Evans, "The Text of Dryden's *Mac Flecknoe,*" *Harvard Library Bull.*, VII (1953). 32-54; Vinton A. Dearing, "Dryden's *Mac Flecknoe:* The Case for Authorial Revision," *Stud. in Bibliography*, VII (1955). 85-102; George McFadden, "Elkanah Settle and the Genesis of *Mac Flecknoe,*" *PQ*, XLIII (1964). 55-72.

On *Religio Laici:* Edward N. Hooker, "Dryden and the Atoms of Epicurus," *ELH*, XXIV (1957). 177-190; David R. Brown, "Dryden's 'Religio Laici' and the 'Judicious and Learned Friend' [Tillotson]," *MLR*, LVI (1961). 66-69; Elias J. Chiasson, "Dryden's Apparent Scepticism in *Religio Laici,*" *Harvard Theological Rev.*, LIV (1961). 207-221; Thomas H. Fujimura, "Dryden's *Religio Laici:* An Anglican Poem," *PMLA*, LXXVI (1961). 205-217; Victor M. Hamm, "Dryden's *Religio Laici* and Roman Catholic Apologetics," *PMLA*, LXXX (1965). 190-198.

728   Clarence H. Miller, "The Styles of *The Hind and the Panther,*" *JEGP*, LXI (1962). 511-527; Earl Miner, "The Wolf's Progress in *The Hind and the Panther,*" *Bull. N.Y. Public Library*, LXVII (1963). 512-516; Donald R. Benson, "Theology and Politics in Dryden's Conversion," *SEL*, IV (1964). 393-412.

730   A. D. Hope, "Anne Killigrew or the Art of Modulating," *Southern Rev.* [Adelaide], I (1963), 4-14; Mother Mary Eleanor, S. H. C. J. *"Anne Killigrew* and *Mac Flecknoe,*" *PQ*, XLIII (1964). 47-54; David M. Vieth, "Irony in Dryden's Ode to Anne Killigrew," *SP*, LXII (1965). 91-100.—Jay Arnold Levine, "Dryden's *Song for St. Cecilia's Day, 1687,*" *PQ*, XLIV (1965). 38-50.

731   William Frost, *Dryden and the Art of Translation* (New Haven, 1955); L. Proudfoot, *Dryden's "Aeneid" and its Seventeenth-Century Predecessors* (Manchester, 1960); Wolfgang B. Fleischmann, *Lucretius and English Literature* (*1680-1740*) (*Paris*, 1964); Mary Gallagher, "Dryden's Translations of Lucretius," *HLQ*, XXVIII (1964), 19-29.

IV. Minor Poets of the Restoration

734   Josephine Bauer, "Some Verse Fragments and Prose *Characters* by Samuel Butler not included in the *Complete Works,*" *MP*, XLV (1948). 160-168; Norma Bentley, "Another Butler Manuscript," *MP*, XLVI (1948). 132-135; Ricardo Quintana, "Samuel Butler: A Restoration Figure in a Modern Light," *ELH*, XVII (1951). 7-13; Ward S. Miller, "The Allegory in Part I of *Hudibras,*" *HLQ*, XXI (1958). 323-343.

739   Cooper R. Mackin, "The Satiric Technique of John Oldham's *Satyrs upon the Jesuits,*" *SP*, LXII (1965). 78-90.

740   On the Court Poets: John Harold Wilson, *The Court Wits of the Restoration: An Introduction* (Princeton, 1948).—V. de Sola Pinto's *Rochester* appeared in a revised edition (1962) as *Enthusiast in Wit: A Portrait of John Wilmot, Earl of Rochester, 1647-1680*. *Rochester's Poems on Several Occasions* (a facsimile of the Huntington Library copy), ed. James Thorpe (Princeton, 1950); *Poems by John Wilmot, Earl of Rochester*, ed. Vivian de Sola Pinto (1953; 2 ed, 1964; *Muses' Library*); *The Famous Pathologist, or, The Noble Mountebank* [by Rochester and Thomas Alcock], ed. Vivian de Sola Pinto (Nottingham, 1961). On Rochester: Lucyle Hook, "The Publication Date of Rochester's *Valentinian*," *HLQ*, XIX (1956). 401-407; Thomas H. Fujimura, "Rochester's 'Satyr against Mankind': An Analysis," *SP*, LV (1958). 576-590; Jean Auffret, "Rochester's *Farewell*," *Études anglaises*, XII (1959). 142-150; David M. Vieth, *Attribution in Restoration Poetry: A Study of Rochester's "Poems" of 1680* (New Haven, 1963; rev. by V. de S. Pinto in *PQ*, XLIII (1964). 381-384, and in *MLR*, LX (1965). 253-256); Ronald Berman, "Rochester and the Defeat of the Senses," *Kenyon Rev.*, XXVI (1964). 354-368.

743   Margaret P. Boddy, "The 1692 *Fourth Book of Virgil*," *RES*, n.s. XV (1964). 364-380 (evidence for Sedley's authorship).

745   *Poems of Charles Cotton*, ed. John Buxton (1958, Muses' Library).

746   *Poems on Affairs of State: Augustan Satirical Verse, 1660-1714* (New Haven, 1963—). Vol. I, *1660-1678*, ed. George de F. Lord (1963); Vol. II, *1678-1681*, ed. Elias F. Mengel, Jr. (1965). See Ruth Nevo, *The Dial of Virtue: A Study of Poems on Affairs of State in the Seventeenth Century* (Princeton, 1963).

747   Additional minor Restoration poets: Richard Leigh: *Poems, 1675*. Repr. with Introduction by Hugh Macdonald (Oxford, 1947). George Stepney: *George Stepney's Translation of the Eighth Satire of Juvenal*, ed. Thomas and Elizabeth Swedenberg (Berkeley, 1948). See also H. T. Swedenberg, Jr., "George Stepney, my Lord Dorset's Boy," *HLQ*, X (1946). 1-33.

V. Restoration Drama: I. Heroic Plays and Tragedies

748   The most valuable addition to our knowledge of Restoration and eighteenth-century drama is *The London Stage, 1660-1800: A Calendar of Plays, Entertainments & Afterpieces, together with Casts, Box-Receipts and Contemporary Comment, compiled from the Playbills, Newspapers and Theatrical Diaries of the Period*, ed. William Van Lennep, Emmett L. Avery, Arthur H. Scouten, George Winchester Stone, Jr., and Charles Beecher Hogan (Carbondale, Ill., 1960—). Vol. I (1965) ed. by William Van Lennep covers the period of the Restoration. Harbage's *Annals of English Drama, 975-1700* has appeared in a revised edition by S. Schoenbaum (1964). The histories by Allardyce Nicoll have been reissued in revised form as *A History of English Drama 1660-1900* (6v, Cambridge, 1952-1959); Vol. VI: *A Short-title Alphabetical Catalogue of Plays produced or printed in England from 1660-1900* (1959). Also useful is *A Check List of English Plays, 1641-1700* by Gertrude L. Woodward and James G. McManaway (Chicago, 1945); *Supplement* by Fredson Bowers (Charlottesville, Va., 1949). See also William S. Clark, *The Early Irish Stage: The Beginnings to*

1720 (Oxford, 1955). A much-needed *Biographical Dictionary of Actors and Actresses* is in preparation by the editors of *The London Stage*. A good account of the actresses of the Restoration is to be found in John Harold Wilson's *All the King's Ladies* (Chicago, 1958). On the general aims of the drama of the period see Sarup Singh, *The Theory of Drama in the Restoration Period* (Calcutta, 1963).

752 Kathleen Lynch, *Roger Boyle, First Earl of Orrery* (Knoxville, 1965).— Vol. VIII of the California edition of Dryden includes *The Wild Gallant, The Rival Ladies, The Indian Queen,* ed. John Harrington Smith and Dougald MacMillan (1962); cf. review by V. de Sola Pinto in *PQ*, XLII (1963). 342-344. On Dryden's heroic plays and early tragedies: Dougald MacMillan, "The Sources of Dryden's *The Indian Emperour*," *HLQ*, XIII (1950). 355-370; Scott C. Osborn, "Heroical Love in Dryden's Heroic Drama," *PMLA*, LXXIII (1958). 480-490; John A. Winterbottom, "The Place of Hobbesian Ideas in Dryden's Tragedies," *JEGP*, LVII (1958). 665-683; Thomas H. Fujimura, "The Appeal of Dryden's Heroic Plays," *PMLA*, LXXV (1960). 37-45; Michael W. Alssid, "The Perfect Conquest: A Study of Theme, Structure and Characters in Dryden's *The Indian Emperor*," *SP*, LIX (1962). 539-559; Jean Gagen, "Love and Honor in Dryden's Heroic Plays," *PMLA*, LXXVII (1962). 208-220; Bruce King, "Heroic and Mock-Heroic Plays," *Sewanee Rev.*, LXX (1962). 514-517; Arthur C. Kirsch, "Dryden, Corneille, and the Heroic Play," *MP*, LIX (1962). 248-264; Eugene M. Waith, *The Herculean Hero in Marlowe, Shakespeare and Dryden* (1962); John A. Winterbottom, "Stoicism in Dryden's Tragedies," *JEGP*, LXI (1962). 868-883; Arthur C. Kirsch, *Dryden's Heroic Drama* (Princeton, 1965); Bruce King, "Dryden, Tillotson, and *Tyrannic Love*," *RES*, n.s. XVI (1965). 364-377; Selma Zebouni, *Dryden: A Study in Heroic Characterization* (Baton Rouge, 1965).

755 On Buckingham and *The Rehearsal:* Hester W. Chapman, *Great Villiers: A Study of George Villiers, Second Duke of Buckingham, 1628-1687* (1949); V. C. Clinton-Baddeley, *The Burlesque Tradition in the English Theatre after 1660* (1952); John Harold Wilson, *A Rake and his Times: George Villiers, 2nd Duke of Buckingham* (1954). On *Aureng-Zebe:* Arthur C. Kirsch, "The Significance of Dryden's *Aureng-Zebe*," *ELH*, XXIX (1962). 160-174; Michael W. Alssid, "The Design of Dryden's *Aureng-Zebe*," *JEGP*, LXIV (1965). 452-469.

756 On Dryden's later plays: John Robert Moore, "Political Allusions in Dryden's Later Plays," *PMLA*, LXXIII (1958). 36-42; Otto Reinert, "Passion and Pity in *All for Love:* A Reconsideration," in *The Hidden Sense and Other Essays,* by Maren-Sofie Røstvig and others (Oslo, 1963), pp. 159-195; L. P. Goggin, "This Bow of Ulysses," *Essays and Stud. in Lang. and Lit.* (Pittsburgh, 1964; *Duquesne Stud., Philol. Ser.,* 5), p. 49-86; Bruce King, "The Significance of Dryden's *State of Innocence*," *SEL*, IV (1964). 371-391; D. T. Starnes, "Imitation of Shakespeare in Dryden's *All for Love*," *Texas Stud. in Lit. and Lang.*, VI (1964). 39-46.

757 On John Banks see the monograph by Hans Hochuli (Bern, 1952). *The Works of Nathaniel Lee* have been edited by Thomas B. Stroup and Arthur L. Cooke (2v, New Brunswick, N.J., 1954-55). On this edition see the review by Fredson Bowers in *PQ*, XXXV (1956). 310-314.

758 Aline M. Taylor, *Next to Shakespeare: Otway's Venice Preserved and*

The Orphan and their History on the London Stage (Durham, N.C., 1950); David R. Hauser, "Otway Preserved: Theme and Form in *Venice Preserv'd*," *SP*, LV (1958). 481-493; William H. McBurney, "Otway's Tragic Muse Debauched: Sensuality in *Venice Preserv'd*," *JEGP*, LVIII (1959). 380-399; André Lefèvre, "Racine en Angleterre au XVIIᵉ siècle: 'Titus and Berenice' de Thomas Otway," *RLC*, XXXIV (1960). 251-257.

VI. Restoration Drama: II. Comedy

762 On Restoration Comedy: John Harrington Smith, *The Gay Couple in Restoration Comedy* (Cambridge, Mass., 1948); David S. Berkeley, "The Penitent Rake in Restoration Comedy," *MP*, XLIX (1952). 223-233; Thomas H. Fujimura, *The Restoration Comedy of Wit* (Princeton, 1952); a series of articles by David S. Berkeley: "The Art of 'Whining' Love," *SP*, LII (1955). 478-496; "Préciosité and the Restoration Comedy of Manners," *HLQ*, XVIII (1955). 109-128; "Some Notes on Probability in Restoration Drama," *N&Q*, CC (1955). 237-239, 342-344, 432; C. D. Cecil, "Libertine and Précieux Elements in Restoration Comedy," *EIC*, IX (1959). 239-253; Norman H. Holland, *The First Modern Comedies: The Significance of Etherege, Wycherley, and Congreve* (Cambridge, Mass., 1959); P. F. Vernon, "Marriage of Convenience and the Mode of Restoration Comedy," *EIC*, XII (1962). 370-387; Irène Simon, "Restoration Comedy and the Critics," *Revue des langues vivantes*, XXIX (1963). 397-430; Charles O. McDonald, "Restoration Comedy as Drama of Satire: An Investigation into Seventeenth-Century Aesthetics," *SP*, LXI (1964). 522-544; D. R. M. Wilkinson, *The Comedy of Habit: An Essay on the Use of Courtesy Literature in a Study of Restoration Comic Drama* (The Hague, 1964); R. C. Sharma, *Themes and Conventions in the Comedy of Manners* (1965). *Restoration Theatre* (*Stratford-upon-Avon Stud.*, 6), ed. John Russell Brown and Bernard Harris (1965) contains first-rate papers on Etherege, Wycherley, Dryden, and Congreve, as well as studies of relevant subjects including the influence of Molière. Jean E. Gagen's *The New Woman: Her Emergence in English Drama, 1600-1730* (1954) also deals in part with Restoration drama.

764 H. J. Oliver, *Sir Robert Howard (1626-1698): A Critical Biography* (Durham, N.C., 1963).

765 Dryden: Frank Harper Moore, *The Nobler Pleasure: Dryden's Comedy in Theory and Practice* (Chapel Hill, 1963).—Etherege: Thomas H. Fujimura, "Etherege at Constantinople," *PMLA*, LXII (1956). 465-481; Dale Underwood, *Etherege and the Seventeenth-Century Comedy of Manners* (New Haven, 1957); *The Poems of Sir George Etherege*, ed. James Thorpe (Princeton, 1963).

766 Wycherley: T. W. Craik, "Some Aspects of Satire in Wycherley's Plays," *ES*, XLI (1960). 168-179; K. M. Rogers, "Fatal Inconsistency: Wycherley and *The Plain-Dealer*," *ELH*, XXVIII (1961). 148-162; J. Auffret, "Wycherley et ses maîtres les moralistes," *Études anglaises*, XV (1962). 375-388; Carl Wooten, "*The Country Wife* and Contemporary Comedy: A World Apart," *Drama Survey*, II (1963). 333-343; Rose A. Zimbardo, *Wycherley's Drama: A Link in the Development of English Satire* (New Haven, 1965).

769 Shadwell: John Harrington Smith, "Shadwell, the Ladies, and Change in Comedy," *MP*, xlvi (1948). 22-33; P. F. Vernon, "Social Satire in Shadwell's *Timon*," *Studia Neophil.*, xxxv (1963). 221-226; Gunnar Sorelius, "Shadwell Deviating into Sense: *Timon of Athens* and the Duke of Buckingham," *Ibid.*, xxxvi (1964). 232-244.

772 Congreve: *The Way of the World*, ed. Kathleen M. Lynch (Lincoln, Nebr., 1965). Emmett L. Avery, *Congreve's Plays on the Eighteenth-Century Stage* (1951); Kathleen M. Lynch, *A Congreve Gallery* (Cambridge, Mass., 1951); John C. Hodges, *The Library of William Congreve* (1955); Paul and Miriam Mueschke, *A New View of Congreve's "Way of the World"* (Ann Arbor, 1958); Robert G. Noyes, "Congreve and his Comedies in the Eighteenth-Century Novel," *PQ*, xxxix (1960). 464-480; Clifford Leech, "Congreve and the Century's End," *PQ*, xli (1962). 275-293; Paul T. Nolan, "Congreve's Lovers: Art and the Critic," *Drama Survey*, i (1962). 330-339; *William Congreve: Letters and Documents*, ed. John C. Hodges (1964); John Barnard, "Did Congreve Write *A Satyr against Love?*" *Bull. N.Y. Public Library*, lxviii (1964). 308-322 [with text of the Satyr]; Jean Gagen, "Congreve's Mirabell and the Ideal of the Gentleman," *PMLA*, lxxix (1964). 422-427; Charles R. Lyons, "Congreve's Miracle of Love," *Criticism*, vi (1964). 331-348 [on *Love for Love*].

776 Farquhar: *The Beaux' Stratagem*, ed. Vincent F. Hopper and Gerald B. Lahey (Great Neck, N.Y., 1963); Willard Connely, *Young George Farquhar: The Restoration Drama at Twilight* (1949); Kaspar Spinner, *George Farquhar als Dramatiker* (Bern, 1956); Eric Rothstein, "Farquhar's *Twin-Rivals* and the Reform of Comedy," *PMLA*, lxxix (1964). 33-41; Eugene N. James, "The Burlesque of Restoration Comedy in *Love and a Bottle*," *SEL*, v (1965). 469-490.

VII. Patterns in Historical Writing

780 Pepys: *The Letters of Samuel Pepys and his Family Circle*, ed. Helen Truesdell Heath (Oxford, 1955); John Harold Wilson, *The Private Life of Mr. Pepys* (1959); Cecil S. Emden, *Pepys Himself* (1963); Ivan E. Taylor, "Mr. Pepy's Use of Colloquial English," *Coll. Lang Assoc. Jour*, vii (1963). 22-36; Marjorie H. Nicolson, *Pepys' "Diary" and the New Science* (Charlottesville, 1965).

784 Evelyn: *The Diary of John Evelyn*, ed. E. S. de Beer (6v, Oxford, 1955; also in 1 vol. (Oxford, 1959); W. G. Hiscock, *John Evelyn and Mrs. Godolphin* (1951) and *John Evelyn and his Family Circle* (1955).

786 William Matthews, *British Diaries: An Annotated Bibliography of British Diaries written between 1442 and 1942* (Berkeley, 1950).—Clarendon: Herbert Davis, "The Augustan Conception of History," *Nicolson Festschrift* (1962), pp. 213-229 [discusses Clarendon, but is mainly on Swift and Pope].

788 Burnet: W. Rees Mogg, "Some Reflections on the Bibliography of Gilbert Burnet," *Library*, iv (1949). 100-113.

790 Autobiography: Wayne Shumaker, *English Autobiography: Its Emergence, Materials, and Form* (Berkeley, 1954); William Matthews, *British Autobiographies: An Annotated Bibliography of British Autobiographies Published or Written before 1951* (Berkeley, 1955); Margaret Bottral, *Every Man a Phoenix:*

Studies in Seventeenth-Century Autobiography (1958).—Duchess of Newcastle: Douglas Grant, *Margaret the First: A Biography of Margaret Cavendish, Duchess of Newcastle, 1623-1673* (1956); Jean Gagen, "Honor and Fame in the Works of the Duchess of Newcastle," *SP*, LVI (1959). 519-538.

791 Winstanley, *Lives of the Most Famous English Poets (1687):* Facsimile Reproduction, with Introduction by William R. Parker (Gainesville, Fla., 1963).

792 Petty: Emil Strauss, *Sir William Petty: Portrait of a Genius* (1954).—Aubrey: *Aubrey's Brief Lives,* ed. Oliver L. Dick (1949; Ann Arbor, 1957); John Powell, *John Aubrey and his Friends* (1948).

VIII. Types of Prose Fiction

793 Charles C. Mish, *English Prose Fiction, 1600-1700: A Chronological Checklist* (Charlottesville, Va., 1952); Sidney Gecker, *English Fiction to 1820 in the University of Pennsylvania Library* (Philadelphia, 1954).

795 *The Adventures of Lindamira, A Lady of Quality,* ed. Benjamin Boyce (Minneapolis, 1949).

796 Strickland Gibson, *A Bibliography of Francis Kirkman, with his Prefaces, Dedications and Commendations (1652-80)* (Oxford, 1950).

797 Bunyan: *The Pilgrim's Progress,* ed. Wharey (rev. ed. by Roger Sharrock, Oxford, 1960); *Grace Abounding,* ed. Roger Sharrock (Oxford, 1962); Henri A. Talon, *John Bunyan, l'homme et l'oeuvre* (Paris, 1948; trans. Barbara Wall, 1951); Vera Brittain, *In the Steps of John Bunyan: An Excursion into Puritan England* (1950; U.S. title: *Valiant Pilgrim: The Story of John Bunyan and Puritan England*); Roger Sharrock, *John Bunyan* (1954); Berta Haferkamp, *Bunyan als Künstler: Stilkritische Studien zu seinem Hauptwerk "The Pilgrim's Progress"* (Tübingen, 1963).

804 Mrs. Behn: George Woodcock, *The Incomparable Aphra* (1948); Emily Hahn, *Aphra Behn* (1951); W. J. Cameron, *New Light on Aphra Behn* (Auckland, 1961); R. T. Sheffey, "Some Evidence for a New Source of Aphra Behn's *Oroonoko*," *SP*, LIX (1962). 52-63; G. M. Laborde, "Du nouveau sur Aphra Behn," *Études anglaises,* XVI (1963). 364-368 [a review of Cameron's monograph]. —Henry Neville: A. O. Aldridge, "Polygamy in Early Fiction: Henry Neville and Denis Veiras," *PMLA*, LXV (1950). 464-472.

IX. The Essay and Allied Forms

807 Cowley's Essays: Robert B. Hinman, *Abraham Cowley's World of Order* (Cambridge, Mass., 1960).

808 *Five Miscellaneous Essays by Sir William Temple,* ed. Samuel H. Monk (Ann Arbor, 1963); William Roberts, "Sir William Temple on Orinda: Neglected Publications," *Papers of the Bibl. Soc. of America,* LVII (1963). 328-336.

811 Glanvill: Richard H. Popkin, "The Development of the Philosophical Reputation of Joseph Glanvill," *JHI*, XV (1954). 305-311; Jackson I. Cope, *Joseph*

Glanvill: Anglican Apologist (St. Louis, 1956).—Burnet: H. V. S. Ogden, "Thomas Burnet's *Telluris theoria sacra* and Mountain Scenery," *ELH*, XIV (1947). 139-150; Ernest Tuveson, "The Origins of the 'Moral Sense,'" *HLQ*, XI (1948). 241-259.—Ray: Geoffrey Keynes, *John Ray: A Bibliography* (1951).

812 Halifax: Donald R. Benson, "Halifax and the Trimmers," *HLQ*, XXVII (1964). 115-134; Harold E. Pagliaro, "Paradox in the Aphorisms of La Rochefoucauld and Some Representative English Followers," *PMLA*, LXXIX (1964). 42-50.

813 The Character: Benjamin Boyce, *The Theophrastan Character in England to 1642* (Cambridge, Mass., 1947) and *The Polemic Character, 1640-1661: A Chapter in English Literary History* (Lincoln, Neb., 1955). Henry Gally's "Critical Essay on Characteristic-Writings" [the introduction to his translation of Theophrastus in 1725] is No. 33 of the *ARS*, with an Introduction by Alexander H. Chorney (1952).

815 P. M. Handover, *A History of the London Gazette, 1665-1965* (1965).

816 Jean Honoré, "Charles Gildon rédacteur du *British Mercury* (1711-1712): les attaques contre Pope, Swift, et les wits," *Études anglaises*, XV (1962). 347-364. See also the same writer's "Charles Gildon et la Grammaire de Brightland," *Ibid.*, XVIII (1965). 145-165.

817 *The Turkish Spy*: William H. McBurney, "The Authorship of *The Turkish Spy*," *PMLA*, LXXII (1957). 915-935; Joseph E. Tucker, "The *Turkish Spy* and its French Background," *RLC*, XXXII (1958). 74-91, and "On the Authorship of the *Turkish Spy*: An *État Présent*," *Papers of the Bibl. Soc. of America*, LII (1958). 34-47.
The London Spy: The London Spy, by Ned Ward, ed. Kenneth Fenwick (1955; Folio Society).

819 For *The Adventures of Lindamira*, see above, suppl. to p. 795.

Part II: Classicism and Journalism

I. Eighteenth-Century Quality

823 There is no Short Title Catalogue for the eighteenth century, but for the early years much bibliographical information is to be had from Vol. III of Arber's reprint of the *Term Catalogues, 1668-1711* and from William T. and Chloe S. Morgan's *Bibliography of Bri h History (1700-1715)* (5v, Bloomington, Ind., 1934-42). The incomplete but valuable registers of books in the *Bibliotheca Annua* (1699-1703), the *Monthly Catalogues* (1714-17, 1723-30), and the *Register of Books* (1728-32) from the *Monthly Chronicle*, have been reprinted (1964) under the editorship of David Foxon. *The Rothschild Library*—the catalogue of eighteenth-century books and manuscripts formed by Lord Rothschild—(2v, Cambridge, 1954) is also of great value. See further Stanley Pargellis and D.J. Medley, *Bibliography of British History: The Eighteenth Century, 1714-1789* (Oxford, 1951). Additional surveys of the literature: John Butt, *The Augustan Age* (1950); Roger P. McCutcheon, *Eighteenth-Century English Literature*

(1950); R. C. Churchill, *English Literature of the Eighteenth Century* (1953); A. R. Humphreys, *The Augustan World: Life and Letters in Eighteenth-Century England;* (1954; 2ed, 1964); and Vol. VII of the *Oxford History of English Literature*: Bonamy Dobrée, *English Literature in the Early Eighteenth Century, 1700-1740* (Oxford, 1959), for which see the review by Donald F. Bond in *MP*, LX (1962). 138-141. A useful survey of recent scholarship is contained in the article by James L. Clifford, "The Eighteenth Century," *MLQ* XXVI (1965). 111-134. For recent works on various aspects of the background see Leon Radzinowicz, *A History of English Criminal Law and its Administration from 1750* (Vol. I, 1948); Ernest Cassirer, *The Philosophy of the Enlightenment*, trans. F.C.A. Koelln and J. P. Pettegrove (Princeton, 1951); G.M. Trevelyan, *Illustrated English Social History* (Vol. III, 1951); Ronald N. Stromberg, *Religious Liberalism in Eighteenth-Century England* (1954); L. W. Hanson, *Contemporary Printed Sources for British and Irish Economic History, 1701-1750* (Cambridge, 1963). M. D. George's *London Life in the XVIIIth Century* reached a 3rd rev. ed. in 1951. *Aspects of the Eighteenth Century*, ed. Earl R. Wasserman (Baltimore, 1965), contains several important essays dealing with this period: George Boas, "In Search of the Age of Reason"; J. A. Passmore, "The Malleability of Man in Eighteenth-Century Thought"; René Wellek, "The Term and Concept of 'Classicism' in Literary History"; R. Wittkower, "Imitation, Electicism, and Genius"; Edward E. Lowinsky, "Taste, Style, and Ideology in Eighteenth Century Music"; Henry Guerlac, "Where the Statue Stood: Divergent Loyalties to Newton in the Eighteenth Century."

825   On Shaftesbury see the articles by A. O. Aldridge: "Shaftesbury, Christianity, and Friendship," *Anglican Theological Rev.* XXXII (1950). 121-136; "Two Versions of Shaftesbury's *Inquiry concerning Virtue,*" *HLQ*, XIII (1950). 207-214; "Shaftesbury and the Deist Manifesto," *Trans. Amer. Philos. Soc.*, XLI (1951). 297-385; and "Shaftesbury and Bolingbroke," *PQ*, XXXI (1952). 1-16; R. L. Brett, *The Third Earl of Shaftesbury: A Study in Eighteenth-Century Literary Theory* (1951); Ernest Tuveson, "The Importance of Shaftesbury," *ELH*, XX (1953). 267-299; Robert B. Voitle, "Shaftesbury's Moral Sense," *SP*, LII (1955). 17-38; Erwin Wolff, *Shaftesbury und seine Bedeutung für die englische Literatur des 18. Jahrhunderts: der Moralist und die literarische Form* (Tübingen, 1960) (cf. Irène Simon in *Revue des langues vivantes*, XXVII (1961). 200-215); Jerome Stolnitz, "On the Significance of Lord Shaftesbury in Modern Aesthetic Theory," *Philosophical Quar.* XI (1961). 97-113; J. B. Broadbent, "Shaftesbury's Horses of Religion," *Willey Festschrift* (Cambridge, 1964) pp. 79-89; Robert Marsh, *Four Dialectical Theories of Poetry* (Chicago, 1965); Ernest Tuveson, "Shaftesbury on the not so simple Plan of Human Nature," *SEL*, V (1965). 403-434. The pioneering article by Cecil A. Moore (1916) has been reprinted in Moore's *Backgrounds of English Literature, 1700-1760* (Minneapolis, 1953).

826   F. B. Kaye's edition of Mandeville (2v, Oxford, 1924) is still authoritative. The *Fable* has also been edited by Irwin Primer (1962). See further, J. C. Maxwell, "Ethics and Politics in Mandeville," *Philosophy*, XXVI (1951), 242-252; Thomas R. Edwards, Jr., "Mandeville's Moral Prose," *ELH*, XXXI (1964). 195-212.

828   Berkeley's *Works* have now been edited by A. A. Luce and T. E. Jessop

(9v, 1948-1957). Luce is also author of a biography (1949) and *The Dialectic of Immaterialism: An Account of the Making of Berkeley's "Principles"* (1963). See also Paul Kaufman, "Establishing Berkeley's Authorship of 'Guardian' Papers," *Papers of the Bibl. Soc. of America*, LIV (1960). 181-183; Donald Davie, "Berkeley and the Style of Dialogue," *Willey Festschrift* (Cambridge, 1964), pp. 90-106. There is a useful survey of scholarship by Claude Lehec, "Trente années d'études berkeleyennes," *Revue Philosophique*, CXLIII (1953). 244-265.

829 William Law: Henri Talon, *William Law: A Study in Literary Craftsmanship* (1948); P. Malekin, "Jacob Boeheme's Influence on William Law," *Studia Neophil.* XXXVI (1964). 245-260.—Byrom: *Selections from the Journals and Papers of John Byrom, Poet, Diarist, Shorthand Writer, 1691-1763*, ed. Henri Talon (1950).

831 The Arts and Gardening: Margaret Jourdain, *The Work of William Kent* (1948); Dorothy Stroud, *Capability Brown* (1950, rev. 1957); Laurence Whistler, *The Imagination of Vanbrugh and his Fellow Artists* (1954); Miles Hadfield, *Gardening in Britain* (1960); Edward Hyams, *The English Garden* (1964).—Hogarth: *The Analysis of Beauty, with the Rejected Passages from the Manuscript Drafts and Autobiographical Notes*, ed. Joseph Burke (Oxford, 1955); Robert E. Moore, *Hogarth's Literary Relationships* (Minneapolis, 1948); Peter Quennel, *Hogarth's Progress* (1955); Frederick Antal, *Hogarth and his Place in European Art* (1962).

832 E. F. Carritt, *A Calendar of British Taste from 1600-1800* (1949).

II. The Critical Temper and Doctrine, 1700-1750

833 *Eighteenth-Century Critical Essays*, ed. Scott Elledge (2v, Ithaca, N.Y., 1961); Samuel Kliger, *The Goths in England: A Study in Seventeenth and Eighteenth Century Thought* (Cambridge, Mass., 1952) (cf. review by Alan D. McKillop in *PQ*, XXXII (1953). 247-250); A. Bosker, *Literary Criticism in the Age of Johnson* (rev. ed:, Groningen, 1953); Emerson R. Marks, *Relativist and Absolutist: The Early Neoclassical Debate in England* (New Brunswick, N.J., 1955); A. M. Kinghorn, "Literary Aesthetics and the Sympathetic Emotions— A Main Trend in Eighteenth-Century Scottish Criticism," *Studies in Scottish Literature*, I (1963). 35-47; Martin Price, *To the Palace of Wisdom: Studies in Order and Energy from Dryden to Blake* (Garden City, N.Y., 1964); Paul Fussell, *The Rhetorical World of Augustan Humanism: Ethics and Imagery from Swift to Burke* (Oxford, 1965); Robert Marsh, *Four Dialectical Theories of Poetry: An Aspect of English Neoclassical Criticism* (Chicago, 1965) [Shaftesbury, Akenside, Hartley, and James Harris].

834 Hooker's edition of Dennis' *Critical Works* has been reprinted (2v, Baltimore, 1965).

837 Shaftesbury as Critic. See above, suppl. to p. 825.

839 Lee A. Elioseff, *The Cultural Milieu of Addison's Literary Criticism* (Austin, Texas, 1963).

840 On Hutcheson see Alfred Owen Aldridge, "A French Critic of Hutcheson's Aesthetics," *MP*, XLV (1948). 169-184 [Charles Louis de Villette]; William Frankena, "Hutcheson's Moral Sense Theory," *JHI*, XVI (1955). 356-375; George Dickie, "An Examination of Hutcheson's Alleged Emotivism," *Research Stud. of the State College of Washington*, XXVI (1958). 55-73.

841 Raymond D. Havens, "Simplicity, a Changing Concept," *JHI*, XIV (1953). 3-32. On ballad criticism see Albert B. Friedman, *The Ballad Revival* (Chicago, 1961), chap. IV.

842 Pope as Critic: Edward N. Hooker, "Pope on Wit: the *Essay on Criticism,*" *Jones Festschrift* (Stanford, 1951), pp. 225-246; Robert M. Schmitz, *Pope's Essay on Criticism, 1709: A Study of the Bodleian Manuscript Text, with Facsimiles, Transcripts, and Variants* (St. Louis, 1962). Vol. I of the Twickenham Edition, containing the *Essay on Criticism*, appeared in 1961 (see below, suppl. to p. 921).

844 Donald M. Foerster, *Homer in English Criticism: The Historical Approach in the Eighteenth Century* (New Haven, 1947); Douglas Duncan, *Thomas Ruddiman: A Study in Scottish Scholarship of the Early Eighteenth Century* (1965).

845 Gildon and others: Corbyn Morris' *Essay towards fixing the True Standards of Wit, Humour, Raillery, Satire, and Ridicule . . .* (1744) appeared as No. 10 of the *ARS*, with an Introduction by James L. Clifford (1947); Part 1 of Bysshe's *Art of English Poetry* as No. 40, with an Introduction by A. Dwight Culler (1953); and John Oldmixon's *Essay on Criticism* (1728) as Nos. 107/8), with an Introduction by R. J. Madden, C.S.B. (1964); H. Rossiter Smith, "Matthew Green, 1696-1737," *N&Q*, CXCIX (1954). 250-253, 284-287. See also Paul Fussell, Jr., *Theory of Prosody in Eighteenth-Century England* (New London, Conn., 1954); Beate Wackwitz, *Die Theorie des Prosastils im England des 18. Jahrhunderts* (Hamburg, 1962).

III. Defoe and Journalism

847 Ian Watt, "Publishers and Sinners: The Augustan View," *Stud. in Bibliography*, XII (1958). 3-20.

848 Rodney M. Baine, "The Apparition of Mrs. Veal: A Neglected Account," *PMLA*, LXIX (1954). 523-541, and "Defoe and Mrs. Bargrave's Story," *PQ*, XXXIII (1954). 388-395 (both articles reviewed by Arthur W. Secord in *PQ*, XXXIV (1955). 282); Arthur H. Scouten, "An Early Printed Report on the Apparition of Mrs. Veal," *RES*, n.s. VI (1955). 259-263; Arthur W. Secord, "A September Day in Canterbury: The Veal-Bargrave Story," *JEGP*, LIV (1955). 639-650; Arthur H. Scouten, "At that Moment of Time: Defoe and the Early Accounts of the Apparition of Mistress Veal," *Ball State Teachers College Forum*, II, No. 2 (1961/2), pp. 44-51; Rodney M. Baine, "Daniel Defoe and *The History and Reality of Apparitions,*" *Proc. Amer. Philos. Soc.*, CVI (1962). 335-347.

849 For surveys of Defoe scholarship see the articles by Gerhard Jacob in *Wissenschaftliche Zeitschrift der Karl-Marx-Universität Leipzig (Gesellschafts— und sprachwiss. Reihe,* Heft 5), IV (1954/55). 517-526, and *Archiv,* CXCVII (1960). 126-35. For Defoe bibliography see John Robert Moore, *A Checklist of* *the Writings of Daniel Defoe* (Bloomington, Ind., 1960) and reviews of this by William B. Todd in *Book-Collector,* x (1961). 493-494, 497-498, and by James Sutherland in *Library,* xvii (1963). 323-325. *Meditations,* ed. George H. Healey (Cummington, Mass., 1946); *An Essay on the Regulation of the Press,* ed. John Robert Moore (Oxford, 1948); *Letters,* ed. George H. Healey (Oxford, 1955) (cf. review by A. W. Secord in *MP,* liv (1955). 45-52). See also Bonamy Dobrée, "Some Aspects of Defoe's Prose," *Sherburn Festschrift* (Oxford, 1949), pp. 171-184; William Freeman, *The Incredible Defoe* (1950); Francis Watson, *Daniel Defoe* (1952); Benjamin Boyce, "The Question of Emotion in Defoe," *SP,* l (1953). 45-58; Brian Fitzgerald, *Daniel Defoe: A Study in Conflict* (1954); Spiro Peterson, "Defoe's Yorkshire Quarrel," *HLQ,* xix (1955). 57-79; John Robert Moore, *Daniel Defoe: Citizen of the Modern World* (Chicago, 1958); Arthur W. Secord, *"Robert Drury's Journal" and Other Studies* (Urbana, 1961); Maximillian E. Novak, *Economics and the Fiction of Daniel Defoe* (Berkeley, 1962) and *Defoe and the Nature of Man* (1963); John Robert Moore, "Daniel Defoe: Precursor of Samuel Richardson," *McKillop Festschrift* (Chicago, 1963), pp. 351-369; Richard Gerber, "Zur Namengebung bei Defoe," *Festschrift für Walter Hübner* (Berlin, 1964), pp. 227-233; Maximillian E. Novak, "Defoe's Theory of Fiction," *SP,* lxi (1964). 650-668; G. A. Starr, *Defoe & Spiritual Autobiography* (Princeton, 1965).

850 Godfrey Davies, "Daniel Defoe's *A Tour thro' the Whole Island of Great Britain,*" *MP,* xlviii (1950). 21-36.

852 On *The Review* see the three books by William L. Payne: *Mr. Review: Daniel Defoe as Author of the "Review"* (1947); *Index to Defoe's Review* (1948); *The Best of Defoe's "Review": An Anthology* (1951).

853 *Robinson Crusoe:* Edward D. Seeber, "Oroonoko and Crusoe's Man Friday," *MLQ,* xii (1951). 286-291; Ian Watt, *"Robinson Crusoe as a Myth,"* *EIC,* i (1951). 95-119; Dewey Ganzel, "Chronology in *Robinson Crusoe,*" *PQ,* xl (1961). 495-512; Maximillian E. Novak, "Crusoe the King and the Political Evolution of his Island," *SEL,* ii (1962). 337-350; J. Paul Hunter, "Friday as a Convert: Defoe and the Accounts of Indian Missionaries," *RES,* n.s. xiv (1963). 243-248; Maximillian E. Novak, "Robinson Crusoe and Economic Utopia," *Kenyon Rev.* xxv (1963). 474-490; William H. Halewood, "Religion and Invention in *Robinson Crusoe,*" *EIC,* xiv (1964). 339-351.—*Captain Singleton:* Gary J. Scrimgeour, "The Problem of Realism in Defoe's *Captain Singleton,*" *HLQ,* xxvii (1963). 21-37.—*Moll Flanders:* Terence Martin, "The Unity of *Moll Flanders,*" *MLQ,* xxii (1961). 115-124; Robert R. Columbus, "Conscious Artistry in *Moll Flanders,*" *SEL,* iii (1963). 415-432; Denis Donoghue, "The Values of *Moll Flanders,*" *Sewanee Rev.,* lxxi (1963). 287-303; Howard L. Koonce, "Moll's Muddle: Defoe's Use of Irony in *Moll Flanders,*" *ELH,* xxx (1963). 377-394; Arnold Kettle, "In Defence of *Moll Flanders,*" *Of Books and Humankind: Essays and Poems presented to Bonamy Dobrée* (1964), pp. 55-67; Maximillian E. Novak, "Conscious Irony in *Moll Flanders,*" *College English,* xxvi (1964). 198-204.—*Journal of the Plague Year:* Ernst Gerhard Jacob, "Die medizingeschichtliche Bedeutung des Robinsondichters," *Die Medizinische Welt,* i (1962). 1-20; F. Bastian, "Defoe's *Journal of the Plague Year* Reconsidered," *RES,* n.s. xvi (1965). 151-173.—*Colonel Jacque:* There is an ed. by Samuel H. Monk (1965);

William H. McBurney, "Colonel Jacque: Defoe's Definition of the Complete Gentleman," *SEL,* II (1962). 321-336.—*Roxana,* ed. with Introduction by Jane Jack (1964); Spiro Peterson, "The Matrimonial Theme of Defoe's *Roxana*," *PMLA,* LXX (1955). 166-191.

855 The Picaresque Tradition: Robert Alter, *Rogue's Progress: Studies in ;he Picaresque Novel* (Cambridge, Mass., 1964).

IV. Jonathan Swift

857 Scholarship on Swift is surveyed critically in Milton Voigt's *Swift and the Twentieth Century* (Detroit, 1964), which also contains an introductory chapter on "Nineteenth-Century Views." See also Harold Williams' essay, "Swift's Early Biographers," *Sherburn Festschrift* (Oxford, 1949), pp. 114-128. H. Teerink's *Bibliography of the Writings of Jonathan Swift* has now appeared in a second edition, revised and corrected, by Arthur H. Scouten (Philadelphia, 1963), reviewed by George P. Mayhew in *PQ,* XLIII (1964). 394-396. The Guthkelch-Nichol Smith edition of the *Tale of a Tub* has appeared in a revised edition (Oxford, 1958). Herbert Davis has edited the *Prose Works* (Oxford, 1939-1962) in 13 volumes, with an index volume to follow. A second edition of the *Poems,* ed. by Sir Harold Williams was published in 1958; in the same year the *Collected Poems,* ed. Joseph Horrell, appeared in the *Muses' Library* (2v). Other important editions: the *Journal to Stella,* ed. Harold Williams (2v, Oxford, 1948); *An Enquiry into the Behaviour of the Queen's Last Ministry,* ed. Irvin Ehrenpreis (Bloomington, Ind., 1956); *Swift's Polite Conversation,* ed. Eric Partridge (1963); and the *Correspondence,* ed. Sir Harold Williams (5v, Oxford, 1963-65).

Vol. 1 of *Swift: The Man, his Works, and the Age,* by Irvin Ehrenpreis (the standard life), was published in 1962. Among general studies may be cited: F. R. Leavis, "The Irony of Swift" in *The Common Pursuit* (1952); John M. Bullitt, *Jonathan Swift and the Anatomy of Satire* (Cambridge, Mass., 1953); Martin Price, *Swift's Rhetorical Art* (New Haven, 1953); William B. Ewald, Jr., *The Masks of Jonathan Swift* (Cambridge, Mass., 1954); Louis A. Landa, *Swift and the Church of Ireland* (Oxford, 1954); J. Middleton Murry, *Jonathan Swift* (1954); R. Quintana, *Swift: An Introduction* (1955); Irvin Ehrenpreis, *The Personality of Jonathan Swift* (1958); Kathleen Williams, *Jonathan Swift and the Age of Compromise* (Lawrence, Kans., 1958); Oliver W. Ferguson, *Jonathan Swift and Ireland* (Urbana, 1962); Edward W. Rosenheim, Jr., *Swift and the Satirist's Art* (Chicago, 1963); Herbert Davis, *Jonathan Swift: Essays on his Satire and Other Studies* [contains *Stella, The Satire of Jonathan Swift,* and shorter reprinted pieces] (1964).

859 James L. Clifford, "Swift's *Mechanical Operation of the Spirit,*" *Sherburn Festschrift* (Oxford, 1949), pp. 135-146; Miriam K. Starkman, *Swift's Satire on Learning in "A Tale of a Tub"* (Princeton, 1950); Robert C. Elliott, "Swift's *Tale of a Tub:* An Essay in Problems of Structure," *PMLA,* LXVI (1951). 441-455; Harold D. Kelling, "Reason in Madness: *A Tale of a Tub,*" *PMLA,* LXIX (1954). 198-222; Ronald Paulson, *Theme and Structure in Swift's "Tale of a Tub"* (New Haven, 1960); Phillip Harth, *Swift and Anglican Ra-*

tionalism: The Religious Background of "A Tale of a Tub" (Chicago, 1961); Curtis C. Smith, "Metaphor Structure in Swift's *A Tale of a Tub*," *Thoth*, v (1964). 22-41; Ricardo Quintana, "Emile Pons and the Modern Study of Swift's *Tale of a Tub*," *Études anglaises*, XVIII (1965). 5-17; William J. Roscelli, "*A Tale of a Tub* and the 'Cavils of the Sour,'" *JEGP*, LXIV (1965). 41-56.

860 On the Bickerstaff pamphlets see George P. Mayhew, "The Early Life of John Partridge," *SEL*, I (1961). 31-42; Richmond P. Bond, "John Partridge and the Company of Stationers," *Stud. in Bibliography*, XVI (1963). 61-80; George P. Mayhew, "Swift's Bickerstaff Hoax as an April Fools' Joke," *MP*, LXI (1964). 270-280.

860 On Swift's pamphleteering 1708-14: J. Béranger, "Swift en 1714: position politique et sentiments personnels," *Études anglaises*, XV (1962). 233-247; and the articles by Richard I. Cook: "The 'Several Ways of Abusing One Another,'" *Speech Monographs*, XXIX (1962). 260-273; "Swift as a Tory Rhetorician," *Texas Stud. in Lit. and Lang.* IV (1962). 72-86; "The Uses of *Saeva Indignatio*," *SEL*, II (1962). 287-307; "The Audience of Swift's Tory Tracts, 1710-1714," *MLQ*, XXIV (1963). 31-41; "Swift's Polemical Characters," *Discourse*, VI (1962-3). 30-38, 43-48.

861 Swift's helpers on the *Examiner*: Gwendolyn B. Needham, "Mary de la Rivière Manley: Tory Defender," *HLQ*, XII (1949). 253-288, and "Mrs. Manley: An Eighteenth-Century Wife of Bath," *HLQ*, XIV (1951). 259-284; Robert J. Allen, "William Oldisworth: 'the Author of *The Examiner*,'" *PQ*, XXVI (1947). 159-180.

862 Irvin Ehrenpreis, "Swift's 'Little Language' in the *Journal to Stella*," *SP*, XLV (1948). 80-88.

864 Among the numerous (and frequently controversial) items on *Gulliver* may be cited: Harold Williams, *The Text of "Gulliver's Travels"* (Cambridge, 1952); Paul O. Clark, "A *Gulliver* Dictionary," *SP*, L (1953). 592-624; Ellen D. Leyburn, *Satiric Allegory: Mirror of Man* (New Haven, 1956); Irvin Ehrenpreis, "The Origins of *Gulliver's Travels*," *PMLA*, LXXII (1957). 880-899; George Sherburn, "Errors concerning the Houyhnhnms," *MP*, LVI (1958). 92-97; Edward Wasiolek, "Relativity in *Gulliver's Travels*," *PQ*, XXXVII (1958). 110-116; Pierre Danchin, "The Text of *Gulliver's Travels*," *Texas Stud. in Lit. and Lang.*, II (1960). 233-250; R. S. Crane, "The Rationale of the Fourth Voyage," in *Gulliver's Travels*, ed. Robert A. Greenberg (1961), pp. 300-307, and "The Houyhnhnms, the Yahoos, and the History of Ideas," *Nicolson Festschrift* (1962), pp. 231-253; W. B. Carnochan, "The Complexity of Swift: Gulliver's Fourth Voyage," *SP*, LX (1963). 23-44, and "*Gulliver's Travels*: An Essay on the Human Understanding?" *MLQ*, XXV (1964). 5-21; E. Pons, "Gulliver ou l'Utopie-Bouffe: les 'Voyages travestis' d'un philosophe du moi," *Carré Festschrift* (Paris, 1964), pp. 429-439.

866 On the poems: Herbert Davis, "A Modest Defence of 'The Lady's Dressing Room,'" *McKillop Festschrift* (Chicago, 1963), pp. 39-48; Barry Slepian, "The Ironic Intention of Swift's Verses on his own Death," *RES*, n.s. XIV (1963). 249-256; Marshall Waingrow, "*Verses on the Death of Dr. Swift*," *SEL*, v (1965). 513-518.

867 On Vanessa: Sybil Le Brocquy, *Cadenus: A Reassessment in the Light*

of New Evidence of the Relationships between Swift, Stella and Vanessa (Dublin, 1963), on which see the review by E. Pons in *Études anglaises*, XVI (1963). 187-188; Peter Ohlin, " 'Cadenus and Vanessa': Reason and Passion," *SEL*, IV (1964). 485-496.

V. Addison, Steele, and the Periodical Essay

870 On the Periodical Essay see Melvin R. Watson, *Magazine Serials and the Essay Tradition, 1746-1820* (Baton Rouge, 1956), and Richmond P. Bond, Introduction to *Studies in the Early English Periodical* (Chapel Hill, 1957). The last-named contains six essays on eighteenth-century periodicals: Robert W. Achurch, "Richard Steele, Gazeteer and Bickerstaff"; William F. Belcher, "The Sale and Distribution of the *British Apollo*"; Nicholas Joost, "The Authorship of the *Free Thinker*"; W. O. S. Sutherland, Jr., "Essay Forms in the *Prompter*"; James Hodges, "The *Female Spectator*, a Courtesy Periodical"; and George P. Winship, Jr., "The Printing History of the *World*."

871 Rae Blanchard has ably edited *The Occasional Verse of Richard Steele* (Oxford, 1952) as well as *The Englishman: A Political Journal* (Oxford, 1955) and *Richard Steele's Periodical Journalism, 1714-16: The Lover, The Reader, Town-Talk* (Oxford, 1959). *The Theatre, 1720*, has been edited by John Loftis (Oxford, 1962). For *The Spectator* see below, suppl. to p. 875. On Steele see also: John Loftis, *Steele at Drury Lane* (Berkeley, 1952); Rae Blanchard, "Richard Steele and the Secretary of the S.P.C.K.," *McKillop Festschrift* (Chicago, 1963), pp. 287-295; Calhoun Winton, *Captain Steele: The Early Career of Richard Steele* (Baltimore, 1964).

872 Robert D. Horn, "Addison's *Campaign* and Macaulay" *PMLA*, LXIII (1948). 886-902, and "The Early Editions of Addison's *Campaign*," *Stud. in Bibliography*, III (1950/1). 256-261; Lillian D. Bloom, "Addison as Translator," *SP*, XLVI (1949). 31-53; Edward A. and Lillian D. Bloom, "Addison's 'Enquiry after Truth,'" *PMLA*, LXV (1950). 198-220; J. Lannering, *Studies in the Prose Style of Joseph Addison* (Uppsala, 1951); Peter Smithers, *The Life of Joseph Addison* (Oxford, 1954); Edward A. and Lillian D. Bloom, "Addison on 'Moral Habits of the Mind,'" *JHI*, XXI (1960), 409-427; Jean Wilkinson, "Some Aspects of Addison's Philosophy of Art," *HLQ*, XXVIII (1964). 31-44; John C. Stephens, Jr., "Addison as Social Critic," *Emory Univ. Quar.* XXI (1965). 157-172.

873 William B. Todd, "Early Editions of *The Tatler*," *Stud. in Bibliography*, XV (1962). 121-133; Donald F. Bond, "Armand de la Chapelle and the First French Version of the *Tatler*," *McKillop Festschrift* (Chicago, 1963), pp. 161-184; Richmond P. Bond, "Isaac Bickerstaff, Esq.," *Ibid.*, pp. 103-124, and "The Pirate and the *Tatler*," *Library*, XVIII (1963). 257-274. On the *Tatler* and *Spectator* Fritz Rau has two important articles: "Texte, Ausgaben und Verfasser des 'Tatler,' und 'Spectator': Forschungsbericht," *Germanisch-Romanische Monatsschrift*, VIII (1958). 126-144, and "Zur Gestalt des 'Tatler' und 'Spectator': Kritischer Bericht," *Ibid.*, X (1960). 401-419.

875 *The Spectator*, ed. Donald F. Bond (5v, Oxford, 1965). See also Robert D. Chambers, "Addison at Work on the *Spectator*," *MP*, LVI (1959). 145-153.

879 On continuators and imitators of the *Tatler* see Robert C. Elliott, "Swift's 'little' Harrison, Poet and Continuator of the *Tatler*," *SP*, XLIV (1949). 544-559; John Harrington Smith, "Thomas Baker and the *Female Tatler*," *MP*, XLIX (1952). 182-188.

881 *The True Patriot* of Fielding: Facsimile Text, ed. Miriam A. Locke (University, Ala., 1964).—*The Champion*: The 13 "Job Vinegar" essays comprise No. 67 of the *ARS*, with Introduction by S. J. Sackett (1958). See also William B. Coley, "The 'Remarkable Queries' in the *Champion*," *PQ*, XLI (1962). 426-436; John B. Shipley, "A New Fielding Essay from the *Champion*," *PQ*, XLII (1963). 417-422; "Henry Fielding's 'Defense of the Stage Licensing Act," *ELN*, II (1965). 193-96.

VI. The Drama, 1700-1740

883 Parts 2 and 3 of *The London Stage* (see above, suppl. to p. 748) are of first importance here: Part 2, *1700-1729*, ed. Emmett L. Avery (2v, 1960); Part 3, *1729-1747*, ed. A. H. Scouten (2v, 1961). See further Charles B. Hogan, *Shakespeare in the Theatre, 1701-1800: A Record of Performances in London* (2v, Oxford, 1952-57); Richard Southern, *Changeable Scenery: Its Origin and Development in the British Theatre* (1952); F. S. Boas, *An Introduction to Eighteenth-Century Drama, 1700-1780* (Oxford, 1953); James J. Lynch, *Box, Pit, and Gallery: Stage and Society in Johnson's London* (Berkeley, 1953); George Speaight, *The History of the English Puppet Theatre* (1955); George C. Branam, *Eighteenth-Century Adaptations of Shakespearean Tragedy* (Berkeley, 1956); Leo Hughes, *A Century of English Farce* (Princeton, 1956); John Loftis, *Comedy and Society from Congreve to Fielding* (Stanford, 1959), and *The Politics of Drama in Augustan England* (Oxford, 1963); William S. Clark, *The Irish Stage in the County Towns, 1720-1800* (Oxford, 1965).

884 On Sentimental Comedy (and Tragedy) see Lewis M. Magill, "Poetic Justice: The Dilemma of the Early Creators of Sentimental Tragedy," *Research Stud. of the State College of Washington*, xxv (1957). 24-32; Arthur Sherbo, *English Sentimental Drama* (East Lansing, Mich., 1957); Richard H. Tyre, "Versions of Poetic Justice in the Early Eighteenth Century," *SP*, LIV (1957). 29-44; Paul E. Parnell, "The Sentimental Mask," *PMLA*, LXXVIII (1963). 529-535.

885 Paul E. Parnell, "Equivocation in Cibber's *Love's Last Shift*," *SP*, LVII (1960). 519-534; Albert E. Karlson, "The Chronicles in Cibber's *Richard III*," *SEL*, III (1963). 253-267. Leonard R. N. Ashley, *Colley Cibber* (1965).

886 Rae Blanchard, "The Songs in Steele's Plays," *Sherburn Festschrift* (Oxford, 1949), pp. 185-200.

889 Mrs. Centlivre: John W. Bowyer, *The Celebrated Mrs. Centlivre* (Durham, N.C., 1952); J. E. Norton, "Some Uncollected Authors. XIV: Susanna Centlivre," *Book-Collector*, VI (1957). 172-178, 280-285.—Fielding's Plays: L. P. Goggin, "Development of Techniques in Fielding's Comedies," *PMLA*, LXVII (1952). 769-781, and "Fielding and the *Select Comedies of Mr. de Moliere*," *PQ*, XXXI (1952). 344-350; Sheridan Baker, "Political Allusion in Fielding's *Author's Farce, Mock Doctor*, and *Tumble-Down Dick*," *PMLA*, LXXVII (1962).

221-231; Edgar V. Roberts, "Henry Fielding's Lost Play *Deborah, or A Wife for You All* (1733)," *Bull. N.Y. Public Library*, LXVI (1962). 576-588; and articles by Charles B. Woods: "The 'Miss Lucy' Plays of Fielding and Garrick," *PQ*, XLI (1962). 294-310; "Cibber in Fielding's *Author's Farce*," *PQ*, XLIV (1965). 145-151; "Theobald and Fielding's 'Don Tragedio,'" *ELN*, II (1965). 266-271.

891　Edgar V. Roberts, "Fielding's Ballad Opera *The Lottery* (1732) and the English State Lottery of 1731," *HLQ*, XXVII (1963). 39-52.

893　Alfred Schwarz, "An Example of Eighteenth-Century Pathetic Tragedy: Rowe's *Jane Shore*," *MLQ*, XXII (1961). 236-247; Lindley A. Wyman, "The Tradition of the Formal Meditation in Rowe's *The Fair Penitent*," *PQ*, XLII (1963). 412-416.

894　Paul E. Parnell, "*The Distrest Mother*, Ambrose Philips' Morality Play," *CL*, XI (1959). 111-123.

895　John Robert Moore, "Hughes's Source for *The Siege of Damascus*," *HLQ*, XXI (1958). 362-366.

896　*Le Marchand de Londres:* Edition critique, traduction, préface et notes de J. Hamard (Paris, 1962); *The London Merchant*, ed. W. H. McBurney (Lincoln, Nebr., 1965). Lawrence M. Price, "George Barnwell Abroad," *CL*, II (1950). 126-156.

VII. Traditions in Early Eighteenth-Century Poetry

898　James Sutherland, *A Preface to Eighteenth-Century Poetry* (Oxford, 1948), the best general treatment of the subject; Bonamy Dobrée, *The Theme of Patriotism in the Poetry of the Early Eighteenth Century* (1949); Donald J. Greene, "'Logical Structure' in Eighteenth-Century Poetry," *PQ*, XXXI (1952). 315-336; Norman Maclean, "From Action to Image: Theories of the Lyric in the Eighteenth Century," *Critics and Criticism* (Chicago, 1952), pp. 408-460; W. K. Wimsatt, Jr., "The Augustan Mode in English Poetry," *ELH*, XX (1953). 1-14; Geoffrey Tillotson, *Augustan Poetic Diction* (1964) (four chapters, reprinted with corrections from Tillotson's *Augustan Studies*, 1961).

899　Satire: Ian Jack, *Augustan Satire: Intention and Idiom in English Poetry, 1660-1750* (Oxford, 1952); Bertrand A. Goldgar, "Satires on Man and 'The Dignity of Human Nature,'" *PMLA*, LXXX (1965). 535-541; Alvin B. Kernan, *The Plot of Satire* (New Haven, 1965) discusses Dryden, Gay, Swift, and Pope; Howard D. Weinbrot, "The Pattern of Formal Verse Satire in the Restoration and the Eighteenth Century," *PMLA*, LXXX (1965). 394-401.—Blackmore: Richard C. Boys, *Sir Richard Blackmore and the Wits* (Ann Arbor, 1949); Albert Rosenberg, *Sir Richard Blackmore* (Lincoln, Nebr., 1953); W. J. Cameron, "The Authorship of 'Commendatory Verses,' 1700," *N&Q*, CCVIII (1963). 63-66.

900　Pastoral: Thomas Purney's *Full Enquiry into the True Nature of Pastoral* (1717), with Introduction by Earl R. Wasserman (1948; *ARS*, No. 11). See also J. E. Congleton, *Theories of Pastoral Poetry in England, 1684-1798* (Gainesville, Fla., 1952) and review of this by L. P. Goggin in *MP*, LI (1953). 137-140; Dorothy S. McCoy, *Tradition and Convention: A Study of Periphrasis in English Pastoral Poetry from 1557-1715* (The Hague, 1965).

901   Aaron Hill's Preface to *The Creation* has been reproduced by the *ARS* (No. 18), with an Introduction by Gretchen Graf Pahl (1949).

902   On Ramsay's possible share in the *Collection of Old Ballads* see Albert B. Friedman, *The Ballad Revival* (Chicago, 1961), chap. v. Ramsay's *Works* have been edited: Vols. I, II, ed. Burns Martin and John W. Oliver (Edinburgh, 1951-3); Vol. III (*Poems: Miscellaneous and Uncollected*), ed. Alexander Kinghorn and Alexander Law (Edinburgh, 1963).

904   Harry Escott, *Isaac Watts, Hymnographer: A Study of the Beginnings, Development, and Philosophy of the English Hymn* (1962); Peter B. Steese, "Dennis's Influence on Watts's Preface to *Horae Lyricae*," *PQ*, XLII (1963). 275-277.

908   W. J. Cameron, "Two New Poems by Ambrose Philips (1674-1749)," *N&Q*, CCII (1957), 469-470.—Welsted: Daniel A. Fineman, *Leonard Welsted, Gentleman Poet of the Augustan Age* (Philadelphia, 1950).—Prior: *The Literary Works of Matthew Prior*, ed. H. Bunker Wright and Monroe K. Spears (2v, Oxford, 1959); cf. review by Maynard Mack in *Sewanee Rev.*, LXVIII (1960). 165-176. See also the articles by Spears: "Matthew Prior's Attitude toward Natural Science," *PMLA*, LXIII (1948), 485-507; "Matthew Prior's Religion," *PQ*, XXVII (1948). 159-180; "Some Ethical Aspects of Matthew Prior's Poetry," *SP*, XLV (1948), 606-629.

914   Additional Poet: William Diaper. *The Complete Works of William Diaper*, ed. Dorothy Broughton (1951).

VIII. Pope and His Group

916   Phyllis Freeman, "William Walsh and Dryden: Recently Discovered Letters," *RES*, XXIV (1948). 195-202, and "Two Fragments of Walsh Manuscripts," *RES*, n.s. VIII (1957). 390-401.

917   *Memoirs of the Extraordinary Life, Works, and Discoveries of Martinus Scriblerus*, ed. Charles Kerby-Miller (New Haven, 1950); Robert A. Erickson, "Situations of Identity in the *Memoirs of Martinus Scriblerus*," *MLQ*, XXVI (1965). 388-400.

918   Gay: *The Present State of Wit* (1711) was reproduced as No. 7 of the *ARS*, with Introduction by Donald F. Bond (1947). Two editions of *Three Hours after Marriage* (by Gay, Pope, and Arbuthnot) were published in 1961, one by Richard Morton and William M. Peterson (Painesville, Ohio) and the other by John Harrington Smith (*ARS*, Nos. 91-92). Both are reviewed by Curt A. Zimansky in *PQ*, XLI (1962). 593-595. See also James Sutherland, "John Gay," *Sherburn Festschrift* (Oxford, 1949), pp. 201-214; Sven M. Armens, *John Gay, Social Critic* (1954); John M. Aden, "The 1720 Version of *Rural Sports* and the Georgic Tradition," *MLQ*, XX (1959). 228-232; William D. Ellis, Jr., "Thomas D'Urfey, the Pope-Philips Quarrel, and *The Shepherd's Week*," *PMLA*, LXXIV (1959). 203-212; John Fuller, "Cibber, *The Rehearsal at Goatham*, and the Suppression of *Polly*," *RES*, n.s. XIII (1962). 125-134; C. F. Burgess,

"The Ambivalent Point of View in John Gay's *Trivia,*" *Cithara,* IV (1964). 53-65; Adina Forsgren, *John Gay, Poet "of a Lower Order": Comments on his Rural Poems and Other Early Writings* (Stockholm, 1964), and "Some Complimentary Epistles by John Gay," *Studia Neophil.* XXXVI (1964). 82-100; Bertrand H. Bronson, "The True Proportions of Gay's *Acis and Galatea,*" *PMLA,* LXXX (1965). 325-331; Patricia M. Spacks, *John Gay* (1965).

921 The Twickenham edition (6v in 7, Oxford, 1939-61) is now complete, except for the translations of Homer which are to be added. Some of the volumes have appeared in revised editions, and there is a one volume edition of the Twickenham text with selected annotations ed. by John Butt (1963). Another major edition is the *Correspondence,* ed. George Sherburn (5v, Oxford, 1956): reviews by Donald F. Bond in *MP,* LVI (1958). 55-59; by John Butt in *N&Q,* CCII (1957). 463-466; by Maynard Mack in *PQ,* XXXVI (1957). 389-399; by Robert W. Rogers in *JEGP,* LVI (1957). 615-619. Additional letters, chiefly to Sir William Trumbull, were published by Sherburn in *RES,* n.s. IX (1958). 388-406. A critical edition by Edna L. Steeves of *The Art of Sinking in Poetry* appeared in 1952. For criticism see Norman Ault, *New Light on Pope* (1949), with review by George Sherburn in *RES,* n.s. II (1951). 84-86; Maynard Mack, " 'Wit and Poetry and Pope': Some Observations on his Imagery," *Sherburn Festschrift* (Oxford, 1949), pp. 20-40; " 'The Shadowy Cave': Some Speculations on a Twickenham Grotto," *McKillop Festschrift* (Chicago, 1963), pp. 69-88; "A Poet in his Landscape: Pope at Twickenham," *Pottle Festschrift* (1965). pp. 3-29; and "*Secretum Iter*: Some Uses of Retirement Literature in the Poetry of Pope," in *Aspects of the Eighteenth Century,* ed. Earl R. Wasserman (Baltimore, 1965), pp. 207-243; Agnes M. Sibley, *Alexander Pope's Prestige in America, 1725-1835* (1949); George Sherburn, "Pope and 'the Great Shew of Nature',*" Jones Festschrift* (Stanford, 1951), pp. 306-315; John Butt, "Pope's Poetical Manuscripts," *Proc. Brit. Acad.* XL (1954). 23-39; Rebecca P. Parkin, *The Poetic Workmanship of Alexander Pope* (Minneapolis, 1955); Robert W. Rogers, *The Major Satires of Alexander Pope* (Urbana, 1955); Malcolm Goldstein, *Pope and the Augustan Stage* (Stanford, 1958); Goeffrey Tillotson, *Pope and Human Nature* (Oxford, 1958); Reuben A. Brower, *Alexander Pope: The Poetry of Allusion* (Oxford, 1959); Benjamin Boyce, *The Character Sketches in Pope's Poems* (Durham, N.C., 1962) and "Mr. Pope, in Bath, Improves the Design of his Grotto," *McKillop Festschrift* (Chicago, 1963), pp. 143-153; Thomas R. Edwards, Jr., *This Dark Estate: A Reading of Pope* (Berkeley, 1963); Jacob H. Adler, *The Reach of Art: A Study in the Prosody of Pope* (Gainesville, Fla., 1964); Peter Dixon, " 'Talking upon Paper': Pope and Eighteenth Century Conversation," *ES,* XLVI (1965). 36-44; Donald J. Greene, " 'Dramatic Texture' in Pope," *Pottle Festschrift* (1965), pp. 31-53; W. K. Wimsatt, Jr., *The Portraits of Alexander Pope* (New Haven, 1965).

922 Robert M. Schmitz, *Pope's "Windsor Forest," 1712: A Study of the Washington University Holograph* (St. Louis, 1952); Earl R. Wasserman, *The Subtler Language* (1959), chap. IV.

923 Aubrey Williams, "The 'Fall' of China and *The Rape of the Lock,*" *PQ,* XLI (1962). 412-425; L. P. Goggin, "La Caverne aux Vapeurs," *PQ,* XLII (1963). 404-411.

924 Douglas Knight, *Pope and the Heroic Tradition: A Critical Study of his "Iliad"* (New Haven, 1951); Norman Callan, "Pope's *Iliad:* A New Document," *RES,* n.s. IV (1953). 109-121 [the proof-sheets of Books I-VIII, with Pope's corrections]; R. Sühnel, *Homer und die englische Humanität* (Tübingen, 1958); R. M. Schmitz, "The 'Arsenal' Proof Sheets of Pope's Iliad: A Third Report," *MLN,* LXXIV (1959). 486-489.

925 Theobald's Preface to Shakespeare forms No. 20 of the *ARS,* with an Introduction by Hugh G. Dick (1949). See also P. Dixon, "Pope's Shakespeare," *JEGP,* LXIII (1964). 191-203.

926 Aubrey L. Williams, *Pope's "Dunciad": A Study of its Meaning* (1955); Charles D. Peavy, "The Pope-Cibber Controversy: A Bibliography," *Restoration and 18th Century Theatre Research,* III (1964). 51-55.
On the "Moral Essays" see H. C. Collins Baker and Muriel I. Baker, *The Life and Circumstances of James Brydges, First Duke of Chandos* (Oxford, 1949); Earl R. Wasserman, *Pope's "Epistle to Bathurst": A Critical Reading with an Edition of the Manuscripts* (Baltimore, 1960).

928 *An Essay on Man: Reproduction of the Manuscripts in the Pierpont Morgan Library and the Houghton Library, with the Printed Text of the Original Edition,* with Introduction by Maynard Mack (1962; *Roxburgh Club*); Robert W. Rogers, "Critiques of the 'Essay on Man' in France and Germany, 1736-1755," *ELH,* xv (1948). 176-193, and "Alexander Pope's *Universal Prayer,*" *JEGP,* LIV (1955). 612-624; Ernest Tuveson, "*An Essay on Man* and 'The Way of Ideas,' " *ELH,* xxvi (1959). 368-386; F. E. L. Priestley, "Pope and the Great Chain of Being," *Woodhouse Festschrift* (Toronto, 1964), pp. 213-228.

929 Maynard Mack, "The Muse of Satire," *Yale Rev.,* XLI (1951). 80-92 (repr. in *Studies in the Literature of the Augustan Age,* ed. R. C. Boys [1952]); Aubrey L. Williams, "Pope and Horace: The Second Epistle of the Second Book," *McKillop Festschrift* (Chicago, 1963), pp. 309-321; Thomas E. Maresca, "Pope's Defense of Satire: The First Satire of the Second Book of Horace, Imitated," *ELH,* xxxi (1964). 336-394.

930 *The Nonsense of Common-Sense, 1737-1738,* ed. Robert Halsband (Evanston, 1947). See also Robert Halsband, *The Life of Lady Mary Wortley Montagu* (Oxford, 1956) and "Lady Mary Wortley Montagu as Letter Writer," *PLMA,* LXXX (1965). 155-163. Professor Halsband is editing Lady Mary's correspondence. (Vol. I, covering the years 1708-1720, has appeared [Oxford, 1965]).

IX. New Voices in Poetry

933 John Arthos, *The Language of Natural Description in Eighteenth-Century Poetry* (Ann Arbor, 1949); Bertrand Bronson, "The Pre-Romantic or Post-Augustan Mode [in English Poetry]," *ELH,* xx (1953). 15-28; Chester F. Chapin, *Personification in Eighteenth-Century English Poetry* (1955); Marjorie H. Nicolson, *Mountain Gloom and Mountain Glory: The Development of the Aesthetics of the Infinite* (Ithaca, N.Y., 1959); Patricia M. Spacks, *The Insistence of Horror: Aspects of the Supernatural in Eighteenth-Century Poetry*

(Cambridge, Mass., 1962); Geoffrey Tillotson, "The Methods of Description in Eighteenth- and Nineteenth-Century Poetry," *McKillop Festschrift* (Chicago, 1963), pp. 235-238; Karl Heinz Göller, "Die *Poetic Diction* des 18. Jahrhunderts in England," *Deutsche Viertelpahrsschrift für Literaturwissenschaft und Geistesgeschichte,* xxxviii (1964). 24-39.

934 *The Poetical Works of Richard Savage,* ed. Clarence Tracy (Cambridge, 1962). Professor Tracy is also author of the standard life of Savage (*The Artificial Bastard,* Toronto and Cambridge, Mass., 1953) and an article on the bibliography of Savage (*Book-Collector,* xii [1963]. 340-349). *An Author to be Lett* (1729) is reprinted with Introduction by James Sutherland by the *ARS,* No. 84 (1960).

935 *James Thomson (1700-1748): Letters and Documents,* ed. Alan D. McKillop (Lawrence, Kans., 1958); see also McKillop, "Two More Thomson Letters," *MP,* lx (1962). 128-130. The best general study is Douglas Grant's *James Thomson: Poet of "The Seasons"* (1951).

936 Patricia M. Spacks, *The Varied God: A Critical Study of Thomson's "The Seasons"* (Berkeley, 1959); Ralph Cohen, "Literary Criticism and Artistic Interpretation: Eighteenth-Century English Illustrations of *The Seasons,*" *Nicolson Festschrift* (1962), pp. 279-306; John Chalker, "Thomson's *Seasons* and Virgil's *Georgics,*" *Studia Neophil.* xxxv (1963). 41-56; Ralph Cohen, *The Art of Discrimination: Thomson's "The Seasons" and the Language of Criticism* (Berkeley, 1964).

938 F. E. L. Priestley, "Newton and the Romantic Concept of Nature," *UTQ,* xvii (1948). 323-336; William Powell Jones, "Newton Further Demands the Muse," *SEL,* iii (1963). 287-306 [stresses the *Principia* rather than the *Opticks*].

939 Alan D. McKillop, *The Background of Thomson's "Liberty"* (Houston, 1951).

940 *The Castle of Indolence and Other Poems,* ed. Alan D. McKillop (Lawrence, Kans., 1961). See also William B. Todd, "The Text of *The Castle of Indolence,*" *ES,* xxxiv (1953). 115-121.

942 Ralph M. Williams, *Poet, Painter, and Parson: The Life of John Dyer* (1956).

945 Henry Pettit, "A Check-List of Young's 'Night-Thoughts' in America," *Papers of the Bibl. Soc. of America,* xlii (1948). 150-156 (additions in xliii. 348-349, and xliv. 192-195). Professor Pettit is also author of *A Bibliography of Young's Night-Thoughts* (Boulder, Col., 1954), *The English Rejection of Young's "Night-Thoughts"* (Boulder, 1957), "Edward Young and the Case of *Lee v. D'Aranda,*" *Proc. Amer. Philos. Soc.,* cvii (1963). 145-159, and has in preparation an edition of Young's correspondence. See further C. V. Wicker, *Edward Young and the Fear of Death: A Study in Romantic Melancholy* (Albuquerque, 1952); Catharine K. Firman, "An Unrecorded Poem by Edward Young," *N&Q,* ccviii (1963). 218-219; H. B. Forester, "The Ordination of Edward Young," *ELN,* i (1963). 24-28.

947 Allan D. McKillop, "Nature and Science in the Works of James Hervey," *Univ. of Texas Stud. in English,* xxviii (1949). 124-138.

X. The Mid-Century Novel

950 On the eighteenth-century novel two important surveys have appeared: Alan D. McKillop, *The Early Masters of English Fiction* (Lawrence, Kans., 1956) and Ian Watt, *The Rise of the Novel: Studies in Defoe, Richardson, and Fielding* (Berkeley, 1957). William H. McBurney has published *A Check List of English Prose Fiction, 1700-1739* (Cambridge, Mass., 1960) (additions and corrections by Donald F. Bond in *MP*, LIX (1962). 231-234) and (with assistance of Charlene M. Taylor) a check-list of *English Prose Fiction 1700-1800 in the University of Illinois Library* (Urbana, 1965). He has also edited *Four Before Richardson: Selected English Novels, 1720-1727* (Lincoln, Nebr., 1963), including Mrs. Haywood's *Philidore and Placentia* and Mary Davies' *Accomplished Rake*. See also Robert D. Mayo, *The English Novel in the Magazines, 1740-1815, with a Catalogue of 1375 Magazine Novels and Novelettes* (Evanston, 1962); Sheridan Baker, "The Idea of Romance in the Eighteenth-Century Novel," *Papers of the Michigan Acad.* XLIX (1964). 507-522; Robert B. Pierce, "Moral Education in the Novel of the 1750's," *PQ*, XLIV (1965). 73-87.

951 William H. McBurney, "Mrs. Penelope Aubin and the Early Eighteenth-Century English Novel," *HLQ*, XX (1957). 245-267, and "Edmund Curll, Mrs. Jane Barker, and the English Novel," *PQ*, XXXVII (1958). 385-399.

952 *Selected Letters of Samuel Richardson*, ed. John Carroll (Oxford, 1964). A complete edition of the correspondence is in preparation by T. C. D. Eaves and Ben Kimpel. On Richardson: William M. Sale, Jr., "From *Pamela* to *Clarissa*," *Tinker Festschrift* (New Haven, 1949), pp. 127-138; Frank Kermode, "Richardson and Fielding," *Cambridge Jour.*, IV (1950). 106-114; William M. Sale, Jr., *Samuel Richardson, Master Printer* (Ithaca, N.Y., 1950) (cf. review by A. D. McKillop in *PQ*, XXX (1951). 285-287); T. C. Duncan Eaves, "Graphic Illustrations of the Novels of Samuel Richardson," *HLQ*, XIV (1951). 349-383; Alan D. McKillop, "Epistolary Technique in Richardson's Novels," *Rice Institute Pamphlet*, XXXVIII (1951). 36-54; George Sherburn, "Samuel Richardson's Novels and the Theatre: A Theory Sketched," *PQ*, XLI (1962). 325-329, and "Writing to the Moment: One Aspect," *McKillop Festschrift* (Chicago, 1963), pp. 201-209; John Carroll, "Richardson on Pope and Swift," *UTQ*, XXXIII (1963). 19-29; Morris Golden, *Richardson's Characters* (Ann Arbor, 1963); Leo Hughes, "Theatrical Convention in Richardson: Some Observations on a Novelist's Technique," *McKillop Festschrift* (Chicago, 1963), pp. 239-250.

953 *Pamela*: Richardson's Introduction, omitted in most recent editions, is reproduced as No. 48 of the *ARS*, with Introduction by Sheridan W. Baker, Jr. (1954). See also Robert A. Donovan, "The Problem of Pamela, or, Virtue Unrewarded," *SEL*, III (1963). 377-395; Owen Jenkins, "Richardson's *Pamela* and Fielding's 'Vile Forgeries,'" *PQ*, XLIV (1965). 200-210 [on the second part of *Pamela* as a reply to *Shamela*].

954 *Clarissa, or the History of a Young Lady*, abridged and ed. with an Introduction by George Sherburn (Boston, 1962). Richardson's Preface, "Hints of Prefaces for Clarissa," and Postscript, comprise No. 103 of the *ARS*, with an

Introduction by R. F. Brissenden (1964). See also *Critical Remarks on Sir Charles Grandison, Clarissa and Pamela* (1754) [by Alexander Campbell?], with an Introduction by A. D. McKillop (1950; *ARS*, No. 21); Norman Rabkin, "*Clarissa*: A Study in the Nature of Convention," *ELH*, XXIII (1956). 204-217; William J. Farrell, "The Style and the Action in *Clarissa*," *SEL*, III (1963). 365-375; Christina Van Heyningen, *Clarissa: Poetry and Morals* (Pietermaritzburg, 1963; Mystic, Conn., 1965).

955 E. L. McAdam, Jr., "A New Letter from Fielding," *Yale Rev.*, XXXVIII (1948). 300-310 [to Richardson, on *Clarissa*]; James A. Work, "Henry Fielding, Christian Censor," *Tinker Festschrift* (New Haven, 1949), pp. 139-148; F. Homes Dudden, *Henry Fielding: His Life, Works, and Times* (2v, Oxford, 1952) (rev. by George Sherburn in *Sewanee Rev.*, LXI (1953). 316-321); A. B. Shepperson, "Additions and Corrections to Facts about Fielding," *MP*, LI (1954). 217-224; George Sherburn, "Fielding's Social Outlook," *PQ*, XXXV (1956). 1-23; Maurice Johnson, *Fielding's Art of Fiction* (Philadelphia, 1961); Dietrich Rolle, *Fielding und Sterne: Untersuchungen über die Funktion des Erzählers* (Münster, 1963); Sheldon Sacks, *Fiction and the Shape of Belief: A Study of Henry Fielding, with Glances at Swift, Johnson and Richardson* (Berkeley, 1964); Philip Stevick, "Fielding and the Meaning of History," *PMLA*, LXXIX (1964). 561-568; W. B. Coley, "Fielding's Two Appointments to the Magistracy," *MP*, LXIII (1965). 144-149; Andrew Wright, *Henry Fielding: Mask and Feast* (Berkeley, 1965).

956 *An Apology for the Life of Mrs. Shamela Andrews* has had two recent editions: by Sheridan W. Baker, Jr. (Berkeley, 1953) and by Ian Watt (1956; *ARS*, No. 57).

On *Joseph Andrews* see Martin C. Battestin's *The Moral Basis of Fielding's Art: A Study of "Joseph Andrews"* (Middletown, Conn., 1959) and the same author's articles: "Fielding's Changing Politics and *Joseph Andrews*," *PQ*, XXXIX (1960). 39-55; "Fielding's Revisions of *Joseph Andrews*," *Stud. in Bibliography*, XVI (1963). 81-117; "Lord Hervey's Role in *Joseph Andrews*," *PQ*, XLII (1963). 226-241. See further Homer Goldberg, "Comic Prose Epic or Comic Romance: The Argument of the Preface to *Joseph Andrews*," *PQ*, XLIII (1964). 193-215; J. T. McCullen, "Fielding's Beau Didapper," *ELN*, II (1964). 98-100; Bernard N. Schilling, *The Comic Spirit* (Detroit, 1965) contains two essays on *Joseph Andrews*.

On the *Miscellanies* and *Jonathan Wild*: Bernard Shea, "Machiavelli and Fielding's *Jonathan Wild*," *PMLA*, LXII (1957). 55-73 (cf. review by R. S. Crane in *PQ*, XXXVII (1958). 328-333); Allan Wendt, "The Moral Allegory of *Jonathan Wild*," *ELH*, XXIV (1957). 306-320; Henry Knight Miller, *Essays on Fielding's "Miscellanies": A Commentary on Volume One* (Princeton, 1961); Donald D. Eddy, "The Printing of Fielding's *Miscellanies* (1743)," *Stud. in Bibliography*, XV (1962). 247-256.

On *Tom Jones*: R. S. Crane, "The Plot of *Tom Jones*," *Jour. of General Education*, IV (1950). 112-130 (repr. as "The Concept of Plot and the Plot of *Tom Jones*" in *Critics and Criticism* (Chicago, 1952), pp. 616-647); William Empson, "*Tom Jones*," *Kenyon Rev.*, XX (1958). 217-249; Alan D. McKillop, "Some Recent Views of *Tom Jones*," *College English*, XXI (1959). 17-22; Lyall H. Powers, "*Tom Jones* and Jacob de la Vallée [Marivaux, *Le Paysan parvenu*],"

Papers of the Michigan Acad., xlvii (1962). 659-697; Michael Bliss, "Fielding's Bill of Fare in *Tom Jones*," *ELH*, xxx (1963). 236-243; I. Ehrenpreis, *Fielding: "Tom Jones"* (1964); Oliver W. Ferguson, "Partridge's Vile Encomium: Fielding and Honest Billy Mills," *PQ*, xliii (1964). 73-78; Eleanor N. Hutchens, *Irony in Tom Jones* (University, Ala., 1965).

959 A. R. Towers, "*Amelia* and the State of Matrimony," *RES*, n.s. v (1954). 144-157; John S. Coolidge, "Fielding and 'Conservation of Character,'" *MP*, lvii (1960). 245-259; Arthur Sherbo, "The Time-Scheme in *Amelia*," *Boston Univ. Stud. in English*, iv (1960). 223-228; Allan Wendt, "The Naked Virtue of Amelia," *ELH*, xxvii (1960). 131-148; E. D. H. Johnson, "*Vanity Fair* and *Amelia*," *MP*, lix (1961). 100-113; Sheridan Baker, "Fielding's *Amelia* and the Materials of Romance," *PQ*, xli (1962). 437-449; D. S. Thomas, "The Publication of Henry Fielding's *Amelia*," *Library*, xviii (1963). 303-307, and "Fortune and the Passions in Fielding's *Amelia*," *MLR*, lx (1965). 176-187.

960 *The Journal of a Voyage to Lisbon*, ed. Harold E. Pagliaro (1963).

961 Fred W. Boege, *Smollett's Reputation as a Novelist* (Princeton, 1947); Lewis M. Knapp, *Tobias Smollett: Doctor of Men and Manners* (Princeton, 1949), the standard life; Carmine R. Linsalata, *Smollett's Hoax: "Don Quixote" in English* (Stanford, 1956); cf. review by Lewis M. Knapp in *JEGP*, lvii (1958). 553-555; M. A. Goldberg, *Smollett and the Scottish School* (Albuquerque, 1959); Ronald Paulson, "Satire in the Early Novels of Smollett," *JEGP*, lix (1960). 381-402; C. Aubrun, "Smollet et Cervantès," *Études anglaises*, xv (1962). 122-129; William B. Piper, "The Large Diffused Picture of Life in Smollett's Early Novels," *SP*, lx (1963). 45-56; Donald Bruce, *Radical Doctor Smollett* (1964); Lewis M. Knapp, "Smollett's Translation of Fénelon's *Télémaque*," *PQ*, xliv (1965). 405-407.

962 *Peregrine Pickle*, ed. James L. Clifford (1964). See also Ronald Paulson, "Smollett and Hogarth: The Identity of Pallet," *SEL*, iv (1964). 351-359.

963 James R. Foster, "Smollett and the *Atom*," *PMLA*, lxviii (1953). 1032-1046; Lewis M. Knapp, "The Keys to Smollett's *Atom*," *ELN*, ii (1964). 100-102. —Sheridan Baker, "*Humphry Clinker* as Comic Romance," *Papers of the Michigan Acad.*, xlvi (1961). 645-654; Byron Gassman, "The *Briton* and *Humphry Clinker*," *SEL*, iii (1963). 397-414; Thomas R. Preston, "Smollett and the Benevolent Misanthrope Type," *PMLA*, lxxix (1964). 51-57.

Part III: The Disintegration of Classicism

I. Accentuated Tendencies

967 E. S. de Beer, "Gothic: Origin and Diffusion of the Term; the Idea of Style in Architecture," *Jour. Warburg and Courtauld Inst.*, xi (1948). 142-162; A. O. Aldridge, "The Pleasures of Pity," *ELH*, xvi (1949). 76-87; René Wellek, "The Concept of 'Romanticism' in Literary History," *CL*, i (1949). 1-23, 147-172 [cf. review by R. S. Crane in *PQ*, xxix (1950). 257-259]; Erik Erämetsä, *A Study of the Word 'Sentimental' and of Other Linguistic Characteristics of*

Eighteenth Century Sentimentalism in England (Helsinki, 1951); Northrop Frye, "Towards Defining an Age of Sensibility," *ELH*, xxiii (1956). 144-152; Stuart M. Tave, *The Amiable Humorist: A Study in the Comic Theory and Criticism of the Eighteenth and Early Nineteenth Centuries* (Chicago, 1960).

968 R. A. Knox, *Enthusiasm: A Chapter in the History of Religion, with Special Reference to the Seventeenth and Eighteenth Centuries* (Oxford, 1950).

969 Betsy Rodgers, *Cloak of Charity: Studies in Eighteenth-Century Philanthropy* (1949). On the Adam brothers: James Lees-Milne, *The Age of Adam* (1948).

970 *Portraits by Sir Joshua Reynolds: Character Sketches of Oliver Goldsmith, Samuel Johnson, and David Garrick, together with Other Manuscripts of Reynolds Recently Discovered among the Boswell Papers and Now First Published*, ed. Frederick W. Hilles (1952); *Sir Joshua Reynolds: Discourses on Art*, ed. Robert R. Wark (San Marino, Calif., 1959); Frederick W. Hilles, "Sir Joshua's Prose," *Tinker Festschrift* (New Haven, 1949), pp. 49-60.—Allan Ramsay the Younger: Alastair Smart, *The Life and Art of Allan Ramsay* (1952). —Gainsborough: Mary Woodall, *Thomas Gainsborough: His Life and Work* (1949).

974 Thomas Leland: *Longsword, Earl of Salisbury: An Historical Romance,* ed. John C. Stephens, Jr. (1957).—Medievalism: A. L. Owen, *The Famous Druids* (Oxford, 1962); Arthur Johnston, *Enchanted Ground: The Study of Medieval Romance in the Eighteenth Century* (1964).

II. Opinions of Critics

977 Scott Elledge, "The Background and Development in English Criticism of the Theories of Generality and Particularity," *PMLA*, lxii (1947). 147-182; Earl R. Wasserman, *Elizabethan Poetry in the Eighteenth Century* (Urbana, 1947); W. K. Wimsatt, Jr., "The Structure of the 'Concrete Universal' in Literature," *PMLA*, lxii (1947). 262-280; Gordon McKenzie, *Critical Responsiveness: A Study of the Psychological Current in Later Eighteenth-Century Criticism* (Berkeley, 1949); M. H. Abrams, *The Mirror and the Lamp: Romantic Theory and the Critical Tradition* (1953); René Wellek, *A History of Modern Criticism, 1750-1950:* Vol. 1, *The Later Eighteenth Century* (New Haven, 1955); Walter J. Hipple, Jr., *The Beautiful, the Sublime, & the Picturesque in Eighteenth-Century British Aesthetic Theory* (Carbondale, Ill., 1957); Ernest L. Tuveson, *The Imagination as a Means of Grace: Locke and the Aesthetics of Romanticism* (Berkeley, 1960); Martin Price, "The Picturesque Moment," *Pottle Festschrift* (1965), pp. 259-292.

980 Jean H. Hagstrum, *The Sister Arts: The Tradition of Literary Pictorialism and English Poetry from Dryden to Gray* (Chicago, 1958).

981 *William Duff: An Essay on Original Genius:* Facsimile Reproduction, ed. with an Introduction by John L. Mahoney (Gainesville, Fla., 1964; *SF&R*).

982 Wilma L. Kennedy, *The English Heritage of Coleridge of Bristol, 1798: The Basis in Eighteenth-Century English Thought for his Distinction between*

Imagination and Fancy (New Haven, 1947); Earl R. Wasserman, "Another Eighteenth-Century Distinction between Fancy and Imagination," *MLN*, LXIV (1949). 23-25; Marjorie Nicolson, *Science and Imagination* (Ithaca, N.Y., 1956), containing her 1935 essay, "The Microscope and English Imagination."

983 Frances Reynolds [sister of Sir Joshua], *An Enquiry concerning the Principles of Taste, and of the Origin of our Ideas of Beauty* (1785), with an Introduction by James L. Clifford (1951; *ARS*, No. 27).

984 George Campbell, *The Philosophy of Rhetoric*, ed. Lloyd F. Bitzer (Carbondale, Ill., 1963).

985 Carl Paul Barbier, *William Gilpin: His Drawings, Teaching and Theory of the Picturesque* (Oxford, 1963).—Lord Kames: Leroy R. Shaw, "Henry Home of Kames: Precursor of Herder," *Germanic Rev.* XXXV (1960). 16-27; András Horn, "Kames and the Anthropological Approach to Criticism," *PQ*, XLIV (1965). 211-233.

986 John Baillie, *An Essay on the Sublime*, 1747, with an Introduction by Samuel H. Monk (1953; *ARS*, No. 43). Burke, *A Philosophical Enquiry into the Origin of our Ideas of the Sublime and Beautiful*, ed. J. T. Boulton (1958). Alexander Gerard, *An Essay on Taste (1759), together with Observations concerning the Imitative Nature of Poetry:* Facsimile Reproduction of the Third Edition (1780), with an Introduction by Walter J. Hipple, Jr. (Gainesville, Fla., 1963; *SF&R*).

987 Priestley: *A Course of Lectures on Oratory and Criticism*, ed. Vincent M. Bevilacqua and Richard Murphy (Carbondale, Ill., 1965); *Writings on Philosophy, Science, and Politics*, ed. John A. Passmore (1965). Homeric criticism: Donald M. Foerster, *Homer in English Criticism* (New Haven, 1947); Gustavo Costa, *La Critica omerica di Thomas Blackwell (1701-1757)* (Florence, 1959).

988 Richard Hurd, *Letters on Chivalry and Romance*, with an Introduction by Hoyt Trowbridge (1963; *ARS*, Nos. 101-2).

III. Dr. Johnson

989 For bibliography see R. W. Chapman, *Two Centuries of Johnsonian Scholarship* (Glasgow, 1945); James L. Clifford, *Johnsonian Studies, 1887-1950* (Minneapolis, 1951); "Johnsonian Studies, 1950-60," compiled by James L. Clifford and Donald J. Greene in *Johnsonian Studies*, ed. Magdi Wahba (Cairo, 1962), pp. 263-350.—Three volumes of the new Yale Edition of the *Works* have appeared: Vol. I: *Diaries, Prayers, and Annals*, ed. E. L. McAdam, Jr., with Donald and Mary Hyde (1958); Vol. II: *"The Idler" and "The Adventurer,"* ed. W. J. Bate, John M. Bullitt, and L. F. Powell (1963); Vol. III: *Poems*, ed. E. L. McAdam, with George Milne (1964).—*The Letters of Samuel Johnson, with Mrs. Thrale's Genuine Letters to Him*, ed. R. W. Chapman (3v, Oxford, 1952). For new letters see Mary Hyde, " 'Not in Chapman,' " *Powell Festschrift* (Oxford, 1965), pp. 286-319.—Biographies and general studies: L. F. Powell's revision of the Hill edition of Boswell has been completed with Vols. V-VI (Oxford, 1950; 2 ed., 1964). (For Boswell see also below, suppl. to p. 1066.) Part xi of Reade's *Johnsonian Gleanings (Consolidated Index of Persons to Parts I-X)* was published in 1952. An abridged edition, by Bertram H. Davis, of Sir John Hawkins' *Life* appeared in 1961. Other biographical and general studies: Katharine C. Balderston, "Johnson's Vile Melancholy," *Tinker Festschrift* (New Haven, 1949), pp. 3-14; Bertrand H. Bronson, "The Double Tradition of Dr. Johnson," *ELH*, xviii (1951). 90-106; E. L. McAdam, Jr., *Dr. Johnson and the English Law* (Syracuse, N.Y., 1951); R. W. Chapman, *Johnsonian and Other Essays and Reviews* (Oxford, 1953); Walter J. Bate, *The Achievement of Samuel Johnson* (1955); Hesketh Pearson, *Johnson and Boswell: The Story of their Lives* (1958); *New Light on Dr. Johnson: Essays on the Occasion of his 250th Birthday*, ed. Frederick W. Hilles (New Haven, 1959) [twenty papers, some of them reprinted, by specialists]; Bertram H. Davis, *Johnson before Boswell: A Study of Sir John Hawkins' "Life of Samuel Johnson"* (New Haven, 1960); Donald J. Greene, *The Politics of Samuel Johnson* (New Haven, 1960); Robert Voitle, *Samuel Johnson the Moralist* (Cambridge, Mass., 1961); M. J. C. Hodgart, *Samuel Johnson* (1962).

990 The early and middle years: Benjamin B. Hoover, *Samuel Johnson's Parliamentary Reporting* (Berkeley, 1953); James L. Clifford, *Young Sam Johnson* (1955), and "Some Problems of Johnson's Obscure Middle Years," *Powell Festschrift* (Oxford, 1965), pp. 99-110; Edward A. Bloom, *Samuel Johnson in Grub Street* (Providence, R.I., 1957); Joel L. Gold, "Johnson's Translation of Lobo," *PMLA*, lxxx (1965). 51-61. Marshall Waingrow, "The Mighty Moral of *Irene*," *Pottle Festschrift* (1965), pp. 79-92. *The Vanity of Human Wishes*: Susie I. Tucker and Henry Gifford, "Johnson's Poetic Imagination," *RES*, n.s. viii (1957). 241-248; Frederick W. Hilles, "Johnson's Poetic Fire," *Pottle Festschrift* (1965), pp. 67-77.

991 James H. Sledd and Gwin J. Kolb, *Dr. Johnson's Dictionary: Essays in the Biography of a Book* (Chicago, 1955); Katharine C. Balderston, "Dr. Johnson's Use of William Law in the *Dictionary*," *PQ*, xxxix (1960). 379-388; *Johnson's Dictionary: A Modern Selection*, ed. E. L. McAdam, Jr. and George Milne (1963).

993 *Johnson's Notes to Shakespeare* [the 1773 text], ed. with an Introduction by Arthur Sherbo (*ARS*, Nos. 59-60, 65-66, 71-73, 1956-58); W. R. Keast, "The Preface to *A Dictionary* . . . : Johnson's Revision and the Establishment of the Text," *Stud. in Bibliography*, v (1952/3), 129-146; Arthur Sherbo, *Samuel Johnson, Editor of Shakespeare, with an Essay on "The Adventurer"* (Urbana, 1956); Robert W. Scholes, "Dr. Johnson and the Bibliographical Criticism of Shakespeare," *SQ*, xi (1960). 163-171; Donald D. Eddy, "Samuel Johnson's Editions of Shakespeare (1765)," *Papers of the Bibl. Soc. of America*, lvi (1962). 428-444; D. Nichol Smith (ed.) *Eighteenth Century Essays on Shakespeare* (2 ed., Oxford, 1963).

994 Gwin J. Kolb, "The Structure of *Rasselas*," *PMLA*, lxvi (1951). 698-717, and "The 'Paradise' in Abyssinia and the 'Happy Valley' in *Rasselas*," *MP*, lvi (1958). 10-16; William Kenney, "*Rasselas* and the Theme of Diversification," *PQ*, xxxviii (1959). 84-89; George Sherburn, "Rasselas Returns—to What?" *PQ*, xxxviii (1959). 383-384; *Bicentenary Essays on Rasselas*, ed. Magdi Wahba (Cairo, 1959); Gwin J. Kolb, "*Rasselas:* Purchase Price, Proprietors, and Printings," *Stud. in Bibliography*, xv (1962). 256-259; Donald M. Lockhart, " 'The Fourth Son of the Mighty Emperor': The Ethiopian Background of Johnson's *Rasselas*," *PMLA*, LXXVIII (1963). 516-528; Frederick W. Hilles, "*Rasselas*, an 'Uninstructive Tale,' " *Powell Festschrift* (Oxford, 1965, pp. 111-121.

995 Mary Lascelles, "Notions and Facts: Johnson and Boswell on their Travels," *Powell Festschrift* (Oxford, 1965), pp. 215-229.

996 Benjamin Boyce, "Johnson's *Life of Savage* and its Literary Background," *SP*, LIII (1956). 576-598; William R. Keast, "Johnson and 'Cibber's' *Lives of the Poets*, 1753," *McKillop Festschrift* (Chicago, 1963), pp. 89-101; John Lawrence Abbott, "Dr. Johnson, Fontenelle, Le Clerc, and Six 'French' Lives," *MP*, LXIII (1965). 121-127.

997 Lewis P. Curtis and Herman W. Liebert, *Esto Perpetua: The Club of Dr. Johnson and his Friends, 1764-1784* (Hamden, Conn., 1963).

998 Chester F. Chapin, "Samuel Johnson's Religious Development," *SEL*, IV (1964). 457-474; Maurice J. Quinlan, *Samuel Johnson: A Layman's Religion* (Madison, 1964); Arieh Sachs, "Reason and Unreason in Johnson's Religion," *MLR*, LIX (1964). 519-526; John Hardy, "Johnson and Raphael's Counsel to Adam," *Powell Festschrift* (Oxford, 1965), pp. 122-136.

1000 E. L. McAdam, Jr., "Johnson, Walpole, and Public Order," *Powell Festschrift* (Oxford, 1965), pp. 93-98; Robert Shackleton, "Johnson and the Enlightenment," *Ibid.*, pp. 76-92.

1001 W. K. Wimsatt, Jr., *Philosophic Words: A Study of Style and Meaning in the "Rambler" and "Dictionary" of Samuel Johnson* (New Haven, 1948); Jean H. Hagstrum, *Samuel Johnson's Literary Criticism* (Minneapolis, 1952); W. R. Keast, "The Theoretical Foundations of Johnson's Criticism," *Critics and Criticism* (Chicago, 1952), pp. 389-407; Donald J. Greene, " 'Pictures to the Mind': Johnson and Imagery," *Powell Festschrift* (Oxford, 1965), pp. 137-158; Arieh Sachs, "Generality and Particularity in Johnson's Thought," *SEL*, V (1965). 491-511.

1004 Donald J. Greene, "The Development of the Johnson Canon," *McKillop Festschrift* (Chicago, 1963), pp. 407-427; Gwin J. Kolb, "Johnson's 'Little Pompadour': A Textual Crux and a Hypothesis," *Ibid.*, pp. 125-142; J. D. Fleeman, "Dr. Johnson and Henry Thrale, M. P.," *Powell Festschrift* (Oxford, 1965), pp. 170-189 [Johnson's assistance in Thrale's election addresses].

IV. Mid-Century Poets

1005 Wallace Cable Brown, *The Triumph of Form: A Study of the Later Masters of the Heroic Couplet* (Chapel Hill, 1948); Earl R. Wasserman, "The Inherent Values of Eighteenth-Century Personification," *PMLA*, LXV (1950). 435-463.

1007 *Drafts & Fragments of Verse*, ed. J. S. Cunningham (Oxford, 1956) (rev. by Alan D. McKillop in *PQ*, XXXVI (1957). 352-354); Alan D. McKillop, "Collins's *Ode to Evening*—Background and Structure," *Tennessee Stud. in Lit.* V (1960). 73-83; Merle E. Brown, "On William Collins' 'Ode to Evening,' "

EIC, XI (1961). 136-153; John R. Crider, "Structure and Effect in Collins' Progress Poems," *SP*, LX (1963). 57-72; R. Quintana, "The Scheme of Collins's *Odes on Several . . . Subjects*," *McKillop Festschrift* (Chicago, 1963), pp. 371-380; Oliver F. Sigworth, *William Collins* (1965); A. S. P. Woodhouse, "The Poetry of Collins Reconsidered," *Pottle Festschrift* (1965), pp. 93-137.

1009 Christopher Smart's *Collected Poems* have been edited by Norman Callan in 2v, 1949 (*Muses' Library*); and the *Poems* (a selection) by Robert Brittain (Princeton, 1950). Of major importance: *Jubilate Agno*, re-edited from the Original Manuscript by W. H. Bond (Cambridge, Mass., 1954). *A Song to David* is edited by J. B. Broadbent (1960). See also Cecil Price, "Six Letters by Christopher Smart," *RES*, n.s. VIII (1957). 144-148; Arthur Sherbo, "Christopher Smart's Knowledge of Occult Literature," *JHI*, XVIII (1957). 233-241; Charles Ryskamp, "Problems in the Text of Smart," *Library*, XIV (1959). 293-298; Karina Williamson, "Christopher Smart's *Hymns and Spiritual Songs*," *PQ*, XXXVIII (1959). 413-424; Christopher Devlin, *Poor Kit Smart* (1961); Charles Parish, "Christopher Smart's Knowledge of Hebrew," *SP*, LVIII (1961). 516-532; K. M. Rogers, "The Pillars of the Lord: Some Sources of 'A Song to David,'" *PQ*, XL (1961). 525-534; Albert J. Kuhn, "Christopher Smart: The Poet as Patriot of the Lord," *ELH*, XXX (1963). 121-136; Charles Parish, "Christopher Smart's 'Pillars of the Lord,'" *MLQ* XXIV (1963). 158-163.

1010 A. M. Kinghorn, "Warton's *History* and Early English Poetry," *ES*, XLIV (1963). 197-204.

1011 Jeffrey Hart, "Akenside's Revision of *The Pleasures of Imagination*," *PMLA*, LXXIV (1959). 67-74; Robert Marsh, "Akenside and Addison: The Problem of Ideational Debt," *MP*, LIX (1961). 36-48.—*Shenstone's Miscellany, 1759-1763*, ed. Ian A. Gordon (Oxford, 1952); Roy Lewis, "William Shenstone and Edward Knight: Some New Letters," *MLR*, XLII (1947). 422-433.

1012 Herbert W. Starr, *A Bibliography of Thomas Gray, 1917-1951, with Material supplementary to C. S. Northup's Bibliography* (Philadelphia, 1953); R. W. Ketton-Cremer, *Thomas Gray: A Biography* (Cambridge, 1955); Rintaro Fukuhara, *Essays on Thomas Gray* (Tokyo, 1960); Alastair Macdonald, "The Poet Gray in Scotland," *RES*, n.s. XIII (1962). 245-256; Morris Golden, *Thomas Gray* (1964); Patricia M. Spacks, "Statement and Artifice in Thomas Gray," *SEL*, V (1965). 519-532.

1014 Odell Shepard, "A Youth to Fortune and to Fame Unknown," *MP*, XX (1923). 347-373; Cleanth Brooks, "Gray's Storied Urn," *The Well Wrought Urn* (1947), pp. 96-113; H. W. Starr, "'A Youth to Fortune and to Fame Unknown': A Reestimation," *JEGP*, XLVIII (1949). 97-107; Frank H. Ellis, "Gray's *Elegy*: The Biographical Problem in Literary Criticism," *PMLA*, LXVI (1951). 971-1008; Morse Peckham, "Gray's 'Epitaph' Revisited," *MLN*, LXXI (1956). 409-411; John H. Sutherland, "The Stonecutter in Gray's 'Elegy,'" *MP*, LV (1957). 11-13; Mark Roberts, "A Note on Gray's Elegy," *ES*, XXXIX (1958). 251-256; Francis Berry, "The Sound of Personification in Gray's Elegy," *EIC*, XII (1962). 442-445; and three essays in the *Pottle Festschrift* (1965): Frank Brady, "Structure and Meaning in Gray's *Elegy*," pp. 177-189; Bertrand H. Bronson, "On a Special Decorum in Gray's *Elegy*," pp. 171-176; Ian Jack, "Gray's *Elegy* Reconsidered," pp. 139-169.

1015 Derick S. Thomson, *The Gaelic Sources of Macpherson's "Ossian"* (Edinburgh, 1952).

1016 *The Poems of Robert Fergusson,* ed. Matthew P. McDiarmid (2v, Edinburgh, 1955-7); *The Unpublished Poems,* ed. William E. Gillis (Edinburgh, 1955); Sydney Goodsir Smith (ed.), *Robert Fergusson, 1750-1774: Essays by Various Hands to Commemorate the Bicentenary of his Birth* (1952). See further: David Daiches, *The Paradox of Scottish Culture: The Eighteenth-Century Experience* (1964); John Butt, "The Revival of Vernacular Scottish Poetry in the Eighteenth Century," *Pottle Festschrift* (1965), pp. 219-237. On Hugh Blair see the book by Robert M. Schmitz, *Hugh Blair* (1948).

1017 Four more volumes of *The Percy Letters* have been published (correspondence with Thomas Warton, Lord Hailes, Evan Evans, and George Paton). For an account of the Percy books and papers see D. Nichol Smith, "The Constance Meade Collection and the University Press Museum," *Bodleian Library Record,* VI (1958). 427-433. On the *Reliques* see Albert B. Friedman, *The Ballad Revival* (Chicago, 1961), chap. VII.

1018 Beattie's *London Diary, 1773* and the *Day-Book, 1773-1798* have both been edited by Ralph S. Walker (Aberdeen, 1946-9). See also two articles by Ernest C. Mossner: "Beattie's 'The Castle of Scepticism': An Unpublished Allegory against Hume, Voltaire, and Hobbes," *Texas Stud. in English,* XXVII (1948). 108-145, and "Beattie on Voltaire: An Unpublished Manuscript," *Romanic Rev.,* XLI (1950). 26-32.—Chatterton: Bertrand H. Bronson, "Thomas Chatterton," *Tinker Festschrift* (New Haven, 1949), pp. 239-255.

1019 *The Poetical Works of Charles Churchill,* ed. Douglas Grant (Oxford, 1956); *Correspondence of John Wilkes and Charles Churchill,* ed. Edward H. Weatherly (1954); Wallace Cable Brown, *Charles Churchill: Poet, Rake, and Rebel* (Lawrence, Kans., 1953); Irène Simon, "An Eighteenth-Century Satirist: Charles Churchill," *Revue belge de philologie et d'histoire,* XXXVII (1959). 645-682; William F. Cunningham, Jr., "Charles Churchill and the Satiric Portrait," *Essays and Stud. in Lang. and Lit.* (Pittsburgh, 1964; *Duquesne Stud., Philol. Ser.,* 5), pp. 110-132.

1020 Additional poets:

Christopher Anstey: William C. Powell, *Christopher Anstey: Bath Laureate* (Philadelphia, 1944); Martin S. Day, "Anstey and Anapestic Satire in the Late Eighteenth Century," *ELH,* XV (1948). 122-146.

William Falconer: M. K. Joseph, "William Falconer," *SP,* XLVII (1950). 72-101; Gordon W. Couchman, "Editions of Falconer's 'Shipwreck,'" *N&Q,* CXCVIII (1953). 439-440.

William Hamilton: Nelson S. Bushnell, *William Hamilton of Bangour, Poet and Jacobite* (Aberdeen, 1957).

V. The Novel after 1760

1021 B. G. MacCarthy, *The Later Women Novelists, 1744-1818* (Oxford, 1948); James R. Foster, *History of the Pre-romantic Novel in England* (1949); Henri Roddier, *J.-J. Rousseau en Angleterre au XVIIIᵉ siècle: l'oeuvre et l'homme* (Paris, 1950).

1022 Mrs. Sarah Scott: *A Description of Millenium Hall,* ed. Walter M. Crittenden (1955).—Charlotte Smith: Alan D. McKillop, "Charlotte Smith's Letters," *HLQ,* XV (1952). 237-255.

1023 Ernest N. Dilworth, *The Unsentimental Journey of Laurence Sterne* (1948); Lansing van der Heyden Hammond, *Laurence Sterne's "Sermons of Mr. Yorick"* (New Haven, 1948); Earl R. Wasserman, "Unedited Letters by Sterne, Hume, and Rousseau," *MLN*, LXVI (1951). 73-80; J. C. T. Oates, "On Collecting Sterne," *Book Collector*, I (1952). 247-258; Alan D. McKillop, "The Reinterpretation of Laurence Sterne," *Études anglaises*, VII (1954). 36-47; Alice G. Fredman, *Diderot and Sterne* (1955); Margaret R. B. Shaw, *Laurence Sterne: The Making of a Humorist, 1713-1762* (1957); Willard Connely, *Laurence Sterne as Yorick* (1958); Alan B. Howes, *Yorick and the Critics: Sterne's Reputation in England, 1760-1868* (New Haven, 1958); L. P. Curtis, "New Light on Sterne," *MLN*, LXXVI (1961). 498-501; Henri Fluchère, *Laurence Sterne, de l'homme à l'oeuvre: Biographie critique et essai d'interprétation de "Tristram Shandy"* (Paris, 1961) (trans. and abridged by Barbara Bray, 1965); A. E. Dyson, "Sterne: The Novelist as Jester," *Critical Quar.* IV (1962). 309-320; Peter Michelsen, *Laurence Sterne und der deutsche Roman des achtzehnten Jahrhunderts* (Göttingen, 1962); Christian Pons, "Laurence Sterne ou le génie de l'humour," *Cahiers du Sud*, LIII (1962). 425-446; Dietrich Rolle, *Fielding und Sterne* (Münster, 1963); William B. Piper, *Laurence Sterne* (1965); Arthur H. Cash, "Some New Sterne Letters," *LTLS*, April 8, 1965, p. 284; James M. Kuist, "New Light on Sterne: An Old Man's Recollections of the Young Vicar," *PMLA*, LXXX (1965). 549-553.

1024 John M. Yoklavich, "Notes on the Early Editions of *Tristram Shandy*," *PMLA*, LXIII (1948). 508-519; Wayne Booth, "Did Sterne Complete *Tristram Shandy?*" *MP*, XLVIII (1951). 172-183, and "The Self-Conscious Narrator in Comic Fiction before *Tristram Shandy*," *PMLA*, LXVII (1952). 163-185 [cf. also Booth's *The Rhetoric of Fiction* (Chicago, 1961), chap. VIII]; John Traugott, *Tristram Shandy's World: Sterne's Philosophical Rhetoric* (Berkeley, 1954); Arthur H. Cash, "The Lockean Psychology of *Tristram Shandy*," *ELH*, XXII (1955). 125-135; J. M. Stedmond, "Genre and *Tristram Shandy*," *PQ*, XXXVIII (1959). 37-51, "Style and *Tristram Shandy*," *MLQ*, XX (1959). 243-251, and "Satire and *Tristram Shandy*," *SEL*, I (1961). 53-63; Sigurd Burckhardt, "*Tristram Shandy*'s Law of Gravity," *ELH*, XXVIII (1961). 70-88; William B. Piper, "*Tristram Shandy*'s Digressive Artistry," *SEL*, I (1961). 65-76, and "*Tristram Shandy*'s Tragi-comical Testimony," *Criticism*, III (1961). 171-185; Ernest Tuveson, "Locke and Sterne," *Nicolson Festschrift* (1962). pp. 255-277; William J. Farrell, "Nature versus Art as a Comic Pattern in *Tristram Shandy*," *ELH*, XXX (1963). 16-36; Joan J. Hall, "The Hobbyhorsical World of *Tristram Shandy*," *MLQ*, XXIV (1963). 131-143; Louis A. Landa, "The Shandean Homunculus," *McKillop Festschrift* (Chicago, 1963), pp. 49-68; Arthur H. Cash, "The Sermon in *Tristram Shandy*," *ELH*, XXXI (1964). 395-417; Gardner D. Stout, Jr., "Sterne's Borrowings from Bishop Joseph Hall's *Quo Vadis?*" *ELN*, II (1965). 196-200.

1026 Gardner D. Stout, Jr., "Yorick's *Sentimental Journey*: A Comic 'Pilgrim's Progress' for the Man of Feeling," *ELH*, XXX (1963). 395-412.

1027 Dale Kramer, "The Structural Unity of 'The Man of Feeling,'" *Studies in Short Fiction*, I (1964). 191-199.

1028 Walpole: *The Castle of Otranto*, ed. W. S. Lewis (1964); Arthur L. Cooke, "Some Side Lights on the Theory of the Gothic Romance," *MLQ*, XII (1951). 429-436.

1030 William W. Appleton, *A Cycle of Cathay: The Chinese Vogue in England during the Seventeenth and Eighteenth Centuries* (1951).

1030 John H. Sutherland, "Robert Bage: Novelist of Ideas," *PQ*, xxxvi (1957). 211-220; K. H. Hartley, "Un Roman philosophique anglais: *Hermsprong* de Robert Bage," *RLC*, xxxviii (1964). 558-563.—*The Journal of William Beckford in Portugal and Spain, 1787-1788*, ed. Boyd Alexander (1954); *Excursion à Alcobaça et Batalha*, ed. André Parreaux (Paris & Lisbon, 1956): *Life at Fonthill, 1807-1822, with Interludes in Paris and London: From the Correspondence of William Beckford*, trans. and ed. Boyd Alexander (1957); *Vathek et les Episodes*, ed. Ernest Giddey (Lausanne, 1962); Sacheverell Sitwell, *Beckford and Beckfordism* (1930); H. A. N. Brockman, *The Caliph of Fonthill* (1956); André Parreaux, *William Beckford, auteur de "Vathek" (1760-1844): Etude de la création littéraire* (Paris, 1960); Fatma Moussa Mahmoud (ed.), *William Beckford of Fonthill, 1760-1844: Bicentenary Essays* (Cairo, 1961); Boyd Alexander, *England's Wealthiest Son: A Study of William Beckford* (1962); James Rieger, "Au Pied de la Lettre: Stylistic Uncertainty in *Vathek*," *Criticism*, iv (1962). 302-312; James K. Folsom, "Beckford's 'Vathek' and the Tradition of Oriental Satire," *Criticism*, vi (1964). 53-69; Reinhold Grimm, "*Vathek* in Deutschland," *RLC*, xxxviii (1964). 127-135.

1031 Garland H. Cannon, Jr.: *Sir William Jones, Orientalist: An Annotated Bibliography of his Works* (Honolulu, 1952), *Oriental Jones: A Biography of Sir William Jones (1746-1794)* (1964), and "Sir William Jones and Dr. Johnson's Literary Club," *MP*, lxiii (1965). 20-37.

1032 *Edwy and Elgiva*, ed. Miriam J. Benkovitz (Hamden, Conn., 1957); Joyce Hemlow, "Fanny Burney and the Courtesy Books," *PMLA*, lxv (1950). 732-761, and "Fanny Burney: Playwright," *UTQ*, xix (1950). 170-189; Emily Hahn, *A Degree of Prudery* (1951); Joyce Hemlow, *The History of Fanny Burney* (Oxford, 1958), the standard life; Miriam Benkovitz, "Dr. Burney's Memoirs," *RES*, n.s. x (1959). 257-268; Eugene White, *Fanny Burney, Novelist: A Study in Technique* (Hamden, Conn., 1960); Winifred Gérin, *The Young Fanny Burney: A Biography* (1961); S. Bugnot, "*The Wanderer*, de Fanny Burney: Essai de réhabilitation," *Études anglaises*, xv (1962). 225-232; James P. Erickson, "*Evelina* and *Betsy Thoughtless*," *Texas Stud. in Lit. and Lang.*, vi (1964). 96-103; Kemp Malone, "*Evelina* Revisited," *Papers on English Lang. and Lit.* (So. Illinois Univ.), i (1965). 3-19. On Dr. Burney see Roger Lonsdale, "Dr. Burney and the *Monthly Review*," *RES*, xiv (1963). 346-358; xv (1964). 27-37; and *Dr. Charles Burney: A Literary Biography* (Oxford, 1965).

VI. The Drama 1740-1785

1035 Part 4 of *The London Stage*, (*1747-1776*, ed. George Winchester Stone, Jr., 3v. 1962) deals with this period (see above, suppl. to p. 748). See also Bertrand Evans, *Gothic Drama from Walpole to Shelley* (Berkeley, 1947); Earl R. Wasserman, "The Pleasures of Tragedy," *ELH*, xiv (1947). 283-307, and "The Sympathetic Imagination in Eighteenth-century Theories of Acting," *JEGP*, xlvi (1947). 264-272; Harry W. Pedicord, *The Theatrical Public in the Time of Garrick* (1954); William W. Appleton, *Charles Macklin: An Actor's Life* (Cambridge, Mass., 1960).—Garrick: *The Letters of David Garrick*, ed. David M. Little and George M. Kahrl (3v, Cambridge, Mass., 1963); Margaret Barton, *Garrick* (1948); Dougald MacMillan, "David Garrick, Manager," *SP*, XLV (1948). 630-646; Mary E. Knapp, *A Checklist of Verse by David Garrick* (Charlottesville, Va., 1955); Carola Oman, *David Garrick* (1958); Kalman A. Burnim, *David Garrick, Director* (Pittsburgh, 1961). On Garrick's treatment of Shakespeare see three articles by George Winchester Stone, Jr.: *SP*, XLV (1948). 89-103; *J. Q. Adams Memorial Studies* (Washington, 1948), pp. 115-128; and *PMLA*, LXV (1950). 183-197. On the Shakespeare Jubilee of 1769 see Martha W. England, *Garrick and Stratford* (1962) and *Garrick's Jubilee* (Columbus, Ohio, 1964); Christian Deelman, *The Great Shakespeare Jubilee* (1964); Johanne M. Stochholm, *Garrick's Folly: The Shakespeare Jubilee of 1769 at Stratford and Drury Lane* (1964).

1039 *"The Way to Keep him" and Five Other Plays by Arthur Murphy*, ed. John P. Emery (1956); *New Essays by Arthur Murphy*, ed. Arthur Sherbo (East Lansing, Mich., 1963).

1043 Byron Gassman, "French Sources of Goldsmith's *The Good Natur'd Man*," *PQ*, XXXIX (1960). 56-65.

1044 Jean Dulck, *Les Comédies de R. B. Sheridan: Étude littéraire* (Paris, 1962).

1047 Andrew Schiller, "*The School for Scandal:* The Restoration Unrestored," *PMLA*, LXII (1956). 694-704; Cecil Price, "The Columbia Manuscript of *The School for Scandal*," *Columbia Library Columns*, XI (1961). 25-29; Christian Deelman, "The Original Cast of *The School for Scandal*," *RES*, n.s. XIII (1962). 257-266; Arthur C. Sprague, "In Defence of a Masterpiece: 'The School for Scandal' Re-examined," *English Studies Today*, 3rd ser. (Edinburgh, 1964), pp. 125-135.

1048 Jeremy F. Bagster-Collins, *George Colman the Younger, 1762-1836* (1946).

VII. The Periodicals and Oliver Goldsmith

1050 A. T. Elder, "Irony and Humour in the *Rambler*," *UTQ*, XXX (1960). 57-71.

1051 W. Powell Jones, "The Romantic Bluestocking, Elizabeth Carter," *HLQ*, XII (1948). 85-98.

1052 Randolph Hudson, "Henry Mackenzie, James Beattie *et al.*, and the Edinburgh *Mirror*," *ELN*, I (1963). 104-108. Dr. Horst W. Drescher has in preparation a study of Mackenzie's periodical essays.

Newspapers: Katherine K. Weed and Richmond P. Bond, *Studies of British Newspapers and Periodicals from their Beginning to 1800: A Bibliography* (Chapel Hill, 1946); Robert L. Haig, "*The Gazetteer*," *1735-1797: A Study in the Eighteenth-Century English Newspaper* (Carbondale, Ill., 1960); G. A. Cranfield, *The Development of the Provincial Newspaper, 1700-1760* (Oxford, 1962); Robert R. Rea, *The English Press in Politics, 1760-1774* (Lincoln, Nebr., 1963); Lucyle Werkmeister, *The London Daily Press, 1772-1792* (Lincoln, Nebr., 1963);

Roy M. Wiles, *Freshest Advices: Early Provincial Newspapers in England* (Columbus, O., 1965).—Bonnell Thornton: Wallace C. Brown, "A Belated Augustan: Bonnell Thornton, Esq.," *PQ*, xxxiv (1955). 335-348.

1053 Albert H. Smith, "John Nichols, Printer and Publisher," *Library*, xviii (1963). 169-190; William B. Todd, "A Bibliographical Account of the *Gentleman's Magazine*, 1731-1754," *Stud. in Bibliography*, xviii (1965). 81-109.

1055 Benjamin C. Nangle, *The Monthly Review, Second Series, 1790-1815: Indexes of Contributors and Articles* (Oxford, 1955); Edward A. Bloom, "Labors of the Learned: Neoclassic Book Reviewing Aims and Techniques," *SP*, liv (1957). 537-563; Paul F. Fussell, Jr., "William Kenrick, Eighteenth-Century Scourge and Critic," *Jour. Rutgers Univ. Library*, xx (1957). 42-49.

1056 Arthur Friedman, "Goldsmith's Contributions to the *Critical Review*," *MP*, xliv (1946). 23-52; Edward L. McAdam, Jr., "Goldsmith, the Good-Natured Man," *Tinker Festschrift* (New Haven, 1949), pp. 41-47; Ralph M. Wardle, *Oliver Goldsmith* (Lawrence, Kans., 1957); Earl Miner, "The Making of *The Deserted Village*," *HLQ*, xxii (1959). 125-141; Macdonald Emslie, *Goldsmith: "The Vicar of Wakefield"* (1963); Arthur Friedman, "The Time of Composition of Goldsmith's *Edwin and Angelina*," *McKillop Festschrift* (Chicago, 1963), pp. 155-159; R. Quintana, "Oliver Goldsmith as a Critic of the Drama," *SEL*, v (1965). 435-454. Professor Friedman's edition of Goldsmith's *Works* is to appear in 1966 (5v).

1059 Alan D. McKillop, "Local Attachment and Cosmopolitanism—the Eighteenth-Century Pattern," *Pottle Festschrift* (1965), pp. 191-218.

VIII. Biography and Letter-Writing

1063 R. W. Ketton-Cremer, "Roger North," *E&S*, n.s., xii (1959). 73-86; James L. Clifford, "Roger North and the Art of Biography," *McKillop Festschrift* (Chicago, 1963), pp. 275-285.

1064 William Mason: Philip Gaskell, *The First Editions of William Mason* (Cambridge, 1951).—Austin Wright, "The Veracity of Spence's *Anecdotes*," *PMLA*, lxii (1947). 123-129, and *Joseph Spence: A Critical Biography* (Chicago, 1950); James M. Osborn, "The First History of English Poetry," *Sherburn Festschrift* (Oxford, 1949), pp. 230-250. Mr. Osborn is preparing a definitive edition of Spence's *Anecdotes*.

Several volumes of the Yale Boswell papers have been published, ed. by Frederick A. Pottle and others: the *London Journal, 1762-1763* (1950); *Boswell in Holland, 1763-1764* (1952); *Boswell on the Grand Tour: Germany and Switzerland, 1764* (1953); *Boswell on the Grand Tour: Italy, Corsica, and France, 1765-1766* (1955); *Boswell in Search of a Wife, 1766-1769* (1956); *Boswell for the Defence, 1769-1774* (1959); *Boswell: The Ominous Years, 1774-1776* (1963). *The Hypochondriack* has been reprinted (1951) under the title, *Boswell's Column*. See also the articles by Frederick A. Pottle: "James Boswell, Journalist," *Tinker Festschrift* (New Haven, 1949), pp. 15-25; "Boswell as Icarus" [Boswell and the College of Arcadia], *McKillop Festschrift* (Chicago, 1963), pp. 389-406; "Boswell Revalued," *Literary Views:*

Critical and Historical Essays, ed. Carroll Camden (Chicago, 1964), pp. 79-91; and "Boswell's University Education," *Powell Festschrift* (Oxford, 1965), pp. 230-253. Further: C. N. Fifer, "Boswell and the Decorous Bishop" [Boswell and Percy], *JEGP,* LXI (1962). 48-56; Donald J. Greene, "Reflections on a Literary Anniversary," *Queen's Quar.,* LXX (1963). 198-208; Douglas Day, "Boswell, Corsica, and Paoli," *ES,* XLV (1964). 1-20; James L. Golden, "James Boswell on Rhetoric and Belles-Lettres," *Quar. Jour. of Speech,* L (1964). 266-276; Ian Ross, "Boswell in Search of a Father? or a Subject?" *REL,* V (1964). 19-34; Mary M. Stewart, "Boswell and the Infidels," *SEL,* IV (1964). 475-483; Frank Brady, *Boswell's Political Career* (New Haven, 1965); Thomas I. Rae and William Beattie, "Boswell and the Advocates' Library," *Powell Festschrift* (Oxford, 1965), pp. 254-267. On the *Life of Johnson:* Edward Hart, "The Contributions of John Nichols to Boswell's *Life of Johnson," PMLA,* LXVII (1952). 391-410; James M. Osborn, "Edmond Malone and Dr. Johnson," *Powell Festschrift* (Oxford, 1965), pp. 1-20.

1067 Bernard Martin, *John Newton* (1950); James M. Osborn, "Travel Literature and the Rise of Neo-Hellenism in England," *Bull. N.Y. Public Library,* LXVII (1963). 279-300; George B. Parks, "The Turn to the Romantic in the Travel Literature of the Eighteenth Century," *MLQ,* XXV (1964). 22-33; Franz K. Stanzel, "Das Bild der Alpen in der englischen Literatur des 17. und 18. Jahrhunderts," *Germanisch-Romanische Monatsschrift,* XIV (1964). 121-138.

1068 Gibbon: Roy Pascal, *Design and Truth in Autobiography* (1960); Georges A. Bonnard, "Gibbon at Work on his *Memoirs," English Studies presented to R. W. Zandvoort* (Amsterdam, 1964), pp. 207-213.—*Lord Hervey's Memoirs,* ed. Romney Sedgwick (1952) [a selection from the 1931 edition]; *Lord Hervey and his Friends, 1726-1738: based on Letters from Holland House, Melbury, and Ickworth,* ed. Earl of Ilchester (1950).

1069 Mabel R. Brailsford, *A Tale of Two Brothers: John and Charles Wesley* (1954); James L. Golden, "John Wesley on Rhetoric and Belles Lettres," *Speech Monographs,* XXVIII (1961). 250-264; George Lawton, *John Wesley's English: A Study of his Literary Style* (1962).

1070 *Thraliana* (2 ed, 2v, Oxford, 1951).

1071 William H. Irving, *The Providence of Wit in the English Letter Writers* (Durham, N.C., 1955); Herbert Davis, "The Correspondence of the Augustans," *Woodhouse Festschrift* (Toronto, 1964), pp. 195-212.

1072 Katherine G. Hornbeak, "New Light on Mrs. Montagu," *Tinker Festschrift* (New Haven, 1949), pp. 349-361.—C. Price, "Five Unpublished Letters by Chesterfield," *Life and Letters,* LIX (1948). 3-10; Samuel Shellabarger, *Lord Chesterfield and his World* (Boston, 1951); Harold E. Pagliaro, "Paradox in the Aphorisms of La Rochefoucauld and Some Representative English Followers," *PMLA,* LXXIX (1964). 42-50.

1073 *The Antiquities of Selborne,* ed. Walter S. Scott (1950); Walter S. Scott, *White of Selborne* (1950); Ronald M. Lockley, *Gilbert White* (1954).

1075 Ilse D. Lind, *Richard Jago: A Study in Eighteenth Century Localism* (Philadelphia, 1945).

1076 The Yale edition of the Walpole *Correspondence* continues to appear.

To date 29 volumes have been published, the latest the three volumes of correspondence with the Countess of Upper Ossory, ed. W. S. Lewis and A. Dayle
Wallace (1965). See further: Allen T. Hazen, *A Bibliography of Horace Walpole*
(New Haven, 1948); Wilmarth S. Lewis, *Horace Walpole's Library* (Cambridge, 1958); Bonamy Dobrée, "Horace Walpole," *McKillop Festschrift* (Chicago, 1963), pp. 185-200.

IX. Intellectual Prose

1081   *New Letters of David Hume*, ed. Raymond Klibansky and Ernest C.
Mossner (Oxford, 1954); *An Inquiry concerning Human Understanding*, ed.
Charles W. Hendel (1955); *Writings on Economics*, ed. Eugene Rotwein (1955);
The Natural History of Religion, ed. H. E. Root (1956); *An Inquiry concerning
the Principles of Morals: With a Supplement: A Dialogue*, ed. Charles W. Hendel
(1957). See also "Hume's Early Memoranda, 1729-40: The Complete Text," ed.
E. C. Mossner, *JHI*, IX (1948). 492-518; E. C. Mossner, "Hume's *Four Disserta-
tions:* An Essay in Biography and Bibliography," *MP*, XLVIII (1950). 37-57; Teddy
Brunius, *David Hume on Criticism* (Stockholm, 1952); André-Louis Leroy,
David Hume (Paris, 1953); Ernest C. Mossner, *The Life of David Hume* (1954);
Antony Flew, *Hume's Philosophy of Belief: A Study of his First "Inquiry"*
(1961); Ralph Cohen, "The Transformation of Passion: A Study of Hume's
Theories of Tragedy," *PQ*, XLI (1962). 450-464; Ernest C. Mossner, "New Hume
Letters to Lord Elibank, 1748-1776," *Texas Stud. in Lit. and Lang.*, IV (1962).
431-460; and "Adam Ferguson's 'Dialogue on a Highland Jaunt' with Robert
Adam, William Cleghorn, David Hume, and William Wilkie," *McKillop Fest-
schrift* (Chicago, 1963), pp. 297-308; John B. Stewart, *The Moral and Political
Philosophy of David Hume* (1963); R. T. Broiles, *The Moral Philosophy of
David Hume* (The Hague, 1964); Sebastian A. Matczak, "A Select and Classified
Bibliography of David Hume," *Modern Schoolman*, XLII (1964). 70-81; Raymond
Williams, "David Hume: Reasoning and Experience," *Willey Festschrift* (Cam-
bridge, 1964), pp. 123-145; John V. Price, *The Ironic Hume* (Austin, Tex., 1965).

1085   Bolingbroke: Walter M. Merrill, *From Statesman to Philosopher: A
Study in Bolingbroke's Deism* (1949); J. H. Burns, "Bolingbroke and the Concept of Constitutional Government," *Political Stud.*, X (1962). 263-276; George
H. Nadel, "New Light on Bolingbroke's Letters on History," *JHI*, XXIII (1962).
550-557.—Gibbon: *Le Journal de Gibbon à Lausanne, 17 août 1763-19 avril 1764*,
ed. Georges A. Bonnard (Lausanne, 1945); *The Letters of Edward Gibbon*, ed.
J. E. Norton (3v, 1956); *Gibbon's Journey from Geneva to Rome: His Journal
from 20 April to 2 October 1764*, ed. Georges A. Bonnard (1961); Herbert
Weisinger, "The Middle Ages and the Late Eighteenth-Century Historians," *PQ*,
XXVII (1948). 63-79; Lewis P. Curtis, "Gibbon's Paradise Lost," *Tinker Festschrift*
(New Haven, 1949), pp. 73-90; Gavin R. De Beer, Georges A. Bonnard, and
Louis Junod, *Miscellanea Gibboniana* (Lausanne, 1952); Per Fuglum, *Edward
Gibbon: His View of Life and his Conception of History* (Oslo and Oxford,
1953); Michael Joyce, *Edward Gibbon* (1953); Giuseppe Giarrizzo, *Edward
Gibbon e la cultura europea del settecento* (Bari, 1954); Harold L. Bond, *The
Literary Art of Edward Gibbon* (Oxford, 1960); Nicolas Barker, "A Note on

the Bibliography of Gibbon, 1776-1802," *Library,* xviii (1963). 40-50; J. J. Saunders, "The Debate on the Fall of Rome," *History,* xlviii (1963). 1-17.

1089 *A Note-Book of Edmund Burke: Poems, Characters, Essays and Other Sketches,* ed. H. V. F. Somerset (Cambridge, 1957). The *Correspondence,* ed. Thomas W. Copeland and others (Cambridge and Chicago, 1958—) has now reached its fifth volume: *July 1782-June 1789,* ed. Holden Furber, with assistance of P. J. Marshall (1965). (For Burke's essay on the sublime and beautiful see above, suppl. to p. 986.) On Burke: Thomas W. Copeland, *Our Eminent Friend Edmund Burke: Six Essays* (New Haven, 1949); Carl B. Cone, "Edmund Burke's Library," *Papers of the Bibl. Soc. of America,* xliv (1950). 153-172; Charles Parkin, *The Moral Basis of Burke's Political Thought* (Cambridge, 1956); Carl B. Cone, *Burke and the Nature of Politics* (2v, Lexington, Ky., 1957-64); Peter J. Stanlis, *Edmund Burke and the Natural Law* (Ann Arbor, 1958); Thomas H. D. Mahoney, *Edmund Burke and Ireland* (Cambridge, Mass., 1960); Donald C. Bryant, "Edmund Burke: A Generation of Scholarship and Discovery," *Jour. of British Stud.,* ii (1962). 91-114; James T. Boulton, *The Language of Politics in the Age of Wilkes and Burke* (1963); C. P. Courtney, *Montesquieu and Burke* (Oxford, 1963); Peter P. Stanlis (ed.), *The Relevance of Edmund Burke* (1964); William B. Todd, *A Bibliography of Edmund Burke* (1964); Harvey C. Mansfield, Jr., *Statesmanship and Party Government: A Study of Burke and Bolingbroke* (Chicago, 1965).

1092 Lennart Ågvist, *The Moral Philosophy of Richard Price* (Lund, 1960).

1094 Other prose writers:
Catharine Macaulay. Lucy M. Donnelly, "The Celebrated Mrs. Macaulay," *William and Mary Quar.,* vi (1949). 173-207.

Adam Smith. *Lectures on Rhetoric and Belles Lettres,* ed. John M. Lothian (1963). John Rae's *Life* (1895) has been reissued with an important Introduction by Jacob Viner (1965). See also C. R. Fay, *Adam Smith and the Scotland of his Day* (Cambridge, 1956).

X. Cowper and Burns

1096 "Memoir of William Cowper: An Autobiography," ed. Maurice J. Quinlan, *Proc. Amer. Philos. Soc.,* xcvii (1953). 359-382 (cf. review by Charles Ryskamp in *MP,* liii (1955). 67-70, and ensuing corespondence (liii [1956]. 213-216; liv [1957]. 284); *The Cast-Away: The Text of the Original Manuscript and the First Printing of Cowper's Latin Translation,* ed. Charles Ryskamp (Princeton, 1963). Professor Ryskamp is preparing an edition of the correspondence. On Cowper: Lodwick Hartley, *William Cowper: A List of Critical and Biographical Studies Published from 1895 to 1949* (Raleigh, N.C., 1950); Norman Nicholson, *William Cowper* (1951); Donald A. Davie, "The Critical Principles of William Cowper," *Cambridge Jour.,* vii (1953). 182-188; Maurice J. Quinlan, *William Cowper: A Critical Life* (Minneapolis, 1953); Charles Ryskamp, *William Cowper of the Inner Temple, Esq.: A Study of his Life and Works to the Year 1768* (Cambridge, 1959); Morris Golden, *In Search of Stability: The Poetry of William Cowper* (1960); Lodwick Hartley, *William Cowper: The Continuing Revalua-*

tion: An Essay and a Bibliography of Cowperian Studies from 1895 to 1960 (Chapel Hill, 1960); Harry P. Kroitor, "Cowper, Deism, and the Divinization of Nature," *JHI*, xxi (1960). 511-526, and "The Influence of Popular Science on William Cowper," *MP*, lxi (1964). 281-287; Norma Russell, *A Bibliography of William Cowper to 1837* (Oxford, 1963); Frederick M. Link, "Two Cowper Letters," *MP*, lxii (1964). 137-138.

1102   David Daiches, *Robert Burns* (1950); Maurice Lindsay, *Robert Burns: The Man, his Work, the Legend* (1954); Christina Keith, *The Russet Coat: A Critical Study of Burns' Poetry and of its Background* (1956); Thomas Crawford, *Burns: A Study of the Poems and Songs* (1960); Alan D. McKillop, "The Living Burns," *Rice Institute Pamphlet*, xlvii (1960). 1-16; G. Ross Roy, "French Translations of Robert Burns (to 1893)," *RLC*, xxxvii (1963). 279-297, 437-453, and "French Critics of Robert Burns to 1893," *RLC*, xxxviii (1964). 264-285; Joel W. Egerer, *A Bibliography of Robert Burns* (Edinburgh, 1964; Carbondale, Ill., 1965); Raymond Bentman, "Robert Burns's Use of Scottish Diction," *Pottle Festschrift* (1965), pp. 239-258.

BOOK IV:
THE NINETEENTH CENTURY
AND AFTER (1789-1939)

I. The Background of Revolution, Repression, and Reform: 1789-1832

1111 On England in the period of the French Revolution: J. Steven Watson, *The Reign of George III, 1760-1815* (Oxford, 1960); Asa Briggs, *The Age of Improvement 1783-1867* (1959); Muriel Jaeger, *Before Victoria* (1956); S. Maccoby, *English Radicalism, 1786-1832: From Paine to Cobbett* (1955); R. K. Webb, *The British Working-Class Reader, 1790-1848: Literacy and Social Tension* (1955); *The British Political Tradition*, Vol. II: *The Debate on the French Revolution, 1789-1800*, ed. Alfred Cobban (1950); *English Historical Documents*, Vol. XI, 1783-1832, ed. A. Aspinall and E. A. Smith (1959).

1112 Ralph M. Wardle, *Mary Wollstonecraft: A Critical Biography* (Lawrence, Kan., 1951). On Mackintosh, Samuel Parr, Joseph Fawcett, and other English sympathizers with the French Revolution, including disciples of Godwin and apostles of Pantisocracy, see M. Ray Adams, *Studies in the Literary Backgrounds of English Radicalism* (Lancaster, Pa., 1947).—Paine: *Complete Writings*, ed. Philip S. Foner (1945); *Selected Works*, ed. Howard Fast (1945). Alfred O. Aldridge, *Man of Reason: The Life of Thomas Paine* (Philadelphia, 1959); James T. Boulton, "Tom Paine and the Vulgar Style," *EIC*, XII (1962). 18-33.

1113 Godwin: *Enquiry Concerning Political Justice*, ed. F. E. L. Priestley (3v, Toronto, 1946), important for variant texts. Rosalie Glynn Grylls, *William Godwin and His World* (1953); D. H. Monro, *Godwin's Moral Philosophy* (1953); *Godwin and the Age of Transition*, ed. A. E. Rodway (1952); Doris Fleisher, *William Godwin: A Study in Liberalism* (1951); Burton Ralph Pollin, *Education and Enlightenment in the Works of William Godwin* (1962).

1117 On the period from Waterloo to the First Reform Bill, see, in addition to the works cited above (suppl. to p. 1111): Arthur Bryant, *The Age of Elegance, 1812-1822* (1950); R. J. White, *Waterloo to Peterloo* (1957); T. S. Ashton, *The Industrial Revolution, 1760-1830* (1948); David Thomson, *England in the Nineteenth Century, 1815-1914* (1950), chs. I-III; E. P. Thompson, *The Making of the English Working Class* (1963); Arthur Aspinall, *Politics and the Press, 1780-1850* (1949), important for the journalistic activities of most of the romantic writers. Halévy's *History of the English People in the Nineteenth Century* has appeared in a complete English translation (7v, 1952).

[1111-1117]

1119   Cobbett: *Rural Rides*, ed. S. E. Buckley (1949), an abridgment; ed.
E. W. Martin (1959), text of 1830, with Gillray cartoons. M. L. Pearl, *William
Cobbett: A Bibliographical Account of His Life and Times* (1953); W. Baring
Pemberton, *William Cobbett* (1949).—Herschel M. Sikes, "William Hone:
Regency Patriot, Parodist, and Pamphleteer," *Newberry Library Bull.*, v (1961).
281-294.

1120   Bentham: *A Fragment on Government*, ed. Wilfred Harrison (Oxford,
1948); *Handbook of Political Fallacies*, ed. H. A. Larrabee (Baltimore, 1952).
Mary Mack, *Jeremy Bentham: An Odyssey of Ideas, 1748-92* (1962); David Baum-
gardt, *Bentham and the Ethics of Today* (Princeton, 1952); Robert Preyer,
Bentham, Coleridge, and the Science of History (Bochum-Langendreer, 1958).

II. Romanticism

1122   A revised edition of Bernbaum's *Guide through the Romantic Movement* was published in 1949. Valuable bibliographical reviews of scholarship
and criticism on all the major English romantic authors and on the romantic
movement in general are available in *The English Romantic Poets: A Review
of Research*, ed. Thomas M. Raysor (1950, rev. 1956)—hereafter cited as Raysor
—and *The English Romantic Poets and Essayists: A Review of Research and
Criticism*, ed. C. W. Houtchens and L. H. Houtchens (1957, rev. 1966)—hereafter
cited as Houtchens. The annual bibliography of current writings on the romantic
movement, published in *ELH* from 1937 to 1949 and in *PQ* from 1950 to
1964, is now found in *English Language Notes*. Two volumes of the *Oxford
History of English Literature* are devoted to the period: W. L. Renwick, *English
Literature, 1789-1815* (Oxford, 1963), a sketchy and erratic survey, and Ian
Jack, *English Literature, 1815-1832* (Oxford, 1963), notably readable and well
informed, with excellent bibliographies. See also *The [Pelican] Guide to English
Literature*, ed. Boris Ford: Vol. v, *From Blake to Byron* (1957, rev. 1962).
Other general studies include D. G. James, *The Romantic Comedy* (1948);
Graham Hough, *The Romantic Poets* (1953); Edward E. Bostetter, *The Ro-
mantic Ventriloquists* (Seattle, 1963); and Allan Rodway, *The Romantic Con-
flict* (1963). Walter J. Bate, *From Classic to Romantic* (Cambridge, Mass., 1946)
deals with the transition to the romantic age. On the romantic spirit as it af-
fected later generations: John Heath-Stubbs, *The Darkling Plain* (1950); John
Bayley, *The Romantic Survival* (1957); Morse Peckham, *Beyond the Tragic
Vision: The Quest for Identity in the Nineteenth Century* (1962). On romantic
criticism: M. H. Abrams, *The Mirror and the Lamp* (1953); René Wellek,
History of Modern Criticism, 1750-1950 (New Haven, 1955-   ), Vol. II; *Con-
temporary Reviews of Romantic Poetry*, ed. John Wain (1953); *The Poets and
Their Critics*, ed. Hugh Sykes Davies (1962), Vol. II. On various other aspects
of the romantic movement: Hoxie N. Fairchild, *Religious Trends in English
Poetry*, Vol. III: *1780-1830, Romantic Faith* (1949); John Middleton Murry,
Katherine Mansfield and Other Literary Portraits (1949), essays on five writers;
W. H. Auden, *The Enchafèd Flood* (1950); Mario Praz, *The Romantic Agony*
(rev. 1951); Donald Davie, *Purity of Diction in English Verse* (1952), Part II;
Herbert Read, *The True Voice of Feeling* (1953); Albert Gérard, *L'Idée romanti-*

que de la poésie en Angleterre (Paris, 1955); Josephine Miles, *Eras and Modes in English Poetry* (Berkeley, 1957), chs. IV-VIII; *The Major English Romantic Poets: A Symposium in Reappraisal,* ed. C. D. Thorpe *et al.* (Carbondale, Ill., 1957); C. P. Brand, *Italy and the English Romantics* (Cambridge, 1957); R. A. Foakes, *The Romantic Assertion: A Study in the Language of Nineteenth-Century Poetry* (New Haven, 1958); Eudo C. Mason, *Deutsche und englische Romantik* (Göttingen, 1959); Karl Kroeber, *Romantic Narrative Art* (Madison, Wis., 1960); Harold Bloom, *The Visionary Company* (1961); Upali Amarasinghe, *Dryden and Pope in the Early Nineteenth Century* (Cambridge, 1962); James Benziger, *Images of Eternity: Studies in the Poetry of Religious Vision from Wordsworth to T. S. Eliot* (Carbondale, Ill., 1962); Bernard Blackstone, *The Lost Travellers: A Romantic Theme with Variations* (1962); H. W. Piper, *The Active Universe: Pantheism and the Concept of Imagination in the English Romantic Poets* (1962); *Romanticism Reconsidered (English Institute Essays 1962),* ed. Northrop Frye (1963); *From Sensibility to Romanticism: Essays Presented to Frederick A. Pottle,* ed. F. W. Hilles and Harold Bloom (1965), mainly on the early phase of the movement; Murray Roston, *Prophet and Poet: The Bible and the Growth of Romanticism* (Evanston, Ill., 1965); F. E. L. Priestley, "Newton and the Romantic Concept of Nature," *UTQ,* XVII (1948). 323-336; William K. Wimsatt, Jr., "The Structure of Romantic Nature Imagery," *The Age of Johnson: Essays Presented to Chauncey Brewster Tinker* (New Haven, 1949), pp. 291-303; Wellek, "The Concept of 'Romanticism' in Literary History," *CL,* I (1949). 1-23, 147-172; Raymond D. Havens, "Discontinuity in Literary Development: The Case of English Romanticism," *SP,* XLVII (1950). 102-111; Peckham, "Toward a Theory of Romanticism," *PMLA,* LXVI (1951). 5-23, continued in *Stud. in Romanticism,* I (1961). 1-8; A. S. P. Woodhouse, "Romanticism and the History of Ideas," *English Studies Today,* I (1951). 120-140; C. G. Hoffman, "Whitehead's Philosophy of Nature and Romantic Poetry," *JAAC,* X (1952). 258-263; Georges Poulet, "Timelessness and Romanticism," *JHI,* XV (1954). 3-22; Gérard, "On the Logic of Romanticism," *EIC,* VII (1957). 262-273; Raymond Williams, *Culture and Society 1780-1950* (1958), pp. 3-70; Herbert M. Schueller, "Romanticism Reconsidered," *JAAC,* XX (1962). 359-368; Earl R. Wasserman, "The English Romantics: The Grounds of Knowledge," *Stud. in Romanticism,* IV (1964). 17-34. Collections of reprinted critical essays: *English Romantic Poets: Modern Essays in Criticism,* ed. Abrams (1960); *Romanticism: Points of View,* ed. R. F. Gleckner and G. E. Enscoe (1963).

III. William Blake

1128 *Complete Writings, with All the Variant Readings,* ed. Geoffrey Keynes (1957); *Poetry and Prose,* ed. David V. Erdman (1965), two admirable editions; *The Portable Blake,* ed. Alfred Kazin (1946); *Selected Poetry and Prose,* ed. Northrop Frye (1953); *A Selection of Poems and Letters,* ed. J. Bronowski (1958); *Poems* (selections), ed. Ruthven Todd (1949), F. W. Bateson (1957), Stanley Gardner (1962); *Letters,* ed. Keynes (1956).—G. E. Bentley, Jr., and Martin K. Nurmi, *A Blake Bibliography: Annotated Lists of Works, Studies, and Blakeana* (Minneapolis, 1965); Keynes and E. Wolf, *Blake's Illuminated*

Books: A Census (1953); bibliography of scholarly and critical work in Houtch-
ens, ch. I. Mona Wilson's *Life*, rev. 1948, remains standard. W. P. Witcutt,
Blake: A Psychological Study (1946); Northrop Frye, *Fearful Symmetry* (Prince-
ton, 1947); J. G. Davies, *The Theology of William Blake* (Oxford, 1948);
Keynes, *Blake Studies* (1949); Bernard Blackstone, *English Blake* (1949); Mar-
garet Bottrall, *The Divine Image: A Study of Blake's Interpretation of Christianity*
(Rome, 1950); H. M. Margoliouth, *William Blake* (1951); Margaret Rudd,
Divided Image (1953) and *Organiz'd Innocence: The Story of Blake's Prophetic
Books* (1956); David V. Erdman, *Blake: Prophet Against Empire* (Princeton,
1954); Stanley Gardner, *Infinity on the Anvil* (Oxford, 1954); Hazard Adams,
Blake and Yeats: The Contrary Vision (Ithaca, 1955) and *William Blake: A
Reading of the Shorter Poems* (Seattle, 1963); George W. Digby, *Symbol and
Image in William Blake* (Oxford, 1957); *The Divine Vision: Studies in the
Poetry and Art of Blake,* ed. Vivian de Sola Pinto (1957); Anthony Blunt,
The Art of William Blake (1959); Robert F. Gleckner, *The Piper and the Bard*
(Detroit, 1959); Peter F. Fisher, *The Valley of Vision: Blake as Prophet and
Revolutionary* (Toronto, 1961); George M. Harper, *The Neoplatonism of Wil-
liam Blake* (Chapel Hill, 1961); Harold Bloom, *Blake's Apocalypse: A Study
in Poetic Argument* (1963); Jean H. Hagstrum, *William Blake, Poet and
Painter: An Introduction to the Illuminated Verse* (Chicago, 1964); Alicia
Ostriker, *Vision and Verse in William Blake* (Madison, Wis., 1965); Frye,
"Poetry and Design in William Blake," *JAAC*, x (1951). 35-42, and "Blake
After Two Centuries," *UTQ*, XXVII (1957). 10-21; Karl Kiralis, "A Guide to
the Intellectual Symbolism of William Blake's Later Prophetic Writings," *Criti-
cism*, I (1959). 190-210; E. D. Hirsch, Jr., "The Two Blakes," *RES*, n.s. XII
(1961). 373-390; Kathleen Raine, "Blake's Debt to Antiquity," *Sewanee Rev.*,
LXXI (1963). 352-450; essays by Josephine Miles, Frye, and Erdman in *English
Institute Essays 1950*, ed. Alan S. Downer (1951); *Discussions of William
Blake*, ed. John E. Grant (Boston, 1961).—S. Foster Damon, *A Blake Dictionary* (Providence, R.I., 1965).

1130 C. M. Bowra, "*Songs of Innocence and Experience*," *The Romantic
Imagination* (Cambridge, Mass., 1949), ch. II. The single poem in *Songs of
Experience* which has received most critical attention has been *The Tyger*. See
Kathleen Raine, "Who Made the Tyger?", *Encounter*, II, no. 6 (1954). 43-50;
Martin K. Nurmi, "Blake's Revisions of *The Tyger*," *PMLA*, LXXI (1956).
669-685; Hazard Adams, "Reading Blake's Lyrics: *The Tyger*," *Texas Stud.
in Lit. and Lang.*, II (1960). 18-37; John E. Grant, "The Art and Argument of
The Tyger," *ibid.*, II (1960). 38-60; Paul Miner, "*The Tyger*: Genesis and Evo-
lution in the Poetry of William Blake," *Criticism*, IV (1962). 59-73.—Martin K.
Nurmi, *Blake's "Marriage of Heaven and Hell": A Critical Study* (Kent, Ohio,
1957).

1131 *Vala, or The Four Zoas*, ed. H. M. Margoliouth (Oxford, 1956) and
Gerald E. Bentley, Jr. (Oxford, 1963). Bentley, "The Failure of Blake's *Four
Zoas*," *Texas Stud. in English*, XXXVII (1958). 102-113.

1132 Karl Kiralis, "The Theme and Structure of William Blake's *Jerusalem*,"
ELH, XXIII (1956). 127-143; W. H. Stevenson, "Blake's *Jerusalem*," *EIC*, IX
(1959). 245-264.—Morchard Bishop [pseudonym of Oliver Stoner], *Blake's
Hayley* (1951).

IV. William Wordsworth

1136   De Selincourt's and Helen Darbishire's edition of the *Poetical Works* was completed with the publication of Vol. v in 1949. The de Selincourt edition of *The Prelude* was revised by Miss Darbishire, 1959. *Poems*, ed. Philip Wayne (1955); *Poetry and Prose*, ed. W. M. Merchant (1955); *"The Prelude" with a Selection from the Shorter Poems and Sonnets*, ed. Carlos Baker (1948); *Selected Poetry*, ed. Mark Van Doren (1950); *Selected Poems*, ed. G. W. Meyer (1964); *Selected Poems and Prefaces*, ed. Jack Stillinger (Boston, 1965); *Critical Opinions*, ed. M. L. Peacock, Jr. (Baltimore, 1950); *Political Tracts of Wordsworth, Coleridge, and Shelley*, ed. R. J. White (Cambridge, 1953); *Letters*, ed. Wayne (1954), a selection.—James V. Logan, *Wordsworthian Criticism, A Guide and Bibliography* (Columbus, Ohio, 1947), supplemented by Elton F. Henley and David H. Stam, *Wordsworthian Criticism 1945-1964* (1965); Raysor, ch. II. Mary Moorman, *William Wordsworth* (2v, Oxford, 1957-1965), the most authoritative biography; F. W. Bateson, *Wordsworth: A Re-Interpretation* (1954, rev. 1956), a Freudian speculation; Newton P. Stallknecht, *Strange Seas of Thought* (Durham, N. C., 1945); Jane Worthington, *Wordsworth's Reading of Roman Prose* (New Haven, 1946); de Selincourt, *Wordsworthian and Other Studies* (Oxford, 1947), chs. I-II; Norman Lacey, *Wordsworth's View of Nature* (Cambridge, 1948); Darbishire, *The Poet Wordsworth* (Oxford, 1950); Kenneth MacLean, *Agrarian Age: A Background for Wordsworth* (New Haven, 1950); *Tribute to Wordsworth: A Miscellany of Opinion for the Centenary of the Poet's Death*, ed. Muriel Spark and Derek Stanford (1950); *Wordsworth: Centenary Studies*, ed. G. T. Dunklin (Princeton, 1951); Lascelles Abercrombie, *The Art of Wordsworth* (1952); Florence Marsh, *Wordsworth's Imagery* (New Haven, 1952); C. N. Coe, *Wordsworth and the Literature of Travel* (1953); Geoffrey Hartman, *The Unmediated Vision* (New Haven, 1954), and *Wordsworth's Poetry, 1787-1814* (New Haven, 1964); John Jones, *The Egotistical Sublime: A History of Wordsworth's Imagination* (1954); J. C. Smith, *A Study of Wordsworth* (1955); F. M. Todd, *Politics and the Poet: A Study of Wordsworth* (1957); David Ferry, *The Limits of Mortality* (Middletown, Conn., 1959); David Perkins, *The Quest for Permanence: The Symbolism of Wordsworth, Shelley, and Keats* (Cambridge, Mass., 1959), and *Wordsworth and the Poetry of Sincerity* (Cambridge, Mass., 1964); E. D. Hirsch, Jr., *Wordsworth and Schelling: A Typological Study of Romanticism* (New Haven, 1960); John F. Danby, *The Simple Wordsworth: Studies in the Poems, 1797-1807* (1960); C. C. Clarke, *Romantic Paradox: An Essay on the Poetry of Wordsworth* (1962); Karl Kroeber, *The Artifice of Reality: Poetic Style in Wordsworth, Foscolo, Keats, and Leopardi* (Madison, Wis., 1964); Carl R. Woodring, *Wordsworth* (Boston, 1965); Christopher Salvesen, *The Landscape of Memory: A Study of Wordsworth's Poetry* (1965); Darbishire, "Wordsworth's Belief in the Doctrine of Necessity," *RES*, XXIV (1948). 121-125, and "Wordsworth and the Weather," *REL*, I, no. 3 (1960), 39-49; R. H. Bowers, "Wordsworthian Solitude," *MLQ*, X (1949). 389-399; Herbert Read, "Wordsworth's Philosophical Faith," *Sewanee Rev.*, LVIII (1950). 563-585; Kenneth Muir, "Centenary Eclogue: A Conversation About Wordsworth," *EIC*, I (1951). 17-37; Roger Sharrock, "Wordsworth's Revolt Against Literature," *EIC*, III (1953).

396-412; James R. Baird, "Wordsworth's 'Inscrutable Workmanship' and the Emblems of Reality," *PMLA*, LXVIII (1953). 444-457; Charles J. Smith, "The Contrarieties: Wordsworth's Dualistic Imagery," *PMLA*, LXIX (1954). 1181-1199; Kathleen Coburn, "Coleridge and Wordsworth and 'the Supernatural,' " *UTQ*, XXV (1956). 121-130; Patrick Cruttwell, "Wordsworth, the Public and the People," *Sewanee Rev.*, LXIV (1956). 71-80; Stallknecht, "On Poetry and Geometric Truth," *Kenyon Rev.*, XVIII (1956). 1-20; John Wain, "The Liberation of Wordsworth," *Preliminary Essays* (1957), pp. 78-92; Carl R. Sonn, "An Approach to Wordsworth's Earlier Imagery," *ELH*, XXVII (1960). 208-222; Bennett Weaver, "Wordsworth: Poet of the Unconquerable Mind," *PMLA*, LXXV (1960). 231-237; Paul de Man, "Symbolic Landscape in Wordsworth and Yeats," *In Defense of Reading*, ed. R. A. Brower and W. R. Poirier (1962), pp. 22-37; Lionel Stevenson, "The Unfinished Gothic Cathedral: A Study of the Organic Unity of Wordsworth's Poetry," *UTQ*, XXXII (1963). 170-183; Michael Irwin, "Wordsworth's 'Dependency Sublime,' " *EIC*, XIV (1964). 352-362; Alex Swerdling, "Wordsworth and Greek Myth," *UTQ*, XXXIII (1964). 341-354; Seymour Lainoff, "Wordsworth's Final Phase: Glimpses of Eternity," *SEL*, I, no. 4 (1961). 63-79; essays by Josephine Miles, Stallknecht, and Darbishire in *The Major English Romantic Poets*, ed. Thorpe *et al.*, chs. IV-VI; *Discussions of William Wordsworth*, ed. Jack Davis (Boston, 1964).

1138 Ben Ross Schneider, Jr., *Wordsworth's Cambridge Education* (Cambridge, 1957); Christopher Wordsworth, *The Early Wordsworthian Milieu*, ed. Z. S. Fink (Oxford, 1958).

1139 Z. S. Fink, "Wordsworth and the English Republican Tradition," *JEGP*, XLVII (1948). 107-126.

1140 D. E. Hayden, "Toward an Understanding of Wordsworth's *The Borderers*," *MLN*, LXVI (1951). 1-6; Geoffrey H. Hartman, "Wordsworth, *The Borderers*, and 'Intellectual Murder,' " *JEGP*, LXII (1963). 761-768.—H. M. Margoliouth, *Wordsworth and Coleridge, 1795-1834* (1953).

1142 *Lyrical Ballads . . . The Text of the 1798 Edition with the Additional 1800 Poems and the Prefaces*, ed. R. L. Brett and A. R. Jones (1963); W. J. B. Owen, *Wordsworth's Preface to the "Lyrical Ballads"* (Copenhagen, 1957); Robert Mayo, "The Contemporaneity of the Lyrical Ballads," *PMLA*, LXIX (1954). 486-522; Stephen M. Parrish, "Dramatic Technique in the *Lyrical Ballads*," *PMLA*, LXXV (1959). 85-97; John E. Jordan, "De Quincey on Wordsworth's Theory of Diction," *PMLA*, LXVIII (1953). 764-778; M. H. Abrams, "Wordsworth and Coleridge on Diction and Figures," *English Institute Essays 1952*, ed. Alan S. Downer (1954), pp. 171-201; George Whalley, "Preface to *Lyrical Ballads*: A Portent," *UTQ*, XXV (1956). 467-483; Roger Sharrock, "Wordsworth on Science and Poetry," *REL*, III, no. 4 (1962). 42-50; Mark L. Reed, "Wordsworth, Coleridge, and the 'Plan' of the *Lyrical Ballads*," *UTQ*, XXXIV (1965). 238-253; Max F. Schulz, "Coleridge, Wordsworth, and the 1800 Preface to *Lyrical Ballads*," *SEL*, V (1965). 619-639.—James Benziger, "*Tintern Abbey* Revisited," *PMLA*, LXV (1950). 154-162; Albert S. Gérard, "Dark Passages: Exploring *Tintern Abbey*," *Stud. in Romanticism*, III (1963). 10-23. Abbie F. Potts, *Wordsworth's "Prelude": A Study of Its Literary Form* (Ithaca, 1953); Herbert Lindenberger, *On Wordsworth's "Prelude"* (Princeton, 1963); Francis Christensen, "Creative Sensibility in Wordsworth," *JEGP*, XLV (1946).

361-368; Kenneth MacLean, "The Water Symbol in *The Prelude*," *UTQ*, XVII (1948). 372-389; C. Clarke, "Nature's Education of Man," *Philosophy*, XXIII (1948). 302-316; Ellen D. Leyburn, "Recurrent Words in *The Prelude*," *ELH*, XVI (1949). 284-298; George W. Meyer, "The Early History of *The Prelude*," *Tulane Stud. in English*, I (1949). 119-156; William Empson, "Sense in *The Prelude*," *Kenyon Rev.*, XIII (1951). 285-302; Edwin Morgan, "A Prelude to *The Prelude*," *EIC*, V (1955). 341-353; Barbara Everett, "*The Prelude*," *Critical Quar.*, I (1959). 338-350; Jonathan Bishop, "Wordsworth and the 'Spots of Time'," *ELH*, XXVI (1959). 45-65; J. R. MacGillivray, "The Three Forms of *The Prelude*, 1798-1805," *Essays in English Literature . . . Presented to A. S. P. Woodhouse* (Toronto, 1964), pp. 229-244; Francis Christensen, "Intellectual Love: the Second Theme of *The Prelude*," *PMLA*, LXXX (1965). 69-75.

1143 George W. Meyer, "*Resolution and Independence*: Wordsworth's Answer to Coleridge's *Dejection: An Ode*," *Tulane Stud. in English*, II (1950). 49-74; W. W. Robson, "*Resolution and Independence*," *Interpretations*, ed. John Wain (1955), pp. 117-128; Anthony E. M. Conran, "The Dialectic of Experience: A Study of Wordsworth's *Resolution and Independence*," *PMLA*, LXXV (1960). 66-74; Alan Grob, "Process and Permanence in *Resolution and Independence*," *ELH*, XXVIII (1961). 89-100.—Cleanth Brooks, "Wordsworth and the Paradox of the Imagination," *The Well-Wrought Urn* (1947), pp. 114-138; John K. Mathison, "Wordsworth's *Ode: Intimations of Immortality*," *SP*, XLVI (1949). 419-439; Bowra, *The Romantic Imagination*, ch. IV; George W. Meyer, "A Note on the Sources and Symbolism of the *Intimations Ode*," *Tulane Stud. in English*, III (1952). 33-45; Thomas M. Raysor, "The Themes of Immortality and Natural Piety in Wordsworth's *Immortality Ode*," *PMLA*, LXIX (1954). 861-875; Robert L. Schneider, "The Failure of Solitude: Wordsworth's *Immortality Ode*," *JEGP*, LIV (1955). 625-633; Alan Grob, "Wordsworth's *Immortality Ode* and the Search for Identity," *ELH*, XXXII (1965). 32-61.

1144 Note 40: See also Peter Coveney, *Poor Monkey: The Child in Literature* (1957), ch. III.

1145 Judson S. Lyon, "*The Excursion*": A Study (New Haven, 1950).

1147 Ellen D. Leyburn, "Radiance in *The White Doe of Rylstone*," *SP*, XLVII (1950). 629-633; Martin Price, "Imagination in *The White Doe of Rylstone*," *PQ*, XXXIII (1954). 189-199.—Stewart C. Wilcox, "Wordsworth's River Duddon Sonnets," *PMLA*, LXIX (1954). 131-141.—Melvin R. Watson, "The Redemption of *Peter Bell*," *SEL*, IV (1964). 519-530.—Note 52: *Diary of Benjamin Robert Haydon*, ed. Willard Bissell Pope (5v, Cambridge, Mass., 1960-1963); *Autobiography and Journals*, ed. Malcolm Elwin (1950). Eric George, *The Life and Death of Benjamin Robert Haydon, 1786-1846* (1948); Clark Olney, *Benjamin Robert Haydon: Historical Painter* (Athens, Ga., 1952); Varley Long, "Benjamin Robert Haydon," *PQ*, XXVI (1947). 235-247.

V. Samuel Taylor Coleridge

1149 *Philosophical Lectures* (1949); *Notebooks* (IIV, 1957-   ); *Inquiring Spirit* (1951), selections from "his published and unpublished prose writings"

—all ed. Kathleen Coburn; *Coleridge on the Seventeenth Century,* ed. Roberta F. Brinkley (Durham, N. C., 1955); *Political Tracts of Wordsworth, Coleridge, and Shelley,* ed. R. J. White (Cambridge, 1953); *Writings on Shakespeare,* ed. Terence Hawkes (1959); *Shakespearean Criticism,* ed. T. M. Raysor (1960); *The Portable Coleridge,* ed. I. A. Richards (1950); *Selected Poetry and Prose,* ed. Elisabeth Schneider (1951); *Poems and Prose,* ed. Kathleen Raine (1957); *Poems,* ed. Geoffrey Grigson (1951), Morchard Bishop (1954); *Selected Poems,* ed. James Reeves (1959); *Collected Letters,* ed. Earl L. Griggs (6v, Oxford, 1956-   ).—Bibliography in Raysor, ch. iii. Malcolm Elwin, *The First Romantics* (1947); Wilma Kennedy, *The English Heritage of Coleridge of Bristol, 1798* (New Haven, 1947); H. M. Margoliouth, *Wordsworth and Coleridge, 1795-1834* (1953); D. G. James, *The Romantic Comedy* (1948), Part iii; Humphry House, *Coleridge* (1953); Elio Chinol, *Il Pensiero di S. T. Coleridge* (Venice, 1953); James V. Baker, *The Sacred River: Coleridge's Theory of the Imagination* (Baton Rouge, 1957); J. B. Beer, *Coleridge the Visionary* (1959); John A. Colmer, *Coleridge: Critic of Society* (Oxford, 1959); James D. Boulger, *Coleridge as Religious Thinker* (New Haven, 1961); Carl R. Woodring, *Politics in the Poetry of Coleridge* (Madison, Wis., 1961); Richard H. Fogle, *The Idea of Coleridge's Criticism* (Berkeley, 1962); Werner W. Beyer, *The Enchanted Forest* (1963), on the influence of Wieland's *Oberon;* Max F. Schulz, *The Poetic Voices of Coleridge* (Detroit, 1963); Paul Deschamps, *La Formation de la pensée de Coleridge, 1772-1804* (Paris, 1964); Herbert Read, "Coleridge as Critic," *Sewanee Rev.,* lvi (1948). 597-624; W. J. Bate, "Coleridge on the Function of Art," *Perspectives of Criticism,* ed. Harry Levin (Cambridge, Mass., 1950), pp. 125-159; Albert Gérard, "Coleridge, Keats and the Modern Mind," *EIC,* i (1951). 249-261; Barbara Hardy, "Distinction Without Difference: Coleridge's Fancy and Imagination," *EIC,* i (1951). 336-344, and " 'I Have a Smack of Hamlet': Coleridge and Shakespeare's Characters," *EIC,* viii (1958). 238-255; Margaret L. Wiley, "Coleridge and the Wheels of Intellect," *PMLA,* lxvii (1952). 101-112; George Watson, "Contributions to a Dictionary of Critical Terms: *Imagination* and *Fancy,*" *EIC,* iii (1953). 201-214; Howard H. Creed, "Coleridge's Metacriticism," *PMLA,* lxix (1954). 1160-1180; Frederick B. Rainsberry, "Coleridge and the Paradox of the Poetic Imperative," *ELH,* xxi (1954). 114-145; D. B. Lang, "Point Counterpoint: The Emergence of Fancy and Imagination in Coleridge," *JAAC,* xvi (1958). 384-397; Richard Haven, "Coleridge, Hartley, and the Mystics," *JHI,* xx (1959). 477-494; Emerson R. Marks, "Means and Ends in Coleridge's Critical Method," *ELH,* xxvi (1959). 387-401; Herbert Piper, "The Pantheistic Sources of Coleridge's Early Poetry," *JHI,* xx (1959). 47-59; Lucyle Werkmeister, "Coleridge on Science, Philosophy, and Poetry," *Harvard Theological Rev.,* lii (1959). 85-118, and "The Early Coleridge: His 'Rage for Metaphysics,' " *ibid.,* liv (1961). 99-123; M. M. Badawi, "Coleridge's Formal Criticism of Shakespeare's Plays," *EIC,* x (1960). 148-162; Leonard W. Deen, "Coleridge and the Radicalism of Religious Dissent," *JEGP,* lxi (1962). 496-510; Craig W. Miller, "Coleridge's Concept of Nature," *JHI,* xxv (1964). 77-96; essays by Herbert M. McLuhan, D. G. James, and Kathleen Coburn in *The Major English Romantic Poets,* ed. Thorpe *et al.,* chs. vii-ix; Basil Willey, *Nineteenth Century Studies* (1949), ch. i; Wellek, *History of Modern Criticism,* ii. ch. vi.

1153   The Rime of the Ancient Mariner has attracted much critical attention in recent years, some of it owing to the provocative introduction Robert Penn Warren wrote for an edition of the poem (1946). Bernard Martin, "The Ancient Mariner" and the "Authentic Narrative" (1949) and C. S. Wilkinson, The Wake of the "Bounty" (1953)—both on additional sources of the poem; George Whalley, "The Mariner and the Albatross," UTQ, xvi (1947). 381-398; E. E. Stoll, "Symbolism in Coleridge," PMLA, lxiii (1948). 214-233; E. M. W. Tillyard, "The Rime of the Ancient Mariner," Five Poems 1470-1870 (1948), pp. 66-86; Bowra, The Romantic Imagination, ch. iii; Lionel Stevenson, "The Ancient Mariner as a Dramatic Monologue," Personalist, xxx (1949). 34-44; Coleman O. Parsons, "The Mariner and the Albatross," Virginia Quar. Rev., xxvi (1950). 102-123; Tristram P. Coffin, "Coleridge's Use of the Ballad Stanza in The Rime of the Ancient Mariner," MLQ, xii (1951). 437-445; J. W. R. Purser, "Interpretation of The Ancient Mariner," RES, n.s. viii (1957). 249-256; Richard H. Fogle, "The Genre of The Ancient Mariner," Tulane Stud. in English, vii (1957). 111-124; Elliott B. Gose, Jr., "Coleridge and the Luminous Gloom: An Analysis of the 'Symbolic Language' in The Rime of the Ancient Mariner," PMLA, lxxv (1960). 238-244; R. L. Brett, "Coleridge's The Rime of the Ancient Mariner," Reason and Imagination (1960), pp. 78-107; Ward Pafford, "Coleridge's Wedding Guest," SP, lx (1963). 618-626; Gayle S. Smith, "A Reappraisal of the Moral Stanzas in The Rime of the Ancient Mariner," Stud. in Romanticism, iii (1963). 42-52; A. M. Buchan, "The Sad Wisdom of the Mariner," SP, lxi (1964). 669-688; Daniel McDonald, "Too Much Reality: A Discussion of The Rime of the Ancient Mariner," SEL, iv (1964). 543-554; "The Rime of the Ancient Mariner," A Handbook, ed. Royal A. Gettmann (San Francisco, 1961).

1154   Edgar Jones, "A New Reading of Christabel," Cambridge Jour., v (1951). 97-110; Charles Tomlinson, "Christabel," Interpretations, ed. John Wain (1956), pp. 103-112; Virginia L. Radley, "Christabel: Directions Old and New," SEL, iv (1964). 531-541.

1155   Marshall Suther, Visions of Xanadu (1965); Dorothy F. Mercer, "The Symbolism of Kubla Khan," JAAC, xii (1953). 44-66; Carl R. Woodring, "Coleridge and The Khan," EIC, ix (1959). 361-368; Warren U. Ober, "Southey, Coleridge and Kubla Khan," JEGP, lviii (1959). 414-422; R. H. Fogle, "The Romantic Unity of Kubla Khan," College English, xxii (1960). 112-116; S. K. Heninger, Jr., "A Jungian Reading of Kubla Khan," JAAC, xviii (1960). 358-367; George Watson, "The Meaning of Kubla Khan," REL, ii, no. 1 (1961). 21-29; Alan C. Purves, "Formal Structure in Kubla Khan," Stud. in Romanticism, i (1962). 187-191; Richard Gerber, "Keys to Kubla Khan," ES, xliv (1963). 321-341.—On the group of "conversation poems" to which Frost at Midnight belongs, see Richard H. Fogle, "Coleridge's Conversation Poems," Tulane Stud. in English, v (1955). 103-110; Albert Gérard, "The Systolic Rhythm: The Structure of Coleridge's Conversation Poems," EIC, x (1960). 307-319.—Note 24: Miss Schneider's article is superseded by her book, Coleridge, Opium, and "Kubla Khan" (Chicago, 1953).

1156   Richard H. Fogle, "The Dejection of Coleridge's Ode," ELH, xvii (1950). 71-77; Stephen F. Fogle, "The Design of Coleridge's Dejection," SP, xlviii (1951). 49-55; Charles S. Bouslog, "Structure and Theme in Coleridge's

Dejection: An Ode," MLQ, xxiv (1963). 42-52.—Note 27. See George Whalley, *Coleridge and Sara Hutchinson and the Asra Poems* (Toronto, 1955).

1157 *Biographia Literaria,* ed. George Watson (1956), with useful apparatus.

VI. Robert Southey, Walter Savage Landor, and Other Poets

1159 Southey: *New Letters,* ed. Kenneth Curry (2v, 1965); *Letters from England by Don Manuel Espriella,* ed. Jack Simmons (1952); *Journals of a Residence in Portugal 1800-1801 and a Visit to France 1838,* ed. Adolfo Cabral (Oxford, 1960); *Life of Nelson,* ed. E. R. H. Harvey (1953).—Bibliography in Houtchens, ch. v. Geoffrey Carnall, *Robert Southey and His Age* (Oxford, 1960); Rose Macaulay, "A Romantic Among Philistines," *They Went to Portugal* (1946), pp. 143-165; Malcolm Elwin, *The First Romantics* (1947); George Whalley, "Coleridge and Southey in Bristol, 1795," *RES,* n.s. 1 (1950). 324-340; Kenneth Hopkins, *The Poets Laureate* (1954), ch. xi.

1162 Landor: *Poetry and Prose,* ed. E. K. Chambers (Oxford, 1946); *Poems,* ed. Geoffrey Grigson (1964), a selection.—Bibliography in Houtchens, ch. viii; Robert H. Super, *The Publication of Landor's Works* (1954). Super, *Walter Savage Landor: A Biography* (1954); Malcolm Elwin, *Landor: A Replevin* (1958), not the same book as his *Savage Landor* (1941); Pierre Vitoux, *L'Oeuvre de Walter Savage Landor* (Paris, 1964).

1164 Ernest de Selincourt, "Landor's Prose," *Wordsworthian and Other Studies* (Oxford, 1947), ch. iv.

1166 *The Shorter Poems,* ed. J. B. Sidgwick (Cambridge, 1946). Donald A. Davie, "The Shorter Poems of Walter Savage Landor," *EIC,* 1 (1951). 345-355 (cf. discussion, *ibid.,* 11 [1952]. 214-219).

1167 Crabbe: *New Poems,* ed. Arthur Pollard (Liverpool, 1960). The biography by Crabbe's son was reprinted, with an introduction by Edmund Blunden, in 1947. Lilian Haddakin, *The Poetry of Crabbe* (1955); Oliver F. Sigworth, *Nature's Sternest Painter: Five Essays on the Poetry of George Crabbe* (Tucson, 1964); R. L. Chamberlain, *George Crabbe* (1965); Ian Gregor, "The Last Augustan," *Dublin Rev.,* ccxxix (1955). 37-50; W. K. Thomas, "The Flavour of Crabbe," *Dalhousie Rev.,* xl (1961). 489-504; Walter E. Broman, "Factors in Crabbe's Eminence in the Early Nineteenth Century," *MP,* li (1953). 42-49.

1169 *Recollections of the Table-Talk of Samuel Rogers,* ed. Morchard Bishop (1952); *Italian Journal,* ed. J. R. Hale (1956), first publication. Carl P. Barbier, *Samuel Rogers and William Gilpin: Their Friendship and Correspondence* (1959); Donald Weeks, "Samuel Rogers: Man of Taste," *PMLA,* lxii (1947). 472-486.

1170 Virtually no significant scholarly or critical work has been published on Campbell in recent decades. There is a bibliography in Houtchens, ch. vi.

1171 Moore: *Letters*, ed. Wilfred Dowden (2v, Oxford, 1965). Bibliography in Houtchens, ch. VII. Robert Birley, "Thomas Moore: *Lalla Rookh,*" *Sunk Without Trace: Some Forgotten Masterpieces Reconsidered* (1962), ch. v; Hoover H. Jordan, "Thomas Moore: Artistry in the Song Lyric," *SEL*, II (1962). 403-440.

1172 Leigh Hunt: *Dramatic Criticism, 1808-1831* (1949), *Literary Criticism* (1956), *Political and Occasional Essays* (1962)—all ed. L. H. and C. W. Houtchens.—Bibliography in Houtchens, ch. IX. Clarence D. Thorpe, "Leigh Hunt as Man of Letters," *Literary Criticism*, just cited, pp. 3-73; Carl R. Woodring, "Leigh Hunt as a Political Essayist," *Political and Occasional Essays*, just cited, pp. 3-71; George D. Stout, *The Political History of Leigh Hunt's "Examiner"* (St. Louis, 1949); Jeffrey Fleece, "Leigh Hunt's Shakespearean Criticism," *Essays in Honor of Walter Clyde Curry* (Nashville, 1954), pp. 181-195; Stout, "Leigh Hunt's Shakespeare: A 'Romantic' Concept," *Studies in Memory of Frank Martindale Webster* (St. Louis, 1951), pp. 14-33; Alba H. Warren, *English Poetic Theory, 1825-1865* (Princeton, 1950), ch. VI; Wellek, *History of Modern Criticism*, III. 120-125.

1173 Note 48: A. Lytton Sells, *The Italian Influence in English Poetry* (Bloomington, Ind., 1955); Oswald Doughty, "Dante and the English Romantic Poets," *English Miscellany*, II (1951). 125-169.

1174 William H. Marshall, *Byron, Shelley, Hunt, and "The Liberal"* (Philadelphia, 1960). *Autobiography*, ed. J. E. Morpurgo (1949), well annotated; *Leigh Hunt's Autobiography: The Earliest Sketches*, ed. Stephen F. Fogle (Gainesville, Fla., 1959).

VII. Reviews and Magazines: 1802-1830; The Essayists

1176 John Clive, *Scotch Reviewers: The Edinburgh Review, 1802-1815* (Cambridge, Mass., 1957); Irwin Griggs, John D. Kern, and Elisabeth Schneider, "Early *Edinburgh* Reviewers: A New List," *MP*, XLIII (1946). 192-210; Frank W. Fetter, "The Authorship of Economic Articles in the *Edinburgh Review*, 1802-47," *Jour. of Political Economy*, LXI (1953). 232-259; Thomas Crawford, "The *Edinburgh Review* and Romantic Poetry (1802-29)," *Auckland Univ. College Bull.*, No. 47 (1955).

1177 James A. Greig, *Francis Jeffrey of the Edinburgh Review* (Edinburgh, 1948); J. R. Derby, "The Paradox of Francis Jeffrey: Reason Versus Sensibility," *MLQ*, VII (1946). 489-500; Byron Guyer, "Francis Jeffrey's *Essay on Beauty,*" *HLQ*, XIII (1949). 71-85, and "The Philosophy of Francis Jeffrey," *MLQ*, XI (1950). 17-26.—Frances Hawes, *Henry Brougham* (1957); Chester W. New, *The Life of Henry Brougham to 1830* (Oxford, 1961); Elisabeth Schneider, Irwin Griggs, and John D. Kern, "Brougham's Early Contributions to the *Edinburgh Review*: A New List," *MP*, XLII (1945). 152-173.

1178 *Letters of Sydney Smith*, ed. Nowell C. Smith (2v, Oxford, 1953); *Selected Writings*, ed. W. H. Auden (1956). Gerald Bullett, *Sydney Smith. A Biography and a Selection* (1951).—Hill Shine and Helen C. Shine, *The Quarterly Review under Gifford: Identification of Contributors, 1809-1824* (Chapel

Hill, 1949).—F. O. Tredrey, *The House of Blackwood, 1804-1954* (Edinburgh, 1954); A. L. Strout, *A Bibliography of Articles in Blackwood's Magazine, 1817-1825* (Lubbock, Tex., 1959).

1180 Josephine Bauer, *The London Magazine, 1820-29* (Copenhagen, 1953). —Note 13: On Mahony, see Ethel Mannin, *Two Studies in Integrity* (1954).— Note 14: Studies of Victorian periodicals: *A Century of Punch Cartoons*, ed. R. E. Williams (1955); R. G. G. Price, *A History of Punch* (1957); Diderik Roll-Hansen, *The Academy: 1869-1879* (Copenhagen, 1957); Cyprian Blagden, *"Longman's Magazine," REL*, IV, no. 2 (1963). 9-22; A. J. Gurr, *"Macmillan's Magazine," REL*, VI, no. 1 (1965). 39-55.

1180-1181 *The Portable Charles Lamb*, ed. John Mason Brown (1949); *Essays of Elia*, ed. Malcolm Elwin (1952), both with useful introductions; *Selected Essays, Letters, Poems*, ed. J. L. May (1953); *Letters*, ed. G. Woodcock (1950), a selection; *Selected Letters*, ed. T. S. Matthews (1956). On the deficiencies of Lucas' still unsuperseded edition of the Lambs' letters, see George L. Barnett in *MLQ*, IX (1948). 303-314, and *HLQ*, XVIII (1955). 147-158.—Bibliography in Houtchens, ch. II. J. E. Morpurgo, *Charles Lamb and Elia* (1948); Barnett, *Charles Lamb: The Evolution of Elia* (Bloomington, Ind., 1964); Charles I. Patterson, "Charles Lamb's Insight into the Nature of the Novel," *PMLA*, LXVII (1952). 375-382; Bertram Jessup, "The Mind of Elia," *JHI*, XV (1954). 246-259; Sylvan Barnet, "Charles Lamb's Contributions to the Theory of Dramatic Illusion," *PMLA*, LXIX (1954). 1150-1159; Richard Haven, "The Romantic Art of Charles Lamb," *ELH*, XXX (1963). 137-146; Daniel J. Mulcahy, "Charles Lamb: The Antithetical Manner and the Two Planes," *SEL*, III (1963). 517-542; René Fréchet, "Lamb's 'Artificial Comedy,'" *REL*, V, no. 3 (1964). 27-41; Donald H. Reiman, "Thematic Unity in Lamb's Familiar Essays," *JEGP*, LXIV (1965). 470-476. On the genre to which Hunt and Hazlitt, as well as Lamb, contributed, see Melvin R. Watson, "The *Spectator* Tradition and the Development of the Familiar Essay," *ELH*, XIII (1946). 189-215.

1185 Hazlitt: *Essays*, ed. Catherine M. Maclean (1949), a selection; Maclean, *Hazlitt Painted by Himself* (1948), a synthetic autobiography.—Bibliography in Houtchens, ch. III. Herschel Baker, *William Hazlitt* (Cambridge, Mass., 1962), especially valuable for Hazlitt's intellectual milieu; William P. Albrecht, *William Hazlitt and the Malthusian Controversy* (Albuquerque, 1950) and *Hazlitt and the Creative Imagination* (Lawrence, Kan., 1965); John W. Bullitt, "Hazlitt and the Romantic Conception of the Imagination," *PQ*, XXIV (1945). 343-361; Clarence D. Thorpe, "Keats and Hazlitt," *PMLA*, LXII (1947). 487-502; Charles I. Patterson, "William Hazlitt as a Critic of Prose Fiction," *PMLA*, LXVIII (1953). 1001-1016; Alvin Whitley, "Hazlitt and the Theater," *Univ. of Texas Stud. in English*, XXXIV (1955). 67-100; Albrecht, "Hazlitt's Preference for Tragedy," *PMLA*, LXXI (1956). 1042-1051, and "Hazlitt on the Poetry of Wit," *PMLA*, LXXV (1960). 245-249; G. D. Klingopulos, "Hazlitt as Critic," *EIC*, VI (1956). 386-403; Wellek, *History of Modern Criticism*, II. 188-212; Joseph W. Donohue, Jr., "Hazlitt's Sense of the Dramatic Actor as Tragic Character," *SEL*, V (1965). 705-721.

1187 *Liber Amoris and Dramatic Criticisms*, ed. Charles Morgan (1948), with a long introduction; *Conversations of James Northcote*, ed. Frank Swinnerton (1949).—Robert E. Robinson, *William Hazlitt's Life of Napoleon Buona-parte: Its Sources and Characteristics* (Geneva, 1959).

1188 DeQuincey: *Recollections of the Lake Poets*, ed. E. Sackville-West (1948), John E. Jordan (1961, as *Reminiscences of the English Lake Poets*); *Confessions of an English Opium Eater*, ed. Sackville-West (1950), Malcolm Elwin (1956), Jordan (1960); *The English Mail Coach and Other Essays*, ed. Jordan (1961). (The volumes by Jordan, in Everyman's Library, are noteworthy for the authority of their editing.) *Selected Writings*, ed. Philip Van Doren Stern (1949). —Bibliography in Houtchens, ch. x. Jordan, *Thomas DeQuincey: Literary Critic* (Berkeley, 1952) and *DeQuincey to Wordsworth: A Biography of a Relationship* (Berkeley, 1962); Albert Goldman, *The Mine and the Mint* (Carbondale, Ill., 1965), on De Quincey's sources; Jordan, "DeQuincey's Dramaturgic Criticism," *ELH*, XVIII (1951). 32-49; Charles I. Patterson, "DeQuincey's Conception of the Novel as Literature of Power," *PMLA*, LXX (1955). 375-389; Clifford Leech, "DeQuincey as Literary Critic," *REL*, II, no. 1 (1961). 38-48; Geoffrey Carnall, "DeQuincey on the Knocking at the Gate," *ibid.*, pp. 49-57; J. Hillis Miller, *The Disappearance of God* (Cambridge, Mass., 1963), ch. II.

1190 Note 33: See also Elisabeth Schneider, *Coleridge, Opium, and "Kubla Khan"* (Chicago, 1953), pp. 72-80.

1191 Shozo Kobayashi, *Rhythm in the Prose of Thomas DeQuincey* (Tokyo, 1956); Ian Jack, "DeQuincey Revises His *Confessions*," *PMLA*, LXXII (1957). 122-146; Richard H. Byrns, "DeQuincey's Revisions in the *Dream-Fugue*," *PMLA*, LXXVII (1962). 97-101.

VIII. Gothic Romance and the Novel of Doctrine

1192 On fiction in general during the romantic period, see Walter Allen, *The English Novel* (1954), ch. III; Lionel Stevenson, *The English Novel* (Boston, 1960), chs. VII-VIII.—Devendra P. Varma, *The Gothic Flame, Being a History of the Gothic Novel in England* (1957); Lowry Nelson, Jr., "Night Thoughts on the Gothic Novel," *Yale Rev.*, LII (1962). 236-257.

1193 Alan D. McKillop, "Charlotte Smith's Letters," *HLQ*, XV (1952). 237-255.

1194 Aline Grant, *Ann Radcliffe* (Denver, 1951); R. D. Havens, "Ann Radcliffe's Nature Descriptions," *MLN*, LXVI (1951). 251-255; William Ruff, "Ann Radcliffe, or the Hand of Taste," *The Age of Johnson: Essays Presented to C. B. Tinker* (New Haven, 1949), pp. 183-193.
Note 7: William Powell Jones, "New Light on Sir Egerton Brydges," *Harvard Library Bull.*, XI (1957). 102-116.

1195 *The Monk*, original text ed. Louis F. Peck (1952); Karl S. Guthke, "M. G. Lewis' *The Twins*," *HLQ*, XXV (1962). 189-223, first printing of a farce. Peck, *A Life of Matthew G. Lewis* (Cambridge, Mass., 1961).—Note 13: *Singular Travels, Campaigns and Adventures of Baron Münchhausen*, ed. John Carswell (1948). Carswell, *The Prospector: Being the Life and Times of Rudolf Erich Raspe* (1950).

1196 Mary Shelley: *Mathilda*, ed. Elizabeth Nitchie (Chapel Hill, 1959);

Journal, ed. Frederick L. Jones (Norman, Okla., 1947); *My Best Mary: The Selected Letters,* ed. Muriel Spark and Derek Stanford (1953).—Spark, *Child of Light* (1952); Nitchie, *Mary Shelley* (New Brunswick, 1953); Ernest J. Lovell, Jr., "Byron and the Byronic Hero in the Novels of Mary Shelley," *Univ. of Texas Stud. in English,* xxx (1951). 158-183, and "Byron and Mary Shelley," *KSJ,* II (1953). 35-49; Burton R. Pollin, "Philosophical and Literary Sources of *Franken-stein,*" *CL,* xvii (1965). 97-108.

Maturin: *Melmoth the Wanderer,* ed. W. F. Axton (Lincoln, Neb., 1961). H. W. Piper and A. Norman Jeffares, "Maturin the Innovator," *HLQ,* xxi (1958). 261-284.

1197 Godwin: *Imogen: A Pastoral Romance from the Ancient British,* ed. Jack Marken *et al.* (1963), reprinted from the 1784 edition.—P. N. Furbank, "Godwin's Novels," *EIC,* v (1955). 214-228; Patrick Cruttwell, "On *Caleb Williams,*" *Hudson Rev.,* xi (1958). 87-95; Harvey Gross, "The Pursuer and the Pursued: A Study of *Caleb Williams,*" *Texas Stud. in Lit. and Lang.,* i (1959). 401-411; George Sherburn, "Godwin's Later Novels," *Stud. in Romanticism,* i (1962). 65-82.—Note 23: Rodney M. Baine, *Thomas Holcroft and the Revolutionary Novel* (Athens, Ga., 1965); V. R. Stallbaumer, "Thomas Holcroft as a Novelist," *ELH,* xv (1948). 194-218.

1198 Maria Edgeworth: *Castle Rackrent,* ed. George Watson (1964), scholarly text.—Isabel C. Clarke, *Maria Edgeworth* (1950); P. H. Newby, *Maria Edgeworth* (1950); Elisabeth Inglis-Jones, *The Great Maria* (1959); W. H. G. Armytage, "Little Woman," *Queen's Quar.,* lvi (1949). 248-257.

IX. Jane Austen

1200 The definitive Oxford Edition of Jane Austen's works, ed. R. W. Chapman, was completed in 1954 with the publication of Vol. vi, *Minor Works,* incorporating *Volume the First* (first published 1933), *Love and Freindship* (1922, retitled *Volume the Second* when edited from manuscript by B. C. Southam, 1963), and *Volume the Third* (1951). Chawton Edition (6v, 1948); *The Watsons,* a fragment "continued and completed" by John Coates (1958); *Letters to Her Sister Cassandra and Others,* ed. Chapman (rev. 1952), *Letters 1796-1817,* ed. Chapman (1955), a selection.—Chapman, *Jane Austen: A Critical Bibliography* (Oxford, 1953, rev. 1955). Chapman, *Jane Austen: Facts and Problems* (Oxford, 1948); Elizabeth Jenkins, *Jane Austen* (1949); Marvin Mudrick, *Jane Austen: Irony as Defense and Discovery* (Princeton, 1952); Andrew Wright, *Jane Austen's Novels: A Study in Structure* (1953); Howard S. Babb, *Jane Austen's Novels: The Fabric of Dialogue* (Columbus, Ohio, 1962); Robert Liddell, *The Novels of Jane Austen* (1963); Southam, *Jane Austen's Literary Manuscripts* (1964); W. A. Craik, *Jane Austen: The Six Novels* (1965); A. Walton Litz, *Jane Austen: A Study of Her Artistic Development* (1965); Louise D. Cohen, "Insight, the Essence of Jane Austen's Artistry," *NCF,* viii (1953). 213-224; Frank O'Connor, "Jane Austen and the Flight from Fancy," *The Mirror in the Roadway* (1956), pp. 17-41; Frank W. Bradbrook, "The Letters of Jane Austen," *Cambridge Jour.,* vii (1954). 259-276; Langdon Elsbree, "Jane Austen and the Dance of Fidelity and Complaisance," *NCF,* xv (1960). 113-136; Cynthia

Griffin, "The Development of Realism in Jane Austen's Early Novels," *ELH,* xxx (1963). 36-52; Frederick R. Karl, "Jane Austen: The Necessity of Wit," *An Age of Fiction: The Nineteenth Century British Novel* (1964), pp. 27-62; *Discussions of Jane Austen,* ed. William Heath (Boston, 1961); *Jane Austen: A Collection of Critical Essays,* ed. Ian Watt (1963).

Sense and Sensibility, ed. David Daiches (1950), Lord David Cecil (1957).— Christopher Gillie, "*Sense and Sensibility:* An Assessment," *EIC,* ix (1959). 1-9.

Pride and Prejudice, ed. David Daiches (1950), Mark Schorer (Boston, 1956), Robert Daniel (1960), Bradford A. Booth (1963), the last-named with excerpts from the criticism.—Samuel Kliger, "Jane Austen's *Pride and Prejudice* in the Eighteenth Century Mode," *UTQ,* xvi (1947). 357-370; Mark Schorer, "Pride Unprejudiced," *Kenyon Rev.,* xviii (1956). 72-91; Howard S. Babb, "Dialogue with Feeling: A Note on *Pride and Prejudice,*" *Kenyon Rev.,* xx (1958). 203-216; E. M. Halliday, "Narrative Perspective in *Pride and Prejudice,*" *NCF,* xv (1960). 65-71; Charles J. McCann, "Setting and Character in *Pride and Prejudice,*" *NCF,* xix (1964). 65-75; Dorothy Van Ghent, *The English Novel: Form and Function* (1953), pp. 99-111—hereafter cited as Van Ghent.

Mansfield Park, ed. Mark Schorer (1959), R. A. Brower (Boston, 1965).— Lionel Trilling, "*Mansfield Park,*" *Partisan Rev.,* xxi (1954). 492-511; Joseph M. Duffy, Jr., "Moral Integrity and Moral Anarchy in *Mansfield Park,*" *ELH,* xxiii (1956). 71-91; Charles Murrah, "The Background of *Mansfield Park,*" *From Jane Austen to Joseph Conrad: Essays Collected in Memory of James T. Hillhouse,* ed. Robert C. Rathburn and Martin Steinmann (Minneapolis, 1958), pp. 23-34 (this collection is cited hereafter by title alone); David Lodge, "A Question of Judgment: The Theatricals at Mansfield Park," *NCF,* xvii (1962). 275-282; Thomas R. Edwards, Jr., "The Difficult Beauty of *Mansfield Park,*" *NCF,* xx (1965). 51-67; Joseph W. Donohue, Jr., "Ordination and the Divided House at Mansfield Park," *ELH,* xxxii (1965). 169-178.

Emma, ed. Trilling (Boston, 1957).—F. W. Bradbrook, *Jane Austen: "Emma"* (1961); E. N. Hayes, "*Emma:* A Dissenting Opinion," *NCF,* iv (1949). 1-20; Joseph M. Duffy, Jr., "*Emma:* The Awakening from Innocence," *ELH,* xxi (1954). 39-53; Edgar F. Shannon, Jr., "*Emma:* Character and Construction," *PMLA,* lxxi (1956). 637-650; Wayne C. Booth, "Point of View and Control of Distance in *Emma,*" *NCF,* xvi (1961). 95-116; R. E. Hughes, "The Education of Emma Woodhouse," *NCF,* xvi (1961). 69-74; G. Armour Craig, "Jane Austen's *Emma:* The Truths and Disguises of Human Disclosure," *In Defense of Reading,* ed. R. A. Brower and W. R. Poirier (1962), pp. 235-255; Malcolm Bradbury, "Jane Austen's *Emma,*" *Critical Quar.,* iv (1962). 335-346; Edward M. White, "*Emma* and the Parodic Point of View," *NCF,* xviii (1963). 55-63; Ward Hellstrom, "Francophobia in *Emma,*" *SEL,* v (1965). 607-617; Arnold Kettle, "*Emma,*" *An Introduction to the English Novel* (2v, 1951), i. 90-104—hereafter cited as Kettle.

John K. Mathison, "*Northanger Abbey* and Jane Austen's Conception of the Value of Fiction," *ELH,* xxiv (1957). 138-152; Alan D. McKillop, "Critical Realism in *Northanger Abbey,*" *From Jane Austen to Joseph Conrad,* pp. 35-45.

Persuasion, ed. David Daiches (1958), Andrew Wright (1965), D .W. Harding (1965).—Joseph M. Duffy, Jr., "Structure and Idea in Jane Austen's *Persuasion,*" *NCF,* viii (1954). 272-289; Paul N. Zietlow, "Luck and Fortuitous Circumstance in *Persuasion:* Two Interpretations," *ELH,* xxxii (1965). 179-195.

X. Sir Walter Scott

1207 Scott's *Private Letters of the Seventeenth Century* was first published in full, ed. Douglas Grant (Oxford, 1947). *Selections from the Prose,* ed. J. C. Trewin (1952). Tait's edition of Scott's *Journal* was completed with the publication of Vol. III (Edinburgh, 1946).—Bibliography in Houtchens, ch. IV. Una Pope-Hennessy, *Sir Walter Scott* (1948); Hesketh Pearson, *Walter Scott: His Life and Personality* (1954); *Sir William Gell's Reminiscences of Sir Walter Scott's Residence in Italy,* ed. G. H. Needler (Toronto, 1953; rev. J. C. Corson, 1957), first publication from the manuscript; Needler, *Goethe and Scott* (Toronto, 1950); *Sir Walter Scott Lectures, 1940-1948* (Edinburgh, 1950), by Sir Herbert Grierson, Edwin Muir, G. M. Young, and S. C. Roberts; George Lukács, *The Historical Novel* (English trans., 1962), Part 1; Alexander Welsh, *The Hero of the Waverley Novels* (New Haven, 1963); Coleman O. Parsons, *Witchcraft and Demonology in Scott's Fiction* (1964); Christina Keith, *The Author of Waverley: A Study in the Personality of Sir Walter Scott* (1964); David Daiches, "Scott's Achievement as a Novelist," *Literary Essays* (Edinburgh, 1956), pp. 88-121; John Lauber, "Scott on the Art of Fiction," *SEL,* III (1963). 543-554; Duncan Forbes, "The Rationalism of Sir Walter Scott," *Cambridge Jour.,* VII (1953). 20-35; Paul Roberts, "Sir Walter Scott's Contributions to the English Vocabulary," *PMLA,* LXVIII (1953). 189-210; Richard French, "The Religion of Sir Walter Scott," *Stud. in Scottish Lit.,* II (1964). 32-44; Alice Chandler, "Sir Walter Scott and the Medieval Revival," *NCF,* XIX (1965). 315-332.

1208 William Montgomerie, "Sir Walter Scott as Ballad Editor," *RES,* n.s. VII (1956). 158-163.

1210 On *Harold the Dauntless* see J. T. Hillhouse, "Sir Walter's Last Long Poem," *HLQ,* XVI (1952). 53-73.

1211 S. Stewart Gordon, "*Waverley* and the 'Unified Design,'" *ELH,* XVIII (1951). 107-122; Nelson S. Bushnell, "Walter Scott's Advent as a Novelist of Manners," *Stud. in Scottish Lit.,* I (1963). 15-34.—*Rob Roy,* ed. Edgar Johnson (Boston, 1956).—Note 14: This theory was finally disposed of by Robert D. Mayo, "The Chronology of the Waverley Novels: The Evidence of the Manuscripts," *PMLA,* LXIII (1948). 935-949.

1212 *The Heart of Midlothian,* ed. David Daiches (1948).—P. F. Fisher, "Providence, Fate, and the Historical Imagination in Scott's *The Heart of Midlothian,*" *NCF,* X (1955). 99-114; Robin Mayhead, "*The Heart of Midlothian:* Scott as Artist," *EIC,* VI (1956). 266-277 (cf. David Craig, *ibid.,* VIII [1958]. 217-255); Winifred Lynskey, "The Drama of the Elect and the Reprobate in Scott's *Heart of Midlothian,*" *Boston Univ. Stud. in English,* IV (1960). 39-48; William H. Marshall, "Point of View and Structure in *The Heart of Midlothian,*" *NCF,* XVI (1961). 257-262; Van Ghent, pp. 113-124.—Robert C. Gordon, "*The Bride of Lammermoor:* A Novel of Tory Pessimism," *NCF,* XII (1957). 110-124.—Joseph E. Duncan, "The Anti-Romantic in *Ivanhoe,*" *NCF,* IX (1955). 293-300.

1213 David Daiches, "Scott's *Redgauntlet,*" *From Jane Austen to Joseph Conrad,* pp. 46-59; D. D. Devlin, "Scott and *Redgauntlet,*" *REL,* IV, no. 1 (1963). 91-103.

1218   Donald Davie, *The Heyday of Sir Walter Scott* (1961); John Henry Raleigh, "What Scott Meant to the Victorians," *VS*, VII (1963). 7-34; Francis R. Hart, *"The Fair Maid,* Manzoni's *Betrothed,* and the Grounds of Waverley Criticism," *NCF*, XVIII (1963). 103-118.

XI. Lord Byron

1219   *Poems,* ed. Guy Pocock (3v, 1948); *Selections,* ed. Peter Quennell (1949); *Selected Poetry,* ed. Leslie A. Marchand (1951); *Selected Poetry and Letters,* ed. E. E. Bostetter (1951); *Byron: A Self-Portrait,* ed. Quennell (2v, 1950), a selection from the letters and journals; *His Very Self and Voice: Collected Conversations,* ed. Ernest J. Lovell, Jr. (1954); *Selected Letters,* ed. Jacques Barzun (1953).—Bibliography in Raysor, ch. IV, and annually in *KSJ.* Marchand, *Byron: A Biography* (3v, 1957), the standard life; Lovell, *Byron: The Record of a Quest* (Austin, Tex., 1949); G. Wilson Knight, *Lord Byron: Christian Virtues* (1952); Paul West, *Byron and the Spoiler's Art* (1960); Andrew Rutherford, *Byron: A Critical Study* (Edinburgh, 1961); William H. Marshall, *The Structure of Byron's Major Poems* (Philadelphia, 1962); Peter L. Thorslev, Jr., *The Byronic Hero: Types and Prototypes* (Minneapolis, 1962); M. K. Joseph, *Byron the Poet* (1964); Marchand, *Byron's Poetry: A Critical Introduction* (1965); Marius Bewley, "The Colloquial Mode of Byron," *Scrutiny,* XVI (1949). 8-23; Carl Lefevre, "Lord Byron's Fiery Convert of Revenge," *SP,* XLIX (1952). 468-487; W. W. Robson, "Byron as Poet," *Proc. Brit. Acad.,* XLIII (1957). 25-62; West, "Byronic Romance and Nature's Frailty," *Dalhousie Rev.,* XXXIX (1959). 219-229, and "Byron's Farce with Language," *Twentieth Century,* CLXV (1959). 138-151; Bernard Blackstone, "Guilt and Retribution in Byron's Sea Poems," *REL,* II, no. 1 (1961). 58-69; David V. Erdman, "Byron and 'the New Force of the People,'" *KSJ,* XI (1962). 47-64; Frederick L. Beaty, "Byron's Concept of Ideal Love," *KSJ,* XII (1963). 37-54; essays by W. W. Pratt and Marchand in *The Major English Romantic Poets,* ed. Thorpe *et al.,* chs. XI-XII; *Byron: A Collection of Critical Essays,* ed. West (1963).

1220   William A. Borst, *Lord Byron's First Pilgrimage* (New Haven, 1948). —Note 5: Michael Joyce, *My Friend H* (1948); E. R. Vincent, *Byron, Hobhouse, and Foscolo* (Cambridge, 1949); Andrew Rutherford, "The Influence of Hobhouse on *Childe Harold's Pilgrimage,* Canto IV," *RES,* n.s. XII (1961). 391-397.

1222   See G. Wilson Knight, *Lord Byron's Marriage: The Evidence of the Asterisks* (1957), a highly controversial treatment.

1223   Bertrand Evans, "Manfred's Remorse and Dramatic Tradition," *PMLA,* LXII (1947). 752-773; Maurice J. Quinlan, "Byron's *Manfred* and Zoroastrianism," *JEGP,* LVII (1958). 726-738; Ward Pafford, "Byron and the Mind of Man: *Childe Harold III-IV* and *Manfred,*" *Stud. in Romanticism,* I (1962). 105-127.

1224   *Don Juan,* ed. T. G. Steffan and W. W. Pratt (4v, Austin, Tex., 1957), Vols. II-IV providing a variorum text of the poem and full notes; ed. Peter Quennell (1949), Louis Kronenberger (1949), L. A. Marchand (Boston, 1958), with valuable apparatus.—Steffan, *The Making of a Masterpiece* (Vol. 1 of the edition first cited), describes in detail Byron's composing and revising of *Don Juan;* see also his articles in *MP*, xliv (1947). 141-164, and xlvi (1949). 217-241; *Texas Stud. in English*, xxvi (1947). 108-168; and *SP*, xlvi (1949). 440-452. Andràs Horn, *Byron's "Don Juan" and the Eighteenth Century English Novel* (Bern, 1962); George M. Ridenour, *The Style of "Don Juan"* (New Haven, 1960), and "The Mode of Byron's *Don Juan*," *PMLA*, lxxix (1964). 442-446; W. H. Auden, *"Don Juan," The Dyer's Hand* (1962), pp. 386-406; C. N. Stavrou, "Religion in Byron's *Don Juan*," *SEL*, iii (1963). 567-594; Bowra, *The Romantic Imagination*, ch. vii; Lovell, "Irony and Image in Byron's *Don Juan*," *The Major English Romantic Poets*, ed. Thorpe *et al.*, ch. x.

1226 Much new light is thrown on Byron's liaison with the Countess Guiccioli in Iris Origo, *The Last Attachment* (1949). See also Leslie A. Marchand, "Lord Byron and Count Alborghetti," *PMLA*, lxiv (1949). 976-1007.

1228 See C. L. Cline, *Byron, Shelley, and Their Pisan Circle* (Cambridge, Mass., 1952).—The acrimonious aftermath of Byron's death is described in detail in Doris Langley Moore, *The Late Lord Byron* (1961).

XII. Percy Bysshe Shelley

1230 *Shelley's Prose, or The Trumpet of a Prophecy*, ed. David Lee Clark (Albuquerque, 1954), important for texts; *The Esdaile Notebook: A Volume of Early Poems*, ed. Kenneth N. Cameron (1964); *The Esdaile Poems*, ed. Neville Rogers (1966). Volumes of selections by H. J. Stenning (1948), Morchard Bishop (1949), Richard Church (1949), John Heath-Stubbs (1949), A. S. B. Glover (1951), Carlos Baker (1951), Cameron (1951), Edmund Blunden (1954), John Holloway (1960), G. M. Matthews (1964). *Letters*, ed. Frederick L. Jones (2v, Oxford, 1964), replacing the Ingpen edition; *Shelley and His Circle, 1773-1822*, ed. Cameron (8v, Cambridge, Mass., 1961-   ), an important assemblage of documents.—Bibliography in Raysor, ch. v, and annually in *KSJ*. Cameron, *The Young Shelley: Genesis of a Radical* (1950); *Mary Shelley's Journal*, ed. Jones (Norman, Okla., 1947); Joseph Barrell, *Shelley and the Thought of His Time* (New Haven, 1947); A. M. D. Hughes, *The Nascent Mind of Shelley* (Oxford, 1947); Baker, *Shelley's Major Poetry: The Fabric of a Vision* (Princeton, 1948); D. G. James, *The Romantic Comedy* (1948), Part ii; Anthony Durand, *Shelley on the Nature of Poetry* (Quebec, 1948); James A. Notopoulos, *The Platonism of Shelley* (Durham, N.C., 1949); Richard H. Fogle, *The Imagery of Keats and Shelley* (Chapel Hill, 1949); Sylva Norman, *Flight of the Skylark: The Development of Shelley's Reputation* (Norman, Okla., 1954); Peter Butter, *Shelley's Idols of the Cave* (Edinburgh, 1954); C. E. Pulos, *The Deep Truth: A Study of Shelley's Skepticism* (Lincoln, Neb., 1954); Bice Chiappelli, *Il Pensiero religioso di Shelley* (Rome, 1956); Neville Rogers, *Shelley at Work: A Critical Inquiry* (Oxford, 1956); David Perkins, *The Quest for Permanence: The Symbolism of Wordsworth, Shelley, and Keats* (Cambridge, Mass., 1959); Desmond King-Hele, *Shelley: His Thought and Work* (1960); Hélène Lemaître, *Shelley, Poète des éléments* (Paris, 1962)—these two important for scientific matters; Glenn O'Malley, *Shelley and Synesthesia* (Evanston, Ill., 1964); Raymond D. Havens, "Structure and Prosodic Pattern in Shelley's Lyrics," *PMLA*, lxv (1950). 1076-1087; Frederick A. Pottle, "The Case of

Shelley," *PMLA*, LXVII (1952). 589-608; Matthews, "A Volcano's Voice in Shelley," *ELH*, XXIV (1957). 191-228; three articles by Newell F. Ford, "Paradox and Irony in Shelley's Poetry," *SP*, LVII (1960). 648-662, "The Wit in Shelley's Poetry," *SEL*, I, no. 4 (1961). 1-22, and "The Symbolism of Shelley's Swans," *Stud. in Romanticism*, I (1962). 175-183; Ross G. Woodman, "Shelley's Changing Attitude to Plato," *JHI*, XXI (1960). 497-510; Daniel Hughes, "Kindling and Dwindling: The Poetic Process in Shelley," *KSJ*, XIII (1964). 13-28; essays by Havens, Baker, S. C. Wilcox, and Herbert Read in *The Major English Romantic Poets*, ed. Thorpe *et al.*, chs. XIII-XVI; *Shelley: A Collection of Critical Essays*, ed. George M. Ridenour (1965).

1231 Winifred Scott, *Jefferson Hogg* (1951).

1232 The life and character of Harriet Westbrook Shelley are sympathetically studied in Louise S. Boas, *Harriet Shelley: Five Long Years* (1962).

1234 Frederick L. Jones, "The Inconsistency of Shelley's *Alastor*," *ELH*, XIII (1946). 291-298, and "The Vision Theme in Shelley's *Alastor* and Related Works," *SP*, XLIV (1947). 108-125; Evan K. Gibson, "*Alastor*: A Reinterpretation," *PMLA*, LXII (1947). 1022-1045; A. M. D. Hughes, "*Alastor, or the Spirit of Solitude*," *MLR*, XLIII (1948). 465-470; Albert Gérard, "*Alastor*, or the Spirit of Solipsism," *PQ*, XXXIII (1954). 164-177.

1235 Note 19: W. M. Parker, "The Stockbroker Author," *Quarterly Rev.*, CCXC (1952). 121-134.

1236 Carlos Baker, "Shelley's Ferrarese Maniac," *English Institute Essays 1946* (1947), pp. 41-73; G. M. Matthews, "*Julian and Maddalo*: the Draft and the Meaning," *Studia Neophil.*, XXXV (1963). 57-84, the best text.
Prometheus Unbound: A Variorum Edition, ed. Lawrence J. Zillman (Seattle, 1959).—Bennett Weaver, "*Prometheus Unbound*" (Ann Arbor, 1957), "Pre-Promethean Thought in the Prose of Shelley," *PQ*, XXVII (1948). 193-208, and "*Prometheus Bound* and *Prometheus Unbound*," *PMLA*, LXIV (1949). 115-133; Earl R. Wasserman, *Shelley's "Prometheus Unbound": A Critical Reading* (Baltimore, 1965); Bowra, *The Romantic Imagination*, ch. V; Richard H. Fogle, "Image and Imagelessness: A Limited Reading of *Prometheus Unbound*," *KSJ*, I (1952). 23-36; D. J. Hughes, "Potentiality in *Prometheus Unbound*," *Stud. in Romanticism*, II (1963). 107-126.

1238 Richard H. Fogle, "The Imaginal Design of Shelley's *Ode to the West Wind*," *ELH*, XV (1948). 219-226; Stewart C. Wilcox, "Imagery, Ideas, and Design in Shelley's *Ode to the West Wind*," *SP*, XLVII (1950). 634-649; W. Schrickx, "Shelley's *Ode to the West Wind*: An Analysis," *Revue des langues vivantes*, XIX (1953). 396-404; Neville Rogers, "Shelley and the West Wind," *London Mag.*, III, no. 6 (1956). 56-68.—Stewart C. Wilcox, "The Sources, Symbolism, and Unity of Shelley's *Skylark*," *SP*, XLVI (1949). 560-576.—On Shelley's last years see Ivan Roe, *Shelley: The Last Phase* (1953) and Milton Wilson, *Shelley's Later Poetry: A Study of His Prophetic Imagination* (1959).

1239 Kenneth N. Cameron, "The Planet-Tempest Passage in *Epipsychidion*," *PMLA*, LXIII (1948). 950-972; D. J. Hughes, "Coherence and Collapse in Shelley, with Particular Reference to *Epipsychidion*," *ELH*, XXVIII (1961). 260-283.—Melvin R. Watson, "The Thematic Unity of *Adonais*," *KSJ*, I (1952). 41-46; Earl R. Wasserman, "*Adonais*: Progressive Revelation as a Poetic Mode," *ELH*, XXI (1954). 274-326; Patrick J. Mahony, "An Analysis of Shelley's Craftsmanship in

Adonais," SEL, IV (1964). 555-568.—Donald H. Reiman, *Shelley's "The Triumph of Life": A Critical Study* (Urbana, Ill., 1965), including variorum text; G. M. Mathews, *"The Triumph of Life:* A New Text," *Studia Neophil.*, XXXII (1960). 271-309; P. H. Butter, "Sun and Shape in Shelley's *The Triumph of Life," RES*, n.s. XIII (1962). 40-51.

1240 The many inconsistencies and inaccuracies in Trelawny's successive narratives of Shelley's death and cremation are pointed out by L. A. Marchand, "Trelawny on the Death of Shelley," *Keats-Shelley Memorial Bull.*, IV (1952). 9-34.

XIII. John Keats

1241 Garrod's definitive ed. of Keats's *Poetical Works* was revised in 1958. There are numerous convenient editions of the poems, most of them selections: John Middleton Murry (1948), Richard Church (1948), Lawrence Whistler (1950), George H. Ford (1950), R. Vallance and B. Ifor Evans (1950), Richard H. Fogle (1951), Harold E. Briggs (1951), J. E. Morpurgo (1953), J. H. Walsh (1954), J. R. Caldwell (1954), Douglas Bush (Boston, 1959). *Letters,* ed. Hyder E. Rollins (2v, Cambridge, Mass., 1958), superseding the Buxton Forman edition; *Selected Letters,* ed. Lionel Trilling (1951, rev. 1956); *Letters,* ed. Frederick Page (1954), another selection.—James R. MacGillivray, *John Keats: A Bibliography and Reference Guide* (Toronto, 1949); Raysor, ch. VI; annual bibliography in *KSJ.* Walter J. Bate, *John Keats* (Cambridge, Mass., 1963); Aileen Ward, *John Keats: The Making of a Poet* (1963)—the two best biographical studies; Dorothy Hewlett, *Adonais, A Life of John Keats* (rev. 1949); three books by Rollins, *The Keats Circle* (2v, Cambridge, Mass., 1948), *More Letters and Poems of the Keats Circle* (Cambridge, Mass., 1955)—reissued together (2v, Cambridge, Mass., 1965)—and *Keats's Reputation in America to 1848* (Cambridge, Mass., 1946); Robert Gittings, *John Keats: The Living Year* (1954) and *The Mask of Keats: A Study of Problems* (1956), both controversial but often stimulating and illuminating; J. R. Caldwell, *John Keats' Fancy* (Ithaca, 1945); Lord Gorell, *John Keats: The Principle of Beauty* (1948); D. G. James, *The Romantic Comedy* (1948), Part II; Murry, *The Mystery of Keats* (1949) and *Keats* (1955), two more revisions of his *Studies in Keats;* Richard H. Fogle, *The Imagery of Keats and Shelley* (Chapel Hill, 1949); Newell F. Ford, *The Prefigurative Imagination of Keats* (Stanford, 1951); Earl Wasserman, *The Finer Tone* (Baltimore, 1953), highly sophisticated readings of five poems; Guy Murchie, *The Spirit of Place in Keats* (1955); Michele Renzulli, *John Keats: L'Uomo e il poeta* (Rome, 1956); E. C. Pettet, *On the Poetry of Keats* (Cambridge, 1957); Bernice Slote, *Keats and the Dramatic Principle* (Lincoln, Neb., 1958); *John Keats: A Reassessment,* ed. Kenneth Muir (Liverpool, 1958), essays by various writers; David Perkins, *The Quest for Permanence: The Symbolism of Wordsworth, Shelley, and Keats* (Cambridge, Mass., 1959); Bernard Blackstone, *The Consecrated Urn: An Interpretation of Keats in Terms of Growth and Form* (1959); Walter H. Evert, *Aesthetic and Myth in the Poetry of Keats* (Princeton, 1965); Robert W. Stallman, "Keats the Apollinian: The Time-and-Space Logic of His Poems as Paintings," *UTQ*, XVI (1947). 143-156; Ford, "Keats, Empathy, and 'the Poetical Character,'" *SP*, XLV (1948). 477-490; R. D. Havens, "Of Beauty and Reality in Keats," *ELH*, xvii (1950). 206-213; Albert Gérard, "Coleridge, Keats, and the Modern Mind," *EIC*, i (1951). 249-261, and "Keats and the Romantic *Sehnsucht*," *UTQ*, xxviii (1959). 160-175; Jacob D. Wigod, "Negative Capability and Wise Passiveness," *PMLA*, lxvii (1952). 383-390; Dorothy Van Ghent, "Keats's Myth of the Hero," *KSJ*, iii (1954). 7-25; Roberta D. Cornelius, "Keats as a Humanist," *KSJ*, v (1956). 87-96; James D. Boulger, "Keats's Symbolism," *ELH*, xxviii (1961). 244-259; John Bayley, "Keats and Reality," *Proc. Brit. Acad.*, xlviii (1962). 91-125; essays by Bate, Bush, Cleanth Brooks, and Murry in *The Major English Romantic Poets*, ed. Thorpe *et al.*, chs. xvii-xx; *Keats: A Collection of Critical Essays*, ed. Bate (1964).

1244   Newell F. Ford, "*Endymion*—a Neo-Platonic Allegory?", *ELH*, xiv (1947). 64-76, and "The Meaning of 'Fellowship with Essence' in *Endymion*," *PMLA*, lxii (1947). 1061-1076; Jacob I. Wigod, "The Meaning of *Endymion*," *PMLA*, lxviii (1953). 779-790; Carroll Arnett, "Thematic Structure in Keats's *Endymion*," *Texas Stud. in English*, xxxvi (1957). 100-109; Glen O. Allen, "The Fall of Endymion: A Study in Keats's Intellectual Growth," *KSJ*, vi (1957). 37-57; Robert Harrison, "Symbolism of the Cyclical Myth in *Endymion*," *Texas Stud. in Lit. and Lang.*, i (1960). 538-554; Paul Haeffner, "Keats and the Faery Myth of Seduction," *REL*, iii, no. 2 (1962). 20-31; Stuart M. Sperry, Jr., "The Allegory of *Endymion*," *Stud. in Romanticism*, ii (1962). 38-53; Bruce E. Miller, "On the Meaning of Keats's *Endymion*," *KSJ*, xiv (1965). 33-54.

1247   Kenneth Muir, "The Meaning of *Hyperion*," *EIC*, ii (1952). 54-75; Bernard Blackstone, "*Poetical Sketches* and *Hyperion*," *Cambridge Jour.*, vi (1952). 160-168; Barbara Garlitz, "Egypt and *Hyperion*," *PQ*, xxxiv (1955). 189-196; Stuart M. Sperry, Jr., "Keats, Milton, and *The Fall of Hyperion*," *PMLA*, lxxvii (1962). 77-84.

1248   Arthur Carr, "Keats's Other Urn," *Univ. of Kansas City Rev.*, xx (1954). 237-242.

1248-1249   On Keats's odes generally: John Holloway, "The Odes of Keats," *Cambridge Jour.*, v (1952). 416-425; David Perkins, "Keats's Odes and Letters: Recurrent Diction and Imagery," *KSJ*, ii (1953). 51-60; Edmund Blunden, "Keats's Odes: Further Notes," *KSJ*, iii (1954). 39-46.—Kenneth Allott, "Keats's *Ode to Psyche*," *EIC*, vi (1956). 278-301; Max F. Schulz, "Keats's Timeless Order of Things: A Modern Reading of the *Ode to Psyche*," *Criticism*, ii (1960). 55-65. —Richard H. Fogle, "Keats's *Ode to a Nightingale*," *PMLA*, lxviii (1953). 211-222; Janet Spens, "A Study of Keats's *Ode to a Nightingale*," *RES*, n.s. iii (1952). 234-243.—Harvey T. Lyon, *Keats's Well-Read Urn* (1958), eighty-six critics quoted on the *Ode on a Grecian Urn;* Cleanth Brooks, "Keats's Sylvan Historian," *The Well-Wrought Urn* (1947), ch. viii; Bowra, *The Romantic Imagination*, ch. vi; Robert Daniel, "Odes to Dejection," *Kenyon Rev.*, xv (1953). 129-140; Charles I. Patterson, "Passion and Permanence in Keats's *Ode on a Grecian Urn*," *ELH*, xxi (1954). 208-220; Martha Hale Shackford, "The *Ode on a Grecian Urn*," *KSJ*, iv (1955). 7-13; Jacob D. Wigod, "Keats's Ideal in the *Ode on a Grecian Urn*," *PMLA*, lxxii (1957). 113-121; Albert Gérard, "Romance and Reality: Continuity and Growth in Keats's View of Art," *KSJ*, xi (1962). 17-29.—Ernest J. Lovell, Jr., "The Genesis of Keats's Ode *To Autumn*," *Univ. of Texas Stud. in English*,

XXIX (1950). 204-221; B. C. Southam, "The Ode *To Autumn,*" *KSJ,* IX (1960). 91-98.

O. B. Hardison, Jr., "The Decorum of *Lamia,*" *MLQ,* XIX (1958). 33-42.

XIV. Thomas Hood, Thomas Lovell Beddoes, and Other Poets

1253 Hood: *Poems,* ed. C. Dyment (1948), a selection.—John C. Reid, *Thomas Hood* (1963); N. Hardy Wallis, "Thomas Hood," *Essays by Divers Hands* (Royal Soc. of Lit.), n.s. XXIII (1946). 103-115; Alvin Whitley, "Thomas Hood as a Dramatist," *Univ. of Texas Stud. in English,* XXX (1951). 184-201; "Thomas Hood: The Language of Poetry," *LTLS,* Sept. 19, 1952, pp. 605-606; Edmund Blunden, "The Poet Hood," *REL,* I, no. 1 (1960). 26-34; William G. Lane, "A Chord in Melancholy: Hood's Last Years," *KSJ,* XIII (1964). 43-60; Heath-Stubbs, *The Darkling Plain,* pp. 49-59.

1254 Note 4: *The Ingoldsby Legends, Selected,* ed. J. Tanfield and G. Boas (1951). William G. Lane, "The Primitive Muse of Thomas Ingoldsby," *Harvard Library Bull.,* XII (1958). 47-83, 220-241.—*Complete Nonsense of Edward Lear,* ed. Holbrook Jackson (1947); *Teapots and Quails, and Other New Nonsenses,* ed. Angus Davidson and Philip Hofer (Cambridge, Mass., 1953); *Indian Journal,* ed. Ray Murphy (1953); *Edward Lear in Southern Italy,* ed. Peter Quennell (1964); *Edward Lear in Greece* (1965); *Journals,* ed. Herbert van Thal (1952), a selection. Elizabeth Sewell, *The Field of Nonsense* (1952).

1255 Elliott: "Corn Law Rhymer," *LTLS,* Dec. 2, 1949, p. 794; Asa Briggs, "Ebenezer Elliott, the Corn Law Rhymer," *Cambridge Jour.,* III (1950). 686-695. Praed: *Selected Poems,* ed. Kenneth Allott (1953).

1256 Beddoes: *Plays and Poems,* ed. H. W. Donner (1950). Geoffrey Wagner, "Centennial of a Suicide: Thomas Lovell Beddoes," *Horizon,* XIX (1949). 417-435; Louis O. Coxe, "Beddoes: The Mask of Parody," *Hudson Rev.,* VI (1953). 252-265; Donner, "Echoes of Beddoesian Rambles: Edgeworthstown to Zürich," *Studia Neophil.,* XXXIII (1961). 219-264, including new facts; Charles A. Hoyt, "Theme and Imagery in the Poetry of T. L. Beddoes," *ibid.,* XXXV (1963). 85-103; Heath-Stubbs, *The Darkling Plain,* pp. 37-49.

1259 George C. Haddow, "George Darley: A Centenary Sketch," *Queen's Quar.,* LIII (1946). 491-501; "The Poet of Solitude," *LTLS,* Nov. 23, 1946, p. 580; Graham Greene, "George Darley," *The Lost Childhood and Other Essays* (1951), pp. 143-152; Heath-Stubbs, *The Darkling Plain,* pp. 22-37.

1260 Cyril Pearl, *Always Morning: The Life of Richard Henry "Orion" Horne* (Melbourne, 1960).

Aytoun: *Stories and Verse,* ed. W. L. Renwick (Chicago, 1964). Erik Frykman, *W. E. Aytoun, Pioneer Professor of English at Edinburgh* (Stockholm, 1963).

1261 W. J. A. M. Beek, *John Keble's Literary and Religious Contribution to the Oxford Movement* (Nijmegen, 1959); Georgina Battiscombe, *John Keble: A Study in Limitations* (1963); Warren, *English Poetic Theory,* ch. III.

Arthur G. Lough, *The Influence of John Mason Neale* (1962). On nineteenth-century hymnody in general, see the relevant chapters in Fairchild, *Religious Trends in English Poetry*, Vols. III-IV.

1262 *Poems of John Clare's Madness*, ed. Geoffrey Grigson (1949); *The Shepherd's Calendar* (1964) and *The Later Poems of John Clare* (Manchester, 1964), pieces hitherto unpublished, both ed. Eric Robinson and Geoffrey Summerfield; *Selected Poems*, ed. Grigson (1950), James Reeves (1954); *Prose*, ed. J. W. and Anne Tibble (1951); *Letters*, ed. J. W. and Anne Tibble (1951).—June Wilson, *Green Shadows* (1951); J. W. and Anne Tibble, *John Clare: His Life and Poetry* (1956), revision of their 1932 biography; Frederick Martin, *The Life of John Clare* (1964); John Middleton Murry, *John Clare and Other Studies* (1950), pp. 7-24, and "Clare Revisited," *Unprofessional Essays* (1956), pp. 53-111; Rayner Unwin, *The Rural Muse* (1954), pp. 121-142; Heath-Stubbs, *The Darkling Plain*, pp. 65-75.

1263 Helen Ashton, *Letty Landon* (1951); Lionel Stevenson, "Miss Landon, 'the Milk-and-Watery Moon of our Darkness,' 1824-30," *MLQ*, VIII (1947). 355-363.—Note 40: On Montgomery, see Kenneth Hopkins, "Reflections on Satan Montgomery," *Texas Stud. in Lit. and Lang.*, IV (1962). 351-366.

XV. The Drama in Decline

1264 *Nineteenth Century Plays*, ed. George Rowell (1953); Allardyce Nicoll, *A History of English Drama* (6v, Cambridge, 1952-59), Vols. IV-V; Rowell, *The Victorian Theatre: A Survey* (1956); Bertrand Evans, *Gothic Drama from Walpole to Shelley* (Berkeley, 1947); M. Wilson Disher, *Blood and Thunder: Mid-Victorian Melodrama and Its Origins* (1949).

1268 Richard D. Altick, "Dion Boucicault Stages *Mary Barton*," *NCF*, XIV (1959). 129-141.—M. Norton, "The Plays of Joanna Baillie," *RES*, XXIII (1947). 131-143.

1269 Vera Watson, *Mary Russell Mitford* (1949); Jack, pp. 338-344.—*Bulwer and Macready: A Chronicle of the Early Victorian Theater*, ed. Charles H. Shattuck (Urbana, Ill., 1958).

XVI. The Novel Between Scott and Dickens

1271 Peacock: *Novels*, ed. David Garnett (1948); *The Pleasures of Peacock*, ed. Ben Ray Redman (1947); *Nightmare Abbey* and *Crotchet Castle*, introduction by J. B. Priestley (1948).—Bill Read, "Thomas Love Peacock: An Enumerative Bibliography," *Bull. of Bibliography*, XXIV (1963-64). 32-34, 70-72, 88-91. Olwen W. Campbell, *Thomas Love Peacock* (1953); Sidney J. Black, "The Peacockian Essence," *Boston Univ. Stud. in English*, III (1957). 231-242.

1272 Sandor Baumgarten, *Le Crépuscule néo-classique: Thomas Hope* (Paris, 1958).—Morier: *Hajji Baba in Ispahan*, ed. Richard D. Altick (1954).

1273 *The Last Days of Shelley and Byron: Being the Complete Text of Trelawny's "Recollections,"* ed. "with additions from contemporary sources" by J. E.

Morpurgo (1952).—R. Glynn Grylls, *Trelawny* (1950); Lady Anne Hill, "Trelawny's Family Background and Naval Career," *KSJ*, v (1956). 11-32.
Marryat: *Diary in America*, ed. Jules Zanger (Bloomington, Ind., 1960). Oliver Warner, *Captain Marryat: A Rediscovery* (1953).
Lockhart: *John Bull's Letter to Lord Byron*, ed. A. L. Strout (Norman, Okla., 1947). Marion Lochhead, *John Gibson Lockhart* (1954).

1274 Hogg: *Private Memoirs and Confessions of a Justified Sinner*, with introduction by André Gide (1947). Louis Simpson, *James Hogg* (Edinburgh, 1962); Alan L. Strout, "James Hogg's *Chaldee Manuscript*," *PMLA*, LXV (1950). 695-718.

1276 Thomas J. B. Flanagan, *The Irish Novelists, 1800-1850* (1959). On Carleton: Benedict Kiely, *Poor Scholar* (1947).—Marcel Ian Moraud, *Une Irlandaise libérale en France sous la Restauration, Lady Morgan* (Paris, 1954).— On Gerald Griffin: Ethel Mannin, *Two Studies in Integrity* (1954).

1277 Leonard Cooper, *R. S. Surtees* (1952); Robert L. Collison, *A Jorrocks Handbook* (1964). (Inadvertently omitted from the text is mention of Surtees' most famous novel, *Jorrocks' Jaunts and Jollities* [serialized 1831-1834, book publication 1838].)

1278 Note 36: See also Friedrich Schubel, *Die "Fashionable Novels"* (Uppsala, 1952).

XVII. The Background: 1832-1868
The Progress of Reform

1279 Woodward's *The Age of Reform* appeared in a revised ed. (Oxford, 1962). One further volume of Halévy's *Histoire du peuple anglais au XIXᵉ siècle* appeared after the author's death: *The Age of Peel and Cobden* (1947). David Thomson, *England in the Nineteenth Century* (1950); *English Historical Documents*, Vol. XII (1), 1833-1874, ed. G. M. Young and W. D. Handcock (1956); Asa Briggs, *The Age of Improvement, 1783-1867* (1959); Anthony Wood, *Nineteenth Century Britain, 1815-1914* (1960); W. L. Burn, *The Age of Equipoise: A Study of the Mid-Victorian Generation* (1964).—General studies of the intellectual, cultural, and social background: Bernard N. Schilling, *Human Dignity and the Great Victorians* (1946); *Ideas and Beliefs of the Victorians*, ed. Harman Grisewood (1949); Basil Willey, *Nineteenth Century Studies* (1949) and *More Nineteenth Century Studies* (1956); Jerome H. Buckley, *The Victorian Temper* (Cambridge, Mass., 1951); John W. Dodds, *The Age of Paradox: A Biography of England, 1841-1851* (1952); L. E. Elliott-Binns, *English Thought, 1860-1900* (1956); Walter E. Houghton, *The Victorian Frame of Mind* (New Haven, 1957); Raymond Williams, *Culture and Society, 1780-1950* (1958), Part I; G. M. Young, *Victorian Essays*, ed. Handcock (1962); G. Kitson Clark, *The Making of Victorian England* (1962).—General works on Victorian literature: There is an annual bibliography of books and articles in *MP* (to 1957) and *VS* (1958-   ). Issues for 1932-1944 were gathered into one volume, ed. W. D. Templeman, and those for 1945-1954 into another, ed. Austin Wright (Urbana, Ill., 1945, 1956). Two convenient reviews of scholarship and criticism are *The Victorian Poets: A Guide to Research*, ed. Frederic E. Faverty (Cambridge,

Mass., 1956)—hereafter cited as Faverty—and *Victorian Fiction: A Guide to Research,* ed. Lionel Stevenson (Cambridge, Mass., 1964)—hereafter cited as Stevenson. *The [Pelican] Guide to English Literature,* ed. Boris Ford: Vol. vi, *From Dickens to Hardy* (1958, rev. 1963); *The Reinterpretation of Victorian Literature,* ed. Joseph E. Baker (Princeton, 1950); Sherard Vines, *100 Years of English Literature* [1830-1940] (1950); Clarence R. Decker, *The Victorian Conscience* (1952), on the reaction to realism; Richard D. Altick, *The English Common Reader: A Social History of the Mass Reading Public, 1800-1900* (Chicago, 1957); Geoffrey Tillotson, *Criticism and the Nineteenth Century* (1951), essays on various topics; *Victorian Literature: Modern Essays in Criticism,* ed. Austin Wright (1961).

XVIII. The Religious Revival and Its Expression in Literature

1288 L. E. Elliott-Binns, *The Early Evangelicals* (1953); Ford K. Brown, *Fathers of the Victorians: The Age of Wilberforce* (Cambridge, 1961); Oliver Warner, *William Wilberforce and His Times* (1962); E. M. Forster, *Marianne Thornton* (1956), a biography of a leading member of the Clapham sect; David Spring, "The Clapham Sect: Some Social and Political Aspects," *VS,* v (1961). 35-48.—M. G. Jones, *Hannah More* (Cambridge, 1952), the definitive life; Mary Alden Hopkins, *Hannah More and Her Circle* (1947).

1290 Thomas Arnold: *Principles of Church Reform,* with introduction by M. J. Jackson and J. Rogan (1962).—Norman Wymer, *Dr. Arnold of Rugby* (1953); Frances J. Woodward, *The Doctor's Disciples* (1954); T. W. Bamford, *Thomas Arnold* (1960); David Newsome, *Godliness and Good Learning* (1961); Eugene L. Williamson, *The Liberalism of Thomas Arnold* (University, Ala., 1964); Willey, *Nineteenth Century Studies,* ch. ii.

1291 A projected definitive edition of Newman's works was left incomplete at the death of the editor, Charles Frederick Harrold. The volumes published (1947-1949) were: *Apologia pro Vita Sua, An Essay in Aid of a Grammar of Assent, The Idea of a University, Sermons and Discourses* (2v), *Essays and Sketches* (3v) and *An Essay on the Development of Christian Doctrine.* A number of volumes have presented Newman's previously unpublished or uncollected writings: *University Sketches,* ed. Michael Tierney (Dublin, 1952); *Faith and Prejudice, and Other Unpublished Sermons* (1956); *Catholic Sermons* (1957); *The Argument from Conscience to the Existence of God,* ed. Adrian J. Boekraad and Henry Tristram (Louvain, 1961); *Realizations: Newman's Selection of His Parochial and Plain Sermons,* ed. Vincent F. Blehl (1964). *A Newman Anthology,* ed. W. S. Lilly (1949); *Prose and Poetry,* ed. Geoffrey Tillotson (1957), a selection; *A Newman Reader,* ed. Francis X. Connolly (1964); *Autobiographical Writings,* ed. Tristram (1956); *Letters and Diaries,* ed. Charles S. Dessain and others (1961-   ), a monumental editorial project; *Letters, a Selection,* ed. Derek Stanford and Muriel Spark (1957); Meriol Trevor, *Newman: The Pillar of the Cloud* and *Newman: Light in Winter* (both 1962), the best biography; Eleanor Ruggles, *Journey into Faith* (1948); Maisie Ward, *Young Mr. Newman*

(1948); Seán O'Faoláin, *Newman's Way: The Odyssey of John Henry Newman* (1952); *John Henry Newman: Centenary Essays* (1945); Robert D. Middleton, *Newman and Bloxam: An Oxford Friendship* (1947) and *Newman at Oxford: His Religious Development* (1950); *American Essays for the Newman Centennial*, ed. J. K. Ryan and E. D. Benard (Washington, 1947); Boekraad, *The Personal Conquest of Truth According to Newman* (Louvain, 1955); Owen Chadwick, *From Bossuet to Newman: The Idea of Doctrinal Development* (Cambridge, 1957); Terence Kenney, *The Political Thought of John Henry Newman* (1957); J. H. Walgrave, *Newman the Theologian* (Tournai, 1957, as *Newman: le Développement du dogme;* English trans. 1960); Louis Bouyer, *Newman: His Life and Spirituality* (1958); Ernest E. Reynolds, *Three Cardinals: Newman-Wiseman-Manning* (1958); Thomas S. Bokenkotter, *Cardinal Newman as an Historian* (Louvain, 1959); Tillotson, "Newman's *Essay on Poetry:* an Exposition and Comment," *Perspectives of Criticism*, ed. Harry Levin (Cambridge, Mass., 1950), pp. 161-195 (on the same topic, see also Warren, *English Poetic Theory*, ch. 11); Russell Kirk, "The Conservative Mind of Newman," *Sewanee Rev.,* lx (1952). 659-676; Merritt E. Lawlis, "Newman on the Imagination," *MLN*, lxviii (1953). 73-80; J. M. Cameron, "The Night Battle: Newman and Empiricism," *VS*, iv (1960). 99-117; John Holloway, *The Victorian Sage* (1953), ch. vi.

1294   Note 27: Newman's *Idea of a University*, considerably more important than is implied by its relegation to a note, was edited by George N. Shuster (1959) and Martin J. Svaglic (1960). See A. Dwight Culler, *The Imperial Intellect: A Study of Newman's Educational Ideal* (New Haven, 1955) and Fergal McGrath, *Newman's University: Idea and Reality* (1951).

1295   *Apologia pro Vita Sua*, ed. A. Dwight Culler (Boston, 1956), Philip Hughes (1956), Basil Willey (1964).—As a work of literary art, the *Apologia* has been perhaps more intensively studied than any other example of Victorian non-fictional prose. See Walter E. Houghton, *The Art of Newman's "Apologia"* (New Haven, 1945), and articles by Martin J. Svaglic in *PMLA*, lxvi (1951). 138-148, and *MP*, l (1952). 43-49; by Robert A. Colby in *Jour. of Religion*, xxxiii (1953). 47-57, and *Dublin Rev.*, ccxxvii (1953). 140-156; and by Leonard W. Deen, *ELH*, xxix (1962). 224-238. On the ideas of the *Apologia*, see *Newman's "Apologia": A Classic Reconsidered*, ed. Vincent F. Blehl and Francis X. Connolly (1964).

1296   *The Mind of the Oxford Movement*, ed. Owen Chadwick (1960); Willey, *Nineteenth Century Studies*, ch. iii.—Note 38: See also Margaret M. Maison, *The Victorian Vision: Studies in the Religious Novel* (1962; English title, *Search Your Soul, Eustace*).

1297   On F. W. Newman: Willey, *More Nineteenth Century Studies*, ch. i.— Kingsbury Badger, "The Ordeal of Anthony Froude, Protestant Historian," *MLQ*, xiii (1952). 41-55; Willey, *More Nineteenth Century Studies*, ch. iii.—Florence M. G. Higham, *Frederick Denison Maurice* (1947); Herbert G. Wood, *Frederick Denison Maurice* (Cambridge, 1950); A. M. Ramsey, *F. D. Maurice and the Conflicts of Modern Theology* (Cambridge, 1951); W. Merlin Davies, *An Introduction to F. D. Maurice's Theology* (1964); Olive Brose, "F. D. Maurice and the Victorian Crisis of Belief," *VS*, iii (1960). 227-248.

XIX. The Theory of Evolution and Its Repercussions

1299 Douglas Bush, *Science and English Poetry, A Historical Sketch, 1590-1950* (1950), ch. v; Charles C. Gillispie, *Genesis and Geology* (Cambridge, Mass., 1951); Ruth E. Moore, *Man, Time, and Fossils* (1953); Georg Roppen, *Evolution and Poetic Belief* (Oslo, 1956); Loren Eiseley, *Darwin's Century: Evolution and the Men Who Discovered It* (1957); *Forerunners of Darwin, 1745-1859,* ed. Bentley Glass, Owsei Temkin, and William L. Straus, Jr. (Baltimore, 1959).

1303 Milton Millhauser, *Just Before Darwin: Robert Chambers and "Vestiges"* (Middletown, Conn., 1959).

1305 *The Origin of Species: A Variorum Text,* ed. Morse Peckham (Philadelphia, 1959); *Charles Darwin and the Voyage of The Beagle,* ed. Nora Barlow (1945), the first full publication of his letters and notebooks from the expedition; *Autobiography,* ed. Sir Francis Darwin (1949) and Barlow (1958), the latter "with original omissions restored"; *The Darwin Reader,* ed. Marston Bates and Philip S. Humphrey (1956); *Darwin for Today: The Essence of His Works,* ed. Stanley E. Hyman (1963).—William Irvine, *Apes, Angels, and Victorians* (1955), a dual biography of Darwin and Huxley; Paul Bigelow Sears, *Charles Darwin: The Naturalist as a Cultural Force* (1950); Ruth E. Moore, *Charles Darwin* (1955); Sir Arthur Keith, *Darwin Revalued* (1955); *A Century of Darwin,* ed. Samuel A. Barnett (Cambridge, Mass., 1958), a collection of fifteen essays; Alvar Ellegård, *Darwin and the General Reader* (Göteborg, 1958), on Darwin's reception in the Victorian press; Gertrude Himmelfarb, *Darwin and the Darwinian Revolution* (1959); Darwin centenary issues of *Antioch Rev.,* xix (Spring, 1959) and *VS,* iii (Sept., 1959); *Evolution After Darwin: the University of Chicago Centennial,* ed. Sol Tax (3v, Chicago, 1960); Hyman, *The Tangled Bank: Darwin, Marx, Frazer and Freud as Imaginative Writers* (1962); Irvine, "The Influence of Darwin on Literature," *Proc. Amer. Philos. Soc.,* ciii (1959). 616-628; James Collins, "Darwin's Impact on Philosophy," *Thought,* xxxiv (1959). 185-248; Lionel Stevenson, "Darwin and the Novel," *NCF,* xv (1960). 29-38; Donald Fleming, "Charles Darwin, the Anesthetic Man," *VS,* iv (1961). 219-236.

1307 Huxley: *Touchstone for Ethics 1893-1943* (1947), Romanes Lectures by T. H. Huxley and Julian Huxley.—Cyril Bibby, *T. H. Huxley: Scientist, Humanist, and Educator* (1959), and three articles by Bibby: "Thomas Henry Huxley's Idea of a University," *Universities Quar.,* x (1956). 377-389, "The Prince of Controversialists," *Twentieth Century,* clxi (1957). 268-276, and "Huxley and the Reception of the *Origin*," *VS,* iii (1959). 76-86; William Irvine, "Carlyle and T. H. Huxley," *Booker Memorial Studies* (Chapel Hill, 1950), ch. v; Walter E. Houghton, "The Rhetoric of Huxley," *UTQ,* xviii (1949). 159-175; three articles by Charles S. Blinderman: "Thomas Henry Huxley," *Scientific Mo.,* lxxxiv (1957). 171-182, with new material; "Semantic Aspects of T. H. Huxley's Literary Style," *Jour. of Communication,* xii (1962). 171-178; "T. H. Huxley's Theory of Aesthetics: Unity in Diversity," *JAAC,* xxi (1962). 49-55; Sydney Eisen, "Huxley and the Positivists," *VS,* vii (1964). 337-358.

XX. Thomas Carlyle

1309 *Carlyle's Unfinished History of German Literature*, ed. Hill Shine (Lexington, Ky., 1951); *Letters to William Graham*, ed. John Graham, Jr. (Princeton, 1950); *Letters to His Wife*, ed. Trudy Bliss (1953); *The Correspondence of Emerson and Carlyle*, ed. Joseph Slater (1964); *Jane Welsh Carlyle: A New Selection of Her Letters*, ed. Bliss (1950). A complete edition of the Carlyle correspondence is being prepared by Charles Richard Sanders. *Carlyle: An Anthology*, ed. G. M. Trevelyan (1953); *Selected Works, Reminiscences, and Letters*, ed. Julian Symons (1956).—Symons, *Thomas Carlyle: The Life and Ideas of a Prophet* (1952), the best modern life; Lawrence and Elisabeth Hanson, *Necessary Evil* (1952), a life of Jane Carlyle; Hill Shine, *Carlyle's Early Reading, to 1834* (Lexington, Ky., 1953); Richard Pankhurst, *The Saint Simonians, Mill, and Carlyle* (1957); Raymond Williams, *Culture and Society* (1958), pp. 77-93; Robert M. Estrich and Hans Sperber, *Three Keys to Language* (1952), pp. 108-125, on Carlyle's influence on contemporary language; Sanders, "Carlyle, Poetry, and the Music of Humanity," *Western Humanities Rev.*, xvi (1962). 53-66; G. B. Tennyson, "Carlyle's Poetry to 1840: A Checklist and Discussion," *VP*, i (1963). 161-181; Willey, *Nineteenth Century Studies*, ch. iv; Warren, *English Poetic Theory*, ch. v, on "The Hero as Poet"; Holloway, *The Victorian Sage*, chs. ii-iii; Gaylord LeRoy, *Perplexed Prophets* (Philadelphia, 1953), ch. ii; Wellek, *History of Modern Criticism*, iii. 92-100.

1310 Hill Shine, "Carlyle's Early Writings and Herder's *Ideen:* The Concept of History," *Booker Memorial Studies* (Chapel Hill, 1950), ch. i; J. W. Smeed, "Thomas Carlyle and Jean Paul Richter," *CL*, xvi (1964). 226-253.

1313 *Past and Present*, ed. Richard D. Altick (Boston, 1965). Grace Calder, *The Making of "Past and Present"* (New Haven, 1949), a valuable study of Carlyle's habits of composition.

1316 Study of Carlyle's literary artistry has recently centered on *Sartor Resartus* and the works that led up to it. See Marjorie P. King, "*Illudo Chartis:* An Initial Study in Carlyle's Mode of Composition," *MLR*, xlix (1954). 164-175; Francis X. Roellinger, Jr., "The Early Development of Carlyle's Style," *PMLA*, lxxii (1957). 936-951; articles by Daniel P. Deneau and John Lindberg in *Victorian Newsletter*, No. 17 (Spring, 1960), pp. 17-23; Leonard W. Deen, "Irrational Form in *Sartor Resartus*," *Texas Stud. in Lit. and Lang.*, v (1963). 438-451; George Levine, "*Sartor Resartus* and the Balance of Fiction," *VS*, viii (1964). 131-160; G. B. Tennyson, *Sartor Called Resartus* (Princeton, 1965). Other aspects of *Sartor* are studied in Carlisle Moore, "*Sartor Resartus* and the Problem of Carlyle's 'Conversion,'" *PMLA*, lxx (1955). 662-681, and C. R. Sanders, "The Byron Closed in *Sartor Resartus*," *Stud. in Romanticism*, iii (1964). 77-108. (Inadvertently omitted from note 28 is C. F. Harrold's edition of *Sartor* [1937], with a long and indispensable introduction to its ideas.)

1320 H. Ben-Israel, "Carlyle and the French Revolution," *Historical Jour.*,

1 (1958). 115-135; Alfred Cobban, "Carlyle's *French Revolution*," *History*, n.s. XLVIII (1963). 306-316.

XXI. Philosophy, History, and Miscellaneous Prose

1322 Mill: *Prefaces to Liberty: Selected Writings*, ed. Bernard Wisby (Boston, 1959); *Essays on Politics and Culture*, ed. Gertrude Himmelfarb (1962); *Mill on Bentham and Coleridge*, ed. F. R. Leavis (1950); *The Early Draft of John Stuart Mill's Autobiography*, ed. Jack Stillinger (Urbana, Ill., 1961); *Earlier Letters, 1812-1848*, ed. Francis E. Mineka (2v, Toronto, 1963), the first volumes of a projected complete edition of the works; *John Mill's Boyhood Visit to France*, ed. Anna Jean Mill (Toronto, 1960).—Ney MacMinn, J. R. Hainds, and James McN. McCrimmon, *Bibliography of the Published Writings of John Stuart Mill* (Evanston, 1945); Michael St. John Packe, *The Life of John Stuart Mill* (1954), an outstanding biography; F. A. Hayek, *John Stuart Mill and Harriet Taylor: Their Correspondence and Subsequent Marriage* (Chicago, 1951); R. P. Anschutz, *The Philosophy of J. S. Mill* (Oxford, 1953); Karl Britton, *John Stuart Mill* (1953); Iris W. Mueller, *John Stuart Mill and French Thought* (Urbana, Ill., 1956); Richard Pankhurst, *The Saint Simonians, Mill, and Carlyle* (1957); Dorothea Krook, *Three Traditions of Moral Thought* (Cambridge, 1959); Maurice Cowling, *Mill and Liberalism* (Cambridge, 1963); John B. Ellery, *John Stuart Mill* (1964); Britton, "John Stuart Mill: the Ordeal of an Intellectual," *Cambridge Jour.*, II (1948). 96-105; Hainds, "John Stuart Mill's *Examiner* Articles on Art," *JHI*, XI (1950). 215-234; Walter J. Ong, "J. S. Mill's Pariah Poet," *PQ*, XXIX (1950). 333-344; R. V. Sampson, "J. S. Mill: An Interpretation," *Cambridge Jour.*, III (1950). 232-239; R. J. White, "John Stuart Mill," *ibid.*, V (1951). 86-96; Robert Preyer, "The Utilitarian Poetics: John Stuart Mill," *Univ. of Kansas City Rev.*, XIX (1952). 131-136; Keith Rinehart, "John Stuart Mill's *Autobiography*: Its Art and Appeal," *ibid.*, XIX (1953). 265-273; Bertrand Russell, "John Stuart Mill," *Proc. Brit. Acad.*, XLI (1955). 43-59; John M. Robson, "J. S. Mill's Theory of Poetry," *UTQ*, XXIX (1960). 420-438; Robert Carr, "The Religious Thought of John Stuart Mill," *JHI*, XXIII (1962). 475-495; Willey, *Nineteenth Century Studies*, ch. VI; Warren, *English Poetic Theory*, ch. IV.

1327 Macaulay: *Prose and Poetry*, ed. G. M. Young (Cambridge, Mass., 1952; *Essays*, ed. Hugh Trevor-Roper (1965).—Robert L. Schuyler, "Macaulay and His *History*—a Hundred Years After," *Political Science Quar.*, LXIII (1948). 161-193; J. H. Plumb, "Thomas Babington Macaulay," *UTQ*, XXVI (1956). 17-31; Andrew Browning, "Lord Macaulay, 1800-59," *Historical Jour.*, II (1959). 149-160; John Clive, "Macaulay, History, and the Historians," *History Today*, IX (1959). 830-836; Edwin M. Yoder, Jr., "Macaulay Revisited," *So. Atl. Quar.*, LXIII (1964). 542-551. The special Macaulay number of *REL*, I, no. 4 (Oct., 1960) contains several useful articles.

1330 Waldo H. Dunn, *James Anthony Froude: A Biography* (2v, Oxford, 1961-1963).

1332 Giles St. Aubyn, *A Victorian Eminence: The Life and Works of Henry Thomas Buckle* (1958).—Lecky: *A Victorian Historian: Private Letters, 1859-1878,* ed. H. M. Hyde (1947); J. J. Auchmuty, *Lecky: A Biographical and Critical Essay* (1946).—W. G. Addison, *J. R. Green* (1946); Robert L. Schuyler, "John Richard Green and his *Short History*," *Political Science Quar.,* LXIV (1949). 321-354; L. M. Angus-Butterworth, "John Richard Green," *So. Atl. Quar.,* XLVI (1947). 109-118.—Acton: *Essays on Freedom and Power,* ed. Gertrude Himmelfarb (Boston, 1948); *Essays on Church and State,* ed. Douglas Woodruff (1952); David Mathew, *Acton: the Formative Years* (1946); George E. Fasnacht, *Acton's Political Philosophy* (1952); Himmelfarb, *Lord Acton: A Study in Conscience and Politics* (Chicago, 1952); Lionel Kochan, *Acton on History* (1954); W. Watkin Davies, "The Politics of Lord Acton," *Hibbert Jour.,* XLV (1946). 21-30; Harold Acton, "Lord Acton," *Chicago Rev.,* XV (1961). 31-44; E. D. Watt, "Ethics and Politics: The Example of Lord Acton," *UTQ,* XXXIII (1964). 279-290.

1333 Bagehot: *Complete Works,* ed. Norman St. John-Stevas (8v, 1965-   ); *Physics and Politics,* ed. Jacques Barzun (1948); *The English Constitution,* ed. with a long introduction by R. H. S. Crossman (1963).— Alastair Buchan, *The Spare Chancellor* (1959); St. John-Stevas, *Walter Bagehot: A Study of His Life and Thought* (Bloomington, Ind., 1959); St. John-Stevas, "Walter Bagehot as a Writer," *Wiseman Rev.,* CCXXXVII (1963). 38-65; Wellek, *History of Modern Criticism,* IV. 180-185.

Kinglake: *Eothen,* ed. Robin Fedden (1948), P. H. Newby (1949).—Gordon Waterfield, *Layard of Nineveh* (1963); Nora B. Kubie, *Road to Nineveh: The Adventures and Excavations of Sir Austen Henry Layard* (1964); Robert Silverberg, *The Man Who Found Nineveh* (1964).—Burton: *The Perfumed Garden of the Shaykh Nefzawi* (1963); *The City of the Saints,* ed. Fawn M. Brodie (1963). Byron Farwell, *Burton* (1963); Allen Edwardes, *Death Rides a Camel: A Biography of Sir Richard Burton* (1963); Thomas J. Assad, *Three Victorian Travellers: Burton, Blunt, Doughty* (1964); Jonathan Bishop, "The Identities of Sir Richard Burton: The Explorer as Actor," *VS,* I (1957). 119-135.

1334 Borrow: *Lavengro* and *The Romany Rye,* both ed. Walter Starkie (1948); *The Bible in Spain,* ed. Peter Quennell (1959).—Martin Armstrong, *George Borrow* (1950); Eileen Bigland, *In the Steps of George Borrow* (1951); Brian Vesey-Fitzgerald, *Gypsy Borrow* (1953); René Fréchet, *George Borrow* (Paris, 1956); John E. Tilford, Jr., "The Critical Approach to *Lavengro-Romany Rye,*" *SP,* XLVI (1949). 79-96, and "The Formal Artistry of *Lavengro-Romany Rye,*" *PMLA,* LXIV (1949). 369-384; Andrew Boyle, "Portraiture in *Lavengro,*" *N&Q,* various issues, 1951-1952; Fréchet, "George Borrow devant la critique," *Études anglaises,* VII (1954). 257-270.

Carroll: *The Annotated Alice,* ed. Martin Gardner (1960, rev. 1964); *The Annotated Snark,* ed. Gardner (1962); *Useful and Instructive Poetry,* ed. Derek Hudson (1954); *Diaries,* ed. Roger Lancelyn Green (2v, 1954).—Sidney H. Williams and Falconer Madan, *The Lewis Carroll Handbook* (1962), a revision by R. L. Green of a volume first published in 1931; Alexander Taylor, *The White Knight* (Edinburgh, 1952); Derek Hudson, *Lewis Carroll* (1954); Phyllis Greenacre, *Swift and Carroll* (1955), a psychoanalytic study; Elizabeth Sewell, *The Field of Nonsense* (1952); Green, "The Real Lewis Carroll," *Quarterly Rev.,* CCXCII (1954). 85-97.

XXII. John Ruskin

1336 *Selected Writings,* ed. Peter Quennell (1952); *The Lamp of Beauty: Writings on Art,* ed. Joan Evans (1959); *The Genius of John Ruskin: Selections,* ed. John D. Rosenberg (1963); *Ruskin Today,* ed. Sir Kenneth Clark (1963); *Diaries,* ed. Joan Evans and J. H. Whitehouse (3v, Oxford, 1956-1959); *The Gulf of Years: Letters from John Ruskin to Kathleen Olander,* ed. Rayner Unwin (1953); *Ruskin's Letters from Venice, 1851-52,* ed. John L. Bradley (New Haven, 1955); *Letters to Lord and Lady Mount-Temple,* ed. Bradley (Columbus, Ohio, 1964).—Quennell, *John Ruskin: The Portrait of a Prophet* (1949); Derrick Leon, *Ruskin: The Great Victorian* (1949); Evans, *John Ruskin* (1954); Helen G. Viljoen, *Ruskin's Scottish Heritage* (Urbana, Ill., 1956); Francis G. Townsend, *Ruskin and the Landscape Feeling* (Urbana, Ill., 1951); John T. Fain, *Ruskin and the Economists* (Nashville, 1956); Rosenberg, *The Darkening Glass* (1961); Quentin Bell, *Ruskin* (Edinburgh, 1963); Buckley, *The Victorian Temper,* ch. VIII; Robert Kimbrough, "Calm Between Crises: Pattern and Direction in Ruskin's Mature Thought," *Trans. Wisconsin Acad.,* XLIX (1960). 219-227; LeRoy, *Perplexed Prophets,* ch. IV; Graham Hough, *The Last Romantics* (1947), ch. I; Wellek, *History of Modern Criticism,* III. 136-149.

1337 On *Modern Painters,* see Warren, *English Poetic Theory,* ch. X, and the following articles by Van Akin Burd: "Another Light on the Writing of *Modern Painters,*" *PMLA,* LXVIII (1953). 755-763; "Ruskin's Quest for a Theory of Imagination," *MLQ,* XVII (1956). 60-72; "Ruskin's Defense of Turner: The Imitative Phase," *PQ,* XXXVII (1958). 465-483; and "Background to *Modern Painters:* The Tradition and the Turner Controversy," *PMLA,* LXXIV (1959). 254-267.

1338 Note 10: The circumstances of the annulment are controversially dealt with in Admiral Sir William James, *John Ruskin and Effie Gray* (1947; English title, *The Order of Release*) and J. H. Whitehouse, *Vindication of Ruskin* (1950).

XXIII. Charles Dickens, Wilkie Collins, and Charles Reade

1344 On Victorian fiction generally: Michael Sadleir, *XIX Century Fiction: A Bibliographical Record Based on His Own Collection* (2v, 1951); *Victorian Fiction: A Guide to Research,* ed. Lionel Stevenson (Cambridge, Mass., 1964); Lucien Leclaire, *A General Analytical Bibliography of the Regional Novelists of the British Isles (1800-1950)* (Clermont-Ferrand, 1954); Leo J. Henkin, "Problems and Digressions in the Victorian Novel (1860-1900)," *Bull. of Bibliography,* XVIII (1943)-XX (1950). Walter Allen, *The English Novel* (1954), chs. IV-V; Lionel Stevenson, *The English Novel: A Panorama* (Boston, 1960), chs. IX-XV; Frederick R. Karl, *An Age of Fiction: The Nineteenth Century British Novel* (1964). Richard Stang, *The Theory of the Novel in England, 1850-1870* (1959);

Kenneth Graham, *English Criticism of the Novel, 1865-1900* (1965); Irène Simon, *Formes du roman anglais de Dickens à Joyce* (Liége, 1949); Frank O'Connor, *The Mirror in the Roadway: A Study of the Modern Novel* (1956); V. S. Pritchett, *The Living Novel* (1946); *From Jane Austen to Joseph Conrad,* ed. R. C. Rathburn and Martin Steinmann (Minneapolis, 1958), a large collection of critical essays; Leclaire, *Le Roman régionaliste dans les Iles Britanniques (1800-1950)* (Clermont-Ferrand, 1954); Margaret Dalziel, *Popular Fiction 100 Years Ago* (1957); Louis James, *Fiction for the Working Man 1830-1850* (1963); Patricia Thomson, *The Victorian Heroine: A Changing Ideal, 1837-1873* (1956); Mario Praz, *The Hero in Eclipse in Victorian Fiction* (1956); Mortimer R. Proctor, *The English University Novel* (Berkeley, 1957); Margaret M. Maison, *The Victorian Vision: Studies in the Religious Novel* (1962); Kathleen Tillotson, *Novels of the Eighteen-Forties* (1954), especially Part I, on the authors, publishers, and readers of fiction in the period; Gilbert Phelps, *The Russian Novel in English Fiction* (1956); Stevenson, "The Intellectual Novel in the Nineteenth Century," *Personalist,* xxxi (1950). 42-57, 157-166; G. Armour Craig, "The Unpoetic Compromise: On the Relation between Private Vision and Social Order in Nineteenth-Century English Fiction," *Society and Self in the Novel (English Institute Essays 1955),* ed. Mark Schorer (1956), pp. 26-50, and "Victims and Spokesmen: The Image of Society in the Novel," *1859: Entering an Age of Crisis,* ed. Philip Appleman *et al.* (Bloomington, Ind., 1959), pp. 229-246.

New Oxford Illustrated Dickens (21v, 1947-1958). A long-needed edition with textual authority and scholarly apparatus is being published by the Clarendon Press. *Speeches,* ed. K. J. Fielding (Oxford, 1960); Pilgrim edition of *Letters,* ed. Madeline House and Graham Storey (11v, Oxford, 1965-   ); *The Heart of Charles Dickens,* ed. Edgar Johnson (1952; English title, *Letters from Charles Dickens to Angela Burdett-Coutts); Selected Letters,* ed. F. W. Dupee (1960).—William Miller, *The Dickens Student and Collector: A List of Writings Relating to Charles Dickens and His Works, 1836-1945* (Cambridge, Mass., 1946), the fullest bibliography but very inaccurate; cf. severe review in *Papers of the Bibl. Soc. of America,* xli (1947). 293-320. Extensive bibliography of recent criticism in Stevenson, ch. III. Edgar Johnson, *Charles Dickens, His Tragedy and Triumph* (2v, 1952), the standard modern biography; Hesketh Pearson, *Dickens: His Character, Comedy, and Career* (1949); Jack Lindsay, *Charles Dickens: A Biographical and Critical Study* (1950); Julian Symons, *Charles Dickens* (1951); Sylvère Monod, *Dickens Romancier* (Paris, 1953); George H. Ford, *Dickens and His Readers: Aspects of Novel-Criticism Since 1836* (Princeton, 1955); John Butt and Kathleen Tillotson, *Dickens at Work* (1957), an illuminating study of Dickens' manuscripts and work sheets; K. J. Fielding, *Charles Dickens: A Critical Introduction* (1958, rev. Boston, 1964); J. Hillis Miller, *Charles Dickens: The World of His Novels* (Cambridge, Mass., 1958); Monroe Engel, *The Maturity of Dickens* (Cambridge, Mass., 1959); John Manning, *Dickens and Education* (Toronto, 1959); A. O. J. Cockshut, *The Imagination of Charles Dickens* (1961); P. W. Collins, *Dickens and Crime* (1962) and *Dickens and Education* (1963); J. C. Reid, *The Hidden World of Charles Dickens (Univ. of Auckland Bulletin,* lxi [1962]); *Dickens and the Twentieth Century,* ed. John Gross and Gabriel Pearson (1962), a collection of original essays on all of the novels; Steven Marcus, *Dickens from Pickwick to Dombey* (1965); Robert Garis, *The Dickens Theatre: A Reassessment of the Novels* (Oxford, 1965); Taylor Stoehr, *Dickens: The Dreamer's Stance* (Ithaca, 1965). A small selection of essays and chapters on various topics: Richard Aldington, "The Underworld of Young Dickens," *Four English Portraits* (1948), pp. 147-189; Warrington Winters, "Dickens and the Psychology of Dreams," *PMLA*, LXIII (1948). 984-1006; Dorothy Van Ghent, "The Dickens World: A View from Todgers's," *Sewanee Rev.*, LVIII (1950). 419-438; Graham Greene, "The Young Dickens," *The Lost Childhood and Other Essays* (1951), pp. 51-57; Frank O'Connor, "Dickens: The Intrusion of the Audience," *The Mirror in the Roadway* (1956), pp. 70-82; Peter Coveney, "The Child in Dickens," *Poor Monkey* (1957), ch. v; Douglas Bush, "A Note on Dickens' Humor," *From Jane Austen to Joseph Conrad*, pp. 82-91; Lauriat Lane, Jr., "Dickens' Archetypal Jew," *PMLA*, LXXIII (1958). 94-100 (cf. Harry Stone, "Dickens and the Jews," *VS*, II [1959]. 223-253); R. D. McMaster, "Dickens and the Horrific," *Dalhousie Rev.*, XXXVIII (1958). 18-28; John Henry Raleigh, "Dickens and the Sense of Time," *NCF*, XIII (1958). 127-137; Stone, "Dickens and Interior Monologue," *PQ*, XXXVIII (1959). 52-65; Ellen Moers, *The Dandy* (1960), ch. x; Barbara Hardy, "The Change of Heart in Dickens' Novels," *VS*, V (1961). 49-67; Randolph Quirk, "Some Observations on the Language of Dickens," *REL*, II, no. 3 (1961). 19-28; *The Dickens Critics*, ed. Ford and Lane (Ithaca, 1961); *Discussions of Charles Dickens*, ed. William Ross Clark (Boston, 1961).

1345 Note 2: Ada Nisbet, *Dickens and Ellen Ternan* (Berkeley, 1952), confirms the story of the liaison beyond reasonable doubt. Felix Aylmer, *Dickens Incognito* (1959) adds more evidence, although his most sensational "discovery" —that of the birth of a child to Ellen Ternan—has since been disproved.

1346 General treatments of *The Pickwick Papers* in the perspective of Dickens' subsequent career are found in Miller, *Charles Dickens: The World of His Novels*, ch. 1; Marcus, *Dickens from Pickwick to Dombey*, ch. 1. Special aspects of the book are examined in H. N. MacLean, "Mr. Pickwick and the Seven Deadly Sins," *NCF*, VIII (1953). 198-212; David M. Bevington, "Seasonal Relevance in *The Pickwick Papers*," *NCF*, XVI (1961). 219-230; William Axton, "Unity and Coherence in *The Pickwick Papers*," *SEL*, V (1965). 663-676.

1347 *Oliver Twist*, ed. J. Hillis Miller (1962). V. S. Pritchett, "*Oliver Twist*," *Books in General* (1953), pp. 191-196; Kathleen Tillotson, "*Oliver Twist*," *E&S*, n.s. XII (1959). 87-105; Alec Lucas, "*Oliver Twist* and the Newgate Novel," *Dalhousie Rev.*, XXXIV (1955). 381-387; Keith Hollingsworth, *The Newgate Novel* (Detroit, 1963), pp. 111-130; Kettle, I. 123-138.

1348 James K. Gottshall, "Devils Abroad: The Unity and Significance of *Barnaby Rudge*," *NCF*, XVI (1961). 133-146; Harold F. Folland, "The Doer and the Deed: Theme and Pattern in *Barnaby Rudge*," *PMLA*, LXXIV (1959). 406-417.—Edwin B. Benjamin, "The Structure of *Martin Chuzzlewit*," *PQ*, XXXIV (1955). 39-47.—*Dombey and Son*, ed. Edgar Johnson (1963). Kathleen Tillotson, "*Dombey and Son*," *Novels of the Eighteen-Forties*, pp. 157-201; William Axton, "Tonal Unity in *Dombey and Son*," *PMLA*, LXXVIII (1963). 341-348; F. R. Leavis, "*Dombey and Son*," *Sewanee Rev.*, LXX (1962). 177-201.

1349 *David Copperfield*, ed. E. K. Brown (1950), George H. Ford (Boston,

1958), Edgar Johnson (1962). Brown, *"David Copperfield,"* *Yale Rev.,* xxxvii (1948). 651-666; Gwendolyn B. Needham, "The Undisciplined Heart of David Copperfield," *NCF,* ix (1954). 81-107; Arnold Kettle, "Thoughts on *David Copperfield,"* *REL,* ii, no. 3 (1961). 65-74; Roger Gard, *"David Copperfield,"* *EIC,* xv (1965). 313-325.—*Bleak House,* ed. Morton D. Zabel (1956). George H. Ford, "Self-Help and the Helpless in *Bleak House," From Jane Austen to Joseph Conrad,* pp. 92-105; Norman Friedman, "The Shadow and the Sun: Notes Toward a Reading of *Bleak House," Boston Univ. Stud. in English,* iii (1957). 147-166; Louis Crompton, "Satire and Symbolism in *Bleak House," NCF,* xii (1958). 284-303; James H. Broderick and John E. Grant, "The Identity of Esther Summerson," *MP,* lv (1958). 252-258; Robert A. Donovan, "Structure and Idea in *Bleak House," ELH,* xxix (1962). 175-201; articles by Trevor Blount on the novel's topicality, in *RES,* n.s. xiv (1963). 370-378; *MLQ,* xxv (1964). 295-307; *MP,* lxii (1965). 325-339; *MLR,* lx (1965). 340-351; and *EIC,* xv (1965). 414-427.—*Hard Times,* ed. W. W. Watt (1958). F. R. Leavis, "*Hard Times:* An Analytic Note," *The Great Tradition* (1948), pp. 227-248 (cf. reply by David H. Hirsch, *Criticism,* vi [1964]. 1-16).

1350 Lionel Trilling, *"Little Dorrit," Kenyon Rev.,* xv (1953). 577-590; Edmund Bergler, "*Little Dorrit* and Dickens' Intuitive Knowledge of Psychic Masochism," *American Imago,* xiv (1957). 371-388; John Butt, "The Topicality of *Little Dorrit," UTQ,* xxix (1959). 1-10; R. D. McMaster, "*Little Dorrit:* Experience and Design," *Queen's Quar.,* lxvii (1961). 530-538.—*A Tale of Two Cities,* ed. Edward Wagenknecht (1950), Morton D. Zabel (1958).—*Great Expectations,* ed. Earle Davis (1948), Louis Crompton (Indianapolis, 1964), Angus Calder (1965). Van Ghent, pp. 125-138 (cf. Ruth M. Vande Kieft, "Patterns of Communication in *Great Expectations," NCF,* xv [1961]. 325-334, and George Levine, "Communication in *Great Expectations," NCF,* xviii [1963]. 175-181); G. Robert Stange, "Expectations Well Lost: Dickens' Fable for His Time," *College English,* xvi (1954). 9-17; Julian Moynahan, "The Hero's Guilt: The Case of *Great Expectations," EIC,* x (1960). 60-79; John H. Hagan, Jr., "The Poor Labyrinth: The Theme of Social Injustice in Dickens's *Great Expectations," NCF,* ix (1954). 169-178, and "Structural Patterns in Dickens's *Great Expectations," ELH,* xxi (1954). 54-66; Howard Mumford Jones, "On Rereading *Great Expectations," Southwest Rev.,* xxxix (1954). 328-335; Thomas E. Connolly, "Technique in *Great Expectations," PQ,* xxxiv (1955). 48-55; Arnold P. Drew, "Structure in *Great Expectations," Dickensian,* lii (1956). 123-127; K. J. Fielding, "The Critical Autonomy of *Great Expectations," REL,* ii, no. 3 (1961). 75-88; Charles R. Forker, "The Language of Hands in *Great Expectations," Texas Stud. in Lit. and Lang.,* iii (1961). 280-293; Barbara Hardy, "Food and Ceremony in *Great Expectations," EIC,* xiii (1963). 351-363; Harry Stone, "Fire, Hand, and Gate: Dickens' *Great Expectations," Kenyon Rev.,* xxiv (1962). 662-691; Joseph A. Hynes, "Image and Symbol in *Great Expectations," ELH,* xxx (1963). 258-292. A number of these articles are reprinted in *Assessing "Great Expectations,"* ed. Richard Lettis and William E. Morris (San Francisco, 1960).—Robert Morse, *"Our Mutual Friend," Partisan Rev.,* xvi (1949). 277-289; Sylvère Monod, "L'Expression dans *Our Mutual Friend:* manière ou maniérisme?", *Études anglaises,* x (1957). 37-48; R. D. McMaster, "Birds of Prey: A Study of *Our Mutual Friend," Dalhousie Rev.,* xl (1960). 372-381; Robert Barnard, "The Choral Symphony: *Our Mutual Friend," REL,* ii, no. 3 (1961). 89-99; Sister M. Corona Sharp, "The Archetypal

Feminine: *Our Mutual Friend,*" Univ. of Kansas City Rev., xxvii (1961). 307-311, xxviii (1961). 74-80.

1351 *The Mystery of Edwin Drood,* ed. "Michael Innes" [J. I. M. Stewart] (1950), C. Day Lewis (1956). Richard M. Baker, *The Drood Murder Case* (Berkeley, 1951); Felix Aylmer, *The Drood Case* (1964).

1353 Collins: Bibliography in Stevenson, pp. 277-284. Kenneth Robinson, *Wilkie Collins* (1951), the best biography; Robert Ashley, *Wilkie Collins* (1952); Nuel P. Davis, *The Life of Wilkie Collins* (Urbana, Ill., 1956); Bradford A. Booth, "Wilkie Collins and the Art of Fiction," *NCF*, vi (1951). 131-143.—Le Fanu: *In a Glass Darkly,* ed. V. S. Pritchett (1947); *A Strange Adventure in the Life of Miss Laura Mildmay* (1947); *Uncle Silas,* ed. Elizabeth Bowen (1948); *The Diabolical Genius,* ed. Michael Eenhoorn (1959), a collection of his writings. Nelson Browne, *Sheridan Le Fanu* (1951).—Eileen Bigland, *Ouida: The Passionate Victorian* (1950).

1354 Reade: Bibliography in Stevenson, pp. 284-293. Wayne Burns, *Charles Reade: A Study in Victorian Authorship* (1961); Royal A. Gettmann, "The Serialization of Reade's *A Good Fight,*" *NCF*, vi (1951). 21-32; J. B. Price, "Charles Reade and Charles Kingsley," *Contemporary Rev.,* clxxxiii (1953). 161-166; Sheila M. Smith, "Propaganda and Hard Facts in Charles Reade's Didactic Novels," *Renaissance and Mod. Stud.,* iv (1960). 135-149.

XXIV. Thackeray and Trollope

1355 Thackeray: Bibliography in Stevenson, ch. iv. Gordon N. Ray, *Thackeray: The Uses of Adversity, 1811-1846* (1955) and *Thackeray: The Age of Wisdom, 1847-1863* (1958), the standard biography; Ray, *The Buried Life: A Study of the Relation between Thackeray's Fiction and His Personal History* (Cambridge, Mass., 1952); J. Y. T. Greig, *Thackeray: A Reconsideration* (1950); Lambert Ennis, *Thackeray, the Sentimental Cynic* (Evanston, Ill., 1950); Geoffrey Tillotson, *Thackeray the Novelist* (Cambridge, 1954); John Loofbourow, *Thackeray and the Form of Fiction* (Princeton, 1964); Eva B. Touster, "The Literary Relationship of Thackeray and Fielding," *JEGP*, xlvi (1947). 383-394; John A. Lester, Jr., "Thackeray's Narrative Technique," *PMLA*, lxix (1954). 392-409; Ralph W. Rader, "Thackeray's Injustice to Fielding," *JEGP*, lvi (1957). 203-212; Greig, "Thackeray, a Novelist by Accident," *From Jane Austen to Joseph Conrad,* pp. 72-81; Myron Taube, "Thackeray and the Reminiscential Vision," *NCF*, xviii (1963). 247-259.

1356 *Contributions to the "Morning Chronicle,"* ed. Gordon N. Ray (Urbana, Ill., 1955).—On the background of *Catherine,* and Thackeray's intentions, see Keith Hollingsworth, *The Newgate Novel* (Detroit, 1963), pp. 148-165, and Robert A. Colby, "*Catherine:* Thackeray's Credo," *RES,* n.s. xv (1965). 381-396. —Note 3: The list is extended by Gordon N. Ray, "Thackeray and *Punch:* Forty-Four Newly Identified Contributions," *LTLS,* Jan. 1, 1939, p. 16.

1357 *The Rose and the Ring,* ed. G. N. Ray (1947), a facsimile reproduction of the manuscript.—*Vanity Fair,* ed. Joseph Warren Beach (1950), John W. Dodds (1955), Lionel Stevenson (1958), Geoffrey and Kathleen Tillotson (1963), the last-named important for text. Kathleen Tillotson, *"Vanity Fair," Novels of* *the Eighteen-Forties,* pp. 224-256; Russell A. Fraser, "Pernicious Casuistry: A Study of Character in *Vanity Fair,*" *NCF,* XII (1957). 137-147; G. Armour Craig, "On the Style of *Vanity Fair,*" *Style in Prose Fiction (English Institute Essays 1958),* ed. H. C. Martin (1959), pp. 87-113; E. D. H. Johnson, "*Vanity Fair* and *Amelia:* Thackeray in the Perspective of the Eighteenth Century," *MP,* LIX (1961). 100-113; Myron Taube, "Contrast as a Principle of Structure in *Vanity Fair,*" *NCF,* XVIII (1963). 119-135; A. E. Dyson, "*Vanity Fair:* an Irony against Heroes," *Critical Quar.,* VI (1964). 11-32; Joan Stevens, "Thackeray's *Vanity Fair,*" *REL,* VI, no. 1 (1965). 19-38; Ann Y. Wilkinson, "The Tomeavesian Way of Knowing the World: Technique and Meaning in *Vanity Fair,*" *ELH,* XXXII (1965). 370-387; Edgar F. Harden, "The Field of Mars in *Vanity Fair,*" *Tennessee Stud. in Lit.,* X (1965). 123-132; Van Ghent, pp. 139-152.

1358 Martin Fido, "*The History of Pendennis:* A Reconsideration," *EIC,* XIV (1964). 363-379.—*Henry Esmond,* ed. Gordon N. Ray (1950), G. Robert Stange (1962). Howard O. Brogan, "Rachel Esmond and the Dilemma of the Victorian Ideal of Womanhood," *ELH,* XIII (1946). 223-232; John E. Tilford, Jr., "The Love Theme of *Henry Esmond,*" *PMLA,* LXVII (1952). 684-701; William H. Marshall, "Dramatic Irony in *Henry Esmond,*" *Revue des langues vivantes,* XXVII (1961). 35-42; George J. Worth, "The Unity of *Henry Esmond,*" *NCF,* XV (1961). 345-353; Henri-A. Talon, "Time and Memory in Thackeray's *Henry Esmond,*" *RES,* n.s. XIII (1962). 147-156.

1359 Russell A. Fraser, "Sentimentality in Thackeray's *The Newcomes,*" *NCF,* IV (1949). 187-196.

1361 Oxford Illustrated Trollope, ed. Michael Sadleir and Frederick Page (1948-1954), abandoned after the publication of only eight volumes. Crown Edition of the political novels, also ed. Sadleir and Page (15v, 1948-1954); *North America,* ed. Donald Smalley and Bradford Booth (1951); *Hunting Sketches,* ed. L. Edwards (1952); *Did He Steal It?,* ed. R. H. Taylor (Princeton, 1952); *The Two Heroines of Plumplington* (1953); *The Trollope Reader,* ed. Esther C. Dunn and M. E. Dodd (1947); *Letters,* ed. Booth (1951).—Bibliography in Stevenson, ch. v. Elizabeth Bowen, *Anthony Trollope: A New Judgement* (1946); Beatrice C. Brown, *Anthony Trollope* (1950); A. O. J. Cockshut, *Anthony Trollope: A Critical Study* (1955); Rafael Helling, *A Century of Trollope Criticism* (Helsingfors, 1956); Booth, *Anthony Trollope: Aspects of His Life and Art* (Bloomington, Ind., 1958); Chauncey B. Tinker, "Trollope," *Yale Rev.,* XXXVI (1947). 424-434; W. L. Burn, "Anthony Trollope's Politics," *Nineteenth Century and After,* CXLIII (1948). 161-171; Mario Praz, "Anthony Trollope," *English Miscellany,* I (1950). 93-143; Asa Briggs, "Trollope, Bagehot, and *The English Constitution,*" *Cambridge Jour.,* V (1952). 327-338; John Hagan, "The Divided Mind of Anthony Trollope," *NCF,* XIV (1959). 1-26; Hugh Sykes Davies, "Trollope and His Style," *REL,* I, no. 4 (1960). 73-85; Jerome Thale, "The Problem of Structure in Trollope," *NCF,* XV (1960). 147-157; Audrey L. Laski, "Myths of Character: An Aspect of the Novel," *NCF,* XIV (1960). 333-343; Gerald Warner Brace, "The World of Trollope," *Texas Quar.,* IV, no. 3 (1961). 180-189; John E. Dustin, "Thematic Alternation in Trollope," *PMLA,* LXXVII (1962). 280-287; William Cadbury, "Shape and Theme: Determinants of Trollope's Forms," *PMLA,* LXXVIII (1963). 326-332; Winifred G. Gerould and James T. Gerould, *A*

Guide to Trollope (Princeton, 1948).—Of the Barchester novels, *The Warden* has been edited by Booth (1962), *Barchester Towers* by Booth (1949) and Sadleir (1956), the two together by Harlan Hatcher (1950), *Dr. Thorne* by Elizabeth Bowen (Boston, 1959), and *The Last Chronicles of Barset* by Gerald Warner Brace (1964) and Arthur Mizener (Boston, 1964). Sherman Hawkins, "Mr. Harding's Church Music," *ELH*, xxix (1962). 202-223; M. A. Goldberg, "Trollope's *The Warden:* A Commentary on the 'Age of Equipoise,'" *NCF*, xvii (1963). 381-390; William Cadbury, "Character and the Mock Heroic in *Barchester Towers*," *Texas Stud. in Lit. and Lang.*, v (1964). 509-519. The contemporary scandals utilized in *The Warden* are discussed by G. F. A. Best, "The Road to Hiram's Hospital," *VS*, v (1961). 135-150; Ralph Arnold, *The Whiston Matter* (1961); and R. B. Martin, *Enter Rumour* (1962), ch. iii.—*Autobiography*, ed. Booth (Berkeley, 1947) and Page (1950: part of the Oxford Illustrated Trollope).—Note 8: *Domestic Manners of the Americans*, ed. Donald Smalley (1949). W. H. Chaloner, "Mrs. Trollope and the Early Factory System," *VS*, iv (1960). 159-166.

XXV. Other Novelists of the Mid-Century

1364 Bulwer-Lytton: *The Last Days of Pompeii*, ed. Edgar Johnson (1957).— Bibliography in Stevenson, pp. 35-43. The Earl of Lytton, *Bulwer-Lytton* (1948); Curtis Dahl, "Bulwer-Lytton and the School of Catastrophe," *PQ*, xxxii (1953). 428-442, and "History on the Hustings: Bulwer-Lytton's Historical Novels of Politics," *From Jane Austen to Joseph Conrad*, pp. 72-81; Michael Lloyd, "Bulwer-Lytton and the Idealizing Principle," *English Miscellany*, vii (1956). 25-39; Joseph I. Fradin, " 'The Absorbing Tyranny of Every-day Life': Bulwer-Lytton's *A Strange Story*," *NCF*, xvi (1961). 1-16; Geoffrey Wagner, "A Forgotten Satire: Bulwer-Lytton's *The Coming Race*," *NCF*, xix (1965). 379-385; Ellen Moers, *The Dandy* (1960), ch. iii; Keith Hollingsworth, *The Newgate Novel* (Detroit, 1963), ch. iv.

1365 Disraeli: Bibliography in Stevenson, pp. 22-35. Hesketh Pearson, *Dizzy* (1951); Cecil Roth, *Benjamin Disraeli* (1952); Bernard R. Jerman, *The Young Disraeli* (Princeton, 1960); Muriel Masefield, *Peacocks and Primroses: A Survey of Disraeli's Novels* (1953); Robert Hamilton, "Disraeli and the Two Nations," *Quarterly Rev.*, cclxxxviii (1950). 102-115, on *Sybil;* Eric Forbes-Boyd, "Disraeli, the Novelist," *E&S*, n.s. iii (1950). 100-117; Maurice Edelman, "A Political Novel [*Coningsby*]," *LTLS*, Aug. 7, 1959, pp. x-xi; Holloway, *The Victorian Sage*, ch. iv; Ellen Moers, *The Dandy* (1960), ch. iv.

1367 Kingsley: *Westward Ho!* (1953) and *Hereward the Wake* (1955), both ed. L. A. G. Strong; *American Notes: Letters from a Lecture Tour*, ed. Robert B. Martin (Princeton, 1958).—Bibliography in Stevenson, pp. 263-276. Guy Kendall, *Charles Kingsley and His Ideas* (1947); Una Pope-Hennessy, *Canon Charles Kingsley* (1948); Martin, *The Dust of Combat* (1960); Gillian Beer, "Charles Kingsley and the Literary Image of the Countryside," *VS*, viii (1965). 243-254.

1369 Gaskell: *Cranford* and *Cousin Phillis*, ed. Elizabeth Jenkins (1947);

Mary Barton, ed. Lettice Cooper (1947) and Myron F. Brightfield (1958); *Wives and Daughters,* ed. Rosamond Lehmann (1948); *North and South,* ed. Elizabeth Bowen (1952); *Letters,* ed. J. A. V. Chapple and Arthur Pollard (Manchester, 1965).—Bibliography in Stevenson, pp. 245-263. Yvonne ffrench, *Mrs. Gaskell* (1949); Annette B. Hopkins, *Elizabeth Gaskell* (1952); Edgar Wright, *Mrs. Gaskell: The Basis for Reassessment* (1965); Pollard, *Mrs. Gaskell* (Manchester, 1965); John G. Sharps, *Mrs. Gaskell's Observation and Invention* (Linden Press, 1970); H. P. Collins, "The Naked Sensibility: Elizabeth Gaskell," *EIC,* iii (1953). 60-72; Tillotson, *Novels of the Eighteen-Forties,* pp. 202-223, on *Mary Barton;* Pollard, "The Novels of Mrs. Gaskell," *Bulletin of the John Rylands Lib.,* xliii (1961). 403-425; Martin Dodsworth, "Women Without Men at Cranford," *EIC,* xiii (1963). 132-145.

Note 8: Angela Thirkell, "Henry Kingsley, 1830-1876," *NCF,* v (1950). 175-187, and "The Works of Henry Kingsley," *NCF,* v (1951). 273-293; Robert Lee Wolff, "Henry Kingsley," *Harvard Library Bull.,* xiii (1959). 195-226.—Edward C. Mack and W. H. G. Armytage, *Thomas Hughes* (1953).

1370 Note 11: Joseph B. Rivlin, *Harriet Martineau: A Bibliography of Her Separately Printed Books* (1947); Vera Wheatley, *The Life and Work of Harriet Martineau* (1957); Robert K. Webb, *Harriet Martineau: A Radical Victorian* (1960).—Margaret Mare and Alicia C. Percival, *Victorian Best-Seller: The World of Charlotte Mary Yonge* (1948).

1370-1371 Heather Edition of the Brontës' novels, ed. Phyllis Bentley (6v, 1949); Charlotte Brontë's novels, ed. Margaret Lane (4v, 1953-1957). Emily's *Complete Poems,* ed. Philip Henderson (1951); *Gondal's Queen,* ed. Fannie E. Ratchford (Austin, Tex., 1955), eighty-four of Emily's poems rearranged into a coherent narrative; *Letters of the Brontës,* ed. Muriel Spark (Norman, Okla., 1954), a selection.—Bibliography in Stevenson, ch. vi. Bentley, *The Brontës* (1947); Lawrence and Elisabeth Hanson, *The Four Brontës* (1949); Muriel Spark and Derek Stanford, *Emily Brontë: Her Life and Work* (1953); C. Day Lewis, "Emily Brontë and Freedom," *Notable Images of Virtue* (Toronto, 1954), ch. 1; Jacques Blondel, *Emily Brontë: Expérience spirituelle et création poétique* (Paris, 1955); Ada Harrison and Derek Stanford, *Anne Brontë: Her Life and Work* (1959); Winifred Gérin, *Anne Brontë* (1959); Margaret Lane, *The Brontë Story: A Reconsideration of Mrs. Gaskell's "Life of Charlotte Brontë"* (1953); Richard Chase, "The Brontës: A Centennial Observance," *Kenyon Rev.,* ix (1947). 487-506; Melvin R. Watson, "Form and Substance in the Brontë Novels," *From Jane Austen to Joseph Conrad,* pp. 106-117; Robert B. Heilman, "Charlotte Brontë's 'New' Gothic," *ibid.,* pp. 118-132, and "Charlotte Brontë, Reason, and the Moon," *NCF,* xiv (1960). 283-302; J. Hillis Miller, *The Disappearance of God,* ch. iv (on Emily); Philip Momberger, "Self and the World in the Works of Charlotte Brontë," *ELH,* xxxii (1965). 349-369.

1371 Note 15: Daphne du Maurier, *The Infernal World of Branwell Brontë* (1960); Winifred Gérin, *Branwell Brontë* (1961)—neither very satisfactory.—Note 16: See also Mrs. Harrison's *The Clue to the Brontës* (1948), on the influence of Evangelicalism.—Note 19: Annette B. Hopkins, *The Father of the Brontës* (Baltimore, 1958); John Lock and W. T. Dixon, *A Man of Sorrow* (1965).

1374 *Jane Eyre,* ed. Joe Lee Davis (1950), William Peden (1950), Mark

Schorer (Boston, 1959). Kathleen Tillotson, *"Jane Eyre," Novels of the Eighteen-Forties*, pp. 257-313; M. H. Scargill, " 'All Passion Spent': A Revaluation of *Jane Eyre," UTQ*, xix (1950). 120-125; Edgar F. Shannon, Jr., "The Present Tense in *Jane Eyre," NCF*, x (1955). 141-145; William H. Marshall, "The Self, the World, and the Structure of *Jane Eyre," Revue des langues vivantes*, xxvii (1961). 416-425; R. E. Hughes, *"Jane Eyre:* The Unbaptized Dionysos," *NCF*, xviii (1964). 347-364.

1375 Jacob Korg, "The Problem of Unity in *Shirley," NCF*, xii (1957). 125-136; Asa Briggs, "Private and Social Themes in *Shirley," Brontë Soc. Trans.*, xiii (1958). 203-219; J. M. S. Tompkins, "Caroline Helstone's Eyes," *ibid.*, xiv (1961). 18-28.—Robert A. Colby, *"Villette* and the Life of the Mind," *PMLA*, lxxv (1960). 410-419.

1377 *Wuthering Heights*, ed. Bruce McCullough (1950), Mark Schorer (1950), Royal A. Gettmann (1950), Bonamy Dobrée (1955), V. S. Pritchett (Boston, 1956), Thomas Moser (1962), T. Crehan (1962), William Sale (1963), David Daiches (1965).—Mary Visick, *The Genesis of "Wuthering Heights"* (1958); D. G. Klingopulos, "The Novel as Dramatic Poem: *Wuthering Heights," Scrutiny*, xiv (1947). 269-286; Derek Traversi, *"Wuthering Heights* After a Hundred Years," *Dublin Rev.*, ccxxii (1949). 154-168; Melvin R. Watson, "Tempest in the Soul: The Theme and Structure of *Wuthering Heights," NCF*, iv (1949). 87-100; Schorer, "Fiction and the 'Matrix of Analogy,' " *Kenyon Rev.*, xi (1949). 539-560; B. H. Lehman, "Of Material, Subject, and Form: *Wuthering Heights," The Image of the Work* (Berkeley, 1955), pp. 3-17; John K. Mathison, "Nelly Dean and the Power of *Wuthering Heights," NCF*, xi (1956). 106-129; Carl R. Woodring, "The Narrators of *Wuthering Heights," NCF*, xi (1957). 298-305; James Hafley, "The Villain in *Wuthering Heights," NCF*, xiii (1958). 199-215; Miriam Allott, *"Wuthering Heights:* The Rejection of Heathcliff?", *EIC*, viii (1958). 27-47; Edgar F. Shannon, Jr., "Lockwood's Dreams and the Exegesis of *Wuthering Heights," NCF*, xiv (1959). 95-109; Robert C. McKibben, "The Image of the Book in *Wuthering Heights," NCF*, xv (1960). 159-169; Moser, "What is the Matter with Emily Jane? Conflicting Impulses in *Wuthering Heights," NCF*, xvii (1962). 1-19; Wade Thompson, "Infanticide and Sadism in *Wuthering Heights," PMLA*, lxxviii (1963). 69-74; Philip Drew, "Charlotte Brontë as a Critic of *Wuthering Heights," NCF*, xviii (1964). 365-381; John E. Jordan, "The Ironic Vision of Emily Brontë," *NCF*, xx (1965). 1-18; F. H. Langman, *"Wuthering Heights," EIC*, xv (1965). 294-312; Van Ghent, pp. 153-170.

1378 Eliot: *Essays*, ed. Thomas Pinney (1963); *Letters*, ed. Gordon S. Haight (7v, New Haven, 1954-1955).—Bibliography in Stevenson, ch. ix. Gerald Bullett, *George Eliot: Her Life and Books* (1947); Lawrence and Elisabeth Hanson, *Marian Evans and George Eliot* (1952); Joan Bennett, *George Eliot: Her Mind and Her Art* (Cambridge, 1948; rev. 1962); Robert Speaight, *George Eliot* (1954); Barbara Hardy, *The Novels of George Eliot* (1959); Reva Stump, *Movement and Vision in George Eliot's Novels* (Seattle, 1959); Jerome Thale, *The Novels of George Eliot* (1959); Charles B. Cox, *The Free Spirit: A Study of Liberal Humanism in the Novels of George Eliot* [and others] (1963); Walter Allen, *George Eliot* (1964); U. C. Knoepflmacher, *Religious Humanism and the Victorian Novel* (Princeton, 1965), chs. ii-iii; Bernard J. Paris, *Experiments in*

Life: George Eliot's Quest for Values (Detroit, 1965); F. R. Leavis, "George Eliot," *The Great Tradition* (1948), pp. 28-125; Walter Naumann, "The Architecture of George Eliot's Novels," *MLQ*, IX (1948). 37-50; Graham Hough, "Novelist-Philosophers: George Eliot," *Horizon*, XVII (1948). 50-62; Claude T. Bissell, "Social Analysis in the Novels of George Eliot," *ELH*, XVIII (1951). 221-239; Martin J. Svaglic, "Religion in the Novels of George Eliot," *JEGP*, LIII (1954). 145-159; Alice R. Kaminsky, "George Eliot, George Henry Lewes, and the Novel," *PMLA*, LXX (1955). 997-1013; James D. Rust, "The Art of Fiction in George Eliot's Reviews," *RES*, n.s. VII (1956). 164-172; William J. Hyde, "George Eliot and the Climate of Realism," *PMLA*, LXXII (1957). 147-164; Haight, "George Eliot's Originals," *From Jane Austen to Joseph Conrad*, pp. 177-193; Alexander Welsh, "George Eliot and the Romance," *NCF*, XIV (1959). 241-254; Miriam Allott, "George Eliot in the 1860's," *VS*, V (1961). 94-108; George Levine, "Determinism and Responsibility in the Works of George Eliot," *PMLA*, LXXVII (1962). 268-279; N. N. Feltes, "George Eliot and the Unified Sensibility," *PMLA*, LXXIX (1964). 130-136; Darrel Mansell, Jr., "George Eliot's Conception of 'Form,'" *SEL*, V (1965). 651-662; Ian Adam, "Character and Destiny in George Eliot's Fiction," *NCF*, XX (1965). 127-143; Willey, *Nineteenth Century Studies*, chs. VIII-IX; Holloway, *The Victorian Sage*, ch. V; *Discussions of George Eliot*, ed. Richard Stang (Boston, 1960); *A Century of George Eliot Criticism*, ed. Haight (Boston, 1965).

1379   Thomas S. Noble, *George Eliot's "Scenes of Clerical Life"* (New Haven, 1965).—*Adam Bede*, ed. Gordon S. Haight (1948), Maxwell Goldberg (1956). Maurice Hussey, "Structure and Imagery in *Adam Bede*," *NCF*, X (1955). 115-129; George R. Creeger, "An Interpretation of *Adam Bede*," *ELH*, XXIII (1956). 218-238; Ian Gregor, "The Two Worlds of *Adam Bede*," *The Moral and the Story* (1962), pp. 13-32; Van Ghent, pp. 171-181.—*The Mill on the Floss*, ed. Haight (Boston, 1961). W. R. Steinhoff, "Intent and Fulfillment in the Ending of *The Mill on the Floss*," *The Image of the Work* (Berkeley, 1955), pp. 231-251; Bernard J. Paris, "Toward a Revaluation of George Eliot's *The Mill on the Floss*," *NCF*, XI (1956). 18-31.—*Silas Marner*, ed. Jerome Thale (1962). Robert B. Heilman, "Return to Raveloe," *English Jour.*, XLVI (1957). 1-10; Fred C. Thomson, "The Theme of Alienation in *Silas Marner*," *NCF*, XX (1965). 69-84.—M. Tosello, *Le Fonti italiane della "Romola" di George Eliot* (Turin, 1956); Carole Robinson, "*Romola*: A Reading of the Novel," *VS*, VI (1962). 29-42.—*Felix Holt*: Raymond Williams, *Culture and Society* (1958), pp. 102-109; Fred C. Thomson, "The Genesis of *Felix Holt*," *PMLA*, LXXIV (1959). 576-584, and "*Felix Holt* as Classic Tragedy," *NCF*, XVI (1961). 47-58; David R. Carroll, "Felix Holt: Society as Protagonist," *NCF*, XVII (1962). 237-252.—*Middlemarch*, ed. Haight (1956), W. J. Harvey (1965). *Quarry for "Middlemarch*," ed. Anna T. Kitchel (Berkeley, 1950); Jerome Beaty, *"Middlemarch" from Notebook to Novel* (Urbana, Ill., 1960); David Daiches, *George Eliot: "Middlemarch"* (1963); Mark Schorer, "Fiction and the 'Matrix of Analogy,'" *Kenyon Rev.*, XI (1949). 539-560; F. George Steiner, "A Preface to *Middlemarch*," *NCF*, IX (1955). 262-279; Beaty, "History by Indirection: The Era of Reform in *Middlemarch*," *VS*, I (1957). 173-179; Sumner J. Ferris, "*Middlemarch*: George Eliot's Masterpiece," *From Jane Austen to Joseph Conrad*, pp. 194-207; David R. Carroll, "Unity Through Analogy: An Interpretation of *Middlemarch*," *VS*, II (1959). 305-316; Sylvère

Monod, "George Eliot et les personnages de *Middlemarch*," *Études anglaises*, XII (1959). 306-314; Newton P. Stallknecht, "Resolution and Independence: A Reading of *Middlemarch*," *Twelve Original Essays on Great English Novels*, ed. Charles Shapiro (Detroit, 1960), pp. 125-152; John Hagan, "*Middlemarch*: Narrative Unity in the Story of Dorothea Brooke," *NCF*, XVI (1961). 17-31; Lloyd Fernando, "George Eliot, Feminism and Dorothea Brooke," *REL*, IV, no. 1 (1963). 76-90; Neil D. Isaacs, "*Middlemarch*: Crescendo of Obligatory Drama," *NCF*, XVIII (1963). 21-34; Kettle, I. 170-190.—*Daniel Deronda*, ed. F. R. Leavis (1961). Maurice Beebe, " 'Visions Are Creators': The Unity of *Daniel Deronda*," *Boston Univ. Stud. in English*, I (1955). 166-177; D. R. Carroll, "The Unity of *Daniel Deronda*," *EIC*, IX (1959). 369-380; Jerome Beaty, "*Daniel Deronda* and the Question of Unity in Fiction," *Victorian Newsletter*, No. 15 (1959), pp. 16-19; Robert Preyer, "Beyond the Liberal Imagination: Vision and Unreality in *Daniel Deronda*," *VS*, IV (1960). 33-54; Carole Robinson, "The Severe Angel: A Study of *Daniel Deronda*," *ELH*, XXXI (1964). 278-300.—Note 37: *Literary Criticism*, ed. Alice R. Kaminsky (Lincoln, Neb., 1965); three articles by Morris Greenhut, "George Henry Lewes and the Classical Tradition in English Criticism," *RES*, XXIV (1948). 126-137; "George Henry Lewes as a Critic of the Novel," *SP*, XLV (1948). 491-511; "G. H. Lewes's Criticism of the Drama," *PMLA*, LXIV (1949). 350-368; Jack Kaminsky, "The Empirical Metaphysics of George Henry Lewes," *JHI*, XIII (1952). 314-332; R. L. Brett, "George Henry Lewes: Dramatist, Novelist and Critic," *E&S*, n.s. XI (1958). 101-120.

1381 Mrs. Oliphant: Katharine Moore, "A Valiant Victorian," *Blackwood's Mag.*, CCLXXXIII (1958). 231-243; Robert and Vineta Colby, "*A Beleaguered City: A Fable for the Victorian Age*," *NCF*, XVI (1962). 283-301.

XXVI. Alfred Tennyson

1382 *Poems and Plays* (Oxford, 1953); selections by F. L. Lucas (1947), Sir John Squire (1947), John Heath-Stubbs (1949), Stephen Gwynn (1950), Douglas Bush (1951), Herbert M. McLuhan (1956), Jerome H. Buckley (Boston, 1958); *Poems, 1832-1842*, ed. J. H. Fowler (1950).—Bibliography in Faverty, ch. II. Charles Tennyson, *Alfred Tennyson* (1949), the best biography, and *Six Tennyson Essays* (1954); Ralph W. Rader, *Tennyson's "Maud": The Biographical Genesis* (Berkeley, 1963), important biographical information for the period 1833-1854; George O. Marshall, *A Tennyson Handbook* (1963), to be used with caution; Paull F. Baum, *Tennyson Sixty Years After* (Chapel Hill, 1948), unsympathetic; Edgar F. Shannon, Jr., *Tennyson and the Reviewers* [1830-1850] (Cambridge, Mass., 1952); Buckley, *Tennyson: the Growth of a Poet* (Cambridge, Mass., 1960); Valerie Pitt, *Tennyson Laureate* (Toronto, 1962); Elton E. Smith, *The Two Voices: A Tennyson Study* (Lincoln, Neb., 1964); McLuhan, "Tennyson and Picturesque Poetry," *EIC*, I (1951). 262-282; E. D. H. Johnson, *The Alien Vision of Victorian Poetry* (Princeton, 1952), pp. 3-68; Milton Millhauser, "Tennyson: Artifice and Image," *JAAC*, XIV (1956). 333-338; Allan Danzig, "The Contraries: A Central Concept in Tennyson's Poetry," *PMLA*, LXXVII (1962). 577-585; James Kissane, "Tennyson: the Passion of the Past and the Curse of Time," *ELH*, XXXII (1965). 85-109; *Critical Essays on the Poetry of*

Tennyson, ed. John Killham (1960); Willey, *More Nineteenth Century Studies*, ch.ii.—Note 2: Charles Tennyson-Turner: *A Hundred Sonnets*, ed. John Betjeman and Charles Tennyson (1960). Harold Nicolson, *Tennyson's Two Brothers* (Cambridge, 1947); Charles Tennyson, "The Vicar of Grasby," *English*, viii (1950). 117-120, and "The Somersby Tennysons," *VS* (Christmas Supplement, 1963), pp. 14-16.

1383-1385 Tennyson's earlier poems are studied in Lionel Stevenson, "The 'High-born Maiden' Symbol in Tennyson," *PMLA*, lxiii (1948). 234-243; Robert Preyer, "Tennyson as an Oracular Poet," *MP*, lv (1958). 239-251; Carl R. Sonn, "Poetic Vision and Religious Certainty in Tennyson's Earlier Poetry," *MP*, lvii (1959). 83-93; G. Robert Stange, "Tennyson's Garden of Art: A Study of *The Hesperides*," *PMLA*, lxvii (1952). 732-743; Alan Grob, "Tennyson's *The Lotos-Eaters*: Two Versions of Art," *MP*, lxii (1964). 118-129.

1385 John Killham, *Tennyson and "The Princess": Reflections of an Age* (1958); Milton Millhauser, "Tennyson's *Princess* and *Vestiges*," *PMLA*, lxix (1954). 337-343; Ryals, "The 'Weird Seizures' in *The Princess*," *Texas Stud. in Lit. and Lang.*, iv (1962). 268-275.

1386 Eleanor B. Mattes, *"In Memoriam": The Way of a Soul* (1951); Graham Hough, "The Natural Theology of *In Memoriam*," *RES*, xxiii (1947). 244-256; E. D. H. Johnson, "*In Memoriam*: The Way of a Poet," *VS*, ii (1958). 139-148; John D. Rosenberg, "The Two Kingdoms of *In Memoriam*," *JEGP*, lviii (1959). 228-240; Jonathan Bishop, "The Unity of *In Memoriam*," *Victorian Newsletter*, No. 21 (1962). 9-14; Stephen Allen Grant, "The Mystical Implications of *In Memoriam*," *SEL*, ii (1962). 481-495; Carlisle Moore, "Faith, Doubt, and Mystical Experience in *In Memoriam*," *VS*, vii (1963). 155-169; J. C. C. Mays, "*In Memoriam*: An Aspect of Form," *UTQ*, xxxv (1965). 22-46.

1387 Edgar F. Shannon, "The History of a Poem: Tennyson's *Ode on the Death of the Duke of Wellington*," *Stud. in Bibliography*, xiii (1960). 149-177.—Roy P. Basler, "Tennyson's *Maud*," *Sex, Symbolism, and Psychology in Literature* (New Brunswick, N.J., 1948), pp. 73-93; E. D. H. Johnson, "The Lily and the Rose: Symbolic Meaning in Tennyson's *Maud*," *PMLA*, lxiv (1949). 1222-1227. —Note 12: Jerome Thale, "Sydney Dobell's *Roman*: The Poet's Experience and His Work," *American Imago*, xii (1955). 87-113; Robert Preyer, "Sidney Dobell and the Victorian Epic," *UTQ*, xxx (1961). 163-179. There is a good treatment of the Spasmodics in Buckley, *The Victorian Temper*, ch. iii.

1388 F. E. L. Priestley, "Tennyson's *Idylls*," *UTQ*, xix (1949). 35-49; Samuel C. Burchell, "Tennyson's 'Allegory in the Distance,' " *PMLA*, lxviii (1953). 418-424; Edward Engelberg, "The Beast Image in Tennyson's *Idylls of the King*," *ELH*, xxii (1955). 287-292; Charles Tennyson, "*The Idylls of the King*," *Twentieth Century*, clxi (1957). 277-286; Ryals, "The Moral Paradox of the Hero in *The Idylls of the King*," *ELH*, xxx (1963). 53-69.

1389-1390 Note 17: Brooks Wright, *Interpreter of Buddhism to the West: Sir Edwin Arnold* (1957).—Norton B. Crowell, *Alfred Austin: Victorian* (Albuquerque, 1953).—Derek Hudson, *Martin Tupper: His Rise and Fall* (1949).

1390 On the style of *The Revenge*, see Robert M. Estrich and Hans Sperber, *Three Keys to Language* (1952), ch. xiv.

XXVII. The Brownings

1392 Robert Browning: Selected poems, ed. Humphrey Milford (Oxford, 1949), Simon Nowell-Smith (1950), Kenneth L. Knickerbocker (1951), Horace Gregory (1956), Donald Smalley (Boston, 1956); *New Letters*, ed. William C. DeVane and Knickerbocker (New Haven, 1950); *Dearest Isa*, ed. Edward C. McAleer (Austin, Tex., 1951), replacing Armstrong's edition of *Letters to Isa Blagden; Letters of the Brownings to George Barrett*, ed. Paul Landis and Ronald E. Freeman (Urbana, Ill., 1958); *Browning to His American Friends: Letters Between the Brownings, the Storys and James Russell Lowell, 1841-1890*, ed. Gertrude R. Hudson (1965).—L. N. Broughton, C. S. Northup, and Robert Pearsall, *Robert Browning: A Bibliography, 1830-1950* (Ithaca, 1953); Faverty, ch. III. DeVane's *Browning Handbook* appeared in a revised ed., 1955. There is no really satisfactory life of Browning; until one appears, Betty Miller, *Robert Browning: A Portrait* (1952) will serve despite its Freudian bias. W. O. Raymond, *The Infinite Moment and Other Essays in Browning* (Toronto, 1950; rev. 1965); J. M. Cohen, *Robert Browning* (1952); Roma J. King, Jr., *The Bow and the Lyre* (Ann Arbor, 1957), "new critical" readings of five poems; Park Honan, *Browning's Characters: A Study in Poetic Technique* (New Haven, 1961); Norton B. Crowell, *The Triple Soul: Browning's Theory of Knowledge* (Albuquerque, 1963); DeVane, "The Virgin and the Dragon," *Yale Rev.*, XXXVII (1947). 33-46; "A Version of Browning," *LTLS*, Dec. 30, 1949, p. 856; Hoxie N. Fairchild, "Browning the Simple-Hearted Casuist," *UTQ*, XVIII (1949). 234-240; E. D. H. Johnson, *The Alien Vision of Victorian Poetry*, pp. 71-143; Richard D. Altick, "The Private Life of Robert Browning," *Yale Rev.*, XLI (1952). 247-262; "The Browning Puzzle," *LTLS*, Nov. 14, 1952, p. 742; J. A. Boulton, "Browning—a Potential Revolutionary," *EIC*, III (1953). 165-176; Joseph E. Duncan, "The Intellectual Kinship of John Donne and Robert Browning," *SP*, L (1953). 81-100; G. Robert Stange, "Browning and Modern Poetry," *Pacific Spectator*, VIII (1954). 218-228; J. Hillis Miller, *The Disappearance of God* (Cambridge, Mass., 1963), ch. III; William Cadbury, "Lyric and Anti-Lyric Form: A Method for Judging Browning," *UTQ*, XXXIV (1964). 49-67; Robert Preyer, "Two Styles in the Verse of Robert Browning," *ELH*, XXXII (1965). 62-84; *The Browning Critics*, ed. Boyd Litzinger and Knickerbocker (Lexington, Ky., 1965); *Robert Browning: A Collection of Critical Essays*, ed. Philip Drew (1966).

1393 Robert Preyer, "Robert Browning: A Reading of the Early Narratives," *ELH*, XXVI (1959). 531-548.—F. E. L. Priestley, "The Ironic Pattern of Browning's *Paracelsus*," *UTQ*, XXXIV (1964). 68-81.—Earl Hilton, "Browning's *Sordello* as a Study of the Will," *PMLA*, LXIX (1954). 1127-1134; Daniel Stempel, "Browning's *Sordello*: the Art of the Makers-See," *PMLA*, LXXX (1965). 554-561.

1394 James P. McCormick, "Browning and the Experimental Drama," *PMLA*, LXVIII (1953). 982-991.—Robert Langbaum, *The Poetry of Experience: The Dramatic Monologue in Modern Literary Tradition* (1957), important not only for Browning; Benjamin W. Fuson, "Browning and His English

Predecessors in the Dramatic Monolog," *State Univ. of Iowa Humanistic Stud.*, VIII (1948).

1395 The so-called "Essay on Shelley" is not Browning's "only work in prose": see the *Essay on Chatterton*, ed. Donald Smalley (Cambridge, Mass., 1948)—first published in the *Foreign Quar. Rev.*, 1842. On the critique of Shelley, see Warren, *English Poetic Theory*, ch. VII; Philip Drew, "Browning's *Essay on Shelley*," *VP*, I (1963). 1-6 (cf. reply by Thomas J. Collins, *VP*, II [1964]. 119-124).—Note 13: As noted above, Armstrong's edition of the letters to Isa Blagden is superseded by *Dearest Isa*, ed. McAleer.

1396 Charlotte C. Watkins, "The 'Abstruser Themes' of Browning's *Fifine at the Fair*," *PMLA*, LXXIV (1959). 426-437, and "Browning's *Red Cotton Night-Cap Country* and Carlyle," *VS*, VII (1964). 359-374.

1397 Note 19: See also Hoxie N. Fairchild, "*La Saisiaz* and *The Nineteenth Century*," *MP*, XLVIII (1950). 104-111.

1399-1401 William Whitla, *The Central Truth: The Incarnation in Robert Browning's Poetry* (Toronto, 1963); Kingsbury Badger, " 'See the Christ Stand!': Browning's Religion," *Boston Univ. Stud. in English*, I (1955). 53-73; Joseph E. Baker, "Religious Implications in Browning's Poetry," *PQ*, XXXVI (1957). 436-452; H. N. Fairchild, "Browning's Heaven," *Rev. of Religion*, XIV (1949). 30-37.

1401 Note 31: *The Ring and the Book*, with introduction by Wylie Sypher (1961). Beatrice Corrigan, *Curious Annals: New Documents Relating to Browning's Roman Murder Story* (Toronto, 1956); Paul A. Cundiff, "The Clarity of Browning's Ring Metaphor," *PMLA*, LXIII (1948). 1276-1282 (cf. the discussion of this metaphor in *Victorian Newsletter*, Nos. 16-17 [1959-1960], and George R. Wasserman, "The Meaning of Browning's Ring-Figure," *MLN*, LXXVI [1961]. 420-426).

1403 Elizabeth Barrett Browning: *Sonnets from the Portuguese: Centennial Variorum Edition*, ed. Fannie Ratchford (1950), important for text; *Elizabeth Barrett to Miss Mitford*, ed. Betty Miller (1954); *Elizabeth Barrett to Mr. [Hugh Stuart] Boyd*, ed. Barbara P. McCarthy (New Haven, 1955).—Bibliography in Faverty, pp. 84-92. Dorothy Hewlett, *Elizabeth Barrett Browning* (1952); Gardner B. Taplin, *Life of Elizabeth Barrett Browning* (New Haven, 1957); Alethea Hayter, *Mrs. Browning: A Poet's Work and Its Setting* (1962).

XXVIII. Matthew Arnold and Arthur Hugh Clough; Edward FitzGerald and James Thomson ("B. V.")

1405 Clough: *Poems*, ed. H. F. Lowry, A. L. P. Norrington, and F. L. Mulhauser (Oxford, 1951)—cf. criticism by Richard M. Gollin, *MP*, LX (1962). 120-127; *Correspondence*, ed. Mulhauser (2v, Oxford, 1957).—Bibliography in Faverty, pp. 104-110; Walter E. Houghton, "The Prose Works of Arthur Hugh Clough: A Checklist and Calendar," *Bull. N.Y. Library*, LXIV (1960) 377-394. Katherine Chorley, *Arthur Hugh Clough: The Uncommitted Mind* (Oxford, 1962); Houghton, *The Poetry of Clough* (New Haven, 1963); Paul

Veyriras, *Arthur Hugh Clough* (Paris, 1965); Kingsbury Badger, "Arthur Hugh Clough as Dipsychus," *MLQ*, XII (1951). 39-56; Doris N. Dalglish, "Arthur Hugh Clough: the Shorter Poems," *EIC*, II (1952). 38-53; three articles by Michael Timko, "The 'True Creed' of Arthur Hugh Clough," *MLQ*, XXI (1960). 208-222, "The Poetic Theory of Arthur Hugh Clough," *ES*, XLIII (1962). 240-247, and "The Satiric Poetry of Arthur Hugh Clough," *VP*, I (1963). 104-114; Clyde de L. Ryals, "An Interpretation of Clough's *Dipsychus*," *VP*, I (1963). 182-188; Masao Miyosho, "Clough's Poems of Self-Irony," *SEL*, v (1965). 691-704.

1406 Note 5: Robert Birley, "Philip James Bailey: *Festus*," *Sunk Without Trace* (1962), ch. VI.

1407 Arnold: *Complete Prose Works*, ed. Robert H. Super (Ann Arbor, 1960-   ); *Poetical Works*, ed. C. B. Tinker and Howard F. Lowry (1950); *Poems*, ed. Kenneth Allott (1965); *The Portable Matthew Arnold*, ed. Lionel Trilling (1949); *Poetry and Criticism*, ed. A. Dwight Culler (Boston, 1961); *Selected Poetry and Prose*, ed. Frederick W. Mulhauser (1953); *Poetry and Prose*, ed. John Bryson (Cambridge, Mass., 1954); *Matthew Arnold: an Introduction and a Selection* (1948) and *Poems* (1949), both ed. C. Dyment; *Selected Essays*, ed. Noel Annan (1964); *Five Uncollected Essays*, ed. Allott (Liverpool, 1953); *Essays, Letters, and Reviews*, ed. Fraser Neiman (Cambridge, Mass., 1960), pieces hitherto unreprinted; *England and the Italian Question*, ed. Merle M. Bevington (Durham, N.C., 1953); *Notebooks*, ed. Lowry, Karl Young, and Waldo H. Dunn (1952).—Bibliography, mainly on Arnold the poet, in Faverty, ch. v. Louis Bonnerot, *Matthew Arnold, Poète: Essai de biographie psychologique* (Paris, 1947); Edmund Chambers, *Matthew Arnold* (Oxford, 1947); E. K. Brown, *Matthew Arnold: A Study in Conflict* (Chicago, 1948); W. F. Connell, *The Educational Thought and Influence of Matthew Arnold* (1950); J. D. Jump, *Matthew Arnold* (1955); John Henry Raleigh, *Matthew Arnold and American Culture* (Berkeley, 1957); William A. Jamison, *Arnold and the Romantics* (Copenhagen, 1958); Paull F. Baum, *Ten Studies in the Poetry of Matthew Arnold* (Durham, N.C., 1958); William Robbins, *The Ethical Idealism of Matthew Arnold* (Toronto, 1959); David G. James, *Matthew Arnold and the Decline of English Romanticism* (Oxford, 1961); Wendell S. Johnson, *The Voices of Matthew Arnold* (New Haven, 1961); H. C. Duffin, *Arnold the Poet* (1962); Leon Gottfried, *Matthew Arnold and the Romantics* (1963); Patrick J. McCarthy, *Matthew Arnold and the Three Classes* (1964); Edward Alexander, *Matthew Arnold and John Stuart Mill* (1965); Warren D. Anderson, *Matthew Arnold and the Classical Tradition* (Ann Arbor, 1965); Harold Nicolson, "On Re-reading Matthew Arnold," *Essays by Divers Hands* (Royal Soc. of Lit.), n.s. XXIV (1948). 124-134; John Holloway, "Matthew Arnold and the Modern Dilemma," *EIC*, I (1951). 1-16; E. D. H. Johnson, *The Alien Vision of Victorian Poetry*, pp. 147-213; Kathleen Tillotson, "Matthew Arnold and Carlyle," *Proc. Brit. Acad.*, XLII (1956). 133-153; Neiman, "The Zeitgeist of Matthew Arnold," *PMLA*, LXXII (1957). 977-996; E. N. Greenwood, "Matthew Arnold: Thoughts on a Centenary," *Twentieth Century*, CLXII (1957). 469-479; W. S. Johnson, "Matthew Arnold's Dialogue," *Univ. of Kansas City Rev.*, XXVII (1960). 109-116; Albert J. Lubell, "Matthew Arnold: Between Two Worlds," *MLQ*, XXII (1961). 248-263; Walter J. Hipple, Jr., "Matthew Arnold, Dialectician," *UTQ*, xxxii (1962). 1-26; N. N. Feltes, "Matthew Arnold and the Modern Spirit: A Reassessment," *ibid.*, pp. 27-36; J. Hillis Miller, *The Disappearance of God*, ch. v; Willey, *Nineteenth Century Studies*, ch. x; Holloway, *The Victorian Sage*, ch. vii; LeRoy, *Perplexed Prophets*, ch. iii.—*Concordance to the Poems*, ed. Stephen M. Parrish (Ithaca, 1959).

1408 W. S. Johnson, "Matthew Arnold's Sea of Life," *PQ*, xxxi (1952). 195-207; Allan Brick, "Equilibrium in the Poetry of Matthew Arnold," *UTQ*, xxx (1960). 45-56; John M. Wallace, "Landscape and 'The General Law': The Poetry of Matthew Arnold," *Boston Univ. Stud. in English*, v (1961). 91-106; Alan H. Roper, "The Moral Landscape of Arnold's Poetry," *PMLA*, lxxvii (1962). 289-296; U. C. Knoepflmacher, "Dover Revisited: The Wordsworthian Matrix in the Poetry of Matthew Arnold," *VP*, i (1963). 17-26; Herbert R. Coursen, Jr., " 'The Moon Lies Fair': The Poetry of Matthew Arnold," *SEL*, iv (1964). 569-581.

On specific poems: Leon A. Gottfried, "Matthew Arnold's *The Strayed Reveller*," *RES*, n.s. xi (1960). 403-409; Howard W. Fulweiler, "Matthew Arnold: The Metamorphosis of a Merman," *VP*, i (1963). 208-222, on *The Forsaken Merman* and *The Neckan*; M. G. Sundell, "The Intellectual Background and Structure of Arnold's *Tristram and Iseult*," *VP*, i (1963). 272-283; Louis Bonnerot, introduction to his translation of *Empedocles on Etna* (Paris, 1947); Walter E. Houghton, "Arnold's *Empedocles on Etna*," *VS*, i (1958). 311-336; S. Nagarajan, "Arnold and the *Bhagavad Gita*: A Reinterpretation of *Empedocles on Etna*," *CL*, xii (1960). 335-347; Fred L. Burwick, "Hölderlin and Arnold: *Empedocles on Etna*," *CL*, xvii (1965). 24-42; Kathleen Tillotson, " 'Yes: in the Sea of Life,' " *RES*, n.s. iii (1952). 346-364; G. Wilson Knight, "*The Scholar Gypsy*: An Interpretation," *RES*, n.s. vi (1955). 53-62 (cf. reply by A. E. Dyson, "The Last Enchantments," *RES*, n.s. viii [1957]. 257-265); Murray Krieger, "*Dover Beach* and the Tragic Sense of Eternal Recurrence," *Univ. of Kansas City Rev.*, xxiii (1956). 73-79; Norman N. Holland, "Psychological Depths and *Dover Beach*," *VS*, ix (1965), supplement, pp. 5-28; Harvey Kerpneck, "The Road to *Rugby Chapel*," *UTQ*, xxxiv (1965). 178-196.

1409 Sidney M. B. Coulling, "Matthew Arnold's 1853 Preface: Its Origin and Aftermath," *VS*, vii (1964). 233-263; Warren, *English Poetic Theory*, ch. ix.

1412-1413 Frederic E. Faverty, *Matthew Arnold, the Ethnologist* (Evanston, Ill., 1951); John V. Kelleher, "Matthew Arnold and the Celtic Revival," *Perspectives of Criticism*, ed. Harry Levin (Cambridge, Mass., 1950), pp. 197-221.

John S. Eels, *The Touchstones of Matthew Arnold* (1955); F. J. W. Harding, *Matthew Arnold, The Critic and France* (Geneva, 1964); David Perkins, "Arnold and the Function of Literature," *ELH*, xviii (1951). 287-309; Wayne Shumaker, "Matthew Arnold's Humanism: Literature as a Criticism of Life," *SEL*, ii (1962). 387-402; Wellek, *History of Modern Criticism*, iv. 155-180.

Robert A. Donovan, "The Method of Arnold's *Essays in Criticism*," *PMLA*, lxxi (1956). 922-931; Sidney M. B. Coulling, "The Background of *The Function of Criticism at the Present Time*," *PQ*, xlii (1963). 36-54.

1413 Geoffrey Carnall, "Matthew Arnold's 'Great Critical Effort'," *EIC*, viii

(1958). 256-268; Sidney M. B. Coulling, "The Evolution of *Culture and Anarchy*," *SP*, LX (1963). 637-668.

1414 On *Literature and Dogma:* Dorothea Krook, *Three Traditions of Moral Thought* (Cambridge, 1959), pp. 202-225.

1416 FitzGerald: *Selected Works*, ed. Joanna Richardson (1962); *FitzGerald's Rubáiyát: Centennial Edition,* ed. Carl J. Weber (Waterville, Maine, 1959), and A. J. Arberry, *The Romance of the Rubáiyát* (1959), both with the text of the first edition; Arberry, *FitzGerald's Salámán and Absál* (Cambridge, 1956), the texts of 1856 and 1879; *Letters,* ed. J. M. Cohen (Carbondale, Ill., 1960), a selection. The definitive edition of FitzGerald's correspondence is being prepared by A. McKinley Terhune.—Bibliography in Faverty, pp. 92-103. Terhune, *Life of Edward FitzGerald* (New Haven, 1947); Arberry, *Omar Khayyám* (New Haven, 1952), translation of a manuscript from 1207.

1418 Thomson: *Poems and Some Letters,* ed. Anne Ridler (Carbondale, Ill., 1963).—Imogene B. Walker, *James Thomson (B. V.): A Critical Study* (Ithaca, 1950); William D. Schaefer, *James Thomson (B. V.)* (Berkeley, 1965); R. A. Forsyth, "Evolutionism and the Pessimism of James Thomson," *EIC*, XII (1962). 148-166; Jerome J. McGann, "James Thomson (B. V.): The Woven Hymns of Night and Day," *SEL*, III (1963). 493-507; Heath-Stubbs, *The Darkling Plain,* pp. 111-121; LeRoy, *Perplexed Prophets,* ch. v.

1419 George M. Harper, "Blake's *Nebuchadnezzar* in *The City of Dreadful Night*," *SP*, L (1953). 68-80.

XXIX. Rossetti and His Circle

1421 Rossetti: *Poems,* ed. Oswald Doughty (1957); *Jan Van Hunks,* ed. John Robert Wahl (1952), the only scholarly text; *Letters,* ed. Doughty and Wahl (4v, 1965-   ); *The Rossetti-Macmillan Letters* (written by Dante Gabriel, William Michael, and Christina), ed. Lona Mosk Packer (Berkeley, 1963).—The bibliographical treatment of Rossetti in Faverty, ch. VII, is unsystematic; but much Rossetti material is listed in Fredeman, *Pre-Raphaelitism,* cited below. Doughty, *Dante Gabriel Rossetti* (1949, new ed. 1960), the standard biography; Helen R. Angeli, *Dante Gabriel Rossetti: His Friends and Enemies* (1949); Jacques Savarit, *Tendences mystiques et ésotériques chez Dante Gabriel Rossetti* (Paris, 1961), a psychological treatment; Doughty, "Rossetti's Conception of the 'Poetic' in Poetry and Painting," *Essays by Divers Hands* (Royal Soc. of Lit.), n.s. XXVI (1953). 89-102; Clyde K. Hyder, "Rossetti's *Rose Mary:* A Study in the Occult," *VP*, I (1963). 197-207; Harold L. Weatherby, "Problems of Form and Content in the Poetry of Dante Gabriel Rossetti," *VP*, II (1964). 11-19; LeRoy, *Perplexed Prophets,* ch. VI; Hough, *The Last Romantics,* ch. II.

Note 4: On William Michael Rossetti, see Jerome Thale, "The Third Rossetti," *Western Humanities Rev.,* X (1956). 277-284.

1422 William E. Fredeman, *Pre-Raphaelitism: A Bibliocritical Study* (Cambridge, Mass., 1965), is comprehensive and valuable. *The Pre-Raphaelites in Literature and Art,* ed. D. S. R. Welland (1953); Rayner Unwin, "Keats and Pre-Raphaelitism," *English*, VIII (1951). 229-235; Humphry House, "Pre-Raphaelite Poetry," *All in Due Time* (1955), pp. 151-158.

1423 Note 13: John A. Cassidy, "Robert Buchanan and the Fleshly Controversy," *PMLA*, LXVII (1952). 65-93 (cf. reply by George G. Storey, "Robert Buchanan's Critical Principles," *PMLA*, LXVIII [1953]. 1228-1232).

1424 On Hall Caine: Samuel Norris, *Two Men of Manxland* (Douglas, I.o.M., 1947).—On *The House of Life*: W. E. Fredeman, "Rossetti's 'In Memoriam': An Elegiac Reading of *The House of Life*," *Bull. John Rylands Library*, XLVII (1965). 298-341; Bowra, *The Romantic Imagination*, ch. IX.

1426 Marya Zaturenska, *Christina Rossetti* (1949); Lona Mosk Packer, *Christina Rossetti* (Berkeley, 1963); Barbara Garlitz, "Christina Rossetti's *Sing-Song* and Nineteenth-Century Children's Poetry," *PMLA*, LXX (1955). 539-543; Packer, "Symbol and Reality in Christina Rossetti's *Goblin Market*," *PMLA*, LXXIII (1958). 375-385; Bowra, *The Romantic Imagination*, ch. XI.

1428 Note 32: Madison C. Bates, "'That Delightful Man': A Study of Frederick Locker," *Harvard Library Bull.*, XIII (1959). 92-113, 265-291, 444-470.

1429 James K. Robinson, "Austin Dobson and the Rondeliers," *MLQ*, XIV (1953). 31-42.—Anthony W. Preston, "Calverley of Cambridge," *Queen's Quar.*, LIV (1947). 47-60.

XXX. William Morris

1430 *Selected Writings and Designs*, ed. Asa Briggs (1963); *On Art and Socialism*, ed. Holbrook Jackson (1947); *Letters to His Family and Friends*, ed. Philip Henderson (1950).—Esther Meynell, *Portrait of William Morris* (1947); Lloyd Eric Grey, *William Morris, Prophet of England's New Order* (1949), identical with L. W. Eshelman, *A Victorian Rebel* (1940); Robert P. Arnot, *William Morris: the Man and the Myth* (1964); Hough, *The Last Romantics*, ch. III.

1430-1431 Laurence Perrine, "Morris' *Guenevere*: An Interpretation," *PQ*, XXXIX (1960). 234-241; Curtis Dahl, "Morris's *The Chapel in Lyoness*: An Interpretation," *SP*, LI (1954). 482-491.

1432 Oscar Maurer, "Morris's Treatment of Greek Legend in *The Earthly Paradise*," *Univ. of Texas Stud. in English*, XXXIII (1954). 103-118.

1434 Edward P. Thompson, *William Morris: Romantic to Revolutionary* (1955); Margaret Cole, "The Fellowship of William Morris," *Virginia Quar. Rev.*, XXIV (1948). 260-277.

1436 Charles H. Kegel, "William Morris's *A Dream of John Ball*: A Study in Reactionary Liberalism," *Papers of the Michigan Acad.*, XL (1954). 303-312.

XXXI. Algernon Charles Swinburne

1439 *Novels*, with introduction by Edmund Wilson (1962); selections, ed. H. Treece (1948), Humphrey Hare (1950), Edward Shanks (1950), Kenelm

Foss (1955), Edith Sitwell (1960), Bonamy Dobrée (1961); *Lesbia Brandon,* ed. Randolph Hughes (1952), first publication; *New Writings,* ed. Cecil Y. Lang (Syracuse, N.Y., 1964); *Letters,* ed. Lang (6v, New Haven, 1959-1962). —Bibliography in Faverty, ch. vi. Hare, *Swinburne: A Biographical Approach* (1949); John A. Cassidy, *Algernon C. Swinburne* (1964); Robert L. Peters, *The Crowns of Apollo: Swinburne's Principles of Literature and Art* (Detroit, 1965); Thomas E. Connolly, *Swinburne's Theory of Poetry* (Yellow Springs, Ohio, 1965); Wellek, *History of Modern Criticism,* iv. 371-381.

1440 The story of the origin of *The Triumph of Time* has been entirely discredited. See John S. Mayfield, *Swinburne's Boo* (privately printed, 1954), and Cecil Y. Lang, "Swinburne's Lost Love," *PMLA,* lxxiv (1959). 123-130.— On *Atalanta in Calydon,* see Bowra, *The Romantic Imagination,* ch. x.

XXXII. The Background: The Victorian Decline (1868-1901) and the Aftermath (1901-1939)

1448 The history of the period is traced in J. A. R. Marriott, *Modern England, 1885-1945* (1948); Herman Ausubel, *The Late Victorians: A Short History* (1955); Henry M. Pelling, *Modern Britain, 1885-1955* (Edinburgh, 1960); Thomas L. Jarman, *A Short History of Twentieth-Century England* (1963); and A. J. P. Taylor, *England, 1914-1945* (Oxford, 1965). See also *Edwardian England,* ed. Simon Nowell-Smith (1964) and Raymond Williams, *Culture and Society* (1958), Part ii ("Interregnum").—General studies of the literature of the era include William Y. Tindall, *Forces in Modern British Literature* (1947, rev. 1956), Vivian de Sola Pinto, *Crisis in English Poetry, 1880-1940* (1951), and H. N. Fairchild, *Religious Trends in English Poetry,* Vol. v: *Gods of a Changing Poetry, 1880-1920* (1962). The persistence and revival of "romantic" elements in the literature of the time are discussed, from differing points of view, in Graham Hough, *The Last Romantics* (1949), John Heath-Stubbs, *The Darkling Plain* (1950), Frank Kermode, *Romantic Image* (1957), and John Bayley, *The Romantic Survival* (1957). *Edwardians and Late Victorians (English Institute Essays 1959),* ed. Richard Ellmann (1960) contains seven essays on "the literature written shortly before or shortly after 1900."

S. Marandon, "Frederic Harrison (1831-1923)," *Études anglaises,* xiii (1960). 415-426; Martha S. Vogeler, "Matthew Arnold and Frederic Harrison: The Prophet of Culture and the Prophet of Positivism," *SEL,* ii (1962). 441-462.

Stephen: *Men, Books, and Mountains,* ed. S. O. A. Ullmann (Minneapolis, 1956), previously uncollected essays.—Noel Annan, *Leslie Stephen: His Thought and Character in Relation to His Time* (1951); Gertrude Himmelfarb, "Mr. Stephen and Mr. Ramsay: the Victorian as Intellectual," *Partisan Rev.,* xix (1952). 664-679; Oscar Maurer, "Leslie Stephen and the *Cornhill Magazine,* 1871-82," *Univ. of Texas Stud. in English,* xxxii (1953). 67-95; John W. Bicknell, "Leslie Stephen's *English Thought in the Eighteenth Century:* A Tract for the Times," *VS,* vi (1962). 103-120.

1449 I. F. Clarke, "*The Battle of Dorking*, 1871-1914," *VS*, VIII (1965). 309-328.

1451 On John Morley: Willey, *More Nineteenth Century Studies*, ch. VI.

XXXIII. George Meredith

1455 *Selected Poems*, ed. Graham Hough (1962).—Bibliography in Stevenson, ch. x, and Faverty, pp. 232-236. Siegfried Sassoon, *Meredith* (1948); Lionel Stevenson, *The Ordeal of George Meredith* (1953); Walter F. Wright, *Art and Substance in Meredith* (Lincoln, Neb., 1953); Jack Lindsay, *George Meredith: His Life and Work* (1956), a strongly Marxist interpretation; Norman Kelvin, *A Troubled Eden: Nature and Society in the Works of George Meredith* (Stanford, 1961); J. Gordon Eaker, "Meredith's Human Comedy," *NCF*, v (1951). 253-272; Joseph C. Landis, "George Meredith's Comedy," *Boston Univ. Stud. in English*, II (1956). 17-35; Deborah S. Austin, "Meredith on the Nature of Metaphor," *UTQ*, XXVII (1957). 96-102; Stevenson, "Meredith and the Problem of Style in the Novel," *Zeitschrift für Anglistik und Amerikanistik*, VI (1958). 181-189; Phyllis Bartlett, "The Novels of George Meredith," *REL*, III, no. 2 (1962). 31-46; Donald Fanger, "Meredith as Novelist," *NCF*, XVI (1962). 317-328; Jean Sudrann, " 'The Linked Eye and Mind': A Concept of Action in the Novels of Meredith," *SEL*, IV (1964). 617-635.

1456 *The Ordeal of Richard Feverel*, ed. Lionel Stevenson (1950), Norman Kelvin (1961), Charles J. Hill (1964).—William R. Mueller, "Theological Dualism and the 'System' in *Richard Feverel*," *ELH*, XVIII (1951). 138-154; Frank D. Curtin, "Adrian Harley: The Limits of Meredith's Comedy," *NCF*, VII (1953). 272-282; Phyllis Bartlett, "Richard Feverel, Knight-Errant," *Bull. N.Y. Public Library*, LXIII (1959). 329-340; Irving H. Buchen, "The Importance of the Minor Characters in *The Ordeal of Richard Feverel*," *Boston Univ. Stud. in English*, v (1961). 154-166; John W. Morris, "Inherent Principles of Order in *Richard Feverel*," *PMLA*, LXXVIII (1963). 333-340; Henri-A. Talon, "Le Comique, le tragique, et le romanesque dans *The Ordeal of Richard Feverel*," *Études anglaises*, XVII (1964). 241-261.

1457 Royal A. Gettmann, "Serialization and *Evan Harrington*," *PMLA*, LXIV (1949). 963-975.—*Modern Love*, ed. C. Day Lewis (1948). Lewis, "George Meredith and Responsibility," *Notable Images of Virtue* (Toronto, 1954), ch. II; Norman Friedman, "The Jangled Harp: Symbolic Structure in *Modern Love*," *MLQ*, XVII (1957). 9-26; Elizabeth Cox Wright, "The Significance of the Image Patterns in Meredith's *Modern Love*," *Victorian Newsletter*, No. 13 (1958). 1-9.—On *Rhoda Fleming*: Charles J. Hill, "Meredith's 'Plain Story,' " *NCF*, VII (1952). 90-102; Lionel Stevenson, "Meredith's Atypical Novel," *The Image of the Work* (Berkeley, 1955), pp. 89-109.

Note 3: Royal A. Gettmann, "Meredith as Publisher's Reader," *JEGP*, XLVIII (1949). 45-56.

1458 Barbara Hardy, " 'A Way to Your Hearts through Fire or Water': The Structure of Imagery in *Harry Richmond*," *EIC*, x (1960). 163-180; L. T Hergenhan, "Meredith's Revisions of *Harry Richmond*," *RES*, n.s. XIV (1963)

24-32.—*Beauchamp's Career*, ed. G. M. Young (1950). Charles J. Hill, "The Portrait of the Author in *Beauchamp's Career*," *JEGP*, LII (1953). 332-339.

1459 *The Egoist*, ed. Lord Dunsany (1947), Lionel Stevenson (Boston, 1958). Richard B. Hudson, "The Meaning of Egoism in George Meredith's *The Egoist*," *Trollopian*, III (1948). 163-176; C. J. Hill, "Theme and Image in *The Egoist*," *Univ. of Kansas City Rev.*, XX (1954). 281-285; Irving H. Buchen, "The Egoists in *The Egoist:* The Sensualists and the Ascetics," *NCF*, XIX (1964). 255-269; Van Ghent, pp. 183-194.—Gillian Beer, "Meredith's Revisions of *The Tragic Comedians*," *RES*, n.s. XIV (1963). 33-53, and "Meredith's Idea of Comedy: 1876-1880," *NCF*, XX (1965). 165-176.

1460 On Mrs. Norton, see Alice Acland, *Caroline Norton* (1948).—Joseph E. Kruppa, "Meredith's Late Novels: Suggestions for a Critical Approach," *NCF*, XIX (1964). 271-286.—Fabian Gudas, "George Meredith's *One of Our Conquerors*," *From Jane Austen to Joseph Conrad*, pp. 222-233; Fred C. Thomson, "The Design of *One of Our Conquerors*," *SEL*, II (1962). 463-480.— Bernard A. Brunner, "Meredith's Symbolism: *Lord Ormont and His Aminta*," *NCF*, VIII (1953). 124-133.

XXXIV. Thomas Hardy

1464 *Selected Poems*, ed. John Crowe Ransom (1961); *Our Exploits at West Poley*, ed. Richard L. Purdy (1952), first published in *The Household*, 1892-1893; *Love Poems*, ed. Carl J. Weber (1964); *Letters*, ed. Weber (Waterville, Maine, 1954), limited to the letters at Colby College; *"Dearest Emmie"*: *Hardy's Letters to His First Wife*, ed. Weber (1963); *Notebooks*, ed. Evelyn Hardy (1955).—Purdy, *Thomas Hardy: A Bibliographical Study* (1954); bibliographies of Hardy criticism in Stevenson, ch. XI, Faverty, pp. 238-241, and Maurice Beebe *et al.*, "Criticism of Thomas Hardy: A Selected Checklist," *Mod. Fiction Stud.*, VI (1960). 258-279. Weber's *Hardy of Wessex* had been revised, 1965. Evelyn Hardy, *Thomas Hardy: A Critical Biography* (1954); Emma Lavinia Hardy, *Some Recollections*, ed. Evelyn Hardy and Robert Gittings (1961); James G. Southworth, *The Poetry of Thomas Hardy* (1947); Harvey C. Webster, *On a Darkling Plain* (Chicago, 1947); Albert Guerard, *Thomas Hardy: the Novels and Stories* (Cambridge, Mass., 1949); Desmond Hawkins, *Thomas Hardy* (1951); Douglas Brown, *Thomas Hardy* (1954, rev. 1961); Thomas Hardy number of *Mod. Fiction Stud.*, VI (Autumn, 1960); Samuel Hynes, *The Pattern of Hardy's Poetry* (Chapel Hill, 1961); George Douglas Wing, *Thomas Hardy* (1963); three articles by James O. Bailey, "Hardy's 'Mephistophelian Visitants,'" *PMLA*, LXI (1946). 1146-1184, "Hardy's Visions of the Self," *SP*, LVI (1959). 74-101, and "Evolutionary Meliorism in the Poetry of Thomas Hardy," *SP*, LX (1963). 569-587; J. I. M. Stewart, "The Integrity of Hardy," *English Stud.* (*E&S*, n.s.), I (1948). 1-27; C. Day Lewis, "The Lyrical Poetry of Thomas Hardy," *Proc. Brit. Acad.*, XXXVII (1951). 155-174; Carol R. Andersen, "Time, Space and Perspective in Thomas Hardy," *NCF*, IX (1954). 192-208; C. M. Bowra, "The Lyrical Poetry of Thomas Hardy," *Inspiration and Poetry* (1955), pp. 220-241; Eugene Goodheart, "Thomas Hardy and the Lyrical Novel," *NCF*, XII (1957). 215-225; John Holloway, "Hardy's Major

Fiction," *From Jane Austen to Joseph Conrad*, pp. 234-245; William J. Hyde, "Hardy's View of Realism: A Key to the Rustic Characters," *VS*, ii (1958). 45-59; David Perkins, "Hardy and the Poetry of Isolation," *ELH*, xxvi (1959). 253-270; Roy Morrell, "Hardy in the Tropics: Some Implications of Hardy's Attitude towards Nature," *REL*, iii, no. 1 (1962). 7-30; James F. Scott, "Thomas Hardy's Use of the Gothic: An Examination of Five Representative Works," *NCF*, xvii (1962). 363-380; Richard Beckman, "A Character Typology for Hardy's Novels," *ELH*, xxx (1963). 70-87; Guerard, "The Illusion of Simplicity: The Shorter Poems of Thomas Hardy," *Sewanee Rev.*, lxxii (1964). 363-388; Holloway, *The Victorian Sage*, ch. viii; Stewart, *Eight Modern Writers* (Oxford, 1963), ch. ii; *Hardy: A Collection of Critical Essays*, ed. Guerard (1963).

1466 Lawrence O. Jones, "*Desperate Remedies* and the Victorian Sensation Novel," *NCF*, xx (1965). 35-50.—John F. Danby, "*Under the Greenwood Tree*," *Critical Quar.*, 1 (1959). 5-13; Harold E. Toliver, "The Dance under the Greenwood Tree: Hardy's Bucolics," *NCF*, xvii (1962). 57-68.—*Far from the Madding Crowd*, ed. Carl J. Weber (1959), Richard L. Purdy (Boston, 1957). Richard C. Carpenter, "The Mirror and the Sword: Imagery in *Far from the Madding Crowd*," *NCF*, xviii (1964). 331-345; Howard Babb, "Setting and Theme in *Far from the Madding Crowd*," *ELH*, xxx (1963). 147-161.—Clarice Short, "In Defense of *Ethelberta*," *NCF*, xiii (1958). 48-57.—*The Return of the Native*, ed. Albert Guerard (1950). John Paterson, *The Making of "The Return of the Native"* (Berkeley, 1960); Robert W. Stallman, "Hardy's Hour-Glass Novel," *Sewanee Rev.*, lv (1947). 283-296; M. A. Goldberg, "Hardy's Double-Visioned Universe," *EIC*, vii (1957). 374-382; S. F. Johnson, "Hardy and Burke's 'Sublime,' " *Style in Prose Fiction (English Institute Essays 1958)*, ed. H. C. Martin (1959), pp. 55-86; Paterson, "*The Return of the Native* as Antichristian Document," *NCF*, xiv (1959). 111-127; Otis B. Wheeler, "Four Versions of *The Return of the Native*," *NCF*, xiv (1959). 27-44; Leonard W. Deen, "Heroism and Pathos in Hardy's *Return of the Native*," *NCF*, xv (1960). 207-219; Louis Crompton, "The Sunburnt God: Ritual and Tragic Myth in *The Return of the Native*," *Boston Univ. Stud. in English*, iv (1960). 229-240; Charles C. Walcutt, "Character and Coincidence in *The Return of the Native*," *Twelve Original Essays on Great English Novels*, ed. C. Shapiro (Detroit, 1960), pp. 153-173; John Hagan, "A Note on the Significance of Diggory Venn," *NCF*, xvi (1961). 147-155; Robert C. Schweik, "Theme, Character, and Perspective in Hardy's *The Return of the Native*," *PQ*, xli (1962). 757-767.—George H. Thomson, "The *Trumpet-Major* Chronicle," *NCF*, xvii (1962). 45-56.

1467 *The Mayor of Casterbridge*, ed. Harvey C. Webster (1948), S. C. Chew (1950), Albert Guerard (1956), Robert B. Heilman (1962). Douglas Brown, *Thomas Hardy: "The Mayor of Casterbridge"* (1961); Howard O. Brogan, "'Visible Essences' in *The Mayor of Casterbridge*," *ELH*, xvii (1950). 307-323; D. A. Dike, "A Modern Oedipus: *The Mayor of Casterbridge*," *EIC*, ii (1952). 169-179; John Paterson, "*The Mayor of Casterbridge* as Tragedy," *VS*, iii (1959). 151-172; Heilman, "Hardy's *Mayor* and the Problem of Intention," *Criticism*, v (1963). 199-213, and "Hardy's *Mayor*: Notes on Style," *NCF*, xviii (1964). 307-329.—William H. Matchett, "*The Woodlanders*, or Realism in Sheep's Clothing," *NCF*, ix (1955). 241-261; George S. Fayen, Jr., "*The Woodlanders*: Inwardness and Memory," *SEL*, i, no. 4 (1961). 81-100.—*Tess of the d'Urber-*

villes, ed. Carl J. Weber (1951), William E. Buckler (Boston, 1960), Scott Elledge (1965). Allan Brick, "Paradise and Consciousness in Hardy's *Tess,*" *NCF,* xvii (1962). 115-134; Ian Gregor, "The Novel as Moral Protest: *Tess of the d'Urbervilles,*" *The Moral and the Story* (1962), pp. 135-150; Philip M. Griffith, "The Image of the Trapped Animal in Hardy's *Tess of the d'Urbervilles,*" *Tulane Stud. in English,* xiii (1963). 85-94; Elliott B. Gose, Jr., "Psychic Evolution: Darwinism and Initiation in *Tess of the d'Urbervilles,*" *NCF,* xviii (1963). 261-272; Van Ghent, pp. 195-209.

1468 *Jude the Obscure,* ed. William E. Buckler (1959), Irving Howe (Boston, 1965). Emma Clifford, "The Child: the Circus: and *Jude the Obscure,*" *Cambridge Jour.,* vii (1954). 531-546; Norman Holland, Jr., "*Jude the Obscure:* Hardy's Symbolic Indictment of Christianity," *NCF,* ix (1954). 50-60; Ted R. Spivey, "Thomas Hardy's Tragic Hero," *NCF,* ix (1954). 179-191; John Paterson, "The Genesis of *Jude the Obscure,*" *SP,* lvii (1960). 87-98; Arthur Mizener, "The Novel of Doctrine in the Nineteenth Century: Hardy's *Jude the Obscure,*" *The Sense of Life in the Modern Novel* (Boston, 1964), pp. 55-77; Lewis B. Horne, "Fawley's Quests: A Reading of *Jude the Obscure,*" *Tennessee Stud. in Lit.,* ix (1964). 117-127; William J. Hyde, "Theoretic and Practical Unconventionality in *Jude the Obscure,*" *NCF,* xx (1965). 155-164.

1469 Note 13: Barnes: *Poems,* ed. Bernard Jones (2v, 1962), the first collected edition; *Poems Grave and Gay,* ed. Giles Dugdale (Dorchester, 1949); *Selected Poems,* ed. Geoffrey Grigson (1950).—Willis D. Jacobs, *William Barnes, Linguist* (Albuquerque, 1952); Dugdale, *William Barnes of Dorset* (1953); William Turner Levy, *William Barnes: The Man and the Poems* (1960); Rayner Unwin, *The Rural Muse* (1954), pp. 150-164; R. A. Forsyth, "The Conserving Myth of William Barnes," *VS,* vi (1963). 325-354.—On T. E. Brown, see Samuel Norris, *Two Men of Manxland* (Douglas, I. o. M., 1947).— Note 14: See G. W. Sherman, "Thomas Hardy and the Agricultural Laborer," *NCF,* vii (1952). 111-118.

1471-1472 Note 23: Waldo H. Dunn, *Richard D. Blackmore, the Author of "Lorna Doone"* (1956); Kenneth Budd, *The Last Victorian* (1960).—W. E. Purcell, *Onward Christian Soldier: A Life of Sabine Baring-Gould* (1957); William J. Hyde, "The Stature of Baring-Gould as a Novelist," *NCF,* xv (1960). 1-16.—Jefferies: *The Story of My Heart,* ed. Samuel J. Looker (1947); *The Gamekeeper at Home,* ed. C. Henry Warren (1948); *The Essential Richard Jefferies,* ed. Malcolm Elwin (1948); *The Jefferies Companion* and *The Nature Diaries and Notebooks,* both ed. Looker (1948). A number of additional volumes of Jefferies' writings have been edited by Looker and others.—Reginald Arkell, *Richard Jefferies and His Countryside* (1947); W. J. Keith, *Richard Jefferies: A Critical Study* (1965); Samuel J. Looker and Crichton Porteous, *Richard Jefferies, Man of the Fields* (1965); J. W. Blench, "The Novels of Richard Jefferies," *Cambridge Jour.,* vii (1954). 361-377; William J. Hyde, "Richard Jefferies and the Naturalistic Peasant," *NCF,* xi (1956). 207-217.—*Eden Phillpotts: An Assessment and a Tribute,* ed. Waverly Girvan (1953).

1473 James O. Bailey, *Hardy and the Cosmic Mind: A New Reading of "The Dynasts"* (Chapel Hill, 1956); Harold Orel, *Thomas Hardy's Epic-Drama* (Lawrence, Kan., 1963); Emma Clifford, "The *'Trumpet-Major* Notebook' and

The Dynasts," RES, n.s. VIII (1957). 149-161, and "The Impressionistic View of History in *The Dynasts," MLQ*, XXII (1961). 21-31; Roy Morrell, *"The Dynasts* Reconsidered," *MLR*, LVIII (1963). 161-171.

XXXV. Aestheticism and "Decadence"

1475 *The Religion of Beauty: Selections from the Aesthetes,* ed. Richard Aldington (1950). Ruth Z. Temple, *The Critic's Alchemy: A Study of the Introduction of French Symbolism into England* (1953); Barbara Charlesworth, *Dark Passages: The Decadent Consciousness in Victorian Literature* (Madison, Wis., 1965); James K. Robinson, "A Neglected Phase of the Aesthetic Movement: English Parnassianism," *PMLA*, LXVIII (1953). 733-754; John Wilcox, "The Beginning of *l'art pour l'art," JAAC*, XI (1953). 360-377; Clyde de L. Ryals, "Toward a Definition of *Decadent* as Applied to British Literature of the Nineteenth Century," *JAAC*, XVII (1958). 85-92 (cf. Robert L. Peters, *JAAC*, XVIII [1959]. 258-264, and Russell M. Goldfarb, *ibid.*, XX [1962]. 369-373); Temple, "The Ivory Tower as Lighthouse," *Edwardians and Late Victorians* (1960), pp. 28-49; Buckley, *The Victorian Temper*, chs. IX, XI-XII; Hough, *The Last Romantics*, ch. V.

Pater: *Selected Works,* ed. Richard Aldington (1948); *Selected Writings,* ed. Derek Patmore (1949); *The Renaissance,* ed. Kenneth Clark (1961); *Imaginary Portraits: A New Collection,* ed. Eugene Brzenk (1964).—Germain d'Hangest, *Walter Pater: l'Homme et l'oeuvre* (2v, Paris, 1961); Edmund Chandler, *Pater on Style* (Copenhagen, 1958); Wolfgang Iser, *Walter Pater: die Autonomie des ästhetischen* (Tübingen, 1960); R. V. Johnson, *Walter Pater: A Study of His Critical Outlook and Achievement* (Cambridge, 1961); Bernard F. Huppé, "Walter Pater on Plato's Aesthetics," *MLQ*, IX (1948). 315-321; C. M. Bowra, "Walter Pater," *Sewanee Rev.*, LVII (1949). 378-400; Geoffrey Tillotson, "Arnold and Pater: Critics Historical, Aesthetic and Otherwise," *E&S*, n.s. III (1950). 47-68; Milton Millhauser, "Walter Pater and the Flux," *JAAC*, XI (1953). 214-223; Derek Stanford, "Pater's Ideal Aesthetic Type," *Cambridge Jour.*, VII (1954). 488-494; Lord David Cecil, *Walter Pater: the Scholar-Artist* (Cambridge, 1955); Angelo P. Bertocci, "French Criticism and the Pater Problem," *Boston Univ. Stud. in English*, I (1955). 178-194; Paul West, "Pater and the Tribulations of Taste," *UTQ*, XXVII (1958). 424-432; R. T. Lenaghan, "Pattern in Walter Pater's Fiction," *SP*, LVIII (1961). 69-91; Wendell V. Harris, "Pater as Prophet," *Criticism*, VI (1964). 349-360; U. C. Knoepflmacher, *Religion and Humanism in the Victorian Novel*, chs. V-VI; Hough, *The Last Romantics*, ch. IV; Wellek, *History of Modern Criticism*, IV. 381-399.

1476 R. V. Osbourn, *"Marius the Epicurean," EIC*, I (1951). 387-403; Jean Sudrann, "Victorian Compromise and Modern Revolution," *ELH*, XXVI (1959). 425-444; Bernard Duffey, "The Religion of Pater's *Marius," Texas Stud. in Lit. and Lang.*, II (1960). 103-114; Billie A. Inman, "The Organic Structure of *Marius the Epicurean," PQ*, XLI (1962). 475-491; Louise M. Rosenblatt, "The Genesis of Pater's *Marius the Epicurean," CL*, XIV (1962). 242-260; Martha S. Vogeler, "The Religious Meaning of *Marius the Epicurean," NCF*, XIX (1964). 287-299.

Note 8: *The New Republic,* ed. J. Max Patrick (Gainesville, Fla., 1950).—Charles C. Nickerson, "The Novels of W. H. Mallock: Notes toward a Bibliography" and "A Bibliography of the Novels of W. H. Mallock," *English Lit. in Transition*, vi, no. 4 (1963). 182-198. Carl R. Woodring, "William H. Mallock: A Neglected Wit," *More Books*, xxii (1947). 243-256; P. M. Yarker, "Voltaire among the Positivists: A Study of W. H. Mallock's *The New Paul and Virginia*," *E&S*, n.s. viii (1955). 21-39, and "W. H. Mallock's Other Novels," *NCF*, xiv (1959). 189-205; Patrick, "The Portrait of Huxley in Mallock's *New Republic*," *NCF*, xi (1956). 61-69; Albert V. Turner, "W. H. Mallock and Late Victorian Conservatism," *UTQ*, xxxi (1962). 223-241.

1477 Note 12: Phyllis Grosskurth, *John Addington Symonds* (1964); Robert L. Peters, "Athens and Troy: Notes on John Addington Symonds' Aestheticism," *English Fiction in Transition*, v, no. 5 (1962). 14-26; Grosskurth, "The Genesis of Symonds's Elizabethan Criticism," *MLR*, lix (1964). 183-193.—Paget: *The Snake Lady and Other Stories*, ed. Horace Gregory (1954). Peter Gunn, *Vernon Lee: Violet Paget, 1856-1935* (1964).

1479-1480 Wilde: *Works*, ed. G. F. Maine (1948); *Essays*, ed. Hesketh Pearson (1950); *The Portable Oscar Wilde*, ed. Richard Aldington (1946); *Plays; Prose Writings, and Poems*, ed. Pearson (1955); *Selected Writings*, ed. Richard Ellmann (1961); *Letters*, ed. Rupert Hart-Davis (1962).—Edouard Roditi, *Oscar Wilde* (Norfolk, Conn., 1947); Robert Merle, *Oscar Wilde* (Paris, 1948); *The Trials of Oscar Wilde*, ed. H. Montgomery Hyde (1948); George Woodcock, *The Paradox of Oscar Wilde* (1949); St. John Ervine, *Oscar Wilde* (1951); Vyvyan Holland, *Son of Oscar Wilde* (1954); Aatos Ojala, *Aestheticism and Oscar Wilde* (2v, Helsinki, 1954-55); Hyde, *Oscar Wilde: The Aftermath* (1963); "Oscar Wilde After Fifty Years," *LTLS*, Nov. 24, 1950, pp. 737-739; Alan Harris, "Oscar Wilde as Playwright: A Centenary Review," *Adelphi*, xxx (1954). 212-240; Arthur Ganz, "The Divided Self in the Society Comedies of Oscar Wilde," *Modern Drama*, iii (1960). 16-23; Ted R. Spivey, "Damnation and Salvation in *The Picture of Dorian Gray*," *Boston Univ. Stud. in English*, iv (1960). 162-170; Ellmann, "Romantic Pantomime in Oscar Wilde," *Partisan Rev.*, xxx (1963). 342-355; LeRoy, *Perplexed Prophets*, ch. vii.

1481 *The Importance of Being Earnest*, ed. Sarah A. Dickson (2v, 1956), the texts of the original manuscript and the corrected typescript.— Note 25: William Freeman, *The Life of Lord Alfred Douglas: Spoilt Child of Genius* (1948); Marie C. Stopes, *Lord Alfred Douglas: His Poetry and Personality* (1949); Rupert Croft-Cooke, *Bosie: The Story of Lord Alfred Douglas, His Friends and Enemies* (1963).—Note 27: The first full edition of the text of *De Profundis* was published in 1950, ed. Vyvyan Holland.

1482 *The Yellow Book: A Selection*, ed. Norman Denny (1949); Katherine L. Mix, *A Study in Yellow: the Yellow Book and Its Contributors* (Lawrence, Kan., 1960).—*The Savoy: Nineties Experiment*, ed. Stanley Weintraub (University Park, Pa., 1966), an anthology. Wendell Harris, "Innocent Decadence: the Poetry of the *Savoy*," *PMLA*, lxxvii (1962). 629-636.—*The Best of Beardsley* (1948) and *A Beardsley Miscellany* (1949), both ed. R. A. Walker. Robin Ironside, "Aubrey Beardsley," *Horizon*, xiv (1946). 190-202; "Pierrot of the Minute," *LTLS*, March 19, 1949, p. 184.—Note 29: Cecil Woolf has edited Baron Corvo's *The Cardinal Prefect of Propaganda and Other Stories* (1957), *Nicholas Crabbe* (1958), *Don Renato* (1963), *Letters* (1959-   , various titles); as well as *A*

Bibliography of Frederick Rolfe, Baron Corvo (1957) and, with Brocard Sewell, *Corvo, 1860-1960* (Aylesford, 1961), a collection of eleven essays.

1483 Beerbohm: *Mainly on the Air* (1946; enlarged ed. 1957); *Max in Verse: Rhymes and Parodies*, ed. J. G. Riewald (Brattleboro, Vt., 1963); *The Incomparable Max*, ed. S. C. Roberts (1962), an anthology; *Letters to Reggie Turner*, ed. Rupert Hart-Davis (1964).—A. E. Gallatin and L. M. Oliver, *A Bibliography of the Works of Sir Max Beerbohm* (Cambridge, Mass., 1952). Riewald, *Sir Max Beerbohm* (The Hague, 1953); S. N. Behrman, *Portrait of Max* (1960; English title, *Conversation with Max*); Lord David Cecil, *Max: A Biography* (1964); Derek Stanford, "The Writings of Sir Max Beerbohm," *The Month*, XIII (1955). 325-365; Ellen Moers, *The Dandy* (1960), ch. XIV.

Roger Lhombreaud, *Arthur Symons: A Critical Biography* (1963); Arnold B. Sklare, "Arthur Symons: An Appreciation of the Critic of Literature," *JAAC*, IX (1951). 316-322; Ian Fletcher, "Symons, Yeats and the Demonic Dance," *London Mag.*, VII, no. 6 (1960). 46-60; John M. Munro, "Arthur Symons as Poet: Theory and Practice," *English Lit. in Transition*, VI (1963). 212-222; Edward Baugh, "Arthur Symons, Poet: A Centenary Tribute," *REL*, VI, no. 3 (1965). 70-80.

Richard Whittington-Egan and Geoffrey Smerdon, *The Quest of the Golden Boy: The Life and Letters of Richard LeGallienne* (1960).

Dowson: *Stories* (Philadelphia, 1947) and *Poems* (Philadelphia, 1963), both ed. Mark Longaker. Thomas B. Swann, *Ernest Dowson* (1964).

XXXVI. The Novel: Naturalism and Romance

1485 On the fiction of this period and later see, in addition to some of the books cited above (suppl. to p. 1344), Madeleine M. Cazamian, *Le Roman et les idées en Angleterre, 1860-1914*, Vol. III: *Les Doctrines d'action et d'aventure, 1880-1914* (Paris, 1955). Earlier volumes of this work were published at Strasbourg in 1923 and 1935.

Butler: *Notebooks*, ed. Geoffrey Keynes and Brian Hill (1951), selections; *The Essential Samuel Butler*, ed. G. D. H. Cole (1950); *Correspondence of Samuel Butler with his Sister Mary*, ed. Daniel F. Howard (Berkeley, 1962); *The Family Letters of Samuel Butler*, ed. Arnold Silver (Stanford, 1962).—Stanley B. Harkness, *The Career of Samuel Butler (1835-1902): A Bibliography* (1955). P. N. Furbank, *Samuel Butler* (Cambridge, 1948); Philip Henderson, *Samuel Butler, the Incarnate Bachelor* (1953); Lee Holt, *Samuel Butler* (1964); Basil Willey, *Darwin and Butler: Two Versions of Evolution* (1960); Angus Wilson, "The Revolt of Samuel Butler," *Atl. Mo.*, CC (Nov., 1957). 190-198; Robert E. Shoenberg, "The Literal-Mindedness of Samuel Butler," *SEL*, IV (1964). 601-616; U. C. Knoepflmacher, *Religious Humanism and the Victorian Novel* (Princeton, 1965), chs. VII-VIII.

1486 Joseph J. Jones, *The Cradle of "Erewhon": Samuel Butler in New Zealand* (Austin, Tex., 1959).

1487 *The Way of All Flesh*, ed. William Y. Tindall (1950), Royal A. Gettmann (1948), Morton D. Zabel (1950), A. J. Hoppé (1954), Daniel F. Howard (Boston, 1964), the last-named printing Butler's original, uncut text. G. D. H. Cole, *Samuel Butler and "The Way of All Flesh"* (1947); Kettle, II. 35-48.

1488 Wilfred H. Stone, *Religion and the Art of William Hale White* (Stanford, 1954); Catherine M. Maclean, *Mark Rutherford: A Biography of William Hale White* (1955); Irvin Stock, *William Hale White* (1956); E. S. Merton, "The Autobiographical Novels of Mark Rutherford," *NCF*, v (1950). 189-207 and "The Personality of Mark Rutherford," *NCF*, vi (1951). 1-20; Patricia Thomson, "The Novels of Mark Rutherford," *EIC*, xiv (1964). 256-267; Willey, *More Nineteenth Century Studies*, ch. v.

1489 Vera Buchanan-Gould, *Not Without Honour: the Life and Writings of Olive Schreiner* (1949); D. L. Hobman, *Olive Schreiner: Her Friends and Times* (1955); Lyndall Gregg, *Memories of Olive Schreiner* (1957).

On Mrs. Humphry Ward: Basil Willey, "How *Robert Elsmere* Struck Some Contemporaries," *E&S*, n.s. x (1957). 53-68; Clara Lederer, "Mary Arnold Ward and the Victorian Ideal," *NCF*, vi (1951). 201-208.

On Shorthouse: Morchard Bishop, *"John Inglesant* and Its Author," *Essays by Divers Hands* (Royal Soc. of Lit.), n.s. xxix (1958). 73-86.

1490 Gissing: *Commonplace Book*, ed. Jacob Korg (1962); *Letters to Eduard Bertz, 1887-1903*, ed. Arthur C. Young (New Brunswick, N.J., 1961); *George Gissing and H. G. Wells: Their Friendship and Correspondence*, ed. Royal A. Gettmann (Urbana, Ill., 1961); *Letters to Gabrielle Fleury*, ed. Pierre Coustillas (1964).—Bibliography in Stevenson, pp. 401-413, and Joseph J. Wolff, "George Gissing: An Annotated Bibliography of Writings about Him," *English Fiction in Transition*, iii, no. 2 (1960). 3-33. Morley Roberts, *The Private Life of Henry Maitland* was reissued in 1958 with extensive annotations by Morchard Bishop. Mabel C. Donnelly, *George Gissing: Grave Comedian* (Cambridge, Mass., 1954); Korg, *George Gissing* (Seattle, 1963); "The Permanent Stranger," *LTLS*, Feb. 14, 1948, p. 92; Russell Kirk, "Who Knows George Gissing?", *Western Humanities Rev.*, iv (1950). 213-222; Korg, "George Gissing's Outcast Intellectuals," *Amer. Scholar*, xix (1950). 194-202, and "Division of Purpose in George Gissing," *PMLA*, lxx (1955). 323-336; Jackson I. Cope, "Definition as Structure in Gissing's *Ryecroft Papers*," *Modern Fiction Studies*, iii (1957). 127-140; John Middleton Murry, "George Gissing," *Katherine Mansfield and Other Literary Studies* (1959), pp. 3-68; C. J. Francis, "Gissing and Schopenhauer," *NCF*, xv (1960). 53-63.

1492 Jacob Korg, "The Spiritual Theme of George Gissing's *Born in Exile*," *From Jane Austen to Joseph Conrad*, pp. 246-256.—*New Grub Street*, ed. Irving Howe (Boston, 1962).

1493 Fred W. Boege, "Sir Walter Besant: Novelist," *NCF*, x (1956). 249-280, xi (1956). 32-60; Ernest Boll, "Walter Besant on the Art of the Novel," *English Fiction in Transition*, ii, no. 1 (1959). 28-35.

1493-1494 *Letters to Lady Cunard, 1895-1933*, ed. Rupert Hart-Davis (1957). —Bibliography in Stevenson, pp. 389-401, and Helmut E. Gerber, "George Moore: An Annotated Bibliography of Writings about Him," *English Fiction in Transition*, ii, no. 2 (1959). 1-91; iii, no. 2 (1960). 34-46; iv, no. 2 (1961). 30-42. Nancy Cunard, *GM: Memories of George Moore* (1956); Sonja Nejdefors-Frisk, *George Moore's Naturalistic Prose* (Uppsala, 1952); Malcolm Brown, *George Moore: A Reconsideration* (Seattle, 1955); Georges-Paul Collet, *George Moore et la France* (Geneva, 1957); Max Beerbohm, "George Moore," *Atl. Mo.*, clxxxvi

(Dec., 1950). 34-39; J[oseph] H[one], "George Moore: The Making of a Writer," *LTLS*, Feb. 29, 1952, pp. 149-150; Wayne Shumaker, "The Autobiographer as Artist: George Moore's *Hail and Farewell," The Image of the Work* (Berkeley, 1955), pp. 159-185; Graham Hough, "George Moore and the Nineties," *Edwardians and Late Victorians* (1960), pp. 1-27, and "George Moore and the Novel," *REL*, I, no. 1 (1960). 35-44.

1495 *Esther Waters,* ed. Malcolm Brown (1958), Lionel Stevenson (Boston, 1963).

1498 Stevenson: *Collected Poems,* ed. Janet Adam Smith (1950), authoritative texts; *Novels and Stories,* ed. V. S. Pritchett (1945); *Selected Writings,* ed. Saxe Commins (1947); *The Stevenson Companion,* ed. John Hampden (1950); *Essays,* ed. Malcolm Elwin (1950); *Tales and Essays,* ed. G. B. Stern (1950); *Selected Essays,* ed. George Scott-Moncrieff (1959); *The Mind of Robert Louis Stevenson: Selected Essays, Letters and Prayers,* ed. Roger Ricklefs (1963); *Edinburgh: Picturesque Notes,* ed. Smith (1954); *Henry James and Robert Louis Stevenson: A Record of Friendship and Criticism,* ed. Smith (1948); *RLS: Stevenson's Letters to Charles Baxter,* ed. DeLancey Ferguson and Marshall Waingrow (New Haven, 1956). A comprehensive edition of Stevenson's letters is being prepared by Bradford A. Booth.—George L. McKay, *A Stevenson Library . . . Formed by Edwin J. Beinecke* (6v, New Haven, 1951-1964). J. C. Furnas, *Voyage to Windward* (1951), the best biography; Lettice Cooper, *Robert Louis Stevenson* (1947); Malcolm Elwin, *The Strange Case of Robert Louis Stevenson* (1950); Laura L. Hinkley, *The Stevensons: Louis and Fanny* (1950); Richard Aldington, *Portrait of a Rebel* (1957). Additional biographical material is in Anne B. Fisher, *No More a Stranger* (Stanford, 1946); A. R. Issler, *Happier for His Presence* (Stanford, 1949) and *Our Mountain Heritage* (Stanford, 1950); Joseph W. Ellison, *Tusitala of the South Seas* (1953); *Our Samoan Adventure,* ed. Charles Neider (1955), Mrs. Stevenson's diary; and Elsie N. Caldwell, *Last Witness for Robert Louis Stevenson* (Norman, Okla., 1960). David Daiches, *Robert Louis Stevenson* (Norfolk, Conn., 1947); Robert Kiely, *Robert Louis Stevenson and the Fiction of Adventure* (Cambridge, Mass., 1964); H. W. Garrod, "The Poetry of R. L. Stevenson," *Essays, Mainly on the Nineteenth Century, Presented to Sir Humphrey Milford* (1948), pp. 42-57.

1501 George Blake, *Barrie and the Kailyard School* (1951).
J. E. Scott, *A Bibliography of the Works of Sir Henry Rider Haggard* (1947). Lilias Rider Haggard, *The Cloak That I Left* (1951); Morton Cohen, *Rider Haggard: His Life and Works* (1960).
"Q" Anthology, ed. F. Brittain (1948). Brittain, *Arthur Quiller-Couch: A Biographical Study* (Cambridge, 1947).
John Dickson Carr, *The Life of Sir Arthur Conan Doyle* (1949); Pierre Nardon, *Sir Arthur Conan Doyle* (Paris, 1965); Hugh Kenner, "Baker Street to Eccles Street: the Odyssey of a Myth," *Hudson Rev.,* I (1949). 481-499, on the Holmes "myth" and its analogues in Joyce. See also the files of the *Baker Street Journal* (1946-   ) and the numerous books and brochures issued by Holmesian enthusiasts.
S. Gorley Putt, "The Prisoner of *The Prisoner of Zenda:* Anthony Hope and the Novel of Society," *EIC,* VI (1956). 38-59.—Note 37: "Ellery Queen," *Queen's Quorum: A History of the Detective Crime Short Story* (Boston, 1951); Suther-

land Scott, *Blood in Their Ink: the March of the Modern Mystery Novel* (1953); special issue of *LTLS*, Feb. 25, 1955; A. E. Murch, *The Development of the Detective Novel* (1958).

1502   *A Choice of Kipling's Prose,* with introd. by W. Somerset Maugham (1952). *The Best Short Stories of Rudyard Kipling,* with introd. by Randall Jarrell (1961).—James McG. Stewart, *Rudyard Kipling: A Bibliographical Catalogue* (Toronto, 1959); Helmut E. Gerber and Edward Lauterbach, "Rudyard Kipling: An Annotated Bibliography of Writings about Him," *English Fiction in Transition,* III, nos. 3-5 (1960). 1-235; VIII, nos. 3-4 (1965). 136-241. C. E. Carrington, *The Life of Rudyard Kipling* (1955), the authorized biography; Rupert Croft-Cooke, *Rudyard Kipling* (1948); Robert Escarpit, *Rudyard Kipling: Servitudes et grandeurs impériales* (Paris, 1955); Francis Léaud, *La Poétique de Rudyard Kipling* (Paris, 1958); J. M. S. Tompkins, *The Art of Rudyard Kipling* (1959); C. A. Bodelsen, *Aspects of Kipling's Art* (Manchester, 1964); Roger L. Green, *The Reader's Guide to Rudyard Kipling's Work* (Canterbury, 1961) and *Kipling and the Children* (1965); Lionel Trilling, "Kipling," *The Liberal Imagination* (1950), pp. 118-128; H. L. Varley, "Imperialism and Rudyard Kipling," *JHI,* XIV (1953). 124-135; Michael Edwardes, "Rudyard Kipling and the Imperial Imagination," *Twentieth Century,* CLIII (1953). 443-454; Noel Annan, "Kipling's Place in the History of Ideas," *VS,* III (1960). 323-348; *Kipling's Mind and Art: Selected Critical Essays,* ed. Andrew Rutherford (Stanford, 1964); *Kipling and the Critics,* ed. Elliot L. Gilbert (1965); Stewart, *Eight Modern Writers,* ch. VI.

1504   A. W. Yeats, "The Genesis of *The Recessional*," *Univ. of Texas Stud. in English,* XXXI (1952). 97-108.

1506   Note 49: See also Donald L. Hill, "Kipling in Vermont," *NCF,* VII (1952). 153-170.

XXXVII. The Irish Literary Renaissance

1507   *One Thousand Years of Irish Poetry,* ed. Kathleen Hoagland (1947); *Irish Poets of the Nineteenth Century,* ed. Geoffrey Taylor (Cambridge, Mass., 1951); *One Thousand Years of Irish Prose.* Part I: *The Literary Revival,* ed. Vivian Mercier and David H. Greene (1952).—Benedict Kiely, *Modern Irish Fiction: A Critique* (Dublin, 1950); Estella R. Taylor, *The Modern Irish Writers: Cross Currents of Criticism* (Lawrence, Kan., 1954); Herbert Howarth, *The Irish Writers, 1880-1940: Literature under Parnell's Star* (1958). *The Genius of the Irish Theater,* ed. Sylvan Barnet, Morton Berman, and William Burto (1960), an anthology of plays. Peter Kavanagh, *The Story of the Abbey Theatre* (1950); *Ireland's Abbey Theatre: A History, 1899-1951,* ed. Lennox Robinson (1951); Jan Setterquist, *Ibsen and the Beginnings of Anglo-Irish Drama* (2v, Cambridge, Mass., 1951-60); Gerard Fay, *The Abbey Theatre: Cradle of Genius* (1958).

1508   Yeats: *Collected Plays* (1952); *Poems* (2v, 1949), definitive edition; *Variorum Edition of the Poems,* ed. Peter Allt and Russell Alspach (1957); *Poems,* ed. A. Norman Jeffares (1962); *Selected Poems,* ed. M. L. Rosenthal

(1962); *Essays and Introductions* (1961); *Senate Speeches,* ed. Donald R. Pearce (Bloomington, Ind., 1960); *Explorations,* ed. Mrs. W. B. Yeats (1962); *Autobiography* (1953); *W. B. Yeats and T. Sturge Moore: Their Correspondence 1901-1937,* ed. Ursula Bridge (1953); *Letters to Katharine Tynan,* ed. Roger J. McHugh (1953); *Letters,* ed. Allan Wade (1954).—Wade, *A Bibliography of the Writings of W. B. Yeats* (1951, rev. 1958); George B. Saul, *Prolegomena to the Study of Yeats's Poems* (Philadelphia, 1957) and *Prolegomena to the Study of Yeats's Plays* (Philadelphia, 1958); John Unterecker, *A Reader's Guide to W. B. Yeats* (1959). Richard Ellmann, *Yeats: The Man and the Masks* (1948) and *The Identity of Yeats* (1954); Jeffares, *W. B. Yeats, Man and Poet* (New Haven, 1949, rev. 1962); Monk Gibbon, *The Masterpiece and the Man: Yeats as I Knew Him* (1959); three books by Peter Ure, *Towards a Mythology: Studies in the Poetry of W. B. Yeats* (1946), *Yeats the Playwright: A Commentary on Character and Design in the Major Plays* (1963), and *Yeats* (Edinburgh, 1963); Donald A. Stauffer, *The Golden Nightingale: Essays on Some Principles of Poetry in the Lyrics of William Butler Yeats* (1949); Thomas R. Henn, *The Lonley Tower: Studies in the Poetry of W. B. Yeats* (1950, rev. 1965); Birgit Bjersby, *The Interpretation of the Cuchulain Legend in the Works of W. B. Yeats* (Dublin, 1950); Vivienne Koch, *Yeats: The Tragic Phase: A Study of the Last Poems* (1951); Thomas F. Parkinson, *W. B. Yeats, Self-Critic: A Study of His Early Verse* (Berkeley, 1951), and *W. B. Yeats: The Later Poetry* (Berkeley, 1964); Arland Ussher, *Three Great Irishmen: Shaw, Yeats, Joyce* (1952); Margaret Rudd, *Divided Image: A Study of William Blake and W. B. Yeats* (1953); Virginia Moore, *The Unicorn: Yeats's Search for Reality* (1954); Hazard Adams, *Blake and Yeats: The Contrary Vision* (Ithaca, 1955); Francis A. C. Wilson, *W. B. Yeats and Tradition* (1958) and *Yeats's Iconography* (1960); Giorgio Melchiori, *The Whole Mystery of Art* (1960); George T. Wright, *The Poet in the Poem: The Personae of Eliot, Yeats and Pound* (Berkeley, 1960); Benjamin L. Reid, *W. B. Yeats: The Lyric of Tragedy* (Norman, Okla., 1961); Amy G. Stock, *W. B. Yeats: His Poetry and Thought* (Cambridge, 1961); Morton I. Seiden, *William Butler Yeats: The Poet as Mythmaker* (East Lansing, Mich., 1962); Richard M. Kain, *Dublin in the Age of William Butler Yeats and James Joyce* (Norman, Okla., 1962); Jon Stallworthy, *Between the Lines: Yeats's Poetry in the Making* (Oxford, 1963); Helen H. Vendler, *Yeats's Vision and the Later Plays* (Cambridge, Mass., 1963); Edward Engelberg, *The Vast Design: Patterns in W. B. Yeats's Aesthetic* (Toronto, 1964); Priscilla W. Shaw, *Rilke, Valéry, and Yeats: The Domain of the Self* (New Brunswick, N. J., 1964); Thomas R. Whitaker, *Swan and Shadow: Yeats's Dialogue with History* (Chapel Hill, 1964); Leonard Nathan, *The Tragic Drama of William Butler Yeats* (1965); Suheil B. Bushrui, *Yeats' Verse Plays: The Revisions, 1900-1910* (1965); Donald Torchiana, *W. B. Yeats and Georgian Ireland* (Evanston, Ill., 1966); Alex Zwerdling, *Yeats and the Heroic Ideal* (1965); Balachandra Rajan, *W. B. Yeats: A Critical Introduction* (1965); *W. B. Yeats, 1865-1965: Centenary Essays,* ed. D. E. S. Maxwell and S. B. Bushrui (Ibadan, 1965); *In Excited Reverie: A Centenary Tribute,* ed. Jeffares and K. G. W. Cross (1965); *The Permanence of Yeats: Selected Criticism,* ed. James Hall and Martin Steinmann (1950); *Yeats: A Collection of Critical Essays,* ed. Unterecker (1963); *The Integrity of Yeats,* ed. Denis Donoghue (Cork, 1964); *The World of W. B. Yeats: Essays in Perspective,* ed. Robin Skelton and Ann Saddlemyer (Seattle, 1965); Bayley,

The Romantic Survival, ch. VIII; Hough, *The Last Romantics,* ch. VI; Stewart, *Eight Modern Writers,* ch. VII (see selected list of chapters and essays on Yeats, pp. 677-679).—*Concordance to the Poems of W. B. Yeats,* ed. Stephen M. Parrish (Ithaca, 1963).

1510 Lady Gregory: *Selected Plays,* ed. Elizabeth Coxhead (1962); *Journals, 1916-1930,* ed. Lennox Robinson (1946). Coxhead, *Lady Gregory: A Literary Portrait* (1961); Ann Saddlemyer, *In Defense of Lady Gregory, Playwright* (1965).—Note 14: Sister Marie-Thérèse Courtney, *Edward Martyn and the Irish Theater* (1957); Jan Setterquist, *Ibsen and the Beginnings of Anglo-Irish Drama.* 2. *Edward Martyn* (Cambridge, Mass., 1960).

1512 *Letters from Æ,* ed. Alan Denson (1961). Denson, *Printed Writings by George W. Russell (Æ): A Bibliography* (Evanston, Ill., 1961). "John Eglinton" [William Magee], "The Poetry of Æ," *Dublin Mag.,* n.s. XXVI, no. 3 (1951). 5-9.

1513 Synge: *Collected Works* (5v, 1962-   ); *Plays and Poems,* ed. T. R. Henn (1963); *Translations,* ed. Robin Skelton (Dublin, 1961); *Autobiography,* ed. Alan Price (Dublin, 1965).—Jan Setterquist, *Ibsen and the Beginnings of Anglo-Irish Drama. 1. John Millington Synge* (Cambridge, Mass., 1951); David H. Greene and Edward M. Stephens, *J. M. Synge, 1871-1909* (1959); Price, *Synge and the Anglo-Irish Drama* (1961); Donna Gerstenberger, *John Millington Synge* (1964); Roger McHugh, "Yeats, Synge and the Abbey Theatre," *Studies,* XLI (1952). 333-340; Norman Podhoretz, "Synge's *Playboy:* Morality and the Hero," *EIC,* III (1953). 337-344; Ellen Douglass Leyburn, "The Theme of Loneliness in the Plays of Synge," *Modern Drama,* I (1958). 84-90; O'Casey and Synge number of *Modern Drama,* IV (Dec., 1961). There are also short contributions by Greene in *PMLA,* LXII (1947). 233-238, 824-827, and LXIII (1948). 1314-1321.

1514 Michael J. O'Neill, *Lennox Robinson* (1964).
O'Casey's six autobiographical volumes were collected as *Mirror in My House* (2v, 1956).—Jules Koslow, *The Green and the Red: Sean O'Casey, the Man and His Plays* (1950); Robert G. Hogan, *The Experiments of Sean O'Casey* (1960); David Krause, *Sean O'Casey: The Man and His Work* (1960); Saros Cowasjee, *Sean O'Casey: The Man Behind the Plays* (Edinburgh, 1963); O'Casey and Synge number of *Modern Drama,* IV (Dec., 1961).

1515 Note 20: *Collected Poems* (1954); *A James Stephens Reader* (1962) and *James, Seumas and Jacques: Unpublished Writings of James Stephens* (1964), both ed. Lloyd Frankenberg; *Memoirs,* ed. Merle M. Bevington (1954). Birgit Bramsbäck, *James Stephens: A Literary and Bibliographical Study* (Uppsala, 1959); Hilary Pyle, *James Stephens: His Work and An Account of His Life* (1965); Augustine Martin, "James Stephens: Lyric Poet," *Studies,* XLIX (1960). 173-182, L (1961). 75-87.

XXXVIII. Modern Drama

1516 On antecedents of the modern period see suppl. to p. 1264 above. *Edwardian Plays,* ed. Gerald Weales (1962); *The Genius of the Later English*

Theater, ed. Sylvan Barnet *et al.* (1962). Ernest Reynolds, *Modern English Drama: A Survey of the Theatre from 1900* (1950); John C. Trewin, *Theatre Since 1900* (1951); Albert E. Wilson, *Edwardian Theatre* (1951); Frederick Lumley, *Trends in Twentieth-Century Drama* (1956, rev. 1960); Weales, *Religion in Modern English Drama* (Philadelphia, 1961), and "The Edwardian Theater and the Shadow of Shaw," *Edwardians and Late Victorians* (1960), pp. 160-187; Raymond Williams, "Criticism into Drama, 1888-1950," *EIC*, 1 (1951). 120-138.

1517 Maynard Savin, *Thomas William Robertson, His Plays and Stagecraft* (Providence, R. I., 1950).—*The Savoy Operas*, ed. Derek Hudson (2v, 1962-63). C. L. Purdy, *Gilbert and Sullivan, Masters of Mirth and Melody* (1947); William A. Darlington, *The World of Gilbert and Sullivan* (1950); Leslie Baily, *The Gilbert and Sullivan Book* (1952, rev. 1956); Audrey Williamson, *Gilbert and Sullivan Opera: A New Assessment* (1953); Hesketh Pearson, *Gilbert: His Life and Strife* (1957); *Crowell's Handbook of Gilbert and Sullivan*, ed. Frank L. Moore (1962).—Jan Setterquist, *Ibsen and the Beginnings of Anglo-Irish Drama* (2v, Cambridge, Mass., 1951-1960).

1518 James O. Bailey, "Science in the Dramas of Henry Arthur Jones," *Booker Memorial Studies* (Chapel Hill, 1950), pp. 155-183.

1520 *The Theatre of Bernard Shaw*, ed. Alan S. Downer (1961), ten plays; *Selected Prose*, ed. Diarmuid Russell (1952); *Selected Non-Dramatic Writings*, ed. Dan H. Laurence (Boston, 1965); *Bernard Shaw: A Prose Anthology*, ed. H. M. Burton (1959); *Sixteen Self-Sketches* (1949); *The Quintessence of G. B. S.*, ed. Stephen Winsten (1949); *Shaw and Society: An Anthology and a Symposium*, ed. C. E. M. Joad (1953); *An Unfinished Novel*, ed. Stanley Weintraub (1958); *Shaw on Education*, ed. Louis Simon (1958); *Shaw on Theatre*, ed. E. J. West (1958); *Dramatic Criticism (1895-98)*, ed. John F. Matthews (1959); *How to Become a Musical Critic*, ed. Dan H. Laurence (1961); *Platform and Pulpit*, ed. Laurence (1961); *On Shakespeare*, ed. Edwin Wilson (1961); *The Matter with Ireland*, ed. Dan H. Laurence and David H. Greene (1962); *On Language*, ed. Abraham Tauber (1963); *Religious Speeches*, ed. Warren S. Smith (University Park, Pa., 1963); *The Rationalization of Russia*, ed. Harry M. Geduld (Bloomington, Ind., 1964). *Collected Letters*, ed. Dan H. Laurence (4v, 1965-   ); *Bernard Shaw and Mrs. Patrick Campbell: Their Correspondence*, ed. Alan Dent (1952); *Advice to a Young Critic and Other Letters*, ed. West (1955); *Letters to Granville-Barker*, ed. C. B. Purdom (1957); *To a Young Actress: The Letters of Bernard Shaw to Molly Tompkins*, ed. Peter Tompkins (1960).—Earl Farley and Marvin Carlson, "George Bernard Shaw: A Selected Bibliography (1945-1955)," *Modern Drama*, II (1959). 188-202, 295-325. Archibald Henderson, *George Bernard Shaw: Man of the Century* (1956), the third and final version of this "authorized" biography; St. John Ervine, *Bernard Shaw: His Life, Work, and Friends* (1956); Hesketh Pearson, *Bernard Shaw: His Life and Personality* (1961), combining his 1942 biography and *G.B.S.: A Postscript* (1950); three books by Stephen Winsten, *Days with Bernard Shaw* (1948), *Shaw's Corner* (1952), and *Jesting Apostle: The Life of Bernard Shaw* (1956); *Shaw the Villager and Human Being*, ed. Allan Chappelow (1961), like Winsten's books typical of the large literature of personalia surrounding Shaw's figure; Lawrence

Langner, *G.B.S. and the Lunatic* (1963); Weintraub, *Private Shaw and Public Shaw: A Dual Portrait of Lawrence of Arabia and G.B.S.* (1963); Audrey Williamson, *Bernard Shaw: Man and Writer* (1963); B. C. Rosset, *Shaw of Dublin: The Formative Years* (University Park, Pa., 1964); Eric Bentley, *Bernard Shaw: A Reconsideration* (Norfolk, Conn., 1947; rev. 1957); William Irvine, *The Universe of G.B.S.* (1949); Joad, *Shaw* (1949); Edmund Fuller, *George Bernard Shaw: Critic of Western Morale* (1950); Alick West, *George Bernard Shaw: A Good Man Fallen Among Fabians* (1950); Desmond MacCarthy, *Shaw's Plays in Review* (1951); A. C. Ward, *Bernard Shaw* (1951); Arland Ussher, *Three Great Irishmen: Shaw, Yeats, Joyce* (1952); Arthur H. Nethercot, *Men and Supermen: The Shavian Portrait Gallery* (Cambridge, Mass., 1954); Julian B. Kaye, *Bernard Shaw and the Nineteenth Century Tradition* (Norman, Okla., (1958); Richard M. Ohmann, *Shaw: the Style and the Man* (Middletown, Conn., 1962); C. B. Purdom, *A Guide to the Plays of Bernard Shaw* (1963); Martin Meisel, *Shaw and the Nineteenth-Century Theater* (Princeton, 1963); Homer E. Woodbridge, *George Bernard Shaw* (Carbondale, Ill., 1963); Barbara B. Watson, *A Shavian Guide to the Intelligent Woman* (1964); *G. B. S. 90: Aspects of Bernard Shaw's Life and Work,* ed. Winsten (1946), a symposium; *George Bernard Shaw: A Critical Survey,* ed. Louis Kronenberger (1953); Stewart, *Eight Modern Writers,* ch. iv; *The Shaw Bulletin,* later *The Shaw Review* (1951-   ); *The Independent Shavian,* later *The Shavian* (1963-   ).

1525 Charles B. Purdom, *Harley Granville-Barker: Man of the Theatre, Dramatist and Scholar* (1955); Margery M. Morgan, *A Drama of Political Man: A Study in the Plays of Harley Granville-Barker* (1961); Alan S. Downer, "Harley Granville-Barker," *Sewanee Rev.,* LV (1947). 627-645.

1528 Richard A. Cordell, "The Theatre of Somerset Maugham," *Modern Drama,* I (1959). 211-227.—Cynthia Asquith, *Portrait of Barrie* (1954); Roger L. Green, *Fifty Years of "Peter Pan"* (1954), on the play's theatrical tradition.

1530 Bottomley: *Poems and Plays,* ed. C. C. Abbott (1953); *A Stage for Poetry: My Purposes with Plays* (Kendal, 1948); *Poet and Painter, Being the Correspondence between Gordon Bottomley and Paul Nash, 1910-1946,* ed. C. C. Abbott and Anthony Bertram (1955). A. J. Farmer, "Gordon Bottomley," *Études anglaises,* IX (1956). 323-327.—Muriel Spark, *John Masefield* (1953).

XXXIX. Other Late-Victorian Poets

1532 Patmore: *Poems,* ed. Frederick Page (Oxford, 1949); *A Selection of Poems,* ed. Derek Patmore (rev. of 1931 vol., 1949); *The Rod, the Root, and the Flower,* ed. D. Patmore (1950); *Essay on English Metrical Law,* ed. Sister Mary Roth (Washington, D. C., 1961).—Augusto Guidi, *Coventry Patmore* (Brescia, 1946); D. Patmore, *The Life and Times of Coventry Patmore* (1949), a complete revision of his *Portrait of My Family* (1935); Edward J. Oliver, *Coventry Patmore* (1956); John C. Reid, *The Mind and Art of Coventry Patmore* (1957); J. M. Cohen, "Prophet without Responsibility," *EIC,* I (1951). 283-297; Heath-Stubbs, *The Darkling Plain,* pp. 128-140.

1533 Francis Thompson: *Literary Criticisms* (1948), [reviews of] *Minor*

Poets (Los Angeles, 1949), *The Man Has Wings: New Poems and Plays* (1957), and *The Real Robert Louis Stevenson and Other Critical Essays* (1959), all ed. Terence L. Connolly.—Myrtle P. Pope, *A Critical Bibliography of Works by and about Francis Thompson* (1959). Viola Meynell, *Francis Thompson and Wilfrid Meynell: A Memoir* (1952); John C. Reid, *Francis Thompson* (1959); Pierre Danchin, *Francis Thompson: la Vie et l'oeuvre d'un poète* (Paris, 1959); Paul Van K. Thomson, *Francis Thompson* (1961); Danchin, "Francis Thompson (1859-1907): À propos d'un centenaire," *Études anglaises,* XIII (1960). 427-443; Peter Butter, "Francis Thompson," *REL,* II, no. 1 (1961). 87-94.

1535   Meynell: *Prose and Poetry, Centenary Volume,* ed. Frederick Page *et al.* (1947); *Essays* (Westminster, Md., 1947) and *Poems* (1948), both ed. Francis Meynell. *Alice Meynell Centenary Tribute, 1847-1947,* ed. Terence L. Connolly (Boston, 1948); "An Idyll of Life and Letters," *LTLS,* Oct. 18, 1947, p. 534.— Johnson: *Complete Poems,* ed. Iain Fletcher (1953). A. Bronson Feldman, "The Art of Lionel Johnson," *Poet Lore,* LVII (1953). 140-160.

1536   James Sambrook, *A Poet Hidden: The Life of Richard Watson Dixon, 1833-1900* (1962).—Mary Coleridge: *Collected Poems,* ed. Theresa Whistler (1954). Beatrice White, "Mary Coleridge: An Appreciation," *E&S,* XXXI (1945). 81-94.

1536-1537   Hopkins: *Poems,* ed. W. H. Gardner (1948, enlarged ed. 1956), superseding earlier editions; *Sermons and Devotional Writings,* ed. Christopher Devlin (1949, rev. 1959); *Selected Poems,* ed. James Reeves (1953); *A Hopkins Reader,* ed. John Pick (1953); *Poems and Prose,* ed. Gardner (1954). The *Note-Books and Papers,* ed. House, appeared in an enlarged edition (as *Journals and Papers*), ed. Graham Storey (1959), as did the *Further Letters,* ed. Abbott (1956).—Bibliography in Faverty, ch. VIII. Vol. II of Gardner's *Gerard Manley Hopkins* appeared in 1949. *Immortal Diamond: Studies in Gerard Manley Hopkins,* ed. Norman Weyand and R. V. Schoder (1949), an important collection of critical essays by American Jesuits; Sister Marcella Marie Holloway, *The Prosodic Theory of Gerard Manley Hopkins* (Washington, D.C., 1947); W. A. M. Peters, *Gerard Manley Hopkins: A Critical Essay towards the Understanding of His Poetry* (1948); Geoffrey H. Hartman, *The Unmediated Vision* (New Haven, 1954); Alan Heuser, *The Shaping Vision of Gerard Manley Hopkins* (1958); Robert R. Boyle, *Metaphor in Hopkins* (Chapel Hill, 1961); Jean-Georges Ritz, *Le Poète Gerard Manley Hopkins: sa vie et son oeuvre* (Paris, 1964); two identically titled articles by Selma Jeanne Cohen and John K. Mathison, "The Poetic Theory of Gerard Manley Hopkins," *PQ,* XXVI (1947). 1-20, 21-35; James Collins, "Philosophical Themes in G. M. Hopkins," *Thought,* XXII (1947). 67-106; Yvor Winters, "The Poetry of Gerard Manley Hopkins," *Hudson Rev.,* I (1949). 455-476, II (1949). 61-93 (a severe judgment; cf. reply by J. H. Johnston in *Renascence,* II [1950]. 117-125); Marjorie D. Coogan, "Inscape and Instress: Further Analogies with Scotus," *PMLA,* LXV (1950). 66-74; Donald A. Davie, "Hopkins as a Decadent Critic," *Purity of Diction in English Verse* (1952), pp. 160-182; Lois W. Pitchford, "The Curtal Sonnets of Gerard Manley Hopkins," *MLN,* LXVII (1952). 165-169; J. Hillis Miller, "The Creation of the Self in Gerard Manley Hopkins," *ELH,* XXII (1955). 293-319; Walker Gibson, "Sound and Sense in G. M. Hopkins," *MLN,* LXXIII (1958). 95-100; Paull F. Baum, "Sprung

Rhythm," *PMLA*, LXXIV (1959). 418-425; John Wain, "Gerard Manley Hopkins: An Idiom of Desperation," *Proc. Brit. Acad.*, XLV (1959). 173-197; Carl Wooton, "The Terrible Fire of Gerard Manley Hopkins," *Texas Stud. in Lit. and Lang.*, IV (1962). 367-375; Miller, *The Disappearance of God* (1963), ch. VI; Elisabeth W. Schneider, "Sprung Rhythm: A Chapter in the Evolution of Nineteenth-Century Verse," *PMLA*, LXXX (1965). 237-253.

1537   Note 19: See Philip M. Martin, *Mastery and Mercy: A Study of Two Religious Poems* (1957), on *The Wreck of the Deutschland* and Eliot's *Ash Wednesday,* and John E. Keating, *"The Wreck of the Deutschland": an Essay and a Commentary* (Kent, Ohio, 1963).—Note 20: Among the many explications and analyses of *The Windhover* since 1948 are those of F. N. Lees, *Scrutiny,* XVII (1950). 32-37; Carl R. Woodring, *Western Rev.,* XV (1950). 61-64; F. L. Gwynn, *MLN*, LXVI (1951). 366-370; Archibald A. Hill, *PMLA*, LXX (1955). 968-978; Robert W. Ayers, *MLN*, LXXI (1956). 577-584; Thomas J. Assad, *Tulane Stud. in English*, XI (1961). 87-95; John F. Huntley, *Renascence*, XV (1964). 154-162; F. X. Shea, *VP*, II (1964). 219-239. References to additional commentary on this and other poems of Hopkins may be found in the annual check lists in *The Explicator.*

1538   Bridges: *Poetry and Prose*, ed. John Sparrow (Oxford, 1955). Jean-Georges Ritz, *Robert Bridges and Gerard Hopkins, 1863-1889* (1960); J. M. Cohen, "The Road Not Taken: A Study in the Poetry of Robert Bridges," *Cambridge Jour.*, IV (1951). 555-564.

1540   Elizabeth C. Wright, *Metaphor, Sound, and Meaning in Bridges' "The Testament of Beauty"* (Philadelphia, 1951).

1541   Doughty: Thomas J. Assad, *Three Victorian Travellers: Burton, Blunt, Doughty* (1964); John Holloway, "Poetry and Plain Language: The Verse of C. M. Doughty," *EIC*, IV (1954). 58-70; Barker Fairley, *"The Dawn in Britain* after Fifty Years," *UTQ*, XXVI (1957). 149-164; Heath-Stubbs, *The Darkling Plain,* pp. 188-199.

1542   Gordon Pitts, "Lord de Tabley: Poet of Frustration," *West Virginia Univ. Phil. Papers*, XIV (1963). 57-73.

The Earl of Lytton, *Wilfred Scawen Blunt: A Memoir* (1961); T. J. Assad, *Three Victorian Travellers* (1964); William T. Going, "Wilfred Scawen Blunt, Victorian Sonneteer," *VP*, II (1964). 67-85.

1543   George MacBeth, "Lee-Hamilton and the Romantic Agony," *Critical Quar.*, IV (1962). 141-150.

1544   W. M. Parker, "William Ernest Henley: Twenty-Five New Poems," *Poetry Rev.*, XL (1949). 188-199. Jerome H. Buckley, *William Ernest Henley* (Princeton, 1945); "John Connell" [John Henry Robertson], *W. E. Henley* (1949).

Davidson: *Poems and Ballads*, ed. Robert Macleod (1959); *John Davidson: A Selection of His Poems*, ed. Maurice Lindsay (1961).—John A. Lester, Jr., *John Davidson: A Grub Street Bibliography* (Charlottesville, Va., 1958). John B. Townsend, *John Davidson: Poet of Armageddon* (New Haven, 1961); Paul Turner, "John Davidson: The Novels of a Poet," *Cambridge Jour.*, V (1952). 499-504; Lester, "Friedrich Nietzsche and John Davidson: A Study in Influence,"

JHI, xviii (1957). 411-429, and "Prose-Poetry Transmutation in the Poetry of John Davidson," *MP*, lvi (1958). 38-44.

1545 Housman: *Complete Poems*, ed. Tom Burns Haber (1959); *The Manuscript Poems of A. E. Housman*, ed. Haber (Minneapolis, 1955); *Selected Prose*, ed. John Carter (Cambridge, 1961).—*A. E. Housman: An Annotated Hand-List*, ed. John Carter and John Sparrow (1952, rev. 1957). George L. Watson, *A. E. Housman: A Divided Life* (1957); Maude M. Hawkins, *A. E. Housman: Man Behind a Mask* (Chicago, 1958); Norman Marlow, *A. E. Housman: Scholar and Poet* (Minneapolis, 1958); Oliver Robinson, *Angry Dust: the Poetry of A. E. Housman* (Boston, 1950); Robert Hamilton, *Housman the Poet* (Exeter, 1953); Edmund Wilson, "A. E. Housman," *The Triple Thinkers* (1948), pp. 60-71; John W. Stevenson, "The Pastoral Setting in the Poetry of A. E. Housman," *So. Atl. Quar.*, lv (1956). 487-500; Christopher Ricks, "The Nature of Housman's Poetry," *EIC*, xiv (1964). 268-284.

1546 Note 37: Faith Mackenzie, *William Cory: A Biography, with a Selection of Poems* (1950).

XL. The Modern Novel

1547 General works on twentieth-century English literature, of pertinence to this and the following chapters, include: William York Tindall, *Forces in Modern British Literature* (1947, rev. 1956); B. Ifor Evans, *English Literature Between the Wars* (1948); A. S. Collins, *English Literature of the Twentieth Century* (1951, enlarged 1960); R. A. Scott-James, *Fifty Years of English Literature, 1900-1950* (1951); Raymond Tschumi, *Thought in Twentieth-Century English Literature* (1951); J. Isaacs, *The Assessment of Twentieth-Century Literature* (1951); G. S. Fraser, *The Modern Writer and His World* (1953, rev. 1964); A. C. Ward, *Twentieth-Century English Literature, 1901-1960* (1964); Giorgio Melchiori, *The Tightrope Walkers: Studies of Mannerism in Modern English Literature* (1956); David Daiches, *The Present Age: After 1920* (1958); Graham Hough, *Image and Experience: Reflections on a Literary Revolution* (1960); *The [Pelican] Guide to English Literature*, ed. Boris Ford, Vol. vii: *The Modern Age* (1961, rev. 1964).

Works on the twentieth-century English novel: D. S. Savage, *The Withered Branch: Six Studies in the Modern Novel* (1950); Arnold Kettle, *Introduction to the English Novel*, Vol. ii: *Henry James to the Present Day* (1953); Seán O'Faoláin, *The Vanishing Hero: Studies in Novelists of the Twenties* (1956); Frederick R. Karl and Marvin Magalaner, *A Reader's Guide to Great Twentieth-Century English Novels* (1959); *Modern British Fiction*, ed. Mark Schorer (1961), a collection of critical essays; David Daiches, *The Novel and the Modern World* (Chicago, 1960), a revision of his 1939 volume; Walter Allen, *The English Novel* (1954), chs. vi-vii, and *Tradition and Dream: The English and American Novel from the Twenties to Our Time* (1964); Lionel Stevenson, *The English Novel* (1960), chs. xvi-xvii.

Henry James: *Complete Tales* (12v, 1962-1964), *Complete Plays* (1949), both ed. Leon Edel. Most of the major novels are available in well edited reprints, too numerous to list here. James's journalism and other fugitive writings have been assembled in a number of volumes, including *The Art of Fiction and Other Essays*, ed. Morris Roberts (1948); *The Scenic Art: Notes on Acting and the Drama, 1872-1901*, ed. Allan Wade (New Brunswick, N.J., 1948); *Eight Uncollected Tales*, ed. Edna Kenton (New Brunswick, 1950); *The Painter's Eye: Notes and Essays on the Pictorial Arts*, ed. John L. Sweeney (Cambridge, Mass., 1956); *Parisian Sketches*, ed. Leon Edel and Ilse D. Lind (1957); *Literary Reviews and Essays*, ed. Albert Mordell (1957); *The Art of Travel*, ed. Morton Dauwen Zabel (1958). Anthologies containing some of the better-known stories and criticism are: *American Novels and Stories*, ed. F. O. Matthiessen (1947); *Ghostly Tales* (New Brunswick, 1948), *American Essays* (1956), *The Future of the Novel* (1956), *The House of Fiction* (1957)—all ed. Edel; *The Portable Henry James* (1951) and *Fifteen Short Stories* (1961), both ed. Zabel; *Selected Literary Criticism*, ed. Morris Schapira (1963); *Americans and Europe: Selected Tales*, ed. Napier Wilt and John Lucas (Boston, 1965). *Autobiography*, ed. F. W. Dupee (1956), including *A Small Boy and Others, Notes of a Son and Brother*, and *The Middle Years; Notebooks*, ed. Matthiessen and Kenneth B. Murdock (1947); *Henry James and Robert Louis Stevenson: A Record of Friendship and Criticism*, ed. Janet Adam Smith (1948); *Henry James and H. G. Wells: A Record of Their Friendship*, ed. Edel and Gordon N. Ray (Urbana, Ill., 1958); *Henry James and John Hay: The Record of a Friendship*, ed. George Monteiro (Providence, R. I., 1965). Leon Edel (ed. *Selected Letters*, 1955) is preparing a definitive edition of James's letters.—Edel and Dan H. Laurence, *A Bibliography of Henry James* (1957, rev. 1961); Maurice Beebe and William T. Stafford, "Criticism of Henry James: A Selected Checklist," *Mod. Fiction Stud.*, III (1957-58). 73-96. The fullest lists of current publications on James are found in the quarterly bibliography in *American Lit.* and the annual bibliography in *PMLA*. Edel, *Henry James* (4v, Philadelphia, 1953-   ), the standard biography; *The Legend of the Master*, ed. Simon Nowell-Smith (1947), contemporary records of James's personality; Matthiessen, *The James Family* (1947); Elizabeth Stevenson, *The Crooked Corridor: A Study of Henry James* (1949); Dupee, *Henry James* (1951, rev. 1956); Robert C. LeClair, *Young Henry James: 1843-1870* (1955); Quentin Anderson, *The American Henry James* (New Brunswick, N.J., 1957); Osborn Andreas, *Henry James and the Expanding Horizon* (Seattle, 1948); Edwin T. Bowden, *The Themes of Henry James* (New Haven, 1956); Frederick C. Crews, *The Tragedy of Manners: Moral Drama in the Later Novels of Henry James* (New Haven, 1957); Leo B. Levy, *Versions of Melodrama: A Study of the Fiction and Drama of Henry James, 1865-1897* (Berkeley, 1957); Christof Wegelin, *The Image of Europe in Henry James* (Dallas, 1958); Harold T. McCarthy, *Henry James: The Creative Process* (1958); Alexander Holder-Barrell, *The Development of Imagery and Its Functional Significance in Henry James's Novels* (Bern, 1959); D. W. Jefferson, *Henry James* (1960) and *Henry James and the Modern Reader* (1964); Richard Poirier, *The Comic Sense of Henry James* (1960); Robert Marks, *James's Later Novels: An Interpretation* (1960); Oscar Cargill, *The Novels of Henry James* (1961); J. A. Ward, *The Imagination of Disaster: Evil in the Fiction of Henry James* (Lincoln, Neb., 1961); Dorothea Krook, *The Ordeal of Consciousness in Henry James* (Cambridge, 1962); Walter F. Wright, *The Madness of Art: A Study of Henry James* (Lincoln, Neb., 1962); Maxwell Geismar, *Henry James and the Jacobites* (Boston, 1963); Sister M. Corona Sharp,

The Confidante in Henry James (South Bend, Ind., 1963); Joseph Wiesenfarth, Henry James and the Dramatic Analogy (1963); Robert L. Gale, The Caught Image: Figurative Language in the Fiction of Henry James (Chapel Hill, 1964); Laurence B. Holland, The Expense of Vision: Essays on the Craft of Henry James (Princeton, 1964); Krishna Vaid, Technique in the Tales of Henry James (Cambridge, Mass., 1964); Edward Stone, The Battle and the Books (Athens, Ohio, 1965); The Question of Henry James, ed. Dupee (1945); Henry James: A Collection of Critical Essays, ed. Edel (1963); Discussions of Henry James, ed. Naomi Lebowitz (Boston, 1962); Stewart, Eight Modern Writers, ch. III (see also pp. 647-649 for a selected list of chapters and articles in periodicals).

1551 The Portable Conrad, ed. Morton Dauwen Zabel (1947); Joseph Conrad on Fiction, ed. Walter F. Wright (Lincoln, Neb., 1964); Letters to William Blackwood and David S. Meldrum, ed. William Blackburn (Durham, N.C., 1958); Conrad's Polish Background: Letters to and from Polish Friends, ed. Zdzislaw Najder (1964).—Kenneth A. Lohf and Eugene P. Sheehy, Joseph Conrad at Mid-Century: Editions and Studies, 1895-1955 (Minneapolis, 1957); Maurice Beebe, "Criticism of Joseph Conrad: A Selected Checklist," Mod. Fiction Stud., x (1964). 81-106. Jocelyn Baines, Joseph Conrad: A Critical Biography (1960), the best biography, replacing G. Jean-Aubry, The Sea Dreamer: A Definitive Biography of Joseph Conrad (1957), which in turn superseded Jean-Aubry's 1927 life. Wright, Romance and Tragedy in Conrad (Lincoln, Neb., 1949); Douglas Hewitt, Conrad: A Reassessment (Cambridge, 1952); Paul L. Wiley, Conrad's Measure of Man (Madison, Wis., 1954); E. H. Visiak, The Mirror of Conrad (1955); Thomas Moser, Joseph Conrad: Achievement and Decline (Cambridge, Mass., 1957); Robert F. Haugh, Joseph Conrad: Discovery in Design (Norman, Okla., 1957); Albert J. Guerard, Conrad the Novelist (Cambridge, Mass., 1958); Osborn Andreas, Conrad: A Study in Nonconformity (1959); Adam Gillon, The Eternal Solitary: A Study of Joseph Conrad (1960); The Art of Joseph Conrad: A Critical Symposium, ed. R. W. Stallman (East Lansing, Mich., 1960); Joseph Conrad: Centennial Essays, ed. Ludwik Krzyzanowski (1960); Leo Gurko, Joseph Conrad: Giant in Exile (1962); Eloise Knapp Hay, The Political Novels of Joseph Conrad (Chicago, 1963); Frederick R. Karl, A Reader's Guide to Joseph Conrad (Chicago, 1963); Conrad number of Mod. Fiction Stud. (Spring, 1964); Stewart, Eight Modern Writers, ch. v (see also pp. 662-664 for a selected list of chapters and articles in periodicals).

1553 The Nigger of the "Narcissus," ed. Morton Dauwen Zabel (1951), Douglas Brown (1960), Albert Guerard (1960, with The End of the Tether).—Youth, ed. Zabel (1959, with The End of the Tether).—Heart of Darkness, ed. Guerard (1950, with The Secret Sharer); ed. Robert Kimbrough (1963), authoritative text with critical essays. "Heart of Darkness" and the Critics, ed. Bruce Harkness (San Francisco, 1960); "Heart of Darkness": Backgrounds and Criticisms, ed. Leonard F. Dean (1960).—Lord Jim, ed. Robert B. Heilman (1957), Zabel (1958), Walter Wright (1958). Tony Tanner, Conrad: "Lord Jim": A Critical Study (1963).—Nostromo, ed. Robert Penn Warren (1951), F. R. Leavis (1960), Dorothy Van Ghent (1961).

Note 13: In the 1960's there was a considerable revival of critical interest in Ford Madox Ford. The Bodley Head Ford Madox Ford (4v, 1962-1963); Parade's End (1950), a tetralogy composed of Some Do Not (1924), No More Parades

(1925), *A Man Could Stand Up* (1926), and *Last Post* (1927); *The Good Soldier*, ed. Mark Schorer (1951); *Critical Writings*, ed. Frank MacShane (Lincoln, Neb., 1964); *Letters*, ed. Richard M. Ludwig (Princeton, 1965).—David D. Harvey, *Ford Madox Ford 1873-1939: A Bibliography of Works and Criticism* (Princeton, 1962). Douglas Goldring, *The Last Pre-Raphaelite* (1948); Richard A. Cassell, *Ford Madox Ford: A Study of His Novels* (Baltimore, 1962); John A. Meixner, *Ford Madox Ford's Novels* (Minneapolis, 1962); Paul L. Wiley, *Novelist of Three Worlds: Ford Madox Ford* (Syracuse, N.Y., 1962); Carol Ohmann, *Ford Madox Ford: From Apprentice to Craftsman* (Middletown, Conn., 1964); R. W. Lid, *Ford Madox Ford: The Essence of His Art* (Berkeley, 1964); Frank MacShane, *The Life and Work of Ford Madox Ford* (1965).

1554   *Under Western Eyes* (1951), *The Shadow-Line* (1959), and *The Mirror of the Sea* (1960, with *A Personal Record*), all edited by Zabel.—Note 15: *Conrad's "Secret Sharer" and the Critics*, ed. Bruce Harkness (San Francisco, 1962).

1555   *The Man of Property*, ed. Lionel Stevenson (1949). Helmut E. Gerber *et al.*, "John Galsworthy: An Annotated Checklist of Writings About Him," *English Fiction in Transition*, 1, no. 3 (1958). 7-29, VII (1964). 93-100.—R. H. Mottram, *For Some We Loved: An Intimate Portrait of Ada and John Galsworthy* (1956); Dudley Barker, *The Man of Principle: A View of John Galsworthy* (1963); Jan Henry Smit, *The Short Stories of John Galsworthy* (Rotterdam, 1948); J. Gordon Eaker, "Galsworthy and the Modern Mind," *PQ*, XXIX (1950). 31-48; Drew B. Pallett, "Young Galsworthy: The Forging of a Satirist," *MP*, LVI (1959). 178-186.

1557   *Journals*, ed. Frank Swinnerton (1954), a selection; *Arnold Bennett and H. G. Wells: A Record of a Personal and Literary Friendship*, ed. Harris Wilson (Urbana, Ill., 1960).—Reginald Pound, *Arnold Bennett: A Biography* (1952); Walter Allen, *Arnold Bennett* (1948); Vittoria Sanna, *Arnold Bennett e i romanzi delle Cinque Citta* (Florence, 1953); James Hall, *Arnold Bennett: Primitivism and Taste* (Seattle, 1959); John Wain, "The Quality of Bennett," *Preliminary Essays* (1957), pp. 121-156; James G. Hepburn, *The Art of Arnold Bennett* (Bloomington, Ind., 1963); Kettle, II. 82-89 (on *The Old Wives' Tale*).

1558   Wells: *Collected Short Stories* (1960); *The History of Mr. Polly*, ed. Gordon N. Ray (Boston, 1960); *The Outline of History*, revised by Raymond Postgate (1961); *Henry James and H. G. Wells: A Record of Their Friendship* ed. Leon Edel and G. N. Ray (Urbana, Ill., 1958); *Arnold Bennett and H. G. Wells: A Record of a Personal and Literary Friendship*, ed. Harris Wilson (Urbana, Ill., 1960).—Vincent Brome, *H. G. Wells: A Biography* (1951); Antonia Vallentin, *H. G. Wells: Prophet of Our Day* (1950); Bernard Bergonzi, *The Early H. G. Wells: A Study of the Scientific Romances* (Manchester, 1961); Ingvald Raknem, *H. G. Wells and His Critics* (Oslo, 1962); Kettle, II. 89-95 (on *Tono-Bungay*).

1560   Joyce: *Chamber Music*, ed. William Y. Tindall (1954); *Exiles* (1951) and *Dubliners* (1954), both ed. Padraic Colum; *Stephen Hero, with Additional Manuscript Pages*, ed. Theodore Spencer (Norfolk, Conn., 1955); *Critical Writings*, ed. Ellsworth Mason and Richard Ellmann (1959); *The Portable James Joyce*, ed. Harry Levin (1947); *Letters*, ed. Stuart Gilbert (1957).—John J. Slocum and Herbert Cahoon, *A Bibliography of James Joyce, 1882-1941* (1953);

Maurice Beebe and A. Walton Litz, "Criticism of James Joyce: A Selected Checklist," *Mod. Fiction Stud.*, IV (1958-59). 71-99. Ellmann, *James Joyce* (1959), the standard biography; Mary and Padraic Colum, *Our Friend James Joyce* (1958); Stanislaus Joyce, *My Brother's Keeper: James Joyce's Early Years* (1958); Sylvia Beach, *Shakespeare and Company* (1959). Levin's *James Joyce: A Critical Introduction* was revised in 1960 and Kain's *Fabulous Voyager* in 1959. L. A. G. Strong, *The Sacred River: An Approach to James Joyce* (1949); Patricia Hutchins, *James Joyce's Dublin* (1950) and *James Joyce's World* (1957); three books by Tindall, *James Joyce: His Way of Interpreting the Modern World* (1950), *A Reader's Guide to James Joyce* (1959), and *The Joyce Country* (University Park, Pa., 1960); Arland Ussher, *Three Great Irishmen: Shaw, Yeats, and Joyce* (1952); William Powell Jones, *James Joyce and the Common Reader* (Norman, Okla., 1955); Kristan Smidt, *James Joyce and the Cultic Use of Fiction* (Oslo, 1955); Marvin Magalaner and Richard M. Kain, *Joyce, the Man, the Work, the Reputation* (1956); Hugh Kenner, *Dublin's Joyce* (Bloomington, Ind., 1956); William T. Noon, *Joyce and Aquinas* (New Haven, 1957); Kevin Sullivan, *Joyce among the Jesuits* (1958); Matthew Hodgart and Mabel P. Worthington, *Songs in the Works of James Joyce* (Philadelphia, 1959); J. Mitchell Morse, *The Sympathetic Alien: James Joyce and Catholicism* (1959); Magalaner, *Time of Apprenticeship: The Fiction of Young James Joyce* (1960); Samuel L. Goldberg, *Joyce* (Edinburgh, 1962); Kain, *Dublin in the Age of William Butler Yeats and James Joyce* (Norman, Okla., 1962); Helmut Bonheim, *Joyce's Benefictions* (Berkeley, 1964); Joseph Prescott, *Exploring James Joyce* (Carbondale, Ill., 1964); Joseph G. Brennan, *Three Philosophical Novelists: James Joyce, André Gide, Thomas Mann* (1964); Anthony Burgess, *Here Comes Everybody* (1965); *A James Joyce Miscellany*, ed. Magalaner (1st ser., New York, 1957; 2nd and 3rd ser., Carbondale, Ill., 1959, 1962); *James Joyce: Two Decades of Criticism*, ed. Seon Givens (1948, rev. 1963); *James Joyce Rev.* (1957-1959); *James Joyce Quar.* (1963-   ); Stewart, *Eight Modern Writers*, ch. VIII (see also pp. 684-686 for selected list of chapters and articles in periodicals).

1561   Robert S. Ryf, *A New Approach to Joyce: "The Portrait of the Artist" as a Guidebook* (Berkeley, 1962); *The Workshop of Daedalus: James Joyce and the Raw Materials for "A Portrait of the Artist as a Young Man,"* ed. Robert E. Scholes and R. M. Kain (Evanston, Ill., 1965); *Joyce's "Portrait": Criticism and Critiques,* ed. Thomas E. Connolly (1962).

A. Walton Litz, *The Art of James Joyce: Method and Design in "Ulysses" and "Finnegans Wake"* (1961); S. L. Goldberg, *The Classical Temper: A Study of Joyce's "Ulysses"* (1961); Robert M. Adams, *Surface and Symbol: The Consistency of James Joyce's "Ulysses"* (1962).—*Word Index to James Joyce's "Ulysses,"* comp. Miles E. Hanley (Madison, Wis., 1951).

1562   *A First-Draft Version of "Finnegans Wake,"* ed. David Hayman (Austin, Tex., 1963); Adaline Glasheen, *A Census of "Finnegans Wake": An Index to the Characters and Their Roles* (Evanston, Ill., 1956, enlarged ed. 1963); Frances M. Boldereff, *Reading "Finnegans Wake"* (1959); James S. Atherton, *The Books at the Wake* (1959); Fred H. Higginson, *Anna Livia Plurabell: The Making of a Chapter* (Minneapolis, 1960); *Scribbledehobble: The Ur-Workbook for "Finnegans Wake",* ed. Thomas E. Connolly (Evanston, Ill., 1961); Clive Hart, *Structure and Motif in "Finnegans Wake"* (1962); Bernard Benstock,

Joyce-Agains Wake: An Analysis of "Finnegans Wake" (Seattle, 1966); *Twelve and a Tilly,* ed. Jack P. Dalton and Clive Hart (Evanston, Ill., 1966), a collection of essays.—*A Concordance to "Finnegans Wake,"* ed. Hart (Minneapolis, 1963).

   1563   D. H. Lawrence: *Complete Short Stories* (3v, 1955); *Short Novels* (2v, 1956); *Complete Poems,* ed. Vivian de Sola Pinto and Warren Roberts (2v, 1964); selections of poems, ed. Kenneth Rexroth (1947), W. E. Williams (1950), J. Reeves (1951); *Selected Poetry and Prose,* ed. T. R. Barnes (1957); *Selected Literary Criticism,* ed. Anthony Beal (1955); *The Portable D. H. Lawrence,* ed. Diana Trilling (1947); *Sex, Literature, and Censorship,* ed. Harry T. Moore (1953); *The Symbolic Meaning,* ed. Armin Arnold (1962), early versions of *Studies in Classic American Literature; A D. H. Lawrence Miscellany,* ed. Moore (Carbondale, Ill., 1959); *Collected Letters,* ed. Moore (2v, 1962); *Letters,* ed. Richard Aldington (1950), a selection; *The Plumed Serpent,* ed. William Y. Tindall (1951); *Sons and Lovers,* ed. Mark Schorer (1951).—Roberts, *A Bibliography of D. H. Lawrence* (1963); Maurice Beebe and Anthony Tommasi, "Criticism of D. H. Lawrence: A Selected Checklist of Criticism," *Mod. Fiction Stud.,* II (1959-60). 83-98. Moore, *The Life and Works of D. H. Lawrence* (1951, rev. 1964), and *The Intelligent Heart: The Story of D. H. Lawrence* (1954, rev. 1960), the standard biography; *D. H. Lawrence: A Composite Biography,* ed. Edward Nehls (3v, Madison, Wis., 1957-59), a collection of primary source material; Piero Nardi, *La Vita di D. H. Lawrence* (Milan, 1947); Aldington, *Portrait of a Genius, But—*(1950); Witter Bynner, *Journey with Genius: Recollections and Reflections Concerning the D. H. Lawrences* (1951); Eliot Fay, *Lorenzo in Search of the Sun* (1953); *Frieda Lawrence: The Memoirs and Correspondence,* ed. E. W. Tedlock, Jr. (1961); Anthony West, *D. H. Lawrence* (1950); "William Tiverton" [Martin Jarrett-Kerr], *D. H. Lawrence and Human Existence* (1951); Kenneth Young, *D. H. Lawrence* (1952); Mark Spilka, *The Love Ethic of D. H. Lawrence* (Bloomington, Ind., 1955); F. R. Leavis, *D. H. Lawrence: Novelist* (1955); Mary Freeman, *D. H. Lawrence: A Basic Study of His Ideas* (Gainesville, Fla., 1955); Graham Hough, *The Dark Sun: A Study of D. H. Lawrence* (1956); Arnold, *D. H. Lawrence and America* (1958); Richard Rees, *Brave Men: A Study of D. H. Lawrence and Simone Weil* (1958); F. J. Temple, *David Herbert Lawrence, l'Oeuvre et la vie* (Paris, 1960); Eliseo Vivas, *D. H. Lawrence: The Failure and the Triumph of Art* (Evanston, Ill., 1960); Beal, *D. H. Lawrence* (Edinburgh, 1961); Anaïs Nin, *D. H. Lawrence, An Unprofessional Study* (1962), first published in limited edition, 1932; Julian Moynahan, *The Deed of Life: The Novels and Tales of D. H. Lawrence* (Princeton, 1963); Kingsley Widmer, *The Art of Perversity: D. H. Lawrence's Shorter Fictions* (Seattle, 1963); Eugene Goodheart, *The Utopian Vision of D. H. Lawrence* (Chicago, 1963); Ronald P. Draper, *D. H. Lawrence* (1964); Tedlock, *D. H. Lawrence, Artist and Rebel: A Study of Lawrence's Fiction* (Albuquerque, 1964); H. M. Daleski, *The Forked Flame* (1965); George H. Ford, *Double Measure: A Study of the Novels and Stories of D. H. Lawrence* (1965); *The Achievement of D. H. Lawrence,* ed. Frederick J. Hoffman and Harry T. Moore (Norman, Okla., 1953); *D. H. Lawrence: A Collection of Critical Essays,* ed. Spilka (1963); Stewart, *Eight Modern Writers,* ch. IX (see also pp. 692-694 for a selected list of chapters and articles in periodicals).

   1565   Huxley: *Collected Short Stories* (1957); *Collected Essays* (1959); *Point*

Counter Point, ed. H. H. Watts (1947); *Antic Hay* and *The Gioconda Smile* (1957) and *Brave New World* and *Brave New World Revisited* (1960), both vols. ed. C. J. Rolo; *The World of Aldous Huxley,* ed. Rolo (1947).—Claire J. Eschelbach and Joyce L. Shober, *Aldous Huxley: A Bibliography, 1916-1959* (Berkeley, 1961). Teddy Brunius, *Aldous Huxley* (Stockholm, 1947); Pierre Jouguelet, *Aldous Huxley* (Paris, 1948); John A. Atkins, *Aldous Huxley: A Literary Study* (1956); S. K. Ghose, *Aldous Huxley: A Cynical Salvationist* (Bombay, 1961); Derek S. Savage, "Aldous Huxley and the Dissociation of Personality," *Sewanee Rev.,* LV (1947). 537-568; Geoffrey Bullough, "Aspects of Aldous Huxley," *ES,* xxx (1949). 233-243; Charles I. Glicksberg, "Aldous Huxley: Art and Mysticism," *Prairie Schooner,* xxvii (1953). 344-353, and "Huxley, the Experimental Novelist," *So. Atl. Quar.,* LII (1953). 98-110; Carlyle King, "Aldous Huxley's Way to God," *Queen's Quar.,* LXI (1954). 80-100, and "Aldous Huxley and Music," *ibid.,* LXX (1963). 336-351; Colin Wilson, "Existential Criticism and the Work of Aldous Huxley," *London Mag.,* v, no. 9 (1958). 46-59; Rudolf B. Schmerl, "Aldous Huxley's Social Criticism," *Chicago Rev.,* XIII, no. 1 (1959). 37-58, and "The Two Future Worlds of Aldous Huxley," *PMLA,* LXXVII (1962). 328-334; A. E. Dyson, "Aldous Huxley and the Two Nothings," *Critical Quar.,* III (1961). 293-309; Charles M. Holmes, "Aldous Huxley's Struggle with Art," *Western Humanities Rev.,* xv (1961). 149-156.

Note 25: *The Bodley Head Saki* (1963); *The Best of Saki,* ed. Graham Greene (1950); *Short Stories,* ed. Christopher Morley (1951).—Robert Drake, " 'Saki': Some Problems and a Bibliography," *English Fiction in Transition,* v, no. 1 (1962). 6-26, and "Saki's Ironic Stories," *Texas Stud. in Lit. and Lang.,* v (1963). 374-388.

Note 26: *Norman Douglas: A Selection from His Works,* ed. D. M. Low (1955); *In the Beginning,* ed. Constantine FitzGibbon (1953), first complete publication.—Cecil Woolf, *A Bibliography of Norman Douglas* (1954). R. M. Dawkins, *Norman Douglas* (1952); FitzGibbon, *Norman Douglas: A Pictorial Record* (1953); Richard Aldington, *Pinorman* (1954); Nancy Cunard, *Grand Man: Memories of Norman Douglas* (1954); "Portrait of Norman Douglas," *LTLS,* July 4, 1952, pp. 429-431.

1566 Gloria Glikin, "A Checklist of Writings by Dorothy M. Richardson" and "An Annotated Bibliography of Writings About Her," *English Lit. in Transition,* VIII, no. 1 (1965). 1-35. Caesar Blake, *Dorothy Richardson* (Ann Arbor, 1960); Leon Edel, "Dorothy Richardson, 1882-1957," *Mod. Fiction Stud.,* IV (1958). 165-168; Shiv K. Kumar, "Dorothy Richardson and the Dilemma of 'Being versus Becoming,'" *MLN,* LXXIV (1959). 494-501; Grace Tomkinson, "Dorothy M. Richardson, Pioneer," *Dalhousie Rev.,* xxxviii (1959). 465-471; Glikin, "Dorothy M. Richardson: The Personal 'Pilgrimage,'" *PMLA,* LXXVIII (1963). 586-600.—Robert Humphrey, *Stream of Consciousness in the Modern Novel* (Berkeley, 1954); Melvin Friedman, *Stream of Consciousness: A Study in Literary Method* (New Haven, 1955).

1567 *Virginia Woolf and Lytton Strachey: Letters,* ed. Leonard Woolf and James Strachey (1956).—B. J. Kirkpatrick, *A Bibliography of Virginia Woolf* (1957, rev. 1965); Maurice Beebe, "Criticism of Virginia Woolf: A Selected Checklist," *Mod. Fiction Stud.,* II (1956-57). 36-45. Revised editions of Daiches' and Bennett's studies were published in 1963 and 1964, respectively. Aileen Pippett,

The Moth and the Star (Boston, 1955); L. Woolf, *Beginning Again: An Auto-biography of the Years 1911-18* (1964); R. L. Chambers, *The Novels of Virginia Woolf* (Edinburgh, 1947); Bernard Blackstone, *Virginia Woolf: A Commentary* (1949); Vittoria Sanna, *Il Romanzo di Virginia Woolf: Inspirazione e motivi fondamentale* (Florence, 1951); Irma Rantavaara, *Virginia Woolf and Blooms-bury* (Helsinki, 1953) and *Virginia Woolf's "The Waves"* (Helsinki, 1960); James R. Hafley, *The Glass Roof: Virginia Woolf as Novelist* (Berkeley, 1954); Monique Nathan, *Virginia Woolf par elle-même* (Paris, 1956; Eng. trans. 1961), noteworthy for expert use of photographs; Dorothy Brewster, *Virginia Woolf's London* (1959) and *Virginia Woolf* (1962); Jean Guiguet, *Virginia Woolf et son oeuvre: l'art et la quêt du réel* (Paris, 1962; Eng. trans. 1965); A. D. Moody, *Virginia Woolf* (1963); N. C. Thakur, *The Symbolism of Virginia Woolf* (1965); Josephine O. Schaefer, *The Three-Fold Nature of Reality in the Novels of Virginia Woolf* (1965).

Note 29: Katherine Mansfield: *Selected Stories,* ed. D. M. Davin (1953); *Journal* (rev. 1954), *Letters to John Middleton Murry, 1913-1922* (1951), both ed. J. M. Murry.—Antony Alpers, *Katherine Mansfield: A Biography* (1953); Odette Lenoël, *La Vocation de Katherine Mansfield* (Paris, 1946); Sylvia L. Berkman, *Katherine Mansfield: A Critical Study* (New Haven, 1951); Anne-Marie Monnett, *Katherine Mansfield* (Paris, 1960); Saralyn R. Daly, *Katherine Mansfield* (1965); Murry, *Katherine Mansfield and Other Literary Studies* (1959), ch. II.

1568   H. M. Tomlinson: *A Selection from His Writings,* ed. Kenneth Hopkins (1953).

Maugham: *Complete Short Stories* (3v, 1951); *Collected Plays* (3v, 1952); *Selected Novels* (3v, 1953); *The Travel Books* (1955); *The Maugham Reader* (1950); *The Maugham Enigma: An Anthology,* ed. Klaus W. Jonas (1954); *Of Human Bondage,* ed. Richard A. Cordell (1956).—Jonas, *A Bibliography of the Works of W. Somerset Maugham* (1950); Raymond T. Stott, *The Writings of W. Somerset Maugham* (1956, supplement 1961). Helmut Papejewski, *Die Welt-, Lebens- und Kunstanschauung Maughams* (Cologne, 1952); Karl G. Pfeiffer, *W. Somerset Maugham: A Candid Portrait* (1959); Cordell, *Somerset Maugham: A Biographical and Critical Study* (Bloomington, Ind., 1961), superseding his 1937 volume; Laurence Brander, *Somerset Maugham: A Guide* (1963).

1569   B. J. Kirkpatrick, *A Bibliography of E. M. Forster* (1965); Helmut E. Gerber, "E. M. Forster: An Annotated Checklist of Writings about Him," *English Fiction in Transition,* II, no. 1 (1959). 4-27; Maurice Beebe and Joseph Brogunier, "Criticism of E. M. Forster: A Selected Checklist," *Mod. Fiction Stud.,* VII (1961). 284-292. James McConkey, *The Novels of E. M. Forster* (Ithaca, 1957); H. J. Oliver, *The Art of E. M. Forster* (Melbourne, 1960); J. B. Beer, *The Achievement of E. M. Forster* (1962); Frederick C. Crews, *E. M. Forster: The Perils of Humanism* (Princeton, 1962); K. W. Gransden, *E. M. Forster* (1962); Alan Wilde, *Art and Order: A Study of E. M. Forster* (1964); David Shusterman, *The Quest for Certitude in E. M. Forster's Fiction* (Bloomington, Ind., 1965); *E. M. Forster: A Tribute, with Selections from His Writings on India,* ed. K. Natwar-Singh (1964).

Leo Robertson, *Compton Mackenzie: An Appraisal of His Literary Work* (1955).—Rupert Hart-Davis, *Hugh Walpole: A Biography* (1952).

1570 Jessica B. Young, *Francis Brett Young: A Biography* (1962).
"The Pleasures of Knowing Rose Macaulay," *Encounter*, XII (1959). 23-31, tributes from many leading writers. (She was born in 1887 and died in 1958.)

XLI. Poetry in the Twentieth Century

1572 J. Isaacs, *The Background of Modern Poetry* (1951); Lawrence Durrell, *A Key to Modern British Poetry* (Norman, Okla., 1952); Anthony Thwaite, *Contemporary English Poetry* (1959); J. M. Cohen, *Poetry of This Age, 1908-1958* (1960); M. L. Rosenthal, *The Modern Poets: A Critical Introduction* (1960); H. N. Fairchild, *Religious Trends in English Poetry*, Vol. v: *Gods of a Changing Poetry* (1962); C. K. Stead, *The New Poetic* (1964).

1573 "Edwardian Poets," *LTLS*, March 20, 1953, p. 186, on Binyon and Bottomley.

1574 De la Mare: *Collected Tales*, ed. Edward Wagenknecht (1949); *Walter de la Mare: A Selection from His Writings*, ed. Kenneth Hopkins (1956); *A Choice of De La Mare's Verse*, ed. W. H. Auden (1963). Leonard Clark, "A Handlist of the Writings in Book Form (1902-1953) of Walter de la Mare," *Stud. in Bibliography*, VI (1954). 197-218. John Atkins, *Walter de la Mare: an Exploration* (1947); Henry C. Duffin, *Walter de la Mare: A Study of His Poetry* (1949); N. J. Endicott, "Walter de la Mare, 1873-1956," *UTQ*, XXVI (1957). 109-121.—*W. B. Yeats and T. Sturge Moore: Their Correspondence, 1901-1937*, ed. Ursula Bridge (1953). Frederick L. Gwynn, *Sturge Moore and the Life of Art* (Lawrence, Kan., 1951).

1577 Davies: *Complete Poems* (1963);*The Essential W. H. Davies*, ed. Brian Waters (1951). Richard J. Stonesifer, *W. H. Davies* (1963).

1578 Edward Thomas: *Selected Poems*, ed. Robin Skelton (1962). H. Coombes, *Edward Thomas* (1956); Eleanor Farjeon, *Edward Thomas: the Last Four Years* (1958); Coombes, "The Poetry of Edward Thomas," *EIC*, III (1953). 191-200; C. Day Lewis, "The Poetry of Edward Thomas," *Essays by Divers Hands* (Royal Soc. of Lit.), n.s. XXVIII (1956). 75-92; John Burrow, "Keats and Edward Thomas," *EIC*, VII (1957). 404-415; John F. Danby, "Edward Thomas," *Critical Quar.*, I (1959). 308-317.—Squire: *Collected Poems* (1959).

1579 *Georgian Poetry*, ed. James Reeves (1962). Christopher Hassall, *Sir Edward Marsh* (1959); Robert H. Ross, *The Georgian Revolt 1910-1922: Rise and Fall of a Poetic Ideal* (Carbondale, Ill., 1965); George MacBeth, "Georgian Poetry: 1912-1922," *London Mag.*, n.s.II (1962). 74-80.
Murry: *Selected Criticism, 1916-1957*, ed. Richard Rees (1960). F. A. Lea, *The Life of John Middleton Murry* (1959); Derek Stanford, "Middleton Murry as Literary Critic," *So. Atl. Quar.*, LVIII (1959). 196-205; J. B. Beer, "John Middleton Murry," *Critical Quar.*, III (1961). 59-66; André Crépin, "John Middleton Murry et le sens allégorique de la vie," *Études anglaises*, XIV (1961). 321-330.

1580 Stanley K. Coffman, Jr., *Imagism: A Chapter for the History of Modern Poetry* (Norman, Okla., 1951).
Hulme: *Further Speculations*, ed. Sam Hynes (Minneapolis, 1955; enlarged ed., Lincoln, Neb., 1962). Alun R. Jones, *The Life and Opinions of T. E. Hulme*

(1960); Murray Krieger, "T. E. Hulme: Classicism and the Imagination," *The New Apologists for Poetry* (Minneapolis, 1956), ch. 1.

LeRoy C. Breunig, "F. S. Flint, Imagism's Maître d'École," *CL*, IV (1952). 118-136.

Alister Kershaw, *A Bibliography of the Works of Richard Aldington from 1915 to 1948* (Burlingame, Cal., 1950); *Richard Aldington: An Intimate Portrait,* ed. Kershaw and F. J. Temple (Carbondale, Ill., 1965).

Thomas B. Swann, Jr., *The Classical World of H. D.* (Lincoln, Neb., 1962).

1581 John H. Johnston, *English Poetry of the First World War* (Princeton, 1964); Bernard Bergonzi, *Heroes' Twilight: A Study of the Literature of the Great War* (1965).

Brooke: *Poetical Works,* ed. Geoffrey Keynes (1946); *Prose,* ed. Christopher Hassall (1956). Keynes, *A Bibliography of Rupert Brooke* (1954, rev. 1959). Arthur Stringer, *The Red Wine of Youth: A Life of Rupert Brooke* (Indianapolis, 1948); Hassall, *Rupert Brooke: A Biography* (1964).

Owen: *Poems,* ed. Edmund Blunden (1947). D. S. R. Welland, *Wilfred Owen: A Critical Study* (1960); Harold Owen, *Journey from Obscurity: Memoirs of the Owen Family* (Oxford, 1963-); Hilda D. Spear, "Wilfred Owen and Poetic Truth," *Univ. of Kansas City Rev.,* XXV (1958). 110-116; Samuel J. Hazo, "The Passion of Wilfred Owen," *Renascence,* XI (1959). 201-208; Rosemary Freeman, "Parody as a Literary Form: George Herbert and Wilfred Owen," *EIC,* XIII (1963). 307-322.

1582 Blunden: *Poems of Many Years,* ed. Rupert Hart-Davis (1957); *Edmund Blunden: A Selection of His Poetry and Prose,* ed. Kenneth Hopkins (1950).

Sassoon: *Collected Poems* (1947, enlarged ed., 1961). Geoffrey Keynes, *A Bibliography of Siegfried Sassoon* (1962). Joseph Cohen, "The Three Roles of Siegfried Sassoon," *Tulane Stud. in English,* VII (1957). 169-185.

Graves: *Collected Poems* (1965).—J. M. Cohen, *Robert Graves* (1961); Douglas T. Day, III, *Swifter Than Reason: The Poetry and Criticism of Robert Graves* (Chapel Hill, 1963); Horace Gregory, "Robert Graves: A Parable for Writers," *Partisan Rev.,* XX (1953). 44-54; Ronald Hayman, "Robert Graves," *EIC,* V (1955). 32-43; George Steiner, "The Genius of Robert Graves," *Kenyon Rev.,* XXII (1960). 340-365; D. J. Enright, "Robert Graves and the Decline of Modernism," *EIC,* XI (1961). 319-337; Ronald Gaskell, "The Poetry of Robert Graves," *Critical Quar.,* III (1961). 213-222; Robert Graves number of *Shenandoah,* XIII (Winter, 1962), with essays by W. H. Auden, Enright, G. S. Fraser, and others.

1584 Campbell: *Collected Poems* (3v, 1949-1960). Victor M. Hamm, "Roy Campbell: Satirist," *Thought,* XXXVII (1962). 194-210; Harold R. Collins, "Roy Campbell: The Talking Bronco," *Boston Univ. Stud. in English,* IV (1960). 49-63. —Richard Fifoot, *A Bibliography of Edith, Osbert, and Sacheverell Sitwell* (1963). C. M. Bowra, *Edith Sitwell* (Monaco, 1947); *A Celebration for Edith Sitwell,* ed. Jose García Villa (Norfolk, Conn., 1948); Geoffrey Singleton, *Edith Sitwell, "The Hymn to Life"* (1961); Ihab H. Hassan, "Edith Sitwell and the Symbolist Tradition," *CL,* VII (1955). 240-251; Ralph J. Mills, Jr., "The Poetic Roles of Edith Sitwell," *Chicago Rev.,* XIV, no. 4 (1961). 33-64.—Osbert Sitwell's autobiography was continued by *Great Morning!* (1947), *Laughter in the Next Room* (1948), and *Noble Essences* (1950); *Tales My Father Taught Me* (1962) is an appendage. *Collected Stories* (1953). André Guimbretière, "La Satire dans

les nouvelles de Sir Osbert Sitwell," *Études anglaises*, XIII (1960). 346-358.—
There are two distinct editions of the *Selected Works of Sacheverell Sitwell*
(Indianapolis, 1953, and London, 1955). *Selected Poems* (1948). Joseph Warren
Beach, "Rococo: The Poetry of Sacheverell Sitwell," *Poetry*, LXXIV (1949). 217-233.

1585   Eliot: *Collected Plays* (1962); *Collected Poems* (1963).—Donald Gallup,
T. S. Eliot: A Bibliography (1952). Matthiessen's *The Achievement of T. S. Eliot*
appeared in revised and enlarged editions, 1947 and 1958. George Williamson,
A Reader's Guide to T. S. Eliot (1953); *T. S. Eliot: A Study of His Writings
by Several Hands,* ed. B. Rajan (1947); *T. S. Eliot: A Symposium,* ed. Richard
March and Tambimuttu (1948); V. H. Brombert, *The Criticism of T. S. Eliot*
(New Haven, 1949); Elizabeth Drew, *T. S. Eliot: The Design of His Poetry*
(1949); Helen Gardner, *The Art of T. S. Eliot* (1949); Kristian Smidt, *Poetry
and Belief in the Works of T. S. Eliot* (Oslo, 1949; rev. London, 1961); Rossell
H. Robbins, *The T. S. Eliot Myth* (1951); Desmond E. S. Maxwell, *The Poetry
of T. S. Eliot* (1952); David Morris, *The Poetry of Gerard Manley Hopkins and
T. S. Eliot in the Light of the Donne Tradition* (Bern, 1953); Grover Smith,
Jr., *T. S. Eliot's Poetry and Plays: A Study in Sources and Meaning* (Chicago,
1956); G. Cattaui, *T. S. Eliot* (Paris, 1957); C. A. Bodelsen, *T. S. Eliot's "Four
Quartets"* (Copenhagen, 1958); *T. S. Eliot: A Symposium for His Seventieth
Birthday,* ed. Neville Braybrooke (1958); Hugh Kenner, *The Invisible Poet:
T. S. Eliot* (1959); Staffan Bergsten, *Time and Eternity* (Stockholm, 1960), on
Four Quartets; David E. Jones, *The Plays of T. S. Eliot* (1960); Seán Lucy, *T. S.
Eliot and the Idea of Tradition* (1960); George T. Wright, *The Poet in the
Poem: the Personae of Eliot, Yeats, and Pound* (Berkeley, 1960); Charles Moor-
man, *Arthurian Triptych: Mythic Materials in Charles Williams, C. S. Lewis,
and T. S. Eliot* (Berkeley, 1960); Lewis Freed, *T. S. Eliot: Aesthetics and History*
(La Salle, Ill., 1962); Northrop Frye, *T. S. Eliot* (1963); Eric Thompson, *T. S.
Eliot: The Metaphysical Perspective* (Carbondale, Ill., 1963); Carol H. Smith,
*T. S. Eliot's Dramatic Theory and Practice, from "Sweeney Agonistes" to "The
Elder Statesman"* (Princeton, 1963); Philip Headings, *T. S. Eliot* (1964);
Genesius Jones, *Approach to the Purpose* (1964); *T. S. Eliot: A Selected Critique,*
ed. Leonard Unger (1948); *T. S. Eliot: A Collection of Critical Essays,* ed.
Kenner (1962).

1588   B. C. Bloomfield, *W. H. Auden: A Bibliography: The Early Years
Through 1955* (Charlottesville, Va., 1964). Francis Scarfe, *W. H. Auden* (1949);
Richard Hoggart, *Auden: An Introductory Essay* (1951); Joseph Warren Beach,
The Making of the Auden Canon (Minneapolis, 1957); Monroe K. Spears, *The
Poetry of W. H. Auden: The Disenchanted Island* (1963); John G. Blair, *The
Poetic Art of W. H. Auden* (Princeton, 1965); Bayley, *The Romantic Survival,*
ch. IX; *Auden: A Collection of Critical Essays,* ed. Spears (1964).

XLII. Anthropology; Travel; History; Criticism

1589   Arthur Calder-Marshall, *Havelock Ellis* (1959); John Stewart Collis,
Havelock Ellis (1959).

1590   Frazer: Stanley E. Hyman, *The Tangled Bank: Darwin, Marx, Frazer
and Freud as Imaginative Writers* (1962); M. J. C. Hodgart, "In the Shade of

The Golden Bough," Twentieth Century, CLVII (1955). 111-119; John B. Vickery, *"The Golden Bough:* Impact and Archetype," *Virginia Quar. Rev.*, XXXIX (1963). 37-57.

1593　*The Essential T. E. Lawrence*, ed. David Garnett (1951); *The Home Letters of T. E. Lawrence and His Brothers*, ed. M. R. Lawrence (1954); *Letters to T. E. Lawrence*, ed. A. W. Lawrence (1962); *Selected Letters*, ed. Garnett (1952).—Victoria Ocampo, *338171 T. E. (Lawrence of Arabia)* (Paris, 1947; English trans. 1963); Richard Aldington, *Lawrence of Arabia: A Biographical Enquiry* (1955); Flora Armitage, *The Desert and the Stars* (1955); Jean Beraud-Villars, *T. E. Lawrence, or The Search for the Absolute* (1958); Anthony Nutting, *Lawrence of Arabia: The Man and the Motive* (1961); Stanley Weintraub, *Private Shaw and Public Shaw* (1963); Gordon Mills, "T. E. Lawrence as a Writer," *Texas Quar.*, v, no. 3 (1962). 35-45.

1594　*The Essential R. B. Cunninghame Graham*, ed. Paul Bloomfield (1952). A. F. Tschiffely, *Tornado Cavalier* (1955).

1595　Hudson: *Works*, Uniform Edition (7v, 1951-1954); *The Best of W. H. Hudson*, ed. Odell Shepard (1949).—Robert Hamilton, *W. H. Hudson: the Vision of Earth* (1946); F. Liandrat, *W. H. Hudson, 1841-1922, Naturaliste: sa vie et son oeuvre* (Lyons, 1946); Richard E. Haymaker, *From Pampas to Hedgerows and Downs* (1954); Ruth Tomalin, *W. H. Hudson* (1954); Carlos Baker, "The Source-Book for Hudson's *Green Mansions*," *PMLA*, LXI (1946). 252-257; Hoxie N. Fairchild, "Rima's Mother," *PMLA*, LXVIII (1953). 357-370.

1596　Beatrice Webb: *Our Partnership*, ed. Barbara Drake and Margaret I. Cole (1948); *Diaries, 1912-1924* (1952) and *Diaries, 1924-1932* (1956), both ed. Cole. Cole, *The Webbs and Their Work* (1949).

1598　*Concerning Andrew Lang*, ed. A. B. Webster (Oxford, 1949). Oscar Maurer, "Andrew Lang and *Longman's Magazine*, 1882-1905," *Univ. of Texas Stud. in English*, XXXIV (1955). 152-178.

Belloc: *One Thing and Another: A Miscellany from His Uncollected Essays*, ed. Patrick Cahill (1955); *Selected Essays*, ed. J. B. Morton (1948); *An Anthology of His Prose and Verse*, ed. W. N. Roughead (1951); *Verse*, ed. Roughead (1954); *Letters*, ed. Robert Speaight (1958). Morton, *Hilaire Belloc: A Memoir* (1955); Speaight, *The Life of Hilaire Belloc* (1957); *Testimony to Hilaire Belloc*, ed. Eleanor and Reginald Jebb (1956); Bernard Bergonzi, "Chesterton and/or Belloc," *Critical Quar.*, I (1959). 64-71.

1599　John Sullivan, *G. K. Chesterton: A Bibliography* (1958). Hugh Kenner, *Paradox in Chesterton* (1948); Maisie Ward, *Return to Chesterton* (1952); Garry Willis, *Chesterton: Man and Mask* (1961); Elizabeth Sewell, "G. K. Chesterton: the Giant Upside-Down," *Thought*, xxx (1955-1956). 555-576; Jeffrey Hart, "In Praise of Chesterton," *Yale Rev.*, LIII (1963). 49-60.

1600　Strachey: *Collected Works* (6v, 1948-1952); *Virginia Woolf and Lytton Strachey: Letters*, ed. Leonard Woolf and James Strachey (1956).—Martin Kallich, "Lytton Strachey: An Annotated Bibliography of Writings About Him," *English Fiction in Transition*, v, no. 3 (1962). 1-77. Charles R. Sanders, *Lytton Strachey: His Mind and Art* (New Haven, 1957); Kallich, *The Psychological Milieu of Lytton Strachey* (1961). For Strachey's importance in the history of modern biography, see Richard D. Altick, *Lives and Letters: A History of Literary Biography in England and America* (1965), ch. IX.

1601 *Essays, Poems and Tales of H. W. Nevinson*, ed. H. N. Brailsford (1948).

Gilbert Murray: An Unfinished Autobiography, ed. Jean Smith and Arnold Toynbee (1960).

Laura Lovat, *Maurice Baring: A Postscript* (1947); David Lodge, "Maurice Baring, Novelist: A Reappraisal," *Dublin Rev.*, CCXXXIV (1960). 262-270.

1602 Richard Garnett: see Carolyn G. Heilbrun, *The Garnett Family* (1961).

1603 Lily B. Campbell, "Bradley Revisited: Forty Years After," *SP*, XLIV (1947). 174-194, a reappraisal of *Shakespearean Tragedy*.

A Saintsbury Miscellany: Selections from His Essays and Scrap Books (1947), including biographical material; *A Last Vintage: Essays and Papers*, ed. John W. Oliver *et al.* (1950). Wellek, *History of Modern Criticism*, IV. 416-428.

Gosse: *Father and Son*, ed. William Irvine (Boston, 1965); *The Correspondence of André Gide and Edmund Gosse, 1904-1928*, ed. Linette F. Brugmans (1959); *Correspondence with Scandinavian Writers*, ed. Elias Bredsdorff (Copenhagen, 1960); *Transatlantic Dialogue: Selected American Correspondence*, ed. Paul F. Mattheisen and Michael Millgate (Austin, Tex., 1965); Osbert Sitwell, *Noble Essences* (1950), ch. II; Mattheisen, "Gosse's Candid 'Snapshots,'" *VS*, VIII (1965). 329-354.

1604 Ker: *On Modern Literature: Lectures and Addresses*, ed. Terence Spencer and James Sutherland (Oxford, 1955). J. H. P. Pafford, *W. P. Ker, 1855-1923: A Bibliography* (1950).

INDEX

i